NEW RIDERS' OFFICIAL
INTERNET
DIRECTORY

New Riders Publishing, Indianapolis, Indiana

New Riders' Official Internet Directory

By Christine Maxwell and Czeslaw Jan Grycz

Published by:
New Riders Publishing
201 West 103rd Street
Indianapolis, IN 46290 USA

All rights reserved. No part of this book may be reproduced or transmitted in any form or by any means, electronic or mechanical, including photocopying, recording, or by any information storage and retrieval system, without written permission from the publisher, except for the inclusion of brief quotations in a review.

Copyright©1994 by New Riders Publishing

Printed in the United States of America 2 3 4 5 6 7 8 9 10

```
Maxwell, Christine.
    New Riders' Official Internet Directory / Christine Maxwell, Czeslaw Jan Grycz. — 2nd ed.
      p.  cm.
    Includes bibliographical references (p.  ) and index.
    1. Internet (Computer network) — Directories.    I. Grycz, Czeslaw
Jan.  II. New Riders Publishing.    III. Title.
 TK5105.875.I75M368     1994b
 011'.3 — dc20
                                                                   94-34785
                                                                        CIP
```

Warning and Disclaimer

This book is designed to provide information about the Internet. Every effort has been made to make this book as complete and as accurate as possible, but no warranty or fitness is implied.

The information is provided on an "as is" basis. The authors and New Riders Publishing shall have neither liability nor responsibility to any person or entity with respect to any loss or damages arising from the information contained in this book or from the use of the disks or programs that may accompany it.

Publisher
Lloyd J. Short

Associate Publisher
Tim Huddleston

Product Development Manager
Rob Tidrow

Marketing Manager
Ray Robinson

Director of Special Projects
Cheri Robinson

Managing Editor
Matthew Morrill

About the Authors

Christine Maxwell is Director of Internet Research and Development and Publisher of McKinley Group, Inc. (The McKinley Group specializes in Internet directory publishing and helping companies attain a strong market presence on the Internet.) She also is President and CEO of Research on Demand Inc., a Berkeley based information broker company. Maxwell has been in the information brokering business more than 12 years. Previously, she worked in senior positions in international scientific and educational publishing. She also is a trained elementary school teacher and has taught for several years in British public schools.

Maxwell has written several books including *The Pergamon Dictionary of Perfect Spelling* and *Spelling...Spelling Basics*. Maxwell particularly likes to focus her writing skills on books that deal with problems of information access. Her eclectic background has proved well-suited to exploring all the riches of the Internet and helping those riches to become more accessible to everyone.

Czeslaw (Chet) Jan Grycz is the Director of Advisory Board and Database Development for the McKinley Group. He also is a lecturer in the School of Library Science and Information Technology at the University of California at Berkeley Extension, where he teaches two of the required courses in the Certificate of Publishing program. Grycz also is on permanent faculty of the Denver Publishing Institute, and has conducted workshops and lectured throughout the world, especially in Central and Eastern Europe.

Grycz is an author, consultant, writer, and editor. His special interests are in developing electronic models for publishers, especially in distributed digital network environments. He was instrumental in initiating the 1992 "Red Sage" project, a collaborative electronic publishing effort involving the University of California at San Francisco, Springer-Verlag Publishers, and AT&T Bell Laboratories. In 1994, he helped consolidate a partnership between the University of California System and the Institute for Electrical and Electronics Engineers (IEEE) to similarly prototype electronic publishing mechanisms for engineering information.

Lead Editor
Lisa Wilson

Production Editors
Cliff Shubs
Amy Bezek
Suzanne Snyder
Sarah Kearns

Copy Editors
Rob Lawson
Tad Ringo
Steve Weiss
Lillian Yates

Book Production
Roger S. Morgan
Matthew Morrill
Lisa Wilson

Indexer
Suzanne Snyder

Graphics Image Specialists
Dennis Sheehan
Jeff Yesh

Publisher's Assistant
Melissa Lynch

Editorial Assistant
Karen Opal

Trademark Acknowledgments

All terms mentioned in this book that are known to be trademarks or service marks have been appropriately capitalized. New Riders Publishing cannot attest to the accuracy of this information. Use of a term in this book should not be regarded as affecting the validity of any trademark or service mark.

Acknowledgments

We would like to thank the individuals who have tirelessly assisted us in making the major changes needed to bring about this second edition of our directory. In particular, we are very grateful to the McKinley Group's Managing Editor, Susanna Camp, for her dedication, professionalism, and extremely hard work. We would also like to sincerely thank our Editorial Advisory Board for its expert evaluation assistance. Special thanks are also due to:

> Alex Cohen for both his excellent technical and surfing support; Patrick de Harveng and Suresh Thakur for their invaluable help in programming and developing our database.
>
> Wes Thomas of Mondo for his much-appreciated surfing skills.
>
> Rick Wilson, Intelligent Tool & Eye, San Francisco, for his vision in creating a much improved design.
>
> Laurie Abbott for her special expertise on OPACs.

We would also like to thank the following people for their help in specific areas:

> Jim Terragno and Steve Macintosh: Online Systems Specialists
>
> Helene Atkin: Public Relations

We are very conscious of the important work that was accomplished by all the other experts who "surfed" the Internet on our behalf, gathering resources from all over the world in an ever-growing range of subject areas. Other surfers helped in sorting, cataloging, and verifying the massive amounts of data and Internet URLs that were ultimately e-mailed to our Berkeley, California, headquarters, where all the entries were assembled.

Creating a directory such as this involves much professionalism and an equal amount of generous volunteerism! The following Internet Specialists contributed both in abundance:

> Kasey Asberry
> John Barrie
> Andrew Bernick
> Matisse Enzer
> Antonella Fruscione
> Jack Kessler
> Joel Kohn
> Sean Malloy
> Robert Porter
> Tony Safina

We also wish to acknowledge the important contributions of the following individuals who helped us locate additional resources and shared their Internet navigational experiences with us:

> John Bernard Condant
> Anna Couey
> Larry Dieterich
> Nancy Gusack
> Craig Harris
> Joel Levine
> Judy Malloy
> Joe Paska
> Brian Tanaka
> Eric Theise
> Caius van Nouhuys
> Marla Wilson
> Bob Zimmerman

For their special efforts, we are indebted to Lisa Bornstein and Barbara Lee Williams, our Consulting Editors. We would also like to express much gratitude to the rest of the editorial staff:

> Judith Abrams
> Kathleen Benafel
> Theresa Bergen
> Will Crain
> Nicholas Cronbach
> Diane Gibbs
> Helen Yoon

Putting together a book that literally has no beginning, no middle, and no end (until it is all assembled) poses a particularly tough challenge. Our special thanks go to Darek Milewski, for his unstinting technical support.

We wish to acknowledge the numerous administrative and data-entry-related services supplied by the following individuals, without whose assistance, total dedication, and perseverance this project would not have been possible. Special thanks are due to:

> Jeremy Bled
> Robyn Gregg
> Stephanie Gregg
> Hillary Hayden
> Kaethin Prizer
> Lisa Sorenson

Thanks are also due to:

> Yu-ling Chang
> Michael Coleman
> Greg Drinkwater
> Apolinar Flores
> Roberta Kane
> Dayhawk Kim
> David Schneer
> Irene Sidera
> Neal Skapura

Among our friends at New Riders, we would like to thank Cheri Robinson, Director of Special Projects. Special thanks also go to Matthew Morrill and his team of talented editors, in particular the editing team of Lisa Wilson, Cliff Shubs, Amy Bezek, Suzanne Synder, and Sarah Kearns. Special thanks also goes to Roger Morgan, our page layout specialist.

Thanks are also due to *The McKinley Group* and *Stokes•Hayden, Inc.*, both of Berkeley, California, for their technical and office support and to The Wladyslaw Poniecki Foundation for providing Internet access and connectivity for the project. (The latter nonprofit organization will continue to provide a registry service for new listings.)

Finally, we would like to give special thanks to our long-suffering spouses, Roger and Monica, and to our children, Xavier, Yuri, and Giselle Malina, and Stefan and Krysia Grycz, for putting up once again with our long absences from family life. A special thank you also to Isabel and David Hayden for their inestimable contributions, which included database development and logistical help, and to Ian Maxwell for his advice and support during the many months it took to compile this work.

Disclaimer

An environment as dynamic as the Internet, where change occurs continually, can never be fixed in a book such as this. While every effort has been made to check the factual information contained in this directory, we are very conscious that many changes will have inevitably taken place between the time of this compilation and the date of its publication. We therefore welcome and solicit reader feedback in correcting inaccuracies or in suggesting improvements and additions for subsequent editions of this directory. Forms have been provided at the back of the directory for these purposes. We look forward to your comments.

Table of Contents

Foreword

    Introduction ix
        Internet Editorial Advisory Board
        New Internet Resource Rating System
        Increased Selection of Internet Resources
    Commercial Access to the Internet Gives Business a Competitive Advantage
    This Book is for Internet Novices and Experts Alike

1   Making the Internet More Accessible 1
    Improved Features
        Increased Number of Listings
        Expanded International Coverage
        Expanded Audience Fields
        Expanded Ratings
        Expanded Coverage of Resources that Contain Image, Sound, and Multimedia Files
        Improved Appendixes
        Improved Library Listings
        Advertising

2   The Internet Has Resources of Interest to Everyone 5
        Business and Commerce Come To the Internet
        Advertising Comes to the Internet
        Resources of Interest

3   The Role of the Editorial Advisory Boards 13

4   Getting Connected: What Are the Basics? 17
        Hardware
        Software
        Access to the Internet
        Differences among Providers
        Business Connectivity
        Client/Server Programs

5   Internet Access Tools 21
        Telnet
        Viruses
        FTP (File Transfer Protocol)
        STARS™ (Subject and Topic Access Rater)
        Internet Tools

6   Internet Addresses Explained 27
        Communications on the Internet
        Understanding Internet Addresses
        Dissecting a URL

7		E-mail on the Internet	29
		Electronic Mail	
		Anatomy of an E-mail Message	
		Using E-mail to Subscribe to ListServs	
		ListServs	
		Bulletin Board Systems (BBSs)	
		Usenet Newsgroups	
	A	List of Keywords	729
	B	List of Audience Fields	739
	C	Internet Service Providers	745
	D	Glossary	747
	E	Bibliography	755
	F	A Whimsical Tour of the Internet	757
	G	Making Your Voice Heard	761
	H	Internet Ads	769
Index			773

Forward

Once the preserve of the research and education community, the global Internet has emerged from its academic cocoon to become a vital new infrastructure for electronic commerce. As the pages of this book vividly illustrate, an almost unfathomable wealth of information and services lies below the rolling surface of the Internet ocean.

Navigating its waters and mining its riches are still tasks for the hardy and the brave—not unlike the pioneers who blazed trails across the endless prairies of the American West. But even the unruly frontiers must someday be settled, and the authors of this much-needed guide provide a civilizing influence on the exponentially growing global Internet. New with names such as gopher, World Wide Web, Archie, Mosaic, and Wide Area Information Service (WAIS) are emerging as the basis for new information-browsing and indexing tools. Stable information repositories are emerging that can be cataloged and indexed in various ways. Distributed searching tools based on intelligent agents, Knowbot™ programs, and the like are appearing in both the research and commercial worlds.

Although still somewhat novel today, the application of computers to everyday living and commerce, particularly in connection with the Internet, provides a basis for new product development over the next few years. Mail-enabled applications will increase in popularity, as will combinations of print and online advertising and order fulfillment. Monetary transactions are also finding fertile ground in the Internet landscape.

It should be very apparent to anyone reading this book that the Internet community has diverse interest and skill, which, by their very heterogeneity, suggest an extraordinary breadth of potential. So much communication today is carried digitally that it seems all but inescapable that computer-managed communication and application services will become the norm.

Although the future of the Internet and its technology is still difficult to discern with certainty, it is now deeply embedded not only in the US telecommunications infrastructure, but also in that of other nations. As a global telecommunications service provider and key player in the development of the US Internet infrastructure, MCI Corporation is deeply aware of the needs of Internet users. This massive, globe-girdling, and exponentially growing resource offers almost unlimited opportunities for information service providers and users. In keeping with MCI's network philosophy, MCI is committed to helping the networking technology, including the global Internet.

Vinton Cerf
President, The Internet Society
Senior Vice President, Data Architecture
MCI Corporation

Introduction

In the first edition of this directory, we wrote that INFORMATION ACCESS and PEOPLE ACCESS are what the "Internet" is all about. The Internet now has 10 times as much traffic as six months ago, and 50 times as many information and data resources. Every month, approximately 1 million new subscribers sign on to the Internet. This traffic, along with the daily increase in the enormous volume of information available on the Internet, has made it virtually impossible—even for a proficient Internet user—to zero in easily and quickly on the best resources. Once you get to a site, you now must navigate through increased layers of intermediate menu structures before actually reaching the information required. This is true for all disciplines, regardless of what time of day (or night) you are searching.

This Internet Reference Work is for Internet Novices and Experts Alike

Whether novice or expert, readers soon discover how helpful it is to have this value-added directory (and its updates) close at hand while searching the Internet.

The entries chosen for this second edition still represent only a fraction of the resources available on the Internet. We have striven to correct omissions of coverage in some areas and have expanded the range and scope of many others, as well as reassessing resources originally listed in the first edition. In many cases, we have replaced old listings with brand new entries judged to be of superior quality in both content and coverage.

Key Features from the First Edition

Listed below are features that were carried over from the first edition because readers reported finding them particularly useful.

Embedded Index: A unique feature of *New Riders' Official Internet Directory* is that entries are repeated under their relevant keyword headings. The directory therefore functions as its own index.

Provision of Non-Technical, Factual Resource Descriptions: Short descriptions and profiles for each resource are written in non-technical, plain English.

Template Format: Descriptive fields are consistent with the first edition: Title, Short Description, Keywords, Sponsor, Audience, Contact, Details, Notes, and URL (Internet address).

Titles of Listings: Sorted alphabetically by a series of keywords as well as by title.

Keywords: Provided to help readers focus quickly on the most relevant resources suitable to a given inquiry.

Audience Fields: These are provided to help organize and classify Internet resources for specific audiences and constituencies.

Short Descriptions and Profiles: The content of each resource has been carefully analyzed, enabling precise, factual descriptions for each resource to be compiled.

Access Info: Additional navigation information is provided (where applicable) to assist the reader in accessing a resource as efficiently as possible.

Details: This field identifies whether access to a selected resource is free of charge or has a cost associated with it. Resources can be moderated, and have image, sound or multimedia files.

Internet addresses (or URLs): These are supplied at the bottom of each listing to give quick and easy access to each resource. Whenever available, alternative addresses are given to ensure that as many people as possible can navigate their way to a given resource, even if they don't have a high-speed modem or sufficient bandwidth to be able to access such sites using more sophisticated search tools like Lynx or Mosaic. (See Chapter 5 for an explanation of these and other Internet Access Tools.)

Expanded Features in the Second Edition

International Editorial Advisory Boards Provide Independent The Assessment of Resources. Following the well-established scientific publishing tradition of "peer review," we have greatly expanded our teams of experts and editorial advisors to help review and evaluate the Internet resources published in this new edition. We are particularly pleased that editors representing the Advisory Board of Annual Reviews—the premier international review body of published articles in 57 scientific disciplines—and world-class editors from leading international scientific and educational journals have agreed to serve on newly established Editorial Advisory Boards. Their participation helps us provide the quality-assurance factor that is so vital for today's Internet users.

Each resource listed in this directory has been reviewed and carefully evaluated. We have put into place a system to allow for ongoing evaluations of resources by our Advisory Boards. This system focuses on rating the relative importance of resources, according to a set list of criteria. This is the source of the Subject/Topic Ranking System (STAR) described in detail in Chapter 3. The ranking system is unique and is of inestimable value to professionals and individuals who want to proceed directly to the most useful resources in their interest areas.

Even with artificially intelligent "knowbots"(TM) executing automated resource searches, a directory providing an independent review of Internet resources is essential. For example, if you were to search the Internet for resources dealing with "accounting," you would end up with a list of over 2,000 references! Your productivity would decrease rather than increase while you searched for what you needed—exactly the opposite of what the Internet promises and can deliver!

Increased Selection of Internet Resources. We have increased the selection of listings in this second edition by 40 percent, and have updated the navigational instructions for all the listings appearing in the first edition. One of the most challenging realities of the Internet today continues to be its volatility. Resources made available by a provider one day may be moved or transported to another network site the next day. It is, therefore, quite difficult to keep up with these changes. Until the Internet matures and stabilizes, constant surveillance is necessary. We continue to provide that surveillance on a daily basis in our efforts to produce the most up-to-date information available in subsequent editions of this directory.

More International Resources. The Internet continues to expand globally, even as it penetrates into more communities and remote locations in the United States. Mindful of the global reach of the Internet, we have gone to special lengths to expand the number of international resources listed. In addition, our Advisory Boards are international in scope and have been specifically requested to help us identify international Internet resources wherever they exist and to evaluate them for us.

Commercial Access to the Internet Gives Business a Competitive Advantage

The recent opening of the Internet information highway for commercial use has resulted in far-reaching opportunities for every kind of business—both large and small. Companies can research new markets and track existing ones, increase their level of direct customer contact, make new business connections, and get instant feedback (through e-mail) from internal staff and customers alike.

With the use of the Internet, communities no longer need to be defined entirely by where people live and where businesses are situated. Individual consumers find that shopping on the Internet is an exploding field, and opportunities abound for learning, being entertained, and pursuing every kind of hobby or interest imaginable.

The Two-Way Flow of Information

The Internet is "interactive." This means it is two-directional. People use the Internet to access information, but they also use it to provide information for others to seek out and find.

It is important for both individuals and businesses to realize that the higher the quality of information provided to the Internet, the greater the value received back. In keeping with this simple truth, we want to encourage readers to provide us with feedback on existing and new listings. We have provided in Appendix H a series of forms titled "Making Your Voice Heard."

The forms cover:

- How to Register a New Listing
- How to Update a Current Listing
- How to Recommend a Listing
- How to Become a Resource Evaluator

The comprehensive cataloging of Internet content can never be completed. It is impossible to get "ahead" of the Internet: we can only strive consistently and conscientiously to locate and document in this directory the best resources in every field of endeavor. To that end, we constantly are adding to our Advisory Boards, whose members are at the cutting edge of their given fields.

The Internet is a new world community, with businesses now joining educational and research institutions in embracing its electronic reach. On the Internet, people help one another from across the world—working collaboratively to solve problems, sharing insights, or providing each other with information, solutions, and fresh ideas. The Internet contains a treasure trove that needs to be open to all people. We are committed not only to providing the best information about the contents of the Internet, but also to setting quality standards by which those contents can be evaluated and used.

Finally, the special format we have devised for all entries in the directory ensures that readers do not drown in information overload, but are able to swim gracefully and precisely to where they need to go.

The Elements of the Internet

Some people draw a diagram of a cloud to represent the Internet. In fact, it is a hierarchical assembly of networks: a network of networks. It could be diagrammed in schematic form like this:

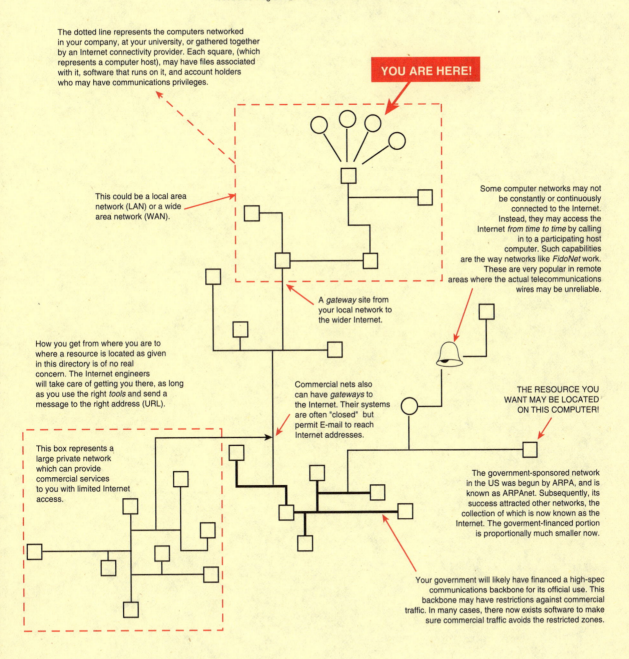

The dotted line represents the computers networked in your company, at your university, or gathered together by an Internet connectivity provider. Each square, (which represents a computer host), may have files associated with it, software that runs on it, and account holders who may have communications privileges.

YOU ARE HERE!

This could be a local area network (LAN) or a wide area network (WAN).

Some computer networks may not be constantly or continuously connected to the Internet. Instead, they may access the Internet *from time to time* by calling in to a participating host computer. Such capabilities are the way networks like *FidoNet* work. These are very popular in remote areas where the actual telecommunications wires may be unreliable.

A *gateway* site from your local network to the wider Internet.

How you get from where you are to where a resource is located as given in this directory is of no real concern. The Internet engineers will take care of getting you there, as long as you use the right *tools* and send a message to the right address (URL).

Commercial nets also can have *gateways* to the Internet. Their systems are often "closed" but permit E-mail to reach Internet addresses.

THE RESOURCE YOU WANT MAY BE LOCATED ON THIS COMPUTER!

This box represents a large private network which can provide commercial services to you with limited Internet access.

The government-sponsored network in the US was begun by ARPA, and is known as ARPAnet. Subsequently, its success attracted other networks, the collection of which is now known as the Internet. The goverment-financed portion is proportionally much smaller now.

Your government will likely have financed a high-spec communications backbone for its official use. This backbone may have restrictions against commercial traffic. In many cases, there now exists software to make sure commercial traffic avoids the restricted zones.

1

Making the Internet More Accessible

The second edition of *New Riders' Official Internet Directory* has expanded original features and added new ones to make it even easier to access the Internet. These upgraded features continue to set the standard for ease of use among content-specific Internet directories.

With thousands of resources being added to the Internet daily from locations around the world, it has become more crucial and urgent than ever before to have informative and concise guideposts to the content and the value of each Internet resource.

Increased Number of Listings

This second edition contains 45 percent more listings than the first edition. Given the constant increase in substantive information that is coming onto the Internet, our resource specialists and editorial advisory boards felt it imperative to provide a high level of increased coverage in this second edition.

Every effort has been made to mirror the breadth of the Internet's coverage and to take into account the major new content areas of commerce and business. Resources that pertain to people of all ages, cultures, and religious persuasions, as well as those that originate from other countries and focus on international issues have been carefully sought out to ensure broad coverage.

Expanded International Coverage

The largest increase in Internet access is coming from countries outside the United States. This increased international Internet activity is reflected in the quality of resources being put onto the Internet from many countries around the world. Representative examples of international resources include:

CEDAR (Central European Environmental Data Request) Facility

CEDAR (Central European Environmental Data Request) Facility

This gopher site provides information about the environmental and scientific community in Central and Eastern Europe (CEE), with access to environmental information located throughout the world on various international computer networks and hosts.

Keywords: Europe, EEC, Environment
Sponsor: The International Society for Environmental Protection, and The Austrian Federal Ministry for Environment, Youth and Family (BMUJF)
Audience: Environmentalists, Educators, Students, Urban Planners
Contact: cedar-info@cedar.univie.ac.at
Notes: CEDAR Marxergasse 3/20, A-1030 Vienna, Austria Tel.: +43-1-715 58 79

`gopher://pan.cedar.univie.ac.at`

Medical and Biological Research in Laboratories Institutions (Israel)

Medical and Biological Research in Laboratories Institutions (Israel)

A descriptive listing of medical research and diagnostic laboratories in Israel. This site also has information on medical research being carried out in Israeli universities and hospitals.

Keywords: Medical Research, Biological Research, Israel
Audience: Medical Researchers, Biomedical Researchers, Medical Professionals
Profile: MATIMOP, The Israeli Industry Center for Health Care Research And Development, is a non-profit service organization, founded by an Israeli association of hospitals, universities, and other medical researchers, aiming their activities at promoting cooperation of Israeli entrepreneurs and manufacturers with qualified business firms abroad. This gopher details specific medical and biological research projects in progress in every department of every major Israeli health care institution: including universities, The General Federation of

Labour, public hospitals, government-municipal hospitals, government hospitals, as well as medical and biological research in the Israeli laboratories and research institutes.

Contact: rdinfo@matimop.org.il

gopher://gopher.matimop.org.il

Refined Keyword List

The keyword list has been carefully refined to take into account all new resources that have been added.

- Appendix A provides a complete list of keywords under which resources have been organized along with page numbers to help locate the appearance of each keyword in the directory.
- On the first page of each alphabetical section, a complete index of all the keywords associated with that letter also can be found.
- All resources continue to be listed alphabetically by title, as well as under the keyword headings associated with their content. A new page design makes the directory easier for readers to quickly locate specific resources, while simultaneously discovering other potentially relevant ones.

Expanded Audience Fields

The audience fields also have been refined and expanded to take into account the increasing breadth and complexity of the directory. An additional 300+ audience categories have been added.

- Appendix B provides a complete list of audience fields under which the resources have been organized.
- Audience terms in the Appendix are provided with page numbers to their references in the Directory listings.

Expanded Ratings

The criteria for rating entries have been extended and clarified. (See Chapter 3 for detailed information.) A rating system using stars and four levels has been instituted to make each resources value instantly visible and easily understood. This system is called STAR (Subject and Topic Access Rater).

A star rating appears at the top right of the entry. If an entry does not have a star, the resource is either quite narrow in scope and likely to change rapidly in coverage, is experimental, or is in development. The resource also might have come to our attention with insufficient time for a proper evaluation. In the latter case, the resource was judged by us to be of sufficient importance to be listed while the evaluation process is underway.

Expanded Coverage of Resources that Contain Image, Sound, and Multimedia Files

The expanding acceptance of the World Wide Web has resulted in a major increase in the availability of files with images, sounds, and multimedia. The following is an example of this:

Leonardo Electronic Almanac

Leonardo Electronic Almanac

The Leonardo Electronic Almanac (LEA) is a monthly, edited journal and an electronic archive dedicated to providing current perspectives in the art, science, and technology domains.

Keywords: Art, Multimedia, Music, Electronic Media

Sponsor: International Society for the Arts, Sciences, and Technology

Audience: New Media Artists, Researchers, Art Educators, Art Professionals

Profile: LEA is an international, interdisciplinary forum for people interested in the use of new media in contemporary artistic expression, especially involving 20th century science and technology. Material is contributed by artists, scientists, philosophers and educators. LEA is published by the MIT Press for Leonardo, the International Society for the Arts, Sciences and Technology (ISAST).

Contact: Craig Harris
craig@well.sf.ca.us

Details: Costs, Moderated, Images, Sounds, Multimedia

mail to:journals-orders@mit.edu

ftp://mitpress.mit.edu/pub/Leonardo-Elec-Almanac

Improved Appendices

In this second edition, the appendixes have been improved to offer more information. They are as follows:

- Appendix A—List of Keywords. All keywords are now listed alphabetically, with referenced page numbers alongside.
- Appendix B—List of Audience Fields. All audience fields are now listed alphabetically, with referenced page numbers alongside.
- Appendix C—Internet Service Providers. Appendix C offers a list of Internet access providers.
- Appendix D—Glossary. Provides an expanded glossary of terms.
- Appendix E—Further Readings. This appendix offers an expanded reading list.
- Appendix F—A Whimsical Tour of the Internet. This appendix provides numerous suggestions about where to travel on the Internet
- Appendix G—Making Your Voice Heard. This is a new section that has evolved to make it easy for readers to register reader feedback, to register new listings, update a current listing, recommend a listing, or apply to become an Internet resource evaluator.
- Appendix H—List of Advertisements.

Improved Library Listings

Emphasis has been placed on expanding the coverage of those major Internet library resources that are superior gateways to thousands of other national and international online public access catalogs, known as OPACs. The following is an example:

Libraries

MELVYL

MELVYL is the University of California's catalog of books and periodicals for the university and the California State Library. It also permits access to database systems around the world.

Keywords:	Libraries, Databases, OPACS, Internet Surfers
Audience:	General Interest, Students, Teachers, Librarians
Producer:	University of California
Contact:	Genny Engel, MELVYL System Users Services email:gen@dla.ucop.edu
Profile:	The MELVYL system is a centralized information system that can be reached from terminals in libraries at all nine campuses of the University of California. The system can also be reached by any terminal or microcomputer with dialup access to UC computers connected to the MELVYL system. The system includes a library card catalog database, a periodicals database, article citation databases, and other files.
Details:	Free
Notes:	All these databases are searched using the same basic commands.

`telnet://melvyl.ucop.edu`

Advertising

In recognition of the growing presence of commerce and business on the Internet, we have decided to allow advertisements to appear in this directory. In keeping with the low key approach to the presence of commercial messages on the Internet, advertisements have been restricted to an unobtrusive and informative style. The intention is to make them subsidiary to the directory text itself. Advertisements appear in the directory with a tinted background and are not rated.

A
B
C
D
E
F
G
H
I
J
K
L
M
N
O
P
Q
R
S
T
U
V
W
X
Y
Z

2

The Internet Has Resources of Interest to Everyone

A common vision is developing in the US and around the world that views the Internet as a vital purveyor of information. The new resources listed in this second edition have been chosen because they:

- Help to expand the contents of resources into new fields not yet covered in the first edition
- Provide expanded coverage of existing subject areas
- Provide updated or more complete coverage of selected subject fields

Every day, people confront situations in which they are required to find some piece of information. Businesses, individuals, organizations, and schools are learning that they all can benefit from having the ability to access the global resources available on the Internet.

The following examples demonstrate the breadth and depth of content. Thumbing through the directory listings will give readers an immediate feel for the breadth of topics covered from A-Z.

Global Change Information Gateway

Global Change Information Gateway

This gateway was created to address environmental data management issues raised by the US Congress, the Administration, and the advisory arms of the Federal policy community. It contains documents related to the UN conference on Environment and Development.

Keywords: UN, Environment, Development, Oceans, Atmosphere

Audience: Environmentalists, Scientists, Researchers, Environmentalists

Details: Free
Select from menu as appropriate.

`gopher://scilibx.ucsc.edu`

ACM SIGGRAPH Online Bibliography Project

ACM SIGGRAPH Online Bibliography Project

This is a collection of computer-graphics bibliographic references.

Keywords: Multimedia, Interactive, Computer Graphics, Programming

Sponsor: Association of Computing Machinery (ACM), Special Interest Group on Computer Graphics (SIGGRAPH)

Audience: Developers, Designers, Producers, Educators, Programmers, Graphic Artists

Profile: The goal of this project is to maintain an up-to-date database of computer-graphics literature, in a format that is accessible to as many members of the computer-graphics community as possible. The database includes references from conferences and workshops worldwide and from a variety of publications dating back as far as the late-19th century. The majority of the major journals and conference proceedings from the mid-1970s to the present are listed.

Contact: bibadmin@siggraph.org

Details: Free, Moderated, Multimedia

`ftp://siggraph.org/publications`

Many Internet resource sites contain such a variety of resources that, any one group of individuals might access the same resource and be able to find totally different information and adapt it to their own particular advantage.

Astronomy

Astronomical Information on the Internet

This FTP site contains pointers to potentially relevant resources available via the Internet.

Keywords: Astronomy, Astrophysics, Astronomical Software, Astronomical Instrumentation

Sponsor: European Space Organization (ESO) and Space Telescope European Coordinating Facility (ST-ECF)

Audience: Astronomers, Physicists, Students (college, graduate), Educators

Profile: This is the entry point for most astronomical resources available online categorized by function. More than 100 resources are accessible concerning general astronomical information, software, and publications. The following are just a few examples of the resources available as of January 1994:

- Online publications from CERN, SISSA, STSCI, NASA, PASP, Cfa, and so on.
- Conferences and meetings
- Metereological information
- Access to over 30 observatories and institutes
- Data archives from over 20 previous and current satellite missions, observatories, and astronomy data centers
- Astronomical images
- Astronomical software
- Jobs

Contact: Hans-Martin Adorf
adorf@eso.org

Details: Free, Moderated; Image, Sound, and Multimedia files available.

`ftp://ecf.hq.eso.org/pub/WWW/astro-resources.html`

Business and Commerce Come to the Internet

The Internet has started to make substantive changes to conventional ways of doing business. However there is still a long way to go before it becomes a place where people feel comfortable doing business and buying or selling products and services. The issues of security, private fiscal transactions, and appropriate pricing mechanisms need to be resolved before the Internet market place fulfills its global potential.

For many companies, the Internet already represents a good, cheap communications link to geographically distant work sites. Technology companies (and increasingly, other types of companies), see the Internet as providing an excellent communications channel between customers and vendors, allowing for expanded and improved customer support, at the same time as it enables operational efficiencies. Publishers by the hundreds (self-publishers and professional publishers alike), and companies with consumer products and services, are making their catalogs available on the Internet, allowing anyone with an Internet connection to peruse them and order desired titles, products and services. Some, like The Online Bookstore, even make the complete text of many books available online.

Online Books

Online BookStore (OBS)

Offers full text (fiction and nonfiction) in a variety of electronic formats, free and for a fee.

Keywords: Online Books, Books, ShareWord, Fiction, Nonfiction Books
Sponsor: Editorial Inc./OBS
Audience: General Public, Reading Enthusiasts
Profile: Started in 1992, the OBS offers a variety of full-text titles.
Contact: Laura Fillmore
laura@editorial.com
Details: Costs, Moderated, Images, Multimedia
User Info: To subscribe to the list, send an e-mail message requesting a subscription to the URL address below.

`http://marketplace.com/0/obs`

No single marketing, or advertising channel is going to reach 100 percent of the Internet market; but even a fraction of that market can represent millions of people. Those companies who can quickly master the rules of online commerce and find a niche market to exploit, can immediately do very good business on the Internet. Many are already doing so.

In line with this growing business emphasis, many commercial sites have been the focus of close scrutiny by other companies, to analyze and keep a close eye on what is succeeding and why. At this time, some companies have developed "home pages" (the opening menu item at all www sites). They often contain a solid body of information of general business interest and are also equipped with instrumentation by which the home page producer can learn how many searches page have been made to the home . (In Chapter 7, the section "Understanding Internet Addresses" will help to clarify further the type of information one can glean from an Internet (URL) address.) An example of a company's home page is given below.

AT&T

AT&T Bell Laboratories WWW Information Page

This web site provides information on research and development at AT&T Bell Laboratories.

Keywords: Telecommunications, Technology, AT&T, Cellular Technology
Sponsor: AT&T Bell Laboratories
Audience: Engineers, Educators, Communications Specialists
Contact: webmaster@research.att.com
Details: Free

`http://www.research.att.com`

Advertising Comes to the Internet

Fun, games, hobbies, sports, and recreation are to be found in abundance on the Internet.

As resistance to traditional advertising on the part of Internet users diminishes, new opportunities for advertising are increasing. The advantages for advertising on the Internet are the opportunity to present more information—unlike advertisements in traditional media. The Internet culture encourages vendors to offer significant amounts of information about the product or service being advertised. There is no lead time between the placement of an ad and its being immediately received by an enormous percent market.

Many shopping malls are beginning to spring up on the Internet. An example of one is shown below. These shopping malls offer a series of services, such as press release services and are busy developing other innovative ways to curry favor with businesses and Internet browsers alike.

Internet Shopping Network

Internet Shopping Network

A shopping network on the Infobahn

Keywords: Business, Electronic Commerce
Sponsor: Internet Shopping Network
Audience: Business Users, Commercial Internet Users, General Public
Profile: The Internet Shopping Network aims to conduct research and develop products and services that commercialize the Internet, for the purpose of retailing and mass merchandising. The stores within this network offer approximately 20,000 products from 1000 vendors.

`http://www.internet.net`

The Internet Has Resources of Interest to Everyone

Telemedia, Networks, and Systems Group

Telemedia, Networks, and Systems Group

A list of commercial services on the Web (and Net).

Keywords:	Business, Electronic Commerce
Sponsor:	MIT Laboratory for Computer Science, Cambridge, MA 02139
Audience:	Business Professionals, Commercial Internet Users, General Public
Profile:	This list of commercial Internet services is well-maintained and frequently updated.
Contact:	hhh@mit.edu

`http://tns-www.lcs.mit.edu/commerce.html`

`http://tns-www.lcs.mit.edu`

Resources of Interest to . . . Businesses

Virtually any resource can be viewed as having potentially useful business applications, and useful market intelligence. The following Internet resources point to the variety of information that can be found.

Business

Business News-Singapore

This gopher site focuses on business in Singapore.

Keywords:	Singapore, Economics, Business
Audience:	Economists, Business Professionals
Details:	Free

`gopher://gopher.cic.net/11/e-serials/alphabetic/b/business-news`

`http://gopher.cic.net`

Environment

ESRI (Environmental Systems Research Institute)

Environmental Systems Research Institute, Inc. is the world leader in GIS technology. ARC/INFO is ESRI's powerful and flexible flagship GIS software.

Keywords:	Geographic Information Systems (GIS), Environment, Software, Computers
Audience:	Geographers, Environmentalists, Computer Users

Details:	Costs
	For product information, call (909) 793-2853, X1475.
	For training information, call (909) 793-2853, X1585, or fax (909) 793-5953.

Sun Microsystems, Inc.

Sun Microsystems, Inc.

This site provides a directory of Sun Microsystems products and services, including a company profile, announcements, financial statements, marketing reports, and international sales and support access.

Keywords:	Computer Systems, Sun Microsystems
Sponsor:	Sun Microsystems, Inc., Mountain View, California, USA
Audience:	Sun Microsystems Users
Profile:	Languages: English
Contact:	webmaster@sun.com
Details:	Free

`http://www.sun.com`

Resources of Interest to . . . People of All Ages and Cultures

With people from all over the world rushing on to the Internet, it is important to realize that its content mirrors that of the people who use it.

One can discover and access thousands of diverse resources from all over the world, as exemplified below:

Chicano Culture

Chicano/LatinoNet

An electronic mechanism that brings together Chicano/Latino research, as well as linguistic minority and educational research efforts being carried out at the University of California and elsewhere. It serves as a gateway between faculty, staff, and students who are engaged in research and curricular efforts in these areas.

Keywords:	Culture, Race, Hispanics
Sponsor:	Chicano Studies Research Center, University of California at Los Angeles
Audience:	Students, Mexican-Americans, Latinos
Contact:	Richard Chabran Chabran@latino.sscnet.ucla.ed
Details:	Free

`gopher://latino.sscnet.ucla.edu`

un.wcw.doc.eng

This is a read-only conference comprised of official UN documents for the United Nations Fourth World Conference on Women: Action for Equality, Development and Peace, scheduled to take place at the Beijing International Convention Center, Beijing, China, from 4-15 September 1995. The documents are provided by the official Conference Secretariat, are posted as received by the UN Non-Governmental Liaison Service (NGLS).

Keywords:	Women, Development (International), Peace, UN, World Conference on Women
Audience:	Women, Activists, Non-Governmental Organizations, Feminists
Contact:	United Nations Non-Governmental Liaison Service/Edie Farwell ngls@igc.apc.org, efarwell@igc.apc.org
Details:	Costs, Moderated
User Info:	Establish an account on the nearest APC node. Login, type c for conferences, then type go un.wcw.doc.eng.
	For information on the nearest APC node, contact: APC International Secretariat IBASE E-mail: apcadmin@apc.org

`telnet://igc.apc.org`

NativeNet

NativeNet

Provides information about and discusses issues relating to indigenous people around the world, including threats to their cultures and habitats (for example, rainforests).

Keywords:	Indigenous People, Environment, Anthroplogy
Audience:	Anthropologists, Environmentalists, Indigenous People
Contact:	Gary S. Trujillo gst@gnosys.svle.ma.us
Details:	Free
User info:	To subscribe to the list, send an e-mail message requesting a subscription to the URL address below.

`mailto:gst@gnosys.svle.ma.us`

Resources of Interest to... Disabled

Many resources on the Internet are especially useful for disabled people. Examples of such resources are:

Cornucopia of Disability Information (CODI)

Cornucopia of Disability Information (CODI)

A large collection of disability-related information available via gopher.

Keywords: Disabilities, Health

Sponsor: State University of New York (SUNY) at Buffalo

Audience: Disabled People, Activists, Rehabilitation Counselors, Health Care Professionals

Profile: This site provides a wide variety of information resources concerning people with disabilities, ranging from legal information to a directory of computer resources aimed at the disabled consumer. Includes state, local, and national information and government documents such as the Americans with Disabilities Act. Also has links to many other related resources on the Internet, such as the National Rehabilitation Information Center.

Contact: Jay Leavitt
leavitt@ubvmsb.cc.buffalo.edu

`gopher://val-dor.cc.buffalo.edu`

Disability Information

A collection of information about and links to sources of disability-related information from around the world. Includes archives of many related mailing lists and electronic newsletters, as well as legal and technical help for the disabled, and information about the Parkinson's Disease Information Exchange Network.

Keywords: Disabilities, Health, Diseases

Sponsor: Computing & Information Services at Texas A&M University, Galveston, Texas, USA

Audience: Disabled People, Rehabilitation Counselors, Health Care Professionals, Activists

Contact: Computing & Information Services at Texas A&M University
gopher@tamu.edu

`gopher://gopher.tamu.edu/.dir/disability.dir`

National Library of Medicine Gopher

World Health Organization (WHO)

This gopher provides information about the National Library of Medicine, the world's largest single-topic library.

Keywords: Medicine, Health, World Health

Sponsor: National Library of Medicine, Massachusetts

World Health Organization, Geneva, Switzerland

Audience: Health-care Professionals, Medical Professionals, Researchers

Profile: The National Library of Medicine (NLM) cares for over 4.5 million holdings (inncluding books, journals, reports, manuscripts, and audio-visual items). The NLM offers extensive online information services dealing with clinical care, toxicology, environmental health, and basic biomedical research. It has several active research and development components, including an extramural grants program, houses an extensive history of medicine collection, and provides several programs designed to improve the nation's medical library system.

Contact: R. P. C. Rodgers
rodgers@nlm.nih.gov
akazawa@who.ch

Details: Free

`gopher://el-gopher.med.utah.edu`

`gopher://gopher.who.ch`

Resources of Interest to... Children and Teachers

As education moves into the 21st century students of all age groups and ability levels (and their teachers) will find enormous quantities of resources on the Internet to:

- Support independent as well as cooperative learning efforts
- Provide tools and projects to promote connectivity with classrooms and individuals worldwide
- Supply information about any topic or curriculum issue

K12Net is an example of a strong educational resources. It is a loosely organized network of school-based electronic bulletin board systems throughout North America, Australia, Europe, and the former USSR, which share curriculum-related conferences, making them available to students and educators at no cost. Other examples of the breadth and depth of educational resources accessible over the Internet are:

EDNET

EDNET

This forum explores the educational potential of the Internet.

Keywords: Education, Internet

Audience: Students, Educators

Profile: This independent, unmoderated mailing-list interest group is open and free of charge to all participants. Ednet links educators with common interests, and introduces students to a number of fields and sources of information, while offering criticism and suggestions.

Contact: Prescott Smith
pgsmith@educ.umass.edu

Details: Free

User info: To subscribe to the list, send an e-mail message to the address shown below consisting of a single line reading:

SUB Ednet YourFirstName YourLastName

To send a message to the entire list, address it to:
ednet@nic.umass.edu.

`gopher://ericir.syr.edu/00/AskERIC/FullText/Lists/Messages/`

`EDNET-List/README`

`mailto:listserv@nic.umass.edu`

K12 Net

K12 Net

Decentralized network of school-based bulletin board systems (BBSs).

Keywords: Education (K-12), Networks

Audience: Educators (K-12), School Children

Profile: K12 Net provides millions of teachers, students, and parents in metropolitan and rural areas throughout the world with the ability to meet and talk with each other to discuss educational issues, exchange information, and share resources on a global scale.

Contact: Jack Crawford, Janet Murray
jack@k12net.org or jmurray@psg.com

Details: Free

`gopher://woonext.dsrd.ornl.gov/11/Docs/k12net`

Today students range in all ages, with many older adults continuing in life-long education or retraining. Administrators, parents, teachers, and educational planners will find here the tools needed to transform their schools into environments that avail themselves of the Information Age with vital forums in cyberspace where ideas can be explored, designs shared, and solutions developed.

Resources of Interest to . . . Researchers, Academics, and the Intellectually Curious

The Internet was founded, originally, to provide operational efficiencies to researcher and academics so they could connect with each other at various remote sites and laboratories. As the Internet grew, this successful pattern was replicated by countries around the world and has resulted in the Internet becoming the single largest network in the world.

The resources now available over the Internet have the potential to fulfill a researcher's highest aspirations or create their worst nightmare. A cyberspace "heaven and hell" where the information one seeks is probably there, but the effort to find it is often equivalent to that needed to find a needle in a haystack!

Further examples of the international nature of many Internet resources are shown below.

LabStat

LabStat

The public database of the Bureau of Labor Statistics.

Keywords: Economics, Labor, Census Data
Sponsor: United States Government, Bureau of Labor Statistics
Audience: General Public, Statisticians, Researchers
Profile: LABSTAT provides current and historical data, as well as numerous press releases. This site is composed of individual databases (in flat file format) corresponding to each of 26 surveys.
Contact: labstat.helpdesk@bls.gov.
Details: Free
Login: anonymous; use e-mail address as password.

Notes: For each news release published by the Bureau of Labor Statistics, the two most current are stored in the /news.release directory. The documentation provides a list of the abbreviations used to identify the news releases, and a description of the sub-directories available to the user.

`ftp://stats.bls.gov`

The Growth of Online Public Access Catalogs (OPACS)

A recent development within the library community has been the rush to put library catalogs online, (known as OPACS). Libraries have for the past several years engaged themselves in the process of converting paper library card catalog systems to computerized ones. The advent of being able to access OPACS on the Internet allows libraries to reach beyond their normal constituencies, and provide considerably more flexible searching capabilities than were available from the paper card catalogs. This makes their collections accessible to the widest number of researchers, academics, and the intellectually curious from anywhere in the world.

Following is the listing for the Internet Library of Congress Catalog. Having access to this, on one's computer means having the collections catalog of the largest library in the world at one's desk. At present, it does not mean you have actual books themselves, although efforts to provide textual matter behind the catalog citations are taking place in various experimental sites in many libraries around the world.

The most visible of the online public access catalogs (OPACs) are contained in the HYTELNET list and the Yale Directory of Internet Libraries. Between these two, alone, there is a huge amount of information readily accessible to anyone with telnet or gopher capabilities on their computer.

Yale Directory of Internet Libraries is a comprehensive listing of worldwide libraries (of which HYTELNET is subset) that provides connection information for all its entries (usually automatic-just hit return) via telnet or gopher and provides subject information for many of its entries, and for all of its major academic research entries.

HYTELNET

HYTELNET

A shareware application database directory to libraries.

Keywords: Computer Systems, Libraries, Shareware
Audience: General Audience
Profile: HYTELNET is a guide to library catalogs from the Americas, Europe
Contact: Peter Scott
aa375@freenet.carleton.ca
Details: Free
Notes: HYTELNET is in English, but the interface to some international

`gopher://gophlib@gopher.yale.edu`

Yale Directory of Internet Libraries

Yale Directory of Internet Libraries

An online directory of international library catalogs.

Keywords: Libraries
Sponsor: Yale University, New Haven, Connecticut, USA
Audience: General Audience
Profile: The Yale Directory of Internet Libraries is a comprehensive
Notes: The Yale Directory of Internet Libraries is in English, but the

`gopher://gophlib@gopher.yale.edu`

Resources of Interest to...Cybernauts of All Persuasions.

The diversity of resources can be clearly seen in Appendix G, "A Whimsical Tour of the Internet." We hope you will enjoy this compilation as a fun expression of some of the more lighthearted directory listings to be found among these pages.

Suffice it to say that whatever your interests, whatever your concerns, wherever your imagination leads you, the Internet is ready to satisfy your curiosity and to empower you with information you can put to productive, entertaining, educational, or profitable use.

The following examples should serve to wet anyone's appetite for information.

Astronomy

Center for Extreme Ultraviolet Astrophysics

A department of the University of California at Berkeley devoted to research in extreme ultraviolet astronomy. It is the ground-based institution of EUVE (the Extreme Ultraviolet Explorer), a NASA satellite launched in 1992.

Keywords: Astronomy, Astrophysics, EUVE, NASA, Satellite
Sponsor: NASA and University of California at Berkeley
Audience: Astronomers, Astrophysicists
Profile: Provides access to details about the EUVE Guest Observer (EGO) Center, the EUVE Public Archive of Mission Data and Information, satellite operation information, and so on. The EUVE Guest Observer Center provides information, software, and data to EUVE Guest Observers.
Contact: egoinfo@cea.berkeley.edu
archive@cea.berkeley.edu
Details: Free

`http://cea-ftp.cea.berkeley.edu`

UC Berkeley Museum of Paleontology and the WWW Subway

UC Berkeley Museum of Paleontology and the WWW Subway

This web site provides a multimedia museum display from UC Berkeley's Museum of Paleontology. Also features an interactive Subway, a tool linking users to other museums and WWW sites around the world.

Keywords: WWW, Museums, Paleontology
Sponsor: University of California at Berkeley, Museum of Paleontology, Berkeley, California, USA
Audience: Paleontologists, Internet Surfers, General Public
Contact: David Polly, Robert Guralnick
davip@ucmp1.berkeley.edu
robg@fossil.berkeley.edu

`http://ucmp1.berkeley.edu/subway.html`

Women

Women's Wire

Women's Wire is an online interactive network focusing on women's issues and interests.

Keywords: Networking, Women's Issues, Online Services
Audience: Women, Internet Users
Profile: This service acts as an international clearinghouse for resources and networking on a broad range of topics including news, politics, careers, education, parenting, health, and arts. Provides e-mail and access to thousands of resources, including Usenet newsgroups.
Details: Costs

Access via an easy-to-use graphical interface for Macintosh and Windows platforms, or a text-based interface for DOS and Unix platforms. Local access numbers available throughout the US and in most countries.

`mailto:info@wwire.net`

MUDs

MUD

A discussion list for the exchange of information about new and recommended Multiuser Dungeons and Dragons (MUDs).

Keywords: MUDs, Games
Audience: MUD Users
Contact: Joseph Wisdom
jwisdom@gnu.ai.mit.edu
Details: Free
User Info: To subscribe to the list, send an e-mail message requesting subscription to the URL address below.

`mailto:jwisdom@gnu.ai.mit.edu`

alt.romance.chat

alt.romance.chat

A Usenet newsgroup providing discussion about the romantic side of love.

Keywords: Chat Groups, Romance
Audience: General Public
User Info: To subscribe to this Usenet newsgroup, you need access to a newsreader.

`news:alt.romance.chat`

rec.arts.tv

rec.arts.tv

A Usenet newsgroup providing information and discussion about past and present TV shows and related trivia.

Keywords: Television, Trivia
Audience: General Public, Television Viewers, Trivia Enthusiasts
User Info: To subscribe to this Usenet newsgroup, you need access to a newsreader.

`news:rec.arts.tv`

Online Career Center

Online Career Center

The Online Career Center gopher provides access to job listings and employment information to member companies and to the public.

Keywords: Employment, Internships
Sponsor: Online Career Center
Audience: Job Seekers
Profile: Online Career Center is a not-for-profit organization funded by its member companies. It is devoted to distributing and exchanging employment and career information between its member companies, human resource professionals, and perspective employees.
Contact: OCC Operator
occ@msen.com

`gopher://gopher.msen.com`

Blues

Blues-L

A mailing list for the discussion of Blues music and the culture surrounding the genre of the Blues.

Keywords: Blues Music, Musical Genres
Audience: Blues Enthusiasts
Contact: listserv@brownvm.brown.edu
Details: Free
User Info: To subscribe to the list, send an e-mail message to the URL address below, consisting of a single line reading:

SUB blues-l YourFirstName YourLastName

To send a message to the entire list, address it to:
blues-l@brownvm.brown.edu

Notes:	To receive the list in digest form: once you get acknowledgment from the listserver that you are on the list, send another message to the URL address below with the message:
	SET Blues-L Dig

`mailto:listserv@brownvm.brown.edu`

Cards

Cards

This list is for people interested in collecting, speculating, and investing in baseball, football, basketball, hockey, and other trading cards and/or memorabilia. Discussion and want/sell lists are welcome.

Keywords:	Trading Cards, Collectibiles, Memorabilia
Audience:	Sports Card Collectors, Sports Card Traders, Memorabilia Collectors
Contact:	Keane Arase cards-request@tanstaafl.uchicago.edu
Details:	Free
	To subscribe to the list, send an e-mail message requesting a subscription to the URL address below.
	To send a message to the entire list, address it to:cards@tanstaafl.uchicago.edu
Notes:	The list is open to anyone.

`mailto:cards-request@tanstaafl.uchicago.edu`

3
The Role of the Editorial Advisory Boards

The second edition of *The New Riders' Official Internet Directory* includes an expanded and simplified star rating system for Internet resources. These stars act as guides to the size and relative importance of each resource.

Criteria developed in cooperation with our Editorial Advisory Boards has been tailored for rating specific varieties of Internet data resources. Those that apply, for example, to a Gopher-compliant database will not necessarily apply to an electronic discussion group. Tailored ratings help you save time, and focus on those listings that are most likely to help you keep up-to-date when you're in a hurry. Information resources on the Internet adjust rapidly to the real world—that means they are continually changing. By concentrating on the resources ranked with a high number of stars, the reader who is pressed for time will find the most comprehensive or dynamic sources of information.

About Our Editorial Advisory Boards

Because the emphasis (and distinguishing feature) of this directory is on the content and value of Internet resources, the Editorial Advisory Boards, composed of recognized specialists in specific subject areas, has been formed to help evaluate the listings selected for publication in this directory.

Getting expert advice about the information you find is always helpful, but often not readily available. Being confident in the reliability of information on an expanding Internet may be more difficult as the Internet includes an ever-expanding array. If you know a specific data provider or the author of the materials you chose to download to your computer, you may feel comfortable about the reliability of the information. If you, as millions of other Internet users, will be referring to resources about which you actually know very little about, then a guide to help you may be crucial. In many instances, predictably, you will have no idea whether the information available is valid, biased, complete, or trustworthy.

In the print world, scientific publishers have developed mechanisms for "peer review," by which articles and manuscripts were subjected to a rigorous evaluation process by the author's peers who are experts in the subject. This process ensured objectivity and critical judgment.

Similar conventions can be applied to the evaluation of Internet resources. Members of the Editorial Advisory Boards are asked to help evaluate Internet resources within their specific areas of expertise. It is intended that the combined judgments of such experts will help save you time. The STAR (H) ratings system informs you of the relative merit assigned a resource.

Gaining the cooperation of external specialist evaluators is an expanding and ongoing process because the evaluation and ranking of resources is one of the most important contributions that can be made to fulfill the promise of the Internet to its various constituencies.

Coverage

Because it would be impractical to establish advisory boards for all the keywords under which individual listings may be found, "umbrella" fields have been established. These are the following:

- Business
- Communications
- Economy
- Education
- Energy
- Engineering
- Government and Politics
- Health and Family
- Humanities and Arts
- Information Science
- International Affairs
- Law
- Life Sciences
- Materials Sciences and Technology
- Physical Sciences
- Popular Culture
- Recreation and Sports
- Religion and Spirituality
- Science (General)
- Social and Behavioral Sciences

The process of evaluating Internet resources "by hand," so to speak, is laborious, but we feel there is no technological substitute for it. Some listings arrived too late for formal review, but were deemed important enough to be included in the directory; these listings have no stars.

The Rating System

Working with our Editorial Advisory Boards, we have developed criteria for rating specific varieties of Internet data resources; this is particularly important as the criteria that is relevant, for example, to a gopher compliant database will not necessarily apply to an electronic discussion group. Tailored ratings help you save time, and allow you to focus on those listings that are most likely to keep you up-to-date.

If a resource has been given a single STAR ★ it has been judged important enough to be included in our directory. A single star designation usually indicates that the information provided in the resource is:

- quite specific in scope
- likely to change rapidly in coverage
- under development

The single STAR ★ ratings are important and valuable resources, and often represent the wide range of coverage represented by Internet resources. The following examples testify to this.

Multimedia

Multimedia, Telecommunications, and Art Project

A project to promote online art that will be implemented as gopher site and on the World-Wide Web.

Keywords: Multimedia, Electronic Art, Telecommunications
Sponsor: CISR (Centre for Image and Sound Research), Vancouver, B.C., Canada
Audience: Artists, Writers
Contact: Derek Dowden
Derek_Dowden@mindlink.bc.ca
For more information, send an e-mail message to the URL address below.
Details: Free

`mailto:Derek_Dowden@mindlink.bc.ca`

rec.pets

rec.pets

★

A Usenet newsgroup providing information and discussion about pets and pet care.

Keywords: Pets, Animals
Audience: Pet Owners
To subscribe to this Usenet newsgroup, you need access to a newsreader.

`news:rec.pets`

Economics

CERRO (Central European Regional Research Organization)

CERRO provides access to information about the economic restructuring of Central Europe, including a discussion list, papers, news summaries, and pointers to other gophers in Central Europe.

Keywords: Central Europe, Economics, News
Audience: Economists, Researchers, Journalists
Contact: gunther.maier@wu-wien.ac.at
Details: Free

`gopher://osiris.wu.wein.ac.at`

Evaluation Criteria

Other resources may be given higher ratings. This will indicate that they provide access to proportionally larger amounts of information or are resources of significance. They might:

- contain essential or unique information
- have been developed in a particularly careful way
- be the product of established and reputable entities

If a resource has been assigned a greater number of stars, this means that the Editorial Advisory Boards found the following:

- the resource is more focused or part of a clearly defined subject area
- the resource has important institutional backing
- the resource contained essential or unique information

The following are examples:

Astrophysics

Center for Extreme Ultraviolet Astrophysics

A department of the University of California at Berkeley devoted to research in extreme ultraviolet astronomy. It is the ground-based institution of EUVE (the Extreme Ultraviolet Explorer), a NASA satellite launched in 1992.

Keywords: Astronomy, Astrophysics, EUVE, NASA, Satellite
Sponsor: NASA and University of California at Berkeley
Audience: Astronomers, Astrophysicists
Profile: Provides access to details about the EUVE Guest Observer (EGO) Center, the EUVE Public Archive of Mission Data and Information, satellite operation information, and so on. The EUVE Guest Observer Center provides information, software, and data to EUVE Guest Observers.
Contact: egoinfo@cea.berkeley.edu, archive@cea.berkeley.edu
Details: Free

`http://cea-ftp.cea.berkeley.edu/`

The highest, or 4-star, rating is reserved for resources of truly outstanding merit. Information in these resources might:

- contain unique information not found anywhere else
- be prepared by institutions or agencies of considerable stature
- point to a wide range of additional resources on the Internet
- consist of layer upon layer of detailed information about a given topic

The following are some examples of 4-star Internet resources, which are important both as resources and as pointers to hundreds of other related materials and files.

Politics

White House Information Service

An outstanding database of current White House information, from 1992 to the present.

Keywords: White House, Politics, President (US), Database

Sponsor: Texas A & M University

Audience: General Public

Profile: Much of the older information on this site was obtained from the clinton@marist.bitnet listserv list or the alt.politics.clinton Usenet newsgroup, both of which receive the information indirectly via the MIT White House information server. Newer and current material is received directly from the MIT distribution list. The menu includes a searchable database and headings such as Domestic Affairs (Health Care, Technology, and so on), Press Briefings and Conferences, the President's Daily Schedule, and many more.

Contact: whadmin@tamu.edu

Details: Free

`gopher://tamuts.tamu.edu/11/.dir/president.dir`

Black/African Related Online Information

Black/African Related Online Information

This is a list of online information storage sites that contain a significant amount of information pertaining to Black or African people, culture, and issues around the world.

Keywords: Culture, Race, Africa, African Studies

Sponsor: AfriInfo

Audience: Students, African-Americans, Africans

Contact: McGee

Contact: mcgee@epsilon.eecs.nwu.edu

Details: Free

`ftp://ftp.netcom.com/pub/amcgee/my_african_related_lists/afrisite.msg`

Music Resources

University of California Santa Barbara Virtual Library

This source provides detailed lists of Internet music resources.

Keywords: Music Resources

Sponsor: University of California at Santa Barbara

Audience: Musicians

Profile: This site contains lists pointing to music resources on the Internet, including ftp sites, gopher servers, newsgroups, and list servers.

Details: Free

Path is The Subject Collections/The Arts Collections/Music

`gopher://ucsbuxa.ucsb.edu`

4

Getting Connected: What Are the Basics?

In theory, getting connected to the Internet is relatively easy. It can, however, be frustrating. In this chapter, we've tried to organize the information you'll need to begin accessing the Internet with a minimum of frustration.

The essential components of connecting to the Internet are not complicated. You will need the following:

- Hardware (personal computer, modem, and hard drive)
- Software (telecommunications software, TCP/IP software, and virus protection software)
- Access to the Internet

Hardware

- A personal computer. This can be of any size or type. It doesn't need to be a fancy model with bells and whistles—a computer that can run a conventional communications program will suffice.
- A modem. This device converts what is typed on a personal computer into signals that can be transmitted across standard telephone wires or data lines. (Modems usually are distinguished by their speed of transmission, which is rated at bits per second, or baud rate. The higher the baud rate, the faster the transmission.)

  If you simply intend to exchange e-mail, a modem with relatively low transmission speeds, like 2400 baud will suffice. Today's modems, however, deliver considerable functionality for their price. Purchasing a modem with the highest available baud rate you can afford is advisable. This means that the transferring and receiving of files can be done much more quickly.

- A hard drive. The hard drive is where you store the files of information taken off the Internet. Buying a hard drive with the most capacity is highly advisable. If you become active in one or more discussion groups, you will quickly find yourself storing a large number of messages. It is likely that the more interesting and complex files and any image or sound files will take up a great deal of space. The prices of hard-disk storage have dropped substantially, and sizes formerly reserved for institutional use (1 gigabyte or more) are now popular for individual purchase.

Software

- A telecommunications program. Communications programs are software programs that permit your computer to send data across a modem. In an increasing number of business and office environments, local area networks (LANS) are being established, through which Internet access is available. If you work from home, you will need a software program to permit your home computer to make a phone connection across telephone lines to another computer connected directly to the Internet.

  Frequently, the people who specialize in modems can recommend an appropriate communications software program. They also can answer questions about setup and provide initial trouble-shooting help.

- TCP/IP software. Standard communications programs are useful for connecting your computer to a variety of online services and bulletin board systems. They also make it possible to connect your computer to other computers.

  If you intend to spend much time on the Internet, however, you will need an additional set of enabling software tools. This is the software that permits the transmissions from your computer to conform to the widely adopted standard for communicating on the Internet. This is known as TCP/IP (Transfer Control Protocol/Internet Protocol). Check the Internet Resources listed in this directory to help you understand how to get the software tools you need.

  Fortunately, a variety of packages are available; many are inexpensive, and many are even free. Check with your software vendor about the specific programs you will need for your model computer. Ask for the software that will help you establish a SLIP (Serial Line Internet Protocol) or a PPP (Point-to-Point) connection to the Internet. Also look around for various commercially available packages that include all the software you will need for Internet connectivity. Increasingly, the IP tools come bundled with the major communications software packages that are available, or they can be provided by your Internet service provider.

- Virus Protection Software. Computer viruses can be conveyed on program files that are downloaded to your computer. Because the Internet holds many programs that will be of interest to you, it is wise to purchase high-quality virus protection software. This software scans incoming files and uses a variety of methods to identify files that might harbor viruses that could harm or disable your computer. No virus protection software is foolproof, so you should be cautious about the files you download onto your hard disk. Caution, coupled with high-quality virus protection software, can protect your investment.

Access to the Internet

All Internet users must establish an Internet address. To do so, you must contact a company specializing in providing Internet communications access. Known as Internet Providers, many are listed in Appendix C of this directory. You must pay one of the Internet providers a monthly fee for an electronic account. (This is just like having to pay the phone company for your telephone number.)

Electronic accounts also can be obtained from universities or research institutions (if you happen to be affiliated with one), or from businesses (many companies are already installing or investigating electronic networking). You might want to check these sources, as they might be able to supply you with additional information and assistance for your particular set of requirements.

Differences Between Providers

When looking around for an authorized access account to the Internet, it is important to be aware that some electronic network providers give subscribers access to a suite of services easily confused with the real Internet. Some might provide restricted gateways to the Internet, but not to the full suite of Internet access tools. Be sure to know what you are getting as you investigate the various access points to the Internet.

There is tremendous ongoing volatility in the marketplace for online connectivity and services. There are, however, identifiable differences among certain providers. One group of companies only provides Internet connectivity, another group provides access to a set of individual online databases, and yet another group provides proprietary online database access *and* a minimum of e-mail access to the Internet. These differences can be confusing, since many of the services seem to overlap.

- Internet Providers. Providers who were once primarily interested in the technical aspects of providing Internet connectivity exclusively to institutions are now beginning to compete with one another for the individual customer. This means that they are providing a greater degree of customer service, troubleshooting, software installation advice, and general hand-holding. These are the companies providing basic access.

- Service Providers. Companies like CompuServ, America Online, GEnie, and Prodigy (all headquartered in the US), Minitel (headquartered in France), and other producers in other countries provide broad menus of electronic services, which they package in an overall user-interface. These companies may not, however, actually be on the Internet. In most cases, they still only provide e-mail access to the Internet, allowing customers to send and receive electronic mail from anyone anywhere on the Internet. This is called providing a gateway to the Internet.

    Minitel in France allows full access to the Internet from Minitel, but not vice versa. As of the time of this writing, Delphi is the only commercial access provider with a full Internet gateway. CompuServ has just given notice that it will also be going to full Internet connectivity. America Online has a partial gateway. It is obvious that the trend is for commercial providers to open up more gateways to the Internet.

- Proprietary Database Vendors. These are companies like Dialog, Data Star, Questel, Orbit, Mead (Nexis/Lexis), and CD Plus (now part of CD Plus).

Business Connectivity

Businesses wanting to use the Internet for commercial or operational advantage must understand the types of available connections to the Internet. While most individual consumers will be satisfied with a SLIP connection, businesses may require greater throughput speeds, particularly if they want to connect their companys local area networks (and thus provide Internet access to all of their employees at one time.)

Universities and large corporations rent dedicated lines from the phone company that are directly connected to the Internet. These lines come in different categories, depending on the speed with which communications can be passed through the wires. This is commonly described as bandwidth. The smallest of these is a 56 KB line, but you can also lease 128 KB transmission capability, all the way up to T1 and T3 speeds.

The educational aspects of Internet connectivity have also spurred an interest in ISDN (Integrated Switching Data Network), which has the capability to provide both data and video channels. The prices for these connections vary enormously (in one sample quotation, including distance education, prices ranged from $45 to $2,500 per month). It is worth spending some time comparing services and vendors with your requirements and needs to obtain the right level of service and connectivity for the best price.

Client/Server Programs

The way one works on a personal computer and the way one works on the Internet are different. Because these differences are fundamental to understanding how the Internet works, we want to close this chapter by addressing some of them.

People used to working with personal computers know that their application programs reside on their computers hard disk and that document files are created every time a Save command is issued. The interaction from the user to the program and from the program to the saved documents seems instantaneous even if it actually isn't.

The Internet's various computer nodes are connected to disks containing numerous programs. Each of the computer nodes is governed by a set of programs. On the Internet, you have the option of running a local program, downloading a program from a remote computer, or, in some cases, actually running a program on a distant computer. This is the case, for example, with the online public access library catalogs (OPACs) in which the actual searching of a very large library database is done by a program located at the site of the OPAC.

For many activities, it doesn't matter whether a program is available locally or at a distance, but imagine the scale of the Internet and the millions of users sending commands and instructions to distant programs, and you can envision some of the traffic bottlenecks and time lags that could result.

This situation has led to the development of a variety of software programs known as client/server. While it isnt necessary to know about client/server technology in any detail, you may run across the term, and it is useful to have a general understanding of what it means because using these new programs can result in a more efficient use of the Internet.

In general, data providers on the Internet realize they can't anticipate all the various equipment configurations and models that may be used to access information. Instead, they have concentrated on establishing standards to provide the information in consistent, regularized, and reliable formats.

Programmers can produce software specific to individual computer platforms when they know that the servers they intend to access contain information in predictable formats. Once servers are known to be reliable, client software can be designed to conform to the special needs of individual hardware configurations. Thus, the Internet access tools described in the following chapter are available for a wide variety of computers. This is why we can talk about SLIP connections and Gopher software later, confident that readers who have Macintosh computers will be able to find client software appropriate for their computers, while DOS users will be able to find similar software for the various operating systems, including OS/2 and Windows, which are particular to their computers.

5

Internet Access Tools

Considering the size of the Internet, the numbers of computers connected to it (over three million at press time), and the sheer amount of data and information resources available, it's easy to imagine that it's impossible to get around on the Internet without getting lost. Although it's true that the Internet's scale and volume are enormous, there are a number of software tools available that help overcome the problems and make it possible and certainly easier to move around.

The following section describes the most common Internet Access Tools. The descriptions are not intended to be definitive, but descriptive. For detailed or technical information you might want to consult books that focus specifically on the How-Tos of the Internet. Appendix E, "Further Readings," gives a list of useful books in this regard.

Moving into and onto the Internet puts one into *cyberspace*, the term coined by William Gibson in his science fiction classic, *Neuromancer*. Cyberspace refers to an electronic place where people and programs work, learn, and coexist. Each of the tools described here have a specialized set of capabilities to help you navigate your way around cyberspace when your computer is connected to the Net.

Telnet

Telnet is one of the earliest Internet Access Tools. This software permits a connection to be made to a remote computer to read the directory of files located on that remote computer and use its programs. Using Telnet software, an authorized user can log on to a computer and have much the same access to it as if he were actually sitting at his own keyboard console.

To use Telnet, you need to know the Internet address of the computer to which you want to establish a connection. If you don't know its address, but do know its common name, you can sometimes use the name in place of the formal Internet address. Simply type the word `telnet` followed by the sequence `ComputerName.ComputerLocation` all in one line with no spaces. For example:

`telnet: olorin.uchicago.edu`

The Internet Telnet software is a tool that has proven to be beneficial to scientific and engineering research and development. This tool makes it possible for people all over the world to work together and share resources in ways otherwise unthinkable without the connectivity that the Internet provides.

Guest Access to Remote Computers

Most computers on the Internet are protected by passwords (at minimum, their important files are protected by some security measures). Only authorized users can have access to protected files. Many of the computers that allow a Telnet connection will permit temporary access (usually restricted to some specific set of functions). In such cases, you might be asked to supply your computer account as a password. In other cases, you will be asked to use the word anonymous or guest as a login. You might have to try several options before being successfully connected to the remote computer. Reading the information on your screen returned by the remote computer during a Telnet session also can provide information about procedures established at a given site.

Telnet-How To

Telnet-How To

An introduction to telnet, an Internet access tool.

Keywords: Internet Tools, Telnet
Sponsor: SURAnet Network Information Center
Audience: Internet Surfers
Contact: info@sura.net
Details: Free

File is: pub/nic/network.service.guides/how.to.telnet.guide

`ftp://ftp.sura.net`

Viruses

It is crucial to point out that most computer viruses are obtained from downloaded program files. Viruses don't come attached to documents or text files but are exclusively associated with executable or program files. If you intend to use FTP (or any other Internet Access Tool) to download executable files to your own computer, make absolutely certain that you know the reliability of the source of the executable program, and that your own computer is protected by a sufficiently capable virus protection program that will scan, evaluate, and intercept all incoming files to check for viruses.

Telnet is a useful command structure with which to interact with computers on the Internet. Many commercial programs now incorporate basic Telnet programming structures, making it possible to use this facility from a variety of telecommunications software programs.

Virus-L

Virus-L

Virus-L is a forum for the discussion of computer virus experiences, protection software, and other virus-related topics. It includes archives and files that list a number of viruses, trojan horses, and pirated programs for the IBM PC.

Keywords: Computer Viruses, Security
Audience: Computer Users
Contact: Kenneth R. van Wyk
luken@vax1.cclehigh.edu
Details: Free

To subscribe to the list, send an e-mail message to the URL address below consisting of a single line reading:

SUB virus-l YourFirstNameYourLastName

To send a message to the entire list, address it to: virus-l@ibml.cc.lehigh.edu

`mailto:listserv@ibm1.cc.lehigh.edu`

Internet Tools

Telnet-How To

An introduction to Telnet, an Internet access tool.
Keywords: Internet, Tools, Telnet
Audience: Internet Users
Producer: SURAnet Network Information Center
Contact: info@sura.net
Details: Free
User Info: File is: pub/nic/network.service.guides/how.to.telnet.guide

`ftp://ftp.sura.net`

FTP (File Transfer Protocol)

FTP is more specific. Its special job is retrieving (downloading) files from remote computers. An FTP Internet Access Tool also enables you to place (upload) files on a remote computer. The files that are transferred can be text files, application programs, binary code, software updates, various utilities, and any of an assortment of helpful or useful computing aids.

To use an FTP Access Tool, you need to know the computer address of the site to which you want to have access, or its common name. Many FTP sites are listed in this directory because they represent a popular way of archiving information that is frequently requested and often downloaded.

Although FTP sites often require passwords, many have been established for the purpose of archiving files, programs, and utilities that are specifically produced for the benefit of the Internet community as freeware (no cost for obtaining or using them for non-commercial purposes). These are known as Anonymous FTP sites, and they enable you to log in with *anonymous* as your login name, and the computer account as the password. Because many of these Anonymous FTP sites are popular, you might experience difficulty logging them at the first try. Persevere, because the information available on many of the Anonymous FTP sites is quite useful.

The difference between an FTP Internet Access Tool and a Telnet tool is that some of the functions for exchanging files have been incorporated into the FTP software. Anything done by FTP software can be done during a Telnet session. The FTP software simply incorporates the command language into various menu items or selections, making it easier for individuals without a working knowledge of Internet protocols to download or upload files.

What you will receive upon login will be a directory listing of the files available. You will need to scroll through these file names looking for items of interest. Many FTP sites have organized files into general categories, but FTP is not designed to provide anything more elaborate than a file name for your guidance. It is a powerful, but simple, retrieval tool.

You should know whether the file you want to move is an executable program or a text file. If it is an executable program, it frequently needs to be identified as a *binary* file, as contrasted with an *ASCII* or *text* identification appropriate for readable files. The FTP software can sometimes make a judgement about what is appropriate (based on a series of algorithms), but if you can supply the information, the transfer may go more smoothly.

FTP FAQ

FTP FAQ

Common questions and answers about FTP (File Transfer Protocol), FTP sites, and anonymous FTP. General information for the novice FTP user.

Keywords: FTP, Internet Reference
Audience: Students, Computer Scientists, Researchers
Contact: Perry Rovers
perry.rovers@kub.nl

`ftp://ftp.ifh.de/pub/FAQ/ftp.faq`

Using FTP requires an individual to know (or learn) what resource is available at which site. There is another Internet Access Tool that has been developed to index all FTP sites, producing a long list of file names and addresses, and which can be enormously useful to those who want to look for specific programs or files and learn where the files actually are located. This service is known as Archie.

Archie

Archie is a software program with a specific function on the Internet. Archie's job is to query all the registered anonymous FTP sites on the Internet in a standardized manner and to create a composite index of the files located on these sites, arranging them in alphabetical order. Because there are thousands of anonymous FTP sites, it could be impossible to find a specific file if you didn't know where it was located. Archie solves the problem by producing a single comprehensive index. Now, if you know a file name, Archie can tell you where such a file is located.

Archie is a software tool that—on an ongoing basis—scans anonymous FTP sites and builds an index of those sites, making it easier to find specific items.

Internet Tools

Archie

A description of Archie, an electronic directory service for the Internet, which allows the user to find files remotely.

Keywords: Internet Tools
Audience: Internet Users
Producer: Computing Centre, McGill University, Montreal, Quebec, Canada
Contact: archie-group@archie.mcgill.ca
Details: Free
User Info: File is: pub/archie/doc/whatis.archie

`http://web-co.uk`

Archie is accessible on the Internet. Directions and instructions can be obtained from the Internet resources listed in the appropriate sections of the directory.

Gopher

Gopher is an extremely popular Internet tool, representing an improved level of ease of use. Gopher was developed at the University of Minnesota. Once connected to a gopher site, you are provided with an opening menu,

Internet Access Tools

followed by a practically unlimited number of submenus. Gopher permits you to access data without knowing precisely what you are looking for. In other words, gopher navigation is based on an inquiry about a subject and does not depend on your knowledge of computer addresses or locations, making it an ideal introductory tool for new Internet users. The links among the gopher sites are more or less invisible to the user, which has made gopher a very popular Internet Access Tool.

Most of the Internet tools can be retrieved from FTP sites. These types of tools often are also carried on local sites, so you might check with your local administrator to find out if a copy is already available to you through your home account provider.

Internet Tools

gopher

A guide to using gopher, an Internet access tool that locates and retrieves resources using a graph of menus.

Keywords: Internet Tools
Audience: Internet Users
Contact: gopher@boombox.micro.umn.edu
Details: Free
User Info: File is: pub/gopher/00README

`ftp://boombox.micro.umn.edu/pub/gopher`

You should locate the appropriate gopher software for your particular computer so that you can pursue those gopher sites that are of interest to you. Frequently, the same site that provides the actual Internet tools will have ancillary files available that provide explanations, demonstrations, or operations manuals.

Internet Tools

Gopher FAQ

Answers to frequently asked questions (FAQs) about gophers from the USENET newsgroup comp.infosystems.gopher

Keywords: Internet, Tools, Gopher
Audience: Internet Users
Contact: Paul Lindner
lindner@boombox.micro.umn.edu
Details: Free
User Info: File is: pub/usenet/news.answers/gopher-faq

`ftp://pit-manager.mit.edu/pub`

Veronica

Veronica is a gopher service analagous to Archie for anonymous FTP sites. The difference is that Veronica has been designed to locate keywords at the various gopher sites that have been established on the Internet. Going to a Veronica site can speed up a search for information. Veronica usually contains information about a large number of sites dealing with a specific keyword, permitting the user to find an Internet resource location that is specific to her interests quickly, rather than making her go through a hierarchical path-searching process.

Veronica is an augmentation of gopher and provides keyword searches of the titles of gopher items. This is a major help to finding where a given file or program not only can be found among the various gopher Internet sites but also can be retrieved. You can often get to Veronica by going through a normal gopher client, either your own or one supplied by your Internet service provider if you don't have your own.

Internet Tools

Veronica Introduction

Veronica (Very Easy Rodent-Oriented Net-wide Index to Computerized Archives) is an Internet access tool that locates titles of gopher items by keyword search.

Keywords: Internet, Tools, Veronica
Audience: Internet Users
Details: Free
User Info: File is: pub/com.archives/bionet.software/veronica

`ftp://cs.dal.ca`

Wide Area Information Servers (WAIS)

WAIS is another information locating tool that enables users to search and access different types of information from a single interface. The information being sought can be in any format (for example, text, sound, or images) and can reside anywhere on the network.

When WAIS finds the information, it ranks the results and delivers a document with the search matches ranked by relevance. You can use the results of your search to modify your original search even further. Thus, if the fourth-ranked file is closer to what you want than the first-ranked file, you can add it to your query parameters, saying, in effect, Get me more like this but including this topic.

WAIS is an example of a tool that provides an enhanced retrieval mechanism through ranking of items according to their relevance to a constructed query.

Internet Tools

WAIS

WAIS (Wide Area Information Servers) is an Internet access tool that retrieves resources by searching indexes of databases.

Keywords: Internet, Tools, WAIS
Audience: Internet Users
Details: Free
User Info: Read wais/README first.

`http://server.wais`

World Wide Web (WWW)

Another characteristic of the Internet is its capability to link documents at one location with files at another. This type of network linking is known as *hypertext*, and a special tool has been developed to pursue hypertextual links among disparate files.

World Wide Web (WWW) is an Internet software tool for network navigation similar to gopher. It also is menu-driven. Unlike gopher, WWW follows hypertext links between related sources rather than files related to one another by server identification. WWW enables you to pursue the strands of a web of information distributed across the Network. Using WWW you might locate an interesting document, notice a citation in it, and use WWW to look up the source document.

This popular Internet navigation software can be obtained from a site in Europe.

Internet Tools

World Wide Web (WWW)

World Wide Web (WWW) is an Internet access tool that retrieves resources through a hypertext browser of databases.

Keywords: Internet, Tools, World Wide Web
Audience: Internet Users
Producer: CERN (European Laboratory for Particle Physics)
Details: Free
User Info: Documents and guides are in: pub/www/doc

`ftp://info.cern.ch`

Though a relative newcomer, WWW holds great promise for navigating the Internet electronically.

Cello and Lynx

Cello and Lynx are useful interfaces to WWW because they are powerful, small, and simple programs. As a result, they are good introductory tools to the World Wide Web of databases on the Internet. The look and feel of these programs is text-based. They lack the elegance of a more polished program like Mosaic, but the navigation capabilities are quick, and the programs provide straightforward and easy ways of obtaining information from WWW sites.

Cello

Cello

A DOS-based Internet browser incorporating WWW (World-Wide Web), Gopher, FTP, Telnet, and usenet.

Keywords: Internet Tools, Cello, DOS
Audience: Internet Surfers
Details: Free

```
ftp://fatty.law.cornell.edu/pub/ldd/cello
```

```
gopher://fatty.law.cornell.edu
```

```
http://fatty.law.cornell.edu/cello/cellotop/html
```

Cello FAQ

A site containing common questions and answers about Cello, a multipurpose Internet browser which allows access to the myriad information resources of the Internet. It supports World Wide Web, Gopher, FTP, CSO/pf/qi, and Usenet News retrievals natively, and other protocols (WAIS, Hytelnet, Telnet, and TN3270) through external clients and public gateways.

Keywords: Internet Tools, Internet Reference
Sponsor: Cornell Law School, New York, USA
Audience: Students, Computer Scientists, Researchers

```
http://www.law.cornell.edu/cello/cellofaq.html
```

Lynx FAQ

A resource providing common questions and answers about Cello, a distributed hypertext browser with full WWW capabilities.

Keywords: Internet Reference
Sponsor: University of Kansas, Distributed Computing Group, Kansas, USA
Audience: Students, Computer Scientists, Researchers
Contact: Garrett Blythe, Lou Montulli
doslynx@falcon.cc.ukans.edu,
montulli@mcom.com
lynx-help@ukanaix.cc.ukans.edu

```
http://ftp2.cc.ukans.edu/about_lynx
```

```
http://ftp2.cc.ukans.edu/lynx_help
```

```
http://ftp2.cc.ukans.edu/lynx_writeup
```

Mosaic

Mosaic was invented by the National Center for Supercomputing Applications at the University of Chicago at Urbana-Champaign, Illinois. It is among the most popular of the recently available Internet searching tools. It comes in many flavors for various computing platforms. Be sure to download the version of Mosaic that matches your computer.

Internet Tools

Mosaic

Mosaic provides a network-distributed hypermedia system for information discovery. It is Internet-based and is free for academic, research, and internal use.

Keywords: Internet, Tools, Mosaic
Audience: Internet Users
Contact: mosaic-x@ncsa.uiuc.edu
Details: Free
User Info: File is: Mosaic/README.Mosaic

```
ftp://ftp.ncsa.uiuc.edu
```

Mosaic understands the protocols of many of the most-used graphical user interfaces. It unifies the searching capacities of many Internet retrieval tools and adds the capability to display images in a variety of graphic formats. This means that Mosaic can retrieve a variety of image files and show them to you on your computer even if you don't own the original graphics program from which the images were generated. Of course, your computer must be able to display graphics (that is, it must have a windowing capability of some sort).

Mosaic is very popular due to its flexibility and its comprehensiveness as an Internet navigator and retriever of a wide variety of types of files. As with many such specialized tools, finding out what can be retrieved by Mosaic can be a problem. Just before publication of this directory, an Internet announcement heralded the appearance of World Wide Web (Worm) WWW(W). The worm accomplishes a function similar to that of Veronica. It scours the Internet, locating WWW sites and indexing their contents so that people can more easily find information they are seeking.

Mosaic

Mosaic Home Page

This is the welcome page to the National Center for Supercomputing Applications (NCSA) World Wide Web server, which features the Mosaic application. Mosaic provides a network-distributed hypermedia system for information discovery. It is Internet-based and is free for academic, research, and internal commercial use.

Keywords: Internet Tools, Mosaic, WWW
Audience: Internet Surfers
Contact: mosaic-x@ncsa.uiuc.edu
Details: Free

```
http://www.ncsa.uiuc.edu/SDG/Software/Mosaic/NCSAMosaicHome.html
```

Newsreaders

Newsreader programs have been created specifically to give people easy ways to read postings made to specific Usenet newsgroups, a specific variety of electronic discussion group. Usenet is a type of loosely organized network, stemming from the period in the Internet's development when programmers designed software for their own use. The programs created to make it easy to keep in touch with one another on a variety of topics became known as *newsgroups*, which became very popular and proliferated. Newsreader software was created when the number of newsgroups grew to unmanageable proportions.

Newsreaders are programs that permit you to specify those newsgroups that are of interest to you. Having been configured in this manner, the program then collects information only from the specified sources, making it a burdenless process to keep abreast of one or several discussions at a time. There is a way to post messages to newsgroups through e-mail (see the following example).

Internet

E-mail Usenet

E-mail Usenet allows the user to post to a newsgroup via e-mail.

Keywords: Internet, Services, E-mail, Usenet
Audience: Internet Surfers
Details: Free

```
mailto://hierarchy-group-name@cs.utexas.edu
```

Internet Access Tools

The following listing contains instructions on retrieving newsreader software. Routine postings on Usenet lists contain information about subscribing to them. Comprehensive and frequently updated lists of currently active newsgroups also are available. These form a dynamic and active portion of the Internet. Changes are frequent, with some newsgroup topics emerging while others are dying off for lack of sustained interest.

Newsreaders

Usenet Newsreaders

Usenet newsreader programs have been created to give people ways to read the thousands of Usenet newsgroups available on the Internet. Among the most popular are: tin, rn, nn, and trn.

Keywords: Newsreaders, Usenet

Audience: Internet Users

Profile: The rn interface uses full-screen display with direct positioning. It includes reading, discarding, and/or processing of articles based on user-definable patterns, and the ability of the user to develop customized macros for display and keyboard interaction.

trn allows readers to follow "threads of discussions" in newsgroups. Trn can be obtained from ftp.coe.montana.edu in the /pub/trn directory, from uunet in the news subdirectory, and from many other archive servers world-wide.

"nn" is different in that it presents a menu of article subject and sender-name lines, allowing you to preselect articles to read. nn is also a very fast newsreader

tin" is a reader that operates with threads, has different article organization methods, and is full-screen oriented. tin also works on a local news spool and has an extensive list of features.,

User Info: rn software can be obtained from:
ftp://lib.tmc.edu
trn can be obtained from:
ftp://ftp.coe.montana.edu in the /pub/trn directory and from manyother Archie servers worldwide.
nn can be obtained via anonymous FTP from: ftp://dkuug.dk, uop.uop.edu
tin can be retrieved by accessing the newsgroup: news:alt.sources

Details: Free

Notes: Each of thse newsreaders can be access from a variety of sources. Further information regarding tin is available from Iain Lea (iain%anl433.uucp@Germany.EU.net).

See the URL information given in the User Info.field above.

Usenet is not centrally organized, so there is no control over who gets a particular newsfeed or how individual articles are sent out. But the bottom line is that whatever your interest may be, there's bound to be a discussion group dedicated to that very subject.

Finger: Finding People on the Internet

Finger helps you locate other people on the Internet. The Finger tool can provide the e-mail addresses, full name, telephone numbers, and other information about a particular user at a specified site. Because Finger enables you to search the user log on a computer connected to the Internet, you can find someone's e-mail address provided you know the name of the computer he or she uses. Even if you don't know a person's login name, you can type part of a person's name and Finger will produce a list of possibilities.

Finger (Internet Database)

Finger Database

This service allows access to a database facility via finger.

Keywords: Internet Services, Finger (Internet Database)

Audience: Internet Surfers

Contact: http://www.usyd.edu.au

Details: Free

`finger://help@dir.su.oz.au`

Service or resource providers on the Internet will often provide help facilities that explain the service or resource. Such is the case with the Internet Finger Database. It is worth trying an address a few times if at first you dont succeed in getting through. You also can experiment with the possibility of reaching a resource using other Internet tools if the first tool doesn't work.

Internet Services

Finger Database

This service allows access to a database facility via Finger.

Keywords: Internet, Services, Finger

Audience: Internet Users

Details: Free

`finger://help@dir.su.oz.au`

Finger enables you to access other types of information contained in text files. For instance you can reach NASA's *Headline News* by typing:

`finger://nasanews@space.mit.edu`

Or you can find the *Top 40* on the pop music charts by typing:

`finger://buckmr@aix.rpi.edu`

STAR (Subject and Topic Access Rater)

What each of these electronic Internet Access Tools lacks is an evaluation of the resource by subject experts. In that context, the STAR ratings are an important Internet access tool because they provide an analytical judgement in a familiar format.

Brown University Library

Brown University Library

The Brown libraries contain approximately 1.5 million volumes, including historical archives of early American imprints and biomedical engineering holdings.

Keywords: Libraries, Research

Audience: General Public, Researchers

Contact: Howard Pasternick
blips15@brownvm.brown.edu

Details: Free

Notes: At the Brown logon screen: tab to command field, Enter Dial Josiah, tab to Josiah choice on the screen.

`telnet://brownvm.brown.edu`

`telnet://library.brown.edu`

`http://stanley.cis.brown.edu/university-library`

6

Internet Addresses Explained

Each of the resources listed in *The New Riders Official Internet Directory* includes at least one Internet address referred to as a Uniform Resource Locator (URL). The URL appears at the bottom of each listing and is the unique electronic address on the Internet that identifies the location of that specific site and the method(s) for gaining access to it.

It is common now to refer to Internet addresses as URLs. *The New Riders Official Internet Directory* adopts this standard for all addresses listed.

Communications on the Internet

Information moves across the Internet in much the same way as mail moves through post offices. Just as your letter is carried in a mail truck, your electronic message is transported through a packet-switching network. In either instance, the message travels along with thousands of other unrelated messages. In the case of the Internet, the destination computer picks up and reassembles the pieces of your message before delivering it to your personal mailbox.

The Internet URL is made up of specific address parts that guarantee a unique address code for each information packet or file. The Transmission Control Protocol (TCP) is the set of rules guaranteeing that packets sent through the Internet are properly packaged, efficiently transmitted, and properly received at their destination.

Understanding Internet Addresses

When you first see an Internet URL, it can appear incomprehensible, as in the following example:

`telnet://purple-crayon.media.mit.edu:8888`

Instead of separating parts of an address by lines as on an envelope, an Internet address separates elements typographically using periods, slashes, and colons. Just as the world is divided up into continents, countries, and regions, Internet addresses are divided up into domains and subdomains. Countries have domain names, and these are known as top-level domains. India's domain name is *in*, for example, Japan's is *jp*, and the United Kingdom's is *uk*.

Internet addresses are built up from left to right, beginning with the most specific piece of information (a users personal and individual identification) and proceeding to the most general (the highest level domain within which the user can be found).

URLs provide one additional important piece of information. They identify the access tools you need to use when attempting to reach a particular Internet resource. These tools have been explained in more detail in the chapter on Internet access tools. They have names like telnet, gopher, FTP, MOSAIC, and WAIS. To reach a specific Internet resource, you need to know which primary access tool will gain you access to it.

Thus at the beginning of each URL address in this directory, the first item of information identifies the appropriate tool to use in accessing that particular resource. Depending on your software, you may have to type the research tool words as commands. These may be summarized as follows:

- telnet://—use a standard telnet tool to access the resource.
- gopher://—use any of the variety of gopher software that is available for your computer.
- ftp://—use File Transfer Protocol tools.

The situation, however, is different for mailto or http. The tools for accessing those types of resources instruct you on how to proceed.

- mailto:—use telnet or standard e-mail management software. (Do not type the word mailto.)
- http://—use Mosaic.

Dissecting a Uniform Resource Locator (URL)

Following is a typical URL address and a description of what each element means.

`telnet://purple-crayon.media.mit.edu:8888`

The :// that follows the research tool is the standard way of separating the name of the research tool from the remainder of the URL address. If your host computer runs UNIX (which most host computers do), then for research tools like telnet and gopher you do not need to physically type :// into the computer when you are trying to access the resource. Instead, you leave a space between the command and the address.

`purple-crayon.media.mit.edu` actually is a specific computer! On the Internet, computers have distinguishing numerical identifiers, known as IP addresses (for example, 18.85.0.48). These addresses are hard to remember, so to make things simpler, the computers have also been assigned easier-to-remember names. Both the name of the computer and its IP number can be used interchangeably in an Internet address. At each major site, a computer acts as a domain name server, which translates any alphabetic IP address into its proper numerical one.

In this example, the purple-crayon computer is located on a subnet of other computers that are all collected together in the network media. In turn, the subnet media is located at mit, which stands for the Massachusetts Institute of Technology, located in Boston Massachussetts.

The .edu at the end of the address reveals that this address represents an educational institution. Certain types of messages (for example, those that are strictly business or commercial) are prohibited from traveling from computers dedicated to research or teaching. Similarly, you cant use military computers to exchange stock market information. While the laws regarding appropriate use have relaxed over time, the individual institutional policies governing these uses, and—perhaps more important—the culture of the Internet user community, is very good at policing itself and taking violators to task. This is especially true for those who appear to be posting messages of a purely marketing or advertising content.

Within the US, higher level domains have been established that are based on different kinds of organizations instead of on geographical location. These include .com (commercial), .edu (education and research), .gov (government agencies), .mil (military), .net (network support centers), and .org (other organizations).

Because the Internet began in the United States, *users* within the US do not presently need to identify the top-level domain *us* in an Internet address. As usage of the Internet continues to expand internationally, it eventually may be necessary to add this final suffix to addresses even within the US. It is, however, required for countries outside the United States. If the example were an address within the educational sector of the Czech Republic, it would be written with the final suffix showing the top-level domain of that country.

Finally, the :8888 is the port number. This instructs your computer to connect not only to a specific address, but to one special port at that address. Whereas Mosaic sites and Telnet sites might not include any port numbers at all, gopher servers have been designated to use port 70. If you were typing the command at a UNIX prompt, it would look like this:

`telnet purple-crayon.media.mit.edu 8888`

Notice that spaces separate those parts of the address that were marked as colons in the URL.

The Internet addressing system may seem complicated at first, but after a while, you will begin to recognize domain names and be able to tell not only where resources lie, but which types of organizations they are associated with.

7

E-Mail on the Internet

Sending and receiving electronic mail (e-mail) is one of the Internet's most frequently used functions. At one time, it was thought that letter-writing would go the way of the horse and buggy, but e-mail has revived and transformed it into something new.

Instead of being delivered by the Post Office, e-mail messages are sent directly to your computer. This not only vastly accelerates the speed with which messages can be transmitted, but provides numerous advantages to individuals as well as businesses.

People use e-mail for the same reasons they use postal mail. In addition, e-mail can be used to transfer and receive copies of files and document; to subscribe to electronic discussion groups, electronic journals, and electronic newsgroups; to obtain free copies of computer software; and to obtain copies of sounds, graphics, and multimedia over the Internet. E-mail is not only faster, but the cost is a fraction of what it is to send and receive mail through traditional means.

There are any number of useful e-mail management software packages available. Many have built in functions that facilitate sending and receiving messages, attaching other files from your computer, and replying to messages that you might have received. With speed and convenience, however, come the danger of new forms of miscommunication.

Using the Reply Function

Most e-mail software packages permit you to easily reply to an incoming message. Every message has a header. The header contains information about the time a message was sent, where it came from, and what path it took to reach you. When you use the Reply function built in to the software, it assumes you want to respond to the sender and uses the information from the header to address your reply.

While this is easy, there are two common situations you should be cautious about.

cc: [carbon copies]. Some software picks up the names of any individuals who have been copied on the original incoming message, or you may have received a copy of a message sent to someone else. Know how your e-mail software treats a "reply." Some packages pick up only the address of the original sender; others pick up all the names of those receiving the message. You may (or may not) want your reply to go to all the individuals who received the original message. Be sure to check which it is that you want.

ListServs. Similarly, when a message comes to you from an electronic discussion group, it is sent by the software that provides mail management functions for a list of individuals. The most common of such software is known as ListServ or MajorDomo. If you post a message to the list management software, the message is sent to all subscribers to the list. But if you use the Reply function, your message also goes to everyone on the discussion list. If you don't want that to happen, pay particular attention to the address line before sending your message

Perhaps the only true drawback of e-mail is that the system is not secure. This means that others may be able to read the mail you send or receive. If you want your mail to remain private, don't risk sending it e-mail.

E-mail Software Programs

To be able to write and receive e-mail messages, you need to have an e-mail software program. The purpose of this software is to enable you to see incoming e-mail messages and to provide an editor for outgoing messages. Check with your local computer software support staff for advice on which e-mail software is most suitable for you.

Using E-mail To Subscribe to ListServs, Mailing Lists, and Discussion Groups

Any listing that has a URL beginning with `mailto:` can be subscribed to via e-mail. Simply "write" to the contact person of the resource, and they "write back." It is just like sending a letter through the post office, except it all happens electronically.

To subscribe to a ListServ group, you first need to send an e-mail message to the URL address. Sometimes the transaction takes place between software programs. Other times, you will be dealing directly with someone. Knowing the difference between a list that has a moderator and one that is controlled by software is useful. You can usually tell by the URL. If the address contains the information listserv@, the resource is handled by a computer; if it contains the information -request@ there is an intermediary who handles the subscription and information requests and maintains the distribution list manually.

Other mailing lists and discussion groups can be subscribed to simply by sending a message to the contact e-mail address supplied.

A Note on Passwords. Security issues on the Internet have frequently made headline news. Individual Internet users can minimize their risks of being victimized by installing and using virus protection software on their computers and by choosing a password that is not easily determined. Passwords also should be changed frequently.

ListServs. ListServs are software programs that enable and maintain e-mail discussion groups. Each ListServ is dedicated to a specific topic. ListServ software permits Internet users to subscribe to a list. After you do so, you will receive copies of any message sent to the list.

To subscribe to a ListServ list, send an e-mail message to the software (called, *ListServ*) that governs the subscription requests and maintains the distribution records for the discussion list in which you are interested. The software governing a list will be located on the same computer host on which a particular discussion group is located. The subscription request is sent as a message containing the single line: `<SUB ListName YourFirstName YourLastName>`

(Substitute your real first name and your real last name for the phrases YourFirstName and YourLastName above.)

To unsubscribe is easier. Send a message containing the single line: `UNSUB ListName>`

In this case, the computer software will determine your first name and last name based on the records it has kept about who has subscribed to the list. It is, however, important to send these messages from the same computer from which you subscribed in the first place, otherwise the records wont match.

To send a message to everyone on the list, simply address an e-mail message to the list instead of to the ListServ software. Thus, if you wanted to join a list called Wonderful-L located at rloc.bernard.edu, you would send a subscription request to: `ListServ@rloc.bernard.edu`

If you intended to send a message to all the subscribers of the list you would address your message to: `Wonderful-L@rloc.bernard.edu`

The computer host, domain, and type (everything following the @ sign) are identical in both instances. You simply are addressing the software manager (ListServ) in the first case, and the distribution list (Wonderful-L) in the second.

ListServs are free. You do not need to pay a subscription fee. But there may be a price associated with subscribing to too many ListServs (or ones that are very active). You should be aware that some ListServs generate a lot of interest and a lot of mail. If you subscribe to several ListServs, be prepared for a substantial increase in mail. This can be difficult to review, but it can also take up disk space on your own computer until you can decide whether or not you wish to keep individual messages. Keep records of the lists to which you have subscribed so that you can easily unsubscribe from a list that inundates you with more messages than you care to (or are able to) handle.

Bulletin Board Systems (BBSs).
Newsgroups distributed worldwide are broken down into the following seven traditional classifications. Each newsgroup is geared to a specific subject. Some newsgroups may literally have thousands of subscribers whereas others may exist with only a dozen or so subscribers.

news	Groups concerned with the news about network and administration topics.
soc	Groups that primarily address social issues and socializing.
talk	Groups largely debate-oriented that tend to feature long exploratory discussions on individual topics with little resolution.
misc	Groups that address themes that are not easily classified under any other headings, or that incorporate themes from multiple headings.
sci	Groups concerned with discussing practical knowledge, usually related to research in or the application of established sciences.
comp	Groups that discuss topics of interest to computer professionals and hobbyists. Hardware and software systems are also discussed.
rec	Groups oriented toward the arts, hobbies, and recreational activities.

In addition, there is a rapidly growing category of newsgroups with alternative grouped names. These involve subjects or communities that are less formal and less traditional, such as the following:

alt	Groups that deal with ephemeral, frivolous, or highly controversial topics.
biz	Groups that are for business and commercial topics.
Ieee	Groups that are for discussions related to engineering and electronics.
k12	Groups that are for discussions of primary school educational topics.

BBSs are software tools for providing bulletin board services. BBSs differ only slightly from e-mail ListServs. Any given BBS can provide e-mail, but it will also provide access to collections of data and documents that are available for downloading. BBSs offer an alternative to ListServs in that you can choose whether you want to obtain information from a BBS, whereas by subscribing to a ListServ you automatically receive all messages from the ListServ. Non-Internet BBSs frequently involve a fee for access, while most Internet-based BBS are free.

Usenet (Users Network). Usenet refers to a worldwide collection of thousands of computers (not all on the Internet) that host and receive Usenet newsgroup information and exchanges. Youll find many of these in *The New Riders' Official Internet Directory* as they have become immensely popular. There are thousands of newsgroups that function as forums for the exchange of questions and answers by their users concerning a selected topic.

A

AACIS-L (American Association for Collegiate Independent Study)

AACIS-L (American Association for Collegiate Independent Study)

The focus of this list is on correspondence, independent study, and distance learning.

Keywords:	Education (Adult), Education (Distance), Education (Continuing)
Sponsor:	American Association for Collegiate Independent Study (AACIS)
Audience:	Faculty Administrators
Details:	Free
User Info:	To subscribe to the list, send an e-mail message to the URL address shown below consisting of a single line reading:
	SUB aacis-l YourFirstName YourLastName
	To send a message to the entire list, address it to: aacis-l@bgu.edu

`mailto:listserv@bgu.edu`

AARNet Guide

AARNet Guide

This is the Australian Network Sites and Resources Guide.

Keywords:	Internet, Internet Guides, Australia
Sponsor:	Australian Academic and Research Network
Audience:	Internet Surfers
Details:	Free

Files are in: pub/resource-guide

`ftp://aarnet.edu.au/pub/resource-guide`

ABC Programming Language

ABC

Discussion of the ABC Programming Language and its implementations.

Keywords:	Programming Languages, ABC Programming Language
Audience:	Programmers
Contact:	Steven Pemberton abc-list-request@cwi.nl
Details:	Free
User Info:	To subscribe to the list, send an e-mail message requesting a subscription to the URL address below.
	To send a message to the entire list, address it to: ABC@cwi.nl

`mailto:abc-list-request@cwi.nl`

ABI/Inform

ABI/Inform

ABI/Inform is a comprehensive source for business and management information, containing abstracts from close to 1,000 publications and the full-text from over 100 publications. The database covers trends, corporate strategies and tactics, management techniques, competitive information and product information

Keywords:	Business, Business Management, Management
Sponsor:	UMI, Ann Arbor, Michigan, US
Audience:	General Public, Researchers, Librarians
Profile:	A few of the thousands of business subjects that can searched in ABI/Inform include: company news and analysis, market conditions and strategies, employee management and compensation, international trade and investment, management styles and corporate cultures, and economic conditions and forecasts.
Contact:	CDP Technologies Sales Department (800)950-2035, extension 400
User Info:	To subscribe, contact CDP Technologies directly

`telnet://cdplus@cdplus.com`

Abolitionism

Johns Hopkins University Library

The library's's holdings are large and wide-ranging and contain significant collections in many fields.

Keywords:	Literature (English), Economics, Classics, Drama (German), Slavery, Trade Unions, Incunabula, Bibles, Diseases (History of), Nursing (History of), Abolitionism
Audience:	General Public, Researchers, Librarians, Historians
Details:	Free

`telnet://jhuvm.hcf.jhu.edu`

The University of Illinois at Chicago Library

The library's holdings are large and wide-ranging and contain significant collections in many fields.

Keywords:	Health Science, Chicago, Industry, Slavery, Abolitionism, Roosevelt (Franklin D.)
Audience:	General Public, Researchers, Librarians, Historians
Details:	Free
User Info:	Expect: introductory screen, Send: Clear key; Expect: UIC flame screen, Send: Enter key; Expect: Logon screen, Send: DIAL PVM; Expect: PVM (Passthru) screen, Send: Type: Move cursor to NOTIS and press Enter key Response: One line message about port in use Type: Enter key

`telnet://uicvm.uic.edu`

U.S. Civil War Reading List

A major directory on abolitionism, providing access to a broad range of resources (library catalogs, databases, and servers) via the Internet.

Keywords:	History (US), Abolitionism
Audience:	General Public, Historians
Profile:	The Suggested Civil War Reading List contains 61 books, several of them with multiple volumes, as well as an 11-hour documentary film and a CD of Civil War era songs. The material is sorted into general categories: General Histories of the War, Causes of the War and History to 1861, Slavery and Southern Society, Reconstruction, Biographies and Autobiographies, Source Documents and official Records, Unit Histories and Soldiers' Reminiscences, Fiction, Specific Battles and Campaigns, Strategies and Tactics, The Experience of Soldiers.
Contact:	Stephen Schmidt whale@leland.Stanford.edu

`http://www.cis.ohio-state.edu/hypertext/faq/usenet/civil-war-usa/reading-list/faq.html`

Abortion

Abortion and Reproductive Rights

A major directory on abortion, providing access to a broad range of related resources (library catalogs, databases, and servers) via the Internet.

Keywords:	Abortion, Activism, Women's Issues
Sponsor:	The WELL Computer Conference System
Audience:	Activists, Feminists
Profile:	Choice-Net Report is a weekly update on reproductive rights issues distributed through E-mail, Women's Wire, gopher.WELL.com, Usenet groups alt.activism, talk.abortion, soc.women, and other Internet channels.
Details:	Free

`http://gopher.well.sf.ca.us`

alt.feminism

A Usenet newsgroup providing information and discussion about feminism.

Keywords:	Feminism, Women's Studies, Abortion, Activism
Audience:	Women, General Public, Feminists
User Info:	To subscribe to this Usenet newsgroup, you need access to a newsreader.

`news:alt.feminism`

table.abortion

A Usenet newsgroup providing information and discussion about all sides of the abortion issue.

Keywords:	Abortion, Women's Issues, Health
Audience:	Women, Activists, Health Care Professionals
Details:	Free
User Info:	To subscribe to this Usenet newsgroup, you need access to a newsreader.

`news:table.abortion`

Women.health

This conference features articles, documents, news, announcements, policy statements, and other information about women's health around the world. Topics include breast cancer, ovarian cancer, alcohol, abortion, pregnancy, sterilization of women, pesticides, Quinacrine, HIV, disability.

Keywords:	Women, Abortion, AIDS, Disability, Feminism, Health
Audience:	Activists, Family Planners, Health Professionals, Non-Governmental Organizations, Women
Details:	Costsosts
User Info.:	Establish an account on the nearest APC node. Login, type c for conferences, then type go women.health. For information on the nearest APC node, contact: APC International Secretariat IBASE.
E-mail:	apcadmin@apc.org

`telnet://igc.apc.org`

Academia

Academia Latinoamericana de Espanol

This program is specifically designed for those interested in learning to speak Spanish through a fully immersive trip to Ecuador.

Keywords:	Spanish Language, Education (Bilingual)
Sponsor:	Academia Latinoamericana de Espanol, Quito, Ecuador
Audience:	Researchers, Students, Language Teachers
Contact:	Webmaster webmaster@comnet.com

`http://www.comnet.com/ecuador/learnSpanish.html`

Academic Freedom Statements

A major directory on academic freedom, providing access to a broad range of related resources (library catalogs, databases, and servers) via the Internet.

Keywords:	Academia
Audience:	Professors, Students (College/Graduate), General Public
Profile:	An online collection of general academic freedom statements, including the Statement on the Rights and Freedoms of Students. Examples of statements include: Academic Freedom and Artistic Expression; an official statement of the American Association of University Professors; The Lima Declaration on Academic Freedom and Autonomy of Institutions of Higher Education; an international declaration by the World University Service; A Statement on the Freedom to Read, Queen's University (Canada); The Yale University (Connecticut) Policy on Freedom of Expression.
Contact:	J.S. Greenfield greeny@eff.org

`gopher://gopher.ef.org/00/CAF/academic/README`

Academic Institution Information of Western Countries

A major directory of information on academic institutions, providing access to a broad range of related resources (library catalogs, databases, and servers) via the Internet.

Keywords:	Academic Research, Information Retrieval, Academia
Audience:	Students, Educators, Researchers
Profile:	Includes information on financial aid, and address for academic institutions in Australia, Canada, Europe, New Zealand, and Hong Kong.

`gopher://ifcss.org/11/cal-aeic/info-World.Inst`

Academic Job Listings All Over the World

A major directory on academic institution information, providing access to a broad range of related resources (library catalogs, databases, and servers) via the Internet.

Keywords: Academia, Employment

Audience: Academics, General Public
Contact: Prentiss Riddle cwis@rice.edu

`gopher://riceinfo.rice.edu/11/Subject/Jobs`

alt.usage.english ★

A Usenet newsgroup providing information and discussion about English grammar, word usages, and related topics.

Keywords: Lexicology, Academia, Linguistics, Education
Audience: English Educators
User Info: To subscribe to this Usenet newsgroup, you need access to a newsreader.

`news:alt.usage.english`

CAF Archive

A source of information relating to Computers and Academic Freedom (CAF).

Keywords: Education, Computers, Academia
Audience: Educators, Researchers
Contact: kadie@eff.org

`http://www.eff.org/CAF/cafhome.html`

The English Server ★★★

A large and eclectic collection of humanities resources.

Keywords: Humanities, Academia, English, Popular Culture, Feminism
Sponsor: Carnegie Mellon University English Department, Pittsburgh, Pennsylvania, USA
Audience: General Public, University Students, Educators (College/University), Researchers (Humanities)
Profile: Contains archives of conventional humanities materials, such as historical documents and classic books in electronic form. Also offers more unusual and hard-to-find resources, particularly in the field of popular culture and media. Features access to many humanities and culture-related online journals such as Bad Subjects, FineArt Forum, and Postmodern Culture. Also has links to a wide variety of related Internet sites and resources.
Contact: Geoff Sauer postmaster@english-server.hss.cmu.edu

`gopher://english-server.hss.cmu.edu`

`http://english-server.hss.cmu.edu`

The MIT Press Online Catalogs ★★

A descriptive listing of recent books and current journals published by the MIT Press.

Keywords: Academia, Books, Publishing, Technology
Sponsor: The MIT Press, Cambridge, Massachusetts, USA.
Audience: Reseachers, Scholars, University Students, Technical Professionals
Profile: Contains a keyword-searchable index of books published in the years 1993 to 1994, as well as current journals covering computational and cognitive sciences, architecture, photography, art and literary theory, economics, environmental science, and linguistics.
Contact: ehling@mitpress.mit.edu
Notes: Coverage: 1993 to present; updated semiannually. MIT Press can also be accessed by calling (800) 356-0343.

`http://www-mitpress.mit.edu`

`gopher://gopher.mit.edu`

Research Databases and Resources by Subject ★★

A collection of databases on over forty subjects, ranging from Anthropology to Women's Studies.

Keywords: Databases, Academia
Sponsor: University of California at Berkeley
Audience: Researchers, General Public
Contact: Gopher Manager gophcom@infolib.lib.berkeley.edu

`gopher://umslvma.umsl.edu/Library/Subjects/Biology/Bioformt/Biodbs`

`gopher://infolib.lib.berkeley.edu`

Academics

Academic Computing Training & User Support

This directory is a compilation of information resources focusing on academic computer training and user support.

Keywords: Computing, Academics
Audience: Computer Users

`ftp://una.hh.lib.umich.edu/70/inetdirsstacks/acadcomp:kovacsm`

Academic Institution Informations of Western Countries ★★★

A major directory of information on academic institutions, providing access to a broad range of related resources (library catalogs, databases, and servers) via the Internet.

Keywords: Academics, Information Retrieval
Audience: Students, Educators, Researchers
Profile: Includes information on financial aid, and address on academic institutions in Australia, Canada, Europe, New Zealand, and Hong Kong.

`gopher://ifcss.org/11/cal-aeic/info-World.Inst`

Accounting

Financial Economics Network (FEN) ★★★★

A mailing list dedicated to recent research in financial economics.

Keywords: Accounting, Economics, Finance
Audience: Business Professionals, Investors, Economists, Accountants
Contact: Wayne Marr Email:marrm@clemson.clemson.edu
Profile: FEN is the largest network of business and economics scholars and practitioners in the world. FEN is a 40+-channel electronic network linking teachers, scholars, and practitioners in investment banks, banks, companies of all sizes, government agencies, international agencies, and universities.
User Info: Access to the network is free, but you must request a subscription to be included in the mailing list.
Details: Free, Moderated

`URL:mailto:marrm@clemson.clemson.edu`

NAARS (National Automated Accounting Research System)

The National Automated Accounting Research System (NAARS) library, provided as a service by agreement with the American Institute of Certified Public Accountants (AICPA) contains a variety of accounting information.

Keywords: Accounting, Auditing, Filings, Publications
Audience: Accountants
Profile: The NAARS library contains annual reports of public corporations and accounting literature and publications for the accounting professional. Annual reports are annotated with descriptive terms assigned by the AICPA. These terms allow the user to search for annual report footnotes that illustrate one or more recognized accounting practices.
Contact: Mead New Sales Group at (800) 227-4908 or (513) 859-5398 inside the US, or (513) 865-7981 for all inquiries outside the US.
User Info: To subscribe, contact Mead directly.

To examine the Nexis user guide, you can access it at the ftp site of the University of Texas at Austin at the URL address: ftp://ftp.cc.utexas.edu

The files are in: /pub/ref-services/LEXIS

`telnet://nex.meaddata.com`

`http://www.meaddata.com`

Utah Valley Community College Library

The library's holdings are large and wide-ranging and contain significant collections in many fields.

Keywords: Accounting, Automobiles, Cabinetry, Child Care, Drafting, Electronics, Home Building, Local History, Refrigeration, Air Conditioning
Audience: General Public, Researchers, Librarians, Document Delivery Professionals
Details: Free
User Info: Expect: Login; Send: Opub

`telnet://uvlib.uvcc.edu`

Accri-l

Accri-l

A mailing list providing information on anesthesia and critical care resources available via the Internet.

Keywords: Health Care, Medical Treatment, Medicine
Audience: Health Care Professionals, Health Care Providers
Contact: A.J. Wright
meds002@uabdpo.dpo.uab.edu
User Info: To subscribe, send an e-mail message to the URL address below consisting of a single line reading:

SUB accri-l YourFirstName YourLastName

To send a message to the entire list, address it to: accri-l@uabdpo.dpo.uab.edu

`mailto:listserv@uabdpo.dpo.uab.edu`

ACDGIS-L

ACDGIS-L

GIS discussions for German speakers.

Keywords: Germany, Geographic Information Systems, Geography
Audience: Germans, Geographers, Cartographers
Details: Costs

Inquire through wigeoarn@awiwuw11.bitnet

`mailto:acdgis-l@awiwuw11.bitnet`

ACEN (Art Com Electronic Network)

ACEN (Art Com Electronic Network)

A conference on the WELL for art, technology, and text-based artworks.

Keywords: Art, Literature (Contemporary), Multimedia
Sponsor: Art Com Electronic Network
Audience: Artists, Musicians, Writers
Profile: Started in 1986, ACEN is a seminal art BBS that includes actual artworks, discussion on topics such as software as art, and on line published works by John Cage, Fred Truck, Jim Rosenberg, Judy Malloy, and others.
Contact: Carl Loeffler
artcomtv@well.sf.ca.us
User Info: To participate in a conference on the WELL, you must first establish an account on the WELL. To do so, start by typing: telnet://well.sf.ca.us

`telnet://well.sf.ca.us`

ACLU

ACLU Free Reading Room

A gopher site containing information relating to the ACLU (American Civil Liberties Union), including the current issue of the ACLU newsletter, Civil Liberties; a growing collection of recent public policy reports and action guides; Congressional voting records for the 103rd Congress; and an archive of news releases from the ACLU's national headquarters.

Keywords: ACLU, Civil Liberties, Congress (US), Activism
Sponsor: ACLU (American Civil Liberties Union)
Audience: Privacy Activists, Civil Libertarians, Activists
Contact: infoaclu@aclu.org

`gopher://aclu.org`

ACM SIGGRAPH Online Bibliography Project

ACM SIGGRAPH Online Bibliography Project

This is a collection of computer-graphics bibliographic references.

Keywords: Multimedia, Interactive, Computer Graphics, Programming
Sponsor: Association of Computing Machinery (ACM), Special Interest Group on Computer Graphics (SIGGRAPH)
Audience: Developers, Designers, Producers, Educators, Programmers, Graphic Artists
Profile: The goal of this project is to maintain an up-to-date database of computer-graphics literature, in a format that is accessible to as many members of the computer-graphics community as possible. The database includes references from conferences and workshops worldwide and from a variety of publications dating back as far as the late-19th century. The majority of the major journals and conference proceedings from the mid-1970s to the present are listed.
Contact: bibadmin@siggraph.org
Details: Free, Moderated, Multimedia

`ftp://siggraph.org/publications`

Acoustical Engineering

CEC

CEC (Canadian Electro-Acoustics Community).

Keywords: Engineering, Acoustical Engineering, Canada, Canadian Electro-Acoustics Community
Audience: Engineers
Contact: Peter Gross
GROSSPA@QUCDN
Details: Free
User Info: To subscribe to the list, send an e-mail message to the URL address below, consisting of a single line reading:

SUB cec YourFirstName YourLastName

To send a message to the entire list, address it to: ced@qucdn.queensu.ca

`mailto:listserv@qucdn.queensu.ca`

Activism

Abortion and Reproductive Rights

A major directory on abortion, providing access to a broad range of related resources (library catalogs, databases, and servers) via the Internet.

Keywords: Abortion, Activism, Women's Issues

Sponsor:	The WELL Computer Conference System
Audience:	Activists, Feminists
Profile:	Choice-Net Report is a weekly update on reproductive rights issues distributed through E-mail, Women's Wire, gopher.WELL.com, Usenet groups alt.activism, talk.abortion, soc.women, and other Internet channels.
Details:	Free

`http://gopher.well.sf.ca.us`

ACLU Free Reading Room

A gopher site containing information relating to the ACLU (American Civil Liberties Union), including the current issue of the ACLU newsletter, Civil Liberties; a growing collection of recent public policy reports and action guides; Congressional voting records for the 103rd Congress; and an archive of news releases from the ACLU's national headquarters.

Keywords:	ACLU, Civil Liberties, Congress (US), Activism
Sponsor:	ACLU (American Civil Liberties Union)
Audience:	Privacy Activists, Civil Libertarians, Activists
Contact:	infoaclu@aclu.org

`gopher://aclu.org`

Act-up

A mailing list for discussion of the work being done by various Act-Up chapters worldwide.

Keywords:	AIDS, Health Care, Activism
Audience:	AIDS Activists, Health Science Researchers
Contact:	Lenard Diggins act-up-request@world.std.com
User Info:	To subscribe to the list, send an e-mail message to the URL address below. To send a message to the entire list, address it to: act-up-request@world.std.com

`mailto:act-up-request@world.std.com`

Activ-L

A mailing list for the discussion of peace, empowerment, justice, and environmental issues.

Keywords:	Peace, Justice, Environment, Activism
Audience:	Activists, Students
Contact:	Rich Winkel harelb@math.cornell.edu
User Info:	To subscribe to the list, send an e-mail message to the URL address below consisting of a single line reading: SUB activ-l YourFirstName YourLastName. To send a message to the entire list, address it to: active-l@mizzou1.missouri.edu

`mailto:listserv@mizzou1.missouri.edu`

alt.activism

A Usenet newsgroup providing information and discussion about activities for activists.

Keywords:	Activism
Audience:	Activists
User Info:	To subscribe to this Usenet newsgroup, you need access to a newsreader.

`news:alt.activism`

alt.censorship

A Usenet newsgroup providing information and discussion about freedom of speech and freedom of the press.

Keywords:	Censorship, Freedom of Speech, Constitution (US), Activism
Audience:	Press, Students, Educators, Activists
User Info:	To subscribe to this Usenet newsgroup, you need access to a newsreader.

`news:alt.censorship`

alt.feminism

A Usenet newsgroup providing information and discussion about feminism.

Keywords:	Feminism, Women's Studies, Abortion, Activism
Audience:	Women, General Public
User Info:	To subscribe to this Usenet newsgroup, you need access to a newsreader.

`news:alt.feminism`

Amend2-discuss

A mailing list for discussion of the implications and issues surrounding the passage of Colorado's Amendment 2, which revokes any existing homosexual civil rights legislation and prohibits the drafting of any new legislation.

Keywords:	Activism, Gay Rights, Lesbians, Bisexuality
Audience:	Gay Rights Activists
Contact:	amend2-mod@cs.colorado.edu
User Info:	To subscribe to the list, send an e-mail message to the URL address below consisting of a single line reading: subscribe amend2-discuss

`mailto:majordomo@cs.colorado.edu`

Amend2-info

Colorado voted in an amendment to their state constitution which revokes any existing gay/lesbian/bisexual civil rights legislation and prohibits the drafting of any new legislation. This moderated list is for information on the implication and issues of this amendment.

Keywords:	Activists, Gay, Lesbian, Bisexual, Constitutional Amendments, Colorado, Civil Rights
Audience:	General Public, Gays, Lesbians, Bisexuals, Activists
Contact:	amend2-info@cs.colorado.edu
User Info:	To subscribe to the list, send an e-mail message requesting a subscription to the URL address below. To send a message to the entire list, address it to: amend2-info@cs.colorado.edu

`mailto:majordomo@cs.colorado.edu`

Amnesty International

A site containing information about Amnesty International, an organization focused strictly and specifically on human rights around the world.

Keywords:	Government, Human Rights, Politics (International), Activism
Sponsor:	Amnesty International
Audience:	Students, Activists
Contact:	Catherine Hampton ariel@netcom.com

`ftp://ftp.netcom.com/pub/ariel/www/human.rights/amnesty.international/ai.html`

AR-news

A public news wire for items relating to animal rights and animal welfare.

Keywords:	Activism, Animal Rights
Audience:	Activists, Animal Lovers
Contact:	Ian Lance Taylor, Chip Roberson taylor@think.com or csr@nic.aren.com
User Info:	To subscribe to the list, send an e-mail message to the URL address below. To send a message to the entire list, address it to: ar-news@think.com
Notes:	Appropriate postings to ar-news include posting a news item, requesting information on some event, or responding to a request for information. Discussions on ar-news are not allowed.

`mailto:ar-news@think.com`

AR-talk

An unmoderated list for the discussion of animal rights and related issues, such as animal liberation, consumer product testing, cruelty-free products, vivisection and dissection, and vegan lifestyles.

Keywords: Activism, Animal Rights
Audience: Activists, Animal Lovers, Researchers
Contact: Ian Lance Taylor, Chip Roberson
taylor@think.com or csr@nic.aren.com
User Info: To subscribe to the list, send an e-mail message to the URL address below.
To send a message to the entire list, address it to: ar-talk@think.com

`mailto:ar-talk-request@think.com`

ARlist

An open, unmoderated mailing list to provide a forum for discussing action research and its use in a variety of disciplines and situations. Topics include philosophical and methodological issues in action research, the use of action research for evaluation, actual case studies, and discourse on increasing the rigor of action research.

Keywords: Activism, Research, Politics
Audience: Activists, Researchers
Profile: Arlist is an open unmoderated mailing list to provide a forum for discussing action research and its use in a variety of disciplines and situations. It is usually (but perhaps not always) cyclic, participative, and qualitative.
Contact: Bob Dick
arlist@psych.psy.uq.oz.au
Details: Free
User Info: To subscribe to the list, send an e-mail message to the URL address below.
To send a message to the entire list, address it to: arlist@psych.psy.uq.oz.au

`mailto:arlist-request@psych.psy.uq.oz.au`

`ftp://psych.psy.uq.oz.au/dir/lists/arlist`

Arts Wire

A national communications network for the arts located on the Meta Network.

Keywords: Art, Writing, Activism, Music
Sponsor: New York Foundation for the Arts
Audience: Art Activists, Art Organizations, Artists, Composers, Foundations, Government Arts Agencies, Writers
Profile: Arts Wire provides immediate access to news, information, and dialogue on conditions affecting the arts and artists, as well as private conferences for organizations. Core features include Money, a searchable resource of grant deadlines; Hotwire, a summary of arts news; and conferences about new music, interactive art, literature, AIDS, and Latino art.
Contact: Judy Malloy
artswire@tmn.com

`telnet://tmn.com`

freedom

Mailing list of people organizing against the Idaho Citizens Alliance antigay ballot initiative.

Keywords: Gay Rights, Activism, Gays
Audience: Gays, Lesbians, Bisexuals, Idaho Citizens, Activists
Details: Free
User Info: To subscribe to the list, send an e-mail message to the URL address shown below consisting of a single line reading:
SUB freedom YourFirstName YourLastName.
To send a message to the entire list, address it to: freedom@idbsu.idbsu.edu

`mailto:listserv@idbsu.idbsu.edu`

HungerWeb

This web site focuses on the political, economic, agricultural, and ethical implications of world hunger.

Keywords: World Health, Activism
Sponsor: Oxfam
Audience: Activists, Financial Planners
Contact: Daniel Zalik
Daniel_Zalik@cs.brown.edu
Details: Free

`http://www.hunger.brown.edu/oxfam`

Mother Jones

A web site containing online electronic issues of Mother Jones magazine (and Zine), making possible instant electronic feedback to the publishers regarding articles.

Keywords: Zines, Ethics, Public Policy, Activism
Sponsor: Mother Jones
Audience: Students, General Public
Contact: Webserver
webserver@mojones.com

`http://www.mojones.com/motherjones.html`

People Using Networks Can Have an Impact on Government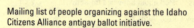

Statement by community networker Anne Fallis, who emphasizes the need for easy-to-use interfaces and inexpensive access to worldwide information. She lists many examples of local communities using networking.

Keywords: Community, Networking, Activism
Audience: Activists, Policymakers, Community Leaders, Network Users
Contact: Anne Fallis
afallis@silver.sdsmt.edu
Details: Free

`http://nearnet.gnn.com/mag/articles/oram/bio.fallis.html`

Qn

A mailing list for Queer Nation activists and for anyone interested in Queer Nation, an activist group devoted to furthering gay rights. The purpose of qn is to network among various Queer Nation chapters, to discuss actions and tactics to bring about Queer Liberation.

Keywords: Homosexuality, Gay Rights, Activism
Audience: Gay Rights Activists, Political Activists
Contact: Roger Klorese
qn-request@queernet.org
Details: Free
User Info: To subscribe to the list, send an e-mail message requesting a subscription to the URL address below.
To send a message to the entire list, address it to: qn@queernet.org

`mailto:qn-request@queernet.org`

Stonewall25

A mailing list for discussion and planning of the "Stonewall 25," an international gay/lesbian/bisexual rights march in New York City on Sunday, June 26, 1994, and the events accompanying it.

Keywords: Gay Rights, Lesbian, Bisexual, Activism
Audience: Gays, Lesbians, Bisexuals, Activists
Contact: stonewall25-request@queernet.org
Details: Free
User Info: To subscribe to the list, send an e-mail message requesting a subscription to the URL address below.
To send a message to the entire list, address it to: stonewall25@queernet.org

`mailto:stonewall25-request@queernet.org`

talk.origins

A Usenet newsgroup providing information and discussion about evolution versus creationism.

Keywords: Evolution, Creationism, Activism
Audience: General Public, Evolutionists, Creationists, Activists
Details: Free
User Info: To subscribe to this Usenet newsgroup, you need access to a newsreader.

`news:talk.origins`

Ada (Programming Language)

info-Ada ★

Discussion of the Ada programming language.

Keywords: Programming Languages, Ada (Programming Language)
Audience: Programmers
Contact: Karl A. Nyberg
Karl@grebyn.com
Details: Free
User Info: To subscribe to the list, send an e-mail message requesting a subscription to the URL address below

`mailto:info-Ada-request@sei.cmu.edu`

ADA-Law

ADA-Law ★★

A mailing list for the discussion of the Americans with Disabilities Act (ADA) and other disability-related legislation both in the US and abroad.

Keywords: Disabilities, Law (US)
Audience: Disabled People, Legal Professionals
Contact: wtm@bunker.afd.olivetti.com
User Info: To subscribe to the list, send an e-mail message to the URL address below consisting of a single line reading:

SUB ADA-Law YourFirstName YourLastName.

To send a message to the entire list, address it to: ADA-Law@vm1.nodak.edu

`mailto:listserv@vm1.nodak.edu`

Ada-sw

Ada-sw ★

A list for users who access and contribute software to the Ada Repository on SIMTEL20.

Keywords: Programming
Audience: Programmers
Details: Free
User Info: To subscribe to the list, send an e-mail message requesting a subscription to the URL address below.

To send a message to the entire list, address it to Ada-sw@wsmr-simtel20.army.mil

`mailto:ada-sw-request@wsmr-simtel20.army.mil`

ADD (Attention Deficit/ Hyperactivity Disorder)

ADD-parents ★★

A mailing list intended to provide support and information to parents of children with Attention Deficit/Hyperactivity Disorder.

Keywords: Parenting, ADD (Attention Deficit/ Hyperactivity Disorder)
Audience: Parents, Educators, Health Care Providers
Contact: add-parents-request@mv.mv.com
User Info: To subscribe to the list, send an e-mail message to the URL address below.

To send a message to the entire list, address it to: add-parents@mv.mv.com

`mailto:add-parents-request@mv.mv.com`

ADLTED-L (Canadian Adult Education Network)

ADLTED-L (Canadian Adult Education Network) ★

The Canadian Adult Continuing Education Network list is a broad, worldwide discussion group.

Keywords: Education (Adult), Education (Distance), Education (Continuing)
Sponsor: Canadian Adult Education Network
Audience: Researchers, Educators, Faculty Administrators
Details: Free
User Info: To subscribe to the list, send an e-mail message to the URL address shown below, consisting of a single line reading:

SUB alted-l YourFirstName YourLastName

To send a message to the entire list, address it to: adlted-l@uregina.bitnet

`mailto:listserv@uregina1.uregina.ca`

Adoption

Adoptees ★★

The adoptees mailing list is a forum for discussion among adult adoptees of any topic related to adoption.

Keywords: Adoption
Audience: Adoptees
Contact: adoptees-request@ucsd.edu
User Info: To subscribe to the list, send an e-mail message to the URL address below.

To send a message to the entire list, address it to: adoptees@ucsd.edu
Notes: This list is not intended to be a general discussion forum for adoption among non-adoptees.

`mailto:adoptees-request@ucsd.edu`

Adoption ★★

A mailing list for discussion of anything and everything connected with adoption.

Keywords: Adoption
Audience: Adoptees, Adoptive Parents
Contact: adoption-request@think.com
User Info: To subscribe to the list, send an e-mail message to the URL address below consisting of a single line reading:

SUB adoption YourFirstName YourLastName.

To send a message to the entire list, address it to: adoption@think.com

`mailto:listserv@think.com`

Bethany Christian Services ★★

A major directory on adoption, providing access to a broad range of related resources (library catalogs, databases, and servers) via the Internet.

Keywords: Adoption, Christianity, Pregnancy, Abortion Rights
Sponsor: Bethany Christian Services, Grand Rapids, Michigan, USA
Audience: Pregnant Women
Profile: The gopher server of Bethany, a pro-life, pro-family agency reaching out to women with unplanned pregnancies and adoptive couples. Contains a large amount of information about national and international adoption, the adoption process, African-American adoptions, and adoption of children with special needs. Also contains information for pregnant women, such as birth father rights and responsibilities, pregnancy counceling, and so on.
Contact: gophermaster@bethany.org

`gopher://gopher.bethany.org/11`

Birthmother ★

A mailing list for any birthmother who has relinquished a child for adoption.

Keywords: Adoption
Audience: Parents, Adoptees

Contact: nadir@acca.nmsu.edu
Details: Free
To join the mailing list, send a message to the URL address below with your E-mail address and brief information about your situation (i.e. bmom who relinquished x years ago and does/does not have contact, has/has not been reunited).

`mailto:nadir@acca.nmsu.edu`

Adult/Distance Education

Adult/Distance Education

This directory is a compilation of information resources focused on adult/distance education. The directory is sponsored by The American Association for Collegiate Independent Study, and focuses on correspondence, independent study and distance learning.

Keywords: Education (Adult), Education (Distance), Education (Continuing)
Audience: Educators, Researchers
Details: Free

`ftp://una.hh.lib.umich.edu/70/inetdirsstacks/disted:ellsworth`

Adv-Eli

Adv-Eli

Adv-Eli discusses the latest advances in electrical engineering. It is sponsored by the IEEE Student Branch of Santa Maria University (Chile).

Keywords: Electrical Engineering, Engineering, Electronics
Audience: Engineers, Educators, Students
Contact: Francisco Javier Fernandez
ffernand@utfsm
Details: Free
User Info: To subscribe to the list, send an e-mail message to the URL address shown below consiting of a single line reading:

SUB adv-eli YourFirstName YourLastName

To send a message to the entire list, address it to: adv-eli@loa.disca.utfsm.cl

`listserv@loa.disca.utfsm.cl`

Adv-Elo

Adv-Elo

Discusses the latest advances in electronics. Sponsored by the IEEE Student Branch of Santa Maria University (Chile).

Keywords: Electrical Engineering, Engineering, Electronics, Technological Advances
Audience: Engineers, Educators, Students
Contact: Rodrigo E. Rodriguez
rrodrigu@utfsm
Details: Free
User Info: To subscribe to the list, send an e-mail message to the URL address shown below consiting of a single line reading:

SUB adv-elo YourFirstName YourLastName

To send a message to the entire list, address it to: adv-elo@loa.disca.utfsm.cl

`listserv@loa.disca.utfsm.cl`

Advanced Product Centers (APC)

APC-Open

A mailing list for the interchange of information relevant to Advanced Product Centers (APC).

Keywords: Advanced Product Centers
Audience: APC-OPEN Members
Contact: Fred Rump
fred@compu.com
User Info: To subscribe to the list, send an e-mail message requesting a subscription to the URL address below.

To send a message to the entire list, address it to: apc-open@compu.com

Notes: Membership restricted to APC-OPEN members or those specifically invited.

`mailto:apc-open-request@compu.com`

Advanced Workshops

MICnews

Microcomputer and advanced workstation computing news relevant to the computing populace at the University of California, Los Angeles (UCLA).

Keywords: Microcomputing, Advanced Workshops, UCLA
Sponsor: Microcomputer Information Center, UCLA
Audience: UCLA Students
Contact: Bob Cooper
csmibob@mvs.oac.ucla.edu
Details: Free
User Info: To subscribe to the list, send an e-mail message to the URL address below, consisting of a single line reading:

SUB micnews YourFirstName YourLastName

To send a message to the entire list, address it to: micnews@uclacn1.ucla.edu

`mailto:listserv@uclacn1.ucla.edu`

Advertising

Apollo Advertising

A major directory on advertising, providing access to a broad range of related resources (library catalogs, databases, and servers) via the Internet.

Keywords: Advertising, Business
Audience: Advertisers, Business Professionals, General Public
Profile: A new web service for advertisers and information providers, which maintains the philosophy that consumers will choose to look for goods and services where it is easy and convenient to locate them. This involves the development of a database of short advertisements, many having hypertext links to more substantial advertisements. These can range from text documents to hypermedia commercials. The Apollo directory can be searched, using logical sorting methods, to identify items of interest. Additional information, including hypermedia, may be connected to the entries. This service encompasses short, stand-alone advertisements, as well as entries with hypertext links to other Internet resources.
Contact: apollo@apollo.co.uk

`gopher://apollo.co.uk`

Communication and Mass Communication Resources

An archive of materials related to mass communications and the media.

Keywords: Mass Communications, Media, Journalism, Telecommunications, Advertising
Sponsor: The University of Iowa
Audience: Mass Communications Students and Teachers, Journalists, Broadcasting Professionals
Contact: Karla Tonella
Karla_Tonella@uiowa.edu

`gopher://iam41.arcade.uiowa.edu`

The Branch Mall, an Electronic Shopping Mall

Branch Information Services offers shopping to customers and leases storefronts and electronic catalogs to vendors.

Keywords: Mall, Shopping, Gifts, Advertising, Mailorder
Sponsor: Branch Information Services

Audience:	Consumers, Merchants
Contact:	Jon Zeeff jon@branch.com
Details:	Free
Notes:	Free for consumers.

`http://branch.com`

Advisory

INTER-L

A list for members of the National Association of Foreign Student Advisors.

Keywords:	Advisory, Education (Bilingual), Educational Policy
Sponsor:	National Association of Foreign Student Advisors (NAFSA)
Audience:	Foreign Students, NAFSA Members
Details:	Free
User Info:	To subscribe to the list, send an e-mail message to the address below consisting of a single line reading:

`mailto:listserv@vtm1.cc.vt.edu`

AEC

Architecture, Building

This directory is a compilation of information resources focused on architecture.

Keywords:	Architecture, Building, Construction, AEC
Audience:	Architects, Builders, Civil Engineers
Contact:	J. Brown
Details:	Free

`ftp://una.hh.lib.umich.edu/70/inetdirsstacks/archi:brown`

AEDNET (Adult Education Network)

AEDNET (Adult Education Network)

This is an international electronic network for those involved in distance education.

Keywords:	Education (Adult), Education (Distance), Education (Continuing)
Sponsor:	Adult Education Network
Audience:	Educators, Researchers, Faculty Administrators
Details:	Free

User Info:	To subscribe to the list, send an e-mail message to the URL address shown below consisting of a single line reading:
	SUB aednet YourFirstName YourLastName
	To send a message to the entire list, address it to: AEDNET@alpha.acast.nova.edu

`mailto:listserv@alpha.acast.nova.edu`

Aeronautics

Aelflow

A mailing list for the discussion of aerospace and aeronautical engineering.

Keywords:	Aerospace, Aeronautics, Engineering
Sponsor:	The Aerospace Engineering Fluid Group
Audience:	Engineers, Educators, Students
Contact:	Dr. Yakov Cohen aer8601@technion.ac.il.edu
Details:	Free
User Info:	To subscribe to the list, send an e-mail message to the URL address shown below consiting of a single line reading:SUB aelflow YourFirstName YourLastName
	To send a message to the entire list, address it to: Aelflow@technion.ac.il ed

`listserv@technion.ac.il edu`

Aeronautics

A moderated discussion-group dealing with atmospheric flight, aerodynamics, flying qualities, simulation, structures, systems, propulsion, and design human factors.

Keywords:	Aeronautics
Audience:	Aeronautical Engineers
Contact:	aeronautics-request@rascal.ics.utexas.edu
User Info:	To subscribe to the list, send an e-mail message to the URL address below.
	To send a message to the entire list, address it to: aeronautics@rascal.ics.utexas.edu
Notes:	The aeronautics mailing list is a news-to-mail feed of the sci.aeronautics newsgroup. Subscribers can participate in real-time with the main group.

`mailto:aeronautics-request@rascal.ics.utexas.edu`

Aeronautics (History of)

Massachusetts Institute of Technology Library

The library's holdings are large and wide-ranging and contain significant collections in many fields.

Keywords:	Aeronautics (History of), Linguistics, Mathematics (History of), Microscopy, Spectroscopy, Aeronautics, Mathematics, Glass
Audience:	General Public, Researchers, Librarians, Document Delivery Professionals
Details:	Free
User Info:	Expect: Mitek Server..., Send: Enter or Return; Expect: prompt, Send: hollis

`telnet://library.mit.edu`

European Space Agency

A major directory on aeronautics, providing access to a broad range of related resources (library catalogs, databases, and servers) via the Internet.

Keywords:	Space Science, Aeronautics
Audience:	Space Science Researchers
Profile:	The home page of the European Space Agency, including information about ESA's mission, specific ESA programs (Science, Manned Spaceflight and Microgravity, Earth Observation, Telecommunications, Launchers), and issues related to the space and aeronautics industry.
Contact:	webmaster@esa.it

`http://www.esrin.esa.it`

Massachusetts Institute of Technology Library

The library's holdings are large and wide-ranging and contain significant collections in many fields.

Keywords:	Aeronautics (History of), Linguistics, Mathematics (History of), Microscopy, Spectroscopy, Aeronautics, Mathematics, Glass
Audience:	General Public, Researchers, Librarians, Document Delivery Professionals
Details:	Free
User Info:	Expect: Mitek Server..., Send: Enter or Return; Expect: prompt, Send: hollis

`telnet://library.mit.edu`

Princeton University Library

The library's holdings are large and wide-ranging. They contain significant collections in many fields.

Aeronautics (History of)

Keywords: China, Japan, Classics, History (Ancient), Near Eastern Studies, Literature (American), Literature (English), Aeronautics, Middle Eastern Studies, Mormonism, Publishing

Audience: General Public, Researchers, Librarians, Document Delivery Professionals

Details: Free

User Info: Expect: Connect message, blank screen, Send: <cr>; Expect: #, Send: Call 500

`telnet://pucable.princeton.edu`

Rascal Aviation Archives

A major directory on aeronautics, providing access to a broad range of related resources (library catalogues, databases, and servers) via the Internet.

Keywords: Aeronautics, Aviation

Audience: Aviators, Aeronautical Engineers

Contact: rdd@rascal.ics.utexas.edu

`ftp://rascal.ics.utexas.edu/explore-me/Aviation-stuff`

Spacelink

This contains information about NASA and its activities, including a large number of curricular activities for elementary and secondary science classes.

Keywords: NASA, Aeronautics, Education (K-12)

Audience: Students (K-12), Educators, General Public

Details: Free

`telnet://newuser@spacelink.msfc.nasa.gov`

Ssi_mail

A moderated list for topics related to Space Studies Institute programs—past, present, and future.

Keywords: Space Studies, Space Science, Aeronautics

Audience: Space Students, Space Scientists

Contact: Mitchell James
mjames@link.com
mitchellj@aol.com

Details: Free, Moderated

User Info: To subscribe to the list, send an e-mail message requesting a subscription to the URL address below.

To send a message to the entire list, address it to: ssi_mail@link.com

Notes: Archives available.

`mailto:listprocessor@link.com`

Aerospace

Aerospace Engineering

This directory is a compilation of information resources focused on aerospace engineeering.

Keywords: Aerospace, Engineering, Aviation, Space

Audience: Aerospace Engineers, Space Scientists

Profile: This is a guide to Internet resources that contain information pertaining to aerospace engineering. Originally the guide was to cover the area of aerospace engineering as applied to lower atmospheric flight. However, it is difficult to narrow the sites down to specific subject areas. As the guide evolved, sites were included with a broader scope of information.The guide is by no means comprehensive and exhaustive; there are sites that are not included and those the authors were not aware of, and they welcome suggestions. The directory lists sites on FTP, Gopher, Listserv, OPAC, Telnet, Usenet, and WWW.

Details: Free

`ftp://una.hh.lib.umich.edu/70/inetdirsstacks/aerospace:potsiedalq`

DMS/FI Market Intelligence Reports

DMS/FI Market Intelligence Reports is the largest collection of unclassified defense and aerospace information available from any single source.

Keywords: Defense, Aerospace

Sponsor: Forecast International/DMS, Newtown, CT, USA

Audience: Defense Analysts

Profile: This file contains the most comprehensive and up-to-date full-text data and analysis for the industry and provides users with valuable information on defense budgets, aerospace and weapons programs, power systems, companies (US and international), agencies, or countries that are involved in the aerospace/defense industry. File 589 contains a great deal of information relative to civil and commercial programs. Reports provide detailed and extensive information such as forecasts, major activity, funding, inventories, location, and much more. This information is gathered from such diverse sources as government documents, civil and defense journals, manufacturers, and field interviews with key industry people. This database is vital to anyone involved in market research, business development, or program management in the aerospace/defense industry.

Contact: Dialog in the US at (800) 334-2564, Dialog internationally at country-specific locations.

User Info: To subscribe, contact Dialog directly.

Notes: Coverage: Current; updated weekly.

`telnet://dialog.com`

Jane's Defense & Aerospace News/Analysis

This file provides articles that summarize, highlight, and interpret worldwide events in the defense and aerospace industry.

Keywords: Defense, Aerospace, News Media

Sponsor: Jane's Information Group, Alexandria, VA US

Audience: Aerospace Industry Professionals

Profile: The database contains the complete text of the following publications: Jane's Defense Weekly, International Defense Review, Jane's Intelligence Review (formerly Jane's Soviet Intelligence Review), Interavia Aerospace Review, and Jane's Airport Review. File 587 also contains the complete text of DMS newsletters, which ceased publication in 1989.

Contact: Dialog in the US at (800) 334-2564, Dialog internationally at country-specific locations.

User Info: To subscribe, contact Dialog directly.

Notes: Coverage: 1982 to the present; updated weekly.

`telnet://dialog.com`

Lockheed Missiles & Space Company

A web site containing information about Lockheed Missiles and Space Company, a major aerospace and defense company specializing in the development of space systems, missiles and other high technology products. Includes company information and press releases.

Keywords: Defense, Aerospace

Sponsor: The Lockheed Palo Alto Artificial Intelligence Center

Audience: Aerospace Industry Professionals

`http://www.lmsc.lockheed.com`

McDonnell Douglas Aerospace

A web site providing information about McDonnell Douglas, including a company profile and related discussion about technology.

Keywords: Aerospace, Space, Aviation, Technology

Audience: Aerospace Engineers

Contact: Zook@pat.mdc.com

`http://pat.mdc.com`

af

af

A mailing list for discussion of AudioFile, a client/server, network-transparent, device-independent audio system.

Keywords: Audio Electronics, Electrical Engineering
Audience: Audio Enthusiasts, Electrical Engineers
Contact: af-request@crl.dec.com
User Info: To subscribe to the list, send an e-mail message to the URL address below.

To send a message to the entire list, address it to: af@crl.dec.com

`mailto:af-request@crl.dec.com`

Africa

Africa in the CIA World Fact Book

A gopher site containing geographical and political information about individual countries in Africa.

Keywords: Africa, Intelligence, Project Gutenberg
Sponsor: Project Gutenberg
Audience: Africans, General Public

`gopher://hoshi.cic.sfu.ca/11/dlam/cia/Africa`

Africa-n

A moderated mailing list dedicated to the exchange of news and information on Africa, including correspondence from many sources worldwide.

Keywords: News Media, Africa
Audience: Africans, Students
Contact: Faraz Rabbani
frabbani@epas.utoronto.ca
User Info: To subscribe to the list, send an e-mail message to the URL address below consisting of a single line reading:

SUB africa-n YourFirstName YourLastName

To send a message to the entire list, address it to: africa-n@utoronto.bitnet

`mailto:listserv@utoronto.bitnet`

African Art Exhibit and Tutorial

This web site provides images of African art and an overview of African aesthetics.

Keywords: Art, Africa, Cultural Studies
Sponsor: University of Virginia
Audience: Artists, Art Students, Educators, Historians

`http://www.lib.virginia.edu`

African Education Research Network

This gopher contains various links to African studies programs at select universities, and other archived information of interest to the African studies scholar.

Keywords: Cultural Studies, Africa, African Studies
Sponsor: Ohio University, African Education Research Network
Audience: Students, African-Americans, Africans
Contact: Milton E. Ploghoft
mperdreau@ohiou.edu
Details: Free

`gopher://gopher.ohiou.edu/00/dept.servers/aern`

Black/African Related Online Information

This is a list of online information storage sites that contain a significant amount of information pertaining to Black or African people, culture, and issues around the world.

Keywords: Culture, Race, Africa, African Studies
Sponsor: AfriInfo
Audience: Students, African-Americans, Africans
Contact: McGee
mcgee@epsilon.eecs.nwu.edu
Details: Free

`ftp://ftp.netcom.com/pub/amcgee/my_african_related_lists/afrisite.msg`

MDEAFR

The Middle East and Africa (MDEAFR) library contains detailed information about every country in the Mideast and Africa. Structured for those who want to follow the unfolding events in the Gulf states, as well as in North and South Africa, this library contains a broad array of sources, including international research reports from InvestextR.

Keywords: News, Analysis, Companies, Middle East, Africa
Audience: Journalists, Business Professionals
Profile: The MDEAFR library contains a wide array of pertinent sources. Among the information sources are newspapers and wire services, trade and business journals, company reports, country and region background, industry and product analysis, business opportunities, and selected legal texts. News sources range from the world-renowned Associated Press and Christian Science Monitor to the regionally important Jerusalem Post and Africa News. Company information is contained in the EXTEL cards as well as ICC. Providers of country background and industry analysis include Associated Banks of Europe, Bank of America, Business International, IBC USA, and the US Department of Commerce. Customers interested in new business opportunities can check OPIC and Foreign Trade Opportunities (FTO).

Contact: Mead New Sales Group at (800) 227-4908 or (513) 859-5398 inside the US, or (513) 865-7981 for all inquiries outside the US.
User Info: To subscribe, contact Mead directly.

To examine the Nexis user guide, you can access it at the ftp site of the University of Texas at Austin at the URL address: ftp://ftp.cc.utexas.edu

The files are in: /pub/ref-services/LEXIS

`telnet://nex.meaddata.com`

`http://www.meaddata.com`

Northwestern University Library

The library's holdings are large and wide-ranging and contain significant collections in many fields.

Keywords: Africa, Wright (Frank Lloyd), Women's Studies, Art, Literature (American), Contemporary Music, Government (US State), UN Documents, Music
Audience: General Public, Researchers, Librarians, Document Delivery Professionals
Details: Free
User Info: Expect: COMMAND:, Send: DIAL VTAM

`telnet://nuacvm.acns.nwu.edu`

South Africa

A major directory on Africa, providing access to a broad range of related resources (library catalogues, databases, and servers) via the Internet.

Keywords: Africa, South Africa
Audience: General Public
Profile: South Africa's home page, containing information about different regions and major cities, weather conditions, vital statistics, and information about the University of South Africa.
Contact: Aleksandar Radovanovic
radova@osprey.unisa.ac.za

`http://osprey.unisa.ac.za/0/docs/south-africa.html`

African American Studies

soc.culture.african.american

A Usenet newsgroup providing information and discussion about African American culture.

Keywords: African American Studies, Sociology, Minorities
Audience: Sociologists, Researchers, General Public

African American Studies

Details:	Free
User Info:	To subscribe to this Usenet newsgroup, you need access to a newsreader.

`news:soc.culture.african.american`

African Studies

African Education Research Network

Various links to African studies programs at select universities, and other archived information of interest to the African studies scholar.

Keywords:	Culture, Race, Africa, African Studies
Sponsor:	Ohio University, African Education Research Network
Audience:	Students, African-Americans, Africans
Contact:	Milton E. Ploghoft mperdreau@ohiou.edu
Details:	Free

`gopher://gopher.ohiou.edu/00/dept.servers/aern`

Black/African Related Online Information

This is a list of online information storage sites that contain a significant amount of information pertaining to Black or African people, culture, and issues around the world.

Keywords:	Culture, Race, Africa, African Studies
Sponsor:	AfriInfo
Audience:	Students, African-Americans, Africans
Contact:	McGee mcgee@epsilon.eecs.nwu.edu
Details:	Free

`ftp://ftp.netcom.com/pub/amcgee/my_african_related_lists/afrisite.msg`

Afrikaans

Harvard University Library

The library's holdings are large and wide-ranging and contain significant collections in many fields.

Keywords:	Afrikaans, Alchemy, Arabic Culure (History of), Celtic Philology, Congo Languages, Folklore, Hebraica, Mormonism, Numismatics, Quakers, Sanskrit, Witchcraft, Arabic Philology
Audience:	General Public, Researchers, Librarians, Document Delivery Professionals
Details:	Free
User Info:	Expect: Mitek Server..., Send: Enter or Return; Expect: prompt, Send: hollis

`telnet://hollis.harvard.edu`

Agence FrancePresse International French Wire

Agence FrancePresse International French Wire

Agence FrancePresse International French Wire provides full-text articles in French relating to national, international, business, and sports news.

Keywords:	News Media, Europe, Third World, French
Sponsor:	Agence FrancePresse, Paris, France
Audience:	Market Researchers, Journalists, Francophiles
Profile:	Agence FrancePresse distributes its French service worldwide, including Western and Eastern Europe, Canada, northern and western Africa, the Middle East, Vietnam, French Guiana, the West Indies, and the French Pacific islands. Agence FrancePresse International French Wire has extensive coverage of the European countries, including every aspect of economic, political, and general business news. It also provides excellent industrial and market news from both developed countries and from the Third World.
Contact:	Dialog in the US at (800) 334-2564; Dialog internationally at country-specific locations.
Details:	Costs
User Info:	To subscribe, contact Dialog directly.
	Coverage: September 1991 to the present; updated daily.

`telnet://dialog.com`

Aging

AgeLine

The AgeLine database is produced by the American Association of Retired Persons (AARP) and provides bibliographic coverage of social gerontology—the study of aging in social, psychological, health-related, and economic contexts.

Keywords:	Gerontology, Retirement, Public Policy, Aging
Sponsor:	American Association of Retired Persons, Washington, DC, USA
Audience:	Retired Persons, Health Care Providers, Researchers
Profile:	AgeLine covers the delivery of health care for the older population and its associated costs and policies, as well as public policy, employment, and consumer issues. Literature covered is of interest to researchers, health professionals, service planners, policy makers, employers, older adults and their families, and consumer advocates.
Contact:	Dialog in the US at (800) 334-2564; Dialog internationally at country-specific locations.
Details:	Costs
User Info:	To subscribe, contact Dialog directly.
Notes:	Coverage: 1978 to the present (selected coverage back to 1966); updated bimonthly.

`telnet://dialog.com`

agora

agora

A forum for Hungarian speakers to discuss a wide variety of subjects.

Keywords:	Hungary
Audience:	Hungarian Speakers
Contact:	Zoli Fekete fekete@bcvms.bc.edu
Details:	Free

Inquiries and contributions to the list can be sent to the personal address of the contact above (place word AGORA in the subject field), or to the world.std.com address below (place word $SEGIT in the subject field).

`mailto:agora@world.std.com`

Agoraphobia

Panic

This is a support group for panic disorders. Discussion involving phobias resulting from panic (agoraphobia and others). Also a place to meet people who have gone through the disorder as well.

Keywords:	Panic Disorders, Agoraphobia
Audience:	Panic Disorder Sufferers
Contact:	Panic-Request@gnu.ai.mit.edu
Details:	Free
User Info:	To subscribe to the list, send an e-mail message requesting a subscription to the URL address below.
	To send a message to the entire list, address it to: panic@gnu.ai.mit.edu

`mailto:Panic-Request@gnu.ai.mit.edu`

Agriculture

agmodels-l

A forum for the discussion of agricultural simulation models of all types. Issues include plant growth, micro-meteorology, soil hydrology, transport, farm economy, and farm systems.

Keywords:	Agriculture, Farm Economy
Audience:	Agronomists
Contact:	Jerome Pier jp@unl.edu
User Info:	To subscribe to the list, send an e-mail message to the URL address below consisting of a single line reading: SUB agmodels-l YourFirstName YourLastName To send a message to the entire list, address it to: agmodels-l@unl.edu

`mailto:listserv@unl.edu`

AGRICOLA

The AGRICOLA database of the National Agricultural Library (NAL) provides comprehensive coverage of worldwide journal literature and monographs on agriculture and related subjects.

Keywords:	Agriculture, Animal Studies, Botany, Entomology
Sponsor:	US National Agricultural Library, Beltsville, MD, USA
Audience:	Agronomists, Botanists, Chemists, Entomologists
Profile:	Related subjects include: animal studies, botany, chemistry, entomology, fertilizers, forestry, hydroponics, soils, and more.
Contact:	Dialog in the US at (800) 334-2564, Dialog internationally at country-specific locations.
User Info:	To subscribe, contact Dialog directly.
Notes:	Coverage: 1970 to the present; updated monthly.

`telnet://dialog.com`

Agricultural Guide

A specialized guide, entitled "Not Just Cows," to the Internet/Bitnet resources in agriculture and related science.

Keywords:	Agriculture, Internet, Internet Guide
Sponsor:	University of North Carolina
Audience:	Internet Surfers
Contact:	Wilfred Drew
Details:	Free

`ftp://sunsite.unc.edu/pub/docs/about-the-net/libsoft/agguide.dos`

`gopher://sunsite.unc.edu`

`http://sunsite.unc.edu/pub/docs/about-the-net/libsoft/agguide.dos`

Agriculture

This directory is a compilation of information resources focused on agriculture.

Keywords:	Agriculture, Economics
Audience:	Farmers, Agronomists, Agriculturalists
Contact:	Wilfred Drew drewwe@snymorva.cs.snymor.edu
Details:	Free

`ftp://una.hh.lib.umich.edu`

`gopher://snymorvb.cs.snymor.edu`

Agriculture, Veterinary Science & Zoology

This directory is a compilation of information resources focused on agriculture, veterinary science, and zoology.

Keywords:	Agriculture, Veterinary Science, Zoology
Audience:	Farmers, Agronomists, Veterinarians, Zoologists
Details:	Free

`ftp://una.hh.lib.umich.edu/70/inetdirsstacks/agvetzoo:haas`

AGRIS International

This database serves as a comprehensive inventory of worldwide agricultural literature that reflects research results, food production, and rural development.

Keywords:	Agriculture, Rural Development, Food Production, Development
Sponsor:	US National Agricultural Library, Beltsville, MD, USA
Audience:	Agronomists, Market Researchers, Agricultural Economists
Profile:	Designed to help users identify problems involved in all aspects of world food supply, the file corresponds in part to Agr Index, published monthly by the Food and Agriculture Organization (FAO) of the United Nations. Subject coverage focuses on many topics: general agriculture; geography and history; education, extension, and advisory work; administration and legislation; economics, development, and rural sociology; plant production; protection of plants and stored products; forestry; animal production; aquatic sciences and fisheries; machinery and buildings; natural resources; food science; home economics; human nutrition; pollution; and more.
Contact:	Dialog in the US at (800) 334-2564
Details:	Costs
User Info:	To subscribe, contact Dialog directly.

`telnet://dialog.com`

Biosis Previews

The database encompasses the entire field of life sciences and covers original research reports and reviews in biological and biomedical areas. This includes field, laboratory, clinical, experimental and theoretical work. The traditional areas of biology, including botany, zoology and microbiology are covered, as well as the related fields such as plant and animal science, agriculture, pharmacology and ecology.

Keywords:	Biology, Botany, Zoology, Microbiology, Plant Science, Animal Science, Agriculture, Pharmacology, Ecology, Biochemistry, Biophysics, Bioengineering
Sponsor:	Biosis
Audience:	Librarians, Researchers, Students, Biologists, Botanists, Zoologists, Scientists, Taxonomists
Contact:	CDP Technologies Sales Department (800)950-2035, extension 400
User Info:	To subscribe, contact CDP Technologies directly

`telnet://cdplus@cdplus.com`

Food Industry Investext

The world's largest database of company, industry, topical, and geographic analysis.

Keywords:	Food Industry, Agriculture
Sponsor:	Thomson Financial Networks, Boston, MA US
Audience:	Business Professionals, Market Researchers
Profile:	The database is composed of more than 320,000 full-text reports written by analysts at 180 investment banks and research firms worldwide. The research can be used for a wide range of business intelligence activities, including competitive analysis, evaluation of companies, and strategic planning. Coverage includes 14,000 companies worldwide and 53 industry groups.
User Info:	To subscribe, contact Dialog directly.
Notes:	Coverage: July 1982 to the present; updated daily.

`telnet://dialog.com`

Iowa State University

The library's holdings contain significant collections in many fields.

Keywords:	Agriculture, Veterinary Medicine, Statistics, Labor, Soil Conservation, Film
Audience:	General Public, Researchers, Librarians, Document Delivery Professionals
Details:	Free
User Info:	Expect: DIAL, Send: LIB

`telnet://isn.iastate.edu`

Ogphre - SunSITE

A collection of Internet resources organized by subject. Particular strengths include agriculture, religious texts, poetry, creative writing, and US politics. The ftp site has a set of more general Internet guides.

Agriculture

Keywords: Agriculture, Politics (US), Religion, Internet
Sponsor: The University of North Carolina - Chapel Hill and Sun Microsystems, USA
Audience: General Public, Internet Surfers, Researchers
Contact: Darlene Fladager, Elizabeth Lyons
Darlene_Fladager@unc.edu
Elizabeth_Lyons@unc.edu

`gopher://sunsite.unc.edu`

`ftp://sunsite.unc.edu`

University of Maryland, College Park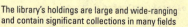

The library's holdings are large and wide-ranging and contain significant collections in many fields.
Keywords: Agriculture, Coastal Marine Biology, Fisheries, Water Quality, Oceanography
Audience: Researchers, Students, General Public
Contact: Janet McLeod
mcleod@umail.umd.edu
Details: Free
User Info: Expect: Login; Send: Atdu

`telnet://info.umd.edu`

University of Puerto Rico Library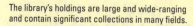

The library's holdings are large and wide-ranging and contain significant collections in many fields.
Keywords: Computer Science, Education, Nursing, Agriculture, Economics
Audience: Researchers, Students, General Public
Details: Free
After Locator: telnet://, press Tab twice. Type DIAL VTAM.
Enter NOTIS. Press Return. On the blank screen, type LUUP.

`telnet://136.145.2.10`

University of Wisconsin River Falls Library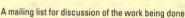

The library's holdings are large and wide-ranging and contain significant collections in many fields.
Keywords: Agriculture, Education, History (US)
Audience: Researchers, Students, General Public
Details: Free
User Info: Expect: Service Name, Send: Victor

`telnet://davee.dl.uwrf.edu`

USDA Agricultural Extension Service

Includes information from the USDA (United States Department of Agriculture) Extension Service, National Agriculture Library, and Americans Communicating Electronically (ACE).
Keywords: Agriculture
Audience: Farmers, Agriculturalists, Educators
Details: Free

`gopher://cyfer.esusda.gov`

Washington State University at Puyallup Library

The library's holdings are large and wide-ranging and contain significant collections in many fields.
Keywords: Agriculture, Scientific Research
Audience: Researchers, Students, General Public
Details: Free
User Info: Expect: Login; Send: Lib

`telnet://wsuvm1.cscwsu.edu`

AIDS

Act-up

A mailing list for discussion of the work being done by various Act-Up chapters worldwide.
Keywords: AIDS, Health Care, Activism
Audience: AIDS Activists, Health Science Researchers
Contact: Lenard Diggins
act-up-request@world.std.com
User Info: To subscribe to the list, send an e-mail message to the URL address below.
To send a message to the entire list, address it to: act-up-request@world.std.com

`mailto:act-up-request@world.std.com`

Aids

A forum for the discussion of AIDS, predominantly from a medical perspective, but also with some discussion of political and social issues.
Keywords: AIDS, Medicine, Politics
Sponsor: UCLA
Audience: AIDS Researchers, AIDS Activists, Health Care Providers
Contact: Daniel R. Greening
aids-request@cs.ucla.edu
User Info: To subscribe to the list, send an e-mail message to the URL address below.
To send a message to the entire list, address it to: aids@cs.ucla.edu

`mailto:aids-request@cs.ucla.edu`

AIDS Treatment News

A newsletter on AIDS treatment.
Keywords: AIDS, Health, Medicine
Sponsor: IGC (Institute for Global Communications)
Audience: AIDS Researchers, Health Workers, AIDS Sufferers
Profile: This newsletter contains interviews, reports on new and existing treatment modalities, announcements of clinical drug testing trials, and more.
Contact: atn@igc.apc.org
Details: Free

`gopher://odie.niaid.nih.gov/11/aids`

AIDS/HIV Information

A clearinghouse for AIDS/HIV-related information. Contains Internet connections to WWW and gopher servers, and archives of AIDS server FAQ's, including an archive of AIDS treatment news.
Keywords: AIDS, Medicine, Health
Sponsor: Queer Resources Directory, USA
Audience: AIDS Sufferers, Gays, Activists
Contact: QRD Staff
QRDstaff@vector.casti.com
Details: AIDS Treatment News

`http://vector.casti.com/QRD/.html/AIDS.html`

AIDSLINE

The AIDSLINE database is a bibliography of research and clinical information as well as health policy issues concerning AIDS. The citations in AIDSLINE are primarily derived from MEDLINE, Health Planning & Administration, CancerLit, CATLINE, AVLINE, the meeting abstracts from the International Conferences on AIDS, the Symposia on Non-human Models of AIDS, and AIDS-related abstracts from the Annual Meetings of the American Society of Microbiology.
Keywords: AIDS, Medicine
Sponsor: U.S. National Library of Medicine
Audience: AIDS Researchers, Epidemiologists, Clinicians, AIDS Sufferers
Contact: CDP Technologies Sales Department (800)950-2035, extension 400
User Info: To subscribe, contact CDP Technologies directly

`telnet://cdplus@cdplus.com`

National Institutes of Health Gopher ★★★★

Provides access to a broad range of National Institutes of Health (NIH) resources (library catalogues, databases) via the Internet.

- Keywords: Health, AIDS, Molecular Biology, Grants
- Sponsor: National Institutes of Health
- Audience: Health Professionals, Molecular Biologists, Researchers
- Profile: This gopher provides access to NIH resources, including institute phone books and calendars, library catalogs, molecular biology databases, the full text of the NIH Guide for Grants and Contracts, files containing AIDS and cancer information and more.
- Contact: gopher@gopher.nih.gov
- Details: Free
- User Info: Expect: Login; Enter: Gopher

`telnet://gopher.nih.gov`

`gopher://gopher.nih.gov`

`gopher://odie.niaid.nih.gov`

South East Florida AIDS Information Network (SEFAIN) ★

Contains a wide range of information on AIDS research(ers), organizations, and services in searchable databases.

- Keywords: AIDS, Medicine
- Sponsor: This project is sponsored in part by the National Library of Medicine
- Audience: Medical Professionals, Scientists, Educators, Health Care Providers
- Details: Free
  Select L on main menu, then select 1 on next menu

`telnet://library@callcat.med.miami.edu`

Women.health ★

This conference features articles, documents, news, announcements, policy statements, and other information about women's health around the world. Topics include breast cancer, ovarian cancer, alcohol, abortion, pregnancy, sterilization of women, pesticides, Quinacrine, HIV, disability.

- Keywords: Women, Abortion, AIDS, Disability, Feminism, Health
- Audience: Activists, Family Planners, Health Professionals, Non-Governmental Organizations, Women
- Details: Costs

- User Info: Establish an account on the nearest APC node. Login, type c for conferences, then type go women.health. For information on the nearest APC node, contact: APC International Secretariat IBASE.
  E-mail: apcadmin@apc.org

`telnet://igc.apc.org`

Aikido

Aikido Information ★

An FTP site containing aikido dojo addresses from around the world, plus a calendar of events, FAQs, and lists of books and periodicals related to aikido.

- Keywords: Aikido, Martial Arts, Sports, Japan
- Sponsor: University of California at San Diego, San Diego, CA, USA
- Audience: Martial Arts Enthusiasts
- Contact: aikido@cs.ucsd.edu
- Details: Free

`ftp://cs.ucsd.edu/pub/aikido`

aikido-l

A discussion group and information exchange on the Japanese martial art Aikido.

- Keywords: Aikido, Martial Arts, Sports, Japan
- Sponsor: Gerry Santoro
- Audience: Martial Arts Enthusiasts
- Contact: aikido-l-request@psuvm.psu.edu
- User Info: To subscribe to the list, send an e-mail message to the URL address below consisting of a single line reading:
  SUB aikido-l YourFirstName YourLastName
  To send a message to the entire list, address it to: aikido-l@psuvm.psu.edu

`mailto:listserv@psuvm.psu.edu`

Physical Education & Recreation

A collection of information on sporting and recreational activities from aikido to windsurfing.

- Keywords: Sports, Recreation, Aikido, Cycling, Scuba Diving, Windsurfing
- Audience: Sports Enthusiasts, Fitness Enthusiasts
- Contact: ctcadmin@ctc.ctc.edu

`gopher://ctc.ctc.edu`

Air Conditioning

Utah Valley Community College Library

The library's holdings are large and wide-ranging and contain significant collections in many fields.

- Keywords: Accounting, Automobiles, Cabinetry, Child Care, Drafting, Electronics, Home Building, Local History, Refrigeration, Air Conditioning
- Audience: General Public, Researchers, Librarians, Document Delivery Professionals
- Details: Free
- User Info: Expect: Login; Send: Opub

`telnet://uvlib.uvcc.edu`

Airplanes

Airplane-clubs

A mailing list for discussion of all matters relating to the management and organization of groups operating aircraft.

- Keywords: Airplanes, Aviation
- Audience: Aviators
- Contact: Matthew Waugh
  airplane-clubs-request@dg-rtp.dg.com
- User Info: To subscribe to the list, send an e-mail message to the URL address below.
  To send a message to the entire list, address it to: airplane-clubs@dg-rtp.dg.com

`mailto:airplane-clubs-request@dg-rtp.dg.com`

Alaska

Information About Alaska

This collection contains information on Alaska's government and politics, as well as historical documents about Alaska's neighbors, Russia and Canada. It also has cultural information, including literature and sports in the Land of the Midnight Sun.

- Keywords: Alaska, Travel
- Sponsor: University of Alaska Computer Network (UACN), Alaska, USA
- Audience: Alaskans, Travelers, General Public
- Contact: Douglas Toelle
  sxinfo@orca.alaska.edu

`gopher://info.alaska.edu`

Alchemy

Harvard University Library ★★★★

The library's holdings are large and wide-ranging and contain significant collections in many fields.

Keywords: Afrikaans, Alchemy, Arabic Culture (History of), Celtic Philology, Congo Languages, Folklore, Hebraica, Mormonism, Numismatics, Quakers, Sanskrit, Witchcraft, Arabic Philology

Audience: General Public, Researchers, Librarians, Document Delivery Professionals

Details: Free

User Info: Expect: Mitek Server..., Send: Enter or Return; Expect: prompt, Send: hollis

`telnet://hollis.harvard.edu`

Aldus Pagemaker

PAGEMAKER ★

The PageMaker ListServ is dedicated to the discussion of desktop publishing in general, with emphasis on the use of Aldus PageMaker. The list discusses PageMaker's use in both the PC and Macintosh realms. The list also maintains an extensive archive of help files that are extremely useful for the modern desktop publisher.

Keywords: Desktop Publishing, Aldus Pagemaker, IBM PC, Macintosh

Audience: Desktop Publishers, Computer Users

Contact: Geoff Peters
gwp@cs.purdue.edu

Details: Free

User Info: To subscribe to the list, send an e-mail message to the URL address shown below consisting of a single line reading:

SUB pagemaker YourFirstName YourLastName

To send a message to the entire list, address it to: gwp@cs.purdue.edu

`mailto:listserv@cs.purdue.edu`

Alex

Alex Description ★

An NIR (Network Information Retrieval) description of Alex, an Internet access tool.

Keywords: Internet Tools, Internet, Alex

Audience: Internet Surfers

Details: Free

`ftp://alex.sp.cs.cmu.edu/usr0/anon/doc/NIR.Tool`

Aliens

alt.alien.visitors ★

A Usenet newsgroup providing information and discussion about space aliens on Earth and related stories.

Keywords: UFOs, Aliens, Extraterrestrial Life

Audience: Alien Enthusiasts

User Info: To subscribe to this Usenet newsgroup, you need access to a newsreader.

`news:alt.alien.visitors`

The University of California Search for Extraterrestrial Civilizations ★

A web site containing information on the UC Berkeley SETI Program, SERENDIP (Search for Extraterrestrial Radio Emmisions from Nearby Developed Intelligent Populations), an ongoing scientific research effort aimed at detecting radio signals from extraterrestrial civilizations. Details about the program and updates on current research activities are also accessible.

Keywords: Extraterrestrial Life, Astronomy, Aliens

Audience: Astronomers, Physicists, Students, Educators, Engineers, General Public

Contact: Dan Werthimer
sereninfo@ssl.berkeley.edu

Details: Free

If Mosaic is available, use the http address below. Otherwise, please send a request for information to the contact address provided.

`http://sereninfo.ssl.berkeley.edu`

Alife

Alife ★★

The alife mailing list is for communications regarding artificial life, a formative interdisciplinary field involving computer science, the natural sciences, mathematics, and medicine.

Keywords: Artificial Life, Science, Mathematics

Sponsor: UCLA

Audience: Scientists, Biologists, Mathematicians

Contact: alife-request@cognet.ucla.edu

User Info: To subscribe to the list, send an e-mail message to the URL address below.

To send a message to the entire list, address it to: alife@cognet.ucla.edu

`mailto:alife-request@cognet.ucla.edu`

Allergies

National Institute for Allergy & Infectious Disease (NIAID) ★

This is a resource into other databases for searching many medical fields, such as the NIAID network userlist or a databank of AIDS-related information.

Keywords: Medicine, Infectious Diseases, Allergies

Sponsor: NIAID

Audience: Health Care Professionals, Researchers, Students

Contact: Brent Sessions
sessions@odie.niaid.nih.gov

Details: Free

`gopher://gopher.niaid.nih.gov/1`

Alliance Marketing Systems

Alliance Marketing Systems

Develops marketing strategies for new business on those in need of turn-around. Designs advertising/marketing plans to prequalify the buying public.

Keywords: Business Marketing, Sales

Audience: Business Professionals, Marketing Professionals, Sales Executives

Details: Costs

`mailto:prftmaker@secretsams.win.net`

Allied and Alternative Medicine (AMED)

Allied and Alternative Medicine (AMED) ★★★

The Allied and Alternative Medicine database covers the fields of contemporary and alternative medicine.

Keywords: Medicine, Alternative Medicine

Sponsor: Medical Information Service, British Library, Boston Spa, West Yorkshire, UK

Audience: Doctors, Nurses, Health Care Providers, Medical Practitioners, Health Care Industry, General Public

Profile: The AMED database will be of interest to all those who need to know more about alternatives to conventional medicine, such as doctors, nurses and other medical practitioners, therapists, health care libraries, specialist colleges, self-help groups, and the pharmaceutical industry. Coverage includes acupuncture, homeopathy, hypnosis, chiropractic, osteopathy, psychotherapy, diet therapy, herbalism, holistic treatment, traditional Chinese medicine, occupational therapy, physiotherapy, rehabilitation, ayurvedic medicine, reflexology, iridology, moxibustion, meditation, yoga, healing research, and the Alexander Technique.

Contact: Data-star through Dialog in the US at (800) 334-2564; Dialog internationally at country-specific locations.
Details: Costs
User Info: To subscribe, contact Dialog directly.

`telnet://dialog.com`

Alloys

METADEX

International literature covering metals and alloys.

Keywords: Material Science, Metals, Alloys
Sponsor: Materials Information, a joint information service of ASM International and the Institute of Materials
Audience: Materials Scientists, Researchers
Profile: Contains more than 925,000 records from the international literature on metals and alloys concerning processes, properties, materials classes, applications, specific alloy designations, intermetallic compounds and metallurgical systems. Updated monthly.
Contact: paul.albert@neteast.com
User Info: To subscribe contact Orbit-Questel directly.

`telnet://orbit.com`

Almost 2001 Archive

Almost 2001 Archive

Archive of transcripts of Almost 2001, a series on computer communications of the future, produced by NBC (National Broadcasting Company).

Keywords: Computers, Communications, Internet
Sponsor: The WELL (Whole Earth 'Lectronic Link)
Audience: Computer Users, Internet Surfers
Details: Free, Moderated
User Info: To participate in a conference on the WELL, you must first establish an account on the WELL. To do so, start by typing: telnet://well.sf.ca.us

`gopher://gopher.well.sf.ca.us//11/Communications/2001`

alpha-osf-managers

alpha-osf-managers

This list is intended to be a quick-turnaround trouble shooting aid for those who administer and manage DEC Alpha AXP systems running OSF/1.

Keywords: Computer Systems, Computer Administration
Sponsor: Oakridge National Laboratory
Audience: Computer Programmers
User Info: To subscribe to the list, send an e-mail message to the URL address below consisting of a single line reading: subscribe alpha-osf-managers.
Notes: Alpha-osf-managers archived at ftp/kpc.com: /pub/list/alpha-osf-managers

`mailto:majordomo@ornl.gov`

Alspa Computer

Alspa

Discussion by users of the CP/M machines made by (now defunct) Alspa Computer, Inc.

Keywords: Computers, Alspa Computer, Inc., CP/M
Audience: CP/M Users
Contact: Brad Allen
alspa-users-request@ssyx.ucsc.edu
Details: Free
User Info: To subscribe to the list, send an e-mail message requesting a subscription to the URL address below.
To send a message to the entire list, address it to: alspa-users@ssyx.ucsc.edu

`mailto:alspa-users-request@ssyx.ucsc.edu`

alt.3d

alt.3d

A Usenet newsgroup providing information and discussion about three-dimensional imaging.

Keywords: Imaging, 3-D
Audience: Graphic Artists, Artists
User Info: To subscribe to this Usenet newsgroup, you need access to a newsreader.

`news:alt.3d`

alt.activism

alt.activism

A Usenet newsgroup providing information and discussion about activities for activists.

Keywords: Activism
Audience: Activists
User Info: To subscribe to this Usenet newsgroup, you need access to a newsreader.

`news:alt.activism`

alt.alien.visitors

alt.alien.visitors

A Usenet newsgroup providing information and discussion about space aliens on Earth and related stories.

Keywords: UFOs, Aliens, Extraterrestrial Life
Audience: Alien Enthusiasts
User Info: To subscribe to this Usenet newsgroup, you need access to a newsreader.

`news:alt.alien.visitors`

alt.aquaria

alt.aquaria

A Usenet newsgroup providing information and discussion about the aquarium as a hobby.

Keywords: Aquariums, Fish, Hobbies
Audience: Aquarium Keepers, Fish Lovers
User Info: To subscribe to this Usenet newsgroup, you need access to a newsreader.

`news:alt.aquaria`

alt.artcom

alt.artcom

A Usenet newsgroup providing information and discussion about contemporary art and technology. Discussion ranges from GIF files to Australian alternative cinema.

Keywords: Art, Technology
Audience: Artists, Writers
User Info: To subscribe to this Usenet newsgroup, you need access to a newsreader.

`news:alt.artcom`

alt.arts.nomad

alt.arts.nomad

A Usenet conference that focuses on group disembodied art projects.

Keywords: Art
Sponsor: Media Arts, Banff Centre, Canada
Audience: Artists

`news:alt.arts.nomad`

alt.atheism

A Usenet newsgroup providing information and discussion about atheism.

Keywords: Religion, Divinity, God
Audience: Philosophers, Clergy, Atheists
User Info: To subscribe to this Usenet newsgroup, you need access to a newsreader.

`news:alt.atheism`

alt.bbs

A Usenet newsgroup providing information and discussion about computer BBS systems & software.

Keywords: BBS, Cyberspace, Computers
Audience: BBS Users
User Info: To subscribe to this Usenet newsgroup, you need access to a newsreader.

`news:alt.bbs`

alt.beer

A Usenet newsgroup providing information and discussion about beer and ale.

Keywords: Beer
Audience: Brewers, Beer Enthusiasts
User Info: To subscribe to this Usenet newsgroup, you need access to a newsreader.

`news:alt.beer`

alt.binaries.pictures.cartoons

A Usenet newsgroup devoted to cartoon illustrations.

Keywords: Cartoons
Audience: Animators, General Public, Animation Enthusiasts
User Info: To subscribe to this Usenet newsgroup, you need access to a newsreader.

`news:alt.binaries.pictures.cartoons`

alt.bonsai

A Usenet newsgroup providing information and discussion about Bonsai gardening.

Keywords: Bonsai Trees, Japan, Gardening, Landscaping
Audience: Gardeners, Bonsai Enthusiasts
User Info: To subscribe to this Usenet newsgroup, you need access to a newsreader.

`news:alt.bonsai`

alt.books.reviews

A Usenet conference devoted to reviews of books, especially science fiction and computer science books.

Keywords: Literature (General), Computer Science, Science Fiction, Books
Audience: General Public, Publishers, Educators, Librarians, Booksellers
Profile: Alt.books.reviews (a.b.r. for short) is a forum for posting reviews of books of interest to readers, school and public librarians, bookstores, publishers, teachers and professors, and others who desire an "educated opinion" about particular books. This is an unmoderated newsgroup.
Contact: sbrock@csn.org.
Details: Free
To participate in a Usenet newsgroup, you need access to a newsreader
Notes: The reviews in alt.books.reviews are archived at csn.org. Ftp to csn.org; login: anonymous; password: your complete E-mail address. At the ftp prompt, type: cd pub/alt.books.reviews

`news:alt.books.reviews`

alt.california

A Usenet newsgroup providing information and discussion about California and Californian lifestyles.

Keywords: California
Audience: Californians, General Public
User Info: To subscribe to this Usenet newsgroup, you need access to a newsreader.

`news:alt.california`

alt.callahans

A Usenet newsgroup providing information and discussion about Callahan's bar for puns and fellowship.

Keywords: Humor, Word Play
Audience: Punsters, Comedians
User Info: To subscribe to this Usenet newsgroup, you need access to a newsreader.

`news:alt.calahans`

alt.caving

A Usenet newsgroup dedicating to discussions of caving and related issues, including cave locations, equipment, spelunking techniques, and other caving information.

Keywords: Spelunking, Caves
Audience: Spelunkers
User Info: To subscribe to this Usenet newsgroup, you need access to a newsreader.

`news:alt.caving`

alt.censorship

A Usenet newsgroup providing information and discussion about freedom of speech and freedom of the press.

Keywords: Censorship, Freedom of Speech, Constitution (US), Activism
Audience: Press, Students, Educators, Activists
User Info: To subscribe to this Usenet newsgroup, you need access to a newsreader.

`news:alt.censorship`

alt.feminism

alt.chinese.text

alt.chinese.text

A Usenet newsgroup providing information and discussion about Chinese language software.

Keywords: Chinese Language, Language Software
Audience: Chinese, Linguists, Computer Users
User Info: To subscribe to this Usenet newsgroup, you need access to a newsreader.

`news:alt.chinese.text`

alt.christnet

alt.christnet

This Usenet newsgroup is a gathering place for Christian ministers and other users.

Keywords: Religion, Christianity, Bibles, Divinity
Audience: Christians, Ministers
User Info: To subscribe to this Usenet newsgroup, you need access to a newsreader.

`news:alt.christnet`

alt.christnet.bible

alt.christnet.bible

A Usenet newsgroup providing information and discussion about bible discussion and research.

Keywords: Bibles, Christianity, Religion, Divinity
Audience: Biblical Scholars, Bible Readers
User Info: To subscribe to this Usenet newsgroup, you need access to a newsreader.

`news:alt.christnet.bible`

alt.config

alt.config

A Usenet newsgroup providing information and discussion about alternative subnet discussions and connectivity.

Keywords: Internet, Computer Networks, Connectivity
Audience: Network Administrators
User Info: To subscribe to this Usenet newsgroup, you need access to a newsreader.

`news:alt.config`

alt.conspiracy

alt.conspiracy

A Usenet newsgroup providing discussion about conspiracy and paranoia.

Keywords: Conspiracy, Paranoia
Audience: Paranoid Persons, General Public
User Info: To subscribe to this Usenet newsgroup, you need access to a newsreader.

`news:alt.conspiracy`

alt.cult-movies

alt.cult-movies

A Usenet newsgroup providing information and discussion about popular movies.

Keywords: Film, Popular Culture
Audience: Film Enthusiasts, Critics
User Info: To subscribe to this Usenet newsgroup, you need access to a newsreader.

`news:alt.cult-movies`

alt.cyberpunk

alt.cyberpunk

A Usenet newsgroup providing information and discussion about the high-tech low-life.

Keywords: Computers, Cyberspace
Audience: Hackers, Cybernauts, General Public
User Info: To subscribe to this Usenet newsgroup, you need access to a newsreader.

`news:alt.cyberpunk`

alt.drugs

alt.drugs

A Usenet newsgroup providing information and discussion about the use of mind, body, and behavior drugs, and about popular drug awareness.

Keywords: Drugs
Audience: Drug Users, Drug Educators
User Info: To subscribe to this Usenet newsgroup, you need access to a newsreader.

`news:alt.drugs`

alt.fan.monty-python

alt.fan.monty-python

A Usenet newsgroup providing an electronic fan club for those wacky Brits.

Keywords: Humor, Entertainment, Comedy, Satire
Audience: Monty Python Enthusiasts, General Public
User Info: To subscribe to this Usenet newsgroup, you need access to a newsreader.

`news:alt.fan.monty-python`

alt.fan.rush-limbaugh

alt.fan.rush-limbaugh

A Usenet newsgroup providing information and discussion about Rush Limbaugh, a politically conservative American figure.

Keywords: Limbaugh (Rush), Politics (Conservative), Comedy
Audience: Rush Limbaugh Enthusiasts
User Info: To subscribe to this Usenet newsgroup, you need access to a newsreader.

`news:alt.fan.rush-limbaugh`

alt.fashion

alt.fashion

A Usenet newsgroup providing information and discussion about all facets of the fashion industry.

Keywords: Fashion Industry, Style
Audience: Designers, General Public
User Info: To subscribe to this Usenet newsgroup, you need access to a newsreader.

`news:alt.fashion`

alt.feminism

alt.feminism

A Usenet newsgroup providing information and discussion about feminism.

Keywords: Feminism, Women's Studies, Abortion, Activism
Audience: Women, General Public
User Info: To subscribe to this Usenet newsgroup, you need access to a newsreader.

`news:alt.feminism`

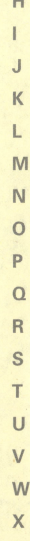

alt.folklore.computers

alt.folklore.computers

A Usenet newsgroup providing information and discussion concerning stories and anecdotes about computers.

Keywords: Computers, Folklore
Audience: Computer Users, Storytellers
User Info: To subscribe to this Usenet newsgroup, you need access to a newsreader.

news:alt.folklore.computers

alt.folklore.urban

A Usenet newsgroup providing information and discussion about urban legends and urban myths.

Keywords: Urban Studies, Folklore
Audience: Story Tellers, General Public
User Info: To subscribe to this Usenet newsgroup, you need access to a newsreader.

news:alt.folklore.urban

alt.guitar

A Usenet newsgroup providing information and discussion about guitar playing.

Keywords: Guitar, Musical Instruments
Audience: Guitarists
User Info: To subscribe to this Usenet newsgroup, you need access to a newsreader.

news:alt.guitar

alt.housing.nontrad

This newsgroup is for discussion of all forms of "nontraditional housing," including cohousing and communes.

Keywords: Community, Housing, Communes
Audience: General Public, Community Activists
Details: Free
User Info: To subscribe to this Usenet newsgroup, you need access to a newsreader.

news:alt.housing.nontrad

alt.hypertext

A Usenet newsgroup devoted to hyperfiction and hypertext documents. Postings range from information about and reviews of both recent hyperfiction and recent nonfiction hypertext documents, to information and/or reviews of software for creating hypertext.

Keywords: Literature (General), Hyperfiction, Hypertext
Audience: General Public, Writers, Computer Programmers
Details: Free
User Info: To subscribe to this Usenet newsgroup, you need access to a newsreader.

news:alt.hypertext

alt.kids-talk

A Usenet newsgroup that provides a place for the pre-collegiate to chat.

Keywords: Chat Groups, Children, Education (K-12)
Audience: Students (K-12)
User Info: To subscribe to this Usenet newsgroup, you need access to a newsreader.

news:alt.kids-talk

alt.music.alternative

A Usenet newsgroup providing information and discussion about alternative music.

Keywords: Musical Genres, Rock Music
Audience: Alternative Music Listeners, Musicians
User Info: To subscribe to this Usenet newsgroup, you need access to a newsreader.

news:alt.music.alternative

alt.music.progressive

A Usenet newsgroup providing information and discussion about progressive music, including the groups Marillion, Asia, King Crimson, and many others.

Keywords: Musical Genres, Pop Music
Audience: Progressive Music Listeners
User Info: To subscribe to this Usenet newsgroup, you need access to a newsreader.

news:alt.music.progressive

alt.pagan

A Usenet newsgroup providing information and discussion about paganism and religion.

Keywords: Paganism, Religion
Audience: Cult Members, Religion Students
User Info: To subscribe to this Usenet newsgroup, you need access to a newsreader.

news:alt.pagan

alt.peeves

A Usenet newsgroup providing information and discussion about peeves, complaints, and whining.

Keywords: Humor, Comedy
Audience: General Public, Complainers
User Info: To subscribe to this Usenet newsgroup, you need access to a newsreader.

news:alt.peeves

alt.personals.ads

A Usenet newsgroup providing a forum for singles.

Keywords: Personals, Singles
Audience: Singles
User Info: To subscribe to this Usenet newsgroup, you need access to a newsreader.

news:alt.personals.ads

alt.politics.clinton

A Usenet newsgroup providing information and discussion about President Bill Clinton and the White House. Perspective tends to be anti-Clinton.

Keywords: Politics (US), Clinton (Bill)
Audience: Politicians, General Public
User Info: To subscribe to this Usenet newsgroup, you need access to a newsreader.

news:alt.politics.clinton

alt.politics.election

alt.politics.election

A Usenet newsgroup organized to help people in the process of running for office.

Keywords: Politics (US), Government
Audience: Politicians, Campaign Managers
User Info: To subscribe to this Usenet newsgroup, you need access to a newsreader.

`news:alt.politics.election`

alt.politics.libertarian

alt.politics.libertarian

A Usenet newsgroup providing information and discussion about the libertarian ideology.

Keywords: Libertarian Party, Politics
Audience: Libertarians, Politicians
User Info: To subscribe to this Usenet newsgroup, you need access to a newsreader.

`news:alt.politics.libertarian`

alt.rap

alt.rap

A Usenet newsgroup providing information and discussion for fans of rap music, including talk about rap performers, new albums, concerts and other aspects of rap.

Keywords: Musical Genres, Rap Music
Audience: Rap Listeners, Rappers
User Info: To subscribe to this Usenet newsgroup, you need access to a newsreader.

`news:alt.rap`

alt.religion.kibology

alt.religion.kibology

A Usenet newsgroup consisting of followers of a god named Kibo, who is, in fact, a human being living in Boston. This newsgroup is highly humorous and hardly religious.

Keywords: Satire, Humor, Religion
Audience: Kibologists
User Info: To subscribe to this Usenet newsgroup, you need access to a newsreader.

`news:alt.religion.kibology`

alt.rock-n-roll

alt.rock-n-roll

A Usenet newsgroup providing information and general discussion about Rock & Roll.

Keywords: Musical Genres, Rock and Roll Music
Audience: Rock Music Listeners
User Info: To subscribe to this Usenet newsgroup, you need access to a newsreader.

`news:alt.rock-n-roll`

alt.rock-n-roll.metal

alt.rock-n-roll.metal

A Usenet newsgroup providing information and discussion about heavy metal music.

Keywords: Musical Genres
Audience: Heavy Metal Listeners
User Info: To subscribe to this Usenet newsgroup, you need access to a newsreader.

`news:alt.rock-n-roll.metal`

alt.romance.chat

alt.romance.chat

A Usenet newsgroup providing discussion about the romantic side of love.

Keywords: Chat Groups, Romance
Audience: General Public
User Info: To subscribe to this Usenet newsgroup, you need access to a newsreader.

`news:alt.romance.chat`

alt.security.pgp

alt.security.pgp

A Usenet newsgroup providing information and discussion about the Pretty Good Privacy package, a privately-developed encryption technique.

Keywords: Privacy, Encryption, Security, Firewalls, Computers
Audience: Internet Surfers
User Info: To subscribe to this Usenet newsgroup, you need access to a newsreader.

`news:alt.security.pgp`

alt.sex

alt.sex

A Usenet newsgroup with many categories providing discussion about sex.

Keywords: Sex
Audience: Adults
User Info: To subscribe to this Usenet newsgroup, you need access to a newsreader.

`news:alt.sex`

alt.sexual.abuse.recovery

alt.sexual.abuse.recovery

A Usenet newsgroup providing information and discussion about sexual abuse recovery and helping others deal with traumatic experiences.

Keywords: Sexual Abuse, Psychotherapy
Audience: Victims
User Info: To subscribe to this Usenet newsgroup, you need access to a newsreader.

`news:alt.sexual.abuse.recovery`

alt.tasteless

alt.tasteless

A Usenet newsgroup providing information and discussion about tasteless jokes.

Keywords: Humor, Comedy
Audience: General Interest, Jokers
User Info: To subscribe to this Usenet newsgroup, you need access to a newsreader.

`news:alt.tasteless`

alt.usage.english

alt.usage.english

A Usenet newsgroup providing information and discussion about English grammar, word usages and related topics.

Keywords: Lexicology, Academia, Linguistics, Education
Audience: English Educators
User Info: To subscribe to this Usenet newsgroup, you need access to a newsreader.

`news:alt.usage.english`

Alternate Tuning Mailing List

Alternate Tuning Mailing List ★★

This mailing list is intended for exchanging ideas relevant to alternate tunings.

Keywords:	Musical Instruments, MIDI
Sponsor:	Mills College
Audience:	Musicians
Profile:	This list deals with just intonation, paratactical tunings, experimental music instrument design, non-standard equal temperaments, MIDI tuning system exclusive specifications, concert postings, non-Western tunings, and the experimental tunings of such people as Harry Partch, Lou Harrison, Martin Bartlett, James Tenney and others.
Contact:	Greg Higgs Higgs@Mills.edu
Details:	Free
User Info:	To subscribe to the list, send an e-mail message to the URL address below, consisting of a single line reading: SUB tuning YourFirstName YourLastName

mailto:listproc@varese.mills.edu

Alternates

Alternates

A mailing list for people who advocate and/or practice an open sexual lifestyle. Its members are primarily bisexual people and their significant others. It serves as a forum and support group for adult men and women who espouse their freedom of choice and imagination in human sexual relations, no matter what their orientaion.

Keywords:	Sexuality, Bisexuality, Sexual Orientation
Audience:	Bisexuals, General Public
Contact:	alternates-request@ns1.rutgers.edu
User Info:	To subscribe to the list, send an e-mail message requesting a subscription to the URL address below. To send a message to the entire list, address it to: alternates@ns1.rutgers.edu

mailto:alternates-request@ns1.rutgers.edu

Alternative Management

AltInst

A mailing list for proposing and critiquing alternative institutions and ways of life. Topics include alternative ways to run conversations, countries, households, markets, offices, romances, and schools.

Keywords:	Institutions, Alternative Management
Audience:	General Public
Contact:	Robin Hanson altinst-request@cs.cmu.edu
Details:	Free
User Info:	To subscribe to the list, send an e-mail message requesting a subscription to the URL address below. To send a message to the entire list, address it to: altinst@cs.cmu.edu
Notes:	AltInst is open to people from any political persuasion, but general political flaming/discussion is forbidden.

mailto:altinst-request@cs.cmu.edu

Alternative Medicine

Allied and Alternative Medicine (AMED)

The Allied and Alternative Medicine database covers the fields of contemporary and alternative medicine.

Keywords:	Medicine, Alternative Medicine
Sponsor:	Medical Information Service, British Library, Boston Spa, West Yorkshire, UK
Audience:	Doctors, Nurses, Health Care Providers, Medical Practitioners, Health Care Industry, General Public
Profile:	The AMED database will be of interest to all those who need to know more about alternatives to conventional medicine, such as doctors, nurses and other medical practitioners, therapists, health care libraries, specialist colleges, self-help groups, and the pharmaceutical industry. Coverage includes acupuncture, homeopathy, hypnosis, chiropractic, osteopathy, psychotherapy, diet therapy, herbalism, holistic treatment, traditional Chinese medicine, occupational therapy, physiotherapy, rehabilitation, ayurvedic medicine, reflexology, iridology, moxibustion, meditation, yoga, healing research, and the Alexander Technique.
Contact:	Data-star through Dialog in the US at (800) 334-2564; Dialog internationally at country-specific locations.
Details:	Costs
User Info:	To subscribe, contact Dialog directly.

telnet://dialog.com

Alternative Medicine, The Definitive Guide

A one-stop reference covering common health problems and leading alternative therapies.

Keywords:	Alternative Medicine, Medicine, Health Care
Sponsor:	Future Medicine Publishing, Inc.
Audience:	General Public, Health Care Professionals
Profile:	Spanning a global effort of 4 years and including input from nearly 400 health care professionals, this one-stop reference offers 1100 pages of in-depth explanations to 43 of the leading alternative therapies. In addition to covering over 200 of the most common health problems, this site offers a wide range of choices for maintaining and regaining your health, highlighted with graphic illustrations. This is truly the "Voice of Alternative Medicine."
Details:	Costs

mailto:futuremd@crl.com

Alternative Press

Prog-Pubs

A mailing list for people interested in progressive and/or alternative publications and other media. Discussions include issues pertaining to all kinds of small-scale, independent, progressive, and/or alternative media, including newspapers, newsletters, and radio and video shows.

Keywords:	Media, Alternative Press, Communications
Audience:	Students (college/university), Independent Media Professionals
Contact:	prog-pubs-request@fuggles.acc.virginia.edu
Details:	Free
User Info:	To subscribe to the list, send an e-mail message requesting a subscription to the URL address below. To send a message to the entire list, address it to:prog-pubs@fuggles.acc.virginia.edu

mailto:prog-pubs@fuggles.acc.virginia.edu

Altlearn (Alternative Approaches to Learning Discussion)

Altlearn (Alternative Approaches to Learning Discussion)

A discussion list that is broadly concerned with learning strategies at all levels.

Keywords:	Education (Adult), Education (Distance), Education (Alternative)
Sponsor:	Alternative Approaches to Learning Discussion
Audience:	Educators, Administrators, Researchers
Details:	Free
User Info:	To subscribe to the list, send an e-mail message to the URL address below, consisting of a single line reading:
	SUB Altlearn YourFirstName YourLastName
	To send a message to the entire list, address it to: altlearn@sjuvm.bitnet

`mailto:listserv@sjuvm.bitnet`

AM/FM

AM/FM

A mailing list for the AM/FM Online Edition, a monthly compilation of news stories concerning the UK radio industry.

Keywords:	Radio, United Kingdom, Communications
Audience:	Radio Enthusiasts (UK), Communications Specialists, Students (College, University)
Contact:	Stephen Hebditch listserv@orbital.demon.co.uk
User Info:	To subscribe to the list, send an e-mail message to the URL addres below, consisting of a single line reading:
	SUB am/fm YourFirstName YourLastName
	To send a message to the entire list, address it to: AM/FM@orbital.demon.co.uk

`mailto:listserv@orbital.demon.co.uk`

AMALGAME

AMALGAME

A resource containing Macintosh demos and XFCN PrintZ files on the subject of health.

Keywords:	Health
Sponsor:	University of Montreal
Audience:	Medical Researchers
Contact:	benoit@medent.umontreal.ca
Details:	Free

`ftp://amalgame.Medent.Umontreal.Ca`

Amazons International

Amazons International

An electronic digest newsletter for and about Amazons (physically and psychologically strong, assertive women who are challenging traditional ideas about gender roles, femininity, and the female physique).

Keywords:	Gender, Feminism, Women's Issues
Audience:	Women, Feminists, Writers, Art Historians
Profile:	The digest is dedicated to the image of the female hero in fiction and in fact, as it is expressed in art and literature, in the physiques and feats of female athletes,and in sexual values and practices; it also provides information, discussion, and a supportive environment for these values and issues.
Contact:	Thomas Gramstad amazons-request@math.uio.no
Details:	Free
User Info:	To subscribe to the list, send an e-mail message requesting a subscription to the URL address below.
	To send a message to the entire list, address it to: amazons@math.uio.no

`mailto:amazons-request@math.uio.no`

Ambulatory Care

University of Texas Health Science Center at San Antonio Library

The library's holdings are large and wide-ranging and contain significant collections in many fields.

Keywords:	Allied Health, Dentistry, Nursing, Veterinary Science, Ambulatory Care, Obstetrics/Gynecology, Pediatrics
Audience:	Researchers, Students, General Public
Details:	Free
User Info:	Expect: Login, Send: LIS

`telnet://athena.uthscsa.edu`

Amend2-discuss

Amend2-discuss

A mailing list for discussion of the implications and issues surrounding the passage of Colorado's Amendment 2, which revokes any existing homosexual civil rights legislation and prohibits the drafting of any new legislation.

Keywords:	Activism, Gay Rights, Lesbians, Bisexuality
Audience:	Gay Rights Activists
Contact:	amend2-mod@cs.colorado.edu
User Info:	To subscribe to the list, send an e-mail message to the URL address below consisting of a single line reading: subscribe amend2-discuss

`mailto:majordomo@cs.colorado.edu`

Amend2-info

Amend2-info

Colorado voted in an amendment to their state constitution which revokes any existing gay/lesbian/bisexual civil rights legislation and prohibits the drafting of any new legislation. This moderated list is for information on the implication and issues of this amendment.

Keywords:	Activists, Gay, Lesbian, Bisexual, Constitutional Amendments, Colorado, Civil Rights
Audience:	General Public, Gays, Lesbians, Bisexuals, Activists
Contact:	amend2-info@cs.colorado.edu
User Info:	To subscribe to the list, send an e-mail message requesting a subscription to the URL address below.
	To send a message to the entire list, address it to: amend2-info@cs.colorado.edu

`mailto:majordomo@cs.colorado.edu`

AmerCath (History of American Catholicism)

AmerCath (History of American Catholicism)

This mailing list focuses on the history of American Catholicism.

Keywords:	Catholicism, Christianity, Religion
Sponsor:	Jefferson Community College, University of Kentucky, Louisville, KY, USA

AmerCath (History of American Catholism)

Audience:	Researchers, Educators, Students, Catholics
Profile:	Since AMERCATH can be accessed internationally, it thus forms a global network of people who research and teach the history of American Catholicism. AMERCATH facilitates communication among faculty, students, and researchers.
Contact:	Anne Kearney jccannek@ukcc.uky.edu
Details:	Free
User Info:	To subscribe to the list, send an e-mail message to the address below, consisting of a single line reading: Sub AmerCath YourFirstName YourLastName To send a message to the entire list, address it to: AmerCath@ukcc.uky.edu

`mailto:listserv@ukcc.uky.edu`

America

America

For people interested in how the United States is dealing with foreign trade policies, congressional status, and other inside information about the government that is freely distributable.

Keywords:	Foreign Trade, Government (US), Congress (US), Business (US)
Audience:	General Public, Researchers, Journalists, Political Scientists, Students
Contact:	subscribe@xamiga.linet.org
User Info:	To subscribe to the list, send an e-mail message to the URL address below, consisting of a single line reading: SUB america YourFirstName YourLastName To send a message to the entire list, address it to: america@xamiga.linet.org
Notes:	This list has monthly postings that are generally in large batches, with posts exceeding a few hundred lines.

`mailto:subscribe@xamiga.linet.org`

American Banker Full Text

American Banker Full Text

This database corresponds to the authoritative print publication American Banker.

Keywords:	Banking, International Finance, Foreign Trade
Sponsor:	American Banker-Bond Buyer, New York, NY, USA
Audience:	Financial Analysts, Bankers
Profile:	Specific coverage is given to local, regional, and international financial services, technology applications, legal commentary and court actions, international trade, government regulations, Washington events, marketing of financial services, general economic overviews, personnel issues, and profiles and movements of industry personnel. Statistical rankings of all types of financial institutions (from thrifts to commercial banks, US and worldwide) are included beginning with the October 1987 editions. Other special features include quarterly bank earnings, results of American Banker surveys, and the complete text of speeches and articles by the industry professionals that are unavailable in the printed paper.
Contact:	Dialog in the US at (800) 334-2564; Dialog internationally at country-specific locations.
Details:	Costs
User Info:	To subscribe, contact Dialog directly.

`telnet://dialog.com`

American Chemical Society

American Chemical Society

This is the gopher site of the American Chemical Society.

Keywords:	Chemistry, Chemical Engineering
Sponsor:	The American Chemical Society
Audience:	Chemists, Chemical Engineers
Profile:	This site contains supplemental material pages from the Journal of the American Chemical Society. Instructions for authors' submissions are also to be found here, as well as general information about the Society.
Contact:	Gopher Operator gopher@acsinfo.acs.org
Details:	Free

`gopher://acsinfo.acs.org`

American Drama

University of Chicago Library

The library's holdings are large and wide-ranging and contain significant collections in many fields.

Keywords:	English Bibles, Lincoln (Abraham), Kentucky & Ohio River Valley (History of), Balzac (Honore de), American Drama, Cromwell (Oliver), Goethe, Judaica, Italy, Chaucer (Geoffrey), Wells (Ida, Personal Papers of), Douglas (Stephen A.), Italy, Literature (Children's)
Audience:	General Public, Researchers, Librarians, Document Delivery Professionals
Details:	Free
User Info:	Expect: ENTER CLASS, Send: LIB48 3; Expect: CONNECTED, Send: RETURN

`telnet://olorin.uchicago.edu`

American Hockey League

American Hockey League

This list is for people interested in discussing and following the activities of The American Hockey League.

Keywords:	Sports, Hockey
Audience:	Hockey Enthusiasts, Sports Enthusiasts
Contact:	ahl-news-request@andrew.cmu.edu
Details:	Free
User Info:	To subscribe to the list, send an e-mail message requesting a subscription to the URL address below. To send a message to the entire list, address it to: ahl-news@andrew.cmu.edu

`mailto:ahl-news-request@andrew.cmu.edu`

American Studies

Summit of the Americas Internet Gopher

A gopher containing supporting materials for the Summit of the Americas, a meeting of the Western Hemisphere's democratically elected heads of state, to be held in Miami in December of 1994.

Keywords:	American Studies, International Relations, Haiti, Latin America
Sponsor:	The Florida University Latin American and Caribbean Center
Audience:	Government Officials, Journalists, NGOs, General Public
Contact:	Rene Ramos summit@SERVAX.FIU.EDU

`gopher://summit.fiu.edu`

Americana

soc.culture.usa

A Usenet newsgroup providing information and discussion about the culture of the United States.

Keywords:	Americana, Sociology, Popular Culture

Audience: Sociologists, General Public
Details: Free
User Info: To subscribe to this Usenet newsgroup, you need access to a newsreader.

`news:soc.culture.usa`

Americana (Western)

University of the Pacific Library

The library's holdings are large and wide-ranging and contain significant collections in many fields.
Keywords: Pharmacology, Americana (Western)
Audience: Researchers, Students, General Public
Details: Free
User Info: Expect: Login, Send: Library

`telnet://pacificat.lib.uop.edu`

Williams College Library ★★★

The library's holdings are large and wide-ranging and contain significant collections in many fields.
Keywords: Americana, Graphic Arts, Printing (History of), Performing Arts, Printing
Audience: General Public, Researchers, Librarians, Document Delivery Professionals
Contact: Jim Cubit
Details: Free
User Info: Expect: Mitek Server..., Send: Enter or Return; Expect: prompt, Send: hollis

`telnet://library.williams.edu`

Americans with Disabilities Act

Americans with Disabilities Act ★

Gives access to the full text of the Americans with Disabilities Act (ADA) and all the related legislation.
Keywords: Disabilities, Legislation (US), Government (US)
Audience: General Public, Disabled People, Differently Abled People, Politicians, Journalists, Students
Profile: The purpose of ADA is to provide a clear and comprehensive national mandate to end discrimination against individuals with disabilities and to bring them into the economic and social mainstream of American life; to provide enforceable standards addressing discrimination against individuals with disabilities; and to ensure that the federal government plays a central role in enforcing these standards on behalf of individuals with disabilities.
Details: Free

`gopher://val-dor.cc.buffalo.edu/11/.legislation/`

Amiga

Amiga CD-ROM ★

For Amiga users who are interested in CD-ROM drives and discs.
Keywords: Computers, Amiga, CD-ROM
Audience: Computer Users, Amiga Users
Contact: ben@ben.com
Details: Free
User Info: To subscribe to the list, send an e-mail message requesting a subscription to the URL address below.

To send a message to the entire list, address it to: cdrom-list@ben.com

`mailto:cdrom-list-request@ben.com`

Amiga Files ★

Archive of files of interest to Amiga users.
Keywords: Amiga
Audience: Computer Users, Amiga Users
Details: Free

`ftp://archive.umich.edu`

AMOS ★

For the AMOS programming language on Amiga computers. Features source, bug reports, and help from users around the world, but mainly from European users. Most posts will be in English, but there are no language limitations.
Keywords: Computers, Programming Languages, AMOS, Amiga
Audience: Programmers, Computer Users, Amiga Users
Contact: subscribe@xamiga.linet.org
Details: Free
User Info: To subscribe to the list, send an e-mail message to the URL address below, consisting of a single line reading:

SUB YourFirstName YourLastName

To send a message to the entire list, address it to: amos@xamiga.linet.org

`mailto:subscribe@xamiga.linet.org`

comp.sys.amiga

A Usenet newsgroup providing information and discussion about Amiga systems. There are many categories within this group.
Keywords: Computer Systems, Amiga
Audience: Computer Users, Amiga Users
User Info: To subscribe to this Usenet newsgroup, you need access to a newsreader.

`news:comp.sys.amiga`

amlat.mujeres

amlat.mujeres

This conference serves as a forum for interchange between organizations and women's movements in Latin America and the Caribbean.
Keywords: Women Issues, Latin America, Caribbean, Feminism
Audience: Women, Feminists, Activists
Contact: Agencia Latinoamericana de Informacion
info@alai.ec
uualai@ecuanex.ec
Details: Costs
User Info: Establish an account on the nearest APC node. Login, type c for conferences, then type: go amlat.mujeres.

For information on the nearest APC node, contact: APC International Secretariat, IBASE.

E-mail: apcadmin@apc.org

`telnet://igc.apc.org`

Amnesty International

Amnesty International

A site containing information about Amnesty International, an organization focused strictly and specifically on human rights around the world.
Keywords: Government, Human Rights, Politics (International), Activism
Sponsor: Amnesty International
Audience: Students, Activists
Contact: Catherine Hampton
ariel@netcom.com

`ftp://ftp.netcom.com/pub/ariel/`

`http:www/human.rights/amnesty.international/ai.html`

An NREN That Includes Everyone

An NREN That Includes Everyone

In this article, community networker Tom Grundner (founder of Free-Net), advocates a National Community Network, one that treats patients looking for health care information as researchers. He advocates expanding our definition of educational access to include people of all ages—senior citizens as well as kindergarteners.

Keywords: Community Networking, Networking, Government (US)

Audience: Activists, Policymakers, Community Leaders

Contact: Tom Grundner
tmg@nptn.org

Details: Free

Notes: This document contains hypertext links to the NPTN (National Public Telecomputing Network).

http://nearnet.gnn.com/mag/articles/oram/bio.grundner.html

Analog Equipment

Analog Heaven

The Analog Heaven mailing list caters to people interested in vintage analog electronic music equipment. Topics include items for sale, repair tips, equipment modifications, ASCII & GIF schematics, and a general discussion of new and old analog equipment. There is an FTP/Gopher site located at cs.uwp.edu with discussions on various machines, a definitive guide to Roland synths, patch editors, modification schematics, and GIFs/JPEGs of vintage synths, as well as a few sound samples of some of the gear itself.

Keywords: Music, Synthesizers, Sequencers, Analog Equipment, Electronic Music

Audience: Electronic Music Enthusiasts, Musicians

Contact: Todd Sines
analogue-request@magnus.acs.ohio-state.edu

Details: Free, Sound files available.

User Info: To subscribe to the list, send an e-mail message requesting a subscription to the URL address below.

To send a message to the entire list, address it to:
analogue@magnus.acs.ohio-state.edu

mailto:analogue-request@magnus.acs.ohio-state.edu

Analysis

CANADA (Canadian News and Information Library)

The Canadian News and Information library (CANADA) contains Canadian legal news, business and company information.

Keywords: News, Analysis, Companies, Canada

Audience: Canadians

Profile: The CANADA library contains respected Canadian news publications such as The Toronto Star, The Vancouver Sun, Ottawa Business News and the Montreal Gazette. The CANADA library also offers Canadian company profiles, country reports, and Canada's financial database, CANCORP Plus.

Contact: Mead New Sales Group at (800) 227-4908 or (513) 859-5398 inside the US, or (513) 865-7981 for all inquiries outside the US.

User Info: To subscribe, contact Mead directly.

To examine the Nexis user guide, you can access it at the ftp site of the University of Texas at Austin at the URL address: ftp://ftp.cc.utexas.edu

The files are in: /pub/ref-services/LEXIS

telnet://nex.meaddata.com

http://www.meaddata.com

ENVIRN (Environment Library)
★★★

The Environment (ENVIRN) Library contains a variety of environment-related news and legal information.

Keywords: News, Analysis, Law, Environment

Audience: Environmental Researchers, Business Professionals

Profile: The ENVIRN library contains a combination of environmental information that can provide critical insight into environmental hazards, EPA ratings, specific company investigations, evaluations on potentially hazardous chemicals, and parties responsible for cleanup of specific hazardous sites. Additionally, ENVIRN provides a wealth of environment-related information—legislation, regulations, and court and agency decisions at both the federal and state levels; news; the Environmental Law Reporter, and American Law Reports.

Contact: Mead New Sales Group at (800) 227-4908 or (513) 859-5398 inside the US, or (513) 865-7981 for all inquiries outside the US.

User Info: To subscribe, contact Mead directly.

To examine the Nexis user guide, you can access it at the ftp site of the University of Texas at Austin at the URL address: ftp://ftp.cc.utexas.edu

The files are in: /pub/ref-services/LEXIS

telnet://nex.meaddata.com

http://www.meaddata.com

FEDTAX (Federal Tax Library)
★★★

The Federal Tax library offerers a comprehensive, up-to-date collection of tax-related materials, including case law, agency materials, legislative and regulatory materials, and so on.

Keywords: Law, Analysis, Tax

Audience: Lawyers

Profile: The Federal Tax library offers a comprehensive, up-to-date collection of tax-related materials. This library includes federal and state tax case law, Internal Revenue Service rulings and releases, state tax administrative decisions and rulings, the Internal Revenue Code, federal tax regulations, international news and treaties, tax looseleaf services, tax periodicals, tax law reviews, tax dailies, pending state legislation, and state property records.

Contact: New Sales Group at 800-227-4908 or 513-859-5398 inside the US, or 1-513-865-7981 for all inquires outside the US.

User Info: To subscribe, contact Mead directly.

To examine the Lexis user guide, you can access it at the ftp site of the University of Texas at Austin at the URL address: ftp://ftp.cc.utexas.edu

The files are in: /pub/ref-services/LEXIS

telnet://nex.meaddata.com

http://www.meaddata.com

INSURE (Insurance)

The Insurance (INSURE) library contains specific full-text and abstract news and legal information sources focusing on the insurance industry.

Keywords: News, Analysis, Law, Insurance

Audience: Insurance Professionals, Lawyers

Profile: The INSURE library contains leading insurance industry news sources, legal and regulatory materials from NILS Publishing Company's INSURLAW, analyst reports on the insurance industry from InvestextR, and insurance company financial reports. Federal and state case law and federal regulations are also available.

Contact: Mead New Sales Group @ (800) 227-4908 or (513) 859-5398 inside the US, or (513) 865-7981 for all inquiries outside the US.

Analysis

User Info: To subscribe, contact Mead directly.

To examine the Nexis user guide, you can access it at the ftp site of the University of Texas at Austin at the URL address: ftp://ftp.cc.utexas.edu

The files are in: /pub/res-services/LEXIS

`telnet://nex.meaddata.com`

INVEST (Investment News and Information) ★★★

The INVEST library contains company and industry research reports provided through the Investext(R) database. These reports are created by industry experts who are employed for their accurate and insightful evaluation. Only the most recent 12 months of data will be displayed.

Keywords: Companies, Financials, Analysis

Audience: Business Researchers, Analysts, Entrepreneurs

Profile: INVEST is categorized by type. Selections can be made using these categories: Industry (more than 50 industries are available), State (where a specific company is located), Country (Country in which the company is located), US Broker or International Broker. The INVEST library provides an automatic display following the selection of a file. For industry reports, a menu will appear providing definitions as they relate to the industries. All remaining files will provide a confirmation of the file selected.

Contact: Mead New Sales Group at (800) 227-4908 or (513) 859-5398 inside the US, or (513) 865-7981 for all inquiries outside the US.

User Info: To subscribe, contact Mead directly.

To examine the Nexis user guide, you can access it at the ftp site of the University of Texas at Austin at the URL address: ftp://ftp.cc.utexas.edu

The files are in: /pub/ref-services/LEXIS

`telnet://nex.meaddata.com`

`http://www.meaddata.com`

LAWREV (Law Review Library) ★★★

The Law Review library contains law reviews, American Bar Association publications, American Institute of Certified Public Accountants periodicals, and other materials. The present focus concentrates on both state and national issues of legal significance.

Keywords: US Law, Analysis, Law Reviews, Journals

Audience: Lawyers

Profile: The Law Review library currently consists of over 70 law reviews, several American Bar Association publicatons and American Institute of Certified Public Accountants periodicals, an Environmental Law Institute publication, ALR and LEd2d articles, two leading legal indices and a number of Warren Gorham & Lamont tax journals. The present focus concentrates on both state and national issues of legal significance.

Contact: New Sales Group at 800-227-4908 or 513-859-5398 inside the US, or 1-513-865-7981 for all inquires outside the US.

User Info: To subscribe, contact Mead directly.

To examine the Lexis user guide, you can access it at the ftp site of the University of Texas at Austin at the URL address: ftp://ftp.cc.utexas.edu

The files are in: /pub/ref-services/LEXIS

`telnet://nex.meaddata.com`

`http://www.meaddata.com`

MARKET (Markets and Industries News and Information) ★★★

The Markets and Industries News and Information (MARKET) library contains sources covering developments in a wide variety of markets and industries.

Keywords: News, Analysis, Industry, Marketing

Audience: Business Professionals, Researchers

Profile: The MARKET library contains a wide selection of sources ranging from trade and industry sources to InvestextR industry reports to company profiles. To round out the offering, MARKET also covers advertising, marketing, public opinion polls, market research, public relations, sales and selling, promotions, consumer attitudes, trends and behaviors, demographics, product announcements and product reviews. In addition, Predicasts Overview of Markets and Technology (PROMT), Marketing and Advertising Reference Service (MARS), US and International Forecast Databases (UFRCST and IFRCST) and the US Time Series (USTIME), all from Information Access Company, are available.

Contact: Mead New Sales Group at (800) 227-4908 or (513) 859-5398 inside the US, or (513) 865-7981 for all inquiries outside the US.

User Info: To subscribe, contact Mead directly.

To examine the Nexis user guide, you can access it at the ftp site of the University of Texas at Austin at the URL address: ftp://ftp.cc.utexas.edu

The files are in: /pub/ref-services/LEXIS

`telnet://nex.meaddata.com`

`http://www.meaddata.com`

MDEAFR ★★★★

The Middle East and Africa (MDEAFR) library contains detailed information about every country in the Mideast and Africa. Structured for those who want to follow the unfolding events in the Gulf states, as well as in North and South Africa, this library contains a broad array of sources, including international research reports from InvestextR.

Keywords: News, Analysis, Companies, Middle East, Africa

Audience: Journalists, Business Professionals

Profile: The MDEAFR library contains a wide array of pertinent sources. Among the information sources are newspapers and wire services, trade and business journals, company reports, country and region background, industry and product analysis, business opportunities, and selected legal texts. News sources range from the world-renowned Associated Press and Christian Science Monitor to the regionally important Jerusalem Post and Africa News. Company information is contained in the EXTEL cards as well as ICC. Providers of country background and industry analysis include Associated Banks of Europe, Bank of America, Business International, IBC USA, and the US Department of Commerce. Customers interested in new business opportunities can check OPIC and Foreign Trade Opportunities (FTO).

Contact: Mead New Sales Group at (800) 227-4908 or (513) 859-5398 inside the US, or (513) 865-7981 for all inquiries outside the US.

User Info: To subscribe, contact Mead directly.

To examine the Nexis user guide, you can access it at the ftp site of the University of Texas at Austin at the URL address: ftp://ftp.cc.utexas.edu

The files are in: /pub/ref-services/LEXIS

`telnet://nex.meaddata.com`

`http://www.meaddata.com`

NEWS (General News) ★★★

The General News (NEWS) library includes more than 2,300 sources. Full-text news from national and international newspapers, magazines, newsletters, and wire services and abstract information are both available.

Keywords: News, Analysis, People, Companies

Audience: Journalists, General Public

Profile: The General News (NEWS) library contains a number of publications and wire services of general interest, as well as others that specialize in particular areas of business . The NEWS library is organized into individual files, group files by source or subject, and user-defined combination files for full-text information sources. Abstracts are also available as individual files or can be searched together in one group file. The NEWS library includes such prestigious full-text sources as the New York Times and more than more than 30 major newspapers from around the US and the world.

Contact: Mead New Sales Group at (800) 227-4908 or (513) 859-5398 inside the US, or (513) 865-7981 for all inquiries outside the US.

User Info: To subscribe, contact Mead directly.

To examine the Nexis user guide, you can access it at the ftp site of the University of Texas at Austin at the URL address: ftp://ftp.cc.utexas.edu

The files are in: /pub/ref-services/LEXIS

`telnet://nex.meaddata.com`

`http://www.meaddata.com`

NSAMER (North and South America Library)

The North and South America library contains detailed information about every country in North and South America (except the United States). The US-Canada Free Trade Agreement, the North American Free Trade Agreement, relations with Mexico and events in such countries as Brazil, Peru, and Nicaragua are among the topics covered by a variety of business, news and legal sources. International research reports from InvestextR are also included. The United States is not covered in this library.

Keywords: News, Analysis, Companies, North America, South America

Audience: Journalists, Business Professionals

Profile: The North and South America library contains a broad array of sources. Among the information sources are newspapers and wire services, trade and business journals, company reports, country and region backgrounds, industry and product analyses, business opportunities, and selected legal texts. News sources range from the world-renowned Washington Post and Christian Science Monitor to the regionally important Toronto Star and Latin American Newsletters. Canadian Business and Maclean's represent a portion of the array of business and trade journals. Company information is contained in the EXTEL cards as well as ICC. Providers of country background and industry analyses include Associated Banks of Europe, Bank of America, Business International, IBC USA and the US Department of Commerce. Among the specialized resources are IBC's Mexico and Brazil Services as well as BI's Business Latin America. Researchers interested in new business opportunities can check OPIC and Foreign Trade Opportunities (FTO).And selected legal texts covering the US-Canada Free Trade Agreement and other international agreements planners and advisors to better assess the business climate in North and South America.

Contact: Mead New Sales Group at (800) 227-4908 or (513) 859-5398 inside the US, or (513) 865-7981 for all inquiries outside the US.

User Info: To subscribe, contact Mead directly.

To examine the Nexis user guide, you can access it at the ftp site of the University of Texas at Austin at the URL address: ftp://ftp.cc.utexas.edu

The files are in: /pub/ref-services/LEXIS

`telnet://nex.meaddata.com`

`http://www.meaddata.com`

SPORTS (Sports News)

The Sports News (SPORTS) library contains a variety of sports-related news and information.

Keywords: News, Analysis, Sports, Biographies

Audience: Sports Enthusiasts, Journalists

Profile: The SPORTS library is a specialized news library that contains the full text of Sports Illustrated and The Sporting News and selected sports-related stories from many major US newspapers and wire services. Biographical information and 1992 Olympic facts are also part of this library.

Contact: Mead New Sales Group at (800) 227-4908 or (513) 859-5398 inside the US, or (513) 865-7981 for all inquiries outside the US.

User Info: To subscribe, contact Mead directly.

To examine the Nexis user guide, you can access it at the ftp site of the University of Texas at Austin at the URL address: ftp://ftp.cc.utexas.edu

The files are in: /pub/ref-services/LEXIS

`telnet://nex.meaddata.com`

`http://www.meaddata.com`

STATES (States Library)

★★★

The combined States library contains case law, code and agency materials from the 53 individual US state libraries (50 states plus the District of Columbia, Puerto Rico and the Virgin Islands), all in the same library.

Keywords: Law, Analysis, Case, States

Audience: Lawyers

Profile: The combined States library contains case law, code and agency materials from the 53 individual state libraries (50 states plus the District of Columbia, Puerto Rico and the Virgin Islands), all in the same library. The States library also features many large group files which allow several individual files to be accessed in the same search. Many of the group files involve case law, including files that cover all state case law available on the LEXIS service plus ALR material and files that combine all federal and state case law available on the LEXIS service.

Contact: New Sales Group at 800-227-4908 or 513-859-5398 inside the US, or 1-513-865-7981 for all inquires outside the US.

User Info: To subscribe, contact Mead directly.

To examine the Lexis user guide, you can access it at the ftp site of the University of Texas at Austin at the URL address: ftp://ftp.cc.utexas.edu

The files are in: /pub/ref-services/LEXIS

`telnet://nex.meaddata.com`

`http://www.meaddata.com`

TOPNWS (Top News)

The Top News (TOPNWS) library contains today's news today for selected key sources from around the world.

Keywords: News, Analysis

Audience: Journalists, General Public

Profile: In the Top News (TOPNWS) library newswires are collected and updated every 60 minutes. Newspapers and other daily publications are updated throughout the day on the day of publication. Transcripts are updated within three hours of broadcast. Two weeks worth of data from more than 40 major publications may be searched as individual files or in specialized group files. The TODAY group file contains today's published information from all sources. the 2WEEK group file expands the window of current information from all sources to two weeks. Specialized section files, designed to be like sections of a newspaper, contain stories from each publication that pertain to the section or topic selected.

Contact: Mead New Sales Group at (800) 227-4908 or (513) 859-5398 inside the US, or (513) 865-7981 for all inquiries outside the US.

User Info: To subscribe, contact Mead directly.

To examine the Nexis user guide, you can access it at the ftp site of the University of Texas at Austin at the URL address: ftp://ftp.cc.utexas.edu

The files are in: /pub/ref-services/LEXIS

`telnet://nex.meaddata.com`

`http://www.meaddata.com`

Animal Rights

AR-news

A public news wire for items relating to animal rights and animal welfare.

Keywords: Activism, Animal Rights, Veterinarians

Audience: Activists, Animal Lovers

Animals

Contact: Ian Lance Taylor, Chip Roberson
taylor@think.com or csr@nic.aren.com

User Info: To subscribe to the list, send an e-mail message to the URL address below.

To send a message to the entire list, address it to: ar-news@think.com

Notes: Appropriate postings to ar-news include posting a news item, requesting information on some event, or responding to a request for information. Discussions on ar-news are not allowed.

`mailto:ar-news@think.com`

AR-talk

An unmoderated list for the discussion of animal rights and related issues, such as animal liberation, consumer product testing, cruelty-free products, vivisection and dissection, and vegan lifestyles.

Keywords: Activism, Animal Rights

Audience: Activists, Animal Lovers, Researchers

Contact: Ian Lance Taylor, Chip Roberson
taylor@think.com or csr@nic.aren.com

User Info: To subscribe to the list, send an e-mail message to the URL address below.

To send a message to the entire list, address it to: ar-talk@think.com

`mailto:ar-talk-request@think.com`

Animal Science

Biosis Previews

The database encompasses the entire field of life sciences and covers original research reports and reviews in biological and biomedical areas. This includes field, laboratory, clinical, experimental and theoretical work. The traditional areas of biology, including botany, zoology and microbiology are covered, as well as the related fields such as plant and animal science, agriculture, pharmacology, and ecology.

Keywords: Biology, Botany, Zoology, Microbiology, Plant Science, Animal Science, Agriculture, Pharmacology, Ecology, Biochemistry, Biophysics, Bioengineering

Sponsor: Biosis

Audience: Librarians, Researchers, Students, Biologists, Botanists, Zoologists, Scientists, Taxonomists

Contact: CDP Technologies Sales Department (800)950-2035, extension 400

User Info: To subscribe, contact CDP Technologies directly

`telnet://cdplus@cdplus.com`

Animal Studies

AGRICOLA

The AGRICOLA database of the National Agricultural Library (NAL) provides comprehensive coverage of worldwide journal literature and monographs on agriculture and related subjects.

Keywords: Agriculture, Animal Studies, Botany, Entomology

Sponsor: US National Agricultural Library, Beltsville, MD, USA

Audience: Agronomists, Botanists, Chemists, Entomologists

Profile: Related subjects include: animal studies, botany, chemistry, entomology, fertilizers, forestry, hydroponics, soils, and more.

Contact: Dialog in the US at (800) 334-2564, Dialog internationally at country-specific locations.

User Info: To subscribe, contact Dialog directly.

Notes: Coverage: 1970 to the present; updated monthly.

`telnet://dialog.com`

Animal Welfare

NetVet Veterinary Resources

An Internet server for veterinary and animal resources.

Keywords: Veterinary Medicine, Animal Welfare, Animals

Sponsor: Washington University, St. Louis, Division of Comparative Medicine

Audience: Veterinarians, Animal Lovers

Profile: A collection of veterinary and animal-related computer resources that includes archives of animal legislation and regulation, listings for colleges of Veterinary Medicine, conference information, and animal-related databases, including the Electronic Zoo. Also has links to other animal and veterinary-related systems.

Contact: Dr. Ken Boshert
ken@wudcm.wustl.edu

`gopher://netvet.wustl.edu`

`http://netvet.wustl.edu`

Animals

Animals

This directory is a compilation of information resources focused on animals.

Keywords: Animals, Electronic Media

Audience: Animal Lovers, Veterinarians, Activists

Contact: Ken Boschert
ken@wudcm.wustl.edu

Details: Free

`ftp://una.hh.lib.umich.edu/70/inetdirsstacks/animals:boschert`

NetVet Veterinary Resources

An Internet server for veterinary and animal resources.

Keywords: Veterinary Medicine, Animal Welfare, Animals

Sponsor: Washington University, St. Louis, Division of Comparative Medicine

Audience: Veterinarians, Animal Lovers

Profile: A collection of veterinary and animal-related computer resources that includes archives of animal legislation and regulation, listings for colleges of Veterinary Medicine, conference information, and animal-related databases, including the Electronic Zoo. Also has links to other animal and veterinary-related systems.

Contact: Dr. Ken Boshert
ken@wudcm.wustl.edu

`gopher://netvet.wustl.edu`

`http://netvet.wustl.edu`

rec.equestrian

A Usenet newsgroup providing information and discussion about all things pertaining to horses.

Keywords: Horses, Equestrians, Animals, Sports

Audience: Horse Riders, Horse Trainers, Horse Owners

User Info: To subscribe to this Usenet newsgroup, you need access to a newsreader.

`news:rec.equestrian`

rec.pets

A Usenet newsgroup providing information and discussion about pets and pet care.

Keywords: Pets, Animals

Audience: Pet Owners

User Info: To subscribe to this Usenet newsgroup, you need access to a newsreader.

`news:rec.pets`

rec.pets.cats ⭐

A Usenet newsgroup providing information and discussion about domestic cats.

Keywords: Pets, Animals
Audience: Cat Owners
User Info: To subscribe to this Usenet newsgroup, you need access to a newsreader.

`news:rec.pets.cats`

rec.pets.dogs ⭐

A Usenet newsgroup providing information and discussion about dogs.

Keywords: Pets, Animals
Audience: Dog Owners
User Info: To subscribe to this Usenet newsgroup, you need access to a newsreader.

`news:rec.pets.dogs`

Animation

ANIME-L ⭐

This discussion list covers animation news, with a special emphasis on Japanese "animedia."

Keywords: Animation, Film, Japan
Audience: Animation Enthusiasts, Animators
Details: Free
User Info: To subscribe to the list, send an e-mail message to the address below, consisting of a single line reading:

Sub anime-l YourFirstName YourLastName

To send a message to the entire list, address it to: anime-l@vtvm1.cc.vt.edu

`mailto:listserv@vtvm1.cc.vt.edu`

OTIS (Operative Term Is Stimulate) ⭐

An image-based electronic art gallery.

Keywords: Art, Graphics, Electronic Art, Animation
Audience: Graphic Artists
Profile: OTIS is a public-access library containing hundreds of images, animations, and information files.

Within the sunsite ftp, the directory is: /pub/multimedia/pictures/OTIS. Use the bin command to insure you're in binary transfer mode.

`ftp://sunsite.unc.edu`

rec.arts.anime ⭐

A Usenet newsgroup providing information and discussion about Japanese animation fen.

Keywords: Animation, Fen, Japan
Audience: Animators
Details: Free
User Info: To subscribe to this Usenet newsgroup, you need access to a newsreader.

`news:rec.arts.anime`

Annealing

Anneal ⭐⭐

A mailing list for the discussion of simulated annealing techniques and analysis, as well as related issues such as stochastic optimization, Boltzmann machines, and metricity of NP-complete move spaces.

Keywords: Mathematics, Simulation, Annealing
Sponsor: UCLA
Audience: Mathematicians, Physicists
Contact: Daniel R. Greening
anneal-request@cs.ucla.edu
User Info: To subscribe to the list, send an e-mail message to the URL address below.

To send a message to the entire list, address it to: anneal@cs.ucla.edu

Notes: Membership is restricted to those doing active research in simulated annealing or related areas.

`mailto:anneal-request@cs.ucla.edu`

Annual Reports

CIA World Factbook ⭐

Annual report of CIA (Central Intelligence Agency) research in over 247 nations.

Keywords: CIA, Intelligence, Annual Reports
Audience: Governments, Lawyers, FBI
Details: Free

`gopher://marvel.loc.gov`

Anthropology

Anthropology, Cross Cultural Studies, & Archaeology ⭐⭐⭐

This directory is a compilation of information resources focused on anthropology, cross cultural studies, and archaeology.

Keywords: Anthropology, Cultural Studies, Archaeology
Audience: Anthropologists, Archaeologists, Students, Educators
Contact: G. Bell
Details: Free

`ftp://una.hh.lib.umich.edu/70/inetdirsstacks/anthro:bell`

Indigenous ⭐

A collection of various on-line resources about indigenous peoples.

Keywords: Indigenous Peoples, Anthropology
Audience: Reseachers, Anthropologists
Details: Free

`ftp://netcom.com`

NativeNet ⭐⭐⭐

Provides information about and discusses issues relating to indigenous people around the world, including threats to their cultures and habitats (e.g. rainforests).

Keywords: Indigenous People, Environment, Anthroplogy
Audience: Anthropologists, Environmentalists, Indigenous People
Contact: Gary S. Trujillo
gst@gnosys.svle.ma.us
Details: Free
User Info: To subscribe to the list, send an e-mail message requesting a subscription to the URL address below.

`mailto:gst@gnosys.svle.ma.us`

Smithsonian Institution Natural History Gopher ⭐⭐⭐

The Smithsonian Natural History Gopher Server provides access to data associated with the Institutions museum collections (natural history and anthropology).

Keywords: Smithsonian, Natural History, Anthropology
Sponsor: Museum of Natural History, Smithsonian Institution, Washington, DC.
Audience: Anthropologists, Biologists, Natural History Scientists, Researchers
Profile: With over 120 million collections and 135 professional scientists, the National Museum of Natural History is one of the worlds largest museums devoted to natural history and anthropology. This server provides access to data associated with the collections, and to information and tools for the study of the natural world. The Department of Vertebrate Zoology includes checklists

of known species names. Currently the Mammal Species of the World have been posted. Plans to expand this to include Amphibians, Fishes, and so on, are under way.

Contact: Don Gourley
don@smithson.si.edu

Details: Free

gopher://nmnhgoph.si.edu

Anti-Semitism

The Israel Information Service

A gopher server containing information on Israel.

Keywords: Israel, Middle East, Political Science, Anti-Semitism, Holocaust, Archaeology

Sponsor: Israeli Foreign Ministry

Audience: Israelis, Jews, Tourists, General Public

Profile: This server features updates on the Middle East peace process, including text of the latest Israel-PLO accord, as well as general political, diplomatic, cultural and economic information on the state of Israel. Also includes archives on archaeology in Israel, anti-Semitism and the Holocaust, and current excerpts from Israeli newspapers.

Contact: Chaim Shacham
shacham@israel-info.gov.il

gopher://israel-info.gov.il

Antiquarian Books

Indiana University Libraries

The library's holdings are large and wide-ranging and contain significant collections in many fields.

Keywords: Literature (English), Literature (American), 1640-Present, British Plays (19th-C.), Western Americana, Railway History, Aristotle (Texts of), Lafayette (Marquis de), Handel (G.F.), Austrian History, Antiquarian Books, Rare Books, French Opera (19th-C.), Drama (British),

Audience: General Public, Researchers, Librarians, Document Delivery Professionals

Details: Free

User Info: Expect: User ID prompt, Send: GUEST

telnet://iuis.ucs.indiana.edu

ANU (Australian National University) Asian-Settlements Database

ANU (Australian National University) Asian-Settlements Database

A searchable database containing abstracts of theses and research studies provided by the Asian Institute of Technology, relating to issues of demography and social geography in Asia.

Keywords: Asian Studies, Demography, Geography

Sponsor: The COOMBSQUEST Social Sciences & Humanities Information Facility at ANU (Australian National University), Canberra, Australia

Audience: Asia Studies Instructors, Demographers, Geographers

Contact: Dr. T. Matthew Ciolek
coombspapers@coombs.anu.edu.au

Details: Free

gopher://cheops.anu.edu.au/Coombs-db/ANU-Asian-Settlements.src

http://coombs.anu.edu.au/WWWVL-AsianStudies.html

ANU (Australian National University) Buddhism Database

ANU (Australian National University) Buddhism Database

A searchable database of messages from the BUDDHA-L listserv, an academic forum for the discussion of Buddhism. It currently contains archives for messages posted in 1993-94.

Keywords: Religion, Asian Studies, Buddhism

Sponsor: COOMBSQUEST Social Sciences & Humanities Information Facility at ANU (Australian National University), Canberra, Australia

Audience: Buddhists, Religious Studies Instructors, Asian Studies Educators

Contact: Dr. T.Matthew Ciolek
coombspapers@coombs.anu.edu.au

gopher://cheops.anu.edu.au/Coombs-db/ANU-Buddha-1.src

http://coombs.anu.edu.au/WWWVL-AsianStudies.html

ANU (Australian National University) Demography and Publications Database

ANU (Australian National University) Demography and Publications Database

A WAIS database of publications on demography by researchers from Australian National University.

Keywords: Demography

Sponsor: Research Schools of Social Sciences & Pacific and Asian Studies, ANU (Australian National University), Canberra, Australia

Audience: Demographers

Contact: demography@anu.edu.au

waissrc:/Coombs-db/ANU-Demography-Publications.src

gopher://cheops.anu.edu.au/7waissrc/Coombs-db/ANU-Demography-Publications.src

ANU (Australian National University) Vietnam-SciTech-L Database

ANU (Australian National University) Vietnam-SciTech-L Database

A WAIS database of information on the development of science and technology in Vietnam

Keywords: Vietnam, Science, Technology

Sponsor: Australia Vietnam Science-Technology Link

Audience: Vietnamese, Scientists, Technology Professionals

Contact: Vern Weitzel
vern@coombs.anu.edu.au

waissrc:/Coombs-db/ANU-Vietnam-SciTech-L.src

gopher://cheops.anu.edu.au/7waissrc/Coombs-db/ANU-Vietnam-SciTech-L.src

APC-Open

APC-Open

A mailing list for the interchange of information relevant to Advanced Product Centers (APC).

Keywords:	Advanced Product Centers (APC)
Audience:	APC-OPEN Members
Contact:	Fred Rump fred@compu.com
User Info:	To subscribe to the list, send an e-mail message requesting a subscription to the URL address below.
	To send a message to the entire list, address it to: apc-open@compu.com
Notes:	Membership restricted to APC-OPEN members or those specifically invited.

mailto:apc-open-request@compu.com

ApE-info

ApE-info

A mailing list for the discussion of the scientific visualization software package ApE, its usage, development, and implementation.

Keywords:	Computers, Visualization, Science
Audience:	ApE Software Users, Computer Programmers
Contact:	Jim Lick ape-info-request@ferkel.ucsb.edu
User Info:	To subscribe to the list, send an e-mail message to the URL address below.
	To send a message to the entire list, address it to: ape-info@ferkel.ucsb.edu

mailto:ape-info-request@ferkel.ucsb.edu

APEX-J (Asia-Pacific Exchange Electronic Journal)

APEX-J (Asia-Pacific Exchange Electronic Journal)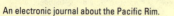

An electronic journal about the Pacific Rim.

Keywords:	Asian Studies
Sponsor:	Published by the University of Hawaii at Kapiolani Community College, Hawaii, USA
Audience:	Educators, Students
Contact:	Jim Shimabukuro JamesS@Hawaii.edu
Notes:	login anonymous;password your email address; cd outgoing; get file.name; bye

ftp://ftp.hawaii.edu

API Energy Business News Index (APIBIZ)

API Energy Business News Index (APIBIZ)

Worldwide coverage of commercial, financial, marketing and regulatory information affecting the petroleum and energy industries.

Keywords:	Petroleum, Business
Sponsor:	The American Petroleum Institute - Central Abstracting and Information Services
Audience:	Researchers, Librarians
Profile:	Twenty-two major news and economics publications are the primary sources for worldwide coverage of information affecting the petroleum and energy industries. Contains more than 600,000 records. Updated weekly.
Contact:	paul.albert@neteast.com
User Info:	To subscribe contact Orbit-Questel directly.

telnet://orbit.com

APL (Programming Language)

APL-L

Discussion of the APL language, its implementation, application, and use. Contributions on teaching APL are particularly welcome.

Keywords:	Programming Languages, APL (Programming Language)
Audience:	Programmers
Contact:	David G. Macneil dgm@unb.cat
Details:	Free
User Info:	To subscribe to the list, send an e-mail message to the URL address below, consisting of a single line reading: SUB APL-L YourFirstName YourLastName
	To send a message to the entire list, address it to: PL-L@cis.vutbr.cs

mailto:listserv@cis.vutbr.cs

Apngowid.meet

Apngowid.meet

A conference on plans by Asia Pacific regional women's groups for the United Nations Fourth World Conference on Women to be held in Beijing in September 1995.

Keywords:	Women, Asia, Pacific, Feminists, Development, United Nations, World Conference on Women
Audience:	Women, Feminists, Nongovernmental Organizations
Contact:	AsPac Info, Docu and Communication Committee AP-IDC@p95.f401.n751.z6.g
Details:	Costs, Moderated
	Establish an account on the nearest APC node. Login, type c for conferences, then type: go apngowid.meet.
	For information on the nearest APC node, contact: APC International Secretariat, IBASE
	E-mail: apcadmin@apc.org

http://www.igc.apc.org/igc/www.women.html

Apollo Advertising

Apollo Advertising

A major directory on advertising, providing access to a broad range of related resources (library catalogs, databases, and servers) via the Internet.

Keywords:	Advertising, Business
Audience:	Advertisers, Business Professionals, General Public
Profile:	A new web service for advertisers and information providers, which maintains the philosophy that consumers will choose to look for goods and services where it is easy and convenient to locate them. This involves the development of a database of short advertisements, many having hypertext links to more substantial advertisements. These can range from text documents to hypermedia commercials. The Apollo directory can be searched, using logical sorting methods, to identify items of interest. Additional information, including hypermedia, may be connected to the entries. This service encompasses short, stand-alone advertisements, as well as entries with hypertext links to other Internet resources.
Contact:	apollo@apollo.co.uk

gopher://apollo.co.uk

Apple Computer

Apple II Files

This FTP site contains the archive of files relating to Apple II computers.

Keywords: Apple Computers, Computers

Audience: Programmers, Computer Users, Apple II Users
Details: Free
`ftp://archive.umich.edu`

Apple Computer Higher Education Gopher Server

This directory is maintained by Apple Computer to provide information about products from Apple Computer.

Keywords: Computer Systems, Computer-Aided Instruction, Apple Computer
Sponsor: Apple Computer, Cupertino, CA
Audience: General Public
Profile: This directory also contains promotional material, such as Apple Press Releases, extensive product information, Apple publications, regional market information, higher education marketing Information and support information.
Contact: feedback@info.hed.apple.com
`http://www.apple.com`

Apple Computer WWW Server

A web site containing information about Apple Computer. The resource is designed to provide timely product information, including press releases on Apple's technology and research. Also contains links to Freeware and Shareware sites, and includes information for developers and programmers.

Keywords: Computer Systems, Technology, Apple Computer, Shareware
Audience: General Public
`http://www.apple.com`

comp.sys.apple2

A Usenet newsgroup providing information and discussion about Apple II systems. There are several categories within this group.

Keywords: Computer Systems, Apple Computer
Audience: Computer Users, Apple II Users
User Info: To subscribe to this Usenet newsgroup, you need access to a newsreader.
`news:comp.sys.apple2`

AppWare Programming Language

AppWare-info

A forum for discussion of issues relating to AppWare software. Topics include simple programming questions, tips for program efficiency, quirks of and complaints about, the environment or tools, the process of writing new ALMs or functions, third party enhancements, and any other question.

Keywords: Programming Languages, AppWare Programming Language
Sponsor: Novell Inc.
Audience: AppWare Users, Computer Programmers
Contact: Novell Inc.
appware-info@serius.uchicago.edu
User Info: To subscribe to the list, send an e-mail message to the URL address below.
To send a message to the entire list, address it to: appware-info@serius.uchicago.edu
`mailto:appware-info-request@serius.uchicago.edu`
`ftp://serius.uchicago.edu`

Aquaculture

University of Maine System Library Catalog
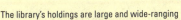

The library's holdings are large and wide-ranging and contain significant collections in many fields.

Keywords: Ucadian Studies, St. John Valley (History of), Canadian-American Studies, Geology, Aquaculture, Maine
Audience: General Public, Researchers, Librarians, Document Delivery Professionals
Contact: Elaine Albright, Marilyn Lutz
Details: Free
User Info: Expect: login, Send: ursus
`telnet://ursus.maine.edu`

University of Maryland System Library

The library's holdings are large and wide-ranging and contain significant collections in many fields.

Keywords: Medicine (History of), Nursing, Pharmacology, Microbiology, Aquaculture, Aquatic Chemistry, Toxicology
Audience: General Public, Researchers, Librarians, Document Delivery Professionals
Contact: Ron Larsen
Details: Free
User Info: Expect: Available Services menu; Send: PAC
`telnet://victor.umd.edu`

Aquariums

alt.aquaria

A Usenet newsgroup providing information and discussion about the aquarium as a hobby.

Keywords: Aquariums, Fish, Hobbies
Audience: Aquarium Keepers, Fish Lovers
User Info: To subscribe to this Usenet newsgroup, you need access to a newsreader.
`news:alt.aquaria`

Aquatic Biology

The University of Notre Dame Library

The library's holdings are large and wide-ranging and contain significant collections in many fields.

Keywords: Music (Irish), Ireland, Botany (History of), Ecology, Entomology, Parasitology, Aquatic Biology, Universities (History of), Paleography
Audience: General Public, Researchers, Librarians, Document Delivery Professionals
Details: Free
User Info: Expect: ENTER COMMAND OR HELP:, Send: library; To leave, type x on the command line and press the enter key. At the ENTER COMMAND OR HELP: prompt, type bye and press the enter key.
`telnet://irishmvs.cc.nd.edu`

Aquatic Chemistry

University of Maryland System Library

The library's holdings are large and wide-ranging and contain significant collections in many fields.

Keywords: Medicine (History of), Nursing, Pharmacology, Microbiology, Aquaculture, Aquatic Chemistry, Toxicology
Audience: General Public, Researchers, Librarians, Document Delivery Professionals
Contact: Ron Larsen
Details: Free
User Info: Expect: Available Services menu; Send: PAC
`telnet://victor.umd.edu`

Aquatic Science

Aquatic Sciences and Fisheries

This database is a comprehensive database on the science, technology, and management of marine and freshwater environments.

Aquatic Science

Keywords: Aquatic Science, Marine Biology
Sponsor: US National Oceanic and Atmospheric Administration (NOAA)/Cambridge Scientific Abstracts, Bethesda, MD, US
Audience: Marine Biologists, Environmentalists
Profile: The database corresponds to the print Aquatic Sciences and Fisheries Abstracts; Part 1: Biological Sciences and Living Resources; Part 2: Ocean Technology, Policy, and Non-Living Resources; and Part 3: Aquatic Pollution and Environmental Quality. ASFA includes citations to 5,000 primary journals, monographs, conference proceedings, and technical reports.
Contact: Dialog in the US at (800) 334-2564, Dialog internationally at country specific locations.
User Info: To subscribe, contact Dialog directly.

`telnet://dialog.com`

rec.aquaria

A Usenet newsgroup providing information and discussion about pet fish and aquaria.

Keywords: Fish, Aquatic Science
Audience: Fish Enthusiasts
Details: Free
User Info: To subscribe to this Usenet newsgroup, you need access to a newsreader.

`news:rec.aquaria`

AR-news

AR-news

A public news wire for items relating to animal rights and animal welfare.

Keywords: Activism, Animal Rights, Veterinarians
Audience: Activists, Animal Lovers
Contact: Ian Lance Taylor, Chip Roberson taylor@think.com or csr@nic.aren.com
User Info: To subscribe to the list, send an e-mail message to the URL address below.
To send a message to the entire list, address it to: ar-news@think.com
Notes: Appropriate postings to ar-news include posting a news item, requesting information on some event, or responding to a request for information. Discussions on ar-news are not allowed.

`mailto:ar-news@think.com`

AR-talk

AR-talk

An unmoderated list for the discussion of animal rights and related issues, such as animal liberation, consumer product testing, cruelty-free products, vivisection and dissection, and vegan lifestyles.

Keywords: Activism, Animal Rights
Audience: Activists, Animal Lovers, Researchers
Contact: Ian Lance Taylor, Chip Roberson taylor@think.com or csr@nic.aren.com
User Info: To subscribe to the list, send an e-mail message to the URL address below.
To send a message to the entire list, address it to: ar-talk@think.com

`mailto:ar-talk-request@think.com`

Arabic Culture (History of)

Harvard University Library

The library's holdings are large and wide-ranging and contain significant collections in many fields.

Keywords: Afrikaans, Alchemy, Arabic Culure (History of), Celtic Philology, Congo Languages, Folklore, Hebraica, Mormonism, Numismatics, Quakers, Sanskrit, Witchcraft, Arabic Philology
Audience: General Public, Researchers, Librarians, Document Delivery Professionals
Details: Free
User Info: Expect: Mitek Server…, Send: Enter or Return; Expect: prompt, Send: hollis

`telnet://hollis.harvard.edu`

Arabic Philology

Harvard University Library

The library's holdings are large and wide-ranging and contain significant collections in many fields.

Keywords: Afrikaans, Alchemy, Arabic Culure (History of), Celtic Philology, Congo Languages, Folklore, Hebraica, Mormonism, Numismatics, Quakers, Sanskrit, Witchcraft, Arabic Philology
Audience: General Public, Researchers, Librarians, Document Delivery Professionals
Details: Free
User Info: Expect: Mitek Server…, Send: Enter or Return; Expect: prompt, Send: hollis

`telnet://hollis.harvard.edu`

Arachnophilia: Florida Institute of Technology's WWW server.

Arachnophilia: Florida Institute of Technology's WWW server.

Provides pointers to information resources and search tools around the Web. Specifically for use by educators and researchers.

Keywords: Internet Tools
Audience: Educators, Researchers
Contact: www@sci-ed.fit.edu
Details: Free

`http://sci-ed.fit.edu`

Archaeology

Anthropology, Cross Cultural Studies, & Archaeology

This directory is a compilation of information resources focused on anthropology, cross cultural studies, and archaeology.

Keywords: Anthropology, Cross Cultural Studies, Archaeology
Audience: Anthropologists, Archaeologists, Students, Educators
Contact: G. Bell
Details: Free

`ftp://una.hh.lib.umich.edu/70/inetdirsstacks/anthro:bell`

Archaeology, Historic Preservation

This directory is a compilation of information resources focused on archaeology, historic preservation, and heritage conservation.

Keywords: Archaeology, Historic Preservation
Audience: Archaeologists, Historians, Architects
Details: Free

`ftp://una.hh.lib.umich.edu/70/inetdirsstacks/archpres:stott`

The Israel Information Service

A gopher server containing information on Israel.

Keywords: Israel, Middle East, Political Science, Anti-Semitism, Holocaust, Archaeology
Sponsor: Israeli Foreign Ministry
Audience: Israelis, Jews, Tourists, General Public

Profile: This server features updates on the Middle East peace process, including text of the latest Israel-PLO accord, as well as general political, diplomatic, cultural and economic information on the state of Israel. Also includes archives on archaeology in Israel, anti-Semitism and the Holocaust, and current excerpts from Israeli newspapers.

Contact: Chaim Shacham
shacham@israel-info.gov.il

`gopher://israel-info.gov.il`

Archie

Archie ★

A description of Archie, an electronic directory service for the Internet, which allows the user to find files remotely.

Keywords: Internet Tools, Archie
Sponsor: Computing Centre, McGill University, Montreal, Quebec, Canada
Audience: Internet Surfers
Contact: archie-group@archie.mcgill.ca
Details: Free
File is: pub/archie/doc/whatis.archie

`ftp://archie.ans.net`

Archie Demo ★

A Telnet demonstration of Archie, an Internet access tool.

Keywords: Internet Tools, Archie
Audience: Internet Surfers
Details: Free
Notes: login; Send: archie

`telnet://archie@archie.ans.net`

Archie Hypertext Servers ★

A list of hypertext Archie servers around the world.

Keywords: Internet Tools, Archie
Sponsor: NEXOR
Audience: Internet Surfers
Contact: Martijn Koster
m.koster@nexor.co.uk
Details: Free

`http://web.nexor.co.uk.archie.html`

Archie Manual ★

A reference manual for Archie, an Internet access tool.

Keywords: Internet Tools, Archie
Audience: Internet Surfers

Contact: R. Rodgers, Nelson N. Beebe
rodgers@maxwell.mmwb.ucsf.edu
beebe@math.utah.edu
Details: Free
File is: pub/archie/doc/archie.man.txt

`ftp://archie.ans.net`

Architecture

ArchiGopher ★★

A server dedicated to architectural knowledge. It includes The Kandinsky archive and the Palladio archive as well as images such as Hellenic architecture.

Keywords: Art, Architecture
Sponsor: University of Michigan, College of Architecture and Urban Planning
Audience: Architects, Artists
Contact: Wassim M. Jabi
wjabi@libra.arch.umich.edu

`gopher://libra.arch.umich.edu`

Architecture, Building ★

This directory is a compilation of information resources focused on architecture.

Keywords: Architecture, Building, Construction
Audience: Architects, Builders, Civil Engineers
Details: Free

`ftp://una.hh.lib.umich.edu/70/inetdirsstacks/archi:brown`

Art & Architecture ★★

This directory is a compilation of information resources focused on art and architecture.

Keywords: Art, Architecture
Audience: Artists, Architects, Art Historians, Architectural Historians
Details: Free

`ftp://una.hh.lib.umich.edu/70/inetdirsstacks/artarch:robinson`

McGill University, Montreal Canada, INFOMcGILL Library ★★★

The library's holdings are large and wide-ranging and contain significant collections in many fields.

Keywords: Architecture, Entomology, Biology, Science (History of), Medicine (History of), Napoleon, Shakespeare (William)
Audience: Researchers, Students, General Public

Contact: Roy Miller
ccrmmus@mcgillm (Bitnet)
ccrmmus@musicm.mcgill.ca (Internet)
User Info: Expect: VM logo; Send: Enter; Expect: prompt; Send: PF3 or type INFO

`telnet://vm1.mcgill.ca`

Universite de Montreal UDEMATIK Library ★★★

The library's holdings are large and wide-ranging and contain significant collections in many fields.

Keywords: Art, Architecture, Economy, Sexology, Social Law, Science, Technology, Literary Studies
Audience: Researchers, Students, General Public
Contact: Joelle or Sebastien Roy
udematik@ere.umontreal.ca
stemp@ere.umontreal.ca
roys@ere.umontreal.ca
User Info: Expect: Login; Send: Application id INFO

`telnet:// udematik.umontreal.ca`

University of New Mexico Unminfo Library ★★

The library's holdings are large and wide-ranging and contain significant collections in many fields.

Keywords: Photography (History of), Architecture, Native American Affairs, Land Records
Audience: Researchers, Students, General Public
Contact: Art St. George
stgeorge@unmb.bitnet
Details: Free
User Info: Expect: Login; Send: Unminfo

`telnet://unminfo.unm.edu`

University of Rochester Library ★★

The library's holdings are large and wide-ranging and contain significant collections in many fields.

Keywords: Architecture, Art History, Photography, Literature (Asian), Lasers, Geology, Statistics, Optics, Medieval Studies
Audience: Researchers, Students, General Public
Details: Free
User Info: Expect: Login; Send: Library

`telnet://128.151.226.71`

University of Wisconsin at Milwaukee Library ★★

The library's holdings are large and wide-ranging and contain significant collections in many fields.

Keywords: Art, Architecture, Business, Cartography, Geography, Geology, Urban Studies, Literature (English), Literature (American)

Audience:	Researchers, Students, General Public	
Details:	Free	
User Info:	Expect: Login, Send: Lib; Expect: vDIAL prompt, Send: Library	

`telnet://uwmcat.lib.uwm.edu`

Archive of Biology Software and Data

Archive of Biology Software and Data ★★★★

The main area of concentration of this archive is molecular biology. It contains software for the Macintosh, MS-DOS, VAX-VMS, and UNIX platforms.

Keywords:	Health, Biology, Molecular Biology
Sponsor:	Indiana University
Audience:	Biologists, Students
Contact:	archive@bio.indiana.edu
Details:	Free
Notes:	It is recommended that the file Archive.doc be transferred and read first. This file gives considerable information about and instructions for using the archive.

`ftp://ftp.bio.indiana.edu`

Archosaurs

dinosaur ★

Discussion of dinosaurs and their reptilian contemporaries.

Keywords:	Dinosaurs, Archosaurs
Audience:	Dinosaur Enthusiasts, Paleontologists
Contact:	John Matrow dinosaur-request@donald.WichitaKS.NCR.COM
Details:	Free
User Info:	To subscribe to the list, send an e-mail message requesting a subscription to the URL address below. To send a message to the entire list, address it to: dinosaur-request@donald.WichitaKS.NCR.COM

`mailto:dinosaur-request@donald.WichitaKS.NCR.COM`

Argentina

Argentina ★★

Mailing list for general discussion and information about Argentina, including Argentine culture and politics.

Keywords:	Argentina, Politics, Culture
Sponsor:	Carlos G. Mendioroz
Audience:	Spanish Speakers, Students
Contact:	Carlos G. Mendioroz argentina-request@ois.db.toronto.edu
User Info:	To subscribe to the list, send an e-mail message to the URL address below. To send a message to the entire list, address it to: argentina@ois.db.toronto.edu

`mailto:argentina-request@ois.db.toronto.edu`

Aristotle (Texts of)

Indiana University Libraries ★★

The library's holdings are large and wide-ranging and contain significant collections in many fields.

Keywords:	Literature (English), Literature (American), 1640-Present, British Plays (19th-C.), Western Americana, Railway History, Aristotle (Texts of), Lafayette (Marquis de), Handel (G.F.), Austrian History, Antiquarian Books, Rare Books, French Opera (19th-C.), Drama (British) ,
Audience:	General Public, Researchers, Librarians, Document Delivery Professionals
Details:	Free
User Info:	Expect: User ID prompt, Send: GUEST

`telnet://iuis.ucs.indiana.edu`

University of Pennsylvania PENNINFO Library ★★★

The library's holdings are large and wide-ranging and contain significant collections in many fields.

Keywords:	Church History, Spanish Inquisition, Witchcraft, Shakespeare (William), Bibles, Aristotle (Texts of), Fiction, Whitman (Walt), French Revolution, Drama (French), Literature (English), Literature (Spanish)
Audience:	Researchers, Students, General Public
Contact:	Al DSouza penninfo-admin@dccs.upenn.edu dsouza@dccs.upenn.edu
Details:	Free
User Info:	Expect: Login; Send: Public

`telnet://penninfo.upenn.edu`

ARlist

ARlist ★★

An open, unmoderated mailing list to provide a forum for discussing action research and its use in a variety of disciplines and situations. Topics include philosophical and methodological issues in action research, the use of action research for evaluation, actual case studies, and discourse on increasing the rigor of action research.

Keywords:	Activism, Research, Politics
Audience:	Activists, Researchers
Profile:	Arlist is an open unmoderated mailing list to provide a forum for discussing action research and its use in a variety of disciplines and situations. It is usually (but perhaps not always) cyclic, participative, and qualitative.
Contact:	Bob Dick arlist@psych.psy.uq.oz.au
Details:	Free
User Info:	To subscribe to the list, send an e-mail message to the URL address below. To send a message to the entire list, address it to: arlist@psych.psy.uq.oz.au

`mailto:arlist-request@psych.psy.uq.oz.au`

`ftp://psych.psy.uq.oz.au/dir/lists/arlist`

Armadillo's World Wide Web Page

Armadillo's World Wide Web Page

This site provides resources and instructional material for an interdisciplinary Texan culture course.

Keywords:	History (US), Texas, Cultural Studies, Education
Sponsor:	Rice University, Houston, Texas, USA
Audience:	Educators, Students
Contact:	armadillo@rice.edu

`http://chico.rice.edu/armadillo`

ars magica

ars magica ★★

A mailing list for the discussion of White Wolf's role-playing game, Ars Magica.

Keywords:	Role-Playing, Games
Audience:	Role-playing Enthusiasts, Game Players
Contact:	ars-magica-request@soda.berkeley.edu
User Info:	To subscribe to the list, send an e-mail message to the URL address below. To send a message to the entire list, address it to: ars-magica-request@soda.berkeley.edu
Notes:	Also available upon request as a nightly digest.

`mailto:ars-magica-request@soda.berkeley.edu`

Art

ACEN (Art Com Electronic Network)

A conference on the WELL for art, technology, and text-based artworks.

Keywords:	Art, Literature (Contemporary), Multimedia
Sponsor:	Art Com Electronic Network
Audience:	Artists, Musicians, Writers
Profile:	Started in 1986, ACEN is a seminal art BBS that includes actual artworks, discussion on topics such as software as art, and on line published works by John Cage, Fred Truck, Jim Rosenberg, Judy Malloy, and others.
Contact:	Carl Loeffler artcomtv@well.sf.ca.us
User Info:	To participate in a conference on the WELL, you must first establish an account on the WELL. To do so, start by typing: telnet://well.sf.ca.us

`telnet://well.sf.ca.us`

African Art Exhibit and Tutorial

This web site provides images of African art and an overview of African aesthetics.

Keywords:	Art, Africa, Cultural Studies
Sponsor:	University of Virginia
Audience:	Artists, Art Students, Educators, Historians

`http://www.lib.virginia.edu`

alt.artcom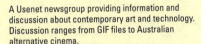

A Usenet newsgroup providing information and discussion about contemporary art and technology. Discussion ranges from GIF files to Australian alternative cinema.

Keywords:	Art, Technology
Audience:	Artists, Writers
User Info:	To subscribe to this Usenet newsgroup, you need access to a newsreader.

`news:alt.artcom`

alt.arts.nomad

A Usenet conference that focuses on group disembodied art projects.

Keywords:	Art
Sponsor:	Media Arts, Banff Centre, Canada
Audience:	Artists
Details:	disembodied art projects.
Notes:	Art

`news:alt.arts.nomad`

ArchiGopher

A server dedicated to architectural knowledge. It includes The Kandinski archive and the Palladio archive as well as images such as Hellenic architecture.

Keywords:	Art, Architecture
Sponsor:	University of Michigan, College of Architecture and Urban Planning
Audience:	Architects, Artists
Contact:	Wassim M. Jabi wjabi@libra.arch.umich.edu

`gopher://libra.arch.umich.edu`

Art & Architecture

This directory is a compilation of information resources focused on art and architecture.

Keywords:	Art, Architecture
Audience:	Artists, Architects, Art Historians, Architectural Historians
Details:	Free

`ftp://una.hh.lib.umich.edu/70/inetdirsstacks/artarch:robinson`

Art-support

A UK Mailbase forum for the discussion of art-related matters.

Keywords:	Art, Fine Arts
Audience:	Artists, Art Enthusiasts, Art Students
Notes:	Login guest; password mailbase

`gopher://mailbase@mailbase.ac.uk`

`mailto:art-support-request@mailbase.ac.uk`

`telnet://mailbase.ac.uk`

artist-users

A discussion group for users and potential users of software tools from Cadence Design Systems.

Keywords:	Computers, Computer Art, Art
Sponsor:	Cadence Design Systems
Audience:	Computer Artists
Contact:	Jeff Putsch artist-users-request@uicc.com
User Info:	To subscribe to the list, send an e-mail message to the URL address below. To send a message to the entire list, address it to: artist-users-request@uicc.com
Notes:	This mailing list is bi-directionally gatewayed to the Usenet newsgroup

`mailto:artist-users-request@uicc.com`

Arts

An umbrella arts conference on the WELL.

Keywords:	Art, Music, Dance
Audience:	Artists, Dancers, Musicians, Photographers
Profile:	A genereal arts conference thet includes listings of show opportunities, books, and events, as well as discussion about art and art criticism.
Contact:	Tim Collins
Notes:	To participate in a conference on the WELL, you must first establish an account on the WELL. To do so, start by typing: telnet well.sf.ca.us

`telnet://well.sf.ca.us`

Arts Wire

A national communications network for the arts located on the Meta Network.

Keywords:	Art, Writing, Activism, Music
Sponsor:	New York Foundation for the Arts
Audience:	Art Activists, Art Organizations, Artists, Composers, Foundations, Government Arts Agencies, Writers
Profile:	Arts Wire provides immediate access to news, information, and dialogue on conditions affecting the arts and artists, as well as private conferences for organizations. Core features include Money, a searcable resource of grant deadlines; Hotwire, a summary of arts news; and conferences about new music, interactive art, literature, AIDS, and Latino art.
Contact:	Judy Malloy artswire@tmn.com

`telnet://tmn.com`

California Museum of Photography: Network Exhibitions

This is a collection of digital images for educational and general use.

Keywords:	Photography, Art, Education
Sponsor:	University of California, Riverside, California, USA
Audience:	Photographers, Artists, Educators (esp. K-12), Historians
Profile:	The California Museum of Photography is in the process of selecting groups of images from the collections as thematic exhibitions. Instead of displays on the walls, these exhibitions comprise a group of digital images with associated text. Particular emphasis is on the utility of these images in class projects for elementary and secondary school students. However, the digital images

also have potential value for more advanced scholarly research in preparation of papers in the Humanities, Social Sciences and the Arts.

Contact: Russ Harvey
russ@cornucopia.ucr.edu

`gopher://gopher.ucr.edu`

comp.graphics

A Usenet newsgroup providing information and discussion about computer graphics, art, animation and more.

Keywords: Computer Graphics, Art
Audience: Computer Users
User Info: To subscribe to this Usenet newsgroup, you need access to a newsreader.

`news:comp.graphics`

Conference about Virtual Reality (The)

A conference on the WELL about cyberspace and virtual reality.

Keywords: Virtual Reality, Art, Cyberspace
Audience: Artists, Computer Programmers, Cyberpunks
Contact: Peter Rothman
avatarp@well.sf.ca.us

`telnet://well.sf.ca.us`

ecto

Information and discussion about singer/songwriter Happy Rhodes, and other music, art, books, and films of common (or singular) interest.

Keywords: Music, Art, Rhodes (Happy)
Audience: Music Enthusiasts, Art Enthusiasts
Contact: Jessica Dembski
ecto-request@ns1.rutgers.edu
Details: Free
User Info: To subscribe to the list, send an e-mail message requesting a subscription to the URL address below.

To send a message to the entire list, address it to: ecto-request@ns1.rutgers.edu

`mailto:ecto-request@ns1.rutgers.edu`

Electronic Cafe

A seminal art and telecommunications group that specializes in video transmission.

Keywords: Art, Video, Telecommunications
Audience: Artists

Profile: This combines performance, communication, and community outreach by making telecommunications equipment available in a cafe-style artists' space.

Contact: Kit Galloway and Sherrie Rabinowitz, 1641 18th St., Santa Monica, CA 90404, USA

`mailto:ecafe@netcom.com`

FineArt Forum

A monthly newsletter that includes listings of art and technology events, showcases, conferences, and jobs.

Keywords: Art, Multimedia
Sponsor: The International Society for the Arts, Sciences, and Technology
Audience: Art Educators, Art Professionals, Artists
Profile: Published by the National Science Foundation Engineering Research Center for Computational Field Simulation, Mississippi State University. FineArt Forum has provided timely information to a large international audience since 1988. The subscriber list consists of individuals working in the realm where art, science, and technology converge. Issues provide information about conferences and competitions, calls for presentations and research, and notices about performances. FineArt_Online is both an archive of FineArt Forum, ISEA News, Leonardo Electronic News, and a variety of longer postings. In January 1994 it began posting an online gallery.

Contact: Paul Brown
brown@erc.msstate.edu
User Info: To subscribe, send E-mail to: brown@erc.msstate.edu, with the message
SUB FAST; also give your name, postal address, and E-mail address.

`http://www.msstate.edu/Fineart_Online/home.html`

IMAGELAB

An unmoderated bulletin board for the discussion of image databases in libraries. Its purpose is to raise questions, solicit input, and share ideas. Another function of the list is to serve as a clearinghouse to announce image databases.

Keywords: Images, Art
Sponsor: University of Arizona Library
Audience: Arts Community
Contact: Stuart Glogoff
User Info: To subscribe to the list, send an e-mail message to the URL address shown below consisting of a single line reading:
SUB imagelab YourFirstName YourLastName

`listserv@arizvm1.ccit.arizona.edu`

Images from Various Sources

This site serves as a link to some 35 image archives throughout the world. A wide variety of images is available, with a particularly large number of weather, geological, and biological collections from government and private sources.

Keywords: Computer Graphics, Photography, Art
Sponsor: The University of Alaska
Audience: General Public
Contact: Douglas Toelle
sxinfo@orca.alaska.edu
Details: Free, Images

`gopher://gopher.uacn.alaska.edu`

`http://info.alaska.edu:70`

Interactive

A conference on Arts Wire about interactive art that includes a library of artists' statements about artworks, texts, and publications, as well as discussion.

Keywords: Art, Interactive Art
Sponsor: New York Foundation for the Arts
Audience: Artists, Writers
Contact: Anna Couey, Judy Malloy
couey@tmn.com, jmalloy@tmn.com

`telnet://tmn.com`

Internet Art Gallery

An online art collection in the form of JPEG files, including the works of 85 artists ranging from Dali to Van Eyck.

Keywords: Art, Fine Art, Art History
Sponsor: New York State Education Department
Audience: Artists, Art Students, Art Teachers, General Public
Contact: Steve Richter, George Casler
steve@unix5.nysed.gov
gcasler@unix5.nysed.gov

`gopher://unix5.nysed.gov`

ISEA (Inter-Society on Electronic Arts) Online

An online forum for discussion of topics related to ISEA-94, the 5th International Symposium on Electronic Art which will take place in Finland in August, 1994.

Keywords: Art, Electronic Art, Technology
Audience: Artists, Art Enthusiasts
Details: Free

`ftp://ftp.ncsa.uiuc.edu`

Kaleidospace ★★

This is a new web server that provides a multimedia showcase for artists, performers, CD-ROM authors, musicians, writers, animators, filmmakers and software developers.

Keywords: Art, Computer Art, Multimedia

Audience: Artists, Performers, CD-ROM Authors, Musicians, Writers, Animators, Filmmakers, Software Developers

Profile: This site was created to support independent artists. The site has similarities to other web servers such as IUMA, but differs in that it works with all kinds of artists, and that it processes orders for the artist's material.

Contact: Jeannie Novak, Peter Markiewicz
jeannienov@aol.com peterm@ewald.mbi.ucla.edu

`http://kspace.com`

`http://fire.kspace.com`

Leonardo Electronic Almanac ★★★★

The Leonardo Electronic Almanac (LEA) is a monthly, edited journal and an electronic archive dedicated to providing current perspectives in the art, science and technology domains.

Keywords: Art, Multimedia, Music, Electronic Media

Sponsor: International Society for the Arts, Sciences, and Technology

Audience: New Media Artists, Researchers, Developers, Art Educators, Art Professionals

Profile: LEA is an international, interdisciplinary forum for people interested in the use of new media in contemporary artistic expression, especially involving 20th century science and technology. Material is contributed by artists, scientists, philosophers and educators. LEA is published by the MIT Press for Leonardo, the International Society for the Arts, Sciences, and Technology (ISAST).

Contact: Craig Harris
craig@well.sf.ca.us

Details: Costs, Moderated, Images, Sounds, Multimedia

`mail to:journals-orders@mit.edu`

`ftp://mitpress.mit.edu/pub/Leonardo-Elec-Almanac`

Muchomedia Conference

A conference on the WELL about multimedia with topics ranging from products and software to multimedia for beginners.

Keywords: Multimedia, Art

Audience: Artists, Computer Programmers, Producers

Contact: Douglas Crockford
crock@well.sf.ca.us

To participate in a conference on the WELL, you must first establish an account on the WELL. To do so, start by typing: telnet well.sf.ca.us

`telnet://well.sf.ca.us`

naplps-list ★

This is a mailing list for people interested in NAPLPS graphics.

Keywords: Computer Graphics, Art

Audience: Graphic Artists, Artists

Contact: Dave Hughes
oldcolo@goldmill.uucp

`naplps-list@oldcolo.com`

Northwestern University Library ★★★

The library's holdings are large and wide-ranging and contain significant collections in many fields.

Keywords: Africa, Wright (Frank Lloyd), Women's Studies, Art, Literature (American), Contemporary Music, Government (US State), UN Documents, Music

Audience: General Public, Researchers, Librarians, Document Delivery Professionals

Details: Free

User Info: Expect: COMMAND:, Send: DIAL VTAM

`telnet://nuacvm.acns.nwu.edu`

NYAL (New York Art Line) ★★★

A gopher containing selected resources on the arts.

Keywords: Art, Audio-Visual Materials, Multimedia, Computer Art

Sponsor: Panix Public Access Unix & Internet Gopher Server, New York, USA

Audience: Artists, Art Enthusiasts

Profile: NYAL features a wide variety of arts resources. The primary focus of this site is visual art, particularly in the New York city area. Information includes online access to selected galleries, image archives, and New York city arts groups. Beyond visual art, information on dance, music, and techno art (with a special section on Internet art) is also available. It also features links to various electronic journals, museums, and schools.

Contact: Kenny Greenberg
kgreen@panix.com

`gopher://gopher.panix.com`

`http://gopher.panix.com/nyart/Kpage/kg`

OTIS (Operative Term Is Stimulate) ★

An image-based electronic art gallery.

Keywords: Art, Graphics, Electronic Art, Animation

Audience: Graphic Artists

Profile: OTIS is a public-access library containing hundreds of images, animations, and information files.

Within the sunsite ftp, the directory is: /pub/multimedia/pictures/OTIS. Use the bin command to insure you're in binary transfer mode.

`ftp://sunsite.unc.edu`

rec.arts.fin ★

A Usenet newsgroup providing information and discussion about the visual arts. Discussions range from archival materials to Ansel Adams, Mary Cassat and Andy Warhol.

Keywords: Art, Fine Art

Audience: Artists, Art Educators, Art Professionals

User Info: To subscribe to this Usenet newsgroup, you need access to a newsreader.

`news:rec.arts.fin`

rec.photo ★

A Usenet newsgroup providing information and discussion about photography.

Keywords: Photography, Art, Crafts

Audience: Photographers, Artists

User Info: To subscribe to this Usenet newsgroup, you need access to a newsreader.

`news:rec.photo`

rec.video ★

A Usenet newsgroup providing information and discussion about video.

Keywords: Video, Art, Film, Computer Art

Audience: Cinematographers, Video Artists

User Info: To subscribe to this Usenet newsgroup, you need access to a newsreader.

`news:rec.video`

Rosen Sculpture Exhibition ★★

This web site contains various examples of sculpture movements.

Keywords: Art, Fine Arts

Sponsor: Visual Resources Curator of the Department of Art at Appalachian State University, Boone, North Carolina, USA

Audience: Art Educators, Art Students

`http://www.acs.appstate.edu/art`

UCSB Library Reference Guide

A list of art references including indexes, dictionaries, bilbiographies and biographical materials.

Keywords: Art, History (World), Libraries
Sponsor: University of California at Santa Barbara
Audience: Artists, Historians, Librarians

`gopher://ucsbuxa.ucsb.edu`

Universite de Montreal UDEMATIK Library

The library's holdings are large and wide-ranging and contain significant collections in many fields.

Keywords: Art, Architecture, Economy, Sexology, Social Law, Science, Technology, Literary Studies
Audience: Researchers, Students, General Public
Contact: Joelle or Sebastien Roy
udematik@ere.umontreal.ca
stemp@ere.umontreal.ca
roys@ere.umontreal.ca
User Info: Expect: Login; Send: Application id INFO

`telnet://udematik.umontreal.ca`

University of Northern Iowa Library

The library's holdings are large and wide-ranging and contain significant collections in many fields.

Keywords: Art, Business Information, Education, Music, Fiction
Audience: Researchers, Students, General Public
Contact: Mike Yohe
yohe@uni.edu
Details: Free
User Info: Expect: Login; Send: Public

`telnet://infosys.uni.edu`

University of Wisconsin at Milwaukee Library

The library's holdings are large and wide-ranging and contain significant collections in many fields.

Keywords: Art, Architecture, Business, Cartography, Geography, Geology, Urban Studies, Literature (English), Literature (American)
Audience: Researchers, Students, General Public
Details: Free
User Info: Expect: Login, Send: Lib; Expect: vDIAL prompt, Send: Library

`telnet://uwmcat.lib.uwm.edu`

Virginia Commonwealth University Library

The library's holdings are large and wide-ranging and contain significant collections in many fields.

Keywords: Art, Biology, Humanities, Journalism, Music, Urban Planning
Audience: Researchers, Students, General Public
Details: Free
User Info: Expect: Login; Send: Opub

`telnet://vcuvm1.ucc.vcu.edu`

WWW Paris

A web site created as a collaborative effort among individuals in both Paris and the United States.

Keywords: Paris, Culture, Art, Travel, French, Tourism
Audience: Students, Educators, Travelers, Researchers
Profile: Contains an extensive collection of images and text regarding all of the major monuments and museums of Paris, including maps of the Metro and the RER; calendars of events and current expositions; promotional images and text relating to local department stores; there is also a visitors' section with up-to-date tourist information on hotels, restaurants, telephones, airport schedules, a basic Paris glossary, and the latest weather images. Includes an extensive collection of links to other resources about Paris and France, and a selected bibliography of history and architecture in Paris.
Contact: Norman Barth, Eric Pouliquen
nbarth@ucsd.edu
epouliq@ucsd.edu

`http://meteora.ucsd.edu/~norman/paris`

Art & Architecture

Art & Architecture

This directory is a compilation of information resources focused on art and architecture.

Keywords: Art, Architecture
Audience: Artists, Architects
Details: Free

`ftp://una.hh.lib.umich.edu/70/inetdirsstacks/artarch:robinson`

Art Com Magazine

Art Com Magazine

A newsletter about art and technology (subjects covered include robotics, artists' software, hyperfiction) that is guest-edited by individual artists.

Keywords: Computer Art, Literature (Contemporary), Technology, Hyperfiction
Sponsor: Art Com Electronic Network
Audience: Artists, Writers
Contact: Fred Truck
fjt@well.sf.ca.us
User Info: To participate in a conference on the WELL, you must first establish an account on the WELL. To do so, start by typing: telnet://well.sf.ca.us

`mailto:artcomtv@well.sf.ca.us`

Art Exhibitions

Smithsonian Online

Located on America Online (with partial access by ftp), this allows online access to the Institution's resources.

Keywords: Museums, Art Exhibitions
Sponsor: Smithsonian Institution, Washington DC
Audience: Educators, Students, General Public
Profile: Smithsonian Online includes resources for teachers and students in the form of bulletin boards about Smithsonian museums, photographs, listings of events in Washington and other communities, and excerpts from Smithsonian and Air & Space/Smithsonian.

`ftp://photo1.si.edu`

Art History

Internet Art Gallery

An online art collection in the form of JPEG files, including the works of 85 artists ranging from Dali to Van Eyck.

Keywords: Art, Fine Art, Art History
Sponsor: New York State Education Department
Audience: Artists, Art Students, Art Teachers, General Public
Contact: Steve Richter, George Casler
steve@unix5.nysed.gov,
gcasler@unix5.nysed.gov

`gopher://unix5.nysed.gov`

University of Rochester Library

The library's holdings are large and wide-ranging and contain significant collections in many fields.

Keywords:	Architecture, Art History, Photography, Literature (Asian), Lasers, Geology, Statistics, Optics, Medieval Studies
Audience:	Researchers, Students, General Public
Details:	Free
User Info:	Expect: Login; Send: Library

`telnet://128.151.226.71`

Artificial Intelligence

Artificial Intelligence, Expert Sys., Virtual Reality

This directory is a compilation of information resources focused on computer science research, artificial intelligence, expert systems, and virtual reality.

Keywords:	Computer Science, Artificial Intelligence, Expert Systems, Virtual Reality
Audience:	Computer Scientists, Engineers
Details:	Free

`ftp://una.hh.lib.umich.edu/70/inetdirsstacks/csaiesvr:kovacsm`

Computists' Communique

A weekly newsletter serving professionals in artificial intelligence, information science, and computer science.

Keywords:	Artificial Intelligence, Information Science, Computer Science
Audience:	Computer Scientists, Information Scientists, Computists International Members
Profile:	Content is career oriented and depends partly on contributions from members. The moderator filters submissions, reports and comments on industry news, collects common knowledge about academia and industry, and helps track people and projects. The Communique is only available to members of Computists International, a networking association for computer and information scientists. It is an association for mutual mentoring about grant and funding sources, information channels, applications, text, software publishing, and the sociology of work.
Contact:	Kenneth I. Laws laws@ari.sri.com
Details:	Costs, Moderated

`mailto:laws@ari.sri.com`

Artificial Life

Alife

The alife mailing list is for communications regarding artificial life, a formative interdisciplinary field involving computer science, the natural sciences, mathematics, and medicine.

Keywords:	Artificial Life, Science, Mathematics
Sponsor:	UCLA
Audience:	Scientists, Biologists, Mathematicians
Contact:	alife-request@cognet.ucla.edu
User Info:	To subscribe to the list, send an e-mail message to the URL address below.
	To send a message to the entire list, address it to: alife@cognet.ucla.edu

`mailto:alife-request@cognet.ucla.edu`

Artificial Life

A forum for the accumulation and dissemination of information about all aspects of the Artificial Life enterprise. Services provided include an FTP site containing preprints and software, a bibliographic database on Artificial Life, and links to various Usenet services.

Keywords:	Artificial Life, Chaos Theory
Sponsor:	MITPress, Cambridge, Massachusetts, USA
Audience:	Mathematical Biologists, Researchers, Theoretical Biologists
Contact:	Chris Langton cgl@santafe.edu

`http://alife.santafe.edu`

artist-users

artist-users

A discussion group for users and potential users of software tools from Cadence Design Systems.

Keywords:	Computers, Computer Art, Art
Sponsor:	Cadence Design Systems
Audience:	Computer Artists, Graphics Designers
Contact:	Jeff Putsch artist-users-request@uicc.com
User Info:	To subscribe to the list, send an e-mail message to the URL address below.
	To send a message to the entire list, address it to: artist-users-request@uicc.com
Notes:	This mailing list is bi-directionally gatewayed to the Usenet newsgroup

`mailto:artist-users-request@uicc.com`

Asat-eva (Distance Education Evaluation Group)

Asat-eva (Distance Education Evaluation Group)

This mailing list addresses issues in evaluating all forms of distance learning and programs.

Keywords:	Education (Adult), Education (Distance), Education (Continuing)
Sponsor:	Agricultural Satellite Corporation
Audience:	Educators, Administrators, Researchers
Details:	Free
User Info:	To subscribe to the list, send an e-mail message to the URL address below, consisting of a single line reading:
	SUB asat-evaYourFirstName YourLastName
	To send a message to the entire list, address it to: asat-eva@unlvm.unl.edu

`mailto:listserv@unlvm.unl.edu`

ASCII

Gopher-Based ASCII Clipart Collection

A collection of more than 500 individual pictures.

Keywords:	ASCII, Clipart
Sponsor:	Texas Tech Computer Sciences Gopher Server
Audience:	Computer Users, General Public
Contact:	Abdul Malik Yoosufan gripe@cs.ttu.edu
Details:	Free, Images

`gopher://cs4sun.cs.ttu.edu`

`ftp://ftp.cs.ttu.edu:/pub/asciiar`

Asia

apngowid.meet

A conference on plans by Asia Pacific regional women's groups for the United Nations Fourth World Conference on Women to be held in Beijing in September 1995.

Keywords:	Women, Asia, Pacific, Feminists, Development, United Nations, World Conference on Women
Audience:	Women, Feminists, Nongovernmental Organizations

Asia

Contact:	AsPac Info, Docu and Communication Committee AP-IDC@p95.f401.n751.z6.g
Details:	Costs, Moderated
	Establish an account on the nearest APC node. Login, type c for conferences, then type: go apngowid.meet.
	For information on the nearest APC node, contact: APC International Secretariat, IBASE.
	E-mail: apcadmin@apc.org

`http://www.igc.apc.org/igc/www.women.html`

Asia-Pacific

The database covers the business, economics, and new industries of the Pacific Rim nations, including East Asia, Southeast Asia, the Indian Subcontinent, the Middle East, Australia, and the Pacific Island nations.

Keywords:	Asia, Pacific, Business, Economy
Sponsor:	Aristarchus Knowledge Industries, Seattle, WA, USA
Audience:	Market Researchers, Economists, Market Analysts
Profile:	Records are of two types: main records consisting of abstracts or citations for journal articles and other publications; and company thesaurus records. Detailed abstracts are provided for selected journal articles, monographs, selected papers in conference proceedings, dissertations, and government documents. Shorter citations with briefer indexing are provided for a wide variety of journal articles, newspapers, government documents, and annual report publications. Asia-Pacific also includes an extensive Corporate Thesaurus subfile, which provides detailed coverage of the corporate players in the Pacific Rim, including thousands of companies traded on the stock exchanges of Southeast and East Asia.
Contact:	Dialog in the US at (800) 334-2564; Dialog internationally at country-specific locations.
Details:	Costs
User Info:	To subscribe, contact Dialog directly.

`telnet://dialog.com`

Asian American FAQ

Document of FAQs for the soc.culture.asian.american Usenet newsgroup. Includes information concerning terminology, publications, dating, and references.

Keywords:	Asia, Asian Studies
Audience:	Students, Asian-Americans, Asians
Contact:	Bryan Wu bwu@panix.com
Details:	Free

`ftp://rtfm.mit.edu/pub/usenet/soc.culture.asian.american/FAQ_for_soc.culture.asian.american`

Asian and Pacific Economic Literature

A list of economic literature covering Asia and the Pacific region.

Keywords:	Asia, Pacific, Economics
Audience:	Economists, Business Professionals
Details:	Free

`ftp://coombs.anu.edu`

Asian Pacific Business and Marketing Resources

A forum on business and marketing in the Pacific Rim region.

Keywords:	Asia, Pacific, Business, Management
Audience:	Business Professionals, Market Researchers
Details:	Free

`gopher://hoshi.cic.sfu.ca/11/dlam/business/forum`

Chiba University Gopher

The Chiba University gopher, including files from the university's library.

Keywords:	Japan, Asia, Libraries
Sponsor:	Chiba University, Chiba, Japan
Audience:	Japan Residents, Computer Programmers, Librarians, Linguists
Contact:	hasimoto@chiba-u.ac.jp

`gopher://himawari.ipc.chiba-u.ac.jp`

University of Hawaii Library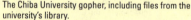

The library's holdings are large and wide-ranging and contain significant collections in many fields.

Keywords:	Asia, European Documents, Book Arts, Hawaii
Audience:	General Public, Researchers, Librarians, Document Delivery Professionals
Details:	Free
User Info:	Expect: enter class, Send: LIB

`telnet://starmaster.uhcc.hawaii.edu`

University of Michigan Library

The library's holdings are large and wide-ranging and contain significant collections in many fields.

Keywords:	Asia, Astronomy, Transportation, Lexicology, Math, Zoology, Geography
Audience:	Researchers, Students, General Public
Contact:	info@merit.edu
Details:	Free
User Info:	Expect: Which Host; Send: Help

`telnet://cts.merit.edu`

Asian American Studies

soc.culture.asian.american

A Usenet newsgroup providing information and discussion about Asian American culture.

Keywords:	Asian American Studies, Sociology
Audience:	Sociologists
Details:	Free
User Info:	To subscribe to this Usenet newsgroup, you need access to a newsreader.

`news:soc.culture.asian.american`

Asian Studies

ANU (Australian National University) Asian-Settlements Database

A searchable database containing abstracts of theses and research studies provided by the Asian Institute of Technology, relating to issues of demography and social geography in Asia.

Keywords:	Asian Studies, Demography, Geography
Sponsor:	The COOMBSQUEST Social Sciences & Humanities Information Facility at ANU (Australian National University), Canberra, Australia
Audience:	Asia Studies Instructors, Demographers, Geographers
Contact:	Dr. T. Matthew Ciolek coombspapers@coombs.anu.edu.au
Details:	Free

`gopher://cheops.anu.edu.au/Coombs-db/ANU-Asian-Settlements.src`

`http://coombs.anu.edu.au/WWWVL-AsianStudies.html`

ANU (Australian National University) Buddhism Database ★★★

A searchable database of messages from the BUDDHA-L listserv, an academic forum for the discussion of Buddhism. It currently contains archives for messages posted in 1993-94.

Keywords: Religion, Asian Studies, Buddhism
Sponsor: COOMBSQUEST Social Sciences & Humanities Information Facility at ANU (Australian National University), Canberra, Australia
Audience: Buddhists, Religious Studies Instructors, Asian Studies Educators
Contact: Dr. T.Matthew Ciolek
coombspapers@coombs.anu.edu.au

gopher://cheops.anu.edu.au /Coombs-db/ANU-Buddha-l.src

http://coombs.anu.edu.au/WWWVL-AsianStudies.html

APEX-J (Asia-Pacific Exchange Electronic Journal) ★

An electronic journal about the Pacific Rim.

Keywords: Asian Studies
Sponsor: Published by the University of Hawaii at Kapiolani Community College, Hawaii, USA
Audience: Educators, Students
Contact: Jim Shimabukuro
JamesS@Hawaii.edu
Notes: login anonymous;password your email address; cd outgoing; get file.name; bye

ftp://ftp.hawaii.edu

Asian American FAQ ★★

Document of FAQs for the soc.culture.asian.american Usenet newsgroup. Includes information concerning terminology, publications, dating, and references.

Keywords: Asia, Asian Studies
Audience: Students, Asian-Americans, Asians
Contact: Bryan Wu
bwu@panix.com
Details: Free

ftp://rtfm.mit.edu/pub/usenet/soc.culture.asian.american/FAQ

_for_soc.culture.asian.american

AskERIC Virtual Library

AskERIC Virtual Library ★★★★

This gopher is part of a federally-funded system to provide public access to educational resources.

Keywords: Education (K-12), Computer-Aided Learning, Libraries, Electronic Books
Sponsor: Educational Resources Information Center (ERIC)
Audience: K-12 Teachers, Administrators
Profile: This gopher contains a wide range of educational aids including pre-prepared lesson plans, guides to Internet resources for the classroom organized by subject, updates on conferences for educators, and archives of education-related listservs. Also allows access to outside gophers, libraries, and sources of electronic books and journals.
Contact: Nancy A. Morgan
nmorgan@ericir.syr.edu
askeric@ericir.syr.edu

gopher://ericir.syr.edu

ASSETS (Real Estate Tax Assessor and Deed Transfer Records)

ASSETS (Real Estate Tax Assessor and Deed Transfer Records) ★★★

The Real Estate Tax Assessor and Deed Transfer Records (ASSETS) library contains information compiled from real property records.

Keywords: Real Estate, Property, Taxes
Audience: Lawyers
Profile: The ASSETS library contains a variety of real estate information, including asset ownership, property address, owner's mailing address, assessed valuation, current market value, and recent property sales and deed transfers. Information is collected from county tax assessors' and recorders' offices nationwide and compiled by TRW REDI Property Data. The ASSETS library also contains a variety of boat and aircraft registration information.
Contact: Mead New Sales Group at (800) 227-4908 or (513) 859-5398 inside the US, or (513) 865-7981 for all inquiries outside the US.
User Info: To subscribe, contact Mead directly.
To examine the Nexis user guide, you can access it at the ftp site of the University of Texas at Austin at the URL address: ftp://ftp.cc.utexas.edu

The files are in: /pub/ref-services/LEXIS

telnet://nex.meaddata.com

http://www.meaddata.com

Assignees

LEXPAT (Patents US) ★★★

The LEXPAT library contains the full text of US patents issued since 1975, the US Patent and Trademark Office Manual of Classification, and the Index to US Patent Classification. The approximately 1,500 patents added to the library each week appear online within four days of their issue.

Keywords: Patents, Inventors, Assignees, Litigants
Audience: Lawyers, Business Researchers, Analysts, Entrepreneurs
Profile: LEXPAT may be searched by individual files for the full text of utility, design or plant patents, or you can combine the files in one 'omni' search. The Manual, Index and Class files can be used to supplement your full-text patent searches. LEXPAT is a valuable tool for both patent professionals and for anyone who needs to access to technical information. More than 80 percent of the information contained in patents is unavailable in any other form.
Contact: Mead New Sales Group at (800) 227-4908 or (513) 859-5398 inside the US, or (513) 865-7981 for all inquiries outside the US.
User Info: To subscribe, contact Mead directly.
User Info: To examine the Nexis user guide, you can access it at the ftp site of the University of Texas at Austin at the URL address: ftp://ftp.cc.utexas.edu

The files are in: /pub/ref-services/LEXIS

telnet://nex.meaddata.com

http://www.meaddata.com

ASTRA-UG

ASTRA-UG ★★

A mailing list for the discussion of Italian and European GIS (Geographical Information Systems).

Keywords: GIS (Geographic Information Systems), Europe, Italy
Audience: Geographers, Cartographers, Europeans
Details: Free
User Info: To subscribe to the list, send an e-mail mesage to the URL address below, consisting of a single line reading:
SUB ASTRA-UG YourFirstName YourLastName

astra-ug@icnucevm

Astronomy

Astronomical Information on the Internet

This FTP site contains pointers to potentially relevant resources available via the Internet.

Keywords: Astronomy, Astrophysics, Astronomical Software, Astronomical Instrumentation

Sponsor: European Space Organization (ESO) and Space Telescope European Coordinating Facility (ST-ECF)

Audience: Astronomers, Physicists, Students (college, graduate), Educators

Profile: This is the entry point for most astronomical resources available online categorized by function. More than 100 resources are accessible concerning general astronomical information, software, and publications. The following are just a few examples of the resources available as of January 1994:

- On-line Publications from CERN, SISSA, STSCI, NASA, PASP, Cfa, and so on.
- Conferences and meetings
- Metereological information
- Access to over 30 observatories and institutes
- Data archives from over 20 previous and current satellite missions, observatories, and astronomy data centers
- Astronomical images
- Astronomical software
- Jobs

Contact: Hans-Martin Adorf

adorf@eso.org

Details: Free, Moderated; Image, Sound, and Multimedia files available.

ftp://ecf.hq.eso.org/pub/WWW/astro-resources.html

Astronomical Publications Resources (APR)

Contains pointers to many relevant resources available via the Internet.

Keywords: Astronomy, Astrophysics, Physics

Sponsor: Space Telescope Science Institute

Audience: Astronomers, Physicists, Students (college, graduate), Educators

Profile: APR is a useful starting point to most of the astronomical publication resources available online. It is conviently divided by type of access (gopher, wais, www, telnet, ftp). As of January 1994, resources include:

- Astrophysics Preprints—SISSA
- ADC Documents
- NOAO News
- NRAO Preprint Database
- STECF Newsletter
- STELAR ApJ, ApJS, AJ, PASP, A&A, A&AS, MNRAS, and JGR Abstracts
- STScI Preprint Database
- IAU Circulars Astronomical Union
- CfA Index of ApJ, AJ, PASP
- DIRA2 Database
- Electronic Journal of Astronomical Society of the Atlantic

Contact: rrpss@stsci.edu

Details: Free, Moderated

http://stsci.edu/net-publications.html

gopher://stsci.edu

Astronomical Software Resources (ASR)

Contains pointers to many relevant resources available via the Internet.

Keywords: Astronomy, Astrophysics, Astronomical Software

Sponsor: Space Telescope Science Institute

Audience: Astronomers, Physicists, Students (College, Graduate), Educators

Profile: ASR is a useful starting point to most of the astronomical software resources available on line. It is conviently divided by type of access (www, wais, gopher, telnet, ftp). As of January 1994, resources include:

- Computer Software Management and Information Center
- IRAF Information System
- Software Support Laboratory SSL
- Starlink Help Browser
- Space Telescope Science Data Analysis System (STSDAS)
- FITS Archive
- NAG Bulletin Board Services
- Numerical Recipes Software
- STSDAS Software
- Working Group on Astronomical Software Archives
- FITS Documents

Contact: rpss@stsci.edu.

Details: Free, Moderated; Image, Sound, and Multimedia files available.

http://stsci.edu/net-software.html

Astronomy

This directory is a compilation of information resources focused on astronomy.

Keywords: Astronomy, Astrophysics, Space

Audience: Astronomers, Astrophysicists, Space Enthusiasts

Details: Free

ftp://una.hh.lib.umich.edu/70/inetdirstacks/astron:parkmiller

Astrophysics Data System (ADS)

A distributed processing software that provides its users with access to over 190 astronomical catalogs and approximately 125,000 astronomical abstracts.

Keywords: Astronomy, Astrophysics,

Sponsor: Smithsonian Astrophysical Observatory

Audience: Astronomers, Physicists, Students (College, Graduate), Educators

Profile: ADS is a suite of information management, manipulation, visualization, and access tools that facilitate user selection of, and access to, data in a distributed environment. These data can be imported to or exported from analysis systems through the use of the ASCII and FITS I/O standards. ADS also provides direct access to the HEASARC Browse tool, NSSDC's Online Data and Information Service (NODIS), the NASA/IPAC Extragalactic Database (NED), SIMBAD (Set of Identifications, Measurements, and Bibliography for Astronomical Data). The user is able to access all of this information via a simple-to-use Graphical User Interface (GUI).

Contact: ads@cuads.colorado.edu

Details: Free, Image files available.

Notes: To become a registered user and get ADS, request a registration form from ads@cuads.colorado.edu.

http://adswww.colorado.edu/adswww/adshomepg.htlm

CADC (Canadian Astronomy Data Center) Home Page

The CADC maintains archives of scientific data from the Hubble Space Telescope and the Canada France Hawaii Telescope. It also serves as a distribution point for various astronomy-related software packages.

Keywords: Astronomy, Hubble Telescope

Sponsor: Dominional Astrophysical Observatory, Victoria, British Columbia, Canada

Audience: Astronomers

Contact: Dennis Crabtree
crabtree@dao.nrc.ca

http://ucluelet.dao.nrc.ca

Canopus

Newsletter of the Space Science and Astronomy Technical Committee of the American Institute of Aeronautics and Astronautics. Its objective is to provide an insider's perspective on issues in space science and astronomy.

Keywords:	Space Science, Astronomy
Sponsor:	NASA (National Aeronautics and Space Administration)
Audience:	Astronomers, Space Scientists
Contact:	William W. L. Taylor wtaylor@nhqvax.hq.nasa.gov
Details:	Costs
User Info:	To subscribe to the list, send an e-mail message to the URL address below.

`mailto:wtaylor@nhqvax.hq.nasa.gov`

Center for Extreme Ultraviolet Astrophysics

A department of the University of California at Berkeley devoted to research in extreme ultraviolet astronomy. It is the ground-based institution of EUVE (the Extreme Ultraviolet Explorer), a NASA satellite launched in 1992.

Keywords:	Astronomy, Astrophysics, EUVE, NASA, Satellite
Sponsor:	NASA and University of California at Berkeley
Audience:	Astronomers, Astrophysicists
Profile:	Provides access to details about the EUVE Guest Observer (EGO) Center, the EUVE Public Archive of Mission Data and Information, satellite operation information, and so on. The EUVE Guest Observer Center provides information, software, and data to EUVE Guest Observers.
Contact:	egoinfo@cea.berkeley.edu, archive@cea.berkeley.edu
Details:	Free

`http://cea-ftp.cea.berkeley.edu`

Earth and Sky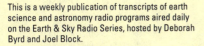

This is a weekly publication of transcripts of earth science and astronomy radio programs aired daily on the Earth & Sky Radio Series, hosted by Deborah Byrd and Joel Block.

Keywords:	Earth Sciences, Astronomy
Audience:	General Public, Earth Scientists, Astronomers
Contact:	majordomo@lists.utexas.edu
Details:	Free

User Info:	To subscribe to the list, send an e-mail message to the URL address shown below consisting of a single line reading: SUB earth-and-sky YourFirstName YourLastName To send a message to the entire list, address it to: earth-and-sky@lists.utexas.edu

`mailto:majordomo@lists.utexas.edu`

Extraterrestrials

A forum for academics, scientists and others interested in questions about the existence of intelligent life in the universe.

Keywords:	Astronomy, Extraterrestrial Life, Space
Sponsor:	University of Kent at Canterbury, United Kingdom
Audience:	Scientists, Astronomers, General Public
Contact:	Dr. Peter Moore pgm@ukc.ac.uk
User Info:	To subscribe to the list, send an e-mail message to the URL address shown below consisting of a single line reading: SUB extraterrestrials YourFirstName YourLastName To send a message to the entire list, address it to: extraterrestrials@mailbase.ac.uk

`mailbase@mailbase.ac.uk`

IUCAA (Inter-University Centre for Astronomy and Astrophysics)

The IUCAA was set up to promote the growth of active groups in astronomy and astrophysics in India. The Centre runs vigorous visitor programs involving short and long-term visits of scientists from India and abroad.

Keywords:	Astronomy, Astrophysics, Physics, Education
Sponsor:	Centre for Astronomy and Astrophysics (IUCAA)
Audience:	Researchers, Astronomers, Physicists, Students
Contact:	Postmaster amk@iucaa.ernet.in

`http://iucaa.iucaa.ernet.in/welcome.html`

Library of Congress, Astronomy, Astrophysics, and Physics Resources

Pointers to important remote databases relating to astronomy and physics.

Keywords:	Astronomy, Astrophysics, NASA
Sponsor:	Library of Congress, Washington, DC
Audience:	Astronomers, Educators (Post-Secondary), Physicists, Students
Profile:	The Library of Congress has pointers to many important remote databases including Astronomy, Astrophysics, and Physics Journals, the Aerospace Directory from Rice University, The American Astronomical Society, The Astronomical Internet Resources Directory, The Cold Fusion Bibliography, The Electromagnetic Wave Research Institute of NRC (Florence, Italy), LANL Physics Information, The Lunar/Planetary Institute Database of Geology, Geophysics, and Astronomy, The NASA Extragalactic Database, The NASA Network Applications and Information Center (NAIC), The National Institute of Standards and Technology (NIST), The Physics Resource Directory from University of California, Irvine, and The Space Telescope Electronic Information System (STEIS).
Contact:	lcmarvel@seq1.loc.gov
Details:	Costs
User info:	Can be accessible via telnet://marvel.loc.gov (login: marvel).

`gopher://marvel.loc.gov/11/global/sci/astro`

NASA/IPAC Extragalactic Database (NED)

Contains positions, basic data, and over 500,000 names for 250,000 extragalactic objects, as well as some 450,000 bibliographic references to 21,000 published papers, and 25,000 notes from catalogs and other publications.

Keywords:	Astronomy, Databases
Sponsor:	Jet Propulsory Lab/ Infrared Processing and Analysis Center
Audience:	Astronomers, Scientists
Profile:	Uses a VT100 or X-based interface.
Contact:	G. Helou, B. Madore, M. Schmitz ned@ipac.caltech.edu
Details:	Free
User Info:	Telnet to URL address below; Expect: login; Send: ned
Notes:	sshare@cscns.comservice@cscns.com

`telnet://ned@ned.ipac.caltech.edu`

`ftp://ned.ipac.caltech.edu/pub/ned`

sci.astro

A Usenet newsgroup providing information and discussion about astronomy.

Keywords:	Astronomy, Space
Audience:	Astronomers
User Info:	To subscribe to this Usenet newsgroup, you need access to a newsreader.

`news:sci.astro`

Astronomy

Sci.astro.fits

Discussions of the Flexible Image Transport System (FITS), a widely used standard for transporting astronomical data.

- Keywords: Astronomy
- Audience: Astronomers
- Details: Free, Images
- User Info: To subscribe to this Usenet newsgroup, you need access to a newsreader.

`news:sci.astro.fits`

Sci.astro.hubble

Information about all subjects concerning NASA's Hubble space telescope.

- Keywords: Hubble Telescope, Astronomy, Space, NASA, Stargazing, Telescopes
- Audience: Astronomers, General Public, Science Teachers, Stargazers
- Contact: Paul A. Scowen scowen@wfpc3.la.asu.edu
- Details: Free, Moderated, Images
- User Info: To subscribe to this Usenet newsgroup, you need access to a newsreader.

`news:sci.astro.hubble`

Sci.astro.planetarium

A group catering to the planetarium operations community.

- Keywords: Astronomy, Planetariums
- Audience: Educators, Astronomers, Planetarium Operators
- Details: Free
- User Info: To subscribe to this Usenet newsgroup, you need access to a newsreader.

`news:sci.astro.planetarium`

The Curiosity Club

This web site offers both an astrophysics exploration and a playspace for young scientists.

- Keywords: Astronomy, Mythology, Children
- Sponsor: Center for Extreme Ultraviolet Astrophysics, Berkeley, California, and The San Francisco Unified School District, San Francisco, California
- Audience: Educators, Students, Astronomers,
- Contact: Kasey Rios Asberry jasberry@sfsuvax1.sfsu.edu
- Details: Free

`http://nisus.sfusd.k12.ca.us/curiosity_club/bridge1.html`

The University of California Search for Extraterrestrial Civilizations

A web site containing information on the UC Berkeley SETI Program, SERENDIP (Search for Extraterrestrial Radio Emmisions from Nearby Developed Intelligent Populations), an ongoing scientific research effort aimed at detecting radio signals from extraterrestrial civilizations. Details about the program and updates on current research activities are also accessible.

- Keywords: Extraterrestrial Life, Astronomy, Aliens
- Audience: Astronomers, Physicists, Students, Educators, Engineers, General Public
- Contact: Dan Werthimer sereninfo@ssl.berkeley.edu
- Details: Free

If Mosaic is available, use the http address below. Otherwise, please send a request for information to the contact address provided.

`http://sereninfo.ssl.berkeley.edu`

University of Michigan Library

The library's holdings are large and wide-ranging and contain significant collections in many fields.

- Keywords: Asia, Astronomy, Transportation, Lexicology, Math, Zoology, Geography
- Audience: Researchers, Students, General Public
- Contact: info@merit.edu
- Details: Free
- User Info: Expect: Which Host; Send: Help

`telnet:// cts.merit.edu`

Astrophysics

Astronomical Information on the Internet

This FTP site contains pointers to potentially relevant resources available via the Internet.

- Keywords: Astronomy, Astrophysics
- Sponsor: European Space Organization (ESO) and Space Telescope European Coordinating Facility (ST-ECF)
- Audience: Astronomers, Physicists, Students (College, Graduate), Educators
- Profile: This is the entry point for most astronomical resources available online categorized by function. More than 100 resources are accessible concerning general astronomical information, software, and publications. The following are just a few examples of the resources available as of January 1994:

  - Online Publications from CERN, SISSA, STSCI, NASA, PASP, Cfa, and so on.
  - Conferences and meetings
  - Metereological information
  - Access to over 30 observatories and institutes
  - Data archives from over 20 previous and current satellite missions, observatories, and astronomy data centers
  - Astronomical images
  - Astronomical software
  - Jobs

- Contact: Hans-Martin Adorf adorf@eso.org
- Details: Free, Moderated. Images, Sounds, and Multimedia files available.

`ftp://ecf.hq.eso.org/pub/WWW/astro-resources.html`

Astronomical Publications Resources (APR)

Contains pointers to many relevant resources available via the Internet.

- Keywords: Astronomy, Astrophysics, Physics
- Sponsor: Space Telescope Science Institute
- Audience: Astronomers, Physicists, Students (College, Graduate), Educators
- Profile: APR is a useful starting point to most of the astronomical publication resources available online. It is conviently divided by type of access (gopher, wais, www, telnet, ftp). As of January 1994, resources include:

  - Astrophysics Preprints—SISSA
  - ADC Documents
  - NOAO News
  - NRAO Preprint Database
  - STECF Newsletter
  - STELAR ApJ, ApJS, AJ, PASP, A&A, A&AS, MNRAS, and JGR Abstracts
  - STScI Preprint Database
  - IAU Circulars Astronomical Union
  - CfA Index of ApJ, AJ, PASP
  - DIRA2 Database
  - Electronic Journal of Astronomical Society of the Atlantic

- Contact: rrpss@stsci.edu
- Details: Free, Moderated

`http://stsci.edu/net-publications.html`

`gopher://stsci.edu`

Astrophysics

Astronomical Software Resources (ASR) ★★★★

Contains pointers to many relevant resources available via the Internet.

Keywords: Astronomy, Astrophysics, Astronomical Software
Sponsor: Space Telescope Science Institute
Audience: Astronomers, Physicists, Students (college, graduate), Educators
Profile: ASR is a useful starting point to most of the astronomical software resources available on line. It is conviently divided by type of access (www, wais, gopher, telnet, ftp). As of January 1994, resources include:
- Computer Software Management and Information Center
- IRAF Information System
- Software Support Laboratory SSL
- Starlink Help Browser
- Space Telescope Science Data Analysis System (STSDAS)
- FITS Archive
- NAG Bulletin Board Services
- Numerical Recipes Software
- STSDAS Software
- Working Group on Astronomical Software Archives
- FITS Documents.

Contact: rpss@stsci.edu.
Details: Free, Moderated, Image, Sounds and Multimedia files available.

`http://stsci.edu/net-software.html`

Astronomy

This directory is a compilation of information resources focused on astronomy.

Keywords: Astronomy, Stars, Astrophysics, Space
Audience: Astronomers, Astrophysicists, Space Enthusiasts
Contact: A. Park, J. Miller
Details: Free

`ftp://una.hh.lib.umich.edu/70/`
`inetdirsstacks/astron:parkmiller`

Astrophysics Data System (ADS) ★★★★

A distributed processing software that provides its users with access to over 190 astronomical catalogs and approximately 125,000 astronomical abstracts.

Keywords: Astronomy, Astrophysics, Astronomical Software, Astronomical Catalogs
Sponsor: Smithsonian Astrophysical Observatory
Audience: Astronomers, Physicists, Students (college, graduate), Educators
Profile: ADS is a suite of information management, manipulation, visualization, and access tools that facilitate user selection of, and access to, data in a distributed environment. These data can be imported to or exported from analysis systems through the use of the ASCII and FITS I/O standards. ADS also provides direct access to the HEASARC Browse tool, NSSDC's Online Data and Information Service (NODIS), the NASA/IPAC Extragalactic Database (NED), SIMBAD (Set of Identifications, Measurements, and Bibliography for Astronomical Data). The user is able to access all of this information via a simple-to-use Graphical User Interface (GUI).
Contact: ads@cuads.colorado.edu
Details: Free, Image files available.

To become a registered user and get ADS, request a registration form from ads@cuads.colorado.edu.

`http://adswww.colorado.edu/adswww/`
`adshomepg.htlm`

Center for Extreme Ultraviolet Astrophysics ★★★

A department of the University of California at Berkeley devoted to research in extreme ultraviolet astronomy. It is the ground-based institution of EUVE (the Extreme Ultraviolet Explorer), a NASA satellite launched in 1992.

Keywords: Astronomy, Astrophysics, EUVE, NASA, Satellite
Sponsor: NASA and University of California at Berkeley
Audience: Astronomers, Astrophysicists
Profile: Provides access to details about the EUVE Guest Observer (EGO) Center, the EUVE Public Archive of Mission Data and Information, satellite operation information, and so on. The EUVE Guest Observer Center provides information, software, and data to EUVE Guest Observers.
Contact: egoinfo@cea.berkeley.edu, archive@cea.berkeley.edu
Details: Free

`http://cea-ftp.cea.berkeley.edu/`

IUCAA (Inter-University Centre for Astronomy and Astrophysics) ★

The IUCAA was set up to promote the growth of active groups in astronomy and astrophysics in India. The Centre runs vigorous visitor programs involving short and long-term visits of scientists from India and abroad.

Keywords: Astronomy, Astrophysics, Physics, Education
Sponsor: Centre for Astronomy and Astrophysics (IUCAA)
Audience: Reseachers, Astronomers, Physicists, Students
Contact: Postmaster amk@iucaa.ernet.in

`http://iucaa.iucaa.ernet.in/`
`welcome.html`

Library of Congress, Astronomy, Astrophysics, and Physics Resources ★★★★

Pointers to important remote databases relating to astronomy and physics.

Keywords: Astronomy, Astrophysics, NASA
Sponsor: Library of Congress, Washington, DC
Audience: Astronomers, Educators (Post-Secondary), Physicists, Students
Profile: The Library of Congress has pointers to many important remote databases including Astronomy, Astrophysics, and Physics Journals, the Aerospace Directory from Rice University, The American Astronomical Society, The Astronomical Internet Resources Directory, The Cold Fusion Bibliography, The Electromagnetic Wave Research Institute of NRC (Florence, Italy), LANL Physics Information, The Lunar/Planetary Institute Database of Geology, Geophysics, and Astronomy, The NASA Extragalactic Database, The NASA Network Applications and Information Center (NAIC), The National Institute of Standards and Technology (NIST), The Physics Resource Directory from University of California, Irvine, and The Space Telescope Electronic Information System (STEIS).
Contact: lcmarvel@seq1.loc.gov
Details: Costs
User info: Can be accessible via telnet://marvel.loc.gov (login: marvel).

`gopher://marvel.loc.gov/11/global/`
`sci/astro`

NSSDC (National Space Science Data Center)'s Online Data & Information Service ★★★

The NSSDC (National Space Science Data Center) is the NASA facility charged with archiving the data from all of NASA's science missions.

Keywords: Space, Astrophysics, Software, NASA, Science
Sponsor: NASA
Audience: Scientists, Space Scientists, Astronomers, Engineers

Profile:	This resource contains information about NASA's missions and analysis of their data.	
Details:	Free	
User Info:	Expect: Login, Send: nssdc	
	See the menu entries in your particular area of interest.	

`telnet://nssdc.gsfc.nasa.gov`

Physics

A newly created digest covering current developments in theoretical and experimental physics. Topics might include particle physics, plasma physics, or astrophysics.

Keywords:	Physics, Astrophysics, Plasma Physics
Audience:	Physicists, Astrophysicists
Contact:	Mike Miskulin physics-request@qedqcd.rye.ny.us
Details:	Free
User Info:	To subscribe to the list, send an e-mail message requesting a subscription to the URL address below.
	To send a message to the entire list, address it to: physics@qedqcd.rye.ny.u

`mailto:physics-request@qedqcd.rye.ny.us`

AT&T

AT&T Bell Laboratories WWW Information Page

This web site provides information on research and development at AT&T Bell Laboratories.

Keywords:	Telecommunications, Technology, AT&T, Cellular Technology
Sponsor:	AT&T Bell Laboratories
Audience:	Engineers, Educators, Communications Specialists
Contact:	webmaster@research.att.com
Details:	Free

`http://www.research.att.com`

att-pc+

A mailing list for users and potential users of the AT&T PC 63xx series of systems.

Keywords:	Computers, AT&T
Audience:	Computer Programmers
Contact:	Bill Kennedy bill@ssbn.wlk.com
User Info:	To subscribe to the list, send an e-mail message to the URL address below.
	To send a message to the entire list, address it to: att-pc+@ssbn.wlk.com
Notes:	Sub-lists are maintained for MS-DOS-only and Simul-Task mailings as well as the full list for items of general interest. Membership must be requested and mail path verification is required before membership is granted.

`mailto:att-pc+@ssbn.wlk.com`

Atari

ST viruses

This list is to provide fast and efficient help with computer viruses infecting the Atari ST/TT/Falcon only.

Keywords:	Computer Viruses, Atari
Audience:	Computer Users
Contact:	r.c.karsmakers@stud.let.ruu.nl
Details:	Free
User Info:	To subscribe to the list, send an e-mail message requesting a subscription to the URL address below.
	To send a message to the entire list, address it to: r.c.karsmakers@stud.let.ruu.nl

`mailto:r.c.karsmakers@stud.let.ruu.nl`

Atmosphere

Global Change Information Gateway

This gatewas was created to address environmental data management issues raised by the US Congress, the Administration, and the advisory arms of the Federal policy community. It contains documents related to the UN conference on Environment and Development.

Keywords:	UN, Environment, Development, Oceans, Atmosphere
Audience:	Environmentalists, Scientists, Researchers, Environmentalists
Profile:	[profile needed]
Details:	Free
	Select from menu as appropriate.

`gopher://scilibx.ucsc.edu`

Atmospheric Science

National Oceanic & Atmospheric Administration (NOAA), Office of Environmental Safety and Health, Department of Energy

The NOAA catalog provides keyword access to sources of environmental information in the US. Gopher for resources pertaining to health and environmental safety.

Keywords:	Environment, Oceans, Atmospheric Science, Health, Environmental Safety
Sponsor:	National Oceanic & Atmospheric Administration (NOAA), Department of Energy (USA)
Audience:	Environmental Scientists, Researchers, Environmentalists, Epidemiologists, Public Health Officials
Profile:	[profile needed]
Details:	Free

`gopher://scilibx.ucsc.edu`

`gopher://gopher.ns.doc.gov`

Purdue University Library

The library's holdings are large and wide-ranging. They contain significant collections in many fields.

Keywords:	Economics (History of), Literature (English), Literature (American), Indiana, Rogers (Bruce), Engineering (History of), Aviation, Earth Science, Atmospheric Science, Consumer Science, Family Science, Chemistry (History of), Physics, Veterinary Science
Audience:	General Public, Researchers, Librarians, Document Delivery Professionals
Contact:	Dan Ferrer dan@asterix.lib.purdue.edu
Details:	Free
User Info:	Expect: User ID prompt, Send: GUEST

`telnet://lib.cc.purdue.edu`

AUC TeX

auc-TeX

Discussion and information exchange about the AUC TeX package, which runs under GNU Emacs.

Keywords:	Computers, TeX, AUC TeX, Emacs
Audience:	Computer Users
Contact:	Kresten Krab Thorup auc-tex-request@iesd.auc.dk

Details: Free

User Info: To subscribe to the list, send an e-mail message requesting a subscription to the URL address below.

To send a message to the entire list, address it to: auc-tex@iesd.auc.dk

`mailto:auc-tex-request@iesd.auc.dk`

Audio Electronics

af

A mailing list for discussion of AudioFile, a client/server, network-transparent, device-independent audio system.

Keywords: Audio Electronics, Electrical Engineering

Audience: Audio Enthusiasts, Electrical Engineers

Contact: af-request@crl.dec.com

User Info: To subscribe to the list, send an e-mail message to the URL address below.

To send a message to the entire list, address it to: af@crl.dec.com

`mailto:af-request@crl.dec.com`

rec.audio

A Usenet newsgroup providing information and discussion about audio products, including troubleshooting advice.

Keywords: Audio Electronics, Stereo Electronics

Audience: Stereo Owners, Music Listeners

User Info: To subscribe to this Usenet newsgroup, you need access to a newsreader.

`news:rec.audio`

rec.music.cd

A Usenet newsgroup providing information and discussion about Compact Discs.

Keywords: Music, Audio Electronics

Audience: Compact Disc Users

User Info: To subscribe to this Usenet newsgroup, you need access to a newsreader.

`news:rec.music.cd`

rec.music.makers.synth

A Usenet newsgroup providing information and discussion about synthesizers.

Keywords: Music, Audio Electronics

Audience: Synthesizer Users

User Info: To subscribe to this Usenet newsgroup, you need access to a newsreader.

`news:rec.music.makers.synth`

Audio Reproduction

Bass

The purpose of this list is to discuss the reproduction and enjoyment of deep bass, primarily in consumer audio.

Keywords: Audio Reproduction

Audience: Stereo Enthusiasts, General Public

Contact: bass-request@gsbcs.uchicago.edu

Details: Free

User Info: To subscribe to the list, send an e-mail message requesting a subscription to the URL address below.

To send a message to the entire list, address it to: bass@gsbcs.uchicago.edu

Notes: Ownership of a subwoofer is not required—membership is open to anyone with an interest in deep bass reproduction.

`mailto:bass-request@gsbcs.uchicago.edu`

Audio-Visual Materials

NYAL (New York Art Line)

A gopher containing selected resources on the arts.

Keywords: Art, Audio-Visual Materials, Multimedia, Computer Art

Sponsor: Panix Public Access Unix & Internet Gopher Server, New York, USA

Audience: Artists, Art Enthusiasts

Profile: NYAL features a wide variety of arts resources. The primary focus of this site is visual art, particularly in the New York city area. Information includes online access to selected galleries, image archives, and New York city arts groups. Beyond visual art, information on dance, music, and techno art (with a special section on Internet art) is also available. It also features links to various electronic journals, museums, and schools.

Contact: Kenny Greenberg
kgreen@panix.com

`gopher://gopher.panix.com`

`http://gopher.panix.com/nyart/Kpage/kg`

Auditing

NAARS (National Automated Accounting Research System)

The National Automated Accounting Research System (NAARS) library, provided as a service by agreement with the American Institute of Certified Public Accountants (AICPA) contains a variety of accounting information.

Keywords: Accounting, Auditing, Filings, Publications

Audience: Accountants

Profile: The NAARS library contains annual reports of public corporations and accounting literature and publications for the accounting professional. Annual reports are annotated with descriptive terms assigned by the AICPA. These terms allow the user to search for annual report footnotes that illustrate one or more recognized accounting practices.

Contact: Mead New Sales Group at (800) 227-4908 or (513) 859-5398 inside the US, or (513) 865-7981 for all inquiries outside the US.

User Info: To subscribe, contact Mead directly.

To examine the Nexis user guide, you can access it at the ftp site of the University of Texas at Austin at the URL address: ftp://ftp.cc.utexas.edu

The files are in: /pub/ref-services/LEXIS

`telnet://nex.meaddata.com`

`http://www.meaddata.com`

AUGLBC-L

AUGLBC-L

The American University Gay, Lesbian, and Bisexual Community (AUGLBC) is a support group for lesbian, gay, bisexual, transsexual, and supportive students. The group is also connected with the International Gay and Lesbian Youth Organization (known as IGLYO).

Keywords: Gays, Lesbians, Bisexuality, Transsexuality, Sexuality

Audience: Gays, Lesbians, Bisexuals, Transsexuals, Students (college)

Contact: Erik G. Paul

User Info: To subscribe to the list, send an e-mail message to the URL address below, consisting of a single line reading:

SUB AUGLBC-l YourFirstName YourLastName

To send a message to the entire list, address it to: AUGLBC-l@american.edu

`mailto:listserv@american.edu`

Australia

AusGBLF

An Australian-based mailing list for gays, bisexuals, lesbians, and friends.

Keywords:	Australia, Gays, Lesbians, Bisexuality
Audience:	Gays, Lesbians, Bisexuals
Contact:	zglc@minyos.xx.rmit.oz.au
Details:	Free
User Info:	To subscribe to the list, send an e-mail message requesting a subscription to the URL address below.
	To send a message to the entire list, address it to: ausgblf@minyos.xx.rmit.oz.au

`mailto:ausgblf-request@minyos.xx.rmit.oz.au`

AusRave (Australian Raves)

A regional rave-related mailing list covering the Australian continent. AusRave contains both discussions and informational postings.

Keywords:	Music, Raves, Australia
Audience:	Ravers (Australian)
Contact:	Simon Rumble ausrave@lsupoz.apana.org.au
Details:	Free, Moderated
User Info:	To subscribe to the list, send an e-mail message requesting a subscription to the URL address below.
	To send a message to the entire list, address it to: ausrave@lsupoz.apana.org.au
Notes:	The mailing list Best of AusRave provides information only.
	Postings to AusRave are not archived, but the list does have an FTP site at: elecsun4.elec.uow.edu.au

`mailto:ausrave-request@lsupoz.apana.org.au`

Australia

Full-text versions of Australian legislation.

Keywords:	Australia, Law (International)
Audience:	Australians, Environmentalists
Details:	Free
Notes:	Select from menu as appropriate

`gopher://wiretap.spies.com`

Australian Environmental Resources Information Network (ERIN)

This gopher contains a wide range of Australian environmental information.

Keywords:	Environment, Australia, Ecology
Audience:	Environmentalists, Ecologists, Researchers, Australians
Profile:	Coverage includes biodiversity, protected areas, terrestrial and marine environments, environmental protection and legislation, international agreements, and general information about ERIN.
Contact:	gopher@erin.gov.au
Details:	Free

`gopher://kaos.erin.gov.au`

`http://kaos.erin.gov.au/erin.html`

Best-of-AusRave (Australian Raves)

A regional rave-related mailing list covering the Australian continent, for people who want Australian rave information without the side discussions and social chatter from the regular list.

Keywords:	Music, Raves, Australia
Audience:	Ravers (Australian)
Contact:	Simon Rumble best-of-ausrave-request@lsupoz.apana.org.au
Details:	Free, Moderated
User Info:	To subscribe to the list, send an e-mail message to the URL address below, consisting of a single line reading:
	SUB ausrave YourFirstName YourLastName
	To send a message to the entire list, address it to: best-of-ausrave@lsupoz.apana.org.au

`mailto:best-of-ausrave-request@lsupoz.apana.org.au`

ELISA (Electronic Library Service)

An information delivery service of the Library of the Australian National University.

Keywords:	OPAC System, Australia
Sponsor:	Australian National University
Audience:	General Public
Profile:	This information delivery service contains Australian mirrors of major gopher directories, and is a national entry point for Australian gopher services.
Contact:	infodesk@info.anu.edu.au
Details:	Free

`gopher://info.anu.edu.au`

news: aus.films

Discussion of films and the film industry from an Australian perspective.

Keywords:	Film, Australia
Audience:	Australia Enthusiasts, Film Enthusiasts
Details:	Free
User Info:	To subscribe to a Usenet newsgroup, you need access to a "newsreader."

`news:aus.films`

Resodlaa (Research SIG of the Open and Distance Learning Association of Australia)

The purpose of this list is to foster electronic discussion, symposia, and conferences on topical issues in distance education and open-learning research.

Keywords:	Education (Adult), Education (Distance), Education (Continuing), Australia
Sponsor:	Research Special Interest Group (SIG) of the Open and Distance Learning Association of Australia
Audience:	Educators, Administrators, Researchers
Details:	Free
User Info:	To subscribe to the list, send an e-mail message to the URL address below ,consisting of a single line reading:
	SUB resodlaa YourFirstName YourLastName
	To send a message to the entire list, address it to: resodlaa@usq.edu.au

`mailto:listserv@usq.edu.au`

Austrian History

Indiana University Libraries

The library's holdings are large and wide-ranging and contain significant collections in many fields.

Keywords:	Literature (English), Literature (American), 1640-Present, British Plays (19th-C.), Western Americana, Railway History, Aristotle (Texts of), Lafayette (Marquis de), Handel (G.F.), Austrian History, Antiquarian Books, Rare Books, French Opera (19th-C.), Drama (British) ,
Audience:	General Public, Researchers, Librarians, Document Delivery Professionals
Details:	Free
User Info:	Expect: User ID prompt, Send: GUEST

`telnet://iuis.ucs.indiana.edu`

Autocrossing

autox

A mailing list for the discussion of autocrossing and other SCCA (Sports Car Club of America) Solo events.

Keywords:	Automobiles, Autocrossing
Sponsor:	SCCA (Sports Car Club of America)
Audience:	Autocross Drivers
Contact:	autox-request@autox.team.net
	autox-request@hoosier.cs.utah.edu
User Info:	To subscribe to the list, send an e-mail message to the URL address below.
	To send a message to the entire list, address it to: autox-request@autox.team.net
	Also available upon request as a digest.

mailto:autox-request@autox.team.net

mailto:autox-request@hoosier.cs.utah.edu

Automobiles

autox

A mailing list for the discussion of autocrossing and other SCCA (Sports Car Club of America) Solo events.

Keywords:	Automobiles, Autocrossing
Sponsor:	SCCA (Sports Car Club of America)
Audience:	Autocross Drivers
Contact:	autox-request@autox.team.net
	autox-request@hoosier.cs.utah.edu
User Info:	To subscribe to the list, send an e-mail message to the URL address below.
	To send a message to the entire list, address it to: autox-request@autox.team.net
Notes:	Also available upon request as a digest.

mailto:autox-request@autox.team.net

mailto:autox-request@hoosier.cs.utah.edu

BMW

This is a discussion of cars made by BMW. Both regular and digest forms are available.

Keywords:	BMW, Automobiles
Audience:	Automobile Enthusiasts, Automobile Racers, BMW Enthusiasts
Contact:	Richard Welty
	bmw-request@balltown.cma.com
Details:	Free
User Info:	To subscribe to the list, send an e-mail message requesting a subscription to the URL address below.
	To send a message to the entire list, address it to: bmw@balltown.cma.com

mailto:bmw-request@balltown.cma.com

British-Cars

This is a discussion of owning, repairing, racing, cursing, and loving British cars, predominantly sports cars, with some talk of Land Rovers and sedans. Also available as a digest.

Keywords:	Automobiles
Audience:	British Automobile Enthusiasts, Automobile Enthusiasts
Contact:	Mark Bradakis
	british-cars-request@autox.team.net
	british-cars-request@hoosier.cs.utah.edu
Details:	Free
User Info:	To subscribe to the list, send an e-mail message requesting a subscription to the URL address below.
	To send a message to the entire list, address it to: british-cars@autox.team.net

mailto:british-cars-request@autox.team.net

datsun-roadsters

A mailing list for discussing any and all aspects of the owning, showing, repairing, driving, and so on, of Datsun roadsters.

Keywords:	Datsuns, Automobiles
Audience:	Datsun Owners, Automobile Enthusiasts
Contact:	Mark J. Bradakis
	datsun-roadsters-request@autox.team.net
	datsun-roadsters-request@hoosier.utah.edu
Details:	Free
User Info:	To subscribe to the list, send an e-mail message requesting a subscription to the URL address below.
	To send a message to the entire list, address it to: datsun-roadsters-request@autox.team.net

mailto:datsun-roadsters-request@autox.team.net

Fordnatics

This unmoderated forum discusses high-performance Fords or Ford-powered vehicles, focusing on modifications and driving techniques for competition or track use.

Keywords:	Automobiles, Fords
Audience:	Automobile Enthusiasts, Ford Drivers, Racers
Details:	Free
User Info:	To subscribe to the list, send an e-mail message requesting a subscription to the URL address below.
	To send a message to the entire list, address it to: fordnatics@freud.arc.nasa.gov

mailto:fordnatics-request@freud.arc.nasa.gov

Miata

An open forum for Mazda Miata owners.

Keywords:	Automobiles
Audience:	Drivers
Details:	Free
User Info:	To subscribe to the list, send an e-mail message requesting subscription to the URL address below.

mailto:miata-request@jhunix.hcf.jhu.edu

Mustangs

A forum for the discussion of technical issues, problems, solutions, and modifications relating to late-model (1980 and later) Ford Mustangs.

Keywords:	Automobiles
Audience:	Drivers
Details:	Free
User Info:	To subscribe to the list, send an e-mail message requesting a subscription to the URL address below.

mailto:mustangs-request@cup.hp.com

Porschephiles

This list is for people who own, operate, work on, or covet various models of Porsche automobiles. Discussion topics include features, functionality, and purchasing advice.

Keywords:	Porsche, Automobiles, Sports Cars
Audience:	Porsche Owners, Sports Car Owners, Automobile Mechanics
Contact:	porschephiles-request@tta.com
Details:	Free
User Info:	To subscribe to the list, send an e-mail message requesting a subscription to the URL address below.
	To send a message to the entire list, address it to: porschephiles@tta.com

mailto:porschephiles-request@tta.com

Quattro

A mailing list for discussions pertaining to Audi automobiles, especially the AWD (all wheel drive) Quattro models. It also includes news, opinions, maintenance procedures, and parts sources.

Keywords:	Automobiles

Audience:	Automobile Enthusiasts
Contact:	David Tahajian quattro-request@aries.east.sun.com
Details:	Free
User Info:	To subscribe to the list, send an e-mail message requesting a subscription to the URL address below.
	To send a message to the entire list, address it to: quattro@aries.east.sun.com

`mailto:quattro-request@aries.east.sun.com`

rec.autos.driving

A Usenet newsgroup providing information and discussion about driving, traffic laws, and car buying.

Keywords:	Automobiles
Audience:	Drivers, Automobile Buyers
User Info:	To subscribe to this Usenet newsgroup, you need access to a newsreader.

`news:rec.autos.driving`

rec.autos.sport

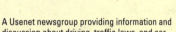

A Usenet newsgroup providing information and discussion about automobile competition.

Keywords:	Automobiles, Automobile Racing, Sports
Audience:	Automobile Racing Enthusiasts
User Info:	To subscribe to this Usenet newsgroup, you need access to a newsreader.

`news:rec.autos.sports`

rec.autos.tech

★

A Usenet newsgroup providing information and discussion about the technical aspects of automobiles.

Keywords:	Automobiles, Technology
Audience:	Automobile Users
User Info:	To subscribe to this Usenet newsgroup, you need access to a newsreader.

`news:rec.autos.tech`

rec.autos.vw

★

A Usenet newsgroup providing information and discussion about Volkswagon products.

Keywords:	Automobiles
Audience:	Volkswagon Drivers
User Info:	To subscribe to this Usenet newsgroup, you need access to a newsreader.

`news:rec.autos.vw`

Stealth

★

Discussion of anything related to Dodge Stealth and Mitsubishi 3000GT cars.

Keywords:	Automobiles
Audience:	Car Enthusiasts
Contact:	stealth-request%jim.uucp@wupost.wustl.edu
Details:	Free
User Info:	Expect: Username prompt, Send: tcucat
	To subscribe to the list, send an e-mail message requesting a subscription to the URL address below.
	To send a message to the entire list, address it to: stealth-request96jim.uucp@wupost.wustl.edu

`mailto:stealth-request%jim.uucp@wupost.wustl.edu`

Utah Valley Community College Library

★

The library's holdings are large and wide-ranging and contain significant collections in many fields.

Keywords:	Accounting, Automobiles, Cabinetry, Child Care, Drafting, Electronics, Home Building, Local History, Refrigeration, Air Conditioning
Audience:	General Public, Researchers, Librarians, Document Delivery Professionals
Details:	Free
User Info:	Expect: Login; Send: Opub

`telnet://uvlib.uvcc.edu`

Autopoiesis

(The) Observer

The central scope of the group covers the theory of autopoiesis (of Humberto Maturana and Francisco Varela) and enactive cognitive science. The extended scope includes applications of the above theoretical work and other relevant work (e.g. systems theory, cognitive science, phenomenology, artificial life, and so on). This is an edited electronic newsletter issued (approximately) twice monthly.

Keywords:	Autopoiesis, Systems Theory, Cognitive Science
Audience:	Systems Theorists, Researchers
Contact:	Randall Whitaker rwhit@cs.umu.se
User Info:	To subscribe to the list, send an e-mail message to the URL address below consisting of a single line reading:
	SUB the observer YourFirstName YourLastName
	To send a message to the entire list, address it to: rwhit@cs.umu.se

`mailto:listserv@cs.umu.se`

Aviation

Aerospace Engineering

This directory is a compilation of information resources focused on aerospace engineeering.

Keywords:	Aerospace, Engineering, Aviation, Space
Audience:	Aerospace Engineers, Space Scientists
Profile:	This is a guide to Internet resources that contain information pertaining to aerospace engineering. Originally the guide was to cover the area of aerospace engineering as applied to lower atmospheric flight. However, it is difficult to narrow the sites down to specific subject areas. As the guide evolved, sites were included with a broader scope of information. The guide is by no means comprehensive and exhaustive; there are sites that are not included and those the authors were not aware of, and they welcome suggestions. The directory lists sites on FTP, Gopher, Listserv, OPAC, Telnet, Usenet, and WWW.
Details:	Free

`ftp://una.hh.lib.umich.edu/70/inetdirsstacks/aerospace:potsiedalq`

Aviator

A mailing list for users of Aviator™, the flight-simulation program from Artificial Horizons, Inc.

Keywords:	Aviation, Simulation, Computers
Audience:	Software Users
Contact:	Jim Hickstein aviator@icdwest.Teradyne.com
Details:	Free
User Info:	To subscribe to the list, send an e-mail message requesting a subscription to the URL address below.
	To send a message to the entire list, address it to: aviator@ICDwest.Teradyne.COM
Notes:	Aviator runs on Sun workstations with the GX graphics accelerator option. Its charter is simply to facilitate communication among users of Aviator. It is not intended for communication with the "providers" of Aviator. All mail received at the submission address is reflected to all the subscribers of the list.

`mailto:aviator-request@ICDwest.Teradyne.COM`

Current Weather Maps and Movies

This web site is updated hourly, and provides links to downloadable software sites instrumental in accessing interactive weather browsers. International information is available, and visual and infrared maps are supplied from satellites.

Keywords: Weather, Meteorology, Aviation
Sponsor: Michigan State University, Michigan, USA
Audience: General Public, Oceanography, Pilots
Contact: Charles Henrich
henrich@crh.cl.msu.edu

`http://rs560.cl.msu.edu/weather`

McDonnell Douglas Aerospace

A web site providing information about McDonnell Douglas, including a company profile and related discussion about technology.

Keywords: Aerospace, Space, Aviation, Technology
Audience: Aerospace Engineers
Contact: Zook@pat.mdc.com

`http://pat.mdc.com`

News, Weather, and Travel Advisories

A major directory of news, weather, and travel advisories, providing access to a broad range of related resources (library catalogues, databases, and servers) via the Internet.

Keywords: Travel, Weather, Aviation
Sponsor: Kennesaw State College, Georgia, USA
Audience: General Public, Travellers
Profile: This collection includes CNN news sources, the National Weather Service Forecast, and the US State Department Travel Advisory, among other sources.
Details: Free

`gopher://kscsuna1.kennesaw.edu`

Purdue University Library

The library's holdings are large and wide-ranging. They contain significant collections in many fields.

Keywords: Economics (History of), Literature (English), Literature (American), Indiana, Rogers (Bruce), Engineering (History of), Aviation, Earth Science, Atmospheric Science, Consumer Science, Family Science, Chemistry (History of), Physics, Veterinary Science
Audience: General Public, Researchers, Librarians, Document Delivery Professionals
Contact: Dan Ferrer
dan@asterix.lib.purdue.edu
Details: Free
User Info: Expect: User ID prompt, Send: GUEST

`telnet://lib.cc.purdue.edu`

Rascal Aviation Archives

A major directory on aeronautics, providing access to a broad range of related resources (library catalogues, databases, and servers) via the Internet.

Keywords: Aeronautics, Aviation
Audience: Aviators, Aeronautical Engineers
Contact: rdd@rascal.ics.utexas.edu

`ftp://rascal.ics.utexas.edu/explore-me/Aviation-stuff`

Aviation Industry

TRANS (The Transportation Library)

The Transportation library contains federal transportation cae law, statutes and agency decisions.

Keywords: Transportation Law, US Government Regulations, Aviation Industry, Railroad Industry, Trucking Industry
Audience: Lawyers
Profile: The Transportation library contains federal transportation case law, statutes and agency decisions. The major emphasis of the library is on three modes of transportation (aviation, railroad and trucking) and how those modes are regulated by the federal government. Agency decisions are provided from the Interstate Commerce Commission, Department of Transportation and the National Transportation Safety Board (NTSB).
Contact: New Sales Group at 800-227-4908 or 513-859-5398 inside the US, or 1-513-865-7981 for all inquires outside the US.
User Info: To subscribe, contact Mead directly.
To examine the Lexis user guide, you can access it at the ftp site of the University of Texas at Austin at the URL address: ftp://ftp.cc.utexas.edu
The files are in: /pub/res-services/LEXIS

`telnet://nex.meaddata.com`

Ayurveda

Ayurveda

Ayurveda is the ancient science of life that originated in India. This mailing list provides information about Ayurveda, such as lectures, workshops, and stores that sell Ayurvedic herbs.

Keywords: Spirituality, Ayurveda, India
Audience: General Public
Contact: ayurveda-request@netcom.com
Details: Free
User Info: To subscribe to the list, send an e-mail message requesting a subscription to the URL address below.
To send a message to the entire list, address it to: ayurveda@netcom.com

`mailto:ayurveda-request@netcom.com`

B

ba-Firearms

ba-Firearms

This list is an announcement and discussion of firearms legislation and related issues. The ca- list is for California statewide issues; the ba- list is for the San Francisco Bay Area and gets all messages sent to the ca- list. Prospective members should subscribe to one or the other, generally depending on whether they are San Francisco Bay Area residents.

Keywords:	Firearms, Gun Control Legislation, San Francisco Bay Area
Audience:	Politicians, General Public, Gun Users, San Francisco Bay Area Residents
Contact:	Jeff Chan ba-firearms-request@shell.portal.com
Details:	Free
User Info:	To subscribe to the list, send an e-mail message requesting a subscription to the URL address below. To send a message to the entire list, address it to: ba-firearms@shell.portal.com

mailto:ba-firearms-request@shell.portal.com

ba-Liberty

ba-Liberty

This list is an announcement of local Libertarian meetings, events, activities, and so on. The ca- list is for California statewide issues; the ba- list is for the San Francisco Bay Area and it gets all messages sent to the ca- list. Prospective members should subscribe to one or the other, generally depending on whether or not they are San Francisco Bay Area residents.

Keywords:	Libertarian Party, Politics, San Francisco Bay Area
Audience:	Libertarians, Political Scientists, Politicians, General Public
Contact:	Jeff Chan ba-liberty-request@shell.portal.com
Details:	Free
User Info:	To subscribe to the list, send an e-mail message requesting a subscription to the following URL address. To send a message to the entire list, address it to: ba-liberty@shell.portal.com

mailto:ba-liberty-request@shell.portal.com

ba-Poker

ba-Poker

Discussion of poker as it is available to residents of and visitors to the San Francisco Bay Area (broadly defined), in home games as well as in licensed card rooms. Topics include upcoming events, unusual games, strategies, comparisons of various venues, and player "networking".

Keywords:	Poker, Card Games, San Francisco Bay Area
Audience:	Poker Players
Contact:	Martin Veneroso ba-poker-request@netcom.com
Details:	Free
User Info:	To subscribe to the list, send an e-mail message requesting a subscription to the URL address below. To send a message to the entire list, address it to: ba-poker@netcom.com

mailto:ba-poker-request@netcom.com

ba-Sappho

ba-Sappho

Ba-Sappho is a San Francisco Bay Area lesbian mailing list intended for local networking and announcements. Ba-Sappho is not a discussion group.

Keywords:	Lesbians, San Francisco Bay Area
Audience:	Lesbians
Contact:	ba-sappho-request@labrys.mti.sgi.com
Details:	Free
User Info:	To subscribe to the list, send an e-mail message requesting a subscription to the following URL address. To send a message to the entire list, address it to: ba-sappho@labrys.mti.sgi.com

mailto:ba-sappho-request@labrys.mti.sgi.com

ba-Volleyball

ba-Volleyball

This list is used for announcements about San Francisco Bay Area volleyball events, clinics, tournaments, and so on.

Keywords:	Volleyball, San Francisco Bay Area, Sports
Audience:	Volleyball Enthusiasts

Contact:	ba-volleyball-request@klerk.cup.hp.com
User Info:	To subscribe to the list, send an e-mail message requesting a subscription to the URL address below.
	To send a message to the entire list, address it to: ba-volleyball@klerk.cup.hp.com

mailto:ba-volleyball-request@klerk.cup.hp.com

ba.general

ba.general

A Usenet newsgroup providing general information and discussion about the San Francisco Bay Area.

Keywords:	California
Audience:	Tourists, Visitors, Bay Area Residents
User Info:	To subscribe to this Usenet newsgroup, you need access to a newsreader.

news:ba.general

Baby Boomer Culture

30something

A mailing list for discussion of the TV show 30something.

Keywords:	Television, Baby Boomer Culture
Audience:	Television Viewers, Baby Boomers
Contact:	Marc Rouleau 30something-request@fuggles.acc.virginia.edu
User Info:	To subscribe to the list, send an e-mail message to the URL address below. To send a message to the entire list, address it to: 30something@fuggles.acc.virginia.edu

mailto:30something-request@fuggles.acc.virginia.edu

Backstreets

Backstreets

Discussion of Bruce Springsteen's music.

Keywords:	Rock Music, Springsteen (Bruce), Musical Groups
Audience:	Bruce Springsteen Fans
Contact:	Kevin Kinder backstreets-request@virginia.edu
Details:	Free

User Info:	To subscribe to the list, send an e-mail message requesting a subscription to the URL address below.
	To send a message to the entire list, address it to: backstreets@virginia.edu

mailto:backstreets-request@virginia.edu

Bagpipes

Pipes

A mailing list of people interested in any topic related to bagpipes, most generally defined as any instrument where air is forced manually from a bellows or bag through drones and/or over reeds. All manner of Scottish, Irish, English, and other instruments are discussed.

Keywords:	Musical Instruments, Bagpipes
Audience:	Bagpipe Enthusiasts
Contact:	pipes-request@sunapee.dartmouth.edu
Details:	Free
User Info:	To subscribe to the list, send an e-mail message requesting a subscription to the URL address below.
	To send a message to the entire list, address it to: pipes@sunapee.dartmouth.edu

mailto:pipes-request@sunapee.dartmouth.edu

Balloon Art

Balloon Sculpting

This list is for the discussion of balloon sculpting. Anyone interested in balloon art is welcome to join. New sculpture designs and suggestions for improving old ones are exchanged. Other topics discussed include entertaining with balloons, health issues, various types of balloons, and book reviews.

Keywords:	Balloon Art
Audience:	Balloon Artists, Balloonists
Contact:	Larry Moss balloon-request@ent.rochester.edu
Details:	Free
User Info:	To subscribe to the list, send an e-mail message requesting a subscription to the URL address below.
	To send a message to the entire list, address it to: balloon@ent.rochester.edu

mailto:balloon-request@ent.rochester.edu

Ballooning

Balloon

This is a list for balloonists of any sort. Discussion covers all types of balloons including hot air, gas, commercial, or sport, and just about anything related to ballooning.

Keywords:	Ballooning, Hot Air Balloons
Audience:	Balloonists
Contact:	Phil Herbert balloon-request@lut.ac.uk
User Info:	To subscribe to the list, send an e-mail message requesting a subscription to the URL address below.
	To send a message to the entire list, address it to: balloon@lut.ac.uk

mailto:balloon-request@lut.ac.uk

Ballroom Dancing

Ballroom

Discussion of any aspect of ballroom dancing, including places to dance, special events, clubs, ballroom dance music, dances, and steps.

Keywords:	Ballroom Dancing, Dancing
Audience:	Ballroom Dancers
Contact:	Shahrukh Merchant ballroom-request@athena.mit.edu
Details:	Free
User Info:	To subscribe to the list, send an e-mail message requesting a subscription to the URL address below.
	To send a message to the entire list, address it to: ballroom@athena.mit.edu

mailto:ballroom-request@athena.mit.edu

Baltic Republics

Balt-L

A forum devoted to communications to and about the Baltic Republics of Lithuania, Latvia, and Estonia.

Keywords:	Lithuania, Latvia, Estonia, Baltic Republics
Audience:	Researchers, Baltic Nationals
Contact:	Jean-Michel Thizy jmyhg@uottawa.edu
Details:	Free
User Info:	To subscribe to the list, send an e-mail message to the URL address below, consisting of a single line reading: SUB balt-l YourFirstName YourLastName

mailto:listserv@ubvm.cc.buffalo.edu

Mideur-l ★

A list containing the history, culture, politics, and current affairs of those countries lying between the Mediterranean/Adriatic and the Baltic Seas, and between the German/Austrian borders and the former Soviet Union.

Keywords: Soviet Union, Baltic Republics, Eastern Europe, News
Audience: Political Scientists, Researchers, Historians, General Public
Contact: Jan George Frajkor
mideur-1@ubvm.cc.buffalo.edu
Details: Free
User Info: To subscribe to the list, send an e-mail message to the URL address below consisting of a single line reading:

SUB mideur-l YourFirstName YourLastName

To send a message to the entire list, address it to: mideur-1@ubvm.cc.buffalo.edu

`mailto:listserv@ubvm.cc.buffalo.edu`

Balzac (Honore de)

University of Chicago Library ★★★

The library's holdings are large and wide-ranging and contain significant collections in many fields.

Keywords: English Bibles, Lincoln (Abraham), Kentucky & Ohio River Valley (History of), Balzac (Honore de), American Drama, Cromwell (Oliver), Goethe, Judaica, Italy, Chaucer (Geoffrey), Wells (Ida, Personal Papers of), Douglas (Stephen A.), Italy, Literature (Children's)
Audience: General Public, Researchers, Librarians, Document Delivery Professionals
Details: Free
Expect: ENTER CLASS, Send: LIB48 3; Expect: CONNECTED, Send: RETURN

`telnet://olorin.uchicago.edu`

Banking

American Banker Full Text

This database corresponds to the authoritative print publication American Banker.

Keywords: Banking, International Finance, International Trade
Sponsor: American Banker-Bond Buyer, New York, NY, USA
Audience: Financial Analysts, Bankers
Profile: Specific coverage is given to local, regional, and international financial services, technology applications, legal commentary and court actions, international trade, government regulations, Washington events, marketing of financial services, general economic overviews, personnel issues, and profiles and movements of industry personnel. Statistical rankings of all types of financial institutions (from thrifts to commercial banks, US and worldwide) are included beginning with the October 1987 editions. Other special features include quarterly bank earnings, results of American Banker surveys, and the complete text of speeches and articles by the industry professionals that are unavailable in the printed paper.
Contact: Dialog in the US at (800) 334-2564; Dialog internationally at country-specific locations.
Details: Costs
User Info: To subscribe, contact Dialog directly.

`telnet://dialog.com`

Banking News Library

The Banking News library provides you with specific banking industry sources. More than 40 full-text documents and selected full-text sources that focus on the banking related news and issues.

Keywords: Banking, Financial News, Regulation
Audience: Journalists, Banking Industry Analysts
Profile: This library contains news, Investext Industry Reports, and legal/regulatory information. Also included in an abstract file is the Financial Industry Information Service (FINIS). The S&L file includes documents from newspapers and magazines which are specific to the S&L crisis.
Contact: Mead New Sales Group at (800) 227-4908 or (513) 859-5398 inside the US, or (513) 865-7981 for all inquiries outside the US.
User Info: To subscribe, contact Mead directly.
Notes: To examine the Nexis user guide, you can access it at the ftp site of the University of Texas at Austin at the URL address: ftp://ftp.cc.utexas.edu

The files are in: /pub/ref-services/LEXIS

`telnet://nex.meaddata.com`

`http://www.meaddata.com`

Bankruptcy

BKRTCY (Bankruptcy Library) ★★★★

The Federal Bankruptcy library is a comprehensive collection of primary and secondary legal research materials pertaining to bankruptcy issues.

Keywords: Law, Filings, Bankruptcy
Audience: Lawyers, Bankers
Profile: The Federal Bankruptcy library is a comprehensive collection of primary and secondary legal research materials that includes case law, rules, statutory and regulatory materials, legal publications, accounting literature, and other resources pertaining to bankruptcy issues.
Contact: New Sales Group at (800) 227-4908 or (513) 859-5398 inside the US, or (513) 865-7981 for all inquires outside the US.
User Info: To subscribe, contact Mead directly.

To examine the Lexis user guide, you can access it at the ftp site of the University of Texas at Austin at the URL address: ftp://ftp.cc.utexas.edu

The files are in: /pub/ref-services/LEXIS

`telnet://nex.meaddata.com`

`http://www.meaddata.com`

Barron's Guide to Accessing On-Line Bibliographic Databases

Barron's Guide to Accessing On-Line Bibliographic Databases

A comprehensive listing of publicly-accessible online libraries, including login instructions for each site.

Keywords: Libraries, Databases
Sponsor: University of North Texas
Audience: Researchers, Library Users, Librarians
Contact: Billy Barron
billy@unt.edu

`gopher://alf.zfn.uni-bremen.de/Allgemeine`

Base de Dados Tropical (BDT)

Base de Dados Tropical (BDT)

Base de Dados Tropical (Tropical Data Base) is a collection of information related to biodiversity and biotechnology.

Keywords: Biodiversity, Biotechnology, Brazil
Sponsor: Fundacao Tropical de Pesquisas e Tecnologia "Andre Tosello", Campinas, SP, Brazil
Audience: Biotechnologists, Scientists, Researchers
Contact: manager@bdt.ftpt.br
Details: Free

`gopher://bdt.ftpt.br`

Base-Jumping

Base-Jumping

An open discussion of fixed-object skydiving. Topics include equipment, sites, packing techniques, and related publications.

Keywords:	Skydiving, Sports
Audience:	Skydivers
Contact:	base-request@lunatix.lex.ky.us
Details:	Free
User Info:	To subscribe to the list, send an e-mail message requesting a subscription to the URL address below.
	To send a message to the entire list, address it to: base@lunatix.lex.ky.us
Notes:	Membership is open to anyone who has made at least one base jump or skydive.

`mailto:base-request@lunatix.lex.ky.us`

Baseball

Minors

Issues affecting minor league baseball, including new stadium standards, minor league franchise status and changes, road trips and groups, schedules, team and league status, players and teams to watch, and collectibles.

Keywords:	Baseball, Minor League
Audience:	Minor League Baseball Fans
Details:	Free
User Info:	To subscribe to the list, send an e-mail message requesting subscription to the URL address below.

`mailto:minors-request@medrant.apple.com`

Professional Sports Schedules

Sports schedules for major professional sports.

Keywords:	Sports, Baseball, Hockey, Football, Basketball
Sponsor:	Colorado University, Boulder, CO
Audience:	Sports Fans, Football Fans, Hockey Fans, Baseball Enthusiasts, Basketball Enthusiasts
Profile:	The Colorado University gopher maintains an interactive online database of schedules for all major US professional sports teams (NBA, NFL, NHL, NBA). The database is indexed by both team name and dates of games, and can be searched accordingly.
Contact:	gopher@gopher.colorado.edu
Details:	Free

`gopher://gopher.colorado.edu/11/professional/sports/schedules`

rec.sport.baseball

A Usenet newsgroup providing information and discussion about professional baseball.

Keywords:	Baseball, Sports
Audience:	Baseball Fans, Sports Fans
User Info:	To subscribe to this Usenet newsgroup, you need access to a newsreader.

`news:rec.sport.baseball`

Basketball

Professional Sports Schedules

Sports schedules for major professional sports.

Keywords:	Sports, Baseball, Hockey, Football, Basketball
Sponsor:	Colorado University, Boulder, CO
Audience:	Sports Fans, Football Fans, Hockey Fans, Baseball Enthusiasts, Basketball Enthusiasts
Profile:	The Colorado University gopher maintains an interactive online database of schedules for all major US professional sports teams (NBA, NFL, NHL, NBA). The database is indexed by both team name and dates of games, and can be searched accordingly.
Contact:	gopher@gopher.colorado.edu
Details:	Free

`gopher://gopher.colorado.edu/11/professional/sports/schedules`

rec.sport.basketball.college

A Usenet newsgroup providing information and discussion about college basketball.

Keywords:	Basketball, College, Sports
Audience:	Basketball Fans, Sport Fans
User Info:	To subscribe to this Usenet newsgroup, you need access to a newsreader.

`news:rec.sport.basketball.college`

rec.sport.basketball.pro

A Usenet newsgroup providing information and discussion about professional basketball.

Keywords:	Basketball, Sports
Audience:	Basketball Fans, Sports Fans
User Info:	To subscribe to this Usenet newsgroup, you need access to a newsreader.

`news:rec.sport.basketball.pro`

Basque Studies

University of Nevada at Reno Library

The library's holdings are large and wide-ranging and contain significant collections in many fields.

Keywords:	Basque Studies, Nevada, UN Army Map Service, Patents
Audience:	General Public, Researchers, Librarians, Document Delivery Professionals
Details:	Free
	Expect: login, Send: wolfpac

`telnet://wolfpac.lib.unr.edu`

Bass

Bass

The purpose of this list is to discuss the reproduction and enjoyment of deep bass, primarily in consumer audio equipment.

Keywords:	Audio Reproduction
Audience:	Stereo Enthusiasts, General Public
Contact:	bass-request@gsbcs.uchicago.edu
Details:	Free
User Info:	To subscribe to the list, send an e-mail message requesting a subscription to the URL address below.
	To send a message to the entire list, address it to: bass@gsbcs.uchicago.edu
Notes:	Ownership of a subwoofer is not required—membership is open to anyone with an interest in deep bass reproduction.

`mailto:bass-request@gsbcs.uchicago.edu`

Bbones

Bbones

A list discussing the construction of e-mail backbones for organizations and campuses.

Keywords:	E-mail, Networking
Audience:	Internet Surfers
Contact:	mail-bbones-request@yorku.ca
Details:	Free
User Info:	To subscribe to the list, send an e-mail message requesting a subscription to the URL address below.
	To send a message to the entire list, address it to: mail-bbones@yorku.ca

`mailto:mail-bbones-request@yorku.ca`

BBS

alt.bbs ★

A Usenet newsgroup providing information and discussion about computer BBS systems and software.

Keywords: BBS, Cyberspace, Computers
Audience: BBS Users
User Info: To subscribe to this Usenet newsgroup, you need access to a newsreader.

`news:alt.bbs`

Government-Sponsored Electronic Bulletin Boards ★★★★

A list of U.S. Government-sponsored electronic bulletin boards (BBSs) for various agencies and departments.

Keywords: Government (US Federal), Law (US Federal), BBS
Sponsor: United States Government
Audience: General Public, Researchers
Profile: EBBs provide a wide and ever-changing assortment of government information, including text files, statistics, software, and graphics. Some of the information also is available in printed form. Depository librarians may find government-sponsored EBBs useful in answering reference questions and in obtaining electronic versions of government publications, regardless of whether those publications were distributed to depository libraries.
Details: Free

`gopher://gopher.ncsu.edu`

bcdv

bcdv ★

A mailing list to discuss issues related to bicycling in the greater Philadelphia metropolitan region, and the advocacy work of the Bicycle Coalition of the Delaware Valley (BCDV), including current efforts to ensure that an appropriate amount of Federal ISTEA and Congestion Mitigation and Air Quality grants are spent on removing barriers to bicycling.

Keywords: Bicycling
Audience: Bicyclists
Contact: bike-request@bcdv.drexel.edu
Details: Free
User Info: To subscribe to the list, send an e-mail message requesting a subscription to the URL address below.
To send a message to the entire list, address it to: bike@bcdv.drexel.edu

`mailto:bike-request@bcdv.drexel.edu`

Bears

Bears ★

A mailing list in digest format for gay and bisexual men who are bears themselves and for those who enjoy the company of bears. The definition of "bears" encompasses men who are variously cuddly, furry, perhaps stocky, or bearded. Mail.bears is designed to be a forum to bring together folks with similar interests for conversation, friendship, and sharing of experiences.

Keywords: Gays, Bisexuality
Audience: Gays, Bisexuals
Contact: Steve Dyer, Brian Gollum
bears-request@spdcc.COM
Details: Free
User Info: To subscribe to the list, send an e-mail message requesting a subscription to the URL address below.
To send a message to the entire list, address it to: bears@spdcc.COM

`mailto:bears-request@spdcc.COM`

Beer

alt.beer ★

A Usenet newsgroup providing information and discussion about beer and ale.

Keywords: Beer
Audience: Brewers, Beer Enthusiasts
User Info: To subscribe to this Usenet newsgroup, you need access to a newsreader.

`news:alt.beer`

rec.crafts.brewing ★

A Usenet newsgroup providing information and discussion about making beers and meads.

Keywords: Beer, Crafts
Audience: Beer Brewers
User Info: To subscribe to this Usenet newsgroup, you need access to a newsreader.

`news:rec.crafts.brewing`

Behavior

PsycINFO

PsycINFO is a leading research database providing bibliographic access to the international literature in psychology, as well as the related behavioral and social sciences.

Keywords: Psychology, Psychiatry, Behavioral Science
Sponsor: American Psychological Association
Audience: Social workers, Psychologists, Psychiatrists, Librarians, Students
Contact: CDP Technologies Sales Department (800) 950-2035, extension 400
User Info: To subscribe, contact CDP Technologies directly

`telnet:\\cdplus@cdplus.com`

Behavioral Science

Eastern Washington University Library ★★

The library's holdings are large and wide-ranging and contain significant collections in many fields.

Keywords: Education, Music, Social Science, Behavioral Science
Audience: Researchers, Students, General Public
Details: Free
Expect: Login; Send: Lib

`telnet:// wsduvm12.csc.wsu.edu`

University of Texas at Austin Library ★★

The library's holdings are large and wide-ranging and contain significant collections in many fields.

Keywords: Music, Natural Science, Nursing, Science Technology, Behavioral Science, Social Work, Computer Science, Engineering, Latin American Studies, Middle Eastern Studies
Audience: Researchers, Students, General Public
Details: Free
Expect: Blank Screen, Send: Return; Expect: Go, Send: Return; Expect: Enter Terminal Type, Send: vt100
Notes: Some databases are restricted to UT Austin users only.

`telnet://utcat.utexas.edu`

Washington University Library ★★

The library's holdings are large and wide-ranging and contain significant collections in many fields.

Keywords: Technology, Literature (German), Social Science, Behavioral Science
Audience: Researchers, Students, General Public
Contact: services@wugate.wustl.edu
Details: Free
Expect: Login; Send: Services

`telnet://wugate.wustl.edu`

Bel Canto

Bel Canto

A mailing list for the discussion of the music, lyrics, and shows of the group Bel Canto, and solo projects of group members, or even the work of related artists if appropriate.

Keywords: Musical Groups, Music
Audience: Music Enthusiasts
Contact: dewy-fields-request@ifi.uio.no
Details: Free
User Info: To subscribe to the list, send an e-mail message requesting a subscription to the URL address below.

To send a message to the entire list, address it to: dewy-fields@ifi.uio.no

mailto:dewy-fields-request@ifi.uio.no

Belgium

BFU (Brussels Free Universities) ★★★

The gopher server of the Brussels Free Universities VUB /ULB is the national entry point for EMBnet in Belgium and provides links to university library systems and EMBnet databases.

Keywords: Computing, EMBnet, Belgium, Europe
Audience: Scientists, Biologists, Biotechnologists
Contact: support@vub.ac.be
Details: Free

gopher://gopher.vub.ac.be

Beloved

Beloved

A mailing list for the discussion of the Beloved, an English pop group with strong ambient and techno influences.

Keywords: Musical Groups, Music
Audience: Music Enthusiasts
Contact: Jyrki Sarkkinen
beloved-request@phoenix.oulu.fi
Details: Free
User Info: To subscribe to the list, send an e-mail message requesting a subscription to the URL address below.

To send a message to the entire list, address it to: beloved@phoenix.oulu.fi

mailto:beloved-request@phoenix.oulu.fi

Berlin Wall

9nov89-l

A discussion list relating to recent events in the former German Democratic Republic.

Keywords: German Democratic Republic, Germany, Berlin Wall
Audience: Researchers, Political Scientists
Contact: Axel Mahler
Contact: axel@avalanche.cs.tu.berlin.de
User Info: To subscribe to the list, send an e-mail message to the URL address shown below, consisting of a single line reading:

SUB 9nov89-l YourFirstName YourLastName

To send a message to the entire list, address it to: 9nov89-1@tubvm.cs.tu.berlin.de

mailto:listserv@tubvm.cs.tu-berlin.de

Berne Convention Implementation Act of 1988

Berne Convention Implementation Act of 1988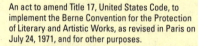

An act to amend Title 17, United States Code, to implement the Berne Convention for the Protection of Literary and Artistic Works, as revised in Paris on July 24, 1971, and for other purposes.

Keywords: Legislation (US), Government (US), Politics (US), Copyright
Audience: Lawyers, Students, Politicians, Journalists
Details: Free

gopher://wiretap.spies.com/00/Gov/Copyright/US.Berne.Convention.txt

Best of the Web '94

Best of the Web '94

This web site highlights those places that were judged as the best sites (based on the criteria of quality, versatility, and power) on the World Wide Web.

Keywords: Internet, WWW
Audience: Internet Surfers
Contact: Brandon Plewe
plewe@acsu.buffalo.edu
Details: Free

http://wings.buffalo.edu/contest

Best-of-AusRave (Australian Raves)

Best-of-AusRave (Australian Raves)

A regional rave-related mailing list covering the Australian continent, for people who want Australian rave information without the side discussions and social chatter from the regular list.

Keywords: Music, Raves, Australia
Audience: Ravers (Australian)
Contact: Simon Rumble
best-of-ausrave-request@lsupoz.apana.org.au
Details: Free
User Info: To subscribe to the list, send an e-mail message to the URL address below, consisting of a single line reading:

SUB ausrave YourFirstName YourLastName

To send a message to the entire list, address it to: best-of-ausrave@lsupoz.apana.org.au

mailto:best-of-ausrave-request@lsupoz.apana.org.au

BETA

BETA

A discussion forum for BETA users. BETA is a modern object-oriented programming language.

Keywords: Programming Languages, Object-Oriented Programming, BETA
Audience: Programmers
Contact: Elmer Soerensen Sandvad
usergroup-request@mjolner.dk
Details: Free
User Info: To subscribe to the list, send an e-mail message requesting a subscription to the URL address below.

To send a message to the entire list, address it to: usergroup@mjolner.dk

mailto:usergroup-request@mjolner.dk

Bethany Christian Services

Bethany Christian Services

A major directory on adoption, providing access to a broad range of related resources (library catalogs, databases, and servers) throughout the Internet.

Keywords: Adoption, Christianity, Pregnancy

Sponsor:	Bethany Christian Services, Grand Rapids, Michigan, USA
Audience:	Pregnant Women
Profile:	The gopher server of Bethany, a pro-life, pro-family agency reaches out to women with unplanned pregnancies and adoptive couples. It contains a large amount of information about national and international adoption, the adoption process, African-American adoptions, and adoption of children with special needs. Also contains information for pregnant women, such as birth father rights and responsibilities, pregnancy counseling, and so on.
Contact:	gophermaster@bethany.org

`gopher://gopher.bethany.org/11`

BiAct-L

BiAct-L

A discussion list for bisexual activists.

Keywords:	Bisexuality, Activism
Audience:	Bisexual Activists
Contact:	Elaine Brennan EL406010@brownvm.brown.edu
Details:	Free
User Info:	To subscribe to the list, send an e-mail message requesting a subscription to the URL address below. Directions for posting to the list will be sent to you when you are added to the list.

`mailto:EL406010@brownvm.brown.edu`

Bible

alt.christnet

This Usenet newsgroup is a gathering place for Christian ministers and users.

Keywords:	Religion, Christianity, Bible, Divinity
Audience:	Christians, Ministers
User Info:	To subscribe to this Usenet newsgroup, you need access to a newsreader.

`news:alt.christnet`

alt.christnet.bible

A Usenet newsgroup providing information and discussion about bible discussion and research.

Keywords:	Bible, Christianity, Religion, Divinity
Audience:	Biblical Scholars, Bible Readers
User Info:	To subscribe to this Usenet newsgroup, you need access to a newsreader.

`news:alt.christnet.bible`

Bible (King James Version)

The Bible (King James Version) includes the complete text of the modern Thomas Nelson revision of the 1769 edition of the King James version of the Bible.

Keywords:	Bible, Religion, Christianity
Sponsor:	Thomas Nelson Publishers, Nashville, TN, USA
Audience:	Christians, Theologians, Historians, Moralists
Profile:	The King James version originated from translations ordered by King James of England in 1604 at the Hampton Court Conference. Both the Old and New Testaments are included in this version. Records in the database represent both chapters and verses.
Contact:	Dialog in the US at (800) 334-2564, Dialog internationally at country specific locations.
Details:	Costs
User Info:	To subscribe, contact Dialog directly.

`telnet://dialog.com`

Bibles

Johns Hopkins University Library

The library's holdings are large and wide-ranging and contain significant collections in many fields.

Keywords:	Literature (English), Economics, Classics, Drama (German), Slavery, Trade Unions, Incunabula, Bibles, Diseases (History of), Nursing (History of), Abolitionism
Audience:	General Public, Researchers, Librarians, Document Delivery Professionals
Details:	Free

`telnet://jhuvm.hcf.jhu.edu`

University of Pennsylvania PENNINFO Library

The library's holdings are large and wide-ranging and contain significant collections in many fields.

Keywords:	Church History, Spanish Inquisition, Witchcraft, Shakespeare (William), Bibles, Aristotle (Texts of), Fiction, Whitman (Walt), French Revolution, Drama (French), Literature (English), Literature (Spanish)
Audience:	Researchers, Students, General Public
Contact:	Al DSouza penninfo-admin@dccs.upenn.edu

`dsouza@dccs.upenn.edu`

Details:	Free
	Expect: Login; Send: Public

`telnet://penninfo.upenn.edu`

Bibliographies

Bibliographies of US Senate Hearings

The US Senate produces a series of committee hearings, prints, and publications as part of the legislative process. The Documents department at North Carolina State University contains files for the 99th through 103rd Congresses, which also can be searched through a WAIS searchable database.

Keywords:	Senate (US), Politics (US), Legislation (US), Bibliographies, Government (US)
Audience:	General Public, Journalists, Students, Politicians, US Citizens
Contact:	Jack McGeachy Jack_McGeachy@ncsu.edu
Details:	Free

`gopher://dewey.lib.ncsu.edu/11/library/disciplines/government/senate`

Music Library Association Mailing List

This is a mail distribution service for the Music Library Association (MLA).

Keywords:	Music Library, Bibliographies
Sponsor:	Indiana University
Audience:	Music Librarians
Profile:	The services provided for the MLA include mail distribution, mail archiving, and file/document serving. This is a list server implementation, and the list managers intend that these services be used for various activities of the MLA that can benefit by wide-scale distribution, such as announcements of deadlines for NOTES and the MLA Newsletter, news items, general inquiries about MLA activities, and so on.
Contact:	Ralph Papkhian Papakhi@iubvm.ucs.Indiana.edu
Details:	Free
User Info:	To subscribe to the list, send an e-mail message to the URL address below, consisting of a single line reading:
	SUB mla-u YourFirstName YourLastName

`mailto:listserv@iubvm.ucs.Indiana.edu`

Style Sheets from the Online Writers' Workshop.

This gopher provides information and examples on how to write bibliographies using three formats: MLA (Modern Language Association), Old-MLA, and APA (American Psychological Association).

Keywords:	Bibliographies, Writing, Lexicology
Sponsor:	University of Illinois at Urbana-Champaign

Bicycling

bcdv

A mailing list to discuss issues related to bicycling in the greater Philadelphia metropolitan region, and the advocacy work of the Bicycle Coalition of the Delaware Valley (BCDV), including current efforts to ensure that an appropriate amount of Federal ISTEA and Congestion Mitigation and Air Quality grants are spent on removing barriers to bicycling.

Keywords: Bicycling
Audience: Bicycling Enthusiasts
Contact: bike-request@bcdv.drexel.edu
Details: Free
User Info: To subscribe to the list, send an e-mail message requesting a subscription to the URL address below.

To send a message to the entire list, address it to: bike@bcdv.drexel.edu

`mailto:bike-request@bcdv.drexel.edu`

Bikecommute

This list's discussion centers around bicycle transportation and the steps necessary for improved bicycling conditions in (sub)urban areas. Participants include local members (Silicon Valley) as well as a few national organizations (League of American Wheelmen, Bikecentennial, and the Bicycle Federation of America).

Keywords: Bicycling
Audience: Bicyclists
Contact: bikecommute-request@bike2work.eng.sun.com
Details: Free
User Info: To subscribe to the list, send an e-mail message requesting a subscription to the URL address below.

To send a message to the entire list, address it to: bikecommute@bike2work.eng.sun.com

`mailto:bikecommute-request@bike2work.eng.sun.com`

Bikepeople

Bicycle activists, primarily from Santa Cruz County, CA, discuss bicycle issues on local, state, and national levels. Public hearings and government meetings are announced and reported on, and messages occasionally are cross-posted with the bikecommute mailing list.

Keywords: Bicycling
Audience: Activists, Bicyclists
Contact: Kevin Karplus
karplus@ce.ucsc.edu
Details: Free
User Info: To subscribe, send an e-mail message requesting a subscription to the URL address below.

`mailto:karplus@ce.ucsc.edu`

Biking

Information on biking events and maintenance, including an FAQ from rec.bicycles.

Keywords: Sports, Bicycling, Fitness
Audience: Bicyclists, Fitness Enthusiasts
Contact: Joern Yngve Dahl-Stamnes
dahls@fysel.unit.no
Details: Free

`ftp://ugle.unit.no/local/biking`

Biking in Canada

A repository of information for bicyclists, including utility programs, events, FAQs, and how-to guides; some with Canadian-specific details.

Keywords: Sports, Bicycling, Canada
Sponsor: Habitat Ecology Division at the Bedford Institute of Oceanography
Audience: Cyclists, Fitness Enthusiasts
Contact: sysop@biome.bio.ns.ca
Details: Free

`gopher://gopher.biome.bio.dfo.ca/pub/biking`

ebikes

New York City Bicycle discussion list.

Keywords: Bicycling, New York
Audience: Bicyclists
Contact: Danny Lieberman
ebikes-request@panix.com
Details: Free
User Info: To subscribe to the list, send an e-mail message requesting a subscription to the URL address below.

To send a message to the entire list, address it to: ebikes-request@panix.com

`mailto:ebikes-request@panix.com`

Velo News Experimental Tour de France Web Page

This web site provides background information on the Tour de France, including press coverage from this year's race.

Keywords: Bicycling, Sports
Sponsor: Velo News
Audience: Bicyclists, Sports Fans
Contact: VeloNews@aol.com

`http://cob.fsu.edu/velonews/`

World Cycling Championship 1994

This web site contains information about events surrounding the 1994 World Cycling Championship.

Keywords: Bicycling
Audience: Bicyclists, Sports Fans

`http://www-worldbike.iunet.it/`

BiFem-L

BiFem-L

A mailing list for bisexual women and bi-friendly women.

Keywords: Bisexuality
Audience: Bisexual Women
Contact: Elaine Brennan
listserv@brownvm.brown.edu
Details: Free
User Info: To subscribe, send an e-mail message requesting a subscription to the URL address below, consisting of a single line reading:

SUB BiFem-L YourFirstName YourLastName

To send a message to the entire list, address it to: BiFem-L@brownvm.brown.edu

`mailto:listserv@brownvm.brown.edu`

Big Dummy's Guide

Big Dummy's Guide

A comprehensive guide to the Internet for people with little or no experience with network communications.

Keywords: Internet, Internet Guides
Sponsor: Electronic Frontier Foundation
Audience: Internet Surfers
Contact: Shari Steele
ssteele@eff.org
Details: Free
Notes: Big Dummy's Guide to the Internet is available in: /pub/Net_info/Big_Dummy, in several versions. The basic text version is bigdummy.txt

`ftp://ftp.eff.org`

Big-DB

Big-DB

Discussions pertaining to large databases (generally greater than 1 million records) and large database management systems such as IMS, DB2, and CCA's Model/204.

Keywords:	Databases, Database Management
Audience:	Database Users, Database Managers
Contact:	Fareed Asad-Harooni big-DB@midway.uchicago.edu
Details:	Free
User Info:	To subscribe to the list, send an e-mail message requesting a subscription to the URL address below.

mailto:big-DB@midway.uchicago.edu

Bilingual Education Network

Bilingual Education Network

This gopher site contains bilingual and bicultural, ESL (English as a Second Language), and Foreign Language resources and curriculum guidelines.

Keywords:	ESL (English as a Second Language), Education (Bilingual)
Sponsor:	California Department of Education, California, USA
Audience:	Educators, Administrators, Parents

gopher://goldmine.cde.ca.gov

Biochemistry

Biosis Previews

The database encompasses the entire field of life sciences and covers original research reports and reviews in biological and biomedical areas. This includes field, laboratory, clinical, experimental and theoretical work. The traditional areas of biology, including botany, zoology, and microbiology are covered, as well as the related fields such as plant and animal science, agriculture, pharmacology, and ecology.

Keywords:	Biology, Botany, Zoology, Microbiology, Plant Science, Animal Science, Agriculture, Pharmacology, Ecology, Biochemistry, Biophysics, Bioengineering
Sponsor:	Biosis
Audience:	Librarians, Researchers, Students, Biologists, Botanists, Zoologists, Scientists, Taxonomists
Contact:	CDP Technologies Sales Department (800)950-2035, extension 400.
User Info:	To subscribe, contact CDP Technologies directly.

telnet://cdplus@cdplus.com

University of Texas Health Science Center at Tyler Library

The library's holdings are large and wide-ranging and contain significant collections in many fields.

Keywords:	Biochemistry, Cardiopulmonary Medicine, Cell Biology, Family Practice, Molecular Biology
Audience:	Researchers, Students, General Public
Details:	Free Expect: Username Prompt, Send: LIS

telnet://athena.uthscsa.edu

Biodiversity

Base de Dados Tropical (BDT)

Base de Dados Tropical (Tropical Data Base) is a collection of information related to biodiversity and biotechnology.

Keywords:	Biodiversity, Biotechnology, Brazil
Sponsor:	Fundacao Tropical de Pesquisas e Tecnologia "Andre Tosello," Campinas, SP, Brazil
Audience:	Biotechnologists, Scientists, Researchers
Contact:	manager@bdt.ftpt.br
Details:	Free

gopher://bdt.ftpt.br

Biodiv-L

This list discusses technical opportunities, administrative and economic issues, and practical limitations and scientific goals, leading to recommendations for the establishment of a biodiversity network. Individual contributions are requested, not only as to network capabilities but also as to existing databases of interest to biodiversity.

Keywords:	Biodiversity
Audience:	Ecologists
Contact:	listserv@bdt.ftpt.ansp.br
Details:	Free
User Info:	To subscribe to the list, send an e-mail message to the URL address below, consisting of a single line reading: SUB biodiv-l YourFirstName YourLastName
	To send a message to the entire list, address it to: biodiv-l@bdt.ftpt.ansp.br
Notes:	For those interested in receiving a summary of all contributions that have been sent to this list, please send the following message get biodiv-l readme.first to the URL address shown below.

mailto:listserv@bdt.ftpt.ansp.br

Bioengineering

Biosis Previews

The database encompasses the entire field of life sciences and covers original research reports and reviews in biological and biomedical areas. This includes field, laboratory, clinical, experimental and theoretical work. The traditional areas of biology, including botany, zoology, and microbiology are covered, as well as the related fields such as plant and animal science, agriculture, pharmacology, and ecology.

Keywords:	Biology, Botany, Zoology, Microbiology, Plant Science, Animal Science, Agriculture, Pharmacology, Ecology, Biochemistry, Biophysics, Bioengineering
Sponsor:	Biosis
Audience:	Librarians, Researchers, Students, Biologists, Botanists, Zoologists, Scientists, Taxonomists
Contact:	CDP Technologies Sales Department (800) 950-2035, ext. 400.
User Info:	To subscribe, contact CDP Technologies directly.

telnet://cdplus@cdplus.com

Biographies

Bowker Biographical Directory

This is a collection of biographical directories that correspond to certain Bowker print publications.

Keywords:	Biographies
Sponsor:	R.R. Bowker, a Reed Reference Publishing Company, a division of Reed Publishing (US) Inc., New Providence, NJ, US
Audience:	General Public, Writers, Researchers
Profile:	The database corresponds to the Bowker print publications as follows: American Men and Women of Science, covering over 122,500 leading US and Canadian scientists and engineers in the physical, biological, and related sciences; Who's Who in American Art, covering some 7,000 North American artists, critics, curators, administrators, librarians, historians, collectors, and dealers; and Who's Who in American Politics, covering over 25,400 American political decision-makers at all levels from federal to local government.

Contact: Dialog in the US at (800) 334-2564, Dialog internationally at country specific locations.
Details: Costs
User Info: To subscribe, contact Dialog directly.

telnet://dialog.com

SPORTS (Sports News)

The Sports News (SPORTS) library contains a variety of sports-related news and information.

Keywords: News, Analysis, Sports, Biographies
Audience: Sports Enthusiasts, Journalists
Profile: The SPORTS library is a specialized news library that contains the full text of *Sports Illustrated* and *The Sporting News* and selected sports-related stories from many major US newspapers and wire services. Biographical information and 1992 Olympic facts also are part of this library.
Contact: Mead New Sales Group at (800) 227-4908 or (513) 859-5398 inside the US, or (513) 865-7981 for all inquiries outside the US.
User Info: To subscribe, contact Mead directly.
To examine the Nexis user guide, you can access it at the ftp site of the University of Texas at Austin at the URL address: ftp://ftp.cc.utexas.edu
The files are in: /pub/ref-services/LEXIS

telnet://nex.meaddata.com

http://www.meaddata.com

Supreme Court Judges

Biographies from the sitting Justices, and a few former Justices.

Keywords: Judiciary, Supreme Court, Judges, Biographies
Audience: General Public, Lawyers, Judges, Journalists
Details: Free

gopher://info.umd.edu

Bioinformatics

Bioinformatics

This gopher server provides data and software related to bioinformatics, including public-domain software for biology and mirror storage for the main databases of the Human Genome Project and Molecular Biology.

Keywords: Bioinformatics, Biology, Molecular Biology
Sponsor: Weizmann Institute of Science, Israel
Audience: Scientists, Biologists

Contact: lsprilus@weizmann.weizmann.ac.il
Details: Free

gopher://bioinformatics.weizmann.ac.il

http://bioinformatics.weizman.act.il

Marshall University School of Medicine (MUSOM) RuralNet Gopher

A gopher server dedicated to the improvement of rural health care.

Keywords: Rural Development, Health Care, Medical Treatment, Bioinformatics
Sponsor: Marshall University School of Medicine
Audience: Health Care Professionals, Medical Students, Rural Residents
Profile: A collection of health care resources, with particular emphasis on rural health care. Includes listings of clinical resources by subject area, information on state and federal rural health care initiatives, and links to local and national health and education services.
Contact: Mike McCarthy, Andy Jarrell
mmccarth@muvms6.wvnet.edu, jarrell@musom01.mu.wvnet.edu

gopher://ruralnet.mu.wvnet.edu

Virus Gopher Server

This server contains names of virus families/groups and members now available online from the Australian National University's bioinformatics facility.

Keywords: Viruses, Bioinformatics, Biology
Sponsor: Research School of Biological Research, Australian National University, Canberra, Australia
Audience: Researchers, Biologists, Health Professionals
Details: Free

gopher://life.anu.edu.au

Biological Research

CVNet (Color and Vision Network)

The network provides a means of communications for scientists working in biological color and vision research. Members' e-mail addresses are maintained and sent to others in the network. CVNet distributes notices of jobs, meetings, and some other special announcements to all registrants. Members can post bulletins, announcements, and so on.

Keywords: Optics, Biological Research, Psychology
Sponsor: York University, North York, Ontario, Canada

Audience: Psychologists, Color/Vision Researchers
Contact: Peter K. Kaiser
cvnet@vm1.yorkU.ca
Details: Free
User Info: To subscribe, send an e-mail message requesting a subscription to the URL address below.

mailto:cvnet@vm1.yorkU.ca

Medical and Biological Research in Laboratories Institutions (Israel)

A descriptive listing of medical research and diagnostic laboratories in Israel. This site also has information on medical research being carried out in Israeli universities and hospitals.

Keywords: Medical Research, Biological Research, Israel
Audience: Medical Researchers, Biomedical Researchers, Medical Professionals
Profile: MATIMOP, The Israeli Industry Center for Health Care Research And Development, is a non-profit service organization, founded by an Israeli association of hospitals, universities, and other medical researchers, aiming their activities at promoting cooperation of Israeli entrepreneurs and manufacturers with qualified business firms abroad. This gopher details specific medical and biological research projects in progress in every department of every major Israeli health care institution including universities, The General Federation of Labour, public hospitals, government-municipal hospitals, and government hospitals, as well as medical and biological research in the Israeli laboratories and research institutes.

Contact: rdinfo@matimop.org.il

gopher://gopher.matimop.org.il

Neuron

This is a moderated list (in digest form) that deals with all aspects of neural networks (and any type of network or neuromorphic system). Topics include both connectionist models (artificial neural networks) and biological systems ("wetware").

Keywords: Neural Networks, Biological Research
Audience: Neuroscientists, Neurobiologists
Contact: Peter Marvit
neuron-request@cattell.psych.upenn.edu
Details: Free
User Info: To subscribe to the list, send an e-mail message requesting a subscription to the URL address below.
Notes: Back issues and limited software are available through FTP from cattell.psych.upenn.edu. The Digest is gatewayed to Usenet's comp.ai.neural-nets.

mailto:neuron-request@cattell.psych.upenn.edu

Biology

Archive of Biology Software and Data

The main area of concentration of this archive is molecular biology. It contains software for the Macintosh, MS-DOS, VAX-VMS, and UNIX.

Keywords: Health, Biology, Molecular Biology
Sponsor: Indiana University
Audience: Biologists, Students
Contact: archive@bio.indiana.edu
Details: Free
Notes: It is recommended that the file ARCHIVE.DOC be transferred and read first. This file gives considerable information about and instructions for using the archive.

ftp://ftp.bio.indiana.edu

Bioinformatics

This gopher server provides data and software related to bioinformatics, including public-domain software for biology and mirror storage for the main databases of the Human Genome Project and Molecular Biology.

Keywords: Bioinformatics, Biology, Molecular Biology
Sponsor: Weizmann Institute of Science, Israel
Audience: Scientists, Biologists
Contact: lsprilus@weizmann.weizmann.ac.il
Details: Free

gopher://bioinformatics.weizmann.ac.il

http://bioinformatics.weizman.act.il

Biomedical Computer Laboratory (BCL)

A resource for biomedical computing.

Keywords: Health, Biomedical Research, Biology, Medicine
Sponsor: Washington University School of Medicine
Audience: Medical Researchers, Biologists
Profile: A significant portion of the activities at BCL are supported by the National Center for Research Resources' Biomedical Research Technology Program (BRTP), which promotes the application of advances in computer science and technology, engineering, mathematics, and the physical sciences, to research problems in biology and medicine by supporting the development of advanced research technologies.
Contact: Kenneth W. Clark
info@wubcl.wustl.edu
Details: Free
Notes: login; Send: anonymous
Investigators wishing to explore the possibility of interactions with BCL at Washington University should send e-mail (preferred).

ftp://wubcl.wustl.edu

bionet.molbio.genbank.updates ★

A Usenet newsgroup providing information and discussion about the GenBank Nucleic acid database.

Keywords: Molecular Biology, Biology, Genetics
Audience: Molecular Biologists, Researchers
User Info: To subscribe to this Usenet newsgroup, you need access to a newsreader.

news:bionet.molbio.genbank.updates

bionet.software ★

A Usenet newsgroup providing information and discussion about software for use in biological research.

Keywords: Computers, Biology
Audience: Students, Educators, Biologists
User Info: To subscribe to this Usenet newsgroup, you need access to a newsreader.

news:bionet.software

Biosis Previews

The database encompasses the entire field of life sciences and covers original research reports and reviews in biological and biomedical areas. This includes field, laboratory, clinical, experimental, and theoretical work. The traditional areas of biology, including botany, zoology, and microbiology are covered, as well as the related fields such as plant and animal science, agriculture, pharmacology, and ecology.

Keywords: Biology, Botany, Zoology, Microbiology, Plant Science, Animal Science, Agriculture, Pharmacology, Ecology, Biochemistry, Biophysics, Bioengineering
Sponsor: Biosis
Audience: Librarians, Researchers, Students, Biologists, Botanists, Zoologists, Scientists, Taxonomists
Contact: CDP Technologies Sales Department (800)950-2035, extension 400.
User Info: To subscribe, contact CDP Technologies directly.

telnet://cdplus@cdplus.com

BOING (Bio-Oriented INternet Gophers)

A searchable gopher index, BOING is used to search through the titles of items in bio-gopher space and to access the items returned.

Keywords: Biology, Health, Medicine
Audience: Health Professionals, Biomedical Researchers, Students (college, graduate)
Details: Free

gopher://gopher.gdb.org

CSU Entomology WWW Site

A web site containing online photos of insects, entomology educational programs, and extensive Internet entomology links.

Keywords: Bioscience, Biology, Entomology
Sponsor: Colorado State University, Denver, Colorado, USA
Audience: Students, Researchers, Entomologists
Contact: Lou Bjostad
lbjostad@lamar.colorado.edu

http://www.colostate.edu/Depts/Entomology/ent.html

Drosophila Information Newsletter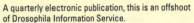

A quarterly electronic publication, this is an offshoot of Drosophila Information Service.

Keywords: Drosophila, Biology, Genetics
Audience: Biologists, Geneticists
Contact: Kathy Matthews
matthewk@ucs.indiana.edu
Details: Free
User Info: To subscribe, send an e-mail message to the address below consisting of a single line reading:

SUB drosophila-information-newsletter YourFirstName Your Last Name

To send a message to the entire list, address it to:

drosophila.information.newsletter@ucs.indiana.edu

mailto:listserv@iubvm.ucs.indiana.edu

EMBnet (European Molecular Biology Network)

A group of European Internet sites that provide computational molecular biology services to both national and international researchers.

Keywords: Biology, Bioscience, Molecular Biology
Sponsor: The EC Funding Program (BRIDGE)
Audience: Biologists, Molecular Biologists, Researchers

Contact: Rodrigo Lopez, Robert Herzog
rodrigol@biotek.uio.no,
rherzog@ulb.ac.be

http://biomaster.uio.no/embnet-www.html

Harvard Biosciences Online Journals

A resource containing selected online journals and periodicals in biology and medicine. Includes peer-reviewed e-journals, journal indexes, and databases.

Keywords: Biology, Bioscience, Molecular Biology
Sponsor: Harvard Biolabs, Harvard University, Cambridge, Massachusetts, USA
Audience: Biologists, Molecular Biologists, Researchers
Contact: Keith Robinson, Steve Brenner
krobinson@nucleus.harvard.edu
s.e.brenner@bioc.cam.ac.uk

http://golgi.harvard.edu/journals.html

Institute for Molecular Virology

A unique virology resource for students, scientists, computer visualization experts, and the general public.

Keywords: Disease, Viruses, Biology
Sponsor: University of Wisconsin-Madison, Madison, Wisconsin, USA
Audience: Virologists, Biologists, Researchers
Contact: Stephen Spencer
sspencer@rhino.bocklabs.wisc.edu

http://www.bocklabs.wisc.edu/Welcome.html

Interactive Frog Dissection Kit

An interactive simulation of the dissection of a computer-generated frog.

Keywords: Biology, Simulation, Interactive Learning
Sponsor: Lawrence Berkeley Laboratory-Whole Frog Project, Berkeley, California, USA
Audience: Students, Educators, Biologists
Contact: David Robertson
dwrobertson@lbl.gov
Notes: Copyrighted (commercial uses require permission)

http://george.1bl.gov/ITG.hm.pg.docs/dissect/info.html

Johns Hopkins Genetic Databases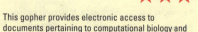

This gopher provides electronic access to documents pertaining to computational biology and a number of different genetic databases.

Keywords: Genetics, Molecular Biology, Medicine, Biology
Sponsor: Johns Hopkins University
Audience: Geneticists, Researchers, Scientists, Molecular Biologists
Profile: The databases accessible from this entry point include GenBank, Swiss-Prot, PDB, PIR, LiMB, TFD, AAtDB, ACEDB, CompoundKB, PROSITE EC Enzyme Database, NRL_3D Protein-Sequence-Structure Database, Eukaryotic Promoter Database (EPD), Cloning Vector Database, Expressed Sequence Tag Database (ESTDB), Online Mendelian Inheritance Man (OMIM), Sequence Analysis Bibliographic Reference Data Bank (Seqanalref), and Database Taxonomy (GenBank, Swiss-Prot). The gopher also provides direct links to other gophers with information relevant to biology.

Contact: Dan Jacobson
danj@mail.gdb.org
Details: Free

gopher://merlot.welch.jhu.edu

McGill University, Montreal Canada, INFOMcGILL Library

The library's holdings are large and wide-ranging and contain significant collections in many fields.

Keywords: Architecture, Entomology, Biology, Science (History of), Medicine (History of), Napolean, Shakespeare (William)
Audience: Researchers, Students, General Public
Contact: Roy Miller
ccrmmus@mcgillm (Bitnet) or
ccrmmus@musicm.mcgill.ca (Internet)
Expect: VM logo; Send: Enter; Expect: prompt; Send: PF3 or type INFO

telnet:// vm1.mcgill.ca

MegaGopher

This is the gopher at the University of Montreal. It supports the software and information requirements for the MegaSequencing project. It also serves as a repository of data for organellar genome and molecular evolution research and acts as the focal point for the GDE (Genetic Data Environment) package.

Keywords: Biology, Canada
Audience: Biologists
Contact: Tim Littlejohn
tim@bch.umontreal.ca
Details: Free

gopher://megasun.bch.umontreal.ca

MGD (Mouse Genome Database)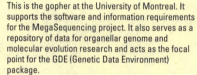

This site provides a comprehensive database of genetic information on the laboratory mouse.

Keywords: Biology, Genetics
Sponsor: The Jackson Laboratory
Audience: Biologists, Researchers, Educators, Students
Contact: mgi-help@informatics.jax.org
Details: Free
Notes: Contact Mouse Genome Informatics User Support by telephone at (207) 288-3371, X 1900, or by FAX at (207) 288-2516.

http://www.informatics.jax.org/mgd.html

National Science Foundation Center for Biological Timing

Vertebrate Museum and Virus Gopher Server

This gopher accesses investigative research pertaining to various aspects of biological timing. The goal of this gopher is to make the Museum's Collections information available over the Internet. This server contains names of virus families/groups and members now available online from the Australian National University's bioinformatics facility.

Keywords: Biology, Vertebrates
Sponsor: Reasearch School of Biological Research, Australian National University, Canberra, Australia
Audience: Biologists, Educators, Researchers
Profile: The center combines the efforts of several universities pertaining to research in biological timing. This includes Vistudies, the internal timing mechanisms that control cycles of sleep and waking, hormone pulsatility, neural excitability, and reproductive rhythmicity. Investigators are involved with research from behavior testing to molecular genetics.

The center also supports educational and outreach programs to industry, universities, and high schools. The center also hosts an annual scientific symposium and a number of mini-symposia.

Details: Free

gopher://gopher.virginia.edu/11/pubs/biotimin

NIBNews - A Monthly Electronic Bulletin About Medical Informatics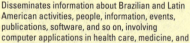

Disseminates information about Brazilian and Latin American activities, people, information, events, publications, software, and so on, involving computer applications in health care, medicine, and biology.

Keywords: Health Care, Biology, Brazil, Latin America, South America, Medicine
Audience: Health Care Professionals, Biologists
Contact: Renato M. E. Sabbatini
sabbatini@bruc.bitnet
Details: Free
e-mail a short notice to

mailto:sabbatini@ccvax.unicamp.br

Biomedical Research

Smbnet (Society for Mathematical Biology Digest)

Keywords: Mathematical Biology, Biology
Audience: Mathematical Biologists, Biologists
Contact: Ray Mejia
Details: Free
User Info: To subscribe to the list, send an e-mail message to the URL address below consisting of a single line reading:

SUB smbnet YourFirstName YourLastName

To send a message to the entire list, address it to: smbnet@fconvx.ncifcrf.gov

`mailto:listserv@fconvx.ncifcrf.gov`

SOCINSCT (Social Insect Biology Research List)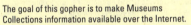

SOCINSCT is dedicated to communication among investigators active in the discipline of social insect biology.

Keywords: Biology, Insect Biology
Audience: Biologists, Researchers (college, graduate)
Profile: It is restricted to discussions of research at the university level. Social insects (bees, wasps, ants, and termites) are the main interest but information can include any area of sociobiology, or solitary bees and wasps. Such areas could include: orientation, navigation, adaptation/selection/evolution, superorganism concept, behavior, physiology and biochemistry, pheromones, flight and energetics, taxonomy and systematics, ecology, genetics, pollination, and nectar/pollen biology. Announcements of meetings and professional opportunities, requests for research help, sharing of literature references, sharing research topics and discussion of ideas are welcome.
Contact: Erik Seielstad
erik@acspr1.acs.brockport.edu
Details: Free
User Info: To subscribe to the list, send an e-mail message to the address below consisting of a single line reading:

SUB socinsct YourFirstName YourLastName

To send message to the entire list, address it to: socinsct@albany.edu

`mailto:listserv@albany.edu`

taxacom

Discussion list on biological systematics.
Keywords: Biology
Audience: Biologists
Contact: James H. Beach
beach@huh.harvard.edu
Details: Free
User Info: To subscribe to the list, send an e-mail message to the URL address below, consisting of a single line reading:

SUB taxacom YourFirstName YourLastName

To send a message to the entire list, address it to:
taxacom@harvarda.harvard.edu

`mailto:listserv@harvarda.harvard.edu`

US Geological Survey Server

This resource containis publications, USGS research programs, technology transfer partnerships, and fact sheets about geology.

Keywords: Biology, Geology, Natural Science
Sponsor: US Geological Survey
Audience: Biologists, Geologists, Researchers, Naturalists
Contact: Systems Operator
webmaster@info.er.usgs.gov

`http://info.er.usgs.gov`

Vertebrate Museum

The goal of this gopher is to make Museums Collections information available over the Internet.

Keywords: Vertebrates, Biology
Sponsor: The Museum of Vertebrate Zoology, University of California at Berkeley
Audience: Natural Scientists, Biologists, Researchers
Details: Free

`gopher://ucmp1.berkeley.edu`

Virginia Commonwealth University Library

The library's holdings are large and wide-ranging and contain significant collections in many fields.

Keywords: Art, Biology, Humanities, Journalism, Music, Urban Planning
Audience: Researchers, Students, General Public
Details: Free
Expect: Login; Send: Opub

`telnet://vcuvm1.ucc.vcu.edu`

Virus Gopher Server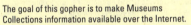

This server contains names of virus families/groups and members now available online from the Australian National University's bioinformatics facility.

Keywords: Viruses, Bioinformation, Biology
Sponsor: Research School of Biological Research, Australian National University, Canberra, Australia
Audience: Researchers, Biologists, Health Professionals
Details: Free

`gopher://life.anu.edu.au`

WWW Biological Science Servers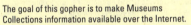

A web site containing Internet links to many gopher servers and other web sites pertaining to bioscience.

Keywords: Bioscience, Biology
Sponsor: U.S. Department of the Interior Survey
Audience: Biologists, Researchers.
Contact: Systems Operator
webmaster@info.er.usgs.gov

`http://info.er.usgs.gov/network/science/biology/index.html`

Biomechanics

Biomch-L

This list is intended for members of the International, European, American, Canadian, and other Societies of Biomechanics, and for members of ISEK (International Society of Electrophysiological Kinesiology), as well as for all others with an interest in the general field of biomechanics and human or animal movement.

Keywords: Biomechanics, Kinesiology, Movement
Sponsor: International Society of Biomechanics
Audience: Kinesiologists
Contact: Ton van den Bogert
listserv@nic.surfnet.nl
Details: Free
User Info: To subscribe to the list, send an e-mail message to the URL address below, consisting of a single line reading:

SUB biomch-l YourFirstName YourLastName

To send a message to the entire list, address it to: biomch-l@nic.surfnet.nl
Notes: To obtain technical help, send the command send biomch-l guide to listserv@nic.surfnet.nl.

`mailto:listserv@nic.surfnet.nl`

Biomedical Research

Biomedical Computer Laboratory (BCL)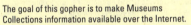

A resource for biomedical computing.
Keywords: Health, Biomedical Research, Biology, Medicine

Sponsor:	Washington University School of Medicine
Audience:	Medical Researchers, Biologists
Profile:	A significant portion of the activities at BCL are supported by the National Center for Research Resources' Biomedical Research Technology Program (BRTP), which promotes the application of advances in computer science and technology, engineering, mathematics, and the physical sciences to research problems in biology and medicine by supporting the development of advanced research technologies.
Contact:	Kenneth W. Clark info@wubcl.wustl.edu
Details:	Free Expect: login; Send: anonymous
Notes:	Investigators who want to explore the possibility of interactions with BCL at Washington University should send e-mail (preferred).

`ftp://wubcl.wustl.edu`

MEDLARS (MEDical Literature Analysis and Retrieval System) ★★★★

MEDLARS is the computerized system of databases and databanks pertinent to biomedical research and patient care, including MEDLINE, the largest and one of the most-used biomedical databases ever.

Keywords:	Medicine, MEDLINE, Biomedical Research
Sponsor:	National Library of Medicine
Audience:	Health Care Providers, Scientists, Biomedical Researchers
Profile:	The computer files can be searched either to produce a list of publications (bibliographic citations) or to retrieve factual information on a specific question. MEDLARS comprises two computer subsystems, ELHISS and TOXNET (TOXicology data NETwork), on which reside over 40 online databases containing about 16 million references. MEDLINE is the largest database and corresponds to three print indexes: Index Medicus, Index to Dental Literature, and Internatonal Nursing Index.
Details:	Costs
User Info:	To subscribe to the service, send e-mail requesting an account to: medlars@nlm.nih.gov

An account is needed for entry and a fee is charged for use. Many university library computers have free link to the MEDLINE database.

`telnet://medlars.nlm.nih.gov`

NIH (National Institute of Health) ★★★★

This server is a network-based computer service operated by the Division of Computer Research and Technology (DCRT) to distribute information for and about the NIH (National Institutes of Health).

Keywords:	NIH, Health Sciences, Biomedical Research, Medicine
Sponsor:	Division of Computer Research and Technology (DCRT), National Institute of Health
Audience:	Scientists, Biomedical Researchers, Health CareProfessionals, General Public
Profile:	This server provides Internet access to information about NIH health and clinical issues (including CancerNet and a variety of AIDS information), NIH-funded grants and research projects, and a variety of research resources in support of NIH and worldwide biomedical researchers. The major molecular biology databases (GenBank, SWISSPROT, PIR, PDB, TFD, Prosite, LiMB), for example, can be accessed through keyword searches from this gopher.
Details:	Free

`gopher://gopher.nih.gov`

NIH Grant Line (Drgline Bulletin Board) ★★★★

The purpose of the NIH Grant Line is to make program and policy information from the Public Health Service (PHS) agencies rapidly available to the biomedical research community.

Keywords:	Biomedical Research, NIH, Grants
Sponsor:	The National Institute of Health
Audience:	Scientists, Researchers, Students
Profile:	Most of the research opportunity information available on this bulletin board is derived from the weekly publication NIH Guide for Grants and Contracts and consists of notices, RFAs, RFPs (announcements of availability), numbered program announcements, and statements of PHS policy. The information found on the NIH Grant Line is grouped into three main sections: short news flashes that appear without any prompting shortly after you have logged on, bulletins that are for reading, and files that are intended mainly for downloading. The E-Guide is available for electronic transmission each week. The material consists predominantly of statements about the research interests of the PHS agencies, institutes, and national centers that have funds to support research in the extramural community. Currently under development are two new files: one will be a monthly listing of new NIH Awards, and the other will be an order form to obtain NIH publications from DRG's Office of Grants Inquiries.
Details:	Free

To access the NIH Grant Line, telnet to the URL address below and when a message has been received that the connection is open, type: ,GEN1 (the comma is mandatory). At the INITIALS? prompt, type BB5 and at the ACCOUNT? prompt, type CCS2

The NIH Guide to Grants and Contracts also can be accessed through gopher://helix.nih.gov/11/res/nih-guide

`telnet://wylbur.cu.nih.gov`

The Tumor Gene Database ★★

A database containing information about genes associated with tumorigenesis and cellular transformation.

Keywords:	Genetics, Diseases, Biomedical Research, Databases
Sponsor:	Department of Cell Biology, Baylor College of Medicine
Audience:	Biomedical Researchers
Contact:	David Steffen, Ph.D. steffen@bcm.tmc.edu

`gopher://mbcr.bcm.tmc.edu`

University of Texas Southwestern Medical Center Library ★★

The library's holdings are large and wide-ranging and contain significant collections in many fields.

Keywords:	Biomedical Research
Audience:	Researchers, Students, General Public
Details:	Free Expect: Login, Send: TIntutsw; Expect: Password, Send: Library

`telnet://library.swmed.edu`

Biomedicine

MEDLINE

MEDLINE is a major source of bibliographic biomedical literature. The MEDLINE database encompasses information from three printed indexes (Index Medicus, Index to Dental Literature and the International Nursing Index) as well as additional information not published in the Index Medicus.

Keywords:	Biomedicine, Dentistry, Nursing, Medicine
Sponsor:	U.S. National Library of Medicine
Audience:	Librarians, Researchers, Physicians, Students
Contact:	CDP Technologies Sales Department (800) 950-2035, ext. 400
User Info:	To subscribe, contact CDP Technologies directly

`telnet://cdplus@cdplus.com`

sci.engr.biomed ★

A Usenet newsgroup providing information and discussion about the field of biomedical engineering.

Keywords: Biomedicine, Engineering (Biomedical)

Audience:	Engineers (Biomedical), Biomedical Researchers
Details:	Free
User Info:	To subscribe to this Usenet newsgroup, you need access to a newsreader.

`news:sci.engr.biomed`

The National Library of Medicine (NLM) Online Catalog System

Catalog of library holdings.

Keywords:	Medicine, Health Sciences, Biomedicine, Rare Books
Sponsor:	National Library of Medicine
Audience:	Health Professionals, Medical Educators, Students
Profile:	The National Library of Medicine (NLM) is the world's largest biomedical library with a collection of over 4.9 million items. NLM is a national resource for all US health sciences libraries and fills over a quarter of a million interlibrary loan requests each year for these libraries. The library is open to the public, but its collection is designed primarily for health professionals. The library collects materials comprehensively in all major areas of the health sciences. Housed within the library is one of the world's finest medical history collections of pre-1914 and rare medical texts, manuscripts, and incunabula.
Contact:	ref@nlm.nih.gov
Details:	Free

The NLM can be accessed also through the WWW at http://www.nlm.nih.gov

`telnet://locator@locator.nlm.nih.gov`

University of Texas at Galveston (Medical Branch) Library

The library's holding's are large and wide-ranging and contain significant collections in many fields.

Keywords:	Health Sciences, Biomedicine, Nursing
Audience:	Researchers, Students, General Public
Details:	Free
	Expect: Login, Send: Library

`telnet://ibm.gal.utexas.edu`

Biophysics

Biosis Previews

The database encompasses the entire field of life sciences and covers original research reports and reviews in biological and biomedical areas. This includes field, laboratory, clinical, experimental, and theoretical work. The traditional areas of biology, including botany, zoology, and microbiology are covered, as well as the related fields such as plant and animal science, agriculture, pharmacology, and ecology.

Keywords:	Biology, Botany, Zoology, Microbiology, Plant Science, Animal Science, Agriculture, Pharmacology, Ecology, Biochemistry, Biophysics, Bioengineering
Sponsor:	Biosis
Audience:	Librarians, Researchers, Students, Biologists, Botanists, Zoologists, Scientists, Taxonomists
Contact:	CDP Technologies Sales Department (800) 950-2035, ext. 400.
User Info:	To subscribe, contact CDP Technologies directly.

`telnet://cdplus@cdplus.com`

Bioscience

CSU Entomology WWW Site

A web site containing online photos of insects, entomology educational programs, and extensive Internet entomology links.

Keywords:	Bioscience, Biology, Entomology
Sponsor:	Colorado State University, Denver, Colorado, USA
Audience:	Students, Researchers, Entomologists
Contact:	Lou Bjostad lbjostad@lamar.colorado.edu

`http://www.colostate.edu/Depts/Entomology/ent.html`

EMBnet (European Molecular Biology Network)

A group of European Internet sites that provide computational molecular biology services to both national and international researchers.

Keywords:	Biology, Bioscience, Molecular Biology
Sponsor:	The EC Funding Program (BRIDGE)
Audience:	Biologists, Molecular Biologists, Researchers
Contact:	Rodrigo Lopez, Robert Herzog rodrigol@biotek.uio.no, rherzog@ulb.ac.be

`http://biomaster.uio.no/embnet-www.html`

Harvard Biosciences Online Journals

A resource containing selected online journals and periodicals in biology and medicine. Includes peer-reviewed e-journals, journal indexes, and databases.

Keywords:	Biology, Bioscience, Molecular Biology
Sponsor:	Harvard Biolabs, Harvard University, Cambridge, Massachusetts, USA
Audience:	Biologists, Molecular Biologists, Researchers
Contact:	Keith Robinson, Steve Brenner krobinson@nucleus.harvard.edu, s.e.brenner@bioc.cam.ac.uk

`http://golgi.harvard.edu/journals.html`

Poisons Information Database

Directories of antivenoms, toxicologists, poison control centers, and poisons from around the world.

Keywords:	Medical Research, Bioscience
Sponsor:	Venom and Toxin Research Group, Department of Anatomy, National University of Singapore, Singapore
Audience:	Biologists, Researchers, Medical Professionals, Toxicologists
Contact:	Professor P. Gopalkrishnakone antgopal@leonis.nus.sg

`http://biomed.nus.sg/PID/PID.html`

WWW Biological Science Servers

A web site containing Internet links to many gopher servers and other web sites pertaining to bioscience.

Keywords:	Bioscience, Biology
Sponsor:	U.S. Department of the Interior Survey
Audience:	Biologists, Researchers.
Contact:	Systems Operator webmaster@info.er.usgs.gov

`http://info.er.usgs.gov/network/science/biology/index.html`

Biosym Technologies Software

Biosym

For users of Biosym Technologies software, including the products Insight II, Discover, Dmol, Homology, Delphi, and Polymer. The list is not run by Biosym.

Keywords:	Biosym Technologies Software, Software
Audience:	Software Users

Contact:	Reinhard Doelz dibug-request@comp.bioz.unibas.ch
Details:	Free
User Info:	To subscribe to the list, send an e-mail message requesting a subscription to the URL address below. To send a message to the entire list, address it to: dibug@comp.bioz.unibas.ch

`mailto:dibug-request@comp.bioz.unibas.ch`

Biotechnet Electronic Buyer's Guide

Biotechnet Electronic Buyer's Guide

Biotechnet is a global computer network created specially for research biologists. It is intended to be a valuable source of information and data, a communications resource, a forum to foster the exchange of current ideas, and an international marketplace for relevant goods and service.

Keywords:	Molecular Biology, Electrophoresis, Chromatography
Audience:	Molecular Biologists, Chemists, Laboratory Suppliers
Profile:	One of the services offered by Biotechnet is the Electronic Buyer's Guide, which is divided into five individual databases for specific product categories: Molecular Biology, Electrophoresis, Chromatography, Liquid Handling, and Instruments & Apparatus. After selecting one of the guides at the prompt, you can search through each database to find either product names and applications or the name and address of the company that manufactures the product you wish to locate.
Details:	Free
Notes:	Password: bguide

`telnet://biotech@biotechnet.com`

Biotechnology

Base de Dados Tropical (BDT)

Base de Dados Tropical (Tropical Data Base) is a collection of information related to biodiversity and biotechnology.

Keywords:	Biodiversity, Biotechnology, Brazil
Sponsor:	Fundacao Tropical de Pesquisas e Tecnologia "Andre Tosello," Campinas, SP, Brazil
Audience:	Biotechnologists, Scientists, Researchers
Contact:	manager@bdt.ftpt.br
Details:	Free

`gopher://bdt.ftpt.br`

Health Periodicals Database

This source covers a broad range of health subjects and issues.

Keywords:	Health, Biotechnology, Medicine, Nutrition
Sponsor:	Information Access Company, Foster City, CA, US
Audience:	Health Professionals, Dieticians, Librarians
Profile:	The database provides indexing and full text of journals covering a broad range of health subjects and issues including: prenatal care, dieting, drug abuse, AIDS, biotechnology, cardiovascular disease, environment, public health, safety, paramedical professions, sports medicine, substance abuse, toxicology, and much more.
Contact:	Dialog in the US at (800) 334-2564, Dialog internationally at country-specific locations.
User Info:	To subscribe, contact Dialog directly.
Notes:	Coverage: 1988 to the present; updated weekly.

`telnet://dialog.com`

ICGEBnet

This is the information server of the International Centre for Genetic Engineering and Molecular Biology (ICGEB), Trieste, Italy.

Keywords:	Molecular Biology, Biotechnology, Italy, Europe
Audience:	Molecular Biotechnologists, Molecular Biologists
Profile:	The primary purpose of the ICGEB computer resource is to disseminate the best of currently available computational technology to the molecular biologists of the ICGEB research community.
Contact:	postmaster@icgeb.trieste.it
Details:	Free

`gopher://icgeb.trieste.it`

IST BioGopher

This is the gopher server of the National Institute for Cancer Research (IST) and of the Advanced Biotechnology Center of Genoa, Italy.

Keywords:	Cancer, Biotechnology, Italy, Europe
Audience:	Biologists, Medical Researchers
Profile:	The server includes data from the Interlab Project Databases (biological materials availability in European laboratories) and the Bio-Media Bulletin Board System (biotechnology researchers, projects, fundings and products).
Contact:	gophman@istge.ist.unige.it
Details:	Free

`gopher://istge.ist.unige.it`

Birds

TitNeT Titnews Titnotes

The network of the International Tit Society (TITS),

Keywords:	Ornithology, Birds
Sponsor:	International Tit Society
Audience:	Bird Watchers
Profile:	The network of the International Tit Society (TITS), Titnet posts three formal series: TITNET, which is the listing of e-mail subscribers, and includes their e-mail addresses, institutional affiliations, and research interests; TITNEWS, which is the forum for exchange concerning academic activities, and consists of single-topic issues and multiple announcements; and TITNOTES, which is the forum for exchange of information about tits (and other hole-nesting birds).
Contact:	Jack P. Hailman jhailman@vms.macc.wisc.edu
Details:	Free
User Info:	To subscribe, send an e-mail message requesting a subscription to the URL address below. Provide: Full name, e-mail address, institutional affiliation, species studied, and topics studied.

`mailto:jhailman@vms.macc.wisc.edu`

titnet (Paridae and Hole-nesting Bird Discussion List)

Promotes communication among scientists working on tits (Paridae) and other hole-nesting birds.

Keywords:	Birds, Ornithology
Audience:	Bird Watchers
Profile:	Titnet is a publication listing e-mail addresses of conference members. Titnews contains announcements and discussions of activities such as bibliographic systems and hence serves as the e-mail newsletter. Titnotes contains material on the biology of the birds and hence serves as a kind of e-mail journal.
Contact:	Jack P. Hailman jhailman@macc.wisc.edu
Details:	Free
User Info:	To subscribe to the list, send an e-mail message requesting a subscription to the URL address below. To send a message to the entire list, address it to: jhailman@macc.wisc.edu
Notes:	Send full name, mailing address, which is forwarded to Dr. Ficken for PARUS INTERNATIONAL, e-mail address(es), species studied, and types of studies (population dynamics, general ecology, vocalizations, nesting, behavior, and so on.).

`mailto:jhailman@macc.wisc.edu`

Birthmother

Birthmother

A mailing list for any birthmother who has relinquished a child for adoption.

- Keywords: Adoption
- Audience: Parents, Adoptees
- Contact: nadir@acca.nmsu.edu
- Details: Free
- User Info: To join the mailing list, send a message to the URL address below with your e-mail address and brief information about your situation (i.e. bmom who relinquished x years ago and does/does not have contact, has/has not been reunited).

mailto:nadir@acca.nmsu.edu

Bisexuality

Alternates

A mailing list for people who advocate and practice an open sexual lifestyle. Its members are primarily bisexual people and their significant others. It serves as a forum and support group for adult men and women who espouse their freedom of choice and imagination in human sexual relations, no matter what their orientaion.

- Keywords: Sexuality, Bisexuality, Sexual Orientation
- Audience: Bisexuals, General Public
- Contact: alternates-request@ns1.rutgers.edu
- User Info: To subscribe to the list, send an e-mail message requesting a subscription to the URL address below.

    To send a message to the entire list, address it to: alternates@ns1.rutgers.edu

mailto:alternates-request@ns1.rutgers.edu

Amend2-discuss

A mailing list for discussion of the implications and issues surrounding the passage of Colorado's Amendment 2, which revokes any existing homosexual civil rights legislation and prohibits the drafting of any new legislation.

- Keywords: Activism, Gay Rights, Lesbians, Bisexuality
- Audience: Gay Rights Activists
- Contact: amend2-mod@cs.colorado.edu
- User Info: To subscribe to the list, send an e-mail message to the URL address below, consisting of a single line reading: subscribe amend2-discuss

mailto:majordomo@cs.colorado.edu

Amend2-info

Colorado voted in an amendment to their state constitution which revokes any existing gay/lesbian/bisexual civil rights legislation and prohibits the drafting of any new legislation. This moderated list is for information on the implication and issues of this amendment.

- Keywords: Activists, Gay, Lesbian, Bisexuality, Constitutional Amendments, Colorado, Civil Rights
- Audience: General Public, Gays, Lesbians, Bisexuals, Activists
- Contact: amend2-info@cs.colorado.edu
- User Info: To subscribe to the list, send an e-mail message requesting a subscription to the URL address below.

    To send a message to the entire list, address it to: amend2-info@cs.colorado.edu

mailto:majordomo@cs.colorado.edu

AUGLBC-l

The American University Gay, Lesbian, and Bisexual Community (AUGLBC) is a support group for lesbian, gay, bisexual, transsexual, and supportive students. The group also is connected with the International Gay and Lesbian Youth Organization (known as IGLYO).

- Keywords: Gay, Lesbian, Bisexual, Transsexual, Sexuality
- Audience: Gays, Lesbians, Bisexuals, Transsexuals, Students (college)
- User Info: To subscribe to the list, send an e-mail message to the URL address below, consisting of a single line reading:

    SUB AUGLBC-l YourFirstName YourLastName

    To send a message to the entire list, address it to: AUGLBC-l@american.edu

mailto:listserv@american.edu

AusGBLF

An Australian-based mailing list for gays, bisexuals, lesbians, and friends.

- Keywords: Australia, Gay, Lesbian, Bisexuality
- Audience: Gays, Lesbians, Bisexuals
- Contact: zglc@minyos.xx.rmit.oz.au
- Details: Free
- User Info: To subscribe to the list, send an e-mail message requesting a subscription to the URL address below.

    To send a message to the entire list, address it to: ausgblf@minyos.xx.rmit.oz.au

mailto:ausgblf-request@minyos.xx.rmit.oz.au

Bears

A mailing list in digest format for gay and bisexual men who are bears themselves and for those who enjoy the company of bears. The definition of "bears" encompasses men who are variously cuddly, furry, perhaps stocky, or bearded. Mail.bears is designed to be a forum to bring together folks with similar interests for conversation, friendship, and sharing of experiences.

- Keywords: Gay, Bisexuality
- Audience: Gays, Bisexual Men
- Contact: Steve Dyer, Brian Gollum
  bears-request@spdcc.COM
- Details: Free
- User Info: To subscribe to the list, send an e-mail message requesting a subscription to the URL address below.

    To send a message to the entire list, address it to: bears@spdcc.COM

mailto:bears-request@spdcc.COM

BiAct-L

A discussion list for bisexual activists.

- Keywords: Bisexuality, Activism
- Audience: Bisexual Activists
- Contact: Elaine Brennan
  EL406010@brownvm.brown.edu
- Details: Free
- User Info: To subscribe to the list, send an e-mail message requesting a subscription to the URL address below. Directions for posting to the list will be sent to you when you are added to the list.

mailto:EL406010@brownvm.brown.edu

BiFem-L

A mailing list for bisexual women and bi-friendly women.

- Keywords: Bisexuality
- Audience: Women, Bisexuals
- Contact: Elaine Brennan
  listserv@brownvm.brown.edu
- Details: Free
- User Info: To subscribe, send an e-mail message requesting a subscription to the URL address below, consisting of a single line reading:

    SUB BiFem-L YourFirstName YourLastName

    To send a message to the entire list, address it to: BiFem-L@brownvm.brown.edu

mailto:listserv@brownvm.brown.edu

Bisexuality

Bisexu-L

This list is for the discussion of issues of bisexuality and the civilized exchange of relevant ideas, opinions, and experiences between members of all orientations. There is no discrimination on the basis of orientation, religion, gender, race, and so on.

- **Keywords:** Bisexuality, Gender
- **Audience:** Bisexuals, General Public
- **Contact:** Bill Sklar
  listserv@brownvm.brown.edu
- **Details:** Free
- **User Info:** To subscribe to the list, send an e-mail message to the URL address below, consisting of a single line reading:

  SUB Bisexu-L YourFirstName YourLastName

  To send a message to the entire list, address it to: bisexu-l@brownvm.brown.edu

mailto:listserv@brownvm.brown.edu

BITHRY-L

This list is for the theoretical discussion of bisexuality and gender issues. It is not a social group, a support group, or an announcement or news forum.

- **Keywords:** Bisexuality, Gender
- **Audience:** Bisexuals, Sex Therapists, Psychologists, Psychiatrists
- **Contact:** Elaine Brennan
  listserv@brownvm.brown.edu
- **Details:** Free
- **User Info:** To subscribe to the list, send an e-mail message to the URL address below, consisting of a single line reading:

  SUB bithry-l YourFirstName YourLastName

  To send a message to the entire list, address it to: bithry-l@brownvm.brown.edu

mailto:listserv@brownvm.brown.edu

DC-MOTSS

DC-MOTSS is a social mailing list for the gay, lesbian, and bisexual folks who live in the Washington Metropolitan Area—everything within approximately 50 miles of The Mall.

- **Keywords:** Gay, Lesbian, Bisexuality, Washington DC
- **Audience:** Gays, Lesbians, Bisexuals, Washington DC Residents
- **Contact:** DC-MOTSS-request@vector.intercon.com
- **Details:** Free
- **User Info:** To subscribe to the list, send an e-mail message requesting a subscription to the URL address below.

  To send a message to the entire list, address it to: DC-MOTSS-request@vector.intercon.com

mailto:DC-MOTSS-request@vector.intercon.com

gay-libn

A network for gay, lesbian, and bisexual librarians.

- **Keywords:** Libraries, Gay, Lesbian, Bisexuality
- **Audience:** Librarians, Gays, Lesbians, Bisexuals
- **Details:** Free
- **User Info:** To subscribe to the list, send an e-mail message to the URL address below consisting of a single line reading:

  SUB gay-libn YourFirstName YourLastName

  To send a message to the entire list, address it to: gay-libn@vm.usc.edu

mailto:listserv@vm.usc.edu

Ne-social-motss

Announcements of lesbian/gay/bisexual social events and other happenings in the Northeastern US.

- **Keywords:** Social Events, Lesbian, Gay, Bisexuality
- **Audience:** Lesbians, Gays, Bisexuals
- **Contact:** ne-social-motss-request@plts.org
- **Details:** Free
- **User Info:** To subscribe to the list, send an e-mail message requesting a subscription to the URL address below.

mailto:ne-social-motss-request@plts.org

NJ-motss

Mailing list for gay, lesbian, and bisexual issues in New Jersey.

- **Keywords:** Gay, Lesbian, Bisexuality, New Jersey
- **Audience:** Gays, Lesbians, Bisexuals
- **Contact:** majordomo@plts.org
- **Details:** Free
- **User Info:** To subscribe to the list, send an e-mail message to the URL address shown below consisting of a single line reading:

  SUB NJ-motss YourFirstName YourLastName

  To send a message to the entire list, address it to: NJ-motss@plts.org

mailto:majordomo@plts.org

NJ-motss-announce

Announcements of interests to New Jersey's gay, lesbian, and bisexual population.

- **Keywords:** Gay, Lesbian, Bisexuality, New Jersey
- **Audience:** Gays, Lesbians, Bisexuals
- **Contact:** majordomo@plts.org
- **Details:** Free
- **User Info:** To subscribe to the list, send an e-mail message to the URL address shown below consisting of a single line reading:

  SUB NJ-motss-announce YourFirstName YourLastName

  To send a message to the entire list, address it to: NJ-motss-announce@plts.org

mailto:majordomo@plts.org

OUTIL (Out in Linguistics)

The list is open to lesbian, gay, bisexual, transsexual linguists and their friends. The only requirement is that you be willing to be out to everyone on the list. The purposes of the group are to be visible and to gather occasionally to enjoy one another's company.

- **Keywords:** Linguistics, Gays, Lesbians, Bisexuality, Transsexuals
- **Audience:** Linguists, Gays, Lesbians, Bisexuals, Transsexuals
- **Contact:** Arnold Zwicky
  outil-request@csli.stanford.edu
- **Details:** Free
- **User Info:** To subscribe to the list, send an e-mail message requesting a subscription to the URL address below.

  To send a message to the entire list, address it to: outil@csli.stanford.edu

mailto:outil-request@csli.stanford.edu

soc.bi

A Usenet newsgroup providing information and discussion about bisexuality.

- **Keywords:** Bisexuality, Social and Behavioral Science
- **Audience:** Bisexuals, Bisexual Activists, Sociologists, Social Scientists
- **Details:** Free
- **User Info:** To subscribe to this Usenet newsgroup, you need access to a newsreader.

news:soc.bi

soc.motss

A Usenet newsgroup providing information and discussion about homosexuality.

- **Keywords:** Homosexuality, Gays, Lesbians, Bisexuality

Audience:	Gays, Lesbians, Bisexuals	
Details:	Free	
User Info:	To subscribe to this Usenet newsgroup, you need access to a newsreader.	

`news:soc.motss`

Stonewall25

A mailing list for discussion and planning of the "Stonewall 25," an international gay/lesbian/bisexual rights march in New York City on Sunday, June 26, 1994, and the events accompanying it.

Keywords:	Gay Rights, Lesbian, Bisexuality, Activism
Audience:	Gays, Lesbians, Bisexuals, Activists
Contact:	stonewall25-request@queernet.org
Details:	Free
User Info:	To subscribe to the list, send an e-mail message requesting a subscription to the URL address below.
	To send a message to the entire list, address it to: stonewall25@queernet.org

`mailto:stonewall25-request@queernet.org`

bit.general

bit.general

A Usenet newsgroup providing information and discussion about Bitnet or Usenet. Contained in the bit. category are many bit.listserv discussion lists.

Keywords:	Internet, Bitnet
Audience:	General Public, Internet Surfers
User Info:	To subscribe to this Usenet newsgroup, you need access to a newsreader.

`news:bit.general`

Bitnet

LIST REVIEW SERVICE ★★★

Explores e-mail distribution lists (primarily bitnet and ListServ lists).

Keywords:	E-mail, Bitnet, Listserv
Audience:	E-mail Users
Profile:	Akin to book and restaurant reviews, each issue begins with a narrative description of usually one weeks worth of monitoring, then presents simple statistical data, such as the number of messages and lines, number of queries and nonqueries, number of subscribers and countries represented, list owner, location, and how to subscribe.
Contact:	Raleigh C. Muns srcmuns@umslvma.bitnet

Details:	Free
User Info:	To subscribe, send an e-mail message to the address below, consisting of a single line reading:
	SUB listreviewservice YourFirstName YourLastName
	To send a message to the entire list, address it to:

`listreviewservice@kentvm.kent.edu`

`mailto:listserv@kentvm.kent.edu`

NetMonth ★

An independant guide to Bitnet.

Keywords:	Bitnet, Networking
Audience:	Computer Users, Internet Surfers
Contact:	Philip Baczewski nmonthed@vm.marist.edu
Details:	Costs
User Info:	To subscribe, send an e-mail message to the address below, consisting of a single line reading:
	netmonth YourFirstName YourLastName
	To send a message to the entire list, address it to: netmonth@vm.marist.edu

`mailto:listserv@vm.marist.edu`

BIVERSITY

BIVERSITY

A mailing list for announcements of Boston-area events and organizations.

Keywords:	Boston
Audience:	Boston Residents
Contact:	liz@ai.mit.edu
Details:	Free
User Info:	To subscribe to the list, send an e-mail message requesting a subscription to the URL address below.

`mailto:liz@ai.mit.edu`

BKRTCY (Bankruptcy Library)

BKRTCY (Bankruptcy Library) ★★★★

The Federal Bankruptcy library is a comprehensive collection of primary and secondary legal research materials pertaining to bankruptcy issues.

Keywords:	Law, Filings, Bankruptcy
Audience:	Lawyers, Bankers

Profile:	The Federal Bankruptcy library is a comprehensive collection of primary and secondary legal research materials that includes case law, rules, statutory and regulatory materials, legal publications, accounting literature, and other resources pertaining to bankruptcy issues.
Contact:	New Sales Group at (800) 227-4908 or (513) 859-5398 inside the US, or (513) 865-7981 for all inquires outside the US.
User Info:	To subscribe, contact Mead directly.
	To examine the Lexis user guide, you can access it at the ftp site of the University of Texas at Austin at the URL address: ftp://ftp.cc.utexas.edu
	The files are in: /pub/ref-services/LEXIS

`telnet://nex.meaddata.com`

`http://www.meaddata.com`

Black/African Related Online Information

Black/African Related Online Information

This is a list of online information storage sites that contain a significant amount of information pertaining to Black or African people, culture, and issues around the world.

Keywords:	Cultural Studies, Race, Africa, African Studies
Sponsor:	AfriInfo
Audience:	Students, African-Americans, Africans
Contact:	McGee mcgee@epsilon.eecs.nwu.edu
Details:	Free

`ftp://ftp.netcom.com/pub/amcgee/my_african_related_lists/afrisite.msg`

Blacksburg Electronic Village Gopher

Blacksburg Electronic Village Gopher

The Blacksburg Electronic Village is a project to link an entire town in southwestern Virginia with a 21st-century telecommunications infrastructure. This infrastructure will bring a useful set of information services and interactive communications facilities into the daily activities of citizens and businesses.

Keywords:	Community Networking, Networking, Telecommunications
Sponsor:	Town of Blacksburg, Virginia, USA
Audience:	Activists, Policymakers, Community Leaders, Government

Profile: This community gopher server, run by the town of Blacksburg, contains information about Blacksburg and how it is building its electronic infrastructure. It includes a list of Blacksburg-area BBSs, instructions for local residents to get an account on the town's BBS, and a section called "Village Schoolhouse."

Details: Costs

gopher://morse.cns.vt.edu

Blindness

Blind News Digest

This is a moderated mailing list in digest format that deals with all aspects of visual impairment and blindness.

Keywords: Blindness, Disabilities
Audience: Blind People, Health Care Providers, Therapists
Contact: wtm@bunker.afd.olivetti.com
Details: Free
User Info: To subscribe to the list, send the message:

SUB BlindNws YourFirstName YourLastName to listserv@vm1.nodak.edu

Or send e-mail requesting a subscription to wtm@bunker.afd.olivetti.com

mailto:wtm@bunker.afd.olivetti.com

BlindFam

The Blindness and Family Life mailing list is devoted to a discussion of the day-to-day impact of this disability on families, and the patterns of domestic life associated with blindness.

Keywords: Blindness, Disabilities, Family
Audience: Blind People, Families, Health Care Professionals, Therapists
Contact: Roger Myers, Patt Bromberger Meyers@ab.wvnet.edu, Patt@squid.tram.com
User Info: To subscribe, send an e-mail message to the URL address below, consisting of a single line reading:

SUB BlindFam YourFirstName YourLastName.

To send a message to the entire list, address it to: BlindFam@sjuvm.stjohns.edu

mailto:listserv@sjuvm.stjohns.edu

Disability-Related Resources

A collection of information that includes newsletters for deaf/blind issues, electronic resources for the deaf, and a section on Chronic Fatigue Syndrome.

Keywords: Disabilities, Deafness, Blindness, Chronic Fatigue Syndrome

Sponsor: University of Washington DO-IT Program
Audience: Deaf and Disabled People, Health Care Professionals
Contact: Sheryl Burgstahler, Ph.D. doit@u.washington.edu

gopher://hawking.u.washington.edu

Blues

Blues (St. Louis Blues)

Provides information, game reports, stats, discussion, and more on the St. Louis Blues of the National Hockey League.

Keywords: Hockey, Sports
Audience: Hockey Enthusiasts
Contact: Joe Ashkar blues@medicine.wustl.edu
User Info: To subscribe to the list, send an e-mail message requesting a subscription to the URL address below.

To send a message to the entire list, address it to: blues@medicine.wustl.edu

mailto:blues@medicine.wustl.edu

Blues-L

A mailing list for the discussion of Blues music and the culture surrounding the genre of the Blues.

Keywords: Blues Music, Musical Genres
Audience: Blues Enthusiasts
Contact: listserv@brownvm.brown.edu
Details: Free
User Info: To subscribe to the list, send an e-mail message to the URL address below, consisting of a single line reading:

SUB blues-l YourFirstName YourLastName

To send a message to the entire list, address it to: blues-l@brownvm.brown.edu

Notes: To receive the list in digest form: once you get acknowledgment from the listserver that you are on the list, send another message to the URL address below with the message: SET Blues-L Dig

mailto:listserv@brownvm.brown.edu

BMW

BMW

This is a discussion of cars made by BMW. Both regular and digest forms are available.

Keywords: BMW, Automobiles

Audience: Automobile Enthusiasts, Automobile Racers, BMW Enthusiasts, Automobile Mechanics
Contact: Richard Welty bmw-request@balltown.cma.com
Details: Free
User Info: To subscribe to the list, send an e-mail message requesting a subscription to the URL address below.

To send a message to the entire list, address it to: bmw@balltown.cma.com

mailto:bmw-request@balltown.cma.com

BMW Motorcycles

This is a discussion of all years and models of BMW motorcycles.

Keywords: BMW, Motorcycles
Audience: Motorcycle Enthusiasts, BMW Enthusiasts
Contact: bmw-request@rider.cactus.org
Details: Free
User Info: To subscribe to the list, send an e-mail message requesting a subscription to the URL address below.

To send a message to the entire list, address it to: bmw@rider.cactus.org

mailto:bmw-request@rider.cactus.org

Boating

The Nautical Bookshelf

Catalog and ordering information for Nautical Bookshelf's collection of books on Sailing and other water sports.

Keywords: Boating, Power Boating, Sailing, Sports
Sponsor: Nautical Bookshelf
Audience: Boating Enthusiasts, Sailors
Contact: staff@nautical.com

gopher://gopher.nautical.com

Boise State University Library

Boise State University Library

The library's holdings are large and wide-ranging and contain significant collections in many fields.

Keywords: Jordan (Len, Senatorial Papers of), Church (Frank, Senatorial Papers of), Poetry (American)
Audience: General Public, Researchers, Librarians, Document Delivery Professionals
Details: Free
Notes: Expect: login; Send: catalyst

telnet://catalyst.idbsu.edu

Bong (Depeche Mode)

Bong (Depeche Mode)

Bong is for the discussion of the mostly electronic band Depeche Mode and related projects like Recoil. Depeche Mode incorporate synth-pop, industrial dance, Kraftwerkian electro, ambient, techno, and rock influences in a dark blend of innovative alternative music.

Keywords:	Musical Groups, Pop Music, Electronic Music
Audience:	Pop Music Enthusiasts, Depeche Mode Enthusiasts, Musicians
Contact:	Colin Smiley bong-request@lestat.compaq.com
Details:	Free
User Info:	To subscribe to the list, send an e-mail message requesting a subscription to the URL address below.
	To send a message to the entire list, address it to: bong@lestat.compaq.com

`mailto:bong-request@lestat.compaq.com`

Bonsai

alt.bonsai ★

A Usenet newsgroup providing information and discussion about Bonsai gardening.

Keywords:	Bonsai Trees, Japan, Gardening, Landscaping
Audience:	Gardeners, Bonsai Enthusiasts
User Info:	To subscribe to this Usenet newsgroup, you need access to a newsreader.

`news:alt.bonsai`

Bonsai ★

This list has been set up to facilitate discussion of the art and craft of bonsai (the Oriental art of miniaturizing trees and plants into forms that mimic nature) and related art forms.

Keywords:	Bonsai Trees, Japan, Gardening, Landscaping
Audience:	Bonsai Enthusiasts, Horticulturists, Gardeners
Contact:	Dan@foghorn.pass.wayne.edu
Details:	Free
User Info:	To subscribe to the list, send an e-mail message to the URL address below, consisting of a single line reading:
	SUB bonsai YourFirstName YourLastName
	To send a message to the entire list, address it to: bonsai@cms.cc.wayne.edu
Notes:	Everyone interested, whether novice or professional, is invited to subscribe.

`mailto:listserv@cms.cc.wayne.edu`

Book Arts

University of Hawaii Library ★★

The library's holdings are large and wide-ranging and contain significant collections in many fields.

Keywords:	Asia, European Documents, Book Arts, Hawaii
Audience:	General Public, Researchers, Librarians, Document Delivery Professionals
Details:	Free
	Expect: enter class, Send: LIB

`telnet://starmaster.uhcc.hawaii.edu`

Book Reviews

alt.books.reviews

A Usenet conference devoted to reviews of books, especially science fiction and computer science books.

Keywords:	Literature (General), Computer Science, Science Fiction, Book Reviews
Audience:	General Public, Publishers, Educators, Librarians, Booksellers
Profile:	Alt.books.reviews (a.b.r. for short) is a forum for posting reviews of books of interest to readers, school and public librarians, bookstores, publishers, teachers and professors, and others who desire an "educated opinion" of a book. This is an unmoderated newsgroup.
Contact:	sbrock@csn.org.
Details:	Free
	To participate in a Usenet newsgroup, you need access to a "newsreader."
Notes:	The reviews in alt.books.reviews are archived at csn.org. Ftp to csn.org; login: anonymous; password: your complete e-mail address. At the ftp prompt, type: cd pub/alt.books.reviews

`news:alt.books.reviews`

Book Review Index ★★

This database contains references to more than 2.5 million citations to reviews of approximately 1.5 million distinct book and periodical titles.

Keywords:	Book Reviews, Periodicals, Publications
Sponsor:	Gale Research, Inc., Detroit, MI, USA
Audience:	Publishing Professionals, Writers, Researchers
Profile:	The database covers every review published since 1969 in nearly 500 periodicals and newspapers. Each record includes the author and title of the work being reviewed, journal name, date of review, and page number. Document type indications are also included if the work is a periodical; a reference work; a children's book, periodical, or reference book; or a young adult book, periodical, or reference book. Book Review Index corresponds to the print publication of the same name. Periodicals indexed range from the Harvard Business Review to the Center for Children's Books: Bulletin, and from the American Scholar to Psychology Today. General interest magazines such as *Ms.*, *Time*, *The New Yorker*, and *Atlantic* are covered, as are specialized periodicals like *Flying*, *Yachting*, and *National Genealogical Society Quarterly*.
Contact:	Dialog in the US at (800) 334-2564, Dialog internationally at country specific locations.
Details:	Costs
User Info:	To subscribe, contact Dialog directly.

`telnet://dialog.com`

Erofile

This newsletter provides reviews of the latest books associated with French and Italian studies in fields such as literary criticism, cultural studies, film studies, pedagogy, and software.

Keywords:	Italian Studies, French Studies, Book Reviews
Audience:	French Students, Italian Students, Book Reviewers
Details:	Free

`mailto:erofile@ucsbuxa.ucsb.edu`

Books

Books In Print ★★

This is a major source of information on books currently published and in-print in the United States.

Keywords:	Books, Publications
Sponsor:	R.R. Bowker, New York, NY, US
Audience:	General Public, Writers, Researchers
Profile:	The database provides a record of forthcoming books, books in-print, and books out-of-print. Scientific, technical, medical, scholarly, and popular works, as well as children's books, are included in the file. The file corresponds to several print publications: Books in Print, Subject Guide to Books in Print, Books in Print Supplement, Paperbound Books in Print, Forthcoming Books, Law Books in Print, Subject Guide to Forthcoming Books, and Scientific and Technical Books & Serials in Print. Records in Books In Print include basic bibliographic information (author, title, publisher, date), as well as L.C. card number, International Standard Book Number (ISBN), and price.

A
B
C
D
E
F
G
H
I
J
K
L
M
N
O
P
Q
R
S
T
U
V
W
X
Y
Z

Contact: Dialog in the US at (800) 334-2564, Dialog internationally at country specific locations.

User Info: To subscribe, contact Dialog directly.

`telnet://dialog.com`

Books Online

This web site contains hundreds of full-text online books, including many classics such as *Anna Karenina* and *The Complete Works of William Shakespeare*. Also provides links to other book resources and has a searchable index.

Keywords: Books, Electronic Media
Audience: Readers, Literary Scholars
Contact: spok@cs.cmu.edu

`gopher://calypso-2.oit.unc.edu/11/sunsite.d/book.d`

`http://www.cs.cmu.edu/Web/books.html`

Electronic Books

A collection of books available as ASCII text files, including classics of antiquity (Aristotle, Virgil, Sophocles, the Bible), as well as more contemporary works of fiction and nonfiction by authors ranging from Dostoevsky to Martin Luther King, Jr.

Keywords: Books, Online Books, Literature (Contemporary), Literature (General)
Sponsor: The Blacksburg Electronic Village (BEV) at Virginia Tech
Audience: General Public, Historians
Contact: BEV Gopher Administrators gopher@gopher.vt.edu

`gopher://gopher.vt.edu`

Moon Travel Handbooks

Moon Publications' gopher features a travel newsletter, as well as excerpts and ordering information for their travel guides.

Keywords: Travel, Books
Sponsor: Moon Publications
Audience: International Travelers, General Public
Contact: gopher@moon.com
Notes: Also see Moon Publications' hypertext exhibit, Big Island of Hawaii Handbook, at http://bookweb.cwis.uci.edu:8042.

`gopher://gopher.moon.com`

Mystery

This mailing list reviews and discusses mystery and detective fiction, including works on film, television, and radio.

Keywords: Mystery Fiction, Detective Fiction, Books
Audience: Mystery Enthusiasts
Details: Free

User Info: To subscribe to the list, send an e-mail message requesting a subscription to the URL address below.

`mailto:mystery-request@introl.com`

Online BookStore (OBS)

Offers full text (fiction and nonfiction) in a variety of electronic formats, free and for a fee.

Keywords: Online Books, Books, ShareWord, Fiction, Nonfiction Books
Sponsor: Editorial Inc./OBS
Audience: General Public, Reading Enthusiasts
Profile: Started in 1992, the OBS offers a variety of full-text titles.
Contact: Laura Fillmore laura@editorial.com
Details: Costs

User Info: To subscribe to the list, send an e-mail message requesting a subscription to the URL address below.

`mailto:laura@editorial.com`

Publishing

This directory is a compilation of information resources focused on publishing.

Keywords: Publishing, Books
Audience: Publishers, Book Dealers, Book Readers
Details: Free

`ftp://una.hh.lib.umich.edu/70/inetdirsstacks/publishing:robinson`

rec.arts.books

A Usenet newsgroup providing information and discussion about a wide variety of books.

Keywords: Books
Audience: Readers, Writers
Details: Free

User Info: To subscribe to this Usenet newsgroup, you need access to a newsreader.

`news:rec.arts.books`

rec.arts.comics.misc

A Usenet newsgroup providing information and discussion about comic books and graphic novels.

Keywords: Comic Books, Books
Audience: Comics Enthusiasts, Readers, Writers
Details: Free

User Info: To subscribe to this Usenet newsgroup, you need access to a newsreader.

`news:rec.arts.comics.misc`

The MIT Press Online Catalogs

A descriptive listing of recent books and current journals published by the MIT Press.

Keywords: Academia, Books, Publishing, Technology
Sponsor: The MIT Press, Cambridge, Massachusetts, USA.
Audience: Researchers, Scholars, University Students, Technical Professionals
Profile: Contains a keyword-searchable index of books published in the years 1993 to 1994, as well as current journals covering computational and cognitive sciences, architecture, photography, art and literary theory, economics, environmental science, and linguistics.
Contact: ehling@mitpress.mit.edu
Notes: Coverage: 1993 to present; updated semiannually. MIT Press can also be accessed by calling (800) 356-0343.

`http://www-mitpress.mit.edu`

`gopher://gopher.mit.edu`

Books (Antiquarian)

Princeton University Online Manuscripts Catalog Library

The library's holdings are large and wide-ranging. They contain significant collections in many fields.

Keywords: Books (Antiquarian), Dickens (Charles), Disraeli (Benjamin), Eliot (George), Hardy (Thomas), Kingsley (Charles), Trollope (Anthony)
Audience: General Public, Researchers, Librarians, Document Delivery Professionals
Details: Free

Expect: VM370 logo, Send: <cr>; Expect: Welcome screen, Send: folio <cr>; Expect: Welcome screen for FOLIO, Send: <cr>; Expect: List of choices, Send: 3 <cr>; To exit: type: logoff

`telnet://pucc.princeton.edu`

Bosnia

BosNet

BosNet is a group/forum run by volunteers. Its goals are to present and distribute information relevant to the events in/about the Republic of Bosnia-Herzegovina (RB&H) and to initiate and coordinate various initiatives, and so on.

Keywords: Bosnia, Herzegovina
Audience: Bosnians, Political Scientists, Students
Contact: listproc@cu23.crl.aecl.ca

Details:	Free
User Info:	To subscribe to the list, send an e-mail message requesting a subscription to the URL address below.
	To send a message to the entire list, address it to: BosNet@cu23.crl.aecl.ca
Notes:	The contributions/opinions presented on BosNet do not necessarily reflect the personal opinions of the moderator or the member(s) of the Editorial Board. To participate in a discussion on a specific topic related to RB&H, please consider Usenet newsgroup soc.culture.bosna-herzegovina.

`mailto:listproc@cu23.crl.aecl.ca`

Boston

BIVERSITY

A mailing list for announcements of Boston-area events and organizations.

Keywords:	Boston
Audience:	Boston Residents
Contact:	liz@ai.mit.edu
Details:	Free
User Info:	To subscribe to the list, send an e-mail message requesting a subscription to the URL address below.

`mailto:liz@ai.mit.edu`

Boston Bruins

This list is for discussion of the Boston Bruins of the National Hockey League and their farm teams. Also available as a digest.

Keywords:	Boston, Hockey, Sports
Audience:	Hockey Enthusiasts, Boston Residents, Sports Enthusiasts
Contact:	Garry Knox bruins-request@cristal.umd.edu
Details:	Free
User Info:	To subscribe to the list, send an e-mail message requesting a subscription to the URL address below.
	To send a message to the entire list, address it to: bruins@cristal.umd.edu

`mailto:bruins-request@cristal.umd.edu`

Botanical Taxonomy

The University of Minnesota Library System (LUMINA)

The library's holdings are large and wide-ranging and contain significant collections in many fields.

Keywords:	Immigration (History of), Ethnic Studies, Horticulture, Equine Research, Botanical Taxonomy, Quantum Physics, Native American Studies, Holmes (Sherlock)
Audience:	General Public, Researchers, Librarians, Document Delivery Professionals
Contact:	Craig D. Rice cdr@acc.stolaf.edu
Details:	Free

`telnet://lumina.lib.umn.edu`

Botany

AGRICOLA

The AGRICOLA database of the National Agricultural Library (NAL) provides comprehensive coverage of worldwide journal literature and monographs on agriculture and related subjects.

Keywords:	Agriculture, Animal Studies, Botany, Entomology
Sponsor:	US National Agricultural Library, Beltsville, MD, USA
Audience:	Agronomists, Botanists, Chemists, Entomologists
Profile:	Related subjects include: animal studies, botany, chemistry, entomology, fertilizers, forestry, hydroponics, soils, and more.
Contact:	Dialog in the US at (800) 334-2564, Dialog internationally at country-specific locations.
User Info:	To subscribe, contact Dialog directly.
Notes:	Coverage: 1970 to the present; updated monthly.

`telnet://dialog.com`

Biosis Previews

The database encompasses the entire field of life sciences and covers original research reports and reviews in biological and biomedical areas. This includes field, laboratory, clinical, experimental, and theoretical work. The traditional areas of biology, including botany, zoology, and microbiology are covered, as well as the related fields such as plant and animal science, agriculture, pharmacology, and ecology.

Keywords:	Biology, Botany, Zoology, Microbiology, Plant Science, Animal Science, Agriculture, Pharmacology, Ecology, Biochemistry, Biophysics, Bioengineering
Sponsor:	Biosis
Audience:	Librarians, Researchers, Students, Biologists, Botanists, Zoologists, Scientists, Taxonomists
Contact:	CDP Technologies Sales Department (800) 950-2035, ext. 400.
User Info:	To subscribe, contact CDP Technologies directly.

`telnet://cdplus@cdplus.com`

CP

Topics of interest to the group include the cultivation and propagation of CP's (carnivorous plants), field observations of CP's, sources of CP material, and CP trading between members. The discussion is not moderated, and usually consists of short messages offering plants for trade, asking CP questions and advice, relating experiences with plant propagation, and so on. The group also maintains archives of commercial plant sources and members growing lists.

Keywords:	Carnivorous Plants, Botany
Audience:	Horticulturists, Botanists
Contact:	Rick Walker walker@hpl-opus.hpl.hp.com
User Info:	To subscribe to the list, send an e-mail message to the address below consisting of a single line reading:
	SUB CP YourFirstName YourLastName
	To send a message to the entire list, address it to: CP@hpl-opus.hpl.hp.com

`mailto:listserv@hpl-opus.hpl.hp.com`

The University of Kansas Library

The library's holdings are large and wide-ranging and contain significant collections in many fields.

Keywords:	Botany, Chinese Studies, Cartography (History of), Kansas, Opera, Ornithology, Joyce (James), Yeats (William Butler), Walpole (Sir Robert, Collections of)
Audience:	General Public, Researchers, Librarians, Document Delivery Professionals
Contact:	John S. Miller
Details:	Free
	Expect: Username, Send: relay

`telnet://kuhub.cc.ukans.edu`

Botany (History of)

The University of Notre Dame Library

The library's holdings are large and wide-ranging and contain significant collections in many fields.

Keywords:	Music (Irish), Ireland, Botany (History of), Ecology, Entomology, Parasitology, Aquatic Biology, Universities (History of), Paleography
Audience:	General Public, Researchers, Librarians, Document Delivery Professionals
Details:	Free
	Expect: ENTER COMMAND OR HELP:, Send: library; To leave, type x on the command line and press the enter key. At the ENTER COMMAND OR HELP: prompt, type bye and press the enter key.

`telnet://irishmvs.cc.nd.edu`

Bowker Biographical Directory

Bowker Biographical Directory

This is a collection of biographical directories that correspond to certain Bowker print publications.

Keywords: Biographies

Sponsor: R.R. Bowker, a Reed Reference Publishing Company; a division of Reed Publishing (US) Inc., New Providence, NJ, US

Audience: General Public, Writers, Researchers

Profile: The database corresponds to the Bowker print publications as follows: American Men and Women of Science, covering over 122,500 leading US and Canadian scientists and engineers in the physical, biological, and related sciences; Who's Who in American Art, covering some 7,000 North American artists, critics, curators, administrators, librarians, historians, collectors, and dealers; and Who's Who in American Politics, covering over 25,400 American political decision-makers at all levels from federal to local government.

Contact: Dialog in the US at (800) 334-2564, Dialog internationally at country specific locations.

Details: Costs

User Info: To subscribe, contact Dialog directly.

`telnet://dialog.com`

Boy Scouts

Eagles

This list provides a forum for Boy Scouts, Scouters, and former Scouts who are gay/bisexual to discuss how they can apply pressure to the BSA to change their homophobic policies.

Keywords: Boy Scouts, Gays, Lesbians

Audience: Gays, Lesbians, Boy Scouts, Former Boy Scouts

Contact: eagles-request@flash.usc.edu

Details: Free

User Info: To subscribe to the list, send an e-mail message requesting a subscription to the URL address below.

To send a message to the entire list, address it to: eagles-request@flash.usc.edu

`mailto:eagles-request@flash.usc.edu`

Boyler-Moore Theorem Prover

nqthm-users

Discussion of theorem proving using the Boyler-Moore theorem prover, NQTHM. Offers lore, advice, information, discussion, and help.

Keywords: Computer Programs, NQTHM, Boyler-Moore Theorem Prover

Audience: NQTHM Theorem Users

Contact: nqthm-users-request@cli.com

Details: Free

User Info: To subscribe to the list, send an e-mail message requesting a subscription to the URL address below.

To send a message to the entire list, address it to: nqthm-users@cli.com

`mailto:nqthm-users@cli.com`

BPM

BPM

This list is for novice and professional DJs. Discussion often covers music releases, DJing techniques, and turntable maintenance.

Keywords: Disk Jockeys, Music

Audience: Disk Jockeys, Music Enthusiasts

Contact: Simon Gatrall
bpm-request@andrew.cmu.edu

Details: Free

User Info: To subscribe to the list, send an e-mail message requesting a subscription to the URL address below.

To send a message to the entire list, address it to: bpm@andrew.cmu.edu

`mailto:bpm-request@andrew.cmu.edu`

Brain Research

Neurosciences Internet Resource Guide

A comprehensive Internet resource addressing biological, chemical, medical, engineering, and computer science aspects of neurobiology.

Keywords: Neurobiology, Neuroscience, Brain Research

Sponsor: The University of Michigan School of Information and Library

Audience: Neuroscientists, Neurobiologists

Profile: This resource provides links to journal articles, tutorials on neuroimaging and neurobiology, moderated newsgroups, and international forums, all of which address issues surrounding the field of neuroscience.

Contact: Sheryl Cormicle, Steve Bonario
sherylc@sils.umich.edu,
sbonario@umich.edu

`http://http2.sils.umich.edu/Public/nirg/nirg1.html`

Brazil

Base de Dados Tropical (BDT)

Base de Dados Tropical (Tropical Data Base) is a collection of information related to biodiversity and biotechnology.

Keywords: Biodiversity, Biotechnology, Brazil

Sponsor: Fundacao Tropical de Pesquisas e Tecnologia ÒAndre ToselloÓ, Campinas, SP, Brazil

Audience: Biotechnologists, Scientists, Researchers

Contact: manager@bdt.ftpt.br

Details: Free

`gopher://bdt.ftpt.br`

Brasil

This is a mailing list for general discussion about and information on Brazil. Portuguese is the main language of discussion.

Keywords: Brazil, Portuguese Language

Audience: Brazilians, Portuguese Speakers

Contact: B. R. Araujo Neto
bras-net-request@cs.ucla.edu

Details: Free

User Info: To subscribe to the list, send an e-mail message requesting a subscription to the URL address below. Include your name, e-mail, phone number, address, and topics of interest.

To send a message to the entire list, address it to: bras-net@cs.ucla.edu

`mailto:bras-net-request@cs.ucla.edu`

NIBNews - A Monthly Electronic Bulletin About Medical Informatics

Disseminates information about Brazilian and Latin American activities, people, information, events, publications, software, and so on, involving computer applications in health care, medicine, and biology.

Keywords: Health Care, Biology, Brazil, Latin America, South America, Medicine

Audience: Health Care Professionals, Biologists

Contact: Renato M. E. Sabbatini
SABBATINI@BRUC.BITNET
Details: Free
E-mail a short notice to:
`mailto:sabbatini@ccvax.unicamp.br`

BRIDGE

BRIDGE ★

An online public access catalog, this PALS-based resource provides access to the collections of two institutions, St. Boniface University and the Manitoba General Hospital.

Keywords: Medicine, Library
Sponsor: St. Boniface University, and the Manitoba General Hospital Libraries
Audience: Health Professionals, Students, Medical Educators
Details: Free

`telnet://BE@umopac.umanitoba.ca`

Brit-Iron

Brit-Iron ★

The purpose of this list is to provide a friendly forum in which riders, owners, and admirers of British motorcycles can share information and experiences. A list of parts sources and shops that repair these classic machines is maintained. All makes are welcome, from AJS to Vellocette.

Keywords: Motorcycles
Audience: British Motorcycle Enthusiasts, Motorcycle Enthusiasts
Contact: cstringe@indiana.edu
Details: Free
User Info: To subscribe to the list, send an e-mail message requesting a subscription to the URL address below.
To send a message to the entire list, address it to: Brit-Iron@indiana.edu

`mailto:Brit-Iron@indiana.edu`

Britain

British Online Yellow Pages ★

A directory of British firms and organizations; searches of the database are possible by firm, location, or product.

Keywords: Britain, Business (British)
Sponsor: British Telecom
Audience: General Public, Market Researchers
Details: Free

`telnet://sun.nsf.ac.uk`

veggies ★

Vegetarian matters in Britain.
Keywords: Vegetarianism, Britain, Food
Audience: Vegetarians
Details: Free
User Info: To subscribe to the list, send an e-mail message requesting a subscription to the URL address below.
To send a message to the entire list, address it to: veggies@ncl.ak.uk

`mailto:veggies-request@ncl.ac.uk`

Britannica Online

Britannica Online ★

This web site provides an information service for Encyclopaedia Britannica, Inc. Its database allows for keyword searches, and also includes experimental articles.

Keywords: Information Retrieval, Databases
Sponsor: Encyclopaedia Britannica, Inc.
Audience: Researchers, Educators, Students
Contact: support@eb.com
Details: Costs

`http://www.eb.com`

British

British-Cars ★

This is a discussion of owning, repairing, racing, cursing, and loving British cars, predominantly sports cars, with some talk of Land Rovers and sedans. Also available as a digest.

Keywords: Automobiles, Britiain
Audience: British Automobile Enthusiasts, Automobile Enthusiasts, Automobile Mechanics
Contact: Mark Bradakis
british-cars-request@autox.team.net,
british-cars-request@hoosier.cs.utah.edu
Details: Free
User Info: To subscribe to the list, send an e-mail message requesting a subscription to the URL address below.
To send a message to the entire list, address it to: british-cars@autox.team.net

`mailto:british-cars-request@autox.team.net`

British National Register of Archives ★★

A multi-volume electronic guide to accessing a wide-variety of archival materials and repositories in the United Kingdom.

Keywords: United Kingdom, History, Business (British), Information Retrieval
Sponsor: Coombspapers Social Sciences Research Data Bank at ANU (Australian National University).
Audience: Researchers, Anglophiles, Archioists
Contact: Dr. T. Matthew Ciolek
tmciolek@coombs.anu.edu.au

`gopher://coombs.anu.edu.au`

`ftp://coombs.anu.edu.au/coombspapers/otherarchives/uk-nra-archives/`

`http://coombs.anu.edu.au/CoombsHome.html`

British Commonwealth Law

University of Texas at Austin Tarlton Law Library ★★

The library's holdings are large and wide-ranging and contain significant collections in many fields.

Keywords: British Commonwealth Law, Constitutional Law, Law (International), Human Rights
Audience: Researchers, Students, General Public
Details: Free
Expect: Login, Send: Library

`telnet://tallons.law.utexas.edu`

British Plays (19th-C.)

Indiana University Libraries ★★

The library's holdings are large and wide-ranging and contain significant collections in many fields.

Keywords: Literature (English), Literature (American), 1640-Present, British Plays (19th-C.), Western Americana, Railway History, Aristotle (Texts of), Lafayette (Marquis de), Handel (G.F.), Austrian History, Antiquarian Books, Rare Books, French Opera (19th-C.), Drama (British) ,
Audience: General Public, Researchers, Librarians, Document Delivery Professionals
Details: Free
Expect: User ID prompt, Send: GUEST

`telnet://iuis.ucs.indiana.edu`

Broadcasting

FM-10

A discussion of modifications, enhancements, and uses of the Ramsey FM-10 and other BA-1404 based FM Stereo broadcasters; some discussion of the FM pirate radio, as well.

Keywords: Radio, Broadcasting
Audience: Broadcasters, Radio Broadcasters
Details: Free
User Info: To subscribe to the list, send an e-mail message requesting a subscription to the URL address below.
To send a message to the entire list, address it to: fm-10@dg-rtp.dg.com

`mailto:fm-10-request@dg-rtp.dg.com`

Multicast

Discussion of multicast and broadcast issues in an open systems interconnection environment.

Keywords: Multicasting, Broadcasting
Audience: Multicasters, Broadcasting Professionals
Details: Free
User Info: To subscribe to the list, send an e-mail message requesting subscription to the URL address below.

`mailto:multicast-request@arizona.edu`

Brown University Library

Brown University Library

The Brown libraries contain approximately 1.5 million volumes, including historical archives of early American imprints and biomedical engineering holdings.

Keywords: Libraries, Research
Audience: General Public, Researchers
Contact: Howard Pasternick
blips15@brownvm.brown.edu
Details: Free
Notes: At the Brown logon screen: tab to command field, Enter Dial Josiah, tab to Josiah choice on the screen.

`telnet://brownvm.brown.edu`

`telnet://library.brown.edu`

BTHS-ENews-L

BTHS-ENews-L

This list provides an open forum for students, teachers, and alumni of Brooklyn Technical High School.

Keywords: New York, Education (K-12)
Audience: Teachers, Students, Educators
Contact: listserv@Cornell.edu
Details: Free
User Info: To subscribe to the list, send an e-mail message to the URL address below, consisting of a single line reading:
SUB BTHS-ENews-l YourFirstName YourLastName
To send a message to the entire list, address it to: BTHS-ENews-l@Cornell.edu

`mailto:listserv@Cornell.edu`

Buddhism

ANU (Australian National University) Buddhism Database

A searchable database of messages from the BUDDHA-L listserv, an academic forum for the discussion of Buddhism. It currently contains archives for messages posted in 1993-94.

Keywords: Religion, Asian Studies, Buddhism
Sponsor: COOMBSQUEST Social Sciences & Humanities Information Facility at ANU (Australian National University), Canberra, Australia
Audience: Buddhists, Religious Studies Instructors, Asian Studies Educators
Contact: Dr. T.Matthew Ciolek
coombspapers@coombs.anu.edu.au

`gopher://cheops.anu.edu.au/Coombs-db/ANU-Buddha-l.src`

`http://coombs.anu.edu.au/WWWVL-AsianStudies.html`

Budget

Budget of the United States (1994)

Provides the full-text of the 1994 budget of the United States.

Keywords: Budget, Government (US), Finance
Audience: Politicians, Lawyers, Journalists, Economists, Students, US Citizens
Details: Free
Notes: This document is over one megabyte in size and thus takes a couple of minutes to load onto the screen.

`gopher://wiretap.spies.com/00/Gov/US-Gov/budget.94`

Bugs-386bsd

Bugs-386bsd

This list is for 386bsd bugs, patches, and ports.

Keywords: Operating Systems, 386bsd
Audience: Computer Operators, Computer Scientists, Computer Engineers
Contact: bugs-386bsd-request@ms.uky.edu
Details: Free
User Info: To subscribe to the list, send an e-mail message requesting a subscription to the URL address below.
To send a message to the entire list, address it to: bugs-386bsd@ms.uky.edu
Notes: Requirement to join: an interest in actively working on 386bsd to improve the operating system for use by yourself and others.

`mailto:bugs-386bsd-request@ms.uky.edu`

Builder Xcessory

BX-Talk

BX-talk has been created for users of Builder Xcessory (BX) to discuss problems (and solutions) and ideas for using BX, which is a graphical user interface builder for Motif applications, and is sold by ICS. Note that this list is not associated with ICS (the authors of BX) in any way.

Keywords: Builder Xcessory, Graphical User Interfaces
Audience: Graphics Experts, Computer Operators
Contact: Darci L. Chapman
bx-talk-request@qiclab.scn.rain.com
Details: Free
User Info: To subscribe to the list, send an e-mail message requesting a subscription to the URL address below.
To send a message to the entire list, address it to: bx-talk@qiclab.scn.rain.com
Notes: This list is unmoderated.

`mailto:bx-talk-request@qiclab.scn.rain.com`

Building

Architecture, Building

This directory is a compilation of information resources focused on architecture.

Keywords: Architecture, Building, Construction, AEC
Audience: Architects, Builders, Civil Engineers
Contact: J. Brown
Details: Free

`ftp://una.hh.lib.umich.edu/70/inetdirsstacks/archi:brown`

Bulgaria

CEE Environmental Libraries Database

A directory of over 300 libraries and environmental information centers in Central Eastern Europe that specalize in, or maintain significant collections of information about, the environment, ecology, sustainable living, or conservation. The database concentrates on six Central Eastern European countries: Bulgaria, Czech Republic, Hungary, Romania, Slovakia, and Poland.

Keywords: Central Eastern Europe, Environment, Sustainable Living, Bulgaria, Czech Republic, Hungary, Romania, Slovakia, Poland.
Sponsor: The Wladyslaw Poniecki Charitable Foundation, Inc.
Audience: Environmentalists, Green Movement, Librarians, Community Builders, Sustainable Living Specialists.
Profile: This database is the product of an Environmental Training Project (ETP) that was funded in 1992 by the US Agency for International Development as a 5-year cooperative agreement with a consortium headed by the University of Minnesota (US AID Cooperative Agreement Number EUR-0041-A-002-2020). Other members of the consortium include the University of PittsburghÕs Center for Hazardous Materials Research, The Institute for Sustainable Communities, and the World Wildlife Fund. The Wladyslaw Poniecki Charitable Foundation, Inc., was a subcontractor to the World Wildlife Fund and published the Directory of Libraries and Environmental Information Centers in Central Eastern Europe: A Locator/Directory . This gopher database consists of an electronic version of the printed directory, subsequently modified and updated online. Access to the data is facilitated by a WAIS search engine that makes it possible to retrieve information about libraries, subject area specializations, personnel, and so on.

Contact: Doug Kahn, CEDAR
kahn@pan.cedar.univie.ac.at

`gopher://gopher.poniecki.berkeley.edu`

Business

ABI/Inform

ABI/Inform is a comprehensive source for business and management information, containing abstracts from close to 1,000 publications and the full-text from over 100 publications. The database covers trends, corporate strategies and tactics, management techniques, competitive information and product information

Keywords: Business, Business Management, Management
Sponsor: UMI, Ann Arbor, Michigan, US
Audience: General Public, Researchers, Librarians
Profile: A few of the thousands of business subjects that can searched in ABI/Inform include: company news and analysis, market conditions and strategies, employee management and compensation, international trade and investment, management styles and corporate cultures, and economic conditions and forecasts.
Contact: CDP Technologies Sales Department (800) 950-2035, ext. 400
User Info: To subscribe, contact CDP Technologies directly

`telnet://cdplus@cdplus.com`

API Energy Business News Index (APIBIZ)

Worldwide coverage of commercial, financial, marketing and regulatory information affecting the petroleum and energy industries.

Keywords: Petroleum, Business
Sponsor: The American Petroleum Institute - Central Abstracting and Information Services
Audience: Researchers, Librarians
Profile: Twenty-two major news and economics publications are the primary sources for worldwide coverage of information affecting the petroleum and energy industries. Contains more than 600,000 records. Updated weekly.
Contact: PAUL.ALBERT@NETEAST.COM
User Info: To subscribe contact Orbit-Questel directly.

`telnet://orbit.com`

Apollo Advertising

A major directory on advertising, providing access to a broad range of related resources (library catalogs, databases, and servers) through the Internet.

Keywords: Advertising, Business
Audience: Advertisers, Business Professionals, General Public
Profile: A new web service for advertisers and information providers that maintains the philosophy that consumers will choose to look for goods and services where it is easy and convenient to locate them. This involves the development of a database of short advertisements, many having hypertext links to more substantial advertisements. These can range from text documents to hypermedia commercials. The Apollo directory can be searched, using logical sorting methods, to identify items of interest. Additional information, including hypermedia, may be connected to the entries. This service encompasses short, stand-alone advertisements, as well as entries with hypertext links to other Internet resources.
Contact: apollo@apollo.co.uk

`gopher://apollo.co.uk`

Asia-Pacific

The database covers the business, economics, and new industries of the Pacific Rim nations, including East Asia, Southeast Asia, the Indian Subcontinent, the Middle East, Australia, and the Pacific Island nations.

Keywords: Asia, Pacific, Business, Economy
Sponsor: Aristarchus Knowledge Industries, Seattle, WA, USA
Audience: Market Researchers, Economists, Market Analysts
Profile: Records are of two types: main records consisting of abstracts or citations for journal articles and other publications; and company thesaurus records. Detailed abstracts are provided for selected journal articles, monographs, selected papers in conference proceedings, dissertations, and government documents. Shorter citations with briefer indexing are provided for a wide variety of journal articles, newspapers, government documents, and annual report publications. Asia-Pacific also includes an extensive Corporate Thesaurus subfile, which provides detailed coverage of the corporate players in the Pacific Rim, including thousands of companies traded on the stock exchanges of Southeast and East Asia.
Contact: Dialog in the US at (800) 334-2564; Dialog internationally at country-specific locations.
Details: Costs
User Info: To subscribe, contact Dialog directly.

`telnet://dialog.com`

Asian Pacific Business and Marketing Resources

A forum on business and marketing in the Pacific Rim region.

Keywords: Asia, Pacific, Business, Management

Audience: Business Professionals, Market Researchers

Details: Free

`gopher://hoshi.cic.sfu.ca/11/dlam/business/forum`

British National Register of Archives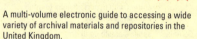

A multi-volume electronic guide to accessing a wide variety of archival materials and repositories in the United Kingdom.

Keywords: United Kingdom, History, Business(British), Information Retrieval

Sponsor: Coombspapers Social Sciences Research Data Bank at ANU (Australian National University).

Audience: Researchers, Anglophiles, Archivists

Contact: Dr. T. Matthew Ciolek
tmciolek@coombs.anu.edu.au

`gopher://coombs.anu.edu.au`

`ftp:/coombs.anu.edu.au/coombspapers/otherarchives/uk-nra-archives/`

`http://coombs.anu.edu.au/CoombsHome.html`

Business Dateline

The database contains the full-text of articles from more than 350 local and regional business publications from the United States and Canada.

Keywords: Business, Regional Business, Market Research

Sponsor: UMI, Louisville, KY, USA

Audience: Business Analysts, Market Researchers, Writers

Profile: Sources include city business journals, daily newspapers, regional business magazines, and wire services. Subjects include city economic conditions, new product announcements, manufacturing methods, executive profiles, quality control, company histories, market conditions, service industries, regulations, litigation, and legislation.

Contact: Dialog in the US at (800) 334-2564, Dialog internationally at country specific locations.

Details: Costs

User Info: To subscribe, contact Dialog directly.

`telnet://dialog.com`

Business News-Singapore ★

This gopher site focuses on business in Singapore.

Keywords: Singapore, Economics, Business

Audience: Economists, Business Professionals

Details: Free

`gopher://gopher.cic.net/11/e-serials/alphabetic/b/business-news`

`http://gopher.cic.net`

Business Sources on the Net

A list of business-related Internet resources organized by subject.

Keywords: Business

Audience: Business Professionals

Profile: A project undertaken by librarians at Kent State to catalog business-related Internet resources, this guide currenty has 13 chapters on aspects ranging from accounting to statistics.

Contact: Leslie M. Haas
lhaas@kentvm.kent.edu

`gopher://refmac.kent.edu`

Business Wire

The database contains the unedited text of news releases from over 10,000 diverse news sources: companies, public relations firms, government agencies, political organizations, colleges and universities, and research institutes.

Keywords: Business, Finance, and Industry

Sponsor: Business Wire, San Francisco, CA, USA

Audience: Business Analysts, Market Researchers, General Public

Profile: Approximately 90 percent of all releases carried by Business Wire are business/financial related, covering essentially every category of business and industry. News releases include all information on earnings, dividend announcements, mergers and acquisitions, major contract awards, new products, new security offerings, takeovers, restructurings, and more. Business Wire transmits the full, unedited text of these releases, complete with financial statements and other details that are not generally made available by the press. In addition, all releases carry the name and telephone number of a contact person within that company. Also contains news on other subjects, such as entertainment, travel, sports, politics, medicine and science, and lifestyles.

Contact: Dialog in the US at (800) 334-2564, Dialog internationally at country specific locations.

Details: Costs

User Info: To subscribe, contact Dialog directly.

`telnet://dialog.com`

Business, Economics

This directory is a compilation of information resources focused on business and economics.

Keywords: Business, Economics

Audience: Business Professionals, Business Students, Economists

Details: Free

`ftp://una.hh.lib.umich.edu/70/inetdirsstacks/govdocs:tsangaustin`

BUSREF (Business Reference)

The Business Refernce (BUSREF) library contains a variety of reference materials covering business and industry.

Keywords: Reference, Business, Government

Audience: Business Professionals, Business Analysts

Profile: The BUSREF library contains company directories, reference publications, information on business opportunities, and biographical information on political candidates, Congressional members, celebrities, and international decision makers.

Contact: Mead New Sales Group at (800) 227-4908 or (513) 859-5398 inside the US, or (513) 865-7981 for all inquiries outside the US.

User Info: To subscribe, contact Mead directly.

To examine the Nexis user guide, you can access it at the ftp site of the University of Texas at Austin at the URL address: ftp://ftp.cc.utexas.edu

The files are in: /pub/ref-services/LEXIS

`telnet://nex.meaddata.com`

`http://www.meaddata.com`

Chemical Industry Notes

Citations to worldwide chemical business news.

Keywords: Chemistry, Business

Sponsor: Chemical Abstracts Service, American Chemical Society

Audience: Researchers, Librarians, Chemists

Profile: Contains worldwide chemical business news related to production, pricing, sales, facilities, products and processes, corporate activities, government activities, and people. Contains over 950,000 records. Update weekly.

Contact: PAUL.ALBERT@NETEAST.COM

User Info: To subscribe contact Orbit-Questel directly.

`telnet://orbit.com`

CommerceNet

An open, internet-based infrastructure for electronic commerce, created by a coalition of Silicon Valley organizations.

Keywords: Business, Electronic Commerce
Sponsor: CommerceNet, Inc. 800 El Camino Real, Menlo Park, CA 94025.
Audience: Business Professionals, Commercial Internet Users, General Public
Profile: Services include basic enabling services required by virtually every user and application (generic directories, secure multimedia messaging, network access control, and payment facilities). Applications include a framework for the developmentof compelling applications and services targeted to electronic commerce among companies in the region. Applications are designed to address the varied business and community needs of CommerceNet users; these are developed by third-party providers, in compliance with protocols established by CommerceNet. Connectivity is high-quality and affordable, with minimal on-site equipment or network expertise required of the user.
Contact: feedback@commerce.net

http://www.commerce.net

Computer-Mediated Marketing Environments

A web site devoted to research aimed at understanding the ways in which computer-mediated marketing environments (CMEs), especially the Internet, are revolutionizing the way firms conduct business.

Keywords: WWW, Information Retrieval, Internet, Marketing, Business
Sponsor: Vanderbilt University, Owen Graduate School of Management, Nashville, Tennessee, USA
Audience: General Public, Entrepeneurs, Financial Planners, Marketers
Contact: Donna Hoffman, Tom Novak
hoffman@colette.ogsm.vanderbilt.edu,
novak@moe.ogsm.vanderbilt.edu

http://colette.ogsm.vanderbilt.edu

D&B - Duns Financial Records Plus

This database provides up to three years of comprehensive financial statements for over 650,000 private and public companies.

Keywords: Finance, Business, Dun & Bradstreet
Sponsor: Dun & Bradstreet Information Services, Parsippany, NJ, USA
Audience: Business Professionals
Profile: Information provided includes balance sheet, income statement, and 14 of the most widely used business ratios for measuring solvency, efficiency, and profitability. A companyÕs financial position can be compared to those of others in the same industry as determined by industry norm percentages. In addition, there are over 1.2 million records included that contain company history and operations background only. DFR also contains company identification data, such as company name, address, primary and secondary SIC codes, D-U-N-S number, and number of employees. Textual paragraphs cover the history and operations background of a firm. Coverage: Current; updated quarterly.
Contact: Dialog in the US at (800) 334-2564, Dialog internationally at country-specific locations.
Details: Costs
User Info: To subscribe, contact Dialog directly.

telnet://dialog.com

D&B - Dun's Electronic Business Directory

Keywords: Finance, Business, Dun & Bradstreet
Sponsor: Dun & Bradstreet Information Services, Parsippany, NJ, USA
Audience: Business Professionals, Business Analysts
Profile: A full directory listing is provided for each entry, including address, telephone number, SIC codes and descriptions, and number of employees. The file covers both public and private US companies of all sizes and types. Fifteen broad business categories are indexed as industry groups: agriculture, business services, communication, construction, finance, insurance, manufacturing, mining, professional services, public administration, real estate, retail, transportation, utilities, and wholesale. Data for the file is compiled and maintained primarily through Dun & BradstreetÕs intensive credit interviewing process. Dun's staff of 1,300 business analysts actively interviews millions of entrepreneurs each year. This information is supplemented with data from large-volume telemarketing and direct mail campaigns. Coverage: Current; updated quarterly.
Contact: Dialog in the US at (800) 334-2564, Dialog internationally at country-specific locations.
Details: Costs
User Info: To subscribe, contact Dialog directly.

telnet://dialog.com

D&B - European Dun's Market (EDMI)

This database presents detailed information on over 2.5 million businesses located in 26 European countries.

Keywords: Dun & Bradstreet, Europe, Business
Sponsor: Dun & Bradstreet Information Services, Parsippany, NJ, USA
Audience: Business Professionals
Profile: EDMI provides directory listings, sales volume and marketing data, and references to parent companies. Companies are selected for inclusion based on sales volume, national prominence, and international interest. Names, addresses, SIC codes, D-U-N-S numbers, and other data are given in each record. Both public and private companies are included.
Contact: Dialog in the US at (800) 334-2564, Dialog internationally at country-specific locations.
User Info: To subscribe, contact Dialog directly.
Notes: Coverage: Current; updated quarterly.

telnet://dialog.com

Delphes European Business

This is a French database that provides information on international markets, products, industries, and companies from a European perspective.

Keywords: Business, Europe
Sponsor: Chamber of Commerce and Industry of Paris and The French Assembly of the Chambers of Commerce and Industry, Paris, France
Audience: Business Professionals
Profile: Abstracts are produced by approximately 60 local organizations grouped into two networks, CCIP (Chamber of Commerce and Industry of Paris) and ACFCI (French Assembly of the Chambers of Commerce and Industry), which collect and consolidate the information into the Delphes database. Delphes contains bibliographic citations and informative abstracts from over 900 European trade journals, newspapers, and business periodicals, in French, English, Italian, German, or Spanish. Titles are in the original language; abstracts are in French. A comprehensive classification scheme in English, French, and Spanish is used to index documents covered. Geographic coverage is 45% France, 35% Europe, and 20 percent is devoted to other countries. In addition, about 1,000 new books, corporate and business directories, and reports are reviewed each year.

Contact: Dialog in the US at (800) 334-2564, Dialog internationally at country-specific locations.
User Info: To subscribe, contact Dialog directly.
Notes: Coverage: 1980 to the present; updated weekly.

`telnet://dialog.com`

Dun & Bradstreet Corporation ★★

Dun and Bradstreet's home page contains examples of existing services, services in development, and business and financial information, advising and so on.

Keywords: Finance, Business
Audience: General Public, Business Professionals
Profile: Files include company news, related industry information, product descriptions, and discussions of IBM's services.

`http://www.corp.dnb.com`

e-europe ★

The electronic communications network for doing business in Eastern Europe. Its purpose is to help these countries in their transition to market economies.

Keywords: Eastern Europe, Economics, Business
Audience: Business Profesionals, Investors, Economists
Contact: James W. Reese r505040@univ scvm or e-europe@pucc.princeton.edu
Details: Free
User Info: To subscribe to the list, send an e-mail message to the URL address shown below consisting of a single line reading:
SUB e-europe YourFirstName YourLastName
To send a message to the entire list, address it to: e-europe@indycms.iupui.edu

`mailto:listserv@indycms.iupui.edu`

econ-dev ★

This mailing list is for sharing with economic development professionals who are helping small, innovative companies compete in the new global environment.

Keywords: Economic Development, Business
Audience: Economic Development Experts, Business Professionals
Contact: majordomo@csn.org
Details: Free
User Info: To subscribe to the list, send an e-mail message to the URL address shown below consisting of a single line reading:
SUB econ-dev YourFirstName YourLastName
To send a message to the entire list, address it to: econ.dev@csn.org

`mailto:majordomo@csn.org`

Esbdc-l ★★

A mailing list intended to facilitate discussion between small business development centers, focusing on such topics as performance standards, business behavior, products, specific industry information access, deficit reduction plans, and private cost sharing.

Keywords: Business, Small Business
Sponsor: Association of Small Business Development Centers, USA
Audience: State Officials, Educators, Certified Public Accountants, Investors
User Info: To subscribe to the list, send an e-mail message to the URL address below consisting of a single line reading:
SUB esbdc-l YourFirstName YourLastName
To send a message to the entire list, address it to: esbdc-l@ferris.bitnet

`mailto:listserv@ferris.bitnet`

EUROPE (European News Library) ★★★

The Europe library contains detailed information about every country in Eastern, Central, and Western Europe.

Keywords: Business, Europe
Audience: Business Researchers, Analysts, Entrepreneurs, Regulatory Agencies
Profile: EUROPE is designed for those who need to monitor countries of the European Community, the European Free Trade Association, or emerging European market economies. This library includes a wide array of sources: Among the information sources are: newspapers and wire services, trade and business journals, company reports, country and region background, industry and product analyses, business opportunities, and selected legal texts. News sources range from the world-renowned Financial Times and Reuters to the regionally important PAP and CTK newswires. EIS's European newsletters and Euroscipe from Coopers and Lybrand help analyze the legal and business environment in Western Europe. Company information is contained in the EXTEL cards as well as ICC.
Contact: Mead New Sales Group at (800) 227-4908 or (513) 859-5398 inside the US, or (513) 865-7981 for all inquiries outside the US.
User Info: To subscribe, contact Mead directly.
To examine the Nexis user guide, you can access it at the ftp site of the University of Texas at Austin at the URL address: ftp://ftp.cc.utexas.edu
The files are in: /pub/ref-services/LEXIS

`telnet://nex.meaddata.com`

`http://www.meaddata.com`

GC-L ★

Project for international business and management curricula.

Keywords: Business, Management, Language
Sponsor: Global Classroom
Audience: Linguists, Language Teachers, Language Students, International Business Educators
Details: Free
User Info: To subscribe to the list, send an e-mail message to the address below, consisting of a single line reading:
SUB gc-l YourFirstName YourLastName

`mailto:listserv@uriacc.uri.edu`

International Business Machines

This is IBM's main WWW server and it contains extensive links to information about the company and its products.

Keywords: Computers, Business
Audience: General Public
Profile: Contains: Industry Solutions, Products and Services, Technology information and News about the company.
Contact: mail to: askibm@www.ibm.com

`http://www.ibm.com`

Internet Shopping Network

A shopping network on the Infobahn

Keywords: Business, Electronic Commerce
Sponsor: Internet Shopping Network
Audience: Business Users, Commercial Internet Users, General Public
Profile: The Internet Shopping Network aims to conduct research and develop products and services that commercialize the Internet, for the purpose of retailing and mass merchandising. The stores within this network offer approximately 20,000 products from 1000 vendors.

`xxx@xxx.xxx`

Materials Business File

Covers all commercial aspects of iron and steel, non-ferrous metals and non-metallic materials.

Keywords: Materials Science, Business, Iron, Steel
Sponsor: Materials Information, a joint information service of ASM International and the Institute of Materials
Audience: Materials Scientists, Researchers
Profile: Articles are abstracted from over 2,000 worldwide technical and trade journals to create more than 65,000 records. Updated monthly.
Contact: PAUL.ALBERT@NETEAST.COM
User Info: To subscribe, contact Orbit-Questel directly.

`telnet://orbit.com`

National Export Strategy ★★

This site provides the complete text of a report presented to Congress by the Trade Promotion Coordinating Committee, describing ways to develop U.S. export promotion efforts.

Keywords: Commerce, Trade, Exports, Business
Sponsor: United States Government, Trade Promotion Coordinating Committee
Audience: Exporters, Business Professionals, Trade Specialists
Details: Free

`ftp://sunny.stat-usa.gov`

`http://sunny.stat-usa.gov`

National Technology Transfer Center (NTTC) ★★

A federally-funded national network to apply government research to commercial applications.

Keywords: Technology, Research and Development, Business, Industry, Defense, Government (US)
Sponsor: National Technology Transfer Center
Audience: Business Professionals, Entrepreneurs, Manufactures, Technology Enthusiasts
Profile: Features state-by-state listings of agencies designed to facilitate the adaptation of new technologies to industry. Also provides updates on conferences, and a current list of Department of Defense projects soliciting private assistance from small businesses. Allows limited access to NTTC databases.
Contact: Charles Monfradi
cmonfra@nttc.edu, info@nttc.edu

`gopher://iron.nttc.edu`

`http://iridium.nttc.edu/nttc.hmtl`

NetEc ★★★

An electronic forum for published academic papers relating to economics.

Keywords: Economics, Business
Audience: Economists, Business Professionals

Contact: netec@uts.mcc.ac.uk
Details: Free
User Info: To subscribe to the list, send an e-mail message to the address below, consisting of a single line reading:

SUB netec YourFirstName YourLastName

To send a message to the entire list, address it to: netec@hasara11.bitnet

`mailto:listserv@hasara11.bitnet`

Overseas Business Reports ★★

Full-text of U.S. International Trade Administration reports, discussing the economic and commercial climate in various countries around the world.

Keywords: Business, Trade, Commerce
Sponsor: U.S. Government, International Trade Administration
Audience: Business Professionals, Trade Specialists, Investors
Details: Free

`gopher://umslvma.umsl.edu/11/library/govdocs/obr`

Special Chemicals Update Program ★★

Comprehensive reports covering 32 specialty chemical industry segments.

Keywords: Chemistry, Business
Sponsor: Chemical Marketing Research Center
Audience: Librarians, Researchers, Chemists
Profile: Coverage of chemical industry segments, plus more than a dozen reports of general interest on the management of specialty chemical businesses.
Contact: PAUL.ALBERT@NETEAST.COM
User Info: To subscribe, contact Orbit-Questel directly.

`telnet://orbit.com`

St. Petersburg Business News ★★★

Contains a digest of business information extracted from Russian and St. Petersburg morning newspapers, stock exchange reports, reports from the News own correspondents.

Keywords: Business, St. Petersburg
Audience: Russians, Business Professionals
Contact: Elena Artemova
esa@cfea.ecc.spb.su
spbeac@sovamsu.sovusa.com
Details: Costs

User Info: To subscribe to the list, send an e-mail message to the URL address below, consisting of a single line reading:

SUB spbeac YourFirstName YourLastName

`mailto:listserv@sovamsu.sovusa.com`

State Small Business Profiles ★★★

This site contains Small Business Administration reports, which provide statistics on the small business sector in each state.

Keywords: Business, Statistics, United States
Sponsor: U.S. Government, Small Business Administration, in conjunction with the Reference Department of the Thomas Jefferson Library of the University of Missouri-St. Louis
Audience: Business Professionals, Researchers
Profile: The 1993 State Business Profiles bring together an array of statistics on the small business sector in each state. Included is data on small business income and employment trends; women-owned and minority-owned businesses; business closings and formations; and state exports.
Contact: Raleigh Muns
srcmuns@umslvma.umsl.edu
Details: Free
Notes: For additional information, call the Small Business Administration toll free at (800) 359-2777, or the SBA District Office in Washington, D.C. at (202) 205-6600.

`gopher://umslvma.umsl.edu/11/library/govdocs/states`

Telemedia, Networks, and Systems Group

A list of commercial services on the Web (and Net).

Keywords: Business, Electronic Commerce
Sponsor: MIT Laboratory for Computer Science, Cambridge, MA 02139
Audience: Business Professionals, Commercial Internet Users, General Public
Profile: This list of commercial Internet services is well-maintained and frequently updated.
Contact: hhh@mit.edu

`http://tns-www.lcs.mit.edu/commerce.html`

`http://tns-www.lcs.mit.edu`

The Management Archive ★★★

This is an electronic forum for management ideas and information.

Keywords: Management, Business, Economics

Audience: Managers, Business Professionals, Economists

Profile: The Archive arranges working papers, teaching materials, and so on, in directories by subject. All materials in the Archive are fully indexed and searchable. If you have material that you would like to see receive worldwide network exposure and distribution, submit them to the Archive.

Contact: Jim Goes
goes@chimera.sph.umn.edu

Details: Free

Expect: login, Send: anonymous; Expect: password, Send: your e-mail address.

`ftp://chimera.sph.umn.edu`

The Teleputing Hotline And Field Computing Source Letter

A leading voice in covering telephone connections worldwide. Plans to expand coverage of a worldwide revolution called Field Computing.

Keywords: Business, Telecomputing, Telecommunications

Audience: Industry, Telecommunications Experts, Business Professionals

Profile: Field Computing involves linking workers outside the office—in sales, repair, and delivery functions—to central computer systems with handheld terminals and wireless data networks. The Teleputing Hotline has covered this trend since its inception.

Contact: Dana Blankenhorn
MCI: 409-8960 GEnie: nb.atl CompuServe

Details: Costs

User Info: To subscribe to the list, send an e-mail message requesting a subscription to the URL address below.

`mailto:sfer request@mthvax.cs.miami.edu`

Total Quality Management Gopher

A collection of materials relating to the elimination of defects through comprehensive quality control in industry, government, and universities.

Keywords: Quality Control, Management, Business

Sponsor: The Clemson University Department of Industrial Engineering, Clemson, South Carolina, USA

Audience: Managers, Administrators

Contact: quality@eng.clemson.edu

`gopher://deming.eng.clemson.edu`

`http://deming.eng.clemson.edu`

TRADSTAT

TRADSTAT is a comprehensive online source of national trade statistics.

Keywords: Trade, Commerce, Business

Sponsor: TRADSTAT Ltd., London, UK

Audience: Importers, Exporters, Business Professionals

Profile: TRADSTAT covers over 90 percent of world trade. Every month the latest trade figures are loaded into the database from over 20 countries worldwide and all their trading partners. Trade is reported by countries in the EC, EFTA, North and South America, and the Far East. TRADSTAT gives annual trends back to 1981; and monthly reports can be produced at any time for the latest 25 months' trade. The data is made available on average three to eight weeks after the month of trade. This is often weeks, even months, ahead of the equivalent printed data.

User Info: To subscribe, contact Dialog directly.

`telnet://dialog.com`

U.S. Patent and Trademark Office Database

A database of patents issued in 1994 by the U.S. Patent and Trademark Office, including a searchable index.

Keywords: Patents, Databases, Inventions, Business

Sponsor: New York University School of Business

Audience: Inventors, General Public

Contact: questions@town.hall.org

`gopher://town.hall.org/patent`

University of Toledo Library

The library's holdings are large and wide-ranging and contain significant collections in many fields.

Keywords: Business, Great Lakes Area, Humanities, International Relations, Psychology, Science

Audience: Researchers, Students, General Public

Details: Free

Expect: Enter one of the following commands ... , Send: DIAL MVS; Expect: dialed to mvs ####; Send: UTMOST

`telnet://uofto1.utoledo.edu`

University of Wisconsin at Milwaukee Library

The library's holdings are large and wide-ranging and contain significant collections in many fields.

Keywords: Art, Architecture, Business, Cartography, Geography, Geology, Urban Studies, Literature (English), Literature (American)

Audience: Researchers, Students, General Public

Details: Free

Expect: Login, Send: Lib; Expect: vDIAL prompt, Send: Library

`telnet://uwmcat.lib.uwm.edu`

University of Wisconsin at Oshkosh Library

The library's holdings are large and wide-ranging and contain significant collections in many fields.

Keywords: Business, Liberal Education, Nursing

Audience: Researchers, Students, General Public

Details: Free

Expect: Login; Send: Lib; Expect: vDIAL Prompt, Send: Library

`telnet://polk.cis.uwosh.edu`

University of Wisconsin at Platteville Library

The library's holdings are large and wide-ranging and contain significant collections in many fields.

Keywords: Business, Industry

Audience: Researchers, Students, General Public

Details: Free

Expect: Login, Send: Lib; Expect: vDIAL Prompt, Send: Library

`telnet://137.104.128.44`

University of Wisconsin at Stout Library

The library's holdings are large and wide-ranging and contain significant collections in many fields.

Keywords: Mathematics, Business, Fashion Merchandising, Home Economics, Hospitality, Tourism, Hotel Administration, Restaurant Management, Microelectronics

Audience: Researchers, Students, General Public

Details: Free

Expect: Login, Send: Lib; Expect: vDIAL Prompt, Send: Library

`telnet://lib.uwstout.edu`

University of Wisconsin Eau Claire Library

The library's holdings are large and wide-ranging and contain significant collections in many fields.

Keywords: Health Sciences, Business, Nursing, Education

Audience: Researchers, Students, General Public
Details: Free
Expect: Service Name, Send: Victor

`telnet://lib.uwec.edu`

WORLD (World News and Information)

★★★★

This library contains detailed information about every country in Europe, Asia, the Pacific Rim, Africa, the Middle East, and North and South America. Designed for those who need to monitor world events, organizations, and leaders, this library provides a global view of any subject or topic.

Keywords: Business, News
Audience: Business Researchers, Analysts, Entrepreneurs
Profile: WORLD includes information from newspapers and wire services, trade and business journals, company reports, country and region background, industry and product analysis, business opportunities, and selected legal texts. News sources range from the world-renowned Christian Science Monitor, Financial Times, Reuters and Associated Press to the regionally important eastern European CTK, MTI and PAP newswires, The Toronto Star, Jerusalem Post, and Xinhua News Agency. Business and trade information include a wide variety of sources, such as EIS's European newsletters and Euroscope from Coopers and Lybrand, Canada's Maclean's, Japan's Comline Daily News Service, BNA's international dailies and the Soviet Union's SovData DiaLine servicesÑall help analyze the political and economic climate around the globe. Company information is contained in the EXTEL cards as well as ICC. Providers of country background and industry analysis include Associated Banks of Europe, Bank of America, Business International, IBC USA and the US Department of Commerce. Economic risk can be assessed with the Economist's Economic Risk Services, IBC's International Reports and International Country Risk Guide and many of Business International's Country Reports. Political risk is forecast in IBC's Political Risk Services as well as BOA's World Information Services' Country RiskOutlooks, Monitors and Forecasts.
Contact: Mead New Sales Group at (800) 227-4908 or (513) 859-5398 inside the US, or (513) 865-7981 for all inquiries outside the US.
User Info: To subscribe, contact Mead directly.
To examine the Nexis user guide, you can access it at the ftp site of the University of Texas at Austin at the URL address: ftp://ftp.cc.utexas.edu
The files are in: /pub/ref-services/LEXIS

`telnet://nex.meaddata.com`

`http://www.meaddata.com`

Yahoo Market and Investments

★★★

A comprehensive look at the current economic status, with a wide range of coverage, from brokers to stocks.

Keywords: Business, Stock Market, Investment, Economy
Sponsor: Stanford University, Palo Alto, California, USA
Audience: Investors, Economists
Contact: jerry@akebono.stanford.edu

`http://akebono.stanford.edu/yahoo/Economy/Markets_and_Investments`

Business (British)

British Online Yellow Pages

★

A directory of British firms and organizations; searches of the database are possible by firm, location, or product.

Keywords: Britain, Business (British)
Sponsor: British Telecom
Audience: General Public, Market Researchers
Details: Free

`telnet://sun.nsf.ac.uk`

ICC British Company Directory

★★★

The database is a comprehensive reference source for companies registered in England, Wales, Scotland, and Northern Ireland.

Keywords: UK Companies, Business (British)
Sponsor: ICC Information Group Ltd., London, UK
Audience: Business Professionals
Profile: The database contains a record for each company included on the Index of Companies maintained by the official Companies Registration Offices in the UK. Companies that have been dissolved since 1968 are listed. The total number of records in the ICC British Company Directory is over 2 million. Reference data includes name, registered number, registered address, issued and nominal-share capital, dates of incorporation and document filings at the Companies Registration Office. Document filings include latest filed annual accounts and annual returns, changes of directors or registered address, special resolutions, mergers of public (PLC) companies, winding-up orders, appointment of liquidators, and so on.
Contact: Dialog in the US at (800) 334-2564, Dialog internationally at country-specific locations.
User Info: To subscribe, contact Dialog directly.
Notes: Coverage: Current; updated weekly.

`telnet://dialog.com`

Business (US)

America

For people interested in how the United States is dealing with foreign trade policies, congressional status, and other inside information about the government that is freely distributable.

Keywords: Trade, Government (US), Congress (US), Business (International)
Audience: General Public, Researchers, Journalists, Political Scientists, Students
Contact: subscribe@xamiga.linet.org
User Info: To subscribe to the list, send an e-mail message to the URL address below, consisting of a single line reading:
SUB america YourFirstName YourLastName
To send a message to the entire list, address it to: america@xamiga.linet.org
Notes: This list has monthly postings that generally are in large batches, with posts exceeding a few hundred lines.

`mailto:subscribe@xamiga.linet.org`

Commerce Business Daily

★

The Commerce Business Daily is a publication that announces invitations to bid on proposals requested by the US Federal Government. This gopher is updated every business day.

Keywords: Business (US), Economics, Commerce, Trade, Government (US)
Sponsor: CNS and Softshare Government Information Systems
Audience: Economists, Business Professionals, General Public, Journalists, Students, Politicians.
Profile: Invitations via Internet email that apply only to specific companies can be arranged.
Contact: Melissa Allensworth
sshare@cscns.com
service@cscns.com
Details: Free

`gopher://cns.cscns.com/cbd/About the CBD`

Business Information

Uniform Commercial Code (UCC)

★

Articles 1 and 2 of the UCC, adopted with some variations in all 50 states (USA).

Keywords: Commerce, Business Information, Standards

University of Northern Iowa Library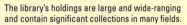

The library's holdings are large and wide-ranging and contain significant collections in many fields.

Keywords: Art, Business Information, Education, Music, Fiction
Audience: Researchers, Students, General Public
Contact: Mike Yohe
yohe@uni.edu
Details: Free
Expect: Login; Send: Public

`telnet://infosys.uni.edu`

Business Management

ABI/Inform

ABI/Inform is a comprehensive source for business and management information, containing abstracts from close to 1,000 publications and the full-text from over 100 publications. The database covers trends, corporate strategies and tactics, management techniques, competitive information, and product information

Keywords: Business, Business Management, Management
Sponsor: UMI, Ann Arbor, Michigan, US
Audience: General Public, Researchers, Librarians
Profile: A few of the thousands of business subjects that can searched in ABI/Inform include: company news and analysis, market conditions and strategies, employee management and compensation, international trade and investment, management styles and corporate cultures, and economic conditions and forecasts.
Contact: CDP Technologies Sales Department (800) 950-2035, ext. 400
User Info: To subscribe, contact CDP Technologies directly

`telnet://cdplus@cdplus.com`

Business Marketing

Alliance Marketing Systems

Develops marketing strategies for new business on those in need of turn-around. Designs advertising/marketing plans to prequalify the buying public.

Keywords: Business Marketing, Sales
Audience: Business Professionals, Marketing Professionals, Sales Executives
Details: Costs

`xx@xx.xxx`

Buyers' Guide to Micro Software

Buyers' Guide to Micro Software

The database contains a directory of business and professional microcomputer software available in the United States.

Keywords: Buyers' Guides, Microcomputing, Software
Sponsor: Online, Inc., Weston, CT, USA
Audience: Computer Users
Profile: Provided are directory, product, technical, and bibliographic information on leading software packages, integrated into one succinct composite record. The database can help professionals locate suitable packages compatible with specified hardware, without having to sift through large numbers of records.

The file is highly selective, listing packages rated at least "good" by the technical press; all packages from major software producers, even if negatively reviewed; and packages unique to specific business segments, with special emphasis placed on library and medical software. Each record includes directory information; technical specifications, including required hardware and operating systems; an abstracted product description, and, when available, a full citation of representative reviews.

Contact: Dialog in the US at (800) 334-2564, Dialog internationally at country-specific locations.
Details: Costs
User Info: To subscribe, contact Dialog directly.
Notes: Coverage: current; updated monthly.

`telnet://dialog.com`

BX-Talk

BX-Talk

BX-talk has been created for users of Builder Xcessory (BX) to discuss problems (and solutions) and ideas for using BX, which is a graphical user interface builder for Motif applications, and is sold by ICS. Please note that this list is not associated with ICS (the authors of BX) in any way.

Keywords: Builder Xcessory, Graphical User Interfaces
Audience: Graphics Experts, Computer Operators
Contact: Darci L. Chapman
bx-talk-request@qiclab.scn.rain.com
Details: Free
User Info: To subscribe to the list, send an e-mail message requesting a subscription to the URL address below.

To send a message to the entire list, address it to: bx-talk@qiclab.scn.rain.com
Notes: This list is unmoderated.

`mailto:bx-talk-request@qiclab.scn.rain.com`

C

C Programming Language

info-C

Discussions about C programming and the C programming language.

Keywords:	Programming, C Programming Language
Audience:	C Programmers
Contact:	Mark Plotnick info-C-request@research.att.com
Details:	Free
User Info:	To subscribe to the list, send an e-mail message requesting a subscription to the URL address below.

`mailto:info-C-request@research.att.com`

C-IBM-370

The C on IBM mainframes mailing list is a place to discuss aspects of using the C programming language on s/370-architecture computers—especially under IBM's operating systems for that environment.

Keywords:	C Programming Language, Programming Languages, IBM
Audience:	IBM Users, Computer Users, Computer Programmers
Contact:	David Wolfskill C-IBM-370-request@dhw68k.cts.com
Details:	Free
User Info:	To subscribe to the list, send an e-mail message requesting a subscription to the URL address below. To send a message to the entire list, address it to: C-IBM-370@dhw68k.cts.com

`mailto:C-IBM-370-request@dhw68k.cts.com`

C-L

Discussion of C programming.

Keywords:	Programming Languages
Audience:	C Programmers
Contact:	George Foster, Katie Hanson igaf400@indyvax, abh100@indycms
Details:	Free
User Info:	To subscribe to the list, send an e-mail message to the URL address below, consisting of a single line reading: SUB C-L YourFirstName YourLastName To send a message to the entire list, address it to: C-L@indycms.iupui.edu

`mailto:listserv@indycms.iupui.edu`

C-SPAN (Cable-Satellite Public Affairs Network) Gopher

C-SPAN (Cable-Satellite Public Affairs Network) Gopher

Online information from C-SPAN, the public affairs television network.

Keywords:	News Media, Government, Congress (US), Television
Sponsor:	C-SPAN
Audience:	Journalists, Government Officials, Educators (K-12), General Public
Profile:	Comprehensive listings of C-SPAN's programming and coverage of events in Washington D.C. and beyond. In addition to the programming notes and schedules, this site also features online educational resources sponsored by C-SPAN, text of historic documents and speeches, and background political information on the House of Representatives and the Supreme Court.
Contact:	cspanviewr@aol.com
Details:	Free

`gopher://c-span.org`

c2man

c2man

This is a discussion of Graham Stoney's c2man program, which parses comments from C and C++ programs and produces documentation for man pages, info files, and so on.

Keywords:	Computer Programs, c2man
Audience:	Computer Programmers
Contact:	listserv@research.canon.oz.au
User Info:	To subscribe to the list, send an e-mail message to the URL address below, consisting of a single line reading: SUB c2man YourFirstName YourLastName To send a message to the entire list, address it to: c2man@research.canon.oz.au
Notes:	This list is archived and unmoderated.

`mailto:listserv@research.canon.oz.au`

Cabinetry

Utah Valley Community College Library

The library's holdings are large and wide-ranging and contain significant collections in many fields.

Keywords: Accounting, Automobiles, Cabinetry, Child Care, Drafting, Electronics, Home Building, Local History, Refrigeration, Air Conditioning

Audience: General Public, Researchers, Librarians, Document Delivery Professionals

Details: Free
Expect: Login; Send: Opub

`telnet://uvlib.uvcc.edu`

Cabot (Sebastian)

Cabot

This is the official mailing list of the New York State Institute for Sebastian Cabot Studies.

Keywords: Cabot (Sebastian)
Audience: Scholars, Students, Historians
Contact: Richard Welty
cabot-request@sol.crd.ge.com
User Info: To subscribe to the list, send an e-mail message requesting a subscription to the URL address below.
To send a message to the entire list, address it to:
cabot@sol.crd.ge.com

`mailto:cabot-request@sol.crd.ge.com`

CADC (Canadian Astronomy Data Center) Home Page

CADC (Canadian Astronomy Data Center) Home Page

The CADC maintains archives of scientific data from the Hubble Space Telescope and the Canada France Hawaii Telescope. It also serves as a distribution point for various astronomy-related software packages.

Keywords: Astronomy, Hubble Telescope
Sponsor: Dominional Astrophysical Observatory, Victoria, British Columbia, Canada
Audience: Astronomers
Contact: Dennis Crabtree
crabtree@dao.nrc.ca

`http://ucluelet.dao.nrc.ca`

CAEDS-L

CAEDS-L

A mailing list for the discussion of CAED (Computer Aided Engineering Design) products.

Keywords: Computer-Aided Design, Engineering, Computer Graphics
Audience: Engineers
Contact: netman@suvm.acs.syr.edu
Details: Free
User Info: To subscribe to the list, send an e-mail message to the URL address shown below consisting of a single line reading:
SUB caeds-l YourFirstName YourLastName
To send a message to the entire list, address it to:
CaeDS-1@suvm.ACS.SYR.EDU

`mailto:listserv@suvm.acs.syr.edu`

CAF Archive

CAF Archive

A source of information relating to Computers and Academic Freedom (CAF).

Keywords: Education, Computers, Academic Freedom
Audience: Educators, Researchers
Contact: kadie@eff.org

`http://www.eff.org/CAF/cafhome.html`

Calendars

On-this-day

Subscribers receive a daily listing of notable birthdays, events, religious holidays, astronomical events, and other items of interest. The messages are sent out in the wee hours of the morning.

Keywords: Calendars
Audience: General Public
Contact: Wayne Geiser
geiser@pictel.com
Details: Free
User Info: To subscribe to the list, send an e-mail message requesting a subscription to the URL address below.
To send a message to the entire list, address it to: geiser@pictel.com

`mailto:geiser@pictel.com`

California

alt.california

A Usenet newsgroup providing information and discussion about California and Californian lifestyles.

Keywords: California
Audience: Californians, General Public
User Info: To subscribe to this Usenet newsgroup, you need access to a newsreader.

`news:alt.california`

ba.general

A Usenet newsgroup providing general information and discussion about the San Francisco Bay area.

Keywords: California
Audience: Tourists, Visitors, Bay area Residents
User Info: To subscribe to this Usenet newsgroup, you need access to a newsreader.

`news:ba.general`

ca-Firearms

This is an announcement and discussion of firearms legislation and related issues. The ca- list is for California statewide issues; the ba- list is for the San Francisco Bay area and gets all messages sent to the ca- list. Prospective members should subscribe to one or the other, generally depending on whether or not they are SF Bay area residents.

Keywords: Firearms, Gun Control Legislation, California
Audience: Politicians, General Public, Gun Users, California Residents
Contact: Jeff Chan
ca-firearms-request@shell.portal.com
Details: Free
User Info: To subscribe to the list, send an e-mail message requesting a subscription to the URL address below.
To send a message to the entire list, address it to:
ca-firearms@shell.portal.com

`mailto:ca-firearms-request@shell.portal.com`

ca-Liberty

This is an announcement of area-based Libertarian meetings, events, activities, and so on. The ca- list is for California statewide issues; the ba- list is for the San Francisco Bay area and gets all messages sent to the ca- list. Prospective members should subscribe to one or the other, generally depending on whether or not they are SF Bay area residents.

Keywords: Libertarian Party, Politics, California

Audience:	Libertarians, Political Scientists, Politicians, General Public
Contact:	Jeff Chan ca-liberty-request@shell.portal.com
Details:	Free
User Info:	To subscribe to the list, send an e-mail message requesting a subscription to the URL address below. To send a message to the entire list, address it to: ca-liberty@shell.portal.com

`mailto:ca-liberty-request@shell.portal.com`

California State Senate Gopher

This is a gopher site accessing California state government records and providing links to related gophers.

Keywords:	California, Government (US), Law (US State)
Sponsor:	California State Senate, California, USA
Audience:	Californians, General Public
Profile:	The California State Senate Gopher provides access to state government records, pending bills, laws, state statistics, budgets, and related matters. The gopher also provides links to related gophers inside and outside state government.
Contact:	Gopher Provider gopher@sen.ca.gov

`gopher://gopher.sen.ca.gov`

California Museum of Photography: Network Exhibitions

This is a collection of digital images for educational and general use.

Keywords:	Photography, Art, Education, California
Sponsor:	University of California, Riverside, California, USA
Audience:	Photographers, Artists, Educators (esp. K-12), Historians
Profile:	The California Museum of Photography is in the process of selecting groups of images from the collections as thematic exhibitions. Instead of displays on the walls, these exhibitions comprise a group of digital images with associated text. Particular emphasis is on the utility of these images in class projects for elementary and secondary school students. However, the digital images also have potential value for more advanced scholarly research in preparation of papers in the Humanities, Social Sciences, and the Arts.
Contact:	Russ Harvey russ@cornucopia.ucr.edu

`gopher://gopher.ucr.edu`

California Privacy Act 1992

Text of the California Privacy Act of 1992.

Keywords:	Law, California
Audience:	General Public, Lawyers
Details:	Free

`gopher://wiretap.spies.com`

CERFnet Guide

A comprehensive guide to the CERFnet (California Education and Research Federation Network), a data-communications regional network that operates throughout California. The purpose of CERFnet is to advance science and education by assisting the interchange of information among research and educational institutions.

Keywords:	Internet, Science, Education, California
Audience:	Internet Surfers, Researchers, Educators
Contact:	CERFnet Hotline help@cerf.net
Details:	Free Files are in: cerfnet/cerfnet_info/cerfnet_guide/

`ftp://nic.cerf.net`

CERFNet News

This is a mid-level network linking academic, government, and industrial research facilities throughout California.

Keywords:	Education, California
Sponsor:	California Education and Research Federation Network
Audience:	Researchers, Students (college, graduate)
Contact:	help@cerf.net
Details:	Free

`gopher://gopher.cerf.net/11/cerfnet`

CAMIS (Center for Advanced Medical Informatics at Stanford)

CAMIS (Center for Advanced Medical Informatics at Stanford)

CAMIS is a shared computing resource supporting research activities in biomedical informatics.

Keywords:	Medical Informatics, Heuristics, Health Sciences
Sponsor:	Stanford University School of Medicine, Palo Alto, CA, USA
Audience:	Medical Informatics, Health Science Researchers
Profile:	The CAMIS gopher includes an Internet-wide title search, computing information, and technical reports for the Section on Medical Informatics (SMI) community as well as that of the Knowledge Systems Laboratory (KSL), information on the Heuristic Programming Project, pointers to various online library catalogs, and more.
Contact:	Torsten_Heycke@med.stanford.edu

`gopher://camis.stanford.edu/00/gopherdoc`

Canada

1991 Census of Population Documentation

This gopher provides Canadian Census information from 1991 including geographic and demographic information.

Keywords:	Census Data, Canada, Demography, Geography
Audience:	Canadians, Researchers, Demographers
Contact:	David McCallum carl@acadvm1.uottawa.ca

`gopher://alpha.epas.utoronto.ca/Data Library/Census of Population`

1994 Federal Budget (Canada)

This site offers full-text of Canada's federal budget. It also has a wealth of information on Canadian industry and industrial policy, including Provincial and Sectorial GATT opportunities and briefs from the Information Highway Advisory Council.

Keywords:	Canada, Government (International), Industry, Foreign Trade
Sponsor:	Industry Canada, Canada
Audience:	Canadians, Government Officials, Businesspeople, Researchers
Contact:	Tyson Macaulay tyson@debra.dgbt.doc.ca

`gopher://debra.dgbt.doc.ca/industry canada documents/isc.news.releases`

Biking in Canada

A repository of information for bicyclists, including utility programs, events, FAQs, and how-to guides; some with Canadian-specific details.

Keywords:	Sports, Bicycling, Canada
Sponsor:	Habitat Ecology Division at the Bedford Institute of Oceanography
Audience:	Cyclists, Fitness Enthusiasts
Contact:	sysop@biome.bio.ns.ca
Details:	Free

`gopher://gopher.biome.bio.dfo.ca/pub/biking`

Can-Stud-Assoc

This is a mailing list for anyone who might wish to discuss Canadian postsecondary education and student associations' involvement in it.

Keywords:	Canada, Education (Post-Secondary)
Audience:	Canadians, Students (college)
Contact:	can-stud-assoc-request@unixg.ubc.ca
Details:	Free
User Info:	To subscribe to the list, send an e-mail message requesting a subscription to the URL address below.
	To send a message to the entire list, address it to:
	can-stud-assoc@unixg.ubc.ca

`mailto:can-stud-assoc-request@unixg.ubc.ca`

Canada

The wiretap gopher provides access to a range of Canadian documents in full-text format in French.

Keywords:	Canada, French
Audience:	Canadian Citizens, Lawyers
Details:	Free

`gopher://wiretap.spies.com`

CANADA (Canadian News and Information Library)

The Canadian News and Information Library (CANADA) contains Canadian legal news, business and company information.

Keywords:	News, Analysis, Companies, Canada
Audience:	Canadians
Profile:	The CANADA library contains respected Canadian news publications such as *The Toronto Star*, *The Vancouver Sun*, *Ottawa Business News*, and the *Montreal Gazette*. The CANADA library also offers Canadian company profiles, country reports, and Canada's financial database, CANCORP Plus.
Contact:	Mead New Sales Group at (800) 227-4908 or (513) 859-5398 inside the US, or (513) 865-7981 for all inquiries outside the US.
User Info:	To subscribe, contact Mead directly.
	To examine the Nexis user guide, you can access it at the ftp site of the University of Texas at Austin at the URL address: ftp://ftp.cc.utexas.edu
	The files are in: /pub/ref-services/LEXIS

`telnet://nex.meaddata.com`

`http://www.meaddata.com`

Canadian Geographical WWW Index Travel

This web site provides weekly weather information.

Keywords:	Weather, Travel, Canada, Geography
Sponsor:	University of Manitoba, Canada
Audience:	Travelers, Educators, Students
Contact:	www@umanitoba.ca
Details:	Free

`http://www.umanitoba.ca`

CCES-L

A mailing list for the national communication branch of the CFES (Canadian Federation of Engineering Students).

Keywords:	Engineering, Canada
Audience:	Engineers, Students
Contact:	Canadian Federation of Engineering Students cfes@jupiter.sun.csd.unb.ca
Details:	Free
User Info:	To subscribe to the list, send an e-mail message to the URL address below consisting of a single line reading:
	SUB cces-l YourFirstName YourLastName
	To send a message to the entire list, address it to: cces-l@unb.ca

`mailto:listserv@unb.ca`

CEC

CEC (Canadian Electro-Acoustics Community).

Keywords:	Engineering, Acoustical Engineering, Canada, Canadian Electro-Acoustics Community
Audience:	Engineers
Contact:	Peter Gross GROSSPA@QUCDN
Details:	Free
User Info:	To subscribe to the list, send an e-mail message to the URL address below, consisting of a single line reading:
	SUB cec YourFirstName YourLastName
	To send a message to the entire list, address it to: cec@qucdn.queensu.ca

`mailto:listserv@qucdn.queensu.ca`

CFES-L

National communication branch of the CFES (Canadian Federation of Engineering Students).

Keywords:	Engineering, Students, Canada
Audience:	Engineers, Students
Contact:	Canadian Federation of Engineering Students cfes@jupiter.sun.csd.unb.ca
Details:	Free
User Info:	To subscribe to the list, send an e-mail message to the URL address below consisting of a single line reading:
	SUB cfes-l YourFirstName YourLastName
	To send a message to the entire list, address it to: CfES-L@UNB.CA

`mailto:listserv@unb.ca`

Freedom of Information Directory of Records (Canada)

A database compiled by the Canadian federal government listing documents available to the public under The Freedom of Information and Protection of Privacy Act. It can be searched by keyword, or browsed through a menuing system.

Keywords:	Canada, Government (International), Freedom of Information Act
Sponsor:	British Columbia Systems Corporation, British Columbia, Canada
Audience:	Canadians, Journalists, Activists
Contact:	Office of the Information and Privacy Commissione tcphelp@bcsc02.gov.bc.ca

`gopher://bcsc02.gov.bc.ca`

MegaGopher

This is the gopher at the University of Montreal. It supports the software and information requirements for the MegaSequencing project. It also serves as a repository of data for organellar genome and molecular evolution research and acts as the focal point for the GDE (Genetic Data Environment) package.

Keywords:	Biology, Canada
Audience:	Biologists
Contact:	Tim Littlejohn tim@bch.umontreal.ca
Details:	Free

`gopher://megasun.bch.umontreal.ca`

Natural Resources Canada (NRCan) Gopher

This site offers information on forests, energy, mining, and geomatics from the Canadian government. Also has reports from the Geological Survey of Canada and an overview of NRCan statutes, organization, and personnel. Provides links to other Canadian environmental and government gophers.

Keywords:	Canada, Environment, Geology, Forestry
Sponsor:	The Department of Natural Resources, Canada
Audience:	Canadians, Environmentalists, Environmental Researchers, Geologists

Canadian Documents

Contact: Bob Fillmore
fillmore@emr.ca

Notes: NRCan maintains a toll-free hotline (800) 267-5166

`gopher://gopher.emr.ca`

`http://www.emr.ca/`

NLC (National Library of Canada)

A Canadian library gopher in French and English.

Keywords: Canada, Libraries, Library Science
Sponsor: National Library of Canada (NLC), Canada
Audience: Canadians, Librarians, Publishers
Profile: This site provides a gateway to Canadian library and Internet resources linking users to the National Library, which offers a bibliographic database, a list of NLC publications, and other services for libraries and publishers. It also has links to many other Canadian libraries and Internet services, as well as a large selection of general information from and about the Government of Canada and its provinces.
Contact: Nancy Brodie, Lynn Herbert
Nancy.Brodie@nlc-bnc.ca,
Lynn.Herbert@nlc-bnc.ca

`gopher://gopher.nlc-bnc.ca`

North American Free Trade Agreement (NAFTA) ★

The agreement between the governments of Canada, the United Mexican States, and the United States of America to establish a free trade area in North America.

Keywords: Trade, US, Mexico, Canada, Free Trade, NAFTA
Audience: Journalists, Politicians, Economists, Students
Details: Free

`gopher://wiretap.spies.com/00/Gov/NAFTA`

Open Government Pilot ★★

This web site provides information concerning the Canadian government, including information on Canadian infrastructure, industry, communications, provinces, and parliament.

Keywords: Canada, Government (International)
Sponsor: Canadian Federal Government
Audience: Canadians, Educators, Students
Details: Free

`http://debra.dgbt.doc.ca/opengov`

Open Government Project (Canada)

This site provides online audio-visual and text information on the Canadian government.

Keywords: Canada, Government
Sponsor: Directorate of Communications Development, Industry Canada, Canada
Audience: Canadians, Government Officials, Journalists
Profile: This bilingual (French/English) site has detailed information on members of the Canadian Senate and House of Commons, as well as Supreme Court rulings and biographies of the justices. It features a number of pictures, maps, and links to other Canadian information servers.
Contact: Tyson Macaulay
tyson.macaulay@crc.doc.ca

`http://debra.dgbt.doc.ca/ogp.html`

`gopher://debra.dgbt.doc.ca/open_government_project`

PEI (Prince Edward Island, Canada) Crafts Council Gopher ★★

A gopher devoted to all manner of crafts, from weaving to glass blowing. Information includes a database of tools, services, and materials for crafts enthusiasts, as well as FAQs and pointers to other crafts resources. Also provides background on the PEI Craft Council's activities and on Prince Edward Island.

Keywords: Crafts, Hobbies, Canada
Sponsor: PEI Crafts Council, Prince Edward Island, Canada
Audience: Crafts Enthusiasts
Details: Free

`gopher://crafts-council.pe.ca`

soc.culture.canada ★

A Usenet newsgroup providing information and discussion about Canada and its people.

Keywords: Culture, Canada, Sociology
Audience: Sociologists, Canadians
Details: Free
User Info: To subscribe to this Usenet newsgroup, you need access to a newsreader.

`news:soc.culture.canada`

Statistics Canada Gopher ★★★★

A repository of information from the National Statistical Agency of Canada.

Keywords: Statistics, Canada, Canadian Documents
Sponsor: Statistics Canada, Canada
Audience: Canadians, Researchers
Profile: Updated daily, this site allows users to search Statistics Canada documents and provides updates of upcoming statistical conferences and publications in Canada. It also allows access to Statistics Canada FTP and list servers.
Contact: Michael Thoen, Jackie Godfrey
thoemic@statcan.ca,
godfrey@statcan.ca

`gopher://talon.statcan.ca`

Supreme Court of Canada ★★

This gopher allows access to Canadian Supreme Court rulings from 1993 forward. Documents are available as full-text and searchable by keyword. This site also has information on Canadian statute and case law.

Keywords: Law (International), Canada
Sponsor: Universite de Montreal Law Gopher Project, Montreal, Canada
Audience: Lawyers, General Public
Contact: Pablo Fuentes
fuentesp@droit.umontreal.ca

`gopher://gopher.droit.umontreal.ca/English/SCC`

University of Saskatchewan Libraries ★★

A major Canadian University library with access to library catalogs archives, and Canadian Government documents.

Keywords: Canada, Government (International)
Sponsor: University of Saskatchewan
Audience: Canadians, General Public
Profile: The University of Saskatchewan Libraries maintain online databases of their collections archives, and catalogs. The libraries are a voluminous resource for the study of Canada, Canadian government, and Canadian-American issues.

Login: sonia

`telnet://sklib.usask.ca`

Canadian Documents

Statistics Canada Gopher ★★★★

A repository of information from the National Statistical Agency of Canada.

Keywords: Statistics, Canada, Canadian Documents
Sponsor: Statistics Canada, Canada
Audience: Canadians, Researchers

124 Canadian Documents

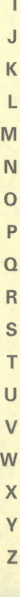

Profile: Updated daily, this site allows users to search Statistics Canada documents and provides updates of upcoming statistical conferences and publications in Canada. It also allows access to Statistics Canada FTP and list servers.

Contact: Michael Thoen, Jackie Godfrey
thoemic@statcan.ca
godfrey@statcan.ca

`gopher://talon.statcan.ca`

University of Nevada, Las Vegas Library - Las Vegas, NV ★★

The library's holdings are large and wide-ranging and contain significant collections in many fields.

Keywords: Gaming, Hotel Administration, Nevadiana, Canadian Documents, Nevada State Documents

Audience: General Public, Researchers, Librarians, Document Delivery Professionals

Contact: Myoung-ja Lee Kwon
kwon@nevada.edu.

Details: Free

Expect: login; Send: library

`telnet://library.lv-lib.nevada.edu`

Canadian Electro-Acoustics Community

CEC

CEC (Canadian Electro-Acoustics Community).

Keywords: Engineering, Acoustical Engineering, Canada, Canadian Electro-Acoustics Community

Audience: Engineers

Contact: Peter Gross
grosspa@qucdn

Details: Free

User Info: To subscribe to the list, send an e-mail message to the URL address below, consisting of a single line reading:

SUB cec YourFirstName YourLastName

To send a message to the entire list, address it to:

cec@qucdn.queensu.ca

`mailto:listerv@qucdn.queensu.ca`

Canadian University Consortium on Health in International Development (CANCHID)

Canadian University Consortium on Health in International Development (CANCHID) ★

CANCHID is a multi-campus consortium that includes medical schools and other educational institutions devoted to research and projects dealing with health care issues in developing countries.

Keywords: Health, International Development

Audience: Public Health, Medicine, International Aid Agencies

Contact: Sam Lanfranco
lanfran@vm1.yorku.ca

Details: Free

User Info: To subscribe to the list, send an e-mail message to the URL address below, consisting of a single line reading:

SUB canchid YourFirstName YourLastName

To send a message to the entire list, address it to:

canchid@vm1.yorku.ca

`mailto:listserv@vm1.yorku.ca`

Canadian-American Studies

University of Maine System Library Catalog ★★

The library's holdings are large and wide-ranging and contain significant collections in many fields.

Keywords: Ucadian Studies, St. John Valley (History of), Canadian-American Studies, Geology, Aquaculture, Maine

Audience: General Public, Researchers, Librarians, Document Delivery Professionals

Contact: Elaine Albright, Marilyn Lutz

Details: Free

Expect: login, Send: ursus

`telnet://ursus.maine.edu`

Cancer

IST BioGopher ★

This is the gopher server of the National Institute for Cancer Research (IST) and of the Advanced Biotechnology Center of Genoa, Italy.

Keywords: Cancer, Biotechnology, Italy, Europe

Audience: Biologists, Medical Researchers

Profile: The server includes data from the Interlab Project Databases (biological materials availability in European laboratories) and the Bio-Media Bulletin Board System (biotechnology researchers, projects, fundings and products).

Contact: gophman@istge.ist.unige.it

Details: Free

`gopher://istge.ist.unige.it`

National Cancer Center, Tokyo, Japan ★

This is the information service for the National Cancer Center in Tokyo, Japan, as well as the entry point for the Japanese Cancer Research Resources Bank (JCRB).

Keywords: Cancer, Japan

Audience: Biologists, Medical Researchers

Contact: ncc-gopher-news@gan.ncc.go.jp

Details: Free

`gopher://ncc.go.jp`

Canopus

Canopus ★★★

Newsletter of the Space Science and Astronomy Technical Committee of the American Institute of Aeronautics and Astronautics. Its objective is to provide an insider's perspective on issues in space science and astronomy.

Keywords: Space Science, Astronomy

Sponsor: NASA (National Aeronautics and Space Administration)

Audience: Astronomers, Space Scientists

Contact: William W. L. Taylor
wtaylor@nhqvax.hq.nasa.gov

Details: Costs

User Info: To subscribe to the list, send an e-mail message to the URL address below.

`mailto:wtaylor@nhqvax.hq.nasa.gov`

Cantus

Cantus

This gopher site accesses the Gregorian Chant Database, which is maintained by the Catholic University of America.

Keywords: Gregorian Chants, Music, Liturgy
Sponsor: Catholic University of America (CUA)
Audience: Vocalists, Educators, Students
Profile: The database contains an introduction to the Cantus Gopher at the CUA, and has a searchable index.

`gopher://vmsgopher.cua.edu`

Card Games

ba-Poker ★

Discussion of poker as it is available to residents of and visitors to the San Francisco Bay area (broadly defined), in home games as well as in licensed card rooms. Topics include upcoming events, unusual games, strategies, comparisons of various venues, and player "networking."

Keywords: Poker, Card Games, San Francisco Bay Area
Audience: Poker Players
Contact: Martin Veneroso
ba-poker-request@netcom.com
Details: Free
User Info: To subscribe to the list, send an e-mail message requesting a subscription to the URL address below.
To send a message to the entire list, address it to: ba-poker@netcom.com

`mailto:ba-poker-request@netcom.com`

Cards ★

This list is for people interested in collecting, speculating, and investing in baseball, football, basketball, hockey, and other trading cards memorabilia. Discussion and want/sell lists are welcome.

Keywords: Trading Cards, Collectibiles, Memorabilia
Audience: Sports Card Collectors, Sports Card Traders, Memorabilia Collectors
Contact: Keane Arase
cards-request@tanstaafl.uchicago.edu
Details: Free
User Info: To subscribe to the list, send an e-mail message requesting a subscription to the URL address below.
To send a message to the entire list, address it to:
cards@tanstaafl.uchicago.edu
Notes: The list is open to anyone.

`mailto:cards-request@tanstaafl.uchicago.edu`

rec.gambling

Discussion of card games, gambling, and gambling sites.

Keywords: Card Games, Gambling
Audience: Card Players, Gamblers
Profile: Discussion in this group covers gambling, and card games, the rules of various card games, odds, betting, and the pros and cons of various gambling and card playing sites. The archived FAQ is a lengthy card game resource.
Contact: rec.gambling Moderator
jacobs@cs.utah.edu
Notes: The rec.gambling FAQ is accessible via anonymous ftp at soda.berkeley.edu through the path pub/rec.gambling.

`news:rCardiopulmonary Medicine`

Cardopulmonary Medicine

University of Texas Health Science Center at Tyler Library ★★

The library's holdings are large and wide-ranging and contain significant collections in many fields.

Keywords: Biochemistry, Cardiopulmonary Medicine, Cell Biology, Family Practice, Molecular Biology
Audience: Researchers, Students, General Public
Details: Free
Expect: Username Prompt, Send: LIS

`telnet://athena.uthscsa.edu`

`ec.gambling`

Careers

CAREER (Career Library)

The LEXIS Career Library contains job and job-related information.

Keywords: Employment, Careers
Audience: Lawyers, Law Students
Profile: The LEXIS Career Library contains job and job-related information designed to assist the student and attorney in finding the right job. The Career Library contains a number of helpful directories, many of which have an "Address" feature that enables users to generate a mailing list from their answer set.
Contact: Mead New Sales Group at (800) 227-4908 or (513) 859-5398 inside the US, or (513) 865-7981 for all inquires outside the US.
Details: Costs
User Info: To subscribe, contact Mead directly.
To examine the Lexis user guide, you can access it at the ftp site of the University of Texas at Austin at the URL address: ftp://ftp.cc.utexas.edu
The files are in: /pub/res-services/LEXIS

`telnet://nex.meaddata.com`

Occupational Outlook Handbook 1992-93

An annual U.S. Department of Labor publication that provides detailed information for more than 320 occupations, including job descriptions, typical salaries, education and training requirements, working conditions, job outlook, and more.

Keywords: Careers, Employment, Labor
Sponsor: U.S. Deptartment of Labor
Audience: General Public, Job Seekers, Business Professionals
Details: Free

`gopher://umslvma.umsl.edu/11/library/govdocs/ooha`

Caribbean

amlat.mujeres

This conference serves as a forum for interchange between organizations and women's movements in Latin America and the Caribbean.

Keywords: Women, Latin America, Caribbean, Feminism
Audience: Women, Feminists, Activists
Contact: Agencia Latinoamericana de Informacion
info@alai.ec, uualai@ecuanex.ec
Details: Costs
Establish an account on the nearest APC node. Login, type c for conferences, then type: **go amlat.mujeres**.
For information on the nearest APC node, contact:
APC International Secretariat IBASE
E-mail: apcadmin@apc.org
Contact: Carlos Afonso (cafonso@ax.apc.org) or APC North American Regional Office e-mail: apcadmin@apc.org
Edie Farwell (efarwell@igc.apc.org)

`telnet://igc.apc.org`

cread (Latin American & Caribbean Distance & Continuing Education)

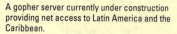

This is a digest list of distance education information primarily focused on Latin America and the Caribbean.

Keywords: Latin America, Caribbean, Education (Distance)

Audience: Educators, Administrators, Faculty

Details: Free

User Info: To subscribe to the list, send an e-mail message to the URL address below consisting of a single line reading: SUB cread YourFirstName YourLastName.

To send a message to the entire list, address it to: cread@yorkvm1.bitnet

`mailto:listserv@yorkvm1.bitnet`

Latin America & Caribbean Network Gopher server

A gopher server currently under construction providing net access to Latin America and the Caribbean.

Keywords: Caribbean, Latin America

Sponsor: Lacnet Corporation

Audience: Caribbean Enthusiasts

Profile: The Latin America & Caribbean Network Gopher server is a gopher server currently under construction. When finished it will provide gopher access to gopher servers throughout Latin America and the Caribbean providing government and institutional information on various countries.

Contact: Luis Rodriguez or Javier Hidalgo lrodriguez@mia.lac.net or jhidalgo@mia.lac.net

Notes: Currently under construction.

`gopher://mia.lac.net`

Carnivorous Plants

CP

Topics of interest to the group include the cultivation and propagation of CP's (carnivorous plants), field observations of CP's, sources of CP material, and CP trading between members. The discussion is not moderated, and usually consists of short messages offering plants for trade, asking CP questions and advice, relating experiences with plant propagation, and so on. The group also maintains archives of commercial plant sources and members growing lists.

Keywords: Carnivorous Plants, Botany

Audience: Horticulturists, Botanists

Contact: Rick Walker walker@hpl-opus.hpl.hp.com

User Info: To subscribe to the list, send an e-mail message to the address below consisting of a single line reading:

SUB CP YourFirstName YourLastName

To send a message to the entire list, address it to: CP@hpl-opus.hpl.hp.com

`mailto:listserv@hpl-opus.hpl.hp.com`

Carter (Hodding)

Mississippi State University Library

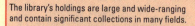

The library's holdings are large and wide-ranging and contain significant collections in many fields.

Keywords: History (US), Forestry, Energy, Carter (Hodding, Papers of), Mississippi

Audience: General Public, Researchers, Librarians, Document Delivery Professionals

Contact: Stephen Cunetto shc1@ra.msstate.edu

Details: Free

Expect: username, Send: msu; Expect: password, Send: library

Cartography

next-gis

Discussion of Geographical Information Systems (GIS) and cartography-related topics on the NeXT and other workstation computers. Some moderated reposting of comp.infosys.gis occurs as well.

Keywords: Geography, Cartography, GIS, NeXT

Audience: GIS Users, NeXT Users

Contact: Steven R. Staton sstaton@deltos.com

Details: Free

User Info: To subscribe to the list, send an e-mail message to the URL address shown below consisting of a single line reading:

SUB next-gis YourFirstName YourLastName

To send a message to the entire list, address it to: next-gis@DistributionAddress

`mailto:listserv@deltos.com`

The University of Kansas Library

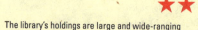

The library's holdings are large and wide-ranging and contain significant collections in many fields.

Keywords: Botany, Chinese Studies, Cartography, Kansas, Opera, Ornithology, Joyce (James), Yeats (William Butler), Walpole (Sir Robert, Collections of)

Audience: General Public, Researchers, Librarians, Document Delivery Professionals

Contact: John S. Miller

Details: Free

Expect: Username, Send: relay <cr>

`telnet://kuhub.cc.ukans.edu`

University of Wisconsin at Milwaukee Library

The library's holdings are large and wide-ranging and contain significant collections in many fields.

Keywords: Art, Architecture, Business, Cartography, Geography, Geology, Urban Studies, Literature (English), Literature (American)

Audience: Researchers, Students, General Public

Details: Free

Expect: Login, Send: Lib; Expect: vDIAL prompt, Send: Library

`telnet://uwmcat.lib.uwm.edu`

USGS (United States Geological Survey) Gopher

A gopher site covering issues related to the United State Geological Survey.

Keywords: Cartography, Geology

Sponsor: United States Geological Survey

Audience: Geologists, Cartologists

Profile: The USGS gopher was established to provide general information about USGS, information about USGS Divisions, publications, data, and briefings, USGS's Network resources, and other data on geology, hydrology, and cartography.

Contact: Gopher Operator webmaster@info.er.usgs.gov

`gopher://info.er.usgs.gov`

`telnet://libserv.msstate.edu`

Cartoons

alt.binaries.pictures.cartoons

A Usenet newsgroup devoted to cartoon illustrations.

Keywords: Cartoons

Audience: Animators, General Public

User Info: To subscribe to this Usenet newsgroup, you need access to a newsreader.

`news://alt.binaries.pictures.cartoons`

The University of Iowa Libraries

The library's holdings are large and wide-ranging and contain significant collections in many fields.

Keywords: Hunt (Leigh), Native American Studies, Typography, Railroads, Cartoons, French Revolution, NASA, Hydraulics

Audience: General Public, Researchers, Librarians, Document Delivery Professionals

Details: Free

Send <RETURN> to display a menu of available systems. Type 1 for OASIS access and press <RETURN> to display the Welcome to OASIS screen.

`telnet://oasis.uiowa.edu`

Case Law (US)

MEGA (Combined Federal/State Case Law)

The Federal/State Case Law combined library contains files that allow one-stop searching of combined federal and state case law on the LEXIS service. American Law Reports (ALR)) and Lawyers' Edition, 2d articles are also included.

Keywords: Case Law (US), Law (US State), Law (US Federal)

Audience: Lawyers

Profile: The MEGA file is a one-stop search of all available federal and state case law on the LEXIS service. The circuit-base MEGA files combine federal and state case law from federal and state courts within the geographical area defined by the federal circuit. The state-based MEGA files combine case law from the courts of the state plus case law from the federal circuit for that state and the federal district courts within the state. Two chronological files restrict combined federal and state case law searches to particular date ranges. Each MEGA file includes all available U.S. Supreme Court cases. American Law Reports (ALR) and Lawyers' Edition, 2d (LEd2) articles are also included.

Contact: New Sales Group @ (800) 227-4908 or (513) 859-5398 inside the US, or (413) 865-7981 for all inquires outside the US.

User Info: To subscribe, contact Mead directly.

To examine the Lexis user guide, you can access it at the ftp site of the University of Texas at Austin at the URL address: ftp://ftp.cc.utexas.edu

The files are in: /pub/res-services/LEXIS

`telnet://nex.meaddata.com`

STATES (States Library)

The combined States Library contains case law, code, and agency materials from the 53 individual US state libraries (50 states plus the District of Columbia, Puerto Rico, and the Virgin Islands), all in the same library.

Keywords: Law, Analysis, Case Law, States

Audience: Lawyers

Profile: The combined States Library contains case law, code, and agency materials from the 53 individual state libraries (50 states plus the District of Columbia, Puerto Rico and the Virgin Islands), all in the same library. The States library also features many large group files which allow several individual files to be accessed in the same search. Many of the group files involve case law, including files that cover all state case law available on the LEXIS service plus ALR material and files that combine all federal and state case law available on the LEXIS service.

Contact: New Sales Group at 800-227-4908 or 513-859-5398 inside the US, or 1-513-865-7981 for all inquires outside the US.

User Info: To subscribe, contact Mead directly.

To examine the Lexis user guide, you can access it at the ftp site of the University of Texas at Austin at the URL address: ftp://ftp.cc.utexas.edu

The files are in: /pub/ref-services/LEXIS

`telnet://nex.meaddata.com`

`http://www.meaddata.com`

Catalyst

Catalyst

This is the electronic version of Catalyst, a refereed print journal for community college educators.

Keywords: Education (Adult), Education (Distance), Education (Continuing), Education (International)

Audience: Educators, Administrators, Faculty, Researchers

Details: Free

User Info: To subscribe to the journal, send an e-mail message to the URL address below, consisting of a single line reading:

SUB catalyst YourFirstName YourLastName

To send a message to the entire list, address it to: catalyst@vtvm1.bitnet

`mailto:listserv@vtvm1.cc.vt.edu`

Catholicism

AmerCath (History of American Catholicism)

This mailing list focuses on the history of American Catholicism.

Keywords: Catholicism, Christianity, Religion

Sponsor: Jefferson Community College, University of Kentucky, Louisville, KY, USA

Audience: Researchers, Educators, Students, Catholics

Profile: Since AMERCATH can be accessed internationally, it thus forms a global network of people who research and teach the history of American Catholicism. AMERCATH facilitates communication among faculty, students, and researchers.

Contact: Anne Kearney
jccannek@ukcc.uky.edu

Details: Free

User Info: To subscribe to the list, send an e-mail message to the address below, consisting of a single line reading:

Sub AmerCath YourFirstName YourLastName

To send a message to the entire list, address it to:

AmerCath@ukcc.uky.edu

`mailto:listserv@ukcc.uky.edu`

Catholic

The Catholic mailing list is a forum for Catholics who wish to discuss their discipleship to Jesus Christ in terms of the Catholic approach to Christianity. "Catholic" is loosely defined as anyone embracing the Catholic approach to Christianity whether Roman Catholic, Anglo-Catholic, or Orthodox. Discussions on ecumenism are encouraged.

Keywords: Catholicism, Ecumenism, Religion

Audience: Catholics, Priests, Theologians

Contact: Cindy Smith
cms@dragon.com

Details: Free

User Info: To subscribe to the list, send an e-mail message to the address below, consisting of a single line reading:

SUB Catholic YourFirstName YourLastName

To send a message to the entire list, address it to:

Catholic@american.edu

Notes: This list is also bi-directionally forwarded to the newsgroup bit.listserv.catholic.

`mailto:listserv@american.edu`

Catholic Doctrine

This is for discussions of orthodox Catholic theology by everyone under the jurisdiction of the Holy Father, John Paul II. No attacks on the Catholic Church here, please.

Keywords:	Theology, Catholocism
Audience:	Catholics, Priests, Theologians
Contact:	catholic-request@sarto.gaithersburg.md.us
Details:	Free
User Info:	To subscribe to the list, send an e-mail message requesting a subscription to the URL address below.
	To send a message to the entire list, address it to:
	catholic@sarto.gaithersburg.md.us
Notes:	There is an archive server (containing Catholic art and magisterial documents) associated with this list. Send mail to the URL address below to get details about the archive server.

mailto:catholic-request@sarto.gaithersburg.md.us

Catholic University of America Gopher

Gopher server of the Catholic University of America.

Keywords:	Catholicism, Libraries
Sponsor:	Catholic University of America
Audience:	Catholics
Profile:	The Catholic University of America gopher provides access to CUA's libraries and archived material as well as providing links to outside, and foreign, related gophers, and electronic resources.

gopher://gopher.cua.edu

Catholic-action

Catholic-action is a moderated list concerned with Catholic evangelism, church revitalization, and preservation of Catholic teachings, traditions, and values, and the vital effort to decapitate modernist heresy.

Keywords:	Catholicism, Evangelism, Religion
Audience:	Catholics, Priests
Contact:	Richard Freeman rfreeman@vpnet.chi.il.us
Details:	Free
User Info:	To subscribe to the list, send an e-mail message requesting a subscription to the URL address below.

mailto:rfreeman@vpnet.chi.il.us

CAUCE-L (Canadian Association for University Continuing Education)

CAUCE-L (Canadian Association for University Continuing Education)

Provides an electronic forum for the discussion of issues (broad, narrow, practical, theoretical, controversial, or mundane) related to university continuing education.

Keywords:	Education (Adult), Education (Distance), Education (Continuing)
Sponsor:	Canadian Association for University Continuing Education
Audience:	Educators, Administrators, Faculty
Details:	Free
User Info:	To subscribe to the list, send an e-mail message to the URL address below, consisting of a single line reading:
	SUB cauce-l YourFirstName YourLastName
	To send a message to the entire list, address it to: cauce@max.cc.uregina.ca

mailto:listserv@max.cc.uregina.ca

Caves

alt.caving

A Usenet newsgroup dedicated to discussions of caving and related issues, including cave locations, equipment, spelunking techniques, and other caving information.

Keywords:	Spelunking, Caves
Audience:	Spelunkers
User Info:	To subscribe to this Usenet newsgroup, you need access to a newsreader.

news://alt.caving

Cavers

This is an information resource and forum for anyone interested in exploring caves.

Keywords:	Caves, Spelunking
Audience:	Cave Explorers, Spelunkers
Contact:	John D. Sutter cavers-request@vlsi.bu.edu
Details:	Free
User Info:	To subscribe to the list, send an e-mail message requesting a subscription to the URL address below.
	To send a message to the entire list, address it to:
	cavers@vlsi.bu.edu

mailto:cavers-request@vlsi.bu.edu

CBDS-l

CBDS-l

A mailing list for the discussion of CBDS (Circuit Board Design System).

Keywords:	Engineering, Computer-Aided Design, Electronics
Audience:	Engineers
Contact:	netman@suvm.acs.syr.edu
Details:	Free
User Info:	To subscribe to the list, send an e-mail message to the URL address below consisting of a single line reading:
	SUB cbds-l YourFirstName YourLastName
	To send a message to the entire list, address it to:
	cbds-l@suvm.acs.syr.edu

mailto:listserv@suvm.acs.syr.edu

CCES-L

CCES-L

A mailing list for the national communication branch of the CFES (Canadian Federation of Engineering Students).

Keywords:	Engineering, Canada
Audience:	Engineers, Students
Contact:	Canadian Federation of Engineering Students cfes@jupiter.sun.csd.unb.ca
Details:	Free
User Info:	To subscribe to the list, send an e-mail message to the URL address below consisting of a single line reading:
	SUB cces-l YourFirstName YourLastName
	To send a message to the entire list, address it to: cces-l@unb.ca

mailto:listserv@unb.ca

CCNEWS

CCNEWS ★★★

An electronic forum for campus-computing newsletter editors and other publications specialists.

Keywords: Computers, Editors, Students, Newsletters
Audience: Students (college), Editors
Profile: CCNEWS consists of a biweekly newsletter that focuses on the writing, editing, designing, and producing of campus-computing publications, and an articles abstracts published on alternating weeks that describes new contributions to the articles archive.
Contact: Wendy Rickard Bollentin
ccnews@educom.bitnet
Details: Free
User Info: To subscribe to the list, send an e-mail message to the URL address below consisting of a single line reading:
SUB ccnews YourFirstName YourLastName
To send a message to the entire list, address it to: ccnews@educom.bitnet
Inquire about needing a password.

`mailto:listserv@bitnic.cren.net`

Cd-Forum

Cd-Forum ★

The purpose of this list is to provide support and to discuss/share experiences about gender-related issues, including cross dressing, transvestism, and transsexualism.

Keywords: Transsexualism, Transvestism, Sexuality, Gender
Audience: Transsexuals, Transvestites
Contact: Valerie
cd-request@valis.biocad.com
Details: Free
User Info: To subscribe to the list, send an e-mail message requesting a subscription to the URL address below.
To send a message to the entire list, address it to: cd@valis.biocad.com
Notes: This list is in digest format.

`mailto:cd-request@valis.biocad.com`

CD-ROM

Amiga CD-ROM ★

For Amiga users who are interested in CD-ROM drives and discs.

Keywords: Computers, Amiga, CD-ROM
Audience: Computer Users
Contact: ben@ben.com
Details: Free
User Info: To subscribe to the list, send an e-mail message requesting a subscription to the URL address below.
To send a message to the entire list, address it to: cdrom-list@ben.com

`mailto:cdrom-list-request@ben.com`

CDPub ★

CDPub is an electronic mailing list for those engaged or interested in CD-ROM publishing in general, and in desktop CD-ROM recorders and publishing systems in particular. Topics of interest to the list include information on the various desktop publishing systems for premastering using CD-ROM media and tapes (for example, DAT), replication services, various standards of interest to publishers (for example, ISO9660, RockRidge), retrieval engines, and platform independence issues. Discussions on all platforms are welcome.

Keywords: CD-ROM, Electronic Publishing, Desktop Publishing
Audience: CD-ROM Publishers, Desktop Publishers, Publishers
Contact: CDPub-Info@knex.via.mind.org
Details: Free
User Info: To subscribe to the list, send an e-mail message requesting a subscription to the URL address below.
To send a message to the entire list, address it to: CDPub@knex.via.mind.org

`mailto:mail-server@knex.via.mind.org`

CE Software

CE Software ★

Technical support for CE Software Products, such as QuickKeys for the Macintosh.

Keywords: Software, Technical Support, Macintosh
Audience: Software users
Details: Free
User Info: To subscribe to the list, send an e-mail message requesting a subscription to the URL address below.

`mailto:ce_info%cedsm@uunet.uu.net`

CEC

CEC ★

CEC (Canadian Electro-Acoustics Community).

Keywords: Engineering, Acoustical Engineering, Canada, Canadian Electro-Acoustics Community
Audience: Engineers
Contact: Peter Gross
grosspa@qucdn
Details: Free
User Info: To subscribe to the list, send an e-mail message to the URL address below, consisting of a single line reading:
SUB cec YourFirstName YourLastName
To send a message to the entire list, address it to:
cec@qucdn.queensu.ca

`mailto:listserv@qucdn.queensu.ca`

CEDAR (Central European Environmental Data Request) Facility

CEDAR (Central European Environmental Data Request) Facility ★★★

This gopher site provides information about the environmental and scientific community in Central and Eastern Europe (CEE), with access to environmental information located throughout the world on various international computer networks and hosts.

Keywords: Europe, EEC, Environment
Sponsor: The International Society for Environmental Protection, and The Austrian Federal Ministry for Environment, Youth and Family (BMUJF)
Audience: Environmentalists, Educators, Students, Urban Planners
Contact: cedar-info@cedar.univie.ac.at
Notes: CEDAR Marxergasse 3/20, A-1030 Vienna, Austria Tel.: +43-1-715 58 79

`gopher://pan.cedar.univie.ac.at`

CEE Environmental Libraries Database

CEE Environmental Libraries Database

A directory of over 300 libraries and environmental information centers in Central Eastern Europe that specalize in, or maintain significant collections of information about, the environment, ecology, sustainable living, or conservation. The database concentrates on six Central Eastern European countries: Bulgaria, Czech Republic, Hungary, Romania, Slovakia, and Poland.

Keywords: Central Eastern Europe, Environment, Sustainable Living, Bulgaria, Czech Republic, Hungary, Romania, Slovakia, Poland.

Sponsor: The Wladyslaw Poniecki Charitable Foundation, Inc.

Audience: Environmentalists, Green Movement, Librarians, Community Builders, Sustainable Living Specialists.

Profile: This database is the product of an Environmental Training Project (ETP) that was funded in 1992 by the US Agency for International Development as a 5-year cooperative agreement with a consortium headed by the University of Minnesota (US AID Cooperative Agreement Number EUR-0041-A-002-2020). Other members of the consortium include the University of Pittsburgh's Center for Hazardous Materials Research, The Institute for Sustainable Communities, and the World Wildlife Fund. The Wladyslaw Poniecki Charitable Foundation, Inc., was a subcontractor to the World Wildlife Fund and published the Directory of Libraries and Environmental Information Centers in Central Eastern Europe: A Locator/Directory. This gopher database consists of an electronic version of the printed directory, subsequently modified and updated online. Access to the data is facilitated by a WAIS search engine which makes it possible to retrieve information about libraries, subject area specializations, personnel, and so on.

Contact: Doug Kahn, CEDAR
kahn@pan.cedar.univie.ac.at

`gopher://gopher.poniecki.berkeley.edu`

Cell Biology

University of Texas Health Science Center at Tyler Library ★★

The library's holdings are large and wide-ranging and contain significant collections in many fields.

Keywords: Biochemistry, Cardiopulmonary Medicine, Cell Biology, Family Practice, Molecular Biology

Audience: Researchers, Students, General Public

Details: Free

Expect: Username Prompt, Send: LIS

`telnet://athena.uthscsa.edu`

Cell Church Discussion Group

Cell Church Discussion Group ★

A list for Christians who are in cell churches or in churches that are in transition to becoming cell churches, as well as anyone interested in learning more about cell churches. A cell church is a nontraditional form of church life in which small groups of Christians (cells) meet in a special way in their homes for the evangelism of the unchurched, the bonding of believers, their nurture, and ministry to one another.

Keywords: Cell Churches, Christianity, Evangelism, Religion

Audience: Christians, Theologians, Evangelists

Contact: Jon Reid
reid@cei.com

Details: Free

User Info: To subscribe to the list, send an e-mail message to the URL address below with the single word SUBSCRIBE in the body (not subject) of your message.

To send a message to the entire list, address it to: cell-church@bible.acu.edu

Notes: The group archives, FAQ, and helpful articles are available by anonymous FTP from bible.acu.edu; they can also be retrieved by sending mail to cell-church-archives@bible.acu.edu with the single word LIST for a list of files, or HELP for more information.

`mailto:cell-church-request@bible.acu.edu`

Cello

Cello ★

A DOS-based Internet browser incorporating WWW (World Wide Web), gopher, ftp, telnet, and usenet.

Keywords: Internet Tools, Cello, DOS

Audience: Internet Surfers

Details: Free

`ftp://fatty.law.cornell.edu`

`gopher://fatty.law.cornell.edu`

`http://fatty.law.cornell.edu`

Cello FAQ ★★★★

A site containing common questions and answers about Cello, a multipurpose Internet browser that allows access to the myriad information resources of the Internet. It supports World Wide Web, Gopher, FTP, CSO/pf/qi, and Usenet News retrievals natively, and other protocols (WAIS, Hytelnet, Telnet, and TN3270) through external clients and public gateways.

Keywords: Internet Tools, Internet Reference

Sponsor: Cornell Law School, New York, USA

Audience: Students, Computer Scientists, Researchers.

`http://www.law.cornell.edu/cello/cellofaq.html`

Cellular Technology

AT&T Bell Laboratories WWW Information Page ★★

This web site provides information on research and development at AT&T Bell Laboratories.

Keywords: Telecommunications, Technology, AT&T, Cellular Technology

Sponsor: AT&T Bell Laboratories

Audience: Engineers, Educators, Communications Specialists

Contact: webmaster@research.att.com

Details: Free

`http://www.research.att.com`

Celtic Culture

soc.culture.celtic ★

A Usenet newsgroup providing information and discussion about Irish Scottish, Britain, and Cornish culture.

Keywords: Celtic Culture, Sociology

Audience: Sociologists, Celts

Details: Free

User Info: To subscribe to this Usenet newsgroup, you need access to a newsreader.

`news:soc.culture.celtic`

Celtic Philology

Harvard University Library ★★

The library's holdings are large and wide-ranging and contain significant collections in many fields.

Keywords: Afrikaans, Alchemy, Arabic Culure (History of), Celtic Philology, Congo Languages, Folklore, Hebraica, Mormonism, Numismatics, Quakers, Sanskrit, Witchcraft, Arabic Philology

Audience: General Public, Researchers, Librarians, Document Delivery Professionals

Details: Free

Expect: Mitek Server..., Send: Enter or Return; Expect: prompt, Send: hollis

`telnet://hollis.harvard.edu`

Celtic Studies

soc.cultures.celtic

This Usenet newsgroup discusses all issues related to Celtic culture, including its history, language, art, and religion.

Keywords:	Celtic Studies
Sponsor:	Mo dhachaidh, Edinburgh, Scotland
Audience:	Anthropologists, Celtic Enthusiasts
Contact:	Godfrey Nolan godfrey@itc.icl.ie
User Info:	To subscribe to this Usenet newsgroup, you need access to a newsreader.
Notes:	The soc.culture.celtic FAQ is particularly large and contains many references to other online resources — it is posted to the newsgroup regularly.

`news://alt.cultures.celtic`

CEM-L

CEM-L

A mailing list for discussion surrounding the UTD (University of Texas at Dallas) Center for Engineering Mathematics.

Keywords:	Engineering, Mathematics
Audience:	Engineers, Mathematicians, Educators, Students
Contact:	David Lippke lippke@utdallas
Details:	Free
User Info:	To subscribe to the list, send an e-mail message to the URL address below, consisting of a single line reading: SUB cem-l YourFirstName YourLastName To send a message to the entire list, address it to: cem-l@utdallas.edu

`mailto:listserv@utdallas.edu`

Censorship

alt.censorship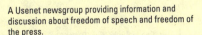

A Usenet newsgroup providing information and discussion about freedom of speech and freedom of the press.

Keywords:	Censorship, Freedom of Speech, Constitution (US), Activism
Audience:	Press, Students, Educators, Activists
User Info:	To subscribe to this Usenet newsgroup, you need access to a newsreader.

`news:alt.censorship`

Census Data

1991 Census of Population Documentation

This gopher provides Canadian census information from 1991 including geographic and demographic information.

Keywords:	Census Data, Canada, Demography, Geography
Audience:	Canadians, Researchers, Demographers
Contact:	David McCallum carl@acadvm1.uottawa.ca

`gopher://alpha.epas.utoronto.ca/Data Library/Census of Population`

LabStat

The public database of the Bureau of Labor Statistics.

Keywords:	Economics, Labor, Census Data
Sponsor:	United States Government, Bureau of Labor Statistics
Audience:	General Public, Statisticians, Researchers
Profile:	LABSTAT provides current and historical data, as well as numerous press releases. This site is composed of individual databases (in flat file format) corresponding to each of 26 surveys.
Contact:	labstat.helpdesk@bls.gov.
Details:	Free Login: anonymous; use e-mail address as password.
Notes:	For each news release published by the Bureau of Labor Statistics, the two most current are stored in the /news.release directory. The documentation provides a list of the abbreviations used to identify the news releases, and a description of the sub-directories available to the user.

`ftp://stats.bls.gov`

The Texas Information Highway

Access to the public information resources of the state of Texas.

Keywords:	Texas, States, Government, Census Data, Tourism
Sponsor:	Texas Department of Information Resources
Audience:	Texans, General Public
Profile:	Still under construction as we go to press, this is a model program to make state and local information resources available to Internet users. The current collection features city, country, and state political information, including full-text of bills before the Texas state legislature. Materials related to Texas history and tourism are also provided, along with links to Texas-area user groups and other state and federal information servers.
Contact:	Wayne McDilda wayne@dir.texas.gov

`gopher://info.texas.gov`

U.S. Bureau of the Census Gopher

A gopher offering official census data and services direct from the Census Bureau.

Keywords:	Census Data, Demography, Statistics
Sponsor:	U.S. Census Bureau
Audience:	Journalists, Government Officials, General Public
Profile:	A wealth of demographic and economic data from the Census Bureau. Information available includes population estimates, financial data from state and local governments, and assorted statistical briefs. This gopher also has details on the offices, programs, and personnel of the Bureau itself, as well as links to other federal information systems and sources of Census data.
Contact:	gatekeeper@census.gov
Details:	Free, Images

`gopher://gopher.census.gov`

`http://www.census.gov`

Center for Biomedical Informatics, Brazil

Center for Biomedical Informatics, Brazil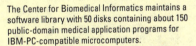

The Center for Biomedical Informatics maintains a software library with 50 disks containing about 150 public-domain medical application programs for IBM-PC-compatible microcomputers.

Keywords:	Health Sciences, Public Domain Software
Sponsor:	Center for Biomedical Informatics, Brazil
Audience:	Physicians, Nurses, Dentists, University Biomedical Researchers, Students
Details:	Costs To receive the catalogue in electronic form, send the following one-line message to infomed@ccvax.unicamp.br or infomed@bruc.bitnet: get public-domain p (for version in Portuguese) get public-domain e (for version in English). Instructions on how to acquire the software are included.

`ftp://ccsun.unicamp.br`

Center for Extreme Ultraviolet Astrophysics

Center for Extreme Ultraviolet Astrophysics

A department of the University of California at Berkeley devoted to research in extreme ultraviolet astronomy. It is the ground-based institution of EUVE (the Extreme Ultraviolet Explorer), a NASA satellite launched in 1992.

- Keywords: Astronomy, Astrophysics, EUVE, NASA, Satellite
- Sponsor: NASA and University of California at Berkeley
- Audience: Astronomers, Astrophysicists
- Profile: Provides access to details about the EUVE Guest Observer (EGO) Center, the EUVE Public Archive of Mission Data and Information, satellite operation information, and so on. The EUVE Guest Observer Center provides information, software, and data to EUVE Guest Observers.
- Contact: egoinfo@cea.berkeley.edu, archive@cea.berkeley.edu
- Details: Free

http://cea-ftp.cea.berkeley.edu/

Central Eastern Europe

CEE Environmental Libraries Database

A directory of over 300 libraries and environmental information centers in Central Eastern Europe that specalize in, or maintain significant collections of information about the environment, ecology, sustainable living, or conservation. The database concentrates on six Central Eastern European countries: Bulgaria, Czech Republic, Hungary, Romania, Slovakia, and Poland.

- Keywords: Central Eastern Europe, Environment, Sustainable Living, Bulgaria, Czech Republic, Hungary, Romania, Slovakia, Poland.
- Sponsor: The Wladyslaw Poniecki Charitable Foundation, Inc.
- Audience: Environmentalists, Green Movement, Librarians, Community Builders, Sustainable Living Specialists.
- Profile: This database is the product of an Environmental Training Project (ETP) that was funded in 1992 by the US Agency for International Development as a 5-year cooperative agreement with a consortium headed by the University of Minnesota (US AID Cooperative Agreement Number EUR-0041-A-002-2020). Other members of the consortium include the University of Pittsburgh's Center for Hazardous Materials Research, The Institute for Sustainable Communities, and the World Wildlife Fund. The Wladyslaw Poniecki Charitable Foundation, Inc., was a subcontractor to the World Wildlife Fund and published the Directory of Libraries and Environmental Information Centers in Central Eastern Europe: A Locator/Directory . This gopher database consists of an electronic version of the printed directory, subsequently modified and updated online. Access to the data is facilitated by a WAIS search engine which makes it possible to retrieve information about libraries, subject area specializations, personnel, and so on.
- Contact: Doug Kahn, CEDAR
  kahn@pan.cedar.univie.ac.at

gopher://gopher.poniecki.berkeley.edu

Central Europe

Central European Environment Data Report (CEDAR) Facility

This gopher site provides information about the environmental and scientific community in Central and Eastern Europe, with access to environmental information located throughout the world on various international computer networks and hosts.

- Keywords: Europe, Central Europe, Eastern Europe, Environment
- Sponsor: The International Society for Environmental Protection, and The Austrian Federaloerer), a NASA satellite launched in 1992.
- Keywords:
- Audience: Environmentalists, Educators, Students, Urban Planners, Environmental Scientists
- Profile: The CEDAR Facility, established in 1991, is administered by the International Society for Environmental Protection (ISEP). The Facility is designed to provide regional groups and individuals with access to its information retrieval and higher computing resources, technical advice and database and network access support. In addition, CEDAR works to facilitate information and dialogue exchange with organizations in other parts of the world and in partner countries; and to promote training forums, including the joint development of seminars and conferences with ISEP on environmental and network topics. Finally, CEDAR develops and manages environmental reference data sets, including a US EPA bibliographic reference on hazardous waste treatment, CEDAR databases on Central and Eastern European environmental expertise and information, and the holdings of the Regional Environmental Center Library at Budapest.
- Contact: cedar-info@cedar.univie.ac.at

gopher://pan.cedar.univie.ac.at

CERRO (Central European Regional Research Organization)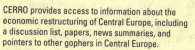

CERRO provides access to information about the economic restructuring of Central Europe, including a discussion list, papers, news summaries, and pointers to other gophers in Central Europe.

- Keywords: Central Europe, Economics, News
- Audience: Economists, Researchers, Journalists
- Contact: gunther.maier@wu-wien.ac.at
- Details: Free

gopher://osiris.wu.wein.ac.at

EcoDirectory

A directory of libraries and Environmental Information Centers in Central Eastern Europe.

- Keywords: Environment, Eastern Europe, Central Europe
- Sponsor: The Wladyslaw Poniecki Charitable Foundation, Inc.
- Audience: Environmentalists, Librarians, International Development Specialists
- Profile: This database is the product of an Environmental Training Project (ETP) that was founded in 1992 by the US Agency for International Development. The project concentrated on six Central and Eastern European countries: Bulgaria, Czech Republic, Hungary, Romania, Slovakia, and Poland.

  It contains information on over 300 libraries and Environmental Information Centers in those countries. Access to the data is facilitated by a WAIS search engine that makes it possible to retrieve information about libraries, subject area specializations, personnel, and so on.
- Contact: Joerg Findeisen, CEDAR
  findeisen@pan.cedar.univie.ac.at

gopher://gopher.poniecki.berkeley.edu

Cerebi

Cerebi

This list discusses the Cerebus comic book by Dave Sim. Anything relating to Cerebus or Sim is welcome.

- Keywords: Comic Books, Sim (Dave)
- Audience: Comics Enthusiasts
- Contact: Christian Walters
  cerebi-request@tomservo.b23b.ingr.com

Details: Free

User Info: To subscribe to the list, send an e-mail message requesting a subscription to the URL address below.

To send a message to the entire list, address it to: cerebi@tomservo.b23b.ingr.com

Notes: It's just an echo list, so anything that gets mailed is bounced to everyone.

`mailto:cerebi-request@tomservo.b23b.ingr.com`

CERFnet Guide

CERFnet Guide ★

A comprehensive guide to the CERFnet (California Education and Research Federation Network), a data-communications regional network that operates throughout California. The purpose of CERFnet is to advance science and education by assisting the interchange of information among research and educational institutions.

Keywords: Internet, Science, Education, California
Audience: Internet Surfers, Researchers, Educators
Contact: CERFnet Hotline
help@cerf.net
Details: Free
Files are in: cerfnet/cerfnet_info/cerfnet_guide/

`ftp://nic.cerf.net`

CERFNet News

CERFNet News ★

This is a mid-level network linking academic, government, and industrial research facilities throughout California.

Keywords: Education, California
Sponsor: California Education and Research Federation Network
Audience: Researchers, Students (college, graduate)
Contact: help@cerf.net
Details: Free

`gopher://gopher.cerf.net/11/cerfnet`

CERT (Computer Emergency Response Team) Advisory

CERT (Computer Emergency Response Team) Advisory ★★

A major directory on computer advisory, providing access to a broad range of related resources (library catalogs, databases, and servers) via the Internet.

Keywords: Computers, Security, Computer Networking
Audience: Computer Users
Profile: Profides information on how to obtain a patch or details of a workaround for a known computer security problem. CERT works with vendors to produce a workaround or a patch for a problem, and does not publish vulnerability information until a workaround or patch is available. A CERT advisory may also be a warning about ongoing attacks to network systems.
Contact: cert@cert.org

`ftp://cert.org/pub/cert_advisories`

Cervantes (Miguel de)

Dartmouth College Library ★★

The library's holdings are large and wide-ranging and contain significant collections in many fields.

Keywords: American Calligraphy, Cervantes (Miguel de), Railroads, Polar Regions, Frost (Robert), Shakespeare (William), Spanish Plays
Audience: General Public, Researchers, Librarians, Document Delivery Professionals
Contact: Katharina Klemperer
kathy.klemperer@dartmouth.edu
Details: Free
Expect: login, Send: wolfpac

`telnet://lib.dartmouth.edu`

CEXPRESS (Computer Express Internet Superstore)

CEXPRESS (Computer Express Internet Superstore) ★

Computer Express offers over 3,000 software titles and hardware products, available for immediate delivery.

Keywords: Computer Products
Audience: Consumers

`mailto:info@cexpress.com`

`gopher cexpress.com`

`http://cexpress.com`

cfcp-members

cfcp-members ★

The Confederation of Future Computer Professionals (CFCP) is a group of users on the Internet who are interested enough in various fields of computers to consider computers as their future. The Confederation exists to foster education and stimulate communication.

Keywords: Internet, Computers
Audience: Internet Surfers, Computer Users
Contact: mlindsey@nyx.cs.du.edu
Details: Free
User Info: To subscribe to the list, send an e-mail message requesting a subscription to the URL address below.

`mailto:mlindsey@nyx.cs.du.edu`

CFD

CFD

CFD (Computational Fluid Dynamics Group).
Keywords: Engineering, Fluid Dynamics
Audience: Engineers
Contact: justin@ukcc.uky.edu
justin@engr.uky.edu
Details: Free
User Info: To subscribe to the list, send an e-mail message to the URL address below, consisting of a single line reading:

SUB cfd YourFirstName YourLastName

To send a message to the entire list, address it to:

cfd@ukcc.uky.edu

`justin@ukcc.uky.edu`

CFES-L

CFES-L

National communication branch of the CFES (Canadian Federation of Engineering Students).

Keywords:	Engineering, Students, Canada
Audience:	Engineers, Students
Contact:	Canadian Federation of Engineering Students cfes@jupiter.sun.csd.unb.ca
Details:	Free
User Info:	To subscribe to the list, send an e-mail message to the URL address below consiting of a single line reading: SUB cfes-l YourFirstName YourLastName To send a message to the entire list, address it to: cfes-l@unb.ca

`mailto:listserv@unb.ca`

CGN (Christian Growth Newsletter)

CGN (Christian Growth Newsletter) ★

This site is intended to help Christians in personal growth, and includes testimonials and encouraging articles.

Keywords:	Christianity, Religion
Audience:	Christians
Contact:	Laura Smith bible@olsen.ch

`mailto:bible@olsen.ch`

Chalkhills

Chalkhills ★

A mailing list for the discussion of the music and records of XTC (the band).

Keywords:	Pop Music, XTC
Audience:	Pop Music Enthusiasts, XTC Enthusiasts
Contact:	John M. Relph chalkhills-request@presto.ig.com
Details:	Free
User Info:	To subscribe to the list, send an e-mail message requesting a subscription to the URL address below. To send a message to the entire list, address it to: chalkhills@presto.ig.com
Notes:	Chalkhills is moderated and distributed in a digest format.

`mailto:chalkhills-request@presto.ig.com`

Chaos Theory

Artificial Life

A forum for the accumulation and dissemination of information about all aspects of the Artificial Life enterprise. Services provided include an FTP site containing preprints and software, a bibliographic database on Artificial Life, and links to various Usenet services.

Keywords:	Artificial Life, Chaos Theory
Sponsor:	MITPress, Cambridge, Massachusetts, USA
Audience:	Mathematical Biologists, Researchers, Theoretical Biologists
Contact:	Chris Langton cgl@santafe.edu

`http://alife.santafe.edu`

Spanky Fractal Database ★★★★

This web site provides a collection of fractals and fractal-related material for free distribution on the Internet.

Keywords:	Mathematics, Chaos Theory, Computer Programming, Computer Graphics
Audience:	Mathematicians, Computer Programmers
Profile:	Contains information on dynamical systems, software, distributed fractal generators, galleries, and databases from all over the world.
Contact:	Noel Giffin noel@triumf.ca
Details:	Free

`http://spanky.triumf.ca`

Chat Groups

alt.kids-talk ★

A Usenet newsgroup that provides a place for the pre-collegiate to chat.

Keywords:	Chat Groups, Children
Audience:	Kids, Students (K-12)
User Info:	To subscribe to this Usenet newsgroup, you need access to a newsreader.

`news:alt.kids-talk`

alt.romance.chat ★

A Usenet newsgroup providing discussion about the romantic side of love.

Keywords:	Chat Groups, Romance
Audience:	General Public
User Info:	To subscribe to this Usenet newsgroup, you need access to a newsreader.

`news:alt.romance.chat`

k12.chat.junior ★

A Usenet newsgroup providing information and discussion for and about students in junior high school.

Keywords:	Students, Chat Groups
Audience:	Students (K-8)
Details:	Free
User Info:	To subscribe to this Usenet newsgroup, you need access to a newsreader.

`news:k12.chat.junior`

k12.chat.senior ★

A Usenet newsgroup providing information and discussion for and about students in senior high school.

Keywords:	Students, Chat Groups
Audience:	Students (K-12)
Details:	Free
User Info:	To subscribe to this Usenet newsgroup, you need access to a newsreader.

`news:k12.chat.senior`

Chaucer (Geoffrey)

Chaucer ★★

A discussion list on the subject of Medieval English literature, especially that of Chaucer.

Keywords:	Chaucer (Geoffrey), Literature (English)
Audience:	Chaucer Fans, English Teachers
Contact:	Dan Mosser mosserd@vtm1.cc.vt.edu

`mailto: CHAUCER@VTM1.CC.VT.EDU`

University of Chicago Library ★★

The library's holdings are large and wide-ranging and contain significant collections in many fields.

Keywords:	English Bibles, Lincoln (Abraham), Kentucky & Ohio River Valley (History of), Balzac (Honore de), American Drama, Cromwell (Oliver), Goethe, Judaica, Italy, Chaucer (Geoffrey), Wells (Ida, Personal Papers of), Douglas (Stephen A.), Italy, Literature (Children's)
Audience:	General Public, Researchers, Librarians, Document Delivery Professionals

Details: Free
          Expect: ENTER CLASS, Send: LIB48 3;
          Expect: CONNECTED, Send: RETURN
`telnet://olorin.uchicago.edu`

ChE Electronic Newsletter

ChE Electronic Newsletter

This newsletter contains information of interest to chemical engineers.

Keywords: Chemical Engineering, Chemistry, Engineering
Audience: Chemical Engineers
Contact: Martyn S. Ray
           trayms@cc.curtin.edu.au
Details: Free
           Inquire about needing a password.

`mailto:trayms@cc.curtin.edu.au`

Chemical Engineering

American Chemical Society

This is the gopher site of the American Chemical Society.

Keywords: Chemistry, Chemical Engineering
Sponsor: The American Chemical Society
Audience: Chemists, Chemical Engineers
Profile: This site contains supplemental material pages from the Journal of the American Chemical Society. Instructions for authors' submissions are also to be found here, as well as general information about the Society.
Contact: Gopher Operator
           gopher@acsinfo.acs.org
Details: Free

`gopher://acsinfo.acs.org`

ChE Electronic Newsletter

This newsletter contains information of interest to chemical engineers.

Keywords: Chemical Engineering, Chemistry, Engineering
Audience: Chemical Engineers
Contact: Martyn S. Ray
           trayms@cc.curtin.edu.au
Details: Free
           Inquire about needing a password.

`mailto:trayms@cc.curtin.edu.au`

Chemistry (History of)

Purdue University Library

The library's holdings are large and wide-ranging. They contain significant collections in many fields.

Keywords: Economics (History of), Literature (English), Literature (American), Indiana, Rogers (Bruce), Engineering (History of), Aviation, Earth Science, Atmospheric Science, Consumer Science, Family Science, Chemistry (History of), Physics, Veterinary Science
Audience: General Public, Researchers, Librarians, Document Delivery Professionals
Contact: Dan Ferrer
           dan@asterix.lib.purdue.edu
Details: Free
           Expect: User ID prompt, Send: GUEST

`telnet://lib.cc.purdue.edu`

University of Delaware Libraries (DELCAT)

The library's holdings are large and wide-ranging and contain significant collections in many fields.

Keywords: Literature (American), Hemingway (Ernest), Papermaking (History of), Chemistry (History of), Literature (Irish), Delaware
Audience: General Public, Researchers, Librarians, Document Delivery Professionals
Contact: Stuart Glogoff
           epo27855@udacsvm.bitnet
Details: Free
           Expect: prompt, Send: RETURN 2-3 times

`telnet://delcat.udel.edu or delcat.acs.udel.edu`

Chemistry

American Chemical Society

This is the gopher site of the American Chemical Society.

Keywords: Chemistry, Chemical Engineering
Sponsor: The American Chemical Society
Audience: Chemists, Chemical Engineers
Profile: This site contains supplemental material pages from the Journal of the American Chemical Society. Instructions for authors' submissions are also to be found here, as well as general information about the Society.
Contact: Gopher Operator
           gopher@acsinfo.acs.org
Details: Free

`gopher://acsinfo.acs.org`

ChE Electronic Newsletter

This newsletter contains information of interest to chemical engineers.

Keywords: Chemical Engineering, Chemistry, Engineering
Audience: Chemical Engineers
Contact: Martyn S. Ray
           trayms@cc.curtin.edu.au
Details: Free
           Inquire about needing a password.

`mailto:trayms@cc.curtin.edu.au`

Chem-Talk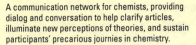

A communication network for chemists, providing dialog and conversation to help clarify articles, illuminate new perceptions of theories, and sustain participants' precarious journies in chemistry.

Keywords: Chemistry
Audience: Chemists, Scientists, Researchers
Contact: Manus Monroe
           ...!{ames,cbosgd}!pacbell!unicom!manus
Details: Free
User Info: To subscribe to the list, send an e-mail message requesting a subscription to the URL address below.

`mailto:...!{ames,cbosgd}!pacbell!unicom!manus`

Chemical Abstracts

Worldwide coverage of the chemical sciences literature.

Keywords: Chemistry, Engineering
Sponsor: Chemical Abstracts Service, American Chemical Society
Audience: Researchers, Librarians, Chemists
Profile: Provides coverage of chemical sciences literature from over 9,000 journals, patents from 27 countries, and 2 international property organizations, new books, conference proceedings, and government research reports. Updated every two weeks.
Contact: PAUL.ALBERT@NETEAST.COM
User Info: To subscribe contact Orbit-Questel directly.

`telnet://orbit.com`

Chemical Abstracts Service Source Index

Listing of bibliographic and library holdings information for scientific and technical primary literature relevant to the chemical sciences.

Chemistry

Keywords: Chemistry
Sponsor: Chemical Abstracts Service, American Chemical Society
Audience: Researchers, Librarians, Chemists
Profile: Approximately 65,000 records. Titles listed in CASSI represent all publications covered by CAS since 1907. Updated quarterly.
Contact: PAUL.ALBERT@NETEAST.COM
User Info: To subscribe contact Orbit-Questel directly.

`telnet://orbit.com`

Chemical Dictionary

Companion files to the Chemical Abstracts databases.

Keywords: Chemistry
Sponsor: Chemical Abstracts Service, American Chemical Society
Audience: Researchers, Chemists, Librarians
Profile: All compounds cited in the literature from 1957 to date are contained in these files. Each of the over 11 million records contains a CAS Registry Number, the molecular formula, CAS nomenclature for a specific compound, and many common synonyms.
Contact: PAUL.ALBERT@NETEAST.COM
User Info: To subscribe contact Orbit-Questel directly.

`telnet://orbit.com`

Chemical Industry Notes

Citations to worldwide chemical business news.

Keywords: Chemistry, Business
Sponsor: Chemical Abstracts Service, American Chemical Society
Audience: Researchers, Librarians, Chemists
Profile: Contains worldwide chemical business news related to production, pricing, sales, facilities, products and processes, corporate activities, government activities, and people. Contains over 950,000 records. Update weekly.
Contact: PAUL.ALBERT@NETEAST.COM
User Info: To subscribe contact Orbit-Questel directly.

`telnet://orbit.com`

Chemistry

This directory is a compilation of information resources focused on chemistry.

Keywords: Chemistry, Science

Audience: Chemical Engineers, Chemistry Teachers, Students
Details: Free

`ftp://una.hh.lib.umich.edu/70/inetdirsstacks/chemistry:wiggins`

Chemistry Tutorial Information

This site provides chemistry tutorial information in the form of text, data, pictures, source code, and executable programs for Macintosh computers.

Keywords: Chemistry, Tutorials, Macintosh, Education
Sponsor: University of Michigan
Audience: Chemistry Students (high school up)
Contact: comments@mac.archive.umich.edu
Details: Free

`gopher://plaza.aarnet.edu.au@/micros/mac/umich/misc/chemistry/00index.txt`

Imperial College Gopher Server

A gopher server pertaining to the Imperial College Chemistry Department.

Keywords: Chemistry
Sponsor: Imperial College, United Kingdom
Audience: Chemists
Profile: This gopher server provides access the Imperial College Chemistry Department's extensive online facilities. The server provides links to outside chemistry gophers, and contains files related to chemistry software, biochemistry, organic chemistry, and much more.
Contact: Gopher Operator
gopher@argon.ch.ic.ac.uk

`gopher://argon.ch.ic.ac.uk`

ISIS/Draw

ISIS/Draw provides a chemical drawing package from MDL Information Systems and the American Chemical Society.

Keywords: Chemistry, Graphics
Sponsor: MDL Information Systems, Inc., ACS
Audience: Chemists, Chemistry Professors, Chemistry Students
Profile: ISIS/Draw, the premier chemical drawing package from MDL Information Systems, Inc., is now available to chemistry students and professors at a special academic price through the American Chemical Society (ACS). Used by major pharmaceutical, agrochemical, and chemical companies worldwide, ISIS/Draw has the chemical intelligence to know that a line is a bond, and a letter is an atom. It can be used to: build queries for a structure-searching database; create presentation-quality sketches of chemical structures, reactions, and a wide range of other graphics; cut and paste annotated chemical structure drawings into popular word processing programs to create instructional materials and reports.

Details: Costs
Call ACS at (800) 227-5558. When placing an order, use the following catalog numbers: 2152-9-151 (Windows) or 2156-1-151 (Macintosh).

dmg96@acs.org

Special Chemicals Update Program

Comprehensive reports covering 32 specialty chemical industry segments.

Keywords: Chemistry, Business
Sponsor: Chemical Marketing Research Center
Audience: Librarians, Researchers, Chemists
Profile: Coverage of chemical industry segments, plus more than a dozen reports of general interest on the management of specialty chemical businesses.
Contact: PAUL.ALBERT@NETEAST.COM
User Info: To subscribe contact Orbit-Questel directly.

`telnet://orbit.com`

WWW Chemistry Sites

This is a major 'departure' site for a vast array of chemical resources. Provides a list of WWW chemistry sites at academic institutions.

Keywords: Chemistry
Audience: Chemists, Chemistry Students, Chemical Engineers
Contact: Max Kopelevich
mik@chem.ucla.edu
Details: Free

`http://www.chem.ucla.edu/chempointers.html`

Chess

Chessnews

A mailing list for the discussion of chess and related events.

Keywords: Chess, Games
Audience: Chess Enthusiasts
Contact: Michael Nolan
chessnews-request@tssi.com

Details:	Free
User Info:	To subscribe to the list, send an e-mail message requesting a subscription to the URL address below. To send a message to the entire list, address it to: chessnews@tssi.com
Notes:	The Chessnews mailing list is a repeater for the usenet newsgroup rec.games.chess. This is a bidirectional repeater. Postings originating from usenet are sent to the list, and those originating from the list are sent to re

`mailto:chessnews-request@tssi.com`

Internet Chess Library

An FTP and gopher site containing all kinds of chess-related files.

Keywords:	Chess
Audience:	Chess Players
Profile:	The Internet Chess Library is an FTP and gopher site with archives containing all kinds of chess-related files. The library contains chess software of different types, schedules, international chess announcements, rating guides, and anything else relating to chess.
Contact:	Chris Petroff chris@chess.uaknor.edu

`gopher://chess.uaknor.edu`

`ftp://chess.uaknor.edu`

rec.games.chess

A Usenet newsgroup providing information and discussion about chess strategies, organized computer chess playing events, and software.

Keywords:	Chess, Games, Recreation
Audience:	Chess Players, Game Players
User Info:	To subscribe to this Usenet newsgroup, you need access to a newsreader.

`news:rec.games.chess`

Chiba University Gopher

Chiba University Gopher

The Chiba University gopher, including files from the university's library.

Keywords:	Japan, Asia, Libraries
Sponsor:	Chiba University, Chiba, Japan
Audience:	Japan Residents, Computer Programmers, Librarians, Linguists
Contact:	hasimoto@chiba-u.ac.jp

`gopher://himawari.ipc.chiba-u.ac.jp`

Chicago

The University of Illinois at Chicago Library

The library's holdings are large and wide-ranging and contain significant collections in many fields.

Keywords:	Health Science, Chicago, Industry, Slavery, Abolitionism, Roosevelt (Franklin D.)
Audience:	General Public, Researchers, Librarians, Document Delivery Professionals
Details:	Free
	Expect: introductory screen, Send: Clear key; Expect: UIC flame screen, Send: Enter key; Expect: Logon screen, Send: DIAL PVM; Expect: PVM (Passthru) screen, Send: Type: Move cursor to NOTIS and press Enter key Response: One line message about port in use Type: Enter key

`telnet://uicvm.uic.edu`

Chicano Culture

Chicano/LatinoNet

An electronic mechanism that brings together Chicano/Latino research, as well as linguistic minority and educational research efforts being carried out at the University of California and elsewhere. It serves as a gateway between faculty, staff, and students who are engaged in research and curricular efforts in these areas.

Keywords:	Culture, Race, Chicano Culture, Latino Culture
Sponsor:	Chicano Studies Research Center, University of California at Los Angeles
Audience:	Students, Mexican-Americans, Latinos
Contact:	Richard Chabran Chabran@latino.sscnet.ucla.ed
Details:	Free

`gopher://latino.sscnet.ucla.edu`

Mexican Culture FAQ

This is the FAQ from the soc.culture.mexican newsgroup. Provides information on Mexican culture, history, society, language, and tourism.

Keywords:	Culture, Race, Chicano Culture, Latino Culture
Sponsor:	News Group Moderators for soc.culture.mexican
Audience:	Students, Latinos, Chicanos
Contact:	News Group Moderator mendoza-grado@att.com
Details:	Free

`ftp://ftp.mty.itesm.ms/pub/mexico/faqs`

`http://www.cis.ohio-state.edu/hypertext/faq/usenet/mexican-faq/faq.html`

Child Care

ACS Gopher

A gopher relating to the Department of Health and Human Services Administration for Children and Families. Provides access to ACS documents, the Department of Health and Human Services information, and other Federal Government documentation relating to children, families, and child care.

Keywords:	Children, Child Care
Sponsor:	Department of Health and Human Services Administration for Children and Families, USA
Audience:	Child Care Providers
Contact:	Tim Link linkt@gopher.acf.dhhs.gov

`gopher://spike.acf.dhhs.gov`

misc.kids

A Usenet newsgroup providing information and discussion about children and their behavior.

Keywords:	Children, Child Care
Audience:	Parents, Child Development Professionals, Children
Details:	Free
User Info:	To subscribe to this Usenet newsgroup, you need access to a newsreader.

`news:misc.kids`

UNICEF Gopher

The gopher site of the United Nations Children's Fund.

Keywords:	Children, Child Care
Sponsor:	United Nations
Audience:	Child Care Providers, Children's Rights Activists
Profile:	This gopher provides access to full-text UNICEF publications such as the State of the World's Children report and the Progress of Nations, the UNICEF Annual Report, UNICEF Features, the First Call for Children newsletter, press releases, information notes and other advocacy and information booklets, brochures, and pamphlets. The gopher also contains the full-text of the Convention on the Rights of the Child and the Declaration and Plan of Action of the 1990 World Summit for Children.

Contact: UNICEF Gopher Host
rpadolina@unicef.org

gopher://hqfaus01.unicef.org

Utah Valley Community College Library

The library's holdings are large and wide-ranging and contain significant collections in many fields.

Keywords: Accounting, Automobiles, Cabinetry, Child Care, Drafting, Electronics, Home Building, Local History, Refrigeration, Air Conditioning

Audience: General Public, Researchers, Librarians, Document Delivery Professionals

Details: Free
Expect: Login; Send: Opub

telnet:// uvlib.uvcc.edu

Childbirth

Midwifery Resources on the Net

A resource list for helping find information about midwifery on the Internet.

Keywords: Midwifery, Childbirth, Medicine, Nursing
Audience: Midwives, Medical professionals
Details: Free

gopher://una.hh.lib.umich.edu

Children

ACS Gopher

A gopher relating to the Department of Health and Human Services Administration for Children and Families. Provides access to ACS documents, the Department of Health and Human Services information, and other Federal Government documentation relating to children, families, and child care.

Keywords: Children, Child Care
Sponsor: Department of Health and Human Services Administration for Children and Families, USA
Audience: Child Care Providers
Contact: Tim Link
linkt@gopher.acf.dhhs.gov

gopher://spike.acf.dhhs.gov

alt.kids-talk

A Usenet newsgroup that provides a place for the pre-collegiate to chat.

Keywords: Chat Groups, Children
Audience: Kids, Students (K-12)
User Info: To subscribe to this Usenet newsgroup, you need access to a newsreader.

news:alt.kids-talk

Children's Rights

Contains files from the Children's Rights Council, the Central Ohio Organization, Fathers and Children for Equality, and the National Congress for Men and Children.

Keywords: Children, Law
Audience: Lawyers, Social Workers, Children's Rights Activists
Details: Free

telnet://cwgk4.chem.cwru.edu

FrEd Mail Foundation

This foundation specializes in establishing innovative and educationally rewarding collaborative projects using the Internet for the K-12 community.

Keywords: Children, Education (K-12)
Audience: Educators (K-12)
Contact: Al Rogers
arogers@bonita.cerf.fred.org
Details: Free

gopher://gopher.cerf.net/11/fredmail

KIDLINK and KIDCAFE

This discussion group is designed to act as a structured forum for e-mail exchanges between children aged 10-15.

Keywords: Education, Children
Audience: Children
Profile: A dialog is set up each year called 'KIDS-XX' where 'XX' is the current year. Each participating child posts an e-mail message answering the following four questions before he or she can engage in the dialog: 1. Who am I? 2. What do I want to be when I grow up? 3. How do I want the world to be better when I grow up? 4. What can I do to make this happen?

KIDLINK operates the following free discussion lists and services:

- KIDLINK: discussion group for children aged 10-15.
- RESPONSE: the destination for answers to the four questions above.
- KIDCAFE: a forum for children aged 10-15. Read-only for people outside this age group.
- KIDCAFEP: a Portuguese-language version of KIDCAFE.
- KIDCAFEJ: a Japanese-language version of KIDCAFE.
- KIDCAFEN: a Scandinavian-language (Nordic) version of KIDCAFE.
- KIDFORUM: a showcase of works by kids on a series of topics specified to promote exchange between classrooms. Teachers can plan for class participation in monthly topics.
- KIDPROJ: a forum enabling teachers/youth group leaders to design projects for children through the KIDLINK network.
- KIDLEADR: an informal meeting place for exchanging ideas, networking, asking for help, requesting hello messages, and so on, for teachers, coordinators, parents, social workers, and others interested in KIDS-94.
- KIDLEADP: a Portuguese-language version of KIDLEADR.
- KIDLEADS: a Spanish-language version of KIDLEADR.
- KIDLEADN: a Scandinavian-language (Nordic) version of KIDLEADR.

Contact: Odd de Presno
opresno@extern.uio.no
Details: Free

For information about the projects, subscribe to the KIDLINK announcement service: send an e-mail message to: listserv@vm1.NoDak.edu with the following command in the text of your message: SUB KIDLINK Yourfirstname Yourlastname.

Notes: For more information, read the 'WHAT IS KIDLINK / KIDS-94' page at gopher://kids.ccit.duq.edu/00/about/kidlink-general.

gopher://kids.ccit.duq.edu

Lego Information

A web site containing pictures, sets, and instructions for building with Legos. Also discusses various ideas, activities, and history pertaining to Legos, as well as information about clubs for Lego enthusiasts.

Keywords: Construction, Toys, Children
Sponsor: Lego
Audience: Children, General Public
Contact: David Koblas
koblas@netcom.com

http://legowww.itek.norut.no

misc.kids

A Usenet newsgroup providing information and discussion about children and their behavior.

Keywords:	Children, Child Care
Audience:	Parents, Child Development Professionals, Children
Details:	Free
User Info:	To subscribe to this Usenet newsgroup, you need access to a newsreader.

`news:misc.kids`

Pen-pals

This mailing list provides a forum for children to correspond with each other electronically. Although the list is not moderated, it is monitored for content and is managed by listproc.

Keywords:	Computing, Children, Writing
Audience:	Computer Users, Children, Student Writers
Contact:	pen-pals-request@mainstream.com
Details:	Free
User Info:	To subscribe to the list, send an e-mail message requesting a subscription to the URL address below.
	To send a message to the entire list, address it to: pen-pals@mainstream.com

`mailto:pen-pals@mainstream.com`

The Curiosity Club

This web site offers both an astrophysics exploration and a playspace for young scientists

Keywords:	Astronomy, Mythology, Children
Sponsor:	Center for Extreme Ultraviolet Astrophysics, Berkeley, California, and The San Francisco Unified School District, San Francisco, California
Audience:	Educators, Students, Astronomers,
Contact:	Kasey Rios Asberry jasberry@sfsuvax1.sfsu.edu
Details:	Free

`http://nisus.sfusd.k12.ca.us/curiosity_club/bridge1.html`

UNICEF Gopher

The gopher site of the United Nations Children's Fund.

Keywords:	Children, Child Care
Sponsor:	United Nations
Audience:	Child Care Providers, Children's Rights Activists
Profile:	This gopher provides access to full-text UNICEF publications such as the State of the World's Children report and the Progress of Nations, the UNICEF Annual Report, UNICEF Features, the First Call for Children newsletter, press releases, information notes and other advocacy

and information booklets, brochures, and pamphlets. The gopher also contains the full-text of the Convention on the Rights of the Child and the Declaration and Plan of Action of the 1990 World Summit for Children.

Contact:	UNICEF Gopher Host rpadolina@unicef.org

`gopher://hqfaus01.unicef.org`

Children's Books

University of North Carolina at Greensboro MINERVA Library

The library's holdings are large and wide-ranging and contain significant collections in many fields.

Keywords:	Herbert (George), Film, Dickinson (Emily), Children's Books
Audience:	Researchers, Students, General Public
Details:	Free
	Expect: Login; Send: Info or MINERVA

`telnet://steffi.acc.uncg.edu`

Chile

edista (Educación a Distancia)

The University Distance Program (UNIDIS) at the University of Santiago, Chile, sponsors Educación a Distancia (Education at a Distance).

Keywords:	Education (Adult), Education (Distance), Education (Continuing), Chile
Sponsor:	The University Distance Program (UNIDIS) at the University of Santiago, Chile
Audience:	Educators, Researchers
Details:	Free
User Info:	To subscribe to the list, send an e-mail message to the URL address shown below consisting of a single line reading:
	SUB edista YourFirstName YourLastName
	To send a message to the entire list, address it to: edista@usachvm1.bitnet

`mailto:listserv@usachvm1.bitnet`

China

INTLAW (International Law Library)

The International Law Library provides comprehensive international law materials.

Keywords:	International Law, EEC, Commonwealth, China
Audience:	Lawyers, International Lawyers
Profile:	The International Law Library provides comprehensive international law materials. The International Law library contains federal case law, European Community materials, treaties and agreements, Commonwealth law materials, topical and professional journals, French law materials (in French), China law materials, plus relevant topical publications.
Contact:	New Sales Group at (800) 227-4908 or (513) 859-5398 inside the US, or (513) 865-7981 for all inquires outside the US.
User Info:	To subscribe, contact Mead directly.
	To examine the Lexis user guide, you can access it at the ftp site of the University of Texas at Austin at the URL address: ftp://ftp.cc.utexas.edu
	The files are in: /pub/ref-services/LEXIS

`telnet://nex.meaddata.com`

`http://www.meaddata.com`

Princeton University Library

The library's holdings are large and wide-ranging. They contain significant collections in many fields.

Keywords:	China, Japan, Classics, History (Ancient), Near Eastern Studies, Literature (American), Literature (English), Aeronautics, Middle Eastern Studies, Mormonism, Publishing
Audience:	General Public, Researchers, Librarians, Document Delivery Professionals
Details:	Free
	Expect: Connect message, blank screen, Send: <cr>; Expect: #, Send: Call 500

`telnet://pucable.princeton.edu`

soc.culture.china

A Usenet newsgroup providing information and discussion about China and Chinese culture.

Keywords:	China, Sociology
Audience:	Sociologists, Chinese, Sinologists
Details:	Free
User Info:	To subscribe to this Usenet newsgroup, you need access to a newsreader.

`news:soc.culture.china`

Chinapats

Chinapats

Covers all patent applications published under the patent law of People's Republic of China.

Keywords:	Patents, Intellectual Property, Trademarks
Sponsor:	European Patent Office
Audience:	Patent Attorneys, Patent Agents, Librarians, Researchers
Profile:	English language abstracts are included for all applications filed by Chinese applicants. Contains more than 59,000 records. Updated monthly.
Contact:	paul.albert@neteast.com
User Info:	To subscribe contact Orbit-Questel directly.

`telnet://orbit.com`

Chinese Language

alt.chinese.text

A Usenet newsgroup providing information and discussion about Chinese language software.

Keywords:	Chinese Language, Language Software
Audience:	Chinese, Chinese Speakers, Computer Users
User Info:	To subscribe to this Usenet newsgroup, you need access to a newsreader.

`news:alt.chinese.text`

Chinese Studies

The University of Kansas Library

The library's holdings are large and wide-ranging and contain significant collections in many fields.

Keywords:	Botany, Chinese Studies, Cartography (History of), Kansas, Opera, Ornithology, Joyce (James), Yeats (William Butler), Walpole (Sir Robert, Collections of)
Audience:	General Public, Researchers, Librarians, Document Delivery Professionals
Contact:	John S. Miller
Details:	Free
	Expect: Username, Send: relay <cr>

`telnet://kuhub.cc.ukans.edu`

Choral Singing

Chorus

This is the lesbian and gay chorus mailing list, formed November 1991 by John Schrag (jschrag@alias.com) and Brian Jarvis (jarvis@psych.toronto.edu). Membership includes artistic directors, singers, chorus officers, interpreters, and support staff and friends. Topics of discussion include repertoire, arrangements, staging, costuming, management, fundraising, music, events and concerts.

Keywords:	Singing, Choral Singing, Homosexuality, Gay, Lesbian
Audience:	Lesbian Singers, Gay Singers, Chorus Officers, Lesbians, Gays, Choral Singers
Contact:	chorus-request@psych.toronto.edu
Details:	Free
User Info:	To subscribe to the list, send an e-mail message requesting a subscription to the URL address below.
	To send a message to the entire list, address it to: chorus@psych.toronto.edu

`mailto:chorus-request@psych.toronto.edu`

`news:alt.christnet.bible`

Christianity

alt.christnet

This Usenet newsgroup is a gathering place for Christian ministers and users.

Keywords:	Religion, Christianity, Bible, Divinity
Audience:	Christians, Ministers
User Info:	To subscribe to this Usenet newsgroup, you need access to a newsreader.

`news:alt.christnet`

Christian

alt.christnet.bible

A Usenet newsgroup providing information and discussion about bible discussion and research.

Keywords:	Bible, Christian, Religion, Divinity
Audience:	Biblical Scholars, Bible Readers
User Info:	To subscribe to this Usenet newsgroup, you need access to a newsreader.

AmerCath (History of American Catholicism)

This mailing list focuses on the history of American Catholicism.

Keywords:	Catholicism, Christianity, Religion
Sponsor:	Jefferson Community College, University of Kentucky, Louisville, KY, USA
Audience:	Researchers, Educators, Students, Catholics
Profile:	Because AMERCATH can be accessed internationally, it forms a global network of people who research and teach the history of American Catholicism. AMERCATH facilitates communication among faculty, students, and researchers.
Contact:	Anne Kearney jccannek@ukcc.uky.edu
Details:	Free
User Info:	To subscribe to the list, send an e-mail message to the address below, consisting of a single line reading:
	Sub AmerCath YourFirstName YourLastName
	To send a message to the entire list, address it to:
	AmerCath@ukcc.uky.edu

`mailto:listserv@ukcc.uky.edu`

Bethany Christian Services

A major directory on adoption, providing access to a broad range of related resources (library catalogs, databases, and servers) via the Internet.

Keywords:	Adoption, Christianity, Pregnancy, Abortion Rights
Sponsor:	Bethany Christian Services, Grand Rapids, Michigan, USA
Audience:	Pregnant Women
Profile:	The gopher server of Bethany, a pro-life, pro-family agency reaching out to women with unplanned pregnancies and adoptive couples contains a large amount of information about national and international adoption, the adoption process, African-American adoptions, and adoption of children with special needs. Also contains information for pregnant women, such as birth father rights and responsibilities, pregnancy counceling, and so on.
Contact:	gophermaster@bethany.org

`gopher://gopher.bethany.org/11`

Cell Church Discussion Group

A list for Christians who are in cell churches or in churches that are in transition to becoming cell churches, as well as anyone interested in learning more about cell churches. A cell church is a nontraditional form of church life in which small groups of Christians (cells) meet in a special way in their homes for the evangelism of the unchurched, the bonding of believers, their nurture, and ministry to one another.

Keywords:	Cell Churches, Christianity, Evangelism, Religion
Audience:	Christians, Theologians, Evangelists
Contact:	Jon Reid reid@cei.com
Details:	Free
User Info:	To subscribe to the list, send an e-mail message to the URL address below with the single word SUBSCRIBE in the body (not subject) of your message.
	To send a message to the entire list, address it to: cell-church@bible.acu.edu

Notes: The group archives, FAQ, and helpful articles are available by anonymous FTP from bible.acu.edu; they can also be retrieved by sending mail to cell-church-archives@bible.acu.edu with the single word LIST for a list of files, or HELP for more information.

`mailto:cell-church-request@bible.acu.edu`

CGN (Christian Growth Newsletter)

This site is intended to help Christians in personal growth, and includes testimonials and encouraging articles.

Keywords: Christianity, Religion
Audience: Christians
Contact: Laura Smith
bible@olsen.ch

`mailto:bible@olsen.ch`

Christian

The purpose of this list is to provide a nonhostile environment for discussion among Christians. Non-Christians may join the list and "listen in," but full-blown debates between Christians and non-Christians are best carried out in talk.religion.misc or soc.religion.christian.

Keywords: Christianity
Audience: Christians, Theologians
Contact: mailjc-request@grian.cps.altadena.ca.us
Details: Free
User Info: To subscribe to the list, send an e-mail message requesting a subscription to the URL address below.

To send a message to the entire list, address it to:

mailjc@grian.cps.altadena.ca.us

`mailto:mailjc-request@grian.cps.altadena.ca.us`

Christian Growth Newsletter (CGN)

Intended to help Christians in personal growth. It includes testimonies and encouraging articles.

Keywords: Christianity, Religion
Audience: Christians
Contact: Laura Smith
bible@olsen.ch
Details: Free

`mailto:bible@olsen.ch`

Ecchst-l

A discussion list for scholars of Ecclesiastical history, including those interested both in the history of the church and in the examination of theology in an historical context.

Keywords: Religion, Ecclesiastical History, Christianity, Theology
Audience: Historians, Theologians
Contact: Gregory H. Singleton
ugsingle@uxa.ecn.bgu.edu
User Info: To subscribe, send an e-mail message to the URL address below consisting of a single line reading: SUB ecchst-l YourFirstName YourLastName.

To send a message to the entire list, address it to: ecchst-l@bgu.edu

`mailto:listserv@bgu.edu`

Shakers

A forum on the United Society of Believers for those interested in the history, culture, artifacts, and beliefs of the Shakers (United Society of Believers). Discussions cover a broad range of subject matter.

Keywords: Shakers, Christianity, Religion
Audience: Shakers, Theologians
Contact: Marc Rhorer
rhorer@ukcc.uky.edu
Details: Free
User Info: To subscribe to the list, send an e-mail message to the URL address shown below consisting of a single line reading:

SUB shaker YourFirstName YourLastName

To send a message to the entire list, address it to: shaker@ukcc.uky.edu

`mailto:listserv@ukcc.uky.edu`

soc.religion.christian

A Usenet newsgroup providing information and discussion about Christianity and related issues.

Keywords: Christianity, Religion
Audience: Christians, Theologians
Details: Free
User Info: To subscribe to this Usenet newsgroup, you need access to a newsreader.

`news:soc.religion.christian`

Chromatography

Biotechnet Electronic Buyer's Guide

Biotechnet is a global computer network created specially for research biologists. It is intended to be a valuable source of information and data, a communications resource, a forum to foster the exchange of current ideas, and an international marketplace for relevant goods and service.

Keywords: Molecular Biology, Electrophoresis, Chromatography
Audience: Molecular Biologists, Chemists, Laboratory Suppliers
Profile: One of the services offered by Biotechnet is the Electronic Buyer's Guide, which is divided into five individual databases for specific product categories: Molecular Biology, Electrophoresis, Chromatography, Liquid Handling, and Instruments & Apparatus. After selecting one of the guides at the prompt, you can search through each database to find either product names and applications or the name and address of the company that manufactures the product you wish to locate.
Details: Free
Password: bguide

`telnet://biotech@biotechnet.com`

Chronic Fatigue Syndrome

Disability-Related Resources

A collection of information that includes newsletters for deaf/blind issues, electronic resources for the deaf, and a section on Chronic Fatigue Syndrome.

Keywords: Disabilities, Deafness, Blindness, Chronic Fatigue Syndrome
Sponsor: University of Washington DO-IT Program
Audience: Deaf and Disabled People, Health Care Professionals
Contact: Sheryl Burgstahler, Ph.D.
doit@u.washington.edu

`gopher://hawking.u.washington.edu`

Church (Frank)

Boise State University Library

The library's holdings are large and wide-ranging and contain significant collections in many fields.

Keywords: Jordan (Len, Senatorial Papers of), Church (Frank, Senatorial Papers of), Poetry (American)
Audience: General Public, Researchers, Librarians, Document Delivery Professionals
Contact: Dan Lester
Details: Free

Expect: login; Send: catalyst

`telnet://catalyst.idbsu.edu`

Church History

University of Pennsylvania PENNINFO Library ★★

The library's holdings are large and wide-ranging and contain significant collections in many fields.

Keywords: Church History, Spanish Inquisition, Witchcraft, Shakespeare (William), Bibles, Aristotle (Texts of), Fiction, Whitman (Walt), French Revolution, Drama (French), Literature (English), Literature (Spanish)
Audience: Researchers, Students, General Public
Contact: Al DSouza
penninfo-admin@dccs.upenn.edu
dsouza@dccs.upenn.edu
Details: Free
Expect: Login; Send: Public

`telnet://penninfo.upenn.edu`

CIA

CIA World Factbook ★

Annual report of CIA (Central Intelligence Agency) research in over 247 nations.

Keywords: CIA, Intelligence, Annual Reports
Audience: Governments, Lawyers, FBI
Details: Free

`gopher://marvel.loc.gov`

CILEA (Consorzio Interuniversitario Lombardo per la Elaborazione Automatica)

CILEA (Consorzio Interuniversitario Lombardo per la Elaborazione Automatica) ★

The gopher for the InterUniversity Computer Center, Milan, Italy, provides access to CILEA hosts, databases in Europe, CERN (European Laboratory for Particle Physics) services such as WWW and ALICE, Usenet newsgroups, PostScript documentation on various items, Italian research network information, and more.

Keywords: Informatics, Italy, Europe
Audience: Particle physicists, Researchers
Contact: Luciano Guglielm
guglielm@imicilea.cilea.it
Details: Free

`gopher://imicilea.cilea.it`

Cinema

CinemaSpace ★★★

CinemaSpace, from the Film Studies Program at UC Berkeley, is devoted to all aspects of Cinema and New Media.

Keywords: Cinema, Film, Multimedia
Sponsor: Film Studies Program at UC Berkeley
Audience: Students, Film researchers
Profile: Projects for CinemaSpace include academic papers on film and new media, film theory and critique. multimedia lectures, and sources of film clips and references to other sites.
Contact: xcohen@garnet.berkeley.edu
Details: Free

`http://remarque.berkeley.edu/~xcohen`

Circle K International

Circle K International ★

This list is for members and alumni of the worldwide collegiate service organization sponsored by Kiwanis International.

Keywords: Kiwanis International
Audience: Kiwanis Members
Contact: Jeffrey M. Wolff
jwolff@nyx.cs.du.edu
Details: Free
User Info: To subscribe to the list, send an e-mail message requesting a subscription to the URL address below.

`mailto:jwolff@nyx.cs.du.edu`

CIRCUITS-L

CIRCUITS-L

This list discusses all aspects of the introductory course in circuit analysis for electrical engineering undergraduates.

Keywords: Engineering, Electrical Engineering, Teaching, Electric Circuit Analysis
Audience: Engineers, Students (college)
Contact: Paul E. Gray
mailto:GRAY@MAPLE.UCS.UWPLATT.EDU
Details: Free
User Info: To subscribe to the list, send an e-mail message to the URL address below, and include: name; E-mail address; home phone, business phone, and FAX numbers (including area code); and US postal address (including ZIP code)

To send a message to the entire list, address it to:
CIRCUITS-L@UWPLATT.EDU

`mailto:CIRCUITS-REQUEST@UWPLATT.EDU`

CIS (Commonwealth of Independent States)

soc.culture.soviet ★

A Usenet newsgroup providing information and discussion about topics relating to Russia or the former Soviet Union.

Keywords: Russia, CIS (Commonwealth of Independent States), Communism, Sociology
Audience: Sociologists, Russians
Details: Free
User Info: To subscribe to this Usenet newsgroup, you need access to a newsreader.

`news:soc.culture.soviet`

talk.politics.soviet ★

A Usenet newsgroup providing information and discussion about Soviet, domestic and international politics.

Keywords: Communism, Russia, Politics, CIS (Commonwealth of Independent States)
Audience: Political Scientists
Details: Free
User Info: To subscribe to this Usenet newsgroup, you need access to a newsreader.

`news:talk.politics.soviet`

Cisco Systems

Cisco ★

This list is for discussion of the network products from Cisco Systems, Inc (primarily the AGS gateway, but also the ASM terminal multiplex) and any other relevant products. Discussions about operation, problems, features, topology, configuration, protocols, routing, loading, serving, and so on, are all encouraged. Other topics include vendor relations, new product announcements, availability of fixes and new features, and discussion of new requirements and desirables.

Keywords: Cisco Systems, Networks
Audience: Cisco Employees, Cisco Users, Distributors
Contact: David Wood
cisco-request@spot.colorado.edu
Details: Free

User Info: To subscribe to the list, send an e-mail message requesting a subscription to the URL address below.

To send a message to the entire list, address it to: cisco@spot.colorado.edu

```
mailto:cisco-
request@spot.colorado.edu
```

Citation Authority

Citation Authority

Legal citation authority expected to be used in the highest US appellate state courts, based on a 1985 survey (revised March 1991).

Keywords: Law (US), State Courts
Audience: Lawyers
Details: Free
Expect: login; Send: lawlib

```
gopher://liberty.uc.wlu.edu/00/
library/law/lawftp/citation.txt
```

Citizens Project

Citizens Project

A grass-roots community group in the Pikes Peak region of Colorado.

Keywords: Community, Networking, Colorado
Audience: Activists, Policymakers, Community Leaders, Government
Profile: Based in Colorado Springs, Colorado, the Citizens Project makes use of the online world in pursuit of its mission to investigate, inform, and advocate issues affecting the Pikes Peak region. It maintains an extensive gopher server, FTP site, and a ListServ (for people who have only e-mail access).
Contact: Citizens Project
citizens@cscns.com
Details: Free
User Info: To subscribe to the list, send an e-mail message to the URL address below, consisting of a single line reading:

SUB cns-citizens-pub YourFirstName YourLastName

```
mailto:listserv@cscns.com
```

City of San Carlos World Wide Web Fire Safety Tutorial

City of San Carlos World Wide Web Fire Safety Tutorial

This WWW site offers fire prevention information, with a special emphasis on preventing wildland fires. Also includes color diagram on how to create a proper firebreak.

Keywords: Disaster Relief, Safety
Sponsor: The City of San Carlos, California, USA
Audience: Students, Educators, Environmentalists, Community Groups

```
http://www.abag.ca.gov/abag/
local_gov/city/san_carlos/schome.html
```

CIUWInfo (Centrum Informacyj ny Uniwersyetu Warzawskiego)

CIUWInfo (Centrum Informacyj ny Uniwersyetu Warzawskiego)

Provides data from the Informatics Center information service of Warsaw University, Warsaw, Poland.

Keywords: Informatics, Poland
Audience: Researchers
Contact: chomac@plearn.edu.pl
Details: Free

```
gopher://chomac@plearn.edu.pl
```

Civil Liberties

ACLU Free Reading Room

A gopher site containing information relating to the ACLU (American Civil Liberties Union), including the current issue of the ACLU newsletter, Civil Liberties; a growing collection of recent public policy reports and action guides; Congressional voting records for the 103rd Congress; and an archive of news releases from the ACLU's national headquarters.

Keywords: ACLU, Civil Liberties, Congress (US), Activism
Sponsor: ACLU (American Civil Liberties Union)
Audience: Privacy Activists, Civil Libertarians, Activists
Contact: infoaclu@aclu.org

```
gopher://aclu.org
```

Civil Rights

amend2-info

Colorado voted in an amendment to their state constitution to revoke any existing gay/lesbian/bisexual civil rights legislation and prohibit the drafting of any new legislation. This moderated list is for information on the implication and issues of this amendment.

Keywords: Activists, Gay, Lesbian, Bisexual, Constitutional Amendments, Colorado, Civil Liberties
Audience: General Public, Gays, Lesbians, Bisexuals, Activists
Contact: amend2-info@cs.colorado.edu
User Info: To subscribe to the list, send an e-mail message requesting a subscription to the URL address below.

To send a message to the entire list, address it to: amend2-info@cs.colorado.edu

```
mailto:majordomo@cs.colorado.edu
```

Civil War

University of Tennessee at Chatanooga Library

The library's holdings are large and wide-ranging and contain significant collections in many fields.

Keywords: Civil War, Literature (American)
Audience: Researchers, Students, General Public
Contact: Randy Whitson
rwhitson@utcvmutc.edu
Details: Free
Expect: OK prompt; Send: Login pub1;
Expect: Password, Send: Usc

```
telnet://library.utc.edu
```

Civil-L

Civil-L

A mailing list for the discussion of Civil Engineering Research and Education.

Keywords: Engineering (Civil), Computer-Aided Instruction
Audience: Engineers, Educators, Students
Contact: Eldo Hildebrand
ELDO@UNB.CA

CJI (Computer Jobs in Israel)

CJI (Computer Jobs in Israel) ★

Computer Jobs in Israel (CJI) is a one-way list that will automatically send you the monthly updated computer jobs document. This list will also send you other special documents or announcements regarding finding computer work in Israel. Eventually this list will be an open, moderated list for everyone to exchange information about computer jobs in Israel.

- Keywords: Israel, Computer, Jobs
- Audience: Computer Users, Jews, Israelis, Israel Residents
- Contact: Jacob Richman
  listserv@jerusalem1.datasrv.co.il
- Details: Free
- User Info: To subscribe to the list, send an e-mail message to the address below, consisting of a single line reading:
  SUB CJI YourFirstName YourLastName
  To send a message to the entire list, address it to:
  CJI@jerusalem1.datasrv.co.il

mailto:listserv@jerusalem1.datasrv.co.il

CLAIMS

CLAIMS

Provides access to over 2.3 million U.S. patents issued by the U.S. Patent and Trademark Office.

- Keywords: Patents, Intellectual Property, Trademarks
- Sponsor: IFI/Plenum Data Corporation
- Audience: Patent Attorneys, Patent Agents, Librarians, Researchers
- Profile: Chemical patents are covered from 1950 forward; mechanical and electrical patents from 1963 forward; design patents from 1980 forward.
- Contact: PAUL.ALBERT@NETEAST.COM
- User Info: To subscribe contact Orbit-Questel directly.

telnet://orbit.com

Clarissa

Clarissa ★

This list discusses the Nickelodeon TV show "Clarissa Explains It All."

- Keywords: Television Shows, Nickelodeon
- Audience: Nickelodeon Viewers, TV Viewers
- Contact: Jim Lick
  clarissa-request@tcp.com
- Details: Free
- User Info: To subscribe to the list, send an e-mail message requesting a subscription to the URL address below.
  To send a message to the entire list, address it to: clarissa@tcp.com

mailto:clarissa-request@tcp.com

Class Four Relay Magazine

Class Four Relay Magazine ★★★

A magazine by Relay Ops for the relay community.

- Keywords: Relays, Magazines, Electronics
- Sponsor: Carnegie Mellon University, Pittsburg, PA, USA
- Audience: Relay Community
- Profile: Includes articles on general questions and issues of relay usage, information for and about relay ops, discussion of policy issues and guidelines, and technical issues and new developments.
- Contact: Joey J. Stanford
  stjs@vm.marist.edu
- Details: Free

mailto:stjs@vm.marist.edu

Classics

History at the University of Virginia ★★

A collection of online history resources, with particular emphasis on medieval and classical studies. Links to other systems, including the Library of Congress.

- Keywords: History (World), Classics, Medieval Studies
- Sponsor: University of Virginia, Charlottesville, Virginia, USA
- Audience: Historians, Students (College/University)
- Contact: mssbks@virginia.edu
- Details: Free

gopher://gopher.lib.virginia.edu

Johns Hopkins University Library ★★

The library's holdings are large and wide-ranging and contain significant collections in many fields.

- Keywords: Literature (English), Economics, Classics, Drama (German), Slavery, Trade Unions, Incunabula, Bibles, Diseases (History of), Nursing (History of), Abolitionism
- Audience: General Public, Researchers, Librarians, Document Delivery Professionals
- Details: Free

telnet://jhuvm.hcf.jhu.edu

Princeton University Library ★★

The library's holdings are large and wide-ranging. They contain significant collections in many fields.

- Keywords: China, Japan, Classics, History (Ancient), Near Eastern Studies, Literature (American), Literature (English), Aeronautics, Middle Eastern Studies, Mormonism, Publishing
- Audience: General Public, Researchers, Librarians, Document Delivery Professionals
- Details: Free
  Expect: Connect message, blank screen, Send: <cr>; Expect: #, Send: Call 500

telnet://pucable.princeton.edu

Cleveland FreeNet

Cleveland FreeNet ★★

A network designed for community access and education.

- Keywords: Networks, Community Access
- Sponsor: The Cleveland FreeNet Project, Case Western Reserve University, Cleveland, Ohio, USA
- Audience: Educators, Researchers, Students, Parents
- Profile: A prototypical user-friendly city FreeNet, containing complete historical documents, an up-to-date news service, extensive info on the arts, sciences, technology, medicine, business, and education.
- Notes: Registration is required, and information on registration is included.

telnet://freenet-in-a.cwru.edu

Cleveland Sports

Cleveland Sports ★

A forum for people to discuss their favorite Cleveland sports teams/personalities, and to obtain news and information about those teams that most out-of-towners couldn't get otherwise. Teams discussed include the Cleveland Indians, the Cleveland Browns, the Cleveland Cavaliers, and the teams from Ohio State University.

Keywords: Cleveland Sports, Ohio State Universiry
Audience: Cleveland Sports Enthusiasts, Sports Enthusiasts, Cleveland Residents
Contact: Richard Kowicki
aj755@cleveland.freenet.edu
Details: Free
User Info: To subscribe to the list, send an e-mail message requesting a subscription to the URL address below.

`mailto:aj755@cleveland.freenet.edu`

Climatology

Energy and Climate Information Exchange (ECIX) Newsletter

This newsletter focuses on energy and climate issues, and contains summaries of network postings, updates on national and international policy initiatives, full-length articles, information on new network resources, and a calendar of upcoming events.

Keywords: Energy, Meteorology, Climatology
Audience: Meteorologists, Geologists, Energy Researchers, Climatologists
Contact: econet@igc.org

`mailto:larris@igc.org`

Clinton (Bill)

alt.politics.clinton

A Usenet newsgroup providing information and discussion about President Bill Clinton and the White House. Perspective tends to be anti-Clinton.

Keywords: Politics (US), Clinton (Bill)
Audience: Politicians, General Public
User Info: To subscribe to this Usenet newsgroup, you need access to a newsreader.

`news:alt.politics.clinton`

Clinton's Economic Plan ★

The contents of US President Clinton's economic plan.

Keywords: Economics, Government (US), Clinton (Bill)
Audience: Economists, General Public

Details: Free
The data contained on the President's Economic Plan diskette is now available via anonymous FTP at cu.nih.gov. The data can be found in a directory named USDOC-OBA-INFO.

`gopher://wiretap.spies.com/11/Gov/Economic`

White House Frequently Asked Questions ★★★★

This document is a good starting point for answering questions such as: How do I send e-mail to President Clinton? How do I get current news updates from the White House? Where can I get White House documents from?

Keywords: Clinton (Bill), Government (US), Politics (US), FAQs
Audience: General Public, Researchers
Details: Free
Expect: login; Send: anonymous; Expect: password; Send: your e-mail address; Expect: directory; Send: /pub/nic; Expect: file; Send: whitehouse FAQ.

`ftp://ftp.sura.net`

Clinton Watch

A regular political column devoted to a critical examination of the Clinton Administration.

Keywords: Politics, Clinton(Bill), Satire, Government (US)
Sponsor: Informatics Resource
Audience: Republicans, General Public, Citizens
Contact: clintonwatch@dolphin.gulf.net

`gopher://dolphin.gulf.net`

Clip Art

Gopher-Based ASCII Clip Art Collection

A collection of over 500 individual pictures, ranging from images of food to Star Wars, created with ASCII characters. Organized by subject, and including archives of the Usenet group alt.ascii-art. Also contains links to other ASCII collections.

Keywords: Clip Art, Design
Sponsor: Texas Tech Computer Sciences Gopher Server
Audience: Computer Users, General Public
Contact: Abdul Malik Yoosufan
gripe@cs.ttu.edu
Details: Free, Images

`gopher://cs4sun.cs.ttu.edu`

`ftp://ftp.cs.ttu.edu:/pub/asciiart`

The ASCII Bazaar

An extensive collection of ASCII art, organized by subject. Also includes FAQ files, software tools, ASCII art discussion lists, and links to other collections of ASCII art.

Keywords: Clip Art, Computer Art
Sponsor: Department of Computer and Information Sciences, University of Alabama at Birmingham, Birmingham, Alabama, USA
Audience: Computer Users, General Public
Contact: R. L. Samuell
samuell@cis.uab.edu

`gopher://twinbrook.cis.uab.edu`

Clp.x

Clp.x

Devoted to discussion of concurrent logic programming languages, concurrent constraint programming languages, semantics, proof techniques and program transformations, parallel Prolog systems, implementations, and programming techniques and idioms.

Keywords: Programming, Programming Languages, Concurrent Logic
Audience: Concurrent Logic Programmers
Contact: Jacob Levy
jlevy.pa@xerox.com
Details: Free
User Info: To subscribe to the list, send an e-mail message requesting a subscription to the URL address below.
To send a message to the entire lst, address it to: clp.x@xerox.com

`mailto:clp-request.x@xerox.com`

CMPCOM (Computers and Communications) Libraryzzzz

CMPCOM (Computers and Communications) Libraryzzzz

The Computers and Communications Library provides you industry-specific sources. More than 40 full-text sources that concentrate on computers and communications are available. Full-text files can be searched in a variety of ways: as an individual file, by major-subject group file, or as a user-defined group file.

Keywords: Computers, Communications, Technology, Electronics

Audience:	Business Researchers, Analysts, Entrepreneurs
Profile:	This library can be used to gain insight on new products and technologies being introduced; monitor industry news for high technology systems, electronics, engineering, communications, and computer hardware and software; and locate product evaluations for both the professional as well as the casual personal computer user.
Contact:	Mead New Sales Group at (800) 227-4908 or (513) 859-5398 inside the US, or (513) 865-7981 for all inquiries outside the US.
User Info:	To subscribe, contact Mead directly.
	To examine the Nexis user guide, you can access it at the ftp site of the University of Texas at Austin at the URL address: ftp://ftp.cc.utexas.edu
	The files are in: /pub/ref-services/LEXIS

telnet://nex.meaddata.com

http://www.meaddata.com

CMPGN (Campaign Library)

CMPGN (Campaign Library)

The CMPGN Library contains information and news about US Congressional, Senatorial, Gubernatorial and Presidential elections. The media, political campaigns, and others whose responsibilities include monotoring activity on the campaign trail will find CMPGN to be a unique and comprehensive source of information for campaign research.

Keywords:	Politics (US), Congress (US)
Audience:	Journalists, Political Researchers
Profile:	CMPGN allows searching of individual files or group files that cover topics such as candidate and incumbent profiles; Honoraria, PACs, and demographic and media profiles; Committee and Floor voting records and floor statement indexes for all House and Senate incumbents; and reputable sources of news that are known for their in-depth campaign coverage, including the Hotline, the Cook Political Report, ABC news Transcripts, Roll Call, States News Service, US Newswire, Federal News Service, and much more.
Contact:	Mead New Sales Group at (800) 227-4908 or (513) 859-5398 inside the US, or (513) 865-7981 for all inquiries outside the US.
User Info:	To subscribe, contact Mead directly.

	To examine the Nexis user guide, you can access it at the ftp site of the University of Texas at Austin at the URL address: ftp://ftp.cc.utexas.edu
	The files are in: /pub/ref-services/LEXIS

telnet://nex.meaddata.com

http://www.meaddata.com

CNI

CNI

CNI (Coalition for Networked Information) is an Internet information retrieval service. The CNI promotes the creation of and access to information resources in networked environments in order to enrich scholarship and to enhance intellectual productivity.

Keywords:	Internet, Information Retrieval, CNI
Audience:	Internet Surfers
Details:	Free
	The readme file is: CNI/info.packet/README

ftp://ftp.cni.org/CNI (/info.packet/README)

gopher://ftp.cni.org

http://www.cni.org/CNI.homepage.html

CNI Gopher

The gopher for CNI (Coalition for Networked Information), an Internet information retrieval service. The CNI promotes the creation of and access to information resources in networked environments in order to enrich scholarship and to enhance intellectual productivity.

Keywords:	Internet, Information Retrieval, CNI
Audience:	Internet Surfers
Contact:	Craig A. Summerhill Craig@cni.org
Details:	Free

gopher://gopher.cni.org

CNI TopNode Project

Part of CNI (Coalition for Networked Information) directories and resource information service.

Keywords:	Internet, Information Retrieval, CNI
Audience:	Internet Surfers
Details:	Free

ftp://ftp.cni.org/CNI/projects/topnode

gopher://ftp.cni.org

http://www.cni.org/CNI.homepage.html

CNI-Copyright Mailing List Archives

CNI-Copyright Mailing List Archives

An archive of lists related to copyright and intellectual property law.

Keywords:	Copyright Law, Intellectual Property
Sponsor:	CNI (The Coalition for Networked Information)
Audience:	Entrepreneurs, Lawyers, Journalists
Contact:	Craig Summerhill, Joan K. Lippincott craig@cni.org, joan@cni.org

gopher://gopher.cni.org

CNN Headline News Gopher

CNN Headline News Gopher

Latest news as read by the CNN anchorpersons. Searchable index of subject matter.

Keywords:	News Media, Politics (International), Journalism
Sponsor:	CNN Newsource Service
Audience:	General Public, Students, Journalists
Contact:	Chet Rhodes cr9@umail.umd.edu
Details:	Free

gopher://info.umd.edu:925/

Coastal Marine Biology

University of Maryland, College Park

The library's holdings are large and wide-ranging and contain significant collections in many fields. Agriculture, Coastal Marine Biology, Fisheries, Water Quality, Oceanography

Keywords:	Agriculture, Coastal Marine Biology, Fisheries, Water Quality, Oceanography
Audience:	Researchers, Students, General Public
Contact:	Janet McLeod mcleod@umail.umd.edu
Details:	Free
	Expect: Login; Send: Atdu

telnet://info.umd.edu

CoCo

CoCo

This is a discussion related to the Tandy Color Computer (any model) OS-9 Operating System, and any other topics relating to the "CoCo," as this computer is affectionately known.

Keywords:	Tandy Computers, Computers
Audience:	Tandy Computer Users, Computer Users
Contact:	Paul E. Campbell pecampbe@mtus5.BITNET
Details:	Free
User Info:	To subscribe to the list, send an e-mail message requesting a subscription to the URL address below.

`mailto:listserv@pucc.princeton.edu`

CODES (Codes Library)

CODES (Codes Library)

The Codes Library offers access to US federal and state legislative materials, in codified, slip law, and bill form, plus federal and state regulatory materials and a statutes archive.

Keywords:	Statutes, Codes, State, Federal
Audience:	(US) Lawyers
Profile:	The Codes library contains an extensive compilation of federal and state statutory materials, in codified as well as slip law form, from all 50 states, the District of Columbia, Puerto Rico, the Virgin Islands and the United States Code Service. The library also contains federal and state regulatory materials plus a statues archive. Pending legislation can be found with 50-state and federal fill tracking, the full text of federal bills, the Congressional Record, and the full text of bills for a growing number of states. Administrative materials include the Code of Federal Regulations, the Federal Register, 50-state regulation tracking, and the administrative codes for a selected number of states.
Contact:	New Sales Group at (800) 227-4908 or (513) 859-5398 inside the US, or (513) 865-7981 for all inquires outside the US.
User Info:	To subscribe, contact Mead directly. To examine the Lexis user guide, you can access it at the ftp site of the University of Texas at Austin at the URL address: ftp://ftp.cc.utexas.edu The files are in: /pub/ref-services/LEXIS

`telnet://nex.meaddata.com`

`http://www.meaddata.com`

Cognitive Science

(The) Observer

The central scope of the group covers the theory of autopoiesis (of Humberto Maturana and Francisco Varela) and enactive cognitive science. The extended scope includes applications of the above theoretical work and other relevant work (for example, systems theory, cognitive science, phenomenology, artificial life, and so on). This is an edited electronic newsletter issued (approximately) twice monthly.

Keywords:	Autopoiesis, Systems Theory, Cognitive Science
Audience:	Systems Theorists, Researchers
Contact:	Randall Whitaker rwhit@cs.umu.se
User Info:	To subscribe to the list, send an e-mail message to the URL address below consisting of a single line reading: SUB the observer YourFirstName YourLastName. To send a message to the entire list, address it to: rwhit@cs.umu.se

`mailto:listserv@cs.umu.se`

Cognitive and Psychological Sciences on the Internet

A resource containing links to academic programs, organizations and conference lists, journals and magazines, Usenet newsgroups, discussion lists, and other general information regarding cognitive science.

Keywords:	Cognitive Science, Psychology, Neuroscience
Sponsor:	The Stanford University Psychology Department
Audience:	Cognitive Scientists, Neuroscientists, Psychologists, Psychiatrists
Contact:	Scott Mainwaring sdm@psych.stanford.edu

`http://matia.stanford.edu/cogsci.html`

ELSNET (European Network in Language and Speech)

A web site addressing the development of language technology in Europe and abroad by helping to coordinate progress on both scientific and technological fronts.

Keywords:	Linguistics, Cognitive Science, Communication
Sponsor:	The University of Edinburgh Centre for Cognitive Science, Edinburgh, Scotland
Audience:	Linguists, Cognitive Scientists
Contact:	Ewan Klein klein@ed.ac.uk

`http://www.cogsci.ed.ac.uk/elsnet/home.html`

COHOUSING-L

COHOUSING-L

A list for discussion of Cohousing, the name of a type of collaborative housing that has been developed primarily in Denmark since 1972 where it is known as bofoellesskaber. Cohousing is housing designed to foster community and cooperation while preserving independence. Private residences are clustered near shared facilities. The members design and manage all aspects of their community.

Keywords:	Community, Housing, Cooperatives
Audience:	Urban Planners, Architects, General Contractors
Contact:	fholson@uci.com
Details:	Free
User Info:	To subscribe to the list, send an e-mail message to the address below consisting of a single line reading: SUB COHOUSING-L YourFirstName YourLastName To send a message to the entire list, address it to: COHOUSING-L@uci.com

`mailto:listserv@uci.com`

Coins

coins

A forum for discussions on numismatic topics, including US and world coins, paper money, tokens, and medals.

Keywords:	Coins, Numismatics
Audience:	Coin Collectors
Contact:	Daniel J. Power COINS-REQUEST@ISCSVAX.UNI.EDU
Details:	Free
User Info:	To subscribe to the list, send an e-mail message requesting a subscription to the URL address below. To send a message to the entire list, address it to: COINS@ISCSVAX.UNI.EDU

`mailto:COINS-REQUEST@ISCSVAX.UNI.EDU`

Colby College Library

Colby College Library

The library's holdings are large and wide-ranging and contain significant collections in many fields.

Keywords:	Contemporary Letters, Hardy (Thomas), James (Henry), Mann (Thomas, Collections of), Housman (A.E., Letters of), Maine Authors, Irish History (Modern)

Audience: General Public, Researchers, Librarians, Document Delivery Professionals
Details: Free
Expect: login, Send: library

`telnet://library.colby.edu`

Collectibiles

Cards

This list is for people interested in collecting, speculating, and investing in baseball, football, basketball, hockey, and other trading cards and/or memorabilia. Discussion and want/sell lists are welcome.

Keywords: Trading Cards, Collectibiles, Memorabilia
Audience: Sports Card Collectors, Sports Card Traders, Memorabilia Collectors
Contact: Keane Arase
cards-request@tanstaafl.uchicago.edu
Details: Free
User Info: To subscribe to the list, send an e-mail message requesting a subscription to the URL address below.

To send a message to the entire list, address it to:
cards@tanstaafl.uchicago.edu

Notes: The list is open to anyone.

`mailto:cards-request@tanstaafl.uchicago.edu`

Collections (of)

Colby College Library ★★

The library's holdings are large and wide-ranging and contain significant collections in many fields.

Keywords: Contemporary Letters, Hardy (Thomas), James (Henry), Mann (Thomas), Collections (of), Housman (A.E., Letters of), Maine Authors, Irish History (Modern)
Audience: General Public, Researchers, Librarians, Document Delivery Professionals
Details: Free
Expect: login, Send: library

`telnet://library.colby.edu`

Georgia State University Library ★★

The library's holdings are large and wide-ranging and contain significant collections in many fields.

Keywords: Labor (History of), Multimedia, Mercer (Johnny, Collection of)

Audience: General Public, Researchers, Librarians, Document Delivery Professionals
Contact: Phil Williams
isgpew@gsuvm1.gsu.edu
Details: Free
Expect: VM screen, Send: RETURN;
Expect: CP READ, Send: DIAL VTAM, press RETURN; Expect: CICS screen, Send: PF1

`telnet://library.gsu.edu`

University of New Hampshire Videotex Library

The library's holdings are large and wide-ranging and contain significant collections in many fields.

Keywords: Dance, Folk Music, Milne (A.A., Collection of), Galway (Ireland)
Audience: Researchers, Students, General Public
Contact: Robin Tuttle
r_tuttle1@unhh.unh.edu
Details: Free
Expect: USERNAME; Send: Student (no password required). Control-z to log off.

`telnet://unhvt@unh.edu`

The University of Kansas Library ★★

The library's holdings are large and wide-ranging and contain significant collections in many fields.

Keywords: Botany, Chinese Studies, Cartography (History of), Kansas, Opera, Ornithology, Joyce (James), Yeats (William Butler), Walpole (Sir Robert, Collections of)
Audience: General Public, Researchers, Librarians, Document Delivery Professionals
Contact: John S. Miller
Details: Free
Expect: Username, Send: relay <cr>

`telnet://kuhub.cc.ukans.edu`

College

rec.sport.basketball.college ★

A Usenet newsgroup providing information and discussion about college basketball.

Keywords: Basketball, College, Sports
Audience: Basketball Fans, Sport Fans
User Info: To subscribe to this Usenet newsgroup, you need access to a newsreader.

`news:rec.sport.basketball.college`

College E-mail Addresses

College E-mail Addresses ★

Information on e-mail addresses at graduate offices.

Keywords: Internet, E-mail
Audience: Internet Surfers, Students, College/University Educators
Details: Free
File is: pub/usenet/soc.college/Admission_Office_Email_Address_List

`ftp://pit-manager.mit.edu/pub/usenet-by-group/soc.college`

`gopher://sipb.mit.edu`

rec.sport.football.college ★

A Usenet newsgroup providing information and discussion about college football.

Keywords: Football, College, Sports
Audience: Football Fans, Sports Fans
User Info: To subscribe to this Usenet newsgroup, you need access to a newsreader.

`news:rec.sport.football.college`

Colorado

amend2-info

Colorado voted in an amendment to their state constitution that revoke any existing gay/lesbian/bisexual civil rights legislation and prohibit the drafting of any new legislation. This moderated list is for information on the implication and issues of this amendment.

Keywords: Activists, Gay, Lesbian, Bisexual, Constitutional Amendments, Colorado, Civil Rights
Audience: General Public, Gays, Lesbians, Bisexuals, Activists
Contact: amend2-info@cs.colorado.edu
User Info: To subscribe to the list, send an e-mail message requesting a subscription to the URL address below.

To send a message to the entire list, address it to: amend2-info@cs.colorado.edu

`mailto:majordomo@cs.colorado.edu`

Citizens Project

A grass-roots community group in the Pikes Peak region of Colorado.

Keywords:	Community, Networking, Colorado	Details:	Free Send an e-mail message to the URL address below asking for further information.	Keywords:	Humor, Comedy		
Audience:	Activists, Policymakers, Community Leaders, Government			Audience:	General Public, Complainers		
Profile:	Based in Colorado Springs, Colorado, the Citizens Project makes use of the online world in pursuit of its mission to investigate, inform, and advocate issues affecting the Pikes Peak region. It maintains an extensive gopher server, FTP site, and a ListServ (for people who have only e-mail access).			User Info:	To subscribe to this Usenet newsgroup, you need access to a newsreader.		

`mailto:tellinst@csn.org`

Columbia University Libraries

`news:alt.peeves`

alt.tasteless

Columbia University Libraries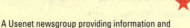

A Usenet newsgroup providing information and discussion about tasteless jokes.

Keywords:	Humor, Comedy
Audience:	General Interest, Jokers
User Info:	To subscribe to this Usenet newsgroup, you need access to a newsreader.

The Columbia libraries include a medical library and a mathematics library.

Contact:	Citizens Project citizens@cscns.com
Details:	Free
User Info:	To subscribe to the list, send an e-mail message to the URL address below, consisting of a single line reading: SUB cns-citizens-pub YourFirstName YourLastName

Keywords:	Libraries, Research
Audience:	General Public, Researchers
Details:	Free When connected, hit return, enter terminal type: **vt100**.

`news:alt.tasteless`

Comic Books

Cerebi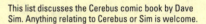

This list discusses the Cerebus comic book by Dave Sim. Anything relating to Cerebus or Sim is welcome.

`mailto:listserv@cscns.com`

`telnet://clio.cul.columbia.edu`

Colorado Document Citations

Comedians

Keywords:	Comic Books, Sim (Dave)
Audience:	Comics Enthusiasts
Contact:	Christian Walters cerebi-request@tomservo.b23b.ingr.com
Details:	Free
User Info:	To subscribe to the list, send an e-mail message requesting a subscription to the URL address below. To send a message to the entire list, address it to: cerebi@tomservo.b23b.ingr.com
Notes:	It's just an echo list, so anything that gets mailed is bounced to everyone.

A list of publications from all Colorado statutory government agencies. The wiretap gopher provides access to a range of world documents in full-text format.

alt.fan.monty-python

A Usenet newsgroup providing an electronic fan club for those wacky Brits.

Keywords:	Colorado, Government (US)
Audience:	Researchers, Lawyers, Colorado Residents, Governments, historians, Researchers, General Public Select from Menu as appropriate

Keywords:	Humor, Entertainment, Comedians, Satire
Audience:	Monty Python Enthusiasts, General Public
User Info:	To subscribe to this Usenet newsgroup, you need access to a newsreader.

`telnet://pac.carl.org`

Telluride Institute

`news:alt.fan.monty-python`

`mailto:cerebi-request@tomservo.b23b.ingr.com`

alt.fan.rush-limbaugh

comix

This is a community organization involved in building an electronic dimension in rural Colorado. The vision of Telluride Institute includes linking rural residents to each other and outside resources, creating new opportunities for education, jobs, and arts.

A Usenet newsgroup providing information and discussion about Rush Limbaugh, a politically conservative American figure.

This list is intended for talking about non-mainstream and independent comic books. There is little talk about superheroes, and none about Marvel Mutants.

Keywords:	Limbaugh (Rush), Politics (Conservative), Comedians
Audience:	Followers of Rush Limbaugh
User Info:	To subscribe to this Usenet newsgroup, you need access to a newsreader.

Keywords:	Comic Books
Audience:	Comics Enthusiasts
Contact:	Elizabeth Lear Newman comix-request@world.std.com
Details:	Free
User Info:	To subscribe to the list, send an e-mail message requesting a subscription to the URL address below. To send a message to the entire list, address it to: comix@world.std.com

Keywords:	Community, Networking, Virtual Community, Rural Development, Colorado
Sponsor:	The Telluride Institute, Telluride, Colorado
Audience:	Activists, Policymakers, Community Leaders, Students, Colorado Residents
Profile:	The Telluride Institute is a local community-based organization that produces arts, environmental, and educational events in the Telluride area of Colorado. The Institite is committed to the creation of what it calls the "InfoZone": it wants to use modern telecommunications to link together the local community and to connect to the rest of the world to exchange ideas, commerce, arts, and inspiration.
Contact:	Richard Lowenberg tellinst@CSN.ORG

`news:alt.fan.rush-limbaugh`

Comedy

alt.peeves

A Usenet newsgroup providing information and discussion about peeves, complaints, and whining.

`mailto:comix-request@world.std.com`

A
B
C
D
E
F
G
H
I
J
K
L
M
N
O
P
Q
R
S
T
U
V
W
X
Y
Z

modesty-blaise

A discussion forum on Peter O'Donnell's Modesty Blaise books and comics. Topics include character, plot, artists, and relevant articles.

Keywords: Comic Books, Comics
Audience: Modesty Blaise Enthusiasts
Contact: Thomas Gramstad
modesty-blaise-request@math.uio.no
User Info: To subscribe to the list, send an e-mail message to the URL address below consisting of a single line reading:
SUB modesty-blaise YourFirstName YourLastName

`mailto: modesty-blaise-request@math.uio.no`

rec.arts.comics.misc

A Usenet newsgroup providing information and discussion about comic books and graphic novels.

Keywords: Comic Books, Books
Audience: Comics Enthusiasts, Readers, Writers
Details: Free
User Info: To subscribe to this Usenet newsgroup, you need access to a newsreader.

`news:rec.arts.comics.misc`

Comics

disney-comics

A forum for discussion of Disney comics.

Keywords: Comics, Disney
Audience: Comics Enthusiasts, Disney
Contact: Per Starbuck
disney-comics-request@student.docs.uu.se
Details: Free
User Info: To subscribe to the list, send an e-mail message requesting a subscription to the URL address below.

To send a message to the entire list, address it to: disney-comics-request@student.docs.uu.se

`mailto:disney-comics-request@student.docs.uu.se`

modesty-blaise

A discussion forum on Peter O'Donnell's Modesty Blaise books and comics. Topics include character, plot, artists, and relevant articles.

Keywords: Comic Books, Comics
Audience: Modesty Blaise Enthusiasts
Contact: Thomas Gramstad
modesty-blaise-request@math.uio.no
User Info: To subscribe to the list, send an e-mail message to the URL address below consisting of a single line reading: SUB modesty-blaise YourFirstName YourLastName

`mailto: modesty-blaise-request@math.uio.no`

Commcoll

Commcoll

A mailing list providing a forum for faculty, staff, and administrators at two-year institutions.

Keywords: Education (Continuing), Community Colleges
Sponsor: Jefferson Community College at the University of Kentucky, Kentucky, USA
Audience: Educators, Administrators
User Info: To subscribe to the list, send an e-mail message to the URL address below consisting of a single line reading: SUB commcoll YourFirstName YourLastName.

To send a message to the entire list, address it to: commcoll@ukcc.uky.edu

`mailto: listserv@ukcc.uky.edu`

Commerce Business Daily

Commerce Business Daily

The Commerce Business Daily is a publication that announces invitations to bid on proposals requested by the US Federal Government. This gopher is updated every business day.

Keywords: Business (US), Economics, Commerce, Trade, Government (US)
Sponsor: CNS and Softshare Government Information Systems
Audience: Economists, Business Professionals, General Public, Journalists, Students, Politicians
Profile: Invitations via Internet email that apply only to specific companies can be arranged.
Contact: Melissa Allensworth
sshare@cscns.com
service@cscns.com
Details: Free

`gopher://cns.cscns.com/cbd/About the CBD`

Ireland-Related Online Resources

This is a list of network-accessible online resources (documents, images, information, access mechanisms for off-line material, and so on) of Irish interest. Coverage includes some Bulletin Board Services, some commercial information systems such as CompuServe and commercial bibliographic services.

Keywords: Ireland, Travel, Commerce, Geography
Audience: Irish, General Public, Tourists, Businesses
Contact: fmurtagh@eso.org

`http://http.hq.eso.org/~fmurtagh/ireland-resources.html`

National Export Strategy

This site provides the complete text of a report presented to Congress by the Trade Promotion Coordinating Committee, describing ways to develop U.S. export promotion efforts.

Keywords: Commerce, Trade, Exports, Business
Sponsor: United States Government, Trade Promotion Coordinating Committee
Audience: Exporters, Businesspeople, Trade Specialists
Details: Free

`ftp://sunny.stat-usa.gov`

`http://sunny.stat-usa.gov`

Overseas Business Reports

Full-text of U.S. International Trade Administration reports, discussing the economic and commercial climate in various countries around the world.

Keywords: Business, Trade, Commerce
Sponsor: U.S. Government, International Trade Administration
Audience: Businesspeople, Trade Specialists, Investors
Details: Free

`gopher://umslvma.umsl.edu/11/library/govdocs/obr`

Trademark Act of the US

The US Trademark Act of 1946 (the "Lanham Act"), Title 15, United States Code, Sections 1051–1127.

Keywords: Trademarks, Laws (US), Government (US), Commerce
Audience: Journalists, Politicians, Students, Lawyers, Business Professionals, Designers, Marketers
Details: Free

`http://www.law.cornell.edu/lanham/lanham.table.html`

TRADSTAT

TRADSTAT is a comprehensive online source of national trade statistics.

Keywords: Trade, Commerce, Business
Sponsor: TRADSTAT Ltd., London, UK
Audience: Importers, Exporters, Businesses
Profile: TRADSTAT covers over 90 percent of world trade. Every month the latest trade figures are loaded into the database from over 20 countries worldwide and all their trading partners. Trade is reported by countries in the EC, EFTA, North and South America, and the Far East. TRADSTAT gives annual trends back to 1981, and monthly reports can be produced at any time for the latest 25 months' trade. The data is made available on average three to eight weeks after the month of trade. This is often weeks, even months, ahead of the equivalent printed data.
User Info: To subscribe, contact Dialog directly.

`telnet://dialog.com`

Uniform Commercial Code (UCC)

Articles 1 and 2 of the UCC, adopted with some variations in all 50 states (USA).

Keywords: Commerce, Business Info, Standards
Audience: Politicians, Marketers, Students, Retailers, Lawyers
Details: Free

`http://www.law.cornell.edu/ucc/ucc.table.html`

CommerceNet

CommerceNet

An open, internet-based infrastructure for electronic commerce, created by a coalition of Silicon Valley organizations.

Keywords: Business, Electronic Commerce
Sponsor: CommerceNet, Inc. 800 El Camino Real, Menlo Park, CA 94025.
Audience: Businesses, Commercial Internet Users, General Public
Profile: Services include basic enabling services required by virtually every user and application (generic directories, secure multimedia messaging, network access control, and payment facilities). Applications include a framework for the development of compelling applications and services targeted to electronic commerce among companies in the region. Applications are designed to address the varied business and community needs of CommerceNet

users; these are developed by third-party providers; in compliance with protocols established by CommerceNet. Connectivity is high-quality and affordable, with minimal on-site equipment or network expertise required of the user.

Contact: feedback@commerce.net

`http://www.commerce.net`

Commercial Real Estate

Commercial Real Estate

Users can send and receive listings on property for sale, ask and answer questions, send press releases, receive editorial material, and do networking on commercial property.

Keywords: Real Estate
Audience: Real Estate Brokers, General Public
Contact: commercial.realestate@data-base.com
Details: Free
User Info: To subscribe to the list, send an e-mail message requesting a subscription to the URL address below.

`mailto:commercial.realestate@data-base.com`

Commodore-Amiga

Commodore-Amiga

This list is for Commodore Amiga computer users. Weekly postings include hardware reviews, news briefs, system information, company progress, and information for finding out more about the Commodore and Amiga.

Keywords: Commodore-Amiga, Computers
Audience: Computer Users
Contact: subscribe@xamiga.linet.org
Details: Free
Send subscription requests to the URL address below using this format:
#commodore username@domain

`mailto:subscribe@xamiga.linet.org`

Commodore-Amiga Computers

CSAA

The Comp.Sys.Amiga.Announce mailing list has been created for those who have no access to USENET. It provides the gate between the USENET newsgroup C.S.A.A. and e-mail. This group distributes announcements of importance to people using the Commodore brand Amiga computers. Announcements contain information on new products, disk library releases, software updates, reports of major bugs or dangerous viruses, notices of meetings or upcoming events, and so forth. A large proportion of posts announce the upload of software packages to anonymous FTP archive sites.

Keywords: Commodore-Amiga Computers, Computers
Audience: Commodore-Amiga Users
Contact: Carlos Amezaga
announce-request@cs.ucdavis.edu
Details: Free
User Info: To subscribe to the list, send an e-mail message requesting a subscription to the URL address below.

To send a message to the entire list, address it to:announce@cs.ucdavis.edu

`mailto:announce-request@cs.ucdavis.edu`

Commonwealth of Independent States (CIS)

Sovokinform

CIS news, events, general information; usually in transliterated Russian.

Keywords: Commonwealth of Independent States (CIS)
Audience: Journalists, Political Scientists
Contact: burkov@drfmc.ceng.cea.fr
Details: Free
User Info: To subscribe to the list, send an e-mail message requesting a subscription to the URL address below.

To send a message to the entire list, address it to:
sovokinform@drfmc.ceng.cea.fr

`mailto:burkov@drfmc.ceng.cea.fr`

Commonwealth

INTLAW (International Law Library)

The International Law Library provides comprehensive international law materials.

Keywords: International Law, EEC, Commonwealth, China
Audience: Lawyers, International Lawyers
Profile: The International Law library provides comprehensive international law materials. The International Law library contains federal case law, European Community materials, treaties and agreements, Commonwealth law

152 Commonwealth

materials, topical and professional journals, French law materials (in French) China law materials, plus relevant topical publications.

Contact: New Sales Group at (800) 227-4908 or (513) 859-5398 inside the US, or (513) 865-7981 for all inquires outside the US.

User Info: To subscribe, contact Mead directly.

To examine the Lexis user guide, you can access it at the ftp site of the University of Texas at Austin at the URL address: ftp://ftp.cc.utexas.edu

The files are in: /pub/ref-services/LEXIS

`telnet://nex.meaddata.com`

`http://www.meaddata.com`

Communes

alt.housing.nontrad ★

This newsgroup is for discussion of all forms of "nontraditional housing," including cohousing and communes.

Keywords: Community, Housing, Communes
Audience: General Public, Community Activists
Details: Free

To participate in a USENET newsgroup, you need access to a "newsreader."

`news:alt.housing.nontrad`

commune ★

The purpose of this list is to discuss the COMMUNE protocol, a Telnet replacement.

Keywords: Communes, Telnet
Audience: Commune Protocol Users
Contact: Dan Bernstein
commune-request@stealth.acf.nyu.edu
Details: Free
User Info: To subscribe to the list, send an e-mail message requesting a subscription to the URL address below.

To send a message to the entire list, address it to:
commune-list@stealth.acf.nyu.edu

`mailto:commune-request@stealth.acf.nyu.edu`

Communication

ELSNET (European Network in Language and Speech)

A web site addressing the development of language technology in Europe and abroad by helping to coordinate progress on both scientific and technological fronts.

Keywords: Linguistics, Cognitive Science, Communication
Sponsor: The University of Edinburgh Centre for Cognitive Science, Edinburgh, Scotland
Audience: Linguists, Cognitive Scientists
Contact: Ewan Klein
klein@ed.ac.uk

`http://www.cogsci.ed.ac.uk/elsnet/home.html`

Journal of Technology Education ★

Electronic journal devoted to educational issues in technology.

Keywords: Communication, Education, Technology,
Audience: Educators
Details: Free

Send an e-mail message to the URL address below with the request: GET MISCELLA JTE-V5N1. This file will give you access information for additional issues.

`mailto:listserv@vtvm1.cc.vt.edu`

Communication and Mass Communication Resources

Communication and Mass Communication Resources ★★

An archive of materials related to mass communications and the media.

Keywords: Mass Communications, Media, Journalism, Telecommunications, Advertising
Sponsor: The University of Iowa
Audience: Mass Communications Students and Teachers, Journalists, Broadcasting Professionals
Contact: Karla Tonella
Karla_Tonella@uiowa.edu

`gopher://iam41.arcade.uiowa.edu`

Communications

Almost 2001 Archive ★

Archive of transcripts of Almost 2001, a series on computer communications of the future, produced by NBC (National Broadcasting Company).

Keywords: Computers, Communications, Internet
Sponsor: The WELL (Whole Earth 'Lectronic Link)
Audience: Computer Users, Internet Surfers
Details: Free

To participate in a conference on the WELL, you must first establish an account on the WELL. To do so, start by typing: telnet://well.sf.ca.us

`gopher://gopher.well.sf.ca.us//11/Communications/2001`

AM/FM

A mailing list for the AM/FM Online Edition, a monthly compilation of news stories concerning the UK radio industry.

Keywords: Radio, United Kingdom, Communications
Audience: Radio Enthusiasts (UK), Communications Specialists, Students (college, graduate)
Contact: Stephen Hebditch
listserv@orbital.demon.co.uk
User Info: To subscribe to the list, send an e-mail message to the URL addres below, consisting of a single line reading:

SUB am/fm YourFirstName YourLastName

To send a message to the entire list, address it to: AM/FM@orbital.demon.co.uk

`mailto:listserv@orbital.demon.co.uk`

CMPCOM (Computers and Communications) Libraryzzzz

The Computers and Communications Library provides you industry-specific sources. More than 40 full-text sources that concentrate on computers and communications are available. Full-text files can be searched in a variety of ways: as an individual file, by major-subject group file, or as a user-defined group file.

Keywords: Computers, Communications, Technology, Electronics
Audience: Business Researchers, Analysts, Entrepreneurs
Profile: This library can be used to gain insight on new products and technologies being introduced; monitor industry news for high technology systems, electronics, engineering, communications, and computer hardware and software; and locate product evaluations for both the professional as well as the casual personal computer user.
Contact: Mead New Sales Group at (800) 227-4908 or (513) 859-5398 inside the US, or (513) 865-7981 for all inquiries outside the US.
User Info: To subscribe, contact Mead directly.

To examine the Nexis user guide, you can access it at the ftp site of the University of Texas at Austin at the URL address: ftp://ftp.cc.utexas.edu

The files are in: /pub/ref-services/LEXIS

`telnet://nex.meaddata.com`

`http://www.meaddata.com`

ejcrec 'Electronic Journal of Communications/La Revue électronique de communication'

This journal is a quarterly bilingual (English and French) journal for the communications field broadly.

Keywords:	Communications
Audience:	Educators, Administrators, Communications Professionals
Details:	Free
User Info:	To subscribe to the journal, send an e-mail message to the URL address shown below consisting of a single line reading
	Join edupage YourFirstName YourLastName

mailto:comserve@rpitsvm.bitnet

Electronic Communications Privacy Act of 1986

This is the act to amend Title 18, United States Code, with respect to the interception of certain communications, other forms of surveillance, and for other purposes. This act affects every USENET, Bitnet, BBS, shortwave listener, TV viewer, and so on.

Keywords:	Communications, Privacy, Government (US Federal), Laws (US Federal)
Audience:	Journalists, Privacy Activists, Students, Politicians
Details:	Free

gopher://wiretap.spies.com/00/Gov/ecpa.act

Newsline

An electronic newsletter describing additions to or changes in Comserve, the electronic information and discussion service for communications faculty and students.

Keywords:	Communications, Comserve
Audience:	Communications Students, Communications Specialists
Profile:	The information includes announcements of additions to Comserve's database, new services offered through Comserve's electronic conferences, or fundamental changes in the services offered by Comserve.
Contact:	Timothy Stephen, Teresa Harrison
	Support@RpiecsSupport@Vm.Ecs.Rpi.Edu
User Info:	To subscribe, send an e-mail message to the URL address below consisting of a single line reading:
	SUB NEWSLINE YourFirstName YourLastName

mailto:Comserve@Vm.Ecs.Rpi.Edu

PRL

The Pirate Radio SWL list is for the distribution of questions, answers, information, and loggings of Pirate Radio Stations.

Keywords:	Radio, Communications
Audience:	Radio Listeners, Radio Pirates
Contact:	John Brewer
	brewer@ace.enet.dec.com
User Info:	To subscribe to the list, send an e-mail message to the URL address below, consisting of a single line reading:
	SUB PRLYourFirstName YourLastName.
	To send a message to the entire list, address it to: brewer@ace.enet.dec.com

mailto:listserv@ace.enet.dec.com

Prog-Pubs

A mailing list for people interested in progressive or alternative publications and other media. Discussions include issues pertaining to all kinds of small-scale, independent, progressive, and/or alternative media, including newspapers, newsletters, and radio and video shows.

Keywords:	Media, Alternative Press, Communications
Audience:	Students (college/university), Independent Media Professionals
Contact:	prog-pubs-request@fuggles.acc.virginia.edu
Details:	Free
User Info:	To subscribe to the list, send an e-mail message requesting a subscription to the URL address below.
	To send a message to the entire list, address it to:prog-pubs@fuggles.acc.virginia.edu

mailto:prog-pubs@fuggles.acc.virginia.edu

Scit-L

A list for those interested in information and communications science.

Keywords:	Communications, Information Sciences
Audience:	Communications Specialists, Communications Students, Information Scientists
Contact:	Elia Zureik
	Scitdoc@qucdn.queensu.ca
User Info:	To subscribe to this list, send an e-mail message to the URL address below, consisting of a single line reading:
	SUB scit-l YourFirstName YourLastName
	To send a message to the entire list, address it to: scit-l@qucdn.queensu.ca

mailto:listserv@qucdn.queensu.ca

Stutt-L

A list for the clinical discussion of stuttering, a speech disorder.

Keywords:	Communications, Speech Disorders, Disabilities
Audience:	Communications Specialists, Speech Pathologists
Contact:	Woody Starkweather
	v5002e@vm.temple.edu
User Info:	To subscribe to this list, send an e-mail message to the URL address below, consisting of a single line reading:
	SUB Stutt-L YourFirstName YourLastName
	To send a message to the entire list, address it to: stutt-l@rm.temple.edu

mailto:listserv@vm.temple.edu

The Black Box Catalog

The Black Box Catalog, the industry's most complete source for data communication equipment, is now available on the Internet. The complete range of products, technical references, and application briefs are available on the Black Box World Wide Web Server.

Keywords:	Communications, Networking, Telecommunication, Computers
Sponsor:	Black Box Corporation, Lawrence, PA
Audience:	Engineers, Network Administration, LAN Administrators, Communication Specialists
Profile:	Black Box Corporation is a leading international supplier of data communications networking and related computer connectivity products. Black Box's commitment to providing effective solutions that substantially enhance the capabilities of communications systems is backed by a technical support staff that is available around the clock, a liberal 45-day return policy, and same day shipment of its 6000 products.
Contact:	Webmaster
	webmaster@blackbox.com
Details:	Costs

http://www.blackbox.com

Communism

Emory University Library

The library's holdings are large and wide-ranging and contain significant collections in many fields.

Keywords:	Health Sciences, Theology, History (US), Communism, Economics (History of), Literature (American)
Audience:	General Public, Researchers, Librarians, Document Delivery Professionals

Communism

A B **C** D E F G H I J K L M N O P Q R S T U V W X Y Z

Details: Free

Expect: VM screen, Send: RETURN;
Expect: CP READ, Send: DIAL VTAM,
press RETURN; Expect: CICS screen,
Send: PF1

`telnet://emuvm1.cc.emory.edu`

soc.culture.soviet

A Usenet newsgroup providing information and discussion about topics relating to Russia or the former Soviet Union.

Keywords: Russia, CIS (Commonwealth of Independent States), Communism, Sociology

Audience: Sociologists, Russians

Details: Free

User Info: To subscribe to this Usenet newsgroup, you need access to a newsreader.

`news:soc.culture.soviet`

talk.politics.soviet

A Usenet newsgroup providing information and discussion about Soviet politics, domestic and international.

Keywords: Communism, Russia, Politics, CIS (Commonwealth of Independent States)

Audience: Political Scientists

Details: Free

User Info: To subscribe to this Usenet newsgroup, you need access to a newsreader.

`news:talk.politics.soviet`

val-l

Discussion on changes in the Communist countries, ranging from Cuba and Vietnam to the former Soviet Union.

Keywords: Communism, Soviet Union, Political Science

Audience: Political Scientists

Contact: cdell@umkcax1 or cdell@umkcvax1.bitnet

Details: Free

User Info: To subscribe to the list, send an e-mail message to the URL address below consisting of a single line reading:

SUB val-l YourFirstName YourLastName

To send a message to the entire list, address it to: val-l@ucflvm.cc.ucf.edu

`mailto:listserv@ucflvm.cc.ucf.edu`

Community Access

Cleveland FreeNet

A network designed for community access and education.

Keywords: Networks, Community Access

Sponsor: The Cleveland FreeNet Project, Case Western Reserve University, Cleveland, Ohio, USA

Audience: Educators, Researchers, Students, Parents

Profile: A prototypical user-friendly city FreeNet, containing complete historical documents, an up-to-date news service, extensive info on the arts, sciences, technology, medicine, business, and education.

Notes: Registration is required, and information on registration is included.

`telnet://freenet-in-a.cwru.edu`

Community Colleges

Commcoll

A mailing list providing a forum for faculty, staff, and administrators at two-year institutions.

Keywords: Education (Continuing), Community Colleges

Sponsor: Jefferson Community College at the University of Kentucky, Kentucky, USA

Audience: Educators, Administrators

User Info: To subscribe to the list, send an e-mail message to the URL address below consisting of a single line reading:

SUB commcoll YourFirstName YourLastName.

To send a message to the entire list, address it to: commcoll@ukcc.uky.edu

`mailto:listserv@ukcc.uky.edu`

Community Networking

Free-Net Working Papers

An FTP site with a collection of articles and papers about community networking.

Keywords: Community Networking, Networking

Sponsor: Carleton University, National Clearinghouse for Machine Readable Texts

Audience: Activists, Government, General Public

Profile: Project Guttenburg's goal is to provide a collection of 10,000 of the most used books by the year 2001.

Contact: Jay Weston, Michael S. Hart

jweston@carleton.ca

Details: Free

Login anonymous; cd text

`ftp://alfred.carleton.ca/pub/freenet/working.papers`

FreeNets

This resource provides extensive information about FreeNets, which are public access Internet sites at no-charge or for donations.

Keywords: Internet Access, Community Networking

Audience: Individuals, Communities, Libraries

Profile: FreeNets, community computing services providing Internet access, exist internationally and include such systems as LA FreeNet, Buffalo FreeNet, Cleveland FreeNet, FreeNet Erlangen-Nuernburg, Victoria FreeNet, Vaasa FreePort (Finland), CapAccess (D.C.), and many more.

Details: Free

URL (gopher path) below contains pointers to all FreeNets.

`gopher path: 1/internet/freenets marvel.loc.gov`

Community

(The) Electronic Public Interest versus the Private Good

Statement by community networker Dave Hughes, sounding the warning that the federal goverment may be leaving the marketplace too much control over who gets access to the information infrastructure.

Keywords: Community, Networking, Government (US)

Audience: Activists, Policymakers, Community Leaders

Contact: Dave Hughes

dave@oldcolo.com

Details: Free

`http://nearnet.gnn.com/mag/articles/oram/bio.hughes.html`

(The) WELL (Whole Earth 'Lectronic Link)

The WELL is a computer conferencing system, a virtual community, and an electronic coffee shop.

Keywords: Community, Networking, Computer Conferencing, Virtual Community
Sponsor: Whole Earth 'Lectronic Link
Audience: General Public, Internet Surfers
Profile: The WELL is a classic example of an online community that uses what is called 'conferencing' to bring a myriad of people together for intense interactions without them having to be connected at the same time. At the end of 1993, the WELL had about 8,000 users (about 90% from all over the USA and about 10% from other locations) and approximately 200 public discussion areas ('conferences'), and 200 private discussion areas. It is a place rich in diverse 'neighborhoods.'
Contact: The WELL Support Staff
info@well.sf.ca.us
Direct dial access through: +1 (415) 332-4335
To participate in a conference on the WELL, you must first establish an account on the WELL. To do so, start by typing: `telnet well.sf.ca.us`

`telnet://well.sf.ca.us`

(The) Worldwide Impact of Network Access

This is an article by community networker Felipe Rodriquez. In this statement Rodriquez argues that developed countries should help less developed countries build their information infrastructures, and that governments should not censor the content of network traffic.

Keywords: Community, Networking, Europe, Development (International)
Audience: Activists, Policymakers, Community Leaders
Contact: Felipe Rodriquez
felipe@hacktic.nl

`http://nearnet.gnn.com/mag/articles/oram/bio.rodriquez.html`

alt.housing.nontrad

This newsgroup is for discussion of all forms of "nontraditional housing," including cohousing and communes.

Keywords: Community, Housing, Communes
Audience: General Public, Community Activists
Details: Free
To participate in a USENET newsgroup, you need access to a "newsreader."

`news:alt.housing.nontrad`

An NREN That Includes Everyone

In this article, community networker Tom Grundner (founder of Free-Net), advocates a National Community Network, one that treats parents looking for health-care information as researchers. He advocates expanding our definition of educational access to include people of all ages—senior citizens as well as kindergarteners.

Keywords: Community, Networking, Government (US)
Audience: Activists, Policymakers, Community Leaders
Contact: Tom Grundner
tmg@nptn.org
Details: Free
Notes: This document contains hypertext links to the NPTN (National Public Telecomputing Network).

`http://nearnet.gnn.com/mag/articles/oram/bio.grundner.html`

Blacksburg Electronic Village Gopher

The Blacksburg Electronic Village is a project to link an entire town in southwestern Virginia with a 21st-century telecommunications infrastructure. This infrastructure will bring a useful set of information services and interactive communications facilities into the daily activities of citizens and businesses.

Keywords: Community, Networking, Telecommunications
Sponsor: Town of Blacksburg, Virginia, USA
Audience: Activists, Policymakers, Community Leaders, Government
Profile: This community gopher server run by the town of Blacksburg contains information about Blacksburg and how it is building its electronic infrastructure. It includes a list of Blacksburg-area BBSs, instructions for local residents to get an account on the town's BBS, and a section called "Village Schoolhouse."
Details: Costs

`gopher://morse.cns.vt.edu`

Citizens Project

A grass-roots community group in the Pikes Peak region of Colorado.

Keywords: Community, Networking, Colorado
Audience: Activists, Policymakers, Community Leaders, Government
Profile: Based in Colorado Springs, Colorado, the Citizens Project makes use of the online world in pursuit of its mission to investigate, inform, and advocate issues affecting the Pikes Peak region. It maintains an extensive gopher server, FTP site, and a ListServ (for people who have only e-mail access).
Contact: Citizens Project
citizens@cscns.com
Details: Free
User Info: To subscribe to the list, send an e-mail message to the URL address below, consisting of a single line reading:
SUB cns-citizens-pub YourFirstName YourLastName

`mailto:listserv@cscns.com`

Civic Promise of the National Information Infrastructure (NII)

Community networker Richard Civille (founder of EcoNet and director of the Center for Civic Networking) describes several experiments in community networking.

Keywords: Community, Networking, Government (US)
Audience: Activists, Policymakers, Community Leaders, Government
Contact: Richard Civille
rciville@civicnet.org
Details: Free

`http://nearnet.gnn.com/mag/articles/oram/bio.civille.html`

COHOUSING-L

A list for discussion of cohousing, the name of a type of collaborative housing that has been developed primarily in Denmark since 1972 where it is known as bofoellesskaber. Cohousing is housing designed to foster community and cooperation while preserving independence. Private residences are clustered near shared facilities. The members design and manage all aspects of their community.

Keywords: Community, Housing, Cooperatives
Audience: Urban Planners, Architects, General Contractors
Contact: fholson@uci.com
Details: Free
User Info: To subscribe to the list, send an e-mail message to the address below consisting of a single line reading:
SUB COHOUSING-L YourFirstName YourLastName
To send a message to the entire list, address it to: COHOUSING-L@uci.com

`mailto:listserv@uci.com`

Community Networks Benefit Federal Goals ★

Statement by community networker Frank Odasz, founder and director of Big Sky Telegraph, a network of rural BBSs throughout Montana. In this article he makes the case that the federal goverment will benefit from the widespread rural employment of networking technology.

Keywords: Community, Networking, Rural Development, Development

Audience: Activists, Policy Analysts, Community Leaders, Government, Citizens, Rural Residents, Native Americans

Contact: Frank Odasz

franko@bigsky.dillon.mt.us,

Details: Free

`http://nearnet.gnn.com/mag/articles/oram/bio.odasz.html`

CSF: Communications for a Sustainable Future ★★★★

A gopher server for the distribution of Conflict Resolution Materials.

Keywords: Conflict Resolution, Community, Politics

Sponsor: Communications for a Sustainable Future

Audience: Activists, Policy Analysts, Community Leaders, Mediators, Lawyers

Profile: Communications for a Sustainable Future is a collective effort of several scholars. CSF does research, education, and applied work. Its main subject areas are: Intractable Conflicts and Constructive Confrontation, Environmental and Public Policy Dispute Resolution, Social/Political Conflicts, International Conflicts.

Contact: roper@csf.colorado.edu

Details: Free

`gopher://csf.colorado.edu`

ECHO ★★★★

A computer conferencing system based in New York City.

Keywords: Community, Networking, Women's Issues

Sponsor: East Coast Hang Out

Audience: Activists, Policy Makers, Community Leaders, Governments, Students, Feminists, Educators, Health-Care Professionals, Artists, Communicators, General Public

Profile: ECHO was started by Stacy Horn, as an East Coast counterpart to the WELL. ECHO makes an effort to be hospitable to women and has one of the highest percentages of women in an online community.

Contact: Stacy Horn

horn@echonyc.com,

Details: Costs

`telnet://echonyc.com`

Electronic Democracy Must Come from Us ★

Article about government policy and community networks by community networker Evelyn Pine (former national director of Computer Professionals for Social Responsibility). A short critique of the promises of electronic networking contrasted with the realities of political control.

Keywords: Community, Networking, Government (US)

Audience: Activists, Community Leaders, Governments

Contact: Evelyn Pine

evy@well.sf.ca.us

Details: Free

`http://nearnet.gnn.com/mag/articles/oram/bio.pine.html`

Leaders of Community Networking: People Who Create Online Communities ★

A WWW document with links to several important community networking resources. A brief overview of community networking is provided, as are links to statements by several leaders in the movement.

Keywords: Community, Networking, Government (US Federal)

Audience: Activists, Policymakers, Community Leaders, Government, Citizens

Details: Free

`http://nearnet.gnn.com/mag/articles/oram/introduction.html`

Networks & Communities ★★

This directory is a compilation of information resources focused on networks and communities.

Keywords: Community, Networking, Privacy

Audience: Network Developers, Community Activists, Free-net Organizers, Fundraisers

Details: Free

`ftp://una.hh.lib.umich.edu/70/inetdirsstacks/nets:sternberg`

People Using Networks Can Have an Impact on Government ★★★★

Statement by community networker Anne Fallis, who emphasizes the need for easy-to-use interfaces and inexpensive access to worldwide information. She lists many examples of local communities using networking.

Keywords: Community, Networking, Activism

Audience: Activists, Policymakers, Community Leaders, Network Users

Contact: Anne Fallis

afallis@silver.sdsmt.edu

Details: Free

`http://nearnet.gnn.com/mag/articles/oram/bio.fallis.html`

Telluride Institute ★

This is a community organization involved in building an electronic dimension in rural Colorado. The vision of Telluride Institute includes linking rural residents to each other and outside resources, creating new opportunities for education, jobs, and arts.

Keywords: Community, Networking, Virtual Community, Rural Development, Colorado

Sponsor: The Telluride Institute, Telluride, Colorado

Audience: Activists, Policymakers, Community Leaders, Students, Colorado Residents

Profile: The Telluride Institute is a local community-based organization that produces arts, environmental, and educational events in the Telluride area of Colorado. The Institite is committed to the creation of what it calls the "InfoZone": it wants to use modern telecommunications to link together the local community and to connect to the rest of the world to exchange ideas, commerce, arts, and inspiration.

Contact: Richard Lowenberg

tellinst@CSN.ORG

Details: Free

Send an e-mail message to the URL address below asking for further information.

`mailto:tellinst@csn.org`

TWICS ★★★★

This is an English-language computer conferencing system in Japan.

Keywords: Community, Networking, Computer Conferencing, Japan, Virtual Community

Sponsor: TWICS Co., Ltd.

Audience: Internationalists, General Public, Journalists, Policymakers

Profile: TWICS is a computer conferencing system that has a reputation for being a thriving electronic community. It recently obtained a full Internet connection and is currently one of the few places in Japan accessible via the Internet. Unlike a database or a gopher server, TWICS is a place to visit for interaction with actual people.
Contact: Tim Buress
twics@twics.co.jp,
Details: Free
`telnet://tanuki.twics.co.jp`

Community Service

Community Services Catalyst

This electronic journal provides information concerning community services around the country, especially those dealing with continuing education. The journal is published quarterly.
Keywords: Education (Continuing), Community Service
Sponsor: National Council on Community Services and Continuing Education (an affiliate council of the American Association of Community Colleges), USA
Audience: Educators, Administrators
User Info: To subscribe to the list, send an e-mail message to the URL address below consisting of a single line reading:

SUB catalyst YourFirstName YourLastName

To send a message to the entire list, address it to: catalyst@vtvm1.cc.vt.edu
`mailto: listserv@vtvml.cc.vt.edu`

comp.compression

comp.compression ★

A Usenet newsgroup providing information and discussion about data compression algorithms and theory.
Keywords: Computers, Mathematics (Algorithims)
Audience: Computer Users
User Info: To subscribe to this Usenet newsgroup, you need access to a newsreader.
`news:comp.compression`

comp.databases

comp.databases ★

A Usenet newsgroup providing information and discussion about databases and data management issues.

Keywords: Computing, Computer Databases
Audience: Computer Users
User Info: To subscribe to this Usenet newsgroup, you need access to a newsreader.
`news:comp.databases`

comp.graphics

comp.graphics ★

A Usenet newsgroup providing information and discussion about computer graphics, art, animation and more.
Keywords: Computer Graphics, Art
Audience: Computer Users
User Info: To subscribe to this Usenet newsgroup, you need access to a newsreader.
`news:comp.graphics`

comp.infosystems.gopher

comp.infosystems.gopher ★

A Usenet newsgroup providing information and discussion about the gopher information search tool.
Keywords: Gopher, Internet Reference, Information Retrieval
Audience: Internet Surfers
User Info: To subscribe to this Usenet newsgroup, you need access to a newsreader.
`news:comp.infosystems.gopher`

comp.infosystems.wais

comp.infosystems.wais ★

A Usenet newsgroup providing information and discussion about the WAIS full-text search tool.
Keywords: WAIS, Internet Reference, Information Retrieval
Audience: Internet Surfers
User Info: To subscribe to this Usenet newsgroup, you need access to a newsreader.
`news:comp.infosystems.wais`

comp.infosystems.www

comp.infosystems.www ★

A Usenet newsgroup providing information and discussion about the World Wide Web.

Keywords: WWW, Internet Reference, Information Retrieval
Audience: Internet Surfers
User Info: To subscribe to this Usenet newsgroup, you need access to a newsreader.
`news:comp.infosystems.www`

comp.lang.c

comp.lang.c ★

A Usenet newsgroup providing information and discussion about the C programming language.
Keywords: Computer Programming, Programming Languages
Audience: Computer Users, C Programmers
User Info: To subscribe to this Usenet newsgroup, you need access to a newsreader.
`news:comp.lang.c`

comp.lang.c++

comp.lang.c++ ★

A Usenet newsgroup providing information and discussion about the object-oriented C++ programming language.
Keywords: Computers, Programming Languages
Audience: Computer Users, C++ Programmers
User Info: To subscribe to this Usenet newsgroup, you need access to a newsreader.
`news:comp.lang.c++`

comp.org.eff.talk

comp.org.eff.talk ★

A Usenet newsgroup organized by the EFF (Electronic Frontier Foundation) providing information and discussion about the political, social, and legal issues surrounding the Internet.
Keywords: Computers, Intellectual Property, Security, Internet
Audience: Internet Surfers
User Info: To subscribe to this Usenet newsgroup, you need access to a newsreader.
`news:comp.org.eff.talk`

comp.os

comp.os

A Usenet newsgroup providing information and discussion about computer operating systems. There are many categories within this group.

Keywords: Computer Systems
Audience: Computer Users
User Info: To subscribe to this Usenet newsgroup, you need access to a newsreader.

news:comp.os

comp.os.ms-windows.apps

A Usenet newsgroup providing information and discussion about applications in Windows.

Keywords: Computers Systems
Audience: Computer Users, Windows Users
User Info: To subscribe to this Usenet newsgroup, you need access to a newsreader.

news:comp.os.ms-windows.apps

comp.os.os2.misc

A Usenet newsgroup providing information and discussion about miscellaneous topics concerning O/S2.

Keywords: Computer Systems
Audience: Computer Users, O/S2 Users
User Info: To subscribe to this Usenet newsgroup, you need access to a newsreader.

news:comp.os.os2.misc

comp.security.misc

A Usenet newsgroup providing information and discussion about security issues of computers and networks.

Keywords: Computers, Security, Firewalls
Audience: Computer Users
User Info: To subscribe to this Usenet newsgroup, you need access to a newsreader.

news:comp.security.misc

comp.sys.amiga

comp.sys.amiga

A Usenet newsgroup providing information and discussion about Amiga systems. There are many categories within this group.

Keywords: Computer Systems, Amiga Aystems
Audience: Computer Users, Amiga Users
User Info: To subscribe to this Usenet newsgroup, you need access to a newsreader.

news:comp.sys.amiga

comp.sys.apple2

A Usenet newsgroup providing information and discussion about Apple II systems. There are several categories within this group.

Keywords: Computer Systems, Apple Computer
Audience: Computer Users, Apple II Users
User Info: To subscribe to this Usenet newsgroup, you need access to a newsreader.

news:comp.sys.apple2

comp.sys.atari.st

A Usenet newsgroup providing information and discussion about 16-bit Atari.

Keywords: Computer Systems
Audience: Computer Users, Atari Users
User Info: To subscribe to this Usenet newsgroup, you need access to a newsreader.

news:comp.sys.atari.st

comp.sys.ibm.pc

A Usenet newsgroup providing information and discussion about the IBM PC computer. There are many categories within this group.

Keywords: Computer Systems, IBM
Audience: Computer Users, IBM Users
User Info: To subscribe to this Usenet newsgroup, you need access to a newsreader.

news:comp.sys.ibm.pc

comp.sys.mac

comp.sys.mac

A Usenet newsgroup providing information and discussion about the Macintosh computer. There are many categories within this group.

Keywords: Computer Systems, Macintosh Computers
Audience: Computer Users, Macintosh Users
User Info: To subscribe to this Usenet newsgroup, you need access to a newsreader.

news:comp.sys.mac

comp.sys.next

A Usenet newsgroup providing information and discussion about NeXT computers. There are several categories within this group.

Keywords: Computer Systems, NeXT
Audience: Computer Users, NeXT Users
User Info: To subscribe to this Usenet newsgroup, you need access to a newsreader.

news:comp.sys.next

comp.sys.sgi

A Usenet newsgroup providing information and discussion about Silicon Graphic systems. There are several categories within this group.

Keywords: Computer Systems
Audience: Computer Users, Silicon Graphics Users
User Info: To subscribe to this Usenet newsgroup, you need access to a newsreader.

news:comp.sys.sgi

comp.sys.sun

A Usenet newsgroup providing information and discussion about Sun systems. There are several categories within this group.

Keywords: Computer Systems, Sun
Audience: Computer Users, Sun Users
User Info: To subscribe to this Usenet newsgroup, you need access to a newsreader.

news:comp.sys.sun

comp.text.tex

comp.text.tex

A Usenet newsgroup providing information and discussion about the TeX and LaTeX systems.

Keywords: Text Processing, Internet
Audience: Computer Users, TeX and LaTeX Users
User Info: To subscribe to this Usenet newsgroup, you need access to a newsreader.

`news:comp.text.tex`

comp.unix.aix

comp.unix.aix

A Usenet newsgroup providing information and discussion about IBM's version of UNIX.

Keywords: Computer System, Internet, UNIX
Audience: Computer Users, UNIX Users, IBM Users
User Info: To subscribe to this Usenet newsgroup, you need access to a newsreader.

`news:comp.unix.aix`

comp.unix.questions

comp.unix.questions

A Usenet newsgroup providing discussion and questions for those learning UNIX.

Keywords: Computers, UNIX
Audience: Computer Users, UNIX Users
User Info: To subscribe to this Usenet newsgroup, you need access to a newsreader.

`news:comp.unix.questions`

comp.unix.wizards

comp.unix.wizards

A Usenet newsgroup providing discussion and questions for true UNIX wizards.

Keywords: Computers, UNIX
Audience: Computer Users, Unix Users
User Info: To subscribe to this Usenet newsgroup, you need access to a newsreader.

`news:comp.unix.wizards`

comp.windows.x

comp.windows.x

A Usenet newsgroup providing information and discussion about the X Window systems.

Keywords: Computer Systems
Audience: Computer Users, Windows Users
User Info: To subscribe to this Usenet newsgroup, you need access to a newsreader.

`news:comp.windows.x`

comp.windows.x.motif

comp.windows.x.motif

A Usenet newsgroup providing information and discussion about the Motif GUI for the X Window systems.

Keywords: Computer Graphics
Audience: Computer Users, Windows Users
User Info: To subscribe to this Usenet newsgroup, you need access to a newsreader.

`news:comp.windows.x.motif`

Companies

CANADA (Canadian News and Information Library)

The Canadian News and Information Library (CANADA) contains Canadian legal news, business, and company information.

Keywords: News, Analysis, Companies, Canada
Audience: Canadians
Profile: The CANADA Library contains respected Canadian news publications such as *The Toronto Star*, *The Vancouver Sun*, *Ottawa Business News* and the *Montreal Gazette*. The CANADA Library also offers Canadian company profiles, country reports, and Canada's financial database, CANCORP Plus.
Contact: Mead New Sales Group at (800) 227-4908 or (513) 859-5398 inside the US, or (513) 865-7981 for all inquiries outside the US.
User Info: To subscribe, contact Mead directly.

To examine the Nexis user guide, you can access it at the ftp site of the University of Texas at Austin at the URL address: ftp://ftp.cc.utexas.edu

The files are in: /pub/ref-services/LEXIS

`telnet://nex.meaddata.com`

`http://www.meaddata.com`

COMPNY

The COMPNY library contains more than 75 files of business and financial information, including thousands of in-depth company and industry research reports from leading national and international investments banks and brokerage houses.

Keywords: Companies, Financials, Filings, Disclosure
Audience: Business and Financial Researchers, Analysts, Entrepreneurs and Regulators.
Profile: COMPNY includes the following types of information:

- Full-text 10-Q, 10-K, Annual Reports to Shareholders, and Proxy filings
- Extracts of filings for more than 11,000 public companies whose securities are traded on the major exchanges as well as over-the-counter
- Abstracts of S-registration statements, 13-Ds, 14-Ds, 8Ks, Form 4s, and other SEC filings updated on a daily basis
- Business news abstracts from more than 400 information sources
- Daily US economic trends and forecasts.

The materials may be searched in individual files, such as brokerage house reports, or in group files organized by subject, such as SEC filings.

Contact: Mead New Sales Group at (800) 227-4908 or (513) 859-5398 inside the US, or (513) 865-7981 for all inquiries outside the US.
User Info: To subscribe, contact Mead directly.

To examine the Nexis user guide, you can access it at the ftp site of the University of Texas at Austin at the URL address: ftp://ftp.cc.utexas.edu

The files are in: /pub/ref-services/LEXIS

`telnet://nex.meaddata.com`

`http://www.meaddata.com`

INVEST (Investment News and Information)

The INVEST library contains company and industry research reports provided through the Investext(R) database. These reports are created by industry experts who are employed for their accurate and insightful evaluation. Only the most recent 12 months of data will be displayed.

Keywords: Companies, Financials, Analysis
Audience: Business Researchers, Analysts, Entrepreneurs
Profile: INVEST is categorized by type. Selections can be made using these categories: Industry (more than 50 industries are available), State (where a

160 Companies

specific company is located), Country (Country in which the company is located), US Broker or International Broker. The INVEST library provides an automatic display following the selection of a file. For industry reports, a menu will appear providing definitions as they relate to the industries. All remaining files will provide a confirmation of the file selected.

Contact: Mead New Sales Group at (800) 227-4908 or (513) 859-5398 inside the US, or (513) 865-7981 for all inquiries outside the US.

User Info: To subscribe, contact Mead directly.

To examine the Nexis user guide, you can access it at the ftp site of the University of Texas at Austin at the URL address: ftp://ftp.cc.utexas.edu

The files are in: /pub/ref-services/LEXIS

telnet://nex.meaddata.com

http://www.meaddata.com

MDEAFR

The Middle East and Africa (MDEAFR) library contains detailed information about every country in the Mideast and Africa. Structured for those who want to follow the unfolding events in the Gulf states, as well as in North and South Africa, this library contains a broad array of sources, including international research reports from InvestextR.

Keywords: News, Analysis, Companies, Middle East, Africa

Audience: Journalists, Businesspeople

Profile: The MDEAFR library contains a wide array of pertinent sources. Among the information sources are newspapers and wire services, trade and business journals, company reports, country and region background, industry and product analysis, business opportunities, and selected legal texts. News sources range from the world-renowned Associated Press and Christian Science Monitor to the regionally important Jerusalem Post and Africa News. Company information is contained in the EXTEL cards as well as ICC. Providers of country background and industry analysis include Associated Banks of Europe, Bank of America, Business International, IBC USA, and the US Department of Commerce. Customers interested in new business opportunities can check OPIC and Foreign Trade Opportunities (FTO).

Contact: Mead New Sales Group at (800) 227-4908 or (513) 859-5398 inside the US, or (513) 865-7981 for all inquiries outside the US.

User Info: To subscribe, contact Mead directly.

To examine the Nexis user guide, you can access it at the ftp site of the University of Texas at Austin at the URL address: ftp://ftp.cc.utexas.edu

The files are in: /pub/ref-services/LEXIS

telnet://nex.meaddata.com

http://www.meaddata.com

NEWS (General News)

The General News (NEWS) library includes more than 2,300 sources. Full-text news from national and international newspapers, magazines, newsletters, and wire services and abstract information are both available.

Keywords: News, Analysis, People, Companies

Audience: Journalists, General Public

Profile: The General News (NEWS) library contains a number of publications and wire services of general interest, as well as others that specialize in particular areas of business. The NEWS library is organized into individual files, group files by source or subject, and user-defined combination files for full-text information sources. Abstracts are also available as individual files or can be searched together in one group file. The NEWS library includes such prestigious full-text sources as the New York Times and more than more than 30 major newspapers from around the US and the world.

Contact: Mead New Sales Group at (800) 227-4908 or (513) 859-5398 inside the US, or (513) 865-7981 for all inquiries outside the US.

User Info: To subscribe, contact Mead directly.

To examine the Nexis user guide, you can access it at the ftp site of the University of Texas at Austin at the URL address: ftp://ftp.cc.utexas.edu

The files are in: /pub/ref-services/LEXIS

telnet://nex.meaddata.com

http://www.meaddata.com

NSAMER (North and South America Library)

The North and South America library contains detailed information about every country in North and South America (except the United States). The US-Canada Free Trade Agreement, the North American Free Trade Agreement, relations with Mexico and events in such countries as Brazil, Peru, and Nicaragua are among the topics covered by a variety of business, news and legal sources. International research reports from InvestextR are also included. The United States is not covered in this library.

Keywords: News, Analysis, Companies, North America, South America

Audience: Journalists, Businesspeople

Profile: The North and South America library contains a broad array of sources. Among the information sources are newspapers and wire services, trade and business journals, company reports, country and region backgrounds, industry and product analyses, business opportunities, and selected legal texts. News sources range from the world-renowned Washington Post and Christian Science Monitor to the regionally important Toronto Star and Latin American Newsletters. Canadian Business and Maclean's represent a portion of the array of business and trade journals. Company information is contained in the EXTEL cards as well as ICC. Providers of country background and industry analyses include Associated Banks of Europe, Bank of America, Business International, IBC USA and the US Department of Commerce. Among the specialized resources are IBC's Mexico and Brazil Services as well as BI's Business Latin America. Researchers interested in new business opportunities can check OPIC and Foreign Trade Opportunities (FTO).And selected legal texts covering the US-Canada Free Trade Agreement and other international agreements planners and advisors to better assess the business climate in North and South America.

Contact: Mead New Sales Group at (800) 227-4908 or (513) 859-5398 inside the US, or (513) 865-7981 for all inquiries outside the US.

User Info: To subscribe, contact Mead directly.

To examine the Nexis user guide, you can access it at the ftp site of the University of Texas at Austin at the URL address: ftp://ftp.cc.utexas.edu

The files are in: /pub/ref-services/LEXIS

telnet://nex.meaddata.com

http://www.meaddata.com

Company Name

DIALOG Company Name Finder

This database is a search aid designed to locate company information in DIALOG databases.

Keywords: Company Name

Sponsor: Dialog Information Services, Inc., Palo Alto, CA, USA

Audience: Business Professionals, Market Researchers

Profile: Company name records are created for unique entries in the company name indexes of the DIALOG files included. Company names are shown in the form in which they appear in the original database index, including abbreviations, punctuation (commas and periods are stripped out), and spelling variations, and are limited to 46 characters. Long company names may be truncated because of the 46-character maximum.

Contact: Dialog in the US at (800) 334-2564, Dialog internationally at country-specific locations.

User Info: To subscribe, contact Dialog directly.

Notes: Coverage: Dialog databases indexing company name; updated quarterly.

telnet://dialog.com

Composition

Computer Music Journal Archive and World Wide Web Home Page.

This resource reinforces material available in the hardcopy version of Computer Music Journal, published by the MIT Press

Keywords:	Computer Music, Composition, Synthesis, Interaction
Sponsor:	The MIT Press
Audience:	Computer Musicians
Profile:	The archive includes the tables of contents, abstracts, and editor's notes for the last several volumes of CMJ (including the recent bibliography, diskography, and taxonomy of the field), a number of useful CM-related documents such as the full MIDI and AIFF format specifications, a lengthy reference list, the guidelines for manuscript submission, and the full-text of several recent articles.
Contact:	Stephen Pope cmj@cnmat.Berkeley.edu
Details:	Free

`ftp://mitpress.mit.edu:/pub/Computer-Music-Journal`

IRCAM DSP and musical software

This site offers a variety of computer music resources.

Keywords:	Computer Music, Sound Synthesis, Composition, DSP
Sponsor:	IRCAM
Audience:	Computer Music Researchers and Computer Musicians
Profile:	Contains a list and brief description of IRCAM software (digital signal processing, voice and sound synthesis, music composition, wind instrument making, and other programs). There are also calendars of the IRCAM-EIC concerts and tours, and links to various other music servers.
Contact:	Michel Fingerhut fingerhu@ircam.fr
Details:	Free

`http://www.ircam.fr`

Computational Chemistry

Theoretical Journal Abstract And Bibliographic Files

Abstract and bibliographic information for several theoretical chemistry journals.

Keywords:	Theoretical Chemistry, Quantum Chemistry, Quantum Mechanics, Computational Chemistry.
Sponsor:	Online, Inc., Weston, CT, US
Audience:	Chemists, Librarians, Students , (College up)
Profile:	Provided are directory, product, technical, and bibliographic information on leading software packages, integrating this information into one succinct composite record. The database can help professionals locate suitable packages compatible with specified hardware without sifting through large numbers of records.
Contact:	Dialog in the US at (800) 334-2564, Dialog internationally at country specific locations. Mailserv@osc.edu
Details:	Free
User Info:	To subscribe, contact Dialog directly. Select Other OSC Gopher Servers then select OSC Chemistry Gopher Server

`telnet://dialog.com`

`gopher://infomeister.osc.edu`

Computational Neuroscience

Purkinje Park

A server maintained by CalTech to support the sharing of information between users of the GENESIS neural simulator, and to address topics of general interest to the Computational Neuroscience community.

Keywords:	Computational Neuroscience, GENESIS, Neural Simulation.
Sponsor:	Cal Tech
Audience:	Neuroscientists, Computational Neuroscientists
Contact:	Dave Beeman dbeeman@smaug.bbb.caltech.edu

`http://www.bbb.caltech.edu/index.html`

Computer

CJI (Computer Jobs in Israel)

Computer Jobs in Israel (CJI) is a one-way list that will automatically send you the monthly updated computer jobs document. This list will also send you other special documents or announcements regarding finding computer work in Israel. Eventually this list will be an open, moderated list for everyone to exchange information about computer jobs in Israel.

Keywords:	Israel, Computer, Jobs
Audience:	Computer Users, Jews, Israelis, Israel Residents
Contact:	Jacob Richman listserv@jerusalem1.datasrv.co.il
Details:	Free
User Info:	To subscribe to the list, send an e-mail message to the address below, consisting of a single line reading: SUB CJI YourFirstName YourLastName To send a message to the entire list, address it to: CJI@jerusalem1.datasrv.co.il

`mailto:listserv@jerusalem1.datasrv.co.il`

Georgia-Computer Systems Protection Act

Lists full text of the Georgia Computer Systems Protection Act.

Keywords:	Computer, Crime
Audience:	Lawyers, Computer Programmers, Computer Operators
Details:	Free

`gopher://wiretap.spies.com`

Computer Administration

alpha-osf-managers

This list is intended to be a quick-turnaround trouble shooting aid for those who administer and manage DEC Alpha AXP systems running OSF/1.

Keywords:	Computer Systems, Computer Administration
Sponsor:	Oakridge National Laboratory
Audience:	Computer Programmers
User Info:	To subscribe to the list, send an e-mail message to the URL address below consisting of a single line reading: subscribe alpha-osf-managers.
Notes:	Alpha-osf-managers archived at ftp/ kpc.com: /pub/list/alpha-osf-managers

`mailto:majordomo@ornl.gov`

cm5-Managers ★

This is a discussion of administrating the Thinking Machines CM5 parallel supercomputer.

Keywords:	Supercomputers, Computer Administration
Audience:	Supercomputer Users, Supercomputer Administrators
Contact:	J. Eric Townsend jet@nas.nasa.gov
Details:	Free
User Info:	To subscribe to the list, send an e-mail message to the address below, consisting of a single line reading: SUB cm5-managers YourFirstName YourLastName To send a message to the entire list, address it to: cm5-managers@boxer.nas.nasa.gov

`mailto:listserv@boxer.nas.nasa.gov`

LLTI ★

The Language Learning Technology International (LLTI) forum is a discussion of computer-assisted language learning.

Keywords:	Language, Linguistics, Computer Aided Instruction
Audience:	Linguists, Language Teachers, Language Students
Details:	Free
User Info:	To subscribe to the list, send an e-mail message to the URL address below, consisting of a single line reading: SUB llti YourFirstName YourLastName To send a message to the entire list, address it to: llti@dartcms1.dartmouth.edu

`mailto:listserv@dartcms1.dartmouth.edu`

OE-CALL: Old English Computer Assisted Language Learning Newsletter ★

A newsletter for persons interested in computer assisted language-learning methods for teaching Old English.

Keywords:	Old English, Computer-Aided Instruction
Audience:	English Teachers, Educators
Contact:	Clare Lees, Patrick W. Conner mailto:u47c2@wvnvm.bitnet
Details:	Free

`mailto:lees@fordmurh.bitnet`

Vetcai-L ★

Discussion of veterinary medicine computer assisted instruction.

Keywords:	Veterinary Medicine, Computer Aided Instruction
Audience:	Veterinarians, Medical Educators
Contact:	Pat Oblander oblandr@ksuvm.ksu.edu
User Info:	To subscribe to the list, send an e-mail message to the URL address below consisting of a single line reading: SUB vetcai'l YourFirstName YourLastName To send a message to the entire list, address it to: vetcai-l@ksuvm.ksu.edu

`mailto:listserv@ksuvm.ksu.edu`

Computer Aided Learning

AskERIC Virtual Library ★★★★

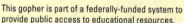

This gopher is part of a federally-funded system to provide public access to educational resources.

Keywords:	Education (K-12), Computer-Aided Learning, Libraries, Electronic Books
Sponsor:	Educational Resources Information Center (ERIC)
Audience:	K-12 Teachers, Administrators
Profile:	This gopher contains a wide-range of educational aids including pre-prepared lesson plans, guides to Internet resources for the classroom organized by subject, updates on conferences for educators, and archives of education-related listservs. Also allows access to outside gophers, libraries, and sources of electronic books and journals.
Contact:	Nancy A. Morgan nmorgan@ericir.syr.edu askeric@ericir.syr.edu

`gopher://ericir/syr.edu`

Computer Applications

CUSSNET ★

Computer Users in the Social Sciences (CUSS) is a discussion group devoted to issues of interest to social workers, counselors, and human service workers of all disciplines. The discussion frequently involves computer applications in treatment, agency administration, and research. Students, faculty, community-based professionals, and casual observers join in the discussion. Software, hardware, and ethical issues associated with their use in the human services generate lively and informative discussions.

Keywords:	Social Sciences, Computers, Computer Applications
Audience:	Social Workers, Human Services Workers, General Public
Contact:	cussnet-request@stat.com
Details:	Free
User Info:	To subscribe to the list, send an e-mail message to the address below consisting of a single line reading: SUB cussnet YourFirstName YourLastName. To send a message to the entire list, address it to: cussnet@stat.com

`mailto:listserv@stat.com`

Computer Art

Art Com Magazine

A newsletter about art and technology (subjects covered include robotics, artists' software, hyperfiction) that is guest-edited by individual artists.

Keywords:	Computer Art, Literature (Contemporary), Technology, Hyperfiction
Sponsor:	Art Com Electronic Network
Audience:	Artists, Writers
Contact:	Fred Truck fjt@well.sf.ca.us To participate in a conference on the WELL, you must first establish an account on the WELL. To do so, start by typing: telnet://well.sf.ca.us

`mailto:artcomtv@well.sf.ca.us`

artist-users ★★

A discussion group for users and potential users of software tools from Cadence Design Systems.

Keywords:	Computers, Computer Art
Sponsor:	Cadence Design Systems
Audience:	Computer Artists
Contact:	Jeff Putsch artist-users-request@uicc.com
User Info:	To subscribe to the list, send an e-mail message to the URL address below. To send a message to the entire list, address it to: artist-users-request@uicc.com
Notes:	This mailing list is bi-directionally gatewayed to the Usenet newsgroup

`mailto:artist-users-request@uicc.com`

Kaleidospace

This is a new web server that provides a multimedia showcase for artists, performers, CD-ROM authors, musicians, writers, animators, filmmakers, and software developers.

Keywords: Art, Computer Art, Multimedia
Audience: Artists, Performers, CD-ROM Authors, Musicians, Writers, Animators, Filmmakers, Software Developers
Profile: This site was created to support independent artists. The site has similarities to other web servers such as IUMA, but differs in that it works with all kinds of artists, and that it processes orders for the artist's material.
Contact: Jeannie Novak, Peter Markiewicz
jeannienov@aol.com,
peterm@ewald.mbi.ucla.edu

`http://kspace.com`

`http://fire.kspace.com`

NYAL (New York Art Line)

A gopher containing selected resources on the arts.

Keywords: Art, Audio-Visual Materials, Multimedia, Computer Art
Sponsor: Panix Public Access Unix & Internet Gopher Server, New York, USA
Audience: Artists, Art Enthusiasts
Profile: NYAL features a wide variety of arts resources. The primary focus of this site is visual art, particularly in the New York city area. Information includes online access to selected galleries, image archives, and New York city arts groups. Beyond visual art, information on dance, music, and techno art (with a special section on Internet art) is also available. It also features links to various electronic journals, museums, and schools.
Contact: Kenny Greenberg
kgreen@panix.com

`gopher://gopher.panix.com`

`http://gopher.panix.com/nyart/Kpage/kg`

rec.video

A Usenet newsgroup providing information and discussion about video.

Keywords: Video, Art, Film, Computer Art
Audience: Cinematographers, Video Artists
User Info: To subscribe to this Usenet newsgroup, you need access to a newsreader.

`news:rec.video`

The ASCII Bazaar

An extensive collection of ASCII art, organized by subject. Also includes FAQ files, software tools, ASCII art discussion lists, and links to other collections of ASCII art.

Keywords: Clip Art, Computer Art
Sponsor: Department of Computer and Information Sciences, University of Alabama at Birmingham, Birmingham, Alabama, USA
Audience: Computer Users, General Public
Contact: R. L. Samuell
samuell@cis.uab.edu

`gopher://twinbrook.cis.uab.edu`

Computer Communications

EFFector Online-The Electronic Frontier Foundation, Inc.

Established to make the electronic frontier truly useful and accessible to everyone, emphasizing the free and open flow of information and communication.

Keywords: Computer Communications, Electronic Media, Intellectual Property, Privacy
Audience: Computer Users, Civil Libertarians
Profile: EFFector Online presents news, information, and discussion about the world of computer-based communications media that constitute the electronic frontier. It covers issues such as freedom of speech in digital media, privacy rights, censorship, and standards of responsibility for users and operators of computer systems, as well as policy issues such as the development of a national information infrastructure, and intellectual property.
Contact: Gerard Van der Leun, Mike Godwin
gerard@eff.org
mnemonic@eff.org
Details: Free
User Info: To subscribe, send an e-mail message requesting a subscription to:
request@eff.org
Notes: This takes you to the front door of the eff gopher server which contains much more information than just Effector online.

`gopher://gopher.eff.org/1`

Computer Conferencing

(The) WELL (Whole Earth 'Lectronic Link)

The WELL is a computer conferencing system, a virtual community, and an electronic coffee shop.

Keywords: Community, Networking, Computer Conferencing, Virtual Community
Sponsor: Whole Earth 'Lectronic Link
Audience: General Public, Internet Surfers
Profile: The WELL is a classic example of an online community that uses what is called "conferencing" to bring a myriad of people together for intense interactions without them having to be connected at the same time. At the end of 1993, the WELL had about 8,000 users (about 90% from all over the USA and about 10% from other locations) and approximately 200 public discussion areas ('conferences'), and 200 private discussion areas. It is a place rich in diverse 'neighborhoods.'
Contact: The WELL Support Staff
info@well.sf.ca.us
Direct dial access through: +1 (415) 332-4335
To participate in a conference on the WELL, you must first establish an account on the WELL. To do so, start by typing: telnet well.sf.ca.us

`telnet://well.sf.ca.us`

TWICS

This is an English-language computer conferencing system in Japan.

Keywords: Community, Networking, Computer Conferencing, Japan, Virtual Community
Sponsor: TWICS Co., Ltd.
Audience: Internationalists, General Public, Journalists, Policymakers
Profile: TWICS is a computer conferencing system that has a reputation for being a thriving electronic community. It recently obtained a full Internet connection and is currently one of the few places in Japan accessible via the Internet. Unlike a database or a gopher server, TWICS is a place to visit for interaction with actual people.
Contact: Tim Buress
twics@twics.co.jp,
Details: Free

`telnet://tanuki.twics.co.jp`

Computer Databases

comp.databases

A Usenet newsgroup providing information and discussion about databases and data management issues.

Keywords: Computing, Computer Databases
Audience: Computer Users
User Info: To subscribe to this Usenet newsgroup, you need access to a newsreader.

`news:comp.databases`

Computer Ethics

IMPACT ONLINE

The electronic version of IMPACT, the newsletter of the Social Impact group of the Boston Computer Society.

Keywords: Information Technology, Computer Ethics, Computers
Sponsor: Boston Computer Society, Boston, MA
Audience: Computer Users
Profile: The purpose of the Social Impact group is to provide a forum for the discussion of social and ethical concerns related to information technology.
Contact: Ian Wells
bcs-ssi@compass.com

Read on comp.society

You will need access to a newsreader.

`news:comp.society`

Computer Games

crossfire

To discuss the developement of the game Crossfire. The official anonymous FTP-site is ftp.ifi.uio.no in the directory /pub/crossfire. Old mails to the list are archived there. Crossfire is a multiplayer arcade and adventure game made for the X-window environment.

Keywords: Computer Games
Audience: Crossfire specialists, Computer Game Enthusiasts
Contact: Frank Tore Johansen
crossfire-request@ifi.uio.no
Details: Free
User Info: To subscribe to the list, send an e-mail message requesting a subscription to the URL address below.
To send a message to the entire list, address it to: crossfire@ifi.uio.no

`mailto:crossfire-request@ifi.uio.no`

Digital Games Review ★

Reviews of video and computer entertainment titles for the entire industry.

Keywords: Computer Games, Games, Video Games
Audience: Computer Game Players, Computer Game Developers
Profile: Reviews are written by computer game enthusiasts, with an eye to accessibility, enjoyment, and fun, as well as to graphics, technical sophistication, and complexity.
Contact: Dave Taylor
taylor@intuitive.com
Details: Free

`mailto:digital-games-request@intuitive.com`

Rec.arts.int-fiction ★

A USENET newsgroup about interactive literature and interactive computer games.

Keywords: Literature (General), Interactive Media, Computer Games
Audience: General Public, Computer Games Players
Details: Free
To participate in a USENET newsgroup, you need access to a 'newsreader'.

`news:rec.arts.int-fiction`

The Chaosium Digest ★

This is a weekly digest for the discussion of Chaosium's many games, including Call of Cthulhu, Elric!, Elfquest, and Pendragon.

Keywords: Computer Games
Audience: Chaosium Enthusiasts, Computer Users
Contact: appel@erzo.berkeley.edu
Details: Free
User Info: To subscribe to the list, send an e-mail message requesting a subscription to the URL address below.
To send a message to the entire list, address it to: appel@erzo.berkeley.edu

`mailto:appel@erzo.berkeley.edu`

Computer Graphics

ACM SIGGRAPH Online Bibliography Project ★★★★

This is a collection of computer-graphics bibliographic references.

Keywords: Multimedia, Interactive, Computer Graphics, Programming
Sponsor: Association of Computing Machinery (ACM), Special Interest Group on Computer Graphics (SIGGRAPH)
Audience: Developers, Designers, Producers, Educators, Programmers, Graphic Artists
Profile: The goal of this project is to maintain an up-to-date database of computer-graphics literature, in a format that is accessible to as many members of the computer-graphics community as possible. The database includes references from conferences and workshops worldwide and from a variety of publications dating back as far as the late-19th century. The majority of the major journals and conference proceedings from the mid-1970s to the present are listed.
Contact: bibadmin@siggraph.org
Details: Free

`ftp://siggraph.org/publications`

CAEDS-L ★★

A mailing list for the discussion of CAED (Computer Aided Engineering Design) Products.

Keywords: Computer-Aided Design, Engineering, Computer Graphics
Audience: Engineers
Contact: netman@suvm.acs.syr.edu
Details: Free
User Info: To subscribe to the list, send an e-mail message to the URL address shown below consisting of a single line reading:
SUB caeds-l YourFirstName YourLastName
To send a message to the entire list, address it to:
caeds-l@suvm.acs.syr.edu

`mailto:listserv@suvm.acs.syr.edu`

comp.graphics ★

A Usenet newsgroup providing information and discussion about computer graphics, art, animation and more.

Keywords: Computer Graphics, Art
Audience: Computer Users
User Info: To subscribe to this Usenet newsgroup, you need access to a newsreader.

`news:comp.graphics`

comp.windows.x.motif ★

A Usenet newsgroup providing information and discussion about the Motif GUI for the X Window systems.

Keywords: Computer Graphics
Audience: Computer Users, Windows Users
User Info: To subscribe to this Usenet newsgroup, you need access to a newsreader.

`news:comp.windows.x.motif`

DISSPLA (Display Integrated Software System and Plotting Language)

News and information exchange concerning DISSPLA.

Keywords:	Computer Graphics, Programming
Audience:	DISSPLA Users, Computer Programmers
Profile:	DISSPLA is a high-level FORTRAN graphics subroutine library designed for programmers in engineering, science and business.
Contact:	Zvika Bar-Deroma er7101@technion.technion.ac.il
Details:	Free
User Info:	To subscribe to the list, send an e-mail message to the URL address shown below consisting of a single line reading: SUB disspla YourFirstName YourLastName
	To send a message to the entire list, address it to: disspla@taunivm.tau.ac.il

`mailto:listserv@taunivm.tau.ac.il`

Images from Various Sources

This site serves as a link to some 35 image archives throughout the world. A wide variety of images is available, with a particularly large number of weather, geological, and biological collections from government and private sources.

Keywords:	Computer Graphics, Photography, Art
Sponsor:	The University of Alaska
Audience:	General Public
Contact:	Douglas Toelle sxinfo@orca.alaska.edu
Details:	Free, Images

`gopher://gopher.uacn.alaska.edu`

`http://info.alaska.edu:70`

INGRAFX

This E-conference is for discussion of all matters relating to information graphics.

Keywords:	Computer Graphics, Graphic Design, Scientific Visualization
Audience:	Graphic Designers, Cartographers, Animators
Contact:	Jeremy Crampton http://info.cern.ch/hypertext/WWW/The Project.html
User Info:	To subscribe to the list, send an e-mail message to the URL address below consisting of a single line reading: SUB ingrafx YourFirstName YourLastName
	To send a message to the entire list, address it to: ingrafx@psuvm.psu.edu

`mailto:listserv@psuvm.psu.edu`

naplps-list

This is a mailing list for people interested in NAPLPS graphics.

Keywords:	Computer Graphics, Art
Audience:	Graphic Artists, Artists
Contact:	Dave Hughes oldcolo@goldmill.uucp

`naplps-list@oldcolo.com`

PERQ-fanatics

This mailing list is for users of PERQ graphics workstations.

Keywords:	PERQ workstations, Computer Graphics
Audience:	PERQ Users, Graphic Artists
Contact:	perq-fanatics-request@alchemy.com
Details:	Free
User Info:	To subscribe to the list, send an e-mail message requesting a subscription to the URL address below.
	To send a message to the entire list, address it to: perq-fanatics@alchemy.com

`mailto:perq-fanatics-request@alchemy.com`

PHOTO-CD

This list provides libraries of information on Kodak CD products or technology and closely related products.

Keywords:	Photography, Photo-CD, Computer Graphics
Sponsor:	Eastman Kodak, Rochester, NY
Audience:	Photographers, General Public
Contact:	Don Cox listmgr@info.kodak.com
User Info:	To subscribe to the list, send an e-mail message to the address below, consisting of a single line reading: SUB photo-cd Your First Name Your Last Name
	To send a message to the entire list, address it to: photo-cd@info.kodak.com

`mailto:listserv@info.kodak.com`

picasso-users

A mailing list for users of the Picasso Graphical User Interface Development System.

Keywords:	Computing, Computer Graphics
Audience:	Computer Users, Computer Graphic Designers, Graphics
Contact:	picasso-users@postgres.berkeley.edu
Details:	Free
User Info:	To subscribe to the list, send an e-mail message requesting a subscription to the URL address below.
	To send a message to the entire list, address it to: picasso-users@postgres.berkeley.edu

`mailto:picasso-users@postgres.berkeley.edu`

Spanky Fractal Database

This web site provides a collection of fractals and fractal-related material for free distribution on the Internet.

Keywords:	Mathematics, Chaos Theory, Computer Programming, Computer Graphics
Audience:	Mathematicians, Computer Programmers
Profile:	Contains information on dynamical systems, software, distributed fractal generators, galleries, and databases from all over the world.
Contact:	Noel Giffin noel@triumf.ca
Details:	Free

`http://spanky.triumf.ca`

VTcad-L

This E-conference is for discussion of CAD by Va Tech users. Discussion includes: CAD applications, CAD hardware, CAD networking.

Keywords:	Computer Graphics, Computers
Audience:	Computer Graphic Designers, Engineers, Architects
Contact:	Darrell A. Early bestuur@VTVM1.cc.vt.edu
Details:	Free
User Info:	To subscribe to the list, send an e-mail message to the URL address below consisting of a single line reading: SUB vtcad-L YourFirstName YourLastName
	To send a message to the entire list, address it to: vtcad-L@vtvm1.cc.vt.edu

`mailto:listserv@vtvm1.cc.vt.edu`

Computer Hardware

dg-users

The mailing list is concerned with the technical details of Data General, its O/Ss, and the cornucopia of hardware they supply and support.

Keywords:	Computer Hardware, Data General

Audience: Computer Hardware Users
Contact: brian@ilinx.wimsey.com
User Info: To subscribe to the list, send an e-mail message requesting a subscription to the URL address below.

To send a message to the entire list, address it to: dg-users-request@ilinx.wimsey.com

`mailto:dg-users-request@ilinx.wimsey.com`

numeric-interest ★

Discussion of issues of floating-point correctness and performance with respect to hardware, operating systems, languages, and standard libraries.

Keywords: Computers, Computer Hardware
Audience: Computer Users
Contact: David Hough numeric-interest-request@validgh.com
Details: Free
User Info: To subscribe to the list, send an e-mail message requesting a subscription to the URL address below.

To send a message to the entire list, address it to: numeric-interest@validgh.com

`mailto:numeric-interest-request@validgh.com`

Computer Music

Computer Music Journal Archive and World Wide Web Home Page ★★★★

This resource reinforces material available in the hardcopy version of Computer Music Journal, published by the MIT Press.

Keywords: Computer Music, Composition, Synthesis, Interaction
Sponsor: The MIT Press
Audience: Computer Musicians
Profile: The archive includes the tables of contents, abstracts, and editor's notes for the last several volumes of CMJ (including the recent bibliography, diskography, and taxonomy of the field), a number of useful CM-related documents such as the full MIDI and AIFF format specifications, a lengthy reference list, the guidelines for manuscript submission, and the full-text of several recent articles.
Contact: Stephen Pope cmj@cnmat.Berkeley.edu
Details: Free

`ftp://mitpress.mit.edu:/pub/Computer-Music-Journal`

IRCAM DSP and musical software ★★

This site offers a variety of computer music resources.

Keywords: Computer Music, Sound Synthesis, Composition, DSP
Sponsor: IRCAM
Audience: Computer Music Researchers and Computer Musicians
Profile: Contains a list and brief description of IRCAM software (digital signal processing, voice and sound synthesis, music composition, wind instrument making, and other programs). There are also calendars of the IRCAM-EIC concerts and tours, and links to various other music servers.
Contact: Michel Fingerhut fingerhu@ircam.fr
Details: Free

`http://www.ircam.fr`

Computer Network Conferencing

Computer Network Conferencing ★

Discussions on the topic of computer network conferencing. The memo is intended to make more people aware of the present developments in the computer conferencing field as well as to put forward ideas on what should be done to formalize this work.

Keywords: Internet, Conferencing Systems
Audience: Internet Surfers
Contact: Darren Reed avalon@coombs.anu.edu.au
Details: Free
File is: documents/rfc/rfc1324.txt

`ftp://nic.merit.edu`

Computer Networking

CERT (Computer Emergency Response Team) Advisory ★★

A major directory on computer advisory, providing access to a broad range of related resources (library catalogs, databases, and servers) via the Internet.

Keywords: Computers, Security, Computer Networking
Audience: Computer Users
Profile: Profides information on how to obtain a patch or details of a workaround for a known computer security problem. CERT works with vendors to produce a workaround or a patch for a problem, and does not publish vulnerability information until a workaround or patch is available. A CERT advisory may also be a warning about ongoing attacks to network systems.
Contact: cert@cert.org

`ftp://cert.org/pub/cert_advisories`

NCSA (National Center for Supercomputing Applications) ★★★★

A high-performance computing and communications facility and research center designed to serve the US computational science and engineering community.

Keywords: Supercomputing, Computer Networking, Computer Science, Mosaic
Sponsor: University of Illinois at Urbana-Champaign, Champaign, Illinois, USA
Audience: Students, Researchers, Computer Scientists, General Public
Contact: Systems Operator pubs@ncsa.uiuc.edu

`http://www.ncsa.uiuc.edu/General/NCSAHome.html`

The Scout Report ★★★★

The Scout Report is a weekly publication offered by InterNIC Information Services to the Internet community as a fast, convenient way to stay informed on network activities.

Keywords: WWW, Information Retrieval, Internet, Computer Networking
Sponsor: National Science Foundation, USA
Audience: Researchers, Students, General Public
Profile: The purpose of this resource is to combine in one place the highlights of new resource announcements and other news that occurred on the Internet during the previous week. The Report is released every Friday. Categories included each week will vary depending on content, and the report will evolve with time and with input from the networking community.
Contact: InfoGuide scout@is.internic.net, guide@is.internic.net

`http://www.internic.net/scout-report`

Computer Networks

alt.config ★

A Usenet newsgroup providing information and discussion about alternative subnet discussions and connectivity.

Keywords: Internet, Computer Networks, Connectivity
Audience: Network Administrators
User Info: To subscribe to this Usenet newsgroup, you need access to a newsreader.

`news:alt.config`

Computer Science Center Link ★

This is a newsletter about academic computing, located at the University of Maryland, College Park campus, featuring articles about networking, new trends in computing, and innovative uses of computing.

Keywords: Computer Science, Computer Networks
Sponsor: University of Maryland
Audience: Computer Students
Contact: Link Editor
yellow_pages@umail.umd.edu
Details: Free
Request a free subscription by sending e-mail to: yellow_pages@umail.umd.edu

`mailto:yellow_pages@umail.umd.edu`

Computing and Network News ★

A newsletter published 10 times a year for the Kansas State University community.

Keywords: Computers, Computer Networks, Computer Science
Sponsor: Kansas State University
Audience: Kansas State University Students, Educators
Contact: Betsy Edwards
betsy@ksuvm.ksu.edu
Details: Free

`mailto:editor@ksuvm.ksu.edu`

MichNet News (previously Merit Network News) ★

Newsletter of MichNet (Michigan Networks), Michigan's regional computer network. It contains information about MichNet, as well as hosts and services that can be reached through MichNet.

Keywords: Computer Networks, Michigan Networks
Sponsor: MichNet
Audience: Michigan Network Users, Network Users
Contact: Pat McGregor
patmcg@merit.edu
Details: Free
Contact the MichNet News at mnn-request@merit.edu. Available by anonymous FTP from the address below.

`ftp://nis.nsf.net`

Computer News

CUD (Computer Underground Digest) ★

USA Today of cyberspace and the computer underground. Contains information relating to the computer underground.

Keywords: Hacking, Computer News, Cyberculture
Audience: Hackers, Reality Hackers, Computer Underground Enthusiasts
Contact: Gordon Meyer, Jim Thomas
tk0jut2@niu.bitnet or
pumpcon@mindvox.phantom.com
Details: Free

`ftp://etext.archive.umich.edu/pub/Zines/CUD`

Computer Products

CEXPRESS (Computer Express Internet Superstore) ★

Computer Express offers over 3,000 software titles and hardware products, available for immediate delivery.

Keywords: Computer Products
Audience: Consumers

`mailto:info@cexpress.com`

`gophercexpress.com`

`http://cexpress.com`

gateway2000 ★

This list is a source of information about Gateway2000 products.

Keywords: Computer Products, Software, Hardware
Audience: Computer Users, Hardware Engineers, Software Engineers
Details: Free
User Info: To subscribe to the list, send an e-mail message requesting a subscription to the URL address below.
To send a message to the entire list, address it to: gateway2000@sei.cmu.edu

`gateway2000-request@sei.cmu.edu`

Hewlett-Packard Computers ★

This web site provides information on Hewlett Packard products, news, contacts, and services.

Keywords: Computer Products, Hewlett-Packard
Sponsor: Hewlett-Packard
Audience: Computer Users, Educators, Distributors
Contact: webmaster@www.hp.com
Details: Free

`http://www.hp.com`

Computer Professionals

CPSR/PDX Newsletter ★

This is the newsletter of the Portland chapter of Computer Professionals for Social Responsibility.

Keywords: Computer Professionals, Social Responsibility
Audience: Computer Professionals
Contact: Erik Nilsson
ERIKN@Goldfish.mitron.tek.com
Details: Free

`mailto:erikn@goldfish.mitron.tek.com`

Computer Programming

comp.lang.c ★

A Usenet newsgroup providing information and discussion about the C programming language.

Keywords: Computer Programming, Programming Languages
Audience: Computer Users, C Programmers
User Info: To subscribe to this Usenet newsgroup, you need access to a newsreader.

`news:comp.lang.c`

PERL (Practical Extraction and Report Language)

An HTML-formatted and highly indexed PERL programming reference document.

Keywords: Programming Languages, Computer Programming

Audience:	Computer Programmers, Students, Researchers
Contact:	Larry Wall lwall@netlabs.com

`http://www.cs.cmu.edu/Web/People/rgs/perl.html`

Python

A mailing list for discussion of and questions about all aspects of the design and use of the Python programming language.

Keywords:	Computer Programming Languages
Audience:	Computer Programmers, Python Language Users
Contact:	Guido van Rossum python-list-request@cwi.nl
Details:	Free
User Info:	To subscribe to the list, send an e-mail message requesting a subscription to the URL address below. To send a message to the entire list, address it to: python-list@cwi.nl
Notes:	The source of the latest Python release is always available by anonymous FTP from ftp.cwi.nl, in directory /pub/python.

`mailto:python-list-request@cwi.nl`

Spanky Fractal Database

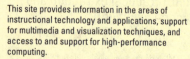

This web site provides a collection of fractals and fractal-related material for free distribution on the Internet.

Keywords:	Mathematics, Chaos Theory, Computer Programming, Computer Graphics
Audience:	Mathematicians, Computer Programmers
Profile:	Contains information on dynamical systems, software, distributed fractal generators, galleries, and databases from all over the world.
Contact:	Noel Giffin noel@triumf.ca
Details:	Free

`http://spanky.triumf.ca`

UTIRC (University of Toronto Instructional and Research Computing)

This site provides information in the areas of instructional technology and applications, support for multimedia and visualization techniques, and access to and support for high-performance computing.

Keywords:	Computing, Computer Programming, Computer-Aided Design
Sponsor:	University of Toronto, Division of Computing, Toronto, Canada
Audience:	Programmers, Designers
Details:	Free

`http://www.utirc.utoronto.ca/HTMLdocs/NewHTML/intro.html`

Computer Programs

c2man

This is a discussion of Graham Stoney's c2man program, which parses comments from C and C++ programs and produces documentation for man pages, info files, and so on.

Keywords:	Computer Programs, c2man
Audience:	Computer Programmers
Contact:	listserv@research.canon.oz.au
User Info:	To subscribe to the list, send an e-mail message to the URL address below, consisting of a single line reading: SUB c2man YourFirstName YourLastName To send a message to the entire list, address it to: c2man@research.canon.oz.au
Notes:	This list is archived and unmoderated.

`mailto:listserv@research.canon.oz.au`

nqthm-users

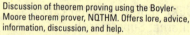

Discussion of theorem proving using the Boyler-Moore theorem prover, NQTHM. Offers lore, advice, information, discussion, and help.

Keywords:	Computer Programs, NQTHM, Boyler-Moore Theorem Prover
Audience:	NQTHM Theorem Users
Contact:	nqthm-users-request@cli.com
Details:	Free
User Info:	To subscribe to the list, send an e-mail message requesting a subscription to the URL address below. To send a message to the entire list, address it to: nqthm-users@cli.com

`mailto:nqthm-users@cli.com`

Computer Resources

DIGIT

A bimonthly publication containing information aimed at users of computing resources at the University of Colorado, Boulder.

Keywords:	Computers, Computer Resources
Audience:	University of Colorado Students, Computer Students
Contact:	Suzanne Kincaid kincaid@spot.colorado.edu
Details:	Free

`mailto:kincaid@spot.colorado.edu`

Computer Science

alt.books.reviews

A Usenet conference devoted to reviews of books, especially science fiction and computer science books.

Keywords:	Literature (General), Computer Science, Science Fiction, Book Reviews
Audience:	General Public, Publishers, Educators, Librarians, Booksellers
Profile:	Alt.books.reviews (a.b.r. for short) is a forum for posting reviews of books of interest to readers, school and public librarians, bookstores, publishers, teachers and professors, and others who desire an "educated opinion" of a book. This is an unmoderated newsgroup.
Contact:	sbrock@csn.org.
Details:	Free
	To participate in a Usenet newsgroup, you need access to a newsreader.
Notes:	The reviews in alt.books.reviews are archived at csn.org. Ftp to csn.org; login: anonymous; password: your complete e-mail address. At the ftp prompt, type: cd pub/alt.books.reviews

`news:alt.books.reviews`

Artificial Intelligence, Expert Sys., Virtual Reality

This directory is a compilation of information resources focused on computer science research, artificial intelligence, expert systems, and virtual reality.

Keywords:	Computer Science, Artificial Intelligence, Expert Systems, Virtual Reality
Audience:	Computer Scientists, Engineers
Contact:	M. Kovacs
Details:	Free

`ftp://una.hh.lib.umich.edu/70/inetdirsstacks/csaiesvr:kovacsm`

Computer Science Center Link

This is a newsletter about academic computing, located at the University of Maryland, College Park campus, featuring articles about networking, new trends in computing, and innovative uses of computing.

Keywords:	Computer Science, Computer Networks	
Sponsor:	University of Maryland	
Audience:	Computer Students	
Contact:	Link Editor yellow_pages@umail.umd.edu	
Details:	Free Request a free subscription by sending e-mail to: yellow_pages@umail.umd.edu	

mailto:yellow_pages@umail.umd.edu

Computing and Network News ★

A newsletter published 10 times a year for the Kansas State University community.

Keywords:	Computers, Computer Networks, Computer Science
Sponsor:	Kansas State University
Audience:	Kansas State University Students, Educators
Contact:	Betsy Edwards betsy@ksuvm.ksu.edu
Details:	Free

mailto:editor@ksuvm.ksu.edu

Computists' Communique ★★★

A weekly newsletter serving professionals in artificial intelligence, information science, and computer science.

Keywords:	Artificial Intelligence, Information Science, Computer Science
Audience:	Computer Scientists, Information Scientists, Computists International Members
Profile:	Content is career oriented and depends partly on contributions from members. The moderator filters submissions, reports and comments on industry news, collects common knowledge about academia and industry, and helps track people and projects. The Communique is only available to members of Computists International, a networking association for computer and information scientists. It is an association for mutual mentoring about grant and funding sources, information channels, applications, text, software publishing, and the sociology of work.
Contact:	Kenneth I. Laws laws@ari.sri.com
Details:	Costs

mailto:laws@ari.sri.com

ctf-discuss ★

This mailing list aims to stimulate discussion of issues critical to the computer science community in the United States (and, by extension, the world). The Computer Science and Telecommunications Board (CSTB) of the National Research Council (NRC) is charged with identifying and initiating studies in areas critical to the health of the field. Recently one such study, Computing the Future, has generated a major discussion in the community and has motivated the establishment of this mailing list in order to involve broader participation. This list will be used in the future to report and discuss the activities of the CSTB and to solicit opinions in a variety of areas.

Keywords:	Computer Science, Telecommunications
Audience:	Computer Scientists, Telecommunications Experts
Contact:	Dave Farber ctf-discuss-request@cis.upenn.edu
Details:	Free
User Info:	To subscribe to the list, send an e-mail message requesting a subscription to the URL address below. To send a message to the entire list, address it to: ctf-discuss@cis.upenn.edu

mailto:ctf-discuss-request@cis.upenn.edu

National Centre for Software Technology ★★

The National Centre for Software Technology (NCST) is an autonomous R&D unit in Bombay and Bangalore. Specialty areas of research include graphics, CAD, real time systems, knowledge-based systems, and software engineering.

Keywords:	Computer Science, Engineering, Computer-Aided Design
Sponsor:	National Centre for Software Technology, Bombay, India
Audience:	Researchers, Computer Scientists, Engineers, Students
Contact:	Postmaster postmaster@saathi.ncst.ernet.in

gopher://shakti.ncst.ernet.in

NCSA (National Center for Supercomputing Applications) ★★★★

A high-performance computing and communications facility and research center designed to serve the US computational science and engineering community.

Keywords:	Supercomputing, Computer Networking, Computer Science, Mosaic
Sponsor:	University of Illinois at Urbana-Champaign, Champaign, Illinois, USA
Audience:	Students, Researchers, Computer Scientists, General Public
Contact:	Systems Operator pubs@ncsa.uiuc.edu

http://www.ncsa.uiuc.edu/General/NCSAHome.html

The InterNIC Home Page

This is the home page for the InterNIC networking organization.

Keywords:	WWW, Information Retrieval, Computer Science, Internet Resources
Sponsor:	National Science Foundation, USA
Audience:	Researchers, Students, General Public
Profile:	The InterNIC is a collaborative project of three organizations, which work together to offer the Internet community a full scope of network information services. These services include providing information about accessing and using the Internet, assistance in locating resources on the network, and registering network components for Internet connectivity. The overall goal of the InterNIC is to make networking and networked information more easily accessible to researchers, educators, and the general public. The term InterNIC signifies cooperation between Network Information Centers, or NICS.
Contact:	InfoGuide guide@internic.net
Details:	InterNIC signifies cooperation between Network Information Centers

http://www.internic.net

University of Puerto Rico Library ★★

The library's holdings are large and wide-ranging and contain significant collections in many fields.

Keywords:	Computer Science, Education, Nursing, Agriculture, Economics
Audience:	Researchers, Students, General Public
Details:	Free After Locator: telnet://, press Tab twice. Type DIAL VTAM. Enter NOTIS. Press Return. On the blank screen, type LUUP.

telnet://136.145.2.10

University of Texas at Austin Library ★★

The library's holdings are large and wide-ranging and contain significant collections in many fields.

Keywords:	Music, Natural Science, Nursing, Science Technology, Behavioral Science, Social Work, Computer Science, Engineering, Latin American Studies, Middle Eastern Studies
Audience:	Researchers, Students, General Public
Details:	Free Expect: Blank Screen, Send: Return; Expect: Go, Send: Return; Expect: Enter Terminal Type, Send: vt100
Notes:	Some databases are restricted to UT Austin users only.

telnet://utcat.utexas.edu

Computer Specialists

Posix-ada

To discuss the Ada binding of the POSIX standard. This is the IEEE P1003.5 working group.

- Keywords: Poxis, Computer Specialists
- Audience: Posix Users, Software Developers
- Contact: Karl Nyberg
  posix-ada-request@grebyn.com
- Details: Free
- User Info: To subscribe to the list, send an e-mail message requesting a subscription to the URL address below.

  To send a message to the entire list, address it to: posix-ada@grebyn.com

mailto:posix-ada-request@grebyn.com

Computer Speech Interfaces

ECTL

A list dedicated to researchers interested in Computer Speech Interfaces.

- Keywords: Computer Speech Interfaces
- Audience: Computer Speech Researchers
- Contact: David Leip
  ectl-request@snowhite.cis.uoguelph.ca
- Details: Free
- User Info: To subscribe to the list, send an e-mail message requesting a subscription to the URL address below.

  To send a message to the entire list, address it to: ectl-request@snowhite.cis.uoguelph.ca

mailto:ectl-request@snowhite.cis.uoguelph.ca

Computer Systems

alpha-osf-managers

This list is intended to be a quick-turnaround trouble shooting aid for those who administer and manage DEC Alpha AXP systems running OSF/1.

- Keywords: Computer Systems, Computer Administration
- Sponsor: Oakridge National Laboratory
- Audience: Computer Programmers
- User Info: To subscribe to the list, send an e-mail message to the URL address below consisting of a single line reading:

  subscribe alpha-osf-managers.
- Notes: Alpha-osf-managers archived at ftp/kpc.com: /pub/list/alpha-osf-managers

mailto:majordomo@ornl.gov

Apple Computer Higher Education Gopher Server

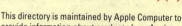

This directory is maintained by Apple Computer to provide information about products from Apple Computer.

- Keywords: Computer Systems, Computer-Aided Instruction, Apple Computer
- Sponsor: Apple Computer, Cupertino, CA
- Audience: General Public
- Profile: This directory also contains promotional material, such as Apple Press Releases, extensive product information, Apple publications, regional market information, Higher Education Marketing Information and support information.
- Contact: mail to:
  feedback@info.hed.apple.com

http://www.apple.com

Apple Computer WWW Server

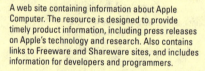

A web site containing information about Apple Computer. The resource is designed to provide timely product information, including press releases on Apple's technology and research. Also contains links to Freeware and Shareware sites, and includes information for developers and programmers.

- Keywords: Computer Systems, Technology, Apple Computer, Shareware
- Audience: General Public

http://www.apple.com

comp.os

A Usenet newsgroup providing information and discussion about computer operating systems. There are many categories within this group.

- Keywords: Computer Systems
- Audience: Computer Users
- User Info: To subscribe to this Usenet newsgroup, you need access to a newsreader.

news:comp.os

comp.os.ms-windows.apps

A Usenet newsgroup providing information and discussion about applications in Windows.

- Keywords: Computers Systems
- Audience: Computer Users, Windows Users
- User Info: To subscribe to this Usenet newsgroup, you need access to a newsreader.

news:comp.os.ms-windows.apps

comp.os.os2.misc

A Usenet newsgroup providing information and discussion about miscellaneous topics concerning O/S2.

- Keywords: Computer Systems
- Audience: Computer Users, O/S2 Users
- User Info: To subscribe to this Usenet newsgroup, you need access to a newsreader.

news:comp.os.os2.misc

comp.sys.amiga

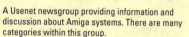

A Usenet newsgroup providing information and discussion about Amiga systems. There are many categories within this group.

- Keywords: Computer Systems, Amiga Aystems
- Audience: Computer Users, Amiga Users
- User Info: To subscribe to this Usenet newsgroup, you need access to a newsreader.

news:comp.sys.amiga

comp.sys.apple2

A Usenet newsgroup providing information and discussion about Apple II systems. There are several categories within this group.

- Keywords: Computer Systems, Apple Computer
- Audience: Computer Users, Apple II Users
- User Info: To subscribe to this Usenet newsgroup, you need access to a newsreader.

news:comp.sys.apple2

comp.sys.atari.st

A Usenet newsgroup providing information and discussion about 16-bit Atari.

- Keywords: Computer Systems
- Audience: Computer Users, Atari Users
- User Info: To subscribe to this Usenet newsgroup, you need access to a newsreader.

news:comp.sys.atari.st

comp.sys.ibm.pc

A Usenet newsgroup providing information and discussion about the IBM PC computer. There are many categories within this group.

- Keywords: Computer Systems, IBM
- Audience: Computer Users, IBM Users

Computer Systems

User Info: To subscribe to this Usenet newsgroup, you need access to a newsreader.

`news:comp.sys.ibm.pc`

comp.sys.mac ★

A Usenet newsgroup providing information and discussion about the Macintosh computer. There are many categories within this group.

Keywords: Computer Systems, Macintosh Computers
Audience: Computer Users, Macintosh Users
User Info: To subscribe to this Usenet newsgroup, you need access to a newsreader.

`news:comp.sys.mac`

comp.sys.next ★

A Usenet newsgroup providing information and discussion about NeXT computers. There are several categories within this group.

Keywords: Computer Systems, NeXT
Audience: Computer Users, NeXT Users
User Info: To subscribe to this Usenet newsgroup, you need access to a newsreader.

`news:comp.sys.next`

comp.sys.sgi ★

A Usenet newsgroup providing information and discussion about Silicon Graphic systems. There are several categories within this group.

Keywords: Computer Systems
Audience: Computer Users, Silicon Graphics Users
User Info: To subscribe to this Usenet newsgroup, you need access to a newsreader.

`news:comp.sys.sgi`

comp.sys.sun ★

A Usenet newsgroup providing information and discussion about Sun systems. There are several categories within this group.

Keywords: Computer Systems, Sun
Audience: Computer Users, Sun Users
User Info: To subscribe to this Usenet newsgroup, you need access to a newsreader.

`news:comp.sys.sun`

comp.unix.aix ★

A Usenet newsgroup providing information and discussion about IBM's version of UNIX.

Keywords: Computer Systems, Internet, UNIX
Audience: Computer Users, UNIX Users, IBM Users
User Info: To subscribe to this Usenet newsgroup, you need access to a newsreader.

`news:comp.unix.aix`

comp.windows.x ★

A Usenet newsgroup providing information and discussion about the X Window Systems.

Keywords: Computer Systems
Audience: Computer Users, Windows Users
User Info: To subscribe to this Usenet newsgroup, you need access to a newsreader.

`news:comp.windows.x`

Digital Equipment WWW Information Server ★★

Digital Equipment's server contains product and service information, and includes archives to public domain software. Also includes an online catalog resource for purchasing products from Digital Equipment.

Keywords: Computer Systems, Digital Equipment
Audience: Digital Equipment Users
Contact: Steve Painter
steve_painter@mro.mts.dec.com

`http://www.service.digital.com/home.html`

Digital's World Wide Web Server ★★

Digital World Wide Web server provides product and service information, back issues of the Digital Technical Journal, performance reports, buyers guides, and product catalogs.

Keywords: Digital Equipment Corporation, Computer Systems
Audience: Computer Users, Computing Consultants
Contact: Russ Jones
webmaster@pa.dec.com
Details: Free

`http://www.digital.com/home.html`

HYTELNET ★★★★

A shareware application database directory to libraries.

Keywords: Computer Systems, Libraries, Shareware
Audience: General Audience
Profile: HYTELNET is a guide to library catalogs from the Americas, Europe
Contact: Peter Scott
aa375@freenet.carleton.ca
Details: Free
Notes: HYTELNET is in English, but the interface to some international

`gopher://gophlib@gopher.yale.edu`

Info-tandem ★★

Info-tandem is an e-mail list for users of systems from Tandem Computers, Inc.

Keywords: Computer Systems, Tandem Computers
Audience: Programmers, Analysts
Contact: Scott Hazen Mueller
scott@zorch.sf-bay.org
Details: Free
User Info: To subscribe to the list, send an e-mail message requesting

`mailto:info-tandem-request@zorch.sf-bay.org`

Pcbuild ★

An open, unmoderated E-conference for discussion of PC hardware, including such topics as upgrading your PC, building your own PC, hardware problems, questions, and businesses from which to buy hardware cheaply.

Keywords: Computer Systems
Audience: PC Users
Contact: Dave Gomberg
gomberg@ucsfvm.edu
Details: Free
User Info: To subscribe to the list, send an e-mail message to the URL address below, consisting of a single line reading: SUB pcbuild YourFirstName YourLastName

To send a message to the entire list, address it to:
pcbuild@tsclion.trenton.edu

`mailto:listserv@tsclion.trenton.edu`

Posix-testing ★

A forum for discussion of issues related to testing operating systems for conformance to the various POSIX standards and proposed standards. Issues include problems related to test suites in general, testability of various features of the standards, and portability of the test suites to the many very different POSIX implementations anticipated in the near future.

Keywords: COmputer Systems
Audience: Posix Testers
Contact: Chuck Karish
posix-testing-request@mindcraft.com
Details: Free
User Info: To subscribe to the list, send an e-mail message requesting a subscription to the URL address below.

To send a message to the entire list, address it to: posix-testing@mindcraft.com

`mailto:posix-testing-request@mindcraft.com`

Pubnet

A mailing list for the discussion of administration and use of public-access computer systems, primarily UNIX systems. The list also answers questions about setting up or running a public-access system

Keywords:	Computer Systems, UNIX
Audience:	Computer System Designers, UNIX Users
Contact:	Chip Rosenthal pubnet-request@chinacat.unicom.com
Details:	Free
User Info:	To subscribe to the list, send an e-mail message requesting a subscription to the URL address below. To send a message to the entire list, address it to: pubnet@chinacat.unicom.com

`mailto:pubnet-request@chinacat.unicom.com`

Sun Microsystems, Inc.

This site provides a directory of Sun Microsystems products and services, including a company profile, announcements, financial statements, marketing reports, and international sales and support access.

Keywords:	Computer Systems, Sun Microsystems
Sponsor:	Sun Microsystems, Inc., Mountain View, California, USA
Audience:	Sun Microsystems Users
Profile:	Languages: English
Contact:	webmaster@sun.com
Details:	Free

`http://www.sun.com`

Computer Technology

Current Cites

A monthly publication of the Library Technology Watch Program at the library, University of California, Berkeley.

Keywords:	Computer Technology, Libraries
Sponsor:	The Library, University of California, Berkeley, CA
Audience:	Librarians, Computer Programmers
Profile:	Over 30 journals in librarianship and computer technology are scanned for articles on optical-disk technologies,

computer networks and networking, information transfer, expert systems and artificial intelligence, and hypermedia and multimedia.

Contact:	David Robison drobison@library.berkeley.edu
Details:	Free

`telnet://melvyl.ucop.edu`

Hot off the Tree (HOTT)

HOTT contains excerpts and abstracts of articles from trade journals, popular periodicals, online news services, and electronic bulletin boards.

Keywords:	Computer Technology, Technology
Sponsor:	University of California, San Diego Library's Technology Watch Information Group (TWIG)
Audience:	Computer Programmers, Technology Enthusiasts, General Public
Contact:	Susan Jurist sjurist@ucsd.edu or sjurist@ucsd.bitnet
Details:	Free
	Available on MELVYL, the University of California online catalog. Anyone with access to telnet, can telnet MELVYL (31.0.0.13) and show hott.

`telnet://melvyl.berkeley.edu/showhott`

Computer Underground

High Weirdness by E-Mail

Guide to some interesting sources of information online.

Keywords:	Technology, Hacking, Computer Underground
Audience:	Mystics, Reality Hackers, Weirdos
Profile:	This file focuses mainly on bizarre philosophies, such as Discordia and SubGenius. Contents include: offbeat religions and 'spirituality' paganism and magic, occultism, UFOs and paranormal phenomena.
Details:	Free

`ftp://etext.archive.umich.edu/pub/Zines/Weirdness`

Computer Users

Futurebus+ Users

This discussion group focuses on the design, implementation, integration, and operation of hardware and software related to Futurebus+.

Keywords:	Computer Users, Hardware, Software
Audience:	Computer Users, Software Engineers, Hardware Engineers
Contact:	majordomo@theus.rain.com
Details:	Free
User Info:	To subscribe to the list, send an e-mail message to the URL address below consisting of a single line reading: SUB fbus_users YourFirstName YourLastName To send a message to the entire list, address it to: fbus_users+@theus.rain.com

`mailto:majordomo@theus.rain.com`

Computer Viruses

ST viruses

This list is to provide fast and efficient help with computer viruses infecting the Atari ST/TT/Falcon only.

Keywords:	Computer Viruses, Atari
Audience:	Computer Users
Contact:	r.c.karsmakers@stud.let.ruu.nl
Details:	Free
User Info:	To subscribe to the list, send an e-mail message requesting a subscription to the URL address below. To send a message to the entire list, address it to: r.c.karsmakers@stud.let.ruu.nl

`mailto:r.c.karsmakers@stud.let.ruu.nl`

Virus-L

Virus-l is a forum for the discussion of computer virus experiences, protection software, and other virus-related topics. This list includes archives and files that list a number of viruses, trojan horses, and pirated programs for the IBM PC.

Keywords:	Computer Viruses, Security
Audience:	Computer Users
Contact:	Kenneth R. van Wyk luken@vax1.cc.lehigh.edu
Details:	Free
User Info:	To subscribe to the list, send an e-mail message to the URL address below consisting of a single line reading: SUB virus-l YourFirstName YourLastName To send a message to the entire list, address it to: virus-l@ibml.cc.lehigh.edu

`mailto:listserv@ibm1.cc.lehigh.edu`

CBDS-l ★★

A mailing list for the discussion of CBDS (Circuit Board Design System).

Keywords:	Engineering, Computer-Aided Design, Electronics
Audience:	Engineers
Contact:	NETMAN@suvm.ACS.SYR.EDU
Details:	Free
User Info:	To subscribe to the list, send an e-mail message to the URL address below consisting of a single line reading:
	SUB cbds-l YourFirstName YourLastName
	To send a message to the entire list, address it to:
	CbDS-L@suvm.ACS.SYR.EDU

`mailto:listserv@suvm.ACS.SYR.EDU`

Free Art For HTML Page ★

This web site provides copyrighted graphics for the Mosaic program.

Keywords:	Computer-Aided Design, Graphics
Audience:	Designers, Educators
Contact:	Harlan Wallach wallach@mcs.com
Details:	Free

`http://www.mcs.net/wallach/Fart/buttons.html`

National Centre for Software Technology ★★

The National Centre for Software Technology (NCST) is an autonomous R&D unit in Bombay and Bangalore. Specialty areas of research include graphics, CAD, real time systems, knowledge-based systems, and software engineering.

Keywords:	Computer Science, Engineering, Computer-Aided Design
Sponsor:	National Centre for Software Technology, Bombay, India
Audience:	Reseachers, Computer Scientists, Engineers, Students
Contact:	Postmaster postmaster@saathi.ncst.ernet.in

`gopher://shakti.ncst.ernet.in`

UTIRC (University of Toronto Instructional and Research Computing ★★

This site provides information in the areas of instructional technology and applications, support for multimedia and visualization techniques, and access to and support for high-performance computing.

Keywords:	Computing, Computer Programming, Computer-Aided Design
Sponsor:	University of Toronto, Division of Computing, Toronto, Canada
Audience:	Programmers, Designers
Details:	Free

`http://www.utirc.utoronto.ca/HTMLdocs/NewHTML/intro.html`

Civil-L ★★

A mailing list for the discussion of civil engineering Research and Education.

Keywords:	Engineering (Civil), Computer-Aided Instruction
Audience:	Engineers, Educators, Students
Contact:	Eldo Hildebrand eldo@unb.ca
Details:	Free
User Info:	To subscribe to the list, send an e-mail message to the URL address shown below consisting of a single line reading:
	SUB civil-l YourFirstName YourLastName
	To send a message to the entire list, address it to:
	civil-l@unb.ca

`mailto:listserv@unb.ca`

Computer-Human Interactions

Loughborough University of Technology Computer-Human Interaction (LUTCHI) Research Centre ★★★★

This server contains general information on computer-human interaction.

Keywords:	Interface Design, Ergonomics, Computer-Human Interactions, Programming
Sponsor:	Loughborough University of Technology, Leicestershire, UK
Audience:	Software Developers, Software Designers, Programmers
Profile:	The LUTCHI Research Centre is based within the Department of Computer Studies at the Loughborough University of Technology, Leicestershire, UK. This server contains information about LUTCHI research projects, official LUTCHI publicity releases, as well as documents, images, and movies associated with those projects.
Contact:	Ben Anderson b.anderson@lut.ac.uk

Details:	Free, Moderated, Image and Sound files available. Multimedia files available.
	Use a World-Wide Web (Mosaic) client and open a connection to the resource.

`http://pipkin.lut.ac.uk`

Computer-Mediated Marketing Environments

Computer-Mediated Marketing Environments ★★

A web site devoted to research aimed at understanding the ways in which computer-mediated marketing environments (CMEs), especially the Internet, are revolutionizing the way firms conduct business.

Keywords:	WWW, Information Retrieval, Internet, Marketing, Business
Sponsor:	Vanderbilt University, Owen Graduate School of Management, Nashville, Tennessee, USA
Audience:	General Public, Entrepreneurs, Financial Planners, Marketers
Contact:	Donna Hoffman, Tom Novak hoffman@colette.ogsm.vanderbilt.edu novak@moe.ogsm.vanderbilt.edu

`http://colette.ogsm.vanderbilt.edu`

Computers

Almost 2001 Archive ★

Archive of transcripts of Almost 2001, a series on computer communications of the future, produced by NBC (National Broadcasting Company).

Keywords:	Computers, Communications, Internet
Sponsor:	The WELL (Whole Earth 'Lectronic Link)
Audience:	Computer Users, Internet Surfers
Details:	Free, Moderated.
	To participate in a conference on the WELL, you must first establish an account on the WELL. To do so, start by typing: telnet://well.sf.ca.us

`gopher://gopher.well.sf.ca.us//11/Communications/2001`

Alspa ★

Discussion by users of the CP/M machines made by (now defunct) Alspa Computer, Inc.

Keywords:	Computers, Alspa Computer, Inc., CP/M
Audience:	CP/M Users
Contact:	Brad Allen alspa-users-request@ssyx.ucsc.edu

Details:	Free
User Info:	To subscribe to the list, send an e-mail message requesting a subscription to the URL address below.
	To send a message to the entire list, address it to: alspa-users@ssyx.ucsc.edu

`mailto:alspa-users-request@ssyx.ucsc.edu`

alt.bbs ★

A Usenet newsgroup providing information and discussion about computer BBS systems and software.

Keywords:	BBS Systems, Cyberspace, Computers
Audience:	BBS Users
User Info:	To subscribe to this Usenet newsgroup, you need access to a newsreader.

`news:alt.bbs`

alt.cyberpunk ★

A Usenet newsgroup providing information and discussion about the high-tech low-life.

Keywords:	Computers, Cyberspace
Audience:	Hackers, Cybernauts, General Public
User Info:	To subscribe to this Usenet newsgroup, you need access to a newsreader.

`news:alt.cyberpunk`

alt.folklore.computers ★

A Usenet newsgroup providing information and discussion concerning stories and anecdotes about computers.

Keywords:	Computers, Folklore
Audience:	Computer Users, Storytellers
User Info:	To subscribe to this Usenet newsgroup, you need access to a newsreader.

`news:alt.folklore.computers`

alt.security.pgp ★

A Usenet newsgroup providing information and discussion about the Pretty Good Privacy package, a privately-developed encryption technique.

Keywords:	Privacy, Encryption, Security Firewalls, Computers
Audience:	Internet Surfers
User Info:	To subscribe to this Usenet newsgroup, you need access to a newsreader.

`news:alt.security.pgp`

Amiga CD-ROM ★

For Amiga users who are interested in CD-ROM drives and discs.

Keywords:	Computers, Amiga, CD-ROM
Audience:	Computer Users
Contact:	ben@ben.com
Details:	Free
User Info:	To subscribe to the list, send an e-mail message requesting a subscription to the URL address below.
	To send a message to the entire list, address it to: cdrom-list@ben.com

`mailto:cdrom-list-request@ben.com`

AMOS ★

For the AMOS programming language on Amiga computers. Features source, bug reports, and help from users around the world, but mainly from European users. Most posts will be in English, but there are no language limitations.

Keywords:	Computers, Programming Languages, AMOS, Amiga
Audience:	Programmers, Computer Users
Contact:	subscribe@xamiga.linet.org
Details:	Free
User Info:	To subscribe to the list, send an e-mail message to the URL address below, consisting of a single line reading:
	SUB #amos userneame@domain
	To send a message to the entire list, address it to: subscribe@xamiga.linet.org

`mailto:subscribe@xamiga.linet.org`

ApE-info

A mailing list for the discussion of the scientific visualization software package ApE, its usage, development, and implementation.

Keywords:	Computers, Visualization, Science
Sponsor:	Jim Lick
Audience:	ApE Software Users, Computer Programmers
Contact:	Jim Lick ape-info-request@ferkel.ucsb.edu
User Info:	To subscribe to the list, send an e-mail message to the URL address below.
	To send a message to the entire list, address it to: ape-info@ferkel.ucsb.edu

`mailto:ape-info-request@ferkel.ucsb.edu`

Apple II Files ★

This FTP site contains the archive of files relating to Apple II computers.

Keywords:	Apple Computers, Computers
Audience:	Programmers, Computer Users, Apple II Users
Details:	Free

`ftp://archive.umich.edu`

AppWare-info

A forum for discussion of issues relating to AppWare software. Topics include simple programming questions, tips for program efficiency, quirks of, and complaints about the environment or tools, the process of writing new ALMs or functions, third party enhancements, and any other question.

Keywords:	Computers, Programming Languages
Sponsor:	Novell Inc.
Audience:	AppWare Users, Computer Programmers
Contact:	Novell Inc. appware-info@serius.uchicago.edu
User Info:	To subscribe to the list, send an e-mail message to the URL address below.
	To send a message to the entire list, address it to: appware-info@serius.uchicago.edu

`mailto:appware-info-request@serius.uchicago.edu`

`ftp://serius.uchicago.edu`

artist-users ★★

A discussion group for users and potential users of software tools from Cadence Design Systems.

Keywords:	Computers, Computer Art
Sponsor:	Cadence Design Systems
Audience:	Computer Artists
Contact:	Jeff Putsch artist-users-request@uicc.com
User Info:	To subscribe to the list, send an e-mail message to the URL address below.
	To send a message to the entire list, address it to: artist-users-request@uicc.com
Notes:	This mailing list is bi-directionally gatewayed to the Usenet newsgroup

`mailto:artist-users-request@uicc.com`

att-pc+

A mailing list for users and potential users of the AT&T PC 63xx series of systems.

Keywords:	Computers, AT&T Computer Systems
Audience:	Computer Programmers
Contact:	Bill Kennedy bill@ssbn.wlk.com
User Info:	To subscribe to the list, send an e-mail message to the URL address below.
	To send a message to the entire list, address it to: att-pc+@ssbn.wlk.com
Notes:	Sub-lists are maintained for MS-DOS-only and Simul-Task mailings as well as the full list for items of general interest. Membership must be requested and mail path verification is required before membership is granted.

`mailto:att-pc+@ssbn.wlk.com`

auc-TeX

Discussion and information exchange about the AUC TeX package, which runs under GNU Emacs.

Keywords:	Computers, TeX, AUC TcX, Emacs
Audience:	Computer Users
Contact:	Kresten Krab Thorup auc-tex-request@iesd.auc.dk
Details:	Free
User Info:	To subscribe to the list, send an e-mail message requesting a subscription to the URL address below.
	To send a message to the entire list, address it to: auc-tex@iesd.auc.dk

`mailto:auc-tex-request@iesd.auc.dk`

Aviator

A mailing list for users of Aviator™, the flight-simulation program from Artificial Horizons, Inc.

Keywords:	Aviation, Simulation, Computers, Flight Simulation
Audience:	Software Users
Contact:	Jim Hickstein aviator@Icdwest.teradyne.com
Details:	Free
User Info:	To subscribe to the list, send an e-mail message requesting a subscription to the URL address below.
	To send a message to the entire list, address it to: aviator@ICDwest.Teradyne.COM
Notes:	Aviator runs on Sun workstations with the GX graphics accelerator option. Its charter is simply to facilitate communication among users of Aviator. It is not intended for communication with the "providers" of Aviator. All mail received at the submission address is reflected to all the subscribers of the list.

`mailto:aviator-request@ICDwest.Teradyne.COM`

bionet.software

A Usenet newsgroup providing information and discussion about software for use in biological research.

Keywords:	Computers, Biology
Audience:	Students, Educators, Biologists
User Info:	To subscribe to this Usenet newsgroup, you need access to a newsreader.

`news:bionet.software`

Buyer's Guide to Micro Software

The database contains a directory of business and professional microcomputer software available in the United States.

Keywords:	Buyer's Guides, Microcomputers, Computers, Software
Sponsor:	Online, Inc., Weston, CT, USA
Audience:	Computer Users
Profile:	Provided are directory, product, technical, and bibliographic information on leading software packages, integrated this information into one succinct composite record. The database can help professionals locate suitable packages compatible with specified hardware, without having to sift through large numbers of records. The file is highly selective, listing packages rated at least "good" by the technical press; all packages from major software producers, even if negatively reviewed; and packages unique to specific business segments, with special emphasis placed on library and medical software. Each record includes directory information; technical specifications, including required hardware and operating systems; an abstracted product description, and, when available, a full citation of representative reviews.
Contact:	Dialog in the US at (800) 334-2564, Dialog internationally at country-specific locations.
Details:	Costs
User Info:	To subscribe, contact Dialog directly.
Notes:	Coverage: current; updated monthly.

`telnet://dialog.com`

CAF Archive

A source of information relating to Computers and Academic Freedom (CAF).

Keywords:	Education, Computers, Academic Freedom
Audience:	Educators, Researchers
Contact:	kadie@eff.org http://www.eff.org/CAF/cafhome.html

CCNEWS

An electronic forum for campus-computing newsletter editors and other publications specialists.

Keywords:	Computers, Editors, Students, Newsletters
Audience:	Students (college), Editors
Profile:	CCNEWS consists of a biweekly newsletter that focuses on the writing, editing, designing, and producing of campus-computing publications, and an articles abstracts published on alternating weeks that describes new contributions to the articles archive.
Contact:	Wendy Rickard Bollentin ccnews@educom.bitnet
Details:	Free
User Info:	To subscribe to the list, send an e-mail message to the URL address below consisting of a single line reading: SUB ccnews YourFirstName YourLastName To send a message to the entire list, address it to: ccnews@educom.bitnet Inquire about needing a password.

`mailto:listserv@bitnic.cren.net`

CERT (Computer Emergency Response Team) Advisory

A major directory on computer advisory, providing access to a broad range of related resources (library catalogs, databases, and servers) via the Internet.

Keywords:	Computers, Security, Computer Networking
Audience:	Computer Users
Profile:	Profides information on how to obtain a patch or details of a workaround for a known computer security problem. CERT works with vendors to produce a workaround or a patch for a problem, and does not publish vulnerability information until a workaround or patch is available. A CERT advisory may also be a warning about ongoing attacks to network systems.
Contact:	cert@cert.org

`ftp://cert.org/pub/cert_advisories`

cfcp-members

The Confederation of Future Computer Professionals (CFCP) is a group of users on the Internet who are interested enough in various fields of computers to consider computers as their future. The Confederation exists to foster education and stimulate communication.

Keywords:	Internet, Computers
Audience:	Internet Surfers, Computer Users
Contact:	mlindsey@nyx.cs.du.edu
Details:	Free
User Info:	To subscribe to the list, send an e-mail message requesting a subscription to the URL address below.

`mailto:mlindsey@nyx.cs.du.edu`

CMPCOM (Computers and Communications) Libraryzzzz

The Computers and Communications Library provides you industry-specific sources. More than 40 full-text sources that concentrate on computers and communications are available. Full-text files can be searched in a variety of ways: as an individual file, by major-subject group file, or as a user-defined group file.

Keywords:	Computers, Communications, Technology, Electronics
Audience:	Business Researchers, Analysts, Entrepreneurs
Profile:	This library can be used to gain insight on new products and technologies being introduced; monitor industry news for high technology systems, electronics, engineering, communications, and computer hardware and software; and locate product evaluations for both the professional as well as the casual personal computer user.
Contact:	Mead New Sales Group at (800) 227-4908 or (513) 859-5398 inside the US, or (513) 865-7981 for all inquiries outside the US.
User Info:	To subscribe, contact Mead directly.
	To examine the Nexis user guide, you can access it at the ftp site of the University of Texas at Austin at the URL address: ftp://ftp.cc.utexas.edu
	The files are in: /pub/ref-services/LEXIS

`telnet://nex.meaddata.com`

`http://www.meaddata.com`

CoCo

This is a discussion related to the Tandy Color Computer (any model) OS-9 Operating System, and any other topics relating to the "CoCo," as this computer is affectionately known.

Keywords:	Tandy Computers, Computers
Audience:	Tandy Computer Users, Computer Users
Contact:	Paul E. Campbell pecampbe@mtus5.BITNET
Details:	Free
User Info:	To subscribe to the list, send an e-mail message requesting a subscription to the URL address below.

`mailto:listserv@pucc.princeton.edu`

Commodore-Amiga

This list is for Commodore Amiga computer users. Weekly postings include hardware reviews, news briefs, system information, company progress, and information for finding out more about the Commodore and Amiga.

Keywords:	Commodore-Amiga, Computers
Audience:	Computer Users
Contact:	subscribe@xamiga.linet.org
Details:	Free
	Send subscription requests to the URL address below using this format:
	#commodore username@domain

`mailto:subscribe@xamiga.linet.org`

comp.compression

A Usenet newsgroup providing information and discussion about data compression algorithms and theory.

Keywords:	Computers, Mathematics (Algorithims)
Audience:	Computer Users
User Info:	To subscribe to this Usenet newsgroup, you need access to a newsreader.

`news:comp.compression`

comp.lang.c++

A Usenet newsgroup providing information and discussion about the object-oriented C++ programming language.

Keywords:	Computers, Programming Languages
Audience:	Computer Users, C++ Programmers
User Info:	To subscribe to this Usenet newsgroup, you need access to a newsreader.

`news:comp.lang.c++`

comp.org.eff.talk

A Usenet newsgroup organized by the EFF (Electronic Frontier Foundation) providing information and discussion about the political, social, and legal issues surrounding the Internet.

Keywords:	Computers, Intellectual Property, Security, Internet
Audience:	Internet Surfers
User Info:	To subscribe to this Usenet newsgroup, you need access to a newsreader.

`news:comp.org.eff.talk`

comp.security.misc

A Usenet newsgroup providing information and discussion about security issues of computers and networks.

Keywords:	Computers, Security, Firewalls
Audience:	Computer Users
User Info:	To subscribe to this Usenet newsgroup, you need access to a newsreader.

`news:comp.security.misc`

comp.unix.questions

A Usenet newsgroup providing discussion and questions for those learning UNIX.

Keywords:	Computers, UNIX
Audience:	Computer Users, UNIX Users
User Info:	To subscribe to this Usenet newsgroup, you need access to a newsreader.

`news:comp.unix.questions`

comp.unix.wizards

A Usenet newsgroup providing discussion and questions for true UNIX wizards.

Keywords:	Computers, UNIX
Audience:	Computer Users, Unix Users
User Info:	To subscribe to this Usenet newsgroup, you need access to a newsreader.

`news:comp.unix.wizards`

Computing and Network News

A newsletter published 10 times a year for the Kansas State University community.

Keywords:	Computers, Computer Networks, Computer Science
Sponsor:	Kansas State University
Audience:	Kansas State University Students, Educators
Contact:	Betsy Edwards betsy@ksuvm.ksu.edu
Details:	Free

`mailto:editor@ksuvm.ksu.edu`

Convex Customer Satisfaction Information Server

An online customer help server for Convex computer users.

Keywords:	Computers, Convex Computers
Sponsor:	Convex Computer Corporation
Audience:	Convex Computer Users
Contact:	iserv_admin@convex.com
Details:	Free
Notes:	Convex has its own gopher client, called "cxgopher."

`gopher://iserv.convex.com`

CSAA

The Comp.Sys.Amiga.Announce mailing list has been created for those who have no access to USENET. It provides the gate between the USENET newsgroup C.S.A.A. and e-mail. This group distributes announcements of importance to people using the Commodore brand Amiga computers. Announcements contain information on new products, disk library releases, software updates, reports of major bugs or dangerous viruses, notices of meetings or upcoming events, and so forth. A large proportion of posts announce the upload of software packages to anonymous FTP archive sites.

Keywords:	Commodore-Amiga Computers, Computers
Audience:	Commodore-Amiga Users
Contact:	Carlos Amezaga announce-request@cs.ucdavis.edu

Details: Free
User Info: To subscribe to the list, send an e-mail message requesting a subscription to the URL address below.

To send a message to the entire list, address it to:announce@cs.ucdavis.edu

`mailto:announce-request@cs.ucdavis.edu`

ctree

A forum for the discussion of FairCom's C-Tree, R-Tree, and D-Tree products. This mailing list is not associated with FairCom. Discussion covers virtually all hardware and operating system ports.

Keywords: Computers, FairCom
Audience: Computer Operators
Contact: Tony Olekshy
alberta!oha!ctree-request
Details: Free
User Info: To subscribe to the list, send an e-mail message requesting a subscription to the URL address below.

To send a message to the entire list, address it to: ctree

`mailto:alberta!oha!ctree-request`

CUSSNET

Computer Users in the Social Sciences (CUSS) is a discussion group devoted to issues of interest to social workers, counselors, and human service workers of all disciplines. The discussion frequently involves computer applications in treatment, agency administration, and research. Students, faculty, community-based professionals, and casual observers join in the discussion. Software, hardware, and ethical issues associated with their use in the human services generate lively and informative discussions.

Keywords: Social Sciences, Computers, Computer Applications
Audience: Social Workers, Human Services Workers, General Public
Contact: cussnet-request@stat.com
Details: Free
User Info: To subscribe to the list, send an e-mail message to the address below consisting of a single line reading:

SUB cussnet YourFirstName YourLastName.

To send a message to the entire list, address it to: cussnet@stat.com

`mailto:listserv@stat.com`

data-exp

The mail list server provides an open forum for users to discuss the Visualization Data Explorer Package. It contains three files at the moment: a. FAQ, b. summary, and c. forum.

Keywords: Computers, Software, Hardware, Visualization Data Explorer Package
Audience: Computer Users
User Info: To subscribe to the list, send an e-mail message requesting a subscription to the URL address below.

To send a message to the entire list, address it to: stein@watson.ibm.com

`mailto:stein@watson.ibm.com`

DECNEWS for Education and Research

Monthly electronic newsletter from Digital Equipment Corporation (DEC) summarizing announcements of its products, programs, and applications of interest to computer users in the academic and research communities.

Keywords: Computers, Education,
Sponsor: Digital Equipment Corp.
Audience: Computer Users, Educators, Researchers
Contact: Mary Hoffmann
decnews@mr4dec.enet.dec.com
Details: Free
User Info: To subscribe to the list, send an e-mail message to the address below consisting of a single line reading:

SUB DECNews YourFirstName YourLastName

To send a message to the entire list, address it to:
decnews@ubvm.buffalo.edu

`mailto:listserv@ubvm.buffalo.edu`

DECnews-EDU

DECNEWS for Education and Research is a monthly electronic publication from Digital Equipment Corporation's Education Business Unit for the education and research communities worldwide.

Keywords: Education, Computers, Digital Equipment Corporation
Audience: Educators, Researchers
Contact: Anne Marie McDonald
decnews@mr4dec.enet.dec.com
Details: Free
User Info: To subscribe to the list, send an e-mail message requesting a subscription to the URL address below.

To send a message to the entire list, address it to:
decnews@mr4dec.enet.dec.com

`mailto:decnews@mr4dec.enet.dec.com`

DECnews-PR

DECnews for Press and Analysts is an Internet-based distribution of all Digital Equipment Corporation press releases. This is a one-way mailing list. There are approximately 8 press releases per week.

Keywords: DEC, Computers
Audience: Computing Consultants, Computing Analysts
Contact: Russ Jones
decnews-pr-request@pa.dec.com
User Info: To subscribe to the list, send an e-mail message requesting a subscription to the URL address below.

To send a message to the entire list, address it to: decnews-pr-request@pa.dec.com

Notes:User Info: To subscribe, send e-mail to decnews-pr@pa.dec.com with a subject line of
Subject: subscribe. Please include your name and telephone number in the body of the subscription request.

`mailto:decnews-pr-request@pa.dec.com`

DECnews-UNIX

DECnews for UNIX is published by Digital Equipment Corporation every three weeks and contains product and service information of interest to the Digital UNIX community.

Keywords: DEC, UNIX, Computers
Audience: UNIX Users
Contact: Russ Jones
decnews-unix-request@pa.dec.com
User Info: To subscribe to the list, send an e-mail message requesting a subscription to the URL address below.

To send a message to the entire list, address it to: decnews-unix-request@pa.dec.com

Notes:User Info: To subscribe, send e-mail to decnews-unix@pa.dec.com with a subject line of Subject: subscribe abstract. Please include your name and telephone number in the body of the subscription request.

`mailto:decnews-unix-request@pa.dec.com`

DECstation-managers

Fast-turnaround troubleshooting tool for managers of RISC DECstations.

Keywords: DEC, Computers
Audience: Computer Systems Analysts/ Programmers, Engineers
Contact: decstation-managers-request@ornl.gov
User Info: To subscribe to the list, send an e-mail message to the URL address shown below consisting of a single line reading:

SUB decstation-manager YourFirstName YourLastName

To send a message to the entire list, address it to: decstation-manager@msu.edu

`mailto:majordomo@ornl.gov`

DIGIT

A bimonthly publication containing information aimed at users of computing resources at the University of Colorado, Boulder.

Keywords:	Computers, Computer Resources
Audience:	University of Colorado Students, Computer Students
Contact:	Suzanne Kincaid kincaid@spot.colorado.edu
Details:	Free

`mailto:kincaid@spot.colorado.edu`

dirt-users

Dirt is an X11-based UIMS.

Keywords:	Computers
Audience:	UIMS Users
Contact:	dirt-users-request@ukc.ac.uk
User Info:	To subscribe to the list, send an e-mail message requesting a subscription to the URL address below. To send a message to the entire list, address it to: dirt-users@ukc.ac.uk

`mailto:dirt-users@ukc.ac.uk`

dist-users

This list is for discussions of issues related to the dist 3.0 package and its components: metaconfig, jmake, patch tools, and so on. The dist package was posted on comp.sources.misc (August 1993).

Keywords:	dist, Computers
Audience:	dist Users
Contact:	Shigeya Suzuki Raphael Manfredi
Contact:	shigeya@foretune.co.jp ram@acri.fr
User Info:	To subscribe to the list, send an e-mail message to the URL address shown below consisting of a single line reading: SUB dist-users YourFirstName YourLastName To send a message to the entire list, address it to: dist-users@msu.edu

`mailto:majordomo@foretune.co.jp`

dp-friends

This is a list for discussing Decision Power, a product of ICL Computers Limited composed of the logic programming language Prolog, the constraint handling system Chip, the database interface Seduce (runs on top of Ingres), the development environment Kegi (runs on X) and the end-user graphical display environment KHS (also runs on X).

Keywords:	Computers
Audience:	Computer Users
Contact:	Ken Johnson dp-friends-request@aiai.ed.ac.uk
User Info:	To subscribe to the list, send an e-mail message requesting a subscription to the URL address below. To send a message to the entire list, address it to: dp-friends-request@aiai.ed.ac.uk

`mailto:dp-friends-request@aiai.ed.ac.uk`

ESRI (Environmental Systems Research Institute)

Environmental Systems Research Institute, Inc. is the world leader in GIS technology. ARC/INFO is ESRI's powerful and flexible flagship GIS software.

Keywords:	Geographic Information Systems (GIS), Environment, Software, Computers
Audience:	Geographers, Environmentalists, Computer Users
Details:	Costs For product information, call (909)793-2853, X1475. For training information, call (909)793-2853, X1585, or fax (909)793-5953.

Fam-Med

An Internet resource and discussion group on computers in family medicine.

Keywords:	Medicine, Computers, Telecommunications
Sponsor:	Gustavus Adolphus College, Minnesota
Audience:	Health-CareProfessionals, Family Physicians
Profile:	Fam-Med is an electronic conference and file area that focuses on the use of computer and telecommunication technologies in the teaching and practice of family medicine. The conference and files are accessible to anyone able to send e-mail. The discussion on Fam-Med is distributed in two ways: by an unmoderated mail echo in which all posted messages are immediately distributed to subscribers without human intervention, and by a digest where messages accumulated over several days are assembled into a single document with erroneous posts deleted.
Contact:	Paul Kleeberg paul@gac.edu
Details:	Free To join either the unmoderated list or the digest, send e-mail to the contact above. To post to Fam-Med, send e-mail to Fam-Med@GAC.Edu

`gopher://ftp.gac.edu/00/pub/E-mail-archives/fam-med/`

foxpro-l

This mailing list is designed to foster information sharing between users of the FoxPro™ database development environment now owned and distributed by Microsoft. Both new and experienced users of FoxPro are welcome to join in the discussions.

Keywords:	Databases, Computers, Microsoft Corp.
Audience:	Database Users, Microsoft FoxPro Users, Software Engineers
Contact:	Chris O'Neill coneill@heaven.polarbear.rankin-inlet.nt.ca
Details:	Free
User Info:	To subscribe to the list, send an e-mail message requesting a subscription to the URL address below. To send a message to the entire list, address it to: foxpro-l@polarbear.rankin-inlet.nt.ca

`mailto:fileserv@polarbear.rankin-inlet.nt.ca`

General Hacking Info

Files on the topic of hacking.

Keywords:	Hacking, Computers
Audience:	Hackers, Computer Users
Details:	Free Expect: login,Send: anonymous; Expect: Password,Send: Your e-mail Address

`ftp://ftp.eff.org`

GlobeTrotter

File concerning hacking from an international perspective.

Keywords:	Hacking, Computers
Audience:	Hackers, Computer Users
Details:	Free Expect: login,Send: anonymous; Expect: Password,Send: Your e-mail Address

`ftp://ftp.eff.org`

Hacker's Network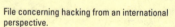

File of hacking, published in Britain.

Keywords:	Hacking, Computers
Audience:	Hackers, Computer Users
Details:	Free Expect: login,Send: anonymous; Expect: Password,Send: Your e-mail Address

`ftp://ftp.eff.org`

IMPACT ONLINE

The electronic version of IMPACT, the newsletter of the Social Impact group of the Boston Computer Society.

Keywords: Information Technology, Computer Ethics, Computers
Sponsor: Boston Computer Society, Boston, MA
Audience: Computer Users
Profile: The purpose of the Social Impact group is to provide a forum for the discussion of social and ethical concerns related to information technology.
Contact: Ian Wells
bcs-ssi@compass.com
Read on comp.society
You will need access to a newsreader.

`news:comp.society`

International Business Machines

This is IBM's main WWW server and it contains extensive links to information about the company and its products.

Keywords: Computers, Business
Audience: General Public
Profile: Industry Solutions, Products and Services, Technology information and News about the company.
Contact: mail to: askibm@www.ibm.com

`http://www.ibm.com`

Legion of Doom/Hackers Technical Journals

Technical journals of the infamous hacking ring Legion of Doom.

Keywords: Hacking, Computers
Audience: Hackers, Computer Users
Details: Free
Expect: login,Send: anonymous;
Expect: Password,Send: Your e-mail Address

`ftp://ftp.eff.org`

Microsoft FTP Site

Microsoft's file repository.

Keywords: Computers, Microsoft Corporations
Sponsor: Microsoft
Audience: Software Developers, Microsoft Product Users
Details: Free

`ftp://ftp.microsoft.com`

Nihon Sun Microsystems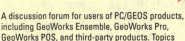

This site provides a directory for Sun Microsystems in Japan. Includes the Rolling Stones Official Server WWW site, with access to Rolling Stones music, merchandise, and information. Also provides multimedia links to the Science University of Tokyo and other Asia-Pacific resources.

Keywords: Computers, Rolling Stones
Sponsor: Sun Microsystems, Inc., Tokyo, Japan
Audience: Computer Users, Rolling Stones Fans
Contact: www-admin@sun.co.jp
Details: Multimedia, Free, Sounds. Images

`http://www.sun.co.jp`

numeric-interest

Discussion of issues of floating-point correctness and performance with respect to hardware, operating systems, languages, and standard libraries.

Keywords: Computers, Computer Hardware
Audience: Computer Users
Contact: David Hough
numeric-interest-request@validgh.com
Details: Free
User Info: To subscribe to the list, send an e-mail message requesting a subscription to the URL address below.
To send a message to the entire list, address it to: numeric-interest@validgh.com

`mailto:numeric-interest-request@validgh.com`

Online Radio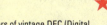

Transcripts and promotional information from Online Radio, a weekly radio program of Perth's Curtin University devoted to reporting the latest developments in the computing world.

Keywords: Computers, Internet, Radio
Sponsor: Curtin University Computing Center, Perth, Australia
Audience: Computer Enthusiasts
Contact: Onno Benschop
online@info.curtin.edu.au

`gopher://ob1.curtin.edu.au`

Pc532

A mailing list for people interested in the pc532 project, a National Semiconductor NS32532-based system, offered at a low cost.

Keywords: Computers, Hardware, Software
Audience: Computer Users, Software Developers
Contact: Dave Rand
pc532-request@bungi.com
Details: Free
User Info: To subscribe to the list, send an e-mail message requesting a subscription to the URL address below.
To send a message to the entire list, address it to: pc532@bungi.com

`mailto:pc532-request@bungi.com`

Pcgeos-list

A discussion forum for users of PC/GEOS products, including GeoWorks Ensemble, GeoWorks Pro, GeoWorks POS, and third-party products. Topics include general information, tips, techniques, applications, and experiences.

Keywords: Computers, Software
Audience: Computer Users, Software Developers
Contact: listserv@pandora.sf.ca.us
Details: Free
User Info: To subscribe to the list, send an e-mail message to the URL address below, consisting of a single line reading:

SUB pcgeos-list YourFirstName YourLastName

To send a message to the entire list, address it to: pcgeos@pandora.sf.ca.us

`mailto:listserv@pandora.sf.ca.us`

Pdp8-lovers

A mailing list for owners of vintage DEC (Digital Equipment Corp.) computers, especially the PDP-8 series. Discussion topics include hardware, software, and programming techniques.

Keywords: Computers, Hardware, Software
Audience: Computer Users, Product Analysts
Contact: Robert E. Seastrom
pdp8-lovers-request@mc.lcs.mit.edu
Details: Free
User Info: To subscribe to the list, send an e-mail message requesting a subscription to the URL address below.
To send a message to the entire list, address it to: pdp8-lovers@mc.lcs.mit.edu

`mailto:pdp8-lovers@mc.lcs.mit.edu`

Prompt

Contains news tips and briefs for the NCSU (North Carolina State University) campus community. Complementing the paper newsletter Connect, Prompt is designed to provide timely, up-to-date information concerning all platforms of computing.

Computers

Keywords: Computers
Audience: NCSU Computer Students, Educators, Computer Users
Contact: Sarah Noell
sarah_noell@ncsu.edu
Details: Free
User Info: To subscribe to the list, send an e-mail message to the URL address below, consisting of a single line reading:
prompt YourFirstName YourLastName
To send a message to the entire list, address it to: prompt@cc.ncsu.edu

`mailto:listserv@cc.ncsu.edu`

REACH (Research and Educational Applications of Computers in the Humanities)

Newsletter of the Humanities Computing Facility of the University of California, Santa Barbara. Contains material of general interest to computing humanists, including announcements of new listservers, projects, and conferences.

Keywords: Computers
Audience: Computer Users
Contact: Eric Dahlin
HCF1DAHL@UCSBvm.bitnet
Details: Free
listserv@ucsbvm.bitnet
reach@ucsbvm.bitnet

`mailto:listserv@ucsbvm.bitnet`

SUMEX-AIM

An FTP archive of software, demonstration programs, and various applications, especially for Macintosh computers.

Keywords: Computers, Macintosh, Software
Audience: Computer Users, Macintosh Users
Details: Free

`ftp://sumex-aim.Stanford.edu`

Texas: Computer Crimes Statute

Lists text of the Texas Computer Crimes Statute.

Keywords: Computers, Crime, Texas
Audience: Lawyers, Computer Programmers, Computer Operators
Details: Free
Select from menu as appropriate

`gopher://wiretap.spies.com`

The Black Box Catalog

The Black Box Catalog, the industry's most complete source for data communication equipment, is now available on the Internet. The complete range of products, technical references, and application briefs are available on the Black Box World Wide Web Server.

Keywords: Communications, Networking, Telecommunication, Computers
Sponsor: Black Box Corporation, Lawrence, PA
Audience: Engineers, Network Administration, LAN Administrators, Communication Specialists
Profile: Black Box Corporation is a leading international supplier of data communications networking and related computer connectivity products. Black Box's commitment to providing effective solutions that substantially enhance the capabilities of communications systems is backed by a technical support staff that is available around the clock, a liberal 45-day return policy, and same day shipment of its 6000 products.
Contact: Webmaster
webmaster@blackbox.com
Details: Costs

`http://www.blackbox.com`

VapourWare

A column of speculation about new computers and computer-related products that are not yet available for sale (and may never be).

Keywords: Computers
Audience: Computer Users
Contact: Murphy Sewall
sewall@UConnVM.UConn.Edu
Details: Free

`mailto:sewall@uconnvm.uconn.edu`

VTcad-L

This E-conference is for discussion of CAD by Va Tech users. Discussion includes: CAD applications, CAD hardware, CAD networking.

Keywords: Computer Graphics, Computers
Audience: Computer Graphic Designers, Engineers, Architects
Contact: Darrell A. Early
bestuur@VTVM1.cc.vt.edu
Details: Free
User Info: To subscribe to the list, send an e-mail message to the URL address below consisting of a single line reading:
SUB vtcad-L YourFirstName YourLastName
To send a message to the entire list, address it to: vtcad-L@vtvm1.cc.vt.edu

`mailto:listserv@vtvm1.cc.vt.edu`

Works

Works discusses personal workstation computers, such as the Sun2, Sun3, Apollo, Silicon Graphics, and AT&T workstations. Works provides a way for interested members of the Internet community to discuss and share useful insights about these kinds of systems.

Keywords: Workstations, Computers
Audience: Workstation Users, Computer Users
Contact: Dave Steiner
steiner@rutgers.edu
Details: Free
User Info: To subscribe to the list, send an e-mail message requesting a subscription to the URL address below.

`mailto:works@rutgers.edu`

Computing

Academic Computing Training & User Support

This directory is a compilation of information resources focusing on academic computer training and user support.

Keywords: Computing, Academics
Audience: Computer Users

`ftp://una.hh.lib.umich.edu/70/inetdirsstacks/acadcomp:kovacsm`

BFU (Brussels Free Universities)

The gopher server of the Brussels Free Universities VUB /ULB is the national entry point for EMBnet in Belgium and provides links to university library systems and EMBnet databases.

Keywords: Computing, EMBnet, Belgium, Europe
Audience: Scientists, Biologists, Biotechnologists
Contact: support@vub.ac.be
Details: Free

`gopher://gopher.vub.ac.be`

comp.databases

A Usenet newsgroup providing information and discussion about databases and data management issues.

Keywords: Computing, Computer Databases
Audience: Computer Users
User Info: To subscribe to this Usenet newsgroup, you need access to a newsreader.

`news:comp.databases`

ETHCSE-L

A mailing list for the discussion of ethical issues in software engineering, dealing with subjects of interest to professional software engineers.

Keywords: Engineering, Computing, Ethics
Audience: Engineers, Software Engineers, Researchers
Contact: Margaret Mason MASON@UTKVml.utk.edu
Details: Free
User Info: To subscribe to the list, send an e-mail message to the URL address shown below consisting of a single line reading:
SUB ethcse-l YourFirstName YourLastName
To send a message to the entire list, address it to:
ethcse-l@utkvm1.utk.edu

`mailto: listserv@utkvm1.UTK.EDU`

High-Performance Computing Act of 1991

This is a Senate bill to provide for a coordinated federal research program to ensure continued US leadership in high-performance computing.

Keywords: Computing, Government (US Federal), Law (US Federal)
Audience: General Public, Journalists, Politicians, Scientists
Details: Free
File is: /internet/nren/hpca.1991/gorebill.1991-txt

`ftp://nis.nsf.net`

Imperial College Department of Computing

This is the home of the department of Computing, Imperial College, United Kingdom, the UKUUG (UK UNIX User Group) Archive and the DoC Information Service.

Keywords: Computing, United Kingdom, Europe
Audience: Computer Scientists
Contact: imjm@doc.ic.ac.uk
Details: Free

`gopher://src.doc.ic.ac.uk`

`http://src.doc.ic.ac.uk`

INSPEC

IINSPEC corresponds to the three Science Abstracts print publications: Physics Abstracts, Electrical and Electronics Abstracts, and Computer and Control Abstracts.

Keywords: Physics, Electronic, Computing
Sponsor: Institution of Electrical Engineers, London, UK
Audience: Physicists, Electrical Engineers, Computer Specialists
Profile: Approximately 16 percent of the database's source publications are in languages other than English, but all articles are abstracted and indexed in English. The special DIALOG online thesaurus feature is available to assist searchers in determining appropriate subject terms and codes.
Contact: Dialog in the US at (800) 334-2564, Dialog internationally at country-specific locations.
User Info: To subscribe, contact Dialog directly.
Notes: Coverage: April 1969 to the present; updated weekly.

`telnet://dialog.com`

Metacard-list

Discussion of the MetaCard product from MetaCard Corp. MetaCard is an application-development system similar to Apple's HyperCard product; it runs on a variety of popular platforms in a UNIX/X11/Motif environment.

Keywords: MetaCard, Computing, UNIX
Audience: MetaCard Users, Computer Users
Contact: metacard-list-owner@grot.starconn.com
Details: Free
Notes:User Info: To subscribe to the list, send an e-mail message requesting a subscription to the URL address below.

`mailto:metacard-list@grot.starconn.com`

Pen-pals

This mailing list provides a forum for children to correspond with each other electronically. Although the list is not moderated, it is monitored for content and is managed by listproc.

Keywords: Computing, Children, Writing
Audience: Computer Users, Children, Student Writers
Contact: pen-pals-request@mainstream.com
Details: Free
User Info: To subscribe to the list, send an e-mail message requesting a subscription to the URL address below.
To send a message to the entire list, address it to: pen-pals@mainstream.com

`mailto:pen-pals@mainstream.com`

picasso-users

A mailing list for users of the Picasso Graphical User Interface Development System.

Keywords: Computing, Computer Graphics
Audience: Computer Users, Computer Graphic Designers, Graphics
Contact: picasso-users@postgres.berkeley.edu
Details: Free
User Info: To subscribe to the list, send an e-mail message requesting a subscription to the URL address below.
To send a message to the entire list, address it to: picasso-users@postgres.berkeley.edu

`mailto:picasso-users@postgres.berkeley.edu`

Progress

Discussion of the Progress RDBMS (Relational Database Management System).

Keywords: Databases, Computing
Audience: Computer Users, Business Students
Contact: Progress-list-request@math.niu.edu
Details: Free
User Info: To subscribe to the list, send an e-mail message requesting a subscription to the URL address below.
To send a message to the entire list, address it to: progress-list@math.niu.edu

`mailto:Progress-list-request@math.niu.edu`

Project-management

The aim of the list is to discuss project-management techniques generally, as well as project-management software and programs.

Keywords: Project Management, Computing, Software
Audience: Business Professionals, Business Students
Contact: project-management-request@smtl.demon.co.uk
Details: Free
User Info: To subscribe to the list, send an e-mail message requesting a subscription to the URL address below.
To send a message to the entire list, address it to: project-management@smtl.demon.co.uk

`mailto:project-management-request@smtl.demon.co.uk`

Proof-users

Discussion of the left-associative natural language "parser proof."

Keywords:	Computing, Programming
Audience:	Computer Programmers
Contact:	Craig Latta proof-request@xcf.berkeley.edu
Details:	Free
	To join, e-mail proof-request@xcf.berkeley.edu with the subject line "add me".

`mailto:proof-request@xcf.berkeley.edu`

Qnx2

Discussion of all aspects of the QNX real-time operating systems. Topics include compatible hardware, available third-party software, software reviews, available PD/free software, QNX platform-specific programming discussions, and QNX and FLEET networking.

Keywords:	Computing, Hardware, Software
Audience:	Computer Users, Hardware/Software Designers, Product Analysts
Contact:	Martin Zimmerman camz@dlogtech.cuc.ab.ca
Details:	Free
User Info:	To subscribe to the list, send an e-mail message requesting a subscription to the URL address below. To send a message to the entire list, address it to: qnx2@dlogtech.cuc.ab.ca

`mailto:qnx2@dlogtech.cuc.ab.ca`

Qnx4

A mailing list for discussion of all aspects of the QNX real-time operating systems. Topics include compatible hardware, available third-party software, software reviews, available PD/free software, QNX and FLEET networking, process control, and so on.

Keywords:	Computing, Hardware, Software, Networking
Audience:	Computer Users, Hardware/Software Designers, Product Analysts
Contact:	Martin Zimmerman camz@dlogtech.cuc.ab.ca
Details:	Free
User Info:	To subscribe to the list, send an e-mail message requesting a subscription to the URL address below. To send a message to the entire list, address it to: qnx4@dlogtech.cuc.ab.ca

`mailto:qnx4@dlogtech.cuc.ab.ca`

soc.penpals

A Usenet newsgroup providing information and discussion for people in search of Net pals and other online correspondence.

Keywords:	Computing, Writing
Audience:	Computer Users, Writers
Details:	Free
User Info:	To subscribe to this Usenet newsgroup, you need access to a newsreader.

`news:soc.penpals`

Supercomputers

Weekly mailing list of the world's most powerful computing sites.

Keywords:	Supercomputers, Computing
Audience:	Supercomputer Users, computer scientists
Contact:	gunter@yarrow.wt.uwa.oz.au
Details:	Free
User Info:	To subscribe to the list, send an e-mail message requesting a subscription to the URL address below. To send a message to the entire list, address it to: gunter@yarrow.wt.uwa.oz.au

`mailto:gunter@yarrow.wt.uwa.oz.au`

UTIRC (University of Toronto Instructional and Research Computing

This site provides information in the areas of instructional technology and applications, support for multimedia and visualization techniques, and access to and support for high-performance computing.

Keywords:	Computing, Computer Programming, Computer-Aided Design
Sponsor:	University of Toronto, Division of Computing, Toronto, Canada
Audience:	Programmers, Designers
Details:	Free

`http://www.utirc.utoronto.ca/HTMLdocs/NewHTML/intro.html`

Computing and Network News

Computing and Network News

A newsletter published 10 times a year for the Kansas State University community.

Keywords:	Computers, Computer Networks, Computer Science
Sponsor:	Kansas State University
Audience:	Kansas State University Students, Educators
Contact:	Betsy Edwards betsy@ksuvm.ksu.edu
Details:	Free

`mailto:editor@ksuvm.ksu.edu`

Computists' Communique

Computists' Communique

A weekly newsletter serving professionals in artificial intelligence, information science, and computer science.

Keywords:	Artificial Intelligence, Information Science, Computer Science
Audience:	Computer Scientists, Information Scientists, Computists International Members
Profile:	Content is career oriented and depends partly on contributions from members. The moderator filters submissions, reports and comments on industry news, collects common knowledge about academia and industry, and helps track people and projects. The Communique is only available to members of Computists International, a networking association for computer and information scientists. It is an association for mutual mentoring about grant and funding sources, information channels, applications, text, software publishing, and the sociology of work.
Contact:	Kenneth I. Laws laws@ari.sri.com
Details:	Costs

`mailto:laws@ari.sri.com`

Comserve

Newsline

An electronic newsletter describing additions to or changes in Comserve, the electronic information and discussion service for communications faculty and students.

Keywords:	Communications, Comserve
Audience:	Communications Students, Communications Specialists
Profile:	The information includes announcements of additions to Comserve's database, new services offered through Comserve's electronic conferences, or fundamental changes in the services offered by Comserve.
Contact:	Timothy Stephen, Teresa Harrison Support@RpiecsSupport@Vm.Ecs.Rpi.Edu
User Info:	To subscribe, send an e-mail message to the URL address below consisting of a single line reading: SUB NEWSLINE YourFirstName YourLastName

`mailto:Comserve@Vm.Ecs.Rpi.Edu`

Concrete Blonde

concrete-blonde

This list discusses the rock group Concrete Blonde and related artists and issues.

Keywords: Pop Music, Concrete Blonde
Audience: Concrete Blonde Enthusiasts, Pop Music Enthusiasts
Contact: Robert Earl
concrete-blonde-request@piggy.ucsb.edu
Details: Free
User Info: To subscribe to the list, send an e-mail message requesting a subscription to the URL address below.

To send a message to the entire list, address it to:

concrete-blonde@piggy.ucsb.edu

`mailto:concrete-blonde-request@piggy.ucsb.edu`

Concurrent Logic

Clp.x

Devoted to discussion of concurrent logic programming languages, concurrent constraint programming languages, semantics, proof techniques and program transformations, parallel Prolog systems, implementations, and programming techniques and idioms.

Keywords: Programming, Programming Languages, Concurrent Logic
Audience: Concurrent Logic Programmers
Contact: Jacob Levy
jlevy.pa@xerox.com
Details: Free
User Info: To subscribe to the list, send an e-mail message requesting a subscription to the URL address below.

To send a message to the entire lst, address it to: clp.x@xerox.com

`mailto:clp-request.x@xerox.com`

Conference about Virtual Reality (The)

Conference about Virtual Reality (The)

A conference on the WELL about cyberspace and virtual reality.

Keywords: Virtual Reality, Art, Cyberspace
Audience: Artists, Computer Programmers, Cyberpunks
Contact: Peter Rothman
avatarp@well.sf.ca.us

To participate in a conference on the WELL, you must first establish an account on the WELL. To do so, start by typing: telnet well.sf.ca.us

`telnet://well.sf.ca.us`

Conferences

news.announce.conferences

A Usenet newsgroup providing information and discussion about conferences, as well as calls for papers.

Keywords: Conferences, Papers, Writing
Audience: Writers, General Public
Details: Free
User Info: To subscribe to this Usenet newsgroup, you need access to a newsreader.

`news:news.announce.conferences`

Scholarly Communication

These quarterly technical reports contain information and discussion about the role of network-based electronic resources in scholarly communication.

Keywords: Education, Scholarly Communication, Conferences
Audience: Educators, Researchers
Details: Free
File is: pub/vpiej-l/reports

`ftp://borg.lib.vt.edu/pub/vpiej-1/reports`

`http://borg.lib.vt.edu/scholar.info.html`

Conferencing Systems

Computer Network Conferencing

Discussions on the topic of computer network conferencing. The memo is intended to make more people aware of the present developments in the computer conferencing field as well as to put forward ideas on what should be done to formalize this work.

Keywords: Internet, Conferencing Systems
Audience: Internet Surfers
Contact: Darren Reed
avalon@coombs.anu.edu.au
Details: Free
File is: documents/rfc/rfc1324.txt

`ftp://nic.merit.edu`

DECuserve-journal

A monthly digest of technical discussions that take place on the DECUS conferencing system, open to anyone who is interested in Digital Equipment topics, "3rd party" topics, and connectivity topics.

Keywords: DECUS, Conferencing Systems
Audience: Conferencing System Users
Contact: Sharon Frey
frey@eisner.decus.org
User Info: To subscribe to the list, send an e-mail message requesting a subscription to the URL address below.

To send a message to the entire list, address it to: frey@eisner.decus.org

`mailto:frey@eisner.decus.org`

Conflict Resolution

CSF: Communications for a Sustainable Future

A gopher server for the distribution of Conflict Resolution Materials.

Keywords: Conflict Resolution, Community, Politics
Sponsor: Communications for a Sustainable Future
Audience: Activists, Policy Analysts, Community Leaders, Mediators, Lawyers
Profile: Communications for a Sustainable Future is a collective effort of several scholars. CSF does research, education, and applied work. Its main subject areas are: Intractable Conflicts and Constructive Confrontation, Environmental and Public Policy Dispute Resolution, Social/Political Conflicts, International Conflicts.
Contact: roper@csf.colorado.edu
Details: Free

`gopher://csf.colorado.edu`

NAME (National Association for Mediation in Education) Publications and Resources List

This is a tax-exempt clearinghouse of information promoting conflict resolution, mediation, and violence prevention in schools. NAME also publishes a newsletter and has a directory of over 120 resources, including guidelines for conflict resolution, and technical assistance.

Keywords:	Conflict Resolution, Mediation, Education (K-12)
Sponsor:	National Association for Mediation in Education, University of Massachusetts, Amherst, Massachusetts, USA
Audience:	Counselors, Educators, Administrators, Parents
Contact:	Clarinda Merripen ConflictNet@agc.ipc.org
	Request introductory packet from address below.

mailto:ConflictNet@agc.ipc.org

Congo Languages

Harvard University Library ★★

The library's holdings are large and wide-ranging and contain significant collections in many fields.

Keywords:	Afrikaans, Alchemy, Arabic Culure (History of), Celtic Philology, Congo Languages, Folklore, Hebraica, Mormonism, Numismatics, Quakers, Sanskrit, Witchcraft, Arabic Philology
Audience:	General Public, Researchers, Librarians, Document Delivery Professionals
Details:	Free
	Expect: Mitek Server..., Send: Enter or Return; Expect: prompt, Send: hollis

telnet://hollis.harvard.edu

Congress (US)

ACLU Free Reading Room ★★★

A gopher site containing information relating to the ACLU (American Civil Liberties Union), including the current issue of the ACLU newsletter, Civil Liberties; a growing collection of recent public policy reports and action guides; Congressional voting records for the 103rd Congress; and an archive of news releases from the ACLU's national headquarters.

Keywords:	ACLU, Civil Liberties, Congress (US), Activism
Sponsor:	ACLU (American Civil Liberties Union)
Audience:	Privacy Activists, Civil Libertarians, Activists
Contact:	infoaclu@aclu.org

gopher://aclu.org

America

For people interested in how the United States is dealing with foreign trade policies, congressional status, and other inside information about the government that is freely distributable.

Keywords:	Trade, Government (US), Congress (US), Business (International)
Audience:	General Public, Researchers, Journalists, Political Scientists, Students
Contact:	subscribe@xamiga.linet.org
User Info:	To subscribe to the list, send an e-mail message to the URL address below, consisting of a single line reading: SUB america YourFirstName YourLastName To send a message to the entire list, address it to: america@xamiga.linet.org
Notes:	This list has monthly postings that are generally in large batches, with posts exceeding a few hundred lines.

mailto:subscribe@xamiga.linet.org

C-SPAN (Cable-Satellite Public Affairs Network) Gopher ★★★

Online information from C-SPAN, the public affairs television network.

Keywords:	News Media, Government, Congress (US), Television
Sponsor:	C-SPAN
Audience:	Journalists, Government Officials, Educators (K-12), General Public
Profile:	Comprehensive listings of C-SPAN's programming and coverage of events in Washington D.C. and beyond. In addition to the programming notes and schedules, this site also features online educational resources sponsored by C-SPAN, text of historic documents and speeches, and background political information on the House of Representatives and the Supreme Court.
Contact:	cspanviewr@aol.com
Details:	Free

gopher://c-span.org

CMPGN (Campaign Library)

The CMPGN library contains information and news about US Congressional, Senatorial, Gubernatorial and Presidentail elections. The media, political campaigns, and others whose responsibilities include monotoring activity on the campaign trail will find CMPGN to be a unique and comprehensive source of information for campaign research.

Keywords:	Politics (US), Congress (US)
Audience:	Journalists, Political Researchers
Profile:	CMPGN allows searching of individual files or group files that cover topics such as candidate and incumbent profiles; Honoraria, PACs, and demographic and media profiles; Committee and Floor voting records and floor statement indexes for all House and Senate incumbents; and reputable sources of news that are known for their in-depth campaign coverage, including the Hotline, the Cook Political Report, ABC news Transcripts, Roll Call, States News Service, US Newswire, Federal News Service, and much more.
Contact:	Mead New Sales Group at (800) 227-4908 or (513) 859-5398 inside the US, or (513) 865-7981 for all inquiries outside the US.
User Info:	To subscribe, contact Mead directly. To examine the Nexis user guide, you can access it at the ftp site of the University of Texas at Austin at the URL address: ftp://ftp.cc.utexas.edu The files are in: /pub/ref-services/LEXIS

telnet://nex.meaddata.com

http://www.meaddata.com

Congressional Contact Information ★

The US Senate and 103rd Congress phone and fax numbers are accessible and searchable from this server.

Keywords:	Congress (US), Directories, Government (US)
Sponsor:	Library of Congress
Audience:	General Public, Journalists, Students, Politicians
Details:	Free

gopher://marvel.loc.gov/11/congress/directory

Congressional Quarterly Gopher

Online Information from Congressional Quarterly (CQ), the premier journal covering events on Capitol Hill.

Keywords:	Congress (US), Government (US Federal), Laws (US Federal)
Sponsor:	Congressional Quarterly
Audience:	Journalists, Government Officials, Educators, General Public
Profile:	This gopher allows access to weekly stories and news briefs from CQ, as well as providing information on legislation before Congress, Congressional voting records, and results of recent federal elections. Also has catalogs of CQ's publications and schedules of their professional education seminars.
Contact:	gopher_admin@cqalert.com
Details:	Free

gopher://gopher.cqalert.com

GAO

Files intended to provide Congress and Administration with an overview of health problems facing the nation.

Keywords: Health, Congress (US)
Audience: US Congress, Journalists, General Public
Profile: These files concern health-care reform and human services and date from December 1992. They are provided by the government to familiarize the reader with the health issues confronting the administration.
Details: Free
Login: anonymous
Notes: ABSTRACT.FIL is a file with abstracts for each of the 28 reports.

`ftp://cu.nig.gov`

University of Tennessee at Knoxville Library

The library's holdings are large and wide-ranging and contain significant collections in many fields.
Keywords: Native American Affairs, Congress (US), Folklore, Travel (History of)
Audience: Researchers, Students, General Public
Details: Free
Expect: OK Prompt; Send: Login pub1; Expect: Password, Send: Usc

`telnet://opac.lib.utk.edu`

US House of Representatives Gopher

The online service of the U.S. House of Representatives.
Keywords: Congress (US), Federal Law (US), Government Records (US)
Sponsor: House Administration Committee Internet Working Group
Audience: Government Officials, Journalists, Educators (K-12), General Public
Profile: Provides access to information on members and committees of the House of Representatives, as well as full-text of bills before the House. Includes education resources on the legislative process, Congressional directories, and House schedules. Also has information for visitors (including area maps), as well as access to other federal information systems.
Contact: House Internet Working Group househlp@hr.house.gov

`gopher://gopher.house.gov`

Connectivity

alt.config

A Usenet newsgroup providing information and discussion about alternative subnet discussions and connectivity.

Keywords: Internet, Computer Networks, Connectivity
Audience: Network Administrators
User Info: To subscribe to this Usenet newsgroup, you need access to a newsreader.

`news:alt.config`

Conservation

consgis

A discussion list for those using GIS (Geographic Information Systems) in the interest of conservation.
Keywords: Conservation, Environment, GIS (Geographic Information Systems)
Audience: Geographers, Environmentalists, Cartographers
Contact: Dr. Peter August pete@edcserv.edc.uri.edu
Details: Free
User Info: To subscribe to the list, send an e-mail message to the URL address below consisting of a single line reading:

SUB consgis YourFirstName YourLastName.

To send a message to the entire list, address it to: consgis@uriacc.uri.edu

`mailto:listserv@uriacc.uri.edu`

Conspiracy

alt.conspiracy

A Usenet newsgroup providing discussion about conspiracy and paranoia.
Keywords: Conspiracy, Paranoia
Audience: Paranoid Persons, General Public
User Info: To subscribe to this Usenet newsgroup, you need access to a newsreader.

`news:alt.conspiracy`

Constitution

alt.censorship

A Usenet newsgroup providing information and discussion about freedom of speech and freedom of the press.
Keywords: Censorship, Freedom of Speech, Constitution, Activism
Audience: Press, Students, Educators, Activists
User Info: To subscribe to this Usenet newsgroup, you need access to a newsreader.

`news:alt.censorship`

Utah State Constitution

Lists full text of the Utah State Constitution 1991.
Keywords: Utah, Constitution
Audience: Utah Residents, Historians

`gopher://wiretap.spies.com`

Constitutional Amendments

Amend2-info

Colorado voted in an amendment to their state constitution which revokes any existing gay/lesbian/bisexual civil rights legislation and prohibits the drafting of any new legislation. This moderated list is for information on the implication and issues of this amendment.
Keywords: Activists, Gay, Lesbian, Bisexual, Constitutional Amendments, Colorado, Civil Rights
Audience: General Public, Gays, Lesbians, Bisexuals, Activists
Contact: amend2-info@cs.colorado.edu
User Info: To subscribe to the list, send an e-mail message requesting a subscription to the URL address below.

To send a message to the entire list, address it to: amend2-info@cs.colorado.edu

`mailto:majordomo@cs.colorado.edu`

Constitutional Law

University of Texas at Austin Tarlton Law Library

The library's holdings are large and wide-ranging and contain significant collections in many fields. British Commonwealth Law, Constitutional Law, International Law, Human Rights
Keywords: British Commonwealth Law, Constitutional Law, Law (International), Human Rights
Audience: Researchers, Students, General Public
Details: Free
Expect: Login, Send: Library

`telnet://tallons.law.utexas.edu`

Construction

Architecture, Building

This directory is a compilation of information resources focused on architecture.

Keywords: Architecture, Building, Construction, AEC
Audience: Architects, Builders, Civil Engineers
Contact: J. Brown
Details: Free

`ftp://una.hh.lib.umich.edu/70/inetdirsstacks/archi:brown`

Lego Information

A web site containing pictures, sets, and instructions for building with Legos. Also discusses various ideas, activities, and history pertaining to Legos, as well as information about clubs for Lego enthusiasts.

Keywords: Construction, Toys, Children
Sponsor: Lego
Audience: Children, General Public
Contact: David Koblas
koblas@netcom.com

`http://legowww.itek.norut.no`

Consumer Goods

Consumer News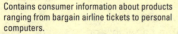

Contains consumer information about products ranging from bargain airline tickets to personal computers.

Keywords: Consumer Goods
Audience: Consumers
Details: Free

`gopher://gopher.cic.net/00/e-serials/alphabetic/c/consumer-news/AboutIndex.gz`

`http://gopher.cis.net`

misc.forsale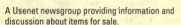

A Usenet newsgroup providing information and discussion about items for sale.

Keywords: Consumer Goods
Audience: General Public
Details: Free
User Info: To subscribe to this Usenet newsgroup, you need access to a newsreader.

`news:misc.forsale`

Consumer Rights

Privacy Rights Clearinghouse (PRC)

A collection of materials related to privacy issues.

Keywords: Privacy, Legislation, Consumer Rights, Freedom of Information
Sponsor: University of San Diego
Audience: Citizens, Privacy Activists, Journalists
Profile: This site contains fact sheets (in English and Spanish) on privacy issues ranging from wiretapping to credit reporting. Also includes federal and state privacy legislation as well as related position papers and press releases.
Contact: prc@teetot.acusd.edu
Expect: Login; Send: Privacy

`gopher://teetot.acusd.edu`

`telnet://teetot.acusd.edu`

Consumer Science

Purdue University Library

The library's holdings are large and wide-ranging. They contain significant collections in many fields.

Keywords: Economics (History of), Literature (English), Literature (American), Indiana, Rogers (Bruce), Engineering (History of), Aviation, Earth Science, Atmospheric Science, Consumer Science, Family Science, Chemistry (History of), Physics, Veterinary Science
Audience: General Public, Researchers, Librarians, Document Delivery Professionals
Contact: Dan Ferrer
dan@asterix.lib.purdue.edu
Details: Free
Expect: User ID prompt, Send: GUEST

`telnet://lib.cc.purdue.edu`

Consumerism

misc.consumers

A Usenet newsgroup providing information and discussion about consumer interests, including product reviews.

Keywords: Consumerism
Audience: Consumers, General Public
Details: Free
User Info: To subscribe to this Usenet newsgroup, you need access to a newsreader.

`news:misc.consumers`

misc.wanted

A Usenet newsgroup providing information and discussion about items, excluding software, that are wanted or needed.

Keywords: Consumerism
Audience: General Public
Details: Free
User Info: To subscribe to this Usenet newsgroup, you need access to a newsreader.

`news:misc.wanted`

U.S. Consumer Product Safety Commission (CPSC)

The CPSC's mission is to protect the public from defective and potentially dangerous consumer products. This gopher has archives of CPSC press releases and action reports from 1990-1994, as well as a calendar of upcoming events and guidelines for reporting potentially dangerous products to the CPSC.

Keywords: Safety, Consumerism, Laws (US Federal)
Sponsor: US Consumer Product Safety Commission
Audience: Consumers, Activists
Contact: pweddle@cpsc.gov
Notes: You can call the CPSC at their toll-free hotline at (800) 638-2772.

`gopher://cpsc.gov`

Contemporary Letters

Colby College Library

The library's holdings are large and wide-ranging and contain significant collections in many fields.

Keywords: Contemporary Letters, Hardy (Thomas), James (Henry), Mann (Thomas, Collections of), Housman (A.E., Letters of), Maine Authors, Irish History (Modern)
Audience: General Public, Researchers, Librarians, Document Delivery Professionals
Details: Free
Expect: login, Send: library

`telnet://library.colby.edu`

Contemporary Music

Northwestern University Library ★★

The library's holdings are large and wide-ranging and contain significant collections in many fields.

Keywords: Africa, Wright (Frank Lloyd), Women's Studies, Art, Literature (American), Contemporary Music, Government (US State), UN Documents, Music

Audience: General Public, Researchers, Librarians, Document Delivery Professionals

Details: Free
Expect: COMMAND:, Send: DIAL VTAM

`telnet://nuacvm.acns.nwu.edu`

Convex Computers

Convex Customer Satisfaction Information Server

An online customer help server for Convex computer users.

Keywords: Computers, Convex Computers
Sponsor: Convex Computer Corporation
Audience: Convex Computer Users
Contact: iserv_admin@convex.com
Details: Free
Notes: Convex has its own gopher client, called "cxgopher."

`gopher://iserv.convex.com`

Cooking

rec.food.cooking

A Usenet newsgroup providing information and discussion about cooking.

Keywords: Food, Cooking
Audience: General Public, Cooks, Chefs
User Info: To subscribe to this Usenet newsgroup, you need access to a newsreader.

`news:rec.food.cooking`

rec.food.veg

A Usenet newsgroup providing information and discussion about vegetarian cooking.

Keywords: Vegetarianism, Food, Cooking
Audience: Vegetarians, Cooks, Chefs
User Info: To subscribe to this Usenet newsgroup, you need access to a newsreader.

`news:rec.food.veg`

Recipe Archive

This is an archive of recipes organized by main ingredient or title.

Keywords: Cooking, Food
Audience: General Public, Cooks, Chefs
Profile: Here are a few intriguing examples from the archive:

Advokaat: Advokaat is the Dutch word for egg cognac. It is highly recommended for A. I. (Alcohol Imbibing) meetings. This recipe is a modification of a recipe obtained in Poland. It makes a potent, superb advokaat (or egg cognac). The milk and eggs are healthy, the sugar and alcohol are not!

Berlinerkranzer: Norwegian wreath cookies are decorative holiday cookies that add quite a bright, colorful, aromatic touch to your plate of cookies.

Bouillabaisse: This recipe for Marseille-style fish soup represents a combination of several recipes derived from old Gourmets, Julia Child, the Playboy Gourmet Cookbook, and "Gee, that sounds good, let's add it.." The accompanying rouille is a garlic/hot pepper mayonnaise condiment traditional to Marseille-style fish soup.

Details: Free

`gopher://calypso.oit.unc.edu/7waissrc%3a/ref.d/indexes.d/recipes.src`

`gopher://calypso.oit.unc.edu/7waissrc%3a/ref.d/indexes.d/usenet-cookbook.sr`

They can also be accessed through mosaic at the URL address shown below or from the calypso.oit.unc.edu gopher in the subdirectories: Internet Dog-Eared Pages (Frequently used resources)/ Search Many WAIS Indices

Notes: There are two searchable gopher Indexes containing recipes that have passed through the rec.food.cooking and rec.food.recipes newsgroups. They can be found at the following URL addresses:

`ftp://gatekeeper.dec.com/pub/recipes`

The World Wide Web rec.food.recipes archive

World-Wide Web archive of recipes posted to Usenet newsgroup rec.food.recipes. Updated weekly.

Keywords: Food, Recipes, Cooking
Audience: Cooks, General Public
Contact: Amy Gale
mara@kauri.vuw.ac.nz
User Info: Use a World-Wide Web (WWW) client such as lynx

`http://www.vuw.ac.nz/non-local/recipes-archive/recipe-archive.html`

COOMBSQUEST Social Sciences and Humanities Information Facility

COOMBSQUEST Social Sciences and Humanities Information Facility

This is the worldwide Social Sciences and Humanities Information Service of the Coombs Computing Unit, Research Schools of Social Sciences and Pacific Studies, Australian National University, Canberra, Australia.

Keywords: Social Science Humanities Australia
Sponsor: Australian National University
Audience: Social Scientists, Humanists, Researchers, Educators, Students
Profile: COOMBSQUEST provides direct access to the Coombspapers Social Sciences Research Data Bank. The databank was established in December 1991 to act as the world's major electronic repository of social science and humanities papers, and other high-grade research material dealing with Australia, the Pacific region, and Southeast and Northeast Asia, Buddhism, Taoism, and other Oriental religions.

Contact: T. Matthew Ciolek
tmciolek@coombs.anu.edu.au

Details: Free

`gopher://coombs.anu.edu.au`

`http://combs.anu.edu.au/CoombsHome.html`

Cooperatives

COHOUSING-L

A list for discussion of cohousing, the name of a type of collaborative housing that has been developed primarily in Denmark since 1972 where it is known as bofoellesskaber. Cohousing is housing designed to foster community and cooperation while preserving independence. Private residences are clustered near shared facilities. The members design and manage all aspects of their community.

Keywords: Community, Housing, Cooperatives
Audience: Urban Planners, Architects, General Contractors
Contact: fholson@uci.com
Details: Free
User Info: To subscribe to the list, send an e-mail message to the address below consisting of a single line reading:

Cooperatives

```
SUB COHOUSING-L YourFirstName
YourLastName
```
To send a message to the entire list, address it to: COHOUSING-L@uci.com

`mailto:listserv@uci.com`

Copyright

Berne Convention Implementation Act of 1988 ★

An act to amend Title 17, United States Code, to implement the Berne Convention for the Protection of Literary and Artistic Works, as revised in Paris on July 24, 1971, and for other purposes.

Keywords: Legislation (US), Government (US), Politics (US), Copyright
Audience: Lawyers, Students, Politicians, Journalists
Details: Free

`gopher://wiretap.spies.com/00/Gov/Copyright/US.Berne.Convention.txt`

Copyright Act ★

The full text of the Copyright Act of 1976, Title 17, United States Code, Sections 101–810.

Keywords: Politics (US), Government (US Federal), Laws (US Federal), Copyright
Audience: Lawyers, Students, Politicians, Journalists
Details: Free

`gopher://wiretap.spies.com/00/Gov/Copyright/US.Copyright.1976.tx`

Copyright Basics ★

This information is from Circular 1 issued by the Copyright Office, Library of Congress, January 1991. It explains what copyright is, who can claim copyright, the principles of copyrights, what works are protected, how to secure a copyright, and so on.

Keywords: Copyright, Government (US Federal), Laws (US Federal)
Audience: Lawyers, Students, Politicians, Journalists
Details: Free

`gopher://wiretap.spies.com/00/Gov/Copyright/US.Copyright.Basics.txt`

CNI-Copyright Mailing List Archives ★★

An archive of lists related to copyright and intellectual property law.

Keywords: Copyright Law, Intellectual Property

Sponsor: CNI (The Coalition for Networked Information)
Audience: Entrepreneurs, Lawyers, Journalists
Contact: Craig Summerhill, Joan K. Lippincott
craig@cni.org, joan@cni.org

`gopher://gopher.cni.org`

Universal Copyright Convention ★★

The Universal Copyright Convention as revised at Paris (1971). Convention and protocols were done at Paris on July 24, 1971. It was ratified by the President of the United States of America on August 28, 1972.

Keywords: Copyright, Laws (US), Government (US), Politics (US)
Audience: Lawyers, Students, Politicians, Journalists
Details: Free

`gopher://wiretap.spies.com/00/Gov/Copyright/US.Universal.Copyright.Conv.txt`

Cornell Law School Gopher

Cornell Law School Gopher ★★★

A gopher server providing extensive access to Cornell Law School's online archives.

Keywords: Law (US)
Sponsor: The Legal Information Institute
Audience: Legal Professionals, Students
Profile: The Cornell Law School Gopher provides access to Cornell Law School's extensive online archives. Areas covered by the gopher include case law, copyright law, trademark law, commercial law, and information about the admissions and events at the Cornell Law school.
Contact: Thomas R. Bruce or Peter W. Martin
feedback@fatty.law.cornell.edu

`gopher://fatty.law.cornell.edu`

Cornell University Libraries

Cornell University Libraries ★★★★

This library system maintains special collections in engineering, nuclear engineering, textile engineering, agriculture, medicine, Africana, entomology, hotels, ILR, mathematics, physical sciences, and veterinary medicine.

Keywords: Libraries, Research

Audience: General Public, Researchers
Details: Free

When userid/password screen appears, press return. When cp read appears on the screen, type library.

`telnet://cornellc.cit.cornell.edu`

Cornucopia of Disability Information (CODI)

Cornucopia of Disability Information (CODI) ★★★

A large collection of disability-related information available via gopher.

Keywords: Disabilities, Health
Sponsor: State University of New York (SUNY) at Buffalo
Audience: Disabled People, Activists, Rehabilitation Counselors, Health Care Professionals
Profile: This site provides a wide variety of information resources concerning people with disabilities, ranging from legal information to a directory of computer resources aimed at the disabled consumer. Includes state, local, and national information and government documents such as the Americans with Disabilities Act. Also has links to many other related resources on the Internet, such as the National Rehabilitation Information Center.
Contact: Jay Leavitt
leavitt@ubvmsb.cc.buffalo.edu

`gopher://val-dor.cc.buffalo.edu`

Corporations

INCORPR (Corporation and Partnership Records)

The Corporation and Partnership Records (INCORP) library contains current US corporation and partnership filings.

Keywords: Corporations, Partnerships, Filings, Trademarks
Audience: Corporations, Lawyers, Researchers
Profile: The INCORP library contains current records on corporations and limited partnerships registered with the office of the Secretary or Department of State. These records include information extracted by the state's staff from articles of incorporation, annual reports, amendments, and other public filings.
Contact: Mead New Sales Group at (800) 227-4908 or (513) 859-5398 inside the US, or (513) 865-7981 for all inquiries outside the US.

User Info:	To subscribe, contact Mead directly.	
	To examine the Nexis user guide, you can access it at the ftp site of the University of Texas at Austin at the URL address: ftp://ftp.cc.utexas.edu	
	The files are in: /pub/ref-services/LEXIS	

`telnet://nex.meaddata.com`

`http://www.meaddata.com`

Corpse/Respondents

Corpse/Respondents

This is a gothic pen-pal zine in digest form with small traffic mailing list.

Keywords:	Gothic Rock, Rock Music
Audience:	Gothic Rock Enthusiasts
Contact:	carriec@eskimo.com
Details:	Free
User Info:	To subscribe send an e-mail message to the URL address below with "subscribe corpse <yournameandaddress>" in the text.

`mailto:carriec@eskimo.com`

Correct Time

Correct Time/NBS

Correct Time/NBS tells the correct time from the National Bureau of Standards (NBS).

Keywords:	Internet, Services, Correct Time
Audience:	Internet Surfers
Details:	Free

`ftp://india.colorado.edu/pub`

Cosmic Update

Cosmic Update

Internet notice identifying new computer software from the National Aeronautics and Space Administration (NASA) made available for international use.

Keywords:	NASA, Software, Space
Audience:	Space Scientists, Astronomers
Profile:	COSLINE is a 24-hour electronic information service to COSMIC's customers. The principal feature of COSLINE is the catalog Search facility. A separate help file is available for browsing from the Search main menu option.

Contact:	Pat Mortenson service@cossack.cosmic.uga.edu
Details:	Free
User Info:	To subscribe, send an e-mail message requesting a subscription to the URL address below.

`mailto:service@cossack.cosmic.uga.edu`

Counterev-L

Counterev-L

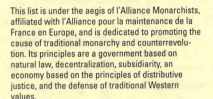

This list is under the aegis of l'Alliance Monarchists, affiliated with l'Alliance pour la maintenance de la France en Europe, and is dedicated to promoting the cause of traditional monarchy and counterrevolution. Its principles are a government based on natural law, decentralization, subsidiarity, an economy based on the principles of distributive justice, and the defense of traditional Western values.

Keywords:	Monarchy, Government (International)
Audience:	Monarchists, Counterrevolutionaries
Contact:	Jovan Weismiller ae852@yfn.ysu.edu
Details:	Free
User Info:	To subscribe to the list, send an e-mail message requesting a subscription to the URL address below.

`mailto:ae852@yfn.ysu.edu`

CP

CP

Topics of interest to the group include the cultivation and propagation of CP's (carniverous plants), field observations of CP's, sources of CP material, and CP trading between members. The discussion is not moderated, and usually consists of short messages offering plants for trade, asking CP questions and advice, relating experiences with plant propagation, and so on. The group also maintains archives of commercial plant sources and members growing lists.

Keywords:	Carnivorous Plants, Botany
Audience:	Horticulturists, Botanists
Contact:	Rick Walker walker@hpl-opus.hpl.hp.com
User Info:	To subscribe to the list, send an e-mail message to the address below consisting of a single line reading:
	SUB CP YourFirstName YourLastName
	To send a message to the entire list, address it to: CP@hpl-opus.hpl.hp.com

`mailto:listserv@hpl-opus.hpl.hp.com`

CP/M

Alspa

Discussion by users of the CP/M machines made by (now defunct) Alspa Computer, Inc.

Keywords:	Computers, Alspa Computer, Inc., CP/M
Audience:	CP/M Users
Contact:	Brad Allen alspa-users-request@ssyx.ucsc.edu
Details:	Free
User Info:	To subscribe to the list, send an e-mail message requesting a subscription to the URL address below.
	To send a message to the entire list, address it to: alspa-users@ssyx.ucsc.edu

`mailto:alspa-users-request@ssyx.ucsc.edu`

CPSR/PDX Newsletter

CPSR/PDX Newsletter

This is the newsletter of the Portland chapter of Computer Professionals for Social Responsibility.

Keywords:	Computer Professionals, Social Responsibility
Audience:	Computer Professionals
Contact:	Erik Nilsson ERIKN@Goldfish.mitron.tek.com
Details:	Free

`mailto:erikn@goldfish.mitron.tek.com`

Crafts

PEI (Prince Edward Island, Canada) Crafts Council Gopher

A gopher devoted to all manner of crafts, from weaving to glass blowing. Information includes a database of tools, services, and materials for crafts enthusiasts, as well as FAQs and pointers to other crafts resources. Also provides background on the PEI Craft Council's activities and on Prince Edward Island.

Keywords:	Crafts, Hobbies, Canada
Sponsor:	PEI Crafts Council, Prince Edward Island, Canada
Audience:	Crafts Enthusiasts
Details:	Free

`gopher://crafts-council.pe.ca`

rec.crafts.brewing

A Usenet newsgroup providing information and discussion about making beers and meads.

Keywords: Beer, Crafts
Audience: Beer Brewers
User Info: To subscribe to this Usenet newsgroup, you need access to a newsreader.

news:rec.crafts.brewing

rec.photo

A Usenet newsgroup providing information and discussion about photography.

Keywords: Photography, Art, Crafts
Audience: Photographers, Artists
User Info: To subscribe to this Usenet newsgroup, you need access to a newsreader.

news:rec.photo

rec.woodworking

A Usenet newsgroup providing information and discussion about woodworking.

Keywords: Woodworking, Crafts, Hobbies
Audience: Woodworkers
User Info: To subscribe to this Usenet newsgroup, you need access to a newsreader.

news:rec.woodworking

cread (Latin American & Caribbean Distance & Continuing Education)

cread (Latin American & Caribbean Distance & Continuing Education)

This is a digest list of distance education information primarily focused on Latin America and the Caribbean.

Keywords: Latin America, Caribbean, Education (Distance)
Audience: Educators, Administrators, Faculty
Details: Free
User Info: To subscribe to the list, send an e-mail message to the URL address below consisting of a single line reading: SUB cread YourFirstName YourLastName.

To send a message to the entire list, address it to: cread@yorkvm1.bitnet

mailto:listserv@yorkvm1.bitnet

Creationism

talk.origins

A Usenet newsgroup providing information and discussion about evolution versus creationism.

Keywords: Evolution, Creationism, Activism
Audience: General Public, Evolutionists, Creationists, Activists
Details: Free
User Info: To subscribe to this Usenet newsgroup, you need access to a newsreader.

news:talk.origins

Creativity

de Bono

This is a discussion list concerning the work of Edward de Bono. Also provides help with teaching the CoRT Thinking Program, and Six Thinking Hats.

Keywords: de Bono (Edward), Education (Alternative), Creativity
Audience: Teachers, Students, Management Trainers
Contact: Rosa Casarez
Casarez@netcom.net

mailto:casarez@netcom.com

Creighton University Library Online Catalogue

Creighton University Library Online Catalogue

This site maintains a catalog of the Creighton University library's holdings.

Keywords: Health Sciences, Libraries
Sponsor: Creighton University, Omaha, Nebraska, USA
Audience: Health-Care Professionals, Medical Educators, Students
Details: Free
At the prompt type <lib hsl>for Health Sciences Library.

telnet://attachpals@owl.creighton.edu

Crew

rec.sport.rowing

A Usenet newsgroup providing information and discussion about recreational and competitive rowing. It provides information from the United States Rowing Association, the latest race results, equipment sales, coaching positions and more.

Keywords: Rowing, Crew, Sports
Audience: Rowers, Coaches, Athletes
Profile: This newsgroup covers technical, training and nutritional aspects as well as the latest race results, National Team information, equipment sales, coaching positions, information from the United States Rowing Association and more.
User Info: To subscribe to this Usenet newsgroup, you need access to a newsreader.

news:rec.sport.rowing

Cricket

rec.sport.cricket

A Usenet newsgroup providing information and discussion about cricket.

Keywords: Cricket, Sports
Audience: Cricket Fans, Sports Fans
User Info: To subscribe to this Usenet newsgroup, you need access to a newsreader.

news:rec.sport.cricket

University of Glasgow Information Service (GLANCE)

GLANCE provides subject-based information services, including an extensive section on European and world sports.

Keywords: Sports, Soccer, Motor Racing, Mountaineering, Squash, Cricket, Golf, Tennis, Europe, Scotland
Sponsor: University of Glasgow, Glasgow, Scotland
Audience: Sport Enthusiasts, Fitness Enthusiasts, Nature Lovers
Profile: Information at this site includes schedules, results, and statistics for sports such as cricket and soccer. There is also a selection of items on mountaineering.
Contact: Alan Dawson
a.dawson@uk.ac.gla.compserv
Details: Free

gopher://govan.cent.gla.ac.uk/ Subject/Sports and Rec

Crime

Georgia-Computer Systems Protection Act ★

Lists full text of the Georgia Computer Systems Protection Act.

Keywords: Computer, Crime
Audience: Lawyers, Computer Programmers, Computer Operators
Details: Free

`gopher://wiretap.spies.com`

Investigators and Detectives ★★★

This resource provides information files for individuals involved with investigative research, as well as a free monthly newsletter.

Keywords: Detectives, Crime, Information Retrieval, Security
Audience: Investigators, Detectives, Information Brokers, General Public
Profile: Investigators and Detectives provides access to information covering topics such as private investigative research, strategies, sources, the art and science of investigating, theft deterrents, and electronic PI schematics and plans. Also offers a free sample of a newsletter covering various topics of interest to Private Investigators, such as techniques and strategies, security, and tracing.
Contact: Mike Enlow
menlow@Intec.win.net
michael@enlow.com
Details: Inside Secrets.

`mailto:info@enlow.com`

Texas: Computer Crimes Statute ★

Lists text of the Texas Computer Crimes Statute.

Keywords: Computers, Crime, Texas
Audience: Lawyers, Computer Programmers, Computer Operators
Details: Free
Select from menu as appropriate

`gopher://wiretap.spies.com`

UN Criminal Justice Country Profiles ★

UN profiles of world crime in 113 countries.
Keywords: Crime, UN
Sponsor: United Nations

Audience: Lawyers, Legal Professionals, Librarians, Governments
Details: Free
Select from menu as appropriate.

`gopher://uacsc2.albany.edu`

Croatia

Cro-News/SCYU-Digest ★

This unmoderated list is the distribution point for the news coming from Croatia. The list carries articles from Novi Vjesnik, Vecernji List, Croatia Monitor, Slobodna Dalmacija, Novi Danas, Radio Free Europe/Radio Luxemburg bulletins, and UPI reports.

Keywords: Croatia, News Media
Audience: Croats, Journalists, General Public
Contact: Nino Margetic
cro-news-request@medphys.ucl.ac.uk
Details: Free
User Info: To subscribe to the list, send an e-mail message requesting a subscription to the URL address below.
To send a message to the entire list, address it to: cro-news@medphys.ucl.ac.uk

`mailto:cro-news-request@medphys.ucl.ac.uk`

Cro-Views ★

Cro-Views is an opinion service that consists of discussions relating to Croatia and other former Yugoslav republics. The main objective is to give people who cannot access the news network (for example, via <rn>command in UNIX a chance to read and voice their own opinions about these issues.

Keywords: Croatia, News
Audience: Croats, Journalists, General Public
Contact: Joe Stojsic
Joe@Mullara.Met.UniMelb.Edu.AU
Details: Free
User Info: To subscribe to the list, send an e-mail message requesting a subscription to the URL address below.
Notes: Cro-Views is an unmoderated service, but abusive language and name-calling is not tolerated.

`mailto:Joe@Mullara.Met.UniMelb.Edu.AU`

Croatian-News/Hrvatski-Vjesnik ★

News from and related to Croatia, run by volunteers. These are actually two news distributions: one in Croatian (occasionally an article might be in some other South Slavic language) and one in English.

Keywords: Croatia, News
Audience: Croats, Journalists, General Public
Contact: Croatian-News-Request@Andrew.CMU.Edu, Hrvatski-Vjesnik-Zamolbe@Andrew.CMU.Edu
Details: Free
User Info: To subscribe to the list, send an e-mail message to the URL address below with the following information: your name, your e-mail address, and state/country where your account is. Please put the state/country information in the Subject: line of your letter. If you would like to receive the news in Croatian as well, please indicate that in your message. If you would prefer to receive the news in Croatian only, please send a message to the following address: Hrvatski-Vjesnik-Zamolbe@Andrew.CMU.Edu

To send a message to the entire list, address it to:Croatian-News@Andrew.CMU.Edu

`mailto:Croatian-News-Request@Andrew.CMU.Edu`

Cromwell (Oliver)

University of Chicago Library ★★

The library's holdings are large and wide-ranging and contain significant collections in many fields.

Keywords: English Bibles, Lincoln (Abraham), Kentucky & Ohio River Valley (History of), Balzac (Honore de), American Drama, Cromwell (Oliver), Goethe, Judaica, Italy, Chaucer (Geoffrey), Wells (Ida, Personal Papers of), Douglas (Stephen A.), Italy, Literature (Children's)
Audience: General Public, Researchers, Librarians, Document Delivery Professionals
Details: Free
Expect: ENTER CLASS, Send: LIB48 3;
Expect: CONNECTED, Send: RETURN

`telnet://olorin.uchicago.edu`

Cross Cultural Studies

Anthropology, Cross Cultural Studies, & Archaeology

This directory is a compilation of information resources focused on anthropology, cross cultural studies, and archaeology.

Keywords: Anthropology, Cross Cultural Studies, Archaeology
Audience: Anthropologists, Archaeologists, Students, Educators
Contact: G. Bell
Details: Free

`ftp://una.hh.lib.umich.edu/70/inetdirsstacks/anthro:bell`

crossfire

crossfire ★

To discuss the developement of the game Crossfire. The official anonymous FTP-site is ftp.ifi.uio.no in the directory /pub/crossfire. Old mails to the list are archived there. Crossfire is a multiplayer arcade and adventure game made for the X-window environment.

Keywords: Computer Games
Audience: Crossfire specialists, Computer Game Enthusiasts
Contact: Frank Tore Johansen
crossfire-request@ifi.uio.no
Details: Free
User Info: To subscribe to the list, send an e-mail message requesting a subscription to the URL address below.

To send a message to the entire list, address it to: crossfire@ifi.uio.no

`mailto:crossfire-request@ifi.uio.no`

Crowes

Crowes ★

To provide a forum for discussion about the rock band the Black Crowes. Topics include the group's music and lyrics, as well as the band's participation with NORML, concert dates and playlists, and bootlegs (audio and video).

Keywords: Rock Music, Pop Music
Audience: Rock Music Enthusiasts, Pop Music Enthusiasts
Contact: rstewart@unex.ucla.edu
Details: Free
User Info: To subscribe, mail to the address below with the command SUBSCRIBE in the first line.

`mailto:rstewart@unex.ucla.edu`

Cryonics

cryonics ★

Cryonic suspension is an experimental procedure whereby patients who can no longer be kept alive with today's medical abilities are preserved at low temperatures for treatment in the future. This list is a forum for topics related to cryonics, including biochemistry of memory, low temperature biology, legal status of cryonics and cryonically suspended people, nanotechnology and cell repair machines, philosophy of identity, mass media coverage of cryonics, new research and publications, conferences, and local cryonics group meetings.

Keywords: Cryonics
Audience: Doctors, Biologists, Biochemists
Contact: Kevin Q. Brown
kqb@whscad1.att.com
Details: Free
User Info: To subscribe to the list, send an e-mail message requesting a subscription to the URL address below.

`mailto:kqb@whscad1.att.com`

CSAA

CSAA ★

The Comp.Sys.Amiga.Announce mailing list has been created for those who have no access to USENET. It provides the gate between the USENET newsgroup C.S.A.A. and e-mail. This group distributes announcements of importance to people using the Commodore brand Amiga computers. Announcements contain information on new products, disk library releases, software updates, reports of major bugs or dangerous viruses, notices of meetings or upcoming events, and so forth. A large proportion of posts announce the upload of software packages to anonymous FTP archive sites.

Keywords: Commodore-Amiga Computers, Computers
Audience: Commodore-Amiga Users
Contact: Carlos Amezaga
announce-request@cs.ucdavis.edu
Details: Free
User Info: To subscribe to the list, send an e-mail message requesting a subscription to the URL address below.

To send a message to the entire list, address it to:announce@cs.ucdavis.edu

`mailto:announce-request@cs.ucdavis.edu`

CSF: Communications for a Sustainable Future

CSF: Communications for a Sustainable Future ★★★★

A gopher server for the distribution of Conflict Resolution Materials.

Keywords: Conflict Resolution, Community, Politics
Sponsor: Communications for a Sustainable Future
Audience: Activists, Policy Analysts, Community Leaders, Mediators, Lawyers
Profile: Communications for a Sustainable Future is a collective effort of several scholars. CSF does research, education, and applied work. Its main subject areas are: Intractable Conflicts and Constructive Confrontation, Environmental and Public Policy Dispute Resolution, Social/Political Conflicts, International Conflicts.
Contact: roper@csf.colorado.edu
Details: Free

`gopher://csf.colorado.edu`

CSORG (Clearinghouse for Subject-Oriented Internet Resource Guides)

CSORG (Clearinghouse for Subject-Oriented Internet Resource Guides) ★★★

The goal of CSORG is to collect and make widely available guides to Internet resources which are subject-oriented. These guides are produced by members of the Internet community, and by SILS students who participate in the Internet Resource Discovery project.

Keywords: WWW, Information Retrieval, Internet
Sponsor: University of Michigan, School of Information and Library Studies, Michigan, USA
Audience: Reseachers, Students, General Public
Contact: Louis Rosenfeld
i-guides@umich.edu

`gopher://una.hh.lib.umich.edu/11/inetdirs`

CSU Entomology WWW Site

CSU Entomology WWW Site ★★★★

A web site containing online photos of insects, entomology educational programs, and extensive Internet entomology links.

Keywords: Bioscience, Biology, Entomology
Sponsor: Colorado State University, Denver, Colorado, USA
Audience: Students, Researchers, Entomologists
Contact: Lou Bjostad
lbjostad@lamar.colorado.edu

`http://www.colostate.edu/Depts/Entomology/ent.html`

ctf-discuss

ctf-discuss ★

This mailing list aims to stimulate discussion of issues critical to the computer science community in the United States (and, by extension, the world). The Computer Science and Telecommunications Board (CSTB) of the National Research Council (NRC) is charged with identifying and initiating studies in areas critical to the health of the field. Recently one such study, Computing the Future, has generated a major discussion in the community and has motivated the establishment of this mailing list in order to involve broader participation. This list will be used in the future to report and discuss the activities of the CSTB and to solicit opinions in a variety of areas.

Keywords: Computer Science, Telecommunications
Audience: Computer Scientists, Telecommunications Experts
Contact: Dave Farber
ctf-discuss-request@cis.upenn.edu
Details: Free
User Info: To subscribe to the list, send an e-mail message requesting a subscription to the URL address below.
To send a message to the entire list, address it to: ctf-discuss@cis.upenn.edu

mailto:ctf-discuss-request@cis.upenn.edu

CTN News

CTN News ★

This is a list covering news on Tibet.
Keywords: Tibet, New Media
Audience: Tibetans, Journalists, General Public
Contact: ctn-editors@utcc.utoronto.ca
Details: Free
User Info: To subscribe to the list, send an e-mail message requesting a subscription to the URL address below.
To send a message to the entire list, address it to: CTN_News@utcc.utoronto.ca

mailto:ctn-editors@utcc.utoronto.ca

Cuba

INFOMED ★

Provides yearly statistical information in the form of tables (in ASCII format) listing the principal indicators of health in Cuba.

Keywords: Cuba, Health Statistics, Public Health
Sponsor: Cuban Ministry of Health
Audience: Medical Professionals, Researchers, Public Health Professionals
Details: Free
To obtain a table from the yearbook, send an electronic message to the URL address below without a subject and with the following content in the body of the message:
GET ANUARIO <name of table>
Examples of tables are CMT-11: Death rates by age group; CMT-15: Infant mortality by province, and so on. For a listing of the available tables request the help file.

mailto:listserv@infomed.cu

CUD (Computer Underground Digest)

CUD (Computer Underground Digest) ★

USA Today of cyberspace and the computer underground. Contains information relating to the computer underground.
Keywords: Hacking, Computer News, Cyberculture
Audience: Hackers, Reality Hackers, Computer Underground Enthusiasts
Contact: Gordon Meyer, Jim Thomas
tk0jut2@niu.bitnet
pumpcon@mindvox.phantom.com.
Details: Free

ftp://etext.archive.umich.edu/pub/Zines/CUD

Culinary (Collection of)

University of Denver Library ★★

The library's holdings are large and wide-ranging and contain significant collections in many fields.
Keywords: Folklore Collection, Husted (Margaret), Culinary (Collection of)
Audience: Researchers, Students, General Public
Contact: Bob Stocker
bstocker@ducair.bitnet
Details: Free
Expect: Login; Send: Atdu

telnet://du.edu

Cults

The Purple Thunderbolt of Spode (PURPS)

Magazine of the OTISian faith (a small but growing cult worshiping OTIS, the ancient Sumerian goddess of life) carrying news, fiction, poetry, humor, and the pure, unadulterated Secrets of the Universe to its subscribers.
Keywords: Religion, Cults
Audience: OTIS Followers
Contact: barker@acc.fau.edu
User Info: To subscribe, send an e-mail message requesting a subscription to the URL address below.

mailto:barker@acc.fau.edu

Cultural Studies

African Art Exhibit and Tutorial ★★

This web site provides images of African art and an overview of African aesthetics.
Keywords: Art, Africa, Cultural Studies
Sponsor: University of Virginia
Audience: Artists, Art Students, Educators, Historians

http://www.lib.virginia.edu

Armadillo's World Wide Web Page

This site provides resources and instructional material for an interdisciplinary Texan culture course.
Keywords: History (US), Texas, Cultural Studies, Education
Sponsor: Rice University, Houston, Texas, USA
Audience: Educators, Students
Contact: armadillo@rice.edu

http://chico.rice.edu/armadillo

Culture

African Education Research Network ★★

Various links to African studies programs at select universities, and other archived information of interest to the African studies scholar.

Culture

Keywords: Culture, Race, Africa, African Studies
Sponsor: Ohio University, African Education Research Network
Audience: Students, African-Americans, Africans
Contact: Milton E. Ploghoft
Contact: mperdreau@ohiou.edu
Details: Free

gopher://gopher.ohiou.edu/00/dept.servers/aern

Argentina

Mailing list for general discussion and information about Argentina, including Argentine culture and politics.

Keywords: Argentina, Politics, Culture
Sponsor: Carlos G. Mendioroz
Audience: Spanish Speakers, Students
Contact: Carlos G. Mendioroz
argentina-request@ois.db.toronto.edu
User Info: To subscribe to the list, send an e-mail message to the URL address below.
To send a message to the entire list, address it to:
argentina@ois.db.toronto.edu

mailto:argentina-request@ois.db.toronto.edu

Black/African Related Online Information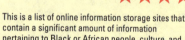

This is a list of online information storage sites that contain a significant amount of information pertaining to Black or African people, culture, and issues around the world.

Keywords: Culture, Race, Africa, African Studies
Sponsor: AfriInfo
Audience: Students, African-Americans, Africans
Contact: McGee
mcgee@epsilon.eecs.nwu.edu
Details: Free

ftp://ftp.netcom.com/pub/amcgee/my_african_related_lists/afrisite.msg

Chicano/LatinoNet

An electronic mechanism which brings together Chicano/Latino research, as well as linguistic minority and educational research efforts being carried out at the University of California and elsewhere. It serves as a gateway between faculty, staff, and students who are engaged in research and curricular efforts in these areas.

Keywords: Culture, Race, Chicano Culture, Latino Culture
Sponsor: Chicano Studies Research Center, University of California at Los Angeles
Audience: Students, Mexican-Americans, Latinos
Contact: Richard Chabran
Chabran@latino.sscnet.ucla.ed
Details: Free

gopher://latino.sscnet.ucla.edu/

Japanese Information

This web site contains extensive information on the geography, culture, law, and tourism of Japan. Includes archived Japanese newsgroup information and FAQs.

Keywords: Culture, Race, Japan, Japanese Culture
Sponsor: Nippon Telegraph and Telephone
Audience: Students, Tourists, Japanese, Japanese-Americans
Contact: Webmaster
www-admin@seraph.ntt.jp
Details: Free

http://www.ntt.jp/japan/index.html

Mexican Culture FAQ

This is the FAQ from the soc.culture.mexican newsgroup. Provides information on Mexican culture, history, society, language, and tourism.

Keywords: Culture, Race, Chicano Culture, Latino Culture
Sponsor: News Group Moderators for soc.culture.mexican
Audience: Students, Latinos, Chicanos
Contact: News Group Moderator
mendoza-grado@att.com
Details: Free

ftp://ftp.mty.itesm.ms/pub/mexico/faqs

http://www.cis.ohio-state.edu/hypertext/faq/usenet/mexican-faq/faq.html

Poland-I

A mailing list devoted to discussion of Polish culture and events.

Keywords: Poland, Culture
Audience: Researchers
Contact: Micahl Prussak
michal@gs58.sp.cs.cmu.edu
Details: Free
User Info: To subscribe to the list, send an e-mail message to the URL address below, consisting of a single line reading:
SUB poland-I YourFirstName YourLastName
To send a message to the entire list, address it to: poland-1@ubvm.cc.buffalo.edu

mailto:listserv@ubvm.cc.buffalo.edu

Reggae Down Babylon

A collection of links to sources of information about reggae music on the World Wide Web and the Internet. Site includes reggae FAQs, and listings of reggae radio shows, lyrics, pictures, and news group archives.

Keywords: Reggae, Culture, Music
Sponsor: Reggae Down Babylon
Audience: Music Fans, Musicians, Reggae Enthusiasts
Contact: ReggaeMaster
damjohns@nyx10.cs.du.edu
Details: Free

ftp://jammin.nosc.mil/pub/reggae

SCS

A discussion of the culture of the former Soviet Union.

Keywords: Soviet Union, Culture
Audience: Researchers, Slavicists, General Public
Contact: John B. Harlan
ijph200@indycms.iupui.edu
Details: Free
User Info: To subscribe to the list, send an e-mail message to the URL address below consisting of a single line reading:
SUB scs YourFirstName YourLastName
To send a message to the entire list, address to: scs@indycms.iupui.edu

mailto:listserv@indycms.iupui.edu

slovak-I

A mailing list for discussion of Slovak culture, and so on.

Keywords: Slovakia, Culture
Audience: Researchers, Students, Slovaks
Contact: Jan George Frajkor
gfrajkor@ccs.carleton.ca
User Info: To subscribe to the list, send an e-mail message to the URL address below consisting of a single line reading:
SUB slovak-I YourFirstName YourLastName
To sen a message to the entire list, address it to: slovak-1@ubvm.cc.buffalo.edu

mailto:listserv@ubvm.cc.buffalo.edu

soc.culture.canada

A Usenet newsgroup providing information and discussion about Canada and its people.

Keywords: Culture, Canada, Sociology
Audience: Sociologists, Canadians

Details: Free
User Info: To subscribe to this Usenet newsgroup, you need access to a newsreader.

`news:soc.culture.canada`

Spojrzenia

A weekly E-journal devoted to Polish culture, history and politics.

Keywords: Poland, News (international), Culture
Audience: Poles, Students
Contact: Jerzy Krzystek
krzystek@u.washington.edu
Details: Free
User Info: To subscribe to the list, send an e-mail message requesting a subscription to the URL address below.

To send a message to the entire list, address it to:

spojrzenia@u.washington.edu

`mailto:krzystek@u.washington.edu`

WWW Paris

A web site created as a collaborative effort among individuals in both Paris and the United States.

Keywords: Paris, Culture, Art, Travel, French, Tourism
Audience: Students, Educators, Travelers, Researchers
Profile: Contains an extensive collection of images and text regarding all of the major monuments and museums of Paris, including maps of the Metro and the RER; calendars of events and current expositions; promotional images and text relating to local department stores; there is also a visitors' section with up-to-date tourist information on hotels, restaurants, telephones, airport schedules, a basic Paris glossary, and the latest weather images. Includes an extensive collection of links to other resources about Paris and France, and a selected bibliography of history and architecture in Paris.
Contact: Norman Barth, Eric Pouliquen
nbarth@ucsd.edu, epouliq@ucsd.edu

`http://meteora.ucsd.edu/~norman/paris`

Current Cites

Current Cites

A monthly publication of the Library Technology Watch Program at The Library, University of California, Berkeley.

Keywords: Computer Technology, Libraries
Sponsor: The Library, University of California, Berkeley, CA
Audience: Librarians, Computer Programmers
Profile: Over 30 journals in librarianship and computer technology are scanned for articles on optical-disk technologies, computer networks and networking, information transfer, expert systems and artificial intelligence, and hypermedia and multimedia.
Contact: David Robison
drobison@library.berkeley.edu
Details: Free

`telnet://melvyl.ucop.edu`

Current Contents

Current Contents

Current Contents provides access to the tables of contents from the current issues of leading domestic and international scientific journals. Every discipline within the sciences is represented. The database provides complete bibliographic information for each article, review, letter, note and editorial.

Keywords: Sciences, Scientific Journals
Sponsor: Institute for Scientific Information
Audience: General Public, Researchers, Librarians, Physicians
Contact: CDP Technologies Sales Department (800)950-2035, extension 400
User Info: To subscribe, contact CDP Technologies directly

`telnet://cdplus@cdplus.com`

Current Events

misc.headlines

A Usenet newsgroup providing information and discussion about current events and issues.

Keywords: Current Events
Audience: General Public
Details: Free
User Info: To subscribe to this Usenet newsgroup, you need access to a newsreader.

`news:misc.headlines`

Current Weather Maps and Movies

Current Weather Maps and Movies

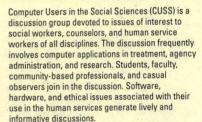

This web site is updated hourly, and provides links to downloadable software sites instrumental in accessing interactive weather browsers. International information is available, and visual and infrared maps are supplied from satellites.

Keywords: Weather, Meteorology, Aviation
Sponsor: Michigan State University, Michigan, USA
Audience: General Public, Oceanography, Pilots
Contact: Charles Henrich
henrich@crh.cl.msu.edu

`http://rs560.cl.msu.edu/weather`

CUSSNET

CUSSNET

Computer Users in the Social Sciences (CUSS) is a discussion group devoted to issues of interest to social workers, counselors, and human service workers of all disciplines. The discussion frequently involves computer applications in treatment, agency administration, and research. Students, faculty, community-based professionals, and casual observers join in the discussion. Software, hardware, and ethical issues associated with their use in the human services generate lively and informative discussions.

Keywords: Social Sciences, Computers, Computer Applications
Audience: Social Workers, Human Services Workers, General Public
Contact: cussnet-request@stat.com
Details: Free
User Info: To subscribe to the list, send an e-mail message to the address below consisting of a single line reading:

SUB cussnet YourFirstName YourLastName.

To send a message to the entire list, address it to: cussnet@stat.com

`mailto:listserv@stat.com`

CVNet (Color and Vision Network)

CVNet (Color and Vision Network)

The network provides a means of communications for scientists working in biological color vision research. Members' e-mail addresses are maintained and sent to others in the network. CVNet distributes notices of jobs, meetings, and some other special announcements to all registrants. Members can post bulletins, announcements, and so on.

Keywords:	Optics, Biological Research, Psychology
Sponsor:	York University, North York, Ontario, Canada
Audience:	Psychologists, Color/Vision Researchers
Contact:	Peter K. Kaiser cvnet@vm1.yorkU.ca
Details:	Free
User Info:	To subscribe, send an e-mail message requesting a subscription to the URL address below.

`mailto:cvnet@vm1.yorkU.ca`

Cyberculture

CUD (Computer Underground Digest)

USA Today of cyberspace and the computer underground. Contains information relating to the computer underground.

Keywords:	Hacking, Computer News, Cyberculture
Audience:	Hackers, Reality Hackers, Computer Underground Enthusiasts
Contact:	Gordon Meyer, Jim Thomas tk0jut2@niu.bitnet or pumpcon@mindvox.phantom.com.
Details:	Free

`ftp://etext.archive.umich.edu/pub/Zines/CUD`

fringeware

A moderated mailing list devoted to cyberculture and the like.

Keywords:	Cyberculture
Audience:	Cyberculture Enthusiasts
Details:	Free
User Info:	To subscribe to the list, send an e-mail message to the URL address shown below.
	To send a message to the entire list, address it to: fringeware@illuminati.io.com

`mailto:fringeware-request@illuminati.io.com`

FutureCulture FAQ (Frequently Asked Questions) File ★★★

List of online and offline items of interest to subscribers of FutureCulture, a mailing list on 'technoculture' or 'new edge' or 'cyberculture.'

Keywords:	Technology, Cyberculture, Postmodernism, Sci-Fi, Zines
Audience:	Reality Hackers, Cyberculture Enthusiasts
Profile:	This list discusses cyberpunk culture, rave culture, industrial music, virtual reality, drugs, computer underground, Net sociology, and virtual communities.
Contact:	Alias Datura (adatura on IRC) adatura@uafhp.uark.edu
Details:	Free

`ftp://etext.archive.umich.edu/pub`

Internet Wiretap ★★

A resource containing electronic books, zines, and government documents, White House press releases, and links to worldwide gopher and WAIS servers.

Keywords:	Electronic Media, Cyberculture, Zines
Sponsor:	Internet Wiretap
Audience:	Cyberculture Enthusiasts, Civil Libertarians, Educators

`gopher://wiretap.spies.com/11/`

`http://wiretap.spies.com`

Cyberpunk Games

flashlife

A mailing list for general managers of Shadowrun and other cyberpunk role-playing games to discuss rules and scenarios, ask questions, and make up answers.

Keywords:	Games, Cyberpunk Games
Audience:	Game Players
Details:	Free
User Info:	To subscribe to the list, send an e-mail message requesting a subscription to the URL address below.
	To send a message to the entire list, address it to: flashlife@netcom.com

`mailto:flashlife-request@netcom.com`

Cyberspace

alt.bbs

A Usenet newsgroup providing information and discussion about computer BBS systems & software.

Keywords:	BBS Systems, Cyberspace, Computers
Audience:	BBS Users
User Info:	To subscribe to this Usenet newsgroup, you need access to a newsreader.

`news:alt.bbs`

alt.cyberpunk

A Usenet newsgroup providing information and discussion about the high-tech low-life.

Keywords:	Computers, Cyberspace
Audience:	Hackers, Cybernauts, General Public
User Info:	To subscribe to this Usenet newsgroup, you need access to a newsreader.

`news:alt.cyberpunk`

Conference about Virtual Reality (The)

A conference on the WELL about cyberspace and virtual reality.

Keywords:	Virtual Reality, Art, Cyberspace
Audience:	Artists, Computer Programmers, Cyberpunks
Contact:	Peter Rothman avatarp@well.sf.ca.us
	To participate in a conference on the WELL, you must first establish an account on the WELL. To do so, start by typing: telnet well.sf.ca.us

`telnet://well.sf.ca.us`

THINKNET

Electronic newsletter on philosophy, systems theory, interdisciplinary studies, and thoughtful conversation in cyberspace.

Keywords:	Cyberspace, Systems Theory, Philosophy
Audience:	Philosophers, System Theorists
Contact:	Kent D. Palmer Ph.D. Internet: palmer@world.std.com
Details:	Free
User Info:	To subscribe, send an e-mail message to the URL address below consisting of a single line reading:
	SUB THINKNET YourFirstName YourLastName

`mailto:palmer@world.std.com`

Vigis-L ★★

A mailing list for the discussion of Virtual Reality and GIS (Geographic Information Systems).

Keywords: Virtual Reality, Geography, GIS (Geographic Information Systems), Cyberspace

Audience: Geographers, Cartographers, Cybernauts

Contact: Tom Edwards
navanax.u.washington.edu

User Info: To subscribe to the list, send an e-mail message to the URL address below consisting of a single line reading:

SUB vigis-l YourFirstName YourLastName.

To send a message to the entire list, address it to:
vigis@uwavm.u.washington.edu

`mailto:listserv@uwavm.u.washington.edu`

Virtual Reality Space ★★★

A collection of virtual reality information, including downloadable software tools from Silicon Graphics.

Keywords: Virtual Reality, Cyberspace, Software, Silicon Graphics

Sponsor: The University of Texas, Austin, Texas, USA

Audience: Virtual Reality Enthusiasts, Programmers

Contact: Jay Ashcraft
ashcraft@ccwf.cc.utexas.edu

`gopher://ftp.cc.utexas.edu`

`ftp://cc.utexas.edu`

Cycling

Physical Education & Recreation

A collection of information on sporting and recreational activities from aikido to windsurfing.

Keywords: Sports, Recreation, Aikido, Cycling, Scuba Diving, Windsurfing

Audience: Sports Enthusiasts, Fitness Enthusiasts

Contact: ctcadmin@ctc.ctc.edu

`gopher://ctc.ctc.edu`

CYFERNET (Child, Youth, and Family Education Network)

CYFERNET (Child, Youth, and Family Education Network)

This public information service supports child, youth, and family development programs.

Keywords: Education, Networks

Sponsor: Youth Development Information Center at the National Agricultural Library

Audience: Educators, Children, Families

Profile: CYFERNET contains information useful to child, youth, and family development professionals. Features include programs for children aged 5-8 years, youth-at-risk programs, community projects, and education.

Contact: jkane@nalusda.gov

Details: Free

`gopher://ra.esusda.gov/11/CYFER-net`

Czech Republic

CEE Environmental Libraries Database

A directory of over 300 libraries and environmental information centers in Central Eastern Europe that specialize in, or maintain significant collections of information about, the environment, ecology, sustainable living, or conservation. The database concentrates on six Central Eastern European countries: Bulgaria, Czech Republic, Hungary, Romania, Slovakia, and Poland.

Keywords: Central Eastern Europe, Environment, Sustainable Living, Bulgaria, Czech Republic, Hungary, Romania, Slovakia, Poland.

Sponsor: The Wladyslaw Poniecki Charitable Foundation, Inc.

Audience: Environmentalists, Green Movement, Librarians, Community Builders, Sustainable Living Specialists.

Profile: This database is the product of an Environmental Training Project (ETP) that was funded in 1992 by the US Agency for International Development as a 5-year cooperative agreement with a consortium headed by the University of Minnesota (US AID Cooperative Agreement Number EUR-0041-A-002-2020). Other members of the consortium include the University of Pittsburgh's Center for Hazardous Materials Research, The Institute for Sustainable Communities, and the World Wildlife Fund. The Wladyslaw Poniecki Charitable Foundation, Inc., was a subcontractor to the World Wildlife Fund and published the Directory of Libraries and Environmental Information Centers in Central Eastern Europe: A Locator/Directory. This gopher database consists of an electronic version of the printed directory, subsequently modified and updated online. Access to the data is facilitated by a WAIS search engine which makes it possible to retrieve information about libraries, subject area specializations, personnel, and so on.

Contact: Doug Kahn, CEDAR
kahn@pan.cedar.univie.ac.at

`gopher://gopher.poniecki.berkeley.edu`

EUnet Czechia

This is the information service of EUnet Czechia, the network service provider in the Czech Republic and contains information about top-level domains.

Keywords: Czech Republic

Audience: Czechs, General Public

Contact: gopher.eunet.cz

Details: Free

`http://www.eunet.cz`

Prague University of Economics Gopher Service ★★

Includes information about the University, integrative studies of economy, economic information, and public domain software.

Keywords: Czech Republic, Economics, Europe

Audience: Czechs, Economists

Contact: gopher@pub.vse.cz

Details: Free

`gopher://pub.vse.cz`

University of Nebraska at Lincoln Library

The library's holdings are large and wide-ranging and contain significant collections in many fields..

Keywords: Slovak Republic, Czech Republic, Folklore, Military History, Latvia, Law (Tax), Law (US)

Audience: General Public, Researchers, Librarians, Document Delivery Professionals

Contact: Anita Cook

Details: Free
Expect: login, Send: library

`telnet://unllib.unl.edu`

D

Dallas Stars

Dallas Stars ★

Discussion of the Dallas Stars (of the National Hockey League) and their farm clubs.

Keywords: Hockey, Sports

Audience: NHL Enthusiasts

Details: Free

User Info: To subscribe to the list, send an e-mail message requesting a subscription to the URL address below.

To send a message to the entire list, address it to: hamlet@u.washington.edu

Notes: Please include the word "DSTARS" in your subject line and include your name and preferred e-mail address in the body of your message.

mailto:hamlet@u.washington.edu

Dance

Arts

An umbrella arts conference on the WELL.

Keywords: Art, Music, Dance

Audience: Artists, Dancers, Musicians, Photographers

Profile: A general arts conference that includes listings of show opportunities, books, and events, as well as discussion about art and art criticism.

Contact: Tim Collins

telnet://well.sf.ca.us

Ballroom ★

Discussion of any aspect of ballroom dancing, including places to dance, special events, clubs, ballroom dance music, dances, and steps.

Keywords: Ballroom Dancing, Dancing

Audience: Ballroom Dancers

Contact: Shahrukh Merchant
ballroom-request@athena.mit.edu

Details: Free

User Info: To subscribe to the list, send an e-mail message requesting a subscription to the URL address below.

To send a message to the entire list, address it to: ballroom@athena.mit.edu

mailto:ballroom-request@athena.mit.edu

Folk-dancing

A discussion of folk dancing, including contra, square, western square, morris, cajun, and barn dancing.

Keywords: Dance, Folk Dance

Audience: Dancers, Folk Dancers

Contact: Terry J. Wood
tjw+@pitt.edu

Details: Free

User Info: To subscribe to the list, send an e-mail message requesting a subscription to the URL address below

To send a message to the entire list, address it to: fdml@pitt.edu

Notes: Please note that the Folk Dancing Mailing List (fdml) operates in conjunction with the Usenet newsgroup rec.folk-dancing. When subscribing to the FDML, please include several computer mail addresses and a postal mail address (or phone number).

mailto:tjw+@pitt.edu

Morris ★

A discussion list related to Morris Dancing, including Cotswold, Border, Northwest, Rapper, Longsword, Abbots Bromley, Garland, and similar forms of English dance along with the accompanying music and traditions.

Keywords: Morris Dancing, England, Dance

Audience: Morris Dancers

Details: Free

User Info: To subscribe to the list, send an e-mail message requesting subscription to the URL address below.

mailto:morris@suvm.acs.syr.edu

rec.arts.dance ★

A Usenet newsgroup providing information and discussion about all types of dance.

Keywords: Dance, Fine Arts

Audience: Dancers, Dance Enthusiasts, Choreographers

User Info: To subscribe to this Usenet newsgroup, you need access to a newsreader.

news: rec.arts.dance

Strathspey ★

A forum for the discussion of all aspects of Scottish Country Dancing, e.g. dancing technique.

Keywords: Dance, Scotland, Scottish Dance

Audience: Dancers, Dance Historians
Contact: owner-strathspey@math.uni-frankfurt.de
Details: Free
User Info: To subscribe to the list, send an e-mail message requesting a subscription to the URL address below.

To send a message to the entire list, address it to: strathspey@math.uni-frankfurt.de

`mailto:strathspey-request@math.uni-frankfurt.de`

University of New Hampshire Videotex Library ★★

The library's holdings are large and wide-ranging and contain significant collections in many fields.

Keywords: Dance, Folk Music, Milne (A.A., Collection of), Galway (Ireland)
Audience: Researchers, Students, General Public
Contact: Robin Tuttle r_tuttle1@unhh.unh.edu
Details: Free
Expect: USERNAME; Send: Student (no password required). Control-z to log off.

`telnet://unhvt@unh.edu`

Dante

Dartmouth Dante Database Library ★★

This database is focused entirely on the works of Dante.

Keywords: Dante
Audience: Dante Scholars, Educators (College, University)
Details: Free
User Info: User Info: Expect: login, Send: wolfpac

`telnet://dartmouth.edu`

Dark Shadows

dark-shadows ★

Dark Shadows was a daily soap opera that ran on ABC in the late Sixties (ending in 1971). It had a Gothic feel to it and featured storylines involving the supernatural.

Keywords: Television, Television Series
Audience: Horror Enthusiasts, Soap Opera Enthusiasts
Contact: Bernie Roehl shadows-request@sunee.waterloo.ca

Details: Free
User Info: To subscribe to the list, send an e-mail message requesting a subscription to the URL address below.

To send a message to the entire list, address it to: shadows@usunee.waterloo.ca

`news:alt.horror`

`news:rec.arts.tv.soaps`

Dartmouth College Library

Dartmouth College Library ★★★

The library's holdings are large and wide-ranging and contain significant collections in many fields.

Keywords: Calligraphy, Cervantes (Miguel de), Railroads, Polar Regions, Frost (Robert), Shakespeare (William), Spanish Plays
Audience: General Public, Researchers, Librarians, Document Delivery Professionals
Contact: Katharina Klemperer kathy.klemperer@dartmouth.edu
Details: Free
User Info: User Info: Expect: login, Send: wolfpac

`telnet://lib.dartmouth.edu`

Data General

dg-users

The mailing list is concerned with the technical details of Data General, its O/Ss, and the cornucopia of hardware they supply and support.

Keywords: Computer Hardware, Data General
Audience: Computer Hardware Users
Contact: brian@ilinx.wimsey.com
User Info: To subscribe to the list, send an e-mail message requesting a subscription to the URL address below.

To send a message to the entire list, address it to: dg-users-request@ilinx.wimsey.com

`mailto:dg-users-request@ilinx.wimsey.com`

data-exp

data-exp

The mail list server provides an open forum for users to discuss the Visualization Data Explorer Package. It contains three files at the moment: a. FAQ, b. summary, and c. forum.

Keywords: Computing, Software, Hardware, Visualization Data Explorer Package
Audience: Computer Users
User Info: To subscribe to the list, send an e-mail message requesting a subscription to the URL address below.

To send a message to the entire list, address it to: stein@watson.ibm.com

`mailto:stein@watson.ibm.com`

Database Management

Big-DB ★

Discussions pertaining to large databases (generally greater than 1 million records) and large database management systems such as IMS, DB2, and CCA's Model/204.

Keywords: Databases, Database Management
Audience: Database Users, Database Managers
Contact: Fareed Asad-Harooni big-DB@midway.uchicago.edu
Details: Free
User Info: To subscribe to the list, send an e-mail message requesting a subscription to the URL address below.

`mailto:big-DB@midway.uchicago.edu`

Databases

Barron's Guide to Accessing On-Line Bibliographic Databases ★★

A comprehensive listing of publicly-accessible online libraries, including login instructions for each site.

Keywords: Libraries, Databases
Sponsor: University of North Texas
Audience: Researchers, Library Users, Librarians
Contact: Billy Barron billy@unt.edu

`gopher://alf.zfn.uni-bremen.de/Allgemeine`

Big-DB ★

Discussions pertaining to large databases (generally greater than 1 million records) and large database management systems such as IMS, DB2, and CCA's Model/204.

Keywords: Databases, Database Management
Audience: Database Users, Database Managers
Contact: Fareed Asad-Harooni big-DB@midway.uchicago.edu

User Info:	To subscribe to the list, send an e-mail message requesting a subscription to the URL address below.
Details:	Free

`mailto:big-DB@midway.uchicago.edu`

Britannica Online

This web site provides an information service for Encyclopaedia Britannica, Inc. Its database allows for keyword searches, and also includes experimental articles.

Keywords:	Information Retrieval, Databases
Sponsor:	Encyclopaedia Britannica, Inc.
Audience:	Researchers, Educators, Students
Contact:	support@eb.com
Details:	Costs

`http://www.eb.com`

DIALOG Bluesheets

This database contains records representing the Bluesheet documentation issued for all databases on the DIALOG Information Retrieval Service.

Keywords:	Databases
Sponsor:	Dialog Information Services, Inc., Palo Alto, CA, USA
Audience:	Dialog Users, Market Researchers
Profile:	All databases are represented, including bibliographic files, complete-text files, menu-driven files, and gateway services. Each record represents a Bluesheet and contains traditional first-page information, including a file description, subject coverage, sources, file data, origin, and legal terms and conditions. All searchable indexes, display codes, field names, examples, sorts, limits, report fields, map fields, predefined formats, and direct record access information are included. Source information for the DIALOG Bluesheets database is derived from print Bluesheet documentation. Additional information not found on the printed Bluesheets is also included, such as the availability of DIALOG AlertSM service, Classroom Instruction Program databases, type of data in the file, document types indexed in the database represented, DIALINDEX category acronyms, and annual accession number ranges for files having accession number limits.
Contact:	Dialog in the US at (800) 334-2564, Dialog internationally at country-specific locations.
User Info:	To subscribe, contact Dialog directly.
Notes:	Coverage: same as for all Dialog databases; updated weekly.

`telnet://dialog.com`

ERIC (Educational Resources Information Center)

ERIC is a database of short abstracts and information about education-related topics of interest to teachers and administrators.

Keywords:	Education, Databases
Sponsor:	(Office of Educational Research and Development), US Department of Education, Department of Education (ED)
Audience:	Educators, Administrators
Profile:	ERIC is the complete database on educational materials from the Educational Resources Information Center in Washington, DC. The database corresponds to two print indexes: Resources in Education, which is concerned with identifying the most significant and timely education research reports; and Current Index to Journals in Education, an index of more than 700 periodicals of interest to every segment of the teaching profession.
Details:	Costs
	ERIC can be accessed in a variety of ways, for example, through CARL (Colorado Alliance of Research Libraries), through the University of Saskatchewan
	(Request: sklib username: sonia)
	ERIC can also be accessed by WAIS if you have WAIS installed on your local computer.

`telnet://pac.carl.org`

`telnet://skdevel12.usask.ca`

foxpro-l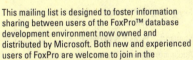

This mailing list is designed to foster information sharing between users of the FoxPro™ database development environment now owned and distributed by Microsoft. Both new and experienced users of FoxPro are welcome to join in the discussions.

Keywords:	Databases, Computers, Microsoft Corp.
Audience:	Database Users, Microsoft FoxPro Users, Software Engineers
Contact:	Chris O'Neill coneill@heaven.polarbear.rankin-inlet.nt.ca
Details:	Free
User Info:	To subscribe to the list, send an e-mail message requesting a subscription to the URL address below.
	To send a message to the entire list, address it to: foxpro-l@polarbear.rankin-inlet.nt.ca

`mailto:fileserv@polarbear.rankin-inlet.nt.ca`

GIS Master Bibliography Project

A bibliography of GIS literature encompassing journal articles, conference proceedings, books, and technical reports.

Keywords:	GIS, Databases
Sponsor:	Ohio State University - Department of Geography and others
Audience:	GIS Users, Researchers, Students
Contact:	Dr. Duane Marble marble.1@osu.edu
Details:	Free

`ftp://128.146.209.34/biblio`

Internet Libraries (Gopher)

The site maintains the most current possible list of all library catalogs accessible on the Internet.

Keywords:	Libraries, Databases, Internet, Information Retrieval
Audience:	Reseacher, Students, Librarians
Contact:	Gopherlib gopherlib@gopher.yale.edu

`gopher://yaleinfo.yale.edu`

Links to Many Databases

A collection of links to over 40 databases covering a wide variety of subjects ranging from Postmodern Culture to the 1990 Census.

Keywords:	Databases, Research
Sponsor:	University of Texas, Austin, Texas, USA
Audience:	Researchers, General Public
Contact:	remark@ftp.cc.utexas.edu

`gopher://ftp.cc.utexas.edu`

MS-Access

A list for the discussion of MS (Microsoft) Access topics, including Access Basic questions, reviews, rumors, and so on.

Keywords:	Microsoft Access Program, Databases
Audience:	MS-Access Users
Details:	Free
User Info:	To subscribe to the list, send an e-mail message requesting subscription to the URL address below.

`mailto:ms-access-request@eunet.co.at`

NASA/IPAC Extragalactic Database (NED)

Contains positions, basic data, and over 500,000 names for 250,000 extragalactic objects, as well as some 450,000 bibliographic references to 21,000 published papers, and 25,000 notes from catalogs and other publications.

Keywords:	Astronomy, Databases	
Sponsor:	Jet Propulsory Lab/ Infrared Processing and Analysis Center	
Audience:	Astronomers, Scientists	
Profile:	Uses a VT100 or X-based interface.	
Contact:	G. Helou, B. Madore, M. Schmitz ned@ipac.caltech.edu	
Details:	Free	
User Info:	Telnet to URL address below; Expect: login; Send: ned	
Notes:	sshare@cscns.com service@cscns.com	

`telnet://ned@ned.ipac.caltech.edu`

`ftp://ned.ipac.caltech.edu/pub/ned`

Progress

Discussion of the Progress RDBMS (Relational Database Management System).

Keywords:	Databases, Computing
Audience:	Computer Users, Business Students
Contact:	Progress-list-request@math.niu.edu
Details:	Free
User Info:	To subscribe to the list, send an e-mail message requesting a subscription to the URL address below. To send a message to the entire list, address it to: progress-list@math.niu.edu

`mailto:Progress-list-request@math.niu.edu`

Research Databases and Resources by Subject

A collection of databases on over forty subjects, ranging from Anthropology to Women's Studies.

Keywords:	Databases, Academic Research
Sponsor:	University of California at Berkeley
Audience:	Researchers, General Public
Contact:	Gopher Manager gophcom@infolib.lib.berkeley.edu

`gopher://umslvma.umsl.edu/library/Subjects/Biology/Bioformt/Biodbs<Heads Classification>`

`gopher://infolib.lib.berkeley.edu`

SABINET (South African Bibliographic and Information Network)

This gopher offers information searches from a variety of electronic databases, as well as for library locations and availability of books and periodicals.

Keywords:	South Africa, Databases, Networks
Audience:	South African Internet Surfers
Contact:	hennie@info1.sabinet.co.za
Details:	Free

`gopher://info2.sabinet.co.za`

The Tumor Gene Database ★★

A database containing information about genes associated with tumorigenesis and cellular transformation.

Keywords:	Genetics, Diseases, Biomedical Research, Databases
Sponsor:	Department of Cell Biology, Baylor College of Medicine
Audience:	Biomedical Researchers
Contact:	David Steffen, Ph.D. steffen@bcm.tmc.edu

`gopher://mbcr.bcm.tmc.edu`

U.S. Patent and Trademark Office Database ★★

A database of patents issued in 1994 by the U.S. Patent and Trademark Office, including a searchable index.

Keywords:	Patents, Databases, Inventions, Business
Sponsor:	New York University School of Business
Audience:	Inventors, General Public
Contact:	questions@town.hall.org

`gopher://town.hall.org/patent`

White House Information Service ★★★★

An outstanding database of current White House information, from 1992 to the present.

Keywords:	White House, Politics, President (US), Database
Sponsor:	Texas A & M University
Audience:	General Public
Profile:	Much of the older information on this site was obtained from the clinton@marist.bitnet listserv list or the alt.politics.clinton Usenet newsgroup, both of which receive the information indirectly via the MIT White House information server. Newer and current material is received directly from the MIT distribution list. The menu includes a searchable database and headings such as Domestic Affairs (Health Care, Technology, and so on), Press Briefings and Conferences, the President's Daily Schedule, and many more.
Contact:	whadmin@tamu.edu
Details:	Free

`gopher://tamuts.tamu.edu/11/.dir/president.dir`

Datsuns

datsun-roadsters

A mailing list for discussing any and all aspects of the owning, showing, repairing, driving, and so on, of Datsun roadsters.

Keywords:	Datsuns, Automobiles
Audience:	Datsun Owners, Automobile Enthusiasts
Contact:	Mark J. Bradakis datsun-roadsters-request@autox.team.net datsun-roadsters-request@hoosier.utah.edu
Details:	Free
User Info:	To subscribe to the list, send an e-mail message requesting a subscription to the URL address below. To send a message to the entire list, address it to: datsun-roadsters-request@autox.team.net

`mailto:datsun-roadsters-request@autox.team.net`

DC-MOTSS

DC-MOTSS

DC-MOTSS is a social mailing list for the gay, lesbian, and bisexual folks who live in the Washington Metropolitan Area—everything within approximately 50 miles of The Mall.

Keywords:	Gays, Lesbians, Bisexuality, Washington DC
Audience:	Gays, Lesbians, Bisexuals, Washington DC Residents
Contact:	DC-MOTSS-request@vector.intercon.com
Details:	Free
User Info:	To subscribe to the list, send an e-mail message requesting a subscription to the URL address below. To send a message to the entire list, address it to: DC-MOTSS-request@vector.intercon.com

`mailto:DC-MOTSS-request@vector.intercon.com`

DCRaves

DCRaves

One of several regional rave-related mailing lists, DCRaves covers the Washington, DC, area exclusively. Archives are available through the listserv, FTP, or gopher at american.edu.

Keywords:	Raves, Washington DC

Audience:	Ravers
Details:	Free
User Info:	To subscribe to the list, send an e-mail message to the URL address shown below consisting of a single line reading: SUB dcraves YourFirstName YourLastName To send a message to the entire list, address it to: dcraves@american.edu

`mailto:listserv@american.edu`

DDN (Defense Data Network)

DDN Management Bulletin ★

A means of communicating official policy, procedures, and other information of concern to management personnel at DDN facilities.

Keywords:	Defense, DDN
Sponsor:	DDN Network Info Center
Audience:	Defense Analysts
Contact:	nic@nic.ddn.mil
Details:	Free

`ftp://nic.ddn.mil`

DDN New User Guide ★

Defense Data Network (DDN) guide for new users.

Keywords:	Internet, Internet Guides, Defense, Security, DDN
Audience:	Internet Surfers
Details:	Free
	File is: netinfo/nug.doc

`ftp://nic.ddn.mil/netinfo`

DDTs-Users

DDTs-Users

The DDTs-Users mailing list is for discussions of issues related to the DDTs defect-tracking software from QualTrak, including software, methods, mechanisms, techniques, general usage tips, policies, bugs, and bug workarounds.

Keywords:	Software, Software Defects
Audience:	Computer Users
Contact:	ddts-users-request@bigbird.bu.edu
User Info:	To subscribe to the list, send an e-mail message requesting a subscription to the URL address below. To send a message to the entire list, address it to: ddts-users-request@bigbird.bu.edu

`mailto:ddts-users-request@bigbird.bu.edu`

de Bono (Edward)

de Bono

This is a discussion list concerning the work of Edward de Bono. Also provides help with teaching the CoRT Thinking Program, and Six Thinking Hats.

Keywords:	de Bono (Edward), Education (Alternative), Creativity
Audience:	Teachers, Students, Management Trainers
Contact:	Rosa Casarez Casarez@netcom.net

`mailto: casarez@netcom.com`

dead-runners

dead-runners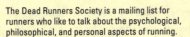

The Dead Runners Society is a mailing list for runners who like to talk about the psychological, philosophical, and personal aspects of running.

Keywords:	Running, Sports
Audience:	Runners, Athletes
Contact:	Christopher Mark Conn dead-runners-request@unx.sas.com
Details:	Free
User Info:	To subscribe to the list, send an e-mail message requesting a subscription to the URL address below. To send a message to the entire list, address it to: dead-runners-request@unx.sas.com

`mailto:dead-runners-request@unx.sas.com`

Deafness

Deaf Gopher ★★

Gopher menu of deaf resources in the State of Michigan.

Keywords:	Disabilities, Deafness, Health
Sponsor:	Michigan State University
Audience:	Deaf and Disabled People, Health Care Professionals, Activists, Policy Makers, Rehabilitation Counselors, Therapists
Profile:	A small but useful menu of deaf resources that includes a collection of files in essay and/or report form about a variety of historical and cultural aspects of deafness.
Contact:	Gary LaPointe deafgopher@ah3.cal.msu.edu
Details:	Free

`gopher://cl.msu.edu/11/msu/dept/deaf`

Disability-Related Resources ★★

A collection of information that includes newsletters for deaf/blind issues, electronic resources for the deaf, and a section on Chronic Fatigue Syndrome.

Keywords:	Disabilities, Deafness, Blindness, Chronic Fatigue Syndrome
Sponsor:	University of Washington DO-IT Program
Audience:	Deaf and Disabled People, Health Care Professionals
Contact:	Sheryl Burgstahler, Ph.D. doit@u.washington.edu

`gopher://hawking.u.washington.edu`

Deborah Harry and Blondie Information Service

Deborah Harry and Blondie Information Service ★

An information service on everything and anything regarding Deborah Harry and Blondie, including tour information, recordings/films release information, and so on.

Keywords:	Rock Music, Harry (Deborah), Musical Groups
Audience:	Rock Music Enthusiasts, Deborah Harry Enthusiasts
Contact:	gunter@yarrow.wt.uwa.oz.au
Details:	Free
User Info:	To subscribe to the list, send an e-mail message requesting a subscription to the URL address below. To send a message to the entire list, address it to: gunter@yarrow.wt.uwa.oz.au

`mailto:gunter@yarrow.wt.uwa.oz.au`

DEC

DECNEWS for Education and Research ★★★

Monthly electronic newsletter from Digital Equipment Corporation (DEC) summarizing announcements of its products, programs, and applications of interest to computer users in the academic and research communities.

Keywords:	Computers, Education
Sponsor:	Digital Equipment Corp.
Audience:	Computer Users, Educators, Researchers
Contact:	Mary Hoffmann decnews@mr4dec.enet.dec.com
Details:	Free

User Info:	To subscribe, send an e-mail message to the address below consisting of a single line reading:
	SUB DECNews YourFirstName YourLastName
	To send a message to the entire list, address it to: DECNews@ubvm.buffalo.edu

`mailto:listserv@ubvm.buffalo.edu`

DECnews-EDU

DECNEWS for Education and Research is a monthly electronic publication from Digital Equipment Corporation's Education Business Unit for the education and research communities worldwide.

Keywords:	Education, Computers, DEC
Audience:	Educators, Researchers
Contact:	Anne Marie McDonald decnews@mr4dec.enet.dec.com
Details:	Free
User Info:	To subscribe to the list, send an e-mail message requesting a subscription to the URL address below.
	To send a message to the entire list, address it to: decnews@mr4dec.enet.dec.com

`mailto:decnews@mr4dec.enet.dec.com`

DECnews-PR

DECnews for Press and Analysts is an Internet-based distribution of all Digital Equipment Corporation press releases. This is a one-way mailing list. Approximately eight press releases per week.

Keywords:	DEC, Computers
Audience:	Computing Consultants, Computing Analysts
Contact:	Russ Jones decnews-pr-request@pa.dec.com
User Info:	To subscribe to the list, send an e-mail message requesting a subscription to the URL address below.
	To send a message to the entire list, address it to: decnews-pr-request@pa.dec.com
User Info:	To subscribe, send e-mail to decnews-pr@pa.dec.com with a subject line of Subject: subscribe. Please include your name and telephone number in the body of the subscription request.

`mailto:decnews-pr-request@pa.dec.com`

DECnews-UNIX

DECnews for UNIX is published by Digital Equipment Corporation every three weeks and contains product and service information of interest to the Digital UNIX community.

Keywords:	DEC, UNIX, Computers
Audience:	UNIX Users
Contact:	Russ Jones decnews-unix-request@pa.dec.com
User Info:	To subscribe to the list, send an e-mail message requesting a subscription to the URL address below.
	To send a message to the entire list, address it to: decnews-unix-request@pa.dec.com
User Info:	To subscribe, send e-mail to decnews-unix@pa.dec.com with a subject line of Subject: subscribe abstract. Please include your name and telephone number in the body of the subscription request.

`mailto:decnews-unix-request@pa.dec.com`

DECstation-managers

Fast-turnaround troubleshooting tool for managers of RISC DECstations.

Keywords:	DEC, Computers
Audience:	Computer Systems Analysts/Programmers, Engineers
Contact:	decstation-managers-request@ornl.gov
User Info:	To subscribe to the list, send an e-mail message to the URL address shown below consisting of a single line reading:
	SUB decstation-manager YourFirstName YourLastName
	To send a message to the entire list, address it to: decstation-manager@msu.edu

`mailto:majordomo@ornl.gov`

DECUS

DECuserve-journal

A monthly digest of technical discussions that take place on the DECUS conferencing system, open to anyone who is interested in Digital Equipment topics, "3rd party" topics, and connectivity topics.

Keywords:	DECUS, Conferencing System
Audience:	Conferencing System Users
Contact:	Sharon Frey frey@eisner.decus.org
User Info:	To subscribe to the list, send an e-mail message requesting a subscription to the URL address below.
	To send a message to the entire list, address it to: frey@eisner.decus.org

`mailto:frey@eisner.decus.org`

Deed Transfers

ASSETS (Real Estate Tax Assessor and Deed Transfer Records)

The RealEstate Tax Assessor and Deed Transfer Records (ASSETS) library contains information compiled from real property records.

Keywords:	Real Estate, Property, Tax Assessor, Deed Transfers, Records
Audience:	Lawyers
Profile:	The ASSETS library contains a variety of real estate information, including asset ownership, property address, owner's mailing address, assessed valuation, current market value, and recent property sales and deed transfers. Information is collected from county tax assessors' and recorders' offices nationwide and compiled by TRW REDI Property Data. The ASSETS library also contains a variety of boat and aircraft registration information.
Contact:	Mead New Sales Group at (800) 227-4908 or (513) 859-5398 inside the US, or (513) 865-7981 for all inquiries outside the US.
User Info:	To subscribe, contact Mead directly.
	To examine the Nexis user guide, you can access it at the ftp site of the University of Texas at Austin at the URL address: ftp://ftp.cc.utexas.edu
	The files are in: /pub/ref-services/LEXIS

`telnet://nex.meaddata.com`

`http://www.meaddata.com`

Defense

DDN Management Bulletin

A means of communicating official policy, procedures, and other information of concern to management personnel at DDN facilities.

Keywords:	Defense, DDN
Sponsor:	DDN Network Info Center
Audience:	Defense Industry Followers
Contact:	NIC@NIC.DDN.MIL
Details:	Free

`ftp//nic.ddn.mil`

DDN New User Guide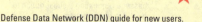

Defense Data Network (DDN) guide for new users.

Keywords: Internet, Internet Guides, Defense, Security

Audience: Internet Surfers
Details: Free
File is: netinfo/nug.doc
`ftp://nic.ddn.mil/netinfo`

DMS/FI Market Intelligence Reports

DMS/FI Market Intelligence Reports is the largest collection of unclassified defense and aerospace information available from any single source.

Keywords: Defense, Aerospace
Sponsor: Forecast International/DMS, Newtown, CT, USA
Audience: Defense Analysts
Profile: This file contains the most comprehensive and up-to-date full-text data and analysis for the industry and provides users with valuable information on defense budgets, aerospace and weapons programs, power systems, companies (US and international), agencies, or countries that are involved in the aerospace/defense industry. File 589 contains a great deal of information relative to civil and commercial programs. Reports provide detailed and extensive information such as forecasts, major activity, funding, inventories, location, and much more. This information is gathered from such diverse sources as government documents, civil and defense journals, manufacturers, and field interviews with key industry people. This database is vital to anyone involved in market research, business development, or program management in the aerospace/defense industry.
Contact: Dialog in the US at (800) 334-2564, Dialog internationally at country-specific locations.
User Info: To subscribe, contact Dialog directly.
Notes: Coverage: Current; updated weekly.
`telnet://dialog.com`

Jane's Defense & Aerospace News/Analysis

This file provides articles that summarize, highlight, and interpret worldwide events in the defense and aerospace industry.

Keywords: Defense, Aerospace, News Media
Sponsor: Jane's Information Group, Alexandria, VA US
Audience: Aerospace Industry Professionals
Profile: The database contains the complete text of the following publications: Jane's Defense Weekly, International Defense Review, Jane's Intelligence Review (formerly Jane's Soviet Intelligence Review), Interavia Aerospace Review, and Jane's Airport Review. File 587 also contains the complete text of DMS newsletters, which ceased publication in 1989.

Contact: Dialog in the US at (800) 334-2564, Dialog internationally at country-specific locations.
User Info: To subscribe, contact Dialog directly.
Notes: Coverage: 1982 to the present; updated weekly.
`telnet://dialog.com`

Lockheed Missiles & Space Company

A web site containing information about Lockheed Missiles and Space Company, a major aerospace and defense company specializing in the development of space systems, missiles, and other high technology products. Includes company information and press releases.

Keywords: Defense, Aerospace
Sponsor: The Lockheed Palo Alto Artificial Intelligence Center
Audience: Aerospace Industry Professionals
`http://www.lmsc.lockheed.com`

NATO

Online version of The NATO Handbook, which recommends changes for the future of the North Atlantic Treaty Organization in light of decreasing defense resources.

Keywords: NATO, Guidelines, Defense
Sponsor: The NATO Office of Information and Press
Audience: Governent Officials, Military Personnel, Historians
Details: Free
Select from menu as appropriate.
`gopher://wiretap.spies.com`

Delaware

University of Delaware Libraries (DELCAT)

The library's holdings are large and wide-ranging and contain significant collections in many fields.

Keywords: Literature (American), Hemingway (Ernest), Papermaking (History of), Chemistry (History of), Literature (Irish), Delaware
Audience: General Public, Researchers, Librarians, Document Delivery Professionals
Contact: Stuart Glogoff
epo27855@udacsvm.bitnet
Details: Free
User Info: Expect: prompt, Send: RETURN 2-3 times
`telnet://delcat.udel.edu`

`telnet://delcat.acs.udel.edu`

Delphes European Business

Delphes European Business

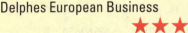

This is a French database that provides information on international markets, products, industries, and companies from a European perspective.

Keywords: Business, Europe
Sponsor: Chamber of Commerce and Industry of Paris and The French Assembly of the Chambers of Commerce and Industry, Paris, France
Audience: Business Professionals, Business Analysts
Profile: Abstracts are produced by approximately 60 local organizations grouped into two networks, CCIP (Chamber of Commerce and Industry of Paris) and ACFCI (French Assembly of the Chambers of Commerce and Industry), which collect and consolidate the information into the Delphes database. Delphes contains bibliographic citations and informative abstracts from over 900 European trade journals, newspapers, and business periodicals, in French, English, Italian, German, or Spanish. Titles are in the original language; abstracts are in French. A comprehensive classification scheme in English, French, and Spanish is used to index documents covered. Geographic coverage is 45% France, 35% Europe, and 20% is devoted to other countries. In addition, about 1,000 new books, corporate and business directories, and reports are reviewed each year.
Contact: Dialog in the US at (800) 334-2564, Dialog internationally at country-specific locations.
User Info: To subscribe, contact Dialog directly.
Notes: Coverage: 1980 to the present; updated weekly.
`telnet://dialog.com`

Delphi

Delphi

Delphi is an online service provider.
Keywords: Internet
Sponsor: Delphi, NewsCorp. Technologies
Audience: Internet Users
Details: Costs
`telnet://delphi.com`

Democracy

Historical Documents

A collection of historical documents (with particular emphasis on freedom and democracy) ranging from the Magna Carta to Nelson Mandela's Inauguration Speech.

Keywords: History (World), Democracy
Sponsor: The Queens Borough Public Library
Audience: Historians, Activists, General Public

gopher://vax.queens.lib.ny.us/Social Sciences/Historical Documents

Political Platforms of the US

Full text of various documents including the Democratic platform of 1992, the Jerry Brown positions of 1992, the Libertarian platform of 1990, and more.

Keywords: Politics (US), Government (US Federal), Democracy, Libertarian Politics
Audience: Politicians, Grass-Roots Organizers, Journalists
Details: Free

gopher://wiretap.spies.com/11/Gov/Platform

Democratic Socialists of America

DSA-LGB

DSA-LGB is a mailing list for members of the Lesbian/Gay/Bisexual Commission of the Democratic Socialists of America, and for others interested in similar concerns.

Keywords: Democratic Socialists of America, Gay, Lesbian
Audience: Democratic Socialists, Gays, Lesbians
Contact: DSA-LGB-request@midway.uchicago.edu
User Info: To subscribe to the list, send an e-mail message requesting a subscription to the URL address below.

To send a message to the entire list, address it to: DSA-LGB-request@midway.uchicago.edu

mailto:DSA-LGB-request@midway.uchicago.edu

Demography

1991 Census of Population Documentation

This gopher provides Canadian Census information from 1991 including geographic and demographic information.

Keywords: Census Data, Canada, Demography, Geography
Audience: Canadians, Researchers, Demographers
Contact: David McCallum
carl@acadvm1.uottawa.ca

gopher://alpha.epas.utoronto.ca/Data Library/Census of Population

ANU (Australian National University) Asian-Settlements Database

A searchable database containing abstracts of theses and research studies provided by the Asian Institute of Technology, relating to issues of demography and social geography in Asia.

Keywords: Asian Studies, Demography, Geography
Sponsor: The COOMBSQUEST Social Sciences & Humanities Information Facility at ANU (Australian National University), Canberra, Australia
Audience: Asia Studies Instructors, Demographers, Geographers
Contact: Dr. T. Matthew Ciolek
coombspapers@coombs.anu.edu.au
Details: Free

gopher://cheops.anu.edu.au/Coombs-db/ANU-Asian-Settlements.src

http://coombs.anu.edu.au/WWWVL-AsianStudies.html

ANU (Australian National University) Demography and Publications Database

A WAIS database of publications on demography by researchers from Australian National University.

Keywords: Demography
Sponsor: Research Schools of Social Sciences & Pacific and Asian Studies, ANU (Australian National University), Canberra, Australia
Audience: Demographers
Contact: demography@anu.edu.au

waissrc:/Coombs-db/ANU-Demography-Publications.src

gopher://cheops.anu.edu.au/7waissrc/Coombs-db/ANU-Demography-Publications.src

U.S. Bureau of the Census Gopher

A gopher offering official Census data and services direct from the Census Bureau.

Keywords: Census, Demography, Statistics
Sponsor: U.S. Census Bureau
Audience: Journalists, Government Officials, General Public
Profile: A wealth of demographic and economic data from the Census Bureau. Information available includes population estimates, financial data from state and local governments, and assorted statistical briefs. This gopher also has details on the offices, programs, and personnel of the Bureau itself, as well as links to other federal information systems and sources of Census data.
Contact: gatekeeper@census.gov
Details: Images, Free

gopher://gopher.census.gov

http://www.census.gov

Denmark

DENet Information Server

This is the gopher of the Danish national academic network, which is located at the Danish Computer Centre for Research and Education (UNI-C).

Keywords: Education, Denmark, Libraries
Audience: Researchers, Educators
Profile: This gopher provides DENet information and statistics, UNI-C information, directory services and phone books, pointers to Danish electronic libraries and gophers, an index of major Danish FTP archives, and news in Danish.
Contact: Steen.Linden@uni-c.dk
Details: Free

gopher://gopher.denet.dk

Denmark's Library for Medicine and Science

Keywords: Science, Medicine, Libraries, Denmark
Audience: Scientists, Health Care Professionals, Medical Researchers
Details: Free
At the CCL>prompt type DIA ENG for English interface.

telnet://cosmos.bib.dk

Dentistry

Dental Information Area

A collection of dental information, including a selection of related educational software and dental informatics materials.

Keywords: Dentistry, Health Care, Informatics
Sponsor: Columbia School of Oral and Dental Surgery
Audience: Dentists, Medical Students, Health Care Professionals
Contact: Dr. John Zimmerman
jlz4@columbia.edu

`gopher://cuhsla.cpmc.columbia.edu/health.sci/dental.toc`

MEDLINE

MEDLINE is a major source of bibliographic biomedical literature. The MEDLINE database encompasses information from three printed indexes (Index Medicus, Index to Dental Literature and the International Nursing Index) as well as additional information not published in the Index Medicus.

Keywords: Biomedicine, Dentistry, Nursing, Medicine
Sponsor: U.S. National Library of Medicine
Audience: Librarians, Researchers, Physicians, Students
Contact: CDP Technologies Sales Department (800)950-2035, extension 400
User Info: To subscribe, contact CDP Technologies directly

`telnet://cdplus@cdplus.com`

University of Texas Health Science Center at San Antonio Library

The library's holdings are large and wide-ranging and contain significant collections in many fields.

Keywords: Allied Health, Dentistry, Nursing, Veterinary Science, Ambulatory Care, Obstetrics/Gynecology, Pediatrics
Audience: Researchers, Students, General Public
Details: Free
User Info: Expect: Login, Send: LIS

`telnet://athena.uthscsa.edu`

Deos-L

Deos-L

A mailing list intended to promote communication among distance educators, to disseminate information and requests about distance education around the world, and to discuss issues raised in the electronic journal DEOSNEWS.

Keywords: Education (Distance), Education (Continuing)
Sponsor: The American Center for the Study of Distance Education, Pennsylvania State University, Pennsylvania, USA
Audience: Distance Educators, Administrators
User Info: To subscribe to the list, send an e-mail message to the URL address below consisting of a single line reading:

SUB deos-l YourFirstName YourLastName

To send a message to the entire list, address it to: deos-l@psuvm.psu.edu

`mailto:listserv@psuvm.psu.edu`

deosnews (Distance Education Online Symposium)

deosnews (Distance Education Online Symposium)

The Distance Education Online Symposium publishes The American Journal of Distance Education.

Keywords: Education (Adult), Education (Distance), Education (Continuing)
Sponsor: Distance Education Online Symposium, American Center for the Study of Distance Education, Pennsylvania State University, State College, PA
Audience: Educators, Administrators, Researchers
Details: Free
User Info: To subscribe to the journal, send an e-mail message to the URL address shown below consisting of a single line reading:

SUB deosnews YourFirstName YourLastName

`mailto:listserv@psuvm.bitnet`

Department of Defense

National Technology Transfer Center (NTTC)

A federally-funded national network to apply government research to commercial applications.

Keywords: Technology, Technology Transfer, Research and Development, Business and Industry, Department of Defense, Government (US)
Sponsor: National Technology Transfer Center
Audience: Business People, Entrepreneurs, Manufactures, Technology Enthusiasts
Profile: Features state-by-state listings of agencies designed to facilitate the adaptation of new technologies to industry. Also provides updates on conferences, and a current list of Department of Defense projects soliciting private assistance from small businesses. Allows limited access to NTTC databases.
Contact: Charles Monfradi
cmonfra@nttc.edu, info@nttc.edu

`gopher://iron.nttc.edu`

`http://iridium.nttc.edu/nttc.hmtl`

Department of Justice Gopher

Department of Justice Gopher

A gopher containing online information from the Justice Department.

Keywords: Federal Laws (US), Government (US), Justice Department
Sponsor: United States Department of Justice
Audience: Lawyers, Citizens
Profile: The Department of Justice (DOJ) gopher features DOJ criminal and law enforcement statistics, as well as agency procurement requests, job listings, and press releases. Also has links to other US government online systems.
Contact: gopher@usdoj.gov

`gopher://gopher.usdoj.gov`

Department of Labor

NLSNews Newsletter (National Longitudinal Surveys of Labor Market Experience)

Issued by the Center for Human Resource Research (Ohio State University); distributed to researchers using NLS data, as well as to other interested persons.

Keywords: Labor, Government (US), Department of Labor
Sponsor: Bureau of Labor Statistics, US Department of Labor
Audience: Statisticians, Researchers (Labor)
Profile: A typical issue contains updates on the status and availability of NLS data tapes and CD-ROMs for the six NLS cohorts (Older Men, Mature Women, Young Men, Young Women, Youth, and Children), notices to researchers of data-file or documentation errors, summaries of in-progress and completed NLS research, and other information of general interest to the NLS research community.
Contact: Gale James
james@ohsthr.bitnet
A description of the subscription service that enables users to automatically receive, as soon as it becomes available, the latest issue of the NLS Newsletter and/or error updates can be found in the file subscribe.info, available via nlserve@ohsthr.bitnet, the Center's file server.

`mailto:james@ohsthr.bitnet`

derby

derby

To discuss various aspects and strategies of horseracing, primarily dealing with, but not limited to, handicapping.

Keywords: Horseracing, Handicapping
Audience: Horseracing Enthusiasts
Contact: John Wilkes
derby-request@ekrl.com
User Info: To subscribe to the list, send an e-mail message requesting a subscription to the URL address below.
To send a message to the entire list, address it to: derby-request@ekrl.com

`mailto:derby-request@ekrl.com`

Dermatology

rxderm-l

A mailing list intended for promoting the discussion of dermatologic treatment among practicing dermatologists.

Keywords: Dermatology, Skin, Disease, Doctors
Audience: Dermatologists
Contact: A.C. Huntley
achuntley@ucdavis.edu
User Info: To subscribe to the list, send an e-mail message to the URL address below consisting of a single line reading:
SUB rxderm-l YourFirstName YourLastName. To send a message to the entire list, address it to: rxderm-l@ucdavis.edu

`mailto:listserv@ucdavis.edu`

Derwent World Patents Index

Derwent World Patents Index

Patent specifications issued by the patent offices of 33 major issuing authorities.

Keywords: Patents, Intellectual Property, Trademarks
Sponsor: Derwent Publications, Ltd.
Audience: Patent Attorneys, Patent Agents, Librarians, Researchers
Profile: Includes European Patent Office and Patent Cooperation Treaty published applications, plus Research Disclosure and International Technology Disclosure. Each patent is extensively indexed from the complete patent specifications. Abstracts are included.
Contact: paul.albert@neteast.com
User Info: To subscribe contact Orbit-Questel directly.

`telnet://orbit.com`

Deryni-L

Deryni-L

A list for readers and fans of Katernine Kurtz's novels and other works.

Keywords: Science Fiction, Kurtz (Katernine)
Audience: Science Fiction Readers
Contact: Edward J. Branley
elendil@mintir.new-orleans.la.us
User Info: To subscribe to the list, send an e-mail message requesting a subscription to the URL address below.
To send a message to the entire list, address it to: deryni-l@mintir.new-orleans.la.us

`mailto:deryni-l@mintir.new-orleans.la.us`

Design

Engineering-Design

Supports researchers at the five national Engineering Design Centres.

Keywords: Engineering, Design
Audience: Engineers, Researchers
Contact: engineering-design-request@mailbase.ac.uk
Details: Free
User Info: To subscribe to the list, send an e-mail message to the URL address shown below consiting of a single line reading:
SUB engineering-design YourFirstName YourLastName
To send a message to the entire list, address it to:
engineering-design@mailbase.ac.uk

`mailbase@mailbase.ac.uk`

Engineering; A. Park, J. Miller

This directory is a compilation of information resources focused on engineering.

Keywords: Engineering, Design
Audience: Engineers, Students, Educators
Details: Free

`ftp://una.hh.lib.umich.edu/70/inetdirstacks/engin:parkmiller`

Geodesic

A mailing list for the discussion of Buckminster Fuller's works.

Keywords: Geodesic Quantum Physics, Design, Fuller (Buckminster)
Audience: Designers, Physicists
Contact: Patrick G. Salsbury
salsbury@acsu.buffalo.edu
Details: Free
User Info: To subscribe to the list, send an e-mail message to the URL address shown below consisting of a single line reading:
SUB geodesic YourFirstName YourLastName
To send a message to the entire list, address it to:
geodesic@ubvm.cc.buffalo.edu

`mailto:listserv@ubvm.cc.buffalo.edu`

Gopher-Based ASCII Clip Art Collection ★★

A collection of over 500 individual pictures, ranging from images of food to Star Wars, created with ASCII characters. Organized by subject, and including archives of the Usenet group alt.ascii-art. Also contains links to other ASCII collections.

Keywords: Clip Art, Design
Sponsor: Texas Tech Computer Sciences Gopher Server
Audience: Computer Users, General Public
Contact: Abdul Malik Yoosufan
gripe@cs.ttu.edu
Details: Free, Images

gopher://cs4sun.cs.ttu.edu

ftp://ftp.cs.ttu.edu:/pub/asciiart

Desktop Publishing

(The) DTP Direct Catalog ★

DTP Direct specializes in Macintosh hardware and software tools for desktop publishers and graphics professionals.

Keywords: Macintosh, Desktop Publishing, Graphic Design
Sponsor: InterNex Server Bureau
Audience: Graphic Designers, Artists, Desktop Publishers
Details: Free, Moderated, Image and Sound files available. Multimedia files available.

http://www.internex.net/DTP/home.html

CDPub ★

CDPub is an electronic mailing list for those engaged or interested in CD-ROM publishing in general, and in desktop CD-ROM recorders and publishing systems in particular. Topics of interest to the list include information on the various desktop publishing systems for premastering using CD-ROM media and tapes (e.g. DAT), replication services, various standards of interest to publishers (e.g. ISO9660, RockRidge), retrieval engines, and platform independence issues. Discussions on all platforms are welcome.

Keywords: CD-ROM, Electronic Publishing, Desktop Publishing
Audience: CD-ROM Publishers, Desktop Publishers, Publishers
Contact: CDPub-Info@knex.via.mind.org
Details: Free
User Info: To subscribe to the list, send an e-mail message requesting a subscription to the URL address below.
To send a message to the entire list, address it to: CDPub@knex.via.mind.org

mailto:mail-server@knex.via.mind.org

framers ★

This is a forum to share experiences and information about the FrameMaker desktop-publishing package from Frame Technology.

Keywords: Desktop Publishing
Audience: Desktop Publishers, Publishers
Details: Free
User Info: To subscribe to the list, send an e-mail message requesting a subscription to the URL address below.
To send a message to the entire list, address it to: framers@uunet.uu.net

mailto:framers-request@uunet.uu.net

journet ★★

An electronic conference for the discussion of topics of interest to journalists and journalism educators.

Keywords: Journalism, Writing, Desktop Publishing, Electronic Publishing <Standard Audience>Journalists, Writers, Publishers, Educators
Audience: Journalism, Writing, Desktop Publishing, Electronic Publishing <Standard Audience>Journalists, Writers, Publishers, Educators
Contact: George Frajkor
gfrajkor@ccs.carleton.ca
User Info: To subscribe to the list, send an e-mail message to the URL address below consisting of a single line reading:
SUB journet YourFirstName YourLastName
To send a message to the entire list, address it to: journet@qucdn.queensu.ca

mailto:listserv@qucdn.queensu.ca

PAGEMAKER ★

The PageMaker ListServ is dedicated to the discussion of desktop publishing in general, with emphasis on the use of Aldus PageMaker. The list discusses PageMaker's use in both the PC and Macintosh realms. The list also maintains an extensive archive of help files that are extremely useful for the modern desktop publisher.

Keywords: Desktop Publishing, Aldus Pagemaker, IBM PC, Macintosh
Audience: Desktop Publishers, Computer Users
Contact: Geoff Peters
gwp@cs.purdue.edu
Details: Free
User Info: To subscribe to the list, send an e-mail message to the URL address shown below consisting of a single line reading:
SUB pagemaker YourFirstName YourLastName
To send a message to the entire list, address it to: gwp@cs.purdue.edu

mailto:listserv@cs.purdue.edu

Detective Fiction

Mystery ★

This mailing list reviews and discusses mystery and detective fiction, including works on film, television, and radio.

Keywords: Mystery Fiction, Detective Fiction, Books
Audience: Mystery Enthusiasts
Details: Free
User Info: To subscribe to the list, send an e-mail message requesting a subscription to the URL address below.

mailto:mystery-request@introl.com

Detectives

Investigators and Detectives ★★★

This resource provides information files for individuals involved with investigative research, as well as a free monthly newsletter.

Keywords: Detectives, Crime, Information Retrieval, Security
Audience: Investigators, Detectives, Information Brokers, General Public
Profile: Investigators and Detectives provides access to information covering topics such as private investigative research, strategies, sources, the art and science of investigating, theft deterrents, and electronic PI schematics and plans. Also offers a free sample of a newsletter covering various topics of interest to Private Investigators, such as techniques and strategies, security, and tracing.
Contact: Mike Enlow
menlow@Intec.win.net
michael@enlow.com
Details: Inside Secrets.

mailto:info@enlow.com

Development

AGRIS International ★★★

This database serves as a comprehensive inventory of worldwide agricultural literature that reflects research results, food production, and rural development.

Keywords: Agriculture, Rural Development, Food Production, Development
Sponsor: US National Agricultural Library, Beltsville, MD, USA
Audience: Agronomists, Market Researchers

Profile: Designed to help users identify problems involved in all aspects of world food supply, the file corresponds in part to Agr Index, published monthly by the Food and Agriculture Organization (FAO) of the United Nations. Subject coverage focuses on many topics; general agriculture; geography and history; education, extension, and advisory work; administration and legislation; economics, development, and rural sociology; plant production; protection of plants and stored products; forestry; animal production; aquatic sciences and fisheries; machinery and buildings; natural resources; food science; home economics; human nutrition; pollution; and more.

Contact: Dialog in the US at (800) 334-2564
Details: Costs
User Info: To subscribe, contact Dialog directly.

`telnet://dialog.com`

apngowid.meet ★

A conference on plans by Asia Pacific regional women's groups for the United Nations Fourth World Conference on Women to be held in Beijing in September 1995.

Keywords: Women, Asia, Pacific, Feminists, Development, United Nations, World Conference on Women
Audience: Women, Feminists, Nongovernmental Organizations
Contact: AsPac Info, Docu and Communication Committee
AP-IDC@p95.f401.n751.z6.g
Details: Costs, Moderated.

Establish an account on the nearest APC node. Login, type c for conferences, then type: go apngowid.meet.

For information on the nearest APC node, contact: APC International Secretariat IBASE e-mail: apcadmin@apc.org

`http://www.igc.apc.org/igc/www.women.html`

Community Networks Benefit Federal Goals ★

Statement by community networker Frank Odasz, founder and director of Big Sky Telegraph, a network of rural BBSs throughout Montana. In this article he makes the case that the federal government will benefit from the widespread rural employment of networking technology.

Keywords: Community, Networking, Rural Development, Development
Audience: Activists, Policy Analysts, Community Leaders, Government, Citizens, Rural Residents, Native Americans
Contact: Frank Odasz
franko@bigsky.dillon.mt.us,
Details: Free

`http://nearnet.gnn.com/mag/articles/oram/bio.odasz.html`

devel-l ★

Discussion forum on technology transfer in international development.

Keywords: Development, Technology
Sponsor: Volunteers in Technical Assistance (VITA)
Audience: Technology Professionals
Contact: vita@gmuvax.gmu.edu
Details: Free
User Info: To subscribe to the list, send an e-mail message to the URL address shown below consisting of a single line reading:
SUB devel-l YourFirstName YourLastName

`mailto:listserv@auvm.american.edu`

DevelopNet News ★

A monthly newsletter on technology transfer in international development.

Keywords: Nonprofits, Technology, Development
Sponsor: Volunteers in Technical Assistance
Audience: Technology Professionals
Contact: R.R. Ronkin
vita@gmuvax.gmu.edu
Details: Free
User Info: To subscribe, send an e-mail message to the address below.
Inquire about needing a password.

`mailto:vita@gmuvax.gmu.edu`

Global Change Information Gateway ★★★★

This gateway was created to address environmental data management issues raised by the US Congress, the Administration, and the advisory arms of the Federal policy community. It contains documents related to the UN conference on Environment and Development.

Keywords: UN, Environment, Development, Oceans, Atmosphere
Audience: Environmentalists, Scientists, Researchers, Environmentalists
Profile: [profile needed]????????????
Details: Free
Select from menu as appropriate.

`gopher://scilibx.ucsc.edu`

World Bank Gopher Server ★★★

A collection of online information from the World Bank.

Keywords: Government (International), Development, International Finance, Foreign Trade

Sponsor: The World Bank
Audience: Nongovernmental Organizations, Activists, Government Officials, Environmentalists
Profile: A collection of World Bank information including a list of publications, environmental assessments, economic reports, and updates on current projects being funded by the World Bank.
Contact: webmaster@www.worldbank.org
gopher://gopher.worldbank.org

`http://www.worldbank.org`

Development (International)

(The) Worldwide Impact of Network Access

This is an article by community networker Felipe Rodriquez. In this statement Rodriquez argues that developed countries should help less developed countries build their information infrastructures, and that governments should not censor the content of network traffic.

Keywords: Community, Networking, Europe, Development (International)
Audience: Activists, Policymakers, Community Leaders
Contact: Felipe Rodriquez
felipe@hacktic.nl

`http://nearnet.gnn.com/mag/articles/oram/bio.rodriquez.html`

un.wcw.doc.eng ★

This is a read-only conference comprised of official UN documents for the United Nations Fourth World Conference on Women: Action for Equality, Development and Peace, scheduled to take place at the Beijing International Convention Center, Beijing, China, from 4-15 September 1995. The documents are provided by the official Conference Secretariat, are posted as received by the UN Non-Governmental Liaison Service (NGLS).

Keywords: Women, Development (International), Peace, UN, World Conference on Women
Audience: Women, Activists, Non-Governmental Organizations, Feminists
Contact: United Nations Non-Governmental Liaison Service/Edie Farwell
ngls@igc.apc.org, efarwell@igc.apc.org
Details: Costs, Moderated
User Info: Establish an account on the nearest APC node. Login, type c for conferences, then type go un.wcw.doc.eng.

For information on the nearest APC node, contact:
APC International Secretariat IBASE e-mail: apcadmin@apc.org

`telnet://igc.apc.org`

United Nations

Includes full text of UN press releases, UN Conference on Environment and Development reports, UN Development Programme documents, U.N. telephone directories.

- Keywords: UN, Environment, Development (International)
- Audience: Researchers, Educators, Political Scientists, Environmentalists
- Details: Free

`gopher://nywork1.undp.org`

Women.dev

Conference for information about local, regional, and international development as it relates to women. The conference includes bibliographies, statements, news, articles, and announcements about development and women in Africa, South America, and South Asia.

- Keywords: Women, Development (International), International Politics
- Audience: Women, Activists, Non-governmental Organizations, Feminists
- Details: Free, Sound files available.
- User Info: Establish an account on the nearest APC node. Login, type c for conferences, then type go women.dev.

  For information on the nearest APC node, contact:

  APC International Secretariat IBASE e-mail: apcadmin@apc.org
- Contact: Carlos Afonso (cafonso@ax.apc.org) or
  APC North American Regional Office e-mail: apcadmin@apc.org
  Edie Farwell (efarwell@igc.apc.org)

`telnet://igc.apc.org`

Deviance

deviants

The workings of the Great Wok and all things deviant from social norms are discussed here.

- Keywords: Deviance
- Audience: Curiosity Seekers, Researchers, Deviants
- Contact: deviants-request@csv.warwick.ac.uk
- Details: Free
- User Info: To subscribe to the list, send an e-mail message requesting a subscription to the URL address below.

  To send a message to the entire list, address it to: deviants-request@csv.warwick.ac.uk

`mailto:deviants-request@csv.warwick.ac.uk`

dg-users

dg-users

The mailing list is concerned with the technical details of Data General, its O/Ss, and the cornucopia of hardware they supply and support.

- Keywords: Computer Hardware, Data General
- Audience: Computer Hardware Users
- Contact: brian@ilinx.wimsey.com
- User Info: To subscribe to the list, send an e-mail message requesting a subscription to the URL address below.

  To send a message to the entire list, address it to: dg-users-request@ilinx.wimsey.com

`mailto:dg-users-request@ilinx.wimsey.com`

dh.mujer

dh.mujer

The Association for Progressive Communications conference for women and human rights issues throughout the world, contains news and announcements.

- Keywords: Feminism, Human Rights
- Audience: Feminists, Activists
- Contact: Debra Guzman
  hrcoord@igc.apc.org
- Details: Costs
- User Info.: Establish an account on the nearest APC node. Login, type c for conferences, then type go dh.mujer.

  For information on the nearest APC node, contact: APC International Secretariat IBASE
  e-mail: apcadmin@apc.org

`gopher://gopher.telnet://igc.apc.org`

`http://igc.apc.org`

DIALOG Company Name Finder

DIALOG Company Name Finder

This database is a search aid designed to locate company information in DIALOG databases.

- Keywords: Companies
- Sponsor: Dialog Information Services, Inc., Palo Alto, CA, USA
- Audience: Business Professionals, Market Researchers
- Profile: Company name records are created for unique entries in the company name indexes of the DIALOG files included. Company names are shown in the form in which they appear in the original database index, including abbreviations, punctuation (commas and periods are stripped out), and spelling variations, and are limited to 46 characters. Long company names may be truncated because of the 46-character maximum.
- Contact: Dialog in the US at (800) 334-2564, Dialog internationally at country-specific locations.
- User Info: To subscribe, contact Dialog directly.
- Notes: Coverage: Dialog databases indexing company name; updated quarterly.

`telnet://dialog.com`

Dick (Philip K.)

Pkd-list

A discussion of the works and life of Philip K. Dick (1928-82), science fiction writer. Topics also include the nature of reality, consciousness, and religious experience.

- Keywords: Science Fiction, Dick (Philip K.)
- Audience: Philip K. Dick Readers, Science Fiction Enthusiasts
- Contact: pkd-list-request@wang.com
- Details: Free
- User Info: To subscribe to the list, send an e-mail message requesting a subscription to the URL address below. To send a message to the entire list, address it to: pkd-list@wang.com

`mailto:pkd-list@wang.com`

Dickens (Charles)

Princeton University Online Manuscripts Catalog Library

The library's holdings are large and wide-ranging. They contain significant collections in many fields.

- Keywords: Books (Antiquarian), Dickens (Charles), Disraeli (Benjamin), Eliot (George), Hardy (Thomas), Kingsley (Charles), Trollope (Anthony)
- Audience: General Public, Researchers, Librarians, Document Delivery Professionals
- Details: Free

Dickinson (Emily)

University of North Carolina at Greensboro MINERVA Library ★★

The library's holdings are large and wide-ranging and contain significant collections in many fields.

Keywords: Herbert (George), Film, Dickinson (Emily), Children's Books
Audience: Researchers, Students, General Public
Details: Free
User Info: Expect: Login; Send: Info or MINERVA

telnet://steffi.acc.uncg.edu

Dictionaries

Online-dict

A mailing list devoted to a discussion of online dictionaries and related issues including installation, modification, and maintenance of their databases, search engines, and user interfaces.

Keywords: Dictionaries, Information Technology, Lexicology
Audience: Librarians, Information Scientists, Systems Operators
Contact: Jack Lynch
jlynch@dept.english.upenn.edu
Details: Free
User Info: To subscribe, send an e-mail message to the URL address below consisting of a single line reading:

SUB online-dict YourFirstName YourLastName.

To send a message to the entire list, address it to: online-dict@dept.english.upenn.edu

mailto:listserv@dept.english.upenn.edu

Diet

International Food and Nutrition (INFAN) Database ★★★

A database covering all aspects of nutrition, health and food, as for example, weight control, food safety, eating patterns, and more.

Keywords: Nutrition, Health, Diet

User Info: Expect: VM370 logo, Send: <cr>; Expect: Welcome screen, Send: folio <cr>; Expect: Welcome screen for FOLIO, Send: <cr>; Expect: List of choices, Send: 3 <cr>; To exit: type: logoff

telnet://pucc.princeton.edu

Sponsor: Pennsylvania State University Nutrition Center
Audience: Nutritionists, Health Care Professionals, Consumers
Details: Free

To access the database, select PENpages (1), then General Information (3), and finally INFAN Database (4).

telnet://penpages@psupen.psu.edu

DIGIT

DIGIT ★

A bimonthly publication containing information aimed at users of computing resources at the University of Colorado, Boulder.

Keywords: Computing, Computer Resources
Audience: University of Colorado Students, Computer Students
Contact: Suzanne Kincaid
kincaid@spot.colorado.edu
Details: Free

mailto:kincaid@spot.colorado.edu

Digital Equipment Corporation

DECnews-EDU ★

DECNEWS for Education and Research is a monthly electronic publication from Digital Equipment Corporation's Education Business Unit for the education and research communities worldwide.

Keywords: Education, Computers, Digital Equipment Corporation
Audience: Educators, Researchers
Contact: Anne Marie McDonald
decnews@mr4dec.enet.dec.com
Details: Free
User Info: To subscribe to the list, send an e-mail message requesting a subscription to the URL address below.

To send a message to the entire list, address it to:
decnews@mr4dec.enet.dec.com

mailto:decnews@mr4dec.enet.dec.com

Digital's World Wide Web Server ★★

Digital World Wide Web server provides product and service information, back issues of the Digital Technical Journal, performance reports, buyers guides and product catalogs.

Keywords: Digital Equipment Corporation, Computer Systems
Audience: Computer Users, Computing Consultants

Contact: Russ Jones
webmaster@pa.dec.com
Details: Free

http://www.digital.com/home.html

Digital Equipment WWW Information Server

Digital Equipment WWW Information Server ★★

Digital Equipment's server contains product and service information, and includes archives to public domain software. Also includes an online catalog resource for purchasing products from Digital Equipment.

Keywords: Computer Systems, Digital Equipment
Audience: Digital Equipment Users
Contact: Steve Painter
steve_painter@mro.mts.dec.com

http://www.service.digital.com/home.html

Digital Games Review

Digital Games Review ★

Reviews of video and computer entertainment titles for the entire industry.

Keywords: Computer Games, Games, Video Games
Audience: Computer Game Players, Computer Game Developers
Profile: Reviews are written by computer game enthusiasts, with an eye to accessibility, enjoyment, and fun, as well as to graphics, technical sophistication, and complexity.
Contact: Dave Taylor
taylor@intuitive.com
Details: Free

mailto:digital-games-request@intuitive.com

DIMUND

DIMUND FTP ★

DIMUND (Document Image Understanding) is an Internet information retrieval service.

Keywords: Internet, Information Retrieval, DIMUND, Documents
Sponsor: Document Processing Group, University of Maryland
Audience: Internet Surfers
Contact: gopher@dimund.cfar.umd.edu
Details: Free

gopher://dimund.umd.edu

dinosaur

dinosaur

Discussion of dinosaurs and their reptilian contemporaries.

Keywords:	Dinosaurs, Archosaurs
Audience:	Dinosaur Enthusiasts, Paleontologists
Contact:	John Matrow dinosaur-request@donald.WichitaKS.NCR.COM
Details:	Free
User Info:	To subscribe to the list, send an e-mail message requesting a subscription to the URL address below.
	To send a message to the entire list, address it to: dinosaur-request@donald.WichitaKS.NCR.COM

`mailto:dinosaur-request@donald.WichitaKS.NCR.COM`

Diogenes

Diogenes

Diogenes provides access to the US Food and Drug Administration (FDA) regulatory information needed by the health care industry.

Keywords:	Food, Drugs
Sponsor:	Diogenes, Rockville, MD, USA
Audience:	Health Care Professionals
Profile:	The database contains news stories and unpublished documents relating to the United States regulation of pharmaceuticals and medical devices. The complete text is provided for materials that are substantive and timely. Diogenes covers information relating to the Food and Drug Administration regulation of drugs and medical devices, including listings of approved products, experience reports for devices, documentation of the approval process for specific products, recall and regulatory action documentation, and more.
Contact:	Dialog in the US at (800) 334-2564, Dialog internationally at country-specific locations.
User Info:	To subscribe, contact Dialog directly.
Notes:	Coverage: 1976 to the present; updated weekly.

`telnet://dialog.com`

Dire Straits

dire-straits

Discussion of the musical group Dire Straits and associated side projects.

Keywords:	Rock Music, Dire Straits, Music
Audience:	Rock Music Enthusiasts, Dire Straits Enthusiasts
Contact:	Rand P. Hall dire-straits-request@merrimack.edu
Details:	Free
User Info:	To subscribe to the list, send an e-mail message requesting a subscription to the URL address below.
	To send a message to the entire list, address it to: dire-straits-request@merrimack.edu

`Anonymous ftp to: merrimack.edu`
`(f=ANONYMOUS/DIRE-STRAITS)`

Mail list probably exists.

Direct

Direct

Discussion of the work of the musical artist Vangelis.

Keywords:	New Age Music, Musical Groups
Audience:	Musicians, Music Enthusiasts, Vangelis Fans
Contact:	Keith Gregoire direct-request@celtech.com
User Info:	To subscribe to the list, send an e-mail message requesting a subscription to the URL address below. To send a message to the entire list, address it to: direct@celtech.com
	Both bounce and daily digest modes are available; specify your preference when subscribing.

`mailto:direct-request@celtech.com`

Directories

Congressional Contact Information

The US Senate and 103rd Congress phone and fax numbers are accessible and searchable from this server.

Keywords:	Congress (US), Directories, Government (US)
Sponsor:	Library of Congress
Audience:	General Public, Journalists, Students, Politicians
Details:	Free

`gopher://marvel.loc.gov/11/congress/directory`

Internet Resources for Earth Sciences

A document detailing Internet resources for a variety of earth science disciplines, including GIS.

Keywords:	Directory, GIS, Geology, Geography, GPS, Mapping, Earth Science
Sponsor:	Bill Thoen
Audience:	Earth Scientists, Researchers
Profile:	A complete document detailing the types of information available in earth sciences and the mechanisms to retrieve needed information.
Contact:	Bill Thoen bthoen@gisnet.com
Details:	Free

`ftp://ftp.csn.org/COGS/ores.text`

dirt-users

dirt-users

Dirt is an X11-based UIMS.

Keywords:	Computer Applications
Audience:	UIMS Users
Contact:	dirt-users-request@ukc.ac.uk
User Info:	To subscribe to the list, send an e-mail message requesting a subscription to the URL address below.
	To send a message to the entire list, address it to: dirt-users@ukc.ac.uk

`mailto:dirt-users@ukc.ac.uk`

Disabilities

ADA-Law

A mailing list for discussion of the Americans with Disabilities Act (ADA) and other disability-related legislation both in the US and abroad.

Keywords:	Disabilities, Law (US)
Audience:	Disabled People, Legal Professionals
Contact:	wtm@bunker.afd.olivetti.com
User Info:	To subscribe to the list, send an e-mail message to the URL address below consisting of a single line reading:
	SUB ADA-Law YourFirstName YourLastName
	To send a message to the entire list, address it to: ADA-Law@vm1.nodak.edu

`mailto:listserv@vm1.nodak.edu`

Americans with Disabilities Act ★

Gives access to the full text of the Americans with Disabilities Act (ADA) and all the related legislation.

Keywords: Disabilities

Audience: General Public, Disabled People, Differently Abled People, Politicians, Journalists, Students

Profile: The purpose of ADA is to provide a clear and comprehensive national mandate to end discrimination against individuals with disabilities and to bring them into the economic and social mainstream of American life; to provide enforceable standards addressing discrimination against individuals with disabilities; and to ensure that the federal government plays a central role in enforcing these standards on behalf of individuals with disabilities.

Details: Free

`gopher://val-dor.cc.buffalo.edu/11/.legislation/`

BlindFam ★★

The Blindness and Family Life mailing list is devoted to a discussion of the day-to-day impact of this disability on families, and the patterns of domestic life associated with blindness.

Keywords: Blindness, Disabilities, Family

Audience: Blind People, Families, Health Care Professionals, Rehabilitation Counselors

Contact: Roger Myers, Patt Bromberger
Meyers@ab.wvnet.edu
Patt@squid.tram.com

User Info: To subscribe, send an e-mail message to the URL address below consisting of a single line reading:

SUB BlindFam YourFirstName YourLastName

To send a message to the entire list, address it to:
BlindFam@sjuvm.stjohns.edu

`mailto:listserv@sjuvm.stjohns.edu`

Cornucopia of Disability Information (CODI)

A large collection of disability-related information available via gopher.

Keywords: Disabilities, Health

Sponsor: State University of New York (SUNY) at Buffalo

Audience: Disabled People, Activists, Rehabilitation Counselors, Health Care Professionals

Profile: This site provides a wide variety of information resources concerning people with disabilities, ranging from legal information to a directory of computer resources aimed at the disabled consumer. Includes state, local, and national information and government documents such as the Americans with Disabilities Act. Also has links to many other related resources on the Internet, such as the National Rehabilitation Information Center.

Contact: Jay Leavitt
leavitt@ubvmsb.cc.buffalo.edu

`gopher://val-dor.cc.buffalo.edu`

Deaf Gopher

Gopher menu of deaf resources in the State of Michigan.

Keywords: Disabilities, Deafness, Health

Sponsor: Michigan State University

Audience: Deaf and Disabled People, Health Care Professionals, Activists, Policy Makers, Rehabilitation Counselors, Therapists

Profile: A small but useful menu of deaf resources that includes a collection of files in essay and/or report form about a variety of historical and cultural aspects of deafness.

Contact: Gary LaPointe
deafgopher@ah3.cal.msu.edu

Details: Free

`gopher://cal.msu.edu/11/msu/dept/deaf`

Disability Information

A collection of information about and links to sources of disability-related information from around the world. Includes archives of many related mailing lists and electronic newsletters, as well as legal and technical help for the disabled, and information about the Parkinson's Disease Information Exchange Network.

Keywords: Disabilities, Health, Diseases

Sponsor: Computing & Information Services at Texas A&M University, Galveston, Texas, USA

Audience: Disabled People, Rehabilitation Counselors, Health Care Professionals, Activists

Contact: Computing & Information Services at Texas A&M University
gopher@tamu.edu

`gopher://gopher.tamu.edu/.dir/disability.dir`

Disability Reading Room

Gopher menu of all kinds of reading material on disabilities.

Keywords: Disabilities, Health

Sponsor: University of Maryland

Audience: Deaf and Disabled People, Health Care Professionals, Activists, Policy Analysts, Rehabilitation Counselors, Therapists

Profile: A fascinating collection of reading material on disabilities and related issues, including first-person stories of dealing with chronic pain, detailed descriptions of laws involving the disabled, relevant press releases, and a large selection of journals on disabilities and related matters.

Contact: UMD Computer Science Center
consult@umail.umd.edu

Details: Free

`gopher://info.umd.edu`

Disability-Related Resources

A collection of information that includes newsletters for deaf/blind issues, electronic resources for the deaf, and a section on Chronic Fatigue Syndrome.

Keywords: Disabilities, Deafness, Blindness, Chronic Fatigue Syndrome

Sponsor: University of Washington DO-IT Program

Audience: Deaf and Disabled People, Health Care Professionals

Contact: Sheryl Burgstahler, Ph.D.
doit@u.washington.edu

`gopher://hawking.u.washington.edu`

Down's Syndrome

For discussion of any issue related to Down's Syndrome.

Keywords: Down's Syndrome, Disabilities

Audience: Down's Syndrome Community

Contact: wtm@bunker.afd.olivetti.com

Details: Free

User Info: To subscribe to the list, send an e-mail message to the URL address shown below consisting of a single line reading:

SUB downs-syndrome YourFirstName YourLastName

To send a message to the entire list, address it to:
downs-syndrome@vm1.nodak.edu

`mailto:listserv@vm1.nodak.edu`

Handicap

An anonymous data site containing disability-related files or programs.

Keywords: Health, Disabilities

Audience: Disabled People

Profile: There are about 40 directories with 500 files/programs covering all types of disabilities. The "Handicap BBS List" originates here.

Details: Free

Login: anonymous

`ftp://handicap.shel.isc-br.com`

History and Analysis of Disabilities Newsletter

Covers the history of disabilities, disabled persons, and disability issues.

Keywords: Disabilities, Disabled Persons
Sponsor: History of Disabilities Network, Centre for Independent Living, Toronto, and International Society for the History of Disabilities, Paris.
Audience: Disabled persons, Doctors, Historians
Contact: Gary Woodill
fcty731@ryerson
Details: Free

`mailto:fcty7310@ryerson.bitnet`

misc.handicap

A Usenet newsgroup providing information and discussion for and about handicapped individuals.

Keywords: Disabilities
Audience: Disabled
Details: Free
User Info: To subscribe to this Usenet newsgroup, you need access to a newsreader.

`news:misc.handicap`

Stutt-L

A list for the clinical discussion of stuttering, a speech disorder.

Keywords: Communications, Speech Disorders, Disabilities
Audience: Communications Specialists, Speech Pathologists
Contact: Woody Starkweather
v5002e@vm.temple.edu
User Info: To subscribe to this list, send an e-mail message to the URL address below, consisting of a single line reading:

SUB Stutt-L YourFirstName YourLastName

To send a message to the entire list, address it to: stutt-l@rm.temple.edu

`mailto: listserv@vm.temple.edu`

Women.health

This conference features articles, documents, news, announcements, policy statements, and other information about women's health around the world. Topics include breast cancer, ovarian cancer, alcohol, abortion, pregnancy, sterilization of women, pesticides, Quinacrine, HIV, disability.

Keywords: Women, Abortion, AIDS, Disabilities, Feminism, Health
Audience: Activists, Family Planners, Health Professionals, Non-Governmental Organizations, Women
Details: Costs
User Info: Establish an account on the nearest APC node. Login, type c for conferences, then type go women.health. For information on the nearest APC node, contact: APC International Secretariat IBASE e-mail: apcadmin@apc.org Contact: Carlos Afonso (cafonso@ax.apc.org) or APC North American Regional Office e-mail: apcadmin@apc.org Contact: Edie Farwell (efarwell@igc.apc.org)
Notes: ALAI: Agencia Latinoamericana de Informacion e-mail message to APCadmin@apc.org

`telnet://igc.apc.org`

Disaster Relief

City of San Carlos World Wide Web Fire Safety Tutorial

This WWW site offers fire prevention information, with a special emphasis on preventing wildland fires. Also includes color diagram on how to create a proper firebreak.

Keywords: Disaster Relief, Safety
Sponsor: The City of San Carlos, California, USA
Audience: Students, Educators, Environmentalists, Community Groups

`http://www.abag.ca.gov/abag/local_gov/city/san_carlos/schome.html`

Tornado Warnings

Gopher site providing up-to-the-minute tornado warnings for the United States.

Keywords: Disaster Relief
Sponsor: University of Illinois at Urbana-Champaign, Department of Atmospheric Sciences
Audience: Weather Forecasters, General Public, News Media
Contact: John Kemp
johnkemp@uiuc.edu
Details: Free

`gopher://wx.atmos.uiuc.edu/11/Severe/Tornado_Warnings`

Disaster Research

Disaster Research

This newsletter deals with hazards and disasters. It includes articles on recent events and policy developments, plus updates on ongoing research and upcoming meetings; it also fields queries, responses, and ongoing discussion among readers.

Keywords: Disaster Research
Audience: Health Care Professionals, Public Servants
Contact: mailserv@vaxf.colorado.edu (Internet).
Details: Free

`mailto:hazards@vaxf.colorado.edu`

Disclosure Database

Disclosure Database

Disclosure Database provides in-depth financial information on over 12,500 companies.

Keywords: Securities, Stock Market
Sponsor: Disclosure Incorporated, Bethesda, MD, USA
Audience: Business Professionals
Profile: The information is derived from reports filed with the US Securities and Exchange Commission (SEC) by publicly owned companies. These reports provide detailed and reliable financial information on the companies included. Extracts of 10-K and 10-Q financial reports are included, as well as 20-F financial reports and registration reports for new registrants. Disclosure provides an online source of information for marketing intelligence, corporate planning, accounting research, and corporate finance. Contents of the records include management discussion and president's letter on past-year performance, footnotes to the financials, significant events, and market conditions affecting a particular company.
Contact: Dialog in the US at (800) 334-2564, Dialog internationally at country-specific locations.
User Info: To subscribe, contact Dialog directly.
Notes: Coverage: Current; updated weekly.

`telnet://dialog.com`

Disclosure

COMPNY

The COMPNY library contains more than 75 files of business and financial information, including thousands of in-depth company and industry research reports from leading national and international investments banks and brokerage houses.

Keywords: Companies, Financials, Filings, Disclosure
Audience: Business and Financial Researchers, Analysts, Entrepreneurs and Regulators.
Profile: COMPNY includes the following types of information: Full-text 10-Q, 10-K, Annual Reports toShareholders and Proxy filings; Extracts of filings for more than 11,000 public companies whose

216 Disclosure

securities are traded on the major exchanges as well as over-the-counter Abstracts of S-registration statements, 13-Ds, 14-Ds, 8Ks, Form 4s and other SEC filings updated on a daily basis; Business news abstracts from more than 400 information sources; Daily US economic trends and forecasts.

The materials may be searched in individual files, such as brokerage house reports, or in group files organized by subject, such as SEC filings.

Contact: Mead New Sales Group at (800) 227-4908 or (513) 859-5398 inside the US, or (513) 865-7981 for all inquiries outside the US.

User Info: To subscribe, contact Mead directly.

To examine the Nexis user guide, you can access it at the ftp site of the University of Texas at Austin at the URL address: ftp://ftp.cc.utexas.edu

The files are in: /pub/ref-services/LEXIS

`telnet://nex.meaddata.com`

`http://www.meaddata.com`

Diseases

Disability Information ★★★

A collection of information about and links to sources of disability-related information from around the world. Includes archives of many related mailing lists and electronic newsletters, as well as legal and technical help for the disabled, and information about the Parkinson's Disease Information Exchange Network.

Keywords: Disabilities, Health, Diseases

Sponsor: Computing & Information Services at Texas A&M University, Galveston, Texas, USA

Audience: Disabled People, Rehabilitation Counselors, Health Care Professionals, Activists

Contact: Computing & Information Services at Texas A&M University

gopher@tamu.edu

`gopher://gopher.tamu.edu/.dir/disability.dir`

Discipline and Disease Specific Sources

This database contains links to sources of Medical and Health Care information. Has disease-specific resources for AIDS, Cancer, Parkinson's Disease, and Sudden Infant Death Syndrome, among others. Also covers over 30 discipline-specific sources, ranging from anesthesiology to tropical medicine.

Keywords: Medicine, Diseases, Medical Research

Sponsor: University of Miami Biomedical Gopher Project, Miami, Florida, USA

Audience: Medical Professionals, Medical Researchers

Contact: Thomas Williams, Michael Cutherell
twilliam@mednet.med.miami.edu
mcuthere@mednet.med.miami.edu

Details: Free

`gopher://caldmed.med.miami.edu`

Institute for Molecular Virology ★

A unique virology resource for students, scientists, computer visualization experts, and the general public.

Keywords: Diseases, Viruses, Biology

Sponsor: University of Wisconsin-Madison, Madison, Wisconsin, USA

Audience: Virologists, Biologists, Researchers

Contact: Stephen Spencer
sspencer@rhino.bocklabs.wisc.edu

`http://www.bocklabs.wisc.edu/Welcome.html`

rxderm-l ★★

A mailing list intended for promoting the discussion of dermatologic treatment among practicing dermatologists.

Keywords: Dermatology, Skin, Disease, Doctors

Audience: Dermatologists

Contact: A.C. Huntley
achuntley@ucdavis.edu

User Info: To subscribe to the list, send an e-mail message to the URL address below consisting of a single line reading:

SUB rxderm-l YourFirstName YourLastName

To send a message to the entire list, address it to: rxderm-l@ucdavis.edu

`mailto:listserv@ucdavis.edu`

The Tumor Gene Database ★★

A database containing information about genes associated with tumorigenesis and cellular transformation.

Keywords: Genetics, Disease, Biomedical Research, Databases

Sponsor: Department of Cell Biology, Baylor College of Medicine

Audience: Biomedical Researchers

Contact: David Steffen, Ph.D.
steffen@bcm.tmc.edu

`gopher://mbcr.bcm.tmc.edu`

Diseases (History of)

Johns Hopkins University Library ★★

The library's holdings are large and wide-ranging and contain significant collections in many fields, including the following:

Keywords: Literature (English), Economics, Classics, Drama (German), Slavery, Trade Unions, Incunabula, Bibles, Diseases (History of), Nursing (History of), Abolitionism

Audience: General Public, Researchers, Librarians, Document Delivery Professionals

Details: Free

`telnet://jhuvm.hcf.jhu.edu`

Disk Jockeys

BPM ★

This list is for novice and professional DJs. Discussion often covers music releases, DJ'ing techniques, and turntable maintenance.

Keywords: Disk Jockeys, Music

Audience: Disk Jockeys, Music Enthusiasts

Contact: Simon Gatral
bpm-request@andrew.cmu.edu

Details: Free

User Info: To subscribe to the list, send an e-mail message requesting a subscription to the URL address below.

To send a message to the entire list, address it to:

bpm@andrew.cmu.edu

`mailto:bpm-request@andrew.cmu.edu`

Disney

disney-afternoon ★

Discussion of The Disney Afternoon and other related topics. This is a very high-volume, low-noise mailing list.

Keywords: Disney, Television

Audience: Disney Enthusiasts, Television Viewers

Contact: Stephanie da Silva
ranger-list-request@taronga.com

Details: Free, Moderated

User Info: To subscribe to the list, send an e-mail message requesting a subscription to the URL address below.

To send a message to the entire list, address it to: ranger-list-request@taronga.com

`mailto:ranger-list-request@taronga.com`

disney-comics

A forum for discussion of Disney comics.

Keywords:	Comics, Disney
Audience:	Comics Enthusiasts, Disney Enthusiasts
Contact:	Per Starbuck disney-comics-request@student.docs.uu.se
Details:	Free
User Info:	To subscribe to the list, send an e-mail message requesting a subscription to the URL address below.
	To send a message to the entire list, address it to: disney-comics-request@student.docs.uu.se

`mailto:disney-comics-request@student.docs.uu.se`

rec.arts.disney

A Usenet newsgroup providing information and discussion about Disney and related topics.

Keywords:	Disney
Audience:	Disney Fans
Details:	Free
User Info:	To subscribe to this Usenet newsgroup, you need access to a newsreader.

`news:rec.arts.disney`

Disraeli (Benjamin)

Princeton University Online Manuscripts Catalog Library

The library's holdings are large and wide-ranging. They contain significant collections in many fields.

Keywords:	Books (Antiquarian), Dickens (Charles), Disraeli (Benjamin), Eliot (George), Hardy (Thomas), Kingsley (Charles), Trollope (Anthony)
Audience:	General Public, Researchers, Librarians, Document Delivery Professionals
Details:	Free
User Info:	Expect: VM370 logo, Send: <cr>; Expect: Welcome screen, Send: folio <cr>; Expect: Welcome screen for FOLIO, Send: <cr>; Expect: List of choices, Send: 3 <cr>; To exit: type: logoff

`telnet://pucc.princeton.edu`

DISSPLA (Display Integrated Software System and Plotting Language)

DISSPLA (Display Integrated Software System and Plotting Language)

News and information exchange concerning DISSPLA.

Keywords:	Computer Graphics, Programming
Audience:	DISSPLA Users, Computer Programmers
Profile:	DISSPLA is a high-level FORTRAN graphics subroutine library designed for programmers in engineering, science and business.
Contact:	Zvika Bar-Deroma er7101@technion.technion.ac.il
Details:	Free
User Info:	To subscribe to the list, send an e-mail message to the URL address shown below consisting of a single line reading:
	SUB disspla YourFirstName YourLastName
	To send a message to the entire list, address it to: disspla@taunivm.tau.ac.il

`mailto:listserv@taunivm.tau.ac.il`

Dist

Dist-users

This list is for discussions of issues related to the dist 3.0 package and its components: metaconfig, jmake, patch tools, and so on. The dist package was posted on comp.sources.misc (August 1993).

Keywords:	Dist, Programming, Computer Applications
Audience:	dist Users
Contact:	Shigeya Suzuki, Raphael Manfredi shigeya@foretune.co.jp ram@acri.fr
User Info:	To subscribe to the list, send an e-mail message to the URL address shown below consisting of a single line reading:
	SUB dist-users YourFirstName YourLastName
	To send a message to the entire list, address it to: dist-users@msu.edu

`mailto:majordomo@foretune.co.jp`

Distance Education

Distance Education

This gopher site takes advantage of New Brunswick's advanced telecommunications infrastructure to provide leading edge technology-based learning environments. A computer-based teleconferencing system forms the core of the network complemented by computer-aided communications, electronic data links and other multimedia technologies.

Keywords:	Education (Distance), Independent Study
Sponsor:	TeleEducation New Brunswick, Department of Advanced Education and Labor
Audience:	Educators, Students

`gopher://gopher.ollc.mta.ca`

Theater

This directory is a compilation of information resources focused on theater.

Keywords:	Theater, Drama, Performing Arts
Audience:	Theater Personnel, Drama Personnel, Performers
Contact:	Deborah Torres Martha Vander Kolk dtorres@umich.edu mjvk@umich.edu
Details:	Free

`ftp://una.hh.lib.umich.edu/70/inetdirsstacks/theater:torresmjvk`

Drama (British)

Indiana University Libraries

The library's holdings are large and wide-ranging and contain significant collections in many fields.

Keywords:	Literature (English), Literature (American), 1640-Present, British Plays (19th-C.), Western Americana, Railway History, Aristotle (Texts of), Lafayette (Marquis de), Handel (G.F.), Austrian History, Antiquarian Books, Rare Books, French Opera (19th-C.), Drama (British),
Audience:	General Public, Researchers, Librarians, Document Delivery Professionals
Details:	Free
Expect:	User ID prompt, Send: GUEST

`telnet://iuis.ucs.indiana.edu`

Drama (French)

University of Pennsylvania PENNINFO Library

The library's holdings are large and wide-ranging and contain significant collections in many fields.

Keywords: Church History, Spanish Inquisition, Witchcraft, Shakespeare (William), Bibles, Aristotle (Texts of), Fiction, Whitman (Walt), French Revolution, Drama (French), Literature (English), Literature (Spanish)
Audience: Researchers, Students, General Public
Contact: Al DSouza
 penninfo-admin@dccs.upenn.edu
 dsouza@dccs.upenn.edu
Details: Free
User Info: Expect: Login; Send: Public

`telnet://penninfo.upenn.edu`

Drama (German)

Johns Hopkins University Library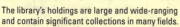

The library's holdings are large and wide-ranging and contain significant collections in many fields.

Keywords: Literature (English), Economics, Classics, Drama (German), Slavery, Trade Unions, Incunabula, Bibles, Diseases (History of), Nursing (History of), Abolitionism
Audience: General Public, Researchers, Librarians, Document Delivery Professionals
Details: Free

`telnet://jhuvm.hcf.jhu.edu`

Drew University

Drewids

This is the mailing list for Drew University alumni to chat.

Keywords: Drew University
Audience: Drew University Alumni
Contact: drewids-approval@plts.org
Details: Free
User Info: To subscribe to the list, send an e-mail message to the URL address shown below consisting of a single line reading:

 SUB drewids YourFirstName YourLastName

 To send a message to the entire list, address it to: drewids@Warren.MentorG.com

Notes: There is a similar mailing list called drewids-news. When you subscribe to either, we ask that you write to the mailing list (drewids@Warren.MentorG.COM) and tell us what school and class (for example, CLA'91, THEO'66, or GRA'95) you were in.

`mailto:majordomo@Warren.MentorG.com`

Drewids-news

This is the "announcements only" version of the "drewids" (Drew University Alumni) mailing list.

Keywords: Drew University
Audience: Drew University Alumni
Contact: drewids-approval@plts.org
Details: Free
User Info: To subscribe to the list, send an e-mail message to the URL address shown below consisting of a single line reading:

 SUB drewids-news YourFirstName YourLastName

 To send a message to the entire list, address it to: drewids-news@Warren.MentorG.com

`mailto:majordomo@Warren.MentorG.com`

Drone On...

Drone On...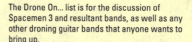

The Drone On... list is for the discussion of Spacemen 3 and resultant bands, as well as any other droning guitar bands that anyone wants to bring up.

Keywords: Rock Music, Musical Groups
Audience: Spacemen 3 Enthusiasts, Rock Music Enthusiasts
Contact: droneon-request@ucsd.edu
Details: Free
User Info: To subscribe to the list, send an e-mail message requesting a subscription to the URL address below.

 To send a message to the entire list, address it to: droneon-request@ucsd.edu

`mailto:droneon-request@ucsd.edu`

Drosophila

Drosophila Information Newsletter

A quarterly electronic publication, this is an offshoot of Drosophila Information Service.

Keywords: Drosophila, Biology, Genetics
Audience: Biologists, Geneticists
Contact: Kathy Matthews
 matthewk@ucs.indiana.edu
Details: Free
User Info: To subscribe, send an e-mail message to the address below consisting of a single line reading:

 SUB drosophila-information-newsletter YourFirstName Your Last Name

 To send a message to the entire list, address it to:

 drosophila.information.newsletter@ucs.indiana.edu

`mailto:listserv@iubvm.ucs.indiana.edu`

DRT EC and Eastern Europe Business Database

DRT EC and Eastern Europe Business Database

DRTE's comprehensive full-text coverage of business and industry in the EC is combined with in-depth reporting on doing business in Eastern Europe.

Keywords: European Community, Eastern Europe
Sponsor: DRT Europe Services Brussels, Belgium
Audience: Market Analysts, Business Professionals, Market Researchers
Profile: DRTE reports provide comprehensive and detailed coverage of all EC proposals, laws and policy directions and their commercial applications, and unique, country-specific information on the regulatory framework for business development and expansion in Eastern Europe. These are continually updated to reflect the rapidly changing nature of the political and administrative structure of these emerging economies as they affect business undertakings with EC concerns.
Contact: Data-star through Dialog in the US at (800) 334-2564, Dialog internationally at country-specific locations.
User Info: To subscribe, contact Dialog directly.
Notes: Coverage: The database is updated weekly to enable it to offer exceptionally current full-text information.

`telnet://dialog.com`

Drug Regulations

Federal Food and Drug Administration

The Federal Food and Drug Administration (FDA) databank contains reports and articles related to the FDA.

Keywords: FDA, Drug Regulations, Nutrition
Sponsor: Federal Food and Drug Administration

Audience:	Researchers, Nutritionists, Consumers, Health Care Providers
Profile:	The topics covered include the drug and device product-approvals list, FDA federal register summaries by subject, text from drug bulletins, current information on AIDS, FDA consumer magazine index and selected articles, summaries of FDA information, text of testimony at FDA congressional hearings, and speeches given by the FDA commissioner and deputy.
Details:	Free

`telnet://bbs@fdabbs.fda.gov`

Drugs

alt.drugs ★

A Usenet newsgroup providing information and discussion about the use of mind, body and behavior drugs, and about popular drug awareness.

Keywords:	Drugs
Audience:	Drug Users, Drug Educators
User Info:	To subscribe to this Usenet newsgroup, you need access to a newsreader.

`news:alt.drugs`

Diogenes

Diogenes provides access to the US Food and Drug Administration (FDA) regulatory information needed by the health care industry.

Keywords:	Food, Drugs
Sponsor:	Diogenes, Rockville, MD, USA
Audience:	Health Care Professionals
Profile:	The database contains news stories and unpublished documents relating to the United States regulation of pharmaceuticals and medical devices. The complete text is provided for materials that are substantive and timely. Diogenes covers information relating to the Food and Drug Administration regulation of drugs and medical devices, including listings of approved products, experience reports for devices, documentation of the approval process for specific products, recall and regulatory action documentation, and more.
Contact:	Dialog in the US at (800) 334-2564, Dialog internationally at country-specific locations.
User Info:	To subscribe, contact Dialog directly.
Notes:	Coverage: 1976 to the present; updated weekly.

`telnet://dialog.com`

Drug Information Fulltext

Drug Information Fulltext corresponds to two print publications: AHFS Drug Information, which contains information on 1,000 drugs available commercially in the United States, and the Handbook on Injectable Drugs, which covers 217 commercially available and 57 investigational drugs in use in the US.

Keywords:	Drugs, Pharmaceuticals
Sponsor:	American Society of Hospital Pharmacists, Washington, DC, USA
Audience:	Health Care Professionals, Pharmacists
Profile:	Drug Information Fulltext can be searched for information on the stability, chemistry, and pharmaco-kinetics of drugs, as well as on their action, usage, dosage, and administration. The file also covers compatibility and interactions of drugs and cautions for use.
Contact:	Dialog in the US at (800) 334-2564, Dialog internationally at country-specific locations.
User Info:	To subscribe, contact Dialog directly.
Notes:	Coverage: Current; updated quarterly.

`telnet://dialog.com`

Drugs of the Future

Drugs of the Future contains descriptions of drugs in the earliest stages of development. It includes details about synthesis, uses, pharmacological actions, and clinical tests and also provides a monthly summary of drugs whose status has changed.

Keywords:	Drugs
Sponsor:	J.R. Prous, S.A., Barcelona, Spain
Audience:	Health Care Professionals
Profile:	The file is drawn from the prestigious print publication Drugs of the Future.
Contact:	Dialog in the US at (800) 334-2564, Dialog internationally at country-specific locations.
User Info:	To subscribe, contact Dialog directly.
Notes:	Coverage: 1989 to the present; updated monthly.

`telnet://dialog.com`

Recreational Pharmacology Server

★★★★

Very extensive collection of drug FAQs, data sheets, net articles, resources, and electronic books. Complete list of Internet links to related sites.

Keywords:	Pharmacology, Drugs, Neuroscience
Sponsor:	University of Washington, Seattle, Washington, USA
Audience:	Students, General Public, Pharmacologists, Neuroscientists
Contact:	Webmaster lamontg@u.washington.edu
Details:	Free

`http://stein1.u.washington.edu:2012/pharm/pharm.html`

Drum Machines

DR-660

The DR-660 mailing list is for the discussion of practical applications of and technical matters relating to the Boss DR-660 drum machine.

Keywords:	Drum Machines
Audience:	Musicians
Contact:	Mike Perkowitz dr-660-request@cs.washington.edu
Details:	Free
User Info:	To subscribe to the list, send an e-mail message requesting a subscription to the URL address below.
	To send a message to the entire list, address it to: dr-660-request@cs.washington.edu

`mailto:dr-660-request@cs.washington.edu`

DSA-LGB

DSA-LGB

DSA-LGB is a mailing list for members of the Lesbian/Gay/Bisexual Commission of the Democratic Socialists of America, and for others interested in similar concerns.

Keywords:	Democratic Socialists of America, Gay, Lesbians
Audience:	Democratic Socialists, Gays, Lesbians
Contact:	DSA-LGB-request@midway.uchicago.edu
User Info:	To subscribe to the list, send an e-mail message requesting a subscription to the URL address below.
	To send a message to the entire list, address it to: DSA-LGB-request@midway.uchicago.edu

`mailto:DSA-LGB-request@midway.uchicago.edu`

dts-l (Dead Teachers Society Discussion List)

dts-l (Dead Teachers Society Discussion List)

This list is for broad discussions of teaching and learning.

Keywords: Education (Adult), Education (Distance), Education (Continuing)
Audience: Educators (K-12), Educational Administrators
Details: Free
User Info: To subscribe to the list, send an e-mail message to the URL address shown below consisting of a single line reading:
SUB dts-l YourFirstName YourLastName
To send a message to the entire list, address it to: dts-l@iubvm.bitnet

`mailto:listserv@iubvm.bitnet`

Dual-Personalities

Dual-Personalities

Discussion, maintenance/survival tips, and commercial offerings for the System/83 UNIX box made by the now-defunct DUAL Systems Corp. of Berkeley, as well as similar machines using the IEEE-696 bus (such as the CompuPro 8/16E with Root/Unisoft UNIX).

Keywords: UNIX
Audience: UNIX Users
Contact: dual-personalities-request@darwin.uucp
Details: Free
User Info: To subscribe to the list, send an e-mail message requesting a subscription to the URL address below.
To send a message to the entire list, address it to: dual-personalities-request@darwin.uucp

`mailto:dual-personalities-request@darwin.uucp`

Dun & Bradstreet

D&B - Duns Financial Records Plus

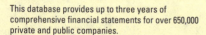

This database provides up to three years of comprehensive financial statements for over 650,000 private and public companies.

Keywords: Finance, Business, Dun & Bradstreet
Sponsor: Dun & Bradstreet Information Services, Parsippany, NJ, USA
Audience: Business Professionals
Profile: Information provided includes balance sheet, income statement, and 14 of the most widely used business ratios for measuring solvency, efficiency, and profitability. A company's financial position can be compared to those of others in the same industry as determined by industry norm percentages. In addition, there are over 1.2 million records included that contain company history and operations background only. DFR also contains company identification data, such as company name, address, primary and secondary SIC codes, D-U-N-S number, and number of employees. Textual paragraphs cover the history and operations background of a firm.
Notes: Coverage: Current; updated quarterly.
Contact: Dialog in the US at (800) 334-2564, Dialog internationally at country-specific locations.
Details: Costs
User Info: To subscribe, contact Dialog directly.

`telnet://dialog.com`

D&B - Dun's Electronic Business Directory

This database provides online information for over 8.9 million business and professionals throughout the US.

Keywords: Finance, Business, Dun & Bradstreet
Sponsor: Dun & Bradstreet Information Services, Parsippany, NJ, USA
Audience: Business Professionals, Business Analysts
Profile: A full directory listing is provided for each entry, including address, telephone number, SIC codes and descriptions, and number of employees. The file covers both public and private US companies of all sizes and types. Fifteen broad business categories are indexed as industry groups: agriculture, business services, communication, construction, finance, insurance, manufacturing, mining, professional services, public administration, real estate, retail, transportation, utilities, and wholesale. Data for the file is compiled and maintained primarily through Dun & Bradstreet's intensive credit interviewing process. Dun's staff of 1,300 business analysts actively interviews millions of entrepreneurs each year. This information is supplemented with data from large-volume telemarketing and direct mail campaigns.
Notes: Coverage: Current; updated quarterly.
Contact: Dialog in the US at (800) 334-2564, Dialog internationally at country-specific locations.
Details: Costs
User Info: To subscribe, contact Dialog directly.

`telnet://dialog.com`

D&B - European Dun's Market (EDMI)

This database presents detailed information on over 2.5 million businesses located in 26 European countries.

Keywords: Dun & Bradstreet, Europe, Business
Sponsor: Dun & Bradstreet Information Services, Parsippany, NJ, USA
Audience: Business Professionals
Profile: EDMI provides directory listings, sales volume and marketing data, and references to parent companies. Companies are selected for inclusion based on sales volume, national prominence, and international interest. Names, addresses, SIC codes, D-U-N-S numbers, and other data are given in each record. Both public and private companies are included.
Contact: Dialog in the US at (800) 334-2564, Dialog internationally at country-specific locations.
User Info: To subscribe, contact Dialog directly.
Notes: Coverage: Current; updated quarterly.

`telnet://dialog.com`

Dun & Bradstreet Corporation

Dun and Bradstreet's home page contains examples of existing services, services in development, and business and financial information, advising and so on.

Keywords: Finance, Business, Dun & Bradstreet
Audience: General Public, Business Professionals
Profile: Files include company news, related industry information, product descriptions, and discussions of IBM's services.

`http://www.corp.dnb.com`

DVI-list

DVI-list

This mailing list is intended for discussions about Intel's DVI (Digital Video Interactive) system. These discussions cover both applications and programming with DVI.

Keywords: Interactive Computing, Multimedia
Audience: Interactive Program Developers, Computer Programmers, Multimedia Users
Contact: Andrew Patrick
dvi-list-request@calvin.dgbt.doc.ca

User Info: To subscribe to the list, send an e-mail message requesting a subscription to the URL address below.

To send a message to the entire list, address it to: dvi-list-request@calvin.dgbt.doc.ca

`mailto:dvi-list-request@calvin.dgbt.doc.ca`

DYNSYS-L

DYNSYS-L

The Dynamical System exchanges information among people working in ergodic theory and dynamical systems.

Keywords: Entropy, Systems Theory

Audience: Engineers

Details: Free

`mailto:newserv@uhcvm1.oit.uhc.edu`

e-europe

e-europe

The electronic communications network for doing business in Eastern Europe. Its purpose is to help these countries in their transition to market economies.

Keywords: Eastern Europe, Economics, Business
Audience: Business Professionals, Investors, Economists
Contact: James W. Reese
r505040@univ scvm
e-europe@pucc.princeton.edu
Details: Free
User info: To subscribe to the list, send an e-mail message to the URL address shown below consisting of a single line reading:
SUB e-europe YourFirstName YourLastName.
To send a message to the entire list, address it to: e-europe@indycms.iupui.edu

`mailto:listserv@indycms.iupui.edu`

E-Mail

Bbones

A list discussing the construction of e-mail backbones for organizations and campuses.

Keywords: E-mail, Networking
Audience: Internet Surfers
Contact: mail-bbones-request@yorku.ca
Details: Free
User Info: To subscribe to the list, send an e-mail message requesting a subscription to the URL address below.
To send a message to the entire list, address it to: mail-bbones@yorku.ca

`mailto:mail-bbones-request@yorku.ca`

College E-mail Addresses

Information on e-mail addresses at graduate offices.

Keywords: Internet, E-mail
Audience: Internet Surfers, Students, College/University Educators
Details: Free
File is: pub/usenet/soc.college/Admission_Office_Email_Address_List

`ftp://pit-manager.mit.edu/pub/usenet-by-group/soc.college`

`gopher://sipb.mit.edu`

E-mail 101

E-mail 101 describes how to use e-mail as well as other Internet features.

Keywords: Internet, E-mail
Audience: Internet Surfers
Details: Free

`gopher://mrcnext.cso.uiuc.edu`

`http://mrcnext.cso.uiuc.edu`

E-mail Gopher

E-mail Gopher allows the use of a gopher via e-mail.

Keywords: Internet, Services, E-mail, Gopher
Audience: Internet Surfers
Details: Free
Include the word "help" in the Email.
(This is the National Cancer Center of Japan Server)

`gopher://gopher.ncc.go.jp/11/INFO/gopher`

E-mail Services

A list of services available by e-mail.

Keywords: Internet, E-mail, Services
Audience: Internet Surfers
Contact: David DeSimone
an207@cleveland.freenet.edu
Details: Free
File is: pub/docs/about-the-net/libsoft/email_services.txt

`ftp://sunsite.unc.edu/pub/docs/about-the-net/libsoft/email_services.txt`

`http://sunsite.unc.edu/pub/docs/about-the-net/libsoft/email_services.txt`

E-mail Understanding

A special issue of the University of Illinois publication UIUC net describing electronic mail.

Keywords: Internet, E-mail
Audience: Internet Surfers
Details: Free
File is: doc/net/uiucnet/vol2no2.txt

`ftp://ftp.cso.uiuc.edu/doc/net/uiucnet`

E-mail Usenet

E-mail Usenet allows the user to post to a newsgroup via e-mail.

E-Mail

Keywords: Internet, Services, E-mail, Usenet
Audience: Internet Surfers
Details: Free

`mailto://hierarchy-group-name@cs.utexas.edu`

E-mail WWW

E-mail WWW allows the user to obtain a web file via e-mail.

Keywords: Internet Services, E-mail, WWW
Audience: Internet Surfers
Details: Free
Include the words "www URL" in the e-mail.

`http://info.cern.ch/hypertext/WWW/TheProject.html`

E-mail-How To

An introductory guide to the UNIXMail System and to the procedures for sending and receiving mail, sending files by mail, and adding messages to files that are sent by mail.

Keywords: Internets Tools, Internet Guides, E-mail
Sponsor: SURAnet Network Information Center
Audience: Internet Surfers
Contact: info@sura.net
Details: Free
File is: pub/nic/network.service.guides/how.to.email.guide

`ftp://ftp.sura.net`

Educator's Guide to E-mail Lists

A guide to help educators find e-mail lists. Includes a very large list of e-mail addresses related to education.

Keywords: Education, E-mail, Internet
Sponsor: University of Massachusetts, Amherst, MA
Audience: Educators, Researchers
Contact: Prescott Smith
pgsmith@educ.umass.edu
Details: Free

`ftp://nic.umass.edu`

FAXNET

FAXNET allows the user to send faxes via e-mail.

Keywords: Internet Services, E-mail
Audience: Internet Surfers
Details: Free
Include the word "help" in the e-mail.

`mailto:info@awa.com`

Finding E-mail Addresses

Tips on finding e-mail addresses.

Keywords: Internet, E-mail
Audience: Internet Surfers
Contact: Jonathan Kamens
jib@MIT.Edu
Details: Free
File is: pub/docs/about-the-net/libsoft/email_address.txt

`ftp://sunsite.unc.edu`

Internet Phone Books

A collection of Internet phone books and e-mail directories.

Keywords: Phone Books, Internet Guides, E-mail
Sponsor: Texas Tech University
Audience: Internet Surfers, General Public
Profile: This gopher includes a number of resources for finding people on the Internet. In addition to the standard Netfind, WHOIS, and Inter-NIC services, it also has information on finding college and international e-mail addresses. Also features snail mail information from the U.S. Post Office on Zip codes, as well as an international directory of telephone area codes.
Contact: Abdul Malik Yoosufani
gripe@cs.ttu.edu

`gopher://cs4sun.cs.ttu.edu`

Internet Policy

An article entitled "What Should We Plan Given the Dilemma of the Network?" by G. Cook.

Keywords: Internet, E-mail
Audience: Internet Surfers
Details: Free

`ftp://pit-manager.mit.edu`

LIST REVIEW SERVICE

Explores e-mail distribution lists (primarily bitnet and ListServ lists).

Keywords: E-mail, Bitnet Lists, Listserv
Audience: Email Users
Profile: Akin to book and restaurant reviews, each issue begins with a narrative description of usually one week's worth of monitoring, then presents simple statistical data, such as the number of messages and lines, number of queries and nonqueries, number of subscribers and countries represented, list owner, location, and how to subscribe.
Contact: Raleigh C. Muns
srcmuns@umslvma.bitnet

Details: Free
User Info: To subscribe, send an e-mail message to the address below.
To send a message to the entire list, address it to:
listreviewservice@kentvm.kent.edu

`mailto:listserv@kentvm.kent.edu`

MetaMail

This resource contains information about MetaMail, which allows existing mail readers to read multimedia e-mail in the MIME (Multipurpose Internet Mail Extensions) format.

Keywords: Internet, E-mail
Audience: Internet Surfers
Contact: Nathaniel S. Borenstein
nsb@nsb.fv.com
Readme file is pub/nsb/README

`ftp://thumper.bellcore.com`

MIME (Multipurpose Internet Mail Extensions)

This resource contains information about the MIME (Multipurpose Internet Mail Extensions) protocol.

Keywords: Internet, E-Mail
Audience: Internet Surfers
Contact: Nathaniel S. Borenstein
nsb@nsb.fv.com
File is: documents/rfc/rfc1521.txt

`ftp://nic.merit.edu`

Netfind

Netfind is a way of finding Internet e-mail addresses.

Keywords: WWW, Information Retrieval, E-mail
Sponsor: Emory University, Georgia, USA
Audience: Reseachers, Students, General Public
Profile: This service relies on common but not universal programs, and thus may not find some people with valid addresses. The most foolproof way of finding someone's e-mail address remains to call them on the phone and ask. All Netfind sites are functionally equivalent. Multiple ones are listed here in case some are overloaded or down with technical problems.
Contact: Netfind Help
schwartz@cs.colorado.edu

`gopher://emoryu1.cc.emory.edu/11/internet/General/netfind`

news.newusers.questions

A Usenet newsgroup providing information and discussion.

Keywords: Usenet, E-mail, Internet Resources
Audience: Usenet Users, E-mail Users
Details: Free
User info: To subscribe to this Usenet newsgroup, you need access to a newsreader.

`news:news.newusers.questions`

PGP Mail

Information regarding the use of PGP (Pretty Good Privacy) mail, a public key.

Keywords: Internet, E-mail
Audience: Internet Surfers
Details: Free

`ftp://ftp.uu.net/networking/mail`

Pine E-mail

A description of the Program for Internet News and E-mail (PINE), a tool for reading, sending, and managing electronic messages.

Keywords: Internet Tools, E-mail
Audience: Internet Surfers
Details: Free
File is: mail/pine.blur

`ftp://ftp.cac.washington.edu`

E-mail-How To

E-mail-How To

An introductory guide to the UNIXMail System and to the procedures for sending and receiving mail, sending files by mail, and adding messages to files that are sent by mail.

Keywords: Internets Tools, Internet Guides, E-mail
Sponsor: SURAnet Network Information Center
Audience: Internet Surfers
Contact: info@sura.net
Details: Free
File is: pub/nic/network.service.guides/how.to.email.guide

`ftp://ftp.sura.net`

eagles

eagles

This list provides a forum for Boy Scouts, Scouters, and former Scouts who are gay/bisexual to discuss how they can apply pressure to the BSA to change their homophobic policies.

Keywords: Boy Scouts, Gays, Lesbians
Audience: Gays, Lesbians, Boy Scouts, Former Boy Scouts
Contact: eagles-request@flash.usc.edu
Details: Free
User info: To subscribe to the list, send an e-mail message requesting a subscription to the URL address below.

To send a message to the entire list, address it to: eagles-request@flash.usc.edu

`mailto:eagles-request@flash.usc.edu`

Earth Science

Earth and Sky

This is a weekly publication of transcripts of earth science and astronomy radio programs aired daily on the Earth & Sky Radio Series, hosted by Deborah Byrd and Joel Block.

Keywords: Earth Science, Astronomy
Audience: General Public, Earth Scientists, Astronomers
Contact: majordomo@lists.utexas.edu
Details: Free
User Info: To subscribe to the list, send an e-mail message to the URL address shown below consisting of a single line reading:

SUB earth-and-sky YourFirstName YourLastName

To send a message to the entire list, address it to: earth-and-sky@lists.utexas.edu

Notes: To add yourself to the EARTHANDSKY mailing list send

subscribe EARTHANDSKY

yourname@host.domain.name in an e-mail message to:

`mailto:majordomo@lists.utexas.edu`

Internet Resources for Earth Sciences

A document detailing Internet resources for a variety of earth science disciplines, including GIS.

Keywords: Directory, GIS, Geology, Geography, GPS, Mapping, Earth Science
Sponsor: Bill Thoen
Audience: Earth Scientists, Researchers
Profile: A complete document detailing the types of information available in earth sciences and the mechanisms to retrieve needed information.
Contact: Bill Thoen
bthoen@gisnet.com
Details: Free

`ftp://ftp.csn.org/COGS/ores.text`

Purdue University Library

The library's holdings are large and wide-ranging. They contain significant collections in many fields.

Keywords: Economics (History of), Literature (English), Literature (American), Indiana, Rogers (Bruce), Engineering (History of), Aviation, Earth Science, Atmospheric Science, Consumer Science, Family Science, Chemistry (History of), Physics, Veterinary Science
Audience: General Public, Researchers, Librarians, Document Delivery Professionals
Contact: Dan Ferrer
dan@asterix.lib.purdue.edu
Details: Free
User Info: Expect: User ID prompt, Send: GUEST

`telnet://lib.cc.purdue.edu`

East Asian Studies

University of Pennsylvania Library- Philadelphia Pa.

The library's holdings are large and wide-ranging and contain significant collections in many fields.

Keywords: Literature (English), Literature (American), History (World), Medieval Studies, East Asian Studies, Middle Eastern Studies, South Asian Studies, Judaica, Lithuania.
Audience: Educators, Students, Researchers
Profile: Access to the central Van Pelt Library and to most of the departmental libraries is restricted to members of the University community on weekends and holidays. Online visitors are advised to call (215) 898-7554 for information on hours and access restrictions.
Contact: Patricia Renfro, Associate Director of Libraries
Details: Free

`telnet://library.upenn.edu`

Eastern Europe

Central European Environment Data Report (CEDAR) Facility

This gopher site provides information about the environmental and scientific community in Central and Eastern Europe, with access to environmental information located throughout the world on various international computer networks and hosts.

Keywords: Europe, Central Europe, Eastern Europe, Environment

Sponsor:	The International Society for Environmental Protection, and The Austrian Federal Ministry for Environment, Youth and Family (BMUJF)
Audience:	Environmentalists, Educators, Students, Urban Planners, Environmental Scientists
Profile:	The CEDAR Facility, established in 1991, is administered by the International Society for Environmental Protection (ISEP). The Facility is designed to provide regional groups and individuals with access to its information retrieval and higher computing resources, technical advice and database and network access support. In addition, CEDAR works to facilitate information and dialogue exchange with organizations in other parts of the world and in partner countries; and to promote training forums, including the joint development of seminars and conferences with ISEP on environmental and network topics. Finally, CEDAR develops and manages environmental reference data sets, including a US EPA bibliographic reference on hazardous waste treatment, CEDAR databases on Central and Eastern European environmental expertise and information, and the holdings of the Regional Environmental Center Library at Budapest.
Contact:	cedar-info@cedar.univie.ac.at

`gopher://pan.cedar.univie.ac.at`

DRT EC and Eastern Europe Business Database

DRTE's comprehensive full-text coverage of business and industry in the EC is combined with in-depth reporting on doing business in Eastern Europe.

Keywords:	European Community, Eastern Europe
Sponsor:	DRT Europe Services Brussels, Belgium
Audience:	Market Analysts, Business Professionals, Market Researchers
Profile:	DRTE reports provide comprehensive and detailed coverage of all EC proposals, laws and policy directions and their commercial applications, and unique, country-specific information on the regulatory framework for business development and expansion in Eastern Europe. These are continually updated to reflect the rapidly changing nature of the political and administrative structure of these emerging economies as they affect business undertakings with EC concerns.
Contact:	Data-star through Dialog in the US at (800) 334-2564, Dialog internationally at country-specific locations.
User info:	To subscribe, contact Dialog directly.
Notes:	Coverage: The database is updated weekly to enable it to offer exceptionally current full-text information.

`telnet://dialog.com`

e-europe

The electronic communications network for doing business in Eastern Europe. Its purpose is to help these countries in their transition to market economies.

Keywords:	Eastern Europe, Economics, Business
Audience:	Business Professionals, Investors, Economists
Contact:	James W. Reese r505040@univ scvm or e-europe@pucc.princeton.edu
Details:	Free
User info:	To subscribe to the list, send an e-mail message to the URL address shown below consisting of a single line reading: SUB e-europe YourFirstName YourLastName. To send a message to the entire list, address it to: e-europe@indycms.iupui.edu

`mailto:listserv@indycms.iupui.edu`

EcoDirectory

A directory of Libraries and Environmental Information Centers in Central Eastern Europe.

Keywords:	Environment, Eastern Europe, Central Europe
Sponsor:	The Wladyslaw Poniecki Charitable Foundation, Inc.
Audience:	Environmentalists, Librarians, International Development Specialists
Profile:	This database is the product of an Environmental Training Project (ETP) which was founded in 1992 by the US Agency for International Development. The project concentrated on six Central and Eastern European countries: Bulgaria, Czech Republic, Hungary, Romania, Slovakia, and Poland. It contains information on over 300 Libraries and Environmental Information Centers in those countries. Access to the data is facilitated by a WAIS search engine which makes it possible to retrieve information about libraries, subject area specializations, personnel, and so on.
Contact:	Joerg Findeisen, CEDAR findeisen@pan.cedar.univie.ac.at

`gopher://gopher.poniecki.berkeley.edu`

Hungary

This discussion list circulates timely information about Hungary.

Keywords:	Hungary, Eastern Europe, News
Audience:	Researchers, Observers, Political Scientists
Contact:	Eric Dahlin hcf2hung@iucsbuxa
Details:	Free
User info:	To subscribe to the list, send an e-mail message to the URL address shown below consisting of a single line reading: SUB hungary YourFirstName YourLastName

`mailto:listserv@gwuvm.gwu.edu`

Mideur-l

A list containing the history, culture, politics, and current affairs of those countries lying between the Mediterranean/Adriatic and the Baltic Seas, and between the German/Austrian borders and the former Soviet Union.

Keywords:	Soviet Union, Baltic Republics, Eastern Europe, News
Audience:	Political Scientists, Researchers, Historians, General Public
Contact:	Jan George Frajkor mideur-1@ubvm.cc.buffalo.edu
Details:	Free
User info:	To subscribe to the list, send an e-mail message to the URL address below consisting of a single line reading: SUB mideur-l YourFirstName YourLastName To send a message to the entire list, address it to: mideur-1@ubvm.cc.buffalo.edu

`mailto:listserv@ubvm.cc.buffalo.edu`

Pigulki

This is an English-language digest concerning the Net news from Poland.

Keywords:	Poland, Eastern Europe
Audience:	Poles, Poland Observers, Journalists
Contact:	Marek Zielinski zielinski@acfcluster.nyu.edu
Details:	Free
User info:	To subscribe to the list, send an e-mail message requesting a subscription to the URL address below. To send a message to the entire list, address it to: davep@acsu.buffalo.edu

`mailto:davep@acsu.buffalo.edu`

Russian and East European Studies Home Pages

Keywords:	Russia, Eastern Europe, Government, Political Science
Sponsor:	University of Pittsburgh
Audience:	Researchers, Politicians

Contact:	Casey Palowitch cjp@acid.library.pitt.edu

`http://www.pitt.edu/cjp/rspubl.html`

Eastern European Business

DRT EC and Eastern Europe Business Database

DRTE's comprehensive full-text coverage of business and industry in the EC is combined with in-depth reporting on doing business in Eastern Europe.

Keywords:	European Community, Eastern Europe
Sponsor:	DRT Europe Services Brussels, Belgium
Audience:	Market Analysts, Business Professionals, Market Researchers
Profile:	DRTE reports provide comprehensive and detailed coverage of all EC proposals, laws and policy directions and their commercial applications, and unique, country-specific information on the regulatory framework for business development and expansion in Eastern Europe. These are continually updated to reflect the rapidly changing nature of the political and administrative structure of these emerging economies as they affect business undertakings with EC concerns.
Contact:	Data-star through Dialog in the US at (800) 334-2564, Dialog internationally at country-specific locations.
User info:	To subscribe, contact Dialog directly.
Notes:	Coverage: The database is updated weekly to enable it to offer exceptionally current full-text information.

`telnet://dialog.com`

Eastern Washington University Library

Eastern Washington University Library

The library's holdings are large and wide-ranging and contain significant collections in many fields.

Keywords:	Education, Music, Social Science, Behavioral Science
Audience:	Researchers, Students, General Public
Details:	Free
User Info:	Expect: Login; Send: Lib

`telnet://wsduvm12.csc.wsu.edu`

ebikes

ebikes

New York City Bicycle discussion list.

Keywords:	Bicycling, New York
Audience:	Bicyclists
Contact:	Danny Lieberman ebikes-request@panix.com
Details:	Free
User info:	To subscribe to the list, send an e-mail message requesting a subscription to the URL address below. To send a message to the entire list, address it to: ebikes-request@panix.com

`mailto:ebikes-request@panix.com`

EC

EC

Dedicated to discussion of the European Community (EC).

Keywords:	European Community, Europe
Audience:	Europeans, Researchers, General Public, Economists
Contact:	John B. Harlan ijbh200@indyvax.iupui.edu or ec@vm.cc.metu.edu.tr
Details:	Free
User info:	To subscribe to the list, send an e-mail message to the URL address shown below consisting of a single line reading: SUB ec YourFirstName YourLastName

`mailto:listserv@linycms.iupiu.edu`

Ecclesiastical History

Ecchst-l

A discussion list for scholars of Ecclesiastical history, including those interested both in the history of the Church and in the examination of theology in an historical context.

Keywords:	Religion, Ecclesiastical History, Christianity, Theology
Audience:	Historians, Theologians
Contact:	Gregory H. Singleton ugsingle@uxa.ecn.bgu.edu
User info:	To subscribe, send an e-mail message to the URL address below consisting of a single line reading: SUB ecchst-l YourFirstName YourLastName. To send a message to the entire list, address it to: ecchst-l@bgu.edu

`mailto:listserv@bgu.edu`

Echinoderm

Starnet (Echinoderm Newsletter)

The Starnet echinoderm electronic newsletter is distributed quarterly.

Keywords:	Echinoderm, Starfish, Marine Biology
Audience:	Marine Biologists
Contact:	Win Hide whide@matrix.bchs.uh.edu
Details:	Free
User info:	To subscribe to the list, send an e-mail message requesting a subscription to the URL address below.

`mailto:whide@matrix.bchs.uh.edu`

echl-news

echl-news

For people interested in discussing and following the East Coast Hockey League.

Keywords:	Hockey, Sports
Audience:	Hockey Enthusiasts
Contact:	echl-news-request@andrew.cmu.edu
Details:	Free
User info:	To subscribe to the list, send an e-mail message requesting a subscription to the URL address below. To send a message to the entire list, address it to: echl-news-request@andrew.cmu.edu

`mailto:echl-news-request@andrew.cmu.edu`

ECHO

ECHO

A computer conferencing system based in New York City.

Keywords:	Community, Networking, Women's Issues
Sponsor:	East Coast Hang Out

Audience:	Activists, Policy Makers, Community Leaders, Governments, Students, Feminists, Educators, Health Care Professionals, Artists, Communicators, General Public
Profile:	ECHO was started by Stacy Horn, as an East Coast counterpart to the WELL. ECHO makes an effort to be hospitable to women and has one of the highest percentages of women in an online community.
Contact:	Stacy Horn horn@echonyc.com,
Details:	Costs

`telnet://echonyc.com`

echoes

echoes

Info and commentary on the musical group Pink Floyd, as well as other projects members of the group have been involved with.

Keywords:	Rock Music, Pink Floyd
Audience:	Rock Music Enthusiasts, Pink Floyd Enthusiasts
Contact:	H. W. Neff echoes-request@fawnya.tcs.com
Details:	Free
User Info:	To subscribe to the list, send an e-mail message requesting a subscription to the URL address below. To send a message to the entire list, address it to: echoes-request@fawnya.tcs.com

`mailto:echoes-request@fawnya.tcs.com`

EcoDirectory

EcoDirectory

A directory of Libraries and Environmental Information Centers in Central Eastern Europe.

Keywords:	Environment, Eastern Europe, Central Europe
Sponsor:	The Wladyslaw Poniecki Charitable Foundation, Inc.
Audience:	Environmentalists, Librarians, International Development Specialists
Profile:	This database is the product of an Environmental Training Project (ETP) which was founded in 1992 by the US Agency for International Development. The project concentrated on six Central and Eastern European countries: Bulgaria, Czech Republic, Hungary, Romania, Slovakia, and Poland.

It contains information on over 300 Libraries and Environmental Information Centers in those countries. Access to the data is facilitated by a WAIS search engine which makes it possible to retrieve information about libraries, subject area specializations, personnel, and so on.

Contact:	Joerg Findeisen, CEDAR findeisen@pan.cedar.univie.ac.at

`gopher://gopher.poniecki.berkeley.edu`

Ecology

Australian Environmental Resources Information Network (ERIN)

This gopher contains a wide range of Australian environmental information.

Keywords:	Environment, Australia, Ecology
Audience:	Environmentalists, Ecologists, Researchers, Australians
Profile:	Coverage includes biodiversity, protected areas, terrestrial and marine environments, environmental protection and legislation, international agreements, and general information about ERIN.
Contact:	gopher@erin.gov.au
Details:	Free

`gopher://kaos.erin.gov.au`

`http://kaos.erin.gov.au/erin.html`

Biosis Previews

The database encompasses the entire field of life sciences and covers original research reports and reviews in biological and biomedical areas. This includes field, laboratory, clinical, experimental and theoretical work. The traditional areas of biology, including botany, zoology, and microbiology, are covered, as well as the related fields such as plant and animal science, agriculture, pharmacology, and ecology.

Keywords:	Biology, Botany, Zoology, Microbiology, Plant Science, Animal Science, Agriculture, Pharmacology, Ecology, Biochemistry, Biophysics, Bioengineering
Sponsor:	Biosis
Audience:	Librarians, Researchers, Students, Biologists, Botanists, Zoologists, Scientists, Taxonomists
Contact:	CDP Technologies Sales Department (800)950-2035, extension 400.
User info:	To subscribe, contact CDP Technologies directly.

`telnet://cdplus@cdplus.com`

sci.environment

A Usenet newsgroup providing information and discussion about the environment and ecology.

Keywords:	Environment, Ecology
Audience:	Environmentalists, ecologists, Earth Scientists
Details:	Free
User info:	To subscribe to this Usenet newsgroup, you need access to a newsreader.

`news:sci.environment`

Sense of Place

An electronic environmentalists magazine. The magazine incorporates graphics and text in a format specifically designed to be read on a Macintosh screen. You must have Hypercard version 2.1 or later.

Keywords:	Environment, Ecology
Audience:	Environmentalists
Contact:	SOP@dartmouth.edu
Details:	Costs
User info:	To subscribe send electronic mail to SOP@dartmouth.edu

`gopher://gopher.dartmouth.edu/1/anonftp/pub/sop`

The University of Notre Dame Library

The Library's holdings are large and wide-ranging and contain significant collections in many fields, including the following: Irish Music, Maps of Ireland, History of Botany, Ecology, Entomology, Parasitology, Aquatic Biology, History of Universities, Manuscript Studies, Paleography, Botany, Ireland

Keywords:	Music (Irish), Ireland, Botany (History of), Ecology, Entomology, Parasitology, Aquatic Biology, Universities (History of), Paleography
Audience:	General Public, Researchers, Librarians, Document Delivery Professionals
Details:	Free
User Info:	Expect: ENTER COMMAND OR HELP:, Send: library; To leave, type x on the command line and press the enter key. At the ENTER COMMAND OR HELP: prompt, type bye and press the enter key.

`telnet://irishmvs.cc.nd.edu`

Western Lands

A collection of articles and reports relating to environmental and land use issues in the Western United States.

Keywords:	Environmentalism, Ecology, Forests, The Western United States
Sponsor:	The Institute for Global Communications (IGC)

Economics   229

Audience: Environmentalists, Ecologists, Activists, Foresters, Citizens
Contact: Dan Yurman, IGC User Support
dyurman@igc.apc.com
support@igc.apc.com
Notes: User submissions encouraged.

`gopher://gopher.igc.apc.org/11/environment/forests/western.lands`

Economic Development

econ-dev

This mailing list is for sharing with economic development professionals who are helping small, innovative companies compete in the new global environment.

Keywords: Economic Development, Business
Audience: Economic Development Experts, Business Professionals
Contact: majordomo@csn.org
Details: Free
User info: To subscribe to the list, send an e-mail message to the URL address shown below consisting of a single line reading:

SUB econ-dev YourFirstName YourLastName

To send a message to the entire list, address it to: econ.dev@csn.org

`mailto:majordomo@csn.org`

Economic Policy

Economic Policy Research

A forum for the exchange of papers and information on economic-policy research.

Keywords: Economics, Economic Policy
Audience: Economists, Policy Analysts
Details: Free

`gopher://cis.anu.edu.au`

`http://coombs.anu.edu.au/CoombsHome.html`

Economics

Asian and Pacific Economic Literature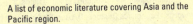

A list of economic literature covering Asia and the Pacific region.

Keywords: Asia, Pacific, Economics
Audience: Economists, Business Professionals
Details: Free

`ftp://coombs.anu.edu`

Business News—Singapore

This gopher site focuses on business in Singapore.

Keywords: Singapore, Economics, Business
Audience: Economists, Business Professionals
Details: Free

`gopher://gopher.cic.net/11/e-serials/alphabetic/b/business-news`

`http://gopher.cic.net`

Business, Economics

This directory is a compilation of information resources focused on business and economics.

Keywords: Business, Economics
Audience: Business Professionals, Business Students, Economists
Details: Free

`ftp://una.hh.lib.umich.edu/70/inetdirsstacks/govdocs:tsangaustin`

CERRO (Central European Regional Research Organization)

CERRO provides access to information about the economic restructuring of Central Europe, including a discussion list, papers, news summaries, and pointers to other gophers in Central Europe.

Keywords: Central Europe, Economics, News
Audience: Economists, Researchers, Journalists
Contact: gunther.maier@wu-wien.ac.at
Details: Free

`gopher://osiris.wu.wein.ac.at`

Clinton's Economic Plan

The contents of US President Clinton's economic plan.

Keywords: Economics, Government (US), Clinton (Bill)
Audience: Economists, General Public
Details: Free
The data contained on the President's Economic Plan diskette is now available via anonymous FTP at cu.nih.gov. The data can be found in a directory named USDOC-OBA-INFO.

`gopher://wiretap.spies.com/11/Gov/Economic`

Commerce Business Daily

The Commerce Business Daily is a publication that announces invitations to bid on proposals requested by the US Federal Government. This gopher is updated every business day.

Keywords: Business (US), Economics, Commerce, Trade, Government (US)
Sponsor: CNS and Softshare Government Information Systems
Audience: Economists, Business Professionals, General Public, Journalists, Students, Politicians.
Profile: Invitations via Internet email that apply only to specific companies can be arranged.
Contact: Melissa Allensworth
sshare@cscns.com
service@cscns.com
Details: Free

`gopher://cns.cscns.com/cbd/About the CBD`

e-europe

The electronic communications network for doing business in Eastern Europe. Its purpose is to help these countries in their transition to market economies.

Keywords: Eastern Europe, Economics, Business
Audience: Business Professionals, Investors, Economists
Contact: James W. Reese
r505040@univ scvm
e-europe@pucc.princeton.edu
Details: Free
User info: To subscribe to the list, send an e-mail message to the URL address shown below consisting of a single line reading:

SUB e-europe YourFirstName YourLastName.

To send a message to the entire list, address it to: e-europe@indycms.iupui.edu

`mailto:listserv@indycms.iupui.edu`

Economic Policy Research

A forum for the exchange of papers and information on economic-policy research.

Keywords: Economics, Economic Policy
Audience: Economists, Policy Analysts
Details: Free

`gopher://cis.anu.edu.au`

`http://coombs.anu.edu.au/CoombsHome.html`

Info-South (Latin American News)

The database provides citations and abstracts of materials relating to contemporary economic, political, and social issues in Latin America.

Keywords: International News, Economics, International Politics, Latin America
Sponsor: University of Miami, Coral Gables, FL, US

Audience:	General Public	
Profile:	Coverage includes a wide range of topics assessing the current situation in Latin America.	
Contact:	Dialog in the US at (800) 334-2564, Dialog internationally at country-specific locations.	
User info:	To subscribe, contact Dialog directly.	
Notes:	Coverage: 1988 to the present; updated weekly.	

`telnet://dialog.com`

Internet Economics

An article entitled "Some Economics of the Internet" by Jeffrey K. Mackie-Mason.

Keywords:	Economics, Internet
Audience:	Internet Surfers
Contact:	Jeffrey K. Mackie-Mason
Details:	Free

`ftp://gopher.econ.lsa.umich.edu`

Internet Pricing

An article entitled "Pricing the Internet."

Keywords:	Internet, Economics
Audience:	Internet Surfers
Contact:	Mackie-Mason and Varian
Details:	Free

`gopher://gopher.econ.lsa.umich.edu`

Johns Hopkins University Library

The library's holdings are large and wide-ranging and contain significant collections in many fields.

Keywords:	Literature (English), Economics, Classics, Drama (German), Slavery, Trade Unions, Incunabula, Bibles, Diseases (History of), Nursing (History of), Abolitionism
Audience:	General Public, Researchers, Librarians, Document Delivery Professionals
Details:	Free

`telnet://jhuvm.hcf.jhu.edu`

LabStat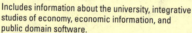

The public database of the Bureau of Labor Statistics.

Keywords:	Economics, Labor, Census Data
Sponsor:	United States Government, Bureau of Labor Statistics
Audience:	General Public, Statisticians, Researchers
Profile:	LABSTAT provides current and historical data, as well as numerous press releases. This site is composed of individual databases (in flat file format) corresponding to each of 26 surveys.
Contact:	labstat.helpdesk@bls.gov
Details:	Free
Login:	anonymous; use e-mail address as password.
Notes:	For each news release published by the Bureau of Labor Statistics, the two most current are stored in the /news.release directory. The documentation provides a list of the abbreviations used to identify the news releases and a description of the sub-directories available to the user.

`ftp://stats.bls.gov`

NetEc

An electronic forum for published academic papers relating to economics.

Keywords:	Economics, Business
Audience:	Economists, Business People
Contact:	netec@uts.mcc.ac.uk
Details:	Free
User info:	To subscribe to the list, send an e-mail message to the address below consisting of a single line reading: SUB netec YourFirstName YourLastName To send a message to the entire list, address it to: netec@hasara11.bitnet

`mailto:listserv@hasara11.bitnet`

Prague University of Economics Gopher Service

Includes information about the university, integrative studies of economy, economic information, and public domain software.

Keywords:	Czech Republic, Economics, Europe
Audience:	Czechs, Economists
Contact:	gopher@pub.vse.cz
Details:	Free

`gopher://pub.vse.cz`

The Management Archive

This is an electronic forum for management ideas and information.

Keywords:	Management, Business, Economics
Audience:	Managers, Business Professionals, Economists
Profile:	The Archive arranges working papers, teaching materials, and so on, in directories by subject. All materials in the Archive are fully indexed and searchable. If you have material that you would like to see receive worldwide network exposure and distribution, submit them to the Archive.
Contact:	Jim Goes goes@chimera.sph.umn.edu
Details:	Free
User Info:	Expect: login, Send: anonymous; Expect: password, Send: your e-mail address.

`ftp://chimera.sph.umn.edu`

University of Puerto Rico Library

The library's holdings are large and wide-ranging and contain significant collections in many fields.

Keywords:	Computer Science, Education, Nursing, Agriculture, Economics
Audience:	Researchers, Students, General Public
Details:	Free
	After Locator: telnet://, press Tab twice. Type DIAL VTAM. Enter NOTIS. Press Return. On the blank screen, type LUUP.

`telnet://136.145.2.10`

University of Wisconsin Green Bay Library

The library's holdings are large and wide-ranging and contain significant collections in many fields.

Keywords:	Economics, Environmental Studies, Music, Natural Science
Audience:	Researchers, Students, General Public
Details:	Free
User Info:	Expect: Service Name, Send: Victor

`telnet://gbls2k.uwgb.edu`

Economics (History of)

Emory University Library

The library's holdings are large and wide-ranging and contain significant collections in many fields.

Keywords:	Health Sciences, Theology, History (US), Communism, Economics (History of), Literature (American)
Audience:	General Public, Researchers, Librarians, Document Delivery Professionals
Details:	Free
User Info:	Expect: VM screen, Send: RETURN; Expect: CP READ, Send: DIAL VTAM, press RETURN; Expect: CICS screen, Send: PF1

`telnet://emuvm1.cc.emory.edu`

Purdue University Library

The library's holdings are large and wide-ranging. They contain significant collections in many fields.

Keywords:	Economics (History of), Literature (English), Literature (American), Indiana, Rogers (Bruce), Engineering (History of), Aviation, Earth Science, Atmospheric Science, Consumer Science, Family Science, Chemistry (History of), Physics, Veterinary Science

Audience:	General Public, Researchers, Librarians, Document Delivery Professionals
Contact:	Dan Ferrer dan@asterix.lib.purdue.edu
Details:	Free
User Info:	Expect: User ID prompt, Send: GUEST

`telnet://lib.cc.purdue.edu`

Economy

Asia-Pacific

The database covers the business, economics, and new industries of the Pacific Rim nations, including East Asia, Southeast Asia, the Indian Subcontinent, the Middle East, Australia, and the Pacific Island nations.

Keywords:	Asia, Pacific, Business, Economy
Sponsor:	Aristarchus Knowledge Industries, Seattle, WA, USA
Audience:	Market Researchers, Economists, Market Analysts
Profile:	Records are of two types: main records consisting of abstracts or citations for journal articles and other publications; and company thesaurus records. Detailed abstracts are provided for selected journal articles, monographs, selected papers in conference proceedings, dissertations, and government documents. Shorter citations with briefer indexing are provided for a wide variety of journal articles, newspapers, government documents, and annual report publications. Asia-Pacific also includes an extensive Corporate Thesaurus subfile, which provides detailed coverage of the corporate players in the Pacific Rim, including thousands of companies traded on the stock exchanges of Southeast and East Asia.
Contact:	Dialog in the US at (800) 334-2564; Dialog internationally at country-specific locations.
Details:	Costs
User info:	To subscribe, contact Dialog directly.

`telnet://dialog.com`

Universite de Montreal UDEMATIK Library

The library's holdings are large and wide-ranging and contain significant collections in many fields.

Keywords:	Art, Architecture, Economy, Sexology, Social Law, Science, Technology, Literary Studies
Audience:	Researchers, Students, General Public
Contact:	Joelle or Sebastien Roy udematik@ere.umontreal.ca stemp@ere.umontreal.ca roys@ere.umontreal.ca
User Info:	Expect: Login; Send: Application id INFO

`telnet://udematik.umontreal.ca`

Yahoo Market and Investments

A comprehensive look at the current economic status, with a wide range of coverage, from brokers to stocks.

Keywords:	Business, Stock Market, Investment, Economy
Sponsor:	Stanford University, Palo Alto, California, USA
Audience:	Investors, Economists
Contact:	jerry@akebono.stanford.edu

`http://akebono.stanford.edu/yahoo/Economy/Markets_and_Investments`

ECTL

ECTL

A list dedicated to researchers interested in Computer Speech Interfaces.

Keywords:	Computer Speech Interfaces
Audience:	Computer Speech Researchers
Contact:	David Leip ectl-request@snowhite.cis.uoguelph.ca
Details:	Free
User Info:	To subscribe to the list, send an e-mail message requesting a subscription to the URL address below. To send a message to the entire list, address it to: ectl-request@snowhite.cis.uoguelph.ca

`mailto:ectl-request@snowhite.cis.uoguelph.ca`

ecto

ecto

Information and discussion about singer/songwriter Happy Rhodes, and other music, art, books, and films of common (or singular) interest.

Keywords:	Music, Art, Rhodes (Happy)
Audience:	Music Enthusiasts, Art Enthusiasts
Contact:	Jessica Dembski ecto-request@ns1.rutgers.edu
Details:	Free
User Info:	To subscribe to the list, send an e-mail message requesting a subscription to the URL address below. To send a message to the entire list, address it to: ecto-request@ns1.rutgers.edu

`mailto:ecto-request@ns1.rutgers.edu`

Ecumenism

Catholic

The CATHOLIC mailing list is a forum for Catholics who wish to discuss their discipleship to Jesus Christ in terms of the Catholic approach to Christianity. "Catholic" is loosely defined as anyone embracing the Catholic approach to Christianity whether Roman Catholic, Anglo-Catholic, or Orthodox. Discussions on ecumenism are encouraged.

Keywords:	Catholicism, Ecumenism, Religion
Audience:	Catholics, Priests, Theologians
Contact:	Cindy Smith cms@dragon.com
Details:	Free
User info:	To subscribe to the list, send an e-mail message to the address below, consisting of a single line reading: SUB Catholic YourFirstName YourLastName To send a message to the entire list, address it to: Catholic@american.edu
Notes:	This list is also bi-directionally forwarded to the newsgroup bit.listserv.catholic.

`mailto:listserv@american.edu`

edista (Educacin a Distancia)

edista (Educacin a Distancia)

The University Distance Program (UNIDIS) at the University of Santiago, Chile, sponsors Educacin a Distancia (Education at a Distance).

Keywords:	Education (Adult), Education (Distance), Education (Continuing), Chile
Sponsor:	The University Distance Program (UNIDIS) at the University of Santiago, Chile
Audience:	Educators, Researchers
Details:	Free
User info:	To subscribe to the list, send an e-mail message to the URL address shown below consisting of a single line reading: SUB edistaYourFirstName YourLastName To send a message to the entire list, address it to: edista@usachvm1.bitnet

`mailto:listserv@usachvm1.bitnet`

Editors

CCNEWS

An electronic forum for campus-computing newsletter editors and other publications specialists.

Keywords: Computers, Editors, Students, Newsletters
Audience: Students (college), Editors
Profile: CCNEWS consists of a biweekly newsletter that focuses on the writing, editing, designing, and producing of campus-computing publications, and an articles abstracts published on alternating weeks that describes new contributions to the articles archive.
Contact: Wendy Rickard Bollentin
ccnews@educom.bitnet
Details: Free
User info: To subscribe to the list, send an e-mail message to the URL address below consisting of a single line reading:

SUB ccnews YourFirstName YourLastName

To send a message to the entire list, address it to: ccnews@educom.bitnet

Inquire about needing a password.

`mailto:listserv@bitnic.cren.net`

EDNET

EDNET ★

This forum explores the educational potential of the Internet.

Keywords: Education, Internet
Audience: Students, Educators
Profile: This independent, unmoderated mailing-list interest group is open and free of charge to all participants. Ednet links educators with common interests, and introduces students to a number of fields and sources of information, while offering criticism and suggestions.
Contact: Prescott Smith
pgsmith@educ.umass.edu
Details: Free
User info: To subscribe to the list, send an e-mail message to the address shown below consisting of a single line reading:

SUB Ednet YourFirstName YourLastName

To send a message to the entire list, address it to:

ednet@nic.umass.edu.

`gopher://ericir.syr.edu/00/AskERIC/FullText/Lists/Messages/`

EDNET-List/README

`mailto:listserv@nic.umass.edu`

edpolyan (Educational Policy Analysis)

edpolyan (Educational Policy Analysis) ★

This list focuses on educational policy analysis. This is an active, broad list, where issues surrounding all levels of education are discussed. This list takes a relatively philosophical approach to the issue.

Keywords: Education (Continuing), Educational Policy
Audience: University Administrators, K-12 Educators, Postsecondary Educators
Details: Free
User info: To subscribe to the list, send an e-mail message to the URL address shown below consisting of a single line reading:

SUB edpolyan YourFirstName YourLastName

To send a message to the entire list, address it to: edpolyan@asuacad.bitnet

`mailto:listserv@asuacad.bitnet`

edpolyar (Educational Policy Analysis Archive)

edpolyar (Educational Policy Analysis Archive) ★

The Educational Policy Analysis Archive, an outgrowth of the edpolyan scholarly discussion list, publishes peer-reviewed articles of between 500 and 1,500 lines in length on all aspects of education policy analysis.

Keywords: Education (Continuing), Educational Policy
Audience: K-12 Educators, University Administrators, Postsecondary Educators
Details: Free, Moderated
User info: To subscribe to the archive, send an e-mail message to the URL address shown below consisting of a single line reading

SUB edpolyar YourFirstName YourLastName

`mailto:listserv@asuacad.bitnet`

edstyle (Learning Styles Theory and Research List)

edstyle (Learning Styles Theory and Research List) ★

This list discusses all forms of information about learning styles.

Keywords: Education (Continuing)
Audience: Educators, Educational Administrators, Researchers
Details: Free
User info: To subscribe to the list, send an e-mail message to the URL address shown below consisting of a single line reading:

SUB edstyle YourFirstName YourLastName

To send a message to the entire list, address it to: edstyle @sjuvm.bitnet

`mailto:listserv@sjuvm.bitnet`

Education (Adult)

AACIS-L (American Association for Collegiate Independent Study)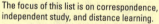

★

The focus of this list is on correspondence, independent study, and distance learning.

Keywords: Education (Adult), Education (Distance), Education (Continuing)
Sponsor: American Association for Collegiate Independent Study (AACIS)
Audience: Faculty Administrators
Details: Free
User info: To subscribe to the list, send an e-mail message to the URL address shown below consisting of a single line reading:

SUB aacis-l YourFirstName YourLastName

To send a message to the entire list, address it to: aacis-l@bgu.edu

`mailto:listserv@bgu.edu`

ADLTED-L (Canadian Adult Education Network)

★

The Canadian Adult Continuing Education Network list is a broad, worldwide discussion group.

Keywords: Education (Adult), Education (Distance), Education (Continuing)
Sponsor: Canadian Adult Education Network
Audience: Researchers, Educators, Administrators, Faculty
Details: Free

Education (Adult)

User info: To subscribe to the list, send an e-mail message to the URL address shown below, consisting of a single line reading:

SUB adlted-l YourFirstName YourLastName

To send a message to the entire list, address it to: adletd-L@uregina1.bitnet

mailto:listserv@uregina1.uregina.ca

Adult/Distance Education

This directory is a compilation of information resources focused on adult/distance education. The directory is sponsored by The American Association for Collegiate Independent Study, and focuses on correspondence, independent study and distance learning.

Keywords: Education (Adult), Education (Distance), Education (Continuing)
Audience: Educators, Researchers
Details: Free

ftp://una.hh.lib.umich.edu/70/inetdirsstacks/disted:ellsworth

AEDNET (Adult Education Network) ★★★★

This is an international electronic network for those involved in distance education.

Keywords: Education (Adult), Education (Distance), Education (Continuing)
Sponsor: Adult Education Network
Audience: Educators, Researchers, Administrators, Faculty
Details: Free
User info: To subscribe to the list, send an e-mail message to the URL address below consisting of a single line reading:

SUB aednet YourFirstName YourLastName

To send a message to the entire list, address it to: AEDNET@alpha.acast.nova.edu

mailto:listserv@alpha.acast.nova.edu

Altlearn (Alternative Approaches to Learning Discussion)

A discussion list that is broadly concerned with learning strategies at all levels.

Keywords: Education (Adult), Education (Distance), Education (Alternative)
Sponsor: Alternative Approaches to Learning Discussion
Audience: Educators, Administrators, Researchers
Details: Free

User info: To subscribe to the list, send an e-mail message to the URL address below, consisting of a single line reading:

SUB Altlearn YourFirstName YourLastName

To send a message to the entire list, address it to: altlearn@sjuvm.bitnet

mailto:listserv@sjuvm.bitnet

Asat-eva (Distance Education Evaluation Group) ★

This mailing list addresses issues in evaluating all forms of distance learning and programs.

Keywords: Education (Adult), Education (Distance), Education (Continuing)
Sponsor: Agricultural Satellite Corporation
Audience: Educators, Administrators, Researchers
Details: Free
User info: To subscribe to the list, send an e-mail message to the URL address below, consisting of a single line reading:

SUB asat-eva YourFirstName YourLastName

To send a message to the entire list, address it to: asat-eva@unlvm.unl.edu

mailto:listserv@unlvm.unl.edu

Catalyst ★

This is the electronic version of Catalyst, a refereed print journal for community college educators.

Keywords: Education (Adult), Education (Distance), Education (Continuing), Education (International)
Audience: Educators, Administrators, Faculty, Researchers
Details: Free, Moderated
User info: To subscribe to the journal, send an e-mail message to the URL address below, consisting of a single line reading:

SUB catalyst YourFirstName YourLastName

To send a message to the entire list, address it to: catalyst@vtvm1.bitnet

mailto:listserv@vtvm1.cc.vt.edu

CAUCE-L (Canadian Association for University Continuing Education) ★

Provides an electronic forum for the discussion of issues (broad, narrow, practical, theoretical, controversial, or mundane) related to university continuing education.

Keywords: Education (Adult), Education (Distance), Education (Continuing)
Sponsor: Canadian Association for University Continuing Education
Audience: Educators, Administrators, Faculty

Details: Free
User info: To subscribe to the list, send an e-mail message to the URL address below, consisting of a single line reading:

SUB cauce-l YourFirstName YourLastName

To send a message to the entire list, address it to: cauce@max.cc.uregina.ca

mailto:listserv@max.cc.uregina.ca

deos-l (International Discussion Forum for Distance Learning)

A large, diverse distance education list, which currently has 1,325 subscribers in 48 countries.

Keywords: Education (Adult), Education (Distance), Education (Continuing)
Sponsor: American Center for the Study of Distance Education
Audience: Educators, Administrators
Details: Free
User info: To subscribe to the list, send an e-mail message to the URL address shown below consisting of a single line reading:

SUB deos-l YourFirstName YourLastName

To send a message to the entire list, address it to: deos-l@psuvm.bitnet

mailto:listserv@psuvm.bitnet

deosnews (Distance Education Online Symposium) ★★★

The Distance Education Online Symposium publishes The American Journal of Distance Education.

Keywords: Education (Adult), Education (Distance), Education (Continuing)
Sponsor: Distance Education Online Symposium, American Center for the Study of Distance Education, Pennsylvania State University, State College, PA
Audience: Educators, Administrators, Researchers
Details: Free
User info: To subscribe to the journal, send an e-mail message to the URL address shown below consisting of a single line reading:

SUB deosnews YourFirstName YourLastName

mailto:listserv@psuvm.bitnet

dts-l (Dead Teachers Society Discussion List)

This list is for broad discussions of teaching and learning.

Keywords: Education (Adult), Education (Distance), Education (Continuing)
Audience: Educators (K-12), Educational Administrators

Education (Adult)

Details: Free

User info: To subscribe to the list, send an e-mail message to the URL address shown below consisting of a single line reading:

SUB dts-l YourFirstName YourLastName

To send a message to the entire list, address it to: dts-l@iubvm.bitnet

mailto:listserv@iubvm.bitnet

edista (Educacin a Distancia)

The University Distance Program (UNIDIS) at the University of Santiago, Chile, sponsors Educacin a Distancia (Education at a Distance).

Keywords: Education (Adult), Education (Distance), Education (Continuing), Chile

Sponsor: The University Distance Program (UNIDIS) at the University of Santiago, Chile

Audience: Educators, Researchers

Details: Free

User info: To subscribe to the list, send an e-mail message to the URL address shown below consisting of a single line reading:

SUB edistaYourFirstName YourLastName

To send a message to the entire list, address it to: edista@usachvm1.bitnet

mailto:listserv@usachvm1.bitnet

hilat-l (Higher Education in Latin America)

Provides a means of interchange about research on higher education in Latin America. Postings are mostly in English, but are also welcome in Spanish and Portuguese.

Keywords: Education (Adult), Education (Distance), Education (Continuing), Latin America

Audience: Educators, Administrators, Faculty

Details: Free

User info: To subscribe to the list, send an e-mail message to the URL address shown below consisting of a single line reading:

SUB hilat-l YourFirstName YourLastName

To send a message to the entire list, address it to: hilat-l@bruspvm.bitnet

mailto:listserv@bruspvm.bitnet

horizons 'New Horizons in Adult Education'

A journal transmitted to educators around the world.

Keywords: Education (Adult), Education (Distance), Education (Continuing)

Audience: Educators, Administrators, Faculty, Researchers

Details: Free

User info: To subscribe to the journal, send an e-mail message to the URL address shown below consisting of a single line reading:

SUB horizonsYourFirstName YourLastName

mailto:listserv@alpha.acast.nova.edu

ipct-j 'Interpersonal Computing and Technology: An Electronic Journal for the 21st Century'

Interpersonal Computing and Technology Journal is an outgrowth of the IPCT-L discussion group.

Keywords: Education (Adult), Education (Distance), Education (Continuing), Information Technology

Sponsor: Interpersonal Computing and Technology

Audience: Educators, Administrators, Faculty

Details: Free

User info: To subscribe to the journal, send an e-mail message to the URL address shown below consisting of a single line reading:

SUB ipct-j YourFirstName YourLastName

mailto:listserv@guvm.bitnet

joe 'The Journal of Extension'

This is the peer-reviewed publication of the Cooperative Extension System; it covers all phases of extension education, including adult and distance education.

Keywords: Education (Adult), Education (Distance), Education (Continuing)

Audience: Educators (K-12), Faculty Administrators

Details: Free

User info: To subscribe to the journal, send an e-mail message requesting a subscription to the URL address shown below.

mailto:almanac@joe.uwex.edu

Jte-l 'Journal of Technology Education'

The Journal of Technology Education provides a forum for all topics relating to technology in education.

Keywords: Education (Adult), Education (Distance), Education (Continuing), Information Technology

Audience: Faculty, Administrators, Educators (K-12)

Details: Free

User info: To subscribe to the journal, send an e-mail message to the URL address below consisting of a single line reading:

SUB jte-l YourFirstName YourLastName

mailto:listserv@vtvm1.cc.vt.edu

Newedu-l (New Paradigms in Education List)

This list discusses education broadly, including delivery systems, media, collaborative learning, learning styles, and distance education.

Keywords: Education (Adult), Education (Distance), Education (Continuing)

Audience: Educators (k-12), Administrators, Researchers

Details: Free

User info: To subscribe to the list, send an e-mail message to the URL address below consisting of a single line reading:

SUB newedu-l YourFirstName YourLastName

To send a message to the entire list, address it to: newedu-l@uscvm.bitnet

mailto:listserv@uscvm.bitnet

POD (Professional Organizational Development)

The POD network is aimed at faculty, instructional, and organizational development in higher education.

Keywords: Education (Adult), Education (Distance), Education (Continuing)

Audience: Educators, Administrators, Researchers

Details: Free

User info: To subscribe to the list, send an e-mail message to the URL address shown below consisting of a single line reading:

SUB pod YourFirstName YourLastName

To send a message to the entire list, address it to: pod@lists.acs.ohio-state.edu

mailto:listserv@lists.acs.ohio-state.edu

Pubs-IAT (Institute for Academic Technology newsletter)

This newsletter shares information on publications, programs, courses, and other activities of the Institute for Academic Technology.

Keywords: Education (Adult), Education (Distance), Education (Continuing), Information Technology

Sponsor: Institute for Academic Technology

Audience: Educators, Administrators, Researchers

Details: Free

User info: To subscribe to the list, send an e-mail message to the URL address below, consisting of a single line reading:

SUB pubs-iat YourFirstName YourLastName

To send a message to the entire list, address it to: pubs-iat@gibbs.oit.unc.edu

mailto:listserv@gibbs.oit.unc.edu

Education (Bilingual)

Resodlaa (Research SIG of the Open and Distance Learning Association of Australia)

The purpose of this list is to foster electronic discussion, symposia, and conferences on topical issues in distance education and open-learning research.

Keywords:	Education (Adult), Education (Distance), Education (Continuing), Australia
Sponsor:	Research Special Interest Group (SIG) of the Open and Distance Learning Association of Australia
Audience:	Educators, Administrators, Researchers
Details:	Free
User info:	To subscribe to the list, send an e-mail message to the URL address below, consisting of a single line reading: SUB resodlaa YourFirstName YourLastName To send a message to the entire list, address it to: resodlaa@usq.edu.au

`mailto:listserv@usq.edu.au`

Stlhe-l (Forum for Teaching & Learning in Higher Education)

This list focuses on postsecondary education teaching and learning.

Keywords:	Education (Adult), Education (Distance), Education (Continuing), Education (Post Secondary)
Audience:	Educators, Faculty, Administrators, Researchers
Details:	Free
User info:	To subscribe to the list, send an e-mail message to the URL address below consisting of a single line reading: SUB stlhe-l YourFirstName YourLastName To send a message to the entire list, address it to: stlhe-l@unbvm1.bitnet

`mailto:listserv@unbvm1.bitnet`

teacheft (Teaching Effectiveness)

This list treats teaching effectiveness and a broad range of teaching and learning interests.

Keywords:	Education (Adult), Education (Distance), Education (Continuing)
Audience:	Educators, Educational Administrators, Researchers
Details:	Free
User info:	To subscribe to the list, send an e-mail message to the URL address shown below consisting of a single line reading: SUB stlhe-l YourFirstName YourLastName To send a message to the entire list, address it to: stlhe-l@wcu.bitnet

`mailto:listserv@wcu.bitnet`

teslit-l (Adult Education & Literacy Test Literature)

This is a sublist of tesl-l (Teaching English as a Second Language). Discussions focus primarily on issues of literacy and the teaching of English as a second language.

Keywords:	Education (Adult), Education (Distance), Education (Continuing), Literacy
Audience:	Educators (K-12), Educational Administrators, Researchers
Details:	Free
User info:	To subscribe to the list, send an e-mail message to the URL address below consisting of a single line reading: SUB teslit-l YourFirstName YourLastName To send a message to the entire list, address it to: teslit-l@cunyvm.bitnet
Notes:	Members of teslit-l must be members of tesl-l.

`mailto:listserv@cunyvm.bitnet`

Education (Alternative)

Altlearn (Alternative Approaches to Learning Discussion)

A discussion list that is broadly concerned with learning strategies at all levels.

Keywords:	Education (Adult), Education (Distance), Education (Alternative)
Sponsor:	Alternative Approaches to Learning Discussion
Audience:	Educators, Administrators, Researchers
Details:	Free
User info:	To subscribe to the list, send an e-mail message to the URL address below, consisting of a single line reading: SUB Altlearn YourFirstName YourLastName To send a message to the entire list, address it to: altlearn@sjuvm.bitnet

`mailto:listserv@sjuvm.bitnet`

de Bono

This is a discussion list concerning the work of Edward de Bono. Also provides help with teaching the CoRT Thinking Program, and Six Thinking Hats.

Keywords:	de Bono (Edward), Education (Alternative), Creativity
Audience:	Teachers, Students, Management Trainers
Contact:	Rosa Casarez Casarez@netcom.net

`mailto: casarez@netcom.com`

Marimed Foundation

This foundation provides therapy and education to adjudicated and emotionally impaired teens. Therapies include wilderness experiences on a square-rigged sail ship, boat building, and traditional therapies.

Keywords:	Education (Alternative), Sailing
Audience:	Educators, Alternative Educators, Social Workers
Contact:	Dr. Robert Grossman marimed@holonet.net
Details:	Free

`mailto:marimed@holonet.net`

Education (Bilingual)

Academia Latinoamericana de Espanol

This program is specifically designed for those interested in learning to speak Spanish through a fully immersive trip to Ecuador.

Keywords:	Spanish Language, Education (Bilingual)
Sponsor:	Academia Latinoamericana de Espanol, Quito, Ecuador
Audience:	Reseachers, Students, Language Teachers
Contact:	Webmaster webmaster@comnet.com

`http://www.comnet.com/ecuador/learnSpanish.html`

Bilingual Education Network

This gopher site contains bilingual and bicultural, ESL (English as a Second Language), and Foreign Language resources and curriculum guidelines.

Keywords:	ESL (English as a Second Language), Education (Bilingual)
Sponsor:	California Department of Education, California, USA
Audience:	Educators, Administrators, Parents

`gopher://goldmine.cde.ca.gov`

Felipe's Bilingual WWW Pages

An interactive web site containing gopher and web links to various Latin American resources.

Keywords:	Latin America, Education (Bilingual)
Sponsor:	University of Texas, Texas, USA
Audience:	Educators, Language Students, Translators
Contact:	Felipe Campos felipe@bongo.utexas.edu

`http://edb518ea.edb.utexas.edu`

Education (Bilingual)

INTER-L ★

A list for members of the National Association of Foreign Student Advisors.

- **Keywords:** Advisory, Education (Bilingual), Educational Policy
- **Sponsor:** National Association of Foreign Student Advisors (NAFSA)
- **Audience:** Foreign Students, NAFSA Members
- **Details:** Free
- **User info:** To subscribe to the list, send an e-mail message to the address below consisting of a single line reading:

`mailto:listserv@vtm1.cc.vt.edu`

KFLC-L

A mailing list for distributing information on the meetings and proceedings of the Kentucky Foreign Language Conferences (KFCL).

- **Keywords:** Language, Linguistics, Education (Bilingual)
- **Audience:** Linguists, Educators
- **Contact:** John Greenway engjlg@ukcc.uky.edu
- **User info:** To subscribe, send an e-mail message to the URL address below consisting of a single line reading:

  SUB kflc-l YourFirstName YourLastName.

  To send a message to the entire list, address it to: kflc-l@ukcc.uky.edu

`mailto:listserv@ukcc.uky.edu`

The University of Michigan Library ★★

The library's holdings are large and wide-ranging and contain significant collections in many fields, including the following: Bilingual Education, Linguistics, Neuroscience, Michigan History, Temperance and Prohibition, African Government, Prohibition

- **Keywords:** Education (Bilingual), Linguistics, Neuroscience, Michigan, Prohibition, Government (African)
- **Audience:** General Public, Researchers, Librarians, Document Delivery Professionals
- **Details:** Free
- **User Info:** Expect: nothing, Send: <cr>

`telnet://cts.merit.edu`

Education (College/University)

soc.college ★

A Usenet newsgroup providing information and discussion about college life, activities, campus, and so on.

- **Keywords:** Sociology, Social Science, Education (College/University)
- **Audience:** Sociologists, Social Scientists, Educators (College/University), Students (College/University)
- **Details:** Free
- **User info:** To subscribe to this Usenet newsgroup, you need access to a newsreader.

`news:soc.college`

University of Minnesota Gopher Server ★★

The University of Minnesota Gopher server provides information about Minnesota University, as well as providing access to other universities' gopher servers.

- **Keywords:** Universities, Education (College/University)
- **Sponsor:** University of Minnesota, Minnesota, USA
- **Audience:** Students
- **Contact:** Gopher Development Team gopher@boombox.micro.umn.edu

`gopher://gopher.tc.umn.edu`

Education (Continuing)

AACIS-L (American Association for Collegiate Independent Study) ★

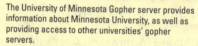

The focus this list is on correspondence, independent study, and distance learning.

- **Keywords:** Education (Adult), Education (Distance), Education (Continuing)
- **Sponsor:** American Association for Collegiate Independent Study (AACIS)
- **Audience:** Faculty Administrators
- **Details:** Free
- **User Info:** To subscribe to the list, send an e-mail message to the URL address shown below consisting of a single line reading:

  SUB aacis-l YourFirstName YourLastName

  To send a message to the entire list, address it to: aacis-l@bgu.edu

`mailto:listserv@bgu.edu`

ADLTED-L (Canadian Adult Education Network) ★

The Canadian Adult Continuing Education Network list is a broad, worldwide discussion group.

- **Keywords:** Education (Adult), Education (Distance), Education (Continuing)
- **Sponsor:** Canadian Adult Education Network
- **Audience:** Researchers, Educators, Administrators, Faculty
- **Details:** Free
- **User info:** To subscribe to the list, send an e-mail message to the URL address shown below, consisting of a single line reading:

  SUB adlted-l YourFirstName YourLastName

  To send a message to the entire list, address it to: adlted-L@uregina1.bitnet

`mailto:listserv@uregina1.uregina.ca`

AEDNET (Adult Education Network) ★★★★

This is an international electronic network for those involved in distance education.

- **Keywords:** Education (Adult), Education (Distance), Education (Continuing)
- **Sponsor:** Adult Education Network
- **Audience:** Educators, Researchers, Administrators, Faculty
- **Details:** Free
- **User info:** To subscribe to the list, send an e-mail message to the URL address below consisting of a single line reading:

  SUB aednet YourFirstName YourLastName

  To send a message to the entire list, address it to: AEDNET@alpha.acast.nova.edu

`mailto:listserv@alpha.acast.nova.edu`

Adult/Distance Education

This directory is a compilation of information resources focused on adult/distance education. The directory is sponsored by The American Association for Collegiate Independent Study, and focuses on correspondence, independent study and distance learning.

- **Keywords:** Education (Adult), Education (Distance), Education (Continuing)
- **Audience:** Educators, Researchers
- **Details:** Free

`ftp://una.hh.lib.umich.edu/70/inetdirsstacks/disted:ellsworth`

Education (Continuing)

Asat-eva (Distance Education Evaluation Group) ★

This mailing list addresses issues in evaluating all forms of distance learning and programs.

- Keywords: Education (Adult), Education (Distance), Education (Continuing)
- Sponsor: Agricultural Satellite Corporation
- Audience: Educators, Administrators, Researchers
- Details: Free
- User info: To subscribe to the list, send an e-mail message to the URL address below, consisting of a single line reading:

    SUB asat-eva YourFirstName YourLastName

    To send a message to the entire list, address it to: asat-eva@unlvm.unl.edu

mailto:listserv@unlvm.unl.edu

Catalyst ★

This is the electronic version of Catalyst, a refereed print journal for community college educators.

- Keywords: Education (Adult), Education (Distance), Education (Continuing), Education (International)
- Audience: Educators, Administrators, Faculty, Researchers
- Details: Free, Moderated
- User info: To subscribe to the journal, send an e-mail message to the URL address below, consisting of a single line reading:

    SUB catalyst YourFirstName YourLastName

    To send a message to the entire list, address it to: catalyst@vtvm1.bitnet

mailto:listserv@vtvm1.cc.vt.edu

CAUCE-L (Canadian Association for University Continuing Education) ★

Provides an electronic forum for the discussion of issues (broad, narrow, practical, theoretical, controversial, or mundane) related to university continuing education.

- Keywords: Education (Adult), Education (Distance), Education (Continuing)
- Sponsor: Canadian Association for University Continuing Education
- Audience: Educators, Administrators, Faculty
- Details: Free
- User info: To subscribe to the list, send an e-mail message to the URL address below, consisting of a single line reading:

    SUB cauce-l YourFirstName YourLastName

    To send a message to the entire list, address it to: cauce@max.cc.uregina.ca

mailto:listserv@max.cc.uregina.ca

Commcoll

A mailing list providing a forum for faculty, staff and administrators at two-year institutions.

- Keywords: Education (Continuing), Community Colleges
- Sponsor: Jefferson Community College at the University of Kentucky, Kentucky, USA
- Audience: Educators, Administrators
- User info: To subscribe to the list, send an e-mail message to the URL address below consisting of a single line reading:

    SUB commcoll YourFirstName YourLastName

    To send a message to the entire list, address it to: commcoll@ukcc.uky.edu

mailto:listserv@ukcc.uky.edu

Community Services Catalyst

This electronic journal provides information concerning community services around the country, especially those dealing with continuing education. The journal is published quarterly.

- Keywords: Education (Continuing), Community Service
- Sponsor: National Council on Community Services and Continuing Education (an affiliate council of the American Association of Community Colleges), USA
- Audience: Educators, Administrators
- User info: To subscribe to the list, send an e-mail message to the URL address below consisting of a single line reading:

    SUB catalyst YourFirstName YourLastName

    To send a message to the entire list, address it to: catalyst@vtvm1.cc.vt.edu

mailto:listserv@vtvm1.cc.vt.edu

Deos-L

A mailing list intended to promote communication among distance educators, to disseminate information and requests about distance education around the world, and to discuss issues raised in the electronic journal DEOSNEWS.

- Keywords: Education (Distance), Education (Continuing)
- Sponsor: The American Center for the Study of Distance Education, Pennsylvania State University, Pennsylvania, USA
- Audience: Distance Educators, Administrators
- User info: To subscribe to the list, send an e-mail message to the URL address below consisting of a single line reading:

    SUB deos-l YourFirstName YourLastName

    To send a message to the entire list, address it to: deos-l@psuvm.psu.edu

mailto:listserv@psuvm.psu.edu

deos-l (International Discussion Forum for Distance Learning)

A large, diverse distance education list, which currently has 1,325 subscribers in 48 countries.

- Keywords: Education (Adult), Education (Distance), Education (Continuing)
- Sponsor: American Center for the Study of Distance Education
- Audience: Educators, Administrators
- Details: Free
- User info: To subscribe to the list, send an e-mail message to the URL address shown below consisting of a single line reading:

    SUB deos-l YourFirstName YourLastName

    To send a message to the entire list, address it to: deos-l@psuvm.bitnet

mailto:listserv@psuvm.bitnet

deosnews (Distance Education Online Symposium) ★★★

The Distance Education Online Symposium publishes The American Journal of Distance Education.

- Keywords: Education (Adult), Education (Distance), Education (Continuing)
- Sponsor: Distance Education Online Symposium, American Center for the Study of Distance Education, Pennsylvania State University, State College, PA
- Audience: Educators, Administrators, Researchers
- Details: Free
- User info: To subscribe to the journal, send an e-mail message to the URL address shown below consisting of a single line reading:

    SUB deosnews YourFirstName YourLastName

mailto:listserv@psuvm.bitnet

dts-l (Dead Teachers Society Discussion List) ★

This list is for broad discussions of teaching and learning.

- Keywords: Education (Adult), Education (Distance), Education (Continuing)
- Audience: Educators K-12, Educational Administrators
- Details: Free
- User info: To subscribe to the list, send an e-mail message to the URL address shown below consisting of a single line reading:

    SUB dts-l YourFirstName YourLastName

    To send a message to the entire list, address it to: dts-l@iubvm.bitnet

mailto:listserv@iubvm.bitnet

edista (Educacin a Distancia) ★

The University Distance Program (UNIDIS) at the University of Santiago, Chile, sponsors Educacin a Distancia (Education at a Distance).

Keywords: Education (Adult), Education (Distance), Education (Continuing), Chile
Sponsor: The University Distance Program (UNIDIS) at the University of Santiago, Chile
Audience: Educators, Researchers
Details: Free
User info: To subscribe to the list, send an e-mail message to the URL address shown below consisting of a single line reading:
SUB edistaYourFirstName YourLastName
To send a message to the entire list, address it to: edista@usachvm1.bitnet

mailto:listserv@usachvm1.bitnet

edpolyan (Educational Policy Analysis) ★

This list focuses on educational policy analysis. This is an active, broad list, where issues surrounding all levels of education are discussed. This list takes a relatively philosophical approach to the issue.

Keywords: Education (Continuing), Educational Policy
Audience: University Administrators, K-12 Educators, Postsecondary Educators
Details: Free
User info: To subscribe to the list, send an e-mail message to the URL address shown below consisting of a single line reading:
SUB edpolyan YourFirstName YourLastName
To send a message to the entire list, address it to: edpolyan@asuacad.bitnet

mailto:listserv@asuacad.bitnet

edpolyar (Educational Policy Analysis Archive) ★

The Educational Policy Analysis Archive, an outgrowth of the edpolyan scholarly discussion list, publishes peer-reviewed articles of between 500 and 1,500 lines in length on all aspects of education policy analysis.

Keywords: Education (Continuing), Educational Policy
Audience: K-12 Educators, University Administrators, Postsecondary Educators
Details: Free, Moderated
User info: To subscribe to the archive, send an e-mail message to the URL address shown below consisting of a single line reading
SUB edpolyar YourFirstName YourLastName

mailto:listserv@asuacad.bitnet

edstyle (Learning Styles Theory and Research List) ★

This list discusses all forms of information about learning styles.

Keywords: Education (Continuing)
Audience: Educators, Educational Administrators, Researchers
Details: Free
User info: To subscribe to the list, send an e-mail message to the URL address shown below consisting of a single line reading:
SUB edstyle YourFirstName YourLastName
To send a message to the entire list, address it to: edstyle@sjuvm.bitnet

mailto:listserv@sjuvm.bitnet

edupage (A News Update from EDUCOM) ★★★★

A newsletter put out by EDUCOM summarizing information technology news.

Keywords: Education (Continuing), Information Technology
Sponsor: EDUCOM
Audience: Educators, Administrators
Details: Free
User info: To subscribe to the newsletter, send an e-mail message requesting a subscription to the URL address shown below and include your name, institutional affiliation, and e-mail address.

mailto:edupage@educom.edu

euitnews (Educational Uses of Information Technology) ★★★

EDUCOM's newsletter for the Educational Uses of Information Technology program encompasses distance learning, self-paced instruction, computer-aided instruction, video, and other information technologies for teaching and learning.

Keywords: Education (Continuing), Information Technology
Audience: Administrators, K-12 Educators
Details: Free
User info: To subscribe to the newsletter, send an e-mail message to the URL address shown below consisting of a single line reading:
SUB euitnews YourFirstName YourLastName

mailto:listserv@bitnic.educom.edu

hilat-l (Higher Education in Latin America) ★

Provides a means of interchange about research on higher education in Latin America. Postings are mostly in English, but are also welcome in Spanish and Portuguese.

Keywords: Education (Adult), Education (Distance), Education (Continuing), Latin America
Audience: Educators, Administrators, Faculty
Details: Free
User info: To subscribe to the list, send an e-mail message to the URL address shown below consisting of a single line reading:
SUB hilat-l YourFirstName YourLastName
To send a message to the entire list, address it to: hilat-l@bruspvm.bitnet

mailto:listserv@bruspvm.bitnet

horizons 'New Horizons in Adult Education' ★★★★

A journal transmitted to educators around the world.

Keywords: Education (Adult), Education (Distance), Education (Continuing)
Audience: Educators, Administrators, Faculty, Researchers
Details: Free
User info: To subscribe to the journal, send an e-mail message to the URL address shown below consisting of a single line reading:
SUB horizonsYourFirstName YourLastName

mailto:listserv@alpha.acast.nova.edu

ipct-j 'Interpersonal Computing and Technology: An Electronic Journal for the 21st Century' ★

Interpersonal Computing and Technology Journal is an outgrowth of the IPCT-L discussion group.

Keywords: Education (Adult), Education (Distance), Education (Continuing), Information Technology
Sponsor: Interpersonal Computing and Technology
Audience: Educators, Administrators, Faculty
Details: Free
User info: To subscribe to the journal, send an e-mail message to the URL address shown below consisting of a single line reading:
SUB ipct-j YourFirstName YourLastName

mailto:listserv@guvm.bitnet

joe 'The Journal of Extension' ★★★

This is the peer-reviewed publication of the Cooperative Extension System; it covers all phases of extension education, including adult and distance education.

Keywords: Education (Adult), Education (Distance), Education (Continuing)
Audience: Educators (K-12), Faculty Administrators
Details: Free
User info: To subscribe to the journal, send an e-mail message requesting a subscription to the URL address shown below.

mailto:almanac@joe.uwex.edu

Jte-l 'Journal of Technology Education' ★

The Journal of Technology Education provides a forum for all topics relating to technology in education.

Keywords: Education (Adult), Education (Distance), Education (Continuing), Information Technology
Audience: Faculty, Administrators, Educators (K-12)
Details: Free
User info: To subscribe to the journal, send an e-mail message to the URL address below consisting of a single line reading:

SUB jte-l YourFirstName YourLastName

mailto:listserv@vtvm1.cc.vt.edu

Newedu-l (New Paradigms in Education List)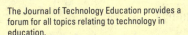

This list discusses education broadly, including delivery systems, media, collaborative learning, learning styles, and distance education.

Keywords: Education (Adult), Education (Distance), Education (Continuing)
Audience: Educators (k-12), Administrators, Researchers
Details: Free
User info: To subscribe to the list, send an e-mail message to the URL address below consisting of a single line reading:

SUB newedu-l YourFirstName YourLastName

To send a message to the entire list, address it to: newedu-l@uscvm.bitnet

mailto:listserv@uscvm.bitnet

POD (Professional Organizational Development) ★★★

The POD network is aimed at faculty, instructional, and organizational development in higher education.

Keywords: Education (Adult), Education (Distance), Education (Continuing)

Audience: Educators, Administrators, Researchers
Details: Free
User info: To subscribe to the list, send an e-mail message to the URL address shown below consisting of a single line reading:

SUB pod YourFirstName YourLastName

To send a message to the entire list, address it to: pod@lists.acs.ohio-state.edu

mailto:listserv@lists.acs.ohio-state.edu

Pubs-IAT (Institute for Academic Technology newsletter) ★★★★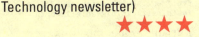

This newsletter shares information on publications, programs, courses, and other activities of the Institute for Academic Technology.

Keywords: Education (Adult), Education (Distance), Education (Continuing), Information Technology
Sponsor: Institute for Academic Technology
Audience: Educators, Administrators, Researchers
Details: Free
User info: To subscribe to the list, send an e-mail message to the URL address below, consisting of a single line reading:

SUB pubs-iat YourFirstName YourLastName

To send a message to the entire list, address it to: pubs-iat@gibbs.oit.unc.edu

mailto:listserv@gibbs.oit.unc.edu

Resodlaa (Research SIG of the Open and Distance Learning Association of Australia) ★

The purpose of this list is to foster electronic discussion, symposia, and conferences on topical issues in distance education and open-learning research.

Keywords: Education (Adult), Education (Distance), Education (Continuing), Australia
Sponsor: Research Special Interest Group (SIG) of the Open and Distance Learning Association of Australia
Audience: Educators, Administrators, Researchers
Details: Free
User info: To subscribe to the list, send an e-mail message to the URL address below, consisting of a single line reading:

SUB resodlaa YourFirstName YourLastName

To send a message to the entire list, address it to: resodlaa@usq.edu.au

mailto:listserv@usq.edu.au

Stlhe-l (Forum for Teaching & Learning in Higher Education) ★

This list focuses on postsecondary education teaching and learning.

Keywords: Education (Adult), Education (Distance), Education (Continuing), Education (Post Secondary)
Audience: Educators, Faculty, Administrators, Researchers
Details: Free
User info: To subscribe to the list, send an e-mail message to the URL address below consisting of a single line reading:

SUB stlhe-l YourFirstName YourLastName

To send a message to the entire list, address it to: stlhe-l@unbvm1.bitnet

mailto:listserv@unbvm1.bitnet

teacheft (Teaching Effectiveness) ★

This list treats teaching effectiveness and a broad range of teaching and learning interests.

Keywords: Education (Adult), Education (Distance), Education (Continuing)
Audience: Educators, Educational Administrators, Researchers
Details: Free
User info: To subscribe to the list, send an e-mail message to the URL address shown below consisting of a single line reading:

SUB stlhe-l YourFirstName YourLastName

To send a message to the entire list, address it to: stlhe-l@wcu.bitnet

mailto:listserv@wcu.bitnet

teslit-l (Adult Education & Literacy Test Literature) ★

This is a sublist of tesl-l (Teaching English as a Second Language). Discussions focus primarily on issues of literacy and the teaching of English as a second language.

Keywords: Education (Adult), Education (Distance), Education (Continuing), Literacy
Audience: Educators K-12, Educational Administrators, Researchers
Details: Free
User info: To subscribe to the list, send an e-mail message to the URL address below consisting of a single line reading:

SUB teslit-l YourFirstName YourLastName

To send a message to the entire list, address it to: teslit-l@cunyvm.bitnet

Notes: Members of teslit-l must be members of tesl-l.

mailto:listserv@cunyvm.bitnet

Education (Continuing)

The Electronic AIR ★★★

Biweekly (nominal schedule) electronic newsletter for the Association for Institutional Research members, as well as college and university planners.

Keywords:	Education (Continuing), Institutional Research
Sponsor:	Association for Institutional Research (AIR)
Audience:	College/University Planners, University Administrators
Contact:	Larry Nelson NELSON_L@PLU.bitnet
Details:	Free

`mailto:nelson_l@plu.bitnet`

Education (Distance)

AACIS-L (American Association for Collegiate Independent Study) ★

The focus of this list is on correspondence, independent study, and distance learning.

Keywords:	Education (Adult), Education (Distance), Education (Continuing)
Sponsor:	American Association for Collegiate Independent Study (AACIS)
Audience:	Faculty Administrators
Details:	Free
User Info:	To subscribe to the list, send an e-mail message to the URL address shown below consisting of a single line reading: SUB aacis-l YourFirstName YourLastName. To send a message to the entire list, address it to: aacis-l@bgu.edu

`mailto:listserv@bgu.edu`

ADLTED-L (Canadian Adult Education Network) ★

The Canadian Adult Continuing Education Network list is a broad, worldwide discussion group.

Keywords:	Education (Adult), Education (Distance), Education (Continuing)
Sponsor:	Canadian Adult Education Network
Audience:	Researchers, Educators, Administrators, Faculty
Details:	Free
User info:	To subscribe to the list, send an e-mail message to the URL address shown below, consisting of a single line reading: SUB adlted-l YourFirstName YourLastName. To send a message to the entire list, address it to: adlted-l@uregina1.bitnet

`mailto:listserv@uregina1.uregina.ca`

Adult/Distance Education

This directory is a compilation of information resources focused on adult/distance education. The directory is sponsored by The American Association for Collegiate Independent Study, and focuses on correspondence, independent study and distance learning.

Keywords:	Education (Adult), Education (Distance), Education (Continuing)
Audience:	Educators, Researchers
Details:	Free

`ftp://una.hh.lib.umich.edu/70/inetdirsstacks/disted:ellsworth`

AEDNET (Adult Education Network) ★★★★

This is an international electronic network for those involved in distance education.

Keywords:	Education (Adult), Education (Distance), Education (Continuing)
Sponsor:	Adult Education Network
Audience:	Educators, Researchers, Administrators, Faculty
Details:	Free
User info:	To subscribe to the list, send an e-mail message to the URL address below consisting of a single line reading: SUB aednet YourFirstName YourLastName. To send a message to the entire list, address it to: AEDNET@alpha.acast.nova.edu

`mailto:listserv@alpha.acast.nova.edu`

Altlearn (Alternative Approaches to Learning Discussion) ★

A discussion list that is broadly concerned with learning strategies at all levels.

Keywords:	Education (Adult), Education (Distance), Education (Alternative)
Sponsor:	Alternative Approaches to Learning Discussion
Audience:	Educators, Administrators, Researchers
Details:	Free
User info:	To subscribe to the list, send an e-mail message to the URL address below, consisting of a single line reading: SUB Altlearn YourFirstName YourLastName. To send a message to the entire list, address it to: altlearn@sjuvm.bitnet

`mailto:listserv@sjuvm.bitnet`

Asat-eva (Distance Education Evaluation Group) ★

This mailing list addresses issues in evaluating all forms of distance learning and programs.

Keywords:	Education (Adult), Education (Distance), Education (Continuing)
Sponsor:	Agricultural Satellite Corporation
Audience:	Educators, Administrators, Researchers
Details:	Free
User info:	To subscribe to the list, send an e-mail message to the URL address below, consisting of a single line reading: SUB asat-evaYourFirstName YourLastName. To send a message to the entire list, address it to: asat-eva@unlvm.unl.edu

`mailto:listserv@unlvm.unl.edu`

Catalyst ★

This is the electronic version of Catalyst, a refereed print journal for community college educators.

Keywords:	Education (Adult), Education (Distance), Education (Continuing), Education (International)
Audience:	Educators, Administrators, Faculty, Researchers
Details:	Free, Moderated
User info:	To subscribe to the journal, send an e-mail message to the URL address below, consisting of a single line reading: SUB catalyst YourFirstName YourLastName. To send a message to the entire list, address it to: catalyst@vtvm1.bitnet

`mailto:listserv@vtvm1.cc.vt.edu`

CAUCE-L (Canadian Association for University Continuing Education) ★

Provides an electronic forum for the discussion of issues (broad, narrow, practical, theoretical, controversial, or mundane) related to university continuing education.

Keywords:	Education (Adult), Education (Distance), Education (Continuing)
Sponsor:	Canadian Association for University Continuing Education
Audience:	Educators, Administrators, Faculty
Details:	Free
User info:	To subscribe to the list, send an e-mail message to the URL address below, consisting of a single line reading: SUB cauce-l YourFirstName YourLastName. To send a message to the entire list, address it to: cauce@max.cc.uregina.ca

`mailto:listserv@max.cc.uregina.ca`

Education (Distance)

cread (Latin American & Caribbean Distance & Continuing Education)

This is a digest list of distance education information primarily focused on Latin America and the Caribbean.

Keywords: Latin America, Caribbean, Education (Distance)
Audience: Educators, Administrators, Faculty
Details: Free
User info: To subscribe to the list, send an e-mail message to the URL address below consisting of a single line reading:

SUB cread YourFirstName YourLastName.

To send a message to the entire list, address it to: cread@yorkvm1.bitnet

mailto:listserv@yorkvm1.bitnet

Deos-L

A mailing list intended to promote communication among distance educators, to disseminate information and requests about distance education around the world, and to discuss issues raised in the electronic journal DEOSNEWS.

Keywords: Education (Distance), Education (Continuing)
Sponsor: The American Center for the Study of Distance Education, Pennsylvania State University, Pennsylvania, USA
Audience: Distance Educators, Administrators
User info: To subscribe to the list, send an e-mail message to the URL address below consisting of a single line reading:

SUB deos-l YourFirstName YourLastName

To send a message to the entire list, address it to: deos-l@psuvm.psu.edu

mailto:listserv@psuvm.psu.edu

deos-l (International Discussion Forum for Distance Learning)

A large, diverse distance education list, which currently has 1,325 subscribers in 48 countries.

Keywords: Education (Adult), Education (Distance), Education (Continuing)
Sponsor: American Center for the Study of Distance Education
Audience: Educators, Administrators
Details: Free
User info: To subscribe to the list, send an e-mail message to the URL address below consisting of a single line reading:

SUB deos-l YourFirstName YourLastName

To send a message to the entire list, address it to: deos-l@psuvm.bitnet

mailto:listserv@psuvm.bitnet

deosnews (Distance Education Online Symposium)

The Distance Education Online Symposium publishes The American Journal of Distance Education.

Keywords: Education (Adult), Education (Distance), Education (Continuing)
Sponsor: Distance Education Online Symposium, American Center for the Study of Distance Education, Pennsylvania State University, State College, PA
Audience: Educators, Administrators, Researchers
Details: Free
User info: To subscribe to the journal, send an e-mail message to the URL address shown below consisting of a single line reading:

SUB deosnews YourFirstName YourLastName

mailto:listserv@psuvm.bitnet

Distance Education

This gopher site takes advantage of New Brunswick's advanced telecommunications infrastructure to provide leading edge technology-based learning environments. A computer-based teleconferencing system forms the core of the network complemented by computer-aided communications, electronic data links and other multimedia technologies.

Keywords: Education (Distance), Independent Study
Sponsor: TeleEducation New Brunswick, Department of Advanced Education and Labor
Audience: Educators, Students, Professionals

gopher://gopher.ollc.mta.ca

dts-l (Dead Teachers Society Discussion List)

This list is for broad discussions of teaching and learning.

Keywords: Education (Adult), Education (Distance), Education (Continuing)
Audience: Educators K-12, Educational Administrators
Details: Free
User info: To subscribe to the list, send an e-mail message to the URL address shown below consisting of a single line reading:

SUB dts-l YourFirstName YourLastName

To send a message to the entire list, address it to: dts-l@iubvm.bitnet

mailto:listserv@iubvm.bitnet

edista (Educacin a Distancia)

The University Distance Program (UNIDIS) at the University of Santiago, Chile, sponsors Educacin a Distancia (Education at a Distance).

Keywords: Education (Adult), Education (Distance), Education (Continuing), Chile
Sponsor: The University Distance Program (UNIDIS) at the University of Santiago, Chile
Audience: Educators, Researchers
Details: Free
User info: To subscribe to the list, send an e-mail message to the URL address shown below consisting of a single line reading:

SUB edistaYourFirstName YourLastName

To send a message to the entire list, address it to: edista@usachvm1.bitnet

mailto:listserv@usachvm1.bitnet

hilat-l (Higher Education in Latin America)

Provides a means of interchange about research on higher education in Latin America. Postings are mostly in English, but are also welcome in Spanish and Portuguese.

Keywords: Education (Adult), Education (Distance), Education (Continuing), Latin America
Audience: Educators, Administrators, Faculty
Details: Free
User info: To subscribe to the list, send an e-mail message to the URL address shown below consisting of a single line reading:

SUB hilat-l YourFirstName YourLastName

To send a message to the entire list, address it to: hilat-l @bruspvm.bitnet

mailto:listserv@bruspvm.bitnet

horizons 'New Horizons in Adult Education'

A journal transmitted to educators around the world.

Keywords: Education (Adult), Education (Distance), Education (Continuing)
Audience: Educators, Administrators, Faculty, Researchers
Details: Free
User info: To subscribe to the journal, send an e-mail message to the URL address shown below consisting of a single line reading:

SUB horizonsYourFirstName YourLastName

mailto:listserv@alpha.acast.nova.edu

Education (Distance)

International Centre for Distance Learning

This site is a distance education database.

Keywords: Education (Distance)

Sponsor: International Centre for Distance Learning, The Open University, United Kingdom

Audience: Educators, Students, Researchers

Profile: The database is exensive, and provides information about courses, related institutions, and relevant literature, with over 30,000 entries, including the following: study skills, agriculture, fisheries, architecture, building, surveying, planning, arts, humanities and social sciences,business, services, management, economics, education and training, applied science, technology, computers, environment, pure science and mathematics, medicine, health, social welfare, law, law enforcement, regulations and standards, personal, home and family affairs

User Info: Expect: Login; Send: icdl; Send: <Country>; Password: AAA

`telnet://acsvax.open.ac.uk`

ipct-j 'Interpersonal Computing and Technology: An Electronic Journal for the 21st Century'

Interpersonal Computing and Technology Journal is an outgrowth of the IPCT-L discussion group.

Keywords: Education (Adult), Education (Distance), Education (Continuing), Information Technology

Sponsor: Interpersonal Computing and Technology

Audience: Educators, Administrators, Faculty

Details: Free, Moderated

User info: To subscribe to the journal, send an e-mail message to the URL address shown below consisting of a single line reading:

SUB ipct-j YourFirstName YourLastName

`mailto:listserv@guvm.bitnet`

joe 'The Journal of Extension'

This is the peer-reviewed publication of the Cooperative Extension System; it covers all phases of extension education, including adult and distance education.

Keywords: Education (Adult), Education (Distance), Education (Continuing)

Audience: Educators (K-12), Faculty Administrators

Details: Free, Moderated

User info: To subscribe to the journal, send an e-mail message requesting a subscription to the URL address shown below.

`mailto:almanac@joe.uwex.edu`

Jte-l 'Journal of Technology Education'

The Journal of Technology Education provides a forum for all topics relating to technology in education.

Keywords: Education (Adult), Education (Distance), Education (Continuing), Information Technology

Audience: Faculty, Administrators, Educators (K-12)

Details: Free

User info: To subscribe to the journal, send an e-mail message to the URL address below consisting of a single line reading:

SUB jte-l YourFirstName YourLastName

`mailto:listserv@vtvm1.cc.vt.edu`

Newedu-l (New Paradigms in Education List)

This list discusses education broadly, including delivery systems, media, collaborative learning, learning styles, and distance education.

Keywords: Education (Adult), Education (Distance), Education (Continuing)

Audience: Educators (K-12), Administrators, Researchers

Details: Free

User info: To subscribe to the list, send an e-mail message to the URL address below consisting of a single line reading:

SUB newedu-l YourFirstName YourLastName

To send a message to the entire list, address it to: newedu-l @uscvm.bitnet

`mailto:listserv@uscvm.bitnet`

POD (Professional Organizational Development)

The POD network is aimed at faculty, instructional, and organizational development in higher education.

Keywords: Education (Adult), Education (Distance), Education (Continuing)

Audience: Educators, Administrators, Researchers

Details: Free

User info: To subscribe to the list, send an e-mail message to the URL address shown below consisting of a single line reading:

SUB pod YourFirstName YourLastName

To send a message to the entire list, address it to: pod@lists.acs.ohio-state.edu

`mailto:listserv@lists.acs.ohio-state.edu`

Pubs-IAT (Institute for Academic Technology newsletter)

This newsletter shares information on publications, programs, courses, and other activities of the Institute for Academic Technology.

Keywords: Education (Adult), Education (Distance), Education (Continuing), Information Technology

Sponsor: Institute for Academic Technology

Audience: Educators, Administrators, Researchers

Details: Free

User info: To subscribe to the list, send an e-mail message to the URL address below, consisting of a single line reading:

SUB pubs-iat YourFirstName YourLastName

To send a message to the entire list, address it to: pubs-iat@gibbs.oit.unc.edu

`mailto:listserv@gibbs.oit.unc.edu`

Resodlaa (Research SIG of the Open and Distance Learning Association of Australia)

The purpose of this list is to foster electronic discussion, symposia, and conferences on topical issues in distance education and open-learning research.

Keywords: Education (Adult), Education (Distance), Education (Continuing), Australia

Sponsor: Research Special Interest Group (SIG) of the Open and Distance Learning Association of Australia

Audience: Educators, Administrators, Researchers

Details: Free

User info: To subscribe to the list, send an e-mail message to the URL address below, consisting of a single line reading:

SUB resodlaa YourFirstName YourLastName

To send a message to the entire list, address it to: resodlaa @usq.edu.au

`mailto:listserv@usq.edu.au`

Stlhe-l (Forum for Teaching & Learning in Higher Education)

This list focuses on postsecondary education teaching and learning.

Keywords: Education (Adult), Education (Distance), Education (Continuing), Education (Post Secondary)

Audience: Educators, Faculty, Administrators, Researchers

Details: Free

Education (K-12)   243

User info:	To subscribe to the list, send an e-mail message to the URL address below consisting of a single line reading:
	SUB stlhe-l YourFirstName YourLastName
	To send a message to the entire list, address it to: stlhe-l@unbvm1.bitnet

mailto:listserv@unbvm1.bitnet

teacheft (Teaching Effectiveness)

This list treats teaching effectiveness and a broad range of teaching and learning interests.

Keywords:	Education (Adult), Education (Distance), Education (Continuing)
Audience:	Educators, Educational Administrators, Researchers
Details:	Free
User info:	To subscribe to the list, send an e-mail message to the URL address shown below consisting of a single line reading:
	SUB stlhe-l YourFirstName YourLastName
	To send a message to the entire list, address it to: stlhe-l@wcu.bitnet

mailto:listserv@wcu.bitnet

teslit-l (Adult Education & Literacy Test Literature)

This is a sublist of tesl-l (Teaching English as a Second Language). Discussions focus primarily on issues of literacy and the teaching of English as a second language.

Keywords:	Education (Adult), Education (Distance), Education (Continuing), Literacy
Audience:	Educators K-12, Educational Administrators, Researchers
Details:	Free
User info:	To subscribe to the list, send an e-mail message to the URL address below consisting of a single line reading:
	SUB teslit-l YourFirstName YourLastName
	To send a message to the entire list, address it to: teslit-l@cunyvm.bitnet
Notes:	Members of teslit-l must be members of tesl-l.

mailto:listserv@cunyvm.bitnet

University of Wisconsin Extension Program in Independent Study

A gopher containing information about courses of study at the University of Wisconsin Extension Program in Independent Study. Over fifty-five disciplines, from Arabic to Womens Studies, are represented.

Keywords: Education (Distance), Independent Study

Sponsor:	University of Wisconsin Extension Program in Independent Study, Madison, Wisconsin, USA
Audience:	Professionals, Educators, Students
Notes:	Information is free, but fees are charged for courses. Contact the Advisor to Students at 608-263-2055, or write University of Wisconsin Extension Program in Independent Study, 104 Extension Building, 432 North Lake Street, Madison, WI 53706-1498

gopher.uwex.edu

Virtual Hospital

The Virtual Hospital (VH) is a continuously updated medical multimedia database accessible 24 hours a day. The site provides distance learning to practicing physicians and may be used for Continuing Medical Education (CME).

Keywords:	Medicine, Education (Distance)
Sponsor:	The Electronic Differential Multimedia Laboratory, Department of Radiology, University of Iowa College of Medicine, USA
Audience:	Biologists, Researchers, Medical Professionals, Health Care Professionals
Contact:	Librarian librarian@vh.radiology.uiowa.edu

http://indy.radiology.uiowa.edu/VirtualHospital.html

Education (International)

Catalyst

This is the electronic version of Catalyst, a refereed print journal for community college educators.

Keywords:	Education (Adult), Education (Distance), Education (Continuing), Education (International)
Audience:	Educators, Administrators, Faculty, Researchers
Details:	Free, Moderated
User info:	To subscribe to the journal, send an e-mail message to the URL address below, consisting of a single line reading:
	SUB catalyst YourFirstName YourLastName
	To send a message to the entire list, address it to: catalyst@vtvm1.bitnet

mailto:listserv@vtvm1.cc.vt.edu

Education (K-12)

AskERIC Virtual Library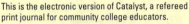

This gopher is part of a federally-funded system to provide public access to educational resources.

Keywords:	Education (K-12), Computer-Aided Learning, Libraries, Electronic Books
Sponsor:	Educational Resources Information Center (ERIC)
Audience:	K-12 Teachers, Administrators
Profile:	This gopher contains a wide range of educational aids including pre-prepared lesson plans, guides to Internet resources for the classroom organized by subject, updates on conferences for educators, and archives of education-related listservs. Also allows access to outside gophers, libraries, and sources of electronic books and journals.
Contact:	Nancy A. Morgan nmorgan@ericir.syr.edu askeric@ericir.syr.edu

gopher://ericir/syr.edu

FrEd Mail Foundation

This foundation specializes in establishing innovative and educationally rewarding collaborative projects using the Internet for the K-12 community.

Keywords:	Children, Education (K-12)
Audience:	Educators (K-12)
Contact:	Al Rogers arogers@bonita.cerf.fred.org
Details:	Free

gopher://gopher.cerf.net/11/fredmail

Incomplete Guide to the Internet (K12-Netzanleitung)

An Internet guide created especially for teachers and students in grades K-12.

Keywords:	Education (K-12), Internet
Audience:	Educators (K-12), Students (K-12)
Contact:	Chuck Farmer cfarmer@ncsa.uiuc.edu
Details:	Free

ftp://ncsa.uiuc.edu

K-12 School Libraries

This directory is a compilation of information resources focused on K-12 Education.

Keywords:	Libraries, Education (K-12)
Audience:	Librarians, Educators (K-12)

ftp://una.hh.lib.umich.edu/70/inetdirsstacks/k12schmed:troselius

K12 Net

Decentralized network of school-based bulletin board systems (BBSs).

Keywords:	Education (K-12), Networks
Audience:	Educators (K-12), School Children

Education (K-12)

Profile: K12 Net provides millions of teachers, students, and parents in metropolitan and rural areas throughout the world with the ability to meet and talk with each other to discuss educational issues, exchange information, and share resources on a global scale.

Contact: Jack Crawford, Janet Murray
jack@k12net.org or jmurray@psg.com

Details: Free

gopher://woonext.dsrd.ornl.gov/11/Docs/k12net

NAME (National Association for Mediation in Education) Publications and Resources List ★★

This is a tax-exempt clearinghouse of information promoting conflict resolution, mediation, and violence prevention in schools. NAME also publishes a newsletter and has a directory of over 120 resources, including guidelines for conflict resolution, and technical assistance.

Keywords: Conflict Resolution, Mediation, Education (K-12)

Sponsor: National Association for Mediation in Education, University of Massachusetts, Amherst, Massachusetts, USA

Audience: Counselors, Educators, Administrators, Parents

Contact: Clarinda Merripen
ConflictNet@agc.ipc.org

Request introductory packet from address below.

mailto:ConflictNet@agc.ipc.org

NIH EDNET ★

EdNet is set up as a free electronic bulletin board at the Bethesda, Maryland campus of the National Institute of Health (NIH). Its purpose is to allow high school students to ask questions of NIH scientists about current research.

Keywords: NIH, Education (Post-Secondary), Education (K-12), Science

Sponsor: National Institute of Health (NIH)

Audience: Students (high school and up), Educators

Details: Free

To receive an EDNET User's Guide and account, send an e-mail message with your name and mailing address to the URL address below.

mailto:vt5@cu.nih.gov

NWNet Internet Guide ★

An introductory guide to the Internet. Details the basic Internet tools of electronic mail, FTP (File Transfer Protocol), and Telnet. Covers types of resources found on the Internet, and how to use them. Includes information directed toward supercomputer users and the K-12 community.

Keywords: Internet, Internet Guides, Supercomputers, Education (K-12)

Sponsor: NorthWestNet

Audience: Internet Surfers, Supercomputer Users, Students (K-12)

Contact: Jonathan Kochmer
nusirg@nwnet.net

Details: Free

File is: /user-docs/nusirg/nusirg.whole-guide.ps

ftp://ftphost.nwnet.net

Sais-l (Science Awareness and Promotion) ★

The SAIS list creates a forum for exchanging innovative ideas about making science more appealing to students.

Keywords: Science, Education (K-12), Education (Secondary)

Audience: Students (K-12), Students (high school up), Science Teachers

Contact: Keith W. Wilson
sais@unb.ca

Details: Free

User info: To subscribe to the list, send an e-mail message to the URL address below consisting of a single line reading:

SUB sais-l YourFirstName YourLastName

To send a message to the entire list, address it to: sais-l@unb.ca

mailto:listserv@unb.ca

Spacelink ★★★★

This contains information about NASA and its activities, including a large number of curricular activities for elementary and secondary science classes.

Keywords: NASA, Aeronautics, Education (K-12)

Audience: Students (K-12), Educators, General Public

Details: Free

telnet://newuser@spacelink.msfc.nasa.gov

Education (Post-Graduate)

The PSYCHGRAD Project and Psychology-Related Information ★★

An electronic forum for the communication and dissemination of information among psychology graduate students.

Keywords: Psychology, Education (Post-Graduate)

Sponsor: University of Ottawa, Canada

Audience: Psychologists, Psychology Graduate Students

Profile: Designed to facilitate electronic communications and networking between psychology graduate students, this site contains archives of psychology listserv groups, and directories of psychology associations, along with related electronic journals and software. Also has links to other gopher and WWW sites related to psychology.

Contact: Matthew Simpson
054340@acadvm1.uottawa.ca
054340@uottawa.bitnet

gopher://panda1.uottawa.ca

Education (Post-Secondary)

Can-Stud-Assoc ★

This is a mailing list for anyone who might wish to discuss Canadian post-secondary education and student associations' involvement in it.

Keywords: Canada, Education (Post-Secondary)

Audience: Canadians, Students (college)

Contact: can-stud-assoc-request@unixg.ubc.ca

Details: Free

User info: To subscribe to the list, send an e-mail message requesting a subscription to the URL address below.

To send a message to the entire list, address it to:

can-stud-assoc@unixg.ubc.ca

mailto:can-stud-assoc-request@unixg.ubc.ca

disted 'Journal of Distance Education and Communication'

This online journal covers distance education broadly, including formal and informal education, geographically disadvantaged learners, and both K-12 and post-secondary education.

Keywords: Education (Adult), Education (Distance), Education (Continuing), K-12 Education (K-12), Education (Post-Secondary)

Audience: K-12 Educators, K-12 Administrators

Details: Free

User info: To subscribe to the journal, send an e-mail message to the URL address shown below consisting of a single line reading:

SUB disted YourFirstName YourLastName

mailto:listserv@uwavm.bitnet

don't-tell ★

The don't-tell list is for people concerned about the effects that the new military policy known as "don't ask/don't tell" will have at academic institutions, whether military or ROTC-affiliated.

Keywords:	Sexuality, Military Policy, Education (Post-Secondary)
Audience:	Students, Gays, Lesbians, Military Personnel, Civil Libertarians
Contact:	dont-tell-request@choice.princeton.edu
Details:	Free
User info:	To subscribe to the list, send an e-mail message requesting a subscription to the URL address below.
	To send a message to the entire list, address it to: dont-tell-request@choice.princeton.edu

`mailto:dont-tell-request@choice.princeton.edu`

NIH EDNET

EdNet is set up as a free electronic bulletin board at the Bethesda, Maryland campus of the National Institute of Health (NIH). Its purpose is to allow high school students to ask questions of NIH scientists about current research.

Keywords:	NIH, Education (Post-Secondary), Education (K-12), Science
Sponsor:	National Institute of Health (NIH)
Audience:	Students (high school and up), Educators
Details:	Free
	To receive an EDNET User's Guide and account, send an e-mail message with your name and mailing address to the URL address below.

`mailto:vt5@cu.nih.gov`

Stlhe-I (Forum for Teaching & Learning in Higher Education)

This list focuses on post-secondary education teaching and learning.

Keywords:	Education (Adult), Education (Distance), Education (Continuing), Education (Post Secondary)
Audience:	Educators, Faculty, Administrators, Researchers
Details:	Free
User info:	To subscribe to the list, send an e-mail message to the URL address below consisting of a single line reading:
	SUB stlhe-I YourFirstName YourLastName
	To send a message to the entire list, address it to: stlhe-I@unbvm1.bitnet

`mailto:listserv@unbvm1.bitnet`

Education (Secondary)

Sais-I (Science Awareness and Promotion)

The SAIS list creates a forum for exchanging innovative ideas about making science more appealing to students.

Keywords:	Science, Education (K-12), Education (Secondary)
Audience:	Students (K-12), Students (high school up), Science Teachers
Contact:	Keith W. Wilson sais@unb.ca
Details:	Free
User info:	To subscribe to the list, send an e-mail message to the URL address below consisting of a single line reading:
	SUB sais-I YourFirstName YourLastName
	To send a message to the entire list, address it to: sais-I@unb.ca

`mailto:listserv@unb.ca`

Education

alt.usage.english

A Usenet newsgroup providing information and discussion about English grammar, word usages and related topics.

Keywords:	Lexicology, Academia, Linguistics, Education
Audience:	English Educators
User info:	To subscribe to this Usenet newsgroup, you need access to a newsreader.

`news:alt.usage.english`

Armadillo's World Wide Web Page

This site provides resources and instructional material for an interdisciplinary Texan culture course.

Keywords:	History (US), Texas, Cultural Studies, Education
Sponsor:	Rice University, Houston, Texas, USA
Audience:	Educators, Students
Contact:	armadillo@rice.edu

`http://chico.rice.edu/armadillo`

CAF Archive

A source of information relating to Computers and Academic Freedom (CAF).

Keywords:	Education, Computers, Academic Freedom
Audience:	Educators, Researchers
Contact:	kadie@eff.org

`http://www.eff.org/CAF/cafhome.html`

California Museum of Photography: Network Exhibitions

This is a collection of digital images for educational and general use.

Keywords:	Photography, Art, Education
Sponsor:	University of California, Riverside, California, USA
Audience:	Photographers, Artists, Educators (esp. K-12), Historians
Profile:	The California Museum of Photography is in the process of selecting groups of images from the collections as thematic exhibitions. Instead of displays on the walls, these exhibitions comprise a group of digital images with associated text. Particular emphasis is on the utility of these images in class projects for elementary and secondary school students. However, the digital images also have potential value for more advanced scholarly research in preparation of papers in the Humanities, Social Sciences and the Arts.
Contact:	Russ Harvey russ@cornucopia.ucr.edu

`gopher://gopher.ucr.edu`

CERFnet Guide

A comprehensive guide to the CERFnet (California Education and Research Federation Network), a data-communications regional network that operates throughout California. The purpose of CERFnet is to advance science and education by assisting the interchange of information among research and educational institutions.

Keywords:	Internet, Science, Education, California
Audience:	Internet Surfers, Researchers, Educators
Contact:	CERFnet Hotline help@cerf.net
Details:	Free
	Files are in: cerfnet/cerfnet_info/cerfnet_guide/

`ftp://nic.cerf.net`

CERFNet News

This is a mid-level network linking academic, government, and industrial research facilities throughout California.

Keywords:	Education, California
Sponsor:	California Education and Research Federation Network
Audience:	Researchers, Students (college, graduate)

Contact: help@cerf.net
Details: Free
`gopher://gopher.cerf.net/11/cerfnet`

Chemistry Tutorial Information ★

This site provides chemistry tutorial information in the form of text, data, pictures, source code, and executable programs for Macintosh computers.

Keywords: Chemistry, Tutorials, Macintosh, Education
Sponsor: University of Michigan
Audience: Chemistry Students (high school up)
Contact: comments@mac.archive.umich.edu
Details: Free, Images

`gopher://plaza.aarnet.edu.au@/micros/mac/umich/misc/chemistry/00index.txt`

CYFERNET (Child, Youth, and Family Education Network) ★

This public information service supports child, youth, and family development programs.

Keywords: Education, Networks
Sponsor: Youth Development Information Center at the National Agricultural Library
Audience: Educators, Children, Families
Profile: CYFERNET contains information useful to child, youth, and family development professionals. Features include programs for children aged 5-8 years, youth-at-risk programs, community projects, and education.
Contact: jkane@nalusda.gov
Details: Free

`gopher://ra.esusda.gov/11/CYFER-net`

DECNEWS for Education and Research ★★

Monthly electronic newsletter from Digital Equipment Corporation (DEC) summarizing announcements of its products, programs, and applications of interest to computer users in the academic and research communities.

Keywords: Computing, Education, DEC
Sponsor: Digital Equipment Corp.
Audience: Computer Users, Educators, Researchers
Contact: Mary Hoffmann
decnews@mr4dec.enet.dec.com
Details: Free
User info: To subscribe, send an e-mail message to the address below consisting of a single line reading:

SUB DECNews YourFirstName YourLastName

To send a message to the entire list, address it to:
DECNews@ubvm.buffalo.edu

`mailto:listserv@ubvm.buffalo.edu`

DECnews-EDU ★

DECNEWS for Education and Research is a monthly electronic publication from Digital Equipment Corporation's Education Business Unit for the education and research communities worldwide.

Keywords: Education, Computers, Digital Equipment Corporation
Audience: Educators, Researchers
Contact: Anne Marie McDonald
decnews@mr4dec.enet.dec.com
Details: Free
User info: To subscribe to the list, send an e-mail message requesting a subscription to the URL address below.

To send a message to the entire list, address it to:
decnews@mr4dec.enet.dec.com

`mailto:decnews@mr4dec.enet.dec.com`

DENet Information Server ★★★

This is the gopher of the Danish national academic network, which is located at the Danish Computer Centre for Research and Education (UNI-C).

Keywords: Education, Denmark, Libraries
Audience: Researchers, Educators
Profile: This gopher provides DENet information and statistics, UNI-C information, directory services and phone books, pointers to Danish electronic libraries and gophers, an index of major Danish FTP archives, and news in Danish.
Contact: Steen.Linden@uni-c.dk
Details: Free

`gopher://gopher.denet.dk`

Diversity U ★

Diversity University is an experiment in interactive learning.

Keywords: Education, Interactive Learning, Multimedia
Audience: Educators, Researchers
Details: Free

`gopher://erau.db.erau.edu`

Eastern Washington University Library ★★

The library's holdings are large and wide-ranging and contain significant collections in many fields.

Keywords: Education, Music, Social Science, Behavioral Science
Audience: Researchers, Students, General Public
Details: Free
User Info: Expect: Login; Send: Lib

`telnet://wsduvm12.csc.wsu.edu`

EDNET ★

This forum explores the educational potential of the Internet.

Keywords: Education, Internet
Audience: Students, Educators
Profile: This independent, unmoderated mailing-list interest group is open and free of charge to all participants. Ednet links educators with common interests, and introduces students to a number of fields and sources of information, while offering criticism and suggestions.
Contact: Prescott Smith
pgsmith@educ.umass.edu
Details: Free
User info: To subscribe to the list, send an e-mail message to the address shown below consisting of a single line reading:

SUB Ednet YourFirstName YourLastName

To send a message to the entire list, address it to:
ednet@nic.umass.edu.

`gopher://ericir.syr.edu/00/AskERIC/FullText/Lists/Messages/`

`EDNET-List/README`

`mailto:listserv@nic.umass.edu`

Education Gopher ★

Florida Tech's gopher relating to education. Includes information on search tools, libraries, electronic texts, and selected education-related gophers and information servers.

Keywords: Education, Gopher
Audience: Educators, Researchers
Contact: Kevin Barry
barry@sci-ed.fit.edu
Details: Free

`gopher://sci-ed.fit.edu`

Educator's Guide to E-mail Lists ★

A guide to help educators find e-mail lists. Includes a very large list of e-mail addresses related to education.

Keywords: Education, E-mail, Internet
Sponsor: University of Massachusetts, Amherst, MA
Audience: Educators, Researchers
Contact: Prescott Smith
pgsmith@educ.umass.edu
Details: Free

`ftp://nic.umass.edu`

EDUCOM ★

A large source of information relating to education.

Keywords: Education
Audience: Educators, Researchers
Contact: inquiry@educom.edu
Details: Free

`gopher://ivory.educom.edu/11/`

ERIC (Educational Resources Information Center) ★★★

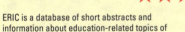

ERIC is a database of short abstracts and information about education-related topics of interest to teachers and administrators.

Keywords: Education, Databases
Sponsor: (Office of Educational Research and Development), US Department of Education
Department of Education (ED)
Audience: Educators, Administrators
Profile: ERIC is the complete database on educational materials from the Educational Resources Information Center in Washington, DC. The database corresponds to two print indexes: Resources in Education, which is concerned with identifying the most significant and timely education research reports; and Current Index to Journals in Education, an index of more than 700 periodicals of interest to every segment of the teaching profession.
Details: Costs
ERIC can be accessed in a variety of ways, for example, through CARL (Colorado Alliance of Research Libraries), through the University of Saskatchewan
(Request: sklib username: sonia)
ERIC can also be accessed by WAIS if you have WAIS installed on your local computer.

`telnet://pac.carl.org`

`telnet://skdevel12.usask.ca`

GLOSAS News (Global Systems Analysis and Simulating Association) ★

Newsletter of GLOSAS in the US, which is dedicated to global electronic education and simulation as a tool for promoting peace and the care of the natural environment.

Keywords: Education, Simulation, Peace
Audience: Educators, Environmentalists
Contact: Anton Ljutic
anton@vax2.concordia.ca
Details: Free
User info: To subscribe, send an e-mail message to the address below consisting of a single line reading:
SUB glosas YourFirstName YourLastName
To send a message to the entire list, address it to: glosas@ vm/.mcgill.ca

`mailto:listserv@vm1.mcgill.ca`

Information Infrastructure and Technology Act of 1992 ★

The Information Infrastructure and Technology Act of 1992 builds on the High-Performance Computing Act. The newer bill will ensure that the technology developed by the High-Performance Computing Program is applied widely in K-12 education, libraries, health care, and industry, particularly manufacturing. It will authorize a total of $1.15 billion over the next five years.

Keywords: Government (US Federal), Law (US Federal), Information Technology, Education, Health Care
Audience: Journalists, Politicians, Scientists, Manufacturers, Educators
Details: Free
File is: /internet/nren/iita.1992/gorebill.1992.txt

`ftp://nis.nsf.net`

IUCAA (Inter-University Centre for Astronomy and Astrophysics) ★

The IUCAA was set up to promote the growth of active groups in astronomy and astrophysics in India. The Centre runs vigorous visitor programs involving short and long-term visits of scientists from India and abroad.

Keywords: Astronomy, Astrophysics, Physics, Education
Sponsor: Centre for Astronomy and Astrophysics (IUCAA)
Audience: Reseachers, Astronomers, Physicists, Students
Contact: Postmaster
amk@iucaa.ernet.in

`http://iucaa.iucaa.ernet.in/welcome.html`

Journal of Technology Education ★

Electronic journal devoted to educational issues in technology.

Keywords: Communication, Education, Technology,
Audience: Educators
Details: Free
Send an e-mail message to the URL address below with the request: GET MISCELLA JTE-V5N1. This file will give you access information for additional issues.

`mailto:listserv@vtvm1.cc.vt.edu`

KIDLINK and KIDCAFE ★

This discussion group is designed to act as a structured forum for e-mail exchanges between children aged 10-15.

Keywords: Education, Children
Audience: Children
Profile: A dialog is set up each year called 'KIDS-XX' where 'XX' is the current year. Each participating child posts an e-mail message answering the following four questions before he or she can engage in the dialog: 1. Who am I? 2. What do I want to be when I grow up? 3. How do I want the world to be better when I grow up? 4. What can I do to make this happen?

KIDLINK operates the following free discussion lists and services:
- KIDLINK: discussion group for children aged 10-15.
- RESPONSE: the destination for answers to the four questions above.
- KIDCAFE: a forum for children aged 10-15. Read-only for people outside this age group.
- KIDCAFEP: a Portuguese-language version of KIDCAFE.
- KIDCAFEJ: a Japanese-language version of KIDCAFE.
- KIDCAFEN: a Scandinavian-language (Nordic) version of KIDCAFE.
- KIDFORUM: a showcase of works by kids on a series of topics specified to promote exchange between classrooms. Teachers can plan for class participation in monthly topics.
- KIDPROJ: a forum enabling teachers/youth group leaders to design projects for children through the KIDLINK network.
- KIDLEADR: an informal meeting place for exchanging ideas, networking, asking for help, requesting hello messages, and so on, for teachers, coordinators, parents, social workers, and others interested in KIDS-94.

- KIDLEADP: a Portuguese-language version of KIDLEADR.
- KIDLEADS: a Spanish-language version of KIDLEADR.
- KIDLEADN: a Scandinavian-language (Nordic) version of KIDLEADR.

Contact: Odd de Presno
opresno@extern.uio.no

Details: Free

For information about the projects, subscribe to the KIDLINK announcement service: send an e-mail message to: listserv@vm1.NoDak.edu with the following command in the text of your message:

SUB KIDLINK Yourfirstname Yourlastname.

Notes: For more information, read the 'WHAT IS KIDLINK / KIDS-94' page at gopher://kids.ccit.duq.edu/00/about/kidlink-general.

gopher://kids.ccit.duq.edu

NCTM-L ★★

A mailing list for the discussion of standards applying to the National Council of Teachers of Mathematics.

Keywords: Education, Mathematics
Audience: Mathematics Educators
Contact: barry@sci-ed.fit.edu
Details: Free
User info: To subscribe to this list, send an e-mail message to the URL address below, consisting of a single line reading:

SUB nctm-l YourFirstName YourLastName

To send a message to the entire list, address it to: nctm-l@sci-ed.fit.edu

mailto:listproc@sci-ed.fit.edu

PENPages

This easy-to-use general-interest database contains articles and brochures.

Keywords: Food, Employment, Education
Sponsor: Pennsylvania State University, PA
Audience: General Public
User Info: Expect: login; Send: your state's two-letter code (or "world" if sent from outside the USA)

telnet://psunet.psu.edu

Scholarly Communication ★

These quarterly technical reports contain information and discussion about the role of network-based electronic resources in scholarly communication.

Keywords: Education, Scholarly Communication, Conferences
Audience: Educators, Researchers
Details: Free
File is: pub/vpiej-l/reports

ftp://borg.lib.vt.edu/pub/vpiej-1/reports

http://borg.lib.vt.edu/scholar.info.html

Thailand: The Big Picture ★★

A web site maintaining a complete list of Internet servers pertaining to and found within Thailand. General information concerning Thailand and extensive Internet connections to Thai academic institutions.

Keywords: Thailand, Education, Travel Research
Sponsor: National Electronics and Computer Center at the National Science and Technology Development Agency, USA
Audience: Researchers, Exchange Students
Contact: Trin Tantsetthi
webmaster@www.nectec.or.th

http://www.nectec.or.th

UNC-CH Info system ★★

The University of North Carolina at Chapel Hill's campus-wide information server, providing access to a wide range of campus information and to electronic information services worldwide.

Keywords: Education, Internet Services
Sponsor: University of North Carolina at Chapel Hill
Audience: Educators, Researchers, Internet Surfers
Contact: info@unc.edu
Details: Free

gopher://gibbs.oit.unc.edu

University of Northern Iowa Library ★★

The library's holdings are large and wide-ranging and contain significant collections in many fields.

Keywords: Art, Business Information, Education, Music, Fiction
Audience: Researchers, Students, General Public
Contact: Mike Yohe
yohe@uni.edu
Details: Free
User Info: Expect: Login; Send: Public

telnet://infosys.uni.edu

University of Puerto Rico Library ★★

The library's holdings are large and wide-ranging and contain significant collections in many fields.

Keywords: Computer Science, Education, Nursing, Agriculture, Economics
Audience: Researchers, Students, General Public
Details: Free

After Locator: telnet://, press Tab twice. Type DIAL VTAM. Enter NOTIS.
Press Return. On the blank screen, type LUUP.

telnet://136.145.2.10

University of Puget Sound Library ★★

The library's holdings are large and wide-ranging and contain significant collections in many fields.

Keywords: Education, Literature (General), Music, Natural Science, Theology
Audience: Researchers, Students, General Public
Details: Free
User Info: Expect: Login; Send: Library

telnet://192.124.98.2

University of Wisconsin Eau Claire Library ★★

The library's holdings are large and wide-ranging and contain significant collections in many fields.

Keywords: Health Sciences, Business, Nursing, Education
Audience: Researchers, Students, General Public
Details: Free
User Info: Expect: Service Name, Send: Victor

telnet://lib.uwec.edu

University of Wisconsin River Falls Library ★★

The library's holdings are large and wide-ranging and contain significant collections in many fields.

Keywords: Agriculture, Education, History (US)
Audience: Researchers, Students, General Public
Details: Free
User Info: Expect: Service Name, Send: Victor

telnet://davee.dl.uwrf.edu

University of Wisconsin Stevens Point Library ★★

The library's holdings are large and wide-ranging and contain significant collections in many fields.

Keywords: Education, Environmental Studies, Ethnic Studies, History (US)
Audience: Researchers, Students, General Public
Details: Free
User Info: Expect: Login; Send: Lib; Expect: vDIAL Prompt, Send: Library

telnet://lib.uwsp.edu

US Department of Education Online Library ★★★

A resource for information on federal programs, including full-text of the GOALS 2000, Educate America Act, The Prisoners of Time Report, and other documents regarding education legislation, reports, and information.

Keywords: Education, Law (US)
Sponsor: US Department of Education
Audience: Educators, Students, Legislators, Researchers

`http://www.ed.gov/`

`gopher://gopher.ed.gov`

`ftp://ftp.ed.gov`

Usenet University ★

An archive of Usenet university groups that are currently active on the Internet.

Keywords: Education, Universities
Audience: University Students, Educators, Researchers
Details: Free
 File is: pub/doc/uu/FAQ

`ftp://nic.funet.fi`

Virginia's PEN (Public Education Network) ★

This is a statewide educational network.

Keywords: Education, Community Networking, Virginia
Sponsor: Virginia Department of Education
Audience: Educators
Profile: Educators throughout Virginia can access PEN via a local telephone call or through a toll-free line. The network includes discussion groups, news reports, study guides, and curriculum resources. In one of the features, History OnLine, students and teachers query historical figures such as Thomas Jefferson, and historians will answer in character.
Contact: Harold Cathern
 hcathern@vdoe386.vak12.edu
Details: Free
Password: Guest

`telnet://guest@vdoe386.vak12.edu`

Educational Policy

edpolyan (Educational Policy Analysis) ★

This list focuses on educational policy analysis. This is an active, broad list, where issues surrounding all levels of education are discussed. This list takes a relatively philosophical approach to the issue.

Keywords: Education (Continuing), Educational Policy
Audience: University Administrators, K-12 Educators, Postsecondary Educators
Details: Free
User info: To subscribe to the list, send an e-mail message to the URL address shown below consisting of a single line reading:
 SUB edpolyan YourFirstName YourLastName
 To send a message to the entire list, address it to: edpolyan@asuacad.bitnet

`mailto:listserv@asuacad.bitnet`

edpolyar (Educational Policy Analysis Archive) ★

The Educational Policy Analysis Archive, an outgrowth of the edpolyan scholarly discussion list, publishes peer-reviewed articles of between 500 and 1,500 lines in length on all aspects of education policy analysis.

Keywords: Education (Continuing), Educational Policy
Audience: K-12 Educators, University Administrators, Postsecondary Educators
Details: Free, Moderated
User info: To subscribe to the archive, send an e-mail message to the URL address shown below consisting of a single line reading:
 SUB edpolyar YourFirstName YourLastName

`mailto:listserv@asuacad.bitnet`

INTER-L ★

A list for members of the National Association of Foreign Student Advisors.

Keywords: Advisory, Education (Bilingual), Educational Policy
Sponsor: National Association of Foreign Student Advisors (NAFSA)
Audience: Foreign Students, NAFSA Members
Details: Free
User info: To subscribe to the list, send an e-mail message to the address below consisting of a single line reading:

`mailto:listserv@vtm1.cc.vt.edu`

University of Wisconsin Superior Library ★★

The library's holdings are large and wide-ranging and contain significant collections in many fields.

Keywords: Educational Policy, Government (US)
Audience: Researchers, Students, General Public
Details: Free
User Info: Expect: Login, Send: Lib; Expect: vDIAL Prompt, Send: Library

`telnet://sail.uwsuper.edu`

Educators

journet ★★

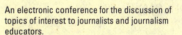

An electronic conference for the discussion of topics of interest to journalists and journalism educators.

Keywords: Journalism, Writing, Desktop Publishing, Electronic Publishing
Audience: Journalists, Writers, Publishers, Educators
Contact: George Frajkor
 gfrajkor@ccs.carleton.ca
User info: To subscribe to the list, send an e-mail message to the URL address below consisting of a single line reading:
 SUB journet YourFirstName YourLastName
 To send a message to the entire list, address it to: journet@qucdn.queensu.ca

`mailto:listserv@qucdn.queensu.ca`

Educator's Guide to E-mail Lists

Educator's Guide to E-mail Lists ★

A guide to help educators find e-mail lists. Includes a very large list of e-mail addresses related to education.

Keywords: Education, E-mail, Internet
Sponsor: University of Massachusetts, Amherst, MA
Audience: Educators, Researchers
Contact: Prescott Smith
 pgsmith@educ.umass.edu
Details: Free

`ftp://nic.umass.edu`

EDUCOM

EDUCOM

A large source of information relating to education.

Keywords: Education
Audience: Educators, Researchers
Contact: inquiry@educom.edu
Details: Free

`gopher://ivory.educom.edu/11`

edupage (A News Update from EDUCOM)

edupage (A News Update from EDUCOM)

A newsletter put out by EDUCOM summarizing information technology news.

Keywords: Education (Continuing), Information Technology
Sponsor: EDUCOM
Audience: Educators, Administrators
Details: Free
User info: To subscribe to the newsletter, send an e-mail message requesting a subscription to the URL address shown below and include your name, institutional affiliation, and e-mail address.

`mailto:edupage@educom.edu`

EEC

CEDAR (Central European Environmental Data Request) Facility

This gopher site provides information about the environmental and scientific community in Central and Eastern Europe (CEE), with access to environmental information located throughout the world on various international computer networks and hosts.

Keywords: Europe, EEC, Environment
Sponsor: The International Society for Environmental Protection, and The Austrian Federal Ministry for Environment, Youth and Family (BMUJF)
Audience: Environmentalists, Educators, Students, Urban Planners
Contact: cedar-info@cedar.univie.ac.at
Notes: CEDAR Marxergasse 3/20, A-1030 Vienna, Austria Tel.: +43-1-715 58 79

`gopher://pan.cedar.univie.ac.at`

INTLAW (International Law Library)

The International Law library provides comprehensive international law materials.

Keywords: International Law, EEC, Commonwealth, China
Audience: Lawyers, International Lawyers
Profile: The International Law library provides comprehensive international law materials. The International Law library contains federal case law, European Community materials, treaties and agreements, Commonwealth law materials, topical and professional journals, French law materials (in French), China law materials, plus relevant topical publications.
Contact: New Sales Group at 800-227-4908 or 513-859-5398 inside the US, or 1-513-865-7981 for all inquires outside the US.
User info: To subscribe, contact Mead directly.

To examine the Lexis user guide, you can access it at the ftp site of the University of Texas at Austin at the URL address: ftp://ftp.cc.utexas.edu

The files are in: /pub/ref-services/LEXIS

`telnet://nex.meaddata.com`

`http://www.meaddata.com`

EEJobs

EEJobs

Discusses and advertises positions available and positions desired in the electrical and electronic engineering fields. Discussion and tips on how to find jobs are also welcome.

Keywords: Engineering, Electrical Engineering, Employment
Audience: Engineers, Students
Contact: Jerome Grimmer
st6267@aix370.siu.edu
Details: Free
User info: To subscribe to the list, send an e-mail messagel with a subject of SERVER.COMMANDS to ST6267@AIX370.SIU.EDU

In the body of the mail, type on the first line, /BBOARD SUB EEJOBS or /BBOARD SIGNON EEJOBS to be added to the EEJOBS list.

`st6267@aix370.siu.edu`

Eerie, Indiana

Eerie, Indiana

The list is for the discussion of the critically acclaimed but short-lived TV series "Eerie, Indiana" which originally aired on NBC in 1991-1992 and is now distributed internationally.

Keywords: Eerie, Indiana
Audience: Television Viewers
Contact: Corey Kirk
owner-eerie-indiana@sfu.ca
Details: Free
User Info: To subscribe to the list, send an e-mail message requesting a subscription to the URL address below.

To send a message to the entire list, address it to: owner-eerie-indiana@sfu.ca

`mailto:owner-eerie-indiana@sfu.ca`

EFFector Online—The Electronic Frontier Foundation, Inc.

EFFector Online—The Electronic Frontier Foundation, Inc.

Established to make the electronic frontier truly useful and accessible to everyone, emphasizing the free and open flow of information and communication.

Keywords: Computer Communications, Electronic Media, Intellectual Property, Privacy
Audience: Computer Users, Civil Libertarians
Profile: EFFector Online presents news, information, and discussion about the world of computer-based communications media that constitute the electronic frontier. It covers issues such as freedom of speech in digital media, privacy rights, censorship, and standards of responsibility for users and operators of computer systems, as well as policy issues such as the development of a national information infrastructure, and intellectual property.
Contact: Gerard Van der Leun, Mike Godwin
gerard@eff.org mnemonic@eff.org
Details: Free
User info: To subscribe, send an e-mail message requesting a subscription to: request@eff.org
Notes: This takes you to the front door of the eff gopher server which contains much more information than just Effector online.

`gopher://gopher.eff.org/1`

Ei Compendex Plus

Ei Compendex Plus

The Ei Compendex Plus database is the machine-readable version of The Engineering Index (monthly/annual), which provides abstracted information from the world's significant literature of engineering and technology.

Keywords:	Engineering, Technology
Sponsor:	Engineering Information Inc. (Ei), Hoboken, NJ, USA
Audience:	Engineers
Profile:	Ei Compendex Plus provides worldwide coverage of approximately 4,500 journals and selected government reports and books. Subjects covered include: civil, energy, environmental, geological, and biological engineering; electrical, automotive, nuclear, and aerospace engineering; and computers, robotics, and industrial robots.
Contact:	Dialog in the US at (800) 334-2564, Dialog internationally at country-specific locations.
User info:	To subscribe, contact Dialog directly.
Notes:	Coverage: 1970 to the present; updated weekly.

`telnet://dialog.com`

EINet Galaxy

EINet Galaxy

EINet Galaxy is a guide to world-wide information and services. It includes public information as well as commercial information and services provided by EINet customers and affiliates. The information is organized by topic, and can be searched.

Keywords:	WWW, Information Retrieval, Internet
Sponsor:	Microelectronic and Computer Technology Corporation (MCC)
Audience:	Reseachers, Students
Contact:	Wayne Allen, Bruce Speyer WA@EINet.net, Speyer@EINet.net

`http://galaxy.einet.net/galaxy.html`

ejcrec 'Electronic Journal of Communications/La Revue _lectronique de communication'

ejcrec 'Electronic Journal of Communications/La Revue _lectronique de communication'

This journal is a quarterly bilingual (English and French) journal for the communications field broadly.

Keywords:	Communications
Audience:	Educators, Administrators, Communications Professionals
Details:	Free
User info:	To subscribe to the journal, send an e-mail message to the URL address shown below consisting of a single line reading: Join edupage YourFirstName YourLastName

`mailto:comserve@rpitsvm.bitnet`

Electric

Electric Power Database

Electric Power Database provides references to research and development projects of interest to the electric power industry, and corresponds to the print Digest of Research in the Electric Utility Industry.

Keywords:	Energy, Electric
Sponsor:	Electric Power Research Institute (EPRI), Palo Alto, CA, USA
Audience:	Engineers
Profile:	The database covers US and Canadian research on 13 major categories related to issues in electric power, including hydroelectric power, fossil fuels, nuclear power, transmission, economics, advanced power systems, and environmental assessment. The records include abstracts of project summaries for past and ongoing research projects. Such projects are conducted largely by companies under contract to EPRI or to other utilities, and by EPRI itself. Research from other corporate and utility sources is also covered.
Contact:	Dialog in the US at (800) 334-2564, Dialog internationally at country-specific locations.
User info:	To subscribe, contact Dialog directly.
Notes:	Coverage: 1972 to the present; updated monthly.

`telnet://dialog.com`

Electric Circuit Analysis

CIRCUITS-L

This list discusses all aspects of the introductory course in circuit analysis for electrical engineering undergraduates.

Keywords:	Engineering, Electrical Engineering, Teaching, Electric Circuit Analysis
Audience:	Engineers, Students (college)
Contact:	Paul E. Gray gray@maple.ucs.uwplatt.edu
Details:	Free
User info:	To subscribe to the list, send an e-mail message to the URL address below, and include: name; e-mail address; home phone, business phone, and FAX numbers (including area code); and US postal address (including ZIP code) To send a message to the entire list, address it to: circuits-l@uwplatt.edu

`mailto:circuits-request@uwplatt.edu`

Electric Light Orchestra

Electric Light Orchestra

Discussion of the music of Electric Light Orchestra and later solo efforts by band members and former members.

Keywords:	Electric Light Orchestra, Rock Music
Audience:	Rock Music Enthusiasts
Contact:	elo-list-request@andrew.cmu.edu
Details:	Free
User Info:	To subscribe to the list, send an e-mail message requesting a subscription to the URL address below. To send a message to the entire list, address it to: elo-list-request@andrew.cmu.edu

`mailto:elo-list-request@andrew.cmu.edu`

Electric Vehicles

EV

General list for discussion of all aspects of electric vehicles.

Keywords:	Electric Vehicles
Audience:	Electric Vehicle Enthusiasts
Contact:	Clyde Visser listserv@sjsuvm1.sjsu.edu

User info: To subscribe to the list, send an e-mail message to the URL address below consisting of a single line reading:

SUB electric-vehicle YourFirstName YourLastName

To send a message to the entire list, address it to: electric-vehicle@sjsuvm1.sjsu.edu

mailto:listserv@sjsuvm1.sjsu.edu

Electrical Engineering

Adv-Eli

Adv-Eli discusses the latest advances in electrical engineering. It is sponsored by the IEEE Student Branch of Santa Maria University (Chile).

Keywords: Electrical Engineering, Engineering, Electronics
Audience: Engineers, Educators, Students
Contact: Francisco Javier Fernandez ffernand@utfsm
Details: Free
User info: To subscribe to the list, send an e-mail message to the URL address shown below consiting of a single line reading:

SUB adv-eli YourFirstName YourLastName

To send a message to the entire list, address it to: adv-eli@loa.disca.utfsm.cl

listserv@loa.disca.utfsm.cl

Adv-Elo

Discusses the latest advances in electronics. Sponsored by the IEEE Student Branch of Santa Maria University (Chile).

Keywords: Electrical Engineering, Engineering, Electronics, Technological Advances
Audience: Engineers, Educators, Students
Contact: Rodrigo E. Rodriguez rrodrigu@utfsm
Details: Free
User info: To subscribe to the list, send an e-mail message to the URL address shown below consiting of a single line reading:

SUB adv-elo YourFirstName YourLastName

To send a message to the entire list, address it to: adv-elo@loa.disca.utfsm.cl

listserv@loa.disca.utfsm.cl

CIRCUITS-L

This list discusses all aspects of the introductory course in circuit analysis for electrical engineering undergraduates.

Keywords: Engineering, Electrical Engineering, Teaching, Electric Circuit Analysis
Audience: Engineers, Students (college)
Contact: Paul E. Gray gray@maple.ucs.uwplatt.edu
Details: Free
User info: To subscribe to the list, send an e-mail message to the URL address below, and include: name; e-mail address; home phone, business phone, and FAX numbers (including area code); and US postal address (including ZIP code)

To send a message to the entire list, address it to:

circuits-l@uwplatt.edu

mailto:circuits-request@uwplatt.edu

EEJobs

Discusses and advertises positions available and positions desired in the electrical and electronic engineering fields. Discussion and tips on how to find jobs are also welcome.

Keywords: Engineering, Electrical Engineering, Employment
Audience: Engineers, Students
Contact: Jerome Grimmer st6267@aix370.siu.edu
Details: Free
User info: To subscribe to the list, send an e-mail messagel with a subject of SERVER.COMMANDS to st627@aix370.siu.edu

In the body of the mail, type on the first line, /BBOARD SUB EEJOBS or /BBOARD SIGNON EEJOBS to be added to the EEJOBS list.

st6267@aix370.siu.edu

IEEE-L

Serves as a forum for all IEEE student branch officers and members.

Keywords: Engineering, Electrical Engineering
Audience: Engineers, Electrical Engineers, Students
Contact: Paul D. Kroculick or Chas Elliot tjwo465@bingtjw.cc.binghamton.edu ba0803@bingsuns.cc.binghamton.edu
Details: Free
User info: To subscribe to the list, send an e-mail message to the URL address below consisting of a single line reading:

SUB ieee-l YourFirstName YourLastName.

To send a message to the entire list, address it to: IEEE-l@bingvmb.cc.binghamton.edu

mailto:listserv@bingvmb.cc.binghamton.edu

Electronic

INSPEC

IINSPEC corresponds to the three Science Abstracts print publications: Physics Abstracts, Electrical and Electronics Abstracts, and Computer and Control Abstracts.

Keywords: Physics, Electronic, Computing
Sponsor: Institution of Electrical Engineers, London, UK
Audience: Physicists, Electrical Engineers, Computer Specialists
Profile: Approximately 16 percent of the database's source publications are in languages other than English, but all articles are abstracted and indexed in English. The special DIALOG online thesaurus feature is available to assist searchers in determining appropriate subject terms and codes.
Contact: Dialog in the US at (800) 334-2564, Dialog internationally at country-specific locations.
User info: To subscribe, contact Dialog directly.
Notes: Coverage: April 1969 to the present; updated weekly.

telnet://dialog.com

Electronic Art

ISEA (Inter-Society on Electronic Arts) Online

An online forum for discussion of topics related to ISEA-94, the 5th International Symposium on Electronic Art which will take place in Finland in August, 1994.

Keywords: Art, Electronic Art, Technology
Audience: Artists, Art Enthusiasts
Details: Free

ftp://ftp.ncsa.uiuc.edu

Multimedia, Telecommunications, and Art Project

A project to promote online art that will be implemented as gopher site and on the World-Wide Web.

Keywords: Multimedia, Electronic Art, Telecommunications
Sponsor: CISR (Centre for Image and Sound Research), Vancouver, B.C., Canada
Audience: Artists, Writers
Contact: Derek Dowden Derek_Dowden@mindlink.bc.ca

For more information, send an e-mail message to the URL address below.

mailto:Derek_Dowden@mindlink.bc.ca

OTIS (Operative Term Is Stimulate)

An image-based electronic art gallery.

Keywords: Art, Graphics, Electronic Art, Animation
Audience: Graphic Artists
Profile: OTIS is a public-access library containing hundreds of images, animations, and information files.

Within the sunsite ftp, the directory is: /pub/multimedia/pictures/OTIS. Use the bin command to insure you're in binary transfer mode.

`ftp://sunsite.unc.edu`

Electronic Books

AskERIC Virtual Library

This gopher is part of a federally-funded system to provide public access to educational resources.

Keywords: Education (K-12), Computer-Aided Learning, Libraries, Electronic Books
Sponsor: Educational Resources Information Center (ERIC)
Audience: K-12 Teachers, Administrators
Profile: This gopher contains a wide range of educational aids including pre-prepared lesson plans, guides to Internet resources for the classroom organized by subject, updates on conferences for educators, and archives of education-related listservs. Also allows access to outside gophers, libraries, and sources of electronic books and journals.
Contact: Nancy A. Morgan
nmorgan@ericir.syr.edu
askeric@ericir.syr.edu

`gopher://ericir.syr.edu`

Electronic Books

A collection of books available as ASCII text files, including classics of antiquity (Aristotle, Virgil, Sophocles, the Bible), as well as more contemporary works of fiction and nonfiction by authors ranging from Dostoevsky to Martin Luther King, Jr.

Keywords: Books, Online Books, Literature (Contemporary), Literature (General)
Sponsor: The Blacksburg Electronic Village (BEV) at Virginia Tech
Audience: General Public, Historians
Contact: BEV Gopher Administrators
gopher@gopher.vt.edu

`gopher://gopher.vt.edu`

Electronic Cafe

Electronic Cafe

A seminal art and telecommunications group that specializes in video transmission.

Keywords: Art, Video, Telecommunications
Audience: Artists
Profile: This combines performance, communication, and community outreach by making telecommunications equipment available in a cafe-style artists' space.
Contact: Kit Galloway and Sherrie Rabinowitz, 1641 18th St., Santa Monica, CA 90404, USA

`mailto:ecafe@netcom.com`

Electronic Commerce

CommerceNet

An open, internet-based infrastructure for electronic commerce, created by a coalition of Silicon Valley organizations.

Keywords: business, electronic commerce
Sponsor: CommerceNet, Inc. 800 El Camino Real, Menlo Park, CA 94025.
Audience: businesses, commercial internet users, general public
Profile: Services include basic enabling services required by virtually every user and application (generic directories, secure multimedia messaging, network access control, and payment facilities). Applications include a framework for the development of compelling applications and services targeted to electronic commerce among companies in the region. Applications are designed to address the varied business and community needs of CommerceNet users; these are developed by third-party providers, in compliance with protocols established by CommerceNet. Connectivity is high-quality and affordable, with minimal on-site equipment or network expertise required of the user.
Contact: feedback@commerce.net

`http://www.commerce.net`

Internet Shopping Network

A shopping network on the Infobahn

Keywords: Business, Electronic Commerce
Sponsor: Internet Shopping Network
Audience: Business Users, Commercial Internet Users, General Public
Profile: The Internet Shopping Network aims to conduct research and develop products and services that commercialize the Internet, for the purpose of retailing and mass merchandising. The stores within this network offer approximately 20,000 products from 1000 vendors.

Telemedia, Networks, and Systems Group

A list of commercial services on the Web (and Net)

Keywords: Business, Electronic Commerce
Sponsor: MIT Laboratory for Computer Science, Cambridge, MA 02139
Audience: Business Professionals, Commercial Internet Users, General Public
Profile: This list of commercial Internet services is well-maintained and frequently updated.
Contact: hhh@mit.edu

`http://tns-www.lcs.mit.edu/commerce.html`

`http://tns-www.lcs.mit.edu`

Electronic Communications Privacy Act of 1986

Electronic Communications Privacy Act of 1986

This is the act to amend Title 18, United States Code, with respect to the interception of certain communications, other forms of surveillance, and for other purposes. This act affects every Usenet, Bitnet, BBS, shortwave listener, TV viewer, and so on.

Keywords: Communications, Privacy, Government (US Federal), Laws (US Federal)
Audience: Journalists, Privacy Activists, Students, Politicians
Details: Free

`gopher://wiretap.spies.com/00/Gov/ecpa.act`

Electronic Democracy Must Come from Us

Electronic Democracy Must Come from Us

Article about government policy and community networks by community networker Evelyn Pine (former national director of Computer Professionals for Social Responsibility). A short critique of the promises of electronic networking contrasted with the realities of political control.

Keywords: Community, Networking, Government (US)
Audience: Activists, Community Leaders, Governments
Contact: Evelyn Pine
evy@well.sf.ca.us
Details: Free

`http://nearnet.gnn.com/mag/articles/oram/bio.pine.html`

Electronic Hebrew Users Newsletter (E-Hug)

Electronic Hebrew Users Newsletter (E-Hug) ★

This newsletter is electronic only, and is mandated, like the original, to cover everything relating to the use of Hebrew, Yiddish, Judesmo, and Aramaic on computers.

Keywords: Judaism, Religion, Hebrew Language
Sponsor: Berkeley Hillel Foundation
Audience: Jews, Judaism Students
Contact: Ari Davidow
well!ari@apple.com
Details: Free
User info: To subscribe, send an e-mail message to the address below consisting of a single line reading:

To send a message to the entire list,

`mailto:listserv@dartcms1.bitnet`

Electronic Media

Animals

This directory is a compilation of information resources focused on animals.

Keywords: Animals, Electronic Media
Audience: Animal Lovers, Veterinarians, Activists

Contact: Ken Boschert
ken@wudcm.wustl.edu
Details: Free

`ftp://una.hh.lib.umich.edu/70/inetdirsstacks/animals:boschert`

Books Online

This web site contains hundreds of full-text online books, including many classics such as *Anna Karenina* and *The Complete Works of William Shakespeare*. Also provides links to other book resources and has a searchable index.

Keywords: Books, Electronic Media
Audience: Readers, Literary Scholars
Contact: spok@cs.cmu.edu

`gopher://calypso-2.oit.unc.edu/11/sunsite.d/book.d`

`http://www.cs.cmu.edu/Web/books.html`

EFFector Online—The Electronic Frontier Foundation, Inc.

Established to make the electronic frontier truly useful and accessible to everyone, emphasizing the free and open flow of information and communication.

Keywords: Computer Communications, Electronic Media, Intellectual Property, Privacy
Audience: Computer Users, Civil Libertarians
Profile: EFFector Online presents news, information, and discussion about the world of computer-based communications media that constitute the electronic frontier. It covers issues such as freedom of speech in digital media, privacy rights, censorship, and standards of responsibility for users and operators of computer systems, as well as policy issues such as the development of a national information infrastructure, and intellectual property.
Contact: Gerard Van der Leun, Mike Godwin
gerard@eff.org mnemonic@eff.org
Details: Free
User info: To subscribe, send an e-mail message requesting a subscription to:
request@eff.org
Notes: This takes you to the front door of the eff gopher server which contains much more information than just Effector online.

`gopher://gopher.eff.org/1`

GameBytes magazine

This monthly electronic magazine provides reviews (with graphics) of electronic games.

Keywords: Games, Electronic Media, Entertainment
Sponsor: Game Bytes Magazine

Audience: Game Players, Computer Game Developers, Computer Graphics Designers
Contact: Ross Erickson
rwericks@ingr.com
Details: Free

`http://wcl-rs.bham.ac.uk/GameBytes`

Internet Wiretap

A resource containing electronic books, zines, and government documents, White House press releases, and links to worldwide gopher and WAIS servers.

Keywords: Electronic Media, Cyberculture, Zines
Sponsor: Internet Wiretap
Audience: Cyberculture Enthusiasts, Civil Libertarians, Educators

`gopher://wiretap.spies.com/11/`
`http://wiretap.spies.com`

Leonardo Electronic Almanac

The Leonardo Electronic Almanac (LEA) is a monthly, edited journal and an electronic archive dedicated to providing current perspectives in the art, science and technology domains.

Keywords: Art, Multimedia, Music, Electronic Media
Sponsor: International Society for the Arts, Sciences, and Technology
Audience: New Media Artists, Researchers, Developers, Art Educators, Art Professionals
Profile: LEA is an international, interdisciplinary forum for people interested in the use of new media in contemporary artistic expression, especially involving 20th century science and technology. Material is contributed by artists, scientists, philosophers and educators. LEA is published by the MIT Press for Leonardo, the International Society for the Arts, Sciences, and Technology (ISAST).
Contact: Craig Harris
craig@well.sf.ca.us
Details: Costs, Moderated, Images, Sounds, Multimedia

`mailto:journals-orders@mit.edu`

`ftp://mitpress.mit.edu/pub/Leonardo-Elec-Almanac`

News

This directory is a general compilation of information resources focused on news.

Keywords: News Media, Electronic Media, Journalism
Audience: Newsreaders, Journalists, General Public
Details: Free

`ftp://una.hh.lib.umich.edu/70/inetdirsstacks/news:robinson`

Electronic Music

Analog Heaven

The Analog Heaven mailing list caters to people interested in vintage analog electronic music equipment. Topics include items for sale, repair tips, equipment modifications, ASCII & GIF schematics, and a general discussion of new and old analog equipment. There is an FTP/Gopher site located at cs.uwp.edu with discussions on various machines, a definitive guide to Roland synths, patch editors, modification schematics, and GIFs/JPEGs of vintage synths, as well as a few sound samples of some of the gear itself.

- Keywords: Music, Synthesizers, Sequencers, Analog Equipment, Electronic Music
- Audience: Electronic Music Enthusiasts, Musicians
- Contact: Todd Sines analogue-request@magnus.acs.ohio-state.edu
- Details: Free, Sound files available.
- User info: To subscribe to the list, send an e-mail message requesting a subscription to the URL address below.

    To send a message to the entire list, address it to: analogue@magnus.acs.ohio-state.edu

mailto:analogue-request@magnus.acs.ohio-state.edu

Space-music

This mailing list is for the discussion of artists who use primarily electronic instruments to create 'sound spaces' or sound atmospheres that fall into categories defined as 'floating,' 'cosmic,' or 'noncommercial' and demand an active listener.

- Keywords: Music, Electronic Music
- Audience: Electronic Music Enthusiasts
- Contact: Dave Datta space-music-request@cs.uwp.edu
- Details: Free
- User info: To subscribe to the list, send an e-mail message requesting a subscription to the URL address below.

    To send a message to the entire list, address it to: space-music@cs.uwp.edu

mailto:space-music-request@cs.uwp.edu

Synth-l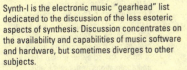

Synth-l is the electronic music "gearhead" list dedicated to the discussion of the less esoteric aspects of synthesis. Discussion concentrates on the availability and capabilities of music software and hardware, but sometimes diverges to other subjects.

- Keywords: Electronic Music, Music Software
- Audience: Electronic Music Enthusiasts, Musicians, Software Designers
- Contact: Joe McMahon Synth-L@american.edu
- Details: Free
- User info: To subscribe to the list, send an e-mail message to the address shown below consisting of a single line reading:

    SUB Synth-L YourFirstName YourLastName

    To send a message to the entire list, address it to: Synth-L@american.edu

mailto:listserv@american.edu

Electronic Publications

(The) Scientist Newsletter

Electronic newsletter pertaining to science.
- Keywords: Science, Electronic Publications
- Audience: Scientists, Educators, Researchers, General Public

gopher://internic.net

The Internet Press

A guide to electronic journals about the Internet.
- Keywords: Internet Guides, Electronic Publications
- Audience: General Public
- Profile: Publications discussed include the following: NSF Network News, Meta Magazine, Bits and Bytes, The Network Observer, HotWIRED, Scout Report, Netsurfer Digest, and The Internet Informer.
- Contact: Kevin M. Savetz
- User info: To subscribe to the list, send an e-mail message to the URL address below, with the subject line subscribe ipress. (Leave the body of the message blank.)

mailto:savetz@rahul.net

Electronic Publishing

CDPub

CDPub is an electronic mailing list for those engaged or interested in CD-ROM publishing in general, and in desktop CD-ROM recorders and publishing systems in particular. Topics of interest to the list include information on the various desktop publishing systems for premastering using CD-ROM media and tapes (e.g. DAT), replication services, various standards of interest to publishers (e.g. ISO9660, RockRidge), retrieval engines, and platform independence issues. Discussions on all platforms are welcome.

- Keywords: CD-ROM, Electronic Publishing, Desktop Publishing
- Audience: CD-ROM Publishers, Desktop Publishers, Publishers
- Contact: CDPub-Info@knex.via.mind.org
- Details: Free
- User info: To subscribe to the list, send an e-mail message requesting a subscription to the URL address below.

    To send a message to the entire list, address it to: CDPub@knex.via.mind.org

mailto:mail-server@knex.via.mind.org

Electronic Newsstand Gopher ★★★

This gopher contains tables of contents, selected full-text articles, and assorted other information from many mainstream print journals.

- Keywords: Journals, Electronic Publishing, Publishing, News
- Audience: News Enthusiasts, Publishers, Publishing Professionals, Journalists
- Profile: This gopher was compiled with the collaboration of the American Journal of International Law, Policy Review, Technology Review, Business Week, Current History, The Economist, Foreign Affairs, National Review, The New Yorker, The New Republic, Mother Jones, among other distinguished publications.
- Contact: William Love love@enews.com

gopher://gopher.enews.com

journet

An electronic conference for the discussion of topics of interest to journalists and journalism educators.

- Keywords: Journalism, Writing, Desktop Publishing, Electronic Publishing
- Audience: Journalists, Writers, Publishers, Educators
- Contact: George Frajkor gfrajkor@ccs.carleton.ca
- User info: To subscribe to the list, send an e-mail message to the URL address below consisting of a single line reading:

    SUB journet YourFirstName YourLastName. To send a message to the entire list, address it to: journet@qucdn.queensu.ca

mailto:listserv@qucdn.queensu.ca

Electronics

Adv-Eli

Adv-Eli discusses the latest advances in electrical engineering. It is sponsored by the IEEE Student Branch of Santa Maria University (Chile).

- Keywords: Electrical Engineering, Engineering, Electronics
- Audience: Engineers, Educators, Students

Adv-Elo

Contact:	Francisco Javier Fernandez ffernand@utfsm
Details:	Free
User info:	To subscribe to the list, send an e-mail message to the URL address shown below consiting of a single line reading: SUB adv-eli YourFirstName YourLastName To send a message to the entire list, address it to: adv-eli@loa.disca.utfsm.cl

listserv@loa.disca.utfsm.cl

Adv-Elo

Discusses the latest advances in electronics. Sponsored by the IEEE Student Branch of Santa Maria University (Chile).

Keywords:	Electrical Engineering, Engineering, Electronics, Technological Advances
Audience:	Engineers, Educators, Students
Contact:	Rodrigo E. Rodriguez rrodrigu@utfsm
Details:	Free
User info:	To subscribe to the list, send an e-mail message to the URL address shown below consiting of a single line reading: SUB adv-elo YourFirstName YourLastName To send a message to the entire list, address it to: adv-elo@loa.disca.utfsm.cl

listserv@loa.disca.utfsm.cl

CBDS-l

A mailing list for the discussion of CBDS (Circuit Board Design System).

Keywords:	Engineering, Computer-Aided Design, Electronics
Audience:	Engineers
Contact:	NETMAN@SUVM.ACS.SYR.EDU
Details:	Free
User info:	To subscribe to the list, send an e-mail message to the URL address below consisting of a single line reading: SUB cbds-l YourFirstName YourLastName To send a message to the entire list, address it to: CbDS-L@SUVM.ACS.SYR.EDU

mailto: LISTSERV@SUVM.ACS.SYR.EDU

Class Four Relay Magazine

A magazine by Relay Ops for the relay community.

Keywords:	Relays, Magazines, Electronics
Sponsor:	Carnegie Mellon University, Pittsburg, PA, USA
Audience:	Relay Community
Profile:	Includes articles on general questions and issues of relay usage, information for and about relay ops, discussion of policy issues and guidelines, and technical issues and new developments.
Contact:	Joey J. Stanford stjs@vm.marist.edu
Details:	Free

mailto:stjs@vm.marist.edu

CMPCOM (Computers and Communications) Library

The Computers and Communications Library provides you industry-specific sources. More than 40 full-text sources that concentrate on computers and communications are available. Full-text files can be searched in a variety of ways: as an individual file, by major-subject group file, or as a user-defined group file.

Keywords:	Computers, Communications, Technology, Electronics
Audience:	Business Researchers, Analysts, Entrepreneurs
Profile:	This library can be used to gain insight on new products and technologies being introduced; monitor industry news for high technology systems, electronics, engineering, communications, and computer hardware and software; and locate product evaluations for both the professional as well as the casual personal computer user.
Contact:	Mead New Sales Group at (800) 227-4908 or (513) 859-5398 inside the US, or (513) 865-7981 for all inquiries outside the US.
User info:	To subscribe, contact Mead directly. To examine the Nexis user guide, you can access it at the ftp site of the University of Texas at Austin at the URL address: ftp://ftp.cc.utexas.edu The files are in: /pub/ref-services/LEXIS

telnet://nex.meaddata.com
http://www.meaddata.com

rec.radio.amateur.misc

A Usenet newsgroup providing information and discussion about ham radios.

Keywords:	Radio, Electronics
Audience:	Ham Radio Users
User info:	To subscribe to this Usenet newsgroup, you need access to a newsreader.

news:rec.radio.amateur.misc

rec.radio.shortwave

A Usenet newsgroup providing information and discussion about shortwave radio.

Keywords:	Radio, Electronics
Audience:	Shortwave Radio Users
User info:	To subscribe to this Usenet newsgroup, you need access to a newsreader.

news:rec.radio.shortwave

sci.electronics

A Usenet newsgroup providing information and discussion about circuits, theory and electrons.

Keywords:	Electronics, Engineering
Audience:	Electrical Engineers
Details:	Free
User info:	To subscribe to this Usenet newsgroup, you need access to a newsreader.

news:sci.electronics

Utah Valley Community College Library

The library's holdings are large and wide-ranging and contain significant collections in many fields.

Keywords:	Accounting, Automobiles, Cabinetry, Child Care, Drafting, Electronics, Home Building, Local History, Refrigeration, Air Conditioning
Audience:	General Public, Researchers, Librarians, Document Delivery Professionals
Details:	Free
User Info:	Expect: Login; Send: Opub

telnet:// uvlib.uvcc.edu

Electrophoresis

Biotechnet Electronic Buyer's Guide

Biotechnet is a global computer network created specially for research biologists. It is intended to be a valuable source of information and data, a communications resource, a forum to foster the exchange of current ideas, and an international marketplace for relevant goods and service.

Keywords:	Molecular Biology, Electrophoresis, Chromatography
Audience:	Molecular Biologists, Chemists, Laboratory Suppliers
Profile:	One of the services offered by Biotechnet is the Electronic Buyer's Guide, which is divided into five individual databases for specific product categories: Molecular Biology, Electrophoresis, Chromatography, Liquid Handling, and Instruments & Apparatus. After selecting one of the guides at the prompt, you can search through each database to find either product names and applications or the name and address of the company that manufactures the product you wish to locate.

Details: Free
Notes: Password: bguide
`telnet://biotech@biotechnet.com`

Eliot (George)

Princeton University Online Manuscripts Catalog Library

The library's holdings are large and wide-ranging. They contain significant collections in many fields.

Keywords: Books (Antiquarian), Dickens (Charles), Disraeli (Benjamin), Eliot (George), Hardy (Thomas), Kingsley (Charles), Trollope (Anthony)
Audience: General Public, Researchers, Librarians, Document Delivery Professionals
Details: Free
User Info: Expect: VM370 logo, Send: <cr>; Expect: Welcome screen, Send: folio <cr>; Expect: Welcome screen for FOLIO, Send: <cr>; Expect: List of choices, Send: 3 <cr>; To exit: type: logoff

`telnet://pucc.princeton.edu`

ELISA (Electronic Library Service)

ELISA (Electronic Library Service)

An information delivery service of the Library of the Australian National University.

Keywords: OPAC System, Australia
Sponsor: Australian National University
Audience: General Public
Profile: This information delivery service contains Australian mirrors of major gopher directories, and is a national entry point for Australian gopher services.
Contact: infodesk@info.anu.edu.au
Details: Free

`gopher://info.anu.edu.au`

ELSNET (European Network in Language and Speech)

ELSNET (European Network in Language and Speech)

A web site addressing the development of language technology in Europe and abroad by helping to coordinate progress on both scientific and technological fronts.

Keywords: Linguistics, Cognitive Science, Communication
Sponsor: The University of Edinburgh Centre for Cognitive Science, Edinburgh, Scotland
Audience: Linguists, Cognitive Scientists
Contact: Ewan Klein
klein@ed.ac.uk

`http://www.cogsci.ed.ac.uk/elsnet/home.html`

Emacs

auc-TeX

Discussion and information exchange about the AUC TeX package, which runs under GNU Emacs.

Keywords: Computers, TeX, AUC TeX, Emacs
Audience: Computer Users
Contact: Kresten Krab Thorup
auc-tex-request@iesd.auc.dk
Details: Free
User info: To subscribe to the list, send an e-mail message requesting a subscription to the URL address below.

To send a message to the entire list, address it to: auc-tex@iesd.auc.dk

`mailto:auc-tex-request@iesd.auc.dk`

NotGNU

There are three lists associated with the NotGNU Emacs editor. NotGNU-list is an interactive list dedicated to miscellaneous discussions, problems, and suggestions for NotGNU. NotGNU-announce is used for announcing new versions of NotGNU, notification of new services, bug reports, amd so on. NotGNU-distribution is a list to which new NotGNU binaries will be sent unencoded upon release.

Keywords: NotGNU, Emacs
Audience: NotGNU Users
Contact: notgnu-request@netcom.com
Details: Free
User info: To subscribe to the list, send an e-mail message requesting a subscription to the URL address below.

To send a message to the entire list, address it to: notgnu@netcom.com

`mailto:notgnu-request@netcom.com`

EMBASE

EMBASE

EMBASE is an acclaimed comprehensive index of international literature on medicine, science and pharmacology.

Keywords: Medicine, Science, Pharmacology
Sponsor: Elsevier Science Publishers
Audience: Librarians, Researchers, Students, Physicians
Contact: CDP Technologies Sales Department (800)950-2035, extension 400
User info: To subscribe, contact CDP Technologies directly

`telnet://cdplus@cdplus.com`

EMBnet (European Molecular Biology Network)

EMBnet (European Molecular Biology Network)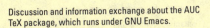

A group of European Internet sites which provide computational molecular biology services to both national and international researchers.

Keywords: Biology, Bioscience, Molecular Biology
Sponsor: The EC Funding Program (BRIDGE)
Audience: Biologists, Molecular Biologists, Researchers
Contact: Rodrigo Lopez, Robert Herzog
rodrigol@biotek.uio.no
rherzog@ulb.ac.be

`http://biomaster.uio.no/embnet-www.html`

EMBnet

BFU (Brussels Free Universities)

The gopher server of the Brussels Free Universities VUB/ULB is the national entry point for EMBnet in Belgium and provides links to university library systems and EMBnet databases.

Keywords: Computing, EMBnet, Belgium, Europe
Audience: Scientists, Biologists, Biotechnologists
Contact: support@vub.ac.be
Details: Free

`gopher://gopher.vub.ac.be`

Emergency Preparedness

Disaster Research

This newsletter deals with hazards and disasters. It includes articles on recent events and policy developments, plus updates on ongoing research and upcoming meetings; it also fields queries, responses, and ongoing discussion among readers.

Keywords: Disaster Research, Emergency Preparedness
Audience: Health Care Professionals, Public Servants
Contact: mailserv@vaxf.colorado.edu (Internet).
Details: Free

`mailto:hazards@vaxf.colorado.edu`

Emory University Library

Emory University Library

The library's holdings are large and wide-ranging and contain significant collections in many fields.

Keywords: Health Sciences, Theology, History (US), Communism, Economics (History of), Literature (American)
Audience: General Public, Researchers, Librarians, Document Delivery Professionals
Details: Free
User Info: Expect: VM screen, Send: RETURN; Expect: CP READ, Send: DIAL VTAM, press RETURN; Expect: CICS screen, Send: PF1

`telnet://emuvm1.cc.emory.edu`

Employment

Academic Job Listings All Over the World

A major directory on academic institution information, providing access to a broad range of related resources (library catalogs, databases, and servers) via the Internet.

Keywords: Academia, Employment
Audience: Academics, General Public
Contact: Prentiss Riddle
cwis@rice.edu

`gopher://riceinfo.rice.edu/11/Subject/Jobs`

CAREER (Career Library)

The LEXIS Career Library contains job and job-related information.

Keywords: Employment
Audience: Lawyers, Law Students
Profile: The LEXIS Career Library contains job and job-related information designed to assist the student and attorney in finding the right job. The Career Library contains a number of helpful directories, many of which have an "Address" feature that enables users to generate a mailing list from their answer set.
Contact: Mead New Sales Group at 800-227-4908 or 513-859-5398 inside the US, or 1-513-865-7981 for all inquires outside the US.
Details: Costs
User info: To subscribe, contact Mead directly.
To examine the Lexis user guide, you can access it at the ftp site of the University of Texas at Austin at the URL address: ftp://ftp.cc.utexas.edu
The files are in: /pub/res-services/LEXIS

`telnet://nex.meaddata.com`

EEJobs

Discusses and advertises positions available and positions desired in the electrical and electronic engineering fields. Discussion and tips on how to find jobs are also welcome.

Keywords: Engineering, Electrical Engineering, Employment
Audience: Engineers, Students
Contact: Jerome Grimmer
st6267@aix370.siu.edu
Details: Free
User info: To subscribe to the list, send an e-mail messagel with a subject of SERVER.COMMANDS to st6267@aix370.siu.edu
In the body of the mail, type on the first line, /BBOARD SUB EEJOBS or /BBOARD SIGNON EEJOBS to be added to the EEJOBS list.

`mailto:st626@aix370.siu.edu`

misc.jobs.misc

A Usenet newsgroup providing information and discussion about miscellaneous available jobs.

Keywords: Employment
Audience: Job Seekers, General Public
Details: Free
User info: To subscribe to this Usenet newsgroup, you need access to a newsreader.

`news:misc.jobs.misc`

misc.jobs.offered

A Usenet newsgroup providing information and discussion about job openings, listed by subject.

Keywords: Employment
Audience: Job Seekers, General Public
Details: Free
User info: To subscribe to this Usenet newsgroup, you need access to a newsreader.

`news:misc.jobs.offered`

misc.jobs.resumes

A Usenet newsgroup providing information and discussion about resumes.

Keywords: Employment
Audience: Job Seekers, General Public
Details: Free
User info: To subscribe to this Usenet newsgroup, you need access to a newsreader.

`news:misc.jobs.resumes`

Occupational Outlook Handbook 1992-93

An annual U.S. Department of Labor publication that provides detailed information for more than 320 occupations, including job descriptions, typical salaries, education and training requirements, working conditions, job outlook, and more.

Keywords: Careers, Employment, Labor
Sponsor: U.S. Deptartment of Labor
Audience: General Public, Job Seekers, Business Professionals
Details: Free

`gopher://umslvma.umsl.edu/11/library/govdocs/ooha`

Online Career Center

The Online Career Center gopher provides access to job listings and employment information to member companies and to the public.

Keywords: Employment, Internships
Sponsor: Online Career Center
Audience: Job Seekers
Profile: Online Career Center is a not-for-profit organization funded by its member companies. It is devoted to distributing and exchanging employment and career information between its member companies, human resource professionals, and perspective employees.
Contact: OCC Operator
occ@msen.com

`gopher://gopher.msen.com`

PENPages

This easy-to-use general-interest database contains articles and brochures.

Keywords: Food, Employment, Education
Sponsor: Pennsylvania State University, PA

Audience: General Public
User Info: Expect: login; Send: your state's two-letter code (or "world" if sent from outside the USA)

`telnet://psunet.psu.edu`

Encryption

alt.security.pgp

A Usenet newsgroup providing information and discussion about the Pretty Good Privacy package, a privately-developed encryption technique.

Keywords: Privacy, Encryption, Security, Firewalls, Computers
Audience: Internet Surfers
User info: To subscribe to this Usenet newsgroup, you need access to a newsreader.

`news:alt.security.pgp`

Encyclopedia of Associations

Encyclopedia of Associations

The Encyclopedia of Associations database is a comprehensive source of detailed information on over 88,000 nonprofit membership organizations worldwide.

Keywords: Nonprofit Organizations
Sponsor: Gale Research Inc., Detroit, MI, USA
Audience: Researchers
Profile: The database corresponds to the print Encyclopedia of Associations family of publications as follows: National Organizations of the US, covering more than 23,000 American associations of national scope; International Organizations, covering some 11,000 multinational, binational, and non-US national organizations; and Regional, State, and Local Organizations, covering more than 54,000 US associations with interstate, state, intrastate, city, or local scope or membership.
Contact: Dialog in the US at (800) 334-2564, Dialog internationally at country-specific locations.
User info: To subscribe, contact Dialog directly.
Notes: Coverage: Current editions; updated semiannually.

`telnet://dialog.com`

Energy

Electric Power Database

Electric Power Database provides references to research and development projects of interest to the electric power industry, and corresponds to the print Digest of Research in the Electric Utility Industry.

Keywords: Energy, Electric
Sponsor: Electric Power Research Institute (EPRI), Palo Alto, CA, USA
Audience: Engineers
Profile: The database covers US and Canadian research on 13 major categories related to issues in electric power, including hydroelectric power, fossil fuels, nuclear power, transmission, economics, advanced power systems, and environmental assessment. The records include abstracts of project summaries for past and ongoing research projects. Such projects are conducted largely by companies under contract to EPRI or to other utilities, and by EPRI itself. Research from other corporate and utility sources is also covered.
Contact: Dialog in the US at (800) 334-2564, Dialog internationally at country-specific locations.
User info: To subscribe, contact Dialog directly.
Notes: Coverage: 1972 to the present; updated monthly.

`telnet://dialog.com`

ENERGY

The Energy News and Information (ENERGY) library consists of news, legal, and regulatory information.

Keywords: Energy, News, Law, Regulations
Audience: Energy Researchers
Profile: The ENERGY library contains more than 50 full-text sources concentrating on energy-related news and issues. Also available are decisions and orders of the United States Federal Power Commission, Federal Energy Regulatory Commission, and Nuclear Regulatory Commission. At the state level, it covers administrative decisions and orders for 17 states. Energy industry research reports from InvestextR are also available.
Contact: Mead New Sales Group at (800) 227-4908 or (513) 859-5398 inside the US, or (513) 865-7981 for all inquiries outside the US.
User info: To subscribe, contact Mead directly.
To examine the Nexis user guide, you can access it at the ftp site of the University of Texas at Austin at the URL address: ftp://ftp.cc.utexas.edu
The files are in: /pub/ref-services/LEXIS

`telnet://nex.meaddata.com`

`http://www.meaddata.com`

Energy and Climate Information Exchange (ECIX) Newsletter

This newsletter focuses on energy and climate issues, and contains summaries of network postings, updates on national and international policy initiatives, full-length articles, information on new network resources, and a calendar of upcoming events.

Keywords: Energy, Meteorology, Climatology
Audience: Meteorologists, Geologists, Energy Researchers, Climatologists
Contact: econet@igc.org

`mailto:larris@igc.org`

Energy Research in Israel Newsletter

This newsletter on Bitnet is for people interested in energy research, and is meant to allow important local and international energy information to be disseminated efficiently.

Keywords: Energy, Israel
Audience: Energy Researchers, Utility Professionals, Conservationists
Contact: Michael Wolff
WOLFF@ILNCRD.bitnet
Details: Free
User info: To subscribe, send an e-mail message to the address below consisting of a single line reading:
To send a message to the entire list,

`mailto:listserv@taunivm.bitnet`

Energy-L

A mailing list for the discussion of all relevant information on the subject of energy in Israel.

Keywords: Engineering, Energy, Israel
Audience: Engineers, Researchers
Contact: Jo van Zwaren, Dr Michael Wolff
jo%ilncrd.bitnet@cunyvm.cuny.edu
wolff@ilncrd
Details: Free
User info: To subscribe to the list, send an e-mail message to the URL addres below consisting of a single line reading:
SUB energy-l YourFirstName YourLastName
To send a message to the entire list, address it to: energy-i@taunivm.tau.ac.il

`mailto:listserv@taunivm.tau.ac.il`

Martin Marietta Energy Systems Gopher

Information on Martin Marietta's energy projects and technologies for both government and commercial applications.

Keywords: Technology, Energy, Industry
Sponsor: Martin Marietta
Audience: Business Professionals, Entrepreneurs, Manufactures, Energy Researchers, Technology Enthusiasts
Profile: This gopher contains a list of technologies currently being developed at Martin Marietta as well as detailing facilities available to university, government, and commercial researchers. Also includes updates on employment openings, and a list of current publications.
Contact: gopher@ornl.gov

`gopher://gopher.ornl.gov`

`http://www.ornl.gov/mmes.html`

Mississippi State University Library

The library's holdings are large and wide-ranging and contain significant collections in many fields.

Keywords: History (US), Forestry, Energy, Carter (Hodding, Papers of), Mississippi
Audience: General Public, Researchers, Librarians, Document Delivery Professionals
Contact: Stephen Cunetto shc1@ra.msstate.edu
Details: Free
User Info: Expect: username, Send: msu; Expect: password, Send: library

`telnet://libserv.msstate.edu`

Solstice ★★★★

This file server provides state-of-the-art information on renewable energy, energy efficiency, the environment, and sustainable community development.

Keywords: Energy, Environment
Sponsor: The Center for Renewable Energy and Sustainable Technology (CREST)
Audience: Environmentalists, Urban Planners, Educators, Students
Contact: www-content@solstice.crest.org
Details: Free
Login: anonymous, Password: e-mail

`http://solstice.crest.org`

Energy and Climate Information Exchange (ECIX) Newsletter

Energy and Climate Information Exchange (ECIX) Newsletter

This newsletter focuses on energy and climate issues, and contains summaries of network postings, updates on national and international policy initiatives, full-length articles, information on new network resources, and a calendar of upcoming events.

Keywords: Energy, Meteorology, Climatology
Audience: Meteorologists, Geologists, Energy Researchers, Climatologists
Contact: econet@igc.org

`mailto:larris@igc.org`

Energy Research in Israel Newsletter

Energy Research in Israel Newsletter

This newsletter on Bitnet is for people interested in energy research, and is meant to allow important local and international energy information to be disseminated efficiently.

Keywords: Energy, Israel
Audience: Energy Researchers, Utility Professionals, Conservationists
Contact: Michael Wolff WOLFF@ILNCRD.bitnet
Details: Free
User info: To subscribe, send an e-mail message to the address below consisting of a single line reading:

To send a message to the entire list,
`mailto:listserv@taunivm.bitnet`

Engineering

Adv-Eli

Adv-Eli discusses the latest advances in electrical engineering. It is sponsored by the IEEE Student Branch of Santa Maria University (Chile).

Keywords: Electrical Engineering, Engineering, Electronics
Audience: Engineers, Educators, Students
Contact: Francisco Javier Fernandez ffernand@utfsm
Details: Free
User info: To subscribe to the list, send an e-mail message to the URL address shown below consiting of a single line reading:
SUB adv-eli YourFirstName YourLastName
To send a message to the entire list, address it to: adv-eli@loa.disca.utfsm.cl

`listserv@loa.disca.utfsm.cl`

Adv-Elo

Discusses the latest advances in electronics. Sponsored by the IEEE Student Branch of Santa Maria University (Chile).

Keywords: Electrical Engineering, Engineering, Electronics, Technological Advances
Audience: Engineers, Educators, Students
Contact: Rodrigo E. Rodriguez rrodrigu@utfsm
Details: Free
User info: To subscribe to the list, send an e-mail message to the URL address shown below consiting of a single line reading:
SUB adv-elo YourFirstName YourLastName
To send a message to the entire list, address it to: adv-elo@loa.disca.utfsm.cl

`listserv@loa.disca.utfsm.cl`

Aelflow

A mailing list for the discussion of aerospace and aeronautical engineering.

Keywords: Aerospace, Aeronautics, Engineering
Sponsor: The Aerospace Engineering Fluid Group
Audience: Engineers, Educators, Students
Contact: Dr. Yakov Cohen aer8601@technion.ac.il.edu
Details: Free
User info: To subscribe to the list, send an e-mail message to the URL address shown below consiting of a single line reading:
SUB aelflow YourFirstName YourLastName
To send a message to the entire list, address it to: aelflow@technion.ac.il ed

`listserv@technion.ac.il edu`

Aerospace Engineering

This directory is a compilation of information resources focused on aerospace engineeering.

Keywords: Aerospace, Engineering, Aviation, Space
Audience: Aerospace Engineers, Space Scientists
Profile: This is a guide to Internet resources that contain information pertaining to aerospace engineering. Originally the guide was to cover the area of aerospace engineering as applied to

lower atmospheric flight. However, it is difficult to narrow the sites down to specific subject areas. As the guide evolved, sites were included with a broader scope of information. The guide is by no means comprehensive and exhaustive; there are sites that are not included and those the authors were not aware of, and they welcome suggestions. The directory lists sites on FTP, Gopher, Listserv, OPAC, Telnet, Usenet, and WWW.

Details: Free

ftp://una.hh.lib.umich.edu/70/inetdirsstacks/aerospace:potsiedalq

CAEDS-L

A mailing list for the discussion of CAED (Computer Aided Engineering Design) Products.

Keywords: Computer-Aided Design, Engineering, Computer Graphics
Audience: Engineers
Contact: NETMAN@SUVM.acs.syr.edu
Details: Free
User info: To subscribe to the list, send an e-mail message to the URL address shown below consisting of a single line reading:

SUB caeds-l YourFirstName YourLastName

To send a message to the entire list, address it to:

cae-l@suvm.acs.syr.edu

mailto:listserv@suvm.acs.syr.edu

CBDS-l

A mailing list for the discussion of CBDS (Circuit Board Design System).

Keywords: Engineering, Computer-Aided Design, Electronics
Audience: Engineers
Contact: netman@suv.acs.syr.edu
Details: Free
User info: To subscribe to the list, send an e-mail message to the URL address below consisting of a single line reading:

SUB cbds-l YourFirstName YourLastName

To send a message to the entire list, address it to:

cbds-l@suvm.acs.syr.edu

mailto:listserv@suvm.acs.syr.edu

CCES-L

A mailing list for the national communication branch of the CFES (Canadian Federation of Engineering Students).

Keywords: Engineering, Canada
Audience: Engineers, Students
Contact: Canadian Federation of EngineeringStudents
cfes@jupiter.sun.csd.unb.ca
Details: Free
User info: To subscribe to the list, send an e-mail message to the URL address below consisting of a single line reading:

SUB cces-l YourFirstName YourLastName

To send a message to the entire list, address it to:

cces-l@unb.ca

mailto:listserv@unb.ca

CEC

CEC (Canadian Electro-Acoustics Community).

Keywords: Engineering, Acoustical Engineering, Canada, Canadian Electro-Acoustics Community
Audience: Engineers
Contact: Peter Gross
grosspa@qucdn
Details: Free
User info: To subscribe to the list, send an e-mail message to the URL address below, consisting of a single line reading:

SUB cec YourFirstName YourLastName

To send a message to the entire list, address it to: cec@qucdn.queensu.ca

mailto:listserv@qucdn.queensu.ca

CEM-L

A mailing list for discussion surrounding the UTD (University of Texas at Dallas) Center for Engineering Mathematics.

Keywords: Engineering, Mathematics
Audience: Engineers, Mathematicians, Educators, Students
Contact: David Lippke
LIPPKE@UTDALLAS
Details: Free
User info: To subscribe to the list, send an e-mail message to the URL address below, consisting of a single line reading:

SUB cem-l YourFirstName YourLastName

To send a message to the entire list, address it to: cem-l@utdallas.edu

mailto:listserv@utdallas.edu

CFD

CFD (Computational Fluid Dynamics Group).

Keywords: Engineering, Fluid Dynamics
Audience: Engineers
Contact: JUSTIN@UKCC.UKY.EDU
justin@engr.uky.edu
Details: Free
User info: To subscribe to the list, send an e-mail message to the URL address below, consisting of a single line reading:

SUB cfd YourFirstName YourLastName

To send a message to the entire list, address it to:

cfd@ukcc.uky.edu

mailto:justin@ukcc.uky.edu

CFES-L

National communication branch of the CFES (Canadian Federation of Engineering Students).

Keywords: Engineering, Students, Canada
Audience: Engineers, Students
Contact: Canadian Federation of EngineeringStudents
cfes@jupiter.sun.csd.unb.ca
Details: Free
User info: To subscribe to the list, send an e-mail message to the URL address below consisting of a single line reading:

SUB cfes-l YourFirstName YourLastName

To send a message to the entire list, address it to:

cfes-l@unb.ca

mailto:listserv@unb.ca

ChE Electronic Newsletter

This newsletter contains information of interest to chemical engineers.

Keywords: Chemical Engineering, Chemistry, Engineering
Audience: Chemical Engineers
Contact: Martyn S. Ray
trayms@cc.curtin.edu.au
Details: Free
Inquire about needing a password.

mailto:trayms@cc.curtin.edu.au

Chemical Abstracts

Worldwide coverage of the chemical sciences literature.

Keywords: Chemistry, Engineering
Sponsor: Chemical Abstracts Service, American Chemical Society
Audience: Researchers, Librarians, Chemists
Profile: Provides coverage of chemical sciences literature from over 9,000 journals, patents from 27 countries, and 2 international property organizations, new books, conference proceedings, and government research reports. Updated every two weeks.

CIRCUITS-L

This list discusses all aspects of the introductory course in circuit analysis for electrical engineering undergraduates.

- **Keywords:** Engineering, Electrical Engineering, Teaching, Electric Circuit Analysis
- **Audience:** Engineers, Students (college)
- **Contact:** Paul E. Gray
  mailto:gray@maple.ucs.uwplatt.edu
- **Details:** Free
- **User info:** To subscribe to the list, send an e-mail message to the URL address below, and include: name; e-mail address; home phone, business phone, and FAX numbers (including area code); and US postal address (including ZIP code)

  To send a message to the entire list, address it to:
  circuits-l@uwplatt.edu

mailto:circuits-request@uwplatt.edu

EEJobs

Discusses and advertises positions available and positions desired in the electrical and electronic engineering fields. Discussion and tips on how to find jobs are also welcome.

- **Keywords:** Engineering, Electrical Engineering, Employment
- **Audience:** Engineers, Students
- **Contact:** Jerome Grimmer
  st6267@aix370.siu.edu
- **Details:** Free
- **User info:** To subscribe to the list, send an e-mail messagel with a subject of SERVER.COMMANDS to st6267@aix370.siu.edu

  In the body of the mail, type on the first line, /BBOARD SUB EEJOBS or /BBOARD SIGNON EEJOBS to be added to the EEJOBS list.

st626@aix370.siu.edu

Ei Compendex Plus

The Ei Compendex Plus database is the machine-readable version of The Engineering Index (monthly/annual), which provides abstracted information from the world's significant literature of engineering and technology.

- **Keywords:** Engineering, Technology
- **Sponsor:** Engineering Information Inc. (Ei), Hoboken, NJ, USA
- **Audience:** Engineers
- **Profile:** Ei Compendex Plus provides worldwide coverage of approximately 4,500 journals and selected government reports and books. Subjects covered include: civil, energy, environmental, geological, and biological engineering; electrical, automotive, nuclear, and aerospace engineering; and computers, robotics, and industrial robots.
- **Contact:** Dialog in the US at (800) 334-2564, Dialog internationally at country-specific locations.
- **User info:** To subscribe, contact Dialog directly.
- **Notes:** Coverage: 1970 to the present; updated weekly.

telnet://dialog.com

Energy-L

A mailing list for the discussion of all relevant information on the subject of energy in Israel.

- **Keywords:** Engineering, Energy, Israel
- **Audience:** Engineers, Researchers
- **Contact:** Jo van Zwaren, Dr Michael Wolff
  jo%ilncrd.bitnet@cunyvm.cuny.edu
  wolff@ilncrd
- **Details:** Free
- **User info:** To subscribe to the list, send an e-mail message to the URL addres below consisting of a single line reading:

  SUB energy-l YourFirstName YourLastName

  To send a message to the entire list, address it to: energy-l@TAUNIVM.TAU.AC.IL

mailto:listserv@taunivm.tau.ac.il

Engineering-Design

Supports researchers at the five national Engineering Design Centres.

- **Keywords:** Engineering, Design
- **Audience:** Engineers, Researchers
- **Contact:** engineering-design-request@mailbase.ac.uk
- **Details:** Free
- **User info:** To subscribe to the list, send an e-mail message to the URL address shown below consiting of a single line reading:

  SUB engineering-design YourFirstName YourLastName

  To send a message to the entire list, address it to:
  engineering-design@mailbase.ac.uk

mailbase@mailbase.ac.uk

Engineering; A. Park, J. Miller

This directory is a compilation of information resources focused on engineering.

- **Keywords:** Engineering, Design
- **Audience:** Engineers, Students, Educators
- **Details:** Free

ftp://una.hh.lib.umich.edu/70/inetdirsstacks/engin:parkmiller

ETHCSE-L

A mailing list for the discussion of Ethical Issues in Software Engineering, dealing with subjects of interest to professional software engineers.

- **Keywords:** Engineering, Computing, Ethics
- **Audience:** Engineers, Software Engineers, Researchers
- **Contact:** Margaret Mason
  mason@utkvm1.utk.edu
- **Details:** Free
- **User info:** To subscribe to the list, send an e-mail message to the URL address shown below consisting of a single line reading:

  SUB ethcse-l YourFirstName YourLastName

  To send a message to the entire list, address it to:
  ethcse-l@utkvm1.utk.edu

mailto:listerv@utkvm1.utk.edu

IEEE-L

Serves as a forum for all IEEE student branch officers and members.

- **Keywords:** Engineering, Electrical Engineering
- **Audience:** Engineers, Electrical Engineers, Students
- **Contact:** Paul D. Kroculick or Chas Elliot
  tjw0465@bingtjw.cc.binghamton.edu
  ba08034@bingsuns.cc.binghamton.edu
- **Details:** Free
- **User info:** To subscribe to the list, send an e-mail message to the URL address below consisting of a single line reading:

  SUB ieee-l YourFirstName YourLastName. To send a message to the entire list, address it to:

  iee-l@bingvmb.cc.binghamton.edu

mailto:listserv@bingvb.cc.binghamton.edu

IHS International Standards and Specifications

The database contains references to industry standards, and military and federal specifications and standards covering all aspects of engineering and related disciplines.

- **Keywords:** Engineering, Military Specifications, Federal Standards
- **Sponsor:** Information Handling Services, Englewood, CO, US
- **Audience:** Engineers, Military Hisorians, Lawyers

Profile:	The file includes 90% of the world's most referenced standards from over 70 domestic, foreign, and international standardizing bodies. Also included is the world's largest commercially available collection of unclassified active and historical US military and federal specifications and standards.
Contact:	Dialog in the US at (800) 334-2564, Dialog internationally at country-specific locations.
User info:	To subscribe, contact Dialog directly.
Notes:	Coverage: Current; updated weekly for MILSPECS, every two months.

`telnet://dialog.com`

National Centre for Software Technology

The National Centre for Software Technology (NCST) is an autonomous R&D unit in Bombay and Bangalore. Specialty areas of research include graphics, CAD, real time systems, knowledge-based systems, and software engineering.

Keywords:	Computer Science, Engineering, Computer-Aided Design
Sponsor:	National Centre for Software Technology, Bombay, India
Audience:	Reseachers, Computer Scientists, Engineers, Students
Contact:	Postmaster postmaster@saathi.ncst.ernet.in

`gopher://shakti.ncst.ernet.in`

sci.electronics

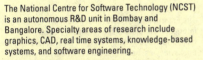

A Usenet newsgroup providing information and discussion about circuits, theory and electrons.

Keywords:	Electronics, Engineering
Audience:	Electrical Engineers
Details:	Free
User info:	To subscribe to this Usenet newsgroup, you need access to a newsreader.

`news:sci.electronics`

University of Texas at Austin Library

The library's holdings are large and wide-ranging and contain significant collections in many fields. Music, Natural Science, Nursing, Science Technology, Behavioral Science, Social Work, Computer Science, Engineering, Latin American Studies, Middle Eastern Studies

Keywords:	Music, Natural Science, Nursing, Science Technology, Behavioral Science, Social Work, Computer Science, Engineering, Latin American Studies, Middle Eastern Studies
Audience:	Researchers, Students, General Public
Details:	Free
User Info:	Expect: Blank Screen, Send: Return; Expect: Go, Send: Return; Expect: Enter Terminal Type, Send: vt100
	note: Some databases are restricted to UT Austin users only.

`telnet://utcat.utexas.edu`

US Army Corps of Engineers

This site provides information on the organization, programs, news, facilities, and activities of the US Army Corps of Engineers.

Keywords:	Military, Engineering
Sponsor:	Cold Regions Research and Engineering Laboratory, under
Audience:	Military Personnel, Engineers, Researchers
Contact:	www@usace.mil
Details:	Free

`http://www.usace.mil/usace.html`

Engineering (Biomedical)

sci.engr.biomed

A Usenet newsgroup providing information and discussion about the field of biomedical engineering.

Keywords:	Biomedicine, Engineering (Biomedical)
Audience:	Engineers (Biomedical), Biomedical Researchers
Details:	Free
User info:	To subscribe to this Usenet newsgroup, you need access to a newsreader.

`news:sci.engr.biomed`

Engineering (Chemical)

chem-eng

This is an electronic newsletter on chemical engineering.

Keywords:	Engineering (Chemical)
Audience:	Chemical Engineers, Chemists, Engineers
Contact:	Martyn Ray trayms@cc.curtin.edu.au
Details:	Free
User info:	To subscribe to the list, send an e-mail message requesting a subscription to the URL address below.

`mailto:trayms@cc.curtin.edu.au`

Engineering (Civil)

Civil-L

A mailing list for the discussion of Civil Engineering Research and Education.

Keywords:	Engineering (Civil), Computer-Aided Instruction
Audience:	Engineers, Educators, Students
Contact:	Eldo Hildebrand ELDO@UNB.CA
Details:	Free
User info:	To subscribe to the list, send an e-mail message to the URL address shown below consisting of a single line reading:
	SUB civil-l YourFirstName YourLastName
	To send a message to the entire list, address it to:
	civil-l@unb.ca

`mailto:listserv@unb.ca`

Engineering (Electrical)

af

A mailing list for discussion of AudioFile, a client/server, network-transparent, device-independent audio system.

Keywords:	Audio Electronics, Electrical Engineering
Audience:	Audio Enthusiasts, Electrical Engineers
Contact:	af-request@crl.dec.com
User info:	To subscribe to the list, send an e-mail message to the URL address below.
	To send a message to the entire list, address it to: af@crl.dec.com

`mailto:af-request@crl.dec.com`

Engineering (History of)

Purdue University Library

The library's holdings are large and wide-ranging. They contain significant collections in many fields.

Keywords:	Economics (History of), Literature (English), Literature (American), Indiana, Rogers (Bruce), Engineering (History of), Aviation, Earth Science, Atmospheric Science, Consumer Science, Family Science, Chemistry (History of), Physics, Veterinary Science
Audience:	General Public, Researchers, Librarians, Document Delivery Professionals
Contact:	Dan Ferrer dan@asterix.lib.purdue.edu

A
B
C
D
E
F
G
H
I
J
K
L
M
N
O
P
Q
R
S
T
U
V
W
X
Y
Z

Details: Free
User Info: Expect: User ID prompt, Send: GUEST

`telnet://lib.cc.purdue.edu`

Engineering (Mechanical)

MECH-L

A mailing list for the discussion of mechanical engineering.

Keywords: Engineering (Mechanical)
Audience: Engineers, Mechanical Engineers
Contact: S. Nomura
b470ssn@utarlvm1.uta.edu
Details: Free
User info: To subscribe to the list, send an e-mail message to the URL address below consisting of a single line reading:

SUB mech-l YourFirstName YourLastName

To send a message to the entire list, address it to: mech-l@utarlvm1.uta.edu

`mailto:listserv@utarlvm1.uta.edu`

England

Morris

A discussion list related to Morris Dancing, including Cotswold, Border, Northwest, Rapper, Longsword, Abbots Bromley, Garland, and similar forms of English dance along with the accompanying music and traditions.

Keywords: Morris Dancing, England, Dance
Audience: Morris Dancers
Details: Free
User info: To subscribe to the list, send an e-mail message requesting subscription to the URL address below.

`mailto:morris@suvm.acs.syr.edu`

English

The English Server

A large and eclectic collection of humanities resources.

Keywords: Humanities, Academia, English, Popular Culture, Feminism
Sponsor: Carnegie Mellon University English Department, Pittsburgh, Pennsylvania, USA
Audience: General Public, University Students, Educators (College/University), Researchers (Humanities)

Profile: Contains archives of conventional humanities materials, such as historical documents and classic books in electronic form. Also offers more unusual and hard-to-find resources, particularly in the field of popular culture and media. Features access to many humanities and culture-related online journals such as Bad Subjects, FineArt Forum, and Postmodern Culture. Also has links to a wide variety of related Internet sites and resources.
Contact: Geoff Sauer
postmaster@english-server.hss.cmu.edu

`gopher://english-server.hss.cmu.edu`

`http://english-server.hss.cmu.edu`

English Bibles

University of Chicago Library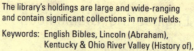

The library's holdings are large and wide-ranging and contain significant collections in many fields.

Keywords: English Bibles, Lincoln (Abraham), Kentucky & Ohio River Valley (History of), Balzac (Honore de), American Drama, Cromwell (Oliver), Goethe, Judaica, Italy, Chaucer (Geoffrey), Wells (Ida, Personal Papers of), Douglas (Stephen A.), Italy, Literature (Children's)
Audience: General Public, Researchers, Librarians, Document Delivery Professionals
Details: Free
User Info: Expect: ENTER CLASS, Send: LIB48 3;
Expect: CONNECTED, Send: RETURN

`telnet://olorin.uchicago.edu`

Entering the WWW

Entering the WWW

An article entitled "Entering the World-Wide Web: A Guide to Cyberspace."

Keywords: Internet Tools, WWW
Sponsor: Honolulu Community College
Audience: Internet Surfers
Contact: Kevin Hughes
kevinh@pulua.hcc.hawaii.edu
Details: Free

`http://www.hcc.hawaii.edu/guide/www.guide.html`

Entertainment

alt.fan.monty-python

A Usenet newsgroup providing an electronic fan club for those wacky Brits.

Keywords: Humor, Entertainment, Comedy, Satire
Audience: Monty Python Enthusiasts, General Public
User info: To subscribe to this Usenet newsgroup, you need access to a newsreader.

`news:alt.fan.monty-python`

ENTERT (Entertainment News Library)

The Entertainment News library contains sources of information about the entertainment industry, including broadcasting, cable TV, theater, television, books, movies, ballet and dance, video, radio, music, and the record industry.

Keywords: Entertainment, News
Audience: Business Researchers, Analysts, Entrepreneurs
Profile: ENTERT includes the full text of publications such as Variety, Daily Variety, Communications Daily and People, as well as documents about entertainment-related topics from premier NEXIS sources such as the Los Angeles Times and USA Today. Additionally, ENTERT has the premier source database covering the entertainment industry, BASELINE, which provides daily updates of the financial status of movies, background on actors and details on works in production.
Contact: Mead New Sales Group at (800) 227-4908 or (513) 859-5398 inside the US, or (513) 865-7981 for all inquiries outside the US.
User info: To subscribe, contact Mead directly.

To examine the Nexis user guide, you can access it at the ftp site of the University of Texas at Austin at the URL address: ftp://ftp.cc.utexas.edu

The files are in: /pub/ref-services/LEXIS

`telnet://nex.meaddata.com`

`http://www.meaddata.com`

Film and Video

This directory is a compilation of information resources focused on film and video.

Keywords: Film, Video, Entertainment
Audience: Students, Producers, Artists
Details: Free

`ftp://una.hh.lib.umich.edu/70/inetdirsstacks/filmvideo:woodgarlock`

GameBytes magazine ★★

This monthly electronic magazine provides reviews (with graphics) of electronic games.

- Keywords: Games, Electronic Media, Entertainment
- Sponsor: Game Bytes Magazine
- Audience: Game Players, Computer Game Developers, Computer Graphics Designers
- Contact: Ross Erickson
  rwericks@ingr.com
- Details: Free

http://wcl-rs.bham.ac.uk/GameBytes

Zarf's List of Interactive Games on the Web

A list containing links to games and toys that can be played on the Internet.

- Keywords: Games, Toys, Entertainment, Recreation
- Sponsor: Carnegie Mellon University, School of Computer Science, Pittsburgh, Pennsylvania, USA
- Audience: General Public, Game Players, Kids
- Contact: Andrew Plotkin
  zarf@cs.cmu.edu, apli@andrew.cmu.edu

http://www.cs.cmu.edu/:8001/afs/cs.cmu.edu/user/zarf/www/games.html

Entomology

AGRICOLA

The AGRICOLA database of the National Agricultural Library (NAL) provides comprehensive coverage of worldwide journal literature and monographs on agriculture and related subjects.

- Keywords: Agriculture, Animal Studies, Botany, Entomology
- Sponsor: US National Agricultural Library, Beltsville, MD, USA
- Audience: Agronomists, Botanists, Chemists, Entomologists
- Profile: Related subjects include: animal studies, botany, chemistry, entomology, fertilizers, forestry, hydroponics, soils, and more.
- Contact: Dialog in the US at (800) 334-2564, Dialog internationally at country-specific locations.
- User info: To subscribe, contact Dialog directly.
- Notes: Coverage: 1970 to the present; updated monthly.

telnet://dialog.com

CSU Entomology WWW Site

A web site containing online photos of insects, entomology educational programs, and extensive Internet entomology links.

- Keywords: Bioscience, Biology, Entomology
- Sponsor: Colorado State University, Denver, Colorado, USA
- Audience: Students, Researchers, Entomologists
- Contact: Lou Bjostad
  lbjostad@lamar.colorado.edu

http://www.colostate.edu/Depts/Entomology/ent.html

McGill University, Montreal Canada, INFOMcGILL Library

The library's holdings are large and wide-ranging and contain significant collections in many fields.

- Keywords: Architecture, Entomology, Biology, Science (History of), Medicine (History of), Napolean, Shakespeare (William)
- Audience: Researchers, Students, General Public
- Contact: Roy Miller
  ccrmmus@mcgillm (Bitnet)
  ccrmmus@musicm.mcgill.ca (Internet)
- User Info: Expect: VM logo; Send: Enter; Expect: prompt; Send: PF3 or type INFO

telnet://vm1.mcgill.ca

The University of Notre Dame Library

The library's holdings are large and wide-ranging and contain significant collections in many fields.

- Keywords: Music (Irish), Ireland, Botany (History of), Ecology, Entomology, Parasitology, Aquatic Biology, Universities (History of), Paleography
- Audience: General Public, Researchers, Librarians, Document Delivery Professionals
- Details: Free
- User Info: Expect: ENTER COMMAND OR HELP:, Send: library; To leave, type x on the command line and press the enter key. At the ENTER COMMAND OR HELP: prompt, type bye and press the enter key.

telnet://irishmvs.cc.nd.edu

Entropy

DYNSYS-L

The Dynamical System exchanges information among people working in ergodic theory and dynamical systems.

- Keywords: Entropy, Systems Theory
- Audience: Engineers
- Details: Free

mailto:newserv@uncvm1.oit.unc.edu

ENVIRN (Environment Library)

ENVIRN (Environment Library)

The Environment (ENVIRN) Library contains a variety of environment-related news and legal information.

- Keywords: News, Analysis, Law, Environment
- Audience: Environmental Researchers, Business Professionals
- Profile: The ENVIRN library contains a combination of environmental information that can provide critical insight into environmental hazards, EPA ratings, specific company investigations, evaluations on potentially hazardous chemicals, and parties responsible for cleanup of specific hazardous sites. Additionally, ENVIRN provides a wealth of environment-related information—legislation, regulations, and court and agency decisions at both the federal and state levels; news; the Environmental Law Reporter, and American Law Reports.
- Contact: Mead New Sales Group at (800) 227-4908 or (513) 859-5398 inside the US, or (513) 865-7981 for all inquiries outside the US.
- User info: To subscribe, contact Mead directly.

  To examine the Nexis user guide, you can access it at the ftp site of the University of Texas at Austin at the URL address: ftp://ftp.cc.utexas.edu

  The files are in: /pub/ref-services/LEXIS

telnet://nex.meaddata.com

http://www.meaddata.com

Enviroethics

Enviroethics

A mailing list for the scholarly discussion of environmental ethics and philosophy.

- Keywords: Environment, Environmental Studies
- Audience: Environmental Researchers, Environmental Scientists, Environmentalists
- Contact: Clare Palmer, Ian Tilsed
  C.A.Palmer@greenwich.ac.uk, I.J.Tilsed@exeter.ac.uk

User info: To subscribe, send an e-mail message to the URL address below consisting of a single line reading:

    join enviroethics YourFirstName YourLastName

To obtain a list of archived files, send an e-mail message with the body 'index enviroethics' to the same address.

mailto:mailbase@mailbase.ac.uk

Environment

Activ-L

A mailing list for the discussion of peace, empowerment, justice and environmental issues.

Keywords: Peace, Justice, Environment, Activism

Audience: Activists, Students

Contact: Rich Winkel
harelb@math.cornell.edu

User info: To subscribe to the list, send an e-mail message to the URL address below consisting of a single line reading:

    SUB activ-l YourFirstName YourLastName

To send a message to the entire list, address it to: active-l@mizzou1.missouri.edu

mailto:listserv@mizzou1.missouri.edu

Australian Environmental Resources Information Network (ERIN)

This gopher contains a wide range of Australian environmental information.

Keywords: Environment, Australia, Ecology

Audience: Environmentalists, Ecologists, Researchers, Australians

Profile: Coverage includes biodiversity, protected areas, terrestrial and marine environments, environmental protection and legislation, international agreements, and general information about ERIN.

Contact: gopher@erin.gov.au

Details: Free

gopher://kaos.erin.gov.au

http://kaos.erin.gov.au/erin.html

CEDAR (Central European Environmental Data Request) Facility

This gopher site provides information about the environmental and scientific community in Central and Eastern Europe (CEE), with access to environmental information located throughout the world on various international computer networks and hosts.

Keywords: Europe, EEC, Environment

Sponsor: The International Society for Environmental Protection, and The Austrian Federal Ministry for Environment, Youth and Family (BMUJF)

Audience: Environmentalists, Educators, Students, Urban Planners

Contact: cedar-info@cedar.univie.ac.at

Notes: CEDAR Marxergasse 3/20, A-1030 Vienna, Austria Tel.: +43-1-715 58 79

gopher://pan.cedar.univie.ac.at

CEE Environmental Libraries Database

A directory of over 300 libraries and environmental information centers in Central Eastern Europe that specalize in, or maintain significant collections of information about, the environment, ecology, sustainable living, or conservation. The database concentrates on six Central Eastern European countries: Bulgaria, Czech Republic, Hungary, Romania, Slovakia, and Poland.

Keywords: Central Eastern Europe, Environment, Sustainable Living, Bulgaria, Czech Republic, Hungary, Romania, Slovakia, Poland.

Sponsor: The Wladyslaw Poniecki Charitable Foundation, Inc.

Audience: Environmentalists, Green Movement, Librarians, Community Builders, Sustainable Living Specialists.

Profile: This database is the product of an Environmental Training Project (ETP) that was funded in 1992 by the US Agency for International Development as a 5-year cooperative agreement with a consortium headed by the University of Minnesota (US AID Cooperative Agreement Number EUR-0041-A-002-2020). Other members of the consortium include the University of Pittsburgh's Center for Hazardous Material Research, The Institute for Sustainable Communities, and the World Wildlife Fund. The Wladyslaw Poniecki Charitable Foundation, Inc., was a subcontractor to the World Wildlife Fund and published the Directory of Libraries and Environmental Information Centers in Central Eastern Europe: A Locator/Directory . This gopher database consists of an electronic version of the printed directory, subsequently modified and updated online. Access to the data is facilitated by a WAIS search engine which makes it possible to retrieve information about libraries, subject area specializations, personnel, and so on.

Contact: Doug Kahn, CEDAR
kahn@pan.cedar.univie.ac.at

gopher://gopher.poniecki.berkeley.edu

Central European Environment Data Report (CEDAR) Facility

This gopher site provides information about the environmental and scientific community in Central and Eastern Europe, with access to environmental information located throughout the world on various international computer networks and hosts.

Keywords: Europe, Central Europe, Eastern Europe, Environment

Sponsor: The International Society for Environmental Protection, and The Austrian Federal Ministry for Environment, Youth and Family (BMUJF)

Audience: Environmentalists, Educators, Students, Urban Planners, Environmental Scientists

Profile: The CEDAR Facility, established in 1991, is administered by the International Society for Environmental Protection (ISEP). The Facility is designed to provide regional groups and individuals with access to its information retrieval and higher computing resources, technical advice and database and network access support. In addition, CEDAR works to facilitate information and dialogue exchange with organizations in other parts of the world and in partner countries; and to promote training forums, including the joint development of seminars and conferences with ISEP on environmental and network topics. Finally, CEDAR develops and manages environmental reference data sets, including a US EPA bibliographic reference on hazardous waste treatment, CEDAR databases on Central and Eastern European environmental expertise and information, and the holdings of the Regional Environmental Center Library at Budapest.

Contact: cedar-info@cedar.univie.ac.at

gopher://pan.cedar.univie.ac.at

consgis

A discussion list for those using GIS (Geographic Information Systems) in the interest of conservation.

Keywords: Conservation, Environment, GIS (Geographic Information Systems)

Audience: Geographers, Environmentalists, Cartographers

Contact: Dr. Peter August
pete@edcserv.edc.uri.edu

Details: Free
User info: To subscribe to the list, send an e-mail message to the URL address below consisting of a single line reading:

SUB consgis YourFirstName YourLastName.

To send a message to the entire list, address it to: consgis@uriacc.uri.edu

`mailto:listserv@uriacc.uri.edu`

EcoDirectory

A directory of Libraries and Environmental Information Centers in Central Eastern Europe.

Keywords: Environment, Eastern Europe, Central Europe
Sponsor: The Wladyslaw Poniecki Charitable Foundation, Inc.
Audience: Environmentalists, Librarians, International Development Specialists
Profile: This database is the product of an Environmental Training Project (ETP) which was founded in 1992 by the US Agency for International Development. The project concentrated on six Central and Eastern European countries: Bulgaria, Czech Republic, Hungary, Romania, Slovakia, and Poland.

It contains information on over 300 Libraries and Environmental Information Centers in those countries. Access to the data is facilitated by a WAIS search engine which makes it possible to retrieve information about libraries, subject area specializations, personnel, and so on.
Contact: Joerg Findeisen, CEDAR findeisen@pan.cedar.univie.ac.at

`gopher://gopher.poniecki.berkeley.edu`

ENVIRN (Environment Library)

The Environment (ENVIRN) Library contains a variety of environment-related news and legal information.

Keywords: News, Analysis, Law, Environment
Audience: Environmental Researchers, Business Professionals
Profile: The ENVIRN library contains a combination of environmental information that can provide critical insight into environmental hazards, EPA ratings, specific company investigations, evaluations on potentially hazardous chemicals, and parties responsible for cleanup of specific hazardous sites. Additionally, ENVIRN provides a wealth of environment-related information—legislation, regulations, and court and agency decisions at both the federal and state levels; news; the Environmental Law Reporter, and American Law Reports.
Contact: Mead New Sales Group at (800) 227-4908 or (513) 859-5398 inside the US, or (513) 865-7981 for all inquiries outside the US.

User info: To subscribe, contact Mead directly.

To examine the Nexis user guide, you can access it at the ftp site of the University of Texas at Austin at the URL address: ftp://ftp.cc.utexas.edu

The files are in: /pub/ref-services/LEXIS

`telnet://nex.meaddata.com`

`http://www.meaddata.com`

Enviroethics

A mailing list for the scholarly discussion of environmental ethics and philosophy.

Keywords: Environment, Environmental Studies
Audience: Environmental Researchers, Environmental Scientists, Environmentalists
Contact: Clare Palmer, Ian Tilsed
C.A.Palmer@greenwich.ac.uk, I.J.Tilsed@exeter.ac.uk
User info: To subscribe, send an e-mail message to the URL address below consisting of a single line reading:

join enviroethics YourFirstName YourLastName

To obtain a list of archived files, send an e-mail message with the body 'index enviroethics' to the same address.

`mailto:mailbase@mailbase.ac.uk`

ESRI (Environmental Systems Research Institute)

Environmental Systems Research Institute, Inc. is the world leader in GIS technology. ARC/INFO is ESRI's powerful and flexible flagship GIS software.

Keywords: Geographic Information Systems (GIS), Environment, Software, Computers
Audience: Geographers, Environmentalists, Computer Users
Details: Costs

For product information, call (909)793-2853, X1475.

For training information, call (909)793-2853, X1585, or fax (909)793-5953.

GIS-L ★★

A forum for the discussion of all issues pertaining to GIS (Geographic Information Systems), including hydrological modeling, environmental issues, and available software packages.

Keywords: Geography, Environment, GIS (Geographical Information Systems)
Audience: Geographers, Cartographers
Contact: David Mark
dmark@acsu.buffalo.edu

User info: To subscribe to the list, send an e-mail message to the URL address below consisting of a single line reading:

SUB gis-l YourFirstName YourLastName

To send a message to the entire list, address it to: gis-l@ubvm.cc.buffalo.edu

`mailto:listserv@ubvm.cc.buffalo.edu`

Global Change Information Gateway ★★★★

This gateway was created to address environmental data management issues raised by the US Congress, the Administration, and the advisory arms of the Federal policy community. It contains documents related to the UN conference on Environment and Development.

Keywords: United Nations, Environment, Development, Oceans, Atmosphere
Audience: Environmentalists, Scientists, Researchers
Details: Free
Notes: Select from menu as appropriate.

`gopher://scilibx.ucsc.edu`

National Oceanic & Atmospheric Administration (NOAA) Office of Environmental Safety and Health, Department of Energy ★★★★

The NOAA catalog provides keyword access to sources of environmental information in the US. Gopher for resources pertaining to health and environmental safety.

Keywords: Environment, Oceans, Atmospheric Science, Health, Environmental Safety
Sponsor: National Oceanic & Atmospheric Administration (NOAA)

Department of Energy (USA)
Audience: Environmental Scientists, Researchers, Environmentalists, Epidemiologists, Public Health Officials
Details: Free

`gopher://scilibx.ucsc.edu`

`gopher://gopher.ns.doc.gov`

NativeNet ★

Provides information about and discusses issues relating to indigenous people around the world, including threats to their cultures and habitats (e.g. rainforests).

Keywords: Indigenous People, Environment, Anthroplogy
Audience: Anthropologists, Environmentalists, Indigenous People
Contact: Gary S. Trujillo
gst@gnosys.svle.ma.us

Details:	Free
User info:	To subscribe to the list, send an e-mail message requesting a subscription to the URL address below.

`mailto:gst@gnosys.svle.ma.us`

Natural Resources Canada (NRCan) Gopher

This site offers information on forests, energy, mining, and geomatics from the Canadian government. Also has reports from the Geological Survey of Canada and an overview of NRCan statutes, organization, and personnel. Provides links to other Canadian environmental and government gophers.

Keywords:	Canada, Environment, Geology, Forestry
Sponsor:	The Department of Natural Resources, Canada
Audience:	Canadians, Environmentalists, Environmental Researchers, Geologists
Contact:	Bob Fillmore fillmore@emr.ca
Notes:	NRCan maintains a toll-free hotline - 1-800-267-5166

`gopher://gopher.emr.ca`

`http://www.emr.ca/`

sci.environment

A Usenet newsgroup providing information and discussion about the environment and ecology.

Keywords:	Environment, Ecology
Audience:	Environmentalists, ecologists, Earth Scientists
Details:	Free
User info:	To subscribe to this Usenet newsgroup, you need access to a newsreader.

`news:sci.environment`

Sense of Place

An electronic environmentalists magazine. The magazine incorporates graphics and text in a format specifically designed to be read on a Macintosh screen. You must have Hypercard version 2.1 or later.

Keywords:	Environment, Ecology
Audience:	Environmentalists
Contact:	SOP@dartmouth.edu
Details:	Costs
User info:	To subscribe send electronic mail to SOP@dartmouth.edu

`gopher://gopher.dartmouth.edu/1/anonftp/pub/sop`

Solstice

This file server provides state-of-the-art information on renewable energy, energy efficiency, the environment, and sustainable community development.

Keywords:	Energy, Environment
Sponsor:	The Center for Renewable Energy and Sustainable Technology (CREST)
Audience:	Environmentalists, Urban Planners, Educators, Students
Contact:	www-content@solstice.crest.org
Details:	Free Login: anonymous, Password: e-mail

`http://solstice.crest.org/`

South Florida Environmental Reader

Newsletter distributing information on the environment of South Florida.

Keywords:	Environment, Florida
Audience:	Environmentalists
Contact:	aem@mthvax.cs.miami.edu
Details:	Free
User info:	To subscribe to the list, send an e-mail messgae requesting a subscription to the URL address below. To send a mesage to the entire USL, address it to: sfer@mthvax.cs.miami.edu

`mail to:sfer-requesti@mthvax.cs.miami.edu`

United Nations

Includes full text of UN press releases, UN Conference on Environment and Development reports, UN Development Programme documents, U.N. telephone directories.

Keywords:	UN, Environment, Development (International)
Audience:	Researchers, Educators, Political Scientists, Environmentalists
Details:	Free

`gopher://nywork1.undp.org`

US/Mexico Border Discussion List

This group provides a forum for the discussion of issues pertaining to the US/Mexico border environment.

Keywords:	Mexico, Environment, Latin American Culture
Sponsor:	The US Environmental Protection Agency
Audience:	Activists, Environmentalists, Urban Planners
Details:	Free
User info:	To subscribe to the list, send a message to the URL address below consisting of a single line reading: SUB us_mexborder YourFirstName YourLastName To send a message to the entire list, address it to: us_mexborder@unixmail.rtpnc.epa.gov

`mailto:listserver@unixmail.rtpnc.epa.gov`

Environmental Health

Safety (Environmental Health and Safety Discussion List)

E-conference for people interested in the various environmental health and safety issues on college and university campuses.

Keywords:	Environmental Health, Safety, Health
Audience:	Students (College/University), Educators (college/University)
Contact:	Ralph Stuart, Dayna Flath rstuart@moose.uvm.edu dmf@uvmvm.uvm.edu
Details:	Free
User info:	To subscribe to the list, send an e-mail message to the URL address below, consisting of a single line reading: SUB safety YourFirstName YourLastName To send a message to the entire list, address it to: safety@uvmvm.uvm.edu

`mailto:listserv@uvmvm.uvm.edu`

Environmental Policies

US Department of the Interior

This resource contains Internet links to the Bureau of Indian Affairs, Bureau of Land Management, Bureau of Reclamation, National Biological Survey, National Park Service, and the US Fish and Wildlife Service.

Keywords:	Government (US), Environmental Policies
Sponsor:	US Department of the Interior Survey, Office of Public Affairs
Audience:	Biologists, Geologists, Researchers, Environmentalists

`http://info.er.usgs.gov/doi/doi.html`

Environmental Safety

National Oceanic & Atmospheric Administration (NOAA)
Office of Environmental Safety and Health, Department of Energy

The NOAA catalog provides keyword access to sources of environmental information in the US. Gopher for resources pertaining to health and environmental safety.

Keywords: Environment, Oceans, Atmospheric Science, Health, Environmental Safety
Sponsor: National Oceanic & Atmospheric Administration (NOAA)
Department of Energy (USA)
Audience: Environmental Scientists, Researchers, Environmentalists, Epidemiologists, Public Health Officials
Details: Free

`gopher://scilibx.ucsc.edu`

`gopher://gopher.ns.doc.gov`

Office of Environmental Safety and Health, Department of Energy

Gopher for resources pertaining to health and environmental safety.

Keywords: Health, Environmental Safety
Sponsor: Department of Energy (US)
Audience: Epidemiologists, Public Health Policymakers, General Public
Details: Free

`gopher://gopher.ns.doc.gov`

Environmental Studies

Enviroethics

A mailing list for the scholarly discussion of environmental ethics and philosophy.

Keywords: Environment, Environmental Studies
Audience: Environmental Researchers, Environmental Scientists, Environmentalists
Contact: Clare Palmer, Ian Tilsed
C.A.Palmer@greenwich.ac.uk, I.J.Tilsed@exeter.ac.uk
User info: To subscribe, send an e-mail message to the URL address below consisting of a single line reading:

join enviroethics YourFirstName YourLastName
To obtain a list of archived files, send an e-mail message with the body 'index enviroethics' to the same address.

`mailto:mailbase@mailbase.ac.uk`

Solid Waste Recycling

The text of an eight-lesson correspondence class designed to teach the basics of setting up a successful recycling program.

Keywords: Recycling, Environmental Studies
Sponsor: University of Wisconsin
Audience: Environmentalists, Educators, Students
Contact: Judy Faber
faber@engr.wisc.edu

`gopher://wissago.uwex.edu/11/uwex/course/recycling`

University of Wisconsin Green Bay Library

The library's holdings are large and wide-ranging and contain significant collections in many fields.

Keywords: Economics, Environmental Studies, Music, Natural Science
Audience: Researchers, Students, General Public
Details: Free
User Info: Expect: Service Name, Send: Victor

`telnet://gbls2k.uwgb.edu`

University of Wisconsin Stevens Point Library

The library's holdings are large and wide-ranging and contain significant collections in many fields.

Keywords: Education, Environmental Studies, Ethnic Studies, History (US)
Audience: Researchers, Students, General Public
Details: Free
User Info: Expect: Login; Send: Lib; Expect: vDIAL Prompt, Send: Library

`telnet://lib.uwsp.edu`

Environmentalism

Western Lands

A collection of articles and reports relating to environmental and land use issues in the Western United States.

Keywords: Environmentalism, Ecology, Forests, The Western United States
Sponsor: The Institute for Global Communications (IGC)
Audience: Environmentalists, Ecologists, Activists, Foresters, Citizens
Contact: Dan Yurman, IGC User Support
dyurman@igc.apc.com
support@igc.apc.com
Notes: User submissions encouraged.

`gopher://gopher.igc.apc.org/11/environment/forests/western.lands`

Enzymes

REBASE (Restriction Enzyme Database)

The Restriction Enzyme Database contains both data and literature citations. It can be searched for enzyme names, species, authors, journals, and recognition sequences.

Keywords: Physiology, Enzymes
Sponsor: New England Biolabs
Audience: Scientists, Molecular Biologists
Contact: Richard Roberts
roberts@cshl.org
Details: Free

`gopher://gopher.gdb.org/77/.INDEX/rebase`

EPPD-L

EPPD-L

Engineering and Public Policy Discussion List.

Keywords: Engineering, Public Policy
Audience: Engineers
Contact: Ken Sollows
listserv@unb.ca
Details: Free
User info: To subscribe to the list, send an e-mail message to the URL address shown below consiting of a single line reading:

SUB eppd-l YourFirstName YourLastName

To send a message to the entire list, address it to:

EPPD-L@UNB.CA

"Contact the Moderator" (ie: Contact's Email)

Equestrians

rec.equestrian

A Usenet newsgroup providing information and discussion about all things pertaining to horses.

Keywords: Horses, Equestrians, Animals, Sports

Audience: Horse Riders, Horse Trainers, Horse Owners
User info: To subscribe to this Usenet newsgroup, you need access to a newsreader.

`news:rec.equestrian`

Equine Research

The University of Minnesota Library System (LUMINA)

The library's holdings are large and wide-ranging and contain significant collections in many fields.

Keywords: Immigration (History of), Ethnic Studies, Horticulture, Equine Research, Botanical Taxonomy, Quantum Physics, Native American Studies, Holmes (Sherlock)
Audience: General Public, Researchers, Librarians, Document Delivery Professionals
Contact: Craig D. Rice
cdr@acc.stolaf.edu
Details: Free

`telnet://lumina.lib.umn.edu`

Ergonomics

HFS-L

Human Factors and Ergonomics Society, Virginia Tech Chapter.

Keywords: Ergonomics, Physical Therapy
Audience: Researchers, Physical Therapists, Designers
Contact: Cortney Vargo
CORTV@VTVM1.CC.VT.EDU
Details: Free
User info: To subscribe to the list, send an e-mail message to the URL address shown below consiting of a single line reading:
SUB hfs-l YourFirstName YourLastName
To send a message to the entire list, address it to: hfs-l@vtvm1.cc.vt.edu

`listserv@vtvm1.cc.vt.edu`

Loughborough University of Technology Computer-Human Interaction (LUTCHI) Research Centre

This server contains general information on computer-human interaction.

Keywords: Interface Design, Ergonomics, Computer-Human Interactions, Programming
Sponsor: Loughborough University of Technology, Leicestershire, UK
Audience: Software Developers, Software Designers, Programmers
Profile: The LUTCHI Research Centre is based within the Department of Computer Studies at the Loughborough University of Technology, Leicestershire, UK. This server contains information about LUTCHI research projects, official LUTCHI publicity releases, as well as documents, images, and movies associated with those projects.
Contact: Ben Anderson
B.Anderson@lut.ac.uk
Details: Free, Moderated, Image and Sound files available. Multimedia files available.
Use a World-Wide Web (Mosaic) client and open a connection to the resource.

`http://pipkin.lut.ac.uk`

ERIC (Educational Resources Information Center)

ERIC (Educational Resources Information Center)

ERIC is a database of short abstracts and information about education-related topics of interest to teachers and administrators.

Keywords: Education, Databases
Sponsor: (Office of Educational Research and Development), US Department of Education
Department of Education (ED)
Audience: Educators, Administrators
Profile: ERIC is the complete database on educational materials from the Educational Resources Information Center in Washington, DC. The database corresponds to two print indexes: Resources in Education, which is concerned with identifying the most significant and timely education research reports; and Current Index to Journals in Education, an index of more than 700 periodicals of interest to every segment of the teaching profession.
Details: Costs
ERIC can be accessed in a variety of ways, for example, through CARL (Colorado Alliance of Research Libraries), through the University of Saskatchewan
(Request: sklib username: sonia)
ERIC can also be accessed by WAIS if you have WAIS installed on your local computer.

`telnet://pac.carl.org`

`telnet://skdevel2.usask.ca`

Erofile

Erofile

This newsletter provides reviews of the latest books associated with French and Italian studies in fields such as literary criticism, cultural studies, film studies, pedagogy, and software.

Keywords: Italian Studies, French Studies, Book Reviews
Audience: French Students, Italian Students, Book Reviewers
Details: Free

`mailto:erofile@ucsbuxa.ucsb.edu`

Esbdc-l

Esbdc-l

A mailing list intended to facilitate discussion between small business development centers, focusing on such topics as performance standards, business behavior, products, specific industry information access, deficit reduction plans, and private cost sharing.

Keywords: Business, Small Business
Sponsor: Association of Small Business Development Centers, USA
Audience: State Officials, Educators, Certified Public Accountants, Investors
User info: To subscribe to the list, send an e-mail message to the URL address below consisting of a single line reading:
SUB esbdc-l YourFirstName YourLastName
To send a message to the entire list, address it to: esbdc-l@ferris.bitnet

`mailto:listserv@ferris.bitnet`

ESL (English as a Second Language)

Bilingual Education Network

This gopher site contains bilingual and bicultural, ESL (English as a Second Language), and Foreign Language resources and curriculum guidelines.

Keywords: ESL (English as a Second Language), Education (Bilingual)
Sponsor: California Department of Education, California, USA
Audience: Educators, Administrators, Parents

`gopher://goldmine.cde.ca.gov`

ESRI (Environmental Systems Research Institute)

ESRI (Environmental Systems Research Institute)

Environmental Systems Research Institute, Inc. is the world leader in GIS technology. ARC/INFO is ESRIÕs powerful and flexible flagship GIS software.

Keywords: Geographic Information Systems (GIS), Environment, Software, Computers

Audience: Geographers, Environmentalists, Computer Users

Details: Costs

For product information, call (909)793-2853, X1475.

For training information, call (909)793-2853, X1585, or fax (909)793-5953.

Essence

Essence ★

A description of Essence, an Internet resource discovery system based on semantic file indexing.

Keywords: Internet Tools, Essence (Internet Resource Directory)

Sponsor: University of Colorado, Boulder, CO

Audience: Internet Surfers

Contact: Darren R. Hardy, Michael F. Schwartz
hardy@cs.colorado.edu
schwartz@cs.colorado.edu

Details: Free

File is: pub/cs/distribs/essence/README

`ftp://.cs.colorado.edu`

Estonia

Balt-L ★

A forum devoted to communications to and about the Baltic Republics of Lithuania, Latvia, and Estonia.

Keywords: Lithuania, Latvia, Estonia, Baltic Republics

Audience: Researchers, Baltic Nationals

Contact: Jean-Michel Thizy
jmyhg@uottawa.edu

Details: Free

User info: To subscribe to the list, send an e-mail message to the URL address below, consisting of a single line reading:

SUB balt-l YourFirstName YourLastName

`mailto:listserv@ubvm.cc.buffalo.edu`

Ethics

ETHCSE-L

A mailing list for the discussion of Ethical Issues in Software Engineering, dealing with subjects of interest to professional software engineers.

Keywords: Engineering, Computing, Ethics

Audience: Engineers, Software Engineers, Researchers

Contact: Margaret Mason
mason@utkvml.utk.edu

Details: Free

User info: To subscribe to the list, send an e-mail message to the URL address shown below consisting of a single line reading:

SUB ethcse-l YourFirstName YourLastName

To send a message to the entire list, address it to:

ethsce-l@utkvm1.utk.edu

`mailto:listserv@utkvm1.utk.edu`

misc.legal ★

A Usenet newsgroup providing information and discussion about law and ethics.

Keywords: Law, Ethics

Audience: Lawyers, Legal Professionals, General Public

Details: Free

User info: To subscribe to this Usenet newsgroup, you need access to a newsreader.

`news:misc.legal`

Mother Jones

A web site containing online electronic issues of Mother Jones magazine (and Zine), making possible instant electronic feedback to the publishers regarding articles.

Keywords: Zines, Ethics, Public Policy, Activism

Sponsor: Mother Jones

Audience: Students, General Public

Contact: Webserver
webserver@mojones.com

`http://www.mojones.com/motherjones.html`

talk.religion.misc

A Usenet newsgroup providing information and discussion about religious, ethical, and moral implications.

Keywords: Religion, Ethics

Audience: General Public, Researchers, Students

Details: Free

User info: To subscribe to this Usenet newsgroup, you need access to a newsreader.

`news:talk.religion.misc`

Ethnic Studies

Geneology

A large collection of geneology resources for both beginners and specialists. Includes archives of geneology lists, FAQs, helper software, and specific geneological information for a number of national and ethnic groups.

Keywords: Geneology, Ethnic Studies

Sponsor: Go M-Link at the University of Michigan

Audience: Geneologists, General Public, Researchers

Contact: Sue Davidsen
davidsen@umich.edu

`gopher://vienna.hh.lib.umich.edu`

The University of Minnesota Library System (LUMINA)

The library's holdings are large and wide-ranging and contain significant collections in many fields.

Keywords: Immigration (History of), Ethnic Studies, Horticulture, Equine Research, Botanical Taxonomy, Quantum Physics, Native American Studies, Holmes (Sherlock)

Audience: General Public, Researchers, Librarians, Document Delivery Professionals

Contact: Craig D. Rice
cdr@acc.stolaf.edu

Details: Free

`telnet://lumina.lib.umn.edu`

University of Wisconsin Stevens Point Library

The library's holdings are large and wide-ranging and contain significant collections in many fields.

Keywords: Education, Environmental Studies, Ethnic Studies, History (US)

Audience: Researchers, Students, General Public

Details: Free

User Info: Expect: Login; Send: Lib; Expect: vDIAL Prompt, Send: Library

`telnet://lib.uwsp.edu`

Ethnicity

POS302-L

A discussion list created for the "Race, Ethnicity, and Social Inequality" seminar offered at Illinois State University (spring 1994). The general purposes of the list are to create an e-mail audience for the written work of enrolled students and to invite a broad audience to participate in the seminar.

Keywords: Race, Ethnicity, Minorities
Audience: Ethnic Studies Students, Sociologists, Educators
Details: Free
User info: To subscribe to the list, send an e-mail message to the URL address below, consisting of a single line reading:

SUB pos302-l YourFirstName YourLastName

To send a message to the entire list, address it to: pos302-l@ilstu.edu

`mailto:listserv@ilstu.edu`

Ethnomusicology Research Digest

Ethnomusicology Research Digest

For subscribers with a professional interest in ethnomusicology, including news, discussion, queries, bibliographies, and archives. Subscription by permission only.

Keywords: Musicians, Ethnomusicology
Audience: Ethnomusicologists, Educators, Librarians, Researchers, Students
Contact: Karl Signell
signell@umdd.umd.edu
Details: Free
User info: To subscribe, send an e-mail message to the address below consisting of a single line reading:

SUB ethmus-l YourFirstName YourLastName

To send a message to the entire list, address it to: ethmus-l@umdd.vmd.edu

`mailto:listserv@umdd.umd.edu`

Ethnomusicology

Ethnomusicology Research Digest

For subscribers with a professional interest in ethnomusicology, including news, discussion, queries, bibliographies, and archives. Subscription by permission only.

Keywords: Musicians, Ethnomusicology
Audience: Ethnomusicologists, Educators, Librarians, Researchers, Students
Contact: Karl Signell
signell@umdd.umd.edu
Details: Free
User info: To subscribe, send an e-mail message to the address below consisting of a single line reading:

SUB ethmus-l YourFirstName YourLastName

To send a message to the entire list, address it to: ethmus-l@umdd.vmd.edu

`mailto:listserv@umdd.umd.edu`

Etiquette

Net Etiquette Guide

Guidelines and netiquette for the Net user.

Keywords: Internet, Etiquette, Netiquette
Sponsor: SURAnet Network Information Center
Audience: Internet Surfers
Contact: info@sura.net
Details: Free
File is: pub/nic/internet.literature/netiquette.txt

`ftp://ftp.sura.net`

euitnews (Educational Uses of Information Technology)

euitnews (Educational Uses of Information Technology)

EDUCOM's newsletter for the Educational Uses of Information Technology program encompasses distance learning, self-paced instruction, computer-aided instruction, video, and other information technologies for teaching and learning.

Keywords: Education (Continuing), Information Technology
Audience: Administrators, K-12 Educators
Details: Free
User info: To subscribe to the newsletter, send an e-mail message to the URL address below consisting of a single line reading:

SUB euitnews YourFirstName YourLastName

`mailto:listserv@bitnic.educom.edu`

EUnet

EUnet

A global Internet Service Provider with national providers in almost 30 countries. Applications such as customer support, remote diagnosis, software development tools, and product information are available through this net.

Keywords: Internet
Sponsor: EUnet Information Services
Audience: Internet Surfers
Contact: info@eu.net
Details: Free

`http://www.eu.net`

EUnet Czechia

EUnet Czechia

This is the information service of EUnet Czechia, the network service provider in the Czech Republic and contains information about top-level domains.

Keywords: Czech Republic
Audience: Czechs, General Public
Contact: gopher.eunet.cz
Details: Free

`http://www.eunet.cz`

Euromath

Euromath Center Gopher Server

A gopher server providing information about the Euromath Center, the Euromath Project, and related activities.

Keywords: Europe, Mathematics, Euromath
Sponsor: University of Copenhagen
Audience: Mathematicians, Europeans
Contact: Klaus Harbo
emc@euromath.dk
Details: Free

`gopher://laurel.euromath.dk`

Europe

(The) Worldwide Impact of Network Access

This is an article by community networker Felipe Rodriquez. In this statement Rodriquez argues that developed countries should help less developed countries build their information infrastructures, and that governments should not censor the content of network traffic.

Keywords: Community, Networking, Europe, Development (International)

Audience: Activists, Policymakers, Community Leaders

Contact: Felipe Rodriquez
felipe@hacktic.nl

`http://nearnet.gnn.com/mag/articles/oram/bio.rodriquez.html`

Agence FrancePresse International French Wire ★★★

Agence FrancePresse International French Wire provides full-text articles in French relating to national, international, business, and sports news.

Keywords: News Media, Europe, Third World, French

Sponsor: Agence FrancePresse, Paris, France

Audience: Market Researchers, Journalists, Francophiles

Profile: Agence FrancePresse distributes its French service worldwide, including Western and Eastern Europe, Canada, northern and western Africa, the Middle East, Vietnam, French Guiana, the West Indies, and the French Pacific islands. Agence FrancePresse International French Wire has extensive coverage of the European countries, including every aspect of economic, political, and general business news. It also provides excellent industrial and market news from both developed countries and from the Third World.

Coverage: September 1991 to the present; updated daily.

Contact: Dialog in the US at (800) 334-2564; Dialog internationally at country-specific locations.

Details: Costs

Notes: To subscribe, contact Dialog directly.

`telnet://dialog.com`

ASTRA-UG

A mailing list for the discussion of Italian and European GIS.

Keywords: (Geographical Information Systems), Europe, Italy

Audience: Geographers, Cartographers, Europeans

Details: Free

User info: To subscribe to the list, send an e-mail mesage to the URL address below, consisting of a single line reading:

SUB ASTRA-UG YourFirstName YourLastName

`astra-ug@icnucevm`

BFU (Brussels Free Universities) ★

The gopher server of the Brussels Free Universities VUB /ULB is the national entry point for EMBnet in Belgium and provides links to university library systems and EMBnet databases.

Keywords: Computing, EMBnet, Belgium, Europe

Audience: Scientists, Biologists, Biotechnologists

Contact: support@vub.ac.be

Details: Free

`gopher://gopher.vub.ac.be`

CEDAR (Central European Environmental Data Request) Facility ★★★

This gopher site provides information about the environmental and scientific community in Central and Eastern Europe (CEE), with access to environmental information located throughout the world on various international computer networks and hosts.

Keywords: Europe, EEC, Environment

Sponsor: The International Society for Environmental Protection, and The Austrian Federal Ministry for Environment, Youth and Family (BMUJF)

Audience: Environmentalists, Educators, Students, Urban Planners

Contact: cedar-info@cedar.univie.ac.at

Notes: CEDAR Marxergasse 3/20, A-1030 Vienna, Austria Tel.: +43-1-715 58 79

`gopher://pan.cedar.univie.ac.at`

Central European Environment Data Report (CEDAR) Facility ★★★★

This gopher site provides information about the environmental and scientific community in Central and Eastern Europe, with access to environmental information located throughout the world on various international computer networks and hosts.

Keywords: Europe, Central Europe, Eastern Europe, Environment

Sponsor: The International Society for Environmental Protection, and The Austrian Federal Ministry for Environment, Youth and Family (BMUJF)

Audience: Environmentalists, Educators, Students, Urban Planners, Environmental Scientists

Profile: The CEDAR Facility, established in 1991, is administered by the International Society for Environmental Protection (ISEP). The Facility is designed to provide regional groups and individuals with access to its information retrieval and higher computing resources, technical advice and database and network access support. In addition, CEDAR works to facilitate information and dialogue exchange with organizations in other parts of the world and in partner countries; and to promote training forums, including the joint development of seminars and conferences with ISEP on environmental and network topics. Finally, CEDAR develops and manages environmental reference data sets, including a US EPA bibliographic reference on hazardous waste treatment, CEDAR databases on Central and Eastern European environmental expertise and information, and the holdings of the Regional Environmental Center Library at Budapest.

Contact: cedar-info@cedar.univie.ac.at

`gopher://pan.cedar.univie.ac.at`

CILEA (Consorzio Interuniversitario Lombardo per la Elaborazione Automatica) ★

The gopher for the InterUniversity Computer Center, Milan, Italy, provides access to CILEA hosts, databases in Europe, CERN (European Laboratory for Particle Physics) services such as WWW and ALICE, Usenet newsgroups, PostScript documentation on various items, Italian research network information, and more.

Keywords: Informatics, Italy, Europe

Audience: Particle physicists, Researchers

Contact: Luciano Guglielm
guglielm@imicilea.cilea.it

Details: Free

`gopher://imicilea.cilea.it`

D&B - European Dun's Market (EDMI) ★★★★

This database presents detailed information on over 2.5 million businesses located in 26 European countries.

Keywords: Dun & Bradstreet, Europe, Business

Sponsor: Dun & Bradstreet Information Services, Parsippany, NJ, USA

Audience: Business Professionals, Business Analysts

Profile: EDMI provides directory listings, sales volume and marketing data, and references to parent companies. Companies are selected for inclusion based on sales volume, national prominence, and international interest. Names, addresses, SIC codes, D-U-N-S numbers, and other data are given in each record. Both public and private companies are included.

Europe

```
A
B
C
D
E
F
G
H
I
J
K
L
M
N
O
P
Q
R
S
T
U
V
W
X
Y
Z
```

Contact: Dialog in the US at (800) 334-2564, Dialog internationally at country-specific locations.
User info: To subscribe, contact Dialog directly.
Notes: Coverage: Current; updated quarterly.

`telnet://dialog.com`

Delphes European Business ★★★★

This is a French database that provides information on international markets, products, industries, and companies from a European perspective.

Keywords: Business, Europe
Sponsor: Chamber of Commerce and Industry of Paris and The French Assembly of the Chambers of Commerce and Industry, Paris, France
Audience: Business Professionals, Business Analysts
Profile: Abstracts are produced by approximately 60 local organizations grouped into two networks, CCIP (Chamber of Commerce and Industry of Paris) and ACFCI (French Assembly of the Chambers of Commerce and Industry), which collect and consolidate the information into the Delphes database. Delphes contains bibliographic citations and informative abstracts from over 900 European trade journals, newspapers, and business periodicals, in French, English, Italian, German, or Spanish. Titles are in the original language; abstracts are in French. A comprehensive classification scheme in English, French, and Spanish is used to index documents covered. Geographic coverage is 45% France, 35% Europe, and 20% is devoted to other countries. In addition, about 1,000 new books, corporate and business directories, and reports are reviewed each year.
Contact: Dialog in the US at (800) 334-2564, Dialog internationally at country-specific locations.
User info: To subscribe, contact Dialog directly.
Notes: Coverage: 1980 to the present; updated weekly.

`telnet://dialog.com`

EC ★

Dedicated to discussion of the European Community (EC).

Keywords: European Community, Europe
Audience: Europeans, Researchers, General Public, Economists
Contact: John B. Harlan
ijbh200@indyvax.iupui.edu
ec@vm.cc.metu.edu.tr
Details: Free
User info: Io subscribe to the list, send an e-mail message to the URL address shown below consisting of a single line reading:
SUB ec YourFirstName YourLastName

`mailto:listserv@linycms.iupui.edu`

Euromath Center Gopher Server ★

A gopher server providing information about the Euromath Center, the Euromath Project, and related activities.

Keywords: Europe, Mathematics, Euromath
Sponsor: University of Copenhagen
Audience: Mathematicians, Europeans
Contact: Klaus Harbo
emc@euromath.dk
Details: Free

`gopher://laurel.euromath.dk`

EUROPE (European News Library)

The Europe library contains detailed information about every country in Eastern, Central and Western Europe.

Keywords: Business, Europe
Audience: Business Researchers, Analysts, Entrepreneurs, Regulatory Agencies
Profile: EUROPE is designed for those who need to monitor countries of the European Community, the European Free Trade Association, or emerging European market economies. This library includes a wide array of sources: Among the information sources are: newspapers and wire services, trade and business journals, company reports, country and region background, industry and product analyses, business opportunities, and selected legal texts. News sources range from the world-renowned Financial Times and Reuters to the regionally important PAP and CTK newswires. EIS's European newsletters and Euroscipe from Coopers and Lybrand help analyze the legal and business environment in Western Europe. Company information is contained in the EXTEL cards as well as ICC.
Contact: Mead New Sales Group at (800) 227-4908 or (513) 859-5398 inside the US, or (513) 865-7981 for all inquiries outside the US.
User info: To subscribe, contact Mead directly.
To examine the Nexis user guide, you can access it at the ftp site of the University of Texas at Austin at the URL address: ftp://ftp.cc.utexas.edu
The files are in: /pub/ref-services/LEXIS

`telnet://nex.meaddata.com`

`http://www.meaddata.com`

European Patents Fulltext

European Patents Fulltext contains the complete text of European published applications and patents and European PCT published applications.

Keywords: Patents, Europe, Law (International)
Sponsor: European Patent Office, Vienna, Austria
Audience: Patent Researchers
Profile: It contains bibliographic, administrative, and legal information from the European Patent Registry. Records have abstracts, patent specifications including all claims, and the search report, including cited patents and other references.
Contact: Dialog in the US at (800) 334-2564, Dialog internationally at country-specific locations.
User info: To subscribe, contact Dialog directly.
Notes: Coverage: 1978 to the present; updated weekly.

`telnet://dialog.com`

European Root Gopher ★

A root gopher server and registry for European gophers run by the Swedish University Network to serve European users.

Keywords: Europe, Gophers
Sponsor: Swedish University Computer Network (SUNET)
Audience: European Internet Surfers
Contact: gopher-info@sunic.sunet.se
Details: Free

`gopher://gopher@sunet.se`

Hungarian Gopher—Hollosi Information Exchange (HIX) ★

This is the main Hungarian gopher, providing information for and about residents of Hungary and Hungarian speakers.

Keywords: Hungary, Europe
Sponsor: Stanford University, Palo Alto, CA
Audience: Hungarian Internet Surfers
Contact: hollosi@andrea.standford.edu
Details: Free

`gopher://hix.elte.hu`

ICGEBnet ★

This is the information server of the International Centre for Genetic Engineering and Molecular Biology (ICGEB), Trieste, Italy.

Keywords: Molecular Biology, Biotechnology, Italy, Europe
Audience: Molecular Biotechnologists, Molecular Biologists
Profile: The primary purpose of the ICGEB computer resource is to disseminate the best of currently available computational technology to the molecular biologists of the ICGEB research community.
Contact: postmaster@icgeb.trieste.it
Details: Free

`gopher://icgeb.trieste.it`

ICTP (International Centre for Theoretical Physics) ★

ICTP's gopher disseminates information regarding the many scientific activities carried out at ICTP (Trieste, Italy). Information is also provided on the scientific publications, courses, and other services offered by ICS (International Centre for Science and High Technology) and TWAS (Third World Academy of Sciences) at Trieste.

Keywords: Theoretical Physics, Italy, Europe
Audience: Physicists
Profile: Topics include programming techniques, theoretical aspects, Icon in relation to other languages, applications of Icon, implementation issues, porting, and bugs.
Contact: admin@ictp.trieste.it
Details: Free

`gopher://gopher.ictp.trieste.it`

`http://gopher.ictp.trieste.it`

Imperial College Department of Computing ★★

This is the home of the department of Computing, Imperial College, United Kingdom, the UKUUG (UK UNIX User Group) Archive and the DoC Information Service.

Keywords: Computing, United Kingdom, Europe
Audience: Computer Scientists
Contact: imjm@doc.ic.ac.uk
Details: Free

`gopher://src.doc.ic.ac.uk`

`http://src.doc.ic.ac.uk`

Information Services in Germany ★

This gopher is an informal entry point for Germany, together with some hints to specialties in German information systems.

Keywords: Germany, Information, Europe
Audience: German Internet Surfers
Contact: lange@rz.tu-clausthal.de
Details: Free

`gopher://gopher.tu-clausthal.de`

IST BioGopher ★

This is the gopher server of the National Institute for Cancer Research (IST) and of the Advanced Biotechnology Center of Genoa, Italy.

Keywords: Cancer, Biotechnology, Italy, Europe
Audience: Biologists, Medical Researchers
Profile: The server includes data from the Interlab Project Databases (biological materials availability in European laboratories) and the Bio-Media Bulletin Board System (biotechnology researchers, projects, fundings and products).
Contact: gophman@istge.ist.unige.it
Details: Free

`gopher://istge.ist.unige.it`

Lysator's Gopher Service ★

Lysator is the name of the Academic Computer Society at Linkoping University, Linkoping, Sweden. It relies on voluntary efforts by students, and any service of activity runs as long as they think it is fun—content always reflects their personal interests.

Keywords: Sweden, Students, Europe
Audience: Swedish Students
Contact: Lars Aronsson@lysator.liu.se
Details: Free

`gopher://gopher.lysator.liu.se`

`http://dla.ucop.edu`

Maastricht Treaty ★

The file contains the text of the latest edition of the Treaty on European Union, also known as the Maastricht Treaty, signed on February 7, 1992.

Keywords: Europe, European Union, Maastricht Treaty
Audience: Politicians, Historians, Europeans, Political Scientists, General Public
Details: Free
 Select from menu as appropriate.

`gopher://wiretap.spies.com`

NORDUnet region Root Gopher ★

The Nordic University and Research Network is a collaboration by the national research networks in Denmark, Finland, Iceland, Norway, and Sweden. It provides the national research and education communities with an efficient networking service that ensures the coherence of the national networks and connects these to similar networks in the rest of Europe and the world.

Keywords: Nordic University, Europe
Audience: Nordic Internet Surfers
Contact: hostmaster@nic.nordu.net
Details: Free

`gopher://gopher.nordu.net`

OLIS (Oxford University Library Information Service) Gopher ★★

OLIS is a network of libraries. It contains all the books from the English, Modern Languages, Social Studies, and Hooke libraries. It also contains books and journals cataloged since September 1988 in the Bodleian and Dependant libraries and the Taylor Institution. Books can be searched in any OLIS library from any location.

Keywords: Libraries, United Kingdom, Europe
Audience: Library Users
Contact: jose@olis.lib.ox.ac.uk
Details: Free

`gopher://gopher.lib.ox.ac.uk/00/Info/OLIS`

Prague University of Economics Gopher Service ★★

Includes information about the University, integrative studies of economy, economic information, and public domain software.

Keywords: Czech Republic, Economics, Europe
Audience: Czechs, Economists
Contact: gopher@pub.vse.cz
Details: Free

`gopher://pub.vse.cz`

RIPE Network Coordination Centre Gopher ★

RIPE (Reseaux IP Europeens) is a collaborative organization open to all European Internet service providers. RIPE coordinates the operation of a pan-European IP network. In November 1993, more than 500,000 hosts throughout Europe were reachable via networks coordinated by RIPE.

Keywords: Europe, Networks
Audience: European Internet Surfers
Contact: ncc@ripe.net
Details: Free

`gopher://gopher.ripe.net`

soc.culture.europe ★

A Usenet newsgroup providing information and discussion about all aspects of Europe.

Keywords: Europe, Sociology
Audience: Sociologists, Europeans
Details: Free
User info: To subscribe to this Usenet newsgroup, you need access to a newsreader.

`news:soc.culture.europe`

SURFnet—KB InfoServer

InfoService is a joint project by SURFnet (National Network Organization for Research and Higher Education) and the Koninklijke Bibliotheek (National Library of the Netherlands).

Keywords: Netherlands, Networks, Europe
Audience: European Internet Surfers
Contact: infoservices@surfnet.nl
Details: Free

`gopher://gopher.nic.surfnet.nl`

Swiss Scientific Supercomputing Center (CSCS) Info Server ★

The Centro Svizzero di Calcolo Scientifico (CSCS) info server is the national scientific computing center in Switzerland.

Keywords: Switzerland, Supercomputing, Europe
Audience: Swiss Internet Surfers
Contact: mgay@cscs.ch
Details: Free

`gopher://pobox.cscs.ch`

University of Glasgow Information Service (GLANCE) ★★★★

GLANCE provides subject-based information services, including an extensive section on European and world sports.

Keywords: Sports, Soccer, Motor Racing, Mountaineering, Squash, Cricket, Golf, Tennis, Europe, Scotland
Sponsor: University of Glasgow, Glasgow, Scotland
Audience: Sport Enthusiasts, Fitness Enthusiasts, Nature Lovers
Profile: Information at this site includes schedules, results, and statistics for sports such as cricket and soccer. There is also a selection of items on mountaineering.
Contact: Alan Dawson
A.Dawson@uk.ac.gla.compserv
Details: Free

`gopher://govan.cent.gla.ac.uk/Subject/Sports and Rec`

EUROPE (European News Library)

EUROPE (European News Library)

The Europe library contains detailed information about every country in Eastern, Central and Western Europe.

Keywords: Business, Europe
Audience: Business Researchers, Analysts, Entrepreneurs, Regulatory Agencies
Profile: EUROPE is designed for those who need to monitor countries of the European Community, the European Free Trade Association, or emerging European market economies. This library includes a wide array of sources: Among the information sources are: newspapers and wire services, trade and business journals, company reports, country and region background, industry and product analyses, business opportunities, and selected legal texts. News sources range from the world-renowned Financial Times and Reuters to the regionally important PAP and CTK newswires. EIS's European newsletters and Euroscipe from Coopers and Lybrand help analyze the legal and business environment in Western Europe. Company information is contained in the EXTEL cards as well as ICC.
Contact: Mead New Sales Group at (800) 227-4908 or (513) 859-5398 inside the US, or (513) 865-7981 for all inquiries outside the US.
User info: To subscribe, contact Mead directly.

To examine the Nexis user guide, you can access it at the ftp site of the University of Texas at Austin at the URL address: ftp://ftp.cc.utexas.edu

The files are in: /pub/ref-services/LEXIS

`telnet://nex.meaddata.com`

`http://www.meaddata.com`

European Community

DRT EC and Eastern Europe Business Database

DRTE's comprehensive full-text coverage of business and industry in the EC is combined with in-depth reporting on doing business in Eastern Europe.

Keywords: European Community, Eastern Europe.
Sponsor: DRT Europe Services Brussels, Belgium
Audience: Market Analysts, Business Professionals, Market Researchers
Profile: DRTE reports provide comprehensive and detailed coverage of all EC proposals, laws and policy directions and their commercial applications, and unique, country-specific information on the regulatory framework for business development and expansion in Eastern Europe. These are continually updated to reflect the rapidly changing nature of the political and administrative structure of these emerging economies as they affect business undertakings with EC concerns.
Contact: Data-star through Dialog in the US at (800) 334-2564, Dialog internationally at country-specific locations.
User info: To subscribe, contact Dialog directly.
Notes: Coverage: The database is updated weekly to enable it to offer exceptionally current full-text information.

`telnet://dialog.com`

EC ★

Dedicated to discussion of the European Community (EC).

Keywords: European Community, Europe
Audience: Europeans, Researchers, General Public, Economists
Contact: John B. Harlan
ijbh200@indyvax.iupiu.edu
ec@vm.cc.metu.edu.tr
Details: Free
User info: To subscribe to the list, send an e-mail message to the URL address shown below consisting of a single line reading:

SUB ec YourFirstName YourLastName

`mailto:listserv@linycms.iupiu.edu`

INTNAT (International Library)

The International library contains all French treaties, conventions and agreements that are effective today, as well as decisions from the Cour Europenne des Droits de l'Homme and the Cour de Justice des Communautes Europennes plus the Journal Officiel des Communautes Europenne.

Keywords: French Law, European Community
Audience: International Lawyers
Profile: The International library contains all French treaties, conventions and agreements published before 1958 that are in effect today, as well as decisions from the European Court of Human Rights (Cour Europeenne des Droits del'Homme), the European Court of Justice (Cour de Justice des Communautes Europeennes) and the Journal Officiel des Communautes Europeenne, the daily record of the European Community.
Contact: New Sales Group at 800-227-4908 or 513-859-5398 inside the US, or 1-513-865-7981 for all inquires outside the US.
User info: To subscribe, contact Mead directly.
To examine the Lexis user guide, you can access it at the ftp site of the University of Texas at Austin at the URL address: ftp://ftp.cc.utexas.edu

The files are in: /pub/ref-services/LEXIS

`telnet://nex.meaddata.com`

`http://www.meaddata.com`

European Documents

University of Hawaii Library

The library's holdings are large and wide-ranging and contain significant collections in many fields.

Keywords: Asia, European Documents, Book Arts, Hawaii
Audience: General Public, Researchers, Librarians, Document Delivery Professionals
Details: Free
User Info: Expect: enter class, Send: LIB

`telnet://starmaster.uhcc.hawaii.edu`

European Patents Fulltext

European Patents Fulltext

European Patents Fulltext contains the complete text of European published applications and patents and European PCT published applications.

Keywords: Patents, Europe, Law (International)
Sponsor: European Patent Office, Vienna, Austria
Audience: Patent Researchers
Profile: It contains bibliographic, administrative, and legal information from the European Patent Registry. Records have abstracts, patent specifications including all claims, and the search report, including cited patents and other references.
Contact: Dialog in the US at (800) 334-2564, Dialog internationally at country-specific locations.
User info: To subscribe, contact Dialog directly.
Notes: Coverage: 1978 to the present; updated weekly.

`telnet://dialog.com`

European Root Gopher

European Root Gopher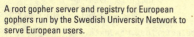

A root gopher server and registry for European gophers run by the Swedish University Network to serve European users.

Keywords: Europe, Gophers
Sponsor: Swedish University Computer Network (SUNET)
Audience: European Internet Surfers
Contact: gopher-info@sunic.sunet.se
Details: Free

`gopher://gopher@sunet.se`

European Space Agency

European Space Agency

A major directory on aeronautics, providing access to a broad range of related resources (library catalogs, databases, and servers) via the Internet.

Keywords: Space Science, Aeronautics
Audience: Space Science Researchers
Profile: The home page of the European Space Agency, including information about ESA's mission, specific ESA programs (Science, Manned Spaceflight and Microgravity, Earth Observation, Telecommunications, Launchers), and issues related to the space and aeronautics industry.
Contact: webmaster@esa.it

`http://www.esrin.esa.it`

European Union

Maastricht Treaty

The file contains the text of the latest edition of the Treaty on European Union, also known as the Maastricht Treaty, signed on February 7, 1992.

Keywords: Europe, European Union, Maastricht Treaty
Audience: Politicians, Historians, Europeans, Political Scientists, General Public
Details: Free
        Select from menu as appropriate.

`gopher://wiretap.spies.com`

EUVE

Center for Extreme Ultraviolet Astrophysics

A department of the University of California at Berkeley devoted to research in extreme ultraviolet astronomy. It is the ground-based institution of EUVE (the Extreme Ultraviolet Explorer), a NASA satellite launched in 1992.

Keywords: Astronomy, Astrophysics, EUVE, NASA, Satellite
Sponsor: NASA and University of California at Berkeley
Audience: Astronomers, Astrophysicists
Profile: Provides access to details about the EUVE Guest Observer (EGO) Center, the EUVE Public Archive of Mission Data and Information, satellite operation information, and so on. The EUVE Guest Observer Center provides information, software, and data to EUVE Guest Observers.
Contact: egoinfo@cea.berkeley.edu
         archive@cea.berkeley.edu
Details: Free

`http://cea-ftp.cea.berkeley.edu/`

EV

EV

General list for discussion of all aspects of electric vehicles.

Keywords: Electric Vehicles
Audience: Electric Vehicle Enthusiasts
Contact: Clyde Visser
         listserv@sjsuvm1.sjsu.edu
User info: To subscribe to the list, send an e-mail message to the URL address below consisting of a single line reading:

    SUB electric-vehicle YourFirstName YourLastName

    To send a message to the entire list, address it to: electric-vehicle@sjsuvm1.sjsu.edu

`mailto:listserv@sjsuvm1.sjsu.edu`

Evangelism

Catholic-action

Catholic-action is a moderated list concerned with Catholic evangelism, church revitalization, and preservation of Catholic teachings, traditions and values, and the vital effort to decapitate modernist heresy.

Keywords: Catholicism, Evangelism, Religion
Audience: Catholics, Priests
Contact: Richard Freeman
         rfreeman@vpnet.chi.il.us
Details: Free
User info: To subscribe to the list, send an e-mail message requesting a subscription to the URL address below.

`mailto:rfreeman@vpnet.chi.il.us`

Cell Church Discussion Group ★

A list for Christians who are in cell churches or in churches that are in transition to becoming cell churches, as well as anyone interested in learning more about cell churches. A cell church is a nontraditional form of church life in which small groups of Christians (cells) meet in a special way in their homes for the evangelism of the unchurched, the bonding of believers, their nurture, and ministry to one another.

Keywords: Cell Churches, Christianity, Evangelism, Religion
Audience: Christians, Theologians, Evangelists
Contact: Jon Reid
reid@cei.com
Details: Free
User info: To subscribe to the list, send an e-mail message to the URL address below with the single word SUBSCRIBE in the body (not subject) of your message.

To send a message to the entire list, address it to: cell-church@bible.acu.edu
Notes: The group archives, FAQ, and helpful articles are available by anonymous FTP from bible.acu.edu; they can also be retrieved by sending mail to cell-church-archives@bible.acu.edu with the single word LIST for a list of files, or HELP for more information.

`mailto:cell-church-request@bible.acu.edu`

Evolution

talk.origins ★

A Usenet newsgroup providing information and discussion about evolution versus creationism.

Keywords: Evolution, Creationism, Activism
Audience: General Public, Evolutionists, Creationists, Activists
Details: Free
User info: To subscribe to this Usenet newsgroup, you need access to a newsreader.

`news:talk.origins`

Executive Branch

EXEC (Executive Branch News US)

The EXEC library contains information and news about the Executive Branch of the Federal Government. From the Department of Agriculture to the White House, this file is a comprehensive source of information that will be especially useful to those whose responsibilities include monitoring federal regulations, Agency and Department activity, and the people and issues involved.

Keywords: News, Legislation, Regulation, Politics, Executive Branch
Audience: Journalists, Lobbyists, Business Executives, Analysts, Entrepreneurs
Profile: The EXEC library allows the searching of individual files or group files that cover topics such as the Federal Register and Code of Federal Regulations; public laws; proposed treasury regulation; and over 50 news sources, including BNAÕs Daily Report for Executives, the Dept. of State Dispatch, ABC News transcripts, Federal News Service Daybook, Government Executive, MacNeil/Lehrer Newshour, New Leader, National Review, the Washington Post, the Washington Times, Presidential Documents, and many others.
Contact: Mead New Sales Group at (800) 227-4908 or (513) 859-5398 inside the US, or (513) 865-7981 for all inquiries outside the US.
User info: To subscribe, contact Mead directly.

To examine the Nexis user guide, you can access it at the ftp site of the University of Texas at Austin at the URL address: ftp://ftp.cc.utexas.edu

The files are in: /pub/ref-services/LEXIS

`telnet://nex.meaddata.com, http://www.meaddata.com`

Experimental Stock Market Data

Experimental Stock Market Data ★★★

This is an experimental page that provides a link to the latest stock market information.

Keywords: Stock Market, Investments, Finance
Audience: General Public, Investors, Stock Brokers
Profile: This site is updated automatically, to reflect the current day's closing information. Provides general market news and quotes for selected stocks, although prices are not guaranteed. Also includes recent prices for many mutual funds, as well as technical analysis charts for a large number of stocks and mutual funds.
Contact: Mark Torrance
stockmaster@ai.mit.edu
Details: Free

`http://www.ai.mit.edu/stocks.html`

Expert Systems

Artificial Intelligence, Expert Sys., Virtual Reality

This directory is a compilation of information resources focused on computer science research, artificial intelligence, expert systems, and virtual reality.

Keywords: Computer Science, Artificial Intelligence, Expert Systems, Virtual Reality
Audience: Computer Scientists, Engineers
Details: Free

`ftp://una.hh.lib.umich.edu/70/inetdirstacks/csaiesvr:kovacsm`

Exports

ITRADE (International Trade Library)

The International Trade library contains materials related to the importing of goods and services, exporting of goods and services, licensing of intellectual property, payment of taxes, or investment and banking at the international level.

Keywords: Law, Import, Exports, International Banking
Audience: Lawyers
Profile: ITRADE contains a comprehensive collection of federal case law, statutes, regulations, and agency decisions all related to the importing of goods and services, exporting of goods and services, licensing of intellectual property, payment of taxes, or investment and banking at the international level.
Contact: New Sales Group at 800-227-4908 or 513-859-5398 inside the US, or 1-513-865-7981 for all inquires outside the US.
User info: To subscribe, contact Mead directly.

To examine the Lexis user guide, you can access it at the ftp site of the University of Texas at Austin at the URL address: ftp://ftp.cc.utexas.edu

The files are in: /pub/ref-services/LEXIS

`telnet://nex.meaddata.com`

`http://www.meaddata.com`

National Export Strategy ★★

This site provides the complete text of a report presented to Congress by the Trade Promotion Coordinating Committee, describing ways to develop U.S. export promotion efforts.

Keywords: Commerce, Trade, Exports, Business

Sponsor:	United States Government, Trade Promotion Coordinating Committee
Audience:	Exporters, Business Professionals, Trade Specialists
Details:	Free

`ftp://sunny.stat-usa.gov`

`http://sunny.stat-usa.gov`

PIERS Exports (US Ports)

Keywords:	Trade, Exports, Maritime
Sponsor:	The Journal of Commerce/PIERS, New York, NY, USA
Audience:	Importers, Exporters, Business, Trade Specialists
Profile:	Principal applications include identification of new sources of supply, monitoring exports of products whose details are lost in traditional government reports, and identification of potential trade partners. PIERS covers virtually all maritime movements in and out of the continental US and Puerto Rico. Details on each individual shipment are stored in the database.
Contact:	Dialog in the US at (800) 334-2564, Dialog internationally at country specific locations.
User info:	To subscribe, contact Dialog directly.
Notes:	Coverage: current 15 months, excluding data in file 571.

`telnet://dialog.com`

EXPRESS Information Modeling Language

EXPRESS-Users

Discussion of topics pertaining to the EXPRESS information modeling language, such as information sources, how to download information, information modeling techniques, and sample models.

Keywords:	Programming, EXPRESS Information Modeling Language
Audience:	EXPRESS Programmers
Contact:	Steve Clark, Charlie Lindahl EXPRESS-users-request@cme.nist.gov
Details:	Free
User info:	To subscribe to the list, send an e-mail message requesting a subscription to the URL address below.

`mailto:EXPRESS-users-request@cme.nist.gov`

Extraterrestrial Life

alt.alien.visitors

A Usenet newsgroup providing information and discussion about space aliens on Earth and related stories.

Keywords:	UFOs, Aliens, Extraterrestrial Life
Audience:	Alien Enthusiasts
User info:	To subscribe to this Usenet newsgroup, you need access to a newsreader.

`news:alt.alien.visitors`

Extraterrestrials

A forum for academics, scientists and others interested in questions about the existence of intelligent life in the universe.

Keywords:	Astronomy, Extraterrestrial Life, Space
Sponsor:	University of Kent at Canterbury, United Kingdom
Audience:	Scientists, Astronomers, General Public
Contact:	Dr. Peter Moore pgm@ukc.ac.uk
User info:	To subscribe to the list, send an e-mail message to the URL address shown below consisting of a single line reading: SUB extraterrestrials YourFirstName YourLastName To send a message to the entire list, address it to: extraterrestrials@mailbase.ac.uk

`mailbase@mailbase.ac.uk`

The University of California Search for Extraterrestrial Civilizations

A web site containing information on the UC Berkeley SETI Program, SERENDIP (Search for Extraterrestrial Radio Emmisions from Nearby Developed Intelligent Populations), an ongoing scientific research effort aimed at detecting radio signals from extraterrestrial civilizations. Details about the program and updates on current research activities are also accessible.

Keywords:	Extraterrestrial Life, Astronomy, Aliens
Audience:	Astronomers, Physicists, Students, Educators, Engineers, General Public
Contact:	Dan Werthimer sereninfo@ssl.berkeley.edu
Details:	Free If Mosaic is available, use the http address below. Otherwise, please send a request for information to the contact address provided.

`http://sereninfo.ssl.berkeley.edu`

F

FairCom

ctree

A forum for the discussion of FairCom's C-Tree, R-Tree, and D-Tree products. This mailing list is not associated with FairCom. Discussion covers virtually all hardware and operating system ports.

Keywords:	Computers, FairCom
Audience:	Computer Operators
Contact:	Tony Olekshy alberta!oha!ctree-request
Details:	Free
User Info:	To subscribe to the list, send an e-mail message requesting a subscription to the URL address below. To send a message to the entire list, address it to: ctree

`mailto:alberta!oha!ctree-request`

Fam-Med

Fam-Med

An Internet resource and discussion group on computers in family medicine.

Keywords:	Medicine, Computers, Telecommunications
Sponsor:	Gustavus Adolphus College, Minnesota
Audience:	Health Care Professionals, Family Physicians
Profile:	Fam-Med is an electronic conference and file area that focuses on the use of computer and telecommunication technologies in the teaching and practice of family medicine. The conference and files are accessible to anyone able to send e-mail. The discussion on Fam-Med is distributed in two ways: by an unmoderated mail echo in which all posted messages are immediately distributed to subscribers without human intervention, and by a digest where messages accumulated over several days are assembled into a single document with erroneous posts deleted.
Contact:	Paul Kleeberg Paul@GAC.Edu
Details:	Free To join either the unmoderated list or the digest, send e-mail to the contact above. To post to Fam-Med, send e-mail to Fam-Med@GAC.Edu

`gopher://ftp.gac.edu/00/pub/E-mail-archives/fam-med/`

Family

BlindFam

The Blindness and Family Life mailing list is devoted to a discussion of the day-to-day impact of this disability on families, and the patterns of domestic life associated with blindness.

Keywords:	Blindness, Disabilities, Family
Audience:	Blind People, Families, Health Care Professionals, Rehabilitation Counselors
Contact:	Roger Myers, Patt Bromberger Meyers@ab.wvnet.edu, Patt@squid.tram.com
User Info:	To subscribe, send an e-mail message to the URL address below consisting of a single line reading: SUB BlindFam YourFirstName YourLastName. To send a message to the entire list, address it to: BlindFam@sjuvm.stjohns.edu

`mailto:listserv@sjuvm.stjohns.edu`

National Family Database—MAPP

This database contains family sociological and health data, including research briefs, bibliographies, census data, program ideas, reference materials, media materials, and publications.

Keywords:	Sociology, Family, Health
Sponsor:	Department of Agriculture Economics and Rural Sociology, Pennsylvania State University
Audience:	Sociologists, Public Health Policymakers, Health Care Providers
	To access the database select PENpages (1), then General Information (3) and finally Information on MAPP - National Family Database (5)

`telnet://penpages@psupen.psu.edu`

Family and Legal Status (INPADOC)

Family and Legal Status (INPADOC)

The database includes a listing of patents issued in 56 countries and patenting organizations.

Keywords:	Patents, Technlogy
Sponsor:	European Patent Office (EPO), Vienna, Austria

Family and Legal Status

Audience: Patent Researchers, Inventors

Profile: INPADOC contains bibliographic data consisting of title, inventor, and assignee for most patents. In addition, this file brings together information on priority-application numbers, countries and dates, and equivalent patents (for instance, patent families) for patents. This file also contains the legal status information for patents in some countries.

Contact: Dialog in the US at (800) 334-2564, Dialog internationally at country-specific locations.

User Info: To subscribe, contact Dialog directly.

Notes: Coverage: April 1968 to the present; updated weekly.

`telnet://dialog.com`

Family Practice

University of Texas Health Science Center at Tyler Library

The library's holdings are large and wide-ranging and contain significant collections in many fields.

Keywords: Biochemistry, Cardiopulmonary Medicine, Cell Biology, Family Practice, Molecular Biology

Audience: Researchers, Students, General Public

Details: Free

User Info: Expect: Username Prompt, Send: LIS

`telnet://athena.uthscsa.edu`

Family Science

Purdue University Library

The library's holdings are large and wide-ranging. They contain significant collections in many fields.

Keywords: Economics (History of), Literature (English), Literature (American), Indiana, Rogers (Bruce), Engineering (History of), Aviation, Earth Science, Atmospheric Science, Consumer Science, Family Science, Chemistry (History of), Physics, Veterinary Science

Audience: General Public, Researchers, Librarians, Document Delivery Professionals

Contact: Dan Ferrer
dan@asterix.lib.purdue.edu

Details: Free

User Info: Expect: User ID prompt, Send: GUEST

`telnet://lib.cc.purdue.edu`

FAQs

Internet Services FAQ

General information and answers to frequently asked questions (FAQs) about the Internet.

Keywords: Internet, Internet Guides, FAQs

Audience: Internet Surfers

Details: Free

User Info: File is: pub/usenet/news.answers/internet-services/faq

`ftp://rtfm.mit.edu`

Sci.space.news

Keywords: Space, FAQs

Audience: Space Flight Enthusiasts

Profile: This newsgroup carries recent information about the world's space programs. Reading the FAQ set is recommended before asking questions on the other sci.space. groups.

Contact: Peter Yee
yee@atlas.arc.nasa.gov

Details: Free, Moderated

To participate in a Usenet newsgroup you need access to a newsreader.

`news:sci.space.news`

Sex FAQ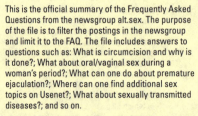

This is the official summary of the Frequently Asked Questions from the newsgroup alt.sex. The purpose of the file is to filter the postings in the newsgroup and limit it to the FAQ. The file includes answers to questions such as: What is circumcision and why is it done?; What about oral/vaginal sex during a woman's period?; What can one do about premature ejaculation?; Where can one find additional sex topics on Usenet?; What about sexually transmitted diseases?; and so on.

Keywords: Sex, FAQ

Audience: General Public

Contact: David Johnson, Snugglebunny
superdj@cs.mcgill.ca

Details: Free

`ftp://pit-manager.mit.edu/pub/usenet/news.answers/alt-sex/faq`

White House Frequently Asked Questions

This document is a good starting point for answering questions such as: How do I send e-mail to President Clinton? How do I get current news updates from the White House? Where can I get White House documents from?

Keywords: Clinton (Bill), Government (US), Politics (US), FAQs

Audience: General Public, Researchers

Details: Free

User Info: Expect: login; Send: anonymous; Expect: password; Send: your e-mail address; Expect: directory; Send: /pub/nic; Expect: file; Send: whitehouse FAQ.

`ftp://ftp.sura.net`

WWW FAQ

Answers to frequently-asked questions (FAQs) about World Wide Web (WWW), an Internet access tool.

Keywords: Internet Tools, WWW, FAQs

Audience: Internet Surfers

Details: Free

`ftp://info.cern.ch`

Farming

agmodels-l

A forum for the discussion of agricultural simulation models of all types. Issues include plant growth, micro-meteorology, soil hydrology, transport, farm economy, and farm systems.

Keywords: Agriculture, Farming

Audience: Agronomists

Contact: Jerome Pier
jp@unl.edu

User Info: To subscribe to the list, send an e-mail message to the URL address below consisting of a single line reading:

SUB agmodels-l YourFirstName YourLastName.

To send a message to the entire list, address it to: agmodels-l@unl.edu

`mailto:listserv@unl.edu`

Agriculture

This directory is a compilation of information resources focused on agriculture.

Keywords: Agriculture, Farming

Audience: Farmers, Agronomists, Agriculturalists

Contact: Wilfred Drew
drewwe@snymorva.cs.snymor.edu

Details: Free

`ftp://una.hh.lib.umich.edu`

`gopher://snymorvb.cs.snymor.edu`

`gopher://SNYMORVB.cs.snymor.edu`

Fashion Industry

alt.fashion

A Usenet newsgroup providing information and discussion about all facets of the fashion industry.

Keywords: Fashion Industry, Style
Audience: Designers, General Public
User Info: To subscribe to this Usenet newsgroup, you need access to a newsreader.

`news:alt.fashion`

Fashion Photography Conference

A conference on the WELL about photography; topics range from products and technical information to aesthetics and fashion photography.

Keywords: Photography, Fashion Industry
Audience: Photographers, Fashion Enthusiasts
Contact: Ralph E. Bedwell
ralf@well.sf.ca.us
To participate in a conference on the WELL, you must first establish an account on the WELL. To do so, start by typing: telnet well.sf.ca.us

`telnet://well.sf.ca.us`

Fashion Merchandising

University of Wisconsin at Stout Library

The library's holdings are large and wide-ranging and contain significant collections in many fields.

Keywords: Mathematics, Business, Fashion Merchandising, Home Economics, Hospitality, Tourism, Hotel Administration, Restaurant Management, Microelectronics
Audience: Researchers, Students, General Public
Details: Free
User Info: Expect: Login, Send: Lib; Expect: vDIAL Prompt, Send: Library

`telnet://lib.uwstout.edu`

FAX

SupraFAX

This list was created to help people who are using the SupraFAX v.32bis modem.

Keywords: Modem, FAX
Audience: Modem Users, FAX Users
Contact: David Tiberio
subscribe@xamiga.linet.org
Details: Free
User Info: To subscribe to the list, send an e-mail message requesting a subscription to the URL address below. To send a message to the entire list, address it to: subscribe@xamiga.linet.org

`mailto:subscribe@xamiga.linet.org`

FAXNET

FAXNET

FAXNET allows the user to send faxes via e-mail.

Keywords: Internet Services, E-mail
Audience: Internet Surfers, E-mail Users
Details: Free
User Info: Include the word "help" in the e-mail.

`mailto:info@awa.com`

FDA

Federal Food and Drug Administration

The Federal Food and Drug Administration (FDA) databank contains reports and articles related to the FDA.

Keywords: FDA, Drug Regulations, Nutrition
Sponsor: Federal Food and Drug Administration
Audience: Researchers, Nutritionists, Consumers, Health Care Providers
Profile: The topics covered include the drug and device product-approvals list, FDA federal register summaries by subject, text from drug bulletins, current information on AIDS, FDA consumer magazine index and selected articles, summaries of FDA information, text of testimony at FDA congressional hearings, and speeches given by the FDA commissioner and deputy.
Details: Free

`telnet://bbs@fdabbs.fda.gov`

Seafood Internet Network

A mailing list to facilitate information exchange about the HACCP Alliance and the implementation of the FDA seafood HACCP program.

Keywords: Food, FDA
Audience: Seafood Industry Professionals
Contact: Robert J. Price
rjprice@dale.ucdavis.edu
User Info: To subscribe, send an e-mail message to: listproc@ucdavis.edu Leave the subject blank and place in the body of the note: subscribe seafood YourFirstName YourLastName

`mailto:seafood@ucdavis.edu`

Federal Databases

GPO Gateway to Government Act of 1992: Senator Al Gore

A bill to establish an electronic gateway in the Government Printing Office (GPO) to provide public access to a wide range of Federal databases containing public information stored electronically.

Keywords: Government (US Federal), Federal Databases
Audience: General Public, Journalists, Politicians
Details: Free
User Info: File is: /pub/nic/NREN/GPO.bill.6-92

`ftp://ftp.sura.net`

A Grant Getter's Guide to the Internet

A summary of Internet-accessible information regarding federal grants.

Keywords: Grants, Federal Register (US), Federal Databases
Sponsor: University of Idaho, Moscow, Idaho, USA
Audience: Researchers, Scientists, Public Health Professionals, Students
Profile: This site is intended to provide federal grant information on the Internet. The focus is federal grant resources, including those sponsored by the National Institute of Health (NIH), the National Science Foundation (NSF), and the National Telecommunications and Information Administration (NTIA). This server also includes supplemental education-related information. This guide is searchable by keyword and contains pointers to such grant sources as the Federal Register, the National Science Foundation, the National Institutes of Health, and the Catalog of Federal Domestic Assistance. This same site allows direct access to many of the systems mentioned in the guide.
Contact: James Kearney, Marty Zimmerman
jkearney@raven.csrv.uidaho.edu,
martyz@uidaho.edu

`gopher://gopher.uidaho.edu/Science, Research, & Grant Information/Grant Information`

Questions and Answers about the GPO Gateway to Government Act

Questions and answers dealing with the bill GPO Gateway to Government Act of 1992. Questions such as, "What will the gateway do?," "Why is this gateway needed?," "What types of Information will be available through the Gateway?," and more.

Keywords: Laws (US Federal), Government (US Federal), Federal Databases
Audience: General Public, Journalists, Politicians
Details: Free
File is: /pub/nic/NREN/GPO.questions

`ftp://ftp.sura.net`

Federal Documents (US)

Miscellaneous Federal Documents

This directory includes documents such as the Civil Rights Act of 1991, the Computer Fraud and Abuse Act, the High-Performance Computing Senate Report, and more.

Keywords: Government (US Federal), Federal Documents (US)
Audience: Politicians, Journalists, Students (high school and up)
Details: Free

`gopher://wiretap.spies.com/11/Gov/US-Docs`

The Old Dominion University Library

★★

The library's holdings are large and wide-ranging and contain significant collections in many fields.

Keywords: Virginia, Federal Documents (US)
Audience: General Public, Researchers, Librarians, Document Delivery Professionals
Details: Free

`telnet://geac.lib.odu.edu`

Federal Government (US)

FinanceNet (National Performance Review)

★★★★

FinanceNet is intended to act as a forum for discussing the "reinvention" of government, to make it more cost effective and efficient.

Keywords: Finance, Federal Documents (US), Federal Register (US), Federal Government (US)
Sponsor: National Performance Review (NPR)
Audience: Government Officials, Journalists, Financial Analysts
Profile: FinanceNet is associated with Vice President Al Gore's National Performance Review (NPR). Available resources include text of Congressional testimony, agency reports, publications and announcements of upcoming events, all related to the improvement of federal money-managing and government accounting. It also has links to a number of other federal systems, including the NPR, Congressional Quarterly, and the Federal Register.
Contact: B. Preston Rich or Linda L. Hoogeveen Preston.Rich@nsf.gov or lhoog@tmn.com
Details: Free
Notes: Send a blank message to info@financenet.gov to receive more information about this project.

`gopher://gopher.financenet.gov`
`http://www.financenet.gov`

U.S. Army Area Handbooks

★★★

This gopher provides detailed political, cultural, historical, military, and economic information on hot spots in world affairs, everywhere from China to Yugoslavia.

Keywords: Military (US), Politics (International), Federal Government (US)
Sponsor: The Thomas Jefferson Library at the University of Missouri at St. Louis, St. Louis, Missouri, USA
Audience: Journalists, Government Officials, Travelers/Tourists
Profile: The Army Area Handbooks, which provide a comprehensive overview of several important countries including Japan, China, Israel, Egypt, South Korea, and Somalia, are only one of the many government resources available at this site. Other full-text documents include the proposed 1995 federal budget, the CIA world fact book, the NAFTA agreement, health care proposals currently before Congress, and statistics for the U.S. industrial outlook. Also has links to many federal gophers and information systems.
Contact: Joe Rottman rottman@umslvma.umsl.edu
Details: Free

`gopher://umslvma.umsl.edu/11/library/govdocs`

Federal Law (US)

Publications of the Office of Environment, Safety and Health

A collection of government safety information including updates, bulletins, and hazard alerts. Topics are diverse, covering everything from 'Employee Hit on Head by Falling Steel Wheel' to 'New Regulations to Control the Speed of Bloodborne Diseases.'

Keywords: Safety, Government (US), Federal Laws (US)
Sponsor: U.S. Department of Energy
Audience: Government Officials, General Public
Details: Free

`gopher://dewey.tis.inel.gov`

US House of Representatives Gopher

The online service of the U.S. House of Representatives.

Keywords: Congress (US), Federal Law (US), Government Records (US)
Sponsor: House Administration Committee Internet Working Group
Audience: Government Officials, Journalists, Educators (K-12), General Public
Profile: Provides access to information on members and committees of the House of Representatives, as well as full text of bills before the House. Includes education resources on the legislative process, Congressional directories, and House schedules. Also has information for visitors (including area maps), as well as access to other federal information systems.
Contact: House Internet Working Group househlp@hr.house.gov

`gopher://gopher.house.gov`

Federal Register

CODES (Codes Library)

The Codes Library offers access to US federal and state legislative materials, in codified, slip law, and bill form, plus federal and state regulatory materials and a statutes archive.

Keywords: Statutes, Codes, State, Federal Registry

Audience: (US) Lawyers

Profile: The Codes Library contains an extensive compilation of federal and state statutory materials, in codified as well as slip law form, from all 50 states, the District of Columbia, Puerto Rico, the Virgin Islands and the United States Code Service. The library also contains federal and state regulatory materials plus a statues archive. Pending legislation can be found with 50-state and federal fill tracking, the full text of federal bills, the Congressional Record, and the full text of bills for a growing number of states. Administrative materials include the Code of Federal Regulations, the Federal Register, 50-state regulation tracking, and the administrative codes for a selected number of states.

Contact: New Sales Group at (800) 227-4908 or (513) 859-5398 inside the US, or (513) 865-7981 for all inquires outside the US.

User Info: To subscribe, contact Mead directly.

To examine the Lexis user guide, you can access it at the ftp site of the University of Texas at Austin at the URL address: ftp://ftp.cc.utexas.edu

The files are in: /pub/ref-services/LEXIS

`telnet://nex.meaddata.com`

`http://www.meaddata.com`

A Grant Getter's Guide to the Internet

A summary of Internet-accessible information regarding federal grants.

Keywords: Grants, Federal Register, Federal Databases (US)

Sponsor: University of Idaho, Moscow, Idaho, USA

Audience: Researchers, Scientists, Public Health Professionals, Students

Profile: This site is intended to provide federal grant information on the Internet. The focus is federal grant resources, including those sponsored by the National Institute of Health (NIH), the National Science Foundation (NSF), and the National Telecommunications and Information Administration (NTIA). This server also includes supplemental education-related information. This guide is searchable by keyword and contains pointers to such grant sources as the Federal Register, the National Science Foundation, the National Institutes of Health, and the Catalog of Federal Domestic Assistance. This same site allows direct access to many of the systems mentioned in the guide.

Contact: James Kearney, Marty Zimmerman
jkearney@raven.csrv.uidaho.edu
martyz@uidaho.edu

`gopher://gopher.uidaho.edu/Science, Research, & Grant Information/Grant Information`

Internet Federal Register (IFR)

The full text of the US Federal Register.

Keywords: Federal Register, Government (US Federal), Law (US Federal)

Sponsor: Counterpoint Publishing

Audience: General Public, Journalists, Students, Politicians, Citizens

Contact: fedreg@internet.com

Details: Costs

`gopher://gopher.internet.com`

Federal Standards

IHS International Standards and Specifications

The database contains references to industry standards, and military and federal specifications and standards covering all aspects of engineering and related disciplines.

Keywords: Engineering, Military Specifications, Federal Standards

Sponsor: Information Handling Services, Englewood, CO, US

Audience: Engineers, Military Hisorians, Lawyers

Profile: The file includes 90% of the world's most referenced standards from over 70 domestic, foreign, and international standardizing bodies. Also included is the world's largest commercially available collection of unclassified active and historical US military and federal specifications and standards.

Contact: Dialog in the US at (800) 334-2564, Dialog internationally at country-specific locations.

User Info: To subscribe, contact Dialog directly.

Notes: Coverage: Current; updated weekly for MILSPECS, every two months.

`telnet://dialog.com`

FEDSEC (Federal Securities Library)

FEDSEC (Federal Securities Library)

The US Federal Securities library covers federal case law, Securities Exchanges Commission (SEC) materials, Commodities Futures Trading Commision (CFTC) materials and other legal and legislative materials relevant to the securities industry, as well as company information, news and analysis.

Keywords: Law, Filings, Securities, SEC

Audience: Lawyers, Bankers, Stock Brokers

Profile: The Federal Securities library contains over 60 separately searchable files covering federal case law: Securities Exchange Commision (SEC) no-action letters, decisions, orders, releases, and SEC filings (both full text and abstracts); Commodities Futures Trading Commision (CFTC) decisions, orders, releases; legislative materials; statutory and regulatory materials; selected RICO, class derivative, and collateralized mortgage obligations case law, rules and regulations; Federal Reserve Board materials; AICPA annual reports and accounting & audit literature files; Standard & Poors company information; state administrative decisions, orders, and releases; and company news and analysis information.

Contact: New Sales Group at (800) 227-4908 or 513-859-5398 inside the US, or 1-513-865-7981 for all inquires outside the US.

User Info: To subscribe, contact Mead directly.

To examine the Lexis user guide, you can access it at the ftp site of the University of Texas at Austin at the URL address: ftp://ftp.cc.utexas.edu

The files are in /pub/ref-services/LEXIS

`telnet://nex.meaddata.com`

`http://www.meaddata.com`

FEDTAX (Federal Tax Library)

FEDTAX (Federal Tax Library)

The Federal Tax Library offerers a comprehensive, up-to-date collection of tax-related materials, including case law, agency materials, legislative and regulatory materials, and so on.

Keywords: Law, Analysis, Tax

Audience: Lawyers

Profile:	The Federal Tax Library offers a comprehensive, up-to-date collection of tax-related materials. This library includes federal and state tax case law, Internal Revenue Service rulings and releases, state tax administrative decisions and rulings, the Internal Revenue Code, federal tax regulations, international news and treaties, tax looseleaf services, tax periodicals, tax law reviews, tax dailies, pending state legislation, and state property records.	Audience:	Educators, Language Students, Translators	Details:	Costs
		Contact:	Felipe Campos felipe@bongo.utexas.edu		Establish an account on the nearest APC node. Login, type c for conferences, then type: go amlat.mujeres.
		http://edb518ea.edb.utexas.edu		For information on the nearest APC node, contact: APC International Secretariat IBASE E-mail: apcadmin@apc.org

Feminism

alt.feminism

Contact:	New Sales Group at (800) 227-4908 or (513) 859-5398 inside the US, or (513) 865-7981 for all inquires outside the US.
User Info:	To subscribe, contact Mead directly.
	To examine the Lexis user guide, you can access it at the ftp site of the University of Texas at Austin at the URL address: ftp://ftp.cc.utexas.edu
	The files are in: /pub/ref-services/LEXIS

telnet://nex.meaddata.com

http://www.meaddata.com

A Usenet newsgroup providing information and discussion about feminism.

Keywords:	Feminism, Women's Studies, Abortion, Activism
Audience:	Women, General Public
User Info:	To subscribe to this Usenet newsgroup, you need access to a newsreader.

news:alt.feminism

Amazons International

An electronic digest newsletter for and about Amazons (physically and psychologically strong, assertive women who are challenging traditional ideas about gender roles, femininity, and the female physique).

Keywords:	Gender, Amazons, Feminism
Audience:	Women, Feminists, Writers, Art Historians
Profile:	The digest is dedicated to the image of the female hero in fiction and in fact, as it is expressed in art and literature, in the physiques and feats of female athletes, and in sexual values and practices; it also provides information, discussion, and a supportive environment for these values and issues.
Contact:	Thomas Gramstad amazons-request@math.uio.no
Details:	Free
User Info:	To subscribe to the list, send an e-mail message requesting a subscription to the URL address below.
	To send a message to the entire list, address it to: amazons@math.uio.no

mailto:amazons-request@math.uio.no

amlat.mujeres

This conference serves as a forum for interchange between organizations and women's movements in Latin America and the Caribbean.

Keywords:	Women, Latin America, Caribbean, Feminism
Audience:	Women, Feminists, Activists
Contact:	Agencia Latinoamericana de Informacion info@alai.ec, uualai@ecuanex.ec

FedWorld Bulletin Board

FedWorld Bulletin Board

A BBS run by the National Technical Information Service, with many databases of government documents, job announcements, and connections to other federal government online services.

Keywords:	US Federal Government, Government Documents
Sponsor:	US National Technical Information Service
Audience:	General Public, Researchers
Profile:	This is the place to begin any kind of search for US federal government records and publications. The GateWay option connects you to the Library of Congress, Supreme Court opinions, government job listing, the various Federal Reserve Banks, Congressional Bills and studies, and so on.
	To establish an account: Expect: login, Send: new
Notes:	Mail to sysop once you have an account.

telnet://fedworld.gov

Felipe's Bilingual WWW Pages

Felipe's Bilingual WWW Pages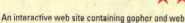

An interactive web site containing gopher and web links to various Latin American resources.

| Keywords: | Latin America, Education (Bilingual) |
| Sponsor: | University of Texas, Texas, USA |

telnet://igc.apc.org

apngowid.meet

A conference on plans by Asia Pacific regional women's groups for the United Nations Fourth World Conference on Women to be held in Beijing in September 1995.

Keywords:	Women, Asia, Pacific, Feminists, Development, United Nations, World Conference on Women
Audience:	Women, Feminism, Nongovernmental Organizations
Contact:	AsPac Info, Docu and Communication Committee AP-IDC@p95.f401.n751.z6.g
Details:	Costs, Moderated
	Establish an account on the nearest APC node. Login, type c for conferences, then type: go apngowid.meet.
	For information on the nearest APC node, contact: APC International Secretariat IBASE E-mail: apcadmin@apc.org

http://www.igc.apc.org/igc/www.women.html

dh.mujer

The primary Association for Progressive Communications conference for women and human rights issues throughout the world, contains news and announcements.

Keywords:	Women's Issues, Feminism, Human Rights
Audience:	Feminists, Activists
Contact:	Debra Guzman hrcoord@igc.apc.org
Details:	Costs
	Establish an account on the nearest APC node. Login, type c for conferences, then type go dh.mujer.
	For information on the nearest APC node, contact: APC International Secretariat IBASE E-mail: apcadmin@apc.org

Contact: Carlos Afonso (cafonso@ax.apc.org) or
APC North American Regional Office
E-mail: apcadmin@apc.org
Edie Farwell (efarwell@igc.apc.org)

gopher://gopher.telnet://igc.apc.org

http://igc.apc.org

The English Server

A large and eclectic collection of humanities resources.

Keywords: Humanities, Academia, English, Popular Culture, Feminism
Sponsor: Carnegie Mellon University English Department, Pittsburgh, Pennsylvania, USA
Audience: General Public, University Students, Educators (College/University), Researchers (Humanities)
Profile: Contains archives of conventional humanities materials, such as historical documents and classic books in electronic form. Also offers more unusual and hard-to-find resources, particularly in the field of popular culture and media. Features access to many humanities and culture-related online journals such as Bad Subjects, FineArt Forum, and Postmodern Culture. Also has links to a wide variety of related Internet sites and resources.
Contact: Geoff Sauer
postmaster@english-server.hss.cmu.

gopher://english-server.hss.cmu.edu

http://english-server.hss.cmu.edu

Forum for Women's Issues

A forum for issues relating to women.

Keywords: Women, General Interest, Feminism
Audience: Women
Contact: Reva Basch
reva@well.sf.ca.us
Details: Free
To participate in a conference on the WELL, you must first establish an account on the WELL. To do so, start by typing: telnet://well.sf.ca.us

telnet://well.sf.ca.us

hr.women

A conference on human rights issues pertaining to women.

Keywords: Women, Feminism, Human Rights
Audience: Women, Feminists, Activists
Contact: Jillaine Smith
jillaine@igc.apc.org

Details: Costs
Establish an account on the nearest APC node. Login, type c for conferences, then type go hr.women.
For information on the nearest APC node, contact: APC International Secretariat IBASE E-mail: apcadmin@apc.org
Contact: Carlos Afonso (cafonso@ax.apc.org) or
APC North American Regional Office
E-mail: apcadmin@apc.org
Edie Farwell (efarwell@igc.apc.org)

telnet://igc.apc.org

InforM Women's Studies Database

A gopher- or FTP-accessible archive of documents, opportunities, and resources pertaining to women's studies and women's issues.

Keywords: Women's Studies, Feminism, Women
Audience: Women, Women's Studies Students, Women's Studies Educators, Other Women's Issues Observers
Profile: This women's studies database is an easily navigable archive of files on women's studies and women's issues. It includes information such as health, employment opportunities, political issues, gender issues in the workplace and in education, reproductive rights, sex discrimination, sexual harassment, violence, work and family, women and computers, feminist film reviews, and poetry. InforM contains a compilation of electronic forums (listservs and newsgroups) for the discussion of male/female relations, societal problems, and for women of diverse cultures and sexual persuasions.
Contact: Paula Gaber
Gaber@info.umd.edu
Details: Free
Gopher or telnet to Inform.umd.edu, select Educational Resources/Women's Studies/. Or FTP to Inform.umd.edu, log in as anonymous, then cd /inforM/Educational_Resources/WomensStudies/
This source is also accessible through gopher, ftp, or telnet.

gopher://inform.umd.edu

http://inform.umd.edu/welcome.html

Notable Women

A database listing some important and notable women through the ages. Available for online searching by keyword, or as a full-text file.

Keywords: Women's Studies, History (Women's), Feminism
Sponsor: Estrella Mountain Community College (Arizona)

Audience: Women's Studies Educators, Historians, Researchers, Feminists
Contact: EMC Gopher Team
root@gopher.emc.maricopa.edu

gopher://gopher.emc.maricopa.edu

Women's Studies and Resources

A collection of materials related to women's studies and issues.

Keywords: Women's Studies, Feminism
Sponsor: Peripatetic Eclectic Gopher (PEG) at UC Irvine
Audience: Women, Feminists, Activists, Women's Studies Educators and Students
Profile: Contains bibliographies, listserv archives, conference announcements, and other resources related to women's studies. Also has links to other groups and sites related to women's issues.
Contact: Calvin Boyer
cjboyer@uci.edu

gopher://peg.cwis.uci.edu

Women.forum

Conference for discussion of women's issues.

Keywords: Women, Feminism, Women's Issues
Audience: Women, Feminists
Contact: Corina Hughes
corina@igc.apc.org
Details: Costs
User Info.: Establish an account on the nearest APC node. Login, type c for conferences, then type go women.forum. For information on the nearest APC node, contact: APC International Secretariat IBASE E-mail: apcadmin@apc.org Contact: Carlos Afonso (cafonso@ax.apc.org) or APC North American Regional Office E-mail: apcadmin@apc.org Contact: Edie Farwell (efarwell@igc.apc.org)
Notes: ALAI: Agencia Latinoamericana de Informacion E-mail message to APCadmin@apc.org

telnet://igc.apc.org

Women.health

This conference features articles, documents, news, announcements, policy statements, and other information about women's health around the world. Topics include breast cancer, ovarian cancer, alcohol, abortion, pregnancy, sterilization of women, pesticides, Quinacrine, HIV, disability.

Keywords: Women, Abortion, AIDS, Disability, Feminism, Health
Audience: Activists, Family Planners, Health Professionals, Non-Governmental Organizations, Women

Feminism

Details:	Costs	
	Establish an account on the nearest APC node. Login, type c for conferences, then type go women.health. For information on the nearest APC node, contact: APC International Secretariat IBASE E-mail: apcadmin@apc.org Contact: Carlos Afonso (cafonso@ax.apc.org) or APC North American Regional Office E-mail: apcadmin@apc.org Contact: Edie Farwell (efarwell@igc.apc.org)	
Notes:	ALAI: Agencia Latinoamericana de Informacion e-mail message to APCadmin@apc.org	

`telnet://igc.apc.org`

Women.news

This conference features news and action alerts about women and women's issues around the world, including human rights, feminism, health, sexual abuse, workers, population, abortion, activism, development, and peace.

Keywords:	Feminism, Gender, Women
Audience:	Women, Feminists, Activists
Contact:	Debra Guzman, Sue VanHattum hrcoord@igc.apc.org or suev@igc.apc.org
Details:	Free
	Establish an account on the nearest APC node. Login, type c for conferences, then type go women.news. For information on the nearest APC node, contact: APC International Secretariat IBASE E-mail: apcadmin@apc.org
Contact:	Carlos Afonso (cafonso@ax.apc.org) or APC North American Regional Office E-mail: apcadmin@apc.org or Edie Farwell (efarwell@igc.apc.org)
Notes:	Alai: Agencia Latinoamericana De Informacion E-mail message to APCadmin@apc.org

`telnet://igc.apc.org`

Fen

rec.arts.anime ★

A Usenet newsgroup providing information and discussion about Japanese animation fen.

Keywords:	Animation, Fen, Japan
Audience:	Animators
Details:	Free
User Info:	To subscribe to this Usenet newsgroup, you need access to a newsreader.

`news:rec.arts.anime`

Fiction

Online BookStore (OBS) ★★★

Offers full text (fiction and nonfiction) in a variety of electronic formats, free and for a fee.

Keywords:	Online Books, Books, ShareWord, Fiction, Nonfiction Books
Sponsor:	Editorial Inc./OBS
Audience:	General Public, Reading Enthusiasts
Profile:	Started in 1992, the OBS offers a variety of full-text titles.
Contact:	Laura Fillmore laura@editorial.com
Details:	Costs, Moderated, Images, Multimedia
User Info:	To subscribe to the list, send an e-mail message requesting a subscription to the URL address below.

`mailto:laura@editorial.com`

University of Northern Iowa Library

The library's holdings are large and wide-ranging and contain significant collections in many fields.

Keywords:	Art, Business Information, Education, Music, Fiction
Audience:	Researchers, Students, General Public
Contact:	Mike Yohe yohe@uni.edu
Details:	Free
User Info:	Expect: Login; Send: Public

`telnet://infosys.uni.edu`

University of Pennsylvania PENNINFO Library

The library's holdings are large and wide-ranging and contain significant collections in many fields.

Keywords:	Church History, Spanish Inquisition, Witchcraft, Shakespeare (William), Bibles, Aristotle (Texts of), Fiction, Whitman (Walt), French Revolution, Drama (French), Literature (English), Literature (Spanish)
Audience:	Researchers, Students, General Public
Contact:	Al DSouza penninfo-admin@dccs.upenn.edu dsouza@dccs.upenn.edu
Details:	Free
User Info:	Expect: Login; Send: Public

`telnet://penninfo.upenn.edu`

Filings

BKRTCY (Bankruptcy Library)

The Federal Bankruptcy library is a comprehensive collection of primary and secondary legal research materials pertaining to bankruptcy issues.

Keywords:	Law, Filings, Bankruptcy
Audience:	Lawyers, Bankers
Profile:	The Federal Bankruptcy library is a comprehensive collection of primary and secondary legal research materials that includes case law, rules, statutory and regulatory materials, legal publications, accounting literature and other resources pertaining to bankruptcy issues.
Contact:	New Sales Group at (800) 227-4908 or (513) 859-5398 inside the US, or (513) 865-7981 for all inquires outside the US.
User Info:	To subscribe, contact Mead directly.
	To examine the Lexis user guide, you can access it at the ftp site of the University of Texas at Austin at the URL address: ftp://ftp.cc.utexas.edu
	The files are in /pub/ref-services/LEXIS

`telnet://nex.meaddata.com`

`http://www.meaddata.com`

COMPNY

The COMPNY library contains more than 75 files of business and financial information, including thousands of in-depth company and industry research reports from leading national and international investments banks and brokerage houses.

Keywords:	Companies, Financials, Filings, Disclosure
Audience:	Business and Financial Researchers, Analysts, Entrepreneurs and Regulators.
Profile:	COMPNY includes the following types of information:

- Full-text 10-Q, 10-K, Annual Reports to Shareholders and Proxy filings.
- Extracts of filings for more than 11,000 public companies whose securities are traded on the major exchanges as well as over-the-counter.
- Abstracts of S-registration statements, 13-Ds, 14-Ds, 8Ks, Form 4s and other SEC filings updated on a daily basis.
- Business news abstracts from more than 400 information sources.
- Daily US economic trends and forecasts.

The materials may be searched in individual files, such as brokerage house reports, or in group files organized by subject, such as SEC filings.

Contact:	Mead New Sales Group at (800) 227-4908 or (513) 859-5398 inside the US, or (513) 865-7981 for all inquiries outside the US.
User Info:	To subscribe, contact Mead directly.
	To examine the Nexis user guide, you can access it at the ftp site of the University of Texas at Austin at the URL address: ftp://ftp.cc.utexas.edu
	The files are in: /pub/ref-services/LEXIS

telnet://nex.meaddata.com

http://www.meaddata.com

FEDSEC (Federal Securities Library)

The US Federal Securities library covers federal case law, Securities Exchanges Commission (SEC) materials, Commodities Futures Trading Commision (CFTC) materials and other legal and legislative materials relevant to the securities industry, as well as company information, news and analysis.

Keywords:	Law, Filings, Securities, SEC
Audience:	Lawyers, Bankers, Stockbrokers
Profile:	The Federal Securities library contains over 60 separately searchable files covering federal case law: Securities Exchange Commision (SEC) no-action letters, decisions, orders, releases, and SEC filings (both full text and abstracts); Commodities Futures Trading Commision (CFTC) decisions, orders, releases; legislative materials; statutory and regulatory materials; selected RICO, class derivative, and collateralized mortgage obligations case law, rules and regulations; Federal Reserve Board materials; AICPA annual reports and accounting and audit literature files; Standard & Poors company information; state administrative decisions, orders, and releases; and company news and analysis information.
Contact:	New Sales Group at (800) 227-4908 or 513-859-5398 inside the US, or 1-513-865-7981 for all inquires outside the US.
User Info:	To subscribe, contact Mead directly.
	To examine the Lexis user guide, you can access it at the ftp site of the University of Texas at Austin at the URL address: ftp://ftp.cc.utexas.edu
	The files are in: /pub/ref-services/LEXIS

telnet://nex.meaddata.com

http://www.meaddata.com

INCORPR (Corporation and Partnership Records)

The Corporation and Partnership Records (INCORP) library contains current US corporation and partnership filings.

Keywords:	Corporations, Partnerships, Filings, Trademarks
Audience:	Corporations, Lawyers, Researchers
Profile:	The INCORP library contains current records on corporations and limited partnerships registered with the office of the Secretary or Department of State. These records include information extracted by the state's staff from articles of incorporation, annual reports, amendments, and other public filings.
Contact:	Mead New Sales Group at (800) 227-4908 or (513) 859-5398 inside the US, or (513) 865-7981 for all inquiries outside the US.
User Info:	To subscribe, contact Mead directly.
	To examine the Nexis user guide, you can access it at the ftp site of the University of Texas at Austin at the URL address: ftp://ftp.cc.utexas.edu
	The files are in: /pub/ref-services/LEXIS

telnet://nex.meaddata.com

http://www.meaddata.com

NAARS (National Automated Accounting Research System)

The National Automated Accounting Research System (NAARS) library, provided as a service by agreement with the American Institute of Certified Public Accountants (AICPA) contains a variety of accounting information.

Keywords:	Accounting, Auditing, Filings, Publications
Audience:	Accountants
Profile:	The NAARS library contains annual reports of public corporations and accounting literature and publications for the accounting professional. Annual reports are annotated with descriptive terms assigned by the AICPA. These terms allow the user to search for annual report footnotes that illustrate one or more recognized accounting practices.
Contact:	Mead New Sales Group at (800) 227-4908 or (513) 859-5398 inside the US, or (513) 865-7981 for all inquiries outside the US.
User Info:	To subscribe, contact Mead directly.
	To examine the Nexis user guide, you can access it at the ftp site of the University of Texas at Austin at the URL address: ftp://ftp.cc.utexas.edu
	The files are in: /pub/ref-services/LEXIS

telnet://nex.meaddata.com

http://www.meaddata.com

SEC (Securities and Exchange Commission) EDGAR (Electronic Data Gathering, Analysis and Retrieval) System

Provides free access to 1994 SEC filings for approximately 2,300 companies.

Keywords:	Securities, Filings, SEC, Stock Market
Sponsor:	New York University School of Business
Audience:	Business Professionals, Investors
Profile:	This expanding project aims to make available current, public SEC filings that are filed electronically. The system is searchable by company name and is updated and indexed daily. Many types of SEC forms, including 10-K and 10-Q financial reports, are available in a number of different electronic formats. The site also provides some explanatory documentation on the EDGAR program and on the types of SEC forms and information available to the public.
Contact:	Ajit Kambil piotr@edgar.stern.nyu.edu
Details:	Free

ftp://town.hall.org/edgar

http://www.town.hall.org

Film

alt.cult-movies

A Usenet newsgroup providing information and discussion about popular movies.

Keywords:	Film, Popular Culture
Audience:	Movie Watchers, Critics
User Info:	To subscribe to this Usenet newsgroup, you need access to a newsreader.

news:alt.cult-movies

ANIME-L

This discussion list covers animation news, with a special emphasis on Japanese "animedia."

Keywords:	Animation, Film, Japan
Audience:	Animation Enthusiasts, Animators
Details:	Free
User Info:	To subscribe to the list, send an e-mail message to the address below, consisting of a single line reading:
	Sub anime-l YourFirstName YourLastName
	To send a message to the entire list, address it to: anime-l@vtvm1.bitnet

mailto:listserv@vtvm1.cc.vt.edu

CinemaSpace

CinemaSpace, from the Film Studies Program at UC Berkeley, is devoted to all aspects of Cinema and New Media.

Keywords:	Cinema, Film, Multimedia
Sponsor:	Film Studies Program at UC Berkeley
Audience:	Students, Film researchers

Profile: Projects for CinemaSpace include academic papers on film and new media, film theory and critique, multimedia lectures, and sources of film clips and references to other sites.
Contact: xcohen@garnet.berkeley.edu
Details: Free

http://remarque.berkeley.edu/~xcohen

Film and Video

This directory is a compilation of information resources focused on film and video.
Keywords: Film, Video, Entertainment
Audience: Students, Producers, Artists
Details: Free

ftp://una.hh.lib.umich.edu/70/inetdirsstacks/filmvideo:woodgarlock

Filmmaking Conference

A conference on the WELL about the technical, theoretical, and aesthetic issues of filmmaking; includes listings of film and video festivals.
Keywords: Film, Filmmaking, Video
Audience: Filmmakers
Contact: Sandy Santra
trevor@well.sf.ca.us
Details: Costs
To participate in a conference on the WELL, you must first establish an account on the WELL. To do so, start by typing: telnet well.sf.ca.us

telnet://well.sf.ca.us

Iowa State University

The library's holdings contain significant collections in many fields.
Keywords: Agriculture, Veterinary Medicine, Statistics, Labor, Soil Conservation, Film
Audience: General Public, Researchers, Librarians, Document Delivery Professionals
Details: Free
User Info: Expect: DIAL, Send: LIB

telnet://isn.iastate.edu

National Broadcasting Society— Alpha Epsilon Rho

Forum for mass media professionals to share experiences and ideas.
Keywords: Film, Television, Radio, Mass Media
Sponsor: National Broadcasting Society-Alpha Epsilon Rho
Audience: Journalists, Students, Educators, Broadcasting Professionals

Contact: Reg Gamar
regbc@cunyvm.bitnet
Details: Free
User Info: To subscribe to the list, send an e-mail message to the address shown below consisting of a single line reading:
SUB NBS-AER YourFirstName YourLastName
To send a message to the entire list, address it to: nbs-aer@cunyvm.bitnet

mailto:listserv@cunyvm.bitnet

news: aus.films

Discussion of films and the film industry from an Australian perspective.
Keywords: Film, Australia
Audience: Australia Enthusiasts, Film Enthusiasts
Details: Free
User Info: To subscribe to a Usenet newsgroup, you need access to a "newsreader."

news:aus.films

rec.arts.movies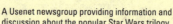

A Usenet newsgroup providing information and discussion about films and film making.
Keywords: Film
Audience: Film Enthusiasts, Filmmakers
Details: Free
User Info: To subscribe to this Usenet newsgroup, you need access to a newsreader.

news:rec.arts.movies

rec.arts.sf.starwars

A Usenet newsgroup providing information and discussion about the popular Star Wars trilogy.
Keywords: Science Fiction, Film
Audience: Star Wars Enthusiasts, Movie Viewers
User Info: To subscribe to this Usenet newsgroup, you need access to a newsreader.

news:rec.arts.sf.starwars

rec.arts.startrek.misc

A Usenet newsgroup providing general information and discussion about all aspects of Star Trek, including its various television and film reviews.
Keywords: Television, Film
Audience: Trekkies, Television Viewers, Movie Viewers
User Info: To subscribe to this Usenet newsgroup, you need access to a newsreader.

news:rec.arts.startrek.misc

rec.video

A Usenet newsgroup providing information and discussion about video.
Keywords: Video, Art, Film, Computer Art
Audience: Cinematographers, Video Artists
User Info: To subscribe to this Usenet newsgroup, you need access to a newsreader.

news:rec.video

Theater, Film & Television

This directory is a compilation of information resources focused on theater, film & television.
Keywords: Theater, Film, Television
Audience: Theater Personnel, Film Personnel, Television Personnel
Details: Free

ftp://una.hh.lib.umich.edu/70/inetdirsstacks/filmtv:robinson

University of North Carolina at Greensboro MINERVA Library

The library's holdings are large and wide-ranging and contain significant collections in many fields.
Keywords: Herbert (George), Film, Dickinson (Emily), Children's Books
Audience: Researchers, Students, General Public
Details: Free
User Info: Expect: Login; Send: Info or MINERVA

telnet://steffi.acc.uncg.edu

Filmmaking

Filmmaking Conference

A conference on the WELL about the technical, theoretical, and aesthetic issues of filmmaking; includes listings of film and video festivals.
Keywords: Film, Filmmaking, Video
Audience: Filmmakers
Contact: Sandy Santra
trevor@well.sf.ca.us
Details: Costs
To participate in a conference on the WELL, you must first establish an account on the WELL. To do so, start by typing: telnet well.sf.ca.us

telnet://well.sf.ca.us

FINALE

FINALE Discussion List

Discussion list targeted towards people who use the FINALE music notation program.

Keywords:	Music Notation, FINALE
Sponsor:	CODA
Audience:	FINALE Program Users
Profile:	The music notation program FINALE (for Macintosh and Windows) provides the basis for the chief discussion on this list. Other CODA products, as well as various notation programs, are also suitable topics.
Contact:	Henry Howey mus_heh@SHSU.edu
Details:	Free
User Info:	To subscribe to the list, send an e-mail message to the URL address below, consisting of a single line reading: SUB finale YourFirstName YourLastName

`mail to: listserv@shsu.edu`

Finance

Banking News Library

The Banking News library provides you specific banking industry sources. More than 40 full-text and selected full-text sources which focus on the banking related news and issues.

Keywords:	Banking, Finance, Regulation
Audience:	Journalists, Banking Industry Analysts
Profile:	This library contains news, Investext Industry Reports, and legal/regulatory information. Also included in an abstract files is the Financial Industry Information Service (FINIS). The S&L file includes documents from newspapers and magazines which are specific to the S&L.
Contact:	Mead New Sales Group at (800) 227-4908 or (513) 859-5398 inside the US, or (513) 865-7981 for all inquiries outside the US.
User Info:	To subscribe, contact Mead directly. To examine the Nexis user guide, you can access it at the ftp site of the University of Texas at Austin at the URL address: ftp://fp.cc.utexas.edu The files are in: /pub/ref-services/LEXIS

`telnet://nex.meaddata.com`

`http://www.meaddata.com`

Budget of the United States (1994)

Provides the full text of the 1994 budget of the United States.

Keywords:	Budget, Government (US), Finance
Audience:	Politicians, Lawyers, Journalists, Economists, Students, US Citizens
Details:	Free
Notes:	This document is over one megabyte in size and thus takes a couple of minutes to load onto the screen.

`gopher://wiretap.spies.com/00/Gov/US-Gov/budget.94`

Business Wire

The database contains the unedited text of news releases from over 10,000 diverse news sources: companies, public relations firms, government agencies, political organizations, colleges and universities, and research institutes.

Keywords:	Business, Finance, and Industry
Sponsor:	Business Wire, San Francisco, CA, USA
Audience:	Business Analysts, Market Researchers, General Public
Profile:	Approximately 90% of all releases carried by Business Wire are business/financial, covering essentially every category of business and industry. News releases include all information on earnings, dividend announcements, mergers and acquisitions, major contract awards, new products, new security offerings, takeovers, restructurings, and more. Business Wire transmits the full, unedited text of these releases, complete with financial statements and other details that are not generally made available by the press. In addition, all releases carry the name and telephone number of a contact person within that company. Also contained are news on other subjects, such as entertainment, travel, sports, politics, medicine and science, and lifestyles.
Contact:	Dialog in the US at (800) 334-2564, Dialog internationally at country specific locations.
Details:	Costs
User Info:	To subscribe, contact Dialog directly.

`telnet://dialog.com`

COMPNY

The COMPNY library contains more than 75 files of business and financial information, including thousands of in-depth company and industry research reports from leading national and international investments banks and brokerage houses.

Keywords:	Companies, Finance, Filings, Disclosure
Audience:	Business and Financial Researchers, Analysts, Entrepreneurs and Regulators.
Profile:	COMPNY includes the following types of information: • Full-text 10-Q, 10-K, Annual Reports to Shareholders and Proxy filings. • Extracts of filings for more than 11,000 public companies whose securities are traded on the major exchanges as well as over-the-counter. • Abstracts of S-registration statements, 13-Ds, 14-Ds, 8Ks, Form 4s and other SEC filings updated on a daily basis. • Business news abstracts from more than 400 information sources. • Daily US economic trends and forecasts. The materials may be searched in individual files, such as brokerage house reports, or in group files organized by subject, such as SEC filings.
Contact:	Mead New Sales Group at (800) 227-4908 or (513) 859-5398 inside the US, or (513) 865-7981 for all inquiries outside the US.
User Info:	To subscribe, contact Mead directly. To examine the Nexis user guide, you can access it at the ftp site of the University of Texas at Austin at the URL address: ftp://ftp.cc.utexas.edu The files are in: /pub/ref-services/LEXIS

`telnet://nex.meaddata.com`

`http://www.meaddata.com`

INVEST (Investment News and Information)

The INVEST library contains company and industry research reports provided through the Investext(R) database. These reports are created by industry experts who are employed for their accurate and insightful evaluation. Only the most recent 12 months of data will be displayed.

Keywords:	Companies, Finance, Analysis
Audience:	Business Researchers, Analysts, Entrepreneurs
Profile:	INVEST is categorized by type. Selections can be made using these categories: Industry (more than 50 industries are available), State (where a specific company is located), Country (Country in which the company is located), US Broker or International Broker. The INVEST library provides an automatic display following the selection of a file. For industry reports, a menu will appear providing definitions as they relate to the industries. All remaining files will provide a confirmation of the file selected.
Contact:	Mead New Sales Group at (800) 227-4908 or (513) 859-5398 inside the US, or (513) 865-7981 for all inquiries outside the US.

User Info: To subscribe, contact Mead directly.

To examine the Nexis user guide, you can access it at the ftp site of the University of Texas at Austin at the URL address: ftp://ftp.cc.utexas.edu

The files are in: /pub/ref-services/LEXIS

`telnet://nex.meaddata.com`

`http://www.meaddata.com`

D&B - Duns Financial Records Plus

This database provides up to three years of comprehensive financial statements for over 650,000 private and public companies.

Keywords: Finance, Business, Dun & Bradstreet

Sponsor: Dun & Bradstreet Information Services, Parsippany, NJ, USA

Audience: Business Professionals

Profile: Information provided includes balance sheet, income statement, and 14 of the most widely used business ratios for measuring solvency, efficiency, and profitability. A company's financial position can be compared to those of others in the same industry as determined by industry norm percentages. In addition, there are over 1.2 million records included that contain company history and operations background only. DFR also contains company identification data, such as company name, address, primary and secondary SIC codes, D-U-N-S number, and number of employees. Textual paragraphs cover the history and operations background of a firm. Coverage: Current; updated quarterly.

Contact: Dialog in the US at (800) 334-2564, Dialog internationally at country-specific locations.

Details: Costs

User Info: To subscribe, contact Dialog directly.

`telnet://dialog.com`

D&B - Dun's Electronic Business Directory

Keywords: Finance, Business, Dun & Bradstreet

Sponsor: Dun & Bradstreet Information Services, Parsippany, NJ, USA

Audience: Business Professionals, Business Analysts

Profile: A full directory listing is provided for each entry, including address, telephone number, SIC codes and descriptions, and number of employees. The file covers both public and private US companies of all sizes and types. Fifteen broad business categories are indexed as industry groups: agriculture, business services, communication, construction, finance, insurance, manufacturing, mining, professional services, public administration, real estate, retail, transportation, utilities, and wholesale. Data for the file is compiled and maintained primarily through Dun & Bradstreet's intensive credit interviewing process. Dun's staff of 1,300 business analysts actively interviews millions of entrepreneurs each year. This information is supplemented with data from large-volume telemarketing and direct mail campaigns. Coverage: Current; updated quarterly.

Contact: Dialog in the US at (800) 334-2564, Dialog internationally at country-specific locations.

Details: Costs

User Info: To subscribe, contact Dialog directly.

`telnet://dialog.com`

Dun & Bradstreet Corporation

Dun and Bradstreet's home page contains examples of existing services, services in development, and business and financial information, advising and so on.

Keywords: Finance, Business

Audience: General Public, Business Professionals

Profile: Files include company news, related industry information, product descriptions, and discussions of IBM's services.

`http://www.corp.dnb.com`

Experimental Stock Market Data

This is an experimental page that provides a link to the latest stock market information.

Keywords: Stock Market, Investments, Finance

Audience: General Public, Investors, Stock Brokers

Profile: This site is updated automatically, to reflect the current day's closing information. Provides general market news and quotes for selected stocks, although prices are not guaranteed. Also includes recent prices for many mutual funds, as well as technical analysis charts for a large number of stocks and mutual funds.

Contact: Mark Torrance stockmaster@ai.mit.edu

Details: Free

`http://www.ai.mit.edu/stocks.html`

FinanceNet (National Performance Review)

FinanceNet is intended to act as a forum for discussing the "reinvention" of government, to make it more cost effective and efficient.

Keywords: Finance, Federal Documents (US), Federal Register (US), Federal Government (US)

Sponsor: National Performance Review (NPR)

Audience: Government Officials, Journalists, Financial Analysts

Profile: FinanceNet is associated with Vice President Al Gore's National Performance Review (NPR). Available resources include text of Congressional testimony, agency reports, publications and announcements of upcoming events, all related to the improvement of federal money-managing and government accounting. It also has links to a number of other federal systems, including the NPR, Congressional Quarterly, and the Federal Register.

Contact: B. Preston Rich or Linda L.Hoogeveen Preston.Rich@nsf.gov or lhoog@tmn.com

Details: Free

Notes: Send a blank message to info@financenet.gov to receive more information about this project.

`gopher://gopher.financenet.gov`

`http://www.financenet.gov/`

Global Internet

A full-service Internet provider, offering superior quality Internet access and value-added services to business professionals, researchers, and educational communities.

Keywords: Internet, Finance

Sponsor: Global Internet, Palo Alto, CA (415) 855-1700

Audience: Internet Users, Business Professionals, Financial Analysts, Publishers

Details: Costs

`mailto:sales@gi.net`

misc.invest

A Usenet newsgroup providing information and discussion about how to invest money.

Keywords: Investments, Finance

Audience: General Public

Details: Free

User Info: To subscribe to this Usenet newsgroup, you need access to a newsreader.

`news:misc.invest`

Stock Market Secrets

Publication of a stock market-related daily commentary. Questions are answered on a wide variety of investment and financial topics.

Keywords: Stock Market, Investments, Finance

Audience: Investors, Stock Brokers, Financial Advisors

Contact: smi-request@world.std.com

Details: Free, Moderated

User Info: To subscribe to the list, send an e-mail message requesting a subscription to the URL address below. To send a message to the entire list, address it to: smi@world.std.com

`mailto:smi-request@world.std.com`

US General Accounting Office Transitional Reports

A major directory on accounting, providing access to a broad range of related resources (library catalogs, databases, and servers) via the Internet.

Keywords: Government (US), Finance
Audience: Politicians, Government Workers
Profile: Contains full-text documents of the Transitional Reports for the U.S. General Accounting Office. Reports includes Budget Issues, Investment, Government Management Issues, Financial Management Issues, Health Care Reform, National Security Issues, International Trade Issues, and so on.
Contact: kh3@cu.nih.gov

`gopher://thor.ece.uc.edu`

Finding E-mail Addresses

Finding E-mail Addresses

Tips on finding e-mail addresses.

Keywords: Internet, E-mail
Audience: Internet Surfers
Contact: Jonathan Kamens
jib@MIT.Edu
Details: Free
File is pub/docs/about-the-net/libsoft/email_address.txt

`ftp://sunsite.unc.edu`

Finding Resources on the Internet

Finding Resources on the Internet

A collection of help files introducing the new user to Internet utilities and resources.

Keywords: Internet Reference, Information Retrieval
Sponsor: Proper Publishing
Audience: Internet Surfers
Contact: info@proper.com

`gopher://proper.com`

Fine Arts

Art-support

A UK Mailbase forum for the discussion of art-related matters.

Keywords: Art, Fine Arts
Audience: Artists, Art Enthusiasts, Art Students
Login guest; password mailbase

`gopher://mailbase@mailbase.ac.uk`

`mailto:art-support-request@mailbase.ac.uk`

`telnet://mailbase.ac.uk`

HypArt

This is the site of an International collaborative art project.

Keywords: Art, Fine Art
Sponsor: University of Hamburg
Audience: Artists, Designers
Contact: rosenfeld@rrz.uni-hamburg.de
Details: Free

`http://rzsun01.rrz.uni-hamburg.de/cgi-bin/HypArt.sh`

Internet Art Gallery

An online art collection in the form of JPEG files, including the works of 85 artists ranging from Dali to Van Eyck.

Keywords: Art, Fine Art, Art History
Sponsor: New York State Education Department
Audience: Artists, Art Students, Art Teachers, General Public
Contact: Steve Richter, George Casler
steve@unix5.nysed.gov,
gcasler@unix5.nysed.gov

`gopher://unix5.nysed.gov`

rec.arts.fin

A Usenet newsgroup providing information and discussion about the visual arts. Discussions range from archival materials to Ansel Adams, Mary Cassat, and Andy Warhol.

Keywords: Art, Fine Art
Audience: Artists, Art Educators, Art Professionals
User Info: To subscribe to this Usenet newsgroup, you need access to a newsreader.

`news:rec.arts.fin`

rec.arts.dance

A Usenet newsgroup providing information and discussion about all types of dance.

Keywords: Dance, Fine Arts
Audience: Dancers, Dance Enthusiasts, Choreographers
User Info: To subscribe to this Usenet newsgroup, you need access to a newsreader.

`news:rec.arts.dance`

Rosen Sculpture Exhibition

This web site contains various examples of sculpture movements.

Keywords: Art, Fine Arts
Sponsor: Visual Resources Curator of the Department of Art at Appalachian State University, Boone, North Carolina, USA
Audience: Art Educators, Art Students

`http://www.acs.appstate.edu/art`

FineArt Forum

FineArt Forum

A monthly newsletter that includes listings of art and technology events, showcases, conferences, and jobs.

Keywords: Art, Multimedia
Sponsor: The International Society for the Arts, Sciences, and Technology
Audience: Art Educators, Art Professionals, Artists
Profile: Published by the National Science Foundation Engineering Research Center for Computational Field Simulation, Mississippi State University. FineArt Forum has provided timely information to a large international audience since 1988. The subscriber list consists of individuals working in the realm where art, science, and technology converge. Issues provide information about conferences and competitions, calls for presentations and research, and notices about performances. FineArt_Online is both an archive of FineArt Forum, ISEA News, Leonardo Electronic News, and a variety of longer postings. In January 1994 it began posting an online gallery.
Contact: Paul Brown
brown@erc.msstate.edu
User Info: To subscribe, send e-mail to: brown@erc.msstate.edu, with the message SUB FAST; also give your name, postal address, and e-mail address.

`http://www.msstate.edu/Fineart_Online/home.html`

Finger (Internet Database)

Finger Database

This service allows access to a database facility via finger.

Keywords: Internet Services, Finger (Internet Database)
Audience: Internet Surfers
Contact: http://www.usyd.edu.au
Details: Free

`finger://help@dir.su.oz.au`

Firearms

ba-Firearms

This is an announcement and discussion of firearms legislation and related issues. The ca- list is for California statewide issues; the ba- list is for the San Francisco Bay Area and gets all messages sent to the ca- list. Prospective members should subscribe to one or the other, generally depending on whether or not they are SF Bay Area residents.

Keywords: Firearms, Gun Control Legislation, San Francisco Bay Area
Audience: Politicians, General Public, Gun Users, San Francisco Bay Area Residents
Contact: Jeff Chan
ba-firearms-request@shell.portal.com
Details: Free
User Info: To subscribe to the list, send an e-mail message requesting a subscription to the URL address below.
To send a message to the entire list, address it to:
ba-firearms@shell.portal.com

`mailto:ba-firearms-request@shell.portal.com`

ca-Firearms

This is an announcement and discussion of firearms legislation and related issues. The ca- list is for California statewide issues; the ba- list is for the San Francisco Bay Area and gets all messages sent to the ca- list. Prospective members should subscribe to one or the other, generally depending on whether or not they are SF Bay Area residents.

Keywords: Firearms, Gun Control Legislation, California
Audience: Politicians, General Public, Gun Users, California Residents
Contact: Jeff Chan
ca-firearms-request@shell.portal.com
Details: Free

User Info: To subscribe to the list, send an e-mail message requesting a subscription to the URL address below.
To send a message to the entire list, address it to:
ca-firearms@shell.portal.com

`mailto:ca-firearms-request@shell.portal.com`

rec.guns

A Usenet newsgroup providing information and discussion about firearms.

Keywords: Firearms, Weapons
Audience: Gun Users
User Info: To subscribe to this Usenet newsgroup, you need access to a newsreader.

`news:rec.guns`

Firewalls

comp.security.misc

A Usenet newsgroup providing information and discussion about security issues of computers and networks.

Keywords: Computers, Security, Firewalls
Audience: Computer Users
User Info: To subscribe to this Usenet newsgroup, you need access to a newsreader.

`news:comp.security.misc`

Systems Operators, firewalls

A mailing list to discuss the issues involved in setting up and maintaining Internet security firewall systems.

Keywords: Security, Internet Security, Firewalls
Audience: Security Workers, Network Administrator, System Operators
Contact: Brent Chapman
Brent@GreatCircle.com
Details: Free
User Info: To subscribe to the list, send an e-mail message consisting of a single line reading:
SUB firewalls YourFirstName YourLastName

`mailto:majordomo@greatcircle.com`

Fish

alt.aquaria

A Usenet newsgroup providing information and discussion about the aquarium as a hobby.

Keywords: Aquariums, Fish, Hobbies
Audience: Aquarium Keepers, Fish Lovers
User Info: To subscribe to this Usenet newsgroup, you need access to a newsreader.

`news:alt.aquaria`

FINS (Fish Information Service)

This site provides information on issues relating to fish, including aquarium-building tips, diseases, clubs, newsgroups, movies, and fish trivia from Woods Hole Oceanographic Institute.

Keywords: Fish, Oceanography
Sponsor: Active Window Productions
Audience: Fish Enthusiasts, Ichthyologists
Details: Free

`http://www.actwin.com/fish/index.html`

rec.aquaria

A Usenet newsgroup providing information and discussion about pet fish and aquaria.

Keywords: Fish, Aquatic Sciences
Audience: Fish Enthusiasts
Details: Free
User Info: To subscribe to this Usenet newsgroup, you need access to a newsreader.

`news:rec.aquaria`

Fisheries

University of Maryland, College Park

The library's holdings are large and wide-ranging and contain significant collections in many fields.

Keywords: Agriculture, Coastal Marine Biology, Fisheries, Water Quality, Oceanography
Audience: Researchers, Students, General Public
Contact: Janet McLeod
mcleod@umail.umd.edu
Details: Free
User Info: Expect: Login; Send: Atdu

`telnet://info.umd.edu`

wildnet (Computing and Statistics in Fishers & Wildlife Biology)

This mailing list was established for the exchange of ideas, questions, and solutions in the area of fisheries and wildlife biology computing and statistics.

Keywords: Wildlife, Fisheries, Statistics
Audience: Wildlife Biologists, Environmentalists, Statisticians

Contact: Eric Woodsworth
woodsworth@sask.usask.ca
Details: Free
User Info: To subscribe to the list, send an e-mail message requesting a subscription to the URL address below.

To send a message to the entire list, address it to: wildnet@tribune.usask.ca

mailto:wildnet-request@tribune.usask.ca

Fitness

Biking

Information on biking events and maintenance, including an FAQ from rec.bicycles.
Keywords: Sports, Bicycling, Fitness
Audience: Bicyclists, Fitness Enthusiasts
Contact: Joern Yngve Dahl-Stamnes
dahls@fysel.unit.no
Details: Free

ftp://ugle.unit.no/local/biking

GolfData OnLine

A web site sampling of the information on the subscriber service GolfData OnLine. Provides numerous links to other sites which may be of interest to golfers.
Keywords: Golf, Sports, Fitness
Audience: Golfers, Sports Fans
Contact: david@gdol.com
Notes: GolfData Online is a paid subscriber electronic bulletin board service for golf enthusiasts. More information about how to subscribe can be obtained by accessing the address below.

http://www.gdol.com

Open Computing Facilty (OCF) Gopher, Sports Section

A gopher server offering access to information about a number of sporting activities.
Keywords: Sports, Fitness
Sponsor: Open Computing Facility, University of California, Berkeley
Audience: Sports Fans, Fitness Enthusiasts
Profile: This gopher has information on various sports, including football, cricket, skiing, windsurfing, and basketball, as well as links to WWW. Resources include schedules for some professional and collegiate sports, as well as FAQs and other miscellaneous information.
Contact: general-manager@ocf.berkeley.edu
Details: Free

gopher://gopher.ocf.berkeley.edu/11/gopherspace

The Wellness List

This list is founded for the purpose of discussing issues concerning Health/Nutrition/Wellness/Life Expectancy/Physical Fitness, and the books, experiences, and solutions recommended by the participants.
Keywords: Health, Nutrition, Fitness
Audience: Doctors, Nutritionists, General Public
Profile: This resource provides announcements of and reviews of books that include solutions, nutrition related position papers, requests for information, recommendations of participants, healthy recipes, nutrition and fitness related product announcements, and general discussion of related issues. Health professionals, authors, and nutritionists are encouraged to subscribe and share their knowledge with the participants.
Contact: George Rust, Wellnessmart
george@wellnessmart.com,
info@wellnessmart.com
User Info: To subscribe send an e-mail message to the URL address below consisting of a single line reading: subscribe wellnesslist

mailto:majordomo@wellnessmart.com

FL-Raves (Florida Raves)

FL-Raves (Florida Raves)

One of several regional rave-related mailing lists, this covers the state of Florida. Discussions tend to be social; Floridians may want to check out SERaves as well.
Keywords: Raves, Florida
Audience: Ravers, Florida Residents
Details: Free
User Info: To subscribe to the list, send an e-mail message requesting a subscription to the URL address below.

To send a message to the entire list, address it to: flraves@cybernet.cse.fau.edu

mailto:flraves-request@cybernet.cse.fau.edu

Flags

flags

A discussion about all kinds of flags, including (inter)national, (un)official, political, religious, movements' flags, and others. Topics include the analysis of symbols and colors used on flags, and the history of particular flags.
Keywords: Flags
Audience: Historians
Contact: Giuseppe Bottasini
bottasini@cesi.it
Details: Free
User Info: To subscribe to the list, send an e-mail message requesting a subscription to the URL address below.

To send a message to the entire list, address it to: flags@cesi.it

mailto:bottasi@cesi.it

flamingo

flamingo

This list discusses the series 'Parker Lewis' (formerly 'Parker Lewis Can't Lose') on the Fox television network.
Keywords: Television, Fox Television
Audience: Television Viewers
Details: Free
User Info: To subscribe to the list, send an e-mail message requesting a subscription to the URL address below.

To send a message to the entire list, address it to:
flamingo@lenny.corp.sgi.com

mailto:flamingo-request@lenny.corp.sgi.com

flashlife

flashlife

A mailing list for general managers of Shadowrun and other cyberpunk role-playing games to discuss rules and scenarios, ask questions, and make up answers.
Keywords: Games, Cyberpunk Games, Role Playing
Audience: Game Players, Cyberpunks
Details: Free
User Info: To subscribe to the list, send an e-mail message requesting a subscription to the URL address below.

To send a message to the entire list, address it to: flashlife@netcom.com

mailto:flashlife-request@netcom.com

Flight Simulation

Aviator

A mailing list for users of Aviator™, the flight-simulation program from Artificial Horizons, Inc.
Keywords: Aviation, Simulation, Computers, Flight Simulation
Audience: Compueter Games Users

Contact:	Jim Hickstein
	aviator@ICDwest.Teradyne.COM
Details:	Free
User Info:	To subscribe to the list, send an e-mail message requesting a subscription to the URL address below.
	To send a message to the entire list, address it to: aviator@ICDwest.Teradyne.COM
Notes:	Aviator runs on Sun workstations with the GX graphics accelerator option. Its charter is simply to facilitate communication among users of Aviator. It is not intended for communication with the "providers" of Aviator. All mail received at the submission address is reflected to all the subscribers of the list.

`mailto:aviator-request@ICDwest.Teradyne.COM`

Florida

Florida State University System Library

The library's holdings are large and wide-ranging and contain significant collections in many fields.

Keywords:	Florida, Latin America, Judaica, Literature (Children's), Marine Engineering, Law (Brazilian), Law (British)
Audience:	General Public, Researchers, Librarians, Document Delivery Professionals
Details:	Free
User Info:	Expect: Command ==>, Send: dial vtam; Expect: LUIS User Menu, Send: Your Catalog choice; To log off: Send: %off

`telnet://nervm.nerdc.ufl.edu`

South Florida Environmental Reader

Newsletter distributing information on the environment of South Florida.

Keywords:	Environment, Florida
Audience:	Environmentalists
Contact:	aem@mthvax.cs.miami.edu
Details:	Free
User Info:	To subscribe to the list, send an e-mail messgae requesting a subscription to the URL address below.
	To send a mesage to the entire USL, address it to: sfer@mthvax.cs.miami.edu

`mail to:sfer-requesti@mthvax.cs.miami.edu`

Fluid Dynamics

CFD

CFD (Computational Fluid Dynamics Group).

Keywords:	Engineering, Fluid Dynamics
Audience:	Engineers
Contact:	JUSTIN@UKCC.UKY.EDU
	justin@engr.uky.edu
Details:	Free
User Info:	To subscribe to the list, send an e-mail message to the URL address below, consisting of a single line reading:
	SUB cfd YourFirstName YourLastName
	To send a message to the entire list, address it to: cfd@UKCC.UKY.EDU

`justin@UKCC.UKY.EDU`

FM-10

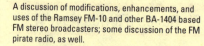

FM-10

A discussion of modifications, enhancements, and uses of the Ramsey FM-10 and other BA-1404 based FM stereo broadcasters; some discussion of the FM pirate radio, as well.

Keywords:	Radio, Broadcasting
Audience:	Broadcasters, Radio Broadcasters
Details:	Free
User Info:	To subscribe to the list, send an e-mail message requesting a subscription to the URL address below.
	To send a message to the entire list, address it to: fm-10@dg-rtp.dg.com

`mailto:fm-10-request@dg-rtp.dg.com`

fogelberg

fogelberg

A discussion of the work of recording artist Dan Fogelberg.

Keywords:	Music, Musicians
Audience:	Dan Fogelberg Enthusiasts
Contact:	ai411@yfn.ysu.edu
Details:	Free
User Info:	To subscribe to the list, send an e-mail message requesting a subscription to the URL address below.
	To send a message to the entire list, address it to: fogelberg@yfn.ysu.edu

`mailto:ai411@yfn.ysu.edu`

Folk Dance

Folk-dancing

A discussion of folk dancing, including contra, square, western square, morris, cajun, and barn dancing.

Keywords:	Dance, Folk Dance
Audience:	Dancers, Folk Dancers
Contact:	Terry J. Wood
	tjw+@pitt.edu
Details:	Free
User Info:	To subscribe to the list, send an e-mail message requesting a subscription to the URL address below.
	To send a message to the entire list, address it to: fdml@pitt.edu
Notes:	Please note that the Folk Dancing Mailing List (fdml) operates in conjunction with the Usenet newsgroup rec.folk-dancing. When subscribing to the FDML, please include several computer mail addresses and a postal mail address (or phone number).

`mailto:tjw+@pitt.edu`

Folk Music

Folk music

This discussion list deals with the music of the recent wave of American singer/songwriters. List traffic includes tour schedules, reviews, album and release information.

Keywords:	Folk Music, Music
Audience:	Folk Musicians, Musicians, Folk Music Enthusiasts
Contact:	Alan Rowoth
	listserv@nysernet.org
Details:	Free
User Info:	To subscribe to the list, send an e-mail message to the URL address below consisting of a single line reading:
	SUB folk_music YourFirstName YourLastName
	To send a message to the entire list, address it to: folk_music@nysernet.org

`mailto:listserv@nysernet.org`

University of New Hampshire Videotex Library

The library's holdings are large and wide-ranging and contain significant collections in many fields.

Keywords:	Dance, Folk Music, Milne (A.A., Collection of), Galway (Ireland)
Audience:	Researchers, Students, General Public

Contact:	Robin Tuttle
	r_tuttle1@unhh.unh.edu
Details:	Free
User Info:	Expect: USERNAME; Send: Student (no password required). Control-z to log off.

`telnet://unhvt@unh.edu`

Folklore

alt.folklore.computers

A Usenet newsgroup providing information and discussion concerning stories and anecdotes about computers.

Keywords:	Computers, Folklore
Audience:	Computer Users, Storytellers
User Info:	To subscribe to this Usenet newsgroup, you need access to a newsreader.

`news:alt.folklore.computers`

alt.folklore.urban

A Usenet newsgroup providing information and discussion about urban legends and urban myths.

Keywords:	Urban Studies, Folklore
Audience:	Story Tellers, General Public
User Info:	To subscribe to this Usenet newsgroup, you need access to a newsreader.

`news:alt.folklore.urban`

Harvard University Library

The library's holdings are large and wide-ranging and contain significant collections in many fields.

Keywords:	Afrikaans, Alchemy, Arabic Culture (History of), Celtic Philology, Congo Languages, Folklore, Hebraica, Mormonism, Numismatics, Quakers, Sanskrit, Witchcraft, Arabic Philology
Audience:	General Public, Researchers, Librarians, Document Delivery Professionals
Details:	Free
User Info:	Expect: Mitek Server..., Send: Enter or Return; Expect: prompt, Send: hollis

`telnet://hollis.harvard.edu`

University of Nebraska at Lincoln Library

The library's holdings are large and wide-ranging and contain significant collections in many fields.

Keywords:	Slovak Republic, Czech Republic, Folklore, Military History, Latvia, Law (Tax), Law (US)
Audience:	General Public, Researchers, Librarians, Document Delivery Professionals
Contact:	Anita Cook
Details:	Free
User Info:	Expect: login, Send: library

`telnet://unllib.unl.edu`

University of Tennessee at Knoxville Library

The library's holdings are large and wide-ranging and contain significant collections in many fields.

Keywords:	Native American Affairs, Congress (US), Folklore, Travel (History of)
Audience:	Researchers, Students, General Public
Details:	Free
User Info:	Expect: OK Prompt; Send: Login pub1; Expect: Password, Send: Usc

`telnet://opac.lib.utk.edu`

Folklore Collection

University of Denver Library

The library's holdings are large and wide-ranging and contain significant collections in many fields.

Keywords:	Folklore Collection, Husted (Margaret, Culinary Collection of)
Audience:	Researchers, Students, General Public
Contact:	Bob Stocker
	bstocker@ducair.bitnet
Details:	Free
User Info:	Expect: Login; Send: Atdu

`telnet:// du.edu`

Food

Diogenes

Diogenes provides access to the US Food and Drug Administration (FDA) regulatory information needed by the health care industry.

Keywords:	Food, Drugs
Sponsor:	Diogenes, Rockville, MD, USA
Audience:	Health Care Professionals
Profile:	The database contains news stories and unpublished documents relating to the United States regulation of pharmaceuticals and medical devices. The complete text is provided for materials that are substantive and timely. Diogenes covers information relating to the Food and Drug Administration regulation of drugs and medical devices, including listings of approved products, experience reports for devices, documentation of the approval process for specific products, recall and regulatory action documentation, and more.
Contact:	Dialog in the US at (800) 334-2564, Dialog internationally at country-specific locations.
User Info:	To subscribe, contact Dialog directly.
Notes:	Coverage: 1976 to the present; updated weekly.

`telnet://dialog.com`

PENPages

This easy-to-use general-interest database contains articles and brochures.

Keywords:	Food, Employment, Education
Sponsor:	Pennsylvania State University, PA
Audience:	General Public
User Info:	Expect: login; Send: your state's two-letter code (or "world" if sent from outside the USA)

`telnet://psunet.psu.edu`

rec.food.cooking

A Usenet newsgroup providing information and discussion about cooking.

Keywords:	Food, Cooking
Audience:	General Public, Cooks, Chefs
User Info:	To subscribe to this Usenet newsgroup, you need access to a newsreader.

`news:rec.food.cooking`

rec.food.veg

A Usenet newsgroup providing information and discussion about vegetarian cooking.

Keywords:	Vegetarianism, Food, Cooking
Audience:	Vegetarians, Cooks, Chefs
User Info:	To subscribe to this Usenet newsgroup, you need access to a newsreader.

`news:rec.food.veg`

Recipe Archive

This is an archive of recipes organized by main ingredient or title.

Keywords:	Cooking, Food
Audience:	General Public, Cooks, Chefs
Profile:	Here are a few intriguing examples from the archive:

Advokaat: Advokaat is the Dutch word for egg cognac. It is highly recommended for A. I. (Alcohol Imbibing) meetings. This recipe is a modification of a recipe obtained in Poland. It makes a potent, superb advokaat (or egg cognac). The milk and eggs are healthy, the sugar and alcohol are not!

Berlinerkranzer: Norwegian wreath cookies are decorative holiday cookies that add quite a bright, colorful, aromatic touch to your plate of cookies.

Bouillabaisse: This recipe for Marseille-style fish soup represents a combination of several recipes derived from old Gourmets, Julia Child, the Playboy Gourmet Cookbook, and "Gee, that sounds good, let's add it.." The accompanying rouille is a garlic/hot pepper mayonnaise condiment traditional to Marseille-style fish soup.

Details: Free

gopher://calypso.oit.unc.edu/7waissrc%3a/ref.d/indexes.d/recipes.src

gopher://calypso.oit.unc.edu/7waissrc%3a/ref.d/indexes.d/usenet-cookbook.sr

They can also be accessed through MOSAIC at the URL address shown below or from the calypso.oit.unc.edu gopher in the subdirectories: Internet Dog-Eared Pages (Frequently used resources)/Search Many WAIS Indices

Notes: There are two searchable gopher Indexes containing recipes that have passed through the rec.food.cooking and rec.food.recipes newsgroups. They can be found at the following URL addresses:

ftp://gatekeeper.dec.com/pub/recipes

Seafood Internet Network

A mailing list to facilitate information exchange about the HACCP Alliance and the implementation of the FDA seafood HACCP program.

Keywords: Food, FDA

Audience: Seafood Industry Professionals

Contact: Robert J. Price
rjprice@dale.ucdavis.edu

User Info: To subscribe , send an e-mail message to: listproc@ucdavis.edu Leave the subject blank and place in the body of the note: subscribe seafood YourFirstName YourLastName

mailto:seafood@ucdavis.edu

The World Wide Web rec.food.recipes archive

World Wide Web archive of recipes posted to Usenet newsgroup rec.food.recipes. Updated weekly.

Keywords: Food, Recipes, Cooking

Audience: Cooks, General Public

Contact: Amy Gale
mara@kauri.vuw.ac.nz

User Info: Use a World-Wide Web (WWW) client such as lynx

http://www.vuw.ac.nz/non-local/recipes-archive/recipe-archive.html

VEGCNY-L (Vegetarians in Central New York area)

VegCNY-L is an open discussion list intended to serve those people living in the Central New York area who are vegetarians, as well as those who are interested in vegetarianism.

Keywords: Vegetarianism, New York, Food

Audience: Vegetarians

Contact: Chuck Goelzer Lyons
cgl1@cornell.edu

Details: Free

User Info: To subscribe to the list, send an e-mail message to the URL address below consisting of a single line reading:

SUB VEGCNY-L YourFirstName Your:LastName

To send a message to the entire list, address it to: VEGCNY-L@cornell.edu

mailto:listserv@cornell.edu

veggie (Vegetarian Issues Discussion List)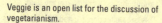

Veggie is an open list for the discussion of vegetarianism.

Keywords: Vegetarianism, Food

Audience: Vegetarians

Details: Free

User Info: To subscribe to the list, send an e-mail message to the URL address below consisting of a single line reading:

SUB veggie YourFirstName YourLastName

mailto:listserv@gibbs.oit.unc.edu

veggies

Vegetarian matters in Britain.

Keywords: Vegetarianism, Britain, Food

Audience: Vegetarians

Details: Free

User Info: To subscribe to the list, send an e-mail message requesting a subscription to the URL address below.

To send a message to the entire list, address it to: veggies@ncl.ak.uk

mailto:veggies-request@ncl.ak.uk

veglife (Vegetarian Life List)

Veglife (formerly Granola) provides a supportive atmosphere for the discussion of issues related to the vegetarian lifestyle.

Keywords: Vegetarianism, Food

Audience: Vegetarians

Contact: Darrell A. Early, Charles Goelzer Lyons

Details: Free

User Info: To subscribe to the list, send an e-mail message to the URL address below consisting of a single line reading:

SUB veglife YourFirstName YourLastName

To send a message to the entire list, address it to: veglife@vtvml.cc.vt.edu

mailto:listserv@vtvm1.cc.vt.edu

Food Production

AGRIS International

This database serves as a comprehensive inventory of worldwide agricultural literature that reflects research results, food production, and rural development.

Keywords: Agriculture, Rural Development, Food Production, Development

Sponsor: US National Agricultural Library, Beltsville, MD, USA

Audience: Agronomists, Market Researchers

Profile: Designed to help users identify problems involved in all aspects of world food supply, the file corresponds in part to Agr Index, published monthly by the Food and Agriculture Organization (FAO) of the United Nations. Subject coverage focuses on many topics, general agriculture; geography and history; education, extension, and advisory work; administration and legislation; economics, development, and rural sociology; plant production; protection of plants and stored products; forestry; animal production; aquatic sciences and fisheries; machinery and buildings; natural resources; food science; home economics; human nutrition; pollution; and more.

Contact: Dialog in the US at (800) 334-2564

Details: Costs

User Info: To subscribe, contact Dialog directly.

telnet://dialog.com

Food Industry Investext

The world's largest database of company, industry, topical, and geographic analysis.

Keywords: Food Production, Agriculture Industry

Sponsor: Thomson Financial Networks, Boston, MA, US

Audience: Business Professionals, Market Researchers

Profile: The database is composed of more than 320,000 full-text reports written by analysts at 180 investment banks and research firms worldwide. The research can be used for a wide range of business intelligence activities, including competitive analysis, evaluation of companies, and strategic planning. Coverage includes 14,000 companies worldwide and 53 industry groups.

Football

NFL Scores, Schedules, and Point Spreads ★

Information on National Football League (NFL) football scores, schedules, and point spreads.

Keywords: Professional Sports, Sports, Football, NFL
Audience: Football Fans
Contact: office@world.std.com
Details: Free

`gopher://world.std.com/News and Weather`

Professional Sports Schedules ★

Sports schedules for major professional sports.

Keywords: Sports, Baseball, Hockey, Football, Basketball
Sponsor: Colorado University, Boulder, CO
Audience: Sports Fans, Football Fans, Hockey Fans, Baseball Enthusiasts, Basketball Enthusiasts
Profile: The Colorado University gopher maintains an interactive online database of schedules for all major US professional sports teams (NBA, NFL, NHL, MLB). The database is indexed by both team name and dates of games, and can be searched accordingly.
Contact: gopher@gopher.colorado.edu
Details: Free

`gopher://gopher.colorado.edu/11/professional/sports/schedules`

rec.sport.football.college ★

A Usenet newsgroup providing information and discussion about college football.

Keywords: Football, College, Sports
Audience: Football Fans, Sports Fans
User Info: To subscribe to this Usenet newsgroup, you need access to a newsreader.

`news:rec.sport.football.college`

rec.sport.football.pro ★

A Usenet newsgroup providing information and discussion about pro football.

Keywords: Football, Sports
Audience: Football Enthusiasts
User Info: To subscribe to this Usenet newsgroup, you need access to a newsreader.

`news:rec.sport.football.pro`

Usenet Sports Groups Archived ★

An archive for Usenet groups, including many related to sports ranging from football to table tennis.

Keywords: Sports, Skydiving, Volleyball, Football, Scuba Diving, Table Tennis
Sponsor: Massachusetts Institute of Technology, Boston, MA
Audience: Sports Enthusiasts
Contact: ftp-bugs@rtfm.mit.edu
Details: Free

`ftp://rtfm.mit.edu/pub/usenet`

Wiretap Sports Archives ★

Sports articles, including information on soccer in the US and Canada, rules for soccer and Australian football, and some rather dated material on American football.

Keywords: Sports, Football, Soccer
Sponsor: The Internet Wiretap Library
Audience: Sports Enthusiasts
Details: Free

`gopher://wiretap.spies.com/library/article/sports`

Ford

Fordnatics ★

This unmoderated forum discusses high-performance Fords or Ford-powered vehicles, focusing on modifications and driving techniques for competition or track use.

Keywords: Automobiles, Fords
Audience: Automobile Enthusiasts, Ford Drivers, Racers
Details: Free
User Info: To subscribe to the list, send an e-mail message requesting a subscription to the URL address below.

To send a message to the entire list, address it to: fordnatics@freud.arc.nasa.gov

`mailto:fordnatics-request@freud.arc.nasa.gov`

Mustangs ★

A forum for the discussion of technical issues, problems, solutions, and modifications relating to late-model (1980 and later) Ford Mustangs.

Keywords: Ford, Automobiles
Audience: Ford Owners
Details: Free
User Info: To subscribe to the list, send an e-mail message requesting a subscription to the URL address below.

`mailto:mustangs-request@cup.hp.com`

Foreign Trade

1994 Federal Budget (Canada) ★★★★

This site offers full-text of Canada's federal budget. Also has a wealth of information on Canadian industry and industrial policy, including Provincial and Sectorial GATT opportunities and briefs from the Information Highway Advisory Council.

Keywords: Canada, Government (International), Industry, Foreign Trade
Sponsor: Industry Canada, Canada
Audience: Canadians, Government Officials, Business Professionals, Researchers
Contact: Tyson Macaulay
tyson@debra.dgbt.doc.ca

`gopher://debra.dgbt.doc.ca/industry canada documents/isc.news.releases`

World Bank Gopher Server ★★★

A collection of online information from the World Bank.

Keywords: Government (International), Development, International Finance, Foreign Trade
Sponsor: The World Bank
Audience: Nongovernmental Organizations, Activists, Government Officials, Environmentalists
Profile: A collection of World Bank information including a list of publications, environmental assessments, economic reports, and updates on current projects being funded by the World Bank.
Contact: webmaster@www.worldbank.org

`gopher://gopher.worldbank.org`

`http://www.worldbank.org`

Forestry

FMDSS-L (Forest Management Decision Support Systems)

This is a forum for the rapid exchange of information, ideas, and opinions related to the topics of DSS (decision support systems) and information systems for forest-management planning.

Keywords:	Forest Management, Forestry
Audience:	Foresters
Contact:	Tom Moore listserv@pnfi.forestry.ca
Details:	Free
User Info:	To subscribe to the list, send an e-mail message to the URL address below consisting of a single line reading: SUB fmdss-l YourFirstName YourLastName To send a message to the entire list, address it to: fmdss-l@pnfi.forestry.ca

`mailto:listserv@pnfi.forestry.ca`

Mississippi State University Library

The library's holdings are large and wide-ranging and contain significant collections in many fields.

Keywords:	History (US), Forestry, Energy, Carter (Hodding, Papers of), Mississippi
Audience:	General Public, Researchers, Librarians, Document Delivery Professionals
Contact:	Stephen Cunetto shc1@ra.msstate.edu
Details:	Free
User Info:	Expect: username, Send: msu; Expect: password, Send: library

`telnet://libserv.msstate.edu`

Natural Resources Canada (NRCan) Gopher

This site offers information on forests, energy, mining, and geomatics from the Canadian government. Also has reports from the Geological Survey of Canada and an overview of NRCan statutes, organization, and personnel. Provides links to other Canadian environmental and government gophers.

Keywords:	Canada, Environment, Geology, Forestry
Sponsor:	The Department of Natural Resources, Canada
Audience:	Canadians, Environmentalists, Environmental Researchers, Geologists
Contact:	Bob Fillmore fillmore@emr.ca
Notes:	NRCan maintains a toll-free hotline - 1-(800) 267-5166

`gopher://gopher.emr.ca`

`http://www.emr.ca/`

Forests

Western Lands

A collection of articles and reports relating to environmental and land use issues in the Western United States.

Keywords:	Environmentalism, Ecology, Forests, The Western United States
Sponsor:	The Institute for Global Communications (IGC)
Audience:	Environmentalists, Ecologists, Activists, Foresters, Citizens
Contact:	Dan Yurman, IGC User Support dyurman@igc.apc.com., support@igc.apc.com
Notes:	User submissions encouraged.

`gopher://gopher.igc.apc.org/11/environment/forests/western.lands`

Four Wheel Drive

Offroad

Discusses and shares experiences with four-wheel and off-road adventures, including driving tips, vehicle modifications, and anything else related to four-wheeling. This list is specifically designed for four-wheel-drive vehicle owners, users, or enthusiasts. Discussions center around technical and mechanical matters, driving techniques, and trip reports.

Keywords:	Four Wheel Drive
Audience:	Off Road Driving Enthusiasts, Four Wheel Drive Enthusiasts
Contact:	Stefan Roth offroad-request@ai.gtri.gatech.edu
Details:	Free
User Info:	To subscribe to the list, send an e-mail message requesting a subscription to the URL address below. To send a message to the entire list, address it to: offroad@ai.gtri.gatech.edu

`mailto:offroad-request@ai.gtri.gatech.edu`

Fox Television

flamingo

This list discusses the series 'Parker Lewis' (formerly 'Parker Lewis Can't Lose') on the Fox television network.

Keywords:	Television, Fox Television
Audience:	Television Viewers
Details:	Free
User Info:	To subscribe to the list, send an e-mail message requesting a subscription to the URL address below. To send a message to the entire list, address it to: flamingo@lenny.corp.sgi.com

`mailto:flamingo-request@lenny.corp.sgi.com`

Melrose-place

Discussion of the Fox television show Melrose Place.

Keywords:	Melrose Place, Fox Television, Television Series
Audience:	Melrose Place Fans, Television Viewers
Details:	Free
User Info:	To subscribe to the list, send an e-mail message requesting a subscription to the URL address below.

`mailto:melrose-place-request@ferkel.ucsb.edu`

foxpro-l

foxpro-l

This mailing list is designed to foster information sharing between users of the FoxPro™ database development environment now owned and distributed by Microsoft. Both new and experienced users of FoxPro are welcome to join in the discussions.

Keywords:	Databases, Computers, Microsoft Corp.
Audience:	Database Users, Microsoft FoxPro Users, Software Engineers
Contact:	Chris O'Neill coneill@heaven.polarbear.rankin-inlet.nt.ca
Details:	Free
User Info:	To subscribe to the list, send an e-mail message requesting a subscription to the URL address below. To send a message to the entire list, address it to: foxpro-l@polarbear.rankin-inlet.nt.ca

`mailto:fileserv@polarbear.rankin-inlet.nt.ca`

framers

framers

This is a forum to share experiences and information about the FrameMaker desktop-publishing package from Frame Technology.

Keywords:	Desktop Publishing
Audience:	Desktop Publishers, Publishers
Details:	Free
User Info:	To subscribe to the list, send an e-mail message requesting a subscription to the URL address below.
	To send a message to the entire list, address it to: framers@uunet.uu.net

`mailto:framers-request@uunet.uu.net`

France

france-foot

Discussions of the French football (soccer) scene. Results and news are posted regularly.

Keywords:	Soccer, Sports, France, Football
Audience:	Soccer Enthusiasts, French Sports Enthusiasts
Contact:	Vincent Habchi, Kent Hedlundh dvlkhh@cs.umu.se
Details:	Free
User Info:	To subscribe to the list, send an e-mail message requesting a subscription to the URL address below.
	To send a message to the entire list, address it to: france-foot@inf.enst.fr

`mailto:france-foot-request@inf.enst.fr`

soc.culture.french

A Usenet newsgroup providing information and discussion about French culture and history.

Keywords:	France, Sociology
Audience:	Sociologists, Francophiles
Details:	Free
User Info:	To subscribe to this Usenet newsgroup, you need access to a newsreader.

`news:soc.culture.french`

Fraud

Scifraud

Scifraud is dedicated to the discussion of fraud in science.

Keywords:	Science, Fraud
Audience:	Scientists
Contact:	Al Higgins, Mike Ramundo ach13@albnyvms.bitnet sysmrr@albnyvm1.bitnet
Details:	Free

User Info:	To subscribe to the list, send an e-mail message to the URL address below consisting of a single line reading:
	SUB scifraud YourFirstName YourLastName
	To send a message to the entire list, address it to: scifraud@uacs2.albany.edu

`mailto:listserv@uacsc2.albany.edu`

freaks

freaks

This mailing list focuses on Marillion and related rock groups.

Keywords:	Music, Rock Music
Audience:	Marillion Enthusiasts
Details:	Free
User Info:	To subscribe to the list, send an e-mail message requesting a subscription to the URL address below.
	To send a message to the entire list, address it to:freaks@bnf.com

`mailto:freaks-request@bnf.com`

FrEd Mail Foundation

FrEd Mail Foundation

This foundation specializes in establishing innovative and educationally rewarding collaborative projects using the Internet for the K-12 community.

Keywords:	Children, Education (K-12)
Audience:	Educators (K-12)
Contact:	Al Rogers arogers@bonita.cerf.fred.org
Details:	Free

`gopher://gopher.cerf.net/11/fredmail`

Free Art For HTML Page

Free Art For HTML Page

This web site provides copyrighted graphics for the MOSAIC program.

Keywords:	Computer-Aided Design, Graphics
Audience:	Designers, Educators
Contact:	Harlan Wallach wallach@mcs.com
Details:	Free

`http://www.mcs.net/wallach/Fart/buttons.html`

Free for All

Free for All

An experiment in a networked hypermedia group bulletin board.

Keywords:	Internet, Group Communications, Multimedia
Audience:	Internet Surfers, Multimedia Enthusiasts
Details:	Free, Multimedia

`http://south.ncsa.uiuc.edu/Free.html`

Free Software

GNUs Bulletin: Newsletter of the Free Software Foundation

Bringing you news about the GNU Project, the Free Software Foundation is dedicated to eliminating restrictions on copying, redistribution, understanding, and modification of computer programs.

Keywords:	Software, Shareware, Free Software
Sponsor:	Free Software Foundation
Audience:	Computer Programmers, Computer Users
Contact:	Leonard H. Tower, Jr. tower@ai.mit.edu
Details:	Free
	news:gnu.announce

`mailto:info-gnu-request@prep.ai.mit.edu`

Free Trade

North American Free Trade Agreement (NAFTA)

The agreement among the governments of Canada, the United Mexican States, and the United States of America to establish a free trade area in North America.

Keywords:	Trade, US, Mexico, Canada, Free Trade, NAFTA
Audience:	Journalists, Politicians, Economists, Students
Details:	Free

`gopher://wiretap.spies.com/00/Gov/NAFTA`

freedom

freedom

Mailing list of people organizing against the Idaho Citizens Alliance antigay ballot initiative.

Keywords: Gay Rights, Activism, Gays
Audience: Gays, Lesbians, Bisexuals, Idaho Citizens, Activists
Details: Free
User Info: To subscribe to the list, send an e-mail message to the URL address shown below consisting of a single line reading:

SUB freedom YourFirstName YourLastName.

To send a message to the entire list, address it to: freedom@idbsu.idbsu.edu

`mailto:listserv@idbsu.idbsu.edu`

Freedom of Information

Freedom of Information Act (FOIA): Guide to Use ★

This is a citizen's guide on using the Freedom of Information Act and the Privacy Act of 1974 to request government records.

Keywords: Privacy, Freedom of Information, Government (US Federal)
Audience: Journalists, Privacy Activists, Students, Politicians, US Citizens
Details: Free

`gopher://wiretap.spies.com/00/Gov/foia.cit`

Freedom of Information Directory of Records (Canada) ★★

A database compiled by the Canadian federal government listing documents available to the public under The Freedom of Information and Protection of Privacy Act. It can be searched by keyword, or browsed through a menuing system.

Keywords: Canada, Government (International), Freedom of Information Act
Sponsor: British Columbia Systems Corporation, British Columbia, Canada
Audience: Canadians, Journalists, Activists
Contact: Office of the Information and Privacy Commissioner
tcphelp@bc02.gov.bc.ca

`gopher://bcsc02.gov.bc.ca`

Privacy Rights Clearinghouse (PRC) ★★

A collection of materials related to privacy issues.

Keywords: Privacy, Legislation, Consumer Rights, Freedom of Information
Sponsor: University of San Diego
Audience: Citizens, Privacy Activists, Journalists
Profile: This site contains fact sheets (in English and Spanish) on privacy issues ranging from wiretapping to credit reporting. Also includes federal and state privacy legislation as well as related position papers and press releases.
Contact: prc@teetot.acusd.edu
User Info: Expect: Login; Send: Privacy

`gopher://teetot.acusd.edu`
`telnet://teetot.acusd.edu`

Freedom of Speech

alt.censorship

A Usenet newsgroup providing information and discussion about freedom of speech and freedom of the press.

Keywords: Censorship, Freedom of Speech, Constitution (US), Activism
Audience: Press, Students, Educators, Activists
User Info: To subscribe to this Usenet newsgroup, you need access to a newsreader.

`news:alt.censorship`

Free Net Working Papers

Free-Net Working Papers

An FTP site with a collection of articles and papers about community networking.

Keywords: Community Networking, Networking
Sponsor: Carleton University, National Clearinghouse for Machine Readable Texts
Audience: Activists, Government, General Public
Profile: Project Guttenburg's goal is to provide a collection of 10,000 of the most used books by the year 2001.
Contact: Jay Weston, Michael S. Hart
jweston@carleton.ca
Details: Free
Login anonymous; cd text

`ftp://alfred.carleton.ca/pub/freenet/working.papers`

FreeNets

FreeNets

This resource provides extensive information about FreeNets, which are public access Internet sites at no charge or for donations.

Keywords: Internet Access, Community Networking
Audience: Individuals, Communities, Libraries
Profile: FreeNets, community computing services providing Internet access, exist internationally and include such systems as LA FreeNet, Buffalo FreeNet, Cleveland FreeNet, FreeNet Erlangen-Nuernburg, Victoria FreeNet, Vaasa FreePort (Finland), CapAccess (D.C.), and many more.
Details: Free

URL (gopher path) below contains pointers to all FreeNets.

`gopher path: 1/internet/freenets marvel.loc.gov`

Freeware

info-GNU-MSDOS

This electronic conference is for the GNUISH MS-DOS Development Group.

Keywords: Shareware, Freeware, MS-DOS Computers
Audience: MS-DOS Users, GNUISH MS-DOS Developers
Contact: David J. Camp
david@wubios.wustl.edu
Details: Free
User Info: To subscribe to the list, send an e-mail message to the URL address below consisting of a single line reading:

SUB info-GNU-MSDOS YourFirstName YourLastName

`mailto:listserv@wugate.wustl.edu`

French

Agence FrancePresse International French Wire

Agence FrancePresse International French Wire provides full-text articles in French relating to national, international, business, and sports news.

Keywords: News, Europe, Third World, French
Sponsor: Agence FrancePresse, Paris, France
Audience: Market Researchers, Journalists, Francophiles

Profile:	Agence FrancePresse distributes its French service worldwide, including Western and Eastern Europe, Canada, northern and western Africa, the Middle East, Vietnam, French Guiana, the West Indies, and the French Pacific islands. Agence FrancePresse International French Wire has extensive coverage of the European countries, including every aspect of economic, political, and general business news. It also provides excellent industrial and market news from both developed countries and from the Third World. Coverage: September 1991 to the present; updated daily.
Contact:	Dialog in the US at (800) 334-2564; Dialog internationally at country-specific locations.
Details:	Costs
User Info:	To subscribe, contact Dialog directly.

`telnet://dialog.com`

Canada

The wiretap gopher provides access to a range of Canadian documents in full-text format in French.

Keywords:	Canada, French
Audience:	Canadian Citizens, Lawyers
Details:	Free

`gopher://wiretap.spies.com`

WWW Paris

A web site created as a collaborative effort among individuals in both Paris and the United States.

Keywords:	Paris, Culture, Art, Travel, French, Tourism
Audience:	Students, Educators, Travelers, Researchers
Profile:	Contains an extensive collection of images and text regarding all of the major monuments and museums of Paris, including maps of the Metro and the RER; calendars of events and current expositions; promotional images and text relating to local department stores; there is also a visitors' section with up-to-date tourist information on hotels, restaurants, telephones, airport schedules, a basic Paris glossary, and the latest weather images. Includes an extensive collection of links to other resources about Paris and France, and a selected bibliography of history and architecture in Paris.
Contact:	Norman Barth, Eric Pouliquen nbarth@ucsd.edu, epouliq@ucsd.edu

`http://meteora.ucsd.edu/~norman/paris`

French Law

INTNAT (International Library)

The International library contains all French treaties, conventions and agreements that are effective today, as well as decisions from the Cour Europ_enne des Droits de l'Homme and the Cour de Justice des Communautes Europ_ennes plus the Journal Officiel des Communautes Europ_enne.

Keywords:	French Law, European Community
Audience:	International Lawyers
Profile:	The International library contains all French treaties, conventions and agreements published before 1958 that are in effect today, as well as decisions from the European Court of Human Rights (Cour Europeenne des Droits de l'Homme), the European Court of Justice (Cour de Justice des Communautes Europeennes) and the Journal Officiel des Communautes Europeenne, the daily record of the European Community.
Contact:	New Sales Group at (800) 227-4908 or 513-859-5398 inside the US, or 1-513-865-7981 for all inquires outside the US.
User Info:	To subscribe, contact Mead directly. To examine the Lexis user guide, you can access it at the ftp site of the University of Texas at Austin at the URL address: ftp://ftp.cc.utexas.edu The files are in: /pub/ref-services/LEXIS

`telnet://nex.meaddata.com`

`http://www.meaddata.com`

French Opera (19th-C.)

Indiana University Libraries

The library's holdings are large and wide-ranging and contain significant collections in many fields.

Keywords:	Literature (English), Literature (American), 1640-Present, British Plays (19th-C.), Western Americana, Railway History, Aristotle (Texts of), Lafayette (Marquis de), Handel (G.F.), Austrian History, Antiquarian Books, Rare Books, French Opera (19th-C.), Drama (British) ,
Audience:	General Public, Researchers, Librarians, Document Delivery Professionals
Details:	Free
User Info:	Expect: User ID prompt, Send: GUEST

`telnet://iuis.ucs.indiana.edu`

French Revolution

The University of Iowa Libraries

The library's holdings are large and wide-ranging and contain significant collections in many fields.

Keywords:	Hunt (Leigh), Native American Studies, Typography, Railroads, Cartoons, French Revolution, NASA, Hydraulics
Audience:	General Public, Researchers, Librarians, Document Delivery Professionals
Details:	Free Send <RETURN>to display a menu of available systems. Type 1 for OASIS access and press <RETURN>to display the Welcome to OASIS screen.

`telnet://oasis.uiowa.edu`

University of Pennsylvania PENNINFO Library

The library's holdings are large and wide-ranging and contain significant collections in many fields.

Keywords:	Church History, Spanish Inquisition, Witchcraft, Shakespeare (William), Bibles, Aristotle (Texts of), Fiction, Whitman (Walt), French Revolution, Drama (French), Literature (English), Literature (Spanish)
Audience:	Researchers, Students, General Public
Contact:	Al DSouza penninfo-admin@dccs.upenn.edu dsouza@dccs.upenn.edu
Details:	Free
User Info:	Expect: Login; Send: Public

`telnet://penninfo.upenn.edu`

French Studies

Erofile

This newsletter provides reviews of the latest books associated with French and Italian studies in fields such as literary criticism, cultural studies, film studies, pedagogy, and software.

Keywords:	Italian Studies, French Studies, Book Reviews
Audience:	French Students, Italian Students, Book Reviewers
Details:	Free

`mailto:erofile@ucsbuxa.ucsb.edu`

Friends of Ohio State

Friends of Ohio State

A forum for alumni and other friends of Ohio State University.

Keywords:	Ohio
Audience:	Ohio State University Alumni
Contact:	Jerry Canterbury antivirus@aol.com
Details:	Free
User Info:	To subscribe to the list, send an e-mail message requesting a subscription to the URL address below.
	To send a message to the entire list, address it to: antivirus@aol.com

`mailto:antivirus@aol.com`

fringeware

fringeware

A moderated mailing list devoted to cyberculture and the like.

Keywords:	Cyberculture
Audience:	Cyberculture Enthusiasts
Details:	Free, Moderated
User Info:	To subscribe to the list, send an e-mail message to the URL address shown below.
	To send a message to the entire list, address it to: fringeware@illuminati.io.com

`mailto:fringeware-request@illuminati.io.com`

Frost (Robert)

Dartmouth College Library

The library's holdings are large and wide-ranging and contain significant collections in many fields.

Keywords:	American Calligraphy, Cervantes (Miguel de), Railroads, Polar Regions, Frost (Robert), Shakespeare (William), Spanish Plays
Audience:	General Public, Researchers, Librarians, Document Delivery Professionals
Contact:	Katharina Klemperer kathy.klemperer@dartmouth.edu
Details:	Free
User Info:	Expect: login, Send: wolfpac

`telnet://lib.dartmouth.edu`

FSP Protocol

fsp-discussion

Discusses the new FSP protocol. FSP is a set of programs that implements a public-access archive similar to an anonymous FTP archive.

Keywords:	FSP Protocol, Public Access Archives
Audience:	Computer Users
Details:	Free
User Info:	To subscribe to the list, send an e-mail message requesting a subscription to the URL address below.
	To send a message to the entire list, address it to: fsp-discussion@germany.eu.net

`mailto:listmaster@germany.eu.net`

fsuucp

fsuucp

The FSUUCP mailing list is for the discussion of bug hunting, feature proposing, and announcements of the availability and release dates of FSUUCP, an MS-DOS UUCP mail news package.

Keywords:	Software, Shareware
Audience:	Students, Computer Users
Details:	Free
User Info:	To subscribe to the list, send an e-mail message requesting a subscription to the URL address below.
	To send a message to the entire list, address it to: fsuucp@polyslo.calpoly.edu

`mailto:fsuucp-request@polyslo.calpoly.edu`

FTP

FTP FAQ

Common questions and answers about FTP (File Transfer Protocol), FTP sites, and anonymous FTP. General information for the novice FTP user.

Keywords:	FTP, Internet Tools
Audience:	Students, Computer Scientists, Researchers
Contact:	Perry Rovers perry.rovers@kub.nl

`ftp://ftp.ifh.de/pub/FAQ/ftp.faq`

FTP-How To

A short guide to using anonymous FTP, an Internet access tool.

Keywords:	Internet Tools, FTP
Sponsor:	SURAnet Network Information Center
Audience:	Internet Surfers
Contact:	info@sura.net
Details:	Free
	File is: pub/nic/network.service.guides/how.to.ftp.guide

`ftp://ftp.sura.net`

FTP Setup

Tips on using FTP, an Internet access tool.

Keywords:	Internet Tools, FTP
Sponsor:	Carnegie Mellon University, Pittsburgh, PA
Audience:	Internet Surfers
Details:	Free
	File is: pub/tech_tips/anonymous_ftp

`ftp://cert.org`

Fuller (Buckminster)

Geodesic

A mailing list for the discussion of Buckminster Fuller's works.

Keywords:	Geodesic Quantum Physics, Design, Fuller (Buckminster)
Audience:	Designers, Physicists
Contact:	Patrick G. Salsbury SALSBURY@ACSU.BUFFALO.EDU
Details:	Free
User Info:	To subscribe to the list, send an e-mail message to the URL address shown below consisting of a single line reading:
	SUB geodesic YourFirstName YourLastName
	To send a message to the entire list, address it to: GEODESIC@UBVM.CC.BUFFALO.EDU

`mailto: LISTSERV@UBVM.CC.BUFFALO.EDU`

Funding

Research (Funding Support List)

The Research list is for people (primarily at educational institutions) interested in applying for funding support from various sources.

Keywords:	Grants, Funding

Audience:	Educators (College, Graduate)	
Profile:	This list assists faculty in locating sources of support from government agencies, corporations, and foundations. It also forwards information regarding the latest news from potential sponsors such as the National Science Foundation and the National Institutes of Health, and provides information on upcoming international seminars on various topics ranging from medicine to artificial intelligence.	
Contact:	Eleanor Cicinsky v2153a@vm.temple.edu	
User Info:	To subscribe to the list, send an e-mail message to the address below consisting of a single line reading: SUB research YourFirstName YourLastName To send a message to the entire list, address it to: research@vm.temple.edu	

mailto:listserv@vm.temple.edu

Funet Sports Information

Funet Sports Information ★★★★

An FTP archive of information on various sports with links to the archive at wuarchive.wustl.edu.

Keywords:	Sports, Hockey, Football, Basketball, Baseball
Sponsor:	Finnish Academic and Research Network (FUNET)
Audience:	Sports Enthusiasts
Profile:	A fairly extensive archive of information on both American (NBA, MLB, NHL, NFL) and worldwide sports (soccer, ice hockey, motor racing, and so on). Includes FAQs for various sports, statistics, pictures, and some sports games for the PC.
Contact:	Jari Pullinen sports-adm@nic.funet.fi
Details:	Free, Images

gopher://ftp.funet.fi/pub/sports

Funk Music

Funky Music

This mailing list covers funk and funk-influenced music, including hip-hop, house party, soul, and rhythm and blues.

Keywords:	Musical Genres, Funk Music
Audience:	Musicians, Funk Music Enthusiasts
Details:	Free
User Info:	To subscribe to the list, send an e-mail message requesting a subscription to the URL address below. To send a message to the entire list, address it to: funky-music@mit.edu

mailto:funky-music-request@mit.edu

Fusion

fusion ★

Fusion is an e-mail redistribution of Usenet sci.physics.fusion newsgroup for sites/users lacking access to Usenet.

Keywords:	Physics, Fusion, Science
Audience:	Physicists, Scientists
Details:	Free
User Info:	To subscribe to the list, send an e-mail message requesting a subscription to the URL address below. To send a message to the entire list, address it to: fusion@zorch.sf-bay.org

mailto:fusion-request@zorch.sf-bay.org

Futurebus+ Users

Futurebus+ Users ★

This discussion group focuses on the design, implementation, integration, and operation of hardware and software related to Futurebus+.

Keywords:	Computer Users, Hardware, Software
Audience:	Computer Users, Software Engineers, Hardware Engineers
Contact:	majordomo@theus.rain.com
Details:	Free
User Info:	To subscribe to the list, send an e-mail message to the URL address below consisting of a single line reading: SUB fbus_users YourFirstName YourLastName To send a message to the entire list, address it to: fbus_users+@theus.rain.com

mailto:majordomo@theus.rain.com

FutureCulture FAQ (Frequently Asked Questions) File

FutureCulture FAQ (Frequently Asked Questions) File ★★★

List of online and offline items of interest to subscribers of FutureCulture, a mailing list on 'technoculture' or 'new edge' or 'cyberculture.'

Keywords:	Technology, Cyberculture, Postmodernism, Sci-Fi, Zines
Audience:	Reality Hackers, Cyberculture Enthusiasts
Profile:	This list discusses cyberpunk culture, rave culture, industrial music, virtual reality, drugs, computer underground, Net sociology, and virtual communities.
Contact:	Alias Datura (adatura on IRC) adatura@uafhp.uark.edu
Details:	Free

ftp://etext.archive.umich.edu/pub

Fuzzy Logic

fuzzy-mail

Discussion of fuzzy logic, fuzzy sets. It is linked with the NAFIPS-L list and the comp.ai.fuzzy newsgroup.

Keywords:	Fuzzy Logic
Audience:	Programmers
Contact:	listserv@vexpert.dbai.tuwien.ac.at
Details:	Free, Moderated
User Info:	To subscribe to the list, send an e-mail message to the URL address below consisting of a single line reading: SUB fuzzy-mail YourFirstName YourLastName To send a message to the entire list, address it to: fuzzy-mail@vexpert.dbai.tuwien.ac.at

mailto:listserv@vexpert.dbai.tuwien.ac.at

fuzzy-ramblings

fuzzy-ramblings

Discussion of the British girl-group "We've Got a Fuzzbox and We're Going to Use It!"

Keywords:	Music
Audience:	Musicians, Music Enthusiasts
Details:	Free
User Info:	To subscribe to the list, send an e-mail message requesting a subscription to the URL address below. To send a message to the entire list, address it to: fuzzy-ramblings@piggy.ucsb.edu

mailto:fuzzy-ramblings-request@piggy.ucsb.edu

fwake-l

fwake-l

A conference and forum for a broad discussion of James Joyce's *Finnegan's Wake*.

Keywords:	Joyce (James), Literature (Irish), Writing
Audience:	Writers, Joyce Scholars, Literary Critics, Literary Theorists

User Info: To subscribe to the list, send an e-mail message to the URL address below consisting of a single line reading:
SUB fwake-l YourFirstName YourLastName

`mailto:listserv@irlearn.ucd.ie`

FYI on Questions and Answers to Commonly asked New Internet User Questions

FYI on Questions and Answers to Commonly asked New Internet User Questions

Answers to questions commonly asked by new Internet users.

Keywords: Internet, Internet Resources
Sponsor: Xylogics, Inc. and SRI International
Audience: Internet Surfers
Contact: Gary Scott Malkin or April N. Marine
gmalkin@Xylogics.com
april@nisc.sri.com
Details: Free
User Info: File is: documents/fyi/RFC_1594.txt

`ftp://nic.merit.edu`

G

gaelic-l

Gaelic-L

A multidisciplinary discussion list that facilitates the exchange of news, views, and information in Scottish Gaelic, Irish, and Manx.

Keywords: Scottish Gaelic, Irish, Manx, Linguistics

Audience: Linguists

Contact: Marion Gunn
mgunn@irlearn.ucd.ie or
caoimhin@smo.ac.uk
lss203@cs.napier.ac.uk

Details: Free

User Info: To subscribe to the list, send an e-mail message to the URL address shown below, consisting of a single line reading:

SUB gaelic-l YourFirstName YourLastName

To send a message to the entire list, address it to: gaelic-l@irlearn.ucd.ie

`mailto:listserv@irlearn.ucd.ie`

Galway (Ireland)

The Complete Guide to Galway

This is a detailed guide to the city of Galway (past and present), covering tourist sites, industry, local transportation, folklore, history, entertainment, drinking and dining. This web site includes maps, photographs and illustrations.

Keywords: Galway (Ireland), Tourism, Travel

Audience: Irish, Tourists, Historians, Businesses

Contact: Joe Desbonnet
joe@epona.physics.ucg.ie

`http://wombatix.physics.ucg.ie/galway/galway.html`

University of New Hampshire Videotex Library

The library's holdings are large and wide-ranging and contain significant collections in many fields.

Keywords: Dance, Folk Music, Milne (A.A., Collection of), Galway (Ireland)

Audience: Researchers, Students, General Public

Contact: Robin Tuttle
r_tuttle1@unhh.unh.edu

Details: Free

Expect: USERNAME; Send: Student (no password required). Control-z to log off.

`telnet://unhvt@unh.edu`

Gambling

rec.gambling

Discussion of card games, gambling, and gambling sites.

Keywords: Cards, Gambling

Audience: Card Players, Gamblers

Profile: Discussion in this group covers gambling and card games, the rules of various card games, odds, betting, and the pros and cons of various gambling and card playing sites. The archived FAQ is a lengthy card game resource.

Contact: rec.gambling Moderator
jacobs@cs.utah.edu

Notes: The rec.gambling FAQ is accessible via anonymous ftp at soda.berkeley.edu through the path pub/rec.gambling.

`news:rec.gambling`

University of Nevada, Las Vegas Library - Las Vegas, NV

The library's holdings are large and wide-ranging and contain significant collections in many fields.

Keywords: Gambling, Hotel Administration, Nevadiana, Canadian Documents, Nevada State Documents

Audience: General Public, Researchers, Librarians, Document Delivery Professionals

Contact: Myoung-ja Lee Kwon
kwon@nevada.edu.

Details: Free

Expect: login; Send: library

`telnet://library.lv-lib.nevada.edu`

Game Theory

Pd-games

A mailing list for people interested in game theory, especially Prisoner's Dilemma types of problems. Discussions include purely technical issues and questions, as well as specific scientific applications and the political and ideological aspects and consequences of game theory.

Keywords: Game Theory, Mathematics

Audience: Game Theorists, Mathematicians

Contact: Thomas Gramstad
pd-games-request@math.uio.no

Details: Free

User Info: To subscribe to the list, send an e-mail message requesting a subscription to the URL address below.

To send a message to the entire list, address it to: pd-games@math.uio.no

`mailto:pd-games-request@math.uio.no`

Games

ars magica

A mailing list for the discussion of White Wolf's role-playing game, Ars Magica.

Keywords:	Role-Playing, Games
Audience:	Role-playing Enthusiasts, Game Players
Contact:	ars-magica-request@soda.berkeley.edu
User Info:	To subscribe to the list, send an e-mail message to the URL address below.
	To send a message to the entire list, address it to: ars-magica-request@soda.berkeley.edu
	Also available upon request as a nightly digest.

mailto:ars-magica-request@soda.berkeley.edu

Chessnews

A mailing list for the discussion of chess and related events.

Keywords:	Chess, Games
Audience:	Chess Enthusiasts
Contact:	Michael Nolan chessnews-request@tssi.com
Details:	Free
User Info:	To subscribe to the list, send an e-mail message requesting a subscription to the URL address below.
	To send a message to the entire list, address it to: chessnews@tssi.com
Notes:	The Chessnews mailing list is a repeater for the USENET newsgroup rec.games.chess. This is a bi-directional repeater. Postings originating from USENET are sent to the list, and those originating from the list are sent to re

mailto:chessnews-request@tssi.com

Digital Games Review

Reviews of video and computer entertainment titles for the entire industry.

Keywords:	Computer Games, Games, Video Games
Audience:	Computer Game Players, Computer Game Developers
Profile:	Reviews are written by computer game enthusiasts, with an eye to accessibility, enjoyment, and fun, as well as to graphics, technical sophistication, and complexity.
Contact:	Dave Taylor taylor@intuitive.com
Details:	Free

mailto:digital-games-request@intuitive.com

flashlife

A mailing list for general managers of Shadowrun and other cyberpunk role-playing games to discuss rules and scenarios, ask questions, and make up answers.

Keywords:	Games, Cyberpunk Games
Audience:	Game Players
Details:	Free
User Info:	To subscribe to the list, send an e-mail message requesting a subscription to the URL address below.
	To send a message to the entire list, address it to: flashlife@netcom.com

mailto:flashlife-request@netcom.com

GameBytes magazine

This monthly electronic magazine provides reviews (with graphics) of electronic games.

Keywords:	Games, Electronic Media, Entertainment
Sponsor:	Game Bytes Magazine
Audience:	Game Players, Computer Game Developers, Computer Graphic Designers
Contact:	Ross Erickson rwericks@ingr.com
Details:	Free

http://wcl-rs.bham.ac.uk/GameBytes

Internet Hunt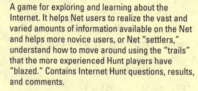

A game for exploring and learning about the Internet. It helps Net users to realize the vast and varied amounts of information available on the Net and helps more novice users, or Net "settlers," understand how to move around using the "trails" that the more experienced Hunt players have "blazed." Contains Internet Hunt questions, results, and comments.

Keywords:	Internet, Internet Guides, Games
Sponsor:	CICnet
Audience:	Internet Surfers
Contact:	Rick Gates rgates@nic.cic.net
Details:	Free

gopher://gopher.cic.net

MUD

A discussion list for the exchange of information about new and recommended Multiuser Dungeons and Dragons (MUDs).

Keywords:	MUDs, Games
Audience:	MUD Users
Contact:	Joseph Wisdom jwisdom@gnu.ai.mit.edu
Details:	Free
User Info:	To subscribe to the list, send an e-mail message requesting subscription to the URL address below.

mailto:jwisdom@gnu.ai.mit.edu

Nero Ashbury

Nero is a live-action, medieval role-playing game with a plot line and characters that continue from one adventure to the next. Nero has been successful in New England for over six years and is growing rapidly.

Keywords:	Medieval Studies, Role-Playing, Games
Audience:	General Public, Role-Playing Enthusiasts
Contact:	lsonko@pearl.tufts.edu
Details:	Free
User Info:	To subscribe to the list, send an e-mail message requesting a subscription to the URL address below.

mailto:lsonko@pearl.tufts.edu

rec.gambling

A Usenet newsgroup providing information and discussion about gambling.

Keywords:	Games, Gambling, Recreation
Audience:	Gamblers
User Info:	To subscribe to this Usenet newsgroup, you need access to a newsreader.

news:rec.gambling

rec.games.board

A Usenet newsgroup providing hints and discussion about board games.

Keywords:	Games, Recreation
Audience:	Game Players
User Info:	To subscribe to this Usenet newsgroup, you need access to a newsreader.

news:rec.games.board

rec.games.chess

A Usenet newsgroup providing information and discussion about chess strategies, organized computer chess playing events, and software.

Keywords:	Chess, Games, Recreation
Audience:	Chess Players, Game Players
User Info:	To subscribe to this Usenet newsgroup, you need access to a newsreader.

news:rec.games.chess

rec.games.programmer

A Usenet newsgroup providing information and discussion about adventure game programming.

Keywords:	Games, Programming, Video Games

Audience: Programmers
User Info: To subscribe to this Usenet newsgroup, you need access to a newsreader.

`news:rec.games.programmer`

rec.games.video.arcade

A Usenet newsgroup providing information and discussion about video games.

Keywords: Games, Video Games
Audience: Game Players
User Info: To subscribe to this Usenet newsgroup, you need access to a newsreader.

`news:rec.games.video.arcade`

rec.puzzles

A Usenet newsgroup providing information and discussion about math puzzles and brain teasers.

Keywords: Games, Puzzles, Recreation
Audience: General Public
User Info: To subscribe to this Usenet newsgroup, you need access to a newsreader.

`news:rec.puzzles`

Zarf's List of Interactive Games on the Web

A list containing links to games and toys that can be played on the Internet.

Keywords: Games, toys, entertainment, recreation
Sponsor: Carnegie Mellon University, School of Computer Science, Pittsburgh, Pennsylvania, USA
Audience: General Public, Game Players, Kids
Contact: Andrew Plotkin
zarf@cs.cmu.edu, apli@andrew.cmu.edu

`http://www.cs.cmu.edu/:8001//afs/cs.cmu.edu/user/zarf/www/games.html`

GAO

GAO

Files intended to provide Congress and Administration with an overview of health problems facing the nation.

Keywords: Health, Congress (US)
Audience: US Congress, Journalists, General Public
Profile: These files concern health-care reform and human services and date from December 1992. They are provided by the government to familiarize the reader with the health issues confronting the administration.
Details: Free
Notes: Login: anonymous ABSTRACT.FIL is a file with abstracts for each of the 28 reports.

`ftp://cu.nig.gov`

Gardening

alt.bonsai

A Usenet newsgroup providing information and discussion about Bonsai gardening.

Keywords: Bonsai Trees, Japan, Gardening, Landscaping
Audience: Gardeners, Bonsai Enthusiasts
User Info: To subscribe to this Usenet newsgroup, you need access to a newsreader.

`news:alt.bonsai`

rec.gardens

A Usenet newsgroup providing information and discussion about gardening.

Keywords: Gardening, Landscaping
Audience: Gardeners
User Info: To subscribe to this Usenet newsgroup, you need access to a newsreader.

`news:rec.gardens`

Gateway2000

Gateway2000

This list is a source of information about Gateway2000 products.

Keywords: Computer Products, Software, Hardware
Audience: Computer Users, Hardware Engineers, Software Engineers
Details: Free
User Info: To subscribe to the list, send an e-mail message requesting a subscription to the URL address below.

To send a message to the entire list, address it to: gateway2000@sei.cmu.edu

`gateway2000-request@sei.cmu.edu`

Gay Rights

Amend2-discuss

A mailing list for discussion of the implications and issues surrounding the passage of Colorado's Amendment 2, which revokes any existing homosexual civil rights legislation and prohibits the drafting of any new legislation.

Keywords: Activism, Gay Rights, Lesbians, Bisexuality
Audience: Gay Rights Activists
Contact: amend2-mod@cs.colorado.edu
User Info: To subscribe to the list, send an e-mail message to the URL address below, consisting of a single line reading:

subscribe amend2-discuss

`mailto:majordomo@cs.colorado.edu`

freedom

Mailing list of people organizing against the Idaho Citizens Alliance antigay ballot initiative.

Keywords: Gay Rights, Activism, Gays
Audience: Gays, Lesbians, Bisexuals, Idaho Citizens, Activists
Details: Free
User Info: To subscribe to the list, send an e-mail message to the URL address shown below, consisting of a single line reading:

SUB freedom YourFirstName YourLastName.

To send a message to the entire list, address it to: freedom@idbsu.idbsu.edu

`mailto:listserv@idbsu.idbsu.edu`

Qn

A mailing list for Queer Nation activists and for anyone interested in Queer Nation, an activist group devoted to furthering gay rights. The purpose of qn is to network among various Queer Nation chapters, to discuss actions and tactics to bring about Queer Liberation.

Keywords: Homosexuality, Gay Rights, Activism
Audience: Gay Rights Activists, Political Activists
Contact: Roger Klorese
qn-request@queernet.org
Details: Free
User Info: To subscribe to the list, send an e-mail message requesting a subscription to the URL address below.

To send a message to the entire list, address it to: qn@queernet.org

`mailto:qn-request@queernet.org`

Stonewall25

A mailing list for discussion and planning of the "Stonewall 25," an international gay/lesbian/bisexual rights march in New York City on Sunday, June 26, 1994, and the events accompanying it.

Keywords: Gay Rights, Lesbian, Bisexual, Activism
Audience: Gays, Lesbians, Bisexuals, Activists
Contact: stonewall25-request@queernet.org
Details: Free
User Info: To subscribe to the list, send an e-mail message requesting a subscription to the URL address below.

To send a message to the entire list, address it to: stonewall25@queernet.org

`mailto:stonewall25-request@queernet.org`

Gays

AUGLBC-l

The American University Gay, Lesbian, and Bisexual Community (AUGLBC) is a support group for lesbian, gay, bisexual, transsexual, and supportive students. The group is also connected with the International Gay and Lesbian Youth Organization (known as IGLYO).

Keywords:	Gays, Lesbians, Bisexuals, Transsexuality, Sexuality
Audience:	Gays, Lesbians, Bisexuals, Transsexuals, Students (college)
Contact:	Erik G. Paul
User Info:	To subscribe to the list, send an e-mail message to the URL address below, consisting of a single line reading:
	SUB AUGLBC-l YourFirstName YourLastName
	To send a message to the entire list, address it to: AUGLBC-l@american.edu

mailto:listserv@american.edu

AusGBLF

An Australian-based mailing list for gays, bisexuals, lesbians, and friends.

Keywords:	Australia, Gays, Lesbians, Bisexuality
Audience:	Gays, Lesbians, Bisexuals
Contact:	zglc@minyos.xx.rmit.oz.au
Details:	Free
User Info:	To subscribe to the list, send an e-mail message requesting a subscription to the URL address below.
	To send a message to the entire list, address it to: ausgblf@minyos.xx.rmit.oz.au

mailto:ausgblf-request@minyos.xx.rmit.oz.au

Bears

A mailing list in digest format for gay and bisexual men who are bears themselves and for those who enjoy the company of bears. The definition of a "bear" encompasses men who are variously cuddly, furry, perhaps stocky, or bearded. Mail.bears is designed to be a forum to bring together folks with similar interests for conversation, friendship, and sharing of experiences.

Keywords:	Gays, Bisexuality
Audience:	Gays, Bisexuals
Contact:	Steve Dyer, Brian Gollum bears-request@spdcc.COM
Details:	Free
User Info:	To subscribe to the list, send an e-mail message requesting a subscription to the URL address below.
	To send a message to the entire list, address it to: bears@spdcc.COM

mailto:bears-request@spdcc.COM

Chorus

This is the lesbian and gay chorus mailing list, formed November 1991 by John Schrag (jschrag@alias.com) and Brian Jarvis (jarvis@psych.toronto.edu). Membership includes artistic directors, singers, chorus officers, interpreters, and support staff and friends. Topics of discussion include repertoire, arrangements, staging, costuming, management, fundraising, music, events, and concerts.

Keywords:	Singing, Choral Singing, Homosexuality, Gays, Lesbians
Audience:	Lesbian Singers, Gay Singers, Chorus Officers, Lesbians, Gays, Choral Singers
Contact:	chorus-request@psych.toronto.edu
Details:	Free
User Info:	To subscribe to the list, send an e-mail message requesting a subscription to the URL address below.
	To send a message to the entire list, address it to: chorus@psych.toronto.edu

mailto:chorus-request@psych.toronto.edu

DC-MOTSS

DC-MOTSS is a social mailing list for the gay, lesbian, and bisexual folks who live in the Washington Metropolitan Area—everything within approximately 50 miles of The Mall.

Keywords:	Gays, Lesbians, Bisexuality, Washington DC
Audience:	Gays, Lesbians, Bisexuals, Washington DC Residents
Contact:	DC-MOTSS-request@vector.intercon.com
Details:	Free
User Info:	To subscribe to the list, send an e-mail message requesting a subscription to the URL address below.
	To send a message to the entire list, address it to: DC-MOTSS-request@vector.intercon.com

mailto:DC-MOTSS-request@vector.intercon.com

DSA-LGB

DSA-LGB is a mailing list for members of the Lesbian/Gay/Bisexual Commission of the Democratic Socialists of America, and for others interested in similar concerns.

Keywords:	Democratic Socialists of America, Gays, Lesbians
Audience:	Democratic Socialists, Gays, Lesbians
Contact:	DSA-LGB-request@midway.uchicago.edu
User Info:	To subscribe to the list, send an e-mail message requesting a subscription to the URL address below.
	To send a message to the entire list, address it to: DSA-LGB-request@midway.uchicago.edu

mailto:DSA-LGB-request@midway.uchicago.edu

eagles

This list provides a forum for Boy Scouts, Scouters, and former Scouts who are gay/bisexual to discuss how they can apply pressure to the BSA to change their homophobic policies.

Keywords:	Boy Scouts, Gays, Lesbians
Audience:	Gays, Lesbians, Boy Scouts, Former Boy Scouts
Contact:	eagles-request@flash.usc.edu
Details:	Free
User Info:	To subscribe to the list, send an e-mail message requesting a subscription to the URL address below.
	To send a message to the entire list, address it to: eagles-request@flash.usc.edu

mailto:eagles-request@flash.usc.edu

gay-libn

A network for gay, lesbian, and bisexual librarians.

Keywords:	Libraries, Gays, Lesbians, Bisexuality
Audience:	Librarians, Gays, Lesbians, Bisexuals
Details:	Free
User Info:	To subscribe to the list, send an e-mail message to the URL address below, consisting of a single line reading:
	SUB gay-libn YourFirstName YourLastName
	To send a message to the entire list, address it to: gay-libn@vm.usc.edu

mailto:listserv@vm.usc.edu

gaynet

This list covers gay, lesbian, and bisexual concerns (with a focus on college campuses), including outreach programs, political action, AIDS education, school administration issues, social programs, and support group exchanges.

Keywords:	Gays, Lesbians
Audience:	Gays, Lesbians, Bisexuals, Students
Contact:	Roger B.A. Klorese gaynet-approval@queernet.org

Details:	Free
User Info:	To subscribe to the list, send an e-mail message to the URL address below, consisting of a single line reading:
	SUB gaynet YourFirstName YourLastName
	To send a message to the entire list, address it to: gaynet@queernet.org

mailto:majordomo@queernet.org

Ne-social-motss

Announcements of lesbian/gay/bisexual social events and other happenings in the Northeastern US.

Keywords:	Social Events, Lesbians, Gays, Bisexuality
Audience:	Lesbians, Gays, Bisexuals
Contact:	ne-social-motss-request@plts.org
Details:	Free
User Info:	To subscribe to the list, send an e-mail message requesting a subscription to the URL address below.

mailto:ne-social-motss-request@plts.org

NJ-motss

Mailing list for gay, lesbian, and bisexual issues in New Jersey.

Keywords:	Gays, Lesbians, Bisexuality, New Jersey
Audience:	Gays, Lesbians, Bisexuals
Contact:	majordomo@plts.org
Details:	Free
User Info:	To subscribe to the list, send an e-mail message to the URL address shown below, consisting of a single line reading:
	SUB NJ-motss YourFirstName YourLastName
	To send a message to the entire list, address it to: NJ-motss@plts.org

mailto: majordomo@plts.org

NJ-motss-announce

Announcements of interests to New Jersey's gay, lesbian, and bisexual population.

Keywords:	Gays, Lesbians, Bisexuality, New Jersey
Audience:	Gays, Lesbians, Bisexuals
Contact:	majordomo@plts.org
Details:	Free
User Info:	To subscribe to the list, send an e-mail message to the URL address shown below, consisting of a single line reading:
	SUB NJ-motss-announce YourFirstName YourLastName
	To send a message to the entire list, address it to: NJ-motss-announce@plts.org

mailto:majordomo@plts.org

noglstp

This list is sponsored by the National Organization of Gay and Lesbian Scientists and Technical Professionals, Inc. (a 501-C3 organization). National office is in Pasadena, CA and can be reached at (818) 791-7689 or P.O. Box 91803, Pasadena, CA 90019. There is also a newsletter that is available to membership.

Keywords:	Gays, Lesbians, Scientists, Technical Professionals
Audience:	Gay Scientists, Lesbian Scientists
Contact:	noglstp-request@elroy.jpl.nasa.gov
Details:	Free
User Info:	To subscribe to the list, send an e-mail message requesting a subscription to the URL address below.
	To send a message to the entire list, address it to: noglstp@elroy.jpl.nasa.gov

mailto:noglstp-request@elroy.jpl.nasa.gov

Oh-motss

The oh-motss (Ohio Members of the Same Sex) mailing list is for open discussion of lesbian, gay, and bisexual issues in and affecting Ohio. The mailing list is not moderated. It is open to all, regardless of location or sexuality. The subscriber list is known only to the list owner.

Keywords:	Gays, Lesbians, Ohio
Audience:	Gays, Lesbians
Contact:	oh-motss-request@cps.udayton.edu
Details:	Free
User Info:	To subscribe to the list, send an e-mail message requesting a subscription to the URL address below.
	To send a message to the entire list, address it to: oh-motss@cps.udayton.edu

mailto:oh-motss-request@cps.udayton.edu

OUTIL (Out in Linguistics)

The list is open to lesbian, gay, bisexual, transsexual linguists and their friends. The only requirement is that you be willing to be out to everyone on the list. The purposes of the group are to be visible and to gather occasionally to enjoy one another's company.

Keywords:	Linguistics, Gays, Lesbians, Bisexuals, Transsexuality
Audience:	Linguists, Gays, Lesbians, Bisexuality, Transsexuals
Contact:	Arnold Zwicky outil-request@csli.stanford.edu
Details:	Free
User Info:	To subscribe to the list, send an e-mail message requesting a subscription to the URL address below.
	To send a message to the entire list, address it to: outil@csli.stanford.edu

mailto:outil-request@csli.stanford.edu

soc.motss

A Usenet newsgroup providing information and discussion about homosexuality.

Keywords:	Homosexuality, Gays, Lesbians, Bisexuality
Audience:	Gays, Lesbians, Bisexuals
Details:	Free
User Info:	To subscribe to this Usenet newsgroup, you need access to a newsreader.

news:soc.motss

GC-L

GC-L

Project for international business and management curricula.

Keywords:	Business, Management, Linguistics
Sponsor:	Global Classroom
Audience:	Linguists, Language Teachers, Language Students, International Business Professionals
Details:	Free
User Info:	To subscribe to the list, send an e-mail message to the address below, consisting of a single line reading:
	SUB gc-l YourFirstName YourLastName
	To send a message to the entire list, address it: gc-l@uriacc.uri.edu

mailto:listserv@uriacc.uri.edu

Gegstaff

Gegstaff

All topics relating to sexuality and gender in geography.

Keywords:	Geography, Sexuality
Audience:	Geographers, Sex Enthusiasts
Details:	Free
User Info:	To subscribe to the list, send an e-mail message to the URL address shown below, consisting of a single line reading:

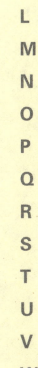

A B C D E F G H I J K L M N O P Q R S T U V W X Y Z

SUB gegstaff YourFirstName YourLastName

To send a message to the entire list, address it to: gegstaff@ukcc.uky.edu

`mailto:listserv@ukcc.uky.edu`

Gender

Amazons International

An electronic digest newsletter for and about Amazons (physically and psychologically strong, assertive women who are challenging traditional ideas about gender roles, femininity, and the female physique).

Keywords:	Gender, Amazons, Feminism
Audience:	Women, Feminists, Writers, Art Historians
Profile:	The digest is dedicated to the image of the female hero in fiction and in fact, as it is expressed in art and literature, in the physiques and feats of female athletes, and in sexual values and practices; it also provides information, discussion, and a supportive environment for these values and issues.
Contact:	Thomas Gramstad amazons-request@math.uio.no
Details:	Free
User Info:	To subscribe to the list, send an e-mail message requesting a subscription to the URL address below.
	To send a message to the entire list, address it to: amazons@math.uio.no

`mailto:amazons-request@math.uio.no`

BITHRY-L

This list is for the theoretical discussion of bisexuality and gender issues. It is not a social group, a support group, or an announcement or news forum.

Keywords:	Bisexuality, Gender
Audience:	Bisexuals
Contact:	Elaine Brennan listserv@brownvm.brown.edu
Details:	Free
User Info:	To subscribe to the list, send an e-mail message to the URL address below, consisting of a single line reading:
	SUB bithry-l YourFirstName YourLastName
	To send a message to the entire list, address it to: bithry-l@brownvm.brown.edu

`mailto:listserv@brownvm.brown.edu`

Cd-Forum

The purpose of this list is to provide support and to discuss/share experiences about gender-related issues, including cross dressing, transvestism, and transsexualism.

Keywords:	Transsexualism, Transvestism, Sexuality, Gender
Audience:	Transsexuals, Transvestites
Contact:	Valerie cd-request@valis.biocad.com
Details:	Free
User Info:	To subscribe to the list, send an e-mail message requesting a subscription to the URL address below.
	To send a message to the entire list, address it to: cd@valis.biocad.com
Notes:	This list is in digest format.

`mailto:cd-request@valis.biocad.com`

soc.men

A Usenet newsgroup providing information and discussion about men, their problems, and their relationships.

Keywords:	Men's Movement, Gender
Audience:	Men, Activists
Details:	Free
User Info:	To subscribe to this Usenet newsgroup, you need access to a newsreader.

`news:soc.men`

Women.news

This conference features news and action alerts about women and women's issues around the world — including human rights, feminism, health, sexual abuse, workers, population, abortion, activism, development, and peace.

Keywords:	Feminism, Gender, Women
Audience:	Women, Feminists, Activists
Contact:	Debra Guzman, Sue VanHattum hrcoord@igc.apc.org suev@igc.apc.org
Details:	Free
User Info:	Establish an account on the nearest APC node. Login, type c for conferences, then type go women.news.
	For information on the nearest APC node, contact: APC International Secretariat IBASE
	E-mail: apcadmin@apc.org

`telnet://igc.apc.org`

Geneology

Geneology

A large collection of geneology resources for both beginners and specialists. Includes archives of geneology lists, FAQs, helper software, and specific geneological information for a number of national and ethnic groups.

Keywords:	Geneology, Ethnic Studies
Sponsor:	Go M-Link at the University of Michigan
Audience:	Geneologists, General Public, Researchers
Contact:	Sue Davidsen davidsen@umich.edu

`gopher://vienna.hh.lib.umich.edu`

General Hacking Info

General Hacking Info

Files on the topic of hacking.

Keywords:	Hacking, Computers
Audience:	Hackers, Computer Users
Details:	Free
	Expect: login, Send: anonymous;
	Expect: Password, Send: Your e-mail Address

`ftp://ftp.eff.org`

GENESIS

Purkinje Park

A server maintained by CalTech to support the sharing of information between users of the GENESIS neural simulator, and to address topics of general interest to the Computational Neuroscience community.

Keywords:	Computational Neuroscience, GENESIS, Neural Simulation.
Sponsor:	Cal Tech
Audience:	Neuroscientists, Computational Neuroscientists
Contact:	Dave Beeman dbeeman@smaug.bbb.caltech.edu

`http://www.bbb.caltech.edu/index.html`

Genetics

bionet.molbio.genbank.updates ★

A Usenet newsgroup providing information and discussion about the GenBank Nucleic acid database.

Keywords: Molecular Biology, Biology, Genetics
Audience: Molecular Biologists, Researchers
User Info: To subscribe to this Usenet newsgroup, you need access to a newsreader.

`news:bionet.molbio.genbank.updates`

Drosophila Information Newsletter ★

A quarterly electronic publication; this is an offshoot of Drosophila Information Service.

Keywords: Drosophila, Biology, Genetics
Audience: Biologists, Geneticists
Contact: Kathy Matthews
MATTHEWK@UCS.INDIANA.EDU
Details: Free
User Info: To subscribe, send an e-mail message to the address below, consisting of a single line reading:

SUB drosophila-information-newsletter YourFirstName Your Last Name

To send a message to the entire list, address it to: drosophila.information.newsletter@ucs.indiana.edu

`mailto:listserv@iubvm.ucs.indiana.edu`

GenBank

The GenBank database provides a collection of nucleotide sequences as well as relevant bibliographic and biological annotation.

Keywords: Genetics, Medicine, Molecular Biology
Sponsor: National Center for Biotechnology Information (NCBI) at the National Library of Medicine (NLM)
Audience: Geneticists, Scientists, Molecular Biologists
Profile: DNA sequence entries are rated by specialized indexers in the Division of Library Operations. Over 325,000 articles per year from 3,400 journals are scanned for sequence data. They are supplemented by journals in plant and veterinary sciences through a collaboration with the National Agricultural Library. These records join the direct submission data stream and submissions from the European Molecular Biology Laboratory (EMBL) Data Library and the DNA Database of Japan (DDBJ).

Contact: info@ncbi.nlm.nih.gov
Details: Free

Send direct submissions to gb-sub@ncbi.nlm.nih.gov and updates and changes to existing GenBank records to update@ncbi.nlm.nih.gov For help in retrieval by e-mail send an e-mail message with the word "help" in the body of the message to retrieve@ncbi.nlm.hih.gov

`gopher://gopher.nih.gov/77/gopherlib/indices/genbank/index`

Johns Hopkins Genetic Databases ★★★

This gopher provides electronic access to documents pertaining to computational biology and a number of different genetic databases.

Keywords: Genetics, Molecular Biology, Medicine, Biology
Sponsor: Johns Hopkins University
Audience: Geneticists, Researchers, Scientists, Molecular Biologists
Profile: The databases accessible from this entry point include GenBank, Swiss-Prot, PDB, PIR, LiMB, TFD, AAtDB, ACEDB, CompoundKB, PROSITE EC Enzyme Database, NRL_3D Protein-Sequence-Structure Database, Eukaryotic Promoter Database (EPD), Cloning Vector Database, Expressed Sequence Tag Database (ESTDB), Online Mendelian Inheritance Man (OMIM), Sequence Analysis Bibliographic Reference Data Bank (Seqanalref), and Database Taxonomy (GenBank, Swiss-Prot). The gopher also provides direct links to other gophers with information relevant to biology.
Contact: Dan Jacobson
danj@mail.gdb.org
Details: Free

`gopher://merlot.welch.jhu.edu`

MGD (Mouse Genome Database)

This site provides a comprehensive database of genetic information on the laboratory mouse.

Keywords: Biology, Genetics
Sponsor: The Jackson Laboratory
Audience: Biologists, Researchers, Educators, Students
Contact: mgi-help@informatics.jax.org
Details: Free
Notes: Contact Mouse Genome Informatics User Support by telephone at (207) 288-3371, X 1900, or by FAX at (207) 288-2516.

`http://www.informatics.jax.org/mgd.html`

The Tumor Gene Database

A database containing information about genes associated with tumorigenesis and cellular transformation.

Keywords: Genetics, Diseases, Biomedical Research, Databases
Sponsor: Department of Cell Biology, Baylor College of Medicine
Audience: Biomedical Researchers
Contact: David Steffen, Ph.D.
steffen@bcm.tmc.edu

`gopher://mbcr.bcm.tmc.edu`

GENFED (General Federal Library)

GENFED (General Federal Library)

The General Federal library is a comprehensive collection of federal legal materials of a general nature, including case law, legislative and regulatory materials, administrative decisions, court rules, and publications.

Keywords: Law (US Case), Law (US Federal)
Audience: Lawyers
Profile: The General Federal library is a comprehensive collection of federal legal materials of a general nature. Case law from all federal courts is available. Legislative materials include the United States Codes Service, United States Public Laws, pending federal legislation, legislative histories, and the Congressional Record. Regulatory materials include the Code of Federal Regulstions and the Federal Register. Administrative decisions, court rules, circuit summaries, sentencing guidelines, and legal publications are also available.
Contact: New Sales Group at 800-227-4908 or 513-859-5398 inside the US, or 1-513-865-7981 for all inquiries outside the US.
Details: Costs
User Info: To subscribe, contact Mead directly.

To examine the Lexis user guide, you can access it at the ftp site of the University of Texas at Austin at the URL address: ftp://ftp.cc.utexas.edu

The files are in: /pub/res-services/LEXIS

`telnet://nex.meaddata.com`

Genius

Mensatalk

A discussion group for members of Mensa.

Keywords: Mensa, Genius
Audience: Mensa Members
Details: Free
User Info: To subscribe to the list, send an e-mail message requesting a subscription to the URL address below.

`mailto:mensatalk-request@psg.com`

GENMED (General Medical Information)

GENMED (General Medical Information)

The General Medical Information (GENMED) library contains a variety of medical care and treatment, toxicology, and hospital administration materials.

Keywords: Medicine, Toxicology, Hospital, Treatment
Audience: Medical Professionals
Profile: The GENMED library contains full-text medical journals and newsletters, as well as drug information, disease, and trauma reviews, Physicians Data Query cancer information, and medical administration journals. GENMED also offers a gateway to the MEDLINE database.
Contact: Mead New Sales Group at (800) 227-4908 or (513) 859-5398 inside the US, or (513) 865-7981 for all inquiries outside the US.
User Info: To subscribe, contact Mead directly.
To examine the Nexis user guide, you can access it at the ftp site of the University of Texas at Austin at the URL address: ftp://ftp.cc.utexas.edu
The files are in: /pub/ref-services/LEXIS

`telnet://nex.meaddata.com`

`http://www.meaddata.com`

Geodesic Quantum Physics

Geodesic

A mailing list for the discussion of Buckminster Fuller's works.

Keywords: Geodesic Quantum Physics, Design, Fuller (Buckminster)
Audience: Designers, Physicists
Contact: Patrick G. Salsbury
salsbury@acsu.buffalo.edu
Details: Free
User Info: To subscribe to the list, send an e-mail message to the URL address shown below consisting of a single line reading:
SUB geodesic YourFirstName YourLastName
To send a message to the entire list, address it to: geodesic@ubvm.cc.buffalo.edu

`mailto:LISTSERV@UBVM.CC.BUFFALO.EDU`

Geographic Information and Analysis Laboratory (GIAL)

Geographic Information and Analysis Laboratory (GIAL)

Server distributing a variety of information related to geography and GIS.

Keywords: Architecture, Geography, GIS, NCGIA
Sponsor: SUNY-Buffalo and the National Center for Geographic Information and Analysis (NCGIA)
Audience: Geographers, GIS Professionals, Researchers, Students
Contact: Brandon Plewe, Reginald O. Carroll, Patricia M. Baumgarten
plewe@geog.buffalo.edu
carrol@geog.buffalo.edu
pmb@geog.buffalo.edu
Details: Free
Images
Notes: Check out the You-are-here server!

`http://zia.geog.buffalo.edu/`

Geography

1991 Census of Population Documentation

This gopher provides Canadian Census information from 1991 including geographic and demographic information.

Keywords: Census Data, Canada, Demography, Geography
Audience: Canadians, Researchers, Demographers
Contact: David McCallum
carl@acadvm1.uottawa.ca

`gopher://alpha.epas.utoronto.ca/Data Library/Census of Population`

ACDGIS-L

GIS discussions for German speakers.

Keywords: Germany, Geographic Information Systems, Geography
Audience: Germans, Geographers, Cartographers
Details: Costsost
Inquire through wigeoarn@awiwuw11.bitnet

`mailto:acdgis-l@awiwuw11.bitnet`

ANU (Australian National University) Asian-Settlements Database

A searchable database containing abstracts of theses and research studies provided by the Asian Institute of Technology, relating to issues of demography and social geography in Asia.

Keywords: Asian Studies, Demography, Geography
Sponsor: The COOMBSQUEST Social Sciences & Humanities Information Facility at ANU (Australian National University), Canberra, Australia
Audience: Asia Studies Instructors, Demographers, Geographers
Contact: Dr. T. Matthew Ciolek
coombspapers@coombs.anu.edu.au
Details: Free

`gopher://cheops.anu.edu.au/Coombs-db/ANU-Asian-Settlements.src`

`http://coombs.anu.edu.au/WWWVL-AsianStudies.html`

Canadian Geographical WWW Index Travel

This web site provides weekly weather information.

Keywords: Weather, Travel, Canada, Geography
Sponsor: University of Manitoba, Canada
Audience: Travelers, Educators, Students
Contact: www@umanitoba.ca
Details: Free

`http://www.umanitoba.ca`

Gegstaff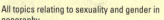

All topics relating to sexuality and gender in geography.

Keywords: Geography, Sexuality
Audience: Geographers, Sex Enthusiasts
Details: Free
User Info: To subscribe to the list, send an e-mail message to the URL address shown below, consisting of a single line reading:

SUB gegstaff YourFirstName YourLastName

To send a message to the entire list, address it to: gegstaff@ukcc.uky.edu

`mailto:listserv@ukcc.uky.edu`

Geographic Information and Analysis Laboratory (GIAL)

Server distributing a variety of information related to geography and GIS.

Keywords: Geography, GIS, NCGIA
Sponsor: SUNY-Buffalo and the National Center for Geographic Information and Analysis (NCGIA)
Audience: Geographers, GIS Professionals, Researchers, Students
Contact: Brandon Plewe, Reginald O. Carroll, Patricia M. Baumgarten
plewe@geog.buffalo.edu,
carrol@geog.buffalo.edu,
pmb@geog.buffalo.edu
Details: Free
Images
Notes: Check out the You-are-here server!

`http://zia.geog.buffalo.edu/`

GIS-L

A forum for the discussion of all issues pertaining to GIS (Geographic Information Systems), including hydrological modeling, environmental issues, and available software packages.

Keywords: Geography, Environment, GIS (Geographic Information Systems)
Audience: Geographers, Cartographers
Contact: David Mark
dmark@acsu.buffalo.edu
User Info: To subscribe to the list, send an e-mail message to the URL address below, consisting of a single line reading:

SUB gis-l YourFirstName YourLastName.

To send a message to the entire list, address it to: gis-l@ubvm.cc.buffalo.edu

`mailto:listserv@ubvm.cc.buffalo.edu`

gis-t

A mailing list for the discussion of GIS (Geographic Information Systems) and transportation.

Keywords: Geography, Transportation, GIS (Geographic Information Systems)
Audience: Geographers, Cartographers
Contact: Jay Sandhu
jsandhu@esri.com

User Info: To subscribe to the list, send an e-mail message to the URL address below, consisting of a single line reading:

SUB gis-t YourFirstName YourLastName.

To send a message to the entire list, address it to: gis-t@esri.com

`mailto:listserv@esri.com`

Internet GIS and RS Information Sites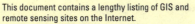

This document contains a lengthy listing of GIS and remote sensing sites on the Internet.

Keywords: GIS, Remote Sensing, Image Processing, Geography
Sponsor: Queen's University Department of Geography
Audience: Researchers, General Public
Contact: Michael McDermott
mcdermom@gisdog.gis.queensu.ca
Details: Free
Notes: ASCII version also available from the same FTP site.

`ftp://gis.queensu.ca/pub/gis/docs/gissites.html`

Internet Resources for Earth Sciences

A document detailing Internet resources for a variety of earth science disciplines including GIS.

Keywords: Directory, GIS, Geology, Geography, GPS, Mapping, Earth Science
Sponsor: Bill Thoen
Audience: Earth Scientists, Researchers
Profile: A complete document detailing the types of information available in earth sciences and the mechanisms to retrieve needed information.
Contact: Bill Thoen
bthoen@gisnet.com
Details: Free

`ftp://ftp.csn.org/COGS/ores.text`

Ireland-Related Online Resources

This is a list of network-accessible online resources (documents, images, information, access mechanisms for offline material, and so on) of Irish interest. Coverage includes some Bulletin Board services, some commercial information systems such as CompuServe and commercial bibliographic services.

Keywords: Ireland, Travel, Commerce, Geography
Audience: Irish, General Public, Tourists, Businesses
Contact: fmurtagh@eso.org

`http://http.hq.eso.org/~fmurtagh/ireland-resources.html`

MAPINFO-L

A mailing list for the discussion of MapInfo.

Keywords: Geographic Information Systems
Audience: Geographers, Cartographers
Contact: Bill Thoen
bthoen@gisnet.com
Details: Free
User Info: To subscribe to the list, send an e-mail message to the URL address below, consisting of a single line reading:

SUB mapinfo-l YourFirstName YourLastName

`mapinfo-l@csn.org`

next-gis

Discussion of Geographical Information Systems (GIS) and cartography-related topics on the NeXT and other workstation computers. Some moderated reposting of comp.infosys.gis occurs as well.

Keywords: Geography, Cartography, GIS, NeXT
Audience: GIS Users, NeXT Users
Contact: Steven R. Staton
sstaton@deltos.com
Details: Free
User Info: To subscribe to the list, send an e-mail message to the URL address shown below, consisting of a single line reading:

SUB next-gis YourFirstName YourLastName

To send a message to the entire list, address it to: next-gis@DistributionAddress

`mailto:listserv@deltos.com`

Sahel-NAFR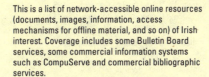

This site contains information about a database of composite satellite images of Sahel and North Africa (known as the Sahelian and NW Africa 14-Day NDVI Composites). The images come from a pilot program defined between the U.S. Geological Survey and the U.S. Agency for International Development (AID) to develop and test a near-real-time monitoring procedure using satellite remote sensing and Geographic Information System technologies in grasshopper and locust control programs in West Africa. Also contains an appendix with information about the Senegalese Grasshoppers.

Keywords: Geology, Geography, GIS (Geographic Information Systems)
Sponsor: U.S. Geological Survey and U.S. Agency for International Development (AID)
Audience: Geologists, Geographers

`http://sun1.cr.usgs.gov/glis/hyper/guide/sahel_nafr`

UIgis-L

A mailing list for the discussion of user interfaces and GIS (Geographic Information Systems).

Keywords:	Geography, GIS (Geographic Information Systems)
Audience:	Geographers, Cartographers
Contact:	David Mark dmark@acsu.buffalo.edu
User Info:	To subscribe to the list, send an e-mail message to the URL address below, consisting of a single line reading: SUB uigis-l YourFirstName YourLastName. To send a message to the entire list, address it to: uigis@ubvm.cc.buffalo.edu

`mailto:listserv@ubvm.cc.buffalo.edu`

United States Geographic Name Server

A database searchable by city name or zip code, this server provides geographic data including population, longitude and latitude, elevation, county, state, and zip codes.

Keywords:	Geography, GIS (Geographical Information Systems)
Audience:	Geographers, General Public
Contact:	pubgopher@pluto.cc.brandeis.edu

`gopher://pluto.cc.brandeis.edu`

United States Geological Survey Home Page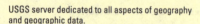

USGS server dedicated to all aspects of geography and geographic data.

Keywords:	USGS, GIS, Geography
Sponsor:	United States Geological Survey
Audience:	Geographers, GIS Professionals, Researchers, Students
Profile:	Probably the most comprehensive geography/GIS server on the net. Features include a GIS tutorial, descriptions (and examples) of available USGS data products, access to online spatial data, and more.
Contact:	webmaster@info.er.usgs.gov
Details:	Free, Images, Sounds, Multimedia
Notes:	The USGS maintains many servers; this page contains links to most of them, such as EROS Data Center, GLIS, and others.

`http://info.er.usgs.gov/USGSHome.html`

University of Michigan Library

The library's holdings are large and wide-ranging and contain significant collections in many fields.

Keywords:	Asia, Astronomy, Transportation, Lexicology, Math, Zoology, Geography
Audience:	Researchers, Students, General Public
Contact:	info@merit.edu
Details:	Free
Expect:	Which Host; Send: Help

`telnet:// cts.merit.edu`

University of Wisconsin at Milwaukee Library

The library's holdings are large and wide-ranging and contain significant collections in many fields.

Keywords:	Art, Architecture, Business, Cartography, Geography, Geology, Urban Studies, Literature (English), Literature (American)
Audience:	Researchers, Students, General Public
Details:	Free
Expect:	Login, Send: Lib; Expect: vDIAL prompt, Send: Library

`telnet://uwmcat.lib.uwm.edu`

Vietnam

This file in the CIA World Factbook provides geographical, political, and cultural information about Vietnam.

Keywords:	Vietnam, Geography
Sponsor:	Central Intelligence Agency
Audience:	Educators, Students, Travellers, Vietnamese Americans
Contact:	Ephraim Vishniac ephraim@think.com
Details:	Free

`gopher://info.und.edu`

vigis-l

A mailing list for the discussion of Virtual Reality and GIS (Geographic Information Systems).

Keywords:	Virtual Reality, Geography, GIS (Geographic Information Systems), Cyberspace
Audience:	Geographers, Cartographers, Cybernauts
Contact:	Tom Edwards navanax.u.washington.edu
User Info:	To subscribe to the list, send an e-mail message to the URL address below, consisting of a single line reading: SUB vigis-l YourFirstName YourLastName. To send a message to the entire list, address it to: vigis@uwavm.u.washington.edu

`mailto:listserv@uwavm.u.washington.edu`

Geology

Internet Resources for Earth Sciences

A document detailing Internet resources for a variety of earth science disciplines, including GIS.

Keywords:	Directory, GIS, Geology, Geography, GPS, Mapping, Earth Science
Sponsor:	Bill Thoen
Audience:	Earth Scientists, Researchers
Profile:	A complete document detailing the types of information available in earth sciences and the mechanisms to retrieve needed information.
Contact:	Bill Thoen bthoen@gisnet.com
Details:	Free

`Ftp://ftp.csn.org/COGS/ores.text`

Natural Resources Canada (NRCan) Gopher

This site offers information on forests, energy, mining, and geomatics from the Canadian government. Also has reports from the Geological Survey of Canada and an overview of NRCan statutes, organization, and personnel. Provides links to other Canadian environmental and government gophers.

Keywords:	Canada, Environment, Geology, Forestry
Sponsor:	The Department of Natural Resources, Canada
Audience:	Canadians, Environmentalists, Environmental Researchers, Geologists
Contact:	Bob Fillmore fillmore@emr.ca
Notes:	NRCan maintains a toll-free hotline - 1-800-267-5166

`gopher://gopher.emr.ca`

`http://www.emr.ca/`

Sahel-NAFR

This site contains information about a database of composite satellite images of Sahel and North Africa (known as the Sahelian and NW Africa 14-Day NDVI Composites). The images come from a pilot program defined between the U.S. Geological Survey and the U.S. Agency for International Development (AID) to develop and test a near-real-time monitoring procedure using satellite remote sensing and Geographic Information System technologies in grasshopper and locust control programs in West Africa. Also contains an appendix with information about the Senegalese Grasshoppers.

Keywords: Geology, Geography, GIS (Geographic Information Systems)
Sponsor: U.S. Geological Survey and U.S. Agency for International Development (AID)
Audience: Geologists, Geographers

`http://sun1.cr.usgs.gov/glis/hyper/guide/sahel_nafr`

University of Maine System Library Catalog

The library's holdings are large and wide-ranging and contain significant collections in many fields.

Keywords: Ucadian Studies, St. John Valley (History of), Canadian-American Studies, Geology, Aquaculture, Maine
Audience: General Public, Researchers, Librarians, Document Delivery Professionals
Contact: Elaine Albright, Marilyn Lutz
Details: Free
         Expect: login, Send: ursus

`telnet://ursus.maine.edu`

University of Rochester Library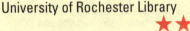

The library's holdings are large and wide-ranging and contain significant collections in many fields.

Keywords: Architecture, Art History, Photography, Literature (Asian), Lasers, Geology, Statistics, Optics, Medieval Studies
Audience: Researchers, Students, General Public
Details: Free
User Info: Expect: Login; Send: Library

`telnet://128.151.226.71`

University of Tulsa Library

The library's holdings are large and wide-ranging and contain significant collections in many fields.

Keywords: Literature (American), Petroleum, Geology
Audience: Researchers, Students, General Public
Details: Free
User Info: Expect: Username Prompt, Send: LIAS

`telnet://vax2.utulsa.edu`

University of Utah Library

The library's holdings are large and wide-ranging and contain significant collections in many fields.

Keywords: Western America, Middle Eastern Studies, Geology, Mining
Audience: Researchers, Students, General Public
Details: Free
Expect: Command Line, Send: Dial Unis

`telnet://lib.utah.edu`

University of Wisconsin at Milwaukee Library

The library's holdings are large and wide-ranging and contain significant collections in many fields.

Keywords: Art, Architecture, Business, Cartography, Geography, Geology, Urban Studies, Literature (English), Literature (American)
Audience: Researchers, Students, General Public
Details: Free
        Expect: Login, Send: Lib; Expect: vDIAL prompt, Send: Library

`telnet://uwmcat.lib.uwm.edu`

US Geological Survey Server

This resource containis publications, USGS research programs, technology transfer partnerships, and fact sheets about geology.

Keywords: Biology, Geology, Natural Science
Sponsor: US Geological Survey
Audience: Biologists, Geologists, Researchers, Naturalists
Contact: Systems Operator
         webmaster@info.er.usgs.gov

`http://info.er.usgs.gov`

USGS (United States Geological Survey) Gopher

A gopher site covering issues related to the United State Geological Survey.

Keywords: Cartography, Geology
Sponsor: United States Geological Survey
Audience: Geologists, Cartologists
Profile: The USGS gopher was established to provide general information about USGS, information about USGS Divisions, publications, data, and briefings, USGS's Network resources, and other data on geology, hydrology, and cartography.
Contact: Gopher Operator
         webmaster@info.er.usgs.gov

`gopher://info.er.usgs.gov`

Georgetown University Medical Center Online Catalogue

Georgetown University Medical Center Online Catalogue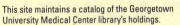

This site maintains a catalog of the Georgetown University Medical Center library's holdings.

Keywords: Medicine, Library
Sponsor: Georgetown University, Washington, DC
Audience: Medical Professionals, Educators, Students
Contact: Jane Banks
         banksj@gumedlib2.georgetown.edu
Details: Free
         The password is dahlgren, then enter netguest, hit RETURN several times and select option 1.

`telnet://medlib@gumedlib.georgetown.edu`

Georgia State University Library

Georgia State University Library

The library's holdings are large and wide-ranging and contain significant collections in many fields.

Keywords: Labor (History of), Multimedia, Mercer (Johnny, Collection of)
Audience: General Public, Researchers, Librarians, Document Delivery Professionals
Contact: Phil Williams
         isgpew@gsuvm1.gsu.edu
Details: Free
Expect: VM screen, Send: RETURN; Expect: CP READ, Send: DIAL VTAM, press RETURN; Expect: CICS screen, Send: PF1

`telnet://library.gsu.edu`

Georgia-Computer Systems Protection Act

Georgia-Computer Systems Protection Act

Lists full text of the Georgia Computer Systems Protection Act.

Keywords: Computer, Crime
Audience: Lawyers, Computer Programmers, Computer Operators
Details: Free

`gopher://wiretap.spies.com`

Geoscience

Geoscience at Texas A&M University

General server with info on all aspects of GIS and remote sensing, especially GPS.

Keywords: GIS (Geographical Information Systems), Image Processing, Remote Sensing, Geoscience
Sponsor: Texas A&M University - Department of Agricultural Engineering
Audience: Researchers, GIS and IP professionals, Students
Contact: Hal Mueller hmueller@diamond.tamu.edu
Details: Free
Images
Notes: Contains links to related Univerity of Texas gophers and WWW servers.

`http://ageninfo.tamu.edu/geoscience.html`

Meetings Calendar (Geosciences)

A collection of meetings and conferences in the geosciences, with a special emphasis on meteorology. The entries are sorted by date and some contain links to Calls for Papers.

Keywords: Geosciences, Meteorology
Sponsor: Freie Universit Berlin, Germany
Audience: Researchers, Meteorologists
Contact: Dennis Schulze dennis@bibo.met.fu-berlin.de
Details: Free
Notes: If there is a conference you want to have included in this list, send an e-mail to dennis@bibo.met.fu-berlin.de

`http://www.met.fu-berlin.de/konferenzen/index.html`

Germany

9nov89-l

A discussion list relating to recent events in the former German Democratic Republic.

Keywords: German Democratic Republic, Germany, Berlin Wall
Audience: Researchers, Political Scientists
Contact: Axel Mahler axel@avalanche.cs.tu-berlin.de
User Info: To subscribe to the list, send an e-mail message to the URL address shown below, consisting of a single line reading:

SUB 9nov89-l YourFirstName YourLastName
To send a message to the entire list, address it to: 9nov89-l@tubvm.cs.tu.berlin.de

`mailto:listserv@tubvm.cs.tu-berlin.de`

ACDGIS-L

GIS discussions for German speakers.

Keywords: Germany, Geographic Information Systems, Geography
Audience: Germans, Geographers, Cartographers
Details: Costsost
Inquire through wigeoarn@awiwuw11.bitnet

`mailto:acdgis-l@awiwuw11.bitnet`

Germany

Full text in German of various German laws and codes.

Keywords: German, Law
Sponsor: Berlin University, Berlin, Germany
Audience: Lawyers, Historians, Germans
Details: Free
Select from menu as appropriate.

`gopher://gate1.zedat.fu-berlin.de`

Hoppenstedt Directory of German Companies

This directory covers 50,000 German companies with sales exceeding 2 million DM or with a minimum of 20 employees.

Keywords: German Companies, International Business, Germany
Sponsor: Hoppenstedt Wirtschaftsdatenbank, Darmstadt, Germany
Audience: Business Professionals, International Market, Researchers, Germans
Profile: Records include current company address, line of business, number of employees, sales, capital stock, branches and subsidiaries, and a listing of executives and directors with positions in the company. The file is bilingual; users can view the records in either German or English.
Contact: Dialog in the US at (800) 334-2564; Dialog internationally at country-specific locations.
User Info: To subscribe, contact Dialog directly.
Notes: Coverage: 1973 to the present; updated semiannually.

`telnet://dialog.com`

Information Services in Germany

This gopher is an informal entry point for Germany, together with some hints to specialties in German information systems.

Keywords: Germany, Information, Europe
Audience: German Internet Surfers
Contact: lange@rz.tu-clausthal.de
Details: Free

`gopher://gopher.tu-clausthal.de`

soc.culture.german

A Usenet newsgroup providing information and discussion about German Culture.

Keywords: Germany, Sociology
Audience: Sociologists, Germans
Details: Free
User Info: To subscribe to this Usenet newsgroup, you need access to a newsreader.

`news:soc.culture.german`

Gerontology

AgeLine

The AgeLine database is produced by the American Association of Retired Persons (AARP) and provides bibliographic coverage of social gerontology—the study of aging in social, psychological, health-related, and economic contexts.

Keywords: Gerontology, Retired, Public Policy, Aging
Sponsor: American Association of Retired Persons, Washington, DC, USA
Audience: Retired Persons, Health Care Providers, Researchers
Profile: AgeLine covers the delivery of health care for the older population and its associated costs and policies, as well as public policy, employment, and consumer issues. Literature covered is of interest to researchers, health professionals, service planners, policy makers, employers, older adults and their families, and consumer advocates.
Coverage: 1978 to the present (selected coverage back to 1966); updated bimonthly.
Contact: Dialog in the US at (800) 334-2564; Dialog internationally at country-specific locations.
Details: Costs

There is no print equivalent of the database. To subscribe, contact Dialog directly.

`telnet://dialog.com`

Gifts

The Branch Mall, an Electronic Shopping Mall

Branch Information Services offers shopping to customers and leases storefronts and electronic catalogs to vendors.

Keywords: Mall, Shopping, Gifts, Advertising, Mailorder
Sponsor: Branch Information Services
Audience: Consumers, Merchants
Contact: Jon Zeeff
jon@branch.com
Details: Free
Notes: Free for consumers.

http://branch.com

GIS (Geographical Information Systems)

ACDGIS-L

GIS discussions for German speakers.

Keywords: Germany, Geographical Information Systems, Geography
Audience: Germans, Geographers, Cartographers
Details: Costsost
Inquire through wigeoarn@awiwuw11.bitnet

mailto:acdgis-l@awiwuw11.bitnet

ASTRA-UG

A mailing list for the discussion of Italian and European GIS

Keywords: GIS (Geographical Information Systems), Europe, Italy
Audience: Geographers, Cartographers, Europeans
Details: Free
User Info: To subscribe to the list, send an e-mail mesage to the URL address below, consisting of a single line reading:
SUB ASTRA-UG YourFirstName YourLastName

astra-ug@icnucevm

consgis

A discussion list for those using GIS (Geographic Information Systems) in the interest of conservation.

Keywords: Conservation, Environment, GIS (Geographical Information Systems)
Audience: Geographers, Environmentalists, Cartographers
Contact: Dr. Peter August
pete@edcserv.edc.uri.edu
Details: Free
User Info: To subscribe to the list, send an e-mail message to the URL address below, consisting of a single line reading:
SUB consgis YourFirstName YourLastName.
To send a message to the entire list, address it to: consgis@uriacc.uri.edu

mailto:listserv@uriacc.uri.edu

ESRI (Environmental Systems Research Institute)

Environmental Systems Research Institute, Inc. is the world leader in GIS technology. ARC/INFO is ESRI's powerful and flexible flagship GIS software.

Keywords: GIS (Geographical Information Systems), Environment, Software, Computers
Audience: Geographers, Environmentalists, Computer Users
Details: Costs
For product information, call (909)793-2853, X1475.
For training information, call (909)793-2853, X1585, or fax (909)793-5953.

xx.xx@xxx

Geographic Information and Analysis Laboratory (GIAL)

Server distributing a variety of information related to geography and GIS.

Keywords: Geography, GIS (Geographical Information Systems), NCGIA
Sponsor: SUNY-Buffalo and the National Center for Geographic Information and Analysis (NCGIA)
Audience: Geographers, GIS Professionals, Researchers, Students
Contact: Brandon Plewe, Reginald O. Carroll, Patricia M. Baumgarten
plewe@geog.buffalo.edu,
carrol@geog.buffalo.edu,
pmb@geog.buffalo.edu
Details: Free, Images
Notes: Check out the You-are-here server!

http://zia.geog.buffalo.edu/

Geoscience at Texas A&M University

General server with info on all aspects of GIS and remote sensing, especially GPS.

Keywords: GIS (Geographical Information Systems), Image Processing, Remote Sensing, Geoscience
Sponsor: Texas A&M University - Department of Agricultural Engineering
Audience: Researchers, GIS and IP professionals, Students
Contact: Hal Mueller
hmueller@diamond.tamu.edu
Details: Free
Images
Notes: Contains links to related Univeristy of Texas gophers and WWW servers.

http://ageninfo.tamu.edu/geoscience.html

GIS Master Bibliography Project

A bibliography of GIS literature encompassing journal articles, conference proceedings, books, and technical reports.

Keywords: GIS (Geographical Information Systems), Databases
Sponsor: Ohio State University - Department of Geography and others
Audience: GIS Users, Researchers, Students
Contact: Dr. Duane Marble
marble.1@osu.edu
Details: Free

ftp://128.146.209.34/biblio

GIS-L

A forum for the discussion of all issues pertaining to GIS (Geographical Information Systems), including hydrological modeling, environmental issues, and available software packages.

Keywords: Geography, Environment, GIS (Geographic Information Systems)
Audience: Geographers, Cartographers
Contact: David Mark
dmark@acsu.buffalo.edu
User Info: To subscribe to the list, send an e-mail message to the URL address below, consisting of a single line reading:
SUB gis-l YourFirstName YourLastName.
To send a message to the entire list, address it to: gis-l@ubvm.cc.buffalo.edu

mailto:listserv@ubvm.cc.buffalo.edu

GIS-L and comp.infosystems.gis FAQ

HTML and/or ASCII document describing all aspects of GIS on the Internet.

Keywords: GIS (Geographical Information Systems), Usenet
Audience: GIS Users
Profile: Contains information on data sources, formats, software info, and pointers to other Internet GIS info sources.
Contact: Lisa Nyman
lnyman@census.gov

GIS-T

A mailing list for the discussion of GIS (Geographical Information Systems) and transportation.

Keywords: Geography, Transportation, GIS (Geographical Information Systems)
Audience: Geographers, Cartographers
Contact: Jay Sandhu
jsandhu@esri.com
User Info: To subscribe to the list, send an e-mail message to the URL address below, consisting of a single line reading:
SUB gis-t YourFirstName YourLastName.
To send a message to the entire list, address it to: gis-t@esri.com

mailto:listserv@esri.com

ingr-en

A mailing list for the discussion of Intergraph products.

Keywords: GIS (Geographical Information Systems), Intergraph
Audience: Geographers, Cartographers
Contact: Dusan Blasko
blasko@svfnov.tuke.sk
User Info: To subscribe to the list, send an e-mail message to the URL address below, consisting of a single line reading:
SUB ingr-en YourFirstName YourLastName.
To send a message to the entire list, address it to: ingr-en@ccsun.tuke.sk

mailto:listserv@ccsun.tuke.sk

Internet GIS and RS Information Sites

This document contains a lengthy listing of GIS and remote sensing sites on the Internet.

Keywords: GIS (Geographical Information Systems), Remote Sensing, Image Processing, Geography
Sponsor: Queen's University Department of Geography
Audience: Researchers, General Public
Contact: Michael McDermott
mcdermom@gisdog.gis.queensu.ca
Details: Free
Notes: ASCII version also available from the same FTP site.

ftp://gis.queensu.ca/pub/gis/docs/gissites.html

Details: Free
Notes: ASCII version also available.

http://www.cencus.gov/geo/gis/faqindex.html

ftp://ftp.cencus.gov/pub/geo/gis-faq.txt

Internet Resources for Earth Sciences

A document detailing Internet resources for a variety of earth science disciplines, including GIS.

Keywords: Directory, GIS, Geology, Geography, GPS, Mapping, Earth Science
Sponsor: Bill Thoen
Audience: Earth Scientists, Researchers
Profile: A complete document detailing the types of information available in earth sciences and the mechanisms to retrieve needed information.
Contact: Bill Thoen
bthoen@gisnet.com
Details: Free

ftp://ftp.csn.org/COGS/ores.text

Internet Resources for Geographic Information and GIS

An HTML document with information on all aspects of GIS.

Keywords: GIS
Sponsor: Bates College- Department of Classical and Romance Languages
Audience: GIS Professionals
Contact: Neel Smith
nsmith@abacus.bates.edu
Details: Free

http://abacus.bates.edu/~nsmith/General/Resources-GIS.html

ITRE Home Page

A server dealing with transportation research and some GIS-related discussion.

Keywords: GIS, Transportation
Sponsor: University of North Carolina Institute for Transportation Research and Education
Audience: GIS Professionals, Transportation Professionals
Profile: The ITRE server address GIS issues regarding transportation, a different flavor than will be found on most servers on the Net. Also features image mapping examples.
Contact: Jay Novello
jay@itre.uncecs.edu
Details: Free, Images, Multimedia

http://itre.uncecs.edu/

mapinfo-l

A mailing list for the discussion of MapInfo Software.

Keywords: GIS (Geographic Information Systems)
Audience: Geographers, Cartographers
Contact: Bill Thoen
bthoen@gisnet.com

mailto:mapinfo-l-request@csn.org

next-gis

Discussion of Geographical Information Systems (GIS) and cartography-related topics on the NeXT and other workstation computers. Some moderated reposting of comp.infosys.gis occurs as well.

Keywords: Geography, Cartography, GIS, NeXT
Audience: GIS Users, NeXT Users
Contact: Steven R. Staton
sstaton@deltos.com
Details: Free
User Info: To subscribe to the list, send an e-mail message to the URL address shown below, consisting of a single line reading:
SUB next-gis YourFirstName YourLastName
To send a message to the entire list, address it to: next-gis@DistributionAddress
Details: Free
User Info: To subscribe to the list, send an e-mail message to the URL address below, consisting of a single line reading:
SUB mapinfo-l YourFirstName YourLastName

mailto:listserv@deltos.com

rrl

A mailing list for the discussion of GIS (Geographic Information Systems) in the United Kingdom.

Keywords: GIS (Geographic Information Systems), United Kingdom
Audience: Geographers, Cartographers
Contact: rrl@uk.ac.leicester

mailto:rrl@uk.ac.leicester

Sahel-NAFR

This site contains information about a database of composite satellite images of Sahel and North Africa (known as the Sahelian and NW Africa 14-Day NDVI Composites). The images come from a pilot program defined between the U.S. Geological Survey and the U.S. Agency for International Development (AID) to develop and test a near-real-time monitoring procedure using satellite remote sensing and Geographic Information System technologies in grasshopper and locust control programs in West Africa. Also contains an appendix with information about the Senegalese Grasshoppers.

Keywords: Geology, Geography, GIS (Geographic Information Systems)
Sponsor: U.S. Geological Survey and U.S. Agency for International Development (AID)
Audience: Geologists, Geographers

http://sun1.cr.usgs.gov/glis/hyper/guide/sahel_nafr

UIgis-L

A mailing list for the discussion of user interfaces and GIS (Geographic Information Systems).

Keywords: Geography, GIS (Geographic Information Systems)
Audience: Geographers, Cartographers
Contact: David Mark
dmark@acsu.buffalo.edu
User Info: To subscribe to the list, send an e-mail message to the URL address below, consisting of a single line reading:

SUB uigis-l YourFirstName YourLastName.

To send a message to the entire list, address it to: uigs@ubvm.cc.buffalo.edu

`mailto:listserv@ubvm.cc.buffalo.edu`

United States Geographic Name Server

A database searchable by city name or zip code, this server provides geographic data including population, longitude and latitude, elevation, county, state, and zip codes.

Keywords: Geography, GIS (Geographical Information Systems)
Audience: Geographers, General Public
Contact: pubgopher@pluto.cc.brandeis.edu

`gopher://pluto.cc.brandeis.edu`

United States Geological Survey Home Page ★★★★

USGS server dedicated to all aspects of geography and geographic data.

Keywords: USGS, GIS, Geography
Sponsor: United States Geological Survey
Audience: Geographers, GIS Professionals, Researchers, Students
Profile: Probably the most comprehensive geography/GIS server on the net. Features include a GIS tutorial, descriptions (and examples) of available USGS data products, access to online spatial data, and more.
Contact: webmaster@info.er.usgs.gov
Details: Free, Images, Sounds, Multimedia
Notes: The USGS maintains many servers; this page contains links to most of them, such as EROS Data Center, GLIS and others.

`http://info.er.usgs.gov/USGSHome.html`

The University of Minnesota Remote Sensing Lab

General information about remote sensing and GIS.

Keywords: GIS, Remote Sensing, Image Processing
Sponsor: University of Minnesota, Department of Forest Resources
Audience: Researchers, GIS and IP professionals, Students
Profile: The RSL server contains information regarding all aspects of image process and GIS. Some features include: home of the GIS Jobs Clearinghouse, archives of ESRI-L, IMAGRS-L and TGIS-L, and the NBS CPSU WWW server.
Contact: Stephen Lime
sdlime@torpedo.forestry.umn.edu
Details: Free, Images
Notes: The RSL also maintains a companion gopher server and anonymous FTP site for the GIS Jobs Clearinghouse.

`http://walleye.forestry.umn.edu/0/www/main.html`

vigis-l

A mailing list for the discussion of Virtual Reality and GIS (Geographic Information Systems).

Keywords: Virtual Reality, Geography, GIS (Geographic Information Systems), Cyberspace
Audience: Geographers, Cartographers, Cybernauts
Contact: Tom Edwards
navanax.u.washington.edu
User Info: To subscribe to the list, send an e-mail message to the URL address below, consisting of a single line reading:

SUB vigis-l YourFirstName YourLastName.

To send a message to the entire list, address it to:
vigis@uwavm.u.washington.edu

`mailto:listserv@uwavm.u.washington.edu`

Germany

Full text in German of various German laws and codes.

Keywords: German, Law
Sponsor: Berlin University, Berlin, Germany
Audience: Lawyers, Historians, Germans
Details: Free
Select from menu as appropriate.

`gopher://gate1.zedat.fu-berlin.de`

Glass

Massachusetts Institute of Technology Library

The library's holdings are large and wide-ranging and contain significant collections in many fields.

Keywords: Aeronautics (History of), Linguistics, Mathematics (History of), Microscopy, Spectroscopy, Aeronautics, Mathematics, Glass
Audience: General Public, Researchers, Librarians, Document Delivery Professionals
Details: Free
Expect: Mitek Server..., Send: Enter or Return; Expect: prompt, Send: hollis

`telnet://library.mit.edu`

Global Change Information Gateway

Global Change Information Gateway

This gateway was created to address environmental data management issues raised by the US Congress, the Administration, and the advisory arms of the Federal policy community. It contains documents related to the UN conference on Environment and Development.

Keywords: United Nations, Environment, Development, Oceans, Atmosphere
Audience: Environmentalists, Scientists, Researchers, Environmentalists
Details: Free
Select from menu as appropriate.

`gopher://scilibx.ucsc.edu`

Global Internet

Global Internet

A full-service Internet provider, offering superior quality Internet access and value-added services to business professionals, researchers, and educational communities.

Keywords: Internet, Finance
Sponsor: Global Internet, Palo Alto, CA (415)855-1700
Audience: Internet Users, Business Professionals, Financial Analysts, Publishers
Details: Costs

`mailto:sales@gi.net`

Global News

News of Earth

Newsletter covering global news.

Keywords: Global News, News
Audience: General Public
Profile: News of Earth consists of: NewsE-A Analysis, an analysis of global news; NewsE-B Bulletins, late-breaking global news; NewsE-C Commentary, a commentary on global news; NewsE-D Distribution, global news monitored from shortwave radio broadcasts; and, the continuation of JBH Online (Online-L), published from 1987 through 1990 (Issues 1-213); NewsE-I Interviews, interviews on global issues; NewsE-L Letters, news and reaction from readers; NewsE-S Supplements, containing additional news and information from electronic and print sources. News of Earth supplements continues JBH News (JBHNewsL), published in 1990 (issues 1-4). NewsE is a "superlist" that includes all components listed above.
Contact: John B. Harlan
jbharlan@indyvax.iupui.edu
Details: Free
User Info: To subscribe, send an e-mail message to the URL address below, consisting of a single line reading:
SUB NEWSE-x (where x is A, B, C, D, I, L or S) YourFirstName YourLastName
To send a message to the entire list, address it to: newse@indyvax.iupui.edu

mailto:listserv@Indyvax.iupui.edu

GlobeTrotter

GlobeTrotter ★

File concerning hacking from an international perspective.

Keywords: Hacking, Computers
Audience: Hackers, Computer Users
Details: Free
Expect: login,Send: anonymous; Password,Send: Your e-mail Address

ftp://ftp.eff.org

GLOSAS News (Global Systems Analysis and Simulating Association)

GLOSAS News (Global Systems Analysis and Simulating Association) ★

Newsletter of GLOSAS in the US, which is dedicated to global electronic education and simulation as a tool for promoting peace and the care of the natural environment.

Keywords: Education, Simulation, Peace
Audience: Educators, Environmentalists
Contact: Anton Ljutic
anton@vax2.concordia.ca
Details: Free
User Info: To subscribe, send an e-mail message to the address below, consisting of a single line reading:
SUB glosas YourFirstName YourLastName
Address it to: glosas@vm/.mcgill.ca
To send a message to the entire list,

mailto:listserv@vm1.mcgill.ca

GNUs Bulletin: Newsletter of the Free Software Foundation

GNUs Bulletin: Newsletter of the Free Software Foundation ★★★

Bringing you news about the GNU Project, the Free Software Foundation is dedicated to eliminating restrictions on copying, redistribution, understanding, and modification of computer programs.

Keywords: Software, Shareware
Sponsor: Free Software Foundation
Audience: Computer Programmers, Computer Users
Contact: Leonard H. Tower, Jr.
tower@ai.mit.edu
Details: Free

mailto:info-gnu-request@prep.ai.mit.edu

God

alt.atheism

A Usenet newsgroup providing information and discussion about atheism.

Keywords: Religion, Divinity, God
Audience: Philosophers, Clergy, Atheists
User Info: To subscribe to this Usenet newsgroup, you need access to a newsreader.

news:alt.atheism

Goethe

University of Chicago Library

The library's holdings are large and wide-ranging and contain significant collections in many fields.

Keywords: English Bibles, Lincoln (Abraham), Kentucky & Ohio River Valley (History of), Balzac (Honore de), American Drama, Cromwell (Oliver), Goethe, Judaica, Italy, Chaucer (Geoffrey), Wells (Ida, Personal Papers of), Douglas (Stephen A.), Italy, Literature (Children's)
Audience: General Public, Researchers, Librarians, Document Delivery Professionals
Details: Free
Expect: ENTER CLASS, Send: LIB48 3; Expect: CONNECTED, Send: RETURN

telnet://olorin.uchicago.edu

Gold in Networks

Gold in Networks

An introductory guide to the Internet.

Keywords: Internet, Internet Guide
Sponsor: Ohio State University
Audience: Internet Surfers
Contact: J. Martin
nic@osu.edu
Details: Free
File is: documents/fyi/fyi_1o.txt

ftp://nic.merit.edu

Golf

GolfData OnLine

A web site sampling of the information on the subscriber service GolfData OnLine. Provides numerous links to other sites that may be of interest to golfers.

Keywords: Golf, Sports, Fitness
Audience: Golfers, Sports Fans
Contact: david@gdol.com
Notes: GolfData Online is a paid subscriber electronic bulletin board service for golf enthusiasts. More information about how to subscribe can be obtained by accessing the address below.

http://www.gdol.com

University of Glasgow Information Service (GLANCE) ★★★★

GLANCE provides subject-based information services, including an extensive section on European and world sports.

Keywords: Sports, Soccer, Motor Racing, Mountaineering, Squash, Cricket, Golf, Tennis, Europe, Scotland
Sponsor: University of Glasgow, Glasgow, Scotland
Audience: Sport Enthusiasts, Fitness Enthusiasts, Nature Lovers
Profile: Information at this site includes schedules, results, and statistics for sports such as cricket and soccer. There is also a selection of items on mountaineering.
Contact: Alan Dawson
A.Dawson@uk.ac.gla.compserv
Details: Free

`gopher://govan.cent.gla.ac.uk/Subject/Sports and Rec`

Gopher

comp.infosystems.gopher ★

A Usenet newsgroup providing information and discussion about the gopher information search tool.

Keywords: Gopher, Internet Reference, Information Retrieval
Audience: Internet Surfers
User Info: To subscribe to this Usenet newsgroup, you need access to a newsreader.

`news:comp.infosystems.gopher`

E-mail Gopher ★

E-mail Gopher allows the use of a gopher via e-mail.

Keywords: Internet, Services, e-mail, Gopher
Audience: Internet Surfers
Details: Free
Include the word "help" in the Email.

`gopher://gopher.ncc.go.jp/11/INFO/gopher`

Education Gopher ★

Florida Tech's gopher relating to education. Includes information on search tools, libraries, electronic texts, and selected education-related gophers and information servers.

Keywords: Education, Gopher
Audience: Educators, Researchers
Contact: Kevin Barry
barry@sci-ed.fit.edu
Details: Free

`gopher://sci-ed.fit.edu`

European Root Gopher ★

A root gopher server and registry for European gophers run by the Swedish University Network to serve European users.

Keywords: Europe, Gophers
Sponsor: Swedish University Computer Network (SUNET)
Audience: European Internet Surfers
Contact: gopher-info@sunic.sunet.se
Details: Free

`gopher://gopher@sunet.se`

French Language Gophers (Les Gophers Francophones) ★★★

A gopher site providing links to over 50 gopher servers in the French-speaking world. Most sites are located in either Canada, Switzerland, or France.

Keywords: Gopher, French Language, French Studies
Sponsor: National Capitol Freenet, Canada
Audience: French Students, Francophiles
Contact: gopher@jussieu.fr

`gopher://freenet.carleton.ca/Les Gopher francophones/`

Gopher ★

A guide to using gopher, an Internet access tool that locates and retrieves resources using a graph of menus.

Keywords: Internet Tools, Gopher
Audience: Internet Surfers
Contact: gopher@boombox.micro.umn.edu
Details: Free
File is: pub/gopher/00README

`ftp://boombox.micro.umn.edu`

Gopher-Based ASCII Clip Art Collection ★★

A collection of over 500 individual pictures, ranging from images of food to Star Wars, created with ASCII characters. Organized by subject, and including archives of the Usenet group alt.ascii-art. Also contains links to other ASCII collections.

Keywords: Clip Art, Design, ASCII, Gopher
Sponsor: Texas Tech Computer Sciences Gopher Server
Audience: Computer Users, General Public
Contact: Abdul Malik Yoosufan
gripe@cs.ttu.edu
Details: Free, Images

`gopher://cs4sun.cs.ttu.edu`

`ftp://ftp.cs.ttu.edu:/pub/asciiart`

Gopher Demo ★

A session demonstrating gopher at the University of Minnesota.

Keywords: Internet Tools, Gopher
Audience: Internet Surfers

`gopher://gopher.micro.umn.edu`

Gopher FAQ ★

Answers to frequently asked questions (FAQs) about gophers from the USENET newsgroup comp.infosystems.gopher.

Keywords: Internet Tools, Gopher
Audience: Internet Surfers
Contact: Paul Lindner
lindner@boombox.micro.umn.edu
Details: Free
File is: pub/usenet/news.answers/gopher-faq

`ftp://pit-manager.mit.edu`

Gopher Jewels ★★★★

A searchable catalog of outstanding gopher sites worldwide.

Keywords: Gopher, Internet Tools
Audience: Internet Surfers, Researchers
Profile: Gopher Jewels, indexed by subject and searchable through WAIS, allows access to more than 2,000 gopher sites. The main server also has archives of the Gopher Jewels listserv, and extensive help and FAQ files on the uses of gopher. It is also available as a WWW site.
Contact: David Riggins
david.riggins@tpoint.com gopherjewels-comment@einet.net
Details: Free

`gopher://cwis.usc.edu/11/Other_Gophers_and_Information_Resources/Gopher_Jewels`

`http://galaxy.einet.net/gopher/gopher.html`

Gopher Sites ★

A list of worldwide gopher sites (sorted by domain structure) available on the Internet.

Keywords: Internet Tools, Gopher
Sponsor: Washington & Lee University, Lexington, VA, USA
Audience: Internet Surfers
Details: Free
File is: pub/lawlib/veronica.gopher.sites

`ftp://liberty.uc.wlu.edu`

Gopher Telnet Demo

A Telnet session demonstrating the use of gopher.

Keywords: Internet Tools, Gopher
Audience: Internet Surfers
Details: Free

`telnet://gopher@consultant.micro.umn.ed`

Gopher/Veronica-How To

A special issue of the University of Illinois publication describing gopher and Veronica.

Keywords: Internet Tools, Gopher, Veronica
Sponsor: University of Illinois, Urbana, IL
Audience: Internet Surfers
Details: Free
File is: doc/net/uiucnet/vol6no1.txt

`ftp://ftp.cso.uiuc.edu`

LIST Gopher

This is a library-related service that enables users to obtain information by using their e-mail accounts.

Keywords: Mailing Lists, Listserv, Libraries, Gopher
Sponsor: North Carolina State University, Raleigh, North Carolina, USA
Audience: Librarians, Library Users, E-mail Users
Profile: LISTGopher enables users to search library-related LISTSERV archives through the Gopher interface. Users enter their e-mail address, the list they want to search, and the keyword(s) they wish to find. LISTGopher then sends the results of their search to the user's e-mail address. Currently, only library-related archives are supported, but more archive types may be added in the future.
Contact: Eric Lease Morgan, Systems Librarian
eric_morgan@ncsu.edu

`http://ericmorgan.lib.ncsu.edu/staff/morgan/morgan.html`

`gopher://dewey.lib.ncsu.edu /library/disciplines/library/listgopher`

Gothic Rock

Corpse/Respondents

This is a gothic pen-pal zine in digest form. Small traffic mailing list.

Keywords: Gothic Rock, Rock Music
Audience: Gothic Rock Enthusiasts
Contact: carriec@eskimo.com
Details: Free

User Info: To subscribe, send an e-mail message to the URL address below, with "subscribe corpse <yournameandaddress>" in the text.

`mailto:carriec@eskimo.com`

Government

alt.politics.election

A Usenet newsgroup organized to help people in the process of running for office.

Keywords: Politics (US), Government
Audience: Politicians, Campaign Managers
User Info: To subscribe to this Usenet newsgroup, you need access to a newsreader.

`news:alt.politics.election`

Amnesty International

A site containing information about Amnesty International, an organization focused strictly and specifically on human rights around the world.

Keywords: Government, Human Rights, Politics (International), Activism
Sponsor: Amnesty International
Audience: Students, Activists
Contact: Catherine Hampton
ariel@netcom.com

`ftp://ftp.netcom.com/pub/ariel/`

`http://www/human.rights/amnesty.international/ai.html`

BUSREF (Business Reference)

The Business Refernce (BUSREF) library contains a variety of reference materials covering business and industry.

Keywords: News, Reference, Business, Government
Audience: Businessmen
Profile: The BUSREF library contains company directories, reference publications, information on business opportunities, and biographical information on political candidates, Congressional members, celebrities, and international decision makers.
Contact: Mead New Sales Group at (800) 227-4908 or (513) 859-5398 inside the US, or (513) 865-7981 for all inquiries outside the US.
User Info: To subscribe, contact Mead directly.

To examine the Nexis user guide, you can access it at the ftp site of the University of Texas at Austin at the URL address: ftp://ftp.cc.utexas.edu

The files are in: /pub/ref-services/LEXIS

`telnet://nex.meaddata.com`

`http://www.meaddata.com`

C-SPAN (Cable-Satellite Public Affairs Network) Gopher

Online information from C-SPAN, the public affairs television network.

Keywords: News Media, Government, Congress (US), Television
Sponsor: C-SPAN
Audience: Journalists, Government Officials, Educators (K-12), General Public
Profile: Comprehensive listings of C-SPAN's programming and coverage of events in Washington D.C. and beyond. In addition to the programming notes and schedules, this site also features online educational resources sponsored by C-SPAN, text of historic documents and speeches, and background political information on the House of Representatives and the Supreme Court.
Contact: cspanviewr@aol.com
Details: Free

`gopher://c-span.org`

Open Government Project (Canada)

This site provides online audio-visual and text information on the Canadian government.

Keywords: Canada, Government
Sponsor: Directorate of Communications Development, Industry Canada, Canada
Audience: Canadians, Government Officials, Journalists
Profile: This bilingual (French/English) site has detailed information on members of the Canadian Senate and House of Commons, as well as Supreme Court rulings and biographies of the justices. It features a number of pictures, maps, and links to other Canadian information servers.
Contact: Tyson Macaulay
tyson.macaulay@crc.doc.ca

`http://debra.dgbt.doc.ca/ogp.html`

`gopher://debra.dgbt.doc.ca/open_government_project`

Russian and East European Studies Home Pages

Keywords: Russia, Eastern Europe, Government, Political Science
Sponsor: University of Pittsburgh
Audience: Researchers, Politicians
Contact: Casey Palowitch
cjp@acid.library.pitt.edu

`http://www.pitt.edu/cjp/rspubl.html`

The Texas Information Highway ★★

Access to the public information resources of the state of Texas.

Keywords:	Texas, States, Government, Census, Tourism
Sponsor:	Texas Department of Information Resources
Audience:	Texans, General Public
Profile:	Still under construction as we go to press, this is a model program to make state and local information resources available to Internet users. The current collection features city, country, and state political information, including full-text of bills before the Texas state legislature. Materials related to Texas history and tourism are also provided, along with links to Texas-area user groups and other state and federal information servers.
Contact:	Wayne McDilda wayne@dir.texas.gov

`gopher://info.texas.gov`

Government (African)

The University of Michigan Library ★★

The library's holdings are large and wide-ranging and contain significant collections in many fields.

Keywords:	Education (Bilingual), Linguistics, Neuroscience, Michigan, Prohibition, Government (African)
Audience:	General Public, Researchers, Librarians, Document Delivery Professionals
Details:	Free
Expect:	nothing, Send: <cr>

`telnet://cts.merit.edu`

Government (International)

1994 Federal Budget (Canada) ★★★★

This site offers full-text of Canada's federal budget. Also has a wealth of information on Canadian industry and industrial policy, including Provincial and Sectorial GATT opportunities and briefs from the Information Highway Advisory Council.

Keywords:	Canada, Government (International), Industry, Foreign Trade
Sponsor:	Industry Canada, Canada
Audience:	Canadians, Government Officials, Businesspeople, Researchers
Contact:	Tyson Macaulay tyson@debra.dgbt.doc.ca

`gopher://debra.dgbt.doc.ca/industry canada documents/isc.news.releases`

Counterev-L ★

This list is under the aegis of l'Alliance Monarchists, affiliated with l'Alliance pour la maintenance de la France en Europe, and is dedicated to promoting the cause of traditional monarchy and counterrevolution. Its principles are a government based on natural law, decentralization, subsidiarity, an economy based on the principles of distributive justice, and the defense of traditional Western values.

Keywords:	Monarchy, Government (International)
Audience:	Monarchists, Counterrevolutionaries
Contact:	Jovan Weismiller ae852@yfn.ysu.edu
Details:	Free
User Info:	To subscribe to the list, send an e-mail message requesting a subscription to the URL address below.

`mailto:ae852@yfn.ysu.edu`

Freedom of Information Directory of Records (Canada) ★★

A database compiled by the Canadian federal government listing documents available to the public under The Freedom of Information and Protection of Privacy Act. It can be searched by keyword, or browsed through a menuing system.

Keywords:	Canada, Government (International), Freedom of Information Act
Sponsor:	British Columbia Systems Corporation, British Columbia, Canada
Audience:	Canadians, Journalists, Activists
Contact:	Office of the Information and Privacy Commissioner TCPHELP@BCSC02.GOV.BC.CA

`gopher://bcsc02.gov.bc.ca`

Government Docs (US & World) ★★

A large and eclectic collection of documents, ranging from the Laws of William the Conqueror to the North American Free Trade Agreement (NAFTA). Particular strengths include 20th century American political documents and international treaties and covenants.

Keywords:	Government (International), History (World), Politics (International)
Sponsor:	The Internet Wiretap
Audience:	Researchers, Historians, Political Scientists, Journalists
Contact:	gopher@wiretap.spies.com

`gopher://wiretap.spies.com/Gov`

Open Government Pilot ★★

This web site provides information concerning the Canadian government, including information on Canadian infrastructure, industry, communications, provinces, and parliament.

Keywords:	Canada, Government (International)
Sponsor:	Canadian Federal Government
Audience:	Canadians, Educators, Students
Details:	Free

`http://debra.dgbt.doc.ca/opengov`

UN Resolutions ★

List of selected US and world government documents and UN resolutions.

Keywords:	Government (International), United Nations, Government (US)
Sponsor:	United Nations
Audience:	Historians, Internationalists, Political Scientists
Details:	Free

`gopher://wiretap.spies.com`

University of Saskatchewan Libraries ★★

A major Canadian University library with access to library catalogs archives, and Canadian Government documents.

Keywords:	Canada, Government (International)
Sponsor:	University of Saskatchewan
Audience:	Canadians, General Public
Profile:	The University of Saskatchewan Libraries maintain online databases of their collections archives, and catalogs. The libraries are a voluminous resource for the study of Canada, Canadian government, and Canadian-American issues.
Login:	sonia

`telnet://sklib.usask.ca`

World Bank Gopher Server ★★★

A collection of online information from the World Bank.

Keywords:	Government (International), Development, International Finance, Foreign Trade
Sponsor:	The World Bank
Audience:	Nongovernmental Organizations, Activists, Government Officials, Environmentalists
Profile:	A collection of World Bank information including a list of publications, environmental assessments, economic reports, and updates on current projects being funded by the World Bank.
Contact:	webmaster@www.worldbank.org

`gopher://gopher.worldbank.org`

`http://www.worldbank.org`

Government (US)

America

For people interested in how the United States is dealing with foreign trade policies, congressional status, and other inside information about the government that is freely distributable.

- **Keywords:** Foreign Trade, Government (US), Congress (US), Business (US)
- **Audience:** General Public, Researchers, Journalists, Political Scientists, Students
- **Contact:** subscribe@xamiga.linet.org
- **User Info:** To subscribe to the list, send an e-mail message to the URL address below, consisting of a single line reading:

    SUB america YourFirstName YourLastName

    To send a message to the entire list, address it to: america@xamiga.linet.org
- **Notes:** This list has monthly postings that are generally in large batches, with posts exceeding a few hundred lines.

`mailto:subscribe@xamiga.linet.org`

Americans with Disabilities Act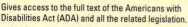

Gives access to the full text of the Americans with Disabilities Act (ADA) and all the related legislation.

- **Keywords:** Disabilities, Legislation (US), Government (US)
- **Audience:** General Public, Disabled People, Differently Abled People, Politicians, Journalists, Students
- **Profile:** The purpose of ADA is to provide a clear and comprehensive national mandate to end discrimination against individuals with disabilities and to bring them into the economic and social mainstream of American life; to provide enforceable standards addressing discrimination against individuals with disabilities; and to ensure that the federal government plays a central role in enforcing these standards on behalf of individuals with disabilities.
- **Details:** Free

`gopher://val-dor.cc.buffalo.edu/11/.legislation/`

An NREN That Includes Everyone

In this article, community networker Tom Grundner (founder of Free-Net), advocates a National Community Network— one that treats parents looking for health-care information as researchers. He advocates expanding our definition of educational access to include people of all ages— senior citizens as well as kindergarteners.

- **Keywords:** Community, Networking, Government (US)
- **Audience:** Activists, Policymakers, Community Leaders
- **Contact:** Tom Grundner
  tmg@nptn.org
- **Details:** Free
- **Notes:** This document contains hypertext links to the NPTN (National Public Telecomputing Network).

`http://nearnet.gnn.com/mag/articles/oram/bio.grundner.html`

Berne Convention Implementation Act of 1988

An act to amend Title 17, United States Code, to implement the Berne Convention for the Protection of Literary and Artistic Works, as revised in Paris on July 24, 1971, and for other purposes.

- **Keywords:** Legislation (US), Government (US), Politics (US), Copyright
- **Audience:** Lawyers, Students, Politicians, Journalists
- **Details:** Free

`gopher://wiretap.spies.com/00/Gov/Copyright/US.Berne.Convention.txt`

Bibliographies of US Senate Hearings

The US Senate produces a series of committee hearings, prints, and publications as part of the legislative process. The Documents department at North Carolina State University contains files for the 99th through 103rd Congresses, which can also be searched through a WAIS searchable database.

- **Keywords:** Senate (US), Politics (US), Legislation (US), Bibliographies, Government (US)
- **Audience:** General Public, Journalists, Students, Politicians, US Citizens
- **Contact:** Jack McGeachy
  Jack_McGeachy@ncsu.edu
- **Details:** Free

`gopher://dewey.lib.ncsu.edu/11/library/disciplines/government/senate`

Budget of the United States (1994)

Provides the full text of the 1994 budget of the United States.

- **Keywords:** Budget, Government (US), Finance
- **Audience:** Politicians, Lawyers, Journalists, Economists, Students, US Citizens
- **Details:** Free
- **Notes:** This document is over one megabyte in size and thus takes a couple of minutes to load onto the screen.

`gopher://wiretap.spies.com/00/Gov/US-Gov/budget.94`

California State Senate Gopher

This is a gopher site accessing California State government records and providing links to related gophers.

- **Keywords:** California, Government (US), Law (US State)
- **Sponsor:** California State Senate, California, USA
- **Audience:** Californians, General Public
- **Profile:** The California State Senate Gopher provides access to state government records, pending bills, laws, state statistics, budgets, and related matters. The gopher also provides links to related gophers inside and outside state government.
- **Contact:** Gopher Provider
  gopher@sen.ca.gov

`gopher://gopher.sen.ca.gov`

Civic Promise of the National Information Infrastructure (NII)

Community networker Richard Civille (founder of EcoNet and director of the Center for Civic Networking) describes several experiments in community networking.

- **Keywords:** Community, Networking, Government (US)
- **Audience:** Activists, Policymakers, Community Leaders, Government
- **Contact:** Richard Civille
  rciville@civicnet.org
- **Details:** Free

`http://nearnet.gnn.com/mag/articles/oram/bio.civille.html`

Clinton Watch

A regular political column devoted to a critical examination of the Clinton Administration.

- **Keywords:** Politics, Clinton(Bill), Satire, Government (US)
- **Sponsor:** Informatics Resource
- **Audience:** Republicans, General Public, Citizens
- **Contact:** clintonwatch@dolphin.gulf.net

`gopher://dolphin.gulf.net`

Clinton's Economic Plan

The contents of US President Clinton's economic plan.

- **Keywords:** Economics, Government (US), Clinton (Bill)
- **Audience:** Economists, General Public

Details: Free

The data contained on the President's Economic Plan diskette is now available via anonymous FTP at cu.nih.gov. The data can be found in a directory named USDOC-OBA-INFO.

`gopher://wiretap.spies.com/11/Gov/Economic`

Colorado Document Citations

A list of publications from all Colorado statutory government agencies.

The wiretap gopher provides access to a range of world documents in full-text format.

Keywords: Colorado, Government (US)

Audience: Researchers, Lawyers, Colorado Residents, Governments, historians, Researchers, General Public

Select from menu as appropriate.

`telnet://pac.carl.org`

Commerce Business Daily

The Commerce Business Daily is a publication that announces invitations to bid on proposals requested by the US Federal Government. This gopher is updated every business day.

Keywords: Business (US), Economics, Commerce, Trade, Government (US)

Sponsor: CNS and Softshare Government Information Systems

Audience: Economists, Business Professionals, General Public, Journalists, Students, Politicians.

Profile: Invitations via Internet e-mail that apply only to specific companies can be arranged.

Contact: Melissa Allensworth
sshare@cscns.com
service@cscns.com

Details: Free

`gopher://cns.cscns.com/cbd/About the CBD`

Congressional Contact Information

The US Senate and 103rd Congress phone and fax numbers are accessible and searchable from this server.

Keywords: Congress (US), Directories, Government (US)

Sponsor: Library of Congress

Audience: General Public, Journalists, Students, Politicians

Details: Free

`gopher://marvel.loc.gov/11/congress/directory`

Department of Justice Gopher

A gopher containing online information from the Justice Department.

Keywords: Federal Law (US), Government (US), Justice Department

Sponsor: United States Department of Justice

Audience: Lawyers, Citizens

Profile: The Department of Justice (DOJ) gopher features DOJ criminal and law enforcement statistics, as well as agency procurement requests, job listings, and press releases. Also has links to other US government online systems.

Contact: gopher@usdoj.gov

`gopher://gopher.usdoj.gov`

Electronic Democracy Must Come from Us

Article about government policy and community networks by community networker Evelyn Pine (former national director of Computer Professionals for Social Responsibility). A short critique of the promises of electronic networking contrasted with the realities of political control.

Keywords: Community, Networking, Government (US)

Audience: Activists, Community Leaders, Governments

Contact: Evelyn Pine
evy@well.sf.ca.us

Details: Free

`http://nearnet.gnn.com/mag/articles/oram/bio.pine.html`

(The) Electronic Public Interest versus the Private Good

Statement by community networker Dave Hughes, sounding the warning that the federal goverment may be leaving to the marketplace too much control over who gets access to the Information infrastructure.

Keywords: Community, Networking, Government (US)

Audience: Activists, Policymakers, Community Leaders

Contact: Dave Hughes
dave@oldcolo.com

Details: Free

`http://nearnet.gnn.com/mag/articles/oram/bio.hughes.html`

National Technology Transfer Center (NTTC)

A federally-funded national network to apply government research to commercial applications.

Keywords: Technology, Technology Transfer, Research and Development, Business and Industry, Department of Defense, Government (US)

Sponsor: National Technology Transfer Center

Audience: Business People, Entrepreneurs, Manufactures, Technology Enthusiasts

Profile: Features state-by-state listings of agencies designed to facilitate the adaptation of new technologies to industry. Also provides updates on conferences, and a current list of Department of Defense projects soliciting private assistance from small businesses. Allows limited access to NTTC databases.

Contact: Charles Monfradi
cmonfra@nttc.edu, info@nttc.edu

`gopher://iron.nttc.edu`

`http://iridium.nttc.edu/nttc.hmtl`

NLSNews Newsletter (National Longitudinal Surveys of Labor Market Experience)

Issued by the Center for Human Resource Research (Ohio State University); distributed to researchers using NLS data, as well as to other interested persons.

Keywords: Labor, Government (US), Department of Labor

Sponsor: Bureau of Labor Statistics, US Department of Labor

Audience: Statisticians, Researchers (Labor)

Profile: A typical issue contains updates on the status and availability of NLS data tapes and CD-ROMs for the six NLS cohorts (Older Men, Mature Women, Young Men, Young Women, Youth, and Children), notices to researchers of data-file or documentation errors, summaries of in-progress and completed NLS research, and other information of general interest to the NLS research community.

Contact: Gale James
james@ohsthr.bitnet

A description of the subscription service that enables users to automatically receive, as soon as it becomes available, the latest issue of the NLS Newsletter and/or error updates can be found in the file subscribe.info, available via nlserve@ohsthr.bitnet, the Center's file server.

`mailto:james@ohsthr.bitnet`

Park Rangers

This list is primarily for anyone working or interested in working as a ranger (general, interpretive, and so on) for the US National Park Service, but rangers from state and county agencies and from other countries are also welcome. The group discusses numerous topics related to this profession.

Keywords:	US National Park Service, Government (US)
Audience:	Park Rangers
Contact:	Cynthia Dorminey 60157903@wsuvm1.csc.wsu.edu
Details:	Free
User Info:	To subscribe to the list, send an e-mail message requesting a subscription to the URL address below.
	To send a message to the entire list, address it to: 60157903@wsuvm1.csc.wsu.edu

`mailto:60157903@wsuvm1.csc.wsu.edu`

Publications of the Office of Environment, Safety and Health ★★★

A collection of government safety information including updates, bulletins, and hazard alerts. Topics are diverse, covering everything from "Employee Hit on Head by Falling Steel Wheel" to "New Regulations to Control the Speed of Bloodborne Diseases."

Keywords:	Safety, Government (US), Federal Laws (US)
Sponsor:	U.S. Department of Energy
Audience:	Government Officials, General Public
Details:	Free

`gopher://dewey.tis.inel.gov`

PVS (Project Vote Smart) ★★

A gopher site containing Federal political information from PVS.

Keywords:	Politics, Government (US)
Sponsor:	Project Vote Smart, Corvallis, Oregon, USA
Audience:	Voters, General Public
Profile:	PVS is a volunteer organization dedicated to providing voters with factual information about candidates for Federal office. Currently, the gopher offers background information, including detailed profiles and legislative analysis of Senators and Representatives for all 50 states.
Contact:	pvs@neu.edu
Notes:	For more information on Project Vote Smart, call their toll free hotline at 1-800-622-SMART. Or write to: Project Vote Smart, 129 NW Fourth St. #240, Corvallis, OR 97330

`gopher://gopher.neu.edu`

Trademark Act of the US

The US Trademark Act of 1946 (the "Lanham Act"), Title 15, United States Code, Sections 1051_1127.

Keywords:	Trademarks, Laws (US), Government (US), Commerce

Audience:	Journalists, Politicians, Students, Lawyers, Business Professionals, Designers, Marketers
Details:	Free

`http://www.law.cornell.edu/lanham/lanham.table.html`

UN Resolutions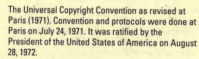

List of selected US and world government documents and UN resolutions.

Keywords:	Government (International), United Nations, Government (US)
Sponsor:	United Nations
Audience:	Historians, Internationalists, Political Scientists
Details:	Free

`gopher://wiretap.spies.com`

Universal Copyright Convention ★★

The Universal Copyright Convention as revised at Paris (1971). Convention and protocols were done at Paris on July 24, 1971. It was ratified by the President of the United States of America on August 28, 1972.

Keywords:	Copyright, Laws (US), Government (US), Politics (US)
Audience:	Lawyers, Students, Politicians, Journalists
Details:	Free

`gopher://wiretap.spies.com/00/Gov/Copyright/US.Universal.Copyright.Conv.txt`

University of Wisconsin Superior Library

The library's holdings are large and wide-ranging and contain significant collections in many fields.

Keywords:	Educational Policy, Government (US)
Audience:	Researchers, Students, General Public
Details:	Free
Expect:	Login, Send: Lib; Expect: vDIAL Prompt, Send: Library

`telnet://sail.uwsuper.edu`

US Department of the Interior

This resource contains Internet links to the Bureau of Indian Affairs, Bureau of Land Management, Bureau of Reclamation, National Biological Survey, National Park Service, and the US Fish and Wildlife Service.

Keywords:	Government (US), Environmental Policies
Sponsor:	US Department of the Interior Survey, Office of Public Affairs
Audience:	Biologists, Geologists, Researchers, Environmentalists

`http://info.er.usgs.gov/doi/doi.html`

US General Accounting Office Transitional Reports

A major directory on accounting, providing access to a broad range of related resources (library catalogs, databases, and servers) via the Internet.

Keywords:	Government (US), Finance
Audience:	Politicians, Government Workers
Profile:	Contains full-text documents of the Transitional Reports for the U.S. General Accounting Office. Reports includes Budget Issues, Investment, Government Management Issues, Financial Management Issues, Health Care Reform, National Security Issues, International Trade Issues, and so on.
Contact:	kh3@cu.nih.gov

`gopher://thor.ece.uc.edu`

War Powers Resolution of 1973 ★

A joint resolution concerning the war powers of Congress and the President resolved by the Senate and the House of Representatives of the United States of America in Congress.

Keywords:	War, Law (International), Government (US)
Audience:	Politicians, Students, Lawyers, Historians
Details:	Free

`gopher://wiretap.spies.com/00/Gov/warpower.act`

White House Frequently Asked Questions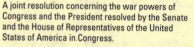

This document is a good starting point for answering questions such as: How do I send e-mail to President Clinton? How do I get current news updates from the White House? Where can I get White House documents from?

Keywords:	Clinton (Bill), Government (US), Politics (US), FAQs
Audience:	General Public, Researchers
Details:	Free
Expect:	login; Send: anonymous; Expect: password; Send: your e-mail address; Expect: directory; Send: /pub/nic; Expect: file; Send: whitehouse FAQ.

`ftp://ftp.sura.net`

Government (US Federal/State)

Congressional Quarterly Gopher

Online Information from Congressional Quarterly (CQ), the premier journal covering events on Capitol Hill.

Government   329

Keywords:	Congress (US), Government (US Federal), Laws (US Federal)
Sponsor:	Congressional Quarterly
Audience:	Journalists, Government Officials, Educators, General Public
Profile:	This gopher allows access to weekly stories and news briefs from CQ, as well as providing information on legislation before Congress, Congressional voting records, and results of recent federal elections. Also has catalogs of CQ's publications and schedules of their professional education seminars.
Contact:	gopher_admin@cqalert.com
Details:	Free

gopher://gopher.cqalert.com

Copyright Act ★

The full text of the Copyright Act of 1976, Title 17, United States Code, Sections 101_810.

Keywords:	Politics (US), Government (US Federal), Laws (US Federal), Copyright
Audience:	Lawyers, Students, Politicians, Journalists
Details:	Free

gopher://wiretap.spies.com/00/Gov/Copyright/US.Copyright.1976.tx

Copyright Basics ★

This information is from Circular 1 issued by the Copyright Office, Library of Congress, January 1991. It explains what copyright is, who can claim copyright, the principles of copyrights, what works are protected, how to secure a copyright, and so on.

Keywords:	Copyright, Government (US Federal), Laws (US Federal)
Audience:	Lawyers, Students, Politicians, Journalists
Details:	Free

gopher://wiretap.spies.com/00/Gov/Copyright/US.Copyright.Basics.txt

Electronic Communications Privacy Act of 1986 ★

This is the act to amend Title 18, United States Code, with respect to the interception of certain communications, other forms of surveillance, and for other purposes. This act affects every USENET, Bitnet, BBS, shortwave listener, TV viewer, and so on.

Keywords:	Communications, Privacy, Government (US Federal), Laws (US Federal)
Audience:	Journalists, Privacy Activists, Students, Politicians
Details:	Free

gopher://wiretap.spies.com/00/Gov/ecpa.act

Freedom of Information Act (FOIA): Guide to Use ★

This is a citizen's guide on using the Freedom of Information Act and the Privacy Act of 1974 to request government records.

Keywords:	Privacy, Freedom of Information, Government (US Federal)
Audience:	Journalists, Privacy Activists, Students, Politicians, US Citizens
Details:	Free

gopher://wiretap.spies.com/00/Gov/foia.cit

GPO Gateway to Government Act of 1992: Senator Al Gore ★

A bill to establish an electronic gateway in the Government Printing Office (GPO) to provide public access to a wide range of Federal databases containing public information stored electronically.

Keywords:	Government (US Federal), Federal Databases
Audience:	General Public, Journalists, Politicians
Details:	Free
	File is: /pub/nic/NREN/GPO.bill.6-92

ftp://ftp.sura.net

Government-Sponsored Electronic Bulletin Boards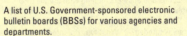

A list of U.S. Government-sponsored electronic bulletin boards (BBSs) for various agencies and departments.

Keywords:	Government (US Federal), Law (US Federal), BBS
Sponsor:	United States Government
Audience:	General Public, Researchers
Profile:	EBBs provide a wide and ever-changing assortment of government information, including text files, statistics, software, and graphics. Some of the information is also available in printed form, but much is not. Depository librarians may find government-sponsored EBBs useful in answering reference questions and in obtaining electronic versions of government publications, regardless of whether those publications were distributed to depository libraries.
Details:	Free

gopher://gopher.ncsu.edu

High-Performance Computing Act of 1991 ★★★

This is a Senate bill to provide for a coordinated federal research program to ensure continued US leadership in high-performance computing.

Keywords:	Computing, Government (US Federal), Law (US Federal)
Audience:	General Public, Journalists, Politicians, Scientists
Details:	Free
	File is: /internet/nren/hpca.1991/gorebill.1991-txt

ftp://nis.nsf.net

Historical Documents of the US ★

A large sample of US historical documents, from the Fundamental Orders of 1639 to the Vietnam Era Documents, including World War II documents, Federalist papers, and more.

Keywords:	Historical Documents (US), Government (US Federal), Law (US Federal)
Audience:	Historians, Journalists, Students, Politicians
Details:	Free

gopher://wiretap.spies.com/11/Gov/US-History

Information Infrastructure and Technology Act of 1992 ★

The Information Infrastructure and Technology Act of 1992 builds on the High-Performance Computing Act. The newer bill will ensure that the technology developed by the High-Performance Computing Program is applied widely in K-12 education, libraries, health care, and industry, particularly manufacturing. It will authorize a total of $1.15 billion over the next five years.

Keywords:	Government (US Federal), Law (US Federal), Information Technology, Education, Health Care
Audience:	Journalists, Politicians, Scientists, Manufacturers, Educators
Details:	Free
	File is: /internet/nren/iita.1992/gorebill.1992.txt

ftp://nis.nsf.net

Internet Federal Register (IFR)

The full text of the US Federal Register.

Keywords:	Federal Register, Government (US Federal), Law (US Federal)
Sponsor:	Counterpoint Publishing
Audience:	General Public, Journalists, Students, Politicians, Citizens
Contact:	fedreg@internet.com
Details:	Costs

gopher://gopher.internet.com

Leaders of Community Networking: People Who Create Online Communities ★

A WWW document with links to several important community networking resources. A brief overview of community networking is provided, as are links to statements by several leaders in the movement.

Keywords: Community, Networking, Government (US Federal)
Audience: Activists, Policymakers, Community Leaders, Government, Citizens
Details: Free

http://nearnet.gnn.com/mag/articles/oram/introduction.html

Miscellaneous Federal Documents ★

This directory includes documents such as the Civil Rights Act of 1991, the Computer Fraud and Abuse Act, the High-Performance Computing Senate Report, and more.

Keywords: Government (US Federal), Federal Documents (US)
Audience: Politicians, Journalists, Students (high school up)
Details: Free

gopher://wiretap.spies.com/11/Gov/US-Docs

Patent Act of the US ★

This resource contains full-text documentation regarding the US Patent Act (Title 35, United States Code, Sections 1 - 376).

Keywords: Patents, Laws (US Federal), Government (US Federal)
Audience: Journalists, Politicians, Economists, Lawyers, Scientists
Details: Free

http://fatty.law.cornell.edu/patent/patent.overview.html

Political Platforms of the US ★

Full text of various documents including the Democratic platform of 1992, the Jerry Brown positions of 1992, the Libertarian platform of 1990, and more.

Keywords: Politics (US), Government (US Federal), Democracy, Libertarian Politics
Audience: Politicians, Grass-Roots Organizers, Journalists
Details: Free

gopher://wiretap.spies.com/11/Gov/Platform

Privacy Act of 1974 ★

The act that regulates the maintenance of privacy and protection of records on individuals.

Keywords: Privacy, Laws (US Federal), Government (US Federal)
Audience: Journalists, Politicians, Lawyers
Details: Free
Choose from menu as appropriate.

gopher://wiretap.spies.com/00/Gov/privacy.act

Northwestern University Library ★★

The library's holdings are large and wide-ranging and contain significant collections in many fields.

Keywords: Africa, Wright (Frank Lloyd), Women's Studies, Art, Literature (American), Contemporary Music, Government (US State), UN Documents, Music
Audience: General Public, Researchers, Librarians, Document Delivery Professionals
Details: Free
Expect: COMMAND:, Send: DIAL VTAM

telnet://nuacvm.acns.nwu.edu

Questions and Answers about the GPO Gateway to Government Act ★

Questions and answers dealing with the bill GPO Gateway to Government Act of 1992. Questions such as, "What will the gateway do?", "Why is this gateway needed?", "What types of information will be available through the gateway?", and more.

Keywords: Laws (US Federal), Government (US Federal), Federal Databases
Audience: General Public, Journalists, Politicians
Details: Free
File is: /pub/nic/NREN/GPO.questions

ftp://ftp.sura.net

Government Documents

FedWorld Bulletin Board

A BBS run by the National Technical Information Service, with many databases of government documents, job announcements, and connections to other federal government online services.

Keywords: US Federal Government, Government Documents
Sponsor: US National Technical Information Service
Audience: General Public, Researchers
Profile: This is the place to begin any kind of search for US federal government records and publications. The GateWay option connects you to the Library of Congress, Supreme Court opinions, government job listing, the various Federal Reserve Banks, Congressional Bills and studies, and so on.
To establish an account: Expect: login, Send: new
Notes: Mail to sysop once you have an account.

telnet://fedworld.gov

Government Docs (US & World)

A large and eclectic collection of documents, ranging from the Laws of William the Conqueror to the North American Free Trade Agreement (NAFTA). Particular strengths include 20th century American political documents and international treaties and covenants.

Keywords: Government (International), Government Documents, History (World), Politics (International)
Sponsor: The Internet Wiretap
Audience: Researchers, Historians, Political Scientists, Journalists
Contact: gopher@wiretap.spies.com

gopher://wiretap.spies.com/Gov

US House of Representatives Gopher ★★★★

The online service of the U.S. House of Representatives.

Keywords: Congress (US), Federal Law (US), Government Documents
Sponsor: House Administration Committee Internet Working Group
Audience: Government Officials, Journalists, Educators (K-12), General Public
Profile: Provides access to information on members and committees of the House of Representatives, as well as full-text of bills before the House. Includes education resources on the legislative process, Congressional directories, and House schedules. Also has information for visitors (including area maps), as well as access to other federal information systems.
Contact: House Internet Working Group househlp@hr.house.gov

gopher://gopher.house.gov

GRANOLA (Vegetarian Discussion List)

GRANOLA (Vegetarian Discussion List) ★

A ListServ for discussion of vegetarian issues, including everything from recipes to animal rights.

Keywords:	Health, Nutrition, Vegetarian, Recipes
Audience:	Vegetarians, Nutritionists, Health Professionals
Details:	Free
User Info:	To subscribe to the list, send an e-mail message to the URL address shown below, consisting of a single line reading: SUB granola YourFirstName YourLastName

`mailto:listserv@gitvm1.bitnet`

Grants

A Grant Getter's Guide to the Internet ★★★★

A summary of Internet-accessible information regarding federal grants.

Keywords:	Grants, Federal Register (US), Federal Databases (US)
Sponsor:	University of Idaho, Moscow, Idaho, USA
Audience:	Researchers, Scientists, Public Health Professionals, Students
Profile:	This site is intended to provide federal grant information on the Internet. The focus is federal grant resources, including those sponsored by the National Institute of Health (NIH), the National Science Foundation (NSF), and the National Telecommunications and Information Administration (NTIA). This server also includes supplemental education-related information. This guide is searchable by keyword and contains pointers to such grant sources as the Federal Register, the National Science Foundation, the National Institutes of Health, and the Catalog of Federal Domestic Assistance. This same site allows direct access to many of the systems mentioned in the guide.
Contact:	James Kearney, Marty Zimmerman jkearney@raven.csrv.uidaho.edu, martyz@uidaho.edu

`gopher://gopher.uidaho.edu/Science, Research, & Grant Information/Grant Information`

National Institutes of Health Gopher ★★★★

Provides access to a broad range of National Institutes of Health (NIH) resources (library catalogues, databases) via the Internet.

Keywords:	Health, AIDS, Molecular Biology, Grants
Sponsor:	National Institutes of Health
Audience:	Health Professionals, Molecular Biologists, Researchers
Profile:	This gopher provides access to NIH resources, including institute phone books and calendars, library catalogs, molecular biology databases, the full text of the NIH Guide for Grants and Contracts, files containing AIDS and cancer information, and more.
Contact:	gopher@gopher.nih.gov
Details:	Free
Expect:	Login; Enter: Gopher

`telnet://gopher.nih.gov`

`gopher://gopher.nih.gov`

`gopher://odie.niaid.nih.gov`

NIH Grant Line (Drgline Bulletin Board) ★★★★

The purpose of the NIH Grant Line is to make program and policy information from the Public Health Service (PHS) agencies rapidly available to the biomedical research community.

Keywords:	Biomedical Research, NIH, Grants
Sponsor:	The National Institute of Health
Audience:	Scientists, Researchers, Students
Profile:	Most of the research opportunity information available on this bulletin board is derived from the weekly publication "NIH Guide for Grants and Contracts," and consists of notices, RFAs, RFPs (announcements of availability), numbered program announcements, and statements of PHS policy. The information found on the NIH Grant Line is grouped into three main sections: (1) short news flashes that appear without any prompting shortly after you have logged on, (2) bulletins that are for reading, and (3) files that are intended mainly for downloading. The E-Guide is available for electronic transmission each week. The material consists predominantly of statements about the research interests of the PHS agencies, institutes, and national centers that have funds to support research in the extramural community. Currently under development are two new files: one will be a monthly listing of new NIH Awards, and the other will be an order form to obtain NIH publications from DRG's Office of Grants Inquiries.
Details:	Free
	To access the NIH Grant Line, telnet to the URL address below and when a message has been received that the connection is open, type: ,GEN1 (the comma is mandatory). At the INITIALS? prompt, type BB5 and at the ACCOUNT? prompt, type CCS2
	The NIH Guide to Grants and Contracts can also be accessed through gopher://helix.nih.gov/11/res/nih-guide

`telnet://wylbur.cu.nih.gov`

Research (Funding Support List) ★★★

The Research list is for people (primarily at educational institutions) interested in applying for funding support from various sources.

Keywords:	Grants, Funding
Audience:	Educators (College, Graduate)
Profile:	This list assists faculty in locating sources of support from government agencies, corporations, and foundations. It also forwards information regarding the latest news from potential sponsors such as the National Science Foundation and the National Institutes of Health, and provides information on upcoming international seminars on various topics ranging from medicine to artificial intelligence.
Contact:	Eleanor Cicinsky v2153a@vm.temple.edu
User Info:	To subscribe to the list, send an e-mail message to the address below consisting of a single line reading: SUB research YourFirstName YourLastName. To send a message to the entire list, address it to: research@vm.temple.edu

`mailto:listserv@vm.temple.edu`

Graphical User Interfaces

BX-Talk ★

BX-talk has been created for users of Builder Xcessory (BX) to discuss problems (and solutions) and ideas for using BX, which is a graphical user interface builder for Motif applications, and is sold by ICS. Please note that this list is not associated with ICS (the authors of BX) in any way.

Keywords:	Builder Xcessory, Graphical User Interfaces
Audience:	Graphics Experts, Computer Operators
Contact:	Darci L. Chapman bx-talk-request@qiclab.scn.rain.com
Details:	Free

User Info:	To subscribe to the list, send an e-mail message requesting a subscription to the URL address below.
	To send a message to the entire list, address it to: bx-talk@qiclab.scn.rain.com
Notes:	This list is unmoderated.

`mailto:bx-talk-request@qiclab.scn.rain.com`

Graphic Arts

Williams College Library ★

The library's holdings are large and wide-ranging and contain significant collections in many fields.

Keywords:	Americana, Graphic Arts, Printing (History of), Performing Arts, Printing
Audience:	General Public, Researchers, Librarians, Document Delivery Professionals
Contact:	Jim Cubit
Details:	Free
Expect:	Mitek Server..., Send: Enter or Return; Expect: prompt, Send: hollis

`telnet://library.williams.edu`

Graphic Design

(The) DTP Direct Catalog ★

DTP Direct specializes in Macintosh hardware and software tools for desktop publishers and graphics professionals.

Keywords:	Macintosh, Desktop Publishing, Graphic Design
Sponsor:	InterNex Server Bureau
Audience:	Graphic Designers, Artists, Desktop Publishers
Details:	Free, Moderated, Image, and Sound files available. Multimedia files available.

`http://www.internex.net/DTP/home.html`

INGRAFX

This E-conference is for discussion of all matters relating to information graphics.

Keywords:	Computer Graphics, Graphic Design, Scientific Visualization
Audience:	Graphic Designers, Cartographers, Animators
Contact:	Jeremy Crampton http://info.cern.ch/hypertext/WWW/The Project.html

User Info:	To subscribe to the list, send an e-mail message to the URL address below, consisting of a single line reading:
	SUB ingrafx YourFirstName YourLastName
	To send a message to the entire list, address it to: ingrafx@psuvm.psu.edu

`mailto:listserv@psuvm.psu.edu`

Graphics

Free Art For HTML Page ★

This web site provides copyrighted graphics for the Mosaic program.

Keywords:	Computer-Aided Design, Graphics
Audience:	Designers, Educators
Contact:	Harlan Wallach wallach@mcs.com
Details:	Free

`http://www.mcs.net/wallach/Fart/buttons.html`

ISIS/Draw

ISIS/Draw provides a chemical drawing package from MDL Information Systems and The American Chemical Society (ACS).

Keywords:	Chemistry, Graphics
Sponsor:	ACS and MDL Information Systems, Inc.
Audience:	Chemists, Chemistry Professors, Chemistry Students
Profile:	ISIS/Draw, the premier chemical drawing package from MDL Information Systems, Inc., is now available to chemistry students and professors at a special academic price through the American Chemical Society (ACS). Used by major pharmaceutical, agrochemical, and chemical companies worldwide, ISIS/Draw has the chemical intelligence to know that a line is a bond, and a letter is an atom. It can be used to: build queries for a structure-searching database; create presentation-quality sketches of chemical structures, reactions, and a wide range of other graphics; cut and paste annotated chemical structure drawings into popular word processing programs to create instructional materials and reports.
Details:	Costs
	Call ACS at 1-800-227-5558. When placing an order, use the following catalog numbers: 2152-9-151 (Windows) or 2156-1-151 (Macintosh).

`dmg96@acs.org`

OTIS (Operative Term Is Stimulate)

An image-based electronic art gallery.

Keywords:	Art, Graphics, Electronic Art, Animation
Audience:	Graphic Artists
Profile:	OTIS is a public-access library containing hundreds of images, animations, and information files.
	Within the sunsite ftp, the directory is: /pub/multimedia/pictures/OTIS. Use the bin command to ensure you're in binary transfer mode.

`ftp://sunsite.unc.edu`

UWP Music Archive (named for the host machine's location: the University of Wisconsin—Parkside)

An extensive repository of files relating to a diverse array of music genres: rock, folk, classical, and so on.

Keywords:	Music, Lyrics, Graphics
Sponsor:	University of Wisconsin—Parkside
Audience:	Musicians, Music Enthusiasts, Musicologists
Profile:	This FTP archive contains a music database, artist discographies, essays about music and particular works, hundreds of image files (mostly .GIF and .JPEG format) of musicians—including album covers and posters, a lyrics archive, and the ever-popular 'Beginner's Introduction to Classical Music.'
Contact:	Dave Datta datta@ftp.uwp.edu
User Info:	Select "Music Archives" from the gopher top-level menu.
Notes:	Also accessible through CMU's "English Server" gopher server. (q.v.)

`gopher://gopher.uwp.edu`

Great Lakes Area

University of Toledo Library ★★

The library's holdings are large and wide-ranging and contain significant collections in many fields.

Keywords:	Business, Great Lakes Area, Humanities, International Relations, Psychology, Science
Audience:	Researchers, Students, General Public
Details:	Free
Expect:	Enter one of the following commands..., Send: DIAL MVS; Expect: dialed to mvs ####; Send: UTMOST

`telnet:/ uofto1.utoledo.edu`

Greece

soc.culture.greek

A Usenet newsgroup providing information and discussion about Greek culture.

Keywords:	Greece, Sociology
Audience:	Sociologists, Greeks
Details:	Free
User Info:	To subscribe to this Usenet newsgroup, you need access to a newsreader.

`news:soc.culture.greek`

Gregorian Chants

Cantus

This gopher site accesses the Gregorian Chant Database, which is maintained by the Catholic University of America.

Keywords:	Gregorian Chants, Music, Liturgy
Sponsor:	Catholic University of America (CUA)
Audience:	Vocalists, Educators, Students
Profile:	The database contains an introduction to the Cantus Gopher at the CUA, and has a searchable index.

`gopher://vmsgopher.cua.edu`

Group Communications

Free for All

An experiment in a networked hypermedia group bulletin board.

Keywords:	Internet, Group Communications, Multimedia
Audience:	Internet Surfers, Multimedia Enthusiasts
Details:	Free, Mm

`http://south.ncsa.uiuc.edu/Free.html`

Hypermedia/Internet

A guide to hypermedia and the Internet.

Keywords:	Internet, Group Communications, Hypermedia
Sponsor:	Australian National University
Audience:	Internet Surfers
Contact:	David Geoffrey Green David.Green@anu.edu.au
Details:	Free

`http://life.anu.edu.au`

irc (Internet Relay Chat)

A multiuser, multichannel chatting network. It enables people all over the Internet to "talk" to one another interactively.

Keywords:	Internet, Group Communications
Audience:	Internet Surfers
Details:	Free
User Info:	Readme file is: irc/README

`ftp://cs.bu.edu`

Guidelines

NATO

Online version of The NATO Handbook, which recommends changes for the future of the North Atlantic Treaty Organization in light of decreasing defense resources.

Keywords:	NATO, Guidelines, Defense
Sponsor:	The NATO Office of Information and Press
Audience:	Governent Officials, Military Personnel, Historians
Details:	Free
	Select from menu as appropriate.

`gopher://wiretap.spies.com`

Guitar

alt.guitar

A Usenet newsgroup providing information and discussion about guitar playing.

Keywords:	Guitar, Musical Instruments
Audience:	Guitarists
User Info:	To subscribe to this Usenet newsgroup, you need access to a newsreader.

`news:alt.guitar`

Gun Control Legislation

BA-Firearms

This is an announcement and discussion of firearms legislation and related issues. The ca- list is for California statewide issues; the ba- list is for the San Francisco Bay Area and gets all messages sent to the ca- list. Prospective members should subscribe to one or the other, generally depending on whether or not they are SF Bay Area residents.

Keywords:	Firearms, Gun Control Legislation, San Francisco Bay Area
Audience:	Politicians, General Public, Gun Users, San Francisco Bay Area Residents
Contact:	Jeff Chan ba-firearms-request@shell.portal.com
Details:	Free
User Info:	To subscribe to the list, send an e-mail message requesting a subscription to the URL address below.
	To send a message to the entire list, address it to: ba-firearms@shell.portal.com

`mailto:ba-firearms-request@shell.portal.com`

ca-Firearms

This is an announcement and discussion of firearms legislation and related issues. The ca- list is for California statewide issues; the ba- list is for the San Francisco Bay Area and gets all messages sent to the ca- list. Prospective members should subscribe to one or the other, generally depending on whether or not they are SF Bay Area residents.

Keywords:	Firearms, Gun Control Legislation, California
Audience:	Politicians, General Public, Gun Users, California Residents
Contact:	Jeff Chan ca-firearms-request@shell.portal.com
Details:	Free
User Info:	To subscribe to the list, send an e-mail message requesting a subscription to the URL address below.
	To send a message to the entire list, address it to: ca-firearms@shell.portal.com

`mailto:ca-firearms-request@shell.portal.com`

GUTENBERG Listserver

GUTENBERG Listserver

A mailing list providing information about Project Gutenberg.

Keywords:	Project Gutenberg, Literature (General), Reference
Sponsor:	National Clearinghouse for Machine Readable Texts
Audience:	General Public, Researchers, Educators, Students
Contact:	Michael S. Hart gutnberg@vmd.cso.uiuc.edu
Details:	Free
User Info:	To subscribe to the list, send an e-mail message to the URL address shown below, consisting of a single line reading:
	SUB GUTBNERG YourFirstName YourLastName

`mailto:listserv@vmd.cso.uiuc.edu`

H

Hacking

CUD (Computer Underground Digest)

USA Today of cyberspace and the computer underground. Contains information relating to the computer underground.

Keywords: Hacking, Computer News, Cyberculture
Audience: Hackers, Reality Hackers, Computer Underground Enthusiasts
Contact: Gordon Meyer, Jim Thomas tk0jut2@niu.bitnet or pumpcon@mindvox.phantom.com.
Details: Free

ftp://etext.archive.umich.edu/pub/Zines/CUD

General Hacking Info

Files on the topic of hacking.

Keywords: Hacking, Computers
Audience: Hackers, Computer Users
Details: Free
Notes: Expect: login, Send: anonymous; Expect: Password, Send: Your E-mail Address

ftp://ftp.eff.org

GlobeTrotter

File concerning hacking from an international perspective.

Keywords: Hacking, Computers
Audience: Hackers, Computer Users
Details: Free
Notes: Expect: login, Send: anonymous; Expect: Password, Send: Your E-mail Address

ftp://ftp.eff.org

Hacker's Network

File of hacking, published in Britain.

Keywords: Hacking, Computers
Audience: Hackers, Computer Users
Details: Free
Notes: Expect: login, Send: anonymous; Expect: Password, Send: Your E-mail Address

ftp://ftp.eff.org

High Weirdness by E-Mail

Guide to some interesting sources of information online.

Keywords: Technology, Hacking, Computer Underground
Audience: Mystics, Hackers, Computer Users
Profile: This file focuses mainly on bizarre philosophies, such as Discordia and SubGenius. Contents include: offbeat religions and 'spirituality' paganism and magic, occultism, UFOs, and paranormal phenomena.
Details: Free

ftp://etext.archive.umich.edu/pub/Zines/Weirdness

Legion of Doom/Hackers Technical Journals

Technical journals of the infamous hacking ring Legion of Doom.

Keywords: Hacking, Computers
Audience: Hackers, Computer Users
Details: Free
Notes: Expect: login, Send: anonymous; Expect: Password, Send: Your E-mail Address

ftp://ftp.eff.org

Haiti

Summit of the Americas Internet Gopher

A gopher containing supporting materials for the Summit of the Americas, a meeting of the Western Hemisphere's democratically elected heads of state, to be held in Miami in December of 1994.

Keywords: American Studies, International Relations, Haiti, Latin America
Sponsor: The Florida University Latin American and Caribbean Center
Audience: Government Officials, Journalists, NGOs, General Public
Contact: Rene Ramos summit@SERVAX.FIU.EDU

gopher://summit.fiu.edu

Hamill (Peter)

Ph7

A mailing list for discussions about Peter Hamill and related rock groups.

Keywords: Rock Music, Hamill (Peter)
Audience: Musicians, Rock Music Enthusiasts
Contact: ph7-request@bnf.com
User Info: To Subscribe to the list, send an e-mail message requesting a subscription to the URL address below.

To send a message to the entire list, address it to: ph7@bnf.com

mailto:ph7-request@bnf.com

Handel (G.F.)

Indiana University Libraries

The library's holdings are large and wide-ranging and contain significant collections in many fields.

Keywords:	Literature (English), Literature (American), 1640-Present, British Plays (19th-C.), Western Americana, Railway History, Aristotle (Texts of), Lafayette (Marquis de), Handel (G.F.), Austrian History, Antiquarian Books, Rare Books, French Opera (19th-C.), Drama (British)
Audience:	General Public, Researchers, Librarians, Document Delivery Professionals
Details:	Free
Notes:	Expect: User ID prompt, Send: GUEST

`telnet://iuis.ucs.indiana.edu`

Handicap

Handicap

An anonymous data site containing disability-related files or programs.

Keywords:	Health, Disability
Audience:	Disabled People
Profile:	There are about 40 directories with 500 files/programs covering all types of disabilities. The "Handicap BBS List" originates here.
Details:	Free
Notes:	Login: anonymous

`ftp://handicap.shel.isc-br.com`

Handicapping

derby

To discuss various aspects and strategies of horseracing, primarily dealing with, but not limited to, handicapping.

Keywords:	Horseracing, Handicapping
Audience:	Horseracing Enthusiasts
Contact:	John Wilkes derby-request@ekrl.com
User Info:	To Subscribe to the list, send an e-mail message requesting a subscription to the URL address below. To send a message to the entire list, address it to: derby-request@ekrl.com

`mailto:derby-request@ekrl.com`

Hardware

data-exp

The mail list server provides an open forum for users to discuss the Visualization Data Explorer Package. It contains three files at the moment: a. FAQ, b. summary, and c. forum.

Keywords:	Computing, Software, Hardware, Visualization Data Explorer Package
Audience:	Computer Users
User Info:	To Subscribe to the list, send an e-mail message requesting a subscription to the URL address below. To send a message to the entire list, address it to: stein@watson.ibm.com

`mailto:stein@watson.ibm.com`

Futurebus+ Users

This discussion group focuses on the design, implementation, integration, and operation of hardware and software related to Futurebus+.

Keywords:	Computer Users, Hardware, Software
Audience:	Computer Users, Software Engineers, Hardware Engineers
Contact:	majordomo@theus.rain.com
Details:	Free
User Info:	To Subscribe to the list, send an e-mail message to the URL address below consisting of a single line reading: SUB fbus_users YourFirstName YourLastName To send a message to the entire list, address it to: fbus_users+@theus.rain.com

`mailto:majordomo@theus.rain.com`

gateway2000

This list is a source of information about Gateway2000 products.

Keywords:	Computer Products, Software, Hardware
Audience:	Computer Users, Hardware Engineers, Software Engineers
Details:	Free
User Info:	To Subscribe to the list, send an e-mail message requesting a subscription to the URL address below. To send a message to the entire list, address it to: gateway2000@sei.cmu.edu

`gateway2000-request@sei.cmu.edu`

Pc532

A mailing list for people interested in the pc532 project, a National Semiconductor NS32532-based system, offered at a low cost.

Keywords:	Computers, Hardware, Software
Audience:	Computer Users, Software Developers
Contact:	Dave Rand pc532-request@bungi.com
Details:	Free
User Info:	To Subscribe to the list, send an e-mail message requesting a subscription to the URL address below. To send a message to the entire list, address it to: pc532@bungi.com

`mailto:pc532-request@bungi.com`

Pdp8-lovers

A mailing list for owners of vintage DEC (Digital Equipment Corp.) computers, especially the PDP-8 series. Discussion topics include hardware, software, and programming techniques.

Keywords:	Computers, Hardware, Software
Audience:	Computer Users, Product Analysts
Contact:	Robert E. Seastrom pdp8-lovers-request@mc.lcs.mit.edu
Details:	Free
User Info:	To Subscribe to the list, send an e-mail message requesting a subscription to the URL address below. To send a message to the entire list, address it to: pdp8-lovers@mc.lcs.mit.edu

`mailto:pdp8-lovers@mc.lcs.mit.edu`

Qnx2

Discussion of all aspects of the QNX real-time operating systems. Topics include compatible hardware, available third-party software, software reviews, available PD/free software, QNX platform-specific programming discussions, and QNX and FLEET networking.

Keywords:	Computing, Hardware, Software
Audience:	Computer Users, Hardware/Software Designers, Product Analysts
Contact:	Martin Zimmerman camz@dlogtech.cuc.ab.ca
Details:	Free
User Info:	To Subscribe to the list, send an e-mail message requesting a subscription to the URL address below. To send a message to the entire list, address it to: qnx2@dlogtech.cuc.ab.ca

`mailto:qnx2@dlogtech.cuc.ab.ca`

Qnx4

A mailing list for discussion of all aspects of the QNX real-time operating systems. Topics include compatible hardware, available third-party software, software reviews, available PD/free software, QNX and FLEET networking, process control, and so on.

Keywords:	Computing, Hardware, Software, Networking

Audience:	Computer Users, Hardware/Software Designers, Product Analysts
Contact:	Martin Zimmerman camz@dlogtech.cuc.ab.ca
Details:	Free
User Info:	To Subscribe to the list, send an e-mail message requesting a subscription to the URL address below.
	To send a message to the entire list, address it to: qnx4@dlogtech.cuc.ab.ca

mailto:qnx4@dlogtech.cuc.ab.ca

Hardy (Thomas)

Colby College Library

The library's holdings are large and wide-ranging and contain significant collections in many fields.

Keywords:	Contemporary Letters, Hardy (Thomas),James (Henry), Mann (Thomas, Collections of), Housman (A.E., Letters of), Maine Authors, Irish History (Modern)
Audience:	General Public, Researchers, Librarians, Document Delivery Professionals
Details:	Free
Notes:	Expect: login, Send: library

telnet://library.colby.edu

Princeton University Online Manuscripts Catalog Library

The library's holdings are large and wide-ranging. They contain significant collections in many fields.

Keywords:	Books (Antiquarian), Dickens (Charles), Disraeli (Benjamin), Eliot (George), Hardy (Thomas), Kingsley (Charles), Trollope (Anthony)
Audience:	General Public, Researchers, Librarians, Document Delivery Professionals
Details:	Free
Notes:	Expect: VM370 logo, Send: <cr>; Expect: Welcome screen, Send: folio <cr>; Expect: Welcome screen for FOLIO, Send: <cr>; Expect: List of choices, Send: 3 <cr>; To exit: type: logoff

telnet://pucc.princeton.edu

Harper (Roy)

Stormcock ★

For general discussion and news concerning the music of Roy Harper, a folk-rock musician with a conscience. Recommendations and news concerning similar artists are encouraged.

Keywords:	Rock Music, Music, Harper (Roy)
Audience:	Music Fans
Contact:	Paul Davison stormcock-request@qmw.ac.uk
Details:	Free
User Info:	To Subscribe to the list, send an e-mail message to the address shown below consisting of a single line reading:
	SUB stormcock YourFirstName YourLastName
	To send a message to the entire list, address it to: stormcock@qmw.ac.uk

mailto: listserv@qmw.ac.uk

Harry (Deborah)

Deborah Harry and Blondie Information Service ★

An information service on everything and anything regarding Deborah Harry and Blondie, including tour information, recordings/films release information, and so on.

Keywords:	Rock Music, Harry (Deborah), Musical Groups
Audience:	Rock Music Enthusiasts, Deborah Harry Enthusiasts
Contact:	gunter@yarrow.wt.uwa.oz.au
Details:	Free
User Info:	To Subscribe to the list, send an e-mail message requesting a subscription to the URL address below.
	To send a message to the entire list, address it to: gunter@yarrow.wt.uwa.oz.au

mailto:gunter@yarrow.wt.uwa.oz.au

Harvard Biosciences Online Journals

Harvard Biosciences Online Journals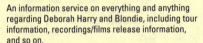

A resource containing selected online journals and periodicals in biology and medicine. Includes peer-reviewed e-journals, journal indexes, and databases.

Keywords:	Biology, Bioscience, Molecular Biology
Sponsor:	Harvard Biolabs, Harvard University, Cambridge, Massachusetts, USA
Audience:	Biologists, Molecular Biologists, Researchers
Contact:	Keith Robinson, Steve Brenner krobinson@nucleus.harvard.edu s.e.brenner@bioc.cam.ac.uk

http://golgi.harvard.edu/ journals.html

Harvard Medical Gopher

Harvard Medical Gopher

This gopher site accesses information from Harvard Medical School. Provides bibliographic information from Harvard Medical Library, basic science and clinical resources, and public health and government statistics.

Keywords:	Medicine, Libraries, Health Care
Sponsor:	Harvard Medical School, Cambridge, Massachusetts, USA
Audience:	Physicians, Health Care Professionals, Educators, Students
Contact:	gopher@warren.med.harvard.edu
Details:	Free

gopher://gopher.med.harvard.edu

Harvard University Library

Harvard University Library

The library's holdings are large and wide-ranging and contain significant collections in many fields.

Keywords:	Afrikaans, Alchemy, Arabic Culture (History of), Celtic Philology, Congo Languages, Folklore, Hebraica, Mormonism, Numismatics, Quakerism, Sanskrit, Witchcraft, Arabic Philology
Audience:	General Public, Researchers, Librarians, Document Delivery Professionals
Details:	Free
Notes:	Expect: Mitek Server..., Send: Enter or Return; Expect: prompt, Send: hollis

telnet://hollis.harvard.edu

Hawaii

Hawaii FYI

A state information system providing a wide range of free legal information.

Keywords:	Hawaii, Law (US)
Audience:	Hawaiians, Lawyers
Details:	Free

telnet://fyi.uhcc.hawaii.edu

University of Hawaii Library

The library's holdings are large and wide-ranging and contain significant collections in many fields.

Keywords:	Asia, European Documents, Book Arts, Hawaii

Audience:	General Public, Researchers, Librarians, Document Delivery Professionals
Details:	Free
Notes:	Expect: enter class, Send: LIB

`telnet://starmaster.uhcc.hawaii.edu`

Health

(The) Center for Biomedical Informatics of the State University of Campinas, Brazil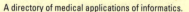

A directory of medical applications of informatics.

Keywords:	Health, Medicine, Informatics
Sponsor:	State University of Campinas, Brazil
Audience:	Medical Professionals, Medical Educators, Medical Researchers
Profile:	Designed to foster educational and practical uses of computers in medicine and the health sciences by providing free international access to resources.
Contact:	Renato M.E. Sabbatini sabbatini@ccvax.unicamp.br
Details:	Free

`ftp://ccsun.unicamp.br`

AIDS Treatment News

A newsletter on AIDS treatment.

Keywords:	AIDS, Health, Medicine
Sponsor:	IGC (Institute for Global Communications)
Audience:	AIDS Researchers, Health Workers, AIDS Sufferers
Profile:	This newsletter contains interviews, reports on new and existing treatment modalities, announcements of clinical drug testing trial, and more.
Contact:	atn@igc.apc.org
Details:	Free

`gopher://odie.niaid.nih.gov/11/aids`

AIDS/HIV Information

A clearinghouse for AIDS/HIV-related information. Contains Internet connections to WWW and gopher servers, and archives of AIDS server FAQs, including an archive of AIDS treatment news.

Keywords:	AIDS, Medicine, Health
Sponsor:	Queer Resources Directory, USA
Audience:	AIDS Sufferers, Gays, Activists
Contact:	QRD Staff QRDstaff@vector.casti.com
Details:	AIDS Treatment News

`http://vector.casti.com/QRD/.html/AIDS.html`

Alternative Medicine, the Definitive Guide

A one-stop reference covering common health problems and leading alternative therapies.

Keywords:	Alternative Medicine, Medicine, Health, Health Care
Sponsor:	Future Medicine Publishing, Inc.
Audience:	General Public, Health Care Professionals
Profile:	Spanning a global effort of 4 years, and including input from nearly 400 health-care professionals, this one-stop reference offers 1100 pages of in-depth explanations to 43 of the leading alternative therapies. In addition to covering over 200 of the most common health problems, the site offers a wide range of choices for maintaining and regaining your health, highlighted with graphic illustrations. This is truly the "Voice of Alternative Medicine."
Details:	Costs

`mailto:FutureMd@CRL.com`

AMALGAME

A resource containing Macintosh demos and XFCN PrintZ files on the subject of health.

Keywords:	Health
Sponsor:	University of Montreal
Audience:	Medical Researchers
Contact:	benoit@medent.umontreal.ca
Details:	Free

`ftp://amalgame.Medent.Umontreal.Ca`

Archive of Biology Software and Data

The main area of concentration of this archive is molecular biology. It contains software for the Macintosh, MS-DOS, VAX-VMS, and UNIX platforms.

Keywords:	Health, Biology, Molecular Biology
Sponsor:	Indiana University
Audience:	Biologists, Students
Contact:	archive@bio.indiana.edu
Details:	Free
Notes:	It is recommended that the file Archive.doc be transferred and read first. This file gives considerable information about and instructions for using the archive.

`ftp://ftp.bio.indiana.edu`

Biomedical Computer Laboratory (BCL)

A resource for biomedical computing.

Keywords:	Health, Biomedical Computing, Biology, Medicine
Sponsor:	Washington University School of Medicine
Audience:	Medical Researchers, Biologists
Profile:	A significant portion of the activities at BCL are supported by the National Center for Research Resources' Biomedical Research Technology Program (BRTP), which promotes the application of advances in computer science and technology, engineering, mathematics, and the physical sciences to research problems in biology and medicine by supporting the development of advanced research technologies.
Contact:	Kenneth W. Clark info@wubcl.wustl.edu
Details:	Free
Notes:	Expect: login; Send: anonymous Investigators wishing to explore the possibility of interactions with BCL at Washington University should send e-mail (preferred).

`ftp://wubcl.wustl.edu`

BOING (Bio-Oriented INternet Gophers)

A searchable gopher index, BOING is used to search through the titles of items in bio-gopher space and to access the items returned.

Keywords:	Biology, Health, Medicine
Audience:	Health Professionals, Biomedical Researchers, Students (college, graduate)
Details:	Free

`gopher://gopher.gdb.org`

Canadian University Consortium on Health in International Development (CANCHID)

CANCHID is a multi-campus consortium that includes medical schools and other educational institutions devoted to research and projects dealing with health care issues in developing countries.

Keywords:	Health, International Development
Audience:	Public Health, Medicine, International Aid Agencies
Contact:	Sam Lanfranco lanfran@vm1.yorku.ca
Details:	Free

User Info:	To Subscribe to the list, send an e-mail message to the URL address below, consisting of a single line reading: SUB canchid YourFirstName YourLastName To send a message to the entire list, address it to: canchid@vm1.yorku.ca	Keywords:	Disabilities, Health, Diseases	Details:	Free
		Sponsor:	Computing & Information Services at Texas A&M University, Galveston, Texas, USA	User Info:	To Subscribe to the list, send an e-mail message to the URL address shown below consisting of a single line reading: SUB granola YourFirstName YourLastName
		Audience:	Disabled People, Rehabilitation Counselors, Health Care Professionals, Activists		
		Contact:	Computing & Information Services at Texas A&M University gopher@tamu.edu		

mailto:listserv@vm1.yorku.ca

mailto:listserv@gitvm1.bitnet

Cornucopia of Disability Information (CODI)

gopher://gopher.tamu.edu/.dir/disability.dir

Handicap

Disability Reading Room

An anonymous data site containing disability-related files or programs.

A large collection of disability-related information available via gopher.

Keywords:	Disabilities, Health
Sponsor:	State University of New York (SUNY) at Buffalo
Audience:	Disabled People, Activists, Rehabilitation Counselors, Health Care Professionals
Profile:	This site provides a wide variety of information resources concerning people with disabilities, ranging from legal information to a directory of computer resources aimed at the disabled consumer. Includes state, local, and national information and government documents such as the Americans with Disabilities Act. Also has links to many other related resources on the Internet, such as the National Rehabilitation Information Center.
Contact:	Jay Leavitt leavitt@ubvmsb.cc.buffalo.edu

Gopher menu of all kinds of reading material on disabilities.

Keywords:	Disabilities, Health
Sponsor:	University of Maryland
Audience:	Deaf and Disabled People, Health Care Professionals, Activists, Policy Analysts, Rehabilitation Counselors, Therapists
Profile:	A fascinating collection of reading material on disabilities and related issues, including first-person stories of dealing with chronic pain, detailed descriptions of laws involving the disabled, relevant press releases, and a large selection of journals on disabilities and related matters.
Contact:	UMD Computer Science Center consult@umail.umd.edu
Details:	Free

Keywords:	Health, Disability
Audience:	Disabled People
Profile:	There are about 40 directories with 500 files/programs covering all types of disabilities. The "Handicap BBS List" originates here.
Details:	Free
Notes:	Login: anonymous

ftp://handicap.shel.isc-br.com

Health News Daily

The database contains all the daily news and full-text articles from Health News Daily, a publication from F-D-C Reports, Inc.

Keywords:	Health, Pharmacology, Medical Research, News
Sponsor:	F-D-C Reports, Inc., Chevy Chase, MD, US
Audience:	Health Professionals, Market Researchers, Pharmacists
Profile:	The database provides specialized, in-depth business, scientific, regulatory, and legal news. Timely coverage of pharmacy and pharmaceuticals is given, as well as coverage of medical devices and diagnostics, medical research, cosmetics, health policy, provider payment policies, and cost containment in national health care. Coverage: 1990 to the present; updated daily.
Contact:	Dialog in the US at (800) 334-2564, Dialog internationally at country-specific locations.
Details:	Costs
User Info:	To Subscribe, contact Dialog directly.

gopher://val-dor.cc.buffalo.edu

Deaf Gopher

gopher://info.umd.edu

GAO

Gopher menu of deaf resources in the state of Michigan.

Files intended to provide Congress and Administration with an overview of health problems facing the nation.

Keywords:	Disabilities, Deafness, Health
Sponsor:	Michigan State University
Audience:	Deaf and Disabled People, Health Care Professionals, Activists, Policy Makers, Rehabilitation Counselors, Therapists
Profile:	A small but useful menu of deaf resources that includes a collection of files in essay and/or report form about a variety of historical and cultural aspects of deafness.
Contact:	Gary LaPointe deafgopher@ah3.cal.msu.edu
Details:	Free

Keywords:	Health, Congress (US)
Audience:	US Congress, Journalists, General Public
Profile:	These files concern health-care reform and human services and date from December 1992. They are provided by the government to familiarize the reader with the health issues confronting the administration.
Details:	Free
Notes:	Login: anonymous ABSTRACT.FIL is a file with abstracts for each of the 28 reports.

telnet://dialog.com

Health Periodicals Database

This source covers a broad range of health subjects and issues.

Keywords:	Health, Biotechnology, Medicine, Nutrition
Sponsor:	Information Access Company, Foster City, CA, US
Audience:	Health Professionals, Dieticians, Librarians

ftp://cu.nig.gov

gopher://cl.msu.edu/11/msu/dept/deaf

GRANOLA (Vegetarian Discussion List)

Disability Information

A ListServ for discussion of vegetarian issues, including everything from recipes to animal rights.

A collection of information about and links to sources of disability-related information from around the world. Includes archives of many related mailing lists and electronic newsletters, as well as legal and technical help for the disabled, and information about the Parkinson's Disease Information Exchange Network.

Keywords:	Health, Nutrition, Vegetarian, Recipes
Audience:	Vegetarians, Nutritionists, Health Professionals

Health

Profile:	The database provides indexing and full text of journals covering a broad range of health subjects and issues including: prenatal care, dieting, drug abuse, AIDS, biotechnology, cardiovascular disease, environment, public health, safety, paramedical professions, sports medicine, substance abuse, toxicology, and much more.
Contact:	Dialog in the US at (800) 334-2564, Dialog internationally at country-specific locations.
User Info:	To Subscribe, contact Dialog directly.
Notes:	Coverage: 1988 to the present; updated weekly.

`telnet://dialog.com`

Health Planning and Administration

The database contains references to nonclinical literature on many aspects of health care.

Keywords:	Health, Health Care
Sponsor:	US National Library of Medicine, Bethesda, MD, US
Audience:	Healthcare professionals
Profile:	Coverage includes: health care planning and facilities, health insurance, and the aspects of financial management, personnel administration, manpower planning, and licensure and accreditation that apply to the delivery of health care.
Contact:	Dialog in the US at (800) 334-2564, Dialog internationally at country-specific locations.
User Info:	To Subscribe, contact Dialog directly.
Notes:	Coverage: 1975 to the present; updated monthly.

`telnet://dialog.com`

HICNet Newsletter (MEDNEWS - The Health InfoCom Newsletter)

Usually published once a week, this is a large newsletter that is broken up into multiple sections to facilitate network movement.

Keywords:	Health, Medical News
Audience:	Health Professionals
Contact:	David Dodell ddodell@stjhmc.fidonet.org
Details:	Free
User Info:	To Subscribe, send an e-mail message to the address below consisting of a single line reading: SUB mednews YourFirstName YourLastName To send a message to the entire list, address it to: mednews@asuacad.bitnet

`mailto:listserv@asuacad.bitnet`

International Food and Nutrition (INFAN) Database

A database covering all aspects of nutrition, health and food, as for example, weight control, food safety, eating patterns, and more.

Keywords:	Nutrition, Health, Diet
Sponsor:	Pennsylvania State University Nutrition Center
Audience:	Nutritionists, Health Care Professionals, Consumers
Details:	Free To access the database, select PENpages (1), then General Information (3), and finally INFAN Database (4).

`telnet://penpages@psupen.psu.edu`

National Family Database— MAPP

This database contains family sociological and health data, including research briefs, bibliographies, census data, program ideas, reference materials, media materials, and publications.

Keywords:	Sociology, Family, Health
Sponsor:	Department of Agriculture Economics and Rural Sociology, Pennsylvania State University
Audience:	Sociologists, Public Health Policymakers, Health Care Providers
	To access the database select PENpages (1), then General Information (3) and finally Information on MAPP - National Family Database (5)

`telnet://penpages@psupen.psu.edu`

National Institutes of Health Gopher

Provides access to a broad range of National Institutes of Health (NIH) resources (library catalogues, databases) via the Internet.

Keywords:	Health, AIDS, Molecular Biology, Grants
Sponsor:	National Institutes of Health
Audience:	Health Professionals, Molecular Biologists, Researchers
Profile:	This gopher provides access to NIH resources, including institute phone books and calendars, library catalogs, molecular biology databases, the full text of the NIH Guide for Grants and Contracts, files containing AIDS and cancer information and more.
Contact:	gopher@gopher.nih.gov
Details:	Free
Notes:	Expect: Login; Enter: Gopher

`telnet://gopher.nih.gov`

`gopher://gopher.nih.gov`

`gopher://odie.niaid.nih.gov`

National Library of Medicine Gopher World Health Organization (WHO)

This gopher provides information about the National Library of Medicine, the world's largest single-topic library.

Keywords:	Medicine, Health, World Health
Sponsor:	National Library of Medicine, Massachusetts
	World Health Organization, Geneva, Switzerland
Audience:	Health-care Professionals, Medical Professionals, Researchers
Profile:	The National Library of Medicine (NLM) cares for over 4.5 million holdings (including books, journals, reports, manuscripts, and audio-visual items). The NLM offers extensive online information services dealing with clinical care, toxicology, environmental health, and basic biomedical research. It has several active research and development components, including an extramural grants program, houses an extensive history of medicine collection, and provides several programs designed to improve the nation's medical library system.
Contact:	R. P. C. Rodgers rodgers@nlm.nih.gov akazawa@who.ch
Details:	Free

`gopher://el-gopher.med.utah.edu`

`gopher://gopher.who.ch`

National Oceanic & Atmospheric Administration (NOAA) Office of Environmental Safety and Health, Department of Energy

The NOAA catalog provides keyword access to sources of environmental information in the US. Gopher for resources pertaining to health and environmental safety.

Keywords:	Environment, Oceans, Atmospheric Science, Health, Environmental Safety
Sponsor:	National Oceanic & Atmospheric Administration (NOAA)
	Department of Energy (USA)
Audience:	Environmental Scientists, Researchers, Environmentalists, Epidemiologists, Public Health Officials
Details:	Free

`gopher://scilibx.ucsc.edu`

`gopher://gopher.ns.doc.gov`

Health Care

Office of Environmental Safety and Health, Department of Energy ★★★★

Gopher for resources pertaining to health and environmental safety.

Keywords:	Health, Environmental Safety
Sponsor:	Department of Energy (US)
Audience:	Epidemiologists, Public Health Policymakers, General Public
Details:	Free

`gopher://gopher.ns.doc.gov`

Prion (Prion Research Digest) ★

Prion Infection Digest discusses current research on prion (slow virus) infection. The Prion Digest was formed as a reference point for the discussion and sharing of current research into prion infection.

Keywords:	Prion, Health
Audience:	Medical Researchers, Health-care Professionals
Contact:	Chris Swanson prion-request@stolaf.edu
Details:	Free
User Info:	To Subscribe to the list, send an e-mail message requesting a subscription to the URL address below.
	To send a message to the entire list, address it to: prion@stolaf.edu

`mailto:prion-request@stolaf.edu`

Safety (Environmental Health and Safety Discussion List) ★

E-conference for people interested in the various environmental health and safety issues on college and university campuses.

Keywords:	Environmental Health, Safety, Health
Audience:	Students (College/University), Educators (college/University)
Contact:	Ralph Stuart, Dayna Flath rstuart@moose.uvm.edu dmf@uvmvm.uvm.edu
Details:	Free
User Info:	To Subscribe to the list, send an e-mail message to the URL address below, consisting of a single line reading:
	SUB safety YourFirstName YourLastName
	To send a message to the entire list, address it to: safety@uvmvm.uvm.edu

`mailto:listserv@uvmvm.uvm.edu`

table.abortion ★

A Usenet newsgroup providing information and discussion about all sides of the abortion issue.

Keywords:	Abortion, Women's Issues, Health
Audience:	Women, Activists, Health Care Professionals
Details:	Free
User Info:	To Subscribe to this Usenet newsgroup, you need access to a newsreader.

`news:table.abortion`

The Wellness List

This list is founded for the purpose of discussing issues concerning Health/Nutrition/Wellness/Life Expectancy/Physical Fitness, and the books, experiences, and solutions recommended by the participants.

Keywords:	Health, Nutrition, Fitness
Audience:	Doctors, Nutritionists, General Public
Profile:	This resource provides announcements of and reviews of books that include solutions, nutrition-related position papers, requests for information, recommendations of participants, healthy recipes, nutrition and fitness related product announcements, and general discussion of related issues. Health professionals, authors, and nutritionists are encouraged to subscribe and share their knowledge with the participants.
Contact:	George Rust, Wellnessmart george@wellnessmart.com, info@wellnessmart.com
User Info:	To Subscribe send an e-mail message to the URL address below consisting of a single line reading: subscribe wellnesslist

`mailto:majordomo@wellnessmart.com`

University of Pennsylvania School of Medicine Library ★★

The library's holdings are large and wide-ranging and contain significant collections in many fields.

Keywords:	Health Care, Nursing, History, Health
Audience:	Researchers, Students, General Public
Details:	Free
Notes:	Expect: Login; Send: Public

`telnet://penninfo.upenn.edu`

Women.health ★

This conference features articles, documents, news, announcements, policy statements, and other information about women's health around the world. Topics include breast cancer, ovarian cancer, alcohol, abortion, pregnancy, sterilization of women, pesticides, Quinacrine, HIV, and disability.

Keywords:	Women, Abortion, AIDS, Disability, Feminism, Health
Audience:	Activists, Family Planners, Health Professionals, Non-Governmental Organizations, Women
Details:	Costs
User Info.:	Establish an account on the nearest APC node. Login, type c for conferences, then type go women.health. For information on the nearest APC node, contact: APC International Secretariat IBASE E-mail: apcadmin@apc.org

`telnet://igc.apc.org`

World Health Organization (WHO) ★★★

This gopher provides access to the databases of the WHO.

Keywords:	World Health Organization, Health, Medicine, Non-governmental organizations
Sponsor:	World Health Organization, Geneva, Switzerland
Audience:	Medical Professionals, Researchers
Contact:	akazawa@who.ch
Details:	Free

`gopher://gopher.who.ch`

Health Care

Accri-l ★★

A mailing list providing information on anesthesia and critical care resources available via the Internet.

Keywords:	Health Care, Medical Treatment, Medicine
Audience:	Health Care Professionals, Health Care Providers
Contact:	A.J. Wright meds002@uabdpo.dpo.uab.edu
User Info:	To Subscribe, send an e-mail message to the URL address below consisting of a single line reading:
	SUB accri-l YourFirstName YourLastName
	To send a message to the entire list, address it to: accri-l@uabdpo.dpo.uab.edu

`mailto:listserv@uabdpo.dpo.uab.edu`

Act-up ★★

A mailing list for discussion of the work being done by various Act-Up chapters worldwide.

Keywords:	AIDS, Health Care, Activism
Audience:	AIDS Activists, Health Science Researchers

Health Care

Contact: Lenard Diggins
act-up-request@world.std.com

User Info: To Subscribe to theist list, send an e-mail message to the URL address below.

To send a message to the entire list, address it to: act-up-request@world.std.com

mailto:act-up-request@world.std.com

Alternative Medicine, the Definitive Guide

A one stop reference covering common health problems and leading alternative therapies.

Keywords: Alternative Medicine, Medicine, Health, Health Care

Sponsor: Future Medicine Publishing, Inc.

Audience: General Public, Health Care Professionals

Profile: Spanning a global effort of 4 years and input from nearly 400 health-care professionals, this one-stop reference offers 1100 pages of in-depth explanations to 43 of the leading alternative therapies. In addition to covering over 200 of the most common health problems, a wide range of choices to maintaining and regaining your health are highlighted with graphic illustrations. This is truly the "Voice of Alternative Medicine."

Details: Costs

URL:FutureMd@CRL.com

Dental Information Area

A collection of dental information, including a selection of related educational software and dental informatics materials.

Keywords: Dentistry, Health Care, Informatics

Sponsor: Columbia School of Oral and Dental Surgery

Audience: Dentists, Medical Students, Health Care Professionals

Contact: Dr. John Zimmerman
jlz4@columbia.edu

gopher://cuhsla.cpmc.columbia.edu/health.sci/dental.toc

Harvard Medical Gopher

This gopher site accesses information from Harvard Medical School. Provides bibliographic information from Harvard Medical Library, basic science and clinical resources, and public health and government statistics.

Keywords: Medicine, Libraries, Health Care

Sponsor: Harvard Medical School, Cambridge, Massachusetts, USA

Audience: Physicians, Health Care Professionals, Educators, Students

Contact: gopher@warren.med.harvard.edu

Details: Free

gopher://gopher.med.harvard.edu

Health and Clinical Information & Bioethics Online Service

A collection of gopher links to servers offering a wide variety of health information.

Keywords: Medicine, Medical Treatment, Health Care

Sponsor: Medical College of Wisconsin (MCW) InfoScope, Wisconsin, USA

Audience: Health Care Professionals, Health Care Providers

Profile: Links include the National Institutes of Health, MedNews Digest, Family Medicine list archives, and full-text of national health plans. Also features the Bioethics Online Service, which provides updates, journal abstracts, alerts, and a forum for discussing medical ethics. Site specific information on MCW physicians and surgeons is also available.

Contact: Dieta Murra
mcw-info@its.mcw.edu

gopher://post.its.mcw.edu

Health Planning and Administration

The database contains references to nonclinical literature on many aspects of health care.

Keywords: Health, Health Care

Sponsor: US National Library of Medicine, Bethesda, MD, US

Audience: Healthcare professionals

Profile: Coverage includes: health care planning and facilities, health insurance, and the aspects of financial management, personnel administration, manpower planning, and licensure and accreditation that apply to the delivery of health care.

Contact: Dialog in the US at (800) 334-2564, Dialog internationally at country-specific locations.

User Info: To Subscribe, contact Dialog directly.

Notes: Coverage: 1975 to the present; updated monthly.

telnet://dialog.com

Information Infrastructure and Technology Act of 1992

The Information Infrastructure and Technology Act of 1992 builds on the High-Performance Computing Act. The newer bill will ensure that the technology developed by the High-Performance Computing Program is applied widely in K-12 education, libraries, health care, and industry, particularly manufacturing. It will authorize a total of $1.15 billion over the next five years.

Keywords: Government (US Federal), Law (US Federal), Information Technology, Education, Health Care

Audience: Journalists, Politicians, Scientists, Manufacturers, Educators

Details: Free

File is: /internet/nren/iita.1992/gorebill.1992.txt

ftp://nis.nsf.net

Marshall University School of Medicine (MUSOM) RuralNet Gopher

A gopher server dedicated to the improvement of rural health care.

Keywords: Rural Development, Health Care, Medical Treatment, Bioinformatics

Sponsor: Marshall University School of Medicine

Audience: Health Care Professionals, Medical Students, Rural Residents

Profile: A collection of health care resources, with particular emphasis on rural health care. Includes listings of clinical resources by subject area, information on state and federal rural health care initiatives, and links to local and national health and education services.

Contact: Mike McCarthy, Andy Jarrell
mmccarth@muvms6.wvnet.edu
jarrell@musom01.mu.wvnet.edu

gopher://ruralnet.mu.wvnet.edu

New York State Department of Health Gopher

An electronic guide to health information from the state of New York.

Keywords: Health Care, Statistics, Health Sciences, New York

Sponsor: New York State Department of Health

Audience: Health Care Professionals, Health Care Consumers

Profile: Information provided includes health statistics for New York State, lists of health care providers, facilities, and publications, as well as New York State Department of Health press releases.

Contact: nyhealth@albnydh2.bitnet

gopher://gopher.health.state.ny.us

Health Sciences

NIBNews - A Monthly Electronic Bulletin About Medical Informatics

⭐

Disseminates information about Brazilian and Latin American activities, people, information, events, publications, software, and so on, involving computer applications in health care, medicine, and biology.

Keywords: Health Care, Biology, Brazil, Latin America, South America, Medicine
Audience: Health Care Professionals, Biologists
Contact: Renato M. E. Sabbatini
SABBATINI@BRUC.BITNET
Details: Free
E-mail a short notice to
`mailto:sabbatini@ccvax.unicamp.br`

sci.med

⭐

A Usenet newsgroup providing information and discussion about medicine and its related products.

Keywords: Medicine, Health Care
Audience: Medical Professionals
Details: Free
User Info: To Subscribe to this Usenet newsgroup, you need access to a newsreader.
`news:sci.med`

sci.med.physics

⭐

A Usenet newsgroup providing information and discussion about physics in medical testing and care.

Keywords: Physics, Medical Research, Health Care
Audience: Physicists, Medical Researchers, Medical Practitioners, Health Care Professionals
Details: Free
User Info: To Subscribe to this Usenet newsgroup, you need access to a newsreader.
`news:sci.med.physics`

Stanford Medical Center Gopher

⭐⭐

This gopher allows extensive access to the Stanford Medical Center's archives.

Keywords: Medicine, Health Care, Health Sciences
Sponsor: Stanford Medical Center, Palo Alto, California, USA
Audience: Health Care Professionals, Health Science Researchers
Contact: Stanford Medical Center
gopher@medisg.stanford.edu
`gopher://med.stanford.edu`

University of Pennsylvania School of Medicine Library

⭐⭐

The library's holdings are large and wide-ranging and contain significant collections in many fields.

Keywords: Health Care, Nursing, History, Health
Audience: Researchers, Students, General Public
Details: Free
Notes: Expect: Login; Send: Public
`telnet://penninfo.upenn.edu`

Health News Daily

Health News Daily

⭐⭐⭐

The database contains all the daily news and full-text articles from Health News Daily, a publication from F-D-C Reports, Inc.

Keywords: Health, Pharmacology, Medical Research, News
Sponsor: F-D-C Reports, Inc., Chevy Chase, MD, US
Audience: Health Professionals, Market Researchers, Pharmacists
Profile: The database provides specialized, in-depth business, scientific, regulatory, and legal news. Timely coverage of pharmacy and pharmaceuticals is given, as well as coverage of medical devices and diagnostics, medical research, cosmetics, health policy, provider payment policies, and cost containment in national health care.
Coverage: 1990 to the present; updated daily.
Contact: Dialog in the US at (800) 334-2564, Dialog internationally at country-specific locations.
Details: Costs
User Info: To Subscribe, contact Dialog directly.
`telnet://dialog.com`

Health Periodicals Database

Health Periodicals Database

This source covers a broad range of health subjects and issues.

Keywords: Health, Biotechnology, Medicine, Nutrition
Sponsor: Information Access Company, Foster City, CA, US
Audience: Health Professionals, Dieticians, Librarians
Profile: The database provides indexing and full text of journals covering a broad range of health subjects and issues including: prenatal care, dieting, drug abuse, AIDS, biotechnology, cardiovascular disease, environment, public health, safety, paramedical professions, sports medicine, substance abuse, toxicology, and much more.
Contact: Dialog in the US at (800) 334-2564, Dialog internationally at country-specific locations.
User Info: To Subscribe, contact Dialog directly.
Notes: Coverage: 1988 to the present; updated weekly.
`telnet://dialog.com`

Health Sciences

CAMIS (Center for Advanced Medical Informatics at Stanford)

CAMIS is a shared computing resource supporting research activities in biomedical informatics.

Keywords: Medical Informatics, Heuristics, Health Sciences
Sponsor: Stanford University School of Medicine, Palo Alto, CA, USA
Audience: Medical Informatics, Health Science Researchers
Profile: The CAMIS gopher includes an Internet-wide title search, computing information, and technical reports for the Section on Medical Informatics (SMI) community as well as that of the Knowledge Systems Laboratory (KSL), information on the Heuristic Programming Project, pointers to various online library catalogs, and more.
Contact: Torsten_Heycke@med.stanford.edu
`gopher://camis.stanford.edu/00/gopherdoc`

Center for Biomedical Informatics, Brazil

⭐

The Center for Biomedical Informatics maintains a software library with 50 disks containing about 150 public-domain medical application programs for IBM-PC-compatible microcomputers.

Keywords: Health Sciences, Public Domain Software
Sponsor: Center for Biomedical Informatics, Brazil

Health Sciences

Audience:	Physicians, Nurses, Dentists, University Biomedical Researchers, Students
Details:	Costs
	To receive the catalogue in electronic form, send the following one-line message to infomed@ccvax.unicamp.br or infomed@bruc.bitnet: get public-domain p (for version in Portuguese) get public-domain e (for version in English). Instructions on how to acquire the software are included.

`ftp://ccsun.unicamp.br`

Creighton University Library Online Catalogue ★★★★

This site maintains a catalog of the Creighton University library's holdings.

Keywords:	Health Sciences, Libraries
Sponsor:	Creighton University, Omaha, Nebraska, USA
Audience:	Health Care Professionals, Medical Educators, Students
Details:	Free
	At the prompt type <lib hsl>for Health Sciences Library.

`telnet://attachpals@owl.creighton.edu`

Emory University Library

The library's holdings are large and wide-ranging and contain significant collections in many fields.

Keywords:	Health Sciences, Theology, History (US), Communism, Economics (History of), Literature (American)
Audience:	General Public, Researchers, Librarians, Document Delivery Professionals
Details:	Free
Notes:	Expect: READ, Send: DIAL VTAM, press RETURN; Expect: CICS screen, Send: PF1

`telnet://emuvm1.cc.emory.edu`

New York State Department of Health Gopher

An electronic guide to health information from the state of New York.

Keywords:	Health Care, Statistics, Health Sciences, New York
Sponsor:	New York State Department of Health
Audience:	Health Care Professionals, Health Care Consumers
Profile:	Information provided includes health statistics for New York State, lists of health care providers, facilities, and publications, as well as New York State Department of Health press releases.
Contact:	nyhealth@albnydh2.bitnet

`gopher://gopher.health.state.ny.us`

NIH (National Institute of Health)

This server is a network-based computer service operated by the Division of Computer Research and Technology (DCRT) to distribute information for and about the NIH (National Institutes of Health).

Keywords:	NIH, Health Sciences, Biomedical Research, Medicine
Sponsor:	Division of Computer Research and Technology (DCRT), National Institute of Health
Audience:	Scientists, Biomedical Researchers, Health CareProfessionals, General Public
Profile:	This server provides Internet access to information about NIH health and clinical issues (including CancerNet and a variety of AIDS information), NIH-funded grants and research projects, and a variety of research resources in support of NIH and worldwide biomedical researchers. For example, the major molecular biology databases (GenBank, SWISSPROT, PIR, PDB, TFD, Prosite, LiMB) can be accessed through keyword searches from this gopher.
Details:	Free

`gopher://gopher.nih.gov`

Stanford Medical Center Gopher ★★

This gopher allows extensive access to the Stanford Medical Center's archives.

Keywords:	Medicine, Health Care, Health Sciences
Sponsor:	Stanford Medical Center, Palo Alto, California, USA
Audience:	Health Care Professionals, Health Science Researchers
Contact:	Stanford Medical Center gopher@medisg.stanford.edu

`gopher://med.stanford.edu`

The National Library of Medicine (NLM) Online Catalog System ★★★★

Catalog of library holdings.

Keywords:	Medicine, Health Sciences, Biomedicine, Rare Books
Sponsor:	National Library of Medicine
Audience:	Health Professionals, Medical Educators, Students
Profile:	The National Library of Medicine (NLM) is the world's largest biomedical library with a collection of over 4.9 million items. NLM is a national resource for all US health sciences libraries and fills over a quarter of a million interlibrary loan requests each year for these libraries. The library is open to the public, but its collection is designed primarily for health professionals. The library collects materials comprehensively in all major areas of the health sciences. Housed within the library is one of the world's finest medical history collections of pre-1914 and rare medical texts, manuscripts, and incunabula.
Contact:	ref@nlm.nih.gov
Details:	Free
	The NLM can be accessed also through the WWW at http://www.nlm.nih.gov

`telnet://locator@locator.nlm.nih.gov`

The University of Illinois at Chicago Library

The library's holdings are large and wide-ranging and contain significant collections in many fields.

Keywords:	Health Science, Chicago, Industry, Slavery, Abolitionism, Roosevelt (Franklin D.)
Audience:	General Public, Researchers, Librarians, Document Delivery Professionals
Details:	Free
Notes:	Expect: introductory screen, Send: Clear key; Expect: UIC flame screen, Send: Enter key; Expect: Logon screen, Send: DIAL PVM; Expect: PVM (Passthru) screen, Send: Type: Move cursor to NOTIS and press Enter key Response: One line message about port in use Type: Enter key

`telnet://uicvm.uic.edu`

University of Texas at Galveston (Medical Branch) Library

The library's holdings are large and wide-ranging and contain significant collections in many fields.

Keywords:	Health Sciences, Biomedicine, Nursing
Audience:	Researchers, Students, General Public
Details:	Free
Notes:	Expect: Login, Send: Library

`telnet://ibm.gal.utexas.edu`

University of Wisconsin Eau Claire Library

The library's holdings are large and wide-ranging and contain significant collections in many fields.

Keywords:	Health Sciences, Business, Nursing, Education
Audience:	Researchers, Students, General Public
Details:	Free
Notes:	Expect: Service Name, Send: Victor

`telnet://lib.uwec.edu`

Health Statistics

INFOMED

Provides yearly statistical information in the form of tables (in ASCII format) listing the principal indicators of health in Cuba.

Keywords: Cuba, Health Statistics, Public Health
Sponsor: Cuban Ministry of Health
Audience: Medical Professionals, Researchers, Public Health Professionals
Details: Free
 To obtain a table from the yearbook, send an electronic message to the URL address below without a subject and with the following content in the body of the message:
 GET ANUARIO <name of table>
 Examples of tables are CMT-11: Death rates by age group; CMT-15: Infant mortality by province, and so on. For a listing of the available tables request the help file.

`mailto:listserv@infomed.cu`

Hebraica

Harvard UniversityLibrary

The library's holdings are large and wide-ranging and contain significant collections in many fields.

Keywords: Afrikaans, Alchemy, Arabic Culture (History of), Celtic Philology, Congo Languages, Folklore, Hebraica, Mormonism, Numismatics, Quakerism, Sanskrit, Witchcraft, Arabic Philology
Audience: General Public, Researchers, Librarians, Document Delivery Professionals
Details: Free
Notes: Expect: Mitek Server..., Send: Enter or Return; Expect: prompt, Send: hollis

`telnet://hollis.harvard.edu`

Hebrew Language

Electronic Hebrew Users Newsletter (E-Hug)

This newsletter is electronic only, and is mandated, like the original, to cover everything relating to the use of Hebrew, Yiddish, Judesmo, and Aramaic on computers.

Keywords: Judaism, Religion, Hebrew Language
Sponsor: Berkeley Hillel Foundation
Audience: Jews, Judaism Students
Contact: Ari Davidow
 well!ari@apple.com
Details: Free
User Info: To Subscribe, send an e-mail message to the address below consisting of a single line reading:
 SUB e-hug YourFirstName YourLastName
 To send a message to the entire list, address it to: e-hug@dartcms1.bitnet

`mailto:listserv@dartcms1.bitnet`

NYIsrael Project of NYSERnet

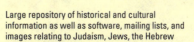

Large repository of historical and cultural information as well as software, mailing lists, and images relating to Judaism, Jews, the Hebrew language, and Israel.

Keywords: Judaism, Jews, Hebrew Language, Israel
Sponsor: The New York Israel Project, NYSERNet, Inc.
Audience: Jewish Organizations
Profile: The purpose of this project is to create a network of diverse Jewish organizations worldwide that can communicate electronically and share information with one another.
Contact: Avrum Goodblatt
 goodblat@israel.nysernet.org
Details: Free

`gopher://israel.nysernet.org`

Hemingway (Ernest)

Papa

A mailing list devoted to discussion of the life and works of Ernest Hemingway.

Keywords: Hemingway (Ernest), Literature (American)
Audience: Ernest Hemingway Readers
Contact: Dave Gross
 dgross@polyslo.calpoly.edu
Details: Free
User Info: To Subscribe to the list, send an e-mail message requesting a subscription to the URL address below. To send a message to the entire list, address it to: dgross@polyslo.calpoly.edu

`mailto:dgross@polyslo.calpoly.edu`

University of Delaware Libraries (DELCAT)

The library's holdings are large and wide-ranging and contain significant collections in many fields.

Keywords: Literature (American), Hemingway (Ernest), Papermaking (History of), Chemistry (History of), Literature (Irish), Delaware
Audience: General Public, Researchers, Librarians, Document Delivery Professionals
Contact: Stuart Glogoff
 epo27855@udacsvm.bitnet
Details: Free
Notes: Expect: prompt, Send: RETURN 2-3 times

`telnet://delcat.udel.edu`

`telnet://delcat.acs.udel.edu`

Herbert (George)

University of North Carolina at Greensboro MINERVA Library

The library's holdings are large and wide-ranging and contain significant collections in many fields.

Keywords: Herbert (George), Film, Dickinson (Emily), Children's Books
Audience: Researchers, Students, General Public
Details: Free
Notes: Expect: Login; Send: Info or MINERVA

`telnet://steffi.acc.uncg.edu`

Herzegovina

BosNet

BosNet is a group/forum run by volunteers. Its goals are to present and distribute information relevant to the events in/about the Republic of Bosnia-Herzegovina (RB&H) and to initiate and coordinate various initiatives, and so on.

Keywords: Bosnia, Herzegovina
Audience: Bosnians, Political Scientists, Students
Contact: listproc@cu23.crl.aecl.ca
Details: Free, Moderated
User Info: To Subscribe to the list, send an e-mail message requesting a subscription to the URL address below. To send a message to the entire list, address it to: BosNet@cu23.crl.aecl.ca
Notes: The contributions/opinions presented on BosNet do not necessarily reflect the personal opinions of the moderator or the member(s) of the Editorial Board. To participate in a discussion on a specific topic related to RB&H, please consider Usenet newsgroup soc.culture.bosnia-herzegovina.

`mailto:listproc@cu23.crl.aecl.ca`

Heuristics

CAMIS (Center for Advanced Medical Informatics at Stanford)

CAMIS is a shared computing resource supporting research activities in biomedical informatics.

Keywords: Medical Informatics, Heuristics, Health Sciences
Sponsor: Stanford University School of Medicine, Palo Alto, CA, USA
Audience: Medical Informatics, Health Science Researchers
Profile: The CAMIS gopher includes an Internet-wide title search, computing information, and technical reports for the Section on Medical Informatics (SMI) community as well as that of the Knowledge Systems Laboratory (KSL), information on the Heuristic Programming Project, pointers to various online library catalogs, and more.
Contact: Torsten_Heycke@med.stanford.edu

`gopher://camis.stanford.edu/00/gopherdoc`

Hewlett-Packard

Hewlett-Packard Computers

This web site provides information on Hewlett Packard products, news, contacts, and services.

Keywords: Computer Products, Hewlett-Packard
Sponsor: Hewlett-Packard
Audience: Computer Users, Educators, Distributors
Contact: webmaster@www.hp.com.
Details: Free

`http://www.hp.com`

HFS-L

HFS-L

Human Factors and Ergonomics Society Virginia Tech Chapter.

Keywords: Ergonomics, Physical Therapy
Audience: Researchers, Physical Therapists, Designers
Contact: Cortney Vargo
courtv@vtvm1.cc.vt.edu
Details: Free
User Info: To Subscribe to the list, send an e-mail message to the URL address shown below consiting of a single line reading:

SUB hfs-l YourFirstName YourLastName
To send a message to the entire list, address it to: hfs-l@vtm1.cc.vt.edu

`mailto:listserv@vtm1.cc.vt.edu`

HICNet Newsletter (MEDNEWS - The Health InfoCom Newsletter)

HICNet Newsletter (MEDNEWS - The Health InfoCom Newsletter)

Usually published once a week, this is a large newsletter that is broken up into multiple sections to facilitate network movement.

Keywords: Health, Medical News
Audience: Health Professionals
Contact: David Dodell
ddodell@stjhmc.fidonet.org
Details: Free
User Info: To Subscribe, send an e-mail message to the address below consisting of a single line reading:

SUBhicnet YourFirstName YourLastName

To send a message to the entire list, address it to: hicnet@asvacad.bitnet

`mailto:listserv@asuacad.bitnet`

High Weirdness by E-Mail

High Weirdness by E-Mail

Guide to some interesting sources of information online.

Keywords: Technology, Hacking, Computer Underground
Audience: Mystics, Hackers, Internet Surfers
Profile: This file focuses mainly on bizarre philosophies, such as Discordia and SubGenius. Contents include: offbeat religions and 'spirituality' paganism and magic, occultism, UFOs, and paranormal phenomena.
Details: Free

`ftp://etext.archive.umich.edu/pub/Zines/Weirdness`

High-Performance Computing Act of 1991

High-Performance Computing Act of 1991

This is a Senate bill to provide for a coordinated federal research program to ensure continued US leadership in high-performance computing.

Keywords: Computing, Government (US Federal), Law (US Federal)
Audience: General Public, Journalists, Politicians, Scientists
Details: Free

File is internet/nren/hpca.1991/gorebill.1991-txt

`ftp://nis.nsf.net`

Highlands and Islands of Scotland

Highlands and Islands of Scotland

This web site provides information on Scotland, including business, leisure, culture, Gaelic language, tourism, distance education, and work opportunities.

Keywords: Scotland, Travel
Sponsor: British Telecom, United Kingdom
Audience: Travelers, Educators, Students
Contact: webmaster@nsa.bt.co.uk
Details: Free

`http://nsa.bt.co.uk/nsa.html`

hilat-l (Higher Education in Latin America)

hilat-l (Higher Education in Latin America)

Provides a means of interchange about research on higher education in Latin America. Postings are mostly in English, but are also welcome in Spanish and Portuguese.

Keywords: Education (Adult), Education (Distance), Education (Continuing), Latin America
Audience: Educators, Administrators, Faculty
Details: Free

History (Ancient) 347

User Info: To Subscribe to the list, send an e-mail message to the URL address shown below consisting of a single line reading:

SUB hilat-l YourFirstName YourLastName

To send a message to the entire list, address it to: hilat-l@bruspvm.bitnet

`mailto:listserv@bruspvm.bitnet`

Hispanic

Latin American Database Historic World Documents ★★★★

International legal files covering 33 nations and article citations from publications relating to Hispanic legal systems. The wiretap gopher provides access to a range of world documents in full-text format.

Keywords: Hispanic, Law, International Law, International Documents
Audience: General Public, Hispanics, Lawyers
Profile: The database includes two files, 1) LAWL containing legislation from 33 nations, mostly Spanish speaking 2) HISS containing Hispanic Legal Article citations.
Details: Free
Select from menu as appropriate.

`gopher://marvel.loc.gov`

Historic Preservation

Archaeology, Historic Preservation ★★

This directory is a compilation of information resources focused on archaeology, historic preservation, and heritage conservation.

Keywords: Archaeology, Historic Preservation
Audience: Archaeologists, Historians, Architects
Details: Free

`ftp://una.hh.lib.umich.edu/70/inetdirsstacks/archpres:stott`

Historical Documents

Historical Documents ★★

A collection of historical documents (with particular emphasis on freedom and democracy) ranging from the Magna Carta to Nelson Mandela's Inauguration Speech.

Keywords: History (World), Democracy, Historical Documents

Sponsor: The Queens Borough Public Library
Audience: Historians, Activists, General Public

`gopher://vax.queens.lib.ny.us/Social Sciences/Historical Documents`

Historic World Documents ★

The wiretap gopher provides access to a range of world documents in full-text format.

Keywords: Historical Documents, Treaties, History (World)
Audience: Governments, Historians, Researchers, General Public
Details: Free
Select from Menu as appropriate

`gopher://wiretap.spies.com`

Historical Documents of the US ★

A large sample of US historical documents, from the Fundamental Orders of 1639 to the Vietnam Era Documents, including World War II documents, Federalist papers, and more.

Keywords: Historical Document, Government (US Federal), Law (US Federal)
Audience: Historians, Journalists, Students, Politicians
Details: Free

`gopher://wiretap.spies.com/11/Gov/US-History`

University of North Carolina at Wilmington SEABOARD Library ★★

The library's holdings are large and wide-ranging and contain significant collections in many fields.

Keywords: Marine Biology, Historical Documents
Audience: Researchers, Students, General Public
Contact: Eddy Cavenaugh
cavenaughd@uncwil.bitnet
cavenaughd@vxc.uncwil.edu
Details: Free
Notes: Expect: Login; Send: Info

`telnet://vxc.uncwil.edu`

History

British National Register of Archives ★★

A multi-volume electronic guide to accessing a wide-variety of archival materials and repositories in the United Kingdom.

Keywords: United Kingdom, History, Business (British), Information Retrieval

Sponsor: Coombspapers Social Sciences Research Data Bank at ANU (Australian National University).
Audience: Researchers, Anglophiles, Archivists
Contact: Dr. T. Matthew Ciolek
tmciolek@coombs.anu.edu.au

`gopher://coombs.anu.edu.au`

`ftp:/coombs.anu.edu.au/coombspapers/otherarchives/uk-nra-archives/`

`http://coombs.anu.edu.au/CoombsHome.html`

University of Pennsylvania School of Medicine Library ★★

The library's holdings are large and wide-ranging and contain significant collections in many fields.

Keywords: Health Care, Nursing, History, Health
Audience: Researchers, Students, General Public
Details: Free
Notes: Expect: Login; Send: Public

`telnet://penninfo.upenn.edu`

History (20th Century)

Vwar-L ★★

An electronic conference on issues relating to the Vietnam War.

Keywords: History (20th Century), History (US), Vietnam
Audience: Historians
Contact: Lydia Fish
fishlm@snybufva.cs.snybuf.edu
User Info: To Subscribe to the list, send an e-mail message to the URL address below consisting of a single line reading:

SUB vwar-l YourFirstName YourLastName

To send a message to the entire list, address it to: vwar-l@ubvm.cc.buffalo.edu

`mailto: listserv@ubvm.cc.buffalo.edu`

History (Ancient)

Princeton University Library ★★

The library's holdings are large and wide-ranging. They contain significant collections in many fields.

Keywords: China, Japan, Classics, History (Ancient), Near Eastern Studies, Literature (American), Literature (English), Aeronautics, Middle Eastern Studies, Mormonism, Publishing

History (Ancient)

Audience: General Public, Researchers, Librarians, Document Delivery Professionals
Details: Free
Notes: Expect: Connect message, blank screen, Send: <cr>; Expect: #, Send: Call 500

`telnet://pucable.princeton.edu`

History (Jewish)

US Holocaust Memorial Museum

The web site of the newly-opened (April, 1993) US Holocaust Memorial Museum in Washington D.C.

Keywords: Jews, Jewish Politics, Holocaust, History (Jewish)
Audience: Jews, Holocaust Researchers, Israelis, Students
Profile: This resource contains files on educational programs, general information about the Holocaust Research Institute, a contact list for the Association of Holocaust Organizations, and a searchable archive of related materials.

`http://www.ushmm.org`

History (US)

Armadillo's World Wide Web Page

This site provides resources and instructional material for an interdisciplinary Texan culture course.

Keywords: History (US), Texas, Cultural Studies, Education
Sponsor: Rice University, Houston, Texas, USA
Audience: Educators, Students
Contact: armadillo@rice.edu

`http://chico.rice.edu/armadillo`

Emory University Library ★★

The library's holdings are large and wide-ranging and contain significant collections in many fields.

Keywords: Health Sciences, Theology, History (US), Communism, Economics (History of), Literature (American)
Audience: General Public, Researchers, Librarians, Document Delivery Professionals
Details: Free
Notes: Expect: VM screen, Send: RETURN; Expect: CP READ, Send: DIAL VTAM, press RETURN; Expect: CICS screen, Send: PF1

`telnet://emuvm1.cc.emory.edu`

Mississippi State University Library ★

The library's holdings are large and wide-ranging and contain significant collections in many fields.

Keywords: History (US), Forestry, Energy, Carter (Hodding, Papers of), Mississippi
Audience: General Public, Researchers, Librarians, Document Delivery Professionals
Contact: Stephen Cunetto
shc1@ra.msstate.edu
Details: Free
Notes: Expect: username, Send: msu; Expect: password, Send: library

`telnet://libserv.msstate.edu`

U.S. Civil War Reading List ★★★

A major directory on abolitionism, providing access to a broad range of resources (library catalogs, databases, and servers) via the Internet.

Keywords: History (US), Abolitionism
Audience: General Public, Historians
Profile: The Suggested Civil War Reading List contains 61 books, several of them with multiple volumes, as well as an 11-hour documentary film and a CD of Civil War era songs. The material is sorted into general categories: General Histories of the War, Causes of the War and History to 1861, Slavery and Southern Society, Reconstruction, Biographies and Autobiographies, Source Documents and official Records, Unit Histories and Soldiers' Reminiscences, Fiction, Specific Battles and Campaigns, Strategies and Tactics, The Experience of Soldiers.
Contact: Stephen Schmidt
whale@leland.Stanford.edu

`http://www.cis.ohio-state.edu/hypertext/faq/usenet/civil-war-usa/reading-list/faq.html`

University of Colorado at Boulder Library ★★

The library's holdings are large and wide-ranging and contain significant collections in many fields.

Keywords: Numismatics, Human Rights, Literature (Children's), Labor Archives, History (US)
Audience: Researchers, Students, General Public
Contact: Donna Pattee
pattee@spot.colorado.edu
Details: Free
Notes: Expect: Login; Send: Culine

`telnet://culine.colorado.edu`

University of Southern Colorado Library ★★

The library's holdings are large and wide-ranging and contain significant collections in many fields.

Keywords: History (US)
Audience: Researchers, Students, General Public
Details: Free
Notes: Expect: OK Prompt, Send: Login Pub1; Expect: Password: usc

`telnet://starburst.uscolo.edu`

University of Wisconsin River Falls Library ★★

The library's holdings are large and wide-ranging and contain significant collections in many fields.

Keywords: Agriculture, Education, History (US)
Audience: Researchers, Students, General Public
Details: Free
Notes: Expect: Service Name, Send: Victor

`telnet://davee.dl.uwrf.edu`

University of Wisconsin Stevens Point Library ★★

The library's holdings are large and wide-ranging and contain significant collections in many fields.

Keywords: Education, Environmental Studies, Ethnic Studies, History (US)
Audience: Researchers, Students, General Public
Details: Free
Notes: Expect: Login; Send: Lib; Expect: vDIAL Prompt, Send: Library

`telnet://lib.uwsp.edu`

Vwar-L ★★

An electronic conference on issues relating to the Vietnam War.

Keywords: History (20th Century), History (US), Vietnam
Audience: Historians
Contact: Lydia Fish
fishlm@snybufva.cs.snybuf.edu
User Info: To Subscribe to the list, send an e-mail message to the URL address below consisting of a single line reading:

SUB vwar-l YourFirstName YourLastName

To send a message to the entire list, address it to: vwar-l@ubvm.cc.buffalo.edu

`mailto: listserv@ubvm.cc.buffalo.edu`

History (Women's)

Notable Women

A database listing some important and notable women through the ages. Available for online searching by keyword, or as a full-text file.

Keywords: Women's Studies, History (Women's), Feminism
Sponsor: Estrella Mountain Community College (Arizona)
Audience: Women's Studies Educators, Historians, Researchers, Feminists
Contact: EMC Gopher Team
root@gopher.emc.maricopa.edu

`gopher://gopher.emc.maricopa.edu`

History (World)

Government Docs (US & World)

A large and eclectic collection of documents, ranging from the Laws of William the Conqueror to the North American Free Trade Agreement (NAFTA). Particular strengths include 20th century American political documents and international treaties and covenants.

Keywords: Government (International), History (World), Politics (International)
Sponsor: The Internet Wiretap
Audience: Researchers, Historians, Political Scientists, Journalists
Contact: gopher@wiretap.spies.com

`gopher://wiretap.spies.com/Gov`

Historic World Documents

The wiretap gopher provides access to a range of world documents in full-text format.

Keywords: Historical Documents, Treaties, History (World)
Audience: Governments, Historians, Researchers, General Public
Details: Free
Notes: Select from Menu as appropriate

`gopher://wiretap.spies.com`

Historical Documents

A collection of historical documents (with particular emphasis on freedom and democracy) ranging from the Magna Carta to Nelson Mandela's Inauguration Speech.

Keywords: History (World), Democracy, Historical Documents
Sponsor: The Queens Borough Public Library
Audience: Historians, Activists, General Public

`gopher://vax.queens.lib.ny.us/Social Sciences/Historical Documents`

History at the University of Virginia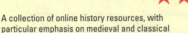

A collection of online history resources, with particular emphasis on medieval and classical studies. Links to other systems, including the Library of Congress.

Keywords: History (World), Classics, Medieval Studies
Sponsor: University of Virginia, Charlottesville, Virginia, USA
Audience: Historians, Students (College/University)
Contact: mssbks@virginia.edu
Details: Free

`gopher://gopher.lib.virginia.edu`

History Discussion Forum

This mailing list is a general starting point for the discussion of history; subscribers include professional historians, graduate students, and history enthusiasts.

Keywords: History (World)
Sponsor: Penn State University
Audience: Historians, History Enthusiasts
User Info: To Subscribe to the list, send an e-mail message requesting a subscription to the URL address below consisting of a single line reading:

SUB history YourFirstName YourLastName

To send a message to the entire list, address it to: history@psuvm.psu.edu

`mailto:listserv@psuvm.psu.edu`

`news:bit.listserv.history`

HNSource

HNSource is an extensive collection of history resources.

Keywords: History (World)
Sponsor: Academic Computer Service and the Department of History of the University of Kansas
Audience: Historians, Researchers, Librarians, Students
Profile: HNSource provides information, announcements, guides, references, and links to related Internet resources, including FTP sites, WAIS sites, OPACs, and gophers
Contact: Lynn Nelson
lhnelson@ukanvm.bitnet

Notes: telnet: Expect: login; Send: history.

`http://history.cc.ukans.edu/history/WWW_history_main.html`

`telnet:history.cc.ukans.edu`

soc.history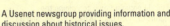

A Usenet newsgroup providing information and discussion about historical issues.

Keywords: History (World)
Audience: Historians
Details: Free
User Info: To Subscribe to this Usenet newsgroup, you need access to a newsreader.

`news:soc.history`

UCSB Library Reference Guide

A list of art references including indexes, dictionaries, bilbiographies and biographical materials.

Keywords: Art, History (World), Libraries
Sponsor: University of California at Santa Barbara
Audience: Artists, Historians, Librarians

`gopher://ucsbuxa.ucsb.edu`

UN Development Program ★

Provides a detailed history of the UN and its development, as well as an outline of UN Internet programs.

Keywords: United Nations, History (World)
Sponsor: United Nations
Audience: General Public, Historians, Internationalists, Researchers
Details: Free

`gopher://nywork1.undp.org`

University of Pennsylvania Library- Philadelphia Pa. ★★★

The library's holdings are large and wide-ranging and contain significant collections in many fields.

Keywords: Literature (English), Literature (American), History (World), Medieval Studies, East Asian Studies, Middle Eastern Studies, South Asian Studies, Judaica, Lithuania
Audience: Educators, Students, Researchers
Profile: Access to the central Van Pelt Library and to most of the departmental libraries is restricted to members of the University community on weekends and holidays. Online visitors are advised to call (215) 898-7554 for information on hours and access restrictions.

Contact:	Patricia Renfro, Associate Director of Libraries
Details:	Free

`telnet://library.upenn.edu`

World Constitutions

A list of world constitutions, containing the constitutions of more than 18 nations including Basic Law of Germany 1949; Constitution of Macedonia (in former Yugoslavia); Magna Carta.

Keywords:	Law (International), History (World), Politics (International)
Audience:	Researchers, Lawyers, Historians
Details:	Free

`gopher://wiretap.spies.com`

History and Analysis of Disabilities Newsletter

History and Analysis of Disabilities Newsletter ★

Covers the history of disabilities, disabled persons, and disability issues.

Keywords:	Disabilities, Disabled Persons
Sponsor:	History of Disabilities Network, Centre for Independent Living, Toronto, and International Society for the History of Disabilities, Paris.
Audience:	Disabled persons, Doctors, Historians
Contact:	Gary Woodill fcty7310@ryerson.bitnet
Details:	Free

`mailto:fcty7310@ryerson.bitnet`

Hitchhiker's Guide

Hitchhiker's Guide ★

A narrative of what the Internet has to offer.

Keywords:	Internet, Internet Guides
Sponsor:	University of Illinois, Urbana, IL
Audience:	Internet Surfers
Contact:	Ed Krol krol@uxc.cso.uiuc.ed
Details:	Free File is: documents/rfc/rfc1118.txt

`ftp://nic.merit.edu`

HIV

AIDS Treatment News ★★★

A newsletter on AIDS treatment.

Keywords:	AIDS, HIV, Health, Medicine
Sponsor:	IGC (Institute for Global Communications)
Audience:	AIDS Researchers, Health Workers, AIDS Sufferers
Profile:	This newsletter contains interviews, reports on new and existing treatment modalities, announcements of clinical drug testing trial, and more.
Contact:	atn@igc.apc.org
Details:	Free

`gopher://odie.niaid.nih.gov/11/aids`

Hobbies

alt.aquaria ★

A Usenet newsgroup providing information and discussion about the aquarium as a hobby.

Keywords:	Aquariums, Fish, Hobbies
Audience:	Aquarium Keepers, Fish Lovers
User Info:	To Subscribe to this Usenet newsgroup, you need access to a newsreader.

`news:alt.aquaria`

Model-horse ★

Discussion of the model-horse hobby. All aspects of showing (live and photo), collecting, re-making/re-painting for all breeds are discussed. All ages and levels of experience welcome.

Keywords:	Model Horses, Hobbies
Audience:	Model Horse Collectors
Details:	Free
User Info:	To Subscribe to the list, send an e-mail message requesting a subscription to the URL address below.

`mailto:model-horse-request@qiclab.scn.rain.com`

PEI (Prince Edward Island, Canada) Crafts Council Gopher ★★

A gopher devoted to all manner of crafts, from weaving to glass blowing. Information includes a database of tools, services, and materials for crafts enthusiasts, as well as FAQs and pointers to other crafts resources. Also provides background on the PEI Craft Council's activities and on Prince Edward Island.

Keywords:	Crafts, Hobbies, Canada
Sponsor:	PEI Crafts Council, Prince Edward Island, Canada
Audience:	Crafts Enthusiasts
Details:	Free

`gopher://crafts-council.pe.ca`

rec.collecting.cards ★

A Usenet newsgroup providing information and discussion about collecting sports and other trading cards.

Keywords:	Trading Cards, Hobbies
Audience:	Card Collectors
User Info:	To Subscribe to this Usenet newsgroup, you need access to a newsreader.

`news:rec.collecting.cards`

rec.woodworking

A Usenet newsgroup providing information and discussion about woodworking.

Keywords:	Woodworking, Crafts, Hobbies
Audience:	Woodworkers
User Info:	To Subscribe to this Usenet newsgroup, you need access to a newsreader.

`news:rec.woodworking`

Hockey

American Hockey League ★

This list is for people interested in discussing and following the activities of The American Hockey League.

Keywords:	Sports, Hockey, American Hockey League
Audience:	Hockey Enthusiasts, Sports Enthusiasts
Contact:	ahl-news-request@andrew.cmu.edu
Details:	Free
User Info:	To Subscribe to the list, send an e-mail message requesting a subscription to the URL address below. To send a message to the entire list, address it to: ahl-news@andrew.cmu.edu

`mailto:ahl-news-request@andrew.cmu.edu`

Blues (St. Louis Blues)

Provides information, game reports, stats, discussion, and so on, on the St. Louis Blues of the National Hockey League.

Keywords:	Hockey, Sports
Audience:	Hockey Enthusiasts
Contact:	Joe Ashkar blues@medicine.wustl.edu

User Info: To Subscribe to the list, send an e-mail message requesting a subscription to the URL address below.

To send a message to the entire list, address it to: blues@medicine.wustl.edu

`mailto:blues@medicine.wustl.edu`

Boston Bruins

This list is for discussion of the Boston Bruins of the National Hockey League and their farm teams. Also available as a digest.

Keywords: Hockey, Sports, Boston

Audience: Hockey Enthusiasts, Boston Residents, Sports Enthusiasts

Contact: Garry Knox
bruins-request@cristal.umd.edu

Details: Free

User Info: To Subscribe to the list, send an e-mail message requesting a subscription to the URL address below.

To send a message to the entire list, address it to: bruins@cristal.umd.edu

`mailto:bruins-request@cristal.umd.edu`

Dallas Stars

Discussion of the Dallas Stars (of the National Hockey League) and their farm clubs.

Keywords: Hockey, Sports

Audience: NHL Enthusiasts

Details: Free

User Info: To Subscribe to the list, send an e-mail message requesting a subscription to the URL address below. To send a message to the entire list, address it to: hamlet@u.washington.edu

Notes: Please include the word "DSTARS" in your subject line and include your name and preferred e-mail address in the body of your message.

`mailto:hamlet@u.washington.edu`

echl-news

For people interested in discussing and following the East Coast Hockey League.

Keywords: Hockey, Sports

Audience: Hockey Enthusiasts

Contact: echl-news-request@andrew.cmu.edu

Details: Free

User Info: To Subscribe to the list, send an e-mail message requesting a subscription to the URL address below.

To send a message to the entire list, address it to: echl-news-request@andrew.cmu.edu

`mailto:echl-news-request@andrew.cmu.edu`

mda

Discussion of the Mighty Ducks of Anaheim of the National Hockey League, including statistics and game summaries.

Keywords: Hockey, Sports

Audience: Ice Hockey Fans

Contact:

Details: Free

User Info: To Subscribe to the list, send an e-mail message to the URL address below, consisting of a single line reading:

SUB mda YourFirstName YourLastName

To send a message to the entire list, address it to: mda@macsch.com

`mailto:mda@macsch.com`

New York Islanders

A discussion of the New York Islanders hockey team, with emphasis on the current season.

Keywords: Hockey, Sports, New York

Audience: New York Islanders Fans, Ice Hockey Fans

Contact: David Strauss
dss2k@virginia.edu

Details: Free

User Info: To Subscribe to the list, send an e-mail message requesting a subscription to the URL address below.

`mailto:dss2k@virginia.edu`

NHL Goalie Stats

A mailing list for the distribution of information regarding NHL goalie statistics.

Keywords: Hockey, Sports Statistics

Audience: Hockey Enthusiasts

Profile: Weekday reports of goalie statistics from the National Hockey League.

Contact: dfa@triple-i.com

Details: Free

User Info: To Subscribe to the list, send an e-mail message requesting a subscription to the URL address below.

To send a message to the entire list, address it to: dfa@triple-i.com

`mailto:dfa@triple-i.com`

Professional Sports Schedules

Sports schedules for major professional sports.

Keywords: Sports, Baseball, Hockey, Football, Basketball

Sponsor: Colorado University, Boulder, CO

Audience: Sports Fans, Football Fans, Hockey Fans, Baseball Enthusiasts, Basketball Enthusiasts

Profile: The Colorado University gopher maintains an interactive online database of schedules for all major US professional sports teams (NBA, NFL, NHL, MLB). The database is indexed by both team name and dates of games, and can be searched accordingly.

Contact: gopher@gopher.colorado.edu

Details: Free

`gopher://gopher.colorado.edu/11/professional/sports/schedules`

Quebec Nordiques

A mailing list to discuss topics concerning the National Hockey League's Quebec Nordiques.

Keywords: Hockey, Quebec (Canada), Sports

Audience: Hockey Enthusiasts

Contact: Danny J. Sohier
nords-request@badaboum.ulaval.ca

Details: Free

User Info: To Subscribe to the list, send an e-mail message requesting a subscription to the URL address below.

To send a message to the entire list, address it to: nords@badaboum.ulaval.ca

`mailto:nords@badaboum.ulaval.ca`

rec.sport.hockey

A Usenet newsgroup providing information and discussion about hockey.

Keywords: Hockey, Sports

Audience: Hockey Fans, Sports Fans

User Info: To Subscribe to this Usenet newsgroup, you need access to a newsreader.

`news:rec.sport.hockey`

Holmes (Sherlock)

The University of Minnesota Library System (LUMINA)

The library's holdings are large and wide-ranging and contain significant collections in many fields.

Keywords: Immigration (History of), Ethnic Studies, Horticulture, Equine Research, Botanical Taxonomy, Quantum Physics, Native American Studies, Holmes (Sherlock)

Audience: General Public, Researchers, Librarians, Document Delivery Professionals

Contact: Craig D. Rice
cdr@acc.stolaf.edu

Details: Free

`telnet://lumina.lib.umn.edu`

A B C D E F G H I J K L M N O P Q R S T U V W X Y Z

Holocaust

The Israel Information Service ★★★

A gopher server containing information on Israel.

Keywords:	Israel, Middle East, Political Science, Anti-Semitism, Holocaust, Archaeology
Sponsor:	Israeli Foreign Ministry
Audience:	Israelis, Jews, Tourists, General Public
Profile:	This server features updates on the Middle East peace process, including text of the latest Israel-PLO accord, as well as general political, diplomatic, cultural, and economic information on the state of Israel. Also includes archives on archaeology in Israel, anti-Semitism and the Holocaust, and current excerpts from Israeli newspapers.
Contact:	Chaim Shacham shacham@israel-info.gov.il

`gopher://israel-info.gov.il`

US Holocaust Memorial Museum

The web site of the newly-opened (April, 1993) US Holocaust Memorial Museum in Washington D.C.

Keywords:	Jews, Jewish Politics, Holocaust, History (Jewish)
Audience:	Jews, Holocaust Researchers, Israelis, Students
Profile:	This resource contains files on educational programs, general information about the Holocaust Research Institute, a contact list for the Association of Holocaust Organizations, and a searchable archive of related materials.

`http://www.ushmm.org`

Home Building

Utah Valley Community College Library ★★

The library's holdings are large and wide-ranging and contain significant collections in many fields.

Keywords:	Accounting, Automobiles, Cabinetry, Child Care, Drafting, Electronics, Home Building, Local History, Refrigeration, Air Conditioning
Audience:	General Public, Researchers, Librarians, Document Delivery Professionals
Details:	Free
Notes:	Expect: Login; Send: Opub

`telnet://uvlib.uvcc.edu`

Home Economics

misc.consumers.house ★

A Usenet newsgroup providing information and discussion about owning and maintaining your house.

Keywords:	Home Economics, Housing
Audience:	Home Owners, General Public
Details:	Free
User Info:	To Subscribe to this Usenet newsgroup, you need access to a newsreader.

`news:misc.consumers.house`

University of Wisconsin at Stout Library ★★

The library's holdings are large and wide-ranging and contain significant collections in many fields.

Keywords:	Mathematics, Business, Fashion Merchandising, Home Economics, Hospitality, Tourism, Hotel Administration, Restaurant Management, Microelectronics
Audience:	Researchers, Students, General Public
Details:	Free
Notes:	Expect: Login, Send: Lib; Expect: vDIAL Prompt, Send: Library

`telnet://lib.uwstout.edu`

Hong Kong

Hong Kong Law ★

Lists the basic Hong Kong Law (1990) and Hong Kong Bill of Rights Ordinance (1991).

Keywords:	Hong Kong, Law (International)
Audience:	Lawyers, Sinologists
Details:	Free

`gopher://marvel.loc.gov`

soc.culture.hongkong ★

A Usenet newsgroup providing information and discussion about Hong Kong and its people.

Keywords:	Hong Kong, Sociology
Audience:	Sociologists
Details:	Free
User Info:	To Subscribe to this Usenet newsgroup, you need access to a newsreader.

`news:soc.culture.hongkong`

Hongkongiana

Hong Kong Polytechnic Library System ★

An index to journal articles about Hong Kong, published in selected Hong Kong periodicals beginning in 1986. The online version is written in English.

Keywords:	Hong Kong, Hongkongiana
Sponsor:	Hong Kong Polytechnic Library, Hong Kong
Audience:	Sinologists, General Public
Details:	Free
Notes:	Expect: Username, Send: Library

`telnet://library.hkp.hk`

Hoppenstedt Directory of German Companies

Hoppenstedt Directory of German Companies

This directory covers 50,000 German companies with sales exceeding 2 million DM or with a minimum of 20 employees.

Keywords:	German Companies, International Business, Germany
Sponsor:	Hoppenstedt Wirtschaftsdatenbank, Darmstadt, Germany
Audience:	Business Professionals, International Market, Researchers, Germans
Profile:	Records include current company address, line of business, number of employees, sales, capital stock, branches and subsidiaries, and a listing of executives and directors with positions in the company. The file is bilingual; users can view the records in either German or English.
Contact:	Dialog in the US at (800) 334-2564, Dialog internationally at country-specific locations.
User Info:	To Subscribe, contact Dialog directly.
Notes:	Coverage: 1973 to the present; updated semiannually.

`telnet://dialog.com`

horizons 'New Horizons in Adult Education'

horizons 'New Horizons in Adult Education'

A journal transmitted to educators around the world.

Keywords: Education (Adult), Education (Distance), Education (Continuing)
Audience: Educators, Administrators, Faculty, Researchers
Details: Free
User Info: To Subscribe to the journal, send an e-mail message to the URL address shown below consisting of a single line reading:

SUB horizonsYourFirstName YourLastName

`mailto:listserv@alpha.acast.nova.edu`

Horseracing

derby ★

To discuss various aspects and strategies of horseracing, primarily dealing with, but not limited to, handicapping.

Keywords: Horseracing, Handicapping
Audience: Horseracing Enthusiasts
Contact: John Wilkes
derby-request@ekrl.com
User Info: To Subscribe to the list, send an e-mail message requesting a subscription to the URL address below.

To send a message to the entire list, address it to: derby-request@ekrl.com

`mailto:derby-request@ekrl.com`

Horses

rec.equestrian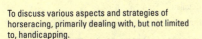

A Usenet newsgroup providing information and discussion about all things pertaining to horses.

Keywords: Horses, Equestrians, Animals, Sports
Audience: Horse Riders, Horse Trainers, Horse Owners
User Info: To Subscribe to this Usenet newsgroup, you need access to a newsreader.

`news:rec.equestrian`

Horticulture

The University of Minnesota Library System (LUMINA)

The library's holdings are large and wide-ranging and contain significant collections in many fields.

Keywords: Immigration (History of), Ethnic Studies, Horticulture, Equine Research, Botanical Taxonomy, Quantum Physics, Native American Studies, Holmes (Sherlock)
Audience: General Public, Researchers, Librarians, Document Delivery Professionals
Contact: Craig D. Rice
cdr@acc.stolaf.edu
Details: Free

`telnet://lumina.lib.umn.edu`

hospex

hospex ★

A bulletin board for people interested in being hosts to foreign visitors.

Keywords: Travel, Hospitality
Audience: International Travelers, General Public
Contact: hospex@plearn.edu.p1
Details: Free
User Info: To Subscribe to the list, send an e-mail message to the URL address shown below consisting of a single line reading:

SUB hospex YourFirstName YourLastName

`mailto:listserv@plearn.bitnet`

Hospital Administration

GENMED (General Medical Information)

The General Medical Information (GENMED) library contains a variety of medical care and treatment, toxicology, and hospital administration materials.

Keywords: Medicine, Toxicology, Hospital Administration, Treatment
Audience: Medical Professionals
Profile: The GENMED library contains full-text medical journals and newsletters, as well as drug information, disease and trauma reviews, Physicians Data Query cancer information, and medical administration journals. GENMED also offers a gateway to the MEDLINE database.
Contact: Mead New Sales Group at (800) 227-4908 or (513) 859-5398 inside the US, or (513) 865-7981 for all inquiries outside the US.
User Info: To Subscribe, contact Mead directly.

To examine the Nexis user guide, you can access it at the ftp site of the University of Texas at Austin at the URL address: ftp://ftp.cc.utexas.edu

The files are in: /pub/ref-services/LEXIS

`telnet://nex.meaddata.com`

`http://www.meaddata.com`

Vetadm-L

A discussion group for those involved in veterinary hospital administration.

Keywords: Hospital Administration, Veterinary Hospitals
Audience: Veterinarians
Contact: Joel Hammond
joel@tamvet.bitnet
Details: Free
User Info: To Subscribe to the list, send an e-mail message to the URL address below consisting of a single line reading:

SUB vetadm-l YourFirstName YourLastName

To send a message to the entire list, address it to: vetadm-l@tamvm1.tamu.edu

`mailto:listserv@tamvm1.tamu.edu`

Hospitality

University of Wisconsin at Stout Library

The library's holdings are large and wide-ranging and contain significant collections in many fields.

Keywords: Mathematics, Business, Fashion Merchandising, Home Economics, Hospitality, Tourism, Hotel Administration, Restaurant Management, Microelectronics
Audience: Researchers, Students, General Public
Details: Free
Notes: Expect: Login, Send: Lib; Expect: vDIAL Prompt, Send: Library

`telnet://lib.uwstout.edu`

Hot Air Balloons

Balloon

This is a list for balloonists of any sort. Discussion covers all types of balloons, be they hot air or gas, commercial or sport, and just about anything related to ballooning.

- Keywords: Ballooning, Hot Air Balloons
- Audience: Balloonists
- Contact: Phil Herbert
  balloon-request@lut.ac.uk
- User Info: To Subscribe to the list, send an e-mail message requesting a subscription to the URL address below.

  To send a message to the entire list, address it to: balloon@lut.ac.uk

`mailto:balloon-request@lut.ac.uk`

Hot off the Tree (HOTT)

Hot off the Tree (HOTT)

HOTT contains excerpts and abstracts of articles from trade journals, popular periodicals, online news services, and electronic bulletin boards.

- Keywords: Computer Technology, Technology
- Sponsor: University of California, San Diego library's Technology Watch Information Group (TWIG)
- Audience: Computer Programmers, Technology Enthusiasts, General Public
- Contact: Susan Jurist
  sjurist@ucsd.edu or sjurist@ucsd.bitnet
- Details: Free

  Available on MELVYL, the University of California online catalog. Anyone with access to telnet, can telnet MELVYL (31.0.0.13) and show hott.

`telnet://melvyl.berkeley.edu/showhott`

Hotel Administration

University of Nevada, Las Vegas Library - Las Vegas, NV

The library's holdings are large and wide-ranging and contain significant collections in many fields.

- Keywords: Gaming, Hotel Administration, Nevadiana, Canadian Documents, Nevada State Documents
- Audience: General Public, Researchers, Librarians, Document Delivery Professionals
- Contact: Myoung-ja Lee Kwon
  kwon@nevada.edu.
- Details: Free
- Notes: Expect: login; Send: library

`telnet://library.lv-lib.nevada.edu`

University of Wisconsin at Stout Library

The library's holdings are large and wide-ranging and contain significant collections in many fields.

- Keywords: Mathematics, Business, Fashion Merchandising, Home Economics, Hospitality, Tourism, Hotel Administration, Restaurant Management, Microelectronics
- Audience: Researchers, Students, General Public
- Details: Free
- Notes: Expect: Login, Send: Lib; Expect: vDIAL Prompt, Send: Library

`telnet://lib.uwstout.edu`

Housing

alt.housing.nontrad

This newsgroup is for discussion of all forms of "nontraditional housing," including cohousing and communes

- Keywords: Community, Housing, Communes
- Audience: General Public, Community Activists
- Details: Free

  To participate in a Usenet newsgroup, you need access to a Önewsreader.Ö

`news:alt.housing.nontrad`

COHOUSING-L

A list for discussion of Cohousing, the name of a type of collaborative housing that has been developed primarily in Denmark since 1972 where it is known as bofoellesskaber. Cohousing is housing designed to foster community and cooperation while preserving independence. Private residences are clustered near shared facilities. The members design and manage all aspects of their community.

- Keywords: Community, Housing, Cooperatives
- Audience: Urban Planners, Architects, General Contractors
- Contact: fholson@uci.com
- Details: Free
- User Info: To Subscribe to the list, send an e-mail message to the address below consisting of a single line reading:

  SUB COHOUSING-L YourFirstName YourLastName

  To send a message to the entire list, address it to: COHOUSING-L@uci.com

`mailto:listserv@uci.com`

misc.consumers.house

A Usenet newsgroup providing information and discussion about owning and maintaining your house.

- Keywords: Home Economics, Housing
- Audience: Home Owners, General Public
- Details: Free
- User Info: To Subscribe to this Usenet newsgroup, you need access to a newsreader.

`news:misc.consumers.house`

Housman (A.E.)

Colby College Library

The library's holdings are large and wide-ranging and contain significant collections in many fields.

- Keywords: Contemporary Letters, Hardy (Thomas),James (Henry), Mann (Thomas, Collections of), Housman (A.E., Letters of), Maine Authors, Irish History (Modern)
- Audience: General Public, Researchers, Librarians, Document Delivery Professionals
- Details: Free
- Notes: Expect: login, Send: library

`telnet://library.colby.edu`

hr.women

hr.women

A conference on human rights issues pertaining to women.

- Keywords: Women's Issues, Feminists, Human Rights
- Audience: Women, Feminists, Activists
- Contact: Jillaine Smith
  jillaine@igc.apc.org
- Details: Costs
- User Info: Establish an account on the nearest APC node. Login, type c for conferences, then type go hr.women. For information on the nearest APC node, contact: APC International Secretariat IBASE E-mail: apcadmin@apc.org

`telnet://igc.apc.org`

HTML FAQ

HTML FAQ

Common questions and answers about HTML (Hypertext Markup Language). The FAQ covers the practices of creating new documents specifically for the WWW format, as well as transforming existing materials into WWW documents.

Keywords:	WWW, Internet Reference, Information Retrieval
Audience:	Students, Computer Scientists, Researchers
Contact:	Iain O'Cain ec@umcc.umich.edu

`http://www.umcc.umich.edu/~ec/www/html_faq.html`

Hubble Telescope

CADC (Canadian Astronomy Data Center) Home Page

The CADC maintains archives of scientific data from the Hubble Space Telescope and the Canada France Hawaii Telescope. It also serves as a distribution point for various astronomy-related software packages.

Keywords:	Astronomy, Hubble Telescope
Sponsor:	Dominional Astrophysical Observatory, Victoria, British Columbia, Canada
Audience:	Astronomers
Contact:	Dennis Crabtree crabtree@dao.nrc.ca

`http://ucluelet.dao.nrc.ca`

Sci.astro.hubble

Information about all subjects concerning NASA's Hubble space telescope.

Keywords:	Hubble Telescope, Astronomy, Space, NASA, Stargazing, Telescopes
Audience:	Astronomers, General Public, Science Teachers, Stargazers
Contact:	Paul A. Scowen scowen@wfpc3.la.asu.edu
Details:	Free, Moderated, Images
User Info:	To Subscribe to this Usenet newsgroup, you need access to a newsreader.

`news:sci.astro.hubble`

Human Behavior

MBI, Music and the Brain Information Center Database (MuSICA)

The intent of this resource is to establish a comprehensive database of scientific research on music.

Keywords:	Music Resources, Human Behavior, Neurology
Sponsor:	Music and the Brain Information Center
Audience:	Researchers, Scientists
Profile:	MuSICA maintains a data base of scientific research (references and abstracts) on music as related to behavior, the brain and allied fields, in order to foster interdisciplinary knowledge. Topics include the auditory system; human and animal behavior; creativity; the neuropsychology of music and the human brain; the effects of music on behavior and physiology; music education, medicine, performance, and therapy; neurobiology; perception and psychophysics. Citations and abstracts are excerpted from the following journals: The Bulletin of the Council for Research in Music Education, The Journal of Research in Music Education, Music Perception, Psychology of Music, Psychomusicology.
Contact:	Norman Weinberger, Gordon Shaw mbic@mila.ps.uci.edu
Details:	Free Expect login: Send mbi Expect password: Send nammbi

`telnet://mila.ps.uci.edu`

Political Analysis and Research Cooperation (PARC) News Bulletin

Newsletter on political analysis, political behavior, political communication, and political culture. The purpose of PARC is to encourage and facilitate scientific research on human behavior in political life.

Keywords:	Politics (US), Human Behavior
Audience:	Political Scientists, Political Analysts
Contact:	Tom Bryde kusftb@vms2.uni-c.dk
Details:	Free
User Info:	To Subscribe, send an e-mail message to the URL address below.

`mailto:kusftb@vms2.uni-c.dk`

Human Communications

CRTNet (Communication Research and Theory Network)

All topics related to human communications.

Keywords:	Communications, Sociology, Human Communications
Audience:	Sociologists, Psychologists, Therapists

`mailto:listserv@psuvm.bitnet`

Human Rights

Amnesty International

A site containing information about Amnesty International, an organization focused strictly and specifically on human rights around the world.

Keywords:	Government, Human Rights, Politics (International), Activism
Sponsor:	Amnesty International
Audience:	Students, Activists
Contact:	Catherine Hampton ariel@netcom.com

`ftp://ftp.netcom.com/pub/ariel`

`http://www/human.rights/amnesty.international/ai.html`

dh.mujer

The primary Association for Progressive Communications conference for women and human rights issues throughout the world, contains news and announcements.

Keywords:	Women's Issues, Feminism, Human Rights
Audience:	Feminists, Activists
Contact:	Debra Guzman hrcoord@igc.apc.org
Details:	Costs
User Info:	Establish an account on the nearest APC node. Login, type c for conferences, then type go dh.mujer. For information on the nearest APC node, contact: APC International Secretariat IBASE E-mail: apcadmin@apc.org

Contact: Carlos Afonso (cafonso@ax.apc.org) or APC North American Regional Office
E-mail: apcadmin@apc.org
Contact: Edie Farwell (efarwell@igc.apc.org)

`gopher://gopher.telnet://igc.apc.org`

`http://igc.apc.org`

hr.women

A conference on human rights issues pertaining to women.

Keywords: Women's Issues, Feminists, Human Rights
Audience: Women, Feminists, Activists
Contact: Jillaine Smith
jillaine@igc.apc.org
Details: Costs
User Info: Establish an account on the nearest APC node. Login, type c for conferences, then type go hr.women. For information on the nearest APC node, contact: APC International Secretariat IBASE E-mail: apcadmin@apc.org

`telnet://igc.apc.org`

University of Colorado at Boulder Library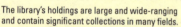

The library's holdings are large and wide-ranging and contain significant collections in many fields.

Keywords: Numismatics, Human Rights, Literature (Children's), Labor Archives, History (US)
Audience: Researchers, Students, General Public
Contact: Donna Pattee
pattee@spot.colorado.edu
Details: Free
Expect: Login; Send: Culine

`telnet://culine.colorado.edu`

University of Texas at Austin Tarlton Law Library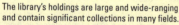

The library's holdings are large and wide-ranging and contain significant collections in many fields.

Keywords: British Commonwealth Law, Constitutional Law, Law (International), Human Rights
Audience: Researchers, Students, General Public
Details: Free
Notes: Expect: Login, Send: Library

`telnet://tallons.law.utexas.edu`

Humanities

The English Server

A large and eclectic collection of humanities resources.

Keywords: Humanities, Academia, English, Popular Culture, Feminism
Sponsor: Carnegie Mellon University English Department, Pittsburgh, Pennsylvania, USA
Audience: General Public, University Students, Educators (College/University), Researchers (Humanities)
Profile: Contains archives of conventional humanities materials, such as historical documents and classic books in electronic form. Also offers more unusual and hard-to-find resources, particularly in the field of popular culture and media. Features access to many humanities and culture-related online journals such as Bad Subjects, FineArt Forum, and Postmodern Culture. Also has links to a wide variety of related Internet sites and resources.
Contact: Geoff Sauer
postmaster@english-server.hss.cmu

`gopher://english-server.hss.cmu.edu`

`http://english-server.hss.cmu.edu/`

University of Toledo Library

The library's holdings are large and wide-ranging and contain significant collections in many fields.

Keywords: Business, Great Lakes Area, Humanities, International Relations, Psychology, Science
Audience: Researchers, Students, General Public
Details: Free
Notes: Expect: Enter one of the following commands . . . , Send: DIAL MVS; Expect: dialed to mvs ####; Send: UTMOST

`telnet://uofto1.utoledo.edu`

Virginia Commonwealth University Library

The library's holdings are large and wide-ranging and contain significant collections in many fields.

Keywords: Art, Biology, Humanities, Journalism, Music, Urban Planning
Audience: Researchers, Students, General Public
Details: Free
Notes: Expect: Login; Send: Opub

`telnet://vcuvm1.ucc.vcu.edu`

Humor

alt.callahans

A Usenet newsgroup providing information and discussion about Callahan's bar for puns and fellowship.

Keywords: Humor, Word Play
Audience: Punsters, Comedians
User Info: To Subscribe to this Usenet newsgroup, you need access to a newsreader.

`news:alt.calahans`

alt.fan.monty-python

A Usenet newsgroup providing an electronic fan club for those wacky Brits.

Keywords: Humor, Entertainment, Comedy, Satire
Audience: Monty Python Enthusiasts, General Public
User Info: To Subscribe to this Usenet newsgroup, you need access to a newsreader.

`news:alt.fan.monty-python`

alt.peeves

A Usenet newsgroup providing information and discussion about peeves, complaints, and whining.

Keywords: Humor, Comedy
Audience: General Public, Complainers
User Info: To Subscribe to this Usenet newsgroup, you need access to a newsreader.

`news:alt.peeves`

alt.religion.kibology

A Usenet newsgroup consisting of followers of a god named Kibo, who is, in fact, a human being living in Boston. This newsgroup is highly humorous and hardly religious.

Keywords: Satire, Humor, Religion
Audience: Kibologists
User Info: To Subscribe to this Usenet newsgroup, you need access to a newsreader.

`news:alt.religion.kibology`

alt.tasteless

A Usenet newsgroup providing information and discussion about tasteless jokes.

Keywords: Humor, Comedy
Audience: General Interest, Jokers
User Info: To Subscribe to this Usenet newsgroup, you need access to a newsreader.

`news:alt.tasteless`

rec.humor

A Usenet newsgroup providing information and discussion about jokes.

Keywords: Jokes, Humor
Audience: General Public, Jokers
User Info: To Subscribe to this Usenet newsgroup, you need access to a newsreader.

`news:rec.humor`

talk.bizarre

A Usenet newsgroup providing information and discussion about the unusual, the bizarre, and the curious.

Keywords: Humor
Audience: General Public
Details: Free
User Info: To Subscribe to this Usenet newsgroup, you need access to a newsreader.

`news:talk.bizarre`

Hungary

agora

A forum for Hungarian speakers to discuss a wide variety of subjects.

Keywords: Hungary
Audience: Hungarian Speakers
Contact: Zoli Fekete
fekete@bcvms.bc.edu,
agora@world.std.com
Details: Free
Notes: Inquiries and contributions to the list can be sent to the personal address of the contact above (place word AGORA in the subject field), or to the world.std.com address below (place word $SEGIT in the subject field).

`mailto:agora@world.std.com`

CEE Environmental Libraries Database

A directory of over 300 libraries and environmental information centers in Central Eastern Europe that specalize in, or maintain significant collections of information about, the environment, ecology, sustainable living, or conservation.

Keywords: Central Eastern Europe, Environment, Sustainable Living, Bulgaria, Czech Republic, Hungary, Romania, Slovakia, Poland
Sponsor: The Wladyslaw Poniecki Charitable Foundation, Inc.
Audience: Environmentalists, Green Movement, Librarians, Community Builders, Sustainable Living Specialists.
Profile: This database is the product of an Environmental Training Project (ETP) that was funded in 1992 by the US Agency for International Development as a 5-year cooperative agreement with a consortium headed by the University of Minnesota (US AID Cooperative Agreement Number EUR-0041-A-002-2020). Other members of the consortium include the University of Pittsburgh's Center for Hazardous Materials Research, The Institute for Sustainable Communities, and the World Wildlife Fund. The Wladyslaw Poniecki Charitable Foundation, Inc., was a subcontractor to the World Wildlife Fund and published the Directory of Libraries and Environmental Information Centers in Central Eastern Europe: A Locator/Directory. This gopher database consists of an electronic version of the printed directory, subsequently modified and updated online. Access to the data is facilitated by a WAIS search engine which makes it possible to retrieve information about libraries, subject area specializations, personnel, and so on.
Contact: Doug Kahn, CEDAR
kahn@pan.cedar.univie.ac.at

`gopher://gopher.poniecki.berkeley.edu`

Hungarian Gopher-Hollosi Information Exchange (HIX)

This is the main Hungarian gopher, providing information for and about residents of Hungary and Hungarian speakers.

Keywords: Hungary, Europe
Sponsor: Stanford University, Palo Alto, CA
Audience: Hungarian Internet Surfers
Contact: hollosi@andrea.standford.edu
Details: Free

`gopher://hix.elte.hu`

Hungary

This discussion list circulates timely information about Hungary.

Keywords: Hungary, Eastern Europe, News
Audience: Researchers, Observers, Political Scientists
Contact: Eric Dahlin
hcf2hung@iucsbuxa
Details: Free
User Info: To Subscribe to the list, send an e-mail message to the URL address shown below consisting of a single line reading:

SUB hungary YourFirstName YourLastName

`mailto:listserv@gwuvm.gwu.edu`

HungerWeb

HungerWeb

This web site focuses on the political, economic, agricultural, and ethical implications of world hunger.

Keywords: World Health, Activism
Sponsor: Oxfam
Audience: Activists, Financial Planners
Contact: Daniel Zalik
Daniel_Zalik@cs.brown.edu
Details: Free

`http://www.hunger.brown.edu/oxfam`

Hunt (Leigh)

The University of Iowa Libraries

The library's holdings are large and wide-ranging and contain significant collections in many fields.

Keywords: Hunt (Leigh), Native American Studies, Typography, Railroads, Cartoons, French Revolution, NASA, Hydraulics
Audience: General Public, Researchers, Librarians, Document Delivery Professionals
Details: Free
Send <RETURN> to display a menu of available systems. Type 1 for OASIS access and press <RETURN> to display the Welcome to OASIS screen.

`telnet://oasis.uiowa.edu`

Husted (Margaret, Culinary Collections of)

University of Denver Library

The library's holdings are large and wide-ranging and contain significant collections in many fields.

Keywords: Folklore Collection, Husted (Margaret, Culinary Collection of)
Audience: Researchers, Students, General Public
Contact: Bob Stocker
bstocker@ducair.bitnet
Details: Free
Notes: Expect: Login; Send: Atdu

`telnet://du.edu`

Hydraulics

Hydraulics

The University of Iowa Libraries

The library's holdings are large and wide-ranging and contain significant collections in many fields.

Keywords:	Hunt (Leigh), Native American Studies, Typography, Railroads, Cartoons, French Revolution, NASA, Hydraulics
Audience:	General Public, Researchers, Librarians, Document Delivery Professionals
Details:	Free
	Send <RETURN> to display a menu of available systems. Type 1 for OASIS access and press <RETURN> to display the Welcome to OASIS screen.

`telnet://oasis.uiowa.edu`

HypArt

HypArt

This is the site of an International collaborative art project.

Keywords:	This is the site of an International collaborative art project.
Sponsor:	University of Hamburg
Audience:	Artists, Designers
Contact:	rosenfeld@rrz.uni-hamburg.de
Details:	Free

`http://rzsun01.rrz.uni-hamburg.de/cgi-bin/HypArt.sh`

Hyperfiction

alt.hypertext

A Usenet newsgroup devoted to hyperfiction and hypertext documents. Postings range from information about and reviews of both recent hyperfiction and recent nonfiction hypertext documents, to information and/or reviews of software for creating hypertext.

Keywords:	Literature (General), Hyperfiction, Hypertext
Audience:	General Public, Writers, Computer Programmers
Details:	Free
User Info:	To subscribe to this Usenet newsgroup, you need access to a newsreader.

`news:alt.hypertext`

Art Com Magazine

A newsletter about art and technology (subjects covered include robotics, artists' software, hyperfiction) that is guest-edited by individual artists.

Keywords:	Computer Art, Literature (Contemporary), Technology, Hyperfiction
Sponsor:	Art Com Electronic Network
Audience:	Artists, Writers
Contact:	Fred Truck fjt@well.sf.ca.us
User Info:	To participate in a conference on the WELL, you must first establish an account on the WELL. To do so, start by typing: telnet://well.sf.ca.us

`mailto:artcomtv@well.sf.ca.us`

Hypermedia

Hypermedia/Internet

A guide to hypermedia and the Internet.

Keywords:	Internet, Group Communications, Hypermedia
Sponsor:	Austrailian National University
Audience:	Internet Surfers
Contact:	David Geoffrey Green David.Green@anu.edu.au
Details:	Free

`http://life.anu.edu.au`

Hypertext

alt.hypertext

A Usenet newsgroup devoted to hyperfiction and hypertext documents. Postings range from information about and reviews of both recent hyperfiction and recent nonfiction hypertext documents, to information and/or reviews of software for creating hypertext.

Keywords:	Literature (General), Hyperfiction, Hypertext
Audience:	General Public, Writers, Computer Programmers
Details:	Free
User Info:	To subscribe to this Usenet newsgroup, you need access to a newsreader.

`news:alt.hypertext`

HYTELNET

HYTELNET

Keywords:	Computer Systems, Libraries, Shareware
Audience:	General Audience
Profile:	HYTELNET is a guide to library catalogs all over the worlde
Contact:	Peter Scott aa375@freenet.carleton.ca
Details:	Free
Notes:	HYTELNET is in English, but the interface to some international

`gopher://gopher.yale.edu/11/libraries`

I.S.P.O.B. Bulletin YSSTI (Yugoslav System for Scientific and Technology Information)

I.S.P.O.B. Bulletin YSSTI (Yugoslav System for Scientific and Technology Information)

The participants in this system can exchange news about the operations and development of YSSTI.

Keywords:	Technology, Yugoslavia, Science
Sponsor:	Institute of Information Sciences, University of Maribor, Yugoslavia
Audience:	Technology Professionals, Librarians
Contact:	Davor Sostaric davor%rcum@yubgef51.bitnet
User Info:	Subscribe by sending an e-mail with a single line containing: SUBSCRIBE P.O.B. to addresses POB%RCUM@YUBGEF51.bitnet

`mailto:pob%rcum@yubgef51.bitnet`

IBM

C-IBM-370

The C on IBM mainframes mailing list is a place to discuss aspects of using the C programming language on s/370-architecture computers—especially under IBM's operating systems for that environment.

Keywords:	C Language, Programming Languages, IBM
Audience:	IBM Users, Computer Users, Computer Programmers
Contact:	David Wolfskill C-IBM-370-request@dhw68k.cts.com
Details:	Free
User Info:	To subscribe to the list, send an e-mail message requesting a subscription to the URL address below. To send a message to the entire list, address it to: C-IBM-370@dhw68k.cts.com

`mailto:C-IBM-370-request@dhw68k.cts.com`

comp.sys.ibm.pc

A Usenet newsgroup providing information and discussion about the IBM PC computer. There are many categories within this group.

Keywords:	Computer Systems, IBM
Audience:	Computer Users, IBM Users
User Info:	To subscribe to this Usenet newsgroup, you need access to a newsreader.

`news:comp.sys.ibm.pc`

PAGEMAKER

The PageMaker ListServ is dedicated to the discussion of desktop publishing in general, with emphasis on the use of Aldus PageMaker. The list discusses PageMaker's use in both the PC and Macintosh realms. The list also maintains an extensive archive of help files that are extremely useful for the modern desktop publisher.

Keywords:	Desktop Publishing, Aldus Pagemaker, Macintosh
Audience:	Desktop Publishers, Computer Users
Contact:	Geoff Peters gwp@cs.purdue.edu
Details:	Free
User Info:	To subscribe to the list, send an e-mail message to the URL address shown below, consisting of a single line reading: SUB pagemaker YourFirstName YourLastName. To send a message to the entire list, address it to: gwp@cs.purdue.edu

`mailto:listserv@cs.purdue.edu`

ICC British Company Directory

ICC British Company Directory

The database is a comprehensive reference source for companies registered in England, Wales, Scotland, and Northern Ireland.

Keywords:	United Kingdom, Business (British)
Sponsor:	ICC Information Group Ltd., London, UK
Audience:	Business Professionals, Business Analysts
Profile:	The database contains a record for each company included on the Index of Companies maintained by the official Companies Registration Offices in the UK. Companies that have been dissolved since 1968 are also listed. The total number of records in the ICC British Company Directory is over 2 million. Reference data includes name, registered number, registered address, issued and nominal-share capital, dates of incorporation and document filings at the Companies Registration Office. Document filings include latest filed annual accounts and annual returns, changes of directors or registered address, special resolutions, mergers of public (PLC) companies, winding-up orders, appointment of liquidators, and so on.

Contact:	Dialog in the US at (800) 334-2564; Dialog internationally at country-specific locations.
User Info:	To subscribe, contact Dialog directly.
Notes:	Coverage: Current; updated weekly.

`telnet://dialog.com`

Ice Hockey

Funet Sports Information

An FTP archive of information on various sports with links to the archive at wuarchive.wustl.edu.

Keywords:	Sports, Professional Sports, Ice Hockey, Motor Racing, NFL, NHL, NBA, MLB
Sponsor:	Finnish Academic and Research Network (FUNET)
Audience:	Sports Enthusiasts
Profile:	A fairly extensive archive of information on both American (NBA, MLB, NHL, NFL) and worldwide sports (soccer, ice hockey, motor racing, and so on). Includes FAQs for various sports, statistics, pictures, and some sports games for the PC.
Contact:	Jari Pullinen sports-adm@nic.funet.fi
Details:	Free, Images

`gopher://ftp.funet.fi/pub/sports`

OlymPuck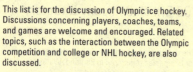

This list is for the discussion of Olympic ice hockey. Discussions concerning players, coaches, teams, and games are welcome and encouraged. Related topics, such as the interaction between the Olympic competition and college or NHL hockey, are also discussed.

Keywords:	Olympics, Ice Hockey, NHL
Audience:	Ice Hockey Players, Olympics Enthusiasts, Ice Hockey Fans
Details:	Free
User Info:	To subscribe to the list, send an e-mail message to the URL address below, consisting of a single line reading: SUB olympuck YourFirstName YourLastName To send a message to the entire list, address it to: olympuck@maine.maine.edu

`mailto:listserv@maine.maine.edu`

ICGEBnet

ICGEBnet

This is the information server of the International Centre for Genetic Engineering and Molecular Biology (ICGEB), Trieste, Italy.

Keywords:	Molecular Biology, Biotechnology, Italy, Europe
Audience:	Molecular Biotechnologists, Molecular Biologists
Profile:	The primary purpose of the ICGEB computer resource is to disseminate the best of currently available computational technology to the molecular biologists of the ICGEB research community.
Contact:	postmaster@icgeb.trieste.it
Details:	Free

`gopher://icgeb.trieste.it`

Icon Programming Language

Icon-group

Discussion of topics related to the Icon programming language

Keywords:	Icon Programming Language, Programming Language String Processing
Audience:	Icon Programmers, Computer Programmers
Profile:	Icon is a high-level, general purpose programming language emphazing string and structure processing. Topics include programming techniques, theoretical aspects, Icon in relation to other languages, applications of Icon, implementation issues, porting, and bugs.
Contact:	Bill Mitchell (Internet) whm@arizona.edu
Details:	Free
User Info:	To subscribe to the list, send an e-mail message requesting a subscription to the URL address below.

`mailto:Icon-group-request@arizona.edu`

ICTP (International Centre for Theoretical Physics)

ICTP (International Centre for Theoretical Physics)

ICTP's gopher disseminates information regarding the many scientific activities carried out at ICTP (Trieste, Italy). Information is also provided on the scientific publications, courses, and other services offered by ICS (International Centre for Science and High Technology) and TWAS (Third World Academy of Sciences) at Trieste.

Keywords:	Theoretical Physics, Italy, Europe, Physics
Audience:	Physicists
Profile:	Topics include programming techniques, theoretical aspects, Icon in relation to other languages, applications of Icon, implementation issues, porting, and bugs.
Contact:	admin@ictp.trieste.it
Details:	Free

`gopher://gopher.ictp.trieste.it`

`http://gopher.ictp.trieste.it`

IEEE-L

IEEE-L

Serves as a forum for all IEEE student branch officers and members.

Keywords:	Engineering, Electrical Engineering
Audience:	Engineers, Electrical Engineers, Students
Details:	Free
User Info:	To subscribe to the list, send an e-mail message to the URL address below, consisting of a single line reading: SUB ieee-l YourFirstName YourLastName. To send a message to the entire list, address it to: ieee-l@bingvmb.cc.binghamton.edu

`mailto:listserv@bingvmb.cc.binghamton.edu`

IHOUSE-L International Voice Newsletter Prototype List

IHOUSE-L International Voice Newsletter Prototype List

Contains articles of interest to international students and scholars, professors, administrators, and other interested staff and groups (on- and off-campus).

Keywords:	International Visitors, Washington University
Sponsor:	International Office of Washington University, St. Louis MO
Audience:	International Students
Contact:	Doyle Cozadd c73221dc@wuvmdwastl.edu
Details:	Free
User Info:	To subscribe, send an e-mail message to the address below, consisting of a single line reading: SUB ihousel@Your First Name Your Last Name To send a message to the entire list, Address it to: ihouse-l@wnvmd 8tl.con

`mailto:listserv@wuvmd.wustl.edu`

IHS International Standards and Specifications

IHS International Standards and Specifications

The database contains references to industry standards, and military and federal specifications and standards covering all aspects of engineering and related disciplines.

Keywords:	Engineering, Military Specifications, Federal Standards
Sponsor:	Information Handling Services, Englewood, CO, US
Audience:	Engineers, Military Hisyorians, Lawyers, Business Professionals
Profile:	The file includes 90 percent of the world's most referenced standards from over 70 domestic, foreign, and international standardizing bodies. Also included is the world's largest commercially available collection of unclassified active and historical US military and federal specifications and standards.
Contact:	Dialog in the US at (800) 334-2564; Dialog internationally at country-specific locations.
User Info:	To subscribe, contact Dialog directly.
Notes:	Coverage: Current; updated weekly for MILSPECS, every two months.

`telnet://dialog.com`

Illinois

Illinois Legislation

This directory contains several Illinois Department of Nuclear Safety Statues and Regulations.

Keywords:	Nuclear Safety, Law, Illinois
Audience:	Lawyers, General Public, Activists
Details:	Free

`gopher://wiretap.spies.com`

Image Processing

Geoscience at Texas A&M University

General server with info on all aspects of GIS and remote sensing, especially GPS.

Keywords:	GIS, Image Processing, Remote Sensing, Geoscience, GPS
Sponsor:	Texas A&M University - Department of Agricultural Engineering
Audience:	Researchers, GIS and IP professionals, Students
Contact:	Hal Mueller hmueller@diamond.tamu.edu
Details:	Free, Images
Notes:	Contains links to related Univeristy of Texas gophers and WWW servers.

`http://ageninfo.tamu.edu/geoscience.html`

Internet GIS and RS Information Sites

This document contains a lengthy listing of GIS and remote sensing sites on the Internet.

Keywords:	GIS, Remote Sensing, Image Processing, Geography
Sponsor:	Queen's University Department of Geography
Audience:	Researchers, General Public
Contact:	Michael McDermott mcdermom@gisdog.gis.queensu.ca
Details:	Free
Notes:	ASCII version also available from the same FTP site.

`ftp://gis.queensu.ca/pub/gis/docs/gissites.html`

The University of Minnesota Remote Sensing Lab

General information about remote sensing and GIS.

Keywords:	GIS, Remote Sensing, Image Processing
Sponsor:	University of Minnesota, Department of Forest Resources
Audience:	Researchers, GIS and IP professionals, Students
Profile:	The RSL server contains information regarding all aspects of image process and GIS. Some features include: home of the GIS Jobs Clearinghouse, archives of ESRI-L, IMAGRS-L, and TGIS-L, and the NBS CPSU WWW server.
Contact:	Stephen Lime sdlime@torpedo.forestry.umn.edu
Details:	Free, Images
Notes:	The RSL also maintains a companion gopher server and anonymous FTP site for the GIS Jobs Clearinghouse.

`http://walleye.forestry.umn.edu/0/www/main.html`

Images from Various Sources

Images from Various Sources

This site serves as a link to some 35 image archives throughout the world. A wide variety of images is available, with a particularly large number of weather, geological, and biological collections from government and private sources.

Keywords:	Computer Graphics, Photography, Art
Sponsor:	The University of Alaska
Audience:	General Public
Contact:	Douglas Toelle sxinfo@orca.alaska.edu
Details:	Free, Images
	The ancient science of life that originated in India. This mailing list provides information about ayurveda, such as lectures, workshops, and stores that sell ayurvedic herbs.
Keywords:	Spirituality, Ayurveda, India
Audience:	General Public, Religion Students
Contact:	ayurveda-request@netcom.com
Details:	Free
User Info:	To subscribe to the list, send an e-mail message requesting a subscription to the URL address below. To send a message to the entire list, address it to: ayurveda@netcom.com

`mailto:ayurveda-request@netcom.com`

soc.culture.indian

A Usenet newsgroup providing information and discussion about India and its people.

Keywords:	India, Sociology
Audience:	Sociologists, Students
Details:	Free
User Info:	To subscribe to this Usenet newsgroup, you need access to a newsreader.

`news:soc.culture.indian`

Indiana

Eerie, Indiana

The list is for the discussion of the critically acclaimed but short-lived TV series "Eerie, Indiana," which originally aired on NBC in 1991-1992 and is now distributed internationally.

Keywords:	Eerie, Indiana
Audience:	Television Viewers
Contact:	Corey Kir owner-eerie-indiana@sfu.ca

Indiana

Details: Free

User Info: To subscribe to the list, send an e-mail message requesting a subscription to the URL address below.

To send a message to the entire list, address it to: owner-eerie-indiana@sfu.ca

`mailto:owner-eerie-indiana@sfu.ca`

Indiana University Libraries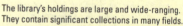

The library's holdings are large and wide-ranging and contain significant collections in many fields.

Keywords: Literature (English), Literature (American), 1640-Present, British Plays (19th-C.), Western Americana, Railway History, Aristotle (Texts of), Lafayette (Marquis de), Handel (G.F.), Austrian History, Antiquarian Books, Rare Books, French Opera (19th-C.), Drama (British),

Audience: General Public, Researchers, Librarians, Historians

Details: Free

Expect: User ID prompt, Send: GUEST

`telnet://iuis.ucs.indiana.edu`

Purdue University Library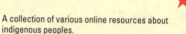

The library's holdings are large and wide-ranging. They contain significant collections in many fields.

Keywords: Economics (History of), Literature (English), Literature (American), Indiana, Rogers (Bruce), Engineering (History of), Aviation, Earth Science, Atmospheric Science, Consumer Science, Family Science, Chemistry (History of), Physics, Veterinary Science

Audience: General Public, Researchers, Librarians, Document Delivery Professionals

Contact: Dan Ferrer
dan@asterix.lib.purdue.edu

Details: Free

Expect: User ID prompt, Send: GUEST

`telnet://lib.cc.purdue.edu`

Indigenous People

Indigenous ★

A collection of various online resources about indigenous peoples.

Keywords: Indigenous Peoples, Anthropology

Audience: Reseachers, Anthropologists, Native Americans

Details: Free

`ftp://netcom.com`

NativeNet ★

Provides information about and discusses issues relating to indigenous people around the world, including threats to their cultures and habitats (e.g. rainforests).

Keywords: Indigenous People, Environment, Anthroplogy

Audience: Anthropologists, Environmentalists, Indigenous People

Contact: Gary S. Trujillo
gst@gnosys.svle.ma.us

Details: Free

User Info: To subscribe to the list, send an e-mail message requesting a subscription to the URL address below.

`mailto:gst@gnosys.svle.ma.us`

Industry

1994 Federal Budget (Canada)

This site offers full-text of Canada's federal budget. Also has a wealth of information on Canadian industry and industrial policy, including Provincial and Sectorial GATT opportunities and briefs from the Information Highway Advisory Council.

Keywords: Canada, Government (International), Industry, Foreign Trade

Sponsor: Industry Canada, Canada

Audience: Canadians, Government Officials, Businesspeople, Researchers

Contact: Tyson Macaulay
tyson@debra.dgbt.doc.ca

`gopher://debra.dgbt.doc.ca/industry canada documents/isc.news.releases`

MARKET (Markets and Industries News and Information)

The Markets and Industries News and Information (MARKET) library contains sources covering developments in a wide variety of markets and industries.

Keywords: News, Analysis, Industry, Marketing

Audience: Businesspeople, Researchers

Profile: The MARKET library contains a wide selection of sources ranging from trade and industry sources to InvestextR industry reports to company profiles. To round out the offering, MARKET also covers advertising, marketing, public opinion polls, market research, public relations, sales and selling, promotions, consumer attitudes, trends and behaviors, demographics, product announcements, and product reviews. In addition, Predicasts Overview of Markets and Technology (PROMT), Marketing and Advertising Reference Service (MARS), US and International Forecast Databases (UFRCST and IFRCST), and the US Time Series (USTIME), all from Information Access Company, are available.

Contact: Mead New Sales Group at (800) 227-4908 or (513) 859-5398 inside the US, or (513) 865-7981 for all inquiries outside the US.

User Info: To subscribe, contact Mead directly.

To examine the Nexis user guide, you can access it at the ftp site of the University of Texas at Austin at the URL address: ftp://ftp.cc.utexas.edu

The files are in: /pub/ref-services/LEXIS

`telnet://nex.meaddata.com`

`http://www.meaddata.com`

Martin Marietta Energy Systems Gopher

Information on Martin Marietta's energy projects and technologies for both government and commercial applications.

Keywords: Technology, Energy, Industry

Sponsor: Martin Marietta

Audience: Businesspeople, Entrepreneurs, Manufactures, Energy Researchers, Technology Enthusiasts

Profile: This gopher contains a list of technologies currently being developed at Martin Marietta, as well as detailing facilities available to university, government, and commercial researchers. Also includes updates on employment openings, and a list of current publications.

Contact: gopher@ornl.gov

`gopher://gopher.ornl.gov`

`http://www.ornl.gov/mmes.html`

Tecbase- Sandia National Laboratory

A catalog of technologies, developed at Sandia National Laboratories, which have potential commercial applications.

Keywords: Technology, Information Technology, Industry

Sponsor: Sandia National Laboratory

Audience: Business People, Entrepreneurs, Manufactures, Technicians

Contact: TechTransfer@ccsmtp.sandia.gov

`gopher://somnet.sandia.gov/Tecbase`

The University of Illinois at Chicago Library ★★

The library's holdings are large and wide-ranging and contain significant collections in many fields.

Keywords: Health Science, Chicago, Industry, Slavery, Abolitionism, Roosevelt (Franklin D.)
Audience: General Public, Researchers, Librarians, Document Delivery Professionals
Details: Free
Expect: introductory screen, Send: Clear key; Expect: UIC flame screen, Send: Enter key; Expect: Logon screen, Send: DIAL PVM; Expect: PVM (Passthru) screen, Send: Type: Move cursor to NOTIS and press Enter key Response: One line message about port in use Type: Enter key

`telnet://uicvm.uic.edu`

University of Wisconsin at Platteville Library ★★

The library's holdings are large and wide-ranging and contain significant collections in many fields.

Keywords: Business, Industry
Audience: Researchers, Students, General Public
Details: Free
Expect: Login, Send: Lib; Expect: vDIAL Prompt, Send: Library

`telnet://137.104.128.44`

Infectious Diseases

National Institute for Allergy & Infectious Disease (NIAID) ★

This is a resource into other databases for searching many medical fields, such as the NIAID network userlist or a databank of AIDS-related information.

Keywords: Medicine, Infectious Diseases, Allergies
Sponsor: NIAID
Audience: Health-care Professionals, Researchers, Students
Contact: Brent Sessions
sessions@odie.niaid.nih.gov
Details: Free

`gopher://gopher.niaid.nih.gov/1`

Infiniti Automobiles

nissan ★

Discusses Nissan and Infiniti automobiles, with the exception of the Sentra SE-R, NX2000, and G20, which are served by the se-r list.

Keywords: Nissan Automobiles, Infiniti Automobiles
Audience: Nissan Owners, Nissan Enthusiasts
Contact: Rich Siegel
nissan-request@world.std.com
Details: Free
User Info: To subscribe to the list, send an e-mail message requesting a subscription to the URL address below.

To send a message to the entire list, address it to: nissan@world.std.com

`mailto:nissan-request@world.std.com`

info-Ada

info-Ada ★

Discussion of the Ada programming language.

Keywords: Programming, Ada (Programming Language)
Audience: Programmers
Contact: Karl A. Nyberg
Karl@grebyn.com
Details: Free
User Info: To subscribe to the list, send an e-mail message requesting a subscription to the URL address below.

`mailto:info-Ada-request@sei.cmu.edu`

info-C

info-C ★

Discussions about C programming and the C programming language.

Keywords: Programming, C (Programming Language)
Audience: Programmers
Contact: Mark Plotnick
info-C-request@research.att.com
Details: Free
User Info: To subscribe to the list, send an e-mail message requesting a subscription to the URL address below.

`mailto:info-C-request@research.att.com`

info-GNU-MSDOS

info-GNU-MSDOS ★

This electronic conference is for the GNUISH MS-DOS Development Group.

Keywords: Shareware, Freeware, MS-DOS Computers
Audience: MS-DOS Users, GNUISH MS-DOS Developers
Contact: David J. Camp
david@wubios.wustl.edu
Details: Free
User Info: To subscribe to the list, send an e-mail message to the URL address below, consisting of a single line reading:

SUB info-GNU-MSDOS YourFirstName YourLastName

`mailto:listserv@wugate.wustl.edu`

info-M2

info-M2 ★

E-conference for the Modula-2 programming language.

Keywords: Programming Languages, Modula-2 (Programming Language)
Audience: Programmers
Contact: Thomas Habernoll
postmast@ucf1vm.cc.ucf.edu (USA);
habernol@tubvm.cs.tu-berlin.de (Europe)
Details: Free
User Info: To subscribe to the list, send an e-mail message to the URL address below, consisting of a single line reading:

SUB info-M2 YourFirstName YourLastName

To send a message to the entire list, address it to: info-M2@ucf1vm.cc.ucf.edu

`mailto:listserv@ucf1vm.cc.ucf.edu`

info-Pascal

info-Pascal ★

Discussions of any Pascal implementation, from mainframe to micro, for Pascal program users.

Keywords: Programming, Pascal
Audience: Pascal Programmers, Pascal Users
Contact: Hernan Lobos *Mitzio*
hlobos@utfsm.bitnet

Details: Free
User Info: To subscribe to the list, send an e-mail message requesting a subscription to the URL address below

`info-Pascal@brl.mil`

Info-South (Latin American News)

Info-South (Latin American News)

The database provides citations and abstracts of materials relating to contemporary economic, political, and social issues in Latin America.

Keywords: International News, Economics, International Politics, Latin America
Sponsor: University of Miami, Coral Gables, FL, US
Audience: General Public
Profile: Coverage includes a wide range of topics assessing the current situation in Latin America.
Contact: Dialog in the US at (800) 334-2564; Dialog internationally at country-specific locations.
User Info: To subscribe, contact Dialog directly.
Notes: Coverage: 1988 to the present; updated weekly.

`telnet://dialog.com`

Info-tandem

Info-tandem

Info-tandem is an e-mail list for users of systems from Tandem Computers, Inc.

Keywords: Computer Systems, Tandem Computers
Audience: Programmers, Analysts, Tandem Computer Users
Contact: Scott Hazen Mueller
scott@zorch.sf-bay.org
Details: Free
User Info: To subscribe to the list, send an e-mail message requesting

`mailto:info-tandem-request@zorch.sf-bay.org`

info-UNIX

info-UNIX

Info-UNIX is intended for Question/Answer discussion, where "novice" system administrators

information and discussion about the gopher information search tool.

Keywords: Gopher, Internet Reference, Information Retrieval
Audience: Internet Surfers
User Info: To subscribe to this Usenet newsgroup, you need access to a newsreader.

`news:comp.infosystems.gopher`

Information Retrieval

comp.infosystems.wais

A Usenet newsgroup providing information and discussion about the WAIS full-text search tool.

Keywords: WAIS, Internet Reference, Information Retrieval
Audience: Internet Surfers
User Info: To subscribe to this Usenet newsgroup, you need access to a newsreader.

`news:comp.infosystems.wais`

comp.infosystems.www

A Usenet newsgroup providing information and discussion about the World Wide Web.

Keywords: WWW, Internet Reference, Information Retrieval
Audience: Internet Surfers
User Info: To subscribe to this Usenet newsgroup, you need access to a newsreader.

`news:comp.infosystems.www`

Computer-Mediated Marketing Environments

A web site devoted to research aimed at understanding the ways in which computer-mediated marketing environments (CMEs), especially the Internet, are revolutionizing the way firms conduct business.

Keywords: WWW, Information Retrieval, Internet, Marketing, Business
Sponsor: Vanderbilt University, Owen Graduate School of Management, Nashville, Tennessee, USA
Audience: General Public, Entrepeneurs, Financial Planners, Marketers
Contact: Donna Hoffman, Tom Novak
hoffman@colette.ogsm.vanderbilt.edu, novak@moe.ogsm.vanderbilt.edu

`http://colette.ogsm.vanderbilt.edu`

CSORG (Clearinghouse for Subject-Oriented Internet Resource Guides)

The goal of CSORG is to collect and make widely available guides to Internet resources that are subject-oriented. These guides are produced by members of the Internet community and by SILS students who participate in the Internet Resource Discovery project.

Keywords: WWW, Information Retrieval, Internet
Sponsor: University of Michigan, School of Information and Library Studies, Michigan, USA
Audience: Reseachers, Students, General Public
Contact: Louis Rosenfeld
i-guides@umich.edu

`gopher://una.hh.lib.umich.edu/11/inetdirs`

DIMUND

DIMUND (Document Image Understanding) is an Internet information retrieval service.

Keywords: Internet, Information Retrieval, DIMUND, Documents
Sponsor: Document Processing Group, University of Maryland
Audience: Internet Surfers
Contact: gopher@dimund.cfar.umd.edu
Details: Free

`gopher:// dimund.umd.edu`

DIMUND FTP

DIMUND (Document Image Understanding) information service FTP archives. Provides access to selected documents.

Keywords: Internet, Information Retrieval, DIMUND, Documents
Sponsor: Document Processing Group, University of Maryland
Audience: Internet Surfers
Contact: gopher@dimund.cfar.umd.edu
Details: Free

`ftp://dimund.umd.edu`

Doc Center

A hard-copy document-delivery service for government and industry specifications and standards.

Keywords: Internet, Information Retrieval
Audience: Internet Surfers, Document Delivery Professionals
Details: Costs

`http://www.service.com/doccenter/home.html`

EINet Galaxy ★★★★

EINet Galaxy is a guide to world-wide information and services. It includes public information as well as commercial information and services provided by EINet customers and affiliates. The information is organized by topic, and can be searched.

Keywords: WWW, Information Retrieval, Internet
Sponsor: Microelectronic and Computer Technology Corporation (MCC)
Audience: Reseachers, Students
Contact: Wayne Allen, Bruce Speyer
WA@EINet.net, Speyer@EINet.net

http://galaxy.einet.net/galaxy.html

Finding Resources on the Internet ★★

A collection of help files introducing the new user to Internet utilities and resources.

Keywords: Internet Reference, Information Retrieval
Sponsor: Proper Publishing
Audience: Internet Surfers
Contact: info@proper.com

gopher://proper.com

HTML FAQ ★★★

Common questions and answers about HTML (Hypertext Markup Language). The FAQ covers the practices of creating new documents specifically for the WWW format, as well as transforming existing materials into WWW documents.

Keywords: WWW, Internet Reference, Information Retrieval
Audience: Students, Computer Scientists, Researchers
Contact: Iain O'Cain
ec@umcc.umich.edu

http://www.umcc.umich.edu/~ec/www/html_faq.html

Internet Libraries (Gopher) ★★★

The site maintains the most current possible list of all library catalogs accessible on the Internet.

Keywords: Libraries, Databases, Internet, Information Retrieval
Audience: Reseacher, Students, Librarians
Contact: Gopherlib
gopherlib@gopher.yale.edu

gopher://yaleinfo.yale.edu

Internet Multicasting ★

Answers to frequently asked questions (FAQs) about the Internet Multicasting Service.

Keywords: Internet, Information Retrieval
Audience: Internet Surfers
Details: Free, Sound files available.
Include "send FAQ" in the e-mail.

mailto:info@radio.com

Internet Sound ★

Internet Sound contains various documents and programs regarding sound.

Keywords: Internet, Information Retrieval
Audience: Internet Surfers
Contact: Guido van Rossum
ftp://ftp.cwi.nl/pub/audio/INDEX
ftp://ftp.cwi.nl/pub/audio/index.html
Details: Free, Sound files available.
The index is: pub/audio/INDEX

ftp://ftp.cwi.nl

Internet Tools HTML ★

An HTML version of a list summarizing Internet tools for network information retrieval (NIR) and computer-mediated communication (CMC) forums; it is useful in a WWW server.

Keywords: Internet Tools, Information Retrieval
Audience: Internet Surfers
Contact: John December
decemj@rpi.edu
Details: Free
Files are located in pub/communications. Read the internet-tools.readme first.

ftp://ftp.rpi.edu

Investigators and Detectives ★★★

This resource provides information files for individuals involved with investigative research, as well as a free monthly newsletter.

Keywords: Detectives, Crime, Information Retrieval, Security
Audience: Investigators, Detectives, Information Brokers, General Public
Profile: Investigators and Detectives provides access to information covering topics such as private investigative research, strategies, sources, the art and science of investigating, theft deterrents, and electronic PI schematics and plans. Also offers a free sample of a newsletter covering various topics of interest to Private Investigators, such as techniques and strategies, security, and tracing.
Contact: Mike Enlow
menlow@Intec.win.net,
michael@enlow.com
Details: Inside Secrets.

mailto:info@enlow.com

Library Special ★

Library Special collections on the Internet.

Keywords: Internet, Information Retrieval
Audience: Internet Surfers
Details: Free

ftp://dla.ucop.edu/pub

http://dla.ucop.edu

LOCIS (LIBRARY Of CONGRESS INFORMATION SYSTEM) ★★★

The Library of Congress (LC) telnet service is a Campus-Wide Information System that combines the vast collection of information available about the Library, with easy access to diverse electronic resources over the Internet. Its goal is to serve the staff of the LC, as well as the U.S. Congress and constituents throughout the world.

Keywords: Information Retrieval, Libraries
Sponsor: Library of Congress, Washington, D.C., USA
Audience: Reseachers, Students, Librarians
Contact: LC MARVEL Design Team
lcmarvel@loc.gov
Notes: The Library of Congress (LC) Machine-Assisted Realization of the Virtual Electronic Library (MARVEL) also exists as a gopher site: gopher://marvel.loc.gov

telnet://locis.loc.gov

Multicast Backbone ★

Live audio and video multicast virtual network on top of the Internet.

Keywords: Internet, Information Retrieval
Audience: Internet Surfers
Details: Free, Sound files available.

ftp://venera.isi.edu

http://venera.isi.edu

Netfind ★

Netfind is a way of finding Internet e-mail addresses.

Keywords: WWW, Information Retrieval, E-mail
Sponsor: Emory University, Georgia, USA
Audience: Reseachers, Students, General Public
Profile: This service relies on common but not universal programs, and thus may not find some people with valid addresses. The most foolproof way of finding someone's e-mail address remains to call them on the phone and ask. All Netfind sites are functionally equivalent.

Information Retrieval

Multiple ones are listed here in case some are overloaded or down with technical problems.

Contact: Netfind Help
schwartz@cs.colorado.edu

gopher://emoryu1.cc.emory.edu/11/internet/General/netfind

NIR Archives

Archives of the NIR (Networked Information Retrieval) service.

Keywords: Internet, Information Retrieval
Audience: Internet Surfers
Details: Free

Files are in: pub/lists/nir

ftp:// mailbase.ac.uk

NIR Gopher

The gopher for the NIR (Networked Information Retrieval) service.

Keywords: Internet, Information Retrieval, NIR
Audience: Internet Surfers
Details: Free

gopher:// mailbase.ac.auk /11/lists-k-o/nic

Retrieval Success

Succesfull stories of using the Internet for reference. In each case, a librarian used Internet resources to answer reference questions. In many cases, particularly for the smaller libraries, the Internet provided information that would otherwise have been inaccessible.

Keywords: Internet, Information Retrieval
Audience: Internet Surfers
Contact: Karen Schneider
kgs@panix.com
Details: Free

File is: pub/lists/unite/files/internet-stories.txt

ftp://mailbase.ac.uk

Searching Gopherspace with Veronica

A resource which conducts Veronica searches over restricted areas of the Internet.

Keywords: WWW, Information Retrieval, Internet
Audience: Reseachers, Students, General Public

gopher://gopher.well.sf.ca.us/11/outbound/veronica.search

The InterNIC Home Page

This is the home page for the InterNIC networking organization.

Keywords: WWW, Information Retrieval, Computer Science, Internet Resources
Sponsor: National Science Foundation, USA
Audience: Reseachers, Students, General Public
Profile: The InterNIC is a collaborative project of three organizations, which work together to offer the Internet community a full scope of network information services. These services include providing information about accessing and using the Internet, assistance in locating resources on the network, and registering network components for Internet connectivity. The overall goal of the InterNIC is to make networking and networked information more easily accessible to researchers, educators, and the general public. The term InterNIC signifies cooperation between Network Information Centers, or NICS.
Contact: InfoGuide
guide@internic.net
Details: InterNIC signifies cooperation between Network Information Centers

http://www.internic.net

The Scout Report

The Scout Report is a weekly publication offered by InterNIC Information Services to the Internet community as a fast, convenient way to stay informed on network activities.

Keywords: WWW, Information Retrieval, Internet, Computer Networking
Sponsor: National Science Foundation, USA
Audience: Reseachers, Students, General Public
Profile: The purpose of this resource is to combine in one place the highlights of new resource announcements and other news that occurred on the Internet during the previous week. The Report is released every Friday. Categories included each week will vary depending on content, and the report will evolve with time and with input from the networking community.
Contact: InfoGuide
scout@is.internic.net
guide@is.internic.net

http://www.internic.net/scout-report

The Wired Librarian

A collection of online resources designed to help library professionals and users keep abreast of current developments in library science and information studies. Includes links to many library and information systems associations and services.

Keywords: Library Science, Libraries, Information Retrieval
Sponsor: Davidson Library, University of California, Santa Barbara, California, USA
Audience: Librarians, Library Users
Contact: Andrea L. Duda
duda@library.ucsb.edu

gopher://ucsbuxa.ucsb.edu

UNITE Archive

The User Network Interface to Everything (UNITE) discussion list. The list is a focus for discussion on the concept of a total solution interface with user-friendly, desktop-integrated access to all network services.

Keywords: Internet, Information Retrieval, Interface Design
Audience: Internet Surfers
Contact: George Munroe, Jill Foster
unite-request@mailbase.ac.uk
Details: Free

Files are in: pub/lists/unite

ftp://mailbase.ac.uk

Veronica FAQ

A gopher containing common questions and answers about Veronica, a title search and retrieval system for use with the Internet Gopher.

Keywords: Internet Reference, Information Retrieval, Veronica
Audience: Students, Computer Scientists, Researchers

gopher://pogonip.scs.unr.edu/00/veronica/veronica-faq

WAIS, Inc.

WAIS, Inc. provides interactive on line publishing systems and services to organizations that publish information over the Internet. The organization's three main goals are: to develop the Internet as a viable means for distributing information electronically; to improve the nature and quality of information available over networks; and to offer better methods to access that information.

Keywords: WWW, Information Retrieval, Publishing, Internet Tools
Sponsor: WAIS, Inc.
Audience: Researchers, Students, General Public, Publishers
Contact: Webmaster
webmaster@wais.com

http://server.wais.com/

World Wide Web FAQ

A web site containing common questions and answers about WWW, a distributed hypermedia system first developed by CERN.

	Keywords:	WWW, Internet Reference, Information Retrieval
	Audience:	Students, Computer Scientists, Researchers
	Contact:	Thomas Boutell, Nathan Torkington boutell@netcom.com, nathan.torckington@vuw.ac.nz

`http://sunsite.unc.edu/boutell/faq/www_faq.html`

World Wide Web Worm (WWWW)

WWWW provides a mechanism to search the WWW in a multitude of ways. It also provides lists of all Home pages and of all URLs cited anywhere. This site contains an exhaustive list of WWW servers nationally and internationally.

	Keywords:	WWW, Information Retrieval, Internet
	Sponsor:	University of Colorado at Boulder, Department of Computer Science, Boulder, Colorado, USA
	Audience:	Researchers, Students, General Public
	Contact:	Oliver McBryan mcbryan@cs.colorado.edu

`http://www.cs.colorado.edu/home/mcbryan/WWWW.html`

Information Sciences

Computists' Communique

A weekly newsletter serving professionals in artificial intelligence, information science, and computer science.

	Keywords:	Artificial Intelligence, Information Science, Computer Science
	Audience:	Computer Scientists, Information Scientists, Computists International Members
	Profile:	Content is career-oriented and depends partly on contributions from members. The moderator filters submissions, reports and comments on industry news, collects common knowledge about academia and industry, and helps track people and projects. The Communique is only available to members of Computists International, a networking association for computer and information scientists. It is an association for mutual mentoring about grant and funding sources, information channels, applications, text, software publishing, and the sociology of work.
	Contact:	Kenneth I. Laws laws@ari.sri.com
	Details:	Costs, Moderated

`mailto:laws@ari.sri.com`

I.S.P.O.B. Bulletin YSSTI (Yugoslav System for Scientific and Technology Information)

The participants in this system can exchange news about the operations and development of YSSTI.

	Keywords:	Information Sciences, Yugoslavia
	Sponsor:	Institute of Information Sciences, University of Maribor, Yugoslavia
	Audience:	Information Scientists
	Contact:	Davor Sostaric davor%rcum@yubgef51.bitnet Subscribe by sending an e-mail with a single line containing: SUBSCRIBE P.O.B. to addresses POB%RCUM@YUBGEF51.bitnet

`mailto:pob%rcum@yubgef51.bitnet`

Scit-L

★

A list for those interested in information and communications science.

	Keywords:	Communications, Information Sciences
	Audience:	Communications Specialists, Communications Students, Information Scientists
	Contact:	Elia Zureik Scitdoc@qucdn.queensu.ca
	User Info:	To subscribe to this list, send an e-mail message to the URL address below, consisting of a single line reading: SUB scit-l YourFirstName YourLastName To send a message to the entire list, address it to: scit-l@qucdn.queensu.ca

`mailto:listserv@qucdn.queensu.ca`

Information Services in Germany

Information Services in Germany

★

This gopher is an informal entry point for Germany, together with some hints to specialties in German information systems.

	Keywords:	Germany, Europe
	Audience:	Germans Internet Surfers
	Contact:	lange@rz.tu-clausthal.de
	Details:	Free

`gopher://gopher.tu-clausthal.de`

Information Sources

Information Sources

These compiled resources provide information describing the Internet and computer-mediated communication technologies, as well as information on related applications, culture, discussion forums, and bibliographies.

	Keywords:	Internet, Networking
	Audience:	Internet Surfers, Computer-Mediated Communication Researchers, Librarians
	User Info:	Files are located in: pub/communications.
	Contact:	John December decemj@rpi.edu
	Details:	Free

`ftp://ftp.rpi.edu`

`http://www.rpi.edu/Internet/Guides/decemj/icmc/top.html`

Information Technology

edupage (A News Update from EDUCOM)

A newsletter put out by EDUCOM summarizing information technology news.

	Keywords:	Education (Continuing), Information Technology
	Sponsor:	EDUCOM
	Audience:	Educators, Administrators
	Details:	Free
	User Info:	To subscribe to the newsletter, send an e-mail message requesting a subscription to the URL address shown below, and include your name, institutional affiliation, and e-mail address.

`mailto:edupage@educom.edu`

euitnews (Educational Uses of Information Technology)

EDUCOM's newsletter for the Educational Uses of Information Technology program encompasses distance learning, self-paced instruction, computer-aided instruction, video, and other information technologies for teaching and learning.

	Keywords:	Education (Continuing), Information Technology
	Audience:	Administrators, K-12 Educators
	Details:	Free

Information Technology

User Info:	To subscribe to the newsletter, send an e-mail message to the URL address below, consisting of a single line reading:
	SUB euitnews YourFirstName YourLastName

`mailto:listserv@bitnic.educom.edu`

IMPACT ONLINE

The electronic version of IMPACT, the newsletter of the Social Impact group of the Boston Computer Society.

Keywords:	Information Technology, Computer Ethics, Social Responsibility
Sponsor:	Boston Computer Society, Boston, MA
Audience:	Computer Users, Boston Residents, Information Scientists
Profile:	The purpose of the Social Impact group is to provide a forum for the discussion of social and ethical concerns related to information technology.
Contact:	Ian Wells bcs-ssi@compass.com
Notes:	Read on comp.society
	You will need access to a newsreader.

`news:comp.society`

Information Infrastructure and Technology Act of 1992

The Information Infrastructure and Technology Act of 1992 builds on the High-Performance Computing Act. The newer bill will ensure that the technology developed by the High-Performance Computing Program is applied widely in K-12 education, libraries, health care, and industry, particularly manufacturing. It will authorize a total of $1.15 billion over the next five years.

Keywords:	Government (US Federal), Law (US Federal), Information Technology, Education
Audience:	Journalists, Politicians, Scientists, Manufacturers, Educators
Details:	Free
	File is: /internet/nren/iita.1992/gorebill.1992.txt

`ftp://nis.nsf.net`

ipct-j 'Interpersonal Computing and Technology: An Electronic Journal for the 21st Century'

Interpersonal Computing and Technology Journal is an outgrowth of the IPCT-L discussion group.

Keywords:	Education (Adult), Education (Distance), Education (Continuing), Information Technology
Sponsor:	Interpersonal Computing and Technology
Audience:	Educators, Administrators, Faculty
Details:	Free, Moderated
User Info:	To subscribe to the journal, send an e-mail message to the URL address shown below, consisting of a single line reading:
	SUB ipct-j YourFirstName YourLastName

`mailto:listserv@guvm.bitnet`

Jte-l 'Journal of Technology Education'

The Journal of Technology Education provides a forum for all topics relating to technology in education.

Keywords:	Education (Adult), Education (Distance), Education (Continuing), Information Technology
Audience:	Faculty, Administrators, Educators (K-12)
Details:	Free
User Info:	To subscribe to the journal, send an e-mail message to the URL address shown below, consisting of a single line reading:
	SUB jte-l YourFirstName YourLastName

`mailto:listserv@vtvm1.cc.vt.edu`

Online-dict

A mailing list devoted to a discussion of online dictionaries and related issues including installation, modification, and maintenance of their databases, search engines, and user interfaces.

Keywords:	Dictionaries, Information Technology, Lexicology
Audience:	Librarians, Information Scientists, Systems Operators
Contact:	Jack Lynch jlynch@dept.english.upenn.edu
Details:	Free
User Info:	To subscribe, send an e-mail message to the URL address below, consisting of a single line reading:
	SUB online-dict YourFirstName YourLastName.
	To send a message to the entire list, address it to: online-dict@dept.english.upenn.edu

`mailto:listserv@dept.english.upenn.edu`

Pubs-IAT (Institute for Academic Technology newsletter)

This newsletter shares information on publications, programs, courses, and other activities of the Institute for Academic Technology.

Keywords:	Education (Adult), Education (Distance), Education (Continuing), Information Technology
Sponsor:	Institute for Academic Technology
Audience:	Educators, Administrators, Researchers
Details:	Free
User Info:	To subscribe to the list, send an e-mail message to the URL address below, consisting of a single line reading:
	SUB pubs-iat YourFirstName YourLastName
	To send a message to the entire list, address it to: pubs-iat@gibbs.oit.unc.edu

`mailto:listserv@gibbs.oit.unc.edu`

Tecbase- Sandia National Laboratory

A catalog of technologies, developed at Sandia National Laboratories, which have potential commercial applications.

Keywords:	Technology, Information Technology, Industry
Sponsor:	Sandia National Laboratory
Audience:	Business People, Entrepreneurs, Manufactures, Technicians
Contact:	TechTransfer@ccsmtp.sandia.gov

`gopher://somnet.sandia.gov/Tecbase`

INGR-EN

INGR-EN

A mailing list for the discussion of Intergraph products.

Keywords:	Geographic Information Systems, Intergraph (GIS)
Audience:	Geographers, Cartographers
Contact:	Dusan Blasko blasko@svfnov.tuke.sk
Details:	Free
User Info:	To subscribe to the list, send an e-mail message to the URL address below, consisting of a single line reading:
	SUB ingr-en YourFirstName YourLastName

`ingr-en@ccsun.tuke.sk`

INGRAFX

INGRAFX

This E-conference is for discussion of all matters relating to information graphics.

Keywords:	Computer Graphics, Graphic Design, Scientific Visualization
Audience:	Graphic Designers, Cartographers, Animators

Contact:	Jeremy Crampton http://info.cern.ch/hypertext/WWW/The Project.html
User Info:	To subscribe to the list, send an e-mail message to the URL address below, consisting of a single line reading: SUB ingrafx YourFirstName YourLastName To send a message to the entire list, address it to: ingrafx@psuvm.psu.edu

`mailto:listserv@psuvm.psu.edu`

INPADOC/INPANEW

INPADOC/INPANEW

Patent documents issued by more than fifty national and international patent offices.

Keywords:	Patents, Intellectual Property, Trademarks
Sponsor:	European Patent Office
Audience:	Patent Attorneys, Patent Agents, Librarians, Researchers
Profile:	Bibliographic information is searchable, including inventor names, assignees, international patent classification codes, and in most cases, titles, as well as complete publications and application data. Contains approximately 20 million records. Updated weekly.
Contact:	PAUL.ALBERT@NETEAST.COM
User Info:	To subscribe, contact Orbit-Questel directly.

`telnet://orbit.com`

Insect Biology

SOCINSCT (Social Insect Biology Research List)

SOCINSCT is dedicated to communication among investigators active in the discipline of social insect biology.

Keywords:	Biology, Insect Biology, Zoology, Entomology
Audience:	Biologists, Researchers
Profile:	It is restricted to discussions of research at the university level. Social insects (bees, wasps, ants, and termites) are the main interest, but information can include any area of sociobiology, or solitary bees and wasps. Such areas could include: orientation, navigation, adaptation/selection/evolution, superorganism concept, behavior, physiology and biochemistry, pheromones, flight and energetics, taxonomy and systematics, ecology, genetics, pollination, and nectar/pollen

biology. Announcements of meetings and professional opportunities, requests for research help, sharing of literature references, sharing research topics, and discussion of ideas are welcome.

Contact:	Erik Seielstad erik@acspr1.acs.brockport.edu
Details:	Free
User Info:	To subscribe to the list, send an e-mail message to the address below, consisting of a single line reading: SUB socinsct YourFirstName YourLastName To send message to the entire list, address it to: socinsct@albany.edu

`mailto:listserv@albany.edu`

Insider Trading

Insider Trading Monitor ★

The database contains the transaction details of all insider-trading filings .

Keywords:	Insider Trading, Securities
Sponsor:	Invest/Net, Inc., Ft. Lauderdale, FL US
Audience:	Stockbrokers , Media
Profile:	This source contains the transaction details of all insider-trading filings, (ownership changes) received by the US Securities and Exchange Commission (SEC) since January 1984. The ownership of securities by over 100,000 officers, directors, and major shareholders (10 percent or more) in over 8,500 US public companies is covered in the file.
Contact:	Dialog in the US at (800) 334-2564; Dialog internationally at country-specific locations.
User Info:	To subscribe, contact Dialog directly.
Notes:	Coverage: April 1984 to the present; updated daily.

`telnet://dialog.com`

insoft-l

insoft-l ★

This list discusses techniques for developing new software and for converting existing software, as well as internationalization tools, announcements of internationalized public-domain software and of foreign-language versions of commercial software, calls for papers, conference announcements, and references to documentation related to the internationalization of software.

Keywords:	Programming, Software Internationalization
Sponsor:	Center for Computing and Information Services, Technical University of Brno
Audience:	Software Developers, Computer Professionals
Contact:	insoft-l-request@cis.vutbr.cs
Details:	Free, Moderated
User Info:	To subscribe to the list, send an e-mail message to the URL address below, consisting of a single line reading: SUB insoft-l YourFirstName YourLastName To send a message to the entire list, address it to: insoft-l@cis.vutbr.cs

`mailto:listserv@cis.vutbr.cs`

INSPEC

INSPEC

IINSPEC corresponds to the three Science Abstracts print publications: Physics Abstracts, Electrical and Electronics Abstracts, and Computer and Control Abstracts.

Keywords:	Physics, Electronics, Computing
Sponsor:	Institution of Electrical Engineers, London, UK
Audience:	Physicists, Electrical Engineers, Computer Specialists
Profile:	Approximately 16 percent of the database's source publications are in languages other than English, but all articles are abstracted and indexed in English. The special DIALOG online thesaurus feature is available to assist searchers in determining appropriate subject terms and codes.
Contact:	Dialog in the US at (800) 334-2564; Dialog internationally at country-specific locations.
User Info:	To subscribe, contact Dialog directly.
Notes:	Coverage: April 1969 to the present; updated weekly.

`telnet://dialog.com`

Institute for Molecular Virology

Institute for Molecular Virology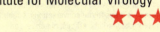

A unique virology resource for students, scientists, computer visualization experts, and the general public.

Keywords:	Disease, Viruses, Biology, Medicine
Sponsor:	University of Wisconsin-Madison, Madison, Wisconsin, USA
Audience:	Virologists, Biologists, Researchers, Medical Students, Medical Researchers
Contact:	Stephen Spencer sspencer@rhino.bocklabs.wisc.edu

`http://www.bocklabs.wisc.edu/Welcome.html`

Institutional Real Estate Newsline

Institutional Real Estate Newsline

Five-page fax briefing with articles regarding institutional real estate, life insurance company, banks, pension fund, real estate investment trust, and commercial mortgage backed securities markets.

Keywords:	Real Estate, Investments, Insurance
Sponsor:	Institutional Real Estate
Audience:	Investors
Details:	Costs

Institutional Research

The Electronic AIR

Biweekly (nominal schedule) electronic newsletter for the Association for Institutional Research members, as well as college and university planners.

Keywords:	Education (Continuing), Institutional Research
Sponsor:	Association for Institutional Research (AIR)
Audience:	College/University Planners, University Administrators
Contact:	Larry Nelson NELSON_L@PLU.bitnet
Details:	Free

`mailto:nelson_l@plu.bitnet`

Institutions

AltInst

A mailing list for proposing and critiquing alternative institutions and ways of life. Topics include alternative ways to run conversations, countries, households, markets, offices, romances, and schools.

Keywords:	Institutions, Alternative Management
Audience:	General Public
Contact:	Robin Hanson AltInst-request@cs.cmu.edu
Details:	Free
User Info:	To subscribe to the list, send an e-mail message requesting a subscription to the URL address below.

To send a message to the entire list, address it to: AltInst@cs.cmu.edu

Notes: AltInst is open to people from any political persuasion, but general political flaming/discussion is forbidden.

`mailto:AltInst-request@cs.cmu.edu`

Insurance

Insurance Periodicals Index

The database indexes and abstracts 35 of the most respected and widely read insurance industry journals and magazines.

Keywords:	Insurance Industry, Law
Sponsor:	NILS Publishing Company, Chatsworth, CA, US
Audience:	Insurance Brokers, Industry Professionals, Lawyers, Researchers
Profile:	The subject coverage of the publications indexed includes the following major groupings: AIDS, alcohol abuse, asbestos, automobile insurance, aviation insurance, banks, bonds, catastrophes, crime, disability insurance, drug abuse, financial services, health insurance, insurance agents and brokers, legislation, liability insurance, life insurance, Lloyds, loss control, marketing, pensions, pollution, product liability, property insurance, rates, regulation, risk management, tort reform, uninsured motorists, workers' compensation, and so on.
Contact:	Dialog in the US at (800) 334-2564, Dialog internationally at country-specific locations.
User Info:	To subscribe, contact Dialog directly.
Notes:	Coverage: 1984 to the present; updated biweekly.

`telnet://dialog.com`

Institutional Real Estate Newsline

Five-page fax briefing with articles regarding institutional real estate, life insurance company, banks, pension fund, real estate investment trust and commercial mortgage backed securities markets.

Keywords:	Real Estate, Investments, Insurance
Sponsor:	Institutional Real Estate
Audience:	Investors
Details:	Costs

INSURE (Insurance)

The Insurance (INSURE) library contains specific full-text and abstract news and legal information sources focusing on the insurance industry.

Keywords:	News, Analysis, Law, Insurance
Audience:	Insurance Professionals, Lawyers, Industry Researchers
Profile:	The INSURE library contains leading insurance industry news sources, legal and regulatory materials from NILS Publishing Company's INSURLAW, analyst reports on the insurance industry from InvestextR, and insurance company financial reports. Federal and state case law and federal regulations are also available.
Contact:	Mead New Sales Group @ (800) 227-4908 or (513) 859-5398 inside the US, or (513) 865-7981 for all inquiries outside the US.
User Info:	To subscribe, contact Mead directly.
	To examine the Nexis user guide, you can access it at the ftp site of the University of Texas at Austin at the URL address: ftp://ftp.cc.utexas.edu
	The files are in: /pub/res-services/LEXIS

`telnet://nex.meaddata.com`

Intellectual Property

Chinapats

Covers all patent applications published under the patent law of People's Republic of China.

Keywords:	Patents, Intellectual Property, Trademarks
Sponsor:	European Patent Office
Audience:	Patent Attorneys, Patent Agents, Librarians, Researchers
Profile:	English language abstracts are included for all applications filed by Chinese applicants. Contains more than 59,000 records. Updated monthly.
Contact:	PAUL.ALBERT@NETEAST.COM
User Info:	To subscribe, contact Orbit-Questel directly.

`telnet://orbit.com`

CLAIMS

Provides access to over 2.3 million U.S. patents issued by the U.S. Patent and Trademark Office.

Keywords:	Patents, Intellectual Property, Trademarks
Sponsor:	IFI/Plenum Data Corporation
Audience:	Patent Attorneys, Patent Agents, Librarians, Researchers
Profile:	Chemical patents are covered from 1950 forward; mechanical and electrical patents from 1963 forward; design patents from 1980 forward.
Contact:	PAUL.ALBERT@NETEAST.COM
User Info:	To subscribe, contact Orbit-Questel directly.

`telnet://orbit.com`

CNI-Copyright Mailing List Archives ★★

An archive of lists related to copyright and intellectual property law.

Keywords:	Copyright Law, Intellectual Property
Sponsor:	CNI (The Coalition for Networked Information)
Audience:	Entrepreneurs, Lawyers, Journalists
Contact:	Craig Summerhill, Joan K. Lippincott craig@cni.org, joan@cni.org

`gopher://gopher.cni.org`

comp.org.eff.talk ★

A Usenet newsgroup organized by the EFF (Electronic Frontier Foundation) providing information and discussion about the political, social, and legal issues surrounding the Internet.

Keywords:	Computers, Intellectual Property, Security, Internet
Audience:	Internet Surfers
User Info:	To subscribe to this Usenet newsgroup, you need access to a newsreader.

`news:comp.org.eff.talk`

Derwent World Patents Index ★

Patent specifications issued by the patent offices of 33 major issuing authorities.

Keywords:	Patents, Intellectual Property, Trademarks
Sponsor:	Derwent Publications, Ltd.
Audience:	Patent Attorneys, Patent Agents, Librarians, Researchers
Profile:	Includes European Patent Office and Patent Cooperation Treaty published applications, plus Research Disclosure and International Technology Disclosure. Each patent is extensively indexed from the complete patent specifications. Abstracts are included.
Contact:	PAUL.ALBERT@NETEAST.COM
User Info:	To subscribe, contact Orbit-Questel directly.

`telnet://orbit.com`

EFFector Online—The Electronic Frontier Foundation, Inc. ★★★

Established to make the electronic frontier truly useful and accessible to everyone, emphasizing the free and open flow of information and communication.

Keywords:	Computer Communications, Electronic Media, Intellectual Property, Privacy
Audience:	Computer Users, Civil Libertarians
Profile:	EFFector Online presents news, information, and discussion about the world of computer-based communications media that constitute the electronic frontier. It covers issues such as freedom of speech in digital media, privacy rights, censorship, and standards of responsibility for users and operators of computer systems, as well as policy issues such as the development of a national information infrastructure, and intellectual property.
Contact:	Gerard Van der Leun, Mike Godwin gerard@eff.org mnemonic@eff.org
Details:	Free
User Info:	To subscribe, send an e-mail message requesting a subscription to: request@eff.org
Notes:	This takes you to the front door of the eff gopher server, which contains much more information than just EFFector online.

`gopher://gopher.eff.org/1`

INPADOC/INPANEW ★★★

Patent documents issued by more than fifty national and international patent offices.

Keywords:	Patents, Intellectual Property, Trademarks
Sponsor:	European Patent Office
Audience:	Patent Attorneys, Patent Agents, Librarians, Researchers
Profile:	Bibliographic information is searchable, including inventor names, assignees, international patent classification codes, and in most cases, titles, as well as complete publications and application data. Contains approximately 20 million records. Updated weekly.
Contact:	PAUL.ALBERT@NETEAST.COM
User Info:	To subscribe, contact Orbit-Questel directly.

`telnet://orbit.com`

JAPIO ★

Comprehensive source of unexamined Japanese patent applications.

Keywords:	Patents, Intellectual Property, Trademarks
Sponsor:	Japan Patent Information Organization
Audience:	Patent Attorneys, Patent Agents, Librarians, Researchers
Profile:	More than 2.8 million records covering all technologies. Unique features include English-language abstracts for many Japanese patent applications
Contact:	PAUL.ALBERT@NETEAST.COM
User Info:	To subscribe, contact Orbit-Questel directly.

`telnet://orbit.com`

Legal Status ★

Records thousands of types of actions that can affect the legal status of a patent document after it is published and after the patent is granted.

Keywords:	Patents, Intellectual Property, Trademarks
Sponsor:	European Patent Office
Audience:	Patent Attorneys, Patent Agents, Librarians, Researchers
Profile:	Information about the disposition of patent applications published under the Patent Cooperation Treaty by the World Intellectual Property Organizations is included as well. Contains more than 8 million records. Updated weekly.
Contact:	PAUL.ALBERT@NETEAST.COM
User Info:	To subscribe, contact Orbit-Questel directly.

`telnet://orbit.com`

US Patents ★

Complete patent information of all claims of U.S. patents issued since 1971.

Keywords:	Patents, Intellectual Property, Trademarks
Sponsor:	Derwent, Inc.
Audience:	Patent Attorneys, Patent Agents, Librarians, Researchers
Profile:	Includes complete front page information, plus all claims of US patents issued since 1971. Merged file contains approximately 1.4 million records. Updated weekly.
Contact:	PAUL.ALBERT@NETEAST.COM
User Info:	To subscribe, contact Orbit-Questel directly.

`telnet://orbit.com`

Intelligence

Africa in the CIA World Fact Book ★★

A gopher site containing geographical and political information about individual countries in Africa.

Keywords:	Africa, Intelligence, Project Gutenberg
Sponsor:	Project Gutenberg
Audience:	Africans, General Public

`gopher://hoshi.cic.sfu.ca/11/dlam/cia/Africa`

CIA World Factbook ★

Annual report of CIA (Central Intelligence Agency) research in over 247 nations.

Keywords:	CIA, Intelligence, Annual Reports

Audience: Governments, Lawyers, FBI
Details: Free
`gopher://marvel.loc.gov`

INTER-L

INTER-L ★

A list for members of the National Association of Foreign Student Advisors.

Keywords: Education (Bilingual), Educational Policy
Sponsor: National Association of Foreign Student Advisors (NAFSA)
Audience: Foreign Students, NAFSA Members
Details: Free
User Info: To subscribe to the list, send an e-mail, message to the address below, consisting of a single line reading:
??missing line here??

`mailto:listserv@vtm1.cc.vt.edu`

Interaction

Computer Music Journal Archive and World Wide Web Home Page. ★★★★

This resource reinforces material available in the hardcopy version of Computer Music Journal, published by the MIT Press

Keywords: Computer Music, Composition, Synthesis, Interaction
Sponsor: The MIT Press
Audience: Computer Musicians
Profile: The archive includes the tables of contents, abstracts, and editor's notes for the last several volumes of CMJ (including the recent bibliography, diskography, and taxonomy of the field), a number of useful CM-related documents such as the full MIDI and AIFF format specifications, a lengthy reference list, the guidelines for manuscript submission, and the full-text of several recent articles.
Contact: Stephen Pope
cmj@cnmat.Berkeley.edu
Details: Free

`ftp://mitpress.mit.edu:/pub/Computer-Music-Journal`

Interactive

ACM SIGGRAPH Online Bibliography Project ★★★★

This is a collection of computer-graphics bibliographic references.

Keywords: Multimedia, Interactive, Computer Graphics, Programming
Sponsor: Association of Computing Machinery (ACM), Special Interest Group on Computer Graphics (SIGGRAPH)
Audience: Developers, Designers, Producers, Educators, Programmers, Graphic Artists
Profile: The goal of this project is to maintain an up-to-date database of computer-graphics literature in a format that is accessible to as many members of the computer-graphics community as possible. The database includes references from conferences and workshops worldwide and from a variety of publications dating back as far as the late-19th century. The majority of the major journals and conference proceedings from the mid-1970s to the present are listed.
Contact: bibadmin@siggraph.org
Details: Free, Moderated, Multimedia

`ftp://siggraph.org/publications`

DVI-list

This mailing list is intended for discussions about Intel's DVI (Digital Video Interactive) system. These discussions cover both applications and programming with DVI.

Keywords: Interactive Computing
Audience: Interactive Program Developers
Contact: Andrew Patrick
dvi-list-request@calvin.dgbt.doc.ca
User Info: To subscribe to the list, send an e-mail message requesting a subscription to the URL address below.
To send a message to the entire list, address it to: dvi-list-request@calvin.dgbt.doc.ca

`mailto:dvi-list-request@calvin.dgbt.doc.ca`

Interactive

A conference on Arts Wire about interactive art that includes a library of artists' statements about artworks, texts, and publications, as well as discussion.

Keywords: Art, Interactive Art
Sponsor: New York Foundation for the Arts
Audience: Artists, Writers
Contact: Anna Couey, Judy Malloy
couey@tmn.com, jmalloy@tmn.com

`telnet://tmn.com`

NIC (Nucleus for Interactive Computing) ★★★★

WWW-based system for interactive computing.

Keywords: Multimedia, Interactive Computing, Interface Design, Scripting Laguages, Programming
Sponsor: BYU Interactive Software Systems Lab
Audience: Software Developers, Educators
Profile: NIC is a system for interactive computing that combines a data model, a user interface model, and a scripting language to create flexible and powerful user interfaces. Documentation still under construction is located here.
Contact: Dan Olsen
olsen@cs.byu.edu
Details: Free, Moderated, Image, and Sound files available. Multimedia files available.
Use a World Wide Web (Mosaic) client and open a connection to the resource.

`ftp://issl.cs.byu.edu/docs/NIC/home.html`

Interactive Learning

Diversity U ★

Diversity University is an experiment in interactive learning.

Keywords: Education, Interactive Learning, Multimedia
Audience: Educators, Researchers
Details: Free

`gopher://erau.db.erau.edu`

Interactive Frog Dissection Kit ★

An interactive simulation of the dissection of a computer-generated frog.

Keywords: Biology, Simulation, Interactive Learning
Sponsor: Lawrence Berkeley Laboratory-Whole Frog Project, Berkeley, California, USA
Audience: Students, Educators, Biologists
Contact: David Robertson
dwrobertson@lbl.gov
Notes: Copyrighted (commercial uses require permission)

`http://george.1b1.gov/ITG.hm.pg.docs/dissect/info.html`

Interactive Media

Index to Multimedia Information Sources

This site provides a guide to multimedia on the Web, including lists of software, companies, research, publications, conferences, archives, and galleries.

Keywords: Multimedia, Interactive Media
Audience: Multimedia Users, Educators
Contact: Simon Gibbs
simon.gibbs@gmd.de
Details: Free

http://cui_www.unige.ch/OSG/MultimediaInfo/index.html

Rec.arts.int-fiction

A Usenet newsgroup about interactive literature and interactive computer games.

Keywords: Literature (General), Interactive Media, Computer Games
Audience: General Public, Computer Games Players
Details: Free
To participate in a Usenet newsgroup, you need access to a newsreader.

news:rec.arts.int-fiction

rec.arts.movies movie database (Cardiff WWW front-end)

An extensive, interactive database covering over 32,000 movies, with more than 370,000 filmography entries, from early cinema to current releases.

Keywords: Movies, Television, Popular Culture, Interactive Media
Audience: Movie Buffs
Profile: A WWW front-end to the rec.arts.movies movie database, complete with form-filling interfaces to add new data and to rate movies (on a scale from 1 through 10). The database includes filmographies for actors, directors, writers, composers, cinematographers, editors, production designers, costume designers, and producers; plot summaries; character names; movie ratings; year of release; running times; movie trivia; quotes; goofs; soundtracks; personal trivia and Academy Award information.
Contact: Rob Hartill
Robert.Hartill@cm.cf.ac.uk
Details: Free

http://www.cm.cf.ac.uk/Movies

http://www.msstate.edu/Movies

Interactivity

INTERCUL

A study of international communication.

Keywords: Languages (international)
Audience: Linguists, Language Teachers, Language Students
Details: Free
User Info: To subscribe to the list, send an e-mail message to the address below, consisting of a single line reading:
??missing line?????

mailto:listserv@vm.its.rpi.edu

Interface Design

Loughborough University of Technology Computer-Human Interaction (LUTCHI) Research Centre

This server contains general information on computer-human interaction.

Keywords: Interface Design, Ergonomics, Computer-Human Interactions, Programming
Sponsor: Loughborough University of Technology, Leicestershire, UK
Audience: Software Developers, Software Designers, Programmers
Profile: The LUTCHI Research Centre is based within the Department of Computer Studies at the Loughborough University of Technology, Leicestershire, UK. This server contains information about LUTCHI research projects, official LUTCHI publicity releases, as well as documents, images, and movies associated with those projects.
Contact: Ben Anderson
B.Anderson@lut.ac.uk
Details: Free, Moderated, Image, and Sound files available. Multimedia files available.
Use a World-Wide Web (Mosaic) client and open a connection to the resource.

http://pipkin.lut.ac.uk

NIC (Nucleus for Interactive Computing)

WWW-based system for interactive computing.

Keywords: Multimedia, Interactive Computing, Interface Design, Scripting Languages, Programming
Sponsor: BYU Interactive Software Systems Lab
Audience: Software Developers, Educators
Profile: NIC is a system for interactive computing that combines a data model, a user interface model, and a scripting language to create flexible and powerful user interfaces. Documentation still under construction is located here.
Contact: Dan Olsen
olsen@cs.byu.edu
Details: Free, Moderated, Image, and Sound files available. Multimedia files available.
Use a World Wide Web (Mosaic) client and open a connection to the resource.

ftp://issl.cs.byu.edu/docs/NIC/home.html

UNITE Archive

The User Network Interface to Everything (UNITE) discussion list. The list is a focus for discussion on the concept of a total solution interface with user-friendly, desktop-integrated access to all network services.

Keywords: Internet, Information Retrieval, Interface Design
Audience: Internet Surfers
Contact: George Munroe, Jill Foster
unite-request@mailbase.ac.uk
Details: Free
Files are in: pub/lists/unite

ftp://mailbase.ac.uk

Intergraph

INGR-EN

A mailing list for the discussion of Intergraph products.

Keywords: Geographic Information Systems, Intergraph
Audience: Geographers, Cartographers
Contact: Dusan Blasko
blasko@svfnov.tuke.sk
Details: Free
User Info: To subscribe to the list, send an e-mail message to the URL address below, consisting of a single line reading:
SUB ingr-en YourFirstName YourLastName

ingr-en@ccsun.tuke.sk

```
A
B
C
D
E
F
G
H
I
J
K
L
M
N
O
P
Q
R
S
T
U
V
W
X
Y
Z
```

International Banking

ITRADE (International Trade Library)

The International Trade library contains materials related to the importing of goods and services, exporting of goods and services, licensing of intellectual property, payment of taxes, or investment and banking at the international level.

Keywords: Law, Imports, International Banking

Audience: Lawyers, Bankers, International Lawyers

Profile: ITRADE contains a comprehensive collection of federal case law, statutes, regulations, and agency decisions all related to the importing of goods and services, exporting of goods and services, licensing of intellectual property, payment of taxes, or investment and banking at the international level.

Contact: New Sales Group at 800-227-4908 or 513-859-5398 inside the US, or (513)-865-7981 for all inquires outside the US.

User Info: To subscribe, contact Mead directly.

Notes: To examine the Lexis user guide, you can access it at the ftp site of the University of Texas at Austin at the URL address: ftp://ftp.cc.utexas.edu

The files are in: /pub/ref-services/LEXIS

`telnet://nex.meaddata.com`

`http://www.meaddata.com`

International Business Machines

International Business Machines

This is IBM's main WWW server and it contains extensive links to information about the company and its products.

Keywords: Computers, Business

Audience: General Public

Profile: Contains: Industry, Solutions, Products and Services, Technology information and News about the company.

Contact: mail to: askibm@www.ibm.com

`http://www.ibm.com`

International Business

Hoppenstedt Directory of German Companies

This directory covers 50,000 German companies with sales exceeding 2 million DM or with a minimum of 20 employees.

Keywords: German Companies, International Business, Germany

Sponsor: Hoppenstedt Wirtschaftsdatenbank, Darmstadt, Germany

Audience: Business Professionals, International Market, Researchers, Germans

Profile: Records include current company address, line of business, number of employees, sales, capital stock, branches and subsidiaries, and a listing of executives and directors with positions in the company. The file is bilingual; users can view the records in either German or English.

Contact: Dialog in the US at (800) 334-2564; Dialog internationally at country-specific locations.

User Info: To subscribe, contact Dialog directly.

Notes: Coverage: 1973 to the present; updated semiannually.

`telnet://dialog.com`

Infomat International Business

The database provides concise English-language abstracts of business news articles appearing in over 600 international business newspapers and journals from more than 20 countries.

Keywords: International Business, International News

Sponsor: Information Access Company, Foster City, CA

Audience: Business Professionals

Profile: Abstracts included are selected to meet the specific information requests of Infomat's client companies, which are major players in key industries, such as biotechnology, communications/telecommunications, construction/civil engineering, electronics, financial services, food and beverages, and others.

Contact: Dialog in the US at (800) 334-2564; Dialog internationally at country-specific locations.

User Info: To subscribe, contact Dialog directly.

Notes: Coverage: April 1984 to the present; updated weekly.

`telnet://dialog.com`

International Centre for Distance Learning

International Centre for Distance Learning

This site is a distance education database.

Keywords: Education (Distance)

Sponsor: International Centre for Distance Learning, The Open University, United Kingdom

Audience: Educators, Students, Researchers

Profile: The database is extensive, and provides information about courses, related institutions, and relevant literature, with over 30,000 entries, including the following: study skills, agriculture, fisheries, architecture, building, surveying, planning, arts, humanities and social sciences, business, services, management, economics, education and training, applied science, technology, computers, environment, pure science and mathematics, medicine, health, social welfare, law, law enforcement, regulations and standards, personal, home, and family affairs

Expect: Login; Send: icdl; Send: <Country>; Password: AAA

`telnet://acsvax.open.ac.uk`

International Communication

Voice of America and Worldnet

A gopher server for the Voice of America and Worldnet. Includes full-text transcripts of VOA news reports, press releases, and announcements.

Keywords: US Government Publications, News Media, Radio, International Communication

Sponsor: United States Information Agency

Audience: Journalists, Government Officials, General Public

Contact: info@voa.gov, letters-usa@VOA.GOV (For correspondence from inside the U.S.)

`gopher://gopher.voa.gov`

International Court of Justice Historical Documents

International Court of Justice Historical Documents

This gopher offers full-text documents from the International Court of Justice, and contains a searchable index.

Keywords: Judicial Process, Law (International)
Audience: Lawyers, Legal Scholars, Legal Professionals, Law Students
Notes: File is in Foreign and International Law/International Court of Justice Historical Documents

`gopher://fatty.law.cornell.edu`

International Development

Canadian University Consortium on Health in International Development (CANCHID) ★

CANCHID is a multi campus consortium that includes medical schools and other educational institutions devoted to research and projects dealing with health care issues in developing countries.

Keywords: Health, International Development
Audience: Public Health, Medicine, International Aid Agencies
Contact: Sam Lanfranco
lanfran@vm1.yorku.ca
Details: Free
User Info: To subscribe to the list, send an e-mail message to the URL address below, consisting of a single line reading:

SUB canchid YourFirstName YourLastName

To send a message to the entire list, address it to: canchid@vm1.yorku.ca

`mailto:listserv@vm1.yorku.ca`

International Documents

Historic World Documents

The wiretap gopher provides access to a range of world documents in full-text format.

Keywords: International Documents, Treaties, History (World)
Audience: Governments, Historians, Researchers, General Public
Details: Free
Select from menu as appropriate.

`gopher://wiretap.spies.com`

Latin American Database Historic World Documents

International legal files covering 33 nations and article citations from publications relating to Hispanic legal systems. The wiretap gopher provides access to a range of world documents in full-text format.

Keywords: Hispanic, Law, International Law, International Documents
Audience: General Public, Hispanics, Lawyers
Profile: The database includes two files, 1) LAWL containing legislation from 33 nations, mostly Spanish speaking 2) HISS containing Hispanic Legal Article citations.
Details: Free
Select from menu as appropriate.

`gopher://marvel.loc.gov`

International Finance

American Banker Full Text

This database corresponds to the authoritative print publication American Banker.

Keywords: Banking, International Finance, International Trade
Sponsor: American Banker-Bond Buyer, New York, NY, USA
Audience: Financial Analysts, Bankers
Profile: Specific coverage is given to local, regional, and international financial services, technology applications, legal commentary and court actions, international trade, government regulations, Washington events, marketing of financial services, general economic overviews, personnel issues, and profiles and movements of industry personnel. Statistical rankings of all types of financial institutions (from thrifts to commercial banks, US and worldwide) are included beginning with the October 1987 editions. Other special features include quarterly bank earnings, results of American Banker surveys, and the complete text of speeches and articles by the industry professionals that are unavailable in the printed paper.
Contact: Dialog in the US at (800) 334-2564; Dialog internationally at country-specific locations.
Details: Costs
User Info: To subscribe, contact Dialog directly.

`telnet://dialog.com`

World Bank Gopher Server

A collection of online information from the World Bank.

Keywords: Government (International), Development, International Finance, Foreign Trade
Sponsor: The World Bank
Audience: Nongovernmental Organizations, Activists, Government Officials, Environmentalists
Profile: A collection of World Bank information, including a list of publications, environmental assessments, economic reports, and updates on current projects being funded by the World Bank.
Contact: webmaster@www.worldbank.org

`gopher://gopher.worldbank.org`

`http://www.worldbank.org`

International Food and Nutrition (INFAN) Database

International Food and Nutrition (INFAN) Database

A database covering all aspects of nutrition, health and food, including weight control, food safety, eating patterns, and more.

Keywords: Nutrition, Health, Diet
Sponsor: Pennsylvania State University Nutrition Center
Audience: Nutritionists, Health-Care Professionals, Consumers
Details: Free
To access the database, select PENpages (1), then General Information (3), and finally INFAN Database (4).

`telnet://penpages@psupen.psu.edu`

International Law

INTLAW (International Law Library)

The International Law Library provides comprehensive international law materials.

Keywords: International Law, EEC, Commonwealth, China
Audience: Lawyers, International Lawyers
Profile: The International Law Library provides comprehensive international law materials. The International Law Library contains federal case law, European Community materials, treaties and agreements, Commonwealth law

materials, topical and professional journals, French law materials (in French) China law materials, plus relevant topical publications.

Contact: New Sales Group at 800-227-4908 or 513-859-5398 inside the US, or (513)-865-7981 for all inquires outside the US.

User Info: To subscribe, contact Mead directly.

To examine the Lexis user guide, you can access it at the ftp site of the University of Texas at Austin at the URL address: ftp://ftp.cc.utexas.edu

The files are in: /pub/ref-services/LEXIS

`telnet://nex.meaddata.com`

`http://www.meaddata.com`

Latin American Database Historic World Documents

International legal files covering 33 nations and article citations from publications relating to Hispanic legal systems. The wiretap gopher provides access to a range of world documents in full-text format.

Keywords: Hispanic, Law, International Law, International Documents

Audience: General Public, Hispanics, Lawyers

Profile: The database includes two files, 1) LAWL containing legislation from 33 nations, mostly Spanish speaking 2) HISS containing Hispanic Legal Article citations.

Details: Free

Select from menu as appropriate.

`gopher://marvel.loc.gov`

International News

Info-South (Latin American News)

The database provides citations and abstracts of materials relating to contemporary economic, political, and social issues in Latin America.

Keywords: International News, Economics, International Politics, Latin America

Sponsor: University of Miami, Coral Gables, FL, US

Audience: General Public

Profile: Coverage includes a wide range of topics assessing the current situation in Latin America.

Contact: Dialog in the US at (800) 334-2564; Dialog internationally at country-specific locations.

User Info: To subscribe, contact Dialog directly.

Notes: Coverage: 1988 to the present; updated weekly.

`telnet://dialog.com`

Infomat International Business

The database provides concise English-language abstracts of business news articles appearing in over 600 international business newspapers and journals from more than 20 countries.

Keywords: International Business, International News

Sponsor: Information Access Company, Foster City, CA, US

Audience: Business Professionals

Profile: Abstracts included are selected to meet the specific information requests of Infomat's client companies that are major players in key industries, such as biotechnology, communications/telecommunications, construction/civil engineering, electronics, financial services, food and beverages, and others.

Contact: Dialog in the US at (800) 334-2564; Dialog internationally at country-specific locations.

User Info: To subscribe, contact Dialog directly.

Notes: Coverage: April 1984 to the present; updated weekly.

`telnet://dialog.com`

International Politics

Info-South (Latin American News)

The database provides citations and abstracts of materials relating to contemporary economic, political, and social issues in Latin America.

Keywords: International News, Economics, International Politics, Latin America

Sponsor: University of Miami, Coral Gables, FL, US

Audience: General Public

Profile: Coverage includes a wide range of topics assessing the current situation in Latin America.

Contact: Dialog in the US at (800) 334-2564; Dialog internationally at country-specific locations.

User Info: To subscribe, contact Dialog directly.

Notes: Coverage: 1988 to the present; updated weekly.

`telnet://dialog.com`

Women.dev

Conference for information about local, regional, and international development as it relates to women. The conference includes bibliographies, statements, news, articles, and announcements about development and women in Africa, South America, and South Asia.

Keywords: Women, Development (International), International Politics

Audience: Women, Activists, Non-governmental Organizations, Feminists

Details: Sound files available, Free.

User Info: Establish an account on the nearest APC node. Login, type c for conferences, then type go women.dev.

For information on the nearest APC node, contact:

APC International Secretariat

IBASE

E-mail: apcadmin@apc.org

Contact: Carlos Afonso (cafonso@ax.apc.org)

or

APC North American Regional Office

E-mail: apcadmin@apc.org

Contact: Edie Farwell (efarwell@igc.apc.org)

Notes: Alai: Agencia Latinoamericana De Informacion

E-mail message to APCadmin@apc.org

`telnet://igc.apc.org`

International Relations

Summit of the Americas Internet Gopher

A gopher containing supporting materials for the Summit of the Americas, a meeting of the Western Hemisphere's democratically elected heads of state, to be held in Miami in December of 1994.

Keywords: American Studies, International Relations, Haiti, Latin America

Sponsor: The Florida University Latin American and Caribbean Center

Audience: Government Officials, Journalists, NGOs, General Public

Contact: Rene Ramos summit@SERVAX.FIU.EDU

`gopher://summit.fiu.edu`

University of Toledo Library

The library's holdings are large and wide-ranging and contain significant collections in many fields.

Keywords: Business, Great Lakes Area, Humanities, International Relations, Psychology, Science

Audience: Researchers, Students, General Public

Details: Free

Expect: Enter one of the following commands . . . , Send: DIAL MVS; Expect: dialed to mvs ####; Send: UTMOST

`telnet:/ uofto1.utoledo.edu`

International Research

Research on Demand

A resource for the provision of market information, strategic information location, product information, and national and international business information.

Keywords:	Market Research, Internet Research, Legal Research, International Research
Audience:	Marketing Specialists, Lawyers, Public Relations Experts, Business Professionals, Researchers, Writers, Producers
Profile:	This resource has special access to unique information resources worldwide. Areas of particular information access include the former Soviet Union, Europe, and the US. Information access also includes access to all the major online systems, including Dialog, BRS, Orbit, DataStar, and so on. Current Awareness Services include research information gathered from the Internet.
Details:	Costs
User Info:	To subscribe, send an e-mail message to the URL address below. In the body of your message, state the nature of your inquiry.
Notes:	Contact ROD directly in the US at: (800) 227-0750; outside the US at: (510) 841-1145.

`mailto:rod@holonet.net`

International Trade

American Banker Full Text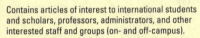

This database corresponds to the authoritative print publication American Banker.

Keywords:	Banking, International Finance, International Trade
Sponsor:	American Banker-Bond Buyer, New York, NY, USA
Audience:	Financial Analysts, Bankers
Profile:	Specific coverage is given to local, regional, and international financial services, technology applications, legal commentary and court actions, international trade, government regulations, Washington events, marketing of financial services, general economic overviews, personnel issues, and profiles and movements of industry personnel. Statistical rankings of all types of financial institutions (from thrifts to commercial banks, US and worldwide) are included beginning with the October 1987 editions. Other special features include quarterly bank earnings, results of American Banker surveys, and the complete text of speeches and articles by the industry professionals that are unavailable in the printed paper.
Contact:	Dialog in the US at (800) 334-2564; Dialog internationally at country-specific locations.
Details:	Costs
User Info:	To subscribe, contact Dialog directly.

`telnet://dialog.com`

International Visitors

IHOUSE-L International Voice Newsletter Prototype List

Contains articles of interest to international students and scholars, professors, administrators, and other interested staff and groups (on- and off-campus).

Keywords:	International Visitors, Washington University
Sponsor:	International Office of Washington University, St. Louis MO
Audience:	International Students
Contact:	Doyle Cozadd C73221DC@WUVMD
Details:	Free
User Info:	To subscribe, send an e-mail message to the address below, consisting of a single line reading: SUB: house-l Your First Name Your Last Name To send a message to the entire list,

`mailto:listserv@wuvmd.wustl.edu`

Internet

AARNet Guide

This is the Australian Network Sites and Resources Guide.

Keywords:	Internet, Internet Guide
Sponsor:	Australian Academic and Research Network
Audience:	Internet Surfers
Details:	Free Files are in: pub/resource-guide

`ftp://aarnet.edu.au/pub/resource-guide`

Agricultural Guide

A specialized guide, entitled "Not Just Cows," to the Internet/Bitnet resources in agriculture and related science.

Keywords:	Agriculture, Internet
Sponsor:	University of North Carolina
Audience:	Internet Surfers
Contact:	Wilfred Drew
Details:	Free File is: pub/docs/about-the-net/libsoft/agguide.dos

`ftp://sunsite.unc.edu/pub/docs/about-the-net/libsoft/agguide.dos`

`gopher://sunsite.unc.edu`

`http://sunsite.unc.edu/pub/docs/about-the-net/libsoft/agguide.dos`

Alex Description

An NIR (Network Information Retrieval) description of Alex, an Internet access tool.

Keywords:	Internet Tools, Internet, Alex
Audience:	Internet Surfers
Details:	Free File is: usr0/anon/doc/NIR.Tool

`ftp://alex.sp.cs.cmu.edu/usr0/anon/doc/NIR.Tool`

Almost 2001 Archive

Archive of transcripts of Almost 2001, a series on computer communications of the future, produced by NBC (National Broadcasting Company).

Keywords:	Computers, Communications, Internet
Sponsor:	The WELL (Whole Earth 'Lectronic Link)
Audience:	Computer Users, Internet Surfers
Details:	Free, Moderated To participate in a conference on the WELL, you must first establish an account on the WELL. To do so, start by typing: telnet://well.sf.ca.us

`gopher://gopher.well.sf.ca.us//11/Communications/2001`

alt.config

A Usenet newsgroup providing information and discussion about alternative subnet discussions and connectivity.

Keywords:	Internet, Computer Networks, Connectivity
Audience:	Network Administrators
User Info:	To subscribe to this Usenet newsgroup, you need access to a newsreader.

`news:alt.config`

Best of the Web '94

This web site highlights those places which were judged as the best sites (based on the criteria of quality, versatility, and power) on the World Wide Web.

Keywords: Internet, WWW
Audience: Internet Surfers
Contact: Brandon Plewe
plewe@acsu.buffalo.edu
Details: Free

http://wings.buffalo.edu/contest

Big Dummy's Guide ★

A comprehensive guide to the Internet for people with little or no experience with network communications.

Keywords: Internet
Sponsor: Electronic Frontier Foundation
Audience: Internet Surfers
Contact: Shari Steele
ssteele@eff.org
Details: Free
Big Dummy's Guide to the Internet is available in: /pub/Net_info/Big_Dummy, in several versions. The basic text version is bigdummy.txt

ftp://ftp.eff.org

bit.general

A Usenet newsgroup providing information and discussion about Bitnet or Usenet. Contained in the bit. category are many bit.listserv discussion lists.

Keywords: Internet, News
Audience: General Public, Internet Surfers
User Info: To subscribe to this Usenet newsgroup, you need access to a newsreader.

news:bit.general

CERFnet Guide ★

A comprehensive guide to the CERFnet (California Education and Research Federation Network), a data-communications regional network that operates throughout California. The purpose of CERFnet is to advance science and education by assisting the interchange of information among research and educational institutions.

Keywords: Internet, Science, Education, California
Audience: Internet Surfers, Researchers, Educators
Contact: CERFnet Hotline
help@cerf.net
Details: Free
Files are in: cerfnet/cerfnet_info/cerfnet_guide/

ftp://nic.cerf.net

cfcp-members ★

The Confederation of Future Computer Professionals (CFCP) is a group of users on the Internet who are interested enough in various fields of computers to consider computers as their future. The Confederation exists to foster education and stimulate communication.

Keywords: Internet, Computers
Audience: Internet Surfers, Computer Users
Contact: mlindsey@nyx.cs.du.edu
Details: Free
User Info: To subscribe to the list, send an e-mail message requesting a subscription to the URL address below.

mailto:mlindsey@nyx.cs.du.edu

CNI ★

CNI (Coalition for Networked Information) is an Internet information retrieval service. The CNI promotes the creation of and access to information resources in networked environments in order to enrich scholarship and to enhance intellectual productivity.

Keywords: Internet, Information Retrieval, CNI
Audience: Internet Surfers
Details: Free
The readme file is: CNI/info.packet/README

ftp://ftp.cni.org/CNI (/info.packet/README)

gopher://ftp.cni.org

http://www.cni.org/CNI.homepage.html

CNI Gopher ★

The gopher for CNI (Coalition for Networked Information), an Internet information retrieval service. The CNI promotes the creation of and access to information resources in networked environments in order to enrich scholarship and to enhance intellectual productivity.

Keywords: Internet, Information Retrieval, CNI
Audience: Internet Surfers
Contact: Craig A. Summerhill
Craig@cni.org
Details: Free

gopher://gopher.cni.org

CNI TopNode Project ★

Part of CNI (Coalition for Networked Information) directories and resource information service.

Keywords: Internet, Information Retrieval, CNI
Audience: Internet Surfers
Details: Free

ftp://ftp.cni.org/CNI/projects/topnode

gopher://ftp.cni.org

http://www.cni.org/CNI.homepage.html

College E-mail Addresses ★

Information on e-mail addresses at graduate offices.

Keywords: Internet, E-mail
Audience: Internet Surfers, Students, College/University Educators
Details: Free
File is: pub/usenet/soc.college/Admission_Office_Email_Address_List

ftp://pit-manager.mit.edu/pub/usenet-by-group/soc.college

gopher://sipb.mit.edu

comp.org.eff.talk ★

A Usenet newsgroup organized by the EFF (Electronic Frontier Foundation) providing information and discussion about the political, social, and legal issues surrounding the Internet.

Keywords: Computers, Intellectual Property, Security, Internet
Audience: Internet Surfers
User Info: To subscribe to this Usenet newsgroup, you need access to a newsreader.

news:comp.org.eff.talk

comp.text.tex ★

A Usenet newsgroup providing information and discussion about the TeX and LaTeX systems.

Keywords: Text Processing, Internet
Audience: Computer Users, TeX and LaTeX Users
User Info: To subscribe to this Usenet newsgroup, you need access to a newsreader.

news:comp.text.tex

comp.unix.aix ★

A Usenet newsgroup providing information and discussion about IBM's version of UNIX.

Keywords: Computer System, Internet, UNIX
Audience: Computer Users, UNIX Users, IBM Users
User Info: To subscribe to this Usenet newsgroup, you need access to a newsreader.

news:comp.unix.aix

Internet 379

Computer Network Conferencing ★

Discussions on the topic of computer network conferencing. The memo is intended to make more people aware of the present developments in the computer conferencing field, as well as to put forward ideas on what should be done to formalize this work.

Keywords: Internet, Conferencing Systems
Audience: Internet Surfers
Contact: Darren Reed
avalon@coombs.anu.edu.au
Details: Free
File is: documents/rfc/rfc1324.txt

`ftp://nic.merit.edu`

Computer-Mediated Marketing Environments ★★

A web site devoted to research aimed at understanding the ways in which computer-mediated marketing environments (CMEs), especially the Internet, are revolutionizing the way firms conduct business.

Keywords: WWW, Information Retrieval, Internet, Marketing, Business
Sponsor: Vanderbilt University, Owen Graduate School of Management, Nashville, Tennessee, USA
Audience: General Public, Entrepeneurs, Financial Planners, Marketers
Contact: Donna Hoffman, Tom Novak
hoffman@colette.ogsm.vanderbilt.edu,
novak@moe.ogsm.vanderbilt.edu

`http://colette.ogsm.vanderbilt.edu`

Correct Time/NBS ★

Correct Time/NBS tells the correct time from the National Bureau of Standards (NBS).

Keywords: Internet, Services, Correct Time
Audience: Internet Surfers
Details: Free

`ftp://india.colorado.edu/pub` (Bogus site!)

CSORG (Clearinghouse for Subject-Oriented Internet Resource Guides) ★★★

The goal of CSORG is to collect and make widely available guides to Internet resources that are subject-oriented. These guides are produced by members of the Internet community, and by SILS students who participate in the Internet Resource Discovery project.

Keywords: WWW, Information Retrieval, Internet,

Sponsor: University of Michigan, School of Information and Library Studies, Michigan, USA
Audience: Reseachers, Students, General Public
Contact: Louis Rosenfeld
i-guides@umich.edu

`gopher://una.hh.lib.umich.edu/11/inetdirs`

DDN New User Guide ★

Defense Data Network (DDN) guide for new users.

Keywords: Internet, Internet Guides, Defense, Security
Audience: Internet Surfers
Details: Free
File is: netinfo/nug.doc

`ftp://nic.ddn.mil/netinfo`

Delphi

Delphi is an online service provider.
Keywords: Internet
Sponsor: Delphi, NewsCorp. Technologies
Audience: Internet Users
Details: Costs

`telnet://delphi.com`

DIMUND

DIMUND (Document Image Understanding) is an Internet information retrieval service.

Keywords: Internet, Information Retrieval, DIMUND, Documents
Sponsor: Document Processing Group, University of Maryland
Audience: Internet Surfers
Contact: gopher@dimund.cfar.umd.edu
Details: Free

`gopher:// dimund.umd.edu`

DIMUND FTP ★

DIMUND (Document Image Understanding) information service FTP archives. Provides access to selected documents.

Keywords: Internet, Information Retrieval, DIMUND, Documents
Sponsor: Document Processing Group, University of Maryland
Audience: Internet Surfers
Contact: gopher@dimund.cfar.umd.edu
Details: Free

`ftp://dimund.umd.edu`

Doc Center ★★★

A hard-copy document-delivery service for government and industry specifications and standards.

Keywords: Internet, Information Retrieval
Audience: Internet Surfers, Document Delivery Professionals
Details: Costs

`http://www.service.com/doccenter/home.html`

E-mail 101 ★

E-mail 101 describes how to use e-mail as well as other Internet features.

Keywords: Internet, E-mail
Audience: Internet Surfers
Details: Free

`gopher://mrcnext.cso.uiuc.edu`

`http://mrcnext.cso.uiuc.edu`

E-mail Gopher ★

E-mail Gopher allows the use of a gopher via e-mail.

Keywords: Internet, Services, E-mail, Gopher
Audience: Internet Surfers
Details: Free
Include the word "help" in the e-mail.

`gopher://gopher.ncc.go.jp/11/INFO/gopher`

E-mail Services ★

A list of services available by e-mail.

Keywords: Internet, E-mail, Services
Audience: Internet Surfers
Contact: David DeSimone
an207@cleveland.freenet.edu
Details: Free
File is: pub/docs/about-the-net/libsoft/email_services.txt

`ftp://sunsite.unc.edu/pub/docs/about-the-net/libsoft/email_services.txt`

`http://sunsite.unc.edu/pub/docs/about-the-net/libsoft/email_services.txt`

E-mail Understanding ★

A special issue of the University of Illinois publication UIUC net describing electronic mail.

Keywords: Internet, E-mail
Audience: Internet Surfers
Details: Free
File is: doc/net/uiucnet/vol2no2.txt

`ftp://ftp.cso.uiuc.edu/doc/net/uiucnet`

E-mail Usenet ★

E-mail Usenet enables the user to post to a newsgroup via e-mail.

Keywords: Internet, Services, E-mail, Usenet
Audience: Internet Surfers
Details: Free

`mailto://hierarchy-group-name@cs.utexas.edu`

EDNET ★

This forum explores the educational potential of the Internet.

Keywords: Education, Internet
Audience: Students, Educators
Profile: This independent, unmoderated mailing-list interest group is open and free of charge to all participants. Ednet links educators with common interests, and introduces students to a number of fields and sources of information, while offering criticism and suggestions.
Contact: Prescott Smith
pgsmith@educ.umass.edu
Details: Free
User Info: To subscribe to the list, send an e-mail message to the address shown below, consisting of a single line reading:
SUB Ednet YourFirstName YourLastName
To send a message to the entire list, address it to: ednet@nic.umass.edu.

`gopher://ericir.syr.edu/00/AskERIC/FullText/Lists/Messages/EDNET-List/README`

`mailto:listserv@nic.umass.edu`

Educator's Guide to E-mail Lists ★

A guide to help educators find e-mail lists. Includes a very large list of e-mail addresses related to education.

Keywords: Education, E-mail, Internet
Sponsor: University of Massachusetts, Amherst, MA
Audience: Educators, Researchers
Contact: Prescott Smith
pgsmith@educ.umass.edu

Details: Free

`ftp://nic.umass.edu`

EINet Galaxy ★★★★

EINet Galaxy is a guide to world-wide information and services. It includes public information as well as commercial information and services provided by EINet customers and affiliates. The information is organized by topic, and can be searched.

Keywords: WWW, Information Retrieval, Internet
Sponsor: Microelectronic and Computer Technology Corporation (MCC)
Audience: Reseachers, Students
Contact: Wayne Allen, Bruce Speyer
WA@EINet.net
Speyer@EINet.net

`http://galaxy.einet.net/galaxy.html`

EUnet ★

A global Internet Service Provider with national providers in almost 30 countries. Applications such as customer support, remote diagnosis, software development tools, and product information are available through this net.

Keywords: Internet
Sponsor: EUnet Information Services
Audience: Internet Surfers
Contact: info@eu.net
Details: Free

`http://www.eu.net`

Finding E-mail Addresses ★

Tips on finding e-mail addresses.

Keywords: Internet, E-mail
Audience: Internet Surfers
Contact: Jonathan Kamens
jik@MIT.Edu
Details: Free
File is: pub/docs/about-the-net/libsoft/email_address.txt

`ftp://sunsite.unc.edu`

Free for All ★

An experiment in a networked hypermedia group bulletin board.

Keywords: Internet, Group Communications, Multimedia
Audience: Internet Surfers, Multimedia Enthusiasts
Details: Free, Multimedia

`http://south.ncsa.uiuc.edu/Free.html`

FYI on Questions and Answer Answers to Commonly asked New Internet User Questions ★★

Answers to questions commonly asked by new Internet users.

Keywords: Internet, Internet Resources
Sponsor: Xylogics, Inc., and SRI International
Audience: Internet Surfers
Profile: File is: documents/fyi/RFC_1594.txt
Contact: Gary Scott Malkin, April N. Marine
gmalkin@Xylogics.com or
april@nisc.sri.com
Details: Free

`ftp://nic.merit.edu`

Global Internet

A full-service Internet provider, offering superior quality Internet access and value-added services to business professionals, researchers, and educational communities.

Keywords: Internet, Finance
Sponsor: Global Internet, Palo Alto, CA (415)855-1700
Audience: Internet Users, Business Professionals, Financial Analysts, Publishers
Details: Costs

`mailto:sales@gi.net`

Gold in Networks ★

An introductory guide to the Internet.

Keywords: Internet
Sponsor: Ohio State University
Audience: Internet Surfers
Contact: J. Martin
nic@osu.edu
Details: Free
File is: documents/fyi/fyi_1o.txt

`ftp://nic.merit.edu`

Hitchhiker's Guide ★

A narrative of what the Internet has to offer.

Keywords: Internet
Sponsor: University of Illinois, Urbana, IL
Audience: Internet Surfers
Contact: Ed Krol
krol@uxc.cso.uiuc.ed
Details: Free
File is: documents/rfc/rfc1118.txt

`ftp://nic.merit.edu`

Hypermedia/Internet

A guide to hypermedia and the Internet.

Keywords:	Internet, Group Communications, Hypermedia
Sponsor:	Australian National University
Audience:	Internet Surfers
Contact:	David Geoffrey Green David.Green@anu.edu.au
Details:	Free

`http:// life.anu.edu.au`

Incomplete Guide to the Internet (K12-Netzanleitung)

An Internet guide created especially for teachers and students in grades K-12.

Keywords:	Education (K-12), Internet
Audience:	Educators (K-12), Students (K-12)
Contact:	Chuck Farmer cfarmer@ncsa.uiuc.edu
Details:	Free

`ftp://ncsa.uiuc.edu`

Infopop

A WINHELP (hypertext) guide to the Internet, CompuServe, BBS systems, and more.

Keywords:	Internet, Internet Guides
Sponsor:	Fenwick Library, George Mason University, Fairfax, VA
Audience:	Internet Surfers
Contact:	Wally Grotophorst wallyg@fen1.gmu.edu
Details:	Free Read the file: library/readme

`ftp://ftp.gmu.edu`

Information Sources

These compiled resources provide information describing the Internet and computer-mediated communication technologies, as well as information on related applications, culture, discussion forums, and bibliographies.

Keywords:	Internet, Networking
Audience:	Internet Surfers, Computer-Mediated Communication Researchers
Contact:	John December decemj@rpi.edu
Details:	Free

`ftp://ftp.rpi.edu`

`http://www.rpi.edu/Internet/Guides/decemj/icmc/top.html`

Internet Browsers

A list of sources for Internet browsers and client software.

Keywords:	Internet, Internet Tools
Sponsor:	ANU Bioinformatics Hypermedia Service
Audience:	Internet Surfers
Contact:	David Green David Green@anu.edu.au
Details:	Free

`http://life.anu.edu.au/links/syslib.html`

Internet Companion

A beginner's guide to global networking.

Keywords:	Internet, Internet Guides
Sponsor:	Software Tool & Die
Audience:	Internet Surfers
Contact:	staff@world.std.com
Details:	Free Files are in: OBS/The.Internet.Companion

`ftp://world.std.com`

Internet Cruise

A computer-based tutorial for new and experienced Internet "navigators." Provides an introduction to Internet resources as diverse as: supercomputing, minorities, multimedia, cooking, and so on. Also provides information about the tools needed to access those resources.

Keywords:	Internet, Internet Guides
Sponsor:	Merit Network Information Center, Ann Arbor, MI
Audience:	Internet Surfers
Contact:	Steve Burdick, Laura Kelleher, Mark Davis-Craig cruise2feedback@merit.edu
Details:	Free File is located in: /internet/resources

`ftp://nic.merit.edu`

Internet Economics

An article entitled "Some Economics of the Internet," by Jeffrey K. Mackie-Mason.

Keywords:	Economics, Internet
Audience:	Internet Surfers
Contact:	Jeffrey K. Mackie-Mason
Details:	Free

`ftp://gopher.econ.lsa.umich.edu`

Internet Growth

Contains figures showing the growth of the Internet, derived from historical figures and published by Mark Lottor and Marten Terpstra.

Keywords:	Internet
Sponsor:	Electronic Frontier Foundation
Audience:	Internet Surfers
Contact:	Free Files are in: matrix/growth/internet

`ftp://tic.com`

Internet Hunt

A game for exploring and learning about the Internet. It helps Net users to realize the vast and varied amounts of information available on the Net and helps more novice users, or Net "settlers," understand how to move around using the "trails" that the more experienced Hunt players have "blazed." Contains Internet Hunt questions, results, and comments.

Keywords:	Internet, Games
Sponsor:	CICnet
Audience:	Internet Surfers
Contact:	Rick Gates rgates@nic.cic.net
Details:	Free

`gopher://gopher.cic.net`

Internet Information Listing

A comprehensive collection of Internet information and utilities. Includes a listing of Internet providers, a large collection of guide books (NSF Resource Guide, Zen and the Art of the Internet, Big Dummy's Guide, and others), as well as specific help files for Internet utilities such as FTP, Telnet, and IRC. This site also features access to many popular gopher destinations.

Keywords:	Internet, Internet Guides
Sponsor:	Phantom Access Technologies, Inc.
Audience:	Internet Surfers
Contact:	root@phantom.com

`gopher://mindvox.phantom.com`

Internet Libraries (Gopher)

The site maintains the most current possible list of all library catalogs accessible on the Internet.

Keywords:	Libraries, Databases, Internet, Information Retrieval
Audience:	Reseacher, Students, Librarians
Contact:	Gopherlib gopherlib@gopher.yale.edu

`gopher://yaleinfo.yale.edu`

Internet Monthly Reports ★

Monthly communications to the Internet Research Group.
Keywords: Internet, Internet Guides
Sponsor: Merit Network Information Center Services
Audience: Internet Surfers
Details: Free
Index is: internet/newsletters/ INDEX.internet.monthly.report

`ftp://nic.merit.edu`

Internet Multicasting ★

Answers to frequently asked questions (FAQs) about the Internet Multicasting Service.
Keywords: Internet, Information Retrieval
Audience: Internet Surfers
Details: Free, Sound
Include "send FAQ" in the e-mail.

`mailto:info@radio.com`

Internet Policy ★

An article entitled "What Should We Plan Given the Dilemma of the Network?" by G. Cook.
Keywords: Internet, E-mail
Audience: Internet Surfers
Details: Free

`ftp://pit-manager.mit.edu`

Internet Pricing ★

An article entitled "Pricing the Internet."
Keywords: Internet, Economics
Audience: Internet Surfers
Details: Free

`gopher://gopher.econ.lsa.umich.edu`

Internet Public Subsidies ★

An article entitled "The Economic Case for Public Subsidy of the Internet."
Keywords: Internet, Economics
Audience: Internet Surfers
Details: Free

`gopher://ssugopher.sonoma.edu`

Internet Services FAQ ★

General information and answers to frequently asked questions (FAQs) about the Internet.

Keywords: Internet, Internet Guides, FAQs
Audience: Internet Surfers
Details: Free
User Info: File is: pub/usenet/news.answers/ internet-services/faq

`ftp://rtfm.mit.edu`

Internet Sound ★

Internet Sound contains various documents and programs regarding sound.
Keywords: Internet, Information Retrieval
Audience: Internet Surfers
User Info: ftp://ftp.cwi.nl/pub/audio/INDEX
ftp://ftp.cwi.nl/pub/audio/index.html
The index is: pub/audio/INDEX
Details: Free, Sound

`ftp://ftp.cwi.nl`

Internet Statistics ★

The latest statistical information about the Internet from the National Science Foundation.
Keywords: Internet
Sponsor: Merit Network Information Center
Audience: Internet Surfers
Details: Free
Index is: nsfnet/statistics/ INDEX.statistics

`ftp://nic.merit.edu`

Internet Systems UNITE ★

A list of tools for use on the Internet, by UNITE (User Network Interface to Everything).
Keywords: Internet, Internet Tools
Audience: Internet Surfers
Contact: unite-request@mailbase.ac.uk
Details: Free
File is: pub/lists/unite/files/systems-list.txt

`ftp://mail.base.ac.uk`

Internet Tools EARN ★

A guide to network research tools by the European Academic Research Network (EARN).
Keywords: Internet, Internet Tools
Audience: Internet Surfers
Contact: listserv@earncc.bitnet
Details: Free
Document is:earn/earn-resource-tool-guide.txt

`ftp://ns.ripe.net`

Internet Tools NIR ★

A status report on Networked Information Retrieval (NIR) tools and groups.
Keywords: Internet, Internet Tools
Sponsor: Joint IETF/RARE/CNI Networked Information Retrieval Working Group
Audience: Internet Surfers
Contact: Jill Foster
jill.foster@newcastle.ac.uk
Details: Free
User Info: File is: pub/lists/nir/files/nir.status.report

`ftp://mail.base.ac.uk`

Internet Tools Summary ★

A list summarizing Internet tools for Network Information Retrieval (NIR) and computer-mediated communication (CMC) forums.
Keywords: Internet, Internet Tools
Audience: Internet Surfers
Contact: John December
decemj@rpi.edu
Details: Free
User Info: Files are located in: pub/communications. Read the internet-tools.readme first.

`ftp://ftp.rpi.edu`

InterNIC Directory Services (White Pages) ★★

This web site provides free access to X.500, WHOIS, and Netfind white pages on the Internet.
Keywords: WWW, Internet, Internet Tools
Sponsor: National Science Foundation, USA
Audience: General Public, Students
Contact: Database Administrator
admin@ds.internic.net

`http://ds.internic.net/ds/dspgwp.html`

irc (Internet Relay Chat) ★

A multiuser, multichannel chatting network. It enables people all over the Internet to "talk" to one another interactively.
Keywords: Internet, Group Communications
Audience: Internet Surfers
Details: Free
User Info: Readme file is: irc/README

`ftp://cs.bu.edu`

Library Resources

A specialized guide to library resources on the Internet, with a focus on strategies for selection and use.

Keywords: Libraries, Internet
Audience: Internet Surfers, Researchers
User Info: File is: pub/internet/libcat-guide

`ftp://dla.ucop.edu/pub/internet/libcat-guide`

Library Special

Library Special collections on the Internet.

Keywords: Internet, Information Retrieval
Audience: Internet Surfers
Details: Free

`ftp://dla.ucop.edu/pub`

`http://dla.ucop.edu`

Merit Network Information Center Services

This site provides a large collection of Internet guides and information.

Keywords: Internet, Internet Guides, Internet Tools
Sponsor: Merit Network, Inc.
Audience: Internet Surfers
Profile: This site serves as a clearinghouse for many Internet guides, documents, and utilities. It includes Internet FAQs, bibliographies, glossaries, and user guides such as Zen and the Art of the Internet and The Internet Companion. It also has archives of various Internet documents listing service providers, acceptable use policies, and resources. Many software programs for navigating the Internet are also available here for a wide variety of platforms
Contact: nic-info@nic.merit.edu

`gopher://nic.merit.edu`

`ftp://nic.merit.edu`

MetaMail

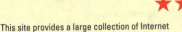

This resource contains information about MetaMail, which allows existing mail readers to read multimedia e-mail in the MIME (Multipurpose Internet Mail Extensions) format.

Keywords: Internet, E-mail
Audience: Internet Surfers
Contact: Nathaniel S. Borenstein
nsb@nsb.fv.com
Readme file is pub/nsb/README

`ftp://thumper.bellcore.com`

MIME (Multipurpose Internet Mail Extensions)

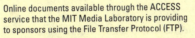

This resource contains information about the MIME (Multipurpose Internet Mail Extensions) protocol.

Keywords: Internet, E-Mail
Audience: Internet Surfers
Contact: Nathaniel S. Borenstein
nsb@nsb.fv.com
File is: documents/rfc/rfc1521.txt

`ftp://nic.merit.edu`

MIT Media Lab

Online documents available through the ACCESS service that the MIT Media Laboratory is providing to sponsors using the File Transfer Protocol (FTP).

Keywords: Internet, Multimedia
Audience: Internet Surfers
Details: Free, Multimedia

`ftp://media-lab.media.mit.edu`

Multicast Backbone

Live audio and video multicast virtual network on top of the Internet.

Keywords: Internet, Information Retrieval
Audience: Internet Surfers
Details: Free, Sound

`ftp://venera.isi.edu`

`http://venera.isi.edu`

Multimedia Index

A list of multimedia information sources on the Internet.

Keywords: Internet, Multimedia
Sponsor: Centre Universitaire d'Informatique, University of Geneva
Audience: Internet Surfers
Contact: Oscar Nierstrasz
oscar@cui.unige.ch
Details: Free, Multimedia

`http://cui_www.unige.ch`

Multimedia Lab BU

Information about the Multimedia Lab at Boston University (BU), investigating issues surrounding the construction of general-purpose distributed multimedia information systems (DMISs).

Keywords: Internet, Multimedia
Sponsor: Boston University
Audience: Internet Surfers
Contact: T.D.C. Little
tdcl@spiderman.bu.edu
Details: Free, Multimedia

`http://spiderman.bu.edu`

Multimedia Survey

A survey of distributed multimedia research, standards, and products by RARE (Associated Networks for European Research).

Keywords: Internet, Multimedia
Audience: Internet Surfers
Details: Free, Multimedia files available.

`ftp://ftp.ed.ac.uk/pub/mmsurvey`

Neci-announce

This is the announcement forum of New England Community Internet, an organization dedicated to making Usenet and Internet accessible to the public without economic or technical barriers. The group is developing ways to bring IP connectivity at low cost into homes and nonprofit organizations.

Keywords: Internet, Usenet
Audience: Internet Surfers, Usenet Users
Contact: neci-announce-request@pioneer.ci.net
Details: Free
User Info: To subscribe to the list, send an e-mail message requesting a subscription to the URL address below.

`mailto:neci-announce-request@pioneer.ci.net`

Neci-digest

This is the daily discussion forum of New England Community Internet, an organization dedicated to making Usenet and Internet accessible to the public without economic or technical-expertise barriers. The group is developing ways to bring IP connectivity at low cost into homes and nonprofit organizations.

Keywords: Internet, Usenet
Audience: Internet Surfers, Usenet Users
Contact: neci-digest-request@pioneer.ci.net
Details: Free
User Info: To subscribe to the list, send an e-mail message requesting a subscription to the URL address below.

`mailto:neci-digest-request@pioneer.ci.net`

Neci-discuss

This is the general discussion forum of New England Community Internet, an organization dedicated to making Usenet and Internet accessible to the public without economic or technical-expertise barriers. The group is developing ways to bring IP connectivity at low cost into homes and nonprofit organizations.

Keywords: Internet, Usenet
Audience: Internet Surfers, Usenet Users
Contact: neci-discuss-request@pioneer.ci.net
Details: Free
User Info: To subscribe to the list, send an e-mail message requesting a subscription to the URL address below.
Notes: To get a daily digestified version, subscribe to neci-digest. To receive organizational announcements only, subscribe to neci-announce.

`mailto:neci-discuss-request@pioneer.ci.net`

Net Etiquette Guide

Guidelines and Netiquette for the Net user.
Keywords: Internet, Etiquette, Netiquette
Sponsor: SURAnet Network Information Center
Audience: Internet Surfers
Contact: info@sura.net
Details: Free
File is: pub/nic/internet.literature/netiquette.txt

`ftp://ftp.sura.net`

Net-News ★★★

A newsletter devoted to library and information resources on the Internet.
Keywords: Information, Libraries, Networking, Internet
Sponsor: Metronet
Audience: Librarians, Researchers
Contact: Dana Noonan
noonan@msus1.msus.edu
Details: Free
Send e-mail request to noonan@msus1.msus.edu or metronet@vz.acs.umn.edu

`gopher://noonan@msus1.msus.edu`

NetCom

NetCom is an Internet provider. It has produced "Net Cruiser" software for Windows.
Keywords: Internet
Audience: Internet Users
Details: Costs

Netcom@netcom.com

New User's Questions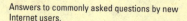

Answers to commonly asked questions by new Internet users.
Keywords: Internet, Internet Guides
Sponsor: Xylogics, Inc., and SRI International
Audience: Internet Surfers
Contact: Gary Scott Malkin, April N. Marine
gmalkin@Xylogics.COM
april@nisc.sri.com
Details: Free
File is: documents/fyi/fyi_04.txt

`ftp://nic.merit.edu`

NIR Archives ★

Archives of the NIR (Networked Information Retrieval) service.
Keywords: Internet, Information Retrieval
Audience: Internet Surfers
Details: Free
Files are in: pub/lists/nir

`ftp:// mailbase.ac.uk`

NIR Gopher ★

The gopher for the NIR (Networked Information Retrieval) service.
Keywords: Internet, Information Retrieval, NIR
Audience: Internet Surfers
Details: Free

`gopher:// mailbase.ac.auk /11/lists-k-o/nic`

NSF Resource Guide ★

A guide to Internet resources from the NSF (National Science Foundation).
Keywords: Internet, Internet Guides
Audience: Internet Surfers
Details: Free
Read the overview in: resource-guide/overview

`ftp://ds.internic.net`

NWNet Internet Guide ★

An introductory guide to the Internet. Details the basic Internet tools of electronic mail, FTP (File Transfer Protocol), and Telnet. Covers types of resources found on the Internet, and how to use them. Includes information directed toward supercomputer users and the K-12 community.
Keywords: Internet, Internet Guides, Supercomputers, Education (K-12)

Sponsor: NorthWestNet
Audience: Internet Surfers, Supercomputer Users, Students (K-12)
Contact: Jonathan Kochmer
nusirg@nwnet.net
Details: Free
File is: /user-docs/nusirg/nusirg.whole-guide.ps

`ftp://ftphost.nwnet.net`

NYSERNet Internet Guide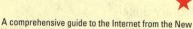

A comprehensive guide to the Internet from the New York State Education and Research Network (NYSERNet). NYSERNet provides access to specialized databases and online libraries, as well as to supercomputing and parallel-processing facilities throughout the US and to many national networks.
Keywords: Internet, Internet Guides, New York, Supercomputers
Sponsor: NYSERNet K-12 Networking Interest Group
Audience: Internet Surfers
Contact: info@nysernet.org
Details: Free

`ftp://nysernet.org`

Ogphre - SunSITE

A collection of Internet resources organized by subject. Particular strengths include agriculture, religious texts, poetry, creative writing, and US politics. The ftp site has a set of more general Internet guides.
Keywords: Agriculture, Politics (US), Religion, Internet
Sponsor: The University of North Carolina - Chapel Hill and Sun Microsystems, USA
Audience: General Public, Internet Surfers, Researchers
Contact: Darlene Fladager, Elizabeth Lyons
Darlene_Fladager@unc.edu,
Elizabeth_Lyons@unc.edu

`gopher://sunsite.unc.edu`

`ftp://sunsite.unc.edu`

Online Radio

Transcripts and promotional information from Online Radio, a weekly radio program of Perth's Curtin University devoted to reporting the latest developments in the computing world.
Keywords: Computers, Internet, Radio
Sponsor: Curtin University Computing Center, Perth, Australia
Audience: Computer Enthusiasts
Contact: Onno Benschop
online@info.curtin.edu.au

`gopher://ob1.curtin.edu.au`

ORA-NEWS

Announcements from O'Reilly & Associates, publishers of books about the Internet, UNIX, and other open systems. Other products and services include The Global Network Navigator (an interactive online magazine) and Internet in a Box. It's gatewayed to the biz.oreilly.announce Usenetnewsgroup.

Keywords: Internet, UNIX, Usenet
Audience: Internet Surfers, Usenet Users, UNIX Users
Contact: listown@online.ora.com
Details: Free, Moderated
User Info: To subscribe to the list, send an e-mail message requesting a subscription to the URL address below.
            To send a message to the entire list, address it to: ora-news@online.ora.com

`mailto:listproc@online.ora.com`

ParNET

To discuss the installation, use, and modification of ParNET, an Amiga<->Amiga networking program.

Keywords: Internet
Audience: ParNet Users
Contact: Ben Jackson
            parnet-list@ben.com
Details: Free
User Info: To subscribe to the list, send an e-mail message requesting a subscription to the URL address below.
            To send a message to the entire list, address it to: parnet-list@ben.com

`mailto:parnet-list-request@ben.com`

PGP Mail

Information regarding the use of PGP (Pretty Good Privacy) mail, a public key.

Keywords: Internet, E-mail
Audience: Internet Surfers
Details: Free

`ftp://ftp.uu.net/networking/mail`

Privacy

An archive about identity, privacy, and anonymity on the Internet, from the Usenet newsgroup alt.privacy.

Keywords: Privacy, Internet
Audience: Internet Surfers
Details: Free
            File is: pub/nic/internet.literature/netiquette.txt

`ftp://pit-manager.mit.edu`

PSI

PSI is an Internet service provider.

Keywords: Internet
Sponsor: PSI
Audience: Internet Users
Details: Costs

`telnet://psi.com`

Retrieval Success

Succesfull stories of using the Internet for reference. In each case, a librarian used Internet resources to answer reference questions. In many cases, particularly for the smaller libraries, the Internet provided information that would otherwise have been inaccessible.

Keywords: Internet, Information Retrieval
Audience: Internet Surfers
Contact: Karen Schneider
            kgs@panix.com
Details: Free
            File is: pub/lists/unite/files/internet-stories.txt

`ftp://mailbase.ac.uk`

Searching Gopherspace with Veronica

A resource that conducts Veronica searches over restricted areas of the Internet.

Keywords: WWW, Information Retrieval, Internet
Audience: Reseachers, Students, General Public

`gopher://gopher.well.sf.ca.us/11/outbound/veronica.search`

Singapore DMC

The Digital Media Center (DMC) home page contains links related to contents about Singapore, the National Computer Board (NCB), and various other National IT (Information Technology) projects.

Keywords: Internet, Networking
Audience: Internet Surfers
Contact: shaopin@ncb.gov.sg
            kianjin@ncb.gov.sg
Details: Free

`http://king.ncb.gov.sg`

Smiley Faces Dictionary

An unofficial list of more than 200 smilies.

Keywords: Internet, Smiley
Audience: Internet Surfers
Details: Free
User Info: File is: /pub/smiley-dictionary

`http://ftp.gsfc.nasa.gov`

Surfing the Internet

An introductory guide to "surfing," or finding information on the Internet.

Keywords: Internet, Internet Guides, Surfing (internet)
Audience: Internet Surfers
Details: Free

`ftp://rtfm.mit.edu`

The Scout Report

The Scout Report is a weekly publication offered by InterNIC Information Services to the Internet community as a fast, convenient way to stay informed on network activities.

Keywords: WWW, Information Retrieval, Internet, Computer Networking
Sponsor: National Science Foundation, USA
Audience: Researchers, Students, General Public
Profile: The purpose of this resource is to combine in one place the highlights of new resource announcements and other news which occurred on the Internet during the previous week. The Report is released every Friday. Categories included each week will vary depending on content, and the report will evolve with time and with input from the networking community.
Contact: InfoGuide
            scout@is.internic.net,
            guide@is.internic.net

`http://www.internic.net/scout-report`

The World Wide Web Acronym Server

This web site is a guide to acronyms and abbreviations used on

Keywords: Internet, Lexicography
Audience: Internet Surfers
Contact: Peter Flynn
            pflynn@curia.ucc.ie
Details: Free

`http://curia.ucc.ie/info/net/acronyms/acro.html`

UNITE Archive

The User Network Interface to Everything (UNITE) discussion list. The list is a focus for discussion on the concept of a total solution interface with user-friendly, desktop-integrated, access to all network services.

A
B
C
D
E
F
G
H
I
J
K
L
M
N
O
P
Q
R
S
T
U
V
W
X
Y
Z

Keywords: Internet, Information Retrieval, Interface Design
Audience: Internet Surfers
Contact: George Munroe, Jill Foster
unite-request@mailbase.ac.uk
Details: Free
Files are in: pub/lists/unite

`ftp://mailbase.ac.uk`

Usenet Repository

★

Regular informational postings and FAQs from various newsgroups on the Usenet, grouped into archives by newsgroup.

Keywords: Internet, Networking, Usenet
Audience: Internet Surfers
Details: Free
File is: pub/usenet-by-group

`ftp://pit-manager.mit.edu`

What is the Internet?

★

An introductory guide to the Internet.

Keywords: Internet
Sponsor: University of Illinois and Merit Network, Inc.
Audience: Internet Surfers
Contact: Ed Krol , Ellen Hoffman
e-krol@uiuc.edu or ellen@merit.edu
Details: Free
File is: documents/fyi/fyi_20.txt

`ftp://nic.merit.edu`

World Wide Web Worm (WWWW)

★★★★

WWWW provides a mechanism to search the WWW in a multitude of ways. It also provides lists of all Home pages and of all URLs cited anywhere. This site contains an exhaustive list of WWW servers nationally and internationally.

Keywords: WWW, Information Retrieval, Internet
Sponsor: University of Colorado at Boulder, Department of Computer Science, Boulder, Colorado, USA
Audience: Researchers, Students, General Public
Contact: Oliver McBryan
mcbryan@cs.colorado.edu

`http://www.cs.colorado.edu/home/mcbryan/WWWW.html`

Zen and the Art of the Internet

★

A beginner's guide to the Internet.

Keywords: Internet
Audience: Internet Surfers

Contact: Brendan Kehoe
guide-bugs@cs.widener.edu
Details: Free
User Info: File is: /net/zen/zen-1.0.txt

`ftp://csn.org`

Internet Access

FreeNets

★★★

This resource provides extensive information about FreeNets, which are public access Internet sites at no-charge or for donations.

Keywords: Internet Access, Community Networking
Audience: Individuals, Communities, Libraries
Profile: FreeNets, community computing services providing Internet access, exist internationally and include such systems as LA FreeNet, Buffalo FreeNet, Cleveland FreeNet, FreeNet Erlangen-Nuernburg, Victoria FreeNet, Vaasa FreePort (Finland), CapAccess (D.C.), and many more.
Details: Free
The URL (gopher path) below, contains pointers to all FreeNets.

`gopher path: 1/internet/freenets marvel.loc.gov`

Internet Art Gallery

Internet Art Gallery

★★

An online art collection in the form of JPEG files, including the works of 85 artists ranging from Dali to Van Eyck.

Keywords: Art, Fine Art, Art History
Sponsor: New York State Education Department
Audience: Artists, Art Students, Art Teachers, General Public
Contact: Steve Richter, George Casler
steve@unix5.nysed.gov,
gcasler@unix5.nysed.gov

`gopher://unix5.nysed.gov`

Internet Browsers

Internet Browsers

★★

A list of sources for Internet browsers and client software.

Keywords: Internet, Internet Tools
Sponsor: ANU Bioinformatics Hypermedia Service
Audience: Internet Surfers

Contact: David Green
David.Green@anu.edu.au
Details: Free

`http://life.anu.edu.au/links/syslib.html`

Internet Chess Library

Internet Chess Library

An FTP and gopher site containing all kinds of chess-related files.

Keywords: Chess
Audience: Chess Players
Profile: The Internet Chess Library is an FTP and gopher site with archives containing all kinds of chess-related files. The library contains chess software of different types, schedules, international chess announcements, rating guides, and anything else relating to chess.
Contact: Chris Petroff
chris@chess.uaknor.edu

`gopher://chess.uaknor.edu`

`ftp://chess.uaknor.edu`

Internet Companion

Internet Companion

★

A beginner's guide to global networking.

Keywords: Internet, Internet Guides
Sponsor: Software Tool & Die
Audience: Internet Surfers
Contact: staff@world.std.com
Details: Free
User Info: Files are in: OBS/
The.Internet.Companion

`ftp://world.std.com`

Internet Cruise

Internet Cruise

★

A computer-based tutorial for new and experienced Internet "navigators." Provides an introduction to Internet resources as diverse as: supercomputing, minorities, multimedia, cooking, and so on. Also provides information about the tools needed to access those resources.

Keywords: Internet, Internet Guides
Sponsor: Merit Network Information Center, Ann Arbor, MI

Audience:	Internet Surfers	
Contact:	Steve Burdick, Laura Kelleher, Mark Davis-Craig cruise2feedback@merit.edu	
Details:	Free	
User Info:	File is located in: /internet/resources	

`ftp://nic.merit.edu`

Internet Directories

The McKinley Group

A resource for the location of US and international data, to assist in the preparation of Geographic Information Systems (GIS). Specializes also in locating copies of old advertisements from anywhere in the world.

Keywords:	Internet Publishing, Internet Directories, Internet Marketing, Internet Research
Audience:	Management Information Specialists, Market Researchers, Lawyers
Profile:	Provision of strategic information to assist organizations and businesses in targeting their markets more effectively. Specializes in obtaining hard-to-locate information for the creation of Geographic Information Systems. Resource include old advertisements from newspapers and magazines worldwide.
Details:	Costs
User Info:	To subscribe, send an e-mail message to the URL address below. In the body of your message, state the nature of your inquiry.

`mailto:mckinley@holonet.net`

Internet Economics

Internet Economics

An article entitled "Some Economics of the Internet," by Jeffrey K. Mackie-Mason.

Keywords:	Economics, Internet
Audience:	Internet Surfers
Contact:	Jeffrey K. Mackie-Mason
Details:	Free

`ftp://gopher.econ.lsa.umich.edu`

Internet FAQs and Guides

Internet FAQs and Guides

A collection of introductory Internet information, including guides to netiquette, jargon, and utilities, such as ftp and telnet.

Keywords:	Internet Resources
Sponsor:	University of Wisconsin - Stevens Point
Audience:	Internet Surfers
Contact:	Peter Zuge gopher@worf.uwsp.edu

`gopher://nt2.uwsp.edu`

Internet Federal Register (IFR)

Internet Federal Register (IFR) ★★★★

The full text of the US Federal Register.

Keywords:	Federal Register, Government (US Federal), Law (US Federal)
Sponsor:	Counterpoint Publishing
Audience:	General Public, Journalists, Students, Politicians, Citizens
Contact:	fedreg@internet.com
Details:	Costs

`gopher://gopher.internet.com`

Internet GIS and RS Information Sites

Internet GIS and RS Information Sites ★★

This document contains a lengthy listing of GIS and remote sensing sites on the Internet.

Keywords:	GIS, Remote Sensing, Image Processing, Geography
Sponsor:	Queen's University Department of Geography
Audience:	Researchers, General Public
Contact:	Michael McDermott mcdermom@gisdog.gis.queensu.ca
Details:	Free
Notes:	ASCII version also available from the same FTP site.

`ftp://gis.queensu.ca/pub/gis/docs/gissites.html`

Internet Guides

AARNet Guide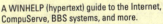

This is the Australian Network Sites and Resources Guide.

Keywords:	Internet, Internet Guide
Sponsor:	Australian Academic and Research Network
Audience:	Internet Surfers
Details:	Free Files are in: pub/resource-guide

`ftp://aarnet.edu.au/pub/resource-guide`

DDN New User Guide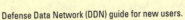

Defense Data Network (DDN) guide for new users.

Keywords:	Internet, Internet Guides, Defense, Security
Audience:	Internet Surfers
Details:	Free File is: netinfo/nug.doc

`ftp://nic.ddn.mil/netinfo`

E-mail-How To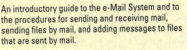

An introductory guide to the e-Mail System and to the procedures for sending and receiving mail, sending files by mail, and adding messages to files that are sent by mail.

Keywords:	Internets Tools, Internet Guides, E-mail
Sponsor:	SURAnet Network Information Center
Audience:	Internet Surfers
Contact:	info@sura.net
Details:	Free File is: pub/nic/network.service.guides/how.to.email.guide

`ftp://ftp.sura.net`

Infopop

A WINHELP (hypertext) guide to the Internet, CompuServe, BBS systems, and more.

Keywords:	Internet, Internet Guides
Sponsor:	Fenwick Library, George Mason University, Fairfax, VA
Audience:	Internet Surfers
Contact:	Wally Grotophorst wallyg@fen1.gmu.edu
Details:	Free
User Info:	Read the file: library/readme

`ftp://ftp.gmu.edu`

Internet Companion

A beginner's guide to global networking.

Keywords:	Internet, Internet Guides
Sponsor:	Software Tool & Die
Audience:	Internet Surfers
Contact:	staff@world.std.com
Details:	Free Files are in: OBS/ The.Internet.Companion

```
ftp://world.std.com
```

Internet Cruise ★

A computer-based tutorial for new and experienced Internet "navigators." Provides an introduction to Internet resources as diverse as: supercomputing, minorities, multimedia, cooking, and so on. Also provides information about the tools needed to access those resources.

Keywords:	Internet, Internet Guides
Sponsor:	Merit Network Information Center, Ann Arbor, MI
Audience:	Internet Surfers
Contact:	Steve Burdick, Laura Kelleher, Mark Davis-Craig cruise2feedback@merit.edu
Details:	Free
User Info:	File is located in: /internet/resources

```
ftp://nic.merit.edu
```

Internet Growth

Contains figures showing the growth of the Internet, derived from historical figures and published by Mark Lottor and Marten Terpstra.

Keywords:	Internet, Internet Guides
Sponsor:	Electronic Frontier Foundation
Audience:	Internet Surfers
Details:	Free
User Info:	Files are in: matrix/growth/internet

```
ftp://tic.com
```

Internet Hunt ★

A game for exploring and learning about the Internet. It helps Net users to realize the vast and varied amounts of information available on the Net and helps more novice users, or Net "settlers," understand how to move around using the "trails" that the more experienced Hunt players have "blazed." Contains Internet Hunt questions, results, and comments.

Keywords:	Internet, Internet Guides, Games
Sponsor:	CICnet
Audience:	Internet Surfers
Contact:	Rick Gates rgates@nic.cic.net
Details:	Free

```
gopher://gopher.cic.net
```

Internet Information Listing ★★★★

A comprehensive collection of Internet information and utilities. Includes a listing of Internet providers, a large collection of guide books (NSF Resource Guide, Zen and the Art of the Internet, Big Dummy's Guide, and others), as well as specific help files for Internet utilities such as FTP, Telnet, and IRC. This site also features access to many popular gopher destinations.

Keywords:	Internet Guides
Sponsor:	Phantom Access Technologies, Inc.
Audience:	Internet Surfers
Contact:	root@phantom.com

```
gopher://mindvox.phantom.com
```

Internet Monthly Reports ★

Monthly communications to the Internet Research Group.

Keywords:	Internet, Internet Guides
Sponsor:	Merit Network Information Center Services
Audience:	Internet Surfers
Details:	Free
Index is:	internet/newsletters/ INDEX.internet.monthly.report

```
ftp://nic.merit.edu
```

Internet Phone Books ★★★

A collection of Internet phone books and e-mail directories.

Keywords:	Phone Books, Internet Guides, E-mail
Sponsor:	Texas Tech University
Audience:	Internet Surfers, General Public
Profile:	This gopher includes a number of resources for finding people on the Internet. In addition to the standard Netfind, WHOIS, and Inter-NIC services, it also has information on finding college and international e-mail addresses. Also features snail mail information from the U.S. Post Office on ZIP codes, as well as an international directory of telephone area codes.
Contact:	Abdul Malik Yoosufani gripe@cs.ttu.edu

```
gopher://cs4sun.cs.ttu.edu
```

Internet Services FAQ ★

General information and answers to frequently asked questions (FAQs) about the Internet.

Keywords:	Internet, Internet Guides, FAQs
Audience:	Internet Surfers
Details:	Free
User Info:	File is: pub/usenet/news.answers/ internet-services/faq

```
ftp://rtfm.mit.edu
```

Internet Statistics ★

The latest statistical information about the Internet from the National Science Foundation.

Keywords:	Internet, Internet Guides
Sponsor:	Merit Network Information Center
Audience:	Internet Surfers
Details:	Free

Index is: /nsfnet/statistics/INDEX.statistics

```
ftp://nic.merit.edu
```

Librarian's Internet Reference ★

Electronic version of "Internet Connections: A Librarian's Guide to Dial-Up Access and Use," written by Engle, Mary E, and Marilyn Lutz, William Jones, Jr., and Genevieve Engel.

Keywords:	Internet Guides, Librarianship
Audience:	Librarians
Contact:	Mary Engle Mary_Engle@ucop.edu

```
gopher://gopher.poniecki.berkeley.edu
```

Poniecki Foundation/Internet Guides

Merit Network Information Center Services ★★

This site provides a large collection of Internet guides and information.

Keywords:	Internet, Internet Guides, Internet Tools
Sponsor:	Merit Network, Inc.
Audience:	Internet Surfers
Profile:	This site serves as a clearinghouse for many Internet guides, documents, and utilities. It includes Internet FAQs, bibliographies, glossaries, and user guides such as Zen and the Art of the Internet and The Internet Companion. It also has archives of various Internet documents listing service providers, acceptable use policies, and resources. Many software programs for navigating the Internet are also available here for a wide variety of platforms
Contact:	nic-info@nic.merit.edu

```
gopher://nic.merit.edu
```

```
ftp://nic.merit.edu
```

New User's Questions ★

Answers to commonly asked questions by new Internet users.

Keywords:	Internet, Internet Guides
Sponsor:	Xylogics, Inc., and SRI International
Audience:	Internet Surfers
Contact:	Gary Scott Malkin, April N. Marine gmalkin@Xylogics.COM april@nisc.sri.com
Details:	Free
	File is: documents/fyi/fyi_04.txt

```
ftp://nic.merit.edu
```

NSF Resource Guide ★

A guide to Internet resources from the NSF (National Science Foundation).

Keywords: Internet, Internet Guides
Audience: Internet Surfers
Details: Free
Read the overview in: resource-guide/overview

`ftp://ds.internic.net`

NWNet Internet Guide ★

An introductory guide to the Internet. Details the basic Internet tools of electronic mail, FTP (File Transfer Protocol), and Telnet. Covers types of resources found on the Internet, and how to use them. Includes information directed toward supercomputer users and the K-12 community.

Keywords: Internet, Internet Guides, Supercomputers, Education (K-12)
Sponsor: NorthWestNet
Audience: Internet Surfers, Supercomputer Users, Students (K-12)
Contact: Jonathan Kochmer
nusirg@nwnet.net
Details: Free
File is: /user-docs/nusirg/nusirg.whole-guide.ps

`ftp://ftphost.nwnet.net`

NYSERNet Internet Guide ★

A comprehensive guide to the Internet from the New York State Education and Research Network (NYSERNet). NYSERNet provides access to specialized databases and online libraries, as well as to supercomputing and parallel-processing facilities throughout the US and to many national networks.

Keywords: Internet, Internet Guides, New York, Supercomputers
Sponsor: NYSERNet K-12 Networking Interest Group
Audience: Internet Surfers
Contact: info@nysernet.org
Details: Free

`ftp://nysernet.org`

Surfing the Internet ★

An introductory guide to "surfing," or finding information on the Internet.

Keywords: Internet, Internet Guides, Surfing (internet)
Audience: Internet Surfers
Details: Free

`ftp://rtfm.mit.edu`

The Internet Press ★★★

A guide to electronic journals about the Internet.
Keywords: Internet Guides, Electronic Publications

Audience: General Public
Profile: Publications discussed include the following: NSF Network News, Meta Magazine, Bits and Bytes, The Network Observer, HotWIRED, Scout Report, Netsurfer Digest, and The Internet Informer.
Contact: Kevin M. Savetz
User Info: To subscribe to the list, send an e-mail message to the URL address below, with the subject line subscribe ipress. (Leave the body of the message blank.)

`mailto:savetz@rahul.net`

Usenet What Is? ★

An article entitled "What Is Usenet?"
Keywords: Internet Guides, Internet Tools, Usenet
Audience: Internet Surfers
Details: Free
File is: pub/usenet/news.answers/what-is/usenet/part1

`ftp://rtfm.mit.edu`

Usenet World ★

A special issue of the Amateur Computerist newsletter about Usenet.
Keywords: Internet Guides, Internet Tools, Usenet
Audience: Internet Surfers
Details: Free
File is: doc/misc/acn/acn4-5.txt

`ftp://wuarchive.wustl.edu`

Internet Hunt

Internet Hunt ★

A game for exploring and learning about the Internet. It helps Net users to realize the vast and varied amounts of information available on the Net and helps more novice users, or Net "settlers," understand how to move around using the "trails" that the more experienced Hunt players have "blazed." Contains Internet Hunt questions, results, and comments.

Keywords: Internet, Internet Guides, Games
Sponsor: CICnet
Audience: Internet Surfers
Contact: Rick Gates
rgates@nic.cic.net
Details: Free

`gopher://gopher.cic.net`

Internet Information Listing

Internet Information Listing ★★★★

A comprehensive collection of Internet information and utilities. Includes a listing of Internet providers, a large collection of guide books (NSF Resource Guide, Zen and the Art of the Internet, Big Dummy's Guide, and others), as well as specific help files for Internet utilities such as FTP, Telnet, and IRC. This site also features access to many popular gopher destinations.

Keywords: Internet, Internet Guides
Sponsor: Phantom Access Technologies, Inc.
Audience: Internet Surfers
Contact: root@phantom.com

`gopher://mindvox.phantom.com`

Internet Libraries (Gopher)

Internet Libraries (Gopher) ★★★

The site maintains the most current possible list of all library catalogs accessible on the Internet.
Keywords: Libraries, Databases, Internet, Information Retrieval
Audience: Reseacher, Students, Librarians
Contact: Gopherlib
gopherlib@gopher.yale.edu

`gopher://yaleinfo.yale.edu`

Internet Marketing

The McKinley Group ★★★

A resource for the location of US and international data, to assist in the preparation of Geographic Information Systems (GIS). Specializes also in locating copies of old advertisements from anywhere in the world.

Keywords: Internet Publishing, Internet Directories, Internet Marketing, Internet Research
Audience: Management Information Specialists, Market Researchers, Lawyers
Profile: Provision of strategic information to assist organizations and businesses in targeting their markets more effectively. Specializes in obtaining hard-to-locate information for the creation of Geographic Information Systems. Resource include old advertisements from newspapers and magazines worldwide.
Details: Costs
To subscribe, send an e-mail message to the URL address below.

`mailto:mckinley@holonet.net`

Internet Monthly Reports

Internet Monthly Reports

Monthly communications to the Internet Research Group.

- **Keywords:** Internet, Internet Guides
- **Sponsor:** Merit Network Information Center Services
- **Audience:** Internet Surfers
- **Details:** Free
- **User Info:** internet/newsletters/ INDEX.internet.monthly.report

`ftp://nic.merit.edu`

Internet Multicasting

Internet Multicasting

Answers to frequently asked questions (FAQs) about the Internet Multicasting Service.

- **Keywords:** Internet, Information Retrieval
- **Audience:** Internet Surfers
- **Details:** Free, Sound Files Available. Include "send FAQ" in the e-mail.

`mailto: info@radio.com`

Internet Nonprofit Center

Internet Nonprofit Center

A clearinghouse of information for nonprofit organizations and those interested in donating to them. Includes annual reports, directories, financial information, and brochures of selected nonprofit organizations, as well as volunteer opportunities and advice for potential donors. The Internet Nonprofit Center is currently located on EnviroLink Network, a gopher dedicated to environmental causes.

- **Keywords:** Nonprofit Organizations, Philanthropy
- **Sponsor:** American Institute of Philanthropy, USA, and The Internet Nonprofit Center, Brooklyn, New York, USA
- **Audience:** Activists, Philanthropists
- **Contact:** Cliff Landesman clandesm@panix.com

`gopher://envirolink.org`

Internet Phone Books

Internet Phone Books

A collection of Internet phone books and e-mail directories.

- **Keywords:** Phone Books, Internet Guides, E-mail
- **Sponsor:** Texas Tech University
- **Audience:** Internet Surfers, General Public
- **Profile:** This gopher includes a number of resources for finding people on the Internet. In addition to the standard Netfind, WHOIS, and Inter-NIC services, it also has information on finding college and international e-mail addresses. Also features snail mail information from the U.S. Post Office on ZIP codes, as well as an international directory of telephone area codes.
- **Contact:** Abdul Malik Yoosufani gripe@cs.ttu.edu

`gopher://cs4sun.cs.ttu.edu`

Internet Policy

Internet Policy

An article entitled "What Should We Plan Given the Dilemma of the Network?" by G. Cook.

- **Keywords:** Internet, E-mail
- **Audience:** Internet Surfers
- **Details:** Free

`ftp://pit-manager.mit.edu`

Internet Pricing

Internet Pricing

An article entitled "Pricing the Internet."

- **Keywords:** Internet, Economics
- **Audience:** Internet Surfers
- **Contact:** Mackie-Mason and Varian
- **Details:** Free

`gopher:// gopher.econ.lsa.umich.edu`

Internet Public Subsidies

Internet Public Subsidies

An article entitled "The Economic Case for Public Subsidy of the Internet."

- **Keywords:** Internet, Pricing
- **Audience:** Internet Surfers
- **Contact:** Sandra Schickele
- **Details:** Free

`gopher://ssugopher.sonoma.edu`

Internet Publishing

The McKinley Group

A resource for the location of US and international data, to assist in the preparation of Geographic Information Systems (GIS). Specializes also in locating copies of old advertisements from anywhere in the world.

- **Keywords:** Internet Publishing, Internet Directories, Internet Marketing, Internet Research
- **Audience:** Management Information Specialists, Market Researchers, Lawyers
- **Profile:** Provision of strategic information to assist organizations and businesses in targeting their markets more effectively. Specializes in obtaining hard-to-locate information for the creation of Geographic Information Systems. Resource include old advertisements from newspapers and magazines worldwide.
- **Details:** Costs

To subscribe, send an e-mail message to the URL address below. In the body of your message, state the nature of your inquiry.

`mailto:mckinley@holonet.net`

Internet Reference

Cello FAQ

A site containing common questions and answers about Cello, a multipurpose Internet browser that allows access to the myriad information resources of the Internet. It supports World Wide Web, Gopher, FTP, CSO/pf/qi, and Usenet News retrievals natively, and other protocols (WAIS, Hytelnet, Telnet, and TN3270) through external clients and public gateways.

- **Keywords:** Internet Tools, Internet Reference
- **Sponsor:** Cornell Law School, New York, USA
- **Audience:** Students, Computer Scientists, Researchers

`http://www.law.cornell.edu/cello/cellofaq.html`

comp.infosystems.gopher

A Usenet newsgroup providing information and discussion about the gopher information search tool.

- **Keywords:** Gopher, Information Retrieval
- **Audience:** Internet Surfers
- **User Info:** To subscribe to this Usenet newsgroup, you need access to a newsreader.

`news:comp.infosystems.gopher`

comp.infosystems.wais

A Usenet newsgroup providing information and discussion about the WAIS full-text search tool.

Keywords: WAIS, Information Retrieval
Audience: Internet Surfers
User Info: To subscribe to this Usenet newsgroup, you need access to a newsreader.

`news:comp.infosystems.wais`

comp.infosystems.www

A Usenet newsgroup providing information and discussion about the World Wide Web.

Keywords: WWW, Information Retrieval
Audience: Internet Surfers
User Info: To subscribe to this Usenet newsgroup, you need access to a newsreader.

`news:comp.infosystems.www`

Finding Resources on the Internet

A collection of help files introducing the new user to Internet utilities and resources.

Keywords: Internet Reference, Information Retrieval
Sponsor: Proper Publishing
Audience: Internet Surfers
Contact: info@proper.com

`gopher://proper.com`

FTP FAQ

Common questions and answers about FTP (File Transfer Protocol), FTP sites, and anonymous FTP. General information for the novice FTP user.

Keywords: FTP, Internet Guides
Audience: Students, Computer Scientists, Researchers
Contact: Perry Rovers
         perry.rovers@kub.nl

`ftp://ftp.ifh.de/pub/FAQ/ftp.faq`

HTML FAQ

Common questions and answers about HTML (Hypertext Markup Language). The FAQ covers the practices of creating new documents specifically for the WWW format, as well as transforming existing materials into WWW documents.

Keywords: WWW, Internet Reference, Information Retrieval
Audience: Students, Computer Scientists, Researchers
Contact: Iain O'Cain
         ec@umcc.umich.edu

`http://www.umcc.umich.edu/~ec/www/html_faq.html`

Lynx FAQ

A resource providing common questions and answers about Cello, a distributed hypertext browser with full WWW capabilities.

Keywords: Internet Reference
Sponsor: University of Kansas, Distributed Computing Group, Kansas, USA
Audience: Students, Computer Scientists, Researchers
Contact: Garrett Blythe, Lou Montulli
         doslynx@falcon.cc.ukans.edu,
         montulli@mcom.com, lynx-help@ukanaix.cc.ukans.edu

`http://ftp2.cc.ukans.edu/about_lynx`

`http://ftp2.cc.ukans.edu/lynx_help`

`http://ftp2.cc.ukans.edu/lynx_writeup`

NCSA Mosaic FAQ

Common questions and answers about NCSA Mosaic, a network information browser (more technically, a World Wide Web Client) that allows one to retrieve documents from the World Wide Web system. There are versions of Mosaic available for Microsoft Windows on IBM PC-compatible machines, the X Window System on UNIX computers, and for the Apple Macintosh.

Keywords: Internet Reference
Sponsor: National Center for Supercomputing Applications at the University of Illinois at Urbana-Champaign, Illinois, USA
Audience: Students, Computer Scientists, Researchers
Contact: Software Development Group
         softdev@ncsa.uiuc.edu

`http://www.ncsa.uiuc.edu/SDG/Software/MacMosaic/FAQ/FAQ-mac.html`

Veronica FAQ

A gopher containing common questions and answers about Veronica, a title search and retrieval system for use with the Internet Gopher.

Keywords: Internet Reference, Information Retrieval, Veronica
Audience: Students, Computer Scientists, Researchers

`gopher://pogonip.scs.unr.edu/00/veronica/veronica-faq`

WAIS FAQ

Common questions and answers about WAIS (Wide Area Information Servers), a networked full-text retrieval system.

Keywords: Internet Reference
Sponsor: Thinking Machines, Apple Computer, Dow Jones, and KPMG Peat Marwick
Audience: Students, Computer Scientists, Researchers
Contact: Aydin Edguer
         edguer.ces.cwru.edu

`ftp://rtfm.mit.edu/pub/usenet-by-group/news.answers/wais-faq/getting-started`

World Wide Web FAQ

A web site containing common questions and answers about WWW, a distributed hypermedia system first developed by CERN.

Keywords: WWW, Internet Reference, Information Retrieval
Audience: Students, Computer Scientists, Researchers
Contact: Thomas Boutell, Nathan Torkington
         boutell@netcom.com,
         nathan.torckington@vuw.ac.nz

`http://sunsite.unc.edu/boutell/faq/www_faq.html`

Internet Research

Research on Demand

A resource for the provision of market information, strategic information location, product information, and national and international business information.

Keywords: Market Research, Internet Research, Legal Research, International Research
Audience: Marketing Specialists, Lawyers, Public Relations Experts, Business Professionals, Researchers, Writers, Producers
Profile: This resource has special access to unique information resources worldwide. Areas of particular information access include the former Soviet Union, Europe, and the US. Information access also includes access to all the major online systems, including Dialog, BRS, Orbit, DataStar, and so on. Current Awareness Services include research information gathered from the Internet.
Details: Costs
User Info: To subscribe, send an e-mail message to the URL address below. In the body of your message, state the nature of your inquiry.
Notes: Contact ROD directly in the US at: (800) 227-0750; outside the US at: (510) 841-1145.

`mailto:rod@holonet.net`

The McKinley Group

A resource for the location of US and international data, to assist in the preparation of Geographic Information Systems (GIS). Specializes also in locating copies of old advertisements from anywhere in the world.

Keywords: Internet Publishing, Internet Directories, Internet Marketing, Internet Research

Audience: Management Information Specialists, Market Researchers, Lawyers

Profile: Provision of strategic information to assist organizations and businesses in targeting their markets more effectively. Specializes in obtaining hard-to-locate information for the creation of Geographic Information Systems. Resource include old advertisements from newspapers and magazines worldwide.

Details: Costs

To subscribe, send an e-mail message to the URL address below. In the body of your message, state the nature of your inquiry.

`mailto:mckinley@holonet.net`

Internet Resources

FYI on Questions and Answer Answers to Commonly asked New Internet User Questions

Answers to questions commonly asked by new Internet users.

Keywords: Directories, Internet Resources
Sponsor: Xylogics, Inc., and SRI International
Audience: Internet Surfers
Profile: File is: documents/fyi/RFC_1594.txt
Contact: Gary Scott Malkin, April N. Marine
gmalkin@Xylogics.com or
april@nisc.sri.com
Details: Free

`ftp://nic.merit.edu`

Internet FAQs and Guides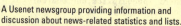

A collection of introductory Internet information, including guides to netiquette, jargon, and utilities, such as ftp and telnet.

Keywords: Internet Resources
Sponsor: University of Wisconsin - Stevens Point
Audience: Internet Surfers
Contact: Peter Zuge
gopher@worf.uwsp.edu

`gopher://nt2.uwsp.edu`

Music

This directory is a general compilation of information resources focused on music.

Keywords: Internet Resources, Music
Audience: Musicians, Music Enthusiasts
Details: Free

`ftp://una.hh.lib.umich.edu/70/inetdirsstacks/music:robinson`

news.announce.newgroups

A Usenet newsgroup providing information and discussion about creating a new newsgroup, changing active newsgroups, and how to access new Usenet groups.

Keywords: Usenet, Internet Resources
Audience: Usenet Users
Details: Free
User Info: To subscribe to this Usenet newsgroup, you need access to a newsreader.

`news:news.announce.newgroups`

news.answers

A Usenet newsgroup providing information and discussion about periodic Usenet articles.

Keywords: Usenet, Internet Resources
Audience: Usenet Users
Details: Free
User Info: To subscribe to this Usenet newsgroup, you need access to a newsreader.

`news:news.answers`

news.groups

A Usenet newsgroup providing information and discussion about lists of existing newsgroups.

Keywords: Usenet, Internet Resources
Audience: Usenet Users
Details: Free
User Info: To subscribe to this Usenet newsgroup, you need access to a newsreader.

`news:news.groups`

news.lists

A Usenet newsgroup providing information and discussion about news-related statistics and lists.

Keywords: Usenet, Internet Resources
Audience: Usenet Users
Details: Free
User Info: To subscribe to this Usenet newsgroup, you need access to a newsreader.

`news:news.lists`

news.newusers.questions

A Usenet newsgroup providing information and discussion about how

Keywords: Usenet, E-mail, Internet Resources
Audience: Usenet Users, E-mail Users
Details: Free
User Info: To subscribe to this Usenet newsgroup, you need access to a newsreader.

`news:news.newusers.questions`

The InterNIC Home Page

This is the home page for the InterNIC networking organization.

Keywords: WWW, Information Retrieval, Computer Science, Internet Resources
Sponsor: National Science Foundation, USA
Audience: Reseachers, Students, General Public
Profile: The InterNIC is a collaborative project of three organizations, which work together to offer the Internet community a full scope of network information services. These services include providing information about accessing and using the Internet, assistance in locating resources on the network, and registering network components for Internet connectivity. The overall goal of the InterNIC is to make networking and networked information more easily accessible to researchers, educators, and the general public. The term InterNIC signifies cooperation between Network Information Centers, or NICS.
Contact: InfoGuide
guide@internic.net
Details: InterNIC signifies cooperation between Network Information Centers

`http://www.internic.net`

Internet Resources for Earth Sciences

Internet Resources for Earth Sciences

A document detailing Internet resources for a variety of earth science disciplines, including GIS.

Keywords: Directory, GIS, Geology, Geography, GPS, Mapping, Earth Science
Sponsor: Bill Thoen
Audience: Earth Scientists, Researchers
Profile: A complete document detailing the types of information available in earth sciences and the mechanisms to retrieve needed information.
Contact: Bill Thoen
bthoen@gisnet.com

Details: Free

```
ftp://ftp.csn.org/COGS/ores.text
```

Internet Resources for Geographic Information and GIS

Internet Resources for Geographic Information and GIS

An HTML document with information on all aspects of GIS.

Keywords: GIS, Geography
Sponsor: Bates College - Department of Classical and Romance Languages
Audience: GIS Professionals
Contact: Neel Smith
nsmith@abacus.bates.edu
Details: Free

```
http://abacus.bates.edu/~nsmith/
General/Resources-GIS.html
```

Internet Security

firewalls

A mailing list to discuss the issues involved in setting up and maintaining Internet security firewall systems.

Keywords: Security, Internet Security, Firewalls
Audience: Security Workers
Contact: Brent Chapman
Brent@GreatCircle.com
Details: Free
User Info: To subscribe to the list, send an e-mail message consisting of a single line reading:

SUB firewalls YourFirstName YourLastName

```
mailto:majordomo@greatcircle.com
```

Internet Services FAQ

Internet Services FAQ

General information and answers to frequently asked questions (FAQs) about the Internet.

Keywords: Internet, Internet Guides, FAQs
Audience: Internet Surfers
Details: Free
User Info: File is: pub/usenet/news.answers/internet-services/faq

```
ftp://rtfm.mit.edu
```

Internet Services

E-mail WWW

E-mail WWW allows the user to obtain a web file via e-mail.

Keywords: Internet Services, E-mail, WWW
Audience: Internet Surfers
Details: Free
Include the words "www URL" in the e-mail.

```
http://info.cern.ch/hypertext/WWW/
TheProject.html
```

FAXNET

FAXNET allows the user to send faxes via e-mail.

Keywords: Internet Services, E-mail
Audience: Internet Surfers
Details: Free
Include the word "help" in the e-mail.

```
mailto:info@awa.com
```

Finger Database

This service allows access to a database facility via finger.

Keywords: Internet Services, Finger (Internet Database)
Audience: Internet Surfers
Contact: http://www.usyd.edu.au
Details: Free

```
finger://help@dir.su.oz.au
```

Knowbot

Knowbot provides a uniform user interface to heterogenous remote information services.

Keywords: Internet Services, Knowbot
Audience: Internet Surfers
Details: Free
Login; Send: email address

```
telnet://info.cnri.reston.va.us
```

MarketBase Gopher

An online catalog of goods and services dedicated to providing a forum where buyers and sellers meet to electronically exchange the attributes of products and services. Free access is provided to product purchasers.

Keywords: Internet Services, MarketBase
Audience: Internet Surfers
Contact: help@mb.com

Details: Free

```
gopher://mb.com
```

UNC-CH Info system

The University of North Carolina at Chapel Hill's campus-wide information server, providing access to a wide range of campus information and to electronic information services worldwide.

Keywords: Education, Internet Services
Sponsor: University of North Carolina at Chapel Hill
Audience: Educators, Researchers, Internet Surfers
Contact: info@unc.edu
Details: Free

```
gopher://gibbs.oit.unc.edu
```

Internet Shopping Network

Internet Shopping Network

A shopping network on the Infobahn.

Keywords: Business, Electronic Commerce
Sponsor: Internet Shopping Network
Audience: Business Users, General Public
Profile: The Internet Shopping Network aims to conduct research and develop products and services that commercialize the Internet, for the purpose of retailing and mass merchandising. The stores within this network offer approximately 20,000 products from 1000 vendors.

```
http://www.internet.net
```

Internet Sound

Internet Sound

Internet Sound contains various documents and programs regarding sound.

Keywords: Internet, Information Retrieval
Audience: Internet Surfers
Contact: Guido van Rossum
ftp://ftp.cwi.nl/pub/audio/INDEX
ftp://ftp.cwi.nl/pub/audio/index.html
Details: Free, Sound files available.
The index is: pub/audio/INDEX

```
ftp://ftp.cwi.nl
```

394 Internet Statistics

Internet Statistics

Internet Statistics ★

The latest statistical information about the Internet from the National Science Foundation.

Keywords: Internet, Internet Guides
Sponsor: Merit Network Information Center
Audience: Internet Surfers
Details: Free
Index is: /nsfnet/statistics/INDEX.statistics

`ftp://nic.merit.edu`

Internet Systems UNITE

Internet Systems UNITE ★

A list of tools for use on the Internet, by UNITE (User Network Interface to Everything).

Keywords: Internet, Internet Tools
Audience: Internet Surfers
Contact: unite-request@mailbase.ac.uk
Details: Free
User Info: File is: pub/lists/unite/files/systems-list.txt

`ftp://mail.base.ac.uk`

Internet Tools

Alex Description ★

An NIR (Network Information Retrieval) description of Alex, an Internet access tool.

Keywords: Internet Tools, Internet, Alex
Audience: Internet Surfers
Details: Free
File is: usr0/anon/doc/NIR.Tool

`ftp://alex.sp.cs.cmu.edu/usr0/anon/doc/NIR.Tool`

Arachnophilia: Florida Institute of Technology's WWW server. ★★

Provides pointers to information resources and search tools around the Web. Specifically for use by educators and researchers.

Keywords: Internet Tools
Audience: Educators, Researchers
Contact: www@sci-ed.fit.edu
Details: Free

`http://sci-ed.fit.edu`

Archie ★

A description of Archie, an electronic directory service for the Internet, which allows the user to find files remotely.

Keywords: Internet Tools, Archie
Sponsor: Computing Centre, McGill University, Montreal, Quebec, Canada
Audience: Internet Surfers
Contact: archie-group@archie.mcgill.ca
Details: Free
File is: pub/archie/doc/whatis.archie

`ftp://archie.ans.net`

Archie Demo ★

A Telnet demonstration of Archie, an Internet access tool.

Keywords: Internet Tools, Archie
Audience: Internet Surfers
Details: Free

`telnet://archie@archie.ans.net (login; Send: archie)`

Archie Hypertext Servers ★

A list of hypertext Archie servers around the world.

Keywords: Internet Tools, Archie
Sponsor: NEXOR
Audience: Internet Surfers
Contact: Martijn Koster
         m.koster@nexor.co.uk
Details: Free

`http://web.nexor.co.uk.archie.html`

Archie Manual ★

A reference manual for Archie, an Internet access tool.

Keywords: Internet Tools, Archie
Audience: Internet Surfers
Contact: R. Rodgers, Nelson N. Beebe, A. Emtage
         rodgers@maxwell.mmwb.ucsf.edu,
         beebe@math.utah.edu
Details: Free
File is: pub/archie/doc/archie.man.txt

`ftp://archie.ans.net`

Cello ★

A DOS-based Internet browser incorporating WWW (World-Wide Web), Gopher, FTP, Telnet, and usenet.

Keywords: Internet Tools, Cello, DOS
Audience: Internet Surfers
Details: Free

`ftp://fatty.law.cornell.edu`
`gopher://fatty.law.cornell.edu`
`http://fatty.law.cornell.edu`

Cello FAQ ★★★★

A site containing common questions and answers about Cello, a multipurpose Internet browser which allows access to the myriad information resources of the Internet. It supports World Wide Web, Gopher, FTP, CSO/pf/qi, and Usenet News retrievals natively, and other protocols (WAIS, Hytelnet, Telnet, and TN3270) through external clients and public gateways.

Keywords: Internet Tools, Internet Reference
Sponsor: Cornell Law School, New York, USA
Audience: Students, Computer Scientists, Researchers

`http://www.law.cornell.edu/cello/cellofaq.html`

Entering the WWW ★

An article entitled "Entering the World-Wide Web: A Guide to Cyberspace."

Keywords: Internet Tools, WWW
Sponsor: Honolulu Community College
Audience: Internet Surfers
Contact: Kevin Hughes
         kevinh@pulua.hcc.hawaii.edu
Details: Free

`http://www.hcc.hawaii.edu/guide/www.guide.html`

E-mail-How To ★

An introductory guide to the UNIXMail System and to the procedures for sending and receiving mail, sending files by mail, and adding messages to files that are sent by mail.

Keywords: Internets Tools, Internet Guides, E-mail
Sponsor: SURAnet Network Information Center
Audience: Internet Surfers
Contact: info@sura.net
Details: Free
File is: pub/nic/network.service.guides/how.to.email.guide

`ftp://ftp.sura.net`

Essence ★

A description of Essence, an Internet resource discovery system based on semantic file indexing.

Keywords: Internet Tools, Essence (Internet Resource Directory)
Sponsor: University of Colorado, Boulder, CO

Audience: Internet Surfers
Contact: Darren R. Hardy, Michael F. Schwartz
hardy@cs.colorado.edu or
schwartz@cs.colorado.edu
Details: Free
File is: pub/cs/distribs/essence/README

`ftp://.cs.colorado.edu`

FTP-How To

A short guide to using anonymous FTP, an Internet access tool.
Keywords: Internet Tools, FTP
Sponsor: SURAnet Network Information Center
Audience: Internet Surfers
Contact: info@sura.net
Details: Free
File is: pub/nic/network.service.guides/how.to.ftp.guide

`ftp://ftp.sura.net`

FTP Setup

Tips on using FTP, an Internet access tool.
Keywords: Internet Tools, FTP
Sponsor: Carnegie Mellon University, Pittsburgh, PA
Audience: Internet Surfers
Details: Free
File is: pub/tech_tips/anonymous_ftp

`ftp://cert.org`

Gopher

A guide to using gopher, an Internet access tool that locates and retrieves resources using a graph of menus.
Keywords: Internet Tools, Gopher
Audience: Internet Surfers
Contact: gopher@boombox.micro.umn.edu
Details: Free
File is: pub/gopher/00README

`ftp://boombox.micro.umn.edu`

Gopher Demo

A session demonstrating gopher at the University of Minnesota.
Keywords: Internet Tools, Gopher
Audience: Internet Surfers

`gopher:// gopher.micro.umn.edu`

Gopher FAQ

Answers to frequently asked questions (FAQs) about gophers from the Usenet newsgroup comp.infosystems.gopher
Keywords: Internet Tools, Gopher
Audience: Internet Surfers
Contact: Paul Lindner
lindner@boombox.micro.umn.edu
Details: Free
File is: pub/usenet/news.answers/gopher-faq

`ftp://pit-manager.mit.edu`

Gopher Jewels

A searchable catalog of outstanding gopher sites worldwide.
Keywords: Gopher, Internet Tools
Audience: Internet Surfers, Researchers
Profile: Gopher Jewels, indexed by subject and searchable through WAIS, allows access to more than 2,000 gopher sites. The main server also has archives of the Gopher Jewels listserv, and extensive help and FAQ files on the uses of gopher. It is also available as a WWW site.
Contact: David Riggins
david.riggins@tpoint.com
gopherjewels-comment@einet.net
Details: Free

`gopher://cwis.usc.edu/11/Other_Gophers_and_Information_Resources/Gopher_Jewels`

`http://galaxy.einet.net/gopher/gopher.html`

Gopher Sites

A list of worldwide gopher sites (sorted by domain structure) available on the Internet.
Keywords: Internet Tools, Gopher
Sponsor: Washington & Lee University, Lexington, VA
Audience: Internet Surfers
Details: Free
File is: pub/lawlib/veronica.gopher.sites

`ftp://liberty.uc.wlu.edu`

Gopher Telnet Demo

A Telnet session demonstrating the use of gopher.
Keywords: Internet Tools, Gopher
Audience: Internet Surfers
Details: Free

`telnet://gopher@consultant.micro.umn.ed`

Gopher/Veronica-How To

A special issue of the University of Illinois publication describing gopher and Veronica.
Keywords: Internet Tools, Gopher, Veronica
Sponsor: University of Illinois, Urbana, IL
Audience: Internet Surfers
Details: Free
File is: doc/net/uiucnet/vol6no1.txt

`ftp://ftp.cso.uiuc.edu`

Hytelnet

A hypertext database of publicly accessible Internet sites.
Keywords: Internet Tools, Hytelnet
Audience: Internet Surfers
Profile: Hytelnet currently lists over 1,400 sites, including libraries, campus-wide information systems, Gopher, WAIS, and WWW systems, and Freenets.
Contact: Earl Fogel
earl.fogel@usask.ca
Details: Free
File is: pub/hytelnet/README

`ftp://ftp.usask.ca`

Internet Browsers

A list of sources for Internet browsers and client software.
Keywords: Internet, Internet Tools
Sponsor: ANU Bioinformatics Hypermedia Service
Audience: Internet Surfers
Contact: David Green
David.Green@anu.edu.au
Details: Free

`http://life.anu.edu.au/links/syslib.html`

Internet Systems UNITE

A list of tools for use on the Internet, by UNITE (User Network Interface to Everything).
Keywords: Internet, Internet Tools
Audience: Internet Surfers
Contact: unite-request@mailbase.ac.uk
Details: Free
File is: pub/lists/unite/files/systems-list.txt

`ftp://mail.base.ac.uk`

Internet Tools EARN

A guide to network research tools by the European Academic Research Network (EARN).

Keywords: Internet, Internet Tools
Audience: Internet Surfers
Contact: listserv@earncc.bitnet
Details: Free
User Info: The file is: earn/earn-resource-tool-guide.txt

`ftp://ns.ripe.net`

Internet Tools HTML

An html version of a list summarizing Internet tools for network information retrieval (NIR) and computer-mediated communication (CMC) forums; it is useful in a WWW server.

Keywords: Internet Tools, Information Retrieval
Audience: Internet Surfers
Contact: John December
decemj@rpi.edu
Details: Free
User Info: Files are located in pub/communications. Read the internet-tools.readme first.

`ftp://ftp.rpi.edu`

Internet Tools NIR

A status report on networked information retrieval (NIR): tools and groups.

Keywords: Internet, Internet Tools
Sponsor: Joint IETF/RARE/CNI Networked Information Retrieval Working Group
Audience: Internet Surfers
Contact: Jill Foster
Jill Foster@newcastle.ac.uk
Details: Free
User Info: File is: pub/lists/nir/files/nir.status.report

`ftp://mail.base.ac.uk`

Internet Tools Summary

A list summarizing Internet tools for network information retrieval (NIR) and computer-mediated communication (CMC) forums.

Keywords: Internet, Internet Tools
Audience: Internet Surfers
Contact: John December
decemj@rpi.edu
Details: Free
User Info: Files are located in: pub/communications. Read the internet-tools.readme first.

`ftp://ftp.rpi.edu`

InterNIC Directory Services (White Pages)

This web site provides free access to X.500, WHOIS, and Netfind white pages on the Internet.

Keywords: WWW Information, Internet, Internet Tools
Sponsor: National Science Foundation, USA
Audience: General Public, Students
Contact: Database Administrator
admin@ds.internic.net

`http://ds.internic.net/ds/dspgwp.html`

Jughead

Jonzy's Universal Gopher Hierarchy Excavation and Display (Jughead) gets menu information from various gopher servers.

Keywords: Internet Tools
Sponsor: University of Utah Computer Center
Audience: Internet Surfers
Contact: Rhett "Jonzy" Jones
jonzy@cc.utah.edu
Details: Free
User Info: File is: pub/gopher/Unix/GopherTools/jughead/jughead.ReadMe

`ftp:// boombox.micro.umn`

List Serv

A mailing list server for group communication.

Keywords: Internet Tools, ListServ
Audience: Internet Surfers
Details: Free

`mailto:listserv@uacsc2.albany`

Merit Network Information Center Services

This site provides a large collection of Internet guides and information.

Keywords: Internet, Internet Guides, Internet Tools
Sponsor: Merit Network, Inc.
Audience: Internet Surfers
Profile: This site serves as a clearinghouse for many Internet guides, documents, and utilities. It includes Internet FAQs, bibliographies, glossaries, and user guides such as Zen and the Art of the Internet and The Internet Companion. It also has archives of various Internet documents listing service providers, acceptable use policies, and resources. Many software programs for navigating the Internet are also available here for a wide variety of platforms.

Contact: nic-info@nic.merit.edu
`gopher://nic.merit.edu`
`ftp://nic.merit.edu`

Mosaic Home Page

This is the welcome page to the National Center for Supercomputing Applications (NCSA) World Wide Web server, which features the Mosaic application. Mosaic provides a network-distributed hypermedia system for information discovery. It is Internet-based and is free for academic, research, and internal commercial use.

Keywords: Internet Tools, Mosaic, WWW
Audience: Internet Surfers
Contact: mosaic-x@ncsa.uiuc.edu
Details: Free

`http://www.ncsa.uiuc.edu/SDG/Software/Mosaic/NCSAMosaicHome.html`

Netfind

Netfind is a service for locating individuals on the Internet.

Keywords: Internet Tools
Sponsor: University of Colorado, Boulder, CO
Audience: Internet Surfers
Contact: Michael F. Schwartz, Panagiotis G. Tsirigotis
schwartz@cs.colorado.edu
panos@cs.colorado.edu
Details: Free
User Info: File is: pub/cs/distribs/netfind/README

`ftp://ftp.cs.colorado.edu`

Pine E-mail

A description of the Program for Internet News and E-mail (PINE), a tool for reading, sending, and managing electronic messages.

Keywords: Internet Tools, E-mail
Audience: Internet Surfers
Details: Free
User Info: File is: mail/pine.blur

`ftp://ftp.cac.washington.edu`

Ping

With Ping, a user requests an "echo" from an Internet host to check status. It is useful for checking to see if a host or gateway is up and functioning.

Keywords: Internet Tools, Ping
Audience: Internet Surfers
Details: Free
User Info: File is: utils/ping/README

`ftp://vixen.cso.uiuc.edu/utils/ping/README`

Prospero

A guide to using Prospero, an Internet access tool that provides a user-centered view of remote files.

Keywords: Internet Tools, Prospero
Audience: Internet Surfers
Contact: info-prospero@ISI.EDU
Details: Free
User Info: Files are in: pub/prospero/doc

`ftp://prospero.isi.edu`

Telnet Access to WWW (World Wide Web)

A server providing free public access to WWW written in both English and Hebrew.

Keywords: WWW, Internet Tools, Jerusalem
Sponsor: Hebrew University of Jerusalem
Audience: Internet Surfers
Contact: RASHTY@www.huji.ac.il
Expect: Username; Send: WWW

`telnet://www.huji.ac.il`

Telnet-How To

An introduction to telnet, an Internet access tool.

Keywords: Internet Tools, Telnet
Sponsor: SURAnet Network Information Center
Audience: Internet Surfers
Contact: info@sura.net
Details: Free
User Info: File is: pub/nic/network.service.guides/how.to.telnet.guide

`ftp://ftp.sura.net`

The Virtual Tourist - WWW Information

This site constitutes an attempt to catalogue and organize WWW sites by geographic location.

Keywords: WWW, Internet Tools
Sponsor: The State University of New York at Buffalo, Buffalo, New York, USA
Audience: Internet Surfers, General Public
Profile: Using CERN's master list of WWW servers, this Mosiac-accessible site is centered around an interactive world map that displays WWW/NIR sites within countries and regions. Multimedia Virtual Tourist guides are available for some countires, providing political, cultural, and historical information.
Contact: Brandon Plewe
plewe@acsu.buffalo.edu

`http://wings.buffalo.edu/world`

Usenet What Is?

An article entitled "What Is Usenet?"

Keywords: Internet Guides, Internet Tools, Usenet
Audience: Internet Surfers
Details: Free
User Info: File is: pub/usenet/news.answers/what-is/usenet/part1

`ftp://rtfm.mit.edu`

Usenet World

A special issue of the Amateur Computerist newsletter about Usenet.

Keywords: Internet Guides, Internet Tools, Usenet
Audience: Internet Surfers
Details: Free
User Info: File is: doc/misc/acn/acn4-5.txt

`ftp://wuarchive.wustl.edu`

Veronica Introduction

Veronica (Very Easy Rodent-Oriented Net-wide Index to Computerized Archives) is an Internet access tool that locates titles of gopher items by keyword search.

Keywords: Internet Tools, Veronica
Audience: Internet Surfers
Details: Free
User Info: File is pub/com.archives/bionet.software/veronica

`ftp://cs.dal.ca`

WAIS

WAIS (Wide Area Information Servers) is an Internet access tool that retrieves resources by searching indexes of databases.

Keywords: Internet Tools, WAIS
Audience: Internet Surfers
Details: Free
User Info: Read wais/README first.

`ftp://think.com`

WAIS, Inc.

WAIS, Inc. provides interactive online publishing systems and services to organizations that publish information over the Internet. The organization's three main goals are: to develop the Internet as a viable means for distributing information electronically; to improve the nature and quality of information available over networks; and to offer better methods to access that information.

Keywords: WWW, Information Retrieval, Publishing, Internet Tools
Sponsor: WAIS, Inc.
Audience: Researchers, Students, General Public, Publishers
Contact: Webmaster
webmaster@wais.com

`http://server.wais.com/`

Whois

Whois is an Internet access tool that provides information on registered network names.

Keywords: Internet Tools, Whois
Sponsor: SRI International Telecommunication Sciences Center
Audience: Internet Surfers
Contact: Nancy C. Fischer
fischer@sri-nic
Details: Free
User Info: File is: documents/rfc/rfc0954.txt

`ftp://nic.merit.edu`

World-Wide Web (WWW)

World-Wide Web (WWW) is an Internet access tool that retrieves resources through a hypertext browser of databases.

Keywords: Internet Tools, WWW
Sponsor: CERN (European Laboratory for Particle Physics)
Audience: Internet Surfers
Details: Free
User Info: Documents and guides are in: pub/www/doc

`ftp://info.cern.ch`

World-Wide Web Demo

A Telnet session demonstrating the World-Wide Web (WWW), an Internet access tool.

Keywords: Internet Tools, WWW
Audience: Internet Surfers
Details: Free
No surname is needed.

`telnet://info.cern.ch`

WWW Catalog

A catalog for World-Wide Web (WWW), an Internet access tool.

Keywords: Internet Tools, WWW
Sponsor: Centre Universitaire d'Informatique, University of Geneva
Audience: Internet Surfers
Details: Free

`http://cui_www.unige.ch`

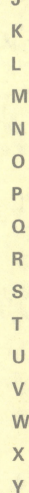

WWW FAQ

Answers to frequently-asked questions (FAQs) about World-Wide Web (WWW), an Internet access tool.

Keywords: Internet Tools, WWW, FAQs
Audience: Internet Surfers
Details: Free

`ftp://info.cern.ch`

X.500

A catalog of available X.500 Implementations, a globally distributed Internet directory service.

Keywords: Internet Tools, X.500
Sponsor: SRI International and Lawrence Berkeley Laboratory
Audience: Internet Surfers
Contact: Ruth Lang, Russ Wright
rlang@nisc.sri.com or wright@lbl.gov
Details: Free
File is: documents/fyi/fyi_11.txt

`ftp://nic.merit.edu`

World-Wide Web Book

A book describing the WWW (World-Wide Web) project.

Keywords: Internet Tools, WWW
Audience: Internet Surfers
Details: Free

`ftp://emx.cc.utexas.edu`

Internet Wiretap

Internet Wiretap

A resource containing electronic books, zines, and government documents, White House press releases, and links to worldwide gopher and WAIS servers.

Keywords: Electronic Media, Cyberculture, Zines
Sponsor: Internet Wiretap
Audience: Cyberculture Enthusiasts, Civil Libertarians, Educators

`gopher://wiretap.spies.com/11/`

`http://wiretap.spies.com`

InterNIC Directory Services (White Pages)

InterNIC Directory Services (White Pages)

This Web site provides free access to X.500, WHOIS, and Netfind white pages on the Internet.

Keywords: WWW Information, Internet, Internet Tools
Sponsor: National Science Foundation, USA
Audience: General Public, Students
Contact: Database Administrator
admin@ds.internic.net

`http://ds.internic.net/ds/dspgwp.html`

Internships

Online Career Center

The Online Career Center gopher provides access to job listings and employment information to member companies and to the public.

Keywords: Employment, Internships
Sponsor: Online Career Center
Audience: Job Seekers
Profile: Online Career Center is a not-for-profit organization funded by its member companies. It is devoted to distributing and exchanging employment and career information between its member companies, human resource professionals, and perspective employees.
Contact: OCC Operator
occ@msen.com

`gopher://gopher.msen.com`

Interpretation

LANTRA-L

A discussion of interpretation and translation.

Keywords: Interpretation, Translation, Language, Linguistics
Audience: Linguists, Interpreters, Translators
Details: Free

`mailto:listserv@searn.bitnet`

InterText

InterText

A network-distributed bimonthly literary magazine.

Keywords: Literature (Contemporary), Journals
Audience: General Public, Writers
Profile: InterText publishes all kinds of material, ranging from mainstream stories to fantasy to horror to science fiction to humor. InterText publishes in both ASCII and PostScript formats, and reaches over 1,000 readers worldwide.
Contact: Jason Snell
jsnell@ocf.berkeley.edu
Details: Free
Select OCF On-Line Library; then select Fiction; then select InterText
Notes: The ASCII version runs approximately 150 KB per issue; if you have tight file gateways, the issue can be split up and squeezed through if need be. The PostScript version runs approximately 500 KB. If you would like to see back issues of InterText, you can FTP them from: network.ucsd.edu(128.54.16.3) in/intertext. Login as anonymous, with your e-mail address as your password.

`gopher://ocf.berkeley.edu`

INTLAW (International Law Library)

INTLAW (International Law Library)

The International Law Library provides comprehensive international law materials.

Keywords: International Law, EEC, Commonwealth, China
Audience: Lawyers, International Lawyers
Profile: The International Law Library provides comprehensive international law materials. The International Law Library contains federal case law, European Community materials, treaties and agreements, Commonwealth law materials, topical and professional journals, French law materials (in French) China law materials, plus relevant topical publications.
Contact: New Sales Group at (800) 227-4908 or 513-859-5398 inside the US, or (513) 865-7981 for all inquires outside the US.
User Info: To subscribe, contact Mead directly.

To examine the Lexis user guide, you can access it at the ftp site of the University of Texas at Austin at the URL address: ftp://ftp.cc.utexas.edu

The files are in: /pub/ref-services/LEXIS

`telnet://nex.meaddata.com`

`http://www.meaddata.com`

INTNAT (International Library)

INTNAT (International Library)

The International Library contains all French treaties, conventions, and agreements that are in effect today, as well as decisions from the Cour Européenne des Droits de l'Homme and the Cour de Justice des Communautes Européennes, and the Journal Officiel des Communautes Européenne.

Keywords: French Law, European Community

Audience: International Lawyers

Profile: The International Library contains all French treaties, conventions, and agreements published before 1958 that are in effect today, as well as decisions from the European Court of Human Rights (Cour Europeenne des Droits de l'Homme), the European Court of Justice (Cour de Justice des Communautes Europeennes) and the Journal Officiel des Communautes Europeenne, the daily record of the European Community.

Contact: New Sales Group at 800-227-4908 or 513-859-5398 inside the US, or (513)-865-7981 for all inquires outside the US.

User Info: To subscribe, contact Mead directly.

To examine the Lexis user guide, you can access it at the ftp site of the University of Texas at Austin at the URL address: ftp://ftp.cc.utexas.edu

The files are in: /pub/ref-services/LEXIS

`telnet://nex.meaddata.com`

`http://www.meaddata.com`

Inventions

Derwent World Patents Index

Derwent World Patents Index and Derwent World Patents Index Latest contain data from nearly 3 million inventions represented in more than 6 million patent documents from 33 patent-issuing authorities around the world.

Keywords: Patents, Inventions

Sponsor: Derwent Publications, Ltd., London, UK

Audience: Science Researchers

Profile: In addition to bibliographic information, the basic patent record includes the full abstract (for new patents issued from 1981 to the present), informative title, International Patent Classification codes, and Derwent subject codes. These files also provide access to equivalent patents, grouped together by patent family in the basic patent record. The use of manual and fragmentation codes is restricted to Derwent subscribers, in accordance with their subscription level.

Pharmaceutical patents are included from 1963 to the present, agricultural chemical patents from 1965 to the present, and polymer and plastics patents from 1966 to the present. Coverage of all chemical patents began in 1970; coverage of all patents, irrespective of subject, began in 1974.

Contact: Dialog in the US at (800) 334-2564, Dialog internationally at country-specific locations.

User Info: To subscribe, contact Dialog directly.

Notes: Coverage: 1963 to the present; updated weekly (file 351) and monthly (file 350).

`telnet://dialog.com`

INVEST (Investment News and Information)

The INVEST library contains company and industry research reports provided through the Investext(R) database. These reports are created by industry experts who are employed for their accurate and insightful evaluation. Only the most recent 12 months of data will be displayed.

Keywords: Companies, Financials, Analysis

Audience: Business Researchers, Analysts, Entrepreneurs

Profile: INVEST is categorized by type. Selections can be made using these categories: Industry (more than 50 industries are available), State (where a specific company is located), Country (Country in which the company is located), and US Broker or International Broker. The INVEST library provides an automatic display following the selection of a file. For industry reports, a menu will appear providing definitions as they relate to the industries. All remaining files will provide a confirmation of the file selected.

Contact: Mead New Sales Group at (800) 227-4908 or (513) 859-5398 inside the US, or (513) 865-7981 for all inquiries outside the US.

User Info: To subscribe, contact Mead directly.

To examine the Nexis user guide, you can access it at the ftp site of the University of Texas at Austin at the URL address: ftp://ftp.cc.utexas.edu

The files are in: /pub/ref-services/LEXIS

`telnet://nex.meaddata.com`

`http://www.meaddata.com`

LEXPAT (Patents US)

The LEXPAT library contains the full text of US patents issued since 1975, the US Patent and Trademark Office Manual of Classification, and the Index to US Patent Classification. The approximately 1,500 patents added to the library each week appear online within four days of their issue.

Keywords: Patents, Inventors, Assignees, Litigants

Audience: Lawyers, Business Researchers, Analysts, Entrepreneurs

Profile: LEXPAT may be searched by individual files for the full text of utility, design, or plant patents, or you can combine the files in one 'omni' search. The Manual, Index, and Class files can be used to supplement your full-text patent searches. LEXPAT is a valuable tool for both patent professionals and for anyone who needs to access to technical information. More than 80 percent of the information contained in patents is unavailable in any other form.

Contact: Mead New Sales Group at (800) 227-4908 or (513) 859-5398 inside the US, or (513) 865-7981 for all inquiries outside the US.

User Info: To subscribe, contact Mead directly.

To examine the Nexis user guide, you can access it at the ftp site of the University of Texas at Austin at the URL address: ftp://ftp.cc.utexas.edu

The files are in: /pub/ref-services/LEXIS

`telnet://nex.meaddata.com`

`http://www.meaddata.com`

U.S. Patent and Trademark Office Database

A database of patents issued in 1994 by the U.S. Patent and Trademark Office, including a searchable index.

Keywords: Patents, Databases, Inventions, Business

Sponsor: New York University School of Business

Audience: Inventors, General Public

Contact: questions@town.hall.org

`gopher://town.hall.org/patent`

Investigators and Detectives

Investigators and Detectives

This resource provides information files for individuals involved with investigative research, as well as a free monthly newsletter.

Keywords: Detectives, Crime, Information Retrieval, Security

Audience: Investigators, Detectives, Information Brokers, General Public

Profile: Investigators and Detectives provides access to information covering topics such as private investigative research, strategies, sources, the art and science of investigating, theft deterrents, and electronic PI schematics and plans. Also offers a free sample of a newsletter covering various topics of interest to Private Investigators, such as techniques and strategies, security, and tracing.

Contact: Mike Enlow
menlow@Intec.win.net,
michael@enlow.com

Details: Inside Secrets.

`mailto:info@enlow.com`

Investments

Experimental Stock Market Data

This is an experimental page that provides a link to the latest stock market information.

Keywords: Stock Market, Investments, Finance

Audience: General Public, Investors, Stock Brokers

Profile: This site is updated automatically to reflect the current day's closing information. Provides general market news and quotes for selected stocks, although prices are not guaranteed. Also includes recent prices for many mutual funds, as well as technical analysis charts for a large number of stocks and mutual funds.

Contact: Mark Torrance
stockmaster@ai.mit.edu

Details: Free

`http://www.ai.mit.edu/stocks.html`

Institutional Real Estate Newsline

Five-page fax briefing with articles regarding institutional real estate, life insurance company, banks, pension fund, real estate investment trust and commercial mortgage backed securities markets.

Keywords: Real Estate, Investments, Insurance

Sponsor: Institutional Real Estate

Audience: Investors

Details: Costs

misc.invest

A Usenet newsgroup providing information and discussion about how to invest money.

Keywords: Investments, Finance

Audience: General Public

Details: Free

User Info: To subscribe to this Usenet newsgroup, you need access to a newsreader.

`news:misc.invest`

misc.invest.real-estate

A Usenet newsgroup providing information and discussion about property investments.

Keywords: Investments, Real Estate

Audience: General Public

Details: Free

User Info: To subscribe to this Usenet newsgroup, you need access to a newsreader.

`news:misc.invest.real-estate`

Stock Market Secrets

Publication of a stock market-related daily commentary. Questions are answered on a wide variety of investment and financial topics.

Keywords: Stock Market, Investments, Finance

Audience: Investors, Stock Brokers, Financial Advisors

Contact: smi-request@world.std.com

Details: Free, Moderated

User Info: To subscribe to the list, send an e-mail message requesting a subscription to the URL address below.

To send a message to the entire list, address it to: smi@world.std.com

`mailto:smi-request@world.std.com`

Yahoo Market and Investments

A comprehensive look at the current economic status, with a wide range of coverage, from brokers to stocks.

Keywords: Business, Stock Market, Investment, Economy

Sponsor: Stanford University, Palo Alto, California, USA

Audience: Investors, Economists

Contact: jerry@akebono.stanford.edu

`http://akebono.stanford.edu/yahoo/Economy/Markets_and_Investments`

Iowa State University

Iowa State University

The library's holdings contain significant collections in many fields.

Keywords: Agriculture, Veterinary Medicine, Statistics, Labor, Soil Conservation, Film

Audience: General Public, Researchers, Librarians, Document Delivery Professionals

Details: Free

Expect: DIAL, Send: LIB

`telnet://isn.iastate.edu`

ipct-j 'Interpersonal Computing and Technology: An Electronic Journal for the 21st Century'

ipct-j 'Interpersonal Computing and Technology: An Electronic Journal for the 21st Century'

Interpersonal Computing and Technology Journal is an outgrowth of the IPCT-L discussion group.

Keywords: Education (Adult), Education (Distance), Education (Continuing), Information Technology

Sponsor: Interpersonal Computing and Technology

Audience: Educators, Administrators, Faculty

Details: Free, Moderated

User Info: To subscribe to the journal, send an e-mail message to the URL address shown below, consisting of a single line reading:

SUB ipct-j YourFirstName YourLastName

`mailto:listserv@guvm.bitnet`

Iran

soc.culture.iranian

A Usenet newsgroup providing information and discussion about Iran and Iranian culture.

Keywords: Iran, Sociology
Audience: Sociologists, Iranians
Details: Free
User Info: To subscribe to this Usenet newsgroup, you need access to a newsreader.

`news:soc.culture.iranian`

irc

irc (Internet Relay Chat)

A multiuser, multichannel chatting network. It allows people all over the Internet to "talk" to one another interactively.

Keywords: Internet, Group Communications
Audience: Internet Surfers
Details: Free
User Info: Readme file is: irc/README

`ftp://cs.bu.edu`

Operlist

A discussion list for everything having to do with IRC (Internet Relay Chat). Its main purpose is irc routing discussions, protocol discussions, and announcements of new versions of IRC clients and servers.

Keywords: irc
Audience: irc Users
Contact: Helen Trillian Rose
operlist-request@eff.org
Details: Free
User Info: To subscribe to the list, send an e-mail message requesting a subscription to the URL address below.
To send a message to the entire list, address it to: operlist@eff.org

`mailto:operlist@eff.org`

IRCAM DSP and musical software

IRCAM DSP and musical software

This site offers a variety of computer music resources.

Keywords: Computer Music, Sound Synthesis, Composition, DSP
Sponsor: IRCAM
Audience: Electronic Music Enthusiasts
Profile: Contains a list and brief description of IRCAM software (digital signal processing, voice and sound synthesis, music composition, wind instrument making, and other programs). There are also calendars of the IRCAM-EIC concerts and tours, and links to various other music servers.
Contact: Michel Fingerhut
fingerhu@ircam.fr
Details: Free

`http://www.ircam.fr`

Ireland

Ireland-Related Online Resources

This is a list of network-accessible online resources (documents, images, information, access mechanisms for offline material, and so on) of Irish interest. Coverage includes some Bulletin Board services, some commercial information systems such as CompuServe, and commercial bibliographic services.

Keywords: Ireland, Travel, Commerce, Geography
Audience: Irish, General Public, Tourists, Businesses
Contact: fmurtagh@eso.org

`http://http.hq.eso.org/~fmurtagh/ireland-resources.html`

The University of Notre Dame Library

The library's holdings are large and wide-ranging and contain significant collections in many fields.

Keywords: Music (Irish), Ireland, Botany (History of), Ecology, Entomology, Parasitology, Aquatic Biology, Universities (History of), Paleography
Audience: General Public, Researchers, Librarians, Document Delivery Professionals
Details: Free
Expect: ENTER COMMAND OR HELP:, Send: library; To leave, type x on the command line and press the Enter key. At the ENTER COMMAND OR HELP: prompt, type bye and press the Enter key.

`telnet://irishmvs.cc.nd.edu`

Irish

gaelic-l

A multidisciplinary discussion list that facilitates the exchange of news, views, and information in Scottish Gaelic, Irish, and Manx.

Keywords: Scottish Gaelic, Irish, Manx, Language
Audience: Linguists
Contact: Marion Gunn
mgunn@irlearn.ucd.ie or
caoimhin@smo.ac.uk
lss203@cs.napier.ac.uk
Details: Free
User Info: To subscribe to the list, send an e-mail message to the URL address shown below, consisting of a single line reading:

SUB gaelic-l YourFirstName YourLastName

To send a message to the entire list, address it to: gaelic-l@irlearn.ucd.ie

`mailto:listserv@irlearn.ucd.ie`

Irish History (Modern)

Colby College Library

The library's holdings are large and wide-ranging and contain significant collections in many fields.

Keywords: Contemporary Letters, Hardy (Thomas), James (Henry), Mann (Thomas, Collections of), Housman (A.E., Letters of), Maine Authors, Irish History (Modern)
Audience: General Public, Researchers, Librarians, Document Delivery Professionals
Details: Free
Expect: login, Send: library

`telnet://library.colby.edu`

Iron

Materials Business File

Covers all commercial aspects of iron and steel, non-ferrous metals and non-metallic materials.

Keywords: Materials Science, Business, Iron, Steel

Sponsor: Materials Information, a joint information service of ASM International and the Institute of Materials
Audience: Materials Scientists, Researchers
Profile: Articles are abstracted from over 2,000 worldwide technical and trade journals to create more than 65,000 records. Update monthly.
Contact: PAUL.ALBERT@NETEAST.COM
User Info: To subscribe, contact Orbit-Questel directly.

`telnet://orbit.com`

IRVL-I (Institute for Research on Visionary Leadership)

IRVL-I (Institute for Research on Visionary Leadership)

The Forum for Research on Visionary Leadership provides continuing substantive discourse on visionary leadership and networked archiving of digests of dialogue.
Keywords: Leadership
Sponsor: Institute for Visionary Leadership
Audience: Administrators
Contact: estepp@byrd.mu.wvnet.edu or m034050@marshall
User Info: To subscribe to the list, send an e-mail message to the address below, consisting of a single line reading:
SUB irvl-I YourFirstName YourLastName.
To send a message to the entire list, address it to: irvl-I@byrd.mu.wvnet.edu

`mailto: listserv@byrd.mu.wvnet.edu`

ISEA (Inter-Society on Electronic Arts) Online

ISEA (Inter-Society on Electronic Arts) Online

★

An online forum for discussion of topics related to ISEA-94, the 5th International Symposium on Electronic Art that will take place in Finland in August, 1994.
Keywords: Art, Electronic Art, Technology
Audience: Artists, Art Enthusiasts
Details: Free

`ftp://ftp.ncsa.uiuc.edu`

ISIS/Draw

ISIS/Draw

ISIS/Draw provides a chemical drawing package from the American Chemical Society (ACS).
Keywords: Chemistry, Graphics
Sponsor: (ACS) and MDL Information Systems, Inc.
Audience: Chemists, Chemistry Professors, Chemistry Students
Profile: ISIS/Draw, the premier chemical drawing package from MDL Information Systems, Inc., is now available to chemistry students and professors at a special academic price through the American Chemical Society (ACS). Used by major pharmaceutical, agrochemical, and chemical companies worldwide, ISIS/Draw has the chemical intelligence to know that a line is a bond, and a letter is an atom. It can be used to: build queries for a structure-searching database; create presentation-quality sketches of chemical structures, reactions, and a wide range of other graphics; cut and paste annotated chemical structure drawings into popular word processing programs to create instructional materials and reports.
Details: Costs
Call ACS at 1-800-227-5558. When placing an order, use the following catalog numbers: 2152-9-151 (Windows) or 2156-1-151 (Macintosh).

`dmg96@acs.org`

Islam

MSA

★

A mailing list to meet the communication needs of Muslim Student Associations (MSA) in North America. Issues related to Islam and MSAs are discussed.
Keywords: Islam, Muslim Student Associations
Audience: Muslim
Details: Free
User Info: To subscribe to the list, send an e-mail message requesting subscription to the URL address below.

`mailto:msa-request@htm3.ee.queensu.ca`

MSA-Net

A mailing list intended to meet the communication needs of Muslim Student Associations (MSA) in North America, and to discuss issues related to Islam and MSAs are discussed.

Keywords: Islam, Muslim Associations
Audience: Muslims
Contact: Aalim Fevens
msa-request@htm3.ee.queensu.ca
User Info: To subscribe to the list, send an e-mail message
Notes: Members must be Muslim.

`mailto:msa-request@htm3.ee.queensu.ca`

Israel

CJI (Computer Jobs in Israel)

Computer Jobs in Israel (CJI) is a one-way list that will automatically send you the monthly updated computer jobs document. This list will also send you other special documents or announcements regarding finding computer work in Israel. Eventually this list will be an open, moderated list for everyone to exchange information about computer jobs in Israel.
Keywords: Israel, Computer, Jobs
Audience: Computer Users, Jews, Israelis, Israel Residents
Contact: Jacob Richman
listserv@jerusalem1.datasrv.co.il
Details: Free
User Info: To subscribe to the list, send an e-mail message to the address below, consisting of a single line reading:
SUB CJI YourFirstName YourLastName
To send a message to the entire list, address it to:
CJI@jerusalem1.datasrv.co.il

`mailto:listserv@jerusalem1.datasrv.co.il`

Energy Research in Israel Newsletter

This newsletter on Bitnet is for people interested in energy research, and is meant to allow important local and international energy information to be disseminated efficiently.
Keywords: Energy, Israel
Audience: Energy Researchers, Utility Professionals, Conservationists
Contact: Michael Wolff
WOLFF@ILNCRD.bitnet
Details: Free
User Info: To subscribe, send an e-mail message to the address below, consisting of a single line reading:
???missing line????
To send a message to the entire list,

`mailto:listserv@taunivm.bitnet`

Energy-L ★★

A mailing list for the discussion of all relevant information on the subject of energy in Israel.

Keywords: Engineering, Energy, Israel

Audience: Engineers, Researchers

Contact: Jo van Zwaren Dr Michael Wolff JO%ILNCRD.BITNET@CUNYVM.CUNY.EDU WOLFF@ILNCRD

Details: Free

User Info: To subscribe to the list, send an e-mail message to the URL addres below, consisting of a single line reading:

SUB energy-l YourFirstName YourLastName

To send a message to the entire list, address it to: energy-l@TAUNIVM.TAU.AC.IL

mailto:LISTSERV@TAUNIVM.TAU.AC.IL

Israel-mideast ★★

This discussion group provides information on and analysis of Israel and the Middle East. Includes news flashes, Israeli leaders briefings, editorials and articles translated from the Israeli press, background papers, press communiques, and economic, environmental and cultural updates.

Keywords: Israel, Middle East, Politics

Sponsor: Israel Information Center, Jerusalem

Audience: General Public, Students

Contact: Israel Information Service ask@israel-info.gov.il

User Info: To subscribe to the list, send an e-mail message to the address below, consisting of a single line reading:

SUB israel mideast YourFirstName YourLastName.

To send a message to the entire list, address it to: israel mideast@vm.tau.ac.il

mailto:listserv@vm.tau.ac.il

Jerusalem-One Network ★★★

A gopher site covering issues concerned with Jews, Jewish politics, and history.

Keywords: Judaism, Israel, Politics (International)

Audience: Political Activists, Holocaust Researchers, Jews, Israelis

Profile: The Jerusalem-One Network was established in May 1993 by the Jewish International Communications Network (JICN), a branch of the Jewish International Association Against Assimilation. Entries include The Jewish Electronic Library, The Holocaust Archives, and JUNK (the Jewish student University Network)

gopher://jerusalem1.datasrv.co.il

jewishnt ★★

A mailing list for the discussion of all things concerning the establishment of the Global Jewish Information Network

Keywords: Judaism, Jews, Israel, Religion

Sponsor: The Global Jewish Information Network Project

Audience: Jews, Israelis, Political Activists

Contact: Dov Winder viner@bguvm.bgu.ac.il

User Info: To subscribe to the list, send an e-mail message to the URL address below, consisting of a single line reading:

SUB jewishnt

mailto: listserv@bguvm.bgu.ac.il

Judaica ★★★

A mailing list for the discussion of Jewish and Near Eastern Studies.

Keywords: Judaica, Israel, Middle Eastern Studies, Religion

Audience: Judaica Scholars, Jews, Middle East Scholars

Contact: Tzvee Zahavy maic@uminn1.bitnet

User Info: To subscribe to the list, send an e-mail message to the URL address below, consisting of a single line reading:

SUB judaica

mailto:listserv@vm1.spcs.umn.edu

Material Science in Israel Newsletter ★

Newsletter on bitnet for people interested in material sciences, established to allow important local and international information to be disseminated efficiently and rapidly to all interested parties.

Keywords: Material Science, Israel

Audience: Material Scientists

Contact: Michael Wolff WOLFF@ILNCRD.bitnet

Details: Free

User Info: To subscribe to the list, send an e-mail message to the URL address below, consisting of a single line reading:

SUB YourFirstName YourLastName

To send a message to the entire list, address it to: @taunivmbitnet

mailto:listserv@taunivmbitnet

Medical and Biological Research in Laboratories Institutions (Israel) ★★

A descriptive listing of medical research and diagnostic laboratories in Israel. This site also has information on medical research being carried out in Israeli universities and hospitals.

Keywords: Medical Research, Biological Research, Israel

Audience: Medical Researchers, Biomedical Researchers, Medical Professionals

Profile: MATIMOP, The Israeli Industry Center for Health Care Research And Development, is a non-profit service organization, founded by an Israeli association of hospitals, universities, and other medical researchers, aiming their activities at promoting cooperation of Israeli entrepreneurs and manufacturers with qualified business firms abroad. This gopher details specific medical and biological research projects in progress in every department of every major Israeli health care institution: including universities, The General Federation of Labour, public hospitals, government-municipal hospitals, government hospitals, as well as medical and biological research in the Israeli laboratories and research institutes.

Contact: rdinfo@matimop.org.il

gopher://gopher.matimop.org.il

NYIsrael Project of NYSERnet ★★★★

Large repository of historical and cultural information as well as software, mailing lists, and images relating to Judaism, Jews, the Hebrew language, and Israel.

Keywords: Judaism, Jews, Hebrew Language, Israel

Sponsor: The New York Israel Project, NYSERNet, Inc.

Audience: Jewish Organizations

Profile: The purpose of this project is to create a network of diverse Jewish organizations worldwide that can communicate electronically and share information with one another.

Contact: Avrum Goodblatt goodblat@israel.nysernet.org

Details: Free

gopher://israel.nysernet.org

Shamash, The New York - Israel Project ★★★

This site is designed to facilitate communications between Jews and Jewish organizations through the medium of the Internet. Information includes archives of Jewish lists, updates of community Jewish events in New York and beyond, a Jewish white pages, and a section on the Holocaust. It also has Hebrew software and access to other Jewish and Israeli information servers.

Keywords: Judaism, Israel, New York
Sponsor: New York - Israel Project (Nysernet), New York, USA
Audience: Jews, Jewish Organizations
Contact: Avrum Goodblatt, Chaim Dworkin
goodblat@israel.nysernet.org,
chaim@israel.nysernet.org.

`gopher://nysernet.org`

The Israel Information Service

A gopher server containing information on Israel.

Keywords: Israel, Middle East, Political Science, Anti-Semitism, Holocaust, Archaeology
Sponsor: Israeli Foreign Ministry
Audience: Israelis, Jews, Tourists, General Public
Profile: This server features updates on the Middle East peace process, including text of the latest Israel-PLO accord, as well as general political, diplomatic, cultural, and economic information on the state of Israel. Also includes archives on archaeology in Israel, anti-Semitism and the Holocaust, and current excerpts from Israeli newspapers.
Contact: Chaim Shacham
shacham@israel-info.gov.il

`gopher://israel-info.gov.il`

IST BioGopher

IST BioGopher

This is the gopher server of the National Institute for Cancer Research (IST) and of the Advanced Biotechnology Center of Genoa, Italy.

Keywords: Cancer, Biotechnology, Italy, Europe
Audience: Biologists, Medical Researchers
Profile: The server includes data from the Interlab Project Databases (biological materials availability in European laboratories) and the Bio-Media Bulletin Board System (biotechnology researchers, projects, fundings, and products).
Contact: gophman@istge.ist.unige.it
Details: Free

`gopher://istge.ist.unige.it`

Italian Studies

Erofile

This newsletter provides reviews of the latest books associated with French and Italian studies in fields such as literary criticism, cultural studies, film studies, pedagogy, and software.

Keywords: Italian Studies, French Studies, Book Reviews
Audience: French Students, Italian Students, Book Reviewers
Details: Free

`mailto:erofile@ucsbuxa.ucsb.edu`

Italy

ASTRA-UG

A mailing list for the discussion of Italian and European GIS.

Keywords: Geographic Information Systems, Europe, Italy
Audience: Geographers, Cartographers, Europeans
Details: Free
User Info: To subscribe to the list, send an e-mail message to the URL address below, consisting of a single line reading:

SUB ASTRA-UG YourFirstName YourLastName

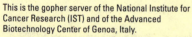
`astra-ug@icnucevm`

CILEA (Consorzio Interuniversitario Lombardo per la Elaborazione Automatica)

The gopher for the InterUniversity Computer Center, Milan, Italy, provides access to CILEA hosts, databases in Europe, CERN (European Laboratory for Particle Physics) services such as WWW and ALICE, Usenet newsgroups, PostScript documentation on various items, Italian research network information, and more.

Keywords: Informatics, Italy, Europe
Audience: Particle physicists, Researchers
Contact: Luciano Guglielm
guglielm@imicilea.cilea.it
Details: Free

`gopher://imicilea.cilea.it`

ICGEBnet

This is the information server of the International Centre for Genetic Engineering and Molecular Biology (ICGEB), Trieste, Italy.

Keywords: Molecular Biology, Biotechnology, Italy, Europe
Audience: Molecular Biotechnologists, Molecular Biologists
Profile: The primary purpose of the ICGEB computer resource is to disseminate the best of currently available computational technology to the molecular biologists of the ICGEB research community.
Contact: postmaster@icgeb.trieste.it
Details: Free

`gopher://icgeb.trieste.it`

ICTP (International Centre for Theoretical Physics)

ICTP's gopher disseminates information regarding the many scientific activities carried out at ICTP (Trieste, Italy). Information is also provided in the scientific publications, courses, and other services offered by ICS (International Centre for Science and High Technology) and TWAS (Third World Academy of Sciences) at Trieste.

Keywords: Theoretical Physics, Italy, Europe
Audience: Physicists
Profile: Topics include programming techniques, theoretical aspects, applications, implementation issues, porting, and bugs of Icon.
Contact: admin@ictp.trieste.it
Details: Free

`gopher://gopher.ictp.trieste.it`

`http://gopher.ictp.trieste.it`

IST BioGopher

This is the gopher server of the National Institute for Cancer Research (IST) and of the Advanced Biotechnology Center of Genoa, Italy.

Keywords: Cancer, Biotechnology, Italy, Europe
Audience: Biologists, Medical Researchers
Profile: The server includes data from the Interlab Project Databases (biological materials availability in European laboratories) and the Bio-Media Bulletin Board System (biotechnology researchers, projects, fundings, and products).
Contact: gophman@istge.ist.unige.it
Details: Free

`gopher://istge.ist.unige.it`

LANGIT

A forum for members of the Italian Linguistics Center (Centri Linguistici Italian).

Keywords: Italy, Linguistics
Audience: Linguists, Educators, Students
Details: Free
User Info: To subscribe to the list, send an e-mail message to the address below.

`mailto:listserv@icineca.bitnet`

soc.culture.italian

A Usenet newsgroup providing information and discussion about the Italian people and their culture.

Keywords: Italy, Sociology
Audience: Sociologists, Italians
Details: Free
User Info: To subscribe to this Usenet newsgroup, you need access to a newsreader.

`news:soc.culture.italian`

University of Chicago Library

The library's holdings are large and wide-ranging and contain significant collections in many fields, including the following:

Keywords: English Bibles, Lincoln (Abraham), Kentucky & Ohio River Valley (History of), Balzac (Honore de), American Drama, Cromwell (Oliver), Goethe, Judaica, Italy, Chaucer (Geoffrey), Wells (Ida, Personal Papers of), Douglas (Stephen A.), Italy, Literature (Children's)
Audience: General Public, Researchers, Librarians, Document Delivery Professionals
Details: Free
Expect: ENTER CLASS, Send: LIB48 3; Expect: CONNECTED, Send: RETURN

`telnet://olorin.uchicago.edu`

ITRADE (International Trade Library)

ITRADE (International Trade Library)

The International Trade Library contains materials related to the import and export of goods and services, licensing of intellectual property, payment of taxes, or investment and banking at the international level.

Keywords: Law, Import, Export, International Banking
Audience: Lawyers
Profile: ITRADE contains a comprehensive collection of federal case law, statutes, regulations, and agency decisions all related to the importing of goods and services, exporting of goods and services, licensing of intellectual property, payment of taxes, or investment and banking at the international level.
Contact: New Sales Group at 800-227-4908 or 513-859-5398 inside the US, or (513)-865-7981 for all inquires outside the US.
User Info: To subscribe, contact Mead directly.

To examine the Lexis user guide, you can access it at the ftp site of the University of Texas at Austin at the URL address: ftp://ftp.cc.utexas.edu

The files are in: /pub/ref-services/LEXIS

`telnet://nex.meaddata.com`

`http://www.meaddata.com`

ITRE Home Page

ITRE Home Page

A server dealing with transportation research and some GIS-related discussion.

Keywords: GIS, Transportation
Sponsor: University of North Carolina Institute for Transportation Research and Education
Audience: GIS Professionals, Transportation Professionals
Profile: The ITRE server address GIS issues regarding transportation, a different flavor than will be found on most servers on the Net. Also features image mapping examples.
Contact: Jay Novello
jay@itre.uncecs.edu
Details: Free, Images, Multimedia

`http://itre.uncecs.edu/`

IUCAA (Inter-University Centre for Astronomy and Astrophysics)

IUCAA (Inter-University Centre for Astronomy and Astrophysics)

The IUCAA was set up to promote the growth of active groups in astronomy and astrophysics in India. The Centre runs vigorous visitor programs involving short and long-term visits of scientists from India and abroad.

Keywords: Astronomy, Astrophysics, Physics, Education
Sponsor: Centre for Astronomy and Astrophysics (IUCAA)
Audience: Reseachers, Astronomers, Physicists, Students
Contact: Postmaster
amk@iucaa.ernet.in

`http://iucaa.iucaa.ernet.in/welcome.html`

J

James (Henry)
Colby College Library

The library's holdings are large and wide-ranging and contain significant collections in many fields.

Keywords:	Contemporary Letters, Hardy (Thomas),James (Henry), Mann (Thomas, Collections of), Housman (A.E., Letters of), Maine Authors, Irish History (Modern)
Audience:	General Public, Researchers, Librarians, Document Delivery Professionals
Details:	Free
User Info:	Expect: login, Send: library

`telnet://library.colby.edu`

Jane's Defense & Aerospace News/Analysis
Jane's Defense & Aerospace News/Analysis

This file provides articles that summarize, highlight, and interpret worldwide events in the defense and aerospace industry.

Keywords:	Defense, Aerospace, News Media
Sponsor:	Jane's Information Group, Alexandria, VAAUS
Audience:	Aerospace Industry Professionals
Profile:	The database contains the complete text of the following publications: Jane's Defense Weekly, International Defense Review, Jane's Intelligence Review (formerly Jane's Soviet Intelligence Review), Interavia Aerospace Review, and Jane's Airport Review. File 587 also contains the complete text of DMS newsletters, which ceased publication in 1989.
Contact:	Dialog in the US at (800) 334-2564, Dialog internationally at country-specific locations.
User Info:	To subscribe, contact Dialog directly.
Notes:	Coverage: 1982 to the present; updated weekly.

`telnet://dialog.com`

Japan
alt.bonsai ★

A Usenet newsgroup providing information and discussion about Bonsai gardening.

Keywords:	Bonsai Trees, Japan, Gardening, Landscaping
Audience:	Gardeners, Bonsai Enthusiasts
User Info:	To subscribe to this Usenet newsgroup, you need access to a newsreader.

`news:alt.bonsai`

ANIME-L

This discussion list covers animation news, with a special emphasis on Japanese "animedia."

Keywords:	Animation, Film, Japan
Audience:	Animation Enthusiasts, Animators
Details:	Free
User Info:	To subscribe to the list, send an e-mail message to the address below, consisting of a single line reading: Sub anime-l YourFirstName YourLastName To send a message to the entire list, address it to: anime-l@vtvm1.bitnet

`mailto:listserv@vtvm1.cc.vt.edu`

Chiba University Gopher

The Chiba University gopher, including files from the university's library.

Keywords:	Japan, Asia, Libraries
Sponsor:	Chiba University, Chiba, Japan
Audience:	Japan Residents, Computer Programmers, Librarians, Linguists
Contact:	hasimoto@chiba-u.ac.jp

`gopher://himawari.ipc.chiba-u.ac.jp`

Japanese Information

This web site contains extensive information on the geography, culture, law, and tourism of Japan. Includes archived Japanese newsgroup information and FAQs.

Keywords:	Cultural Studies, Race, Japan
Sponsor:	Nippon Telegraph and Telephone
Audience:	Students, Tourists, Japanese, Japanese-Americans
Contact:	Webmaster www-admin@seraph.ntt.jp
Details:	Free

`http://www.ntt.jp/japan/index.html`

JAPIO

Comprehensive source of unexamined Japanese patent applications.

Keywords:	Patents, Intellectual Property, Trademarks, Japan
Sponsor:	Japan Patent Information Organization
Audience:	Patent Attorneys, Patent Agents, Librarians, Researchers

Japan

Profile:	More than 2.8 million records covering all technologies. Unique features include English-language abstracts for many Japanese patent applications.
Contact:	paul.albert@neteast.com
User Info:	To subscribe, contact Orbit-Questel directly.

`telnet://orbit.com`

National Cancer Center, Tokyo, Japan ★

This is the information service for the National Cancer Center in Tokyo, Japan, as well as the entry point for the Japanese Cancer Research Resources Bank (JCRB).

Keywords:	Cancer, Japan
Audience:	Biologists, Medical Researchers
Contact:	ncc-gopher-news@gan.ncc.go.jp
Details:	Free

`gopher://ncc.go.jp`

Princeton University Library ★★

The library's holdings are large and wide-ranging. They contain significant collections in many fields.

Keywords:	China, Japan, Classics, History (Ancient), Near Eastern Studies, Literature (American), Literature (English), Aeronautics, Middle Eastern Studies, Mormonism, Publishing
Audience:	General Public, Researchers, Librarians, Document Delivery Professionals
Details:	Free
User Info:	Expect: Connect message, blank screen, Send: <cr>; Expect: #, Send: Call 500

`telnet://pucable.princeton.edu`

rec.arts.anime ★

A Usenet newsgroup providing information and discussion about Japanese animation fen.

Keywords:	Animation, Fen, Japan
Audience:	Animators
Details:	Free
User Info:	To Subscribe to this Usenet newsgroup, you need access to a newsreader.

`news:rec.arts.anime`

soc.culture.japan ★

A Usenet newsgroup providing information and discussion about Japan and the Japanese culture.

Keywords:	Japan, Sociology
Audience:	Sociologists, Japanese
Details:	Free
User Info:	To Subscribe to this Usenet newsgroup, you need access to a newsreader.

`news:soc.culture.japan`

TWICS ★★★★

This is an English-language computer conferencing system in Japan.

Keywords:	Community Networking, Networking, Japan, Virtual Community
Sponsor:	TWICS Co., Ltd.
Audience:	Internationalists, General Public, Journalists, Policy Makers
Profile:	TWICS is a computer conferencing system that has a reputation for being a thriving electronic community. This system maintains a full Internet connection. Unlike a database or a gopher server, TWICS allows real-time online interaction with actual people.
Contact:	Tim Buress twics@twics.co.jp,
Details:	Free

`telnet://tanuki.twics.co.jp`

Jerusalem

Telnet Access to WWW (World Wide Web) ★★

A server providing free public access to WWW, written in both English and Hebrew.

Keywords:	WWW, Internet Tools, Jerusalem
Sponsor:	Hebrew University of Jerusalem
Audience:	Internet Surfers
Contact:	rashty@www.huji.ac.il
User Info:	Expect: Username; Send: WWW

`telnet://www.huji.ac.il`

Jerusalem-One Network

Jerusalem-One Network ★★★

A gopher site covering issues concerned with Jews, Jewish politics, and history.

Keywords:	Judaism, Israel, Politics (International)
Audience:	Political Activists, Holocaust Researchers, Jews, Israelis
Profile:	The Jerusalem-One Network was established in May 1993 by the Jewish International Communications Network (JICN), a branch of the Jewish International Association Against Assimilation. Entries include The Jewish Electronic Library, The Holocaust Archives, and JUNK (the Jewish student University Network)

`gopher://jerusalem1.datasrv.co.il`

Jewish Politics

US Holocaust Memorial Museum

The web site of the newly-opened (April, 1993) US Holocaust Memorial Museum in Washington D.C.

Keywords:	Jews, Jewish Politics, Holocaust, History (Jewish)
Audience:	Jews, Holocaust Researchers, Israelis, Students
Profile:	This resource contains files on educational programs, general information about the Holocaust Research Institute, a contact list for the Association of Holocaust Organizations, and a searchable archive of related materials.

`http://www.ushmm.org`

Jobs

CJI (Computer Jobs in Israel) ★

Computer Jobs in Israel (CJI) is a one-way list that will automatically send you the monthly updated computer jobs document. This list will also send you other special documents or announcements regarding finding computer work in Israel. Eventually this list will be an open, moderated list for everyone to exchange information about computer jobs in Israel.

Keywords:	Israel, Computer, Jobs
Audience:	Computer Users, Jews, Israelis, Israel Residents
Contact:	Jacob Richman listserv@jerusalem1.datasrv.co.il
Details:	Free
User Info:	To subscribe to the list, send an e-mail message to the address below, consisting of a single line reading: SUB CJI YourFirstName YourLastName To send a message to the entire list, address it to: CJI@jerusalem1.datasrv.co.il

`mailto:listserv@jerusalem1.datasrv.co.il`

joe 'The Journal of Extension'

joe 'The Journal of Extension' ★★★

This is the peer-reviewed publication of the Cooperative Extension System; it covers all phases of extension education, including adult and distance education.

Keywords:	Education (Adult), Education (Distance), Education (Continuing)
Audience:	Educators (K-12), Faculty Administrators

Details: Free, Moderated
User Info: To subscribe to the journal, send an e-mail message requesting a subscription to the URL address shown below.

`mailto:almanac@joe.uwex.edu`

Johns Hopkins Genetic Databases

Johns Hopkins Genetic Databases

This gopher provides electronic access to documents pertaining to computational biology and a number of different genetic databases.

Keywords: Genetics, Molecular Biology, Medicine, Biology
Sponsor: Johns Hopkins University
Audience: Geneticists, Researchers, Scientists, Molecular Biologists
Profile: The databases accessible from this entry point include GenBank, Swiss-Prot, PDB, PIR, LiMB, TFD, AAtDB, ACEDB, CompoundKB, PROSITE EC Enzyme Database, NRL_3D Protein-Sequence-Structure Database, Eukaryotic Promoter Database (EPD), Cloning Vector Database, Expressed Sequence Tag Database (ESTDB), Online Mendelian Inheritance Man (OMIM), Sequence Analysis Bibliographic Reference Data Bank (Seqanalref), and Database Taxonomy (GenBank, Swiss-Prot). The gopher also provides direct links to other gophers with information relevant to biology.
Contact: Dan Jacobson
danj@mail.gdb.org
Details: Free

`gopher://merlot.welch.jhu.edu`

Johns Hopkins University Library

Johns Hopkins University Library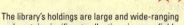

The library's holdings are large and wide-ranging and contain significant collections in many fields.

Keywords: Literature (English), Economics, Classics, Drama (German), Slavery, Trade Unions, Incunabula, Bibles, Diseases (History of), Nursing (History of), Abolitionism
Audience: General Public, Researchers, Librarians, Document Delivery Professionals
Details: Free

`telnet://jhuvm.hcf.jhu.edu`

Jokes

rec.humor

A Usenet newsgroup providing information and discussion about jokes.
Keywords: Jokes, Humor
Audience: General Public, Jokers
User Info: To Subscribe to this Usenet newsgroup, you need access to a newsreader.

`news:rec.humor`

Jordan (Len, Senatorial Papers of)

Boise State University Library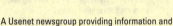

The library's holdings are large and wide-ranging and contain significant collections in many fields.

Keywords: Jordan (Len, Senatorial Papers of), Church (Frank, Senatorial Papers of), Poetry (American)
Audience: General Public, Researchers, Librarians, Document Delivery Professionals
Details: Free
User Info: Expect: login; Send: catalyst

`telnet://catalyst.idbsu.edu`

Journal of Technology Education

Journal of Technology Education

Electronic journal devoted to educational issues in technology.
Keywords: Communication, Education, Technology
Audience: Educators
Details: Free
Send an e-mail message to the URL address below with the request: GET miscella jte-v5n1. This file will give you access information for additional issues.

`mailto:listserv@vtvm1.cc.vt.edu`

Journalism

CNN Headline News Gopher

Latest news as read by the CNN anchorpersons. Searchable index of subject matter.
Keywords: News Media, Politics (International), Journalism
Sponsor: CNN Newsource Service
Audience: General Public, Students, Journalists
Contact: Chet Rhodes
cr9@umail.umd.edu
Details: Free

`gopher://info.umd.edu:925/`

Communication and Mass Communication Resources

An archive of materials related to mass communications and the media.

Keywords: Mass Communications, Media, Journalism, Telecommunications, Advertising
Sponsor: The University of Iowa
Audience: Mass Communications Students and Teachers, Journalists, Broadcasting Professionals
Contact: Karla Tonella
Karla_Tonella@uiowa.edu

`gopher://iam41.arcade.uiowa.edu`

Journet

An electronic conference for the discussion of topics of interest to journalists and journalism educators.

Keywords: Journalism, Writing, Desktop Publishing, Electronic Publishing
Audience: Journalists, Writers, Publishers, Educators
Contact: George Frajkor
gfrajkor@ccs.carleton.ca
User Info: To subscribe to the list, send an e-mail message to the URL address below consisting of a single line reading:

SUB journet YourFirstName YourLastName

To send a message to the entire list, address it to: journet@qucdn.queensu.ca

`mailto:listserv@qucdn.queensu.ca`

News

This directory is a general compilation of information resources focused on news.
Keywords: News Media, Electronic Media, Journalism
Audience: Newsreaders, Journalists, General Public
Details: Free

`ftp://una.hh.lib.umich.edu/70/inetdirsstacks/news:robinson`

ViewPoints

Newsletter of the Visual Communication Division of the Association of Educators in Journalism and Mass Communication.

Journalism

Keywords: Journalism, Mass Communication, Visual Communication
Audience: Educators, Photographers, Desktop Publishers
Contact: Paul Lester
lester@fullerton.edu
Details: Free

`mailto:lester@fullerton.edu`

Virginia Commonwealth University Library

The library's holdings are large and wide-ranging and contain significant collections in many fields.

Keywords: Art, Biology, Humanities, Journalism, Music, Urban Planning
Audience: Researchers, Students, General Public
Details: Free
User Info: Expect: Login; Send: Opub

`telnet://vcuvm1.ucc.vcu.edu`

Journals

Electronic Newsstand Gopher

This gopher contains tables of contents, selected full-text articles, and assorted other information from many mainstream print journals.

Keywords: Journals, Electronic Publishing, Publishing, News
Audience: News Enthusiasts, Publishers, Publishing Professionals, Journalists
Profile: This gopher was compiled with the collaboration of the American Journal of International Law, Policy Review, Technology Review, Business Week, Current History, The Economist, Foreign Affairs, National Review, The New Yorker, The New Republic, Mother Jones, among other distinguished publications.
Contact: William Love
love@enews.com

`gopher://gopher.enews.com`

InterText

A network-distributed bimonthly literary magazine.

Keywords: Literature (Contemporary), Journals
Audience: General Public, Writers
Profile: InterText publishes all kinds of material, ranging from mainstream stories to fantasy to horror to science fiction to humor. InterText publishes in both ASCII and PostScript formats, and reaches over 1,000 readers worldwide.
Contact: Jason Snell
jsnell@ocf.berkeley.edu
Details: Free
Select OCF On-Line Library; then select Fiction; then select InterText
Notes: The ASCII version runs approximately 150K per issue; if you have tight file gateways, the issue can be split up and squeezed through if need be. The PostScript version runs approximately 500K. If you would like to see back issues of InterText, you can FTP them from: network.ucsd.edu (128.54.16.3) in/intertext. Login as anonymous, with your e-mail address as your password.

`gopher://ocf.berkeley.edu`

LAWREV (Law Review Library)

The Law Review library contains law reviews, American Bar Association publications, American Institute of Certified Public Accountants periodicals, and other materials. The present focus concentrates on both state and national issues of legal significance.

Keywords: US Law, Analysis, Law Reviews, Journals
Audience: Lawyers
Profile: The Law Review library currently consists of over 70 law reviews, several American Bar Association publicatons and American Institute of Certified Public Accountants periodicals, an Environmental Law Institute publication, ALR and LEd2d articles, two leading legal indices and a number of Warren Gorham & Lamont tax journals. The present focus concentrates on both state and national issues of legal significance.
Contact: New Sales Group at 800-227-4908 or 513-859-5398 inside the US, or 1-513-865-7981 for all inquires outside the US.
User Info: To subscribe, contact Mead directly.
To examine the Lexis user guide, you can access it at the ftp site of the University of Texas at Austin at the URL address: ftp://ftp.cc.utexas.edu
The files are in: /pub/ref-services/LEXIS

`telnet://nex.meaddata.com`

`http://www.meaddata.com`

Journey-L

Journey-L

Information and discussion of the rock band Journey and any of the band members' outside projects.

Keywords: Musical Groups, Rock Music
Audience: Rock Music Fans
Contact: Hunter Goatley or Britt Pierce
journey-l@wkuvx1.wku.edu
User Info: To subscribe to the list, send an e-mail message to the URL address below, with the body text subscribe journey-l. To subscribe to the digest version, send the message to : journey-l-digest-request@wkuvx1.wku.edu

`mailto:journey-l-request@wkuvx1.wku.edu`

Joyce (James)

fwake-l

A conference and forum for a broad discussion of James Joyce's Finnegan's Wake.

Keywords: Joyce (James), Literature (Irish), Authors, Writing
Audience: Writers, Joyce Scholars, Literary Critics, Literary Theorists
User Info: To Subscribe to the list, send an e-mail message to the URL address below consisting of a single line reading:
SUB fwake-l

`mailto:listserv@irlearn.ucd.ie`

The University of Kansas Library

The library's holdings are large and wide-ranging and contain significant collections in many fields.

Keywords: Botany, Chinese Studies, Cartography (History of), Kansas, Opera, Ornithology, Joyce (James), Yeats (William Butler), Walpole (Sir Robert, Collections of)
Audience: General Public, Researchers, Librarians, Document Delivery Professionals
Contact: John S. Miller
Details: Free
User Info: Expect: Username, Send: relay <cr>

`telnet://kuhub.cc.ukans.edu`

Jte-l 'Journal of Technology Education'

Jte-l 'Journal of Technology Education'

The Journal of Technology Education provides a forum for all topics relating to technology in education.

Keywords: Education (Adult), Education (Distance), Education (Continuing), Information Technology
Audience: Faculty, Administrators, Educators (K-12)
Details: Free
User Info: To subscribe to the journal, send an e-mail message to the URL address below consisting of a single line reading:
SUB jte-l YourFirstName YourLastName

`mailto:listserv@vtvm1.cc.vt.edu`

Judaica

Florida State University System Library ★★

The library's holdings are large and wide-ranging and contain significant collections in many fields.

- Keywords: Florida, Latin America, Judaica, Literature (Children's), Marine Engineering, Law (Brazilian), Law (British)
- Audience: General Public, Researchers, Librarians, Document Delivery Professionals
- Details: Free
- User Info: Expect: Command ==>, Send: dial vtam; Expect: LUIS User Menu, Send: Your Catalog choice; To log off: Send: %off

`telnet://nervm.nerdc.ufl.edu`

Judaica ★★★

A mailing list for the discussion of Jewish and Near Eastern Studies.

- Keywords: Judaica, Israel, Middle Eastern Studies, Religion
- Audience: Judaica Scholars, Jews, Middle East Scholars
- Contact: Tzvee Zahavy
  maic@uminn1.bitnet
- User Info: To subscribe to the list, send an e-mail message to the URL address below consisting of a single line reading:

    SUB judaica YourFirstName YourLastName

`mailto:listserv@vm1.spcs.umn.edu`

University of Chicago Library ★★

The library's holdings are large and wide-ranging and contain significant collections in many fields.

- Keywords: English Bibles, Lincoln (Abraham), Kentucky & Ohio River Valley (History of), Balzac (Honore de), American Drama, Cromwell (Oliver), Goethe, Judaica, Italy, Chaucer (Geoffrey), Wells (Ida, Personal Papers of), Douglas (Stephen A.), Italy, Literature (Children's)
- Audience: General Public, Researchers, Librarians, Document Delivery Professionals
- Details: Free
- User Info: Expect: ENTER CLASS, Send: LIB48 3; Expect: CONNECTED, Send: RETURN

`telnet://olorin.uchicago.edu`

University of Pennsylvania Library - Philadelphia Pa. ★★★

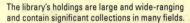

The library's holdings are large and wide-ranging and contain significant collections in many fields.

- Keywords: Literature (English), Literature (American), History (World), Medieval Studies, East Asian Studies, Middle Eastern Studies, South Asian Studies, Judaica, Lithuania.
- Audience: Educators, Students, Researchers
- Profile: Access to the central Van Pelt Library and to most of the departmental libraries is restricted to members of the University community on weekends and holidays. Online visitors are advised to call (215) 898-7554 for information on hours and access restrictions.
- Contact: Patricia Renfro, Associate Director of Libraries
- Details: Free

`telnet://library.upenn.edu`

Judaism

Electronic Hebrew Users Newsletter (E-Hug) ★

This newsletter is electronic only, and is mandated, like the original, to cover everything relating to the use of Hebrew, Yiddish, Judesmo, and Aramaic on computers.

- Keywords: Judaism, Religion, Hebrew Language
- Sponsor: Berkeley Hillel Foundation
- Audience: Jews, Judaism Students
- Contact: Ari Davidow
  well!ari@apple.com
- Details: Free
- User Info: To subscribe, send an e-mail message to the address below consisting of a single line reading:

    To send a message to the entire list,

`mailto:listserv@dartcms1.bitnet`

Jerusalem-One Network ★★★

A gopher site covering issues concerned with Jews, Jewish politics, and history.

- Keywords: Judaism, Israel, Politics (International)
- Audience: Political Activists, Holocaust Researchers, Jews, Israelis
- Profile: The Jerusalem-One Network was established in May 1993 by the Jewish International Communications Network (JICN), a branch of the Jewish International Association Against Assimilation. Entries include The Jewish Electronic Library, The Holocaust Archives, and JUNK (the Jewish student University Network)

`gopher://jerusalem1.datasrv.co.il`

jewishnt ★★

A mailing list for the discussion of all things concerning the establishment of the Global Jewish Information Network

- Keywords: Judaism, Israel, Religion
- Sponsor: The Global Jewish Information Network Project
- Audience: Jews, Israelis, Political Activists
- Contact: Dov Winder
  viner@bguvm.bgu.ac.il
- User Info: To subscribe to the list, send an e-mail message to the URL address below consisting of a single line reading:

    SUB jewishnt YourFirstName YourLastName

`mailto:listserv@bguvm.bgu.ac.il`

NYIsrael Project of NYSERnet ★★★★

Large repository of historical and cultural information as well as software, mailing lists, and images relating to Judaism, Jews, the Hebrew language, and Israel.

- Keywords: Judaism, Jews, Hebrew Language, Israel
- Sponsor: The New York Israel Project, NYSERNet, Inc.
- Audience: Jewish Organizations
- Profile: The purpose of this project is to create a network of diverse Jewish organizations worldwide that can communicate electronically and share information with one another.
- Contact: Avrum Goodblatt
  goodblat@israel.nysernet.org
- Details: Free

`gopher://israel.nysernet.org`

Shamash, The New York - Israel Project ★★★

This site is designed to facilitate communications between Jews and Jewish organizations through the medium of the Internet. Information includes archives of Jewish lists, updates of community Jewish events in New York and beyond, a Jewish white pages, and a section on the Holocaust. It also has Hebrew software and access to other Jewish and Israeli information servers.

- Keywords: Judaism, Israel, New York
- Sponsor: New York - Israel Project (Nysernet), New York, USA
- Audience: Jews, Jewish Organizations
- Contact: Avrum Goodblatt, Chaim Dworkin
  goodblat@israel.nysernet.org,
  chaim@israel.nysernet.org.

`gopher://nysernet.org`

412 Judaism

A
B
C
D
E
F
G
H
I
J
K
L
M
N
O
P
Q
R
S
T
U
V
W
X
Y
Z

soc.culture.jewish

A Usenet newsgroup providing information and discussion about Jewish culture and religion.

Keywords: Judaism, Sociology
Audience: Sociologists, Jews, Jewish Organizations
Details: Free
User Info: To Subscribe to this Usenet newsgroup, you need access to a newsreader.

`news:soc.culture.jewish`

US Holocaust Memorial Museum

The web site of the newly-opened (April, 1993) US Holocaust Memorial Museum in Washington D.C.

Keywords: Jews, Jewish Politics, Holocaust, History (Jewish)
Audience: Holocaust Researchers, Israelis, Students
Profile: This resource contains files on educational programs, general information about the Holocaust Research Institute, a contact list for the Association of Holocaust Organizations, and a searchable archive of related materials.

`http://www.ushmm.org`

Judicial Process

International Court of Justice Historical Documents

This gopher offers full-text documents from the International Court of Justice, and contains a searchable index.

Keywords: Judicial Process, Judgments, Judges, Law (International)
Audience: Lawyers, Legal Scholars, Legal Professionals, Law Students

File is in Foreign and International Law/ International Court of Justice Historical Documents/

`gopher://fatty.law.cornell.edu`

Law and Politics Book Review

Reviews books of interest to political scientists studying US law, the courts, and the judicial process. Reviews are commissioned by the editor.

Keywords: Political Science, Law, Judicial Process
Audience: Political Scientists, Lawyers
Details: Free, Moderated
User Info: To subscribe, send an e-mail message to the address below consisting of a single line reading:

To send a message to the entire list, address it to: listserv@umcvmb.bitnet

`mailto:listserv@umcvmb.bitnet`

LEGNEW (Legal News)

The Legal News Library provides general news information about the domestic legal industry and legal profession.

Keywords: Law (US), Judicial Process, Supreme Court (US)
Audience: Business Researchers, Analysts, Entrepreneurs
Profile: Included are sources which cover materials on law firm management, bar association journals and a hot file of case list summaries on recently decided US Supreme Court cases. LEGNEW is organized very simply. There are individual files, group files, and user-defined combination files.
Contact: Mead New Sales Group at (800) 227-4908 or (513) 859-5398 inside the US, or (513) 865-7981 for all inquiries outside the US.
User Info: To Subscribe, contact Mead directly.

To examine the Nexis user guide, you can access it at the ftp site of the University of Texas at Austin at the URL address: ftp://ftp.cc.utexas.edu

The files are in: /pub/ref-services/LEXIS

`telnet://nex.meaddata.com`

`http://www.meaddata.com`

Supreme Court Decisions (Project Hermes)

US Supreme Court decisions available online as part of 'Project Hermes.'

Keywords: Supreme Court, Judiciary, Law
Sponsor: Case Western Reserve University
Audience: General Public, Lawyers, Students
Profile: Project Hermes was started in May 1990 by the US Supreme Court as an experiment in disseminating its opinions electronically. Starting with the 1993 calendar year, the US Supreme Court began disseminating opinions electronically on an official basis. Each decision consists of a syllabus (summarizing the ruling), the opinion, and optional concurrent and dissenting opinions.
Contact: Peter W. Martin
martin@law.mail.cornell.edu
Details: Free

Anonymous ftp: Expect: login; Send: anonymous; Expect: password; Send: your e-mail address

`ftp://cwru.edu`

`gopher://marvel.loc.gov`

Supreme Court Judges

Biographies from the sitting Justices, and a few former Justices.

Keywords: Judiciary, Supreme Court, Judges, Biography
Audience: General Public, Lawyers, Judges, Journalists
Details: Free

`gopher://info.umd.edu`

VRDCT (Jury Verdicts Library)

The Verdicts library aids litigation preparation by providing quick and convenient access to selected online verdict and settlement information for civil cases nationwide. Case information covered includes verdict and settlement amounts, expert witnesses, case summaries and counsel data.

Keywords: Judicial Process, Law
Audience: Lawyers
Profile: The Verdicts library aids litigation preparation by providing quick and convenient access to selected online verdict and settlement information for civil cases nationwide. Case information covered includes verdict and settlement amounts, expert witnesses, case summaries and counsel data.
Contact: New Sales Group at 800-227-4908 or 513-859-5398 inside the US, or 1-513-865-7981 for all inquires outside the US.
User Info: To Subscribe, contact Mead directly.

To examine the Lexis user guide, you can access it at the ftp site of the University of Texas at Austin at the URL address: ftp://ftp.cc.utexas.edu

The files are in: /pub/ref-services/LEXIS

`telnet://nex.meaddata.com`

`http://www.meaddata.com`

Jughead

Jughead

Jonzy's Universal Gopher Hierarchy Excavation and Display (Jughead) gets menu information from various gopher servers.

Keywords: Internet Tools
Sponsor: University of Utah Computer Center
Audience: Internet Surfers
Contact: Rhett "Jonzy" Jones
jonzy@cc.utah.edu
Details: Free

File is: pub/gopher/Unix/GopherTools/ jughead/jughead.ReadMe

`ftp://boombox.micro.umn`

Jury

VRDCT (Jury Verdicts Library)

The Verdicts library aids litigation preparation by providing quick and convenient access to selected online verdict and settlement information for civil cases nationwide. Case information covered includes verdict and settlement amounts, expert witnesses, case summaries and counsel data.

Keywords:	Judicial Process, Law
Audience:	Lawyers
Profile:	The Verdicts library aids litigation preparation by providing quick and convenient access to selected online verdict and settlement information for civil cases nationwide. Case information covered includes verdict and settlement amounts, expert witnesses, case summaries and counsel data.
Contact:	New Sales Group at 800-227-4908 or 513-859-5398 inside the US, or 1-513-865-7981 for all inquires outside the US.
User Info:	To Subscribe, contact Mead directly.
	To examine the Lexis user guide, you can access it at the ftp site of the University of Texas at Austin at the URL address: ftp://ftp.cc.utexas.edu
	The files are in: /pub/ref-services/LEXIS

`telnet://nex.meaddata.com`

`http://www.meaddata.com`

Justice

Activ-L

A mailing list for the discussion of peace, empowerment, justice, and environmental issues.

Keywords:	Peace, Justice, Environment, Activism
Audience:	Activists, Students
Contact:	Rich Winkel harelb@math.cornell.edu
User Info:	To Subscribe to the list, send an e-mail message to the URL address below consisting of a single line reading:
	SUB activ-l YourFirstName YourLastName.
	To send a message to the entire list, address it to: active-l@mizzou1.missouri.edu

`mailto:listserv@mizzou1.missouri.edu`

Justice Department

Department of Justice Gopher

A gopher containing online information from the Justice Department.

Keywords:	Federal Law (US), Government (US), Justice Department
Sponsor:	United States Department of Justice
Audience:	Lawyers, Citizens
Profile:	The Department of Justice (DOJ) gopher features DOJ criminal and law enforcement statistics, as well as agency procurement requests, job listings, and press releases. Also has links to other US government online systems.
Contact:	gopher@usdoj.gov

`gopher://gopher.usdoj.gov`

414

K

K-12 Education

disted 'Journal of Distance Education and Communication'

This online journal covers distance education broadly, including formal and informal education, geographically disadvantaged learners, and both K-12 and postsecondary education.

Keywords: Education (Adult), Education (Distance), Education (Continuing), K-12 Education (K-12), Education (Post-Secondary)

Audience: K-12 Educators, K-12 Administrators

Details: Free

To subscribe to the journal, send an e-mail message to the URL address shown below consisting of a single line reading:

SUB disted YourFirstName YourLastName

mailto:listserv@uwavm.bitnet

K-12 School Libraries

This directory is a compilation of information resources focused on K-12 Education.

Keywords: Libraries, Education (K-12)

Audience: Librarians, Educators (K-12)

ftp://una.hh.lib.umich.edu/70/inetdirsstacks/k12schmed:troselius

k12.chat.junior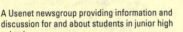

A Usenet newsgroup providing information and discussion for and about students in junior high school.

Keywords: Students, Chat Groups

Audience: Students (K-8)

Details: Free

To subscribe to this Usenet newsgroup, you need access to a newsreader.

news:k12.chat.junior

k12.chat.senior

A Usenet newsgroup providing information and discussion for and about students in senior high school.

Keywords: Students, Chat Groups

Audience: Students (K-12)

Details: Free

To subscribe to this Usenet newsgroup, you need access to a newsreader.

news:k12.chat.senior

K12 Net

Decentralized network of school-based bulletin board systems (BBSs).

Keywords: Education (K-12), Networks

Audience: Educators (K-12), School Children

Profile: K12 Net provides millions of teachers, students, and parents in metropolitan and rural areas throughout the world with the ability to meet and talk with each other to discuss educational issues, exchange information, and share resources on a global scale.

Contact: Jack Crawford, Janet Murray
jack@k12net.org or jmurray@psg.com

Details: Free

gopher://woonext.dsrd.ornl.gov/11/Docs/k12net

Kaleidospace

Kaleidospace

This is a new web server that provides a multimedia showcase for artists, performers, CD-ROM authors, musicians, writers, animators, filmmakers, and software developers.

Keywords: Art, Computer Art, Multimedia

Audience: Artists, Performers, CD-ROM Authors, Musicians, Writers, Animators, Filmmakers, Software Developers

Profile: This site was created to support independent artists. The site has similarities to other web servers, such as IUMA, but differs in that it works with all types of artists, and that it processes orders for the artist's material.

Contact: Jeannie Novak, Peter Markiewicz
jeannienov@aol.com
peterm@ewald.mbi.ucla.edu

http://kspace.com

http://fire.kspace.com

Kansas

The University of Kansas Library

The library's holdings are large and wide-ranging and contain significant collections in many fields.

Keywords: Botany, Chinese Studies, Cartography (History of), Kansas, Opera, Ornithology, Joyce (James), Yeats (William Butler), Walpole (Sir Robert, Collections of)

Audience: General Public, Researchers, Librarians, Document Delivery Professionals

Contact:	John S. Miller
Details:	Free
Expect:	Username, Send: relay <cr>

`telnet://kuhub.cc.ukans.edu`

Kentucky and Ohio River Valley (History of)

University of Chicago Library

The library's holdings are large and wide-ranging and contain significant collections in many fields.

Keywords:	English Bibles, Lincoln (Abraham), Kentucky & Ohio River Valley (History of), Balzac (Honore de), American Drama, Cromwell (Oliver), Goethe, Judaica, Italy, Chaucer (Geoffrey), Wells (Ida, Personal Papers of), Douglas (Stephen A.), Italy, Literature (Children's)
Audience:	General Public, Researchers, Librarians, Document Delivery Professionals
Details:	Free
Expect:	ENTER CLASS, Send: LIB48 3; Expect: CONNECTED, Send: RETURN

`telnet://olorin.uchicago.edu`

KFLC-L

KFLC-L

A mailing list for distributing information on the meetings and proceedings of the Kentucky Foreign Language Conferences (KFCL).

Keywords:	Language, Linguistics, Education (Bilingual)
Audience:	Linguists, Educators
Contact:	John Greenway engjlg@ukcc.uky.edu
	To subscribe, send an e-mail message to the URL address below consisting of a single line reading:
	SUB kflc-l YourFirstName YourLastName.
	To send a message to the entire list, address it to: kflc-l@ukcc.uky.edu

`mailto:listserv@ukcc.uky.edu`

KIDLINK and KIDCAFE

KIDLINK and KIDCAFE

This discussion group is designed to act as a structured forum for e-mail exchanges between children aged 10-15.

Keywords:	Education, Children
Audience:	Children
Profile:	A dialog is set up each year called 'KIDS-XX' where 'XX' is the current year. Each participating child posts an e-mail message answering the following four questions before he or she can engage in the dialog: 1. Who am I? 2. What do I want to be when I grow up? 3. How do I want the world to be better when I grow up? 4. What can I do to make this happen?

KIDLINK operates the following free discussion lists and services:

- KIDLINK: discussion group for children aged 10-15.
- RESPONSE: the destination for answers to the four questions above.
- KIDCAFE: a forum for children aged 10-15. Read-only for people outside this age group.
- KIDCAFEP: a Portuguese-language version of KIDCAFE.
- KIDCAFEJ: a Japanese-language version of KIDCAFE.
- KIDCAFEN: a Scandinavian-language (Nordic) version of KIDCAFE.
- KIDFORUM: a showcase of works by kids on a series of topics specified to promote exchange between classrooms. Teachers can plan for class participation in monthly topics.
- KIDPROJ: a forum enabling teachers/youth group leaders to design projects for children through the KIDLINK network.
- KIDLEADR: an informal meeting place for exchanging ideas, networking, asking for help, requesting hello messages, etc., for teachers, coordinators, parents, social workers, and others interested in KIDS-94.
- KIDLEADP: a Portuguese-language version of KIDLEADR.
- KIDLEADS: a Spanish-language version of KIDLEADR.
- KIDLEADN: a Scandinavian-language (Nordic) version of KIDLEADR.

Contact:	Odd de Presno opresno@extern.uio.no
Details:	Free
	For information about the projects, subscribe to the KIDLINK announcement service: send an e-mail message to: listserv@vm1.NoDak.edu with the following command in the text of your message:
	SUB KIDLINK Yourfirstname Yourlastname.
Notes:	For more information, read the 'WHAT IS KIDLINK / KIDS-94' page at gopher://kids.ccit.duq.edu/00/about/kidlink-general.

`gopher://kids.ccit.duq.edu`

Kinesiology

Biomch-L

This list is intended for members of the International, European, American, Canadian, and other Societies of Biomechanics, and for members of ISEK (International Society of Electrophysiological Kinesiology), as well as for all others with an interest in the general field of biomechanics and human or animal movement.

Keywords:	Biomechanics, Kinesiology, Movement
Sponsor:	International Society of Biomechanics
Audience:	Kinesiologists
Contact:	Ton van den Bogert listserv@nic.surfnet.nl
Details:	Free
	To subscribe to the list, send an e-mail message to the URL address below, consisting of a single line reading:
	SUB biomch-l YourFirstName YourLastName
	To send a message to the entire list, address it to: biomch-l@nic.surfnet.nl
Notes:	To obtain technical help, send the command send biomch-l guide to listserv@hearn or listserv@nic.surfnet.nl.

`mailto:listserv@nic.surfnet.nl`

Kingsley (Charles)

Princeton University Online Manuscripts Catalog Library

The library's holdings are large and wide-ranging. They contain significant collections in many fields.

Keywords:	Books (Antiquarian), Dickens (Charles), Disraeli (Benjamin), Eliot (George), Hardy (Thomas), Kingsley (Charles), Trollope (Anthony)
Audience:	General Public, Researchers, Librarians, Document Delivery Professionals
Details:	Free
Expect:	VM370 logo, Send: <cr>; Expect: Welcome screen, Send: folio <cr>; Expect: Welcome screen for FOLIO, Send: <cr>; Expect: List of choices, Send: 3 <cr>; To exit: type: logoff

`telnet://pucc.princeton.edu`

Kites

(The) Kites FTP Archive

Files pertaining to kites and kite-flying.
Keywords: Kites, Recreation
Sponsor: University of Hawaii
Audience: Kite Enthusiasts, Aeronautical Engineers
Contact: Kevin Mayeshiro
kevin@ftp.hawaii.edu
Details: Free, Moderated, Images

`ftp://ftp.hawaii.edu/pub/rec.kites`

Kiwanis International

Circle K International

This list is for members and alumni of the worldwide collegiate service organization sponsored by Kiwanis International.
Keywords: Kiwanis International
Audience: Kiwanis Members
Contact: Jeffrey M. Wolff
jwolff@nyx.cs.du.edu
Details: Free
To subscribe to the list, send an e-mail message requesting a subscription to the URL address below.

`mailto:jwolff@nyx.cs.du.edu`

Knowbot

Knowbot

Knowbot provides a uniform user interface to heterogenous remote information services.
Keywords: Internet Services, Knowbot
Audience: Internet Surfers
Details: Free
Login; Send: email address

`telnet://info.cnri.reston.va.us`

Knowledge Representation

nl-kr

This E-conference is open to discussion of any topic related to the understanding and generation of natural language and knowledge representation as subfields of artificial intelligence.
Keywords: Programming Languages, Natural Language, Knowledge Representation, Linguistics
Audience: Computer Programmers
Contact: Christopher Welty
weltyc@cs.rpi.edu
Details: Free, Moderated
To subscribe to the list, send an e-mail message requesting a subscription to the URL address below.

`mailto:nl-kr-request@cs.rpi.edu`

Korea

soc.culture.korean

A Usenet newsgroup providing information and discussion about Korea's culture and its people.
Keywords: Korea, Sociology
Audience: Sociologists, Koreans
Details: Free
To subscribe to this Usenet newsgroup, you need access to a newsreader

`news:soc.culture.korean`

Kurtz (Katernine)

Deryni-L

A list for readers and fans of Katernine Kurtz's novels and other works.
Keywords: Science Fiction, Kurtz (Katernine)
Audience: Science Fiction Enthusiasts
Contact: Edward J. Branley
elendil@mintir.new-orleans.la.us
User Info: To subscribe to the list, send an e-mail message requesting a subscription to the URL address below.
To send a message to the entire list, address it to: deryni-l@mintir.new-orleans.la.us

`mailto:deryni-l@mintir.new-orleans.la.us`

L

Labor

Iowa State University

The library's holdings contain significant collections in many fields.

- Keywords: Agriculture, Veterinary Medicine, Statistics, Labor, Soil Conservation, Film
- Audience: General Public, Researchers, Librarians, Document Delivery Professionals
- Details: Free

  Expect: DIAL, Send: LIB

`telnet://isn.iastate.edu`

LabStat

The public database of the Bureau of Labor Statistics.

- Keywords: Economics, Labor, Census Data
- Sponsor: United States Government, Bureau of Labor Statistics
- Audience: General Public, Statisticians, Researchers
- Profile: LABSTAT provides current and historical data, as well as numerous press releases. This site is composed of individual databases (in flat file format) corresponding to each of 26 surveys.
- Contact: labstat.helpdesk@bls.gov.
- Details: Free

  Login: anonymous; use e-mail address as password.
- Notes: For each news release published by the Bureau of Labor Statistics, the two most current are stored in the /news.release directory. The documentation provides a list of the abbreviations used to identify the news releases, and a description of the sub-directories available to the user.

`ftp://stats.bls.gov`

NLSNews Newsletter (National Longitudinal Surveys of Labor Market Experience)

This newsletter issued by the Center for Human Resource Research (Ohio State University); distributed to researchers using NLS data, as well as to other interested persons.

- Keywords: Labor, Government (US), Department of Labor
- Sponsor: Bureau of Labor Statistics, US Department of Labor
- Audience: Statisticians, Researchers (Labor)
- Profile: A typical issue contains updates on the status and availability of NLS data tapes and CD-ROMs for the six NLS cohorts (Older Men, Mature Women, Young Men, Young Women, Youth, and Children), notices to researchers of data-file or documentation errors, summaries of in-progress and completed NLS research, and other information of general interest to the NLS research community.
- Contact: Gale James

  james@ohsthr.bitnet

  A description of the subscription service that enables users to automatically receive, as soon as it becomes available, the latest issue of the NLS Newsletter and error updates can be found in the file subscribe.info, available via nlserve@ohsthr.bitnet, the Center's file server.

`mailto:james@ohsthr.bitnet`

Occupational Outlook Handbook 1992-93

An annual U.S. Department of Labor publication that provides detailed information for more than 320 occupations, including job descriptions, typical salaries, education and training requirements, working conditions, job outlook, and more.

- Keywords: Careers, Employment, Labor
- Sponsor: U.S. Deptartment of Labor
- Audience: General Public, Job Seekers, Business Professionals
- Details: Free

`gopher://umslvma.umsl.edu/11/library/govdocs/ooha`

Labor (History of)

Georgia State University Library

The library's holdings are large and wide-ranging and contain significant collections in many fields.

- Keywords: Labor (History of), Multimedia, Mercer (Johnny, Collection of)
- Audience: General Public, Researchers, Librarians, Document Delivery Professionals
- Contact: Phil Williams

  isgpew@gsuvm1.gsu.edu
- Details: Free

  Expect: VM screen, Send: RETURN; Expect: CP READ, Send: DIAL VTAM, press RETURN; Expect: CICS screen, Send: PF1

`telnet://library.gsu.edu`

Labor Archives

University of Colorado at Boulder Library

The library's holdings are large and wide-ranging and contain significant collections in many fields.

- Keywords: Numismatics, Human Rights, Literature (Children's), Labor Archives, History (US)
- Audience: Researchers, Students, General Public
- Contact: Donna Pattee
  pattee@spot.colorado.edu
- Details: Free
  Expect: Login; Send: Culine

`telnet://culine.colorado.edu`

Laboratory Primate Newsletter

Laboratory Primate Newsletter

Provides a central source of information about nonhuman primates and related matters for scientists who use these animals in their research and for those whose work supports such research.

- Keywords: Primatology, Psychology
- Audience: Primate Researchers, Psychologists
- Contact: Judith E. Schrier
  primate@brownvm.brown.edu
- Details: Free

`mailto:listserv@brownvm.brown.edu`

Lafayette (Marquis de)

Indiana University Libraries

The library's holdings are large and wide-ranging and contain significant collections in many fields.

- Keywords: Literature (English), Literature (American), 1640-Present, British Plays (19th-C.), Western Americana, Railway History, Aristotle (Texts of), Lafayette (Marquis de), Handel (G.F.), Austrian History, Antiquarian Books, Rare Books, French Opera (19th-C.), Drama (British),
- Audience: General Public, Researchers, Librarians, Document Delivery Professionals
- Details: Free
  Expect: User ID prompt, Send: GUEST

`telnet://iuis.ucs.indiana.edu`

Land Records

University of New Mexico UNMinfo Library

The library's holdings are large and wide-ranging and contain significant collections in many fields.

- Keywords: Photography (History of), Architecture, Native American Affairs, Land Records
- Audience: Researchers, Students, General Public
- Contact: Art St. George
  stgeorge@unmb.bitnet
- Details: Free
  Expect: Login; Send: Unminfo

`telnet://unminfo.unm.edu`

Landscaping

alt.bonsai

A Usenet newsgroup providing information and discussion about bonsai gardening.

- Keywords: Bonsai Trees, Japan, Gardening, Landscaping
- Audience: Gardeners, Bonsai Enthusiasts
- User Info: To subscribe to this Usenet newsgroup, you need access to a newsreader.

`news:alt.bonsai`

rec.gardens

A Usenet newsgroup providing information and discussion about gardening.

- Keywords: Gardening, Landscaping
- Audience: Gardeners
- User Info: To subscribe to this Usenet newsgroup, you need access to a newsreader.

`news:rec.gardens`

Lang-Lucid

Lang-Lucid

Discussions on all subjects related to the programming language Lucid, including language design issues, implementations for personal computers, implementations for parallel machines, language extensions, programming environments, products, bug reports, and bug fixes/workarounds.

- Keywords: Programming, Programming Languages
- Audience: Lucid Programmers
- Contact: R. Jagannathan
  lang-lucid-request@csl.sri.com
- Details: Free
- User Info: To subscribe to the list, send an e-mail message requesting a subscription to the URL address below.

`mailto:lang-lucid-request@csl.sri.com`

LANGIT

LANGIT

A forum for members of the Italian Linguistics Center (Centri Linguistici Italian).

- Keywords: Italy, Linguistics
- Audience: Linguists, Educators, Students
- Details: Free
- User Info: To subscribe to the list, send an e-mail message to the URL address below.

`mailto:listserv@icineca.bitnet`

Language

Academia Latinoamericana de Espanol

This program is specifically designed for those interested in learning to speak Spanish through a fully immersive trip to Ecuador.

- Keywords: Spanish, Language, Education (Bilingual)
- Sponsor: Academia Latinoamericana de Espanol, Quito, Ecuador
- Audience: Reseachers, Students, Language Teachers
- Contact: Webmaster
  webmaster@comnet.com

`http://www.comnet.com/ecuador/learnSpanish.html`

gaelic-l

A multidisciplinary discussion list that facilitates the exchange of news, views, and information in Scottish Gaelic, Irish, and Manx.

- Keywords: Scottish Gaelic, Irish, Manx, Language
- Audience: Linguists
- Contact: Marion Gunn
  mgunn@irlearn.ucd.ie or
  caoimhin@smo.ac.uk
  lss203@cs.napier.ac.uk
- Details: Free
- User Info: To subscribe to the list, send an e-mail message to the URL address shown below consisting of a single line reading:

SUB gaelic-l YourFirstName YourLastName

To send a message to the entire list, address it to: gaelic-l@irlearn.ucd.ie

`mailto:listserv@irlearn.ucd.ie`

GC-L

Project for international business and management curricula.

Keywords: Business, Management, Language
Sponsor: Global Classroom
Audience: Linguists, Language Teachers, Language Students, International Business Educators
Details: Free
User Info: To subscribe to the list, send an e-mail message to the address below consisting of a single line reading:

`mailto:listserv@uriacc.uri.edu`

INTERCUL

A study of international communication.

Keywords: Languages (international)
Audience: Linguists, Language Teachers, Language Students
Details: Free

`mailto:listserv@vm.its.rpi.edu`

KFLC-L

A mailing list for distributing information on the meetings and proceedings of the Kentucky Foreign Language Conferences (KFCL).

Keywords: Language, Linguistics, Education (Bilingual)
Audience: Linguists, Educators
Contact: John Greenway
engjlg@ukcc.uky.edu
User Info: To subscribe, send an e-mail message to the URL address below consisting of a single line reading:

SUB kflc-l YourFirstName YourLastName.

To send a message to the entire list, address it to: kflc-l@ukcc.uky.edu

`mailto:listserv@ukcc.uky.edu`

Lantra-L

A discussion of interpretation and translation.

Keywords: Interpretation, Translation, Linguistics
Audience: Linguists, Interpreters, Translators
User Info: To subscribe to the list, send and e-mail message to the URL address below consisting of a single line reading:

SUB lantra-l Your First Name Your Last Name

To send a message to the entire list, address it to: kabtra-l@search.bitnet

Details: Free

`mailto:listserv@searn.bitnet`

LINGUIST

A discussion of language and linguistics.

Keywords: Language, Linguistics
Audience: Linguists, Language Teachers, Language Students
Details: Free
User Info: To subscribe to the list, send an e-mail message to the address shown below consisting of a single line reading:

SUB linguist Your First Name Your Last Name

`mailto:listserv@tamvm1.bitnet`

LLTI

The Language Learning Technology International (LLTI) forum is a discussion of computer-assisted language learning.

Keywords: Linguistics, Computer-Aided Instruction
Audience: Linguists, Language Teachers, Language Students
Details: Free
User Info: To subscribe to the list, send an e-mail message to the URL address below, consisting of a single line reading:

SUB llti YourFirstName YourLastName

To send a message to the entire list, address it to:
llti@dartcms1.dartmouth.edu

`mailto:listserv@dartcms1.dartmouth.edu`

LTEST

A discussion of language-testing research and practice.

Keywords: Linguistics, Translations
Audience: Linguists, Language Teachers, Language Students
Details: Free
User Info: To subscribe to the list, send an e-mail message to the URL address below, consisting of a single line reading:

SUB Ltest YourFirstName YourLastName

To send a message to the entire list, address it to:ltest@uclan1.bitnet

`mailto:listserv@uclan1.bitnet`

Russian

This list is dedicated to the discussion of Russian-language issues, including Russian language, linguistics, grammar, translations, and literature.

Keywords: Language, Literature (Russian), Linguistics
Audience: Slavicists, Linguists, Translators
Contact: Andrew Wollert
ispajw@asuacad
russian@asuvm.inre.asu.edu
Details: Free
User Info: To subscribe to the list, send an e-mail message requesting subscription to the URL address below.

`russian@asuvm.inre.asu.edu`

The Human Languages Page

This site provides language resources from around the world, including dictionaries, language tutorials, and spoken samples of languages.

Keywords: Language, Linguistics
Audience: Linguists, Educators, Students
Profile: Languages covered include Esperanto, Gaelic, Arabic, Hindi, and Kanji. Also provides link to the Gutenberg Project (electronic texts) and to the Library of Congress.
Contact: Tyler Jones
tjones@willamette.edu.
Details: Free

`http://www.willamette.edu/~tjones/Language-Page.html`

Language Software

alt.chinese.text

A Usenet newsgroup providing information and discussion about Chinese language software.

Keywords: Chinese Language, Language Software
Audience: Chinese, Chinese Speakers, Computer Users
User Info: To subscribe to this Usenet newsgroup, you need access to a newsreader.

`news:alt.chinese.text`

Lasers

University of Rochester Library

The library's holdings are large and wide-ranging and contain significant collections in many fields.

Keywords: Architecture, Art History, Photography, Literature (Asian), Lasers, Geology, Statistics, Optics, Medieval Studies

Latin America

amlat.mujeres ★

This conference serves as a forum for interchange between organizations and women's movements in Latin America and the Caribbean.

- Keywords: Women, Latin America, Caribbean, Feminism
- Audience: Women, Feminists, Activists
- Contact: Agencia Latinoamericana de Informacion info@alai.ec, uualai@ecuanex.ec
- Details: Costs

    Establish an account on the nearest APC node. Login, type c for conferences, then type: **go amlat.mujeres**.

    For information on the nearest APC node, contact:

    APC International Secretariat IBASE E-mail: apcadmin@apc.org
- Contact: Carlos Afonso (cafonso@ax.apc.org) or APC North American Regional Office E-mail: apcadmin@apc.org Edie Farwell (efarwell@igc.apc.org)

`telnet://igc.apc.org`

cread (Latin American & Caribbean Distance & Continuing Education) ★

This is a digest list of distance education information primarily focused on Latin America and the Caribbean.

- Keywords: Latin America, Caribbean, Education (Distance)
- Audience: Educators, Administrators, Faculty
- Details: Free
- User Info: To subscribe to the list, send an e-mail message to the URL address below consisting of a single line reading:

    SUB cread YourFirstName YourLastName.

    To send a message to the entire list, address it to: cread@yorkvm1.bitnet

`mailto:listserv@yorkvm1.bitnet`

Felipe's Bilingual WWW Pages ★★

An interactive web site containing gopher and web links to various Latin American resources.

- Keywords: Latin America, Education (Bilingual)
- Audience: Researchers, Students, General Public
- Details: Free

    Expect: Login; Send: Library

`telnet://128.151.226.71`

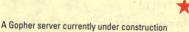

- Sponsor: University of Texas, Texas, USA
- Audience: Educators, Language Students, Translators
- Contact: Felipe Campos felipe@bongo.utexas.edu

`http://edb518ea.edb.utexas.edu`

Florida State University System Library ★★

The library's holdings are large and wide-ranging and contain significant collections in many fields.

- Keywords: Florida, Latin America, Judaica, Literature (Children's), Marine Engineering, Law (Brazilian), Law (British)
- Audience: General Public, Researchers, Librarians, Document Delivery Professionals
- Details: Free

    Expect: Command ==>, Send: dial vtam; Expect: LUIS User Menu, Send: Your Catalog choice; To log off: Send: %off

`telnet://nervm.nerdc.ufl.edu`

hilat-l (Higher Education in Latin America) ★

Provides a means of interchange about research on higher education in Latin America. Postings are mostly in English, but are also welcome in Spanish and Portuguese.

- Keywords: Education (Adult), Education (Distance), Education (Continuing), Latin America
- Audience: Educators, Administrators, Faculty
- Details: Free
- User Info: To subscribe to the list, send an e-mail message to the URL address shown below consisting of a single line reading:

    SUB hilat-l YourFirstName YourLastName

    To send a message to the entire list, address it to: hilat-l@bruspvm.bitnet

`mailto:listserv@bruspvm.bitnet`

Info-South (Latin American News)

The database provides citations and abstracts of materials relating to contemporary economic, political, and social issues in Latin America.

- Keywords: International News, Economics, International Politics, Latin America
- Sponsor: University of Miami, Coral Gables, FL, US
- Audience: General Public
- Profile: Coverage includes a wide range of topics assessing the current situation in Latin America.
- Contact: Dialog in the US at (800) 334-2564, Dialog internationally at country-specific locations.
- User Info: To subscribe, contact Dialog directly.
- Notes: Coverage: 1988 to the present; updated weekly.

`telnet://dialog.com`

Latin America & Caribbean Network Gopher server ★

A Gopher server currently under construction providing Internet access to Latin America and the Caribbean.

- Keywords: Caribbean, Latin America
- Sponsor: Lacnet Corporation
- Audience: Caribbean Enthusiasts
- Profile: The Latin America & Caribbean Network Gopher server is a gopher server currently under construction. When finished it will provide gopher access to gopher servers throughout Latin America and the Caribbean providing government and institutional information on various countries.
- Contact: Luis Rodriguez or Javier Hidalgo lrodriguez@mia.lac.net jhidalgo@mia.lac.net
- Notes: Currently under construction.

`gopher://mia.lac.net`

Latin American Database Historic World Documents ★★★★

International legal files covering 33 nations and article citations from publications relating to Hispanic legal systems. The wiretap gopher provides access to a range of world documents in full-text format.

- Keywords: Latin America, Law (International), International Documents, Latin America
- Audience: General Public, Hispanics, Lawyers
- Profile: The database includes two files, LAWL containing legislation from 33 nations, mostly Spanish speaking, and HISS containing Hispanic Legal Article citations.
- Details: Free
- Notes: Select from menu as appropriate.

`gopher://marvel.loc.gov`

NIBNews - A Monthly Electronic Bulletin About Medical Informatics ★

Disseminates information about Brazilian and Latin American activities, people, information, events, publications, software, and so on, involving computer applications in health care, medicine, and biology.

- Keywords: Health Care, Biology, Brazil, Latin America, South America, Medicine

Audience:	Health-Care Professionals, Biologists
Contact:	Renato M. E. Sabbatini SABBATINI@BRUC.BITNET
Details:	Free E-mail a short notice to

`mailto:sabbatini@ccvax.unicamp.br`

Summit of the Americas Internet Gopher

A gopher containing supporting materials for the Summit of the Americas, a meeting of the Western Hemisphere's democratically elected heads of state, to be held in Miami in December of 1994.

Keywords:	American Studies, International Relations, Haiti, Latin America
Sponsor:	The Florida University Latin American and Caribbean Center
Audience:	Government Officials, Journalists, NGOs, General Public
Contact:	Rene Ramos summit@SERVAX.FIU.EDU

`gopher://summit.fiu.edu`

Latin American Studies

University of Texas at Austin Library

The library's holdings are large and wide-ranging and contain significant collections in many fields.

Keywords:	Music, Natural Science, Nursing, Science Technology, Behavioral Science, Social Work, Computer Science, Engineering, Latin American Studies, Middle Eastern Studies
Audience:	Researchers, Students, General Public
Details:	Free Expect: Blank Screen, Send: Return; Expect: Go, Send: Return; Expect: Enter Terminal Type, Send: vt100
Notes:	Some databases are restricted to UT Austin users only.

`telnet://utcat.utexas.edu`

Latino Culture

Chicano/LatinoNet

An electronic mechanism that brings together Chicano/Latino research, as well as linguistic minority and educational research efforts being carried out at the University of California and elsewhere. It serves as a gateway between faculty, staff, and students who are engaged in research and curricular efforts in these areas.

Keywords:	Culture, Race, Chicano Culture, Latino Culture
Sponsor:	Chicano Studies Research Center, University of California at Los Angeles
Audience:	Students, Mexican-Americans, Latinos
Contact:	Richard Chabran Chabran@latino.sscnet.ucla.ed
Details:	Free

`gopher://latino.sscnet.ucla.edu/`

Mexican Culture FAQ

This is the FAQ from the soc.culture.mexican newsgroup. Provides information on Mexican culture, history, society, language, and tourism.

Keywords:	Culture, Race, Chicano Culture, Latino Culture
Sponsor:	News Group Moderators for soc.culture.mexican
Audience:	Students, Latinos, Chicanos
Contact:	News Group Moderator mendoza-grado@att.com
Details:	Free

`ftp://ftp.mty.itesm.ms/pub/mexico/faqs`

`http://www.cis.ohio-state.edu/hypertext/faq/usenet/mexican-faq/faq.html`

US/Mexico Border Discussion List

This group provides a forum for the discussion of issues pertaining to the US/Mexico border environment.

Keywords:	Mexico, Environment, Latino Culture
Sponsor:	The US Environmental Protection Agency
Audience:	Activists, Environmentalists, Urban Planners
Details:	Free
User Info:	To subscribe to the list, send a message to the URL address below consisting of a single line reading: SUB us_mexborder YourFirstName YourLastName To send a message to the entire list, address it to: us_mexborder@unixmail.rtpnc.epa.gov

`mailto:listserver@unixmail.rtpnc.epa.gov`

Latvia

Balt-L

A forum devoted to communications to and about the Baltic Republics of Lithuania, Latvia, and Estonia.

Keywords:	Lithuania, Latvia, Estonia, Baltic Republics
Audience:	Researchers, Baltic Nationals
Contact:	Jean-Michel Thizy jmyhg@uottawa.edu
Details:	Free
User Info:	To subscribe to the list, send an e-mail message to the URL address below, consisting of a single line reading: SUB balt-l YourFirstName YourLastName

`mailto:listserv@ubvm.cc.buffalo.edu`

University of Nebraska at Lincoln Library

The library's holdings are large and wide-ranging and contain significant collections in many fields.

Keywords:	Slovak Republic, Czech Republic, Folklore, Military History, Latvia, Law (Tax), Law (US)
Audience:	General Public, Researchers, Librarians, Document Delivery Professionals
Contact:	Anita Cook
Details:	Free Expect: login, Send: library

`telnet://unllib.unl.edu`

Law

BKRTCY (Bankruptcy Library)

The Federal Bankruptcy library is a comprehensive collection of primary and secondary legal research materials pertaining to bankruptcy issues.

Keywords:	Law, Filings, Bankruptcy
Audience:	Lawyers, Bankers
Profile:	The Federal Bankruptcy library is a comptrehensive collection of primary and secondary legal research materials that includes case law, rules, statutory and regulatory materials, legal publications, accounting literature and other resources pertaining to bankruptcy issues.
Contact:	New Sales Group at (800) 227-4908 or 513-859-5398 inside the US, or 1-513-865-7981 for all inquires outside the US.
User Info:	To subscribe, contact Mead directly. To examine the Lexis user guide, you can access it at the ftp site of the University of Texas at Austin at the URL address: ftp://ftp.cc.utexas.edu The files are in: pub/ref-services/LEXIS

`telnet://nex.meaddata.com`

`http://www.meaddata.com`

California Privacy Act 1992

Text of the California Privacy Act of 1992.

Keywords: Law, California
Audience: General Public, Lawyers
Details: Free

`gopher://wiretap.spies.com`

Children's Rights

Contains files from the Children's Rights Council, the Central Ohio Organization, Fathers and Children for Equality, and the National Congress for Men and Children.

Keywords: Children, Law
Audience: Lawyers, Social Workers, Children's Rights Activists
Details: Free

`telnet://cwgk4.chem.cwru.edu`

ENERGY

The Energy News and Information (ENERGY) library consists of news, legal, and regulatory information.

Keywords: Energy, News, Law, Regulations
Audience: Energy Researchers
Profile: The ENERGY library contains more than 50 full-text sources concentrating on energy-related news and issues. Also available are decisions and orders of the United States Federal Power Commission, Federal Energy Regulatory Commission, and Nuclear Regulatory Commission. At the state level, it covers administrative decisions and orders for 17 states. Energy industry research reports from InvestextR are also available.
Contact: Mead New Sales Group at (800) 227-4908 or (513) 859-5398 inside the US, or (513) 865-7981 for all inquiries outside the US.
User Info: To subscribe, contact Mead directly.

To examine the Nexis user guide, you can access it at the ftp site of the University of Texas at Austin at the URL address: ftp://ftp.cc.utexas.edu

The files are in: pub/ref-services/LEXIS

`telnet://nex.meaddata.com`

`http://www.meaddata.com`

ENVIRN (Environment Library)

The Environment (ENVIRN) Library contains a variety of environment-related news and legal information.

Keywords: News, Analysis, Law, Environment
Audience: Environmental Researchers, Businesspeople
Profile: The ENVIRN Library contains a combination of environmental information that can provide critical insight into environmental hazards, EPA ratings, specific company investigations, evaluations on potentially hazardous chemicals, and parties responsible for cleanup of specific hazardous sites. Additionally, ENVIRN provides a wealth of environment-related informationÑlegislation, regulations, and court and agency decisions at both the federal and state levels; news; the Environmental Law Reporter, and American Law Reports.
Contact: Mead New Sales Group at (800) 227-4908 or (513) 859-5398 inside the US, or (513) 865-7981 for all inquiries outside the US.
User Info: To subscribe, contact Mead directly.

To examine the Nexis user guide, you can access it at the ftp site of the University of Texas at Austin at the URL address: ftp://ftp.cc.utexas.edu

The files are in: /pub/ref-services/LEXIS

`telnet://nex.meaddata.com`

`http://www.meaddata.com`

FEDSEC (Federal Securities Library)

The US Federal Securities library covers federal case law, Securities Exchanges Commission (SEC) materials, Commodities Futures Trading Commision (CFTC) materials and other legal and legislative materials relevant to the securities industry, as well as company information, news and analysis.

Keywords: Law, Filings, Securities, SEC
Audience: Lawyers, Bankers, Stockbrokers
Profile: The Federal Securities library contains over 60 separately searchable files covering federal case law: Securities Exchange Commision (SEC) no-action letters, decisions, orders, releases, and SEC filings (both full text and abstracts); Commodities Futures Trading Commision (CFTC) decisions, orders, releases; legislative materials; statutory and regulatory materials; selected RICO, class derivative, and collateralized mortgage obligations case law, rules and regulations; Federal Reserve Board materials; AICPA annual reports and accounting & audit literature files; Standard & Poors company information; state administrative decisions, orders, and releases; and company news and analysis information.
Contact: New Sales Group at (800) 227-4908 or 513-859-5398 inside the US, or 1-513-865-7981 for all inquires outside the US.
User Info: To subscribe, contact Mead directly.

To examine the Lexis user guide, you can access it at the ftp site of the University of Texas at Austin at the URL address: ftp://ftp.cc.utexas.edu

The files are in: pub/ref-services/LEXIS

`telnet://nex.meaddata.com`

`http://www.meaddata.com`

FEDTAX (Federal Tax Library)

The Federal Tax library offers a comprehensive, up-to-date collection of tax-related materials, including case law, agency materials, legislative and regulatory materials, and more.

Keywords: Law, Analysis, Tax
Audience: Lawyers
Profile: This library includes federal and state tax case law, Internal Revenue Service rulings and releases, state tax administrative decisions and rulings, the Internal Revenue Code, federal tax regulations, international news and treaties, tax looseleaf services, tax periodicals, tax law reviews, tax dailies, pending state legislation, and state property records.
Contact: New Sales Group at (800) 227-4908 or 513-859-5398 inside the US, or 1-513-865-7981 for all inquires outside the US.
User Info: To subscribe, contact Mead directly.

To examine the Lexis user guide, you can access it at the ftp site of the University of Texas at Austin at the URL address: ftp://ftp.cc.utexas.edu
The files are in: pub/ref-services/LEXIS

`telnet://nex.meaddata.com`

`http://www.meaddata.com`

Germany

Full text in German of various German laws and codes.

Keywords: German, Law
Sponsor: Berlin University, Berlin, Germany
Audience: Lawyers, Historians, Germans
Details: Free

Select from menu as appropriate.

`gopher://gate1.zedat.fu-berlin.de`

Illinois Legislation

This directory contains several Illinois Department of Nuclear Safety Statues and Regulations.

Keywords: Nuclear Safety, Law, Illinois
Audience: Lawyers
Details: Free

`gopher://wiretap.spies.com`

Hawaii FYI

A state information system providing a wide range of free legal information.

Keywords: Hawaii, Law
Audience: Hawaiians, Lawyers
Details: Free

`telnet://fyi.uhcc.hawaii.edu`

Hong Kong Law

Lists the basic Hong Kong Law (1990) and Hong Kong Bill of Rights Ordinance (1991).

Keywords: Hong Kong, Law
Audience: Lawyers, Sinologists
Details: Free

`gopher://marvel.loc.gov`

Insurance Periodicals Index

The database indexes and abstracts 35 of the most respected and widely read insurance industry journals and magazines.

Keywords: Insurance Industry, Law
Sponsor: NILS Publishing Company, Chatsworth, CA, US
Audience: Insurance Brokers
Profile: The subject coverage of the publications indexed includes the following major groupings: AIDS, alcohol abuse, asbestos, automobile insurance, aviation insurance, banks, bonds, catastrophes, crime, disability insurance, drug abuse, financial services, health insurance, insurance agents and brokers, legislation, liability insurance, life insurance, Lloyds, loss control, marketing, pensions, pollution, product liability, property insurance, rates, regulation, risk management, tort reform, uninsured motorists, workers' compensation, and more.
Contact: Dialog in the US at (800) 334-2564, Dialog internationally at country-specific locations.
User Info: To subscribe, contact Dialog directly.
Notes: Coverage: 1984 to the present; updated biweekly.

`telnet://dialog.com`

INSURE (Insurance)

The Insurance (INSURE) library contains specific full-text and abstract news and legal information sources focusing on the insurance industry.

Keywords: News, Analysis, Law, Insurance
Audience: Insurance Professionals, Lawyers
Profile: The INSURE library contains leading insurance industry news sources, legal and regulatory materials from NILS Publishing Company's INSURLAW, analyst reports on the insurance industry from InvestextR, and insurance company financial reports. Federal and state case law and federal regulations are also available.
Contact: Mead New Sales Group @ (800) 227-4908 or (513) 859-5398 inside the US, or (513) 865-7981 for all inquiries outside the US.
User Info: To subscribe, contact Mead directly.
To examine the Nexis user guide, you can access it at the ftp site of the University of Texas at Austin at the URL address: ftp://ftp.cc.utexas.edu The files are in: /pub/res-services/LEXIS

`telnet://nex.meaddata.com`

ITRADE (International Trade Library)

The International Trade Library contains materials related to the importing of goods and services, exporting of goods and services, licensing of intellectual property, payment of taxes, or investment and banking at the international level.

Keywords: Law, Import, Export, International Banking
Audience: Lawyers
Profile: ITRADE contains a comprehensive collection of federal case law, statutes, regulations, and agency decisions all related to the importing of goods and services, exporting of goods and services, licensing of intellectual property, payment of taxes, or investment and banking at the international level.
Contact: New Sales Group at (800) 227-4908 or 513-859-5398 inside the US, or 1-513-865-7981 for all inquires outside the US.
User Info: To subscribe, contact Mead directly.
To examine the Lexis user guide, you can access it at the ftp site of the University of Texas at Austin at the URL address: ftp://ftp.cc.utexas.edu The files are in: /pub/ref-services/LEXIS

`telnet://nex.meaddata.com`

`http://www.meaddata.com`

Latin American Database Historic World Documents

International legal files covering 33 nations and article citations from publications relating to Hispanic legal systems. The wiretap gopher provides access to a range of world documents in full-text format.

Keywords: Hispanic, Law, International Law, International Documents
Audience: General Public, Hispanics, Lawyers
Profile: The database includes two files, 1) LAWL containing legislation from 33 nations, mostly Spanish speaking 2) HISS containing Hispanic Legal Article citations.
Details: Free
Select from menu as appropriate.

`gopher://marvel.loc.gov`

Law and Politics Book Review

Reviews books of interest to political scientists studying US law, the courts, and the judicial process. Reviews are commissioned by the editor.

Keywords: Political Science, Law, Judicial Process
Audience: Political Scientists, Lawyers
Details: Free, Moderated
User Info: To send a message to the entire list, address it to: listserv@umcvmb.bitnet

`mailto:listserv@umcvmb.bitnet`

Maryland

System provides access to a wide range of state information, including the policies and activities of members of Maryland's congress and voting district data.

Keywords: Maryland, Law, Voting
Audience: Maryland Residents, Lawyers
Details: Free
Select from menu as appropriate.

`gopher://info.umd.edu`

misc.legal

A Usenet newsgroup providing information and discussion about law and ethics.

Keywords: Law, Ethics
Audience: Lawyers, Legal Professionals, General Public
Details: Free
User Info: To subscribe to this Usenet newsgroup, you need access to a newsreader.

`news:misc.legal`

Multilateral Treaties

An experimental program to make available to the Internet community the text of a wide variety of multilateral conventions, even those that have not yet been ratified.

Keywords: Multilateral, Treaty, Law
Sponsor: The Fletcher School of Law and Diplomacy, Cornell University, Ithaca, NY

Audience: Government Officials, Researchers, Lawyers

Profile: Almost all treaties listed are available in print form. The program will enable access to even very recent conventions. Primary focus is on Environmental and human rights issues but other fields are also included. The conventions coming out of the 1992 United Nations Conference on the Environment and Development have NOT been included as they are available elsewhere through CIESIN. Those Treaties covered include: Convention on International Trade in Endangered Species of Wild Fa; Montreal Protocol on Substances that Depleate the Ozone Layer; The Berne Convention for the Protection of Literary and Artistic Works; Agreement on the Rescue of Astronauts; the return of Astronauts

Contact: Peter Scott Director, Multilaterals Project, Fletcher School of Law and Diplomacy
pstott@pearl.tufts.edu
pstott@icg.apc.org

Details: Free
Select from menu as appropriate

`gopher://gopher.law.cornell.edu/11/foreign/fletcher-cat`

New Mexico LegalNet

The system makes legal resources available, including state motor vehicle and corporation databases, court dockets, border trade information, and country and city data.

Keywords: Law, New Mexico
Audience: New Mexico Residents, Lawyers, Private Investigators
Contact: inettgen@technet.nm.org
Details: Costs

`telnet://technet.nm.org`

Ohio

Provides access to Ohio State Supreme Court Opinions and Ohio 8th District Court Opinions.

Keywords: Ohio, Law
Sponsor: Case Western University Freenet, Youngstown University Freenet
Audience: Lawyers, General Public, Ohio Residents
Details: Free

`telnet://ytn.ysu.edu`

STATES (States Library)

The combined States Library contains case law, code and agency materials from the 53 individual US state libraries (50 states plus the District of Columbia, Puerto Rico and the Virgin Islands), all in the same library.

Keywords: Law, Analysis, Case, States
Audience: Lawyers
Profile: The States Library features many large group files which allow several individual files to be accessed in the same search. Many of the group files involve case law, including files that cover all state case law available on the LEXIS service plus ALR material and files that combine all federal and state case law available on the LEXIS service.

Contact: New Sales Group at (800) 227-4908 or 513-859-5398 inside the US, or 1-513-865-7981 for all inquires outside the US.

User Info: To subscribe, contact Mead directly.
To examine the Lexis user guide, you can access it at the ftp site of the University of Texas at Austin at the URL address:
ftp://ftp.cc.utexas.edu
The files are in: pub/ref-services/LEXIS

`telnet://nex.meaddata.com`

`http://www.meaddata.com`

Supreme Court Decisions

Full text of Supreme Court decisions issued since 1989, as well as brief biographies of Supreme Court justices.

Keywords: Supreme Court, Law
Audience: Legal Professionals, Educators, Researchers

`gopher://info.umd.edu`

Supreme Court Decisions (Project Hermes)

US Supreme Court decisions available online as part of 'Project Hermes.'

Keywords: Supreme Court, Judiciary, Law
Sponsor: Case Western Reserve University
Audience: General Public, Lawyers, Students
Profile: Project Hermes was started in May 1990 by the US Supreme Court as an experiment in disseminating its opinions electronically. Starting with the 1993 calendar year, the US Supreme Court began disseminating opinions electronically on an official basis. Each decision consists of a syllabus (summarizing the ruling), the opinion, and optional concurrent and dissenting opinions.

Contact: Peter W. Martin
martin@law.mail.cornell.edu
Details: Free
Anonymous ftp: Expect: login; Send: anonymous; Expect: password; Send: your e-mail address

`ftp://cwru.edu`
`gopher://marvel.loc.gov`

Uniform Code of Military Justice

The files in this directory contain the US Uniform Code of Military Justice.

Keywords: Military, Law
Audience: Journalists, Politicians, Students, Military Personnel
Details: Free

`gopher://wiretap.spies.com/00/Gov/UCMJ`

Law (Brazilian)

Florida State University System Library

The library's holdings are large and wide-ranging and contain significant collections in many fields.

Keywords: Florida, Latin America, Judaica, Literature (Children's), Marine Engineering, Law (Brazilian), Law (British)
Audience: General Public, Researchers, Librarians, Document Delivery Professionals
Details: Free
Expect: Command ==>, Send: dial vtam; Expect: LUIS User Menu, Send: Your Catalog choice; To log off: Send: %off

`telnet://nervm.nerdc.ufl.edu`

Law (British)

Florida State University System Library

The library's holdings are large and wide-ranging and contain significant collections in many fields.

Keywords: Florida, Latin America, Judaica, Literature (Children's), Marine Engineering, Law (Brazilian), Law (British)
Audience: General Public, Researchers, Librarians, Document Delivery Professionals
Details: Free
Expect: Command ==>, Send: dial vtam; Expect: LUIS User Menu, Send: Your Catalog choice; To log off: Send: %off

`telnet://nervm.nerdc.ufl.edu`

Law (International)

European Patents Fulltext

European Patents Fulltext contains the complete text of European published applications and patents and European PCT published applications.

- **Keywords:** Patents, Europe, Law (International)
- **Sponsor:** European Patent Office, Vienna, Austria
- **Audience:** Patent Researchers
- **Profile:** It contains bibliographic, administrative, and legal information from the European Patent Registry. Records have abstracts, patent specifications including all claims, and the search report, including cited patents and other references.
- **Contact:** Dialog in the US at (800) 334-2564, Dialog internationally at country-specific locations.
- **User Info:** To subscribe, contact Dialog directly.
- **Notes:** Coverage: 1978 to the present; updated weekly.

`telnet://dialog.com`

International Court of Justice Historical Documents ★★★

This gopher offers full-text documents from the International Court of Justice, and contains a searchable index.

- **Keywords:** Judicial Process, Judgments, Judges, Law (International)
- **Audience:** Lawyers, Legal Scholars, Legal Professionals, Law Students
- File is in Foreign and International Law/International Court of Justice Historical Documents/

`gopher://fatty.law.cornell.edu`

Law and Courts Preprint Archive ★★

An online archive of papers dealing with American and international legal issues presented at major conferences since August 1993.

- **Keywords:** Law (US), Law (International), Legislation, Political Science
- **Sponsor:** American Political Science Association
- **Audience:** Lawyers, Legal Professionals
- **Contact:** Professor Herbert Jacob mzltov@nwu.edu

`gopher://gopher.nwu.edu`

Pre-Law, Legislation, Court Decisions ★★

A collection of legal information including court decisions on abortion, a directory of US Judges, US Supreme Court rulings, and some primary documents relating to US and International law.

- **Keywords:** Law (US Federal), Law, Law (International)
- **Sponsor:** Skidmore College Gopher Project, New York, USA
- **Audience:** Lawyers, Legal Professionals
- **Contact:** Leo Geoffrion, Peggy Seiden ldg@skidmore.edu, pseiden@skidmore.edu

`gopher://grace.skidmore.edu/readings/social-sciences/law`

Supreme Court of Canada ★★

This gopher allows access to Canadian Supreme Court rulings from 1993 forward. Documents are available as full-text and searchable by keyword. This site also has information on Canadian statute and case law.

- **Keywords:** Law (International), Canada
- **Sponsor:** Universite de Montreal Law Gopher Project, Montreal, Canada
- **Audience:** Lawyers, General Public
- **Contact:** Pablo Fuentes fuentesp@droit.umontreal.ca

`gopher://gopher.droit.umontreal.ca/English/SCC`

University of Texas at Austin Tarlton Law Library ★★

The library's holdings are large and wide-ranging and contain significant collections in many fields.

- **Keywords:** British Commonwealth Law, Constitutional Law, Law (International), Human Rights
- **Audience:** Researchers, Students, General Public
- **Details:** Free
- Expect: Login, Send: Library

`telnet://tallons.law.utexas.edu`

War Powers Resolution of 1973 ★

A joint resolution concerning the war powers of Congress and the President resolved by the Senate and the House of Representatives of the United States of America in Congress.

- **Keywords:** War, Law (International), Government (US)
- **Audience:** Politicians, Students, Lawyers, Historians
- **Details:** Free

`gopher://wiretap.spies.com/00/Gov/warpower.act`

World Constitutions ★

A list of world constitutions, containing the constitutions of more than 18 nations including Basic Law of Germany 1949; Constitution of Macedonia (in former Yugoslavia); Magna Carta.

- **Keywords:** Law (International), History (World), Politics (International)
- **Audience:** Researchers, Lawyers, Historians
- **Details:** Free

`gopher://wiretap.spies.com`

Law (Tax)

University of Nebraska at Lincoln Library ★★

The library's holdings are large and wide-ranging and contain significant collections in many fields.

- **Keywords:** Slovak Republic, Czech Republic, Folklore, Military History, Latvia, Law (Tax), Law (US)
- **Audience:** General Public, Researchers, Librarians, Document Delivery Professionals
- **Contact:** Anita Cook
- **Details:** Free
- Expect: login, Send: library

`telnet://unllib.unl.edu`

Law (US)

ADA-Law ★★

A mailing list for discussion of the Americans with Disabilities Act (ADA) and other disability-related legislation both in the US and abroad.

- **Keywords:** Disabilities, Law (US)
- **Audience:** Disabled People, Legal Professionals
- **Contact:** wtm@bunker.afd.olivetti.com
- **User Info:** To subscribe to the list, send an e-mail message to the URL address below consisting of a single line reading:

    SUB ADA-Law YourFirstName YourLastName

    To send a message to the entire list, address it to: ADA-Law@vm1.nodak.edu

`mailto:listserv@vm1.nodak.edu`

California State Senate Gopher ★★

This is a gopher site accessing California State government records and providing links to related gophers.

- **Keywords:** California, Government (US), Law (US State)
- **Sponsor:** California State Senate, California, USA
- **Audience:** Californians, General Public
- **Profile:** The California State Senate Gopher provides access to state government records, pending bills, laws, state statistics, budgets, and related matters. The gopher also provides links to related gophers inside and outside state government.

| Contact: | Gopher Provider
gopher@sen.ca.gov |

gopher://gopher.sen.ca.gov

Citation Authority

Legal citation authority expected to be used in the highest US appellate state courts, based on a 1985 survey (revised March 1991).

Keywords:	Law (US), State Courts
Audience:	Lawyers
Details:	Free
	Expect: login; Send: lawlib

gopher://liberty.uc.wlu.edu/00/library/law/lawftp/citation.txt

Cornell Law School Gopher

A gopher server providing extensive access to Cornell Law School's online archives.

Keywords:	Law (US)
Sponsor:	The Legal Information Institute
Audience:	Legal Professionals, Students
Profile:	The Cornell Law School Gopher provides access to Cornell Law School's extensive online archives. Areas covered by the gopher include case law, copyright law, trademark law, commercial law, and information about the admissions and events at the Cornell Law school.
Contact:	Thomas R. Bruce or Peter W. Martin
feedback@fatty.law.cornell.edu

gopher://fatty.law.cornell.edu

Law and Courts Preprint Archive

An online archive of papers dealing with American and international legal issues presented at major conferences since August 1993.

Keywords:	Law (US), Law (International), Legislation, Political Science
Sponsor:	American Political Science Association
Audience:	Lawyers, Legal Professionals
Contact:	Professor Herbert Jacob
mzltov@nwu.edu

gopher://gopher.nwu.edu

LEGNEW (Legal News)

The Legal News Library provides general news information about the domestic legal industry and legal profession.

Keywords:	Law (US), Justicial Process, Supreme Court (US)
Audience:	Business Researchers, Analysts, Entrepreneurs
Profile:	Included are sources which cover materials on law firm management, bar association journals and a hot file of case list summaries on recently decided US Supreme Court cases. LEGNEW is organized very simply. There are individual files, group files, and user-defined combination files.
Contact:	Mead New Sales Group at (800) 227-4908 or (513) 859-5398 inside the US, or (513) 865-7981 for all inquiries outside the US.
User Info:	To subscribe, contact Mead directly.
To examine the Nexis user guide, you can access it at the ftp site of the University of Texas at Austin at the URL address: ftp://ftp.cc.utexas.edu
The files are in: /pub/ref-services/LEXIS

telnet://nex.meaddata.com

http://www.meaddata.com

MEGA (Combined Federal/State Case Law)

The Federal/State Case Law combined library contains files that allow one-stop searching of combined federal and state case law on the LEXIS service. American Law Reports (ALR) and Lawyers' Edition, 2d articles are also included.

Keywords:	Case Law (US), Law (US State), Law (US Federal)
Audience:	Lawyers
Profile:	The MEGA file is a one-stop search of all available federal and state case law on the LEXIS service. The circuit-base MEGA files combine federal and state case law from federal and state courts within the geographical area defined by the federal circuit. The state-based MEGA files combine case law from the courts of the state plus case law from the federal circuit for that state and the federal district courts within the state. Two chronological files restrict combined federal and state case law searches to particular date ranges. Each MEGA file includes all available U.S. Supreme Court cases. American Law Reports (ALR) and Lawyers' Edition, 2d (LEd2) articles are also included.
Contact:	New Sales Group @ (800) 227-4908 or 513-859-5398 inside the US, or 1-513-865-7981 for all inquires outside the US.
User Info:	To subscribe, contact Mead directly.
To examine the Lexis user guide, you can access it at the ftp site of the University of Texas at Austin at the URL address: ftp://ftp.cc.utexas.edu
The files are in: /pub/res-services/LEXIS

telnet://nex.meaddata.com

Pre-Law, Legislation, Court Decisions

A collection of legal information including court decisions on abortion, a directory of US Judges, US Supreme Court rulings, and some primary documents relating to US and International law.

Keywords:	Law (US Federal), Law (US State), Law (International)
Sponsor:	Skidmore College Gopher Project, New York, USA
Audience:	Lawyers, Legal Professionals
Contact:	Leo Geoffrion, Peggy Seiden
ldg@skidmore.edu,
pseiden@skidmore.edu

gopher://grace.skidmore.edu/readings/social-sciences/law

LAWREV (Law Review Library)

The Law Review Library contains law reviews, American Bar Association publications, American Institute of Certified Public Accountants periodicals, and other materials. The present focus concentrates on both state and national issues of legal significance.

Keywords:	Law (US), Analysis, Journals
Audience:	Lawyers
Profile:	The Law Review Library currently consists of over 70 law reviews, several American Bar Association publicatons and American Institute of Certified Public Accountants periodicals, an Environmental Law Institute publication, ALR and LEd2d articles, two leading legal indices and a number of Warren Gorham & Lamont tax journals. The present focus concentrates on both state and national issues of legal significance.
Contact:	New Sales Group at (800) 227-4908 or 513-859-5398 inside the US, or 1-513-865-7981 for all inquires outside the US.
User Info:	To subscribe, contact Mead directly.
To examine the Lexis user guide, you can access it at the ftp site of the University of Texas at Austin at the URL address: ftp://ftp.cc.utexas.edu
The files are in: pub/ref-services/LEXIS

telnet://nex.meaddata.com

University of Nebraska at Lincoln Library

The library's holdings are large and wide-ranging and contain significant collections in many fields.

| Keywords: | Slovak Republic, Czech Republic, Folklore, Military History, Latvia, Law (Tax), Law (US) |
| Audience: | General Public, Researchers, Librarians, Document Delivery Professionals |

Contact: Anita Cook
Details: Free
Expect: login, Send: library

`telnet://unllib.unl.edu`

US Department of Education Online Library

A resource for information on federal programs, including full-text of the GOALS 2000, Educate America Act, The Prisoners of Time Report, and other documents regarding education legislation, reports, and information.

Keywords: Education, Law (US)
Sponsor: US Department of Education
Audience: Educators, Students, Legislators, Researchers

`http://www.ed.gov/`

`gopher://gopher.ed.gov`

`ftp://ftp.ed.gov`

Law (US Case)

GENFED (General Federal Library)

The General Federal Library is a comprehensive collection of federal legal materials of a general nature, including case law, legislative and regulatory materials, administrative decisions, court rules, and publications.

Keywords: Law (US Case), Law (US Federal)
Audience: Lawyers
Profile: Case law from all federal courts is available. Legislative materials include the United States Codes Service, United States Public Laws, pending federal legislation, legislative histories, and the Congressional Record. Regulatory materials include the Code of Federal Regulstions and the Federal Register. Administrative decisions, court rules, circuit summaries, sentencing guidelines, and legal publications are also available.
Contact: New Sales Group at (800) 227-4908 or 513-859-5398 inside the US, or 1-513-865-7981 for all inquiries outside the US.
Details: Costs
User Info: To subscribe, contact Mead directly.
To examine the Lexis user guide, you can access it at the ftp site of the University of Texas at Austin at the URL address: ftp://ftp.cc.utexas.edu
The files are in: pub/res-services/LEXIS

`telnet://nex.meaddata.com`

Law (US Federal)

GENFED (General Federal Library)

The General Federal Library is a comprehensive collection of federal legal materials of a general nature, including case law, legislative and regulatory materials, administrative decisions, court rules, and publications.

Keywords: Law (US Case), Law (US Federal)
Audience: Lawyers
Profile: Case law from all federal courts is available. Legislative materials include the United States Codes Service, United States Public Laws, pending federal legislation, legislative histories, and the Congressional Record. Regulatory materials include the Code of Federal Regulstions and the Federal Register. Administrative decisions, court rules, circuit summaries, sentencing guidelines, and legal publications are also available.
Contact: New Sales Group at (800) 227-4908 or 513-859-5398 inside the US, or 1-513-865-7981 for all inquiries outside the US.
Details: Costs
User Info: To subscribe, contact Mead directly.
To examine the Lexis user guide, you can access it at the ftp site of the University of Texas at Austin at the URL address: ftp://ftp.cc.utexas.edu
The files are in: /pub/res-services/LEXIS

`telnet://nex.meaddata.com`

Government-Sponsored Electronic Bulletin Boards

A list of U.S. Government-sponsored electronic bulletin boards (BBSs) for various agencies and departments.

Keywords: Government (US Federal), Law (US Federal), BBS
Sponsor: United States Government
Audience: General Public, Researchers
Profile: EBBs provide a wide and ever-changing assortment of government information, including text files, statistics, software, and graphics. Some of the information is also available in printed form but much is not. Depository librarians may find government-sponsored EBBs useful in answering reference questions and in obtaining electronic versions of government publications, regardless of whether those publications were distributed to depository libraries.
Details: Free

`gopher://gopher.ncsu.edu`

High-Performance Computing Act of 1991

This is a Senate bill to provide for a coordinated federal research program to ensure continued US leadership in high-performance computing.

Keywords: Computing, Government (US Federal), Law (US Federal)
Audience: General Public, Journalists, Politicians, Scientists
Details: Free
File is: /internet/nren/hpca.1991/gorebill.1991-txt

`ftp://nis.nsf.net`

Historical Documents of the US

A large sample of US historical documents, from the Fundamental Orders of 1639 to the Vietnam Era Documents, including World War II documents, Federalist papers, and more.

Keywords: Historical Documents (US), Government (US Federal), Law (US Federal)
Audience: Historians, Journalists, Students, Politicians
Details: Free

`gopher://wiretap.spies.com/11/Gov/US-History`

Information Infrastructure and Technology Act of 1992

The Information Infrastructure and Technology Act of 1992 builds on the High-Performance Computing Act. The newer bill will ensure that the technology developed by the High-Performance Computing Program is applied widely in K-12 education, libraries, health care, and industry, particularly manufacturing. It will authorize a total of $1.15 billion over the next five years.

Keywords: Government (US Federal), Law (US Federal), Information Technology, Education, Health Care
Audience: Journalists, Politicians, Scientists, Manufacturers, Educators
Details: Free
File is: /internet/nren/iita.1992/gorebill.1992.txt

`ftp://nis.nsf.net`

Internet Federal Register (IFR)

The full text of the US Federal Register.

Keywords: Federal Register, Government (US Federal), Law (US Federal)
Sponsor: Counterpoint Publishing
Audience: General Public, Journalists, Students, Politicians, Citizens

Contact: fedreg@internet.com
Details: Costs

`gopher://gopher.internet.com`

MEGA (Combined Federal/State Case Law)

The Federal/State Case Law combined library contains files that allow one-stop searching of combined federal and state case law on the LEXIS service. American Law Reports (ALR)) and Lawyers' Edition, 2d articles are also included.

Keywords: Case Law (US), Law (US), Law (US Federal)
Audience: Lawyers
Profile: The MEGA file is a one-stop search of all available federal and state case law on the LEXIS service. The circuit-base MEGA files combine federal and state case law from federal and state courts within the geographical area defined by the federal circuit. The state-based MEGA files combine case law from the courts of the state plus case law from the federal circuit for that state and the federal district courts within the state. Two chronological files restrict combined federal and state case law searches to particular date ranges. Each MEGA file includes all available U.S. Supreme Court cases. American Law Reports (ALR)) and Lawyers' Edition, 2d (LEd2) articles are also included.
Contact: New Sales Group @ (800) 227-4908 or 513-859-5398 inside the US, or 1-513-865-7981 for all inquires outside the US.
User Info: To subscribe, contact Mead directly.
To examine the Lexis user guide, you can access it at the ftp site of the University of Texas at Austin at the URL address: ftp://ftp.cc.utexas.edu
The files are in: pub/res-services/LEXIS

`telnet://nex.meaddata.com`

Pre-Law, Legislation, Court Decisions

A collection of legal information including court decisions on abortion, a directory of US Judges, US Supreme Court rulings, and some primary documents relating to US and International law.

Keywords: Law (US Federal), Law (US), Law (International)
Sponsor: Skidmore College Gopher Project, New York, USA
Audience: Lawyers, Legal Professionals
Contact: Leo Geoffrion, Peggy Seiden
ldg@skidmore.edu,
pseiden@skidmore.edu

`gopher://grace.skidmore.edu/readings/social-sciences/law`

Law and Courts Preprint Archive

Law and Courts Preprint Archive

An online archive of papers dealing with American and international legal issues presented at major conferences since August 1993.

Keywords: Law (US), Law (International), Legislation, Political Science
Sponsor: American Political Science Association
Audience: Lawyers, Legal Professionals
Contact: Professor Herbert Jacob
mzltov@nwu.edu

`gopher://gopher.nwu.edu`

`http://www.meaddata.com`

Laws

Congressional Quarterly Gopher

Online Information from Congressional Quarterly (CQ), the premier journal covering events on Capitol Hill.

Keywords: Congress (US), Government (US Federal), Laws
Sponsor: Congressional Quarterly
Audience: Journalists, Government Officials, Educators, General Public
Profile: This gopher allows access to weekly stories and news briefs from CQ, as well as providing information on legislation before Congress, Congressional voting records, and results of recent federal elections. Also has catalogs of CQ's publications and schedules of their professional education seminars.
Contact: gopher_admin@cqalert.com
Details: Free

`gopher://gopher.cqalert.com`

Copyright Act

The full text of the Copyright Act of 1976, Title 17, United States Code, Sections 101_810.

Keywords: Politics (US), Government (US Federal), Laws, Copyright
Audience: Lawyers, Students, Politicians, Journalists
Details: Free

`gopher://wiretap.spies.com/00/Gov/Copyright/US.Copyright.1976.tx`

Copyright Basics

This information is from Circular 1 issued by the Copyright Office, Library of Congress, January 1991. It explains what copyright is, who can claim copyright, the principles of copyrights, what works are protected, how to secure a copyright, and more.

Keywords: Copyright, Government (US Federal), Laws
Audience: Lawyers, Students, Politicians, Journalists
Details: Free

`gopher://wiretap.spies.com/00/Gov/Copyright/US.Copyright.Basics.txt`

Department of Justice Gopher

A gopher containing online information from the Justice Department.

Keywords: Laws, Government (US), Justice Department
Sponsor: United States Department of Justice
Audience: Lawyers, Citizens
Profile: The Department of Justice (DOJ) gopher features DOJ criminal and law enforcement statistics, as well as agency procurement requests, job listings, and press releases. Also has links to other US government online systems.
Contact: gopher@usdoj.gov

`gopher://gopher.usdoj.gov`

Electronic Communications Privacy Act of 1986

This is the act to amend Title 18, United States Code, with respect to the interception of certain communications, other forms of surveillance, and for other purposes. This act affects every Usenet, Bitnet, BBS, shortwave listener, TV viewer, and so on.

Keywords: Communications, Privacy, Government (US Federal), Laws
Audience: Journalists, Privacy Activists, Students, Politicians
Details: Free

`gopher://wiretap.spies.com/00/Gov/ecpa.act`

Patent Act of the US

This resource contains full-text documentation regarding the US Patent Act (Title 35, United States Code, Sections 1 - 376).

Keywords: Patents, Laws, Government (US Federal)
Audience: Journalists, Politicians, Economists, Lawyers, Scientists
Details: Free

`http://fatty.law.cornell.edu/patent/patent.overview.html`

Privacy Act of 1974 ★

The act that regulates the maintenance of privacy and protection of records on individuals.

Keywords: Privacy, Laws, Government (US Federal)
Audience: Journalists, Politicians, Lawyers
Details: Free
Choose from menu as appropriate.

`gopher://wiretap.spies.com/00/Gov/privacy.act`

Questions and Answers about the GPO Gateway to Government Act ★

Questions and answers dealing with the bill GPO Gateway to Government Act of 1992. Questions such as, "What will the gateway do?," "Why is this gateway needed?," "What types of Information will be available through the Gateway?," and more.

Keywords: Laws (US Federal), Government (US Federal), Federal Databases
Audience: General Public, Journalists, Politicians
Details: Free
File is: pub/nic/NREN/GPO.questions

`ftp://ftp.sura.net`

Trademark Act of the US ★

The US Trademark Act of 1946 (the "Lanham Act"), Title 15, United States Code, Sections 1051_1127.

Keywords: Trademarks, Laws, Government (US), Commerce
Audience: Journalists, Politicians, Students, Lawyers, Business Professionals, Designers, Marketers
Details: Free

`http://www.law.cornell.edu/lanham/lanham.table.html`

Universal Copyright Convention ★★

The Universal Copyright Convention as revised at Paris (1971). Convention and protocols were done at Paris on July 24, 1971. It was ratified by the President of the United States of America on August 28, 1972.

Keywords: Copyright, Laws, Government (US), Politics (US)
Audience: Lawyers, Students, Politicians, Journalists
Details: Free

`gopher://wiretap.spies.com/00/Gov/Copyright US.Universal.Copyright.Conv.txt`

U.S. Consumer Product Safety Commission (CPSC) ★★★

The CPSC's mission is to protect the public from defective and potentially dangerous consumer products. This gopher has archives of CPSC press releases and action reports from 1990-1994, as well as a calendar of upcoming events and guidelines for reporting potentially dangerous products to the CPSC.

Keywords: Safety, Consumerism, Laws
Sponsor: US Consumer Product Safety Commission
Audience: Consumers, Activists
Contact: pweddle@cpsc.gov
Notes: You can call the CPSC at their toll-free hotline at (800) 638-2772.

`gopher://cpsc.gov`

Leaders of Community Networking: People Who Create Online Communities

Leaders of Community Networking: People Who Create Online Communities ★

A WWW document with links to several important community networking resources. A brief overview of community networking is provided, as are links to statements by several leaders in the movement.

Keywords: Community, Networking, Government (US Federal)
Audience: Activists, Policymakers, Community Leaders, Government, Citizens
Details: Free

`http://nearnet.gnn.com/mag/articles/oram/introduction.html`

Leadership

IRVL-l (Institute for Research on Visionary Leadership) ★★

The Forum for Research on Visionary Leadership provides continuing substantive discourse on visionary leadership and networked archiving of digests of dialogue.

Keywords: Leadership
Sponsor: Institute for Visionary Leadership
Audience: Administrators
Contact: estepp@byrd.mu.wvnet.edu or m034050@marshall

User Info: To subscribe to the list, send an e-mail message to the address below consisting of a single line reading:
SUB irvl-l YourFirstName YourLastName
To send a message to the entire list, address it to: irvl-l@byrd.mu.wvnet.edu

`mailto: listserv@byrd.mu.wvnet.edu`

Legal Research

Research on Demand ★★★

A resource for the provision of market information, strategic information location, product information, and national and international business information.

Keywords: Market Research, Internet Research, Legal Research, International Research
Audience: Marketing Specialists, Lawyers, Public Relations Experts, Business Professionals, Researchers, Writers, Producers
Profile: This resource has special access to unique information resources worldwide. Areas of particular information access include the former Soviet Union, Europe, and the US. Information access also includes access to all the major online systems, including Dialog, BRS, Orbit, DataStar, and so on. Current Awareness Services include research information gathered from the Internet.
Details: Costs
User Info: To subscribe, send an e-mail message to the URL address below. In the body of your message, state the nature of your inquiry.
Notes: Contact ROD directly in the US at: (800) 227-0750; outside the US at: (510) 841-1145.

`mailto:rod@holonet.net`

Legal Status

Legal Status

Records thousands of types of actions that can affect the legal status of a patent document after it is published and after the patent is granted.

Keywords: Patents, Intellectual Property, Trademarks
Sponsor: European Patent Office
Audience: Patent Attorneys, Patent Agents, Librarians, Researchers
Profile: Information about the disposition of patent applications published under the Patent Cooperation Treaty by the World

Intellectual Property Organizations is included as well. Contains more than 8 million records. Updated weekly.

Contact: paul.albert@neteast.com

User Info: To subscribe contact Orbit-Questel directly.

`telnet://orbit.com`

Legion of Doom/Hackers Technical Journals

Legion of Doom/Hackers Technical Journals

Technical journals of the infamous hacking ring Legion of Doom.

Keywords: Hacking, Computers

Audience: Hackers, Computer Users

Details: Free

User Info: Expect: login,Send: anonymous; Expect: Password,Send: Your E-mail Address

`ftp://ftp.eff.org`

Legislation

Americans with Disabilities Act

Gives access to the full text of the Americans with Disabilities Act (ADA) and all the related legislation.

Keywords: Disabled People, Differently Abled People, Legislation, Government

Audience: General Public, Disabled People, Differently Abled People, Politicians, Journalists, Students

Profile: The purpose of ADA is to provide a clear and comprehensive national mandate to end discrimination against individuals with disabilities and to bring them into the economic and social mainstream of American life; to provide enforceable standards addressing discrimination against individuals with disabilities; and to ensure that the federal government plays a central role in enforcing these standards on behalf of individuals with disabilities.

Details: Free

`gopher://val-dor.cc.buffalo.edu/11/.legislation/`

Berne Convention Implementation Act of 1988

An act to amend Title 17, United States Code, to implement the Berne Convention for the Protection of Literary and Artistic Works, as revised in Paris on July 24, 1971, and for other purposes.

Keywords: Legislation, Government (US), Politics (US), Copyright

Audience: Lawyers, Students, Politicians, Journalists

Details: Free

`gopher://wiretap.spies.com/00/Gov/Copyright/US.Berne.Convention.txt`

Bibliographies of US Senate Hearings

The US Senate produces a series of committee hearings, prints, and publications as part of the legislative process. The Documents department at North Carolina State University contains files for the 99th through 103rd Congresses, which can also be searched through a WAIS searchable database.

Keywords: Senate (US), Politics (US), Legislation, Bibliographies, Government (US)

Audience: General Public, Journalists, Students, Politicians, US Citizens

Contact: Jack McGeachy
Jack_McGeachy@ncsu.edu

Details: Free

`gopher://dewey.lib.ncsu.edu/11/library/disciplines/government/senate`

EXEC (Executive Branch News US)

The EXEC library contains information and news about the Executive Branch of the Federal Government. From the Department of Agriculture to the White House, this file is a comprehensive source of information that will be especially useful to those whose responsibilities include monitoring federal regulations, Agency and Department activity, and the people and issues involved.

Keywords: News, Legislation, Regulation, Politics, Executive Branch

Audience: Journalists, Lobbyists, Business Executives, Analysts, Entrepreneurs

Profile: The EXEC library allows the searching of individual files or group files that cover topics such as the Federal Register and Code of Federal Regulations; public laws; proposed treasury regulation; and over 50 news sources, including BNA's Daily Report for Executives, the Dept. of State Dispatch, ABC News transcripts, Federal News Service Daybook, Government Executive, MacNeil/Lehrer Newshour, New Leader, National Review, the Washington Post, the Washington Times, Presidential Documents, and many others.

Contact: Mead New Sales Group at (800) 227-4908 or (513) 859-5398 inside the US, or (513) 865-7981 for all inquiries outside the US.

User Info: To subscribe, contact Mead directly.

To examine the Nexis user guide, you can access it at the ftp site of the University of Texas at Austin at the URL address: ftp://ftp.cc.utexas.edu

The files are in: /pub/ref-services/LEXIS

`telnet://nex.meaddata.com`

`http://www.meaddata.com`

Law and Courts Preprint Archive

An online archive of papers dealing with American and international legal issues presented at major conferences since August 1993.

Keywords: Law (US), Law (International), Legislation, Political Science

Sponsor: American Political Science Association

Audience: Lawyers, Legal Professionals

Contact: Professor Herbert Jacob
mzltov@nwu.edu

`gopher://gopher.nwu.edu`

Privacy Rights Clearinghouse (PRC)

A collection of materials related to privacy issues.

Keywords: Privacy, Legislation, Consumer Rights, Freedom of Information

Sponsor: University of San Diego

Audience: Citizens, Privacy Activists, Journalists

Profile: This site contains fact sheets (in English and Spanish) on privacy issues ranging from wiretapping to credit reporting. Also includes federal and state privacy legislation as well as related position papers and press releases.

Contact: prc@teetot.acusd.edu

Expect: Login; Send: Privacy

`gopher://teetot.acusd.edu`

`telnet://teetot.acusd.edu`

Legislation (Australian)

Australia

Full-text versions of Australian legislation.

Keywords: Australia, Legislation (Australian)

Audience: Australian Citizens, Environmentalists, Governments

Details: Free

Select from menu as appropriate

`gopher://wiretap.spies.com`

LEGNEW (Legal News)

LEGNEW (Legal News)

The Legal News Library provides general news information about the domestic legal industry and legal profession.

Keywords:	Law (US), Judicial Process, Supreme Court (US)
Audience:	Business Researchers, Analysts, Entrepreneurs
Profile:	Included are sources which cover materials on law firm management, bar association journals and a hot file of case list summaries on recently decided US Supreme Court cases. LEGNEW is organized very simply. There are individual files, group files, and user-defined combination files.
Contact:	Mead New Sales Group at (800) 227-4908 or (513) 859-5398 inside the US, or (513) 865-7981 for all inquiries outside the US.
User Info:	To subscribe, contact Mead directly. To examine the Nexis user guide, you can access it at the ftp site of the University of Texas at Austin at the URL address: ftp://ftp.cc.utexas.edu The files are in: /pub/ref-services/LEXIS

`telnet://nex.meaddata.com`

`http://www.meaddata.com`

Lego Information

Lego Information ★★★

A web site containing pictures, sets, and instructions for building with Legos. Also discusses various ideas, activities, and history pertaining to Legos, as well as information about clubs for Lego enthusiasts.

Keywords:	Construction, Toys, Children
Sponsor:	Lego
Audience:	Children, General Public
Contact:	David Koblas koblas@netcom.com

`http://legowww.itek.norut.no`

Leonardo Electronic Almanac

Leonardo Electronic Almanac ★★★★

The Leonardo Electronic Almanac (LEA) is a monthly, edited journal and an electronic archive dedicated to providing current perspectives in the art, science, and technology domains.

Keywords:	Art, Multimedia, Music, Electronic Media
Sponsor:	International Society for the Arts, Sciences, and Technology
Audience:	New Media Artists, Researchers, Art Educators, Art Professionals
Profile:	LEA is an international, interdisciplinary forum for people interested in the use of new media in contemporary artistic expression, especially involving 20th century science and technology. Material is contributed by artists, scientists, philosophers and educators. LEA is published by the MIT Press for Leonardo, the International Society for the Arts, Sciences, and Technology (ISAST).
Contact:	Craig Harris craig@well.sf.ca.us
Details:	Costs, Moderated, Images, Sounds, Multimedia

`mail to:journals-orders@mit.edu`

`ftp://mitpress.mit.edu/pub/Leonardo-Elec-Almanac`

Lesbians

amend2-discuss ★★

A mailing list for discussion of the implications and issues surrounding the passage of Colorado's Amendment 2, which revokes any existing homosexual civil rights legislation and prohibits the drafting of any new legislation.

Keywords:	Activism, Gay Rights, Lesbians, Bisexuality
Audience:	Gay Rights Activists
Contact:	amend2-mod@cs.colorado.edu
User Info:	To subscribe to the list, send an e-mail message to the URL address below consisting of a single line reading: subscribe amend2-discuss

`mailto:majordomo@cs.colorado.edu`

amend2-info

Colorado voted in an amendment to their state constitution which revokes any existing gay/lesbian/bisexual civil rights legislation and prohibits the drafting of any new legislation. This moderated list is for information on the implication and issues of this amendment.

Keywords:	Activists, Gays, Lesbians, Bisexuality, Constitutional Amendments, Colorado, Civil Rights
Audience:	General Public, Gays, Lesbians, Bisexuals, Activists
Contact:	amend2-info@cs.colorado.edu
User Info:	To subscribe to the list, send an e-mail message requesting a subscription to the URL address below. To send a message to the entire list, address it to: amend2-info@cs.colorado.edu

`mailto:majordomo@cs.colorado.edu`

AUGLBC-l

The American University Gay, Lesbian, and Bisexual Community (AUGLBC) is a support group for lesbian, gay, bisexual, transsexual, and supportive students. The group is also connected with the International Gay and Lesbian Youth Organization (known as IGLYO).

Keywords:	Gays, Lesbians, Bisexuality, Transsexuality, Sexuality
Audience:	Gays, Lesbians, Bisexuals, Transsexuals, Students (college)
Contact:	Erik G. Paul
User Info:	To subscribe to the list, send an e-mail message to the URL address below, consisting of a single line reading: SUB AUGLBC-l YourFirstName YourLastName To send a message to the entire list, address it to: AUGLBC-l@american.edu

`mailto:listserv@american.edu`

AusGBLF ★

An Australian-based mailing list for gays, bisexuals, lesbians, and friends.

Keywords:	Australia, Gays, Lesbians, Bisexuality
Audience:	Gays, Lesbians, Bisexuals
Contact:	zglc@minyos.xx.rmit.oz.au
Details:	Free
User Info:	To subscribe to the list, send an e-mail message requesting a subscription to the URL address below. To send a message to the entire list, address it to: ausgblf@minyos.xx.rmit.oz.au

`mailto:ausgblf-request@minyos.xx.rmit.oz.au`

ba-Sappho ★

Ba-Sappho is a San Francisco Bay Area lesbian mailing list intended for local networking and announcements. BA-Sappho is not a discussion group.

Keywords:	Lesbians, San Francisco Bay Area
Audience:	Lesbians
Contact:	ba-sappho-request@labrys.mti.sgi.com
Details:	Free

User Info: To subscribe to the list, send an e-mail message requesting a subscription to the URL address below.

To send a message to the entire list, address it to: ba-sappho@labrys.mti.sgi.com

mailto:ba-sappho-request@labrys.mti.sgi.com

Chorus

This is the lesbian and gay chorus mailing list, formed November 1991 by John Schrag (jschrag@alias.com) and Brian Jarvis (jarvis@psych.toronto.edu). Membership includes artistic directors, singers, chorus officers, interpreters, and support staff and friends. Topics of discussion include repertoire, arrangements, staging, costuming, management, fundraising, music, events, and concerts.

Keywords: Singing, Choral Singing, Homosexuality, Gays, Lesbians

Audience: Lesbian Singers, Gay Singers, Chorus Officers, Lesbians, Gays, Choral Singers

Contact: chorus-request@psych.toronto.edu

Details: Free

User Info: To subscribe to the list, send an e-mail message requesting a subscription to the URL address below.

To send a message to the entire list, address it to: chorus@psych.toronto.edu

mailto:chorus-request@psych.toronto.edu

DC-MOTSS

DC-MOTSS is a social mailing list for the gay, lesbian, and bisexual folks who live in the Washington Metropolitan Area—everything within approximately 50 miles of The Mall.

Keywords: Gays, Lesbians, Bisexuality, Washington DC

Audience: Gays, Lesbians, Bisexuals, Washington DC Residents

Contact: DC-MOTSS-request@vector.intercon.com

Details: Free

User Info: To subscribe to the list, send an e-mail message requesting a subscription to the URL address below.

To send a message to the entire list, address it to: DC-MOTSS-request@vector.intercon.com

mailto:DC-MOTSS-request@vector.intercon.com

DSA-LGB

DSA-LGB is a mailing list for members of the Lesbian/Gay/Bisexual Commission of the Democratic Socialists of America, and for others interested in similar concerns.

Keywords: Democratic Socialists of America, Gays, Lesbians

Audience: Democratic Socialists, Gays, Lesbians

Contact: DSA-LGB-request@midway.uchicago.edu

User Info: To subscribe to the list, send an e-mail message requesting a subscription to the URL address below.

To send a message to the entire list, address it to: DSA-LGB-request@midway.uchicago.edu

mailto:DSA-LGB-request@midway.uchicago.edu

eagles

This list provides a forum for Boy Scouts, Scouters, and former Scouts who are gay/bisexual to discuss how they can apply pressure to the BSA to change their homophobic policies.

Keywords: Boy Scouts, Gays, Lesbians

Audience: Gays, Lesbians, Boy Scouts, Former Boy Scouts

Contact: eagles-request@flash.usc.edu

Details: Free

User Info: To subscribe to the list, send an e-mail message requesting a subscription to the URL address below.

To send a message to the entire list, address it to: eagles-request@flash.usc.edu

mailto:eagles-request@flash.usc.edu

gay-libn

A network for gay, lesbian, and bisexual librarians.

Keywords: Libraries, Gays, Lesbians, Bisexual

Audience: Librarians, Gays, Lesbians, Bisexuals

Details: Free

User Info: To subscribe to the list, send an e-mail message to the URL address below consisting of a single line reading:

SUB gay-libn YourFirstName YourLastName

To send a message to the entire list, address it to: gay-libn@vm.usc.edu

mailto:listserv@vm.usc.edu

gaynet

This list covers gay, lesbian, and bisexual concerns (with a focus on college campuses), including outreach programs, political action, AIDS education, school administration issues, social programs, and support group exchanges.

Keywords: Gays, Lesbians

Audience: Gays, Lesbians, Bisexuals, Students

Contact: Roger B.A. Klorese gaynet-approval@queernet.org

Details: Free

User Info: To subscribe to the list, send an e-mail message to the URL address below consisting of a single line reading:

SUB gaynet YourFirstName YourLastName

To send a message to the entire list, address it to: gaynet@queernet.org

mailto:majordomo@queernet.org

Moms

Moms is a list for lesbian mothers.

Keywords: Lesbian, Parenting

Audience: Lesbian Mothers, Lesbians

Contact: moms-request@qiclab.scn.rain.com

Details: Free

User Info: To subscribe to the list, send an e-mail message requesting subscription to the URL address below.

mailto:moms-request@qiclab.scn.rain.com

Ne-social-motss

Announcements of lesbian/gay/bisexual social events and other happenings in the Northeastern US.

Keywords: Social Events, Lesbian, Gay, Bisexuality

Audience: Lesbians, Gays, Bisexuals

Contact: ne-social-motss-request@plts.org

Details: Free

User Info: To subscribe to the list, send an e-mail message requesting a subscription to the URL address below.

mailto:ne-social-motss-request@plts.org

NJ-motss

Mailing list for gay, lesbian, and bisexual issues in New Jersey.

Keywords: Gay, Lesbian, Bisexuality, New Jersey

Audience: Gays, Lesbians, Bisexuals

Contact: majordomo@plts.org

Details: Free

User Info: To subscribe to the list, send an e-mail message to the URL address shown below consisting of a single line reading:

SUB NJ-motss YourFirstName YourLastName

To send a message to the entire list, address it to: NJ-motss@plts.org

mailto:majordomo@plts.org

NJ-motss-announce

Announcements of interests to New Jersey's gay, lesbian, and bisexual population.

Keywords:	Gay, Lesbian, Bisexuality, New Jersey
Audience:	Gays, Lesbians, Bisexuals
Contact:	majordomo@plts.org
Details:	Free
User Info:	To subscribe to the list, send an e-mail message to the URL address shown below consisting of a single line reading:
	SUB NJ-motss-announce YourFirstName YourLastName
	To send a message to the entire list, address it to: NJ-motss-announce@plts.org

`mailto:majordomo@plts.org`

noglstp

This list is sponsored by the National Organization of Gay and Lesbian Scientists and Technical Professionals, Inc. (a 501-C3 organization). National office is in Pasadena, CA and can be reached at (818) 791-7689 or p.o. Box 91803, Pasadena, CA 90019. There is also a newsletter that is available to membership.

Keywords:	Gay, Lesbian, Scientists, Technical Professionals
Audience:	Gay Scientists, Lesbian Scientists
Contact:	noglstp-request@elroy.jpl.nasa.gov
Details:	Free
User Info:	To subscribe to the list, send an e-mail message requesting a subscription to the URL address below.
	To send a message to the entire list, address it to: noglstp@elroy.jpl.nasa.gov

`mailto:noglstp-request@elroy.jpl.nasa.gov`

Oh-motss

The Oh-motss (Ohio Members of the Same Sex) mailing list is for open discussion of lesbian, gay, and bisexual issues in and affecting Ohio. The mailing list is not moderated. It is open to all, regardless of location or sexuality. The subscriber list is known only to the list owner.

Keywords:	Gays, Lesbian, Ohio
Audience:	Gays, Lesbians
Contact:	oh-motss-request@cps.udayton.edu
Details:	Free
User Info:	To subscribe to the list, send an e-mail message requesting a subscription to the URL address below.
	To send a message to the entire list, address it to: oh-motss@cps.udayton.edu

`mailto:oh-motss-request@cps.udayton.edu`

OUTIL (Out in Linguistics)

The list is open to lesbian, gay, bisexual, transsexual linguists, and their friends. The only requirement is that you be willing to be out to everyone on the list. The purposes of the group are to be visible to and to gather occasionally to enjoy one another's company.

Keywords:	Linguistics, Gays, Lesbians, Bisexuals, Transsexuals
Audience:	Linguists, Gays, Lesbians, Bisexuals, Transsexuals
Contact:	Arnold Zwicky outil-request@csli.stanford.edu
Details:	Free
User Info:	To subscribe to the list, send an e-mail message requesting a subscription to the URL address below.
	To send a message to the entire list, address it to: outil@csli.stanford.edu

`mailto:outil-request@csli.stanford.edu`

soc.motss

A Usenet newsgroup providing information and discussion about homosexuality.

Keywords:	Homosexuality, Gays, Lesbians, Bisexuals
Audience:	Gays, Lesbians, Bisexuals
Details:	Free
User Info:	To subscribe to this Usenet newsgroup, you need access to a newsreader.

`news:soc.motss`

Stonewall25

A mailing list for discussion and planning of the "Stonewall 25," an international gay/lesbian/bisexual rights march in New York City on Sunday, June 26, 1994, and the events accompanying it.

Keywords:	Gay Rights, Lesbian, Bisexual, Activism
Audience:	Gays, Lesbians, Bisexuals, Activists
Contact:	stonewall25-request@queernet.org
Details:	Free
User Info:	To subscribe to the list, send an e-mail message requesting a subscription to the URL address below.
	To send a message to the entire list, address it to: stonewall25@queernet.org

`mailto:stonewall25-request@queernet.org`

Lexicography

The World Wide Web Acronym Server

This web site is a guide to acronyms and abbreviations.

Keywords:	Internet, Lexicography
Audience:	Internet Surfers
Contact:	Peter Flynn pflynn@curia.ucc.ie
Details:	Free

`http://curia.ucc.ie/info/net/acronyms/acro.html`

Lexicology

alt.usage.english

A Usenet newsgroup providing information and discussion about English grammar, word usages, and related topics.

Keywords:	Lexicology, Academia, Linguistics, Education
Audience:	English Educators
User Info:	To subscribe to this Usenet newsgroup, you need access to a newsreader.

`news:alt.usage.english`

Online-dict

A mailing list devoted to a discussion of online dictionaries and related issues including installation, modification, and maintenance of their databases, search engines, and user interfaces.

Keywords:	Dictionaries, Information Technology, Lexicology
Audience:	Librarians, Information Scientists, Systems Operators
Contact:	Jack Lynch jlynch@dept.english.upenn.edu
Details:	Free
User Info:	To subscribe, send an e-mail message to the URL address below consisting of a single line reading:
	SUB online-dict YourFirstName YourLastName
	To send a message to the entire list, address it to: online-dict@dept.english.upenn.edu

`mailto:listserv@dept.english.upenn.edu`

Style Sheets from the Online Writers' Workshop.

This gopher provides information and examples on how to write bibliographies using three formats: MLA (Modern Language Association), Old-MLA, and APA (American Psychological Association).

Keywords:	Bibliographies, Writing, Lexicology
Sponsor:	University of Illinois at Urbana-Champaign
Audience:	Writers, Students (High School/College/University)
Contact:	Dr. Michael Pemberton michaelp@ux1.cso.uiuc

`gopher://gopher.uiuc.edu`

University of Michigan Library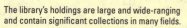

The library's holdings are large and wide-ranging and contain significant collections in many fields.

Keywords:	Asia, Astronomy, Transportation, Lexicology, Mathematics, Zoology, Geography
Audience:	Researchers, Students, General Public
Contact:	info@merit.edu
Details:	Free
	Expect: Which Host; Send: Help

`telnet://cts.merit.edu`

LEXPAT (Patents US)

LEXPAT (Patents US)

The LEXPAT library contains the full text of US patents issued since 1975, the US Patent and Trademark Office Manual of Classification, and the Index to US Patent Classification. The approximately 1,500 patents added to the library each week appear online within four days of their issue.

Keywords:	Patents, Inventors, Assignees, Litigants
Audience:	Lawyers, Business Researchers, Analysts, Entrepreneurs
Profile:	LEXPAT may be searched by individual files for the full text of utility, design or plant patents, or you can combine the files in one 'omni' search. The Manual, Index and Class files can be used to supplement your full-text patent searches. LEXPAT is a valuable tool for both patent professionals and for anyone who needs to access to technical information. More than 80 percent of the information contained in patents is unavailable in any other form.
Contact:	Mead New Sales Group at (800) 227-4908 or (513) 859-5398 inside the US, or (513) 865-7981 for all inquiries outside the US.

User Info:	To subscribe, contact Mead directly.
	To examine the Nexis user guide, you can access it at the ftp site of the University of Texas at Austin at the URL address: ftp://ftp.cc.utexas.edu The files are in: /pub/ref-services/LEXIS

`telnet://nex.meaddata.com`

`http://www.meaddata.com`

Liberal Education

University of Wisconsin at Oshkosh Library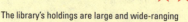

The library's holdings are large and wide-ranging and contain significant collections in many fields.

Keywords:	Business, Liberal Education, Nursing
Audience:	Researchers, Students, General Public
Details:	Free
	Expect: Login; Send: Lib; Expect: vDIAL Prompt, Send: Library

`telnet://polk.cis.uwosh.edu`

Libertarian Politics

alt.politics.libertarian

A Usenet newsgroup providing information and discussion about the libertarian ideology.

Keywords:	Libertarian Politics
Audience:	Libertarians, Politicians
User Info:	To subscribe to this Usenet newsgroup, you need access to a newsreader.

`news:alt.politics.libertarian`

ca-Liberty

This is an announcement of area-based Libertarian meetings, events, activities, etc. The ca- list is for California statewide issues; the ba- list is for the San Francisco Bay Area and gets all messages sent to the ca- list. Prospective members should subscribe to one or the other, generally depending on whether or not they are SF Bay Area residents.

Keywords:	Libertarian Politics, California
Audience:	Libertarians, Political Scientists, Politicians, General Public
Contact:	Jeff Chan ca-liberty-request@shell.portal.com
Details:	Free
User Info:	To subscribe to the list, send an e-mail message requesting a subscription to the URL address below.
	To send a message to the entire list, address it to: ca-liberty@shell.portal.com

`mailto:ca-liberty-request@shell.portal.com`

Political Platforms of the US

Full text of various documents including the Democratic platform of 1992, the Jerry Brown positions of 1992, the Libertarian platform of 1990, and more.

Keywords:	Politics (US), Government (US Federal), Democracy, Libertarian Politics
Audience:	Politicians, Grass-Roots Organizers, Journalists
Details:	Free

`gopher://wiretap.spies.com/11/Gov/Platform`

Librarianship

Librarian's Internet Reference

Electronic version of 'Internet Connections: A Librarian's Guide to Dial-Up Access and Use,' written by Mary E. Engle, and Marilyn Lutz, William Jones, Jr., and Genevieve Engel.

Keywords:	Internet Guides, Librarianship
Audience:	Librarians
Contact:	Mary Engle Mary_Engle@ucop.edu

`gopher://gopher.poniecki.berkeley.edu Poniecki Foundation/Internet Guides`

Newsletter on Serials Pricing Issues

The focus of this newsletter is the pricing of library serials.

Keywords:	Serials Pricing, Librarianship
Audience:	Librarians, Publishers
Profile:	Contributions include examples of titles considered to be overpriced, as well as of publishers' actions to keep prices down, strategies for coping with serials price increases, information about libraries' evaluation and cancellation policies and procedures, announcements of and reports from relevant meetings, and other news of serials prices.
Contact:	Marcia Tuttle tuttle@unc.bitnet
Details:	Free
User Info:	To subscribe, send an e-mail message to the URL address shown below consisting of a single line reading:
	SUB serials_pricing YourFirstName YourLastName

`mailto:listserv@uncvx1.Bitnet`

Libraries

AskERIC Virtual Library ★★★★

This gopher is part of a federally-funded system to provide public access to educational resources.

Keywords:	Education (K-12), Computer-Aided Learning, Libraries, Electronic Books
Sponsor:	Educational Resources Information Center (ERIC)
Audience:	K-12 Teachers, Administrators
Profile:	This gopher contains a wide-range of educational aids including pre-prepared lesson plans, guides to Internet resources for the classroom organized by subject, updates on conferences for educators, and archives of education-related listservs. Also allows access to outside gophers, libraries, and sources of electronic books and journals.
Contact:	Nancy A. Morgan nmorgan@ericir.syr.edu askeric@ericir.syr.edu

`gopher://ericir/syr.edu`

Barron's Guide to Accessing On-Line Bibliographic Databases ★★

A comprehensive listing of publicly-accessible online libraries, including login instructions for each site.

Keywords:	Libraries, Databases
Sponsor:	University of North Texas
Audience:	Researchers, Library Users, Librarians
Contact:	Billy Barron billy@unt.edu

`gopher://alf.zfn.uni-bremen.de/Allgemeine`

BRIDGE ★

An online public access catalogue, the PALS-based catalogue provides access to the collections of two institutions, St. Boniface University and the Manitoba General Hospital.

Keywords:	Medicine, Libraries
Sponsor:	St. Boniface University, and the Manitoba General Hospital Libraries
Audience:	Health Professionals, Students, Medical Educators
Details:	Free

`telnet://BE@umopac.umanitoba.ca`

Brown University Library ★★★★

The Brown libraries contain approximately 1.5 million volumes, including historical archives of early American imprints and the biomedical engineering holdings.

Keywords:	Libraries, Research
Audience:	General Public, Researchers
Contact:	Howard Pasternick blips15@brownvm.brown.edu
Details:	Free At the Brown logon screen: tab to command field, Enter Dial Josiah, tab to Josiah choice on the screen.

`telnet://brownvm.brown.edu`

`telnet://library.brown.edu`

Catholic University of America Gopher ★★

Gopher server of the Catholic University of America

Keywords:	Catholicism, Libraries
Sponsor:	Catholic University of America
Audience:	Catholics
Profile:	The Catholic University of America gopher provides access to CUA's libraries and archived material as well as providing links to outside, and foreign, related gophers, and electronic resources.

`gopher://gopher.cua.edu`

Chiba University Gopher

The Chiba University gopher, including files from the university's library.

Keywords:	Japan, Asia, Libraries
Sponsor:	Chiba University, Chiba, Japan
Audience:	Japan Residents, Computer Programmers, Librarians, Linguists
Contact:	hasimoto@chiba-u.ac.jp

`gopher://himawari.ipc.chiba-u.ac.jp`

Columbia University Libraries ★★★★

The Columbia libraries include a medical library and a mathematics library.

Keywords:	Libraries, Research
Audience:	General Public, Researchers
Details:	Free When connected, hit return, enter terminal type: vt100.

`telnet://clio.cul.columbia.edu`

Cornell University Libraries ★★★★

This library system maintains special collections in engineering, nuclear engineering, textile engineering, agriculture, medicine, Africana, entomology, hotels, ILR, mathematics, physical sciences, and veterinary medicine.

Keywords:	Libraries, Research
Audience:	General Public, Researchers
Details:	Free When userid/password screen appears, press return. When cp read appears on the screen, type library.

`telnet://cornellc.cit.cornell.edu`

Creighton University Library Online Catalogue ★★★★

This site maintains a catalog of the Creighton University library's holdings.

Keywords:	Health Sciences, Libraries
Sponsor:	Creighton University, Omaha, Nebraska, USA
Audience:	Health-Care Professionals, Medical Educators, Students
Details:	Free At the prompt type <lib hsl>for Health Sciences Library.

`telnet://attachpals@owl.creighton.edu`

Current Cites ★★★

A monthly publication of the Library Technology Watch Program at The Library, University of California, Berkeley.

Keywords:	Computer Technology, Libraries
Sponsor:	The Library, University of California, Berkeley, CA
Audience:	Librarians, Computer Programmers
Profile:	Over 30 journals in librarianship and computer technology are scanned for articles on optical-disk technologies, computer networks and networking, information transfer, expert systems and artificial intelligence, and hypermedia and multimedia.
Contact:	David Robison drobison@library.berkeley.edu
Details:	Free

`telnet://melvyl.ucop.edu`

Denmark's Library for Medicine and Science ★

Keywords:	Science, Medicine, Libraries, Denmark
Audience:	Scientists, Health-Care Professionals, Medical Researchers
Details:	Free At the CCL>prompt type DIA ENG for English interface.

`telnet://cosmos.bib.dk`

gay-libn ★

A network for gay, lesbian, and bisexual librarians.

Keywords: Libraries, Gays, Lesbians, Bisexuality

Audience:	Librarians, Gays, Lesbians, Bisexuals
Details:	Free
User Info:	To subscribe to the list, send an e-mail message to the URL address below consisting of a single line reading:
	SUB gay-libn YourFirstName YourLastName
	To send a message to the entire list, address it to: gay-libn@vm.usc.edu

`mailto:listserv@vm.usc.edu`

Georgetown University Medical Center Online Catalogue ★★

This site maintains a catalog of the Georgetown University Medical Center library's holdings.

Keywords:	Medicine, Libraries
Sponsor:	Georgetown University, Washington, DC
Audience:	Medical Professionals, Educators, Students
Contact:	Jane Banks banksj@gumedlib2.georgetown.edu
Details:	Free
	The password is dahlgren, then enter netguest, hit RETURN several times and select option 1.

`telnet://medlib@gumedlib.georgetown.edu`

Harvard Medical Gopher ★★

This gopher site accesses information from Harvard Medical School. Provides bibliographic information from Harvard Medical Library, basic science and clinical resources, and public health and government statistics.

Keywords:	Medicine, Libraries, Health Care
Sponsor:	Harvard Medical School, Cambridge, Massachusetts, USA
Audience:	Physicians, Health-Care Professionals, Educators, Students
Contact:	gopher@warren.med.harvard.edu
Details:	Free

`gopher://gopher.med.harvard.edu`

HYTELNET

A shareware application database directory to libraries.

Keywords:	Computer Systems, Libraries, Shareware
Audience:	General Audience
Profile:	HYTELNET is a guide to library catalogs from the Americas, Europe
Contact:	Peter Scott aa375@freenet.carleton.ca
Details:	Free
Notes:	HYTELNET is in English, but the interface to some international

`gopher://gophlib@gopher.yale.edu`

Internet Libraries (Gopher) ★★★

The site maintains the most current possible list of all library catalogs accessible on the Internet.

Keywords:	Libraries, Databases, Internet, Information Retrieval
Audience:	Reseacher, Students, Librarians
Contact:	Gopherlib gopherlib@gopher.yale.edu

`gopher://yaleinfo.yale.edu`

K-12 School Libraries

This directory is a compilation of information resources focused on K-12 Education.

Keywords:	Libraries, Education (K-12)
Audience:	Librarians, Educators (K-12)

`ftp://una.hh.lib.umich.edu/70/inetdirsstacks/k12schmed:troselius`

Library Resources

A specialized guide to library resources on the Internet, with a focus on strategies for selection and use.

Keywords:	Libraries, Internet, Internet Guide
Audience:	Internet Surfers, Researchers
	File is: pub/internet/libcat-guide

`ftp://dla.ucop.edu/pub/internet/libcat-guide`

Library Special ★

Library special collections on the Internet.

Keywords:	Internet, Information Retrieval
Audience:	Internet Surfers
Details:	Free

`ftp://dla.ucop.edu/pub`

`http://dla.ucop.edu`

LIST Gopher ★★★

This is a library-related service that allows users to obtain information by using their e-mail accounts.

Keywords:	Mailing Lists, Listserv, Libraries, Gopher
Sponsor:	North Carolina State University, Raleigh, North Carolina, USA
Audience:	Librarians, Library Users, e-mail Users
Profile:	LISTGopher allows users to search library-related LISTSERV archives through the Gopher interface. Users enter their Email address, the list they want to search, and the keyword(s) they wish to find. LISTGopher then send the results of their search to the user's e-mail address. Currently, only library-related archives are supported, but more archive types may be added in the future.
Contact:	Eric Lease Morgan, Systems Librarian eric_morgan@ncsu.edu

`http://ericmorgan.lib.ncsu.edu/staff/morgan/morgan.html`

`gopher://dewey.lib.ncsu.edu /library/disciplines/library/listgopher`

LOCIS (LIBRARY Of CONGRESS INFORMATION SYSTEM) ★★★

The Library of Congress (LC) telnet service is a Campus-Wide Information System that combines the vast collection of information available about the Library with easy access to diverse electronic resources over the Internet. Its goal is to serve the staff of LC, as well as the U.S. Congress and it's constituents.

Keywords:	Information Retrieval, Libraries
Sponsor:	Library of Congress, Washington, D.C., USA
Audience:	Reseachers, Students, Librarians
Contact:	LC MARVEL Design Team lcmarvel@loc.gov
Notes:	The Library of Congress (LC) Machine-Assisted Realization of the Virtual Electronic Library (MARVEL) also exists as a gopher site: gopher://marvel.loc.gov

`telnet://locis.loc.gov`

Medical College of Ohio Library Online Catalogue ★★

A catalog of library holdings.

Keywords:	Medicine, Libraries
Sponsor:	Medical College of Ohio
Audience:	Health Professionals, Medical Researchers, Educators, Students
Details:	Free

`telnet://library@136.247.10.14`

Medical College of Wisconsin Library Online Catalogue ★★

Catalog of library holdings.

Keywords:	Medicine, Library
Sponsor:	Medical College of Wisconsin
Audience:	Health Professionals, Medical Researchers, Educators, Students
Details:	Free

`telnet://ils.lib.mcw.edu`

Montefiore Medical Center Library Online Catalog ★

A catalog of library holdings.

Keywords:	Medicine, Libraries
Sponsor:	Montefiore Medical Center at Albert Einstein College of Medicine, New York
Audience:	Health-care Professionals, Medical Researchers, Educators, Students
Details:	Free
	After Telnetting, hit RETURN twice, then select 0 on main menu. Select 2 on locations menu. To exit, hit the Telnet escape key.

telnet://lis.aecom.yu.edu

National Institute of Health Library Online Catalog

This entry point provides access to the books and journal holdings in the NIH Library. Journal articles are not included.

Keywords:	NIH, Medicine, Science, Libraries
Sponsor:	National Institute of Health (NIH)
Audience:	Scientists, Researchers, Educators, Health-care Professionals
Details:	Free

telnet://nih-library.ncrr.nih.gov

Net-News ★★★

A newsletter devoted to library and information resources on the Internet.

Keywords:	Information, Libraries, Networking, Internet
Sponsor:	Metronet
Audience:	Librarians, Researchers
Contact:	Dana Noonan noonan@msus1.msus.edu
Details:	Free
	Send email request to noonan@msus1.msus.edu or metronet@vz.acs.umn.edu

gopher://noonan@msus1.msus.edu

NLC (National Library of Canada) ★★★★

A Canadian library gopher in French and English.

Keywords:	Canada, Libraries, Library Science
Sponsor:	National Library of Canada (NLC), Canada
Audience:	Canadians, Librarians, Publishers
Profile:	This site provides a gateway to Canadian library and Internet resources linking users to the National Library, which offers a bibliographic database, a list of NLC publications, and other services for libraries and publishers. It also has links to many other Canadian libraries and Internet services, as well as a large selection of general information from and about the Government of Canada and its provinces.
Contact:	Nancy Brodie, Lynn Herbert Nancy.Brodie@nlc-bnc.ca, Lynn.Herbert@nlc-bnc.ca

gopher://gopher.nlc-bnc.ca

OLIS (Oxford University Library Information Service) Gopher ★★

OLIS is a network of libraries. It contains all the books from the English, Modern Languages, Social Studies, and Hooke libraries. It also contains books and journals cataloged since September 1988 in the Bodleian and Dependant libraries and the Taylor Institution. Books can be searched in any OLIS library from any location.

Keywords:	Libraries, United Kingdom, Europe
Audience:	Library Users
Contact:	jose@olis.lib.ox.ac.uk
Details:	Free

gopher://gopher.lib.ox.ac.uk/00/Info/OLIS

The Wired Librarian ★★

A collection of online resources designed to help library professionals and users keep abreast of current developments in library science and information studies. Includes links to many library and information systems associations and services.

Keywords:	Libraries, Information Retrieval
Sponsor:	Davidson Library, University of California, Santa Barbara, California, USA
Audience:	Librarians, Library Users
Contact:	Andrea L. Duda duda@library.ucsb.edu

gopher://ucsbuxa.ucsb.edu

UCSB Library Reference Guide ★★

A list of art references including indexes, dictionaries, bilbiographies, and biographical materials.

Keywords:	Art, History (World), Libraries
Sponsor:	University of California at Santa Barbara
Audience:	Artists, Historians, Librarians

gopher://ucsbuxa.ucsb.edu

University of Texas Health Science Center (UTHSCSA) Biomedical Library Information System ★★

Keywords:	Medicine, Libraries
Sponsor:	Audie L. Murphy Memorial Veterans' Administration Hospital, San Antonio, TX
Audience:	Medical Professionals, Medical Educators, Students
Details:	Free

telnet://lis@athena.uthscsa.edu

University of Wales College of Medicine Library Online Catalog ★★

Keywords:	Medicine, Libraries
Sponsor:	University of Wales, United Kingdom
Audience:	Health Care Professionals, Medical Educators, Students
Details:	Free
	Expect: login, Send: 'janet'; Expect: password; Send: 'janet'

telnet://sun.nsf.ac.uk

Vetlib-L (Veterinary Medicine Librarians List) ★

Vetlib-L is an E-mail discussion group for librarians in schools and colleges of veterinary medicine worldwide.

Keywords:	Veterinary Medicine, Libraries
Sponsor:	Virginia Polytechnic Institute and State University
Audience:	Veterinarians, Librarians
Contact:	Victoria T. Kok, James Powell kok@vtvm1.cc.vt.edu or jpowell@vtvm1.cc.vt.edu
Details:	Free
User Info:	To subscribe to the list, send an e-mail message to the URL address below consisting of a single line reading:
	vetlib-l YourFirstName YourLastName
	To send a message to the entire list, address it to: vetlib-l@vtvm1.cc.vt.edu

mailto:listserv@vtvm1.cc.vt.edu

Yale Directory of Internet Libraries ★★★

An online directory of international library catalogs with continuing links to many servers, including several with Internet access tools.

Keywords:	Libraries
Sponsor:	Yale University, New Haven, Connecticut, USA
Audience:	General Audience
Profile:	The Yale Directory of Internet Libraries is a comprehensive listing of international libraries that provide information about the subject area strengths of many of its entries.

`gopher://gophlib@gopher.yale.edu`

Library of Congress, Astronomy, Astrophysics, and Physics Resources

Library of Congress, Astronomy, Astrophysics, and Physics Resources

Pointers to important remote databases relating to astronomy and physics.

Keywords:	Astronomy, Astrophysics, NASA
Sponsor:	Library of Congress, Washington, DC
Audience:	Astronomers, Educators (Post-Secondary), Physicists, Students
Profile:	The Library of Congress has pointers to many important remote databases including Astronomy, Astrophysics, and Physics Journals, the Aerospace Directory from Rice University, The American Astronomical Society, The Astronomical Internet Resources Directory, The Cold Fusion Bibliography, The Electromagnetic Wave Research Institute of NRC (Florence, Italy), LANL Physics Information, The Lunar/Planetary Institute Database of Geology, Geophysics, and Astronomy, The NASA Extragalactic Database, The NASA Network Applications and Information Center (NAIC), The National Institute of Standards and Technology (NIST), The Physics Resource Directory from University of California, Irvine, and The Space Telescope Electronic Information System (STEIS).
Contact:	lcmarvel@seq1.loc.gov
Details:	Costs
User info:	Can be accessible via telnet:// marvel.loc.gov (login: marvel).

`gopher://marvel.loc.gov/11/global/sci/astro`

Limbaugh (Rush)

alt.fan.rush-limbaugh

A Usenet newsgroup providing information and discussion about Rush Limbaugh, a politically conservative American figure.

Keywords:	Limbaugh (Rush), Politics (Conservative), Comedians
Audience:	Followers of Rush Limbaugh
User Info:	To subscribe to this Usenet newsgroup, you need access to a newsreader.

`news:alt.fan.rush-limbaugh`

Lincoln (Abraham)

University of Chicago Library

The library's holdings are large and wide-ranging and contain significant collections in many fields.

Keywords:	English Bibles, Lincoln (Abraham), Kentucky & Ohio River Valley (History of), Balzac (Honore de), American Drama, Cromwell (Oliver), Goethe, Judaica, Italy, Chaucer (Geoffrey), Wells (Ida, Personal Papers of), Douglas (Stephen A.), Italy, Literature (Children's)
Audience:	General Public, Researchers, Librarians, Document Delivery Professionals
Details:	Free
	Expect: ENTER CLASS, Send: LIB48 3; Expect: CONNECTED, Send: RETURN

`telnet://olorin.uchicago.edu`

Linguistics

alt.usage.english

A Usenet newsgroup providing information and discussion about English grammar, word usages, and related topics.

Keywords:	Lexicology, Academia, Linguistics, Education
Audience:	English Educators
User Info:	To subscribe to this Usenet newsgroup, you need access to a newsreader.

`news:alt.usage.english`

ELSNET (European Network in Language and Speech)

A web site addressing the development of language technology in Europe and abroad by helping to coordinate progress on both scientific and technological fronts.

Keywords:	Linguistics, Cognitive Science, Communication
Sponsor:	The University of Edinburgh Centre for Cognitive Science, Edinburgh, Scotland
Audience:	Linguists, Cognitive Scientists
Contact:	Ewan Klein klein@ed.ac.uk

`http://www.cogsci.ed.ac.uk/elsnet/home.html`

KFLC-L

A mailing list for distributing information on the meetings and proceedings of the Kentucky Foreign Language Conferences (KFCL).

Keywords:	Language, Linguistics, Education (Bilingual)
Audience:	Linguists, Educators
Contact:	John Greenway engjlg@ukcc.uky.edu
User Info:	To subscribe, send an e-mail message to the URL address below consisting of a single line reading: SUB kflc-l YourFirstName YourLastName To send a message to the entire list, address it to: kflc-l@ukcc.uky.edu

`mailto:listserv@ukcc.uky.edu`

LANGIT

A forum for members of the Italian Linguistics Center (Centri Linguistici Italian).

Keywords:	Italy, Linguistics
Audience:	Linguists, Educators, Students
Details:	Free
User Info:	To subscribe to the list, send an e-mail message to the address below.

`mailto:listserv@icineca.bitnet`

Lantra-l

A discussion of interpretation and translation.

Keywords:	Interpretation, Translation, Language, Linguistics
Audience:	Linguists, Interpreters, Translators
Details:	Free
User Info:	To subscribe to the list send an e-mail message the the URL address below consisting of a single line reading: SUB landra-l Your First Name Your Last Name To send a message to the entire list, address it to: lantra-l@search.bitnet

`mailto:listserv@searn.bitnet`

Linguist

A discussion of language and linguistics.

Keywords:	Language, Linguistics
Audience:	Linguists, Language Teachers, Language Students
Details:	Free
User Info:	To subscribe to the list, send an e-mail message to the URL address shown below consisting of a single line reading: SUB linguist Your First Name Your Last Name

`mailto:listserv@tamvmi.bitnet`

LLTI

The Language Learning Technology International (LLTI) forum is a discussion of computer-assisted language learning.

Keywords: Linguistics, Computer-Aided Instruction
Audience: Linguists, Language Teachers, Language Students
Details: Free
User Info: To subscribe to the list, send an e-mail message to the URL address below, consisting of a single line reading:
SUB llti YourFirstName YourLastName
To send a message to the entire list, address it to: llti@dartcms1.dartmouth.edu

`mailto:listserv@dartcms1.dartmouth.edu`

LTEST

A discussion of language-testing research and practice.

Keywords: Linguistics
Audience: Linguists, Language Teachers, Language Students
Details: Free
User Info: To subscribe to the list, send an e-mail message to the URL address below, consisting of a single line reading:
SUB Ltest YourFirstName YourLastName
To send a message to the entire list, address it to: ltest@uclan1.bitnet

`mailto:listserv@uclan1.bitnet`

Massachusetts Institute of Technology Library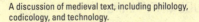

The library's holdings are large and wide-ranging and contain significant collections in many fields.

Keywords: Aeronautics (History of), Linguistics, Mathematics (History of), Microscopy, Spectroscopy, Aeronautics, Mathematics, Glass
Audience: General Public, Researchers, Librarians, Document Delivery Professionals
Details: Free
Expect: Mitek Server..., Send: Enter or Return; Expect: prompt, Send: hollis

`telnet://library.mit.edu`

MEDTEXT-L

A discussion of medieval text, including philology, codicology, and technology.

Keywords: Medieval, Philology, Linguistics
Audience: Linguists, Language Teachers, Language Students, Historians
Details: Free
User Info: To subscribe to the list, send an e-mail message to the URL address below consisting of a single line reading:
medtext-l YourFirstName YourLastName
To send a message to the entire list, address it to: medtext-l@uiucvmd.bitnet

`mailto:listserv@uiucvmd.bitnet`

nl-kr

This E-conference is open to discussion of any topic related to the understanding and generation of natural language and knowledge representation as subfields of artificial intelligence.

Keywords: Programming Languages, Natural Language, Knowledge Representation, Linguistics
Audience: Computer Programmers
Contact: Christopher Welty
weltyc@cs.rpi.edu
Details: Free, Moderated
User Info: To subscribe to the list, send an e-mail message requesting a subscription to the URL address below.

`mailto:nl-kr-request@cs.rpi.edu`

OUTIL (Out in Linguistics)

The list is open to lesbian, gay, bisexual, transsexual linguists, and their friends. The only requirement is that you be willing to be out to everyone on the list. The purposes of the group are to be visible and to gather occasionally to enjoy one another's company.

Keywords: Linguistics, Gays, Lesbians, Bisexuals, Transsexuals
Audience: Linguists, Gays, Lesbians, Bisexuals, Transsexuals
Contact: Arnold Zwicky
outil-request@csli.stanford.edu
Details: Free
User Info: To subscribe to the list, send an e-mail message requesting a subscription to the URL address below.
To send a message to the entire list, address it to: outil@csli.stanford.edu

`mailto:outil-request@csli.stanford.edu`

Russian

This list is dedicated to the discussion of Russian-language issues, including Russian language, linguistics, grammar, translations, and literature.

Keywords: Language, Literature (Russian), Linguistics
Audience: Slavicists, Linguists, Translators
Contact: Andrew Wollert
ispajw@asuacad
russian@asuvm.inre.asu.edu
Details: Free
User Info: To subscribe to the list, send an e-mail message requesting subscription to the URL address below.

`russian@asuvm.inre.asu.edu`

The Human Languages Page

This site provides language resources from around the world, including dictionaries, language tutorials, and spoken samples of languages.

Keywords: Languages, Linguistics
Audience: Linguists, Educators, Students
Profile: Languages covered include Esperanto, Gaelic, Arabic, Hindi, and Kanji. Also provides link to the Gutenberg Project (electronic texts) and to the Library of Congress.
Contact: Tyler Jones
tjones@willamette.edu
Details: Free

`http://www.willamette.edu/~tjones/Language-Page.html`

The University of Michigan Library

The library's holdings are large and wide-ranging and contain significant collections in many fields.

Keywords: Education (Bilingual), Linguistics, Neuroscience, Michigan, Prohibition, Government (African)
Audience: General Public, Researchers, Librarians, Document Delivery Professionals
Details: Free
Expect: nothing, Send: <cr>

`telnet://cts.merit.edu`

Links to Many Databases

Links to Many Databases

A collection of links to over 40 databases covering a wide variety of subjects ranging from Postmodern Culture to the 1990 Census.

Keywords: Databases, Research
Sponsor: University of Texas, Austin, Texas, USA
Audience: Researchers, General Public
Contact: remark@ftp.cc.utexas.edu

`gopher://ftp.cc.utexas.edu`

ListServ

LIST Gopher

This is a library-related service that allows users to obtain information by using their e-mail accounts.

- **Keywords:** Mailing Lists, Listserv, Libraries, Gopher
- **Sponsor:** North Carolina State University, Raleigh, North Carolina, USA
- **Audience:** Librarians, E-mail Users
- **Profile:** LISTGopher allows users to search library-related LISTSERV archives through the Gopher interface. Users enter their Email address, the list they want to search, and the keyword(s) they wish to find. LISTGopher then send the results of their search to the user's Email address. Currently, only library-related archives are supported, but more archive types may be added in the future.
- **Contact:** Eric Lease Morgan, Systems Librarian eric_morgan@ncsu.edu

`http://ericmorgan.lib.ncsu.edu/staff/morgan/morgan.html`

`gopher://dewey.lib.ncsu.edu /library/disciplines/library/listgopher`

LIST REVIEW SERVICE

Explores e-mail distribution lists (primarily bitnet and List Serv lists).

- **Keywords:** Bitnet, ListServ
- **Audience:** Email Users
- **Profile:** Akin to book and restaurant reviews, each issue begins with a narrative description of usually one weeks worth of monitoring, then presents simple statistical data, such as the number of messages and lines, number of queries and nonqueries, number of subscribers and countries represented, list owner, location, and how to subscribe.
- **Contact:** Raleigh C. Muns srcmuns@umslvma.bitnet
- **Details:** Free
- **User Info:** To subscribe, send an e-mail message to the address below consisting of a single line reading:

    SUB listreviewservice Your First Name Your Last Name

    To send a message to the entire list, address it to: listreviewservice@kentvm.kent.edu

`mailto:listserv@kentvm.kent.edu`

ListServ

A mailing list server for group communication.

- **Keywords:** Internet Tools, ListServ
- **Audience:** Internet Surfers
- **Details:** Free

`mailto:listserv@uacsc2.albany`

Literacy

teslit-l (Adult Education & Literacy Test Literature)

This is a sublist of tesl-l (Teaching English as a Second Language). Discussions focus primarily on issues of literacy and the teaching of English as a second language.

- **Keywords:** Education (Adult), Education (Distance), Education (Continuing), Literacy
- **Audience:** K-12 Educators, Administrators, Researchers
- **Details:** Free
- **User Info:** To subscribe to the list, send an e-mail message to the URL address below consisting of a single line reading:

    SUB teslit-l YourFirstName YourLastName

    To send a message to the entire list, address it to: teslit-l @cunyvm.bitnet
- **Notes:** Members of teslit-l must be members of tesl-l.

`mailto:listserv@cunyvm.bitnet`

Literary Criticism

PMC-MOO

A real-time, text-based, virtual-reality environment in which subscribers to Postmodern Culture can interact and participate in live conferences.

- **Keywords:** Literature (Contemporary), Postmodern Culture, Literary Criticism
- **Audience:** General Public, Writers, Literary Critics, Literary Theorists, Researchers
- **Profile:** In addition to providing Postmodern Culture's subscribers with the opportunity to interact and to participate in live conferences, PMC-MOO provides access to texts generated by the journal and by PMC-TALK, as well as the opportunity to experience (or to help design) programs that simulate object lessons in postmodern theory. PMC-MOO is based on the LambdaMOO program, freeware by Pavel Curtis.
- **Contact:** pmc@unity.ncsu.edu
- **Notes:** If your Internet account is on a UNIX machine and you have access to the Emacs editor (type 'man emacs' or 'help emacs' or simply 'emacs' at your command prompt to find out, or ask your user-services people). You can connect to PMC-MOO using a customized Emacs client available from our FTP site. This client provides text-buffering, multiple windows, and many features superior to an unmediated Telnet connection. To retrieve the Emacs client, perform the following ftp transfer: ftp ftp.ncsu.edu; login: ftp; password: [your e-mail address]; cd pub/docs/pmc/pmc-talk; get PMC-MOO.doc; get mud.el; bin; get mud.elc; quit.

`telnet://dewey.lib.ncsu.edu`

Postmodern Culture

Postmodern Culture is a peer-reviewed electronic journal of interdisciplinary criticism on contemporary literature, theory, and culture.

- **Keywords:** Literature (Contemporary), Postmodern Culture, Literary Criticism
- **Sponsor:** Oxford University Press
- **Audience:** General Public, Writers, Literary Critics, Literary Theorists, Researchers
- **Profile:** All back issues of Postmodern Culture are always available; previous issues have included: Andrew Ross, Hacking Away at the Counter-Culture, Bell Hooks, Postmodern Blackness, Laura Kipnis, Marx: The Video (A Politics of Revolting Bodies), Kathy Acker, Dead Doll Humility' and Obsession, Neil Larsen, Postmodernism and Imperialism: Theory and Politics in Latin America, Patrick O'Donnell, His Master's Voice: On William Gaddis's JR, Greg Ulmer, Grammatology Hypemedia, Charles Bernstein, The Second War and Postmodern Memory, Allison Fraiberg, Of AIDS, Cyborgs, and Other Indiscretions: Resurfacing the Body in the Postmodern (with a response by David Porush), Stuart Moulthrop, You Say You Want a Revolution: Hypertext and the Laws of Media, Bob Perelman, The Marginalization of Poetry
- **Details:** Costs
- **User Info:** To subscribe to the list, send an e-mail message requesting a subscription to the URL address below.

`mailto:pmc@ncsvm.cc.ncsu.edu`

Literary Studies

Universite de Montreal UDEMATIK Library

The library's holdings are large and wide-ranging and contain significant collections in many fields.

Keywords: Art, Architecture, Economy, Sexology, Social Law, Science, Technology, Literary Studies
Audience: Researchers, Students, General Public
Contact: Joelle or Sebastien Roy
udematik@ere.umontreal.ca or
stemp@ere.umontreal.ca or
roys@ere.umontreal.ca
Expect: Login; Send: Application id INFO

`telnet://udematik.umontreal.ca`

Literate Programming

Litprog

A network list dealing with topics related to literate programming, both general (is literate programming compatible with writing portable programs), and particular (is it possible to use CWEB with ANSI C).

Keywords: Programming, Literate Programming
Audience: Computer Programmers
Contact: George D. Greenwade
bed_gdg@shsu.edu
Details: Free
User Info: To subscribe to the list, send an e-mail message to the URL address shown below consisting of a single line reading:

SUB litprog YourFirstName YourLastName

To send a message to the entire list, address it to: litprog @shsu.edu

Notes: This list is open to novices and seasoned literate programmers.

`mailto:listserv@shsu.edu`

Literature (American)

Emory University Library

The library's holdings are large and wide-ranging and contain significant collections in many fields.

Keywords: Health Sciences, Theology, History (US), Communism, Economics (History of), Literature (American)
Audience: General Public, Researchers, Librarians, Document Delivery Professionals
Details: Free
Expect: VM screen, Send: RETURN; Expect: CP READ, Send: DIAL VTAM, press RETURN; Expect: CICS screen, Send: PF1

`telnet://emuvm1.cc.emory.edu`

Indiana University Libraries

The library's holdings are large and wide-ranging and contain significant collections in many fields.

Keywords: Literature (English), Literature (American), 1640-Present, British Plays (19th-C.), Western Americana, Railway History, Aristotle (Texts of), Lafayette (Marquis de), Handel (G.F.), Austrian History, Antiquarian Books, Rare Books, French Opera (19th-C.), Drama (British),
Audience: General Public, Researchers, Librarians, Document Delivery Professionals
Details: Free
Expect: User ID prompt, Send: GUEST

`telnet://iuis.ucs.indiana.edu`

Northwestern University Library

The library's holdings are large and wide-ranging and contain significant collections in many fields.

Keywords: Africa, Wright (Frank Lloyd), Women's Studies, Art, Literature (American), Contemporary Music, Government (US State), UN Documents, Music
Audience: General Public, Researchers, Librarians, Document Delivery Professionals
Details: Free
Expect: COMMAND: Send: DIAL VTAM

`telnet://nuacvm.acns.nwu.edu`

Papa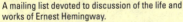

A mailing list devoted to discussion of the life and works of Ernest Hemingway.

Keywords: Hemingway (Ernest), Literature (American)
Audience: Ernest Hemingway Readers
Contact: Dave Gross
dgross@polyslo.calpoly.edu
Details: Free
User Info: To subscribe to the list, send an e-mail message requesting a subscription to the URL address below.

To send a message to the entire list, address it to:
dgross@polyslo.calpoly.edu

`mailto:dgross@polyslo.calpoly.edu`

Princeton University Library

The library's holdings are large and wide-ranging. They contain significant collections in many fields.

Keywords: China, Japan, Classics, History (Ancient), Near Eastern Studies, Literature (American), Literature (English), Aeronautics, Middle Eastern Studies, Mormonism, Publishing
Audience: General Public, Researchers, Librarians, Document Delivery Professionals
Details: Free
Expect: Connect message, blank screen, Send: <cr>; Expect: #, Send: Call 500

`telnet://pucable.princeton.edu`

Purdue University Library

The library's holdings are large and wide-ranging. They contain significant collections in many fields.

Keywords: Economics (History of), Literature (English), Literature (American), Indiana, Rogers (Bruce), Engineering (History of), Aviation, Earth Science, Atmospheric Science, Consumer Science, Family Science, Chemistry (History of), Physics, Veterinary Science
Audience: General Public, Researchers, Librarians, Document Delivery Professionals
Contact: Dan Ferrer
dan@asterix.lib.purdue.edu
Details: Free
Expect: User ID prompt, Send: GUEST

`telnet://lib.cc.purdue.edu`

University of Delaware Libraries (DELCAT)

The library's holdings are large and wide-ranging and contain significant collections in many fields.

Keywords: Literature (American), Hemingway (Ernest), Papermaking (History of), Chemistry (History of), Literature (Irish), Delaware
Audience: General Public, Researchers, Librarians, Document Delivery Professionals
Contact: Stuart Glogoff
epo27855@udacsvm.bitnet
Details: Free
Expect: prompt, Send: RETURN 2-3 times

`telnet://delcat.udel.edu`

`telnet://delcat.acs.udel.edu`

University of Pennsylvania Library- Philadelphia Pa.

The library's holdings are large and wide-ranging and contain significant collections in many fields.

Keywords: Literature (English), Literature (American), History (World), Medieval Studies, East Asian Studies, Middle Eastern Studies, South Asian Studies, Judaica, Lithuania.
Audience: Educators, Students, Researchers
Profile: Access to the central Van Pelt Library and to most of the departmental libraries is restricted to members of the University community on weekends and

holidays. Online visitors are advised to call (215) 898-7554 for information on hours and access restrictions.

Contact: Patricia Renfro, Associate Director of Libraries

Details: Free

telnet://library.upenn.edu

University of Tennessee at Chatanooga Library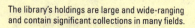

The library's holdings are large and wide-ranging and contain significant collections in many fields.

Keywords: Civil War, Literature (American)
Audience: Researchers, Students, General Public
Contact: Randy Whitson
rwhitson@utcvmutc.edu
Details: Free
Expect: OK prompt; Send: Login pub1; Expect: Password, Send: Usc

telnet://library.utc.edu

University of Tennessee at Memphis Library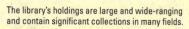

The library's holdings are large and wide-ranging and contain significant collections in many fields.

Keywords: Tennessee, Literature (American)
Audience: Researchers, Students, General Public
Details: Costs
Expect: Username Prompt, Send: Harvey

telnet://utmem1.utmem.edu

University of Tulsa Library

The library's holdings are large and wide-ranging and contain significant collections in many fields.

Keywords: Literature (American), Petroleum, Geology
Audience: Researchers, Students, General Public
Details: Free
Expect: Username Prompt, Send: LIAS

telnet://vax2.utulsa.edu

University of Wisconsin at Milwaukee Library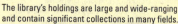

The library's holdings are large and wide-ranging and contain significant collections in many fields.

Keywords: Art, Architecture, Business, Cartography, Geography, Geology, Urban Studies, Literature (English), Literature (American)
Audience: Researchers, Students, General Public
Details: Free
Expect: Login, Send: Lib; Expect: vDIAL prompt, Send: Library

telnet://uwmcat.lib.uwm.edu

Literature (Asian)

University of Rochester Library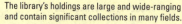

The library's holdings are large and wide-ranging and contain significant collections in many fields.

Keywords: Architecture, Art History, Photography, Literature (Asian), Lasers, Geology, Statistics, Optics, Medieval Studies
Audience: Researchers, Students, General Public
Details: Free
Expect: Login; Send: Library

telnet://128.151.226.71

Literature (Children's)

Florida State University System Library ★★

The library's holdings are large and wide-ranging and contain significant collections in many fields.

Keywords: Florida, Latin America, Judaica, Literature (Children's), Marine Engineering, Law (Brazilian), Law (British)
Audience: General Public, Researchers, Librarians, Document Delivery Professionals
Details: Free
Expect: Command ==>, Send: dial vtam; Expect: LUIS User Menu, Send: Your Catalog choice; To log off: Send: %off

telnet://nervm.nerdc.ufl.edu

University of Chicago Library ★★

The library's holdings are large and wide-ranging and contain significant collections in many fields.

Keywords: English Bibles, Lincoln (Abraham), Kentucky & Ohio River Valley (History of), Balzac (Honore de), American Drama, Cromwell (Oliver), Goethe, Judaica, Italy, Chaucer (Geoffrey), Wells (Ida, Personal Papers of), Douglas (Stephen A.), Italy, Literature (Children's)
Audience: General Public, Researchers, Librarians, Document Delivery Professionals
Details: Free
Expect: ENTER CLASS, Send: LIB48 3; Expect: CONNECTED, Send: RETURN

telnet://olorin.uchicago.edu

University of Colorado at Boulder Library ★★

The library's holdings are large and wide-ranging and contain significant collections in many fields.

Keywords: Numismatics, Human Rights, Literature (Children's), Labor Archives, History (US)
Audience: Researchers, Students, General Public
Contact: Donna Pattee
pattee@spot.colorado.edu
Details: Free
Expect: Login; Send: Culine

telnet://culine.colorado.edu

Literature (Contemporary)

ACEN (Art Com Electronic Network)

A conference on the WELL for art, technology, and text-based artworks.

Keywords: Art, Literature (Contemporary), Multimedia
Sponsor: Art Com Electronic Network
Audience: Artists, Musicians, Writers
Profile: Started in 1986, ACEN is a seminal art BBS that includes actual artworks, discussion on topics such as software as art, and on line published works by John Cage, Fred Truck, Jim Rosenberg, Judy Malloy, and others.
Contact: Carl Loeffler
artcomtv@well.sf.ca.us

To participate in a conference on the WELL, you must first establish an account on the WELL. To do so, start by typing: telnet://well.sf.ca.us

telnet://well.sf.ca.us

Art Com Magazine

A newsletter about art and technology (subjects covered include robotics, artists' software, hyperfiction) that is guest-edited by individual artists.

Keywords: Computer Art, Literature (Contemporary), Technology, Hyperfiction
Sponsor: Art Com Electronic Network
Audience: Artists, Writers
Contact: Fred Truck
fjt@well.sf.ca.us

To participate in a conference on the WELL, you must first establish an account on the WELL. To do so, start by typing: telnet://well.sf.ca.us

mailto:artcomtv@well.sf.ca.us

Electronic Books

A collection of books available as ASCII text files, including classics of antiquity (Aristotle, Virgil, Sophocles, the Bible), as well as more contemporary works of fiction and nonfiction by authors ranging from Dostoevsky to Martin Luther King, Jr.

Keywords: Books, Online Books, Literature (Contemporary), Literature (General)
Sponsor: The Blacksburg Electronic Village (BEV) at Virginia Tech
Audience: General Public, Historians
Contact: BEV Gopher Administrators
gopher@gopher.vt.edu

`gopher://gopher.vt.edu`

InterText

A network-distributed bimonthly literary magazine.

Keywords: Literature (Contemporary), Journals
Audience: General Public, Writers
Profile: InterText publishes all kinds of material, ranging from mainstream stories to fantasy to horror to science fiction to humor. InterText publishes in both ASCII and PostScript formats, and reaches over 1,000 readers worldwide.
Contact: Jason Snell
jsnell@ocf.berkeley.edu
Details: Free
Select OCF On-Line Library; then select Fiction; then select InterText
Notes: The ASCII version runs approximately 150K per issue; if you have tight file gateways, the issue can be split up and squeezed through if need be. The PostScript version runs approximately 500K. If you would like to see back issues of InterText, you can FTP them from:
network.ucsd.edu(128.54.16.3) in/intertext. Login as anonymous, with your e-mail address as your password.

`gopher://ocf.berkeley.edu`

PMC-MOO

A real-time, text-based, virtual-reality environment in which subscribers to Postmodern Culture can interact and participate in live conferences.

Keywords: Literature (Contemporary), Postmodern Culture, Literary Criticism
Audience: General Public, Writers, Literary Critics, Literary Theorists, Researchers
Profile: In addition to providing Postmodern Culture's subscribers with the opportunity to interact and to participate in live conferences, PMC-MOO provides access to texts generated by the journal and by PMC-TALK, as well as the opportunity to experience (or to help design) programs that simulate object lessons in postmodern theory. PMC-MOO is based on the LambdaMOO program, freeware by Pavel Curtis.
Contact: pmc@unity.ncsu.edu
Notes: If your Internet account is on a UNIX machine and you have access to the Emacs editior (type 'man emacs' or 'help emacs' or simply 'emacs' at your command prompt to find out, or ask your user-services people). You can connect to PMC-MOO using a customized Emacs client available from our FTP site. This client provides text-buffering, multiple windows, and many features superior to an unmediated Telnet connection. To retrieve the Emacs client, perform the following ftp transfer: ftp ftp.ncsu.edu; login: ftp; password: [your e-mail address]; cd pub/docs/pmc/pmc-talk; get PMC-MOO.doc; get mud.el; bin; get mud.elc; quit.

`telnet://dewey.lib.ncsu.edu`

Postmodern Culture

Postmodern Culture is a peer-reviewed electronic journal of interdisciplinary criticism on contemporary literature, theory, and culture.

Keywords: Literature (Contemporary), Postmodern Culture, Literary Criticism
Sponsor: Oxford University Press
Audience: General Public, Writers, Literary Critics, Literary Theorists, Researchers
Profile: All back issues of Postmodern Culture are always available; previous issues have included: Andrew Ross, Hacking Away at the Counter-Culture, Bell Hooks, Postmodern Blackness, Laura Kipnis, Marx: The Video (A Politics of Revolting Bodies), Kathy Acker, Dead Doll Humility' and Obsession, Neil Larsen, Postmodernism and Imperialism: Theory and Politics in Latin America, Patrick O'Donnell, His Master's Voice: On William Gaddis's JR, Greg Ulmer, Grammatology Hypemedia, Charles Bernstein, The Second War and Postmodern Memory, Allison Fraiberg, Of AIDS, Cyborgs, and Other Indiscretions: Resurfacing the Body in the Postmodern (with a response by David Porush), Stuart Moulthrop, You Say You Want a Revolution: Hypertext and the Laws of Media, Bob Perelman, The Marginalization of Poetry
Details: Costs
User Info: To subscribe to the list, send an e-mail message requesting a subscription to the URL address below.

`mailto:pmc@ncsvm.cc.ncsu.edu`

Literature (English)

Chaucer

A discussion list on the subject of Medieval English literature, especially that of Chaucer.

Keywords: Chaucer (Geoffrey), Literature (English)
Audience: Chaucer Fans, English Teachers
Contact: Dan Mosser
mosserd@vtm1.cc.vt.edu

`mailto:chaucer@vtm1.cc.vt.edu`

Indiana University Libraries

The library's holdings are large and wide-ranging and contain significant collections in many fields.

Keywords: Literature (English), Literature (American), 1640-Present, British Plays (19th-C.), Western Americana, Railway History, Aristotle (Texts of), Lafayette (Marquis de), Handel (G.F.), Austrian History, Antiquarian Books, Rare Books, French Opera (19th-C.), Drama (British),
Audience: General Public, Researchers, Librarians, Document Delivery Professionals
Details: Free
Expect: User ID prompt, Send: GUEST

`telnet://iuis.ucs.indiana.edu`

Johns Hopkins University Library

The library's holdings are large and wide-ranging and contain significant collections in many fields.

Keywords: Literature (English), Economics, Classics, Drama (German), Slavery, Trade Unions, Incunabula, Bibles, Diseases (History of), Nursing (History of), Abolitionism
Audience: General Public, Researchers, Librarians, Document Delivery Professionals
Details: Free

`telnet://jhuvm.hcf.jhu.edu`

Princeton University Library

The library's holdings are large and wide-ranging. They contain significant collections in many fields.

Keywords: China, Japan, Classics, History (Ancient), Near Eastern Studies, Literature (American), Literature (English), Aeronautics, Middle Eastern Studies, Mormonism, Publishing
Audience: General Public, Researchers, Librarians, Document Delivery Professionals
Details: Free
Expect: Connect message, blank screen, Send: <cr>; Expect: #, Send: Call 500

`telnet://pucable.princeton.edu`

Purdue University Library

The library's holdings are large and wide-ranging. They contain significant collections in many fields.

Keywords: Economics (History of), Literature (English), Literature (American), Indiana, Rogers (Bruce), Engineering (History of), Aviation, Earth Science, Atmospheric

	Science, Consumer Science, Family Science, Chemistry (History of), Physics, Veterinary Science
Audience:	General Public, Researchers, Librarians, Document Delivery Professionals
Contact:	Dan Ferrer dan@asterix.lib.purdue.edu
Details:	Free
	Expect: User ID prompt, Send: GUEST

`telnet://lib.cc.purdue.edu`

University of Pennsylvania Library- Philadelphia Pa. ★★★

The library's holdings are large and wide-ranging and contain significant collections in many fields.

Keywords:	Literature (English), Literature (American), History (World), Medieval Studies, East Asian Studies, Middle Eastern Studies, South Asian Studies, Judaica, Lithuania.
Audience:	Educators, Students, Researchers
Profile:	Access to the central Van Pelt Library and to most of the departmental libraries is restricted to members of the University community on weekends and holidays. Online visitors are advised to call (215) 898-7554 for information on hours and access restrictions.
Contact:	Patricia Renfro, Associate Director of Libraries
Details:	Free

`telnet://library.upenn.edu`

University of Pennsylvania PENNINFO Library ★★

The library's holdings are large and wide-ranging and contain significant collections in many fields.

Keywords:	Church History, Spanish Inquisition, Witchcraft, Shakespeare (William), Bibles, Aristotle (Texts of), Fiction, Whitman (Walt), French Revolution, Drama (French), Literature (English), Literature (Spanish)
Audience:	Researchers, Students, General Public
Contact:	Al DSouza penninfo-admin@dccs.upenn.edu dsouza@dccs.upenn.edu
Details:	Free
	Expect: Login; Send: Public

`telnet://penninfo.upenn.edu`

University of Wisconsin at Milwaukee Library ★★

The library's holdings are large and wide-ranging and contain significant collections in many fields.

Keywords:	Art, Architecture, Business, Cartography, Geography, Geology, Urban Studies, Literature (English), Literature (American)
Audience:	Researchers, Students, General Public
Details:	Free
	Expect: Login, Send: Lib; Expect: vDIAL prompt, Send: Library

`telnet://uwmcat.lib.uwm.edu`

Literature (General)

alt.books.reviews ★

A Usenet conference devoted to reviews of books, especially science fiction and computer science books.

Keywords:	Literature (General), Computer Science, Science Fiction, Book Reviews
Audience:	General Public, Publishers, Educators, Librarians, Booksellers
Profile:	Alt.books.reviews (a.b.r. for short) is a forum for posting reviews of books of interest to readers, school and public librarians, bookstores, publishers, teachers and professors, and others who desire an "educated opinion" of a book. This is an unmoderated newsgroup.
Contact:	sbrock@csn.org.
Details:	Free
	To participate in a Usenet newsgroup, you need access to a newsreader
Notes:	The reviews in alt.books.reviews are archived at csn.org. FTP to csn.org; login: anonymous; password: your complete e-mail address. At the FTP prompt, type: `cd pub/alt.books.reviews`

`news:alt.books.reviews`

alt.hypertext ★

A USENET newsgroup devoted to hyperfiction and hypertext documents. Postings range from information about and reviews of both recent hyperfiction and recent nonfiction hypertext documents, to information reviews of software for creating hypertext.

Keywords:	Literature (General), Hyperfiction, Hypertext
Audience:	General Public, Writers, Computer Programmers
Details:	Free
	To participate in a USENET newsgroup, you need access to a newsreader.

`news:alt.hypertext`

Electronic Books ★★

A collection of books available as ASCII text files, including classics of antiquity (Aristotle, Virgil, Sophocles, the Bible), as well as more contemporary works of fiction and nonfiction by authors ranging from Dostoevsky to Martin Luther King, Jr.

Keywords:	Books, Online Books, Literature (Contemporary), Literature (General)
Sponsor:	The Blacksburg Electronic Village (BEV) at Virginia Tech
Audience:	General Public, Historians
Contact:	BEV Gopher Administrators gopher@gopher.vt.edu

`gopher://gopher.vt.edu`

GUTENBERG Listserver ★

A mailing list providing information about Project Gutenberg.

Keywords:	Project Gutenberg, Literature (General), Reference
Sponsor:	National Clearinghouse for Machine Readable Texts
Audience:	General Public, Researchers, Educators, Students
Contact:	Michael S. Hart gutnberg@vmd.cso.uiuc.edu
Details:	Free
User Info:	To subscribe to the list, send an e-mail message to the URL address shown below consisting of a single line reading: SUB GUTNBERG YourFirstName YourLastName

`mailto:listserv@vmd.cso.uiuc.edu`

Project Gutenberg ★★★★

The purpose of Project Gutenberg is to encourage the creation and distribution of English-language electronic texts.

Keywords:	Literature (General), Reference
Sponsor:	National Clearinghouse for Machine Readable Texts
Audience:	General Public, Researchers, Educators, Students
Profile:	Contents Include: Project Gutenberg's goal is to provide a collection of 10,000 of the most used books by the year 2001, and to reduce the effective costs to the user to a price of approximately one cent per book, plus the cost of media and of shipping and handling. Thus it is hoped that the entire cost of libraries of this nature will be about US$100, plus the price of the disks and CD-ROMs and mailing. Project Gutenberg assists in the selection of hardware and software as well as in their installation and use. It also assists in scanning, spelling checkers, proofreading, etc.

Contact:	Michael S. Hart
	hart@vmd.cso.uiuc.edu
Details:	Costs
	Login anonymous; cd text

`ftp://mrcnext.cso.uiuc.edu`

Rec.arts.int-fiction

A Usenet newsgroup about interactive literature and interactive computer games.

Keywords:	Literature (General), Interactive Media, Computer Games
Audience:	General Public, Computer Games Players
Details:	Free
	To participate in a USENET newsgroup, you need access to a newsreader.

`news:rec.arts.int-fiction`

rec.arts.poems

A Usenet newsgroup providing information and discussion about poetry.

Keywords:	Poetry, Literature (General)
Audience:	Poets, Poetry Readers
User Info:	To subscribe to this Usenet newsgroup, you need access to a newsreader.

`news:rec.arts.poems`

University of Puget Sound Library

The library's holdings are large and wide-ranging and contain significant collections in many fields.

Keywords:	Education, Literature (General), Music, Natural Science, Theology
Audience:	Researchers, Students, General Public
Details:	Free
	Expect: Login; Send: Library

`telnet://192.124.98.2`

Literature (German)

Washington University Library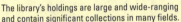

The library's holdings are large and wide-ranging and contain significant collections in many fields.

Keywords:	Technology, Literature (German), Social Science, Behavioral Science
Audience:	Researchers, Students, General Public
Contact:	services@wugate.wustl.edu
Details:	Free
	Expect: Login; Send: Services

`telnet://wugate.wustl.edu`

Literature (Irish)

fwake-l

A conference and forum for a broad discussion of James Joyce's *Finnegan's Wake*.

Keywords:	Joyce (James), Literature (Irish), Authors, Writing
Audience:	Writers, Joyce Scholars, Literary Critics, Literary Theorists
User Info:	To subscribe to the list, send an e-mail message to the URL address below consisting of a single line reading:
	SUB fwake-l

`mailto:listserv@irlearn.ucd.ie`

University of Delaware Libraries (DELCAT)

The library's holdings are large and wide-ranging and contain significant collections in many fields.

Keywords:	Literature (American), Hemingway (Ernest), Papermaking (History of), Chemistry (History of), Literature (Irish), Delaware
Audience:	General Public, Researchers, Librarians, Document Delivery Professionals
Contact:	Stuart Glogoff
	epo27855@udacsvm.bitnet
Details:	Free
	Expect: prompt, Send: RETURN 2-3 times

`telnet://delcat.udel.edu`

`delcat.acs.udel.edu`

Literature (Russian)

Russian

This list is dedicated to the discussion of Russian-language issues, including Russian language, linguistics, grammar, translations, and literature.

Keywords:	Language, Literature (Russian), Linguistics
Audience:	Slavicists, Linguists, Translators
Contact:	Andrew Wollert
	ispajw@asuacad
	russian@asuvm.inre.asu.edu
Details:	Free
User Info:	To subscribe to the list, send an e-mail message requesting subscription to the URL address below.

`russian@asuvm.inre.asu.edu`

Literature (Spanish)

University of Pennsylvania PENNINFO Library

The library's holdings are large and wide-ranging and contain significant collections in many fields.

Keywords:	Church History, Spanish Inquisition, Witchcraft, Shakespeare (William), Bibles, Aristotle (Texts of), Fiction, Whitman (Walt), French Revolution, Drama (French), Literature (English), Literature (Spanish)
Audience:	Researchers, Students, General Public
Contact:	Al DSouza
	penninfo-admin@dccs.upenn.edu
	dsouza@dccs.upenn.edu
Details:	Free
	Expect: Login; Send: Public

`telnet://penninfo.upenn.edu`

Lithuania

Balt-L

A forum devoted to communications to and about the Baltic Republics of Lithuania, Latvia, and Estonia.

Keywords:	Lithuania, Latvia, Estonia, Baltic Republics
Audience:	Researchers, Baltic Nationals
Contact:	Jean-Michel Thizy
	jmyhg@uottawa.edu
Details:	Free
User Info:	To subscribe to the list, send an e-mail message to the URL address below, consisting of a single line reading:
	SUB balt-l YourFirstName YourLastName

`mailto:listserv@ubvm.cc.buffalo.edu`

University of Pennsylvania Library- Philadelphia Pa.

The library's holdings are large and wide-ranging and contain significant collections in many fields.

Keywords:	Literature (English), Literature (American), History (World), Medieval Studies, East Asian Studies, Middle Eastern Studies, South Asian Studies, Judaica, Lithuania
Audience:	Educators, Students, Researchers
Profile:	Access to the central Van Pelt Library and to most of the departmental libraries is restricted to members of the University community on weekends and holidays. Online visitors are advised to call (215) 898-7554 for information on hours and access restrictions.

Litigants

LEXPAT (Patents US)

The LEXPAT library contains the full text of US patents issued since 1975, the US Patent and Trademark Office Manual of Classification, and the Index to US Patent Classification. The approximately 1,500 patents added to the library each week appear online within four days of their issue.

Keywords: Patents, Inventors, Assignees, Litigants
Audience: Lawyers, Business Researchers, Analysts, Entrepreneurs
Profile: LEXPAT may be searched by individual files for the full text of utility, design or plant patents, or you can combine the files in one 'omni' search. The Manual, Index and Class files can be used to supplement your full-text patent searches. LEXPAT is a valuable tool for both patent professionals and for anyone who needs to access to technical information. More than 80 percent of the information contained in patents is unavailable in any other form.
Contact: Mead New Sales Group at (800) 227-4908 or (513) 859-5398 inside the US, or (513) 865-7981 for all inquiries outside the US.
User Info: To subscribe, contact Mead directly.
To examine the Nexis user guide, you can access it at the ftp site of the University of Texas at Austin at the URL address: ftp://ftp.cc.utexas.edu
The files are in: /pub/ref-services/LEXIS

`telnet://nex.meaddata.com`

`http://www.meaddata.com`

Liturgy

Cantus

This gopher site accesses the Gregorian Chant Database, which is maintained by the Catholic University of America.

Keywords: Gregorian Chants, Music, Liturgy
Sponsor: Catholic University of America (CUA)
Audience: Vocalists, Educators, Students
Profile: The database contains an introduction to the Cantus Gopher at the CUA, and has a searchable index.

`gopher://vmsgopher.cua.edu`

Lockheed Missiles & Space Company

Lockheed Missiles & Space Company

A web site containing information about Lockheed Missiles and Space Company, a major aerospace and defense company specializing in the development of space systems, missiles and other high technology products. Includes company information and press releases.

Keywords: Defense, Aerospace
Sponsor: The Lockheed Palo Alto Artificial Intelligence Center
Audience: Aerospace Engineers, Defense Analysts

`http://www.lmsc.lockheed.com`

Loughborough University of Technology Computer-Human Interaction (LUTCHI) Research Centre

Loughborough University of Technology Computer-Human Interaction (LUTCHI) Research Centre

This server contains general information on computer-human interaction.

Keywords: Interface Design, Ergonomics, Computer-Human Interactions, Programming
Sponsor: Loughborough University of Technology, Leicestershire, UK
Audience: Software Developers, Software Designers, Programmers
Profile: The LUTCHI Research Centre is based within the Department of Computer Studies at the Loughborough University of Technology, Leicestershire, UK. This server contains information about LUTCHI research projects, official publicity releases, as well as documents, images, and movies associated with those projects.
Contact: Ben Anderson
B.Anderson@lut.ac.uk
Details: Free, Moderated, Image, Sound, and Multimedia.
Use a World Wide Web (Mosaic) client and open a connection to the resource.

`http://pipkin.lut.ac.uk`

Lower Rio Grande Valley (History of)

University of Texas-Pan American Library

The library's holdings are large and wide-ranging and contain significant collections in many fields.

Keywords: Lower Rio Grande Valley (History of), Mexican-American Studies
Audience: Researchers, Students, General Public
Details: Free
Expect: Username Prompt, Send: packey

`telnet://panam2.panam.edu`

Lynx FAQ

Lynx FAQ

A resource providing common questions and answers about Cello, a distributed hypertext browser with full WWW capabilities.

Keywords: Internet Reference FAQs
Sponsor: University of Kansas, Distributed Computing Group, Kansas, USA
Audience: Students, Computer Scientists, Researchers
Contact: Garrett Blythe, Lou Montulli
doslynx@falcon.cc.ukans.edu
montulli@mcom.com
lynx-help@ukanaix.cc.ukans.edu

`http://ftp2.cc.ukans.edu/about_lynx`

`http://ftp2.cc.ukans.edu/lynx_help`

`http://ftp2.cc.ukans.edu/lynx_writeup`

Lyrics

UWP Music Archive (named for the host machine's location: the University of Wisconsin—Parkside)

An extensive repository of files relating to a diverse array of music genres: rock, folk, classical, etc.

Keywords: Music, Lyrics, Graphics
Sponsor: University of Wisconsin—Parkside
Audience: Musicians, Music Enthusiasts, Musicologists
Profile: This FTP archive contains a music database, artist discographies, essays about music and particular works, hundreds of image files (mostly .GIF and

.JPEG format) of musicians Ñ including album covers and posters, a lyrics archive and the ever-popular 'Beginner's Introduction to Classical Music.'

Contact: Dave Datta
datta@ftp.uwp.edu

User Info: Select Music Archives from the gopher top-level menu.

Notes: Also accessible through CMU's "English Server" gopher server. (q.v.)

`gopher://gopher.uwp.edu`

Lysator's Gopher Service

Lysator's Gopher Service

Lysator is the name of the Academic Computer Society at Linkoping University, Linkoping, Sweden. It relies on voluntary efforts by students, and any service of activity runs as long as they think it is fun—content always reflects their personal interests.

Keywords: Sweden, Europe

Audience: Swedish Students

Contact: Lars Aronsson@lysator.liu.se

Details: Free

`gopher://gopher.lysator.liu.se`

`http://dla.ucop.edu`

450

Maastricht Treaty

Maastricht Treaty

The file contains the text of the latest edition of the Treaty on European Union, also known as the Maastricht Treaty, signed on February 7, 1992.

Keywords:	Europe, European Community, Maastricht Treaty
Audience:	Politicians, Historians, Europeans, Political Scientists, General Public
Details:	Free
	Select from menu as appropriate.

`gopher://wiretap.spies.com`

Macintosh Computer

(The) DTP Direct Catalog

DTP Direct specializes in Macintosh hardware and software tools for desktop publishers and graphics professionals.

Keywords:	Macintosh Computer, Desktop Publishing, Graphic Design
Sponsor:	InterNex Server Bureau
Audience:	Graphic Designers, Artists, Desktop Publishers
Details:	Free, Moderated, Image, Sound, and Multimedia files available.

`http://www.internex.net/DTP/home.html`

CE Software

Technical support for CE Software Products, such as QuickKeys for the Macintosh.

Keywords:	Software, Technical Support, Macintosh Computer
Audience:	Software users
Details:	Free
User Info:	To Subscribe to the list, send an e-mail message requesting a subscription to the URL address below.

`mailto:ce_info%cedsm@uunet.uu.net`

Chemistry Tutorial Information

This site provides chemistry tutorial information in the form of text, data, pictures, source code, and executable programs for Macintosh computers.

Keywords:	Chemistry, Tutorials, Macintosh Computer, Education
Sponsor:	University of Michigan
Audience:	Chemistry Students (high school up)
Contact:	comments@mac.archive.umich.edu
Details:	Free, Image files available.

`gopher://plaza.aarnet.edu.au@/micros/mac/umich/misc/chemistry/00index.txt`

comp.sys.mac

A Usenet newsgroup providing information and discussion about the Macintosh computer. There are many categories within this group.

Keywords:	Computer Systems, Macintosh Computer
Audience:	Computer Users, Macintosh Users
Details:	To subscribe to this Usenet newsgroup, you need access to a newsreader.

`news:comp.sys.mac`

PAGEMAKER

The PageMaker ListServ is dedicated to the discussion of desktop publishing in general, with emphasis on the use of Aldus PageMaker. The list discusses PageMaker's use in both the PC and Macintosh realms. The list also maintains an extensive archive of help files that are extremely useful for the modern desktop publisher.

Keywords:	Desktop Publishing, Aldus Pagemaker, IBM PC, Macintosh Computer
Audience:	Desktop Publishers, Computer Users
Contact:	Geoff Peters gwp@cs.purdue.edu
Details:	Free
User Info:	To Subscribe to the list, send an e-mail message to the URL address shown below consisting of a single line reading: SUB pagemaker YourFirstName YourLastName. To send a message to the entire list, address it to: gwp@cs.purdue.edu

`mailto:listserv@cs.purdue.edu`

SUMEX-AIM

An FTP archive of software, demonstration programs, and various applications, especially for Macintosh computers.

Keywords:	Computers, Macintosh Computer, Software
Audience:	Computer Users, Macintosh Users
Details:	Free

`ftp://sumex-aim.Stanford.edu`

Magazines

(The) Electric Eclectic

A multimedia magazine delivered online that includes pictures, sounds, and text.

Keywords: Magazines, Multimedia
Audience: General Public

`mailto:ee-discuss-request@eitech.cm`

Class Four Relay Magazine

A magazine by Relay Ops for the relay community.
Keywords: Relays, Magazines, Electronics
Sponsor: Carnegie Mellon University, Pittsburgh, PA, USA
Audience: Relay Community
Profile: Includes articles on general questions and issues of relay usage, information for and about relay ops, discussion of policy issues and guidelines, and technical issues and new developments.
Contact: Joey J. Stanford
stjs@vm.marist.edu
Details: Free

`mailto:stjs@vm.marist.edu`

Mailing Lists

LIST Gopher

This is a library-related service that allows users to obtain information by using their e-mail accounts.
Keywords: Mailing Lists, Listserv, Libraries, Gopher
Sponsor: North Carolina State University, Raleigh, North Carolina, USA
Audience: Librarians, Library Users, Email Users
Profile: LISTGopher allows users to search library-related LISTSERV archives through the Gopher interface. Users enter their e-mail address, the list they want to search, and the keyword(s) they want to find. LISTGopher then send the results of their search to the user's Email address. Currently, only library-related archives are supported, but more archive types may be added in the future.
Contact: Eric Lease Morgan, Systems Librarian
eric_morgan@ncsu.edu
http://ericmorgan.lib.ncsu.edu/staff/morgan/morgan.html

`gopher://dewey.lib.ncsu.edu/library/disciplines/library/listgopher`

MLoL

The MLoL (Musical List of Lists) is a list of music-related mailing lists available on the Internet.
Keywords: Music, Mailing Lists
Audience: Musicians, General Public
Details: Free
User Info: To Subscribe to the list, send an e-mail message requesting a subscription to the URL address below.

`mailto:mlol-request@wariat.org`

Newlists

This is a mailing list clearing house for new mailing lists. Subscribers will get announcements of new lists that are mailed to this list.
Keywords: Mailing Lists
Audience: Internet Surfers
Contact: Marty Hoag
info@vm1.nodak.edu
Details: Free
User Info: To Subscribe to the list, send an e-mail message requesting a subscription to the URL address below.

`mailto:info@vm1.nodak.edu`

Maine

University of Maine System Library Catalog

The library's holdings are large and wide-ranging and contain significant collections in many fields.
Keywords: Ucadian Studies, St. John Valley (History of), Canadian-American Studies, Geology, Aquaculture, Maine
Audience: General Public, Researchers, Librarians, Document Delivery Professionals
Contact: Elaine Albright, Marilyn Lutz
Details: Free
Notes: Expect: login, Send: ursus

`telnet://ursus.maine.edu`

Maine Authors

Colby College Library

The library's holdings are large and wide-ranging and contain significant collections in many fields.
Keywords: Contemporary Letters, Hardy (Thomas),James (Henry), Mann (Thomas, Collections of), Housman (A.E., Letters of), Maine Authors, Irish History (Modern)
Audience: General Public, Researchers, Librarians, Document Delivery Professionals
Details: Free
Notes: Expect: login, Send: library

`telnet://library.colby.edu`

Malls

The Branch Mall, an Electronic Shopping Mall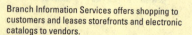

Branch Information Services offers shopping to customers and leases storefronts and electronic catalogs to vendors.
Keywords: Malls, Shopping, Gifts, Advertising
Sponsor: Branch Information Services
Audience: Consumers, Merchants
Contact: Jon Zeeff
jon@branch.com
Details: Free
Notes: Free for consumers.

`http://branch.com`

Management

ABI/Inform

ABI/Inform is a comprehensive source for business and management information, containing abstracts from close to 1,000 publications and the full-text from over 100 publications. The database covers trends, corporate strategies and tactics, management techniques, competitive information and product information
Keywords: Business, Business Management, Management
Sponsor: UMI, Ann Arbor, Michigan, US
Audience: General Public, Researchers, Librarians
Profile: A few of the thousands of business subjects that can searched in ABI/Inform include: company news and analysis, market conditions and strategies, employee management and compensation, international trade and investment, management styles and corporate cultures, and economic conditions and forecasts.
Contact: CDP Technologies Sales Department (800)950-2035, extension 400
User Info: To Subscribe, contact CDP Technologies directly

`telnet://cdplus@cdplus.com`

Asian Pacific Business and Marketing Resources

A forum on business and marketing in the Pacific Rim region.
Keywords: Asia, Pacific, Business, Management
Audience: Business Professionals, Market Researchers
Details: Free

`gopher://hoshi.cic.sfu.ca/11/dlam/business/forum`

GC-L

Project for international business and management curricula.

Keywords: Business, Management, Language
Sponsor: Global Classroom
Audience: Linguists, Language Teachers, Language Students, International Business Educators
Details: Free
User Info: To Subscribe to the list, send an e-mail message to the address below consisting of a single line reading:

mailto:listserv@uriacc.uri.edu

The Management Archive

This is an electronic forum for management ideas and information.

Keywords: Management, Business, Economics
Audience: Managers, Business Professionals, Economists
Profile: The Archive arranges working papers, teaching materials, and so on, in directories by subject. All materials in the Archive are fully indexed and searchable. If you have material that you would like to see receive worldwide network exposure and distribution, submit them to the Archive.
Contact: Jim Goes
goes@chimera.sph.umn.edu
Details: Free
Notes: Expect: login, Send: anonymous; Expect: password, Send: your e-mail address.

ftp://chimera.sph.umn.edu

Total Quality Management Gopher

A collection of materials relating to the elimination of defects through comprehensive quality control in industry, government, and universities.

Keywords: Quality Control, Management, Business
Sponsor: The Clemson University Department of Industrial Engineering, Clemson, South Carolina, USA
Audience: Managers, Administrators
Contact: quality@eng.clemson.edu

gopher://deming.eng.clemson.edu

http://deming.eng.clemson.edu

Mann (Thomas)

Colby College Library

The library's holdings are large and wide-ranging and contain significant collections in many fields.

Keywords: Contemporary Letters, Hardy (Thomas), James (Henry), Mann (Thomas, Collections of), Housman (A.E., Letters of), Maine Authors, Irish History (Modern)
Audience: General Public, Researchers, Librarians, Document Delivery Professionals
Details: Free
Notes: Expect: login, Send: library

telnet://library.colby.edu

Manx

gaelic-l

A multidisciplinary discussion list that facilitates the exchange of news, views, and information in Scottish Gaelic, Irish, and Manx.

Keywords: Scottish Gaelic, Irish, Manx, Language
Audience: Linguists
Contact: Marion Gunn
mgunn@irlearn.ucd.ie or
caoimhin@smo.ac.uk
lss203@cs.napier.ac.uk
Details: Free
User Info: To Subscribe to the list, send an e-mail message to the URL address shown below consisting of a single line reading:

SUB gaelic-l YourFirstName YourLastName

To send a message to the entire list, address it to:

gaelic-l@irlearn.ucd.ie

mailto:listserv@irlearn.ucd.ie

MapInfo-l

MapInfo-l

A mailing list for the discussion of MapInfo Software.

Keywords: GIS (Geographic Information Systems)
Audience: Geographers, Cartographers
Contact: Bill Thoen
bthoen@gisnet.com

mailto:mapinfo-l-request@csn.org

Mapping

Internet Resources for Earth Sciences

A document detailing Internet resources for a variety of earth science disciplines, including GIS.

Keywords: Directory, GIS, Geology, Geography, GPS, Mapping, Earth Science
Sponsor: Bill Thoen
Audience: Earth Scientists, Researchers
Profile: A complete document detailing the types of information available in earth sciences and the mechanisms to retrieve needed information.
Contact: Bill Thoen
bthoen@gisnet.com
Details: Free

ftp://ftp.csn.org/COGS/ores.text

Marimed Foundation

Marimed Foundation

This foundation provides therapy and education to adjudicated and emotionally impaired teens. Therapies include wilderness experiences on a square-rigged sail ship, boat building, and traditional therapies.

Keywords: Education (Alternative), Sailing
Audience: Educators, Social Workers
Contact: Dr. Robert Grossman
marimed@holonet.net
Details: Free

mailto:marimed@holonet.net

Marine Biology

Starnet (Echinoderm Newsletter)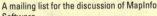

The Starnet echinoderm electronic newsletter is distributed quarterly.

Keywords: Echinoderm, Starfish, Marine Biology
Audience: Marine Biologists
Contact: Win Hide
whide@matrix.bchs.uh.edu
Details: Free
User Info: To Subscribe to the list, send an e-mail message requesting a subscription to the URL address below.

mailto:whide@matrix.bchs.uh.edu

Marine Biology

University of North Carolina at Wilmington SEABOARD Library ★★

The library's holdings are large and wide-ranging and contain significant collections in many fields.

Keywords: Marine Biology, Historical Documents
Audience: Researchers, Students, General Public
Contact: Eddy Cavenaugh
cavenaughd@uncwil.bitnet
cavenaughd@vxc.uncwil.edu
Details: Free
Notes: Expect: Login; Send: Info

`telnet://vxc.uncwil.edu`

Marine Engineering

Florida State University System Library ★★

The library's holdings are large and wide-ranging and contain significant collections in many fields.

Keywords: Florida, Latin America, Judaica, Literature (Children's), Marine Engineering, Law (Brazilian), Law (British)
Audience: General Public, Researchers, Librarians, Document Delivery Professionals
Details: Free
Notes: Expect: Command ==>, Send: dial vtam; Expect: LUIS User Menu, Send: Your Catalog choice; To log off: Send: %off

`telnet://nervm.nerdc.ufl.edu`

Maritime Industry

PIERS Imports (US Ports)

PIERS (Port Import Export Reporting Service) Imports (US Ports), produced by The Journal of Commerce, is a compilation of manifests of vessels loading or discharging cargo at approximately 120 US seaports.

Keywords: Trade, Imports, Maritime Industry
Sponsor: The Journal of Commerce/PIERS, New York, NY, USA
Audience: Business Professionals
Profile: The principal applications of this information include: identification of new sources of supply for imports, monitoring imports of products whose details are lost in traditional government reports, and identification of potential trade partners.
Contact: Dialog in the US at (800) 334-2564, Dialog internationally at country specific locations.

User Info: To Subscribe, contact Dialog directly.
Notes: Coverage: current 15 months, updated monthly.

`telnet://dialog.com`

Research Ship Schedules and Information ★★★

A gopher providing information on research and deep water vessels from more than 45 countries. Includes detailed ship specifications, some with deck plans and photographs available as GIF files. Also has cruise schedules for US ships, as well as some from other countries.

Keywords: Oceanography, Transportation, Maritime Industry, Travel
Sponsor: University of Delaware (The OCEANIC Ocean Information Center), Newark, Delaware, USA
Audience: Oceanographers, General Public
Contact: Ocean Information Center, University of Delaware, College of Marine Studies
oceanic@diu.cms.udel.edu
Details: Free, Images

`gopher://diu.cms.udel.edu`

MARKET (Markets and Industries News and Information)

MARKET (Markets and Industries News and Information) ★★★★

The Markets and Industries News and Information (MARKET) library contains sources covering developments in a wide variety of markets and industries.

Keywords: News, Analysis, Industry, Marketing
Audience: Business Professionals, Researchers
Profile: The MARKET library contains a wide selection of sources ranging from trade and industry sources to InvestextR industry reports to company profiles. To round out the offering, MARKET also covers advertising, marketing, public opinion polls, market research, public relations, sales and selling, promotions, consumer attitudes, trends and behaviors, demographics, product announcements and product reviews. In addition, Predicasts Overview of Markets and Technology (PROMT), Marketing and Advertising Reference Service (MARS), US and International Forecast Databases (UFRCST and IFRCST) and the US Time Series (USTIME), all from Information Access Company, are available.
Contact: Mead New Sales Group at (800) 227-4908 or (513) 859-5398 inside the US, or (513) 865-7981 for all inquiries outside the US.

User Info: To Subscribe, contact Mead directly.
To examine the Nexis user guide, you can access it at the ftp site of the University of Texas at Austin at the URL address: ftp://ftp.cc.utexas.edu
The files are in: /pub/ref-services/LEXIS

`telnet://nex.meaddata.com`

`http://www.meaddata.com`

Market Conditions

Business Dateline ★★★

The database contains the full text of articles from more than 350 local and regional business publications from throughout the United States and Canada.

Keywords: Business, Regional Business, Market Conditions
Sponsor: UMI, Louisville, KY, USA
Audience: Business Analysts, Market Researchers, Writers
Profile: Sources include city business journals, daily newspapers, regional business magazines, and wire services. Subjects include city economic conditions, new product announcements, manufacturing methods, executive profiles, quality control, company histories, market conditions, service industries, regulations, litigation, and legislation.
Contact: Dialog in the US at (800) 334-2564, Dialog internationally at country specific locations.
Details: Costs
User Info: To Subscribe, contact Dialog directly.

`telnet://dialog.com`

Market Research

Research on Demand ★★★

A resource for the provision of market information, strategic information location, product information, and national and international business information.

Keywords: Market Research, Internet Research, Legal Research, International Research
Audience: Marketing Specialists, Lawyers, Public Relations Experts, Business Professionals, Researchers, Writers, Producers
Profile: This resource has special access to unique information resources worldwide. Areas of particular information access include the former Soviet Union, Europe, and the US. Information access also includes access to all the major online systems, including Dialog, BRS, Orbit, DataStar, and so on. Current Awareness Services include research information gathered from the Internet.

Details:	Costs
User Info:	To Subscribe, send an e-mail message to the URL address below. In the body of your message, state the nature of your inquiry.
Notes:	Contact ROD directly in the US at: (800) 227-0750; outside the US at: (510) 841-1145.

`mailto:rod@holonet.net`

Marketing

MarketBase Gopher

An online catalog of goods and services dedicated to providing a forum where buyers and sellers meet to electronically exchange the attributes of products and services. Free access is provided to product purchasers.

Keywords:	Internet Services, Marketing
Audience:	Internet Surfers
Contact:	help@mb.com
Details:	Free

`gopher://mb.com`

Computer-Mediated Marketing Environments

A web site devoted to research aimed at understanding the ways in which computer-mediated marketing environments (CMEs), especially the Internet, are revolutionizing the way firms conduct business.

Keywords:	WWW, Information Retrieval, Internet, Marketing, Business
Sponsor:	Vanderbilt University, Owen Graduate School of Management, Nashville, Tennessee, USA
Audience:	General Public, Entrepeneurs, Financial Planners, Marketers
Contact:	Donna Hoffman, Tom Novak hoffman@colette.ogsm.vanderbilt.edu, novak@moe.ogsm.vanderbilt.edu

`http://colette.ogsm.vanderbilt.edu`

MARKET (Markets and Industries News and Information)

The Markets and Industries News and Information (MARKET) library contains sources covering developments in a wide variety of markets and industries.

Keywords:	News, Analysis, Industry, Marketing
Audience:	Business Professionals, Researchers
Profile:	The MARKET library contains a wide selection of sources ranging from trade and industry sources to InvestextR industry reports to company profiles. To round out the offering, MARKET also covers advertising, marketing, public opinion polls, market research, public relations, sales and selling, promotions, consumer attitudes, trends and behaviors, demographics, product announcements and product reviews. In addition, Predicasts Overview of Markets and Technology (PROMT), Marketing and Advertising Reference Service (MARS), US and International Forecast Databases (UFRCST and IFRCST) and the US Time Series (USTIME), all from Information Access Company, are available.
Contact:	Mead New Sales Group at (800) 227-4908 or (513) 859-5398 inside the US, or (513) 865-7981 for all inquiries outside the US.
User Info:	To Subscribe, contact Mead directly.
	To examine the Nexis user guide, you can access it at the ftp site of the University of Texas at Austin at the URL address: ftp://ftp.cc.utexas.edu
	The files are in: /pub/ref-services/LEXIS

`telnet://nex.meaddata.com`

`http://www.meaddata.com`

Marshall University School of Medicine (MUSOM) RuralNet Gopher

Marshall University School of Medicine (MUSOM) RuralNet Gopher

A gopher server dedicated to the improvement of rural health care.

Keywords:	Rural Development, Health Care, Medical Treatment, Bioinformatics
Sponsor:	Marshall University School of Medicine
Audience:	Health Care Professionals, Medical Students
Profile:	A collection of health care resources, with particular emphasis on rural health care. Includes listings of clinical resources by subject area, information on state and federal rural health care initiatives, and links to local and national health and education services.
Contact:	Mike McCarthy, Andy Jarrell mmccarth@muvms6.wvnet.edu jarrell@musom01.mu.wvnet.edu

`gopher://ruralnet.mu.wvnet.edu`

Martial Arts

Aikido Information

An FTP site containing aikido dojo addresses from around the world, plus a calendar of events, FAQs, and lists of books and periodicals related to aikido.

Keywords:	Aikido, Martial Arts, Sports
Sponsor:	University of California at San Diego, San Diego, CA, USA
Audience:	Aikido Enthusiasts, Martial Artists
Contact:	aikido@cs.ucsd.edu
Details:	Free

`ftp://cs.ucsd.edu/pub/aikido`

aikido-l

A discussion group and information exchange on the Japanese martial art Aikido.

Keywords:	Aikido, Martial Arts
Sponsor:	Gerry Santoro
Audience:	Aikido Enthusiasts
Contact:	aikido-l-request@psuvm.psu.edu
User Info:	To Subscribe to the list, send an e-mail message to the URL address below consisting of a single line reading:
	SUB aikido-l YourFirstName YourLastName.
	To send a message to the entire list, address it to: aikido-l@psuvm.psu.edu

`mailto:listserv@psuvm.psu.edu`

rec.martial-arts

A Usenet newsgroup providing information and discussion about martial arts.

Keywords:	Martial Arts
Audience:	Martial Artists
User Info:	To Subscribe to this Usenet newsgroup, you need access to a newsreader.

`news:rec.martial-arts`

Martin Marietta Energy Systems Gopher

Martin Marietta Energy Systems Gopher

Information on Martin Marietta's energy projects and technologies for both government and commercial applications.

Keywords:	Technology, Energy, Industry
Sponsor:	Martin Marietta
Audience:	Business Professionals, Entrepreneurs, Manufactures, Energy Researchers, Technology Professionals
Profile:	This gopher contains a list of technologies currently being developed at Martin Marietta as well as detailing facilities available to university, government, and commercial researchers. Also includes updates on employment openings, and a list of current publications.

Contact: gopher@ornl.gov

gopher:// gopher.ornl.gov

http://www.ornl.gov/mmes.html

Maryland

Maryland

System provides access to a wide range of state information, including the policies and activities of members of Maryland's congress and voting district data.

Keywords: Maryland, Law (US State), Voting
Audience: Maryland Residents, Lawyers
Details: Free
User Info: Select from menu as appropriate.

gopher://info.umd.edu

Mass Media

Communication and Mass Communication Resources

An archive of materials related to mass communications and the media.

Keywords: Mass Media, Media, Journalism, Telecommunications, Advertising
Sponsor: The University of Iowa
Audience: Mass Communications Students and Teachers, Journalists, Broadcasting Professionals
Contact: Karla Tonella
Karla_Tonella@uiowa.edu

gopher://iam41.arcade.uiowa.edu

National Broadcasting Society— Alpha Epsilon Rho

Forum for mass media professionals to share experiences and ideas.

Keywords: Film, Television, Radio, Mass Media
Sponsor: National Broadcasting Society-Alpha Epsilon Rho
Audience: Journalists, Students, Educators, Broadcasting Professionals
Contact: Reg Gamar
regbc@cunyvm.bitnet
Details: Free
User Info: To Subscribe to the list, send an e-mail message to the address shown below consisting of a single line reading:

SUB NBS-AER YourFirstName YourLastName

To send a message to thhe entire list, address it to: nbs-aer@cunyvm.bitnet

mailto:listserv@cunyvm.bitnet

ViewPoints

Newsletter of the Visual Communication Division of the Association of Educators in Journalism and Mass Communication.

Keywords: Journalism, Mass Media, Visual Communication
Audience: Educators, Photographers, Desktop Publishers
Contact: Paul Lester
lester@fullerton.edu
Details: Free

mailto:lester@fullerton.edu

Massachusetts Institute of Technology Library

Massachusetts Institute of Technology Library

The library's holdings are large and wide-ranging and contain significant collections in many fields.

Keywords: Aeronautics (History of), Linguistics, Mathematics (History of), Microscopy, Spectroscopy, Aeronautics, Mathematics, Glass
Audience: General Public, Researchers, Librarians, Document Delivery Professionals
Details: Free
User Info: Expect: Mitek Server..., Send: Enter or Return; Expect: prompt, Send: hollis

telnet://library.mit.edu

Material Science

Material Science in Israel Newsletter

Newsletter on bitnet, for people interested in material sciences, established to allow important local and international information to be disseminated efficiently and rapidly to all interested parties.

Keywords: Material Science, Israel
Audience: Material Scientists
Contact: Michael Wolff
wolff@ilncrd.bitnet
Details: Free
User Info: To Subscribe to the list, send an e-mail message to the URL address below, consisting of a single line reading:

SUB YourFirstName YourLastName

To send a message to the entire list, address it to: @taunivmbitnet

mailto:listserv@taunivmbitnet

Materials Business File

Covers all commercial aspects of iron and steel, non-ferrous metals and non-metallic materials.

Keywords: Material Science, Business, Iron, Steel
Sponsor: Materials Information, a joint information service of ASM International and the Institute of Materials
Audience: Material Scientists, Researchers
Profile: Articles are abstracted from over 2,000 worldwide technical and trade journals to create more than 65,000 records. Update monthly.
Contact: paul.albert@neteast.com
User Info: To Subscribe contact Orbit-Questel directly.

telnet://orbit.com

METADEX

International literature covering metals and alloys.

Keywords: Material Science, Metals, Alloys
Sponsor: Materials Information, a joint information service of ASM International and the Institute of Materials
Audience: Material Scientists, Researchers
Profile: Contains more than 925,000 records from the international literature on metals and alloys concerning processes, properties, materials classes, applications, specific alloy designations, intermetallic compounds and metallurgical systems. Updated monthly.
Contact: paul.albert@neteast.com
User Info: To Subscribe contact Orbit-Questel directly.

telnet://orbit.com

PIRA - Paper, Printing and Publishing, Packaging, and Nonwovens Abstracts

Coverage of all aspects of paper, pulp, nonwovens, printing, publishing and packaging.

Keywords: Material Science, Paper, Printing, Publishing, Packaging, Nonwovens
Sponsor: PIRA International
Audience: Material Scientists, Researchers
Profile: File contains more than 300,000 records. Special applications: company and market profiles, product and trade name searches, research and technology trends. Updated biweekly.
Contact: paul.albert@neteast.com
User Info: To Subscribe contact Orbit-Questel directly.

telnet://orbit.com

RAPRA Abstracts

Coverage on technical and commercial aspects of the rubber, plastics, and polymer composites industries.

Keywords: Material Science, Rubbers, Plastics, Polymers
Sponsor: Rapra Technology, Ltd.
Audience: Material Scientists, Researchers
Profile: This unique source of information covers the world's polymer literature including journals, conference proceedings, books, specifications, reports and trade literature. Contains over 375,000 records. Updated biweekly.
Contact: paul.albert@neteast.com
User Info: To Subscribe contact Orbit-Questel directly.

`telnet://orbit.com`

Mathematical Biology

Smbnet (Society for Mathematical Biology Digest)

Keywords: Mathematical Biology, Biology
Audience: Mathematical Biologists, Biologists
Contact: Ray Mejia
Details: Free
User Info: To Subscribe to the list, send an e-mail message to the URL address below consisting of a single line reading:

SUB smbnet YourFirstName YourLastName

To send a message to the entire list, address it to: smbnet@fconvx.ncifcrf.gov

`mailto:listserv@fconvx.ncifcrf.gov`

Mathematics (Algorithms)

comp.compression

A Usenet newsgroup providing information and discussion about data compression algorithms and theory.

Keywords: Computers, Mathematics (Algorithms)
Audience: Computer Users
User Info: To Subscribe to this Usenet newsgroup, you need access to a newsreader.

`news:comp.compression`

Mathematics

alife

The alife mailing list is for communications regarding artificial life, a formative interdisciplinary field involving computer science, the natural sciences, mathematics, and medicine.

Keywords: Artificial Life, Science, Mathematics
Sponsor: UCLA
Audience: Scientists, Biologists, Mathematicians
Contact: alife-request@cognet.ucla.edu
User Info: To Subscribe to the list, send an e-mail message to the URL address below.

To send a message to the entire list, address it to: alife@cognet.ucla.edu

`mailto:alife-request@cognet.ucla.edu`

Anneal

A mailing list for the discussion of simulated annealing techniques and analysis, as well as related issues such as stochastic optimization, Boltzmann machines, and metricity of NP-complete move spaces.

Keywords: Mathematics, Simulation, Annealing
Sponsor: UCLA
Audience: Mathematicians, Physicists
Contact: Daniel R. Greening
anneal-request@cs.ucla.edu
User Info: To Subscribe to the list, send an e-mail message to the URL address below.

To send a message to the entire list, address it to: anneal@cs.ucla.edu

Notes: Membership is restricted to those doing active research in simulated annealing or related areas.

`mailto:anneal-request@cs.ucla.edu`

CEM-L

A mailing list for discussion surrounding the UTD (University of Texas at Dallas) Center for Engineering Mathematics.

Keywords: Engineering, Mathematics
Audience: Engineers, Mathematicians, Educators, Students
Contact: David Lippke
lippke@utdallas
Details: Free
User Info: To Subscribe to the list, send an e-mail message to the URL address below, consisting of a single line reading:

SUB cem-l YourFirstName YourLastName

To send a message to the entire list, address it to: CEM-L@UTDALLAS.EDU

`mailto:listserv@utdallas.edu`

Euromath Center Gopher Server

A gopher server providing information about the Euromath Center, the Euromath Project, and related activities.

Keywords: Europe, Mathematics, Euromath
Sponsor: University of Copenhagen
Audience: Mathematicians, Europeans
Contact: Klaus Harbo
emc@euromath.dk
Details: Free

`gopher://laurel.euromath.dk`

Massachusetts Institute of Technology Library

The library's holdings are large and wide-ranging and contain significant collections in many fields.

Keywords: Aeronautics (History of), Linguistics, Mathematics (History of), Microscopy, Spectroscopy, Aeronautics, Mathematics, Glass
Audience: General Public, Researchers, Librarians, Document Delivery Professionals
Details: Free
Notes: Expect: Mitek Server..., Send: Enter or Return; Expect: prompt, Send: hollis

`telnet://library.mit.edu`

NCTM-L

A mailing list for the discussion of standards applying to the National Council of Teachers of Mathematics.

Keywords: Education, Mathematics
Audience: Mathematics Educators
Contact: barry@sci-ed.fit.edu
Details: Free
User Info: To Subscribe to this list, send an e-mail message to the URL address below, consisting of a single line reading:

SUB nctm-l YourFirstName YourLastName.

To send a message to the entire list, address it to: nctm-l@sci-ed.fit.edu

`mailto:listproc@sci-ed.fit.edu`

Pd-games

A mailing list for people interested in game theory, especially Prisoner's Dilemma types of problems. Discussions include purely technical issues and questions, as well as specific scientific applications and the political and ideological aspects and consequences of game theory.

Keywords: Game Theory, Mathematics
Audience: Game Theorists, Mathematicians

Mathematics

Contact:	Thomas Gramstad
	pd-games-request@math.uio.no
Details:	Free
User Info:	To Subscribe to the list, send an e-mail message requesting a subscription to the URL address below.
	To send a message to the entire list, address it to: pd-games@math.uio.no

`mailto:pd-games-request@math.uio.no`

sci.math

A Usenet newsgroup providing information and discussion about mathematics.

Keywords:	Mathematics
Audience:	Mathematicians
Details:	Free

To subscribe to this Usenet newsgroup, you need access to a newsreader.

`news:sci.math`

Spanky Fractal Database ★★★★

This Web site provides a collection of fractals and fractal-related material for free distribution on the Internet.

Keywords:	Mathematics, Chaos Theory, Computer Programming, Computer Graphics
Audience:	Mathematicians, Computer Programmers
Profile:	Contains information on dynamical systems, software, distributed fractal generators, galleries, and databases from all over the world.
Contact:	Noel Giffin
	noel@triumf.ca
Details:	Free

`http://spanky.triumf.ca`

Statlib ★★★

Statlib is an archive of statistics-related materials.

Keywords:	Statistics, Mathematics
Audience:	Statisticians, Mathematicians
Profile:	This archive contains a large collection of statistics software data. The directory lists the source to entire statistics packages, the collection of applied statistics algorithms, the archives of the s-news mailing list, and more.
Contact:	statlib@lib.stat.cmu.edu
Details:	Free

`ftp://lib.stat.cmu.edu`

University of Michigan Library ★★

The library's holdings are large and wide-ranging and contain significant collections in many fields.

Keywords:	Asia, Astronomy, Transportation, Lexicology, Mathamatics, Zoology, Geography
Audience:	Researchers, Students, General Public
Contact:	info@merit.edu
Details:	Free
Notes:	Expect: Which Host; Send: Help

`telnet://cts.merit.edu`

University of Wisconsin at Stout Library ★★

The library's holdings are large and wide-ranging and contain significant collections in many fields.

Keywords:	Mathematics, Business, Fashion Merchandising, Home Economics, Hospitality, Tourism, Hotel Administration, Restaurant Management, Microelectronics
Audience:	Researchers, Students, General Public
Details:	Free
Notes:	Expect: Login, Send: Lib; Expect: vDIAL Prompt, Send: Library

`telnet://lib.uwstout.edu`

May (Julian)

Milieu

Discussion of the works of Julian May, notably the Saga of the Exiles and the Galactic Milieu Trilogy.

Keywords:	May (Julian), Science Fiction
Audience:	Julian May Readers
Contact:	milieu-request@yoyo.cc.monash.edu.au
Details:	Free
User Info:	To subscribe to the list, send an e-mail message requesting a subscription to the URL address below.

`mailto:milieu-request@yoyo.cc.monash.edu.au`

Mazda Miata

Miata

An open forum for Mazda Miata owners.

Keywords:	Mazda Miata, Automobiles
Audience:	Automobile Owners
Details:	Free
User Info:	To Subscribe to the list, send an e-mail message requesting subscription to the URL address below.

`mailto:miata-request@jhunix.hcf.jhu.edu`

MBI, Music and the Brain Information Center Database (MuSICA)

MBI, Music and the Brain Information Center Database (MuSICA) ★★★★

The intent of this resource is to establish a comprehensive database of scientific research on music.

Keywords:	Music Resources, Human Behavior, Neurology
Sponsor:	Music and the Brain Information Center
Audience:	Researchers, Scientists
Profile:	MuSICA maintains a data base of scientific research (references and abstracts) on music as related to behavior, the brain and allied fields, in order to foster interdisciplinary knowledge. Topics include the auditory system; human and animal behavior; creativity; the neuropsychology of music and the human brain; the effects of music on behavior and physiology; music education, medicine, performance, and therapy; neurobiology; perception and psychophysics. Citations and abstracts are excerpted from the following journals: The Bulletin of the Council for Research in Music Education, The Journal of Research in Music Education, Music Perception, Psychology of Music, Psychomusicology.
Contact:	Norman Weinberger, Gordon Shaw
	mbic@mila.ps.uci.edu
Details:	Free
	Expect login: Send mbi Expect password: Send nammbi

`telnet://mila.ps.uci.edu`

McDonnell Douglas Aerospace

McDonnell Douglas Aerospace ★★

A Web site providing information about McDonnell Douglas, including a company profile and related discussion about technology.

Keywords:	Aerospace, Space, Aviation, Technology
Audience:	Aerospace Engineers
Contact:	mail to:
	Zook@pat.mdc.com

`http://pat.mdc.com`

McGill University, Montreal Canada, INFOMcGILL Library

McGill University, Montreal Canada, INFOMcGILL Library

The library's holdings are large and wide-ranging and contain significant collections in many fields.

Keywords: Architecture, Entomology, Biology, Science (History of), Medicine (History of), Napolean, Shakespeare (William)

Audience: Researchers, Students, General Public

Contact: Roy Miller
ccrmmus@mcgillm (Bitnet) or
ccrmmus@musicm.mcgill.ca (Internet)

Notes: Expect: VM logo; Send: Enter; Expect: prompt; Send: PF3 or type INFO

`telnet://vm1.mcgill.ca`

mda

mda

Discussion of the Mighty Ducks of Anaheim of the National Hockey League, including statistics and game summaries.

Keywords: Hockey, Sports

Audience: Hockey Enthusiasts, Hockey Players

Details: Free

User Info: To Subscribe to the list, send an e-mail message to the URL address below, consisting of a single line reading:

SUB mda YourFirstName YourLastName

To send a message to the entire list, address it to: mda@macsch.com

`mailto:mda@macsch.com`

MDEAFR

MDEAFR

The Middle East and Africa (MDEAFR) library contains detailed information about every country in the Mideast and Africa. Structured for those who want to follow the unfolding events in the Gulf states, as well as in North and South Africa, this library contains a broad array of sources, including international research reports from InvestextR.

Keywords: News, Analysis, Companies, Middle East, Africa

Audience: Journalists, Business Professionals

Profile: The MDEAFR library contains a wide array of pertinent sources. Among the information sources are newspapers and wire services, trade and business journals, company reports, country and region background, industry and product analysis, business opportunities, and selected legal texts. News sources range from the world-renowned Associated Press and Christian Science Monitor to the regionally important Jerusalem Post and Africa News. Company information is contained in the EXTEL cards as well as ICC. Providers of country background and industry analysis include Associated Banks of Europe, Bank of America, Business International, IBC USA, and the US Department of Commerce. Customers interested in new business opportunities can check OPIC and Foreign Trade Opportunities (FTO).

Contact: Mead New Sales Group at (800) 227-4908 or (513) 859-5398 inside the US, or (513) 865-7981 for all inquiries outside the US.

User Info: To Subscribe, contact Mead directly.

To examine the Nexis user guide, you can access it at the ftp site of the University of Texas at Austin at the URL address: ftp://ftp.cc.utexas.edu

The files are in: /pub/ref-services/LEXIS

`telnet://nex.meaddata.com`

`http://www.meaddata.com`

MECH-L

MECH-L

A mailing list for the discussion of mechanical engineering.

Keywords: Mechanical Engineering

Audience: Engineers, Mechanical Engineers

Contact: S. Nomura
b470ssn@utarlvm1.uta.edu

Details: Free

User Info: To Subscribe to the list, send an e-mail message to the URL address below consisting of a single line reading:

SUB mech-l YourFirstName YourLastName.

To send a message to the entire list, address it to: mech-l@utarlvm1.uta.edu

`mailto:listserv@utarlvm1.uta.edu`

Media

Communication and Mass Communication Resources

An archive of materials related to mass communications and the media.

Keywords: Mass Communications, Media, Journalism, Telecommunications, Advertising

Sponsor: The University of Iowa

Audience: Mass Communications Students and Teachers, Journalists, Broadcasting Professionals

Contact: Karla Tonella
karla_tonella@uiowa.edu

`gopher://iam41.arcade.uiowa.edu`

Prog-Pubs

A mailing list for people interested in progressive and/or alternative publications and other media. Discussions include issues pertaining to all kinds of small-scale, independent, progressive, and/or alternative media, including newspapers, newsletters, and radio and video shows.

Keywords: Media, Alternative Press, Communications

Audience: Students (college/university), Independent Media Professionals

Contact: prog-pubs-request@fuggles.acc.virginia.edu

Details: Free

User Info: To Subscribe to the list, send an e-mail message requesting a subscription to the URL address below.

To send a message to the entire list, address it to:prog-pubs@fuggles.acc.virginia.edu

`mailto:prog-pubs@fuggles.acc.virginia.edu`

Mediation

NAME (National Association for Mediation in Education) Publications and Resources List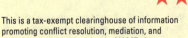

This is a tax-exempt clearinghouse of information promoting conflict resolution, mediation, and violence prevention in schools. NAME also publishes a newsletter and has a directory of over 120 resources, including guidelines for conflict resolution, and technical assistance.

Keywords: Conflict Resolution, Mediation, Education (K-12)

Sponsor: National Association for Mediation in Education, University of Massachusetts, Amherst, Massachusetts, USA

Audience: Counselors, Educators, Administrators, Parents

Contact: Clarinda Merripen
conflictnet@agc.ipc.org

Request introductory packet from address below.

`mailto:conflictnet@agc.ipc.org`

Medical College of Ohio Library Online Catalogue

Medical College of Ohio Library Online Catalogue ★★

Catalog of library holdings.

Keywords: Medicine, Libraries
Sponsor: Medical College of Ohio
Audience: Health Professionals, Medical Researchers, Educators, Students
Details: Free

`telnet://library@136.247.10.14`

Medical College of Wisconsin Library Online Catalogue

Medical College of Wisconsin Library Online Catalogue ★★

Catalog of library holdings.

Keywords: Medicine, Libraries
Sponsor: Medical College of Wisconsin
Audience: Health Professionals, Medical Researchers, Educators, Students
Details: Free

`telnet://ils.lib.mcw.edu`

Medical Informatics

CAMIS (Center for Advanced Medical Informatics at Stanford)

CAMIS is a shared computing resource supporting research activities in biomedical informatics.

Keywords: Medical Informatics, Heuristics, Health Sciences
Sponsor: Stanford University School of Medicine, Palo Alto, CA, USA
Audience: Medical Informatics, Health Science Researchers

Profile: The CAMIS gopher includes an Internet-wide title search, computing information, and technical reports for the Section on Medical Informatics (SMI) community as well as that of the Knowledge Systems Laboratory (KSL), information on the Heuristic Programming Project, pointers to various online library catalogs, and more.

Contact: torsten_heycke@med.stanford.edu

`gopher://camis.stanford.edu/00/gopherdoc`

Medical News

HICNet Newsletter (MEDNEWS - The Health InfoCom Newsletter) ★★★

Usually published once a week, this is a large newsletter that is broken up into multiple sections to facilitate network movement.

Keywords: Health, Medical News
Audience: Health Professionals
Contact: David Dodell
ddodell@stjhmc.fidonet.org
Details: Free

`mailto:listserv@asuacad.bitnet`

Medical Research

Discipline and Disease Specific Sources

This database contains links to sources of Medical and Health Care information. Has disease-specific resources for AIDS, Cancer, Parkinson's Disease, and Sudden Infant Death Syndrome, among others. Also covers over 30 discipline-specific sources, ranging from anesthesiology to tropical medicine.

Keywords: Medicine, Diseases, Medical Research
Sponsor: University of Miami Biomedical Gopher Project, Miami, Florida, USA
Audience: Medical Professionals, Medical Researchers, Medical Practitioners
Contact: Thomas Williams, Michael Cutherell
twilliam@mednet.med.miami.edu
mcuthere@mednet.med.miami.edu
Details: Free

`gopher://caldmed.med.miami.edu`

Health News Daily ★★★

The database contains all the daily news and full-text articles from Health News Daily, a publication from F-D-C Reports, Inc.

Keywords: Health, Pharmacology, Medical Research, News
Sponsor: F-D-C Reports, Inc., Chevy Chase, MD, US

Audience: Health Professionals, Pharmaceutical Industry, Market Researchers

Profile: The database provides specialized, in-depth business, scientific, regulatory, and legal news. Timely coverage of pharmacy and pharmaceuticals is given, as well as coverage of medical devices and diagnostics, medical research, cosmetics, health policy, provider payment policies, and cost containment in national health care.

Coverage: 1990 to the present; updated daily.
Contact: Dialog in the US at (800) 334-2564, Dialog internationally at country-specific locations.
Details: Costs
User Info: To Subscribe, contact Dialog directly.

`telnet://dialog.com`

Medical and Biological Research in Laboratories Institutions (Israel) ★★

A descriptive listing of medical research and diagnostic laboratories in Israel. This site also has information on medical research being carried out in Israeli universities and hospitals.

Keywords: Medical Research, Biological Research, Israel
Audience: Medical Researchers, Biomedical Researchers, Medical Professionals
Profile: MATIMOP, The Israeli Industry Center for Health Care Research And Development, is a non-profit service organization, founded by an Israeli association of hospitals, universities, and other medical researchers, aiming their activities at promoting cooperation of Israeli entrepreneurs and manufacturers with qualified business firms abroad. This gopher details specific medical and biological research projects in progress in every department of every major Israeli health care institution: including universities, The General Federation of Labour, public hospitals, government-municipal hospitals, government hospitals, as well as medical and biological research in the Israeli laboratories and research institutes.

Contact: rdinfo@matimop.org.il

`gopher://gopher.matimop.org.il`

Poisons Information Database ★★

Directories of antivenoms, toxicologists, poison control centers, and poisons from around the world.

Keywords: Medical Research, Bioscience
Sponsor: Venom and Toxin Research Group, Department of Anatomy, National University of Singapore, Singapore
Audience: Biologists, Researchers, Medical Professionals, Toxicologists
Contact: Professor P. Gopalkrishnakone
antgopal@leonis.nus.sg

`http://biomed.nus.sg/PID/PID.html`

sci.med.physics

A Usenet newsgroup providing information and discussion about physics in medical testing and care.

Keywords: Physics, Medical Research, Health Care

Audience: Physicists, Medical Researchers, Medical Practitioners, Health Care Professionals

Details: Free

User Info: To Subscribe to this Usenet newsgroup, you need access to a newsreader.

`news:sci.med.physics`

Medical Treatment

Accri-l

A mailing list providing information on anesthesia and critical care resources available via the Internet.

Keywords: Health Care, Medical Treatment, Medicine

Audience: Health Care Professionals, Health Care Providers

Contact: A.J. Wright
meds002@uabdpo.dpo.uab.edu

User Info: To Subscribe, send an e-mail message to the URL address below consisting of a single line reading:

SUB accri-l YourFirstName YourLastName.

To send a message to the entire list, address it to: accri-l@uabdpo.dpo.uab.edu

`mailto:listserv@uabdpo.dpo.uab.edu`

Health and Clinical Information & Bioethics Online Service

A collection of gopher links to servers offering a wide variety of health information.

Keywords: Medicine, Medical Treatment, Health Care

Sponsor: Medical College of Wisconsin (MCW) InfoScope, Wisconsin, USA

Audience: Health Care Professionals, Health Care Providers

Profile: Links include the National Institutes of Health, MedNews Digest, Family Medicine list archives, and full-text of national health plans. Also features the Bioethics Online Service, which provides updates, journal abstracts, alerts, and a forum for discussing medical ethics. Site specific information on MCW physicians and surgeons is also available.

Contact: Dieta Murra
mcw-info@its.mcw.edu

`gopher://post.its.mcw.edu`

Marshall University School of Medicine (MUSOM) RuralNet Gopher

A gopher server dedicated to the improvement of rural health care.

Keywords: Rural Development, Health Care, Medical Treatment, Bioinformatics

Sponsor: Marshall University School of Medicine

Audience: Health Care Professionals, Medical Students

Profile: A collection of health care resources, with particular emphasis on rural health care. Includes listings of clinical resources by subject area, information on state and federal rural health care initiatives, and links to local and national health and education services.

Contact: Mike McCarthy, Andy Jarrell
mmccarth@muvms6.wvnet.edu
jarrell@musom01.mu.wvnet.edu

`gopher://ruralnet.mu.wvnet.edu`

Medicine

(The) Center for Biomedical Informatics of the State University of Campinas, Brazil

A directory of medical applications of informatics.

Keywords: Health, Medicine, Informatics

Sponsor: State University of Campinas, Brazil

Audience: Medical Professionals, Medical Educators, Medical Researchers

Profile: Designed to foster educational and practical uses of computers in medicine and the health sciences by providing free international access to resources.

Contact: Renato M.E. Sabbatini
sabbatini@ccvax.unicamp.br

Details: Free

`ftp://ccsun.unicamp.br`

Accri-l

A mailing list providing information on anesthesia and critical care resources available via the Internet.

Keywords: Health Care, Medical Treatment, Medicine

Audience: Health Care Professionals, Health Care Providers

Contact: A.J. Wright
meds002@uabdpo.dpo.uab.edu

User Info: To Subscribe, send an e-mail message to the URL address below consisting of a single line reading:

SUB accri-l YourFirstName YourLastName.

To send a message to the entire list, address it to: accri-l@uabdpo.dpo.uab.edu

`mailto:listserv@uabdpo.dpo.uab.edu`

Aids

A forum for the discussion of AIDS, predominantly from a medical perspective, but also with some discussion of political and social issues.

Keywords: AIDS, Medicine, Politics, Society

Sponsor: UCLA

Audience: AIDS Researchers, AIDS Activists, Health Care Providers

Contact: Daniel R. Greening
aids-request@cs.ucla.edu

User Info: To Subscribe to the list, send an e-mail message to the URL address below.

To send a message to the entire list, address it to: aids@cs.ucla.edu

`mailto:aids-request@cs.ucla.edu`

AIDS Treatment News

A newsletter on AIDS treatment.

Keywords: AIDS, HIV, Health, Medicine

Sponsor: IGC (Institute for Global Communications)

Audience: AIDS Researchers, Health Workers, AIDS Sufferers

Profile: This newsletter contains interviews, reports on new and existing treatment modalities, announcements of clinical drug testing trial, and more.

Contact: atn@igc.apc.org

Details: Free

`gopher://odie.niaid.nih.gov/11/aids`

AIDS/HIV Information

A clearinghouse for AIDS/HIV-related information. Contains Internet connections to WWW and gopher servers, and archives of AIDS server FAQ's, including an archive of AIDS treatment news.

Keywords: AIDS, Medicine, Health

Sponsor: Queer Resources Directory, USA

Audience: AIDS Sufferers, Gays, Students, Activists

Contact: QRD Staff
QRDstaff@vector.casti.com

Details: AIDS Treatment News

`http://vector.casti.com/QRD/.html/AIDS.html`

AIDSLINE

The AIDSLINE database is a bibliography of research and clinical information as well as health policy issues concerning AIDS. The citations in AIDSLINE are primarily derived from MEDLINE, Health Planning & Administration, CancerLit, CATLINE, AVLINE, the meeting abstracts from the International Conferences on AIDS, the Symposia on Non-human Models of AIDS, and AIDS-related abstracts from the Annual Meetings of the American Society of Microbiology.

Keywords: AIDS, Medicine
Sponsor: U.S. National Library of Medicine
Audience: AIDS Researchers, Epidemiologists, Clinicians, AIDS Sufferers
Contact: CDP Technologies Sales Department (800)950-2035, extension 400
User Info: To Subscribe, contact CDP Technologies directly

`telnet://cdplus@cdplus.com`

Allied and Alternative Medicine (AMED)

The Allied and Alternative Medicine database covers the fields of contemporary and alternative medicine.

Keywords: Medicine, Alternative Medicine
Sponsor: Medical Information Service, British Library, Boston Spa, West Yorkshire, UK
Audience: Doctors, Nurses, Health Care Providers, Medical Practitioners, Health Care Industry, General Public
Profile: The AMED database will be of interest to all those who need to know more about alternatives to conventional medicine, such as doctors, nurses and other medical practitioners, therapists, health care libraries, specialist colleges, self-help groups, and the pharmaceutical industry. Coverage includes acupuncture, homeopathy, hypnosis, chiropractic, osteopathy, psychotherapy, diet therapy, herbalism, holistic treatment, traditional Chinese medicine, occupational therapy, physiotherapy, rehabilitation, ayurvedic medicine, reflexology, iridology, moxibustion, meditation, yoga, healing research, and the Alexander Technique.
Contact: Data-star through Dialog in the US at (800) 334-2564; Dialog internationally at country-specific locations.
Details: Costs
User Info: To Subscribe, contact Dialog directly.

`telnet://dialog.com`

Alternative Medicine, the Definitive Guide

A one-stop reference covering common health problems and leading alternative therapies.

Keywords: Alternative Medicine, Medicine, Health, Health Care
Sponsor: Future Medicine Publishing, Inc.
Audience: General Public, Health Care Professionals
Profile: Spanning a global effort of 4 years and input from nearly 400 Health Care professionals, this one stop reference offers 1100 pages of in-depth explanations to 43 of the leading alternative therapies. In addition to covering over 200 of the most common health problems, a wide range of choices to maintaining and regaining your health are highlighted with graphic illustrations. This is truly the "Voice of Alternative Medicine."
Details: Costs

FutureMd@CRL.com

Biomedical Computer Laboratory (BCL) ★★★

A resource for biomedical computing.

Keywords: Health, Biomedical Computing, Biology, Medicine
Sponsor: Washington University School of Medicine
Audience: Medical Researchers, Biologists
Profile: A significant portion of the activities at BCL are supported by the National Center for Research Resources' Biomedical Research Technology Program (BRTP), which promotes the application of advances in computer science and technology, engineering, mathematics, and the physical sciences to research problems in biology and medicine by supporting the development of advanced research technologies.
Contact: Kenneth W. Clark info@wubcl.wustl.edu
Details: Free
Notes: Expect: login; Send: anonymous
Notes: Investigators wishing to explore the possibility of interactions with BCL at Washington University should send e-mail (preferred).

`ftp://wubcl.wustl.edu`

BOING (Bio-Oriented INternet Gophers)

A searcheable gopher index, BOING is used to search through the titles of items in bio-gopher space and to access the items returned.

Keywords: Biological Sciences, Health, Medicine
Audience: Health Professionals, Biomedical Researchers, Students (college, graduate)
Details: Free

`gopher://gopher.gdb.org`

BRIDGE

An online public access catalogue, the PALS-based catalog provides access to the collections of two institutions, St. Boniface University and the Manitoba General Hospital.

Keywords: Medicine, Library
Sponsor: St. Boniface University, and the Manitoba General Hospital Libraries
Audience: Health Professionals, Students, Medical Educators
Details: Free

`telnet://BE@umopac.umanitoba.ca`

Denmark's Library for Medicine and Science ★

Keywords: Science, Medicine, Libraries, Denmark
Audience: Scientists, Health Care Professionals, Medical Researchers
Details: Free
At the CCL>prompt type DIA ENG for English interface.

`telnet://cosmos.bib.dk`

Discipline and Disease Specific Sources

This database contains links to sources of Medical and Health Care information. Has disease-specific resources for AIDS, Cancer, Parkinson's Disease, and Sudden Infant Death Syndrome, among others. Also covers over 30 discipline-specific sources, ranging from anesthesiology to tropical medicine.

Keywords: Medicine, Diseases, Medical Research
Sponsor: University of Miami Biomedical Gopher Project, Miami, Florida, USA
Audience: Medical Professionals, Medical Researchers, Medical Practitioners
Contact: Thomas Williams, Michael Cutherell twilliam@mednet.med.miami.edu, mcuthere@mednet.med.miami.edu
Details: Free

`gopher://caldmed.med.miami.edu`

EMBASE

EMBASE is an acclaimed comprehensive index of international literature on medicine, science and pharmacology.

Keywords: Medicine, Science, Pharmacology
Sponsor: Elsevier Science Publishers
Audience: Librarians, Researchers, Students, Physicians
Contact: CDP Technologies Sales Department (800)950-2035, extension 400
User Info: To Subscribe, contact CDP Technologies directly

`telnet://cdplus@cdplus.com`

Medicine   463

Fam-Med

An Internet resource and discussion group on computers in family medicine.

Keywords: Medicine, Computers, Telecommunications
Sponsor: Gustavus Adolphus College, Minnesota
Audience: Health CareProfessionals, Family Physicians
Profile: Fam-Med is an electronic conference and file area that focuses on the use of computer and telecommunication technologies in the teaching and practice of family medicine. The conference and files are accessible to anyone able to send e-mail. The discussion on Fam-Med is distributed in two ways: by an unmoderated mail echo in which all posted messages are immediately distributed to subscribers without human intervention, and by a digest where messages accumulated over several days are assembled into a single document with erroneous posts deleted.
Contact: Paul Kleeberg
paul@gac.edu
Details: Free
To join either the unmoderated list or the digest, send e-mail to the contact above. To post to Fam-Med, send e-mail to fam-med@gac.edu

gopher://ftp.gac.edu/00/pub/e-mail-archives/fam-med/

GenBank

The GenBank database provides a collection of nucleotide sequences as well as relevant bibliographic and biological annotation.

Keywords: Genetics, Medicine, Molecular Biology
Sponsor: National Center for Biotechnology Information (NCBI) at the National Library of Medicine (NLM)
Audience: Geneticists, Scientists, Molecular Biologists
Profile: DNA sequence entries are rated by specialized indexers in the Division of Library Operations. Over 325,000 articles per year from 3,400 journals are scanned for sequence data. They are supplemented by journals in plant and veterinary sciences through a collaboration with the National Agricultural Library. These records join the direct submission data stream and submissions from the European Molecular Biology Laboratory (EMBL) Data Library and the DNA Database of Japan (DDBJ).
Contact: info@ncbi.nlm.nih.gov

Details: Free
Send direct submissions to gb-sub@ncbi.nlm.nih.gov and updates and changes to existing GenBank records to update@ncbi.nlm.nih.gov
For help in retrieval by e-mail send an e-mail message with the word "help" in the the body of the message to retrieve@ncbi.nlm.hih.gov

gopher://gopher.nih.gov/77/gopherlib/indices/genbank/index

GENMED (General Medical Information)

The General Medical Information (GENMED) library contains a variety of medical care and treatment, toxicology, and hospital administration materials.

Keywords: Medicine, Toxicology, Hospital, Treatment
Audience: Medical Professionals
Profile: The GENMED library contains full-text medical journals and newsletters, as well as drug information, disease and trauma reviews, Physicians Data Query cancer information, and medical administration journals. GENMED also offers a gateway to the MEDLINE database.
Contact: Mead New Sales Group at (800) 227-4908 or (513) 859-5398 inside the US, or (513) 865-7981 for all inquiries outside the US.
User Info: To Subscribe, contact Mead directly.
To examine the Nexis user guide, you can access it at the ftp site of the University of Texas at Austin at the URL address: ftp://ftp.cc.utexas.edu
The files are in: /pub/ref-services/LEXIS

telnet://nex.meaddata.com

http://www.meaddata.com

Georgetown University Medical Center Online Catalogue

This site maintains a catalog of the Georgetown University Medical Center library's holdings.

Keywords: Medicine, Library
Sponsor: Georgetown University, Washington, DC
Audience: Medical Professionals, Educators, Students
Contact: Jane Banks
banksj@gumedlib2.georgetown.edu
Details: Free
The password is dahlgren, then enter netguest, hit RETURN several times and select option 1.

telnet://medlib@gumedlib.georgetown.edu

Harvard Medical Gopher

This gopher site accesses information from Harvard Medical School. Provides bibliographic information from Harvard Medical Library, basic science and clinical resources, and public health and government statistics.

Keywords: Medicine, Libraries, Health Care
Sponsor: Physicians, Health Care Professionals, Educators, Students <Standard Producer>Harvard Medical School, Cambridge, Massachusetts, USA
Audience: Physicians, Health Care Professionals, Educators, Students <Standard Producer>Harvard Medical School, Cambridge, Massachusetts, USA
Contact: gopher@warren.med.harvard.edu
Details: Free

gopher://gopher.med.harvard.edu

Health and Clinical Information & Bioethics Online Service

A collection of gopher links to servers offering a wide variety of health information.

Keywords: Medicine, Medical Treatment, Health Care
Sponsor: Medical College of Wisconsin (MCW) InfoScope, Wisconsin, USA
Audience: Health Care Professionals, Health Care Providers
Profile: Links include the National Institutes of Health, MedNews Digest, Family Medicine list archives, and full-text of national health plans. Also features the Bioethics Online Service, which provides updates, journal abstracts, alerts, and a forum for discussing medical ethics. Site specific information on MCW physicians and surgeons is also available.
Contact: Dieta Murra
mcw-info@its.mcw.edu

gopher://post.its.mcw.edu

Health Periodicals Database

This source covers a broad range of health subjects and issues.

Keywords: Health, Biotechnology, Medicine, Nutrition
Sponsor: Information Access Company, Foster City, CA, US
Audience: Health Professionals, Dieticians, Librarians
Profile: The database provides indexing and full text of journals covering a broad range of health subjects and issues including: prenatal care, dieting, drug abuse, AIDS, biotechnology, cardiovascular disease, environment, public health, safety, paramedical professions, sports medicine, substance abuse, toxicology, and much more.

464 Medicine

Contact:	Dialog in the US at (800) 334-2564, Dialog internationally at country-specific locations.
User Info:	To Subscribe, contact Dialog directly.
Notes:	Coverage: 1988 to the present; updated weekly.

telnet://dialog.com

Johns Hopkins Genetic Databases

This gopher provides electronic access to documents pertaining to computational biology and a number of different genetic databases.

Keywords:	Genetics, Molecular Biology, Medicine, Biology
Sponsor:	Johns Hopkins University
Audience:	Geneticists, Researchers, Scientists, Molecular Biologists
Profile:	The databases accessible from this entry point include GenBank, Swiss-Prot, PDB, PIR, LiMB, TFD, AAtDB, ACEDB, CompoundKB, PROSITE EC Enzyme Database, NRL_3D Protein-Sequence-Structure Database, Eukaryotic Promoter Database (EPD), Cloning Vector Database, Expressed Sequence Tag Database (ESTDB), Online Mendelian Inheritance Man (OMIM), Sequence Analysis Bibliographic Reference Data Bank (Seqanalref), and Database Taxonomy (GenBank, Swiss-Prot). The gopher also provides direct links to other gophers with information relevant to biology.
Contact:	Dan Jacobson danj@mail.gdb.org
Details:	Free

gopher://merlot.welch.jhu.edu

Medical College of Ohio Library Online Catalogue

	Catalog of library holdings.
Keywords:	Medicine, Libraries
Sponsor:	Medical College of Ohio
Audience:	Health Professionals, Medical Researchers, Educators, Students
Details:	Free

telnet://library@136.247.10.14

Medical College of Wisconsin Library Online Catalogue

	Catalog of library holdings.
Keywords:	Medicine, Libraries
Sponsor:	Medical College of Wisconsin
Audience:	Health Professionals, Medical Researchers, Educators, Students
Details:	Free

telnet://ils.lib.mcw.edu

MEDLARS (MEDical Literature Analysis and Retrieval System)

MEDLARS is the computerized system of databases and databanks pertinent to biomedical research and patient care, including MEDLINE, the largest and one of the most-used biomedical databases ever.

Keywords:	Medicine, MEDLINE, Biomedical Research
Sponsor:	National Library of Medicine
Audience:	Health Care Providers, Scientists, Biomedical Researchers
Profile:	The computer files can be searched either to produce a list of publications (bibliographic citations) or to retrieve factual information on a specific question. MEDLARS comprises two computer subsystems, ELHISS and TOXNET (TOXicology data NETwork), on which reside over 40 online databases containing about 16 million references. MEDLINE is the largest database and corresponds to three print indexes: Index Medicus, Index to Dental Literature, and Internatonal Nursing Index.
Details:	Costs
User Info:	To Subscribe to the service, send e-mail requesting an account to: medlars@nlm.nih.gov
	An account is needed for entry and a fee is charged for use. Many university library computers have free link to the MEDLINE database.

telnet://medlars.nlm.nih.gov

MEDLINE

MEDLINE is a major source of bibliographic biomedical literature. The MEDLINE database encompasses information from three printed indexes (Index Medicus, Index to Dental Literature and the International Nursing Index) as well as additional information not published in the Index Medicus.

Keywords:	Biomedicine, Dentistry, Nursing, Medicine
Sponsor:	U.S. National Library of Medicine
Audience:	Librarians, Researchers, Physicians, Students
Contact:	CDP Technologies Sales Department (800)950-2035, extension 400
User Info:	To Subscribe, contact CDP Technologies directly

telnet://cdplus@cdplus.com

Midwifery Resources on the Net

A resource list for helping find information about midwifery on the Internet.

Keywords:	Midwifery, Childbirth, Medicine, Nursing
Audience:	Midwives, Medical professionals
Details:	Free

gopher://una.hh.lib.umich.edu

Montefiore Medical Center Library Online Catalog

	Catalog of library holdings.
Keywords:	Medicine, Libraries
Sponsor:	Montefiore Medical Center at Albert Einstein College of Medicine, New York
Audience:	Health Care Professionals, Medical Researchers, Educators, Students
Details:	Free
	After Telnetting, hit RETURN twice, then select 0 on main menu. Select 2 on locations menu. To exit, hit the Telnet escape key.

telnet://lis.aecom.yu.edu

National Institute for Allergy & Infectious Disease (NIAID)

This is a resource into other databases for searching many medical fields, such as the NIAID network userlist or a databank of AIDS-related information.

Keywords:	Medicine, Infectious Diseases, Allergies
Sponsor:	NIAID
Audience:	Health Care Professionals, Researchers, Students
Contact:	Brent Sessions sessions@odie.niaid.nih.gov
Details:	Free

gopher://gopher.niaid.nih.gov/1

National Institute of Health Library Online Catalog

This entry point provides access to the books and journal holdings in the NIH Library. Journal articles are not included.

Keywords:	NIH, Medicine, Science, Libraries
Sponsor:	National Institute of Health (NIH)
Audience:	Scientists, Researchers, Educators, Health Care Professionals
Details:	Free

telnet://nih-library.ncrr.nih.gov

National Library of Medicine Gopher

World Health Organization (WHO)

This gopher provides information about the National Library of Medicine, the world's largest single-topic library.

Keywords:	Medicine, Health, World Health
Sponsor:	National Library of Medicine, Massachusetts
	World Health Organization, Geneva, Switzerland

Audience: Health Care Professionals, Medical Professionals, Researchers

Profile: The National Library of Medicine (NLM) cares for over 4.5 million holdings (including books, journals, reports, manuscripts, and audio-visual items). The NLM offers extensive online information services dealing with clinical care, toxicology, environmental health, and basic biomedical research, It has several active research and development components, including an extramural grants program, houses an extensive history of medicine collection, and provides several programs designed to improve the nation's medical library system.

Contact: R. P. C. Rodgers
rodgers@nlm.nih.gov

akazawa@who.ch

Details: Free

gopher://el-gopher.med.utah.edu

gopher://gopher.who.ch

NIBNews - A Monthly Electronic Bulletin About Medical Informatics

★

Disseminates information about Brazilian and Latin American activities, people, information, events, publications, software, and more, involving computer applications in health care, medicine, and biology.

Keywords: Health Care, Biology, Brazil, Latin America, South America, Medicine

Audience: Health Care Professionals, Biologists

Contact: Renato M. E. Sabbatini
sabbatini@bruc.bitnet

Details: Free
E-mail a short notice to

mailto:sabbatini@ccvax.unicamp.br

NIH (National Institute of Health)

★★★★

This server is a network-based computer service operated by the Division of Computer Research and Technology (DCRT) to distribute information for and about the NIH (National Institutes of Health).

Keywords: NIH, Health Sciences, Biomedical Research, Medicine

Sponsor: Division of Computer Research and Technology (DCRT), National Institute of Health

Audience: Scientists, Biomedical Researchers, Health CareProfessionals, General Public

Profile: This server provides Internet access to information about NIH health and clinical issues (including CancerNet and a variety of AIDS information), NIH-funded grants and research projects, and a variety of research resources in support of NIH and worldwide biomedical researchers. For example, the major molecular biology databases (GenBank, SWISSPROT, PIR, PDB, TFD, Prosite, LiMB) can be accessed through keyword searches from this gopher.

Details: Free

gopher://gopher.nih.gov

sci.med

★

A Usenet newsgroup providing information and discussion about medicine and its related products.

Keywords: Medicine, Health Care

Audience: Medical Professionals

Details: Free

User Info: To Subscribe to this Usenet newsgroup, you need access to a newsreader.

news:sci.med

South East Florida AIDS Information Network (SEFAIN)

★

Contains a wide range of information on AIDS research(ers), organizations, and services in searchable databases.

Keywords: AIDS, Medicine

Sponsor: This project is sponsored in part by the National Library of Medicine

Audience: Medical Professionals, Scientists, Educators, Health Care Providers

Details: Free
Select L on main menu, then select 1 on next menu

telnet://library@callcat.med.miami.edu

Stanford Medical Center Gopher

★★

This gopher allows extensive access to the Stanford Medical Center's archives.

Keywords: Medicine, Health Care, Health Sciences

Sponsor: Stanford Medical Center, Palo Alto, California, USA

Audience: Health Care Professionals, Health Science Researchers

Contact: Stanford Medical Center
gopher@medisg.stanford.edu

gopher://med.stanford.edu

The National Library of Medicine (NLM) Online Catalog System

★★★★

Catalog of library holdings.

Keywords: Medicine, Health Sciences, Biomedicine, Rare Books

Sponsor: National Library of Medicine

Audience: Health Professionals, Medical Educators, Students

Profile: The National Library of Medicine (NLM) is the world's largest biomedical library with a collection of over 4.9 million items. NLM is a national resource for all US health sciences libraries and fills over a quarter of a million interlibrary loan requests each year for these libraries. The library is open to the public, but its collection is designed primarily for health professionals. The library collects materials comprehensively in all major areas of the health sciences. Housed within the library is one of the world's finest medical history collections of pre-1914 and rare medical texts, manuscripts, and incunabula.

Contact: ref@nlm.nih.gov

Details: Free
The NLM can be accessed also through the WWW at http://www.nlm.nih.gov

telnet://locator@locator.nlm.nih.gov

University of Texas Health Science Center (UTHSCSA) Biomedical Library Information System

★★

Keywords: Medicine, Libraries

Sponsor: Audie L. Murphy Memorial Veterans' Administration Hospital, San Antonio, TX

Audience: Medical Professionals, Medical Educators, Students

Details: Free

telnet://lis@athena.uthscsa.edu

University of Wales College of Medicine Library Online Catalog

★★

Keywords: Medicine, Libraries

Sponsor: University of Wales, United Kingdom

Audience: Health Care Professionals, Medical Educators, Students

Details: Free

Notes: Expect: login, Send: 'janet'; Expect: password; Send: 'janet'

telnet://sun.nsf.ac.uk

Virtual Hospital

The Virtual Hospital (VH) is a continuously updated medical multimedia database accessible 24 hours a day. The site provides distance learning to practicing physicians and may be used for Continuing Medical Education (CME).

Keywords: Medicine, Education (Distance)
Sponsor: The Electronic Differential Multimedia Laboratory, Department of Radiology, University of Iowa College of Medicine, USA
Audience: Biologists, Researchers, Medical Professionals, Health Care Professionals
Contact: Librarian
librarian@vh.radiology.uiowa.edu

`http://indy.radiology.uiowa.edu/VirtualHospital.html`

Washington University-St. Louis Medical Library & MembersLibrary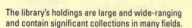

The library's holdings are large and wide-ranging and contain significant collections in many fields.

Keywords: Medicine, Science, Technology
Audience: Researchers, Students, General Public
Details: Free
Notes: Expect: Destination Code Prompt, Send: Catalog

`telnet://mcftcp.wustl.edu`

World Health Organization (WHO)

This gopher provides access to the databases of the WHO.

Keywords: World Health Organization, Health, Medicine, Non-governmental organizations
Sponsor: World Health Organization, Geneva, Switzerland
Audience: Medical Professionals, Researchers
Contact: akazawa@who.ch
Details: Free

`gopher://gopher.who.ch`

Medicine (History of)

McGill University, Montreal Canada, INFOMcGILL Library

The library's holdings are large and wide-ranging and contain significant collections in many fields.

Keywords: Architecture, Entomology, Biology, Science (History of), Medicine (History of), Napolean, Shakespeare (William)
Audience: Researchers, Students, General Public
Contact: Roy Miller
ccrmmus@mcgillm (Bitnet) or
ccrmmus@musicm.mcgill.ca (Internet)
Notes: Expect: VM logo; Send: Enter; Expect: prompt; Send: PF3 or type INFO

`telnet://vm1.mcgill.ca`

University of Maryland System Library

The library's holdings are large and wide-ranging and contain significant collections in many fields.

Keywords: Medicine (History of), Nursing, Pharmacology, Microbiology, Aquaculture, Aquatic Chemistry, Toxicology
Audience: General Public, Researchers, Librarians, Document Delivery Professionals
Contact: Ron Larsen
Details: Free
Notes: Expect: Available Services menu; Send: PAC

`telnet://victor.umd.edu`

Medieval Studies

History at the University of Virginia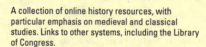

A collection of online history resources, with particular emphasis on medieval and classical studies. Links to other systems, including the Library of Congress.

Keywords: History (World), Classics, Medieval Studies
Sponsor: University of Virginia, Charlottesville, Virginia, USA
Audience: Historians, Students (College/University)
Contact: mssbks@virginia.edu
Details: Free

`gopher://gopher.lib.virginia.edu`

MEDTEXT-L

A discussion of medieval text, including philology, codicology, and technology.

Keywords: Medieval, Philology, Linguistics
Audience: Linguists, Language Teachers, Language Students, Historians
Details: Free
User Info: To Subscribe to the list, send an e-mail message to the URL address below consisting of a single line reading:

medtext-l YourFirstName YourLastName

To send a message to the entire list, address it to: medtext-l@uiucvmd.bitnet

`mailto:listserv@uiucvmd.bitnet`

Nero Ashbury

Nero is a live-action, medieval role-playing game with a plot line and characters that continue from one adventure to the next. Nero has been successful in New England for over six years and is growing rapidly.

Keywords: Medieval Studies, Role-Playing, Games
Audience: General Public, Role-Playing Enthusiasts
Contact: lsonko@pearl.tufts.edu
Details: Free
User Info: To Subscribe to the list, send an e-mail message requesting a subscription to the URL address below.

`mailto:lsonko@pearl.tufts.edu`

rec.org.sca

A Usenet newsgroup providing information and discussion about medieval re-enactments.

Keywords: SCA (Society For Creative Anachronism), Medieval Studies
Audience: General Public
User Info: To Subscribe to this Usenet newsgroup, you need access to a newsreader.

`news:rec.org.sca`

University of Pennsylvania Library- Philadelphia Pa.

The library's holdings are large and wide-ranging and contain significant collections in many fields.

Keywords: Literature (English), Literature (American), History (World), Medieval Studies, East Asian Studies, Middle Eastern Studies, South Asian Studies, Judaica, Lithuania.
Audience: Educators, Students, Researchers
Profile: Access to the central Van Pelt Library and to most of the departmental libraries is restricted to members of the University community on weekends and holidays. Online visitors are advised to call (215) 898-7554 for information on hours and access restrictions.
Contact: Patricia Renfro, Associate Director of Libraries
Details: Free

`telnet://library.upenn.edu`

University of Rochester Library

The library's holdings are large and wide-ranging and contain significant collections in many fields.

Keywords: Architecture, Art History, Photography, Literature (Asian), Lasers, Geology, Statistics, Optics, Medieval Studies
Audience: Researchers, Students, General Public
Details: Free
Notes: Expect: Login; Send: Library

`telnet://128.151.226.71`

Meetings Calendar (Geosciences)

Meetings Calendar (Geosciences)

A collection of meetings and conferences in the geosciences, with a special emphasis on meteorology. The entries are sorted by date and some contain links to Calls for Papers.

Keywords: Geosciences, Meteorology
Sponsor: Freie Universit_t Berlin, Germany
Audience: Researchers, Meteorologists
Contact: Dennis Schulze
dennis@bibo.met.fu-berlin.de
Details: Free
Notes: If there is a conference you want to have included in this list, send an e-mail to dennis@bibo.met.fu-berlin.de

`http://www.met.fu-berlin.de/konferenzen/index.html`

MEGA (Combined Federal/State Case Law)

MEGA (Combined Federal/State Case Law)

The Federal/State Case Law combined library contains files that allow one-stop searching of combined federal and state case law on the LEXIS service. American Law Reports (ALR)) and Lawyers' Edition, 2d articles are also included.

Keywords: Case Law (US), Law (US State), Law (US Federal)
Audience: Lawyers
Profile: The MEGA file is a one-stop search of all available federal and state case law on the LEXIS service. The circuit-base MEGA files combine federal and state case law from federal and state courts within the geographical area defined by the federal circuit. The state-based MEGA files combine case law from the courts of the state plus case law from the federal circuit for that state and the federal district courts within the state. Two chronological files restrict combined federal and state case law searches to particular date ranges. Each MEGA file includes all available U.S. Supreme Court cases. American Law Reports (ALR)) and Lawyers' Edition, 2d (LEd2) articles are also included.
Contact: New Sales Group @ 800-227-4908 or 513-859-5398 inside the US, or 1-513-865-7981 for all inquires outside the US.
User Info: To Subscribe, contact Mead directly.
To examine the Lexis user guide, you can access it at the ftp site of the University of Texas at Austin at the URL address: ftp://ftp.cc.utexas.edu
The files are in: /pub/res-services/LEXIS

`telnet://nex.meaddata.com`

MegaGopher

MegaGopher

This is the gopher at the University of Montreal. It supports the software and information requirements for the MegaSequencing project. It also serves as a repository of data for organellar genome and molecular evolution research and acts as the focal point for the GDE (Genetic Data Environment) package.

Keywords: Biology, Canada
Audience: Biologists
Contact: Tim Littlejohn
tim@bch.umontreal.ca
Details: Free

`gopher://megasun.bch.umontreal.ca`

Melrose Place

Melrose-place

Discussion of the Fox television show Melrose Place.

Keywords: Melrose Place, Fox Television, Television Series
Audience: Melrose Place Enthusiasts, Television Viewers
Details: Free
User Info: To Subscribe to the list, send an e-mail message requesting a subscription to the URL address below.

`mailto:melrose-place-request@ferkel.ucsb.edu`

MELVYL Library System

MELVYL Library System

MELVYL is the University of California's catalog of books and periodicals for the university and the California State Library. It also permits access to database systems around the world.

Keywords: Libraries, Databases, OPACS, Internet Surfers
Audience: General Interest, Students, Teachers, Librarians
Producer: University of California
Contact: Genny Engel, MELVYL System Users Services
email:gen@dla.ucop.edu
Profile: The MELVYL system is a centralized information system that can be reached from terminals in libraries at all nine campuses of the University of California. The system can also be reached by any terminal microcomputer with dialup access to UC computers connected to the MELVYL system. The MELVYL system includes a library catalog database, a periodicals database, article citation databases, and other files. A large number of other libraries and database systems are also accessible from MELVYL.
Details: Free
Notes: All these databases are searched using the same basic commands.

`telnet://melvyl.ucop.edu`

Memorabilia

Cards

This list is for people interested in collecting, speculating, and investing in baseball, football, basketball, hockey, and other trading cards and/or memorabilia. Discussion and want/sell lists are welcome.

Keywords: Trading Cards, Collectibiles, Memorabilia
Audience: Sports Card Collectors, Sports Card Traders, Memorabilia Collectors
Contact: Keane Arase
cards-request@tanstaafl.uchicago.edu
Details: Free
User Info: To Subscribe to the list, send an e-mail message requesting a subscription to the URL address below.
To send a message to the entire list, address it to:
cards@tanstaafl.uchicago.edu
Notes: The list is open to anyone.

`mailto:cards-request@tanstaafl.uchicago.edu`

Sports-cards

For people interested in collection, speculation and investing in baseball, football, basketball, hockey, and other trading cards and/or memorabilia. Discussion and want/sell lists are welcome.

Keywords: Memorabilia, Sports, Trading Cards
Audience: Collectors, Sports Card Traders
Contact: Keane Arase
cards-request@tanstaafl.uchicago.edu
Details: Free
User Info: To Subscribe to the list, send an e-mail message requesting a subscription to the URL address below.
To send a message to the entire list, address it to:
cards@tanstaafl.uchicago.edu

`mailto:cards-request@tanstaafl.uchicago.edu`

Men

Men

This digested mailing list discusses men's issues.

Keywords:	Men, General Interest
Audience:	General Public
Contact:	mail-men-request@summit.novell.com
Details:	Free
User Info:	To Subscribe to the list, send an e-mail message requesting a subscription to the URL address below.

`mailto:mail-men-request@summit.novell.com`

soc.men

A Usenet newsgroup providing information and discussion about men, their problems, and their relationships.

Keywords:	Men, Gender
Audience:	Men, Activists
Details:	Free
User Info:	To Subscribe to this Usenet newsgroup, you need access to a newsreader.

`news:soc.men`

Mensa

Mensatalk

A discussion group for members of Mensa.

Keywords:	Mensa, Genius
Audience:	Mensa Members
Details:	Free
User Info:	To Subscribe to the list, send an e-mail message requesting a subscription to the URL address below.

`mailto:mensatalk-request@psg.com`

Mercer (Johnny, Collection of)

Georgia State University Library

The library's holdings are large and wide-ranging and contain significant collections in many fields.

Keywords:	Labor (History of), Multimedia, Mercer (Johnny, Collection of)
Audience:	General Public, Researchers, Librarians, Document Delivery Professionals
Contact:	Phil Williams isgpew@gsuvm1.gsu.edu
Details:	Free
Notes:	Expect: VM screen, Send: RETURN; Expect: CP READ, Send: DIAL VTAM, press RETURN; Expect: CICS screen, Send: PF1

`telnet://library.gsu.edu`

Merit Network Information Center Services

Merit Network Information Center Services

This site provides a large collection of Internet guides and information.

Keywords:	Internet, Internet Guides, Internet Tools
Sponsor:	Merit Network, Inc.
Audience:	Internet Surfers
Profile:	This site serves as a clearinghouse for many Internet guides, documents, and utilities. It includes Internet FAQs, bibliographies, glossaries, and user guides such as Zen and the Art of the Internet and The Internet Companion. It also has archives of various Internet documents listing service providers, acceptable use policies, and resources. Many software programs for navigating the Internet are also available here for a wide variety of platforms
Contact:	nic-info@nic.merit.edu

`gopher://nic.merit.edu`

`ftp://nic.merit.edu`

MetaCard

Metacard-list

Discussion of the MetaCard product from MetaCard Corp. MetaCard is an application-development system similar to Apple's HyperCard product; it runs on a variety of popular platforms in a UNIX/X11/Motif environment.

Keywords:	MetaCard, Computing, UNIX
Audience:	Computer Users
Contact:	metacard-list-owner@grot.starconn.com
Details:	Free
User Info:	To Subscribe to the list, send an e-mail message requesting a subscription to the URL address below.

`mailto:metacard-list@grot.starconn.com`

Metals

METADEX

International literature covering metals and alloys.

Keywords:	Material Science, Metals, Alloys
Sponsor:	Materials Information, a joint information service of ASM International and the Institute of Materials
Audience:	Material Scientists, Researchers
Profile:	Contains more than 925,000 records from the international literature on metals and alloys concerning processes, properties, materials classes, applications, specific alloy designations, intermetallic compounds and metallurgical systems. Updated monthly.
Contact:	paul.albert@neteast.com
User Info:	To Subscribe contact Orbit-Questel directly.

`telnet://orbit.com`

MetaMail

MetaMail

This resource contains information about MetaMail, which allows existing mail readers to read multimedia e-mail in the MIME (Multipurpose Internet Mail Extensions) format.

Keywords:	Internet, E-mail
Audience:	Internet Surfers
Contact:	Nathaniel S. Borenstein nsb@nsb.fv.com
	Readme file is pub/nsb/readme

`ftp://thumper.bellcore.com`

Meteorology

Current Weather Maps and Movies

This web site is updated hourly, and provides links to downloadable software sites instrumental in accessing interactive weather browsers. International information is available, and visual and infrared maps are supplied from satellites.

Keywords:	Weather, Meteorology, Aviation
Sponsor:	Michigan State University, Michigan, USA
Audience:	General Public, Oceanography, Pilots
Contact:	Charles Henrich henrich@crh.cl.msu.edu

`http://rs560.cl.msu.edu/weather`

Energy and Climate Information Exchange (ECIX) Newsletter

This newsletter focuses on energy and climate issues, and contains summaries of network postings, updates on national and international policy initiatives, full-length articles, information on new network resources, and a calendar of upcoming events.

Keywords: Energy, Meteorology, Climatology
Audience: Meteorologists, Geologists, Energy Researchers, Climatologists
Contact: econet@igc.org

`mailto:larris@igc.org`

Meetings Calendar (Geosciences)

A collection of meetings and conferences in the geosciences, with a special emphasis on meteorology. The entries are sorted by date and some contain links to Calls for Papers.

Keywords: Geosciences, Meteorology
Sponsor: Freie Universit_t Berlin, Germany
Audience: Researchers, Meteorologists
Contact: Dennis Schulze
dennis@bibo.met.fu-berlin.de
Details: Free
Notes: If there is a conference you want to have included in this list, send an e-mail to dennis@bibo.met.fu-berlin.de

`http://www.met.fu-berlin.de/konferenzen/index.html`

Weather-users

Weather-users is a mailing list for developers of programs that access the Weather Underground database at the University of Michigan.

Keywords: Weather, Programming, Meteorology
Audience: Programmers
Contact: Scott Hazen Mueller
scott@zorch.sf-bay.org
Details: Free
User Info: To Subscribe to the list, send an e-mail message

`mailto:weather-users-request@zorch.sf-bay.org`

Meteorology Students ★

A discussion of meteorology, with particular emphasis on student-related topics, such as scholarships, summer schools, conferences, and university meteorology programs.

Keywords: Metereology
Audience: Meteorology Students
Contact: dennis@metw3.met.fu-berlin.de

Details: Free
User Info: To Subscribe to the list, send an e-mail message requesting a subscription to the URL address below.

`mailto:dennis@metw3.met.fu-berlin.de`

Mexican Culture FAQ

Mexican Culture FAQ

This is the FAQ from the soc.culture.mexican newsgroup. Provides information on Mexican culture, history, society, language, and tourism.

Keywords: Cultural Studies, Race, Chicano Culture, Latino Culture
Sponsor: News Group Moderators for soc.culture.mexican
Audience: Students, Hispanics
Contact: News Group Moderator
mendoza-grado@att.com
Details: Free

`ftp://ftp.mty.itesm.ms/pub/mexico/faqs`

`http://www.cis.ohio-state.edu/hypertext/faq/usenet/mexican-faq/faq.html`

Mexican-American Studies

University of Texas-Pan American Library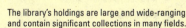

The library's holdings are large and wide-ranging and contain significant collections in many fields.

Keywords: Lower Rio Grande Valley (History of), Mexican-American Studies
Audience: Researchers, Students, General Public
Details: Free
Notes: Expect: Username Prompt, Send: packey

`telnet://panam2.panam.edu`

Mexico

North American Free Trade Agreement (NAFTA) ★

The agreement between the governments of Canada, the United Mexican States, and the United States of America to establish a free trade area in North America.

Keywords: Trade, US, Mexico, Canada, Free Trade, NAFTA

Audience: Journalists, Politicians, Economists, Students
Details: Free

`gopher://wiretap.spies.com/00/Gov/NAFTA`

US/Mexico Border Discussion List ★★

This group provides a forum for the discussion of issues pertaining to the US/Mexico border environment.

Keywords: Mexico, Environment, Latino Culture
Sponsor: The US Environmental Protection Agency
Audience: Activists, Environmentalists, Urban Planners
Details: Free
User Info: To Subscribe to the list, send a message to the URL address below consisting of a single line reading:

SUB us_mexborder YourFirstName YourLastName.

To send a message to the entire list, address it to:
us_mexborder@unixmail.rtpnc.epa.gov

`mailto:listserver@unixmail.rtpnc.epa.gov`

MGD (Mouse Genome Database)

MGD (Mouse Genome Database)

This site provides a comprehensive database of genetic information on the laboratory mouse.

Keywords: Biology, Genetics
Sponsor: The Jackson Laboratory
Audience: Biologists, Researchers, Educators, Students
Contact: mgi-help@informatics.jax.org
Details: Free
User Info: Contact Mouse Genome Informatics User Support by telephone at (207) 288-3371, X 1900, or by FAX at (207) 288-2516.

`http://www.informatics.jax.org/mgd.html`

Miata

Miata

An open forum for Mazda Miata owners.
Keywords: Mazda Miata, Automobiles
Audience: Automobile Owners

Details: Free

User Info: To Subscribe to the list, send an e-mail message requesting subscription to the URL address below.

mailto:miata-request@jhunix.hcf.jhu.edu

Michigan

MichNet News (previously Merit Network News) ★

Newsletter of MichNet (Michigan Networks), Michigan's regional computer network. It contains information about MichNet, as well as hosts and services that can be reached through MichNet.

Keywords: Computer Networks, Michigan

Sponsor: MichNet

Audience: Network Developers

Contact: Pat McGregor
patmcg@merit.edu

Details: Free

Contact the MichNet News at mnn-request@merit.edu. Available by anonymous FTP from the address below.

ftp://nis.nsf.net

The University of Michigan Library ★★

The library's holdings are large and wide-ranging and contain significant collections in many fields. Bilingual Education, Linguistics, Neuroscience, Michigan History, Temperance and Prohibition, African Government, Prohibition

Keywords: Education (Bilingual), Linguistics, Neuroscience, Michigan, Prohibition, Government (African)

Audience: General Public, Researchers, Librarians, Document Delivery Professionals

Details: Free

Notes: Expect: nothing, Send: <cr>

telnet://cts.merit.edu

Microbiology

Biosis Previews

The database encompasses the entire field of life sciences and covers original research reports and reviews in biological and biomedical areas. This includes field, laboratory, clinical, experimental and theoretical work. The traditional areas of biology, including botany, zoology, and microbiology, are covered, as well as the related fields such as plant and animal science, agriculture, pharmacology, and ecology.

Keywords: Biology, Botany, Zoology, Microbiology, Plant Science, Animal Science, Agriculture, Pharmacology, Ecology, Biochemistry, Biophysics, Bioengineering

Sponsor: Biosis

Audience: Librarians, Researchers, Students, Biologists, Botanists, Zoologists, Scientists, Taxonomists

Contact: CDP Technologies Sales Department (800)950-2035, extension 400

User Info: To Subscribe, contact CDP Technologies directly

telnet://cdplus@cdplus.com

University of Maryland System Library ★★

The library's holdings are large and wide-ranging and contain significant collections in many fields.

Keywords: Medicine (History of), Nursing, Pharmacology, Microbiology, Aquaculture, Aquatic Chemistry, Toxicology

Audience: General Public, Researchers, Librarians, Document Delivery Professionals

Contact: Ron Larsen

Details: Free

Notes: Expect: Available Services menu; Send: PAC

telnet://victor.umd.edu

vetmicro ★

Discussion group for veterinary microbiology.

Keywords: Veterinary Microbiology, Veterinary Medicine, Microbiology

Audience: Veterinarians

Contact: James T. Case, Bill Cohen
jcase@ucdcvdls.bitnet or
bcohen@ucdcvdls.bitnet

Details: Free

User Info: To Subscribe to the list, send an e-mail message to the URL address below consisting of a single line reading:

SUB vetmicro YourFirstName YourLastName

To send a message to the entire list, address it to: vetmicro@ucdavis.edu

mailto:listserv@ucdavis.edu

Microcomputing

Buyer's Guide to Micro Software ★★★

The database contains a directory of business and professional microcomputer software available in the United States.

Keywords: Buyer's Guides, Microcomputing, Computers, Software

Sponsor: Online, Inc., Weston, CT, USA

Audience: Computer Users

Profile: Provided are directory, product, technical, and bibliographic information on leading software packages, integrated this information into one succinct composite record. The database can help professionals locate suitable packages compatible with specified hardware, without having to sift through large numbers of records.

The file is highly selective, listing packages rated at least "good" by the technical press; all packages from major software producers, even if negatively reviewed; and packages unique to specific business segments, with special emphasis placed on library and medical software. Each record includes directory information; technical specifications, including required hardware and operating systems; an abstracted product description, and, when available, a full citation of representative reviews.

Contact: Dialog in the US at (800) 334-2564, Dialog internationally at country-specific locations.

Details: Costs

User Info: To Subscribe, contact Dialog directly.

Notes: Coverage: current; updated monthly.

telnet://dialog.com

MICnews ★

Microcomputer and advanced workstation computing news relevant to the computing populace at the University of California, Los Angeles (UCLA).

Keywords: Microcomputing, Advanced Workshops

Sponsor: Microcomputer Information Center, UCLA

Audience: UCLA Students

Contact: Bob Cooper
csmibob@mvs.oac.ucla.edu

Details: Free

User Info: To Subscribe to the list, send an e-mail message to the URL address below, consisting of a single line reading:

SUB micnews YourFirstName YourLastName

To send a message to the entire list, address it to:
micnews@uclacn1.ucla.edu

mailto:listserv@uslach1.edu

Output ★

Newsletter of the Florida State University (FSU) Computing Center. Includes topics such as networking, microcomputing, mainframe computing, and supercomputing on campus, including use of computers in classroom and research computing at FSU.

Keywords:	Networking, Microcomputing, Supercomputing	
Audience:	FSU Computer Science Students, Computer Users	
Contact:	Suzanne C. Nelson nelson@avm.cc.fsu.edu	
Details:	Free Send your request addressed to the Editor.	

mailto:nelson@avm.cc.fsu.edu

Microelectronics

University of Wisconsin at Stout Library ★★

The library's holdings are large and wide-ranging and contain significant collections in many fields.

Keywords:	Mathematics, Business, Fashion Merchandising, Home Economics, Hospitality, Tourism, Hotel Administration, Restaurant Management, Microelectronics
Audience:	Researchers, Students, General Public
Details:	Free
Notes:	Expect: Login, Send: Lib; Expect: vDIAL Prompt, Send: Library

telnet://lib.uwstout.edu

Microscopy

Massachusetts Institute of Technology Library ★★

The library's holdings are large and wide-ranging and contain significant collections in many fields.

Keywords:	Aeronautics (History of), Linguistics, Mathematics (History of), Microscopy, Spectroscopy, Aeronautics, Mathematics, Glass
Audience:	General Public, Researchers, Librarians, Document Delivery Professionals
Details:	Free
Notes:	Expect: Mitek Server..., Send: Enter or Return; Expect: prompt, Send: hollis

telnet://library.mit.edu

Microsoft Corporation

foxpro-l ★

This mailing list is designed to foster information sharing between users of the FoxPro^a database development environment now owned and distributed by Microsoft. Both new and experienced users of FoxPro are welcome to join in the discussions.

Keywords:	Databases, Computers, Microsoft Corporation
Audience:	Database Users, Microsoft FoxPro Users, Software Engineers
Contact:	Chris O'Neill coneill@heaven.polarbear.rankin-inlet.nt.ca
Details:	Free
User Info:	To Subscribe to the list, send an e-mail message requesting a subscription to the URL address below. To send a message to the entire list, address it to: foxpro-l@polarbear.rankin-inlet.nt.ca

mailto:fileserv@polarbear.rankin-inlet.nt.ca

Microsoft Corporation World Wide Web Server 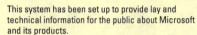★★★★

This system has been set up to provide lay and technical information for the public about Microsoft and its products.

Keywords:	Microsoft, Windows, MS-DOS, Chicago
Sponsor:	Microsoft Corporation
Audience:	Computer Users, Microsoft Product Users, Computer Programmers, Investors
Profile:	The Microsoft Knowledge Base and Software Library is accessible here. Information can be obtained on Windows NT Server, Developer Network News, Windows News, and also Windows Sockets Information. There are sections on Windows 4 (Chicago), Microsoft's new 32-bit TCP/IP VxD stack, a "What's New" page, current employment opportunities at Microsoft, recent speeches given by Microsoft Corporation's CEO Bill Gates, as well as current financial information about Microsoft.
Contact:	Email: www@microsoft.com
Details:	Free, Images
Notes:	The information contained on this server is copyrighted, and may not be distributed, downloaded, modified, reused, reposted, or otherwise used outside the scope of a WWW client without the express written permission of Microsoft Corporation.

http://www.microsoft.com

gopher://gopher.microsoft.com

ftp://ftp.microsoft.com

MS-Access ★

A list for the discussion of MS (Microsoft) Access topics, including Access Basic questions, reviews, rumors, and so on.

Keywords:	Microsoft Corporation, Databases
Audience:	Computer Users, Database Managers
Details:	Free
User Info:	To Subscribe to the list, send an e-mail message requesting subscription to the URL address below.

mailto:ms-access-request@eunet.co.at

Middle East

Israel-mideast ★★

This discussion group provides information on and analysis of Israel and the Middle East. Includes news flashes, briefings by Israeli leaders, editorials and articles translated from the Israeli press, background papers, press communiques and economic, environmental and cultural updates.

Keywords:	Israel, Middle East, Politics
Sponsor:	Israel Information Center, Jerusalem
Audience:	General Public, Students
Contact:	Israel Information Service ask@israel-info.gov.il
User Info:	To Subscribe to the list, send an e-mail message to the address below consisting of a single line reading: SUB israel mideast YourFirstName YourLastName To send a message to the entire list, address it to: israel mideast@vm.tau.ac.il

mailto:listserv@vm.tau.ac.il

MDEAFR ★★★

The Middle East and Africa (MDEAFR) library contains detailed information about every country in the Mideast and Africa. Structured for those who want to follow the unfolding events in the Gulf states, as well as in North and South Africa, this library contains a broad array of sources, including international research reports from InvestextR.

Keywords:	Analysis, Companies, Middle East, Africa
Audience:	Journalists, Business Professionals
Profile:	The MDEAFR library contains a wide array of pertinent sources. Among the information sources are newspapers and wire services, trade and business journals, company reports, country and region background, industry and product analysis, business opportunities, and selected legal texts. News sources range from the world-renowned Associated Press and Christian Science Monitor to the regionally important Jerusalem Post and Africa News. Company information is contained in the EXTEL cards as well as ICC. Providers of country background and industry analysis include Associated Banks of Europe, Bank of America, Business International, IBC USA, and the US Department of Commerce. Customers interested in new business opportunities can check OPIC and Foreign Trade Opportunities (FTO).

Contact:	Mead New Sales Group at (800) 227-4908 or (513) 859-5398 inside the US, or (513) 865-7981 for all inquiries outside the US.
User Info:	To Subscribe, contact Mead directly.
	To examine the Nexis user guide, you can access it at the ftp site of the University of Texas at Austin at the URL address: ftp://ftp.cc.utexas.edu
	The files are in: /pub/ref-services/LEXIS

`telnet://nex.meaddata.com`

`http://www.meaddata.com`

talk.politics.mideast

A Usenet newsgroup providing information and discussion about Middle Eastern topics.

Keywords:	Middle East, Middle Eastern Studies, Politics (Middle Eastern)
Audience:	Political Scientists
Details:	Free
User Info:	To Subscribe to this Usenet newsgroup, you need access to a newsreader.

`news:talk.politics.mideast`

The Israel Information Service

A gopher server containing information on Israel.

Keywords:	Israel, Middle East, Political Science, Anti-Semitism, Holocaust, Archaeology
Sponsor:	Israeli Foreign Ministry
Audience:	Israelis, Jews, Tourists, General Public
Profile:	This server features updates on the Middle East peace process, including text of the latest Israel-PLO accord, as well as general political, diplomatic, cultural and economic information on the state of Israel. Also includes archives on archaeology in Israel, anti-Semitism and the Holocaust, and current excerpts from Israeli newspapers.
Contact:	Chaim Shacham shacham@israel-info.gov.il

`gopher://israel-info.gov.il`

Middle Eastern Studies

Judaica

A mailing list for the discussion of Jewish and Near Eastern Studies.

Keywords:	Judaica, Israel, Middle Eastern Studies, Religion
Audience:	Judaica Scholars, Jews, Middle East Scholars
Contact:	Tzvee Zahavy maic@uminn1.bitnet

User Info:	To Subscribe to the list, send an e-mail message to the URL address below consisting of a single line reading:
	SUB judaica

`mailto:listserv@vm1.spcs.umn.edu`

Princeton University Library

The library's holdings are large and wide-ranging. They contain significant collections in many fields. China, Japan, Classics, Ancient History, Near East Studies, Literature, Aeronautics, Middle East, Mormon History, Publishing

Keywords:	China, Japan, Classics, History (Ancient), Near Eastern Studies, Literature (American), Literature (English), Aeronautics, Middle Eastern Studies, Mormonism, Publishing
Audience:	General Public, Researchers, Librarians, Document Delivery Professionals
Details:	Free
Notes:	Expect: Connect message, blank screen, Send: <cr>; Expect: #, Send: Call 500

`telnet://pucable.princeton.edu`

soc.culture.arabic

A Usenet newsgroup providing information and discussion about Arabic culture and technologies.

Keywords:	Sociology, Middle Eastern Studies
Audience:	Sociologists
Details:	Free
User Info:	To Subscribe to this Usenet newsgroup, you need access to a newsreader.

`news:soc.culture.arabic`

talk.politics.mideast

A Usenet newsgroup providing information and discussion about Middle Eastern topics.

Keywords:	Middle East, Middle Eastern Studies, Politics (Middle Eastern)
Audience:	Political Scientists
Details:	Free
User Info:	To Subscribe to this Usenet newsgroup, you need access to a newsreader.

`news:talk.politics.mideast`

University of Pennsylvania Library- Philadelphia Pa.

The library's holdings are large and wide-ranging and contain significant collections in many fields.

Keywords:	Literature (English), Literature (American), History (World), Medieval Studies, East Asian Studies, Middle Eastern Studies, South Asian Studies, Judaica, Lithuania.
Audience:	Educators, Students, Researchers

Profile:	Access to the central Van Pelt Library and to most of the departmental libraries is restricted to members of the University community on weekends and holidays. Online visitors are advised to call (215) 898-7554 for information on hours and access restrictions.
Contact:	Patricia Renfro, Associate Director of Libraries
Details:	Free

`telnet://library.upenn.edu`

University of Texas at Austin Library

The library's holdings are large and wide-ranging and contain significant collections in many fields.

Keywords:	Music, Natural Science, Nursing, Science Technology, Behavioral Science, Social Work, Computer Science, Engineering, Latin American Studies, Middle Eastern Studies
Audience:	Researchers, Students, General Public
Details:	Free
Notes:	Expect: Blank Screen, Send: Return; Expect: Go, Send: Return; Expect: Enter Terminal Type, Send: vt100
Note:	Some databases are restricted to UT Austin users only.

`telnet://utcat.utexas.edu`

University of Utah Library

The library's holdings are large and wide-ranging and contain significant collections in many fields.

Keywords:	Western America, Middle Eastern Studies, Geology, Mining
Audience:	Researchers, Students, General Public
Details:	Free
Notes:	Expect: Command Line, Send: Dial Unis

`telnet://lib.utah.edu`

Mideur-l

Mideur-L

A list containing the history, culture, politics, and current affairs of those countries lying between the Mediterranean/Adriatic and the Baltic Seas, and between the German/Austrian borders and the former Soviet Union.

Keywords:	Soviet Union, Baltic Republics, Eastern Europe, News
Audience:	Political Scientists, Researchers, Historians, General Public
Contact:	Jan George Frajkor mideur-1@ubvm.cc.buffalo.edu
Details:	Free

User Info: To Subscribe to the list, send an e-mail message to the URL address below consisting of a single line reading:

SUB mideur-l YourFirstName YourLastName

To send a message to the entire list, address it to: mideur-1@ubvm.cc.buffalo.edu

`mailto:listserv@ubvm.cc.buffalo.edu`

MIDI

Alternate Tuning Mailing List ★★

This mailing list is intended for exchanging ideas relevant to alternate tunings.

Keywords: Musical Instruments, MIDI
Sponsor: Mills College
Audience: Musicians
Profile: This list deals with just intonation, paratactical tunings, experimental music instrument design, non-standard equal temperaments, MIDI tuning system exclusive specifications, concert postings, non-Western tunings, and the experimental tunings of such people as Harry Partch, Lou Harrison, Martin Bartlett, James Tenney and others.
Contact: Greg Higgs
Higgs@Mills.edu
Details: Free
User Info: To Subscribe to the list, send an e-mail message to the URL address below, consisting of a single line reading:

SUB tuning YourFirstName YourLastName

`listproc@varese.mills.edu`

Midwifery

Midwifery Resources on the Net ★★

A resource list for helping find information about midwifery on the Internet.

Keywords: Midwifery, Childbirth, Medicine, Nursing
Audience: Midwives, Medical professionals
Details: Free

`gopher://una.hh.lib.umich.edu`

Migration

Migra-list ★

Mailing list on international migration.
Keywords: Migration

Sponsor: US Immigration and Naturalization Service
Audience: Politicians, General Public
Contact: Maurizio Oliva
moliva@cc.utah.edu
Details: Free

`mailto:migra-list@cc.utah.edu`

Milieu

Milieu ★

Discussion of the works of Julian May, notably the Saga of the Exiles, and the Galactic Milieu Trilogy.

Keywords: May (Julian), Science Fiction
Audience: Julian May Readers
Contact: milieu-request@yoyo.cc.monash.edu.au
Details: Free
User Info: To Subscribe to the list, send an e-mail message requesting subscription to the URL address below.

`mailto:milieu-request@yoyo.cc.monash.edu.au`

Military (US)

Uniform Code of Military Justice ★

The files in this directory contain the US Uniform Code of Military Justice.

Keywords: Military, Law
Audience: Journalists, Politicians, Students, Military Personnel
Details: Free

`gopher://wiretap.spies.com/00/Gov/UCMJ`

U.S. Army Area Handbooks ★★★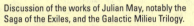

This gopher provides detailed political, cultural, historical, military, and economic information on hot spots in world affairs, everywhere from China to Yugoslavia.

Keywords: Military (US), Politics (International), Federal Government (US)
Sponsor: The Thomas Jefferson Library at the University of Missouri at St. Louis, St. Louis, Missouri, USA
Audience: Journalists, Government Officials, Travelers/Tourists
Profile: The Army Area Handbooks, which provide a comprehensive overview of several important countries including Japan, China, Israel, Egypt, South Korea, and Somalia, are only one of the many government resources available at this site. Other full-text documents include the proposed 1995 federal budget, the CIA world fact book, the NAFTA agreement, health care proposals currently before Congress, and statistics for the U.S. industrial outlook. Also has links to many federal gophers and information systems.

Contact: Joe Rottman
rottman@umslvma.umsl.edu
Details: Free

`gopher://umslvma.umsl.edu/11/library/govdocs`

US Army Corps of Engineers ★★

This site provides information on the organization, programs, news, facilities, and activities of the US Army Corps of Engineers.

Keywords: Military, Engineering
Sponsor: Cold Regions Research and Engineering Laboratory
Audience: Military Personnel, Engineers, Researchers
Contact: www@usace.mil
Details: Free

`http://www.usace.mil/usace.html`

Military History

University of Nebraska at Lincoln Library ★★

The library's holdings are large and wide-ranging and contain significant collections in many fields.

Keywords: Slovak Republic, Czech Republic, Folklore, Military History, Latvia, Law (Tax), Law (US)
Audience: General Public, Researchers, Librarians, Document Delivery Professionals
Contact: Anita Cook
Details: Free
Expect: login, Send: library

`telnet://unllib.unl.edu`

Military Policy

dont-tell ★

The dont-tell list is for people concerned about the effects that the new military policy known as "don't ask/don't tell" will have at academic institutions, whether military or ROTC-affiliated.

Keywords: Sexuality, Military Policy, Education (Post-Secondary)
Audience: Students, Gays, Lesbians, Military Personnel, Civil Libertarians
Contact: dont-tell-request@choice.princeton.edu

Military Policy

Details: Free

User Info: To subscribe to the list, send an e-mail message requesting a subscription to the URL address below.

To send a message to the entire list, address it to: dont-tell-request@choice.princeton.edu

`mailto:dont-tell-request@choice.princeton.edu`

Military Science

sci.military

A Usenet newsgroup providing information and discussion about science and the military.

Keywords: Military Science

Audience: Military Personnel, Military Historians

Details: Free

User Info: To Subscribe to this Usenet newsgroup, you need access to a newsreader.

`news:sci.military`

Military Specifications

IHS International Standards and Specifications

The database contains references to industry standards, and military and federal specifications and standards covering all aspects of engineering and related disciplines.

Keywords: Engineering, Military Specifications, Federal Standards

Sponsor: Information Handling Services, Englewood, CO, US

Audience: Engineers, Military Hisorians, Lawyers

Profile: The file includes 90% of the world's most referenced standards from over 70 domestic, foreign, and international standardizing bodies. Also included is the world's largest commercially available collection of unclassified active and historical US military and federal specifications and standards.

Contact: Dialog in the US at (800) 334-2564, Dialog internationally at country-specific locations.

User Info: To Subscribe, contact Dialog directly.

Notes: Coverage: Current; updated weekly for MILSPECS, every two months.

`telnet://dialog.com`

Milne (A.A.)

University of New Hampshire Videotex Library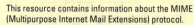

The library's holdings are large and wide-ranging and contain significant collections in many fields.

Keywords: Dance, Folk Music, Milne (A.A., Collection of), Galway (Ireland)

Audience: Researchers, Students, General Public

Contact: Robin Tuttle
r_tuttle1@unhh.unh.edu

Details: Free

Notes: Expect: USERNAME; Send: Student (no password required). Control-z to log off.

`telnet://unhvt@unh.edu`

MIME (Multipurpose Internet Mail Extensions)

MIME (Multipurpose Internet Mail Extensions)

This resource contains information about the MIME (Multipurpose Internet Mail Extensions) protocol.

Keywords: Internet, E-Mail

Audience: Internet Surfers

Contact: Nathaniel S. Borenstein
nsb@nsb.fv.com

User Info: File is: documents/rfc/rfc1521.txt

`ftp://nic.merit.edu`

Mind

Mind-L

A discussion group for people interested in mind-altering techniques, as well as mind machines. Related topics include smart nutrients, hypnosis, relaxation techniques, and subliminal tapes/videos. Does not cover hallucinatory drugs.

Keywords: Mind, Pschiatry, Psychology

Audience: Pschologists, Psychiatrists

Details: Free

User Info: To Subscribe to the list, send an e-mail message requesting subscription to the URL address below.

`mailto:mind-l-request@asylum.sf.ca.us`

Miniatures

Miniatures

The Miniatures Digest is a mailing list for discussion of the painting, sculpting, converting, and displaying of miniature figurines, generally for war games or fantasy role-playing games.

Keywords: Miniatures, Role-Playing

Audience: Miniature Figurine Collectors

Contact: minimallist-request@cs.unc.edu

Details: Free

User Info: To Subscribe to the list, send an e-mail message requesting subscription to the URL address below.

`mailto:minilist@cs.unc.edu`

Miniaturized Plants

Bonsai

This list has been set up to facilitate discussion of the art and craft of bonsai (the Oriental art of miniaturizing trees and plants into forms that mimic nature) and related art forms.

Keywords: Bonsai, Ornamental Plants, Miniaturized Plants

Audience: Bonsai Enthusiasts, Horticulturists, Ornamental Plant Enthusiasts, Nursery Owners

Contact: Dan@foghorn.pass.wayne.edu

Details: Free

User Info: To Subscribe to the list, send an e-mail message to the URL address below, consisting of a single line reading:

SUB bonsai YourFirstName YourLastName

To send a message to the entire list, address it to: bonsai@cms.cc.wayne.edu

Notes: Everyone interested, whether novice or professional, is invited to subscribe.

`mailto:listserv@cms.cc.wayne.edu`

Mining

University of Utah Library

The library's holdings are large and wide-ranging and contain significant collections in many fields.

Keywords: Western America, Middle Eastern Studies, Geology, Mining

Audience: Researchers, Students, General Public

Details: Free

Notes: Expect: Command Line, Send: Dial Unis

`telnet://lib.utah.edu`

Minor League

Minors ★

Issues affecting minor league baseball, including new stadium standards, minor league franchise status and changes, road trips and groups, schedules, team and league status, players and teams to watch, and collectibles.

Keywords: Baseball Enthusiasts
Audience: Baseball Enthusiasts
Details: Free
User Info: To Subscribe to the list, send an e-mail message requesting subscription to the URL address below.

`mailto:minors-request@medrant.apple.com`

Minorities

POS302-L ★

A discussion list created for the "Race, Ethnicity, and Social Inequality" seminar offered at Illinois State University (spring 1994). The general purposes of the list are to create an e-mail audience for the written work of enrolled students and to invite a broad audience to participate in the seminar.

Keywords: Race, Ethnicity, Minorities
Audience: Ethnic Studies Students, Sociologists, Educators
Details: Free
User Info: To Subscribe to the list, send an e-mail message to the URL address below, consisting of a single line reading:

SUB pos302-l YourFirstName YourLastName

To send a message to the entire list, address it to: pos302-l@ilstu.edu

`mailto:listserv@ilstu.edu`

soc.culture.african.american ★

A Usenet newsgroup providing information and discussion about African American culture.

Keywords: African American Studies, Sociology, Minorities
Audience: Sociologists
Details: Free
User Info: To Subscribe to this Usenet newsgroup, you need access to a newsreader.

`news:soc.culture.african.american`

Miracles

Miracles ★

This list provides daily readings from: A Course in Miracles and other selected readings from teachers, lecturers, and Course in Miracles Centers to provide additional reflection, inspiration, and avenues of practical application.

Keywords: Miracles
Audience: General Public
Contact: perry.sills@EBayperrys@spiritlead.Sun.COM
Details: Free
User Info: To Subscribe to the list, send an e-mail message requesting subscription to the URL address below.

`mailto:perry@spiritlead.Sun.COM`

misc.consumers

misc.consumers ★

A Usenet newsgroup providing information and discussion about consumer interests, including product reviews.

Keywords: Consumerism
Audience: Consumers, General Public
Details: Free
User Info: To Subscribe to this Usenet newsgroup, you need access to a newsreader.

`news:misc.consumers`

misc.consumers.house ★

A Usenet newsgroup providing information and discussion about owning and maintaining your house.

Keywords: Home Economics, Housing
Audience: Home Owners, General Public
Details: Free
User Info: To Subscribe to this Usenet newsgroup, you need access to a newsreader.

`news:misc.consumers.house`

misc.forsale

misc.forsale ★

A Usenet newsgroup providing information and discussion about items for sale.

Keywords: Consumerism
Audience: General Public
Details: Free
User Info: To Subscribe to this Usenet newsgroup, you need access to a newsreader.

`news:misc.forsale`

misc.handicap

misc.handicap ★

A Usenet newsgroup providing information and discussion for and about handicapped individuals.

Keywords: Disabilities
Audience: Differently Abled People, Disabled
Details: Free
User Info: To Subscribe to this Usenet newsgroup, you need access to a newsreader.

`news:misc.handicap`

misc.headlines

misc.headlines ★

A Usenet newsgroup providing information and discussion about current events and issues.

Keywords: Current Events
Audience: General Public
Details: Free
User Info: To Subscribe to this Usenet newsgroup, you need access to a newsreader.

`news:misc.headlines`

misc.invest

misc.invest ★

A Usenet newsgroup providing information and discussion about how to invest money.

Keywords: Investments, Finance
Audience: General Public
Details: Free
User Info: To Subscribe to this Usenet newsgroup, you need access to a newsreader.

`news:misc.invest`

misc.invest.real-estate

misc.invest.real-estate ★

A Usenet newsgroup providing information and discussion about property investments.

Keywords: Investments, Real Estate

Audience:	General Public
Details:	Free
User Info:	To Subscribe to this Usenet newsgroup, you need access to a newsreader.

`news:misc.invest.real-estate`

misc.jobs.misc

misc.jobs.misc

A Usenet newsgroup providing information and discussion about miscellaneous available jobs.

Keywords:	Employment
Audience:	Job Seekers, General Public
Details:	Free
User Info:	To Subscribe to this Usenet newsgroup, you need access to a newsreader.

`news:misc.jobs.misc`

misc.jobs.offered

misc.jobs.offered

A Usenet newsgroup providing information and discussion about job openings, listed by subject.

Keywords:	Employment
Audience:	Job Seekers, General Public
Details:	Free
User Info:	To Subscribe to this Usenet newsgroup, you need access to a newsreader.

`news:misc.jobs.offered`

misc.jobs.resumes

misc.jobs.resumes

A Usenet newsgroup providing information and discussion about resumes.

Keywords:	Employment
Audience:	Job Seekers, General Public
Details:	Free
User Info:	To Subscribe to this Usenet newsgroup, you need access to a newsreader.

`news:misc.jobs.resumes`

misc.kids

misc.kids

A Usenet newsgroup providing information and discussion about children and their behavior.

Keywords:	Children, Child Care
Audience:	Parents, Child Development Professionals, Children
Details:	Free
User Info:	To Subscribe to this Usenet newsgroup, you need access to a newsreader.

`news:misc.kids`

misc.legal

misc.legal

A Usenet newsgroup providing information and discussion about law and ethics.

Keywords:	Law, Ethics
Audience:	Lawyers, Legal Professionals, General Public
Details:	Free
User Info:	To Subscribe to this Usenet newsgroup, you need access to a newsreader.

`news:misc.legal`

misc.wanted

misc.wanted

A Usenet newsgroup providing information and discussion about items, excluding software, that are wanted or needed.

Keywords:	Consumerism
Audience:	General Public
Details:	Free
User Info:	To Subscribe to this Usenet newsgroup, you need access to a newsreader.

`news:misc.wanted`

Miscellaneous Federal Documents

Miscellaneous Federal Documents

This directory includes documents such as the Civil Rights Act of 1991, the Computer Fraud and Abuse Act, the High-Performance Computing Senate Report, and more.

Keywords:	Government (US Federal), Federal Documents (US)
Audience:	Politicians, Journalists, Students (high school up)
Details:	Free

`gopher://wiretap.spies.com/11/Gov/US-Docs`

Mississippi State University Library

Mississippi State University Library

The library's holdings are large and wide-ranging and contain significant collections in many fields.

Keywords:	History (US), Forestry, Energy, Carter (Hodding, Papers of), Mississippi
Audience:	General Public, Researchers, Librarians, Document Delivery Professionals
Contact:	Stephen Cunetto shc1@ra.msstate.edu
Details:	Free
User Info:	Expect: username, Send: msu; Expect: password, Send: library

`telnet://libserv.msstate.edu`

MIT Media Lab

MIT Media Lab

Online documents available through the ACCESS service that the MIT Media Laboratory is providing to sponsors using the File Transfer Protocol (FTP).

Keywords:	Internet, Multimedia
Audience:	Internet Surfers
Details:	Free, Multimedia

`ftp://media-lab.media.mit.edu`

MLoL

MLoL

The MLoL (Musical List of Lists) is a list of music-related mailing lists available on the Internet.

Keywords:	Music, Mailing Lists
Audience:	Musicians, General Public
Details:	Free
User Info:	To Subscribe to the list, send an e-mail message requesting a subscription to the URL address below.

`mailto:mlol-request@wariat.org`

Model Horses

Model-horse

Discussion of the model-horse hobby. All aspects of showing (live and photo), collecting, re-making/re-painting for all breeds are discussed. All ages and levels of experience welcome.

Keywords:	Model Horses, Hobbies
Audience:	Model Horse Collectors
Details:	Free
User Info:	To Subscribe to the list, send an e-mail message requesting a subscription to the URL address below.

`mailto:model-horse-request@qiclab.scn.rain.com`

Modem

SupraFAX

This list was created to help people who are using the SupraFAX v.32bis modem.

Keywords:	Modem, FAX
Audience:	Modem Users, FAX Users
Contact:	David Tiberio subscribe@xamiga.linet.org
Details:	Free
User Info:	To Subscribe to the list, send an e-mail message requesting a subscription to the URL address below.
	To send a message to the entire list, address it to: subscribe@xamiga.linet.org

`mailto:subscribe@xamiga.linet.org`

Modern Dance

OMD (Orchestral Manoeuvres In The Dark)

The OMD list is a forum for discussions about the English pop band Orchestral Manoevres In The Dark, which often incorporate modern dance elements into its music. The discussions are not moderated but they should have something to do with the band or with ex-band members.

Keywords:	OMD, Modern Dance
Audience:	OMD Enthusiasts
Contact:	Dave Datta omd-request@cs.uwp.edu
Details:	Free
User Info:	To Subscribe to the list, send an e-mail message requesting a subscription to the URL address below.
	To send a message to the entire list, address it to: omd@cs.uwp.edu
Notes:	The list is available as a daily digest and reflector. Archives are stored at ftp.uwp.edu.

`mailto:omd-request@cs.uwp.edu`

modesty-blaise

modesty-blaise

A discussion forum on Peter O'Donnell's Modesty Blaise books and comics. Topics include character, plot, artists, and relevant articles.

Keywords:	Comic Books, Comics, O'Donnell (Peter)
Audience:	Modesty Blaise Enthusiasts
Contact:	Thomas Gramstad modesty-blaise-request@math.uio.no
User Info:	To Subscribe to the list, send an e-mail message to the URL address below consisting of a single line reading:
	SUB modesty-blaise YourFirstName YourLastName

`mailto: modesty-blaise-request@math.uio.no`

Modula-2 (Programming Language)

info-M2

E-conference for the Modula-2 programming language.

Keywords:	Programming Languages, Modula-2 (Programming Language)
Audience:	Modula-2 Programmers
Contact:	Thomas Habernoll postmast@ucf1vm.cc.ucf.edu (USA); habernol@tubvm.cs.tu-berlin.de (Europe)
Details:	Free
User Info:	To Subscribe to the list, send an e-mail message to the URL address below consisting of a single line reading:
	SUB info-M2 YourFirstName YourLastName
	To send a message to the entire list, address it to: info-M2@ucf1vm.cc.ucf.edu

`mailto:listserv@ucf1vm.cc.ucf.edu`

Molecular Biology

Archive of Biology Software and Data

The main area of concentration of this archive is molecular biology. It contains software for the Macintosh, MS-DOS, VAX-VMS, and UNIX.

Keywords:	Health, Biology, Molecular Biology
Sponsor:	Indiana University
Audience:	Biologists, Students
Contact:	archive@bio.indiana.edu
Details:	Free
Notes:	It is recommended that the file Archive.doc be transferred and read first. This file gives considerable information about and instructions for using the archive.

`ftp://ftp.bio.indiana.edu`

Bioinformatics

This gopher server provides data and software related to bioinformatics, including public-domain software for biology and mirror storage for the main databases of the Human Genome Project and Molecular Biology.

Keywords:	Bioinformatics, Biology, Molecular Biology
Sponsor:	Weizmann Institute of Science, Israel
Audience:	Scientists, Biologists
Contact:	lsprilus@weizmann.weizmann.ac.il
Details:	Free

`gopher://bioinformatics.weizmann.ac.il`

`http://bioinformatics.weizman.act.il`

bionet.molbio.genbank.updates

A Usenet newsgroup providing information and discussion about the GenBank Nucleic acid database.

Keywords:	Molecular Biology, Biology, Genetics
Audience:	Molecular Biologists, Researchers
User Info:	To Subscribe to this Usenet newsgroup, you need access to a newsreader.

`news:bionet.molbio.genbank.updates`

Biotechnet Electronic Buyer's Guide

Biotechnet is a global computer network created specially for research biologists. It is intended to be a valuable source of information and data, a communications resource, a forum to foster the exchange of current ideas, and an international marketplace for relevant goods and service.

Keywords:	Molecular Biology, Electrophoresis, Chromatography
Audience:	Molecular Biologists, Chemists, Laboratory Suppliers
Profile:	One of the services offered by Biotechnet is the Electronic Buyer's Guide, which is divided into five individual databases for specific product categories: Molecular Biology, Electrophoresis, Chromatography, Liquid Handling, and Instruments & Apparatus. After selecting one of the guides at the prompt, you can search through each database to find either product names and applications or the name and address of the company that manufactures the product you wish to locate.

Molecular Biology

Details:	Free	
	Password: bguide	

`telnet://biotech@biotechnet.com`

EMBnet (European Molecular Biology Network)

A group of European Internet sites which provide computational molecular biology services to both national and international researchers.

Keywords:	Biology, Bioscience, Molecular Biology
Sponsor:	The EC Funding Program (BRIDGE)
Audience:	Biologists, Molecular Biologists, Researchers
Contact:	Rodrigo Lopez, Robert Herzog rodrigol@biotek.uio.no rherzog@ulb.ac.be

`http://biomaster.uio.no/embnet-www.html`

GenBank

The GenBank database provides a collection of nucleotide sequences as well as relevant bibliographic and biological annotation.

Keywords:	Genetics, Medicine, Molecular Biology
Sponsor:	National Center for Biotechnology Information (NCBI) at the National Library of Medicine (NLM)
Audience:	Geneticists, Scientists, Molecular Biologists
Profile:	DNA sequence entries are rated by specialized indexers in the Division of Library Operations. Over 325,000 articles per year from 3,400 journals are scanned for sequence data. They are supplemented by journals in plant and veterinary sciences through a collaboration with the National Agricultural Library. These records join the direct submission data stream and submissions from the European Molecular Biology Laboratory (EMBL) Data Library and the DNA Database of Japan (DDBJ).
Contact:	info@ncbi.nlm.nih.gov
Details:	Free
	Send direct submissions to gb-sub@ncbi.nlm.nih.gov and updates and changes to existing GenBank records to update@ncbi.nlm.nih.gov
	For help in retrieval by e-mail send an e-mail message with the word "help" in the body of the message to retrieve@ncbi.nlm.nih.gov

`gopher://gopher.nih.gov/77/gopherlib/indices/genbank/index`

Harvard Biosciences Online Journals

A resource containing selected online journals and periodicals in biology and medicine. Includes peer-reviewed e-journals, journal indexes, and databases.

Keywords:	Biology, Bioscience, Molecular Biology
Sponsor:	Harvard Biolabs, Harvard University, Cambridge, Massachusetts, USA
Audience:	Biologists, Molecular Biologists, Researchers
Contact:	Keith Robinson, Steve Brenner krobinson@nucleus.harvard.edu s.e.brenner@bioc.cam.ac.uk

`http://golgi.harvard.edu/journals.html`

ICGEBnet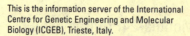

This is the information server of the International Centre for Genetic Engineering and Molecular Biology (ICGEB), Trieste, Italy.

Keywords:	Molecular Biology, Biotechnology, Italy, Europe
Audience:	Molecular Biotechnologists, Molecular Biologists
Profile:	The primary purpose of the ICGEB computer resource is to disseminate the best of currently available computational technology to the molecular biologists of the ICGEB research community.
Contact:	postmaster@icgeb.trieste.it
Details:	Free

`gopher://icgeb.trieste.it`

Johns Hopkins Genetic Databases

This gopher provides electronic access to documents pertaining to computational biology and a number of different genetic databases.

Keywords:	Genetics, Molecular Biology, Medicine, Biology
Sponsor:	Johns Hopkins University
Audience:	Geneticists, Researchers, Scientists, Molecular Biologists
Profile:	The databases accessible from this entry point include GenBank, Swiss-Prot, PDB, PIR, LiMB, TFD, AAtDB, ACEDB, CompoundKB, PROSITE EC Enzyme Database, NRL_3D Protein-Sequence-Structure Database, Eukaryotic Promoter Database (EPD), Cloning Vector Database, Expressed Sequence Tag Database (ESTDB), Online Mendelian Inheritance Man (OMIM), Sequence Analysis Bibliographic Reference Data Bank (Seqanalref), and Database Taxonomy (GenBank, Swiss-Prot). The gopher also provides direct links to other gophers with information relevant to biology.
Contact:	Dan Jacobson danj@mail.gdb.org
Details:	Free

`gopher://merlot.welch.jhu.edu`

National Institutes of Health Gopher

Provides access to a broad range of National Institutes of Health (NIH) resources (library catalogues, databases) via the Internet.

Keywords:	Health, AIDS, Molecular Biology, Grants
Sponsor:	National Institutes of Health
Audience:	Health Professionals, Molecular Biologists, Researchers
Profile:	This gopher provides access to NIH resources, including institute phone books and calendars, library catalogs, molecular biology databases, the full text of the NIH Guide for Grants and Contracts, files containing AIDS and cancer information and more.
Contact:	gopher@gopher.nih.gov
Details:	Free
Notes:	Expect: Login; Enter: Gopher

`telnet://gopher.nih.gov`

`gopher://gopher.nih.gov`

`gopher://odie.niaid.nih.gov`

University of Texas Health Science Center at Tyler Library

The library's holdings are large and wide-ranging and contain significant collections in many fields.

Keywords:	Biochemistry, Cardiopulmonary Medicine, Cell Biology, Family Practice, Molecular Biology
Audience:	Researchers, Students, General Public
Details:	Free
Notes:	Expect: Username Prompt, Send: LIS

`telnet://athena.uthscsa.edu`

Moms

Moms

Moms is a list for lesbian mothers.

Keywords:	Lesbians, Parenting
Audience:	Lesbians
Contact:	moms-request@qiclab.scn.rain.com
Details:	Free
User Info:	To Subscribe to the list, send an e-mail message requesting subscription to the URL address below.

`mailto:moms-request@qiclab.scn.rain.com`

Monarchy

Counterev-L

This list is under the aegis of l'Alliance Monarchists, affiliated with l'Alliance pour la maintenance de la France en Europe, and is dedicated to promoting the cause of traditional monarchy and counterrevolution. Its principles are a government based on natural law, decentralization, subsidiarity, an economy based on the principles of distributive justice, and the defense of traditional Western values.

Keywords: Monarchy, Government (International)
Audience: Monarchists, Counterrevolutionaries
Contact: Jovan Weismiller
ae852@yfn.ysu.edu
Details: Free
User Info: To Subscribe to the list, send an e-mail message requesting a subscription to the URL address below.

mailto:ae852@yfn.ysu.edu

Montefiore Medical Center Library Online Catalog

Montefiore Medical Center Library Online Catalog

Catalog of library holdings.

Keywords: Medicine, Libraries
Sponsor: Montefiore Medical Center at Albert Einstein College of Medicine, New York
Audience: Health Care Professionals, Medical Researchers, Educators, Students
Details: Free
After Telnetting, hit RETURN twice, then select 0 on main menu. Select 2 on locations menu. To exit, hit the Telnet escape key.

telnet://lis.aecom.yu.edu

Moon Travel Handbooks

Moon Travel Handbooks

Moon Publications' gopher features a travel newsletter, as well as excerpts and ordering information for their travel guides.

Keywords: Travel, Books
Sponsor: Moon Publications
Audience: International Travelers, General Public
Contact: gopher@moon.com
Notes: Also see Moon Publications' hypertext exhibit, Big Island of Hawaii Handbook, at http://bookweb.cwis.uci.edu:8042.

gopher://gopher.moon.com

Mormonism

Harvard University Library

The library's holdings are large and wide-ranging and contain significant collections in many fields.

Keywords: Afrikaans, Alchemy, Arabic Culure (History of), Celtic Philology, Congo Languages, Folklore, Hebraica, Mormonism, Numismatics, Quakers, Sanskrit, Witchcraft, Arabic Philology
Audience: General Public, Researchers, Librarians, Document Delivery Professionals
Details: Free
Notes: Expect: Mitek Server..., Send: Enter or Return; Expect: prompt, Send: hollis

telnet://hollis.harvard.edu

Princeton University Library

The library's holdings are large and wide-ranging. They contain significant collections in many fields.

Keywords: China, Japan, Classics, History (Ancient), Near Eastern Studies, Literature (American), Literature (English), Aeronautics, Middle Eastern Studies, Mormonism, Publishing
Audience: General Public, Researchers, Librarians, Document Delivery Professionals
Details: Free
Notes: Expect: Connect message, blank screen, Send: <cr>; Expect: #, Send: Call 500

telnet://pucable.princeton.edu

Morphology

Qmlist (Quantitative Morphology List)

This is an open, unmoderated mailing list to support researchers and clinicians in the field of quantitative morphology.

Keywords: Morphology
Audience: Morphologists, Biologists
Contact: Dean Pentcheff
dean2@tbone.biol.scarolina.edu
Details: Free
User Info: To Subscribe to the list, send an e-mail message to the URL address below, consisting of a single line reading:

SUB qmlist YourFirstName YourLastName

To send a message to the entire list, address it to:
qmlist@tbone.biol.scarolina.edu

mailto:listserv@tbone.biol.scarolina.edu

Morris Dancing

Morris

A discussion list related to Morris Dancing, including Cotswold, Border, Northwest, Rapper, Longsword, Abbots Bromley, Garland, and similar forms of English dance along with the accompanying music and traditions.

Keywords: Morris Dancing, England, Dance
Audience: Morris Dancers
Details: Free
User Info: To Subscribe to the list, send an e-mail message requesting subscription to the URL address below.

mailto:morris@suvm.acs.syr.edu

Mosaic

Mosaic Home Page

This is the welcome page to the National Center for Supercomputing Applications (NCSA) World Wide Web server, which features the Mosaic application. Mosaic provides a network-distributed hypermedia system for information discovery. It is Internet-based and is free for academic, research, and internal commercial use.

Keywords: Internet Tools, Mosaic, WWW
Audience: Internet Surfers
Contact: mosaic-x@ncsa.uiuc.edu
Details: Free

http://www.ncsa.uiuc.edu/sdg/software/mosaic/hcsamosaichome.html

NCSA (National Center for Supercomputing Applications)

A high-performance computing and communications facility and research center designed to serve the US computational science and engineering community.

Keywords: Supercomputing, Computer Networking, Computer Science, Mosaic
Sponsor: University of Illinois at Urbana-Champaign, Champaign, Illinois, USA
Audience: Students, Researchers, Computer Scientists, General Public
Contact: Systems Operator
pubs@ncsa.uiuc.edu

http://www.ncsa.uiuc.edu/general/hcsamome.html

Mother Jones

Mother Jones

A web site containing online electronic issues of Mother Jones magazine (and Zine), making possible instant electronic feedback to the publishers regarding articles.

Keywords:	Zines, Ethics, Public Policy, Activism
Sponsor:	Mother Jones
Audience:	Students, General Public
Contact:	Webserver webserver@mojones.com

`http://www.mojones.com/motherjones.html`

Motor Racing

Funet Sports Information

An FTP archive of information on various sports with links to the archive at wuarchive.wustl.edu.

Keywords:	Sports, Hockey, Motor Racing
Sponsor:	Finnish Academic and Research Network (FUNET)
Audience:	Sports Enthusiasts
Profile:	A fairly extensive archive of information on both American (NBA, MLB, NHL, NFL) and worldwide sports (soccer, ice hockey, motor racing, and so on). Includes FAQs for various sports, statistics, pictures, and some sports games for the PC.
Contact:	Jari Pullinen sports-adm@nic.funet.fi
Details:	Free, Images

`gopher://ftp.funet.fi/pub/sports`

University of Glasgow Information Service (GLANCE)

GLANCE provides subject-based information services, including an extensive section on European and world sports.

Keywords:	Sports, Soccer, Motor Racing, Mountaineering, Squash, Cricket, Golf, Tennis, Europe, Scotland
Sponsor:	University of Glasgow, Glasgow, Scotland
Audience:	Sport Enthusiasts, Fitness Enthusiasts, Nature Lovers
Profile:	Information at this site includes schedules, results, and statistics for sports such as cricket and soccer. There is also a selection of items on mountaineering.
Contact:	Alan Dawson a.dawson@uk.ac.gla.compserv
Details:	Free

`gopher://govan.cent.gla.ac.uk/subject/sports and rec`

Motorcycles

BMW Motorcycles

This is a discussion of all years and models of BMW motorcycles.

Keywords:	BMW Motorcycles, Motorcycles
Audience:	Motorcycle Enthusiasts, BMW Enthusiasts
Contact:	bmw-request@rider.cactus.org
Details:	Free
User Info:	To Subscribe to the list, send an e-mail message requesting a subscription to the URL address below. To send a message to the entire list, address it to: bmw@rider.cactus.org

`mailto:bmw-request@rider.cactus.org`

Brit-Iron

The purpose of this list is to provide a friendly forum in which riders, owners, and admirers of British motorcycles can share information and experiences. A list of parts sources and shops that repair these classic machines is maintained. All makes are welcome, from AJS to Vellocette.

Keywords:	Motorcycles
Audience:	British Motorcycle Enthusiasts, Motorcycle Enthusiasts
Contact:	cstringe@indiana.edu
Details:	Free
User Info:	To Subscribe to the list, send an e-mail message requesting a subscription to the URL address below. To send a message to the entire list, address it to: brit-iron@indiana.edu

`mailto:brit-iron@indiana.edu`

Nedod

Discussion of events, technical issues, and just plain social exchange related to motorcycling in the New England area of the US.

Keywords:	Motorcycles, New England
Audience:	Motorcycle Enthusiasts
Contact:	cookson@mbunix.mitre.org
User Info:	To Subscribe to the list, send an e-mail message requesting a subscription to the URL address below.

`mailto:nedod-request@mbunix.mitre.org`

rec.motorcycles

A Usenet newsgroup providing information and discussion about motorcycles and related products.

Keywords:	Motorcycles
Audience:	Motorcycle Riders
User Info:	To Subscribe to this Usenet newsgroup, you need access to a newsreader.

`news:rec.motorcycles`

Mountaineering

University of Glasgow Information Service (GLANCE)

GLANCE provides subject-based information services, including an extensive section on European and world sports.

Keywords:	Sports, Soccer, Motor Racing, Mountaineering, Squash, Cricket, Golf, Tennis, Europe, Scotland
Sponsor:	University of Glasgow, Glasgow, Scotland
Audience:	Sport Enthusiasts, Fitness Enthusiasts, Nature Lovers
Profile:	Information at this site includes schedules, results, and statistics for sports such as cricket and soccer. There is also a selection of items on mountaineering.
Contact:	Alan Dawson a.dawson@uk.ac.gla.compserv
Details:	Free

`gopher://govan.cent.gla.ac.uk/Subject/Sports and Rec`

Movement

Biomch-L

This list is intended for members of the International, European, American, Canadian, and other Societies of Biomechanics, and for members of ISEK (International Society of Electrophysiological Kinesiology), as well as for all others with an interest in the general field of biomechanics and human or animal movement.

Keywords:	Biomechanics, Kinesiology, Movement
Sponsor:	International Society of Biomechanics
Audience:	Kinesiologists
Contact:	Ton van den Bogert listserv@nic.surfnet.nl
Details:	Free
User Info:	To Subscribe to the list, send an e-mail message to the URL address below, consisting of a single line reading:

SUB biomch-l YourFirstName YourLastName

To send a message to the entire list, address it to: biomch-l@nic.surfnet.nl

Notes: To obtain technical help, send the command send biomch-l guide to listserv@hearn or listserv@nic.surfnet.nl.

`mailto:listserv@nic.surfnet.nl`

Movies

rec.arts.movies movie database

An extensive FTP database covering over 32,000 movies, with more than 370,000 filmography entries, from early cinema to current releases.

Keywords: Movies, Television, Popular Culture
Audience: Movie Buffs
Profile: Interfaces to search the database include Unix, MS-DOS and Amiga (and Windows and Mac versions are in development). The database includes filmographies for actors, directors, writers, composers, cinematographers, editors, production designers, costume designers and producers; plot summaries; character names; movie ratings; year of release; running times; movie trivia; quotes; goofs; soundtracks; personal trivia and Academy Award information.
Contact: Col Needham
cn@ibmpcug.co.uk
Details: Free

`ftp://cathouse.org/pub/cathouse/movies/database`

rec.arts.movies movie database (Cardiff WWW front-end)

An extensive, interactive database covering over 32,000 movies, with more than 370,000 filmography entries, from early cinema to current releases.

Keywords: Movies, Television, Popular Culture, Interactive Media
Audience: Movie Buffs
Profile: A WWW front-end to the rec.arts.movies movie database, complete with form-filling interfaces to add new data and to rate movies (on a scale from 1 through 10). The database includes filmographies for actors, directors, writers, composers, cinematographers, editors, production designers, costume designers and producers; plot summaries; character names; movie ratings; year of release; running times; movie trivia; quotes; goofs; soundtracks; personal trivia and Academy Award information.
Contact: Rob Hartill
Robert.Hartill@cm.cf.ac.uk
Details: Free

`http://www.cm.cf.ac.uk/movies`

`http://www.msstate.edu/movies`

MR2-Interest

Mr2-interest

Discussion of Toyota MR2s, old and new.

Keywords: Automobiles
Audience: Automobile Owners
Details: Free
User Info: To Subscribe to the list, send an e-mail message requesting subscription to the URL address below.

`mailto:mr2-interest-request@validgh.com`

MS-Access

MS-Access

A list for the discussion of MS (Microsoft) Access topics, including Access Basic questions, reviews, rumors, and so on.

Keywords: Microsoft Corporation, Databases
Audience: Computer Users, Database Managers
Details: Free
User Info: To Subscribe to the list, send an e-mail message requesting subscription to the URL address below.

`mailto:ms-access-request@eunet.co.at`

MS-DOS Computers

info-GNU-MSDOS

This electronic conference is for the GNUISH MS-DOS Development Group.

Keywords: Shareware, Freeware, MS-DOS Computers
Audience: MS-DOS Users, GNUISH MS-DOS Developers
Contact: David J. Camp
david@wubios.wustl.edu
Details: Free
User Info: To Subscribe to the list, send an e-mail message to the URL address below consisting of a single line reading:
SUB info-GNU-MSDOS YourFirstName YourLastName

`mailto:listserv@wugate.wustl.edu`

Microsoft Corporation World Wide Web Server

This system has been set up to provide lay and technical information for the public about Microsoft and its products.

Keywords: Microsoft, Windows, MS-DOS, Chicago
Sponsor: Microsoft Corporation
Audience: Computer Users, Microsoft Product Users, Computer Programmers, Investors
Profile: The Microsoft Knowledge Base and Software Library is accessible here. Information can be obtained on Windows NT Server, Developer Network News, Windows News, and also Windows Sockets Information. There are sections on Windows 4 (Chicago), Microsoft's new 32-bit TCP/IP VxD stack, a "What's New" page, current employment opportunities at Microsoft, recent speeches given by Microsoft Corporation's CEO Bill Gates, as well as current financial information about Microsoft.
Contact: Email: www@microsoft.com
Details: Free, Images
Notes: The information contained on this server is copyrighted, and may not be distributed, downloaded, modified, reused, reposted, or otherwise used outside the scope of a WWW client without the express written permission of Microsoft Corporation.

`http://www.microsoft.com`

`gopher://gopher.microsoft.com`

`ftp://ftp.microsoft.com`

MSA-Net

MSA-Net

A mailing list intended to meet the communication needs of Muslim Student Associations (MSA) in North America, and to discuss issues related to Islam and MSAs are discussed.

Keywords: Islam, Muslim Student Associations
Audience: Muslims
Contact: Aalim Fevens
msa-request@htm3.ee.queensu.ca
User Info: To Subscribe to the list, send an e-mail message
Notes: Members must be Muslim.

`mailto:msa-request@htm3.ee.queensu.ca`

Mt. Xinu

Mtxinu-users

Discussion and bug fixes for users of the 4.3+NFS release from the Mt. Xinu folks.

Keywords: Mt. Xinu Computing
Audience: Computer Users

Details:	Free
User Info:	To Subscribe to the list, send an e-mail message requesting subscription to the URL address below.

`mailto:mtxinu-users-request@nike.cair.du.edu`

Muchomedia Conference

Muchomedia Conference

A conference on the WELL about multimedia with topics ranging from products and software to multimedia for beginners.

Keywords:	Multimedia, Art
Audience:	Artists, Computer Programmers, Producers
Contact:	Douglas Crockford crock@well.sf.ca.us
Notes:	To participate in a conference on the WELL, you must first establish an account on the WELL. To do so, start by typing: telnet well.sf.ca.us

`telnet://well.sf.ca.us`

MUDs

MUD

A discussion list for the exchange of information about new and recommended Multiuser Dungeons and Dragons (MUDs).

Keywords:	MUDs, Games
Audience:	MUD Users
Contact:	Joseph Wisdom jwisdom@gnu.ai.mit.edu
Details:	Free
User Info:	To Subscribe to the list, send an e-mail message requesting subscription to the URL address below.

`mailto:jwisdom@gnu.ai.mit.edu`

Multicasting

Multicast

Discussion of multicast and broadcast issues in an open systems interconnection environment.

Keywords:	Multicasting, Broadcasting
Audience:	Multicasters, Broadcasting Professionals
Details:	Free
User Info:	To Subscribe to the list, send an e-mail message requesting subscription to the URL address below.

`mailto:multicast-request@arizona.edu`

Multicast Backbone

Live audio and video multicast virtual network on top of the Internet.

Keywords:	Internet, Information Retrieval, Multitaskingg
Audience:	Internet Surfers
Details:	Free; sound files available.

`ftp://venera.isi.edu`

`http://venera.isi.edu`

Multilateral Treaties

Multilateral Treaties

An experimental program to make available to the Internet community the text of a wide variety of multilateral conventions, even those which have not yet been ratified.

Keywords:	Treaties, Law (International)
Sponsor:	The Fletcher School of Law and Diplomacy, Cornell University, Ithaca, NY
Audience:	Government Officials, Researchers, Lawyers
Profile:	Almost all treaties listed are available in print form. The program will enable access to even very recent conventions. Primary focus is on Environmental and human rights issues but other fields are also included. The conventions coming out of the 1992 United Nations Conference on the Environment and Development have NOT been included as they are available elsewhere through CIESIN. Those Treaties covered include: Convention on International Trade in Endangered Species of Wild Fa; Montreal Protocol on Substances that Depleate the Ozone Layer; The Berne Convention for the Protection of Literary and Artistic Works; Agreement on the Rescue of Astronauts; the return of Astronauts
Contact:	Peter Scott Director, Multilaterals Project, Fletcher School of Law and Diplomacy pstott@pearl.tufts.edu pstott@icg.apc.org
Details:	Free
Notes:	Select from menu as appropriate

`gopher://gopher.law.cornell.edu/11/foreign/fletcher-cat`

Multimedia

(The) Electric Eclectic

A multimedia magazine delivered online that includes pictures, sounds, and text.

Keywords:	Magazines, Multimedia
Audience:	General Public

`mailto:ee-discuss-request@eitech.cm`

ACEN (Art Com Electronic Network)

A conference on the WELL for art, technology, and text-based artworks.

Keywords:	Art, Literature (Contemporary), Multimedia
Sponsor:	Art Com Electronic Network
Audience:	Artists, Musicians, Writers
Profile:	Started in 1986, ACEN is a seminal art BBS that includes actual artworks, discussion on topics such as software as art, and on line published works by John Cage, Fred Truck, Jim Rosenberg, Judy Malloy, and others.
Contact:	Carl Loeffler artcomtv@well.sf.ca.us

To participate in a conference on the WELL, you must first establish an account on the WELL. To do so, start by typing: telnet://well.sf.ca.us

`telnet://well.sf.ca.us`

ACM SIGGRAPH Online Bibliography Project

This is a collection of computer-graphics bibliographic references.

Keywords:	Multimedia, Interactive, Computer Graphics, Programming
Sponsor:	Association of Computing Machinery (ACM), Special Interest Group on Computer Graphics (SIGGRAPH)
Audience:	Developers, Designers, Producers, Educators, Programmers, Graphic Artists
Profile:	The goal of this project is to maintain an up-to-date database of computer-graphics literature, in a format that is accessible to as many members of the computer-graphics community as possible. The database includes references from conferences and workshops worldwide and from a variety of publications dating back as far as the late-19th century. The majority of the major journals and conference proceedings from the mid 1970s to the present are listed.
Contact:	bibadmin@siggraph.org
Details:	Free, Moderated, Multimedia

`ftp://siggraph.org/publications`

CinemaSpace

CinemaSpace, from the Film Studies Program at UC Berkeley, is devoted to all aspects of Cinema and New Media.

Keywords:	Cinema, Film, Multimedia
Sponsor:	Film Studies Program at UC Berkeley

Audience: Students, Film researchers
Profile: Projects for CinemaSpace include academic papers on film and new media, film theory and critique. multimedia lectures, and sources of film clips and references to other sites.
Contact: xcohen@garnet.berkeley.edu
Details: Free

`http://remarque.berkeley.edu/~xcohen`

Diversity U

Diversity University is an experiment in interactive learning.
Keywords: Education, Interactive Learning, Multimedia
Audience: Educators, Researchers
Details: Free

`gopher://erau.db.erau.edu`

FineArt Forum

A monthly newsletter that includes listings of art and technology events, showcases, conferences, and jobs.
Keywords: Art, Multimedia
Sponsor: The International Society for the Arts, Sciences, and Technology
Audience: Art Educators, Art Professionals, Artists
Profile: Published by the National Science Foundation Engineering Research Center for Computational Field Simulation, Mississippi State University. FineArt Forum has provided timely information to a large international audience since 1988. The subscriber list consists of individuals working in the realm where art, science, and technology converge. Issues provide information about conferences and competitions, calls for presentations and research, and notices about performances. FineArt_Online is both an archive of FineArt Forum, ISEA News, Leonardo Electronic News, and a variety of longer postings. In January 1994 it began posting an online gallery.
Contact: Paul Brown
brown@erc.msstate.edu
User Info: To Subscribe, send e-mail to:
brown@erc.msstate.edu, with the message
SUB FAST; also give your name, postal address, and e-mail address.

`http://www.msstate.edu/fineart_online/home.html`

Free for All

An experiment in a networked hypermedia group bulletin board.
Keywords: Internet, Group Communications, Multimedia
Audience: Internet Surfers, Multimedia Enthusiasts

Details: Free, Multimedia

`http://south.ncsa.uiuc.edu/free.html`

Georgia State University Library

The library's holdings are large and wide-ranging and contain significant collections in many fields.
Keywords: Labor (History of), Multimedia, Mercer (Johnny, Collection of)
Audience: General Public, Researchers, Librarians, Document Delivery Professionals
Contact: Phil Williams
isgpew@gsuvm1.gsu.edu
Details: Free
Notes: Expect: VM screen, Send: RETURN; Expect: CP READ, Send: DIAL VTAM, press RETURN; Expect: CICS screen, Send: PF1

`telnet://library.gsu.edu`

Index to Multimedia Information Sources

This site provides a guide to multimedia on the Web, including lists of software, companies, research, publications, conferences, archives, and galleries.
Keywords: Multimedia, Interactive Media
Audience: Designers, Educators
Contact: Simon Gibbs
simon.gibbs@gmd.de
Details: Free

`http://cui_www.unige.ch/osg/multimediainfo/index.html`

Kaleidospace

This is a new Web server that provides a multimedia showcase for artists, performers, CD-ROM authors, musicians, writers, animators, filmmakers and software developers.
Keywords: Art, Computer Art, Multimedia
Audience: Artists, Performers, CD-ROM Authors, Musicians, Writers, Animators, Filmmakers, Software Developers
Profile: This site was created to support independent artists. The site has similarities to other web servers such as IUMA, but differs in that it works with all kinds of artists, and that it processes orders for the artist's material.
Contact: Jeannie Novak, Peter Markiewicz
jeannienov@aol.com
peterm@ewald.mbi.ucla.edu

`http://kspace.com`

`http://fire.kspace.com`

Leonardo Electronic Almanac

The Leonardo Electronic Almanac (LEA) is a monthly, edited journal and an electronic archive dedicated to providing current perspectives in the art, science and technology domains.
Keywords: Art, Multimedia, Music, Electronic Media
Sponsor: International Society for the Arts, Sciences, and Technology
Audience: New Media Artists, Researchers, Developers, Art Educators, Art Professionals
Profile: LEA is an international, interdisciplinary forum for people interested in the use of new media in contemporary artistic expression, especially involving 20th century science and technology. Material is contributed by artists, scientists, philosophers and educators. LEA is published by the MIT Press for Leonardo, the International Society for the Arts, Sciences, and Technology (ISAST).
Contact: Craig Harris
craig@well.sf.ca.us
Details: Costs, Moderated, Images, Sounds, Multimedia

`mail to:journals-orders@mit.edu`

`ftp://mitpress.mit.edu/pub/Leonardo-Elec-Almanac`

MIT Media Lab

Online documents available through the ACCESS service that the MIT Media Laboratory is providing to sponsors using the File Transfer Protocol (FTP).
Keywords: Internet, Multimedia
Audience: Internet Surfers
Details: Free, Multimedia

`ftp://media-lab.media.mit.edu`

Muchomedia Conference

A conference on the WELL about multimedia with topics ranging from products and software to multimedia for beginners.
Keywords: Multimedia, Art
Audience: Artists, Computer Programmers, Producers
Contact: Douglas Crockford
crock@well.sf.ca.us
Notes: To participate in a conference on the WELL, you must first establish an account on the WELL. To do so, start by typing: telnet well.sf.ca.us

`telnet://well.sf.ca.us`

Multimedia Index

A list of multimedia information sources on the Internet.

Keywords: Internet, Multimedia
Sponsor: Centre Universitaire d'Informatique, University of Geneva
Audience: Internet Surfers
Contact: Oscar Nierstrasz
oscar@cui.unige.ch
Details: Free, Multimedia

`http://cui_www.unige.ch`

Multimedia Lab BU

Information about the Multimedia Lab at Boston University (BU), investigating issues surrounding the contruction of general purpose distributed multimedia information systems (DMISs).

Keywords: Internet, Multimedia
Sponsor: Boston University
Audience: Internet Surfers
Contact: T.D.C. Little
tdcl@spiderman.bu.edu
Details: Free, Multimedia

`http://spiderman.bu.edu`

Multimedia Survey

A survey of distributed multimedia research, standards, and products by RARE (Associated Networks for European Research).

Keywords: Internet, Multimedia
Audience: Internet Surfers
Details: Free, Multimedia

`ftp://ftp.ed.ac.uk/pub/mmsurvey`

Multimedia, Telecommunications, and Art Project

A project to promote online art that will be implemented as gopher site and on the World Wide Web.

Keywords: Multimedia, Electronic Art, Telecommunications
Sponsor: CISR (Centre for Image and Sound Research), Vancouver, BC, Canada
Audience: Artists, Writers
Contact: Derek Dowden
Derek_Dowden@mindlink.bc.ca
For more information, send an e-mail message to the URL address below.

`mailto:Derek_Dowden@mindlink.bc.ca`

NIC (Nucleus for Interactive Computing)

WWW-based system for interactive computing.

Keywords: Multimedia, Interactive Computing, Interface Design, Scripting Laguages, Programming
Sponsor: BYU Interactive Software Systems Lab
Audience: Software Developers, Educators
Profile: NIC is a system for interactive computing that combines a data model, a user interface model, and a scripting language to create flexible and powerful user interfaces. Documentation still under construction is located here.
Contact: Dan Olsen
olsen@cs.byu.edu
Details: Free, Moderated, Image, Sound and Multimedia files available.
Use a World Wide Web (Mosaic) client and open a connection to the resource.

`ftp://issl.cs.byu.edu/docs/NIC/home.html`

NYAL (New York Art Line)

A gopher containing selected resources on the arts.

Keywords: Art, Audio-Visual Materials, Multimedia, Computer Art
Sponsor: Panix Public Access Unix & Internet Gopher Server, New York, USA
Audience: Artists, Art Enthusiasts
Profile: NYAL features a wide variety of arts resources. The primary focus of this site is visual art, particularly in the New York city area. Information includes online access to selected galleries, image archives, and New York city arts groups. Beyond visual art, information on dance, music, and techno art (with a special section on Internet art) is also available. It also features links to various electronic journals, museums, and schools.
Contact: Kenny Greenberg
kgreen@panix.com

`gopher://gopher.panix.com`

`http//gopher.panix.com/nyart/Kpage/kg`

Museums

Smithsonian Online

Located on America Online (with partial access by ftp), this allows online access to the Institution's resources.

Keywords: Museums, Art Exhibitions
Sponsor: Smithsonian Institution, Washington DC
Audience: Educators, Students, General Public
Profile: Smithsonian Online includes resources for teachers and students in the form of bulletin boards about Smithsonian museums, photographs, listings of events in Washington and other communities, and excerpts from Smithsonian and Air & Space/ Smithsonian.

`ftp://photo1.si.edu`

UC Berkeley Museum of Paleontology and the WWW Subway

This web site provides a multimedia museum display from UC Berkeley's Museum of Paleontology. Also features an interactive Subway, a tool linking users to other museums and WWW sites around the world.

Keywords: WWW, Museums, Paleontology
Sponsor: University of California at Berkeley, Museum of Paleontology, Berkeley, California, USA
Audience: Paleontologists, Internet Surfers, General Public
Contact: David Polly, Robert Guralnick
davip@ucmp1.berkeley.edu
robg@fossil.berkeley.edu

`http://ucmp1.berkeley.edu/subway.html`

Music

alt.music.alternative

A Usenet newsgroup providing information and discussion about alternative music.

Keywords: Music
Audience: Alternative Music Listeners
User Info: To Subscribe to this Usenet newsgroup, you need access to a newsreader.

`news:alt.music.alternative`

Analog Heaven

The Analog Heaven mailing list caters to people interested in vintage analog electronic music equipment. Topics include items for sale, repair tips, equipment modifications, ASCII & GIF schematics, and a general discussion of new and old analog equipment. There is an FTP/Gopher site located at cs.uwp.edu with discussions on various machines, a definitive guide to Roland synths, patch editors, modification schematics, and GIFs/JPEGs of vintage synths, as well as a few sound samples of some of the gear itself.

Keywords: Music, Synthesizers, Sequencers, Analog Equipment, Electronic Music
Audience: Electronic Music Enthusiasts, Musicians
Contact: Todd Sines
analogue-request@magnus.acs.ohio-state.edu
Details: Free; sound files available.
User Info: To Subscribe to the list, send an e-mail message requesting a subscription to the URL address below.
To send a message to the entire list, address it to:
analogue@magnus.acs.ohio-state.edu

`mailto:analogue-request@magnus.acs.ohio-state.edu`

Music

Arts

An umbrella arts conference on the WELL.

Keywords:	Art, Music, Dance
Audience:	Artists, Dancers, Musicians, Photographers
Profile:	A genereal arts conference that includes listings of show opportunities, books, and events, as well as discussion about art and art criticism.
Contact:	Tim Collins

`telnet://well.sf.ca.us`

Arts Wire

A national communications network for the arts located on the Meta Network.

Keywords:	Art, Writing, Activism, Music
Sponsor:	New York Foundation for the Arts
Audience:	Art Activists, Art Organizations, Artists, Composers, Foundations, Government Arts Agencies, Writers
Profile:	Arts Wire provides immediate access to news, information, and dialogue on conditions affecting the arts and artists, as well as private conferences for organizations. Core features include Money, a searcable resource of grant deadlines; Hotwire, a summary of arts news; and conferences about new music, interactive art, literature, AIDS, and Latino art.
Contact:	Judy Malloy artswire@tmn.com

`telnet://tmn.com`

AusRave (Australian Raves)

A regional rave-related mailing list covering the Australian continent. AusRave contains both discussions and informational postings.

Keywords:	Music, Raves, Australia
Audience:	Ravers (Australian)
Contact:	Simón Rumble ausrave@lsupoz.apana.org.au
Details:	Free, Moderated
User Info:	To Subscribe to the list, send an e-mail message requesting a subscription to the URL address below. To send a message to the entire list, address it to: ausrave@lsupoz.apana.org.au
Notes:	The mailing list Best of AusRave provides information only Postings to AusRave are not archived, but the list does have an FTP site at: elecsun4.elec.uow.edu.au

`mailto:ausrave-request@lsupoz.apana.org.au`

Bagpipe

A mailing list of people interested in any topic related to bagpipes, most generally defined as any instrument where air is forced manually from a bellows or bag through drones and/or over reeds. All manner of Scottish, Irish, English, and other instruments are discussed.

Keywords:	Music, Bagpipes
Audience:	Bagpipe Enthusiasts
Contact:	pipes-request@sunapee.dartmouth.edu
Details:	Free
User Info:	To Subscribe to the list, send an e-mail message requesting a subscription to the URL address below. To send a message to the entire list, address it to: pipes@sunapee.dartmouth.edu

`mailto:pipes-request@sunapee.dartmouth.edu`

Bel Canto

A mailing list for the discussion of the music, lyrics, and shows of the group Bel Canto, and solo projects of group members, or even the work of related artists if appropriate.

Keywords:	Music, Pop Groups
Audience:	Music Enthusiasts
Contact:	dewy-fields-request@ifi.uio.no
Details:	Free
User Info:	To Subscribe to the list, send an e-mail message requesting a subscription to the URL address below. To send a message to the entire list, address it to: dewy-fields@ifi.uio.no

`mailto:dewy-fields-request@ifi.uio.no`

Beloved

A mailing list for the discussion of the Beloved, an English pop group with strong ambient and techno influences.

Keywords:	Music, Pop Groups
Audience:	Music Enthusiasts
Contact:	Jyrki Sarkkinen beloved-request@phoenix.oulu.fi
Details:	Free
User Info:	To Subscribe to the list, send an e-mail message requesting a subscription to the URL address below. To send a message to the entire list, address it to: beloved@phoenix.oulu.fi

`mailto:beloved-request@phoenix.oulu.fi`

Best-of-AusRave (Australian Raves)

A regional rave-related mailing list covering the Australian continent, for people who want Australian rave information without the side discussions and social chatter from the regular list.

Keywords:	Music, Raves, Australia
Audience:	Ravers (Australian)
Contact:	Simon Rumble best-of-ausrave-request@lsupoz.apana.org.au
Details:	Free, Moderated
User Info:	To Subscribe to the list, send an e-mail message to the URL address below, consisting of a single line reading: SUB ausrave YourFirstName YourLastName To send a message to the entire list, address it to: best-of-ausrave@lsupoz.apana.org.au

`mailto:best-of-ausrave-request@lsupoz.apana.org.au`

Blues-L

A mailing list for the discussion of Blues music and the culture surrounding the genre of the Blues.

Keywords:	Blues, Music
Audience:	Blues Enthusiasts
Contact:	listserv@brownvm.brown.edu
Details:	Free
User Info:	To Subscribe to the list, send an e-mail message to the URL address below, consisting of a single line reading: SUB blues-l YourFirstName YourLastName To send a message to the entire list, address it to: blues-l@brownvm.brown.edu
Notes:	To receive the list in digest form: once you get acknowledgment from the listserver that you are on the list, send another message to the URL address below with the message: SET BLUES-L DIG

`mailto:listserv@brownvm.brown.edu`

BPM

This list is for novice and professional DJs. Discussion often covers music releases, DJ'ing techniques, and turntable maintenance.

Keywords:	Disk Jockeys, Music
Audience:	Disk Jockeys, Music Enthusiasts
Contact:	Simon Gatrall bpm-request@andrew.cmu.edu
Details:	Free

Music

A B C D E F G H I J K L M N O P Q R S T U V W X Y Z

User Info:	To Subscribe to the list, send an e-mail message requesting a subscription to the URL address below.
	To send a message to the entire list, address it to: bpm@andrew.cmu.edu

`mailto:bpm-request@andrew.cmu.edu`

Cantus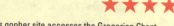

This gopher site accesses the Gregorian Chant Database, which is maintained by the Catholic University of America.

Keywords:	Gregorian Chants, Music, Liturgy
Sponsor:	Catholic University of America (CUA)
Audience:	Vocalists, Educators, Students
Profile:	The database contains an introduction to the Cantus Gopher at the CUA, and has a searchable index.

`gopher://vmsgopher.cua.edu`

dire-straits ★

Discussion of the musical group Dire Straits and associated side projects.

Keywords:	Rock Music, Dire Straits, Music
Audience:	Rock Music Enthusiasts, Dire Straits Enthusiasts
Contact:	Rand P. Hall dire-straits-request@merrimack.edu
Details:	Free
User Info:	To subscribe to the list, send an e-mail message requesting a subscription to the URL address below.
	To send a message to the entire list, address it to: dire-straits-request@merrimack.edu

Anonymous ftp to: merrimack.edu (Ä=ANONYMOUS/DIRE-STRAITS)

Mail list probably exists.

Drake University ★★

The library's holdings are large and wide-ranging and contain significant collections in many fields.

Keywords:	Music, Pharmacology, Theology
Audience:	General Public, Researchers, Librarians, Document Delivery Professionals
Details:	Free, Moderated
	Send: COWLES to access the main library, and LAWLIB to access the Law Library. To leave the system, enter CTRL-Z

`telnet://lib.drake.edu`

Eastern Washington University Library ★★

The library's holdings are large and wide-ranging and contain significant collections in many fields.

Keywords:	Education, Music, Social Science, Behavioral Science
Audience:	Researchers, Students, General Public
Details:	Free
Notes:	Expect: Login; Send: Lib

`telnet://wsduvm12.csc.wsu.edu`

ecto ★

Information and discussion about singer/songwriter Happy Rhodes, and other music, art, books, and films of common (or singular) interest.

Keywords:	Music, Art, Rhodes (Happy)
Audience:	Music Enthusiasts, Art Enthusiasts
Contact:	Jessica Dembski ecto-request@ns1.rutgers.edu
Details:	Free
User Info:	To subscribe to the list, send an e-mail message requesting a subscription to the URL address below.
	To send a message to the entire list, address it to: ecto-request@ns1.rutgers.edu

`mailto:ecto-request@ns1.rutgers.edu`

fogelberg ★

A discussion of the work of recording artist Dan Fogelberg.

Keywords:	Music, Musicians
Audience:	Dan Fogelberg Enthusiasts
Contact:	ai411@yfn.ysu.edu
Details:	Free
User Info:	To Subscribe to the list, send an e-mail message requesting a subscription to the URL address below.
	To send a message to the entire list, address it to: fogelberg@yfn.ysu.edu

`mailto:ai411@yfn.ysu.edu`

Folk music ★

This discussion list deals with the music of the recent wave of American singer/songwriters. List traffic includes tour schedules, reviews, album and release information.

Keywords:	Folk Music, Music
Audience:	Folk Musicians, Musicians, Folk Music Fans
Contact:	Alan Rowoth listserv@nysernet.org
Details:	Free
User Info:	To Subscribe to the list, send an e-mail message to the URL address below consisting of a single line reading:
	SUB folk_music YourFirstName YourLastName
	To send a message to the entire list, address it to: folk_music@nysernet.org

`mailto:listserv@nysernet.org`

freaks ★

This mailing list focuses on Marillion and related rock groups.

Keywords:	Music, Rock Music
Audience:	Marillion Enthusiasts
Details:	Free
User Info:	To Subscribe to the list, send an e-mail message requesting a subscription to the URL address below.
	To send a message to the entire list, address it to:freaks@bnf.com

`mailto:freaks-request@bnf.com`

fuzzy-ramblings ★

Discussion of the British girl-group "We've Got a Fuzzbox and We're Going to Use It!"

Keywords:	Music
Audience:	Musicians, Music Enthusiasts
Details:	Free
User Info:	To Subscribe to the list, send an e-mail message requesting a subscription to the URL address below.
	To send a message to the entire list, address it to: fuzzy-ramblings@piggy.ucsb.edu

`mailto:fuzzy-ramblings-request@piggy.ucsb.edu`

Impulse

This is the online site of Impulse Magazine, a monthly comprehensive journal of contemporary music news, reviews, information, and opinion.

Keywords:	Music (Contemporary)
Sponsor:	Impulse Magazine
Audience:	Musicians, Music Fans
Contact:	Bill Paige impulse@dsigroup.com
Details:	Free
User Info:	To Subscribe, send a message to the URL address below with the message: subscribe impulse

`mailto:impulse@dsigroup.com`

Leonardo Electronic Almanac

The Leonardo Electronic Almanac (LEA) is a monthly, edited journal and an electronic archive dedicated to providing current perspectives in the art, science and technology domains.

Keywords:	Art, Multimedia, Music, Electronic Media
Sponsor:	International Society for the Arts, Sciences, and Technology
Audience:	New Media Artists, Researchers, Developers, Art Educators, Art Professionals

Profile: LEA is an international, interdisciplinary forum for people interested in the use of new media in contemporary artistic expression, especially involving 20th century science and technology. Material is contributed by artists, scientists, philosophers and educators. LEA is published by the MIT Press for Leonardo, the International Society for the Arts, Sciences, and Technology (ISAST).

Contact: Craig Harris
craig@well.sf.ca.us

Details: Costs, Moderated, Images, Sounds, Multimedia

`mail to:journals-orders@mit.edu`

`ftp://mitpress.mit.edu/pub/Leonardo-Elec-Almanac`

Middle-eastern-music

Discussion of music from the Middle East.

Keywords: Middle Eastern Music, Music, Middle East

Audience: Music Enthusiasts, Musicians

Details: Free

User Info: To Subscribe to the list, send an e-mail message requesting a subscription to the URL address below.

`mailto:middle-eastern-music-request@nic.funet.fi`

MLoL

The MLoL (Musical List of Lists) is a list of music-related mailing lists available on the Internet.

Keywords: Music, Mailing Lists

Audience: Musicians, General Public

Details: Free

User Info: To Subscribe to the list, send an e-mail message requesting a subscription to the URL address below.

`mailto:mlol-request@wariat.org`

Music

This directory is a general compilation of information resources focused on music.

Keywords: Internet Resources, Music

Audience: Musicians, Music Enthusiasts

Details: Free

`ftp://una.hh.lib.umich.edu/70/inetdirsstacks/music:robinson`

mw-raves

One of several rave-related lists, MW-Raves (Midwest Raves) covers the Midwestern US. Postings are usually informational, but discussions of scene-related issues can also be expected.

Keywords: Raves, Music

Audience: Ravers

Contact: Andy Crosby
mw-raves-request@engin.umich.edu

Details: Free

User Info: To Subscribe to the list, send an e-mail message to the URL address below consisting of a single line reading:

SUB mw-raves YourFirstName YourLastName.

To send a message to the entire list, address it to: mw-raves@csd.uwm.edu

`mailto:mw-raves@csd.uwm.edu`

NetJam

NetJam provides a means for people to collaborate on musical compositions by sending Musical Instrument Digital Interface (MIDI) and other files to each other.

Keywords: Music, Musicians

Audience: Musicians

Contact: Craig Latta
netjam-request@xcf.berkeley.edu

Details: Free

User Info: To Subscribe to the list, send an e-mail message requesting a subscription to the URL address below.

`mailto:netjam-request@xcf.berkeley.edu`

Network-Audio-Bits

A bimonthly electronic magazine that features reviews and news of current music in rock, pop, new age, jazz, funk, folk, and other genres—including major-label and independent recording artists.

Keywords: Music Reviews, Music

Audience: Music Fans, General Public

Contact: Michael A. Murphy
murph@maine.bitnet

Details: Free

User Info: To Subscribe to the list, send an e-mail message requesting a subscription to the URL address below.

`mailto:murph@maine.bitnet`

NewMusNet

A place on the Arts Wire to discuss issues concerning composers, performers, and presenters of new music and to access information about new music.

Keywords: Music, New Music

Audience: Composers, Musicians, Performers

Contact: Pauline Oliveros
oliveros@tmn.com

`telnet://tmn.com`

On-u

This mailing list encourages discussions related to Adrian Sherwood's On-U Sound label and to the artists who record on it, including Tack>>Head, Gary Clail, The Dub Syndicate, African Head Charge, Bim Sherman and Mark Stewart.

Keywords: Music, Musicians

Audience: Musicians, Music Fans

Contact: Ben Golding
on-u-request@connect.com.au

Details: Free

User Info: To Subscribe to the list, send an e-mail message requesting a subscription to the URL address below.

To send a message to the entire list, address it to: on-u@connect.com.au

`mailto:on-u@connect.com.au`

Queen

A mailing list to discuss the rock group Queen.

Keywords: Music, Rock Music

Audience: Queen Fans, Music Fans, Musicians

Contact: Dan Blanchard
qms-request@uiuc.edu

Details: Free

User Info: To Subscribe to the list, send an e-mail message requesting a subscription to the URL address below.

To send a message to the entire list, address it to: qms@uiuc.edu

`mailto:qms-request@uiuc.edu`

rec.music.cd

A Usenet newsgroup providing information and discussion about Compact Discs.

Keywords: Music, Audio Electronics

Audience: Compact Disc Users

User Info: To Subscribe to this Usenet newsgroup, you need access to a newsreader.

`news:rec.music.cd`

rec.music.classical

A Usenet newsgroup providing information and discussion about classical music.

Keywords: Music

Audience: Classical Music Listeners

User Info: To Subscribe to this Usenet newsgroup, you need access to a newsreader.

`news:rec.music.classical`

rec.music.gdead

A Usenet newsgroup providing information and discussion about the Grateful Dead.

Keywords: Music, Popular Culture
Audience: Grateful Dead Listeners
User Info: To Subscribe to this Usenet newsgroup, you need access to a newsreader.

`news:rec.music.gdead`

rec.music.makers

A Usenet newsgroup providing information and discussion about music-making.

Keywords: Musical Instruments, Music
Audience: Performers, Music Listeners
User Info: To Subscribe to this Usenet newsgroup, you need access to a newsreader.

`news:rec.music.makers`

rec.music.makers.synth

A Usenet newsgroup providing information and discussion about synthesizers.

Keywords: Music, Audio Electronics
Audience: Synthesizer Users
User Info: To Subscribe to this Usenet newsgroup, you need access to a newsreader.

`news:rec.music.makers.synth`

Reggae Down Babylon

A collection of links to sources of information about reggae music on the World Wide Web and the Internet. Site includes reggae FAQs, and listings of reggae radio shows, lyrics, pictures, and news group archives.

Keywords: Reggae, Culture, Music
Sponsor: Reggae Down Babylon
Audience: Music Fans, Musicians, Reggae Enthusiasts
Contact: ReggaeMaster
damjohns@nyx10.cs.du.edu
Details: Free

`ftp://jammin.nosc.mil/pub/reggae`

Soundtracks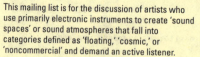

Discussions and reviews of new and older soundtracks (musical and technical aspects). Information about availability of specific soundtracks on different formats in different parts of the world.

Keywords: Music, Recordings
Audience: Audio Enthusiasts, Music Researchers
Contact: Michel Hafner
soundtracks-request@ifi.unizh.ch
User Info: To Subscribe to the list, send an e-mail message requesting a subscription to the URL address below.
To send a message to the entire list, address it to: soundtracks@ifi.unizh.ch

`mailto:soundtracks-request@ifi.unizh.ch`

Space-music

This mailing list is for the discussion of artists who use primarily electronic instruments to create 'sound spaces' or sound atmospheres that fall into categories defined as 'floating,' 'cosmic,' or 'noncommercial' and demand an active listener.

Keywords: Music, Electronic Music
Audience: Electronic Music Enthusiasts
Contact: Dave Datta
space-music-request@cs.uwp.edu
Details: Free
User Info: To Subscribe to the list, send an e-mail message requesting a subscription to the URL address below.
To send a message to the entire list, address it to: space-music@cs.uwp.edu

`mailto:space-music-request@cs.uwp.edu`

Stormcock

For general discussion and news concerning the music of Roy Harper, a folk-rock musician with a conscience. Recommendations and news concerning similar artists are encouraged.

Keywords: Rock Music, Music, Harper (Roy)
Audience: Music Fans
Contact: Paul Davison
stormcock-request@qmw.ac.uk
Details: Free
User Info: To Subscribe to the list, send an e-mail message to the address shown below consisting of a single line reading:
SUB stormcock YourFirstName YourLastName
To send a message to the entire list, address it to: stormcock@qmw.ac.uk

`mailto:listserv@qmw.ac.uk`

University of Northern Iowa Library

The library's holdings are large and wide-ranging and contain significant collections in many fields.

Keywords: Art, Business Information, Education, Music, Fiction
Audience: Researchers, Students, General Public
Contact: Mike Yohe
yohe@uni.edu
Details: Free
Expect: Login; Send: Public

`telnet://infosys.uni.edu`

University of Puget Sound Library

The library's holdings are large and wide-ranging and contain significant collections in many fields.

Keywords: Education, Literature (General), Music, Natural Science, Theology
Audience: Researchers, Students, General Public
Details: Free
Notes: Expect: Login; Send: Library

`telnet://192.124.98.2`

University of Texas at Austin Library

The library's holdings are large and wide-ranging and contain significant collections in many fields.

Keywords: Music, Natural Science, Nursing, Science Technology, Behavioral Science, Social Work, Computer Science, Engineering, Latin American Studies, Middle Eastern Studies
Audience: Researchers, Students, General Public
Details: Free
Notes: Expect: Blank Screen, Send: Return; Expect: Go, Send: Return; Expect: Enter Terminal Type, Send: vt100
Notes: Some databases are restricted to UT Austin users only.

`telnet://utcat.utexas.edu`

University of Wisconsin Green Bay Library

The library's holdings are large and wide-ranging and contain significant collections in many fields.

Keywords: Economics, Environmental Studies, Music, Natural Science
Audience: Researchers, Students, General Public
Details: Free
Notes: Expect: Service Name, Send: Victor

`telnet://gbls2k.uwgb.edu`

UWP Music Archive (named for the host machine's location: the University of Wisconsin-Parkside)

An extensive repository of files relating to a diverse array of music

genres: rock, folk, classical, and so on.

Keywords: Music, Lyrics, Graphics
Sponsor: University of Wisconsin-Parkside
Audience: Musicians, Music Enthusiasts, Musicologists

Profile:	This FTP archive contains a music database, artist discographies, essays about music and particular works, hundreds of image files (mostly .GIF and .JPEG format) of musicians—including album covers and posters, a lyrics archive and the ever-popular 'Beginner's Introduction to Classical Music.'
Contact:	Dave Datta datta@ftp.uwp.edu
User Info:	Select "Music Archives" from the gopher top-level menu.
Notes:	Also accessible through CMU's "English Server" gopher server. (q.v.)

`gopher://gopher.uwp.edu`

Virginia Commonwealth University Library

The library's holdings are large and wide-ranging and contain significant collections in many fields.

Keywords:	Art, Biology, Humanities, Journalism, Music, Urban Planning
Audience:	Researchers, Students, General Public
Details:	Free
Notes:	Expect: Login; Send: Opub

`telnet://vcuvm1.ucc.vcu.edu`

Music Research

Music

This directory is a general compilation of information resources focused on music.

Keywords:	Internet Resources, Music Research
Audience:	Musicians, Music Enthusiasts
Details:	Free

`ftp://una.hh.lib.umich.edu/70/inetdirsstacks/music:robinson`

Music-research

This list provides an effective, efficient means of bringing together musicologists, music analysts, computer scientists, and others working on applications of computers in music research.

Keywords:	Music Research, Music
Audience:	Music Researchers, Musicians, Musicologists
Details:	Free To subscribe to the list, send an e-mail message requesting subscription to the URL address below.

`mailto:music-research-request@prg.oxford.ac.uk`

Northwestern University Library

The library's holdings are large and wide-ranging and contain significant collections in many fields.

Keywords:	Africa, Wright (Frank Lloyd), Women's Studies, Art, Literature (American), Music Research, Government (US State), UN Documents, Music
Audience:	General Public, Researchers, Librarians, Document Delivery Professionals
Details:	Free Expect: COMMAND:, Send: DIAL VTAM

`telnet://nuacvm.acns.nwu.edu`

Music (Irish)

The University of Notre Dame Library

The library's holdings are large and wide-ranging and contain significant collections in many fields.

Keywords:	Music (Irish), Ireland, Botany (History of), Ecology, Entomology, Parasitology, Aquatic Biology, Universities (History of), Paleography
Audience:	General Public, Researchers, Librarians, Document Delivery Professionals
Details:	Free
Notes:	Expect: ENTER COMMAND OR HELP:, Send: library; To leave, type x on the command line and press the enter key. At the ENTER COMMAND OR HELP: prompt, type bye and press the enter key.

`telnet://irishmvs.cc.nd.edu`

Music Library Association Mailing List

Music Library Association Mailing List

This is a mail distribution service for the Music Library Association (MLA).

Keywords:	Music, Libraries, Bibliography
Sponsor:	Indiana University
Audience:	Music Librarians
Profile:	The services provided for the MLA include mail distribution, mail archiving, and file/document serving. This is a list server implementation, and the list managers intend that these services be used for various activities of the MLA that can benefit by wide-scale distribution, such as announcements of deadlines for NOTES and the MLA Newsletter, news items, general inquiries about MLA activities, and so on.
Contact:	Ralph Papkhian Papakhi@iubvm.ucs.Indiana.edu
Details:	Free
User Info:	To Subscribe to the list, send an e-mail message to the URL address below, consisting of a single line reading: SUB mla-u YourFirstName YourLastName

`mailto:listserv@iubvm.ucs.indiana.edu`

Music Notation

FINALE Discussion List

Discussion list targeted towards people who use the FINALE music notation program.

Keywords:	Music Notation, FINALE
Sponsor:	CODA
Audience:	FINALE Program Users
Profile:	The music notation program FINALE (for Macintosh and Windows) provides the basis for the chief discussion on this list. Other CODA products, as well as various notation programs, are also suitable topics.
Contact:	Henry Howey mus_heh@SHSU.edu
Details:	Free To send a message to the list, send an e-mail message to the URL address below, consisting of a single line reading: SUB finale YourFirstName YourLastName

`mail to:listserv@shsu.edu`

Music Resources

MBI, Music and the Brain Information Center Database (MuSICA)

The intent of this resource is to establish a comprehensive database of scientific research on music.

Keywords:	Music Resources, Human Behavior, Neurology
Sponsor:	Music and the Brain Information Center
Audience:	Researchers, Scientists
Profile:	MuSICA maintains a data base of scientific research (references and abstracts) on music as related to behavior, the brain and allied fields, in order to foster interdisciplinary knowledge. Topics include the auditory system; human and animal behavior; creativity; the neuropsychology of music and the human brain; the effects of music on behavior and physiology; music education, medicine, performance, and therapy; neurobiology; perception and psychophysics. Citations and abstracts are excerpted from the following

journals: The Bulletin of the Council for Research in Music Education, The Journal of Research in Music Education, Music Perception, Psychology of Music, Psychomusicology.
Contact: Norman Weinberger, Gordon Shaw mbic@mila.ps.uci.edu
Details: Free
Expect login: Send mbi Expect password: Send nammbi

`telnet://mila.ps.uci.edu`

University of California Santa Barbara Virtual Library

This source provides detailed lists of internet music resources.
Keywords: Music Resources
Sponsor: University of California at Santa Barbara
Audience: Musicians
Profile: This site contains lists pointing to music resources on the internet, including ftp sites, gopher servers, newsgroups, and list servers.
Details: Free
Path is The Subject Collections/The Arts Collections/Music

`gopher://ucsbuxa.ucsb.edu`

Music Reviews

Network-Audio-Bits ★

A bimonthly electronic magazine that features reviews and news of current music in rock, pop, new age, jazz, funk, folk, and other genres—including major-label and independent recording artists.
Keywords: Music Reviews, Music
Audience: Music Fans, General Public
Contact: Michael A. Murphy murph@maine.bitnet
Details: Free
User Info: To Subscribe to the list, send an e-mail message requesting a subscription to the URL address below.

`mailto:murph@maine.bitnet`

Music Software

Synth-l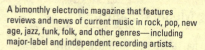

Synth-l is the electronic music "gearhead" list dedicated to the discussion of the less esoteric aspects of synthesis. Discussion concentrates on the availability and capabilities of music software and hardware, but sometimes diverges to other subjects.

Keywords: Electronic Music, Music Software
Audience: Electronic Music Enthusiasts, Musicians, Software Designers
Contact: Joe McMahon Synth-L@american.edu
Details: Free
User Info: To Subscribe to the list, send an e-mail message to the address shown below consisting of a single line reading:
SUB Synth-L YourFirstName YourLastName
To send a message to the entire list, address it to: Synth-L@american.edu

`mailto:listserv@american.edu`

Musical Genres

alt.music.progressive ★

A Usenet newsgroup providing information and discussion about progressive music, including the groups Marillion, Asia, King Crimson, and many others.
Keywords: Musical Genres, Pop Culture
Audience: Progressive Music Listeners
User Info: To Subscribe to this Usenet newsgroup, you need access to a newsreader.

`news:alt.music.progressive`

alt.rap ★

A Usenet newsgroup providing information and discussion for fans of rap music, including talk about rap performers, new albums, concerts and other aspects of rap.
Keywords: Musical Genres
Audience: Rap Listeners, Rappers
User Info: To Subscribe to this Usenet newsgroup, you need access to a newsreader.

`news:alt.rap`

alt.rock-n-roll ★

A Usenet newsgroup providing information and general discussion about Rock & Roll.
Keywords: Musical Genres
Audience: Music Listeners
User Info: To Subscribe to this Usenet newsgroup, you need access to a newsreader.

`news:alt.rock-n-roll`

alt.rock-n-roll.metal ★

A Usenet newsgroup providing information and discussion about heavy metal music.
Keywords: Musical Genres

Audience: Heavy Metal Listeners
User Info: To Subscribe to this Usenet newsgroup, you need access to a newsreader.

`news:alt.rock-n-roll.metal`

Funky Music ★★

This mailing list covers funk and funk-influenced music, including hip-hop, house party, soul, and rhythm and blues.
Keywords: Musical Genres, Funk Music
Audience: Musicians, Funk Music Enthusiasts
Details: Free
User Info: To Subscribe to the list, send an e-mail message requesting a subscription to the URL address below.
To send a message to the entire list, address it to: funky-music@mit.edu

`mailto:funky-music-request@mit.edu`

rec.music.folk ★

A Usenet newsgroup providing information and discussion about folk music.
Keywords: Musical Genres
Audience: Folk Music Listeners
User Info: To Subscribe to this Usenet newsgroup, you need access to a newsreader.

`news:rec.music.folk`

Musical Groups

Direct ★★

Discussion of the work of the musical artist Vangelis.
Keywords: New Age Music, Musical Groups
Audience: Musicians, Music Enthusiasts, Vangelis Fans
Contact: Keith Gregoire direct-request@celtech.com
User Info: To Subscribe to the list, send an e-mail message requesting a subscription to the URL address below.
To send a message to the entire list, address it to: direct@celtech.com
Both bounce and daily digest modes are available; specify your preference when subscribing.

`mailto:direct-request@celtech.com`

Journey-L ★★

Information and discussion of the rock band Journey and any of the band members' outside projects.
Keywords: Musical Groups, Rock & Roll
Audience: Rock Music Fans

Contact:	Hunter Goatley or Britt Pierce journey-l@wkuvx1.wku.edu
User Info:	To Subscribe to the list, send an e-mail message to the URL address below, with the body text subscribe journey-l.
	To Subscribe to the digest version, send the message to : journey-l-digest-request@wkuvx1.wku.edu

`mailto:journey-l-request@wkuvx1.wku.edu`

Prince

A mailing list devoted to discussing the musician formerly named Prince and related artists.

Keywords:	Prince, Musical Groups
Audience:	Musicians, Music Students, Music Fans
Contact:	prince-request@icpsr.umich.edu
Details:	Free
User Info:	To Subscribe to the list, send an e-mail message requesting a subscription to the URL address below.
	To send a message to the entire list, address it to: prince-request@icpsr.umich.edu

`mailto:prince@icpsr.umich.edu`

rec.music.beatles

A Usenet newsgroup providing information and discussion about the Beatles.

Keywords:	Musical Groups, Popular Culture
Audience:	Beatles Listeners
User Info:	To Subscribe to this Usenet newsgroup, you need access to a newsreader.

`news:rec.music.beatles`

rec.music.phish

A Usenet newsgroup providing information and discussion about the band Phish.

Keywords:	Musical Groups, Popular Culture
Audience:	Phish Listeners
User Info:	To Subscribe to this Usenet newsgroup, you need access to a newsreader.

`news:rec.music.phish`

The Beastie Boys' Web Page

This web site features video, audio, magazine articles, lyrics, a discography, and other assorted information relating to the Beastie Boys.

Keywords:	Musical Groups, Rap Music
Audience:	Beastie Boys Fans
Contact:	irogers@ezmail.ucs.indiana.edu

`http://www.nando.net/music/gm`

The Ultimate Gopher for Rush Fans

A collection of lyrics, articles, press releases, concert updates, newsletters, and reviews concerning the musical group Rush.

Keywords:	Musical Groups, Rush, Rock & Roll
Sponsor:	syrinx.umd.edu
Audience:	Rock Music Enthusiasts, Rush Enthusiasts
Contact:	jlang.syrinx.umd.edu

`gopher://syrinx.umd.edu`

Musical Instruments

alt.guitar

A Usenet newsgroup providing information and discussion about guitar playing.

Keywords:	Guitar, Musical Instruments
Audience:	Guitarists
User Info:	To Subscribe to this Usenet newsgroup, you need access to a newsreader.

`news:alt.guitar`

Alternate Tuning Mailing List

This mailing list is intended for exchanging ideas relevant to alternate tunings.

Keywords:	Musical Instruments, MIDI
Sponsor:	Mills College
Audience:	Musicians
Profile:	This list deals with just intonation, paratactical tunings, experimental music instrument design, non-standard equal temperaments, MIDI tuning system exclusive specifications, concert postings, non-Western tunings, and the experimental tunings of such people as Harry Partch, Lou Harrison, Martin Bartlett, James Tenney and others.
Contact:	Greg Higgs Higgs@Mills.edu
Details:	Free
User Info:	To Subscribe to the list, send an e-mail message to the URL address below, consisting of a single line reading:
	SUB tuning YourFirstName YourLastName

`listproc@varese.mills.edu`

rec.music.makers

A Usenet newsgroup providing information and discussion about music-making.

Keywords:	Musical Instruments, Music
Audience:	Performers, Music Listeners
User Info:	To Subscribe to this Usenet newsgroup, you need access to a newsreader.

`news:rec.music.makers`

rec.music.makers.guitar

A Usenet newsgroup providing information and discussion about guitars and guitar playing.

Keywords:	Musical Instruments
Audience:	Guitar Listeners, Guitar Players
User Info:	To Subscribe to this Usenet newsgroup, you need access to a newsreader.

`news:rec.music.makers.guitar`

Musicals

Musicals

This forum is intended for the general discussion of musical theater, in all forms, but related non-musical theater topics are welcome, too.

Keywords:	Musicals, Theater
Audience:	Music, Theater Enthusiasts
Details:	Free
User Info:	To Subscribe to the list, send an e-mail message requesting a subscription to the URL address below.

`mailto:musicals-request@world.std.com`

Musicians

Ethnomusicology Research Digest

For subscribers with a professional interest in ethnomusicology, including news, discussion, queries, bibliographies, and archives. Subscription by permission only.

Keywords:	Musicians, Ethnomusicology, Music Research
Audience:	Ethnomusicologists, Educators, Librarians, Researchers, Students
Contact:	Karl Signell signell@umdd.umd.edu
Details:	Free
User Info:	To Subscribe, send an e-mail message to the address below consisting of a single line reading:
	SUB ethmus-l YourFirstName YourLastName
	To send a message to the entire list, address it to: ethmus-l@umdd.vmd.edu

`mailto:listserv@umdd.umd.edu`

NetJam

NetJam provides a means for people to collaborate on musical compositions by sending Musical Instrument Digital Interface (MIDI) and other files to each other.

Keywords: Music, Musicians
Audience: Musicians
Contact: Craig Latta
netjam-request@xcf.berkeley.edu
Details: Free
User Info: To Subscribe to the list, send an e-mail message requesting a subscription to the URL address below.

mailto:netjam-request@xcf.berkeley.edu

On-u

This mailing list encourages discussions related to Adrian Sherwood's On-U Sound label and to the artists who record on it, including Tack>>Head, Gary Clail, The Dub Syndicate, African Head Charge, Bim Sherman and Mark Stewart.

Keywords: Music, Musicians
Audience: Musicians, Music Fans
Contact: Ben Golding
on-u-request@connect.com.au
Details: Free
User Info: To Subscribe to the list, send an e-mail message requesting a subscription to the URL address below.
To send a message to the entire list, address it to: on-u@connect.com.au

mailto:on-u@connect.com.au

MSA-Net

A mailing list intended to meet the communication needs of Muslim Student Associations (MSA) in North America, and to discuss issues related to Islam and MSAs are discussed.

Keywords: Islam, Muslim Student Associations
Audience: Muslims
Contact: Aalim Fevens
msa-request@htm3.ee.queensu.ca
User Info: To Subscribe to the list, send an e-mail message
Notes: Members must be Muslim.

mailto:msa-request@htm3.ee.queensu.ca

Mustangs

Mustangs

A forum for the discussion of technical issues, problems, solutions, and modifications relating to late-model (1980 and later) Ford Mustangs.

Keywords: Automobiles
Audience: Automobile Owners
Details: Free
User Info: To Subscribe to the list, send an e-mail message requesting a subscription to the URL address below.

mailto:mustangs-request@cup.hp.com

mw-raves

mw-raves

One of several rave-related lists, MW-Raves (Midwest Raves) covers the Midwestern US. Postings are usually informational, but discussions of scene-related issues can also be expected.

Keywords: Raves, Music
Audience: Ravers
Contact: Andy Crosby
mw-raves-request@engin.umich.edu
Details: Free
User Info: To Subscribe to the list, send an e-mail message to the URL address below consisting of a single line reading:
SUB mw-raves YourFirstName YourLastName.
To send a message to the entire list, address it to: mw-raves@csd.uwm.edu

mailto:mw-raves@csd.uwm.edu

Mutual Funds

NETworth (The Internet Resource for Individual Investors)

This is an interactive WWW site, providing information about mutual fund performance, prospecti, and promotional information.

Keywords: Mutual Funds, Investments, Finance
Sponsor: Galt Technologies, Inc.
Audience: Investors
Profile: This WWW site provides registered users free quotes on over 4500 mutual funds; also available is the Morningstar Analysis, financial newsletters, educational forums, financial databases, mutual fund industry news, press releases, and a clipping service.
Contact: Email: admin@atlas.galt.com
Details: Free, I
Notes: For additional information, you can call NETworth at (800)420-GALT

http://networth.galt.com/www/home/start.html

Mycoplasma

vetmycop

Veterinary mycoplasma discussion group.

Keywords: Veterinary Medicine, Mycoplasma
Audience: Veterinarians
Contact: James T. Case, Bill Cohen
jcase@ucdcvdls.bitnet or
bcohen@ucdcvdls.bitnet
Details: Free
User Info: To Subscribe to the list, send an e-mail message to the URL address below consisting of a single line reading:
SUB vetmycop YourFirstName YourLastName
To send a message to the entire list, address it to: vetmycop@ucdavis.edu

mailto:listserv@ucdavis.edu

Mystery

Mystery

This mailing list reviews and discusses mystery and detective fiction, including works on film, television, and radio.

Keywords: Mystery Fiction, Detective Fiction, Books
Audience: Mystery Enthusiasts
Details: Free
User Info: To Subscribe to the list, send an e-mail message requesting a subscription to the URL address below.

mailto:mystery-request@introl.com

Mythology

The Curiosity Club

This web site offers both an astrophysics exploration and a playspace for young scientists

Keywords: Astronomy, Mythology, Children
Sponsor: Center for Extreme Ultraviolet Astrophysics, Berkeley, California, and The San Francisco Unified School District, San Francisco, California
Audience: Educators, Students, Astronomers,
Contact: Kasey Rios Asberry
jasberry@sfsuvax1.sfsu.edu
Details: Free

http://nisus.sfusd.k12.ca.us/curiosity_club/bridge1.html

NA-net

NA-net

This mailing list is a forum for discussions on the subject of numerical analysis.

Keywords: Numerical Analysis

Audience: Numerical Analysts

User Info: To subscribe to the list, send an e-mail message requesting a subscription to the URL address below.

mailto:na.join@na-net.ornl.gov

NAARS (National Automated Accounting Research System)

NAARS (National Automated Accounting Research System)

The National Automated Accounting Research System (NAARS) library, provided as a service by agreement with the American Institute of Certified Public Accountants (AICPA) contains a variety of accounting information.

Keywords: Accounting, Auditing, Filings, Publishing

Audience: Accountants

Profile: The NAARS library contains annual reports of public corporations and accounting literature and publications for the accounting professional. Annual reports are annotated with descriptive terms assigned by the AICPA. These terms allow the user to search for annual report footnotes that illustrate one or more recognized accounting practices.

Contact: Mead New Sales Group at (800) 227-4908 or (513) 859-5398 inside the US, or (513) 865-7981 for all inquiries outside the US.

User Info: To subscribe, contact Mead directly.

To examine the Nexis user guide, you can access it at the ftp site of the University of Texas at Austin at the URL address: ftp://ftp.cc.utexas.edu

The files are in: /pub/ref-services/LEXIS

telnet://nex.meaddata.com

http://www.meaddata.com

NAFTA

North American Free Trade Agreement (NAFTA)

The agreement between the governments of Canada, the United Mexican States, and the United States of America to establish a free trade area in North America.

Keywords: Trade, US, Mexico, Canada, Free Trade, NAFTA

Audience: Journalists, Politicians, Economists, Students

Details: Free

gopher://wiretap.spies.com/00/gov/nafta

NAME (National Association for Mediation in Education) Publications and Resources List

NAME (National Association for Mediation in Education) Publications and Resources List

This is a tax-exempt clearinghouse of information promoting conflict resolution, mediation, and violence prevention in schools. NAME also publishes a newsletter and has a directory of over 120 resources, including guidelines for conflict resolution, and technical assistance.

Keywords: Conflict Resolution, Mediation, Education (K-12)

Sponsor: National Association for Mediation in Education, University of Massachusetts, Amherst, Massachusetts, USA

Audience: Counselors, Educators, Administrators, Parents

Contact: Clarinda Merripen ConflictNet@agc.ipc.org

Notes: Request introductory packet from address below.

mailto:conflictnet@agc.ipc.org

naplps-list

naplps-list

This is a mailing list for people interested in NAPLPS graphics.

Keywords: Computer Graphics, Art

Audience: Graphic Artists

Contact: Dave Hughes
oldcolo@goldmill.uucp
naplps-list@oldcolo.com

Napolean

McGill University, Montreal Canada, INFOMcGILL Library ★

The library's holdings are large and wide-ranging and contain significant collections in many fields.

- Keywords: Architecture, Entomology, Biology, Science (History of), Medicine (History of), Napolean, Shakespeare (William)
- Audience: Researchers, Students, General Public
- Contact: Roy Miller
  ccrmmus@mcgillm (Bitnet)
  ccrmmus@musicm.mcgill.ca (Internet)
- User Info: Expect: VM logo; Send: Enter; Expect: prompt; Send: PF3 or type INFO

`telnet://vm1.mcgill.ca`

NASA

Center for Extreme Ultraviolet Astrophysics ★★★

A department of the University of California at Berkeley devoted to research in extreme ultraviolet astronomy. It is the ground-based institution of EUVE (the Extreme Ultraviolet Explorer), a NASA satellite launched in 1992.

- Keywords: Astronomy, Astrophysics, EUVE, NASA, Satellite
- Sponsor: NASA and University of California at Berkeley
- Audience: Astronomers, Astrophysicists
- Profile: Provides access to details about the EUVE Guest Observer (EGO) Center, the EUVE Public Archive of Mission Data and Information, satellite operation information, and so on. The EUVE Guest Observer Center provides information, software, and data to EUVE Guest Observers.
- Contact: egoinfo@cea.berkeley.edu
  archive@cea.berkeley.edu
- Details: Free

`http://cea-ftp.cea.berkeley.edu`

Cosmic Update ★★★

Internet notice identifying new computer software from the National Aeronautics and Space Administration (NASA) made available for international use.

- Keywords: NASA, Software, Space
- Audience: Space Scientists, Astronomers
- Profile: COSLINE is a 24-hour electronic information service to COSMIC's customers. The principal feature of COSLINE is the catalog Search facility. A separate help file is available for browsing from the Search main menu option.
- Contact: Pat Mortenson
  service@cossack.cosmic.uga.edu
- Details: Free
- User Info: To subscribe, send an e-mail message requesting a subscription to the URL address below.

`mailto:service@cossack.cosmic.uga.edu`

Library of Congress, Astronomy, Astrophysics, and Physics Resources ★★★★

Pointers to important remote databases relating to astronomy and physics.

- Keywords: Astronomy, Astrophysics, NASA
- Sponsor: Library of Congress, Washington, DC
- Audience: Astronomers, Educators (Post-Secondary), Physicists, Students
- Profile: The Library of Congress has pointers to many important remote databases including Astronomy, Astrophysics, and Physics Journals, the Aerospace Directory from Rice University, The American Astronomical Society, The Astronomical Internet Resources Directory, The Cold Fusion Bibliography, The Electromagnetic Wave Research Institute of NRC (Florence, Italy), LANL Physics Information, The Lunar/ Planetary Institute Database of Geology, Geophysics, and Astronomy, The NASA Extragalactic Database, The NASA Network Applications and Information Center (NAIC), The National Institute of Standards and Technology (NIST), The Physics Resource Directory from University of California, Irvine, and The Space Telescope Electronic Information System (STEIS).
- Contact: lcmarvel@seq1.loc.gov
- Details: Costs
- User info: Can be accessible via telnet:// marvel.loc.gov (login: marvel).

`gopher://marvel.loc.gov/11/global/sci/astro`

NASA Ames SPACE Archive ★

This archive contains information about NASA projects. It also has an online CD-ROM jukebox with a rotating selection of NASA mission CD-ROMs.

- Keywords: NASA, Space
- Sponsor: NASA Ames Research Center
- Audience: General Public, Scientists, Technical Writers, Science Teachers
- Profile: This site has access to general space information, including the texts of the press release kits for the space shuttle missions and other NASA press releases. There are also weather images from satellites and other sources in the / pub/weather directory. The /pub/cdrom directory contains information about which NASA mission CD-ROMs are currently mounted.
- Contact: Peter Yee
  yee@atlas.arc.nasa.gov
- User Info: Expect: login, Send: anonymous; Expect: password, Send: your Internet address

`ftp://explorer.arc.nasa.gov`

NASA/IPAC Extragalactic Database (NED) ★★★

Contains positions, basic data, and over 500,000 names for 250,000 extragalactic objects, as well as some 450,000 bibliographic references to 21,000 published papers, and 25,000 notes from catalogs and other publications.

- Keywords: Astronomy, Databases
- Sponsor: Jet Propulsory Lab/ Infrared Processing and Analysis Center
- Audience: Astronomers, Scientists
- Profile: Uses a VT100 or X-based interface.
- Contact: G. Helou, B. Madore, M. Schmitz
  ned@ipac.caltech.edu
- Details: Free
- User Info: Telnet to URL address below; Expect: login; Send: ned
- Notes: sshare@cscns.com
  service@cscns.com

`telnet://ned@ned.ipac.caltech.edu`

`ftp://ned.ipac.caltech.edu/pub/ned`

NSSDC (National Space Science Data Center)'s Online Data & Information Service ★★★

The NSSDC (National Space Science Data Center) is the NASA facility charged with archiving the data from all of NASA's science missions.

- Keywords: Space, Astrophysics, Software, NASA, Science
- Sponsor: NASA
- Audience: Scientists, Space Scientists, Astronomers, Engineers
- Profile: This resource contains information about NASA's missions and analysis of their data.
- Details: Free
- User Info: Expect: Login, Send: nssdc
  See the menu entries in your particular area of interest.

`telnet://nssdc.gsfc.nasa.gov`

Sci.astro.hubble

Information about all subjects concerning NASA's Hubble space telescope.

Keywords:	Hubble Telescope, Astronomy, Space, NASA, Stargazing, Telescopes
Audience:	Astronomers, General Public, Science Teachers, Stargazers
Contact:	Paul A. Scowen scowen@wfpc3.la.asu.edu
Details:	Free, Moderated, Images
User Info:	To subscribe to this Usenet newsgroup, you need access to a newsreader.

`news:sci.astro.hubble`

Spacelink

This contains information about NASA and its activities, including a large number of curricular activities for elementary and secondary science classes.

Keywords:	NASA, Aeronautics, Education (K-12)
Audience:	Students (K-12), Educators, General Public
Details:	Free

`telnet://newuser@spacelink.msfc.nasa.gov`

The University of Iowa Libraries

The library's holdings are large and wide-ranging and contain significant collections in many fields.

Keywords:	Hunt (Leigh), Native American Studies, Typography, Railroads, Cartoons, French Revolution, NASA, Hydraulics
Audience:	General Public, Researchers, Librarians, Document Delivery Professionals
Details:	Free Send <RETURN> to display a menu of available systems. Type 1 for OASIS access and press <RETURN> to display the Welcome to OASIS screen.

`telnet://oasis.uiowa.edu`

National Broadcasting Society—Alpha Epsilon Rho

National Broadcasting Society—Alpha Epsilon Rho

Forum for mass media professionals to share experiences and ideas.

Keywords:	Film, Television, Radio, Mass Media
Sponsor:	National Broadcasting Society-Alpha Epsilon Rho
Audience:	Journalists, Students, Educators, Broadcasting Professionals
Contact:	Reg Gamar regbc@cunyvm.bitnet
Details:	Free
User Info:	To subscribe to the list, send an e-mail message to the address shown below consisting of a single line reading: SUB NBS-AER YourFirstName YourLastName To send a message to the entire list, address it to: nbs-aer@cunyvm.bitnet

`mailto:listserv@cunyvm.bitnet`

National Cancer Center, Tokyo, Japan

National Cancer Center, Tokyo, Japan

This is the information service for the National Cancer Center in Tokyo, Japan, as well as the entry point for the Japanese Cancer Research Resources Bank (JCRB).

Keywords:	Cancer, Japan
Audience:	Biologists, Medical Researchers
Contact:	ncc-gopher-news@gan.ncc.go.jp
Details:	Free

`gopher://ncc.go.jp`

National Centre for Software Technology

National Centre for Software Technology

The National Centre for Software Technology (NCST) is an autonomous R&D unit in Bombay and Bangalore. Specialty areas of research include graphics, CAD, real time systems, knowledge-based systems, and software engineering.

Keywords:	Computer Science, Engineering, Computer-Aided Design
Sponsor:	National Centre for Software Technology, Bombay, India
Audience:	Reseachers, Computer Scientists, Engineers, Students
Contact:	Postmaster postmaster@saathi.ncst.ernet.in

`gopher://shakti.ncst.ernet.in`

National Collegiate Athletic Association

Pac-10-Sports

This mailing list is dedicated to discussing sports of all types that are played competitively within the Pac-10 Athletic Conference.

Keywords:	Pac-10 Sports, National Collegiate Athletic Association, Sports
Audience:	Pac-10 Sports Fans
Contact:	Cliff Slaughterbeck crs@u.washington.edu
Details:	Free
User Info:	To subscribe to the list, send an e-mail message requesting a subscription to the URL address below. To send a message to the entire list, address it to: crs@u.washington.edu

`mailto:crs@u.washington.edu`

National Export Strategy

National Export Strategy

This site provides the complete text of a report presented to Congress by the Trade Promotion Coordinating Committee, describing ways to develop U.S. export promotion efforts.

Keywords:	Commerce, Foreign Trade, Exports, Business
Sponsor:	United States Government, Trade Promotion Coordinating Committee
Audience:	Exporters, Business Professionals, Trade Specialists
Details:	Free

`ftp://sunny.stat-usa.gov`

`http://sunny.stat-usa.gov`

National Family Database—MAPP

National Family Database—MAPP

This database contains family sociological and health data, including research briefs, bibliographies, census data, program ideas, reference materials, media materials, and publications.

Keywords:	Sociology, Family, Health
Sponsor:	Department of Agriculture Economics and Rural Sociology, Pennsylvania State University

Audience:	Sociologists, Public Health Officials, Health Care Providers	
User Info:	To access the database select PENpages (1), then General Information (3) and finally Information on MAPP - National Family Database (5)	

`telnet://penpages@psupen.psu.edu`

National Hockey League (NHL)

Blues (St. Louis Blues)

Provides information, game reports, stats, discussion, and so on, on the St. Louis Blues of the National Hockey League.

Keywords:	Hockey, Sports, National Hockey League (NHL)
Audience:	Hockey Enthusiasts
Contact:	Joe Ashkar blues@medicine.wustl.edu
User Info:	To subscribe to the list, send an e-mail message requesting a subscription to the URL address below. To send a message to the entire list, address it to: blues@medicine.wustl.edu

`mailto:blues@medicine.wustl.edu`

Boston Bruins

This list is for discussion of the Boston Bruins of the National Hockey League and their farm teams. Also available as a digest.

Keywords:	Boston Bruins, Hockey (Ice), National Hockey League (NHL)
Audience:	Hockey Enthusiasts, Boston Residents, Sports Enthusiasts
Contact:	Garry Knox bruins-request@cristal.umd.edu
Details:	Free
User Info:	To subscribe to the list, send an e-mail message requesting a subscription to the URL address below. To send a message to the entire list, address it to: bruins@cristal.umd.edu

`mailto:bruins-request@cristal.umd.edu`

NHL Goalie Stats

Keywords:	Hockey, National Hockey League (NHL), Sports Statistics
Audience:	Hockey Enthusiasts
Profile:	Weekday reports of goalie statistics from the National Hockey League.
Contact:	dfa@triple-i.com
Details:	Free

User Info:	To subscribe to the list, send an e-mail message requesting a subscription to the URL address below. To send a message to the entire list, address it to: dfa@triple-i.com

`mailto:dfa@triple-i.com`

National Institute for Allergy & Infectious Disease (NIAID)

National Institute for Allergy & Infectious Disease (NIAID)

This is a resource into other databases for searching many medical fields, such as the NIAID network user list or a databank of AIDS-related information.

Keywords:	Medicine, Infectious Diseases, Allergies
Sponsor:	NIAID
Audience:	Health Care Professionals, Researchers, Students
Contact:	Brent Sessions sessions@odie.niaid.nih.gov
Details:	Free

`gopher://gopher.niaid.nih.gov/1`

National Institute of Health Library Online Catalog

National Institute of Health Library Online Catalog

This entry point provides access to the books and journal holdings in the NIH Library. Journal articles are not included.

Keywords:	NIH, Medicine, Science, Libraries
Sponsor:	National Institute of Health (NIH)
Audience:	Scientists, Researchers, Educators, Health Care Professionals
Details:	Free

`telnet://nih-library.ncrr.nih.gov`

National Institutes of Health Gopher

National Institutes of Health Gopher

Provides access to a broad range of National Institutes of Health (NIH) resources (library catalogues, databases) via the Internet.

Keywords:	Health, AIDS, Molecular Biology, Grants
Sponsor:	National Institutes of Health
Audience:	Health Care Professionals, Molecular Biologists, Researchers
Profile:	This gopher provides access to NIH resources, including institute phone books and calendars, library catalogs, molecular biology databases, the full text of the NIH Guide for Grants and Contracts, files containing AIDS and cancer information and more.
Contact:	gopher@gopher.nih.gov
Details:	Free
User Info:	Expect: Login; Enter: Gopher

`telnet://gopher.nih.gov`

`gopher://gopher.nih.gov`

`gopher://odie.niaid.nih.gov`

National Library of Medicine Gopher

National Library of Medicine Gopher

This gopher provides information about the National Library of Medicine, the world's largest single-topic library.

Keywords:	Medicine, Health, World Health
Sponsor:	National Library of Medicine, Massachusetts World Health Organization, Geneva, Switzerland
Audience:	Health Care Professionals, Medical Professionals, Researchers
Profile:	The National Library of Medicine (NLM) cares for over 4.5 million holdings (inncluding books, journals, reports, manuscripts, and audio-visual items). The NLM offers extensive online information services dealing with clinical care, toxicology, environmental health, and basic biomedical research, It has several active research and development components, including an extramural grants program, houses an extensive history of medicine collection, and provides several programs designed to improve the nation's medical library system.
Contact:	R. P. C. Rodgers rodgers@nlm.nih.gov akazawa@who.ch
Details:	Free

`gopher://el-gopher.med.utah.edu`

`gopher://gopher.who.ch`

Native American Studies   497

National Oceanic & Atmospheric Administration (NOAA)

National Oceanic & Atmospheric Administration (NOAA)

The NOAA catalog provides keyword access to sources of environmental information in the US. Gopher for resources pertaining to health and environmental safety.

Keywords: Environment, Oceans, Atmospheric Science, Health, Environmental Safety
Sponsor: National Oceanic & Atmospheric Administration (NOAA), Department of Energy (USA)
Audience: Researchers, Environmentalists, Epidemiologists, Public Health Officials
Details: Free

gopher://scilibx.ucsc.edu

gopher://gopher.ns.doc.gov

National Performance Review (NPR)

National Performance Review (NPR)

The Report of the National Performance Review, from the task force led by Vice President Gore, titled 'From Red Tape to Results: Creating a Government that Works Better and Costs Less,' Sept. 7, 1993.

Keywords: President, US Politics, White House
Audience: Political Scientists, General Public
Profile: On March 3, 1993, President Clinton asked Vice President Gore to lead the effort to effect real change in the federal government. Gore's NPR Task Force overview and accompanying reports make specific recommendations for: reducing costs and waste, changing the way government operates, and making government more responsive and effective.
Details: Free

gopher://cyfer.esusda.gov/11/ace/policy/npr/nat

National Science Foundation Center for Biological Timing

National Science Foundation Center for Biological Timing

This gopher accesses investigative research pertaining to various aspects of biological timing. The goal of this gopher is to make the museum's collections information available over the Internet. This server contains names of virus families/groups and members now available online from the Australian National University's Bio-Informatics Facility.

Keywords: Biology, Vertebrates
Sponsor: Reasearch School of Biological Research, Australian National University, Canberra, Australia
Audience: Biologists, Educators, Researchers
Profile: The center combines the efforts of several universities pertaining to research in biological timing. This includes Vistudies, the internal timing mechanisms that control cycles of sleep and waking, hormone pulsatility, neural excitability, and reproductive rhythmicity. Investigators are involved with research from behavior testing to molecular genetics.

The center also supports educational and outreach programs to industry, universities and high schools. The center also hosts an annual scientific symposium and a number of mini-symposia.

Details: Free

gopher://gopher.virginia.edu/11/pubs/biotimin

National Technology Transfer Center (NTTC)

National Technology Transfer Center (NTTC)

A federally-funded national network to apply government research to commercial applications.

Keywords: Technology, Research and Development, Business, Industry, Department of Defense, Government (US)
Sponsor: National Technology Transfer Center
Audience: Business Professionals, Entrepreneurs, Manufacturesr, Technology Professionals
Profile: Features state-by-state listings of agencies designed to facilitate the adaptation of new technologies to industry. Also provides updates on conferences, and a current list of Department of Defense projects soliciting private assistance from small businesses. Allows limited access to NTTC databases.
Contact: Charles Monfradi
cmonfra@nttc.edu, info@nttc.edu

gopher://iron.nttc.edu

http://iridium.nttc.edu/nttc.hmtl

Native American Affairs

University of New Mexico Unminfo Library

The library's holdings are large and wide-ranging and contain significant collections in many fields.

Keywords: Photography (History of), Architecture, Native American Affairs, Land Records
Audience: Researchers, Students, General Public
Contact: Art St. George
stgeorge@unmb.bitnet
Details: Free
User Info: Expect: Login; Send: Unminfo

telnet://unminfo.unm.edu

University of Tennessee at Knoxville Library

The library's holdings are large and wide-ranging and contain significant collections in many fields.

Keywords: Native American Affairs, Congress (US), Folklore, Travel (History of)
Audience: Researchers, Students, General Public
Details: Free
User Info: Expect: OK Prompt; Send: Login pub1; Expect: Password, Send: Usc

telnet://opac.lib.utk.edu

Native American Studies

The University of Iowa Libraries

The library's holdings are large and wide-ranging and contain significant collections in many fields.

Keywords: Hunt (Leigh), Native American Studies, Typography, Railroads, Cartoons, French Revolution, NASA, Hydraulics
Audience: General Public, Researchers, Librarians, Document Delivery Professionals

Details: Free
Send <RETURN> to display a menu of available systems. Type 1 for OASIS access and press <RETURN> to display the Welcome to OASIS screen.

`telnet://oasis.uiowa.edu`

The University of Minnesota Library System (LUMINA)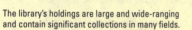

The library's holdings are large and wide-ranging and contain significant collections in many fields.

Keywords: Immigration (History of), Ethnic Studies, Horticulture, Equine Research, Botanical Taxonomy, Quantum Physics, Native American Studies, Holmes (Sherlock)

Audience: General Public, Researchers, Librarians, Document Delivery Professionals

Contact: Craig D. Rice
cdr@acc.stolaf.edu

Details: Free

`telnet://lumina.lib.umn.edu`

NativeNet

NativeNet ★

Provides information about and discusses issues relating to indigenous people around the world, including threats to their cultures and habitats (e.g. rainforests).

Keywords: Indigenous People, Environment, Anthroplogy

Audience: Anthropologists, Environmentalists, Indigenous People

Contact: Gary S. Trujillo
gst@gnosys.svle.ma.us

Details: Free

User Info: To subscribe to the list, send an e-mail message requesting a subscription to the URL address below.

`mailto:gst@gnosys.svle.ma.us`

NATO

NATO ★

Online version of The NATO Handbook, which recommends changes for the future of the North Atlantic Treaty Organization in light of decreasing defense resources.

Keywords: NATO, Guidelines, Defense

Sponsor: The NATO Office of Information and Press

Audience: Government Officials, Military Personnel, Historians

Details: Free
Select from menu as appropriate.

`gopher://wiretap.spies.com`

Natural History

Smithsonian Institution Natural History Gopher

The Smithsonian Natural History Gopher Server provides access to data associated with the Institutions museum collections (natural history and anthropology).

Keywords: Smithsonian, Natural History, Anthropology

Sponsor: Museum of Natural History, Smithsonian Institution, Washington, DC.

Audience: Anthropologists, Biologists, Natural History Scientists, Researchers

Profile: With over 120 million collections and 135 professional scientists, the National Museum of Natural History is one of the worlds largest museums devoted to natural history and anthropology. This server provides access to data associated with the collections, and to information and tools for the study of the natural world. The Department of Vertebrate Zoology includes checklists of known species names. Currently the Mammal Species of the World have been posted. Plans to expand this to include Amphibians, Fishes, and so on, are under way.

Contact: Don Gourley
don@smithson.si.edu

Details: Free

`gopher://nmnhgoph.si.edu`

Natural Language

nl-kr

This E-conference is open to discussion of any topic related to the understanding and generation of natural language and knowledge representation as subfields of artificial intelligence.

Keywords: Programming Languages, Natural Language, Knowledge Representation, Linguistics

Audience: Computer Programmers

Contact: Christopher Welty
weltyc@cs.rpi.edu

Details: Free, Moderated

User Info: To subscribe to the list, send an e-mail message requesting a subscription to the URL address below.

`mailto:nl-kr-request@cs.rpi.edu`

Natural Resources Canada (NRCan) Gopher

Natural Resources Canada (NRCan) Gopher

This site offers information on forests, energy, mining, and geomatics from the Canadian government. Also has reports from the Geological Survey of Canada and an overview of NRCan statutes, organization, and personnel. Provides links to other Canadian environmental and government gophers.

Keywords: Canada, Environment, Geology, Forestry

Sponsor: The Department of Natural Resources, Canada

Audience: Canadians, Environmentalists, Geologists

Contact: Bob Fillmore
fillmore@emr.ca

Notes: NRCan maintains a toll-free hotline (800) 267-5166

`gopher://gopher.emr.ca`

`http://www.emr.ca/`

Natural Science

University of Puget Sound Library

The library's holdings are large and wide-ranging and contain significant collections in many fields.

Keywords: Education, Literature (General), Music, Natural Science, Theology

Audience: Researchers, Students, General Public

Details: Free

User Info: Expect: Login; Send: Library

`telnet://192.124.98.2`

University of Texas at Austin Library

The library's holdings are large and wide-ranging and contain significant collections in many fields.

Keywords: Music, Natural Science, Nursing, Science Technology, Behavioral Science, Social Work, Computer Science, Engineering, Latin American Studies, Middle Eastern Studies

Audience: Researchers, Students, General Public

Details: Free

User Info: Expect: Blank Screen, Send: Return; Expect: Go, Send: Return; Expect: Enter Terminal Type, Send: vt100

Note: Some databases are restricted to UT Austin users only.

`telnet://utcat.utexas.edu`

University of Wisconsin Green Bay Library

The library's holdings are large and wide-ranging and contain significant collections in many fields.

Keywords: Economics, Environmental Studies, Music, Natural Science
Audience: Researchers, Students, General Public
Details: Free
User Info: Expect: Service Name, Send: Victor

`telnet://gbls2k.uwgb.edu`

US Geological Survey Server

This resource contains publications, USGS research programs, technology transfer partnerships, and fact sheets about geology.

Keywords: Biology, Geology, Natural Science
Sponsor: US Geological Survey
Audience: Biologists, Geologists, Researchers, Naturalists
Contact: Systems Operator
webmaster@info.er.usgs.gov

`http://info.er.usgs.gov`

Navy

Navnews

Contains official news and information about fleet operations and exercises, personnel policies, budget actions, and more. This is the same news service that is distributed through Navy circuits to ships at sea and to shore commands around the world. Subscriptions to NAVNEWS by e-mail are available at no charge to anyone with a mailbox on any network reachable through the Internet.

Keywords: Navy, News
Sponsor: The Navy Internal Relations Activity, Washington, DC
Audience: Navy Personnel, Sailors, General Public
Contact: navnews@nctamslant.navy.mil
Details: Free
User Info: To subscribe to the list, send an e-mail message requesting a subscription to the URL address below.

`mailto:navnews@nctamslant.navy.mil`

NBA

Funet Sports Information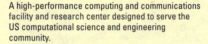

An FTP archive of information on various sports with links to the archive at wuarchive.wustl.edu.

Keywords: Sports, Professional Sports, Ice Hockey, Motor Racing, NFL, NHL, NBA, MLB
Sponsor: Finnish Academic and Research Network (FUNET)
Audience: Sports Enthusiasts
Profile: A fairly extensive archive of information on both American (NBA, MLB, NHL, NFL) and worldwide sports (soccer, ice hockey, motor racing, and so on). Includes FAQs for various sports, statistics, pictures, and some sports games for the PC.
Contact: Jari Pullinen
sports-adm@nic.funet.fi
Details: Free, Images

`gopher://ftp.funet.fi/pub/sports`

NCGIA

Geographic Information and Analysis Laboratory (GIAL)

Server distributing a variety of information related to geography and GIS.

Keywords: Geography, GIS, NCGIA
Sponsor: SUNY-Buffalo and the National Center for Geographic Information and Analysis (NCGIA)
Audience: Geographers, GIS Professionals, Researchers, Students
Contact: Brandon Plewe, Reginald O. Carroll, Patricia M. Baumgarten
plewe@geog.buffalo.edu
carrol@geog.buffalo.edu
pmb@geog.buffalo.edu
Details: Free, Images
Notes: Check out the You-are-here server!

`http://zia.geog.buffalo.edu/`

NCSA (National Center for Supercomputing Applications)

NCSA (National Center for Supercomputing Applications)

A high-performance computing and communications facility and research center designed to serve the US computational science and engineering community.

Keywords: Supercomputing, Computing, Computer Science, Mosaic
Sponsor: University of Illinois at Urbana-Champaign, Champaign, Illinois, USA
Audience: Students, Researchers, Computer Scientists, General Public
Contact: Systems Operator
pubs@ncsa.uiuc.edu

`http://www.ncsa.uiuc.edu/General/NCSAHome.html`

NCSA Mosaic FAQ

NCSA Mosaic FAQ

Common questions and answers about NCSA Mosaic, a network information browser (more technically, a World Wide Web Client) that allows one to retrieve documents from the World Wide Web system. There are versions of Mosaic available for Microsoft Windows on IBM PC-compatible machines, the X Window System on UNIX computers, and for the Apple Macintosh.

Keywords: Internet Reference
Sponsor: National Center for Supercomputing Applications at the University of Illinois at Urbana-Champaign, Illinois, USA
Audience: Students, Computer Scientists, Researchers
Contact: Software Development Group
softdev@ncsa.uiuc.edu

`http://www.ncsa.uiuc.edu/SDG/Software/MacMosaic/FAQ/FAQ-mac.html`

NCTM-L

NCTM-L

A mailing list for the discussion of standards applying to the National Council of Teachers of Mathematics.

Keywords: Education, Mathematics
Audience: Mathematicians
Contact: barry@sci-ed.fit.edu
Details: Free
User Info: To subscribe to this list, send an e-mail message to the URL address below, consisting of a single line reading:

SUB nctm-l YourFirstName YourLastName

To send a message to the entire list, address it to: nctm-l@sci-ed.fit.edu

`mailto:listproc@sci-ed.fit.edu`

Ncube

Ncube

Exchange of information among people using Ncube parallel computers.

Keywords: Ncube, Parallel Computers
Audience: Ncube Users
Contact: David Krumme
ncube-users-request@cs.tufts.edu
Details: Free

User Info: To subscribe to the list, send an e-mail message requesting a subscription to the URL address below.

`mailto:ncube-users-request@cs.tufts.edu`

Ne-social-motss

Ne-social-motss

Announcements of lesbian/gay/bisexual social events and other happenings in the Northeastern US.

Keywords: Social Events, Lesbian, Gay, Bisexuality
Audience: Lesbians, Gays, Bisexuals
Contact: ne-social-motss-request@plts.org
Details: Free
User Info: To subscribe to the list, send an e-mail message requesting a subscription to the URL address below.

`mailto:ne-social-motss-request@plts.org`

Near Eastern Studies

Princeton University Library

The library's holdings are large and wide-ranging. They contain significant collections in many fields.

Keywords: China, Japan, Classics, History (Ancient), Near Eastern Studies, Literature (American), Literature (English), Aeronautics, Middle Eastern Studies, Mormonism, Publishing
Audience: General Public, Researchers, Librarians, Document Delivery Professionals
Details: Free
User Info: Expect: Connect message, blank screen, Send: <cr>; Expect: #, Send: Call 500

`telnet://pucable.princeton.edu`

NEARnet

NEARnet Newsletter

A quarterly publication for users of NEARnet and others who are interested in academic and research networking. The newsletter contains articles about NEARnet services, member organizations, and plans for the future.

Keywords: Networking, NEARnet
Audience: Computer Users, Students
Contact: nearnet-staff@nic.near.net
Details: Free
Available through anonymous FTP at (nic.near.net) in the directory newsletters.

`mailto:nearnet-staff@nic.near.net`

Neci-announce

Neci-announce

This is the announcement forum of New England Community Internet, an organization dedicated to making Usenet and Internet accessible to the public without economic or technical barriers. The group is developing ways to bring IP connectivity at low cost into homes and nonprofit organizations.

Keywords: Internet, Usenet
Audience: Internet Surfers, Usenet Users
Contact: neci-announce-request@pioneer.ci.net
Details: Free
User Info: To subscribe to the list, send an e-mail message requesting a subscription to the URL address below.

`mailto:neci-announce-request@pioneer.ci.net`

Neci-digest

Neci-digest

This is the daily discussion forum of New England Community Internet, an organization dedicated to making Usenet and Internet accessible to the public without economic or technical-expertise barriers. The group is developing ways to bring IP connectivity at low cost into homes and nonprofit organizations.

Keywords: Internet, Usenet
Audience: Internet Surfers, Usenet Users
Contact: neci-digest-request@pioneer.ci.net
Details: Free
User Info: To subscribe to the list, send an e-mail message requesting a subscription to the URL address below.

`mailto:neci-digest-request@pioneer.ci.net`

Neci-discuss

Neci-discuss

This is the general discussion forum of New England Community Internet, an organization dedicated to making Usenet and Internet accessible to the public without economic or technical-expertise barriers. The group is developing ways to bring IP connectivity at low cost into homes and nonprofit organizations.

Keywords: Internet, Usenet
Audience: Internet Surfers, Usenet Users
Contact: neci-discuss-request@pioneer.ci.net
Details: Free
User Info: To subscribe to the list, send an e-mail message requesting a subscription to the URL address below.
Notes: To get a daily digestified version, subscribe to neci-digest. To receive organizational announcements only, subscribe to neci-announce.

`mailto:neci-discuss-request@pioneer.ci.net`

Nedod

Nedod

Discussion of events, technical issues, and just plain social exchange related to motorcycling in the New England area of the US.

Keywords: Motorcycles, New England
Audience: Motorcycle Enthusiasts
Contact: cookson@mbunix.mitre.org
User Info: To subscribe to the list, send an e-mail message requesting a subscription to the URL address below.

`mailto:nedod-request@mbunix.mitre.org`

NERaves (Northeast Raves)

NERaves (Northeast Raves)

One of several regional rave-related mailing lists, NE-Raves covers the Northeastern US.

Keywords: Raves
Audience: Ravers
Details: Free
User Info: To subscribe to the list, send an e-mail message to the URL address below consisting of a single line reading:

SUB neraves YourFirstName YourLastName

To send a message to the entire list, address it to: neraves@umdd.umd.edu

`mailto:listserv@umdd.umd.edu`

Nerdnosh

Nerdnosh

This is a virtual campfire gathering of storytellers. Bring us your tired, your family fables, your journals of yesterday and your imprints on tomorrow.

Keywords: Storytelling
Audience: Storytellers, General Public
Contact: Timothy Bowden
urder@clovis.felton.ca.us

Details:	Free	
User Info:	To subscribe to the list, send an e-mail message requesting a subscription to the URL address below, consisting of a single line reading:	
	SUB nerdnosh YourFirstName YourLastName	
	To send a message to the entire list, address it to: nerdnosh@clovis.felton.ca.us	

mailto:listserv@clovis.felton.ca.us

Nero Ashbury

Nero Ashbury

Nero is a live-action, medieval role-playing game with a plot line and characters that continue from one adventure to the next. Nero has been successful in New England for over six years and is growing rapidly.

Keywords:	Medieval Studies, Role-Playing, Games
Audience:	General Public, Role-Playing Enthusiasts
Contact:	lsonko@pearl.tufts.edu
Details:	Free
User Info:	To subscribe to the list, send an e-mail message requesting a subscription to the URL address below.

mailto:lsonko@pearl.tufts.edu

Net-News

Net-News

A newsletter devoted to library and information resources on the Internet.

Keywords:	Information Science, Libraries, Networking, Internet
Sponsor:	Metronet
Audience:	Librarians, Researchers
Contact:	Dana Noonan noonan@msus1.msus.edu
Details:	Free
User Info:	Send email request to noonan@msus1.msus.edu metronet@vz.acs.umn.edu

gopher://noonan@msus1.msus.edu

Netblazer

Netblazer-users

Provides an unmoderated forum for discussions among users of Telebit NetBlazer products. Topics include known problems and workarounds, features discussions, and configuration advice.

Keywords:	Telebit Computer Products, Netblazer
Audience:	Telebit Netblazer Users
Contact:	netblazer-users-request@telebit.com
Details:	Free
User Info:	To subscribe to the list, send an e-mail message requesting a subscription to the URL address below.

mailto:netblazer-users-request@telebit.com

NetCom

NetCom

NetCom is an Internet provider. It has produced "Net Cruiser" software for Windows.

Keywords:	Internet
Audience:	Internet Users
Details:	Costs

Netcom@netcom.com

NetEc

NetEc

An electronic forum for published academic papers relating to economics.

Keywords:	Economics, Business
Audience:	Economists, Business Professionals
Contact:	netec@uts.mcc.ac.uk
Details:	Free
User Info:	To subscribe to the list, send an e-mail message to the address below consisting of a single line reading:
	SUB netec YourFirstName YourLastName
	To send a message to the entire list, address it to: netec@hasara11.bitnet

mailto:listserv@hasara11.bitnet

Netfind

Netfind

Netfind is a service for locating individuals on the Internet.

Keywords:	Internet Tools
Sponsor:	University of Colorado, Boulder, CO
Audience:	Internet Surfers
Profile:	This service relies on common but not universal programs, and thus may not find some people with valid addresses. The most foolproof way of finding someone's e-mail address remains to call them on the phone and ask. All Netfind sites are functionally equivalent. Multiple ones are listed here in case some are overloaded or down with technical problems.
Contact:	Michael F. Schwartz, Panagiotis G. Tsirigotis schwartz@cs.colorado.edu panos@cs.colorado.edu
Details:	Free
User Info:	File is pub/cs/distribs/netfind/readme

ftp://ftp.cs.colorado.edu

gopher://emoryu1.cc.emory.edu/11/internet/General/netfind

Netherlands

SURFnet—KB InfoServer

InfoService is a joint project by SURFnet (National Network Organization for Research and Higher Education) and the Koninklijke Bibliotheek (National Library of the Netherlands).

Keywords:	Netherlands, Networks, Europe
Audience:	European Internet Surfers
Contact:	infoservices@surfnet.nl
Details:	Free

gopher://gopher.nic.surfnet.nl

Netiquette

Net Etiquette Guide

Guidelines and Netiquette for the Net user.

Keywords:	Internet, Etiquette, Netiquette
Sponsor:	SURAnet Network Information Center
Audience:	Internet Surfers
Contact:	info@sura.net
Details:	Free
User Info:	File is: pub/nic/internet.literature/netiquette.txt

ftp://ftp.sura.net

NetJam

NetJam

NetJam provides a means for people to collaborate on musical compositions by sending Musical Instrument Digital Interface (MIDI) and other files to each other.

Keywords: Music, Musicians
Audience: Musicians
Contact: Craig Latta
netjam-request@xcf.berkeley.edu
Details: Free
User Info: To subscribe to the list, send an e-mail message requesting a subscription to the URL address below.

`mailto:netjam-request@xcf.berkeley.edu`

NetMonth

NetMonth

An independant guide to Bitnet.

Keywords: Bitnet, Networking
Audience: Computer Users, Internet Surfers
Contact: Philip Baczewski
nmonthed@vm.marist.edu
Details: Costs
User Info: To subscribe, send an e-mail message to the address below, consisting of a single line reading:

netmonth YourFirstName YourLastName

To send a message to the entire list, address it to: netmonth@vm.marist.edu

`mailto:listserv@vm.marist.edu`

NetVet Veterinary Resources

NetVet Veterinary Resources

An Internet server for veterinary and animal resources.

Keywords: Veterinary Medicine, Animal Welfare, Animals
Sponsor: Washington University, St. Louis, Division of Comparative Medicine
Audience: Veterinarians, Animal Lovers
Profile: A collection of veterinary and animal-related computer resources that includes archives of animal legislation and regulation, listings for colleges of Veterinary Medicine, conference information, and animal-related databases, including the Electronic Zoo. Also has links to other animal and veterinary-related systems.
Contact: Dr. Ken Boshert
ken@wudcm.wustl.edu

`gopher://netvet.wustl.edu`

`http://netvet.wustl.edu/`

Network-Audio-Bits

Network-Audio-Bits

A bimonthly electronic magazine that features reviews and news of current music in rock, pop, new age, jazz, funk, folk, and other genres—including major-label and independent recording artists.

Keywords: Music Reviews, Music
Audience: Music Entusiasts, General Public
Contact: Michael A. Murphy
murph@maine.bitnet
Details: Free
User Info: To subscribe to the list, send an e-mail message requesting a subscription to the URL address below.

`mailto:murph@maine.bitnet`

Network Servers

The FARNET Gazette

This short monthly electronic newsletter is of interest to network service providers with a research and education focus.

Keywords: Network Servers
Audience: Network Service Providers
Contact: Laura Breeden
breeden@farnet.org
Details: Free

`mailto:gazette-request@farnet.org`

Network Time Protocol

ntp

Discussion of the Network Time Protocol.
Keywords: Network Time Protocol
Audience: Network Time Protocol Users
Contact: ntp-request@trantor.umd.edu
User Info: To subscribe to the list, send an e-mail message requesting a subscription to the URL address below.

To send a message to the entire list, address it to: ntp@trantor.umd.edu

`mailto:ntp-request@trantor.umd.edu`

Networking

(The) Electronic Public Interest versus the Private Good

Statement by community networker Dave Hughes, sounding the warning that the federal goverment may be leaving to the marketplace too much control over who gets access to the Information infrastructure.

Keywords: Community, Networking, Government (US)
Audience: Activists, Policymakers, Community Leaders
Contact: Dave Hughes
dave@oldcolo.com
Details: Free

`http://nearnet.gnn.com/mag/articles/oram/bio.hughes.html`

(The) WELL (Whole Earth 'Lectronic Link)

The WELL is a computer conferencing system, a virtual community, and an electronic coffee shop.

Keywords: Community, Networking, Computer Conferencing, Virtual Community
Sponsor: Whole Earth 'Lectronic Link
Audience: General Public, Internet Surfers
Profile: The WELL is a classic example of an online community that uses what is called "conferencing" to bring a myriad of people together for intense interactions without them having to be connected at the same time. At the end of 1993, the WELL had about 8,000 users (about 90% from all over the USA and about 10% from other locations) and approximately 200 public discussion areas ('conferences'), and 200 private discussion areas. It is a place rich in diverse 'neighborhoods.'
Contact: The WELL Support Staff
info@well.sf.ca.us

Direct dial access through:
(415) 332-4335

To participate in a conference on the WELL, you must first establish an account on the WELL. To do so, start by typing: telnet well.sf.ca.us

`telnet://well.sf.ca.us`

(The) Worldwide Impact of Network Access ★

This is an article by community networker Felipe Rodriquez. In this statement Rodriquez argues that developed countries should help less developed countries build their information infrastructures, and that governments should not censor the content of network traffic.

Keywords: Community, Networking, Europe, Development (International)
Audience: Activists, Policymakers, Community Leaders
Contact: Felipe Rodriquez
felipe@hacktic.nl

http://nearnet.gnn.com/mag/articles/oram/bio.rodriquez.html

An NREN That Includes Everyone ★

In this article, community networker Tom Grundner (founder of Free-Net), advocates a National Community Network, one that treats parents looking for Health Care information as researchers. He advocates expanding our definition of educational access to include people of all ages—senior citizens as well as kindergarteners.

Keywords: Community, Networking, Government (US)
Audience: Activists, Policymakers, Community Leaders
Contact: Tom Grundner
tmg@nptn.org
Details: Free
Notes: This document contains hypertext links to the NPTN (National Public Telecomputing Network).

http://nearnet.gnn.com/mag/articles/oram/bio.grundner.html

Blacksburg Electronic Village Gopher ★★★

The Blacksburg Electronic Village is a project to link an entire town in southwestern Virginia with a 21st-century telecommunications infrastructure. This infrastructure will bring a useful set of information services and interactive communications facilities into the daily activities of citizens and businesses.

Keywords: Community, Networking, Telecommunications
Sponsor: Town of Blacksburg, Virginia, USA
Audience: Activists, Policymakers, Community Leaders, Government
Profile: This community gopher server run by the town of Blacksburg contains information about Blacksburg and how it is building its electronic infrastructure. It includes a list of Blacksburg-area BBSs, instructions for local residents to get an account on the town's BBS, and a section called "Village Schoolhouse."
Details: Costs, Moderated

gopher://morse.cns.vt.edu

Citizens Project

A grass-roots community group in the Pikes Peak region of Colorado.

Keywords: Community, Networking, Colorado
Audience: Activists, Policymakers, Community Leaders, Government
Profile: Based in Colorado Springs, Colorado, the Citizens Project makes use of the online world in pursuit of its mission to investigate, inform, and advocate issues affecting the Pikes Peak region. It maintains an extensive gopher server, FTP site, and a ListServ (for people who have only e-mail access).
Contact: Citizens Project
citizens@cscns.com
Details: Free
User Info: To subscribe to the list, send an e-mail message to the URL address below, consisting of a single line reading:
SUB cns-citizens-pub YourFirstName YourLastName

mailto:listserv@cscns.com

Civic Promise of the National Information Infrastructure (NII) ★

Community networker Richard Civille (founder of EcoNet and director of the Center for Civic Networking) describes several experiments in community networking.

Keywords: Community, Networking, Government (US)
Audience: Activists, Policymakers, Community Leaders, Government
Contact: Richard Civille
rciville@civicnet.org
Details: Free

http://nearnet.gnn.com/mag/articles/oram/bio.civille.html

Community Networks Benefit Federal Goals ★

Statement by community networker Frank Odasz, founder and director of Big Sky Telegraph, a network of rural BBSs throughout Montana. In this article he makes the case that the federal goverment will benefit from the widespread rural employment of networking technology.

Keywords: Community, Networking, Rural Development, Development
Audience: Activists, Policy Analysts, Community Leaders, Government, Citizens, Rural Residents, Native Americans
Contact: Frank Odasz
franko@bigsky.dillon.mt.us,
Details: Free

http://nearnet.gnn.com/mag/articles/oram/bio.odasz.html

ECHO

A computer conferencing system based in New York City.

Keywords: Community, Networking, Women's Issues
Sponsor: East Coast Hang Out
Audience: Activists, Policy Makers, Community Leaders, Governments, Students, Feminists, Educators, Health Care Professionals, Artists, Communicators, General Public
Profile: ECHO was started by Stacy Horn, as an East Coast counterpart to the WELL. ECHO makes an effort to be hospitable to women and has one of the highest percentages of women in an online community.
Contact: Stacy Horn
horn@echonyc.com,
Details: Costs

telnet://echonyc.com

Electronic Democracy Must Come from Us ★

Article about government policy and community networks by community networker Evelyn Pine (former national director of Computer Professionals for Social Responsibility). A short critique of the promises of electronic networking contrasted with the realities of political control.

Keywords: Community, Networking, Government (US)
Audience: Activists, Community Leaders, Governments
Contact: Evelyn Pine
evy@well.sf.ca.us
Details: Free

http://nearnet.gnn.com/mag/articles/oram/bio.pine.html

Free-Net Working Papers

An FTP site with a collection of articles and papers about community networking.

Keywords: Community Networking, Networking
Sponsor: Carleton University, National Clearinghouse for Machine Readable Texts
Audience: Activists, Government, General Public
Profile: Project Guttenburg's goal is to provide a collection of 10,000 of the most used books by the year 2001.
Contact: Jay Weston, Michael S. Hart
jweston@carleton.ca
Details: Free
Login anonymous; cd text

ftp://alfred.carleton.ca/pub/freenet/working.papers

Information Sources

These compiled resources provide information describing the Internet and computer-mediated communication technologies, as well as information on realated applications, culture, discussion forums, and bibliographies.

Keywords: Internet, Networking
Audience: Internet Surfers, Computer-Mediated Communication Researchers
Profile: Files are located in: pub/communications.
Contact: John December
decemj@rpi.edu
Details: Free

ftp://ftp.rpi.edu

http://www.rpi.edu/Internet/Guides/decemj/icmc/top.html

Leaders of Community Networking: People Who Create Online Communities ★

A WWW document with links to several important community networking resources. A brief overview of community networking is provided, as are links to statements by several leaders in the movement.

Keywords: Community, Networking, Government (US Federal)
Audience: Activists, Policymakers, Community Leaders, Government, Citizens
Details: Free

http://nearnet.gnn.com/mag/articles/oram/introduction.html

NEARnet Newsletter ★

A quarterly publication for users of NEARnet and others who are interested in academic and research networking. The newsletter contains articles about NEARnet services, member organizations, and plans for the future.

Keywords: Networking, NEARnet
Audience: Network Users, Students (high school up)
Contact: nearnet-staff@nic.near.net
Details: Free
Available through anonymous FTP at (nic.near.net) in the directory newsletters.

mailto:nearnet-staff@nic.near.net

Net-News

A newsletter devoted to library and information resources on the Internet.

Keywords: Information, Libraries, Networking, Internet
Sponsor: Metronet

Audience: Librarians, Researchers
Contact: Dana Noonan
noonan@msus1.msus.edu
Details: Free
Send email request to noonan@msus1.msus.edu or metronet@vz.acs.umn.edu

gopher://noonan@msus1.msus.edu

NetMonth ★

An independant guide to Bitnet.

Keywords: Bitnet, Networking
Audience: Computer Users, Internet Surfers
Contact: Philip Baczewski
nmonthed@vm.marist.edu
Details: Costs
User Info: To subscribe, send an e-mail message to the address below, consisting of a single line reading:
netmonth YourFirstName YourLastName
To send a message to the entire list, address it to: netmonth@vm.marist.edu

mailto:listserv@vm.marist.edu

Networks & Communities ★★

This directory is a compilation of information resources focused on networks and communities.

Keywords: Community, Networking, Privacy
Audience: Network Developers, Community Activists, Free-Net Organizers, Fundraisers
Details: Free

ftp://una.hh.lib.umich.edu/70/inetdirsstacks/nets:sternberg

Output ★

Newsletter of the Florida State University (FSU) Computing Center. Includes topics such as networking, microcomputing, mainframe computing, and supercomputing on campus, including use of computers in classroom and research computing at FSU.

Keywords: Networking, Microcomputing, Supercomputing
Audience: FSU Computer Science Students, Computer Users
Contact: Suzanne C. Nelson
nelson@avm.cc.fsu.edu
Details: Free
Send your request addressed to the Editor.

mailto:nelson@avm.cc.fsu.edu

People Using Networks Can Have an Impact on Government

Statement by community networker Anne Fallis, who emphasizes the need for easy-to-use interfaces and inexpensive access to worldwide information. She lists many examples of local communities using networking.

Keywords: Community, Networking, Activism
Audience: Activists, Policymakers, Community Leaders, Network Users
Contact: Anne Fallis
afallis@silver.sdsmt.edu
Details: Free

http://nearnet.gnn.com/mag/articles/oram/bio.fallis.html

Polish Archives

Information about Polish Internet gophers and Polish electronic journals.

Keywords: Poland, Telecommunications, Networking
Audience: Historians, Poles
Contact: Darek Milewski
Milewski@poniecki.berkeley.edu
User Info: To subscribe, send an e-mail message requesting a subscription to the URL address below.

gopher://gopher.poniecki.berkeley.edu

Qnx4

A mailing list for discussion of all aspects of the QNX real-time operating systems. Topics include compatible hardware, available third-party software, software reviews, available PD/free software, QNX and FLEET networking, process control, and so on.

Keywords: Computing, Hardware, Software, Networking
Audience: Computer Users, Hardware/Software Designers, Product Analysts
Contact: Martin Zimmerman
camz@dlogtech.cuc.ab.ca
Details: Free
User Info: To subscribe to the list, send an e-mail message requesting a subscription to the URL address below.
To send a message to the entire list, address it to: qnx4@dlogtech.cuc.ab.ca

mailto:qnx4@dlogtech.cuc.ab.ca

Singapore DMC

The Digital Media Center (DMC) home page contains links related to contents about Singapore, the National Computer Board (NCB), and various other National IT (Information Technology) projects.

Keywords: Internet, Networking
Audience: Internet Surfers

Contact: shaopin@ncb.gov.sg
kianjin@ncb.gov.sg

Details: Free

`http://king.ncb.gov.sg`

Telluride Institute

This is a community organization involved in building an electronic dimension in rural Colorado. The vision of Telluride Institute includes linking rural residents to each other and outside resources, creating new opportunities for education, jobs, and arts.

Keywords: Community, Networking, Virtual Community, Rural Development, Colorado

Sponsor: The Telluride Institute, Telluride, Colorado

Audience: Activists, Policymakers, Community Leaders, Students, Colorado Residents

Profile: The Telluride Institute is a local community-based organization that produces arts, environmental, and educational events in the Telluride area of Colorado. The Institite is committed to the creation of what it calls the "InfoZone": it wants to use modern telecommunications to link together the local community and to connect to the rest of the world to exchange ideas, commerce, arts, and inspiration.

Contact: Richard Lowenberg
tellinst@CSN.ORG

Details: Free

Send an e-mail message to the URL address below asking for further information.

`mailto:tellinst@csn.org`

The Black Box Catalog

The Black Box Catalog, the industry's most complete source for data communication equipment, is now available on the Internet. The complete range of products, technical references, and application briefs are available on the Black Box World Wide Web Server.

Keywords: Communications, Networking, Telecommunication, Computers

Sponsor: Black Box Corporation, Lawrence, PA

Audience: Engineers, Network Administration, LAN Administrators, Communication Specialists

Profile: Black Box Corporation is a leading international supplier of data communications networking and related computer connectivity products. Black Box's commitment to providing effective solutions that substantially enhance the capabilities of communications systems is backed by a technical support staff that is available around the clock, a liberal 45-day return policy, and same day shipment of its 6000 products.

Contact: Webmaster
webmaster@blackbox.com

Details: Costs

`http://www.blackbox.com`

TWICS

This is an English-language computer conferencing system in Japan.

Keywords: Community, Networking, Computer Conferencing, Japan, Virtual Community

Sponsor: TWICS Co., Ltd.

Audience: Internationalists, General Public, Journalists, Policymakers

Profile: TWICS is a computer conferencing system that has a reputation for being a thriving electronic community. It recently obtained a full Internet connection and is currently one of the few places in Japan accesible via the Internet. Unlike a database or a gopher server, TWICS is a place to visit for interaction with actual people.

Contact: Tim Buress
twics@twics.co.jp,

Details: Free

`telnet://tanuki.twics.co.jp`

Usenet Repository

Regular informational postings and FAQs from various newsgroups on the Usenet, grouped into archives by newsgroup.

Keywords: Internet, Networking, Usenet

Audience: Internet Surfers

Details: Free

File is: pub/Usenet-by-group

`ftp://pit-manager.mit.edu`

Women's Wire

Women's Wire is an online interactive network focusing on women's issues and interests.

Keywords: Networking, Women's Issues, Online Services

Audience: Women, Internet Users

Profile: This service acts as an international clearinghouse for resources and networking on a broad range of topics including news, politics, careers, education, parenting, health, and arts. Provides e-mail and access to thousands of resources, including Usenet newsgroups.

Details: Costs

Access via an easy-to-use graphical interface for Macintosh and Windows platforms, or a text-based interface for DOS and Unix platforms. Local access numbers available throughout the US and in most countries.

`mailto:info@wwire.net`

Networks

Cisco

This list is for discussion of the network products from Cisco Systems, Inc (primarily the AGS gateway, but also the ASM terminal multiplex) and any other relevant products. Discussions about operation, problems, features, topology, configuration, protocols, routing, loading, serving, and so on, are all encouraged. Other topics include vendor relations, new product announcements, availability of fixes and new features, and discussion of new requirements and desirables.

Keywords: Cisco Systems, Networks

Audience: Cisco Employees, Cisco Users, Distributors

Contact: David Wood
cisco-request@spot.colorado.edu

Details: Free

User Info: To subscribe to the list, send an e-mail message requesting a subscription to the URL address below.

To send a message to the entire list, address it to: cisco@spot.colorado.edu

`mailto:cisco-request@spot.colorado.edu`

Cleveland FreeNet

A network designed for community access and education.

Keywords: Networks, Community Access

Sponsor: The Cleveland FreeNet Project, Case Western Reserve University, Cleveland, Ohio, USA

Audience: Educators, Researchers, Students, Parents

Profile: A prototypical user-friendly city FreeNet, containing complete historical documents, an up-to-date news service, extensive info on the arts, sciences, technology, medicine, business, and education.

Notes: Registration is required, and information on registration is included.

`telnet://freenet-in-a.cwru.edu`

CYFERNET (Child, Youth, and Family Education Network)

This public information service supports child, youth, and family development programs.

Keywords: Education, Networks

Sponsor: Youth Development Information Center at the National Agricultural Library

Audience: Educators, Children, Families

Profile:	CYFERNET contains information useful to child, youth, and family development professionals. Features include programs for children aged 5-8 years, youth-at-risk programs, community projects, and education.
Contact:	jkane@nalusda.gov
Details:	Free

`gopher://ra.esusda.gov/11/CYFER-net`

K12 Net ★

Decentralized network of school-based bulletin board systems (BBSs).

Keywords:	Education (K-12), Networks
Audience:	Educators (K-12), School Children
Profile:	K12 Net provides millions of teachers, students, and parents in metropolitan and rural areas throughout the world with the ability to meet and talk with each other to discuss educational issues, exchange information, and share resources on a global scale.
Contact:	Jack Crawford, Janet Murray jack@k12net.org jmurray@psg.com
Details:	Free

`gopher://woonext.dsrd.ornl.gov/11/Docs/k12net`

Networks & Communities ★★

This directory is a compilation of information resources focused on networks and communities.

Keywords:	Community, Networking, Privacy
Audience:	Network Developers, Community Activists, Free-net Organizers, Fundraisers
Details:	Free

`ftp://una.hh.lib.umich.edu/70/inetdirsstacks/nets:sternberg`

RIPE Network Coordination Centre Gopher ★

RIPE (Reseaux IP Europeens) is a collaborative organization open to all European Internet service providers. RIPE coordinates the operation of a pan-European IP network. In November 1993, more than 500,000 hosts throughout Europe were reachable via networks coordinated by RIPE.

Keywords:	Europe, Networks
Audience:	European Internet Surfers
Contact:	ncc@ripe.net
Details:	Free

`gopher://gopher.ripe.net`

SABINET (South African Bibliographic and Information Network) ★

This gopher offers information searches from a variety of electronic databases, as well as for library locations and availability of books and periodicals.

Keywords:	South Africa, Databases, Networks
Audience:	South African Internet Surfers
Contact:	hennie@info1.sabinet.co.za
Details:	Free

`gopher://info2.sabinet.co.za`

SURFnet—KB InfoServer ★

InfoService is a joint project by SURFnet (National Network Organization for Research and Higher Education) and the Koninklijke Bibliotheek (National Library of the Netherlands).

Keywords:	Netherlands, Networks, Europe
Audience:	European Internet Surfers
Contact:	infoservices@surfnet.nl
Details:	Free

`gopher://gopher.nic.surfnet.nl`

Virginia's PEN (Public Education Network) ★

This is a statewide educational network.

Keywords:	Education, Networks, Virginia
Sponsor:	Virginia Department of Education
Audience:	Educators
Profile:	Educators throughout Virginia can access PEN via a local telephone call or through a toll-free line. The network includes discussion groups, news reports, study guides, and curriculum resources. In one of the features, History OnLine, students and teachers query historical figures such as Thomas Jefferson, and historians will answer in character.
Contact:	Harold Cathernh hcathern@vdoe386.vak12.edu
Details:	Free
	Password: Guest

`telnet://guest@vdoe386.vak12ed.edu`

Neural Networks

Neuron ★

This is a moderated list (in digest form) that deals with all aspects of neural networks (and any type of network or neuromorphic system). Topics include both connectionist models (artificial neural networks) and biological systems ("wetware").

Keywords:	Neural Networks, Biological Research
Audience:	Neuroscientists, Neurobiologists
Contact:	Peter Marvit neuron-request@cattell.psych.upenn.edu
Details:	Free, Moderated
User Info:	To subscribe to the list, send an e-mail message requesting a subscription to the URL address below.
Notes:	Back issues and limited software are available via FTP from cattell.psych.upenn.edu. The Digest is gatewayed to Usenet's comp.ai.neural-nets.

`mailto:neuron-request@cattell.psych.upenn.edu`

Neural Simulation

Purkinje Park ★

A server maintained by CalTech to support the sharing of information between users of the GENESIS neural simulator, and to address topics of general interest to the Computational Neuroscience community.

Keywords:	Computational Neuroscience, GENESIS, Neural Simulation.
Sponsor:	Cal Tech
Audience:	Neuroscientists, Computational Neuroscientists
Contact:	Dave Beeman dbeeman@smaug.bbb.caltech.edu

`http://www.bbb.caltech.edu/index.html`

Neurobiology

Neurosciences Internet Resource Guide ★★★

A comprehensive Internet resource addressing biological, chemical, medical, engineering, and computer science aspects of neurobiology.

Keywords:	Neurobiology, Neuroscience, Brain Research
Sponsor:	The University of Michigan School of Information and Library
Audience:	Neuroscientists, Neurobiologists
Profile:	This resource provides links to journal articles, tutorials on neuroimaging and neurobiology, moderated newsgroups, and international forums, all of which address issues surrounding the field of neuroscience.
Contact:	Sheryl Cormicle, Steve Bonario sherylc@sils.umich.edu sbonario@umich.edu

`http://http2.sils.umich.edu/Public/nirg/nirg1.html`

Neurology

MBI, Music and the Brain Information Center Database (MuSICA)

The intent of this resource is to establish a comprehensive database of scientific research on music.

Keywords: Music Resources, Human Behavior, Neurology
Sponsor: Music and the Brain Information Center
Audience: Researchers, Scientists
Profile: MuSICA maintains a data base of scientific research (references and abstracts) on music as related to behavior, the brain and allied fields, in order to foster interdisciplinary knowledge. Topics include the auditory system; human and animal behavior; creativity; the neuropsychology of music and the human brain; the effects of music on behavior and physiology; music education, medicine, performance, and therapy; neurobiology; perception and psychophysics. Citations and abstracts are excerpted from the following journals: The Bulletin of the Council for Research in Music Education, The Journal of Research in Music Education, Music Perception, Psychology of Music, Psychomusicology.
Contact: Norman Weinberger, Gordon Shaw
mbic@mila.ps.uci.edu
Details: Free
Expect login: Send mbi Expect password: Send nammbi

`telnet://mila.ps.uci.edu`

Neuroscience

Cognitive and Psychological Sciences on the Internet

A resource containing links to academic programs, organizations and conference lists, journals and magazines, Usenet newsgroups, discussion lists, and other general information regarding cognitive science.

Keywords: Cognitive Science, Psychology, Neuroscience
Sponsor: The Stanford University Psychology Department
Audience: Cognitive Scientists, Neuroscientists, Psychologists, Psychiatrists
Contact: Scott Mainwaring
sdm@psych.stanford.edu

`http://matia.stanford.edu/cogsci.html`

Neurosciences Internet Resource Guide

A comprehensive Internet resource addressing biological, chemical, medical, engineering, and computer science aspects of neurobiology.

Keywords: Neurobiology, Neuroscience, Brain Research
Sponsor: The University of Michigan School of Information and Library
Audience: Neuroscientists, Neurobiologists
Profile: This resource provides links to journal articles, tutorials on neuroimaging and neurobiology, moderated newsgroups, and international forums, all of which address issues surrounding the field of neuroscience.
Contact: Sheryl Cormicle, Steve Bonario
sherylc@sils.umich.edu
sbonario@umich.edu

`http://http2.sils.umich.edu/Public/nirg/nirg1.html`

Recreational Pharmacology Server

Very extensive collection of drug FAQs, data sheets, net articles, resources, and electronic books. Complete list of Internet links to related sites.

Keywords: Pharmacology, Drugs, Neuroscience
Sponsor: University of Washington, Seattle, Washington, USA
Audience: Students, General Public, Pharmacologists, Neuroscientists
Contact: Webmaster
lamontg@u.washington.edu
Details: Free

`http://stein1.u.washington.edu:2012/pharm/pharm.html`

The University of Michigan Library

The library's holdings are large and wide-ranging and contain significant collections in many fields.

Keywords: Education (Bilingual), Linguistics, Neuroscience, Michigan, Prohibition, Government (African)
Audience: General Public, Researchers, Librarians, Document Delivery Professionals
Details: Free
User Info: Expect: nothing, Send: <cr>

`telnet://cts.merit.edu`

Nevada

University of Nevada at Reno Library

The library's holdings are large and wide-ranging and contain significant collections in many fields.

Keywords: Basque Studies, Nevada , UN Army Map Service, Patents
Audience: General Public, Researchers, Librarians, Document Delivery Professionals
Details: Free
User Info: Expect: login, Send: wolfpac

`telnet://wolfpac.lib.unr.edu`

Nevada State Documents

University of Nevada, Las Vegas Library - Las Vegas, NV

The library's holdings are large and wide-ranging and contain significant collections in many fields.

Keywords: Gaming, Hotel Administration, Canadian Documents, Nevada State Documents
Audience: General Public, Researchers, Librarians, Document Delivery Professionals
Contact: Myoung-ja Lee Kwon
kwon@nevada.edu.
Details: Free
User Info: Expect: login; Send: library

`telnet://library.lv-lib.nevada.edu`

New Age Music

Direct

Discussion of the work of the musical artist Vangelis.

Keywords: New Age Music, Musical Groups
Audience: Musicians, Music Enthusiasts, Vangelis Fans
Contact: Keith Gregoire
direct-request@celtech.com
User Info: To subscribe to the list, send an e-mail message requesting a subscription to the URL address below.

To send a message to the entire list, address it to: direct@celtech.com

Both bounce and daily digest modes are available; specify your preference when subscribing.

`mailto:direct-request@celtech.com`

New England

Nedod ★

Discussion of events, technical issues, and just plain social exchange related to motorcycling in the New England area of the US.

Keywords: Motorcycles, New England
Audience: Motorcycle Enthusiasts
Contact: cookson@mbunix.mitre.org
User Info: To subscribe to the list, send an e-mail message requesting a subscription to the URL address below.

`mailto:nedod-request@mbunix.mitre.org`

New Jersey

NJ-motss ★

Mailing list for gay, lesbian, and bisexual issues in New Jersey.

Keywords: Gay, Lesbian, Bisexuality, New Jersey
Audience: Gays, Lesbians, Bisexuals
Contact: majordomo@plts.org
Details: Free
User Info: To subscribe to the list, send an e-mail message to the URL address shown below consisting of a single line reading:

SUB NJ-motss YourFirstName YourLastName

To send a message to the entire list, address it to: NJ-motss@plts.org

`mailto:majordomo@plts.org`

NJ-motss-announce ★

Announcements of interests to New Jersey's gay, lesbian, and bisexual population.

Keywords: Gay, Lesbian, Bisexuality, New Jersey
Audience: Gays, Lesbians, Bisexuals
Contact: majordomo@plts.org
Details: Free
User Info: To subscribe to the list, send an e-mail message to the URL address shown below consisting of a single line reading:

SUB NJ-motss-announce YourFirstName YourLastName

To send a message to the entire list, address it to: NJ-motss-announce@plts.org

`mailto:majordomo@plts.org`

New Media

CTN News ★

This is a list covering news on Tibet.

Keywords: Tibet, New Media
Audience: Tibetans, Journalists, General Public
Contact: ctn-editors@utcc.utoronto.ca
Details: Free
User Info: To subscribe to the list, send an e-mail message requesting a subscription to the URL address below.

To send a message to the entire list, address it to: CTN_News@utcc.utoronto.ca

`mailto:ctn-editors@utcc.utoronto.ca`

New Mexico

New Mexico LegalNet ★

The system makes legal resources available, including state motor vehicle and corporation databases, court dockets, border trade information, and country and city data.

Keywords: Law, New Mexico
Audience: New Mexico Residents, Lawyers, Private Investigators
Contact: inettgen@technet.nm.org
Details: Costs

`telnet://technet.nm.org`

New Music

NewMusNet ★

A place on the Arts Wire to discuss issues concerning composers, performers, and presenters of new music and to access information about new music.

Keywords: Music, New Music
Audience: Composers, Musicians, Performers
Contact: Pauline Oliveros
oliveros@tmn.com

`telnet://tmn.com`

New Orleans

New-orleans ★

A list for discussing any and all aspects of the city of New Orleans. History, politics, culture, food, restaurants, music, entertainment, Mardi Gras, and so on, are all fair game.

Keywords: New Orleans, Travel
Audience: New Orleans Residents, Travelers/Tourists
Contact: Edward J. Branley
elendil@mintir.new-orleans.la.us
User Info: To subscribe to the list, send an e-mail message requesting a subscription to the URL address below.

`mailto:mail-server@mintir.new-orleans.la.us`

Neworl-dig ★

This is a digest version of the New Orleans mailing list. It is distributed on a monthly basis, and includes articles from the New Orleans list, minus the "noise."

Keywords: New Orleans, Travel
Audience: New Orleans Residents, New Orleans Visitors
Contact: Edward J. Branley
elendil@mintir.new-orleans.la.us
Details: Free
User Info: To subscribe to the list, send an e-mail message requesting a subscription to the URL address below.

`mailto:mail-server@mintir.new-orleans.la.us`

New Testament

Bible (King James Version) ★★★

The Bible (King James Version) includes the complete text of the modern Thomas Nelson revision of the 1769 edition of the King James version of the Bible.

Keywords: Bible, Religious Text, Old Testament, New Testament
Sponsor: Thomas Nelson Publishers, Nashville, TN, USA
Audience: Christians, Theologians, Historians, Moralists
Profile: The King James version originated from translations ordered by King James of England in 1604 at the Hampton Court Conference. Both the Old and New Testaments are included in this version. Records in the database represent both chapters and verses.

Contact: Dialog in the US at (800) 334-2564, Dialog internationally at country specific locations.
Details: Costs
User Info: To subscribe, contact Dialog directly.

`telnet://dialog.com`

New User's Questions

New User's Questions

Answers to commonly asked questions by new Internet users.
Keywords: Internet, Internet Guides
Sponsor: Xylogics, Inc., and SRI International
Audience: Internet Surfers
Contact: Gary Scott Malkin, April N. Marine
gmalkin@Xylogics.COM
april@nisc.sri.com
Details: Free
Notes: File is: documents/fyi/fyi_04.txt

`ftp://nic.merit.edu`

New York Islanders

New York Islanders

A discussion of the New York Islanders hockey team, with emphasis on the current season.
Keywords: Hockey, Sports, New York
Audience: Ice Hockey Enthusiasts
Contact: David Strauss
dss2k@virginia.edu
Details: Free
User Info: To subscribe to the list, send an e-mail message requesting a subscription to the URL address below.

`mailto:dss2k@virginia.edu`

New York

BTHS-ENews-l

This list provides an open forum for students, teachers, and alumni of Brooklyn Technical High School.
Keywords: New York
Audience: Teachers, Students, Educators
Contact: listserv@Cornell.edu
Details: Free
User Info: To subscribe to the list, send an e-mail message to the URL address below, consisting of a single line reading:
SUB BTHS-ENews-l YourFirstName YourLastName
To send a message to the entire list, address it to: BTHS-ENews-l@Cornell.edu

`mailto:listserv@Cornell.edu`

ebikes

New York City Bicycle discussion list.
Keywords: Bicycling, New York
Audience: Bicyclists
Contact: Danny Lieberman
ebikes-request@panix.com
Details: Free
User Info: To subscribe to the list, send an e-mail message requesting a subscription to the URL address below.
To send a message to the entire list, address it to: ebikes-request@panix.com

`mailto:ebikes-request@panix.com`

Information about New York City

Facts about New York City, including information on museums, restaurants, hotels, bars, and other areas of interest to New Yorkers and visitors alike.
Keywords: New York, Travel
Sponsor: City University of New York (CUNY)
Audience: New York City Residents, Tourists, General Public
Contact: Anil Khullar
gopher@netops.gc.cuny.edu
Notes: Still under construction, some items are incomplete

`gopher://timesq.gc.cuny.edu`

New York Islanders

A discussion of the New York Islanders hockey team, with emphasis on the current season.
Keywords: Hockey, New York Islanders, New York
Audience: New York Islanders Fans, Ice Hockey Fans
Contact: David Strauss
dss2k@virginia.edu
Details: Free
User Info: To subscribe to the list, send an e-mail message requesting a subscription to the URL address below.

`mailto:dss2k@virginia.edu`

New York State Department of Health Gopher

An electronic guide to health information from the state of New York.
Keywords: Health Care, Statistics, Health Sciences, New York
Sponsor: New York State Department of Health
Audience: Health Care Professionals, General Public
Profile: Information provided includes health statistics for New York State, lists of health care providers, facilities, and publications, as well as New York State Department of Health press releases.
Contact: nyhealth@albnydh2.bitnet

`gopher://gopher.health.state.ny.us`

NYSERNet Internet Guide

A comprehensive guide to the Internet from the New York State Education and Research Network (NYSERNet). NYSERNet provides access to specialized databases and online libraries, as well as to supercomputing and parallel-processing facilities throughout the US and to many national networks.
Keywords: Internet, Internet Guides, New York, Supercomputers
Sponsor: NYSERNet K-12 Networking Interest Group
Audience: Internet Surfers
Contact: info@nysernet.org
Details: Free

`ftp://nysernet.org`

Shamash, The New York - Israel Project

This site is designed to facilitate communications between Jews and Jewish organizations through the medium of the Internet. Information includes archives of Jewish lists, updates of community Jewish events in New York and beyond, a Jewish white pages, and a section on the Holocaust. It also has Hebrew software and access to other Jewish and Israeli information servers.
Keywords: Judaism, Israel, New York
Sponsor: New York - Israel Project (Nysernet), New York, USA
Audience: Jews, Jewish Organizations
Contact: Avrum Goodblatt, Chaim Dworkin
goodblat@israel.nysernet.org
chaim@israel.nysernet.org.

`gopher://nysernet.org`

VEGCNY-L (Vegetarians in Central New York area)

VegCNY-L is an open discussion list intended to serve those people living in the Central New York area who are vegetarians, as well as those who are interested in vegetarianism.

Keywords:	Vegetarianism, New York, Food
Audience:	Vegetarians
Contact:	Chuck Goelzer Lyons cgl1@cornell.edu
Details:	Free
User Info:	To subscribe to the list, send an e-mail message to the URL address below consisting of a single line reading: SUB VEGCNY-L YourFirstName Your:LastName To send a message to the entire list, address it to: VEGCNY-L@cornell.edu

mailto:listserv@cornell.edu

Newedu-l (New Paradigms in Education List)

Newedu-l (New Paradigms in Education List)

This list discusses education broadly, including delivery systems, media, collaborative learning, learning styles, and distance education.

Keywords:	Education (Adult), Education (Distance), Education (Continuing)
Audience:	Educators (k-12), Administrators, Researchers
Details:	Free
User Info:	To subscribe to the list, send an e-mail message to the URL address below consisting of a single line reading: SUB newedu-l YourFirstName YourLastName To send a message to the entire list, address it to: newedu-l@uscvm.bitnet

mailto:listserv@uscvm.bitnet

Newlists

Newlists

This is a mailing list clearing house for new mailing lists. Subscribers will get announcements of new lists that are mailed to this list.

Keywords:	Mailing Lists
Audience:	Internet Surfers
Contact:	Marty Hoag info@vm1.nodak.edu
Details:	Free
User Info:	To subscribe to the list, send an e-mail message requesting a subscription to the URL address below.

mailto:info@vm1.nodak.edu

NewMusNet

NewMusNet

A place on the Arts Wire to discuss issues concerning composers, performers, and presenters of new music and to access information about new music.

Keywords:	Music, New Music
Audience:	Composers, Musicians, Performers
Contact:	Pauline Oliveros oliveros@tmn.com

telnet://tmn.com

Neworl-dig

Neworl-dig

This is a digest version of the New Orleans mailing list. It is distributed on a monthly basis, and includes articles from the New Orleans list, minus the "noise."

Keywords:	New Orleans, Travel
Audience:	New Orleans Residents, Travelers/Tourists
Contact:	Edward J. Branley elendil@mintir.new-orleans.la.us
Details:	Free
User Info:	To subscribe to the list, send an e-mail message requesting a subscription to the URL address below.

mailto:mail-server@mintir.new-orleans.la.us

News

Agence FrancePresse International French Wire

Agence FrancePresse International French Wire provides full-text articles in French relating to national, international, business, and sports news.

Keywords:	News, Europe, Third World, French
Sponsor:	Agence FrancePresse, Paris, France
Audience:	Market Researchers, Journalists, Francophiles
Profile:	Agence FrancePresse distributes its French service worldwide, including Western and Eastern Europe, Canada, northern and western Africa, the Middle East, Vietnam, French Guiana, the West Indies, and the French Pacific islands. Agence FrancePresse International French Wire has extensive coverage of the European countries, including every aspect of economic, political, and general business news. It also provides excellent industrial and market news from both developed countries and from the Third World.
Coverage:	September 1991 to the present; updated daily.
Contact:	Dialog in the US at (800) 334-2564; Dialog internationally at country-specific locations.
Details:	Costs
User Info:	To subscribe, contact Dialog directly.

telnet://dialog.com

bit.general

A Usenet newsgroup providing information and discussion about Bitnet or Usenet. Contained in the bit. category are many bit.listserv discussion lists.

Keywords:	Internet, News
Audience:	General Public, Internet Surfers
User Info:	To subscribe to this Usenet newsgroup, you need access to a newsreader.

news:bit.general

BUSREF (Business Reference)

The Business Refernce (BUSREF) library contains a variety of reference materials covering business and industry.

Keywords:	News, Reference, Business, Government
Audience:	Businessmen
Profile:	The BUSREF library contains company directories, reference publications, information on business opportunities, and biographical information on political candidates, Congressional members, celebrities, and international decision makers.
Contact:	Mead New Sales Group at (800) 227-4908 or (513) 859-5398 inside the US, or (513) 865-7981 for all inquiries outside the US
User Info:	To subscribe, contact Mead directly. To examine the Nexis user guide, you can access it at the ftp site of the University of Texas at Austin at the URL address: ftp://ftp.cc.utexas.edu The files are in: /pub/ref-services/LEXIS

telnet://nex.meaddata.com

http://www.meaddata.com

CANADA (Canadian News and Information Library)

The Canadian News and Information library (CANADA) contains Canadian legal news, business and company information.

Keywords: News, Analysis, Companies, Canada

Audience: Canadians

Profile: The CANADA library contains respected Canadian news publications such as The Toronto Star, The Vancouver Sun, Ottawa Business News and the Montreal Gazette. The CANADA library also offers Canadian company profiles, country reports, and Canada's financial database, CANCORP Plus.

Contact: Mead New Sales Group at (800) 227-4908 or (513) 859-5398 inside the US, or (513) 865-7981 for all inquiries outside the US.

User Info: To subscribe, contact Mead directly.

To examine the Nexis user guide, you can access it at the ftp site of the University of Texas at Austin at the URL address: ftp://ftp.cc.utexas.edu

The files are in: /pub/ref-services/LEXIS

telnet://nex.meaddata.com

http://www.meaddata.com

CERRO (Central European Regional Research Organization)

CERRO provides access to information about the economic restructuring of Central Europe, including a discussion list, papers, news summaries, and pointers to other gophers in Central Europe.

Keywords: Central Europe, Economics, News

Audience: Economists, Researchers, Journalists

Contact: gunther.maier@wu-wien.ac.at

Details: Free

gopher://osiris.wu.wein.ac.at

Cro-Views

Cro-Views is an opinion service that consists of discussions relating to Croatia and other former Yugoslav republics. The main objective is to give people who cannot access the news network (e.g. via <rn>command in UNIX) a chance to read and voice their own opinions about these issues.

Keywords: Croatia, News

Audience: Croats, Journalists, General Public

Contact: Joe Stojsic
Joe@Mullara.Met.UniMelb.Edu.AU

Details: Free

User Info: To subscribe to the list, send an e-mail message requesting a subscription to the URL address below.

Notes: Cro-Views is an unmoderated service, but abusive language and name-calling is not tolerated.

mailto:Joe@Mullara.Met.UniMelb.Edu.AU

Croatian-News/Hrvatski-Vjesnik

News from and related to Croatia, run by volunteers. These are actually two news distributions: one in Croatian (occasionally an article might be in some other South Slavic language) and one in English.

Keywords: Croatia, News

Audience: Croats, Journalists, General Public

Contact: Croatian-News-Request@Andrew.CMU.Edu, Hrvatski-Vjesnik-Zamolbe@Andrew.CMU.Edu

Details: Free

User Info: To subscribe to the list, send an e-mail message to the URL address below with the following information: your name, your e-mail address, and state/country where your account is. Please put the state/country information in the Subject: line of your letter. If you would like to receive the news in Croatian as well, please indicate that in your message. If you would prefer to receive the news in Croatian only, please send a message to the following address: Hrvatski-Vjesnik-Zamolbe@Andrew.CMU.Edu

To send a message to the entire list, address it to: Croatian-News@Andrew.CMU.Edu

mailto:Croatian-News-Request@Andrew.CMU.Edu

Electronic Newsstand Gopher

This gopher contains tables of contents, selected full-text articles, and assorted other information from many mainstream print journals.

Keywords: Journals, Electronic Publishing, Publishing, News

Audience: News Enthusiasts, Publishers, Publishing Professionals, Journalists

Profile: This gopher was compiled with the collaboration of the American Journal of International Law, Policy Review, Technology Review, Business Week, Current History, The Economist, Foreign Affairs, National Review, The New Yorker, The New Republic, Mother Jones, among other distinguished publications.

Contact: William Love
love@enews.com

gopher://gopher.enews.com

ENERGY

The Energy News and Information (ENERGY) library consists of news, legal, and regulatory information.

Keywords: Energy, News, Law, Regulations

Audience: Energy Researchers

Profile: The ENERGY library contains more than 50 full-text sources concentrating on energy-related news and issues. Also available are decisions and orders of the United States Federal Power Commission, Federal Energy Regulatory Commission, and Nuclear Regulatory Commission. At the state level, it covers administrative decisions and orders for 17 states. Energy industry research reports from InvestextR are also available.

Contact: Mead New Sales Group at (800) 227-4908 or (513) 859-5398 inside the US, or (513) 865-7981 for all inquiries outside the US.

User Info: To subscribe, contact Mead directly.

To examine the Nexis user guide, you can access it at the ftp site of the University of Texas at Austin at the URL address: ftp://ftp.cc.utexas.edu

The files are in: /pub/ref-services/LEXIS

telnet://nex.meaddata.com

http://www.meaddata.com

ENTERT (Entertainment News Library)

The Entertainment News library contains sources of information about the entertainment industry, including broadcasting, cable TV, theater, television, books, movies, ballet and dance, video, radio, music, and the record industry.

Keywords: Entertainment, News

Audience: Business Researchers, Analysts, Entrepreneurs

Profile: ENTERT includes the full text of publications such as Variety, Daily Variety, Communications Daily and People, as well as documents about entertainment-related topics from premier NEXIS sources such as the Los Angeles Times and USA Today. Additionally, ENTERT has the premier source database covering the entertainment industry, BASELINE, which provides daily updates of the financial status of movies, background on actors and details on works in production.

Contact: Mead New Sales Group at (800) 227-4908 or (513) 859-5398 inside the US, or (513) 865-7981 for all inquiries outside the US.

User Info: To subscribe, contact Mead directly.

To examine the Nexis user guide, you can access it at the ftp site of the University of Texas at Austin at the URL address: ftp://ftp.cc.utexas.edu

The files are in: /pub/ref-services/LEXIS

telnet://nex.meaddata.com

http://www.meaddata.com

ENVIRN (Environment Library)

The Environment (ENVIRN) Library contains a variety of environment-related news and legal information.

Keywords: News, Analysis, Law, Environment

Audience: Environmental Researchers, Business Professionals

Profile: The ENVIRN library contains a combination of environmental information that can provide critical insight into environmental hazards, EPA ratings, specific company investigations, evaluations on potentially hazardous chemicals, and parties responsible for cleanup of specific hazardous sites. Additionally, ENVIRN provides a wealth of environment-related information—legislation, regulations, and court and agency decisions at both the federal and state levels; news; the Environmental Law Reporter, and American Law Reports.

Contact: Mead New Sales Group at (800) 227-4908 or (513) 859-5398 inside the US, or (513) 865-7981 for all inquiries outside the US.

User Info: To subscribe, contact Mead directly.

To examine the Nexis user guide, you can access it at the ftp site of the University of Texas at Austin at the URL address: ftp://ftp.cc.utexas.edu

The files are in: /pub/ref-services/LEXIS

telnet://nex.meaddata.com

http://www.meaddata.com

EXEC (Executive Branch News US)

The EXEC library contains information and news about the Executive Branch of the Federal Government. From the Department of Agriculture to the White House, this file is a comprehensive source of information that will be especially useful to those whose responsibilities include monitoring federal regulations, Agency and Department activity, and the people and issues involved.

Keywords: News, Legislation, Regulation, Politics, Executive Branch

Audience: Journalists, Lobbyists, Business Executives, Analysts, Entrepreneurs

Profile: The EXEC library allows the searching of individual files or group files that cover topics such as the Federal Register and Code of Federal Regulations; public laws; proposed treasury regulation; and over 50 news sources, including BNA's Daily Report for Executives, the Dept. of State Dispatch, ABC News transcripts, Federal News Service Daybook, Government Executive, MacNeil/Lehrer Newshour, New Leader, National Review, the Washington Post, the Washington Times, Presidential Documents, and many others.

Contact: Mead New Sales Group at (800) 227-4908 or (513) 859-5398 inside the US, or (513) 865-7981 for all inquiries outside the US.

User Info: To subscribe, contact Mead directly.

To examine the Nexis user guide, you can access it at the ftp site of the University of Texas at Austin at the URL address: ftp://ftp.cc.utexas.edu

The files are in: /pub/ref-services/LEXIS

telnet://nex.meaddata.com

http://www.meaddata.com

Health News Daily

★★★

The database contains all the daily news and full-text articles from Health News Daily, a publication from F-D-C Reports, Inc.

Keywords: Health, Pharmacology, Medical Research, News

Sponsor: F-D-C Reports, Inc., Chevy Chase, MD, US

Audience: Health Professionals, Pharmaceutical Industry, Market Researchers

Profile: The database provides specialized, in-depth business, scientific, regulatory, and legal news. Timely coverage of pharmacy and pharmaceuticals is given, as well as coverage of medical devices and diagnostics, medical research, cosmetics, health policy, provider payment policies, and cost containment in national health care.

Coverage: 1990 to the present; updated daily.

Contact: Dialog in the US at (800) 334-2564, Dialog internationally at country-specific locations.

Details: Costs

User Info: To subscribe, contact Dialog directly.

telnet://dialog.com

Hungary

This discussion list circulates timely information about Hungary.

Keywords: Hungary, Eastern Europe, News

Audience: Researchers, Observers, Political Scientists

Contact: Eric Dahlin
hcf2hung@iucsbuxa

Details: Free

User Info: To subscribe to the list, send an e-mail message to the URL address shown below consisting of a single line reading:

SUB hungary YourFirstName YourLastName

mailto:listserv@gwuvm.gwu.edu

INSURE (Insurance)

The Insurance (INSURE) library contains specific full-text and abstract news and legal information sources focusing on the insurance industry.

Keywords: News, Analysis, Law, Insurance

Audience: Insurance Professionals, Lawyers

Profile: The INSURE library contains leading insurance industry news sources, legal and regulatory materials from NILS Publishing Company's INSURLAW, analyst reports on the insurance industry from InvestextR, and insurance company financial reports. Federal and state case law and federal regulations are also available.

Contact: Mead New Sales Group @ (800) 227-4908 or (513) 859-5398 inside the US, or (513) 865-7981 for all inquiries outside the US.

User Info: To subscribe, contact Mead directly.

To examine the Nexis user guide, you can access it at the ftp site of the University of Texas at Austin at the URL address: ftp://ftp.cc.utexas.edu The files are in: /pub/res-services/LEXIS

telnet://nex.meaddata.com

MARKET (Markets and Industries News and Information)

The Markets and Industries News and Information (MARKET) library contains sources covering developments in a wide variety of markets and industries.

Keywords: News, Analysis, Industry, Marketing

Audience: Business Professionals, Researchers

Profile: The MARKET library contains a wide selection of sources ranging from trade and industry sources to InvestextR industry reports to company profiles. To round out the offering, MARKET also covers advertising, marketing, public opinion polls, market research, public relations, sales and selling, promotions, consumer attitudes, trends and behaviors, demographics, product announcements and product reviews. In addition, Predicasts Overview of Markets and Technology (PROMT), Marketing and Advertising Reference Service (MARS), US and International Forecast Databases (UFRCST and IFRCST) and the US Time Series (USTIME), all from Information Access Company, are available.

Contact: Mead New Sales Group at (800) 227-4908 or (513) 859-5398 inside the US, or (513) 865-7981 for all inquiries outside the US.

User Info: To subscribe, contact Mead directly.

To examine the Nexis user guide, you can access it at the ftp site of the University of Texas at Austin at the URL address: ftp://ftp.cc.utexas.edu

The files are in: /pub/ref-services/LEXIS

telnet://nex.meaddata.com

http://www.meaddata.com

MDEAFR

The Middle East and Africa (MDEAFR) library contains detailed information about every country in the Mideast and Africa. Structured for those who want to follow the unfolding events in the Gulf states, as well as in North and South Africa, this library contains a broad array of sources, including international research reports from InvestextR.

Keywords:	News, Analysis, Companies, Middle East, Africa
Audience:	Journalists, Business Professionals
Profile:	The MDEAFR library contains a wide array of pertinent sources. Among the information sources are newspapers and wire services, trade and business journals, company reports, country and region background, industry and product analysis, business opportunities, and selected legal texts. News sources range from the world-renowned Associated Press and Christian Science Monitor to the regionally important Jerusalem Post and Africa News. Company information is contained in the EXTEL cards as well as ICC. Providers of country background and industry analysis include Associated Banks of Europe, Bank of America, Business International, IBC USA, and the US Department of Commerce. Customers interested in new business opportunities can check OPIC and Foreign Trade Opportunities (FTO).
Contact:	Mead New Sales Group at (800) 227-4908 or (513) 859-5398 inside the US, or (513) 865-7981 for all inquiries outside the US.
User Info:	To subscribe, contact Mead directly. To examine the Nexis user guide, you can access it at the ftp site of the University of Texas at Austin at the URL address: ftp://ftp.cc.utexas.edu The files are in: /pub/ref-services/LEXIS

telnet://nex.meaddata.com

http://www.meaddata.com

Mideur-l

A list containing the history, culture, politics, and current affairs of those countries lying between the Mediterranean/Adriatic and the Baltic Seas, and between the German/Austrian borders and the former Soviet Union.

Keywords:	Soviet Union, Baltic Republics, Eastern Europe, News
Audience:	Political Scientists, Researchers, Historians, General Public
Contact:	Jan George Frajkor mideur-1@ubvm.cc.buffalo.edu
Details:	Free
User Info:	To subscribe to the list, send an e-mail message to the URL address below consisting of a single line reading: SUB mideur-l YourFirstName YourLastName To send a message to the entire list, address it to: mideur-1@ubvm.cc.buffalo.edu

mailto:listserv@ubvm.cc.buffalo.edu

News

This directory is a general compilation of information resources focused on news.

Keywords:	News Media, Electronic Media, Journalism
Audience:	Newsreaders, Journalists, General Public
Details:	Free

ftp://una.hh.lib.umich.edu/70/inetdirsstacks/news:robinson

NEWS (General News)

The General News (NEWS) library includes more than 2,300 sources. Full-text news from national and international newspapers, magazines, newsletters, and wire services and abstract information are both available.

Keywords:	News, Analysis, People, Companies
Audience:	Journalists, General Public
Profile:	The General News (NEWS) library contains a number of publications and wire services of general interest, as well as others that specialize in particular areas of business . The NEWS library is organized into individual files, group files by source or subject, and user-defined combination files for full-text information sources. Abstracts are also available as individual files or can be searched together in one group file. The NEWS library includes such prestigious full-text sources as the New York Times and more than more than 30 major newspapers from around the US and the world.
Contact:	Mead New Sales Group at (800) 227-4908 or (513) 859-5398 inside the US, or (513) 865-7981 for all inquiries outside the US.
User Info:	To subscribe, contact Mead directly. To examine the Nexis user guide, you can access it at the ftp site of the University of Texas at Austin at the URL address: ftp://ftp.cc.utexas.edu The files are in: /pub/ref-services/LEXIS

telnet://nex.meaddata.com

http://www.meaddata.com

News of Earth

Newsletter covering global news.

Keywords:	Global News, News
Audience:	General Public
Profile:	News of Earth consists of: NewsE-A Analysis, an analysis of global news; NewsE-B Bulletins, late-breaking global news; NewsE-C Commentary, a commentary on global news; NewsE-D Distribution, global news monitored from shortwave radio broadcasts; and, the continuation of JBH Online (Online-L), published from 1987 through 1990 (Issues 1-213); NewsE-I Interviews, interviews on global issues; NewsE-L Letters, news and reaction from readers; NewsE-S Supplements, containing additional news and information from electronic and print sources. News of Earth supplements continues JBH News (JBHNewsL), published in 1990 (issues 1-4). NewsE is a "superlist" that includes all components listed above.
Contact:	John B. Harlan jbharlan@indyvax.iupui.edu
Details:	Free
User Info:	To subscribe, send an e-mail message to the URL address below consisting of a single line reading: SUB NEWSE-x (where x is A, B, C, D, I, L or S) YourFirstName YourLastName To send a message to the entire list, address it to: newse@indyvax.iupui.edu

mailto:listserv@Indyvax.iupui.edu

NewsCommando

This makes available synergies discerned in, and created from, print news media (up to a 12-year time span). The depth of insight possible using the information-mosaic method can be staggering. A form of an electronic magazine, NewsCommando serves as a reference tool, allows access to Medline, PaperChase, or other searches, and, in many ways, is the poor man's IdeaFisher/IdeaBank.

Keywords:	NewsCommando, News
Audience:	NewsCommando Users
Contact:	Lance Sanders starkid@ddsw1.mcs.com
Details:	Free Articles will be deposited in your mailbox with a "NewsCom/Vol.#" Subject header. Most will be in excess of 20K. Please group-save them to a file for later reading.

mailto:starkid@ddsw1.mcs.com

Novice MZT

Novize MZT (News of Ministry for Science and Technology of the Republic of Slovenia) provides easy, accessible news about science, development, universities, and innovative activities to individuals and institutions in research and development areas. Published at least once monthly.

Keywords:	Slovenia, Science, Technology, News
Audience:	Slovenians, Scientists, Technocrats
Contact:	Novice-mzt@krpan.arnes.si or Novice.mzt@uni-lj.si

User Info: To subscribe to the list, send an e-mail message requesting a subscription to the URL address below.

To send a message to the entire list, address it to: Novice-mzt@krpan.arnes.si

`mailto:Novice-MZT@krpan.arnes.si`

NSAMER (North and South America Library)

The North and South America library contains detailed information about every country in North and South America (except the United States). The US-Canada Free Trade Agreement, the North American Free Trade Agreement, relations with Mexico and events in such countries as Brazil, Peru, and Nicaragua are among the topics covered by a variety of business, news and legal sources. International research reports from InvestextR are also included. The United States is not covered in this library.

Keywords: News, Analysis, Companies, North America, South America

Audience: Journalists, Business Professionals

Profile: The North and South America library contains a broad array of sources. Among the information sources are newspapers and wire services, trade and business journals, company reports, country and region backgrounds, industry and product analyses, business opportunities, and selected legal texts. News sources range from the world-renowned Washington Post and Christian Science Monitor to the regionally important Toronto Star and Latin American Newsletters. Canadian Business and Maclean's represent a portion of the array of business and trade journals. Company information is contained in the EXTEL cards as well as ICC. Providers of country background and industry analyses include Associated Banks of Europe, Bank of America, Business International, IBC USA and the US Department of Commerce. Among the specialized resources are IBC's Mexico and Brazil Services as well as BI's Business Latin America. Researchers interested in new business opportunities can check OPIC and Foreign Trade Opportunities (FTO).And selected legal texts covering the US-Canada Free Trade Agreement and other international agreements planners and advisors to better assess the business climate in North and South America.

Contact: Mead New Sales Group at (800) 227-4908 or (513) 859-5398 inside the US, or (513) 865-7981 for all inquiries outside the US.

User Info: To subscribe, contact Mead directly.

To examine the Nexis user guide, you can access it at the ftp site of the University of Texas at Austin at the URL address: ftp://ftp.cc.utexas.edu

The files are in: /pub/ref-services/LEXIS

`telnet://nex.meaddata.com`

`http://www.meaddata.com`

SPORTS (Sports News)

The Sports News (SPORTS) library contains a variety of sports-related news and information.

Keywords: News, Analysis, Sports, Biographies

Audience: Sports Enthusiasts, Journalists

Profile: The SPORTS library is a specialized news library that contains the full text of Sports Illustrated and The Sporting News and selected sports-related stories from many major US newspapers and wire services. Biographical information and 1992 Olympic facts are also part of this library.

Contact: Mead New Sales Group at (800) 227-4908 or (513) 859-5398 inside the US, or (513) 865-7981 for all inquiries outside the US.

User Info: To subscribe, contact Mead directly.

To examine the Nexis user guide, you can access it at the ftp site of the University of Texas at Austin at the URL address: ftp://ftp.cc.utexas.edu

The files are in: /pub/ref-services/LEXIS

`telnet://nex.meaddata.com`

`http://www.meaddata.com`

TOPNWS (Top News)

The Top News (TOPNWS) library contains today's news today for selected key sources from around the world.

Keywords: News, Analysis

Audience: Journalists, General Public

Profile: In the Top News (TOPNWS) library newswires are collected and updated every 60 minutes. Newspapers and other daily publications are updated throughout the day on the day of publication. Transcripts are updated within three hours of broadcast. Two weeks worth of data from more than 40 major publications may be searched as individual files or in specialized group files. The TODAY group file contains today's published information from all sources. the 2WEEK group file expands the window of current information from all sources to two weeks. Specialized section files, designed to be like sections of a newspaper, contain stories from each publication that pertain to the section or topic selected.

Contact: Mead New Sales Group at (800) 227-4908 or (513) 859-5398 inside the US, or (513) 865-7981 for all inquiries outside the US.

User Info: To subscribe, contact Mead directly.

To examine the Nexis user guide, you can access it at the ftp site of the University of Texas at Austin at the URL address: ftp://ftp.cc.utexas.edu

The files are in: /pub/ref-services/LEXIS

`telnet://nex.meaddata.com`

`http://www.meaddata.com`

United Press International News—Sports

Full text of UPI stories and articles.

Keywords: Sports, News

Sponsor: United Press International (UPI)

Audience: Sports Enthusiasts

Profile: This gopher allows access to daily UPI news feeds, including sports news. The most current articles available tend to run three to five days behind. This delay is compensated for by UPIs far-ranging coverage of national and international sporting news. Indexed, with back articles from 1992 onwards available.

Contact: UPI
clarinews@clarinet.com

Details: Free

`gopher://mrfrosty.micro.umn.edu./UPI-data/Today/sports`

WORLD (World News and Information)

This library contains detailed information about every country in Europe, Asia, the Pacific Rim, Africa, the Middle East, and North and South America. Designed for those who need to monitor world events, organizations, and leaders, this library provides a global view of any subject or topic.

Keywords: Business, News

Audience: Business Researchers, Analysts, Entrepreneurs

Profile: WORLD includes information from newspapers and wire services, trade and business journals, company reports, country and region background, industry and product analysis, business opportunities, and selected legal texts. News sources range from the world-renowned Christian Science Monitor, Financial Times, Reuters and Associated Press to the regionally important eastern European CTK, MTI and PAP newswires, The Toronto Star, Jerusalem Post, and Xinhua News Agency. Business and trade information include a wide variety of sources, such as EIS's European newsletters and Euroscope from Coopers and Lybrand, Canada's Maclean's, Japan's Comline Daily News Service, BNA's international dailies and the Soviet Union's SovData DiaLine services—all help analyze the political and economic climate around the globe. Company information is contained in the EXTEL cards as well as ICC. Providers of country background and industry analysis include Associated Banks of Europe, Bank of America, Business International, IBC USA and the US Department of Commerce. Economic risk can be assessed with the Economist's Economic Risk Services, IBC's International Reports and International Country Risk Guide and many of

News Media

Business International's Country Reports. Political risk is forecast in IBC's Political Risk Services as well as BOA's World Information Services' Country RiskOutlooks, Monitors and Forecasts.

Contact: Mead New Sales Group at (800) 227-4908 or (513) 859-5398 inside the US, or (513) 865-7981 for all inquiries outside the US.

User Info: To subscribe, contact Mead directly.

To examine the Nexis user guide, you can access it at the ftp site of the University of Texas at Austin at the URL address: ftp://ftp.cc.utexas.edu

The files are in: /pub/ref-services/LEXIS

`telnet://nex.meaddata.com`

`http://www.meaddata.com`

News (International)

Spojrzenia

A weekly E-journal devoted to Polish culture, history and politics.

Keywords: Poland, News (International), Culture
Audience: Poles, Students
Contact: Jerzy Krzystek
krzystek@u.washington.edu
Details: Free
User Info: To subscribe to the list, send an e-mail message requesting a subscription to the URL address below. To send a message to the entire list, address it to:
spojrzenia@u.washington.edu

`mailto:krzystek@u.washington.edu`

Sri Lanka Net (SLNet)

A moderated mailing list that carries news and other articles about Sri Lanka.

Keywords: Sri Lanka, News (International)
Audience: Sri Lankans, Students
Contact: pkd@fed.frb.gov
slnetad@ganu.colorado.edu
Details: Free, Moderated
User Info: To subscribe to the list, send an e-mail message requesting a subscription to the URL address below.
To send a message to the entire list, address it to:
slnetad@ganu.colorado.edu

`mailto:pkd@fed.frb.gov`

`mailto:slnetad@ganu.colorado.edu`

News Media

Africa-n

A moderated mailing list dedicated to the exchange of news and information on Africa, including correspondence from many sources worldwide.

Keywords: News Media, Africa
Audience: Africans, Students
Contact: Faraz Rabbani
frabbani@epas.utoronto.ca
User Info: To subscribe to the list, send an e-mail message to the URL address below consisting of a single line reading:
SUB africa-n YourFirstName YourLastName
To send a message to the entire list, address it to: africa-n@utoronto.bitnet

`mailto:listserv@utoronto.bitnet`

C-SPAN (Cable-Satellite Public Affairs Network) Gopher

Online information from C-SPAN, the public affairs television network.

Keywords: News Media, Government, Congress (US), Television
Sponsor: C-SPAN
Audience: Journalists, Government Officials, Educators (K-12), General Public
Profile: Comprehensive listings of C-SPAN's programming and coverage of events in Washington D.C. and beyond. In addition to the programming notes and schedules, this site also features online educational resources sponsored by C-SPAN, text of historic documents and speeches, and background political information on the House of Representatives and the Supreme Court.
Contact: cspanviewr@aol.com
Details: Free

`gopher://c-span.org`

CNN Headline News Gopher

Latest news as read by the CNN anchorpersons. Searchable index of subject matter.

Keywords: News Media, Politics (International), Journalism
Sponsor: CNN Newsource Service
Audience: General Public, Students, Journalists
Contact: Chet Rhodes
cr9@umail.umd.edu
Details: Free

`gopher://info.umd.edu:925/`

Cro-News/SCYU-Digest

This unmoderated list is the distribution point for the news coming from Croatia. The list carries articles from Novi Vjesnik, Vecernji List, Croatia Monitor, Slobodna Dalmacija, Novi Danas, Radio Free Europe/Radio Luxemburg bulletins, and UPI reports.

Keywords: Croatia, News Media
Audience: Croats, Journalists, General Public
Contact: Nino Margetic
cro-news-request@medphys.ucl.ac.uk
Details: Free
User Info: To subscribe to the list, send an e-mail message requesting a subscription to the URL address below.
To send a message to the entire list, address it to: cro-news@medphys.ucl.ac.uk

`mailto:cro-news-request@medphys.ucl.ac.uk`

Jane's Defense & Aerospace News/Analysis

This file provides articles that summarize, highlight, and interpret worldwide events in the defense and aerospace industry.

Keywords: Defense, Aerospace, News Media
Sponsor: Jane's Information Group, Alexandria, VA US
Audience: Aerospace Industry Professionals
Profile: The database contains the complete text of the following publications: Jane's Defense Weekly, International Defense Review, Jane's Intelligence Review (formerly Jane's Soviet Intelligence Review), Interavia Aerospace Review, and Jane's Airport Review. File 587 also contains the complete text of DMS newsletters, which ceased publication in 1989.
Contact: Dialog in the US at (800) 334-2564, Dialog internationally at country-specific locations.
User Info: To subscribe, contact Dialog directly.
Notes: Coverage: 1982 to the present; updated weekly.

`telnet://dialog.com`

Navnews

Contains official news and information about fleet operations and exercises, personnel policies, budget actions, and more. This is the same news service that is distributed through Navy circuits to ships at sea and to shore commands around the world. Subscriptions to NAVNEWS by e-mail are available at no charge to anyone with a mailbox on any network reachable through the Internet.

Keywords: Navy, News
Sponsor: The Navy Internal Relations Activity, Washington, DC

News Media

Audience: Navy Personnel, Sailors, General Public
Contact: navnews@nctamslant.navy.mil
Details: Free
User Info: To subscribe to the list, send an e-mail message requesting a subscription to the URL address below.

`mailto:navnews@nctamslant.navy.mil`

News

This directory is a general compilation of information resources focused on news.

Keywords: News, Electronic Media, Journalism
Audience: Newsreaders, Journalists, General Public
Details: Free

`ftp://una.hh.lib.umich.edu/70/inetdirsstacks/news:robinson`

Voice of America and Worldnet

A gopher server for the Voice of America and Worldnet. Includes full-text transcripts of VOA news reports, press releases, and announcements.

Keywords: US Government Publications, News Media, Radio, International Communication
Sponsor: United States Information Agency
Audience: Journalists, Government Officials, General Public
Contact: info@voa.gov, letters-usa@VOA.GOV (for correspondence from inside the U.S.)

`gopher://gopher.voa.gov`

WIRED Online

This is WIRED Magazine's gopher server.

Keywords: Postmodern Culture, News Media
Sponsor: WIRED Magazine
Audience: Internet Surfers, Internet Users, General Public
Profile: Features full-text of WIRED back issues, including the Net Surf column devoted to Internet exploration. Also has archives of the HotWIRED weekly mailing list, some guides to getting started surfing the net, general information about WIRED magazine, and an archive of material on the proposed Clipper federal encryption standard.
Contact: WIRED Online department, WIRED Magazine
online@wired.com, info@wired.com

`gopher://gopher.wired.com`

News, Weather, and Travel Advisories

News, Weather, and Travel Advisories

A major directory of news, weather, and travel advisories, providing access to a broad range of related resources (library catalogues, databases, and servers) via the Internet.

Keywords: Travel, Weather, Aviation
Sponsor: Kennesaw State College, Georgia, USA
Audience: General Public, Travelers/Tourists
Profile: This collection includes CNN news sources, the National Weather Service Forecast, and the US State Department Travel Advisory, among other sources.
Details: Free

`gopher://kscsuna1.kennesaw.edu`

news.announce.conferences

news.announce.conferences

A Usenet newsgroup providing information and discussion about conferences, as well as calls for papers.

Keywords: Conferences, Paper, Writing
Audience: Writers, General Public
Details: Free
User Info: To subscribe to this Usenet newsgroup, you need access to a newsreader.

`news:news.announce.conferences`

news.announce.newgroups

news.announce.newgroups

A Usenet newsgroup providing information and discussion about creating a new newsgroup, changing active newsgroups, and how to access new Usenet groups.

Keywords: Usenet, Internet Resources
Audience: Usenet Users
Details: Free
User Info: To subscribe to this Usenet newsgroup, you need access to a newsreader.

`news:news.announce.newgroups`

news.answers

news.answers

A Usenet newsgroup providing information and discussion about periodic Usenet articles.

Keywords: Usenet, Internet Resources
Audience: Usenet Users
Details: Free
User Info: To subscribe to this Usenet newsgroup, you need access to a newsreader.

`news:news.answers`

news.groups

news.groups

A Usenet newsgroup providing information and discussion about lists of existing newsgroups.

Keywords: Usenet, Internet Resources
Audience: Usenet Users
Details: Free
User Info: To subscribe to this Usenet newsgroup, you need access to a newsreader.

`news:news.groups`

news.lists

news.lists

A Usenet newsgroup providing information and discussion about news-related statistics and lists.

Keywords: Usenet, Internet Resources
Audience: Usenet Users
Details: Free
User Info: To subscribe to this Usenet newsgroup, you need access to a newsreader.

`news:news.lists`

news.newusers.questions

news.newusers.questions

A Usenet newsgroup providing information and discussion about Usenet news groups.

Keywords: Usenet, E-mail, Internet Resources
Audience: Usenet Users, E-mail Users
Details: Free
User Info: To subscribe to this Usenet newsgroup, you need access to a newsreader.

`news:news.newusers.questions`

news.aus.films

news.aus.films

Discussion of films and the film industry from an Australian perspective.

Keywords: Film, Australia
Audience: Australia Enthusiasts, Film Enthusiasts
Details: Free
User Info: To subscribe to a Usenet newsgroup, you need access to a "newsreader."

`news:aus.films`

Newsbrief

Newsbrief

Provides a variety of information and feature articles, primarily for campus users.

Keywords: Information Technology
Sponsor: Office of Information Technology at the University of North Carolina, Chapel Hill (UNC Chapel Hill)
Audience: Students, Educators
Contact: Karen C. Blansfield, Judy Hallman
karen@rhumba.acs.unc.edu
Details: Free
User Info: To subscribe, send an e-mail message to the URL address below consisting of a single line reading:

SUB newsbrief YourFirstName YourLastName

To send a message to the entire list, address it to: newsbrief@uricvmi.bitnet

`mailto:listserv@uncvm1.bitnet`

NewsCommando

NewsCommando

This makes available synergies discerned in, and created from, print news media (up to a 12-year time span). The depth of insight possible using the information-mosaic method can be staggering. A form of an electronic magazine, NewsCommando serves as a reference tool, allows access to Medline, PaperChase, or other searches, and, in many ways, is the poor man's IdeaFisher/IdeaBank.

Keywords: NewsCommando, News
Audience: NewsCommando Users
Contact: Lance Sanders
starkid@ddsw1.mcs.com
Details: Free

User Info: Articles will be deposited in your mailbox with a "NewsCom/Vol.#" Subject header. Most will be in excess of 20K. Please group-save them to a file for later reading.

`mailto:starkid@ddsw1.mcs.com`

Newsletter on Serials Pricing Issues

Newsletter on Serials Pricing Issues

The focus of this newsletter is the pricing of library serials.

Keywords: Serials Pricing, Librarianship
Audience: Librarians, Publishing Professionals
Profile: Contributions include examples of titles considered to be overpriced, as well as of publishers' actions to keep prices down, strategies for coping with serials price increases, information about libraries' evaluation and cancellation policies and procedures, announcements of and reports from relevant meetings, and other news of serials prices.
Contact: Marcia Tuttle
tuttle@unc.bitnet
Details: Free
User Info: To subscribe, send an e-mail message to the URL address shown below consisting of a single line reading:

SUB serials_pricing YourFirstName YourLastName

`mailto:listserv@uncvx1.Bitnet`

Newsletters

CCNEWS

An electronic forum for campus-computing newsletter editors and other publications specialists.

Keywords: Computers, Editors, Students, Newsletters
Audience: Students (college), Editors
Profile: CCNEWS consists of a biweekly newsletter that focuses on the writing, editing, designing, and producing of campus-computing publications, and an articles abstracts published on alternating weeks that describes new contributions to the articles archive.
Contact: Wendy Rickard Bollentin
ccnews@educom.bitnet
Details: Free

User Info: To subscribe to the list, send an e-mail message to the URL address below consisting of a single line reading:

SUB ccnews YourFirstName YourLastName

To send a message to the entire list, address it to: ccnews@educom.bitnet

Inquire about needing a password.

`mailto:listserv@bitnic.cren.net`

Newsline

Newsline

An electronic newsletter describing additions to or changes in Comserve, the electronic information and discussion service for communications faculty and students.

Keywords: Communications, Comserve
Audience: Communications Students, Communications Specialists
Profile: The information includes announcements of additions to Comserve's database, new services offered through Comserve's electronic conferences, or fundamental changes in the services offered by Comserve.
Contact: Timothy Stephen, Teresa Harrison
Support@Rpiecs
Support@Vm.Ecs.Rpi.Edu
User Info: To subscribe, send an e-mail message to the URL address below consisting of a single line reading:

SUB NEWSLINE YourFirstName YourLastName

`mailto:Comserve@Vm.Ecs.Rpi.Edu`

NeXT

comp.sys.next

A Usenet newsgroup providing information and discussion about NeXT computers. There are several categories within this group.

Keywords: Computer Systems, NeXT
Audience: Computer Users, NeXT Users
User Info: To subscribe to this Usenet newsgroup, you need access to a newsreader.

`news:comp.sys.next`

next-gis

Discussion of Geographical Information Systems (GIS) and cartography-related topics on the NeXT and other workstation computers. Some moderated reposting of comp.infosys.gis occurs as well.

Keywords: Geography, Cartography, GIS, NeXT
Audience: GIS Users, NeXT Users

Contact:	Steven R. Staton sstaton@deltos.com	
Details:	Free	
User Info:	To subscribe to the list, send an e-mail message to the URL address shown below consisting of a single line reading: SUB next-gis YourFirstName YourLastName To send a message to the entire list, address it to: next-gis@DistributionAddress	

mailto:listserv@deltos.com

NeXT-icon

Distribute and receive 64 x 64 or 48 x 48 pixel icons, (2-, 12-, 24- and/or 32-bit), compatible with the NeXT Computer's NeXTSTEP software. Nearly all mail is in NeXTmail format.

Keywords:	NeXT, NeXT-icon
Audience:	NeXT Users
Contact:	Timothy Reed next-icon-request@bmt.gun.com
Details:	Free
User Info:	To subscribe to the list, send an e-mail message requesting a subscription to the URL address below. To send a message to the entire list, address it to: next-icon@bmt.gun.com

mailto:next-icon-request@bmt.gun.com

NeXT-Med

NeXT-Med is open to end users and developers interested in medical solutions using NeXT computers and/or 486 systems running NeXTSTEP. Discussions on any topic related to NeXT use in the medical industry or related to health care is encouraged.

Keywords:	NeXT, NeXT-Med
Audience:	NeXT Users, NeXT Developers
Contact:	next-med-request@ms.uky.edu
Details:	Free
User Info:	To subscribe to the list, send an e-mail message requesting a subscription to the URL address below. To send a message to the entire list, address it to: next-med@ms.uky.edu

mailto:next-med@ms.uky.edu

NFL

Funet Sports Information

An FTP archive of information on various sports with links to the archive at wuarchive.wustl.edu.

Keywords:	Sports, Professional Sports, Ice Hockey, Motor Racing, NFL, NHL, NBA, MLB
Sponsor:	Finnish Academic and Research Network (FUNET)
Audience:	Sports Enthusiasts
Profile:	A fairly extensive archive of information on both American (NBA, MLB, NHL, NFL) and worldwide sports (soccer, ice hockey, motor racing, and so on). Includes FAQs for various sports, statistics, pictures, and some sports games for the PC.
Contact:	Jari Pullinen sports-adm@nic.funet.fi
Details:	Free, Images

gopher://ftp.funet.fi/pub/sports

NFL Scores, Schedules, and Point Spreads

Information on National Football League (NFL) football scores, schedules, and point spreads.

Keywords:	Sports, Football, NFL
Audience:	Football Enthusiasts
Contact:	office@world.std.com
Details:	Free

gopher://world.std.com/News and Weather

NHL

Dallas Stars

Discussion of the Dallas Stars (of the National Hockey League) and their farm clubs.

Keywords:	Hockey, NHL
Audience:	NHL Enthusiasts
Details:	Free
User Info:	To subscribe to the list, send an e-mail message requesting a subscription to the URL address below. To send a message to the entire list, address it to: hamlet@u.washington.edu
Notes:	Please include the word "DSTARS" in your subject line and include your name and preferred e-mail address in the body of your message.

mailto:hamlet@u.washington.edu

Funet Sports Information

An FTP archive of information on various sports with links to the archive at wuarchive.wustl.edu.

Keywords:	Sports, Professional Sports, Ice Hockey, Motor Racing, NFL, NHL, NBA, MLB
Sponsor:	Finnish Academic and Research Network (FUNET)
Audience:	Sports Enthusiasts
Profile:	A fairly extensive archive of information on both American (NBA, MLB, NHL, NFL) and worldwide sports (soccer, ice hockey, motor racing, and so on). Includes FAQs for various sports, statistics, pictures, and some sports games for the PC.
Contact:	Jari Pullinen sports-adm@nic.funet.fi
Details:	Free, Images

gopher://ftp.funet.fi/pub/sports

NHL Goalie Stats

A mailing list for the distribution of information regarding goalie stats.

Keywords:	Hockey
Audience:	Hockey Enthusiasts
Profile:	Weekday reports of goalie statistics from the National Hockey League.
Contact:	dfa@triple-i.com
Details:	Free
User Info:	To subscribe to the list, send an e-mail message requesting a subscription to the URL address below. To send a message to the entire list, address it to: dfa@triple-i.com

mailto:dfa@triple-i.com

OlympPuck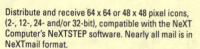

This list is for the discussion of Olympic ice hockey. Discussions concerning players, coaches, teams, and games are welcome and are encouraged. Related topics, such as the interaction between the Olympic competition and college or NHL hockey, are also discussed.

Keywords:	Olympics, Ice Hockey, NHL
Audience:	Ice Hockey Players, Olympics Enthusiasts, Ice Hockey Fans
Details:	Free
User Info:	To subscribe to the list, send an e-mail message to the URL address below, consisting of a single line reading: SUB olympuck YourFirstName YourLastName To send a message to the entire list, address it to: olympuck@maine.maine.edu

mailto:listserv@maine.maine.edu

NIBNews - A Monthly Electronic Bulletin About Medical Informatics

NIBNews - A Monthly Electronic Bulletin About Medical Informatics

Disseminates information about Brazilian and Latin American activities, people, information, events, publications, software, and so on, involving computer applications in health care, medicine, and biology.

Keywords: Health Care, Biology, Brazil, Latin America, South America, Medicine
Audience: Health Care Professionals, Biologists
Contact: Renato M. E. Sabbatini
sabbatini@bruc.bitnet
Details: Free

mailto:sabbatini@ccvax.unicamp.br

NIC (Nucleus for Interactive Computing)

NIC (Nucleus for Interactive Computing)

WWW-based system for interactive computing.

Keywords: Multimedia, Interactive Computing, Interface Design, Scripting Languages, Programming
Sponsor: BYU Interactive Software Systems Lab
Audience: Software Developers, Educators
Profile: NIC is a system for interactive computing that combines a data model, a user interface model, and a scripting language to create flexible and powerful user interfaces. Documentation still under construction is located here.
Contact: Dan Olsen
olsen@cs.byu.edu
Details: Free, Moderated; Sound, Image and Multimedia files available.
Use a World Wide Web (Mosaic) client and open a connection to the resource.

ftp://issl.cs.byu.edu/docs/NIC/home.html

Nickelodeon

Clarissa

This list discusses the Nickelodeon TV show "Clarissa Explains It All."

Keywords: Television Shows, Nickelodeon
Audience: Nickelodeon Viewers, TV Viewers
Contact: Jim Lick
clarissa-request@tcp.com
Details: Free
User Info: To subscribe to the list, send an e-mail message requesting a subscription to the URL address below.
To send a message to the entire list, address it to: clarissa@tcp.com

mailto:clarissa-request@tcp.com

NIH (National Institute of Health)

National Institute of Health Library Online Catalog

This entry point provides access to the books and journal holdings in the NIH Library. Journal articles are not included.

Keywords: NIH, Medicine, Science, Libraries
Sponsor: National Institute of Health (NIH)
Audience: Scientists, Researchers, Educators, Health Care Professionals
Details: Free

telnet://nih-library.ncrr.nih.gov

NIH (National Institute of Health)

This server is a network-based computer service operated by the Division of Computer Research and Technology (DCRT) to distribute information for and about the NIH (National Institutes of Health).

Keywords: NIH, Health Sciences, Biomedical Research, Medicine
Sponsor: Division of Computer Research and Technology (DCRT), National Institute of Health
Audience: Scientists, Biomedical Researchers, Health CareProfessionals, General Public
Profile: This server provides Internet access to information about NIH health and clinical issues (including CancerNet and a variety of AIDS information), NIH-funded grants and research projects, and a variety of research resources in support of NIH and worldwide biomedical researchers. For example, the major molecular biology databases (GenBank, SWISSPROT, PIR, PDB, TFD, Prosite, LiMB) can be accessed through keyword searches from this gopher.
Details: Free

gopher://gopher.nih.gov

NIH EDNET

EdNet is set up as a free electronic bulletin board at the Bethesda, Maryland campus of the National Institute of Health (NIH). Its purpose is to allow high school students to ask questions of NIH scientists about current research.

Keywords: NIH, Education (Post Secondary), Education (K-12), Science
Sponsor: National Institute of Health (NIH)
Audience: Students, Educators
Details: Free
User Info: To receive an EDNET User's Guide and account, send an e-mail message with your name and mailing address to the URL address below.

mailto:vt5@cu.nih.gov

NIH Grant Line (Drgline Bulletin Board)

The purpose of the NIH Grant Line is to make program and policy information from the Public Health Service (PHS) agencies rapidly available to the biomedical research community.

Keywords: Biomedical Research, NIH, Grants
Sponsor: The National Institute of Health
Audience: Scientists, Researchers, Students
Profile: Most of the research opportunity information available on this bulletin board is derived from the weekly publication "NIH Guide for Grants and Contracts,", and consists of notices, RFAs, RFPs (announcements of availability), numbered program announcements, and statements of PHS policy. The information found on the NIH Grant Line is grouped into three main sections: (1) short news flashes that appear without any prompting shortly after you have logged on, (2) bulletins that are for reading, and (3) files that are intended mainly for downloading. The E-Guide is available for electronic transmission each week. The material consists predominantly of statements about the research interests of the PHS agencies, institutes, and national centers that have funds to support research in the extramural community. Currently under development are two new files: one will be a monthly listing of new NIH Awards, and the other will be an order form to obtain NIH publications from DRG's Office of Grants Inquiries.
Details: Free
User Info: To access the NIH Grant Line, telnet to the URL address below and when a message has been received that the connection is open, type: ,GEN1 (the comma is mandatory). At the INITIALS? prompt, type BB5 and at the ACCOUNT? prompt, type CCS2
The NIH Guide to Grants and Contracts can also be accessed through gopher://helix.nih.gov/11/res/nih-guide

telnet://wylbur.cu.nih.gov

Nihon Sun Microsystems

Nihon Sun Microsystems

This site provides a directory for Sun Microsystems in Japan. Includes the Rolling Stones Official Server WWW site, with access to Rolling Stones music, merchandise, and information. Also provides multimedia links to the Science University of Tokyo and other Asia-Pacific resources.

Keywords: Rolling Stones
Sponsor: Sun Microsystems, Inc., Tokyo, Japan
Audience: Computer Users, Rolling Stones Enthusiasts
Contact: www-admin@sun.co.jp
Details: Multimedia, Free, Sounds, Images

`http://www.sun.co.jp`

NIR

NIR Archives

Archives of the NIR (Networked Information Retrieval) service.

Keywords: Internet, Information Retrieval
Audience: Internet Surfers
Details: Free
Notes: Files are in: pub/lists/nir

`ftp:// mailbase.ac.uk`

NIR Gopher

The gopher for the NIR (Networked Information Retrieval) service.

Keywords: Internet, Information Retrieval, NIR
Audience: Internet Surfers
Details: Free

`gopher:// mailbase.ac.auk /11/lists-k-o/nic`

Nissan Automobiles

nissan

Discusses Nissan and Infiniti automobiles, with the exception of the Sentra SE-R, NX2000, and G20, which are served by the SE-R list.

Keywords: Nissan Automobiles, Infiniti Automobiles
Audience: Automobiles Owners, Automobiles Enthusiasts
Contact: Rich Siegel
nissan-request@world.std.com
Details: Free
User Info: To subscribe to the list, send an e-mail message requesting a subscription to the URL address below.
To send a message to the entire list, address it to: nissan@world.std.com

`mailto:nissan-request@world.std.com`

NJ-motss

NJ-motss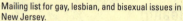

Mailing list for gay, lesbian, and bisexual issues in New Jersey.

Keywords: Gay, Lesbian, Bisexuality, New Jersey
Audience: Gays, Lesbians, Bisexuals
Contact: majordomo@plts.org
Details: Free
User Info: To subscribe to the list, send an e-mail message to the URL address shown below consisting of a single line reading:
SUB NJ-motss YourFirstName YourLastName
To send a message to the entire list, address it to: NJ-motss@plts.org

`mailto: majordomo@plts.org`

NJ-motss-announce

NJ-motss-announce

Announcements of interests to New Jersey's gay, lesbian, and bisexual population.

Keywords: Gays, Lesbians, Bisexuality, New Jersey
Audience: Gays, Lesbians, Bisexuals
Contact: majordomo@plts.org
Details: Free
User Info: To subscribe to the list, send an e-mail message to the URL address shown below consisting of a single line reading:
SUB NJ-motss-announce YourFirstName YourLastName
To send a message to the entire list, address it to: NJ-motss-announce@plts.org

`mailto:majordomo@plts.org`

nl-kr

nl-kr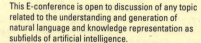

This E-conference is open to discussion of any topic related to the understanding and generation of natural language and knowledge representation as subfields of artificial intelligence.

Keywords: Programming Languages, Natural Language, Knowledge Representation, Linguistics
Audience: Computer Scientists
Contact: Christopher Welty
weltyc@cs.rpi.edu
Details: Free, Moderated
User Info: To subscribe to the list, send an e-mail message requesting a subscription to the URL address below.

`mailto:nl-kr-request@cs.rpi.edu`

NLC (National Library of Canada)

NLC (National Library of Canada)

A Canadian library gopher in French and English.

Keywords: Canada, Libraries, Library Science
Sponsor: National Library of Canada (NLC), Canada
Audience: Canadians, Librarians, Publishing Professionals
Profile: This site provides a gateway to Canadian library and Internet resources linking users to the National Library, which offers a bibliographic database, a list of NLC publications, and other services for libraries and publishers. It also has links to many other Canadian libraries and Internet services, as well as a large selection of general information from and about the Government of Canada and its provinces.
Contact: Nancy Brodie, Lynn Herbert
Nancy.Brodie@nlc-bnc.ca,
Lynn.Herbert@nlc-bnc.ca

`gopher://gopher.nlc-bnc.ca`

NLSNews Newsletter (National Longitudinal Surveys of Labor Market Experience)

NLSNews Newsletter (National Longitudinal Surveys of Labor Market Experience)

Issued by the Center for Human Resource Research (Ohio State University); distributed to researchers using NLS data, as well as to other interested persons.

Keywords: Labor, Government (US), Department of Labor
Sponsor: Bureau of Labor Statistics, US Department of Labor
Audience: Statisticians, Researchers

Profile:	A typical issue contains updates on the status and availability of NLS data tapes and CD-ROMs for the six NLS cohorts (Older Men, Mature Women, Young Men, Young Women, Youth, and Children), notices to researchers of data-file or documentation errors, summaries of in-progress and completed NLS research, and other information of general interest to the NLS research community.
Contact:	Gale James james@ohsthr.bitnet
Notes:	A description of the subscription service that enables users to automatically receive, as soon as it becomes available, the latest issue of the NLS Newsletter and/or error updates can be found in the file subscribe.info, available via nlserve@ohsthr.bitnet, the Center's file server.

`mailto:james@ohsthr.bitnet`

noglstp

noglstp

This list is sponsored by the National Organization of Gay and Lesbian Scientists and Technical Professionals, Inc. (a 501-C3 organization). National office is in Pasadena, CA and can be reached at (818) 791-7689 or p.o. Box 91803, Pasadena, CA 90019. There is also a newsletter that is available to membership.

Keywords:	Gays, Lesbians, Scientists, Technical Professionals
Audience:	Gays, Lesbians, Support
Contact:	noglstp-request@elroy.jpl.nasa.gov
Details:	Free
User Info:	To subscribe to the list, send an e-mail message requesting a subscription to the URL address below. To send a message to the entire list, address it to: noglstp@elroy.jpl.nasa.gov

`mailto:noglstp-request@elroy.jpl.nasa.gov`

Non Serviam

Non Serviam

Non Serviam is an electronic newsletter centered on the philosophy of Max Stirner, author of Der Einzige und Sein Eigentum (The Ego and Its Own) and on his dialectical egoism. The contents, however, are decided by the individual contributors and the editor.

Keywords:	Stirner (Max), Non Serviam, Philosophy
Audience:	Max Stirner Enthusiasts
Contact:	Svein Olav Nyberg solan@math.uio.no
Details:	Free
User Info:	To subscribe to the list, send an e-mail message requesting a subscription to the URL address below. To send a message to the entire list, address it to: solan@math.uio.no

`mailto:solan@math.uio.no`

Non-Governmental Organizations

World Health Organization (WHO)

This gopher provides access to the databases of the WHO.

Keywords:	World Health Organization, Health, Medicine, Non-governmental organizations
Sponsor:	World Health Organization, Geneva, Switzerland
Audience:	Medical Professionals, Researchers
Contact:	akazawa@who.ch
Details:	Free

`gopher://gopher.who.ch`

Nonfiction Books

Online BookStore (OBS)

Offers full text (fiction and nonfiction) in a variety of electronic formats, free and for a fee.

Keywords:	Online Books, Books, ShareWord, Fiction, Nonfiction Books
Sponsor:	Editorial Inc./OBS
Audience:	General Public, Reading Enthusiasts
Profile:	Started in 1992, the OBS offers a variety of full-text titles.
Contact:	Laura Fillmore laura@editorial.com
Details:	Costs, Moderated, Images, Multimedia
User Info:	To subscribe to the list, send an e-mail message requesting a subscription to the URL address below.

`http://marketplace.com/0/obs`

Nonprofit Organizations

DevelopNet News

A monthly newsletter on technology transfer in international development.

Keywords:	Nonprofits, Technology, Development
Sponsor:	Volunteers in Technical Assistance
Audience:	Technology Professionals, International Development Specialists
Contact:	R.R. Ronkin vita@gmuvax.gmu.edu
Details:	Free
User Info:	To subscribe, send an e-mail message to the address below. Inquire about needing a password.

`mailto:vita@gmuvax.gmu.edu`

Encyclopedia of Associations

The Encyclopedia of Associations database is a comprehensive source of detailed information on over 88,000 nonprofit membership organizations worldwide.

Keywords:	Nonprofit Organizations
Sponsor:	Gale Research Inc., Detroit, MI, USA
Audience:	Researchers
Profile:	The database corresponds to the print Encyclopedia of Associations family of publications as follows: National Organizations of the US, covering more than 23,000 American associations of national scope; International Organizations, covering some 11,000 multinational, binational, and non-US national organizations; and Regional, State, and Local Organizations, covering more than 54,000 US associations with interstate, state, intrastate, city, or local scope or membership.
Contact:	Dialog in the US at (800) 334-2564, Dialog internationally at country-specific locations.
User Info:	To subscribe, contact Dialog directly.
Notes:	Coverage: Current editions; updated semiannually.

`telnet://dialog.com`

Internet Nonprofit Center

A clearinghouse of information for nonprofit organizations and those interested in donating to them. Includes annual reports, directories, financial information, and brochures of selected nonprofit organizations, as well as volunteer opportunities and advice for potential donors. The Internet Nonprofit Center is currently located on EnviroLink Network, a gopher dedicated to environmental causes.

Keywords:	Nonprofit Organizations, Philanthropy
Sponsor:	American Institute of Philanthropy, USA, and The Internet Nonprofit Center, Brooklyn, New York, USA
Audience:	Activists, Philanthropists
Contact:	Cliff Landesman clandesm@panix.com

`gopher://envirolink.org`

Nordic Skiing

nordic-skiing

Discussion of Nordic skiing sports. This includes cross-country, biathlon, ski-orienteering, ski jumping, Nordic combined, telemark, and backcountry.

Keywords:	Nordic Skiing
Audience:	Skiers
Contact:	Mitch Collinsworth nordic-ski-request@graphics.cornell.edu
Details:	Free
User Info:	To subscribe to the list, send an e-mail message requesting a subscription to the URL address below. To send a message to the entire list, address it to: nordic-ski@graphics.cornell.edu

`mailto:nordic-ski-request@graphics.cornell.edu`

Nordic University

NORDUnet region Root Gopher

The Nordic University and Research Network is a collaboration by the national research networks in Denmark, Finland, Iceland, Norway, and Sweden. It provides the national research and education communities with an efficient networking service that ensures the coherence of the national networks and connects these to similar networks in the rest of Europe and the world.

Keywords:	Nordic University, Europe
Audience:	Internet Surfers
Contact:	hostmaster@nic.nordu.net
Details:	Free

`gopher://gopher.nordu.net`

North America

NSAMER (North and South America Library)

The North and South America library contains detailed information about every country in North and South America (except the United States). The US-Canada Free Trade Agreement, the North American Free Trade Agreement, relations with Mexico and events in such countries as Brazil, Peru, and Nicaragua are among the topics covered by a variety of business, news and legal sources. International research reports from InvestextR are also included. The United States is not covered in this library.

Keywords:	News, Analysis, Companies, North America, South America
Audience:	Journalists, Business Professionals
Profile:	The North and South America library contains a broad array of sources. Among the information sources are newspapers and wire services, trade and business journals, company reports, country and region backgrounds, industry and product analyses, business opportunities, and selected legal texts. News sources range from the world-renowned Washington Post and Christian Science Monitor to the regionally important Toronto Star and Latin American Newsletters. Canadian Business and Maclean's represent a portion of the array of business and trade journals. Company information is contained in the EXTEL cards as well as ICC. Providers of country background and industry analyses include Associated Banks of Europe, Bank of America, Business International, IBC USA and the US Department of Commerce. Among the specialized resources are IBC's Mexico and Brazil Services as well as BI's Business Latin America. Researchers interested in new business opportunities can check OPIC and Foreign Trade Opportunities (FTO). And selected legal texts covering the US-Canada Free Trade Agreement and other international agreements planners and advisors to better assess the business climate in North and South America.
Contact:	Mead New Sales Group at (800) 227-4908 or (513) 859-5398 inside the US, or (513) 865-7981 for all inquiries outside the US.
User Info:	To subscribe, contact Mead directly. To examine the Nexis user guide, you can access it at the ftp site of the University of Texas at Austin at the URL address: ftp://ftp.cc.utexas.edu The files are in: /pub/ref-services/LEXIS

`telnet://nex.meaddata.com`

`http://www.meaddata.com`

North American Free Trade Agreement (NAFTA)

North American Free Trade Agreement (NAFTA)

The agreement between the governments of Canada, the United Mexican States, and the United States of America to establish a free trade area in North America.

Keywords:	Foreign Trade, Mexico, Canada, Free Trade, NAFTA
Audience:	Journalists, Politicians, Economists, Students
Details:	Free

`gopher://wiretap.spies.com/00/Gov/NAFTA`

North Carolina

Newsbrief

Provides a variety of information and feature articles, primarily for campus users.

Keywords:	University of North Carolina, North Carolina; Information Technology
Sponsor:	Office of Information Technology at the University of North Carolina, Chapel Hill (UNC Chapel Hill)
Audience:	Students, Educators
Contact:	Karen C. Blansfield, Judy Hallman karen@rhumba.acs.unc.edu
Details:	Free
User Info:	To subscribe, send an e-mail message to the URL address below consisting of a single line reading: To send a message to the entire list,

`mailto:listserv@uncvm1.bitnet`

University of North Carolina at Chapel Hill Info Library

The library's holdings are large and wide-ranging and contain significant collections in many fields.

Keywords:	North Carolina; Southern Historical Collection, Rare Books; Books (Antiquarian)
Audience:	Researchers, Students, General Public
Contact:	Judy Hallman hallman@unc.bitnet
Details:	Free
User Info:	Expect: Login; Send: Info

`telnet://info.oit.unc.edu`

Northwestern University Library

Northwestern University Library

The library's holdings are large and wide-ranging and contain significant collections in many fields.

Keywords:	Africa, Wright (Frank Lloyd), Women's Studies, Art, Literature (American), Contemporary Music, Government (US State), UN Documents, Music
Audience:	General Public, Researchers, Librarians, Document Delivery Professionals
Details:	Free
User Info:	Expect: COMMAND:, Send: DIAL VTAM

`telnet://nuacvm.acns.nwu.edu`

Norway

NORWEAVE

Building on the success of NORWAVES, NORWEAVE is an additional e-mail service for Norwegians and friends of Norway. The aim of NORWEAVE is to create a network of people in Norway and abroad who can help each other exchange information and establish contacts across geographical boundaries.

Keywords: Norway
Audience: Norwegians, Travelers/Tourists
Contact: listserv@nki.no
Details: Free
User Info: To subscribe to the list, send an e-mail message to the URL address shown below consisting of a single line reading:

SUB norweave YourFirstName YourLastName

To send a message to the entire list, address it to: norweave@nki.no

mailto:listserv@nki.no

Notable Women

Notable Women

A database listing some important and notable women through the ages. Available for online searching by keyword, or as a full-text file.

Keywords: Women's Studies, History (Women's), Feminism
Sponsor: Estrella Mountain Community College (Arizona)
Audience: Women's Studies Educators, Historians, Researchers, Feminists
Contact: EMC Gopher Team
root@gopher.emc.maricopa.edu

gopher://gopher.emc.maricopa.edu

NotGNU

NotGNU

There are three lists associated with the NotGNU Emacs editor. NotGNU-list is an interactive list dedicated to miscellaneous discussions, problems, and suggestions for NotGNU. NotGNU-announce is used for announcing new versions of NotGNU, notification of new services, bug reports, amd so on. NotGNU-distribution is a list to which new NotGNU binaries will be sent unencoded upon release.

Keywords: NotGNU, Emacs
Audience: NotGNU Users
Contact: notgnu-request@netcom.com
Details: Free
User Info: To subscribe to the list, send an e-mail message requesting a subscription to the URL address below.

To send a message to the entire list, address it to: notgnu@netcom.com

mailto:notgnu-request@netcom.com

Novice MZT

Novice MZT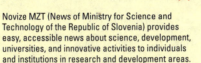

Novize MZT (News of Ministry for Science and Technology of the Republic of Slovenia) provides easy, accessible news about science, development, universities, and innovative activities to individuals and institutions in research and development areas. Published at least once monthly.

Keywords: Slovenia, Science, Technology, News
Audience: Slovenians, Scientists, Technocrats
Contact: Novice-mzt@krpan.arnes.si or Novice.mzt@uni-lj.si
User Info: To subscribe to the list, send an e-mail message requesting a subscription to the URL address below.

To send a message to the entire list, address it to: Novice-mzt@krpan.arnes.si

mailto:Novice-MZT@krpan.arnes.si

NPLC

NPLC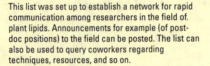

This list was set up to establish a network for rapid communication among researchers in the field of plant lipids. Announcements for example (of post-doc positions) to the field can be posted. The list can also be used to query coworkers regarding techniques, resources, and so on.

Keywords: Plant Lipids
Audience: Researchers
Contact: Walid Tout
tout@genesys.cps.msu.edu
Details: Free
User Info: To subscribe to the list, send an e-mail message requesting a subscription to the URL address below.

To send a message to the entire list, address it to: nplc@genesys.cps.msu.edu

mailto:NPLC@genesys.cps.msu.edu

NQTHM

nqthm-users

Discussion of theorem proving using the Boyler-Moore theorem prover, NQTHM. Offers lore, advice, information, discussion, and help.

Keywords: Computer Programs, NQTHM, Boyler-Moore Theorem Prover
Audience: NQTHM Theorem Users
Contact: nqthm-users-request@cli.com
Details: Free
User Info: To subscribe to the list, send an e-mail message requesting a subscription to the URL address below.

To send a message to the entire list, address it to: nqthm-users@cli.com

mailto:nqthm-users@cli.com

NSAMER (North and South America Library)

NSAMER (North and South America Library)

The North and South America library contains detailed information about every country in North and South America (except the United States). The US-Canada Free Trade Agreement, the North American Free Trade Agreement, relations with Mexico and events in such countries as Brazil, Peru, and Nicaragua are among the topics covered by a variety of business, news and legal sources. International research reports from InvestextR are also included. The United States is not covered in this library.

Keywords: News, Analysis, Companies, North America, South America
Audience: Journalists, Business Professionals
Profile: The North and South America library contains a broad array of sources. Among the information sources are newspapers and wire services, trade and business journals, company reports, country and region backgrounds, industry and product analyses, business opportunities, and selected legal texts. News sources range from the world-renowned Washington Post and Christian Science Monitor to the regionally important Toronto Star and Latin American Newsletters. Canadian Business and Maclean's represent a portion of the array of business and trade journals. Company information is contained in the EXTEL cards as well as ICC. Providers of country background and industry analyses include Associated Banks of Europe, Bank of America, Business International, IBC USA and the US Department of Commerce. Among the specialized resources are IBC's Mexico and Brazil Services as well as BI's Business Latin America. Researchers interested in new business opportunities can check OPIC and Foreign Trade Opportunities (FTO).And selected legal texts covering the US-Canada Free Trade Agreement and other international agreements planners and advisors to better assess the business climate in North and South America.

NSF Resource Guide

NSF Resource Guide ★

A guide to Internet resources from the NSF (National Science Foundation).

- Keywords: Internet, Internet Guides
- Audience: Internet Surfers
- Details: Free
- Note: Read the overview in: resource-guide/overview

`ftp://ds.internic.net`

NSSDC (National Space Science Data Center)'s Online Data & Information Service

NSSDC (National Space Science Data Center)'s Online Data & Information Service ★★★

The NSSDC (National Space Science Data Center) is the NASA facility charged with archiving the data from all of NASA's science missions.

- Keywords: Space, Science, Astrophysics, Software, NASA, Science
- Sponsor: NASA
- Audience: Scientists, Space Scientists, Astronomers, Engineers
- Profile: This resource contains information about NASA's missions and analysis of their data.
- Details: Free
- User Info: Expect: Login, Send: nssdc

  See the menu entries in your particular area of interest.

`telnet://nssdc.gsfc.nasa.gov`

Contact: Mead New Sales Group at (800) 227-4908 or (513) 859-5398 inside the US, or (513) 865-7981 for all inquiries outside the US.

User Info: To subscribe, contact Mead directly.

To examine the Nexis user guide, you can access it at the ftp site of the University of Texas at Austin at the URL address: ftp://ftp.cc.utexas.edu

The files are in: /pub/ref-services/LEXIS

`telnet://nex.meaddata.com`

`http://www.meaddata.com`

NTIS FedWorld

NTIS FedWorld ★

- Keywords: NTIS FedWorld
- Audience: General Public, Researchers, Business Professionals, Politicians
- Contact: Bob Bunge
  webmaster@fedworld.gov

`http://www.fedworld.gov`

`telnet://fedworld.gov`

`ftp://ftp.fedworld.gov`

ntp

ntp ★

Discussion of the Network Time Protocol.

- Keywords: Network Time Protocol
- Audience: Network Time Protocol Users
- Contact: ntp-request@trantor.umd.edu
- User Info: To subscribe to the list, send an e-mail message requesting a subscription to the URL address below.

  To send a message to the entire list, address it to: ntp@trantor.umd.edu

`mailto:ntp-request@trantor.umd.edu`

Nuclear Medicine

nucmed ★

A discussion of nuclear medicine and related issues. Of particular concern is the format of digital images.

- Keywords: Nuclear Medicine
- Audience: Medical Researchers, Doctors
- Contact: Trevor Cradduck
  trevorc@uwovax.uwo.ca
- Details: Free
- User Info: To subscribe to the list, send an e-mail message requesting a subscription to the URL address below.

  To send a message to the entire list, address it to: nucmed@uwovax.uwo.ca

`mailto:nucmed-request@uwovax.uwo.ca`

Nuclear Safety

Illinois Legislation ★

This directory contains several Illinois Department of Nuclear Safety Statues and Regulations.

- Keywords: Nuclear Safety, Law, Illinois
- Audience: Lawyers
- Details: Free

`gopher://wiretap.spies.com`

numeric-interest

numeric-interest ★

Discussion of issues of floating-point correctness and performance with respect to hardware, operating systems, languages, and standard libraries.

- Keywords: Computer Hardware
- Audience: Computer Users
- Contact: David Hough
  numeric-interest-request@validgh.com
- Details: Free
- User Info: To subscribe to the list, send an e-mail message requesting a subscription to the URL address below.

  To send a message to the entire list, address it to: numeric-interest@validgh.com

`mailto:numeric-interest-request@validgh.com`

Numerical Analysis

NA-net ★

This mailing list is a forum for discussions on the subject of numerical analysis.

- Keywords: Numerical Analysis
- Audience: Numerical Analysts
- User Info: To subscribe to the list, send an e-mail message requesting a subscription to the URL address below.

`mailto:na.join@na-net.ornl.gov`

Numismatics

coins ★

A forum for discussions on numismatic topics, including US and world coins, paper money, tokens, and medals.

Keywords: Coins, Numismatics
Audience: Coin Collectors
Contact: Daniel J. Power
coins-request@iscsvax.uni.edu
Details: Free
User Info: To subscribe to the list, send an e-mail message requesting a subscription to the URL address below.

To send a message to the entire list, address it to: coins@iscsvax.uni.edu

`mailto:coins-request@iscsvax.uni.edu`

Harvard University Library ★★

The library's holdings are large and wide-ranging and contain significant collections in many fields.

Keywords: Afrikaans, Alchemy, Arabic Culure (History of), Celtic Philology, Congo Languages, Folklore, Hebraica, Mormonism, Numismatics, Quakers, Sanskrit, Witchcraft, Arabic Philology
Audience: General Public, Researchers, Librarians, Document Delivery Professionals
Details: Free
User Info: Expect: Mitek Server..., Send: Enter or Return; Expect: prompt, Send: hollis

`telnet://hollis.harvard.edu`

University of Colorado at Boulder Library ★★

The library's holdings are large and wide-ranging and contain significant collections in many fields.

Keywords: Numismatics, Human Rights, Literature (Children's), Labor Archives, History (US)
Audience: Researchers, Students, General Public
Contact: Donna Pattee
pattee@spot.colorado.edu
Details: Free
User Info: Expect: Login; Send: Culine

`telnet://culine.colorado.edu`

Nursing

Johns Hopkins University Library ★★

The library's holdings are large and wide-ranging and contain significant collections in many fields.

Keywords: Literature (English), Economics, Classics, Drama (German), Slavery, Trade Unions, Incunabula, Bibles, Diseases (History of), Nursing, Abolitionism
Audience: General Public, Researchers, Librarians, Document Delivery Professionals
Details: Free

`telnet://jhuvm.hcf.jhu.edu`

MEDLINE ★

MEDLINE is a major source of bibliographic biomedical literature. The MEDLINE database encompasses information from three printed indexes (Index Medicus, Index to Dental Literature and the International Nursing Index) as well as additional information not published in the Index Medicus.

Keywords: Biomedicine, Dentistry, Nursing, Medicine
Sponsor: U.S. National Library of Medicine
Audience: Librarians, Researchers, Physicians, Students
Contact: CDP Technologies Sales Department (800)950-2035, extension 400
User Info: To subscribe, contact CDP Technologies directly

`telnet://cdplus@cdplus.com`

Midwifery Resources on the Net ★★

A resource list for helping find information about midwifery on the Internet.

Keywords: Midwifery, Childbirth, Medicine, Nursing
Audience: Midwives, Medical professionals
Details: Free

`gopher://una.hh.lib.umich.edu`

University of Maryland SystemLibrary ★★

The library's holdings are large and wide-ranging and contain significant collections in many fields.

Keywords: Medicine (History of), Nursing, Pharmacology, Microbiology, Aquaculture, Aquatic Chemistry, Toxicology
Audience: General Public, Researchers, Librarians, Document Delivery Professionals
Contact: Ron Larsen
Details: Free
User Info: Expect: Available Services menu; Send: PAC

`telnet://victor.umd.edu`

University of Pennsylvania School of Medicine Library ★★

The library's holdings are large and wide-ranging and contain significant collections in many fields.

Keywords: Health Care, Nursing, History, Health
Audience: Researchers, Students, General Public
Details: Free
User Info: Expect: Login; Send: Public

`telnet://penninfo.upenn.edu`

University of Puerto Rico Library ★★

The library's holdings are large and wide-ranging and contain significant collections in many fields.

Keywords: Computer Science, Education, Nursing, Agriculture, Economics
Audience: Researchers, Students, General Public
Details: Free

After Locator: telnet://, press Tab twice. Type DIAL VTAM. Enter NOTIS.

Press Return. On the blank screen, type LUUP.

`telnet://136.145.2.10`

University of Texas at Austin Library ★★

The library's holdings are large and wide-ranging and contain significant collections in many fields.

Keywords: Music, Natural Science, Nursing, Science Technology, Behavioral Science, Social Work, Computer Science, Engineering, Latin American Studies, Middle Eastern Studies
Audience: Researchers, Students, General Public
Details: Free
User Info: Expect: Blank Screen, Send: Return; Expect: Go, Send: Return; Expect: Enter Terminal Type, Send: vt100

note: Some databases are restricted to UT Austin users only.

`telnet://utcat.utexas.edu`

University of Texas at Galveston (Medical Branch) Library ★★

The library's holdings are large and wide-ranging and contain significant collections in many fields.

Keywords: Health Sciences, Biomedicine, Nursing
Audience: Researchers, Students, General Public
Details: Free
User Info: Expect: Login, Send: Library

`telnet://ibm.gal.utexas.edu`

University of Texas Health Science Center at San Antonio Library ★★

The library's holdings are large and wide-ranging and contain significant collections in many fields.

Keywords: Allied Health, Dentistry, Nursing, Veterinary Science, Ambulatory Care, Obstetrics/Gynecology, Pediatrics
Audience: Researchers, Students, General Public
Details: Free
User Info: Expect: Login, Send: LIS

`telnet://athena.uthscsa.edu`

University of Wisconsin at Oshkosh Library

The library's holdings are large and wide-ranging and contain significant collections in many fields.

Keywords: Business, Liberal Education, Nursing
Audience: Researchers, Students, General Public
Details: Free
User Info: Expect: Login; Send: Lib; Expect: vDIAL Prompt, Send: Library

`telnet://polk.cis.uwosh.edu`

University of Wisconsin Eau Claire Library

The library's holdings are large and wide-ranging and contain significant collections in many fields.

Keywords: Health Sciences, Business, Nursing, Education
Audience: Researchers, Students, General Public
Details: Free
User Info: Expect: Service Name, Send: Victor

`telnet://lib.uwec.edu`

Nutrition

Federal Food and Drug Administration

The Federal Food and Drug Administration (FDA) databank contains reports and articles related to the FDA.

Keywords: FDA, Drug Regulations, Nutrition
Sponsor: Federal Food and Drug Administration
Audience: Researchers, Nutritionists, Consumers, Health Care Providers
Profile: The topics covered include the drug and device product-approvals list, FDA federal register summaries by subject, text from drug bulletins, current information on AIDS, FDA consumer magazine index and selected articles, summaries of FDA information, text of testimony at FDA congressional hearings, and speeches given by the FDA commissioner and deputy.
Details: Free

`telnet://bbs@fdabbs.fda.gov`

GRANOLA (Vegetarian Discussion List)

A ListServ for discussion of vegetarian issues, including everything from recipes to animal rights.

Keywords: Health, Nutrition, Vegetarian, Recipes
Audience: Vegetarians, Nutritionists, Health Professionals

Details: Free
User Info: To subscribe to the list, send an e-mail message to the URL address shown below consisting of a single line reading:

SUB granola YourFirstName YourLastName

`mailto:listserv@gitvm1.bitnet`

Health Periodicals Database

This source covers a broad range of health subjects and issues.

Keywords: Health, Biotechnology, Medicine, Nutrition
Sponsor: Information Access Company, Foster City, CA, US
Audience: Health Professionals, Dieticians, Librarians
Profile: The database provides indexing and full text of journals covering a broad range of health subjects and issues including: prenatal care, dieting, drug abuse, AIDS, biotechnology, cardiovascular disease, environment, public health, safety, paramedical professions, sports medicine, substance abuse, toxicology, and much more.
Contact: Dialog in the US at (800) 334-2564, Dialog internationally at country-specific locations.
User Info: To subscribe, contact Dialog directly.
Notes: Coverage: 1988 to the present; updated weekly.

`telnet://dialog.com`

International Food and Nutrition (INFAN) Database

A database covering all aspects of nutrition, health and food, as for example, weight control, food safety, eating patterns, and more.

Keywords: Nutrition, Health, Diet
Sponsor: Pennsylvania State University Nutrition Center
Audience: Nutritionists, Health Care Professionals, Consumers
Details: Free
To access the database, select PENpages (1), then General Information (3), and finally INFAN Database (4).

`telnet://penpages@psupen.psu.edu`

The Wellness List

This list is founded for the purpose of discussing issues concerning Health/Nutrition/Wellness/Life Expectancy/Physical Fitness, and the books, experiences, and solutions recommended by the participants.

Keywords: Health, Nutrition, Fitness
Audience: Doctors, Nutritionists, General Public

Profile: This resource provides announcements of and reviews of books that include solutions, nutrition related position papers, requests for information, recommendations of participants, healthy recipes, nutrition and fitness related product announcements, and general discussion of related issues. Health professionals, authors, and nutritionists are encouraged to subscribe and share their knowledge with the participants.
Contact: George Rust, Wellnessmart
eorge@wellnessmart.com
info@wellnessmart.com
User Info: To subscribe send an e-mail message to the URL address below consisting of a single line reading:

subscribe wellnesslist

`mailto:majordomo@wellnessmart.com`

NW-Raves (Northwest Raves)

NW-Raves (Northwest Raves)

One of several regional rave-related mailing lists, NW-Raves covers the northwestern US and western Canada. No archives are available.

Keywords: Raves
Audience: Ravers
Contact: Pat Lui
nw-raves-request@wimsey.bc.ca
Details: Free
User Info: To subscribe to the list, send an e-mail message requesting a subscription to the URL address below.

To send a message to the entire list, address it to: nw-raves@wimsey.bc.ca

`mailto:nw-raves-request@wimsey.bc.ca`

NWNet Internet Guide

NWNet Internet Guide

An introductory guide to the Internet. Details the basic Internet tools of electronic mail, FTP (File Transfer Protocol), and Telnet. Covers types of resources found on the Internet, and how to use them. Includes information directed toward supercomputer users and the K-12 community.

Keywords: Internet, Internet Guides, Supercomputing, Education (K-12)
Sponsor: NorthWestNet
Audience: Internet Surfers, Computer Users, Students (K-12)
Contact: Jonathan Kochmer
nusirg@nwnet.net

Details: Free

File is: /user-docs/nusirg/nusirg.whole-guide.ps

`ftp://ftphost.nwnet.net`

NYAL (New York Art Line)

NYAL (New York Art Line)

A gopher containing selected resources on the arts.

Keywords: Art, Audio-Visual Materials, Multimedia, Computer Art

Sponsor: Panix Public Access Unix & Internet Gopher Server, New York, USA

Audience: Artists, Art Enthusiasts

Profile: NYAL features a wide variety of arts resources. The primary focus of this site is visual art, particularly in the New York city area. Information includes online access to selected galleries, image archives, and New York city arts groups. Beyond visual art, information on dance, music, and techno art (with a special section on Internet art) is also available. It also features links to various electronic journals, museums, and schools.

Contact: Kenny Greenberg
kgreen@panix.com

`gopher://gopher.panix.com`

`http://gopher.panix.com/nyart/Kpage/kg`

NYIsrael Project of NYSERnet

NYIsrael Project of NYSERnet

Large repository of historical and cultural information as well as software, mailing lists, and images relating to Judaism, Jews, the Hebrew language, and Israel.

Keywords: Judaism, Hebrew Language, Israel

Sponsor: The New York Israel Project, NYSERNet, Inc.

Audience: Jewish Organizations

Profile: The purpose of this project is to create a network of diverse Jewish organizations worldwide that can communicate electronically and share information with one another.

Contact: Avrum Goodblatt
goodblat@israel.nysernet.org

Details: Free

`gopher://israel.nysernet.org`

NYSERNet Internet Guide

NYSERNet Internet Guide

A comprehensive guide to the Internet from the New York State Education and Research Network (NYSERNet). NYSERNet provides access to specialized databases and online libraries, as well as to supercomputing and parallel-processing facilities throughout the US and to many national networks.

Keywords: Internet, Internet Guides, New York, Supercomputers

Sponsor: NYSERNet K-12 Networking Interest Group

Audience: Internet Surfers

Contact: info@nysernet.org

Details: Free

`ftp://nysernet.org`

O

Object-Oriented Programming

BETA ★

A discussion forum for BETA users. BETA is a modern object-oriented programming language.

Keywords: Programming Languages, Object-Oriented Programming, BETA
Audience: Programmers
Contact: Elmer Soerensen Sandvad
usergroup-request@mjolner.dk
Details: Free, Moderated
User Info: To subscribe to the list, send an e-mail message requesting a subscription to the URL address below. To send a message to the entire list, address it to: usergroup@mjolner.dk

`mailto:usergroup-request@mjolner.dk`

Objectivism

Objectivism ★

A mailing list where students of Objectivism can discuss their ideas, issues, exchange news, and so on. Any issue that may have some relevance to Objectivists is appropriate here.

Keywords: Objectivism
Audience: Objectivists, Philosophers
Contact: Paul Vixie
objectivism-request@vix.com
Details: Free
User Info: To subscribe to the list, send an e-mail message requesting a subscription to the URL address below. To send a message to the entire list, address it to: objectivism@vix.com

`mailto:objectivism-request@vix.com`

Obstetrics/Gynecology

University of Texas Health Science Center at San Antonio Library ★★

The library's holdings are large and wide-ranging and contain significant collections in many fields.

Keywords: Allied Health, Dentistry, Nursing, Veterinary Science, Ambulatory Care, Obstetrics/Gynecology, Pediatrics
Audience: Researchers, Students, General Public
Details: Free
User Info: Expect: Login, Send: LIS

`telnet://athena.uthscsa.edu`

Occupational Outlook Handbook 1992-93

Occupational Outlook Handbook 1992-93 ★★★

An annual U.S. Department of Labor publication that provides detailed information for more than 320 occupations, including job descriptions, typical salaries, education and training requirements, working conditions, job outlook, and more.

Keywords: Careers, Employment, Labor
Sponsor: U.S. Department of Labor
Audience: General Public, Job Seekers, Business Professionals
Details: Free

`gopher://umslvma.umsl.edu/11/library/govdocs/ooha`

Oceanography

FINS (Fish Information Service) ★

This site provides information on issues relating to fish, including aquarium-building tips, diseases, clubs, newsgroups, movies, and fish trivia from Woods Hole Oceanographic Institute.

Keywords: Fish, Oceanography
Sponsor: Active Window Productions
Audience: Fish Enthusiasts, Ichthyologists
Details: Free

`http://www.actwin.com/fish/index.html`

Research Ship Schedules and Information ★★★

A gopher providing information on research and deep water vessels from more than 45 countries. Includes detailed ship specifications, some with deck plans and photographs available as GIF files. Also has cruise schedules for US ships, as well as some from other countries.

Keywords: Oceanography, Transportation, Maritime Industry, Travel
Sponsor: University of Delaware (The OCEANIC Ocean Information Center), Newark, Delaware, USA
Audience: Oceanographers, General Public
Contact: Ocean Information Center, University of Delaware, College of Marine Studies
oceanic@diu.cms.udel.edu
Details: Free, Images

`gopher://diu.cms.udel.edu`

University of Maryland, College Park

The library's holdings are large and wide-ranging and contain significant collections in many fields.

Keywords:	Agriculture, Coastal Marine Biology, Fisheries, Water Quality, Oceanography
Audience:	Researchers, Students, General Public
Contact:	Janet McLeod mcleod@umail.umd.edu
Details:	Free
User Info:	Expect: Login; Send: Atdu

`telnet://info.umd.edu`

Oceans

Global Change Information Gateway

This gateway was created to address environmental data management issues raised by the US Congress, the Administration, and the advisory arms of the Federal policy community. It contains documents related to the UN conference on Environment and Development.

Keywords:	UN, Environment, Development, Oceans, Atmosphere
Audience:	Environmentalists, Scientists, Researchers, Environmentalists
Details:	Free Select from menu as appropriate.

`gopher://scilibx.ucsc.edu`

National Oceanic & Atmospheric Administration (NOAA)

Office of Environmental Safety and Health, Department of Energy

The NOAA catalog provides keyword access to sources of environmental information in the US. Gopher for resources pertaining to health and environmental safety.

Keywords:	Environment, Oceans, Atmospheric Science, Health, Environmental Safety
Sponsor:	National Oceanic & Atmospheric Administration (NOAA) Department of Energy (USA)
Audience:	Environmental Scientists, Researchers, Environmentalists, Epidemiologists, Public Health Officials
Details:	Free

`gopher://scilibx.ucsc.edu`

`gopher://gopher.ns.doc.gov`

ODA

ODA ★

A mailing list for topics related to the ISO 8613 standard for Office Document Architecture and Office Document Interchange Format.

Keywords:	Office Document Architecture
Audience:	Office Document Architects
Contact:	Les Gondor utzoo!trigraph!oda-request
Details:	Free
User Info:	To subscribe to the list, send an e-mail message requesting a subscription to the URL address below. To send a message to the entire list, address it to: utzoo!@trigraph!oda-request

`mailto:utzoo!trigraph!oda-request`

OE-CALL: Old English Computer-Assisted Language Learning Newsletter

OE-CALL: Old English Computer-Assisted Language Learning Newsletter ★

A newsletter for persons interested in computer-assisted language-learning methods for teaching Old English.

Keywords:	Old English, Computer Assisted Instruction
Audience:	English Teachers, Educators
Contact:	Clare Lees, Patrick W. Conner mailto:u47c2@wvnvm.bitnet
Details:	Free

`mailto:lees@fordmurh.bitnet`

Office Document Architecture

ODA ★

A mailing list for topics related to the ISO 8613 standard for Office Document Architecture and Office Document Interchange Format.

Keywords:	Office Document Architecture
Audience:	Architects
Contact:	Les Gondor utzoo!trigraph!oda-request
Details:	Free
User Info:	To subscribe to the list, send an e-mail message requesting a subscription to the URL address below. To send a message to the entire list, address it to: utzoo!@trigraph!oda-request

`mailto:utzoo!trigraph!oda-request`

Office of Environmental Safety and Health, Department of Energy

Office of Environmental Safety and Health, Department of Energy

Gopher for resources pertaining to health and environmental safety.

Keywords:	Health, Environmental Safety
Sponsor:	Department of Energy (US)
Audience:	Epidemiologists, Public Health Officials, General Public
Details:	Free

`gopher://gopher.ns.doc.gov`

Offroad

Offroad ★

Discusses and shares experiences with four-wheel and off-road adventurers, including driving tips, vehicle modifications, and anything else related to four-wheeling. This list is specifically designed for four-wheel-drive vehicle owners, users, or enthusiasts. Discussions center around technical and mechanical matters, driving techniques, and trip reports.

Keywords:	Autmobils
Audience:	Automobile Enthusiasts
Contact:	Stefan Roth offroad-request@ai.gtri.gatech.edu
Details:	Free
User Info:	To subscribe to the list, send an e-mail message requesting a subscription to the URL address below. To send a message to the entire list, address it to: offroad@ai.gtri.gatech.edu

`mailto:offroad-request@ai.gtri.gatech.edu`

Oglasna Deska

Oglasna Deska ⭐

Oglasna Deska (bulletin board) consists of transcripts taken from SLON, which is a nickname for a Decnet connecting several computers in Slovenia. There is a conference similar to a Usenet newsgroup running under SLON and the articles and replies are occasionally saved and sent to the world. The topics cover a wide area.

Keywords:	Slovenia, SLON, Usenet
Audience:	Slovenians, Croatians, Serbians
Contact:	Dean Mozetic oglasna-deska@krpan.arnes.si
Details:	Free
User Info:	To subscribe to the list, send an e-mail message requesting a subscription to the URL address below. To send a message to the entire list, address it to: oglasna-deka@krpan.arnes.si
Notes:	The topics covered are equivalent to Usenet newsgroups such as politics, automobiles, humor, computer networks, climbing, and miscellaneous investments.

`mailto:oglasna-deska@krpan.arnes.si`

Ogphre - SunSITE

Ogphre - SunSITE ⭐⭐

A collection of Internet resources organized by subject. Particular strengths include agriculture, religious texts, poetry, creative writing, and US politics. The ftp site has a set of more general Internet guides.

Keywords:	Agriculture, Politics (US), Religion, Internet, Poetry
Sponsor:	The University of North Carolina - Chapel Hill and Sun Microsystems, USA
Audience:	General Public, Internet Surfers, Researchers
Contact:	Darlene Fladager, Elizabeth Lyons Darlene_Fladager@unc.edu Elizabeth_Lyons@unc.edu

`gopher://sunsite.unc.edu`

`ftp://sunsite.unc.edu`

Ohio

Oh-motss ⭐

The oh-motss (Ohio Members of the Same Sex) mailing list is for open discussion of lesbian, gay, and bisexual issues in and affecting Ohio. The mailing list is not moderated. It is open to all, regardless of location or sexuality. The subscriber list is known only to the list owner.

Keywords:	Gays, Lesbians, Ohio, Bisexuality
Audience:	Gays, Lesbians
Contact:	oh-motss-request@cps.udayton.edu
Details:	Free
User Info:	To subscribe to the list, send an e-mail message requesting a subscription to the URL address below. To send a message to the entire list, address it to: oh-motss@cps.udayton.edu

`mailto:oh-motss-request@cps.udayton.edu`

Ohio ⭐

Provides access to Ohio State Supreme Court Opinions and Ohio 8th District Court Opinions.

Keywords:	Ohio, Law
Sponsor:	Case Western University Freenet, Youngstown University Freenet
Audience:	Lawyers, General Public, Ohio Residents
Details:	Free

`telnet://ytn.ysu.edu`

Cleveland Sports ⭐

A forum for people to discuss their favorite Cleveland sports teams/personalities, and to obtain news and information about those teams that most out-of-towners couldn't get otherwise. Teams discussed include the Cleveland Indians, the Cleveland Browns, the Cleveland Cavaliers, and the teams from Ohio State University.

Keywords:	Cleveland, Sports, Ohio State Universiry
Audience:	Cleveland Sports Enthusiasts, Sports Enthusiasts, Cleveland Residents
Contact:	Richard Kowicki aj755@cleveland.freenet.edu
Details:	Free
User Info:	To subscribe to the list, send an e-mail message requesting a subscription to the URL address below.

`mailto:aj755@cleveland.freenet.edu`

Friends of Ohio State ⭐

A forum for alumni and other friends of Ohio State University.

Keywords:	Ohio
Audience:	Ohio State University Alumni
Contact:	Jerry Canterbury antivirus@aol.com
Details:	Free
User Info:	To subscribe to the list, send an e-mail message requesting a subscription to the URL address below. To send a message to the entire list, address it to: antivirus@aol.com

`mailto:antivirus@aol.com`

Old English

OE-CALL: Old English Computer-Assisted Language Learning Newsletter ⭐

A newsletter for persons interested in computer-assisted language-learning methods for teaching Old English.

Keywords:	Old English, Computer Assisted Instruction
Audience:	English Teachers, Educators
Contact:	Clare Lees, Patrick W. Conner mailto:u47c2@wvnvm.bitnet
Details:	Free

`mailto:lees@fordmurh.bitnet`

Old Testament

Bible (King James Version) ⭐⭐⭐

The Bible (King James Version) includes the complete text of the modern Thomas Nelson revision of the 1769 edition of the King James version of the Bible.

Keywords:	Bible, Religion, Christianity
Sponsor:	Thomas Nelson Publishers, Nashville, TN, USA
Audience:	Christians, Theologians, Historians, Moralists
Profile:	The King James version originated from translations ordered by King James of England in 1604 at the Hampton Court Conference. Both the Old and New Testaments are included in this version. Records in the database represent both chapters and verses.
Contact:	Dialog in the US at (800) 334-2564, Dialog internationally at country-specific locations.
Details:	Costs
User Info:	To subscribe, contact Dialog directly.

`telnet://dialog.com`

Olympics

Olympic Games 1994 at Lillehammer

News, results, and updates every 15 minutes, as well as archive images, from the 1994 Winter Olympic Games at Lillehammer, Norway.

Keywords:	Olympics, Sports, Winter Games
Sponsor:	Sun Microsystem, Skrivervik Data AS, Oslonett AS, Norsk Telegrambyra

Audience:	General Public, Journalists, Skiers, Skaters, Winter Sports Fans
Profile:	This server offers news and results on all the Olympic events in Lillehammer plus a chronological list of all events, a complete schedule day by day, and a very large archive of images. Also flash messages from NTB, a Norwegian news wire, and the opportunity to search in the NTB database.
Contact:	oslonett@oslonett.no

http://www.sun.com

OlympPuck

This list is for the discussion of Olympic ice hockey. Discussions concerning players, coaches, teams, and games are welcome and are encouraged. Related topics, such as the interaction between the Olympic competition and college or NHL hockey, are also discussed.

Keywords:	Olympics, Hockey
Audience:	Hockey Players, Olympics Enthusiasts, Hockey Enthusiasts
Details:	Free
User Info:	To subscribe to the list, send an e-mail message to the URL address below, consisting of a single line reading:
	TAB olympuck YourFirstName YourLastName
	To send a message to the entire list, address it to: olympuck@maine.maine.edu

mailto:listserv@maine.maine.edu

rec.sport.olympics

A Usenet newsgroup providing information and discussion about the summer Olympics Games.

Keywords:	Olympics, Summer Sports
Audience:	Olympic Enthusiasts
User Info:	To subscribe to this Usenet newsgroup, you need access to a newsreader.

news:rec.sport.olympics

OMD

OMD (Orchestral Manoeuvres In The Dark)

The OMD list is a forum for discussions about the English pop band Orchestral Manoeuvres In The Dark, which often incorporate modern dance elements into its music. The discussions are not moderated but they should have something to do with the band or with ex-band members.

Keywords:	Modern Dance, Pop Music
Audience:	Pop Music Enthusiasts
Contact:	Dave Datta omd-request@cs.uwp.edu
Details:	Free
User Info:	To subscribe to the list, send an e-mail message requesting a subscription to the URL address below. To send a message to the entire list, address it to: omd@cs.uwp.edu
Notes:	The list is available as a daily digest and reflector. Archives are stored at ftp.uwp.edu.

mailto:omd-request@cs.uwp.edu

On-this-day

On-this-day

Subscribers receive a daily listing of notable birthdays, events, religious holidays, astronomical events, and other items of interest.

Keywords:	Calendars
Audience:	General Public
Contact:	Wayne Geiser geiser@pictel.com
Details:	Free
User Info:	To subscribe to the list, send an e-mail message requesting a subscription to the URL address below. To send a message to the entire list, address it to: geiser@pictel.com

mailto:geiser@pictel.com

On-u

On-u

This mailing list encourages discussions related to Adrian Sherwood's On-U Sound label and to the artists who record on it, including Tack>>Head, Gary Clail, The Dub Syndicate, African Head Charge, Bim Sherman and Mark Stewart.

Keywords:	Music, Musicians
Audience:	Musicians, Music Enthusiasts
Contact:	Ben Golding on-u-request@connect.com.au
Details:	Free
User Info:	To subscribe to the list, send an e-mail message requesting a subscription to the URL address below. To send a message to the entire list, address it to: on-u@connect.com.au

mailto:on-u@connect.com.au

Online Books

Electronic Books

A collection of books available as ASCII text files, including classics of antiquity (Aristotle, Virgil, Sophocles, the Bible), as well as more contemporary works of fiction and nonfiction by authors ranging from Dostoevsky to Martin Luther King, Jr.

Keywords:	Books, Online Books, Literature (Contemporary), Literature (General)
Sponsor:	The Blacksburg Electronic Village (BEV) at Virginia Tech
Audience:	General Public, Historians
Contact:	BEV Gopher Administrators gopher@gopher.vt.edu

http://marketplace.com/0/OBS

Online BookStore (OBS)

Offers full text (fiction and nonfiction) in a variety of electronic formats, free and for a fee.

Keywords:	Online Books, Books, ShareWord, Fiction, Nonfiction Books
Sponsor:	Editorial Inc./OBS
Audience:	General Public, Reading Enthusiasts
Profile:	Started in 1992, the OBS offers a variety of full-text titles.
Contact:	Laura Fillmore laura@editorial.com
Details:	Costs, Moderated, Images, Multimedia
User Info:	To subscribe to the list, send an e-mail message requesting a subscription to the URL address below.

http://marketplace.com/0/obs

Online Career Center

Online Career Center

The Online Career Center gopher provides access to job listings and employment information to member companies and to the public.

Keywords:	Employment, Internships
Sponsor:	Online Career Center
Audience:	Job Seekers
Profile:	Online Career Center is a not-for-profit organization funded by its member companies. It is devoted to distributing and exchanging employment and career information between its member companies, human resource professionals, and prospective employees.
Contact:	OCC Operator occ@msen.com

gopher://gopher.msen.com

Online Radio

Online Radio

Transcripts and promotional information from Online Radio, a weekly radio program of Perth's Curtin University devoted to reporting the latest developments in the computing world.

Keywords:	Computing, Internet, Radio
Sponsor:	Curtin University Computing Center, Perth, Australia
Audience:	Computer Users
Contact:	Onno Benschop online@info.curtin.edu.au

`gopher://ob1.curtin.edu.au`

Online Services

Women's Wire

Women's Wire is an online interactive network focusing on women's issues and interests.

Keywords:	Networking, Women's Issues, Online Services
Audience:	Women, Internet Users
Profile:	This service acts as an international clearinghouse for resources and networking on a broad range of topics including news, politics, careers, education, parenting, health, and arts. Provides e-mail and access to thousands of resources, including Usenet newsgroups.
Details:	Costs Access via an easy-to-use graphical interface for Macintosh and Windows platforms, or a text-based interface for DOS and Unix platforms. Local access numbers available throughout the US and in most countries.

`mailto:info@wwire.net`

Online-dict

Online-dict

A mailing list devoted to a discussion of online dictionaries and related issues including installation, modification, and maintenance of their databases, search engines, and user interfaces.

Keywords:	Dictionaries, Information Technology, Lexicology
Audience:	Librarians, Information Scientists, Systems Operators
Contact:	Jack Lynch jlynch@dept.english.upenn.edu
Details:	Free

User Info:	To subscribe, send an e-mail message to the URL address below consisting of a single line reading: SUB online-dict YourFirstName YourLastName. To send a message to the entire list, address it to: online-dict@dept.english.upenn.edu

`mailto:listserv@dept.english.upenn.edu`

OPACS

ELISA (Electronic Library Service)

An information delivery service of the Library of the Australian National University.

Keywords:	OPAC System, Australia
Sponsor:	Australian National University
Audience:	General Public
Profile:	This information delivery service contains Australian mirrors of major gopher directories, and is a national entry point for Australian gopher services.
Contact:	infodesk@info.anu.edu.au
Details:	Free

`gopher://info.anu.edu.au`

OLIS (Oxford University Library Information Service) Gopher

OLIS is a network of libraries. It contains all the books from the English, Modern Languages, Social Studies, and Hooke libraries. It also contains books and journals cataloged since September 1988 in the Bodleian and Dependant libraries and the Taylor Institution. Books can be searched in any OLIS library from any location.

Keywords:	Libraries, United Kingdom, Europe, IPACS
Audience:	Researchers
Contact:	jose@olis.lib.ox.ac.uk
Details:	Free

`gopher://gopher.lib.ox.ac.uk/00/Info/OLIS`

Hytelnet

A hypertext database of publicly accessible Internet sites.

Keywords:	Internet Tools, Hytelnet
Audience:	Internet Surfers
Profile:	Hytelnet currently lists over 1,400 sites, including libraries, campus-wide information systems, Gopher, WAIS, and WWW systems, and Freenets.
Contact:	Earl Fogel earl.fogel@usask.ca
Details:	Free
Notes:	File is: pub/hytelnet/README

`ftp://ftp.usask.ca`

LOCIS (LIBRARY Of CONGRESS INFORMATION SYSTEM)

The Library of Congress (LC) telnet service is a Campus-Wide Information System that combines the vast collection of information available about the Library, with easy access to diverse electronic resources over the Internet. Its goal is to serve the staff of LC, as well as the U.S. Congress and constituents throughout the world.

Keywords:	Information Retrieval, Libraries
Sponsor:	Library of Congress, Washington, D.C., USA
Audience:	Researchers, Students, Librarians
Contact:	LC MARVEL Design Team lcmarvel@loc.gov
Notes:	The Library of Congress (LC) Machine-Assisted Realization of the Virtual Electronic Library (MARVEL) also exists as a gopher site: gopher://marvel.loc.gov

`telnet://locis.loc.gov`

MELVYL Library System

MELVYL is the University of California's catalog of books and periodicals for the university and the California State Library. It also permits access to database systems around the world.

Keywords:	Libraries, Databases, OPACS, Internet Surfers
Audience:	General Interest, Students, Teachers, Librarians
Producer:	University of California
Contact:	Genny Engel, MELVYL System Users Services email:gen@dla.ucop.edu
Profile:	The MELVYL system is a centralized information system that can be reached from terminals in libraries at all nine campuses of the University of California. The system can also be reached by any terminal microcomputer with dialup access to UC computers connected to the MELVYL system. The MELVYL system includes a library catalog database, a periodicals database, article citation databases, and other files. A large number of other libraries and database systems are also accessible from MELVYL.
Details:	Free
Notes:	All these databases are searched using the same basic commands.

`telnet://melvyl.ucop.edu`

OLIS (Oxford University Library Information Service) Gopher

OLIS is a network of libraries. It contains all the books from the English, Modern Languages, Social Studies, and Hooke libraries. It also contains books and journals cataloged since September 1988 in the Bodleian and Dependant libraries and the Taylor Institution. Books can be searched in any OLIS library from any location.

Keywords: Libraries, United Kingdom, Europe
Audience: Library Users
Contact: jose@olis.lib.ox.ac.uk
Details: Free

`gopher://gopher.lib.ox.ac.uk/00/Info/OLIS`

Yale Directory of Internet Libraries

An online directory of international library catalogs with

Keywords: Libraries
Sponsor: Yale University, New Haven, Connecticut, USA
Audience: General Audience
Profile: The Yale Directory of Internet Libraries is a comprehensive
Notes: The Yale Directory of Internet Libraries is in English, but the

`gopher://gophlib@gopher.yale.edu`

Open Computing Facility (OCF) Gopher, Sports Section

Open Computing Facilty (OCF) Gopher, Sports Section

A gopher server offering access to information about a number of sporting activities.

Keywords: Sports, Fitness
Sponsor: Open Computing Facility, University of California, Berkeley
Audience: Sports Enthusiasts, Fitness Enthusiasts
Profile: This gopher has information on various sports, including football, cricket, skiing, windsurfing, and basketball, as well as links to WWW. Resources include schedules for some professional and collegiate sports, as well as FAQs and other miscellaneous information.
Contact: general-manager@ocf.berkeley.edu
Details: Free

`gopher://gopher.ocf.berkeley.edu/11/gopherspace`

Open Government Pilot

Open Government Pilot

This web site provides information concerning the Canadian government, including information on Canadian infrastructure, industry, communications, provinces, and parliament.

Keywords: Canada, Government (International)
Sponsor: Canadian Federal Government
Audience: Canadians, Educators, Students
Details: Free

`http://debra.dgbt.doc.ca/opengov`

Open Government Project (Canada)

Open Government Project (Canada)

This site provides online audio-visual and text information on the Canadian government.

Keywords: Canada, Government (International)
Sponsor: Directorate of Communications Development, Industry Canada, Canada
Audience: Canadians, Government Officials, Journalists
Profile: This bilingual (French/English) site has detailed information on members of the Canadian Senate and House of Commons, as well as Supreme Court rulings and biographies of the justices. It features a number of pictures, maps, and links to other Canadian information servers.
Contact: Tyson Macaulay
tyson.macaulay@crc.doc.ca

`http://debra.dgbt.doc.ca/ogp.html`

`gopher://debra.dgbt.doc.ca/open_government_project`

Opera

The University of Kansas Library

The library's holdings are large and wide-ranging and contain significant collections in many fields.

Keywords: Botany, Chinese Studies, Cartography (History of), Kansas, Opera, Ornithology, Joyce (James), Yeats (William Butler), Walpole (Sir Robert, Collections of)
Audience: General Public, Researchers, Librarians, Document Delivery Professionals
Contact: John S. Miller
Details: Free
User Info: Expect: Username, Send: relay <cr>

`telnet://kuhub.cc.ukans.edu`

Operating Systems

Bugs-386bsd

This list is for 386bsd bugs, patches, and ports.

Keywords: Operating Systems, 386bsd
Audience: Computer Operators, Computer Scientists, Computer Engineers
Contact: bugs-386bsd-request@ms.uky.edu
Details: Free
User Info: To subscribe to the list, send an e-mail message requesting a subscription to the URL address below. To send a message to the entire list, address it to:
bugs-386bsd@ms.uky.edu
Notes: Requirement to join: an interest in actively working on 386bsd to improve the operating system for use by yourself and others.

`mailto:bugs-386bsd-request@ms.uky.edu`

Std-UNIX

Discussion of UNIX standards, particularly the IEEE P1003 Portable Operating System Environment draft standard.

Keywords: UNIX, Operating Systems
Audience: UNIX Users
Contact: Sean Eric Fagan
sef@uunet.uu.net
Details: Free, Moderated
User Info: To subscribe to the list, send an e-mail message requesting a subscription to the URL address below.

`mailto:sef@uunet.uu.net`

UNIX-wizards

Distribution list for people maintaining UNIX machines.

Keywords: UNIX, Operating Systems
Audience: UNIX System Administrators
Contact: Mike Muuss
mike@brl.mil
Details: Free
User Info: To subscribe to the list, send an e-mail message requesting a subscription to the URL address below.

`mailto:UNIX-wizards-request@brl.mil`

Operlist

Operlist ★

A discussion list for everything having to do with IRC (Internet Relay Chat). Its main purpose is irc routing discussions, protocol discussions, and announcements of new versions of IRC clients and servers.

Keywords:	irc
Audience:	irc Users
Contact:	Helen Trillian Rose operlist-request@eff.org
Details:	Free
User Info:	To subscribe to the list, send an e-mail message requesting a subscription to the URL address below. To send a message to the entire list, address it to: operlist@eff.org

`mailto:operlist@eff.org`

Optics

CVNet (Color and Vision Network) ★

The network provides a means of communications for scientists working in biological color and/or vision research. Members' e-mail addresses are maintained and sent to others in the network. CVNet distributes notices of jobs, meetings, and some other special announcements to all registrants. Members can post bulletins, announcements, and so on.

Keywords:	Optics, Biological Research, Psychology
Sponsor:	York University, North York, Ontario, Canada
Audience:	Psychologists, Color/Vision Researchers
Contact:	Peter K. Kaiser cvnet@vm1.yorkU.ca
Details:	Free
User Info:	To subscribe, send an e-mail message requesting a subscription to the URL address below.

`mailto:cvnet@vm1.yorkU.ca`

University of Rochester Library ★★

The library's holdings are large and wide-ranging and contain significant collections in many fields.

Keywords:	Architecture, Art History, Photography, Literature (Asian), Lasers, Geology, Statistics, Optics, Medieval Studies
Audience:	Researchers, Students, General Public
Details:	Free
User Info:	Expect: Login; Send: Library

`telnet://128.151.226.71`

ORA-NEWS

ORA-NEWS ★

Announcements from O'Reilly & Associates, publishers of books about the Internet, UNIX and other open systems. Other products and services include The Global Network Navigator (an interactive online magazine) and Internet in a Box. It's gatewayed to the biz.oreilly.announce Usenet newsgroup.

Keywords:	Internet, UNIX, Usenet
Audience:	Internet Surfers, Usenet Users, UNIX Users
Contact:	listown@online.ora.com
Details:	Free, Moderated
User Info:	To subscribe to the list, send an e-mail message requesting a subscription to the URL address below. To send a message to the entire list, address it to: ora-news@online.ora.com

`mailto:listproc@online.ora.com`

Oregon

Oregon-news ★

Mailing list of people organizing against the Oregon Citizens' Alliance. This list will carry news of lawsuits, rallies, events, votes, and so on, that take place in the state of Oregon.

Keywords:	Oregon
Audience:	Oregonians, Activists
Contact:	oregon-news-request@vector.intercon.com
Details:	Free
User Info:	To subscribe to the list, send an e-mail message requesting a subscription to the URL address below.To send a message to the entire list, address it to: oregon-news@vector.intercon.com

`mailto:oregon-news-request@vector.intercon.com`

Orienteering

Orienteering ★

Discusses all aspects of the sport of orienteering.

Keywords:	Orienteering
Audience:	Orienteering Enthusiasts
Contact:	Mitch Collinsworth orienteering-request@graphics.cornell.edu
Details:	Free
User Info:	To subscribe to the list, send an e-mail message requesting a subscription to the URL address below. To send a message to the entire list, address it to: orienteering@graphics.cornell.edu

`mailto:orienteering@graphics.cornell.edu`

Origami

Origami ★

This unmoderated mailing list is for discussion of all facets of origami, the Japanese art of paper folding. Topics include bibliographies, folding techniques, display ideas, descriptions of new folds, creativity, materials, organizations, computer representations of folds, and so on.

Keywords:	Origami
Audience:	Origami Enthusiasts
Contact:	origami-l-request@nstn.ns.ca
Details:	Free Archives available by anonymous ftp from rugcis.rug.nl Start ftp: ftp rugcis.rug.nl
User Info:	Expect: blogin, Send: anonymous; Expect: password, Send: your Internet address. Change dir: cd origami.

`mailto:origami-l-request@nstn.ns.ca`

Ornithology

The University of Kansas Library ★★

The library's holdings are large and wide-ranging and contain significant collections in many fields.

Keywords:	Botany, Chinese Studies, Cartography (History of), Kansas, Opera, Ornithology, Joyce (James), Yeats (William Butler), Walpole (Sir Robert, Collections of)
Audience:	General Public, Researchers, Librarians, Document Delivery Professionals
Contact:	John S. Miller
Details:	Free
User Info:	Expect: Username, Send: relay <cr>

`telnet://kuhub.cc.ukans.edu`

TitNeT Titnews Titnotes ★★★

The network of the International Tit Society (TITS).

Keywords:	Ornithology, Birds
Sponsor:	International Tit Society
Audience:	Bird Watchers

Orinthology

Profile:	The network of the International Tit Society (TITS), Titnet posts three formal series: 1) TITNET is the listing of e-mail subscribers, and includes their e-mail addresses, institutional affiliations, and research interests. 2) TITNEWS is the forum for exchange concerning academic activities, and consists of single-topic issues and multiple announcements. 3) TITNOTES is the forum for exchange of information about tits (and other hole-nesting birds).	
Contact:	Jack P. Hailman jhailman@vms.macc.wisc.edu	
Details:	Free	
User Info:	To subscribe, send an e-mail message requesting a subscription to the URL address below. Provide: (1) Full name, (2) e-mail address, (3) institutional affiliation, (4) species studied, and (5) topics studied.	

`mailto:jhailman@vms.macc.wisc.edu`

titnet (Paridae and Hole-nesting Bird Discussion List)

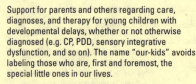

Promotes communication among scientists working on tits (Paridae) and other hole-nesting birds.

Keywords: Birds, Ornithology
Audience: Bird Watchers
Profile: Titnet is a publication listing e-mail addresses of conference members. Titnews contains announcements and discussions of activities such as bibliographic systems and hence serves as the e-mail newsletter. Titnotes contains material on the biology of the birds and hence serves as a kind of e-mail journal.
Contact: Jack P. Hailman
jhailman@macc.wisc.edu
Details: Free
User Info: To subscribe to the list, send an e-mail message requesting a subscription to the URL address below. To send a message to the entire list, address it to: jhailman@macc.wisc.edu
Notes: Send (1) full name, (2) mailing address, which is forwarded to Dr. Ficken for PARUS INTERNATIONAL, (3) e-mail address(es), (4) species studied, and (5) types of studies (population dynamics, general ecology, vocalizations, nesting, behavior, and so on.).

`mailto:jhailman@macc.wisc.edu`

OTIS (Operative Term Is Stimulate)

OTIS (Operative Term Is Stimulate)

An image-based electronic art gallery.

Keywords: Art, Graphics, Electronic Art, Animation
Audience: Graphic Artists
Profile: OTIS is a public-access library containing hundreds of images, animations, and information files.

Within the sunsite ftp, the directory is: /pub/multimedia/pictures/OTIS. Use the bin command to insure you're in binary transfer mode.

`ftp://sunsite.unc.edu`

Our-kids

Our-kids

Support for parents and others regarding care, diagnoses, and therapy for young children with developmental delays, whether or not otherwise diagnosed (e.g. CP, PDD, sensory integrative dysfunction, and so on). The name "our-kids" avoids labeling those who are, first and foremost, the special little ones in our lives.

Keywords: Parenting
Audience: Parents, Child Development Professionals
Contact: our-kids-request@oar.net
Details: Free
User Info: To subscribe to the list, send an e-mail message requesting a subscription to the URL address below. To send a message to the entire list, address it to: our-kids@oar.net

`mailto:our-kids-request@oar.net`

OUTIL (Out in Linguistics)

OUTIL (Out in Linguistics)

The list is open to lesbian, gay, bisexual and, transsexual linguists and their friends. The only requirement is that you be willing to be "out" to everyone on the list. The purposes of the group are to be visible and to gather occasionally to enjoy one another's company.

Keywords: Linguistics, Gays, Lesbians, Bisexuals, Transsexuals
Audience: Linguists, Gays, Lesbians, Bisexuals, Transsexuals
Contact: Arnold Zwicky
outil-request@csli.stanford.edu
Details: Free
User Info: To subscribe to the list, send an e-mail message requesting a subscription to the URL address below. To send a message to the entire list, address it to: outil@csli.stanford.edu

`mailto:outil-request@csli.stanford.edu`

Output

Output

Newsletter of the Florida State University (FSU) Computing Center. Includes topics such as networking, microcomputing, mainframe computing, and supercomputing on campus, including use of computers in classroom and research computing at FSU.

Keywords: Networking, Microcomputing, Supercomputing
Audience: FSU Computer Science Students, Computer Users
Contact: Suzanne C. Nelson
nelson@avm.cc.fsu.edu
Details: Free
Send your request addressed to the editor.

`mailto:nelson@avm.cc.fsu.edu`

Overseas Business Reports

Overseas Business Reports

Full-text of U.S. International Trade Administration reports, discussing the economic and commercial climate in various countries around the world.

Keywords: Business, Foreign Trade, Commerce
Sponsor: U.S. Government, International Trade Administration
Audience: Business Professionals, Trade Specialists, Investors
Details: Free

`gopher://umslvma.umsl.edu/11/library/govdocs/obr`

Oysters

Oysters

For discussion of the British folk-rock band The Oyster Band and related topics.

Keywords: Folk Music
Audience: Folk Music Enthusiasts
Contact: oysters-request@blowfish.taligent.com
Details: Free
User Info: To subscribe to the list, send an e-mail message requesting a subscription to the URL address below. To send a message to the entire list, address it to: oysters@blowfish.taligent.com

`mailto:oysters-request@blowfish.taligent.com`

Pac-10 Sports

Pac-10-Sports

This mailing list is dedicated to discussing sports of all types that are played competitively within the Pac-10 Athletic Conference.

Keywords: Sports
Audience: Sports Enthusiasts
Contact: Cliff Slaughterbeck
crs@u.washington.edu
Details: Free
User Info: To subscribe to the list, send an e-mail message requesting a subscription to the URL address that follows.

To send a message to the entire list, address it to: crs@u.washington.edu

`mailto:crs@u.washington.edu`

Pacific

Apngowid.meet

A conference on plans by Asia Pacific regional women's groups for the United Nations Fourth World Conference on Women to be held in Beijing in September 1995.

Keywords: Women, Asia, Pacific, Feminists, Development, United Nations, World Conference on Women
Audience: Women, Feminists, Nongovernmental Organizations
Contact: AsPac Info, Docu and Communication Committee
AP-IDC@p95.f401.n751.z6.g
Details: Costs, Moderated

Establish an account on the nearest APC node. Login, type c for conferences, then type: go apngowid.meet.

For information on the nearest APC node, contact: APC International Secretariat IBASE

E-mail: apcadmin@apc.org

E-mail message to APCadmin@apc.org

`http://www.igc.apc.org/igc/www.women.html`

Asia-Pacific

The database covers the business, economics, and new industries of the Pacific Rim nations, including East Asia, Southeast Asia, the Indian Subcontinent, the Middle East, Australia, and the Pacific Island nations.

Keywords: Asia, Pacific, Business, Economy
Sponsor: Aristarchus Knowledge Industries, Seattle, WA, USA
Audience: Market Researchers, Economists, Market Analysts
Profile: Records are of two types: main records consisting of abstracts or citations for journal articles and other publications; and company thesaurus records. Detailed abstracts are provided for selected journal articles, monographs, selected papers in conference proceedings, dissertations, and government documents. Shorter citations with briefer indexing are provided for a wide variety of journal articles, newspapers, government documents, and annual report publications. Asia-Pacific also includes an extensive Corporate Thesaurus subfile, which provides detailed coverage of the corporate players in the Pacific Rim, including thousands of companies traded on the stock exchanges of Southeast and East Asia.
Contact: Dialog in the US at (800) 334-2564; Dialog internationally at country-specific locations.
Details: Costs
User Info: To subscribe, contact Dialog directly.

`telnet://dialog.com`

Asian and Pacific Economic Literature

A list of economic literature covering Asia and the Pacific region.

Keywords: Asia, Pacific, Economics
Audience: Economists, Business Professionals
Details: Free

`ftp://coombs.anu.edu`

Asian Pacific Business and Marketing Resources

A forum on business and marketing in the Pacific Rim region.

Keywords: Asia, Pacific, Business, Management
Audience: Business Professionals, Market Researchers
Details: Free

`gopher://hoshi.cic.sfu.ca/11/dlam/business/forum`

Packaging

PIRA - Paper, Printing and Publishing, Packaging, and Nonwovens Abstracts

Coverage of all aspects of paper, pulp, nonwovens, printing, publishing and packaging.

Keywords: Material Science, Paper, Printing, Publishing, Packaging, Nonwovens
Sponsor: PIRA International
Audience: Materials Scientists, Researchers

Packaging

Profile: File contains more than 300,000 records. Special applications: company and market profiles, product and trade name searches, research and technology trends. Updated biweekly.

Contact: paul.albert@neteast.com

User Info: To subscribe, contact Orbit-Questel directly.

`telnet://orbit.com`

Pagan

Pagan

Discusses the religions, philosophy, and other aspects of paganism.

Keywords: Paganism, Religion
Audience: Pagans
Contact: Stacey Greenstein
pagan-request@drycas.club.cc.cmu.edu
Details: Free
User Info: To subscribe to the list, send an e-mail message requesting a subscription to the URL address that follows.
User Info: To send a message to the entire list, address it to: pagan@drycas.club.cc.cmu.edu

`mailto:pagan-request@drycas.club.cc.cmu.edu`

Paganism

alt.pagan

A Usenet newsgroup providing information and discussion about paganism and religion.

Keywords: Paganism, Religion
Audience: Cults, Worshippers, Religion Students
User Info: To subscribe to this Usenet newsgroup, you need access to a newsreader.

`news:alt.pagan`

Pagan

Discusses the religions, philosophy, and other aspects of paganism.

Keywords: Paganism, Religion
Audience: Pagans
Contact: Stacey Greenstein
pagan-request@drycas.club.cc.cmu.edu
Details: Free
User Info: To subscribe to the list, send an e-mail message requesting a subscription to the URL address that follows.
To send a message to the entire list, address it to: pagan@drycas.club.cc.cmu.edu

`mailto:pagan-request@drycas.club.cc.cmu.edu`

PAGEMAKER

PAGEMAKER

The PageMaker ListServ is dedicated to the discussion of desktop publishing in general, with emphasis on the use of Aldus PageMaker. The list discusses PageMaker's use in both the PC and Macintosh realms. The list also maintains an extensive archive of help files that are extremely useful for the modern desktop publisher.

Keywords: Desktop Publishing, Aldus Pagemaker, IBM PC, Macintosh
Audience: Desktop Publishers, Computer Users
Contact: Geoff Peters
gwp@cs.purdue.edu
Details: Free
User Info: To subscribe to the list, send an e-mail message to the URL address shown that follows consisting of a single line reading:
SUB pagemaker YourFirstName YourLastName.
To send a message to the entire list, address it to: gwp@cs.purdue.edu

`mailto:listserv@cs.purdue.edu`

Pakistan

soc.culture.pakistan

A Usenet newsgroup providing information and discussion about Pakistani people and their culture.

Keywords: Pakistan, Sociology
Audience: Sociologists, Pakistanis
Details: Free
User Info: To subscribe to this Usenet newsgroup, you need access to a newsreader.

`news:soc.culture.pakistan`

Paleography

The University of Notre Dame Library

The library's holdings are large and wide-ranging and contain significant collections in many fields.

Keywords: Music (Irish), Ireland, Botany (History of), Ecology, Entomology, Parasitology, Aquatic Biology, Universities (History of), Paleography
Audience: General Public, Researchers, Librarians, Document Delivery Professionals
Details: Free

User Info: Expect: ENTER COMMAND OR HELP:, Send: library; To leave, type x on the command line and press Enter. At the ENTER COMMAND OR HELP: prompt, type bye and press Enter.

`telnet://irishmvs.cc.nd.edu`

Paleontology

UC Berkeley Museum of Paleontology and the WWW Subway

This web site provides a multimedia museum display from UC Berkeley's Museum of Paleontology. Also features an interactive Subway, a tool linking users to other museums and WWW sites around the world.

Keywords: WWW, Museums, Paleontology
Sponsor: University of California at Berkeley, Museum of Paleontology, Berkeley, California, USA
Audience: Paleontologists, Internet Surfers, General Public
Contact: David Polly, Robert Guralnick
davip@ucmp1.berkeley.edu
robg@fossil.berkeley.edu
Details: Subway

`http://ucmp1.berkeley.edu/subway.html`

Panic

Panic

This is a support group for panic disorders. Discussion involving phobias resulting from panic (agoraphobia and others). Also, this is a place to meet people who have gone through the disorder as well.

Keywords: Agoraphobia
Audience: Panic Disorder Sufferers
Contact: Panic-Request@gnu.ai.mit.edu
Details: Free
User Info: To subscribe to the list, send an e-mail message requesting a subscription to the URL address that follows.
To send a message to the entire list, address it to: panic@gnu.ai.mit.edu

`mailto:Panic-Request@gnu.ai.mit.edu`

Papa

Papa

A mailing list devoted to the discussion of the life and works of Ernest Hemingway.

Keywords:	Hemingway (Ernest), Literature (American)
Audience:	Ernest Hemingway Enthusiasts
Contact:	Dave Gross dgross@polyslo.calpoly.edu
Details:	Free
User Info:	To subscribe to the list, send an e-mail message requesting a subscription to the URL address that follows.
	To send a message to the entire list, address it to: dgross@polyslo.calpoly.edu

`mailto:dgross@polyslo.calpoly.edu`

Paper

PIRA - Paper, Printing and Publishing, Packaging, and Nonwovens Abstracts

Coverage of all aspects of paper, pulp, nonwovens, printing, publishing, and packaging.

Keywords:	Material Science, Paper, Printing, Publishing, Packaging, Nonwovens
Sponsor:	PIRA International
Audience:	Material Scientists, Researchers
Profile:	File contains more than 300,000 records. Special applications: company and market profiles, product and trade name searches, research and technology trends. Updated biweekly.
Contact:	paul.albert@neteast.com
User Info:	To subscribe contact, Orbit-Questel directly.

`telnet://orbit.com`

Papermaking (History of)

University of Delaware Libraries (DELCAT)

The library's holdings are large and wide-ranging and contain significant collections in many fields.

Keywords:	Literature (American), Hemingway (Ernest), Papermaking (History of), Chemistry (History of), Literature (Irish), Delaware
Audience:	General Public, Researchers, Librarians, Document Delivery Professionals
Contact:	Stuart Glogoff epo27855@udacsvm.bitnet
Details:	Free
User Info:	Expect: prompt, Send: RETURN 2-3 times

`telnet://delcat.udel.edu or delcat.acs.udel.edu`

Papers (of)

Mississippi State University Library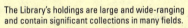

The Library's holdings are large and wide-ranging and contain significant collections in many fields.

Keywords:	History (US), Forestry, Energy, Carter (Hodding, Papers of), Mississippi
Audience:	General Public, Researchers, Librarians, Document Delivery Professionals
Contact:	Stephen Cunetto shc1@ra.msstate.edu
Details:	Free
User Info:	Expect: username, Send: msu; Expect: password, Send: library

`telnet://libserv.msstate.edu`

Papers

news.announce.conferences

A Usenet newsgroup providing information and discussion about conferences, as well as calls for papers.

Keywords:	Conferences, Papers, Writing
Audience:	Writers, General Public
Details:	Free
User Info:	To subscribe to this Usenet newsgroup, you need access to a newsreader.

`news:news.announce.conferences`

Parallel Computers

Ncube

Exchange of information among people using Ncube parallel computers.

Keywords:	Ncube, Parallel Computers
Audience:	Ncube Users
Contact:	David Krumme ncube-users-request@cs.tufts.edu
Details:	Free
User Info:	To subscribe to the list, send an e-mail message requesting a subscription to the URL address that follows.

`mailto:ncube-users-request@cs.tufts.edu`

Paranoia

alt.conspiracy

A Usenet newsgroup providing discussion about conspiracy and paranoia.

Keywords:	Conspiracy, Paranoia
Audience:	Paranoid Persons, General Public
User Info:	To subscribe to this Usenet newsgroup, you need access to a newsreader.

`news:alt.conspiracy`

Parasitology

The University of Notre Dame Library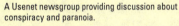

The library's holdings are large and wide-ranging and contain significant collections in many fields.

Keywords:	Music (Irish), Ireland, Botany (History of), Ecology, Entomology, Parasitology, Aquatic Biology, Universities (History of), Paleography
Audience:	General Public, Researchers, Librarians, Document Delivery Professionals
Details:	Free
User Info:	Expect: ENTER COMMAND OR HELP:, Send: library; To leave, type x on the command line and press Enter. At the ENTER COMMAND OR HELP: prompt, type bye and press Enter.

`telnet://irishmvs.cc.nd.edu`

Parenting

ADD-parents

A mailing list intended to provide support and information to parents of children with Attention Deficit/Hyperactivity Disorder.

Keywords:	Parenting, ADD (Attention Deficit/Hyperactivity Disorder)
Audience:	Parents, Educators, Health Care Providers
Contact:	add-parents-request@mv.mv.com
User Info:	To subscribe to the list, send an e-mail message to the URL address that follows.
	To send a message to the entire list, address it to: add-parents@mv.mv.com

`mailto:add-parents-request@mv.mv.com`

Moms

Moms is a list for lesbian mothers.

Keywords:	Lesbian, Parenting
Audience:	Lesbian Mothers, Lesbians
Contact:	moms-request@qiclab.scn.rain.com
Details:	Free
User Info:	To subscribe to the list, send an e-mail message requesting a subscription to the URL address that follows.

`mailto:moms-request@qiclab.scn.rain.com`

Our-kids

Support for parents and others regarding care, diagnoses, and therapy for young children with developmental delays, whether or not otherwise diagnosed (that is, CP, PDD, sensory integrative dysfunction, and so on). The name "our-kids" avoids labeling those who are, first and foremost, the special little ones in our lives.

Keywords:	Parenting
Audience:	Parents, Child Development Professionals
Contact:	our-kids-request@oar.net
Details:	Free
User Info:	To subscribe to the list, send an e-mail message requesting a subscription to the URL address that follows.
	To send a message to the entire list, address it to: our-kids@oar.net

`mailto:our-kids-request@oar.net`

Paris

WWW Paris

A web site created as a collaborative effort among individuals in both Paris and the United States.

Keywords:	Paris, Culture, Art, Travel, French, Tourism
Audience:	Students, Educators, Travelers, Researchers
Profile:	Contains an extensive collection of images and text regarding all of the major monuments and museums of Paris, including maps of the Metro and the RER; calendars of events and current expositions; promotional images and text relating to local department stores; there is also a visitors' section with up-to-date tourist information about hotels, restaurants, telephones, airport schedules, a basic Paris glossary, and the latest weather images. Includes an extensive collection of links to other resources about Paris and France, and a selected bibliography of history and architecture in Paris.

Contact:	Norman Barth, Eric Pouliquen nbarth@ucsd.edu epouliq@ucsd.edu

`http://meteora.ucsd.edu/~norman/paris`

Park Rangers

Park Rangers

This list is primarily for anyone working or interested in working as a ranger (general, interpretive, and so on) for the US National Park Service. However, rangers from state and county agencies and from other countries are also welcome. The group discusses numerous topics related to this profession.

Keywords:	US National Park Service, Government (US)
Audience:	Park Rangers
Contact:	Cynthia Dorminey 60157903@wsuvm1.csc.wsu.edu
Details:	Free
User Info:	To subscribe to the list, send an e-mail message requesting a subscription to the URL address that follows.
	To send a message to the entire list, address it to: 60157903@wsuvm1.csc.wsu.edu

`mailto:60157903@wsuvm1.csc.wsu.edu`

ParNET

ParNET

To discuss the installation, use, and modification of ParNET, an Amiga<->Amiga networking program.

Keywords:	Internet
Audience:	ParNet Users
Contact:	Ben Jackson parnet-list@ben.com
Details:	Free
User Info:	To subscribe to the list, send an e-mail message requesting a subscription to the URL address that follows.
	To send a message to the entire list, address it to: parnet-list@ben.com

`mailto:parnet-list-request@ben.com`

Partners

Partners

Advises the administration of Carnegie Mellon University, Pittsburgh, PA, through the vice-president of Human Resources (who reads the list), of developments in domestic-partnership benefits and makes recommendations about university policy regarding benefits.

Keywords:	Domestic Partnerships
Audience:	Carnegie Mellon Community
Contact:	partners-request@cs.cmu.edu
Details:	Free
User Info:	To subscribe to the list, send an e-mail message requesting a subscription to the URL address that follows.
	To send a message to the entire list, address it to: partners@cs.cmu.edu

`mailto:partners@cs.cmu.edu`

Partnerships

INCORPR (Corporation and Partnership Records)

The Corporation and Partnership Records (INCORP) library contains current US corporation and partnership filings.

Keywords:	Corporations, Partnerships, Filings, Trademarks
Audience:	Corporations, Lawyers, Researchers
Profile:	The INCORP library contains current records on corporations and limited partnerships registered with the office of the Secretary or Department of State. These records include information extracted by the state's staff from articles of incorporation, annual reports, amendments, and other public filings.
Contact:	Mead New Sales Group at (800) 227-4908 or (513) 859-5398 inside the US, or (513) 865-7981 for all inquiries outside the US.
User Info:	To subscribe, contact Mead directly.
Notes:	To examine the Nexis user guide, you can access it at the ftp site of the University of Texas at Austin at the URL address: ftp://ftp.cc.utexas.edu
	The files are in: /pub/ref-services/LEXIS

`telnet://nex.meaddata.com`

`http://www.meaddata.com`

Pascal

info-Pascal

Discussions of any Pascal implementation, from mainframe to micro, for Pascal program users.

Keywords:	Programming, Pascal
Audience:	Pascal Programmers
Contact:	Hernan Lobos *Mitzio* hlobos@utfsm.bitnet
Details:	Free
User Info:	To subscribe to the list, send an e-mail message requesting a subscription to the URL address that follows.

`info-Pascal@brl.mil`

Patents

Chinapats

Covers all patent applications published under the patent law of People's Republic of China.

- Keywords: Patents, Intellectual Property, Trademarks
- Sponsor: European Patent Office
- Audience: Patent Attorneys, Patent Agents, Librarians, Researchers
- Profile: English language abstracts are included for all applications filed by Chinese applicants. Contains more than 59,000 records. Updated monthly.
- Contact: paul.albert@neteast.com
- User Info: To subscribe, contact Orbit-Questel directly.

`telnet://orbit.com`

CLAIMS

Provides access to over 2.3 million U.S. patents issued by the U.S. Patent and Trademark Office.

- Keywords: Patents, Intellectual Property, Trademarks
- Sponsor: IFI/Plenum Data Corporation
- Audience: Patent Attorneys, Patent Agents, Librarians, Researchers
- Profile: Chemical patents are covered from 1950 forward; mechanical and electrical patents from 1963 forward; design patents from 1980 forward.
- Contact: paul.albert@neteast.com
- User Info: To subscribe, contact Orbit-Questel directly.

`telnet://orbit.com`

Derwent World Patents Index

Derwent World Patents Index and Derwent World Patents Index Latest contain data from nearly 3 million inventions represented in more than 6 million patent documents from 33 patent-issuing authorities around the world.

- Keywords: Patents, Inventions
- Sponsor: Derwent Publications, Ltd., London, UK
- Audience: Science Researchers
- Profile: In addition to bibliographic information, the basic patent record includes the full abstract (for new patents issued from 1981 to the present), informative title, International Patent Classification codes, and Derwent subject codes. These files also provide access to equivalent patents, grouped together by patent family in the basic patent record. The use of manual and fragmentation codes is restricted to Derwent subscribers, in accordance with their subscription level.

Pharmaceutical patents are included from 1963 to the present, agricultural chemical patents from 1965 to the present, and polymer and plastics patents from 1966 to the present. Coverage of all chemical patents began in 1970; coverage of all patents, irrespective of subject, began in 1974.

- Contact: Dialog in the US at (800) 334-2564, Dialog internationally at country-specific locations.
- User Info: To subscribe, contact Dialog directly.
- Notes: Coverage: 1963 to the present; updated weekly (file 351) and monthly (file 350).

`telnet://dialog.com`

Derwent World Patents Index/ API Merged

Patents covering petroleum processes, fuels, lubricants, petrochemicals, pipelines, tankers, storage, pollution control, synthetic fuels, synthesis gas, C1 chemistry, and other technologies.

- Keywords: Petroleum, Patents
- Sponsor: Derwent Publications, Ltd. and the American Petroleum Institute Central Abstracting and Indexing Service
- Audience: Researchers, Librarians
- Profile: Unique features include patent family searching, petrochemical patents searching, deep chemical/petroleum indexing.
- Contact: paul.albert@neteast.com
- User Info: To subscribe, contact Orbit-Questel directly.

`telnet://orbit.com`

European Patents Fulltext

European Patents Fulltext contains the complete text of European published applications and patents and European PCT published applications.

- Keywords: Patents, Europe, Law (International)
- Sponsor: European Patent Office, Vienna, Austria
- Audience: Patent Researchers
- Profile: It contains bibliographic, administrative, and legal information from the European Patent Registry. Records have abstracts, patent specifications including all claims, and the search report, including cited patents and other references.
- Contact: Dialog in the US at (800) 334-2564, Dialog internationally at country-specific locations.
- User Info: To subscribe, contact Dialog directly.
- Notes: Coverage: 1978 to the present; updated weekly.

`telnet://dialog.com`

Family and Legal Status (INPADOC)

The database includes a list of patents issued in 56 countries and patenting organizations.

- Keywords: Patents, Technlogy
- Sponsor: European Patent Office (EPO), Vienna, Austria
- Audience: Patent Researchers, Inventors
- Profile: INPADOC contains bibliographic data consisting of title, inventor, and assignee for most patents. In addition, this file brings together information about priority-application numbers, countries and dates, and equivalent patents (that is, patent families) for patents. This file also contains the legal status information for patents in some countries.
- Contact: Dialog in the US at (800) 334-2564, Dialog internationally at country-specific locations.
- User Info: To subscribe, contact Dialog directly.
- Notes: Coverage: April 1968 to the present; updated weekly.

`telnet://dialog.com`

IMSWorld Patents International

The database provides an analysis of the product patent position of more than 1,000 pharmaceutical compounds, either marketed or in active R&D.

- Keywords: Patents, Pharmaceuticals
- Sponsor: IMSWorld Publications, Ltd., London, UK
- Audience: Patent Researchers
- Profile: Each record includes an evaluated entry for all international patents, estimated patent expiration dates, therapeutic class, laboratory code, patent number issued by country, published application number by country, extensions to patent terms for the US and Japan where granted, and US marketing exclusivity information if applicable.
- Contact: Dialog in the US at (800) 334-2564, Dialog internationally at country-specific locations.
- User Info: To subscribe, contact Dialog directly.
- Notes: Coverage: Current; updated monthly.

`telnet://dialog.com`

INPADOC/INPANEW

Patent documents issued by more than fifty national and international patent offices.

- Keywords: Patents, Intellectual Property, Trademarks
- Sponsor: European Patent Office
- Audience: Patent Attorneys, Patent Agents, Librarians, Researchers

JAPIO

Profile:	Bibliographic information is searchable, including inventor names, assignees, international patent classification codes, and in most cases, titles, as well as complete publications and application data. Contains approximately 20 million records. Updated weekly.
Contact:	paul.albert@neteast.com
User Info:	To subscribe, contact Orbit-Questel directly.

`telnet://orbit.com`

JAPIO

Comprehensive source of unexamined Japanese patent applications.

Keywords:	Patents, Intellectual Property, Trademarks
Sponsor:	Japan Patent Information Organization
Audience:	Patent Attorneys, Patent Agents, Librarians, Researchers
Profile:	More than 2.8 million records covering all technologies. Unique features include English-language abstracts for many Japanese patent applications
Contact:	paul.albert@neteast.com
User Info:	To subscribe, contact Orbit-Questel directly.

`telnet://orbit.com`

Legal Status

Records thousands of types of actions that can affect the legal status of a patent document after it is published and after the patent is granted.

Keywords:	Patents, Intellectual Property, Trademarks
Sponsor:	European Patent Office
Audience:	Patent Attorneys, Patent Agents, Librarians, Researchers
Profile:	Information about the disposition of patent applications published under the Patent Cooperation Treaty by the World Intellectual Property Organizations is included as well. Contains more than 8 million records. Updated weekly.
Contact:	paul.albert@neteast.com
User Info:	To subscribe, contact Orbit-Questel directly.

`telnet://orbit.com`

LEXPAT (Patents US)

The LEXPAT library contains the full text of US patents issued since 1975, the US Patent and Trademark Office Manual of Classification, and the Index to US Patent Classification. The approximately 1,500 patents added to the library each week appear online within four days of their issue.

Keywords:	Patents, Inventors, Assignees, Litigants
Audience:	Lawyers, Business Researchers, Analysts, Entrepreneurs
Profile:	LEXPAT may be searched by individual files for the full text of utility, design or plant patents, or you can combine the files in one 'omni' search. The Manual, Index and Class files can be used to supplement your full-text patent searches. LEXPAT is a valuable tool for both patent professionals and for anyone who needs to access to technical information. More than 80 percent of the information contained in patents is unavailable in any other form.
Contact:	Mead New Sales Group at (800) 227-4908 or (513) 859-5398 inside the US, or (513) 865-7981 for all inquiries outside the US.
User Info:	To subscribe, contact Mead directly.
	To examine the Nexis user guide, you can access it at the ftp site of the University of Texas at Austin at the following URL address: ftp://ftp.cc.utexas.edu
	The files are in: /pub/ref-services/LEXIS

`telnet://nex.meaddata.com`

`http://www.meaddata.com`

Patent Act of the US

This resource contains full-text documentation regarding the US Patent Act (Title 35, United States Code, Sections 1 - 376).

Keywords:	Patents, Laws (US Federal), Government (US Federal)
Audience:	Journalists, Politicians, Economists, Lawyers, Scientists
Details:	Free

`http://fatty.law.cornell.edu/patent/patent.overview.html`

U.S. Patent and Trademark Office Database

A database of patents issued in 1994 by the U.S. Patent and Trademark Office, including a searchable index.

Keywords:	Patents, Databases, Inventions, Business
Sponsor:	New York University School of Business
Audience:	Inventors, General Public
Contact:	questions@town.hall.org

`gopher://town.hall.org/patent`

University of Nevada at Reno Library

The Library's holdings are large and wide-ranging and contain significant collections in many fields.

Keywords:	Basque Studies, Nevada , UN Army Map Service, Patents
Audience:	General Public, Researchers, Librarians, Document Delivery Professionals
Details:	Free
User Info:	Expect: login, Send: wolfpac

`telnet://wolfpac.lib.unr.edu`

US Patents

Complete patent information of all claims of U.S. patents issued since 1971.

Keywords:	Patents, Intellectual Property, Trademarks
Sponsor:	Derwent, Inc.
Audience:	Patent Attorneys, Patent Agents, Librarians, Researchers
Profile:	Includes complete front page information, plus all claims of US patents issued since 1971. Merged file contains approximately 1.4 million records. Updated weekly.
Contact:	paul.albert@neteast.com
User Info:	To subscribe, contact Orbit-Questel directly.

`telnet://orbit.com`

PB-Cle-Raves

PB-Cle-Raves

One of several regional rave-related mailing lists, PB-Cle-Raves covers the Pittsburgh, PA, and Cleveland, OH, metropolitan areas exclusively.

Keywords:	Raves
Audience:	Ravers
Contact:	Joe LeSesne pb-cle-raves-request@telerama.lm.com
Details:	Free
User Info:	To subscribe to the list, send an e-mail message requesting a subscription to the URL address that follows.
	To send a message to the entire list, address it to: pb-cle-raves@telerama.lm.com

`mailto:pb-cle-raves-request@telerama.lm.com`

Pc532

Pc532

A mailing list for people interested in the pc532 project, a National Semiconductor NS32532-based system, offered at a low cost.

Keywords:	Computers, Hardware, Software
Audience:	Computer Users, Software Developers
Contact:	Dave Rand pc532-request@bungi.com
Details:	Free

User Info: To subscribe to the list, send an e-mail message requesting a subscription to the URL address that follows.

To send a message to the entire list, address it to: pc532@bungi.com

mailto:pc532-request@bungi.com

Pcbuild

Pcbuild

An open, unmoderated E-conference for discussion of PC hardware, including such topics as upgrading your PC, building your own PC, hardware problems, questions, and businesses from which to buy hardware cheaply.

Keywords: Computer Systems
Audience: PC Users
Contact: Dave Gomberg
gomberg@ucsfvm.edu
Details: Free
User Info: To subscribe to the list, send an e-mail message to the URL address that follows, consisting of a single line reading:

SUB pcbuild YourFirstName YourLastName

To send a message to the entire list, address it to: pcbuild@tsclion.trenton.edu

mailto:listserv@tsclion.trenton.edu

Pcgeos-list

Pcgeos-list

A discussion forum for users of PC/GEOS products, including GeoWorks Ensemble, GeoWorks Pro, GeoWorks POS, and third-party products. Topics include general information, tips, techniques, applications, and experiences.

Keywords: Computers, Software
Audience: Computer Users, Software Developers
Contact: listserv@pandora.sf.ca.us
Details: Free
User Info: To subscribe to the list, send an e-mail message to the URL address that follows, consisting of a single line reading:

SUB pcgeos-list YourFirstName YourLastName

To send a message to the entire list, address it to: pcgeos@pandora.sf.ca.us

mailto:listserv@pandora.sf.ca.us

Pd-games

Pd-games

A mailing list for people interested in game theory, especially Prisoner's Dilemma types of problems. Discussions include purely technical issues and questions, as well as specific scientific applications and the political and ideological aspects and consequences of game theory.

Keywords: Game Theory, Mathematics
Audience: Game Theorists, Mathematicians
Contact: Thomas Gramstad
pd-games-request@math.uio.no
Details: Free
User Info: To subscribe to the list, send an e-mail message requesting a subscription to the URL address that follows.

To send a message to the entire list, address it to: pd-games@math.uio.no

mailto:pd-games-request@math.uio.no

Pdp8-lovers

Pdp8-lovers

A mailing list for owners of vintage DEC (Digital Equipment Corp.) computers, especially the PDP-8 series. Discussion topics include hardware, software, and programming techniques.

Keywords: Computers, Hardware, Software
Audience: Computer Users, Product Analysts
Contact: Robert E. Seastrom
pdp8-lovers-request@mc.lcs.mit.edu
Details: Free
User Info: To subscribe to the list, send an e-mail message requesting a subscription to the URL address that follows.

To send a message to the entire list, address it to: pdp8-lovers@mc.lcs.mit.edu

mailto:pdp8-lovers@mc.lcs.mit.edu

Peace

activ-l

A mailing list for discussion of peace, empowerment, justice, and environmental issues.

Keywords: Peace, Justice, Environment, Activism
Audience: Activists, Students
Contact: Rich Winkel
harelb@math.cornell.edu
User Info: To subscribe to the list, send an e-mail message to the URL address that follows, consisting of a single line reading:

SUB activ-l YourFirstName YourLastName.

To send a message to the entire list, address it to: active-l@mizzou1.missouri.edu

mailto:listserv@mizzou1.missouri.edu

GLOSAS News (Global Systems Analysis and Simulating Association)

Newsletter of GLOSAS in the US, which is dedicated to global electronic education and simulation as a tool for promoting peace and the care of the natural environment.

Keywords: Education, Simulation, Peace
Audience: Educators, Environmentalists
Contact: Anton Ljutic
anton@vax2.concordia.ca
Details: Free
User Info: To subscribe, send an e-mail message to the address that follows.

mailto:listserv@vm1.mcgill.ca

un.wcw.doc.eng

This is a read-only conference comprised of official UN documents for the United Nations Fourth World Conference on Women: Action for Equality, Development and Peace, scheduled to take place at the Beijing International Convention Center, Beijing, China, from 4-15 September 1995. The documents are provided by the official Conference Secretariat, are posted as received by the UN Non-Governmental Liaison Service (NGLS).

Keywords: Women, Development (International), Peace, UN, World Conference on Women
Audience: Women, Activists, Non-Governmental Organizations, Feminists
Contact: United Nations Non-Governmental Liaison Service/Edie Farwell
ngls@igc.apc.org
efarwell@igc.apc.org
Details: Costs, Moderated
User Info: Establish an account on the nearest APC node. Login, type c for conferences, then type go un.wcw.doc.eng.

For information about the nearest APC node, contact: APC International Secretariat IBASE

E-mail: apcadmin@apc.org

E-mail message to APCadmin@apc.org

telnet://igc.apc.org

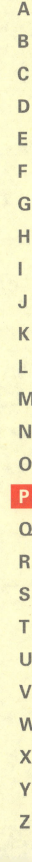

un.wcw.doc.fra

This is a read-only conference comprised of official UN documents for the United Nations Fourth World Conference on Women: Action for Equality, Development and Peace, scheduled to take place at the Beijing International Convention Center, Beijing, China, from 4-15 September 1995. The documents are provided by the official Conference Secretariat, are posted as received by the UN Non-Governmental Liaison Service (NGLS).

Keywords:	Women, Development (International), Peace, UN, World Conference on Women
Audience:	Women, Activists, Non-Governmental Organizations, Feminists
Contact:	United Nations Non-Governmental Liaison Service/Edie Farwell ngls@igc.apc.org or efarwell@igc.apc.org
Details:	Costs, Moderated
User Info:	Establish an account on the nearest APC node. Login, type c for conferences, then type go un.wcw.doc.fra. For information on the nearest APC node, contact: APC International Secretariat IBASE
	E-mail: apcadmin@apc.org
	E-mail message to APCadmin@apc.org

`telnet://igc.apc.org`

Pediatrics

University of Texas Health Science Center at San Antonio Library ★★

The library's holdings are large and wide-ranging and contain significant collections in many fields.

Keywords:	Allied Health, Dentistry, Nursing, Veterinary Science, Ambulatory Care, Obstetrics/Gynecology, Pediatrics
Audience:	Researchers, Students, General Public
Details:	Free
User Info:	Expect: Login, Send: LIS

`telnet://athena.uthscsa.edu`

PEI (Prince Edward Island, Canada) Crafts Council Gopher

PEI (Prince Edward Island, Canada) Crafts Council Gopher

A gopher devoted to all manner of crafts, from weaving to glass blowing. Information includes a database of tools, services, and materials for crafts enthusiasts, as well as FAQs and pointers to other crafts resources. Also provides background on the PEI Craft Council's activities and on Prince Edward Island.

Keywords:	Crafts, Hobbies, Canada
Sponsor:	PEI Crafts Council, Prince Edward Island, Canada
Audience:	Crafts Enthusiasts
Details:	Free

`gopher://crafts-council.pe.ca`

Pen-pals

Pen-pals

This mailing list provides a forum for children to correspond with each other electronically. Although the list is not moderated, it is monitored for content and is managed by listproc.

Keywords:	Computing, Children, Writing
Audience:	Computer Users, Children, Student Writers
Contact:	pen-pals-request@mainstream.com
Details:	Free
User Info:	To subscribe to the list, send an e-mail message requesting a subscription to the URL address that follows.
	To send a message to the entire list, address it to: pen-pals@mainstream.com

`mailto:pen-pals@mainstream.com`

Pennsylvania

PennInfo

PennInfo is a menu-based campus-wide information system whose design offers both the novice and the experienced user access to information of interest to the University of Pennsylvania community. PennInfo currently contains more than 3,500 documents, posted by approximately 70 providers of information. A sampling of the content in PennInfo includes: University of Pennsylvania facts, available grants, fellowships, and research resources; and the entire Penn course register and course timetable.

Keywords:	Pennsylvania
Sponsor:	University of Pennsylvania
Audience:	Researchers, Educators
Details:	Free

`telnet://penninfo.upenn.edu`

PENPages

PENPages

This easy-to-use, general-interest database contains articles and brochures.

Keywords:	Food, Employment, Education
Sponsor:	Pennsylvania State University, PA
Audience:	General Public
Notes:	Expect: login; Send: your state's two-letter code (or "world" if sent from outside the USA)

`telnet://psunet.psu.edu`

People

NEWS (General News)

The General News (NEWS) library includes more than 2,300 sources. Full-text news from national and international newspapers, magazines, newsletters, and wire services and abstract information are both available.

Keywords:	News, Analysis, People, Companies
Audience:	Journalists, General Public
Profile:	The General News (NEWS) library contains a number of publications and wire services of general interest, as well as others that specialize in particular areas of business. The NEWS library is organized into individual files, group files by source or subject, and user-defined combination files for full-text information sources. Abstracts are also available as individual files or can be searched together in one group file. The NEWS library includes such prestigious full-text sources as the New York Times and more than more than 30 major newspapers from around the US and the world.
Contact:	Mead New Sales Group at (000) 227-4908 or (513) 859-5398 inside the US, or (513) 865-7981 for all inquiries outside the US.
User Info:	To subscribe, contact Mead directly.
	To examine the Nexis user guide, you can access it at the ftp site of the University of Texas at Austin at the following URL address: ftp://ftp.cc.utexas.edu
	The files are in: /pub/ref-services/LEXIS

`telnet://nex.meaddata.com`

`http://www.meaddata.com`

People Using Networks Can Have an Impact on Government

People Using Networks Can Have an Impact on Government

Statement by community networker Anne Fallis, who emphasizes the need for easy-to-use interfaces and inexpensive access to worldwide information. She lists many examples of local communities using networking.

Keywords: Community, Networking, Activism

Audience: Activists, Policymakers, Community Leaders, Network Users

Contact: Anne Fallis
afallis@silver.sdsmt.edu

Details: Free

```
http://nearnet.gnn.com/mag/articles/
oram/bio.fallis.html
```

Performing Arts

Theater

This directory is a compilation of information resources focused on theater.

Keywords: Theater, Drama, Performing Arts

Audience: Theater Personnel, Drama Personnel, Performers

Contact: Deborah Torres, Martha Vander Kolk
dtorres@umich.edu
mjvk@umich.edu

Details: Free

```
ftp://una.hh.lib.umich.edu/70/
inetdirsstacks/theater:torresmjvk
```

Williams College Library
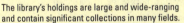

The library's holdings are large and wide-ranging and contain significant collections in many fields.

Keywords: Americana, Graphic Arts, Printing (History of), Performing Arts, Printing

Audience: General Public, Researchers, Librarians, Document Delivery Professionals

Contact: Jim Cubit

Details: Free

User Info: Expect: Mitek Server..., Send: Enter or Return; Expect: prompt, Send: hollis

```
telnet://library.williams.edu
```

Periodicals

Book Review Index

This database contains references to more than 2.5 million citations to reviews of approximately 1.5 million distinct book and periodical titles.

Keywords: Book Reviews, Periodicals, Publications

Sponsor: Gale Research, Inc., Detroit, MI, USA

Audience: Publishing Professionals, Authors

Profile: The database covers every review published since 1969 in nearly 500 periodicals and newspapers. Each record includes the author and title of the work being reviewed, journal name, date of review, and page number. Document type indications are also included if the work is a periodical; a reference work; a children's book, periodical, or reference book; or a young adult book, periodical, or reference book. Book Review Index corresponds to the print publication of the same name. Periodicals indexed range from the Harvard Business Review to the Center for Children's Books: Bulletin, and from the American Scholar to Psychology Today. General interest magazines such as Ms., Time, The New Yorker, and Atlantic are covered, as are specialized periodicals like Flying, Yachting, and National Genealogical Society Quarterly.

Contact: Dialog in the US at (800) 334-2564, Dialog internationally at country specific locations.

Details: Costs

User Info: To subscribe, contact Dialog directly.

```
telnet://dialog.com
```

PERL (Practical Extraction and Report Language)

PERL (Practical Extraction and Report Language)

An HTML-formatted and highly indexed PERL programming reference document.

Keywords: Programming Languages, Computer Programming

Audience: Computer Programmers, Students, Researchers

Contact: Larry Wall
lwall@netlabs.com

```
http://www.cs.cmu.edu/Web/People/rgs/
perl.html
```

PERQ workstations

PERQ-fanatics

This mailing list is for users of PERQ graphics workstations.

Keywords: PERQ workstations, Computer Graphics

Audience: PERQ Users, Graphic Artists

Contact: perq-fanatics-request@alchemy.com

Details: Free

User Info: To subscribe to the list, send an e-mail message requesting a subscription to the URL address that follows.

To send a message to the entire list, address it to: perq-fanatics@alchemy.com

```
mailto:perq-fanatics-
request@alchemy.com
```

Personal Papers

University of Chicago Library

The library's holdings are large and wide-ranging and contain significant collections in many fields.

Keywords: English Bibles, Lincoln (Abraham), Kentucky & Ohio River Valley (History of), Balzac (Honore de), American Drama, Cromwell (Oliver), Goethe, Judaica, Italy, Chaucer (Geoffrey), Wells (Ida, Personal Papers of), Douglas (Stephen A.), Italy, Literature (Children's)

Audience: General Public, Researchers, Librarians, Document Delivery Professionals

Details: Free

Expect: ENTER CLASS, Send: LIB48 3; Expect: CONNECTED, Send: RETURN

```
telnet://olorin.uchicago.edu
```

Personals

alt.personals.ads

A Usenet newsgroup providing a forum for singles.

Keywords: Personals, Singles

Audience: Singles

User Info: To subscribe to this Usenet newsgroup, you need access to a newsreader.

```
news:alt.personals.ads
```

Peru

Peru

A mailing list for the discussion of Peruvian culture and other issues.

- **Keywords:** Peru, South America
- **Audience:** Peruvians, Educators, Researchers
- **Contact:** Herbert Koller owner-peru@cs.sfsu.edu
- **Details:** Free
- **User Info:** To subscribe to the list, send an e-mail message requesting a subscription to the URL address that follows.

  To send a message to the entire list, address it to: owner-peru@cs.sfsu.edu
- **Notes:** This mailing list is simply an echo site, so all posts get bounced from that address to all the people subscribed.

`mailto:owner-peru@cs.sfsu.edu`

Petroleum

API Energy Business News Index (APIBIZ)

Worldwide coverage of commercial, financial, marketing, and regulatory information affecting the petroleum and energy industries.

- **Keywords:** Petroleum, Business
- **Sponsor:** The American Petroleum Institute - Central Abstracting and Information Services
- **Audience:** Researchers, Librarians
- **Profile:** Twenty-two major news and economics publications are the primary sources for worldwide coverage of information affecting the petroleum and energy industries. Contains more than 600,000 records. Updated weekly.
- **Contact:** paul.albert@neteast.com
- **User Info:** To subscribe, contact Orbit-Questel directly.

`telnet://orbit.com`

Derwent World Patents Index/API Merged

Patents covering petroleum processes, fuels, lubricants, petrochemicals, pipelines, tankers, storage, pollution control, synthetic fuels, synthesis gas, C1 chemistry, and other technologies.

- **Keywords:** Petroleum, Patents
- **Sponsor:** Derwent Publications, Ltd. and the American Petroleum Institute Central Abstracting and Indexing Service
- **Audience:** Researchers, Librarians
- **Profile:** Unique features include patent family searching, petrochemical patents searching, deep chemical/petroleum indexing.
- **Contact:** paul.albert@neteast.com
- **User Info:** To subscribe, contact Orbit-Questel directly.

`telnet://orbit.com`

TULSA (Petroleum Abstracts)

References and abstracts to literature and patents related to oil and natural gas exploration, development and production.

- **Keywords:** Petroleum
- **Sponsor:** Petroleum Abstracts, a division of the University of Tulsa
- **Audience:** Researchers, Librarians
- **Profile:** More than 500,000 references. Includes such areas as logging, well drilling, well completion and servicing, petroleum geology, exploration geophysics and geochemistry, oil and gas production, reservoir studies and recovery methods, pollution, alternative fuels, and transportation and storage. Updated weekly.
- **Contact:** paul.albert@neteast.com
- **User Info:** To subscribe, contact Orbit-Questel directly.

`telnet://orbit.com`

University of Tulsa Library

The library's holdings are large and wide-ranging and contain significant collections in many fields.

- **Keywords:** Literature (American), Petroleum, Geology
- **Audience:** Researchers, Students, General Public
- **Details:** Free
- **Expect:** Username Prompt, Send: LIAS

`telnet://vax2.utulsa.edu`

Pets

rec.pets

A Usenet newsgroup providing information and discussion about pets and pet care.

- **Keywords:** Pets, Animals
- **Audience:** Pet Owners
- **User Info:** To subscribe to this Usenet newsgroup, you need access to a newsreader.

`news:rec.pets`

rec.pets.cats

A Usenet newsgroup providing information and discussion about domestic cats.

- **Keywords:** Pets, Animals
- **Audience:** Cat Owners
- **User Info:** To subscribe to this Usenet newsgroup, you need access to a newsreader.

`news:rec.pets.cats`

rec.pets.dogs

A Usenet newsgroup providing information and discussion about dogs.

- **Keywords:** Pets, Animals
- **Audience:** Dog Owners
- **User Info:** To subscribe to this Usenet newsgroup, you need access to a newsreader.

`news:rec.pets.dogs`

PGP Mail

PGP Mail

Information regarding the use of PGP (Pretty Good Privacy) mail, a public key.

- **Keywords:** Internet, e-mail
- **Audience:** Internet Surfers
- **Details:** Free

`ftp://ftp.uu.net/networking/mail`

Ph7

Ph7

A mailing list for discussions about Peter Hamill and related rock groups.

- **Keywords:** Rock Music, Hamill (Peter)
- **Audience:** Musicians, Rock Music Enthusiasts
- **Contact:** ph7-request@bnf.com
- **User Info:** To subscribe to the list, send an e-mail message requesting a subscription to the URL address that follows.

  To send a message to the entire list, address it to: ph7@bnf.com

`mailto:ph7-request@bnf.com`

Pharmaceutical Development

IMSWorld R&D Focus

The database provides information on worldwide pharmaceutical development.

Keywords: Pharmaceutical Development
Sponsor: IMSWorld Publications, Ltd., London, UK
Audience: Pharmacists, Health Care Professionals
Profile: All aspects of drug development are covered, from product discovery to launch. This R&D monitoring database is useful for tracking pharmaceutical products in 48 countries. R&D Focus includes two types of records: 1) profile records that include for each drug the generic name, laboratory code, CAS Registry Number, chemical name, synonyms, therapeutic indications, patents issued, development history, latest stage of worldwide development, commercial potential, and company activity. 2) Drug News records that provide a "quick alert" news service covering international research and pharmaceutical development.
Contact: Dialog in the US at (800) 334-2564, Dialog internationally at country-specific locations.
Details: Costs
User Info: To subscribe, contact Dialog directly.

telnet://dialog.com

Pharmaceuticals

IMSWorld Patents International

The database provides an analysis of the product patent position of more than 1,000 pharmaceutical compounds, either marketed or in active R&D.

Keywords: Patents, Pharmaceuticals
Sponsor: IMSWorld Publications, Ltd., London, UK
Audience: Patent Researchers
Profile: Each record includes an evaluated entry for all international patents, estimated patent expiration dates, therapeutic class, laboratory code, patent number issued by country, published application number by country, extensions to patent terms for the US and Japan where granted, and US marketing exclusivity information if applicable.
Contact: Dialog in the US at (800) 334-2564, Dialog internationally at country-specific locations.
User Info: To subscribe, contact Dialog directly.
Notes: Coverage: Current; updated monthly.

telnet://dialog.com

Pharmacology

Biosis Previews

The database encompasses the entire field of life sciences and covers original research reports and reviews in biological and biomedical areas. This includes field, laboratory, clinical, experimental and theoretical work. The traditional areas of biology, including botany, zoology, and microbiology are covered, as well as the related fields such as plant and animal science, agriculture, pharmacology, and ecology.

Keywords: Biology, Botany, Zoology, Microbiology, Plant Science, Animal Science, Agriculture, Pharmacology, Ecology, Biochemistry, Biophysics, Bioengineering
Sponsor: Biosis
Audience: Librarians, Researchers, Students, Biologists, Botanists, Zoologists, Scientists, Taxonomists
Contact: CDP Technologies Sales Department (800) 950-2035, extension 400.
User Info: To subscribe, contact CDP Technologies directly.

telnet://cdplus@cdplus.com

Drake University

The library's holdings are large and wide-ranging and contain significant collections in many fields.

Keywords: Music, Pharmacology, Theology
Audience: General Public, Researchers, Librarians, Document Delivery Professionals
Details: Free, Moderated
User Info: COWLES to access the main library, and LAWLIB to access the Law Library. To leave the system, enter Ctrl+Z.

telnet://lib.drake.edu

EMBASE

EMBASE is an acclaimed comprehensive index of international literature on medicine, science, and pharmacology.

Keywords: Medicine, Science, Pharmacology
Sponsor: Elsevier Science Publishers
Audience: Librarians, Researchers, Students, Physicians
Contact: CDP Technologies Sales Department (800) 950-2035, extension 400
User Info: To subscribe, contact CDP Technologies directly.

telnet://cdplus@cdplus.com

Health News Daily

The database contains all the daily news and full-text articles from Health News Daily, a publication from F-D-C Reports, Inc.

Keywords: Health, Pharmacology, Medical Research, News
Sponsor: F-D-C Reports, Inc., Chevy Chase, MD, US
Audience: Health Professionals, Pharmaceutical Industry, Market Researchers
Profile: The database provides specialized, in-depth business, scientific, regulatory, and legal news. Timely coverage of pharmacy and pharmaceuticals is given, as well as coverage of medical devices and diagnostics, medical research, cosmetics, health policy, provider payment policies, and cost containment in national health care.
Coverage: 1990 to the present; updated daily.
Contact: Dialog in the US at (800) 334-2564, Dialog internationally at country-specific locations.
Details: Costs
User Info: To subscribe, contact Dialog directly.

telnet://dialog.com

Recreational Pharmacology Server

Very extensive collection of drug FAQs, data sheets, net articles, resources, and electronic books. Complete list of Internet links to related sites.

Keywords: Pharmacology, Drugs, Neuroscience
Sponsor: University of Washington, Seattle, Washington, USA
Audience: Students, General Public, Pharmacologists, Neuroscientists
Contact: Webmaster lamontg@u.washington.edu
Details: Free

http://stein1.u.washington.edu:2012/pharm/pharm.html

University of Maryland System Library

The library's holdings are large and wide-ranging and contain significant collections in many fields.

Keywords: Medicine (History of), Nursing, Pharmacology, Microbiology, Aquaculture, Aquatic Chemistry, Toxicology
Audience: General Public, Researchers, Librarians, Document Delivery Professionals
Contact: Ron Larsen
Details: Free
User Info: Expect:Available Services menu; Send: PAC

telnet://victor.umd.edu

University of the Pacific Library

The library's holdings are large and wide-ranging and contain significant collections in many fields.

Keywords: Pharmacology, Americana (Western)
Audience: Researchers, Students, General Public
Details: Free
User Info: Expect: Login, Send: Library

`telnet://pacificat.lib.uop.edu`

Pharmacy

Svhp-l

A restricted discussion group on veterinary pharmacy issues.

Keywords: Veterinary Pharmacy, Pharmacy, Veterinary Science
Audience: Veterinarians, Veterinary Pharmacists
Contact: Doug Kemp
vetpharm@uga.cc.uga.edu
Details: Free
User Info: To subscribe to the list, send an e-mail message to the URL address shown that follows, consisting of a single line reading:

SUB svhp-l YourFirstName YourLastName

To send a message to the entire list, address it to: svhp-l@uga.cc.uga.edu

`mailto:listserv@uga.cc.uga.edu`

Philanthropy

Internet Nonprofit Center

A clearinghouse of information for nonprofit organizations and those interested in donating to them. Includes annual reports, directories, financial information, and brochures of selected nonprofit organizations, as well as volunteer opportunities and advice for potential donors. The Internet Nonprofit Center is currently located on EnviroLink Network, a gopher dedicated to environmental causes.

Keywords: Nonprofit Organizations, Philanthropy
Sponsor: American Institute of Philanthropy, USA, and The Internet Nonprofit Center, Brooklyn, New York, USA
Audience: Activists, Philanthropists
Contact: Cliff Landesman
clandesm@panix.com

`gopher://envirolink.org`

Philology

MEDTEXT-L

A discussion of medieval text, including philology, codicology, and technology.

Keywords: Medieval, Philology, Linguistics
Audience: Linguists, Language Teachers, Language Students, Historians
Details: Free
User Info: To subscribe to the list, send an e-mail message to the URL address that follows, consisting of a single line reading:

medtext-l YourFirstName YourLastName

To send a message to the entire list, address it to: medtext-l@uiucvmd.bitnet

`mailto:listserv@uiucvmd.bitnet`

Philosophy

Non Serviam

Non Serviam is an electronic newsletter centered on the philosophy of Max Stirner, author of Der Einzige und Sein Eigentum (The Ego and Its Own) and on his dialectical egoism. The contents, however, are decided by the individual contributors and the editor.

Keywords: Max Stirner, Non Serviam, Philosophy
Audience: Max Stirner Fans
Contact: Svein Olav Nyberg
solan@math.uio.no
Details: Free
User Info: To subscribe to the list, send an e-mail message requesting a subscription to the URL address that follows.

To send a message to the entire list, address it to: solan@math.uio.no

`mailto:solan@math.uio.no`

Principia Cybernetica Newsletter

Newsletter for participants in the Principia Cybernetica Project (PCP), as well as for people interested in keeping informed about the project.

Keywords: Philosophy, Worldview
Audience: Philosophers
Profile: PCP is a computer-supported collaborative attempt to develop an integrated evolutionary-systemic philosophy or world view. Its contributors are distributed over several continents and maintain contact primarily through electronic mail (mailing list PRNCYB-L), as well as through annual meetings, the printed (and electronic) newsletter, and postal mail. PCP focuses on the clear formulation of basic concepts and principles of the cybernetic approach.

Contact: Cliff Joslyn, Francis Heylighen
fheyligh@vnet3.vub.ac.be
cjoslyn@bingvaxu.cc.binghamton.edu
Details: Free
Send a 1- to 2- page letter, giving your address and affiliations and motivating your interest in the Project to the List owner (C. Joslyn).

`mailto:cjoslyn@bingvaxu.cc.binghamton.edu`

talk.religion.newage

A Usenet newsgroup providing information and discussion about esoteric and minority religions and philosophies.

Keywords: Religion, Philosophy
Audience: General Public, Researchers, Students
Details: Free
User Info: To subscribe to this Usenet newsgroup, you need access to a newsreader.

`news:talk.religion.newage`

The Electronic Journal of Analytic Philosophy Humanities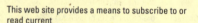

This web site provides a means to subscribe to or read current

Keywords: Philosophy
Sponsor: University of Indiana, Indiana, USA
Audience: Philosophers, Researchers, Educators, Students
Contact: ejap@phil.indiana.edu
Details: Free
User Info: To subscribe, send an e-mail message to: ejap@phil.indiana.edu

`http://www.phil.indiana.edu/ejap/ejap.html`

THINKNET

Electronic newsletter on philosophy, systems theory, interdisciplinary studies, and thoughtful conversation in cyberspace.

Keywords: Cyberspace, Systems Theory, Philosophy
Audience: Philosophers, System Theorists
Contact: Kont D. Palmer Ph.D.
Internet: palmer@world.std.com
Details: Free
User Info: To subscribe, send an e-mail message to the URL address that follows, consisting of a single line reading:

SUB THINKNET YourFirstName YourLastName

`mailto:palmer@world.std.com`

Phone Books

Internet Phone Books

A collection of Internet phone books and e-mail directories.

Keywords: Phone Books, Internet Guides, E-mail
Sponsor: Texas Tech University
Audience: Internet Surfers, General Public
Profile: This gopher includes a number of resources for finding people on the Internet. In addition to the standard Netfind, WHOIS, and Inter-NIC services, it also has information on finding college and international e-mail addresses. Also features snail mail information from the U.S. Post Office on Zip codes, as well as an international directory of telephone area codes.
Contact: Abdul Malik Yoosufani
gripe@cs.ttu.edu

`gopher://cs4sun.cs.ttu.edu`

Photography

3D

A open mailing list for discussion of 3D stereo photography.

Keywords: Photography
Audience: Photographers
Contact: John Bercovitz
JHBercovitz@lbl.gov
User Info: To subscribe to the list, send an e-mail message to the URL address that follows.

To send a message to the entire list, address it to: 3d@lbl.gov

`mailto:3d-request@lbl.gov`

California Museum of Photography: Network Exhibitions

This is a collection of digital images for educational and general use.

Keywords: Photography, Art, Education
Sponsor: University of California, Riverside, California, USA
Audience: Photographers, Artists, Educators, Historians
Profile: The California Museum of Photography is in the process of selecting groups of images from the collections as thematic exhibitions. Instead of displays on the walls, these exhibitions comprise a group of digital images with associated text. Particular emphasis is on the utility of these images in class projects for elementary and secondary school students. However, the digital images also have potential value for more advanced scholarly research in preparation of papers in the Humanities, Social Sciences, and the Arts.
Contact: Russ Harvey
russ@cornucopia.ucr.edu

`gopher://gopher.ucr.edu`

Fashion Photography Conference

A conference on the WELL about photography; topics range from products and technical information to aesthetics and fashion photography.

Keywords: Photography, Fashion
Audience: Photographers, Fashion Enthusiasts
Contact: Ralph E. Bedwell
ralf@well.sf.ca.us
Details: To participate in a conference on the WELL, you must first establish an account on the WELL. To do so, start by typing: telnet well.sf.ca.us

`telnet://well.sf.ca.us`

Images from Various Sources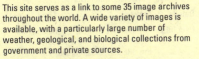

This site serves as a link to some 35 image archives throughout the world. A wide variety of images is available, with a particularly large number of weather, geological, and biological collections from government and private sources.

Keywords: Computer Graphics, Photography, Art
Sponsor: The University of Alaska
Audience: General Public
Contact: Douglas Toelle
sxinfo@orca.alaska.edu
Details: Free, Images

`gopher://gopher.uacn.alaska.edu`

`http://info.alaska.edu:70`

PHOTO-CD

This list provides libraries of information about Kodak CD products or technology and closely related products.

Keywords: Photography, Computer Graphics
Sponsor: Eastman Kodak, Rochester, NY
Audience: Photographers, General Public
Contact: Don Cox
listmgr@info.kodak.com
User Info: To subscribe to the list, send an e-mail message to the address that follows, consisting of a single line reading:
Notes: SUB photo-cd Your First Name Your Last Name

To send a message to the entire list, address it to: photo-cd@info.kodak.com

`mailto:listserv@info.kodak.com`

rec.photo

A Usenet newsgroup providing information and discussion about photography.

Keywords: Photography, Art, Crafts
Audience: Photographers, Artists
User Info: To subscribe to this Usenet newsgroup, you need access to a newsreader.

`news:rec.photo`

University of Rochester Library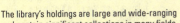

The library's holdings are large and wide-ranging and contain significant collections in many fields.

Keywords: Architecture, Art History, Photography, Literature (Asian), Lasers, Geology, Statistics, Optics, Medieval Studies
Audience: Researchers, Students, General Public
Details: Free
User Info: Expect: Login; Send: Library

`telnet://128.151.226.71`

Photography (History of)

University of New Mexico UNMinfo Library

The library's holdings are large and wide-ranging and contain significant collections in many fields.

Keywords: Photography (History of), Architecture, Native American Affairs, Land Records
Audience: Researchers, Students, General Public
Contact: Art St. George
stgeorge@unmb.bitnet
Details: Free
User Info: Expect: Login; Send: Unminfo

`telnet://unminfo.unm.edu`

Physical Education & Recreation

Physical Education & Recreation

A collection of information on sporting and recreational activities from aikido to windsurfing.

Physical Education

Keywords: Sports, Recreation, Aikido, Cycling, Scuba Diving, Windsurfing
Audience: Sports Enthusiasts, Fitness Enthusiasts
Contact: ctcadmin@ctc.ctc.edu

`gopher://ctc.ctc.edu`

Physical Therapy

HFS-L

Human Factors and Ergonomics Society Virginia Tech Chapter.

Keywords: Ergonomics, Physical Therapy
Audience: Researchers, Physical Therapists, Designers
Contact: Cortney Vargo
CORTV@VTVM1.CC.VT.EDU
Details: Free
User Info: To subscribe to the list, send an e-mail message to the URL address shown that follows consisting of a single line reading:

SUB hfs-l YourFirstName YourLastName

To send a message to the entire list, address it to: hfs-l@tvm1.cc.vt.edu

`listser@vtm1.cc.vt.edu`

Physics

(The) Physics Information Network ★

Distributes papers and software related to the American Institute of Physics and the journal Computers in Physics.

Keywords: Physics
Sponsor: American Institute of Physics (AIP)
Audience: Physicists
Details: Free
User Info: To subscribe to the list, send an e-mail message requesting a subscription to the URL address that follows.

To send a message to the entire list, address it to: admin@pinet.aip.org

`mailto:admin@pinet.aip.org`

Astronomical Publications Resources (APR) ★★★★

Contains pointers to many relevant resources available through the Internet.

Keywords: Astronomy, Astrophysics, Physics
Sponsor: Space Telescope Science Institute
Audience: Astronomers, Physicists, Students (college, graduate), Educators
Profile: APR is a useful starting point to most of the astronomical publication resources available online. It is conviently divided by type of access (gopher, wais, www, telnet, ftp). As of January 1994, resources include:

- Astrophysics Preprints[MD]SISSA
- ADC Documents
- NOAO News
- NRAO Preprint Database
- STECF Newsletter
- STELAR ApJ, ApJS, AJ, PASP, A&A, A&AS, MNRAS, and JGR Abstracts
- STScI Preprint Database
- IAU Circulars Astronomical Union
- CfA Index of ApJ, AJ, PASP
- DIRA2 Database
- Electronic Journal of Astron. Soc. of the Atlantic

Contact: rrpss@stsci.edu
Details: Free, Moderated

`http://stsci.edu/net-publications.html`

`gopher://stsci.edu`

fusion ★

Fusion is an e-mail redistribution of Usenet sci.physics.fusion newsgroup for sites/users lacking access to Usenet.

Keywords: Physics, Fusion, Science
Audience: Physicists, Scientists
Details: Free
User Info: To subscribe to the list, send an e-mail message requesting a subscription to the URL address that follows.

To send a message to the entire list, address it to: fusion@zorch.sf-bay.org

`mailto:fusion-request@zorch.sf-bay.org`

INSPEC

IINSPEC corresponds to the three Science Abstracts print publications: Physics Abstracts, Electrical and Electronics Abstracts, and Computer and Control Abstracts.

Keywords: Physics, Electronic, Computing
Sponsor: Institution of Electrical Engineers, London, UK
Audience: Physicists, Electrical Engineers, Computer Specialists
Profile: Approximately 16 percent of the database's source publications are in languages other than English, but all articles are abstracted and indexed in English. The special DIALOG online thesaurus feature is available to assist searchers in determining appropriate subject terms and codes.

Contact: Dialog in the US at (800) 334-2564, Dialog internationally at country-specific locations.
User Info: To subscribe, contact Dialog directly.
Notes: Coverage: April 1969 to the present; updated weekly.

`telnet://dialog.com`

IUCAA (Inter-University Centre for Astronomy and Astrophysics) ★

The IUCAA was set up to promote the growth of active groups in astronomy and astrophysics in India. The Centre runs vigorous visitor programs involving short and long-term visits of scientists from India and abroad.

Keywords: Astronomy, Astrophysics, Physics, Education
Sponsor: Centre for Astronomy and Astrophysics (IUCAA)
Audience: Reseachers, Astronomers, Physicists, Students
Contact: Postmaster
amk@iucaa.ernet.in

`http://iucaa.iucaa.ernet.in/welcome.html`

Physics ★

A newly created digest covering current developments in theoretical and experimental physics. Topics might include particle physics, plasma physics, or astrophysics.

Keywords: Physics, Astrophysics, Plasma Physics
Audience: Physicists, Astrophysicists
Contact: Mike Miskulin
physics-request@qedqcd.rye.ny.us
Details: Free
User Info: To subscribe to the list, send an e-mail message requesting a subscription to the URL address that follows.

To send a message to the entire list, address it to: physics@qedqcd.rye.ny.u

`mailto:physics-request@qedqcd.rye.ny.us`

PPPL (The Princeton Plasma Physics Laboratory) ★

This web site provides an overview of the projects, mission, physical plant, and history of the PPPL.

Keywords: Physics, Research
Sponsor: U.S. Department of Energy (DOE)
Audience: Physicists, Educators, Students
Contact: Anthony R. De Meo or Jack A. Mervine
pppl_info@pppl.gov
webmaster@pppl.gov
Details: Free

`http://www.pppl.gov`

Purdue University Library ★★

The library's holdings are large and wide-ranging. They contain significant collections in many fields.

Keywords: Economics (History of), Literature (English), Literature (American), Indiana, Rogers (Bruce), Engineering (History of), Aviation, Earth Science, Atmospheric Science, Consumer Science, Family Science, Chemistry (History of), Physics, Veterinary Science
Audience: General Public, Researchers, Librarians, Document Delivery Professionals
Contact: Dan Ferrer
dan@asterix.lib.purdue.edu
Details: Free
Notes: Expect: User ID prompt, Send: GUEST

`telnet://lib.cc.purdue.edu`

Quantum Physics/High Energy Physics ★★★★

A resource containing extensive internet links to international academic and research institutions specializing in high-energy physics. Online links to journals, abstracts, and conference information.

Keywords: Physics, Quantum Physics, Research
Sponsor: Swiss Academic and Research Network, Switzerland
Audience: Students, Physicists, Researchers
Contact: Ingrid Graf
rikv8@cernvm.cern.ch

`http://www.cern.ch/physics/hep.html`

Quark Background Material ★

Background material describing the nature of and current research into quarks and other elementary particles..

Keywords: Quark, Physics
Sponsor: Fermi National Accelerator Laboratory
Audience: Physicists, Students, Researchers
Contact: Webmaster
webmaster@fnal.gov
Details: Free

`http://fnnews.fnal.gov/top_background.html`

sci.med.physics ★

A Usenet newsgroup providing information and discussion about physics in medical testing and care.

Keywords: Physics, Medical Research, Health Care
Audience: Physicists, Medical Researchers, Medical Practitioners, Health Care Professionals
Details: Free
User Info: To subscribe to this Usenet newsgroup, you need access to a newsreader.

`news:sci.med.physics`

sci.physics ★

A Usenet newsgroup providing information and discussion about physical laws and properties.

Keywords: Physics
Audience: Physicists
Details: Free
User Info: To subscribe to this Usenet newsgroup, you need access to a newsreader.

`news:sci.physics`

Physiology

REBASE (Restriction Enzyme Database) ★

The Restriction Enzyme Database contains both data and literature citations. It can be searched for enzyme names, species, authors, journals, and recognition sequences.

Keywords: Physiology, Enzymes
Sponsor: New England Biolabs
Audience: Scientists, Molecular Biologists
Contact: Richard Roberts
roberts@cshl.org
Details: Free

`gopher://gopher.gdb.org/77/.INDEX/rebase`

picasso-users

picasso-users ★

A mailing list for users of the Picasso Graphical User Interface Development System.

Keywords: Computing, Computer Graphics
Audience: Computer Users, Computer Graphic Designers
Contact: picasso-users@postgres.berkeley.edu
Details: Free
User Info: To subscribe to the list, send an e-mail message requesting a subscription to the URL address that follows.

To send a message to the entire list, address it to: picasso-users@postgres.berkeley.edu

`mailto:picasso-users@postgres.berkeley.edu`

PIERS Imports (US Ports)

PIERS Imports (US Ports)

PIERS (Port Import Export Reporting Service) Imports (US Ports), produced by The Journal of Commerce, is a compilation of manifests of vessels loading or discharging cargo at approximately 120 US seaports.

Keywords: Trade, Imports, Maritime
Sponsor: The Journal of Commerce/PIERS, New York, NY, USA
Audience: Business Professionals
Profile: The principal applications of this information include: identification of new sources of supply for imports, monitoring imports of products whose details are lost in traditional government reports, and identification of potential trade partners.
Contact: Dialog in the US at (800) 334-2564, Dialog internationally at country specific locations.
User Info: To subscribe, contact Dialog directly.
Notes: Coverage: current 15 months, updated monthly.

`telnet://dialog.com`

Pigulki

Pigulki ★

This is an English-language digest concerning the Net news from Poland.

Keywords: Poland, Eastern Europe
Audience: Poles, Poland Observers, Journalists
Contact: Marek Zielinski
zielinski@acfcluster.nyu.edu
Details: Free
User Info: To subscribe to the list, send an e-mail message requesting a subscription to the URL address that follows.

To send a message to the entire list, address it to: davep@acsu.buffalo.edu

`mailto:davep@acsu.buffalo.edu`

Pine E-mail

Pine E-mail ★

A description of the Program for Internet News and E-mail (PINE), a tool for reading, sending, and managing electronic messages.

Keywords: Internet Tools, e-mail
Audience: Internet Surfers

Ping

Ping

With Ping, a user requests an "echo" from an Internet host to check status. It is useful for checking to see if a host or gateway is up and functioning.

Keywords: Internet Tools, Ping
Audience: Internet Surfers
Details: Free
User Info: File is: utils/ping/README

`ftp://vixen.cso.uiuc.edu/utils/ping/README`

Pink Floyd

echoes

Info and commentary on the musical group Pink Floyd, as well as other projects members of the group have been involved with.

Keywords: Rock Music, Pink Floyd
Audience: Rock Music Enthusiasts, Pink Floyd Enthusiasts
Contact: H. W. Neff
echoes-request@fawnya.tcs.com
Details: Free
User Info: To subscribe to the list, send an e-mail message requesting a subscription to the URL address that follows.
To send a message to the entire list, address it to: echoes-request@fawnya.tcs.com

`mailto:echoes-request@fawnya.tcs.com`

Pipes

Pipes

A forum for discussing the moderate use and appreciation of fine tobacco, including cigars, pipes, quality cigarettes, pipe making and carving, snuff, publications, and related topics.

Keywords: Pipes, Tobacco, Smoking
Audience: Smokers, Researchers, Market Analysts
Contact: Steve Masticola
masticol@scr.siemens.com
Details: Free, Moderated

Details: Free
User Info: File is mail/pine.blur

`ftp://ftp.cac.washington.edu`

User Info: To subscribe to the list, send an e-mail message requesting a subscription to the URL address that follows.
To send a message to the entire list, address it to: masticol@scr.siemens.com

`mailto:masticol@scr.siemens.com`

PIRA - Paper, Printing and Publishing, Packaging, and Nonwovens Abstracts

PIRA - Paper, Printing and Publishing, Packaging, and Nonwovens Abstracts

Coverage of all aspects of paper, pulp, nonwovens, printing, publishing and packaging.

Keywords: Material Science, Paper, Printing, Publishing, Packaging, Nonwovens
Sponsor: PIRA International
Audience: Material Scientists, Researchers
Profile: File contains more than 300,000 records. Special applications: company and market profiles, product and trade name searches, research and technology trends. Updated biweekly.
Contact: paul.albert@neteast.com
User Info: To subscribe, contact Orbit-Questel directly.

`telnet://orbit.com`

Pisma Bralcev

Pisma Bralcev

An edited mailing list that publishes readers' opinions, questions, inquiries for help, answers, and so on, in Slovene. Also includes travel tips and book reviews.

Keywords: Slovenia
Audience: Slovenians
Contact: Andrej Brodnik
Pisma-Bralcev@krpan.arnes.si
Details: Free
User Info: To subscribe to the list, send an e-mail message requesting a subscription to the URL address that follows.
To send a message to the entire list, address it to: pisma-bralcev@krpan.arnes.si

`mailto:Pisma-Bralcev@krpan.arnes.si`

`mailto:Pisma.Bralcev@uni-lj.si`

Pkd-list

Pkd-list

A discussion of the works and life of Philip K. Dick (1928-82), science fiction writer. Topics also include the nature of reality, consciousness, and religious experience.

Keywords: Science Fiction, Dick (Philip K.)
Audience: Philip K. Dick Readers, Science Fiction Readers
Contact: pkd-list-request@wang.com
Details: Free
User Info: To subscribe to the list, send an e-mail message requesting a subscription to the URL address that follows.
To send a message to the entire list, address it to: pkd-list@wang.com

`mailto:pkd-list@wang.com`

Planetariums

Sci.astro.planetarium

A group catering to the planetarium operations community.

Keywords: Astronomy, Planetariums
Audience: Educators, Astronomers, Planetarium Operators
Details: Free
User Info: To subscribe to this Usenet newsgroup, you need access to a newsreader.

`news:sci.astro.planetarium`

Planning

SCUP BITNET NEWS

Designed to promote the mission of the society and support its activities. Society for College and University Planning (SCUP) Bitnet News provides frequent and timely exchange of information among members as well as nonmembers interested in higher-education planning through the use of bitnet.

Keywords: Planning, University Planning
Sponsor: Society for College and University Planning
Audience: Planners

Profile: Contents of the newsletter are selected on the basis of interest and value to the membership. Particular attention is given to information that advances the state-of-the-art in planning; improves the understanding and application of the tools, techniques, processes and strategies of planning; advances the professional development of the membership; and widens the base of support for planning in higher education.

Contact: Joanne E. MacRae
USERTD8Q@UMICHUM.bitnet

Details: Free

Send an electronic mail note to the editor (Joanne Cate: budlao@uccvma) or the associate editor (Betsey Creekmore: pa94858@utkvm1)

`mailto:Joanne Cate: budlao@uccvma.bitnet`

SCUPMA-L: Society of College and University Planners, Mid-Atlantic Region

This newsletter contains short news pieces and announcements about events of interest to the membership.

Keywords: Planning, University Planning
Audience: University Planners
Contact: Debbie Furlong
OPIR1@AUVM.bitnet
Details: Free

Contact Debbie Furlong at OPIR1@AUVM.bitnet

`mailto:opir1@auvm.bitnet`

Plant Lipids

NPLC

This list was set up to establish a network for rapid communication among researchers in the field of plant lipids. Announcements for example (of post-doc positions) to the field can be posted. The list can also be used to query coworkers regarding techniques, resources, and so on.

Keywords: Plant Lipids
Audience: Plant Lipid Researchers
Contact: Walid Tout
tout@genesys.cps.msu.edu
Details: Free
User Info: To subscribe to the list, send an e-mail message requesting a subscription to the URL address that follows.

To send a message to the entire list, address it to:
nplc@genesys.cps.msu.edu

`mailto:NPLC@genesys.cps.msu.edu`

Plant Science

Biosis Previews

The database encompasses the entire field of life sciences and covers original research reports and reviews in biological and biomedical areas. This includes field, laboratory, clinical, experimental and theoretical work. The traditional areas of biology, including botany, zoology, and microbiology are covered, as well as the related fields such as plant and animal science, agriculture, pharmacology, and ecology.

Keywords: Biology, Botany, Zoology, Microbiology, Plant Science, Animal Science, Agriculture, Pharmacology, Ecology, Biochemistry, Biophysics, Bioengineering
Sponsor: Biosis
Audience: Librarians, Researchers, Students, Biologists, Botanists, Zoologists, Scientists, Taxonomists
Contact: CDP Technologies Sales Department
(800) 950-2035, extension 400
User Info: To subscribe, contact CDP Technologies directly

`telnet://cdplus@cdplus.com`

Plasma Physics

Physics

A newly created digest covering current developments in theoretical and experimental physics. Topics might include particle physics, plasma physics, or astrophysics.

Keywords: Physics, Astrophysics, Plasma Physics
Audience: Physicists, Astrophysicists
Contact: Mike Miskulin
physics-request@qedqcd.rye.ny.us
Details: Free
User Info: To subscribe to the list, send an e-mail message requesting a subscription to the URL address that follows.

To send a message to the entire list, address it to: physics@qedqcd.rye.ny.u

`mailto:physics-request@qedqcd.rye.ny.us`

Plastics

RAPRA Abstracts

Coverage on technical and commercial aspects of the rubber, plastics, and polymer composites industries.

Keywords: Material Science, Rubbers, Plastics, Polymers

Sponsor: Rapra Technology, Ltd.
Audience: Materials Scientists, Researchers
Profile: This unique source of information covers the world's polymer literature including journals, conference proceedings, books, specifications, reports and trade literature. Contains over 375,000 records. Updated biweekly.
Contact: paul.albert@neteast.com
User Info: To subscribe, contact Orbit-Questel directly.

`telnet://orbit.com`

POD (Professional Organizational Development)

POD (Professional Organizational Development)

The POD network is aimed at faculty, instructional, and organizational development in higher education.

Keywords: Education (Adult), Education (Distance), Education (Continuing)
Audience: Educators, Administrators, Researchers
Details: Free
User Info: To subscribe to the list, send an e-mail message to the URL address shown that follows, consisting of a single line reading:

SUB pod YourFirstName YourLastName

To send a message to the entire list, address it to: pod@lists.acs.ohio-state.edu

`mailto:listserv@lists.acs.ohio-state.edu`

Poetry

Poetry Conference

A conference on the WELL about poetry that includes original works.

Keywords: Poetry
Audience: Poets, Writers
Contact: Ron Buck, Sarah Randolph
macbeth@well.sf.ca.us,
stfr@well.sf.ca.us
Details: To participate in a conference on the WELL, you must first establish an account on the WELL. To do so, start by typing: telnet well.sf.ca.us

`telnet://well.sf.ca.us`

rec.arts.poems

A Usenet newsgroup providing information and discussion about poetry.

Keywords: Poetry, Literature (General)
Audience: Poets, Poetry Readers
User Info: To subscribe to this Usenet newsgroup, you need access to a newsreader.

`news:rec.arts.poems`

Poetry (American)

Boise State University Library

The library's holdings are large and wide-ranging and contain significant collections in many fields.

Keywords: Jordan (Len, Senatorial Papers of), Church (Frank, Senatorial Papers of), Poetry (American)
Audience: General Public, Researchers, Librarians, Document Delivery Professionals
Contact: Dan Lester
Details: Free
User Info: Expect: login; Send: catalyst

`telnet://catalyst.idbsu.edu`

Poisons Information Database

Poisons Information Database

Directories of antivenoms, toxicologists, poison control centers, and poisons from around the world.

Keywords: Medical Research, Bioscience
Sponsor: Venom and Toxin Research Group, Department of Anatomy, National University of Singapore, Singapore
Audience: Biologists, Researchers, Medical Professionals, Toxicologists
Contact: Professor P. Gopalkrishnakone
antgopal@leonis.nus.sg

`http://biomed.nus.sg/PID/PID.html`

Poker

ba-Poker

Discussion of poker as it is available to residents of and visitors to the San Francisco Bay area (broadly defined), in home games as well as in licensed card rooms. Topics include upcoming events, unusual games, strategies, comparisons of various venues, and player "networking."

Keywords: Poker, Card Games, San Francisco Bay Area
Audience: Poker Players
Contact: Martin Veneroso
ba-poker-request@netcom.com
Details: Free
User Info: To subscribe to the list, send an e-mail message requesting a subscription to the URL address that follows.

To send a message to the entire list, address it to: ba-poker@netcom.com

`mailto:ba-poker-request@netcom.com`

Poland

CEE Environmental Libraries Database

A directory of over 300 libraries and environmental information centers in Central Eastern Europe that specialize in, or maintain significant collections of information about, the environment, ecology, sustainable living, or conservation. The database concentrates on six Central Eastern European countries: Bulgaria, Czech Republic, Hungary, Romania, Slovakia, and Poland.

Keywords: Central Eastern Europe, Environment, Sustainable Living, Bulgaria, Czech Republic, Hungary, Romania, Slovakia, Poland.
Sponsor: The Wladyslaw Poniecki Charitable Foundation, Inc.
Audience: Environmentalists, Green Movement, Librarians, Community Builders, Sustainable Living Specialists.
Profile: This database is the product of an Environmental Training Project (ETP) that was funded in 1992 by the US Agency for International Development as a 5-year cooperative agreement with a consortium headed by the University of Minnesota (US AID Cooperative Agreement Number EUR-0041-A-002-2020). Other members of the consortium include the University of Pittsburgh's Center for Hazardous Materials Research, The Institute for Sustainable Communities, and the World Wildlife Fund. The Wladyslaw Poniecki Charitable Foundation, Inc., was a subcontractor to the World Wildlife Fund and published the Directory of Libraries and Environmental Information Centers in Central Eastern Europe: A Locator/Directory. This gopher database consists of an electronic version of the printed directory, subsequently modified and updated online. Access to the data is facilitated by a WAIS search engine which makes it possible to retrieve information about libraries, subject area specializations, personnel, and so on.
Contact: Doug Kahn, CEDAR
kahn@pan.cedar.univie.ac.at

`gopher://gopher.poniecki.berkeley.edu`

CIUWInfo (Centrum Informacyjny Uniwersyetu Warszawskiego)

Provides data from the Informatics Center information service of Warsaw University, Warsaw, Poland.

Keywords: Informatics, Poland
Audience: Researchers
Contact: chomac@plearn.edu.pl
Details: Free

`gopher://chomac@plearn.edu.pl`

Donosy

Distribution of a news bulletin from Poland.

Keywords: Poland
Audience: Poles
Contact: Przemek Klosowski
przemek@ndcvx.cc.nd.edu
User Info: To subscribe to the list, send an e-mail message to the URL that follows, consisting of a single line reading:

SUB donosy YourFirstName YourLastName.

To send a message to the entire list, address it to: donosy@fuw.edu.pl

`mailto:listproc@fuw.edu.pl`

Pigulki

This is an English-language digest concerning the Net news from Poland.

Keywords: Poland, Eastern Europe
Audience: Poles, Journalists
Contact: Marek Zielinski
zielinski@acfcluster.nyu.edu
Details: Free
User Info: To subscribe to the list, send an e-mail message requesting a subscription to the URL address that follows.

To send a message to the entire list, address it to: davep@acsu.buffalo.edu

`mailto:davep@acsu.buffalo.edu`

Poland-l

A mailing list devoted to discussion of Polish culture and events.

Keywords: Poland
Audience: Researchers
Contact: Micahl Prussak
michal@gs58.sp.cs.cmu.edu
Details: Free

User Info: To subscribe to the list, send an e-mail message to the URL address that follows, consisting of a single line reading:

SUB poland-l YourFirstName YourLastName

User Info: To send a message to the entire list, address it to: poland-1@ubvm.cc.buffalo.edu

`mailto:listserv@ubvm.cc.buffalo.edu`

Polish Archives

Information about Polish Internet gophers and Polish electronic journals.

Keywords: Poland, Telecommunications, Networking
Audience: Historians, Poles
Contact: Darek Milewski
Milewski@poniecki.berkeley.edu
User Info: To subscribe, send an e-mail message requesting a subscription to the URL address that follows.

`gopher://gopher.poniecki.berkeley.edu`

Spojrzenia

A weekly E-journal devoted to Polish culture, history, and politics.

Keywords: Poland, News (international), Culture
Audience: Poles, Students
Contact: Jerzy Krzystek
krzystek@u.washington.edu
Details: Free
User Info: To subscribe to the list, send an e-mail message requesting a subscription to the URL address that follows.

To send a message to the entire list, address it to: spojrzenia@u.washington.edu

`mailto:krzystek@u.washington.edu`

wroclaw

Distribution of information from weekly Polish bulletin called Society Journal.

Keywords: Poland
Audience: Polish Speakers, Researchers, General Public
Contact: Pawel Misiak
misiak@plwrtu11
Details: Free
User Info: To subscribe to the list, send an e-mail message to the URL address shown that follows, consisting of a single line reading:

SUB wroclaw YourFirstName YourLastName

To send a message to the entire list, address it to: wroclaw@plearn.edu.p1

`mailto:listserv@plearn.edu.p1`

Polar Regions

Dartmouth College Library

The library's holdings are large and wide-ranging and contain significant collections in many fields.

Keywords: American Calligraphy, Cervantes (Miguel de), Railroads, Polar Regions, Frost (Robert), Shakespeare (William), Spanish Plays
Audience: General Public, Researchers, Librarians, Document Delivery Professionals
Contact: Katharina Klemperer
kathy.klemperer@dartmouth.edu
Details: Free
User Info: Expect: login, Send: wolfpac

`telnet://lib.dartmouth.edu`

Police

Police

A mailing list for people interested in the music of the rock group The Police and its members: Sting, Stewart Copeland, and Andy Summers.

Keywords: Police, Sting
Audience: Rock Music Enthusiast
Contact: Pete Ashdown
owner-police@xmission.com
Details: Free
User Info: To subscribe to the list, send an e-mail message to the URL address shown that follows consisting of a single line reading:

SUB police YourFirstName YourLastName.

To send a message to the entire list, address it to: police@xmission.com

`mailto:majordomo@xmission.com`

Political Analysis and Research Cooperation (PARC) News Bulletin

Political Analysis and Research Cooperation (PARC) News Bulletin

Newsletter on political analysis, political behavior, political communication, and political culture. The purpose of PARC is to encourage and facilitate scientific research on human behavior in political life.

Keywords: Politics (US), Human Behavior
Audience: Political Scientists, Political Analysts
Contact: Tom Bryder
kusftb@vms2.uni-c.dk
Details: Free
User Info: To subscribe, send an e-mail message to the URL address that follows.

`mailto:kusftb@vms2.uni-c.dk`

Political Platforms of the US

Political Platforms of the US

Full text of various documents including the Democratic platform of 1992, the Jerry Brown positions of 1992, the Libertarian platform of 1990, and more.

Keywords: Politics (US), Government (US Federal), Democracy, Libertarian Politics
Audience: Politicians, Grass-Roots Organizers, Journalists
Details: Free

`gopher://wiretap.spies.com/11/Gov/Platform`

Political Science

Law and Courts Preprint Archive

An online archive of papers dealing with American and international legal issues presented at major conferences since August 1993.

Keywords: Law (US), Law (International), Legislation, Political Science
Sponsor: American Political Science Association
Audience: Lawyers, Legal Professionals
Contact: Professor Herbert Jacob
mzltov@nwu.edu

`gopher://gopher.nwu.edu`

Law and Politics Book Review

Reviews books of interest to political scientists studying US law, the courts, and the judicial process. Reviews are commissioned by the editor.

Keywords: Political Science, Law, Judicial Process
Audience: Political Scientists, Lawyers
Details: Free, Moderated
User Info: To subscribe, send an e-mail message to the address that follows, consisting of a single line reading:

To send a message to the entire list, address it to:

listserv@umcvmb.bitnet

`mailto:listserv@umcvmb.bitnet`

POSCIM

This mailing list is intended as a forum for those researching, teaching, or studying political science, as well as for politicians.

Keywords: Political Science
Audience: Political Scientists, Educators, Politicians, Researchers
Contact: Markus Schlegel
ups500@vm.gmd.de
Details: Free
User Info: To subscribe to the list, send an e-mail message to the URL address that follows, consisting of a single line reading:

SUB POSCIM YourFirstName YourLastName

To send a message to the entire list, address it to: ups500@vm.gmd.de

`mailto:listserv@vm.gmd.de`

Russian and East European Studies Home Pages

Keywords: Russia, Eastern Europe, Government, Political Science
Sponsor: University of Pittsburgh
Audience: Researchers, Politicians
Contact: Casey Palowitch
cjp@acid.library.pitt.edu

`http://www.pitt.edu/cjp/rspubl.html`

South African Specific Items

A selection of primarily political information on South Africa. Includes ANC (African National Congress) policy statements, as well as an A-Z of South African political figures and the latest issues of South Africa Watch Magazine. Also has weather information and links to gopher and ftp sites in South Africa.

Keywords: South Africa, Political Science
Audience: South Africans, Political Analysts, General Public
Contact: John Dovey
pjcd@maties.sun.ac.za

`gopher://lib.sun.ac.za`

The Israel Information Service

A gopher server containing information on Israel.

Keywords: Israel, Middle East, Political Science, Anti-Semitism, Holocaust, Archaeology
Sponsor: Israeli Foreign Ministry
Audience: Israelis, Jews, Tourists, General Public
Profile: This server features updates on the Middle East peace process, including text of the latest Israel-PLO accord, as well as general political, diplomatic, cultural and economic information on the state of Israel. Also includes archives on archaeology in Israel, anti-Semitism and the Holocaust, and current excerpts from Israeli newspapers.
Contact: Chaim Shacham
shacham@israel-info.gov.il

`gopher://israel-info.gov.il`

val-l

Discussion on changes in the Communist countries, ranging from Cuba and Vietnam to the former Soviet Union.

Keywords: Communism, Soviet Union, Political Science
Audience: Political Scientists
Contact: cdell@umkcax1 or
cdell@umkcvax1.bitnet
Details: Free
User Info: To subscribe to the list, send an e-mail message to the URL address that follows, consisting of a single line reading:

SUB val-l YourFirstName YourLastName

To send a message to the entire list, address it to: val-l@ucflvm.cc.ucf.edu

`mailto:listserv@ucflvm.cc.ucf.edu`

Politics

Aids

A forum for the discussion of AIDS, predominantly from a medical perspective, but also with some discussion of political and social issues.

Keywords: AIDS, Medicine, Politics, Society
Sponsor: UCLA
Audience: AIDS Researchers, AIDS Activists, Health Care Providers
Contact: Daniel R. Greening
aids-request@cs.ucla.edu
User Info: To subscribe to the list, send an e-mail message to the URL address that follows.

To send a message to the entire list, address it to: aids@cs.ucla.edu

`mailto:aids-request@cs.ucla.edu`

alt.politics.libertarian

A Usenet newsgroup providing information and discussion about the libertarian ideology.

Keywords: Libertarian Party, Politics
Audience: Libertarians, Politicians
User Info: To subscribe to this Usenet newsgroup, you need access to a newsreader.

`news:alt.politics.libertarian`

Argentina

Mailing list for general discussion and information about Argentina, including Argentine culture and politics.

Keywords: Argentina, Politics, Culture
Sponsor: Carlos G. Mendioroz
Audience: Spanish Speakers, Students
Contact: Carlos G. Mendioroz
argentina-request@ois.db.toronto.edu
User Info: To subscribe to the list, send an e-mail message to the URL address that follows.

To send a message to the entire list, address it to:
argentina@ois.db.toronto.edu

`mailto:argentina-request@ois.db.toronto.edu`

ARlist

An open, unmoderated mailing list to provide a forum for discussing action research and its use in a variety of disciplines and situations. Topics include philosophical and methodological issues in action research, the use of action research for evaluation, actual case studies, and discourse on increasing the rigor of action research.

Keywords: Activism, Research, Politics
Audience: Activists, Researchers
Profile: Arlist is an open unmoderated mailing list to provide a forum for discussing action research and its use in a variety of disciplines and situations. It is usually (but perhaps not always) cyclic, participative, and qualitative.
Contact: Bob Dick
arlist@psych.psy.uq.oz.au
Details: Free
User Info: To subscribe to the list, send an e-mail message to the URL address that follows.

To send a message to the entire list, address it to: arlist@psych.psy.uq.oz.au

`mailto:arlist-request@psych.psy.uq.oz.au`

`ftp://psych.psy.uq.oz.au/dir/lists/arlist`

ba-Liberty

This is an announcement of local Libertarian meetings, events, activities, and so on. The ca- list is for California statewide issues; the ba- list is for the San Francisco Bay Area and it gets all messages sent to the ca- list. Prospective members should subscribe to one or the other, generally depending on whether or not they are SF Bay Area residents.

Keywords:	Libertarian Party, Politics, San Francisco Bay Area
Audience:	Libertarians, Political Scientists, Politicians, General Public
Contact:	Jeff Chan ba-liberty-request@shell.portal.com
Details:	Free
User Info:	To subscribe to the list, send an e-mail message requesting a subscription to the URL address that follows. To send a message to the entire list, address it to: ba-liberty@shell.portal.com

`mailto:ba-liberty-request@shell.portal.com`

Clinton Watch

A regular political column devoted to a critical examination of the Clinton Administration.

Keywords:	Politics, Clinton(Bill), Satire, Government (US)
Sponsor:	Informatics Resource
Audience:	Republicans, General Public, Citizens
Contact:	clintonwatch@dolphin.gulf.net

`gopher://dolphin.gulf.net`

CSF: Communications for a Sustainable Future

A gopher server for the distribution of Conflict Resolution Materials.

Keywords:	Conflict Resolution, Community, Politics
Sponsor:	Communications for a Sustainable Future
Audience:	Activists, Policy Analysts, Community Leaders, Mediators, Lawyers
Profile:	Communications for a Sustainable Future is a collective effort of several scholars. CSF does research, education, and applied work. Its main subject areas are: Intractable Conflicts and Constructive Confrontation, Environmental and Public Policy Dispute Resolution, Social/Political Conflicts, International Conflicts.
Contact:	roper@csf.colorado.edu
Details:	Free

`gopher://csf.colorado.edu`

EXEC (Executive Branch News US)

The EXEC library contains information and news about the Executive Branch of the Federal Government. From the Department of Agriculture to the White House, this file is a comprehensive source of information that will be especially useful to those whose responsibilities include monitoring federal regulations, Agency and Department activity, and the people and issues involved.

Keywords:	News, Legislation, Regulation, Politics, Executive Branch
Audience:	Journalists, Lobbyists, Business Executives, Analysts, Entrepreneurs
Profile:	The EXEC library allows the searching of individual files or group files that cover topics such as the Federal Register and Code of Federal Regulations; public laws; proposed treasury regulation; and over 50 news sources, including BNA's Daily Report for Executives, the Dept. of State Dispatch, ABC News transcripts, Federal News Service Daybook, Government Executive, MacNeil/Lehrer Newshour, New Leader, National Review, the Washington Post, the Washington Times, Presidential Documents, and many others.
Contact:	Mead New Sales Group at (800) 227-4908 or (513) 859-5398 inside the US, or (513) 865-7981 for all inquiries outside the US.
User Info:	To subscribe, contact Mead directly. To examine the Nexis user guide, you can access it at the ftp site of the University of Texas at Austin at the URL address: ftp://ftp.cc.utexas.edu The files are in: /pub/ref-services/LEXIS

`telnet://nex.meaddata.com`

`http://www.meaddata.com`

Israel-mideast

This discussion group provides information on and analysis of Israel and the Middle East. Includes news flashes, briefings by Israeli leaders, editorials and articles translated from the Israeli press, background papers, press communiques and economic, environmental and cultural updates.

Keywords:	Israel, Middle East, Politics
Sponsor:	Israel Information Center, Jerusalem
Audience:	General Public, Students
Contact:	Israel Information Service ask@israel-info.gov.il
User Info:	To subscribe to the list, send an e-mail message to the address that follows, consisting of a single line reading: SUB israel mideast YourFirstName YourLastName. To send a message to the entire list, address it to: israel mideast@vm.tau.ac.il

`mailto:listserv@vm.tau.ac.il`

National Performance Review (NPR)

The Report of the National Performance Review, from the task force led by Vice President Gore, titled "From Red Tape to Results: Creating a Government that Works Better and Costs Less," Sept. 7, 1993.

Keywords:	President, Politics, White House
Audience:	Political Scientists, General Public
Profile:	On March 3, 1993, President Clinton asked Vice President Gore to lead the effort to effect real change in the federal government. Gore's NPR Task Force overview and accompanying reports make specific recommendations for: reducing costs and waste, changing the way government operates, and making government more responsive and effective.
Details:	Free

`gopher://cyfer.esusda.gov/11/ace/policy/npr/nat`

Presidential Documents

This gopher provides access to the full text of Presidential Proclamations, Executive Orders, Notices, Memoranda, and Determinations dating from December 23, 1992. The documents are listed sequentially by date and number (that is, Proclamation 6520 of December 23, 1992).

Keywords:	Politics, President (US), White House, Documents
Audience:	General Public
Details:	Free Select from menu presented (you will probably follow the following path: Internet Services/US Government/ Presidential Documents.)

`gopher://jupiter.cc.gettysborg.edu`

PVS (Project Vote Smart)

A gopher site containing Federal political information from PVS.

Keywords:	Politics, Government (US)
Sponsor:	Project Vote Smart, Corvallis, Oregon, USA
Audience:	Voters, General Public
Profile:	PVS is a volunteer organization dedicated to providing voters with factual information about candidates for Federal office. Currently, the gopher offers background information, including detailed profiles and legislative analysis of Senators and Representatives for all 50 states.
Contact:	pvs@neu.edu
Notes:	For more information on Project Vote Smart, call their toll free hotline at 1-800-622-SMART. Or write to: Project Vote Smart, 129 NW Fourth St. #240, Corvallis, OR 97330

`gopher://gopher.neu.edu`

talk.politics.soviet

A Usenet newsgroup providing information and discussion about Soviet politics, domestic and international.

Keywords:	Communism, Russia, Politics, CIS (Commonwealth of Independent States)
Audience:	Political Scientists

Politics

```
A
B
C
D
E
F
G
H
I
J
K
L
M
N
O
P
Q
R
S
T
U
V
W
X
Y
Z
```

Details: Free
User Info: To subscribe to this Usenet newsgroup, you need access to a newsreader.

`news:talk.politics.soviet`

Technology Initiatives for the Clinton/Gore Administration

This is a 40-page text of the press release from the Clinton administration on technology initiatives, dated February 22, 1993.

Keywords: Politics, President, White House, Technology
Audience: General Public, Journalists
Details: Free
E-mail to the ListServ and include the following in the body of the message: get cni-bigideas.whouse.paper

`mailto:listserv@cni.org`

The Frog Farm

A forum devoted to the discussion of claiming, exercising, and defending rights in America, past, present, and future. The main topics are issues that involve a free people and their public servants.

Keywords: Rights, Politics
Audience: Activists
Contact: schirado@lab.cc.wmich.edu
User Info: To subscribe to the list, send an e-mail message requesting a subscription to the URL address that follows.
To send a message to the entire list, address it to: schirado@lab.cc.wmich.edu

`mailto:schirado@lab.cc.wmich.edu`

UN Rules

Standards, guidelines, and international instruments promulgated by the UN.

Keywords: Politics, UN, Standards
Sponsor: United Nations Justice Network (UNCJIN)
Audience: Lawyers, General Public, Internationalists
Details: Free
Select from menu as appropriate.

`gopher://uacsc2.albany.edu`

White House Information Service ★★★★

An outstanding database of current White House information, from 1992 to the present.

Keywords: White House, Politics, President (US), Database
Sponsor: Texas A & M University
Audience: General Public

Profile: Much of the older information on this site was obtained from the clinton@marist.bitnet listserv list or the alt.politics.clinton Usenet newsgroup, both of which receive the information indirectly via the MIT White House information server. Newer and current material is received directly from the MIT distribution list. The menu includes a searchable database and headings such as Domestic Affairs (Health Care, Technology, and so on), Press Briefings and Conferences, the President's Daily Schedule, and many more.
Contact: whadmin@tamu.edu
Details: Free

`gopher://tamuts.tamu.edu/11/.dir/president.dir`

White House Phone Numbers ★

A list of names, addresses, e-mail addresses and telephone and fax numbers of the President, First Lady, Vice President, and all the members of the Cabinet.

Keywords: White House, President, Politics
Audience: General Public
Details: Free

`ftp://nifty.andrew.cmu.edu/pub/QRD/info/govt/cabinet`

White House Press Releases

An archive of all the press releases by the Clinton administration organized as Miscellaneous, Briefings by Dee Dee Myers, Executive Orders, Remarks during Photo Opportunities, Remarks of Bill Clinton, Briefings by George Stephanopolous.

Keywords: White House, Politics, President (US)
Audience: General Public
Details: Free

`gopher://wiretap.spies.com/11/Clinton`

Politics (Conservative)

alt.fan.rush-limbaugh

A Usenet newsgroup providing information and discussion about Rush Limbaugh, a politically conservative American figure.

Keywords: Limbaugh (Rush), Politics (Conservative), Comedians
Audience: Followers of Rush Limbaugh
User Info: To subscribe to this Usenet newsgroup, you need access to a newsreader.

`news:alt.fan.rush-limbaugh`

Politics (International)

Amnesty International

A site containing information about Amnesty International, an organization focused strictly and specifically on human rights around the world.

Keywords: Government, Human Rights, Politics (International), Activism
Sponsor: Amnesty International
Audience: Students, Activists
Contact: Catherine Hampton
ariel@netcom.com

`ftp://ftp.netcom.com/pub/ariel/www/human.rights/amnesty.international/ai.html`

CNN Headline News Gopher

Latest news as read by the CNN anchorpersons. Searchable index of subject matter.

Keywords: News Media, Politics (International), Journalism
Sponsor: CNN Newsource Service
Audience: General Public, Students, Journalists
Contact: Chet Rhodes
cr9@umail.umd.edu
Details: Free

`gopher://info.umd.edu:925/`

Government Docs (US & World)

A large and eclectic collection of documents, ranging from the Laws of William the Conqueror to the North American Free Trade Agreement (NAFTA). Particular strengths include 20th century American political documents and international treaties and covenants.

Keywords: Government (International), History (World), Politics (International)
Sponsor: The Internet Wiretap
Audience: Researchers, Historians, Political Scientists, Journalists
Contact: gopher@wiretap.spies.com

`gopher://wiretap.spies.com/Gov`

Jerusalem-One Network

A gopher site covering issues concerned with Jews, Jewish politics and history.

Keywords: Judaism, Israel, Politics (International)
Audience: Political Activists, Holocaust Researchers, Jews, Israelis

Profile: The Jerusalem-One Network was established in May 1993 by the Jewish International Communications Network (JICN), a branch of the Jewish International Association Against Assimilation. Entries include The Jewish Electronic Library, The Holocaust Archives, and JUNK (the Jewish student University Network).

gopher://jerusalem1.datasrv.co.il

U.S. Army Area Handbooks

This gopher provides detailed political, cultural, historical, military, and economic information on hot spots in world affairs, everywhere from China to Yugoslavia.

Keywords: Military (US), Politics (International), Federal Government (US)

Sponsor: The Thomas Jefferson Library at the University of Missouri at St. Louis, St. Louis, Missouri, USA

Audience: Journalists, Government Officials, Travelers/Tourists

Profile: The Army Area Handbooks, which provide a comprehensive overview of several important countries including Japan, China, Israel, Egypt, South Korea, and Somalia, are only one of the many government resources available at this site. Other full-text documents include the proposed 1995 federal budget, the CIA world fact book, the NAFTA agreement, health care proposals currently before Congress, and statistics for the U.S. industrial outlook. Also has links to many federal gophers and information systems.

Contact: Joe Rottman
rottman@umslvma.umsl.edu

Details: Free

gopher://umslvma.umsl.edu/11/library/govdocs

Various Treaties

Provides access to a range of treaties in full-text format.

Keywords: Treaties, Politics (International)
Audience: Governments, Researchers, Lawyers
Details: Free
Select from menu as appropriate

gopher://wiretap.spies.com

World Constitutions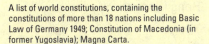

A list of world constitutions, containing the constitutions of more than 18 nations including Basic Law of Germany 1949; Constitution of Macedonia (in former Yugoslavia); Magna Carta.

Keywords: Law (International), History (World), Politics (International)
Audience: Researchers, Lawyers, Historians
Details: Free

gopher://wiretap.spies.com

Politics (Middle Eastern)

talk.politics.mideast

A Usenet newsgroup providing information and discussion about Middle Eastern topics.

Keywords: Middle East, Middle Eastern Studies, Politics (Middle Eastern)
Audience: Political Scientists
Details: Free
User Info: To subscribe to this Usenet newsgroup, you need access to a newsreader.

news:talk.politics.mideast

Politics (US)

alt.politics.clinton

A Usenet newsgroup providing information and discussion about President Bill Clinton and the White House. Perspective tends to be anti-Clinton.

Keywords: Politics (US), Clinton (Bill)
Audience: Politicians, General Public
User Info: To subscribe to this Usenet newsgroup, you need access to a newsreader.

news:alt.politics.clinton

alt.politics.election

A Usenet newsgroup organized to help people in the process of running for office.

Keywords: Politics (US), Government
Audience: Politicians, Campaign Managers
User Info: To subscribe to this Usenet newsgroup, you need access to a newsreader.

news:alt.politics.election

Berne Convention Implementation Act of 1988

An act to amend Title 17, United States Code, to implement the Berne Convention for the Protection of Literary and Artistic Works, as revised in Paris on July 24, 1971, and for other purposes.

Keywords: Legislation (US), Government (US), Politics (US), Copyright
Audience: Lawyers, Students, Politicians, Journalists
Details: Free

gopher://wiretap.spies.com/00/Gov/Copyright/US.Berne.Convention.txt

Bibliographies of US Senate Hearings

The US Senate produces a series of committee hearings, prints, and publications as part of the legislative process. The Documents department at North Carolina State University contains files for the 99th through 103rd Congresses, which can also be searched through a WAIS searchable database.

Keywords: Senate (US), Politics (US), Legislation (US), Bibliographies, Government (US)
Audience: General Public, Journalists, Students, Politicians, US Citizens
Contact: Jack McGeachy
Jack_McGeachy@ncsu.edu
Details: Free

gopher://dewey.lib.ncsu.edu/11/library/disciplines/government/senate

CMPGN (Campaign Library)

The CMPGN library contains information and news about US Congressional, Senatorial, Gubernatorial and Presidential elections. The media, political campaigns, and others whose responsibilities include monotoring activity on the campaign trail will find CMPGN to be a unique and comprehensive source of information for campaign research.

Keywords: Politics (US), Congress (US)
Audience: Journalists, Political Researchers
Profile: CMPGN allows searching of individual files or group files that cover topics such as candidate and incumbent profiles; Honoraria, PACs, and demographic and media profiles; Committee and Floor voting records and floor statement indexes for all House and Senate incumbents; and reputable sources of news that are known for their in-depth campaign coverage, including the Hotline, the Cook Political Report, ABC news Transcripts, Roll Call, States News Service, US Newswire, Federal News Service, and much more.

Contact: Mead New Sales Group at (800) 227-4908 or (513) 859-5398 inside the US, or (513) 865-7981 for all inquiries outside the US.

User Info: To subscribe, contact Mead directly.

To examine the Nexis user guide, you can access it at the ftp site of the University of Texas at Austin at the URL address: ftp://ftp.cc.utexas.edu

The files are in: /pub/ref-services/LEXIS

telnet://nex.meaddata.com

http://www.meaddata.com

Copyright Act

The full text of the Copyright Act of 1976, Title 17, United States Code, Sections 101_810.

Keywords: Politics (US), Government (US Federal), Laws (US Federal), Copyright

Politics (US)

Audience:	Lawyers, Students, Politicians, Journalists
Details:	Free

`gopher://wiretap.spies.com/00/Gov/Copyright/US.Copyright.1976.tx`

Ogphre - SunSITE

A collection of Internet resources organized by subject. Particular strengths include agriculture, religious texts, poetry, creative writing, and US politics. The ftp site has a set of more general Internet guides.

Keywords:	Agriculture, Politics (US), Religion, Internet
Sponsor:	The University of North Carolina - Chapel Hill and Sun Microsystems, USA
Audience:	General Public, Internet Surfers, Researchers
Contact:	Darlene Fladager, Elizabeth Lyons Darlene_Fladager@unc.edu, Elizabeth_Lyons@unc.edu

`gopher://sunsite.unc.edu`

`ftp://sunsite.unc.edu`

Political Analysis and Research Cooperation (PARC) News Bulletin

Newsletter on political analysis, political behavior, political communication, and political culture. The purpose of PARC is to encourage and facilitate scientific research on human behavior in political life.

Keywords:	Politics (US), Human Behavior
Audience:	Political Scientists, Political Analysts
Contact:	Tom Bryder kusftb@vms2.uni-c.dk
Details:	Free
User Info:	To subscribe, send an e-mail message to the URL address that follows.

`mailto:kusftb@vms2.uni-c.dk`

Political Platforms of the US

Full text of various documents including the Democratic platform of 1992, the Jerry Brown positions of 1992, the Libertarian platform of 1990, and more.

Keywords:	Politics (US), Government (US Federal), Democracy, Libertarian Party
Audience:	Politicians, Grass-Roots Organizers, Journalists
Details:	Free

`gopher://wiretap.spies.com/11/Gov/Platform`

Speeches and Addresses in the US

Includes the Clinton State of the Union Speech of 1993, Kennedy's Inaugural Speech, Martin Luther King's "I Have a Dream" speech, and so forth.

Keywords:	Politics (US), Rhetoric
Audience:	Journalists, Writers, Politicians, Students
Details:	Free
	Choose from menu presented.

`gopher://wiretap.spies.com/11/Gov/US-Speech`

Universal Copyright Convention

The Universal Copyright Convention as revised at Paris (1971). Convention and protocols were done at Paris on July 24, 1971. It was ratified by the President of the United States of America on August 28, 1972.

Keywords:	Copyright, Laws (US), Government (US), Politics (US)
Audience:	Lawyers, Students, Politicians, Journalists
Details:	Free

`gopher://wiretap.spies.com/00/Gov/Copyright/US.Universal.Copyright.Conv.txt`

White House Frequently Asked Questions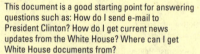

This document is a good starting point for answering questions such as: How do I send e-mail to President Clinton? How do I get current news updates from the White House? Where can I get White House documents from?

Keywords:	Clinton (Bill), Government (US), Politics (US), FAQs
Audience:	General Public, Researchers
Details:	Free
Expect:	login; Send: anonymous; Expect: password; Send: your e-mail address; Expect: directory; Send: /pub/nic; Expect: file; Send: whitehouse FAQ.

`ftp://ftp.sura.net`

Polymers

RAPRA Abstracts

Coverage on technical and commercial aspects of the rubber, plastics, and polymer composites industries.

Keywords:	Material Science, Rubbers, Plastics, Polymers
Sponsor:	Rapra Technology, Ltd.
Audience:	Materials Scientists, Researchers
Profile:	This unique source of information covers the world's polymer literature including journals, conference proceedings, books, specifications, reports and trade literature. Contains over 375,000 records. Updated biweekly.
Contact:	paul.albert@neteast.com
User Info:	To subscribe, contact Orbit-Questel directly.

`telnet://orbit.com`

Pop Groups

Bel Canto

A mailing list for the discussion of the music, lyrics, and shows of the group Bel Canto, and solo projects of group members, or even the work of related artists if appropriate.

Keywords:	Music, Pop Groups
Audience:	Music Enthusiasts
Contact:	dewy-fields-request@ifi.uio.no
Details:	Free
User Info:	To subscribe to the list, send an e-mail message requesting a subscription to the URL address that follows.
	To send a message to the entire list, address it to: dewy-fields@ifi.uio.no

`mailto:dewy-fields-request@ifi.uio.no`

Beloved

A mailing list for the discussion of the Beloved, an English pop group with strong ambient and techno influences.

Keywords:	Music, Pop Groups
Audience:	Music Enthusiasts
Contact:	Jyrki Sarkkinen beloved-request@phoenix.oulu.fi
Details:	Free
User Info:	To subscribe to the list, send an e-mail message requesting a subscription to the URL address that follows.
	To send a message to the entire list, address it to: beloved@phoenix.oulu.fi

`mailto:beloved-request@phoenix.oulu.fi`

Pop Music

Bong (Depeche Mode)

Bong is for the discussion of the mostly electronic band Depeche Mode and related projects like Recoil. Depeche Mode incorporate synth-pop, industrial dance, Kraftwerkian electro, ambient, techno, and rock influences in a dark blend of innovative alternative music.

Keywords:	Depeche Mode, Pop Music	
Audience:	Pop Music Enthusiasts, Depeche Mode Enthusiasts, Musicians	
Contact:	Colin Smiley bong-request@lestat.compaq.com	
Details:	Free	
User Info:	To subscribe to the list, send an e-mail message requesting a subscription to the URL address that follows.	
	To send a message to the entire list, address it to: bong@lestat.compaq.com	

`mailto:bong-request@lestat.compaq.com`

Chalkhills ★

A mailing list for the discussion of the music and records of XTC (the band).

Keywords:	Pop Music, XTC
Audience:	Pop Music Enthusiasts, XTC Enthusiasts
Contact:	John M. Relph chalkhills-request@presto.ig.com
Details:	Free, Moderated
User Info:	To subscribe to the list, send an e-mail message requesting a subscription to the URL address that follows.
	To send a message to the entire list, address it to: chalkhills@presto.ig.com
Notes:	Chalkhills is moderated and distributed in a digest format.

`mailto:chalkhills-request@presto.ig.com`

concrete-blonde ★

This list discusses the rock group Concrete Blonde and related artists and issues.

Keywords:	Pop Music, Concrete Blonde
Audience:	Concrete Blonde Enthusiasts, Pop Music Enthusiasts
Contact:	Robert Earl concrete-blonde-request@piggy.ucsb.edu
Details:	Free
User Info:	To subscribe to the list, send an e-mail message requesting a subscription to the URL address that follows.
	To send a message to the entire list, address it to: concrete-blonde@piggy.ucsb.edu

`mailto:concrete-blonde-request@piggy.ucsb.edu`

Crowes ★

To provide a forum for discussion about the rock band the Black Crowes. Topics include the group's music and lyrics, as well as the band's participation with NORML, concert dates and playlists, and bootlegs (audio and video).

Keywords:	Rock Music, Pop Music
Audience:	Rock Music Enthusiasts, Pop Music Enthusiasts
Contact:	rstewart@unex.ucla.edu
Details:	Free
User Info:	To subscribe, mail to the address that follows with the command SUBSCRIBE in the first line.

`mailto:rstewart@unex.ucla.edu`

Popular Culture

alt.cult-movies ★

A Usenet newsgroup providing information and discussion about popular movies.

Keywords:	Film, Popular Culture
Audience:	Movie Watchers, Critics
User Info:	To subscribe to this Usenet newsgroup, you need access to a newsreader.

`news:alt.cult-movies`

Popular Culture ★★

This directory is a compilation of information resources focused on popular culture.

Keywords:	Popular Culture
Audience:	Popular Culture Enthusiasts, Internet Surfers, Students
Details:	Free

`ftp://una.hh.lib.umich.edu/70/inetdirsstacks/popcult:robinson`

rec.arts.movies movie database ★★★

An extensive FTP database covering over 32,000 movies, with more than 370,000 filmography entries, from early cinema to current releases.

Keywords:	Movies, Television, Popular Culture
Audience:	Movie Buffs
Profile:	Interfaces to search the database include Unix, MS-DOS and Amiga (and Windows and Mac versions are in development). The database includes filmographies for actors, directors, writers, composers, cinematographers, editors, production designers and producers; plot summaries; character names; movie ratings; year of release; running times; movie trivia; quotes; goofs; soundtracks; personal trivia and Academy Award information.
Contact:	Col Needham cn@ibmpcug.co.uk
Details:	Free

`ftp://cathouse.org/pub/cathouse/movies/database`

rec.arts.movies movie database (Cardiff WWW front-end) ★★★

An extensive, interactive database covering over 32,000 movies, with more than 370,000 filmography entries, from early cinema to current releases.

Keywords:	Movies, Television, Popular Culture, Interactive Media
Audience:	Movie Buffs
Profile:	A WWW front-end to the rec.arts.movies movie database, complete with form-filling interfaces to add new data and to rate movies (on a scale from 1 through 10). The database includes filmographies for actors, directors, writers, composers, cinematographers, editors, production designers, costume designers and producers; plot summaries; character names; movie ratings; year of release; running times; movie trivia; quotes; goofs; soundtracks; personal trivia and Academy Award information.
Contact:	Rob Hartill Robert.Hartill@cm.cf.ac.uk
Details:	Free

`http://www.cm.cf.ac.uk/Movies`

`http://www.msstate.edu/Movies`

rec.music.beatles ★

A Usenet newsgroup providing information and discussion about the Beatles.

Keywords:	Musical Groups, Popular Culture
Audience:	Beatles Listeners
User Info:	To subscribe to this Usenet newsgroup, you need access to a newsreader.

`news:rec.music.beatles`

rec.music.gdead ★★

A Usenet newsgroup providing information and discussion about the Grateful Dead.

Keywords:	Music, Popular Culture
Audience:	Grateful Dead Listeners
User Info:	To subscribe to this Usenet newsgroup, you need access to a newsreader.

`news:rec.music.gdead`

rec.music.phish ★

A Usenet newsgroup providing information and discussion about the band Phish.

Keywords:	Musical Groups, Popular Culture
Audience:	Phish Listeners
User Info:	To subscribe to this Usenet newsgroup, you need access to a newsreader.

`news:rec.music.phish`

alt.music.progressive

A Usenet newsgroup providing information and discussion about progressive music, including the groups Marillion, Asia, King Crimson, and many others.

Keywords:	Musical Genres, Popular Culture
Audience:	Progressive Music Listeners
User Info:	To subscribe to this Usenet newsgroup, you need access to a newsreader.

`news:alt.music.progressive`

soc.culture.usa

A Usenet newsgroup providing information and discussion about the culture of the United States.

Keywords:	Americana, Sociology, Popular Culture
Audience:	Sociologists, General Public
Details:	Free
User Info:	To subscribe to this Usenet newsgroup, you need access to a newsreader.

`news:soc.culture.usa`

The English Server

A large and eclectic collection of humanities resources.

Keywords:	Humanities, Academia, English, Popular Culture, Feminism
Sponsor:	Carnegie Mellon University English Department, Pittsburgh, Pennsylvania, USA
Audience:	General Public, University Students, Educators (College/University), Researchers (Humanities)
Profile:	Contains archives of conventional humanities materials, such as historical documents and classic books in electronic form. Also offers more unusual and hard-to-find resources, particularly in the field of popular culture and media. Features access to many humanities and culture-related online journals such as Bad Subjects, FineArt Forum, and Postmodern Culture. Also has links to a wide variety of related Internet sites and resources.
Contact:	Geoff Sauer postmaster@english-server.hss.cmu.

`gopher://english-server.hss.cmu.edu`

`http://english-server.hss.cmu.edu`

Porsche

Porschephiles

This list is for people who own, operate, work on, or covet various models of Porsche automobiles. Discussion topics include features, functionality, and purchasing advice.

Keywords:	Porsche, Automobiles, Sports Cars
Audience:	Automobile Enthusiasts
Contact:	porschephiles-request@tta.com
Details:	Free
User Info:	To subscribe to the list, send an e-mail message requesting a subscription to the URL address that follows.
	To send a message to the entire list, address it to: porschephiles@tta.com

`mailto:porschephiles-request@tta.com`

Portuguese

Brasil

This is a mailing list for general discussion about and information on Brazil. Portuguese is the main language of discussion.

Keywords:	Brazil, Portuguese
Audience:	Brazilians, Portuguese Speakers
Contact:	B. R. Araujo Neto bras-net-request@cs.ucla.edu
Details:	Free
User Info:	To subscribe to the list, send an e-mail message requesting a subscription to the URL address that follows. Include your name, e-mail, phone number, address, and topics of interest.
	To send a message to the entire list, address it to: bras-net@cs.ucla.edu

`mailto:bras-net-request@cs.ucla.edu`

POS302-L

POS302-L

A discussion list created for the "Race, Ethnicity, and Social Inequality" seminar offered at Illinois State University (spring 1994). The general purposes of the list are to create an e-mail audience for the written work of enrolled students and to invite a broad audience to participate in the seminar.

Keywords:	Race, Ethnic Studies, Minorities
Audience:	Ethnic Studies, Students, Sociologists, Educators
Details:	Free
User Info:	To subscribe to the list, send an e-mail message to the URL address that follows, consisting of a single line reading:
	SUB pos302-l YourFirstName YourLastName
	To send a message to the entire list, address it to: pos302-l@ilstu.edu

`mailto:listserv@ilstu.edu`

POSCIM

POSCIM

This mailing list is intended as a forum for those researching, teaching, or studying political science, as well as for politicians.

Keywords:	Political Science
Audience:	Political Scientists, Educators, Politicians, Researchers
Contact:	Markus Schlegel ups500@vm.gmd.de
Details:	Free
User Info:	To subscribe to the list, send an e-mail message to the URL address that follows, consisting of a single line reading:
	SUB POSCIM YourFirstName YourLastName
	To send a message to the entire list, address it to: ups500@vm.gmd.de

`mailto:listserv@vm.gmd.de`

Posix-ada

Posix-ada

To discuss the Ada binding of the POSIX standard. This is the IEEE P1003.5 working group.

Keywords:	Poxis, Computer Specialists
Audience:	Posix Users, Software Developers
Contact:	Karl Nyberg posix-ada-request@grebyn.com
Details:	Free
User Info:	To subscribe to the list, send an e-mail message requesting a subscription to the URL address that follows.
	To send a message to the entire list, address it to: posix-ada@grebyn.com

`mailto:posix-ada-request@grebyn.com`

Posix-testing

Posix-testing

A forum for discussion of issues related to testing operating systems for conformance to the various POSIX standards and proposed standards. Issues include problems related to test suites in general, testability of various features of the standards, and portability of the test suites to the many very different POSIX implementations anticipated in the near future.

Keywords:	COmputer Systems
Audience:	Posix Testers

Postal Services

POP

This list provides an organized source of information for discussion of the Post Office Protocol (POP2 and POP3 - described in RFCs 918, 937, 1081, and 1082) and implementations thereof. Its motivation was the lack of easily obtained knowledge of available POP2 and POP3 servers and clients.

Keywords: Postal Services
Audience: Postal Service Workers
Contact: Andy S. Poling
pop-request@jhunix.hcf.jhu.edu
Details: Free
User Info: To subscribe to the list, send an e-mail message requesting a subscription to the URL address that follows.

To send a message to the entire list, address it to: pop@jhunix.hcf.jhu.edu

`mailto:pop-request@jhunix.hcf.jhu.edu`

Postmodern Culture

PMC-MOO

A real-time, text-based, virtual-reality environment in which subscribers to Postmodern Culture can interact and participate in live conferences.

Keywords: Literature (Contemporary), Postmodern Culture, Literary Criticism
Audience: General Public, Writers, Literary Theorists, Researchers
Profile: In addition to providing Postmodern Culture's subscribers with the opportunity to interact and to participate in live conferences, PMC-MOO provides access to texts generated by the journal and by PMC-TALK, as well as the opportunity to experience (or to help design) programs that simulate object lessons in postmodern theory. PMC-MOO is based on the LambdaMOO program, freeware by Pavel Curtis.
Contact: pmc@unity.ncsu.edu

Notes: If your Internet account is on a UNIX machine and you have access to the Emacs editor (type 'man emacs' or 'help emacs' or simply 'emacs' at your command prompt to find out, or ask your user-services people). You can connect to PMC-MOO using a customized Emacs client available from our FTP site. This client provides text-buffering, multiple windows, and many features superior to an unmediated Telnet connection.

To retrieve the Emacs client, perform the following ftp transfer: ftp ftp.ncsu.edu; login: ftp; password: [your e-mail address]; cd pub/docs/pmc/pmc-talk; get PMC-MOO.doc; get mud.el; bin; get mud.elc; quit.

`telnet://dewey.lib.ncsu.edu`

Postmodern Culture

Postmodern Culture is a peer-reviewed electronic journal of interdisciplinary criticism on contemporary literature, theory, and culture.

Keywords: Literature (Contemporary), Postmodern Culture, Literary Criticism
Sponsor: Oxford University Press
Audience: General Public, Writers, Critics, Literary Theorists, Researchers
Profile: All back issues of Postmodern Culture are always available; previous issues have included:

- Andrew Ross, Hacking Away at the Counter-Culture
- Bell Hooks, Postmodern Blackness
- Laura Kipnis, Marx: The Video (A Politics of Revolting Bodies)
- Kathy Acker, Dead Doll Humility' and Obsession
- Neil Larsen, Postmodernism and Imperialism: Theory and Politics in Latin America
- Patrick O'Donnell, His Master's Voice: On William Gaddis's JR
- Greg Ulmer, Grammatology Hypemedia
- Charles Bernstein, The Second War and Postmodern Memory
- Allison Fraiberg, Of AIDS, Cyborgs, and Other Indiscretions: Resurfacing the Body in the Postmodern (with a response by David Porush)
- Stuart Moulthrop, You Say You Want a Revolution: Hypertext and the Laws of Media
- Bob Perelman, The Marginalization of Poetry

Details: Costs
User Info: To subscribe to the list, send an e-mail message requesting a subscription to the URL address that follows.

`mailto:pmc@ncsvm.cc.ncsu.edu`

WIRED Online

This is WIRED Magazine's gopher server.

Keywords: Postmodern Culture, News Media
Sponsor: WIRED Magazine
Audience: Internet Surfers, Internet Users, General Public
Profile: Features full-text of WIRED back issues, including the Net Surf column devoted to Internet exploration. Also has archives of the HotWIRED weekly mailing list, some guides to getting started surfing the net, general information about WIRED magazine, and an archive of material on the proposed Clipper federal encryption standard.
Contact: WIRED Online department, WIRED Magazine
online@wired.com, info@wired.com

`gopher://gopher.wired.com`

Postmodernism

FutureCulture FAQ (Frequently Asked Questions) File

List of online and offline items of interest to subscribers of FutureCulture, a mailing list on 'technoculture' or 'new edge' or 'cyberculture.'

Keywords: Technology, Cyberculture, Postmodernism, Sci-Fi, Zines
Audience: Reality Hackers, Cyberculture Enthusiasts
Profile: This list discusses cyberpunk culture, rave culture, industrial music, virtual reality, drugs, computer underground, Net sociology, and virtual communities.
Contact: Alias Datura (adatura on IRC)
adatura@uafhp.uark.edu
Details: Free

`ftp://etext.archive.umich.edu/pub`

Power Boating

The Nautical Bookshelf

Catalog and ordering information for Nautical Bookshelf's collection of books on sailing and other water sports.

Keywords: Boating, Power Boating, Sailing, Sports
Sponsor: Nautical Bookshelf
Audience: Boating Enthusiasts, Sailors
Contact: staff@nautical.com

`gopher://gopher.nautical.com`

Poxis

Posix-ada

To discuss the Ada binding of the POSIX standard. This is the IEEE P1003.5 working group.

Keywords: Poxis, Computer Specialists
Audience: Posix Users, Software Developers
Contact: Karl Nyberg
posix-ada-request@grebyn.com
Details: Free
User Info: To subscribe to the list, send an e-mail message requesting a subscription to the URL address that follows.
To send a message to the entire list, address it to: posix-ada@grebyn.com

`mailto:posix-ada-request@grebyn.com`

PPPL (The Princeton Plasma Physics Laboratory)

PPPL (The Princeton Plasma Physics Laboratory)

This web site provides an overview of the projects, mission, physical plant and history of the PPPL.

Keywords: Physics, Research
Sponsor: U.S. Department of Energy (DOE)
Audience: Physicists, Educators, Students
Contact: Anthony R. De Meo or Jack A. Mervine
pppl_info@pppl.gov
webmaster@pppl.gov
Details: Free

`http://www.pppl.gov`

Prague University of Economics Gopher Service

Prague University of Economics Gopher Service

Includes information about the University, integrative studies of economy, economic information, and public domain software.

Keywords: Czech Republic, Economics, Europe
Audience: Czechs, Economists
Contact: gopher@pub.vse.cz
Details: Free

`gopher://pub.vse.cz`

Pre-Law, Legislation, Court Decisions

Pre-Law, Legislation, Court Decisions

A collection of legal information including court decisions on abortion, a directory of US Judges, US Supreme Court rulings, and some primary documents relating to US and International law.

Keywords: Law (US Federal), Law (US State), Law (International)
Sponsor: Skidmore College Gopher Project, New York, USA
Audience: Lawyers, Legal Professionals
Contact: Leo Geoffrion, Peggy Seiden
ldg@skidmore.edu
pseiden@skidmore.edu

`gopher://grace.skidmore.edu/readings/social-sciences/law`

Pregnancy

Bethany Christian Services

A major directory on adoption, providing access to a broad range of related resources (library catalogs, databases, and servers) through the Internet.

Keywords: Adoption, Christianity, Pregnancy, Abortion Rights
Sponsor: Bethany Christian Services, Grand Rapids, Michigan, USA
Audience: Pregnant Women
Profile: The gopher server of Bethany, a pro-life, pro-family agency reaching out to women with unplanned pregnancies and adoptive couples. Contains a large amount of information about national and international adoption, the adoption process, African-American adoptions, and adoption of children with special needs. Also contains information for pregnant women, such as birth father rights and responsibilities, pregnancy counceling, and so on.
Contact: gophermaster@bethany.org

`gopher://gopher.bethany.org/11`

President

National Performance Review (NPR)

The Report of the National Performance Review, from the task force led by Vice President Gore, titled 'From Red Tape to Results: Creating a Government that Works Better and Costs Less,' Sept. 7, 1993.

Keywords: President, Politics, White House
Audience: Political Scientists, General Public
Profile: On March 3, 1993, President Clinton asked Vice President Gore to lead the effort to effect real change in the federal government. Gore's NPR Task Force overview and accompanying reports make specific recommendations for: reducing costs and waste, changing the way government operates, and making government more responsive and effective.
Details: Free

`gopher://cyfer.esusda.gov/11/ace/policy/npr/nat`

Technology Initiatives for the Clinton/Gore Administration

This is a 40-page text of the press release from the Clinton administration on technology initiatives, dated February 22, 1993.

Keywords: Politics, President, White House, Technology
Audience: General Public, Journalists
Details: Free
E-mail to the ListServ and include the following in the body of the message: get cni-bigideas.whouse.paper

`mailto:listserv@cni.org`

White House Phone Numbers

A list of names, addresses, e-mail addresses and telephone and fax numbers of the President, First Lady, Vice President, and all the members of the Cabinet.

Keywords: White House, President, Politics
Audience: General Public
Details: Free

`ftp://nifty.andrew.cmu.edu/pub/QRD/info/govt/cabinet`

President (US)

Presidential Documents

This gopher provides access to the full text of Presidential Proclamations, Executive Orders, Notices, Memoranda, and Determinations dating from December 23, 1992. The documents are listed sequentially by date and number (that is, Proclamation 6520 of December 23, 1992).

Keywords: Politics, President (US), White House, Documents
Audience: General Public
Details: Free
Select from menu presented (probably you will follow the following path: Internet Services/US Government/Presidential Documents.

`gopher://jupiter.cc.gettysborg.edu`

White House Information Service ★★★★

An outstanding database of current White House information, from 1992 to the present.

Keywords: White House, Politics, President (US), Database
Sponsor: Texas A & M University
Audience: General Public
Profile: Much of the older information on this site was obtained from the clinton@marist.bitnet listserv list or the alt.politics.clinton Usenet newsgroup, both of which receive the information indirectly via the MIT White House information server. Newer and current material is received directly from the MIT distribution list. The menu includes a searchable database and headings such as Domestic Affairs (Health Care, Technology, and so on), Press Briefings and Conferences, the President's Daily Schedule, and many more.
Contact: whadmin@tamu.edu
Details: Free

`gopher://tamuts.tamu.edu/11/.dir/president.dir`

White House Press Releases ★★★★

An archive of all the press releases by the Clinton administration organized as Miscellaneous, Briefings by Dee Dee Myers, Executive Orders, Remarks during Photo Opportunities, Remarks of Bill Clinton, Briefings by George Stephanopolous.

Keywords: White House, Politics, President (US)
Audience: General Public
Details: Free

`gopher://wiretap.spies.com/11/Clinton`

Pricing

Internet Public Subsidies ★

An article entitled "The Economic Case for Public Subsidy of the Internet."

Keywords: Internet, Pricing
Audience: Internet Surfers
Contact: Sandra Schickele
Details: Free

`gopher://ssugopher.sonoma.edu`

Primates

Primate-talk (Primate Discussion List) ★★★

Forum for the discussion of primatology and related subjects.

Keywords: Primates, Primatology, Veterinary Medicine
Audience: Primatologists, Veterinarians
Profile: This list is open to any e-mail user with an interest in primatology. Subject matter ranges from, but is not limited to, news items, meeting announcements, research issues, information requests, veterinary/husbandry topics, job notices, animal exchange information, and book reviews.
Contact: Larry Jacobsen
jacobsen@pimate.wisc.edu
Details: Free
User Info: To subscribe to the list, send an e-mail message requesting a subscription to the URL address that follows.

`mailto:primate-talk-request@primate.wisc.edu`

WRPRCC ★★★

Keywords: Primates, Wisconsin
Sponsor: Wisconsin Regional Primate Research Center
Audience: Primatologists, Zoologists
Contact: jacobsen@primate.wisc.edu
Details: Free
User Info: Expect: Login; enter: wiscinfo; choose: UW-Madison Information Servers Wisconsin Primate Research Center Server

`gopher://gopher.primate.wisc.edu`

Primatology

Laboratory Primate Newsletter ★

Provides a central source of information about nonhuman primates and related matters for scientists who use these animals in their research and for those whose work supports such research.

Keywords: Primatology, Psychology
Audience: Primate Researchers, Psychologists
Contact: Judith E. Schrier
primate@brownvm.brown.edu
Details: Free

`mailto:listserv@brownvm.brown.edu`

Primate-talk (Primate Discussion List) ★★★

Forum for the discussion of primatology and related subjects.

Keywords: Primates, Primatology, Veterinary Medicine
Audience: Primatologists, Veterinarians
Profile: This list is open to any e-mail user with an interest in primatology. Subject matter ranges from, but is not limited to, news items, meeting announcements, research issues, information requests, veterinary/husbandry topics, job notices, animal exchange information, and book reviews.
Contact: Larry Jacobsen
jacobsen@pimate.wisc.edu
Details: Free
User Info: To subscribe to the list, send an e-mail message requesting a subscription to the URL address that follows.

`mailto:primate-talk-request@primate.wisc.edu`

Prince

Prince ★

A mailing list devoted to discussing the musician formerly named Prince and related artists.

Keywords: Musical Groups, Rock Music
Audience: Musicians, Music Students, Music Enthusiasts
Contact: prince-request@icpsr.umich.edu
Details: Free
User Info: To subscribe to the list, send an e-mail message requesting a subscription to the URL address that follows.

To send a message to the entire list, address it to: prince-request@icpsr.umich.edu

`mailto:prince@icpsr.umich.edu`

Princeton University Library

Princeton University Library ★★

The library's holdings are large and wide-ranging. They contain significant collections in many fields.

Keywords: China, Japan, Classics, History (Ancient), Near Eastern Studies, Literature (American), Literature (English), Aeronautics, Middle Eastern Studies, Mormonism, Publishing
Audience: General Public, Researchers, Librarians, Document Delivery Professionals

Details:	Free
User Info:	Expect: Connect message, blank screen, Send: <cr>; Expect: #, Send: Call 500

`telnet://pucable.princeton.edu`

Princeton University Online Manuscripts Catalog Library

Princeton University Online Manuscripts Catalog Library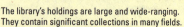

The library's holdings are large and wide-ranging. They contain significant collections in many fields.

Keywords:	Books (Antiquarian), Dickens (Charles), Disraeli (Benjamin), Eliot (George), Hardy (Thomas), Kingsley (Charles), Trollope (Anthony)
Audience:	General Public, Researchers, Librarians, Document Delivery Professionals
Details:	Free
User Info:	Expect: VM370 logo, Send: <cr>; Expect: Welcome screen, Send: folio <cr>; Expect: Welcome screen for FOLIO, Send: <cr>; Expect: List of choices, Send: 3 <cr>; To exit: type: logoff

`telnet://pucc.princeton.edu`

Principia Cybernetica Newsletter

Principia Cybernetica Newsletter

Newsletter for participants in the Principia Cybernetica Project (PCP), as well as for people interested in keeping informed about the project.

Keywords:	Philosophy, Worldview
Audience:	Philosophers
Profile:	PCP is a computer-supported collaborative attempt to develop an integrated evolutionary-systemic philosophy or world view. Its contributors are distributed over several continents and maintain contact primarily through electronic mail (mailing list PRNCYB-L), as well as through annual meetings, the printed (and electronic) newsletter, and postal mail. PCP focuses on the clear formulation of basic concepts and principles of the cybernetic approach.
Contact:	Cliff Joslyn, Francis Heylighen fheyligh@vnet3.vub.ac.be cjoslyn@bingvaxu.cc.binghamton.edu
Details:	Free Send a 1- to 2- page letter, giving your address and affiliations and motivating your interest in the Project to the List owner (C. Joslyn).

`mailto:cjoslyn@bingvaxu.cc.binghamton.edu`

Printing

PIRA - Paper, Printing and Publishing, Packaging, and Nonwovens Abstracts

Coverage of all aspects of paper, pulp, nonwovens, printing, publishing and packaging.

Keywords:	Material Science, Paper, Printing, Publishing, Packaging
Sponsor:	PIRA International
Audience:	Material Scientists, Researchers
Profile:	File contains more than 300,000 records. Special applications: company and market profiles, product and trade name searches, research and technology trends. Updated biweekly.
Contact:	paul.albert@neteast.com
User Info:	To subscribe, contact Orbit-Questel directly.

`telnet://orbit.com`

Prion (Prion Research Digest)

Prion (Prion Research Digest)

Prion Infection Digest discusses current research on prion (slow virus) infection. The Prion Digest was formed as a reference point for the discussion and sharing of current research into prion infection.

Keywords:	Prion, Health
Audience:	Medical Researchers, Health-care Professionals
Contact:	Chris Swanson prion-request@stolaf.edu
Details:	Free
User Info:	To subscribe to the list, send an e-mail message requesting a subscription to the URL address that follows. To send a message to the entire list, address it to: prion@stolaf.edu

`mailto:prion-request@stolaf.edu`

Privacy

alt.security.pgp

A Usenet newsgroup providing information and discussion about the Pretty Good Privacy package, a privately-developed encryption technique.

Keywords:	Privacy, Encryption, Security Firewalls, Computers
Audience:	Internet Surfers
User Info:	To subscribe to this Usenet newsgroup, you need access to a newsreader.

`news:alt.security.pgp`

EFFector Online—The Electronic Frontier Foundation, Inc.

Established to make the electronic frontier truly useful and accessible to everyone, emphasizing the free and open flow of information and communication.

Keywords:	Computer Communications, Electronic Media, Intellectual Property, Privacy
Audience:	Computer Users, Civil Libertarians
Profile:	EFFector Online presents news, information, and discussion about the world of computer-based communications media that constitute the electronic frontier. It covers issues such as freedom of speech in digital media, privacy rights, censorship, and standards of responsibility for users and operators of computer systems, as well as policy issues such as the development of a national information infrastructure, and intellectual property.
Contact:	Gerard Van der Leun, Mike Godwin gerard@eff.org mnemonic@eff.org
Details:	Free
User Info:	To subscribe, send an e-mail message requesting a subscription to: request@eff.org
Notes:	This takes you to the front door of the eff gopher server which contains much more information than just Effector online.

`gopher://gopher.eff.org/1`

Electronic Communications Privacy Act of 1986

This is the act to amend Title 18, United States Code, with respect to the interception of certain communications, other forms of surveillance, and for other purposes. This act affects every Usenet, Bitnet, BBS, shortwave listener, TV viewer, and so on.

Keywords:	Communications, Privacy, Government (US Federal), Laws (US Federal)
Audience:	Journalists, Privacy Activists, Students, Politicians
Details:	Free

`gopher://wiretap.spies.com/00/Gov/ecpa.act`

Freedom of Information Act (FOIA): Guide to Use

This is a citizen's guide on using the Freedom of Information Act and the Privacy Act of 1974 to request government records.

Keywords:	Privacy, Freedom of Information, Government (US Federal)

Audience: Journalists, Privacy Activists, Students, Politicians, US Citizens

Details: Free

gopher://wiretap.spies.com/00/Gov/foia.cit

Networks & Communities

This directory is a compilation of information resources focused on networks and communities.

Keywords: Community, Networking, Privacy

Audience: Network Developers, Community Activists, Free-net Organizers, Fundraisers

Details: Free

ftp://una.hh.lib.umich.edu/70/inetdirsstacks/nets:sternberg

Privacy

An archive about identity, privacy, and anonymity on the Internet, from the Usenet newsgroup alt.privacy.

Keywords: Privacy, Internet

Audience: Internet Surfers

Details: Free

Notes: File is: pub/nic/internet.literature/netiquette.txt

ftp://pit-manager.mit.edu

Privacy Act of 1974

The act that regulates the maintenance of privacy and protection of records on individuals.

Keywords: Privacy, Law (US Federal), Government (US Federal)

Audience: Journalists, Politicians, Lawyers

Details: Free

User Info: Choose from menu as appropriate.

gopher://wiretap.spies.com/00/Gov/privacy.act

Privacy Rights Clearinghouse (PRC)

A collection of materials related to privacy issues.

Keywords: Privacy, Legislation, Consumer Rights, Freedom of Information

Sponsor: University of San Diego

Audience: Citizens, Privacy Activists, Journalists

Profile: This site contains fact sheets (in English and Spanish) on privacy issues ranging from wiretapping to credit reporting. Also includes federal and state privacy legislation as well as related position papers and press releases.

Contact: prc@teetot.acusd.edu

User Info: Expect: Login; Send: Privacy

gopher://teetot.acusd.edu

telnet://teetot.acusd.edu

PRL

PRL

The Pirate Radio SWL list is for the distribution of questions, answers, information, and loggings of Pirate Radio Stations.

Keywords: Radio, Communications

Audience: Radio Broadcasters, Radio Pirates

Contact: John Brewer
brewer@ace.enet.dec.com

User Info: To subscribe to the list, send an e-mail message to the URL address that follows, consisting of a single line reading:

SUB PRLYourFirstName YourLastName

To send a message to the entire list, address it to: brewer@ace.enet.dec.com

mailto:listserv@ace.enet.dec.com

Professional Sports

Funet Sports Information

An FTP archive of information on various sports with links to the archive at wuarchive.wustl.edu.

Keywords: Sports, Professional Sports, Ice Hockey, Motor Racing, NFL, NHL, NBA, MLB

Sponsor: Finnish Academic and Research Network (FUNET)

Audience: Sports Enthusiasts

Profile: A fairly extensive archive of information on both American (NBA, MLB, NHL, NFL) and worldwide sports (soccer, ice hockey, motor racing, and so on). Includes FAQs for various sports, statistics, pictures, and some sports games for the PC.

Contact: Jari Pullinen
sports-adm@nic.funet.fi

Details: Free, Images

gopher://ftp.funet.fi/pub/sports

NFL Scores, Schedules, and Point Spreads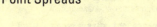

Information on National Football League (NFL) football scores, schedules, and point spreads.

Keywords: Professional Sports, Sports, Football, NFL

Audience: Football Fans

Contact: office@world.std.com

Details: Free

gopher://world.std.com/News and Weather

Professional Sports Schedules

Sports schedules for major professional sports.

Keywords: Sports, Baseball, Hockey, Football, Basketball, Professional Sports

Sponsor: Colorado University, Boulder, CO

Audience: Sports Enthusiasts, Football Enthusiasts, Hockey Enthusiasts, Baseball Enthusiasts, Basketball Enthusiasts

Profile: The Colorado University gopher maintains an interactive online database of schedules for all major US professional sports teams (NBA, NFL, NHL, MLB). The database is indexed by both team name and dates of games, and can be searched accordingly.

Contact: gopher@gopher.colorado.edu

Details: Free

gopher://gopher.colorado.edu/11/professional/sports/schedules

Prog-Pubs

Prog-Pubs

A mailing list for people interested in progressive and/or alternative publications and other media. Discussions include issues pertaining to all kinds of small-scale, independent, progressive, and/or alternative media, including newspapers, newsletters, and radio and video shows.

Keywords: Media, Alternative Press, Communications

Audience: Students (College/University), Media Professionals

Contact: prog-pubs-request@fuggles.acc.virginia.edu

Details: Free

User Info: To subscribe to the list, send an e-mail message requesting a subscription to the URL address that follows.

To send a message to the entire list, address it to: prog-pubs@fuggles.acc.virginia.edu

mailto:prog-pubs@fuggles.acc.virginia.edu

Programming

ABC

Discussion of the ABC Programming Language and its implementations.

Keywords: Programming, ABC Programming Language

Audience: Programmers

Contact: Steven Pemberton
abc-list-request@cwi.nl

Details: Free

User Info: To subscribe to the list, send an e-mail message requesting a subscription to the URL address that follows.

To send a message to the entire list, address it to: ABC@cwi.nl

`mailto:abc-list-request@cwi.nl`

ACM SIGGRAPH Online Bibliography Project ★★★★

This is a collection of computer-graphics bibliographic references.

Keywords: Multimedia, Interactive, Computer Graphics, Programming

Sponsor: Association of Computing Machinery (ACM), Special Interest Group on Computer Graphics (SIGGRAPH)

Audience: Developers, Designers, Producers, Educators, Programmers, Graphic Artists

Profile: The goal of this project is to maintain an up-to-date database of computer-graphics literature, in a format that is accessible to as many members of the computer-graphics community as possible. The database includes references from conferences and workshops worldwide and from a variety of publications dating back as far as the late-19th century. The majority of the major journals and conference proceedings from the mid-1970s to the present are listed.

Contact: bibadmin@siggraph.org

Details: Free, Moderated, Multimedia

`ftp://siggraph.org/publications`

Ada-sw ★

A list for users who access and contribute software to the Ada Repository on SIMTEL20.

Keywords: Programming, Ada

Audience: Programmers

Details: Free

User Info: To subscribe to the list, send an e-mail message requesting a subscription to the URL address that follows.

To send a message to the entire list, address it to Ada-sw@wsmr-simtel20.army.mil

`mailto:ada-sw-request@wsmr-simtel20.army.mil`

APL-L ★

Discussion of the APL language, its implementation, application, and use. Contributions on teaching APL are particularly welcome.

Keywords: Programming, Programming Languages, APL

Audience: Programmers

Contact: David G. Macneil
dgm@unb.cat4327@unb.ca

Details: Free

User Info: To subscribe to the list, send an e-mail message to the URL address that follows, consisting of a single line reading:

SUB APL-L YourFirstName YourLastName

To send a message to the entire list, address it to: APL-L@cis.vutbr.cs

`mailto:listserv@unb.ca`

BETA ★

A discussion forum for BETA users. BETA is a modern object-oriented programming language.

Keywords: Programming, Object-Oriented Programming, BETA

Audience: Programmers

Contact: Elmer Soerensen Sandvad
usergroup-request@mjolner.dk

Details: Free, Moderated

User Info: To subscribe to the list, send an e-mail message requesting a subscription to the URL address that follows.

To send a message to the entire list, address it to: usergroup@mjolner.dk

`mailto:usergroup-request@mjolner.dk`

Clp.x ★

Devoted to discussion of concurrent logic programming languages, concurrent constraint programming languages, semantics, proof techniques and program transformations, parallel Prolog systems, implementations, and programming techniques and idioms.

Keywords: Programming, Programming Languages, Concurrent Logic

Audience: Concurrent Logic Programmers

Contact: Jacob Levy
jlevy.pa@xerox.com

Details: Free

User Info: To subscribe to the list, send an e-mail message requesting a subscription to the URL address that follows.

To send a message to the entire lst, address it to: clp.x@xerox.com

`mailto:clp-request.x@xerox.com`

DISSPLA (Display Integrated Software System and Plotting Language) ★

News and information exchange concerning DISSPLA.

Keywords: Computer Graphics, Programming

Audience: DISSPLA Users, Computer Programmers

Profile: DISSPLA is a high-level FORTRAN graphics subroutine library designed for programmers in engineering, science and business.

Contact: Zvika Bar-Deroma
er7101@technion.technion.ac.il

Details: Free

User Info: To subscribe to the list, send an e-mail message to the URL address shown that follows, consisting of a single line reading:

SUB disspla YourFirstName YourLastName

To send a message to the entire list, address it to: disspla@taunivm.tau.ac.il

`mailto:listserv@taunivm.tau.ac.il`

EXPRESS-Users ★

Discussion of topics pertaining to the EXPRESS information modeling language, such as information sources, how to download information, information modeling techniques, and sample models.

Keywords: Programming, EXPRESS Information Modeling Language

Audience: EXPRESS Programmers

Contact: Steve Clark, Charlie Lindahl
EXPRESS-users-request@cme.nist.gov

Details: Free

User Info: To subscribe to the list, send an e-mail message requesting a subscription to the URL address that follows.

`mailto:EXPRESS-users-request@cme.nist.gov`

Icon-group ★

Discussion of topics related to the Icon programming language

Keywords: Programming, Icon Programming Language, Programming Language, String Processing

Audience: Icon Programmers

Profile: Icon is a high-level, general purpose programming language emphasizing string and structure processing. Topics include programming techniques, theoretical aspects, Icon in relation to other languages, applications of Icon, implementation issues, porting, and bugs.

Contact: Bill Mitchell
whm@arizona.edu

Details: Free

User Info: To subscribe to the list, send an e-mail message requesting a subscription to the URL address that follows.

`mailto:Icon-Group-Request@arizona.edu.`

info-Ada ★

Discussion of the Ada programming language.

Keywords:	Programming, Ada (Programming Language)
Audience:	Programmers
Contact:	Karl A. Nyberg Karl@grebyn.com
Details:	Free
User Info:	To subscribe to the list, send an e-mail message requesting a subscription to the URL address that follows

`mailto:info-Ada-request@sei.cmu.edu`

info-C ★

Discussions about C programming and the C programming language.

Keywords:	Programming, C (Programming Language)
Audience:	C Programmers
Contact:	Mark Plotnick info-C-request@research.att.com
Details:	Free
User Info:	To subscribe to the list, send an e-mail message requesting a subscription to the URL address that follows.

`mailto:info-C-request@research.att.com`

info-M2 ★

E-conference for the Modula-2 programming language.

Keywords:	Programming, Modula-2 (Programming Language)
Audience:	Modula-2 Programmers
Contact:	Thomas Habernoll postmast@ucf1vm.cc.ucf.edu (USA) habernol@tubvm.cs.tu-berlin.de (Europe)
Details:	Free
User Info:	To subscribe to the list, send an e-mail message to the URL address that follows, consisting of a single line reading: SUB info-M2 YourFirstName YourLastName To send a message to the entire list, address it to: info-M2@ucf1vm.cc.ucf.edu

`mailto:listserv@ucf1vm.cc.ucf.edu`

info-Pascal ★

Discussions of any Pascal implementation, from mainframe to micro, for Pascal program users.

Keywords:	Programming, Pascal
Audience:	Pascal Programmers, Pascal Users
Contact:	Hernan Lobos *Mitzio* hlobos@utfsm.bitnet
Details:	Free
User Info:	To subscribe to the list, send an e-mail message requesting a subscription to the following URL address.

`info-Pascal@brl.mil`

insoft-l ★

This list discusses techniques for developing new software and for converting existing software, as well as internationalization tools, announcements of internationalized public-domain software and of foreign-language versions of commercial software, calls for papers, conference announcements, and references to documentation related to the internationalization of software.

Keywords:	Programming, Software Internationalization
Sponsor:	Center for Computing and Information Services, Technical University of Brno
Audience:	Software Developers
Contact:	insoft-l-request@cis.vutbr.cs
Details:	Free, Moderated
User Info:	To subscribe to the list, send an e-mail message to the URL address that follows, consisting of a single line reading: SUB insoft-l YourFirstName YourLastName To send a message to the entire list, address it to: insoft-l@cis.vutbr.cs

`mailto:listserv@cis.vutbr.cs`

Lang-Lucid ★

Discussions on all aspects related to the programming language Lucid, including language design issues, implementations for personal computers, implementations for parallel machines, language extensions, programming environments, products, bug reports, and bug fixes/workarounds.

Keywords:	Programming, Programming Languages
Audience:	Lucid Programmers
Contact:	R. Jagannathan lang-lucid-request@csl.sri.com
Details:	Free
User Info:	To subscribe to the list, send an e-mail message requesting a subscription to the URL address that follows.

`mailto:lang-lucid-request@csl.sri.com`

Litprog ★

A network list dealing with topics related to literate programming, both general (is literate programming compatible with writing portable programs), and particular (is it possible to use CWEB with ANSIC).

Keywords:	Programming, Literate Programming
Audience:	Computer Programmers
Contact:	George D. Greenwade bed_gdg@shsu.edu
Details:	Free
User Info:	To subscribe to the list, send an e-mail message to the URL address that follows, consisting of a single line reading: SUB listprog YourFirstName YourLastName To send a message to the entire list, address it to: listprog @shsu.edu
Notes:	This list is open to novices and seasoned literate programmers.

`mailto:listserv@shsu.edu`

Loughborough University of Technology Computer-Human Interaction (LUTCHI) Research Centre

This server contains general information on computer-human interaction.

Keywords:	Interface Design, Ergonomics, Computer-Human Interactions, Programming
Sponsor:	Loughborough University of Technology, Leicestershire, UK
Audience:	Software Developers, Software Designers, Programmers
Profile:	The LUTCHI Research Centre is based within the Department of Computer Studies at the Loughborough University of Technology, Leicestershire, UK. This server contains information about LUTCHI research projects, official LUTCHI publicity releases, as well as documents, images, and movies associated with those projects.
Contact:	Ben Anderson B.Anderson@lut.ac.uk
Details:	Free, Moderated, Sound, Image, and Multimedia files available. Use a World-Wide Web (Mosaic) client and open a connection to the resource.

`http://pipkin.lut.ac.uk`

NIC (Nucleus for Interactive Computing)

WWW-based system for interactive computing.

Keywords:	Multimedia, Interactive Computing, Interface Design, Scripting Laguages, Programming
Sponsor:	BYU Interactive Software Systems Lab
Audience:	Software Developers, Educators
Profile:	NIC is a system for interactive computing that combines a data model, a user interface model, and a scripting language to create flexible and powerful user interfaces. Documentation still under construction is located here.

Contact: Dan Olsen
olsen@cs.byu.edu

Details: Free, Moderated, Sound, Image, and Multimedia files available.

Use a World Wide Web (Mosaic) client and open a connection to the resource.

`ftp://issl.cs.byu.edu/docs/NIC/home.html`

Proof-users

Discussion of the left-associative natural language "parser proof".

Keywords: Computing, Programming

Audience: Computer Programmers

Contact: Craig Latta
proof-request@xcf.berkeley.edu

Details: Free

To join, e-mail proof-request@xcf.berkeley.edu with the subject line "add me".

`mailto:proof-request@xcf.berkeley.edu`

rec.games.programmer

A Usenet newsgroup providing information and discussion about adventure game programming.

Keywords: Games, Programming, Video Games

Audience: Programmers

User Info: To subscribe to this Usenet newsgroup, you need access to a newsreader.

`news:rec.games.programmer`

Simula

An electronic conference for discussion of the SIMULA programming language.

Keywords: Programming, SIMULA

Audience: SIMULA Programmers

Details: Free

User Info: To subscribe to the list, send an e-mail message to the URL address that follows, consisting of a single line reading:

SUB Simula YourFirstName YourLastName

To send a message to the entire list, address it to: Simula@bitnic.educom.edu

`mailto:listserv@bitnic.educom.edu`

Weather-users

Weather-users is a mailing list for developers of programs that access the Weather Underground database at the University of Michigan.

Keywords: Weather, Programming, Meteorology

Audience: Programmers

Contact: Scott Hazen Mueller
scott@zorch.sf-bay.org

Details: Free

User Info: To subscribe to the list, send an e-mail message

`mailto:weather-users-request@zorch.sf-bay.org`

Programming Languages

AMOS

For the AMOS programming language on Amiga computers. Features source, bug reports, and help from users around the world, but mainly from European users. Most posts will be in English, but there are no language limitations.

Keywords: Computers, Programming Languages, AMOS, Amiga

Audience: Programmers, Computer Users

Contact: subscribe@xamiga.linet.org

Details: Free

User Info: To subscribe to the list, send an e-mail message to the URL address that follows, consisting of a single line reading:

SUB #amos userneame@domain

To send a message to the entire list, address it to: subscribe@xamiga.linet.org

`mailto:subscribe@xamiga.linet.org`

APL-L

Discussion of the APL language, its implementation, application, and use. Contributions on teaching APL are particularly welcome.

Keywords: Programming, Programming Languages, APL

Audience: Programmers

Contact: David G. Macneil
dgm@unb.cat4327@unb.ca

Details: Free

User Info: To subscribe to the list, send an e-mail message to the URL address that follows, consisting of a single line reading:

SUB APL-L YourFirstName YourLastName

To send a message to the entire list, address it to: APL-L@cis.vutbr.cs

`mailto:listserv@unb.ca`

AppWare-info

A forum for discussion of issues relating to AppWare software. Topics include simple programming questions, tips for program efficiency, quirks of, and complaints about the environment or tools, the process of writing new ALMs or functions, third party enhancements, and any other question.

Keywords: Computers, Programming Languages

Sponsor: Novell Inc.

Audience: AppWare Users, Computer Programmers

Contact: Novell Inc.
appware-info@serius.uchicago.edu

User Info: To subscribe to the list, send an e-mail message to the URL address that follows.

To send a message to the entire list, address it to: appware-info@serius.uchicago.edu

`mailto:appware-info-request@serius.uchicago.edu`

`ftp://serius.uchicago.edu`

C-IBM-370

The C on IBM mainframes mailing list is a place to discuss aspects of using the C programming language on s/370-architecture computers—especially under IBM's operating systems for that environment.

Keywords: C Language, Programming Languages, IBM

Audience: IBM Users, Computer Users, Computer Programmers

Contact: David Wolfskill
C-IBM-370-request@dhw68k.cts.com

Details: Free

User Info: To subscribe to the list, send an e-mail message requesting a subscription to the URL address that follows.

To send a message to the entire list, address it to: C-IBM-370@dhw68k.cts.com

`mailto:C-IBM-370-request@dhw68k.cts.com`

C-L

Discussion of C programming.

Keywords: Programming Languages

Audience: C Programmers

Contact: George Foster, Katie Hanson
igaf400@indyvax, abh100@indycms

Details: Free

User Info: To subscribe to the list, send an e-mail message to the URL address that follows, consisting of a single line reading:

SUB C-L YourFirstName YourLastName

To send a message to the entire list, address it to: C-L@indycms.iupui.edu

`mailto:listserv@indycms.iupui.edu`

Clp.x ★

Devoted to discussion of concurrent logic programming languages, concurrent constraint programming languages, semantics, proof techniques and program transformations, parallel Prolog systems, implementations, and programming techniques and idioms.

Keywords:	Programming, Programming Languages, Concurrent Logic
Audience:	Concurrent Logic Programmers
Contact:	Jacob Levy jlevy.pa@xerox.com
Details:	Free
User Info:	To subscribe to the list, send an e-mail message requesting a subscription to the URL address that follows. To send a message to the entire lst, address it to: clp.x@xerox.com

`mailto:clp-request.x@xerox.com`

comp.lang.c ★

A Usenet newsgroup providing information and discussion about the C programming language.

Keywords:	Computer Programming, Programming Languages
Audience:	Computer Users, C Programmers
User Info:	To subscribe to this Usenet newsgroup, you need access to a newsreader.

`news:comp.lang.c`

comp.lang.c++ ★

A Usenet newsgroup providing information and discussion about the object-oriented C++ programming language.

Keywords:	Computers, Programming Languages
Audience:	Computer Users, C++ Programmers
User Info:	To subscribe to this Usenet newsgroup, you need access to a newsreader.

`news:comp.lang.c++`

Icon-group ★

Discussion of topics related to the Icon programming language.

Keywords:	Programming, Icon Programming Language, Programming Language, String Processing
Audience:	Icon Programmers
Profile:	Icon is a high-level, general purpose programming language emphazing string and structure processing. Topics include programming techniques, theoretical aspects, Icon in relation to other languages, applications of Icon, implementation issues, porting, and bugs.
Contact:	Bill Mitchell whm@arizona.edu
Details:	Free
User Info:	To subscribe to the list, send an e-mail message requesting a subscription to the URL address that follows.

`mailto:Icon-Group-Request@arizona.edu.`

Lang-Lucid ★

Discussions on all aspects related to the programming language Lucid, including language design issues, implementations for personal computers, implementations for parallel machines, language extensions, programming environments, products, bug reports, and bug fixes/workarounds.

Keywords:	Programming, Programming Languages
Audience:	Lucid Programmers
Contact:	R. Jagannathan lang-lucid-request@csl.sri.com
Details:	Free
User Info:	To subscribe to the list, send an e-mail message requesting a subscription to the URL address that follows.

`mailto:lang-lucid-request@csl.sri.com`

nl-kr ★

This E-conference is open to discussion of any topic related to the understanding and generation of natural language and knowledge representation as subfields of artificial intelligence.

Keywords:	Programming Languages, Natural Language, Knowledge Representation, Linguistics
Audience:	Computer Programmers
Contact:	Christopher Welty weltyc@cs.rpi.edu
Details:	Free, Moderated
User Info:	To subscribe to the list, send an e-mail message requesting a subscription to the URL address that follows.

`mailto:nl-kr-request@cs.rpi.edu`

PERL (Practical Extraction and Report Language) ★★★

An HTML-formatted and highly indexed PERL programming reference document.

Keywords:	Programming Languages, Computer Programming
Audience:	Computer Programmers, Students, Researchers
Contact:	Larry Wall lwall@netlabs.com

`http://www.cs.cmu.edu/Web/People/rgs/perl.html`

Progress

Progress ★

Discussion of the Progress RDBMS (Relational Database Management System).

Keywords:	Databases, Computing
Audience:	Computer Users, Business Students
Contact:	Progress-list-request@math.niu.edu
Details:	Free
User Info:	To subscribe to the list, send an e-mail message requesting a subscription to the URL address that follows. To send a message to the entire list, address it to: progress-list@math.niu.edu

`mailto:Progress-list-request@math.niu.edu`

Prohibition

The University of Michigan Library ★★

The Library's holdings are large and wide-ranging and contain significant collections in many fields.

Keywords:	Education (Bilingual), Linguistics, Neuroscience, Michigan, Prohibition, Government (African)
Audience:	General Public, Researchers, Librarians, Document Delivery Professionals
Details:	Free
Expect:	nothing, Send: <cr>

`telnet://cts.merit.edu`

Project Gutenberg

Africa in the CIA World Fact Book ★★

A gopher site containing geographial and political information about individual countries in Africa.

Keywords:	Africa, Intelligence, Project Gutenberg
Sponsor:	Project Gutenberg
Audience:	Africans, General Public

`gopher://hoshi.cic.sfu.ca/11/dlam/cia/Africa`

GUTENBERG Listserver ★

A mailing list providing information about Project Gutenberg.

Keywords:	Project Gutenberg, Literature (General), Reference
Sponsor:	National Clearinghouse for Machine Readable Texts

Audience:	General Public, Researchers, Educators, Students
Contact:	Michael S. Hart gutnberg@vmd.cso.uiuc.edu
Details:	Free
User Info:	To subscribe to the list, send an e-mail message to the following URL address consisting of a single line reading: SUB GUTNBERG YourFirstName YourLastName

`mailto:listserv@vmd.cso.uiuc.edu`

Project Gutenberg

The purpose of Project Gutenberg is to encourage the creation and distribution of English-language electronic texts.

Keywords:	Literature (General), Reference
Sponsor:	National Clearinghouse for Machine Readable Texts
Audience:	General Public, Researchers, Educators, Students
Profile:	Contents include: Project Gutenberg's goal is to provide a collection of 10,000 of the most used books by the year 2001, and to reduce the effective costs to the user to a price of approximately one cent per book, plus the cost of media and of shipping and handling. Thus it is hoped that the entire cost of libraries of this nature will be about US$100, plus the price of the disks and CD-ROMS and mailing. Project Gutenberg assists in the selection of hardware and software as well as in their installation and use. It also assists in scanning, spelling checkers, proofreading, and so on.
Contact:	Michael S. Hart hart@vmd.cso.uiuc.edu
Details:	Costs
User Info:	Login anonymous; cd text

`ftp://mrcnext.cso.uiuc.edu`

Project Management

Project-management

The aim of the list is to discuss project-management techniques generally, as well as project-management software and programs.

Keywords:	Project Management, Computing, Software
Audience:	Business Professionals, Business Students
Contact:	project-management-request@smtl.demon.co.uk
Details:	Free

User Info:	To subscribe to the list, send an e-mail message requesting a subscription to the URL address that follows. To send a message to the entire list, address it to: project-management@smtl.demon.co.uk

`mailto:project-management-request@smtl.demon.co.uk`

Prompt

Prompt

Contains news tips and briefs for the NCSU (North Carolina State University) campus community. Complementing the paper newsletter Connect, Prompt is designed to provide timely, up-to-date information concerning all platforms of computing.

Keywords:	Computing
Audience:	NCSU Computer Students, Educators, Computer Users
Contact:	Sarah Noell sarah_noell@ncsu.edu
Details:	Free
User Info:	To subscribe to the list, send an e-mail message to the URL address that follows, consisting of a single line reading: prompt YourFirstName YourLastName To send a message to the entire list, address it to: prompt@cc.ncsu.edu

`mailto:listserv@cc.ncsu.edu`

Proof-users

Proof-users

Discussion of the left-associative natural language "parser proof".

Keywords:	Computing, Programming
Audience:	Computer Programmers
Contact:	Craig Latta proof-request@xcf.berkeley.edu
Details:	Free To join, e-mail proof-request@xct.berkeley.edu with the subject line "add me".

`mailto:proof-request@xcf.berkeley.edu`

Property

ASSETS (Real Estate Tax Assessor and Deed Transfer Records)

The RealEstate Tax Assessor and Deed Transfer Records (ASSETS) library contains information compiled from real property records.

Keywords:	Real Estate, Property, Tax Assessor, Deed Transfers, Records
Audience:	Lawyers
Profile:	The ASSETS library contains a variety of real estate information, including asset ownership, property address, owner's mailing address, assessed valuation, current market value, and recent property sales and deed transfers. Information is collected from county tax assessors' and recorders' offices nationwide and compiled by TRW REDI Property Data. The ASSETS library also contains a variety of boat and aircraft registration information.
Contact:	Mead New Sales Group at (800) 227-4908 or (513) 859-5398 inside the US, or (513) 865-7981 for all inquiries outside the US.
User Info:	To subscribe, contact Mead directly. To examine the Nexis user guide, you can access it at the ftp site of the University of Texas at Austin at the URL address: ftp://ftp.cc.utexas.edu The files are in: /pub/ref-services/LEXIS

`telnet://nex.meaddata.com`

`http://www.meaddata.com`

Prospero

Prospero

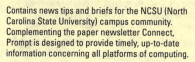

A guide to using Prospero, an Internet access tool that provides a user-centered view of remote files.

Keywords:	Internet Tools, Prospero
Audience:	Internet Surfers
Contact:	info-prospero@ISI.EDU
Details:	Free
Notes:	Files are in: pub/prospero/doc

`ftp://prospero.isi.edu`

PSI

PSI

PSI is an Internet service provider.

Keywords: Internet
Sponsor: PSI
Audience: Internet Users
Details: Costs

`telnet://psi.com`

Psychiatry

PsycINFO

PsycINFO is a leading research database providing bibliographic access to the international literature in psychology, as well as the related behavioral and social sciences.

Keywords: Psychology, Psychiatry, Behavior
Sponsor: American Psychological Association
Audience: Social workers, Psychologists, Psychiatrists, Librarians, Students
Contact: CDP Technologies Sales Department (800)950-2035, extension 400
User Info: To subscribe, contact CDP Technologies directly

`telnet://cdplus@cdplus.com`

Psychology

Cognitive and Psychological Sciences on the Internet

A resource containing links to academic programs, organizations and conference lists, journals and magazines, Usenet newsgroups, discussion lists, and other general information regarding cognitive science.

Keywords: Cognitive Science, Psychology, Neuroscience
Sponsor: The Stanford University Psychology Department
Audience: Cognitive Scientists, Neuroscientists, Psychologists, Psychiatrists
Contact: Scott Mainwaring sdm@psych.stanford.edu

`http://matia.stanford.edu/cogsci.html`

CVNet (Color and Vision Network)

The network provides a means of communications for scientists working in biological color and/or vision research. Members' e-mail addresses are maintained and sent to others in the network. CVNet distributes notices of jobs, meetings, and some other special announcements to all registrants. Members can post bulletins, announcements, and so on.

Keywords: Optics, Biological Research, Psychology
Sponsor: York University, North York, Ontario, Canada
Audience: Psychologists, Color/Vision Researchers
Contact: Peter K. Kaiser cvnet@vm1.yorkU.ca
Details: Free
User Info: To subscribe, send an e-mail message requesting a subscription to the URL address that follows.

`mailto:cvnet@vm1.yorkU.ca`

Laboratory Primate Newsletter

Provides a central source of information about nonhuman primates and related matters for scientists who use these animals in their research and for those whose work supports such research.

Keywords: Primatology, Psychology
Audience: Primate Researchers, Psychologists
Contact: Judith E. Schrier PRIMATE@BROWNVM.brown.edu
Details: Free

`mailto:listserv@brownvm.brown.edu`

PsycINFO

PsycINFO is a leading research database providing bibliographic access to the international literature in psychology, as well as the related behavioral and social sciences.

Keywords: Psychology, Psychiatry, Behavior
Sponsor: American Psychological Association
Audience: Social workers, Psychologists, Psychiatrists, Librarians, Students
Contact: CDP Technologies Sales Department (800) 950-2035, extension 400
User Info: To subscribe, contact CDP Technologies directly

`telnet://cdplus@cdplus.com`

The PSYCHGRAD Project and Psychology-Related Information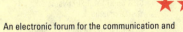

An electronic forum for the communication and dissemination of information among psychology graduate students.

Keywords: Psychology, Education (Post-Graduate)
Sponsor: University of Ottawa, Canada
Audience: Psychologists, Psychology Graduate Students
Profile: Designed to facilitate electronic communications and networking between psychology graduate students, this site contains archives of psychology listserv groups, and directories of psychology associations, along with related electronic journals and software. Also has links to other gopher and WWW sites related to psychology.
Contact: Matthew Simpson 054340@acadvm1.uottawa.ca 054340@uottawa.bitnet

`gopher://panda1.uottawa.ca`

University of Toledo Library

The library's holdings are large and wide-ranging and contain significant collections in many fields.

Keywords: Business, Great Lakes Area, Humanities, International Relations, Psychology, Science
Audience: Researchers, Students, General Public
Details: Free
User Info: Expect: Enter one of the following commands . . . , Send: DIAL MVS; Expect: dialed to mvs ####; Send: UTMOST

`telnet://uofto1.utoledo.edu`

Psychotherapy

alt.sexual.abuse.recovery

A Usenet newsgroup providing information and discussion about sexual abuse recovery and helping others deal with traumatic experiences.

Keywords: Sexual Abuse, Psychotherapy
Audience: Victims
User Info: To subscribe to this Usenet newsgroup, you need access to a newsreader.

`news:alt.sexual.abuse.recovery`

Public Access Archives

fsp-discussion

Discusses the new FSP protocol. FSP is a set of programs that implements a public-access archive similar to an anonymous-FTP archive.

Keywords: FSP Protocol, Public Access Archives
Audience: Computer Users
Details: Free
User Info: To subscribe to the list, send an e-mail message requesting a subscription to the URL address that follows.

To send a message to the entire list, address it to: fsp-discussion@germany.eu.net

`mailto:listmaster@germany.eu.net`

Public Domain Software

Center for Biomedical Informatics, Brazil

★

The Center for Biomedical Informatics maintains a software library with 50 disks containing about 150 public-domain medical application programs for IBM-PC-compatible microcomputers.

Keywords: Health Sciences, Public Domain Software
Sponsor: Center for Biomedical Informatics, Brazil
Audience: Physicians, Nurses, Dentists, University Biomedical Researchers, Students
Details: Costs
User Info: To receive the catalogue in electronic form, send the following one-line message to infomed@ccvax.unicamp.br or infomed@bruc.bitnet: get public-domain p (for version in Portuguese) get public-domain e (for version in English). Instructions on how to acquire the software are included.

`ftp://ccsun.unicamp.br`

Public Health

INFOMED

★

Provides yearly statistical information in the form of tables (in ASCII format) listing the principal indicators of health in Cuba.

Keywords: Cuba, Health Statistics, Public Health
Sponsor: Cuban Ministry of Health
Audience: Medical Professionals, Researchers, Public Health Professionals
Details: Free
User Info: To obtain a table from the yearbook, send an electronic message to the URL address that follows without a subject and with the following content in the body of the message:

GET ANUARIO <name of table>

Notes: Examples of tables are CMT-11: Death rates by age group; CMT-15: Infant mortality by province, and so on. For a listing of the available tables request the help file.

`mailto:listserv@infomed.cu`

Public Policy

AgeLine

The AgeLine database is produced by the American Association of Retired Persons (AARP) and provides bibliographic coverage of social gerontology—the study of aging in social, psychological, health-related, and economic contexts.

Keywords: Gerontology, Retired, Public Policy, Aging
Sponsor: American Association of Retired Persons, Washington, DC, USA
Audience: Retired Persons, Health Care Providers, Researchers
Profile: AgeLine covers the delivery of health care for the older population and its associated costs and policies, as well as public policy, employment, and consumer issues. Literature covered is of interest to researchers, health professionals, service planners, policy makers, employers, older adults and their families, and consumer advocates.

Coverage: 1978 to the present (selected coverage back to 1966); updated bimonthly.

Contact: Dialog in the US at (800) 334-2564; Dialog internationally at country-specific locations.
Details: Costs
User Info: There is no print equivalent of the database. To subscribe, contact Dialog directly.

`telnet://dialog.com`

EPPD-L

Engineering and Public Policy Discussion List.

Keywords: Engineering, Public Policy
Audience: Engineers
Contact: Ken Sollows
listserv@unb.ca
Details: Free
User Info: To subscribe to the list, send an e-mail message to the URL address shown that follows, consiting of a single line reading:

SUB eppd-l YourFirstName YourLastName

To send a message to the entire list, address it to: eppd-l@unb.ca

Mother Jones

A web site containing online electronic issues of Mother Jones magazine (and Zine), making possible instant electronic feedback to the publishers regarding articles.

Keywords: Zines, Ethics, Public Policy, Activism
Sponsor: Mother Jones
Audience: Students, General Public
Contact: Webserver
webserver@mojones.com

`http://www.mojones.com/motherjones.html`

Publications

Book Review Index

This database contains references to more than 2.5 million citations to reviews of approximately 1.5 million distinct book and periodical titles.

Keywords: Book Reviews, Periodicals, Publications
Sponsor: Gale Research, Inc., Detroit, MI, USA
Audience: Publishing Professionals, Authors
Profile: The database covers every review published since 1969 in nearly 500 periodicals and newspapers. Each record includes the author and title of the work being reviewed, journal name, date of review, and page number. Document type indications are also included if the work is a periodical; a reference work; a children's book, periodical, or reference book; or a young adult book, periodical, or reference book. Book Review Index corresponds to the print publication of the same name. Periodicals indexed range from the Harvard Business Review to the Center for Children's Books: Bulletin, and from the American Scholar to Psychology Today. General interest magazines such as Ms., Time, The New Yorker, and Atlantic are covered, as are specialized periodicals like Flying, Yachting, and National Genealogical Society Quarterly.

Contact: Dialog in the US at (800) 334-2564, Dialog internationally at country specific locations.
Details: Costs
User Info: To subscribe, contact Dialog directly.

`telnet://dialog.com`

Books In Print

This is the major source of information on books currently published and in-print in the United States.

Keywords: Books, Publications
Sponsor: R.R. Bowker, New York, NY, US
Audience: General Public, Writers, Researchers
Profile: The database provides the record of forthcoming books, books in-print, and books out-of-print. Scientific, technical, medical, scholarly, and popular works, as well as childrens books, are included in the file. The file corresponds to several print publications: Books in Print, Subject Guide to Books in Print, Books in Print Supplement, Paperbound Books in Print, Forthcoming Books, Law Books in Print, Subject Guide to Forthcoming Books, and Scientific and Technical

Books & Serials in Print. Records in Books In Print include basic bibliographic information (author, title, publisher, date), as well as L.C. card number, International Standard Book Number (ISBN), and price.

Contact: Dialog in the US at (800) 334-2564, Dialog internationally at country specific locations.

User Info: To subscribe, contact Dialog directly.

`telnet://dialog.com`

NAARS (National Automated Accounting Research System)

The National Automated Accounting Research System (NAARS) library, provided as a service by agreement with the American Institute of Certified Public Accountants (AICPA) contains a variety of accounting information.

Keywords: Accounting, Auditing, Filings, Publications

Audience: Accountants

Profile: The NAARS library contains annual reports of public corporations and accounting literature and publications for the accounting professional. Annual reports are annotated with descriptive terms assigned by the AICPA. These terms allow the user to search for annual report footnotes that illustrate one or more recognized accounting practices.

Contact: Mead New Sales Group at (800) 227-4908 or (513) 859-5398 inside the US, or (513) 865-7981 for all inquiries outside the US.

User Info: To subscribe, contact Mead directly.

To examine the Nexis user guide, you can access it at the ftp site of the University of Texas at Austin at the URL address: ftp://ftp.cc.utexas.edu

The files are in: /pub/ref-services/LEXIS

`telnet://nex.meaddata.com`

`http://www.meaddata.com`

Publications of the Office of Environment, Safety and Health

A collection of government safety information including updates, bulletins, and hazard alerts. Topics are diverse, covering everything from 'Employee Hit on Head by Falling Steel Wheel' to 'New Regulations to Control the Speed of Bloodborne Diseases.'

Keywords: Safety, Government (US), Federal Laws (US), Publications

Sponsor: U.S. Department of Energy

Audience: Government Officials, General Public

Details: Free

`gopher://dewey.tis.inel.gov`

Quanta

An electronically distributed science fiction magazine that is published monthly. Each issue contains short fiction, articles, and editorials by authors from around the world and across the Net.

Keywords: Science Fiction, Writing, Publications

Audience: Science Fiction Enthusiasts, Writers

Contact: da1n@andrew.cmu.edu

Details: Free

User Info: To subscribe to the list, send an e-mail message requesting a subscription to the URL address that follows.

To send a message to the entire list, address it to: da1n@andrew.cmu.edu

`mailto:da1n@andrew.cmu.edu`

Scholarly Publishing

Transcript of a paper entitled 'Model University Policy Regarding Faculty Publication in Scientific and Technical Scholarly Journals: A Background Paper and Review of the Issues.'

Keywords: Publications, Scholarly Communication

Sponsor: Triangle Research Libraries Network, Durham, Raleigh, and Chapel Hill, North Carolina

Audience: Educators, Publishers

Details: Free

File is: pub/docs/about-the-net/trln-copyright-paper

`ftp://sunsite.unc.edu`

Publishers

journet

An electronic conference for the discussion of topics of interest to journalists and journalism educators.

Keywords: Journalism, Writing, Desktop Publishing, Electronic Publishing

Audience: Journalists, Writers, Publishers, Educators

Contact: George Frajkor
gfrajkor@ccs.carleton.ca

User Info: To subscribe to the list, send an e-mail message to the URL address that follows, consisting of a single line reading:

SUB journet YourFirstName YourLastName

To send a message to the entire list, address it to: journet@qucdn.queensu.ca

`mailto:listserv@qucdn.queensu.ca`

Publishing

Electronic Newsstand Gopher

This gopher contains tables of contents, selected full-text articles, and assorted other information from many mainstream print journals.

Keywords: Journals, Electronic Publishing, Publishing, News

Audience: News Enthusiasts, Publishers, Publishing Professionals, Journalists

Profile: This gopher was compiled with the collaboration of the American Journal of International Law, Policy Review, Technology Review, Business Week, Current History, The Economist, Foreign Affairs, National Review, The New Yorker, The New Republic, Mother Jones, among other distinguished publications.

Contact: William Love
love@enews.com

`gopher://gopher.enews.com`

PIRA - Paper, Printing and Publishing, Packaging, and Nonwovens Abstracts

Coverage of all aspects of paper, pulp, nonwovens, printing, publishing, and packaging.

Keywords: Material Science, Paper, Printing, Publishing, Packaging

Sponsor: PIRA International

Audience: Materials Scientists, Researchers

Profile: File contains more than 300,000 records. Special applications: company and market profiles, product and trade name searches, research and technology trends. Updated biweekly.

Contact: paul.albert@neteast.com

User Info: To subscribe contact Orbit-Questel directly.

`telnet://orbit.com`

Princeton University Library

The library's holdings are large and wide-ranging. They contain significant collections in many fields.

Keywords: China, Japan, Classics, History (Ancient), Near Eastern Studies, Literature (American), Literature (English), Aeronautics, Middle Eastern Studies, Mormonism, Publishing

Audience: General Public, Researchers, Librarians, Document Delivery Professionals

Details: Free

Expect: Connect message, blank screen, Send: <cr>; Expect: #, Send: Call 500

`telnet://pucable.princeton.edu`

Publishing

This directory is a compilation of information resources focused on publishing.

Keywords:	Publishing, Books
Audience:	Publishing Professionals, Book Readers, Book Sellers
Details:	Free

`ftp://una.hh.lib.umich.edu/70/inetdirsstacks/publishing:robinson`

The MIT Press Online Catalogs

A descriptive listing of recent books and current journals published by the MIT Press.

Keywords:	Academia, Books, Publishing, Technology
Sponsor:	The MIT Press, Cambridge, Massachusetts, USA.
Audience:	Reseachers, Scholars, University Students, Technical Professionals
Profile:	Contains a keyword-searchable index of books published in the years 1993 to 1994, as well as current journals covering computational and cognitive sciences, architecture, photography, art and literary theory, economics, environmental science, and linguistics.
Contact:	ehling@mitpress.mit.edu
Notes:	Coverage: 1993 to present; updated semiannually. MIT Press can also be accessed by calling (800) 356-0343.

`http://www-mitpress.mit.edu`

`gopher://gopher.mit.edu`

WAIS, Inc.

WAIS, Inc. provides interactive on-line publishing systems and services to organizations whcih publish information over the Internet. The organization's three main goals are: to develop the Internet as a viable means for distributing information electronically; to improve the nature and quality of information available over networks; and to offer better methods to access that information.

Keywords:	WWW, Information Retrieval, Publishing, Internet Tools
Sponsor:	WAIS, Inc.
Audience:	Researchers, Students, General Public, Publishers
Contact:	Webmaster webmaster@wais.com

`http://server.wais.com`

Pubnet

Pubnet

A mailing list for the discussion of administration and use of public-access computer systems, primarily UNIX systems. The list also answers questions about setting up or running a public-access system.

Keywords:	Computer Systems, UNIX
Audience:	Computer System Designers, UNIX Users
Contact:	Chip Rosenthal pubnet-request@chinacat.unicom.com
Details:	Free
User Info:	To subscribe to the list, send an e-mail message requesting a subscription to the URL address that follows.
	To send a message to the entire list, address it to: pubnet@chinacat.unicom.com

`mailto:pubnet-request@chinacat.unicom.com`

Pubs-IAT (Institute for Academic Technology newsletter)

Pubs-IAT (Institute for Academic Technology newsletter)

This newsletter shares information on publications, programs, courses, and other activities of the Institute for Academic Technology.

Keywords:	Education (Adult), Education (Distance), Education (Continuing), Information Technology
Sponsor:	Institute for Academic Technology
Audience:	Educators, Administrators, Researchers
Details:	Free
User Info:	To subscribe to the list, send an e-mail message to the URL address that follows, consisting of a single line reading:
	SUB pubs-iat YourFirstName YourLastName
	To send a message to the entire list, address it to: pubs-iat@gibbs.oit.unc.edu

`mailto:listserv@gibbs.oit.unc.edu`

Purdue University Library

Purdue University Library

The library's holdings are large and wide-ranging. They contain significant collections in many fields.

Keywords:	Economics (History of), Literature (English), Literature (American), Indiana, Rogers (Bruce), Engineering (History of), Aviation, Earth Science, Atmospheric Science, Consumer Science, Family Science, Chemistry (History of), Physics, Veterinary Science
Audience:	General Public, Researchers, Librarians, Document Delivery Professionals
Contact:	Dan Ferrer dan@asterix.lib.purdue.edu
Details:	Free
Expect:	User ID prompt, Send: GUEST

`telnet://lib.cc.purdue.edu`

Purkinje Park

Purkinje Park

A server maintained by CalTech to support the sharing of information between users of the GENESIS neural simulator, and to address topics of general interest to the Computational Neuroscience community.

Keywords:	Computational Neuroscience, GENESIS, Neural Simulation.
Sponsor:	Cal Tech
Audience:	Neuroscientists, Computational Neuroscientists
Contact:	Dave Beeman dbeeman@smaug.bbb.caltech.edu

`http://www.bbb.caltech.edu/index.html`

Puzzles

rec.puzzles

A Usenet newsgroup providing information and discussion about math puzzles and brain teasers.

Keywords:	Games, Puzzles, Recreation
Audience:	General Public
User Info:	To subscribe to this Usenet newsgroup, you need access to a newsreader.

`news:rec.puzzles`

PVS (Project Vote Smart)

PVS (Project Vote Smart)

A gopher site containing Federal political information from PVS.

Keywords:	Politics, Government (US)
Sponsor:	Project Vote Smart, Corvallis, Oregon, USA
Audience:	Voters, General Public

Profile: PVS is a volunteer organization dedicated to providing voters with factual information about candidates for Federal office. Currently, the gopher offers background information, including detailed profiles and legislative analysis of Senators and Representatives for all 50 states.

Contact: pvs@neu.edu

Notes: For more information on Project Vote Smart, call their toll free hotline at 1-800-622-SMART. Or write to: Project Vote Smart, 129 NW Fourth St. #240, Corvallis, OR 97330

`gopher://gopher.neu.edu`

Python

Python

A mailing list for discussion of and questions about all aspects of the design and use of the Python programming language.

Keywords: Computer Programming Languages

Audience: Computer Programmers, Python Language Users

Contact: Guido van Rossum
python-list-request@cwi.nl

Details: Free

User Info: To subscribe to the list, send an e-mail message requesting a subscription to the URL address that follows.

To send a message to the entire list, address it to: python-list@cwi.nl

Notes: The source of the latest Python release is always available by anonymous FTP from ftp.cwi.nl, in directory /pub/python.

`mailto:python-list-request@cwi.nl`

Q

Qmlist (Quantitative Morphology List)

Qmlist (Quantitative Morphology List) ★

This is an open, unmoderated mailing list to support researchers and clinicians in the field of quantitative morphology.

Keywords:	Morphology
Audience:	Morphologists, Biologists
Contact:	Dean Pentcheff dean2@tbone.biol.scarolina.edu
Details:	Free
User Info:	To subscribe to the list, send an e-mail message to the URL address below, consisting of a single line reading: SUB qmlist YourFirstName YourLastName To send a message to the entire list, address it to: qmlist@tbone.biol.scarolina.edu

`mailto:listserv@tbone.biol.scarolina.edu`

Qn

Qn ★

A mailing list for Queer Nation activists and for anyone interested in Queer Nation, an activist group devoted to furthering gay rights. The purpose of QN is to network among various Queer Nation chapters, to discuss actions and tactics to bring about Queer Liberation.

Keywords:	Homosexuality, Gay Rights, Activism
Audience:	Gay Rights Activists, Political Activists
Contact:	Roger Klorese qn-request@queernet.org
Details:	Free
User Info:	To subscribe to the list, send an e-mail message requesting a subscription to the URL address below. To send a message to the entire list, address it to: qn@queernet.org

`mailto:qn-request@queernet.org`

Qnx2

Qnx2 ★

Discussion of all aspects of the QNX real-time operating systems. Topics include compatible hardware, available third-party software, software reviews, available public domain or free software, QNX platform-specific programming discussions, and QNX and FLEET networking.

Keywords:	Computing, Hardware, Software
Audience:	Computer Users, Hardware/Software Designers, Product Analysts
Contact:	Martin Zimmerman camz@dlogtech.cuc.ab.ca
Details:	Free
User Info:	To subscribe to the list, send an e-mail message requesting a subscription to the URL address below. To send a message to the entire list, address it to: qnx2@dlogtech.cuc.ab.ca

`mailto:qnx2@dlogtech.cuc.ab.ca`

Qnx4

Qnx4 ★

A mailing list for discussion of all aspects of the QNX real-time operating systems. Topics include compatible hardware, available third-party software, software reviews, available PD/free software, QNX and FLEET networking, process control, and so on.

Keywords:	Computing, Hardware, Software, Networking
Audience:	Computer Users, Hardware/Software Designers, Product Analysts
Contact:	Martin Zimmerman camz@dlogtech.cuc.ab.ca
Details:	Free
User Info:	To subscribe to the list, send an e-mail message requesting a subscription to the URL address below. To send a message to the entire list, address it to: qnx4@dlogtech.cuc.ab.ca

`mailto:qnx4@dlogtech.cuc.ab.ca`

Quakerism

Quaker FTP Archive at ClarkNet ★★

This archive contains extensive writings concerning contemporary Quaker life.

Keywords:	Quakerism, Religion
Sponsor:	Clark Internet Services
Audience:	Quakers
Contact:	George Amoss daruma@clark.net

`ftp://ftp.clark.net/pub/quaker`

`ftp://ftp.univie.ac.at/archive/faq/Quaker-faq`

Harvard University Library ★★

The library's holdings are large and wide-ranging and contain significant collections in many fields.

Keywords:	Afrikaans, Alchemy, Arabic Culture (History of), Celtic Philology, Congo Languages, Folklore, Hebraica, Mormonism, Numismatics, Quakerism, Sanskrit, Witchcraft, Arabic Philology

A B C D E F G H I J K L M N O P **Q** R S T U V W X Y Z

Audience: General Public, Researchers, Librarians, Document Delivery Professionals
Details: Free
User Info: Expect: Mitek Server..., Send: Enter or Return; Expect: prompt, Send: hollis

`telnet://hollis.harvard.edu`

Quality Control

Total Quality Management Gopher

A collection of materials relating to the elimination of defects through comprehensive quality control in industry, government, and universities.

Keywords: Quality Control, Management, Business
Sponsor: The Clemson University Department of Industrial Engineering, Clemson, South Carolina, USA
Audience: Managers, Administrators
Contact: quality@eng.clemson.edu

`gopher://deming.eng.clemson.edu`

`http://deming.eng.clemson.edu`

Quanta

Quanta

An electronically distributed science fiction magazine that is published monthly. Each issue contains short fiction, articles, and editorials by authors from around the world and across the Net.

Keywords: Science Fiction, Writing, Publications
Audience: Science Fiction Enthusiasts, Writers
Contact: da1n@andrew.cmu.edu
Details: Free
User Info: To subscribe to the list, send an e-mail message requesting a subscription to the URL address below. To send a message to the entire list, address it to: da1n@andrew.cmu.edu

`mailto:da1n@andrew.cmu.edu`

Quantum Chemistry

Theoretical Journal Abstract And Bibliographic Files

Abstract and bibliographic information for several theoretical chemistry journals. Coverage includes: Theoretical Chemistry, Quantum Chemistry, Quantum Mechanics, Computational Chemistry.

Keywords: Theoretical Chemistry, Quantum Chemistry, Computational Chemistry.

Sponsor: Online, Inc., Weston, CT, US
Audience: Chemists, Librarians, Students (College/Graduate)
Profile: Provided are directory, product, technical, and bibliographic information on leading software packages, integrating this information into one succinct composite record. The database can help professionals locate suitable packages compatible with specified hardware without sifting through large numbers of records.
Contact: Dialog in the US at (800) 334-2564, Dialog internationally at country-specific locations.
Details: Free
User Info: To subscribe, contact Dialog directly.

`telnet://dialog.com`

Quantum Physics

Quantum Physics/High Energy Physics

A resource containing extensive links to international academic and research institutions specializing in high energy physics and to related to journals, abstracts, and conference information.

Keywords: Physics, Quantum Physics, Research
Sponsor: Swiss Academic and Research Network, Switzerland
Audience: Students, Physicists, Researchers
Contact: Ingrid Graf
rikv8@cernvm.cern.ch

`http://www.cern.ch/Physics/HEP.html`

The University of Minnesota Library System (LUMINA)

The library's holdings are large and wide-ranging and contain significant collections in many fields.

Keywords: Immigration (History of), Ethnic Studies, Horticulture, Equine Research, Botanical Taxonomy, Quantum Physics, Native American Studies, Holmes (Sherlock)
Audience: General Public, Researchers, Librarians, Document Delivery Professionals
Contact: Craig D. Rice
cdr@acc.stolaf.edu
Details: Free

`telnet://lumina.lib.umn.edu`

Quarks

Quark Background Material

Background material describing the nature of and current research into quarks and other elementary particles.

Keywords: Quarks, Physics
Sponsor: Fermi National Accelerator Laboratory
Audience: Physicists, Students, Researchers
Contact: webmaster@fnal.gov
Details: Free

`http://fnnews.fnal.gov/top_background.html`

Quattro

Quattro

A mailing list for discussions pertaining to Audi automobiles, especially the AWD (all wheel drive) Quattro models. It also includes news, opinions, maintenance procedures, and parts sources.

Keywords: Automobiles
Audience: Automobile Enthusiasts
Contact: David Tahajian
quattro-request@aries.east.sun.com
Details: Free
User Info: To subscribe to the list, send an e-mail message requesting a subscription to the URL address below.
To send a message to the entire list, address it to:
quattro@aries.east.sun.com

`mailto:quattro-request@aries.east.sun.com`

Quebec

Rezo, bulletin irregulomadaire du RQSS

E-newsletter of RQSS (Regroupement Quebecois des Sciences Sociales), open to anyone interested in social science research in Quebec and/or about Quebec.

Keywords: Quebec, Social Science
Audience: Social Scientists
Contact: Pierre J. Hamel
HAMEL@INRS-URB.UQUEBEC.CA

Details: Free

User Info: To subscribe, send an e-mail message to the URL address below, consisting of a single line reading:

SUB rezo YourFirstName YourLastName

To send a message to the entire list, address it to: rezo@uquebec.ca

`mailto:listserv@uquebec.ca`

Quebec Nordiques

Quebec Nordiques

A mailing list to discuss topics concerning the National Hockey League's Quebec Nordiques.

Keywords: Hockey, Sports

Audience: Hockey Enthusiasts

Contact: Danny J. Sohier
nords-request@badaboum.ulaval.ca

Details: Free

User Info: To subscribe to the list, send an e-mail message requesting a subscription to the URL address below.

To send a message to the entire list, address it to: nords@badaboum.ulaval.ca

`mailto:nords@badaboum.ulaval.ca`

Queen

Queen

A mailing list to discuss the rock group Queen.

Keywords: Music, Rock Music

Audience: Queen Fans, Music Fans, Musicians

Contact: Dan Blanchard
qms-request@uiuc.edu

Details: Free

User Info: To subscribe to the list, send an e-mail message requesting a subscription to the URL address below.

To send a message to the entire list, address it to: qms@uiuc.edu

`mailto:qms-request@uiuc.edu`

Questions and Answers about the GPO Gateway to Government Act

Questions and Answers about the GPO Gateway to Government Act

Questions and answers dealing with the bill GPO Gateway to Government Act of 1992. Questions such as, "What will the gateway do?," "Why is this gateway needed?," "What types of information will be available through the Gateway?," and more.

Keywords: Laws (US Federal), Government (US Federal), Federal Databases

Audience: General Public, Journalists, Politicians

Details: Free

File is: /pub/nic/NREN/GPO.questions

`ftp://ftp.sura.net`

Quotations

Quotations

A mailing list for the sharing of quotations.

Keywords: Quotations

Audience: General Public

Contact: Jason R. Newquist
jrnewquist@ucdavis.ucdavis.edu

User Info: To subscribe, send an e-mail message to: listproc@ucdavis.edu. Leave the subject blank and place in the body of the note: subscribe quotations YourFirstName YourLastName

`mailto:quotations@ucdavis.edu`

Quotecom Home Page

Quotecom Home Page

QuoteCom is a service dedicated to providing financial market data to Intenet users.

Keywords: Investments, Securities, Finance

Audience: Investors

Producer: QuoteCom, Inc.

Contact: Chris Cooper
Email:chris@quote.com
staff@quote.com
support@quote.com

Profile: This site offers many financial services for a fee. You can register for their free service, which allows you to get up to five quotes per day. Other services available after subscribing include bar charts on historical data, S&P's Stock Guide database, S&P's MarketScope Alerts, Hoover company profiles, historical data, Canadian market data, European market data, and more.

User Info: No services are available without registering. Free services are limited to five quotes per day. Basic service costs $9.95 per month.

Notes: Most of QuoteCom's data is proprietary, and is protected by copyrights of the various providers.

`http://www.quote.com`

R

Race

African Education Research Network ★★

Various links to African studies programs at select universities, and other archived information of interest to the African studies scholar.

Keywords: Culture, Race, Africa, African Studies
Sponsor: Ohio University, African Education Research Network
Audience: Students, African-Americans, Africans
Contact: Milton E. Ploghoft
mperdreau@ohiou.edu
Details: Free

gopher://gopher.ohiou.edu/00/dept.servers/aern

Black/African Related Online Information ★★★★

This is a list of online information storage sites that contain a significant amount of information pertaining to Black or African people, culture, and issues around the world.

Keywords: Culture, Race, Africa, African Studies
Sponsor: AfriInfo
Audience: Students, African-Americans, Africans
Contact: McGee
mcgee@epsilon.eecs.nwu.edu
Details: Free

ftp://ftp.netcom.com/pub/amcgee/my_african_related_lists/afrisite.msg

Chicano/LatinoNet ★★★

An electronic mechanism which brings together Chicano/Latino research, as well as linguistic minority and educational research efforts being carried out at the University of California and elsewhere. It serves as a gateway between faculty, staff, and students who are engaged in research and curricular efforts in these areas.

Keywords: Culture, Race, Chicano Culture, Latino Culture
Sponsor: Chicano Studies Research Center, University of California at Los Angeles
Audience: Students, Mexican-Americans, Latinos
Contact: Richard Chabran
Chabran@latino.sscnet.ucla.ed
Details: Free

gopher://latino.sscnet.ucla.edu

Japanese Information ★★★★

This web site contains extensive information on the geography, culture, law, and tourism of Japan. Includes archived Japanese newsgroup information and FAQs.

Keywords: Culture, Race, Japan, Japanese Culture
Sponsor: Nippon Telegraph and Telephone
Audience: Students, Tourists, Japanese, Japanese-Americans
Contact: Webmaster
www-admin@seraph.ntt.jp
Details: Free

http://www.ntt.jp/japan/index.html

Mexican Culture FAQ ★★★

This is the FAQ from the soc.culture.mexican newsgroup. Provides information on Mexican culture, history, society, language, and tourism.

Keywords: Culture, Race, Chicano Culture, Latino Culture
Sponsor: News Group Moderators for soc.culture.mexican
Audience: Students, Latinos, Chicanos
Contact: News Group Moderator
mendoza-grado@att.com
Details: Free

ftp://ftp.mty.itesm.ms/pub/mexico/faqs

http://www.cis.ohio-state.edu/hypertext/faq/usenet/mexican-faq/faq.html

POS302-L ★

A discussion list created for the "Race, Ethnicity, and Social Inequality" seminar offered at Illinois State University (spring 1994). The general purposes of the list are to create an e-mail audience for the written work of enrolled students and to invite a broad audience to participate in the seminar.

Keywords: Race, Ethnicity, Minorities
Audience: Ethnic Studies Students, Sociologists, Educators
Details: Free
User Info: To subscribe to the list, send an e-mail message to the URL address below, consisting of a single line reading:

SUB pos302-l YourFirstName YourLastName

To send a message to the entire list, address it to: pos302-l@ilstu.edu

mailto:listserv@ilstu.edu

Radio

AM/FM

A mailing list for the AM/FM Online Edition, a monthly compilation of news stories concerning the UK radio industry.

Keywords: Radio, United Kingdom, Communications

Audience: Radio Enthusiasts (UK), Communications Specialists, Students (college, graduate)

Contact: Stephen Hebditch
listserv@orbital.demon.co.uk

User Info: To subscribe to the list, send an e-mail message to the URL addres below, consisting of a single line reading:
SUB am/fm YourFirstName YourLastName
To send a message to the entire list, address it to: AM/FM@orbital.demon.co.uk

`mailto:listserv@orbital.demon.co.uk`

FM-10 ★

A discussion of modifications, enhancements, and uses of the Ramsey FM-10 and other BA-1404 based FM Stereo broadcasters; some discussion of the FM pirate radio, as well.

Keywords: Radio, Broadcasting

Audience: Broadcasters, Radio Broadcasters

Details: Free

User Info: To subscribe to the list, send an e-mail message requesting a subscription to the URL address below. To send a message to the entire list, address it to: fm-10@dg-rtp.dg.com

`mailto:fm-10-request@dg-rtp.dg.com`

National Broadcasting Society— Alpha Epsilon Rho ★

Forum for mass media professionals to share experiences and ideas.

Keywords: Film, Television, Radio, Mass Media

Sponsor: National Broadcasting Society-Alpha Epsilon Rho

Audience: Journalists, Students, Educators, Broadcasting Professionals

Contact: Reg Gamar
regbc@cunyvm.bitnet

Details: Free

User Info: To subscribe to the list, send an e-mail message to the address shown below consisting of a single line reading:
SUB NBS-AER YourFirstName YourLastName
To send a message to the entire list, address it to: nbs-aer@cunyvm.bitnet

`mailto:listserv@cunyvm.bitnet`

Online Radio ★★

Transcripts and promotional information from Online Radio, a weekly radio program of Perth's Curtin University devoted to reporting the latest developments in the computing world.

Keywords: Computers, Internet, Radio

Sponsor: Curtin University Computing Center, Perth, Australia

Audience: Computer Enthusiasts

Contact: Onno Benschop
online@info.curtin.edu.au

`gopher://ob1.curtin.edu.au`

PRL

The Pirate Radio SWL list is for the distribution of questions, answers, information, and loggings of Pirate Radio Stations.

Keywords: Radio, Communications

Audience: Radio Listeners, Radio Pirates

Contact: John Brewer
brewer@ace.enet.dec.com

User Info: To subscribe to the list, send an e-mail message to the URL address below, consisting of a single line reading:
SUB PRL YourFirstName YourLastName.
To send a message to the entire list, address it to: brewer@ace.enet.dec.com

`mailto:listserv@ace.enet.dec.com`

rec.radio.amateur.misc 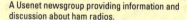★

A Usenet newsgroup providing information and discussion about ham radios.

Keywords: Radio, Electronics

Audience: Ham Radio Operators

User Info: To subscribe to this Usenet newsgroup, you need access to a newsreader.

`news:rec.radio.amateur.misc`

rec.radio.shortwave ★

A Usenet newsgroup providing information and discussion about shortwave radio.

Keywords: Radio, Electronics

Audience: Shortwave Radio Users

User Info: To subscribe to this Usenet newsgroup, you need access to a newsreader.

`news:rec.radio.shortwave`

Voice of America and Worldnet ★★★

A gopher server for the Voice of America and Worldnet. Includes full-text transcripts of VOA news reports, press releases, and announcements.

Keywords: US Government Publications, News Media, Radio, International Communication

Sponsor: United States Information Agency

Audience: Journalists, Government Officials, General Public

Contact: info@voa.gov, letters-usa@VOA.GOV (for correspondence from inside the U.S.)

`gopher://gopher.voa.gov`

Railroads

Dartmouth College Library ★★

The library's holdings are large and wide-ranging and contain significant collections in many fields.

Keywords: American Calligraphy, Cervantes (Miguel de), Railroads, Polar Regions, Frost (Robert), Shakespeare (William), Spanish Plays

Audience: General Public, Researchers, Librarians, Document Delivery Professionals

Contact: Katharina Klemperer
kathy.klemperer@dartmouth.edu

Details: Free
Expect: login, Send: wolfpac

`telnet://lib.dartmouth.edu`

rec.railroad ★

A Usenet newsgroup providing information and discussion about railroads.

Keywords: Railroads, Transportation

Audience: Railroad Enthusiast

User Info: To subscribe to this Usenet newsgroup, you need access to a newsreader.

`news:rec.railroad`

The University of Iowa Libraries ★★

The library's holdings are large and wide-ranging and contain significant collections in many fields.

Keywords: Hunt (Leigh), Native American Studies, Typography, Railroads, Cartoons, French Revolution, NASA, Hydraulics

Audience: General Public, Researchers, Librarians, Document Delivery Professionals

Details: Free
Send <RETURN> to display a menu of available systems. Type 1 for OASIS access and press <RETURN> to display the Welcome to OASIS screen.

`telnet://oasis.uiowa.edu`

TRANS (The Transportation Library)

The Transportation Library contains federal transportation case law, statutes and agency decisions.

Keywords: Transportation Law, US Government Regulations, Aviation Industry, Railroads, Trucking Industry

Audience: Lawyers

Profile: The Transportation Library contains federal transportation case law, statutes and agency decisions. The major emphasis of the library is on three modes of transportation (aviation, railroad and trucking) and how those modes are regulated by the federal government. Agency decisions are provided from the Interstate Commerce Commission, Department of Transportation and the National Transportation Safety Board (NTSB).

Contact: New Sales Group at 800-227-4908 or 513-859-5398 inside the US, or 1-513-865-7981 for all inquires outside the US.

User Info: To subscribe, contact Mead directly.

To examine the Lexis user guide, you can access it at the ftp site of the University of Texas at Austin at the URL address: ftp://ftp.cc.utexas.edu

The files are in: /pub/res-services/LEXIS

`telnet://nex.meaddata.com`

Railway History

Indiana University Libraries

The library's holdings are large and wide-ranging and contain significant collections in many fields.

Keywords: Literature (English), Literature (American), 1640-Present, British Plays (19th-C.), Western Americana, Railway History, Aristotle (Texts of), Lafayette (Marquis de), Handel (G.F.), Austrian History, Antiquarian Books, Rare Books, French Opera (19th-C.), Drama (British) ,

Audience: General Public, Researchers, Librarians, Document Delivery Professionals

Details: Free

Expect: User ID prompt, Send: GUEST

`telnet://iuis.ucs.indiana.edu`

Rap Music

The Beastie Boys' Web Page

This web site features video, audio, magazine articles, lyrics, a discography, and other assorted information relating to the Beastie Boys.

Keywords: Musical Groups, Rap Music

Audience: Beastie Boys Fans

Contact: irogers@ezmail.ucs.indiana.edu

`http://www.nando.net/music/gm`

RAPRA Abstracts

RAPRA Abstracts

Coverage on technical and commercial aspects of the rubber, plastics, and polymer composites industries.

Keywords: Material Science, Rubbers, Plastics, Polymers

Sponsor: Rapra Technology, Ltd.

Audience: Material Scientists, Researchers

Profile: This unique source of information covers the world's polymer literature including journals, conference proceedings, books, specifications, reports and trade literature. Contains over 375,000 records. Updated biweekly.

Contact: paul.albert@neteast.com
To subscribe contact Orbit-Questel directly.

`telnet://orbit.com`

Rare Books

Indiana University Libraries

The library's holdings are large and wide-ranging and contain significant collections in many fields.

Keywords: Literature (English), Literature (American), 1640-Present, British Plays (19th-C.), Western Americana, Railway History, Aristotle (Texts of), Lafayette (Marquis de), Handel (G.F.), Austrian History, Antiquarian Books, Rare Books, French Opera (19th-C.), Drama (British) ,

Audience: General Public, Researchers, Librarians, Document Delivery Professionals

Details: Free

Expect: User ID prompt, Send: GUEST

`telnet://iuis.ucs.indiana.edu`

The National Library of Medicine (NLM) Online Catalog System

Catalog of library holdings.

Keywords: Medicine, Health Sciences, Biomedicine, Rare Books

Sponsor: National Library of Medicine

Audience: Health Professionals, Medical Educators, Students

Profile: The National Library of Medicine (NLM) is the world's largest biomedical library with a collection of over 4.9 million items. NLM is a national resource for all US health sciences libraries and fills over a quarter of a million interlibrary loan requests each year for these libraries. The library is open to the public, but its collection is designed primarily for health professionals. The library collects materials comprehensively in all major areas of the health sciences. Housed within the library is one of the world's finest medical history collections of pre-1914 and rare medical texts, manuscripts, and incunabula.

Contact: ref@nlm.nih.gov

Details: Free

The NLM can be accessed also through the WWW at http://www.nlm.nih.gov

`telnet://locator@locator.nlm.nih.gov`

University of North Carolina at Chapel Hill Info Library

The library's holdings are large and wide-ranging and contain significant collections in many fields.

Keywords: North Carolina; Southern Historical Collection, Rare Books

Audience: Researchers, Students, General Public

Contact: Judy Hallman
hallman@unc.bitnet

Details: Free

Expect: Login; Send: Info

`telnet://info.oit.unc.edu`

Rascal Aviation Archives

Rascal Aviation Archives

A major directory on aeronautics, providing access to a broad range of related resources (library catalogues, databases, and servers) via the Internet.

Keywords: Aeronautics, Aviation

Audience: Aviators, Aeronautical Engineers

Contact: rdd@rascal.ics.utexas.edu

`ftp://rascal.ics.utexas.edu/ explore-me/Aviation-stuff`

Raves

AusRave (Australian Raves)

A regional rave-related mailing list covering the Australian continent. AusRave contains both discussions and informational postings.

Keywords: Music, Raves, Australia

Audience:	Ravers (Australian)
Contact:	Simon Rumble ausrave@lsupoz.apana.org.au
Details:	Free, Moderated
User Info:	To subscribe to the list, send an e-mail message requesting a subscription to the URL address below. To send a message to the entire list, address it to: ausrave@lsupoz.apana.org.au
Notes:	The mailing list Best of AusRave provides information only

Postings to AusRave are not archived, but the list does have an FTP site at: elecsun4.elec.uow.edu.au

`mailto:ausrave-request@lsupoz.apana.org.au`

Best-of-AusRave (Australian Raves)

A regional rave-related mailing list covering the Australian continent, for people who want Australian rave information without the side discussions and social chatter from the regular list.

Keywords:	Music, Raves, Australia
Audience:	Ravers (Australian)
Contact:	Simon Rumble best-of-ausrave-request@lsupoz.apana.org.au
Details:	Free, Moderated
User Info:	To subscribe to the list, send an e-mail message to the URL address below, consisting of a single line reading: SUB ausrave YourFirstName YourLastName To send a message to the entire list, address it to: best-of-ausrave@lsupoz.apana.org.au

`mailto:best-of-ausrave-request@lsupoz.apana.org.au`

DCRaves

One of several regional rave-related mailing lists, DCRaves covers the Washington, DC, area exclusively. Archives are available through the listserv, FTP, or gopher at american.edu.

Keywords:	Raves, Washington DC
Audience:	Rave Enthusiasts
Details:	Free
User Info:	To subscribe to the list, send an e-mail message to the URL address shown below consisting of a single line reading: SUB dcraves YourFirstName YourLastName To send a message to the entire list, address it to: dcraves@american.edu

`mailto:listserv@american.edu`

FL-Raves (Florida Raves)

One of several regional rave-related mailing lists, this covers the state of Florida. Discussions tend to be social; Floridians may want to check out SERaves as well.

Keywords:	Raves
Audience:	Ravers, Florida Residents
Contact:	Steve Smith
Details:	Free
User Info:	To subscribe to the list, send an e-mail message requesting a subscription to the URL address below. To send a message to the entire list, address it to: flraves@cybernet.cse.fau.edu

`mailto:flraves-request@cybernet.cse.fau.edu`

mw-raves

One of several rave-related lists, MW-Raves (Midwest Raves) covers the Midwestern US. Postings are usually informational, but discussions of scene-related issues can also be expected.

Keywords:	Raves, Music
Audience:	Ravers
Contact:	Andy Crosby mw-raves-request@engin.umich.edu
Details:	Free
User Info:	To subscribe to the list, send an e-mail message to the URL address below consisting of a single line reading: SUB mw-raves YourFirstName YourLastName To send a message to the entire list, address it to: mw-raves@csd.uwm.edu

`mailto:mw-raves@csd.uwm.edu`

NERaves (Northeast Raves)

One of several regional rave-related mailing lists, NE-Raves covers the Northeastern US.

Keywords:	Raves
Audience:	Ravers
Details:	Free
User Info:	To subscribe to the list, send an e-mail message to the URLaddress below consisting of a single line reading: SUB neraves YourFirstName YourLastName To send a message to the entire list, address it to: neraves@umdd.umd.edu

`mailto:listserv@umdd.umd.edu`

NW-Raves (Northwest Raves)

One of several regional rave-related mailing lists, NW-Raves covers the northwestern US and western Canada. No archives are available.

Keywords:	Raves
Audience:	Ravers
Contact:	Pat Lui nw-raves-request@wimsey.bc.ca
Details:	Free
User Info:	To subscribe to the list, send an e-mail message requesting a subscription to the URL address below. To send a message to the entire list, address it to: nw-raves@wimsey.bc.ca

`mailto:nw-raves-request@wimsey.bc.ca`

PB-Cle-Raves

One of several regional rave-related mailing lists, PB-Cle-Raves covers the Pittsburgh, PA, and Cleveland, OH, metropolitan areas exclusively.

Keywords:	Raves
Audience:	Ravers
Contact:	Joe LeSesne pb-cle-raves-request@telerama.lm.com
Details:	Free
User Info:	To subscribe to the list, send an e-mail message requesting a subscription to the URL address below. To send a message to the entire list, address it to: pb-cle-raves@telerama.lm.com

`mailto:pb-cle-raves-request@telerama.lm.com`

REACH (Research and Educational Applications of Computers in the Humanities)

REACH (Research and Educational Applications of Computers in the Humanities)

Newsletter of the Humanities Computing Facility of the University of California, Santa Barbara. Contains material of general interest to computing humanists, including announcements of new listservers, projects, and conferences.

Keywords:	Computing
Audience:	Computer Users
Contact:	Eric Dahlin hcf1dahl@ucsbvm.bitnet
Details:	Free
User Info:	listserv@ucsbvm.bitnet reach@ucsbvm.bitnet

`mailto:listserv@ucsbvm.bitnet`

Real Estate

ASSETS (Real Estate Tax Assessor and Deed Transfer Records)

The RealEstate Tax Assessor and Deed Transfer Records (ASSETS) library contains information compiled from real property records.

Keywords:	Real Estate, Property, Tax Assessor, Deed Transfers, Records
Audience:	Lawyers
Profile:	The ASSETS library contains a variety of real estate information, including asset ownership, property address, owner's mailing address, assessed valuation, current market value, and recent property sales and deed transfers. Information is collected from county tax assessors' and recorders' offices nationwide and compiled by TRW REDI Property Data. The ASSETS library also contains a variety of boat and aircraft registration information.
Contact:	Mead New Sales Group at (800) 227-4908 or (513) 859-5398 inside the US, or (513) 865-7981 for all inquiries outside the US.
User Info:	To subscribe, contact Mead directly. To examine the Nexis user guide, you can access it at the ftp site of the University of Texas at Austin at the URL address: ftp://ftp.cc.utexas.edu
	The files are in: /pub/ref-services/LEXIS

`telnet://nex.meaddata.com`

`http://www.meaddata.com`

Commercial Real Estate

Users can send and receive listings on property for sale, ask and answer questions, send press releases, receive editorial material, and do networking on commercial property.

Keywords:	Real Estate
Audience:	Real Estate Brokers, General Public
Contact:	commercial.realestate@data-base.com
Details:	Free
User Info:	To subscribe to the list, send an e-mail message requesting a subscription to the URL address below.

`mailto:commercial.realestate@data-base.com`

Institutional Real Estate Newsline

Five-page fax briefing with articles regarding institutional real estate, life insurance company, banks, pension fund, real estate investment trust and commercial mortgage backed securities markets.

Keywords:	Real Estate, Investments, Insurance
Sponsor:	Institutional Real Estate
Audience:	Investors
Details:	Costs

misc.invest.real-estate

A Usenet newsgroup providing information and discussion about property investments.

Keywords:	Investments, Real Estate
Audience:	General Public
Details:	Free
User Info:	To subscribe to this Usenet newsgroup, you need access to a newsreader.

`news:misc.invest.real-estate`

REBASE (Restriction Enzyme Database)

REBASE (Restriction Enzyme Database)

The Restriction Enzyme Database contains both data and literature citations. It can be searched for enzyme names, species, authors, journals, and recognition sequences.

Keywords:	Physiology, Enzymes
Sponsor:	New England Biolabs
Audience:	Scientists, Molecular Biologists
Contact:	Richard Roberts roberts@cshl.org
Details:	Free

`gopher://gopher.gdb.org/77/.INDEX/rebase`

rec.aquaria

rec.aquaria

A Usenet newsgroup providing information and discussion about pet fish and aquaria.

Keywords:	Fish, Aquatic Sciences
Audience:	Fish Enthusiasts
Details:	Free
User Info:	To subscribe to this Usenet newsgroup, you need access to a newsreader.

`news:rec.aquaria`

rec.arts.anime

rec.arts.anime

A Usenet newsgroup providing information and discussion about Japanese animation fen.

Keywords:	Animation, Fen, Japan
Audience:	Animators
Details:	Free
User Info:	To subscribe to this Usenet newsgroup, you need access to a newsreader.

`news:rec.arts.anime`

rec.arts.books

rec.arts.books

A Usenet newsgroup providing information and discussion about a wide variety of books.

Keywords:	Books
Audience:	Readers, Writers
Details:	Free
User Info:	To subscribe to this Usenet newsgroup, you need access to a newsreader.

`news:rec.arts.books`

rec.arts.comics.misc

rec.arts.comics.misc

A Usenet newsgroup providing information and discussion about comic books and graphic novels.

Keywords:	Comic Books, Books
Audience:	Comics Enthusiasts, Readers, Writers
Details:	Free
User Info:	To subscribe to this Usenet newsgroup, you need access to a newsreader.

`news:rec.arts.comics.misc`

rec.arts.dance

rec.arts.dance

A Usenet newsgroup providing information and discussion about all types of dance.

Keywords:	Dance, Fine Arts
Audience:	Dancers, Dance Enthusiasts, Choreographers
User Info:	To subscribe to this Usenet newsgroup, you need access to a newsreader.

`news:rec.arts.dance`

rec.arts.disney

rec.arts.disney

A Usenet newsgroup providing information and discussion about Disney and related topics.

Keywords: Disney
Audience: Disney Enthusiasts
Details: Free
User Info: To subscribe to this Usenet newsgroup, you need access to a newsreader.

`news:rec.arts.disney`

rec.arts.fin

rec.arts.fin

A Usenet newsgroup providing information and discussion about the visual arts. Discussions range from archival materials to Ansel Adams, Mary Cassat and Andy Warhol.

Keywords: Art, Fine Art
Audience: Artists, Art Educators, Art Professionals
User Info: To subscribe to this Usenet newsgroup, you need access to a newsreader.

`news:rec.arts.fin`

Rec.arts.int-fiction

Rec.arts.int-fiction

A USENET newsgroup about interactive literature and interactive computer games.

Keywords: Literature (General), Interactive Media, Computer Games
Audience: General Public, Computer Games Players
Details: Free
To participate in a USENET newsgroup, you need access to a 'newsreader'.

`news:rec.arts.int-fiction`

rec.arts.movies

rec.arts.movies

A Usenet newsgroup providing information and discussion about films and film making.

Keywords: Film
Audience: Film Enthusiasts, Filmmakers
Details: Free
User Info: To subscribe to this Usenet newsgroup, you need access to a newsreader.

`news:rec.arts.movies`

rec.arts.movies movie database

rec.arts.movies movie database

An extensive FTP database covering over 32,000 movies, with more than 370,000 filmography entries, from early cinema to current releases.

Keywords: Movies, Television, Popular Culture
Audience: Film Enthusiasts
Profile: Interfaces to search the database include Unix, MS-DOS and Amiga (and Windows and Mac versions are in development). The database includes filmographies for actors, directors, writers, composers, cinematographers, editors, production designers, costume designers and producers; plot summaries; character names; movie ratings; year of release; running times; movie trivia; quotes; goofs; soundtracks; personal trivia and Academy Award information.
Contact: Col Needham
cn@ibmpcug.co.uk
Details: Free

`ftp://cathouse.org/pub/cathouse/movies/database`

rec.arts.movies movie database (Cardiff WWW front-end)

rec.arts.movies movie database (Cardiff WWW front-end)

An extensive, interactive database covering over 32,000 movies, with more than 370,000 filmography entries, from early cinema to current releases.

Keywords: Movies, Television, Popular Culture, Interactive Media
Audience: Film Enthusiasts
Profile: A WWW front-end to the rec.arts.movies movie database, complete with form-filling interfaces to add new data and to rate movies (on a scale from 1 through 10). The database includes filmographies for actors, directors, writers, composers, cinematographers, editors, production designers, costume designers and producers; plot summaries; character names; movie ratings; year of release; running times; movie trivia; quotes; goofs; soundtracks; personal trivia and Academy Award information.
Contact: Rob Hartill
Robert.Hartill@cm.cf.ac.uk
Details: Free

`http://www.cm.cf.ac.uk/Movies`

`http://www.msstate.edu/Movies`

rec.arts.poems

rec.arts.poems

A Usenet newsgroup providing information and discussion about poetry.

Keywords: Poetry, Literature (General)
Audience: Poets, Poetry Readers
User Info: To subscribe to this Usenet newsgroup, you need access to a newsreader.

`news:rec.arts.poems`

rec.arts.sf.starwars

rec.arts.sf.starwars

A Usenet newsgroup providing information and discussion about the popular Star Wars trilogy.

Keywords: Science Fiction, Film
Audience: Star Wars Enthusiasts, Movie Viewers
User Info: To subscribe to this Usenet newsgroup, you need access to a newsreader.

`news:rec.arts.sf.starwars`

rec.arts.sf.tv

rec.arts.sf.tv

A Usenet newsgroup providing information and discussion about science fiction television programs.

Keywords: Science Fiction, Television
Audience: Science Fiction Enthusiasts, Television Viewers
User Info: To subscribe to this Usenet newsgroup, you need access to a newsreader.

`news:rec.arts.sf.tv`

rec.arts.sf.written

rec.arts.sf.written

A Usenet newsgroup providing information and discussion about science fiction publications.

Keywords: Science Fiction
Audience: Science Fiction Readers
User Info: To subscribe to this Usenet newsgroup, you need access to a newsreader.

news:rec.arts.sf.written

rec.arts.startrek.current

rec.arts.startrek.current

A Usenet newsgroup providing information and discussion about current Star Trek (The Next Generation) episodes and characters.

Keywords: Television, Science Fiction
Audience: Trekkies, Television Viewers
User Info: To subscribe to this Usenet newsgroup, you need access to a newsreader.

news:rec.arts.startrek.current

rec.arts.startrek.misc

rec.arts.startrek.misc

A Usenet newsgroup providing general information and discussion about all aspects of Star Trek, including its various television and film reviews.

Keywords: Television, Film
Audience: Trekkies, Television Viewers, Film Enthusiasts
User Info: To subscribe to this Usenet newsgroup, you need access to a newsreader.

news:rec.arts.startrek.misc

rec.arts.tv

rec.arts.tv

A Usenet newsgroup providing information and discussion about past and present TV shows and related trivia.

Keywords: Television, Trivia
Audience: General Public, Television Viewers, Trivia Enthusiasts
User Info: To subscribe to this Usenet newsgroup, you need access to a newsreader.

news:rec.arts.tv

rec.arts.tv.soaps

rec.arts.tv.soaps

A Usenet newsgroup providing information and discussion about television soap operas.

Keywords: Television
Audience: Television Viewers, Soap Opera Enthusiasts
User Info: To subscribe to this Usenet newsgroup, you need access to a newsreader.

news:rec.arts.tv.soaps

rec.arts.tv.uk

rec.arts.tv.uk

A Usenet newsgroup providing information and discussion about television shows in the United Kingdom.

Keywords: Television, United Kingdom
Audience: Television Viewers, British
User Info: To subscribe to this Usenet newsgroup, you need access to a newsreader.

news:rec.arts.tv.uk

rec.audio

rec.audio

A Usenet newsgroup providing information and discussion about audio products, including troubleshooting advice.

Keywords: Audio Electronics, Stereo Electronics
Audience: Stereo Owners, Music Listeners
User Info: To subscribe to this Usenet newsgroup, you need access to a newsreader.

news:rec.audio

rec.autos.driving

rec.autos.driving

A Usenet newsgroup providing information and discussion about driving, traffic laws, and car buying.

Keywords: Automobiles
Audience: Drivers, Automobile Buyers
User Info: To subscribe to this Usenet newsgroup, you need access to a newsreader.

news:rec.autos.driving

rec.autos.sport

rec.autos.sport

A Usenet newsgroup providing information and discussion about automobile competition.

Keywords: Automobiles, Automobile Racing, Sports
Audience: Automobile Racing Enthusiasts
User Info: To subscribe to this Usenet newsgroup, you need access to a newsreader.

news:rec.autos.sports

rec.autos.tech

rec.autos.tech

A Usenet newsgroup providing information and discussion about the technical aspects of automobiles.

Keywords: Automobiles, Technology
Audience: Automobile Mechanics
User Info: To subscribe to this Usenet newsgroup, you need access to a newsreader.

news:rec.autos.tech

rec.autos.vw

rec.autos.vw

A Usenet newsgroup providing information and discussion about Volkswagon products.

Keywords: Automobiles
Audience: Volkswagon Drivers
User Info: To subscribe to this Usenet newsgroup, you need access to a newsreader.

news:rec.autos.vw

rec.backcountry

rec.backcountry

A Usenet newsgroup providing information and discussion about wilderness, backpacking, and camping.

Keywords: Recreation, Sports
Audience: Campers, Backpackers, Wilderness Enthusiasts
User Info: To subscribe to this Usenet newsgroup, you need access to a newsreader.

news:rec.backcountry

rec.boats

rec.boats

A Usenet newsgroup providing information and discussion about boating, gear, places to sail, clubs, repairs, and racing.

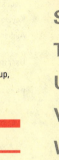

Keywords: Sailing, Sports
Audience: Sailors, Boating Enthusiasts
User Info: To subscribe to this Usenet newsgroup, you need access to a newsreader.

`news:rec.boats`

rec.collecting.cards

rec.collecting.cards

A Usenet newsgroup providing information and discussion about collecting sports and other trading cards.

Keywords: Trading Cards, Hobbies
Audience: Card Collectors
User Info: To subscribe to this Usenet newsgroup, you need access to a newsreader.

`news:rec.collecting.cards`

rec.crafts.brewing

rec.crafts.brewing

A Usenet newsgroup providing information and discussion about making beers and meads.

Keywords: Beer, Crafts
Audience: Beer Brewers
User Info: To subscribe to this Usenet newsgroup, you need access to a newsreader.

`news:rec.crafts.brewing`

rec.equestrian

rec.equestrian

A Usenet newsgroup providing information and discussion about all things pertaining to horses.

Keywords: Horses, Equestrians, Animals, Sports
Audience: Horse Enthusiasts, Horse Trainers, Horse Owners
User Info: To subscribe to this Usenet newsgroup, you need access to a newsreader.

`news:rec.equestrian`

rec.food.cooking

rec.food.cooking

A Usenet newsgroup providing information and discussion about cooking.

Keywords: Food, Cooking
Audience: General Public, Cooks, Chefs
User Info: To subscribe to this Usenet newsgroup, you need access to a newsreader.

`news:rec.food.cooking`

rec.food.veg

rec.food.veg

A Usenet newsgroup providing information and discussion about vegetarian cooking.

Keywords: Vegetarianism, Food, Cooking
Audience: Vegetarians, Cooks, Chefs
User Info: To subscribe to this Usenet newsgroup, you need access to a newsreader.

`news:rec.food.veg`

rec.gambling

rec.gambling

Discussion of card games, gambling, and gambling sites.

Keywords: Cards, Gambling
Audience: Card Players, Gamblers
Profile: Discussion in this group covers gambling, and card games, the rules of various card games, odds, betting, and the pros and cons of various gambling and card playing sites. The archived FAQ is a lengthy card game resource.
Contact: rec.gambling Moderator
jacobs@cs.utah.edu
Notes: The rec.gambling FAQ is accessible via anonymous ftp at soda.berkeley.edu through the path pub/rec.gambling.

`news:rec.gambling`

rec.games.board

rec.games.board

A Usenet newsgroup providing hints and discussion about board games.

Keywords: Games, Recreation
Audience: Game Players
User Info: To subscribe to this Usenet newsgroup, you need access to a newsreader.

`news:rec.games.board`

rec.games.chess

rec.games.chess

A Usenet newsgroup providing information and discussion about chess strategies, organized computer chess playing events, and software.

Keywords: Chess, Games, Recreation
Audience: Chess Players, Game Players
User Info: To subscribe to this Usenet newsgroup, you need access to a newsreader.

`news:rec.games.chess`

rec.games.programmer

rec.games.programmer

A Usenet newsgroup providing information and discussion about adventure game programming.

Keywords: Games, Programming, Video Games
Audience: Programmers
User Info: To subscribe to this Usenet newsgroup, you need access to a newsreader.

`news:rec.games.programmer`

rec.games.video.arcade

rec.games.video.arcade

A Usenet newsgroup providing information and discussion about video games.

Keywords: Games, Video Games
Audience: Game Players
User Info: To subscribe to this Usenet newsgroup, you need access to a newsreader.

`news:rec.games.video.arcade`

rec.gardens

rec.gardens ★

A Usenet newsgroup providing information and discussion about gardening.

Keywords: Gardening, Landscaping
Audience: Gardeners
User Info: To subscribe to this Usenet newsgroup, you need access to a newsreader.

news:rec.gardens

rec.motorcycles

rec.motorcycles ★

A Usenet newsgroup providing information and discussion about motorcycles and related products.

Keywords: Motorcycles
Audience: Motorcycle Enthusiasts
User Info: To subscribe to this Usenet newsgroup, you need access to a newsreader.

news:rec.motorcycles

rec.music.folk

rec.music.folk ★

A Usenet newsgroup providing information and discussion about folk music.

Keywords: Musical Genres
Audience: Folk Music Enthusiasts
User Info: To subscribe to this Usenet newsgroup, you need access to a newsreader.

news:rec.music.folk

rec.guns

rec.guns ★

A Usenet newsgroup providing information and discussion about firearms.

Keywords: Firearms, Weapons
Audience: Gun Users
User Info: To subscribe to this Usenet newsgroup, you need access to a newsreader.

news:rec.guns

rec.music.beatles

rec.music.beatles ★

A Usenet newsgroup providing information and discussion about the Beatles.

Keywords: Musical Groups, Popular Culture
Audience: Beatles Enthusiasts
User Info: To subscribe to this Usenet newsgroup, you need access to a newsreader.

news:rec.music.beatles

rec.music.gdead

rec.music.gdead ★★

A Usenet newsgroup providing information and discussion about the Grateful Dead.

Keywords: Music, Popular Culture
Audience: Grateful Dead Enthusiasts
User Info: To subscribe to this Usenet newsgroup, you need access to a newsreader.

news:rec.music.gdead

rec.humor

rec.humor ★

A Usenet newsgroup providing information and discussion about jokes.

Keywords: Jokes, Humor
Audience: General Public, Jokers
User Info: To subscribe to this Usenet newsgroup, you need access to a newsreader.

news:rec.humor

rec.music.cd

rec.music.cd ★

A Usenet newsgroup providing information and discussion about Compact Discs.

Keywords: Music, Audio Electronics
Audience: Compact Disc Users
User Info: To subscribe to this Usenet newsgroup, you need access to a newsreader.

news:rec.music.cd

rec.music.makers

rec.music.makers ★

A Usenet newsgroup providing information and discussion about music-making.

Keywords: Musical Instruments, Music
Audience: Performers, Musicians
User Info: To subscribe to this Usenet newsgroup, you need access to a newsreader.

news:rec.music.makers

rec.martial-arts

rec.martial-arts ★

A Usenet newsgroup providing information and discussion about martial arts.

Keywords: Martial Arts
Audience: Martial Artist Enthusiasts
User Info: To subscribe to this Usenet newsgroup, you need access to a newsreader.

news:rec.martial-arts

rec.music.classical

rec.music.classical ★

A Usenet newsgroup providing information and discussion about classical music.

Keywords: Music
Audience: Classical Music Listeners
User Info: To subscribe to this Usenet newsgroup, you need access to a newsreader.

news:rec.music.classical

rec.music.makers.guitar

rec.music.makers.guitar ★

A Usenet newsgroup providing information and discussion about guitars and guitar playing.

Keywords: Musical Instruments
Audience: Guitar Players
User Info: To subscribe to this Usenet newsgroup, you need access to a newsreader.

news:rec.music.makers.guitar

rec.music.makers.synth

rec.music.makers.synth ★

A Usenet newsgroup providing information and discussion about synthesizers.

Keywords: Music, Audio Electronics
Audience: Musicians
User Info: To subscribe to this Usenet newsgroup, you need access to a newsreader.

news:rec.music.makers.synth

rec.music.phish

rec.music.phish ★

A Usenet newsgroup providing information and discussion about the band Phish.

Keywords: Musical Groups, Popular Culture
Audience: Phish Enthusiasts
User Info: To subscribe to this Usenet newsgroup, you need access to a newsreader.

news:rec.music.phish

rec.org.sca

rec.org.sca ★

A Usenet newsgroup providing information and discussion about medieval re-enactments.

Keywords: SCA (Society For Creative Anachronism), Medieval Studies
Audience: General Public
User Info: To subscribe to this Usenet newsgroup, you need access to a newsreader.

news:rec.org.sca

rec.pets

rec.pets ★

A Usenet newsgroup providing information and discussion about pets and pet care.

Keywords: Pets, Animals
Audience: Pet Owners
User Info: To subscribe to this Usenet newsgroup, you need access to a newsreader.

news:rec.pets

rec.pets.cats

rec.pets.cats ★

A Usenet newsgroup providing information and discussion about domestic cats.

Keywords: Pets, Animals
Audience: Cat Owners
User Info: To subscribe to this Usenet newsgroup, you need access to a newsreader.

news:rec.pets.cats

rec.pets.dogs

rec.pets.dogs ★

A Usenet newsgroup providing information and discussion about dogs.

Keywords: Pets, Animals
Audience: Dog Owners
User Info: To subscribe to this Usenet newsgroup, you need access to a newsreader.

news:rec.pets.dogs

rec.photo

rec.photo ★

A Usenet newsgroup providing information and discussion about photography.

Keywords: Photography, Art, Crafts
Audience: Photographers
User Info: To subscribe to this Usenet newsgroup, you need access to a newsreader.

news:rec.photo

rec.puzzles

rec.puzzles ★

A Usenet newsgroup providing information and discussion about math puzzles and brain teasers.

Keywords: Games, Puzzles, Recreation
Audience: General Public
User Info: To subscribe to this Usenet newsgroup, you need access to a newsreader.

news:rec.puzzles

rec.radio.amateur.misc

rec.radio.amateur.misc ★

A Usenet newsgroup providing information and discussion about ham radios.

Keywords: Radio, Electronics
Audience: Ham Radio Operators
User Info: To subscribe to this Usenet newsgroup, you need access to a newsreader.

news:rec.radio.amateur.misc

rec.radio.shortwave

rec.radio.shortwave ★

A Usenet newsgroup providing information and discussion about shortwave radio.

Keywords: Radio, Electronics
Audience: Shortwave Radio Users
User Info: To subscribe to this Usenet newsgroup, you need access to a newsreader.

news:rec.radio.shortwave

rec.railroad

rec.railroad ★

A Usenet newsgroup providing information and discussion about railroads.

Keywords: Railroads, Transportation
Audience: Railroad Enthusiast
User Info: To subscribe to this Usenet newsgroup, you need access to a newsreader.

news:rec.railroad

rec.scuba

rec.scuba ★

A Usenet newsgroup providing information and discussion about scuba equipment and techniques.

Keywords: Scuba Sports, Travel, Recreation
Audience: Scuba Divers
User Info: To subscribe to this Usenet newsgroup, you need access to a newsreader.

news:scuba

rec.skiing

rec.skiing

A Usenet newsgroup providing information and discussion about skiing.

Keywords: Sports, Recreation, Skiing
Audience: Skiers
User Info: To subscribe to this Usenet newsgroup, you need access to a newsreader.

`news:rec.skiing`

rec.sport.baseball

rec.sport.baseball

A Usenet newsgroup providing information and discussion about professional baseball.

Keywords: Baseball, Sports
Audience: Baseball Fans, Sports Fans
User Info: To subscribe to this Usenet newsgroup, you need access to a newsreader.

`news:rec.sport.baseball`

rec.sport.basketball.college

rec.sport.basketball.college

A Usenet newsgroup providing information and discussion about college basketball.

Keywords: Basketball, Sports
Audience: Basketball Enthusiasts, Sport Enthusiasts
User Info: To subscribe to this Usenet newsgroup, you need access to a newsreader.

`news:rec.sport.basketball.college`

rec.sport.basketball.pro

rec.sport.basketball.pro

A Usenet newsgroup providing information and discussion about professional basketball.

Keywords: Basketball, Sports
Audience: Basketball Fans, Sports Enthusiasts
User Info: To subscribe to this Usenet newsgroup, you need access to a newsreader.

`news:rec.sport.basketball.pro`

rec.sport.cricket

rec.sport.cricket

A Usenet newsgroup providing information and discussion about cricket.

Keywords: Cricket, Sports
Audience: Cricket Fans, Sports Enthusiasts
User Info: To subscribe to this Usenet newsgroup, you need access to a newsreader.

`news:rec.sport.cricket`

rec.sport.football.college

rec.sport.football.college

A Usenet newsgroup providing information and discussion about college football.

Keywords: Football, Sports
Audience: Football Enthusiasts, Sports Enthusiasts
User Info: To subscribe to this Usenet newsgroup, you need access to a newsreader.

`news:rec.sport.football.college`

rec.sport.football.pro

rec.sport.football.pro

A Usenet newsgroup providing information and discussion about pro football.

Keywords: Football, Sports
Audience: Football Enthusiasts
User Info: To subscribe to this Usenet newsgroup, you need access to a newsreader.

`news:rec.sport.football.pro`

rec.sport.hockey

rec.sport.hockey

A Usenet newsgroup providing information and discussion about hockey.

Keywords: Hockey, Sports
Audience: Hockey Fans, Sports Fans
User Info: To subscribe to this Usenet newsgroup, you need access to a newsreader.

`news:rec.sport.hockey`

rec.sport.olympics

rec.sport.olympics

A Usenet newsgroup providing information and discussion about the summer Olympics Games.

Keywords: Olympic Games, Summer Sports
Audience: Olympic Enthusiasts
User Info: To subscribe to this Usenet newsgroup, you need access to a newsreader.

`news:rec.sport.olympics`

rec.sport.pro-wrestling

rec.sport.pro-wrestling

A Usenet newsgroup providing information and discussion about professional wrestling.

Keywords: Wrestling, Sports
Audience: Wrestling Fans, Sports Fans
User Info: To subscribe to this Usenet newsgroup, you need access to a newsreader.

`news:rec.sport.pro-wrestling`

rec.sport.rowing

rec.sport.rowing

A Usenet newsgroup providing information and discussion about recreational and competitive rowing. It provides information from the United States Rowing Association, the latest race results, equipment sales, coaching positions and more.

Keywords: Rowing, Crew, Sports
Audience: Rowers, Coaches, Athletes
Profile: This newsgroup covers technical, training and nutritional aspects as well as the latest race results, National Team information, equipment sales, coaching positions, information from the United States Rowing Association and more.
User Info: To subscribe to this Usenet newsgroup, you need access to a newsreader.

`news:rec.sport.rowing`

rec.sport.soccer

rec.sport.soccer

A Usenet newsgroup providing information and discussion about soccer.

Keywords:	Soccer, Sports
Audience:	Soccer Enthusiasts, Sports Enthusiasts
User Info:	To subscribe to this Usenet newsgroup, you need access to a newsreader.

`news:rec.sport.soccer`

rec.sport.tennis

rec.sport.tennis

A Usenet newsgroup providing information and discussion about tennis.

Keywords:	Tennis, Sports
Audience:	Tennis Players, Sports Enthusiasts
User Info:	To subscribe to this Usenet newsgroup, you need access to a newsreader.

`news:rec.sport.tennis`

rec.travel

rec.travel

A Usenet newsgroup providing information and discussion about travel.

Keywords:	Travel
Audience:	Travelers
User Info:	To subscribe to this Usenet newsgroup, you need access to a newsreader.

`news:rec.travel`

rec.video

rec.video

A Usenet newsgroup providing information and discussion about video.

Keywords:	Video, Art, Film, Computer Art
Audience:	Cinematographers, Video Artists
User Info:	To subscribe to this Usenet newsgroup, you need access to a newsreader.

`news:rec.video`

rec.video.satellite

rec.video.satellite

A Usenet newsgroup providing information and discussion about satellite television.

Keywords:	Television
Audience:	Television Viewers
User Info:	To subscribe to this Usenet newsgroup, you need access to a newsreader.

`news:rec.video.satellite`

rec.woodworking

rec.woodworking

A Usenet newsgroup providing information and discussion about woodworking.

Keywords:	Woodworking, Crafts, Hobbies
Audience:	Woodworkers
User Info:	To subscribe to this Usenet newsgroup, you need access to a newsreader.

`news:rec.woodworking`

Recipes

GRANOLA (Vegetarian Discussion List)

A ListServ for discussion of vegetarian issues, including everything from recipes to animal rights.

Keywords:	Health, Nutrition, Vegetarian, Recipes
Audience:	Vegetarians, Nutritionists, Health Professionals
Details:	Free
User Info:	To subscribe to the list, send an e-mail message to the URL address shown below consisting of a single line reading: SUB granola YourFirstName YourLastName

`mailto:listserv@gitvm1.bitnet`

Recipe Archive

This is an archive of recipes organized by main ingredient or title.

Keywords:	Cooking, Food, Recipes
Audience:	General Public, Cooks, Chefs
Profile:	Here are a few intriguing examples from the archive:

Advokaat: Advokaat is the Dutch word for egg cognac. It is highly recommended for A. I. (Alcohol Imbibing) meetings. This recipe is a modification of a recipe obtained in Poland. It makes a potent, superb advokaat (or egg cognac). The milk and eggs are healthy, the sugar and alcohol are not!

Berlinerkranzer: Norwegian wreath cookies are decorative holiday cookies that add quite a bright, colorful, aromatic touch to your plate of cookies.

Bouillabaisse: This recipe for Marseille-style fish soup represents a combination of several recipes derived from old Gourmets, Julia Child, the Playboy Gourmet Cookbook, and "Gee, that sounds good, let's add it.." The accompanying rouille is a garlic/hot pepper mayonnaise condiment traditional to Marseille-style fish soup.

| Details: | Free |

`gopher://calypso.oit.unc.edu/7waissrc%3a/ref.d/indexes.d/recipes.src`

`gopher://calypso.oit.unc.edu/7waissrc%3a/ref.d/indexes.d/usenet-cookbook.sr`

They can also be accessed through mosaic at the URL address shown below or from the calypso.oit.unc.edu gopher in the subdirectories: Internet Dog-Eared Pages (Frequently used resources)/ Search Many WAIS Indices

| Notes: | There are two searchable gopher Indexes containing recipes that have passed through the rec.food.cooking and rec.food.recipes newsgroups. They can be found at the following URL addresses: |

`ftp://gatekeeper.dec.com/pub/recipes`

The World Wide Web rec.food.recipes archive

World Wide Web archive of recipes posted to Usenet newsgroup rec.food.recipes. Updated weekly.

Keywords:	Food, Recipes, Cooking
Audience:	Cooks, General Public
Contact:	Amy Gale mara@kauri.vuw.ac.nz
User Info:	Use a World-Wide Web (WWW) client such as lynx

`http://www.vuw.ac.nz/non-local/recipes-archive/recipe-archive.html`

Recordings

Soundtracks

Discussions and reviews of new and older soundtracks (musical and technical aspects). Information about availability of specific soundtracks on different formats in different parts of the world.

Keywords:	Music, Recordings
Audience:	Audio Enthusiasts, Music Researchers
Contact:	Michel Hafner soundtracks-request@ifi.unizh.ch
User Info:	To subscribe to the list, send an e-mail message requesting a subscription to the URL address below. To send a message to the entire list, address it to: soundtracks@ifi.unizh.ch

`mailto:soundtracks-request@ifi.unizh.ch`

Recreation

(The) Kites FTP Archive ★

Files pertaining to kites and kite-flying.

Keywords:	Kites, Recreation
Sponsor:	University of Hawaii
Audience:	Kite Enthusiasts, Aeronautical Engineers
Contact:	Kevin Mayeshiro
	kevin@ftp.hawaii.edu
Details:	Free, Moderated, Images

`ftp://ftp.hawaii.edu/pub/rec.kites`

Physical Education & Recreation ★★

A collection of information on sporting and recreational activities from aikido to windsurfing.

Keywords:	Sports, Recreation, Aikido, Cycling, Scuba Diving, Windsurfing
Audience:	Sports Enthusiasts, Fitness Enthusiasts
Contact:	ctcadmin@ctc.ctc.edu

`gopher://ctc.ctc.edu`

rec.backcountry ★

A Usenet newsgroup providing information and discussion about wilderness, backpacking, and camping.

Keywords:	Recreation, Sports
Audience:	Campers, Backpackers, Wilderness Enthusiasts
User Info:	To subscribe to this Usenet newsgroup, you need access to a newsreader.

`news:rec.backcountry`

rec.gambling ★

A Usenet newsgroup providing information and discussion about gambling.

Keywords:	Games, Gambling, Recreation
Audience:	Gamblers
User Info:	To subscribe to this Usenet newsgroup, you need access to a newsreader.

`news:rec.gambling`

rec.games.board ★

A Usenet newsgroup providing hints and discussion about board games.

Keywords:	Games, Recreation
Audience:	Game Players
User Info:	To subscribe to this Usenet newsgroup, you need access to a newsreader.

`news:rec.games.board`

rec.games.chess ★

A Usenet newsgroup providing information and discussion about chess strategies, organized computer chess playing events, and software.

Keywords:	Chess, Games, Recreation
Audience:	Chess Players, Game Players
User Info:	To subscribe to this Usenet newsgroup, you need access to a newsreader.

`news:rec.games.chess`

rec.puzzles ★

A Usenet newsgroup providing information and discussion about math puzzles and brain teasers.

Keywords:	Games, Puzzles, Recreation
Audience:	General Public
User Info:	To subscribe to this Usenet newsgroup, you need access to a newsreader.

`news:rec.puzzles`

rec.scuba ★

A Usenet newsgroup providing information and discussion about scuba equipment and techniques.

Keywords:	Scuba Sports, Travel, Recreation
Audience:	Scuba Divers
User Info:	To subscribe to this Usenet newsgroup, you need access to a newsreader.

`news:scuba`

rec.skiing ★

A Usenet newsgroup providing information and discussion about skiing.

Keywords:	Sports, Recreation, Skiing
Audience:	Skiers
User Info:	To subscribe to this Usenet newsgroup, you need access to a newsreader.

`news:rec.skiing`

Zarf's List of Interactive Games on the Web

A list containing links to games and toys that can be played on the Internet.

Keywords:	Games, Toys, Entertainment, Recreation
Sponsor:	Carnegie Mellon University, School of Computer Science, Pittsburgh, Pennsylvania, USA
Audience:	General Public, Game Players, Kids
Contact:	Andrew Plotkin
	zarf@cs.cmu.edu, apli@andrew.cmu.edu

`http://www.cs.cmu.edu/afs/cs.cmu.edu/user/zarf/www/games.html`

Recreational Pharmacology Server

Recreational Pharmacology Server ★★★★

Very extensive collection of drug FAQs, data sheets, net articles, resources, and electronic books. Complete list of Internet links to related sites.

Keywords:	Pharmacology, Drugs, Neuroscience
Sponsor:	University of Washington, Seattle, Washington, USA
Audience:	Students, General Public, Neuroscientists, Pharmacists
Contact:	Webmaster
	lamontg@u.washington.edu
Details:	Free

`http://stein1.u.washington.edu:2012/pharm/pharm.html`

Recycling

Solid Waste Recycling ★★

The text of an eight-lesson correspondence class designed to teach the basics of setting up a successful recycling program.

Keywords:	Recycling, Environmental Studies
Sponsor:	University of Wisconsin
Audience:	Environmentalists, Educators, Students
Contact:	Judy Faber
	faber@engr.wisc.edu

`gopher://wissago.uwex.edu/11/uwex/course/recycling`

Reference

BUSREF (Business Reference)

The Business Refernce (BUSREF) library contains a variety of reference materials covering business and industry.

Keywords:	News, Reference, Business, Government
Audience:	Businessmen
Profile:	The BUSREF library contains company directories, reference publications, information on business opportunities, and biographical information on political candidates, Congressional members, celebrities, and international decision makers.
Contact:	Mead New Sales Group at (800) 227-4908 or (513) 859-5398 inside the US, or (513) 865-7981 for all inquiries outside the US.

User Info:	To subscribe, contact Mead directly.
	To examine the Nexis user guide, you can access it at the ftp site of the University of Texas at Austin at the URL address: ftp://ftp.cc.utexas.edu
	The files are in: /pub/ref-services/LEXIS

`telnet://nex.meaddata.com`

`http://www.meaddata.com`

GUTENBERG Listserver

A mailing list providing information about Project Gutenberg.

Keywords:	Project Gutenberg, Literature (General), Reference
Sponsor:	National Clearinghouse for Machine Readable Texts
Audience:	General Public, Researchers, Educators, Students
Contact:	Michael S. Hart gutnberg@vmd.cso.uiuc.edu
Details:	Free
User Info:	To subscribe to the list, send an e-mail message to the URL address shown below consisting of a single line reading: SUB GUTNBERG YourFirstName YourLastName

`mailto:listserv@vmd.cso.uiuc.edu`

Project Gutenberg

The purpose of Project Gutenberg is to encourage the creation and distribution of English-language electronic texts.

Keywords:	Literature (General), Reference
Sponsor:	National Clearinghouse for Machine Readable Texts
Audience:	General Public, Researchers, Educators, Students
Profile:	Contents include:
	Project Gutenberg's goal is to provide a collection of 10,000 of the most used books by the year 2001, and to reduce the effective costs to the user to a price of approximately one cent per book, plus the cost of media and of shipping and handling. Thus it is hoped that the entire cost of libraries of this nature will be about US$100, plus the price of the disks and CD-ROMS and mailing. Project Gutenberg assists in the selection of hardware and software as well as in their installation and use. It also assists in scanning, spelling checkers, proofreading, and so on.
Contact:	Michael S. Hart hart@vmd.cso.uiuc.edu
Details:	Costs
	Login anonymous; cd text

`ftp://mrcnext.cso.uiuc.edu`

Refrigeration

Utah Valley Community College Library

The library's holdings are large and wide-ranging and contain significant collections in many fields.

Keywords:	Accounting, Automobiles, Cabinetry, Child Care, Drafting, Electronics, Home Building, Local History, Refrigeration, Air Conditioning
Audience:	General Public, Researchers, Librarians, Document Delivery Professionals
Details:	Free
	Expect: Login; Send: Opub

`telnet://uvlib.uvcc.edu`

Reggae

Reggae Down Babylon

A collection of links to sources of information about reggae music on the World Wide Web and the Internet. Site includes reggae FAQs, and listings of reggae radio shows, lyrics, pictures, and news group archives.

Keywords:	Reggae, Music, Cultural Studies
Sponsor:	Reggae Down Babylon
Audience:	Music Enthusiasts, Musicians
Contact:	ReggaeMaster damjohns@nyx10.cs.du.edu
Details:	Free

`ftp://jammin.nosc.mil/pub/reggae`

Regional Business

Business Dateline ★★★

The database contains the full text of articles from more than 350 local and regional business publications from throughout the United States and Canada.

Keywords:	Business, Regional Business, Market Conditions
Sponsor:	UMI, Louisville, KY, USA
Audience:	Business Analysts, Market Researchers, Writers
Profile:	Sources include city business journals, daily newspapers, regional business magazines, and wire services. Subjects include city economic conditions, new product announcements, manufacturing methods, executive profiles, quality control, company histories, market conditions, service industries, regulations, litigation, and legislation.
Contact:	Dialog in the US at (800) 334-2564, Dialog internationally at country specific locations.
Details:	Costs
User Info:	To subscribe, contact Dialog directly.

`telnet://dialog.com`

Regulations

Banking News Library

The Banking News library provides you specific banking industry sources. More than 40 full-text and selected full-text sources which focus on the banking related news and issues.

Keywords:	Banking, Financial News, Regulation
Audience:	Journalists, Banking Industry Analysts
Profile:	This library contains news, Investext Industry Reports, and legal/regulatory information. Also included in an abstract file is the Financial Industry Information Service (FINIS). The S&L file includes documents from newspapers and magazines which are specific to the S&L crisis.
Contact:	Mead New Sales Group at (800) 227-4908 or (513) 859-5398 inside the US, or (513) 865-7981 for all inquiries outside the US.
User Info:	To subscribe, contact Mead directly.
	To examine the Nexis user guide, you can access it at the ftp site of the University of Texas at Austin at the URL address: ftp://ftp.cc.utexas.edu
	The files are in: /pub/ref-services/LEXIS

`telnet://nex.meaddata.com`

`http://www.meaddata.com`

ENERGY

The Energy News and Information (ENERGY) library consists of news, legal, and regulatory information.

Keywords:	Energy, News, Law, Regulations
Audience:	Energy Researchers
Profile:	The ENERGY library contains more than 50 full-text sources concentrating on energy-related news and issues. Also available are decisions and orders of the United States Federal Power Commission, Federal Energy Regulatory Commission, and Nuclear Regulatory Commission. At the state level, it covers administrative decisions and orders for 17 states. Energy industry research reports from InvestextR are also available.
Contact:	Mead New Sales Group at (800) 227-4908 or (513) 859-5398 inside the US, or (513) 865-7981 for all inquiries outside the US.

User Info: To subscribe, contact Mead directly.

To examine the Nexis user guide, you can access it at the ftp site of the University of Texas at Austin at the URL address: ftp://ftp.cc.utexas.edu

The files are in: /pub/ref-services/LEXIS

`telnet://nex.meaddata.com`

`http://www.meaddata.com`

EXEC (Executive Branch News US)

The EXEC library contains information and news about the Executive Branch of the Federal Government. From the Department of Agriculture to the White House, this file is a comprehensive source of information that will be especially useful to those whose responsibilities include monitoring federal regulations, Agency and Department activity, and the people and issues involved.

Keywords: News, Legislation, Regulation, Politics, Executive Branch

Audience: Journalists, Lobbyists, Business Executives, Analysts, Entrepreneurs

Profile: The EXEC library allows the searching of individual files or group files that cover topics such as the Federal Register and Code of Federal Regulations; public laws; proposed treasury regulation; and over 50 news sources, including BNA's Daily Report for Executives, the Dept. of State Dispatch, ABC News transcripts, Federal News Service Daybook, Government Executive, MacNeil/Lehrer Newshour, New Leader, National Review, the Washington Post, the Washington Times, Presidential Documents, and many others.

Contact: Mead New Sales Group at (800) 227-4908 or (513) 859-5398 inside the US, or (513) 865-7981 for all inquiries outside the US.

User Info: To subscribe, contact Mead directly.

To examine the Nexis user guide, you can access it at the ftp site of the University of Texas at Austin at the URL address: ftp://ftp.cc.utexas.edu

The files are in: /pub/ref-services/LEXIS

`telnet://nex.meaddata.com`

`http://www.meaddata.com`

Relays

Class Four Relay Magazine

A magazine by Relay Ops for the relay community.

Keywords: Relays, Magazines, Electronics

Sponsor: Carnegie Mellon University, Pittsburg, PA, USA

Audience: Relay Community

Profile: Includes articles on general questions and issues of relay usage, information for and about relay ops, discussion of policy issues and guidelines, and technical issues and new developments.

Contact: Joey J. Stanford
stjs@vm.marist.edu

Details: Free

`mailto:stjs@vm.marist.edu`

Religion

alt.atheism

A Usenet newsgroup providing information and discussion about atheism.

Keywords: Religion, Divinity, God

Audience: Philosophers, Clergy, Atheists

User Info: To subscribe to this Usenet newsgroup, you need access to a newsreader.

`news:alt.atheism`

alt.christnet

This Usenet newsgroup is a gathering place for Christian ministers and users.

Keywords: Religion, Christianity, Bible, Divinity

Audience: Christians, Ministers

User Info: To subscribe to this Usenet newsgroup, you need access to a newsreader.

`news:alt.christnet`

alt.christnet.bible

A Usenet newsgroup providing information and discussion about bible discussion and research.

Keywords: Bible, Christian, Religion, Divinity

Audience: Biblical Scholars, Bible Readers

User Info: To subscribe to this Usenet newsgroup, you need access to a newsreader.

`news:alt.christnet.bible`

alt.pagan

A Usenet newsgroup providing information and discussion about paganism and religion.

Keywords: Paganism, Religion

Audience: Cults, Worshippers, Religion Students

User Info: To subscribe to this Usenet newsgroup, you need access to a newsreader.

`news:alt.pagan`

alt.religion.kibology

A Usenet newsgroup consisting of followers of a god named Kibo, who is, in fact, a human being living in Boston. This newsgroup is highly humorous and hardly religious.

Keywords: Satire, Humor, Religion

Audience: Kibologists

User Info: To subscribe to this Usenet newsgroup, you need access to a newsreader.

`news:alt.religion.kibology`

AmerCath (History of American Catholicism)

This mailing list focuses on the history of American Catholicism.

Keywords: Catholicism, Christianity, Religion

Sponsor: Jefferson Community College, University of Kentucky, Louisville, KY, USA

Audience: Researchers, Educators, Students, Catholics

Profile: Since AMERCATH can be accessed internationally, it thus forms a global network of people who research and teach the history of American Catholicism. AMERCATH facilitates communication among faculty, students, and researchers.

Contact: Anne Kearney
jccannek@ukcc.uky.edu

Details: Free

User Info: To subscribe to the list, send an e-mail message to the address below, consisting of a single line reading:

Sub AmerCath YourFirstName YourLastName

To send a message to the entire list, address it to:

AmerCath@ukcc.uky.edu

`mailto:listserv@ukcc.uky.edu`

ANU (Australian National University) Buddhism Database

A searchable database of messages from the BUDDHA-L listserv, an academic forum for the discussion of Buddhism. It currently contains archives for messages posted in 1993-94.

Keywords: Religion, Asian Studies, Buddhism

Sponsor: COOMBSQUEST Social Sciences & Humanities Information Facility at ANU (Australian National University), Canberra, Australia

Audience:	Buddhists, Religious Studies Instructors, Asian Studies Educators
Contact:	Dr. T.Matthew Ciolek coombspapers@coombs.anu.edu.au

`gopher://cheops.anu.edu.au/Coombs-db/ANU-Buddha-1.src`

`http://coombs.anu.edu.au/WWWVL-AsianStudies.html`

Bible (King James Version)

The Bible (King James Version) includes the complete text of the modern Thomas Nelson revision of the 1769 edition of the King James version of the Bible.

Keywords:	Bible, Religious Text, Old Testament, New Testament
Sponsor:	Thomas Nelson Publishers, Nashville, TN, USA
Audience:	Christians, Theologians, Historians, Moralists
Profile:	The King James version originated from translations ordered by King James of England in 1604 at the Hampton Court Conference. Both the Old and New Testaments are included in this version. Records in the database represent both chapters and verses.
Contact:	Dialog in the US at (800) 334-2564, Dialog internationally at country specific locations.
Details:	Costs
User Info:	To subscribe, contact Dialog directly.

`telnet://dialog.com`

Catholic

The CATHOLIC mailing list is a forum for Catholics who wish to discuss their discipleship to Jesus Christ in terms of the Catholic approach to Christianity. "Catholic" is loosely defined as anyone embracing the Catholic approach to Christianity whether Roman Catholic, Anglo-Catholic, or Orthodox. Discussions on ecumenism are encouraged.

Keywords:	Catholicism, Ecumenism, Religion
Audience:	Catholics, Priests, Theologians
Contact:	Cindy Smith cms@dragon.com
Details:	Free
User Info:	To subscribe to the list, send an e-mail message to the address below, consisting of a single line reading:
	SUB Catholic YourFirstName YourLastName
	To send a message to the entire list, address it to: Catholic@american.edu
Notes:	This list is also bi-directionally forwarded to the newsgroup bit.listserv.catholic.

`mailto:listserv@american.edu`

Catholic-action

Catholic-action is a moderated list concerned with Catholic evangelism, church revitalization, and preservation of Catholic teachings, traditions and values, and the vital effort to decapitate modernist heresy.

Keywords:	Catholicism, Evangelism, Religion
Audience:	Catholics, Priests
Contact:	Richard Freeman rfreeman@vpnet.chi.il.us
Details:	Free
User Info:	To subscribe to the list, send an e-mail message requesting a subscription to the URL address below.

`mailto:rfreeman@vpnet.chi.il.us`

Cell Church Discussion Group

A list for Christians who are in cell churches or in churches that are in transition to becoming cell churches, as well as anyone interested in learning more about cell churches. A cell church is a nontraditional form of church life in which small groups of Christians (cells) meet in a special way in their homes for the evangelism of the unchurched, the bonding of believers, their nurture, and ministry to one another.

Keywords:	Cell Churches, Christianity, Evangelism, Religion
Audience:	Christians, Theologians, Evangelists
Contact:	Jon Reid reid@cei.com
Details:	Free
User Info:	To subscribe to the list, send an e-mail message to the URL address below with the single word SUBSCRIBE in the body (not subject) of your message. To send a message to the entire list, address it to: cell-church@bible.acu.edu
Notes:	The group archives, FAQ, and helpful articles are available by anonymous FTP from bible.acu.edu; they can also be retrieved by sending mail to cell-church-archives@bible.acu.edu with the single word LIST for a list of files, or HELP for more information.

`mailto:cell-church-request@bible.acu.edu`

CGN (Christian Growth Newsletter)

This site is intended to help Christians in personal growth, and includes testimonials and encouraging articles.

Keywords:	Christianity, Religion
Audience:	Christians
Contact:	Laura Smith bible@olsen.ch

`mailto:bible@olsen.ch`

Christian Growth Newsletter (CGN)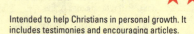

Intended to help Christians in personal growth. It includes testimonies and encouraging articles.

Keywords:	Christianity, Religion
Audience:	Christians
Contact:	Laura Smith bible@olsen.ch
Details:	Free

`mailto:bible@olsen.ch`

Ecchst-l

A discussion list for scholars of Ecclesiastical history, including those interested both in the history of the Church and in the examination of theology in an historical context.

Keywords:	Religion, Ecclesiastical History, Christianity, Theology
Audience:	Historians, Theologians
Contact:	Gregory H. Singleton ugsingle@uxa.ecn.bgu.edu
User Info:	To subscribe, send an e-mail message to the URL address below consisting of a single line reading:
	SUB ecchst-l YourFirstName YourLastName.
	??????missing info?????
	To send a message to the entire list, address it to: ecchst-l@bgu.edu

`mailto:listserv@bgu.edu`

Electronic Hebrew Users Newsletter (E-Hug)

This newsletter is electronic only, and is mandated, like the original, to cover everything relating to the use of Hebrew, Yiddish, Judesmo, and Aramaic on computers.

Keywords:	Judaism, Religion, Hebrew Language
Sponsor:	Berkeley Hillel Foundation
Audience:	Jews, Judaism Students
Contact:	Ari Davidow well!ari@apple.com
Details:	Free
User Info:	To subscribe, send an e-mail message to the address below consisting of a single line reading:
	To send a message to the entire list,

`mailto:listserv@dartcms1.bitnet`

jewishnt

A mailing list for the discussion of all things concerning the establishment of the Global Jewish Information Network

Keywords:	Judaism, Jews, Israel, Religion
Sponsor:	The Global Jewish Information Network Project
Audience:	Jews, Israelis, Political Activists
Contact:	Dov Winder viner@bguvm.bgu.ac.il
User Info:	To subscribe to the list, send an e-mail message to the URL address below consisting of a single line reading: SUB jewishnt

`mailto:listserv@bguvm.bgu.ac.il`

Judaica

A mailing list for the discussion of Jewish and Near Eastern Studies.

Keywords:	Judaica, Israel, Middle Eastern Studies, Religion
Audience:	Judaica Scholars, Jews, Middle East Scholars
Contact:	Tzvee Zahavy maic@uminn1.bitnet
User Info:	To subscribe to the list, send an e-mail message to the URL address below consisting of a single line reading: SUB judaica

`mailto:listserv@vm1.spcs.umn.edu`

Ogphre - SunSITE

A collection of Internet resources organized by subject. Particular strengths include agriculture, religious texts, poetry, creative writing, and US politics. The ftp site has a set of more general Internet guides.

Keywords:	Agriculture, Politics (US), Religion, Internet
Sponsor:	The University of North Carolina - Chapel Hill and Sun Microsystems, USA
Audience:	General Public, Internet Surfers, Researchers
Contact:	Darlene Fladager, Elizabeth Lyons Darlene_Fladager@unc.edu, Elizabeth_Lyons@unc.edu

`gopher://sunsite.unc.edu`

`tp://sunsite.unc.edu`

Pagan ★

Discusses the religions, philosophy, and other aspects of paganism.

Keywords:	Paganism, Religion
Audience:	Pagans
Contact:	Stacey Greenstein pagan-request@drycas.club.cc.cmu.edu
Details:	Free

User Info:	To subscribe to the list, send an e-mail message requesting a subscription to the URL address below. To send a message to the entire list, address it to: pagan@drycas.club.cc.cmu.edu

`mailto:pagan-request@drycas.club.cc.cmu.edu`

Quaker FTP Archive at ClarkNet ★★

Extensive writings concerning contemporary Quaker life.

Keywords:	Quakerism, Religion
Sponsor:	Clark Internet Services
Audience:	Quakers
Contact:	George Amoss daruma@clark.net

`ftp://ftp.clark.net/pub/quaker`

ftp://ftp.univie.ac.at/archive/faq/Quaker-faq

Shakers ★

A forum on the United Society of Believers for those interested in the history, culture, artifacts, and beliefs of the Shakers (United Society of Believers). Discussions cover a broad range of subject matter.

Keywords:	Shakers, Christianity, Religion
Audience:	Shakers, Theologians
Contact:	Marc Rhorer rhorer@ukcc.uky.edu
Details:	Free
User Info:	To subscribe to the list, send an e-mail message to the URL address shown below consisting of a single line reading: SUB shaker YourFirstName YourLastName To send a message to the entire list, address it to: shaker@ukcc.uky.edu

`mailto:listserv@ukcc.uky.edu`

soc.religion.christian

A Usenet newsgroup providing information and discussion about Christianity and related issues.

Keywords:	Christianity, Religion
Audience:	Christians, Theologians
Details:	Free
User Info:	To subscribe to this Usenet newsgroup, you need access to a newsreader.

`news:soc.religion.christian`

talk.religion.misc ★

A Usenet newsgroup providing information and discussion about religious, ethical, and moral implications.

Keywords:	Religion, Ethics
Audience:	General Public, Researchers, Students
Details:	Free
User Info:	To subscribe to this Usenet newsgroup, you need access to a newsreader.

`news:talk.religion.misc`

talk.religion.newage ★

A Usenet newsgroup providing information and discussion about esoteric and minority religions and philosophies.

Keywords:	Religion, Philosophy
Audience:	General Public, Researchers, Students
Details:	Free
User Info:	To subscribe to this Usenet newsgroup, you need access to a newsreader.

`news:talk.religion.newage`

The Purple Thunderbolt of Spode (PURPS)

Magazine of the OTISian faith (a small but growing cult worshiping OTIS, the ancient Sumerian goddess of life) carrying news, fiction, poetry, humor, and the pure, unadulterated Secrets of the Universe to its subscribers.

Keywords:	Religion, Cults
Audience:	OTIS Followers
Contact:	barker@acc.fau.edu
User Info:	To subscribe, send an e-mail message requesting a subscription to the URL address below.

`mailto:barker@acc.fau.edu`

Remote Sensing

Geoscience at Texas A&M University

General server with info on all aspects of GIS and remote sensing, especially GPS.

Keywords:	GIS, Image Processing, Remote Sensing, Geoscience, GPS
Sponsor:	Texas A&M University - Department of Agricultural Engineering
Audience:	Researchers, GIS and IP professionals, Students
Contact:	Hal Mueller hmueller@diamond.tamu.edu
Details:	Free
Images	
Notes:	Contains links to related Univeristy of Texas gophers and WWW servers.

`http://ageninfo.tamu.edu/geoscience.html`

Internet GIS and RS Information Sites

This document contains a lengthy listing of GIS and remote sensing sites on the Internet.

Keywords:	GIS, Remote Sensing, Image Processing, Geography
Sponsor:	Queen's University Department of Geography
Audience:	Researchers, General Public
Contact:	Michael McDermott mcdermom@gisdog.gis.queensu.ca
Details:	Free
Notes:	ASCII version also available from the same FTP site.

ftp://gis.queensu.ca/pub/gis/docs/gissites.html

The University of Minnesota Remote Sensing Lab

General information about remote sensing and GIS.

Keywords:	GIS, Remote Sensing, Image Processing
Sponsor:	University of Minnesota, Department of Forest Resources
Audience:	Researchers, GIS and IP professionals, Students
Profile:	The RSL server contains information regarding all aspects of image process and GIS. Some features include: home of the GIS Jobs Clearinghouse, archives of ESRI-L, IMAGRS-L and TGIS-L and the NBS CPSU WWW server.
Contact:	Stephen Lime sdlime@torpedo.forestry.umn.edu
Details:	Free, Images
Notes:	The RSL also maintains a companion gopher server and anonymous FTP site for the GIS Jobs Clearinghouse.

http://walleye.forestry.umn.edu/0/www/main.html

Research and Development

ARlist

An open, unmoderated mailing list to provide a forum for discussing action research and its use in a variety of disciplines and situations. Topics include philosophical and methodological issues in action research, the use of action research for evaluation, actual case studies, and discourse on increasing the rigor of action research.

Keywords:	Activism, Research, Politics
Audience:	Activists, Researchers
Profile:	Arlist is an open unmoderated mailing list to provide a forum for discussing action research and its use in a variety of disciplines and situations. It is usually (but perhaps not always) cyclic, participative, and qualitative.
Contact:	Bob Dick arlist@psych.psy.uq.oz.au
Details:	Free
User Info:	To subscribe to the list, send an e-mail message to the URL address below. To send a message to the entire list, address it to: arlist@psych.psy.uq.oz.au

mailto:arlist-request@psych.psy.uq.oz.au

ftp://psych.psy.uq.oz.au/dir/lists/arlist

Brown University Library

The Brown libraries contain approximately 1.5 million volumes, including historical archives of early American imprints and the biomedical engineering holdings.

Keywords:	Libraries, Research
Audience:	General Public, Researchers
Contact:	Howard Pasternick blips15@brownvm.brown.edu
Details:	Free At the Brown logon screen: tab to command field, Enter Dial Josiah, tab to Josiah choice on the screen.

telnet://brownvm.brown.edu

telnet://library.brown.edu

Columbia University Libraries

The Columbia Libraries include a medical library and a mathematics library.

Keywords:	Libraries, Research
Audience:	General Public, Researchers
Details:	Free When connected, hit return, enter terminal type: vt100.

telnet://clio.cul.columbia.edu

Cornell University Libraries

This library system maintains special collections in engineering, nuclear engineering, textile engineering, agriculture, medicine, Africana, entomology, hotels, ILR, mathematics, physical sciences, and veterinary medicine.

Keywords:	Libraries, Research
Audience:	General Public, Researchers
Details:	Free When userid/password screen appears, press return. When cp read appears on the screen, type library.

telnet://cornellc.cit.cornell.edu

DENet Information Server

This is the gopher of the Danish national academic network, which is located at the Danish Computer Centre for Research and Education (UNI-C).

Keywords:	Research, Education, Denmark
Audience:	Researchers, Educators
Profile:	This gopher provides DENet information and statistics, UNI-C information, directory services and phone books, pointers to Danish electronic libraries and gophers, an index of major Danish FTP archives, and news in Danish.
Contact:	Steen.Linden@uni-c.dk
Details:	Free

gopher://gopher.denet.dk

Links to Many Databases

A collection of links to over 40 databases covering a wide variety of subjects ranging from Postmodern Culture to the 1990 Census.

Keywords:	Databases, Research
Sponsor:	University of Texas, Austin, Texas, USA
Audience:	Researchers, General Public
Contact:	remark@ftp.cc.utexas.edu

gopher://ftp.cc.utexas.edu

PPPL (The Princeton Plasma Physics Laboratory) ★

This web site provides an overview of the projects, mission, physical plant and history of the PPPL.

Keywords:	Physics, Research
Sponsor:	U.S. Department of Energy (DOE)
Audience:	Physicists, Educators, Students
Contact:	Anthony R. De Meo or Jack A. Mervine pppl_info@pppl.gov, or webmaster@pppl.gov
Details:	Free

http://www.pppl.gov

Quantum Physics/High Energy Physics

A resource containing extensive internet links to international academic and research institutions specializing in high energy physics. Online links to journals, abstracts, and conference information.

Keywords:	Physics, Quantum Physics, Research
Sponsor:	Swiss Academic and Research Network, Switzerland
Audience:	Students, Physicists, Researchers
Contact:	Ingrid Graf rikv8@cernvm.cern.ch

http://www.cern.ch/Physics/HEP.html

Thailand: The Big Picture

A web site maintaining a complete list of Internet servers pertaining to and found within Thailand. General information concerning Thailand and extensive Internet connections to Thai academic institutions.

Keywords: Thailand, Education, Travel, Research
Sponsor: National Electronics and Computer Center at the National Science and Technology Development Agency, USA
Audience: Researchers, Exchange Students
Contact: Trin Tantsetthi
webmaster@www.nectec.or.th

http://www.nectec.or.th

National Technology Transfer Center (NTTC)

A federally-funded national network to apply government research to commercial applications.

Keywords: Technology, Technology Transfer, Research and Development, Business and Industry, Department of Defense, Government (US)
Sponsor: National Technology Transfer Center
Audience: Business People, Entrepreneurs, Manufactures, Technology Enthusiasts
Profile: Features state-by-state listings of agencies designed to facilitate the adaptation of new technologies to industry. Also provides updates on conferences, and a current list of Department of Defense projects soliciting private assistance from small businesses. Allows limited access to NTTC databases.
Contact: Charles Monfradi
cmonfra@nttc.edu, info@nttc.edu

gopher://iron.nttc.edu

http://iridium.nttc.edu/nttc.hmtl

Research Databases and Resources by Subject

A collection of databases on over forty subjects, ranging from Anthropology to Women's Studies.

Keywords: Databases, Academic Research
Sponsor: University of California at Berkeley
Audience: Researchers, General Public
Contact: Gopher Manager
gophcom@infolib.lib.berkeley.edu

gopher://umslvma.umsl.edu/Library/Subjects/Biology/Bioformt/Biodbs

gopher://infolib.lib.berkeley.edu

Research (Funding Support List)

The Research list is for people (primarily at educational institutions) interested in applying for funding support from various sources.

Keywords: Grants, Funding
Audience: Educators (College, University)
Profile: This list assists faculty in locating sources of support from government agencies, corporations, and foundations. It also forwards information regarding the latest news from potential sponsors such as the National Science Foundation and the National Institutes of Health, and provides information on upcoming international seminars on various topics ranging from medicine to artificial intelligence.
Contact: Eleanor Cicinsky
v2153a@vm.temple.edu
User Info: To subscribe to the list, send an Email message to the address below consisting of a single line reading:

SUB research YourFirstName YourLastName

To send a message to the entire list, address it to: research@vm.temple.edu

mailto:listserv@vm.temple.edu

Research on Demand

A resource for the provision of market information, strategic information location, product information, and national and international business information.

Keywords: Market Research, Internet Research, Legal Research, International Research
Audience: Marketing Specialists, Lawyers, Public Relations Experts, Business Professionals, Researchers, Writers, Producers
Profile: This resource has special access to unique information resources worldwide. Areas of particular information access include the former Soviet Union, Europe, and the US. Information access also includes access to all the major online systems, including Dialog, BRS, Orbit, DataStar, and so on. Current Awareness Services include research information gathered from the Internet.
Details: Costs
User Info: To subscribe, send an e-mail message to the URL address below. In the body of your message, state the nature of your inquiry.
Notes: Contact ROD directly in the US at: (800) 227-0750; outside the US at: (510) 841-1145.

mailto:rod@holonet.net

Research Ship Schedules and Information

A gopher providing information on research and deep water vessels from more than 45 countries. Includes detailed ship specifications, some with deck plans and photographs available as GIF files. Also has cruise schedules for US ships, as well as some from other countries.

Keywords: Oceanography, Transportation, Maritime Industry, Travel
Sponsor: University of Delaware (The OCEANIC Ocean Information Center), Newark, Delaware, USA
Audience: Oceanographers, General Public
Contact: Ocean Information Center, University of Delaware of Delaware, College of Marine Studies
oceanic@diu.cms.udel.edu
Details: Free, Images

gopher://diu.cms.udel.edu

Resodlaa (Research SIG of the Open and Distance Learning Association of Australia)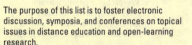

The purpose of this list is to foster electronic discussion, symposia, and conferences on topical issues in distance education and open-learning research.

Keywords: Education (Adult), Education (Distance), Education (Continuing), Australia
Sponsor: Research Special Interest Group (SIG) of the Open and Distance Learning Association of Australia
Audience: Educators, Administrators, Researchers
Details: Free
User Info: To subscribe to the list, send an e-mail message to the URL address below, consisting of a single line reading:

SUB resodlaa YourFirstName YourLastName

To send a message to the entire list, address it to: resodlaa @usq.edu.au

mailto:listserv@usq.edu.au

Restaurant Management

University of Wisconsin at Stout Library

The library's holdings are large and wide-ranging and contain significant collections in many fields.

Keywords: Mathematics, Business, Fashion Merchandising, Home Economics, Hospitality, Tourism, Hotel Administration, Restaurant Management, Microelectronics

Audience: Researchers, Students, General Public
Details: Free
Expect:Login, Send: Lib; Expect: vDIAL Prompt, Send: Library

`telnet://lib.uwstout.edu`

Retirement

AgeLine

The AgeLine database is produced by the American Association of Retired Persons (AARP) and provides bibliographic coverage of social gerontology—the study of aging in social, psychological, health-related, and economic contexts.

Keywords: Gerontology, Retirement, Public Policy, Aging
Sponsor: American Association of Retired Persons, Washington, DC, USA
Audience: Retired Persons, Health Care Providers, Researchers
Profile: AgeLine covers the delivery of health care for the older population and its associated costs and policies, as well as public policy, employment, and consumer issues. Literature covered is of interest to researchers, health professionals, service planners, policy makers, employers, older adults and their families, and consumer advocates.
Coverage: 1978 to the present (selected coverage back to 1966); updated bimonthly.
Contact: Dialog in the US at (800) 334-2564; Dialog internationally at country-specific locations.
Details: Costs
There is no print equivalent of the database. To subscribe, contact Dialog directly.

`telnet://dialog.com`

Retrieval Success

Retrieval Success

Succesful stories of using the Internet for reference. In each case, a librarian used Internet resources to answer reference questions. In many cases, particularly for the smaller libraries, the Internet provided information that would otherwise have been inaccessible.

Keywords: Internet, Information Retrieval
Audience: Internet Surfers
Contact: Karen Schneider
kgs@panix.com
Details: Free
File is: pub/lists/unite/files/internet-stories.txt

`ftp://mailbase.ac.uk`

Rezo, bulletin irregulomadaire du RQSS

Rezo, bulletin irregulomadaire du RQSS

E-newsletter of RQSS (Regroupement Quebecois des Sciences Sociales), open to anyone interested in social science research in Quebec and/or about Quebec.

Keywords: Quebec, Social Science
Audience: Social Scientists
Contact: Pierre J. Hamel
hamel@inrs-urb.uquebec.ca
Details: Free
User Info: To subscribe, send an e-mail message to the URL address below, consisting of a single line reading:
SUB rezo YourFirstName YourLastName
To send a message to the entire list, address it to: rezo@uquebec.ca

`mailto:listserv@uquebec.ca`

Rhetoric

Speeches and Addresses in the US

Includes the Clinton State of the Union Speech of 1993, Kennedy's Inaugural Speech, Martin Luther King's "I Have a Dream" speech, and more.

Keywords: Politics (US), Rhetoric
Audience: Journalists, Writers, Politicians, Students
Details: Free
Choose from menu presented.

`gopher://wiretap.spies.com/11/Gov/US-Speech`

Rhodes (Happy)

ecto

Information and discussion about singer/songwriter Happy Rhodes, and other music, art, books, and films of common (or singular) interest.

Keywords: Music, Art, Rhodes (Happy)
Audience: Music Enthusiasts, Art Enthusiasts
Contact: Jessica Dembski
ecto-request@ns1.rutgers.edu
Details: Free
User Info: To subscribe to the list, send an e-mail message requesting a subscription to the URL address below. To send a message to the entire list, address it to: ecto-request@ns1.rutgers.edu

`mailto:ecto-request@ns1.rutgers.edu`

Rights

The Frog Farm

A forum devoted to the discussion of claiming, exercising, and defending rights in America, past, present, and future. The main topics are issues that involve a free people and their public servants.

Keywords: Rights, Politics
Audience: Activists
Contact: schirado@lab.cc.wmich.edu
User Info: To subscribe to the list, send an e-mail message requesting a subscription to the URL address below. To send a message to the entire list, address it to: schirado@lab.cc.wmich.edu

`mailto:schirado@lab.cc.wmich.edu`

RIPE Network Coordination Centre Gopher

RIPE Network Coordination Centre Gopher

RIPE (Reseaux IP Europeens) is a collaborative organization open to all European Internet service providers. RIPE coordinates the operation of a pan-European IP network. In November 1993, more than 500,000 hosts throughout Europe were reachable via networks coordinated by RIPE.

Keywords: Europe, Networks
Audience: Internet Surfers
Contact: ncc@ripe.net
Details: Free

`gopher://gopher.ripe.net`

Rock Music

Backstreets

Discussion of Bruce Springsteen's music.

Keywords: Rock Music, Springsteen (Bruce)
Audience: Bruce Springsteen Fans
Contact: Kevin Kinder
backstreets-request@virginia.edu

Details:	Free
User Info:	To subscribe to the list, send an e-mail message requesting a subscription to the URL address below. To send a message to the entire list, address it to: backstreets@virginia.edu

`mailto:backstreets-request@virginia.edu`

Corpse/Respondents

This is a gothic pen-pal zine in digest form. Small traffic mailing list.

Keywords:	Gothic Rock, Rock Music
Audience:	Gothic Rock Enthusiasts
Contact:	carriec@eskimo.com
Details:	Free
User Info:	To subscribe send an e-mail message to the URL address below with "subscribe corpse <yournameandaddress>" in the text.

`mailto:carriec@eskimo.com`

Crowes

To provide a forum for discussion about the rock band the Black Crowes. Topics include the group's music and lyrics, as well as the band's participation with NORML, concert dates and playlists, and bootlegs (audio and video).

Keywords:	Rock Music, Pop Music
Audience:	Rock Music Enthusiasts, Pop Music Enthusiasts
Contact:	rstewart@unex.ucla.edu
Details:	Free
User Info:	To subscribe, mail to the address below with the command SUBSCRIBE in the first line.

`mailto:rstewart@unex.ucla.edu`

Deborah Harry and Blondie Information Service

An information service on everything and anything regarding Deborah Harry and Blondie, including tour information, recordings/films release information, and so on.

Keywords:	Rock Music, Harry (Deborah)
Audience:	Rock Music Enthusiasts, Deborah Harry Enthusiasts
Contact:	gunter@yarrow.wt.uwa.oz.au
Details:	Free
User Info:	To subscribe to the list, send an e-mail message requesting a subscription to the URL address below. To send a message to the entire list, address it to: gunter@yarrow.wt.uwa.oz.au

`mailto:gunter@yarrow.wt.uwa.oz.au`

dire-straits

Discussion of the musical group Dire Straits and associated side projects.

Keywords:	Rock Music, Dire Straits, Music
Audience:	Rock Music Enthusiasts, Dire Straits Enthusiasts
Contact:	Rand P. Hall dire-straits-request@merrimack.edu
Details:	Free
User Info:	To subscribe to the list, send an e-mail message requesting a subscription to the URL address below. To send a message to the entire list, address it to: dire-straits-request@merrimack.edu

`Anonymous ftp to: merrimack.edu (f=ANONYMOUS/DIRE-STRAITS)`

Dokken/Lynch Mob

Articles, questions and discussions on Dokken and Lynch Mob.

Keywords:	Rock Music, Dokken, Lynch Mob
Audience:	Rock Music Enthusiasts
Contact:	Kirsten DeNoyelles kydeno00@ukpr.uky.edu
Details:	Free
User Info:	To subscribe to the list, send an e-mail message requesting a subscription to the URL address below. To send a message to the entire list, address it to: kydeno00@ukpr.uky.edu

`mailto:kydeno00@ukpr.uky.edu`

Drone On...

The Drone On... list is for the discussion of Spacemen 3 and resultant bands, as well as any other droning guitar bands that anyone wants to bring up.

Keywords:	Rock Music, Spacemen 3
Audience:	Spacemen 3 Enthusiasts, Rock Music Enthusiasts
Contact:	droneon-request@ucsd.edu
Details:	Free
User Info:	To subscribe to the list, send an e-mail message requesting a subscription to the URL address below. To send a message to the entire list, address it to: droneon-request@ucsd.edu

`mailto:droneon-request@ucsd.edu`

echoes

Info and commentary on the musical group Pink Floyd, as well as other projects members of the group have been involved with.

Keywords:	Rock Music, Pink Floyd
Audience:	Rock Music Enthusiasts, Pink Floyd Enthusiasts
Contact:	H. W. Neff echoes-request@fawnya.tcs.com
Details:	Free
User Info:	To subscribe to the list, send an e-mail message requesting a subscription to the URL address below. To send a message to the entire list, address it to: echoes-request@fawnya.tcs.com

`mailto:echoes-request@fawnya.tcs.com`

Electric Light Orchestra

Discussion of the music of Electric Light Orchestra and later solo efforts by band members and former members.

Keywords:	Electric Light Orchestra, Rock Music
Audience:	Rock Music Enthusiasts
Contact:	elo-list-request@andrew.cmu.edu
Details:	Free
User Info:	To subscribe to the list, send an e-mail message requesting a subscription to the URL address below. To send a message to the entire list, address it to: elo-list-request@andrew.cmu.edu

`mailto:elo-list-request@andrew.cmu.edu`

freaks

This mailing list focuses on Marillion and related rock groups.

Keywords:	Music, Rock Music
Audience:	Marillion Enthusiasts
Details:	Free
User Info:	To subscribe to the list, send an e-mail message requesting a subscription to the URL address below. To send a message to the entire list, address it to:freaks@bnf.com

`mailto:freaks-request@bnf.com`

Journey-L

Information and discussion of the rock band Journey and any of the band members' outside projects.

Keywords:	Musical Groups, Rock Music
Audience:	Rock Music Fans
Contact:	Hunter Goatley or Britt Pierce journey-l@wkuvx1.wku.edu
User Info:	To subscribe to the list, send an e-mail message to the URL address below, with the body text subscribe journey-l. To subscribe to the digest version, send the message to : journey-l-digest-request@wkuvx1.wku.edu

`mailto:journey-l-request@wkuvx1.wku.edu`

Ph7

A mailing list for discussions about Peter Hamill and related rock groups.

Keywords: Rock Music, Hamill (Peter)
Audience: Musicians, Rock Music Enthusiasts
Contact: ph7-request@bnf.com
User Info: To subscribe to the list, send an e-mail message requesting a subscription to the URL address below. To send a message to the entire list, address it to: ph7@bnf.com

mailto:ph7-request@bnf.com

Queen

A mailing list to discuss the rock group Queen.

Keywords: Music, Rock Music
Audience: Queen Fans, Music Fans, Musicians
Contact: Dan Blanchard
qms-request@uiuc.edu
Details: Free
User Info: To subscribe to the list, send an e-mail message requesting a subscription to the URL address below. To send a message to the entire list, address it to: qms@uiuc.edu

mailto:qms-request@uiuc.edu

Stormcock

For general discussion and news concerning the music of Roy Harper, a folk-rock musician with a conscience. Recommendations and news concerning similar artists are encouraged.

Keywords: Rock Music, Music, Harper (Roy)
Audience: Music Fans
Contact: Paul Davison
stormcock-request@qmw.ac.uk
Details: Free
User Info: To subscribe to the list, send an e-mail message to the address shown below consisting of a single line reading:
SUB stormcock YourFirstName YourLastName
To send a message to the entire list, address it to: stormcock@qmw.ac.uk

mailto:listserv@qmw.ac.uk

The Ultimate Gopher for Rush Fans

A collection of lyrics, articles, press releases, concert updates, newsletters, and reviews concerning the musical group Rush.

Keywords: Musical Groups, Rush, Rock Music
Sponsor: syrinx.umd.edu
Audience: Rock Music Enthusiasts, Rush Enthusiasts
Contact: jlang.syrinx.umd.edu

gopher://syrinx.umd.edu

Rogers (Bruce)

Purdue University Library

The library's holdings are large and wide-ranging. They contain significant collections in many fields.

Keywords: Economics (History of), Literature (English), Literature (American), Indiana, Rogers (Bruce), Engineering (History of), Aviation, Earth Science, Atmospheric Science, Consumer Science, Family Science, Chemistry (History of), Physics, Veterinary Science
Audience: General Public, Researchers, Librarians, Document Delivery Professionals
Contact: Dan Ferrer
dan@asterix.lib.purdue.edu
Details: Free
Expect: User ID prompt, Send: GUEST

telnet://lib.cc.purdue.edu

Role-Playing Games

ars magica

A mailing list for the discussion of White Wolf's role-playing game, Ars Magica.

Keywords: Role-Playing Games, Games
Audience: Role-playing Enthusiasts, Game Players
Contact: ars-magica-request@soda.berkeley.edu
User Info: To subscribe to the list, send an e-mail message to the URL address below. To send a message to the entire list, address it to: ars-magica-request@soda.berkeley.edu
Also available upon request as a nightly digest.

mailto:ars-magica-request@soda.berkeley.edu

Miniatures

The Miniatures Digest is a mailing list for discussion of the painting, sculpting, converting, and displaying of miniature figurines, generally for war games or fantasy role-playing games.

Keywords: Miniatures, Role-Playing Games
Audience: Miniature Figurine Entusiasts
Contact: minimallist-request@cs.unc.edu
Details: Free
Notes:User Info: To subscribe to the list, send an e-mail message requesting subscription to the URL address below.

mailto:minilist@cs.unc.edu

Nero Ashbury

Nero is a live-action, medieval role-playing game with a plot line and characters that continue from one adventure to the next. Nero has been successful in New England for over six years and is growing rapidly.

Keywords: Medieval Studies, Role-Playing Games
Audience: General Public, Role-Playing Enthusiasts
Contact: lsonko@pearl.tufts.edu
Details: Free
User Info: To subscribe to the list, send an e-mail message requesting a subscription to the URL address below.

mailto:lsonko@pearl.tufts.edu

Rolling Stones

Nihon Sun Microsystems

This site provides a directory for Sun Microsystems in Japan. Includes the Rolling Stones Official Server WWW site, with access to Rolling Stones music, merchandise, and information. Also provides multimedia links to the Science University of Tokyo and other Asia-Pacific resources.

Keywords: Computers, Rolling Stones
Sponsor: Sun Microsystems, Inc., Tokyo, Japan
Audience: Computer Users, Rolling Stones Fans
Contact: www-admin@sun.co.jp
Details: Multimedia, Free, Sounds, Images

http://www.sun.co.jp

Romance

alt.romance.chat

A Usenet newsgroup providing discussion about the romantic side of love.

Keywords: Chat Groups, Romance
Audience: General Public
User Info: To subscribe to this Usenet newsgroup, you need access to a newsreader.

news:alt.romance.chat

Romania

CEE Environmental Libraries Database

A directory of over 300 libraries and environmental information centers in Central Eastern Europe that specalize in, or maintain significant collections of information about, the environment, ecology, sustainable living, or conservation. The database concentrates on six Central Eastern European countries: Bulgaria, Czech Republic, Hungary, Romania, Slovakia, and Poland.

Keywords: Central Eastern Europe, Environment, Sustainable Living, Bulgaria, Czech Republic, Hungary, Romania, Slovakia, Poland.

Sponsor: The Wladyslaw Poniecki Charitable Foundation, Inc.

Audience: Environmentalists, Green Movement, Librarians, Community Builders, Sustainable Living Specialists.

Profile: This database is the product of an Environmental Training Project (ETP) that was funded in 1992 by the US Agency for International Development as a 5-year cooperative agreement with a consortium headed by the University of Minnesota (US AID Cooperative Agreement Number EUR-0041-A-002-2020). Other members of the consortium include the University of Pittsburgh's Center for Hazardous Materials Research, The Institute for Sustainable Communities, and the World Wildlife Fund. The Wladyslaw Poniecki Charitable Foundation, Inc., was a subcontractor to the World Wildlife Fund and published the Directory of Libraries and Environmental Information Centers in Central Eastern Europe: A Locator/Directory. This gopher database consists of an electronic version of the printed directory, subsequently modified and updated online. Access to the data is facilitated by a WAIS search engine which makes it possible to retrieve information about libraries, subject area specializations, personnel, and so on.

Contact: Doug Kahn, CEDAR
kahn@pan.cedar.univie.ac.at

`gopher://gopher.poniecki.berkeley.edu`

Roosevelt (Franklin D.)

The University of Illinois at Chicago Library ★★

The library's holdings are large and wide-ranging and contain significant collections in many fields.

Keywords: Health Science, Chicago, Industry, Slavery, Abolitionism, Roosevelt (Franklin D.)

Audience: General Public, Researchers, Librarians, Document Delivery Professionals

Details: Free

Expect:introductory screen, Send: Clear key; Expect: UIC flame screen, Send: Enter key; Expect: Logon screen, Send: DIAL PVM; Expect: PVM (Passthru) screen, Send: Type: Move cursor to NOTIS and press Enter key Response: One line message about port in use Type: Enter key

`telnet://uicvm.uic.edu`

Rosen Sculpture Exhibition

Rosen Sculpture Exhibition ★★

This web site contains various examples of sculpture movements.

Keywords: Art, Fine Arts

Sponsor: Visual Resources Curator of the Department of Art at Appalachian State University, Boone, North Carolina, USA

Audience: Art Educators, Art Students

`http://www.acs.appstate.edu/art`

Rowing

rec.sport.rowing ★

A Usenet newsgroup providing information and discussion about recreational and competitive rowing. It provides information from the United States Rowing Association, the latest race results, equipment sales, coaching positions and more.

Keywords: Rowing, Crew, Sports

Audience: Rowers, Coaches, Athletes

Profile: This newsgroup covers technical, training and nutritional aspects as well as the latest race results, National Team information, equipment sales, coaching positions, information from the United States Rowing Association and more.

User Info: To subscribe to this Usenet newsgroup, you need access to a newsreader.

`news:rec.sport.rowing`

rrl

rrl ★★

A mailing list for the discussion of GIS (Geographic Information Systems) in the United Kingdom.

Keywords: GIS (Geographical Information Systems), United Kingdom

Audience: Geographers, Cartographers

Contact: rrl@uk.ac.leicester

`mailto:rrl@uk.ac.leicester`

Rubber

RAPRA Abstracts

Coverage on technical and commercial aspects of the rubber, plastics, and polymer composites industries.

Keywords: Material Science, Rubbers, Plastics, Polymers

Sponsor: Rapra Technology, Ltd.

Audience: Material Scientists, Researchers

Profile: This unique source of information covers the world's polymer literature including journals, conference proceedings, books, specifications, reports and trade literature. Contains over 375,000 records. Updated biweekly.

Contact: paul.albert@neteast.com
To subscribe contact Orbit-Questel directly.

`telnet://orbit.com`

Running

dead-runners ★

The Dead Runners Society is a mailing list for runners who like to talk about the psychological, philosophical, and personal aspects of running.

Keywords: Running, Sports

Audience: Runners

Contact: Christopher Mark Conn
dead-runners-request@unx.sas.com

Details: Free

User Info: To subscribe to the list, send an e-mail message requesting a subscription to the URL address below. To send a message to the entire list, address it to: dead-runners-request@unx.sas.com

`mailto:dead-runners-request@unx.sas.com`

Rural Development

AGRIS International ★★★

This database serves as a comprehensive inventory of worldwide agricultural literature that reflects research results, food production, and rural development.

Keywords:	Agriculture, Rural Development, Food Production, Development
Sponsor:	US National Agricultural Library, Beltsville, MD, USA
Audience:	Agronomists, Market Researchers
Profile:	Designed to help users identify problems involved in all aspects of world food supply, the file corresponds in part to Agr Index, published monthly by the Food and Agriculture Organization (FAO) of the United Nations. Subject coverage focuses on many topics, general agriculture; geography and history; education, extension, and advisory work; administration and legislation; economics, development, and rural sociology; plant production; protection of plants and stored products; forestry; animal production; aquatic sciences and fisheries; machinery and buildings; natural resources; food science; home economics; human nutrition; pollution; and more.
Contact:	Dialog in the US at (800) 334-2564
Details:	Costs
User Info:	To subscribe, contact Dialog directly.

`telnet://dialog.com`

Community Networks Benefit Federal Goals

Statement by community networker Frank Odasz, founder and director of Big Sky Telegraph, a network of rural BBSs throughout Montana. In this article he makes the case that the federal government will benefit from the widespread rural employment of networking technology.

Keywords:	Community, Networking, Rural Development, Development
Audience:	Activists, Policy Analysts, Community Leaders, Government, Citizens, Rural Residents, Native Americans
Contact:	Frank Odasz franko@bigsky.dillon.mt.us,
Details:	Free

`http://nearnet.gnn.com/mag/articles/oram/bio.odasz.html`

Marshall University School of Medicine (MUSOM) RuralNet Gopher

A gopher server dedicated to the improvement of rural health care.

Keywords:	Rural Development, Health Care, Medical Treatment, Bioinformatics
Sponsor:	Marshall University School of Medicine
Audience:	Health Care Professionals, Medical Students, Rural Residents
Profile:	A collection of health care resources, with particular emphasis on rural health care. Includes listings of clinical resources by subject area, information on state and federal rural health care initiatives, and links to local and national health and education services.
Contact:	Mike McCarthy, Andy Jarrell mmccarth@muvms6.wvnet.edu, jarrell@musom01.mu.wvnet.edu

`gopher://ruralnet.mu.wvnet.edu`

Telluride Institute

This is a community organization involved in building an electronic dimension in rural Colorado. The vision of Telluride Institute includes linking rural residents to each other and outside resources, creating new opportunities for education, jobs, and arts.

Keywords:	Community, Networking, Virtual Community, Rural Development, Colorado
Sponsor:	The Telluride Institute, Telluride, Colorado
Audience:	Activists, Policymakers, Community Leaders, Students, Colorado Residents
Profile:	The Telluride Institute is a local community-based organization that produces arts, environmental, and educational events in the Telluride area of Colorado. The Institite is committed to the creation of what it calls the "InfoZone": it wants to use modern telecommunications to link together the local community and to connect to the rest of the world to exchange ideas, commerce, arts, and inspiration.
Contact:	Richard Lowenberg tellinst@CSN.ORG
Details:	Free Send an e-mail message to the URL address below asking for further information.

`mailto:tellinst@csn.org`

Rush

The Ultimate Gopher for Rush Fans

A collection of lyrics, articles, press releases, concert updates, newsletters, and reviews concerning the musical group Rush.

Keywords:	Musical Groups, Rush, Rock & Roll
Sponsor:	syrinx.umd.edu
Audience:	Rock Music Enthusiasts, Rush Enthusiasts
Contact:	jlang.syrinx.umd.edu

`gopher://syrinx.umd.edu`

Russia

Russian

This list is dedicated to the discussion of Russian-language issues, including Russian language, linguistics, grammar, translations, and literature.

Keywords:	Language, Literature (Russian), Linguistics
Audience:	Slavicists, Linguists, Translators
Contact:	Andrew Wollert ispajw@asuacad russian@asuvm.inre.asu.edu
Details:	Free
User Info:	To subscribe to the list, send an e-mail message requesting subscription to the URL address below.

`russian@asuvm.inre.asu.edu`

Russian and East European Studies Home Pages

Keywords:	Russia, Eastern Europe, Government, Political Science
Sponsor:	University of Pittsburgh
Audience:	Researchers, Politicians
Contact:	Casey Palowitch cjp@acid.library.pitt.edu

`http://www.pitt.edu/cjp/rspubl.html`

soc.culture.soviet

A Usenet newsgroup providing information and discussion about topics relating to Russia or the former Soviet Union.

Keywords:	Russia, CIS (Commonwealth of Independent States), Communism, Sociology
Audience:	Sociologists, Russians
Details:	Free
User Info:	To subscribe to this Usenet newsgroup, you need access to a newsreader.

`news:soc.culture.soviet`

talk.politics.soviet

A Usenet newsgroup providing information and discussion about Soviet politics, domestic and international.

Keywords:	Communism, Russia, Politics, CIS (Commonwealth of Independent States)
Audience:	Political Scientists
Details:	Free
User Info:	To subscribe to this Usenet newsgroup, you need access to a newsreader.

`news:talk.politics.soviet`

rxderm-l

rxderm-l

A mailing list intended for promoting the discussion of dermatologic treatment among practicing dermatologists.

Keywords: Dermatology, Skin, Disease, Doctors

Audience: Dermatologists

Contact: A.C. Huntley
achuntley@ucdavis.edu

User Info: To subscribe to the list, send an e-mail message to the URL address below consisting of a single line reading:

SUB rxderm-l YourFirstName YourLastName. To send a message to the entire list, address it to: rxderm-l@ucdavis.edu

`mailto: listserv@ucdavis.edu`

S

SABINET (South African Bibliographic and Information Network)

SABINET (South African Bibliographic and Information Network)

★

This gopher offers information searches from a variety of electronic databases, as well as for library locations and availability of books and periodicals.

Keywords: South Africa, Databases, Networks

Audience: South African Internet Surfers

Contact: hennie@info1.sabinet.co.za

Details: Free

`gopher://info2.sabinet.co.za`

Safety

City of San Carlos World Wide Web Fire Safety Tutorial

★★

This WWW site offers fire prevention information, with a special emphasis on preventing wildland fires. Also includes color diagram on how to create a proper firebreak.

Keywords: Disaster Relief, Safety

Sponsor: The City of San Carlos, California, USA

Audience: Students, Educators, Environmentalists, Community Groups

`http://www.abag.ca.gov/abag/local_gov/city/san_carlos/schome.html`

Publications of the Office of Environment, Safety, and Health

★★★

A collection of government safety information including updates, bulletins, and hazard alerts. Topics are diverse, covering everything from "Employee Hit on Head by Falling Steel Wheel" to "New Regulations to Control the Speed of Bloodborne Diseases."

Keywords: Safety, Government (US), Federal Laws (US)

Sponsor: U.S. Department of Energy

Audience: Government Officials, General Public

Details: Free

`gopher://dewey.tis.inel.gov`

Safety (Environmental Health and Safety Discussion List)

★

E-conference for people interested in the various environmental health and safety issues on college and university campuses.

Keywords: Environmental Health, Safety, Health

Audience: Students (College/University), Educators (college/University)

Contact: Ralph Stuart, Dayna Flath
rstuart@moose.uvm.edu
dmf@uvmvm.uvm.edu

Details: Free

User Info: To subscribe to the list, send an e-mail message to the URL address below, consisting of a single line reading:

SUB safety YourFirstName YourLastName

To send a message to the entire list, address it to: safety@uvmvm.uvm.edu

`mailto:listserv@uvmvm.uvm.edu`

U.S. Consumer Product Safety Commission (CPSC)

★★★

The CPSC's mission is to protect the public from defective and potentially dangerous consumer products. This gopher has archives of CPSC press releases and action reports from 1990-1994, as well as a calendar of upcoming events and guidelines for reporting potentially dangerous products to the CPSC.

Keywords: Safety, Consumerism, Laws (US Federal)

Sponsor: US Consumer Product Safety Commission

Audience: Consumers, Activists

Contact: pweddle@cpsc.gov

Notes: You can call the CPSC at their toll-free hotline at (800) 638-2772.

`gopher://cpsc.gov`

Sahel-NAFR

Sahel-NAFR

★★

This site contains information about a database of composite satellite images of Sahel and North Africa (known as the Sahelian and NW Africa 14-Day NDVI Composites). The images come from a pilot program defined between the U.S. Geological Survey and the U.S. Agency for International Development (AID) to develop and test a near-real-time monitoring procedure using satellite remote sensing and Geographic Information System technologies in grasshopper and locust control programs in West Africa. Also contains an appendix with information about the Senegalese Grasshoppers.

Keywords: Geology, Geography, GIS (Geographic Information Systems)

Sponsor: U.S. Geological Survey and U.S. Agency for International Development (AID)

Audience: Geologists, Geographers

`http://sun1.cr.usgs.gov/glis/hyper/guide/sahel_nafr`

Sailing

Marimed Foundation

This foundation provides therapy and education to adjudicated and emotionally impaired teens. Therapies include wilderness experiences on a square-rigged sail ship, boat building, and traditional therapies.

Keywords: Education (Alternative), Sailing
Audience: Educators, Alternative Educators, Social Workers
Contact: Dr. Robert Grossman
marimed@holonet.net
Details: Free

`mailto:marimed@holonet.net`

rec.boats

A Usenet newsgroup providing information and discussion about boating, gear, places to sail, clubs, repairs, and racing.

Keywords: Sailing, Sports
Audience: Sailors, Boating Enthusiasts
User Info: To subscribe to this Usenet newsgroup, you need access to a newsreader.

`news:rec.boats`

The Nautical Bookshelf

Catalog and ordering information for Nautical Bookshelf's collection of books on sailing and other water sports.

Keywords: Boating, Power Boating, Sailing, Sports
Sponsor: Nautical Bookshelf
Audience: Boating Enthusiasts, Sailors
Contact: staff@nautical.com

`gopher://gopher.nautical.com`

Sais-l (Science Awareness and Promotion)

Sais-l (Science Awareness and Promotion)

The SAIS list creates a forum for exchanging innovative ideas about making science more appealing to students.

Keywords: Science, Education (K-12), Education (Secondary)
Audience: Students (K-12), Students (high school up), Science Teachers
Contact: Keith W. Wilson
sais@unb.ca
Details: Free
User Info: To subscribe to the list, send an e-mail message to the URL address below consisting of a single line reading:
SUB sais-l YourFirstNameYourLastName
To send a message to the entire list, address it to: sais-l@unb.ca

`mailto:listserv@unb.ca`

Sales

Alliance Marketing Systems

Develops marketing strategies for new business on those in need of turn-around. Designs advertising/marketing plans to prequalify the buying public.

Keywords: Business Marketing, Sales
Audience: Business Professionals, Marketing Professionals, Sales Executives
Details: Costs

`xx@xx.xxx`

San Francisco Bay Area

ba-Firearms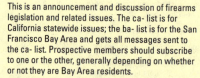

This is an announcement and discussion of firearms legislation and related issues. The ca- list is for California statewide issues; the ba- list is for the San Francisco Bay Area and gets all messages sent to the ca- list. Prospective members should subscribe to one or the other, generally depending on whether or not they are Bay Area residents.

Keywords: Firearms, Gun Control Legislation, San Francisco Bay Area
Audience: Politicians, General Public, Gun Users, San Francisco Bay Area Residents
Contact: Jeff Chan
ba-firearms-request@shell.portal.com
Details: Free
User Info: To subscribe to the list, send an e-mail message requesting a subscription to the URL address below. To send a message to the entire list, address it to: ba-firearms@shell.portal.com

`mailto:ba-firearms-request@shell.portal.com`

ba-Liberty

This is an announcement of local Libertarian meetings, events, activities, and so on. The ca- list is for California statewide issues; the ba- list is for the San Francisco Bay Area and it gets all messages sent to the ca- list. Prospective members should subscribe to one or the other, generally depending on whether or not they are Bay Area residents.

Keywords: Libertarian Party, Politics, San Francisco Bay Area
Audience: Libertarians, Political Scientists, Politicians, General Public
Contact: Jeff Chan
ba-liberty-request@shell.portal.com
Details: Free
User Info: To subscribe to the list, send an e-mail message requesting a subscription to the URL address below. To send a message to the entire list, address it to: ba-liberty@shell.portal.com

`mailto:ba-liberty-request@shell.portal.com`

ba-Poker

Discussion of poker as it is available to residents of and visitors to the San Francisco Bay Area (broadly defined), in home games as well as in licensed card rooms. Topics include upcoming events, unusual games, strategies, comparisons of various venues, and player "networking."

Keywords: Poker, Card Games, San Francisco Bay Area
Audience: Poker Players
Contact: Martin Veneroso
ba-poker-request@netcom.com
Details: Free
User Info: To subscribe to the list, send an e-mail message requesting a subscription to the URL address below. To send a message to the entire list, address it to: ba-poker@netcom.com

`mailto:ba-poker-request@netcom.com`

ba-Sappho

Ba-Sappho is a San Francisco Bay Area lesbian mailing list intended for local networking and announcements. BA-Sappho is not a discussion group.

Keywords: Lesbians, San Francisco Bay Area
Audience: Lesbians
Contact: ba-sappho-request@labrys.mti.sgi.com
Details: Free
User Info: To subscribe to the list, send an e-mail message requesting a subscription to the URL address below. To send a message to the entire list, address it to: ba-sappho@labrys.mti.sgi.com

`mailto:ba-sappho-request@labrys.mti.sgi.com`

ba-Volleyball

This list is used for announcements about San Francisco Bay Area volleyball events, clinics, tournaments, and so on.

Keywords: Volleyball, San Francisco Bay Area
Audience: Volleyball Enthusiasts
Contact: ba-volleyball-request@klerk.cup.hp.com

User Info: To subscribe to the list, send an e-mail message requesting a subscription to the URL address below. To send a message to the entire list, address it to: ba-volleyball@klerk.cup.hp.com

```
mailto:ba-volleyball-
request@klerk.cup.hp.com
```

Sanskrit

Harvard University Library

The library's holdings are large and wide-ranging and contain significant collections in many fields.

Keywords: Afrikaans, Alchemy, Arabic Culure (History of), Celtic Philology, Congo Languages, Folklore, Hebraica, Mormonism, Numismatics, Quakers, Sanskrit, Witchcraft, Arabic Philology
Audience: General Public, Researchers, Librarians, Document Delivery Professionals
Details: Free
User Info: Expect: Mitek Server..., Send: Enter or Return; Expect: prompt, Send: hollis

```
telnet://hollis.harvard.edu
```

Satellite

Center for Extreme Ultraviolet Astrophysics

A department of the University of California at Berkeley devoted to research in extreme ultraviolet astronomy. It is the ground-based institution of EUVE (the Extreme Ultraviolet Explorer), a NASA satellite launched in 1992.

Keywords: Astronomy, Astrophysics, EUVE, NASA, Satellite
Sponsor: NASA and University of California at Berkeley
Audience: Astronomers, Astrophysicists
Profile: Provides access to details about the EUVE Guest Observer (EGO) Center, the EUVE Public Archive of Mission Data and Information, satellite operation information, and so on. The EUVE Guest Observer Center provides information, software, and data to EUVE Guest Observers.
Contact: egoinfo@cea.berkeley.edu, archive@cea.berkeley.edu
Details: Free

```
http://cea-ftp.cea.berkeley.edu/
```

Satire

alt.fan.monty-python

A Usenet newsgroup providing an electronic fan club for those wacky Brits.

Keywords: Humor, Entertainment, Comedians, Satire
Audience: Monty Python Enthusiasts, General Public
User Info: To subscribe to this Usenet newsgroup, you need access to a newsreader.

```
news:alt.fan.monty-python
```

alt.religion.kibology

A Usenet newsgroup consisting of followers of a god named Kibo, who is, in fact, a human being living in Boston. This newsgroup is highly humorous and hardly religious.

Keywords: Satire, Humor, Religion
Audience: Kibologists
User Info: To subscribe to this Usenet newsgroup, you need access to a newsreader.

```
news:alt.religion.kibology
```

Clinton Watch

A regular political column devoted to a critical examination of the Clinton Administration.

Keywords: Politics, Clinton(Bill), Satire, Government (US)
Sponsor: Informatics Resource
Audience: Republicans, General Public, Citizens
Contact: clintonwatch@dolphin.gulf.net

```
gopher://dolphin.gulf.net
```

SCA (Society For Creative Anachronism)

rec.org.sca

A Usenet newsgroup providing information and discussion about medieval reenactments.

Keywords: SCA (Society For Creative Anachronism), Medieval Studies
Audience: General Public
User Info: To subscribe to this Usenet newsgroup, you need access to a newsreader.

```
news:rec.org.sca
```

Scandinavia

soc.culture.nordic

A Usenet newsgroup providing information and discussion about Nordic culture.

Keywords: Scandinavia, Sociology
Audience: Sociologists
Details: Free
User Info: To subscribe to this Usenet newsgroup, you need access to a newsreader.

```
news:soc.culture.nordic
```

Scholarly Communication

Scholarly Communication

These quarterly technical reports contain information and discussion about the role of network-based electronic resources in scholarly communication.

Keywords: Education, Scholarly Communication, Conferences
Audience: Educators, Researchers
Details: Free
File is: pub/vpiej-l/reports

```
ftp://borg.lib.vt.edu/pub/vpiej-1/
reports
```

```
http://borg.lib.vt.edu/
scholar.info.html
```

Scholarly Publishing

Transcript of a paper entitled 'Model University Policy Regarding Faculty Publication in Scientific and Technical Scholarly Journals: A Background Paper and Review of the Issues.'

Keywords: Publications, Scholarly Communication
Sponsor: Triangle Research Libraries Network, Durham, Raleigh, and Chapel Hill, North Carolina
Audience: Educators, Publishers
Details: Free
File is: pub/docs/about-the-net/trln-copyright-paper

```
ftp://sunsite.unc.edu
```

Scholarly Publishing

Scholarly Publishing

Transcript of a paper entitled 'Model University Policy Regarding Faculty Publication in Scientific and Technical Scholarly Journals: A Background Paper and Review of the Issues.'

Keywords:	Publications, Scholarly Communication
Sponsor:	Triangle Research Libraries Network, Durham, Raleigh, and Chapel Hill, North Carolina
Audience:	Educators, Publishers
Details:	Free
	File is: pub/docs/about-the-net/trln-copyright-paper

`ftp://sunsite.unc.edu`

Sci-Fi

FutureCulture FAQ (Frequently Asked Questions) File

List of online and offline items of interest to subscribers of FutureCulture, a mailing list on 'technoculture' or 'new edge' or 'cyberculture.'

Keywords:	Technology, Cyberculture, Postmodernism, Sci-Fi, Zines
Audience:	Reality Hackers, Cyberculture Enthusiasts
Profile:	This list discusses cyberpunk culture, rave culture, industrial music, virtual reality, drugs, computer underground, Net sociology, and virtual communities.
Contact:	Alias Datura (adatura on IRC) adatura@uafhp.uark.edu
Details:	Free

`ftp://etext.archive.umich.edu/pub`

sci.astro

sci.astro

A Usenet newsgroup providing information and discussion about astronomy.

Keywords:	Astronomy, Space
Audience:	Astronomers
User Info:	To subscribe to this Usenet newsgroup, you need access to a newsreader.

`news:sci.astro`

Sci.astro.fits

Sci.astro.fits

Discussions of the Flexible Image Transport System (FITS), a widely used standard for transporting astronomical data.

Keywords:	Astronomy
Audience:	Astronomers
Details:	Free, Images
User Info:	To subscribe to this Usenet newsgroup, you need access to a newsreader.

`news:sci.astro.fits`

Sci.astro.hubble

Sci.astro.hubble

Information about all subjects concerning NASA's Hubble space telescope.

Keywords:	Hubble Telescope, Astronomy, Space, NASA, Stargazing, Telescopes
Audience:	Astronomers, General Public, Science Teachers, Stargazers
Contact:	Paul A. Scowen scowen@wfpc3.la.asu.edu
Details:	Free, Moderated, Images
User Info:	To subscribe to this Usenet newsgroup, you need access to a newsreader.

`news:sci.astro.hubble`

Sci.astro.planetarium

Sci.astro.planetarium

A group catering to the planetarium operations community.

Keywords:	Astronomy, Planetariums
Audience:	Educators, Astronomers, Planetarium Operators
Details:	Free
User Info:	To subscribe to this Usenet newsgroup, you need access to a newsreader.

`news:sci.astro.planetarium`

sci.electronics

sci.electronics

A Usenet newsgroup providing information and discussion about circuits, theory and electrons.

Keywords:	Electronics, Engineering
Audience:	Electrical Engineers
Details:	Free
User Info:	To subscribe to this Usenet newsgroup, you need access to a newsreader.

`news:sci.electronics`

sci.engr.biomed

sci.engr.biomed

A Usenet newsgroup providing information and discussion about the field of biomedical engineering.

Keywords:	Biomedicine, Engineering (Biomedical)
Audience:	Engineers (Biomedical), Biomedical Researchers
Details:	Free
User Info:	To subscribe to this Usenet newsgroup, you need access to a newsreader.

`news:sci.engr.biomed`

sci.environment

sci.environment

A Usenet newsgroup providing information and discussion about the environment and ecology.

Keywords:	Environment, Ecology
Audience:	Environmentalists, ecologists, Earth Scientists
Details:	Free
User Info:	To subscribe to this Usenet newsgroup, you need access to a newsreader.

`news:sci.environment`

sci.math

sci.math

A Usenet newsgroup providing information and discussion about mathematics.

Keywords:	Mathematics
Audience:	Mathematicians
Details:	Free
User Info:	To subscribe to this Usenet newsgroup, you need access to a newsreader.

`news:sci.math`

sci.med

sci.med

A Usenet newsgroup providing information and discussion about medicine and its related products.

Keywords: Medicine, Health Care
Audience: Medical Professionals
Details: Free
User Info: To subscribe to this Usenet newsgroup, you need access to a newsreader.

`news:sci.med`

sci.med.physics

sci.med.physics

A Usenet newsgroup providing information and discussion about physics in medical testing and care.

Keywords: Physics, Medical Research, Health Care
Audience: Physicists, Medical Researchers, Medical Practitioners, Health Care Professionals
Details: Free
User Info: To subscribe to this Usenet newsgroup, you need access to a newsreader.

`news:sci.med.physics`

sci.military

sci.military

A Usenet newsgroup providing information and discussion about science and the military.

Keywords: Military Science
Audience: Military Personnel, Military Historians
Details: Free
User Info: To subscribe to this Usenet newsgroup, you need access to a newsreader.

`news:sci.military`

sci.physics

sci.physics

A Usenet newsgroup providing information and discussion about physical laws and properties.

Keywords: Physics
Audience: Physicists
Details: Free
User Info: To subscribe to this Usenet newsgroup, you need access to a newsreader.

`news:sci.physics`

Sci.space

Sci.space

A wide variety of discussions about space flight.

Keywords: Space, Space Flight
Audience: Space Enthusiasts, General Public
Details: Free
To participate in a Usenet newsgroup you need access to a "newsreader."

`news:sci.space.news`

`news:sci.space.science`

Sci.space.news

Sci.space.news

Keywords: Space, FAQs
Audience: Space Flight Enthusiasts
Profile: This newsgroup carries recent information about the world's space programs. Reading the FAQ set is recommended before asking questions on the other sci.space. groups.
Contact: Peter Yee
yee@atlas.arc.nasa.gov
Details: Free, Moderated
To participate in a Usenet newsgroup you need access to a newsreader.

`news:sci.space.news`

Sci.space.science

Sci.space.science

A place for technical discussions about space exploration and research.

Keywords: Space Exploration, Space
Audience: Space Enthusiasts, Space Professionals
Contact: george william herbert
gwh@crl.com gwh@soda.berkeley.edu
gwh@isu.isunet.edu
Details: Free, Moderated
User Info: To participate in a Usenet newsgroup you need access to a newsreader.

`news:sci.space.science`

Science

(The) Scientist Newsletter

Electronic newsletter pertaining to science.

Keywords: Science, Electronic Publications
Audience: Scientists, Educators, Researchers, General Public

`gopher://internic.net`

alife

The alife mailing list is for communications regarding artificial life, a formative interdisciplinary field involving computer science, the natural sciences, mathematics, and medicine.

Keywords: Artificial Life, Science, Mathematics
Sponsor: UCLA
Audience: Scientists, Biologists, Mathematicians
Contact: alife-request@cognet.ucla.edu
User Info: To subscribe to the list, send an e-mail message to the URL address below. To send a message to the entire list, address it to: alife@cognet.ucla.edu

`mailto:alife-request@cognet.ucla.edu`

ANU (Australian National University) Vietnam-SciTech-L Database

A WAIS databases of information on the development of science and technology in Vietnam

Keywords: Vietnam, Science, Technology
Sponsor: Australia Vietnam Science-Technology Link
Audience: Vietnamese
Contact: Vern Weitzel
vern@coombs.anu.edu.au

`waissrc:/Coombs-db/ANU-Vietnam-SciTech-L.src`

`gopher://cheops.anu.edu.au/7waissrc/Coombs-db/ANU-Vietnam-SciTech-L.src`

ApE-info

A mailing list for the discussion of the scientific visualization software package ApE, its usage, development, and implementation.

Keywords: Computers, Visualization, Science
Sponsor: Jim Lick
Audience: ApE Software Users, Computer Programmers

Science

Contact: Jim Lick
ape-info-request@ferkel.ucsb.edu

User Info: To subscribe to the list, send an e-mail message to the URL address below. To send a message to the entire list, address it to: ape-info@ferkel.ucsb.edu

`mailto:ape-info-request@ferkel.ucsb.edu`

Aquatic Sciences and Fisheries

This database is a comprehensive database on the science, technology, and management of marine and freshwater environments.

Keywords: Aquatic, Science

Sponsor: US National Oceanic and Atmospheric Administration (NOAA)/Cambridge Scientific Abstracts, Bethesda, MD, US

Audience: Marine Biologists, Environmentalists

Profile: The database corresponds to the print Aquatic Sciences and Fisheries Abstracts, Part 1: Biological Sciences and Living Resources, Part 2: Ocean Technology, Policy, and Non-Living Resources, and Part 3: Aquatic Pollution and Environmental Quality. ASFA includes citations to 5,000 primary journals, monographs, conference proceedings, and technical reports.

Contact: Dialog in the US at (800) 334-2564, Dialog internationally at country specific locations.

User Info: To subscribe, contact Dialog directly.

`telnet://dialog.com`

CERFnet Guide

A comprehensive guide to the CERFnet (California Education and Research Federation Network), a data-communications regional network that operates throughout California. The purpose of CERFnet is to advance science and education by assisting the interchange of information among research and educational institutions.

Keywords: Internet, Science, Education, California

Audience: Internet Surfers, Researchers, Educators

Contact: CERFnet Hotline
help@cerf.net

Details: Free
Files are in: cerfnet/cerfnet_info/cerfnet_guide/

`ftp://nic.cerf.net`

Chemistry

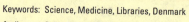

This directory is a compilation of information resources focused on chemistry.

Keywords: Chemistry, Science

Audience: Chemical Engineers, Chemistry Teachers, Students

Details: Free

`ftp://una.hh.lib.umich.edu/70/inetdirsstacks/chemistry:wiggins`

Current Contents

Current Contents provides access to the tables of contents from the current issues of leading domestic and international scientific journals. Every discipline within the sciences is represented. The database provides complete bibliographic information for each article, review, letter, note and editorial.

Keywords: Sciences, Scientific Journals

Sponsor: Institute for Scientific Information

Audience: General Public, Researchers, Librarians, Physicians

Contact: CDP Technologies Sales Department (800)950-2035, extension 400

User Info: To subscribe, contact CDP Technologies directly

`telnet://cdplus@cdplus.com`

Denmark's Library for Medicine and Science

Keywords: Science, Medicine, Libraries, Denmark

Audience: Scientists, Health Care Professionals, Medical Researchers

Details: Free
At the CCL>prompt, type DIA ENG for English interface.

`telnet://cosmos.bib.dk`

EMBASE

EMBASE is an acclaimed comprehensive index of international literature on medicine, science and pharmacology.

Keywords: Medicine, Science, Pharmacology

Sponsor: Elsevier Science Publishers

Audience: Librarians, Researchers, Students, Physicians

Contact: CDP Technologies Sales Department (800) 950-2035, extension 400.

User Info: To subscribe, contact CDP Technologies directly.

`telnet:\\cdplus@cdplus.com`

fusion

Fusion is an e-mail redistribution of Usenet sci.physics.fusion newsgroup for sites/users lacking access to Usenet.

Keywords: Physics, Fusion, Science

Audience: Physicists, Scientists

Details: Free

User Info: To subscribe to the list, send an e-mail message requesting a subscription to the URL address below. To send a message to the entire list, address it to: fusion@zorch.sf-bay.org

`mailto:fusion-request@zorch.sf-bay.org`

National Institute of Health Library Online Catalog

This entry point provides access to the books and journal holdings in the NIH Library. Journal articles are not included.

Keywords: NIH, Medicine, Science, Libraries

Sponsor: National Institute of Health (NIH)

Audience: Scientists, Researchers, Educators, Health Care Professionals

Details: Free

`telnet://nih-library.ncrr.nih.gov`

NIH EDNET

EdNet is set up as a free electronic bulletin board at the Bethesda, Maryland campus of the National Institute of Health (NIH). Its purpose is to allow high school students to ask questions of NIH scientists about current research.

Keywords: NIH, Education (Post-Secondary), Education (K-12), Science

Sponsor: National Institute of Health (NIH)

Audience: Students (high school and up), Educators

Details: Free
To receive an EDNET User's Guide and account, send an e-mail message with your name and mailing address to the URL address below.

`mailto:vt5@cu.nih.gov`

Novice MZT

Novize MZT (News of Ministry for Science and Technology of the Republic of Slovenia) provides easy, accessible news about science, development, universities, and innovative activities to individuals and institutions in research and development areas. Published at least once monthly.

Keywords: Slovenia, Science, Technology, News

Audience: Slovenians, Scientists, Technocrats

Contact: Novice-mzt@krpan.arnes.si or Novice.mzt@uni-lj.si

User Info: To subscribe to the list, send an e-mail message requesting a subscription to the URL address below. To send a message to the entire list, address it to: Novice-mzt@krpan.arnes.si

`mailto:Novice-MZT@krpan.arnes.si`

NSSDC's (National Space Science Data Center) Online Data & Information Service

The NSSDC (National Space Science Data Center) is the NASA facility charged with archiving the data from all of NASA's science missions.

Keywords: Space, Astrophysics, Software, NASA, Science

Sponsor:	NASA
Audience:	Scientists, Space Scientists, Astronomers, Engineers
Profile:	This resource contains information about NASA's missions and analysis of their data.
Details:	Free
User Info:	Expect: Login, Send: nssdc See the menu entries in your particular area of interest.

`telnet://nssdc.gsfc.nasa.gov`

Sais-l (Science Awareness and Promotion)

The SAIS list creates a forum for exchanging innovative ideas about making science more appealing to students.

Keywords:	Science, Education (K-12), Education (Secondary)
Audience:	Students (K-12), Students (high school up), Science Teachers
Contact:	Keith W. Wilson sais@unb.ca
Details:	Free
User Info:	To subscribe to the list, send an e-mail message to the URL address below consisting of a single line reading: SUB sais-l YourFirstName YourLastName To send a message to the entire list, address it to: sais-l@unb.ca

`mailto:listserv@unb.ca`

Scifaq-l

A mailing list to facilitate access to Usenet FAQ documents. It is available to people who have access to local Usenet distributions via NETNEWS or some other medium but do not have USETNET feeds per se. The list contains the latest releases of all Usenet FAQs relating to topics in science.

Keywords:	Science
Audience:	Usenet Users, Scientists
Profile:	The sci.answers newsgroup is moderated, and therefore the gateway between it and the scifaq-l mailing list has been made one-way, from Usenet into the list. The list itself is not moderated, and can be used for relevant discussion or distribution of FAQ-like documents by e-mail subscribers.
Contact:	Una Smith smith-una@yale.edu
Details:	Free
User Info:	To subscribe to the list, send an e-mail message to the URL address below consisting of a single line reading: SUB scifaq-l YourFirstName YourLastName To send a message to the entire list, address it to: scifaq-l@yalevm.cis.yale.edu

`mailto:listserv@yalevm.cis.yale.edu`

Scifraud

Scifraud is dedicated to the discussion of fraud in science.

Keywords:	Science, Fraud
Audience:	Scientists
Contact:	Al Higgins, Mike Ramundo ach13@albnyvms.bitnet sysmrr@albnyvm1.bitnet
Details:	Free
User Info:	To subscribe to the list, send an e-mail message to the URL address below consisting of a single line reading: SUB scifraud YourFirstName YourLastName To send a message to the entire list, address it to: scifraud@uacs2.albany.edu

`mailto:listserv@uacsc2.albany.edu`

Universite de Montreal UDEMATIK Library

The library's holdings are large and wide-ranging and contain significant collections in many fields.

Keywords:	Art, Architecture, Economy, Sexology, Social Law, Science, Technology, Literary Studies
Audience:	Researchers, Students, General Public
Contact:	Joelle or Sebastien Roy udematik@ere.umontreal.ca stemp@ere.umontreal.ca roys@ere.umontreal.ca
User Info:	Expect: Login; Send: Application id INFO

`telnet://udematik.umontreal.ca`

University of Toledo Library

The library's holdings are large and wide-ranging and contain significant collections in many fields.

Keywords:	Business, Great Lakes Area, Humanities, International Relations, Psychology, Science
Audience:	Researchers, Students, General Public
Details:	Free
User Info:	Expect: Enter one of the following commands . . . , Send: DIAL MVS; Expect: dialed to mvs ####; Send: UTMOST

`telnet://uofto1.utoledo.edu`

Washington University-St. Louis Medical Library & MembersLibrary

The library's holdings are large and wide-ranging and contain significant collections in many fields.

Keywords:	Medicine, Science, Technology
Audience:	Researchers, Students, General Public
Details:	Free
User Info:	Expect: Destination Code Prompt, Send: Catalog

`telnet://mcftcp.wustl.edu`

Science Fiction

alt.books.reviews

A Usenet conference devoted to reviews of books, especially science fiction and computer science books.

Keywords:	Literature (General), Computer Science, Science Fiction, Book Reviews
Audience:	General Public, Publishers, Educators, Librarians, Booksellers
Profile:	Alt.books.reviews (a.b.r. for short) is a forum for posting reviews of books of interest to readers, school and public librarians, bookstores, publishers, teachers and professors, and others who desire an "educated opinion" of a book. This is an unmoderated newsgroup.
Contact:	sbrock@csn.org.
Details:	Free To participate in a Usenet newsgroup, you need access to a "newsreader"
Notes:	The reviews in alt.books.reviews are archived at csn.org. FTP to csn.org; login: anonymous; password: your complete e-mail address. At the ftp prompt, type: cd pub/alt.books.reviews

`news:alt.books.reviews`

Deryni-L

A list for readers and fans of Katernine Kurtz's novels and other works.

Keywords:	Science Fiction, Kurtz (Katernine)
Audience:	Science Fiction Enthusiasts
Contact:	Edward J. Branley elendil@mintir.new-orleans.la.us
User Info:	To subscribe to the list, send an e-mail message requesting a subscription to the URL address below. To send a message to the entire list, address it to: deryni-l@mintir.new-orleans.la.us

`mailto:deryni-l@mintir.new-orleans.la.us`

Milieu

Discussion of the works of Julian May, notably the Saga of the Exiles, and the Galactic Milieu Trilogy.

Keywords:	May (Julian), Science Fiction
Audience:	Julian May Readers
Contact:	milieu-request@yoyo.cc.monash.edu.au

Science Fiction

Details: Free
Notes: To subscribe to the list, send an e-mail message requesting subscription to the URL address below.

`mailto:milieu-request@yoyo.cc.monash.edu.au`

Pkd-list ★

A discussion of the works and life of Philip K. Dick (1928-82), science fiction writer. Topics also include the nature of reality, consciousness, and religious experience.

Keywords: Science Fiction, Dick (Philip K.)
Audience: Philip K. Dick Readers, Science Fiction Enthusiasts
Contact: pkd-list-request@wang.com
Details: Free
User Info: To subscribe to the list, send an e-mail message requesting a subscription to the URL address below. To send a message to the entire list, address it to: pkd-list@wang.com

`mailto:pkd-list@wang.com`

Quanta ★

An electronically distributed science fiction magazine that is published monthly. Each issue contains short fiction, articles, and editorials by authors from around the world and across the Net.

Keywords: Science Fiction, Writing, Publications
Audience: Science Fiction Enthusiasts, Writers
Contact: da1n@andrew.cmu.edu
Details: Free
User Info: To subscribe to the list, send an e-mail message requesting a subscription to the URL address below. To send a message to the entire list, address it to: da1n@andrew.cmu.edu

`mailto:da1n@andrew.cmu.edu`

rec.arts.sf.starwars ★

A Usenet newsgroup providing information and discussion about the popular Star Wars trilogy.

Keywords: Science Fiction, Film
Audience: Star Wars Enthusiasts, Movie Viewers
User Info: To subscribe to this Usenet newsgroup, you need access to a newsreader.

`news:rec.arts.sf.starwars`

rec.arts.sf.tv ★

A Usenet newsgroup providing information and discussion about science fiction television programs.

Keywords: Science Fiction, Television

Audience: Science Fiction Enthusiasts, Television Viewers
User Info: To subscribe to this Usenet newsgroup, you need access to a newsreader.

`news:rec.arts.sf.tv`

rec.arts.sf.written ★

A Usenet newsgroup providing information and discussion about science fiction publications.

Keywords: Science Fiction
Audience: Science Fiction Readers
User Info: To subscribe to this Usenet newsgroup, you need access to a newsreader.

`news:rec.arts.sf.written`

rec.arts.startrek.current ★

A Usenet newsgroup providing information and discussion about current Star Trek (The Next Generation) episodes and characters.

Keywords: Television, Science Fiction
Audience: Trekkies, Television Viewers
User Info: To subscribe to this Usenet newsgroup, you need access to a newsreader.

`news:rec.arts.startrek.current`

Star Trek Resources on the Internet ★★★

This extensive resource contains information on mailing lists, news archives, other Internet resources addressing the culture surounding Star Trek fans.

Keywords: Science Fiction, Television
Audience: General Public, Trekkies, Television Viewers
Contact: Brigitte Jellinek
bjelli@cosy.sbg.ac.at

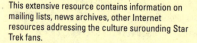

Science (History of)

McGill University, Montreal Canada, INFOMcGILL Library

The library's holdings are large and wide-ranging and contain significant collections in many fields.

Keywords: Architecture, Entomology, Biology, Science (History of), Medicine (History of), Napolean, Shakespeare (William)
Audience: Researchers, Students, General Public
Contact: Roy Miller
ccrmmus@mcgillm (Bitnet)
ccrmmus@musicm.mcgill.ca (Internet)
User Info: Expect: VM logo; Send: Enter; Expect: prompt; Send: PF3 or type INFO

`telnet://vm1.mcgill.ca`

Science Technology

University of Texas at Austin Library ★★

The library's holdings are large and wide-ranging and contain significant collections in many fields.

Keywords: Music, Natural Science, Nursing, Science Technology, Behavioral Science, Social Work, Computer Science, Engineering, Latin American Studies, Middle Eastern Studies
Audience: Researchers, Students, General Public
Details: Free
User Info: Expect: Blank Screen, Send: Return; Expect: Go, Send: Return; Expect: Enter Terminal Type, Send: vt100
Notes: Some databases are restricted to UT Austin users only.

`telnet://utcat.utexas.edu`

Scientific Journals

Current Contents

Current Contents provides access to the tables of contents from the current issues of leading domestic and international scientific journals. Every discipline within the sciences is represented. The database provides complete bibliographic information for each article, review, letter, note, and editorial.

Keywords: Sciences, Scientific Journals
Sponsor: Institute for Scientific Information
Audience: General Public, Researchers, Librarians, Physicians
Contact: CDP Technologies Sales Department (800) 950-2035, extension 400.
User Info: To subscribe, contact CDP Technologies directly.

`telnet://cdplus@cdplus.com`

Scientific Research

Washington State University at Puyallup Library ★★

The library's holdings are large and wide-ranging and contain significant collections in many fields.

Keywords: Agriculture, Scientific Research
Audience: Researchers, Students, General Public
Details: Free
User Info: Expect: Login; Send: Lib

`telnet://wsuvm1.cscwsu.edu`

Scientific Visualization

INGRAFX

This E-conference is for discussion of all matters relating to information graphics.

Keywords:	Computer Graphics, Graphic Design, Scientific Visualization
Audience:	Graphic Designers, Cartographers, Animators
Contact:	Jeremy Crampton http://info.cern.ch/hypertext/WWW/The Project.html
User Info:	To subscribe to the list, send an e-mail message to the URL address below consisting of a single line reading: SUB ingrafx YourFirstName YourLastName To send a message to the entire list, address it to: ingrafx@psuvm.psu.edu

mailto:listserv@psuvm.psu.edu

Scientists

noglstp

This list is sponsored by the National Organization of Gay and Lesbian Scientists and Technical Professionals, Inc. (a 501-C3 organization). National office is in Pasadena, CA and can be reached at (818) 791-7689 or P.O. Box 91803, Pasadena, CA 90019. There is also a newsletter that is available to membership.

Keywords:	Gay, Lesbian, Scientists, Technical Professionals
Audience:	Gay Scientists, Lesbian Scientists
Contact:	noglstp-request@elroy.jpl.nasa.gov
Details:	Free
User Info:	To subscribe to the list, send an e-mail message requesting a subscription to the URL address below. To send a message to the entire list, address it to: noglstp@elroy.jpl.nasa.gov

mailto:noglstp-request@elroy.jpl.nasa.gov

Scit-L

Scit-L

A list for those interested in information and communications science.

Keywords:	Communications, Information Sciences
Audience:	Communications Specialists, Communications Students, Information Scientists
Contact:	Elia Zureik Scitdoc@qucdn.queensu.ca
User Info:	To subscribe to this list, send an e-mail message to the URL address below, consisting of a single line reading: SUB scit-l YourFirstName YourLastName To send a message to the entire list, address it to: scit-l@qucdn.queensu.ca

mailto:listserv@qucdn.queensu.ca

Scotland

Highlands and Islands of Scotland

This web site provides information on Scotland, including business, leisure, culture, Gaelic language, tourism, distance education, and work opportunities.

Keywords:	Scotland, Travel
Sponsor:	British Telecom, United Kingdom
Audience:	Travelers, Educators, Students
Contact:	webmaster@nsa.bt.co.uk
Details:	Free

http://nsa.bt.co.uk/nsa.html

Strathspey

A forum for the discussion of all aspects of Scottish Country Dancing, for example, dancing technique.

Keywords:	Dance, Scotland, Scottish Dance
Audience:	Dancers, Dance Historians
Contact:	owner-strathspey@math.uni-frankfurt.de
Details:	Free
User Info:	To subscribe to the list, send an e-mail message requesting a subscription to the URL address below. To send a message to the entire list, address it to: strathspey@math.uni-frankfurt.de

mailto:strathspey-request@math.uni-frankfurt.de

University of Glasgow Information Service (GLANCE)

GLANCE provides subject-based information services, including an extensive section on European and world sports.

Keywords:	Sports, Soccer, Motor Racing, Mountaineering, Squash, Cricket, Golf, Tennis, Europe, Scotland
Sponsor:	University of Glasgow, Glasgow, Scotland
Audience:	Sport Enthusiasts, Fitness Enthusiasts, Nature Lovers
Profile:	Information at this site includes schedules, results, and statistics for sports such as cricket and soccer. There is also a selection of items on mountaineering.
Contact:	Alan Dawson A.Dawson@uk.ac.gla.compserv
Details:	Free

gopher://govan.cent.gla.ac.uk/Subject/Sports and Rec

Scottish Dance

Strathspey

A forum for the discussion of all aspects of Scottish Country Dancing, for example, dancing technique.

Keywords:	Dance, Scotland, Scottish Dance
Audience:	Dancers, Dance Historians
Contact:	owner-strathspey@math.uni-frankfurt.de
Details:	Free
User Info:	To subscribe to the list, send an e-mail message requesting a subscription to the URL address below. To send a message to the entire list, address it to: strathspey@math.uni-frankfurt.de

mailto:strathspey-request@math.uni-frankfurt.de

Scottish Gaelic

Gaelic-L

A multidisciplinary discussion list that facilitates the exchange of news, views, and information in Scottish Gaelic, Irish, and Manx.

Keywords:	Scottish Gaelic, Irish, Manx, Linguistics
Audience:	Linguists
Contact:	Marion Gunn mgunn@irlearn.ucd.ie caoimhin@smo.ac.uk lss203@cs.napier.ac.uk
Details:	Free
User Info:	To subscribe to the list, send an e-mail message to the URL address shown below consisting of a single line reading: SUB gaelic-l YourFirstName YourLastName To send a message to the entire list, address it to: gaelic-l@irlearn.ucd.ie

mailto:listserv@irlearn.ucd.ie

Scripting Languages

NIC (Nucleus for Interactive Computing)

WWW-based system for interactive computing.

Keywords:	Multimedia, Interactive Computing, Interface Design, Scripting Laguages, Programming

Sponsor: BYU Interactive Software Systems Lab
Audience: Software Developers, Educators
Profile: NIC is a system for interactive computing that combines a data model, a user interface model, and a scripting language to create flexible and powerful user interfaces. Documentation still under construction is located here.
Contact: Dan Olsen
olsen@cs.byu.edu
Details: Free, Moderated; Sound, Image, and Multimedia files available.
Use a World Wide Web (Mosaic) client and open a connection to the resource.

`ftp://issl.cs.byu.edu/docs/NIC/home.html`

Scuba Diving

Physical Education & Recreation

A collection of information on sporting and recreational activities from aikido to windsurfing.
Keywords: Sports, Recreation, Aikido, Cycling, Scuba Diving, Windsurfing
Audience: Sports Enthusiasts, Fitness Enthusiasts
Contact: ctcadmin@ctc.ctc.edu

`gopher://ctc.ctc.edu`

rec.scuba

A Usenet newsgroup providing information and discussion about scuba equipment and techniques.
Keywords: Scuba Sports, Travel, Recreation
Audience: Scuba Divers
User Info: To subscribe to this Usenet newsgroup, you need access to a newsreader.

`news:scuba`

Scuba-d

Digest of the Usenet rec.scuba newsgroup.
Keywords: Scuba Diving
Audience: Scuba Divers
Contact: Catherine Yang, Nick Simicich
cyang@brownvm.brown.edu
njs@watson.ibm.com
Details: Free
User Info: To subscribe to the list, send an e-mail message to the URL address below consisting of a single line reading:

SUB scuba-d YourFirstName YourLastName

To send a message to the entire list, address it to: scuba-d@brownvm.brown.edu

`mailto:listserv@brownvm.brown.edu`

Scuba-l (Scuba Diving Mailing List)

Mailing list for discussion of all aspects of scuba diving.
Keywords: Scuba Diving
Audience: Scuba Divers
Contact: Catherine Yang
cyang@brownvm.brown.edu
Details: Free
User Info: To subscribe to the list, send an e-mail message to the URL address below consisting of a single line reading:

SUB scuba-l YourFirstName YourLastName

To send a message to the entire list, address it to: scuba-l@brownvm.brown.edu

`mailto:listserv@brownvm.brown.edu`

Usenet Sports Groups Archived

An archive for Usenet groups, including many related to sports ranging from football to table tennis.
Keywords: Sports, Skydiving, Volleyball, Football, Scuba Diving, Table Tennis
Sponsor: Massachusetts Institute of Technology, Boston, MA
Audience: Sports Enthusiasts
Contact: ftp-bugs@rtfm.mit.edu
Details: Free

`ftp://rtfm.mit.edu/pub/usenet`

SCUP BITNET NEWS

SCUP BITNET NEWS

Designed to promote the mission of the society and support its activities. Society for College and University Planning (SCUP) Bitnet News provides frequent and timely exchange of information among members as well as nonmembers interested in higher-education planning through the use of bitnet.
Keywords: Planning, University Planning
Sponsor: Society for College and University Planning
Audience: Planners
Profile: Contents of the newsletter are selected on the basis of interest and value to the membership. Particular attention is given to information that advances the state-of-the-art in planning; improves the understanding and application of the tools, techniques, processes and strategies of planning; advances the professional development of the membership; and widens the base of support for planning in higher education.

Contact: Joanne E. MacRae
usertd8q@umichum.bitnet
Details: Free

Send an electronic mail note to the editor (Joanne Cate: budlao@uccvma) or the associate editor (Betsey Creekmore: pa94858@utkvm1)

`mailto:Joanne Cate: budlao@uccvma.bitnet`

SCUPMA-L: Society of College and University Planners, Mid-Atlantic Region

SCUPMA-L: Society of College and University Planners, Mid-Atlantic Region

This newsletter contains short news pieces and announcements about events of interest to the membership.
Keywords: Planning, University Planning
Audience: University Planners
Contact: Debbie Furlong
OPIR1@AUVM.bitnet
Details: Free
Contact: Debbie Furlong at OPIR1@AUVM.bitnet

`mailto:opir1@auvm.bitnet`

Seafood Internet Network

Seafood Internet Network

A mailing list to facilitate information exchange about the HACCP Alliance and the implementation of the FDA seafood HACCP program.
Keywords: Food, FDA
Audience: Seafood Industry Professionals
Contact: Robert J. Price
rjprice@dale.ucdavis.edu
User Info: To subscribe, send an e-mail message to: listproc@ucdavis.edu. Leave the subject blank and place in the body of the note:

subscribe seafood YourFirstName YourLastName

`mailto:seafood@ucdavis.edu`

Searching Gopherspace with Veronica

Searching Gopherspace with Veronica

A resource which conducts Veronica searches over restricted areas of the Internet.

Keywords: WWW, Information Retrieval, Internet
Audience: Reseachers, Students, General Public

`gopher://gopher.well.sf.ca.us/11/outbound/veronica.search`

Securities

Disclosure Database

Disclosure Database provides in-depth financial information on over 12,500 companies.

Keywords: Securities, Stock Market
Sponsor: Disclosure Incorporated, Bethesda, MD, USA
Audience: Business Professionals
Profile: The information is derived from reports filed with the US Securities and Exchange Commission (SEC) by publicly owned companies. These reports provide detailed and reliable financial information on the companies included. Extracts of 10-K and 10-Q financial reports are included, as well as 20-F financial reports and registration reports for new registrants. Disclosure provides an online source of information for marketing intelligence, corporate planning, accounting research, and corporate finance. Contents of the records include management discussion and president's letter on past-year performance, footnotes to the financials, significant events, and market conditions affecting a particular company.
Contact: Dialog in the US at (800) 334-2564, Dialog internationally at country-specific locations.
User Info: To subscribe, contact Dialog directly.
Notes: Coverage: Current; updated weekly.

`telnet://dialog.com`

FEDSEC (Federal Securities Library)

The US Federal Securities library covers federal case law, Securities Exchanges Commission (SEC) materials, Commodities Futures Trading Commision (CFTC) materials and other legal and legislative materials relevant to the securities industry, as well as company information, news and analysis.

Keywords: Law, Filings, Securities
Audience: Lawyers, Bankers, Stockbrokers
Profile: The Federal Securities library contains over 60 separately searchable files covering federal case law: Securities Exchange Commision (SEC) no-action letters, decisions, orders, releases, and SEC filings (both full text and abstracts); Commodities Futures Trading Commision (CFTC) decisions, orders, releases; legislative materials; statutory and regulatory materials; selected RICO, class derivative, and collateralized mortgage obligations case law, rules and regulations; Federal Reserve Board materials; AICPA annual reports and accounting & audit literature files; Standard & Poors company information; state administrative decisions, orders, and releases; and company news and analysis information.
Contact: New Sales Group at (800) 227-4908 or 513-859-5398 inside the US, or 1-513-865-7981 for all inquires outside the US.
User Info: To subscribe, contact Mead directly.

To examine the Lexis user guide, you can access it at the ftp site of the University of Texas at Austin at the URL address: ftp://ftp.cc.utexas.edu. The files are in: pub/ref-services/LEXIS

`telnet://nex.meaddata.com`

`http://www.meaddata.com`

Insider Trading Monitor

The database contains the transaction details of all insider-trading filings.

Keywords: Insider Trading, Securities
Sponsor: Invest/Net, Inc., Ft. Lauderdale, FL US
Audience: Stockbrokers, Media
Profile: This source contains the transaction details of all insider-trading filings, (ownership changes) received by the US Securities and Exchange Commission (SEC) since January 1984. The ownership of securities by over 100,000 officers, directors, and major shareholders (10% or more) in over 8,500 US public companies is covered in the file.
Contact: Dialog in the US at (800) 334-2564, Dialog internationally at country-specific locations.
User Info: To subscribe, contact Dialog directly.
Notes: Coverage: April 1984 to the present; updated daily.

`telnet://dialog.com`

SEC (Securities and Exchange Commission) EDGAR (Electronic Data Gathering, Analysis and Retrieval) System

Provides free access to 1994 SEC filings for approximately 2,300 companies.

Keywords: Securities, Filings, Stock Market
Sponsor: New York University School of Business
Audience: Business Professionals, Investors
Profile: This expanding project aims to make available current, public SEC filings that are filed electronically. The system is searchable by company name and is updated and indexed daily. Many types of SEC forms, including 10-K and 10-Q financial reports, are available in a number of different electronic formats. The site also provides some explanatory documentation on the EDGAR program and on the types of SEC forms and information available to the public.
Contact: Ajit Kambil
piotr@edgar.stern.nyu.edu
Details: Free

`ftp://town.hall.org/edgar`

`http://www.town.hall.org`

Security

CERT (Computer Emergency Response Team) Advisory

A major directory on computer advisory, providing access to a broad range of related resources (library catalogs, databases, and servers) via the Internet.

Keywords: Computers, Security, Computer Networking
Audience: Computer Users
Profile: Profides information on how to obtain a patch or details of a workaround for a known computer security problem. CERT works with vendors to produce a workaround or a patch for a problem, and does not publish vulnerability information until a workaround or patch is available. A CERT advisory may also be a warning about ongoing attacks to network systems.
Contact: cert@cert.org

`ftp://cert.org/pub/cert_advisories`

comp.org.eff.talk

A Usenet newsgroup organized by the EFF (Electronic Frontier Foundation) providing information and discussion about the political, social, and legal issues surrounding the Internet.

Keywords: Computers, Intellectual Property, Security, Internet
Audience: Internet Surfers
User Info: To subscribe to this Usenet newsgroup, you need access to a newsreader.

`news:comp.org.eff.talk`

comp.security.misc

A Usenet newsgroup providing information and discussion about security issues of computers and networks.

- **Keywords:** Computers, Security, Firewalls
- **Audience:** Computer Users
- **User Info:** To subscribe to this Usenet newsgroup, you need access to a newsreader.

`news:comp.security.misc`

DDN New User Guide

Defense Data Network (DDN) guide for new users.

- **Keywords:** Internet, Internet Guides, Defense, Security
- **Audience:** Internet Surfers
- **Details:** Free
- File is: netinfo/nug.doc

`ftp://nic.ddn.mil/netinfo`

firewalls

A mailing list to discuss the issues involved in setting up and maintaining Internet security firewall systems.

- **Keywords:** Security, Internet Security, Firewalls
- **Audience:** Security Workers
- **Contact:** Brent Chapman Brent@GreatCircle.com
- **Details:** Free
- **User Info:** To subscribe to the list, send an e-mail message consisting of a single line reading:
  SUB firewalls YourFirstName YourLastName

`mailto:majordomo@greatcircle.com`

Investigators and Detectives

This resource provides information files for individuals involved with investigative research, as well as a free monthly newsletter.

- **Keywords:** Detectives, Crime, Information Retrieval, Security
- **Audience:** Investigators, Detectives, Information Brokers, General Public
- **Profile:** Investigators and Detectives provides access to information covering topics such as private investigative research, strategies, sources, the art and science of investigating, theft deterrents, and electronic PI schematics and plans. Also offers a free sample of a newsletter covering various topics of interest to Private Investigators, such as techniques and strategies, security, and tracing.
- **Contact:** Mike Enlow menlow@Intec.win.net, michael@enlow.com
- **Details:** Inside Secrets.

`mailto:info@enlow.com`

Security

A forum for discussion of the field of security in general, be it electronic, physical, or computer-related.

- **Keywords:** Security
- **Audience:** Security Workers
- **Contact:** Hobbit@aim.rutgers.edu
- **Details:** Free
- **User Info:** To subscribe to the list, send an e-mail message requesting a subscription to the URL address below.

`mailto:security-request@aim.rutgers.edu.`

Virus-L

Virus-L is a forum for the discussion of computer virus experiences, protection software, and other virus-related topics. This list includes archives and files that list a number of viruses, trojan horses, and pirated programs for the IBM PC.

- **Keywords:** Computer Viruses, Security
- **Audience:** Computer Users
- **Contact:** Kenneth R. van Wyk luken@vax1.cc.lehigh.edu
- **Details:** Free
- **User Info:** To subscribe to the list, send an e-mail message to the URL address below consisting of a single line reading:
  SUB virus-l YourFirstName YourLastName
  To send a message to the entire list, address it to: virus-l@ibm1.cc.lehigh.edu

`mailto:listserv@ibm1.cc.lehigh.edu`

Senate (US)

Bibliographies of US Senate Hearings

The US Senate produces a series of committee hearings, prints, and publications as part of the legislative process. The Documents department at North Carolina State University contains files for the 99th through 103rd Congresses, which can also be searched through a WAIS searchable database.

- **Keywords:** Senate (US), Politics (US), Legislation (US), Bibliographies, Government (US)
- **Audience:** General Public, Journalists, Students, Politicians, US Citizens
- **Contact:** Jack McGeachy Jack_McGeachy@ncsu.edu
- **Details:** Free

`gopher://dewey.lib.ncsu.edu/11/library/disciplines/government/senate`

Senatorial (Papers of)

Boise State University Library

The library's holdings are large and wide-ranging and contain significant collections in many fields.

- **Keywords:** Jordan (Len, Senatorial Papers of), Church (Frank, Senatorial Papers of), Poetry (American)
- **Audience:** General Public, Researchers, Librarians, Document Delivery Professionals
- **Contact:** Dan Lester
- **Details:** Free
- **User Info:** Expect: login; Send: catalyst

`telnet://catalyst.idbsu.edu`

Sense of Place

Sense of Place

An electronic environmentalists magazine. The magazine incorporates graphics and text in a format specifically designed to be read on a Macintosh screen. You must have Hypercard version 2.1 or later.

- **Keywords:** Environment, Ecology
- **Audience:** Environmentalists
- **Contact:** SOP@dartmouth.edu
- **Details:** Costs, Images
- **User Info:** To subscribe send electronic mail to: SOP@dartmouth.edu

`gopher://gopher.dartmouth.edu/1/anonftp/pub/sop`

Sequencers

Analog Heaven

The Analog Heaven mailing list caters to people interested in vintage analog electronic music equipment. Topics include items for sale, repair tips, equipment modifications, ASCII & GIF schematics, and a general discussion of new and old analog equipment. There is an FTP/Gopher site located at cs.uwp.edu with discussions on various machines, a definitive guide to Roland synths, patch editors, modification schematics, and GIFs/JPEGs of vintage synths, as well as a few sound samples of some of the gear itself.

- **Keywords:** Music, Synthesizers, Sequencers, Analog Equipment, Electronic Music

Audience:	Electronic Music Enthusiasts, Musicians
Contact:	Todd Sines analogue-request@magnus.acs.ohio-state.edu
Details:	Free; sound files available.
User Info:	To subscribe to the list, send an e-mail message requesting a subscription to the URL address below. To send a message to the entire list, address it to: analogue@magnus.acs.ohio-state.edu

`mailto:analogue-request@magnus.acs.ohio-state.edu`

Serials Pricing

Newsletter on Serials Pricing Issues

The focus of this newsletter is the pricing of library serials.

Keywords:	Serials Pricing, Librarianship
Audience:	Librarians, Publishers
Profile:	Contributions include examples of titles considered to be overpriced, as well as of publishers' actions to keep prices down, strategies for coping with serials price increases, information about libraries' evaluation and cancellation policies and procedures, announcements of and reports from relevant meetings, and other news of serials prices.
Contact:	Marcia Tuttle tuttle@unc.bitnet
Details:	Free
User Info:	To subscribe, send an e-mail message to the URL address shown below consisting of a single line reading: SUB serials_pricing YourFirstName YourLastName

`mailto:listserv@uncvx1.Bitnet`

Services

Correct Time/NBS

Correct Time/NBS tells the correct time from the National Bureau of Standards (NBS).

Keywords:	Internet, Services, Correct Time
Audience:	Internet Surfers
Details:	Free

`ftp://india.colorado.edu/pub (Bogus site!)`

E-mail Gopher

E-mail Gopher allows the use of a gopher via e-mail.

Keywords:	Internet, Services, E-mail, Gopher
Audience:	Internet Surfers
Details:	Free Include the word "help" in the Email.

`gopher://gopher.ncc.go.jp/11/INFO/gopher`

(This is the National Cancer Center of Japan Server)

E-mail Services

A list of services available by e-mail.

Keywords:	Internet, E-mail, Services
Audience:	Internet Surfers
Contact:	David DeSimone an207@cleveland.freenet.edu
Details:	Free File is: pub/docs/about-the-net/libsoft/email_services.txt

`ftp://sunsite.unc.edu/pub/docs/about-the-net/libsoft/email_services.txt`

`http://sunsite.unc.edu/pub/docs/about-the-net/libsoft/email_services.txt`

E-mail Usenet

E-mail Usenet allows the user to post to a newsgroup via e-mail.

Keywords:	Internet, Services, E-mail, Usenet
Audience:	Internet Surfers
Details:	Free

`mailto://hierarchy-group-name@cs.utexas.edu`

Settlements

VRDCT (Jury Verdicts Library)

The Verdicts Library aids litigation preparation by providing quick and convenient access to selected online verdict and settlement information for civil cases nationwide. Case information covered includes verdict and settlement amounts, expert witnesses, case summaries, and counsel data.

Keywords:	Jury, Verdicts, Judgments, Settlements
Audience:	Lawyers
Profile:	The Verdicts library aids litigation preparation by providing quick and convenient access to selected online verdict and settlement information for civil cases nationwide. Case information covered includes verdict and settlement amounts, expert witnesses, case summaries and counsel data.
Contact:	New Sales Group at (800) 227-4908 or (513) 859-5398 inside the US, or (513) 865-7981 for all inquires outside the US.
User Info:	To subscribe, contact Mead directly. To examine the Lexis user guide, you can access it at the ftp site of the University of Texas at Austin at the URL address: ftp://ftp.cc.utexas.edu. The files are in: pub/ref-services/LEXIS

`telnet://nex.meaddata.com`

`http://www.meaddata.com`

Sex

alt.sex

A Usenet newsgroup with many categories providing discussion about sex.

Keywords:	Sex
Audience:	Adults
User Info:	To subscribe to this Usenet newsgroup, you need access to a newsreader.

`news:alt.sex`

Sex FAQ

This is the official summary of the Frequently Asked Questions from the newsgroup alt.sex. The purpose of the file is to filter the postings in the newsgroup and limit it to the FAQ. The file include answers to questions such as: What is circumcision and why is it done?, What about oral/vaginal sex during a woman's period?, What can one do about premature ejaculation?, Where can one find additional sex topics on Usenet?, What about sexually transmitted diseases?, and more.

Keywords:	Sex, FAQ
Audience:	General Public
Contact:	David Johnson, Snugglebunny superdj@cs.mcgill.ca
Details:	Free

`ftp://pit-manager.mit.edu/pub/usenet/news.answers/alt-sex/faq`

Sexology

Universite de Montreal UDEMATIK Library

The library's holdings are large and wide-ranging and contain significant collections in many fields.

Keywords:	Art, Architecture, Economy, Sexology, Social Law, Science, Technology, Literary Studies
Audience:	Researchers, Students, General Public
Contact:	Joelle or Sebastien Roy udematik@ere.umontreal.ca stemp@ere.umontreal.ca roys@ere.umontreal.ca
User Info:	Expect: Login; Send: Application id INFO

`telnet://udematik.umontreal.ca`

Sexual Abuse

alt.sexual.abuse.recovery

A Usenet newsgroup providing information and discussion about sexual abuse recovery and helping others deal with traumatic experiences.

Keywords: Sexual Abuse, Psychotherapy
Audience: Victims of Sexual Abuse
User Info: To subscribe to this Usenet newsgroup, you need access to a newsreader.

`news:alt.sexual.abuse.recovery`

Sexual Orientation

Alternates

A mailing list for people who advocate and practice an open sexual lifestyle. Its members are primarily bisexual people and their significant others. It serves as a forum and support group for adult men and women who espouse their freedom of choice and imagination in human sexual relations, no matter what their orientaion.

Keywords: Sexuality, Bisexuality, Sexual Orientation
Audience: Bisexuals, General Public
Contact: alternates-request@ns1.rutgers.edu
User Info: To subscribe to the list, send an e-mail message requesting a subscription to the URL address below. To send a message to the entire list, address it to: alternates@ns1.rutgers.edu

`mailto:alternates-request@ns1.rutgers.edu`

Bisexu-L

This list is for the discussion of issues of bisexuality and the civilized exchange of relevant ideas, opinions, and experiences between members of all orientations. There is no discrimination on the basis of orientation, religion, gender, race, and so on.

Keywords: Bisexuality, Sexual Orientation
Audience: Bisexuals, General Public
Contact: Bill Sklar
listserv@brownvm.brown.edu
Details: Free
User Info: To subscribe to the list, send an e-mail message to the URL address below, consisting of a single line reading:

SUB Bisexu-L YourFirstName YourLastName

To send a message to the entire list, address it to: bisexu-l@brownvm.brown.edu

`mailto:listserv@brownvm.brown.edu`

Sexuality

Alternates

A mailing list for people who advocate and practice an open sexual lifestyle. Its members are primarily bisexual people and their significant others. It serves as a forum and support group for adult men and women who espouse their freedom of choice and imagination in human sexual relations, no matter what their orientaion.

Keywords: Sexuality, Bisexuality, Sexual Orientation
Audience: Bisexuals, General Public
Contact: alternates-request@ns1.rutgers.edu
User Info: To subscribe to the list, send an e-mail message requesting a subscription to the URL address below. To send a message to the entire list, address it to: alternates@ns1.rutgers.edu

`mailto:alternates-request@ns1.rutgers.edu`

AUGLBC-l

The American University Gay, Lesbian, and Bisexual Community (AUGLBC) is a support group for lesbian, gay, bisexual, transsexual, and supportive students. The group is also connected with the International Gay and Lesbian Youth Organization (known as IGLYO).

Keywords: Gay, Lesbian, Bisexual, Transsexual, Sexuality
Audience: Gays, Lesbians, Bisexuals, Transsexuals, Students (college)
Contact: Erik G. Paul
User Info: To subscribe to the list, send an e-mail message to the URL address below, consisting of a single line reading:

SUB AUGLBC-l YourFirstName YourLastName

To send a message to the entire list, address it to: AUGLBC-l@american.edu

`mailto:listserv@american.edu`

Cd-Forum

The purpose of this list is to provide support and to discuss/share experiences about gender-related issues, including cross dressing, transvestism, and transsexualism.

Keywords: Transsexualism, Transvestism, Sexuality, Gender
Audience: Transsexuals, Transvestites
Contact: Valerie
cd-request@valis.biocad.com
Details: Free
User Info: To subscribe to the list, send an e-mail message requesting a subscription to the URL address below. To send a message to the entire list, address it to: cd@valis.biocad.com
Notes: This list is in digest format.

`mailto:cd-request@valis.biocad.com`

dont-tell

The don't-tell list is for people concerned about the effects that the new military policy known as "don't ask/don't tell" will have at academic institutions, whether military or ROTC-affiliated.

Keywords: Sexuality, Military Policy, Education (Post-Secondary)
Audience: Students, Gays, Lesbians, Military Personnel, Civil Libertarians
Contact: dont-tell-request@choice.princeton.edu
Details: Free
User Info: To subscribe to the list, send an e-mail message requesting a subscription to the URL address below. To send a message to the entire list, address it to: dont-tell-request@choice.princeton.edu

`mailto:dont-tell-request@choice.princeton.edu`

gegstaff

All topics relating to sexuality and gender in geography.

Keywords: Geography, Sexuality
Audience: Geographers, Sex Enthusiasts
Details: Free
User Info: To subscribe to the list, send an e-mail message to the URL address shown below consisting of a single line reading:

SUB gegstaff YourFirstName YourLastName

To send a message to the entire list, address it to: gegstaff@ukcc.uky.edu

`mailto:listserv@ukcc.uky.edu`

Shakers

Shakers

A forum on the United Society of Believers for those interested in the history, culture, artifacts, and beliefs of the Shakers (United Society of Believers). Discussions cover a broad range of subject matter.

Keywords: Shakers, Christianity, Religion
Audience: Shakers, Theologians
Contact: Marc Rhorer
rhorer@ukcc.uky.edu

Details: Free

User Info: To subscribe to the list, send an e-mail message to the URL address shown below consisting of a single line reading:

SUB shaker YourFirstName YourLastName

To send a message to the entire list, address it to: shaker@ukcc.uky.edu

`mailto:listserv@ukcc.uky.edu`

Shakespeare (William)

Dartmouth College Library ★★

The library's holdings are large and wide-ranging and contain significant collections in many fields.

Keywords: American Calligraphy, Cervantes (Miguel de), Railroads, Polar Regions, Frost (Robert), Shakespeare (William), Spanish Plays

Audience: General Public, Researchers, Librarians, Document Delivery Professionals

Contact: Katharina Klemperer
kathy.klemperer@dartmouth.edu

Details: Free

User Info: Expect: login, Send: wolfpac

`telnet://lib.dartmouth.edu`

McGill University, Montreal Canada, INFOMcGILL Library

The library's holdings are large and wide-ranging and contain significant collections in many fields.

Keywords: Architecture, Entomology, Biology, Science (History of), Medicine (History of), Napolean, Shakespeare (William)

Audience: Researchers, Students, General Public

Contact: Roy Miller
ccrmmus@mcgillm (Bitnet)
ccrmmus@musicm.mcgill.ca (Internet)

User Info: Expect: VM logo; Send: Enter; Expect: prompt; Send: PF3 or type INFO

`telnet://vm1.mcgill.ca`

University of Pennsylvania PENNINFO Library ★★

The library's holdings are large and wide-ranging and contain significant collections in many fields.

Keywords: Church History, Spanish Inquisition, Witchcraft, Shakespeare (William), Bibles, Aristotle (Texts of), Fiction, Whitman (Walt), French Revolution, Drama (French), Literature (English), Literature (Spanish)

Audience: Researchers, Students, General Public

Contact: Al DSouza
penninfo-admin@dccs.upenn.edu
dsouza@dccs.upenn.edu

Details: Free

User Info: Expect: Login; Send: Public

`telnet://penninfo.upenn.edu`

Shamash, The New York - Israel Project

Shamash, The New York - Israel Project ★★★

This site is designed to facilitate communications between Jews and Jewish organizations through the medium of the Internet. Information includes archives of Jewish lists, updates of community Jewish events in New York and beyond, a Jewish white pages, and a section on the Holocaust. It also has Hebrew software and access to other Jewish and Israeli information servers.

Keywords: Judaism, Israel, New York

Sponsor: New York - Israel Project (Nysernet), New York, USA

Audience: Jews, Jewish Organizations

Contact: Avrum Goodblatt, Chaim Dworkin
goodblat@israel.nysernet.org
chaim@israel.nysernet.org.

`gopher://nysernet.org`

Shareware

Apple Computer WWW Server ★★

A web site containing information about Apple Computer. The resource is designed to provide timely product information, including press releases on Apple's technology and research. Also contains links to Freeware and Shareware sites, and includes information for developers and programmers.

Keywords: Computer Systems, Technology, Apple Computer, Shareware

Audience: General Public

`http://www.apple.com`

fsuucp ★

The FSUUCP mailing list is for the discussion of bug hunting, feature proposing, and announcements of the availability and release dates of FSUUCP, an MS-DOS UUCP/mail/ news package.

Keywords: Software, Shareware

Audience: Students, Computer Users

Details: Free

User Info: To subscribe to the list, send an e-mail message requesting a subscription to the URL address below. To send a message to the entire list, address it to: fsuucp@polyslo.calpoly.edu

`mailto:fsuucp-request@polyslo.calpoly.edu`

GNUs Bulletin: Newsletter of the Free Software Foundation ★★★

Bringing you news about the GNU Project, the Free Software Foundation is dedicated to eliminating restrictions on copying, redistribution, understanding, and modification of computer programs.

Keywords: Software, Shareware, Free Software

Sponsor: Free Software Foundation

Audience: Computer Programmers, Computer Users

Contact: Leonard H. Tower, Jr.
tower@ai.mit.edu

Details: Free

`mailto:info-gnu-request@prep.ai.mit.edu`

HYTELNET

A shareware application database directory to libraries.

Keywords: Computer Systems, Libraries, Shareware

Audience: General Audience

Profile: HYTELNET is a guide to library catalogs from the Americas, Europe

Contact: Peter Scott
aa375@freenet.carleton.ca

Details: Free

Notes: HYTELNET is in English, but the interface to some international

`gopher://gophlib@gopher.yale.edu`

info-GNU-MSDOS ★

This electronic conference is for the GNUISH MS-DOS Development Group.

Keywords: Shareware, Freeware, MS-DOS Computers

Audience: MS-DOS Users, GNUISH MS-DOS Developers

Contact: David J. Camp
david@wubios.wustl.edu

Details: Free

User Info: To subscribe to the list, send an e-mail message to the URL address below consisting of a single line reading:

SUB info-GNU-MSDOS YourFirstName YourLastName

`mailto:listserv@wugate.wustl.edu`

ShareWord

Online BookStore (OBS)

Offers full text (fiction and nonfiction) in a variety of electronic formats, free and for a fee.

Keywords:	Online Books, Books, ShareWord, Fiction, Nonfiction Books
Sponsor:	Editorial Inc./OBS
Audience:	General Public, Reading Enthusiasts
Profile:	Started in 1992, the OBS offers a variety of full-text titles.
Contact:	Laura Fillmore laura@editorial.com
Details:	Costs, Moderated, Images, Multimedia
User Info:	To subscribe to the list, send an e-mail message requesting a subscription to the URL address below.

`mailto:laura@editorial.com`

Shopping

The Branch Mall, an Electronic Shopping Mall

Branch Information Services offers shopping to customers and leases storefronts and electronic catalogs to vendors.

Keywords:	Mall, Shopping, Gifts, Advertising, Mailorder
Sponsor:	Branch Information Services
Audience:	Consumers, Merchants
Contact:	Jon Zeeff jon@branch.com
Details:	Free
Notes:	Free for consumers.

`http://branch.com`

Shortwave Radio

Drake-R8

To discuss and share experiences, technical issues, problems, and so on, related to the Drake R8 shortwave receiver.

Keywords:	Shortwave Radio
Audience:	Shortwave Radio Users
Contact:	Mik Butler mik@hpsesuka.pwd.hp.com
User Info:	To subscribe to the list, send an e-mail message requesting a subscription to the URL address below. To send a message to the entire list, address it to: mik@hpsesuka.pwd.hp.com

`mailto:mik@hpsesuka.pwd.hp.com`

Silicon Graphics

Virtual Reality Space

A collection of virtual reality information, including downloadable software tools from Silicon Graphics.

Keywords:	Virtual Reality, Cyberspace, Software, Silicon Graphics
Sponsor:	The University of Texas, Austin, Texas, USA
Audience:	Virtual Reality Enthusiasts, Programmers
Contact:	Jay Ashcraft ashcraft@ccwf.cc.utexas.edu

`gopher://ftp.cc.utexas.edu`

`ftp://cc.utexas.edu`

Sim (Dave)

Cerebi

This list discusses the Cerebus comic book by Dave Sim. Anything relating to Cerebus or Sim is welcome.

Keywords:	Comic Books, Sim (Dave)
Audience:	Comics Enthusiasts
Contact:	Christian Walters cerebi-request@tomservo.b23b.ingr.com
Details:	Free
User Info:	To subscribe to the list, send an e-mail message requesting a subscription to the URL address below. To send a message to the entire list, address it to: cerebi@tomservo.b23b.ingr.com
Notes:	It's just an echo list, so anything that gets mailed is bounced to everyone.

`mailto:cerebi-request@tomservo.b23b.ingr.com`

SIMULA

Simula

An electronic conference for discussion of the SIMULA programming language.

Keywords:	Programming, SIMULA
Audience:	SIMULA Programmers
Details:	Free
User Info:	To subscribe to the list, send an e-mail message to the URL address below consisting of a single line reading: SUB Simula YourFirstName YourLastName To send a message to the entire list, address it to: Simula@bitnic.educom.edu

`mailto:listserv@bitnic.educom.edu`

Simulation

Anneal

A mailing list for the discussion of simulated annealing techniques and analysis, as well as related issues such as stochastic optimization, Boltzmann machines, and metricity of NP-complete move spaces.

Keywords:	Mathematics, Simulation, Annealing
Sponsor:	UCLA
Audience:	Mathematicians, Physicists
Contact:	Daniel R. Greening anneal-request@cs.ucla.edu
User Info:	To subscribe to the list, send an e-mail message to the URL address below. To send a message to the entire list, address it to: anneal@cs.ucla.edu
Notes:	Membership is restricted to those doing active research in simulated annealing or related areas.

`mailto:anneal-request@cs.ucla.edu`

Aviator

A mailing list for users of Aviator™, the flight-simulation program from Artificial Horizons, Inc.

Keywords:	Aviation, Simulation, Computers, Flight Simulation
Audience:	Software Users
Contact:	Jim Hickstein aviator@ICDwest.Teradyne.COM
Details:	Free
User Info:	To subscribe to the list, send an e-mail message requesting a subscription to the URL address below. To send a message to the entire list, address it to: aviator@ICDwest.Teradyne.COM
Notes:	Aviator runs on Sun workstations with the GX graphics accelerator option. Its charter is simply to facilitate communication among users of Aviator. It is not intended for communication with the "providers" of Aviator. All mail received at the submission address is reflected to all the subscribers of the list.

`mailto:aviator-request@ICDwest.Teradyne.COM`

GLOSAS News (Global Systems Analysis and Simulating Association)

Newsletter of GLOSAS in the US, which is dedicated to global electronic education and simulation as a tool for promoting peace and the care of the natural environment.

Keywords:	Education, Simulation, Peace
Audience:	Educators, Environmentalists

Contact:	Anton Ljutic
	anton@vax2.concordia.ca
Details:	Free

`mailto:listserv@vm1.mcgill.ca`

Interactive Frog Dissection Kit

An interactive simulation of the dissection of a computer-generated frog.

Keywords:	Biology, Simulation, Interactive Learning
Sponsor:	Lawrence Berkeley Laboratory-Whole Frog Project, Berkeley, California, USA
Audience:	Students, Educators, Biologists
Contact:	David Robertson
	dwrobertson@lbl.gov
Notes:	Copyrighted (commercial uses require permission)

`http://george.1b1.gov/ITG.hm.pg.docs/dissect/info.html`

Singapore

Business News—Singapore

This gopher site focuses on business in Singapore.

Keywords:	Singapore, Economics, Business
Audience:	Economists, Business Professionals
Details:	Free

`gopher://gopher.cic.net/11/e-serials/alphabetic/b/business-news`

`http://gopher.cic.net`

Singapore DMC

Singapore DMC

The Digital Media Center (DMC) home page contains links related to contents about Singapore, the National Computer Board (NCB), and various other National IT (Information Technology) projects.

Keywords:	Internet, Networking
Audience:	Internet Surfers
Contact:	shaopin@ncb.gov.sg
	kianjin@ncb.gov.sg
Details:	Free

`http://king.ncb.gov.sg`

Singing

Chorus

This is the lesbian and gay chorus mailing list, formed November 1991 by John Schrag (jschrag@alias.com) and Brian Jarvis (jarvis@psych.toronto.edu). Membership includes artistic directors, singers, chorus officers, interpreters, and support staff and friends. Topics of discussion include repertoire, arrangements, staging, costuming, management, fundraising, music, events, and concerts.

Keywords:	Singing, Choral Singing, Homosexuality, Gay, Lesbian
Audience:	Lesbian Singers, Gay Singers, Chorus Officers, Lesbians, Gays, Choral Singers
Contact:	chorus-request@psych.toronto.edu
Details:	Free
User Info:	To subscribe to the list, send an e-mail message requesting a subscription to the URL address below. To send a message to the entire list, address it to: chorus@psych.toronto.edu

`mailto:chorus-request@psych.toronto.edu`

Singles

alt.personals.ads

A Usenet newsgroup providing a forum for singles.

Keywords:	Personals, Singles
Audience:	Singles
User Info:	To subscribe to this Usenet newsgroup, you need access to a newsreader.

`news:alt.personals.ads`

Soc.singles

A Usenet newsgroup for single people discussing their activities and social events.

Keywords:	Singles
Audience:	Single People
	To participate in a Usenet newsgroup you need access to a 'newsreader.'

`news:soc.singles`

Skiing

rec.skiing

A Usenet newsgroup providing information and discussion about skiing.

Keywords:	Sports, Recreation, Skiing
Audience:	Skiers
User Info:	To subscribe to this Usenet newsgroup, you need access to a newsreader.

`news:rec.skiing`

Skiing in Utah

An FTP site maintaining information on skiing sites in Utah, Idaho, and Wyoming.

Keywords:	Sports, Skiing
Sponsor:	Utah University
Audience:	Skiers
Details:	Free

`ftp://ski.utah.edu/skiing`

Skin

rxderm-l

A mailing list intended for promoting the discussion of dermatologic treatment among practicing dermatologists.

Keywords:	Dermatology, Skin, Disease, Doctors
Audience:	Dermatologists
Contact:	A.C. Huntley
	achuntley@ucdavis.edu
User Info:	To subscribe to the list, send an e-mail message to the URL address below consisting of a single line reading:
	SUB rxderm-l YourFirstName YourLastName
	To send a message to the entire list, address it to: rxderm-l@ucdavis.edu

`mailto:listserv@ucdavis.edu`

Skydiving

Base-Jumping

An open discussion of fixed-object skydiving. Topics include equipment, sites, packing techniques, and publications.

Keywords:	Skydiving
Audience:	Skydivers
Contact:	base-request@lunatix.lex.ky.us
Details:	Free
User Info:	To subscribe to the list, send an e-mail message requesting a subscription to the URL address below. To send a message to the entire list, address it to: base@lunatix.lex.ky.us
Notes:	Membership is open to anyone who has made at least one base jump or skydive.

`mailto:base-request@lunatix.lex.ky.us`

Usenet Sports Groups Archived

An archive for Usenet groups, including many related to sports ranging from football to table tennis.

- Keywords: Sports, Skydiving, Volleyball, Football, Scuba Diving, Table Tennis
- Sponsor: Massachusetts Institute of Technology, Boston, MA
- Audience: Sports Enthusiasts
- Contact: ftp-bugs@rtfm.mit.edu
- Details: Free

`ftp://rtfm.mit.edu/pub/usenet`

Slavery

Johns Hopkins University Library

The library's holdings are large and wide-ranging and contain significant collections in many fields.

- Keywords: Literature (English), Economics, Classics, Drama (German), Slavery, Trade Unions, Incunabula, Bibles, Diseases (History of), Nursing (History of), Abolitionism
- Audience: General Public, Researchers, Librarians, Document Delivery Professionals
- Details: Free

`telnet://jhuvm.hcf.jhu.edu`

The University of Illinois at Chicago Library

The library's holdings are large and wide-ranging and contain significant collections in many fields.

- Keywords: Health Science, Chicago, Industry, Slavery, Abolitionism, Roosevelt (Franklin D.)
- Audience: General Public, Researchers, Librarians, Document Delivery Professionals
- Details: Free
- User Info: Expect: introductory screen, Send: Clear key; Expect: UIC flame screen, Send: Enter key; Expect: Logon screen, Send: DIAL PVM; Expect: PVM (Passthru) screen, Send: Type: Move cursor to NOTIS and press Enter key Response: One line message about port in use Type: Enter key

`telnet://uicvm.uic.edu`

SLON

Oglasna Deska

Oglasna Deska (bulletin board) consists of transcripts taken from SLON, which is a nickname for a Decnet connecting several computers in Slovenia. There is a conference similar to a Usenet newsgroup running under SLON and the articles and replies are occasionally saved and sent to the world. The topics cover a wide area.

- Keywords: Slovenia, SLON, Usenet Newsgroup
- Audience: Slovenians, Croatians, Serbians
- Contact: Dean Mozetic
  Oglasna-Deska@krpan.arnes.si
- Details: Free
- User Info: To subscribe to the list, send an e-mail message requesting a subscription to the URL address below. To send a message to the entire list, address it to: oglasna-deka@krpan.arnes.si
- Notes: The topics covered are equivalent to Usenet newsgroups such as politics, automobiles, humor, computer networks, climbing, and miscellaneous investments.

`mailto:Oglasna-Deska@krpan.arnes.si`

Slovak Republic

University of Nebraska at Lincoln Library

The library's holdings are large and wide-ranging and contain significant collections in many fields.

- Keywords: Slovak Republic, Czech Republic, Folklore, Military History, Latvia, Law (Tax), Law (US)
- Audience: General Public, Researchers, Librarians, Document Delivery Professionals
- Contact: Anita Cook
- Details: Free
- User Info: Expect: login, Send: library

`telnet://unllib.unl.edu`

Slovakia

CEE Environmental Libraries Database

A directory of over 300 libraries and environmental information centers in Central Eastern Europe that specalize in, or maintain significant collections of information about, the environment, ecology, sustainable living, or conservation. The database concentrates on six Central Eastern European countries: Bulgaria, Czech Republic, Hungary, Romania, Slovakia, and Poland.

- Keywords: Central Eastern Europe, Environment, Sustainable Living, Bulgaria, Czech Republic, Hungary, Romania, Slovakia, Poland.
- Sponsor: The Wladyslaw Poniecki Charitable Foundation, Inc.
- Audience: Environmentalists, Green Movement, Librarians, Community Builders, Sustainable Living Specialists.
- Profile: This database is the product of an Environmental Training Project (ETP) that was funded in 1992 by the US Agency for International Development as a 5-year cooperative agreement with a consortium headed by the University of Minnesota (US AID Cooperative Agreement Number EUR-0041-A-002-2020). Other members of the consortium include the University of Pittsburgh's Center for Hazardous Materials Research, The Institute for Sustainable Communities, and the World Wildlife Fund. The Wladyslaw Poniecki Charitable Foundation, Inc., was a subcontractor to the World Wildlife Fund and published the Directory of Libraries and Environmental Information Centers in Central Eastern Europe: A Locator/Directory. This gopher database consists of an electronic version of the printed directory, subsequently modified and updated online. Access to the data is facilitated by a WAIS search engine which makes it possible to retrieve information about libraries, subject area specializations, personnel, and so on.
- Contact: Doug Kahn, CEDAR
  kahn@pan.cedar.univie.ac.at

`gopher://gopher.poniecki.berkeley.edu`

slovak-l

A mailing list for discussion of Slovak culture, and more.

- Keywords: Slovakia, Culture
- Audience: Researchers, Students, Slovaks
- Contact: Jan George Frajkor
  gfrajkor@ccs.carleton.ca
- User Info: To subscribe to the list, send an e-mail message to the URL address below consisting of a single line reading:

  SUB slovak-l YourFirstName YourLastName

  To send a message to the entire list, address it to: slovak-1@ubvm.cc.buffalo.edu

`mailto:listserv@ubvm.cc.buffalo.edu`

Slovenia

Novice MZT

Novize MZT (News of Ministry for Science and Technology of the Republic of Slovenia) provides easy, accessible news about science, development, universities, and innovative activities to individuals and institutions in research and development areas. Published at least once monthly.

Keywords: Slovenia, Science, Technology, News
Audience: Slovenians, Scientists, Technocrats
Contact: Novice-mzt@krpan.arnes.si or Novice.mzt@uni-lj.si
User Info: To subscribe to the list, send an e-mail message requesting a subscription to the URL address below. To send a message to the entire list, address it to: Novice-mzt@krpan.arnes.si

mailto:Novice-MZT@krpan.arnes.si

Oglasna Deska

Oglasna Deska (bulletin board) consists of transcripts taken from SLON, which is a nickname for a Decnet connecting several computers in Slovenia. There is a conference similar to a Usenet newsgroup running under SLON and the articles and replies are occasionally saved and sent to the world. The topics cover a wide area.

Keywords: Slovenia, SLON, Usenet Newsgroup
Audience: Slovenians, Croatians, Serbians
Contact: Dean Mozetic
Oglasna-Deska@krpan.arnes.si
Details: Free
User Info: To subscribe to the list, send an e-mail message requesting a subscription to the URL address below. To send a message to the entire list, address it to: oglasna-deka@krpan.arnes.si
Notes: The topics covered are equivalent to Usenet newsgroups such as politics, automobiles, humor, computer networks, climbing, and miscellaneous investments.

mailto:Oglasna-Deska@krpan.arnes.si

Pisma Bralcev

An edited mailing list that publishes readers' opinions, questions, inquiries for help, answers, and so on, in Slovene. Also includes travel tips and book reviews.

Keywords: Slovenia
Audience: Slovenians
Contact: Andrej Brodnik
Pisma-Bralcev@krpan.arnes.si
Details: Free
User Info: To subscribe to the list, send an e-mail message requesting a subscription to the URL address below. To send a message to the entire list, address it to: pisma-bralcev@krpan.arnes.si

mailto:Pisma-Bralcev@krpan.arnes.si
mailto:Pisma.Bralcev@uni-lj.si

Small Business

Esbdc-l

A mailing list intended to facilitate discussion between small business development centers, focusing on such topics as performance standards, business behavior, products, specific industry information access, deficit reduction plans, and private cost sharing.

Keywords: Business, Small Business
Sponsor: Association of Small Business Development Centers, USA
Audience: State Officials, Educators, Certified Public Accountants, Investors
User Info: To subscribe to the list, send an e-mail message to the URL address below consisting of a single line reading:
SUB esbdc-l YourFirstName YourLastName
To send a message to the entire list, address it to: esbdc-l@ferris.bitnet

mailto:listserv@ferris.bitnet

Smbnet (Society for Mathematical Biology Digest)

Smbnet (Society for Mathematical Biology Digest)

Keywords: Mathematical Biology, Biology
Audience: Mathematical Biologists, Biologists
Contact: Ray Mejia
Details: Free
User Info: To subscribe to the list, send an e-mail message to the URL address below consisting of a single line reading:
SUB smbnet YourFirstName YourLastName
To send a message to the entire list, address it to: smbnet@fconvx.ncifcrf.gov

mailto:listserv@fconvx.ncifcrf.gov

Smiley Faces Dictionary

Smiley Faces Dictionary

An unofficial list of more than 200 smilies.

Keywords: Internet, Smiley
Audience: Internet Surfers
Details: Free
User Info: File is pub/smiley-dictionary

http://ftp.gsfc.nasa.gov

Smithsonian

Smithsonian Institution Natural History Gopher

The Smithsonian Natural History Gopher server provides access to data associated with the Institutions museum collections (natural history and anthropology).

Keywords: Smithsonian, Natural History, Anthropology
Sponsor: Museum of Natural History, Smithsonian Institution, Washington, DC.
Audience: Anthropologists, Biologists, Natural History Scientists, Researchers
Profile: With over 120 million collections and 135 professional scientists, the National Museum of Natural History is one of the worlds largest museums devoted to natural history and anthropology. This server provides access to data associated with the collections, and to information and tools for the study of the natural world. The Department of Vertebrate Zoology includes checklists of known species names. Currently the Mammal Species of the World have been posted. Plans to expand this to include Amphibians, Fishes, and so on. are under way.
Contact: Don Gourley
don@smithson.si.edu
Details: Free

gopher://nmnhgoph.si.edu

Smithsonian Online

Located on America Online (with partial access by ftp), this allows online access to the Institution's resources.

Keywords: Museums, Art Exhibitions, Smithsonian
Sponsor: Smithsonian Institution, Washington DC
Audience: Educators, Students, General Public

Profile: Smithsonian Online includes resources for teachers and students in the form of bulletin boards about Smithsonian museums, photographs, listings of events in Washington and other communities, and excerpts from Smithsonian and Air & Space/Smithsonian.

`ftp://photo1.si.edu`

Smoking

Pipes

A forum for discussing the moderate use and appreciation of fine tobacco, including cigars, pipes, quality cigarettes, pipe making and carving, snuff, publications, and related topics.

Keywords: Pipes, Tobacco, Smoking
Audience: Smokers, Researchers, Market Analysts
Contact: Steve Masticola
masticol@scr.siemens.com
Details: Free, Moderated
User Info: To subscribe to the list, send an e-mail message requesting a subscription to the URL address below. To send a message to the entire list, address it to: masticol@scr.siemens.com

`mailto:masticol@scr.siemens.com`

soc.history

soc.history

A Usenet newsgroup providing information and discussion about historical issues.

Keywords: History (World)
Audience: Historians
Details: Free
User Info: To subscribe to this Usenet newsgroup, you need access to a newsreader.

`news:soc.history`

soc.men

soc.men

A Usenet newsgroup providing information and discussion about men, their problems, and their relationships.

Keywords: Men's Movement, Gender
Audience: Men, Activists
Details: Free
User Info: To subscribe to this Usenet newsgroup, you need access to a newsreader.

`news:soc.men`

soc.motss

soc.motss

A Usenet newsgroup providing information and discussion about homosexuality.

Keywords: Homosexuality, Gays, Lesbians, Bisexuals
Audience: Gays, Lesbians, Bisexuals
Details: Free
User Info: To subscribe to this Usenet newsgroup, you need access to a newsreader.

`news:soc.motss`

soc.penpals

soc.penpals

A Usenet newsgroup providing information and discussion for people in search of Net pals and other online correspondence.

Keywords: Computing, Writing
Audience: Computer Users, Writers
Details: Free
User Info: To subscribe to this Usenet newsgroup, you need access to a newsreader.

`news:soc.penpals`

soc.religion.christian

soc.religion.christian

A Usenet newsgroup providing information and discussion about Christianity and related issues.

Keywords: Christianity, Religion
Audience: Christians, Theologians
Details: Free
User Info: To subscribe to this Usenet newsgroup, you need access to a newsreader.

`news:soc.religion.christian`

Soc.singles

Soc.singles

A Usenet newsgroup for single people discussing their activities and social events.

Keywords: Singles
Audience: Single People
         To participate in a Usenet newsgroup you need access to a 'newsreader.'

`news:soc.singles`

Soccer

france-foot

Discussions of the French football (soccer) scene. Results and news are posted regularly.

Keywords: Soccer, Sports, France, Football
Audience: Soccer Enthusiasts, French Sports Enthusiasts
Contact: Vincent Habchi, Kent Hedlundh
dvlkhh@cs.umu.se
Details: Free
User Info: To subscribe to the list, send an e-mail message requesting a subscription to the URL address below. To send a message to the entire list, address it to: france-foot@inf.enst.fr

`mailto:france-foot-request@inf.enst.fr`

rec.sport.soccer

A Usenet newsgroup providing information and discussion about soccer.

Keywords: Soccer, Sports
Audience: Soccer Fans, Sports Fans
User Info: To subscribe to this Usenet newsgroup, you need access to a newsreader.

`news:rec.sport.soccer`

University of Glasgow Information Service (GLANCE)

GLANCE provides subject-based information services, including an extensive section on European and world sports.

Keywords: Sports, Soccer, Motor Racing, Mountaineering, Squash, Cricket, Golf, Tennis, Europe, Scotland
Sponsor: University of Glasgow, Glasgow, Scotland
Audience: Sport Enthusiasts, Fitness Enthusiasts, Nature Lovers
Profile: Information at this site includes schedules, results, and statistics for sports such as cricket and soccer. There is also a selection of items on mountaineering.
Contact: Alan Dawson
A.Dawson@uk.ac.gla.compserv
Details: Free

`gopher://govan.cent.gla.ac.uk/Subject/Sports and Rec`

Wiretap Sports Archives ★

Sports articles, including information on soccer in the US and Canada, rules for soccer and Australian football, and some rather dated material on American football.

Keywords: Sports, Football, Soccer
Sponsor: The Internet Wiretap Library
Audience: Sports Enthusiasts
Details: Free

`gopher://wiretap.spies.com/library/article/sports`

Social and Behavioral Science

soc.bi ★

A Usenet newsgroup providing information and discussion about bisexuality.

Keywords: Bisexuality, Social and Behavioral Science
Audience: Bisexuals, Bisexual Activists, Sociologists, Social Scientists
Details: Free
User Info: To subscribe to this Usenet newsgroup, you need access to a newsreader.

`news:soc.bi`

Social Events

Ne-social-motss ★

Announcements of lesbian/gay/bisexual social events and other happenings in the Northeastern US.

Keywords: Social Events, Lesbian, Gay, Bisexuality
Audience: Lesbians, Gays, Bisexuals
Contact: ne-social-motss-request@plts.org
Details: Free
User Info: To subscribe to the list, send an e-mail message requesting a subscription to the URL address below.

`mailto:ne-social-motss-request@plts.org`

Social Law

Universite de Montreal UDEMATIK Library ★★

The library's holdings are large and wide-ranging and contain significant collections in many fields.

Keywords: Art, Architecture, Economy, Sexology, Social Law, Science, Technology, Literary Studies
Audience: Researchers, Students, General Public
Contact: Joelle or Sebastien Roy
udematik@ere.umontreal.ca
stemp@ere.umontreal.ca
roys@ere.umontreal.ca
User Info: Expect: Login; Send: Application id INFO

`telnet://udematik.umontreal.ca`

Social Responsibility

CPSR/PDX Newsletter ★

This is the newsletter of the Portland chapter of Computer Professionals for Social Responsibility.

Keywords: Computer Professionals, Social Responsibility
Audience: Computer Professionals
Contact: Erik Nilsson
erin@goldfish.mitron.tek.com
Details: Free

`mailto:erikn@goldfish.mitron.tek.com`

Social Science

CUSSNET ★

Computer Users in the Social Sciences (CUSS) is a discussion group devoted to issues of interest to social workers, counselors, and human service workers of all disciplines. The discussion frequently involves computer applications in treatment, agency administration, and research. Students, faculty, community-based professionals, and casual observers join in the discussion. Software, hardware, and ethical issues associated with their use in the human services generate lively and informative discussions.

Keywords: Social Sciences, Computers, Computer Applications
Audience: Social Workers, Human Services Workers, General Public
Contact: cussnet-request@stat.com
Details: Free
User Info: To subscribe to the list, send an e-mail message to the address below consisting of a single line reading:

SUB cussnet YourFirstName YourLastName

To send a message to the entire list, address it to: cussnet@stat.com

`mailto:listserv@stat.com`

Eastern Washington University Library ★★

The library's holdings are large and wide-ranging and contain significant collections in many fields.

Keywords: Education, Music, Social Science, Behavioral Science
Audience: Researchers, Students, General Public
Details: Free
User Info: Expect: Login; Send: Lib

`telnet://wsduvm12.csc.wsu.edu`

Rezo, bulletin irregulomadaire du RQSS ★

E-newsletter of RQSS (Regroupement Quebecois des Sciences Sociales) is open to anyone interested in social science research in Quebec and/or about Quebec.

Keywords: Quebec, Social Science
Audience: Social Scientists
Contact: Pierre J. Hamel
HAMEL@INRS-URB.UQUEBEC.CA
Details: Free
User Info: To subscribe, send an e-mail message to the URL address below, consisting of a single line reading:

SUB rezo YourFirstName YourLastName

To send a message to the entire list, address it to: rezo@uquebec.ca

`mailto:listserv@uquebec.ca`

soc.college ★

A Usenet newsgroup providing information and discussion about college life, activities, campus, and so on.

Keywords: Sociology, Social Science, Education (College/University)
Audience: Sociologists, Social Scientists, Educators (College/University), Students (College/University)
Details: Free
User Info: To subscribe to this Usenet newsgroup, you need access to a newsreader.

`news:soc.college`

Washington University Library ★★

The library's holdings are large and wide-ranging and contain significant collections in many fields.

Keywords: Technology, Literature (German), Social Science, Behavioral Science
Audience: Researchers, Students, General Public
Contact: services@wugate.wustl.edu
Details: Free
User Info: Expect: Login; Send: Services

`telnet://wugate.wustl.edu`

Social Science and Humanities—Australia

COOMBSQUEST Social Sciences and Humanities Information Facility

This is the worldwide Social Sciences and Humanities Information Service of the Coombs Computing Unit, Research Schools of Social Sciences and Pacific Studies, Australian National University, Canberra, Australia.

Keywords: Social Science Humanities Australia
Sponsor: Australian National University
Audience: Social Scientists, Humanists, Researchers, Educators, Students
Profile: COOMBSQUEST provides direct access to the Coombspapers Social Sciences Research Data Bank. The databank was established in December 1991 to act as the world's major electronic repository of social science and humanities papers, and other high-grade research material dealing with Australia, the Pacific region, and Southeast and Northeast Asia, Buddhism, Taoism, and other Oriental religions.
Contact: T. Matthew Ciolek
           tmciolek@coombs.anu.edu.au
Details: Free

`gopher://coombs.anu.edu.au`

`http://combs.anu.edu.au/CoombsHome.html`

Social Work

University of Texas at Austin Library

The library's holdings are large and wide-ranging and contain significant collections in many fields.

Keywords: Music, Natural Science, Nursing, Science Technology, Behavioral Science, Social Work, Computer Science, Engineering, Latin American Studies, Middle Eastern Studies
Audience: Researchers, Students, General Public
Details: Free
User Info: Expect: Blank Screen, Send: Return; Expect: Go, Send: Return; Expect: Enter Terminal Type, Send: vt100

Note: Some databases are restricted to UT Austin users only.

`telnet://utcat.utexas.edu`

Society

Aids

A forum for the discussion of AIDS, predominantly from a medical perspective, but also with some discussion of political and social issues.

Keywords: AIDS, Medicine, Politics, Society
Sponsor: UCLA
Audience: AIDS Researchers, AIDS Activists, Health Care Providers
Contact: Daniel R. Greening
           aids-request@cs.ucla.edu
User Info: To subscribe to the list, send an e-mail message to the URL address below. To send a message to the entire list, address it to: aids@cs.ucla.edu

`mailto:aids-request@cs.ucla.edu`

SOCINSCT (Social Insect Biology Research List)

SOCINSCT (Social Insect Biology Research List)

SOCINSCT is dedicated to communication among investigators active in the discipline of social insect biology.

Keywords: Biology, Insect Biology
Audience: Biologists, Researchers (college, graduate)
Profile: It is restricted to discussions of research at the university level. Social insects (bees, wasps, ants, and termites) are the main interest but information can include any area of sociobiology, or solitary bees and wasps. Such areas could include: orientation, navigation, adaptation/selection/evolution, superorganism concept, behavior, physiology and biochemistry, pheromones, flight and energetics, taxonomy and systematics, ecology, genetics, pollination, and nectar/pollen biology. Announcements of meetings and professional opportunities, requests for research help, sharing of literature references, sharing research topics and discussion of ideas are welcome.
Contact: Erik Seielstad
           erik@acspr1.acs.brockport.edu
Details: Free
User Info: To subscribe to the list, send an e-mail message to the address below consisting of a single line reading:

SUB socinsct YourFirstName YourLastName

To send message to the entire list, address it to: socinsct@albany.edu

`mailto:listserv@albany.edu`

Sociology

CRTNet (Communication Research and Theory Network)

All topics related to human communications.

Keywords: Communications, Sociology, Human Communications
Audience: Sociologists, Psychologists, Therapists
Contact: Tom Benson
           t3b@psuvm.psu.edu

`mailto:listserv@psuvm.bitnet`

National Family Database—MAPP

This database contains family sociological and health data, including research briefs, bibliographies, census data, program ideas, reference materials, media materials, and publications.

Keywords: Sociology, Family, Health
Sponsor: Department of Agriculture Economics and Rural Sociology, Pennsylvania State University
Audience: Sociologists, Public Health Policymakers, Health Care Providers

To access the database select PENpages (1), then General Information (3) and finally Information on MAPP - National Family Database (5)

`telnet://penpages@psupen.psu.edu`

soc.college

A Usenet newsgroup providing information and discussion about college life, activities, campus, and so on.

Keywords: Sociology, Social Science, Education (College/University)
Audience: Sociologists, Social Scientists, Educators (College/University), Students (College/University)
Details: Free
User Info: To subscribe to this Usenet newsgroup, you need access to a newsreader.

`news:soc.college`

soc.culture.african.american

A Usenet newsgroup providing information and discussion about African American culture.

Keywords: African American Studies, Sociology, Minorities

Audience: Sociologists Details: Free User Info: To subscribe to this Usenet newsgroup, you need access to a newsreader. **news:soc.culture.african.american**	Audience: Sociologists, Celts Details: Free User Info: To subscribe to this Usenet newsgroup, you need access to a newsreader. **news:soc.culture.celtic**	Audience: Sociologists, Greeks Details: Free User Info: To subscribe to this Usenet newsgroup, you need access to a newsreader. **news:soc.culture.greek**

soc.culture.arabic ★

soc.culture.china ★

soc.culture.hongkong ★

A Usenet newsgroup providing information and discussion about Arabic culture and technologies.

Keywords: Sociology, Middle Eastern Studies
Audience: Sociologists
Details: Free
User Info: To subscribe to this Usenet newsgroup, you need access to a newsreader.

news:soc.culture.arabic

A Usenet newsgroup providing information and discussion about China and Chinese culture.

Keywords: China, Sociology
Audience: Sociologists, Chinese, Sinologists
Details: Free
User Info: To subscribe to this Usenet newsgroup, you need access to a newsreader.

news:soc.culture.china

A Usenet newsgroup providing information and discussion about Hong Kong and its people.

Keywords: Hong Kong, Sociology
Audience: Sociologists
Details: Free
User Info: To subscribe to this Usenet newsgroup, you need access to a newsreader.

news:soc.culture.hongkong

soc.culture.asian.american ★

soc.culture.europe ★

soc.culture.indian ★

A Usenet newsgroup providing information and discussion about Asian American culture.

Keywords: Asian American Studies, Sociology
Audience: Sociologists
Details: Free
User Info: To subscribe to this Usenet newsgroup, you need access to a newsreader.

news:soc.culture.asian.american

A Usenet newsgroup providing information and discussion about all aspects of Europe.

Keywords: Europe, Sociology
Audience: Sociologists, Europeans
Details: Free
User Info: To subscribe to this Usenet newsgroup, you need access to a newsreader.

news:soc.culture.europe

A Usenet newsgroup providing information and discussion about India and its people.

Keywords: India, Sociology
Audience: Sociologists
Details: Free
User Info: To subscribe to this Usenet newsgroup, you need access to a newsreader.

news:soc.culture.indian

soc.culture.british ★

soc.culture.french ★

soc.culture.iranian ★

A Usenet newsgroup providing information and discussion about Britain and British culture.

Keywords: Sociology, United Kingdom
Audience: Sociologists
Details: Free
User Info: To subscribe to this Usenet newsgroup, you need access to a newsreader.

news:soc.culture.british

A Usenet newsgroup providing information and discussion about French culture and history.

Keywords: France, Sociology
Audience: Sociologists, Francophiles
Details: Free
User Info: To subscribe to this Usenet newsgroup, you need access to a newsreader.

news:soc.culture.french

A Usenet newsgroup providing information and discussion about Iran and Iranian culture.

Keywords: Iran, Sociology
Audience: Sociologists, Iranians
Details: Free
User Info: To subscribe to this Usenet newsgroup, you need access to a newsreader.

news:soc.culture.iranian

soc.culture.canada ★

soc.culture.german ★

soc.culture.italian ★

A Usenet newsgroup providing information and discussion about Canada and its people.

Keywords: Culture, Canada, Sociology
Audience: Sociologists, Canadians
Details: Free
User Info: To subscribe to this Usenet newsgroup, you need access to a newsreader.

news:soc.culture.canada

A Usenet newsgroup providing information and discussion about German culture.

Keywords: Germany, Sociology
Audience: Sociologists, Germans
Details: Free
User Info: To subscribe to this Usenet newsgroup, you need access to a newsreader.

news:soc.culture.german

A Usenet newsgroup providing information and discussion about the Italian people and their culture.

Keywords: Italy, Sociology
Audience: Sociologists, Italians
Details: Free
User Info: To subscribe to this Usenet newsgroup, you need access to a newsreader.

news:soc.culture.italian

soc.culture.celtic ★

soc.culture.greek ★

soc.culture.japan ★

A Usenet newsgroup providing information and discussion about Irish Scottish, Britain, and Cornish culture.

Keywords: Celtic Culture, Sociology

A Usenet newsgroup providing information and discussion about Greek culture.

Keywords: Greece, Sociology

A Usenet newsgroup providing information and discussion about Japan and the Japanese culture.

Keywords: Japan, Sociology

Audience: Sociologists, Japanese
Details: Free
User Info: To subscribe to this Usenet newsgroup, you need access to a newsreader.

news:soc.culture.japan

soc.culture.jewish

A Usenet newsgroup providing information and discussion about Jewish culture and religion.

Keywords: Judaism, Sociology
Audience: Sociologists, Jews, Jewish Organizations
Details: Free
User Info: To subscribe to this Usenet newsgroup, you need access to a newsreader.

news:soc.culture.jewish

soc.culture.korean

A Usenet newsgroup providing information and discussion about Korea's culture and its people.

Keywords: Korea, Sociology
Audience: Sociologists, Koreans
Details: Free
User Info: To subscribe to this Usenet newsgroup, you need access to a newsreader.

news:soc.culture.korean

soc.culture.nordic

A Usenet newsgroup providing information and discussion about Nordic culture.

Keywords: Scandinavia, Sociology
Audience: Sociologists
Details: Free
User Info: To subscribe to this Usenet newsgroup, you need access to a newsreader.

news:soc.culture.nordic

soc.culture.pakistan

A Usenet newsgroup providing information and discussion about Pakistani people and their culture.

Keywords: Pakistan, Sociology
Audience: Sociologists, Pakistanis
Details: Free
User Info: To subscribe to this Usenet newsgroup, you need access to a newsreader.

news:soc.culture.pakistan

soc.culture.soviet

A Usenet newsgroup providing information and discussion about topics relating to Russia or the former Soviet Union.

Keywords: Russia, CIS (Commonwealth of Independent States), Communism, Sociology
Audience: Sociologists, Russians
Details: Free
User Info: To subscribe to this Usenet newsgroup, you need access to a newsreader.

news:soc.culture.soviet

soc.culture.spain

A Usenet newsgroup providing information and discussion about culture on the Iberian peninsula.

Keywords: Spain, Sociology
Audience: Sociologists, Spaniards, Spain Enthusiasts
Details: Free
User Info: To subscribe to this Usenet newsgroup, you need access to a newsreader.

news:soc.culture.spain

soc.culture.taiwan

A Usenet newsgroup providing information and discussion about Taiwanese people and their culture.

Keywords: Taiwan, Sociology
Audience: Sociologists, Taiwanese
Details: Free
User Info: To subscribe to this Usenet newsgroup, you need access to a newsreader.

news:soc.culture.taiwan

soc.culture.turkish

A Usenet newsgroup providing information and discussion about Turkish people and culture.

Keywords: Turkey, Sociology
Audience: Sociologists, Turks
Details: Free
User Info: To subscribe to this Usenet newsgroup, you need access to a newsreader.

news:soc.culture.turkish

soc.culture.usa

A Usenet newsgroup providing information and discussion about the culture of the United States.

Keywords: Americana, Sociology, Popular Culture
Audience: Sociologists, General Public
Details: Free
User Info: To subscribe to this Usenet newsgroup, you need access to a newsreader.

news:soc.culture.usa

soc.culture.vietnamese

A Usenet newsgroup providing information and discussion about the people and culture of Vietnam.

Keywords: Vietnam, Sociology
Audience: Sociologists, Vietnamese
Details: Free
User Info: To subscribe to this Usenet newsgroup, you need access to a newsreader.

news:soc.culture.vietnamese

soc.culture.yugoslavia

A Usenet newsgroup providing information and discussion about the people and culture of Yugoslavia.

Keywords: Yugoslavia, Sociology
Audience: Sociologists, Yugoslavians
Details: Free
User Info: To subscribe to this Usenet newsgroup, you need access to a newsreader.

news:soc.culture.yugoslavia

Software

Biosym

For users of Biosym Technologies software, including the products InsightII, Discover, Dmol, Homology, Delphi, and Polymer. The list is not run by Biosym.

Keywords: Biosym Technologies Software, Software
Audience: Software Users
Contact: Reinhard Doelz
dibug-request@comp.bioz.unibas.ch
Details: Free
User Info: To subscribe to the list, send an e-mail message requesting a subscription to the URL address below. To send a message to the entire list, address it to: dibug@comp.bioz.unibas.ch

mailto:dibug-request@comp.bioz.unibas.ch

Buyer's Guide to Micro Software

The database contains a directory of business and professional microcomputer software available in the United States.

Keywords: Buyer's Guides, Microcomputers, Computers, Software
Sponsor: Online, Inc., Weston, CT, USA
Audience: Computer Users

Profile: Provided are directory, product, technical, and bibliographic information on leading software packages, integrated this information into one succinct composite record. The database can help professionals locate suitable packages compatible with specified hardware, without having to sift through large numbers of records.

The file is highly selective, listing packages rated at least "good" by the technical press; all packages from major software producers, even if negatively reviewed; and packages unique to specific business segments, with special emphasis placed on library and medical software. Each record includes directory information; technical specifications, including required hardware and operating systems; an abstracted product description, and, when available, a full citation of representative reviews.

Contact: Dialog in the US at (800) 334-2564, Dialog internationally at country-specific locations.
Details: Costs
User Info: To subscribe, contact Dialog directly.
Notes: Coverage: current; updated monthly.

`telnet://dialog.com`

CE Software

Technical support for CE Software Products, such as QuickKeys for the Macintosh.
Keywords: Software, Technical Support, Macintosh
Audience: Software users
Details: Free
User Info: To subscribe to the list, send an e-mail message requesting a subscription to the URL address below.

`mailto:ce_info%cedsm@uunet.uu.net`

Cosmic Update

Internet notice identifying new computer software from the National Aeronautics and Space Administration (NASA) made available for international use.
Keywords: NASA, Software, Space
Audience: Space Scientists, Astronomers
Profile: COSLINE is a 24-hour electronic information service to COSMIC's customers. The principal feature of COSLINE is the catalog Search facility. A separate help file is available for browsing from the Search main menu option.
Contact: Pat Mortenson
service@cossack.cosmic.uga.edu
Details: Free
User Info: To subscribe, send an e-mail message requesting a subscription to the URL address below.

`mailto:service@cossack.cosmic.uga.edu`

data-exp

The mail list server provides an open forum for users to discuss the Visualization Data Explorer Package. It contains three files at the moment: a. FAQ, b. summary, and c. forum.
Keywords: Computers, Software, Hardware, Visualization Data Explorer Package
Audience: Computer Users
User Info: To subscribe to the list, send an e-mail message requesting a subscription to the URL address below. To send a message to the entire list, address it to: stein@watson.ibm.com

`mailto:stein@watson.ibm.com`

DDTs-Users

The DDTs-Users mailing list is for discussions of issues related to the DDTs defect-tracking software from QualTrak, including software, methods, mechanisms, techniques, general usage tips, policies, bugs, and bug workarounds.
Keywords: Software, Software Defects
Audience: Computer Users, DDTs Administrators
Contact: DDTs-Users-request@BigBird.BU.EDU
User Info: To subscribe to the list, send an e-mail message requesting a subscription to the URL address below. To send a message to the entire list, address it to: DDTs-Users-request@BigBird.BU.EDU

`mailto:DDTs-Users-request@BigBird.BU.EDU`

ESRI (Environmental Systems Research Institute)

Environmental Systems Research Institute, Inc. is the world leader in GIS technology. ARC/INFO is ESRI's powerful and flexible flagship GIS software.
Keywords: Geographic Information Systems (GIS), Environment, Software, Computers
Audience: Geographers, Environmentalists, Computer Users
Details: Costs
For product information, call (909) 793-2853, X1475.
For training information, call (909) 793-2853, X1585, or fax (909) 793-5953.

fsuucp

The FSUUCP mailing list is for the discussion of bug hunting, feature proposing, and announcements of the availability and release dates of FSUUCP, an MS-DOS UUCP/mail/news package.
Keywords: Software, Shareware
Audience: Students, Computer Users
Details: Free
User Info: To subscribe to the list, send an e-mail message requesting a subscription to the URL address below. To send a message to the entire list, address it to: fsuucp@polyslo.calpoly.edu

`mailto:fsuucp-request@polyslo.calpoly.edu`

Futurebus+ Users

This discussion group focuses on the design, implementation, integration, and operation of hardware and software related to Futurebus+.
Keywords: Computer Users, Hardware, Software
Audience: Computer Users, Software Engineers, Hardware Engineers
Contact: majordomo@theus.rain.com
Details: Free
User Info: To subscribe to the list, send an e-mail message to the URL address below consisting of a single line reading:

SUB fbus_users YourFirstName YourLastName

To send a message to the entire list, address it to: fbus_users+@theus.rain.com

`mailto:majordomo@theus.rain.com`

gateway2000

This list is a source of information about Gateway2000 products.
Keywords: Computer Products, Software, Hardware
Audience: Computer Users, Hardware Engineers, Software Engineers
Details: Free
User Info: To subscribe to the list, send an e-mail message requesting a subscription to the URL address below. To send a message to the entire list, address it to: gateway2000@sei.cmu.edu

`gateway2000-request@sei.cmu.edu`

GNUs Bulletin: Newsletter of the Free Software Foundation

Bringing you news about the GNU Project, the Free Software Foundation is dedicated to eliminating restrictions on copying, redistribution, understanding, and modification of computer programs.
Keywords: Software, Shareware, Free Software
Sponsor: Free Software Foundation
Audience: Computer Programmers, Computer Users
Contact: Leonard H. Tower, Jr.
tower@ai.mit.edu
Details: Free
news:gnu.announce

`mailto:info-gnu-request@prep.ai.mit.edu`

NSSDC's (National Space Science Data Center) Online Data & Information Service

The NSSDC (National Space Science Data Center) is the NASA facility charged with archiving the data from all of NASA's science missions.

Keywords: Space, Astrophysics, Software, NASA, Science
Sponsor: NASA
Audience: Scientists, Space Scientists, Astronomers, Engineers
Profile: This resource contains information about NASA's missions and analysis of their data.
Details: Free
User Info: Expect: Login, Send: nssdc
See the menu entries in your particular area of interest.

`telnet://nssdc.gsfc.nasa.gov`

Pc532

A mailing list for people interested in the pc532 project, a National Semiconductor NS32532-based system, offered at a low cost.

Keywords: Computers, Hardware, Software
Audience: Computer Users, Software Developers
Contact: Dave Rand
pc532-request@bungi.com
Details: Free
User Info: To subscribe to the list, send an e-mail message requesting a subscription to the URL address below. To send a message to the entire list, address it to: pc532@bungi.com

`mailto:pc532-request@bungi.com`

Pcgeos-list

A discussion forum for users of PC/GEOS products, including GeoWorks Ensemble, GeoWorks Pro, GeoWorks POS, and third-party products. Topics include general information, tips, techniques, applications, and experiences.

Keywords: Computers, Software
Audience: Computer Users, Software Developers
Contact: listserv@pandora.sf.ca.us
Details: Free
User Info: To subscribe to the list, send an e-mail message to the URL address below, consisting of a single line reading:
SUB pcgeos-list YourFirstName YourLastName
To send a message to the entire list, address it to: pcgeos@pandora.sf.ca.us

`mailto:listserv@pandora.sf.ca.us`

Pdp8-lovers

A mailing list for owners of vintage DEC (Digital Equipment Corp.) computers, especially the PDP-8 series. Discussion topics include hardware, software, and programming techniques.

Keywords: Computers, Hardware, Software
Audience: Computer Users, Product Analysts
Contact: Robert E. Seastrom
pdp8-lovers-request@mc.lcs.mit.edu
Details: Free
User Info: To subscribe to the list, send an e-mail message requesting a subscription to the URL address below. To send a message to the entire list, address it to: pdp8-lovers@mc.lcs.mit.edu

`mailto:pdp8-lovers@mc.lcs.mit.edu`

Project-management

The aim of the list is to discuss project-management techniques generally, as well as project-management software and programs.

Keywords: Project Management, Computing, Software
Audience: Business Professionals, Business Students
Contact: project-management-request@smtl.demon.co.uk
Details: Free
User Info: To subscribe to the list, send an e-mail message requesting a subscription to the URL address below. To send a message to the entire list, address it to: project-management@smtl.demon.co.uk

`mailto:project-management-request@smtl.demon.co.uk`

Qnx2

Discussion of all aspects of the QNX real-time operating systems. Topics include compatible hardware, available third-party software, software reviews, available PD/free software, QNX platform-specific programming discussions, and QNX and FLEET networking.

Keywords: Computing, Hardware, Software
Audience: Computer Users, Hardware/Software Designers, Product Analysts
Contact: Martin Zimmerman
camz@dlogtech.cuc.ab.ca
Details: Free
User Info: To subscribe to the list, send an e-mail message requesting a subscription to the URL address below. To send a message to the entire list, address it to: qnx2@dlogtech.cuc.ab.ca

`mailto:qnx2@dlogtech.cuc.ab.ca`

Qnx4

A mailing list for discussion of all aspects of the QNX real-time operating systems. Topics include compatible hardware, available third-party software, software reviews, available PD/free software, QNX and FLEET networking, process control, and more.

Keywords: Computing, Hardware, Software, Networking
Audience: Computer Users, Hardware/Software Designers, Product Analysts
Contact: Martin Zimmerman
camz@dlogtech.cuc.ab.ca
Details: Free
User Info: To subscribe to the list, send an e-mail message requesting a subscription to the URL address below. To send a message to the entire list, address it to: qnx4@dlogtech.cuc.ab.ca

`mailto:qnx4@dlogtech.cuc.ab.ca`

SUMEX-AIM

An FTP archive of software, demonstration programs, and various applications, especially for Macintosh computers.

Keywords: Computers, Macintosh, Software
Audience: Computer Users, Macintosh Users
Details: Free

`ftp://sumex-aim.Stanford.edu`

Virtual Reality Space

A collection of virtual reality information, including downloadable software tools from Silicon Graphics.

Keywords: Virtual Reality, Cyberspace, Software, Silicon Graphics
Sponsor: The University of Texas, Austin, Texas, USA
Audience: Virtual Reality Enthusiasts, Programmers
Contact: Jay Ashcraft
ashcraft@ccwf.cc.utexas.edu

`gopher://ftp.cc.utexas.edu`

`ftp://cc.utexas.edu`

Software Defects

DDTs-Users

The DDTs-Users mailing list is for discussions of issues related to the DDTs defect-tracking software from QualTrak, including software, methods, mechanisms, techniques, general usage tips, policies, bugs, and bug workarounds.

Keywords: Software, Software Defects
Audience: Computer Users, DDTs Administrators
Contact: DDTs-Users-request@BigBird.BU.EDU

User Info: To subscribe to the list, send an e-mail message requesting a subscription to the URL address below. To send a message to the entire list, address it to: DDTs-Users-request@bigbird.bu.edu

`mailto:DDTs-Users-request@bigbird.bu.edu`

Software Internationalization

insoft-l

This list discusses techniques for developing new software and for converting existing software, as well as internationalization tools, announcements of internationalized public-domain software and of foreign-language versions of commercial software, calls for papers, conference announcements, and references to documentation related to the internationalization of software.

Keywords: Programming, Software Internationalization
Sponsor: Center for Computing and Information Services, Technical University of Brno
Audience: Software Developers
Contact: insoft-l-request@cis.vutbr.cs
Details: Free, Moderated
User Info: To subscribe to the list, send an e-mail message to the URL address below consisting of a single line reading:

SUB insoft-l YourFirstName YourLastName

To send a message to the entire list, address it to: insoft-l@cis.vutbr.cs

`mailto:listserv@cis.vutbr.cs`

Soil Conservation

Iowa State University

The library's holdings contain significant collections in many fields.

Keywords: Agriculture, Veterinary Medicine, Statistics, Labor, Soil Conservation, Film
Audience: General Public, Researchers, Librarians, Document Delivery Professionals
Details: Free
User Info: Expect: DIAL, Send: LIB

`telnet://isn.iastate.edu`

Solid Waste Recycling

Solid Waste Recycling

The text of an eight-lesson correspondence class designed to teach the basics of setting up a successful recycling program.

Keywords: Recycling, Environmental Studies
Sponsor: University of Wisconsin
Audience: Environmentalists, Educators, Students
Contact: Judy Faber
faber@engr.wisc.edu

`gopher://wissago.uwex.edu/11/uwex/course/recycling`

Solstice

Solstice

This file server provides state-of-the-art information on renewable energy, energy efficiency, the environment, and sustainable community development.

Keywords: Energy, Environment
Sponsor: The Center for Renewable Energy and Sustainable Technology (CREST)
Audience: Environmentalists, Urban Planners, Educators, Students
Contact: www-content@solstice.crest.org
Details: Free
Login: anonymous, Password: e-mail

`http://solstice.crest.org`

Sound Synthesis

IRCAM DSP and musical software

This site offers a variety of computer music resources.

Keywords: Computer Music, Sound Synthesis, Composition, DSP
Sponsor: IRCAM
Audience: Computer Music Researchers and Computer Musicians
Profile: Contains a list and brief description of IRCAM software (digital signal processing, voice and sound synthesis, music composition, wind instrument making, and other programs). There are also calendars of the IRCAM-EIC concerts and tours, and links to various other music servers.
Contact: Michel Fingerhut
fingerhu@ircam.fr
Details: Free

`http://www.ircam.fr`

Soundtracks

Soundtracks

Discussions and reviews of new and older soundtracks (musical and technical aspects). Information about availability of specific soundtracks on different formats in different parts of the world.

Keywords: Music, Recordings
Audience: Audio Enthusiasts, Music Researchers
Contact: Michel Hafner
soundtracks-request@ifi.unizh.ch
User Info: To subscribe to the list, send an e-mail message requesting a subscription to the URL address below. To send a message to the entire list, address it to: soundtracks@ifi.unizh.ch

`mailto:soundtracks-request@ifi.unizh.ch`

South Africa

SABINET (South African Bibliographic and Information Network)

This gopher offers information searches from a variety of electronic databases, as well as for library locations and availability of books and periodicals.

Keywords: South Africa, Databases, Networks
Audience: South African Internet Surfers
Contact: hennie@info1.sabinet.co.za
Details: Free

`gopher://info2.sabinet.co.za`

South Africa

A major directory on Africa, providing access to a broad range of related resources (library catalogs, databases, and servers) via the Internet.

Keywords: Africa, South Africa
Audience: General Public
Profile: South Africa's home page, containing information about different regions and major cities, weather conditions, vital statistics, and information about the University of South Africa.
Contact: Aleksandar Radovanovic
radova@osprey.unisa.ac.za

`http://osprey.unisa.ac.za/0/docs/south-africa.html`

South African Specific Items

A selection of primarily political information on South Africa. Includes ANC (African National Congress) policy statements, as well as an A-Z of South African political figures and the latest issues of South Africa Watch Magazine. Also has weather information and links to gopher and FTP sites in South Africa.

Keywords: South Africa, Political Science

Audience: South Africans, Political Analysts, General Public

Contact: John Dovey
pjcd@maties.sun.ac.za

`gopher://lib.sun.ac.za`

South America

NIBNews - A Monthly Electronic Bulletin About Medical Informatics ★

Disseminates information about Brazilian and Latin American activities, people, information, events, publications, software, and so on, involving computer applications in health care, medicine, and biology.

Keywords: Health Care, Biology, Brazil, Latin America, South America, Medicine

Audience: Health Care Professionals, Biologists

Contact: Renato M. E. Sabbatini
sabbatini@bruc.bitnet

Details: Free
E-mail a short notice to:

`mailto:sabbatini@ccvax.unicamp.br`

NSAMER (North and South America Library)

The North and South America library contains detailed information about every country in North and South America (except the United States). The US-Canada Free Trade Agreement, the North American Free Trade Agreement, relations with Mexico and events in such countries as Brazil, Peru, and Nicaragua are among the topics covered by a variety of business, news and legal sources. International research reports from InvestextR are also included. The United States is not covered in this library.

Keywords: News, Analysis, Companies, North America, South America

Audience: Journalists, Business Professionals

Profile: The North and South America library contains a broad array of sources. Among the information sources are newspapers and wire services, trade and business journals, company reports, country and region backgrounds, industry and product analyses, business opportunities, and selected legal texts. News sources range from the world-renowned Washington Post and Christian Science Monitor to the regionally important Toronto Star and Latin American Newsletters. Canadian Business and Maclean's represent a portion of the array of business and trade journals. Company information is contained in the EXTEL cards as well as ICC. Providers of country background and industry analyses include Associated Banks of Europe, Bank of America, Business International, IBC USA and the US Department of Commerce. Among the specialized resources are IBC's Mexico and Brazil Services as well as BI's Business Latin America. Researchers interested in new business opportunities can check OPIC and Foreign Trade Opportunities (FTO).And selected legal texts covering the US-Canada Free Trade Agreement and other international agreements planners and advisors to better assess the business climate in North and South America.

Contact: Mead New Sales Group at (800) 227-4908 or (513) 859-5398 inside the US, or (513) 865-7981 for all inquiries outside the US.

User Info: To subscribe, contact Mead directly.

To examine the Nexis user guide, you can access it at the ftp site of the University of Texas at Austin at the URL address: ftp://ftp.cc.utexas.edu. The files are in pub/ref-services/LEXIS

`telnet://nex.meaddata.com`

`http://www.meaddata.com`

Peru ★

A mailing list for the discussion of Peruvian culture and other issues.

Keywords: Peru, South America

Audience: Peruvians, Educators, Researchers

Contact: Herbert Koller
owner-peru@cs.sfsu.edu

Details: Free

User Info: To subscribe to the list, send an e-mail message requesting a subscription to the URL address below. To send a message to the entire list, address it to: owner-peru@cs.sfsu.edu

Notes: This mailing list is simply an echo site, so all posts get bounced from that address to all the people subscribed.

`mailto:owner-peru@cs.sfsu.edu`

South Asian Studies

University of Pennsylvania Library- Philadelphia Pa.

The library's holdings are large and wide-ranging and contain significant collections in many fields.

Keywords: Literature (English), Literature (American), History (World), Medieval Studies, East Asian Studies, Middle Eastern Studies, South Asian Studies, Judaica, Lithuania.

Audience: Educators, Students, Researchers

Profile: Access to the central Van Pelt Library and to most of the departmental libraries is restricted to members of the University community on weekends and holidays. Online visitors are advised to call (215) 898-7554 for information on hours and access restrictions.

Contact: Patricia Renfro, Associate Director of Libraries

Details: Free

`telnet://library.upenn.edu`

South East Florida AIDS Information Network (SEFAIN)

South East Florida AIDS Information Network (SEFAIN)

Contains a wide range of information on AIDS research(ers), organizations, and services in searchable databases.

Keywords: AIDS, Medicine

Sponsor: This project is sponsored in part by the National Library of Medicine

Audience: Medical Professionals, Scientists, Educators, Health Care Providers

Details: Free
Select L on main menu, then select 1 on next menu

`telnet://library@callcat.med.miami.edu`

South Florida Environmental Reader

South Florida Environmental Reader

Newsletter distributing information on the environment of South Florida.

Keywords: Environment, Florida

Audience: Environmentalists
Contact: aem@mthvax.cs.miami.edu
Details: Free
User Info: To subscribe to the list, send an e-mail message requesting a subscription to the URL address below.

To send a mesage to the entire USL, address it to: sfer@mthvax.cs.miami.edu

`mail to:sfer-requesti@mthvax.cs.miami.edu`

Soviet Union

Mideur-l

A list containing the history, culture, politics, and current affairs of those countries lying between the Mediterranean/Adriatic and the Baltic Seas, and between the German/Austrian borders and the former Soviet Union.

Keywords: Soviet Union, Baltic Republics, Eastern Europe, News
Audience: Political Scientists, Researchers, Historians, General Public
Contact: Jan George Frajkor
mideur-1@ubvm.cc.buffalo.edu
Details: Free
User Info: To subscribe to the list, send an e-mail message to the URL address below consisting of a single line reading:

SUB mideur-l YourFirstName YourLastName

To send a message to the entire list, address it to: mideur-1@ubvm.cc.buffalo.edu

`mailto:listserv@ubvm.cc.buffalo.edu`

SCS

A discussion of the culture of the former Soviet Union.

Keywords: Soviet Union, Culture
Audience: Researchers, Slavicists, General Public
Contact: John B. Harlan
ijph200@indycms.iupui.edu
Details: Free
User Info: To subscribe to the list, send an e-mail message to the URL address below consisting of a single line reading:

SUB scs YourFirstName YourLastName

To send a message to the entire list, address to: scs@indycms.iupui.edu

`mailto:listserv@indycms.iupui.edu`

val-l

Discussion on changes in the Communist countries, ranging from Cuba and Vietnam to the former Soviet Union.

Keywords: Communism, Soviet Union, Political Science
Audience: Political Scientists
Contact: cdell@umkcax1 or cdell@umkcvax1.bitnet
Details: Free
User Info: To subscribe to the list, send an e-mail message to the URL address below consisting of a single line reading:

SUB val-l YourFirstName YourLastName

To send a message to the entire list, address it to: val-l@ucflvm.cc.ucf.edu

`mailto:listserv@ucflvm.cc.ucf.edu`

Sovokinform

Sovokinform

CIS news, events, general information; usually in transliterated Russian.

Keywords: Commonwealth of Independent States (CIS)
Audience: Journalists, Political Scientists
Contact: burkov@drfmc.ceng.cea.fr
Details: Free
User Info: To subscribe to the list, send an e-mail message requesting a subscription to the URL address below. To send a message to the entire list, address it to: sovokinform@drfmc.ceng.cea.fr

`mailto:burkov@drfmc.ceng.cea.fr`

Space

Aerospace Engineering

This directory is a compilation of information resources focused on aerospace engineeering.

Keywords: Aerospace, Engineering, Aviation, Space
Audience: Aerospace Engineers, Space Scientists
Profile: This is a guide to Internet resources that contain information pertaining to aerospace engineering. Originally the guide was to cover the area of aerospace engineering as applied to lower atmospheric flight. However, it is difficult to narrow the sites down to specific subject areas. As the guide evolved, sites were included with a broader scope of information. The guide is by no means comprehensive and exhaustive; there are sites that are not included and those the authors were not aware of, and they welcome suggestions. The directory lists sites on FTP, Gopher, Listserv, OPAC, Telnet, Usenet, and WWW.
Details: Free

`ftp://una.hh.lib.umich.edu/70/inetdirsstacks/aerospace:potsiedalq`

Astronomy

This directory is a compilation of information resources focused on astronomy.

Keywords: Astronomy, Stars, Astrophysics, Space
Audience: Astronomers, Astrophysicists, Space Enthusiasts
Contact: A. Park, J. Miller
Details: Free

`ftp://una.hh.lib.umich.edu/70/inetdirsstacks/astron:parkmiller`

Cosmic Update

Internet notice identifying new computer software from the National Aeronautics and Space Administration (NASA) made available for international use.

Keywords: NASA, Software, Space
Audience: Space Scientists, Astronomers
Profile: COSLINE is a 24-hour electronic information service to COSMIC's customers. The principal feature of COSLINE is the catalog Search facility. A separate help file is available for browsing from the Search main menu option.
Contact: Pat Mortenson
service@cossack.cosmic.uga.edu
Details: Free
User Info: To subscribe, send an e-mail message requesting a subscription to the URL address below.

`mailto:service@cossack.cosmic.uga.edu`

Extraterrestrials

A forum for academics, scientists and others interested in questions about the existence of intelligent life in the universe.

Keywords: Astronomy, Extraterrestrial Life, Space
Sponsor: University of Kent at Canterbury, United Kingdom
Audience: Scientists, Astronomers, General Public
Contact: Dr. Peter Moore
pgm@ukc.ac.uk
User Info: To subscribe to the list, send an e-mail message to the URL address shown below consisting of a single line reading:

SUB extraterrestrials YourFirstName YourLastName

To send a message to the entire list, address it to: extraterrestrials@mailbase.ac.uk

`mailbase@mailbase.ac.uk`

McDonnell Douglas Aerospace

A web site providing information about McDonnell Douglas, including a company profile and related discussion about technology.

Keywords: Aerospace, Space, Aviation, Technology
Audience: Aerospace Engineers
Contact: mail to: Zook@pat.mdc.com

`http://pat.mdc.com`

NASA Ames SPACE Archive

This archive contains information about NASA projects. It also has an online CD-ROM jukebox with a rotating selection of NASA mission CD-ROMs.

Keywords: NASA, Space, Space Science
Sponsor: NASA Ames Research Center
Audience: General Public, Scientists, Technical Writers, Science Teachers
Profile: This site has access to general space information, including the texts of the press release kits for the space shuttle missions and other NASA press releases. There are also weather images from satellites and other sources in the pub/Weather directory. The pub/cdrom directory contains information about which NASA mission CD-ROMs are currently mounted.
Contact: Peter Yee
yee@atlas.arc.nasa.gov
User Info: User Info: Expect: login, Send: anonymous; Expect: password, Send: your Internet address

`ftp://explorer.arc.nasa.gov`

NSSDC (National Space Science Data Center)'s Online Data & Information Service

The NSSDC (National Space Science Data Center) is the NASA facility charged with archiving the data from all of NASA's science missions.

Keywords: Space, Astrophysics, Software, NASA, Science
Sponsor: NASA
Audience: Scientists, Space Scientists, Astronomers, Engineers
Profile: This resource contains information about NASA's missions and analysis of their data.
Details: Free
Expect: Login, Send: nssdc
See the menu entries in your particular area of interest.

`telnet://nssdc.gsfc.nasa.gov`

sci.astro

A Usenet newsgroup providing information and discussion about astronomy.

Keywords: Astronomy, Space
Audience: Astronomers
User Info: To subscribe to this Usenet newsgroup, you need access to a newsreader.

`news:sci.astro`

Sci.astro.hubble

Information about all subjects concerning NASA's Hubble space telescope.

Keywords: Hubble Telescope, Astronomy, Space, NASA, Stargazing, Telescopes
Audience: Astronomers, General Public, Science Teachers, Stargazers
Contact: Paul A. Scowen
scowen@wfpc3.la.asu.edu
Details: Free, Moderated, Images
User Info: To subscribe to this Usenet newsgroup, you need access to a newsreader.

`news:sci.astro.hubble`

Sci.space

A wide variety of discussions about space flight.

Keywords: Space, Space Flight
Audience: Space Enthusiasts, General Public
Details: Free
To participate in a Usenet newsgroup you need access to a newsreader.

`news:sci.space.news`

`news:sci.space.science`

Sci.space.news

Keywords: Space, FAQs
Audience: Space Flight Enthusiasts
Profile: This newsgroup carries recent information about the world's space programs. Reading the FAQ set is recommended before asking questions on the other sci.space. groups.
Contact: Peter Yee
yee@atlas.arc.nasa.gov
Details: Free, Moderated
To participate in a Usenet newsgroup you need access to a newsreader.

`news:sci.space.news`

Sci.space.science

A place for technical discussions about space exploration and research.

Keywords: Space Exploration, Space
Audience: Space Enthusiasts, Space Professionals
Contact: george william herbert
gwh@crl.com
gwh@soda.berkeley.edu
gwh@isu.isunet.edu
Details: Free, Moderated
User Info: To participate in a Usenet newsgroup you need access to a newsreader.

`news:sci.space.science`

Space Exploration

Sci.space.science

A place for technical discussions about space exploration and research.

Keywords: Space Exploration, Space
Audience: Space Enthusiasts, Space Professionals
Contact: george william herbert
gwh@crl.com
gwh@soda.berkeley.edu
gwh@isu.isunet.edu
Details: Free, Moderated
User Info: To participate in a Usenet newsgroup you need access to a "newsreader."

`news:sci.space.science`

Space Flight

Sci.space

A wide variety of discussions about space flight.

Keywords: Space, Space Flight
Audience: Space Enthusiasts, General Public
Details: Free
To participate in a Usenet newsgroup you need access to a newsreader.

`news:sci.space.news`

`news:sci.space.science`

Space Science

Canopus

Newsletter of the Space Science and Astronomy Technical Committee of the American Institute of Aeronautics and Astronautics. Its objective is to provide an insider's perspective on issues in space science and astronomy.

Keywords:	Space Science, Astronomy	
Sponsor:	NASA (National Aeronautics and Space Administration)	
Audience:	Astronomers, Space Scientists	
Contact:	William W. L. Taylor wtaylor@nhqvax.hq.nasa.gov	
Details:	Costs	
User Info:	To subscribe to the list, send an e-mail message to the URL address below.	

`mailto:wtaylor@nhqvax.hq.nasa.gov`

European Space Agency

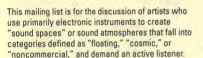

A major directory on aeronautics, providing access to a broad range of related resources (library catalogs, databases, and servers) via the Internet.

Keywords:	Space Science, Aeronautics
Audience:	Space Science Researchers
Profile:	The home page of the European Space Agency, including information about ESA's mission, specific ESA programs (Science, Manned Spaceflight and Microgravity, Earth Observation, Telecommunications, Launchers), and issues related to the space and aeronautics industry.
Contact:	webmaster@esa.it

`http://www.esrin.esa.it`

NASA Ames SPACE Archive

This archive contains information about NASA projects. It also has an online CD-ROM jukebox with a rotating selection of NASA mission CD-ROMs.

Keywords:	NASA, Space, Space Science
Sponsor:	NASA Ames Research Center
Audience:	General Public, Scientists, Technical Writers, Science Teachers
Profile:	This site has access to general space information, including the texts of the press release kits for the space shuttle missions and other NASA press releases. There are also weather images from satellites and other sources in the pub/Weather directory. The pub/cdrom directory contains information about which NASA mission CD-ROMs are currently mounted.
Contact:	Peter Yee yee@atlas.arc.nasa.gov
User Info:	User Info: Expect: login, Send: anonymous; Expect: password, Send: your Internet address

`ftp://explorer.arc.nasa.gov`

Ssi_mail

A moderated list for topics related to Space Studies Institute programs—past, present, and future.

Keywords:	Space Studies, Space Science, Aeronautics
Audience:	Space Students, Space Scientists
Contact:	Mitchell James mjames@link.com mitchellj@aol.com
Details:	Free, Moderated
User Info:	To subscribe to the list, send an e-mail message requesting a subscription to the URL address below. To send a message to the entire list, address it to: ssi_mail@link.com
Notes:	Archives available.

`mailto:listprocessor@link.com`

Space Studies

Ssi_mail

A moderated list for topics related to Space Studies Institute programs—past, present, and future.

Keywords:	Space Studies, Space Science, Aeronautics
Audience:	Space Students, Space Scientists
Contact:	Mitchell James mjames@link.com mitchellj@aol.com
Details:	Free, Moderated
User Info:	To subscribe to the list, send an e-mail message requesting a subscription to the URL address below. To send a message to the entire list, address it to: ssi_mail@link.com
Notes:	Archives available.

`mailto:listprocessor@link.com`

Spacelink

Spacelink

This contains information about NASA and its activities, including a large number of curricular activities for elementary and secondary science classes.

Keywords:	NASA, Aeronautics, Education (K-12)
Audience:	Students (K-12), Educators, General Public
Details:	Free

`telnet://newuser@spacelink.msfc.nasa.gov`

Spacemen 3

Drone On...

The Drone On... list is for the discussion of Spacemen 3 and resultant bands, as well as any other droning guitar bands that anyone wants to bring up.

Keywords:	Rock Music, Spacemen 3
Audience:	Spacemen 3 Enthusiasts, Rock Music Enthusiasts
Contact:	droneon-request@ucsd.edu
Details:	Free
User Info:	To subscribe to the list, send an e-mail message requesting a subscription to the URL address below. To send a message to the entire list, address it to: droneon-request@ucsd.edu

`mailto:droneon-request@ucsd.edu`

Space-music

Space-music

This mailing list is for the discussion of artists who use primarily electronic instruments to create "sound spaces" or sound atmospheres that fall into categories defined as "floating," "cosmic," or "noncommercial," and demand an active listener.

Keywords:	Music, Electronic Music
Audience:	Electronic Music Enthusiasts
Contact:	Dave Datta space-music-request@cs.uwp.edu
Details:	Free
User Info:	To subscribe to the list, send an e-mail message requesting a subscription to the URL address below. To send a message to the entire list, address it to: space-music@cs.uwp.edu

`mailto:space-music-request@cs.uwp.edu`

Spain

soc.culture.spain

A Usenet newsgroup providing information and discussion about culture on the Iberian peninsula.

Keywords:	Spain, Sociology
Audience:	Sociologists, Spaniards, Spain Enthusiasts
Details:	Free
User Info:	To subscribe to this Usenet newsgroup, you need access to a newsreader.

`news:soc.culture.spain`

Spanish

Academia Latinoamericana de Espanol

This program is specifically designed for those interested in learning to speak Spanish through a fully immersive trip to Ecuador.

Keywords:	Spanish, Language, Education (Bilingual)
Sponsor:	Academia Latinoamericana de Espanol, Quito, Ecuador
Audience:	Reseachers, Students, Language Teachers
Contact:	Webmaster
	webmaster@comnet.com

`http://www.comnet.com/ecuador/learnSpanish.html`

Spanish Inquisition

University of Pennsylvania PENNINFO Library ★★

The library's holdings are large and wide-ranging and contain significant collections in many fields.

Keywords:	Church History, Spanish Inquisition, Witchcraft, Shakespeare (William), Bibles, Aristotle (Texts of), Fiction, Whitman (Walt), French Revolution, Drama (French), Literature (English), Literature (Spanish)
Audience:	Researchers, Students, General Public
Contact:	Al DSouza
	penninfo-admin@dccs.upenn.edu
	dsouza@dccs.upenn.edu
Details:	Free
User Info:	Expect: Login; Send: Public

`telnet://penninfo.upenn.edu`

Spanish Plays

Dartmouth College Library ★★

The library's holdings are large and wide-ranging and contain significant collections in many fields.

Keywords:	American Calligraphy, Cervantes (Miguel de), Railroads, Polar Regions, Frost (Robert), Shakespeare (William), Spanish Plays
Audience:	General Public, Researchers, Librarians, Document Delivery Professionals
Contact:	Katharina Klemperer
	kathy.klemperer@dartmouth.edu
Details:	Free
User Info:	Expect: login, Send: wolfpac

`telnet://lib.dartmouth.edu`

Spanky Fractal Database

Spanky Fractal Database ★★★★

This web site provides a collection of fractals and fractal-related material for free distribution on the Internet.

Keywords:	Mathematics, Chaos Theory, Computer Programming, Computer Graphics
Audience:	Mathematicians, Computer Programmers
Profile:	Contains information on dynamical systems, software, distributed fractal generators, galleries, and databases from all over the world.
Contact:	Noel Giffin
	noel@triumf.ca
Details:	Free

`http://spanky.triumf.ca`

Special Chemicals Update Program

Special Chemicals Update Program

Comprehensive reports covering 32 specialty chemical industry segments.

Keywords:	Chemistry, Business
Sponsor:	Chemical Marketing Research Center
Audience:	Librarians, Researchers, Chemists
Profile:	Coverage of chemical industry segments, plus more than a dozen reports of general interest on the management of specialty chemical businesses.
Contact:	PAUL.ALBERT@NETEAST.COM
User Info:	To subscribe, contact Orbit-Questel directly.

`telnet://orbit.com`

Spectroscopy

Massachusetts Institute of Technology Library ★★

The library's holdings are large and wide-ranging and contain significant collections in many fields.

Keywords:	Aeronautics (History of), Linguistics, Mathematics (History of), Microscopy, Spectroscopy, Aeronautics, Mathematics, Glass
Audience:	General Public, Researchers, Librarians, Document Delivery Professionals
Details:	Free
User Info:	Expect: Mitek Server..., Send: Enter or Return; Expect: prompt, Send: hollis

`telnet://library.mit.edu`

Speech Disorders

Stutt-L ★

A list for the clinical discussion of stuttering, a speech disorder.

Keywords:	Communications, Speech Disorders, Disabilities
Audience:	Communications Specialists, Speech Pathologists
Contact:	Woody Starkweather
	v5002e@vm.temple.edu
User Info:	To subscribe to this list, send an e-mail message to the URL address below, consisting of a single line reading:
	SUB Stutt-L YourFirstName YourLastName
	To send a message to the entire list, address it to: stutt-l@rm.temple.edu

`mailto:listserv@vm.temple.edu`

Speeches and Addresses in the US

Speeches and Addresses in the US ★

Includes the Clinton State of the Union Speech of 1993, Kennedy's Inaugural Speech, Martin Luther King's "I Have a Dream" speech, and more.

Keywords:	Politics (US), Rhetoric
Audience:	Journalists, Writers, Politicians, Students
Details:	Free
	Choose from menu presented.

`gopher://wiretap.spies.com/11/Gov/US-Speech`

Spelunking

alt.caving ★

A Usenet newsgroup dedicating to discussions of caving and related issues, including cave locations, equipment, spelunking techniques, and other caving information.

Keywords:	Spelunking, Caves
Audience:	Spelunkers
User Info:	To subscribe to this Usenet newsgroup, you need access to a newsreader.

`news://alt.caving`

Cavers

This is an information resource and forum for anyone interested in exploring caves.

Keywords:	Caves, Spelunking
Audience:	Cave Explorers, Spelunkers
Contact:	John D. Sutter cavers-request@vlsi.bu.edu
Details:	Free
User Info:	To subscribe to the list, send an e-mail message requesting a subscription to the URL address below. To send a message to the entire list, address it to: cavers@vlsi.bu.edu

`mailto:cavers-request@vlsi.bu.edu`

Spirituality

Ayurveda

Ayurveda is the ancient science of life that originated in India. This mailing list provides information about ayurveda, such as lectures, workshops, and stores that sell ayurvedic herbs.

Keywords:	Spirituality, Ayurveda, India
Audience:	General Public
Contact:	ayurveda-request@netcom.com
Details:	Free
User Info:	To subscribe to the list, send an e-mail message requesting a subscription to the URL address below. To send a message to the entire list, address it to: ayurveda@netcom.com

`mailto:ayurveda-request@netcom.com`

Spojrzenia

Spojrzenia

A weekly E-journal devoted to Polish culture, history and politics.

Keywords:	Poland, News (international), Culture
Audience:	Poles, Students
Contact:	Jerzy Krzystek krzystek@u.washington.edu
Details:	Free
User Info:	To subscribe to the list, send an e-mail message requesting a subscription to the URL address below. To send a message to the entire list, address it to: spojrzenia@u.washington.edu

`mailto:krzystek@u.washington.edu`

Sports

Aikido Information

An FTP site containing aikido dojo addresses from around the world, plus a calendar of events, FAQs, and lists of books and periodicals related to aikido.

Keywords:	Aikido, Martial Arts, Sports
Sponsor:	University of California at San Diego, San Diego, CA, USA
Audience:	Aikido Enthusiasts, Martial Artists
Contact:	aikido@cs.ucsd.edu
Details:	Free

`ftp://cs.ucsd.edu/pub/aikido`

American Hockey League

This list is for people interested in discussing and following the activities of the American Hockey League.

Keywords:	Sports, Hockey, American Hockey League
Audience:	Hockey Enthusiasts, Sports Enthusiasts
Contact:	ahl-news-request@andrew.cmu.edu
Details:	Free
User Info:	To subscribe to the list, send an e-mail message requesting a subscription to the URL address below. To send a message to the entire list, address it to: ahl-news@andrew.cmu.edu

`mailto:ahl-news-request@andrew.cmu.edu`

Biking

Information on biking events and maintenance, including an FAQ from rec.bicycles.

Keywords:	Sports, Bicycling, Fitness
Audience:	Bicyclists, Fitness Enthusiasts
Contact:	Joern Yngve Dahl-Stamnes dahls@fysel.unit.no
Details:	Free

`ftp://ugle.unit.no/local/biking`

Biking in Canada

A repository of information for bicyclists, including utility programs, events, FAQs, and how-to guides; some with Canadian-specific details.

Keywords:	Sports, Bicycling, Canada
Sponsor:	Habitat Ecology Division at the Bedford Institute of Oceanography
Audience:	Cyclists, Fitness Enthusiasts
Contact:	sysop@biome.bio.ns.ca
Details:	Free

`gopher://gopher.biome.bio.dfo.ca/pub/biking`

Blues (St. Louis Blues)

Provides information, game reports, stats, discussion, and so on, on the St. Louis Blues of the National Hockey League.

Keywords:	Hockey, Sports, National Hockey League
Audience:	Hockey Enthusiasts
Contact:	Joe Ashkar blues@medicine.wustl.edu
User Info:	To subscribe to the list, send an e-mail message requesting a subscription to the URL address below. To send a message to the entire list, address it to: blues@medicine.wustl.edu

`mailto:blues@medicine.wustl.edu`

Cleveland Sports

A forum for people to discuss their favorite Cleveland sports teams/personalities, and to obtain news and information about those teams that most out-of-towners couldn't get otherwise. Teams discussed include the Cleveland Indians, the Cleveland Browns, the Cleveland Cavaliers, and the teams from Ohio State University.

Keywords:	Cleveland, Sports, Ohio State Universiry
Audience:	Cleveland Sports Enthusiasts, Sports Enthusiasts, Cleveland Residents
Contact:	Richard Kowicki aj755@cleveland.freenet.edu
Details:	Free
User Info:	To subscribe to the list, send an e-mail message requesting a subscription to the URL address below.

`mailto:aj755@cleveland.freenet.edu`

dead-runners

The Dead Runners Society is a mailing list for runners who like to talk about the psychological, philosophical, and personal aspects of running.

Keywords:	Running, Sports
Audience:	Runners
Contact:	Christopher Mark Conn dead-runners-request@unx.sas.com
Details:	Free
User Info:	To subscribe to the list, send an e-mail message requesting a subscription to the URL address below. To send a message to the entire list, address it to: dead-runners-request@unx.sas.com

`mailto:dead-runners-request@unx.sas.com`

dragnet

To discuss strip drag racing from a participant's viewpoint.

Keywords:	Drag Racing, Sports
Audience:	Drag Racers

Contact:	dragnet-request@chiller.compaq.com
User Info:	To subscribe to the list, send an e-mail message requesting a subscription to the URL address below. To send a message to the entire list, address it to: dragnet-request@chiller.compaq.com

mailto:dragnet-request@chiller.compaq.com

echl-news ★

For people interested in discussing and following the East Coast Hockey League.

Keywords:	Hockey, Sports
Audience:	Hockey Enthusiasts
Contact:	echl-news-request@andrew.cmu.edu
Details:	Free
User Info:	To subscribe to the list, send an e-mail message requesting a subscription to the URL address below. To send a message to the entire list, address it to: echl-news-request@andrew.cmu.edu

mailto:echl-news-request@andrew.cmu.edu

france-foot ★

Discussions of the French football (soccer) scene. Results and news are posted regularly.

Keywords:	Soccer, Sports, France, Football
Audience:	Soccer Enthusiasts, French Sports Enthusiasts
Contact:	Vincent Habchi, Kent Hedlundh dvlkhh@cs.umu.se
Details:	Free
User Info:	To subscribe to the list, send an e-mail message requesting a subscription to the URL address below. To send a message to the entire list, address it to: france-foot@inf.enst.fr

mailto:france-foot-request@inf.enst.fr

Funet Sports Information ★★★★

An FTP archive of information on various sports with links to the archive at wuarchive.wustl.edu.

Keywords:	Sports, Professional Sports, Ice Hockey, Motor Racing, NFL, NHL, NBA, MLB
Sponsor:	Finnish Academic and Research Network (FUNET)
Audience:	Sports Enthusiasts
Profile:	A fairly extensive archive of information on both American (NBA, MLB, NHL, NFL) and worldwide sports (soccer, ice hockey, motor racing, and so on). Includes FAQs for various sports, statistics, pictures, and some sports games for the PC.
Contact:	Jari Pullinen sports-adm@nic.funet.fi
Details:	Free, Images

gopher://ftp.funet.fi/pub/sports

GolfData OnLine

A web site sampling of the information on the subscriber service GolfData OnLine. Provides numerous links to other sites which may be of interest to golfers.

Keywords:	Golf, Sports, Fitness
Audience:	Golfers, Sports Fans
Contact:	david@gdol.com
Notes:	GolfData Online is a paid subscriber electronic bulletin board service for golf enthusiasts. More information about how to subscribe can be obtained by accessing the address below.

http://www.gdol.com

mda ★

Discussion of the Mighty Ducks of Anaheim of the National Hockey League, including statistics and game summaries.

Keywords:	Hockey, Sports
Audience:	Ice Hockey Fans
Details:	Free
User Info:	To subscribe to the list, send an e-mail message to the URL address below, consisting of a single line reading: SUB mda YourFirstName YourLastName To send a message to the entire list, address it to: mda@macsch.com

mailto:mda@macsch.com

NFL Scores, Schedules, and Point Spreads ★

Information on National Football League (NFL) football scores, schedules, and point spreads.

Keywords:	Professional Sports, Sports, Football, NFL
Audience:	Football Fans
Contact:	office@world.std.com
Details:	Free

gopher://world.std.com/News and Weather

Olympic Games 1994 at Lillehammer

News, results, and updates every 15 minutes, as well as archive images, from the 1994 Winter Olympic Games at Lillehammer, Norway.

Keywords:	Olympics, Sports, Winter Games
Sponsor:	Sun Microsystem, Skrivervik Data AS, Oslonett AS, Norsk Telegrambyra
Audience:	General Public, Journalists, Skiers, Skaters, Winter Sports Fans
Profile:	This server offers news and results on all the Olympic events in Lillehammer plus a chronological list of all events, a complete schedule day by day, and a very large archive of images. Also flash messages from NTB, a Norwegian news wire, and the opportunity to search in the NTB database.
Contact:	oslonett@oslonett.no

http://www.sun.com

Open Computing Facilty (OCF) Gopher, Sports Section ★★★★

A gopher server offering access to information about a number of sporting activities.

Keywords:	Sports, Fitness
Sponsor:	Open Computing Facility, University of California, Berkeley
Audience:	Sports Fans, Fitness Enthusiasts
Profile:	This gopher has information on various sports, including football, cricket, skiing, windsurfing, and basketball, as well as links to WWW. Resources include schedules for some professional and collegiate sports, as well as FAQs and other miscellaneous information.
Contact:	general-manager@ocf.berkeley.edu
Details:	Free

gopher://gopher.ocf.berkeley.edu/11/gopherspace

Pac-10-Sports ★

This mailing list is dedicated to discussing sports of all types that are played competitively within the Pac-10 Athletic Conference.

Keywords:	Pac-10 Sports, National Collegiate Athletic Association, Sports
Audience:	Pac-10 Sports Fans
Contact:	Cliff Slaughterbeck crs@u.washington.edu
Details:	Free
User Info:	To subscribe to the list, send an e-mail message requesting a subscription to the URL address below. To send a message to the entire list, address it to: crs@u.washington.edu

mailto:crs@u.washington.edu

Physical Education & Recreation ★★

A collection of information on sporting and recreational activities from aikido to windsurfing.

Keywords:	Sports, Recreation, Aikido, Cycling, Scuba Diving, Windsurfing
Audience:	Sports Enthusiasts, Fitness Enthusiasts
Contact:	ctcadmin@ctc.ctc.edu

gopher://ctc.ctc.edu

Professional Sports Schedules

Sports schedules for major professional sports.

Keywords:	Sports, Baseball, Hockey, Football, Basketball
Sponsor:	Colorado University, Boulder, CO
Audience:	Sports Fans, Football Fans, Hockey Fans, Baseball Enthusiasts, Basketball Enthusiasts
Profile:	The Colorado University gopher maintains an interactive online database of schedules for all major US professional sports teams (NBA, NFL, NHL, MLB). The database is indexed by both team name and dates of games, and can be searched accordingly.
Contact:	gopher@gopher.colorado.edu
Details:	Free

`gopher://gopher.colorado.edu/11/professional/sports/schedules`

Quebec Nordiques

A mailing list to discuss topics concerning the National Hockey League's Quebec Nordiques.

Keywords:	Hockey, Quebec (Canada), Sports
Audience:	Hockey Enthusiasts
Contact:	Danny J. Sohier nords-request@badaboum.ulaval.ca
Details:	Free
User Info:	To subscribe to the list, send an e-mail message requesting a subscription to the URL address below. To send a message to the entire list, address it to: nords@badaboum.ulaval.ca

`mailto:nords@badaboum.ulaval.ca`

rec.autos.sport

A Usenet newsgroup providing information and discussion about automobile competition.

Keywords:	Automobiles, Automobile Racing, Sports
Audience:	Automobile Racing Enthusiasts
User Info:	To subscribe to this Usenet newsgroup, you need access to a newsreader.

`news:rec.autos.sports`

rec.backcountry

A Usenet newsgroup providing information and discussion about wilderness, backpacking, and camping.

Keywords:	Recreation, Sports
Audience:	Campers, Backpackers, Wilderness Enthusiasts
User Info:	To subscribe to this Usenet newsgroup, you need access to a newsreader.

`news:rec.backcountry`

rec.boats

A Usenet newsgroup providing information and discussion about boating, gear, places to sail, clubs, repairs, and racing.

Keywords:	Sailing, Sports
Audience:	Sailors, Boating Enthusiasts
User Info:	To subscribe to this Usenet newsgroup, you need access to a newsreader.

`news:rec.boats`

rec.equestrian

A Usenet newsgroup providing information and discussion about all things pertaining to horses.

Keywords:	Horses, Equestrians, Animals, Sports
Audience:	Horse Riders, Horse Trainers, Horse Owners
User Info:	To subscribe to this Usenet newsgroup, you need access to a newsreader.

`news:rec.equestrian`

rec.skiing

A Usenet newsgroup providing information and discussion about skiing.

Keywords:	Sports, Recreation, Skiing
Audience:	Skiers
User Info:	To subscribe to this Usenet newsgroup, you need access to a newsreader.

`news:rec.skiing`

rec.sport.baseball

A Usenet newsgroup providing information and discussion about professional baseball.

Keywords:	Baseball, Sports
Audience:	Baseball Fans, Sports Fans
User Info:	To subscribe to this Usenet newsgroup, you need access to a newsreader.

`news:rec.sport.baseball`

rec.sport.basketball.college

A Usenet newsgroup providing information and discussion about college basketball.

Keywords:	Basketball, College, Sports
Audience:	Basketball Fans, Sport Fans
User Info:	To subscribe to this Usenet newsgroup, you need access to a newsreader.

`news:rec.sport.basketball.college`

rec.sport.basketball.pro

A Usenet newsgroup providing information and discussion about professional basketball.

Keywords:	Basketball, Sports
Audience:	Basketball Fans, Sports Fans
User Info:	To subscribe to this Usenet newsgroup, you need access to a newsreader.

`news:rec.sport.basketball.pro`

rec.sport.cricket

A Usenet newsgroup providing information and discussion about cricket.

Keywords:	Cricket, Sports
Audience:	Cricket Fans, Sports Fans
User Info:	To subscribe to this Usenet newsgroup, you need access to a newsreader.

`news:rec.sport.cricket`

rec.sport.football.college

A Usenet newsgroup providing information and discussion about college football.

Keywords:	Football, College, Sports
Audience:	Football Fans, Sports Fans
User Info:	To subscribe to this Usenet newsgroup, you need access to a newsreader.

`news:rec.sport.football.college`

rec.sport.football.pro

A Usenet newsgroup providing information and discussion about pro football.

Keywords:	Football, Sports
Audience:	Football Enthusiasts
User Info:	To subscribe to this Usenet newsgroup, you need access to a newsreader.

`news:rec.sport.football.pro`

rec.sport.hockey

A Usenet newsgroup providing information and discussion about hockey.

Keywords:	Hockey, Sports
Audience:	Hockey Fans, Sports Fans
User Info:	To subscribe to this Usenet newsgroup, you need access to a newsreader.

`news:rec.sport.hockey`

rec.sport.pro-wrestling

A Usenet newsgroup providing information and discussion about professional wrestling.

Keywords:	Wrestling, Sports
Audience:	Wrestling Fans, Sports Fans
User Info:	To subscribe to this Usenet newsgroup, you need access to a newsreader.

`news:rec.sport.pro-wrestling`

rec.sport.rowing

A Usenet newsgroup providing information and discussion about recreational and competitive rowing. It provides information from the United States Rowing Association, the latest race results, equipment sales, coaching positions, and more.

Keywords: Rowing, Crew, Sports
Audience: Rowers, Coaches, Athletes
Profile: This newsgroup covers technical, training and nutritional aspects as well as the latest race results, National Team information, equipment sales, coaching positions, information from the United States Rowing Association and more.
User Info: To subscribe to this Usenet newsgroup, you need access to a newsreader.

`news:rec.sport.rowing`

rec.sport.soccer

A Usenet newsgroup providing information and discussion about soccer.

Keywords: Soccer, Sports
Audience: Soccer Fans, Sports Fans
User Info: To subscribe to this Usenet newsgroup, you need access to a newsreader.

`news:rec.sport.soccer`

rec.sport.tennis

A Usenet newsgroup providing information and discussion about tennis.

Keywords: Tennis, Sports
Audience: Tennis Fans, Sports Fans
User Info: To subscribe to this Usenet newsgroup, you need access to a newsreader.

`news:rec.sport.tennis`

Skiing in Utah

An FTP site maintaining information on skiing sites in Utah, Idaho, and Wyoming.

Keywords: Sports, Skiing
Sponsor: Utah University
Audience: Skiers
Details: Free

`ftp://ski.utah.edu/skiing`

SPORTS (Sports News)

The Sports News (SPORTS) library contains a variety of sports-related news and information.

Keywords: News, Analysis, Sports, Biographies
Audience: Sports Enthusiasts, Journalists
Profile: The SPORTS library is a specialized news library that contains the full text of Sports Illustrated and The Sporting News and selected sports-related stories from many major US newspapers and wire services. Biographical information and 1992 Olympic facts are also part of this library.
Contact: Mead New Sales Group at (800) 227-4908 or (513) 859-5398 inside the US, or (513) 865-7981 for all inquiries outside the US.
User Info: To subscribe, contact Mead directly.
To examine the Nexis user guide, you can access it at the ftp site of the University of Texas at Austin at the URL address: ftp://ftp.cc.utexas.edu. The files are in: /pub/ref-services/LEXIS

`telnet://nex.meaddata.com`

`http://www.meaddata.com`

Sports-cards

For people interested in collection, speculation and investing in baseball, football, basketball, hockey, and other trading cards and memorabilia. Discussion and want/sell lists are welcome.

Keywords: Memorabilia, Sports, Trading Cards
Audience: Collectors, Sports Card Traders
Contact: Keane Arase
cards-request@tanstaafl.uchicago.edu
Details: Free
User Info: To subscribe to the list, send an e-mail message requesting a subscription to the URL address below. To send a message to the entire list, address it to: cards@tanstaafl.uchicago.edu

`mailto:cards-request@tanstaafl.uchicago.edu`

The Nautical Bookshelf

Catalog and ordering information for Nautical Bookshelf's collection of books on Sailing and other water sports.

Keywords: Boating, Power Boating, Sailing, Sports
Sponsor: Nautical Bookshelf
Audience: Boating Enthusiasts, Sailors
Contact: staff@nautical.com

`gopher://gopher.nautical.com`

Think Wind

An FTP site for information on windsurfing, with FAQs, pictures, details about destinations, and threads from rec.windsurfing.

Keywords: Sports, Windsurfing
Audience: Windsurfers
Contact: phansen@lemming.uvm.edu
Details: Free, Images

`ftp://lemming.uvm.edu/rec.windsurfing`

United Press International News - Sports

Full text of UPI stories and articles.

Keywords: Sports, News
Sponsor: United Press International (UPI)
Audience: Sports Enthusiasts
Profile: This gopher allows access to daily UPI news feeds, including sports news. The most current articles available tend to run three to five days behind. This delay is compensated for by UPIs far-ranging coverage of national and international sporting news. Indexed, with back articles from 1992 onwards available.
Contact: UPI
clarinews@clarinet.com
Details: Free

`gopher://mrfrosty.micro.umn.edu./UPI-data/Today/sports`

University of Glasgow Information Service (GLANCE)

GLANCE provides subject-based information services, including an extensive section on European and world sports.

Keywords: Sports, Soccer, Motor Racing, Mountaineering, Squash, Cricket, Golf, Tennis, Europe, Scotland
Sponsor: University of Glasgow, Glasgow, Scotland
Audience: Sport Enthusiasts, Fitness Enthusiasts, Nature Lovers
Profile: Information at this site includes schedules, results, and statistics for sports such as cricket and soccer. There is also a selection of items on mountaineering.
Contact: Alan Dawson
A.Dawson@uk.ac.gla.compserv
Details: Free

`gopher://govan.cent.gla.ac.uk/Subject/Sports and Rec`

Usenet Sports Groups Archived

An archive for Usenet groups, including many related to sports ranging from football to table tennis.

Keywords: Sports, Skydiving, Volleyball, Football, Scuba Diving, Table Tennis
Sponsor: Massachusetts Institute of Technology, Boston, MA
Audience: Sports Enthusiasts
Contact: ftp-bugs@rtfm.mit.edu
Details: Free

`ftp://rtfm.mit.edu/pub/usenet`

Velo News Experimental Tour de France Web Page

This web site provides background information on the Tour de France, including press coverage from this year's race.

Keywords:	Bicycles, Sports
Sponsor:	Velo News
Audience:	Bicyclists, Sports Fans
Contact:	VeloNews@aol.com

`http://cob.fsu.edu/velonews/`

Wiretap Sports Archives

Sports articles, including information on soccer in the US and Canada, rules for soccer and Australian football, and some rather dated material on American football.

Keywords:	Sports, Football, Soccer
Sponsor:	The Internet Wiretap Library
Audience:	Sports Enthusiasts
Details:	Free

`gopher://wiretap.spies.com/library/article/sports`

Sports Cars

Porschephiles

This list is for people who own, operate, work on, or covet various models of Porsche automobiles. Discussion topics include features, functionality, and purchasing advice.

Keywords:	Porsche, Automobiles, Sports Cars
Audience:	Porsche Owners, Sports Car Owners, Automobile Mechanics
Contact:	porschephiles-request@tta.com
Details:	Free
User Info:	To subscribe to the list, send an e-mail message requesting a subscription to the URL address below. To send a message to the entire list, address it to: porschephiles@tta.com

`mailto:porschephiles-request@tta.com`

Sports Statistics

NHL Goalie Stats

A list of NHL goalie statistics.

Keywords:	Hockey, National Hockey League (NHL), Sports Statistics
Audience:	Hockey Enthusiasts
Profile:	Weekday reports of goalie statistics from the National Hockey League.
Contact:	dfa@triple-i.com
Details:	Free
User Info:	To subscribe to the list, send an e-mail message requesting a subscription to the URL address below. To send a message to the entire list, address it to: dfa@triple-i.com

`mailto:dfa@triple-i.com`

Sports-cards

Sports-cards

For people interested in collection, speculation and investing in baseball, football, basketball, hockey, and other trading cards and/or memorabilia. Discussion and want/sell lists are welcome.

Keywords:	Memorabilia, Sports, Trading Cards
Audience:	Collectors, Sports Card Traders
Contact:	Keane Arase cards-request@tanstaafl.uchicago.edu
Details:	Free
User Info:	To subscribe to the list, send an e-mail message requesting a subscription to the URL address below. To send a message to the entire list, address it to: cards@tanstaafl.uchicago.edu

`mailto:cards-request@tanstaafl.uchicago.edu`

Springsteen (Bruce)

Backstreets

Discussion of Bruce Springsteen's music.

Keywords:	Rock Music, Springsteen (Bruce)
Audience:	Bruce Springsteen Fans
Contact:	Kevin Kinder backstreets-request@virginia.edu
Details:	Free
User Info:	To subscribe to the list, send an e-mail message requesting a subscription to the URL address below. To send a message to the entire list, address it to: backstreets@virginia.edu

`mailto:backstreets-request@virginia.edu`

Squash

University of Glasgow Information Service (GLANCE)

GLANCE provides subject-based information services, including an extensive section on European and world sports.

Keywords:	Sports, Soccer, Motor Racing, Mountaineering, Squash, Cricket, Golf, Tennis, Europe, Scotland
Sponsor:	University of Glasgow, Glasgow, Scotland
Audience:	Sport Enthusiasts, Fitness Enthusiasts, Nature Lovers
Profile:	Information at this site includes schedules, results, and statistics for sports such as cricket and soccer. There is also a selection of items on mountaineering.
Contact:	Alan Dawson A.Dawson@uk.ac.gla.compserv
Details:	Free

`gopher://govan.cent.gla.ac.uk/Subject/Sports and Rec`

Sri Lanka

Sri Lanka Net (SLNet)

A moderated mailing list that carries news and other articles about Sri Lanka.

Keywords:	Sri Lanka, News (International)
Audience:	Sri Lankans, Students
Contact:	pkd@fed.frb.gov slnetad@ganu.colorado.edu
Details:	Free, Moderated
User Info:	To subscribe to the list, send an e-mail message requesting a subscription to the URL address below. To send a message to the entire list, address it to: slnetad@ganu.colorado.edu

`mailto:pkd@fed.frb.gov`

`mailto:slnetad@ganu.colorado.edu`

ST Viruses

ST viruses

This list is to provide fast and efficient help with computer viruses infecting the Atari ST/TT/Falcon only.

Keywords:	Computer Viruses, Atari
Audience:	Computer Users
Contact:	r.c.karsmakers@stud.let.ruu.nl
Details:	Free
User Info:	To subscribe to the list, send an e-mail message requesting a subscription to the URL address below. To send a message to the entire list, address it to: r.c.karsmakers@stud.let.ruu.nl

`mailto:r.c.karsmakers@stud.let.ruu.nl`

St. John Valley (History of)

University of Maine System Library Catalog

The library's holdings are large and wide-ranging and contain significant collections in many fields.

Keywords: Ucadian Studies, St. John Valley (History of), Canadian-American Studies, Geology, Aquaculture, Maine
Audience: General Public, Researchers, Librarians, Document Delivery Professionals
Contact: Elaine Albright, Marilyn Lutz
Details: Free
User Info: Expect: login, Send: ursus

`telnet://ursus.maine.edu`

St. Petersburg

St. Petersburg Business News

Contains a digest of business information extracted from Russian and St. Petersburg morning newspapers, stock exchange reports, reports from the News own correspondents.

Keywords: Business, St. Petersburg
Audience: Russians, Business
Contact: Elena Artemova
esa@cfea.ecc.spb.su
spbeac@sovamsu.sovusa.com
Details: Costs
User Info: To send a message to the entire list, address it to:

`mailto:listserv@sovamsu.sovusa.com`

Stagecraft

Stagecraft

This list is for the discussion of all aspects of stage work, including special effects, sound effects, sound reinforcement, stage management, set design and building, lighting, design, company management, hall management, hall design, and show production.

Keywords: Theater, Drama
Audience: Stage Producers
Contact: Brad Davis
stagecraft-request@zinc.com
User Info: To subscribe to the list, send an Email message requesting a subscription to the URL address below. To send a message to the entire list, address it to: stagecraft@zinc.com
Notes: Also contains archives of list discussions.

`mailto:stagecraft-request@zinc.com`

Standards

UN Rules

Standards, guidelines and international instruments promulgated by the UN.

Keywords: Politics, UN, Standards
Sponsor: United Nations Justice Network (UNCJIN)
Audience: Lawyers, General Public, Internationalists
Details: Free
Select from Menu as appropriate

`gopher://uacsc2.albany.edu`

Uniform Commercial Code (UCC)

Articles 1 and 2 of the UCC, adopted with some variations in all 50 states (USA).

Keywords: Commerce, Business Info, Standards
Audience: Politicians, Marketers, Students, Retailers, Lawyers
Details: Free

`http://www.law.cornell.edu/ucc/ucc.table.html`

Stanford Medical Center Gopher

Stanford Medical Center Gopher

This gopher allows extensive access to the Stanford Medical Center's archives.

Keywords: Medicine, Health Care, Health Sciences
Sponsor: Stanford Medical Center, Palo Alto, California, USA
Audience: Health Care Professionals, Health Science Researchers
Contact: Stanford Medical Center
gopher@medisg.stanford.edu

`gopher://med.stanford.edu`

Starfish

Starnet (Echinoderm Newsletter)

The Starnet echinoderm electronic newsletter is distributed quarterly.

Keywords: Echinoderm, Starfish, Marine Biology
Audience: Marine Biologists
Contact: Win Hide
whide@matrix.bchs.uh.edu
Details: Free
User Info: To subscribe to the list, send an e-mail message requesting a subscription to the URL address below.

`mailto:whide@matrix.bchs.uh.edu`

Stargazing

Sci.astro.hubble

Information about all subjects concerning NASA's Hubble space telescope.

Keywords: Hubble Telescope, Astronomy, Space, NASA, Stargazing, Telescopes
Audience: Astronomers, General Public, Science Teachers, Stargazers
Contact: Paul A. Scowen
scowen@wfpc3.la.asu.edu
Details: Free, Moderated, Images
User Info: To subscribe to this Usenet newsgroup, you need access to a newsreader.

`news:sci.astro.hubble`

Stars

Astronomy

This directory is a compilation of information resources focused on astronomy.

Keywords: Astronomy, Stars, Astrophysics, Space
Audience: Astronomers, Astrophysicists, Space Enthusiasts
Contact: A. Park, J. Miller
Details: Free

`ftp://una.hh.lib.umich.edu/70/inetdirsstacks/astron:parkmiller`

State Courts

Citation Authority ★

Legal citation authority expected to be used in the highest US appellate state courts, based on a 1985 survey (revised March 1991).

Keywords: Law (US), State Courts
Audience: Lawyers
Details: Free
User Info: Expect: login; Send: lawlib

`gopher://liberty.uc.wlu.edu/00/library/law/lawftp/citation.txt`

State Small Business Profiles

State Small Business Profiles ★★★

This site contains Small Business Administration reports, which provide statistics on the small business sector in each state.

Keywords: Business, Statistics, United States
Sponsor: U.S. Government, Small Business Administration, in conjunction with the Reference Department of the Thomas Jefferson Library of the University of Missouri-St. Louis
Audience: Business Professionals, Researchers
Profile: The 1993 State Business Profiles bring together an array of statistics on the small business sector in each state. Included is data on small business income and employment trends; women-owned and minority-owned businesses; business closings and formations; and state exports.
Contact: Raleigh Muns
srcmuns@umslvma.umsl.edu
Details: Free
Notes: For additional information you can call the Small Business Administration toll free at 1-800-359-2777, or the SBA District Office in Washington, D.C. at (202) 205-6600.

`gopher://umslvma.umsl.edu/11/library/govdocs/states`

States

CODES (Codes Library)

The Codes Library offers access to US federal and state legislative materials, in codified, slip law, and bill form, plus federal and state regulatory materials and a statutes archive.

Keywords: Statutes, Codes, State, Federal
Audience: (US) Lawyers
Profile: The Codes library contains an extensive compilation of federal and state statutory materials, in codified as well as slip law form, from all 50 states, the District of Columbia, Puerto Rico, the Virgin Islands and the United States Code Service. The library also contains federal and state regulatory materials plus a statues archive. Pending legislation can be found with 50-state and federal fill tracking, the full text of federal bills, the Congressional Record, and the full text of bills for a growing number of states. Administrative materials include the Code of Federal Regulations, the Federal Register, 50-state regulation tracking, and the administrative codes for a selected number of states.
Contact: New Sales Group at (800) 227-4908 or (513) 859-5398 inside the US, or 1-513-865-7981 for all inquires outside the US.
User Info: To subscribe, contact Mead directly.
To examine the Lexis user guide, you can access it at the ftp site of the University of Texas at Austin at the URL address: ftp://ftp.cc.utexas.edu. The files are in: pub/ref-services/LEXIS

`telnet://nex.meaddata.com`

`http://www.meaddata.com`

STATES (States Library)

The combined States Library contains case law, code and agency materials from the 53 individual US state libraries (50 states plus the District of Columbia, Puerto Rico and the Virgin Islands), all in the same library.

Keywords: Law, Analysis, Case, States
Audience: Lawyers
Profile: The combined States Library contains case law, code and agency materials from the 53 individual state libraries (50 states plus the District of Columbia, Puerto Rico and the Virgin Islands), all in the same library. The States Library also features many large group files which allow several individual files to be accessed in the same search. Many of the group files involve case law, including files that cover all state case law available on the LEXIS service plus ALR material and files that combine all federal and state case law available on the LEXIS service.
Contact: New Sales Group at (800) 227-4908 or (513) 859-5398 inside the US, or 1-513-865-7981 for all inquires outside the US.
User Info: To subscribe, contact Mead directly.
To examine the Lexis user guide, you can access it at the ftp site of the University of Texas at Austin at the URL address: ftp://ftp.cc.utexas.edu. The files are in: pub/ref-services/LEXIS

`telnet://nex.meaddata.com`

`http://www.meaddata.com`

The Texas Information Highway ★★

Access to the public information resources of the state of Texas.

Keywords: Texas, States, Government, Census, Tourism
Sponsor: Texas Department of Information Resources
Audience: Texans, General Public
Profile: Still under construction as we go to press, this is a model program to make state and local information resources available to Internet users. The current collection features city, country, and state political information, including full-text of bills before the Texas state legislature. Materials related to Texas history and tourism are also provided, along with links to Texas-area user groups and other state and federal information servers.
Contact: Wayne McDilda
wayne@dir.texas.gov

`gopher://info.texas.gov`

Statistics

Iowa State University Library ★★

The library's holdings contain significant collections in many fields.

Keywords: Agriculture, Veterinary Medicine, Statistics, Labor, Soil Conservation, Film
Audience: General Public, Researchers, Librarians, Document Delivery Professionals
Details: Free
User Info: Expect: DIAL, Send: LIB

`telnet://isn.iastate.edu`

New York State Department of Health Gopher

An electronic guide to health information from the state of New York.

Keywords: Health Care, Statistics, Health Sciences, New York
Sponsor: New York State Department of Health
Audience: Health Care Professionals, Health Care Consumers
Profile: Information provided includes health statistics for New York State, lists of health care providers, facilities, and publications, as well as New York State Department of Health press releases.
Contact: nyhealth@albnydh2.bitnet

`gopher://gopher.health.state.ny.us`

Statistics

State Small Business Profiles

This site contains Small Business Administration reports, which provide statistics on the small business sector in each state.

Keywords: Business, Statistics, United States

Sponsor: U.S. Government, Small Business Administration, in conjunction with the Reference Department of the Thomas Jefferson Library of the University of Missouri-St. Louis

Audience: Business Professionals, Researchers

Profile: The 1993 State Business Profiles bring together an array of statistics on the small business sector in each state. Included is data on small business income and employment trends; women-owned and minority-owned businesses; business closings and formations; and state exports.

Contact: Raleigh Muns
srcmuns@umslvma.umsl.edu

Details: Free

Notes: For additional information you can call the Small Business Administration toll free at (800) 359-2777, or the SBA District Office in Washington, D.C. at (202) 205-6600.

`gopher://umslvma.umsl.edu/11/library/govdocs/states`

Statistics Canada Gopher

A repository of information from the National Statistical Agency of Canada.

Keywords: Statistics, Canada, Canadian Documents

Sponsor: Statistics Canada, Canada

Audience: Canadians, Researchers

Profile: Updated daily, this site allows users to search Statistics Canada documents and provides updates of upcoming statistical conferences and publications in Canada. It also allows access to Statistics Canada FTP and list servers.

Contact: Michael Thoen, Jackie Godfrey
thoemic@statcan.ca
godfrey@statcan.ca

`gopher://talon.statcan.ca`

Statlib

Statlib is an archive of statistics-related materials.

Keywords: Statistics, Mathematics

Audience: Statisticians, Mathematicians

Profile: This archive contains a large collection of statistics software data. The directory lists the source to entire statistics packages, the collection of applied statistics algorithms, the archives of the s-new mailing list, and more.

Contact: statlib@lib.stat.cmu.edu

Details: Free

`ftp://lib.stat.cmu.edu`

U.S. Bureau of the Census Gopher

A gopher offering official Census data and services direct from the Census Bureau.

Keywords: Census, Demography, Statistics

Sponsor: U.S. Census Bureau

Audience: Journalists, Government Officials, General Public

Profile: A wealth of demographic and economic data from the Census Bureau. Information available includes population estimates, financial data from state and local governments, and assorted statistical briefs. This gopher also has details on the offices, programs, and personnel of the Bureau itself, as well as links to other federal information systems and sources of Census data.

Contact: gatekeeper@census.gov

Details: Free, Images

`gopher://gopher.census.gov`

`http://www.census.gov (CHECK)`

University of Rochester Library ★★

The library's holdings are large and wide-ranging and contain significant collections in many fields.

Keywords: Architecture, Art History, Photography, Literature (Asian), Lasers, Geology, Statistics, Optics, Medieval Studies

Audience: Researchers, Students, General Public

Details: Free

User Info: Expect: Login; Send: Library

`telnet://128.151.226.71`

Wildnet (Computing and Statistics in Fishers & Wildlife Biology)

This mailing list was established for the exchange of ideas, questions, and solutions in the area of fisheries and wildlife biology computing and statistics.

Keywords: Wildlife, Fisheries, Statistics

Audience: Wildlife Biologists, Environmentalists, Statisticians

Contact: Eric Woodsworth
woodsworth@sask.usask.ca

Details: Free

User Info: To subscribe to the list, send an e-mail message requesting a subscription to the URL address below. To send a message to the entire list, address it to: wildnet@tribune.usask.ca

`mailto:wildnet-request@tribune.usask.ca`

Statutes

CODES (Codes Library)

The Codes library offers access to US federal and state legislative materials, in codified, slip law, and bill form, plus federal and state regulatory materials and a statutes archive.

Keywords: Statutes, Codes, State, Federal

Audience: (US) Lawyers

Profile: The Codes library contains an extensive compilation of federal and state statutory materials, in codified as well as slip law form, from all 50 states, the District of Columbia, Puerto Rico, the Virgin Islands and the United States Code Service. The library also contains federal and state regulatory materials plus a statues archive. Pending legislation can be found with 50-state and federal fill tracking, the full text of federal bills, the Congressional Record, and the full text of bills for a growing number of states. Administrative materials include the Code of Federal Regulations, the Federal Register, 50-state regulation tracking, and the administrative codes for a selected number of states.

Contact: New Sales Group at (800) 227-4908 or (513) 859-5398 inside the US, or (513) 865-7981 for all inquires outside the US.

User Info: To subscribe, contact Mead directly.

To examine the Lexis user guide, you can access it at the ftp site of the University of Texas at Austin at the URL address: ftp://ftp.cc.utexas.edu. The files are in: pub/ref-services/LEXIS

`telnet://nex.meaddata.com`

`http://www.meaddata.com`

Std-UNIX

Std-UNIX ★

Discussion of UNIX standards, particularly the IEEE P1003 Portable Operating System Environment draft standard.

Keywords: UNIX, Operating Systems

Audience: UNIX Users

Contact: Sean Eric Fagan
sef@uunet.uu.net

Details: Free, Moderated

User Info: To subscribe to the list, send an e-mail message requesting a subscription to the URL address below.

`mailto:sef@uunet.uu.net`

Stealth

Stealth

Discussion of anything related to Dodge Stealth and Mitsubishi 3000GT cars.

Keywords: Automobile
Audience: Car Enthusiasts
Contact: stealth-request%jim.uucp@wupost.wustl.edu
Details: Free
User Info: Expect: Username prompt, Send: tcucat
User Info: To subscribe to the list, send an e-mail message requesting a subscription to the URL address below. To send a message to the entire list, address it to: stealth-request96jim.uucp@wupost.wustl.edu

`mailto:stealth-request%jim.uucp@wupost.wustl.edu`

Steel

Materials Business File

Covers all commercial aspects of iron and steel, non-ferrous metals and non-metallic materials.

Keywords: Material Science, Business, Iron, Steel
Sponsor: Material Information, a joint information service of ASM International and the Institute of Materials
Audience: Materials Scientists, Researchers
Profile: Articles are abstracted from over 2,000 worldwide technical and trade journals to create more than 65,000 records. Update monthly.
Contact: paul.albert@neteast.com
User Info: To subscribe contact Orbit-Questel directly.

`telnet://orbit.com`

Stereo Electronics

rec.audio

A Usenet newsgroup providing information and discussion about audio products, including troubleshooting advice.

Keywords: Audio Electronics, Stereo Electronics
Audience: Stereo Owners, Music Listeners
User Info: To subscribe to this Usenet newsgroup, you need access to a newsreader.

`news:rec.audio`

Stlhe-l (Forum for Teaching & Learning in Higher Education)

Stlhe-l (Forum for Teaching & Learning in Higher Education)

This list focuses on postsecondary education teaching and learning.

Keywords: Education (Adult), Education (Distance), Education (Continuing), Education (Post Secondary)
Audience: Educators, Faculty, Administrators, Researchers
Details: Free
User Info: To subscribe to the list, send an e-mail message to the URL address below consisting of a single line reading:

SUB stlhe-l YourFirstName YourLastName

To send a message to the entire list, address it to: stlhe-l@unbvm1.bitnet

`mailto:listserv@unbvm1.bitnet`

Stock Market

Disclosure Database

Disclosure Database provides in-depth financial information on over 12,500 companies.

Keywords: Securities, Stock Market
Sponsor: Disclosure Incorporated, Bethesda, MD, USA
Audience: Business Professionals
Profile: The information is derived from reports filed with the US Securities and Exchange Commission (SEC) by publicly owned companies. These reports provide detailed and reliable financial information on the companies included. Extracts of 10-K and 10-Q financial reports are included, as well as 20-F financial reports and registration reports for new registrants. Disclosure provides an online source of information for marketing intelligence, corporate planning, accounting research, and corporate finance. Contents of the records include management discussion and president's letter on past-year performance, footnotes to the financials, significant events, and market conditions affecting a particular company.
Contact: Dialog in the US at (800) 334-2564, Dialog internationally at country-specific locations.
User Info: To subscribe, contact Dialog directly.
Notes: Coverage: Current; updated weekly.

`telnet://dialog.com`

Experimental Stock Market Data

This is an experimental page that provides a link to the latest stock market information.

Keywords: Stock Market, Investments, Finance
Audience: General Public, Investors, Stock Brokers
Profile: This site is updated automatically, to reflect the current day's closing information. Provides general market news and quotes for selected stocks, although prices are not guaranteed. Also includes recent prices for many mutual funds, as well as technical analysis charts for a large number of stocks and mutual funds.
Contact: Mark Torrance stockmaster@ai.mit.edu
Details: Free

`http://www.ai.mit.edu/stocks.html`

SEC (Securities and Exchange Commission) EDGAR (Electronic Data Gathering, Analysis and Retrieval) System

Provides free access to 1994 SEC filings for approximately 2,300 companies.

Keywords: Securities, Filings, SEC, Stock Market
Sponsor: New York University School of Business
Audience: Business Professionals, Investors
Profile: This expanding project aims to make available current, public SEC filings that are filed electronically. The system is searchable by company name and is updated and indexed daily. Many types of SEC forms, including 10-K and 10-Q financial reports, are available in a number of different electronic formats. The site also provides some explanatory documentation on the EDGAR program and on the types of SEC forms and information available to the public.
Contact: Ajit Kambil piotr@edgar.stern.nyu.edu
Details: Free

`ftp://town.hall.org/edgar`

`http://www.town.hall.org`

Stock Market Secrets

Publication of a stock market-related daily commentary. Questions are answered on a wide variety of investment and financial topics.

Keywords: Stock Market, Investments, Finance
Audience: Investors, Stock Brokers, Financial Advisors
Contact: smi-request@world.std.com

Stock Market

Details: Free, Moderated

User Info: To subscribe to the list, send an e-mail message requesting a subscription to the URL address below.

To send a message to the entire list, address it to: smi@world.std.com

`mailto:smi-request@world.std.com`

Yahoo Market and Investments

A comprehensive look at the current economic status, with a wide range of coverage, from brokers to stocks.

Keywords: Business, Stock Market, Investment, Economy

Sponsor: Stanford University, Palo Alto, California, USA

Audience: Investors, Economists

Contact: jerry@akebono.stanford.edu

`http://akebono.stanford.edu/yahoo/Economy/Markets_and_Investments`

Stonewall25

Stonewall25 ★

A mailing list for discussion and planning of the "Stonewall 25," an international gay/lesbian/bisexual rights march in New York City on Sunday, June 26, 1994, and the events accompanying it.

Keywords: Gay Rights, Lesbian, Bisexual, Activism

Audience: Gays, Lesbians, Bisexuals, Activists

Contact: stonewall25-request@queernet.org

Details: Free

User Info: To subscribe to the list, send an e-mail message requesting a subscription to the URL address below. To send a message to the entire list, address it to: stonewall25@queernet.org

`mailto:stonewall25-request@queernet.org`

Stormcock

Stormcock ★

For general discussion and news concerning the music of Roy Harper, a folk-rock musician with a conscience. Recommendations and news concerning similar artists are encouraged.

Keywords: Rock Music, Music, Harper (Roy)

Audience: Music Fans

Contact: Paul Davison
stormcock-request@qmw.ac.uk

Details: Free

User Info: To subscribe to the list, send an e-mail message to the address shown below consisting of a single line reading:

SUB stormcock YourFirstName YourLastName

To send a message to the entire list, address it to: stormcock@qmw.ac.uk

`mailto:listserv@qmw.ac.uk`

Storytelling

Nerdnosh ★

This is a virtual campfire gathering of storytellers. Bring us your tired, your family fables, your journals of yesterday, and your imprints on tomorrow.

Keywords: Storytelling

Audience: Storytellers, General Public

Contact: Timothy Bowden
urder@clovis.felton.ca.us

Details: Free

User Info: To subscribe to the list, send an e-mail message requesting a subscription to the URL address below, consisting of a single line reading:

SUB nerdnosh YourFirstName YourLastName

To send a message to the entire list, address it to:
nerdnosh@clovis.felton.ca.us

`mailto:listserv@clovis.felton.ca.us`

String Processing

Icon-group ★

Discussion of topics related to the Icon programming language.

Keywords: Programming, Icon Programming Language, Programming Language, String Processing

Audience: Icon Programmers

Profile: Icon is a high-level, general purpose programming language emphazing string and structure processing. Topics include programming techniques, theoretical aspects, Icon in relation to other languages, applications of Icon, implementation issues, porting, and bugs.

Contact: Bill Mitchell
whm@arizona.edu

Details: Free

User Info: To subscribe to the list, send an e-mail message requesting a subscription to the URL address below.

`mailto:Icon-Group-Request@arizona.edu`

Students

CCNEWS ★★★

An electronic forum for campus-computing newsletter editors and other publications specialists.

Keywords: Computers, Editors, Students, Newsletters

Audience: Students (college), Editors

Profile: CCNEWS consists of a biweekly newsletter that focuses on the writing, editing, designing, and producing of campus-computing publications, and an articles abstracts published on alternating weeks that describes new contributions to the articles archive.

Contact: Wendy Rickard Bollentin
CCNEWS@EDUCOM.BITNET

Details: Free

User Info: To subscribe to the list, send an e-mail message to the URL address below consisting of a single line reading:

SUB ccnews YourFirstName YourLastName

To send a message to the entire list, address it to: ccnews@educom.bitnet

Inquire about needing a password.

`mailto:listserv@bitnic.cren.net`

CFES-L

National communication branch of the CFES (Canadian Federation of Engineering Students).

Keywords: Engineering, Students, Canada

Audience: Engineers, Students

Contact: Canadian Federation of Engineering Students
cfes@jupiter.sun.csd.unb.ca

Details: Free

User Info: To subscribe to the list, send an e-mail message to the URL address below consiting of a single line reading:

SUB cfes-l YourFirstName YourLastName

To send a message to the entire list, address it to: cfes-l@unb.ca

`mailto:listserv@unb.ca`

k12.chat.junior ★

A Usenet newsgroup providing information and discussion for and about students in junior high school.

Keywords: Students, Chat Groups

Audience: Students (K-8)

Details: Free

User Info: To subscribe to this Usenet newsgroup, you need access to a newsreader.

`news:k12.chat.junior`

k12.chat.senior

A Usenet newsgroup providing information and discussion for and about students in senior high school.

Keywords: Students, Chat Groups
Audience: Students (K-12)
Details: Free
User Info: To subscribe to this Usenet newsgroup, you need access to a newsreader.

`news:k12.chat.senior`

Lysator's Gopher Service

Lysator is the name of the Academic Computer Society at Linkoping University, Linkoping, Sweden. It relies on voluntary efforts by students, and any service of activity runs as long as they think it is fun—content always reflects their personal interests.

Keywords: Sweden, Students, Europe
Audience: Swedish Students
Contact: Lars Aronsson@lysator.liu.se
Details: Free

`gopher://gopher.lysator.liu.se`

`http://dla.ucop.edu`

Style

alt.fashion

A Usenet newsgroup providing information and discussion about all facets of the fashion industry.

Keywords: Fashion Industry, Style
Audience: Designers, General Public
User Info: To subscribe to this Usenet newsgroup, you need access to a newsreader.

`news:alt.fashion`

Style Sheets from the Online Writers' Workshop

Style Sheets from the Online Writers' Workshop

This gopher provides information and examples on how to write bibliographies using three formats: MLA (Modern Language Association), Old-MLA, and APA (American Psychological Association).

Keywords: Bibliographies, Writing, Lexicology
Sponsor: University of Illinois at Urbana-Champaign
Audience: Writers, Students (High School/College/University)
Contact: Dr. Michael Pemberton
michaelp@ux1.cso.uiuc

`gopher://gopher.uiuc.edu`

Subways

Subway Navigator (City Subway Routes)

This service help you find a route in the subway systems of some cities in the world. Estimated times of departure/arrival are also given.

Keywords: Subways, Transit, Travel
Audience: Subway Riders, International Travelers
Profile: Cities covered are:
Frankfurt, Germany
Hong Kong
Lille, France
Lyon, France
Madrid, Spain
Marseille, France
Montreal, Canada
Munich, Germany
New York City, NY, USA*
Paris, France
Toulouse, France

*The network includes all NYCTA (New-York City Transit Authority) subway stations.

Contact: Pierre.David@prism.uvsq.fr
Details: Free

`gopher://gopher.jussieu.fr/11/metro`

`telnet://vishnu.jussieu.fr`

Summer Sports

rec.sport.olympics

A Usenet newsgroup providing information and discussion about the summer Olympics Games.

Keywords: Olympic Games, Summer Sports
Audience: Olympic Enthusiasts
User Info: To subscribe to this Usenet newsgroup, you need access to a newsreader.

`news:rec.sport.olympics`

Summit of the Americas Internet Gopher

Summit of the Americas Internet Gopher

A gopher containing supporting materials for the Summit of the Americas, a meeting of the Western Hemisphere's democratically elected heads of state, to be held in Miami in December of 1994.

Keywords: American Studies, International Relations, Haiti, Latin America
Sponsor: The Florida University Latin American and Caribbean Center
Audience: Government Officials, Journalists, NGOs, General Public
Contact: Rene Ramos
summit@SERVAX.FIU.EDU

`gopher://summit.fiu.edu`

Sun

comp.sys.sun

A Usenet newsgroup providing information and discussion about Sun systems. There are several categories within this group.

Keywords: Computer Systems, Sun
Audience: Computer Users, Sun Users
User Info: To subscribe to this Usenet newsgroup, you need access to a newsreader.

`news:comp.sys.sun`

Sun Microsystems, Inc.

Sun Microsystems, Inc.

This site provides a directory of Sun Microsystems products and services, including a company profile, announcements, financial statements, marketing reports, and international sales and support access.

Keywords: Computer Systems, Sun Microsystems
Sponsor: Sun Microsystems, Inc., Mountain View, California, USA
Audience: Sun Microsystems Users
Profile: Languages: English
Contact: webmaster@sun.com
Details: Free

`http://www.sun.com`

Supercomputers

cm5-Managers

This is a discussion of administrating the Thinking Machines CM5 parallel supercomputer.

Keywords: Supercomputers, Computer Administration
Audience: Supercomputer Users, Supercomputer Administrators
Contact: J. Eric Townsend
jet@nas.nasa.gov
Details: Free
User Info: To subscribe to the list, send an e-mail message to the address below, consisting of a single line reading:
SUB cm5-managers YourFirstName YourLastName
To send a message to the entire list, address it to: cm5-managers@boxer.nas.nasa.gov

mailto:listserv@boxer.nas.nasa.gov

NWNet Internet Guide

An introductory guide to the Internet. Details the basic Internet tools of electronic mail, FTP (File Transfer Protocol), and Telnet. Covers types of resources found on the Internet, and how to use them. Includes information directed toward supercomputer users and the K-12 community.

Keywords: Internet, Internet Guides, Supercomputers, Education (K-12)
Sponsor: NorthWestNet
Audience: Internet Surfers, Supercomputer Users, Students (K-12)
Contact: Jonathan Kochmer
nusirg@nwnet.net
Details: Free
File is user-docs/nusirg/nusirg.whole-guide.ps

ftp://ftphost.nwnet.net

NYSERNet Internet Guide

A comprehensive guide to the Internet from the New York State Education and Research Network (NYSERNet). NYSERNet provides access to specialized databases and online libraries, as well as to supercomputing and parallel-processing facilities throughout the US and to many national networks.

Keywords: Internet, Internet Guides, New York, Supercomputers
Sponsor: NYSERNet K-12 Networking Interest Group
Audience: Internet Surfers
Contact: info@nysernet.org
Details: Free

ftp://nysernet.org

Supercomputers

Weekly mailing list of the world's most powerful computing sites.

Keywords: Supercomputers, Computing
Audience: Supercomputer Users, Computer Scientists
Contact: gunter@yarrow.wt.uwa.oz.au
Details: Free
User Info: To subscribe to the list, send an e-mail message requesting a subscription to the URL address below. To send a message to the entire list, address it to: gunter@yarrow.wt.uwa.oz.au

mailto:gunter@yarrow.wt.uwa.oz.au

Supercomputing

NCSA (National Center for Supercomputing Applications)

A high-performance computing and communications facility and research center designed to serve the US computational science and engineering community.

Keywords: Supercomputing, Computer Networking, Computer Science, Mosaic
Sponsor: University of Illinois at Urbana-Champaign, Champaign, Illinois, USA
Audience: Students, Researchers, Computer Scientists, General Public
Contact: Systems Operator
pubs@ncsa.uiuc.edu

http://www.ncsa.uiuc.edu/General/NCSAHome.html

Output

Newsletter of the Florida State University (FSU) Computing Center. Includes topics such as networking, microcomputing, mainframe computing, and supercomputing on campus, including use of computers in classroom and research computing at FSU.

Keywords: Networking, Microcomputing, Supercomputing
Audience: FSU Computer Science Students, Computer Users
Contact: Suzanne C. Nelson
nelson@avm.cc.fsu.edu
Details: Free
Send your request addressed to the Editor.

mailto:nelson@avm.cc.fsu.edu

Swiss Scientific Supercomputing Center (CSCS) Info Server

The Centro Svizzero di Calcolo Scientifico (CSCS) info server is the national scientific computing center in Switzerland.

Keywords: Switzerland, Supercomputing, Europe
Audience: Swiss Internet Surfers
Contact: mgay@cscs.ch
Details: Free

gopher://pobox.cscs.ch

SupraFAX

SupraFAX

This list was created to help people who are using the SupraFAX v.32bis modem.

Keywords: Modem, FAX
Audience: Modem Users, FAX Users
Contact: David Tiberio
subscribe@xamiga.linet.org
Details: Free
User Info: To subscribe to the list, send an e-mail message requesting a subscription to the URL address below. To send a message to the entire list, address it to: subscribe@xamiga.linet.org

mailto:subscribe@xamiga.linet.org

Supreme Court

Supreme Court Decisions

Full text of Supreme Court decisions issued since 1989, as well as brief biographies of Supreme Court justices.

Keywords: Supreme Court, Law
Audience: Legal Professionals, Educators, Researchers

gopher://info.umd.edu

Supreme Court Decisions (Project Hermes)

US Supreme Court decisions available online as part of 'Project Hermes.'

Keywords: Supreme Court, Judiciary, Law
Sponsor: Case Western Reserve University
Audience: General Public, Lawyers, Students

Supreme Court (US)

Profile: Project Hermes was started in May 1990 by the US Supreme Court as an experiment in disseminating its opinions electronically. Starting with the 1993 calendar year, the US Supreme Court began disseminating opinions electronically on an official basis. Each decision consists of a syllabus (summarizing the ruling), the opinion, and optional concurrent and dissenting opinions.

Contact: Peter W. Martin
martin@law.mail.cornell.edu

Details: Free

Anonymous ftp: Expect: login; Send: anonymous; Expect: password; Send: your e-mail address

`ftp://cwru.edu`

`gopher://marvel.loc.gov`

Supreme Court Judges

Biographies from the sitting Justices, and a few former Justices.

Keywords: Judiciary, Supreme Court, Judges, Biography

Audience: General Public, Lawyers, Judges, Journalists

Details: Free

`gopher://info.umd.edu`

Supreme Court (US)

LEGNEW (Legal News)

The Legal News Library provides general news information about the domestic legal industry and legal profession.

Keywords: Law (US), Justice, Supreme Court (US)

Audience: Business Researchers, Analysts, Entrepreneurs

Profile: Included are sources which cover materials on law firm management, bar association journals and a hot file of case list summaries on recently decided US Supreme Court cases. LEGNEW is organized very simply. There are individual files, group files, and user-defined combination files.

Contact: Mead New Sales Group at (800) 227-4908 or (513) 859-5398 inside the US, or (513) 865-7981 for all inquiries outside the US.

User Info: To subscribe, contact Mead directly.

To examine the Nexis user guide, you can access it at the ftp site of the University of Texas at Austin at the URL address: ftp://ftp.cc.utexas.edu. The files are in pub/ref-services/LEXIS.

`telnet://nex.meaddata.com`

`http://www.meaddata.com`

Supreme Court of Canada

Supreme Court of Canada

This gopher allows access to Canadian Supreme Court rulings from 1993 forward. Documents are available as full-text and searchable by keyword. This site also has information on Canadian statute and case law.

Keywords: Law (International), Canada

Sponsor: Universite de Montreal Law Gopher Project, Montreal, Canada

Audience: Lawyers, General Public

Contact: Pablo Fuentes
fuentesp@droit.umontreal.ca

`gopher://gopher.droit.umontreal.ca/English/SCC`

Surfing (Internet)

Surfing the Internet

An introductory guide to "surfing," or finding information on the Internet.

Keywords: Internet, Internet Guides, Surfing (internet)

Audience: Internet Surfers

Details: Free

`ftp://rtfm.mit.edu`

SURFnet—KB InfoServer

SURFnet—KB InfoServer

InfoService is a joint project by SURFnet (National Network Organization for Research and Higher Education) and the Koninklijke Bibliotheek (National Library of the Netherlands).

Keywords: Netherlands, Networks, Europe

Audience: European Internet Surfers

Contact: infoservices@surfnet.nl

Details: Free

`gopher://gopher.nic.surfnet.nl`

Sustainable Living

CEE Environmental Libraries Database

A directory of over 300 libraries and environmental information centers in Central Eastern Europe that specialize in, or maintain significant collections of information about, the environment, ecology, sustainable living, or conservation. The database concentrates on six Central Eastern European countries: Bulgaria, Czech Republic, Hungary, Romania, Slovakia, and Poland.

Keywords: Central Eastern Europe, Environment, Sustainable Living, Bulgaria, Czech Republic, Hungary, Romania, Slovakia, Poland.

Sponsor: The Wladyslaw Poniecki Charitable Foundation, Inc.

Audience: Environmentalists, Green Movement, Librarians, Community Builders, Sustainable Living Specialists.

Profile: This database is the product of an Environmental Training Project (ETP) that was funded in 1992 by the US Agency for International Development as a 5-year cooperative agreement with a consortium headed by the University of Minnesota (US AID Cooperative Agreement Number EUR-0041-A-002-2020). Other members of the consortium include the University of Pittsburgh's Center for Hazardous Materials Research, The Institute for Sustainable Communities, and the World Wildlife Fund. The Wladyslaw Poniecki Charitable Foundation, Inc., was a subcontractor to the World Wildlife Fund and published the Directory of Libraries and Environmental Information Centers in Central Eastern Europe: A Locator/Directory. This gopher database consists of an electronic version of the printed directory, subsequently modified and updated online. Access to the data is facilitated by a WAIS search engine which makes it possible to retrieve information about libraries, subject area specializations, personnel, and so on.

Contact: Doug Kahn, CEDAR
kahn@pan.cedar.univie.ac.at

`gopher://gopher.poniecki.berkeley.edu`

Svhp-l

Svhp-l

A restricted discussion group on veterinary pharmacy issues.

Keywords: Veterinary Pharmacy, Pharmacy, Veterinary Science

Audience: Veterinarians, Veterinary Pharmacists

Contact: Doug Kemp
vetpharm@uga.cc.uga.edu

Sweden

Lysator's Gopher Service

Lysator is the name of the Academic Computer Society at Linkoping University, Linkoping, Sweden. It relies on voluntary efforts by students, and any service of activity runs as long as they think it is fun; content always reflects their personal interests.

Keywords: Sweden, Students, Europe
Audience: Swedish Students
Contact: Lars Aronsson@lysator.liu.se
Details: Free

`gopher://gopher.lysator.liu.se`

`http://dla.ucop.edu`

Swiss Scientific Supercomputing Center (CSCS) Info Server

Swiss Scientific Supercomputing Center (CSCS) Info Server

The Centro Svizzero di Calcolo Scientifico (CSCS) info server is the national scientific computing center in Switzerland.

Keywords: Switzerland, Supercomputing, Europe
Audience: Swiss Internet Surfers
Contact: mgay@cscs.ch
Details: Free

`gopher://pobox.cscs.ch`

Switzerland

Swiss Scientific Supercomputing Center (CSCS) Info Server

The Centro Svizzero di Calcolo Scientifico (CSCS) info server is the national scientific computing center in Switzerland.

Keywords: Switzerland, Supercomputing, Europe
Audience: Swiss Internet Surfers
Contact: mgay@cscs.ch
Details: Free

`gopher://pobox.cscs.ch`

Synth-l

Synth-l

Synth-l is the electronic music "gearhead" list dedicated to the discussion of the less esoteric aspects of synthesis. Discussion concentrates on the availability and capabilities of music software and hardware, but sometimes diverges to other subjects.

Keywords: Electronic Music, Music Software
Audience: Electronic Music Enthusiasts, Musicians, Software Designers
Contact: Joe McMahon
Synth-L@american.edu
Details: Free
User Info: To subscribe to the list, send an e-mail message to the address shown below consisting of a single line reading:

SUB Synth-L YourFirstName YourLastName

To send a message to the entire list, address it to: Synth-L@american.edu

`mailto:listserv@american.edu`

Synthesis

Computer Music Journal Archive and World Wide Web Home Page.

This resource reinforces material available in the hardcopy version of Computer Music Journal, published by the MIT Press.

Keywords: Computer Music, Composition, Synthesis, Interaction
Sponsor: The MIT Press
Audience: Computer Musicians
Profile: The archive includes the tables of contents, abstracts, and editor's notes for the last several volumes of CMJ (including the recent bibliography, diskography, and taxonomy of the field), a number of useful CM-related documents such as the full MIDI and AIFF format specifications, a lengthy reference list, the guidelines for manuscript submission, and the full-text of several recent articles.

Contact: Stephen Pope
cmj@cnmat.Berkeley.edu
Details: Free

`ftp://mitpress.mit.edu:/pub/Computer-Music-Journal`

Synthesizers

Analog Heaven

The Analog Heaven mailing list caters to people interested in vintage analog electronic music equipment. Topics include items for sale, repair tips, equipment modifications, ASCII & GIF schematics, and a general discussion of new and old analog equipment. There is an FTP/Gopher site located at cs.uwp.edu with discussions on various machines, a definitive guide to Roland synths, patch editors, modification schematics, and GIFs/JPEGs of vintage synths, as well as a few sound samples of some of the gear itself.

Keywords: Music, Synthesizers, Sequencers, Analog Equipment, Electronic Music
Audience: Electronic Music Enthusiasts, Musicians
Contact: Todd Sines
analogue-request@magnus.acs.ohio-state.edu
Details: Free, Sound
User Info: To subscribe to the list, send an e-mail message requesting a subscription to the URL address below. To send a message to the entire list, address it to: analogue@magnus.acs.ohio-state.edu

`mailto:analogue-request@magnus.acs.ohio-state.edu`

Systems Administration

info-UNIX

Info-UNIX is intended for Question/Answer discussion, where "novice" Systems Administrators can pose questions.

Keywords: UNIX (Opersting Systems), Systems Administration
Audience: UNIX Systems Administrators
Contact: Mike Muuss
mike@brl.mil
User Info: To subscribe to the list, send an e-mail message requesting a subscription to the URL address below.

`mailto:info-UNIX@brl.mil`

Systems Theory

(The) Observer

The central scope of the group covers the theory of autopoiesis (of Humberto Maturana and Francisco Varela) and enactive cognitive science. The extended scope includes applications of the above theoretical work and other relevant work (e.g. systems theory, cognitive science, phenomenology, artificial life, and so on). This is an edited electronic newsletter issued (approximately) twice monthly.

Keywords: Autopoiesis, Systems Theory, Cognitive Science

Audience: Systems Theorists, Researchers

Contact: Randall Whitaker
rwhit@cs.umu.se

User Info: To subscribe to the list, send an e-mail message to the URL address below consisting of a single line reading:

SUB the observer YourFirstName YourLastName

To send a message to the entire list, address it to: rwhit@cs.umu.se

mailto: listserv@cs.umu.se

DYNSYS-L

The Dynamical System exchanges information among people working in ergodic theory and dynamical systems.

Keywords: Entropy, Systems Theory

Audience: Engineers

Details: Free

newserv@uhcvm1.oit.uhc.edu

THINKNET

Electronic newsletter on philosophy, systems theory, interdisciplinary studies, and thoughtful conversation in cyberspace.

Keywords: Cyberspace, Systems Theory, Philosophy

Audience: Philosophers, System Theorists

Contact: Kent D. Palmer Ph.D.
Internet: palmer@world.std.com

Details: Free

User Info: To subscribe, send an e-mail message to the URL address below consisting of a single line reading:

SUB THINKNET YourFirstName YourLastName

mailto:palmer@world.std.com

T

Table Tennis

Usenet Sports Groups Archived

An archive for Usenet groups, including many related to sports ranging from football to table tennis.

Keywords:	Sports, Skydiving, Volleyball, Football, Scuba Diving, Table Tennis
Sponsor:	Massachusetts Institute of Technology, Boston, MA
Audience:	Sports Enthusiasts
Contact:	ftp-bugs@rtfm.mit.edu
Details:	Free

`ftp://rtfm.mit.edu/pub/usenet`

table.abortion

table.abortion

A Usenet newsgroup providing information and discussion about all sides of the abortion issue.

Keywords:	Abortion, Women's Issues, Health
Audience:	Women, Activists, Health Care Professionals
Details:	Free
User Info:	To subscribe to this Usenet newsgroup, you need access to a newsreader.

`news:table.abortion`

Taiwan

soc.culture.taiwan

A Usenet newsgroup providing information and discussion about Taiwanese people and their culture.

Keywords:	Taiwan, Sociology
Audience:	Sociologists, Taiwanese
Details:	Free
User Info:User Info:	To subscribe to this Usenet newsgroup, you need access to a newsreader.

`news:soc.culture.taiwan`

talk.bizarre

talk.bizarre

A Usenet newsgroup providing information and discussion about the unusual, the bizarre, and the curious.

Keywords:	Humor
Audience:	General Public
Details:	Free
User Info:	To subscribe to this Usenet newsgroup, you need access to a newsreader.

`news:talk.bizarre`

talk.origins

talk.origins

A Usenet newsgroup providing information and discussion about evolution versus creationism.

Keywords:	Evolution, Creationism, Activism
Audience:	General Public, Evolutionists, Creationists, Activists
Details:	Free
User Info:	To subscribe to this Usenet newsgroup, you need access to a newsreader.

`news:talk.origins`

talk.politics.mideast

talk.politics.mideast

A Usenet newsgroup providing information and discussion about Middle Eastern topics.

Keywords:	Middle East, Middle Eastern Studies, Politics (International)
Audience:	Political Scientists
Details:	Free
User Info:	To subscribe to this Usenet newsgroup, you need access to a newsreader.

`news:talk.politics.mideast`

talk.politics.soviet

talk.politics.soviet

A Usenet newsgroup providing information and discussion about Soviet politics, domestic and international.

Keywords:	Communism, Russia, Politics, Commonwealth of Independent States (CIS)
Audience:	Political Scientists
Details:	Free
User Info:	To subscribe to this Usenet newsgroup, you need access to a newsreader.

`news:talk.politics.soviet`

talk.religion.misc

talk.religion.misc

A Usenet newsgroup providing information and discussion about religious, ethical, and moral implications.

Keywords: Religion, Ethics
Audience: General Public, Researchers, Students
Details: Free
User Info: To subscribe to this Usenet newsgroup, you need access to a newsreader.

`news:talk.religion.misc`

talk.religion.newage

A Usenet newsgroup providing information and discussion about esoteric and minority religions and philosophies.

Keywords: Religion, Philosophy
Audience: General Public, Researchers, Students
Details: Free
User Info: To subscribe to this Usenet newsgroup, you need access to a newsreader.

`news:talk.religion.newage`

Tandem Computers

Info-tandem

Info-tandem is an e-mail list for users of systems from Tandem Computers, Inc.

Keywords: Computer Systems, Tandem Computers
Audience: Programmers, Analysts
Contact: Scott Hazen Mueller
scott@zorch.sf-bay.org
Details: Free
User Info: To subscribe to the list, send an e-mail message requesting

`mailto:info-tandem-request@zorch.sf-bay.org`

Tandy Computers

CoCo

This is a discussion related to the Tandy Color Computer (any model) OS-9 Operating System, and any other topics relating to the "CoCo," as this computer is affectionately known.

Keywords: Tandy Computers, Computers
Audience: Tandy Computer Users, Computer Users
Contact: Paul E. Campbell
pecampbe@mtus5.BITNET
Details: Free
User Info: To subscribe to the list, send an e-mail message requesting a subscription to the URL address below.

`mailto:listserv@pucc.princeton.edu`

Tax

FEDTAX (Federal Tax Library)

The Federal Tax library offers a comprehensive, up-to-date collection of tax-related materials, including case law, agency materials, legislative and regulatory materials, and so on.

Keywords: Law, Analysis, Tax
Audience: Lawyers
Profile: The Federal Tax library offers a comprehensive, up-to-date collection of tax-related materials. This library includes federal and state tax case law, Internal Revenue Service rulings and releases, state tax administrative decisions and rulings, the Internal Revenue Code, federal tax regulations, international news and treaties, tax looseleaf services, tax periodicals, tax law reviews, tax dailies, pending state legislation, and state property records.
Contact: New Sales Group at 800-227-4908 or 513-859-5398 inside the US, or 1-513-865-7981 for all inquires outside the US.
User Info: To subscribe, contact Mead directly.

To examine the Lexis user guide, you can access it at the ftp site of the University of Texas at Austin at the URL address: ftp://ftp.cc.utexas.edu

The files are in: /pub/ref-services/LEXIS

`telnet://nex.meaddata.com`

`http://www.meaddata.com`

Tax Assessor

ASSETS (Real Estate Tax Assessor and Deed Transfer Records)

The Real Estate Tax Assessor and Deed Transfer Records (ASSETS) library contains information compiled from real property records.

Keywords: Real Estate, Property, Taxes
Audience: Lawyers
Profile: The ASSETS library contains a variety of real estate information, including asset ownership, property address, owner's mailing address, assessed valuation, current market value, and recent property sales and deed transfers. Information is collected from county tax assessors' and recorders' offices nationwide and compiled by TRW REDI Property Data. The ASSETS library also contains a variety of boat and aircraft registration information.
Contact: Mead New Sales Group at (800) 227-4908 or (513) 859-5398 inside the US, or (513) 865-7981 for all inquiries outside the US.
User Info: To subscribe, contact Mead directly.

To examine the Nexis user guide, you can access it at the ftp site of the University of Texas at Austin at the URL address: ftp://ftp.cc.utexas.ed

The files are in: /pub/ref-services/LEXIS

`telnet://nex.meaddata.com`

`http://www.meaddata.com`

taxacom

taxacom

Discussion list on biological systematics.

Keywords: Biology
Audience: Biologists
Contact: James H. Beach
beach@huh.harvard.edu
Details: Free
User Info: To subscribe to the list, send an e-mail message to the URL address below, consisting of a single line reading:

SUB taxacom YourFirstName YourLastName

To send a message to the entire list, address it to:
taxacom@harvarda.harvard.edu

`mailto:listserv@harvarda.harvard.edu`

teacheft (Teaching Effectiveness)

teacheft (Teaching Effectiveness)

This list treats teaching effectiveness and a broad range of teaching and learning interests.

Keywords: Education (Adult), Education (Distance), Education (Continuing)
Audience: Educators, Educational Administrators, Researchers

Details: Free

User Info: To subscribe to the list, send an e-mail message to the URL address shown below consisting of a single line reading:

SUB stlhe-l YourFirstName YourLastName

To send a message to the entire list, address it to: stlhe-l@wcu.bitnet

`mailto:listserv@wcu.bitnet`

Teaching

CIRCUITS-L

This list discusses all aspects of the introductory course in circuit analysis for electrical engineering undergraduates.

Keywords: Engineering, Electrical Engineering, Teaching, Electric Circuit Analysis

Audience: Engineers, Students (college)

Contact: Paul E. Gray
mailto:GRAY@MAPLE.UCS.UWPLATT.EDU

Details: Free

User Info: To subscribe to the list, send an e-mail message to the URL address below, and include: name; e-mail address; home phone, business phone, and FAX numbers (including area code); and US postal address (including ZIP code)

To send a message to the entire list, address it to:

CIRCUITS-L@UWPLATT.EDU

`mailto:CIRCUITS-REQUEST@UWPLATT.EDU`

Technical Professionals

noglstp ★

This list is sponsored by the National Organization of Gay and Lesbian Scientists and Technical Professionals, Inc. (a 501-C3 organization). National office is in Pasadena, CA and can be reached at (818) 791-7689 or P.O. Box 91803, Pasadena, CA 90019. There is also a newsletter that is available to members.

Keywords: Gay, Lesbian, Scientists, Technical Professionals

Audience: Gay Scientists, Lesbian Scientists

Contact: noglstp-request@elroy.jpl.nasa.gov

Details: Free

User Info: To subscribe to the list, send an e-mail message requesting a subscription to the URL address below.

To send a message to the entire list, address it to: noglstp@elroy.jpl.nasa.gov

`mailto:noglstp-request@elroy.jpl.nasa.gov`

Technical Writing

techwr-l (Technical Writing List) ★

This is a mailing list for technical communicators. It concerns anything related to any facet of technical communication (practice, research, teaching).

Keywords: Technical Writing

Audience: Technical Writers, Educators, Editors

Contact: Eric J. Ray
ejray@okway.okstate.edu

Details: Free

User Info: To subscribe to the list, send an e-mail message to the URL address below consisting of a single line reading:

SUB techwr-l YourFirstName YourLastName

To send a message to the entire list, address it to:
techwr-l@vm1.ucc.okstate.edu

Notes: Digest version available.

`mailto:listserv@vm1.ucc.okstate.edu`

Technology

alt.artcom ★

A Usenet newsgroup providing information and discussion about contemporary art and technology. Discussion ranges from GIF files to Australian alternative cinema.

Keywords: Art, Technology

Audience: Artists, Writers

User Info: To subscribe to this Usenet newsgroup, you need access to a newsreader.

`news:alt.artcom`

ANU (Australian National University) Vietnam-SciTech-L Database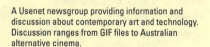

A WAIS databases of information on the development of science and technology in Vietnam

Keywords: Vietnam, Science, Technology

Sponsor: Australia Vietnam Science-Technology Link

Audience: Vietnamese

Contact: Vern Weitzel
vern@coombs.anu.edu.au

`waissrc:/Coombs-db/ANU-Vietnam-SciTech-L.src`

`gopher://cheops.anu.edu.au/7waissrc/Coombs-db/ANU-Vietnam-SciTech-L.src`

Apple Computer WWW Server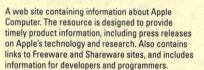

A web site containing information about Apple Computer. The resource is designed to provide timely product information, including press releases on Apple's technology and research. Also contains links to Freeware and Shareware sites, and includes information for developers and programmers.

Keywords: Computer Systems, Technology, Apple Computer, Shareware

Audience: General Public

`http://www.apple.com`

Art Com Magazine

A newsletter about art and technology (subjects covered include robotics, artists' software, hyperfiction) that is guest-edited by individual artists.

Keywords: Computer Art, Literature (Contemporary), Technology, Hyperfiction

Sponsor: Art Com Electronic Network

Audience: Artists, Writers

Contact: Fred Truck
fjt@well.sf.ca.us

To participate in a conference on the WELL, you must first establish an account on the WELL. To do so, start by typing: telnet://well.sf.ca.us

`mailto:artcomtv@well.sf.ca.us`

AT&T Bell Laboratories WWW Information Page

This web site provides information on research and development at AT&T Bell Laboratories.

Keywords: Telecommunications, Technology, AT&T, Cellular Technology

Sponsor: AT&T Bell Laboratories

Audience: Engineers, Educators, Communications Specialists

Contact: webmaster@research.att.com

Details: Free

`http://www.research.att.com`

CMPCOM (Computers and Communications) Library

The Computers and Communications Library provides you industry-specific sources. More than 40 full-text sources that concentrate on computers and communications are available. Full-text files can be searched in a variety of ways: as an individual file, by major-subject group file, or as a user-defined group file.

Keywords: Computers, Communications, Technology, Electronics

Audience: Business Researchers, Analysts, Entrepreneurs

Technology

Profile: This library can be used to gain insight on new products and technologies being introduced; monitor industry news for high technology systems, electronics, engineering, communications, and computer hardware and software; and locate product evaluations for both the professional as well as the casual personal computer user.

Contact: Mead New Sales Group at (800) 227-4908 or (513) 859-5398 inside the US, or (513) 865-7981 for all inquiries outside the US.

User Info: To subscribe, contact Mead directly.

To examine the Nexis user guide, you can access it at the ftp site of the University of Texas at Austin at the URL address: ftp://ftp.cc.utexas.edu

The files are in: /pub/ref-services/LEXIS

`telnet://nex.meaddata.com`

`http://www.meaddata.com`

devel-l ★

Discussion forum on technology transfer in international development.

Keywords: Development, Technology
Sponsor: Volunteers in Technical Assistance (VITA)
Audience: Technical Professionals
Contact: vita@gmuvax.gmu.edu
Details: Free
User Info: To subscribe to the list, send an e-mail message to the URL address shown below consisting of a single line reading:

SUB devel-l YourFirstName YourLastName

`mailto:listserv@auvm.american.edu`

DevelopNet News ★

A monthly newsletter on technology transfer in international development.

Keywords: Nonprofits, Technology, Development
Sponsor: Volunteers in Technical Assistance
Audience: Technology Professionals
Contact: R.R. Ronkin vita@gmuvax.gmu.edu
Details: Free
User Info: To subscribe, send an e-mail message to the address below.

Inquire about needing a password.

`mailto:vita@gmuvax.gmu.edu`

Ei Compendex Plus

The Ei Compendex Plus database is the machine-readable version of The Engineering Index (monthly/annual), which provides abstracted information from the world's significant literature of engineering and technology.

Keywords: Engineering, Technology
Sponsor: Engineering Information Inc. (Ei), Hoboken, NJ, USA
Audience: Engineers
Profile: Ei Compendex Plus provides worldwide coverage of approximately 4,500 journals and selected government reports and books. Subjects covered include: civil, energy, environmental, geological, and biological engineering; electrical, automotive, nuclear, and aerospace engineering; and computers, robotics, and industrial robots.
Contact: Dialog in the US at (800) 334-2564, Dialog internationally at country-specific locations. User Info: To subscribe, contct Dialog directly. Notes: Coverage 1970 to the present; updated weekly.

`telnet://dialog.com`

Family and Legal Status (INPADOC)

The database includes a listing of patents issued in 56 countries and patenting organizations.

Keywords: Patents, Technlogy
Sponsor: European Patent Office (EPO), Vienna, Austria
Audience: Patent Researchers, Inventors
Profile: INPADOC contains bibliographic data consisting of title, inventor, and assignee for most patents. In addition, this file brings together information on priority-application numbers, countries and dates, and equivalent patents (i.e. patent families) for patents. This file also contains the legal status information for patents in some countries.
Contact: Dialog in the US at (800) 334-2564, Dialog internationally at country-specific locations.
User Info: To subscribe, contact Dialog directly.
Notes: Coverage: April 1968 to the present; updated weekly.

`telnet://dialog.com`

FutureCulture FAQ (Frequently Asked Questions) File ★★★

List of online and offline items of interest to subscribers of FutureCulture, a mailing list on 'technoculture' or 'new edge' or 'cyberculture'.

Keywords: Technology, Cyberculture, Postmodernism, Sci-Fi, Zines
Audience: Reality Hackers, Cyberculture Enthuasists
Profile: This list discusses cyberpunk culture, rave culture, industrial music, virtual reality, drugs, computer underground, Net sociology, and virtual communities.
Contact: Alias Datura (adatura on IRC) adatura@uafhp.uark.edu
Details: Free

`ftp://etext.archive.umich.edu/pub`

High Weirdness by E-Mail ★★★

Guide to some interesting sources of information online.

Keywords: Technology, Hacking, Computer Underground
Audience: Mystics, Reality Hackers, Weirdos
Profile: This file focuses mainly on bizarre philosophies, such as Discordia and SubGenius. Contents include: offbeat religions and 'spirituality' paganism and magic, occultism, UFOs and paranormal phenomena.
Details: Free

`ftp://etext.archive.umich.edu/pub/Zines/Weirdness`

Hot off the Tree (HOTT) ★

HOTT contains excerpts and abstracts of articles from trade journals, popular periodicals, online news services, and electronic bulletin boards.

Keywords: Computer Technology, Technology
Sponsor: University of California, San Diego Library's Technology Watch Information Group (TWIG)
Audience: Computer Programmers, Technology Enthusiasts, General Public
Contact: Susan Jurist sjurist@ucsd.edu or sjurist@ucsd.bitnet
Details: Free

Available on MELVYL, the University of California online catalog. Anyone with access to telnet, can telnet MELVYL (31.0.0.13) and show hott.

`telnet://melvyl.berkeley.edu/showhott`

ISEA (Inter-Society on Electronic Arts) Online ★

An online forum for discussion of topics related to ISEA-94, the 5th International Symposium on Electronic Art which will take place in Finland in August, 1994.

Keywords: Art, Electronic Art, Technology
Audience: Artists, Art Enthusiasts
Details: Free

`ftp://ftp.ncsa.uiuc.edu`

Journal of Technology Education ★

Electronic journal devoted to educational issues in technology.

Keywords: Communication, Education, Technology,
Audience: Educators
Details: Free
Send an e-mail message to the URL address below with the request: GET MISCELLA JTE-V5N1. This file will give you access information for additional issues.

mailto:listserv@vtvm1.cc.vt.edu

Martin Marietta Energy Systems Gopher ★★

Information on Martin Marietta's energy projects and technologies for both government and commercial applications.

Keywords: Technology, Energy, Industry
Sponsor: Martin Marietta
Audience: Business Professionals, Entrepreneurs, Manufactures, Energy Researchers, Technology Enthusiasts
Profile: This gopher contains a list of technologies currently being developed at Martin Marietta as well as detailing facilities available to university, government, and commercial researchers. Also includes updates on employment openings, and a list of current publications.
Contact: gopher@ornl.gov

gopher://gopher.ornl.gov

http://www.ornl.gov/mmes.html

McDonnell Douglas Aerospace ★★

A web site providing information about McDonnell Douglas, including a company profile and related discussion about technology.

Keywords: Aerospace, Space, Aviation, Technology
Audience: Aerospace Engineers
Contact: mail to: Zook@pat.mdc.com

http://pat.mdc.com

National Technology Transfer Center (NTTC) ★★

A federally-funded national network to apply government research to commercial applications.

Keywords: Technology, Technology Transfer, Research and Development, Business and Industry, Department of Defense, Government (US)
Sponsor: National Technology Transfer Center
Audience: Business People, Entrepreneurs, Manufactures, Technology Enthusiasts
Profile: Features state-by-state listings of agencies designed to facilitate the adaptation of new technologies to industry. Also provides updates on conferences, and a current list of Department of Defense projects soliciting private assistance from small businesses. Allows limited access to NTTC databases.
Contact: Charles Monfradi
cmonfra@nttc.edu, info@nttc.edu

gopher://iron.nttc.edu

http://iridium.nttc.edu/nttc.hmtl

Novice MZT

Novize MZT (News of Ministry for Science and Technology of the Republic of Slovenia) provides easy, accessible news about science, development, universities, and innovative activities to individuals and institutions in research and development areas. Published at least once monthly.

Keywords: Slovenia, Science, Technology, News
Audience: Slovenians, Scientists, Technocrats
Contact: Novice-mzt@krpan.arnes.si or Novice.mzt@uni-lj.si
User Info: To subscribe to the list, send an e-mail message requesting a subscription to the URL address below.
To send a message to the entire list, address it to: Novice-mzt@krpan.arnes.si

mailto:Novice-MZT@krpan.arnes.si

rec.autos.tech ★

A Usenet newsgroup providing information and discussion about the technical aspects of automobiles.

Keywords: Automobiles, Technology
Audience: Automobile Users
User Info: To subscribe to this Usenet newsgroup, you need access to a newsreader.

news:rec.autos.tech

Tecbase- Sandia National Laboratory ★★

A catalog of technologies developed at Sandia National Laboratories that have potential commercial applications.

Keywords: Technology, Information Technology, Industry
Sponsor: Sandia National Laboratory
Audience: Business Professionals, Entrepreneurs, Manufacturers, Technicians
Contact: TechTransfer@ccsmtp.sandia.gov

gopher://somnet.sandia.gov/Tecbase

Technology Initiatives for the Clinton/Gore Administration ★★★★

This is a 40-page text of the press release from the Clinton Administration on technology initiatives, dated February 22, 1993.

Keywords: Politics, President (US), White House, Technology
Audience: General Public, Journalists
Details: Free
Send e-mail to the URL address below and include the following in the body of the message:
get cni-bigideas.whouse.paper

mailto:listserv@cni.org

The MIT Press Online Catalogs ★★

A descriptive listing of recent books and current journals published by the MIT Press.

Keywords: Academia, Books, Publishing, Technology
Sponsor: The MIT Press, Cambridge, Massachusetts, USA.
Audience: Reseachers, Scholars, University Students, Technical Professionals
Profile: Contains a keyword-searchable index of books published in the years 1993 to 1994, as well as current journals covering computational and cognitive sciences, architecture, photography, art and literary theory, economics, environmental science, and linguistics.
Contact: ehling@mitpress.mit.edu
Notes: Coverage: 1993 to present; updated semiannually. MIT Press can also be accessed by calling (800) 356-0343.

http://www-mitpress.mit.edu

opher://gopher.mit.edu

Universite de Montreal UDEMATIK Library ★★

The library's holdings are large and wide-ranging and contain significant collections in many fields.

Keywords: Art, Architecture, Economy, Sexology, Social Law, Science, Technology, Literary Studies
Audience: Researchers, Students, General Public
Contact: Joelle or Sebastien Roy
udematik@ere.umontreal.ca or stemp@ere.umontreal.ca or roys@ere.umontreal.ca
User Info: Expect: Login; Send: Application id INFO

telnet://udematik.umontreal.ca

Washington University Library ★★

The library's holdings are large and wide-ranging and contain significant collections in many fields.

Keywords:	Technology, Literature (German), Social Science, Behavioral Science
Audience:	Researchers, Students, General Public
Contact:	services@wugate.wustl.edu
Details:	Free
User Info:	Expect: Login; Send: Services

`telnet://wugate.wustl.edu`

Washington University-St. Louis Medical Library & MembersLibrary

The library's holdings are large and wide-ranging and contain significant collections in many fields.

Keywords:	Medicine, Science, Technology
Audience:	Researchers, Students, General Public
Details:	Free
User Info:	Expect: Destination Code Prompt, Send: Catalog

`telnet://mcftcp.wustl.edu`

Technological Advances

Adv-Elo

Discusses the latest advances in electronics. Sponsored by the IEEE Student Branch of Santa Maria University (Chile).

Keywords:	Electrical Engineering, Engineering, Electronics, Technological Advances
Audience:	Engineers, Educators, Students
Contact:	Rodrigo E. Rodriguez rrodrigu@utfsm
Details:	Free
User Info:	To subscribe to the list, send an e-mail message to the URL address shown below consiting of a single line reading: SUB adv-elo YourFirstName YourLastName To send a message to the entire list, address it to: adv-elo@loa.disca.utfsm.cl

`listserv@loa.disca.utfsm.cl`

Technology Transfer

National Technology Transfer Center (NTTC)

A federally-funded national network to apply government research to commercial applications.

Keywords:	Technology, Research and Development, Business and Industry, Department of Defense, Government (US)
Sponsor:	National Technology Transfer Center
Audience:	Business People, Entrepreneurs, Manufactures, Technology Enthusiasts
Profile:	Features state-by-state listings of agencies designed to facilitate the adaptation of new technologies to industry. Also provides updates on conferences, and a current list of Department of Defense projects soliciting private assistance from small businesses. Allows limited access to NTTC databases.
Contact:	Charles Monfradi cmonfra@nttc.edu, info@nttc.edu

`gopher://iron.nttc.edu`

`http://iridium.nttc.edu/nttc.hmtl`

techwr-l (Technical Writing List)

techwr-l (Technical Writing List)

This is a mailing list for technical communicators. It concerns anything related to any facet of technical communication (practice, research, teaching).

Keywords:	Technical Writing
Audience:	Technical Writers, Educators, Editors
Contact:	Eric J. Ray ejray@okway.okstate.edu
Details:	Free
User Info:	To subscribe to the list, send an e-mail message to the URL address below consisting of a single line reading: SUB techwr-l YourFirstName YourLastName To send a message to the entire list, address it to: techwr-l@vm1.ucc.okstate.edu
Notes:	Digest version available.

`mailto:listserv@vm1.ucc.okstate.edu`

Telebit Computer Products

Netblazer-users

Provides an unmoderated forum for discussions among users of Telebit NetBlazer products. Topics include known problems and workarounds, features discussions, and configuration advice.

Keywords:	Telebit Computer Products, Netblazer
Audience:	Telebit Netblazer Users
Contact:	netblazer-users-request@telebit.com
Details:	Free
User Info:	To subscribe to the list, send an e-mail message requesting a subscription to the URL address below.

`mailto:netblazer-users-request@telebit.com`

Telecommunications

AT&T Bell Laboratories WWW Information Page

This web site provides information on research and development at AT&T Bell Laboratories.

Keywords:	Telecommunications, Technology, AT&T, Cellular Technology
Sponsor:	AT&T Bell Laboratories
Audience:	Engineers, Educators, Communications Specialists
Contact:	webmaster@research.att.com
Details:	Free

`http://www.research.att.com`

The Black Box Catalog

The Black Box Catalog, the industry's most complete source for data communication equipment, is now available on the Internet. The complete range of products, technical references, and application briefs are available on the Black Box World Wide Web Server.

Keywords:	Communications, Networking, Telecommunication, Computers
Sponsor:	Black Box Corporation, Lawrence, PA
Audience:	Engineers, Network Administration, LAN Administrators, Communication Specialists
Profile:	Black Box Corporation is a leading international supplier of data communications networking and related computer connectivity products. Black Box's commitment to providing effective solutions that substantially enhance the capabilities of communications systems is backed by a technical support staff that is available around the clock, a liberal 45-day return policy, and same day shipment of its 6000 products.
Contact:	Webmaster webmaster@blackbox.com
Details:	Costs

`http://www.blackbox.com`

Blacksburg Electronic Village Gopher

The Blacksburg Electronic Village is a project to link an entire town in Southwestern Virginia with a 21st-century telecommunications infrastructure. This infrastructure will bring a useful set of information services and interactive communications facilities into the daily activities of citizens and businesses.

Keywords:	Community Networking, Networking Telecommunications
Sponsor:	Town of Blacksburg, Virginia, USA
Audience:	Activists, Policymakers, Community Leaders, Government

Profile: This community gopher server run by the town of Blacksburg contains information about Blacksburg and how it is building its electronic infrastructure. It includes a list of Blacksburg-area BBSs, instructions for local residents to get an account on the town's BBS, and a section called "Village Schoolhouse."

Details: Costs, Moderated

`gopher://morse.cns.vt.edu`

Communication and Mass Communication Resources

An archive of materials related to mass communications and the media.

Keywords: Mass Communications, Media, Journalism, Telecommunications, Advertising

Sponsor: The University of Iowa

Audience: Mass Communications Students and Teachers, Journalists, Broadcasting Professionals

Contact: Karla Tonella
Karla_Tonella@uiowa.edu

`gopher://iam41.arcade.uiowa.edu`

ctf-discuss

This mailing list aims to stimulate discussion of issues critical to the computer science community in the United States (and, by extension, the world). The Computer Science and Telecommunications Board (CSTB) of the National Research Council (NRC) is charged with identifying and initiating studies in areas critical to the health of the field. Recently one such study, Computing the Future, has generated a major discussion in the community and has motivated the establishment of this mailing list in order to involve broader participation. This list will be used in the future to report and discuss the activities of the CSTB and to solicit opinions in a variety of areas.

Keywords: Computer Science, Telecommunications

Audience: Computer Scientists, Telecommunications Experts

Contact: Dave Farber
ctf-discuss-request@cis.upenn.edu

Details: Free

User Info: To subscribe to the list, send an e-mail message requesting a subscription to the URL address below.

To send a message to the entire list, address it to: ctf-discuss@cis.upenn.edu

`mailto:ctf-discuss-request@cis.upenn.edu`

Electronic Cafe

A seminal art and telecommunications group that specializes in video transmission.

Keywords: Art, Video, Telecommunications

Audience: Artists

Profile: This combines performance, communication, and community outreach by making telecommunications equipment available in a cafe-style artists' space.

Contact: Kit Galloway and Sherrie Rabinowitz, 1641 18th St., Santa Monica, CA 90404, USA

`mailto:ecafe@netcom.com`

Fam-Med

An Internet resource and discussion group on computers in family medicine.

Keywords: Medicine, Computers, Telecommunications

Sponsor: Gustavus Adolphus College, Minnesota

Audience: Health Care Professionals, Family Physicians

Profile: Fam-Med is an electronic conference and file area that focuses on the use of computer and telecommunication technologies in the teaching and practice of family medicine. The conference and files are accessible to anyone able to send e-mail. The discussion on Fam-Med is distributed in two ways: by an unmoderated mail echo in which all posted messages are immediately distributed to subscribers without human intervention, and by a digest where messages accumulated over several days are assembled into a single document with erroneous posts deleted.

Contact: Paul Kleeberg
Paul@GAC.Edu

Details: Free

To join either the unmoderated list or the digest, send e-mail to the contact above. To post to Fam-Med, send e-mail to Fam-Med@GAC.Edu.

`gopher://ftp.gac.edu/00/pub/e-mail-archives/fam-med/`

Multimedia, Telecommunications, and Art Project

A project to promote online art that will be implemented as gopher site and on the World-Wide Web.

Keywords: Multimedia, Electronic Art, Telecommunications

Sponsor: CISR (Centre for Image and Sound Research), Vancouver, B.C., Canada

Audience: Artists, Writers

Contact: Derek Dowden
Derek_Dowden@mindlink.bc.ca

For more information, send an e-mail message to the URL address below.

`mailto:Derek_Dowden@mindlink.bc.ca`

Polish Archives

Information about Polish Internet gophers and Polish electronic journals.

Keywords: Poland, Telecommunications, Networking

Audience: Historians, Poles

Contact: Darek Milewski
Milewski@poniecki.berkeley.edu

User Info: To subscribe, send an e-mail message requesting a subscription to the URL address below.

`gopher://gopher.poniecki.berkeley.edu`

Telecom Archives

All of the back issues of Telecom Digest are on file here. Includes many other online articles and resources topical to the telecommunications industry.

Keywords: Telecommunications

Audience: Telecommunications Experts, Researchers, Communications Specialists

Contact: Patrick Townson
telecom-request@eecs.nwu.edu

`http://lcs.mit.edu/telecom-archives`

Telecomputing

The Teleputing Hotline And Field Computing Source Letter

A leading voice in covering telephone connections worldwide. Plans to expand coverage of a worldwide revolution called Field Computing.

Keywords: Business, Telecomputing, Telecommunications

Audience: Industry, Telecommunications Experts, Business Professionals

Profile: Field Computing involves linking workers outside the office -in sales, repair, and delivery functions- to central computer systems with handheld terminals and wireless data networks. The Teleputing Hotline has covered this trend since its inception.

Contact: Dana Blankenhorn
MCI: 409-8960 GEnie: nb.atl CompuServe

Details: Costs

User Info: To subscribe to the list, send an e-mail message requesting a subscription to the URL address below.

`mailto:sfer request@mthvax.cs.miami.edu`

Telemedia, Networks, and Systems Group

Telemedia, Networks, and Systems Group

A list of commercial services on the Web (and Net)

Keywords: Business, Electronic Commerce
Sponsor: MIT Laboratory for Computer Science, Cambridge, MA 02139
Audience: Business Professionals, Commercial Internet Users, General Public
Profile: This list of commercial Internet services is well-maintained and frequently updated.
Contact: hhh@mit.edu

http://tns-www.lcs.mit.edu/commerce.html

http://tns-www.lcs.mit.edu

Telescopes

Sci.astro.hubble

Information about all subjects concerning NASA's Hubble space telescope.

Keywords: Hubble Telescope, Astronomy, Space, NASA, Stargazing, Telescopes
Audience: Astronomers, General Public, Science Teachers, Stargazers
Contact: Paul A. Scowen
scowen@wfpc3.la.asu.edu
Details: Free, Moderated, Images
User Info: To subscribe to this Usenet newsgroup, you need access to a newsreader.

news:sci.astro.hubble

Television

30something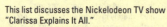

A mailing list for discussion of the TV show 30something.

Keywords: Television, Baby Boomer Culture
Audience: Television Viewers, Baby Boomers
Contact: Marc Rouleau
30something-request@fuggles.acc.virginia.edu
User Info: To subscribe to the list, send an e-mail message to the URL address below. To send a message to the entire list, address it to: 30something@fuggles.acc.virginia.edu

mailto:30something-request@fuggles.acc.virginia.edu

C-SPAN (Cable-Satellite Public Affairs Network) Gopher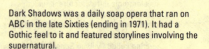

Online information from C-SPAN, the public affairs television network.

Keywords: News Media, Government, Congress (US), Television
Sponsor: C-SPAN
Audience: Journalists, Government Officials, Educators (K-12), General Public
Profile: Comprehensive listings of C-SPAN's programming and coverage of events in Washington D.C. and beyond. In addition to the programming notes and schedules, this site also features online educational resources sponsored by C-SPAN, text of historic documents and speeches, and background political information on the House of Representatives and the Supreme Court.
Contact: cspanviewr@aol.com
Details: Free

gopher://c-span.org

Clarissa

This list discusses the Nickelodeon TV show "Clarissa Explains It All."

Keywords: Television, Nickelodeon
Audience: Nickelodeon Viewers, TV Viewers
Contact: Jim Lick
clarissa-request@tcp.com
Details: Free
User Info: To subscribe to the list, send an e-mail message requesting a subscription to the URL address below.
To send a message to the entire list, address it to: clarissa@tcp.com

mailto:clarissa-request@tcp.com

disney-afternoon ★

Discussion of the Disney Afternoon and other related topics. This is a very high-volume, low-noise mailing list.

Keywords: Disney, Television
Audience: Disney Enthusiasts, Television Viewers
Contact: Stephanie da Silva
ranger-list-request@taronga.com
Details: Free, M
User Info: To subscribe to the list, send an e-mail message requesting a subscription to the URL address below.
To send a message to the entire list, address it to: ranger-list-request@taronga.com

mailto:ranger-list-request@taronga.com

dark-shadows ★

Dark Shadows was a daily soap opera that ran on ABC in the late Sixties (ending in 1971). It had a Gothic feel to it and featured storylines involving the supernatural.

Keywords: Dark Shadows, Television
Audience: Horror Enthusiasts, Soap Opera Enthusiasts
Contact: Bernie Roehl
shadows-request@sunee.waterloo.ca
Details: Free
User Info: To subscribe to the list, send an e-mail message requesting a subscription to the URL address below.
To send a message to the entire list, address it to: shadows@usunee.waterloo.ca

news:alt.horror,
news:rec.arts.tv.soaps

flamingo ★

This list discusses the series 'Parker Lewis' (formerly 'Parker Lewis Can't Lose') on the Fox television network.

Keywords: Television, Television
Audience: Television Viewers, 'Parker Lewis' Enthusiasts'
Details: Free
User Info: To subscribe to the list, send an e-mail message requesting a subscription to the URL address below.
To send a message to the entire list, address it to: flamingo@lenny.corp.sgi.com

mailto:flamingo-request@lenny.corp.sgi.com

Melrose-place ★

Discussion of the Fox television show Melrose Place.

Keywords: Melrose Place, Fox Television, Television
Audience: Melrose Place Fans, Television Viewers
Details: Free
User Info: To subscribe to the list, send an e-mail message requesting a subscription to the URL address below.

mailto:melrose-place-request@ferkel.ucsb.edu

National Broadcasting Society—Alpha Epsilon Rho

Forum for mass media professionals to share experiences and ideas.

Keywords: Film, Television, Radio, Mass Media

Sponsor:	National Broadcasting Society-Alpha Epsilon Rho
Audience:	Journalists, Students, Educators, Broadcasting Professionals
Contact:	Reg Gamar regbc@cunyvm.bitnet
Details:	Free
User Info:	To subscribe to the list, send an e-mail message to the address shown below consisting of a single line reading: SUB NBS-AER YourFirstName YourLastName To send a message to the entire list, address it to: nbs-aer@cunyvm.bitnet

`mailto:listserv@cunyvm.bitnet`

rec.arts.movies movie database

An extensive FTP database covering over 32,000 movies, with more than 370,000 filmography entries, from early cinema to current releases.

Keywords:	Movies, Television, Popular Culture
Audience:	Movie Buffs
Profile:	Interfaces to search the database include Unix, MS-DOS and Amiga (and Windows and Mac versions are in development). The database includes filmographies for actors, directors, writers, composers, cinematographers, editors, production designers, costume designers and producers; plot summaries; character names; movie ratings; year of release; running times; movie trivia; quotes; goofs; soundtracks; personal trivia and Academy Award information.
Contact:	Col Needham cn@ibmpcug.co.uk
Details:	Free

`ftp://cathouse.org/pub/cathouse/movies/database`

rec.arts.movies movie database (Cardiff WWW front-end)

An extensive, interactive database covering over 32,000 movies, with more than 370,000 filmography entries, from early cinema to current releases.

Keywords:	Movies, Television, Popular Culture, Interactive Media
Audience:	Movie Buffs
Profile:	A WWW front-end to the rec.arts.movies movie database, complete with form-filling interfaces to add new data and to rate movies (on a scale from 1 through 10). The database includes filmographies for actors, directors, writers, composers, cinematographers, editors, production designers, costume designers and producers; plot summaries; character names; movie ratings; year of release; running times; movie trivia; quotes; goofs; soundtracks; personal trivia and Academy Award information.
Contact:	Rob Hartill Robert.Hartill@cm.cf.ac.uk
Details:	Free

`http://www.cm.cf.ac.uk/Movies`
`http://www.msstate.edu/Movies`

rec.arts.sf.tv ★

A Usenet newsgroup providing information and discussion about science fiction television programs.

Keywords:	Science Fiction, Television
Audience:	Science Fiction Enthusiasts, Television Viewers
User Info:	To subscribe to this Usenet newsgroup, you need access to a newsreader.

`news:rec.arts.sf.tv`

rec.arts.startrek.current ★

A Usenet newsgroup providing information and discussion about current Star Trek (The Next Generation) episodes and characters.

Keywords:	Television, Science Fiction
Audience:	Trekkies, Television Viewers
User Info:	To subscribe to this Usenet newsgroup, you need access to a newsreader.

`news:rec.arts.startrek.current`

rec.arts.startrek.misc ★

A Usenet newsgroup providing general information and discussion about all aspects of Star Trek, including its various television and film reviews.

Keywords:	Television, Film
Audience:	Trekkies, Television Viewers, Movie Viewers
User Info:	To subscribe to this Usenet newsgroup, you need access to a newsreader.

`news:rec.arts.startrek.misc`

rec.arts.tv ★

A Usenet newsgroup providing information and discussion about past and present TV shows and related trivia.

Keywords:	Television, Trivia
Audience:	General Public, Television Viewers, Trivia Enthusiasts
User Info:	To subscribe to this Usenet newsgroup, you need access to a newsreader.

`news:rec.arts.tv`

rec.arts.tv.soaps ★

A Usenet newsgroup providing information and discussion about television soap operas.

Keywords:	Television
Audience:	Television Viewers, Soap Opera Viewers
User Info:	To subscribe to this Usenet newsgroup, you need access to a newsreader.

`news:rec.arts.tv.soaps`

rec.arts.tv.uk ★

A Usenet newsgroup providing information and discussion about television shows in the United Kingdom.

Keywords:	Television, United Kingdom
Audience:	Television Viewers, British
User Info:	To subscribe to this Usenet newsgroup, you need access to a newsreader.

`news:rec.arts.tv.uk`

rec.video.satellite ★

A Usenet newsgroup providing information and discussion about satellite television.

Keywords:	Television
Audience:	Satellite Television Watchers
User Info:	To subscribe to this Usenet newsgroup, you need access to a newsreader.

`news:rec.video.satellite`

Star Trek Resources on the Internet

This extensive resource contains information on mailing lists, news archives, other Internet resources addressing the culture surounding Star Trek fans.

Keywords:	Science Fiction, Television
Audience:	General Public, Trekkers, Television Viewers
Contact:	Brigitte Jellinek bjelli@cosy.sbg.ac.at

`http://www.cosy.sbg.ac.at/rec/startrek/star_trek_resources.html`

Theater, Film & Television

This directory is a compilation of information resources focused on theater, film, and television.

Keywords:	Theater, Film, Television
Audience:	Entertainment Prols, Actors
Details:	Free

`ftp://una.hh.lib.umich.edu/70/inetdirsstacks/filmtv:robinson`

Telluride Institute

Telluride Institute ★

This is a community organization involved in building an electronic dimension in rural Colorado. The vision of Telluride Institute includes linking rural residents to each other and outside resources, creating new opportunities for education, jobs, and arts.

Keywords: Community Networking, Virtual Community, Rural Development, Colorado
Sponsor: The Telluride Institute, Telluride, Colorado
Audience: Activists, Policy Makers, Community Leaders, Students, Colorado Residents
Profile: The Telluride Institute is a local community-based organization that produces arts, environmental, and educational events in the Telluride area of Colorado. The Institite is committed to the creation of what it calls the "InfoZone": it wants to use modern telecommunications to link together the local community and to connect to the rest of the world to exchange ideas, commerce, arts, and inspiration.
Contact: Richard Lowenberg
tellinst@csn.org
Details: Free
Send an e-mail message to the URL address below asking for further information.

`mailto:tellinst@csn.org`

Telnet Access to WWW (World Wide Web)

Telnet Access to WWW (World Wide Web) ★★

A server providing free public access to WWW written in both English and Hebrew.

Keywords: WWW, Internet Tools, Jerusalem
Sponsor: Hebrew University of Jerusalem
Audience: Internet Surfers
Contact: rashty@www.huji.ac.il
User Info: Expect: Username; Send: WWW

`telnet://www.huji.ac.il`

Telnet

commune ★

The purpose of this list is to discuss the COMMUNE protocol, a Telnet replacement.

Keywords: Commune Protocol, Telnet
Audience: Commune Protocol Users
Contact: Dan Bernstein
commune-request@stealth.acf.nyu.edu
Details: Free
User Info: To subscribe to the list, send an e-mail message requesting a subscription to the URL address below.
To send a message to the entire list, address it to:
commune-list@stealth.acf.nyu.edu

`mailto:commune-request@stealth.acf.nyu.edu`

Telnet-How To ★

An introduction to telnet, an Internet access tool.

Keywords: Internet Tools, Telnet
Sponsor: SURAnet Network Information Center
Audience: Internet Surfers
Contact: info@sura.net
Details: Free
File is: pub/nic/network.service.guides/how.to.telnet.guide

`ftp://ftp.sura.net`

Tennessee

University of Tennessee at Memphis Library ★★

The library's holdings are large and wide-ranging and contain significant collections in many fields.

Keywords: Tennessee, Literature (American)
Audience: Researchers, Students, General Public
Details: Costs
User Info: Expect: Username Prompt, Send: Harvey

`telnet://utmem1.utmem.edu`

Tennis

rec.sport.tennis ★

A Usenet newsgroup providing information and discussion about tennis.

Keywords: Tennis, Sports
Audience: Tennis Fans, Sports Fans
User Info: To subscribe to this Usenet newsgroup, you need access to a newsreader.

`news:rec.sport.tennis`

University of Glasgow Information Service (GLANCE) ★★★★

GLANCE provides subject-based information services, including an extensive section on European and world sports.

Keywords: Sports, Soccer, Motor Racing, Mountaineering, Squash, Cricket, Golf, Tennis, Europe, Scotland
Sponsor: University of Glasgow, Glasgow, Scotland
Audience: Sport Enthusiasts, Fitness Enthusiasts, Nature Lovers
Profile: Information at this site includes schedules, results, and statistics for sports such as cricket and soccer. There is also a selection of items on mountaineering.
Contact: Alan Dawson
A.Dawson@uk.ac.gla.compserv
Details: Free

`gopher://govan.cent.gla.ac.uk/Subject/Sports and Rec`

teslit-l (Adult Education & Literacy Test Literature)

teslit-l (Adult Education & Literacy Test Literature) ★

This is a sublist of tesl-l (Teaching English as a Second Language). Discussions focus primarily on issues of literacy and the teaching of English as a second language.

Keywords: Education (Adult), Education (Distance), Education (Continuing), Literacy
Audience: K-12 Educators, Administrators, Researchers
Details: Free
User Info: To subscribe to the list, send an e-mail message to the URL address below consisting of a single line reading:
SUB teslit-l YourFirstName YourLastName
To send a message to the entire list, address it to: teslit-l@cunyvm.bitnet
Notes: Members of teslit-l must be members of tesl-l.

`mailto:listserv@cunyvm.bitnet`

TeX

auc-TeX ★

Discussion and information exchange about the AUC TeX package, which runs under GNU Emacs.

Keywords: Computers, TeX, AUC TeX, Emacs

Audience:	Computer Users
Contact:	Kresten Krab Thorup auc-tex-request@iesd.auc.dk
Details:	Free
User Info:	To subscribe to the list, send an e-mail message requesting a subscription to the URL address below. To send a message to the entire list, address it to: auc-tex@iesd.auc.dk

mailto:auc-tex-request@iesd.auc.dk

Texas

Armadillo's World Wide Web Page

This site provides resources and instructional material for an interdisciplinary Texan culture course.

Keywords:	History (US), Texas, Cultural Studies, Education
Sponsor:	Rice University, Houston, Texas, USA
Audience:	Educators, Students
Contact:	armadillo@rice.edu

http://chico.rice.edu/armadillo

Texas: Computer Crimes Statute ★

Lists text of the Texas Computer Crimes Statute.

Keywords:	Computing, Crime, Texas
Audience:	Lawyers, Computer Programmers
Details:	Free Select from menu as appropriate

gopher://wiretap.spies.com

The Texas Information Highway ★★

Access to the public information resources of the state of Texas.

Keywords:	Texas, Travel, Government, Census, Pata 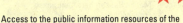
Sponsor:	Texas Department of Information Resources
Audience:	Texans, General Public
Profile:	Still under construction as we go to press, this is a model program to make state and local information resources available to Internet users. The current collection features city, country, and state political information, including full-text of bills before the Texas state legislature. Materials related to Texas history and tourism are also provided, along with links to Texas-area user groups and other state and federal information servers.
Contact:	Wayne McDilda wayne@dir.texas.gov

gopher://info.texas.gov

Text Processing

comp.text.tex ★

A Usenet newsgroup providing information and discussion about the TeX and LaTeX systems.

Keywords:	Text Processing, Internet
Audience:	Computer Users, TeX and LaTeX Users
User Info:	To subscribe to this Usenet newsgroup, you need access to a newsreader.

news:comp.text.tex

Thailand

Thailand: The Big Picture ★★

A web site maintaining a complete list of Internet servers pertaining to and found within Thailand. General information concerning Thailand and extensive Internet connections to Thai academic institutions.

Keywords:	Thailand, Education, Travel
Sponsor:	National Electronics and Computer Center at the National Science and Technology Development Agency, USA
Audience:	Researchers, Exchange Students
Contact:	Trin Tantsetthi webmaster@www.nectec.or.th

http://www.nectec.or.th

Theater

Musicals ★

This forum is intended for the general discussion of musical theater, in all forms, but related non-musical theater topics are welcome, too.

Keywords:	Musicals, Theater
Audience:	Musical Theater Enthusiasts
Details:	Free
User Info:	To subscribe to the list, send an e-mail message requesting a subscription to the URL address below.

mailto:musicals-request@world.std.com

Stagecraft ★★

This list is for the discussion of all aspects of stage work, including special effects, sound effects, sound reinforcement, stage management, set design and building, lighting, design, company management, hall management, hall design, and show production.

Keywords:	Theater, Drama
Audience:	Stage Producers
Contact:	Brad Davis stagecraft-request@zinc.com
User Info:	To subscribe to the list, send an Email message requesting a subscription to the URL address below. To send a message to the entire list, address it to: stagecraft@zinc.com
Notes:	Also contains archives of list discussions.

mailto:stagecraft-request@zinc.com

Theater ★★

This directory is a compilation of information resources focused on theater.

Keywords:	Theater, Drama, Performing Arts
Audience:	Theater Personnel, Drama Personnel, Performers
Contact:	Deborah Torres, Martha Vander Kolk dtorres@umich.edu mjvk@umich.edu
Details:	Free

ftp://una.hh.lib.umich.edu/70/inetdirsstacks/theater:torresmjvk

Theater, Film & Television ★★

This directory is a compilation of information resources focused on theater, film, and television.

Keywords:	Theater, Film, Television
Audience:	Theater Personnel, Film Personnel, Television Personnel
Details:	Free

ftp://una.hh.lib.umich.edu/70/inetdirsstacks/filmtv:robinson

Theology

Catholic Doctrine ★

This is for discussions of orthodox Catholic theology by everyone under the jurisdiction of the Holy Father, John Paul II. No attacks on the Catholic Church here, please.

Keywords:	Catholic Doctrine, Theology
Audience:	Catholics, Priests, Theologians
Contact:	catholic-request@sarto.gaithersburg.md.us
Details:	Free, Moderated
User Info:	To subscribe to the list, send an e-mail message requesting a subscription to the URL address below. To send a message to the entire list, address it to: catholic@sarto.gaithersburg.md.us
Notes:	There is an archive server (containing Catholic art and magisterial documents) associated with this list. Send mail to the URL address below to get details about the archive server.

mailto:catholic-request@sarto.gaithersburg.md.us

Theology

Drake University

The Library's holdings are large and wide-ranging and contain significant collections in many fields.

- Keywords: Music, Pharmacology, Theology
- Audience: General Public, Researchers, Librarians, Document Delivery Professionals
- Details: Free, Moderated
- Send: COWLES to access the main library, and LAWLIB to access the Law Library. To leave the system, enter CTRL-Z

`telnet://lib.drake.edu`

Ecchst-l

A discussion list for scholars of Ecclesiastical history, including those interested both in the history of the Church and in the examination of theology in an historical context.

- Keywords: Religion, Ecclesiastical History, Christianity, Theology
- Audience: Historians, Theologians
- Contact: Gregory H. Singleton ugsingle@uxa.ecn.bgu.edu
- User Info: To subscribe, send an e-mail message to the URL address below consisting of a single line reading:

  SUB ecchst-l YourFirstName YourLastName.

  To send a message to the entire list, address it to: ecchst-l@bgu.edu

`mailto:listserv@bgu.edu`

Emory University Library

The library's holdings are large and wide-ranging and contain significant collections in many fields.

- Keywords: Health Sciences, Theology, History (US), Communism, Economics (History of), Literature (American)
- Audience: General Public, Researchers, Librarians, Document Delivery Professionals
- Details: Free
- User Info: Expect: VM screen, Send: RETURN; Expect: CP READ, Send: DIAL VTAM, press RETURN; Expect: CICS screen, Send: PF1

`telnet://emuvm1.cc.emory.edu`

University of Puget Sound Library

The library's' holdings are large and wide-ranging and contain significant collections in many fields.

- Keywords: Education, Literature (General), Music, Natural Science, Theology
- Audience: Researchers, Students, General Public
- Details: Free
- User Info: Expect: Login; Send: Library

`telnet://192.124.98.2`

Theoretical Chemistry

Theoretical Journal Abstract And Bibliographic Files

Abstract and bibliographic information for several theoretical chemistry journals.

- Keywords: Theoretical Chemistry, Quantum Chemistry, Quantum Mechanics, Computational Chemistry
- Sponsor: Springer-Verlag, and Wiley
- Audience: Chemists, Librarians, Students, (College/University)
- Contact: Dialog in the US at (800) 334-2564, Dialog internationally at country specific locations.

  Mailserv@osc.edu
- Details: Free
- User Info: To subscribe, contact Dialog directly.
- Select: "Other OSC Gopher Servers," then select "OSC Chemistry Gopher Server."

`telnet://dialog.com`

`gopher://infomeister.osc.edu.`

Theoretical Physics

ICTP (International Centre for Theoretical Physics)

ICTP's gopher disseminates information regarding the many scientific activities carried out at ICTP (Trieste, Italy). Information is also provided on the scientific publications, courses, and other services offered by ICS (International Centre for Science and High Technology) and TWAS (Third World Academy of Sciences) at Trieste.

- Keywords: Theoretical Physics, Italy, Europe
- Audience: Physicists
- Profile: Topics include programming techniques, theoretical aspects, Icon in relation to other languages, applications of Icon, implementation issues, porting, and bugs.
- Contact: admin@ictp.trieste.it
- Details: Free

`gopher://gopher.ictp.trieste.it`

`http://gopher.ictp.trieste.it`

Think Wind

Think Wind

An FTP site for information on windsurfing, with FAQs, pictures, details about destinations, and threads from rec.windsurfing.

- Keywords: Sports, Windsurfing
- Audience: Windsurfers
- Contact: phansen@lemming.uvm.edu
- Details: Free, Images

`ftp://lemming.uvm.edu/rec.windsurfing`

THINKNET

THINKNET

Electronic newsletter on philosophy, systems theory, interdisciplinary studies, and thoughtful conversation in cyberspace.

- Keywords: Cyberspace, Systems Theory, Philosophy
- Audience: Philosophers, System Theorists
- Contact: Kent D. Palmer Ph.D. palmer@world.std.com
- Details: Free
- User Info: To subscribe, send an e-mail message to the URL address below consisting of a single line reading:

  SUB THINKNET YourFirstName YourLastName

`mailto:palmer@world.std.com`

Third World

Agence FrancePresse International French Wire

Agence FrancePresse International French Wire provides full-text articles in French relating to national, international, business, and sports news.

- Keywords: News Media, Europe, Third World, French
- Sponsor: Agence FrancePresse, Paris, France
- Audience: Market Researchers, Journalists, Francophiles
- Profile: Agence FrancePresse distributes its French service worldwide, including Western and Eastern Europe, Canada, northern and western Africa, the Middle East, Vietnam, French Guiana, the West Indies, and the French Pacific islands. Agence FrancePresse International French Wire has extensive coverage of the European countries, including every aspect of economic, political, and general business news. It also provides excellent industrial and market news from both developed countries and from the Third World.
- Coverage: September 1991 to the present; updated daily.
- Contact: Dialog in the US at (800) 334-2564; Dialog internationally at country-specific locations.
- Details: Costs
- User Info: To subscribe, contact Dialog directly.

`telnet://dialog.com`

Tibet

CTN News

This is a list covering news on Tibet.

Keywords:	Tibet, New Media
Audience:	Tibetans, Journalists, General Public
Contact:	ctn-editors@utcc.utoronto.ca
Details:	Free
User Info:	To subscribe to the list, send an e-mail message requesting a subscription to the URL address below.
	To send a message to the entire list, address it to: CTN_News@utcc.utoronto.ca

`mailto:ctn-editors@utcc.utoronto.ca`

TitNeT Titnews Titnotes

TitNeT Titnews Titnotes

The network of the International Tit Society (TITS).

Keywords:	Ornithology, Birds
Sponsor:	International Tit Society
Audience:	Bird Watchers
Profile:	The network of the International Tit Society (TITS), Titnet posts three formal series: 1) TITNET is the listing of e-mail subscribers, and includes their e-mail addresses, institutional affiliations, and research interests. 2) TITNEWS is the forum for exchange concerning academic activities, and consists of single-topic issues and multiple announcements. 3) TITNOTES is the forum for exchange of information about tits (and other hole-nesting birds).
Contact:	Jack P. Hailman jhailman@vms.macc.wisc.edu.
Details:	Free
User Info:	To subscribe, send an e-mail message requesting a subscription to the URL address below. Provide: (1) Full name, (2) e-mail address, (3) institutional affiliation, (4) species studied, and (5) topics studied.

`mailto:jhailman@vms.macc.wisc.edu`

titnet (Paridae and Hole-nesting Bird Discussion List)

titnet (Paridae and Hole-nesting Bird Discussion List) ★★★

Promotes communication among scientists working on tits (Paridae) and other hole-nesting birds.

Keywords:	Birds, Ornithology
Audience:	Bird Watchers
Profile:	Titnet is a publication listing e-mail addresses of conference members. Titnews contains announcements and discussions of activities such as bibliographic systems and hence serves as the e-mail newsletter. Titnotes contains material on the biology of the birds and hence serves as a kind of e-mail journal.
Contact:	Jack P. Hailman jhailman@macc.wisc.edu
Details:	Free
User Info:	To subscribe to the list, send an e-mail message requesting a subscription to the URL address below.
	To send a message to the entire list, address it to: jhailman@macc.wisc.edu
Notes:	Send (1) full name, (2) mailing address, which is forwarded to Dr. Ficken for PARUS INTERNATIONAL, (3) e-mail address(es), (4) species studied, and (5) types of studies (population dynamics, general ecology, vocalizations, nesting, behavior, and so on).

`mailto:jhailman@macc.wisc.edu`

Tobacco

Pipes

A forum for discussing the moderate use and appreciation of fine tobacco, including cigars, pipes, quality cigarettes, pipe making and carving, snuff, publications, and related topics.

Keywords:	Pipes, Tobacco, Smoking
Audience:	Smokers, Researchers, Market Analysts
Contact:	Steve Masticola masticol@scr.siemens.com
Details:	Free, M
User Info:	To subscribe to the list, send an e-mail message requesting a subscription to the URL address below. To send a message to the entire list, address it to: masticol@scr.siemens.com

`mailto:masticol@scr.siemens.com`

TOPNWS (Top News)

TOPNWS (Top News)

The Top News (TOPNWS) library contains today's news today for selected key sources from around the world.

Keywords:	News Media, Analysis
Audience:	Journalists, General Public
Profile:	In the Top News (TOPNWS) library newswires are collected and updated every 60 minutes. Newspapers and other daily publications are updated throughout the day on the day of publication. Transcripts are updated within three hours of broadcast. Two weeks' worth of data from more than 40 major publications may be searched as individual files or in specialized group files. The TODAY group file contains today's published information from all sources. the 2WEEK group file expands the window of current information from all sources to two weeks. Specialized section files, designed to be like sections of a newspaper, contain stories from each publication that pertain to the section or topic selected.
Contact:	Mead New Sales Group at (800) 227-4908 or (513) 859-5398 inside the US, or (513) 865-7981 for all inquiries outside the US.
User Info:	To subscribe, contact Mead directly.
	To examine the Nexis user guide, you can access it at the ftp site of the University of Texas at Austin at the URL address: ftp://ftp.cc.utexas.edu
	The files are in: /pub/ref-services/LEXIS

`telnet://nex.meaddata.com`

`http://www.meaddata.com`

Tornado Warnings

Tornado Warnings

Gopher site providing up-to-the-minute tornado warnings for the United States.

Keywords:	Disaster Relief, Weather
Sponsor:	University of Illinois at Urbana-Champaign, Department of Atmospheric Sciences
Audience:	Meteorologists
Contact:	John Kemp johnkemp@uiuc.edu
Details:	Free

`gopher://wx.atmos.uiuc.edu/11/Severe/Tornado_Warnings`

Total Quality Management Gopher

Total Quality Management Gopher

A collection of materials relating to the elimination of defects through comprehensive quality control in industry, government, and universities.

Keywords: Quality Control, Management, Business
Sponsor: The Clemson University Department of Industrial Engineering, Clemson, South Carolina, USA
Audience: Managers, Administrators
Contact: quality@eng.clemson.edu

`gopher://deming.eng.clemson.edu`

`http://deming.eng.clemson.edu`

Tourism

The Complete Guide to Galway

This is a detailed guide to the city of Galway (past and present), covering tourist sites, industry, local transportation, folklore, history, entertainment, drinking and dining. This web site includes maps, photographs, and illustrations.

Keywords: Galway (Ireland), Tourism, Travel
Audience: Irish, Tourists, Historians, Businesses
Contact: Joe Desbonnet
joe@epona.physics.ucg.ie

`http://wombatix.physics.ucg.ie/galway/galway.html`

The Texas Information Highway

Access to the public information resources of the state of Texas.

Keywords: Texas, Government, Census, Data, Travel
Sponsor: Texas Department of Information Resources
Audience: Texans, General Public
Profile: Still under construction as we go to press, this is a model program to make state and local information resources available to Internet users. The current collection features city, county, and state political information, including full-text of bills before the Texas State Legislature. Materials related to Texas history and tourism are also provided, along with links to Texas user groups and other state and federal information servers.
Contact: Wayne McDilda
wayne@dir.texas.gov

`gopher://info.texas.gov`

University of Wisconsin at Stout Library

The library's holdings are large and wide-ranging and contain significant collections in many fields.

Keywords: Mathematics, Business, Fashion Merchandising, Home Economics, Hospitality, Tourism, Hotel Administration, Restaurant Management, Microelectronics
Audience: Researchers, Students, General Public
Details: Free
User Info: Expect: Login, Send: Lib; Expect: vDIAL Prompt, Send: Library

`telnet://lib.uwstout.edu`

WWW Paris

A web site created as a collaborative effort among individuals in both Paris and the United States.

Keywords: Paris, Culture, Art, Travel, French, Tourism
Audience: Students, Educators, Travelers, Researchers
Profile: Contains an extensive collection of images and text regarding all of the major monuments and museums of Paris, including maps of the Metro and the RER; calendars of events and current expositions; promotional images and text relating to local department stores; there is also a visitors' section with up-to-date tourist information on hotels, restaurants, telephones, airport schedules, a basic Paris glossary, and the latest weather images. Includes an extensive collection of links to other resources about Paris and France, and a selected bibliography of history and architecture in Paris.
Contact: Norman Barth, Eric Pouliquen
nbarth@ucsd.edu, epouliq@ucsd.edu

`http://meteora.ucsd.edu/~norman/paris`

Toxicology

GENMED (General Medical Information)

The General Medical Information (GENMED) library contains a variety of medical care and treatment, toxicology, and hospital administration materials.

Keywords: Medicine, Toxicology, Hospital, Treatment
Audience: Medical Professionals
Profile: The GENMED library contains full-text medical journals and newsletters, as well as drug information, disease and trauma reviews, Physicians Data Query cancer information, and medical administration journals. GENMED also offers a gateway to the MEDLINE database.

Contact: Mead New Sales Group at (800) 227-4908 or (513) 859-5398 inside the US, or (513) 865-7981 for all inquiries outside the US.
User Info: To subscribe, contact Mead directly.
To examine the Nexis user guide, you can access it at the ftp site of the University of Texas at Austin at the URL address: ftp://ftp.cc.utexas.edu
The files are in: /pub/ref-services/LEXIS

`telnet://nex.meaddata.com`

`http://www.meaddata.com`

University of Maryland System Library

The library's holdings are large and wide-ranging and contain significant collections in many fields.

Keywords: Medicine (History of), Nursing, Pharmacology, Microbiology, Aquaculture, Aquatic Chemistry, Toxicology
Audience: General Public, Researchers, Librarians, Document Delivery Professionals
Contact: Ron Larsen
Details: Free
User Info: Expect: Available Services menu; Send: PAC

`telnet://victor.umd.edu`

vettox-l (Veterinary Toxicology Discussion List)

A list dedicated to diagnostic toxicology, established at the University of California.

Keywords: Veterinary Medicine, Toxicology
Audience: Veterinarians, Toxicologists
Profile: This list is restricted to those in the practice of diagnostic toxicology, although it will not be an edited list. The goals are to provide an atmosphere of cooperation among those in the field of diagnostic toxicology and to seek solutions to the many challenges that arise during a disease investigation.
Contact: James T. Case, Bill Cohen
jcase@ucdcvdls.bitnet or
bcohen@ucdcvdls.bitnet
Details: Free
User Info: To subscribe to the list, send an e-mail message to the URL address below consisting of a single line reading:
SUB vettox-l YourFirstName YourLastName
To send a message to the entire list, address it to: vettox-l@ucdavis.edu

`mailto:listserv@ucdavis.edu`

Toys

Lego Information

A web site containing pictures, sets, and instructions for building with Legos. Also discusses various ideas, activities, and history pertaining to Legos, as well as information about clubs for Lego enthusiasts.

Keywords: Construction, Toys, Children
Sponsor: Lego
Audience: Children, General Public
Contact: David Koblas
             koblas@netcom.com

`http://legowww.itek.norut.no`

Zarf's List of Interactive Games on the Web

A list containing links to games and toys that can be played on the Internet.

Keywords: Games, toys, entertainment, recreation
Sponsor: Carnegie Mellon University, School of Computer Science, Pittsburgh, Pennsylvania, USA
Audience: General Public, Game Players, Kids
Contact: Andrew Plotkin
             zarf@cs.cmu.edu, apli@andrew.cmu.edu

`http://www.cs.cmu.edu/afs/cs.cmu.edu/user/zarf/www/games.html`

Trade Unions

Johns Hopkins University Library

The library's holdings are large and wide-ranging and contain significant collections in many fields.

Keywords: Literature (English), Economics, Classics, Drama (German), Slavery, Trade Unions, Incunabula, Bibles, Diseases (History of), Nursing (History of), Abolitionism
Audience: General Public, Researchers, Librarians, Document Delivery Professionals
Details: Free

`telnet://jhuvm.hcf.jhu.edu`

Trade

America

For people interested in how the United States is dealing with foreign trade policies, congressional status, and other inside information about the government that is freely distributable.

Keywords: Trade, Government (US), Congress (US), Business (US)
Audience: General Public, Researchers, Journalists, Political Scientists, Students
Contact: subscribe@xamiga.linet.org
User Info: To subscribe to the list, send an e-mail message to the URL address below, consisting of a single line reading:

SUB america YourFirstName YourLastName

To send a message to the entire list, address it to: america@xamiga.linet.org
Notes: This list has monthly postings that are generally in large batches, with posts exceeding a few hundred lines.

`mailto:subscribe@xamiga.linet.org`

Commerce Business Daily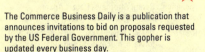

The Commerce Business Daily is a publication that announces invitations to bid on proposals requested by the US Federal Government. This gopher is updated every business day.

Keywords: Business (US), Economics, Commerce, Trade, Government (US)
Sponsor: CNS and Softshare Government Information Systems
Audience: Economists, Business Professionals, General Public, Journalists, Students, Politicians.
Profile: Invitations via Internet email that apply only to specific companies can be arranged.
Contact: Melissa Allensworth
             sshare@cscns.com
             service@cscns.com
Details: Free

`gopher://cns.cscns.com/cbd/About the CBD`

National Export Strategy

This site provides the complete text of a report presented to Congress by the Trade Promotion Coordinating Committee, describing ways to develop U.S. export promotion efforts.

Keywords: Commerce, Trade, Exports, Business
Sponsor: United States Government, Trade Promotion Coordinating Committee
Audience: Exporters, Business Professionals, Trade Specialists
Details: Free

`ftp://sunny.stat-usa.gov`

`http://sunny.stat-usa.gov`

North American Free Trade Agreement (NAFTA)

The agreement between the governments of Canada, the United Mexican States, and the United States of America to establish a free trade area in North America.

Keywords: Trade, US, Mexico, Canada, Free Trade, NAFTA
Audience: Journalists, Politicians, Economists, Students
Details: Free

`gopher://wiretap.spies.com/00/Gov/NAFTA`

Overseas Business Reports

Full-text of U.S. International Trade Administration reports, discussing the economic and commercial climate in various countries around the world.

Keywords: Business, Trade, Commerce
Sponsor: U.S. Government, International Trade Administration
Audience: Business Professionals, Trade Specialists, Investors
Details: Free

`gopher://umslvma.umsl.edu/11/library/govdocs/obr`

PIERS Exports (US Ports)

PIERS (Port Import Export Reporting Service) imports (US Ports), produced by The Journal of Commerce, is a compilation of manifests of vessels loading or discharging caro at approximately 120 US seaports

Keywords: Trade, Exports, Maritime
Sponsor: The Journal of Commerce/PIERS, New York, NY, USA
Audience: Importers, Exporters, Business, Trade Specialists
Profile: Principal applications include identification of new sources of supply, monitoring exports of products whose details are lost in traditional government reports, and identification of potential trade partners. PIERS covers virtually all maritime movements in and out of the continental US and Puerto Rico. Details on each individual shipment are stored in the database.
Contact: Dialog in the US at (800) 334-2564, Dialog internationally at country specific locations.
User Info: To subscribe, contact Dialog directly.
Notes: Coverage: current 15 months, excluding data in file 571.

`telnet://dialog.com`

PIERS Imports (US Ports)

PIERS (Port Import Export Reporting Service) Imports (US Ports), produced by The Journal of Commerce, is a compilation of manifests of vessels loading or discharging cargo at approximately 120 US seaports.

Keywords:	Trade, Imports, Maritime
Sponsor:	The Journal of Commerce/PIERS, New York, NY, USA
Audience:	Business Professionals
Profile:	The principal applications of this information include: identification of new sources of supply for imports, monitoring imports of products whose details are lost in traditional government reports, and identification of potential trade partners.
Contact:	Dialog in the US at (800) 334-2564, Dialog internationally at country specific locations.
User Info:	To subscribe, contact Dialog directly.
Notes:	Coverage: current 15 months, updated monthly.

`telnet://dialog.com`

TRADSTAT

TRADSTAT is a comprehensive online source of national trade statistics.

Keywords:	Trade, Commerce, Business
Sponsor:	TRADSTAT Ltd., London, UK
Audience:	Importers, Exporters, Businesses
Profile:	TRADSTAT covers over 90 percent of world trade. Every month the latest trade figures are loaded into the database from over 20 countries worldwide and all their trading partners. Trade is reported by countries in the EC, EFTA, North and South America, and the Far East. TRADSTAT gives annual trends back to 1981, and monthly reports can be produced at any time for the latest 25 months' trade. The data is made available on average three to eight weeks after the month of trade. This is often weeks, even months, ahead of the equivalent printed data.
User Info:	To subscribe, contact Dialog directly.

`telnet://dialog.com`

Trademarks

Chinapats

Covers all patent applications published under the patent law of People's Republic of China.

Keywords:	Patents, Intellectual Property, Trademarks
Sponsor:	European Patent Office
Audience:	Patent Attorneys, Patent Agents, Librarians, Researchers
Profile:	English language abstracts are included for all applications filed by Chinese applicants. Contains more than 59,000 records. Updated monthly.
Contact:	PAUL.ALBERT@NETEAST.COM
User Info:	To subscribe contact Orbit-Questel directly.

`telnet://orbit.com`

CLAIMS

Provides access to over 2.3 million U.S. patents issued by the U.S. Patent and Trademark Office.

Keywords:	Patents, Intellectual Property, Trademarks
Sponsor:	IFI/Plenum Data Corporation
Audience:	Patent Attorneys, Patent Agents, Librarians, Researchers
Profile:	Chemical patents are covered from 1950 forward; mechanical and electrical patents from 1963 forward; design patents from 1980 forward.
Contact:	PAUL.ALBERT@NETEAST.COM
User Info:	To subscribe contact Orbit-Questel directly.

`telnet://orbit.com`

Derwent World Patents Index

Patent specifications issued by the patent offices of 33 major issuing authorities.

Keywords:	Patents, Intellectual Property, Trademarks
Sponsor:	Derwent Publications, Ltd.
Audience:	Patent Attorneys, Patent Agents, Librarians, Researchers
Profile:	Includes European Patent Office and Patent Cooperation Treaty published applications, plus Research Disclosure and International Technology Disclosure. Each patent is extensively indexed from the complete patent specifications. Abstracts are included.
Contact:	PAUL.ALBERT@NETEAST.COM
User Info:	To subscribe contact Orbit-Questel directly.

`telnet://orbit.com`

INCORPR (Corporation and Partnership Records)

The Corporation and Partnership Records (INCORP) library contains current US corporation and partnership filings.

Keywords:	Corporations, Partnerships, Filings, Trademarks
Audience:	Corporations, Lawyers, Researchers
Profile:	The INCORP library contains current records on corporations and limited partnerships registered with the office of the Secretary or Department of State. These records include information extracted by the state's staff from articles of incorporation, annual reports, amendments, and other public filings.
Contact:	Mead New Sales Group at (800) 227-4908 or (513) 859-5398 inside the US, or (513) 865-7981 for all inquiries outside the US.
User Info:	To subscribe, contact Mead directly.
	To examine the Nexis user guide, you can access it at the ftp site of the University of Texas at Austin at the URL address: ftp://ftp.cc.utexas.edu
	The files are in: /pub/ref-services/LEXIS

`telnet://nex.meaddata.com`

`http://www.meaddata.com`

INPADOC/INPANEW

Patent documents issued by more than 50 national and international patent offices.

Keywords:	Patents, Intellectual Property, Trademarks
Sponsor:	European Patent Office
Audience:	Patent Attorneys, Patent Agents, Librarians, Researchers
Profile:	Bibliographic information is searchable, including inventor names, assignees, international patent classification codes, and in most cases, titles, as well as complete publications and application data. Contains approximately 20 million records. Updated weekly.
Contact:	PAUL.ALBERT@NETEAST.COM
User Info:	To subscribe contact Orbit-Questel directly.

`telnet://orbit.com`

JAPIO

Comprehensive source of unexamined Japanese patent applications.

Keywords:	Patents, Intellectual Property, Trademarks
Sponsor:	Japan Patent Information Organization
Audience:	Patent Attorneys, Patent Agents, Librarians, Researchers
Profile:	More than 2.8 million records covering all technologies. Unique features include English-language abstracts for many Japanese patent applications.
Contact:	PAUL.ALBERT@NETEAST.COM
User Info:	To subscribe contact Orbit-Questel directly.

`telnet://orbit.com`

Legal Status

Records thousands of types of actions that can affect the legal status of a patent document after it is published and after the patent is granted.

Keywords: Patents, Intellectual Property, Trademarks Sponsor: European Patent Office Audience: Patent Atto neys, Pa ent Agents, Librarians, Researcher Profile: Information about the di position f patent applicati ns published under the Patent Cooperation Treaty by the World Intellectual Property Organizations is included as well. Contains more than 8 million records. Updated weekly.

Contact: PAUL.ALBERT@NETEAST.COM
User Info: To subscribe contact Orbit-Questel directly.

`telnet://orbit.com`

Trademark Act of the US

The US Trademark Act of 1946 (The Lanham Act), Title 15, United States Code, Sections 1051_1127.

Keywords: Trademarks, Laws (US), Government (US), Commerce
Audience: Journalists, Politicians, Students, Lawyers, Business Professionals, Designers, Marketers
Details: Free

`http://www.law.cornell.edu/lanham/lanham.table.html`

US Patents

Complete patent information of all claims of U.S. patents issued since 1971.

Keywords: Patents, Intellectual Property, Trademarks
Sponsor: Derwent, Inc.
Audience: Patent Attorneys, Patent Agents, Librarians, Researchers
Profile: Includes complete front page information, plus all claims of US patents issued since 1971. Merged file contains approximately 1.4 million records. Updated weekly.
Contact: PAUL.ALBERT@NETEAST.COM
User Info: To subscribe contact Orbit-Questel directly.

`telnet://orbit.com`

Trading Cards

Cards

This list is for people interested in collecting, speculating, and investing in baseball, football, basketball, hockey, and other trading cards and/or memorabilia. Discussion and want/sell lists are welcome.

Keywords: Trading Cards, Collectibiles, Memorabilia
Audience: Sports Card Collectors, Sports Card Traders, Memorabilia Collectors
Contact: Keane Arase
cards-request@tanstaafl.uchicago.edu
Details: Free
User Info: To subscribe to the list, send an e-mail message requesting a subscription to the URL address below.
To send a message to the entire list, address it to:
cards@tanstaafl.uchicago.edu
Notes: The list is open to anyone.

`mailto:cards-request@tanstaafl.uchicago.edu`

rec.collecting.cards

A Usenet newsgroup providing information and discussion about collecting sports and other trading cards.

Keywords: Trading Cards, Hobbies
Audience: Card Collectors
User Info: To subscribe to this Usenet newsgroup, you need access to a newsreader.

`news:rec.collecting.cards`

Sports-cards

For people interested in collection, speculation and investing in baseball, football, basketball, hockey, and other trading cards and/or memorabilia. Discussion and want/sell lists are welcome.

Keywords: Memorabilia, Sports, Trading Cards
Audience: Collectors, Sports Card Traders
Contact: Keane Arase
cards-request@tanstaafl.uchicago.edu
Details: Free
User Info: To subscribe to the list, send an e-mail message requesting a subscription to the URL address below. To send a message to the entire list, address it to: cards@tanstaafl.uchicago.edu

`mailto:cards-request@tanstaafl.uchicago.edu`

Translation

Lantra-L

A discussion of interpretation and translation.

Keywords: Interpretation, Translation, Language, Linguistics
Audience: Linguists, Interpreters, Translators
Details: Free

`mailto:listserv@searn.bitnet`

Transportation

gis-t

A mailing list for the discussion of GIS (Geographic Information Systems) and transportation.

Keywords: Geography, Transportation, GIS (Geographic Information Systems)
Audience: Geographers, Cartographers
Contact: Jay Sandhu
jsandhu@esri.com
User Info: To subscribe to the list, send an e-mail message to the URL address below consisting of a single line reading:
SUB gis-t YourFirstName YourLastName
To send a message to the entire list, address it to: gis-t@esri.com

`mailto:listserv@esri.com`

ITRE Home Page

A server dealing with transportation research and some GIS-related discussion.

Keywords: GIS, Transportation
Sponsor: University of North Carolina Institute for Transportation Research and Education
Audience: GIS Professionals, Transportation Professionals
Profile: The ITRE server address GIS issues regarding transportation, a different flavor than will be found on most servers on the Net. Also features image mapping examples.
Contact: Jay Novello
jay@itre.uncecs.edu
Details: Free
Images
Multimedia

`http://itre.uncecs.edu`

rec.railroad

A Usenet newsgroup providing information and discussion about railroads.

Keywords:	Railroads, Transportation
Audience:	Railroad Enthusiast
User Info:	To subscribe to this Usenet newsgroup, you need access to a newsreader.

`news:rec.railroad`

Research Ship Schedules and Information

A gopher providing information on research and deep water vessels from more than 45 countries. Includes detailed ship specifications, some with deck plans and photographs available as GIF files. Also has cruise schedules for US ships, as well as some from other countries.

Keywords:	Oceanography, Transportation, Maritime Industry, Travel
Sponsor:	University of Delaware (The OCEANIC Ocean Information Center), Newark, Delaware, USA
Audience:	Oceanographers, General Public
Contact:	Ocean Information Center, University of Delawareof Delaware, College of Marine Studies oceanic@diu.cms.udel.edu
Details:	Free
	Images

`gopher://diu.cms.udel.edu`

Subway Navigator (city subway routes)

This service helps you find a route in the subway systems of some cities in the world. Estimated times of departure/arrival are also given.

Keywords:	Subways, Transit, Travel
Audience:	Subway Riders, International Travelers
Profile:	Cities covered are: •Montreal, Canada •Paris, France •Hong Kong •Lille, France •Toulouse, France •Madrid, Spain •Lyon, France •Frankfurt, Germany •New York City, NY, USA* •Marseille, France •Munich, Germany *The network includes all NYCTA (New-York City Transit Authority) subway stations.
Contact:	Pierre.David@prism.uvsq.fr
Details:	Free

`gopher://gopher.jussieu.fr/11/metro`

`telnet://vishnu.jussieu.fr`

University of Michigan Library

The library's holdings are large and wide-ranging and contain significant collections in many fields.

Keywords:	Asia, Astronomy, Transportation, Lexicology, Math, Zoology, Geography
Audience:	Researchers, Students, General Public
Contact:	info@merit.edu
Details:	Free
User Info:	Expect: Which Host; Send: Help

`telnet://cts.merit.edu`

Transportation Law

TRANS (The Transportation Library)

The Transportation Library contains federal transportation case law, statutes, and agency decisions.

Keywords:	Transportation Law, US Government Regulations, Aviation Industry, Railroad Industry, Trucking Industry
Audience:	Lawyers
Profile:	The Transportation library contains federal transportation case law, statutes and agency decisions. The major emphasis of the library is on three modes of transportation (aviation, railroad and trucking) and how those modes are regulated by the federal government. Agency decisions are provided from the Interstate Commerce Commission, Department of Transportation and the National Transportation Safety Board (NTSB).
Contact:	New Sales Group at 800-227-4908 or 513-859-5398 inside the US, or 1-513-865-7981 for all inquires outside the US.
User Info:	To subscribe, contact Mead directly. To examine the Lexis user guide, you can access it at the ftp site of the University of Texas at Austin at the URL address: ftp://ftp.cc.utexas.edu The files are in: /pub/res-services/LEXIS

`telnet://nex.meaddata.com`

Transsexualism

AUGLBC-l

The American University Gay, Lesbian, and Bisexual Community (AUGLBC) is a support group for lesbian, gay, bisexual, transsexual, and supportive students. The group is also connected with the International Gay and Lesbian Youth Organization (known as IGLYO).

Keywords:	Gays, Lesbians, Bisexuality, Transsexuality, Sexuality
Audience:	Gays, Lesbians, Bisexuals, Transsexuals, Students (College)
Contact:	Erik G. Paul
User Info:	To subscribe to the list, send an e-mail message to the URL address below, consisting of a single line reading: SUB AUGLBC-l YourFirstName YourLastName To send a message to the entire list, address it to: AUGLBC-l@american.edu

`mailto:listserv@american.edu`

Cd-Forum

The purpose of this list is to provide support and to discuss/share experiences about gender-related issues, including cross dressing, transvestism, and transsexualism.

Keywords:	Transsexualism, Transvestism, Sexuality, Gender
Audience:	Transsexuals, Transvestites
Contact:	Valerie cd-request@valis.biocad.com
Details:	Free
User Info:	To subscribe to the list, send an e-mail message requesting a subscription to the URL address below. To send a message to the entire list, address it to: cd@valis.biocad.com
Notes:	This list is in digest format.

`mailto:cd-request@valis.biocad.com`

OUTIL (Out in Linguistics)

The list is open to lesbian, gay, bisexual, transsexual linguists and their friends. The only requirement is that you be willing to be out to everyone on the list. The purposes of the group are to be visible and to gather occasionally to enjoy one another's company.

Keywords:	Linguistics, Gays, Lesbians, Bisexuals, Transsexuals
Audience:	Linguists, Gays, Lesbians, Bisexuals, Transsexuals
Contact:	Arnold Zwicky outil-request@csli.stanford.edu

Details: Free
User Info: To subscribe to the list, send an e-mail message requesting a subscription to the URL address below.

To send a message to the entire list, address it to: outil@csli.stanford.edu

mailto:outil-request@csli.stanford.edu

Travel

The Avid Explorer

A web site providing travel and destination information, including links to a number of other sources of travel information on the Internet.

Keywords: Travel
Sponsor: Explore! Cruises & Expeditions
Audience: General Public
Contact: Richard Reavis
webmaster@explore.com

http://www.explore.com

Canadian Geographical WWW Index Traveler

This web site provides weekly weather information.

Keywords: Weather, Travel, Canada, Geography
Sponsor: University of Manitoba, Canada
Audience: Travelers, Educators, Students
Contact: www@umanitoba.ca
Details: Free

http://www.umanitoba.ca

The Complete Guide to Galway

This is a detailed guide to the city of Galway (past and present), covering tourist sites, industry, local transportation, folklore, history, entertainment, drinking and dining. This web site includes maps, photographs and illustrations.

Keywords: Galway (Ireland), Tourism, Travel
Audience: Irish, Tourists, Historians, Businesses
Contact: Joe Desbonnet
joe@epona.physics.ucg.ie

http://wombatix.physics.ucg.ie/galway/galway.htmlCanadian Geographical WWW Index Travel

Highlands and Islands of Scotland

This web site provides information on Scotland, including business, leisure, culture, Gaelic language, tourism, distance education, and work opportunities.

Keywords: Scotland, Travel
Sponsor: British Telecom, United Kingdom

Audience: Travelers, Educators, Students
Contact: webmaster@nsa.bt.co.uk
Details: Free

http://nsa.bt.co.uk/nsa.html

hospex

A bulletin board for people interested in being hosts to foreign visitors.

Keywords: Travel
Audience: International Travelers, General Public
Contact: hospex@plearn.edu.p1
Details: Free
User Info: To subscribe to the list, send an e-mail message to the URL address shown below consisting of a single line reading:

SUB hospex YourFirstName YourLastName

mailto:listserv@plearn.bitnet

Information About Alaska

This collection contains information on Alaska's government and politics, as well as historical documents about Alaska's neighbors, Russia, and Canada. It also has cultural information, including literature and sports in the Land of the Midnight Sun.

Keywords: Alaska, Travel
Sponsor: University of Alaska Computer Network (UACN), Alaska, USA
Audience: Alaskans, Travelers, General Public
Contact: Douglas Toelle
sxinfo@orca.alaska.edu

gopher://info.alaska.edu

Information about New York City

Facts about New York City, including information on museums, restaurants, hotels, bars, and other areas of interest to New Yorkers and visitors alike.

Keywords: New York, Travel
Sponsor: City University of New York (CUNY)
Audience: New York City Residents, Tourists, General Public
Contact: Anil Khullar
gopher@netops.gc.cuny.edu
Notes: Still under construction, some items are incomplete

gopher://timesq.gc.cuny.edu

Ireland-Related Online Resources

This is a list of network-accessible online resources (documents, images, information, access mechanisms for off-line material, and so on) of Irish interest. Coverage includes some Bulletin Board services, some commercial information systems such as CompuServe and commercial bibliographic services.

Keywords: Ireland, Travel, Commerce, Geography
Audience: Irish, General Public, Tourists, Businesses
Contact: fmurtagh@eso.org

http://http.hq.eso.org/~fmurtagh/ireland-resources.html

Moon Travel Handbooks

Moon Publications' gopher features a travel newsletter, as well as excerpts and ordering information for their travel guides.

Keywords: Travel, Books
Sponsor: Moon Publications
Audience: International Travelers, General Public
Contact: gopher@moon.com
Notes: Also see Moon Publications' hypertext exhibit, Big Island of Hawaii Handbook, at http://bookweb.cwis.uci.edu:8042.

gopher://gopher.moon.com

New-orleans

A list for discussing any and all aspects of the city of New Orleans. History, politics, culture, food, restaurants, music, entertainment, Mardi Gras, and so on, are all fair game.

Keywords: New Orleans, Travel
Audience: New Orleans Residents, New Orleans Visitors
Contact: Edward J. Branley
elendil@mintir.new-orleans.la.us
User Info: To subscribe to the list, send an e-mail message requesting a subscription to the URL address below.

mailto:mail-server@mintir.new-orleans.la.us

Neworl-dig

This is a digest version of the New Orleans mailing list. It is distributed on a monthly basis, and includes articles from the New Orleans list, minus the "noise."

Keywords: New Orleans, Travel
Audience: New Orleans Residents, New Orleans Visitors
Contact: Edward J. Branley
elendil@mintir.new-orleans.la.us
Details: Free
User Info: To subscribe to the list, send an e-mail message requesting a subscription to the URL address below.

mailto:mail-server@mintir.new-orleans.la.us

News, Weather, and Travel Advisories

A major directory of news, weather, and travel advisories, providing access to a broad range of related resources (library catalogues, databases, and servers) via the Internet.

- Keywords: Travel, Weather, Aviation
- Sponsor: Kennesaw State College, Georgia, USA
- Audience: General Public, Travellers
- Profile: This collection includes CNN news sources, the National Weather Service Forecast, and the US State Department Travel Advisory, among other sources.
- Details: Free

`gopher://kscsuna1.kennesaw.edu`

rec.scuba

A Usenet newsgroup providing information and discussion about scuba equipment and techniques.

- Keywords: Scuba Sports, Travel, Recreation
- Audience: Scuba Divers
- User Info: To subscribe to this Usenet newsgroup, you need access to a newsreader.

`news:scuba`

rec.travel

A Usenet newsgroup providing information and discussion about travel.

- Keywords: Travel
- Audience: Travelers
- User Info: To subscribe to this Usenet newsgroup, you need access to a newsreader.

`news:rec.travel`

Research Ship Schedules and Information

A gopher providing information on research and deep water vessels from more than 45 countries. Includes detailed ship specifications, some with deck plans and photographs available as GIF files. Also has cruise schedules for US ships, as well as some from other countries.

- Keywords: Oceanography, Transportation, Maritime Industry, Travel
- Sponsor: University of Delaware (The OCEANIC Ocean Information Center), Newark, Delaware, USA
- Audience: Oceanographers, General Public
- Contact: Ocean Information Center, University of Delaware of Delaware, College of Marine Studies
  oceanic@diu.cms.udel.edu
- Details: Free, Images

`gopher://diu.cms.udel.edu`

Subway Navigator (city subway routes)

This service helps you find a route in the subway systems of some cities in the world. Estimated times of departure/arrival are also given.

- Keywords: Subways, Transportation, Travel
- Audience: Subway Riders, International Travelers
- Profile: Cities covered are:
  - Montreal, Canada
  - Paris, France
  - Hong Kong
  - Lille, France
  - Toulouse, France
  - Madrid, Spain
  - Lyon, France
  - Frankfurt, Germany
  - New York City, NY, USA*
  - Marseille, France
  - Munich, Germany

  *The network includes all NYCTA (New-York City Transit Authority) subway stations
- Contact: Pierre.David@prism.uvsq.fr
- Details: Free

`gopher://gopher.jussieu.fr/11/metro`

`telnet://vishnu.jussieu.fr`

The Texas Information Highway

Access to the public information resources of the state of Texas.

- Keywords: Texas, Government, Census, Data, Travel
- Sponsor: Texas Department of Information Resources
- Audience: Texans, General Public
- Profile: Still under construction as we go to press, this is a model program to make state and local information resources available to Internet users. The current collection features city, county, and state political information, including full-text of bills before the Texas State Legislature. Materials related to Texas history and tourism are also provided, along with links to Texas user groups and other state and federal information servers.
- Contact: Wayne McDilda
  wayne@dir.texas.gov

`gopher://info.texas.gov`

Thailand: The Big Picture

A web site maintaining a complete list of Internet servers pertaining to and found within Thailand. General information concerning Thailand and extensive Internet connections to Thai academic institutions.

- Keywords: Thailand, Education, Travel
- Sponsor: National Electronics and Computer Center at the National Science and Technology Development Agency, USA
- Audience: Researchers, Exchange Students
- Contact: Trin Tantsetthi
  webmaster@www.nectec.or.th

`http://www.nectec.or.th\`

Travelnet

Internet users can gain access here to travel related products and public service announcements pertaining to travel and tourism.

- Keywords: Travel
- Audience: Tourists, Travel Agents
- Producer: TravelWeb
- Profile: Travelnet is a system staffed by professional travel agents who provide accurate and timely information on travel related products. Travelnet also provides travel related news and announcements of general interest free as a public service announcement pertaining to countries globally.
- Access Info: World Wide Web
- Notes: The information contained on this server is copyright and cannot be modified, reposted, or otherwise used outside the policies of the TravelWeb without the permission of the TravelWeb Corporation. The TravelWeb is a resource and referral system only pertaining to travel related products.

`mailto:Travelnet@cruzio.com`

WWW Paris

A web site created as a collaborative effort among individuals in both Paris and the United States.

- Keywords: Paris, Culture, Art, Travel, French, Tourism
- Audience: Students, Educators, Travelers, Researchers
- Profile: Contains an extensive collection of images and text regarding all of the major monuments and museums of Paris, including maps of the Metro and the RER; calendars of events and current expositions; promotional images and text relating to local department stores; there is also a visitors' section with up-to-date tourist information on hotels, restaurants, telephones, airport schedules, a basic Paris glossary, and the latest weather images. Includes an extensive collection of links to other resources about Paris and France, and a selected bibliography of history and architecture in Paris.
- Contact: Norman Barth, Eric Pouliquen
  nbarth@ucsd.edu, epouliq@ucsd.edu

`http://meteora.ucsd.edu/~norman/paris`

Travel (History of)

University of Tennessee at Knoxville Library

The library's holdings are large and wide-ranging and contain significant collections in many fields.

Keywords: Native American Affairs, Congress (US), Folklore, Travel (History of)
Audience: Researchers, Students, General Public
Details: Free
User Info: Expect: OK Prompt; Send: Login pub1; Expect: Password, Send: Usc

`telnet://opac.lib.utk.edu`

Treaties

Historic World Documents

The wiretap gopher provides access to a range of world documents in full-text format.

Keywords: International Documents, Treaties, History (World)
Audience: Governments, Historians, Researchers, General Public
Details: Free
  Select from Menu as appropriate

`gopher://wiretap.spies.com`

Multilateral Treaties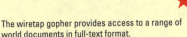

An experimental program to make available to the Internet community the text of a wide variety of multilateral conventions, even those which have not yet been ratified.

Keywords: Multilateral, Treaty, Law
Sponsor: The Fletcher School of Law and Diplomacy, Cornell University, Ithaca, NY
Audience: Government Officials, Researchers, Lawyers
Profile: Almost all treaties listed are available in print form. The program will enable access to even very recent conventions. Primary focus is on Environmental and human rights issues but other fields are also included. The conventions coming out of the 1992 United Nations Conference on the Environment and Development have NOT been included as they are available elsewhere through CIESIN. Those Treaties covered include: Convention on International Trade in Endangered Species of Wild Fa; Montreal Protocol on Substances that Depleate the Ozone Layer; The Berne Convention for the Protection of Literary and Artistic Works; Agreement on the Rescue of Astronauts; the return of Astronauts

Contact: Peter Scott Director, Multilaterals Project, Fletcher School of Law and Diplomacy
  pstott@pearl.tufts.edu
  pstott@icg.apc.org
Details: Free
  Select from menu as appropriate

`gopher://gopher.law.cornell.edu/11/foreign/fletcher-cat`

Various Treaties

Provides access to a range of treaties in full-text format.

Keywords: Treaties, Politics (International)
Audience: Governments, Researchers, Lawyers
Details: Free
  Select from menu as appropriate

`gopher://wiretap.spies.com`

Treatment

GENMED (General Medical Information)

The General Medical Information (GENMED) library contains a variety of medical care and treatment, toxicology, and hospital administration materials.

Keywords: Medicine, Toxicology, Hospital, Treatment
Audience: Medical Professionals
Profile: The GENMED library contains full-text medical journals and newsletters, as well as drug information, disease and trauma reviews, Physicians Data Query cancer information, and medical administration journals. GENMED also offers a gateway to the MEDLINE database.
Contact: Mead New Sales Group at (800) 227-4908 or (513) 859-5398 inside the US, or (513) 865-7981 for all inquiries outside the US.
User Info: To subscribe, contact Mead directly.
  To examine the Nexis user guide, you can access it at the ftp site of the University of Texas at Austin at the URL address: ftp://ftp.cc.utexas.edu
  The files are in: /pub/ref-services/LEXIS

`telnet://nex.meaddata.com`

`http://www.meaddata.com`

Trekkers

Star Trek Resources on the Internet

This extensive resource contains information on mailing lists, news archives, other Internet resources addressing the culture surounding Star Trek fans.

Keywords: Science Fiction, Television, Trekkers
Audience: General Public, Trekkers, Television Viewers
Contact: Brigitte Jellinek
  bjelli@cosy.sbg.ac.at

`http://www.cosy.sbg.ac.at/rec/startrek/star_trek_resources.html`

Trivia

rec.arts.tv

A Usenet newsgroup providing information and discussion about past and present TV shows and related trivia.

Keywords: Television, Trivia
Audience: General Public, Television Viewers, Trivia Enthusiasts
User Info: To subscribe to this Usenet newsgroup, you need access to a newsreader.

`news:rec.arts.tv`

Trollope (Anthony)

Princeton University Online Manuscripts Catalog Library

The library's holdings are large and wide-ranging. They contain significant collections in many fields.

Keywords: Books (Antiquarian), Dickens (Charles), Disraeli (Benjamin), Eliot (George), Hardy (Thomas), Kingsley (Charles), Trollope (Anthony)
Audience: General Public, Researchers, Librarians, Document Delivery Professionals
Details: Free
User Info: Expect: VM370 logo, Send: <cr>; Expect: Welcome screen, Send: folio <cr>; Expect: Welcome screen for FOLIO, Send: <cr>; Expect: List of choices, Send: 3 <cr>; To exit: type: logoff

`telnet://pucc.princeton.edu`

Trucking Industry

TRANS (The Transportation Library)

The Transportation Library contains federal transportation case law, statutes and agency decisions.

Keywords: Transportation Law, US Government Regulations, Aviation, Railroads, Trucking Industry

Audience: Lawyers

Profile: The Transportation library contains federal transportation case law, statutes and agency decisions. The major emphasis of the library is on three modes of transportation (aviation, railroad and trucking) and how those modes are regulated by the federal government. Agency decisions are provided by the Interstate Commerce Commission, Department of Transportation and the National Transportation Safety Board (NTSB).

Contact: New Sales Group at 800-227-4908 or 513-859-5398 inside the US, or 1-513-865-7981 for all inquires outside the US.

User Info: To subscribe, contact Mead directly.

To examine the Lexis user guide, you can access it at the ftp site of the University of Texas at Austin at the URL address: ftp://ftp.cc.utexas.edu

The files are in: /pub/res-services/LEXIS

`telnet://nex.meaddata.com`

TULSA (Petroleum Abstracts)

TULSA (Petroleum Abstracts)

References and abstracts to literature and patents related to oil and natural gas exploration, development and production.

Keywords: Petroleum

Sponsor: Petroleum Abstracts, a division of the University of Tulsa

Audience: Researchers, Librarians

Profile: More than 500,000 references. Includes such areas as logging, well drilling, well completion and servicing, petroleum geology, exploration geophysics and geochemistry, oil and gas production, reservoir studies and recovery methods, pollution, alternative fuels, and transportation and storage. Updated weekly.

Contact: paul.albert@neteast.com

User Info: To subscribe contact Orbit-Questel directly.

`telnet://orbit.com`

Turkey

soc.culture.turkish

A Usenet newsgroup providing information and discussion about Turkish people and culture.

Keywords: Turkey, Sociology

Audience: Sociologists, Turks

Details: Free

User Info: To subscribe to this Usenet newsgroup, you need access to a newsreader.

`news:soc.culture.turkish`

Tutorials

Chemistry Tutorial Information

This site provides chemistry tutorial information in the form of text, data, pictures, source code, and executable programs for Macintosh computers.

Keywords: Chemistry, Tutorials, Macintosh, Education

Sponsor: University of Michigan

Audience: Chemistry Students (high school up)

Contact: comments@mac.archive.umich.edu

Details: Free, Images

`gopher://plaza.aarnet.edu.au@/micros/mac/umich/misc/chemistry/00index.txt`

TWICS

TWICS

This is an English-language computer conferencing system in Japan.

Keywords: Community Networking, Japan, Virtual Community

Sponsor: TWICS Co., Ltd.

Audience: Internationalists, General Public, Journalists, Policy Makers

Profile: TWICS is a computer conferencing system that has a reputation for being a thriving electronic community. This system maintains a full Internet connection. Unlike a database or a gopher server, TWICS enables real-time online interaction with actual people.

Contact: Tim Buress
twics@twics.co.jp.

Details: Free

`telnet://tanuki.twics.co.jp`

Typography

The University of Iowa Libraries

The library's holdings are large and wide-ranging and contain significant collections in many fields.

Keywords: Hunt (Leigh), Native American Studies, Typography, Railroads, Cartoons, French Revolution, NASA, Hydraulics

Audience: General Public, Researchers, Librarians, Document Delivery Professionals

Details: Free

Send <RETURN> to display a menu of available systems. Type 1 for OASIS access and press <RETURN> to display the Welcome to OASIS screen.

`telnet://oasis.uiowa.edu`

UC Berkeley Museum of Paleontology and the WWW Subway

UC Berkeley Museum of Paleontology and the WWW Subway

This web site provides a multimedia museum display from UC Berkeley's Museum of Paleontology. Also features an interactive Subway, a tool linking users to other museums and WWW sites around the world.

Keywords:	WWW, Museums, Paleontology
Sponsor:	University of California at Berkeley, Museum of Paleontology, Berkeley, California, USA
Audience:	Paleontologists, Internet Surfers, General Public
Contact:	David Polly, Robert Guralnick davip@ucmp1.berkeley.edu robg@fossil.berkeley.edu
Details:	Subway

`http://ucmp1.berkeley.edu/subway.html`

Ucadian Studies

University of Maine System Library Catalog

The library's holdings are large and wide-ranging and contain significant collections in many fields.

Keywords:	Ucadian Studies, St. John Valley (History of), Canadian-American Studies, Geology, Aquaculture, Maine
Audience:	General Public, Researchers, Librarians, Document Delivery Professionals
Contact:	Elaine Albright, Marilyn Lutz
Details:	Free
User Info:	Expect: login, Send: ursus

`telnet://ursus.maine.edu`

UCSB Library Reference Guide

UCSB Library Reference Guide

A list of art references including indexes, dictionaries, bibliographies, and biographical materials.

Keywords:	Art, History (World), Libraries
Sponsor:	University of California at Santa Barbara
Audience:	Artists, Historians, Librarians

`gopher://ucsbuxa.ucsb.edu`

UFOs

alt.alien.visitors

A Usenet newsgroup providing information and discussion about space aliens on Earth and related stories.

Keywords:	UFOs, Aliens, Extraterrestrial Life
Audience:	Alien Enthusiasts
User Info:	To subscribe to this Usenet newsgroup, you need access to a newsreader.

`news:alt.alien.visitors`

UIgis-L

UIgis-L

A mailing list for the discussion of user interfaces and GIS (Geographic Information Systems).

Keywords:	Geography, GIS (Geographic Information Systems)
Audience:	Geographers, Cartographers
Contact:	David Mark dmark@acsu.buffalo.edu
User Info:	To subscribe to the list, send an e-mail message to the URL address below consisting of a single line reading: SUB uigis-l YourFirstName YourLastName To send a message to the entire list, address it to: uigis@ubvm.cc.buffalo.edu

`mailto:listserv@ubvm.cc.buffalo.edu`

UN Army Map Service

University of Nevada at Reno Library

The library's holdings are large and wide-ranging and contain significant collections in many fields.

Keywords:	Basque Studies, Nevada, UN Army Map Service, Patents
Audience:	General Public, Researchers, Librarians, Document Delivery Professionals
Details:	Free
User Info:	Expect: login, Send: wolfpac

`telnet://wolfpac.lib.unr.edu`

UN Documents

Northwestern University Library

The library's holdings are large and wide-ranging and contain significant collections in many fields.

Keywords: Africa, Wright (Frank Lloyd), Women's Studies, Art, Literature (American), Contemporary Music, Government (US State), UN Documents, Music

Audience: General Public, Researchers, Librarians, Document Delivery Professionals

Details: Free

User Info: Expect: COMMAND:, Send: DIAL VTAM

`telnet://nuacvm.acns.nwu.edu`

UNC-CH Info system

UNC-CH Info system

The University of North Carolina at Chapel Hill's campus-wide information server, providing access to a wide range of campus information and to electronic information services worldwide.

Keywords: Education, Internet Services

Sponsor: University of North Carolina at Chapel Hill

Audience: Educators, Researchers, Internet Surfers

Contact: info@unc.edu

Details: Free

`gopher://gibbs.oit.unc.edu`

UNICEF Gopher

UNICEF Gopher

The gopher site of the United Nations Children's Fund.

Keywords: Children, Child Care

Sponsor: United Nations

Audience: Child Care Providers, Children's Rights Activists

Profile: This gopher provides access to full-text UNICEF publications such as the State of the World's Children report and the Progress of Nations, the UNICEF Annual Report, UNICEF Features, the First Call for Children newsletter, press releases, information notes and other advocacy and information booklets, brochures and pamphlets. The Gopher also contains the full-text of the Convention on the Rights of the Child and the Declaration and Plan of Action of the 1990 World Summit for Children.

Contact: UNICEF Gopher Host rpadolina@unicef.org

`gopher://hqfaus01.unicef.org`

Uniform Code of Military Justice

Uniform Code of Military Justice

The files in this directory contain the US Uniform Code of Military Justice.

Keywords: Military, Law

Audience: Journalists, Politicians, Students, Military Personnel

Details: Free

`gopher://wiretap.spies.com/00/Gov/UCMJ`

Uniform Commercial Code (UCC)

Uniform Commercial Code (UCC)

Articles 1 and 2 of the UCC, adopted with some variations in all 50 states (USA).

Keywords: Commerce, Business Info, Standards

Audience: Politicians, Marketers, Students, Retailers, Lawyers

Details: Free

`http://www.law.cornell.edu/ucc/ucc.table.html`

Unions

Women.labr

This conference features news, announcements, articles, and other information pertaining to the status of women workers in Europe, Latin America and the Caribbean, and Asia.

Keywords: Women, Unions

Audience: Women, Activists, Unions

Details: Costs

User Info.: Establish an account on the nearest APC node. Login, type c for conferences, then type go women.labr. For information on the nearest APC node, contact: APC International Secretariat IBASE E-mail: apcadmin@apc.org Contact: Carlos Afonso (cafonso@ax.apc.org) or APC North American Regional Office E-mail: apcadmin@apc.org Contact: Edie Farwell (efarwell@igc.apc.org)

Notes: ALAI: Agencia Latinoamericana de Informacion E-mail message to APCadmin@apc.org

`telnet://igc.apc.org`

UNITE Archive

UNITE Archive

The User Network Interface to Everything (UNITE) discussion list. The list is a focus for discussion on the concept of a total solution interface with user-friendly, desktop-integrated, access to all network services.

Keywords: Internet, Information Retrieval, Interface Design

Audience: Internet Surfers

Contact: George Munroe, Jill Foster unite-request@mailbase.ac.uk

Details: Free

Files are in: pub/lists/unite

`ftp://mailbase.ac.uk`

United Kingdom

AM/FM

A mailing list for the AM/FM Online Edition, a monthly compilation of news stories concerning the UK radio industry.

Keywords: Radio, United Kingdom, Communications

Audience: Radio Enthusiasts (UK), Communications Specialists, Students (college, graduate)

Contact: Stephen Hebditch listserv@orbital.demon.co.uk

User Info: To subscribe to the list, send an E-mail message to the URL addres below, consisting of a single line reading:

SUB am/fm YourFirstName YourLastName

To send a message to the entire list, address it to: AM/FM@orbital.demon.co.uk

`mailto:listserv@orbital.demon.co.uk`

British National Register of Archives

A multi-volume electronic guide to accessing a wide-variety of archival materials and repositories in the United Kingdom.

Keywords: United Kingdom, History, Business, Information Retrieval

Sponsor: Coombspapers Social Sciences Research Data Bank at ANU (Australian National University).

Audience: Researchers, Anglophiles

Contact: Dr. T. Matthew Ciolek
tmciolek@coombs.anu.edu.au

gopher://coombs.anu.edu.au

ftp:/coombs.anu.edu.au/coombspapers/
otherarchives/uk-nra-archives/

http://coombs.anu.edu.au/
CoombsHome.html

Imperial College Department of Computing ★★

This is the home of the department of Computing, Imperial College, United Kingdom, the UKUUG (UK UNIX User Group) Archive and the DoC Information Service.

Keywords: Computing, United Kingdom, Europe
Audience: Computer Scientists
Contact: imjm@doc.ic.ac.uk
Details: Free

gopher://src.doc.ic.ac.uk

http://src.doc.ic.ac.uk

OLIS (Oxford University Library Information Service) Gopher ★★

OLIS is a network of libraries. It contains all the books from the English, Modern Languages, Social Studies, and Hooke libraries. It also contains books and journals cataloged since September 1988 in the Bodleian and Dependant libraries and the Taylor Institution. Books can be searched in any OLIS library from any location.

Keywords: Libraries, United Kingdom, Europe
Audience: Library Users
Contact: jose@olis.lib.ox.ac.uk
Details: Free

gopher://gopher.lib.ox.ac.uk/00/Info/
OLIS

rec.arts.tv.uk ★

A Usenet newsgroup providing information and discussion about television shows in the United Kingdom.

Keywords: Television, United Kingdom
Audience: Television Viewers, British
User Info: To subscribe to this Usenet newsgroup, you need access to a newsreader.

news:rec.arts.tv.uk

rrl ★★

A mailing list for the discussion of GIS (Geographic Information Systems) in the United Kingdom.

Keywords: GIS (Geographic Information Systems), United Kingdom

Audience: Geographers, Cartographers
Contact: rrl@uk.ac.leicester

mailto:rrl@uk.ac.leicester

soc.culture.british ★

A Usenet newsgroup providing information and discussion about Britain and British culture.

Keywords: Sociology, United Kingdom
Audience: Sociologists
Details: Free
User Info: To subscribe to this Usenet newsgroup, you need access to a newsreader.

news:soc.culture.british

United Nations

Global Change Information Gateway ★★★★

This gateway was created to address environmental data management issues raised by the US Congress, the Administration, and the advisory arms of the Federal policy community. It contains documents related to the UN conference on Environment and Development.

Keywords: UN, Environment, Development, Oceans, Atmosphere
Audience: Environmentalists, Scientists, Researchers, Environmentalists
Profile: [profile needed]
Details: Free
Select from menu as appropriate.

gopher://scilibx.ucsc.edu

UN Criminal Justice Country Profiles ★

UN profiles of world crime in 113 countries.
Keywords: Crime, UN
Sponsor: United Nations
Audience: Lawyers, Legal Professionals, Librarians, Governments
Details: Free
Select from menu as appropriate.

gopher://uacsc2.albany.edu

UN Development Program ★

Provides a detailed history of the UN and its development, as well as an outline of UN Internet programs.

Keywords: United Nations, History (World)
Sponsor: United Nations

Audience: General Public, Historians, Internationalists, Researchers
Details: Free

gopher://nywork1.undp.org

UN Rules ★

Standards, guidelines and international instruments promulgated by the UN.

Keywords: Politics, UN, Standards
Sponsor: United Nations Justice Network (UNCJIN)
Audience: Lawyers, General Public, Internationalists
Details: Free
Select from Menu as appropriate

gopher://uacsc2.albany.edu

UN Resolutions ★

List of selected US and world government documents and UN resolutions.

Keywords: Government (International), United Nations, Government (US)
Sponsor: United Nations
Audience: Historians, Internationalists, Political Scientists
Details: Free

gopher://wiretap.spies.com

un.wcw.doc.eng

This is a read-only conference comprised of official UN documents for the United Nations Fourth World Conference on Women: Action for Equality, Development and Peace, scheduled to take place at the Beijing International Convention Center, Beijing, China, from 4-15 September 1995. The documents are provided by the official Conference Secretariat, are posted as received by the UN Non-Governmental Liaison Service (NGLS).

Keywords: Women, Development (International), Peace, UN, World Conference on Women
Audience: Women, Activists, Non-Governmental Organizations, Feminists
Contact: United Nations Non-Governmental Liaison Service/Edie Farwell
ngls@igc.apc.org, efarwell@igc.apc.org
Details: Costs, Moderated
User Info: Establish an account on the nearest APC node. Login, type c for conferences, then type go un.wcw.doc.eng.
For information on the nearest APC node, contact:
APC International Secretariat IBASE
E-mail: apcadmin@apc.org

telnet://igc.apc.org

un.wcw.doc.fra

This is a read-only conference comprised of official UN documents for the United Nations Fourth World Conference on Women: Action for Equality, Development and Peace, scheduled to take place at the Beijing International Convention Center, Beijing, China, from 4-15 September 1995. The documents are provided by the official Conference Secretariat, are posted as received by the UN Non-Governmental Liaison Service (NGLS).

- **Keywords:** Women, Development (International), Peace, UN, World Conference on Women
- **Audience:** Women, Activists, Non-Governmental Organizations, Feminists
- **Contact:** United Nations Non-Governmental Liaison Service/Edie Farwell ngls@igc.apc.org or efarwell@igc.apc.org
- **Details:** Costs, Moderated
- **User Info.:** Establish an account on the nearest APC node. Login, type c for conferences, then type go un.wcw.doc.fra. For information on the nearest APC node, contact: APC International Secretariat IBASE E-mail: apcadmin@apc.org Contact: Carlos Afonso (cafonso@ax.apc.org) or APC North American Regional Office E-mail: apcadmin@apc.org Contact: Edie Farwell (efarwell@igc.apc.org)
- **Notes:** ALAI: Agencia Latinoamericana de Informacion E-mail message to APCAdmin@apc.org

`telnet://igc.apc.org`

United Nations

Includes full text of UN press releases, UN Conference on Environment and Development reports, UN Development Programme documents, U.N. telephone directories.

- **Keywords:** UN, Environment, Development (International)
- **Audience:** Researchers, Educators, Political Scientists, Environmentalists
- **Details:** Free

`gopher://nywork1.undp.org`

United Press International News - Sports

United Press International News - Sports

Full text of UPI stories and articles.
- **Keywords:** Sports, News Media
- **Sponsor:** United Press International (UPI)
- **Audience:** Sports Enthusiasts
- **Profile:** This gopher allows access to daily UPI news feeds, including sports news. The most current articles available tend to run three to five days behind. This delay is compensated for by UPIs far-ranging coverage of national and international sporting news. Indexed, with back articles from 1992 onwards available.
- **Contact:** UPI
- **Contact:** clarinews@clarinet.com
- **Details:** Free

`gopher://mrfrosty.micro.umn.edu./UPI-data/Today/sports`

United States

State Small Business Profiles

This site contains Small Business Administration reports, which provide statistics on the small business sector in each state.

- **Keywords:** Business, Statistics, Federal Government (US)
- **Sponsor:** U.S. Government, Small Business Administration, in conjunction with the Reference Department of the Thomas Jefferson Library of the University of Missouri-St. Louis
- **Audience:** Business Professionals, Researchers
- **Profile:** The 1993 State Business Profiles bring together an array of statistics on the small business sector in each state. Included is data on small business income and employment trends; women-owned and minority-owned businesses; business closings and formations; and state exports.
- **Contact:** Raleigh Muns srcmuns@umslvma.umsl.edu
- **Details:** Free
- **Notes:** For additional information you can call the Small Business Administration toll free at 1-800-359-2777, or the SBA District Office in Washington, D.C. at (202) 205-6600.

`gopher://umslvma.umsl.edu/11/library/govdocs/states`

United States Geographic Name Server

United States Geographic Name Server

A database searchable by city name or ZIP code, this server provides geographic data including population, longitude and latitude, elevation, county, state, and ZIP codes.

- **Keywords:** Geography, GIS (Geographical Information Systems)
- **Audience:** Geographers, General Public
- **Contact:** pubgopher@pluto.cc.brandeis.edu

`gopher://pluto.cc.brandeis.edu`

United States Geological Survey Home Page

United States Geological Survey Home Page ★★★★

USGS server dedicated to all aspects of Geography and geographic data.

- **Keywords:** GIS, Geography
- **Sponsor:** United States Geological Survey
- **Audience:** Geographers, GIS Professionals, Researchers, Students
- **Profile:** Probably the most comprehensive geography/GIS server on the net. Features include a GIS tuturial, descriptions (and examples) of available USGS data products, access to online spatial data and more.
- **Contact:** webmaster@info.er.usgs.gov
- **Details:** Free, Images, Sounds, Multimedia
- **Notes:** The USGS maintains many servers, this page contains links to most of them, such as EROS Data Center, GLIS and others.

`http://info.er.usgs.gov/USGSHome.html`

Universal Copyright Convention

Universal Copyright Convention

The Universal Copyright Convention as revised at Paris (1971). Convention and protocols were done at Paris on July 24, 1971. It was ratified by the President of the United States of America on August 28, 1972.

- **Keywords:** Copyright, Laws (US), Government (US), Politics (US)
- **Audience:** Lawyers, Students, Politicians, Journalists
- **Details:** Free

`gopher://wiretap.spies.com/00/Gov/Copyright/US.Universal.Copyright.Conv.txt`

Universite de Montreal UDEMATIK Library

Universite de Montreal UDEMATIK Library

The library's holdings are large and wide-ranging and contain significant collections in many fields.

Keywords: Art, Architecture, Economics, Sexology, Social Law, Science, Technology, Literary Studies
Audience: Researchers, Students, General Public
Contact: Joelle or Sebastien Roy
udematik@ere.umontreal.ca
stemp@ere.umontreal.ca
roys@ere.umontreal.ca
User Info: Expect: Login; Send: Application id INFO

`telnet://udematik.umontreal.ca`

Universities

University of Minnesota Gopher Server

The University of Minnesota gopher server provides information about the University of Minnesota, as well as providing access to other universitygopher servers.

Keywords: Universities, Education (College/ University)
Sponsor: University of Minnesota, Minnesota, USA
Audience: Students
Contact: Gopher Development Team
gopher@boombox.micro.umn.edu

`gopher://gopher.tc.umn.edu`

Usenet University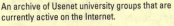

An archive of Usenet university groups that are currently active on the Internet.

Keywords: Education, Universities
Audience: University Students, Educators, Researchers
Details: Free
User Info: File is: pub/doc/uu/FAQ

`ftp://nic.funet.fi`

Universities (History of)

The University of Notre Dame Library

The library's holdings are large and wide-ranging and contain significant collections in many fields.

Keywords: Music (Irish), Ireland, Botany (History of), Ecology, Entomology, Parasitology, Aquatic Biology, Universities (History of), Paleography
Audience: General Public, Researchers, Librarians, Document Delivery Professionals
Details: Free
User Info: Expect: ENTER COMMAND OR HELP:, Send: library; To leave, type x on the command line and press the enter key. At the ENTER COMMAND OR HELP: prompt, type bye and press the enter key.

`telnet://irishmvs.cc.nd.edu`

University of California Santa Barbara Virtual Library

University of California Santa Barbara Virtual Library

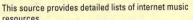

This source provides detailed lists of internet music resources.

Keywords: Music Resources
Sponsor: University of California at Santa Barbara
Audience: Musicians
Profile: This site contains lists pointing to music resources on the internet, including ftp sites, gopher servers, newsgroups, and list servers.
Details: Free
Path is The Subject Collections/The Arts Collections/Music

`gopher://ucsbuxa.ucsb.edu`

University of Chicago Library

University of Chicago Library

The library's holdings are large and wide-ranging and contain significant collections in many fields.

Keywords: Lincoln (Abraham), Kentucky & Ohio River Valley (History of), Balzac (Honore de), American Drama, Cromwell (Oliver), Goethe, Judaica, Italy, Chaucer (Geoffrey), Wells (Ida, Personal Papers of), Douglas (Stephen A.), Italy, Literature (Children's)
Audience: General Public, Researchers, Librarians, Document Delivery Professionals
Details: Free
User Info: Expect: ENTER CLASS, Send: LIB48 3; Expect: CONNECTED, Send: RETURN

`telnet://olorin.uchicago.edu`

University of Colorado at Boulder Library

University of Colorado at Boulder Library

The library's holdings are large and wide-ranging and contain significant collections in many fields.

Keywords: Numismatics, Human Rights, Literature (Children's), Labor Archives, History (US)
Audience: Researchers, Students, General Public
Contact: Donna Pattee
pattee@spot.colorado.edu
Details: Free
User Info: Expect: Login; Send: Culine

`telnet://culine.colorado.edu`

University of Delaware Libraries (DELCAT)

University of Delaware Libraries (DELCAT)

The library's holdings are large and wide-ranging and contain significant collections in many fields.

Keywords: Literature (American), Hemingway (Ernest), Papermaking (History of), Chemistry (History of), Literature (Irish), Delaware
Audience: General Public, Researchers, Librarians, Document Delivery Professionals
Contact: Stuart Glogoff
epo27855@udacsvm.bitnet
Details: Free
User Info: Expect: prompt, Send: RETURN 2-3 times

`telnet://delcat.udel.edu`

`telnet://delcat.acs.udel.edu`

University of Denver Library

University of Denver Library ★★

The library's holdings are large and wide-ranging and contain significant collections in many fields.

Keywords: Folklore Husted (Margaret, Culinary Collection of)
Audience: Researchers, Students, General Public
Contact: Bob Stocker
bstocker@ducair.bitnet
Details: Free
User Info: Expect: Login; Send: Atdu

`telnet://du.edu`

University of Glasgow Information Service (GLANCE) ★★★★

GLANCE provides subject-based information services, including an extensive section on European and world sports.

Keywords: Sports, Soccer, Motor Racing, Mountaineering, Squash, Cricket, Golf, Tennis, Europe, Scotland
Sponsor: University of Glasgow, Glasgow, Scotland
Audience: Sports Enthusiasts, Fitness Enthusiasts, Nature Lovers
Profile: Information at this site includes schedules, results, and statistics for sports such as cricket and soccer. There is also a selection of items on mountaineering.
Contact: Alan Dawson
A.Dawson@uk.ac.gla.compserv
Details: Free

`gopher://govan.cent.gla.ac.uk/Subject/Sports and Rec`

University of Hawaii Library ★★

The library's holdings are large and wide-ranging and contain significant collections in many fields.

Keywords: Asia, European Documents, Book Arts, Hawaii
Audience: General Public, Researchers, Librarians, Document Delivery Professionals
Details: Free
User Info: Expect: enter class, Send: LIB

`telnet://starmaster.uhcc.hawaii.edu`

University of Maine System Library Catalog ★★

The library's holdings are large and wide-ranging and contain significant collections in many fields.

Keywords: Ucadian Studies, St. John Valley (History of), Canadian-American Studies, Geology, Aquaculture, Maine
Audience: General Public, Researchers, Librarians, Document Delivery Professionals
Details: Free
User Info: Expect: login, Send: ursus

`telnet://ursus.maine.edu`

University of Maryland SystemLibrary ★★

The library's holdings are large and wide-ranging and contain significant collections in many fields.

Keywords: Medicine (History of), Nursing, Pharmacology, Microbiology, Aquaculture, Aquatic Chemistry, Toxicology
Audience: General Public, Researchers, Librarians, Document Delivery Professionals
Details: Free
User Info: Expect: Available Services menu; Send: PAC

`telnet://victor.umd.edu`

University of Maryland, College Park ★★

The library's holdings are large and wide-ranging and contain significant collections in many fields.

Keywords: Agriculture, Coastal Marine Biology, Fisheries, Water Quality, Oceanography
Audience: Researchers, Students, General Public
Contact: Janet McLeod
mcleod@umail.umd.edu
Details: Free
User Info: Expect: Login; Send: Atdu

`telnet://info.umd.edu`

University of Michigan Library ★★

The library's holdings are large and wide-ranging and contain significant collections in many fields.

Keywords: Asia, Astronomy, Transportation, Lexicology, Mathematics, Zoology, Geography
Audience: Researchers, Students, General Public
Contact: info@merit.edu
Details: Free
User Info: Expect: Which Host; Send: Help

`telnet://cts.merit.edu`

University of Minnesota Gopher Server ★★

The University of Minnesota gopher server provides information about Minnesota University, as well as providing access to other university gopher servers.

Keywords: Universities, Education (College/University)
Sponsor: University of Minnesota, Minnesota, USA
Audience: Students
Contact: Gopher Development Team
gopher@boombox.micro.umn.edu

`gopher://gopher.tc.umn.edu`

University of Nebraska at Lincoln Library ★★

The library's holdings are large and wide-ranging and contain significant collections in many fields.

Keywords: Slovak Republic, Czech Republic, Folklore, Military History, Latvia, Law (Tax), Law (US)

Audience:	General Public, Researchers, Librarians, Document Delivery Professionals
Details:	Free
User Info:	Expect: login, Send: library

`telnet://unllib.unl.edu`

University of Nevada at Reno Library

University of Nevada at Reno Library ★★

The library's holdings are large and wide-ranging and contain significant collections in many fields.

Keywords:	Basque Studies, Nevada, United Nations, Patents
Audience:	General Public, Researchers, Librarians, Document Delivery Professionals
Details:	Free
User Info:	Expect: login, Send: wolfpac

`telnet://wolfpac.lib.unr.edu`

University of Nevada, Las Vegas Library - Las Vegas, NV

University of Nevada, Las Vegas Library - Las Vegas, NV ★★

The library's holdings are large and wide-ranging and contain significant collections in many fields.

Keywords:	Gambling, Hotel Administration, Nevadiana, Canadian Documents, Nevada State Documents
Audience:	General Public, Researchers, Librarians, Document Delivery Professionals
Contact:	Myoung-Ja Lee Kwon kwon@nevada.edu.
Details:	Free
User Info:	Expect: login; Send: library

`telnet://library.lv-lib.nevada.edu`

University of New Hampshire Videotex Library

University of New Hampshire Videotex Library ★★

The library's holdings are large and wide-ranging and contain significant collections in many fields.

Keywords:	Dance, Folk Music, Milne (A.A. Collection of), Galway (Ireland)
Audience:	Researchers, Students, General Public
Contact:	Robin Tuttle r_tuttle1@unhh.unh.edu
Details:	Free
User Info:	Expect: USERNAME; Send: Student (no password required). Control-z to log off.

`telnet://unhvt@unh.edu`

University of New Mexico Unminfo Library

University of New Mexico Unminfo Library ★★

The library's holdings are large and wide-ranging and contain significant collections in many fields.

Keywords:	Photography (History of), Architecture, Native American Affairs, Land Records
Audience:	Researchers, Students, General Public
Contact:	Art St. George stgeorge@unmb.bitnet
Details:	Free
User Info:	Expect: Login; Send: Unminfo

`telnet://unminfo.unm.edu`

University of North Carolina at Chapel Hill Info Library

University of North Carolina at Chapel Hill Info Library ★★

The library's holdings are large and wide-ranging and contain significant collections in many fields.

Keywords:	North Carolina, Rare Books, Books (Antiquarian)
Audience:	Researchers, Students, General Public
Contact:	Judy Hallman hallman@unc.bitnet
Details:	Free
User Info:	Expect: Login; Send: Info

`telnet://info.oit.unc.edu`

University of North Carolina; Chapel Hill

Newsbrief ★

Provides a variety of information and feature articles, primarily for campus users.

Keywords:	University of North Carolina; Chapel Hill, North Carolina; Information Technology
Sponsor:	Office of Information Technology at the University of North Carolina, Chapel Hill (UNC Chapel Hill)
Audience:	Students, Educators
Contact:	Karen C. Blansfield, Judy Hallman karen@rhumba.acs.unc.edu
Details:	Free
User Info:	To subscribe, send an E-mail message to the URL address below consisting of a single line reading:
	To send a message to the entire list,

`mailto:listserv@uncvm1.bitnet`

University of North Carolina at Greensboro MINERVA Library

University of North Carolina at Greensboro MINERVA Library ★★

The library's holdings are large and wide-ranging and contain significant collections in many fields.

Keywords:	Herbert (George), Film, Dickinson (Emily), Literature (Children's)
Audience:	Researchers, Students, General Public
Details:	Free
User Info:	Expect: Login; Send: Info or MINERVA

`telnet://steffi.acc.uncg.edu`

University of North Carolina at Wilmington SEABOARD Library

University of North Carolina at Wilmington SEABOARD Library ★★

The library's holdings are large and wide-ranging and contain significant collections in many fields.

Keywords:	Marine Biology, Historical Documents
Audience:	Researchers, Students, General Public
Contact:	Eddy Cavenaugh cavenaughd@uncwil.bitnet cavenaughd@vxc.uncwil.edu
Details:	Free
User Info:	Expect: Login; Send: Info

`telnet://vxc.uncwil.edu`

University of Northern Iowa Library

University of Northern Iowa Library ★★

The library's holdings are large and wide-ranging and contain significant collections in many fields.

- Keywords: Art, Business Information, Education, Music, Fiction
- Audience: Researchers, Students, General Public
- Contact: Mike Yohe
  yohe@uni.edu
- Details: Free
- User Info: Expect: Login; Send: Public

`telnet://infosys.uni.edu`

University of Pennsylvania Library- Philadelphia Pa.

University of Pennsylvania Library- Philadelphia Pa. ★★★

The library's holdings are large and wide-ranging and contain significant collections in many fields.

- Keywords: Literature (English), Literature (American), History (World), Medieval Studies, East Asian Studies, Middle Eastern Studies, South Asian Studies, Judaica, Lithuania.
- Audience: Educators, Students, Researchers
- Profile: Access to the central Van Pelt Library and to most of the departmental libraries is restricted to members of the University community on weekends and holidays. Online visitors are advised to call (215) 898-7554 for information on hours and access restrictions.
- Details: Free

`telnet://library.upenn.edu`

University of Pennsylvania PENNINFO Library

University of Pennsylvania PENNINFO Library ★★

The library's holdings are large and wide-ranging and contain significant collections in many fields.

- Keywords: Church History, Spanish Inquisition, Witchcraft, Shakespeare (William), Bibles, Aristotle (Texts of), Fiction, Whitman (Walt), French Revolution, Drama (French), Literature (English), Literature (Spanish)
- Audience: Researchers, Students, General Public
- Contact: Al DSouza
  penninfo-admin@dccs.upenn.edu
  dsouza@dccs.upenn.edu
- Details: Free
- User Info: Expect: Login; Send: Public

`telnet://penninfo.upenn.edu`

University of Pennsylvania School of Medicine Library

University of Pennsylvania School of Medicine Library ★★

The library's holdings are large and wide-ranging and contain significant collections in many fields.

- Keywords: Health Care, Nursing, History, Health
- Audience: Researchers, Students, General Public
- Details: Free
- User Info: Expect: Login; Send: Public

`telnet://penninfo.upenn.edu`

University of Puerto Rico Library

University of Puerto Rico Library ★★

The library's holdings are large and wide-ranging and contain significant collections in many fields.

- Keywords: Computer Science, Education, Nursing, Agriculture, Economics
- Audience: Researchers, Students, General Public
- Details: Free
  After Locator: telnet://, press Tab twice. Type DIAL VTAM. Enter NOTIS. Press Return. On the blank screen, type LUUP.

`telnet://136.145.2.10`

University of Puget Sound Library

University of Puget Sound Library ★★

The library's' holdings are large and wide-ranging and contain significant collections in many fields.

- Keywords: Education, Literature (General), Music, Natural Science, Theology
- Audience: Researchers, Students, General Public
- Details: Free
- User Info: Expect: Login; Send: Library

`telnet://192.124.98.2`

University of Rochester Library

University of Rochester Library ★★

The library's holdings are large and wide-ranging and contain significant collections in many fields.

- Keywords: Architecture, Art History, Photography, Literature (Asian), Lasers, Geology, Statistics, Optics, Medieval Studies
- Audience: Researchers, Students, General Public
- Details: Free
- User Info: Expect: Login; Send: Library

`telnet://128.151.226.71`

University of Saskatchewan Libraries

University of Saskatchewan Libraries ★★

A major Canadian University library with access to library catalogs archives, and Canadian Government documents.

- Keywords: Canada, Government (International)
- Sponsor: University of Saskatchewan
- Audience: Canadians, General Public
- Profile: The University of Saskatchewan Libraries maintain online databases of their collections archives, and catalogs. The libraries are a voluminous resource for the study of Canada, Canadian government, and Canadian-American issues.
- Notes: Login: sonia

`telnet://sklib.usask.ca`

University of Southern Colorado Library

University of Southern Colorado Library ★★

The library's holdings are large and wide-ranging and contain significant collections in many fields.

- Keywords: History (US)
- Audience: Researchers, Students, General Public
- Details: Free
- User Info: Expect: OK Prompt, Send: Login Pub1; Expect: Password: usc

`telnet://starburst.uscolo.edu`

University of Tennessee at Chatanooga Library

University of Tennessee at Chatanooga Library ★★

The library's holdings are large and wide-ranging and contain significant collections in many fields.

- Keywords: Civil War, Literature (American)
- Audience: Researchers, Students, General Public
- Contact: Randy Whitson
  rwhitson@utcvmutc.edu
- Details: Free
- User Info: Expect: OK prompt; Send: Login pub1; Expect: Password, Send: Usc

telnet://library.utc.edu

University of Tennessee at Knoxville Library

University of Tennessee at Knoxville Library ★★

The library's holdings are large and wide-ranging and contain significant collections in many fields.

- Keywords: Native American Affairs, Congress (US), Folklore, Travel (History of)
- Audience: Researchers, Students, General Public
- Details: Free
- User Info: Expect: OK Prompt; Send: Login pub1; Expect: Password, Send: Usc

telnet://opac.lib.utk.edu

University of Tennessee at Memphis Library

University of Tennessee at Memphis Library ★★

The library's holdings are large and wide-ranging and contain significant collections in many fields.

- Keywords: Tennessee, Literature (American)
- Audience: Researchers, Students, General Public
- Details: Costs
- User Info: Expect: Username Prompt, Send: Harvey

telnet://utmem1.utmem.edu

University of Texas at Austin Library

University of Texas at Austin Library ★★

The library's holdings are large and wide-ranging and contain significant collections in many fields.

- Keywords: Music, Natural Science, Nursing, Science Technology, Behavioral Science, Social Work, Computer Science, Engineering, Latin American Studies, Middle Eastern Studies
- Audience: Researchers, Students, General Public
- Details: Free
- User Info: Expect: Blank Screen, Send: Return; Expect: Go, Send: Return; Expect: Enter Terminal Type, Send: vt100

  Note: Some databases are restricted to UT Austin users only.

telnet://utcat.utexas.edu

University of Texas at Austin Tarlton Law Library

University of Texas at Austin Tarlton Law Library ★★

The library's holdings are large and wide-ranging and contain significant collections in many fields.

- Keywords: British Commonwealth Law, Constitutional Law, Law (International), Human Rights
- Audience: Researchers, Students, General Public
- Details: Free
- User Info: Expect: Login, Send: Library

telnet://tallons.law.utexas.edu

University of Texas at Galveston (Medical Branch) Library

University of Texas at Galveston (Medical Branch) Library ★★

The library's holdings are large and wide-ranging and contain significant collections in many fields.

- Keywords: Health Sciences, Biomedicine, Nursing
- Audience: Researchers, Students, General Public
- Details: Free
- User Info: Expect: Login, Send: Library

telnet://ibm.gal.utexas.edu

University of Texas Health Science Center (UTHSCSA) Biomedical Library Information System

University of Texas Health Science Center (UTHSCSA) Biomedical Library Information System ★★

- Keywords: Medicine, Libraries
- Sponsor: Audie L. Murphy Memorial Veterans' Administration Hospital, San Antonio, TX
- Audience: Medical Professionals, Students
- Details: Free

telnet://lis@athena.uthscsa.edu

University of Texas Health Science Center at San Antonio Library

University of Texas Health Science Center at San Antonio Library ★★

The library's holdings are large and wide-ranging and contain significant collections in many fields.

- Keywords: Dentistry, Nursing, Veterinary Science, Ambulatory Care, Obstetrics/Gynecology, Pediatrics
- Audience: Researchers, Students, General Public
- Details: Free
- User Info: Expect: Login, Send: LIS

telnet://athena.uthscsa.edu

University of Texas Health Science Center at Tyler Library

University of Texas Health Science Center at Tyler Library ★★

The library's holdings are large and wide-ranging and contain significant collections in many fields.

- Keywords: Biochemistry, Cardiopulmonary Medicine, Cell Biology, Molecular Biology

Audience: Researchers, Students, General Public
Details: Free
User Info: Expect: Username Prompt, Send: LIS

`telnet://athena.uthscsa.edu`

University of Texas Southwestern Medical Center Library

University of Texas Southwestern Medical Center Library

The library's holdings are large and wide-ranging and contain significant collections in many fields.

Keywords: Biomedical Science
Audience: Researchers, Students, General Public
Details: Free
User Info: Expect: Login, Send: TIntutsw; Expect: Password, Send: Library

`telnet://library.swmed.edu`

University of Texas-Pan American Library

University of Texas-Pan American Library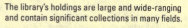

The library's holdings are large and wide-ranging and contain significant collections in many fields.

Keywords: Lower Rio Grande Valley (History of), Mexican-American Studies
Audience: Researchers, Students, General Public
Details: Free
User Info: Expect: Username Prompt, Send: packey

`telnet://panam2.panam.edu`

University of the Pacific Library

University of the Pacific Library

The library's holdings are large and wide-ranging and contain significant collections in many fields.

Keywords: Pharmacology, Americana (Western)
Audience: Researchers, Students, General Public
Details: Free
User Info: Expect: Login, Send: Library

`telnet://pacificat.lib.uop.edu`

University of Toledo Library

University of Toledo Library

The library's holdings are large and wide-ranging and contain significant collections in many fields.

Keywords: Business, Great Lakes Area, Humanities, International Relations, Psychology, Science
Audience: Researchers, Students, General Public
Details: Free
User Info: Expect: Enter one of the following commands..., Send: DIAL MVS; Expect: dialed to mvs ####; Send: UTMOST

`telnet://uofto1.utoledo.edu`

University of Tulsa Library

University of Tulsa Library

The library's holdings are large and wide-ranging and contain significant collections in many fields.

Keywords: Literature (American), Petroleum, Geology
Audience: Researchers, Students, General Public
Details: Free
User Info: Expect: Username Prompt, Send: LIAS

`telnet://vax2.utulsa.edu`

University of Utah Library

University of Utah Library

The library's holdings are large and wide-ranging and contain significant collections in many fields.

Keywords: Western America, Middle Eastern Studies, Geology, Mining
Audience: Researchers, Students, General Public
Details: Free
User Info: Expect: Command Line, Send: Dial Unis

`telnet://lib.utah.edu`

University of Wales College of Medicine Library Online Catalog

University of Wales College of Medicine Library Online Catalog

Keywords: Medicine, Libraries
Sponsor: University of Wales, United Kingdom

Audience: Health Care Professionals, Students
Details: Free
User Info: Expect: login, Send: 'janet'; Expect: password; Send: 'janet'

`telnet://sun.nsf.ac.uk`

University of Wisconsin at Milwaukee Library

University of Wisconsin at Milwaukee Library

The library's holdings are large and wide-ranging and contain significant collections in many fields.

Keywords: Art, Architecture, Business, Cartography, Geography, Geology, Urban Studies, Literature (English), Literature (American)
Audience: Researchers, Students, General Public
Details: Free
User Info: Expect: Login, Send: Lib; Expect: vDIAL prompt, Send: Library

`telnet://uwmcat.lib.uwm.edu`

University of Wisconsin at Oshkosh Library

University of Wisconsin at Oshkosh Library

The library's holdings are large and wide-ranging and contain significant collections in many fields.

Keywords: Business, Liberal Education, Nursing
Audience: Researchers, Students, General Public
Details: Free
User Info: Expect: Login; Send: Lib; Expect: vDIAL Prompt, Send: Library

`telnet://polk.cis.uwosh.edu`

University of Wisconsin at Platteville Library

University of Wisconsin at Platteville Library

The library's holdings are large and wide-ranging and contain significant collections in many fields.

Keywords: Business, Industry

Audience: Researchers, Students, General Public
Details: Free
User Info: Expect: Login, Send: Lib; Expect: vDIAL Prompt, Send: Library

`telnet://137.104.128.44`

University of Wisconsin at Stout Library

University of Wisconsin at Stout Library ★★

The library's holdings are large and wide-ranging and contain significant collections in many fields.

Keywords: Mathematics, Business, Fashion Merchandising, Home Economics, Hospitality, Tourism Industry, Hotel Administration, Restaurant Management, Microelectronics
Audience: Researchers, Students, General Public
Details: Free
User Info: Expect: Login, Send: Lib; Expect: vDIAL Prompt, Send: Library

`telnet://lib.uwstout.edu`

University of Wisconsin Eau Claire Library

University of Wisconsin Eau Claire Library ★★

The library's holdings are large and wide-ranging and contain significant collections in many fields.

Keywords: Health Sciences, Business, Nursing, Education
Audience: Researchers, Students, General Public
Details: Free
User Info: Expect: Service Name, Send: Victor

`telnet://lib.uwec.edu`

University of Wisconsin Extension Program in Independent Study

University of Wisconsin Extension Program in Independent Study

A gopher containing information about courses of study at the University of Wisconsin Extension Program in Independent Study. Over fifty-five disciplines, from Arabic to Womens Studies, are represented.

Keywords: Education (Distance), Independent Study
Sponsor: University of Wisconsin Extension Program in Independent Study, Madison, Wisconsin, USA
Audience: Professionals, Educators, Students
Notes: Information is free, but fees are charged for courses. Contact the Advisor to Students at 608-263-2055, or write University of Wisconsin Extension Program in Independent Study, 104 Extension Building, 432 North Lake Street, Madison, WI 53706-1498

`gopher://gopher.uwex.edu`

University of Wisconsin Green Bay Library

University of Wisconsin Green Bay Library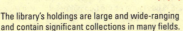

The library's holdings are large and wide-ranging and contain significant collections in many fields.

Keywords: Economics, Environmental Studies, Music, Natural Science
Audience: Researchers, Students, General Public
Details: Free
User Info: Expect: Service Name, Send: Victor

`telnet://gbls2k.uwgb.edu`

University of Wisconsin River Falls Library

University of Wisconsin River Falls Library ★★

The library's holdings are large and wide-ranging and contain significant collections in many fields.

Keywords: Agriculture, Education, History (US)
Audience: Researchers, Students, General Public
Details: Free
User Info: Expect: Service Name, Send: Victor

`telnet://davee.dl.uwrf.edu`

University of Wisconsin Stevens Point Library

University of Wisconsin Stevens Point Library ★★

The library's holdings are large and wide-ranging and contain significant collections in many fields.

Keywords: Education, Environmental Studies, Ethnic Studies, History (US)
Audience: Researchers, Students, General Public
Details: Free
User Info: Expect: Login; Send: Lib; Expect: vDIAL Prompt, Send: Library

`telnet://lib.uwsp.edu`

University of Wisconsin Superior Library

University of Wisconsin Superior Library

The library's holdings are large and wide-ranging and contain significant collections in many fields.

Keywords: Educational Policy, Government (US)
Audience: Researchers, Students, General Public
Details: Free
User Info: Expect: Login, Send: Lib; Expect: vDIAL Prompt, Send: Library

`telnet://sail.uwsuper.edu`

University Planning

SCUP BITNET NEWS ★★★

Designed to promote the mission of the society and support its activities. Society for College and University Planning (SCUP) Bitnet News provides frequent and timely exchange of information among members as well as nonmembers interested in higher-education planning through the use of bitnet.

Keywords: University Planning
Sponsor: Society for College and University Planning
Audience: Planners
Profile: Contents of the newsletter are selected on the basis of interest and value to the membership. Particular attention is given to information that advances the state-of-the-art in planning; improves the understanding and application of the tools, techniques, processes and strategies of planning; advances the professional development of the membership; and widens the base of support for planning in higher education.
Contact: Joanne E. MacRae USERTD8Q@UMICHUM.bitnet
Details: Free
  Send an electronic mail note to the editor (Joanne Cate: budlao@uccvma) or the associate editor (Betsey Creekmore: pa94858@utkvm1)

`mailto:Joanne Cate: budlao@uccvma.bitnet`

SCUPMA-L: Society of College and University Planners, Mid-Atlantic Region

This newsletter contains short news pieces and announcements about events of interest to the membership.

Keywords: University Planning
Audience: University Planners
Contact: Debbie Furlong
OPIR1@AUVM.bitnet
Details: Free

`mailto:opir1@auvm.bitnet`

UNIX (Operating System)

comp.unix.aix

A Usenet newsgroup providing information and discussion about IBM's version of UNIX.

Keywords: Computer Systems, Internet, UNIX
Audience: Computer Users, UNIX Users, IBM Users
User Info: To subscribe to this Usenet newsgroup, you need access to a newsreader.

`news:comp.unix.aix`

comp.unix.questions

A Usenet newsgroup providing discussion and questions for those learning UNIX.

Keywords: Computers, UNIX
Audience: Computer Users, UNIX Users
User Info: To subscribe to this Usenet newsgroup, you need access to a newsreader.

`news:comp.unix.questions`

comp.unix.wizards

A Usenet newsgroup providing discussion and questions for true UNIX wizards.

Keywords: UNIX
Audience: Computer Users, Unix Users
User Info: To subscribe to this Usenet newsgroup, you need access to a newsreader.

`news:comp.unix.wizards`

DECnews-UNIX

DECnews for UNIX is published by Digital Equipment Corporation every three weeks and contains product and service information of interest to the Digital UNIX community.

Keywords: DEC, UNIX
Audience: UNIX Users
Contact: Russ Jones
decnews-unix-request@pa.dec.com
User Info: To subscribe to the list, send an e-mail message requesting a subscription to the URL address below.

To send a message to the entire list, address it to: decnews-unix-request@pa.dec.com

To subscribe, send e-mail to decnews-unix@pa.dec.com with a subject line of Subject: subscribe abstract. Please include your name and telephone number in the body of the subscription request.

`mailto:decnews-unix-request@pa.dec.com`

Dual-Personalities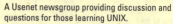

Discussion, maintenance/survival tips, and commercial offerings for the System/83 UNIX box made by the now-defunct DUAL Systems Corp. of Berkeley, as well as similar machines using the IEEE-696 bus (such as the CompuPro 8/16E with Root/Unisoft UNIX).

Keywords: UNIX
Audience: UNIX Users
Contact: dual-personalities-request@darwin.uucp
Details: Free
User Info: To subscribe to the list, send an e-mail message requesting a subscription to the URL address below.

To send a message to the entire list, address it to: dual-personalities-request@darwin.uucp

`mailto:dual-personalities-request@darwin.uucp`

info-UNIX

Info-UNIX is intended for Question/Answer discussion, where "novice" systems administrators can pose questions.

Keywords: UNIX (Operating System), Systems Administration
Audience: UNIX Systems Administrators
Contact: Mike Muuss
mike@brl.mil
User Info: To subscribe to the list, send an e-mail message requesting a subscription to the URL address below.

`mailto:info-UNIX@brl.mil`

Metacard-list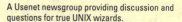

Discussion of the MetaCard product from MetaCard Corp. MetaCard is an application-development system similar to Apple's HyperCard product; it runs on a variety of popular platforms in a UNIX/X11/Motif environment.

Keywords: MetaCard, Computing, UNIX
Audience: MetaCard Users, Computer Users
Contact: metacard-list-owner@grot.starconn.com
Details: Free
User Info: To subscribe to the list, send an e-mail message requesting a subscription to the URL address below.

`mailto:metacard-list@grot.starconn.com`

ORA-NEWS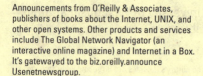

Announcements from O'Reilly & Associates, publishers of books about the Internet, UNIX, and other open systems. Other products and services include The Global Network Navigator (an interactive online magazine) and Internet in a Box. It's gatewayed to the biz.oreilly.announce Usenetnewsgroup.

Keywords: Internet, UNIX, Usenet
Audience: Internet Surfers, Usenet Users, UNIX Users
Contact: listown@online.ora.com
Details: Free, Moderated
User Info: To subscribe to the list, send an e-mail message requesting a subscription to the URL address below.

To send a message to the entire list, address it to: ora-news@online.ora.com

`mailto:listproc@online.ora.com`

Pubnet

A mailing list for the discussion of administration and use of public-access computer systems, primarily UNIX systems. The list also answers questions about setting up or running a public-access system

Keywords: Computer Systems, UNIX
Audience: Computer System Designers, UNIX Users
Contact: Chip Rosenthal
pubnet-request@chinacat.unicom.com
Details: Free
User Info: To subscribe to the list, send an e-mail message requesting a subscription to the URL address below. To send a message to the entire list, address it to: pubnet@chinacat.unicom.com

`mailto:pubnet-request@chinacat.unicom.com`

Std-UNIX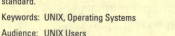

Discussion of UNIX standards, particularly the IEEE P1003 Portable Operating System Environment draft standard.

Keywords: UNIX, Operating Systems
Audience: UNIX Users
Contact: Sean Eric Fagan
sef@uunet.uu.net
Details: Free, Moderated
User Info: To subscribe to the list, send an e-mail message requesting a subscription to the URL address below.

`mailto:sef@uunet.uu.net`

UNIX-wizards ★

Distribution list for people maintaining UNIX machines.

Keywords:	UNIX, Operating Systems
Audience:	UNIX System Administrators
Contact:	Mike Muuss mike@brl.mil
Details:	Free
User Info:	To subscribe to the list, send an e-mail message requesting a subscription to the URL address below.

`mailto:UNIX-wizards-request@brl.mil`

Urban Planning

Virginia Commonwealth University Library ★★

The library's holdings are large and wide-ranging and contain significant collections in many fields.

Keywords:	Art, Biology, Humanities, Journalism, Music, Urban Planning
Audience:	Researchers, Students, General Public
Details:	Free
User Info:	Expect: Login; Send: Opub

`telnet://vcuvm1.ucc.vcu.edu`

Urban Studies

alt.folklore.urban ★

A Usenet newsgroup providing information and discussion about urban legends and urban myths.

Keywords:	Urban Studies, Folklore
Audience:	Story Tellers, General Public
User Info:	To subscribe to this Usenet newsgroup, you need access to a newsreader.

`news:alt.folklore.urban`

University of Wisconsin at Milwaukee Library ★★

The library's holdings are large and wide-ranging and contain significant collections in many fields.

Keywords:	Art, Architecture, Business, Cartography, Geography, Geology, Urban Studies, Literature (English), Literature (American)
Audience:	Researchers, Students, General Public
Details:	Free
User Info:	Expect: Login, Send: Lib; Expect: vDIAL prompt, Send: Library

`telnet://uwmcat.lib.uwm.edu`

US

North American Free Trade Agreement (NAFTA) ★

The agreement between the governments of Canada, the United Mexican States, and the United States of America to establish a free trade area in North America.

Keywords:	Trade, Government (US), Mexico, Canada, Free Trade, NAFTA
Audience:	Journalists, Politicians, Economists, Students
Details:	Free

`gopher://wiretap.spies.com/00/Gov/NAFTA`

U.S. Army Area Handbooks

U.S. Army Area Handbooks ★★★

This gopher provides detailed political, cultural, historical, military, and economic information on hot spots in world affairs, everywhere from China to Yugoslavia.

Keywords:	Military (US), Politics (International), Government (US Federal)
Sponsor:	The Thomas Jefferson Library at the University of Missouri at St. Louis, St. Louis, Missouri, USA
Audience:	Journalists, Government Officials, Travelers/Tourists
Profile:	The Army Area Handbooks, which provide a comprehensive overview of several important countries including Japan, China, Israel, Egypt, South Korea, and Somalia, are only one of the many government resources available at this site. Other full-text documents include the proposed 1995 federal budget, the CIA world fact book, the NAFTA agreement, health care proposals currently before Congress, and statistics for the U.S. industrial outlook. Also has links to many federal gophers and information systems.
Contact:	Joe Rottman rottman@umslvma.umsl.edu
Details:	Free

`gopher://umslvma.umsl.edu/11/library/govdocs`

US Army Corps of Engineers

US Army Corps of Engineers ★★

This site provides information on the organization, programs, news, facilities, and activities of the US Army Corps of Engineers.

Keywords:	Military, Engineering
Sponsor:	Cold Regions Research and Engineering Laboratory, under
Audience:	Military Personnel, Engineers, Researchers
Contact:	www@usace.mil
Details:	Free

`http://www.usace.mil/usace.html`

US Bureau of the Census Gopher

U.S. Bureau of the Census Gopher

A gopher offering official Census data and services directly from the Census Bureau.

Keywords:	Census Data, Demography, Statistics
Sponsor:	US Census Bureau
Audience:	Journalists, Government Officials, General Public
Profile:	A wealth of demographic and economic data from the Census Bureau. Information available includes population estimates, financial data from state and local governments, and assorted statistical briefs. This gopher also has details on the offices, programs, and personnel of the Bureau itself, as well as links to other federal information systems and sources of Census data.
Contact:	gatekeeper@census.gov
Details:	Free, Images

`gopher://gopher.census.gov`

`http://www.census.gov`

US Civil War Reading List

U.S. Civil War Reading List ★★★

A major directory on abolitionism, providing access to a broad range of resources (library catalogs, databases, and servers) via the Internet.

Keywords:	History (US), Abolitionism
Audience:	General Public, Historians

US Civil War Reading List

Profile: The Suggested Civil War Reading List contains 61 books, several of them with multiple volumes, as well as an 11-hour documentary film and a CD of Civil War era songs. The material is sorted into general categories: General Histories of the War, Causes of the War and History to 1861, Slavery and Southern Society, Reconstruction, Biographies and Autobiographies, Source Documents and Official Records, Unit Histories and Soldiers' Reminiscences, Fiction, Specific Battles and Campaigns, Strategies and Tactics, The Experience of Soldiers.

Contact: Stephen Schmidt
whale@leland.Stanford.edu

http://www.cis.ohio-state.edu/hypertext/faq/usenet/civil-war-usa/reading-list/faq.html

US Consumer Product Safety Commission (CPSC)

U.S. Consumer Product Safety Commission (CPSC)

The CPSC's mission is to protect the public from defective and potentially dangerous consumer products. This gopher has archives of CPSC press releases and action reports from 1990-1994, as well as a calendar of upcoming events and guidelines for reporting potentially dangerous products to the CPSC.

Keywords: Safety, Consumerism, Federal Law (US)
Sponsor: US Consumer Product Safety Commission
Audience: Consumers, Activists
Contact: pweddle@cpsc.gov
Notes: You can call the CPSC at their toll-free hotline at (800) 638-2772.

gopher://cpsc.gov

US Department of Education Online Library

US Department of Education Online Library

A resource for information on federal programs, including full-text of the GOALS 2000, Educate America Act, The Prisoners of Time Report, and other documents regarding education legislation, reports, and information.

Keywords: Education, Law (US)
Sponsor: US Department of Education
Audience: Educators, Students, Legislators, Researchers

http://www.ed.gov

gopher://gopher.ed.gov

ftp://ftp.ed.gov

US Department of the Interior

US Department of the Interior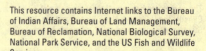

This resource contains Internet links to the Bureau of Indian Affairs, Bureau of Land Management, Bureau of Reclamation, National Biological Survey, National Park Service, and the US Fish and Wildlife Service.

Keywords: Government (US), Environmental Policies
Sponsor: US Department of the Interior Survey, Office of Public Affairs
Audience: Biologists, Geologists, Researchers, Environmentalists

http://info.er.usgs.gov/doi/doi.html

US Federal Government

FedWorld Bulletin Board

A BBS run by the National Technical Information Service, with many databases of government documents, job announcements, and connections to other federal government online services.

Keywords: US Federal Government, Government Documents
Sponsor: US National Technical Information Service
Audience: General Public, Researchers
Profile: This is the place to begin any kind of search for US federal government records and publications. The GateWay option connects you to the Library of Congress, Supreme Court opinions, government job listing, the various Federal Reserve Banks, Congressional Bills and studies, etc.

To establish an account: Expect: login, Send: new

Notes: Mail to sysop once you have an account

telnet://fedworld.gov

US General Accounting Office Transitional Reports

US General Accounting Office Transitional Reports

A major directory on accounting, providing access to a broad range of related resources (library catalogs, databases, and servers) via the Internet.

Keywords: Government (US), Finance
Audience: Politicians, Government Workers

Profile: Contains full-text documents of the Transitional Reports for the U.S. General Accounting Office. Reports includes Budget Issues, Investment, Government Management Issues, Financial Management Issues, Health Care Reform, National Security Issues, International Trade Issues, etc.

Contact: kh3@cu.nih.gov

gopher://thor.ece.uc.edu

US Geological Survey Server

US Geological Survey Server

This resource containis publications, USGS research programs, technology transfer partnerships, and fact sheets about geology.

Keywords: Biology, Geology, Natural Science
Sponsor: US Geological Survey
Audience: Biologists, Geologists, Researchers, Naturalists
Contact: Systems Operator
webmaster@info.er.usgs.gov

http://info.er.usgs.gov

US Government

NTIS FedWorld

Keywords: US Government, Federal Databases
Audience: General Public, Researchers, Business Professionals, Politicians
Contact: Bob Bunge
webmaster@fedworld.gov

http://www.fedworld.gov

telnet://fedworld.gov

ftp://ftp.fedworld.gov

US Government Publications

Voice of America and Worldnet

A gopher server for the Voice of America and Worldnet. Includes full-text transcripts of VOA news reports, press releases, and announcements.

Keywords: US Government Publications, News Media, Radio, International Communication
Sponsor: United States Information Agency

Audience: Journalists, Government Officials, General Public
Contact: info@voa.gov, letters-usa@VOA.GOV (for correspondence from inside the U.S.)

`gopher://gopher.voa.gov`

US Government Regulations

TRANS (The Transportation Library)

The Transportation Library contains federal transportation case law, statutes and agency decisions.

Keywords: Transportation Law, US Government Regulations, Aviation, Railroad, Trucking Industry
Audience: Lawyers
Profile: The Transportation library contains federal transportation case law, statutes and agency decisions. The major emphasis of the library is on three modes of transportation (aviation, railroad and trucking) and how those modes are regulated by the federal government. Agency decisions are provided from the Interstate Commerce Commission, Department of Transportation and the National Transportation Safety Board (NTSB).
Contact: New Sales Group at 800-227-4908 or 513-859-5398 inside the US, or 1-513-865-7981 for all inquires outside the US.
User Info: To subscribe, contact Mead directly.
To examine the Lexis user guide, you can access it at the ftp site of the University of Texas at Austin at the URL address: ftp://ftp.cc.utexas.edu
The files are in: /pub/res-services/LEXIS

`telnet://nex.meaddata.com`

US Holocaust Memorial Museum

US Holocaust Memorial Museum

The web site of the newly-opened (April, 1993) US Holocaust Memorial Museum in Washington D.C.

Keywords: Judaism, Jewish Politics, Holocaust, History (Jewish)
Audience: Jews, Holocaust Researchers, Israelis, Students
Profile: This resource contains files on educational programs, general information about the Holocaust Research Institute, a contact list for the Association of Holocaust Organizations, and a searchable archive of related materials.

`http://www.ushmm.org`

US House of Representatives Gopher

US House of Representatives Gopher

The online service of the U.S. House of Representatives.

Keywords: Congress (US), Federal Law (US), Government Records (US)
Sponsor: House Administration Committee Internet Working Group
Audience: Government Officials, Journalists, Educators (K-12), General Public
Profile: Provides access to information on members and committees of the House of Representatives, as well as full-text of bills before the House. Includes education resources on the legislative process, Congressional directories, and House schedules. Also has information for visitors (including area maps), as well as access to other federal information systems.
Contact: House Internet Working Group househlp@hr.house.gov

`gopher://gopher.house.gov`

US Law

LAWREV (Law Review Library)

The Law Review Library contains law reviews, American Bar Association publications, American Institute of Certified Public Accountants periodicals, and other materials. The present focus concentrates on both state and national issues of legal significance.

Keywords: US Law, Analysis, Law Reviews, Journals
Audience: Lawyers
Profile: The Law Review library currently consists of over 70 law reviews, several American Bar Association publicatons and American Institute of Certified Public Accountants periodicals, an Environmental Law Institute publication, ALR and LEd2d articles, two leading legal indices and a number of Warren Gorham & Lamont tax journals. The present focus concentrates on both state and national issues of legal significance.
Contact: New Sales Group at 800-227-4908 or 513-859-5398 inside the US, or 1-513-865-7981 for all inquires outside the US.
User Info: To subscribe, contact Mead directly.
To examine the Lexis user guide, you can access it at the ftp site of the University of Texas at Austin at the URL address: ftp://ftp.cc.utexas.edu
The files are in: /pub/ref-services/LEXIS

`telnet://nex.meaddata.com`

`http://www.meaddata.com`

US National Park Service

Park Rangers

This list is primarily for anyone working or interested in working as a ranger (general, interpretive, and so on) for the US National Park Service, but rangers from state and county agencies and from other countries are also welcome. The group discusses numerous topics related to this profession.

Keywords: US National Park Service, Government (US)
Audience: Park Rangers
Contact: Cynthia Dorminey 60157903@wsuvm1.csc.wsu.edu
Details: Free
User Info: To subscribe to the list, send an e-mail message requesting a subscription to the URL address below. To send a message to the entire list, address it to: 60157903@wsuvm1.csc.wsu.edu

`mailto:60157903@wsuvm1.csc.wsu.edu`

US Patents

US Patents

Complete patent information of all claims of U.S. patents issued since 1971.

Keywords: Patents, Intellectual Property, Trademarks
Sponsor: Derwent, Inc.
Audience: Patent Attorneys, Patent Agents, Librarians, Researchers
Profile: Includes complete front page information, plus all claims of US patents issued since 1971. Merged file contains approximately 1.4 million records. Updated weekly.
Contact: paul.albert@neteast.com
User Info: To subscribe contact Orbit-Questel directly.

`telnet://orbit.com`

US Patent and Trademark Office Database

U.S. Patent and Trademark Office Database

A database of patents issued in 1994 by the U.S. Patent and Trademark Office, including a searchable index.

Keywords:	Patents, Databases, Inventions, Business
Sponsor:	New York University School of Business
Audience:	Inventors, General Public
Contact:	questions@town.hall.org

`gopher://town.hall.org/patent`

US/Mexico Border Discussion List

US/Mexico Border Discussion List

This group provides a forum for the discussion of issues pertaining to the US/Mexico border environment.

Keywords:	Mexico, Environment, Latin American Culture
Sponsor:	The US Environmental Protection Agency
Audience:	Activists, Environmentalists, Urban Planners
Details:	Free
User Info:	To subscribe to the list, send a message to the URL address below consisting of a single line reading:
	SUB us_mexborder YourFirstName YourLastName
	To send a message to the entire list, address it to: us_mexborder@unixmail.rtpnc.epa.gov

`mailto:listserver@unixmail.rtpnc.epa.gov`

USDA Agricultural Extension Service

USDA Agricultural Extension Service

Includes information from the USDA (United States Department of Agriculture) Extension Service, National Agriculture Library, and Americans Communicating Electronically (ACE)

Keywords:	Agriculture
Audience:	Farmers, Agriculturalists, Educators
Profile:	[profile needed]
Details:	Free

`gopher://cyfer.esusda.gov`

Usenet

E-mail Usenet

E-mail Usenet allows the user to post to a newsgroup via e-mail.

Keywords:	Internet, Services, E-mail, Usenet
Audience:	Internet Surfers
Details:	Free

`mailto://hierarchy-group-name@cs.utexas.edu`

GIS-L and comp.infosystems.gis FAQ

HTML and ASCII document describing all aspects of GIS on the Internet.

Keywords:	GIS, USENET
Audience:	GIS Users
Profile:	Contains information on data sources, formats, software info and pointers to other Internet GIS info sources.
Contact:	Lisa Nyman lnyman@census.gov
Details:	Free
	WWW and FTP
Notes:	ASCII version also available.

`http://www.cencus.gov/geo/gis/faqindex.html`

`ftp://ftp.cencus.gov/pub/geo/gis-faq.txt`

Neci-announce

This is the announcement forum of New England Community Internet, an organization dedicated to making Usenet and Internet accessible to the public without economic or technical barriers. The group is developing ways to bring IP connectivity at low cost into homes and nonprofit organizations.

Keywords:	Internet, Usenet
Audience:	Internet Surfers, Usenet Users
Contact:	neci-announce-request@pioneer.ci.net
Details:	Free
User Info:	To subscribe to the list, send an e-mail message requesting a subscription to the URL address below.

`mailto:neci-announce-request@pioneer.ci.net`

Neci-digest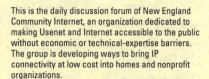

This is the daily discussion forum of New England Community Internet, an organization dedicated to making Usenet and Internet accessible to the public without economic or technical-expertise barriers. The group is developing ways to bring IP connectivity at low cost into homes and nonprofit organizations.

Keywords:	Internet, Usenet
Audience:	Internet Surfers, Usenet Users
Contact:	neci-digest-request@pioneer.ci.net
Details:	Free
User Info:	To subscribe to the list, send an e-mail message requesting a subscription to the URL address below.

`mailto:neci-digest-request@pioneer.ci.net`

Neci-discuss

This is the general discussion forum of New England Community Internet, an organization dedicated to making Usenet and Internet accessible to the public without economic or technical-expertise barriers. The group is developing ways to bring IP connectivity at low cost into homes and nonprofit organizations.

Keywords:	Internet, Usenet
Audience:	Internet Surfers, Usenet Users
Contact:	neci-discuss-request@pioneer.ci.net
Details:	Free
User Info:	To subscribe to the list, send an e-mail message requesting a subscription to the URL address below.
Notes:	To get a daily digestified version, subscribe to neci-digest. To receive organizational announcements only, subscribe to neci-announce.

`mailto:neci-discuss-request@pioneer.ci.net`

news.announce.newgroups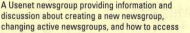

A Usenet newsgroup providing information and discussion about creating a new newsgroup, changing active newsgroups, and how to access new Usenet groups.

Keywords:	Usenet, Internet Resources
Audience:	Usenet Users
Details:	Free
User Info:	To subscribe to this Usenet newsgroup, you need access to a newsreader.

`news:news.announce.newgroups`

news.answers

A Usenet newsgroup providing information and discussion about periodic Usenet articles.

Keywords:	Usenet, Internet Resources

Audience:	Usenet Users
Details:	Free
User Info:	To subscribe to this Usenet newsgroup, you need access to a newsreader.

`news:news.answers`

news.groups

A Usenet newsgroup providing information and discussion about lists of existing newsgroups.

Keywords:	Usenet, Internet Resources
Audience:	Usenet Users
Details:	Free
User Info:	To subscribe to this Usenet newsgroup, you need access to a newsreader.

`news:news.groups`

news.lists

A Usenet newsgroup providing information and discussion about news-related statistics and lists.

Keywords:	Usenet, Internet Resources
Audience:	Usenet Users
Details:	Free
User Info:	To subscribe to this Usenet newsgroup, you need access to a newsreader.

`news:news.lists`

news.newusers.questions

Keywords:	Usenet, E-mail, Internet Resources
Audience:	Usenet Users, E-mail Users
Details:	Free
User Info:	To subscribe to this Usenet newsgroup, you need access to a newsreader.

`news:news.newusers.questions`

ORA-NEWS

Announcements from O'Reilly & Associates, publishers of books about the Internet, UNIX and other open systems. Other products and services include The Global Network Navigator (an interactive online magazine) and Internet in a Box. It's gatewayed to the biz.oreilly.announce Usenetnewsgroup.

Keywords:	Internet, UNIX, Usenet
Audience:	Internet Surfers, Usenet Users, UNIX Users
Contact:	listown@online.ora.com
Details:	Free, Moderated
User Info:	To subscribe to the list, send an e-mail message requesting a subscription to the URL address below. To send a message to the entire list, address it to: ora-news@online.ora.com

`mailto:listproc@online.ora.com`

Usenet Repository

Regular informational postings and FAQs from various newsgroups on the Usenet, grouped into archives by newsgroup.

Keywords:	Internet, Networking, Usenet
Audience:	Internet Surfers
Details:	Free
	File is: pub/usenet-by-group

`ftp://pit-manager.mit.edu`

Usenet Sports Groups Archived

An archive for Usenet groups, including many related to sports ranging from football to table tennis.

Keywords:	Sports, Skydiving, Volleyball, Football, Scuba, Table Tennis, Usenet
Sponsor:	Massachusetts Institute of Technology, Boston, MA
Audience:	Sports Enthusiasts
Contact:	ftp-bugs@rtfm.mit.edu
Details:	Free

`ftp://rtfm.mit.edu/pub/usenet`

Usenet University

An archive of Usenet university groups that are currently active on the Internet.

Keywords:	Education, Universities
Audience:	University Students, Educators, Researchers
Details:	Free
	File is: pub/doc/uu/FAQ

`ftp://nic.funet.fi`

Usenet What Is?

An article entitled "What Is Usenet?"

Keywords:	Internet Guides, Internet Tools, Usenet
Audience:	Internet Surfers
Details:	Free
	File is: pub/usenet/news.answers/what-is/usenet/part1

`ftp://rtfm.mit.edu`

Usenet World

A special issue of the Amateur Computerist newsletter about Usenet.

Keywords:	Internet Guides, Internet Tools, Usenet
Audience:	Internet Surfers
Details:	Free
	File is: doc/misc/acn/acn4-5.txt

`ftp://wuarchive.wustl.edu`

Usenet Newsgroup

Oglasna Deska

Oglasna Deska (Bulletin Board) consists of transcripts taken from SLON, which is a nickname for a Decnet connecting several computers in Slovenia. There is a conference similar to a Usenet newsgroup running under SLON and the articles and replies are occasionally saved and sent to the world. The topics cover a wide area.

Keywords:	Slovenia, SLON, Usenet Newsgroup
Audience:	Slovenians, Croatians, Serbians
Contact:	Dean Mozetic Oglasna-Deska@krpan.arnes.si
Details:	Free
User Info:	To subscribe to the list, send an e-mail message requesting a subscription to the URL address below. To send a message to the entire list, address it to: oglasna-deka@krpan.arnes.si
Notes:	The topics covered are equivalent to Usenet newsgroups such as politics, automobiles, humor, computer networks, climbing, and miscellaneous investments.

`mailto:Oglasna-Deska@krpan.arnes.si`

USGS

United States Geological Survey Home Page

USGS server dedicated to all aspects of Geography and geographic data.

Keywords:	USGS, GIS, Geography
Sponsor:	United States Geological Survey
Audience:	Geographers, GIS Professionals, Researchers, Students
Profile:	Probably the most comprehensive geography/GIS server on the net. Features include a GIS tuturial, descriptions (and examples) of available USGS data products, access to online spatial data and more.
Contact:	webmaster@info.er.usgs.gov
Details:	Free, Images, Sounds, Multimedia
Notes:	The USGS maintains many servers, this page contains links to most of them, such as EROS Data Center, GLIS and others.

`http://info.er.usgs.gov/USGSHome.html`

USGS (United States Geological Survey) Gopher

A gopher site covering issues related to the United State Geological Survey.

| Keywords: | Cartography, Geology, USGS |

Sponsor: United States Geological Survey
Audience: Geologists, Cartologists
Profile: The USGS gopher was established to provide general information about USGS, information about USGS Divisions, publications, data, and briefings, USGS's Network resources, and other data on geology, hydrology, and cartography.
Contact: Gopher Operator
webmaster@info.er.usgs.gov

`gopher://info.er.usgs.gov`

Utah

Utah State Constitution

Lists full text of the Utah State Constitution 1991.
Keywords: Utah, Constitution
Audience: Utah Residents, Historians

`gopher://wiretap.spies.com`

Utah State Constitution

Utah State Constitution

Lists full text of the Utah State Constitution 1991.
Keywords: Utah, Constitution
Audience: Utah Residents, Historians

`gopher://wiretap.spies.com`

Utah Valley Community College Library

Utah Valley Community College Library

The library's holdings are large and wide-ranging and contain significant collections in many fields.
Keywords: Accounting, Automobiles, Cabinetry, Child Care, Drafting, Electronics, Home Building, Refrigeration, Air Conditioning
Audience: General Public, Researchers, Librarians, Document Delivery Professionals
Details: Free
User Info: Expect: Login; Send: Opub

`telnet://uvlib.uvcc.edu`

UTIRC (University of Toronto Instructional and Research Computing

UTIRC (University of Toronto Instructional and Research Computing

This site provides information in the areas of instructional technology and applications, support for multimedia and visualization techniques, and access to and support for high-performance computing.
Keywords: Computing, Computer Programming, Computer-Aided Design
Sponsor: University of Toronto, Division of Computing, Toronto, Canada
Audience: Programmers, Designers
Details: Free

`http://www.utirc.utoronto.ca/htmldocs/hewhtml/intro.html`

UWP Music Archive (named for the host machine's location: the University of Wisconsin—Parkside)

UWP Music Archive (named for the host machine's location: the University of Wisconsin—Parkside)

An extensive repository of files relating to a diverse array of music genres: rock, folk, classical, and more.
Keywords: Music, Lyrics, Graphics
Sponsor: University of Wisconsin—Parkside
Audience: Musicians, Music Enthusiasts, Musicologists
Profile: This FTP archive contains a music database, artist discographies, essays about music and particular works, hundreds of image files (mostly .GIF and .JPEG format) of musicians—including album covers and posters, a lyrics archive and the ever-popular "Beginner's Introduction to Classical Music."
Contact: Dave Datta
datta@ftp.uwp.edu
User Info: Select "Music Archives" from the gopher top-level menu.
Notes: Also accessible through CMU's "English Server" gopher server. (q.v.)

`gopher://gopher.uwp.edu`

Val-L

val-l

Discussion on changes in the Communist countries, ranging from Cuba and Vietnam to the former Soviet Union.

Keywords: Communism, Soviet Union, Political Science

Audience: Political Scientists

Contact: cdell@umkcax1 or cdell@umkcvax1.bitnet

Details: Free

User Info: To subscribe to the list, send an e-mail message to the URL address below consisting of a single line reading:

SUB val-l YourFirstName YourLastName

To send a message to the entire list, address it to: val-l@ucflvm.cc.ucf.edu

`mailto:listserv@ucflvm.cc.ucf.edu`

VapourWare

VapourWare

A column of speculation about new computers and computer-related products that are not yet available for sale (and may never be).

Keywords: Computers

Audience: Computer Users

Contact: Murphy Sewall sewall@uconnvm.uconn.edu

Details: Free

`mailto:sewall@uconnvm.uconn.edu`

Various Treaties

Various Treaties

Provides access to a range of treaties in full-text format.

Keywords: Treaties, Politics (International)

Audience: Governments, Researchers, Lawyers

Details: Free

`gopher://wiretap.spies.com`

Vegetarianism

GRANOLA (Vegetarian Discussion List)

A ListServ for discussion of vegetarian issues, including everything from recipes to animal rights.

Keywords: Health, Nutrition, Vegetarian, Recipes

Audience: Vegetarians, Nutritionists, Health Professionals

Details: Free

User Info: To subscribe to the list, send an e-mail message to the URL address shown below consisting of a single line reading:

SUB granola YourFirstName YourLastName

`mailto:listserv@gitvm1.bitnet`

rec.food.veg

A Usenet newsgroup providing information and discussion about vegetarian cooking.

Keywords: Vegetarianism, Food, Cooking

Audience: Vegetarians, Cooks, Chefs

User Info: To subscribe to this Usenet newsgroup, you need access to a newsreader.

`news:rec.food.veg`

VEGCNY-L (Vegetarians in Central New York area)

VegCNY-L is an open discussion list intended to serve those people living in the Central New York area who are vegetarians, as well as those who are interested in vegetarianism.

Keywords: Vegetarianism, New York, Food

Audience: Vegetarians

Contact: Chuck Goelzer Lyons cgl1@cornell.edu

Details: Free

User Info: To subscribe to the list, send an e-mail message to the URL address below consisting of a single line reading:

SUB VEGCNY-L YourFirstName YourLastName

To send a message to the entire list, address it to: VEGCNY-L@cornell.edu

`mailto:listserv@cornell.edu`

veggie (Vegetarian Issues Discussion List)

Veggie is an open list for the discussion of vegetarianism.

Keywords: Vegetarianism, Food
Audience: Vegetarians
Details: Free
User Info: To subscribe to the list, send an e-mail message to the URL address below consisting of a single line reading:

SUB veggie YourFirstName YourLastName

To send a message to the entire list address it to: veggie@gibbs.oit.unc.edu

`mailto:listserv@gibbs.oit.unc.edu`

veggies

A list for the discussion of vegetarian matters in Britain.

Keywords: Vegetarianism, Britain, Food
Audience: Vegetarians
Details: Free
User Info: To subscribe to the list, send an e-mail message requesting a subscription to the URL address below.

To send a message to the entire list, address it to: veggies@ncl.ak.uk

`mailto:veggies-request@ncl.ac.uk`

veglife (Vegetarian Life List)

Veglife (formerly Granola) provides a supportive atmosphere for the discussion of issues related to the vegetarian lifestyle.

Keywords: Vegetarianism, Food
Audience: Vegetarians
Contact: Darrell A. Early, Charles Goelzer Lyons
Details: Free
User Info: To subscribe to the list, send an e-mail message to the URL address below consisting of a single line reading:

SUB veglife YourFirstName YourLastName

To send a message to the entire list, address it to: veglife@vtvml.cc.vt.edu

`mailto:listserv@vtvm1.cc.vt.edu`

Velo News Experimental Tour de France Web Page

Velo News Experimental Tour de France Web Page

This web site provides background information on the Tour de France, including press coverage from this year's race.

Keywords: Bicycles, Sports
Sponsor: Velo News
Audience: Bicyclists, Sports Fans
Contact: VeloNews@aol.com

`http://cob.fsu.edu/velonews`

Verdicts

VRDCT (Jury Verdicts Library)

The Verdicts Library aids litigation preparation by providing quick and convenient access to selected online verdict and settlement information for civil cases nationwide. Case information covered includes verdict and settlement amounts, expert witnesses, case summaries, and counsel data.

Keywords: Jury, Verdicts, Judgments, Settlements
Audience: Lawyers
Contact: New Sales Group at 800-227-4908 or 513-859-5398 inside the US, or 1-513-865-7981 for all inquires outside the US.
User Info: To subscribe, contact Mead directly.

To examine the Lexis user guide, you can access it at the ftp site of the University of Texas at Austin at the URL address: ftp://ftp.cc.utexas.edu

The files are in: /pub/ref-services/LEXIS

`telnet://nex.meaddata.com`

`http://www.meaddata.com`

Veronica

Gopher/Veronica-How To

A special issue of the University of Illinois publication describing gopher and Veronica.

Keywords: Internet Tools, Gopher, Veronica
Sponsor: University of Illinois, Urbana, IL
Audience: Internet Surfers
Details: Free

File is: doc/net/uiucnet/vol6nol.txt

`ftp://ftp.cso.uiuc.edu`

Veronica FAQ

A gopher containing common questions and answers about Veronica, a title search and retrieval system for use with the Internet gopher.

Keywords: Internet Reference, Information Retrieval, Veronica
Audience: Students, Computer Scientists, Researchers

`gopher://pogonip.scs.unr.edu/00/veronica/veronica-faq`

Veronica Introduction

Veronica (Very Easy Rodent-Oriented Net-wide Index to Computerized Archives) is an Internet access tool that locates titles of gopher items by keyword search.

Keywords: Internet Tools, Veronica
Audience: Internet Surfers
Details: Free

File is: pub/com.archives/bionet.software/veronica

`ftp://cs.dal.ca`

Vertebrates

National Science Foundation Center for Biological Timing Vertebrate Museum and Virus Gopher Server

This gopher accesses investigative research pertaining to various aspects of biological timing. The goal of this gopher is to make the Museum's collection information available over the Internet. This server contains names of virus families/groups and members now available online from the Australian National University's bio-informatics facility.

Keywords: Biology, Vertebrates
Sponsor: Reasearch School of Biological Research, Australian National University, Canberra, Australia
Audience: Biologists, Educators, Researchers
Profile: The center combines the efforts of several universities pertaining to research in biological timing. This includes Vistudies, the internal timing mechanisms that control cycles of sleep and waking, hormone pulsatility, neural excitability, and reproductive rhythmicity. Investigators are involved with research from behavior testing to molecular genetics.

The center also supports educational and outreach programs to industry, universities and high schools. The center also hosts an annual scientific symposium and a number of mini-symposia.

Details: Free

`gopher://gopher.virginia.edu/11/pubs/biotimin`

Vertebrate Museum

The goal of this gopher is to make museum collection information about vertebrates available over the Internet.

Keywords: Vertebrates, Biology
Sponsor: The Museum of Vertebrate Zoology, University of California at Berkeley
Audience: Natural Scientists, Biologists, Researchers
Details: Free

`gopher://ucmp1.berkeley.edu`

Veterinary Hospitals

Vetadm-L

A discussion group for those involved in veterinary hospital administration.

Keywords: Veterinary Hospitals
Audience: Veterinarians
Contact: Joel Hammond
joel@tamvet.bitnet
Details: Free
User Info: To subscribe to the list, send and e-mail message to the URL address below consisting of a single line reading:

SUB vetadm-l YourFirstName YourLastName

To send a message to the entire list, address it to: vetadm-l@tamvml.tamu.edu

`mailto:listserv@tamvm1.tamu.edu`

Vethis-L (Veterinary Hospital Information Systems)

Vethis-L provides a forum for the exchange of information on veterinary hospital information systems.

Keywords: Veterinary Hospitals
Audience: Veterinarians
Profile: Because of the interrelationship between veterinary hospitals and diagnostic laboratories, topics of mutual interest can be discussed here. The forum was created in response to initiatives by members of the American Association of Veterinary Medical Colleges (AAVMC) and the American Academy of Veterinary Informatics (AAVI).

Contact: Ron Smith
r-smith19@uiuc.edu
Details: Free
User Info: To subscribe to the list, send an e-mail message to the URL address below consisting of a single line reading:

SUB vethis-l YourFirstName YourLastName

To send a message to the entire list, address it to: vethis-l@vmd.cso.uiuc.edu

`mailto:listserv@vmd.cso.uiuc.edu`

Veterinary Medicine

Iowa State University

The library's holdings contain significant collections in many fields.

Keywords: Agriculture, Veterinary Medicine, Statistics, Labor, Soil Conservation, Film
Audience: General Public, Researchers, Librarians, Document Delivery Professionals
Details: Free
Expect: DIAL, Send: LIB

`telnet://isn.iastate.edu`

NetVet Veterinary Resources

An Internet server for veterinary and animal resources.

Keywords: Veterinary Medicine, Animal Welfare, Animals
Sponsor: Washington University, St. Louis, Division of Comparative Medicine
Audience: Veterinarians, Animal Lovers
Profile: A collection of veterinary and animal-related computer resources that includes archives of animal legislation and regulation, listings for colleges of Veterinary Medicine, conference information, and animal-related databases, including the Electronic Zoo. Also has links to other animal and veterinary-related systems.
Contact: Dr. Ken Boshert
ken@wudcm.wustl.edu

`gopher://netvet.wustl.edu`

`http://netvet.wustl.edu/`

Primate-talk (Primate Discussion List)

Forum for the discussion of primatology and related subjects.

Keywords: Primates, Primatology, Veterinary Medicine
Audience: Primatologists, Veterinarians
Profile: This list is open to any e-mail user with an interest in primatology. Subject matter ranges from, but is not limited to, news items, meeting announcements, research issues, information requests, veterinary/husbandry topics, job notices, animal exchange information, and book reviews.
Contact: Larry Jacobsen
jacobsen@pimate.wisc.edu
Details: Free
User Info: To subscribe to the list, send an e-mail message requesting a subscription to the URL address below.

`mailto:primate-talk-request@primate.wisc.edu`

Svhp-l

A restricted discussion group on veterinary pharmacy issues.

Keywords: Veterinary Pharmacy, Pharmacy, Veterinary Science
Audience: Veterinarians, Veterinary Pharmacists
Contact: Doug Kemp
vetpharm@uga.cc.uga.edu
Details: Free
User Info: To subscribe to the list, send an e-mail message to the URL address shown below consisting of a single line reading:

SUB svhp-l YourFirstName YourLastName

To send a message to the entire list, address it to: svhp-l@uga.cc.uga.edu

`mailto:listserv@uga.cc.uga.edu`

vetcai-l

Discussion of veterinary medicine computer-assisted instruction.

Keywords: Veterinary Medicine, Computer-Aided Instruction
Audience: Veterinarians, Medical Educators
Contact: Pat Oblander
oblandr@ksuvm.ksu.edu
User Info: To subscribe to the list, send an e-mail message to the URL address below consisting of a single line reading:

SUB vetcai-l YourFirstName YourLastName

To send a message to the entire list, address it to: vetcai-l@ksuvm.ksu.edu

`mailto:listserv@ksuvm.ksu.edu`

vetimm-l

Discussion group for veterinary immunology.

Keywords: Veterinary Medicine, Immunology
Audience: Veterinarians

Veterinary Medicine

Details:	Free
User Info:	To subscribe to the list, send an e-mail message to the URL address below consisting of a single line reading:
	SUB vetimm-l YourFirstName YourLastName
	To send a message to the entire list, address it to: vetimm-l@ucdavis.edu

mailto:listserv@ucdavis.edu

vetinfo (Discussion of Veterinary Informatics)

This list has been created to stimulate discussion in the area of informatics, with special reference to the field of veterinary medicine.

Keywords:	Veterinary Medicine, Informatics
Audience:	Veterinarians
Profile:	Related topics include clinical decision support systems, laboratory information management, imaging, disease nomenclature and coding systems, expert systems, and knowledge bases. Discussions related to specific hardware and software implementations are welcome, as are approaches to specific challenges in veterinary informatics.
Contact:	James T. Case, Bill Cohen jcase@ucdcvdls.bitnet
Details:	Free
User Info:	To subscribe to the list, send an e-mail message to the URL address below consisting of a single line reading:
	SUB vetinfo YourFirstName YourLastName
	To send a message to the entire list, address it to: vetinfo@ucdavis.edu

mailto:listserv@ucdavis.edu

Vetlib-L (Veterinary Medicine Librarians List) ★

Vetlib-L is an E-mail discussion group for librarians in schools and colleges of veterinary medicine worldwide.

Keywords:	Veterinary Medicine, Libraries
Sponsor:	Virginia Polytechnic Institute and State University
Audience:	Veterinarians, Librarians
Contact:	Victoria T. Kok, James Powell kok@vtvm1.cc.vt.edu or jpowell@vtvm1.cc.vt.edu
Details:	Free
User Info:	To subscribe to the list, send an e-mail message to the URL address below consisting of a single line reading:
	SUB vetlib-l YourFirstName YourLastName
	To send a message to the entire list, address it to: vetlib-l@vtvm1.cc.vt.edu

mailto:listserv@vtvm1.cc.vt.edu

Vetmed-L (Veterinary Medicine Discussion List) ★

A discussion group for students, professionals, and others employed, or interested, in the veterinary profession.

Keywords:	Veterinary Medicine
Audience:	Veterinarians, Students (college, graduate), Animal Lovers
Contact:	Harold Pritchett, Doug Kemp, Jean Snow harold@uga.cc.uga.edu or vetpharm@uga.cc.uga.edu or jean@uga.cc.uga.edu
Details:	Free
User Info:	To subscribe to the list, send an e-mail message to the URL address below consisting of a single line reading:
	SUB vetmed-l YourFirstName YourLastName
	To send a message to the entire list, address it to: vetmed-l@uga.cc.uga.edu

mailto:listserv@uga.cc.uga.edu

vetmicro

A discussion group about veterinary microbiology.

Keywords:	Veterinary Medicine, Microbiology
Audience:	Veterinarians
Contact:	James T. Case, Bill Cohen jcase@ucdcvdls.bitnet or bcohen@ucdcvdls.bitnet
Details:	Free
User Info:	To subscribe to the list, send an e-mail message to the URL address below consisting of a single line reading:
	SUB vetmicro YourFirstName YourLastName
	To send a message to the entire list, address it to: vetmicro@ucdavis.edu

mailto:listserv@ucdavis.edu

vetmycop ★

A veterinary mycoplasma discussion group.

Keywords:	Veterinary Medicine, Mycoplasma
Audience:	Veterinarians
Contact:	James T. Case, Bill Cohen jcase@ucdcvdls.bitnet or bcohen@ucdcvdls.bitnet
Details:	Free
User Info:	To subscribe to the list, send an e-mail message to the URL address below consisting of a single line reading:
	SUB vetmycop YourFirstName YourLastName
	To send a message to the entire list, address it to: vetmycop@ucdavis.edu

mailto:listserv@ucdavis.edu

Vettox-L (Veterinary Toxicology Discussion List)

A list dedicated to diagnostic toxicology, established at the University of California.

Keywords:	Veterinary Medicine, Toxicology
Audience:	Veterinarians, Toxicologists
Profile:	This list is restricted to those in the practice of diagnostic toxicology, although it will not be an edited list. The goals are to provide an atmosphere of cooperation among those in the field of diagnostic toxicology and to seek solutions to the many challenges that arise during a disease investigation.
Contact:	James T. Case, Bill Cohen jcase@ucdcvdls.bitnet or bcohen@ucdcvdls.bitnet
Details:	Free
User Info:	To subscribe to the list, send an e-mail message to the URL address below consisting of a single line reading:
	SUB vettox-l YourFirstName YourLastName
	To send a message to the entire list, address it to: vettox-l@ucdavis.edu

mailto:listserv@ucdavis.edu

Veterinary Science

Agriculture, Veterinary Science & Zoology

This directory is a compilation of information resources focused on agriculture, veterinary science, and zoology.

Keywords:	Agriculture, Veterinary Science, Zoology
Audience:	Farmers, Agronomists, Veterinarians, Zoologists
Details:	Free

`ftp://una.hh.lib.umich.edu/70/inetdirsstacks/agvetzoo:haas`

Purdue University Library

The library's holdings are large and wide-ranging. They contain significant collections in many fields.

Keywords:	Economics (History of), Literature (English), Literature (American), Indiana, Rogers (Bruce), Engineering (History of), Aviation, Earth Science, Atmospheric Science, Consumer Science, Family Science, Chemistry (History of), Physics, Veterinary Science
Audience:	General Public, Researchers, Librarians, Document Delivery Professionals

Video

Electronic Cafe

A seminal art and telecommunications group that specializes in video transmission.

Keywords: Art, Video, Telecommunications
Audience: Artists
Profile: This combines performance, communication, and community outreach by making telecommunications equipment available in a cafe-style artists' space.
Contact: Kit Galloway and Sherrie Rabinowitz, 1641 18th St., Santa Monica, CA 90404, USA

`mailto:ecafe@netcom.com`

Film and Video

This directory is a compilation of information resources focused on film and video.

Keywords: Film, Video, Entertainment
Audience: Students, Producers, Artists
Details: Free

`ftp://una.hh.lib.umich.edu/70/inetdirsstacks/filmvideo:woodgarlock`

Filmmaking Conference

A conference on the WELL about the technical, theoretical, and aestheic issues of filmmaking; includes listings of film and video festivals.

Keywords: Film, Filmmaking, Video
Audience: Filmmakers, Film/Video Enthusiasts
Contact: Sandy Santra
trevor@well.sf.ca.us
Details: Costs
To participate in a conference on the WELL, you must first establish an account on the WELL. To do so, start by typing: telnet well.sf.ca.us

`telnet://well.sf.ca.us`

rec.video

A Usenet newsgroup providing information and discussion about video.

Keywords: Video, Art, Film, Computer Art
Audience: Cinematographers, Video Artists
User Info: To subscribe to this Usenet newsgroup, you need access to a newsreader.

`news:rec.video`

(Previous column)

Contact: Dan Ferrer
dan@asterix.lib.purdue.edu
Details: Free
Expect: User ID prompt, Send: GUEST

`telnet://lib.cc.purdue.edu`

Svhp-l

A restricted discussion group on veterinary pharmacy issues.

Keywords: Veterinary Pharmacy, Pharmacy, Veterinary Science
Audience: Veterinarians, Veterinary Pharmacists
Contact: Doug Kemp
vetpharm@uga.cc.uga.edu
Details: Free
User Info: To subscribe to the list, send an e-mail message to the URL address shown below consisting of a single line reading:
SUB svhp-l YourFirstName YourLastName
To send a message to the entire list, address it to: svhp-l@uga.cc.uga.edu

`mailto:listserv@uga.cc.uga.edu`

University of Texas Health Science Center at San Antonio Library

The library's holdings are large and wide-ranging and contain significant collections in many fields.

Keywords: Allied Health, Dentistry, Nursing, Veterinary Science, Ambulatory Care, Obstetrics/Gynecology, Pediatrics
Audience: Researchers, Students, General Public
Details: Free
Expect: Login, Send: LIS

`telnet://athena.uthscsa.edu`

Victims

Victim Help

A discussion list for the purpose of sharing experiences/research in the broad field of victimization and trauma. Assistance of victims of crime or trauma and those who work with them is a primary focus of this group as is helping them to locate workshops and other resources.

Keywords: Victims, Victimization, Violence
Audience: Victims (of crime trauma), Psychologists, Police, Educators
Contact: Dr. R. Casarez

`rcasarez@mercury.sfsu.edu`

Video Games

Digital Games Review

Reviews of video and computer entertainment titles for the entire industry.

Keywords: Computer Games, Games, Video Games
Audience: Computer Game Players, Computer Game Developers
Profile: Reviews are written by computer game enthusiasts, with an eye to accessibility, enjoyment, and fun, as well as to graphics, technical sophistication, and complexity.
Contact: Dave Taylor
taylor@intuitive.com
Details: Free

`mailto:digital-games-request@intuitive.com`

rec.games.programmer

A Usenet newsgroup providing information and discussion about adventure game programming.

Keywords: Games, Programming, Video Games
Audience: Programmers
User Info: To subscribe to this Usenet newsgroup, you need access to a newsreader.

`news:rec.games.programmer`

rec.games.video.arcade

A Usenet newsgroup providing information and discussion about video games.

Keywords: Games, Video Games
Audience: Game Players
User Info: To subscribe to this Usenet newsgroup, you need access to a newsreader.

`news:rec.games.video.arcade`

Vietnam

ANU (Australian National University) Vietnam-SciTech-L Database

A WAIS database of information on the development of science and technology in Vietnam.

Keywords: Vietnam, Science, Technology
Sponsor: Australia Vietnam Science-Technology Link

Vietnam

Audience: Vietnamese, Scientists, Technology Professionals
Contact: Vern Weitzel
vern@coombs.anu.edu.au

`waissrc:/Coombs-db/ANU-Vietnam-SciTech-L.src`

`gopher://cheops.anu.edu.au/7waissrc/Coombs-db/ANU-Vietnam-SciTech-L.src`

soc.culture.vietnamese

A Usenet newsgroup providing information and discussion about the people and culture of Vietnam.

Keywords: Vietnam, Sociology
Audience: Sociologists, Vietnamese
Details: Free
User Info: To subscribe to this Usenet newsgroup, you need access to a newsreader.

`news:soc.culture.vietnamese`

Vietnam

This file (in the CIA World Factbook) provides geographical, political, and cultural information about Vietnam.

Keywords: Vietnam, Geography
Sponsor: Central Intelligence Agency
Audience: Educators, Students, Travellers, Vietnamese Americans
Contact: Ephraim Vishniac
ephraim@think.com
Details: Free

`gopher://info.und.edu`

Vwar-l

An electronic conference on issues relating to the Vietnam War.

Keywords: History (20th Century), History (US), Vietnam
Audience: Historians
Contact: Lydia Fish
fishlm@snybufva.cs.snybuf.edu
User Info: To subscribe to the list, send an e-mail message to the URL address below consisting of a single line reading:

SUB vwar-l YourFirstName YourLastName

To send a message to the entire list, address it to: vwar-l@ubvm.cc.buffalo.edu

`mailto:listserv@ubvm.cc.buffalo.edu`

ViewPoints

ViewPoints

Newsletter of the Visual Communication Division of the Association of Educators in Journalism and Mass Communication.

Keywords: Journalism, Mass Communication, Visual Communication
Audience: Educators, Photographers, Desktop Publishers
Contact: Paul Lester
lester@fullerton.edu
Details: Free

`mailto:lester@fullerton.edu`

vigis-l

Vigis-L

A mailing list for the discussion of Virtual Reality and GIS (Geographic Information Systems).

Keywords: Virtual Reality, Geography, GIS (Geographic Information Systems), Cyberspace
Audience: Geographers, Cartographers, Cybernauts
Contact: Tom Edwards
navanax.u.washington.edu
User Info: To subscribe to the list, send an e-mail message to the URL address below consisting of a single line reading:

SUB vigis-l YourFirstName YourLastName.

To send a message to the entire list, address it to: vigis@uwavm.u.washington.edu

`mailto:listserv@uwavm.u.washington.edu`

Virginia Commonwealth University Library

Virginia Commonwealth University Library

The library's holdings are large and wide-ranging and contain significant collections in many fields.

Keywords: Art, Biology, Humanities, Journalism, Music, Urban Planning
Audience: Researchers, Students, General Public
Details: Free
Expect: Login; Send: Opub

`telnet://vcuvm1.ucc.vcu.edu`

Virginia

The Old Dominion University Library

The library's holdings are large and wide-ranging and contain significant collections in many fields.

Keywords: Virginia, Federal Documents (US)
Audience: General Public, Researchers, Librarians, Document Delivery Professionals
Details: Free

`telnet://geac.lib.odu.edu`

Virginia's PEN (Public Education Network)

This is a statewide educational network.

Keywords: Education, Community Networking, Virginia
Sponsor: Virginia Department of Education
Audience: Educators
Profile: Educators throughout Virginia can access PEN via a local telephone call or through a toll-free line. The network includes discussion groups, news reports, study guides, and curriculum resources. In one of the features, History OnLine, students and teachers query historical figures such as Thomas Jefferson, and historians will answer in character.
Contact: Harold Cathern
hcathern@vdoe386.vak12.edu
Details: Free
Password: Guest

`telnet://guest@vdoe386.vak12ed.edu`

Virtual Community

(The) WELL (Whole Earth 'Lectronic Link)

The WELL is a computer conferencing system, a virtual community, and an electronic coffee shop.

Keywords: Community, Networking, Computer Conferencing, Virtual Community
Sponsor: Whole Earth 'Lectronic Link
Audience: General Public, Internet Surfers
Profile: The WELL is a classic example of an online community that uses what is called "conferencing" to bring a myriad of people together for intense interactions without them having to be connected at the same time. At the end of 1993, the WELL had about 8,000 users (about 90% from all over the USA and about 10% from other locations) and approximately 200 public discussion areas ('conferences'), and 200 private discussion areas. It is a place rich in diverse 'neighborhoods.'

| Contact: | The WELL Support Staff
info@well.sf.ca.us |
|---|---|
| | Direct dial access through:
+1 (415) 332-4335 |
| | To participate in a conference on the WELL, you must first establish an account on the WELL. To do so, start by typing: telnet well.sf.ca.us |

`telnet://well.sf.ca.us`

Telluride Institute

This is a community organization involved in building an electronic dimension in rural Colorado. The vision of Telluride Institute includes linking rural residents to each other and to outside resources, creating new opportunities for education, jobs, and arts.

Keywords:	Community Networking, Virtual Community, Rural Development, Colorado
Sponsor:	The Telluride Institute, Telluride, Colorado
Audience:	Activists, Policy Makers, Community Leaders, Students, Colorado Residents
Profile:	The Telluride Institute is a local community-based organization that produces arts, environmental, and educational events in the Telluride area of Colorado. The Institite is committed to the creation of what it calls the "InfoZone": it wants to use modern telecommunications to link together the local community and to connect to the rest of the world to exchange ideas, commerce, arts, and inspiration.
Contact:	Richard Lowenberg
tellinst@csn.org
Details:	Free
Notes:	Send an e-mail message to the URL address below asking for further information.

`mailto:tellinst@csn.org`

TWICS

This is an English-language computer conferencing system in Japan.

Keywords:	Community Networking, Japan, Virtual Community
Sponsor:	TWICS Co., Ltd.
Audience:	Internationalists, General Public, Journalists, Policy Makers
Profile:	TWICS is a computer conferencing system that has a reputation for being a thriving electronic community. The system maintains a full Internet connection. Unlike a database or a gopher server, TWICS allows real-time online interaction with actual people.
Contact:	Tim Buress
twics@twics.co.jp
Details:	Free

`telnet://tanuki.twics.co.jp`

Virtual Hospital

Virtual Hospital

The Virtual Hospital (VH) is a continuously updated medical multimedia database accessible 24 hours a day. The site provides distance learning to practicing physicians and may be used for Continuing Medical Education (CME).

Keywords:	Medicine, Education (Distance)
Sponsor:	The Electronic Differential Multimedia Laboratory, Department of Radiology, University of Iowa College of Medicine, USA
Audience:	Biologists, Researchers, Medical Professionals, Health Care Professionals
Contact:	Librarian
librarian@vh.radiology.uiowa.edu

`http://indy.radiology.uiowa.edu/VirtualHospital.html`

Virtual Reality

Artificial Intelligence, Expert Sys., Virtual Reality

This directory is a compilation of information resources focused on computer science research, artificial intelligence, expert systems, and virtual reality.

Keywords:	Computer Science, Artificial Intelligence, Expert Systems, Virtual Reality
Audience:	Computer Scientists, Engineers
Contact:	M. Kovacs
Details:	Free

`ftp://una.hh.lib.umich.edu/70/inetdirsstacks/csaiesvr:kovacsm`

Conference about Virtual Reality (The)

A conference on the WELL about cyberspace and virtual reality.

Keywords:	Virtual Reality, Art, Cyberspace
Audience:	Artists, Computer Programmers, Cyberpunks
Contact:	Peter Rothman
avatarp@well.sf.ca.us
	To participate in a conference on the WELL, you must first establish an account on the WELL. To do so, start by typing: telnet well.sf.ca.us

`telnet://well.sf.ca.us`

Vigis-L

A mailing list for the discussion of Virtual Reality and GIS (Geographic Information Systems).

Keywords:	Virtual Reality, Geography, GIS (Geographic Information Systems), Cyberspace
Audience:	Geographers, Cartographers, Cybernauts
Contact:	Tom Edwards
navanax.u.washington.edu
User Info:	To subscribe to the list, send an e-mail message to the URL address below consisting of a single line reading:
SUB vigis-l YourFirstName YourLastName.
To send a message to the entire list, address it to: vigis@uwavm.u.washington.edu

`mailto:listserv@uwavm.u.washington.edu`

Virtual Reality Space

A collection of virtual reality information, including downloadable software tools from Silicon Graphics.

Keywords:	Virtual Reality, Cyberspace, Software, Silicon Graphics
Sponsor:	The University of Texas, Austin, Texas, USA
Audience:	Virtual Reality Enthusiasts, Programmers
Contact:	Jay Ashcraft
ashcraft@ccwf.cc.utexas.edu

`gopher://ftp.cc.utexas.edu`

`ftp://cc.utexas.edu`

Virus-L

Virus-L

Virus-L is a forum for the discussion of computer virus experiences, protection software, and other virus-related topics. It includes archives and files that list a number of viruses, trojan horses, and pirated programs for the IBM PC.

Keywords:	Computer Viruses, Security
Audience:	Computer Users
Contact:	Kenneth R. van Wyk
luken@vax1.cc.lehigh.edu
Details:	Free
User Info:	To subscribe to the list, send an e-mail message to the URL address below consisting of a single line reading:
SUB virus-l YourFirstName YourLastName
To send a message to the entire list, address it to: virus-l@ibml.cc.lehigh.edu

`mailto:listserv@ibm1.cc.lehigh.edu`

Viruses

Institute for Molecular Virology

A unique virology resource for students, scientists, computer visualization experts, and the general public.

Keywords: Disease, Viruses, Biology
Sponsor: University of Wisconsin-Madison, Madison, Wisconsin, USA
Audience: Virologists, Biologists, Researchers
Contact: Stephen Spencer
sspencer@rhino.bocklabs.wisc.edu

http://www.bocklabs.wisc.edu/Welcome.html

Virus Gopher Server

This server contains names of virus families/groups and members now available online from the Australian National University's bioinformatics facility.

Keywords: Viruses, Bioinformation, Biology
Sponsor: Research School of Biological Research, Australian National University, Canberra, Australia
Audience: Researchers, Biologists, Health Professionals
Details: Free

gopher://life.anu.edu.au

Visual Communication

ViewPoints

Newsletter of the Visual Communication Division of the Association of Educators in Journalism and Mass Communication.

Keywords: Journalism, Mass Communication, Visual Communication
Audience: Educators, Photographers, Desktop Publishers
Contact: Paul Lester
lester@fullerton.edu
Details: Free

mailto:lester@fullerton.edu

Visual Impairment

Blind News Digest

This is a moderated mailing list in digest format that deals with all aspects of visual impairment and blindness.

Keywords: Blindness, Disabilities
Audience: Blind People, Health Care Providers, Therapists
Contact: wtm@bunker.afd.olivetti.com
Details: Free, Moderated
User Info: To subscribe to the list, send the message SUB BlindNws YourFirstName YourLastName to listserv@vm1.nodak.edu or send e-mail requesting a subscription to wtm@bunker.afd.olivetti.com

mailto:wtm@bunker.afd.olivetti.com

Visualization Data Explorer Package

data-exp

The mail list server provides an open forum for users to discuss the Visualization Data Explorer Package. It contains three files: a. FAQ, b. summary, and c. forum.

Keywords: Computing, Software, Hardware, Visualization Data Explorer Package
Audience: Computer Users
User Info: To subscribe to the list, send an e-mail message requesting a subscription to the URL address below.

To send a message to the entire list, address it to: stein@watson.ibm.com

mailto:stein@watson.ibm.com

Visualization

ApE-info

A mailing list for the discussion of the scientific visualization software package ApE, its usage, development, and implementation.

Keywords: Computers, Visualization, Science
Audience: ApE Software Users, Computer Programmers
Contact: Jim Lick
ape-info-request@ferkel.ucsb.edu
User Info: To subscribe to the list, send an e-mail message to the URL address below. To send a message to the entire list, address it to: ape-info@ferkel.ucsb.edu

mailto:ape-info-request@ferkel.ucsb.edu

Voice of America and Worldnet

Voice of America and Worldnet

A gopher server for the Voice of America and Worldnet. It includes full-text transcripts of VOA news reports, press releases, and announcements.

Keywords: US Government Publications, News Media, Radio, International Communication
Sponsor: United States Information Agency
Audience: Journalists, Government Officials, General Public
Contact: info@voa.gov, letters-usa@voa.gov (for correspondence from inside the U.S.)

gopher://gopher.voa.gov

Volleyball

ba-Volleyball

This list is used for announcements about San Francisco Bay Area volleyball events, clinics, tournaments, and so on.

Keywords: Volleyball, San Francisco Bay Area, Sports
Audience: Volleyball Enthusiasts
Contact: ba-volleyball-request@klerk.cup.hp.com
User Info: To subscribe to the list, send an e-mail message requesting a subscription to the URL address below.

To send a message to the entire list, address it to: ba-volleyball@klerk.cup.hp.com

mailto:ba-volleyball-request@klerk.cup.hp.com

Usenet Sports Groups Archived

An archive for Usenet groups, including many related to sports ranging from football to table tennis.

Keywords: Sports, Skydiving, Volleyball, Football, Scuba Diving, Table Tennis
Sponsor: Massachusetts Institute of Technology, Boston, MA
Audience: Sports Enthusiasts
Contact: ftp-bugs@rtfm.mit.edu
Details: Free

ftp://rtfm.mit.edu/pub/usenet

Voting

Maryland

System provides access to a wide range of state information, including the policies and activities of members of Maryland's congress and voting district data.

Keywords: Maryland, Law, Voting
Audience: Maryland Residents, Lawyers
Details: Free
Select from menu as appropriate.

gopher://info.umd.edu

VRDCT (Jury Verdicts Library)

VRDCT (Jury Verdicts Library)

The Verdicts Library aids litigation preparation by providing quick and convenient access to selected online verdict and settlement information for civil cases nationwide. Case information covered includes verdict and settlement amounts, expert witnesses, case summaries and counsel data.

Keywords: Judicial Process, Law
Audience: Lawyers
Contact: New Sales Group at 800-227-4908 or 513-859-5398 inside the US, or 1-513-865-7981 for all inquires outside the US.
User Info: To subscribe, contact Mead directly.
To examine the Lexis user guide, you can access it at the ftp site of the University of Texas at Austin at the URL address: ftp://ftp.cc.utexas.edu The files are in: /pub/ref-services/LEXIS

telnet://nex.meaddata.com

http://www.meaddata.com

VTcad-L

VTcad-L

This E-conference is for discussion of CAD by Va Tech users. Discussion includes: CAD applications, CAD hardware, CAD networking.

Keywords: Computer Graphics, Computer Aided Design
Audience: Computer Graphic Designers, Engineers, Architects
Contact: Darrell A. Early
bestuur@VTVM1.cc.vt.edu
Details: Free
User Info: To subscribe to the list, send an e-mail message to the URL address below consisting of a single line reading:

SUB vtcad-l YourFirstName YourLastName

To send a message to the entire list, address it to: vtcad-l@vtvm1.cc.vt.edu

mailto:listserv@vtvm1.cc.vt.edu

WAIS

comp.infosystems.wais ★

A Usenet newsgroup providing information and discussion about the WAIS full-text search tool.

Keywords: WAIS, Internet Reference, Information Retrieval

Audience: Internet Surfers

To subscribe to this Usenet newsgroup, you need access to a newsreader.

`news:comp.infosystems.wais`

WAIS ★

WAIS (Wide Area Information Servers) is an Internet access tool that retrieves resources by searching indexes of databases.

Keywords: Internet Tools, WAIS

Audience: Internet Surfers

Details: Free

Read wais/README first.

`ftp://think.com`

WAIS FAQ ★★

Common questions and answers about WAIS (Wide Area Information Servers), a networked full-text retrieval system.

Keywords: Internet Reference, WAIS

Sponsor: Thinking Machines, Apple Computer, Dow Jones, and KPMG Peat Marwick

Audience: Students, Computer Scientists, Researchers

Contact: Aydin Edguer
edguer.ces.cwru.edu

`ftp://rtfm.mit.edu/pub/usenet-by-group/news.answers/wais-faq/getting-started`

WAIS, Inc. ★★★

WAIS, Inc. provides interactive on-line publishing systems and services to organizations that publish information over the Internet. The organization's three main goals are to develop the Internet as a viable means for distributing information electronically; to improve the nature and quality of information available over networks; and to offer better methods to access that information.

Keywords: WWW, Information Retrieval, Publishing, Internet Tools, WAIS

Sponsor: WAIS, Inc.

Audience: Researchers, Students, General Public, Publishers

Contact: Webmaster
webmaster@wais.com

`http://server.wais.com/`

Walpole (Sir Robert)

The University of Kansas Library ★★

The library's holdings are large and wide ranging and contain significant collections in many fields.

Keywords: Botany, Chinese Studies, Cartography (History of), Kansas, Opera, Ornithology, Joyce (James), Yeats (William Butler), Walpole (Sir Robert)

Audience: General Public, Researchers, Librarians, Document Delivery Professionals

Contact: John S. Miller

Details: Free
Expect: Username, Send: relay <cr>

`telnet://kuhub.cc.ukans.edu`

War

War Powers Resolution of 1973 ★

A joint resolution concerning the war powers of Congress and the President resolved by the Senate and the House of Representatives of the United States of America in Congress.

Keywords: War, Law (International), Government (US)

Audience: Politicians, Students, Lawyers, Historians

Details: Free

`gopher://wiretap.spies.com/00/Gov/warpower.act`

Washington DC

DC-MOTSS ★

DC-MOTSS is a social mailing list for the gay, lesbian, and bisexual folks who live in the Washington Metropolitan Area—everything within approximately 50 miles of The Mall.

Keywords: Gay, Lesbian, Bisexual, Washington DC

Audience: Gays, Lesbians, Bisexuals, Washington DC Residents

Contact: DC-MOTSS-request@vector.intercon.com

Details: Free

To subscribe to the list, send an e-mail message requesting a subscription to the URL address below.

To send a message to the entire list, address it to DC-MOTSS-request@vector.intercon.com

`mailto:DC-MOTSS-request@vector.intercon.com`

DCRaves

One of several regional rave-related mailing lists, DCRaves covers the Washington, DC area exclusively. Archives are available through the listserv, FTP, or gopher at american.edu.

- **Keywords:** Raves, Washington DC
- **Audience:** Rave Enthusiasts
- **Details:** Free

  To subscribe to the list, send an e-mail message to the URL address shown below consisting of a single line reading:

  SUB dcraves YourFirstName YourLastName

  To send a message to the entire list, address it to dcraves@american.edu

`mailto:listserv@american.edu`

Washington State University at Puyallup Library

Washington State University at Puyallup Library

The library's holdings are large and wide-ranging and contain significant collections in many fields.

- **Keywords:** Agriculture, Scientific Research
- **Audience:** Researchers, Students, General Public
- **Details:** Free
  - Expect: Login; Send: Lib

`telnet://wsuvm1.cscwsu.edu`

Washington University

IHOUSE-L International Voice Newsletter Prototype List

Contains articles of interest to international students and scholars, professors, administrators, and other interested staff and groups (on- and off-campus).

- **Keywords:** International Visitors, Washington University
- **Sponsor:** International Office of Washington University, St. Louis, MO
- **Audience:** International Students
- **Contact:** Doyle Cozadd C73221DC@WUVMD
- **Details:** Free

`mailto:listserv@wuvmd.wustl.edu`

Washington University Library

The library's holdings are large and wide ranging and contain significant collections in many fields.

- **Keywords:** Technology, Literature (German), Social Science, Behavioral Science, Washington University
- **Audience:** Researchers, Students, General Public
- **Contact:** services@wugate.wustl.edu
- **Details:** Free
  - Expect: Login; Send: Services

`telnet://wugate.wustl.edu`

Washington University-St. Louis Medical Library & Members Library

The library's holdings are large and wide-ranging and contain significant collections in many fields.

- **Keywords:** Medicine, Science, Technology, Washington University
- **Audience:** Researchers, Students, General Public
- **Details:** Free
  - Expect: Destination Code Prompt, Send: Catalog

`telnet://mcftcp.wustl.edu`

Water Quality

University of Maryland, College Park

The library's holdings are large and wide ranging and contain significant collections in many fields

- **Keywords:** Agriculture, Coastal Marine Biology, Fisheries, Water Quality, Oceanography
- **Audience:** Researchers, Students, General Public
- **Contact:** Janet McLeod mcleod@umail.umd.edu
- **Details:** Free
- **Expect:** Login; Send: Atdu

`telnet://info.umd.edu`

Weapons

rec.guns

A Usenet newsgroup providing information and discussion about firearms.

- **Keywords:** Firearms, Weapons
- **Audience:** Gun Users

  To subscribe to this Usenet newsgroup, you need access to a newsreader.

`news:rec.guns`

Weather

Canadian Geographical WWW Index Travel

This web site provides weekly weather information.

- **Keywords:** Weather, Travel, Canada, Geography
- **Sponsor:** University of Manitoba, Canada
- **Audience:** Travelers, Educators, Students
- **Contact:** www@umanitoba.ca
- **Details:** Free

`http://www.umanitoba.ca`

Current Weather Maps and Movies

This web site is updated hourly, and provides links to downloadable software sites instrumental in accessing interactive weather browsers. International information is available, and visual and infrared maps are supplied from satellites.

- **Keywords:** Weather, Meteorology, Aviation
- **Sponsor:** Michigan State University, Michigan, USA
- **Audience:** General Public, Oceanography, Pilots
- **Contact:** Charles Henrich henrich@crh.cl.msu.edu

`http://rs560.cl.msu.edu/weather`

News, Weather, and Travel Advisories

A major directory of news, weather, and travel advisories, providing access to a broad range of related resources (library catalogues, databases, and servers) via the Internet.

- **Keywords:** Travel, Weather, Aviation
- **Sponsor:** Kennesaw State College, Georgia, USA
- **Audience:** General Public, Travellers
- **Profile:** This collection includes CNN news sources, the National Weather Service forecast, and the US State Department Travel Advisory, among other sources.
- **Details:** Free

`gopher://kscsuna1.kennesaw.edu`

Weather-users

Weather-users is a mailing list for developers of programs that access the Weather Underground database at the University of Michigan.

- **Keywords:** Weather, Programming, Meteorology
- **Audience:** Programmers
- **Contact:** Scott Hazen Mueller scott@zorch.sf-bay.org

Details: Free

To subscribe to the list, send an e-mail message.

`mailto:weather-users-request@zorch.sf-bay.org`

Wells (Ida)

University of Chicago Library

The library's holdings are large and wide ranging and contain significant collections in many fields.

Keywords: English Bibles, Lincoln (Abraham), Kentucky & Ohio River Valley (History of), Balzac (Honore de), American Drama, Cromwell (Oliver), Goethe, Judaica, Italy, Chaucer (Geoffrey), Wells (Ida), Douglas (Stephen A.), Italy, Literature (Children's)

Audience: General Public, Researchers, Librarians, Document Delivery Professionals

Details: Free

Expect: ENTER CLASS, Send: LIB48 3; Expect: CONNECTED, Send: RETURN

`telnet://olorin.uchicago.edu`

Western America

Indiana University Libraries

The library's holdings are large and wide-ranging and contain significant collections in many fields.

Keywords: Literature (English), Literature (American), 1640-Present, British Plays (19th-C.), Western Americana, Railway History, Aristotle (Texts of), Lafayette (Marquis de), Handel (G.F.), Austrian History, Antiquarian Books, Rare Books, French Opera (19th-C.), Drama (British),

Audience: General Public, Researchers, Librarians, Document Delivery Professionals

Details: Free

Expect: User ID prompt, Send: GUEST

`telnet://iuis.ucs.indiana.edu`

University of Utah Library

The library's holdings are large and wide-ranging and contain significant collections in many fields.

Keywords: Western America, Middle Eastern Studies, Geology, Mining

Audience: Researchers, Students, General Public

Details: Free

Expect: Command Line, Send: Dial Unis

`telnet://lib.utah.edu`

Western Lands

Western Lands

A collection of articles and reports relating to environmental and land use issues in the western United States.

Keywords: Environmentalism, Ecology, Forests, The Western United States

Sponsor: The Institute for Global Communications (IGC)

Audience: Environmentalists, Ecologists, Activists, Foresters, Citizens

Contact: Dan Yurman, IGC User Support
dyurman@igc.apc.com
support@igc.apc.com

Notes: User submissions encouraged.

`gopher://gopher.igc.apc.org/11/environment/forests/western.lands`

What is the Internet?

What is the Internet? ★

An introductory guide to the Internet.

Keywords: Internet, Internet Guide

Sponsor: University of Illinois and Merit Network, Inc.

Audience: Internet Surfers

Contact: Ed Krol, Ellen Hoffman
e-krol@uiuc.edu or ellen@merit.edu

Details: Free

File is: documents/fyi/fyi_20.txt

`ftp://nic.merit.edu`

White House

National Performance Review (NPR)

The Report of the National Performance Review, from the task force led by Vice President Gore, titled "From Red Tape to Results: Creating a Government that Works Better and Costs Less," Sept. 7, 1993.

Keywords: President, Politics, White House

Audience: Political Scientists, General Public

Profile: On March 3, 1993, President Clinton asked Vice President Gore to lead the effort to effect real change in the federal government. Gore's NPR Task Force overview and accompanying reports make specific recommendations for reducing costs and waste, changing the way government operates, and making government more responsive and effective.

Details: Free

`gopher://cyfer.esusda.gov/11/ace/policy/npr/nat`

Presidential Documents

This gopher provides access to the full text of Presidential Proclamations, Executive Orders, Notices, Memoranda, and Determinations dating from December 23, 1992. The documents are listed sequentially by date and number (e.g. Proclamation 6520 of December 23, 1992).

Keywords: Politics, President (US), White House, Documents

Audience: General Public

Details: Free

Select from menu presented (probably you will follow the following path: Internet Services/US Government/ Presidential Documents).

`gopher://jupiter.cc.gettysborg.edu`

Technology Initiatives for the Clinton/Gore Administration

This is a 40-page text of the press release from the Clinton administration on technology initiatives, dated February 22, 1993.

Keywords: Politics, President, White House, Technology

Audience: General Public, Journalists

Details: Free

E-mail to the ListServ and include the following in the body of the message: get cni-bigideas.whouse.paper

`mailto:listserv@cni.org`

White House Frequently Asked Questions

This document is a good starting point for answering questions such as: How do I send e-mail to President Clinton? How do I get current news updates from the White House? Where can I get White House documents from?

Keywords: Clinton (Bill), Government (US), Politics (US), FAQs, White House

Audience: General Public, Researchers

Details: Free

Expect: login; Send: anonymous; Expect: password; Send: your e-mail address; Expect: directory; Send: /pub/nic; Expect: file; Send: whitehouse FAQ.

`ftp://ftp.sura.net`

White House Information Service ★★★★

An outstanding database of current White House information, from 1992 to the present.

Keywords: White House, Politics, President (US), Database

Sponsor:	Texas A & M University	
Audience:	General Public	
Profile:	Much of the older information on this site was obtained from the clinton@marist.bitnet listserv list or the alt.politics.clinton Usenet newsgroup, both of which receive the information indirectly via the MIT White House information server. Newer and current material is received directly from the MIT distribution list. The menu includes a searchable database and headings such as Domestic Affairs (Health Care, Technology, etc.), Press Briefings and Conferences, the President's Daily Schedule, and many more.	
Contact:	whadmin@tamu.edu	
Details:	Free	

`gopher://tamuts.tamu.edu/11/.dir/president.dir`

White House Phone Numbers

A list of names, addresses, e-mail addresses, and telephone and fax numbers of the President, First Lady, Vice President, and all the members of the Cabinet.

- Keywords: White House, President, Politics
- Audience: General Public
- Details: Free

`ftp://nifty.andrew.cmu.edu/pub/QRD/info/govt/cabinet`

White House Press Releases

An archive of all the press releases by the Clinton administration organized as Miscellaneous, Briefings by Dee Dee Myers, Executive Orders, Remarks during Photo Opportunities, Remarks of Bill Clinton, and Briefings by George Stephanopolous.

- Keywords: White House, Politics, President (US)
- Audience: General Public
- Details: Free

`gopher://wiretap.spies.com/11/Clinton`

Whitman (Walt)

University of Pennsylvania PENNINFO Library ★★

The library's holdings are large and wide-ranging and contain significant collections in many fields.

- Keywords: Church History, Spanish Inquisition, Witchcraft, Shakespeare (William), Bibles, Aristotle (Texts of), Fiction, Whitman (Walt), French Revolution, Drama (French), Literature (English), Literature (Spanish)
- Audience: Researchers, Students, General Public
- Contact: Al DSouza
  penninfo-admin@dccs.upenn.edu
  dsouza@dccs.upenn.edu
- Details: Free
  Expect: Login; Send: Public

`telnet://penninfo.upenn.edu`

Whois

Whois ★

Whois is an Internet access tool that provides information on registered network names.

- Keywords: Internet Tools
- Sponsor: SRI International Telecommunication Sciences Center
- Audience: Internet Surfers
- Contact: Nancy C. Fischer
  fischer@sri-nic
- Details: Free
  File is: documents/rfc/rfc0954.txt

`ftp://nic.merit.edu`

Wildlife

wildnet (Computing and Statistics in Fisheries & Wildlife Biology) ★

This mailing list was established for the exchange of ideas, questions, and solutions in the area of fisheries and wildlife biology computing and statistics.

- Keywords: Wildlife, Fisheries, Statistics
- Audience: Wildlife Biologists, Environmentalists, Statisticians
- Contact: Eric Woodsworth
  woodsworth@sask.usask.ca
- Details: Free
  To subscribe to the list, send an e-mail message requesting a subscription to the URL address below. To send a message to the entire list, address it to: wildnet@tribune.usask.ca

`mailto:wildnet-request@tribune.usask.ca`

The Wilderness Society ★★

This WWW site provides access to a collection of fact sheets about America's national parks, forests, wildlife refuges, Bureau of Land Management lands, and other natural places.

- Keywords: US National Park Service, Nature, Environment, Wildlife
- Sponsor: Internet Multicasting Service and the Wilderness Society
- Profile: Fact sheets are included for the following subjects: the Adirondacks, America's Public Lands, Ancient Forests of the Pacific Northwest, the Arctic National Wildlife Refuge, Below-cost Timber Sales, the California Desert, Endangered Species, the Everglades, Forest Fires And Forest Health, the Grand Canyon, the General Mining Law of 1872, Grazing On Public Lands, Lifelands, National Park Concessions, the National Wilderness Preservation System, the Northern Forest, the Tongass National Forest, Wetlands, Yellowstone National Park, and Yosemite National Park.
- Contact: email: questions@radio.com
- Details: Free, Images

`http://town.hall.org/environment/wild_soc/wilderness.html`

Williams College Library

Williams College Library

The library's holdings are large and wide-ranging and contain significant collections in many fields.

- Keywords: Americana, Graphic Arts, Printing (History of), Performing Arts, Printing
- Audience: General Public, Researchers, Librarians, Document Delivery Professionals
- Contact: Jim Cubit
- Details: Free
  Expect: Mitek Server..., Send: Enter or Return; Expect: prompt, Send: hollis

`telnet://library.williams.edu`

Windows

Microsoft Corporation World Wide Web Server

This system has been set up to provide lay and technical information for the public about Microsoft and its products.

- Keywords: Microsoft, Windows, MS-DOS, Chicago
- Sponsor: Microsoft Corporation
- Audience: Computer Users, Microsoft Product Users, Computer Programmers, Investors
- Profile: The Microsoft Knowledge Base and Software Library is accessible here. Information can be obtained on Windows NT Server, Developer Network News, Windows News, and also Windows Sockets Information. There are sections on Windows 4 (Chicago), Microsoft's new 32-bit TCP/IP VxD stack, a "What's New" page, current employment opportunities at Microsoft, recent speeches given by Microsoft Corporation's CEO Bill Gates, as well as current financial information about Microsoft.

Contact: email: www@microsoft.com
Details: Free, Images
Notes: The information contained on this server is copyrighted, and may not be distributed, downloaded, modified, reused, reposted, or otherwise used outside the scope of a WWW client without the express written permission of Microsoft Corporation.

http://www.microsoft.com

gopher://gopher.microsoft.com

ftp://ftp.microsoft.com

Windsurfing

Physical Education & Recreation

A collection of information on sporting and recreational activities from aikido to windsurfing.
Keywords: Sports, Recreation, Aikido, Cycling, Scuba Diving, Windsurfing
Audience: Sports Enthusiasts, Fitness Enthusiasts
Contact: ctcadmin@ctc.ctc.edu

gopher://ctc.ctc.edu

Think Wind

An FTP site for information on windsurfing, with FAQs, pictures, details about destinations, and threads from rec.windsurfing.
Keywords: Sports, Windsurfing
Audience: Windsurfers
Contact: phansen@lemming.uvm.edu
Details: Free, Images

ftp://lemming.uvm.edu/rec.windsurfing

Winter Games

Olympic Games 1994 at Lillehammer

News, results, and updates every 15 minutes, as well as archive images, from the 1994 Winter Olympic Games at Lillehammer, Norway.
Keywords: Olympics, Sports, Winter Games
Sponsor: Sun Microsystem, Skrivervik Data AS, Oslonett AS, Norsk Telegrambyra
Audience: General Public, Journalists, Skiers, Skaters, Winter Sports Fans

Profile: This server offers news and results on all the Olympic events in Lillehammer plus a chronological list of all events, a complete schedule day by day, and a very large archive of images. Also flash messages from NTB, a Norwegian news wire, and the opportunity to search in the NTB database.
Contact: oslonett@oslonett.no

http://www.sun.com

WIRED Online

WIRED Online

This is WIRED Magazine's gopher server.
Keywords: Postmodern Culture, News Media
Sponsor: WIRED Magazine
Audience: Internet Surfers, Internet Users, General Public
Profile: Features full-text of WIRED back issues, including the Net Surf column devoted to Internet exploration. Also has archives of the HotWIRED weekly mailing list, some guides to getting started surfing the net, general information about WIRED magazine, and an archive of material on the proposed Clipper federal encryption standard.
Contact: WIRED Online department, WIRED Magazine online@wired.com, info@wired.com

gopher://gopher.wired.com

Wiretap Sports Archives

Wiretap Sports Archives

Sports articles, including information on soccer in the US and Canada, rules for soccer and Australian football, and some rather dated material on American football.
Keywords: Sports, Football, Soccer
Sponsor: The Internet Wiretap Library
Audience: Sports Enthusiasts
Details: Free

gopher://wiretap.spies.com/library/article/sports

Wisconsin

WRPRCC

Keywords: Primates, Wisconsin
Sponsor: Wisconsin Regional Primate Research Center
Audience: Primatologists, Zoologists

Contact: jacobsen@primate.wisc.edu
Details: Free
Expect: Login; enter: wiscinfo; choose: UW-Madison Information Servers Wisconsin Primate Research Center Server

gopher://gopher.primate.wisc.edu

Witchcraft

Harvard University Library

The library's holdings are large and wide ranging and contain significant collections in many fields.
Keywords: Afrikaans, Alchemy, Arabic Culture (History of), Celtic Philology, Congo Languages, Folklore, Hebraica, Mormonism, Numismatics, Quakers, Sanskrit, Witchcraft, Arabic Philology
Audience: General Public, Researchers, Librarians, Document Delivery Professionals
Details: Free
Expect: Mitek Server..., Send: Enter or Return; Expect: prompt, Send: hollis

telnet://hollis.harvard.edu

University of Pennsylvania PENNINFO Library

The library's holdings are large and wide-ranging and contain significant collections in many fields.
Keywords: Church History, Spanish Inquisition, Witchcraft, Shakespeare (William), Bibles, Aristotle (Texts of), Fiction, Whitman (Walt), French Revolution, Drama (French), Literature (English), Literature (Spanish)
Audience: Researchers, Students, General Public
Contact: Al DSouza penninfo-admin@dccs.upenn.edu dsouza@dccs.upenn.edu
Details: Free
Expect: Login; Send: Public

telnet://penninfo.upenn.edu

Women

amlat.mujeres

This conference serves as a forum for interchange between organizations and women's movements in Latin America and the Caribbean.
Keywords: Women, Latin America, Caribbean, Feminism
Audience: Women, Feminists, Activists
Contact: Carlos Afonso (cafonso@ax.apc.org) or APC North American Regional Office
E-mail: apcadmin@apc.org

Edie Farwell (efarwell@igc.apc.org)

Agencia Latinoamericana de Informacion
info@alai.ec
uualai@ecuanex.ec

Establish an account on the nearest APC node. Login, type c for conferences, then type: go amlat.mujeres.

Details: Costs

For information on the nearest APC node, contact APC International Secretariat IBASE

E-mail: apcadmin@apc.org

`telnet://igc.apc.org`

apngowid.meet

A conference on plans by Asia Pacific regional women's groups for the United Nations Fourth World Conference on Women to be held in Beijing in September 1995.

Keywords: Women, Asia, Pacific, Feminists, Development, United Nations, World Conference on Women

Audience: Women, Feminists, Nongovernmental Organizations

Contact: AsPac Info, Docu and Communication Committee
AP-IDC@p95.f401.n751.z6.g

Carlos Afonso (cafonso@ax.apc.org) or APC North American Regional Office

E-mail: apcadmin@apc.org

Edie Farwell (efarwell@igc.apc.org)

Details: Costs, Moderated

Establish an account on the nearest APC node. Login, type c for conferences, then type go apngowid.meet.

For information on the nearest APC node, contact APC International Secretariat IBASE

E-mail: apcadmin@apc.org

`http://www.igc.apc.org/igc/www.women.html`

Forum for Women's Issues

A forum for issues relating to women.

Keywords: Women, General Interest, Feminists
Audience: Women
Contact: Reva Basch
reva@well.sf.ca.us

Details: Free

To participate in a conference on the WELL, you must first establish an account on the WELL.

To do so, start by typing: telnet://well.sf.ca.us

`telnet://well.sf.ca.us`

hr.women

A conference on human rights issues pertaining to women.

Keywords: Women, Feminists, Human Rights
Audience: Women, Feminists, Activists
Contact: Jillaine Smith
jillaine@igc.apc.org

Carlos Afonso (cafonso@ax.apc.org) or APC North American Regional Office

E-mail: apcadmin@apc.org

Edie Farwell (efarwell@igc.apc.org)

Details: Costs
User Info.: Establish an account on the nearest APC node. Login, type c for conferences, then type go hr.women.

For information on the nearest APC node, contact: APC International Secretariat IBASE

E-mail: apcadmin@apc.org

`telnet://igc.apc.org`

InforM Women's Studies Database

A gopher- or FTP-accessible archive of documents, opportunities, and resources pertaining to women's studies and women's issues.

Keywords: Women's Studies, Feminism, Women
Audience: Women, Women's Studies Students, Women's Studies Educators, Other Women's Issues Observers

Profile: This women's studies database is an easily navigable archive of files on women's studies and women's issues. It includes information such as health, employment opportunities, political issues, gender issues in the workplace and in education, reproductive rights, sex discrimination, sexual harassment, violence, work and family, women and computers, feminist film reviews, and poetry. InforM contains a compilation of electronic forums (listservs and newsgroups) for the discussion of male/female relations and societal problems, and for women of diverse cultures and sexual persuasions.

Contact: Paula Gaber
Gaber@info.umd.edu

Details: Free

Gopher or telnet to Inform.umd.edu, select Educational Resources/Women's Studies/. Or FTP to Inform.umd.edu, log in as anonymous, then cd /inforM/Educational_Resources/WomensStudies/

This source is also accessible via gopher, FTP, or Telnet.

`gopher://inform.umd.edu`

`http://inform.umd.edu/welcome.html`

un.wcw.doc.eng

This is a read-only conference comprised of official UN documents for the United Nations Fourth World Conference on Women: Action for Equality, Development and Peace, scheduled to take place at the Beijing International Convention Center, Beijing, China, from 4-15 September 1995. The documents are provided by the official Conference Secretariat, and posted as received by the UN Non-Governmental Liaison Service (NGLS).

Keywords: Women, Development (International), Peace, UN, World Conference on Women

Audience: Women, Activists, Non-Governmental Organizations, Feminists

Contact: United Nations Non-Governmental Liaison Service/Edie Farwell
ngls@igc.apc.org
efarwell@igc.apc.org

Carlos Afonso (cafonso@ax.apc.org) or APC North American Regional Office

E-mail: apcadmin@apc.org

Edie Farwell (efarwell@igc.apc.org)

Details: Costs, Moderated
User Info.: Establish an account on the nearest APC node. Login, type c for conferences, then type go un.wcw.doc.eng.

For information on the nearest APC node, contact: APC International Secretariat IBASE

E-mail: apcadmin@apc.org

`telnet://igc.apc.org`

un.wcw.doc.fra

This is a read-only conference comprised of official UN documents for the United Nations Fourth World Conference on Women: Action for Equality, Development and Peace, scheduled to take place at the Beijing International Convention Center, Beijing, China, from 4-15 September 1995. The documents are provided by the official Conference Secretariat, are posted as received by the UN Non-Governmental Liaison Service (NGLS).

Keywords: Women, Development (International), Peace, UN, World Conference on Women

Women's Issues

Audience: Women, Activists, Non-Governmental Organizations, Feminists
Contact: United Nations Non-Governmental Liaison Service/Edie Farwell
ngls@igc.apc.org or efarwell@igc.apc.org
Carlos Afonso (cafonso@ax.apc.org) or APC North American Regional Office
E-mail: apcadmin@apc.org
Edie Farwell (efarwell@igc.apc.org)
Details: Costs, Moderated
User Info.: Establish an account on the nearest APC node. Login, type c for conferences, then type go un.wcw.doc.fra.
For information on the nearest APC node, contact: APC International Secretariat IBASE
E-mail: apcadmin@apc.org

`telnet://igc.apc.org`

Women.dev ★

Conference for information about local, regional, and international development as it relates to women. The conference includes bibliographies, statements, news, articles, and announcements about development and women in Africa, South America, and South Asia.

Keywords: Women, Development (International), International Politics
Audience: Women, Activists, Non-governmental Organizations, Feminists
Contact: Carlos Afonso (cafonso@ax.apc.org) or APC North American Regional Office
E-mail: apcadmin@apc.org
Edie Farwell (efarwell@igc.apc.org)
Details: Subway, Free
User Info: Establish an account on the nearest APC node. Login, type c for conferences, then type go women.dev.
For information on the nearest APC node, contact: APC International Secretariat IBASE
E-mail: apcadmin@apc.org

`telnet://igc.apc.org`

Women.forum ★

Conference for discussion of women's issues.
Keywords: Women, Feminism, Women's Issues
Audience: Women, Feminists
Contact: Corina Hughes
corina@igc.apc.org
Carlos Afonso (cafonso@ax.apc.org) or APC North American Regional Office
E-mail: apcadmin@apc.org
Edie Farwell (efarwell@igc.apc.org)
Details: Costs
User Info: Establish an account on the nearest APC node. Login, type c for conferences, then type go women.forum.
For information on the nearest APC node, contact: APC International Secretariat IBASE
E-mail: apcadmin@apc.org

`telnet://igc.apc.org`

Women.health ★

This conference features articles, documents, news, announcements, policy statements, and other information about women's health around the world. Topics include breast cancer, ovarian cancer, alcohol, abortion, pregnancy, sterilization of women, pesticides, Quinacrine, HIV, and disabilities.

Keywords: Women, Abortion, AIDS, Disability, Feminism, Health
Audience: Activists, Family Planners, Health Professionals, Non-Governmental Organizations, Women
Contact: Carlos Afonso (cafonso@ax.apc.org) or APC North American Regional Office
E-mail: apcadmin@apc.org
Edie Farwell (efarwell@igc.apc.org)
Details: Costs
User Info: Establish an account on the nearest APC node. Login, type c for conferences, then type go women.health.
For information on the nearest APC node, contact: APC International Secretariat IBASE
E-mail: apcadmin@apc.org

`telnet://igc.apc.org`

Women.labr ★

This conference features news, announcements, articles, and other information pertaining to the status of women workers in Europe, Latin America and the Caribbean, and Asia.

Keywords: Women, Unions
Audience: Women, Activists, Unions
Contact: Carlos Afonso (cafonso@ax.apc.org) or APC North American Regional Office
E-mail: apcadmin@apc.org
Edie Farwell (efarwell@igc.apc.org)
Details: Costs
User Info: Establish an account on the nearest APC node. Login, type c for conferences, then type go women.labr.
For information on the nearest APC node, contact: APC International Secretariat IBASE
E-mail: apcadmin@apc.org

`telnet://igc.apc.org`

Women.news ★

This conference features news and action alerts about women and women's issues around the world—including human rights, feminism, health, sexual abuse, workers, population, abortion, activism, development, and peace.

Keywords: Feminism, Gender, Women
Audience: Women, Feminists, Activists
Contact: Debra Guzman, Sue VanHattum
hrcoord@igc.apc.org or suev@igc.apc.org
Carlos Afonso (cafonso@ax.apc.org) or APC North American Regional Office
E-mail: apcadmin@apc.org
Edie Farwell (efarwell@igc.apc.org)
Details: Free
User Info: Establish an account on the nearest APC node. Login, type c for conferences, then type go women.news.
For information on the nearest APC node, contact: APC International Secretariat IBASE
E-mail: apcadmin@apc.org

`telnet://igc.apc.org`

Women's Issues

Abortion and Reproductive Rights ★★★

A major directory on abortion, providing access to a broad range of related resources (library catalogs, databases, and servers) via the Internet.

Keywords: Abortion Rights, Activism, Women's Issues
Sponsor: The WELL Computer Conference System
Audience: Activists, Feminists
Profile: Choice-Net Report is a weekly update on reproductive rights issues distributed through E-mail; Women's Wire; gopher.WELL.com; Usenet groups alt.activism, talk.abortion; and soc.women, and other Internet channels.
Details: Free

`http://gopher.well.sf.ca.us`

Women's Issues

dh.mujer ★

The primary Association for Progressive Communications conference for women and human rights issues throughout the world. Contains news and announcements.

Keywords: Women's Issues, Feminism, Human Rights
Audience: Feminists, Activists
Contact: Debra Guzman
hrcoord@igc.apc.org
Carlos Afonso (cafonso@ax.apc.org) or APC North American Regional Office
E-mail: apcadmin@apc.org
Edie Farwell (efarwell@igc.apc.org)
Details: Costs
User Info: Establish an account on the nearest APC node. Login, type c for conferences, then type go dh.mujer.
For information on the nearest APC node, contact: APC International Secretariat IBASE
E-mail: apcadmin@apc.org

gopher://gopher.telnet://igc.apc.org (FREE)

http://igc.apc.org (FREE)

ECHO ★★★★

A computer conferencing system based in New York City.

Keywords: Community, Networking, Women's Issues
Sponsor: East Coast Hang Out
Audience: Activists, Policy Makers, Community Leaders, Governments, Students, Feminists, Educators, Health-Care Professionals, Artists, Communicators, General Public
Contact: Stacy Horn
horn@echonyc.com,
Profile: ECHO was started by Stacy Horn as an East Coast counterpart to the WELL. ECHO makes an effort to be hospitable to women and has one of the highest percentages of women in an online community.
Details: Costs

telnet://echonyc.com

table.abortion

A Usenet newsgroup providing information and discussion about all sides of the abortion issue.

Keywords: Abortion, Women's Issues, Health
Audience: Women, Activists, Health-Care Professionals
Details: Free
To subscribe to this Usenet newsgroup, you need access to a newsreader.

news:table.abortion

Women's Wire

Women's Wire is an online interactive network focusing on women's issues and interests.

Keywords: Networking, Women's Issues, Online Services
Audience: Women, Internet Users
Profile: This service acts as an international clearinghouse for resources and networking on a broad range of topics including news, politics, careers, education, parenting, health, and arts. Provides e-mail and access to thousands of resources, including Usenet newsgroups.
Details: Costs
Access via an easy-to-use graphical interface for Macintosh and Windows platforms, or a text-based interface for DOS and Unix platforms. Local access numbers available throughout the US and in most countries.

mailto:info@wwire.net

Women's Studies

alt.feminism ★

A Usenet newsgroup providing information and discussion about feminism.

Keywords: Feminism, Women's Studies, Abortion, Activitism
Audience: Women, General Public
To subscribe to this Usenet newsgroup, you need access to a newsreader.

news:alt.feminism

InforM Women's Studies Database

A gopher- or FTP-accessible archive of documents, opportunities, and resources pertaining to women's studies and women's issues.

Keywords: Women's Studies, Feminism, Women
Audience: Women, Women's Studies Students, Women's Studies Educators, Other Women's Issues Observers
Profile: This women's studies database is an easily navigable archive of files on women's studies and women's issues. It includes information such as health, employment opportunities, political issues, gender issues in the workplace and in education, reproductive rights, sex discrimination, sexual harassment, violence, work and family, women and computers, feminist film reviews, and poetry. InforM contains a compilation of electronic forums (listservs and newsgroups) for the discussion of male/female relations, societal problems, and for women of diverse cultures and sexual persuasions.
Contact: Paula Gaber
Gaber@info.umd.edu
Details: Free
Gopher or telnet to Inform.umd.edu, select Educational Resources/Women's Studies/. Or FTP to Inform.umd.edu, log in as anonymous, then cd /inforM/Educational_Resources/WomensStudies/
This source is also accessible via gopher, FTP, or Telnet.

gopher://inform.umd.edu

http://inform.umd.edu/welcome.html

Northwestern University Library

The library's holdings are large and wide ranging and contain significant collections in many fields.

Keywords: Africa, Wright (Frank Lloyd), Women's Studies, Art, Literature (American), Contemporary Music, Government (US State), UN Documents, Music
Audience: General Public, Researchers, Librarians, Document Delivery Professionals
Details: Free
Expect: COMMAND:, Send: DIAL VTAM

telnet://nuacvm.acns.nwu.edu

Notable Women

A database listing some important and notable women through the ages. Available for online searching by keyword, or as a full-text file.

Keywords: Women's Studies, History (Women's), Feminism
Sponsor: Estrella Mountain Community College (Arizona)
Audience: Women's Studies Educators, Historians, Researchers, Feminists
Contact: EMC Gopher Team
root@gopher.emc.maricopa.edu

gopher://gopher.emc.maricopa.edu

Women's Studies and Resources

A collection of materials related to women's studies and issues.

Keywords: Women's Studies, Feminism
Sponsor: Peripatetic Eclectic Gopher (PEG) at UC Irvine
Audience: Women, Feminists, Activists, Women's Studies Educators and Students

Profile: Contains bibliographies, listserv archives, conference announcements, and other resources related to women's studies. Also has links to other groups and sites related to women's issues.

Contact: Calvin Boyer
cjboyer@uci.edu

`gopher://peg.cwis.uci.edu`

Woodworking

rec.woodworking

A Usenet newsgroup providing information and discussion about woodworking.

Keywords: Woodworking, Crafts, Hobbies
Audience: Woodworkers

To subscribe to this Usenet newsgroup, you need access to a newsreader.

`news:rec.woodworking`

Word Play

alt.callahans

A Usenet newsgroup providing information and discussion about Callahan's bar Members share puns and fellowship.

Keywords: Humor, Word Play
Audience: Punsters, Comedians

To subscribe to this Usenet newsgroup, you need access to a newsreader.

`news:alt.calahans`

Workstations

Works

Works discusses personal workstation computers, such as the Sun2, Sun3, Apollo, Silicon Graphics, and AT&T workstations. Works provides a way for interested members of the Internet community to discuss and share useful insights about these kinds of systems.

Keywords: Workstations, Computers
Audience: Workstation Users, Computer Users
Contact: Dave Steiner
steiner@rutgers.edu
Details: Free

To subscribe to the list, send an E-mail message requesting a subscription to the URL address below.

`mailto:works@rutgers.edu`

WORLD (World News and Information)

WORLD (World News and Information)

This library contains detailed information about every country in Europe, Asia, the Pacific Rim, Africa, the Middle East, and North and South America. Designed for those who need to monitor world events, organizations, and leaders, this library provides a global view of any subject or topic.

Keywords: Business, News
Audience: Business Researchers, Analysts, Entrepreneurs
Profile: WORLD includes information from newspapers and wire services, trade and business journals, company reports, national and regional background, industry and product analysis, business opportunities, and selected legal texts. News sources range from the world-renowned Christian Science Monitor, Financial Times, Reuters and Associated Press to the regionally important eastern European CTK, MTI and PAP newswires, The Toronto Star, Jerusalem Post, and Xinhua News Agency. Business and trade information include a wide variety of sources, such as EIS's European newsletters and Euroscope from Coopers and Lybrand, Canada's Maclean's, Japan's Comline Daily News Service, BNA's international dailies, and the Soviet Union's SovData DiaLine services—all of which help analyze the political and economic climate around the globe. Company information is contained in the EXTEL cards as well as ICC. Providers of national background and industry analysis include Associated Banks of Europe, Bank of America, Business International, IBC USA, and the US Department of Commerce. Economic risk can be assessed with the Economist's Economic Risk Services, IBC's International Reports and International Country Risk Guide, and many of Business International's Country Reports. Political risk is forecast in IBC's Political Risk Services as well as BOA's World Information Services' Country RiskOutlooks, Monitors, and Forecasts.

Contact: Mead New Sales Group at (800) 227-4908 or (513) 859-5398 inside the U.S., or (513) 865-7981 for all inquiries outside the U.S.

To subscribe, contact Mead directly.

To examine the Nexis user guide, you can access it at the ftp site of the University of Texas at Austin at the URL address: ftp://ftp.cc.utexas.edu

The files are in /pub/ref-services/LEXIS

`telnet://nex.meaddata.com`

`http://www.meaddata.com`

World Bank Gopher Server

World Bank Gopher Server

A collection of online information from the World Bank.

Keywords: Government (International), Development, International Finance, Foreign Trade
Sponsor: The World Bank
Audience: Nongovernmental Organizations, Activists, Government Officials, Environmentalists
Profile: A collection of World Bank information including a list of publications, environmental assessments, economic reports, and updates on current projects being funded by the World Bank.
Contact: webmaster@www.worldbank.org

`gopher://gopher.worldbank.org`

`http://www.worldbank.org`

World Conference on Women

apngowid.meet

A conference on plans by Asia Pacific regional women's groups for the United Nations Fourth World Conference on Women to be held in Beijing in September 1995.

Keywords: Women, Asia, Pacific, Feminists, Development, United Nations, World Conference on Women
Audience: Women, Feminists, Nongovernmental Organizations
Contact: AsPac Info, Docu and Communication Committee
AP-IDC@p95.f401.n751.z6.g
Details: Costs, Moderated

Establish an account on the nearest APC node. Login, type c for conferences, then type: go apngowid.meet.

For information on the nearest APC node, contact: APC International Secretariat IBASE

E-mail: apcadmin@apc.org

Contact: Carlos Afonso (cafonso@ax.apc.org) or APC North American Regional Office

E-mail: apcadmin@apc.org

Edie Farwell (efarwell@igc.apc.org)

`http://www.igc.apc.org/igc/www.women.html`

un.wcw.doc.eng

This is a read-only conference comprised of official UN documents for the United Nations Fourth World Conference on Women: Action for Equality, Development and Peace, scheduled to take place at the Beijing International Convention Center, Beijing, China, from 4-15 September 1995. The documents are provided by the official Conference Secretariat, are posted as received by the UN Non-Governmental Liaison Service (NGLS).

Keywords: Women, Development (International), Peace, UN, World Conference on Women
Audience: Women, Activists, Non-Governmental Organizations, Feminists
Contact: United Nations Non-Governmental Liaison Service/Edie Farwell
ngls@igc.apc.org
efarwell@igc.apc.org
Details: Costs, Moderated
User Info: Establish an account on the nearest APC node. Login, type c for conferences, then type go un.wcw.doc.eng. For information on the nearest APC node, contact: APC International Secretariat IBASE
E-mail: apcadmin@apc.org
Contact: Carlos Afonso (cafonso@ax.apc.org) or APC North American Regional Office
E-mail: apcadmin@apc.org
Edie Farwell (efarwell@igc.apc.org)

telnet://igc.apc.org

un.wcw.doc.fra

This is a read-only conference comprised of official UN documents for the United Nations Fourth World Conference on Women: Action for Equality, Development and Peace, scheduled to take place at the Beijing International Convention Center, Beijing, China, from 4-15 September 1995. The documents are provided by the official Conference Secretariat, are posted as received by the UN Non-Governmental Liaison Service (NGLS).

Keywords: Women, Development (International), Peace, UN, World Conference on Women
Audience: Women, Activists, Non-Governmental Organizations, Feminists
Contact: United Nations Non-Governmental Liaison Service/Edie Farwell
ngls@igc.apc.org or efarwell@igc.apc.org
Details: Costs, Moderated
User Info: Establish an account on the nearest APC node. Login, type c for conferences, then type go un.wcw.doc.fra. For information on the nearest APC node, contact: APC International Secretariat IBASE
E-mail: apcadmin@apc.org
Contact: Carlos Afonso (cafonso@ax.apc.org) or APC North American Regional Office
E-mail: apcadmin@apc.org
Contact: Edie Farwell (efarwell@igc.apc.org)

telnet://igc.apc.org

World Constitutions

World Constitutions

A list of world constitutions, containing the constitutions of more than 18 nations including Basic Law of Germany 1949; Constitution of Macedonia (in former Yugoslavia); and Magna Carta.

Keywords: Law (International), History (World), Politics (International)
Audience: Researchers, Lawyers, Historians
Details: Free

gopher://wiretap.spies.com

World Cycling Championship 1994

World Cycling Championship 1994

This web site contains information about events surrounding the 1994 World Cycling Championship.

Keywords: Bicycles
Audience: Bicyclists, Sports Fans

http://www-worldbike.iunet.it/

World Health

HungerWeb

This web site focuses on the political, economic, agricultural, and ethical implications of world hunger.

Keywords: World Health, Activism
Sponsor: Oxfam
Audience: Activists, Financial Planners
Contact: Daniel Zalik
Daniel_Zalik@cs.brown.edu
Details: Free

http://www.hunger.brown.edu/oxfam

National Library of Medicine Gopher

World Health Organization (WHO)

This gopher provides information about the National Library of Medicine, the world's largest single-topic library.

Keywords: Medicine, Health, World Health
Sponsor: National Library of Medicine, Massachusetts
World Health Organization, Geneva, Switzerland
Audience: Health-care Professionals, Medical Professionals, Researchers
Profile: The National Library of Medicine (NLM) cares for over 4.5 million holdings (including books, journals, reports, manuscripts, and audio-visual items). The NLM offers extensive online information services dealing with clinical care, toxicology, environmental health, and basic biomedical research. It has several active research and development components, including an extramural grants program, houses an extensive history of medicine collection, and provides several programs designed to improve the nation's medical library system.
Contact: R. P. C. Rodgers
rodgers@nlm.nih.gov
akazawa@who.ch
Details: Free

gopher://el-gopher.med.utah.edu

gopher://gopher.who.ch

World Health Organization (WHO)

This gopher provides access to the databases of the WHO.

Keywords: World Health, Health, Medicine, Non-governmental organizations
Sponsor: World Health Organization, Geneva, Switzerland
Audience: Medical Professionals, Researchers
Contact: akazawa@who.ch
Details: Free

gopher://gopher.who.ch

World Wide Web (WWW)

WebCrawler (The)

The WebCrawler is a tool for searching the Web.

Keywords: Robots, WWW, Internet Access
Sponsor: The Department of Computer Science and Engineering, University of Washington, Seattle, WA, USA

Audience: Internet Surfers

Profile: The WebCrawler is a tool for searching the Web. It operates by traversing the Web and either building an index for later use, or by searching in real-time for a query. The index built by the WebCrawler is available for searching via the WebCrawler Search Page.

Contact: Brian Pinkerton

User Info: email: bp@cs.washington.edu

Details: Free

`http://www.biotech.washington.edu/WebCrawler/WebQuery.html`

World Wide Web (WWW)

World Wide Web (WWW) is an Internet access tool which retrieves resources through a hypertext browser of databases.

Keywords: Internet Tools, World Wide Web (WWW)

Sponsor: CERN (European Laboratory for Particle Physics)

Audience: Internet Surfers

Details: Free

Documents and guides are in: pub/www/doc

`ftp://info.cern.ch`

World Wide Web Book

A book describing the WWW (World Wide Web) project.

Keywords: Internet Tools, World Wide Web (WWW)

Audience: Internet Surfers

Details: Free

`ftp://emx.cc.utexas.edu`

World Wide Web Demo

A Telnet session demonstrating the World Wide Web (WWW), an Internet access tool.

Keywords: Internet Tools, World Wide Web (WWW)

Audience: Internet Surfers

Details: Free

No surname is needed

`telnet://info.cern.ch`

World Wide Web FAQ

A web site containing common questions and answers about WWW, a distributed hypermedia system first developed by CERN.

Keywords: World Wide Web (WWW), Internet Reference, Information Retrieval

Audience: Students, Computer Scientists, Researchers

Contact: Thomas Boutell, Nathan Torkington
boutell@netcom.com
nathan.torckington@vuw.ac.nz

`http://sunsite.unc.edu/boutell/faq/www_faq.html`

World Wide Web Worm (WWWW)

WWWW provides a mechanism to search the WWW in a multitude of ways. It also provides lists of all Home pages and of all URLs cited anywhere. This site contains an exhaustive list of WWW servers nationally and internationally.

Keywords: World Wide Web, (WWW), Information Retrieval, Internet

Sponsor: University of Colorado at Boulder, Department of Computer Science, Boulder, Colorado, USA

Audience: Researchers, Students, General Public

Contact: Oliver McBryan
mcbryan@cs.colorado.edu

`http://www.cs.colorado.edu/home/mcbryan/WWWW.html`

Worldview

Principia Cybernetica Newsletter

Newsletter for participants in the Principia Cybernetica Project (PCP), as well as for people interested in keeping informed about the project.

Keywords: Philosophy, Worldview

Audience: Philosophers

Profile: PCP is a computer-supported collaborative attempt to develop an integrated evolutionary-systemic philosophy or world view. Its contributors are distributed over several continents and maintain contact primarily through electronic mail (mailing list PRNCYB-L), as well as through annual meetings, the printed (and electronic) newsletter, and postal mail. PCP focuses on the clear formulation of basic concepts and principles of the cybernetic approach.

Contact: Cliff Joslyn, Francis Heylighen
fheyligh@vnet3.vub.ac.be
cjoslyn@bingvaxu.cc.binghamton.edu

Details: Free

Send a 1- to 2-page letter, giving your address and affiliations and explaining your interest in the Project to the List owner (C. Joslyn).

`mailto:cjoslyn@bingvaxu.cc.binghamton.edu`

Wrestling

rec.sport.pro-wrestling

A Usenet newsgroup providing information and discussion about professional wrestling.

Keywords: Wrestling, Sports

Audience: Wrestling Fans, Sports Fans
To subscribe to this Usenet newsgroup, you need access to a newsreader.

`news:rec.sport.pro-wrestling`

Wright (Frank Lloyd)

Northwestern University Library

The library's holdings are large and wide ranging and contain significant collections in many fields.

Keywords: Africa, Wright (Frank Lloyd), Women's Studies, Art, Literature (American), Contemporary Music, Government (US State), UN Documents, Music

Audience: General Public, Researchers, Librarians, Document Delivery Professionals

Details: Free

Expect: COMMAND:, Send: DIAL VTAM

`telnet://nuacvm.acns.nwu.edu`

Writing

Arts Wire

A national communications network for the arts located on the Meta Network.

Keywords: Art, Writing, Activism, Music

Sponsor: New York Foundation for the Arts

Audience: Art Activists, Art Organizations, Artists, Composers, Foundations, Government Arts Agencies, Writers

Profile: Arts Wire provides immediate access to news, information, and dialogue on conditions affecting the arts and artists, as well as private conferences for organizations. Core features include Money, a searchable resource of grant deadlines; Hotwire, a summary of arts news; and conferences about new music, interactive art, literature, AIDS, and Latino art.

Contact: Judy Malloy
artswire@tmn.com

`telnet://tmn.com`

fwake-l

A conference and forum for a broad discussion of James Joyce's Finnegan's Wake.

Keywords: Joyce (James), Literature (Irish), Authors, Writing

Audience: Writers, Joyce Scholars, Literary Critics, Literary Theorists

To subscribe to the list, send an e-mail message to the URL address below consisting of a single line reading: SUB fwake-l

`mailto:listserv@irlearn.ucd.ie`

journet

An electronic conference for the discussion of topics of interest to journalists and journalism educators.

Keywords: Journalism, Writing, Desktop Publishing, Electronic Publishing

Audience: Journalists, Writers, Publishers, Educators

Contact: George Frajkor
gfrajkor@ccs.carleton.ca

To subscribe to the list, send an e-mail message to the URL address below consisting of a single line reading:

SUB journet YourFirstName YourLastName

To send a message to the entire list, address it to: journet@qucdn.queensu.ca

`mailto:listserv@qucdn.queensu.ca`

news.announce.conferences

A Usenet newsgroup providing information and discussion about conferences, as well as calls for papers.

Keywords: Conferences, Papers, Writing

Audience: Writers, General Public

Details: Free

To subscribe to this Usenet newsgroup, you need access to a newsreader.

`news:news.announce.conferences`

Pen-pals

This mailing list provides a forum for children to correspond with each other electronically. Although the list is not moderated, it is monitored for content and is managed by listproc.

Keywords: Computing, Children, Writing

Audience: Computer Users, Children, Student Writers

Contact: pen-pals-request@mainstream.com

Details: Free

To subscribe to the list, send an e-mail message requesting a subscription to the URL address below. To send a message to the entire list, address it to: pen-pals@mainstream.com

`mailto:pen-pals@mainstream.com`

Quanta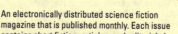

An electronically distributed science fiction magazine that is published monthly. Each issue contains short fiction, articles, and editorials by authors from around the world and across the Net.

Keywords: Science Fiction, Writing, Publications

Audience: Science Fiction Enthusiasts, Writers

Contact: da1n@andrew.cmu.edu

Details: Free

To subscribe to the list, send an e-mail message requesting a subscription to the URL address below.

To send a message to the entire list, address it to: da1n@andrew.cmu.edu

`mailto:da1n@andrew.cmu.edu`

soc.penpals

A Usenet newsgroup providing information and discussion for people in search of Net pals and other online correspondence.

Keywords: Computing, Writing

Audience: Computer Users, Writers

Details: Free

To subscribe to this Usenet newsgroup, you need access to a newsreader.

`news:soc.penpals`

Style Sheets from the Online Writers' Workshop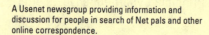

This gopher provides information and examples on how to write bibliographies using three formats: MLA (Modern Language Association), Old-MLA, and APA (American Psychological Association).

Keywords: Bibliographies, Writing, Lexicology

Sponsor: University of Illinois at Urbana-Champaign

Audience: Writers, Students (High School/College/University)

Contact: Dr. Michael Pemberton
michaelp@ux1.cso.uiuc

`gopher://gopher.uiuc.edu`

wroclaw

wroclaw

Distribution of information from weekly Polish bulletin called Society Journal.

Keywords: Poland

Audience: Polish Speakers, Researchers, General Public

Contact: Pawel Misiak
misiak@plwrtu11

Details: Free

To subscribe to the list, send an e-mail message to the URL address shown below consisting of a single line reading:

SUB wroclaw YourFirstName YourLastName

To send a message to the entire list, address it to: wroclaw@plearn.edu.p1

`mailto:listserv@plearn.edu.p1`

WRPRCC

WRPRCC

Keywords: Primates, Wisconsin

Sponsor: Wisconsin Regional Primate Research Center

Audience: Primatologists, Zoologists

Contact: jacobsen@primate.wisc.edu

Details: Free

Expect: Login; enter: wiscinfo; choose: UW-Madison Information Servers Wisconsin Primate Research Center Server

`gopher://gopher.primate.wisc.edu`

WWW

Best of the Web '94

This web site highlights those places which were judged as the best sites (based on the criteria of quality, versatility, and power) on the World Wide Web.

Keywords: Internet, WWW

Audience: Internet Surfers

Contact: Brandon Plewe
plewe@acsu.buffalo.edu

Details: Free

`http://wings.buffalo.edu/contest`

comp.infosystems.www

A Usenet newsgroup providing information and discussion about the World Wide Web.

Keywords: WWW, Internet Reference, Information Retrieval
Audience: Internet Surfers
To subscribe to this Usenet newsgroup, you need access to a newsreader.

`news:comp.infosystems.www`

Computer-Mediated Marketing Environments

A web site devoted to research aimed at understanding the ways in which computer-mediated marketing environments (CMEs), especially the Internet, are revolutionizing the way firms conduct business.

Keywords: WWW, Information Retrieval, Internet, Marketing, Business
Sponsor: Vanderbilt University, Owen Graduate School of Management, Nashville, Tennessee, USA
Audience: General Public, Entrepeneurs, Financial Planners, Marketers
Contact: Donna Hoffman, Tom Novak
hoffman@colette.ogsm.vanderbilt.edu
novak@moe.ogsm.vanderbilt.edu

`http://colette.ogsm.vanderbilt.edu`

CSORG (Clearinghouse for Subject-Oriented Internet Resource Guides)

The goal of CSORG is to collect subject-oriented guides to Internet resources and make them widely available. These guides are produced by members of the Internet community, and by SILS students who participate in the Internet Resource Discovery project.

Keywords: WWW, Information Retrieval, Internet
Sponsor: University of Michigan, School of Information and Library Studies, Michigan, USA
Audience: Reseachers, Students, General Public
Contact: Louis Rosenfeld
i-guides@umich.edu

`gopher://una.hh.lib.umich.edu/11/inetdirs`

E-mail WWW

E-mail WWW allows the user to obtain a web file via E-mail.

Keywords: Internet Services, E-mail, WWW
Audience: Internet Surfers
Details: Free
Include the words "www URL" in the e-mail.

`http://info.cern.ch/hypertext/WWW/TheProject.html`

EINet Galaxy

EINet Galaxy is a guide to world wide information and services. It includes public information as well as commercial information and services provided by EINet customers and affiliates. The information is organized by topic, and can be searched.

Keywords: WWW, Information Retrieval, Internet
Sponsor: Microelectronic and Computer Technology Corporation (MCC)
Audience: Reseachers, Students
Contact: Wayne Allen, Bruce Speyer
WA@EINet.net, Speyer@EINet.net

`http://galaxy.einet.net/galaxy.html`

Entering the WWW

An article entitled "Entering the World-Wide Web: A Guide to Cyberspace."

Keywords: Internet Tools, WWW
Sponsor: Honolulu Community College
Audience: Internet Surfers
Contact: Kevin Hughes
kevinh@pulua.hcc.hawaii.edu
Details: Free

`http://www.hcc.hawaii.edu/guide/www.guide.html`

HTML FAQ

Common questions and answers about HTML (Hypertext Markup Language). The FAQ covers the practices of creating new documents specifically for the WWW format, as well as transforming existing materials into WWW documents.

Keywords: WWW, Internet Reference, Information Retrieval
Audience: Students, Computer Scientists, Researchers
Contact: Iain O'Cain
ec@umcc.umich.edu

`http://www.umcc.umich.edu/~ec/www/html_faq.html`

Mosaic Home Page

This is the welcome page to the National Center for Supercomputing Applications (NCSA) World-Wide Web server, which features the Mosaic application. Mosaic provides a network-distributed hypermedia system for information discovery. It is Internet-based and is free for academic research and internal commercial use.

Keywords: Internet Tools, Mosaic, WWW
Audience: Internet Surfers
Contact: mosaic-x@ncsa.uiuc.edu
Details: Free

`http://www.ncsa.uiuc.edu/SDG/Software/Mosaic/NCSAMosaicHome.html`

Netfind

Netfind is a way of finding Internet e-mail addresses.

Keywords: WWW, Information Retrieval, E-mail
Sponsor: Emory University, Georgia, USA
Audience: Reseachers, Students, General Public
Profile: This service relies on common but not universal programs, and thus may not find some people with valid addresses. The most foolproof way of finding someone's e-mail address remains to call them on the phone and ask. All Netfind sites are functionally equivalent. Multiple ones are listed here in case some are overloaded or down with technical problems.
Contact: Netfind Help
schwartz@cs.colorado.edu

`gopher://emoryu1.cc.emory.edu/11/internet/General/netfind`

Searching Gopherspace with Veronica

A resource which conducts Veronica searches over restricted areas of the Internet.

Keywords: WWW, Information Retrieval, Internet
Audience: Reseachers, Students, General Public

`gopher://gopher.well.sf.ca.us/11/outbound/veronica.search`

Telnet Access to WWW (World-Wide Web)

A server providing free public access to WWW written in both English and Hebrew.

Keywords: WWW, Internet Tools, Jerusalem
Sponsor: Hebrew University of Jerusalem
Audience: Internet Surfers
Contact: RASHTY@www.huji.ac.il
Expect: Username; Send: WWW

`telnet://www.huji.ac.il`

The InterNIC Home Page

This is the home page for the InterNIC networking organization.

Keywords: WWW, Information Retrieval, Computer Science, Internet Resources
Sponsor: National Science Foundation, USA
Audience: Reseachers, Students, General Public

Profile:	The InterNIC is a collaborative project of three organizations, which work together to offer the Internet community a full scope of network information services. These services include providing information about accessing and using the Internet, assistance in locating resources on the network, and registering network components for Internet connectivity. The overall goal of the InterNIC is to make networking and networked information more easily accessible to researchers, educators, and the general public. The term InterNIC signifies cooperation between Network Information Centers, or NICS.
Contact:	InfoGuide guide@internic.net
Details:	InterNIC signifies cooperation between Network Information Centers

`http://www.internic.net`

The Scout Report

The Scout Report is a weekly publication offered by InterNIC Information Services to the Internet community as a fast, convenient way to stay informed on network activities.

Keywords:	WWW, Information Retrieval, Internet, Computer Networking
Sponsor:	National Science Foundation, USA
Audience:	Researchers, Students, General Public
Profile:	The purpose of this resource is to combine in one place the highlights of new resource announcements and other news which occurred on the Internet during the previous week. The Report is released every Friday. Categories included each week will vary depending on content, and the report will evolve with time and with input from the networking community.
Contact:	InfoGuide scout@is.internic.net guide@is.internic.net

`http://www.internic.net/scout-report`

The Virtual Tourist - WWW Information

This site constitutes an attempt to catalogue and organize WWW sites by geographic location.

Keywords:	WWW, Internet Tools
Sponsor:	The State University of New York at Buffalo, Buffalo, New York, USA
Audience:	Internet Surfers, General Public
Profile:	Using CERN's master list of WWW servers, this Mosiac-accessible site is centered around an interactive world map which displays WWW/NIR sites within countries and regions. Multimedia Virtual Tourist guides are available for some countires, providing political, cultural, and historical information.
Contact:	Brandon Plewe plewe@acsu.buffalo.edu

`http://wings.buffalo.edu/world`

UC Berkeley Museum of Paleontology and the WWW Subway

This web site provides a multimedia museum display from UC Berkeley's Museum of Paleontology. Also features an interactive Subway—a tool linking users to other museums and WWW sites around the world.

Keywords:	WWW, Museums, Paleontology
Sponsor:	University of California at Berkeley, Museum of Paleontology, Berkeley, California, USA
Audience:	Paleontologists, Internet Surfers, General Public
Contact:	David Polly, Robert Guralnick davip@ucmp1.berkeley.edu robg@fossil.berkeley.edu
Details:	Subway

`http://ucmp1.berkeley.edu/subway.html`

WAIS, Inc.

WAIS, Inc. provides interactive online publishing systems and services to organizations that publish information over the Internet. The organization's three main goals are to develop the Internet as a viable means for distributing information electronically; to improve the nature and quality of information available over networks; and to offer better methods to access that information.

Keywords:	WWW, Information Retrieval, Publishing, Internet Tools, WAIS
Sponsor:	WAIS, Inc.
Audience:	Researchers, Students, General Public, Publishers
Contact:	Webmaster webmaster@wais.com

`http://server.wais.com/`

World-Wide Web (WWW)

World-Wide Web (WWW) is an Internet access tool which retrieves resources through a hypertext browser of databases.

Keywords:	Internet Tools, WWW
Sponsor:	CERN (European Laboratory for Particle Physics)
Audience:	Internet Surfers
Details:	Free Documents and guides are in pub/www/doc

`ftp://info.cern.ch`

World-Wide Web Book

A book describing the WWW (World-Wide Web) project.

Keywords:	Internet Tools, WWW
Audience:	Internet Surfers
Details:	Free

`ftp://emx.cc.utexas.edu`

World-Wide Web Demo

A Telnet session demonstrating the World-Wide Web (WWW), an Internet access tool.

Keywords:	Internet Tools, WWW
Audience:	Internet Surfers
Details:	Free No surname is needed

`telnet://info.cern.ch`

World Wide Web FAQ

A web site containing common questions and answers about WWW, a distributed hypermedia system first developed by CERN.

Keywords:	WWW, Internet Reference, Information Retrieval
Audience:	Students, Computer Scientists, Researchers
Contact:	Thomas Boutell, Nathan Torkington boutell@netcom.com nathan.torckington@vuw.ac.nz

`http://sunsite.unc.edu/boutell/faq/www_faq.html`

World-Wide Web Worm (WWWW)

WWWW provides a mechanism to search the WWW in a multitude of ways. It also provides lists of all Home pages and of all URLs cited anywhere. This site contains an exhaustive list of WWW servers nationally and internationally.

Keywords:	WWW, Information Retrieval, Internet
Sponsor:	University of Colorado at Boulder, Department of Computer Science, Boulder, Colorado, USA
Audience:	Researchers, Students, General Public
Contact:	Oliver McBryan mcbryan@cs.colorado.edu

`http://www.cs.colorado.edu/home/mcbryan/WWW.html`

WWW Catalog

A catalog for World-Wide Web (WWW), an Internet access tool.

Keywords:	Internet Tools, WWW
Sponsor:	Centre Universitaire d'Informatique, University of Geneva
Audience:	Internet Surfers
Details:	Free

`http://cui_www.unige.ch`

WWW FAQ

Answers to frequently asked questions (FAQs) about World-Wide Web (WWW), an Internet access tool.

Keywords: Internet Tools, WWW, FAQs
Audience: Internet Surfers
Details: Free

`ftp://info.cern.ch`

WWW Biological Science Servers

WWW Biological Science Servers

A web site containing Internet links to many gopher servers and other web sites pertaining to bioscience.

Keywords: Bioscience, Biology
Sponsor: U.S. Department of the Interior Survey
Audience: Biologists, Researchers
Contact: Systems Operator
webmaster@info.er.usgs.gov

`http://info.er.usgs.gov/network/science/biology/index.html`

WWW Chemistry Sites

WWW Chemistry Sites

This is a major departure site for a vast array of chemical resources. Provides a list of WWW chemistry sites at academic institutions.

Keywords: Chemistry
Audience: Chemists, Chemistry Students, Chemical Engineers
Contact: Max Kopelevich
mik@chem.ucla.edu
Details: Free

`http://www.chem.ucla.edu/chempointers.html`

WWW Information

InterNIC Directory Services (White Pages)

This web site provides free access to X.500, WHOIS, and Netfind white pages on the Internet.

Keywords: WWW Information, Internet, Internet Tools
Sponsor: National Science Foundation, USA
Audience: General Public, Students
Contact: Database Administrator
admin@ds.internic.net

`http://ds.internic.net/ds/dspgwp.html`

WWW Paris

WWW Paris

A web site created as a collaborative effort among individuals in both Paris and the United States.

Keywords: Paris, Culture, Art, Travel, French, Tourism
Audience: Students, Educators, Travelers, Researchers
Profile: Contains an extensive collection of images and text regarding all of the major monuments and museums of Paris, including maps of the Métro and the RER; calendars of events and current expositions; and promotional images and text relating to local department stores. There is also a visitors' section with up-to-date tourist information on hotels, restaurants, telephones, airport schedules, a basic Paris glossary, and the latest weather images. Includes an extensive collection of links to other resources about Paris and France, and a selected bibliography of history and architecture in Paris.
Contact: Norman Barth, Eric Pouliquen
nbarth@ucsd.edu
epouliq@ucsd.edu

`http://meteora.ucsd.edu/~norman/paris`

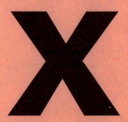

X.500

X.500

A catalog of available X.500 Implementations, a globally distributed Internet directory service.

Keywords:	Internet Tools, X.500
Sponsor:	SRI International and Lawrence Berkeley Laboratory
Audience:	Internet Surfers
Contact:	Ruth Lang, Russ Wright rlang@nisc.sri.com or wright@lbl.gov
Details:	Free File is: documents/fyi/fyi_11.txt

ftp://nic.merit.edu

XTC

Chalkhills

A mailing list for the discussion of the music and records of XTC (the band).

Keywords:	Pop Music, Musical Groups
Audience:	Pop Music Enthusiasts, XTC Enthusiasts
Contact:	John M. Relph chalkhills-request@presto.ig.com
Details:	Free, Moderated To subscribe to the list, send an e-mail message requesting a subscription to the URL address below. To send a message to the entire list, address it to: chalkhills@presto.ig.com
Notes:	Chalkhills is moderated and distributed in a digest format.

mailto:chalkhills-request@presto.ig.com

Yahoo Market and Investments

Yahoo Market and Investments

A comprehensive look at the current economic status, with a wide range of coverage, from brokers to stocks.

Keywords: Business, Stock Market, Investments, Economics

Sponsor: Stanford University, Palo Alto, California, USA

Audience: Investors, Economists

Contact: jerry@akebono.stanford.edu

`http://akebono.stanford.edu/yahoo/Economy/Markets_and_Investments`

Yale Directory of Internet Libraries

Yale Directory of Internet Libraries

An online directory of international library catalogs containing links to many servers, including several with Internet access tools.

Keywords: Libraries, Internet, Resources

Sponsor: Yale University, New Haven, Connecticut, USA

Audience: General Audience

Profile: The Yale Directory of Internet Libraries is a comprehensive listing of international libraries that provides information about the subject area strengths of many of its entries.

`gopher://gophlib@gopher.yale.edu`

Yeats (William Butler)

The University of Kansas Library

The library's holdings are large and wide-ranging and contain significant collections in many fields.

Keywords: Botany, Chinese Studies, Cartography (History of), Kansas, Opera, Ornithology, Joyce (James), Yeats (William Butler), Walpole (Sir Robert, Collections of)

Audience: General Public, Researchers, Librarians, Document Delivery Professionals

Contact: John S. Miller

Details: Free

Expect: Username, Send: relay <cr>

`telnet://kuhub.cc.ukans.edu`

Yugoslavia

I.S.P.O.B. Bulletin YSSTI (Yugoslav System for Scientific and Technology Information)

The participants in this system can exchange news about the operations and development of YSSTI.

Keywords: Information Sciences, Yugoslavia

Sponsor: Institute of Information Sciences, University of Maribor, Yugoslavia

Audience: Information Scientists

Contact: Davor Sostaric
davor%rcum@yubgef51.bitnet

Subscribe by sending an e-mail with a single line containing:

SUBSCRIBE P.O.B. to addresses POB%RCUM@YUBGEF51.bitnet

`mailto:pob%rcum@yubgef51.bitnet`

soc.culture.yugoslavia

A Usenet newsgroup providing information and discussion about the people and culture of Yugoslavia.

Keywords: Yugoslavia, Sociology

Audience: Sociologists, Yugoslavians

Details: Free

To subscribe to this Usenet newsgroup, you need access to a newsreader.

`news:soc.culture.yugoslavia`

726

Z

Zarf's List of Interactive Games on the Web

Zarf's List of Interactive Games on the Web

A list containing links to games and toys that can be played on the Internet.

Keywords: Games, Toys, Entertainment, Recreation
Sponsor: Carnegie Mellon University, School of Computer Science, Pittsburgh, Pennsylvania, USA
Audience: General Public, Game Players, Kids
Contact: Andrew Plotkin
zarf@cs.cmu.edu, apli@andrew.cmu.edu

http://www.cs.cmu.edu/:800/afs/cs.cmu.edu/user/zarf/www/games.html

Zen and the Art of the Internet

Zen and the Art of the Internet

A beginner's guide to the Internet.

Keywords: Internet, Internet Guide
Audience: Internet Surfers
Contact: Brendan Kehoe
guide-bugs@cs.widener.edu
Details: Free
User Info: File is: /net/zen/zen-1.0.txt

ftp://csn.org

'Zines

FutureCulture FAQ (Frequently Asked Questions) File

List of online and offline items of interest to subscribers of FutureCulture, a mailing list on 'technoculture' or 'new edge' or 'cyberculture.'

Keywords: Technology, Cyberculture, Postmodernism, Sci-Fi, Zines
Audience: Reality Hackers, Cyberculture Enthuasists
Profile: This list discusses cyberpunk culture, rave culture, industrial music, virtual reality, drugs, computer underground, Net sociology, and virtual communities.
Contact: Alias Datura (adatura on IRC)
adatura@uafhp.uark.edu
Details: Free

ftp://etext.archive.umich.edu/pub

Internet Wiretap

A resource containing electronic books, zines, and government documents, White House press releases, and links to worldwide gopher and WAIS servers.

Keywords: Electronic Media, Cyberculture, Zines
Sponsor: Internet Wiretap
Audience: Cyberculture Enthusiasts, Civil Libertarians, Educators

gopher://wiretap.spies.com/11/

http://wiretap.spies.com

Mother Jones

A web site containing online electronic issues of Mother Jones magazine (and Zine), making possible instant electronic feedback to the publishers regarding articles.

Keywords: Zines, Ethics, Public Policy, Activism
Sponsor: Mother Jones
Audience: Students, General Public
Contact: Webserver
webserver@mojones.com

http://www.mojones.com/motherjones.html

Zoology

Agriculture, Veterinary Science & Zoology

This directory is a compilation of information resources focused on agriculture, veterinary science, and zoology.

Keywords: Agriculture, Veterinary Science, Zoology
Audience: Farmers, Agronomists, Veterinarians, Zoologists
Details: Free

ftp://una.hh.lib.umich.edu/70/inetdirsstacks/agvetzoo:haas

Biosis Previews

The database encompasses the entire field of life sciences and covers original research reports and reviews in biological and biomedical areas. This includes field, laboratory, clinical, experimental and theoretical work. The traditional areas of biology, including botany, zoology and microbiology are covered, as well as the related fields such as plant and animal science, agriculture, pharmacology and ecology.

Keywords: Biology, Botany, Zoology, Microbiology, Plant Science, Animal Science, Agriculture, Pharmacology, Ecology, Biochemistry, Biophysics, Bio-engineering

Sponsor: Biosis
Audience: Librarians, Researchers, Students, Biologists, Botanists, Zoologists, Scientists, Taxonomists
Contact: CDP Technologies Sales Department (800)950-2035, extension 400.
To subscribe, contact CDP Technologies directly.

`telnet://cdplus@cdplus.com`

University of Michigan Library ★★

The library's holdings are large and wide-ranging and contain significant collections in many fields, including the following:

Keywords: Asia, Astronomy, Transportation, Lexicology, Math, Zoology, Geography
Audience: Researchers, Students, General Public
Contact: info@merit.edu
Details: Free
Expect: Which Host; Send: Help

`telnet://cts.merit.edu`

APPENDIX A

Keywords

ABC Programming Language
Abolitionism
Abortion
Abortion Rights
Academia
Academics
Accounting
ACLU
Acoustical Engineering
Activism
Ada (Programming Language)
ADD (Attention Deficit/Hyperactivity Disorder)
Adoption
APC (Advanced Product Centers)
Advanced Workshops
Advertising
Advisory (Student)
Aeronautics
Aeronautics (History of)
Aerospace
Aerospace Engineering
Africa
African American Studies
African Studies
Afrikaans
Aging
Agoraphobia
Agriculture
AIDS
Aikido
Air Conditioning
Airplanes
Alaska
Alchemy
Aldus PageMaker
Alex
Aliens
Allergies
Alloys
Alspa Computer
Alternative Management
Alternative Medicine
Alternative Press
Ambulatory Care
American Drama
American Studies
Americana
Americana (Western)
Amiga
Analog Equipment
Analysis
Animal Rights
Animal Science
Animal Studies
Animal Welfare
Animals
Animation
Annealing
Annual Reports
Anthropology
Anti-Semitism
Antiquarian Books
APL
Apple Computer
Aquaculture
Aquariums
Aquatic Biology
Aquatic Chemistry
Aquatic Science
Arabic Culture (History of)
Arabic Philology
Archaeology
Archie
Architecture
Archosaurs
Argentina
Aristotle (Texts of)
Art
Art Exhibitions
Art History
Artificial Intelligence
Artificial Life
ASCII
Asia
Asian American Studies
Asian Studies
Assignees
Astronomy
Astrophysics
AT&T
Atari
Atmosphere
Atmospheric Science
AUC TeX
Audio Electronics
Audio Reproduction
Audio-Visual Materials
Auditing
Australia
Austrian History
Autocrossing
Automobiles
Autopoiesis

Aviation
Aviation Industry
Ayurveda
Baby Boomer Culture
Bagpipes
Balloon Art
Ballooning
Ballroom Dancing
Baltic Republics
Balzac (Honore de)
Banking
Bankruptcy
Baseball
Basketball
Basque Studies
BBS
Beer
Behavior
Behavioral Science
Belgium
Berlin Wall
BETA
Bibles
Bibliographies
Bicycling
Biochemistry
Biodiversity
Bioengineering
Biographies
Bioinformatics
Biological Research
Biological Sciences
Biology
Biomechanics
Biomedical Computing
Biomedical Research
Biomedical Science
Biomedicine
Biophysics
Bioscience
Biosym Technologies Software
Biotechnology
Birds
Bisexuality
Bitnet
Blindness
Blues
BMW
Boating
Bonsai Trees
Book Arts
Books

Books (Antiquarian)
Bosnia
Boston
Botanical Taxonomy
Botany
Botany (History of)
Boy Scouts
Boyler-Moore Theorem Prover
Brain Research
Brazil
Britain
British Commonwealth Law
Broadcasting
Buddhism
Builder Xcessory
Building
Bulgaria
Business
Business (British)
Business (International)
Business (US)
Business Information
Business Management
Business Marketing
Buyers' Guides
C (Programming Language)
c2man
Cabinetry
Cabot (Sebastian)
Calendars
California
Canada
Canadian Documents
Canadian-American Studies
Cancer
Card Games
Cardiopulmonary Medicine
Cards
Careers
Caribbean
Carnivorous Plants
Carter (Hodding, Papers of)
Cartography
Cartography (History of)
Cartoons
Catholicism
Caves
CD-ROM
Cell Biology
Cell Churches
Cello
Cellular Technology

Celtic Studies
Celtic Philology
Censorship
Census Data
Central Europe
Cervantes (Miguel de)
Chaos Theory
Chat Groups
Chaucer (Geoffrey)
Chemical Engineering
Chemistry
Chemistry (History of)
Chess
Chicago
Chicano Culture
Child Care
Childbirth
Children
Chile
China
Chinese Language
Chinese Studies
Choral Singing
Christianity
Chromatography
Church (Frank)
Church History
CIA
Cinema
CIS (Commonwealth of Independent States)
Cisco Systems
Civil Liberties
Civil Rights
Civil War
Classics
Cleveland
Climatology
Clinton (Bill)
Clip Art
CNI
Coastal Marine Biology
Cognitive Science
Coins
Collectibles
Colorado
Comedians
Comedy
Comic Books
Comics
Commerce
Commodore-Amiga Computers
Commonwealth

List of Keywords

Commonwealth of Independent States (CIS)
Commune Protocol
Communes
Communications
Communism
Community
Community Networking
Community Service
Companies
Composition
Computational Chemistry
Computational Neuroscience
Computer Administration
Computer Applications
Computer Art
Computer Communications
Computer Conferencing
Computer Databases
Computer Ethics
Computer Games
Computer Graphics
Computer Hardware
Computer Music
Computer Networking
Computer Networks
Computer News
Computer Products
Computer Professionals
Computer Programming
Computer Programming Languages
Computer Programs
Computer Resources
Computer Science
Computer Specialists
Computer Speech Interfaces
Computer System
Computer Systems
Computer Technology
Computer Underground
Computer Viruses
Computer-Aided Design
Computer Aided Instruction
Computer Aided Learning
Computer-Human Interactions
Computer Systems
Computing
Comserve
Concurrent Logic
Conferences
Conferencing Systems
Conflict Resolution
Congo Languages

Congress (US)
Connectivity
Conservation
Conspiracy
Constitution (US)
Construction
Consumer Rights
Consumer Science
Consumerism
Contemporary Letters
Contemporary Music
Convex Computers
Cooking
Cooperatives
Copyright
Corporations
CP/M
Crafts
Creationism
Creativity
Crew
Cricket
Crime
Croatia
Cromwell (Oliver)
Cryonics
Cuba
Cults
Cultural Studies
Culture
Current Events
Cyberculture
Cyberpunk Games
Cyberspace
Cycling
Czech Republic
Dance
Dante
Data General
Database Management
Databases
Datsuns
de Bono (Edward)
Deafness
DEC
DECUS
Deed Transfers
Defense
Delaware
Democracy
Democratic Socialists of America
Demography

Denmark
Dentistry
Department of Defense
Department of Labor
Dermatology
Design
Desktop Publishing
Detective Fiction
Detectives
Development
Development (International)
Deviance
Dialog
Dick (Philip K.)
Dickens (Charles)
Dickinson (Emily)
Dictionaries
Diet
Digital Equipment Corporation
DIMUND
Directories
Disabilities
Disabled People
Disaster Relief
Disaster Research
Disclosure
Diseases
Diseases (History of)
Disk Jockeys
Disney
Disraeli (Benjamin)
Dist Users
Drama (British)
Drama (French)
Drama (German)
Drew University
Drosophila
Drug Regulations
Drugs
Drum Machines
Dun & Bradstreet
E-mail
Earth Science
East Asian Studies
Eastern Europe
Eastern European Business
Ecclesiastical History
Echinoderms
Ecology
Economic Development
Economic Policy
Economics

Appendix A

Economics (History of)	Ethics	Folk Dance
Economy	Ethnic Studies	Folk Music
Ecumenism	Ethnomusicology	Folklore
Education	Etiquette	Food
Education (Adult)	Euromath	Food Production
Education (Alternative)	Europe	Football
Education (Bilingual)	European Community	Ford
Education (College/University)	European Documents	Foreign Trade
Education (Continuing)	Evangelism	Forest Management
Education (Distance)	Evolution	Forestry
Education (International)	Executive Branch	Fox Television
Education (K-12)	Expert Systems	France
Education (Post-Graduate)	Exports	Fraud
Education (Post-Secondary)	EXPRESS Information Modeling Language	Free Software
Education (Secondary)	Extraterrestrial Life	Free Trade
Educational Policy	FairCom	Freedom of Information
EEC	Family	Freedom of Speech
Electric Vehicles	Family Practice	Freeware
Electrical Engineering	Family Science	French
Electronic Art	FAQs (Frequently Asked Questions)	French Language
Electronic Books	Farm Economics	French Law
Electronic Media	Fashion	French Opera (19th-C.)
Electronic Music	Fashion Industry	French Revolution
Electronic Publishing	Fashion Merchandising	French Studies
Electronics	FAX	Frost (Robert)
Electrophoresis	FDA	FSP Protocol
Eliot (George)	Federal	FTP
Emacs	Federal Databases	Fuller (Buckminster)
EMBnet	Federal Documents (US)	Funding
Emergency Preparedness	Federal Government (US)	Funk Music
Employment	Federal Law (US)	Fusion
Encryption	Federal Register	Fuzzy Logic
Energy	Federal Standards	Galway (Ireland)
Engineering	Feminism	Gambling
Engineering (History of)	Fen	Game Theory
England	Fiction	Games
English Bibles	Filings	Gardening
Entertainment	Film	Gay Rights
Entomology	Filmmaking	Gays
Entropy	FINALE	Gender
Environment	Finance	Geneology
Environmental Health	Fine Arts	GENESIS
Environmental Policies	Finger (Internet Database)	Genetics
Environmental Safety	Firearms	Genius
Environmental Studies	Firewalls	Geodesic Quantum Physics
Enzymes	Fish	GIS (Geographic Information Systems)
Equestrians	Fisheries	Geography
Equine Research	Fitness	Geology
Ergonomics	Flags	Geoscience
ESL (English as a Second Language)	Flight Simulation	German
Essence (Internet Resource Directory)	Florida	German Companies
Estonia	Fluid Dynamics	German Democratic Republic

Germany	Heuristics	Incunabula
Gerontology	Hewlett-Packard	Independent Study
Gifts	Hispanic	India
GIS	Historic Preservation	Indiana
Glass	Historical Documents	Indigenous Peoples
Global News	History	Industry
God	History (20th Century)	Infectious Diseases
Goethe	History (Ancient)	Informatics
Golf	History (Jewish)	Information Retrieval
Gopher	History (US)	Information Science
Gophers	History (Women's)	Information Technology
Gothic Rock	History (World)	Insect Biology
Government	Hobbies	Insider Trading
Government (African)	Hockey	Institutional Research
Government (International)	Holmes (Sherlock)	Institutions
Government (US Federal)	Holocaust	Insurance Industry
Government (US)	Home Building	Intellectual Property
Government Documents	Home Economics	Intelligence
Government Records (US)	Homosexuality	Interactive Computing
GPS	Hong Kong	Interactive Learning
Grants	Hongkongiana	Interactive Media
Graphic Arts	Horseracing	Interactivity
Graphic Design	Horses	Interface Design
Graphical User Interfaces	Horticulture	Intergraph
Graphics	Hospital Administration	International Banking
Great Lakes Area	Hospitality	International Business
Greece	Hot Air Balloons	International Communication
Gregorian Chants	Hotel Administration	International Development
Group Communications	Housing	International Documents
Guidelines	Housman (A.E., Letters of)	International Finance
Guitar	Hubble Telescope	International Law
Gun Control Legislation	Human Behavior	International News
Hacking	Human Communications	International Politics
Haiti	Human Rights	International Relations
Hamill (Peter)	Humanities	International Research
Handel (G.F.)	Humor	International Visitors
Handicapping	Hungary	Internet
Hardware	Hunt (Leigh)	Internet Access
Hardy (Thomas)	Husted (Margaret, Culinary Collection of)	Internet Business
Harper (Roy)	Hydraulics	Internet Directories
Harry (Deborah)	Hyperfiction	Internet Guide
Hawaii	Hypermedia	Internet Guides
Health	Hypertext	Internet Marketing
Health Care	Hytelnet	Internet Publishing
Health Insurance	IBM	Internet Reference
Health Sciences	Icon Programming Language	Internet Research
Health Statistics	Illinois	Internet Resources
Hebraica	Image Processing	Internet Security
Hebrew Language	Imaging	Internet Services
Hemingway (Ernest)	Immigration (History of)	Internet Tools
Herbert (George)	Immunology	Internships
Herzegovina	Imports	Interpretation

Inventions
Investments
Iran
irc
Ireland
Irish Language
Irish History (Modern)
Iron
ISDN (Integrated Service Digital Network)
Islam
Israel
Italian Studies
Italy
James (Henry)
Japan
Japanese Culture
Jerusalem
Jewish Politics
Jobs
Jokes
Jordan (Len, Senatorial Papers of)
Journalism
Journals
Joyce (James)
Judaica
Judaism
Judicial Process
Justice Department
Kansas
Kentucky & Ohio River Valley (History of)
Kinesiology
Kingsley (Charles)
Kites
Kiwanis International
Knowbot
Knowledge Representation
Korea
Kurtz (Katernine)
Labor
Labor (History of)
Lafayette (Marquis de)
Land Records
Landscaping
Language Software
Lasers
Latin America
Latin American Studies
Latvia
Law
Law (Brazilian)
Law (British)
Law (International)
Law (Tax)
Law (US Case)
Law (US State)
Law (US)
Law Reviews
Leadership
Legal Research
Legislation
Legislation (Australian)
Legislation (US)
Lesbians
Lexicography
Lexicology
Liberal Education
Libertarian Party
Librarianship
Libraries
Library Science
Limbaugh (Rush)
Lincoln (Abraham)
Linguistics
Listserv
Literacy
Literary Criticism
Literary Studies
Literate Programming
Literature (American)
Literature (Asian)
Literature (Children's)
Literature (Contemporary)
Literature (English)
Literature (General)
Literature (German)
Literature (Irish)
Literature (Russian)
Literature (Spanish)
Lithuania
Litigants
Liturgy
Lower Rio Grande Valley (History of)
Lyrics
Macintosh Computers
Magazines
Mailing Lists
Maine
Maine Authors
Malls
Management
Mann (Thomas, Collections of)
Manx
Mapping
Marine Biology
Marine Engineering
Maritime Industry
Market Conditions
Market Research
MarketBase
Marketing
Martial Arts
Maryland
Mass Communications
Mass Media
Material Science
Math
Mathematical Biology
Mathematics
Mathematics (Algorithms)
Mathematics (History of)
May (Julian)
Media
Mediation
Medical Informatics
Medical News
Medical Research
Medical Treatment
Medicine
Medicine (History of)
Medieval Studies
MEDLINE
Melrose Place
Memorabilia
Men
Men's Movement
Mensa
Mercer (Johnny, Collection of)
MetaCard
Metals
Meteorology
Mexican-American Studies
Mexico
Michigan
Michigan Networks
Microbiology
Microcomputing
Microelectronics
Microscopy
Microsoft Corporation
Middle East
Middle Eastern Music
Middle Eastern Studies
Middlesex (Connecticut)
MIDI
Midwifery
Migration

Military	Mutual Funds	NHL
Military (US)	Mycoplasma	Nickelodeon
Military History	Mystery Fiction	NIH
Military Policy	Mythology	NIR
Military Science	NAFTA	Nissan Automobiles
Military Specifications	Napolean	Non Serviam
Milne (A.A., Collection of)	NASA	Non-governmental organizations
Mind	National Collegiate Athletic Association	Nonfiction Books
Miniatures	Native American Affairs	Nonprofit Organizations
Miniaturized Plants	Native American Studies	Nonprofits
Mining	NATO	Nordic Skiing
Minor League	Natural History	Nordic University
Minorities	Natural Language	North America
Miracles	Natural Science	Norway
Mississippi	Navy	NotGNU
MLB	NBA	NQTHM
Model Horses	NCGIA	Nuclear Medicine
Modem	Ncube	Nuclear Safety
Modern Dance	Near Eastern Studies	Numerical Analysis
Modula-2 (Programming Language)	NEARnet	Numismatics
Molecular Biology	Netblazer	Nursing
Monarchy	Netherlands	Nursing (History of)
Mormonism	Netiquette	Nutrition
Morphology	Network Servers	Object-Oriented Programming
Morris Dancing	Network Time Protocol	Objectivism
Mosaic	Networking	Obstetrics/Gynecology
Motor Racing	Networks	Oceanography
Motorcycles	Neural Networks	Oceans
Mountaineering	Neural Simulation	Office Document Architecture
Movement	Neurobiology	Ohio
Movies	Neurology	Old English
MS-DOS	Neuroscience	Old Testament
Mt. Xinu	Nevada	Olympics
MUDs	Nevada State Documents	OMD
Multicasting	Nevadiana	Online Books
Multilateral Treaties	New Age Music	Online Services
Multimedia	New England	OPAC System
Museums	New Jersey	Opera
Music	New Media	Operating Systems
Music (Contemporary)	New Mexico	Optics
Music (Irish)	New Music	Oregon
Music Notation	New Orleans	Orienteering
Music Resources	New Testament	Origami
Music Reviews	New York	Ornithology
Music Software	News (International)	Pacific
Musical Genres	News Media	Packaging
Musical Groups	NewsCommando	Paganism
Musical Instruments	Newsletters	Pakistan
Musicals	NeXT	Paleography
Musicians	NeXT-icon	Paleontology
Muslim Associations	NeXT-Med	Panic Disorders
Muslim Student Associations	NFL	Paper

Papermaking (History of)
Parallel Computers
Paranoia
Parasitology
Parenting
Paris
Partnerships
Pascal
Patents
Peace
Pediatrics
Pennsylvania
Performing Arts
Periodicals
PERQ workstations
Personals
Peru
Petroleum
Pets
Pharmaceuticals
Pharmacology
Philanthropy
Philology
Philosophy
Phone Books
Photo-CD
Photography
Photography (History of)
Physical Therapy
Physics
Physiology
Ping
Pipes
Planetariums
Plant Lipids
Plant Science
Plasma Physics
Plastics
Poetry
Poetry (American)
Poker
Poland
Polar Regions
Political Science
Politics
Politics (Conservative)
Politics (International)
Politics (US)
Polymers
Pop Music
Popular Culture
Porsche

Portuguese
Postal Services
Postmodern Culture
Postmodernism
Power Boating
Poxis
Pregnancy
President
President (US)
Pricing
Primatology
Prince
Printing
Printing (History of)
Prion
Privacy
Programming
Programming Languages
Prohibition
Project Gutenberg
Project Management
Property
Prospero
Psychiatry
Psychology
Psychotherapy
Public Access Archives
Public Domain Software
Public Health
Public Policy
Publishing
Puzzles
Quakerism
Quality Control
Quantum Chemistry
Quantum Mechanics
Quantum Physics
Quark
Quebec (Canada)
Quotations
Race
Radio
Railroads
Railway History
Rap Music
Rare Books
Raves
Real Estate
Recipes
Recordings
Records
Recreation

Recycling
Reference
Refrigeration
Reggae
Regional Business
Regulation
Regulations
Relays
Religion
Religious Text
Remote Sensing
Research and Development
Restaurant Management
Retirement
Rhetoric
Rhodes (Happy)
Rights
Robots
Rock Music
Rogers (Bruce)
Role-Playing
Rolling Stones
Romance
Romania
Roosevelt (Franklin D.)
Rowing
Rubbers
Running
Rural Development
Rush
Russia
Safety
Sailing
Sales
San Francisco Bay Area
Sanskrit
Satellites
Satire
SCA (Society For Creative Anachronism)
Scandinavia
Scholarly Communication
Science
Science (History of)
Science Fiction
Science Technology
Sciences
Scientific Journals
Scientific Research
Scientific Visualization
Scotland
Scottish Dance
Scottish Gaelic

List of Keywords

Scripting Languages
Scuba
SEC
Securities
Security
Security Firewalls
Senate (US)
Sequencers
Serials Pricing
Services
Settlements
Sex
Sexology
Sexual Abuse
Sexual Orientation
Sexuality
Shakers
Shakespeare (William)
Shareware
ShareWord
Shopping
Shortwave Radio
Silicon Graphics
Sim (Dave)
SIMULA
Simulation
Singapore
Singing
Singles
Skiing
Skin
Skydiving
Slavery
SLON
Slovak Republic
Slovakia
Slovenia
Small Business
Smiley
Smithsonian
Smoking
Soccer
Social Events
Social Law
Social Responsibility
Social Sciences
Social Work
Society
Sociology
Software
Software Defects
Software Internationalization
Soil Conservation
Sound Synthesis
South Africa
South America
South Asian Studies
Soviet Union
Space Science
Spain
Spanish Language
Spanish Inquisition
Spanish Plays
Spectroscopy
Speech Disorders
Spelunking
Spirituality
Sports
Sports Cars
Springsteen (Bruce)
Squash
Sri Lanka
St. John Valley (History of)
St. Petersburg
Standards
Starfish
State Courts
Statistics
Statutes
Steel
Stereo Electronics
Stirner (Max)
Stock Market
Storytelling
String Processing
Style
Subways
Sun Microsystems
Supercomputing
Supreme Court (US)
Surfing (Internet)
Sustainable Living
Sweden
Switzerland
Synthesis
Synthesizers
Systems Administration
Systems Theory
Table Tennis
Taiwan
Tandem Computers
Tandy Computers
Taxes
Teaching
Technical Support
Technical Writing
Technological Advances
Technology
Telebit Computer Products
Telecommunication
Telecommunications
Telecomputing
Television
Telnet
Tennessee
Tennis
TeX
Texas
Text Processing
Thailand
Theater
Theology
Theoretical Chemistry
Theoretical Physics
Third World
Tibet
Tobacco
Tourism
Toxicology
Toys
Trade Unions
Trademarks
Trading Cards
Translation
Transportation
Transportation Law
Transsexualism
Transvestism
Travel
Travel (History of)
Treaties
Treatment
Trivia
Trollope (Anthony)
Trucking Industry
Turkey
Tutorials
Typography
Ucadian Studies
UCLA
UFOs
UN Documents
Unions
United Kingdom
United Nations
University Administration

Universities (History of)
University Planning
UNIX
UNIX (Operating Systems)
Urban Planning
Urban Studies
US Government Publications
US Government Regulations
US National Park Service
Usenet
Utah
Vegetarianism
Verdicts
Veronica
Vertebrates
Veterinary Hospitals
Veterinary Medicine
Veterinary Microbiology
Veterinary Science
Video
Video Games
Vietnam
Virginia
Virtual Community
Virtual Reality
Viruses
Visual Communication
Visual Impairment
Visualization
Visualization Data Explorer Package
Volleyball
Voting
WAIS
Walpole (Sir Robert, Collections of)
War
Washington DC
Washington University
Water Quality
Weapons
Weather
Web
Wells (Ida, Personal Papers of)
Western America
White House
Whitman (Walt)
Whois
Wilderness
Wildlife
Windows
Windsurfing
Winter Games
Wisconsin
Witchcraft
Women's Issues
Women's Studies
Woodworking
Word Play
Workstations
World Health
Worldview
Wrestling
Wright (Frank Lloyd)
Writing
WWW
X.500
Yeats (William Butler)
Yugoslavia
Zines
Zoology

APPENDIX B

Audience Fields

Academics
Accountants
Activists
Actors
Administrators
Adoptees
Adoptive Parents
Adults
Advertisers
Aeronautical Engineers
Aerospace Engineers
Africans
Agricultural Economists
Agriculturalists
Agronomists
Aids Activists
Aids Researchers
Aids Sufferers
Aikido Enthusiasts
Alaskans
Alien Enthusiasts
Alternative Music Listeners
Amiga Users
Anglophiles
Animal Lovers
Animation Enthusiasts
Animators
Anthropologists
APC-Open Members
Ape Software Users
Apple II Users
AppWare Users
Aquarium Keepers
Archaeologists
Architects
Architectural Historians
Archivists
Art Activists
Art Educators
Art Enthusiasts
Art Historians
Art Organizations
Art Professionals
Art Students
Arts Community
Asian Studies Educators
Astronomers
Astrophysicists
Atari Users
Atheists
Athletes
Audio Enthusiasts
Australia Enthusiasts
Australians
Autocross Drivers
Automobile Buyers
Automobile Enthusiasts
Automobile Mechanics
Automobile Owners
Automobile Racers
Automobile Racing Enthusiasts
Aviators
Baby Boomers
Backpackers
Balloon Artists
Balloonists
Ballroom Dancers
Baltic Nationals
Bankers
Banking Industry Analysts
Baseball Enthusiasts
Basketball Enthusiasts
Bay Area Residents
BBS Users
Beastie Boys Enthusiasts
Beatles Listeners
Beer Brewers
Beer Enthusiasts
Bible Readers
Biblical Scholars
Bicycling Enthusiasts
Bicyclists
Biochemists
Biologists
Biomedical Researchers
Biotechnologists
Bird Watchers
Bisexuals
Blind People
Blues Enthusiasts
BMW Enthusiasts
Boating Enthusiasts
Bonsai Enthusiasts
Book Readers
Book Reviewers
Booksellers
Bosnians
Boston Residents
Botanists
Boy Scouts

Brazilians
Brewers
British
British Automobile Enthusiasts
British Motorcycle Enthusiasts
Broadcasters
Broadcasting Professionals
Bruce Springsteen Fans
Buddhists
Builders
Business Analysts
Business Professionals
Business Researchers
Business Students
Californians
Cambridge
Campaign Managers
Campers
Canadians
Card Collectors
Card Players
Caribbean Enthusiasts
Carnegie Mellon Community
Cartographers
Cartologists
Cat Owners
Catholics
Cave Explorers
CD-ROM Authors
CD-ROM Publishers
Celtic Enthusiasts
Celts
Certified Public Accountants
Chaosium Enthusiasts
Chaucer Fans
Chefs
Chemical Engineers
Chemistry Students (High School Up)
Chemistry Teachers
Chemists
Chess Players
Child Care Providers
Child Development Professionals
Children
Children's Rights Activists
Chinese
Choral Singers
Choreographers
Christians
Cinematographers
Cisco Employees
Cisco Users

Citizens
Civil Engineers
Civil Libertarians
Classical Music Listeners
Clergy
Cleveland Residents
Climatologists
Clinicians
Coaches
Cognitive Scientists
Coin Collectors
Collectors
College/University Educators
College/University Planners
Color/Vision Researchers
Colorado Residents
Comedians
Comics Enthusiasts
Commodore-Amiga Users
Commune Protocol Users
Communications Specialists
Communications Students
Community Activists
Community Builders
Community Groups
Community Leaders
Compact Disc Users
Complainers
Composers
Computational Neuroscientists
Computer Engineers
Computer Game Developers
Computer Game Players
Computer Graphic Designers
Computer Hardware Users
Computer Professionals
Computer Programmers
Computer Scientists
Computer Specialists
Computer Speech Researchers
Computer Students
Computer System Designers
Computer Systems Analysts/Programmers
Computer Underground Enthusiasts
Computer Users
Computer-Mediated Communication Researchers
Computing Analysts
Computing Consultants
Computists International Members
Concrete Blonde Enthusiasts
Concurrent Logic Programmers
Conferencing System Users

Conservationists
Consumers
Convex Computer Users
Cooks
Corporations
Counselors
Counterrevolutionaries
CP/M Users
Crafts Enthusiasts
Creationists
Cricket Fans
Critics
Croatians
Crossfire Specialists
Cult Members
Curiosity Seekers
Cyberculture Enthusiasts
Cybernauts
Cyberpunks
Cyclists
Czechs
Dan Fogelberg Enthusiasts
Dancers
Dante Scholars
Database Managers
Deaf and Disabled People
Deborah Harry Enthusiasts
Defense Analysts
Democratic Socialists
Demographers
Dentists
Depeche Mode Enthusiasts
Dermatologists
Designers
Desktop Publishers
Detectives
Deviants
Dialog Subscribers
Dieticians
Differently Abled People
Digital Equipment Users
Dire Straits Enthusiasts
Disabled People
Disk Jockeys
Disney Enthusiasts
Dist Users
Distance Educators
Distributors
Doctors
Document Delivery Professionals
Dog Owners
Down's Syndrome Community

List of Audience Fields

Drag Racers
Dramatists
Drew University Alumni
Drivers
Drug Educators
Drug Users
E-Mail Users
Earth Scientists
Ecologists
Economists
Editors
Educational Administrators
Educators
Educators (College/University)
Educators (K-12)
Electric Vehicle-Drivers
Electrical Engineers
Electronic Music Enthusiasts
Energy Researchers
Engineers
English Teachers
Entomologists
Entrepreneurs
Environmentalists
Epidemiologists
Ernest Hemingway Enthusiasts
Ethnic Studies Students
Ethnomusicologists
Europeans
Evangelists
Evolutionists
Exchange Students
Exporters
Express Programmers
Faculty Administrators
Family Physicians
Family Planners
Farmers
Fashion Enthusiasts
Fax Users
Feminists
Film Enthusiasts
Filmmakers
Finale Program Users
Financial Analysts
Fish Enthusiasts
Fitness Enthusiasts
Florida Residents
Folk Dancers
Folk Music Enthusiasts
Folk Musicians
Football Enthusiasts

Foreign Students
Foresters
Former Boy Scouts
Francophiles
FreeNet Organizers
French Students
Fundraisers
Funk Music Enthusiasts
Gamblers
Game Players
Game Theorists
Gardeners
Gay Rights Activists
Gays
Geneologists
General Public
Geneticists
Geographers
Geologists
Germans
GIS Professionals
GIS Users
Gnuish Ms-Dos Developers
Golfers
Gothic Rock Enthusiasts
Government Officials
Graphic Artists
Graphic Designers
Grass-Roots Organizers
Grateful Dead Enthusiasts
Greeks
Guitar Players
Gun Users
Hackers
Ham Radio Operators
Hardware/Software Designers
Hawaiians
Health Care Professionals
Health Care Providers
Health Science Researchers
Heavy Metal Listeners
Hispanics
Historians
Hockey Enthusiasts
Hockey Players
Holocaust Researchers
Home Owners
Horse Owners
Horse Trainers
Horseracing Enthusiasts
Horticulturists
Humanists

Hungarian Speakers
IBM Users
Ichthyologists
Icon Programmers
Idaho Residents
Importers
Indigenous People
Information Brokers
Information Scientists
Insurance Industry Professionals
International Aid Agencies
International Lawyers
Internationalists
Internet Surfers
Interpreters
Inventors
Investigators
Investors
Iranians
IRC Users
Irish
Israelis
Italian Students
Italians
Japanese
Jewish Organizations
Jews
Job Seekers
Jokers
Journalism
Journalists
Joyce Scholars
Judaica Scholars
Judges
Julian May Readers
Kansas State University Students
Kibologists
Kinesiologists
Kite Enthusiasts
Kiwanis Members
Koreans
Laboratory Suppliers
Language Students
Language Teachers
Law Students
Lawyers
Legal Professionals
Legal Scholars
Legislators
Lesbians
Libertarians
Librarians

- Linguists
- Literary Theorists
- Lobbyists
- Lucid Programmers
- Macintosh Users
- Management Trainers
- Managers
- Manufacturers
- Marillion Enthusiasts
- Marine Biologists
- Market Analysts
- Market Researchers
- Marketing Specialists
- Martial Arts Enthusiasts
- Maryland Residents
- Massachusetts Residents
- Material Scientists
- Mathematical Biologists
- Mathematicians
- Max Stirner Enthusiasts
- Mechanical Engineers
- Media Professionals
- Mediators
- Medical Professionals
- Medical Researchers
- Medical Students
- Melrose Place Enthusiasts
- Memorabilia Collectors
- Mensa Members
- Merchants
- Meteorologists
- Microsoft Product Users
- Middle East Scholars
- Middlesex Alumni
- Middlesex Students
- Midwives
- Military Historians
- Military Personnel
- Miniature Figurine Collectors
- Ministers
- Model Horse Collectors
- Modem Users
- Modesty Blaise Enthusiasts
- Modula-2 Programmers
- Molecular Biologists
- Molecular Biotechnologists
- Monarchists
- Monty Python Enthusiasts
- Moralists
- Morphologists
- Morris Dancers
- Motorcycle Enthusiasts
- MUD Users
- Multicasters
- Multimedia Users
- Music Enthusiasts
- Music Librarians
- Music Researchers
- Music Students
- Musicians
- Muslims
- Mystery Enthusiasts
- Mystics
- Nafsa Members
- Native Americans
- Natural History Scientists
- Natural Scientists
- Naturalists
- Nature Lovers
- Navy Personnel
- NCSU Computer Students
- Ncube Users
- Network Administrators
- Network Developers
- Network Service Providers
- Network Time Protocol Users
- Neurobiologists
- Neuroscientists
- New Media Artists
- New Mexico Residents
- New Orleans Residents
- New York Residents
- News Enthusiasts
- Newscommando Users
- Next Developers
- Next Users
- Norwegians
- Notgnu Users
- Nqthm Theorem Users
- Numerical Analysts
- Nursery Owners
- Nurses
- Nutritionists
- O/S2 Users
- Objectivists
- Oceanographers
- Ohio Residents
- Ohio State University Alumni
- Olympics Enthusiasts
- OMD Enthusiasts
- Oregonians
- Orienteering Enthusiasts
- Origami Enthusiasts
- Ornamental Plant Enthusiasts
- Otis Followers
- Oyster Band Enthusiasts
- Pagans
- Pakistanis
- Paleontologists
- Panic Disorder Sufferers
- Paranoid Persons
- Parents
- Park Rangers
- Parnet Users
- Particle Physicists
- Pascal Programmers
- Patent Agents
- Patent Attorneys
- Patent Researchers
- Perq Users
- Peruvians
- Pet Owners
- Pharmacists
- Philanthropists
- Philip K. Dick Readers
- Philosophers
- Phish Enthusiasts
- Photographers
- Physical Therapists
- Physicians
- Physicists
- Pink Floyd Enthusiasts
- Planetarium Operators
- Planners
- Poetry Readers
- Poets
- Poker Players
- Poles
- Policy Makers
- Polish Speakers
- Political Activists
- Political Analysts
- Political Researchers
- Political Scientists
- Politicians
- Pop Music Enthusiasts
- Popular Culture Enthusiasts
- Portuguese Speakers
- Posix Users
- Postal Service Workers
- Pregnant Women
- Press
- Priests
- Primatologists
- Privacy Activists
- Private Investigators

List of Audience Fields

Programmers
Progressive Music Enthusiasts
Psychiatrists
Psychologists
Public Health Officials
Public Health Professionals
Public Relations Experts
Public Servants
Publishing Professionals
Punsters
Python Language Users
Quakers
Queen Enthusiasts
Radio Broadcasters
Radio Listeners
Railroad Enthusiasts
Rap Enthusiasts
Rappers
Ravers
Readers
Real Estate Brokers
Regulatory Agencies
Rehabilitation Counselors
Religion Students
Republicans
Researchers
Retailers
Retirees
Rock Music Enthusiasts
Role-Playing Enthusiasts
Rolling Stones Enthusiasts
Rowers
Runners
Rush Enthusiasts
Rush Limbaugh Enthusiasts
Russians
Sailors
Sales Professionals
San Francisco Bay Area Residents
Satellite Television Watchers
Scholars
School Children
Science Fiction Readers
Science Teachers
Scientists
Scuba Divers
Securities
Security Workers
Serbians
Sex Researchers
Sex Therapists
Shakers
Shortwave Radio Users
Silicon Graphics Users
Simula Programmers
Singles
Sinologists
Skaters
Skiers
Skydivers
Slavicists
Slovaks
Slovenians
Smokers
Soap Opera Enthusiasts
Soccer Enthusiasts
Social Scientists
Social Workers
Sociologists
Software Designers
Software Developers
South Africans
Space Scientists
Spacemen 3 Enthusiasts
Spaniards
Spanish Speakers
Speech Pathologists
Spelunkers
Sports Card Collectors
Sports Enthusiasts
Sri Lankans
Stage Producers
Star Wars Enthusiasts
State Officials
Statisticians
Stereo Enthusiasts
Stock Brokers
Stockmarket
Storytellers
Students
Students (College/University)
Students (K-12)
Subway Riders
Sun Microsystems Users
Supercomputer Administrators
Systems Operators
Systems Theorists
Taiwanese
Tandy Computer Users
Taxonomists
Teachers
Technical Professionals
Technical Writers
Technicians
Technocrats
Technology Professionals
Telebit Netblazer Users
Telecommunications Experts
Television Professionals
Television Viewers
Tennis Players
Texans
Theologians
Theoretical Biologists
Therapists
Tibetans
Tourists
Toxicologists
Translators
Transportation Professionals
Transsexuals
Transvestites
Travelers/Tourists
Trekkies
Trivia Enthusiasts
Turks
UCLA Students
UIMs Users
Unions
University Administrators
University Biomedical Researchers
University of Colorado Students
University Planners
University Students
Unix System Administrators
Unix Users
Urban Planners
US Citizens
US Congress
USA
Usenet Users
Utah Residents
Utility Professionals
Vangelis Fans
Vegetarians
Veterinarians
Veterinary Pharmacists
Victims of Sexual Abuse
Video Artists
Vietnamese
Vietnamese Americans
Virologists
Virtual Reality Enthusiasts
Visitors
Vocalists
Volkswagon Drivers

Volleyball Enthusiasts
Voters
Washington DC Residents
Wilderness Enthusiasts
Wildlife Biologists
Windows Users
Windsurfers
Winter Sports Fans
Women
Women's Studies Educators
Women's Studies Students
Woodworkers
Workstation Users
Wrestling Fans
Writers
XTC Enthusiasts
Yugoslavians
Zoologists

Appendix C

Internet Service Providers

Following is an updated and expanded list of commercial Internet account providers. The providers listed below run businesses that provide electronic accounts through which you can access the Internet. These include many nonprofit community computing services known as *free-nets*.

Commercial Online Data Vendors

It is important to know about the existence of the major online systems such as Dialog, Nexis/Lexis, Orbit, and CD Plus, that are accessible over the Internet. These private online worlds are complementary to the information available over the Internet, although many are quite costly to access and require specially learned research skills to handle their specific search protocols.

These online systems have been building extraordinary archives of information going back decades in many cases. The following is a chart of the major online system providers. You will need to contact them directly to set up a password to their systems and to find out about the availability of online training.

Provider	Phone	E-mail Address
Dialog (Dialog Information Systems)	telnet://dialog.com	(800) 334-2564
DataStar (Dialog Information Systems)	(800) 334-2564	telnet://dialog.com
Dow Jones News Retrieval (Mead Data)	(800) 227-4908 (513) 859-5398	telnet://nex.meaddata.co
Lexis (Mead Data)	(800) 227-4908 (513) 859-5398	telnet://nex.meaddata.com
BRS (CD Plus)	(800) 950-2035	staff@cdplus.com
Orbit Questel, Inc.	(703) 442-0900	telonet://orbit.com

Private Network Providers with their own Worlds of Information

In addition to actual Internet Access Providers, there are private network providers in the United States, and in other countries, that offer a variety of services including their own worlds of information and proprietary user environments." Some of these maintain and make available elaborate and specialized databases for access by their subscribers. They generally are closed systems, with only e-mail access to the Internet. However, technologies are being developed by which the private and the public Internet can be made seamless. The following provides basic contact information for the major providers that fall in to this category.

America Online provides access to a wide variety of media and reference sources, popular newspapers, magazines, and vendor support. Chat lines are also a major offering (715,000+ subscribers). For more information, call (800) 827-6364.

CompuServe has over 2000 separate resources with many of the largest forums available online. In addition to an array of financial and professional services, CompuServe provides a wide diversity of entertainment services, and a growing shopping service that also offers graphics (1.5 million subscribers). For more information, call (800) 848-8199.

Delphi offers a comprehensive selection of news, reference resources, and computer information as well as full gateway access to the Internet. Special-interest groups, conferences, and online games are major features of this service (200,000 subscribers). For more information, call (800) 544-4005 or contact Delphi via e-mail at `info@delphi.com`

GEnie provides a large menu of news and information services, special-interest groups, games, and databases. GEnie's RoundTables (RTs) provide discussion areas devoted to specific topics; file libraries, bulletin boards, and real-time chat (RTC) are special features of this service (150,000+ subscribers). For more information, contact GEnie at (800) 638-9636.

Prodigy is a "family-oriented" service providing shopping, travel, and personal finance, and specializing in up-to-the minute information such as news, sports, and weather. Prodigy also offers a large collection of shareware programs (1.2 million subscribers).

Ziffnet is an online service with information on buying, using, supporting, and understanding personal computer products. Ziffnet is a major resource for technical support. For more information, contact Ziffnet at (800) 635-6225.

Appendix D

Glossary of Terms, Acronyms, and the Language of the Internet

We are indebted to Hans J. Rocke, University of California at Davis, for his initial work in compiling this glossary.

A

Absolute address An address that indicates, in machine language code, the exact storage location where data or machine instructions are to be found.

access To find or store information in memory or on a peripheral device such as a magnetic tape or disk drive. To communicate in some way with a device.

Access method Any of the data-management techniques available to the user for transferring data from memory to an input/output device, or vice versa.

Access time The time interval between the instant at which data is requested to be retrieved or stored, and the instant at which the operation is carried out.

address A location on a disk or in memory within which a specific piece of information can be stored, or the number assigned to that location. See also absolute address, indirect address.

ADMD Administrative Management Domain.

Anonymous FTP An access command that enables Internet users to retrieve files from various servers without actually having accounts on those servers. A copy of the anonymous FTP list enables users to determine the location of files available on the Internet.

Application A computer program that is applied to performing a specific task.

Archie An information agent that conducts searches against data stored at various anonymous FTP sites, and indexes them for easy access by users.

Archive
1. The storage of files (often in archived and compressed form) for future use, or the storage area that holds those files.
2. To create an archive, to move a file into an archive, or to bundle multiple files together into a larger archive or library file.

ARPA Advanced Research Projects Agency of the United States Department of Defense.

Artificial intelligence Computer programs that perform functions, often by imitation, that are normally associated with human reasoning and knowledge.

ASCII (American Standard Code For Information Interchange) A character encoding standard that uses 7 of the 8 bits of a byte to define the codes for 128 characters (27). For example, in ASCII the number 7 is treated as a character and is encoded as 00010111. Because a byte can have a total of 256 possible values (28), there are an additional 128 possible characters that can be encoded into a byte, but there is no formal ASCII standard for those additional 128 characters. Most IBM-compatible personal computers do use an IBM extended character set that includes international characters, line and box drawing characters, Greek letters, and mathematical symbols.

ASR (Automatic Send and Receive) Having the capability to receive data and produce it on a printer or to send it through a keyboard.

Asynchronous Having a variable time interval between characters, bits, or events.

Automation The implementation of several processes by automatic means.

B

Backbone A single-protocol connection among different systems. Each system has a gateway to the common backbone protocol.

Bandwidth The difference (in hertz) between the upper and lower limits of wave frequencies transmitted over a communications channel.

Baud In communications, a unit of transmission speed of digital signals. It is the reciprocal of the length in seconds of the shortest element of the digital code. Generally a baud will equate to a bit (of data) per second.

BBS (Bulletin Board System) BBSs began as computers running software that permitted people dial-up access, the capability to store messages for other dial-up users, and to retrieve messages left for them. BBSs were the source of the concept of electronic discussion groups, because people could leave and retrieve messages around individual topics.

The concept of the BBS was transferred to the Internet, the software was modified, and now hundreds of Usenet and ListServ discussion groups operate on the same principles: a topic is stated, and people interested in the topic send and receive messages, and conduct discussions from all around the world.

Many programs now archive the discussions so that newcomers can retrieve threads of conversation that took place before they joined a discussion.

Bit Contraction of binary and digit. A bit is the smallest unit of information that a computer can work with. Each bit is either a one or a zero. Often computers work with chunks of bits rather than one bit at a time; the smallest chunk of bits a computer usually works with consists of 8 bits, or a byte.

Bitmapping A digital representation of an image in which all dots or pixels making up the image correspond to specifically assigned bits in memory.

BITNET (Because It's Time Network) A low-cost, low-speed network that was developed to satisfy a need for providing distributed network access beyond the limits of the original ARPAnet network.

Block Physical data consisting of a fixed number of characters or records, and moved as a unit during transmission.

Body/subject The body of an e-mail message is the actual text of a message. The subject is a special field that gives the content of a message. Many SMTP programs take advantage of the Subject line to provide sorting capabilities. Through the clever use of Subject lines, an e-mail handling facility can perform as a small but useful database.

Boolean A system of logic devised by George Boole using a series of symbolic terms such as and, or, and not to express the relationship of data elements to one another.

Bounced message An e-mail message might not reach its destination for any of several reasons. The address might have been typed incorrectly, the Domain Name Server might not recognize an alias, the recipient's computer might be down for maintenance, and so on. In such cases, a message is sent back to the sender to inform them that their message has not been delivered. Sometimes, the information provided in the header reveals why the message was undelivered.

Byte Eight bits. A byte is simply a chunk of 8 ones and zeros. For example 01000001 is a byte. A byte is equal to one column in a file written in character format.

C

CCA
1. Common Cryptographic Architecture; IBM encryption software for MVS and DOS applications.
2. Compatible Communications Architecture; network equipment technology protocol for transmitting asynchronous data over X.25 networks. (See X.25.)
3. Communications Control Architecture; a US Navy network that includes an ISDN backbone called bits.

CCITT (Consultative Committee Of International Telephone And Telegraph) Part of the International Telecommunications Union, a UN treaty organization, setting international standards for worldwide telecommunication, for example, X.25. (see X.25.)

CD-ROM Compact Disk Read Only Memory.

Cello A WWW browser that works under Microsoft Windows and enables people with a connection to the Internet to follow Hypertext (or Hypermedia) links to files and information services all over the world. It displays both regular text files and files that are written in HTML format, and will translate different Internet services such as Gopher, News, and FTP into a format that appears to the user as if it were a hypertext document. It was written by Thomas Bruce of the Legal Information Institute at Cornell Law School. (Extracted from the Cello FAQ.)

You also can use Cello and the WWW-HTML hypertext markup standard to build local hypertext systems on LANs, on single machines, and so on. Cello also permits the post-processing of any file for which you've set up an association in the Windows File Manager—for example, if you download an uncompressed Microsoft Word file from an FTP site, and the appropriate association exists in File Manager, Cello will run MS-Word on it for you. This same capability is used to view graphics and listen to sound files you get from the Net.

Chains In Hypertext, linking randomly located material by means of address information included within the stored item, which cites the location of the succeeding and preceding item in the sequence. Chains permit users to traverse the Internet via links within documents to their origin, or cited materials. The links of the chain provide navigation information, and the user merely needs to click on a link to be moved to a (possibly remote) document whose address is contained in the link.

Channel Any communications pathway between two computers or between a terminal and a computer. It might refer to the physical medium, such as coaxial cable, or to a specific carrier frequency (subchannel) within a larger channel or wireless medium.

Character encoding scheme A method of encoding characters including alphabetic characters (a-z, uppercase and lowercase), numbers 0-9, punctuation and other marks (for example, comma, period, space, &, *), and various control characters (for example, Tab, carriage return, linefeed) using binary numbers. For a computer to print a capital A or a number 7 on the computer screen, for instance, you must have a way to tell the computer that a particular group of bits represents an A or a 7. Standards, commonly called "character sets," exist to establish that a particular byte stands for an A and a different byte stands for a 7. A common standard for representing characters in bytes is known as ASCII.

Character format Any file format in which information is encoded as characters using only a standard character encoding scheme. A file written in "character format" contains only those bytes that are prescribed in the encoding scheme as corresponding to the characters in the scheme (for example, alphabetic and numeric characters, punctuation marks, and spaces). A file written in the ASCII character format would store the number "7" in eight bits (for instance, one byte) 00010111. A file written in EBCDIC would store the number "7" in eight bits as 11110111.

Client The user of a network service; also used to describe a computer that relies upon another computer for some of all of its resources.

Client server
1. Architecture in which the client is the requesting machine (PC or workstation) and the server is the supplying machine (LAN file server, mini or mainframe). The client provides the user interface and performs some or most of the application processing. The server maintains the databases and processes requests from the client to extract data from or update the database. The server also controls the application's integrity and security.
2. Request/supply relationship between programs. Applications can be designed, whether running within the same computer or in multiple computers, in which one program (the client) requests data from another program (the server). In X-window, for example, the server is software that manages the display screen, and the client is the application that asks the server to display something.

Column A single vertical column in a data file that is one byte in length. Fixed-format data files traditionally are described as being arranged in lines and columns. In a fixed-format file, column locations describe the locations of variables.

Compatibility The capability of one device to interconnect or share programs or data with another by means of having the same code, speed, and signal level.

Compress To reduce the size of a file considerably by removing redundant information. Compressed files are more economical to transmit through the Internet or to store. To use the file, it must be exploded, or reconstituted.

Connect time The time during which an operator is in contact with a computer online. This is different from compute time, in which the operator actually is utilizing the computer's resources.

CREN (Corporation for Research and Educational Networking) A merger of BITNET and CSNET networks.

Cyberspace A term coined by William Gibson in his novel Neuromancer that refers to a futuristic computer network that people use by plugging their brains into it.

D

DASD Direct Access Storage Device.

Data
1. A general term for any collection of information, facts, numbers, letters, or symbols that refer to or describe an object, idea, condition, situation, or other factors.
2. Name of an android in Star Trek-The Next Generation.

Data network A telecommunications network built specifically for data transmission, rather than for voice transmission.

database A set of organized data stored in or available to a computer that can be used by the computer or its operator to perform various tasks. The database is not the program; rather it's the information with which the program will work.

Datagram The basic unit of information passed across the Internet. It consists of a source and destination address along with data. Large messages are broken into a sequence of IP datagrams.

Decryption Encoding a message to its original meaningful form by means of a key.

Document delivery A service that provides printed copies (full-text) of articles, reports, and publications, usually by subscription. Some services are connected to the Internet.

Domain A part of the naming hierarchy. Syntactically, a domain name consists of a sequence of names or other words separated by periods (for example, @prep.ai.mit.edu).

Domain name server A computer table that lists the IP numeric addresses of computers on the Internet, and their given common name. Generally, it is easier to remember a computer site by name, but the network stores the numerical address. Domain Name Servers keep track of which name belongs to which numerical address.

Domain Name System (DNS) A global naming system for use in UNIX networking for general-purpose, name-to-resource mapping. While in the Internet the network information center manages the higher-echelon domain names, the bulk of the management is decentralized to the lower-echelon sub-domains. Each name server in an Internet community is responsible for a personal piece of the global name hierarchy over which it has authority.

DOS (disk operating system) Any of a number of widely used operating systems, so-called because a primary function they provide is the control of auxiliary storage in the form of disks.

Download To transmit data from one central computer to another device or to a remote terminal.

Driver A program that controls (drives) the operation of a device or interface. The driver program interprets the computer data, providing the commands and signals required by the device or interface. The driver can output directly to the device or interface, or can provide paper output.

Duplex Pertaining to a transmission system where data can be received and transmitted. Half duplex can only transmit or receive. Full duplex can transmit and receive simultaneously.

E

E-mail See electronic mail.

Electronic mail A message service using electronics and telecommunications to deliver hard- or soft-copy information. These can take the form of text-only messages or of images that include text in font form and graphic material.

Emotives The communication of emotional nuance to a written communication which is otherwise communicated by tone of voice in verbal communication. It is, for example, difficult to convey sarcasm or tongue-in-cheek comments in written fashion. To replicate that capability, a series of emotive symbols (frequently called smileys because they resemble smiling faces, tilted on their side (:-)) have developed. Emotives can convey happiness, sadness, pouting, tongue-in-cheek, and a variety of other nuances that usually are conveyed by tone of voice and body language.

Encryption An algorithm designed to protect the interpretation and use of intellectual property in electronic files against unauthorized use.

End user The person or organization who will directly use a particular set of information or a device.

Error Any discrepancy between the theoretically correct behavior or values in a computer and the actual behavior or values. Most computers have routines specifically designed to detect the presence of errors.

Escape (Esc) A control code that indicates that the next code has a different meaning than it would usually have.

Ethernet A communications protocol developed by Xerox Corporation, widely used for local area networks.

F

FAQ (frequently asked questions) Novices to the Internet commonly face the same problems as their predecessors, and ask similar questions. FAQs are files containing the answers to the most frequently asked questions. FAQs have been expanded to cover a range of topics, so a user may find FAQ files on specific non-Internet related topics.

File A physical unit of storage on a computer disk or tape.

File server A computer that stores files on the Internet, and makes such files available for access by one of the various Internet access tools.

File transfer protocol (FTP) A reliable method of transferring files over the Internet.

Finger A software application whose purpose is to query information files about individual Internet users. The user places information regarding his phone number, address, or affiliation in a file, and the finger software retrieves such files upon request.

Firewall A security program created to prevent incoming access from the Internet to a closed network system.

Firmware Software that is stored in read-only memory (ROM). Firmware functions are not programmable by the user.

Fixed format A file structure consisting of physical records of a constant size within which the precise location of each variable is based on the column location and width of the variable.

Flame This is a pejorative term, signifying a breach of netiquette. Flaming can be losing ones temper, or it can mean calling into question someones personal opinions or observation. If you type your e-mail messages in all caps, you might inadvertently be accused of flaming.

FreeNet An organization whose purpose is to provide access to the Internet to as many people as possible. The first such effort was established by the highly-successful Cleveland FreeNet. Such networks make Internet resources available to the public by providing access at affordable charges. They also frequently provide support and aid in connecting to and navigating across the Internet.

FTP See file transfer protocol.

Full-text Referring to a database that contains entire documents as opposed to citations or abstracts.

G

Gate-keeping system A method of facilitating as well as controlling the process of gathering, organizing, filtering, distributing, and exchanging information in various formats between sources and users.

Gateway The electronic communications node that connects the individual user with specific mainframes or networks.

Glitch A sudden temporary mishap, error, or malfunction in mechanical, electrical, or electronic equipment.

GOPHER A software tool developed at the University of Minnesota. GOPHER enables multiple platform types running a customizable client to access a centralized server that provides coherent translation of information in myriad forms. It also enables a user to retrieve information available from thousands of GOPHER servers, anonymous FTP connections, publicly accessible Telnet connections, World-Wide Web servers, Novell networks, WAIS servers, and many more sources throughout the world.

GOPHER is a menu-driven system. Each gopher server has links to other GOPHER servers so that one can seamlessly bounce from one server to another with no perceived change of environments. GOPHER'S down side is in finding the proper resource. Hundreds of GOPHERS now exist, each with numerous submenus. Somewhere buried in some gopher server on the other side of the world might be an important resource for which you have been looking. Unfortunately, there is no easy way to know about that resource unless you start a lengthy and time-consuming GOPHER tour.

H

Handshake A protocol wherein a transmitting device sends a signal, and then the receiving device sends a ready signal before the transmission continues.

Hard-wired Pertaining to the direct wiring of a terminal to a computer system (or any device to any device), as opposed to devices that communicate through telephone lines or wireless media.

Header Part of an e-mail message generated by the transmission protocols that provide information about who originated a message, when it was posted, its pathway of travel across the Internet, and certain machine identifications along the way.

Hierarchical file A file containing information that is organized in subordinate levels or with a relational structure.

Host A system or subsystem in a network that performs actual processing operations against a database, and with which other network devices communicate.

Host computer The computer and associated database that run as a separate entity, but can be accessed through the network.

Host site The location (station) that receives communications from the other points in the network, performs operations on them through a host computer, and sends communications back to other points.

HTML (Hypertext Mark-up Language) In practical terms, HTML is a collection of styles used to define the various components of a World-Wide Web document. Used in WWW documents to embed style information (fonts, font sizes, and layout), graphics, and hypertext links (URLs) to other Internet files and resources.

HTTP (Hypertext Terminal Protocol) Used as a prefix in a URL, this string of letters tells the application that the address that follows is accessible as a WWW server. (See also URLs.)

Hypertext A term coined by Ted Nelson (Xanadu) to describe a form of relationships that is nonlinear. Most text is intended to be read one paragraph at a time in a serial fashion. Given electronic capabilities, it is possible to link one paragraph with another one in a different location, perhaps even on an entirely different computer. Hypertext describes these more fluid relationships.

I

IF (interactive facsimiles) A computer function that merges voice with facsimile transmissions to be carried over the Internet.

Indirect address An instruction that references an address specified in the content of another address.

Information Agent A software application whose purpose is to act on behalf of a database, updating it from information it retrieves from other databases. Archie and Veronica are examples of Information Agents.

Input
1. The process of entering data through a keyboard or terminal or other device.
2. The material that is entered through a keyboard or other device.

Intelligence The capability of a device to make computational and evaluative decisions under the control of a program.

Interactive
1. Relating to the capability of a device or procedure that enables an operator to make decisions that influence the outcome of a procedure in process.
2. Pertaining to a device that enables an operator to input data or commands and then responds in some way to the operator.

Interface The point and manner in which two separate systems or devices connect and interact with one another.

Internet Yellow Pages
1. A directory of Internet resources maintained in database format by a non-profit institution, for the benefit of the Internet community.
2. The New Riders publication that makes available directory information in printed form.

Internet A concatenation of many individual TCP/IP campus, state, regional, and national networks (such as NSFnet, ARPAnet, and MILnet) into one single logical network all sharing a common addressing scheme.

IP Internet Protocol.

IP address The Internet protocol numerical address assigned to each computer on the network, so that its location and activities can be distinguished from other computers.

ISDN Integrated Services Digital Network.

K

Kernel The level of an operating system or networking system that contains the system-level commands or all of the functions hidden from the user. In a UNIX system, the kernel is a program that contains the device drivers, the memory management routines, the scheduler, and system calls. This program is always running while the system is operating.

L

LAN local area network.

Laser Light amplification by stimulated emission of radiation.

ListServ A feature of e-mail that enables a single message to be "served" or delivered to many addresses simultaneously. The recipients e-mail address must appear on a distribution "list" in order to receive these reflected messages.

Local area network (LAN) A collection of devices and communication channels that connects a group of computers and peripheral devices together so that they can communicate with each other. Typically, local area networks occupy a single building or office area.

Log
1. A record of operations on a file, indicating actions, such as file creation, modification, errors, and other data.
2. To sign on (log on) or off (log off) a computer system or area. Log on procedures might require operator passwords, or might be accomplished simply by designating the desired area.

M

Majordomo Majordomo is a set of programs written in Perl that automate operation of multiple mailing lists. Majordomo automatically handles routine requests to subscribe or unsubscribe; it also has "closed lists" that route all subscription requests to a "list owner" for approval. It also supports "moderated lists" that send all messages to the list owner for approval before they're sent to subscribers.

MAPI Message Application Programming Interface.

MD Management domain.

MELVYL® A centralized information system for all nine campuses of the University of California. It includes a library catalog database, a periodicals database, article citation databases, and other files and can be accessed through UC lines or the Internet.

Memory The internal storage capacity of a computer system. Memory generally is located on some magnetic device such as disk, drum, or core. Data is stored in digitally encoded bytes, and manipulated as needed during calculation processes. The amount of memory a computer has directly affects its capability to perform complex functions.

MHS Message Handling System.

MILNET Military network.

MIME (Multipurpose Internet Mail Extensions) A code to specify the format of Internet messages, identifying text, program, mail-message, image, audio, video, and multipart (mixed media) files.

Mode A particular condition or state under which a computer or other device can operate, such as an insert mode, a communications mode, or a binary mode. Operations or commands can take on different meanings in different modes.

Modem (Modulator/demodulator) Connects computers at remote sites to the telephone system by converting data from the host computer into electronic signals, which are transmitted through the network to the target computer where another modem converts them back into machine-readable data. Modems can send as well as receive data, enabling computers to "converse" with one another.

MOSAIC
1. A free Macintosh client browser for World Wide Web servers. The program can access linked data on Internet servers through many protocols: Archie, gopher, wide area information servers, ftp (file transfer protocol), Telnet, and network news transfer protocol. The program requires system 7 and MacTCP 2.0.2. Mosaic is available through anonymous ftp from `ftp.ncsa.uiuc.edu` in the directory /MAC/mosaic.
2. Netware for Mac developed by Novell Inc. Allows users to share non-PostScript printers connected to the PC portion of a Netware network. The software intercepts the PostScript print job and translates it into PCL (printer control language) before sending it to the Netware server's print services.
3. Acronym for Macro-Connectionist Organization System For Artificial Intelligence Computation. This expert system has two medical applications, one for the diagnosis of kidney graft rejections, and one for the management of hypertension.
4. A program containing a Trojan horse strain that destroys the directories of all available unlocked hard and floppy disks, including the one on which it resides. Even unmounted but available SCSI hard disks are mounted and destroyed by the Trojan.

Mouse A hand-held input device, similar to a keyboard, but limited to such interactions with graphics images on the screen as pointing, clicking, and dragging.

MUD (Multi-User Dungeon) Games have been an important (and sometimes controversial) part of distributed networks. MUDs are sophisticated forms of Dungeons and Dragons in which many individuals can play the game simultaneously, confronting each other in the virtual dungeon made by the software.

MUDs have serious purposes, too. Programming solutions to problems involving multiple simultaneous access (a situation that comes up in many standard workgroup and collaborative applications) are thoroughly tested in such environments.

Multiplex To transmit simultaneously two or more messages over the same communications channel to different receivers.

MX Record (Mail Exchange Record) One of the components through which e-mail that is addressed to you actually gets to you. The MX Record tells domain name servers about routing and location instructions.

N

Network Two or more computers linked together physically or through telecommunications for the purpose of electronically sharing resources such as computer files, programs, and peripheral devices.

Network control program (NCP) A program within the software of a data processing system that controls the performance of a telecommunications network.

Network file system (NFS) A process for mounting magnetic disks on a network so that disks not physically attached to a computer appear as if they were physically attached.

Node A branching or exchange point in a network.

Noise Unwanted signal or signals on an electrical circuit.

Noise immunity The capability of a device to accept valid signals while rejecting invalid signals.

Non-switched line A communications link permanently installed between two points.

NREN (National Research and Education Network) Fiber-optic (improved capacity and transmission speed) network to link all education facilities, including grade schools and libraries, higher education institutions, and government organizations.

NSFNET The National Science Foundation Network The national backbone network, funded by the National Science Foundation and operated by the Merit Corporation, used to interconnect regional (mid-level) networks, such as WestNet, to one another.

Null modem The communications cable used in hardwiring.

Numeric database A database primarily containing numbers.

O

OCR See Optical Character Recognition.

Octet The grouping of eight numbers in a pair and two triplets as used in the domain name system; for example. 35.222.222.

Offline Pertaining to a device or function that is not electronically connected to the main device. Media transmission from an offline device must be by means of manually carried material (disk or tape) or through telephone lines.

Online Pertaining to devices that are electronically connected to the computer. Generally, an online device is treated as if it were an integral part of the computer system.

Online Public Access Catalog (OPAC) A database of bibliographic records to which the public has access, reflecting the material owned by a library or a consortium of libraries.

OPAC Online Public Access Catalog.

Operating system The program or set of programs that control a computer's operations and monitor the functions of the other programs.

Optical Character Recognition (OCR) A method of converting graphic symbols (particularly alphanumeric) to electronic signals by means of a reading device that recognizes character shapes. Until recently, material prepared for optical character recognition had to be typed in a specific format and with a specific type element.

Optical disk A rigid, plastic disk, 4 3/4" in diameter, with an embedded metallic underside on which data are recorded permanently by laser (ROM, read-only-memory). Also known as compact disk, CD, or CD-ROM. Digital information is recorded on a master disk with a strong laser beam. Copies are made by "stamping" 4 3/4 inch disks. They are read by a weaker laser beam. It is a high-density storage medium, with a capacity of 600 MB.

Optical scanner A device that uses light to scan and convert text, graphics, or other visual images into digitized data that can be read by a computer.

OSI Open System Interconnection.

P

Packet An addressed data unit of convenient size for transmission through a network.

Parallel interface A data transmission technique in which a group of binary digits (bits) are transferred simultaneously over multiple lines. Usually, eight bits that correspond to a character are transferred as a single operation.

Parameter
1. A designation for the format of type, as requested by command codes or system defaults. Line length, page depth, typeface, and leading are examples of parameters. Commands that take place as they are entered and do not maintain their effect (such as extra leading, cancel escapement, and so on) are not parameters.
2. (program parameter) A constant or variable that remains unchanged in a subroutine, and fully or partly specifies a process to be performed during the subroutine.
3. (hardware parameter) a parameter characteristic of a machine that establishes certain limitations or capabilities of the machine. For instance, a parameter of a typesetter might be its ability to process 160 lines per minute.

Parity The transmission of data so that all codes have either an even or an odd number of one-bits. Even parity means that one bit has been added to the codes with an odd number of one-bits so that the total is even, and odd parity means that all the even codes have a bit added so that they have an odd number of one-bits.

Parity check A method of verifying the accuracy of a transmitted bit pattern by examining the code to determine whether its value is odd or even.

Password An identification number keyed by the operator and checked by the computer before the database may be accessed.

Pay-by-the-drink A method of charging the user every time a file is accessed, based on the number of connect time units elapsed and records inspected. This is in contrast to paying a subscription or license fee that permits repeated and unlimited access to the files and records for the duration of the stipulated period of time.

Peripheral A device that is external to the system processor but operates under the processor's control, such as a line printer or a communications signal.

Platform A manufacturer's operating system for functions that have not been standardized in the industry and require intermediary programs to interpret the commands across different systems.

Port A communications channel between a computer and another device, such as a terminal, modem, or printer.

POP (Post Office Protocol) A software application that enables individual e-mail users (POP clients) to retrieve mail from a central mail depository (POP server).

PostScript Software made by Adobe for desktop publishing. A page description language that many laser printers understand. The next step is a PostScript-based non-application-specific document-interchange software that will allow searching and indexing.

PPP (Point-to-Point Protocol) Like SLIP, PPP is a software application that allows a computer to use Internet protocols to become a terminal node on the Internet. PPP requires a high-speed modem and standard telephone line.

Printer A peripheral device connected to a computer to render images on paper in black and white or color. Pigments can be transferred from a ribbon pressed against the print surface by an array of wires (matrix or impact printer), heated to sputtering and directed through tiny holes (ink jet) or electrostatically attached to a metal drum and transferred to paper by the xerographic method (laser).

Printout Display of file contents in text or graphics form on paper.

Program Series of instructions to direct the computer to perform specific tasks in a certain order.

Prompt An on-screen processing technique that questions or "prompts" the user of a computer system for responses.

Protocol The proper procedure and sequence of events for data transmission of a particular input device, with regard to code structure, identification of the text stream, and code recognition.

Q

Query A data message structured so as to elicit a response from a computer.

R

RAM Random Access Memory.

Random access Access to data, information, or files without observing any particular order.

Random Access Memory (RAM) A form of volatile memory that allows data (such as documents) to be stored randomly and retrieved directly by an address location. The system accesses the addressed material, with no need to read through intervening data. Information can be retrieved more speedily from random access memory than from serial media such as tape.

Raw data Data that has not been processed, reorganized, or manipulated.

Read-only memory (ROM) Memory that is programmed at the time of manufacture. It can be accessed only and cannot be erased. Non-volatile, read-only memory holds its contents after the power is shut off. It can be used to contain an operating system, language translators, and other "permanent" software.

Real time Pertaining to the performance of a computer in such a way that the operator receives responses quickly enough so that there is no effective delay in the operator's activity.

Remote Pertaining to communication with a device located at some distance from the central device, but connected in some way, with cables, wires, or telephone hookup.

Rich text format (RTF) A text exchange standard proposed by apple to provide an application independent file format including fonts, tab positions, rulers, line breaks, hyphenation, paragraph spacing, embedded objects, such as pictures and sounds, and special text styles.

ROM Read-only memory.

Router A dedicated computer that sends packets from one place to another, paying attention to the current state of the network.

RS-232 Port A standard plug with 25 pins, used to connect computers and I/O devices.

RTF Rich text format.

S

Screen The display surface of a video terminal or cathode ray tube.

Scroll A function available on most video terminals where the display image seems to move up and down (or left and right) on the screen to provide incremental viewing of material earlier or later in the file.

Search The electronic comparison of character strings entered by the operator with those contained in files or databases, arranged in Boolean logic expressions.

Server A network computer that shares its resources, such as files and printer, with other computers; for example, Network file system (NFS).

SFQL Structured Full-Text Query Language.

SGML Standard Generalized Markup Language.

Sign on To connect with a remote computer by providing identification details and performing appropriate procedures.

Signal The electrical quantity that coveys data from one point to another.

Signature
1. One of the requirements for a fully-functional Internet is to provide unique signatures with which to identify individuals (for example, for the purpose of verifying authorization to move funds.) A number of cryptographic solutions to individual signatures have been proposed, most of which depend on a unique encoding pattern that is known only to a single individual.
2. In e-mail, a piece of text that identifies the sender of an e-mail message. Some people develop elaborate and attractive signatures by which their messages are personalized.

Simplex A modem that either sends or receives information but cannot do both during one transmission.

Simultaneous transmission The transmission of data in two directions at one, both sending and receiving, by the same device.

Site license Authorization (usually subject to a fee) to have multiple copies for simultaneous use within a specified organization or location.

SLIP (Serial Line Internet Protocol) A software application that allows a computer to use Internet protocols to become a terminal node on the Internet. SLIP requires a high-speed modem and standard telephone line.

Smiley Symbols by which one can tell the emotional timbre of a given e-mail message. Smileys, such as :), provide emotive qualities in a shorthand fashion.

SMTP (Simple Mail Transport Protocol) The protocol by which e-mail messages are managed by computers on the Internet. It provides the possibility of designing e-mail servers and e-mail clients. Many of the popular e-mail handling programs, such as Eudora, take advantage of the SMTP protocol to make e-mailing easy and efficient.

Software A term coined to contrast computer programs with the hardware of a computer system. Software is a stored set of instructions that governs the operation of a computer system and makes the hardware run.

Stand-alone Referring to a device that is capable of performing the functions for which it is designed without the aid of or connection to another, smarter device. The stand-alone device can receive media from another device for processing.

Standard Generalized Markup Language (SGML) Enables data to move between media by describing documents by their structural elements rather than their visual format and thus permitting further analysis or reuse by various application programs.

Star A network configuration in which a central controller communicates directly with each device or station. A diagram of this configuration looks like a star.

Station One of the input or output points of a communications system or of a multi-user computer.

Stop bit In asynchronous communication, a marker following each character.

String A sequence of entities, such as characters or commands.

Structured Query Language (SQL) A data access language designed to work with relational databases. First used on IBMs dB2, SQL (pronounced sequel) became a de facto standard in the mid-1980s.

Surfing The enjoyable act of browsing for files and interesting gems of information on the Internet. This should be contrasted with the more goal-oriented activity of finding a particular piece of information. The aim of *The New Riders Official Internet Yellow Pages* is to facilitate the latter without limiting any of the pleasure of the former.

Synchronous Occurring concurrently and with a regular or predictable time relationship. In transmission, referring to the capability of the sending and the receiving devices to run continuously at the same frequency.

System A machine or devices using various hardware and software to accomplish certain tasks. Commonly composed of a central processor, with one or more input or output devices, and capable of making decisions about the material that is being processed. Various fields of computer technology tend to define "system" in slightly different ways.

T

TCP/IP Transmission Control Protocol/Internet Protocol

Telecommunication The transmission of signals by telegraph, radio, satellite, or some other means that does not involve physical connection between the sending and receiving devices.

Teleprocessing Computer operations carried out through long- distance communications network.

Teletext A generic term for one-way information retrieval systems that broadcast digitally encoded text and graphics to remote users. Teletext users request pages of transmitted data by means of a keyboard.

TELNET The Internet standard protocol for remote terminal connection service. TELNET enables a user at one site to interact with a remote time-sharing system at another site as if the user's terminal were connected directly to the remote computer.

Terminal A device (usually with a video display) on which an operator can communicate with or receive communication from a computer.

Terminal emulation A software capability in which a computer or terminal can be made to simulate the characteristics of another terminal for communications compatibility.

Terminal server A small, specialized networked computer that connects many terminals to a LAN through one network connection. Any user on the network can then connect to various network hosts.

Text A series of words or characters having some meaning to the reader, as opposed to command codes or instructions.

Throughput The net speed of a device or system, including input, output, and processing speeds together. The throughput speed may be slower than the inherent input or output speeds because input might be slowed by simultaneous output, or vice versa, or input and output might have to take place serially.

Timesharing The use of a computer for two or more purposes during the same time interval. The computer shares its attention among the devices by means of some monitoring program.

Token sharing network A communications network designed so that all computer devices (stations) on the network are connected to a common channel, called a *bus*. A group of bits (a token) is passed from station to station to give each station in turn the opportunity to transmit data.

Transmission Control Protocol (TCP) A set of protocols, resulting from ARPA efforts, used by the Internet to support services such as remote login (TELNET), file transfer (FTP) and mail (SMTP).

Transparent Pertaining to a process that is thoroughly compatible with another process so that a user is not necessarily aware that there is more than one process or function involved. A computer program that can be added to an existing program without retraining or reeducating its users is transparent to the original program.

Tree
1. (tree structure) An arrangement of data in a hierarchical form, with each group of data containing subgroups that present more detail.
2. A network configuration in which a central controller communicates to a number of other devices or stations, each of which in turn communicates to another group of devices or stations in an hierarchy.

U

UNIX A computer operating system developed by Bell Laboratories, written in the C programming language, and distinguished by its portability to different computers. It's widely used in graphics workstations.

Upload The function of sending a file from one computer and transferring it to another. Download, on the other hand, refers to the transfer of a file from another computer onto your own.

URL Uniform Resource Locator.

Usenet An Internet system of discussion groups, some of which may contain thousands of members, and others a mere handful. Most Usenet discussions are archived so that Internet users can query the archives and download threads of discussion centered on specific topics.

User friendly A characterization of computer products that are easy to learn or to use.

V

Value-added Enhancement of documents or data to increase their usefulness, such as gatekeeping and validation (for instance, by peer review), and substantive and copy editing by publishers. Libraries add value by selection, cataloging, archiving, and providing access. Electronic publishing adds value by providing full-text searching, audio, video, animation, large data sets, reducing the time required for publication, and ease of access from workstations.

Veronica An information agent that is used to conduct searches against data stored on various Gopher servers.

Video Display Terminal (VDT) An operator station that includes a display screen as part of its hardware. VDTs at one time were called CRTs (cathode ray tubes).

Virtual library Extends resources through access to bibliographic databases, full-text files, images, and other information in electronic format.

Voice grade Referring to the capability of a data transmission circuit to permit a transfer rate of up to 2400 bits per second (BAUD). A voice-grade circuit uses analog phone lines identical to standard telephone equipment, and encodes digital data into tones for transmission.

W

WAIS Wide Area Information Server.

Wide Area Information Server (WAIS) A method of searching indexed text. You can take a hundred files on the topic of numerical analysis and index them into one SRC file. New resources are announced in a special indexed database called "directory-of-servers," which solves the gopher problem mentioned earlier.

Wide Area Network (WAN) A network spanning hundreds or thousands of miles, in contrast to a local area network.

World Wide Web (WWW) Hypertext that goes beyond gopher by displaying menus and beyond WAIS by allowing pointers and chains within the text. Hypertext links can lead you down a fruitful path or to a dead end.

X

X.25 CCITT standard (1976) for the protocols and message formats that define the interface between a terminal and a packet switching network.

X.400 Global electronic messaging architecture.

Z

Z39.50 Application-layer protocol standard developed by the American National Standards Institute in 1992 for computer-to-computer information retrieval. A number of companies and universities are using it to develop interoperable search-and-retrieval software products for accessing the Internet. The open systems interconnection (OSI) model defines z39.50, but because OSI is not built into the UNIX operating system like TCP/IP, z39.50 was adapted to run over TCP/IP for the Internet.

APPENDIX E

Further Readings

Badget, Tom, and Corey Sandler, *Welcome to... Internet: From Mystery to Mastery,* MIS: Press, NY, a subsidiary of Holt and Co., Inc., 1993, ISBN 1-55828-308-0

Blackman, Josh, *The Legal Researcher's Internet Directory, 1993/1994,* Legal Research of New York, Brooklyn, NY, 1993

Braun, Eric, *The Internet Directory,* Fawcett Columbine, New York, NY, 1994, ISBN 0-449-90898-4

Cronin, Mary J., *Doing Business on the Internet; How the Electronic Highway is Transforming American Companies,* Van Nostrand Reinhold, New York, NY, an International Thomson Publishing Company, 1994, ISBN 0-442-01770-7

Crowe, Elizabeth Powell, *The Electronic Traveller: Exploring Alternative Online Systems,* Windcrest/McGraw-Hill, New York, NY, 1994, ISBN 0-8306-4498-9

Dern, Daniel. *The Internet Guide for New Users.* New York, NY: McGraw-Hill, 1993.

Engst, Adam C., *Internet Starter Kit; Everything You Need to Get on the Internet,* Hayden Books, Division of Prentice Hall Computer Publishing, Indianapolis, IN, 1993, ISBN 1-56830-064-6

Engst, Adam, *Internet Starter Kit for Macintosh,* 2nd Edition, Hayden Books, Division of Prentice Hall Computer Publishing, Indianapolis, IN, 1994, ISBN 1-56830-111-1

Estrada, Susan. *Connecting to the Internet: An OReilly Buyers Guide.* Sebastopol, CA: OReilly & Associates, 1993

Fahey, Tom, *net.speak: the internet dictionary,* Hayden Publishing, a division of Prentice Hall, Indianapolis, IN, 1994, ISBN 1-56830-095-6

Fisher, Sharon, *Riding the Internet Highway; Deluxe Edition,* New Riders Publishing, Indianapolis, IN, 1994, ISBN 1-56205-315-9

Fraase, Michael. *The Mac Internet Tour Guide: Cruising the Internet the Easy Way.* Chapel Hill, NC: Ventana Press, 1993.

Gibbs, Mark, and Richard Smith, *Navigating the Internet,* Sams Publishing, a division of Prentice Hall Publishing, 1993, ISBN 0-672-30362-0

Gibbs, Mark and Richard Smith, *Navigating the Internet: Deluxe Edition,* Sams Publishing, a division of Prentice Hall Publishing, Indianapolis, 1994, ISBN 0-672-30485-6

Gilster, Paul, *The Internet Navigator; The Essential Guide to Network Exploration for the Individual Dial-Up User,* Foreword by Vinton G. Cerf, John Wiley & Sons, New York, NY, 1993, ISBN 0-471-59782-1

Hesslop, Brent. *The Instant Internet Guide: Hands on Global Networking.* New York, NY: McGraw-Hill, 1994

Kehoe, Brendan. *Zen & The Art of the Internet.* New York, NY: Prentice Hall, 1992

Kennedy, Joyce Lain, and Thomas J. Morrow, *Electronic Job Search Revolution; Win With the New Technology That's Reshaping Today's Job Market,* John Wiley & Sons, Inc., New York, 1994, ISBN 0-471-59820-8

Kent, Peter, *The Complete Idiot's Guide to the Internet,* Sams Publishing, a division of Prentice Hall Publishing, Indianapolis, IN, 1994, ISBN 0-672-30519-4

Kochmer, Jonathan, and NorthWestNet, *Internet Passport; NorthWestNet's Guide to Our World Online,* NorthWestNet and Nortwest Academia Computing Consortium, Inc., Bellevue, WA, 1993, 4th Edition, ISBN 0-9635281-0-6

Krol, Ed, *The Whole Internet; User's Guide & Catalog,* O'Reilly & Associates, Inc., Sebastopol, CA, 1992, ISBN 1-56592-025-2

LaQuey, Tracy, and Jeanne C. Ryer, *The Internet Plus Companion; A Beginner's Start-Up Kit for Global Networking,* Foreword by Vice President Al Gore, Addison-Wesley, Boston, MA, 1993, ISBN 0-201-62719-1

Lawley, Elizabeth Lane and Craig Summerhill, *Internet Primer for Information Professionals: Basic Guide to Internet Networking Technology,* Mecklermedia, Westport, 1993, ISBN 0-88736-831-X

Library of Congress; Office for Subject Cataloging Policy Collection and Services, *LC Classification Outline,* Library of Congress, Washington, 1990, 6th edition, ISBN 0-8444-0684-8

Lynch, Daniel and Marshall T. Rose. *Internet System Handbook.* Reading, MA: Addison-Wesley, 1993

Magid, Larry, *Everybody's Online,* Random House, New York, 1993, ISBN O-679-748-82-2

Magid, Larry, *Cruising Online,* Random House, New York, 1994, ISBN 0-679-751-556

Malamud, Carl. *Exploring the Internet: A Technical Travelogue.* New York, NY: Prentice Hall, 1992

Marine, April (Editor). *Internet: Getting Started.* Menlo Park, CA: SRI International, 1992

Marine, April (Editor). *Internet: Getting Started.* Englewood Cliffs, NJ: Prentice Hall, 1994

Newby, Gregory B., *Directory of Directories on the Internet; A Guide to Information Sources,* Meckler, Westport, CT, 1994, ISBN 0-88736-768-2

Otte, Peter, *The Information Superhighway: Beyond the Internet,* Que Corporation, Indianapolis, IN, 1994, ISBN 1-56529-825-X

Pfaffenberger, Bryan, *Que's Computer User's Dictionary*, Que Corporation, Indianapolis, IN, 1993, 4th Edition, ISBN 1-56529-604-4

Que Development Group Staff. *The Hitchhikers Guide to Internet.* Indianapolis, ID: Que, 1993

Resnick, Rosalind and Dave Taylor, *The Internet Business Guide,* Sams Publishing, a division of Prentice-Hall, Indianapolis, IN, 1994, ISBN 0-672-30530-5

Rittner, Don, *Ecolinking; Everyone's Guide to Online Environmental Information,* Peachpit Press, Berkeley, CA, 1992, ISBN 0-938151-35-5

Rugge, Sue and Alfred Glossbrenner, *The Information Broker's Handbook*, Windcrest/McGraw-Hill, New York, NY, 1992, ISBN 0-8306-3797-4

Savetz, Kevin, *Your Internet Consultant: The FAQs of Life Online*, Sams Publishing, Indianapolis, IN, 1994, ISBN 0-672-30520-8

Tweney, Dylan, *The Traveler's Guide to the Information Highway,* Ziff Davis Press, Emeryville, CA, 1994, ISBN 1-56276-206-0

Woods, Lamont and Dana Blankenhorn, *Bulletin Board Systems for Business,* John Wiley & Sons, New York, NY, 1992, ISBN 0-471-55348-4

Appendix F

A Whimsical Tour of the Internet

Following is a whimsical guided tour of the Internet—just another way of enticing you to discover the riches that await you on the Internet!

You can start your online day by accessing the world's first random URL generator! Use your favorite WWW browser to click on an image and be taken to a random URL. You never know where you'll end up!

`http://kuhttp.cc.ukans.edu/cwis/organizations/kucia/uroulette/uroulette.html`

Then you can look for

- An almanac entry:

`<finger://copi@oddjob.uchicago.edu>`

- A verse from the Bible:

`<telnet://138.26.65.78:7777>`

- A virtual fortune cookie

`<telnet://astro.temple.edu:12345>` or
`<telnet://argo.temple.edu:12345>`

With your morning coffee you can

- Read the headlines from USA Today:

`<telnet://freenet-in-[a,b,c].cwru.edu>`

`<telnet://visitor@yfn.ysu.edu>`

- Peruse the Electronic Newsstand:

`<gopher://gopher.cic.net:70/11/e-serials>`

- See how your stocks have been doing:

`<telnet://guest@a2i.rahul.net>`

- Look for a new job at the Online Career Center:

`<gopher://garnet.msen.com:9062/1>`

- Find out about scholarship and minority assistance programs:

`<telnet://fedix.fie.com>`

If you're feeling scholarly, you can check out

- The Library of Congress:

`<gopher://marvel.loc.gov:70/1>`

- The Colorado Alliance of Research Libraries:

`<telnet://pac.carl.org>`

- HYTELNET, which gives access to hundreds of libraries all around the world:

`<telnet://access.usask.ca>`

- An online dictionary:

`<telnet://cs.indiana.edu:2627,` or
`<telnet://guest@wombat.doc.ic.ac.uk>`

Science and Math types can use

- The Scientist, a biweekly newsletter:

`<ftp://ds.internic.net/pub/the-scientist>`

- The Math Gopher, for software, lesson plans, and access to other systems:

`<gopher://archives.math.utk.edu:70>`

- NASA Headline News:

`<finger://nasanews@space.mit.edu>`

- An online periodic table of elements:

`<telnet://camms2.caos.kun.nl:2034>`

For the publisher in you, here are some favorite starting points

- CMU list of Book Publishers & Retailers On-Line:

`<http://www.cs.cmu.edu:8001/web/booksellers.html>`

- CMU list of On-Line Books:

`<http://www.cs.cmu.edu:8001/web/books.html>`

- The Digital Media Center:

`<http://160.96.7.121/>`

- The World Wide Web Virtual Library's Commercial Services:

`<http://info.cern.ch/hypertext/DataSources/bySubject/Yellow/Overview.html>`

- The World Wide Web Virtual Library, literature maintained by the Internet Book Information Center:

`<http://sunsite.unc.edu/ibic/IBIC-homepage.html>`

For the academic in you, you can visit the University Press:

`<gopher://geneva.acs.uci.edu:1070/11/franklin/Libraries/publishers>`

For the geographer in you, visit the map site at Delorme Mapping:

`<http://www.delorme.com/home.htm>`

For the bookworm in you, try Online BookStore (OBS):

`<http://marketplace.com/0/obs/obshome.html>`

Or try Project Gutenberg:

`<http://info.cern.ch/roeber/Misc/Gutenberg.html>` or `<http://med-amsa.bu.edu/Gutenberg/Welcome.html>`

To peruse periodicals and magazines, try

- The Electronic Newsstand:

`<gopher://internet.com:2001/11/>`

- Global Network Navigator (GNN):

`<http://nearnet.gnn.com/gnn.html>`

- Wired Magazine:

`<http://www.wired.com/>`

If you've ever dreamed of visiting far away museums, now's your chance!

- Scrolls from the Dead Sea: an Exhibit at the Library of Congress, Washington, D.C.:

`<http://sunsite.unc.edu/expo/deadsea.scrolls.exhibit/intro.html>`

- The Louvre:

`<http://mistral.enst.fr/~pioch/louvre/>`

Desperate to go downtown in the middle of the night!

- Downtown Anywhere:

`<http://www.awa.com/>`

Want to join a few societies? Try starting with:

- The Internet Society:

`<http://info.isoc.org/home.html>`

- The International Society for Arts, Science and Technology, ISAST

`< leonardo@garnet.berkeley.edu>`

Interested in finding out what's going on in the cyberspace marketplace?

- Marketplace:

`<http://marketplace.com/>`

If you're a history buff, there are:

- Databases:

`<telnet://ukanaix.cc.ukans.edu history>`

- Documents and archives:

`<ftp://byrd.mu.wvnet.edu/pub/history>`

If you want the latest shareware for your MS-DOS, Macintosh, UNIX, Amiga, Apple2, Apollo, or other computer, try one of the enormous software archives on the Internet!

- Shareware depositories:

`<ftp://archive.umich.edu>`

`<ftp://sumex-aim.stanford.edu>`

`<ftp://oak.oakland.edu>`

To see what's been shaking, there's earthquake information at:

`<finger://quake@geophys.washington.edu>`

And the USGS offers land use maps of the United States at:

`<telnet://guest@glis.cr.usgs.gov>`

For legal information try:

- Supreme Court Rulings

`<ftp://ftp.cwru.edu/hermes>`

- Law libraries, offering information by state or subject:

`<telnet://liberty.uc.wlu.edu lawlib>` and `<ftp://sulaw.law.su.oz.au/pub/law>`

- Hypertext access to legal documents:

`<telnet://www.LAW.indiana.edu www>` or `<telnet://fatty.LAW.cornell.edu www>`

For health and clinical information, there's the National Institute of Health:

`<gopher://gopher.nih.gov:70/11/clin>`

Handicapped and disabled users can access medical information, disability assistance, equipment, services, and software at:

`<ftp://handicap.shel.isc-br.com>`

If you're 'Hollywood' inclined, you can get access to a database of actors, directors, and cinematographers:

`<mailto://movie@ibmpcug.co.uk "HELP">`

Home shoppers can access catalogs and place orders for CDs, books, software, and video tapes through home shopping:

`<telnet://columbia.ilc.com cas>`

`<telnet://holonet.net cdc>`

`<telnet://books.com>`

`<telnet://netmark.com>`

If you're a music lover, you can get

- Guitar chords in tablature form:

`<ftp://ftp.nevada.edu/pub/guitar>`

- Lyrics:

`<ftp://ftp.uwp.edu/pub/music>`

- Billboard charts:

`<finger://buckmr@rpi.edu>`

- Cyber-Sleaze reports on pop stars:

`<gopher://metaverse.com>`

If its food from the gods that you're looking for, try accessing Mythology and Folklore in the EINet galaxy catalog. This resource includes pointers to The Gateway of Darkness, books about mythology online, and more.

`<http://www.einet.net/galaxy/Arts-and-Humanities/Religion/Mythology-and-Folklore.html>`

If you're hungry, you can access recipe archives:

`<ftp://gatekeeper.dec.com/pub/recipes>`

`<ftp://mthvax.cs.miami.edu/pub/recipes, <ftp://ftp.neosoft.com/pub/rec.food/recipes>` or

`<ftp://cs.ubc.ca/pub/local/RECIPES>`

And if you're thirsty, you can take a look at the HomeBrew archives:

`<ftp://mthvax.cs.miami.edu/HomebrewDigest>`

If you want to taste the spirit of New York or the spirit of San Francisco, think of becoming a subscriber to:

- **ECHO:**

`phiber@echonyc.com (212) 255-3839`

- **The WELL:**

`telnet://well.sf.ca.us and login as guest. VOICE: +1-415-332-4335`

If you want to play games with partners around the world, your choices include

- **Bolo:**

`<telnet://gwis.circ.gwu.edu:1234>`

- **Go:**

`<telnet://hellspark.wharton.upenn.edu:6969>`

- **Diplomacy:**

`<mailto://judge@morrolan.eff.org>`

`<mailto://judge@dipvax.dsto.gov.au>`

`<mailto://judge@shrike.und.ac.za>`

`<mailto://judge@u.washington.edu>`

- Tetris, Moria, Nethack, MUDs, Text Adventures, and others:

`<telnet://castor.tat.physik.uni-tuebingen.de GAMES>`

Sports fans can get:

- **NBA schedules:**

`<telnet://culine.colorado.edu:859>`

- **NHL schedules:**

`<telnet://culine.colorado.edu:860>`

- **MLB schedules:**

`<telnet://culine.colorado.edu:862>`

- NFL schedules:

`<telnet://culine.colorado.edu:863>`

- **and a variety of others**

`<finger://copi@oddjob.uchicago.edu>`

For access to US Government information, there's the FedWorld Gateway, providing access to scores of government databases:

`<telnet://fedworld.doc.gov>`

And of course, last but not least, you can even find love on the Internet !

`>- mailto://perfect@match.com "SEND FORM"`

And there's much, much more!

Appendix G

Making Your Voice Heard

Making Your Voice Heard

Application to List an Internet Resource

The cooperative nature of the Internet environment is one of its strongest features. If you have discovered a resource that is particularly useful to you and it is not in *The New Riders Official Internet Directory*, you can call it to the attention of the authors, who will endeavor to qualify it for listing in a subsequent edition.

You can make your recommendation by filling in this form and e-mailing or FAXing it to us.

You can e-mail or FAX your recommendation to:

YP@McKinley.com   or   FAX (510) 841-6311

The McKinley Group, Inc., 2421 Fourth St. #D, Berkeley, CA 94710, USA

(Please use a separate form for each entry that you are recommending.)

I would like to recommend the following Internet resource.

Title: _____

Brief Description: _____

_____

_____

_____

Why do you particularly like this resource?

_____

_____

_____

_____

Please supply as much of the following information as possible.

Keywords (up to 4): _____

Producer: _____

Audience (up to 3): _____

Contact Name: _____

Contact's e-mail: _____

URL (up to 3 as appropriate) _____

_____

_____

Profile (up to 10 lines): _____

_____

_____

_____

_____

_____

_____

_____

_____

_____

Your Name: _____

Affiliation: _____

E-mail Address: _____

Telephone: _____

FAX: _____

Snail Mail: _____

_____

_____

Making Your Voice Heard
Notification to Correct a Listing

The volatility of electronic networks is such that addresses and contents change very quickly. To report changes or errors to a listing, please bring them to our attention using the form supplied here.

You may e-mail or FAX the revised information to: **YP@McKinley.com**
or FAX (510) 841-6311

The McKinley Group, Inc., 2421 Fourth St. #D, Berkeley, CA 94710, USA

(Please use a separate form for each entry that you are submitting.)

I would like to point out the following error/change in the Internet resource listing found in the Second Edition of *New Riders' Official Internet Directory.*

Title of Listing: _____

Page Number the Listing Can be Found on: _____

General Observation about this Listing: _____

URL (Confirmation): _____

Correct Information

(Insert Your Changes by the appropriate Field)

Title: _____

Short Description: _____

Keywords: _____

Sponsor: _____

Audience: _____

Profile: _____
_____
_____
_____
_____
_____
_____
_____
_____
_____
_____
_____
_____
_____

Details: _____

Notes: _____
_____
_____

URL: _____
_____
_____

Your Name: _____

Affiliation: _____

E-mail Address: _____

Or SnailMail Address: _____

Telephone: _____

FAX: _____

Date: _____

Making Your Product or Service Known

Application to List an Advertisement

Send this form by e-mail or FAX to:
E-mail: yp@mckinley.com
FAX: (510) 841-6311

Advertisements are being accepted for the *New Riders' Official Internet Directory* as long as they conform to the basic template format as set here.

Each line can be a maximum of 48 characters long (9 point type size).

Title: _____

Brief Description (up to 3 lines): _____

Keywords (2 or up to 4): _____

Sponsor: _____

Contact Name: _____

E-mail: _____

Phone: _____

Profile (up to 10 lines): _____
_____
_____
_____
_____
_____
_____
_____
_____
_____

Details: P (Product) S (Service) IP (Can be ordered over the Internet)

Access Info: (up to 2 lines) _____
_____

Notes: (up to 2 lines) _____
_____

URL: _____

Please fill in the form and return it by fax or e-mail. You will be contacted regarding payment and placement of your advertisement in the next edition.

Costs: $600 per template for 2 placements in the directory; $200 for each additional placement.

Placement: Your ad will automatically be placed in alphabetical order under the two keywords you assign.

Prices are subject to change without notice.

I am interested in advertising, please send further details. _____

I have submitted an ad template, please contact me regarding placement of my ad and payment. _____

Appendix H
Internet Ads

EXPLORE the INTERNET
—— FREE! ——

DELPHI is the only major online service to offer you full access to the Internet. And now you can explore this incredible resource with no risk. You get 5 hours of evening and weekend access to try it out for free!

Use electronic mail to exchange messages with over 30 million people throughout the world. Download programs and files using "FTP" and connect in real-time to other networks using "Telnet." Meet people from around the world with "Internet Relay Chat" and check out "Usenet News," the world's largest bulletin board with over 5,000 topics.

If you're not familiar with these terms, don't worry; DELPHI has expert online assistants and a large collection of help files, books, and other resources to help you get started. After the free trial you can choose from two low-cost membership plans. With rates as low as $1 per hour, no other online service offers so much for so little.

Now supporting 9,600 and 14,400 bps at no extra cost

5-Hour Free Trial!
Dial by modem, 1-800-365-4636
Press return a few times
At *Password*, enter YP9401

DELPHI INTERNET

Offer applies for new members only. A valid credit card is required for immediate access. Other restrictions apply. Complete details are provided during the toll-free registration. Questions? Call 1-800-695-4005 (voice). Send e-mail to INFO@delphi.com

---

MANAGE YOUR INTERNET ACCESS

Only PSI offers managed Internet access to your LAN. If you consider providing information servers like Mosaic, Gopher, Archie, and others on the Internet to provide a public presence for your company or products, you may be interested in controlling what bandwidth is used over your Internet connection.

This control ensures that individual Internet access is available to your company even when the outside world is heavily accessing your information.

56KBPS ACCESS INTERNET ROUTER & INFORMATION SERVER PVC $5,300*

Sign up for our InterFrame Service before December 23, 1994, and receive a 50% discount on our service fees, FREE Internet Router and FREE "Managed Internet" PVC.

To order, call PSI at 1-800-82psi82 today and ask how you can take advantage of this special offer and see how easy it is to get connected.

PSI
PERFORMANCE SYSTEMS INTERNATIONAL, INC.
510 Huntmar Park Drive
Herndon, VA 22070
FaxBack Info: 1.800.FAX.PSI.1
WorldWide Web: http://www.psi.net/

*Restrictions apply. Contact PSI for details.
All trademarks and service marks are used with permission and are the property of their respective owners.

COMPLETE INTERNET
ACCESS
$29 *per Month**

PSI InterRamp

Forget on-line services.
InterRamp℠ connects you *directly* to the Internet. Now you can have the entire worldwide Internet network at your fingertips and tap into an unlimited number of resources like MOSAIC, Gopher, WAIS, Veronica, Archie, ftp, E-Mail, NEWS and much, much more!

PSI brings you InterRamp℠.
Simple and easy-to-use personal Internet access for your PC, Macintosh® or workstation via v.32bis modem and ISDN.

Special Offer Available.
Subscribe to InterRamp by December 31, 1994 and receive special "Pioneer Preference" pricing* and state-of-the-art third party software of *your* choice.

*Restrictions apply. Contact a PSI Sales Representative for details.

Call PSI Today
1.800.psi.3031
(703.709.0300)

Performance Systems International, Inc.
510 Huntmar Park Drive
Herndon, VA 20070
FaxBack Info: 1.800.FAX.PSI.1
Internet E-Mail: interramp-info@psi.com
World Wide Web: http://www.psi.net

FREE
Profit-Making Secrets Report For Your Business

Would you like?
More pre-qualified leads/customers?
More gross sales?
More customer conversions?
More nationwide/international expansion?
More lifetime customer relationships?
and
More Bottom-Line PROFIT?

Contact your Alliance Marketing specialist now for your free report on how you can produce guaranteed results <u>very</u> inexpensively. Send and request Profit-Maker Report #1. Include E-mail and full mailing address.

Mail To: prftmkr@secretsams.win.net

Alliance Marketing Systems
4233 Clark Rd. Ste #8, Sarasota, Fl. 34233

Fast, Easy Internet Access.

New NetCruiser™ For Windows® Software Makes Using The Internet Easy!

- **Easy Point & Click Menus**
  Simple icons and pull-down menus—no Unix
- **FREE 40+ Hours Each Month**
  No charge on 40 prime hours of access time, plus free off-peak and weekend hours
- **Low Cost Service**
  Only $19.95/month, plus a low start-up fee
- **NetCruiser Supports...**
  Usenet News, WWW, Gopher, ftp, Telnet, and more
- **Plus Full Network Connections**
  We also provide dedicated 56kb and T1 links nationwide

CALL TODAY FOR DETAILS
800-353-6600

NETCOM The Leading Internet Service Provider

You can also get more information on NETCOM services via the Internet at *info@netcom.com*. NetCruiser is a trademark of NETCOM. Windows is a trademark of Microsoft Corporation. ©1994 NETCOM Inc.

The Source for Connectivity

Since 1977 the Black Box Catalog has brought unique, hard-to-find computer connectivity products to Fortune 5000 companies, universities, and the military. Now Black Box makes 17 years of accumulated expertise available to you via our own internet web server.

All things for computer connectivity. That's what you'll find in the Black Box internet web server. From PCMCIA technology and ethernet topology overviews to V.34 standards explanation and various application tutorials. All the information—everything you need along with the broadest selection of connectivity equipment available anywhere. All from one source. Black Box Corporation. The Source for Connectivity. Access http://www.blackbox.com

Black Box Corporation
The Source for Connectivity®

Environmental Systems Research Institute, Inc.

Access these resources via the Internet or CompuServe:

- Product Descriptions
- Class Schedules and Descriptions
- Certified Instructors
- Technical Documents
- ARC/INFO AMLs and SMLs

Or, participate in a discussion on our ESRI-L mailing list. See our listing for connect information.

For more product information, call
909-793-2853, extension 1475

For more training information, call
909-793-2853, extension 1585
or fax **909-793-5953**

Just how fast *do* you need it?

When you need a product, you want it on time, to work right, and to come with support you can trust. At Black Box, that's what we deliver every day.

We carry more than 6000 computer connectivity products. And we get them to you fast. We deliver support, too. Our Technical Support is staffed 24 hours a day, seven days a week. Call before you order, during, or after. We're here to help. To get a free subscription to the Black Box Catalog, call 800-552-6816. Or, access Black Box's own internet web server at http://www.blackbox.com

 Black Box Corporation
The Source for Connectivity®

Index

A
Symbols

1991 Census of Population Documentation (Canada), 121, 131, 206, 314
1994 Federal Budget (Canada), 121, 299, 325, 362
30something, 86, 664
3D, 549
9nov89-l, 90, 318

A

A Grant Getter's Guide to the Internet, 283, 285, 331
AACIS-L (American Association for Collegiate Independent Study), 31, 232, 236, 240
AARNet Guide, 31, 377, 387
ABC programming language, 31, 567-568
ABI/Inform, 31, 111, 118, 452
abolitionism
   Johns Hopkins University Library, 31
   The University of Illinois at Chicago Library, 31-32
   U.S. Civil War Reading List, 32
abortion
   Abortion and Reproductive Rights, 32, 34-35, 713
   alt.feminism, 32
   table.abortion, 32
   Women.health, 32
academia
   Academia Latinoamericana de Espanol, 32
   Academic Freedom Statements, 32
   Academic Institution Information of Western Countries, 32
   Academic Job Listings All Over the World, 32-33
   alt.usage.english, 33
   CAF Archive, 33
   The English Server, 33
   The MIT Press Online Catalogs, 33
   Research Databases and Resources by Subject, 33
Academia Latinoamericana de Espanol, 32, 235, 420, 639-640
Academic Computing Training & User Support, 33, 180
Academic Freedom Statements, 32
Academic Institution Information of Western Countries, 32-33
Academic Job Listings All Over the World, 32-33, 258
academics
   Academic Computing Training & User Support, 33
   Academic Institution Informations of Western Countries, 33
accounting
   Financial Economics Network (FEN), 33
   NAARS (National Automated Accounting Research System), 33-34
   Utah Valley Community College Library, 34
Accri-l, 34, 341, 461
ACDGIS-L, 34, 314, 318-319
ACEN (Art Com Electronic Network), 34, 67, 444, 482
ACLU Free Reading Room, 34, 35, 143, 184
ACM SIGGRAPH Online Bibliography Project, 34, 164, 372, 482, 568
acoustical engineering, CEC (Canadian Electro-Acoustics Community), 34
ACS Gopher, 137, 138
Act-up, 35, 44, 341-342
Activ-L, 35, 266, 413, 543
activism, 34-36
Ada (Programming Language), info-Ada, 37
ADA-Law, 37, 213, 427
Ada-sw, 37, 568
ADD (Attention Deficit/Hyperactivity Disorder), ADD-parents, 37, 539
ADLTED-L (Canadian Adult Education Network), 37, 232-233, 236, 240
adoption, 37-38
ADS (Astrophysics Data System), 77
Adult Education Network (AEDNET), 39
Adult/Distance Education, 38, 233, 236, 240
Adv-Eli, 38, 252, 255-256, 260
Adv-Elo, 38, 252, 256, 260, 662
Advanced Product Centers (APC), APC-Open, 38
advanced workshops, MICnews, 38
advertising, 38-39
advisory, INTER-L, 39
AEC, Architecture, Building, 39
AEDNET (Adult Education Network), 39, 233, 236, 240
Aeflow, 39, 260
Aeronautics, 39
aeronautics, history of, 39-40
aerospace, 40-41
Aerospace Engineering, 40, 82, 260-261, 637
af, 41, 79, 263
Africa, 41
Africa in the CIA World Fact Book, 41, 371, 571
Africa-n, 41, 515
African American studies, soc.culture.african.american, 41-42
African Art Exhibit and Tutorial, 41, 67, 193
African Education Research Network, 41-42, 193-194, 583
African government, The University of Michigan Library, 325
African studies, 42
Afrikaans, Harvard University Library, 42
AgeLine, 42, 318, 574, 602
Agence FrancePresse International French Wire, 42, 273, 302-303, 510, 668
aging, AgeLine, 42
agmodels-l, 42-43, 282
agora, 42, 357
agoraphobia, Panic, 42
AGRICOLA, 43, 59, 107, 265
Agricultural Guide, 43, 377
Agriculture, 43, 282
agriculture, 42-44
Agriculture, Veterinary Science & Zoology, 43, 700, 727
AGRIS International, 43, 209-210, 298, 605-606
AIDS (disease), 44-45
Aids, 44, 461, 556, 630
AIDS Treatment News, 44, 338, 350, 461
AIDS/HIV Information, 44, 338, 461
AIDSLINE, 44, 462
Aikido Information, 45, 455, 641
aikido-l, 45, 455
air conditioning, Utah Valley Community College Library, 45
Airplane-clubs, 45
Alaska, Information About Alaska, 45
alchemy, Harvard University Library, 46
Aldus Pagemaker, PAGEMAKER, 46
Alex Description, 46, 377, 394
aliens, 46
alife, 46, 71, 457, 613
allergies, National Institute for Allergy & Infectious Disease (NIAD), 46
Alliance Marketing Systems, 46, 118, 610
Allied and Alternative Medicine (AMED), 46-47, 52, 462
alloys, METADEX, 47
Almost 2001 Archive, 47, 152, 173, 377
alpha-osf-managers, 47, 161, 170
Alspa Computer, Inc., 47, 174, 189
alt.3d, 47
alt.activism, 35, 47
alt.alien.visitors, 46-47, 279, 679
alt.aquaria, 47, 63, 294, 350
alt.artcom, 47, 659
alt.arts.nomad, 48, 67

Index

alt.atheism, 48, 322, 597
alt.bbs, 48, 89, 174, 196
alt.beer, 48, 89
alt.binaries.pictures.cartoons, 48, 126
alt.bonsai, 48, 105, 309, 407, 420
alt.books.reviews, 48, 105, 168, 446, 615
alt.california, 48, 120
alt.callahans, 48, 356, 715
alt.caving, 48, 128, 640
alt.censorship, 35, 48, 131, 185, 302
alt.chinese.text, 49, 140, 421
alt.christnet, 49, 91, 140, 597
alt.christnet.bible, 49, 91, 140, 597
alt.config, 49, 167, 185, 377
alt.conspiracy, 49, 185, 539
alt.cult-movies, 49, 289, 561
alt.cyberpunk, 49, 174, 196
alt.drugs, 49, 219
alt.fan.monty-python, 49, 149, 264, 356, 611
alt.fan.rush-limbaugh, 49, 149, 440, 558
alt.fashion, 49, 283, 651
alt.feminism, 32, 35, 49, 286, 714
alt.folklore.computers, 50, 174, 297
alt.folklore.urban, 50, 297, 691
alt.guitar, 50, 333, 491
alt.housing.nontrad, 50, 152, 155, 354
alt.hypertext, 50, 358, 446
alt.kids-talk, 50, 134, 138
alt.music.alternative, 50, 484
alt.music.progressive, 50, 490, 562
alt.pagan, 50, 538, 597
alt.peeves, 50, 149, 356
alt.personals.ads, 50, 545, 625
alt.politics.clinton, 50, 145, 559
alt.politics.election, 51, 324, 559
alt.politics.libertarian, 51, 436, 556
alt.rap, 51, 490
alt.religion.kibology, 51, 356, 597, 611
alt.rock-n-roll, 51, 490
alt.rock-n-roll.metal, 51, 490
alt.romance.chat, 51, 134, 604
alt.security.pgp, 51, 174, 259, 566
alt.sex, 51, 621
alt.sexual.abuse.recovery, 51, 573, 622
alt.tasteless, 51, 149, 356
alt.usage.english, 33, 51, 245, 435, 440
Alternate Tuning Mailing List, 52, 473, 491
Alternates, 52, 101, 622
Alternative Approaches to Learning Discussion (Altlearn), 53
alternative management, AltInst, 52
alternative medicine
    Allied and Alternative Medicine (AMED), 52
    Alternative Medicine, The Definitive Guide, 52, 338, 342, 462
alternative press, Prog-Pubs, 52
AltInst, 52, 370
Altlearn (Alternative Approaches to Learning Discussion), 53, 240, 235
AM/FM, 53, 152, 584, 680
AMALGAME, 53, 338
Amazons International, 53, 286, 312
ambulatory care, University of Texas Health Science Center at San Antonio Library, 53
AMED (Allied and Alternative Medicine), 46-47, 52
Amend2-discuss, 35, 53, 101, 309, 433
Amend2-info, 35, 53, 101, 143, 148, 185, 433
AmerCath (History of American Catholicism), 53-54, 127, 140, 597
America, 54, 117, 184, 326, 671
American Association for Collegiate Independent Study (AACIS), AACIS-L, 31
American Banker Full Text, 54, 87, 375-377
American Chemical Society, 54, 135
American drama, University of Chicago Library, 54
American Hockey League, 54, 350, 641
American studies, Summit of the Americas Internet Gopher, 54

Americana, soc.culture.usa, 54-55
Americana (Western), 55
Americans with Disabilities Act, 55, 214, 326, 432
Amiga CD-ROM, 55, 129, 174
Amiga computers, 55
amlat.mujeres, 55, 125, 286, 422, 711-712
Amnesty International, 35, 55, 324, 558
AMOS, 55, 174, 570
An NREN That Includes Everyone, 56, 155, 326, 503
Analog Heaven, 56, 255, 484, 620-621, 654
analysis, 56-58
anesthesia, Accri-I, 34
animal rights, 58-59
animal science, Biosis Previews, 59
animal studies, AGRICOLA, 59
animal welfare, NetVet Veterinary Resources, 59
Animals directory, 59, 254
animals, 59-60
animation, 60
ANIME-L, 60, 289, 407
Anneal, 60, 457, 624
annual reports, CIA World Factbook, 60
anthropology, 60-61
Anthropology, Cross Cultural Studies, & Archaeology, 60-61, 64, 191
antiquarian books, 61
ANU (Australian National University)
    Asian Settlements Database, 61
    Asian-Settlements Database, 72, 206, 314
    Buddhism Database, 597-598, 61, 73, 110
    Demography and Publications Database, 61, 206
    Vietnam-SciTech-L Database, 61, 613, 659, 701-702
APC-Open, 38, 61-62
ApE-info, 62, 174, 613-614, 704
APEX-J (Asia-Pacific Exchange Electronic Journal), 62, 73
API Energy Business News Index (APIBIZ), 62, 111, 546
APL programming language, APL-L, 62, 568, 570
Apngowid.meet, 62, 71-72, 210, 286, 537, 712, 715
Apollo Advertising, 38, 62, 111
Apple computer, 62-63
Apple Computer Higher Education Gopher Server, 63, 170
Apple Computer WWW Server, 63, 170, 623, 659
Apple II Files, 62-63, 174
AppWare programming language, AppWare-info, 63, 174, 570
APR (Astronomical Publications Resources), 74-76
aquatics, 63-64
Aquatic Sciences and Fisheries, 63-64, 614
AR-news, 35, 58-59, 64
AR-talk, 36, 59, 64
Arabic culture, Harvard University Library, 64
Arachnophilia: Florida Institute of Technology's WWW Server, 64, 394
Archaeology, Historic Preservation, 64, 347
archeology, 64
Archie, 65, 394
Archie Demo, 65, 394
Archie Hypertext Servers, 65, 394
Archie Manual, 65, 394
ArchiGopher, 65-67
architecture, 65-66
Architecture, Building, 39, 65, 111, 186
Archive of Biology Software and Data, 66, 95, 338, 477
archosaurs, dinosaur, 66
Argentina, 66, 194, 556
Aristotle, texts of, 66
ARlist, 36, 66, 556, 600
Armadillo's World Wide Web Page, 66, 193, 245, 348, 667
ars magica, 66, 308, 604
art, 67-70
Art & Architecture, 65-67, 70
art (balloon), Balloon Sculpting, 86
Art Com Electronic Network (ACEN), 34
Art Com Magazine, 70, 162, 358, 444, 659
art exhibitions, Smithsonian Online, 70
art history, 70-71

Index 775

Art-support, 67, 293
artificial intelligence, 71
Artificial Intelligence, Expert Sys., Virtual Reality, 71, 168, 278, 703
Artificial Life, 71, 134
artificial life, 71
artist-users, 67, 71, 162, 174
Arts, 67, 199, 485
Arts Wire, 36, 67, 485, 717
Asat-eva (Distance Education Evaluation Group), 71, 233, 237, 240
ASCII, Gopher-Based ASCII Clipart Collection, 71
The ASCII Bazaar, 145, 163
Asia, 71-72
Asia-Pacific database, 72, 111, 231, 537
Asian American FAQ, 72-73
Asian American studies, soc.culture.asian.american, 72
Asian and Pacific Economic Literature, 72, 229, 537
Asian Pacific Business and Marketing Resources, 72, 112, 452, 537
Asian studies, 72-73
AskERIC Virtual Library, 73, 162, 243, 253, 437
ASR (Astronomical Software Resources), 74, 77
ASSETS (Real Estate Tax Assessor and Deed Transfer Records), 73, 204, 572, 587, 658
assignees, LEXPAT (Patents US) library, 73
ASTRA-UG, 73, 273, 319, 404
Astronomical Information on the Internet, 74-76
Astronomical Publications Resources (APR), 74-76, 550
Astronomical Software Resources (ASR), 74, 77
Astronomy, 74, 77, 637, 646
astronomy, 74-76
astrophysics, 76-78
Astrophysics Data System (ADS), 74, 77
AT&T Bell Laboratories WWW Information Page, 78, 130, 659, 662
Atari computers, ST viruses, 78
atmosphere, Global Change Information Gateway, 78
atmospheric science, 78
att-pc+, 78, 174
Attention Deficit/Hyperactivity Disorder (ADD), ADD-parents, 37
auc-TeX, 78-79, 175, 257, 666-667
audio electronics, 79
audio reproduction, 79
audio-visual materials, NYAL (New York Art Line), 79
auditing, NAARS (National Automated Accounting Research System), 79
AUGLBC-L, 79
AUGLBC-I, 101, 310, 433, 622, 674
AusGBLF, 80, 101, 310, 433
AusRave (Australian Raves), 80, 485, 585-586
Australia, 80, 433
Australian Environmental Resources Information Network (ERIN), 80, 228, 266
Australian National University (ANU)
   Asian Settlements Database, 61
   Asian-Settlements Database, 72, 206
   Buddhism Database, 61, 73, 110
   Demography and Publications Database, 61, 206
   Vietnam-SciTech-L Database, 61, 613, 659, 701-702
Australian Network Sites and Resources Guide (AARNet Guide), 31
Austrian history, Indiana University Libraries, 80
autocrossing, autox, 81
automobiles, 81-82
autopoiesis, The Observer, 82
autox, 81
aviation, 82-83
aviation industry, TRANS (The Transportation Library), 83
Aviator, 82, 175, 296, 624
The Avid Explorer, 675
Ayurveda, 83, 361, 641

B

The Black Box Catalog, 662
ba-Firearms, 85-118, 294, 333, 610
ba-Liberty, 85-118, 556-557, 610
ba-Poker, 85, 125, 554, 610
ba-Sappho, 85, 433-434, 610
ba-Volleyball, 85-86, 610-611, 704
ba.general, 86, 120
baby boomer culture, 30something, 86
Backstreets, 86, 602-603, 645
bagpipes, 86, 485
Balloon, 86, 354
balloon art, 86
Ballroom, 86, 199
Balt-L, 86, 271, 423, 447
Baltic Republics, 86-87
Balzac (Honore de), University of Chicago Library, 87
banking, 87
Banking News Library, 87, 291, 596
bankruptcy, BKRTCY (Bankruptcy Library), 87
Barron's Guide to Accessing On-Line Bibliographic Databases, 87, 200, 437
Base de Dados Tropical (BDT), 87, 93, 100, 108
Base-Jumping, 88, 625
baseball, 88
basketball, 88
Basque studies, University of Nevada at Reno Library, 88
Bass, 79, 88
Bbones, 88, 223
BBSs, 89
bcdv, 89, 92
BCL (Biomedical Computer Laboratory), 95
BDT (Base de Dados Tropical), 87, 93, 100, 108
Bears, 89, 101, 310
The Beastie Boys' Web Page, 491, 585
beer, 89
behavior, PsycINFO, 89
behavioral science, 89
Bel Canto, 90, 485, 560
Belgium, BFU (Brussels Free Universities), 90
Beloved, 90, 485, 560
Berlin Wall (9nov89-l), 90
Berne Convention Implementation Act of 1988, 90, 188, 326, 432, 559
Best of the Web '94, 90, 377-378, 718
Best-of-AusRave (Australian Raves), 80, 90, 485, 586
BETA, 529, 568
BETA programming language, 90
Bethany Christian Services, 37, 90-91, 140, 564
BFU (Brussels Free Universities), 90, 180, 257, 273
BiAct-L, 91, 101
Bible(s), 91, 508-509, 531, 598
bibliographies, 91-92
Bibliographies of US Senate Hearings, 91, 326, 432, 559, 620
bicycling, 92
BiFem-L, 92, 101
Big Dummy's Guide, 92, 378
Big-DB, 93, 200, 200-201
Bikecommute, 92
Bikepeople, 92
Biking, 92, 295, 641
Biking in Canada, 92, 121, 641
Bilingual Education Network, 93, 235, 270
Bio-Oriented INternet Gophers (BOING), 95
biochemistry, 93
bioengineering, Biosis Previews, 93
biographies, 93-94
Bioinformatics, 94, 95, 477
bioinformatics, 94
biological research, 94
biology, 95-97
biology, aquatic, 63

biology, insect, 369
Biomch-L, 97, 416, 480-481
biomechanics, 97
Biomedical Computer Laboratory (BCL), 95-98, 338, 462
biomedical research, 97-98
biomedicine, 98-99
bionet.molbio.genbank.updates, 95, 313, 477
bionet.software, 95, 175
biophysics, Biosis Previews, 99
bioscience, 99
Biosis Previews, 43, 59, 93-95, 99, 107, 228, 470, 547, 553, 727-728
Biosym (Biosym Technologies Software), 99-100, 632
Biotechnet Electronic Buyer's Guide, 100, 141, 256-257, 477-478
biotechnology, 100
birds, 100
Birthmother, 37-38, 101
Bisexu-L, 102, 622
bisexuality, 101-103
bit.general, 103, 378, 510
BITHRY-L, 102, 312
Bitnet, 103
BIVERSITY, 103, 107
BKRTCY (Bankruptcy Library), 87, 103, 288, 423
The Black Box Catalog, 153, 180, 505
Black/African Related Online Information, 41, 42, 103, 194, 583
Blacksburg Electronic Village Gopher, 103-104, 155, 503, 662-663
Blind News Digest, 104, 704
BlindFam, 104, 214, 281
blindness, 104
Blues (St. Louis Blues), 104, 350-351, 496, 641
Blues-L, 104, 485
BMW, 81, 104
BMW Motorcycles, 104, 480
boating, The Nautical Bookshelf, 104
BOING (Bio-Oriented INternet Gophers), 95, 338, 462
Boise State University Library, 104, 141, 409, 554, 620
Bonaparte, Napoleon, 494
Bong (Depeche Mode), 105, 560-561
Bonsai, 105, 474
bonsai, 105
book arts, 105
Book Review Index, 105, 545, 574
book reviews, 105
books, 105-106
books, antiquarian, 61, 106
books, childrens, 139
Books In Print, 105-106, 574-575
Books Online, 106, 254
BosNet, 106-107, 345
Bosnia, 106-107
Boston, 107
Boston Bruins, 107, 496
botanical taxonomy, 107
botany, 107
Bowker Biographical Directory, 93-94, 108
Boyler-Moore Theorem Prover, nqthm-users, 108
BPM, 108, 216, 485-486
brain research, 108
The Branch Mall, an Electronic Shopping Mall, 624, 38-39, 319, 452
Brasil, 108-109, 562
BRIDGE, 109, 437, 462
Brit-Iron, 109, 480
Britain, 109
Britannica Online, 109, 201
British Commonwealth Law, 109
British National Register of Archives, 109, 112, 347, 680-681
British Online Yellow Pages, 109, 117
British Plays, 19th-century, 109
British-Cars, 81, 109
broadcasting, 110
Brown University Library, 110, 437, 600
Brussels Free Universities (BFU), 90
BTHS-ENews-L, 110, 509

buddhism, 110
Budget of the United States (1994), 110, 291, 326
bug hunting (fsuucp mailing list), 304
Bugs-386bsd, 110, 534
Builder Xcessory, 110
building, 111
Bulgaria, CEE Environmental Libraries Database, 111
business, 111-117
Business Dateline, 112, 454, 596
Business, Economics, 112, 229
business information, 117-118
business management, 118
business marketing, 118
Business News—Singapore, 229, 625
Business News-Singapore, 112
Business Refernce (BUSREF), 510
Business Sources on the Net, 112
Business Wire, 112, 291
BUSREF (Business Reference), 112, 324, 510, 595-596
Buyers' Guide to Micro Software, 118
Buyer's Guide to Micro Software, 175, 470, 632-633
BX-Talk, 110, 118, 331-332

C

C programming language, 119
C-IBM-370, 119, 359, 570
C-L, 119, 570
C-SPAN (Cable-Satellite Public Affairs Network) Gopher, 119, 184, 324, 515, 664
c2man, 119, 168
ca-Firearms, 120, 294, 333
ca-Liberty, 120-121, 436
cabinetry, 120
Cabot (Sebastian), 120
CADC (Canadian Astronomy Data Center) Home Page, 74, 120, 355
CAEDS-L, 120, 164, 261
CAF Archive, 33, 120, 175, 245
calendars, On-this-day, 120
California, 120-121
California Museum of Photography: Network Exhibitions, 67-68, 121, 245, 549
California Privacy Act 1992, 121, 424
California State Senate Gopher, 121, 326, 427-428
CAMIS (Center for Advanced Medical Informatics at Stanford), 121, 343, 346, 460
Can-Stud-Assoc, 122, 244
Canada, 121-123
CANADA (Canadian News and Information Library), 56, 122, 159, 511
Canada (gopher), 122, 303
Canadian Adult Education Network (ADLTED-L), 37
Canadian Association for University Continuing Education (CAUCE-L), 128
Canadian Astronomy Data Center (CADC) Home Page, 74, 120
Canadian documents, 123-124
Canadian Electro-Acoustics Community (CEC), 34, 124, 129
Canadian Federation of Engineering Students (CFES), 133-134, 134
Canadian Geographical WWW Index Traveler, 122, 314, 675, 708
Canadian News and Information Library (CANADA), 122
Canadian University Consortium on Health in
    International Development (CANCHID), 124, 338-339, 375
Canadian-American studies, 124
cancer, 124
CANCHID (Canadian University Consortium on Health
    International Development), 338-339
Canopus, 75, 124, 638-639
Cantus, 125, 333, 448, 486
card games, 125
cardopulmonary medicine, 125
Cards, 125, 148, 467, 673
CAREER (Career Library), 125, 258
careers, 125

Caribbean, 125-126
carnivorous plants, CP, 126
cars, *see automobiles*
Carter (Hodding), 126
cartography, 126
cartoons, 126-127
case law (US), 127
Catalyst, 127, 233, 237, 240, 243
Catholic, 127, 231, 598
Catholic Doctrine, 128, 667
Catholic University of America Gopher, 128, 437
Catholic-action, 128, 277, 598
Catholicism, 127-128
CAUCE-L (Canadian Association for University Continuing Education), 128, 233, 237, 240
Cavers, 128, 641
CBDS (Circuit Board Design System), 256
CBDS-I (Circuit Board Design System), 128, 173, 261
CCES-L, 261
CCNEWS, 129, 175, 232, 517, 650
Cd-Forum, 129, 312, 622, 674-675
CD-ROM, 129
CDPub, 129, 209, 255
CE Software, 129, 451, 633
CEC (Canadian Electro-Acoustics Community), 34, 122-124, 129, 261
CEDAR (Central European Environmental Data Request) Facility, 129, 250, 266, 273
CEE Environmental Libraries Database, 111, 129-132, 197, 266, 357, 554, 605, 626, 653
cell biology, 130
Cell Church Discussion Group, 130, 140-141, 278, 598
Cello, 130, 394
Cello FAQ, 130, 390, 394
cellular technology, 130
Celtic culture/studies, 130-131
CEM-L (Center for Engineering Mathematics), 131, 261, 457
censorship, 131
census data, 131
Center for Advanced Medical Informatics at Stanford (CAMIS), 121
Center for Biomedical Informatics, Brazil
The Center for Biomedical Informatics of the
    State University of Campinas, Brazil, 131, 338, 343-344, 461, 574,
Center for Extreme Ultraviolet Astrophysics, 75-77, 132, 277, 494, 611
Central Eastern Europe, CEE Environmental Libraries Database, 132
Central Europe, 132
Central European Environment Data Report (CEDAR) Facility, 129, 132, 225-226
Cerebi, 132-133, 149, 624
CERFnet Guide, 121, 133, 245, 378, 614
CERFNet News, 121, 133, 245-246
CERRO (Central European Regional Research Organization), 132, 229, 511
CERT (Computer Emergency Response Team) Advisory, 133, 166, 175, 619
Cervantes (Miguel de), 133
CEXPRESS (Computer Express Internet Superstore), 133, 167
cfcp-members, 133, 175, 378
CFD (Computational Fluid Dynamics Group), 133, 261, 296
CFES-L (Canadian Federation of Engineering Students),122, 133-134, 261, 650
CGN (Christian Growth Newsletter), 134, 141, 598
Chalkhills, 134, 561, 723
chaos theory, 134
The Chaosium Digest, 164
chat groups, 134
Chaucer (Geoffrey), 134-135, 445
ChE Electronic Newsletter, 135, 261
chem-eng, 263
Chem-Talk, 135
Chemical Abstracts, 135, 261-262
Chemical Abstracts Service Source Index, 135-136
Chemical Dictionary, 136
chemical engineering, 135
Chemical Industry Notes, 112, 136

Chemistry, 136, 614
chemistry, 135-136
chemistry, aquatic, 63
chemistry, history of, 135
chemistry, theoretical, 668
Chemistry Tutorial Information, 136, 246, 451, 678
chess, 136-137
Chessnews, 136-137, 308
Chiba University Gopher, 72, 137, 437
Chicago, 137
Chicano culture, 137
Chicano/LatinoNet, 137, 194, 423, 583
child care, 137-138
childbirth, Midwifery Resources on the Net, 138
children, 138-139
children's books, 139
Children's Rights, 138, 424
Chile, edista (Educación a Distancia), 139
China, 139-140
Chinapats, 139-140, 370, 541, 672
Chinese language, 140
Chinese studies, 140
Chorus, 140, 310, 434, 625
Christian Growth Newsletter (CGN), 141, 598
Christianity, 140-141
chromatography, Biotechnet Electronic Buyer's Guide, 141
chronic fatigue syndrome, Disability-Related Resources, 141
Church, Frank, 141
church history, 142
CIA World Factbook, 60, 142, 371-372
CILEA (Consorzio Interuniversitario Lombardo per la Elaborazione Automatica), 142, 273, 404
CinemaSpace, 142, 289-290, 482-483
Circle K International, 142, 417
CIRCUITS-L, 142, 251-252, 262, 659
CIS (Commonwealth of Independent States), 142, 151
Cisco Systems, 142-143, 505
Citation Authority, 143, 428, 647
Citizens Project, 143, 148-149, 155, 503
City of San Carlos World Wide Web Fire Safety Tutorial, 143, 215, 609
CIUWInfo (Centrum Informacyj ny Uniwersyetu Warzawskiego), 143, 554
Civic Promise of the National Information Infrastructure (NII), 155, 326, 503
civil liberties, 143
civil rights, 143
Civil War, 143
Civil-L, 143-144, 173, 263
CJI (Computer Jobs in Israel), 144, 161, 402, 408
CLAIMS, 144, 370, 541, 672
Clarissa, 144, 519, 664
Class Four Relay Magazine, 144, 256, 452, 597
classics, 144
Clearinghouse for Subject-Oriented Internet Resource Guides (CSORG), 719
Cleveland FreeNet, 144, 154, 505
Cleveland Sports, 144-145, 531, 641
climatology, 145
Clinton, Bill, 145
Clinton Watch, 145, 326, 557, 611
Clinton's Economic Plan, 145, 229, 326-327
clip art, 145
Clp.x, 145, 183, 568, 571
cm5-Managers, 162, 652
CMPCOM (Computers and Communications) Library, 145-146, 152, , 175-176 256, 659-660
CMPGN (Campaign Library), 146, 184, 559
CNI (Coalition for Networked Information), 146, 378
CNI Gopher, 146, 378
CNI TopNode Project, 146, 378
CNI-Copyright Mailing List Archives, 146, 188, 371
CNN Headline News Gopher, 146, 409, 515, 558
coastal marine biology, 146
CoCo, 147, 176, 658

CODES (Codes Library), 147, 285, 647, 648
Cognitive and Psychological Sciences on the Internet, 147, 573
cognitive science, 147
COHOUSING-L, 147, 155, 187-188, 354
coins, 147, 524-525
Colby College Library, 147-148, 186, 337, 354, 401, 407, 452-453
collectibles, Cards, 148
collections (library), 148
College E-mail Addresses, 148, 223, 378
Color and Vision Network (CVnet), 94
Colorado, 148-149
Colorado Document Citations, 149, 327
Columbia University Libraries, 149, 437, 600
comedians, 149
comedy, 149
comic books, 149-150
comics, 150
comix, 149
Commcoll, 150, 154, 237
commerce, 150-151
Commerce Business Daily, 117, 150, 229, 327, 671
CommerceNet, 113, 151, 253
Commercial Real Estate, 151, 587
Commodore-Amiga computers, 151, 176
    CSAA, 151
Commonwealth of Independent States (CIS), Sovokinform, 151
commonwealths, INTLAW (International Law Library), 151-152
commune, 152, 666
Communication and Mass Communication Resources, 38, 152, 409, 456, 459, 663
communications, 152-153
communications, group, 333
communism, 153-154
community, 154-157
community access, Cleveland FreeNet, 154
community colleges, Commcoll, 154
community networking, 154
Community Networks Benefit Federal Goals, 156, 210, 503, 606
community service, 157
Community Services Catalyst, 157, 237
comp.compression, 157, 176, 457
comp.databases, 157, 163, 180
comp.graphics, 68, 157, 164
comp.infosystems.gopher, 157, 323, 390
comp.infosystems.wais, 157, 364, 391, 707
comp.infosystems.www, 157, 364, 719
comp.lang.c, 157, 167, 571
comp.lang.c++, 157, 176, 571
comp.org.eff.talk, 157, 176, 371, 378, 619
comp.os, 170
comp.os.ms-windows.apps, 158, 170
comp.os.os2.misc, 158, 170
comp.security.misc, 158, 176, 294, 620
comp.sys.amiga, 55, 158, 170
comp.sys.apple2, 63, 158, 170
comp.sys.atari.st, 158, 170
comp.sys.ibm.pc, 158, 170-171, 359
comp.sys.mac, 158, 171, 451
comp.sys.next, 158, 171, 517
comp.sys.sgi, 158, 171
comp.sys.sun, 158, 171, 651
comp.text.tex, 159, 378, 667
comp.unix.aix, 159, 171, 378, 690
comp.unix.questions, 159, 176, 690
comp.unix.wizards, 159, 176, 690
comp.windows.x, 159, 171
comp.windows.x.motif, 159, 164
companies, 159-160
company name, DIALOG Company Name Finder, 160
The Complete Guide to Galway, 307, 670, 675
COMPNY, 159, 215-216, 288-289, 291
composition, music, 161
computational chemistry, 161
computer administration, 161-162

computer applications, 162
computer art, 162-163
computer communications, 163
computer conferencing, 163
computer databases, 163
computer ethics, 164
computer games, 164
computer graphics, 164-165
computer hardware, 165-166
computer music, 166
Computer Music Journal Archive and World Wide Web Home Page, 161, 166, 372, 654
Computer Network Conferencing, 166, 183, 379
computer networking, 166
computer networks, 167
computer news, 167
computer products, 167
computer professionals, 167
computer programming, 167-168
computer programs, 168
computer resources, 168
computer science, 168-169
Computer Science Center Link, 167, 168-169
computer specialists, 170
computer speech interfaces, ECTL, 170
computer systems, 170-172
computer technology, 172
computer underground, 172
computer users, 172
computer viruses, 172
computer-aided design, 173
computer-aided instruction, 162
Computer-Mediated Marketing Environments, 113, 173, 364, 379, 455, 719
computers, 173-180
computing, 180-182
Computing and Network News, 167-169, 176, 182
Computists' Communique, 71, 169, 182, 367
Comserve, Newsline, 182
concrete-blonde, 183, 561
concurrent logic, Clp.x, 183
Confederation of Future Computer Professionals (CFCP), 133
The Conference about Virtual Reality, 68, 703, 183, 196
conferences, 183
conferencing systems, 183
conflict resolution, 183-184
Congo languages, 184
Congress, US, 184-185
Congressional Contact Information, 184, 213, 327
Congressional Quarterly Gopher, 184, 328-329, 430
connectivity, 185
conservation, 185
consgis, 185, 266-267, 319
conspiracy, 185
Constitution, 185
Constitutional amendments, 185
Constitutional law, 185
construction, 186
consumer goods, 186
consumer rights, 186
consumer science, 186
consumerism, 186
contemporary letters, 186
contemporary music, 187
Convex Customer Satisfaction Information Server, 176, 187
cooking, 187
COOMBSQUEST Social Sciences and Humanities Information Facility, 187, 630
cooperatives, 187-188
Copyright Act, 188, 329, 430, 559-560
Copyright Basics, 188, 329, 430
copyrights, 188
Cornell Law School Gopher, 428

Cornell University Libraries, 188, 437, 600
Cornucopia of Disability Information (CODI), 188, 214, 339
corporations, 188-189
Corpse/Respondents, 189, 324, 603
Correct Time/NBS, 189, 379, 621
Cosmic Update, 189, 494, 633, 637
Counterev-L, 189, 325, 479
CP (Carnivorous Plants), 107, 126, 189
CP/M, Alspa, 189
CPSR/PDX Newsletter, 167, 189, 629
crafts, 189-190
cread (Latin American & Caribbean Distance & Continuing Education), 126, 190, 241, 422
creationism, 190
creativity, 190
Creighton University Library Online Catalogue, 190, 344, 437
crew, 190
cricket, 190
crime, 191
Croatia
    Cro-News/SCYU-Digest, 191, 515
    Cro-Views, 191, 511
    Croatian-News/Hrvatski-Vjesnik, 191, 511
Cromwell, Oliver, 191
cross-cultural studies, 191
crossfire, 164, 192
Crowes, 192, 561, 603
CRTNet (Communication Research and Theory Network), 355, 630
cryonics, 192
CSAA, 151, 176-177, 192
CSF: Communications for a Sustainable Future, 156, 183, 192, 557
CSORG (Clearinghouse for Subject-Oriented Internet Resource Guides, 192, 364, 379, 719
CSU Entomology WWW Site, 95, 99, 192, 265
ctf-discuss, 169, 193, 663
CTN News, 193, 508, 669
ctree, 177, 281
Cuba, 193
CUD (Computer Underground Digest), 167, 193, 196, 335
culinary arts, 193
cults, 193
cultural studies, 193
culture, 193-195
The Curiosity Club, 76, 139, 492
Current Cites, 172, 195, 437
Current Contents, 195, 614-616
current events, misc.headlines, 195
Current Weather Maps and Movies, 82-83, 195, 469, 708
CUSSNET, 162, 177, 195, 629
CVNet (Color and Vision Network), 94, 196, 535, 573
cyberculture, 196
cyberpunk games, 196
cyberspace, 196-197
cycling, 197
CYFERNET (Child, Youth, and Family Education Network, 197, 246, 505-506
Czech Republic, 197

D

D&B - Dun's Electronic Business Directory, 113, 220, 292
D&B - Duns Financial Records Plus, 113, 220, 292
D&B - European Dun's Market (EDMI), 113, 220, 273-274
Dallas Stars, 199, 351, 518
dance, 199-200
Dante, 200
dark-shadows, 200, 664
Dartmouth College Library, 133, 200, 304, 555, 584, 623, 640
Dartmouth Dante Database Library, 200
Data General, 200
data-exp, 177, 200, 336, 633, 704
database management, 200

databases
    ANU (Australian National University) Demography and Publications Database, 206
    Barron's Guide to Accessing On-Line Bibliographic Databases, 200
    Big-DB, 200-201
    Britannica Online, 201
    Delphes European Business, 205
    DIALOG Bluesheets, 201
    Disclosure Database, 215
    DRT EC and Eastern Europe Business Database, 218
    ERIC (Educational Resources Information Center), 201
    foxpro-l, 201
    GIS Master Bibliography Project, 201
    International Food and Nutrition (INFAN) Database, 212
    Internet Libraries (Gopher), 201
    Links to Many Databases, 201, 441
    MEDLINE, 207
    MS-Access, 201
    NASA/IPAC Extragalactic Database (NED), 201-202
    Progress, 202
    Research Databases and Resources by Subject, 202
    SABINET (South African Bibliographic and Information Network), 202
    The Tumor Gene Database, 202
    U.S. Patent and Trademark Office Database, 202
    White House Information Service, 202
Datsun automobiles, 81, 202
DC-MOTSS, 102, 202, 310, 434, 707
DCRaves, 202-203, 586, 708
DDN Management Bulletin, 203-204
DDN New User Guide, 203-205, 379, 387, 620
DDTs-Users, 203, 633-635
de Bono, 190, 203, 235
de Bono, Edward, 203
dead-runners, 203, 605, 641
Deaf Gopher, 203, 214, 339
deafness, 203
Deborah Harry and Blondie Information Service, 203, 337, 603
DEC (Digital Equipment Corp.), 203-204
DECNEWS for Education and Research, 177, 203-204, 246
DECnews-EDU, 177, 204, 212, 246
DECnews-PR, 177, 204
DECnews-UNIX, 177, 204, 690
DECstation-managers, 177, 204
DECuserve-journal, 183, 204
deed transfers, 204
defense, 204-205
Delaware, 205
Delphes European Business, 113-114, 205, 274
Delphi, 205, 379
democracy, 206
Democratic Socialists of America, DSA-LGB, 206
demography, 206
DENet Information Server, 206, 246, 600
Denmark's Library for Medicine and Science, 206, 437, 462, 614
Dental Information Area, 207, 342
dentistry, 207
Deos-L, 207, 237, 241
deos-l (International Discussion Forum for Distance Learning), 233, 237, 241
deosnews (Distance Education Online Symposium), 207, 233, 237, 241
Department of Defense National Technology Transfer Center (NTTC), 207
Department of Justice Gopher, 207, 327, 413, 430
Department of Labor, NLSNews Newsletter (National Longitudinal Surveys of Labor Market Experience), 208
derby, 208, 336, 353
dermatology, 208
Derwent World Patents Index, 208, 371, 399, 541, 546, 672
Deryni-L, 208, 417, 615
design, 208-209
desktop publishing, 209
detective fiction, Mystery, 209

detectives, Investigators and Detectives, 209
devel-l, 210, 660
development, 209-210
development, international, 210-211
DevelopNet News, 210, 521, 660
deviants, 211
dg-users, 165-166, 200, 211
dh.mujer, 211, 286-287, 355-356, 714
DIALOG Bluesheets, 201
DIALOG Company Name Finder, 160, 211
Dick, Philip K., 211
Dickens, Charles, 211-212
Dickinson, Emily, 212
dictionaries, 212
diet, 212
DIGIT, 168, 178, 212
Digital Equipment Corp., 212
    see also DEC
Digital Equipment WWW Information Server, 171, 212
Digital Games Review, 164, 212, 308, 701
Digital's World Wide Web Server, 171, 212
DIMUND (Document Image Understanding) FTP, 212, 364, 379
dinosaur, 66, 213
Diogenes (FDA regulations), 213, 219, 297
dire-straits, 213, 486, 603
Direct (Vangelis), 213, 490, 507
directories, 213
dirt-users, 178, 213
disabilities, 213-215
    see also handicapped
Disability Information, 214, 216, 339
Disability Reading Room, 214, 339
Disability-Related Resources, 104, 141, 203, 214
disaster reliefl, 215
Disaster Research, 215, 258
Discipline and Disease Specific Sources, 216, 460, 462
Disclosure Database, 215, 619, 649
disclosures, 215-216
diseases, 216
disk jockeys, 216
disney-afternoon, 216, 664
disney-comics, 150, 217
Disraeli, Benjamin, 217
DISSPLA (Display Integrated Software System and Plotting Language), 165, 217, 568
Dist-users, 178, 217
Distance Education, 217, 241
disted 'Journal of Distance Education and Communication', 244, 415
Diversity U, 246, 372, 483
DMS/FI Market Intelligence Reports, 40, 205
Doc Center, 364, 379
Dokken/Lynch Mob, 603
Donosy, 554
don't-tell, 244-245, 473-474, 622
Down's Syndrome, 214
dp-friends, 178
DR-660 (drum machine), 219
dragnet, 641-642
Drake University, 486, 547, 668
Drake-R8, 624
drama, 217-218
Drew University, 218
Drone On..., 218, 603, 639
Drosophila Information Newsletter, 95, 218, 313
DRT EC and Eastern Europe Business Database, 218, 226-227, 276
Drug Information Fulltext, 219
drug regulations, Federal Food and Drug Administration, 218-219
drugs, 219
Drugs of the Future, 219
drum machines, DR-660, 219
DSA-LGB, 206, 219, 310, 434
The DTP Direct Catalog, 209, 332, 451
dts-l (Dead Teachers Society Discussion List), 220, 233-234, 237, 241
Dual-Personalities, 220, 690

Dun & Bradstreet Corporation, 114, 220, 292
DVI-list (Digital Video Interactive), 220-221, 372
DYNSYS-L, 221, 265, 655

E

e-europe, 114, 223, 226, 229
e-mail, 223-225
E-mail 101, 223, 379
E-mail Gopher, 223, 323, 379, 621
E-mail Services, 223, 379, 621
E-mail Understanding, 223, 379-380
E-mail Usenet, 223-224, 380, 621, 694
E-mail WWW, 224, 393, 719
E-mail-How To, 224-225, 387, 394
Eagles, 108, 225, 310
Earth and Sky, 75, 225
earth sciences, 225
East Asian studies, 225
Eastern Europe, 225-227
Eastern European business, DRT EC and Eastern Europe Business Database, 227
Eastern Washington University Library, 89, 227, 246, 486, 629
ebikes, 92, 227, 509
EC (European Community), 227, 274, 276
Ecchst-l, 141, 227, 668
ecclesiastical history, 227
echinoderms, 227
echl-news, 227, 351, 642
ECHO, 156, 227-228, 503, 714
echoes, 228, 552, 603
EcoDirectory, 132, 226-228, 267
ecology, 228-229
econ-dev, 114, 229
economic policy, 229
Economic Policy Research, 229
economics, 229-230
economics, history of, 230-231
economy, 231
ECTL, 170, 231
ecto, 68, 231, 486, 602
ecumenism, Catholic, 231
edista (Educacin a Distancia), 139, 231, 234, 238, 241
editors, CCNEWS, 232
EDNET, 232, 246, 380
edpolyan (Educational Policy Analysis), 232, 238, 249
edpolyar (Educational Policy Analysis Archive), 232, 238, 249
edstyle (Learning Styles Theory and Research List), 232, 238
education, 245-249
education, adult, 232-235
education, alternative, 235
education, bilingual, 235-236
education, college/university, 236
education, continuing, 236-240
education, distance, 240-243
Education Gopher, 246, 323
education, international, Catalyst, 243
education, K-12, 243-244
education, post-graduate, 244
education, post-secondary, 244-245
education, secondary, 245
educational policy, 249
educators, 249
Educator's Guide to E-mail Lists, 224, 247, 250, 380
EDUCOM, 247, 250
edupage (A News Update from EDUCOM), 238, 250, 367
EEC, 250
EEJobs, 250-252, 258, 262
Eerie, Indiana, 250, 361-362
EFFector Online—The Electronic Frontier Foundation, 163, 250, 254, 371, 566
Ei Compendex Plus, 251, 262, 660

EINet Galaxy, 251, 365, 380, 719
ejcrec 'Electronic Journal of Communications/La Revue
    electronique de communication', 153, 251
electric circuit analysis, 251
The Electric Eclectic, 451-452, 482
Electric Light Orchestra, 251, 603
Electric Power Database, 251, 259
electric vehicles, EV, 251-252
electrical engineering, 252
electronics, INSPEC, 252
The Electronic AIR, 240, 370
electronic arts, 252-253
Electronic Books, 106, 253, 445, 446, 532
Electronic Cafe, 68, 253, 663, 701
electronic commerce, 253
Electronic Communications Privacy Act of 1986, 153, 253, 329, 430, 566
Electronic Democracy Must Come from Us, 156, 254, 327, 503
Electronic Hebrew Users Newsletter (E-Hug), 254, 345, 411, 598
electronic media, 254
electronic music, 255
Electronic Newsstand Gopher, 255, 410, 511, 575
The Electronic Public Interest versus the Private Good, 154, 327, 502
electronic publications, 255
electronic publishing, 255
electronics, 255-256
electrophoresis, 256-257
Eliot, George, 257
ELISA (Electronic Library Service), 80, 257, 533
ELSNET (European Network in Language and Speech), 147, 152, 257, 440
Emacs, 257
EMBASE, 257, 462, 547, 614
EMBnet (European Molecular Biology Network), 95-96, 99, 257, 478
emergency preparedness, 258
Emory University Library, 153-154, 230, 258, 344, 348, 443, 668
employment, 258-259
encryption, 259
Encyclopedia of Associations, 259, 521
ENERGY, 259, 424, 511, 596-597
energy, 259-260
Energy and Climate Information Exchange (ECIX) Newsletter, 145, 259, 260, 469
Energy Research in Israel Newsletter, 259-260, 402
Energy-L, 259, 262, 403
engineering, 260-263
engineering, history of, 263-264
engineering, mechanical, 264
Engineering-Design, 208, 262
Engineering; A. Park, J. Miller, 208, 262
England, 264
English, 264
English Bibles, 264
English, Old, 531
The English Server, 33, 264, 287, 356, 562
Entering the WWW, 264, 394, 719
ENTERT (Entertainment News Library), 264, 511
entertainment, 264-265
entomology, 265
entropy, 265
ENVIRN (Environment Library), 56, 265-267, 424, 511-512
Enviroethics, 265-267, 269
environment, 266-268
Environment Library (ENVIRN), 56
environmental health, 268
environmental policies, 268
environmental safety, 269
environmental studies, 269
environmentalism, 269
enzymes, 269
EPPD-L, 269, 574
equestrians, 269-270
equine research, 270
ergonomics, 270
ERIC (Educational Resources Information Center), 201, 247, 270
ERIN (Australian Environmental Resources Information Network), 80
Erofile, 105, 270, 303, 404
Esbdc-I, 114, 270, 627
ESL (English as a Second Language) Bilingual Education Network, 270
ESRI (Environmental Systems Research Institute), 178, 267, 271, 319, 633
Essence, 271, 394-395
Estonia, 271
ETHCSE-L, 181, 262, 271
ethics, 271
ethnic studies, 271
ethnicity, POS302-L, 272
Ethnomusicology Research Digest, 272, 491
etiquette, Net Etiquette Guide, 272
euitnews (Educational Uses of Information Technology), 238, 272, 367-368
EUnet, 272, 380
EUnet Czechia, 197, 272
Euromath Center Gopher Server, 272-274, 457
Europe, 273-276
EUROPE (European News Library), 114, 274, 276
European community, 276
European documents, 277
European Molecular Biology Network (EMBnet), 95-96, 99
European Patents Fulltext, 274, 277, 427, 541
European Root Gopher, 274, 277, 323
European Space Agency, 39, 277, 639
European union, 277
EUVE (Center for Extreme Ultraviolet Astrophysics), 277
EV (electric vehicles), 251-252, 277
evangelism, 277-278
evolution, 278
EXEC (Executive Branch News US), 278, 432, 512, 557, 597
Executive Branch, EXEC (Executive Branch News US), 278
Experimental Stock Market Data, 278, 292, 400, 649
expert systems, 278
exports, 278-279
EXPRESS information modeling language, EXPRESS-Users, 279, 568
extraterrestrial life, 279
Extraterrestrials, 75, 279, 637

F

FairCom, ctree, 281
Fam-Med, 178, 281, 463, 663
family, 281
Family and Legal Status (INPADOC), 281-282, 541, 660
family practice, 282
family science, 282
FAQs, 282
farming, 282
The FARNET Gazette, 502
fashion industry, 283
fashion merchandising, 283
Fashion Photography Conference, 283, 549
FAX, 283
FAXNET, 224, 283, 393
FDA (Federal Food & Drug Administration) Seafood Internet Network, 283
Federal databases, 283-284
Federal documents (US), 284
Federal Food and Drug Administration, 218-219, 283, 526
Federal government (US), 284
Federal law (US), 284
Federal Register, 285
Federal Securities Library (FEDSEC), 285
federal standards, IHS International Standards and Specifications, 285
Federal Tax Library (FEDTAX), 56
FEDSEC (Federal Securities Library), 285, 289, 424, 619

FEDTAX (Federal Tax Library), 56, 285-286, 424, 658
FedWorld Bulletin Board, 286, 330, 692
Felipe's Bilingual WWW Pages, 235, 286, 422
feminism, 286-288
fen, 288
FEN (Financial Economics Network), 33
fiance, 291
fiction, 288
fiction, detective, 209
filings, 288-289
film, 289-290
Film and Video, 264, 290, 701
Filmmaking Conference, 290, 701
FINALE music notation program, FINALE Discussion List, 291, 489
finance, 291-293
FinanceNet (National Performance Review), 284, 292
Financial Economics Network (FEN), 33
Finding E-mail Addresses, 224, 293, 380
Finding Resources on the Internet, 293, 365, 391
fine arts, 293
FineArt Forum, 68, 293, 483
Finger (Internet Database), 294, 393
FINS (Fish Information Service), 294, 529
firearms, 294
firewalls
    comp.security.misc, 294
    Systems Operators, firewalls, 294
firewalls newsgroup, 393, 620
fish, 294-295
fisheries, 295
fitness, 295
FL-Raves (Florida Raves), 295, 586
flags, 295
flamingo, 295, 300, 664
flashlife, 196, 296, 308
flight simulation, Aviator, 296
Florida, 296
Florida State University System Library, 296, 411, 422, 426, 444, 454
fluid dynamics, 296
fluids, 296
FM-10, 110, 296, 584
FMDSS-L (Forest Management Decision Support Systems), 300
fogelberg, 296, 486
Folk music, 296-297, 486
Folk-dancing, 199, 296
folklore, 297
food, 297-298
Food Industry Investext, 43, 298-299
food production, 298-299
football, 299
Ford automobiles, 299
Fordnatics, 81, 299
foreign trade, 299
forestry, 300
Forum for Women's Issues, 287, 712
four-wheel drive, 300
Fox Television, 300
foxpro-l, 178, 201, 300, 471
framers (Framemaker publishing), 209-301
France
    Counterev-L, 325
    france-foot, 301, 628, 642
    soc.culture.french, 301
    see also French, Paris
fraud, 301
freaks, 301, 486, 603
FrEd Mail Foundation, 138, 243, 301
Free Art For HTML Page, 173, 301, 332
Free for All, 301, 333, 380, 483
free software, 301
free trade, 301
Free-Net Working Papers, 154, 302, 503
freedom, 36, 302, 309
freedom of information, 302

Freedom of Information Act (FOIA): Guide to Use, 302, 329, 566-567
Freedom of Information Directory of Records (Canada), 122, 302, 325
freedom of speech, 302
FreeNets, 154, 302
freeware, 302
French
    Agence FrancePresse International French Wire, 302-303
    Canada gopher, 303
    WWW Paris, 303
    see also France, Paris
French Language Gophers (Les Gophers Francophones), 323
French law, INTNAT (International Library), 303
French opera (19th-century), 303
French Revolution, 303
French studies, 303
Friends of Ohio State, 304, 531
fringeware, 196, 304
The Frog Farm, 558, 602
Frost, Robert, 304
FSP protocol, 304, 573
fsuucp, 304, 623, 633
FTP FAQ, 304, 391
FTP protocol, 304
FTP Setup, 304, 395
FTP-How To, 304, 395
Fuller, Buckminster, 304
funding, 304-305
Funet Sports Information, 305, 360, 480, 499, 518, 567, 642
Funky Music, 305, 490
fusion, 305, 550, 614
Futurebus+ Users, 172, 305, 336, 633
FutureCulture FAQ (Frequently Asked Questions) File, 196, 305, 563, 612, 660, 727
fuzzy logic, 305
fuzzy-mail, 305
fuzzy-ramblings, 305, 486
fwake-l, 305-306, 410, 447, 718
FYI on Questions and Answer Answers to Commonly Asked New Internet User Questions, 306, 380, 392

G

gaelic-l, 307, 401, 420-421, 453, 617
Galway, Ireland, 307
gambling, 307
game theory, 307
GameBytes magazine, 254, 265, 308
games, 308-309
games, role-playing, 308
GAO (health files), 184-185, 309, 339
gardening, 309
gateway2000, 167, 309, 336, 633
gay rights, 309
gay-libn, 102, 310, 434, 437-438
gaynet, 310-311, 434
gays, 310-311
GC-L (Global Classroom), 114, 311, 421, 453
Gegstaff, 311-312, 314-315, 622
GenBank, 313, 463, 478
gender, 312
Geneology, 271, 312
General Hacking Info, 178, 312, 335
GENESIS neural simulator, 312
genetics, 313
GENFED (General Federal Library), 313, 429
genius, Mensatalk, 314
GENMED (General Medical Information), 314, 353, 463, 670, 677
Geodesic, 208, 304, 314
Geographic Information and Analysis Laboratory (GIAL), 314-315, 319, 499
geography, 314-316
geology, 316-317

Georgetown University Medical Center Online Catalog, 317, 438, 463
Georgia State University Library, 148, 317, 419, 468, 483
Georgia-Computer Systems Protection Act, 161, 191, 317
geoscience, 318
Geoscience at Texas A&M University, 318-319, 361, 599
Germany, 318, 424
gerontology, AgeLine, 318
gifts, 319
GIS (Geographical Information Survey), 319-321
GIS Master Bibliography Project, 201, 319
GIS-L (Geographic Information Systems), 267, 319, 315
GIS-L and comp.infosystems.gis FAQ, 319-320, 694
GIS-T, 315, 320, 673
glass, Massachusetts Institute of Technology Library, 321
Global Change Information Gateway, 78, 210, 267, 321, 530, 681
Global Internet, 292, 321, 380
global news, 322
GlobeTrotter, 178, 322, 335
GLOSAS News (Global Systems Analysis and Simulating Association), 247, 322, 543, 624-625
GNUs Bulletin: Newsletter of the Free Software Foundation, 301, 322, 623, 633
God, *see* Christianity, Judaica, Judaism, religion
Goethe, Johann Wolfgang von, 322
Gold in Networks, 322, 380
golf, 322-323
GolfData OnLine, 295, 322, 642
Gopher, 323, 395
Gopher Demo, 323, 395
Gopher FAQ, 323, 395
Gopher Jewels, 323, 395
Gopher Sites, 323, 395
Gopher Telnet Demo, 324, 395
Gopher-Based ASCII Clip Art Collection, 71, 145, 209, 323
Gopher/Veronica-How To, 324, 395, 698
gophers, 323-324
gothic rock, Corpse/Respondents, 324
government, 32-325
government, African, 325
Government Docs (US & World), 325, 330, 349, 558
government documents, 330
government, international, 325
government, US, 326-330
government, US state, 330
Government-Sponsored Electronic Bulletin Boards, 329, 429
GPO Gateway to Government Act of 1992: Senator Al Gore, 283, 329
GRANOLA (Vegetarian Discussion List), 331, 339, 526, 594, 697
 see also veglife (Vegetarian Life List)
grants, 331
graphic arts, 332
graphic design, 332
graphical user interfaces, 331-332
graphics
 Free Art For HTML Page, 332
 INGRAFX, 165
 ISIS/Draw, 332
 naplps-list, 493-494
 OTIS (Operative Term Is Stimulate), 332
 UWP Music Archive, 332
Great Lakes area, 332
Greece, 333
Gregorian chant, 333
group communications, 333
guidelines, 333
guitar, 333
gun control legislation, 333
GUTENBERG Listserver, 333, 446, 596

H

Hacker's Network, 178, 335
hacking, 335
Haiti, Summit of the Americas Internet Gopher, 335

Hamill, Peter, 335
Handel, G. F., 336
Handicap, 214, 336, 339
handicapping, derby, 336
hardware, 336-337
Hardy, Thomas, 337
Harper, Roy, 337
Harry, Deborah, 337
Harvard Biosciences Online Journals, 96, 99, 337, 478
Harvard Medical Gopher, 337, 342, 438, 463
Harvard University Library, 42, 46, 64, 130, 184, 297, 337, 345, 479, 525, 579-580, 611, 711
Hawaii, 337-338
Hawaii FYI, 337, 425
health, 338-341
Health and Clinical Information & Bioethics Online Service, 342, 461-463
health care, 341-343
Health News Daily, 339, 343, 460, 512, 547
Health Periodicals Database, 100, 339-340, 343, 463-464, 526
Health Planning and Administration, 340, 342
health sciences, 343-344
health statistics, 345
Hebraica, 345
Hebrew language, 345
Hemingway, Ernest, 345
Herbert, George, 345
Herzegovina, 345
heuristics, 346
Hewlett-Packard Computers, 167, 346
HFS-L, 270, 346, 550
HICNet Newsletter (MEDNEWS - The Health InfoCom Newsletter), 340, 346, 460
High Weirdness by E-Mail, 172, 335, 346, 660
High-Performance Computing Act of 1991, 181, 329, 346, 429
Highlands and Islands of Scotland, 346, 617, 675
hilat-l (Higher Education in Latin America), 234, 238, 241, 346-347, 422
Hispanic, 347
historic preservation, 347
Historic World Documents, 347, 349, 375, 677
historical documents, 206, 347, 349
Historical Documents of the US, 329, 347, 429
history, 347-348
history, 20th-century, 347
history, ancient, 347-348
History and Analysis of Disabilities Newsletter, 215, 350
history, art, 70-71
History at the University of Virginia, 144, 349, 466
history, Austrian, 80
History Discussion Forum, 349
history, Jewish, 348
history, US, 348
history, women's, 349
history, world, 349-350
Hitchhiker's Guide, 350, 380
HIV, 350
HNSource, 349
hobbies, 350
hockey, 350-351
Holmes, Sherlock, 351
Holocaust, 352
home building, 352
home economics, 352
Hong Kong, 352
Hong Kong Law, 352, 425
Hong Kong Polytechnic Library System, 352
Hoppenstedt Directory of German Companies, 318, 352, 374
horizons 'New Horizons in Adult Education', 234, 238, 241, 353
horseracing, derby, 353
horses, 353
horticulture, 353
hospex, 353, 675
hospital administration, 353
hospitality, 353
hot air balloons, 354

Hot off the Tree (HOTT), 172, 354, 660
hotel administration, 354
housing, 354
Housman, A. E., 354
hr.women, 287, 354-356, 712
HTML FAQ, 355, 365, 391, 719
Hubble Telescope, 355
human behavior, 355
human communications, CRTNet (Communication Research and Theory Network), 355
The Human Languages Page, 421, 441
human rights, 355-356
humanities, 356
humor, 356-357
Hungarian Gopher—Hollosi Information Exchange (HIX), 274, 357
Hungary, 226, 357, 512
HungerWeb, 36, 357, 716
Hunt, Leigh, 357
Husted, Margaret (culinary collections of), 357
hydraulics, 358
HypArt, 293, 358
hyperfiction, 358
hypermedia, 358
Hypermedia/Internet, 333, 358, 381
hypertext, 358
HYTELNET, 171, 358, 438, 623
Hytelnet, 395, 533

I

I.S.P.O.B. Bulletin YSSTI (Yugoslav System for Scientific and Technology Information, 359, 367, 727
IBM (International Business Machines), 114, 359
ICC British Company Directory, 117, 359-360
ice hockey, 360
    see also hockey
ICGEBnet, 100, 274, 360, 404, 478
Icon-group, 360, 568, 571, 650
ICTP (International Centre for Theoretical Physics, 275, 360, 404, 668
IEEE-L, 252, 262, 360
IHOUSE-L International Voice Newsletter Prototype List, 360, 377, 708
IHS International Standards and Specifications, 262-263, 285, 361, 474
Illinois Legislation, 361, 424, 524
image processing, 361
IMAGELAB, 68
Images from Various Sources, 68, 165, 361, 549
IMPACT ONLINE, 164, 179, 368
Imperial College Department of Computing, 181, 275, 681
Imperial College Gopher Server, 136
Impulse, 486
IMSWorld Patents International, 541, 547
IMSWorld R&D Focus, 547
Incomplete Guide to the Internet (K12-Netzanleitung), 243, 381
INCORPR (Corporation and Partnership Records), 188-189, 289, 540, 672
Index to Multimedia Information Sources, 373, 483
India, 361
Indiana, 361-362
Indiana University Libraries, 61, 66, 80, 109, 217, 303, 336, 362, 420, 443-445, 585, 709
Indigenous, 60, 362
industry, 362-363
infectious diseases, 363
Infiniti automobiles, 363
info-Ada, 37, 363, 569
info-C, 119, 363, 569
info-GNU-MSDOS, 302, 363, 481, 623
info-M2, 363, 477, 569
info-Pascal, 363-364, 540, 569
Info-South (Latin American News), 229-230, 364, 376, 422

Info-tandem, 171, 364, 658
info-UNIX, 364, 654, 690
Infomat International Business, 374, 376
INFOMED, 193, 345, 574
Infopop, 381, 387
InforM Women's Studies Database, 287, 712, 714
Information About Alaska, 45, 675
Information about New York City, 509, 675
information, freedom of, 302
Information Infrastructure and Technology Act of 1992, 247, 329, 342, 368, 429
information retrieval, 364-367
information sciences, 367
Information Services in Germany, 275, 318, 367
Information Sources, 367, 381, 504
information technology, 367-368
ingr-en, 320, 368, 373
INGRAFX, 165, 332, 368-369, 617
INPADOC/INPANEW, 369, 371, 541-542, 672
insect biology, SOCINSCT (Social Insect Biology Research List), 369
Insider Trading Monitor, 369, 619
insoft-l, 369, 569, 635
INSPEC, 181, 252, 369, 550
Institute for Molecular Virology, 96, 216, 369, 704
Institutional Real Estate Newsline, 370, 400, 587
institutional research, 370
institutions, 370
insurance, 370
Insurance Periodicals Index, 370, 425
INSURE (Insurance), 56-57, 370, 425, 512
intellectual property, 370-371
intelligence, 371-372
INTER-L, 39, 236, 249, 372
Inter-University Centre for Astronomy and Astrophysics (IUCAA), 77
interaction, 372
Interactive, 68, 372
Interactive Frog Dissection Kit, 96, 372, 625
interactive learning, 372
interactive media, 373
interactivity, 373
INTERCUL, 373, 421
interface design, 373
intergraph, INGR-EN, 373
international banking, 374
international business, 374
International Business Machines (IBM), 114, 179, 374
    see also IBM
International Centre for Distance Learning, 242, 374
international communication, 374
International Court of Justice Historical Documents, 375, 412, 427
international development, 375
international documents, 375
international finance, 375
International Food and Nutrition (INFAN) Database, 212, 340, 375, 526
international government, 325
international law, 375-376
international news, 376
international politics, 376
international relations, 376
international research, 377
international trade, 377
international visitors, 377
Internet, 377-386
Internet Access, 386
Internet Art Gallery, 68, 70, 293, 386
Internet Browsers, 381, 386, 395
Internet Chess Library, 137, 386
Internet Companion, 381, 386, 387
Internet Cruise, 381, 386-387, 388
Internet directories, 387
Internet Economics, 230, 381, 387
Internet FAQs and Guides, 387, 392
Internet Federal Register (IFR), 285, 329, 387, 429-430
Internet GIS and RS Information Sites, 315, 320, 361, 387, 600

Internet Growth, 381, 388
Internet guides, 387-389
Internet Hunt, 308, 381, 388, 389
Internet Information Listing, 381, 388, 389
Internet Libraries (Gopher), 201, 365, 381, 389, 438
Internet marketing, 389
Internet Monthly Reports, 382, 388, 390
Internet Multicasting, 365, 382, 390
Internet Nonprofit Center, 390, 521, 548
Internet Phone Books, 224, 388, 390, 549
Internet Policy, 224, 382, 390
The Internet Press, 389
Internet Pricing, 230, 382, 390
Internet Public Subsidies, 382, 390, 565
Internet publishing, 390
Internet reference, 390-391
Internet research, 391
Internet resources, 392
Internet Resources for Earth Sciences, 213, 225, 315, 316, 320, 392-393, 453
Internet Resources for Geographic Information and GIS, 320, 393
Internet security, 393
Internet services, 393
Internet Services FAQ, 282, 382, 388, 393
Internet Shopping Network, 114, 253, 393
Internet Sound, 365, 382, 393
Internet Statistics, 382, 388, 394
Internet Systems UNITE, 382, 394, 395
Internet tools, 394-398
Internet Tools EARN, 382, 396
Internet Tools HTML, 365, 396
Internet Tools NIR, 382, 396
Internet Tools Summary, 382, 396
Internet Wiretap, 196, 254, 398, 727
InterNIC Directory Services (White Pages), 382, 396, 398, 721
The InterNIC Home Page, 169, 366, 392, 719
internships, 398
interpretation, 398
InterText, 398, 410, 445
INTLAW (International Law Library), 139, 151-152, 250, 375-376, 398-399
INTNAT (International Library), 276, 303, 399
inventions, 399
INVEST (Investment News and Information), 57, 159-160, 291-292, 399
Investigators and Detectives, 191, 209, 365, 400, 620
investments, 400
Iowa State University, 290, 400, 419, 635, 699
Iowa State University Library, 43, 647
ipct-j 'Interpersonal Computing and Technology: An Electronic Journal for the 21st Century', 234, 238, 368, 242, 400
Iran, 401
irc (Internet Relay Chat), 333, 382, 401
IRCAM DSP and musical software, 161, 166, 401, 635
Ireland, 401
Ireland-Related Online Resources, 150, 315, 401, 675
Irish, 401
iron, 401-402
IRVL-I (Institute for Research on Visionary Leadership), 402, 431
ISEA (Inter-Society on Electronic Arts) Online, 68, 252, 402, 660
ISIS/Draw, 136, 332, 402
Islam, 402, 492
Israel, 402-404
The Israel Information Service, 61, 352, 404, 472, 556
Israel-mideast, 403, 471, 557
IST BioGopher, 100, 275, 404
IST BioGopher (National Institute for Cancer Research), 124
Italian studies, Erofile, 404
Italy, 404-405
ITRADE (International Trade Library), 278, 374, 405, 425
ITRE Home Page, 320, 405, 674
IUCAA (Inter-University Centre for Astronomy and Astrophysics), 75, 77, 247, 405, 550

J

James, Henry, 407
Jane's Defense & Aerospace News/Analysis, 40, 205, 407, 515
Japan, 407-408
Japanese Information, 194, 407, 583
JAPIO, 371, 407-408, 542, 673
Jerusalem, 408
Jerusalem-One Network, 403, 408, 411, 558-559
Jewish politics, 408
Jewish, see also Judaica
jewishnt, 403, 411, 599
job listings, see employment
jobs, 408
joe 'The Journal of Extension', 234, 239, 242, 408-409
Johns Hopkins Genetic Databases, 96, 313, 409, 464, 478
Johns Hopkins University Library, 31, 91, 144, 216, 218, 230, 409, 445, 525, 626, 671
jokes, 409
Jordan, Len (senatorial papers of), 409
Journal of Technology Education, 152, 247, 409, 661
journalism, 409-410
journals, 410
journet, 209, 249, 255, 409, 575, 718
Journey-L, 410, 490-491, 603
Joyce, James, 410
Jte-l 'Journal of Technology Education', 234, 239, 242, 368, 410
Judaica, 403, 411, 472, 599
Judaism, 411-412
judicial process, 412
Jughead, 396, 412
jury, VRDCT (Jury Verdicts Library), 413
justice, Activ-L, 413
Justice Department, Department of Justice Gopher, 413

K

K-12 Education, 415
K-12 School Libraries, 243, 415, 438
K12 Net, 243-244, 415, 506
k12.chat.junior, 134, 415, 651
k12.chat.senior, 134, 415, 651
Kaleidospace, 69, 163, 415, 483
Kansas, 415-416
Kentucky and Ohio River Valley, history of, 416
KFLC-L (Kentucky Foreign Language Conferences), 236, 416, 421, 440
KIDLINK and KIDCAFE, 138, 247-248, 416
kinesiology, Biomch-L, 416
Kingsley, Charles, 416
The Kites FTP Archive, 417, 595
Kiwanis International, Circle K International, 417
Knowbot, 393
knowledge representation, nl-kr, 417
Korea. soc.culture.korean, 417
Kurtz, Katernine, 417

L

labor, 419
labor archives, 420
labor, history of, 419
Laboratory Primate Newsletter, 420, 565, 573
LabStat, 131, 230, 419
Lafayette, Marquis de, 420
land records, 420
landscaping, 420
Lang-Lucid, 420, 569, 571
LANGIT, 404, 440
LANGIT (Italian Linguistics Center), 420

language, natural, 498
language software, 421
languages, 420-421
languages, Chinese, 140
languages, Gaelic, 307, 420-421
languages, Hebrew, 345
LANTRA-L, 398, 421, 440, 673
lasers, 421-422
Latin America, 422-423
Latin America & Caribbean Network Gopher server, 126, 422
Latin American Database Historic World Documents, 347, 375-376, 422, 425
Latin American studies, 423
Latino culture, 423
Latvia, 423
law, 423-426
Law and Courts Preprint Archive, 427-432, 555
Law and Politics Book Review, 412, 425, 555
law, international, 303, 424-427
law, military, 426
Law Review Library (LAWREV), 693
law, state, 424-428
law, tax, 427
law, transportation, 674
law, US, 427-429
law, US case, 429
law, US federal, 429-430
LAWREV (Law Review Library), 57, 410, 428, 693
laws, 430-431
LEA (Leonardo Electronic Almanac), 69
Leaders of Community Networking: People Who Create Online Communities, 156, 330, 431, 504
leadership IRVL-I (Institute for Research on Visionary Leadership), 431
legal research, Research on Demand, 431
Legal Status, 371, 431-432, 542, 673
Legion of Doom/Hackers Technical Journals, 179, 335, 432
legislation, 432
legislation, Australian, 433
LEGNEW (Legal News), 412, 428, 433, 653
Lego Information, 138, 186, 433, 671
Leonardo Electronic Almanac, 254, 433, 483, 486-487
Leonardo Electronic Almanac (LEA), 69
lesbians, 433-435
lexicography, 435
lexicology, 435-436
LEXPAT (Patents US), 73, 399, 436, 448, 542
liberal education, 436
libertarian politics, 436
librarians, gay, 437-438
Librarian's Internet Reference, 388, 436
librarianship, 436
Library of Congress, Astronomy, Astrophysics, and Physics Resources, 75-77, 440, 494
Library Resources, 383, 438
Library Special, 365, 383, 438
life, artificial, 71
Limbaugh, Rush, 440
Lincoln, Abraham, 440
LINGUIST, 421
Linguist, 440
linguistics, 440-441
Links to Many Databases, 201, 441, 600
LIST Gopher, 324, 438, 442, 452
LIST REVIEW SERVICE, 103, 224, 442
List Serv, 396, 442
literacy, 442
literary criticism, 442
literary studies, 442-443
literate programming, 443
literature, American, 443-444
literature, Asian, 444
literature, children's, 444
literature, contemporary, 444-445

literature, English, 445-446
literature, general, 446-447
literature, German, 447
literature, Irish, 447
literature, Russian, 447
literature, Spanish, 447
Lithuania, 447-448
litigants, 448
Litprog, 443, 569
liturgy, 448
LLTI (Language Learning Technology International), 162, 421, 441
LOCIS (LIBRARY Of CONGRESS INFORMATION SYSTEM), 365, 438, 533
Lockheed Missiles & Space Company, 40, 205, 448
logic, fuzzy, 305
Loughborough University of Technology, Computer-Human Interaction (LUTCHI) Research Center 173, 270, 373, 448, 569
Lower Rio Grande Valley, history of, 448
LTEST, 421, 441
Lynx FAQ, 391, 448
lyrics, 448-449
Lysator's Gopher Service, 275, 449, 651, 654

M

Maastricht Treaty, 275, 277, 451
Macintosh computers, 451
magazines, 451-452
mailing lists, 452
Maine, 452
Maine authors, 452
malls, 452
management, 452-453
The Management Archive, 115-116, 230, 453
Mann, Thomas, 453
Manx, 453
mapinfo-l, 315, 320, 453
mapping, 453
Marimed Foundation, 235, 453, 610
marine biology, 453-454
marine engineering, Florida State University System Library, 454
maritime industry, 454
MARKET (Markets and Industries News and Information), 57, 362, 454, 455, 512
market conditions, 454
market research, 454-455
MarketBase Gopher, 393, 455
marketing
    Computer-Mediated Marketing Environments, 455
    MARKET (Markets and Industries News and Information), 455
    MarketBase Gopher, 455
Marshall University School of Medicine (MUSOM) RuralNet Gopher, 94, 342, 455, 461, 606
martial arts
    Aikido Information, 455
    aikido-l, 455
    rec.martial-arts, 455
Martin Marietta Energy Systems Gopher, 260, 362, 455-456, 661
Maryland, 425, 456, 705
mass media
    Communication and Mass Communication Resources, 456
    National Broadcasting Society—Alpha Epsilon Rho, 456
    ViewPoints, 456
Massachusetts Institute of Technology Library, 39, 321, 441, 456, 457, 471, 640
Material Science in Israel Newsletter, 403, 456

material sciences
    Material Science in Israel Newsletter, 456
    Materials Business File, 456
    METADEX, 456
    PIRA - Paper, Printing and Publishing,
        Packaging, and Nonwovens Abstracts, 456
    RAPRA Abstracts, 457
Materials Business File, 114-115, 401-402, 456, 649
mathematical biology
    Smbnet (Society for Mathematical Biology
        Digest), 457
mathematics
    alife, 457
    Anneal, 457
    CEM-L, 457
    Euromath Center Gopher Server, 457
    Massachusetts Institute of Technology Library, 457
    NCTM-L, 457
    Pd-games, 457-458
    sci.math, 458
    Spanky Fractal Database, 458
    Statlib, 458
    University of Michigan Library, 458
    University of Wisconsin at Stout Library, 458
mathematics, algorithms
    comp.compression, 457
May, Julien
    Milieu, 458
Mazda automobiles
    Miata, 458
MBI, Music and the Brain Information
    Center Database (MuSICA), 489-490
MBI, Music and the Brain Information Center
    Database (MuSICA), 355, 458, 507
McDonnell Douglas Aerospace, 40-41, 83, 458, 638, 661
McGill University, Montreal Canada,
    INFOMcGILL Library, 459, 466, 494
McGill University, Montreal Canada, INFOMcGILL
    Library, 65, 96, 265, 616, 623
The McKinley Group, 387, 389, 390, 392
mda, 351, 459, 642
MDEAFR, 160, 459, 471-472, 513
MDEAFR (Middle East and Africa Library), 57
MDEAFR (Middle East and Africa), 41
MECH-L, 264, 459
media
    Communication and Mass Communication
        Resources, 459
    Prog-Pubs, 459
mediation
    NAME Publications and Resources List, 459-460
Medical and Biological Research in
    Laboratories Institutions (Israel), 460
Medical and Biological Research in Laboratories
    and Institutions (Israel), 94
    Institutions (Israel), 403
Medical College of Ohio Library Online
    Catalogue, 438, 460, 464
Medical College of Wisconsin Library Online
    Catalogue, 438, 460, 464
medical informatics
    CAMIS (Center for Advanced Medical
        Informatics at Stanford), 460
medical news
    HICNet Newsletter (MEDNEWS -
        The Health InfoCom Newsletter), 460
medical research
    Discipline and Disease Specific Sources, 460
    Health News Daily, 460
    Medical and Biological Research in
        Laboratories Institutions (Israel), 460
    Poisons Information Database, 460
    sci.med.physics, 461

medical treatment
    Accri-I, 461
    Health and Clinical Information & Bioethics
        Online Service, 461
    Marshall University School of Medicine
        (MUSOM) RuralNet Gopher, 461
medicine
    Accri-I, 461
    Aids, 461
    AIDS Treatment News, 461
    AIDS/HIV Information, 461
    AIDSLINE, 462
    Allied and Alternative Medicine (AMED), 462
    Alternative Medicine, the Definitive Guide, 462
    Biomedical Computer Laboratory (BCL), 462
    BOING (Bio-Oriented INternet Gophers), 462
    BRIDGE, 462
    The Center for Biomedical Informatics of the
        State University of Campinas, Brazil, 461
    Denmark's Library for Medicine and Science, 462
    Discipline and Disease Specific Sources, 462
    EMBASE, 462
    Fam-Med, 463
    GenBank, 463
    GENMED (General Medical Information), 463
    Georgetown University Medical Center Online
        Catalogue, 463
    Harvard Medical Gopher, 463
    Health and Clinical Information &
        Biodthics Online Service, 463
    Health Periodicals Database, 463-464
    Johns Hopkins Genetic Databases, 464
    Medical College of Ohio Library Online
        Catalogue, 464
    Medical College of Wisconsin Library Online
        Catalogue, 464
    MEDLARS (MEDical Literature Analysis
        and Retrieval System), 464
    MEDLINE, 464
    Midwifery Resources on the Net, 464
    Montefiore Medical Center Library Online
        Catalog, 464
    National Institute for Allergy &
        Infectious Disease (NIAID), 464
    National Institute of Health Library Online
        Catalog, 464-465
    The National Library of Medicine
        (NLM) Online Catalog System, 465
    National Library of Medicine Gopher
        World Health Organization (WHO), 465
    NIBNews - A Monthly Electronic Bulletin About
        Medical Informatics, 465
    NIH (National Institute of Health), 465
    sci.med, 465
    South East Florida AIDS Information Network
        (SEFAIN), 465
    Stanford Medical Center Gopher, 465
    University of Texas Health Science Center
        (UTHSCSA) Biomedical Library Information Syste, 466
    University of Wales College of Medicine
        Library Online Catalog, 466
    Virtual Hospital, 466
    Washington University-St. Louis Medical
        Library and Members Library, 466
    World Health Organization (WHO), 466
medicine, history of
    McGill University, Montreal Canada,
        INFOMcGILL Library, 466
    University of Maryland System Library, 466
medicine, veterinary
    see veterinary medicine
medieval reenactments
    rec.org.sca, 466

medieval role-playing
    Nero Ashbury, 466
medieval studies
    History at the University of Virginia, 466
    MEDTEXT-L, 466
    University of Pennsylvania Library-
        Philadelphia Pa., 466
    University of Rochester Library, 467
MEDLARS, 464
MEDLARS (MEDical Literature Analysis and
    Retrieval System), 98
MEDLINE, 98, 207, 464, 525
MEDTEXT-L, 441, 466, 548
Meetings Calendar (Geosciences), 318, 467, 469
MEGA (Combined Federal/State Case Law), 127, 428, 430, 467
MegaGopher, 96, 122, 467
Melrose-place, 300, 467, 664
MELVYL Library System, 467, 533
memorabilia
    Cards, 467
    Sports-cards, 468
Men, 468
men
    soc.men, 468
Mensa
    Mensatalk, 468
Mensatalk, 314, 468
Mercer, Johnny (collection of)
    Georgia State University Library, 468
Merit Network Information Center Services, 383, 388, 396, 468
MetaCard
    Metacard-list, 468
Metacard-list, 181, 468, 690
METADEX, 47, 456, 468
metals
    METADEX, 468
MetaMail, 224, 383, 468
meteorology
    Current Weather Maps and Movies, 469
    Energy and Climate Information Exchange
        (ECIX) Newsletter, 469
    Meetings Calendar (Geosciences), 469
    Meteorology Students, 469
    Weather-users, 469
Meteorology Students, 469
Mexican Culture FAQ, 137, 194, 423, 469, 583
Mexican-American studies
    University of Texas-Pan American Library, 469
Mexico
    North American Free Trade Agreement (NAFTA), 469
    US/Mexico Border Discussion List, 469
MGD (Mouse Genome Database), 96, 313, 469
Miata, 81, 458, 469-470
Michigan
    MichNet News (previously Merit Network
        News), 470
    The University of Michigan Library, 470
MichNet News (previously Merit Network
    News), 167, 470
MICnews, 38, 470
microbiology
    Biosis Previews, 470
    University of Maryland System Library, 470
    vetmicro, 470
microcomputing
    Buyer's Guide to Micro Software, 470
    MICnews, 470
    Output, 470-471
microelectronics
    University of Wisconsin at Stout Library, 471
microscopy
    Massachusetts Institute of Technology Library, 471

Microsoft Corporation
    foxpro-l, 471
    Microsoft Corporation World Wide Web Server, 471
    MS-Access, 471
Microsoft Corporation World Wide Web Server, 471, 481, 710-711
Microsoft FTP Site, 179
Middle East
    The Israel Information Service, 472
    Israel-mideast, 471
    MDEAFR, 471-472
    talk.politics.mideast, 472
Middle East and Africa (MDEAFR), 41, 513
Middle Eastern studies
    Judaica, 472
    Princeton University Library, 472
    soc.culture.arabic, 472
    talk.politics.mideast, 472
    University of Pennsylvania Library-
        Philadelphia Pa., 472
    University of Texas at Austin Library, 472
    University of Utah Library, 472
Middle-eastern-music, 487
Mideur-L, 472-473
Mideur-l, 87, 226, 513, 637
MIDI
    Alternate Tuning Mailing List, 473
midwifery
    Midwifery Resources on the Net, 473
Midwifery Resources on the Net, 138, 464, 473, 525
Migra-list, 473
migration
    Migra-list, 473
Milieu, 458, 473, 615-616
military history
    University of Nebraska at Lincoln Library, 473
military policy
    dont-tell, 473-474
military science
    sci.military, 474
military specifications
    IHS International Standards and Specifications, 474
military, US
    U.S. Army Area Handbooks, 473
    Uniform Code of Military Justice, 473
    US Army Corps of Engineers, 473
Milne, A. A.
    University of New Hampshire Videotex Library, 474
MIME (Multipurpose Internet Mail Extensions), 224, 383, 474
mind
    Mind-L, 474
Mind-L, 474
Miniatures, 474, 604
miniatures
    Miniatures, 474
miniaturized plants
    Bonsai, 474
mining
    University of Utah Library, 474
minor leagues
    Minors, 475
minorities
    POS302-L, 475
    soc.culture.african.american, 475
Minors, 88, 475
Miracles, 475
miracles
    Miracles, 475
misc.consumers, 186, 475
misc.consumers.house, 352, 354, 475
misc.forsale, 186, 475
misc.handicap, 215, 475
misc.headlines, 195, 475
misc.invest, 292, 400, 475
misc.invest.real-estate, 400, 475-476, 587

misc.jobs.misc, 258, 476
misc.jobs.offered, 258, 476
misc.jobs.resumes, 258, 476
misc.kids, 137, 138-139, 476
misc.legal, 271, 425, 476
misc.wanted, 186, 476
Miscellaneous Federal Documents, 284, 330, 476
Mississippi State University Library, 126, 260, 300, 348, 476
MIT Media Lab, 383, 476, 483
The MIT Press Online Catalogs, 661, 33, 106, 576
MLoL, 452, 476
MLoL (Musical List of Lists), 487
model horses
    Model-horse, 476-477
Model-horse, 350, 476-477
modems
    SupraFAX, 477
modern dance
    OMD (Orchestral Manoeuvres In The Dark), 477
modesty-blaise, 150, 477
Modula-2 programming language
    info-M2, 477
molecular biology
    Archive of Biology Software and Data, 477
    Bioinformatics, 477
    bionet.molbio.genbank.updates, 477
    Biotechnet Electronic Buyer's Guide, 477-478
    EMBnet (European Molecular Biology Network), 478
    GenBank, 478
    Harvard Biosciences Online Journals, 478
    ICGEBnet, 478
    Johns Hopkins Genetic Databases, 478
    National Institutes of Health Gopher, 478
    University of Texas Health Science Center at Tyler Library, 479
Moms, 434, 479, 540
monarchy
    Counterev-L, 479
Montefiore Medical Center Library Online Catalog, 439, 464, 479
Moon Travel Handbooks, 106, 479, 675
Mormonism
    Harvard University Library, 479
    Princeton University Library, 479
morphology
    Qmlist (Quantitative Morphology List), 479
Morris, 264, 479
Morris (dancing), 199
Morris dancing
    Morris, 479
Mosaic
    Mosaic Home Page, 479
    NCSA (National Center for Supercomputing Applications), 480
Mosaic Home Page, 396, 479, 719
Mother Jones, 36, 271, 480, 574, 727
motor racing
    Funet Sports Information, 480
    University of Glasgow Information Service (GLANCE), 480
motorcycles
    BMW Motorcycles, 480
    Brit-Iron, 480
    Nedod, 480
    rec.motorcycles, 480
mountaineering
    University of Glasgow Information Service (GLANCE), 480
Mouse Genome Database (MGD), 96
movement
    Biomch-L, 480-481
movies
    rec.arts.movies movie database, 481
        (Cardiff WWW front-end), 481

Mr2-interest, 481
MS-Access, 201, 471, 481
MS-DOS computers
    info-GNU-MSDOS, 481
    Microsoft Corporation World Wide Web Server, 481
MSA, 402
MSA-Net, 402, 481, 492
Mt Xinu
    Mtxinu-users, 481-482
Mtxinu-users, 481-482
Muchomedia Conference, 69, 482, 483
MUD (Multi-User Dungeons & Dragons), 308
MUD (Multiuser Dungeons and Dragons), 482
Multicast, 110, 482
Multicast Backbone, 365, 383, 482
multicasting
    Multicast, 482
    Multicast Backbone, 482
Multilateral Treaties, 425-426, 482, 677
multimedia
    ACEN (Art Com Electronic Network), 482
    ACM SIGGRAPH Online Bibliography Project, 482
    CinemaSpace, 482-483
    Diversity U, 483
    The Electric Eclectic, 482
    FineArt Forum, 483
    Free for All, 483
    Georgia State UniversityLibrary, 483
    Index to Multimedia Information Sources, 483
    Kaleidospace, 483
    Leonardo Electronic Almanac, 483
    MIT Media Lab, 483
    Muchomedia Conference, 483
    Multimedia Index, 483-484
    Multimedia Lab BU, 484
    Multimedia Survey, 484
    Multimedia, Telecommunications, and Art Project, 484
    NIC (Nucleus for Interactive Computing), 484
    NYAL (New York Art Line), 484
    UC Berkeley Museum of Paleontology and the WWW Subway, 484
Multimedia Index, 383, 483-484
Multimedia Lab BU, 383, 484
Multimedia Survey, 383, 484
Multimedia, Telecommunications, and Art Project, 484, 663
Multimedia, Telecommunications, and Art Project, 252
museums
    Smithsonian Online, 484
Music, 392
music
    alt.music.alternative, 484
    Analog Heaven, 484
    Arts, 485
    Arts Wire, 485
    AusRave (Australian Raves), 485
    Bagpipe, 485
    Bel Canto, 485
    Beloved, 485
    Best-of-AusRave (Australian Raves), 485
    Blues-L, 485
    BPM, 485-486
    Cantus, 486
    dire-straits, 486
    Drake University, 486
    Eastern Washington University Library, 486
    ecto, 486
    fogelberg, 486
    freaks, 486
    fuzzy-ramblings, 486
    Impulse, 486
    Leonardo Electronic Almanac, 486-487
    MLoL (Musical List of Lists), 487

Music (directory), 487
mw-raves, 487
NetJam, 487
Network-Audio-Bits, 487
NewMusNet, 487
On-u, 487
Queen, 487
rec.music.cd, 487
rec.music.classical, 487
rec.music.gdead, 488
rec.music.makers, 488
rec.music.makers.synth, 488
Reggae Down Babylon, 488
Soundtracks, 488
Space-music, 488
Stormcock, 488
University of Northern Iowa Library, 488
University of Puget Sound Library, 488
University of Texas at Austin Library, 488
University of Wisconsin Green Bay Library, 488
UWP Music Archive, 488-489
Virginia Commonwealth University Library, 489
Music (directory), 487, 489
music, computer
    IRCAM DSP and musical software, 635
music, folk
    Folk music, 486
    University of New Hampshire Videotex Library, 296-297
music, Irish
    The University of Notre Dame Library, 489
Music Library Association Mailing List, 91, 489
music, middle-eastern
    Middle-eastern-music, 487
music notation
    FINALE Discussion List, 489
music research
    Music (directory), 489
    Music-research, 489
    Northwestern University Library, 489
music resources
    MBI, Music and the Brain Information Center Database (MuSICA), 489-490
    University of California Santa Barbara Virtual Library, 490
music reviews
    Network-Audio-Bits, 490
music software
    Synth-l, 490
Music-research, 489
musical genres
    alt.music.progressive, 490
    alt.rap, 490
    alt.rock-n-roll, 490
    Funky Music, 490
    rec.music.folk, 490
musical genres\
    alt.rock-n-roll.metal, 490
musical groups
    The Beastie Boys' Web Page, 491
    Direct, 490
    Journey-L, 490-491
    Prince, 491
    rec.music.beatles, 491
    rec.music.phish, 491
musical instruments
    alt.guitar, 491
    Alternate Tuning Mailing List, 491
    rec.music.makers, 491
    rec.music.makers.guitar, 491
Musicals, 491, 667
musicals
    Musicals, 491

musicians
    Ethnomusicology Research Digest, 491
    MSA-Net, 492
    NetJam, 492
    On-u, 492
Muslims
    MSA-Net, 492
MUSOM (Marshall University School of Medicine)
    RuralNet Gopher, 94
Mustangs, 81, 299, 492
mutual funds
    NETworth (The Internet Resource for *Individual Investors), 492*
mw-raves, 487, 492
mw-raves (Midwest Raves), 586
mycoplasma
    vetmycop, 492
Mystery, 106, 209, 492
mythology
    The Curiosity Club, 492

N

NA-net, 493, 524
NAARS (National Automated Accounting Research System), 33-34, 79, 289, 493, 575
NAFTA
    North American Free Trade Agreement (NAFTA), 493
NAFTA (North American Free Trade Agreement), 123, 301
NAME, 183-184, 244
NAME (National Association for Mediation in Education) Publications and *Resources List, 493*
NAME Publications and Resources List, 459-460
naplps-list, 69, 165, 493-494
Napoleon Bonaparte
    McGill University, Montreal Canada, *INFOMcGILL Library, 494*
NASA
    Center for Extreme Ultraviolet Astrophysics, 494
    Cosmic Update, 494
    Library of Congress, Astronomy, Astrophysics, *and Physics Resources, 494*
    NASA Ames SPACE Archive, 494
    NASA/IPAC Extragalactic Database (NED), 494
    Sci.astro.hubble, 495
    Spacelink, 495
    The University of Iowa Libraries, 495
NASA Ames SPACE Archive, 494, 638, 639
NASA/IPAC Extragalactic Database (NED), 75, 201-202, 494
Nat. Oceanic & Atmospheric Admin. (NOAA)
    Office of Env. Savety & Health, Dep. of Energ, 530
National Aeronautics and Space Administration
    see NASA
National Automated Accounting Research System (NAARS), 33-34, 79, 289
National Broadcasting Society—Alpha Epsilon Rho, 290, 456, 495, 584, 664-665
National Cancer Center, Tokyo, Japan, 124, 408, 495
National Centre for Software Technology, 169, 173, 263, 495
National Collegiate Athletic Association
    Pac-10-Sports, 495
National Export Strategy, 115, 150, 278-279, 495, 671
National Family Database—MAPP, 281, 340, 495-496, 630
National Hockey League (NHL)
    Blues (St. Louis Blues), 496
    Boston Bruins, 496
    NHL Goalie Stats, 496
National Institute for Allergy & Infectious Disease (NIAID), 46
    Infectious Disease (NIAID), 464, 496

National Institute for Allergy & Infectious
    Disease (NIAID), 363
National Institute of Health (NIH), 98
National Institute of Health Library
    Online Catalog, 496
National Institute of Health Library Online
    Catalog, 439, 464-465, 519, 614
National Institutes of Health Gopher, 45, 331, 340, 478, 496
National Library of Canada (NLC), 123
The National Library of Medicine
    (NLM) Online Catalog System, 465
The National Library of Medicine (NLM)
    Online Catalog System, 585, 99, 344
National Library of Medicine Gopher, 496
    World Health Organization (WHO), 465, 716
National Library of Medicine Gopher World
    Health Organization (WHO), 340
National Oceanic & Atmospheric
    Administration (NOAA), 497
National Oceanic & Atmospheric Administration
    (NOAA), 269, 340
    (NOAA) etc, 267
    (NOAA) Office of Environment Safety and Health
    , Department of Energy, 78
National Performance Review (NPR), 497, 557, 564, 709
National Science Foundation Center
    for Biological Timing, 497
National Science Foundation Center for
    Biological Timeing Vertebrate Museum and
        Virus Gopher Server, 96
    Biological Timing, Vertebrate Museum and Virus
        Gopher Server, 698-699
National Space Science Data Center's (NSSDC's)
    Online Data and Information Service, 77-78
National Technology Transfer Center (NTTC), 115, 207, 327, 497, 601, 661, 662
native American affairs
    University of New Mexico Unminfo Library, 497
    University of Tennessee at Knoxville Library, 497
native American studies
    The University of Minnesota Library System
        (LUMINA), 498
    The University of Iowa Libraries, 497-498
NativeNet, 60, 267-268, 362, 498
NATO, 205, 333, 498
natural history
    Smithsonian Institution Natural History Gopher, 498
natural language
    nl-kr, 498
Natural Resources Canada (NRCan) Gopher, 122-123, 268, 300, 316, 498
natural science
    University of Puget Sound Library, 498
    University of Texas at Austin Library, 498
    University of Wisconsin Green Bay Library, 499
    US Geological Survey Server, 499
The Nautical Bookshelf, 104, 563, 610, 644
Navnews, 499, 515-516
navy
    Navnews, 499
NBA
    Funet Sports Information, 499
NCAA
    Pac-10-Sports, 495
NCGIA
    Geographic Information and Analysis
        Laboratory (GIAL), 499
NCSA (National Center for Supercomputing
    Applications), 166, 169, 480, 499, 652
NCSA Mosaic FAQ, 391, 499
NCTM-L, 248, 457, 499
Ncube, 499-500, 539
Ne-social-motss, 102, 311, 434, 500, 629

near eastern studies
    Princeton University Library, 500
NEARnet
    NEARnet Newsletter, 500
NEARnet Newsletter, 500, 504
Neci-announce, 383, 500, 694
Neci-digest, 383, 500, 694
Neci-discuss, 383-384, 500, 694
NED (NASA/IPAC Extragalactic Database), 75
Nedod, 480, 508
Nedod (motorcycling), 500
NERaves (Northeast Raves), 500, 586
Nerdnosh, 650
Nerdnosh (storytelling), 500-501
Nero Ashbury, 308, 466, 501, 604
Net Etiquette Guide, 272, 384, 501
Net-News, 384, 439, 501, 504
Netblazer
    Netblazer-users, 501
Netblazer-users, 501, 662
NetCom, 384, 501
NetEc, 115, 230, 501
Netfind, 224, 365-366, 396, 501, 719
Netherlands
    SURFnet—KB InfoServer, 501
Netiquette
    Net Etiquette Guide, 501
NetJam, 487, 492, 502
NetMonth, 103, 502, 504
NetVet Veterinary Resources, 59, 502, 699
Network servers
    The FARNET Gazette, 502
network servers
    Network Time Protocol, 502
Network Time Protocol, 502
Network-Audio-Bits, 487, 490, 502
networking
    An NREN That Includes Everyone, 503
    The Black Box Catalog, 505
    Blacksburg Electronic Village Gopher, 503
    Citizens Project, 503
    Civic Promise of the National Information
        Infrastructure (NII), 503
    Community Networks Benefit Federal Goals, 503
    ECHO, 503
    Electronic Democracy Must Come from Us, 503
    The Electronic Public Interest versus the Private
        Private Good, 502
    Free-Net Working Papers, 503
    Information Sources, 504
    Leaders of Community Networking:
        People Who Create Online Communities, 504
    NEARnet Newsletter, 504
    Net-News, 504
    NetMonth, 504
    Networks & Communities, 504
    Output, 504
    People Using Networks Can Have
        an Impact on Government, 504
    Polish Archives, 504
    Qnx4, 504
    Singapore DMC, 504-505
    Telluride Institute, 505
    TWICS, 505
    Usenet Repository, 505
    The WELL (Whole Earth 'Lectronic Link), 502
    Women's Wire, 505
    The Worldwide Impact of Network Access, 503
networks
    Cisco, 505
    Cleveland FreeNet, 505
    CYFERNET (Child, Youth, and Family Education
        Network, 505-506
    K12 Net, 506

Index

Networks & Communities, 506
RIPE Network Coordination Centre Gopher, 506
SABINET (South African Bibliographic and *Information Network)*, 506
SURFnet—KB InfoServer, 506
Virginia's PEN (Public Education Network), 506
Networks & Communities, 156, 504, 506, 567
NETworth (The Internet Resource for Individual Investors), 492
neural networks
Neuron, 506
neural simulation
Purkinje Park, 506
neurobiology
Neurosciences Internet Resource Guide, 506
neurology
MBI, Music and the Brain Information Center *Database (MuSICA)*, 507
Neuron, 94, 506
neurosciences
Cognitive and Psychological Sciences on the Internet, 507
Neurosciences Internet Resource Guide, 507
Recreational Pharmacology Server, 507
The University of Michigan Library, 507
Neurosciences Internet Resource Guide, 108, 506, 507
Nevada
University of Nevada at Reno Library, 507
Nevada state documents
University of Nevada, Las Vegas Library - Las Vegas, NV, 507
new age music
Direct, 507
New England
Nedod, 508
New Jersey
NJ-motss, 508
NJ-motss-announce, 508
new media
CTN News, 508
New Mexico
New Mexico LegalNet, 508
New Mexico LegalNet, 426, 508
new music
NewMusNet, 508
New Orleans
New-orleans, 508
Neworl-dig, 508
New Testament
Bible (King James Version), 508-509
New User's Questions, 384, 388, 509
New York
BTHS-ENews-l, 509
ebikes, 509
Information about New York City, 509
New York Islanders, 509
New York State Department of Health Gopher, 509
NYSERNet Internet Guide, 509
Shamash, The New York - Israel Project, 509
VEGCNY-L (Vegetarians in Central New York area), 510
New York Art Line (NYAL), 69, 79
New York Islanders, 351, 509
New York State Department of Health Gopher, 342, 344, 509, 647
New-orleans, 508, 675
Newedu-l (New Paradigms in Education List), 234, 239, 242, 510
Newlists, 452, 510
NewMusNet, 487, 508, 510
Neworl-dig, 508, 510, 676
News, 254, 409, 513, 516
news
Agence FrancePresse International French Wire, 510
bit.general, 510
BUSREF (Business Reference), 510

CANADA (Canadian News and Information *Library)*, 511
CERRO (Central European Regional *Research Organization)*, 511
Cro-Views, 511
Croatian-News/Hrvatski-Vjesnik, 511
Electronic Newsstand Gopher, 511
ENERGY, 511
ENTERT (Entertainment News Library), 511
ENVIRN (Environment Library), 511-512
EXEC (Executive Branch News US), 512
Health News Daily, 512
Hungary, 512
INSURE (Insurance), 512
MARKET (Markets and Industries News and Information), 512
MDEAFR, 513
Mideur-l, 513
News, 513
NEWS (General News), 513
News of Earth, 513
NewsCommando, 513
Novice MZT, 513-514
NSAMER (North and South America Library), 514
SPORTS (Sports News), 514
TOPNWS (Top News), 514
United Press International News—Sports, 514
WORLD (World News and Information), 514-515
NEWS (General News Library), 57-58
NEWS (General News), 160, 513, 544
news, international
Spojrzenia, 515
Sri Lanka Net (SLNet), 515
news media
Africa-n, 515
C-SPAN (Cable-Satellite Public Affairs *Network) Gopher*, 515
CNN Headline News Gopher, 515
Cro-News/SCYU-Digest, 515
Jane's Defense & Aerospace News/Analysis, 515
Navnews, 515-516
News, 516
Voice of America and Worldnet, 516
WIRED Online, 516
News of Earth, 322, 513
News, Weather, and Travel Advisories, 83, 516, 676, 708
news.announce.conferences, 183, 516, 539, 718
news.announce.newgroups, 392, 516, 694
news.answers, 392, 516, 694-695
news.aus.films, 517
news.groups, 392, 516, 695
news.lists, 392, 516, 695
news.newusers.questions, 224-225, 392, 516, 695
news: aus.films, 80, 290
news:comp.infosystems.wais, 391
Newsbrief, 517, 522, 685
NewsCommando, 513, 517
Newsletter on Serials Pricing Issues, 436, 517, 621
newsletters
CCNEWS, 517
Newsline, 153, 182, 517
NeXT
comp.sys.next, 517
next-gis, 517-518
NeXT-icon, 518
NeXT-Med, 518
next-gis, 126, 315, 320, 517-518
NeXT-icon, 518
NeXT-Med, 518
NFL
Funet Sports Information, 518
NFL Scores, Schedules, and Point Spreads, 518
NFL Scores, Schedules, and Point Spreads, 518, 567, 642

NHL
  Dallas Stars, 518
  Funet Sports Information, 518
  NHL Goalie Stats, 518
  OlymPuck, 518
NHL Goalie Stats, 351, 496, 518, 645
NIAD (National Institute for Allergy &
  Infectious Disease), 46
NIBNews, 636
NIBNews - A Monthly Electronic Bulletin
  About Medical Informatics, 96, 422-423
NIBNews - A Monthly Electronic Bulletin About
  Medical Informatics, 108-109, 343, 465, 519
NIC (Nucleus for Interactive Computing), 372, 373, 484, 519, 569-570, 617-618
Nickelodeon
  Clarissa, 519
NIH (National Institute of Health), 98, 344, 465
  National Institute of Health Library Online
    Catalog, 519
  NIH (National Institute of Health) server, 519
  NIH EDNET, 519
  NIH Grant Line (Drgline Bulletin Board), 519
NIH (National Institute of Health) server, 519
NIH EDNET, 244, 245, 519, 614
NIH Grant Line (Drgline Bulletin Board), 98, 331, 519
Nihon Sun Microsystems, 179, 520, 604
NIR (Networked Information Retrieval)
  NIR Archives, 520
  NIR Gopher, 520
NIR Archives, 366, 384, 520
NIR Gopher, 366, 384, 520
nissan, 363, 520
Nissan automobiles
  nissan, 520
NJ-motss, 102, 311, 434, 508, 520
NJ-motss-announce, 102, 311, 435, 508, 520
nl-kr, 417, 441, 498, 520, 571
NLC (National Library of Canada), 123, 439, 520
NLM (The National Library of Medicine)
  Online Catalog System, 99
NLSNews Newsletter, 419
NLSNews Newsletter (National Longitudinal
  Surveys of Labor Market Experience), 208
NLSNews Newsletter (National Longitudinal Surveys
  of Labor Market Experience), 327, 520-521
NOAA, 269
NOAA (National Oceanic & Atmospheric
  Administration, etc., 267
NOAA) National Oceanic & Atmospheric Administratio
  Office of Environment Safety and Health
    , Department of Energy, 78
noglstp, 311, 435, 521, 617, 659
Non Serviam, 521, 548
non-governmental organizations
  World Health Organization (WHO), 521
nonfiction books
  Online BookStore (OBS), 521
nonprofit organizations
  DevelopNet News, 521
  Encyclopedia of Associations, 521
  Internet Nonprofit Center, 521
Nordic skiing
  nordic-skiing, 522
Nordic University
  NORDUnet region Root Gopher, 522
nordic-skiing, 522
NORDUnet region Root Gopher, 275, 522
North America
  NSAMER (North and South America Library), 522
North American Free Trade Agreement (NAFTA), 123, 301, 469, 493, 522, 671, 691

North Carolina
  Newsbrief, 522
  University of North Carolina at
    Chapel Hill Info Library, 522
Northwestern University Library, 41, 69, 187, 330, 443, 489, 522, 679-680, 714, 717
Norway
  NORWEAVE, 523
NORWEAVE, 523
Notable Women, 287, 349, 523, 714
NotGNU, 257, 523
Novice MZT, 513-514, 523, 614, 627, 661
NPLC, 523, 553
NQTHM
  nqthm-users, 523
nqthm-users, 108, 168, 523
NSAMER (North and South America Library), 58, 160, 514, 522, 523-524, 636
NSF Resource Guide, 384, 388-389, 524
NSSDC (National Space Science Data Center)'s
  Online Data & Information Service, 494
  Online Data and Information Service, 77-78, 524
NSSDC's Online Data & Information
  Service, 614-615, 634
NSSDC's Online Data and Information
  Service, 638
NTIS FedWorld, 524, 692
ntp, 524
NTTC (National Technology Transfer Center), 115, 207
nuclear medicine
  nucmed, 524
nuclear safety
  Illinois Legislation, 524
nucmed, 524
numeric-interest, 166, 179, 524
numerical analysis
  NA-net, 524
numismatics
  coins, 524-525
  Harvard University Library, 525
  University of Colorado at Boulder Library, 525
nursing
  Johns Hopkins University Library, 525
  MEDLINE, 525
  Midwifery Resources on the Net, 525
  University of Maryland SystemLibrary, 525
  University of Pennsylvania School of Medicine
    Library, 525
  University of Puerto Rico Library, 525
  University of Texas at Austin Library, 525
  University of Texas at Galveston
    (Medical Branch) Library, 525
  University of Texas Health Science Center
    at San Antonio Library, 525
  University of Wisconsin at Oshkosh Library, 526
  University of Wisconsin Eau Claire Library, 526
nutrition
  Federal Food and Drug Administration, 526
  GRANOLA (Vegetarian Discussion List), 526
  Health Periodicals Database, 526
  International Food and Nutrition (INFAN)
    Database, 526
  The Wellness List, 526
NW-Raves (Northwest Raves), 526, 586
NWNet Internet Guide, 244, 384, 389, 526-527, 652
NYAL (New York Art Line), 69, 79, 163, 484, 527
NYIsrael Project of NYSERnet, 345, 403, 411, 527
NYSERNet Internet Guide, 384, 389, 509, 527, 652

O

object-oriented programming
    BETA, 529
Objectivism, 529
OBS (Online BookStore), 106
The Observer, 82, 147, 654-655
obstetrics/gynacology
    University of Texas Health Science Center
        at San Antonio Library, 529
Occupational Outlook Handbook 1992-93, 125, 258, 419, 529
oceanography
    FINS (Fish Information Service), 529
    Research Ship Schedules and Information, 529
    University of Maryland, College Park, 530
oceans
    Global Change Information Gateway, 530
    Nat. Oceanic & Atmospheric Admin. (NOAA)
        Office of Env. Savety & Health, Dep. of Energ, 530
ODA, 530
ODA (Office Document Architecture), 530
OE-CALL: Old English Computer Assisted
    Language Learning Newsletter, 162
OE-CALL: Old English Computer-Assisted
    Language Learning Newsletter, 530, 531
Office Document Architecture
    ODA, 530
Office of Environmental Safety and Health
    Dept of Energy, 341
Office of Environmental Safety and Health,
    Department of Energy, 269, 530
Offroad, 300, 530
Oglasna Deska, 531, 626, 627, 695
Ogphre - SunSITE, 43-44, 384, 531, 560, 599
Oh-motss, 311, 435, 531
Ohio, 426, 531
    Cleveland Sports, 531
    Friends of Ohio State, 531
    Oh-motss, 531
    Ohio, 531
The Old Dominion University Library, 284, 702
Old English
    OE-CALL: Old English Computer-Assisted
        Language Learning Newsletter, 531
Old Testament
    Bible (King James Version), 531
OLIS (Oxford University Library Information
    Service Gopher, 533, 534, 681
    Service) Gopher, 275, 439
Olympic Games 1994 at Lillehammer, 531-532, 642, 711
Olympics
    Olympic Games 1994 at Lillehammer, 531-532
    OlymPuck, 532
    rec.sport.olympics, 532
OlymPuck, 360, 518, 532
OMD (Orchestral Manoeuvres In The Dark), 477, 532
On-this-day, 120, 532
On-u, 487, 492, 532
online books
    Electronic Books, 532
    Online BookStore (OBS), 532
Online BookStore (OBS), 106, 288, 521, 532, 624
Online Career Center, 258, 398, 532
Online Radio, 179, 384, 533, 584
online services
    Women's Wire, 533
Online-dict, 212, 368, 435, 533
OPAC system
    ELISA (Electronic Library Service), 533
    MELVYL Library System, 533
OPACS
    OLIS (Oxford University Library Information
        Service Gopher, 533

Open Computing Facilty (OCF) Gopher,
    Sports Section, 295, 642
Open Computing Facilty (OCF) Gopher, Sports
    Section, 534
Open Government Pilot, 325, 534
Open Government Pilot (Canada), 123
Open Government Project (Canada), 123, 324, 534
opera
    The University of Kansas Library, 534
opera, French (19th-century)
    Indiana University Libraries, 303
operating systems
    Bugs-386bsd, 534
    Std-UNIX, 534
    UNIX-wizards, 534
Operlist, 401, 535
optics
    CVNet (Color and Vision Network), 535
    University of Rochester Library, 535
ORA-NEWS, 385, 535, 690, 695
Oregon
    Oregon-news, 535
Oregon-news, 535
Orienteering, 535
Origami, 535
ornithology
    titnet (Paridae and Hole-nesting Bird Discussion
        List, 536
    TitNeT Titnews Titnotes, 535-536
    The University of Kansas Library, 535
OTIS (Operative Term Is Stimulate), 60, 69, 253, 332, 536
Our-kids, 536, 540
OUTIL (Out in Linguistics), 102, 311, 435, 441, 536, 675
Output, 470-471, 504, 536, 652
Overseas Business Reports, 115, 150, 536, 671
Oysters, 536

P

The Purple Thunderbolt of Spode (PURPS), 599
Pac-10-Sports, 495, 537, 642
Pacific, 537
packaging, 537-538
Pagan, 538, 599
PAGEMAKER, 46, 209, 359, 451, 538
Pakistan, soc.culture.pakistan, 538
paleography, The University of Notre Dame Library, 538
paleontology, 538
Panic, 42, 538
Papa, 345, 443, 538-539
paper, 539
papermaking, history of, 539
papers, 539
parallel computers, 539
paranoia, alt.conspiracy, 539
parenting, 539-540
Paris, 540
parisitology, 539
Park Rangers, 327-328, 540, 693
ParNET, 385, 540
Partners, 540
partnerships, 540
Pascal, 540
Patent Act of the US, 330, 430, 542
patents, 541-542
PB-Cle-Raves (Pittsburgh/Cleveland Raves), 586
Pc532, 179, 336, 542-543, 634
Pcbuild, 171, 543
Pcgeos-list, 179, 543, 634
Pd-games, 307, 457-458, 543
Pdp8-lovers, 179, 336, 543, 634
peace, 543-544
pediatrics, 544

PEI (Prince Edward Island, Canada) Crafts Council Gopher, 123, 189, 350, 544
Pen-pals, 139, 181, 544, 718
PennInfo, 544
Pennsylvania, PennInfo, 544
PENPages, 248, 258-259, 297, 544
people, NEWS (General News), 544
People Using Networks Can Have an Impact on Government, , 36, 156, 504, 545
performing arts, 545
periodicals, 545
PERL (Practical Extraction and Report Language), 167-168, 545, 571
PERQ-fanatics, 165, 545
personal papers, 545
personals, alt.personals.ads, 545
Peru, 546, 636
petroleum, 546
pets, 546
PGP Mail, 225, 385, 546
Ph7, 335, 546, 604
pharmaceutical development, IMSWorld R&D Focus, 547
pharmaceuticals, 547
pharmacology, 547-548
pharmacy, Svhp-l, 548
philanthropy, Internet Nonprofit Center, 548
philology, MEDTEXT-L, 548
philology, Celtic, 130
philosophy, 548
phone books, Internet Phone Books, 549
PHOTO-CD, 165, 549
photography, 3D, 549
photography, history of, 549
Physical Education & Recreation, 45, 197, 549-550, 595, 618, 642, 711
physical therapy, HFS-L, 550
Physics, 78, 550, 553
physics, 550- 551
physics, geodesic quantum, 314
The Physics Information Network, 550
physics, theoretical, 668
physiology, REBASE (Restriction Enzyme Database), 551
picasso-users, 165, 181, 551
PIERS Exports (US Ports), 279, 671
PIERS Imports (US Ports), 454, 551, 672
Pigulki, 226, 551, 554
Pine E-mail, 225, 396, 551-552
Ping, 396, 552
Pink Floyd, echoes, 552
Pipes, 86, 552, 628, 669
PIRA - Paper, Printing and Publishing, Packaging, and Nonwovens Abstracts, 456, 537-538, 539, 552, 566, 575
Pisma Bralcev, 552, 627
Pkd-list, 211, 552, 616
planetariums, Sci.astro.planetarium, 552
planning, 552-553
plant lipids, NPLC, 553
plant science, Biosis Previews, 553
plasma physics, Physics, 553
plastics, RAPRA Abstracts, 553
plays, Spanish, 640
PMC-MOO, 442, 445, 563
POD (Professional Organizational Development), 234, 239, 242, 553
poetry
    Poetry Conference, 553
    rec.arts.poems, 554
poetry, American, 554
Poetry Conference, 553
Poisons Information Database, 99, 460, 554
poker, 554
Poland, 554-555
Poland-l, 194, 554-555
polar regions, Dartmouth College Library, 555
Police, 555
Polish Archives, 504, 555, 663
Political Analysis and Research Cooperation (PARC) News Bulletin, 355, 555, 560

Political Platforms of the US, 206, 330, 436, 555, 560
political science, 555-556
politics, 556- 558
politics, international, 558-559
politics, libertarian, 436
politics, middle eastern, 559
politics, US, 559-560
polymers, RAPRA Abstracts, 560
POP, 563
pop groups, 560
pop music, 560-561
Popular Culture, 561
popular culture, 561-562
Porschephiles, 81, 562, 645
Portuguese, Brasil, 562
POS302-L, 272, 475, 562, 583
POSCIM, 556, 562
Posix-ada, 170, 562, 564
Posix-testing, 171-172, 562-563
postal services, POP, 563
Postmodern Culture, 442, 445, 563
power boating
    The Nautical Bookshelf, 563
powerboating, The Nautical Bookshelf, 563
PPPL (The Princeton Plasma Physics Laboratory), 550, 564, 600
Prague University of Economics Gopher Service, 197, 230, 275, 564
Pre-Law, Legislation, Court Decisions, 427, 428, 430, 564
pregnancy, Bethany Christian Services, 564
Presidential Documents, 557, 564, 709
presidents, 564-565
pricing, Internet Public Subsidies, 565
Primate-talk (Primate Discussion List), 565, 699
primatology, 565
Prince, 491, 565
Prince Edward Island (Canada) Crafts Council Gopher, 123
Princeton University Library, 39-40, 139, 144, 347-348, 408, 443, 445, 472, 479, 500, 565-566, 575
Princeton University Online Manuscripts Catalog Library, 106, 211-212, 217, 257, 337, 416, 566, 677
Principia Cybernetica Newsletter, 548, 566, 717
printing, 566
Prion (Prion Research Digest), 341, 566
Privacy, 385, 567
privacy, 566-567
Privacy Act of 1974, 431, 567
Privacy Rights Clearinghouse (PRC), 186, 302, 432, 567
PRL, 153, 567, 584
professional sports, 567
Professional Sports Schedules, 88, 299, 351, 567, 643
Prog-Pubs, 52, 153, 459, 567
programming, 567- 570
programming languages, 570-571
programming, literate, 443
Progress, 181, 202, 571
prohibition, 571
Project Gutenberg, 446-447, 571-572, 596
Project-management, 181, 572, 634
Prompt, 179-180, 572
Proof-users, 181-182, 570, 572
property, 572
Prospero, 397, 572
protocols, 304, 502
PSI, 385, 573
The PSYCHGRAD Project and Psychology-Related Information, 244, 573
psychiatry, PsycINFO, 573
psychology, 573
psychotherapy, alt.sexual.abuse.recovery, 573
PsycINFO, 89, 573
public access archives, fsp-discussion, 573
public domain software, 574
public health, 574
public policy, 574
publications, 574-575

Publications of the Office of Environment, Safety and Health, 284, 328, 575, 609
publishers, 575
Publishing, 106, 576
publishing, 575-576
Pubnet, 172, 576, 690
Pubs-IAT (Institute for Academic Technology newsletter), 234, 239, 242, 368, 576
Purdue University Library, 78, 83, 135, 186, 225, 230-231, 263-264, 282, 362, 443, 445-446, 551, 576, 604, 700-701
Purkinje Park, 161, 312, 506, 576
The Purple Thunderbolt of Spode (PURPS), 193
puzzles, 576
PVS (Project Vote Smart), 328, 557, 576-577
Python, 168, 577

Q

Qmlist (Quantitative Morphology List), 479, 579
Qn, 309, 579
Qn (Queer Nation), 36
Qnx2, 182, 336, 579, 634
Qnx4, 182, 336-337, 504, 579, 634
Quaker FTP Archive at ClarkNet, 579, 599
Quakerism, 579-580
quality control, Total Quality Management Gopher, 580
Quanta, 575, 580, 616, 718
quantum chemistry, 580
quantum physics, 580
Quantum Physics/High Energy Physics, 551, 580, 600
Quark Background Material, 551, 580
Quattro, 81-82, 580
Quebec, Rezo, bulletin irregulomadaire du RQSS, 580-581
Quebec Nordiques, 351, 581, 643
Queen, 487, 581, 604
Queer Nation (QN), 36
Questions and Answers about the GPO Gateway to Government Act, 284, 330, 431, 581
Quotations, 581
Quotecom Home Page, 581

R

race, 583-584
radio, 584
railroads, 584-585
railway history, 585
rap music, 585
RAPRA Abstracts, 457, 553, 560, 585, 605
rare books, 585
Rascal Aviation Archives, 40, 83, 585
raves, 585-586
REACH (Research and Educational Applications of Computers in the Humanities), 180, 586
real estate, 587
REBASE (Restriction Enzyme Database), 269, 551, 587
rec.aquaria, 64, 294-295, 587
rec.arts.anime, 60, 288, 408, 587
rec.arts.books, 106, 587
rec.arts.comics.misc, 106, 150, 587
rec.arts.dance, 199, 293, 587
rec.arts.disney, 217, 588
rec.arts.fin, 69, 293, 588
Rec.arts.int-fiction, 164, 373, 447, 588
rec.arts.movies, 290, 588
rec.arts.movies movie database, 481, 561, 588, 665
   (Cardiff WWW front-end), 373, 481, 561, 588, 665
rec.arts.poems, 447, 554, 588
rec.arts.sf.starwars, 290, 588, 616
rec.arts.sf.tv, 588, 616, 665
rec.arts.sf.written, 588-589, 616

rec.arts.startrek.current, 589, 616, 665
rec.arts.startrek.misc, 290, 589, 665
rec.arts.tv, 589, 665, 677
rec.arts.tv.soaps, 589, 665
rec.arts.tv.uk, 589, 665, 681
rec.audio, 79, 589, 649
rec.autos.driving, 82, 589
rec.autos.sport, 82, 589, 643
rec.autos.tech, 82, 589, 661
rec.autos.vw, 82, 589
rec.backcountry, 589, 595, 643
rec.boats, 589-590, 610, 643
rec.collecting.cards, 350, 590, 673
rec.crafts.brewing, 89, 190, 590
rec.equestrian, 59, 269-270, 353, 590, 643
rec.food.cooking, 187, 297, 590
rec.food.veg, 187, 297, 590, 697
rec.gambling, 125, 307, 308, 590, 595
rec.games.board, 308, 590, 595
rec.games.chess, 137, 308, 590, 595
rec.games.programmer, 308-309, 570, 590, 701
rec.games.video.arcade, 309, 590, 701
rec.gardens, 309, 420, 591
rec.guns, 294, 591, 708
rec.humor, 357, 409, 591
rec.martial-arts, 455, 591
rec.motorcycles, 480, 591
rec.music.beatles, 491, 561, 591
rec.music.cd, 79, 487, 591
rec.music.classical, 487, 591
rec.music.folk, 490, 591
rec.music.gdead, 488, 561, 591
rec.music.makers, 488, 491, 591
rec.music.makers.guitar, 491, 591
rec.music.makers.synth, 79, 488, 592
rec.music.phish, 491, 561, 592
rec.org.sca, 466, 592, 611
rec.pets, 59, 546, 592
rec.pets.cats, 60, 546, 592
rec.pets.dogs, 60, 546, 592
rec.photo, 69, 190, 549, 592
rec.puzzles, 309, 576, 592, 595
rec.radio.amateur.misc, 256, 584, 592
rec.radio.shortwave, 256, 584, 592
rec.railroad, 584, 592, 674
rec.scuba, 592, 595, 618, 676
rec.skiing, 593, 595, 625, 643
rec.sport.baseball, 88, 593, 643
rec.sport.basketball.college, 88, 148, 593, 643
rec.sport.basketball.pro, 88, 593, 643
rec.sport.cricket, 190, 593, 643
rec.sport.football.college, 299, 593, 643
rec.sport.football.pro, 299, 593, 643
rec.sport.hockey, 351, 593, 643
rec.sport.olympics, 532, 593, 651
rec.sport.pro-wrestling, 593, 643, 717
rec.sport.rowing, 190, 593, 605, 644
rec.sport.soccer, 593-594, 628, 644
rec.sport.tennis, 594, 644, 666
rec.travel, 594, 676
rec.video, 69, 163, 290, 594, 701
rec.video.satellite, 594, 665
rec.woodworking, 190, 350, 594, 715
Recipe Archive, 187, 297-298, 594
recipes, 594
recordings, 594
recreation, 595
Recreational Pharmacology Server, 219, 507, 547, 595
recycling, Solid Waste Recycling, 595
reference, 595-596
refrigeration, 596
Reggae Down Babylon, 194, 488, 596
regional business, Business Dateline, 596
regulations, 596-597

relays, Class Four Relay Magazine, 597
religion, 597-599
remote sensing, 599-600
research, 600-601
Research (Funding Support List), 304-305, 331, 601
research and development, 600
Research Databases and Resources by Subject, 33, 202, 601
Research on Demand, 377, 391, 431, 454-455, 601
Research Ship Schedules and Information, 454, 529, 601, 674, 676
Research SIG of the Open and Distance Learning Assoc. of Australia (Resodlaa), 80, 235, 239, 242, 601
restaurant management
    University of Wisconsin at Stout Library, 601-602
retirement, AgeLine, 602
Retrieval Success, 366, 385, 602
Rezo, bulletin irregulomadaire du RQSS, 580-581, 602, 629
rhetoric, Speeches and Addresses in the US, 602
Rhodes, Happy, 602
rights, The Frog Farm, 602
RIPE Network Coordination Centre Gopher, 275, 506, 602
rock music, 602-604
Rogers, Bruce, 604
role-playing games, 604
Rolling Stones, Nihon Sun Microsystems, 604
romance, 604
Romania, CEE Environmental Libraries Database, 605
Roosevelt, Franklin D., The University of Illinois at Chicago Library, 605
Rosen Sculpture Exhibition, 69, 293, 605
rowing, rec.sport.rowing, 605
rrl, 320, 605, 681
rubber, RAPRA Abstracts, 605
running, dead-runners, 605
rural development, 605-606
Russia, 606-607
Russian, 421, 441, 447, 606
Russian and East European Studies Home Pages, 226-227, 324, 556, 606
rxderm-l, 208, 216, 607, 625

S

SABINET (South African Bibliographic and Information Network), 202, 506, 609, 635
safety, 609
Safety (Environmental Health and Safety Discussion List), 268, 341, 609
Sahel-NAFR, 315, 317, 320, 609
sailing, 610
Sais-l (Science Awareness and Promotion), 244, 245, 610, 615
sales, Alliance Marketing Systems, 610
San Francisco Bay Area, 610-611
Sanskrit, Harvard University Library, 611
satellite, Center for Extreme Ultraviolet Astrophysics, 611
satire, 611
SCA (Society for Creative Anachronism), rec.org.sca, 611
Scandinavia, soc.culture.nordic, 611
Scholarly Communication, 183, 248, 611
Scholarly Publishing, 575, 612
sci-fi, 612
    see also science fiction
sci.astro, 75, 612, 638
Sci.astro.fits, 76, 612
Sci.astro.hubble, 76, 355, 495, 612, 638, 646, 664
Sci.astro.planetarium, 76, 552, 612
sci.electronics, 256, 263, 612
sci.engr.biomed, 99, 263, 612
sci.environment, 228, 268, 612
sci.math, 458, 612
sci.med, 343, 465, 613
sci.med.physics, 343, 461, 551, 613
sci.military, 474, 613
sci.physics, 551, 613

Sci.space, 613, 638
Sci.space.news, 282, 613, 638
Sci.space.science, 613, 638
science, 613-615
science, aquatic, 64, 614
science, atmospheric, 78
science, behavioral, 89
science fiction, 615-616
    see also sci-fi
science, history of, 616
science technology, 616
sciences, aquatic, 63-64
scientific journals, 616
scientific research, 616
scientific visualization, 617
The Scientist Newsletter, 255, 613
scientists, 617
Scifaq-l, 615
Scifraud, 301, 615
Scit-L, 153, 367, 617
Scotland, 617
The Scout Report, 166, 366, 385, 720
scripting languages, NIC (Nucleus for Interactive Computing), 617-618
SCS, 194, 637
scuba diving, 618
SCUP BITNET NEWS, 552-553, 618, 689
SCUPMA-L: Society of College and University Planners, Mid-Atlantic Region, 553, 618, 690
Seafood Internet Network, 283, 298, 618
Searching Gopherspace with Veronica, 366, 385, 619, 719
SEC (Securities and Exchange Commission) EDGAR (Elect. Data Gathering, Analysis, & Retrieval) System, 289, 619, 649
securities, 619
Security, 620
security, 619-620
Senate, US, 620
Senatorial papers, 620
Sense of Place, 228, 268, 620
sequencers, 620-621
serials pricing, 621
services, 621
settlements, 621
sex, 621
Sex FAQ, 282, 621
sexology, 621
sexual abuse, 622
sexual orientation, 622
sexuality, 622
Shakers, 141, 599, 622-623
Shakespeare, William, 623
Shamash, The New York - Israel Project, 403-404, 411, 509, 623
shareware, 623
ShareWord, Online BookStore (OBS), 624
shopping, 624
shortwave radio, Drake-R8, 624
Silicon Graphics, Virtual Reality Space, 624
Sim, Dave, 624
Simula, 570, 624
simulation, 624-625
simulation, flight, 624
Singapore, 625
Singapore DMC, 385, 504-505, 625
singing, gay, 625
singles, 625
skiing, 625, 644
Skiing in Utah, 625, 644
skin, 625
skydiving, 625-626
slavery, 626
SLON, Oglasna Deska, 626
Slovak Republic, University of Nebraska at Lincoln Library, 626
slovak-l, 194, 626
Slovakia, 626

Slovenia, 627
small business, 627
Smbnet (Society for Mathematical Biology
    Digest), 97, 457, 627
Smiley Faces Dictionary, 385, 627
Smithsonian Institution Natural History Gopher, 60-61, 498, 627
Smithsonian Online, 70, 484, 627-628
smoking, Pipes, 628
soc.bi, 102, 629
soc.college, 236, 629, 630
soc.culture.african.american, 41-42, 475, 630-631
soc.culture.arabic, 472, 631
soc.culture.asian.american, 72, 631
soc.culture.british, 631, 681
soc.culture.canada, 123, 194-195, 631
soc.culture.celtic, 130, 631
soc.culture.china, 139, 631
soc.culture.europe, 275, 631
soc.culture.french, 301, 631
soc.culture.german, 318, 631
soc.culture.greek, 333, 631
soc.culture.hongkong, 352, 631
soc.culture.indian, 361, 631
soc.culture.iranian, 401, 631
soc.culture.italian, 405, 631
soc.culture.japan, 408, 631-632
soc.culture.jewish, 412, 632
soc.culture.korean, 417, 632
soc.culture.nordic, 611, 632
soc.culture.pakistan, 538, 632
soc.culture.soviet, 142, 154, 606, 632
soc.culture.spain, 632, 639
soc.culture.taiwan, 632, 657
soc.culture.turkish, 632, 678
soc.culture.usa, 54-55, 562, 632
soc.culture.vietnamese, 632, 702
soc.culture.yugoslavia, 632, 727
soc.cultures.celtic, 131
soc.history, 349, 628
soc.men, 312, 468, 628
soc.motss, 102-103, 311, 435, 628
soc.penpals, 182, 628, 718
soc.religion.christian, 141, 599, 628
Soc.singles, 625, 628
soccer, 628-629
social and behavioral science, 629
social events, 629
social law, Universite de Montreal UDEMATIK Library, 629
social responsibility, 629
social sciences, 629
social sciences and humanities, Australia COOMBSQUEST Social
    Sciences and Humanities Information Facility, 630
social work, University of Texas at Austin Library, 630
society, Aids, 630
Society for Creative Anachronism, rec.org.sca, 611
SOCINSCT (Social Insect Biology Research List, 97, 369, 630
sociology, 630-632
software, 632-634
software, defects of, 634-635
software, free, 301
software, internationalization of, 635
soil conservation, 635
Solid Waste Recycling, 269, 595, 635
Solstice, 260, 268, 635
sound synthesis, 635
Soundtracks, 488, 594, 635
South Africa, 41, 635, 636
South Africa (directory), 635
South African Specific Items, 556, 636
South America, 636
South Asian studies, 636
South East Florida AIDS Information Network (SEFAIN), 45, 465, 636
South Florida Environmental Reader, 268, 296, 636-637
Soviet Union, 637

Sovokinform, 151, 637
space, 637-638
space exploration, Sci.space.science, 638
space flight, 638
space science, 638-639
space studies, Ssi_mail, 639
Space-music, 255, 488, 639
Spacelink, 40, 244, 495, 639
Spacemen 3, Drone On..., 639
Spain, soc.culture.spain, 639
Spanish, Academia Latinoamericana de Espanol, 639-640
Spanish Inquisition, University of Pennsylvania PENNINFO Library,
    640
Spanish plays, Dartmouth College Library, 640
Spanky Fractal Database, 134, 165, 168, 458, 640
Special Chemicals Update Program, 115, 136, 640
spectroscopy, Massachusetts Institute of Technology Library, 640
speech disorders, Stutt-L, 640
speech, freedom of, 302
Speeches and Addresses in the US, 560, 602, 640
spelunking
    alt.caving, 640
    Cavers, 641
spirituality, Ayurveda, 641
Spojrzenia, 195, 515, 555, 641
sports, 641-645
SPORTS (Sports News Library), 58
SPORTS (Sports News), 94, 514, 644
sports cars, 645
sports statistics, 645
Sports-cards, 468, 644, 645, 673
Springsteen, Bruce, 645
squash, 645
Sri Lanka, 645
Sri Lanka Net (SLNet), 515, 645
Ssi_mail, 40, 639
ST viruses, 78, 172, 645
St. John Valley, history of, 646
St. Petersburg, 646
St. Petersburg Business News, 115, 646
Stagecraft, 646, 667
standards, 646
Stanford Medical Center Gopher, 343, 344, 465, 646
Star Trek Resources on the Internet, 616, 665, 677
starfish, Starnet (Echinoderm Newsletter), 646
stargazing, Sci.astro.hubble, 646
Starnet (Echinoderm Newsletter), 227, 453, 646
stars, Astronomy, 646
state courts, Citation Authority, 647
State Small Business Profiles, 115, 647, 648, 682
states, 647
STATES (States Library), 58, 127, 426, 647
statistics, 647-648
Statistics Canada Gopher, 123, 123-124, 648
Statlib, 458, 648
statutes, CODES (Codes Library), 648
Std-UNIX, 534, 648, 690
Stealth, 82, 649
steel, Materials Business File, 649
stereo electronics, rec.audio, 649
Stlhe-I, 245
Stlhe-I (Forum for Teaching & Learning in Higher Ed), 235, 239, 242-
    243, 649
stock market, 649-650
Stock Market Secrets, 292-293, 400, 649-650
Stonewall25, 36, 103, 309, 435, 650
Stormcock, 337, 488, 604, 650
storytelling, Nerdnosh, 650
Strathspey (dance), 199-200, 617
string processing, Icon-group, 650
students, 650-651
Stutt-L, 153, 215, 640
style, 651
Style Sheets from the Online Writers' Workshop, 91-92, 436, 651, 718

Subway Navigator (city subway routes), 651, 674, 676
SUMEX-AIM, 180, 451, 634
summer sports, rec.sport.olympics, 651
Summit of the Americas Internet Gopher, 54, 335, 376, 423, 651
Sun Microsystems, Inc., 172, 651
Supercomputers, 182, 652
supercomputers, 652
SupraFAX, 283, 477, 652
Supreme Court, 652-653
Supreme Court Decisions, 426, 652
Supreme Court Decisions (Project Hermes), 412, 426, 652-653
Supreme Court Judges, 94, 412, 653
Supreme Court of Canada, 123, 427, 653
Supreme Court, US, 653
Surfing the Internet, 385, 389, 653
SURFnet—KB InfoServer, 276, 501, 506, 653
sustainable living, CEE Environmental Libraries Database, 653
Svhp-l, 548, 653-654, 699, 701
Sweden, Lysator's Gopher Service, 654
Swiss Scientific Supercomputing Center (CSCS) Info Server, 276, 652, 654
Synth-l, 255, 490, 654
synthesis, 654
synthesizers, 654
systems administration, 654
Systems Operators, firewalls, 294
systems theory, 655

T

table tennis, 657
table.abortion, 32, 341, 657, 714
Taiwan, soc.culture.taiwan, 657
talk.bizarre, 357, 657
talk.origins, 36, 190, 278, 657
talk.politics.mideast, 472, 559, 657
talk.politics.soviet, 142, 154, 557-558, 606, 657
talk.religion.misc, 271, 599, 658
talk.religion.newage, 548, 599, 658
Tandem computers, 658
Tandy computers, CoCo, 658
tax assessors, 658
tax law, 427
taxacom, 97, 658
taxes, 658
teacheft (Teaching Effectiveness), 235, 239, 243, 658-659
teaching, 659
Tecbase- Sandia National Laboratory, 362, 368, 661
technical writing, 659
technological advances, 662
technology, 659-662
Technology Initiatives for the Clinton/Gore Administration, 558, 564, 661, 709
technology transfer, National Technology Transfer Center (NTTC), 662
techwr-l (Technical Writing List), 659, 662
Telebit Computer Products, Netblazer-users, 662
Telecom Archives, 663
telecommunications, 662-663
telecomputing, 663
Telemedia, Networks, and Systems Group, 115, 253, 664
The Teleputing Hotline And Field Computing Source Letter, 663
The Teleputing Hotline And Field Computing Source Letter, 116
telescopes, Sci.astro.hubble, 664
television, 664-667
Telluride Institute, 149, 156, 505, 606, 666, 703
Telnet, 666
Telnet Access to WWW (World Wide Web), 397, 408, 666, 719
Telnet-How To, 397, 666
Tennessee, University of Tennessee at Memphis Library, 666
tennis, 666
teslit-l (Adult Education & Literacy Test Literature), 235, 239, 243, 442, 666

TeX, auc-TeX, 666-667
Texas, 667
The Texas Information Highway, 131, 325, 647, 670, 676
Texas: Computer Crimes Statute, 180, 191, 667
text processing, comp.text.tex, 667
Thailand: The Big Picture, 248, 601, 667, 676
The Electronic Journal of Analytic Philosophy Humanities, 548
The Internet Press, 255
The University of Minnesota Library System (LUMINA), 351, 353, 498
The World Wide Web Acronym Server, 385
The World Wide Web rec.food.recipes archive, 187
Theater, 217, 545, 667
theater, 667
Theater, Film & Television, 290, 665, 667
theology, 667-668
theoretical chemistry
Theoretical Journal Abstract And Bibliographic Files, 580, 668
theoretical physics, 668
Think Wind, 644, 668, 711
THINKNET, 196, 548, 655, 668
Third World, Agence FrancePresse International French Wire, 668
Tibet, CTN News, 669
time, correct, 189
titnet (Paridae and Hole-nesting Bird Discussion List,100, 536, 669
TitNeT Titnews Titnotes, 100, 535-536, 669
tobacco, Pipes, 669
TOPNWS (Top News Library), 58, 514, 669
Tornado Warnings, 215, 669
Total Quality Management Gopher, 116, 453, 580, 670
tourism, 670
toxicology, 670
toys, 671
trade, 671-672
trade unions, Johns Hopkins University Library, 671
Trademark Act of the US, 150, 328, 431, 673
trademarks, 672-673
trading cards, 673
TRADSTAT, 116, 151, 672
TRANS (The Transportation Library), 83, 585, 674, 678, 693
translation, Lantra-L, 673
transportation, 673-674
transportation law, TRANS (The Transportation Library), 674
The Transportation Library (TRANS), 83
transsexualism, 674-675
travel, 675-676
travel, history of, University of Tennessee at Knoxville Library, 677
Travelnet, 676
treaties, 677
treatment, GENMED (General Medical Information), 677
trekkers, Star Trek Resources on the Internet, 677
trivia, rec.arts.tv, 677
Trollope, Anthony, 677
trucking industry, TRANS (The Transportation Library), 678
TULSA (Petroleum Abstracts), 546, 678
The Tumor Gene Database, 98, 202, 216, 313
Turkey, soc.culture.turkish, 678
tutorials, Chemistry Tutorial Information, 678
TWICS, 156-157, 163, 408, 505, 678, 703
typography, The University of Iowa Libraries, 678

U

The University of Minnesota Library System (LUMINA, 580
The University of Notre Dame Library, 538
U.S. Army Area Handbooks, 284, 473, 559, 691
U.S. Bureau of the Census Gopher, 131, 206, 648
U.S. Civil War Reading List, 32, 348
U.S. Consumer Product Safety Commission (CPSC), 186, 431, 609, 692
U.S. Patent and Trademark Office Database, 116, 202, 399, 542, 694
UC Berkeley Museum of Paleontology and the WWW Subway, 484, 538, 679, 720
Ucadian studies, 679

UCC (Uniform Commercial Code), 117-118
UCSB Library Reference Guide, 70, 349, 439, 679
UFOs, alt.alien.visitors, 679
UIgis-L, 316, 321, 679
The Ultimate Gopher for Rush Fans, 604, 606
UN Army Map Service, 679
UN Criminal Justice Country Profiles, 191, 681
UN Development Program, 349, 681
UN documents, 679-680
UN Resolutions, 325, 328, 681
UN Rules, 558, 646, 681
un.wcw.doc.eng, 210, 543, 681, 712, 716
un.wcw.doc.fra, 544, 682, 712-713, 716
UNC-CH Info system, 248, 393, 680
UNICEF Gopher, 137-138, 139, 680
Uniform Code of Military Justice, 426, 473, 680
Uniform Commercial Code (UCC), 117-118, 151, 646, 680
unions, Women.labr, 680
UNITE Archive, 366, 373, 385-386, 680
United Kingdom, 680-681
United Nations, 211, 268, 681-682
United Press International News—Sports, 514, 644, 682
United States, 682
United States Geographic Name Server, 316, 321, 682
United States Geological Survey Home Page, 316, 321, 682, 695
Universal Copyright Convention, 188, 328, 431, 560, 682
Universite de Montreal UDEMATIK Library, 65, 231, 442-443, 615, 621, 629, 661, 683
universities, 683
universities, history of, 683
University of California Santa Barbara Virtual Library, 490, 683
The University of California Search for Extraterrestrial Civilizations, 46, 76, 279
University of Chicago Library, 54, 87, 134-135, 191, 264, 322, 405, 411, 416, 440, 444, 545, 683, 709
University of Colorado at Boulder Library, 348, 356, 420, 444, 525, 683
University of Delaware Libraries (DELCAT), 135, 205, 345, 443, 447, 539, 683
University of Denver Library, 193, 297, 357, 684
University of Glasgow Information Service (GLANCE), 190, 276, 323, 480, 617, 628, 644, 645, 666, 684
University of Hawaii Library, 72, 105, 277, 337-338, 684
The University of Illinois at Chicago Library, 605, 344, 31-32, 137, 363, 626
The University of Iowa Libraries, 127, 303, 357, 358, 495, 497-498, 584, 678
The University of Kansas Library, 727, 107, 126, 140, 148, 410, 415-416, 534, 535, 707
University of Maine System Library Catalog, 63, 124, 317, 452, 646, 679, 684
University of Maryland, College Park, 44, 146, 295, 530, 708
University of Maryland System Library, 63, 466, 470, 525, 684, 547, 670
The University of Michigan Library, 72, 76, 236, 316, 325, 436, 441, 458, 470, 507, 571, 674, 684, 728
University of Minnesota Gopher Server, 236, 683, 684
The University of Minnesota Library System (LUMINA), 270, 107, 271, 270
The University of Minnesota Remote Sensing Lab, 321, 361, 600
University of Nebraska at Lincoln Library, 197, 297, 423, 427, 428-429, 473, 626, 684-685
University of Nevada at Reno Library, 88, 507, 542, 679, 685
University of Nevada, Las Vegas Library, 307
  Las Vegas, NV, 124, 354, 507, 685
University of New Hampshire Videotex Library, 148, 200, 296-297, 307, 474, 685
University of New Mexico Unminfo Library, 65, 420, 497, 549, 685
University of North Carolina at Chapel Hill Info Library, 522, 585, 685
University of North Carolina at Greensboro MINERVA Library, 139, 212, 290, 345, 685
University of North Carolina at Wilmington SEABOARD Library, 347, 454, 685
University of North Carolina; Chapel Hill Newsbrief, 685
University of Northern Iowa Library, 70, 118, 248, 288, 488, 686
The University of Notre Dame Library, 228, 63, 107, 265, 401, 489, 539, 683

University of Pennsylvania Library, 225, 636
University of Pennsylvania Library-Philadelphia Pa., 349-350, 411, 443-448, 466, 472,, 686
University of Pennsylvania PENNINFO Library, 66, 91, 142, 218, 288, 303, 446, 447, 623, 640, 686, 710, 711
University of Pennsylvania School of Medicine Library, 341, 343, 347, 525, 686
University of Puerto Rico Library, 44, 169, 230, 248, 525, 686
University of Puget Sound Library, 248, 447, 488, 498, 668, 686
University of Rochester Library, 65, 71, 317, 421-422, 444, 467, 535, 549, 648, 686
University of Saskatchewan Libraries, 123, 325, 686
University of Southern Colorado Library, 348, 686
University of Tennessee at Chatanooga Library, 143, 444, 687
University of Tennessee at Knoxville Library, 185, 297, 497, 677, 687
University of Tennessee at Memphis Library, 444, 666, 687
University of Texas at Austin Library, 89, 169, 263, 423, 472, 488, 498, 525, 616, 630, 687
University of Texas at Austin Tarlton Law Library, 109, 185, 356, 427, 687
University of Texas at Galveston (Medical Branch) Library, 99, 344, 525, 687
University of Texas Health Science Center (UTHSCSA) Biomedical Library Information System, 439, 466, 687
  at San Antonio Library, 53, 207, 525, 529, 544, 687, 701
  at Tyler Library, 93, 125, 130, 282, 479, 687-688
University of Texas Southwestern Medical Center Library, 98, 688
University of Texas-Pan American Library, 448, 469, 688
University of the Pacific Library, 55, 548, 688
University of Toledo Library, 116, 332, 356, 376, 573, 615, 688
University of Tulsa Library, 317, 444, 546, 688
University of Utah Library, 317, 472, 474, 688, 709
University of Wales College of Medicine Library Online Catalog, 439, 466, 688
University of Wisconsin at Milwaukee Library, 65-66, 70, 116, 126, 316, 317, 444, 446, 688, 691
University of Wisconsin at Oshkosh Library, 116, 436, 526, 688
University of Wisconsin at Platteville Library, 116, 363, 688-689
University of Wisconsin at Stout Library, 116, 283, 352, 353, 354, 458, 471, 601-602, 670, 689
University of Wisconsin Eau Claire Library, 116-117, 248, 344, 526, 689
University of Wisconsin Extension Program in Independent Study, 689
University of Wisconsin Extension Program in Independent Study, 243
University of Wisconsin Green Bay Library, 230, 269, 488, 499, 689
University of Wisconsin River Falls Library, 44, 248, 348, 689
University of Wisconsin Stevens Point Library, 248, 269, 271, 348, 689
University of Wisconsin Superior Library, 249, 328, 689
University of Wisconsin—Parkside, 696
university planning, 689-690
UNIX operating system, 690-691
UNIX-wizards, 534, 691
urban planning, Virginia Commonwealth University Library, 691
urban studies, 691
US, North American Free Trade Agreement (NAFTA), 691
US Army Corps of Engineers, 263, 473, 691
US Bureau of the Census Gopher, 691
US Civil War Reading List, 691-692
US Department of Education Online Library, 249, 429, 692
US Department of the Interior, 268, 328, 692
US Federal Government, FedWorld Bulletin Board, 692
US General Accounting Office Transitional Reports, 293, 328, 692
US Geological Survey Server, 97, 317, 499, 692
US Government, NTIS FedWorld, 692
US Government Publications, Voice of America and Worldnet, 692-693
US Government Regulations, TRANS (The Transportation Library), 693
US Holocaust Memorial Museum, 348, 352, 408, 412, 693
US House of Representatives Gopher, 185, 284, 330, 693
US law
  LAWREV (Law Review Library), 693
US National Park Service, Park Rangers, 693

US Patents, 371, 542, 673, 693
US/Mexico Border Discussion List, 268, 423, 469, 694
USDA Agricultural Extension Service, 44, 694
Usenet, 694-695
Usenet Newsgroup, Oglasna Deska, 695
Usenet Repository, 386, 505, 695
Usenet Sports Groups Archived, 299, 618, 626, 644, 657, 695, 704
Usenet University, 249, 683, 695
Usenet What Is?, 389, 397, 695
Usenet World, 389, 397, 695
USGS, United States Geological Survey Home Page, 695
USGS (United States Geological Survey) Gopher, 126, 317, 695-696
Utah State Constitution, 185, 696
Utah Valley Community College Library, 34, 45, 82, 120, 138, 256, 352, 596, 696
UTIRC (University of Toronto Instructional and Research Computing), 168, 173, 182, 696
UWP Music Archive, 332, 448-449, 488-489, 696

V

val-l, 154, 556, 637, 697
VapourWare, 180, 697
Various Treaties, 559, 677, 697
VEGCNY-L (Vegetarians in Central New York area), 298, 510, 697
vegetarianism, 697-698
veggie (Vegetarian Issues Discussion List), 298, 698
veggies, 109, 298, 698
veglife (Vegetarian Life List), 298, 698
Velo News Experimental Tour de France Web Page, 92, 645, 698
verdicts, VRDCT (Jury Verdicts Library), 698
Veronica, 698
Veronica FAQ, 366, 391, 698
Veronica Introduction, 397, 698
Vertebrate Museum, 97, 699
vertebrates, 698-699
    Vertebrate Museum, 699
Vetadm-L, 353, 699
vetcai-l, 162, 699
veterinary hospitals, 699
veterinary medicine, 699-700
veterinary science, 700-701
Vethis-L (Veterinary Hospital Information Systems), 699
vetimm-l, 699-700
vetinfo (Discussion of Veterinary Informatics), 700
Vetlib-L (Veterinary Medicine Librarians List), 439, 700
Vetmed-L (Veterinary Medicine Discussion List), 700
vetmicro, 470, 700
vetmycop, 492, 700
vettox-l (Veterinary Toxicology Discussion List), 670, 700
Victim Help, 701
victims, 701
video, 701
video games, 701
Vietnam, 316, 701-702
Vietnam file (CIA World Factbook), 702
ViewPoints, 409-410, 456, 702, 704
Vigis-L, 197, 316, 321, 702, 703
Virginia, 702
Virginia Commonwealth University Library, 70, 97, 356, 410, 489, 691, 702
Virginia's PEN (Public Education Network), 249, 506, 702
virtual community, 702-703
Virtual Hospital, 243, 466, 703
virtual reality, 703
Virtual Reality Space, 197, 624, 634, 703
The Virtual Tourist - WWW Information, 397, 720
Virus Gopher Server, 94, 97, 704
Virus-L, 172, 620, 703
viruses, 704
visual communication, 704
visual impairment, 704
visualization, 704
Visualization Data Explorer Package, 704
Voice of America and Worldnet, 374, 516, 584, 692-693, 704
volleyball, 704
voting, 705
VRDCT (Jury Verdicts Library), 412, 413, 621, 698, 705
VTcad-L, 165, 180, 705
Vwar-L, 347, 348, 702

W

The WELL (Whole Earth 'Lectronic Link), 155, 163
The World Wide Web rec.food.recipes archive, 594
WAIS, 397
    comp.infosystems.wais, 707
WAIS (Wide Area Information Servers), 707
WAIS FAQ, 391, 707
WAIS, Inc., 366, 397, 576, 707, 720
Walpole, Sir Robert, 707
War Powers Resolution of 1973, 328, 427, 707
Washington DC, 707-708
Washington State University at Puyallup Library , 44, 616, 708
Washington University, 708
Washington University Library, 89, 447, 629, 661-662, 708
Washington University-St. Louis Medical Library & Members Library, 466, 615, 662, 708
water quality, 708
weapons, 708
weather, 708-709
Weather-users, 469, 570, 708-709
weather\Canadian Geographical WWW Index Travel, 708
The WebCrawler, 716-717
The WELL (Whole Earth 'Lectronic Link), 502, 702-703
The Wellness List, 295, 341, 526
Wells, Ida, 709
western America, 709
Western Lands, 228-229, 269, 300, 709
What is the Internet?, 386, 709
White House, 709-710
White House Frequently Asked Questions, 145, 282, 328, 560, 709
White House Information Service, 202, 558, 565, 709-710
White House Phone Numbers, 558, 564, 710
White House Press Releases, 558, 565, 710
Whitman, Walt
    University of Pennsylvania PENNINFO Library, 710
Whois, 397, 710
Wide Area Information Servers, *see* WAIS
The Wilderness Society, 710
wildnet (Computing and Statistics in Fishers & Wildlife Biology), 295, 648, 710
Williams College Library, 55, 332, 545, 710
Windows, 710-711
windsurfing, 711
winter games, 711
The Wired Librarian, 366, 439
WIRED Online, 516, 563, 711
Wiretap Sports Archives, 299, 629, 645, 711
Wisconsin, 711
witchcraft, 711
women, 711-713
Women.dev, 211, 376, 713
Women.forum, 287, 713
Women.health, 32, 45, 215, 287-288, 341, 713
Women.labr, 680, 713
Women.news, 288, 312, 713
women's issues, 713-714
women's studies, 714-715
Women's Studies and Resources, 287, 714-715
Women's Wire, 505, 533, 714
woodworking, 715
word play, alt.callahans, 715
Works, 180, 715
workstations, Works, 715
WORLD (World News and Information), 117, 514-515, 715

World Bank Gopher Server, 210, 299, 325, 375, 715
World Conference on Women, 715-716
World Constitutions, 350, 427, 559, 716
World Cycling Championship 1994, 92, 716
world health, 716
World Health Organization (WHO), 341, 466, 521, 716
World Wide Web (WWW), 717-721
    The Beastie Boys' Web Page, 491
    Best of the Web '94, 718
    Canadian Geographical WWW Index Travel, 314
    City of San Carlos World Wide Web Fire Safety
        Tutorial, 215
    Digital Equipment WWW Information Server, 212
    Digital's World Wide Web Server, 212
    Felipe's Bilingual WWW Pages, 235, 422
    The Human Languages Page, 441
    Lego Information, 433
    Russian and East European Studies Home Pages, 324
    UC Berkeley Museum of Paleontology and the
        WWW Subway, 538, 720
    United States Geological Survey Home Page, 321
    The World Wide Web Acronym Server, 435
    Zarf's List of Interactive Games on the Web, 309
The World Wide Web Acronym Server, 435
World Wide Web Book, 717
World Wide Web Demo, 717
World Wide Web FAQ, 366-367, 391, 717, 720
The World Wide Web rec.food.recipes archive, 298
World Wide Web Worm (WWWW), 367, 386, 717
World-Wide Web (WWW), 397, 720
World-Wide Web Book, 398, 720
World-Wide Web Demo, 397, 720
World-Wide Web Worm (WWWW), 720
Worldview, Principia Cybernetica Newsletter, 717
The Worldwide Impact of Network Access, 155, 210, 273, 503
wrestling, 717
Wright, Frank Lloyd, 717
writing, 717-718
wroclaw, 555, 718
WRPRCC (Wisconsin Regional Primate Research Center), 565, 711, 718
WWW. see World Wide Web (WWW)
WWW Biological Science Servers, 97, 99, 721
WWW Catalog, 397, 720
WWW Chemistry Sites, 136, 721
WWW FAQ, 282, 398, 721
WWW Paris, 70, 195, 303, 540, 670, 676, 721

X

X.500, 398, 723
XTC (the band), Chalkhills, 723

Y

Yahoo Market and Investments, 117, 231, 400, 650, 727
Yale Directory of Internet Libraries, 439-440, 534, 727
Yeats, William Butler, 727
Yugoslavia, 727

Z

Zarf's List of Interactive Games on the Web, 265, 309, 595, 671, 727
Zen and the Art of the Internet, 386, 727
'zines, 727
zoology, 727-728

New Riders' Official Internet Directory
REGISTRATION CARD

Fill out this card to receive information about future Internet books and other New Riders titles!

Name _____ **Title** _____

Company _____

Address _____

City/State/ZIP _____

I bought this book because: _____
_____

I purchased this book from:
- ☐ A bookstore (Name _____)
- ☐ A software or electronics store (Name _____)
- ☐ A mail order (Name of Catalog _____)

I purchase this many computer books each year:
☐ 1–5   ☐ 6 or more

I currently use these applications: _____
_____
_____
_____

I found these chapters to be the most informative: _____
_____

I found these chapters to be the least informative: _____
_____

Additional comments: _____
_____

☐ I would like to see my name in print! You may use my name and quote me in future New Riders products and promotions. My daytime phone number is: _____

New Riders Publishing 201 West 103rd Street • Indianapolis, Indiana 46290 USA

Fold Here

PLACE
STAMP
HERE

New Riders Publishing
201 West 103rd Street
Indianapolis, Indiana 46290
USA